LONDON

A-Z

Geographers' A-Z Map Company Ltd.

Geographers' A-Z Map Company Ltd.

Fairfield Road, Borough Green, Sevenoaks, Kent TN15 8PP
Telephone : 01732 781000 (Enquiries & Trade Sales)
01732 783422 (Retail Sales)

www.a-zmaps.co.uk

Edition 8 2009

Every possible care has been taken to ensure that, to the best of our knowledge, the information contained in this atlas is accurate at the date of publication. However, we cannot warrant that our work is entirely error free and whilst we would be grateful to learn of any inaccuracies, we do not accept any responsibility for loss or damage resulting from reliance on information contained within this publication.

The representation on the maps of a road, track or footpath is no evidence of the existence of a right of way.

The Grid on this map is the National Grid taken from Ordnance Survey mapping with the permission of the Controller of Her Majesty's Stationery Office.

Safety camera locations are publicised by the Safer Roads Partnership who operate them in order to encourage drivers to comply with speed limits at these sites. It is the drivers absolute responsibility to be aware of and to adhere to speed limits at all times.

By showing this safety camera information it is the intention of Geographers' A-Z Map Company Ltd., to encourage safe driving and greater awareness of speed limits and vehicle speed.
Data accurate at time of printing.

The publishers are deeply grateful for the ready co-operation and valuable help given to them in the production of this atlas. They would like to record their obligation to: The Engineers and Surveyors Departments and Planning Offices of all the Local Authorities covered in this atlas, The Department for Transport, Highways Agency, Transport for London, The Post Office, Police Authorities, Fire Brigades, Taxi Drivers, Members of the Public.

Printed and bound in the United Kingdom by Polestar Wheatons Ltd., Exeter.

An AtoZ Publication

CONTENTS

Key to Map Pages	2-3
Super Scale Map Pages @ 5¾" to 1 mile	4-19
Map Pages @ approx. 3" to 1 mile	20-174
West End Theatres Map	175
Index to Streets, Areas & selected Places of Interest	176-434
Index to Hospitals & Hospices	435-438
Index to Stations	439-441
Railway Connections Map	442-443
Underground Railway Map	444-445
Congestion Charging Overview	446
and Information	Inside Back Cover

REFERENCE

Motorway M1

A Road A2

Under Construction

Proposed

B Road B408

Dual Carriageway

One-way

Traffic flow on A Roads is also indicated by a heavy line on the driver's left.

Junction Name MARBLE ARCH

Restricted Access

Pedestrianized Road

Track & Footpath

Residential Walkway

Congestion Charging Zone

Railway — Tunnel, Level Crossing

Stations:

National Rail Network

Docklands Light Railway DLR

Underground — large scale pages

Croydon Tramlink — Tunnel, Stop

The boarding of Tramlink trams at stops may be limited to a single direction,indicated by the arrow.

Postcode Boundary

Built-up Area — BANK, STREET

Map Continuation 62 — Large Scale Map Pages 12

Airport

Car Park Selected

Church or Chapel

Fire Station

Hospital

House Numbers A & B Roads only 51 22 19 48

Information Centre

National Grid Reference 530

Park & Ride Bromley P+

Police Station

Post Office

River Bus Stop

Safety Camera with Speed Limit 30 V

Fixed and long term road works cameras only

Symbols do not indicate camera direction

Fixed Speed Limit — Variable Speed Limit

Toilet

with facilities for the Disabled

Disabled facilities only

Educational Establishment

Hospital or Hospice etc.

Industrial Building

Leisure or Recreational Facility

Place of Interest

Public Building

Shopping Centre or Market

Other Selected Buildings

SCALE

Map Pages 4-19
1:11,000 5¾ inches to 1 Mile
0 — ⅛ — ¼
0 — 100 — 200 — 300 — 400 — 500 Metres
14.62cm to 1 mile 9.1cm to 1 km

Map Pages 20-173
1:22,000 2.88 inches to 1 Mile
0 — ¼ — ½
0 — 250 — 500 — 750 Metres — 1 Kilometre
7.31cm to 1 mile 4.55cm to 1 km

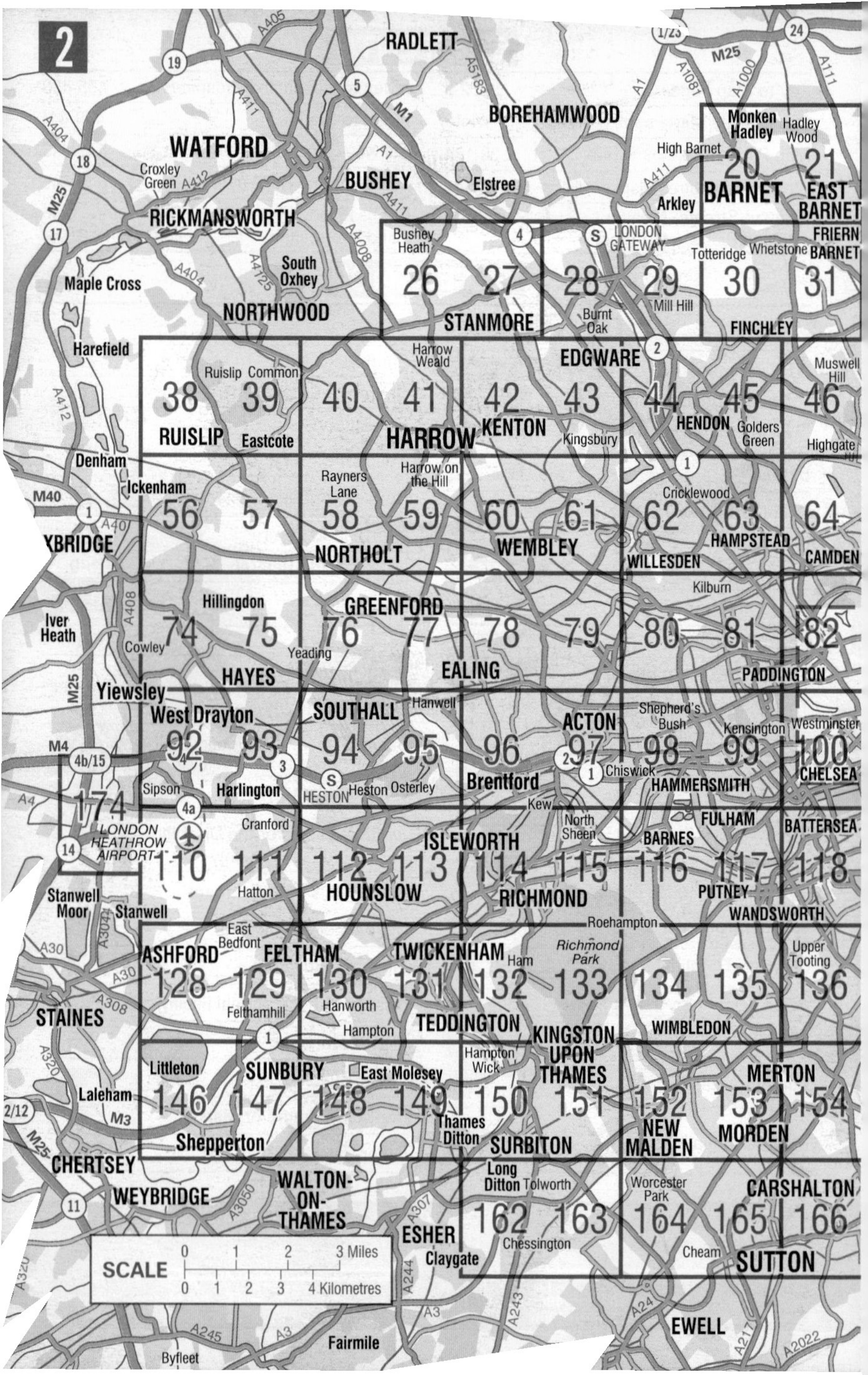
RADLETT
BOREHAMWOOD
WATFORD
Croxley Green
BUSHEY
Elstree
RICKMANSWORTH
Monken Hadley
Hadley Wood
High Barnet
20
21
BARNET
EAST BARNET
Arkley
LONDON GATEWAY
FRIERN BARNET
Totteridge
Whetstone
Bushey Heath
26
27
28
29
30
31
STANMORE
Burnt Oak
Mill Hill
FINCHLEY
South Oxhey
Maple Cross
NORTHWOOD
Harefield
Ruislip Common
Harrow Weald
EDGWARE
Muswell Hill
38
39
40
41
42
43
44
45
46
RUISLIP
Eastcote
HARROW
KENTON
Kingsbury
HENDON
Golders Green
Highgate
Denham
Ickenham
Rayners Lane
Harrow on the Hill
Cricklewood
56
57
58
59
60
61
62
63
64
XBRIDGE
NORTHOLT
WEMBLEY
WILLESDEN
HAMPSTEAD
CAMDEN
Kilburn
Hillingdon
GREENFORD
Iver Heath
74
75
76
77
78
79
80
81
82
Cowley
Yeading
HAYES
EALING
PADDINGTON
Yiewsley
Hanwell
West Drayton
SOUTHALL
ACTON
Shepherd's Bush
Kensington
Westminster
92
93
94
95
96
97
98
99
100
Chiswick
HAMMERSMITH
CHELSEA
Sipson
Harlington
HESTON
Heston
Osterley
Brentford
Kew
174
LONDON HEATHROW AIRPORT
Cranford
North Sheen
FULHAM
BATTERSEA
BARNES
ISLEWORTH
110
111
112
113
114
115
116
117
118
Hatton
HOUNSLOW
RICHMOND
PUTNEY
Stanwell Moor
Stanwell
WANDSWORTH
Roehampton
East Bedfont
ASHFORD
FELTHAM
TWICKENHAM
Ham
Richmond Park
Upper Tooting
128
129
130
131
132
133
134
135
136
STAINES
Felthamhill
Hanworth
Hampton
TEDDINGTON
KINGSTON UPON THAMES
WIMBLEDON
Littleton
SUNBURY
East Molesey
Hampton Wick
MERTON
146
147
148
149
150
151
152
153
154
Laleham
Thames Ditton
SURBITON
NEW MALDEN
MORDEN
Shepperton
CHERTSEY
WALTON-ON-THAMES
Long Ditton
Tolworth
Worcester Park
CARSHALTON
WEYBRIDGE
162
163
164
165
166
ESHER
Claygate
Chessington
Cheam
SUTTON
SCALE
0 1 2 3 Miles
0 1 2 3 4 Kilometres
EWELL
Fairmile
Byfleet
M25
M1
M40
M4
M3
A1
A3
A4
A24
A30
A40
A217
A243
A244
A245
A307
A308
A320
A404
A405
A408
A411
A412
A1000
A1081
A2022
A3044
A3050
A4008
A4125
A5183
A111

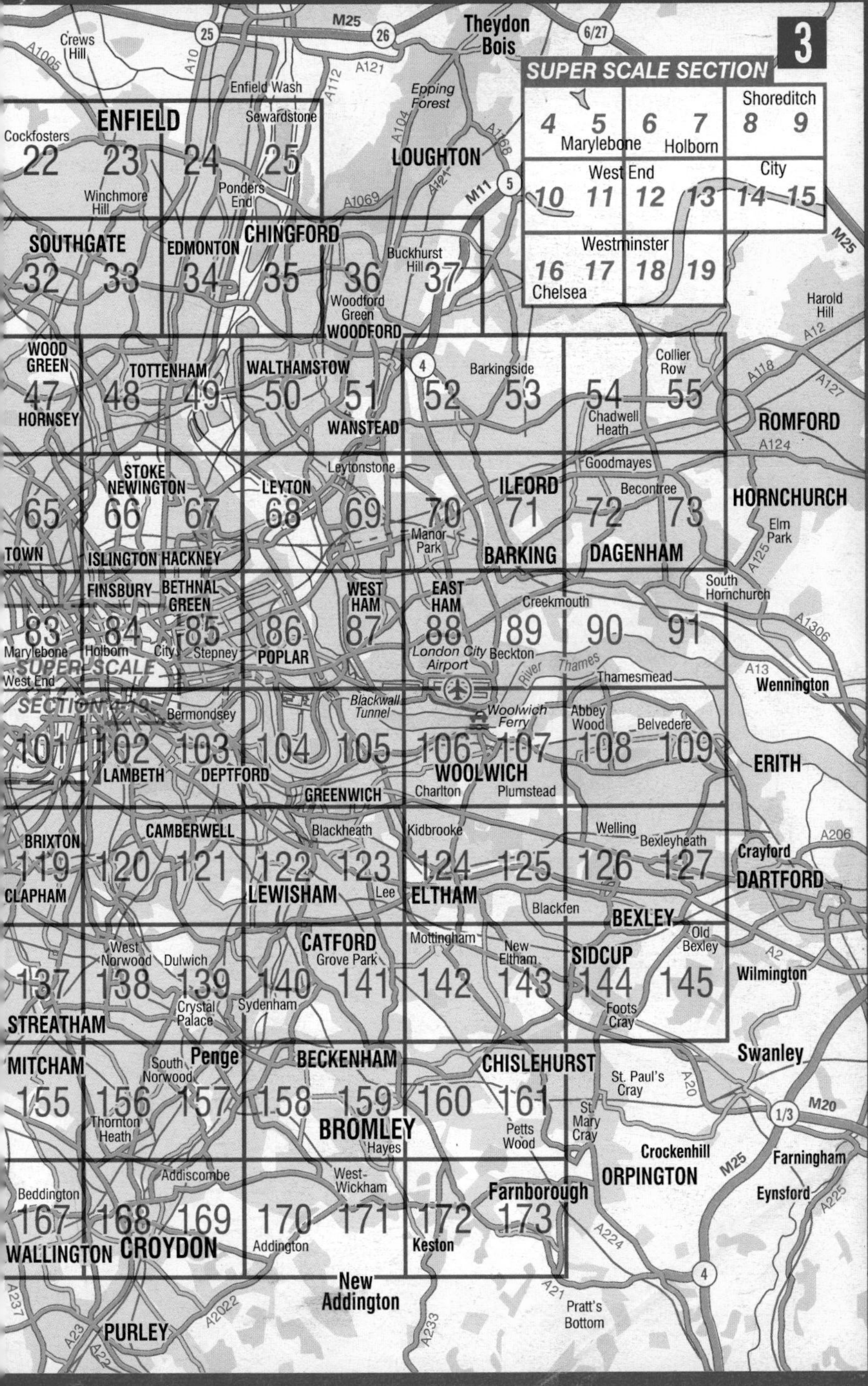
SUPER SCALE SECTION
4 5 6 7 8 9
Marylebone
Holborn
Shoreditch
West End
City
10 11 12 13 14 15
Westminster
16 17 18 19
Chelsea
Theydon Bois
M25
25
26
6/27
Crews Hill
A1005
A10
A121
A112
Enfield Wash
Sewardstone
Epping Forest
A104
A1168
ENFIELD
Cockfosters
22 23 24 25
LOUGHTON
Winchmore Hill
Ponders End
A1069
M11
5
SOUTHGATE
EDMONTON
CHINGFORD
Buckhurst Hill
32 33 34 35 36 37
Woodford Green
WOODFORD
M25
Harold Hill
A12
WOOD GREEN
TOTTENHAM
WALTHAMSTOW
4
Barkingside
Collier Row
A118
A127
47 48 49 50 51 52 53 54 55
HORNSEY
WANSTEAD
Chadwell Heath
ROMFORD
A124
STOKE NEWINGTON
LEYTON
Leytonstone
Goodmayes
ILFORD
Becontree
HORNCHURCH
65 66 67 68 69 70 71 72 73
Manor Park
Elm Park
A125
TOWN
ISLINGTON
HACKNEY
BARKING
DAGENHAM
FINSBURY
BETHNAL GREEN
WEST HAM
EAST HAM
Creekmouth
South Hornchurch
83 84 85 86 87 88 89 90 91
A1306
Marylebone
Holborn
City
Stepney
POPLAR
London City Airport
Beckton
River Thames
Thamesmead
SUPER SCALE SECTION 4-19
West End
A13
Wennington
Blackwall Tunnel
Woolwich Ferry
Abbey Wood
Belvedere
Bermondsey
101 102 103 104 105 106 107 108 109
LAMBETH
DEPTFORD
WOOLWICH
ERITH
GREENWICH
Charlton
Plumstead
CAMBERWELL
Blackheath
Kidbrooke
Welling
Bexleyheath
A206
BRIXTON
119 120 121 122 123 124 125 126 127
Crayford
CLAPHAM
LEWISHAM
Lee
ELTHAM
DARTFORD
Blackfen
BEXLEY
CATFORD
Mottingham
Old Bexley
West Norwood
Dulwich
Grove Park
New Eltham
SIDCUP
A2
137 138 139 140 141 142 143 144 145
Wilmington
Crystal Palace
Sydenham
Foots Cray
STREATHAM
MITCHAM
South Norwood
Penge
BECKENHAM
CHISLEHURST
St. Paul's Cray
A20
Swanley
155 156 157 158 159 160 161
M20
1/3
Thornton Heath
BROMLEY
Petts Wood
St. Mary Cray
Hayes
Crockenhill
Farningham
M25
Addiscombe
West Wickham
ORPINGTON
Beddington
Farnborough
Eynsford
167 168 169 170 171 172 173
A225
A224
WALLINGTON
CROYDON
Addington
Keston
4
New Addington
A21
A237
A2022
Pratt's Bottom
A233
A23
PURLEY
A22

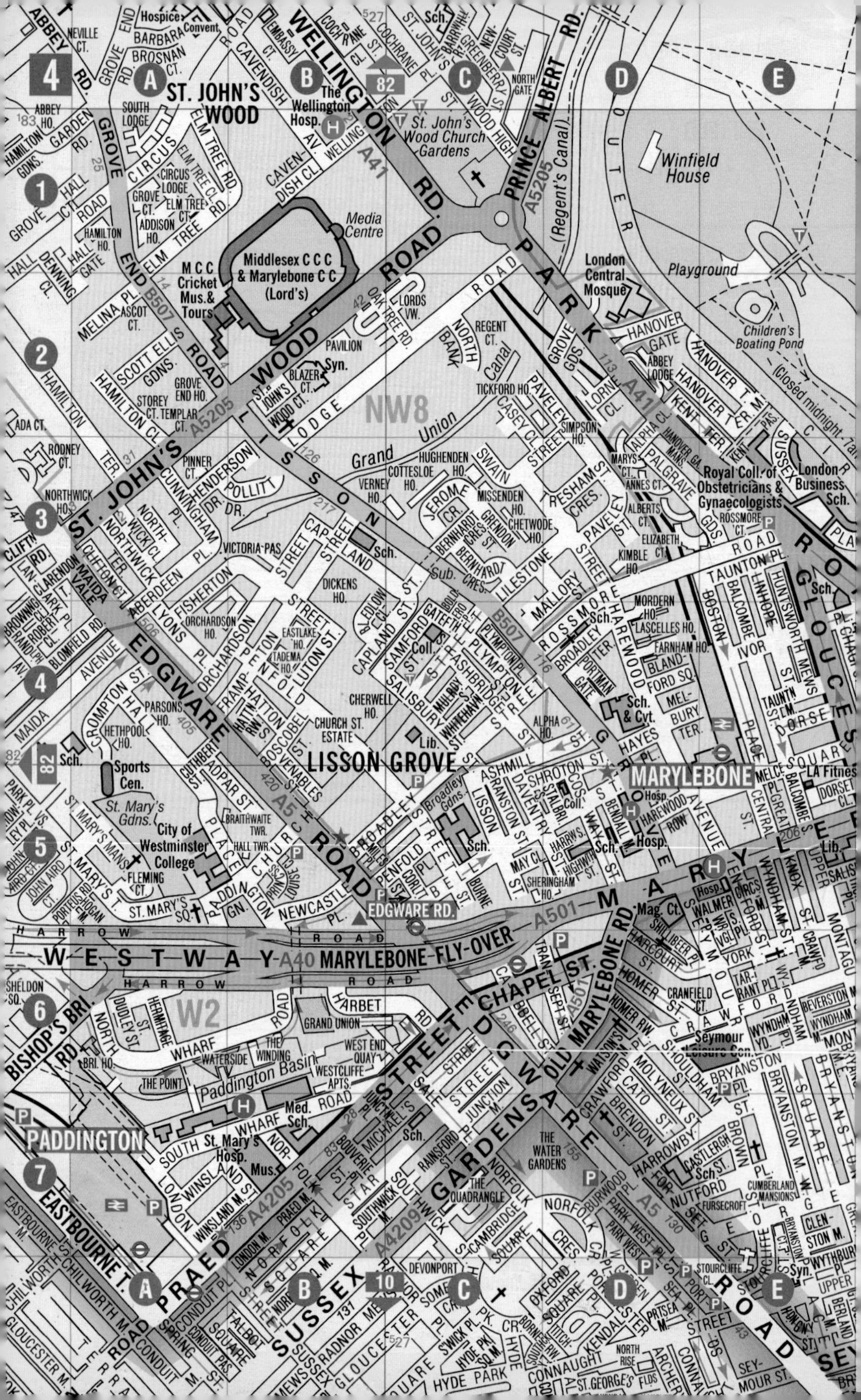
4
82
10
A
B
C
D
E
1
2
3
4
5
6
7
ST. JOHN'S WOOD
WELLINGTON RD.
A41
PRINCE ALBERT RD.
A5205
(Regent's Canal)
OUTER CIRCLE
Winfield House
Playground
Children's Boating Pond
(Closed midnight-7am)
London Central Mosque
PARK RD.
Hospice
Convent
ABBEY RD.
NEVILLE CT.
GROVE END RD.
BARBARA CT.
BROSNAN CT.
CAVENDISH AV.
EMBASSY CT.
The Wellington Hosp.
St. John's Wood Church Gardens
ST. JOHN'S WOOD HIGH ST.
COCHRANE ST.
NORTH GATE
NEWCOURT
ABBEY HO.
HAMILTON GDNS.
GARDEN RD.
SOUTH LODGE
CIRCUS RD.
ELM TREE RD.
CIRCUS LODGE
GROVE CT.
ADDISON HO.
ELM TREE CL.
HAMILTON HO.
HALL GATE
GROVE HALL CT.
HALL RD.
DENNING CL.
CAVENDISH CL.
Media Centre
Middlesex C C C & Marylebone C C (Lord's)
M C C Cricket Mus.& Tours
MELINA PL.
ASCOT CT.
B507
ST. JOHN'S WOOD ROAD
A5205
OAK TREE RD.
LORDS VW.
PAVILION
NORTH BANK
REGENT CT.
Syn.
BLAZER CT.
SCOTT ELLIS GDNS.
GROVE END HO.
STOREY CT.
TEMPLAR CT.
HAMILTON CL.
HAMILTON TER.
ADA CT.
RODNEY CT.
NW8
LODGE RD.
LISSON GROVE
Grand Union Canal
TICKFORD HO.
PAVELEY DR.
CASEY CL.
SIMPSON HO.
HUGHENDEN HO.
COTTESLOE HO.
VERNEY HO.
SWAIN ST.
JEROME CR.
MISSENDEN HO.
GRENDON ST.
CHETWODE HO.
RESHAM CRES.
PAVELEY ST.
HANOVER GATE
HANOVER T.
HANOVER TER. M.
ABBEY LODGE
GROVE GDNS.
LORNE CL.
KENT TER.
KENT PAS.
ALPHA CL.
MARYS CT.
ANNES CT.
ALBERTS CT.
ELIZABETH CT.
PALGRAVE GDNS.
ROSSMORE CT.
Royal Coll. of Obstetricians & Gynaecologists
London Business Sch.
SUSSEX PL.
GLOUCESTER PL.
PINNER CT.
HENDERSON DR.
POLLITT DR.
CUNNINGHAM PL.
NORTHWICK HO.
NORTHWICK CL.
NORTHWICK TER.
CLIFTON RD.
CLIFTON CT.
CLARENDON T.
MAIDA VALE
VICTORIA PAS
ABERDEEN PL.
CAPLAND ST.
Sch.
DICKENS HO.
BERNHARDT CRES.
LILESTONE ST.
ROSSMORE RD.
KIMBLE HO.
MALLORY ST.
MORDERN HO.
LASCELLES HO.
FARNHAM HO.
TAUNTON PL.
BALCOMBE ST.
LINHOPE ST.
HUNTSWORTH MEWS
BOSTON PL.
IVOR PL.
BLANDFORD SQ.
MELBURY TER.
HAREWOOD AV.
BROADLEY TER.
PORTMAN GATE
Sch. & Cvt.
FISHERTON ST.
ORCHARDSON HO.
ORCHARDSON ST.
LYONS PL.
EASTLAKE HO.
TADEMA HO.
LUTON ST.
BLEDLOW CL.
SAMFORD ST.
GATEFORTH ST.
Coll.
PLYMPTON ST.
ASHBRIDGE ST.
SALISBURY ST.
MULBURY ST.
WHITEHAVEN ST.
PENFOLD ST.
FRAMPTON ST.
HATTON RW.
BOSCOBEL ST.
CHERWELL HO.
CHURCH ST. ESTATE
Lib.
ALPHA HO.
HAYES PL.
TAUNTON M.
DORSET SQUARE
MARYLEBONE
MELCOMBE PL.
LA Fitness
DORSET CL.
EDGWARE ROAD
A5
BLOMFIELD RD.
ROBERT CL.
AVENUE
MAIDA AV.
CROMPTON ST.
HALL PL.
PARSONS HO.
HETHPOOL HO.
Sch.
Sports Cen.
St. Mary's Gdns.
City of Westminster College
ST. MARY'S MANS.
FLEMING CT.
CUTHBERT ST.
ADPAR ST.
BRAITHWAITE TWR.
HALL TWR.
HALL PLACE
CHURCH ST.
VENABLES ST.
BROADLEY ST.
Broadley Gdns.
Sch.
ASHMILL ST.
LISSON ST.
RANSTON ST.
DAVENTRY ST.
SHROTON ST.
COSWAY ST.
BENDALL M.
Hosp.
HAREWOOD ROW
CENTRAL ST.
GREAT CENTRAL ST.
BALCOMBE ST.
Lib.
MARYLEBONE RD.
A501
MILES PL.
PENFOLD PL.
CORLT. PL.
BELL ST.
BURNE ST.
MAY CL.
SHERINGHAM HO.
HIGHWITH ST.
HARROWBY ST.
Mag. Ct.
WALMER PL.
SEYMOUR PL.
ENFORD ST.
WYNDHAM ST.
UPPER MONTAGU ST.
ST. MARY'S SQ.
PADDINGTON GN.
NEWCASTLE PL.
EDGWARE RD.
JOHN AIRD CT.
PORTEUS RD.
HOGAN M.
HARROW ROAD
WESTWAY A40
MARYLEBONE FLY-OVER
CHAPEL ST.
TRANSEPT ST.
CAMPBELL ST.
SHILLIBEER PL.
HARCOURT ST.
HOMER ST.
HOMER RW.
YORK ST.
TARRANT PL.
CRANFIELD CT.
CRAWFORD PL.
Seymour Leisure Cen.
WYNDHAM YD.
BEVERSTON M.
SHELDON SQ.
BISHOP'S BRI. RD.
NORTH WHARF RD.
DUDLEY ST.
HERMITAGE ST.
W2
HARBET RD.
GRAND UNION
THE WINDING
WEST END QUAY
WESTCLIFFE APTS.
WATERSIDE
THE POINT
Paddington Basin
BRI. HO.
EDGWARE RD.
OLD MARYLEBONE RD.
WATSON'S M.
MOLYNEUX ST.
CATO ST.
SHOULDHAM ST.
BRYANSTON PL.
BRYANSTON SQUARE
BRYANSTON ST.
PADDINGTON
SOUTH WHARF ROAD
St. Mary's Hosp.
Med. Sch.
Mus.
LONDON ST.
WINSLAND ST.
WINSLAND M.
NORFOLK PL.
SALE PL.
ST. MICHAEL'S ST.
BOUVERIE PL.
Sch.
RAINSFORD ST.
STREET
JUNCTION M.
SUSSEX GARDENS
THE WATER GARDENS
BRENDON ST.
CRAWFORD ST.
CASTLEREAGH ST.
Sch.
NUTFORD PL.
FURSECROFT
BROWN ST.
CUMBERLAND MANSIONS
A5
EASTBOURNE T.
EASTBOURNE M.
PRAED ST.
A4205
LONDON M.
PRAED M.
NORFOLK SQUARE
SOUTHWICK PL.
SOUTHWICK M.
STAR ST.
A4209
THE QUADRANGLE
NORFOLK CRES.
CAMBRIDGE SQUARE
BURWOOD PL.
PARK WEST PL.
PORTSEA PL.
SEYMOUR PL.
CLENSTON M.
WYTHBURN PL.
GEORGE ST.
STOURCLIFFE ST.
STOURCLIFFE CL.
BRYANSTON CT.
Syn.
UPPER BERKELEY ST.
CHILWORTH ST.
CHILWORTH M.
GLOUCESTER TERRACE
SPRING ST.
CONDUIT PL.
CONDUIT M.
CONDUIT PAS
TALBOT SQUARE
SUSSEX PL.
SUSSEX SQUARE
RADNOR M.
GLOUCESTER SQUARE
DEVONPORT
SOMERS CR.
HYDE PK. CR.
SOUTHWICK ST.
SOUTHWICK PL.
HYDE PK. SQ. M.
HYDE PARK
OXFORD SQUARE
CONNAUGHT ST.
KENDAL ST.
NORTH RISE
ARCHERY CL.
PORCHESTER PL.
ST. GEORGE'S FLDS
SEYMOUR ST.
EDGWARE ROAD
SEYMOUR ST.

28
The Hub
F
82
G
H
To London Zoo
J
83
K
5
529
Regent's Park Barracks
CAMBERLEY HO.
PARK VILLAGE EAST
AMBLESIDE
BAGSHOT HO.
REDHILL
REGENT'S PARK
WINDSOR HO.
REGENT'S PARK
Cumberland Gate
St. John's Lodge
Frazer Lodge
Dept. of Environment Parks Dept.
(Closed midnight to 7am)
CHESTER ROAD
ALBANY STREET
A4201
CUMBERLAND MARKET
VARNDELL
ROBERT STREET
COMPTON CL.
CLARENCE GARDENS
Open Air Theatre
Chester Rd. Gates
QUEEN MARY'S GARDENS
INNER CIRCLE
Boating Lake
The Holme
Refreshments
Chester Walk Gate
English Gdns.
CHESTER GA.
CHESTER TERRACE
MUNSTER SQ.
LONGFORD
THE WHITE HO.
EUSTON CENTRE
NW1
Jubilee Gates
New Lodge
Tennis Courts
Regents College
YORK BRIDGE
Royal Coll. of Physicians
Playground
BROAD WALK
OUTER CIRCLE
ULSTER TER.
Clarence Gate
Park Square Gardens
PARK SQ. EAST
PARK SQ. W.
OSNABURGH TER.
ALBANY TER.
30
Sherlock Holmes Mus.
CORNWALL T.
ALLSOP T. M.
YORK TER. WEST
YORK TER. EAST
HARLEY HO.
ULSTER PL.
Cres. Gds.
REGENT'S PARK
GT. PORTLAND ST.
375
BAKER ST.
STATION APP.
Madame Tussaud's
Royal Academy of Music
A501
The London Clinic
PARK CRESCENT
Civil Justice Centre
MELCOMBE ST.
BERKELEY CT.
134
MARYLEBONE ROAD
Univ. of Westminster
NOTTINGHAM PL.
DEVONSHIRE PL.
HARLEY ST.
PORTLAND PLACE
GREAT PORTLAND STREET
B506
BOLSOVER ST.
CARBURTON ST.
BICKENHALL MANSIONS
BICKENHALL ST.
LUXBOROUGH TWR.
MARYLEBONE
PADDINGTON ST.
B524
Public Gdns.
DEVONSHIRE CLOSE
RIBA
HALLAM ST.
CLIPSTONE ST.
FITZROVIA
YORK ST.
MONTAGU MANS.
MOXON ST.
WEYMOUTH ST.
WEYMOUTH MEWS
WIMPOLE ST.
MANSFIELD ST.
CAVENDISH M. S.
BBC Broadcasting Ho.
LANGHAM PL.
ALL SOULS' PL.
DORSET ST.
RODMARTON ST.
BROADSTONE PL.
MANCHESTER STREET
Coll.
VINCENT ST.
NEW CAVENDISH STREET
CROSS KEYS CL.
Queen's Coll.
QUEEN ANNE STREET
CHANDOS ST.
A41
BAKER STREET
W1
BLANDFORD ST.
MANCHESTER M.
SPANISH PL.
THAYER ST.
BULSTRODE ST.
BENTINCK ST.
WELBECK ST.
WIGMORE PL.
Conv.
CAVENDISH PL.
GT. PORTLAND ST.
GLOUCESTER PLACE
ROBERT ADAM ST.
Wallace Colln
HINDE ST.
University
7
PORTMAN CL.
PORTMAN TOWERS
FITZHARDINGE ST.
MANCHESTER SQ.
DUKE'S M.
Wigmore Hall
A5204
HARCOURT HO.
CAVENDISH SQ.
MARGARET ST.
REGENT ST.
PORTMAN SQ.
SEYMOUR M.
WIGMORE ST.
ALDBURGH M.
BOURNE M.
HENRIETTA PL.
CHAPEL PL.
306
HOLLES ST.
GT. CASTLE ST.
Coll.
OXFORD CIRCUS
EDWARDS M.
PICTON PL.
JAMES ST.
11
Selfridges
Oxford St. Restricted Access 7am-7pm. Mon.-Sat.
ORCHARD ST.
Coll.
BOND ST.
OXFORD ST.
WOODSTOCK ST.
UNION YD.
TENTERDEN ST.
Regent Hall
PRINCES ST.
HANOVER SQ.
29
224
SEYMOUR ST.
PORTMAN ST.
PORTMAN M. S.
GRANVILLE PL.
502
Shop!

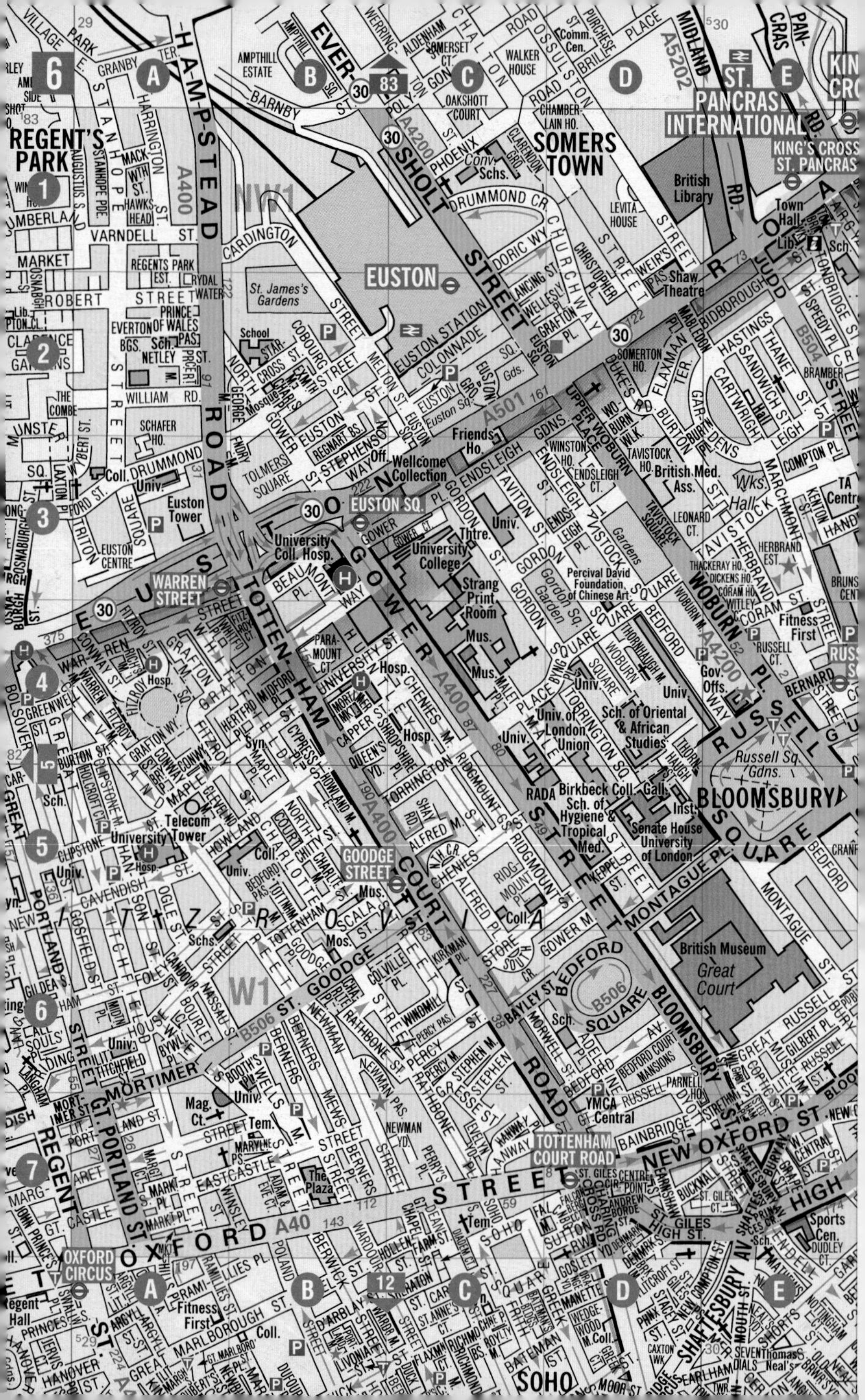
6
REGENT'S PARK
NW1
EUSTON
SOMERS TOWN
British Library
ST. PANCRAS INTERNATIONAL
KING'S CROSS ST. PANCRAS
83
AMPTHILL ESTATE
HAMPSTEAD ROAD
EUSTON ROAD
St. James's Gardens
Euston Tower
WARREN STREET
EUSTON SQ.
University Coll. Hosp.
University College
Wellcome Collection
Friends Ho.
British Med. Ass.
Percival David Foundation of Chinese Art
Gordon Sq. Garden
TAVISTOCK SQUARE
Sch. of Oriental & African Studies
Univ. of London Union
Birkbeck Coll.
Sch. of Hygiene & Tropical Med.
Senate House University of London
BLOOMSBURY
RUSSELL SQUARE
Russell Sq. Gdns.
British Museum
Great Court
TOTTENHAM COURT ROAD
GOODGE STREET
GOWER STREET
Telecom Tower
FITZROVIA
W1
BEDFORD SQUARE
NEW OXFORD ST.
OXFORD STREET
OXFORD CIRCUS
YMCA Central
The Plaza
SOHO
12
SHAFTESBURY AV.
HIGH HOLBORN
Sports Cen.
Shaw Theatre
Town Hall
A B C D E
1 2 3 4 5 6 7

7
8
83
84
13
PENTONVILLE ROAD
A501
KING'S CROSS ROAD
GRAY'S INN ROAD
A5200
A201
FARRINGDON ROAD
CLERKENWELL ROAD
A5201
ROSEBERY AVENUE
A401
THEOBALD'S ROAD
SOUTHAMPTON ROW
HOLBORN
HIGH HOLBORN
A40
KINGSWAY
A4200
CHANCERY LANE
B400
FETTER LANE
NEW FETTER LA.
FLEET ST.
ST. JOHN ST.
GUILFORD STREET
B502
ST. PANCRAS
CLERKENWELL
HOLBORN
WC1
WC2
The Angel Centre
Sadler's Wells
Dame Alice Owen Bldg.
London Inst.
Westminster Kingsway Coll.
The Foundling Museum
The Wolfson Assessment Cen.
Coram's Fields
Mecklenburgh Sq. Gds.
The Eastman Dental Hosp. & Institute
St. Andrew's Gds.
Dickens' Ho.
Post Office Mount Pleasant
London Metropolitan Archives
Family Records Cen.
Spa Fields Open Space
New River Head
The Hydra Building
Great Ormond Street Hosp. for Children
The National Hosp.
Gray's Inn Gdns.
Gray's Inn
Islamic Cen.
Lincoln's Inn Fields
Lincoln's Inn Liby.
Lincoln's Inn Hall
Land Registry Off.
Royal Coll. of Surgeons
Freemasons Hall
King's College Library
Royal Courts of Justice
Temple Bar
Bourne Estate
Budd. Cen.
Min. Offs.
ITN
Holford Gds.
Covered Res.

8
84
14
A
B
C
D
E
1
2
3
4
5
6
7
CITY ROAD
GOSWELL ROAD
GOSWELL RD
City Road Basin
Wenlock Basin
WHARF
A501
EC1
FINSBURY
ST. LUKE'S
OLD STREET
OLD STREET
A5201
CLERKENWELL ROAD
ALDERSGATE
A1
LONDON WALL
A1211
BARBICAN
CHEAPSIDE
NEWGATE ST
V'DUCT
HOLBORN
FARRINGDON ST
FARRINGDON R.
A201
A40
KING EDWARD
ST. MARTIN'S LE-GRAND
CHISWELL STREET
BUNHILL ROW
B144
B100
B501
B502
LEVER STREET
ST. JOHN STREET
Sadler's Wells
Dame Alice Owen Bldg.
City University
Moreland Prim. Sch.
City Forum
Moorfields Eye Hosp.
Baths
Leisure Cen.
Spts. Cen.
The Medical Coll. of St. Bartholomew's Hospital
Charterhouse
St. John's Gardens
FARRINGDON
Central Markets
SMITHFIELD
St. Bartholomew's Hospital
CITY THAMESLINK
Old Bailey
Cen. Crim. Ct.
British Telecom Cen.
St. Paul's Cathedral
ST. PAUL'S
MOORGATE
Guildhall
Museum
Ironmongers Hall
HAC Ground
Bunhill Flds. Burial Grd.
Health Club
TA Cent
Bank of England
BEECH STREET
Fitness First
Golden Lane Estate
Leis. Cen.
Park
Hlth. Cen
THE BREWERY
CITYPOINT
Arts Cen.
Crusoe Ho. Sch.
Spa Green Estate
Finsbury Estate
Kings Bldg.
Lib.

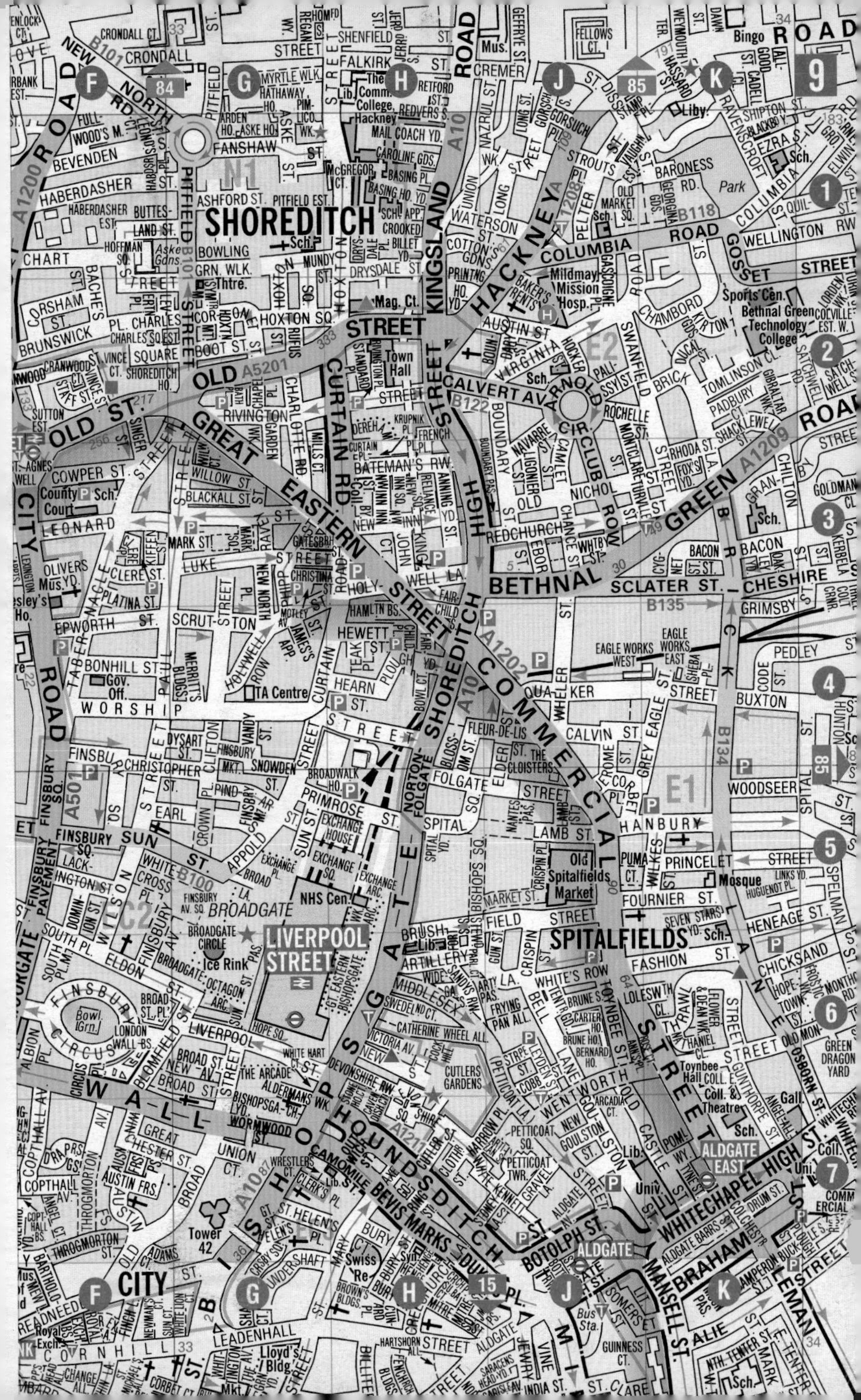
SHOREDITCH
N1
HOXTON
SPITALFIELDS
E1
E2
C2
CITY
LIVERPOOL STREET
ALDGATE
ALDGATE EAST
BROADGATE
9
84
85
15
33
34
F
G
H
J
K
1
2
3
4
5
6
7
NEW NORTH RD.
CRONDALL ST.
SHENFIELD ST.
FALKIRK ST.
CREMER ST.
GEFFRYE ST.
FELLOWS CT.
WEYMOUTH TER.
HASSARD ST.
RAVENSCROFT ST.
COLUMBIA ROAD
Bingo
Liby.
BARONESS RD.
Park
WELLINGTON RW.
GOSSET STREET
FANSHAW ST.
BEVENDEN ST.
HABERDASHER ST.
HABERDASHER EST.
PITFIELD ST.
PITFIELD EST.
ASHFORD ST.
MYRTLE WLK.
HATHAWAY HO.
ASKE ST.
The Comm. College, Hackney
RETFORD ST.
REDVERS ST.
MAIL COACH YD.
CAROLINE GDS.
BASING PL.
KINGSLAND ROAD
A10
STROUTS PL.
HACKNEY RD.
A1208
B118
WATERSON ST.
COTTON'S GDNS.
Mildmay Mission Hosp.
CHAMBORD ST.
SWANFIELD ST.
Sports Cen.
Bethnal Green Technology College
CHART ST.
CORSHAM ST.
BRUNSWICK PL.
CHARLES SQUARE
HOXTON SQ.
HOXTON ST.
OLD STREET
OLD ST.
A5201
Town Hall
CALVERT AV.
ARNOLD CIR.
BOUNDARY ST.
ROCHELLE ST.
CLUB ROW
GREAT EASTERN STREET
CURTAIN RD.
RIVINGTON ST.
CHARLOTTE RD.
BATEMAN'S RW.
REDCHURCH ST.
BETHNAL GREEN ROAD
A1209
SCLATER ST.
CHESHIRE ST.
GRIMSBY ST.
BRICK LANE
B134
B135
CITY ROAD
COWPER ST.
County Court
LEONARD ST.
OLIVERS YD.
TABERNACLE ST.
EPWORTH ST.
SCRUTTON ST.
HOLYWELL ROW
HOLYWELL LA.
SHOREDITCH HIGH STREET
COMMERCIAL STREET
A1202
BONHILL ST.
Gov. Off.
WORSHIP ST.
TA Centre
HEWETT ST.
EAGLE WORKS WEST
EAGLE WORKS EAST
QUAKER STREET
BUXTON ST.
PEDLEY ST.
CALVIN ST.
WOODSEER ST.
FINSBURY SQ.
A501
CHRISTOPHER ST.
EARL ST.
SUN ST.
PRIMROSE ST.
EXCHANGE SQ.
FOLGATE STREET
NORTON FOLGATE
SPITAL SQ.
ELDER ST.
LAMB ST.
HANBURY ST.
PRINCELET STREET
Mosque
Old Spitalfields Market
FOURNIER ST.
FASHION ST.
HENEAGE ST.
CHICKSAND ST.
FINSBURY PAVEMENT
WILSON ST.
BROADGATE CIRCLE
Ice Rink
NHS Cen.
BISHOPSGATE
ARTILLERY LA.
MIDDLESEX ST.
WENTWORTH ST.
TOYNBEE ST.
OLD CASTLE ST.
Toynbee Hall
FINSBURY CIRCUS
LONDON WALL
LIVERPOOL ST.
OLD BROAD ST.
WORMWOOD ST.
HOUNDSDITCH
A1211
CUTLERS GARDENS
PETTICOAT SQ.
GOULSTON ST.
WHITECHAPEL HIGH ST.
ALDGATE HIGH ST.
LEMAN STREET
MANSELL ST.
Tower 42
CAMOMILE ST.
BEVIS MARKS
ST. HELEN'S PL.
UNDERSHAFT
Swiss Re
ST. MARY AXE
DUKE'S PL.
BOTOLPH ST.
MITRE ST.
LEADENHALL ST.
Lloyd's Bldg.
Bus Sta.
GUINNESS CT.
ALIE ST.
Royal Exch.
CORNHILL
THROGMORTON ST.
Tower 42
JEWRY ST.
CRUTCHED FRIARS
FENCHURCH ST.
INDIA ST.
ST. CLARE ST.

PADDINGTON
A
B
C
D
E
1
2
3
4
5
6
7
82
4
100
16
BOURNE TER.
PRAED
ST.
SUSSEX
A4209
SUSSEX GDNS.
LANCASTER TER.
WESTBOURNE ST.
LANCASTER GATE
BAYSWATER ROAD
A402
BAYSWATER
EDGWARE
A5
ROAD
CONNAUGHT
HYDE PARK
STRATHEARN
SQUARE
HYDE PARK GDNS.
HYDE PARK PL.
ALBION GATE
Stanhope Place Gate
Albion Gate
Clarendon Gate
(NORTH CARRIAGE DR.)
Victoria Gate
Westbourne Gate
Marlborough Gate
THE RING
THE RIDE
NORTH
NORTH RIDE
THE FLOWER WALK
NORTH WALK
The Fountains
BUCK HILL WALK
(W. CARRIAGE DR.)
(Closed midnight - 5am)
W2
Nursery
HYDE
PARK
MAGAZINE GATE
The Lookout Education Centre
Rangers Lodge
Speke's Monument
Peter Pan
THE LONG WATER
KENSINGTON
GARDENS
Temple Lodge
Serpentine Bridge
SERPENTINE
RING
Boat Houses
THE SERPENTINE
Boating Lake
Serpentine Gallery
Cafeteria
Princess of Wales Memorial Fountain
Fishermans Keep
(WEST CARRIAGE DR.)
ROTTEN
ROW
Bowling Greens
(Closed midnight - 5am)
LOWER WALK
Albert Memorial
Alexandra Gate
NEW
SOUTH CARRIAGE
Prince of Wales Gate
Rutland Gate
Hyde Park Barracks
A315
KENSINGTON GORE
KENSINGTON ROAD
KNIGHTSBRIDGE
Royal Albert Hall
Royal Coll. of Art
Imperial Coll.
EXHIBITION ROAD
Royal College of Music
Imperial Coll. of Science, Technology
ENNISMORE GDNS.
RUTLAND GATE
MONTPELIER
TREVOR SQUARE
BROMPTON
ROAD
HANS
Harrods
KNIGHTSBRIDGE
A4

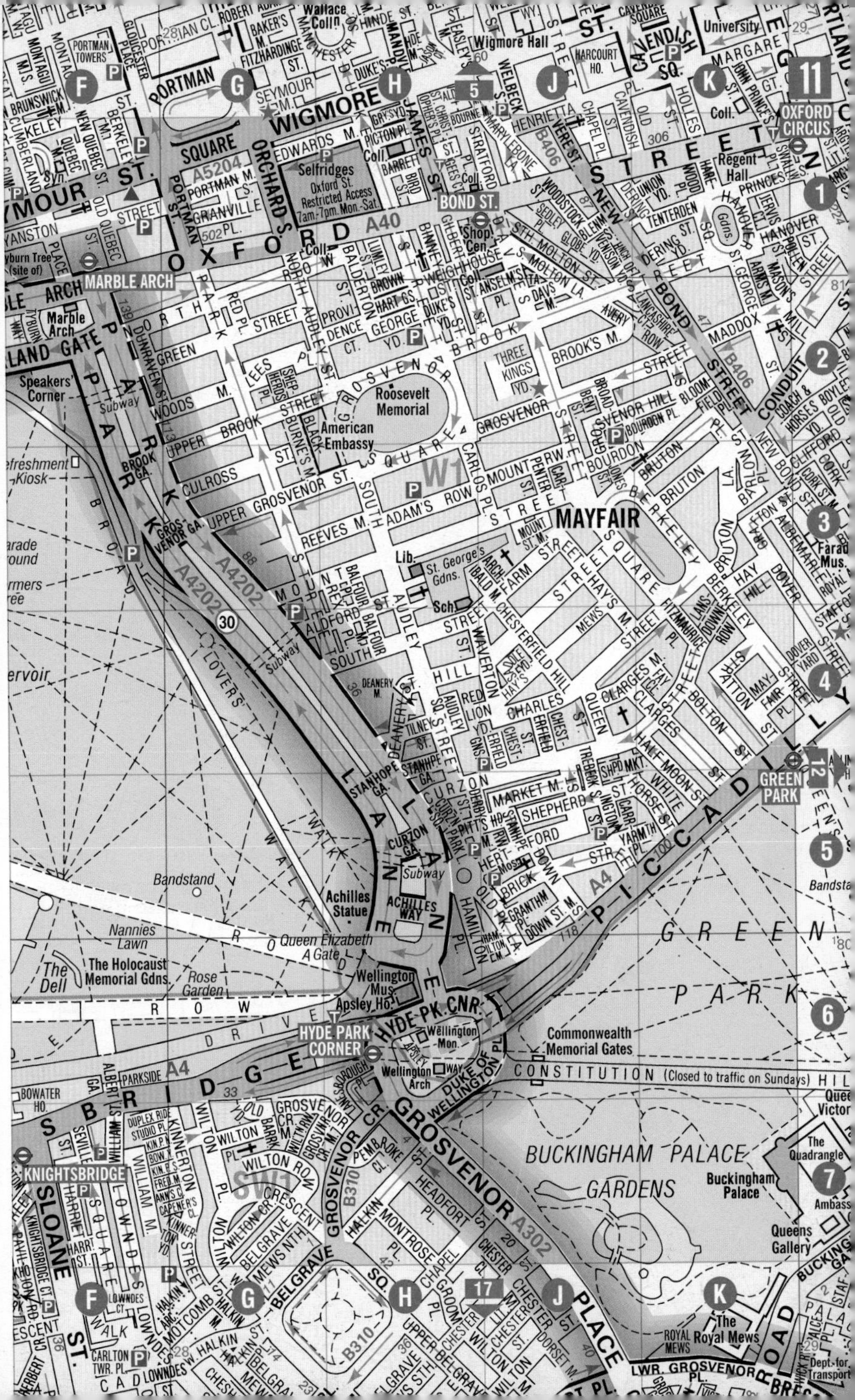

11
12
17
5
F
G
H
J
K
1
2
3
4
5
6
7
Wigmore Hall
Wallace Coll.
University
OXFORD CIRCUS
Regent Hall
WIGMORE
PORTMAN
SQUARE
Selfridges
Oxford St. Restricted Access 7am.-7pm. Mon.-Sat.
OXFORD
A40
BOND ST.
MARBLE ARCH
Marble Arch
Tyburn Tree (site of)
Speakers' Corner
Subway
PARK
LANE
A4202
STREET
NEW
BOND
CONDUIT
GROSVENOR
SQUARE
Roosevelt Memorial
American Embassy
W1
MAYFAIR
BERKELEY
SQUARE
St. George's Gdns.
Lib.
Sch.
CURZON
PICCADILLY
GREEN PARK
Bandstand
Achilles Statue
ACHILLES WAY
Queen Elizabeth Gate
Nannies Lawn
The Dell
The Holocaust Memorial Gdns.
Rose Garden
ROW
DRIVE
Wellington Mus.
Apsley Ho.
HYDE PK. CNR.
HYDE PARK CORNER
Wellington Mon.
Wellington Arch
DUKE OF WELLINGTON PL.
Commonwealth Memorial Gates
CONSTITUTION (Closed to traffic on Sundays) HILL
GREEN
PARK
BUCKINGHAM PALACE
GARDENS
The Quadrangle
Buckingham Palace
Queens Gallery
The Royal Mews
ROYAL MEWS
LWR. GROSVENOR PL.
KNIGHTSBRIDGE
SLOANE
SW1
BELGRAVE
SQ.
GROSVENOR
A302
PLACE
ROAD
WILTON
CRESCENT
LOWNDES
SQUARE
Dept. for Transport

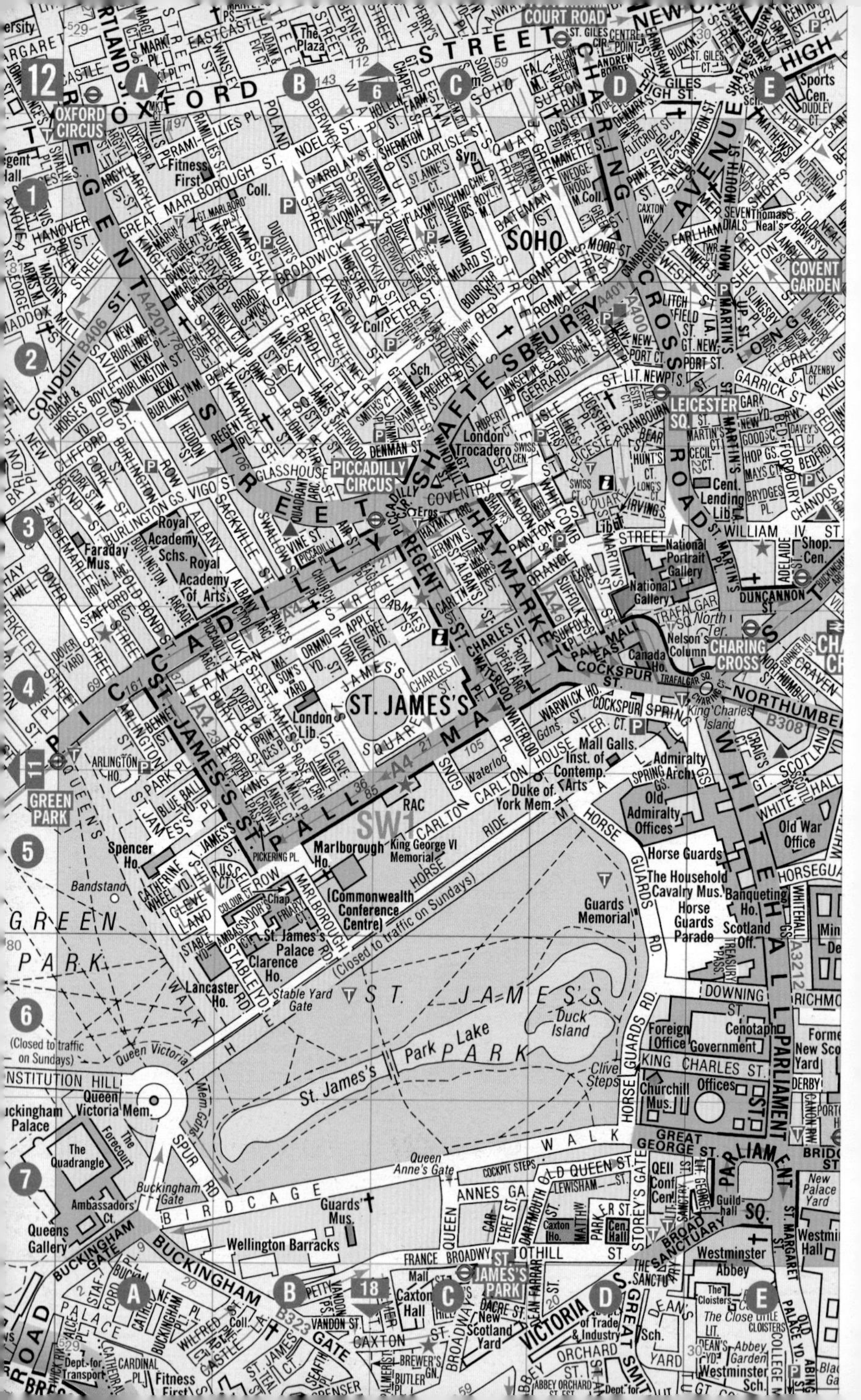

12
OXFORD CIRCUS
OXFORD STREET
COURT ROAD
ST. GILES CIRCUS
CENTRE POINT
HIGH ST.
ST. GILES HIGH ST.
The Plaza
EASTCASTLE
SOHO SQUARE
SOHO
CHARING CROSS ROAD
SHAFTESBURY AVENUE
REGENT STREET
GREAT MARLBOROUGH ST.
CARNABY ST.
BROADWICK ST.
BERWICK ST.
WARDOUR ST.
DEAN ST.
FRITH ST.
GREEK ST.
OLD COMPTON ST.
D'ARBLAY ST.
NOEL ST.
POLAND ST.
CARLISLE ST.
Fitness First
Coll.
Syn.
ST. ANNE'S CT.
CAMBRIDGE CIRCUS
SEVEN DIALS
Thomas Neal's
EARLHAM ST.
SHELTON ST.
NEAL ST.
COVENT GARDEN
LONG ACRE
ST. MARTIN'S LA.
UPPER ST. MARTIN'S LA.
GARRICK ST.
KING ST.
BEDFORD ST.
FLORAL ST.
CONDUIT ST.
NEW BOND ST.
OLD BOND ST.
SAVILE ROW
NEW BURLINGTON ST.
CLIFFORD ST.
CORK ST.
BURLINGTON GS.
VIGO ST.
SACKVILLE ST.
ALBANY
GLASSHOUSE ST.
BEAK ST.
GOLDEN SQ.
BREWER ST.
LEXINGTON ST.
PETER ST.
RUPERT ST.
WINDMILL ST.
DENMAN ST.
GERRARD ST.
LISLE ST.
NEWPORT ST.
LEICESTER SQ.
CRANBOURN ST.
London Trocadero
PICCADILLY CIRCUS
PICCADILLY
COVENTRY ST.
HAYMARKET
Eros
Royal Academy Schs.
Royal Academy of Arts
Faraday Mus.
ALBEMARLE ST.
DOVER ST.
STAFFORD ST.
BERKELEY ST.
VINE ST.
JERMYN ST.
DUKE ST.
BURY ST.
ST. ALBAN'S ST.
ORANGE ST.
CHARLES II ST.
PALL MALL
PALL MALL EAST
COCKSPUR ST.
TRAFALGAR SQ.
Nelson's Column
National Portrait Gallery
National Gallery
Canada Ho.
WILLIAM IV ST.
DUNCANNON ST.
CHARING CROSS
NORTHUMBERLAND AVE.
CRAVEN ST.
Cent. Lending Lib.
ST. JAMES'S
ST. JAMES'S SQUARE
ST. JAMES'S ST.
London Lib.
KING ST.
RYDER ST.
ARLINGTON ST.
GREEN PARK
QUEEN'S WALK
Spencer Ho.
CATHERINE WHEEL YD.
RAC
SW1
Marlborough Ho.
King George VI Memorial
(Commonwealth Conference Centre)
St. James's Palace
Clarence Ho.
Lancaster Ho.
STABLE YD.
Waterloo PL.
CARLTON HOUSE TER.
Mall Galls.
Inst. of Contemp. Arts
Duke of York Mem.
Admiralty Arch
Old Admiralty Offices
Horse Guards
The Household Cavalry Mus.
Horse Guards Parade
Banqueting Ho.
Scotland Off.
Old War Office
WHITEHALL
HORSEGUARDS AVE.
GREAT SCOTLAND YD.
THE MALL
HORSE GUARDS RD.
Guards Memorial
(Closed to traffic on Sundays)
GREEN PARK
Bandstand
Stable Yard Gate
ST. JAMES'S PARK
Duck Island
Park Lake
St. James's
Clive Steps
Queen Victoria Mem.
CONSTITUTION HILL
Buckingham Palace
The Quadrangle
The Forecourt
Ambassadors' Ct.
Queens Gallery
SPUR RD.
Buckingham Gate
BIRDCAGE WALK
Queen Anne's Gate
Guards' Mus.
Wellington Barracks
DOWNING ST.
Foreign Office
Cenotaph
Government Offices
KING CHARLES ST.
Churchill Mus.
PARLIAMENT ST.
GREAT GEORGE ST.
QEII Conf. Cen.
Guildhall
PARLIAMENT SQ.
New Palace Yard
Westminster Hall
Westminster Abbey
BROAD SANCTUARY
THE SANCTUARY
OLD QUEEN ST.
COCKPIT STEPS
LEWISHAM ST.
TOTHILL ST.
Caxton Ho.
Cen. Hall
STOREY'S GATE
ANNES GA.
QUEEN ANNE'S GA.
BROADWAY
ST. JAMES'S PARK
Caxton Hall
CAXTON ST.
New Scotland Yard
VICTORIA ST.
Dept. of Trade & Industry
GREAT SMITH ST.
DEAN'S YARD
Westminster Sch.
The Cloisters
The Close
Abbey Garden
BUCKINGHAM GATE
PALACE ST.
PETTY FRANCE
VANDON ST.
BREWER'S GN.
BUTLER PL.
CARDINAL PL.
Dept. for Transport
Fitness First
ST. JAMES'S CT.
OLD PALACE YD.
ABBEY ORCHARD ST.
ORCHARD ST.
A
B
C
D
E
1
2
3
4
5
6
7
6
11
18

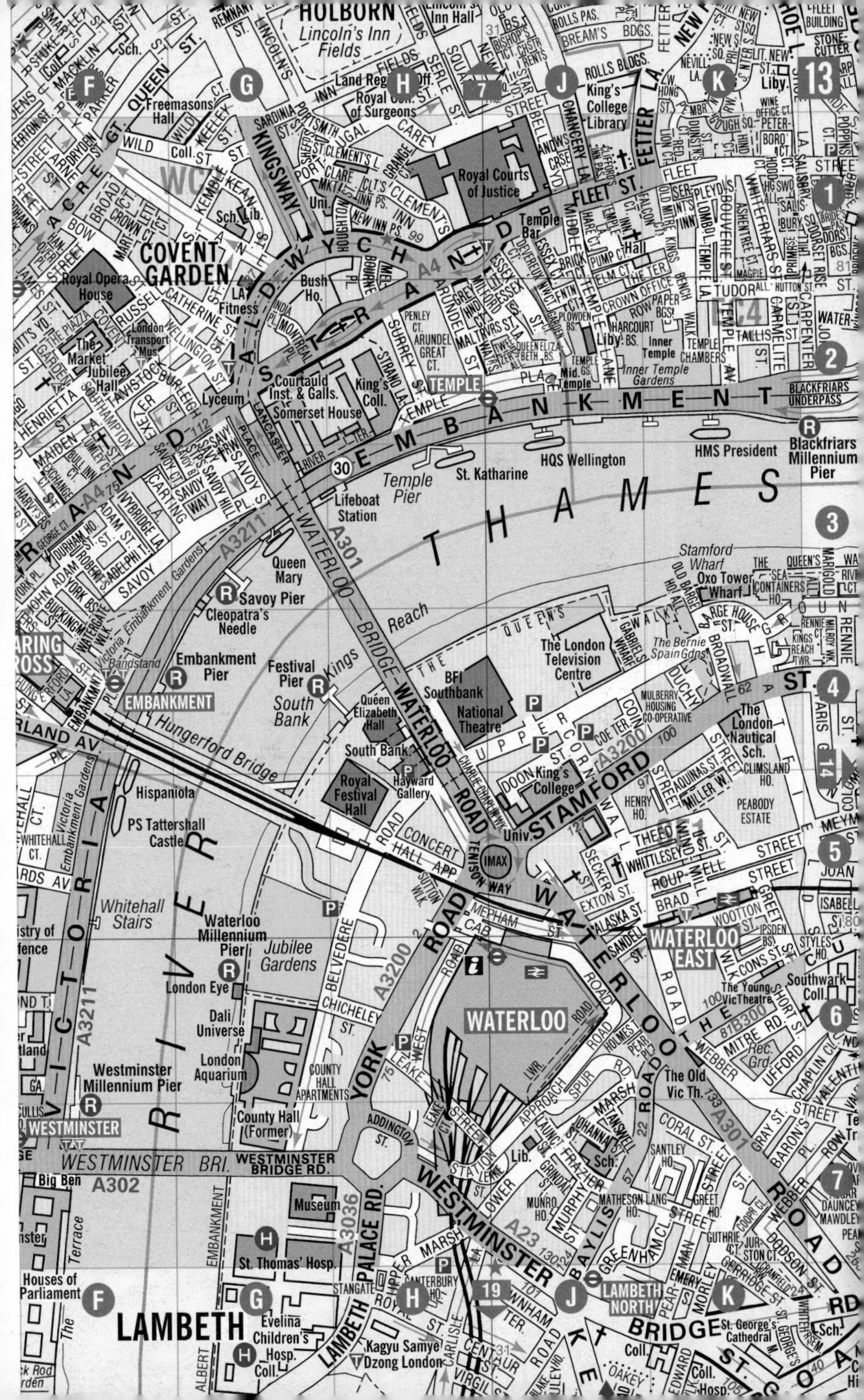

HOLBORN
Lincoln's Inn Fields
Royal Courts of Justice
King's College Library
FLEET ST.
COVENT GARDEN
Royal Opera House
KINGSWAY
ALDWYCH
STRAND
Somerset House
Courtauld Inst. & Galls.
TEMPLE
Inner Temple Gardens
EMBANKMENT
BLACKFRIARS UNDERPASS
Blackfriars Millennium Pier
HMS President
HQS Wellington
Temple Pier
St. Katharine
Lifeboat Station
THAMES
Queen Mary
Savoy Pier
Cleopatra's Needle
Embankment Pier
Festival Pier
South Bank
Oxo Tower Wharf
The London Television Centre
BFI Southbank
National Theatre
Queen Elizabeth Hall
Royal Festival Hall
Hayward Gallery
Hungerford Bridge
Hispaniola
PS Tattershall Castle
Whitehall Stairs
Waterloo Millennium Pier
Jubilee Gardens
London Eye
Dali Universe
London Aquarium
Westminster Millennium Pier
County Hall (Former)
WESTMINSTER
WESTMINSTER BRIDGE RD.
Big Ben
Houses of Parliament
LAMBETH
St. Thomas' Hosp.
Evelina Children's Hosp.
Museum
WATERLOO
WATERLOO EAST
The Old Vic Th.
The Young Vic Theatre
Southwark Coll.
LAMBETH NORTH
St. George's Cathedral
Kagyu Samye Dzong London
VICTORIA EMBANKMENT
RIVER
STAMFORD ST.
WATERLOO BRIDGE
WATERLOO ROAD
YORK ROAD
WESTMINSTER BRIDGE
A4
A301
A3200
A3211
A302
A23
A3036
EMBANKMENT
13
14
19

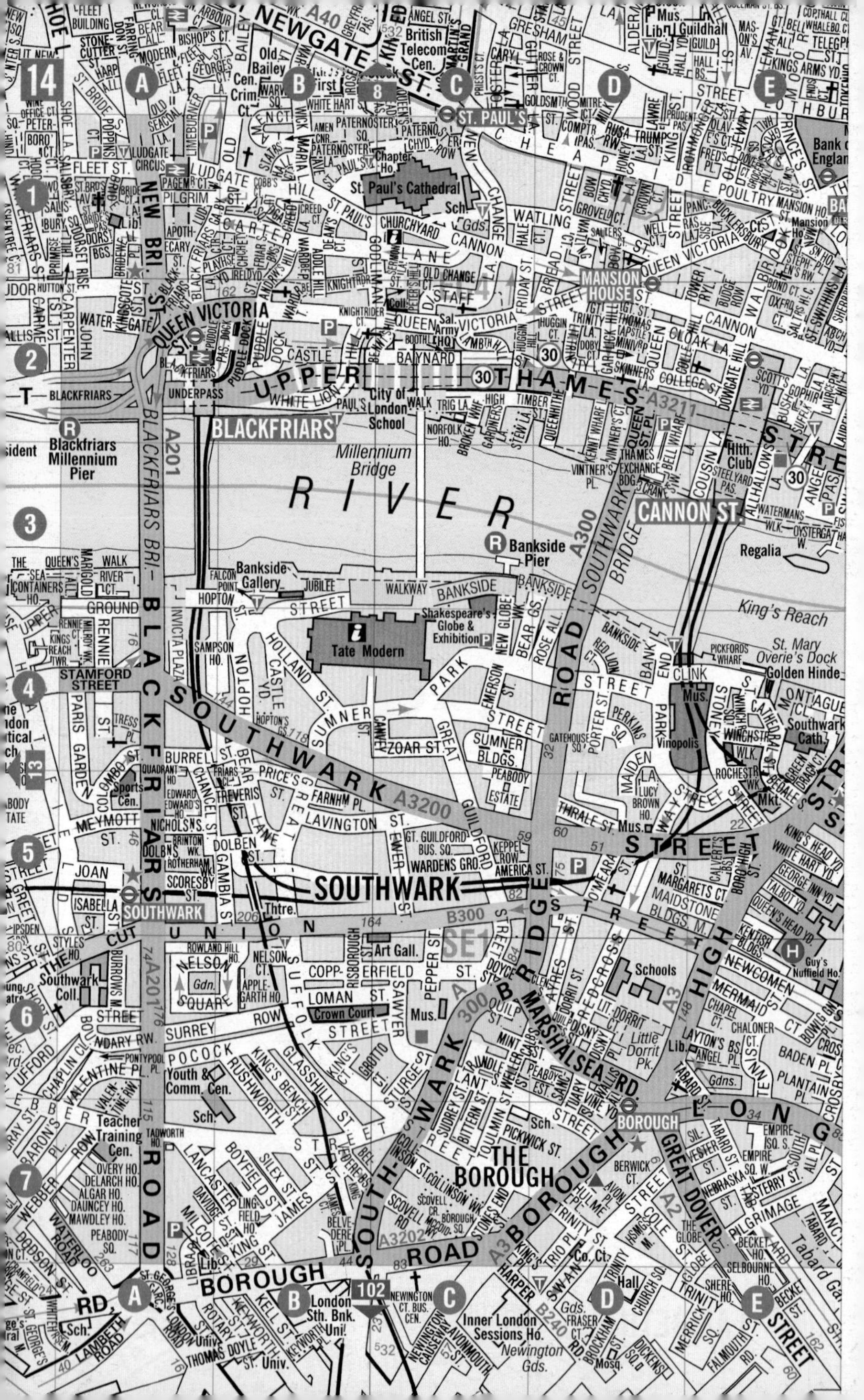
14
A
B
C
D
E
1
2
3
4
5
6
7
8
13
102
NEWGATE ST.
Old Bailey
Cen. Crim. Ct.
British Telecom Cen.
ST. PAUL'S
St. Paul's Cathedral
Chapter Ho.
CHEAPSIDE
POULTRY
Bank of England
MANSION HOUSE
QUEEN VICTORIA ST.
CANNON ST.
LUDGATE CIRCUS
FLEET ST.
NEW BRI. ST.
BLACKFRIARS
UNDERPASS
UPPER THAMES ST.
City of London School
Blackfriars Millennium Pier
Millennium Bridge
RIVER
Bankside Pier
Bankside Gallery
HOPTON STREET
BANKSIDE
Shakespeare's Globe & Exhibition
Tate Modern
King's Reach
St. Mary Overie's Dock
Golden Hinde
CLINK STREET
Vinopolis
Southwark Cath.
SOUTHWARK BRIDGE
SOUTHWARK BRIDGE ROAD
A300
A3200
SOUTHWARK ST.
SOUTHWARK
STAMFORD STREET
BLACKFRIARS ROAD
A201
UNION STREET
THE CUT
Southwark Coll.
Art Gall.
Crown Court
MARSHALSEA RD.
BOROUGH HIGH STREET
BOROUGH
LONG LANE
Guy's Nuffield Ho.
Schools
Little Dorrit Pk.
Youth & Comm. Cen.
Teacher Training Cen.
THE BOROUGH
BOROUGH ROAD
GREAT DOVER ST.
A2
A3
A3202
SE1
London Sth. Bnk. Uni.
Inner London Sessions Ho.
Newington Gds.
LAMBETH ROAD
WATERLOO ROAD
ST. GEORGE'S CIRCUS
Regalia

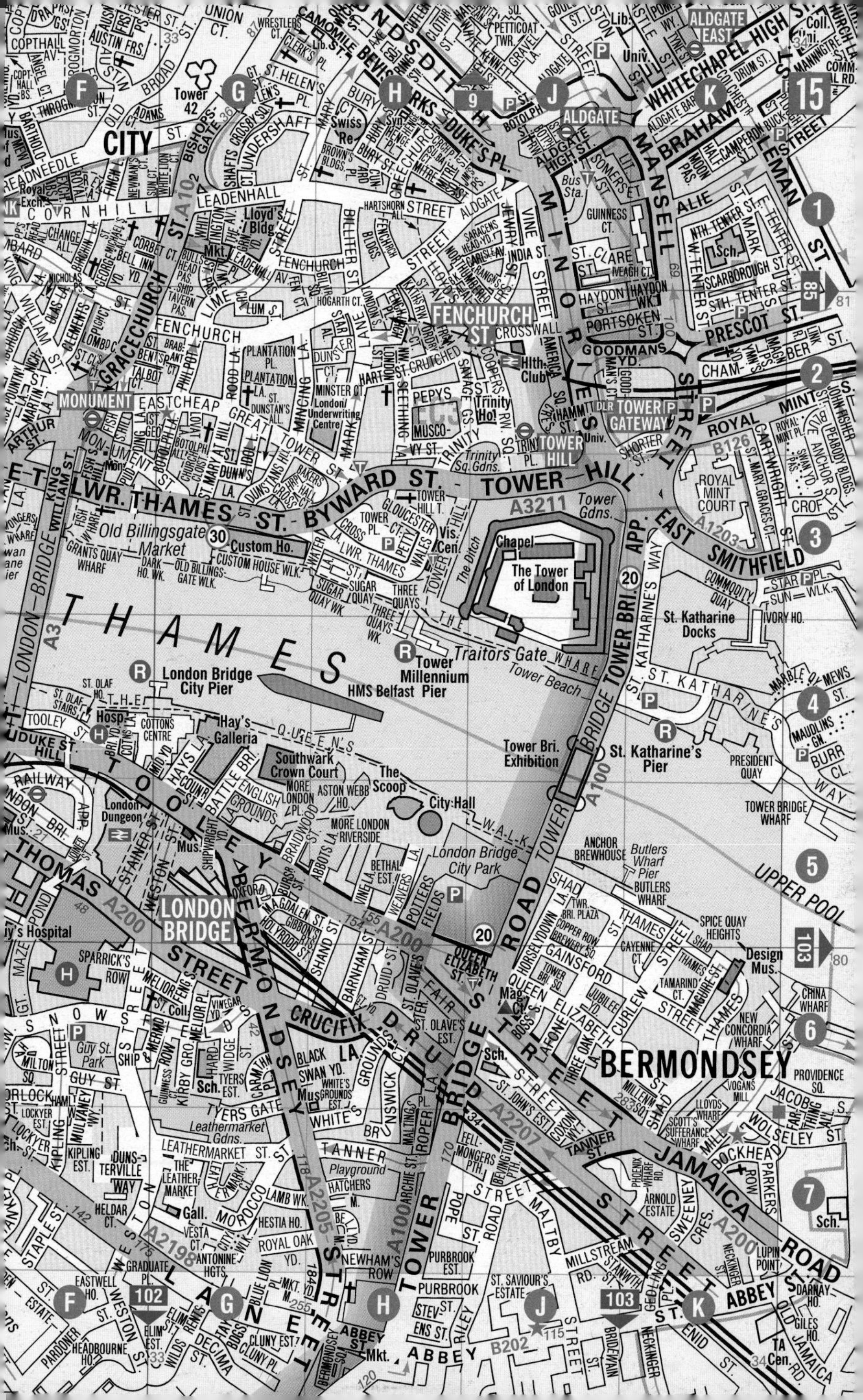

15
F
G
H
J
K
9
1
2
3
4
5
6
7
85
81
103
80
102
CITY
Tower 42
Swiss Re
ALDGATE EAST
ALDGATE
WHITECHAPEL HIGH ST.
BRAHAM
MANSELL
LEMAN ST.
MINORIES
PRESCOT ST.
ALIE
LEADENHALL
Lloyd's Bldg
FENCHURCH
FENCHURCH ST.
GRACECHURCH
MONUMENT
EASTCHEAP
CORNHILL
THREADNEEDLE ST.
BISHOPSGATE
HOUNDSDITCH
DUKE'S PL.
EC3
TOWER HILL
TOWER GATEWAY
ROYAL MINT ST.
ROYAL MINT COURT
EAST SMITHFIELD
LWR. THAMES ST.
BYWARD ST.
Old Billingsgate Market
Custom Ho.
The Tower of London
Chapel
Traitors Gate
Tower Beach
St. Katharine Docks
St. Katharine's Pier
THAMES
London Bridge City Pier
HMS Belfast
Tower Millennium Pier
Hay's Galleria
Southwark Crown Court
The Scoop
City Hall
Tower Bri. Exhibition
TOWER BRIDGE
LONDON BRIDGE
TOOLEY ST.
London Dungeon
Guy's Hospital
ST. THOMAS ST.
BERMONDSEY ST.
CRUCIFIX LA.
DRUID ST.
TOWER BRIDGE ROAD
JAMAICA ROAD
BERMONDSEY
UPPER POOL
Butlers Wharf Pier
SHAD THAMES
Design Mus.
Guy St. Park
Leathermarket Gdns.
LONG LANE
ABBEY ST.
TANNER ST.
GRANGE WALK
A3
A10
A100
A200
A2198
A2205
A2207
A3211
A1203
B126
B202

16
KENSINGTON GORE
Royal Geographical Society
Royal Coll. of Art
Royal Albert Hall
Imperial Coll.
KNIGHTSBRIDGE
10
Harrods
Royal College of Music
Imperial Coll. of Science, Technology & Medicine
Science Mus.
Natural History Museum
Victoria & Albert Museum
Brompton Oratory
CROMWELL RD.
CROMWELL PLACE
THURLOE
Ismaili Cen.
SOUTH KENSINGTON
BROMPTON
LA Fitness
BROMPTON ROAD
OLD BROMPTON RD.
The Royal Marsden Hosp. (Fulham)
Ryl. Brompton Hosp. (Fulham)
CHELSEA
Royal Brompton Hospital
Thamesbrook
Chelsea Cin.
Chelsea Old Town Hall
Sports Cen.
Coll. of Art & Design
FULHAM ROAD
KING'S ROAD
SLOANE AVENUE
KINGS WALK SHOP. CEN.
Carlyle's House
Chelsea Physic Garden
CHELSEA
Cadogan Pier
100

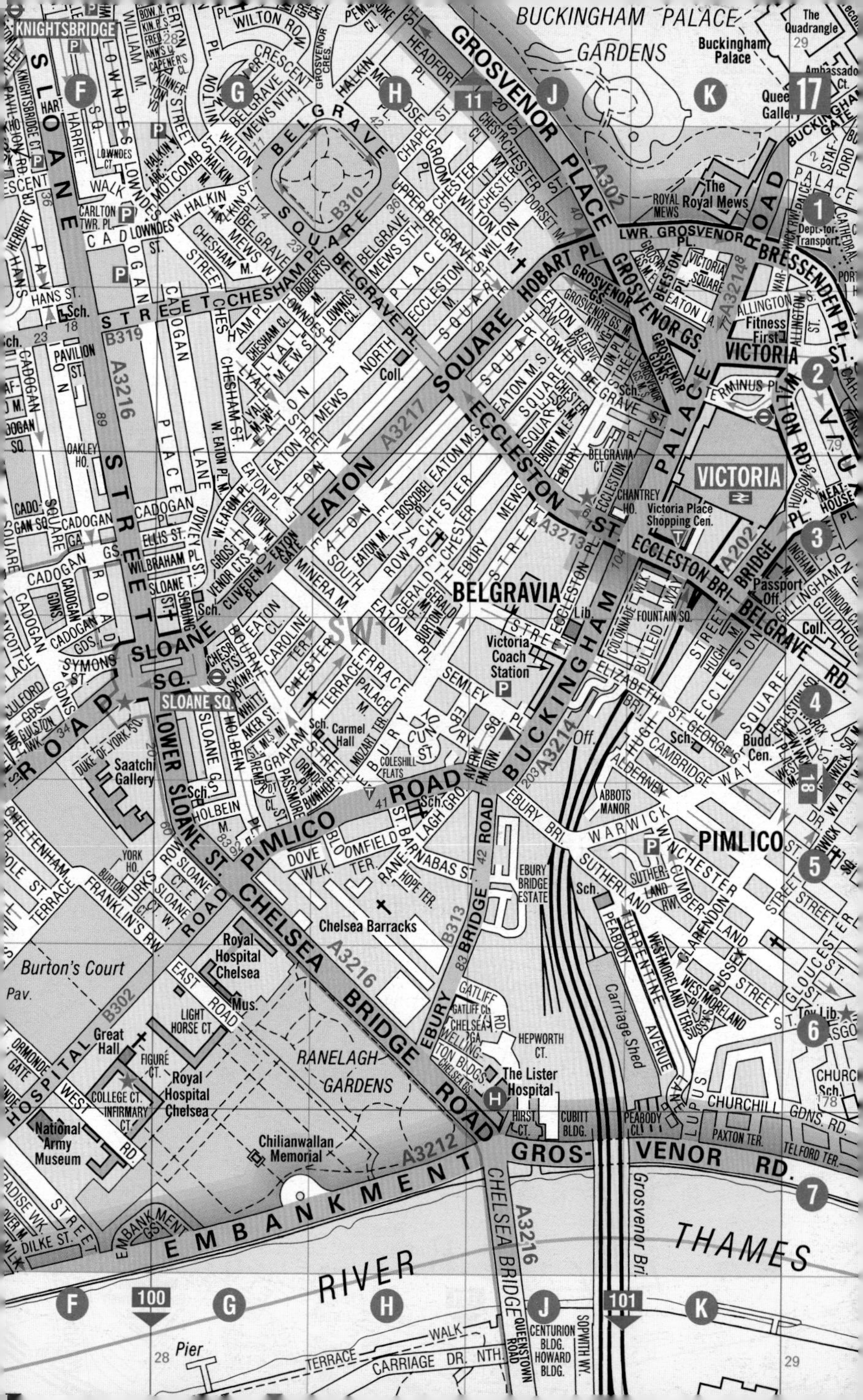

KNIGHTSBRIDGE
BUCKINGHAM PALACE GARDENS
Buckingham Palace
The Quadrangle
Queen's Gallery
17
11
18
100
101
F
G
H
J
K
1
2
3
4
5
6
7
GROSVENOR PLACE
A302
BELGRAVE SQUARE
B310
SLOANE STREET
A3216
B319
CHESHAM PL.
CHESHAM STREET
LOWNDES SQ.
LOWNDES ST.
CADOGAN PLACE
CADOGAN SQUARE
CADOGAN GDNS.
EATON SQUARE
A3217
EATON PLACE
EATON TERRACE
ECCLESTON SQUARE
ECCLESTON ST.
A3213
BELGRAVE PL.
UPPER BELGRAVE ST.
HOBART PL.
LWR. GROSVENOR PL.
GROSVENOR GDNS.
The Royal Mews
ROYAL MEWS
BRESSENDEN PL.
BUCKINGHAM PALACE ROAD
A3214
VICTORIA
Victoria Place Shopping Cen.
ECCLESTON BRI.
A202
BELGRAVE RD.
TERMINUS PL.
WILTON RD.
Fitness First
Dept. for Transport
BELGRAVIA
Victoria Coach Station
SW1
ELIZABETH ST.
CHESTER ROW
EBURY STREET
SEMLEY PL.
BOURNE ST.
SLOANE SQ.
SLOANE SQ.
Saatchi Gallery
DUKE OF YORK SQ.
KING'S ROAD
LOWER SLOANE ST.
HOLBEIN PL.
PIMLICO ROAD
Carmel Hall
EBURY BRIDGE ROAD
B313
EBURY BRIDGE ESTATE
WARWICK WAY
PIMLICO
ST. GEORGE'S DR.
CAMBRIDGE ST.
ALDERNEY ST.
ABBOTS MANOR
WINCHESTER ST.
SUTHERLAND ST.
CLARENDON ST.
SUSSEX ST.
GLOUCESTER ST.
WESTMORELAND TER.
TURPENTINE LANE
PEABODY AVENUE
LUPUS ST.
CHURCHILL GDNS. RD.
Carriage Shed
Chelsea Barracks
CHELSEA BRIDGE ROAD
Royal Hospital Chelsea
Mus.
Burton's Court
Pav.
ROYAL HOSPITAL ROAD
B302
Great Hall
LIGHT HORSE CT.
FIGURE CT.
COLLEGE CT.
INFIRMARY CT.
National Army Museum
EAST ROAD
WEST RD.
RANELAGH GARDENS
Chilianwallah Memorial
The Lister Hospital
HEPWORTH CT.
GATLIFF RD.
FRANKLIN'S RW.
TURKS RW.
CHELTENHAM TERRACE
YORK HO.
BURTON
GROSVENOR RD.
A3212
EMBANKMENT
CHELSEA EMBANKMENT
DILKE ST.
Grosvenor Bri.
CHELSEA BRIDGE
RIVER THAMES
Pier
CARRIAGE DR. NTH.
QUEENSTOWN ROAD
CENTURION BLDG.
HOWARD BLDG.
SOPWITH WY.
28
29

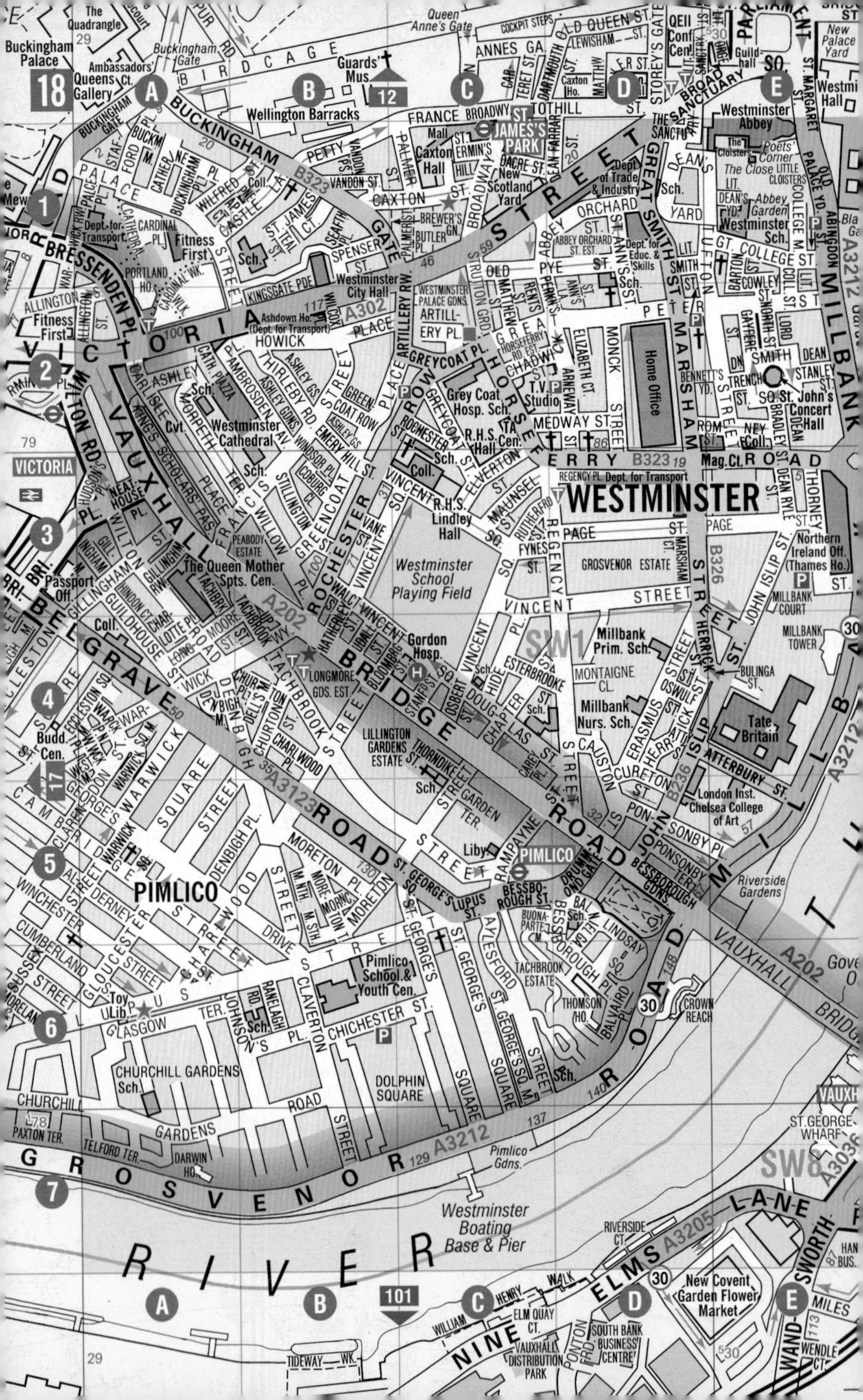

18
Buckingham Palace
The Quadrangle
Queens Gallery
Ambassadors' Ct.
Buckingham Gate
BIRDCAGE
Guards' Mus.
12
Queen Anne's Gate
COCKPIT STEPS
OLD QUEEN ST.
ANNES GA.
LEWISHAM ST.
QEII Conf. Cen.
PARLIAMENT
Guildhall
New Palace Yard
Westmr. Hall
Wellington Barracks
FRANCE
BROADWY
ST. JAMES'S PARK
TOTHILL ST.
BROAD SANCTUARY
THE SANCTUARY
Westminster Abbey
The Cloisters
Poets' Corner
The Close
LITTLE CLOISTERS
Abbey Garden
DEAN'S YARD
Westminster Sch.
BUCKINGHAM
B323
PETTY
VANDON ST.
CAXTON
Caxton Hall
Mall
New Scotland Yard
DACRE ST.
Dept. of Trade & Industry
STREET
ABBEY ORCHARD ST.
GREAT SMITH ST.
Dept. for Educ. & Skills
Dept. for Transport
PALACE PL.
CARDINAL PL.
Fitness First
BRESSENDEN PL.
ALLINGTON ST.
PORTLAND HO.
KINGSGATE PDE.
Westminster City Hall
Ashdown Ho. (Dept. for Transport)
A302
VICTORIA
HOWICK PLACE
ARTILLERY PL.
WESTMINSTER PALACE GDNS.
OLD PYE ST.
GREAT PETER ST.
Home Office
MARSHAM STREET
SMITH SQ.
St. John's Concert Hall
MILLBANK
A3212
VICTORIA
WILTON RD.
VAUXHALL BRIDGE ROAD
ASHLEY PL.
Westminster Cathedral
Sch.
AMBROSDEN AV.
GREYCOAT PL.
Grey Coat Hosp. Sch.
T.V. Studio
MEDWAY ST.
HORSEFERRY ROAD
B323
R.H.S. Hall
R.H.S. Lindley Hall
REGENCY PL.
Dept. for Transport
WESTMINSTER
PAGE ST.
GROSVENOR ESTATE
Northern Ireland Off. (Thames Ho.)
VINCENT SQ.
Westminster School Playing Field
VINCENT STREET
SW1
B326
JOHN ISLIP ST.
MILLBANK COURT
MILLBANK TOWER
Millbank Prim. Sch.
MONTAIGNE CL.
Millbank Nurs. Sch.
The Queen Mother Spts. Cen.
PEABODY ESTATE
Passport Off.
BELGRAVE ROAD
A202
Gordon Hosp.
LONGMORE GDS. EST.
LILLINGTON GARDENS ESTATE
A3123
ROCHESTER ROW
Tate Britain
ATTERBURY ST.
London Inst. Chelsea College of Art
Riverside Gardens
PIMLICO
Liby.
BESSBOROUGH GDNS.
PIMLICO
WARWICK SQUARE
ST. GEORGE'S DRIVE
WINCHESTER STREET
CUMBERLAND STREET
LUPUS STREET
Pimlico School & Youth Cen.
CHICHESTER ST.
TACHBROOK ESTATE
CHURCHILL GARDENS
DOLPHIN SQUARE
CROWN REACH
VAUXHALL BRIDGE
GROSVENOR ROAD
A3212
Pimlico Gdns.
DARWIN HO.
PAXTON TER.
TELFORD TER.
Westminster Boating Base & Pier
RIVER
SW8
NINE ELMS LANE
A3205
RIVERSIDE CT.
New Covent Garden Flower Market
ELM QUAY CT.
VAUXHALL DISTRIBUTION PARK
SOUTH BANK BUSINESS CENTRE
WANDSWORTH
MILES
ST. GEORGE WHARF
TIDEWAY WK.
101
17
A B C D E
1 2 3 4 5 6 7

19
F
G
H
J
K
1
2
3
4
5
6
7
WESTMINSTER BRI.
WESTMINSTER BRIDGE RD.
Big Ben
Houses of Parliament
The Terrace
Museum
St. Thomas' Hosp.
Evelina Children's Hosp.
Coll.
EMBANKMENT
ALBERT
STANGATE
UPPER MARSH
CANTERBURY HO.
ROYAL ST.
WEST-MINSTER BRIDGE RD.
BAYLIS RD.
GREENHAM CL.
LAMBETH NORTH
A23
BRIDGE
St. George's Cathedral
ST. GEORGE'S ROAD
Kagyu Samye Dzong London
CENTAUR ST.
VIRGIL ST.
NEWNHAM TER.
LAMBETH
SE1
COSSER ST.
KING EDWARD WLK.
OAKEY LA.
Coll. Hosp.
BARKHAM T.
Victoria Tower
King's College London (St. Thomas' Campus)
ARCHBISHOP'S PARK
Marine Institute
PENHURST PL.
YORK HO.
CARLISLE LA.
HERCULES RD.
SIDFORD PL.
BRIANT HO.
A3203
LAMBETH TOWERS
Imperial War Museum
Geraldine Mary Harmsworth Park
HARMSWORTH MEWS
Lambeth Palace
Museum of Garden History
Youth Cen.
LAMBETH RD.
BROOK DRIVE
WEDGWOOD HO.
Lambeth Pier
LAMBETH BRI.
A3203
Police H.Q.
JUXON ST.
WALNUT TREE WLK.
WALCOT SQUARE
A3036
PARLIAMENT VW.
OLD PARADISE ST.
GABRIEL HO.
Rec. Grd.
FITZALAN ST.
ST. OLAVE'S MANS.
CULPEPPER CT.
BISHOP'S GDNS.
ST. MARY'S WLK.
SULLIVAN RD.
THAMES
Fire Brigade H.Q.
LAMBETH HIGH ST.
WHITGIFT ST.
LOLLARD ST.
TOMKYNS HO.
KENNINGTON ROAD
A23
Comm. Care Cen.
RENFREW RD.
DRYDEN CT.
KEMPSFORD RD.
EMBANKMENT
BLACK PRINCE ROAD
SE11
MALAM CT.
EMMANUEL HO.
WINCOTT ST.
GILBERT RD.
VANBRUGH CT.
KNIGHT'S WK.
Millbank Millennium Pier
SALAMANCA ST.
RANDALL RD.
CANNON HO.
GROOME HO.
FORTUNE HO.
RUPERT HO.
REEDWORTH ST.
HURLEY HO.
30
CHESTER WAY
TERRITORIAL HO.
EBENEZER HO.
FAIRFORD HO.
102
DENNY CRES.
RESTORMEL HO.
HOTSPUR ST.
MOUNTAIN HO.
BLAND HO.
VAUXHALL ST.
SANCROFT ST.
KENNINGTON LANE
A3204
ISABELLA ST.
OTHELLO CL.
TINWORTH ST.
JONATHAN ST.
PENINSULA HEIGHTS
GLASSHOUSE WALK
ORSETT ST.
KENNINGTON ROAD
Liby
FOWEY HO.
CALSTOCK HO.
CORNWALL SQ.
CARRICK HO.
Sch.
All Nations Centre
VAUXHALL WALK
LAUD ST.
CAMELFORD HO.
COURTENAY ST.
CARDIGAN ST.
STABLES WAY
CLEAVER ST.
CLEAVER SQUARE
Art Sch.
KENNINGS WAY
Spring Gardens
VAUXHALL
DARLEY HO.
TYERS TER.
DOLLAND ST.
WAYLETT HO.
WINDMILL ROW
METHLEY ST.
RAVENSDON ST.
RADCOT ST.
A3
KENNINGTON PARK RD.
VAUXHALL
KENNINGTON LANE
IMPERIAL CT.
HAROLD PL.
MONTFORD PL.
A3204
Superstore
DURHAM ST.
Gas Works
WESTMINSTER BUSINESS SQ.
HARLEYFORD RD.
BONDWAY
SHERWIN HO.
STANNARY ST.
KENNINGTON
KENNINGTON PARK PL.
DE LAUNE ST.
HARMSWORTH ST.
COBALT SQ.
ROSEWOOD HO.
VAUXHALL GRO.
OVAL MANS.
KILNER HO.
PEGASUS PL.
CLAYTON ST.
BOWLING GREEN ST.
LOHMANN HO.
KENNINGTON PARK
Surrey County Cricket Club (The Oval Cricket Grd.)
LANGLEY LA.
BONNINGTON SQ.
PARK MNS.
EBBISHAM DRIVE
KENNINGTON OVAL
LOCKWOOD HO.
LAWN LA.
BANNERMAN HO.
101
Vauxhall Park
St. Peter's Residence
WISDEN HO.
MEADOW RD.
CLAYLANDS RD.
ROTHESAY CT.
ALVERSTONE HO.
102
BRIXTON RD.
HARLEYFORD ST.
SOUTH LAMBETH RD.
FENTIMAN ROAD
RUDOLF PL.
ST. AGNES PL.
Aspen Ho.
MEADCROFT
KENNINGTN PK. GS.

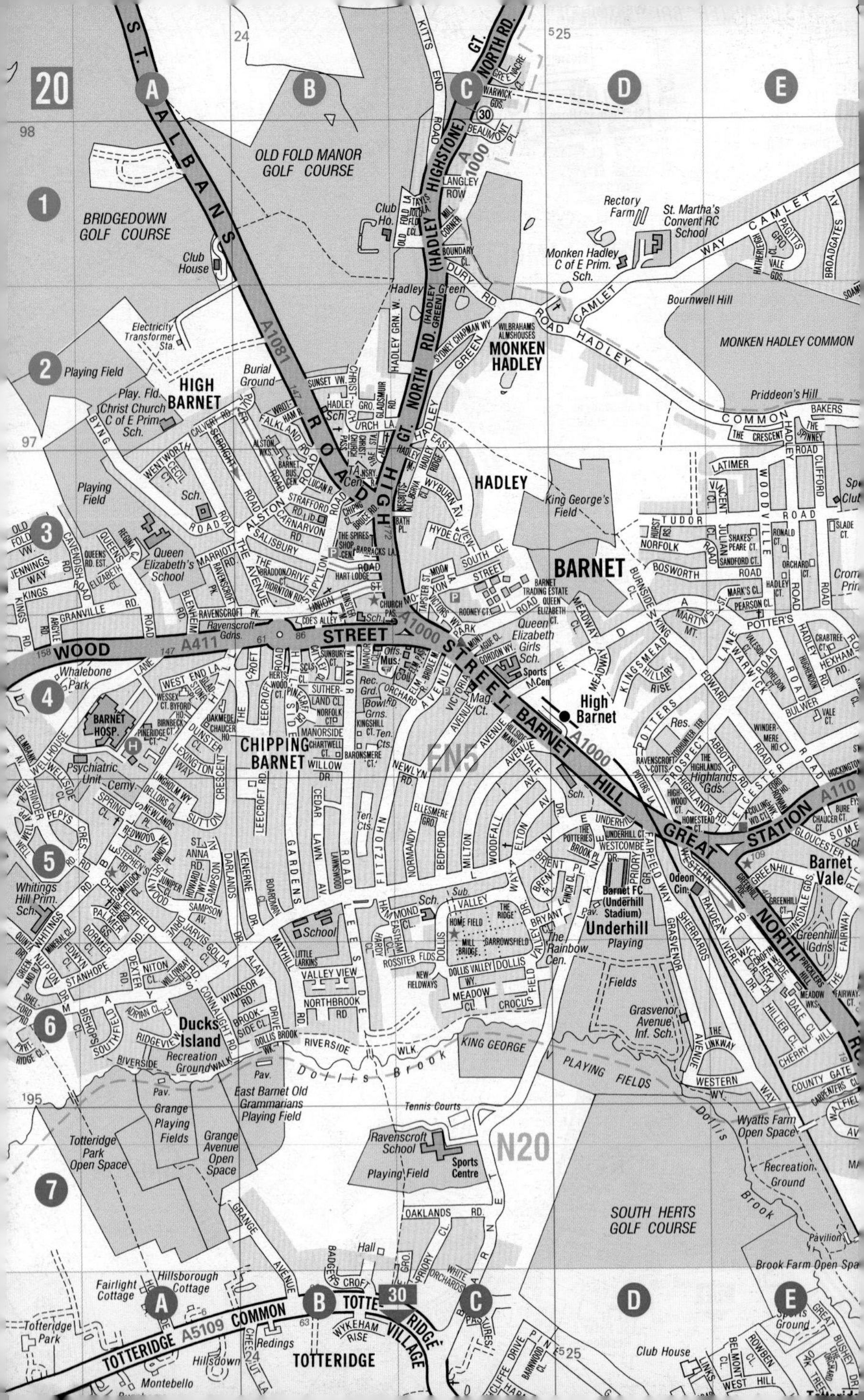
20
A
B
C
D
E
1
2
3
4
5
6
7
98
97
195
24
525
ST. ALBANS ROAD
A1081
GT. NORTH RD.
HIGHSTONE (HADLEY HIGHSTONE)
GT. NORTH RD. (HADLEY GREEN)
A1000
HIGH STREET
WOOD STREET
A411
BARNET HILL
GREAT NORTH ROAD
STATION ROAD
A110
OLD FOLD MANOR GOLF COURSE
BRIDGEDOWN GOLF COURSE
Club House
Club Ho.
Electricity Transformer Sta.
Playing Field
Burial Ground
HIGH BARNET
Play. Fld.
Christ Church C of E Prim. Sch.
Hadley Green
MONKEN HADLEY
WILBRAHAMS ALMSHOUSES
Rectory Farm
St. Martha's Convent RC School
Monken Hadley C of E Prim. Sch.
CAMLET WAY
HADLEY ROAD
Bournwell Hill
MONKEN HADLEY COMMON
Priddeon's Hill
HADLEY COMMON
BAKERS
THE CRESCENT
THE SPINNEY
HADLEY
King George's Field
BARNET
BARNET TRADING ESTATE
Queen Elizabeth Girls Sch.
Sports Cen.
High Barnet
Queen Elizabeth's School
CHIPPING BARNET
EN5
Whalebone Park
BARNET HOSP.
Psychiatric Unit
Cemy.
Whitings Hill Prim. Sch.
Ravenscroft Gdns.
Highlands Gds.
Barnet FC (Underhill Stadium)
Underhill Playing Fields
The Rainbow Cen.
Odeon Cin.
Barnet Vale
Greenhill Gdns.
Ducks Island Recreation Ground
KING GEORGE PLAYING FIELDS
Dollis Brook
Grasvenor Avenue Inf. Sch.
Grange Playing Fields
East Barnet Old Grammarians Playing Field
Grange Avenue Open Space
Totteridge Park Open Space
Tennis Courts
Ravenscroft School
Sports Centre
Playing Field
N20
Wyatts Farm Open Space
Recreation Ground
SOUTH HERTS GOLF COURSE
Pavilion
Brook Farm Open Space
Fairlight Cottage
Hillsborough Cottage
Totteridge Park
Redings
Hillsdown
Montebello
TOTTERIDGE COMMON
A5109
TOTTERIDGE
TOTTERIDGE VILLAGE
30
Hall
Club House
Sports Ground

21
22
31
Hadley Wood
HADLEY WOOD
Lawn Tennis Club
GABLES LODGE
LANCASTER AVENUE
WEST CRESCENT
Great Broadgates Hill
BEECH HILL
WALMAR CL.
Club House
BEECH HILL PARK
HADLEY WOOD GOLF COURSE
Monken Mead Brook
Green Brook
Fish Pond
Hadley Wood Nature Reserve
Sewits Hill
Newmans Hill
HADLEY WOOD RD.
Beech Hill Lake
TUDOR PARK GOLF COURSE
Playing Field East Barnet Sch. 5th. & 6th. Form Centre
Livingstone Prim. Sch.
Play Fld.
COCKFOSTERS ROAD
A111
ENFIELD CHASE
Ash Wood
FERNY HILL
Ferny Hill Cottage
Ferny Hill Farm
Fernyhill Wood
Rough Lot
TRENT PARK (Country Park)
Seedfield Spinney
Water Tower
Oak Wood
Reservoir (covered)
Picnic Area
Monument
Church Wood
Cemetery
FAIRGREEN
GAMES ROAD
Playing Fields
EN4
NEW BARNET
Recreation Ground
Pymmes
COCKFOSTERS
Cockfosters
MOUNT PLEASANT
EAST BARNET
Pleasure Ground
Lib.
CAT HILL
A110
BRAMLEY RD.
Chicken Shed Theatre
Middlesex University
Mus.
Bramley Sports Grd.
Prim. Sch.
Saracens Rugby Football Club
Oaktree Sch.
CHASE SIDE
Southgate Sch. & Sports Cen.
Oakhill College
Oak Hill Woods Nature Reserve
East Barnet Sch.
Play. Fld.
EAST BARNET RD.
BROOKHILL RD.
New Barnet
LA Fitness
Lyonsdown
LONGMORE AV.
B193
Bandstand Playground
OAK HILL PARK
N14
Miniature Golf Course
Pavilion
Bowling Green
Monkfrith Prim. Sch.
Tennis Courts
Oakleigh Park
OAKLEIGH PARK
Playing Field
WHETSTONE
A1000
Playing Field
South Barnet
Pool
Sch.
Warehou
Works
CHANDOS AV.
ALVERSTONE
NORTHUMBERLAND
Oak Hill

TRENT PARK (COUNTRY PARK)
ENFIELD CHASE
Camlet Moat
Moat Wood
Obelisk
Picnic Area
Park Farm
Park Farm Cottages
Reservoir
Parkside Farm
Pumping Station
Vicarage Farm
Wolverton
Camlet Hill
Ride Wood
Leeging Beech Gutter
Fish Pond
Icehouse Wood
Williams Wood
Salmon's Brook
Hog Hill
Noddins Well
Middlesex University (Trent Park Campus)
College Ho.
Shaws Wood Cottages
Shaws Wood
Lodge
The Rookery
Rookery Cotts.
Miniature Rifle Range
Merryhills Brook
Sports Ground
TRENT PARK GOLF COURSE
EN4
Triangular Wood
Trent Park Stables
East Pole Cottages
Trent Park Sports Centre
Depot
Oakwood
Southgate Sch. & Sports Cen.
Chicken Shed Theatre
Bramley Sports Grd.
De Bohun Prim. Sch.
Saracens Rugby Football Club
Oaktree Sch.
Oakhill College
ENFIELD ROAD A110
BRAMLEY ROAD
CHASE SIDE A111
Highlands Village
Nursing Home
Boxer's Lake
Superstore
N14
OAKWOOD PARK
OAKWOOD
Yacht Pond
GROVELANDS PARK
Boating Lake
Bowling Green
Tennis Courts
NORTH LONDON PRIORY HOSP.
Southgate
Osidge Prim. Sch.
Leisure Cen.
Prim. Sch.
21
32

23
FORTY HILL
CHASE FARM HOSPITAL
KING'S OAK BMI HOSP?
CEMETERY
Gordon Hill
Chase Side
Enfield Chase
Enfield Town
ENFIELD TOWN
ENFIELD
EN1
EN2
World's End
ENFIELD GOLF COURSE
GRANGE PARK
Grange Park
BUSH HILL PARK GOLF COURSE
BUSH HILL PARK
Bush Hill Park
WINCHMORE HILL
Winchmore Hill
N21
N9
RIDGEWAY
WINDMILL HILL
SLADES HILL
SOUTHBURY ROAD
LONDON ROAD
VILLAGE RD.
RIDGE AV.
GREEN LANES
GT. CAMBRIDGE RD.
CHURCH ST.
BAKER ST.
SILVER ST.
A1005
A110
A105
A10
B154
F G H J K
1 2 3 4 5 6 7
24
33

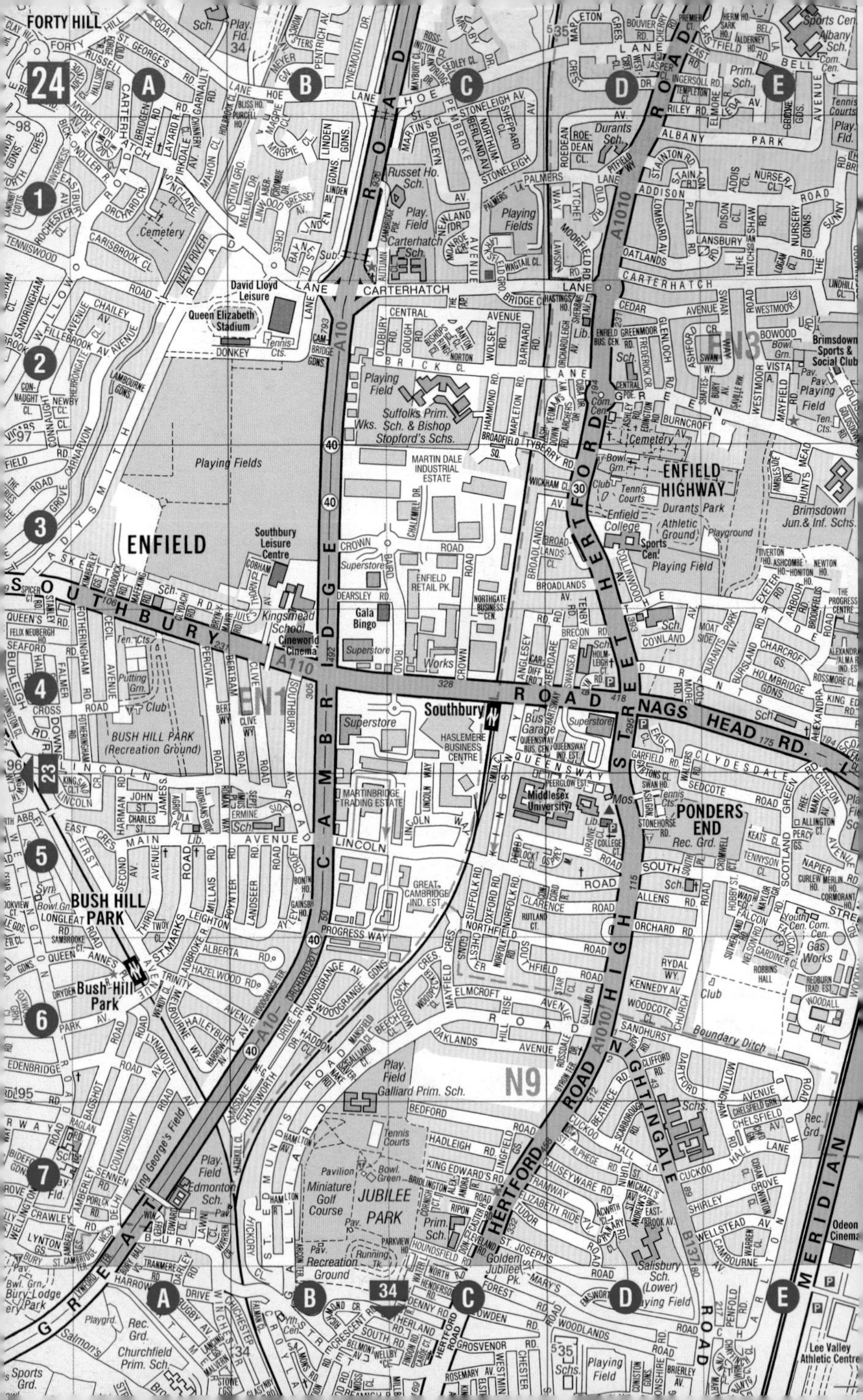
24
FORTY HILL
A
B
C
D
E
1
2
3
4
5
6
7
98
97
96
95
23
34
35
ENFIELD
ENFIELD HIGHWAY
PONDERS END
BUSH HILL PARK
EN1
EN3
N9
Cemetery
David Lloyd Leisure
Queen Elizabeth Stadium
Playing Fields
Southbury Leisure Centre
Kingsmead School
Cineworld Cinema
Gala Bingo
Superstore
MARTIN DALE INDUSTRIAL ESTATE
ENFIELD RETAIL PK.
NORTHGATE BUSINESS CEN.
HASLEMERE BUSINESS CENTRE
MARTINBRIDGE TRADING ESTATE
GREAT CAMBRIDGE IND. EST.
Southbury
Middlesex University
Suffolks Prim. Sch. & Bishop Stopford's Schs.
Russet Ho. Sch.
Carterhatch Sch.
Durants Sch.
Durants Park
Athletic Ground
Enfield College
Sports Cen.
Brimsdown Sports & Social Club
Brimsdown Jun.& Inf. Schs.
BUSH HILL PARK (Recreation Ground)
Putting Grn.
Bush Hill Park
Galliard Prim. Sch.
JUBILEE PARK
Miniature Golf Course
Pavilion
Recreation Ground
Edmonton Sch.
King George's Field
Bury Lodge Park
Churchfield Prim. Sch.
Salisbury Sch. (Lower)
Golden Jubilee Pk.
Odeon Cinema
Lee Valley Athletic Centre
Gas Works
Boundary Ditch
Rec. Grd.
SOUTHBURY ROAD
A110
A10
A1010
B137
GREAT CAMBRIDGE ROAD
HERTFORD ROAD
HIGH STREET
NAGS HEAD RD.
NIGHTINGALE ROAD
MERIDIAN
CARTERHATCH LANE
HOE LANE
ALBANY PARK AVENUE
LINCOLN ROAD
QUEENSWAY
PROGRESS WAY
GREEN STREET
DURANTS ROAD
SOUTH STREET
CARTERHATCH ROAD
LADYSMITH ROAD
NEW RIVER
BRICK CL.
CENTRAL AVENUE
CROWN ROAD
MAIN AVENUE
EAST FIRST CRES.
OAKLANDS AVENUE
HILL RISE ROAD
SOUTH ST.

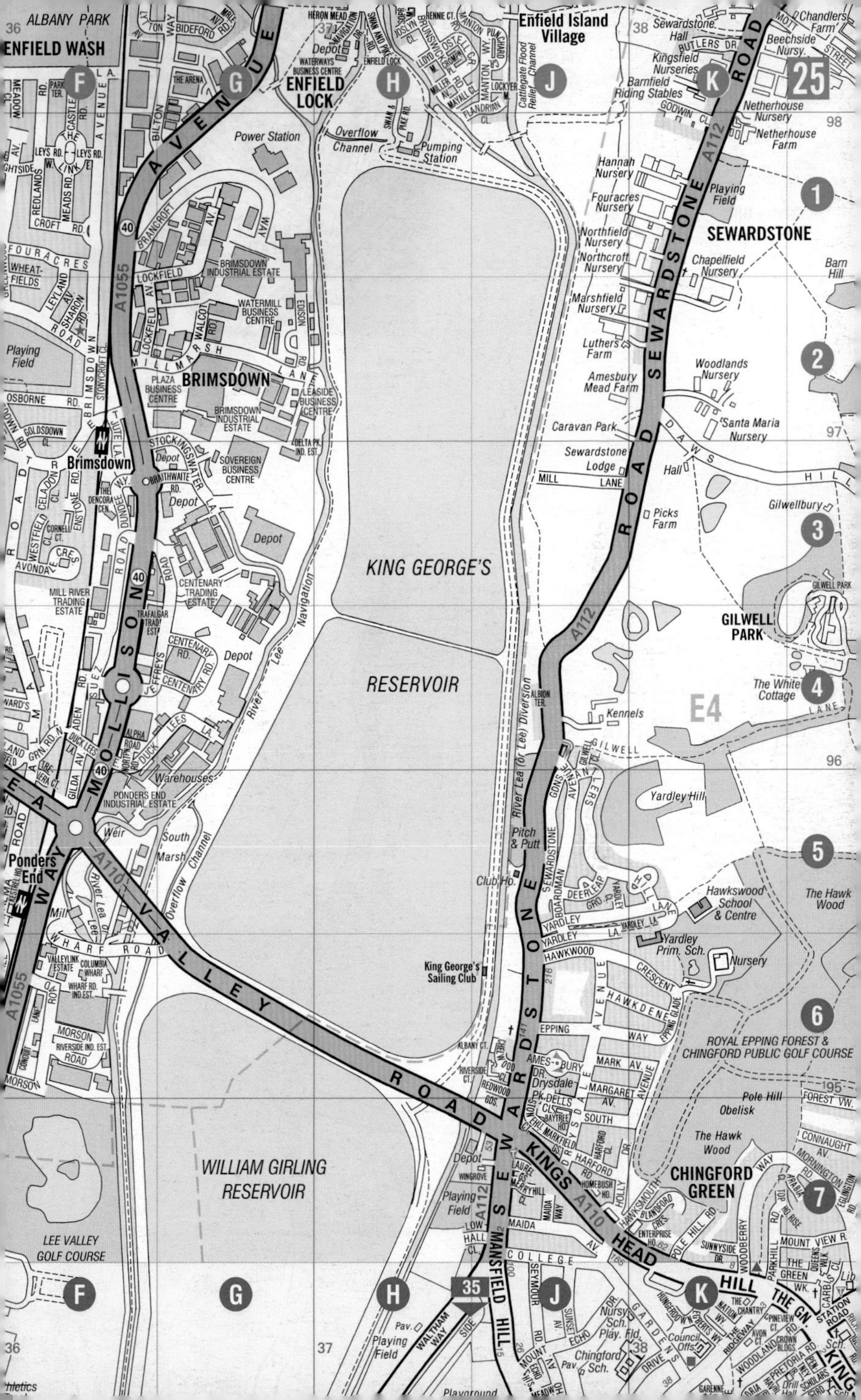

25
ALBANY PARK
ENFIELD WASH
Enfield Island Village
ENFIELD LOCK
Waterways Business Centre
Power Station
Overflow Channel
Pumping Station
Sewardstone Hall
Kingsfield Nurseries
Barnfield Riding Stables
Chandlers' Farm
Beechside Nursy.
Netherhouse Nursery
Netherhouse Farm
Hannah Nursery
Fouracres Nursery
Northfield Nursery
Northcroft Nursery
Marshfield Nursery
Luthers Farm
Amesbury Mead Farm
Caravan Park
Sewardstone Lodge
Picks Farm
Playing Field
SEWARDSTONE
Chapelfield Nursery
Barn Hill
Woodlands Nursery
Santa Maria Nursery
Gilwellbury
GILWELL PARK
The White Cottage
Kennels
Yardley Hill
E4
Hawkswood School & Centre
Yardley Prim. Sch.
Nursery
The Hawk Wood
ROYAL EPPING FOREST & CHINGFORD PUBLIC GOLF COURSE
Pole Hill Obelisk
The Hawk Wood
CHINGFORD GREEN
BRIMSDOWN INDUSTRIAL ESTATE
WATERMILL BUSINESS CENTRE
BRIMSDOWN
PLAZA BUSINESS CENTRE
LEASIDE BUSINESS CENTRE
SOVEREIGN BUSINESS CENTRE
Brimsdown
Depot
CENTENARY TRADING ESTATE
MILL RIVER TRADING ESTATE
Warehouses
PONDERS END INDUSTRIAL ESTATE
Ponders End
Weir
South Marsh
River Lee Navigation
KING GEORGE'S RESERVOIR
River Lea (or Lee) Diversion
Pitch & Putt
Club Ho.
King George's Sailing Club
MOLLISON AVENUE
LEA VALLEY ROAD
SEWARDSTONE ROAD
KINGS HEAD HILL
A1055
A110
A112
WILLIAM GIRLING RESERVOIR
LEE VALLEY GOLF COURSE
VALLEYLINK ESTATE
COLUMBIA WHARF
WHARF RD. IND. EST.
RIVERSIDE IND. EST.
MANSFIELD HILL
35
Chingford Sch.
Council Offs.

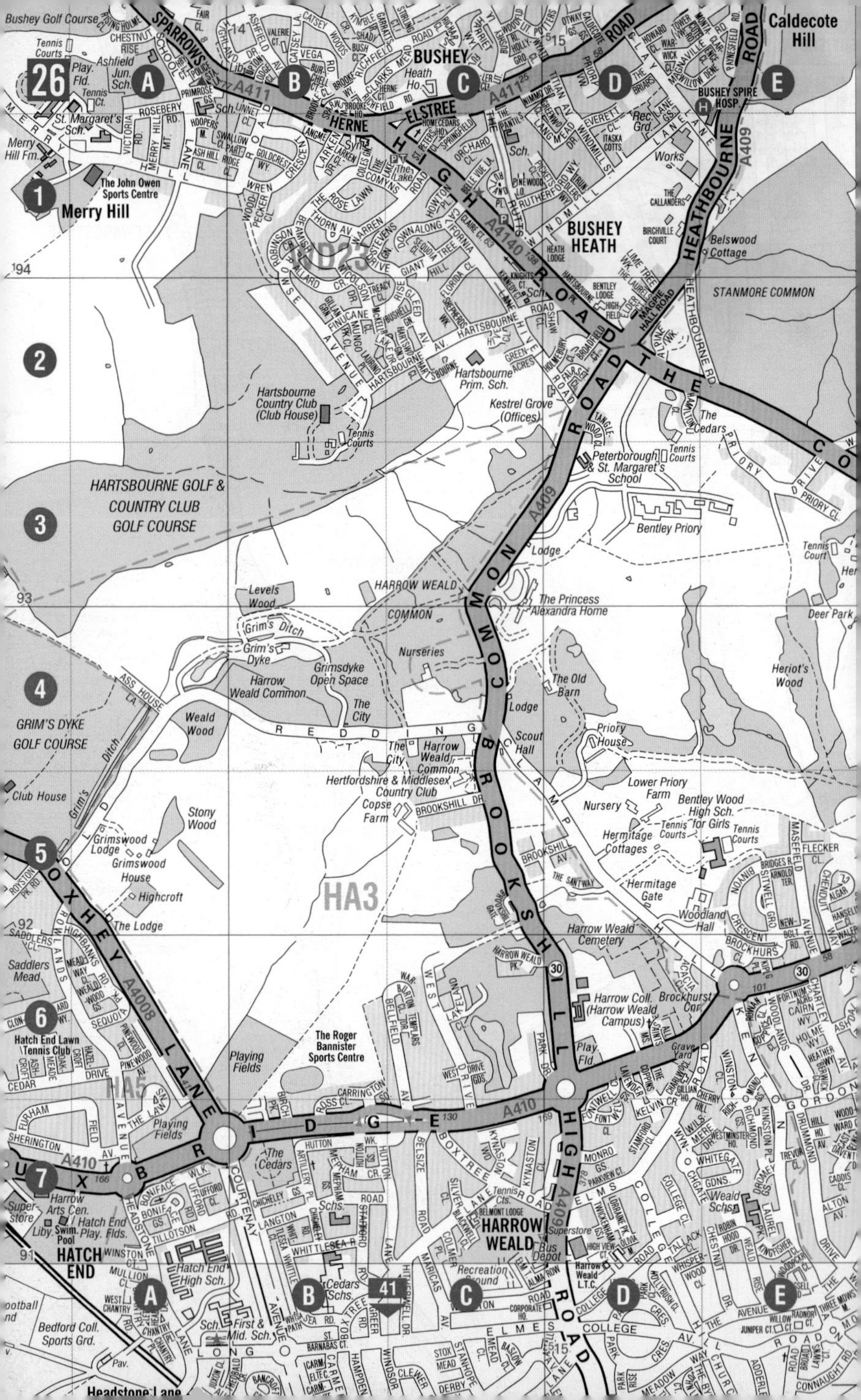
26
Bushey Golf Course
Caldecote Hill
BUSHEY
BUSHEY HEATH
Merry Hill
The John Owen Sports Centre
Ashfield Jun. Sch.
St. Margaret's Sch.
Merry Hill Fm.
SPARROWS HERNE
ELSTREE ROAD
HIGH ROAD
HEATHBOURNE ROAD
BUSHEY SPIRE HOSP.
Belswood Cottage
STANMORE COMMON
Hartsbourne Country Club (Club House)
HARTSBOURNE GOLF & COUNTRY CLUB GOLF COURSE
Hartsbourne Prim. Sch.
Kestrel Grove (Offices)
Peterborough & St. Margaret's School
Bentley Priory
COMMON ROAD
HARROW WEALD COMMON
The Princess Alexandra Home
Deer Park
Heriot's Wood
Levels Wood
Grim's Ditch
Grim's Dyke
Harrow Weald Common
Grimsdyke Open Space
Nurseries
The Old Barn
GRIM'S DYKE GOLF COURSE
Club House
Weald Wood
REDDING
The City
Hertfordshire & Middlesex Country Club
Copse Farm
Priory House
Lower Priory Farm
Bentley Wood High Sch. for Girls
Hermitage Cottages
Hermitage Gate
Woodland Hall
Stony Wood
Grimswood Lodge
Grimswood House
Highcroft
The Lodge
HA3
OXHEY LANE
BROOKSHILL
Harrow Weald Cemetery
Harrow Coll. (Harrow Weald Campus)
Brockhurst Cnr.
Saddlers Mead
Hatch End Lawn Tennis Club
HA5
Playing Fields
The Roger Bannister Sports Centre
UXBRIDGE ROAD
A410
A409
A4008
A4140
A411
HARROW WEALD
HATCH END
Harrow Arts Cen.
Hatch End Play. Flds.
Hatch End High Sch.
Recreation Ground
Harrow Weald L.T.C.
Bus Depot
Superstore
Weald Schs.
Bedford Coll. Sports Grd.
Headstone Lane
COLLEGE ROAD
LONG ELMES
41

27
28
42
16
17
18
F
G
H
J
K
1
2
3
4
5
6
7
WATFORD BY-PASS
A41
M1
50
CENTENNIAL PARK
CENTENNIAL AV.
CENTENNIAL CT.
ELSTREE HILL STH.
ELSTREE HILL SOUTH
A5183
Elstree Open Space
WD6
Norwegian Barn
Penniwells Fm.
Junction 4
EDGWARE
M1-MOTORWAY
WATLING FARM
Brockley Hill Farm
BROCKLEY
Sports Ground
Brockley Grange
ROYAL NATIONAL ORTHOPAEDIC HOSP.
Brockley Hill Ho.
ASPIRE
NUTT GRO.
A41 (WATFORD BY-PASS)
HA8
Pear Wood Cottages
Lodge
Limes House
Wood Farm
Pear Wood
Fish Pond
A5 (WATLING STREET)
Newlands
Cricket Ground
Fish Pond
Grove Field Pavilion
Islamic Centre
Tennis Cts.
Cloisters Wood
Driving Range
Club House
Brockley Hill Golf Course
Club Ho.
Edgwarebury Golf Course
Playing Field
PIPERS GRN. LA.
WAY
Stanmore Hall
LITTLE COMMON
DENNIS
HA7
A4140
STANMORE HILL
A410
SPUR RD.
Pav.
Play. Fld.
Stonegrove
CANONS CORNER
ROAD
STONEGROVE
GLANLEAM RD.
Syn.
St. John's First & Mid. Schs.
Bowling Green
Stanmore Rec. Grd.
Stanmore
LONDON
94
SNARESBROOK DR.
THE SPINNEY
TINTAGEL DR.
PANGBOURNE DR.
Lake Grove Rec. Grd.
A5
Boot Pond
OLD LODGE WAY
THE BROADWAY
Lib.
Tennis Cts.
CHURCH RD.
ROAD
Bernays Gds.
MARSH
Aylward First & Mid. Sch.
Playing Field
DALKEITH
Tennis Courts
North London Collegiate School
The Lake
92
STANMORE
Stanmore College
MANOR HOUSE ESTATE
Temple Pond
King George V Memorial Gdns.
CANONS PARK
HA8
Gas Works
Stanmore Marsh
LANE
Club House
Bowls
Tennis Courts
Pav.
Playing Field
Canons Park
STANMORE GOLF COURSE
Sports Ground
Pav.
Bowling Green
Whitchurch First & Mid. Schs.
Stanburn Schs.
WHITCHURCH LANE
B461
30
Tennis Courts Pav.
Offices
HONEYPOT
Works
LITTLE STANMORE
Little Stanmore First & Middle Sch.
Prince Edward Playing Field
Sports Ground
HONEYPOT BUS. CEN.
WEMBOROUGH RD.
VERNON DRIVE
ST. EDMUNDS
HERMITAGE WAY
BEVERLEY
40

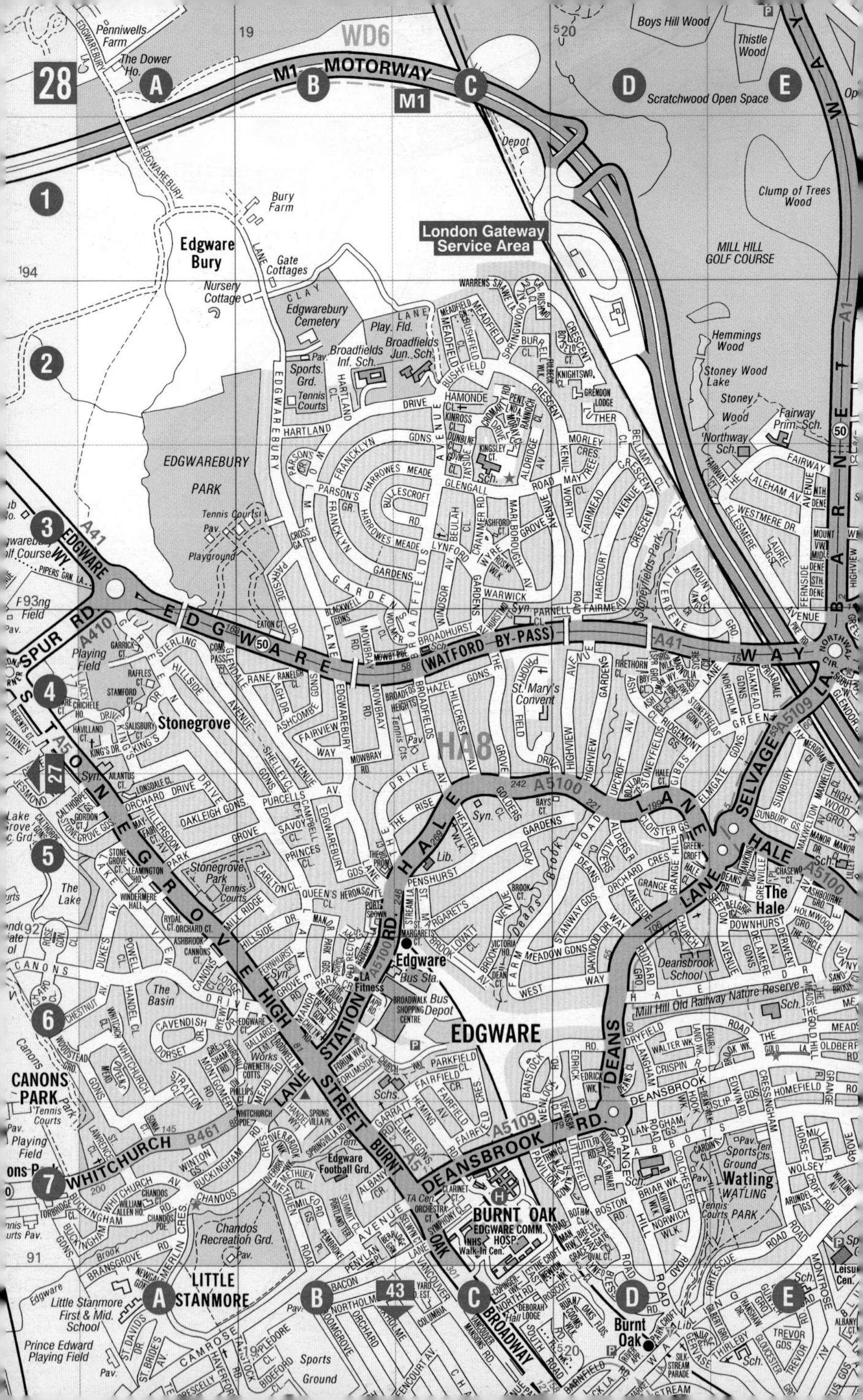

28
Penniwells Farm
The Dower Ho.
WD6
M1 MOTORWAY
M1
Boys Hill Wood
Thistle Wood
Scratchwood Open Space
Depot
Bury Farm
Edgware Bury
Gate Cottages
Nursery Cottage
London Gateway Service Area
Clump of Trees Wood
MILL HILL GOLF COURSE
Edgwarebury Cemetery
Play. Fld.
Broadfields Inf. Sch.
Broadfields Jun. Sch.
Sports Grd.
Tennis Courts
Hemmings Wood
Stoney Wood Lake
Stoney Wood
Fairway Prim. Sch.
Northway Sch.
EDGWAREBURY PARK
Tennis Courts
Playground
EDGWARE WY
A41
SPUR RD.
A410
Playing Field
EDGWARE WAY (WATFORD BY-PASS)
Stoneyfields Park
St. Mary's Convent
HA8
Stonegrove
STONEGROVE
A5
Stonegrove Park
Tennis Courts
HALE LANE
A5100
SELVAGE LA.
A5109
The Hale
HIGH STREET
STATION RD.
Edgware
Bus Sta.
BROADWALK SHOPPING CENTRE
Bus Depot
EDGWARE
Deansbrook School
Mill Hill Old Railway Nature Reserve
DEANS LA.
The Basin
CANONS PARK
Tennis Courts
Playing Field
WHITCHURCH LANE
B461
Edgware Football Grd.
DEANSBROOK RD.
BURNT OAK
EDGWARE COMM. HOSP.
NHS Walk-in Cen.
Watling
WATLING PARK
Sports Ground
Chandos Recreation Grd.
LITTLE STANMORE
Little Stanmore First & Mid. School
Prince Edward Playing Field
Sports Ground
BURNT OAK BROADWAY
Burnt Oak
SILK STREAM PARADE
Leisure Cen.
43
27

29
Hyver Manor
Gravel Pit Wood
Tanglewood
Barnet Gate Wood
HENDON WOOD LANE
BARNET GATE LANE
Brent Lodge Farm
Allendale
EN5
Dollis Brook
F
G
H
J
K
MOAT MOUNT OPEN SPACE
The Shrubbery
Leg of Mutton Pond
Mote End Farm
Mote Mount
Nut Wood
White Lodge
Hendon Park
Hendon Wood Lane Open Space
Sports Ground
Pav.
Totteridge Fields Local Nature Reserve
Boundary House
Farmleigh
N20
Abattoir
St. Edward's College
Oak Lodge
Totteridge Park
Fairlight Cottage
TOTTERIDGE COMMON
A5109
Ellern Mede Nursing Home
Ellern Mede Farm
Totteridge Common
The Lynch House
Fairlawn
1
2
3
4
5
6
7
Tennis Courts
Mill Hill High Sch.
Playing Field
Beech Wood
Highwood Park
The Barn
Highwood Ho.
CLARK'S LANE
Highwood
Highwood Hill
HIGHWOOD HILL
Highwood Hill Cottage
Holcombe Dale
Holcombe Hill
Folly Brook
Folly Farm
MARSH LANE
RAMILLIES RD.
WORCESTER
NORBURY GRO.
GLENWOOD
BRABOURNE HGTS.
THE LINCOLNS
LAWRENCE GDS.
ABBEY VIEW
HORNBEAM CL.
THE REDDINGS
REDDINGS CL.
SUNNYFIELD
AUSTELL GDS.
UPHILL RD.
TRETAWN PK.
TRETAWN GARDENS
LAWRENCE STREET
Pool
Playing Field
Riding School
Belmont Sch.
Belmont Farm
St. Mary's Abbey
The Mill Field
Lawrence Green
Tennis Courts
THE RIDGEWAY
B552
MILLERS CL.
Sports Ground
Cricket Club
Pav.
Cemetery
Nursery
Burtonhole Farm
APEX CORNER
NW7
WATFORD WAY
A1
St. Joseph's RC College
LAWRENCE GROVE
CHALET ESTATE
DRAPERS' COTTAGE HOMES
Leisure Cen.
Spts. Grd.
St. Paul's C of E Prim. Sch.
KINGSHEAD HO.
Mill Hill School
MARSHALL ESTATE
St. Vincent's School
St. Vincent's Convent
Medical Research Laboratory
Works
30
SHAKESPEARE RD.
MILTON RD.
TAYLORSMEAD
TENNYSON RD.
HAMMERS LANE
B1461
MILL HILL CIRCUS
VICTORIA RD.
ALBERT RD.
WILTSHIRE
Ten. Cts.
MILL HILL
Playing Field
HIGH ST.
BURTONHOLE LA.
Oakfield House
St. Vincent's RC Prim. Sch.
Wentworth Hall
Drivers Hill
M1-MOTORWAY
WEYMOUTH AV.
NEWCOMBE
Hall
Sch.
GOODWYN AV.
THE BROADWAY
DAWS LANE
WILLS GROVE
Tennis Court
Ridgeway Ho.
VINERIES BANK
Play. Fld.
The Mount Sch.
Pavilion
Burton Bank
School Park
Arrandene Open Space
MILESPIT HILL
Watch Tower House
BITTACY PARK
LANE
Sub.
Garden Centre
Featherstone Hill
Playground
Univ.
Bus Sta.
SYLVAN AV.
WISTERIA CL.
WOODLAND WAY
(BARNET BY-PASS)
50
Pav.
Cricket Ground
Tennis Courts
MILL HILL PARK
Mill Hill Cemetery
RUSHDEN GDS.
WOODCOTE AVENUE
BITTACY RISE
Mill Hill Broadway
GRANARD BUS. CEN.
Lyndhurst Park
WISE LANE
MELDEX CL.
BROOKFIELD AV.
FEATHERSTONE RD.
MILL HILL IND. EST.
BUNNS LANE
THE RISE
HOLMDENE AV.
GLENMERE AV.
Playing Field
Copthall Sch. & Sports Cen.
Ten. Cts.
BITTACY HILL
SANDERS LA.
WOODCROFT AV.
Woodcroft Park
Sports Ground
Pavilion
GRAHAME PARK WAY
PENTAVIA RETAIL PK.
HILLSIDE GRO.
COPTHALL GDNS.
PURSLEY RD.
Chase Lodge Playing Fields
Powerleague Soccer Cen.
Dollis Jun. & Inf. Schs.
Playgolf Metro
Club House
M1
ROWLANDS CL.
COLENSO
Tennis Courts
Copthall Swimming Pool
NW4
Barnet Copthall Stadium
ABERDARE GDNS.
ASHLEY LANE
LONGFIELD AVENUE
Rugby Club
Pav.
CHAMPIONS WAY
GREENLANDS
Play. Fld.
Hendon Sch.
44
Junction 2
BARNET COPTHALL SPORTS CENTRE
Pavilion
HENDON GOLF COURSE
Play. Field
Tennis Cts.
Barnet Coll.
Grahame Park
THE CONCOURSE
SOUTH MEAD
LYSANDER
LEVERGLADE STRAND
Lib.
22
23

30
A
B
C
D
E
1
2
3
4
5
6
7
20
29
45
TOTTERIDGE COMMON
TOTTERIDGE
A5109
TOTTERIDGE VILLAGE
TOTTERIDGE
SOUTH HERTS GOLF COURSE
Club House
Darland Lake Nature Reserve
Laurel Farmhouse
Woodridge Prim. Sch.
Folly Farm
Burtonhole Lane Farm Estate
Burtonhole Farm
Sports Ground
Mill Hill Sub. Sta.
NW7
N20
N3
Oakfield House
Partingdale Manor
London Equestrian Centre
Frith Manor Ho.
Frith Manor Prim. Sch.
FINCHLEY GOLF COURSE
Nether Court (Club House)
Woodside Park Club
Woodside Park
West Finchley
Mill Hill East
Inglis Barracks
Bittacy Hill Park
Watch Tower House
THE RIDGEWAY
BITTACY HILL
B552
B1462
A598
DOLLIS ROAD
NETHER ST.
BALLARDS
Hendon Crematorium
HENDON CEMETERY
HENDON GOLF COURSE
CHURCH END
FINCHLEY
Finchley Central
Playing Field
Sports Centre
Recreation Ground
Brook Farm Open Space
Fairlight Cottage
Hillsborough Cottage
Redings
Hillsdown
Montebello
Burnhams
Chestnut Cottages
The Warren
Waverley
Windyridge
Dell House
The Croft
Cricket Ground
Victoria Rec. Grd.
Sikh Cen.

Oakleigh Park
Miniature Golf Course
Monkfrith Prim. Sch.
Bowling Green
31
21
F
G
H
J
K
OAKLEIGH PARK
South Barnet
OSIDGE LANE
Brunswick Park Prim. Sch.
Totteridge and Whetstone
OAKLEIGH ROAD
WHETSTONE
NORTH MIDDLESEX GOLF COURSE
Owen's Centre Playing Field
RUSSELL ROAD
A109
B1453
B550
BARNET
EN4
BRUNSWICK PARK
NEW SOUTHGATE CEMETERY
1
2
3
4
5
6
7
OAKLEIGH RD. SOUTH
Friary Park
Bethune Park Recreation Ground
FRIERN BARNET
Curtis Family Centre
32
NORTH FINCHLEY
N12
N11
A1003
WOODHOUSE RD.
FRIERN BARNET RD.
COLNEY HATCH LANE
COLNEY HATCH
Coppetts Wood
Glebelands Local Nature Reserve
A406
NORTH CIRCULAR ROAD
PINKHAM WAY
BOBBY MOORE WAY
Powerleague Soccer Cen.
N10
N2
Refuse Destructor
Wingate & Finchley Rugby FC Grd. Football Ground
Cricket & Football Grounds
Glebe Land Open Space
Finchley Lido
David Lloyd Leisure
FINCHLEY MEM. HOSP.
Fallow Corner
HIGH ROAD
A1000
NEW SOUTHGATE
46
Islington Crematorium
ST. PANCRAS & ISLINGTON CEMETERY
Recreation Ground
Playing Field

32
22
31
47
A
B
C
D
E
1
2
3
4
5
6
7
SOUTHGATE
OSIDGE
NEW SOUTHGATE
N14
N11
N22
N10
Southgate
Arnos Grove
New Southgate
Bounds Green
Bowes Park
Palmers Green
GROVELANDS PARK
North London Priory Hospital
Boating Lake
Pitch & Putt Course
NEW SOUTHGATE CEMETERY
New Southgate Crematorium
ARNOS PARK
Broomfield Park
MUSWELL HILL GOLF COURSE
Hollickwood Park
Scout Park
Southgate Cricket Club Ground
Ashmole Sch. & Sports Cen.
Southgate Coll.
Playing Fields
Pymme's Play. Fld.
Friern Bridge Retail Park
Superstore
Durnsford Spts. Cen.
CHASE SIDE
HIGH STREET
THE BOURNE
BOURNE HILL
CANNON HILL
ALDERMANS HILL
WATERFALL ROAD
BOWES ROAD
BOUNDS GREEN ROAD
TELFORD RD.
POWYS LA.
WILMER WY.
BROWNLOW RD.
DURNSFORD RD.
PINKHAM WAY
FRIERN BARNET RD.
STATION RD.
OAKLEIGH RD. STH.
HAMPDEN WAY
WINCHMORE HILL RD.
GREEN LANES
HIGH RD.
CLOCKHOUSE JUNCTION
A111
A1004
A1003
A109
A1110
A406
B1453
B1452
B106
A105

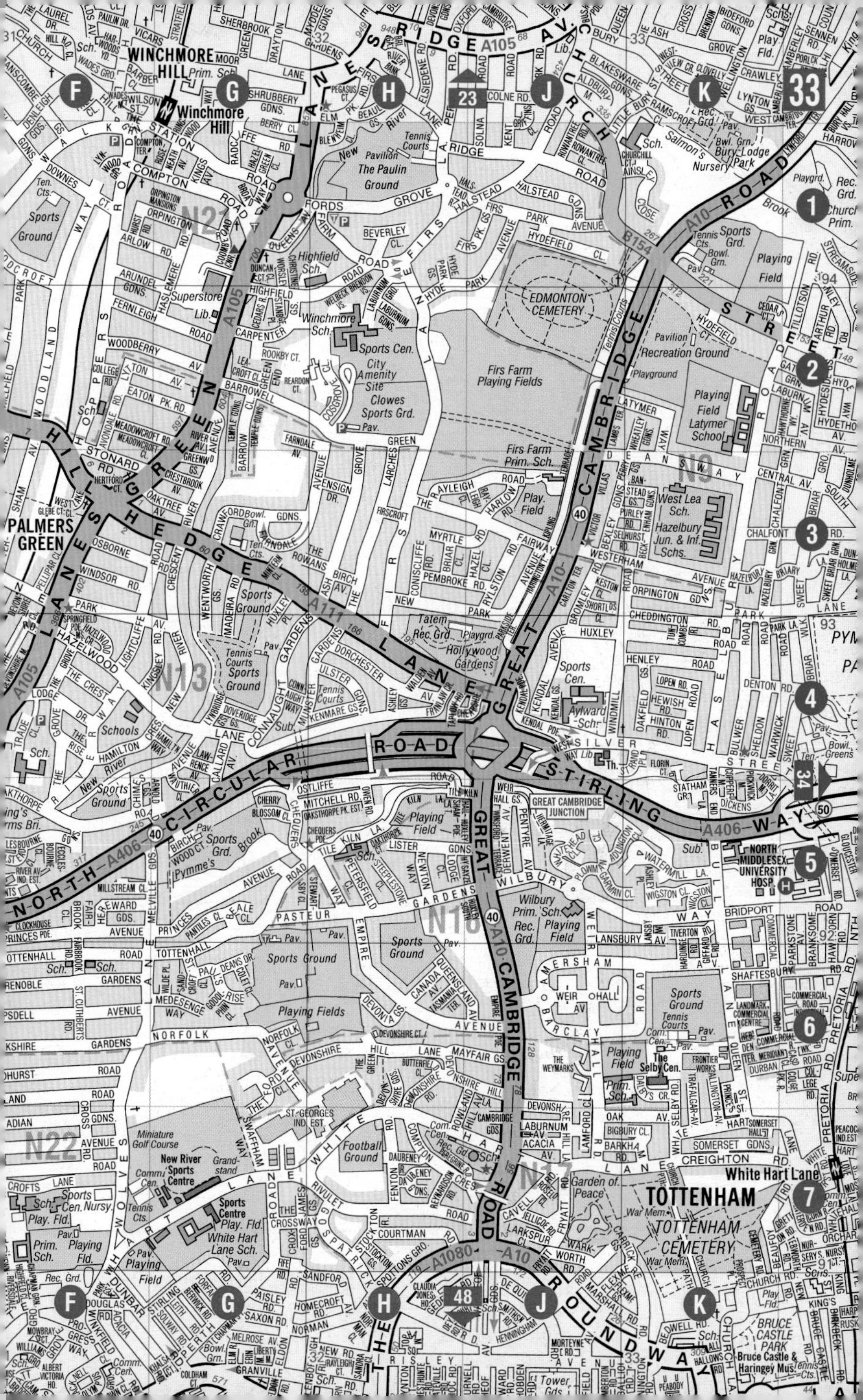

33
23
34
48
F
G
H
J
K
1
2
3
4
5
6
7
WINCHMORE HILL
Winchmore Hill
PALMERS GREEN
TOTTENHAM
N21
N13
N9
N18
N17
N22
GREEN LANES
RIDGE AV.
CHURCH STREET
GREAT CAMBRIDGE ROAD
HEDGE LANE
NORTH CIRCULAR ROAD
SILVER STREET
STIRLING WAY
HERTFORD ROAD
WHITE HART LANE
THE ROUNDWAY
The Paulin Ground
EDMONTON CEMETERY
Firs Farm Playing Fields
Recreation Ground
Latymer School
West Lea Sch.
Hazelbury Jun. & Inf. Schs.
Winchmore Sch.
City Amenity Site
Clowes Sports Grd.
Firs Farm Prim. Sch.
Highfield Sch.
Tatem Rec. Grd.
Hollywood Gardens
Aylward Sch.
GREAT CAMBRIDGE JUNCTION
NORTH MIDDLESEX UNIVERSITY HOSP.
Wilbury Prim. Sch.
The Selby Cen.
Miniature Golf Course
New River Sports Centre
White Hart Lane Sch.
Garden of Peace
TOTTENHAM CEMETERY
BRUCE CASTLE PARK
Bruce Castle & Haringey Mus.
White Hart Lane
Bury Lodge Park
Salmon's Nursery
Superstore

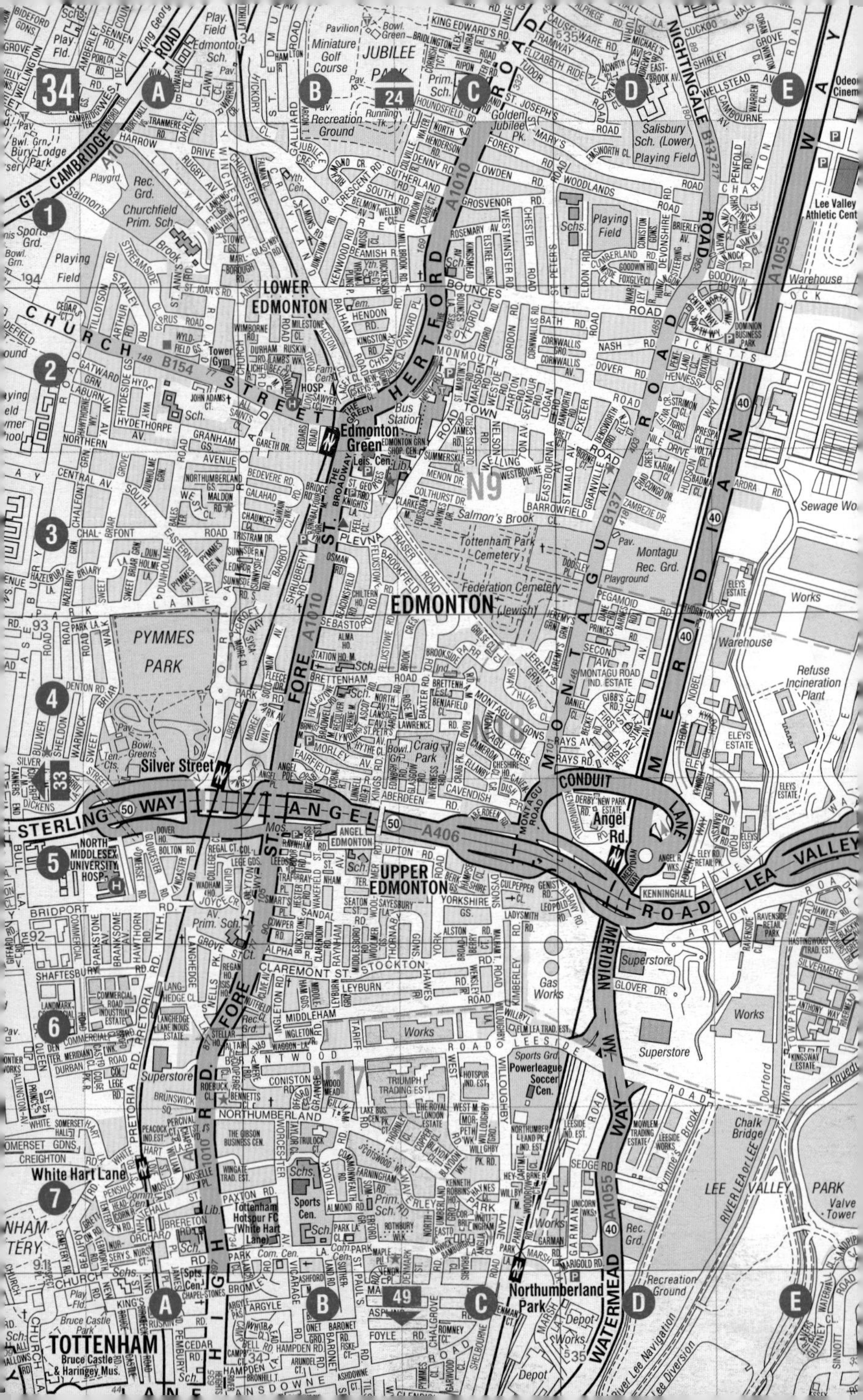

34
A
B
C
D
E
1
2
3
4
5
6
7
24
33
49
JUBILEE PARK
Miniature Golf Course
Recreation Ground
Salisbury Sch. (Lower) Playing Field
Lee Valley Athletic Cent
LOWER EDMONTON
Churchfield Prim. Sch.
Playing Field
CHURCH STREET
B154
Tower Gym
HERTFORD ROAD
A1010
Edmonton Green
Bus Station
N9
Salmon's Brook
Tottenham Park Cemetery
Federation Cemetery (Jewish)
Montagu Rec. Grd.
EDMONTON
PYMMES PARK
MONTAGU ROAD
MERIDIAN WAY
A1055
B137
Refuse Incineration Plant
Sewage Wo
Craig Park
Silver Street
STERLING WAY
ANGEL
A406
CONDUIT LANE
Angel Rd.
NORTH MIDDLESEX UNIVERSITY HOSP.
UPPER EDMONTON
N18
KENNINGHALL ROAD
LEA VALLEY ROAD
Gas Works
Superstore
Works
N17
TRIUMPH TRADING EST.
Powerleague Soccer Cen.
FORE ST.
HIGH ROAD
White Hart Lane
Tottenham Hotspur FC (White Hart Lane)
Northumberland Park
WATERMEAD WAY
LEE VALLEY PARK
River Lea or Lee
Lee Diversion
River Lee Navigation
Recreation Ground
Chalk Bridge
Valve Tower
TOTTENHAM
Bruce Castle & Haringey Mus.
Bruce Castle Park

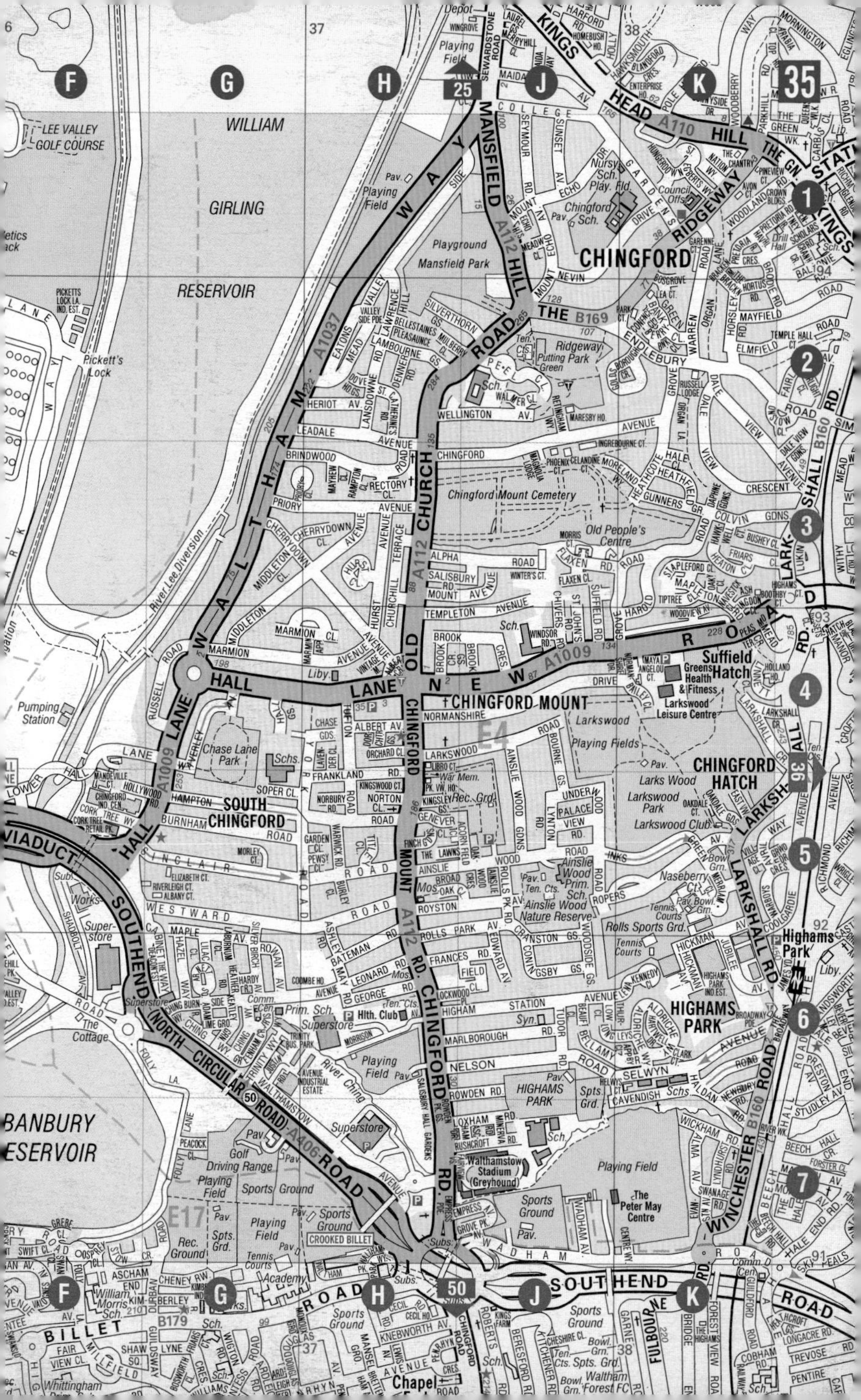

37
38
F
G
H
J
K
1
2
3
4
5
6
7
35
36
25
50
LEE VALLEY GOLF COURSE
WILLIAM GIRLING RESERVOIR
Pickett's Lock
River Lee Diversion
Pumping Station
Playing Field
Playground
Mansfield Park
CHINGFORD
Chingford Sch.
Council Offs.
Nursy. Sch. Play. Fld.
Ridgeway Putting Park Green
Chingford Mount Cemetery
Old People's Centre
CHINGFORD MOUNT
Larkswood Playing Fields
Larkswood Leisure Centre
Greens Health & Fitness
Suffield Hatch
CHINGFORD HATCH
Larks Wood
Larkswood Park
Larkswood Club
Chase Lane Park
SOUTH CHINGFORD
E4
Ainslie Wood Prim. Sch.
Ainslie Wood Nature Reserve
Rolls Sports Grd.
HIGHAMS PARK
Highams Park
Superstore
River Ching
Walthamstow Stadium (Greyhound)
The Peter May Centre
Golf Driving Range
Sports Ground
E17
CROOKED BILLET
BANBURY RESERVOIR
The Cottage
William Morris Sch.
Academy
Chapel
Waltham Forest FC
WALTHAM WAY
A1037
MANSFIELD HILL
A112
OLD CHURCH ROAD
CHINGFORD MOUNT ROAD
CHINGFORD ROAD
NEW ROAD
A1009
HALL LANE
KINGS HEAD HILL
A110
RIDGEWAY
THE RIDGEWAY
B169
LARKSHALL ROAD
B160
WINCHESTER ROAD
NORTH CIRCULAR ROAD
A406
SOUTHEND ROAD
VIADUCT
WALTHAMSTOW AVENUE
BILLET ROAD
B179

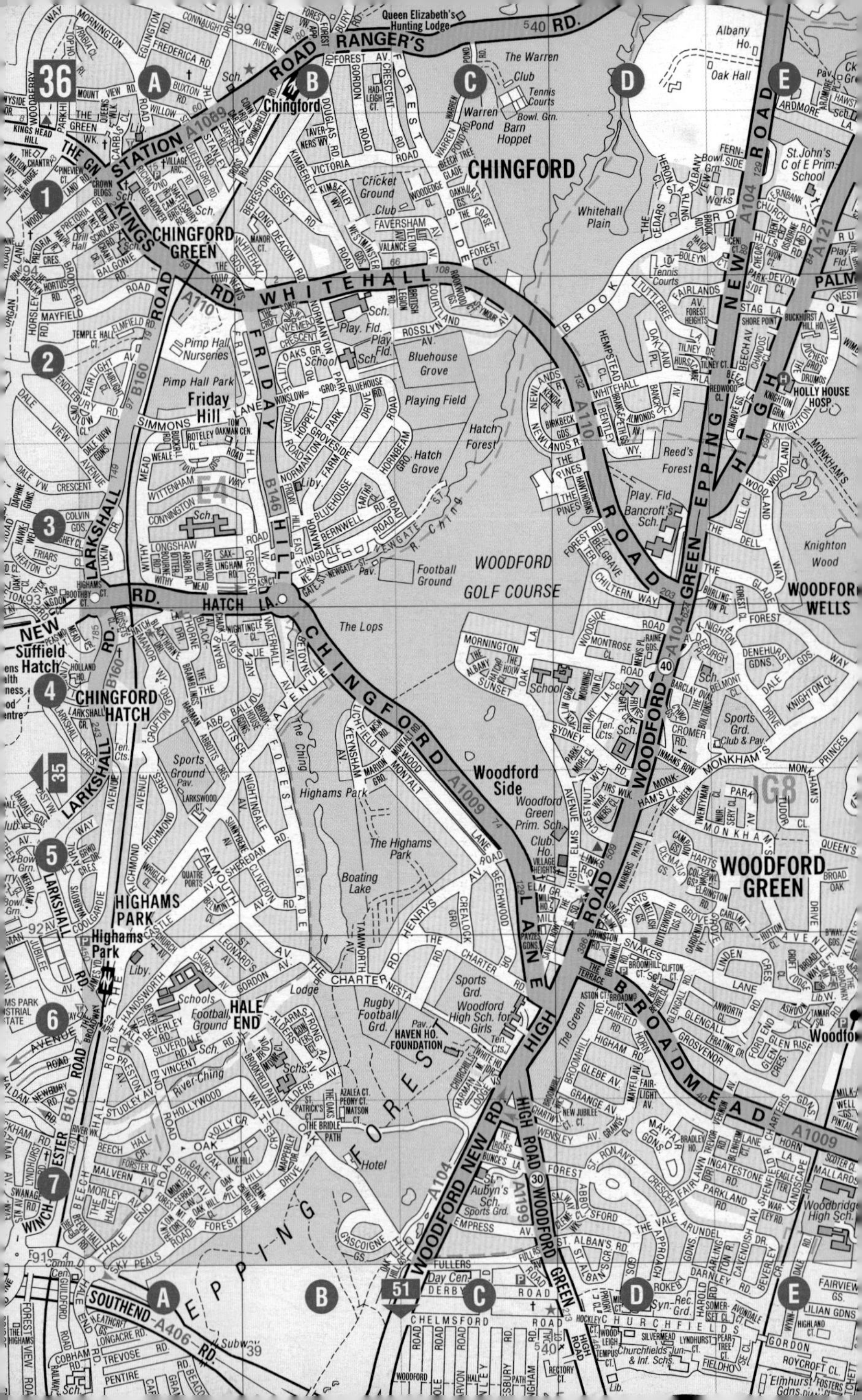
36
35
51
A
B
C
D
E
1
2
3
4
5
6
7
39
40
CHINGFORD
Chingford
CHINGFORD GREEN
Queen Elizabeth's Hunting Lodge
RANGER'S ROAD
STATION ROAD
A1069
KINGS ROAD
THE GN.
The Warren
Club
Tennis Courts
Bowl. Grn.
Warren Pond
Barn Hoppet
Albany Ho.
Oak Hall
Whitehall Plain
Cricket Ground
Club
WHITEHALL RD.
A110
FRIDAY HILL
B146
Friday Hill
Pimp Hall Nurseries
Pimp Hall Park
Play. Fld.
Bluehouse Grove
Playing Field
Hatch Forest
Hatch Grove
R. Ching
Football Ground
WOODFORD GOLF COURSE
The Lops
LARKSHALL ROAD
B160
HATCH LA.
NEW RD.
Suffield Hatch
CHINGFORD HATCH
CHINGFORD LANE
A1009
Woodford Side
Woodford Green Prim. Sch.
Higham's Park
The Highams Park
Boating Lake
HIGHAMS PARK
Highams Park
HALE END
Sports Ground
The Ching
FOREST GLADE
Rugby Football Grd.
Sports Grd.
Woodford High Sch. for Girls
HAVEN HO. FOUNDATION
EPPING FOREST
River Ching
Hotel
WOODFORD NEW RD.
A104
HIGH ROAD WOODFORD GREEN
A1199
St. Aubyn's Sch.
Sports Grd.
Day Cen.
SOUTHEND RD.
A406
Subway
NEWLANDS
Reed's Forest
Play. Fld.
Bancroft's Sch.
EPPING NEW ROAD
St. John's C of E Prim. School
HIGH ROAD
A121
HOLLY HOUSE HOSP.
Knighton Wood
WOODFORD WELLS
WOODFORD GREEN
IG8
E4
Sports Grd. Club & Pav.
BROADMEAD ROAD
Woodbridge High Sch.
Churchfields Jun. & Inf. Schs.
CHURCHFIELDS
CHELMSFORD ROAD
DERBY ROAD
Woodford

37
52
BUCKHURST HILL
Buckhurst Hill
CHIGWELL
Chigwell
WOODFORD BRIDGE
LORD'S BUSHES
RODING VALLEY MEADOWS NATURE RESERVE
IG10
IG9
IG7
IG5
M11 MOTORWAY
M11
RODING LANE
CHIGWELL LANE
CHIGWELL ROAD
MANOR ROAD
HIGH ROAD
LUXBOROUGH LANE
ROEBUCK LANE
STRADBROKE GROVE
QUEEN'S RD.
PRINCES WAY
STATION WAY
BUCKHURST WAY
PROSPECT GROVE
ALBERT RD.
CASCADE RD.
LOUGHTON WAY
STATION WAY
Roding Valley
David Lloyd Leisure
Recreation Ground
Playing Field
Sports Ground
Wakes Hall
Club Ho.
The Rodings
Buckhurst Hill Prim. Sch.
River Roding
New Barns Farm
Old Loughtonians Hockey Club
Rugby Football Ground
Luxborough
Works
Chigwell Sewage Works
Playing Fields
Cedar Park
West Hatch High School
Hill House
Ashton Playing Fields
RODING VALLEY PARK
Running Track
Ray Park
Ray Ho.
Ray Lodge Prim. Sch.
Gas Works
St. John's RC Sch.
Convent
CHIGWELL GOLF COURSE
Club House
Redbridge Ho.
Kennels
Repton Pk
Health Club
Roding Prim. Sch.
Claybury Hall
Claybury Hospital Woods Nature Reserve
Hospital Hill Wood
Hospital Hill
Cocked Hat Plantation
Egg Clump
Ash Plantation
Cemetery
Winn Bridge
Dartnalls Playing Field
Factory
WOODFORD
A113
B170
B173
F
G
H
J
K
1
2
3
4
5
6
7

38
06
07
08
Battlers Wells Wood
A
B
C
D
E
Shepherds Hill Farm
NORTHWOOD ROAD
Shepherds Hill House
Play. Fld.
91
The Harefield Academy
1
2
3
4
5
6
7
HAREFIELD
GROVE
ASH GROVE
ASH CL.
GILBERT RD.
KNIGHTS COTE CL.
Furzefield
Deadman's Grove
Ashain Spring
Scarlet Spring
Kiln Pond
Claypits
Dell
Knightscote Farm
190
Raveners Spring
Badminton Shooting Ground
JACKETS LANE
JACKETS
HURST PL.
MANOR HOUSE DR.
NORTHGATE
BUTTSMEAD
SEVENOAKS CL.
THE COVERT
FRINGEWOOD CL.
DRAKES DR.
FARM END
KINGFISHER CL.
Duck's Hill Farm
Ducks Hill Grange
Duck's Hill
Ashby Cottages
DUCK'S HILL ROAD
A4180
120
COPSE WOOD WAY
NICHOLAS WAY
OAK GLADE
SILVER WOOD CL.
ROGERS RUFF
LOWSWOOD CL.
COPSE CL.
THE BROADWAY
COPSE WOOD
Ashby Farm
Youngwood Farm
YOUNG WOOD
MAD BESS WOOD
NORTH RIDING WOOD
Mad Bess Wood Cottage
BREAKSPEAR ROAD
BREAKSPEAR M.
Bourne Farm
UB9
Breakspear House
Middle Lodge
Nature Reserve
Warren Farm
BAYHURST WOOD COUNTRY PARK
89
Willow Tree Farm
RUISLIP COMMON
Breakspear Crematorium (Ruislip)
The Lodge
Football Ground
WITHY LA.
BRICKETT CL.
HOWLETTS LA.
BURY AV.
FINE BUSH LA.
Oak Cottage
NORTH
Lower Lodge
The Bungalow
HAREFIELD ROAD
NEWYEARS GREEN LANE
The Bungalow
Highway Farm
88
Dewes Farm Cottages
St. Leonard's Farm
Pylon Farm
Elm Tree Farm
High View Farm
Newyears Green
Braemar Farm
Crows Nest Farm
STOWE CR.
LEAHOLME WY.
WYTELEAF CL.
WELLINGTON DR.
ST. CATHERINE'S FARM CT.
MAYFLOWER DR.
CHERWELL CT.
FLEET CL.
WAYBORNE GRO.
THAMES CT.
WYE CL.
ISIS CL.
STANFORD CL.
LADYGATE LA.
WESTWOOD CL.
WESTWOOD CL.
Whiteheath Jun. & Inf. Schs.
ALLINGHAM CL.
GREYSTOKE CL.
CLAYMONT CL.
SANDALWOOD DRIVE
GLOVERS GROVE
LARKSPUR CL.
WHITEHEATH AV.
GRASMERE AV.
FAIRFIELD AV.
ELLESMERE
RAVENS CT.
ARDLEY CL.
WEST CT.
ORCHARD
Old Clack Farm
Newyears Green Covert
SOUTH
TILE KILN LANE
OLD PRIORY
The Corner
Tile Kiln
WOODVILLE GS.
HEATHFIELD RI.
HILL FARM COTTS.
LYMEHURST AV.
FIELD WY.
Grays Cottages
SKIP LANE
Works
Depot
Birch Farm
56
Dunster Cottage
Gatemead Farm
Playground
RUISLIP GOLF COURSE
CLACK LANE
HILL LANE
Brackenbury Barn
Copthall Covert
Moat

39
NORTHWOOD
NORTHWOOD HILLS
Northwood Hills
RICKMANSWORTH ROAD
A404
PINNER ROAD
HIGH ST.
A4125
JOEL STREET
B472
NORTHWOOD GOLF COURSE
HASTE HILL GOLF COURSE
HA6
HA5
HA4
Ruislip Local Nature Reserve
Haste Hill
Poor's Field
Eleanor's
Ruislip Lido Railway
Lakeside
RUISLIP LIDO
Ruislip Woodlands Centre
Woody Bay
Landing Stage
PARK WOOD
Grangewood School
Haydon School
Playing Field
Joel Street Farm
White Cottage
Harlyn Primary Sch.
Nurseries
Miniature Rifle Range
Club House
Health Club
Northwood FC (Northwood Pk.)
Cemetery
Northwood Sports Cen.
Northwood Sch.
Haydon Hall Pk.
Cricket Grd.
EASTCOTE VILLAGE
Eastcote Ho. Gs.
Coteford Sch.
Kings College Playing Fields
Eastcote Hockey & Badminton Club
King's Coll. Play. Flds. Track
Highgrove Swim. Pool
Bishop Ramsey C of E Sch. (Up.)
Warrender Park
Warrender Prim. Sch.
Bishop Ramsey Sch.
High Grove
Offices
RUISLIP
Winston Churchill Hall
Church Field Gdns.
Ruislip Manor
EASTCOTE
Hillingdon Athletic Club
Cannons Bridge Farm
River Pinn
EASTCOTE ROAD
B466
HIGH ROAD
HIGH STREET
A4180
40
57
Pinner Park
Cuckoo Hill
Cavendish Recreation Ground
F
G
H
J
K
1
2
3
4
5
6
7

40
PINNER HILL GOLF COURSE
A
B
C
D
E
Hatch End
HATCH END
Superstore
Rugby Football Ground
Pinnerwood Park
First & Mid. Schs.
PINNER GREEN
Montesole Play. Flds.
UXBRIDGE ROAD
A404
ST. THOMAS' DR.
GEORGE V AVENUE
A410
PINNER
Pinner Park Farm
Pinner Lawn Tennis Club
River Pinn
Paine's Br.
Cemetery
Little Common
Innellan Ho. Sch.
Hlth. Club
Pinner Village Hall
Pinner Memorial Park
Superstore
Pinner
West Lodge Schs.
Tennis Courts
Reddiford Sch.
Nower Hill
Pinner New Cemetery
Nower Hill High Sch.
Woodlands Open Space
North Harrow
HA5
CUCKOO HILL
B466
Cuckoo Hill
HIGH RD.
RICKMANSWORTH ROAD
Superstore
1
2
3
4
5
6
7
39
Pinner Village Gardens (Rec. Grd.)
Yeading Brook Open Space
The Croft Play. Fld.
Cannon Lane First & Mid. Schs. Play. Fld.
Heathfield Sch.
Streamside Rec. Grd.
Longfield Schs.
EASTCOTE
Eastcote
HA4
Roxborough Rough
Roxbourne Park
Playground
58
Rayners Lane
RAYNERS LANE
ALEXANDRA AV.
IMPERIAL DRIVE
A4090
Cavendish Recreation Ground
Sports Ground
EASTCOTE ROAD
VIEW EASTERN
CANNON LANE
RAYNERS LANE
MARSH ROAD
WOODLANDS

41
42
26
59
HARROW WEALD
HA3
HA2
HA1
WEALDSTONE
Harrow & Wealdstone
Headstone Lane
HEADSTONE
GREENHILL
NORTH HARROW
West Harrow
WEST HARROW
Harrow-on-the-Hill
HARROW
HARROW ON THE HILL
Hatch End High Sch.
Cedars Schs.
Headstone Lane Sports Grd.
Headstone Manor Recreation Ground
Harrow Museum & Heritage Cen.
Sports Ground
Open Air Theatre
Harrow Crown Court
Salvatorian Coll.
Belmont First & Mid. Schs.
Recreation Ground
Harrow Leisure Centre
Civic Centre
Harrow Recreation Ground
Harrow Cemetery
St. Ann's Shopping Cen.
The Grove Open Space
Harrow Hill Golf Course
Miniature Rifle Range
Playing Fields
Cricket Ground
Whitmore High Sch.
Whitmore Sports Cen.
Vaughan Schs.
Grange Schs.
Harrow School Playing Fields
A409
A404
A4005
A312
B457
HIGH ROAD
ST. GEORGE GANGE WAY
STATION ROAD
GREENHILL ROAD
LOWLANDS RD.
KENTON RD.
SHEEPCOTE RD.
PINNER VIEW
HARROW VIEW
HEADSTONE GS.
WHITMORE RD.
BESSBOROUGH RD.
WATFORD RD.
ELMES COLLEGE AV.
CHURCH HILL
HIGH ST.
PETERBOROUGH RD.

42
27
41
60
A
B
C
D
E
1
2
3
4
5
6
7
16
17
18
STANMORE GOLF COURSE
Canons Park
WHITCHURCH
Whitchurch First & Mid. Schs.
Stanburn Schs.
Sports Ground
Offices
Works
HONEYPOT LANE
A4140
Prince Edward Playing Field
HA7
BELMONT
Belmont First & Mid. Schs.
Kenton Lane Farm
Centenary Park
Park High Sch.
Pitch & Putt
Priestmead Rec. Grd.
Play. Field Schs.
Byron Recreation Ground
Cemetery
WEALDSTONE
Harrow Leisure Centre
Harrow Driving, Cycling and Road Safety Centre
Elmgrove First & Middle Schools
Kenton Recreation Ground
KENTON
HA3
Glebe Schs.
Hospice
Wealdstone Brook
WOODCOCK PARK
KENTON ROAD
A4006
Kenton
Superstore
Northwick Park
University of Westminster (Harrow Campus)
Univ. of Westminster Sports Centre
NORTHWICK PARK HOSPITAL
ST. MARK'S HOSP.
HARROW HILL GOLF COURSE
HARROW
WATFORD ROAD
A404
HA1
HA9
Mt. Stewart Jun. & Inf. Sch.
John Billam Playing Fields
PRESTON
Preston Road
Northwick Park Playgolf
Harrow School Playing Fields
Playing Fields
Club Ho.

43
28
44
61
F
G
H
J
K
1
2
3
4
5
6
7
19
20
21
88
89
190
BURNT OAK
EDGWARE COMM. HOSP.
Edgware Football Grd.
Watling
WATLING PARK
LITTLE STANMORE
Chandos Recreation Grd.
Sports Ground
Burnt Oak
Silk Stream Park
Montrose Recreation Ground
National Blood Service
Elysian House
COLINDALE
QUEENSBURY
Queensbury
Canons High Sch.
Mecca Burnt Oak
Roe Green
Eton Grove Open Space
Kingsbury High Sch.
Roe Green Park
Kingsbury Manor
Kingsbury Manor Studio
Kingsbury
KINGSBURY
Kingsbury Green
Kingsbury Green Rec. Grd.
Silver Jubilee Park
Kingsbury Town FC Grd.
JFS School
Recreation Ground
St. Robert Southwell Sch.
FRYENT COUNTRY PARK
Barn Hill Open Space
Field Study Centre
Woodfield Sch.
HA8
NW9
HA9
BROADWAY
EDGWARE
OAK
A5
A4140
A4006
B454
KINGSBURY ROAD
FRYENT WAY
CHURCH LANE
STAG LANE
MOLLISON WAY
HOLMSTALL AVENUE
COLINDEEP LA.

A
B
C
D
E
1
2
3
4
5
6
7
29
43
62
Grahame Park
Colindale
COLINDALE
Leisure Cen.
Barnet Coll.
High Sch.
RAF Museum Hendon
Battle of Britain Hall
Beaufort Park
Peel Centre (Metropolitan Police Training Establishment)
Sports Ground
Colindale Park
News-paper Library
Silkstream Unit East
National Blood Service Offices
Elysian House
Montrose Recreation Ground
COLINDEEP LANE
A5150
M1
M1—MOTORWAY
Junction 2
FIVEWAYS CORNER
WATFORD WAY
A41
GREAT (BARNET BY-PASS)
Hasmonean High Sch.
BARNET COPTHALL SPORTS CENTRE
Copthall Swimming Pool
Barnet Copthall Stadium
Chase Lodge Playing Fields
Powerleague Soccer Cen.
Playgolf Metro
Club House
HENDON GOLF COURSE
Rugby Club
SUNNY HILL PARK
Tennis Courts
THE GARDEN BMI HOSP
St. Mary's C of E High Sch.
Museum
The Burroughs
Middlesex University
HENDON
NW4
NW9
Hendon Central
QUEENS ROAD
B551
HENDON PARK
HENDON WAY
CHURCH RD.
BRENT ST.
A502
PARSON ST.
B552
STATION ROAD
A504
THE HYDE
WEST HENDON BROADWAY
A5
EDGWARE ROAD
THE HYDE ROAD
KINGSBURY RD.
A4006
KINGSBURY
Hendon
Malcolm Park
WEST HENDON PLAYING FIELDS
Silver Jubilee Park
Kingsbury Town FC Grd.
Cycle Track
Pavilion
Cool Oak Bridge
COOL OAK LANE
Youth Sailing Base
WEST HENDON
BRENT RESERVOIR
Welsh Harp Nature Reserve
Rifle Range
Woodfield Sch.
Nursery
BRENT CROSS INTERCHANGE
Brent Cross
BRENT CROSS SHOPPING CENTRE
Junc. 1
A406 NORTH CIRCULAR
STAPLES CORNER
STAPLES CORNER RETAIL PARK
CLAREMONT WAY INDUSTRIAL ESTATE
Superstore
GARRICK INDUSTRIAL ESTATE
THE HYDE IND. EST.

45
FINCHLEY
CHURCH END
Finchley Central
Holders Hill
HENDON GOLF COURSE
Hendon Crematorium
HENDON CEMETERY
Windsor Open Space
Avenue House Grounds
Sports Ground
Pentland Centre
N3
College Farm
HENLYS CORNER
St. Marylebone Crematorium
ST. MARYLEBONE CEMETERY
Christ's College
N2
Little Wood
Big Wood
Willifred Green
Temple Fortune
Princes Park
NW11
Jewish Cemetery
Golders Green Crematorium
GOLDERS GREEN
Brent Cross
Golders Green
HAMPSTEAD
HEATH
NW2
Superstores
Sports Cen.
Kisharon Sch.
Mutton Brook
The Decoy
Monastery
Tennis Courts
Clitterhouse Recreation
DOLLIS ROAD
REGENTS PARK ROAD
BALLARDS LANE
EAST END ROAD
NORTH CIRCULAR ROAD
FALLODEN WAY
HENDON WAY
HENDON LANE
HOLDERS HILL ROAD
FINCHLEY ROAD
GOLDERS GREEN RD.
NORTH END RD.
HOLDERS HILL
A598
A504
A406
A1
A502
A41
B552
B1462
30
63
46
F
G
H
J
K
1
2
3
4
5
6
7
24
25
26
88
89
90
91

46
31
45
64
A
B
C
D
E
1
2
3
4
5
6
7
Fallow Corner
FINCHLEY MEM. HOSP.
Finchley Lido
Glebe Open Space
NORTH CIRCULAR ROAD
A406
BOBBY MOORE WAY
COLNEY HATCH LANE
Powerleague Soccer Cen.
Playing Field
Recreation Ground
Islington Crematorium
Strawberry Vale Brook
ST. PANCRAS & ISLINGTON CEM.
Muswell Hill Spts. Grd.
COLDFALL WOOD
Coldfall Prim. Sch.
A1000
HIGH ROAD
EAST FINCHLEY
Martin Jun. & Inf. School
Fortismere Sch.
Our Lady of Muswell RC Prim. Sch.
FORTIS GREEN
A504
St. Marylebone Crem.
ST. MARYLEBONE CEMETERY
EAST END ROAD
Oak Lodge Sch.
East Finchley
N2
N12
N6
NW11
ST. LUKE'S WOODSIDE HOSP.
Cherry Tree Wood
St. James CE Prim. Sch.
HIGHGATE WOOD
Sports Ground
Stormont Lawn Tennis & Squash Club
LYTTELTON ROAD
A1
AYLMER ROAD
GREAT NORTH RD.
ARCHWAY ROAD
HAMPSTEAD GARDEN SUBURB
HIGHGATE GOLF COURSE
Club House
HIGHGATE
HIGHGATE HOSPITAL
Mallinson Sports Centre
Highgate School Playing Field
NORTH HILL
B519
B550
SOUTHWOOD LANE
HAMPSTEAD GOLF COURSE
Bunkers Hill
HAMPSTEAD HEATH
HAMPSTEAD LANE
Turners Wood
North Wood
Kenwood House
Ken Wood Towers Farm
The Spaniards
WILDWOOD RD.
Yth. Hostel
Open Air Stage
Bowling Green
Mount
Sandy

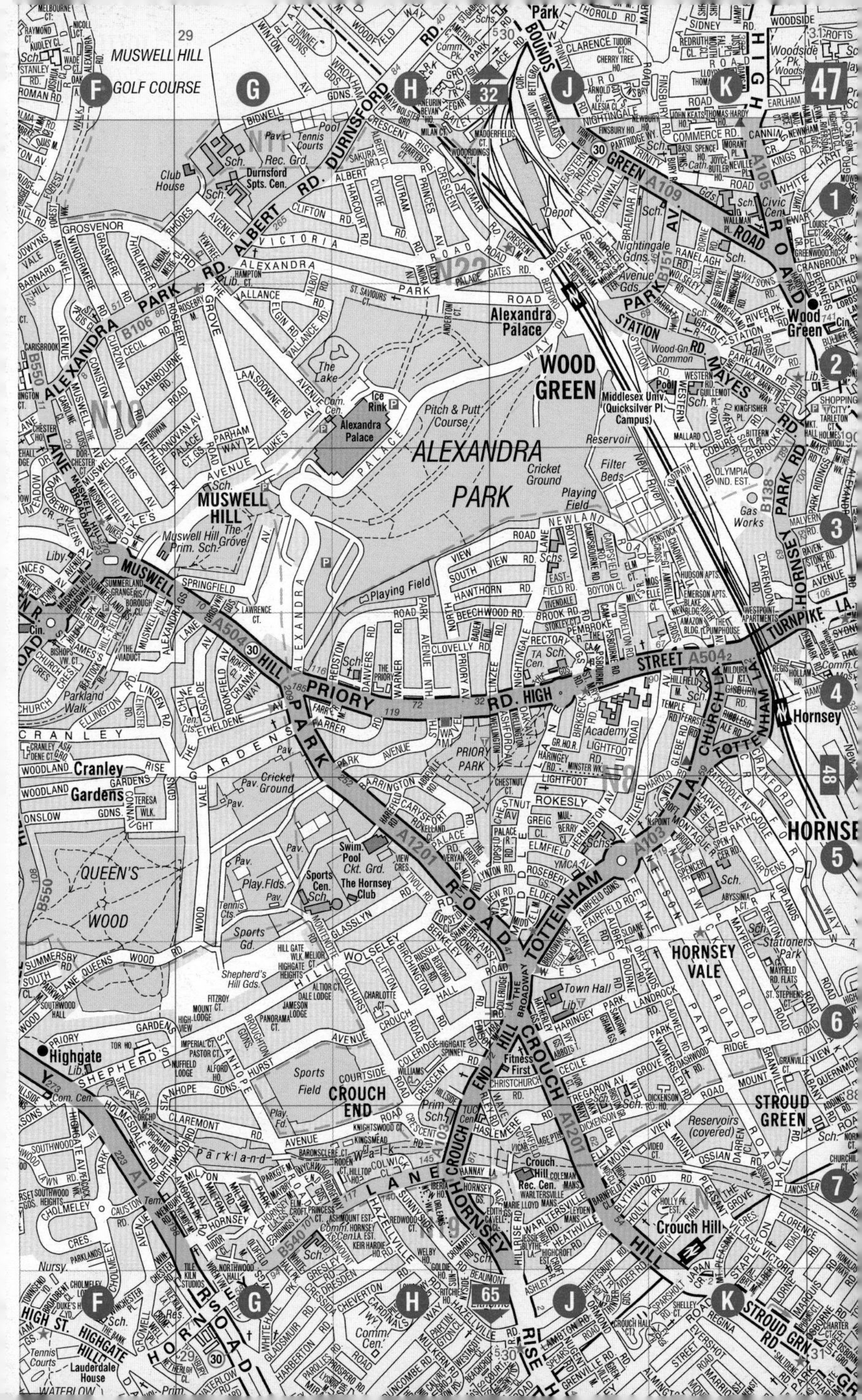

47
48
32
65
F
G
H
J
K
1
2
3
4
5
6
7
MUSWELL HILL GOLF COURSE
ALEXANDRA PARK
Alexandra Palace
WOOD GREEN
Wood Green
MUSWELL HILL
Cranley Gardens
QUEEN'S WOOD
CROUCH END
HORNSEY VALE
STROUD GREEN
Highgate
HORNSEY
Hornsey
Crouch Hill
Middlesex Univ. (Quicksilver Pl. Campus)
Pitch & Putt Course
Cricket Ground
Playing Field
Filter Beds
Reservoir
Reservoirs (covered)
Gas Works
Wood-Gn. Common
The Lake
Ice Rink
Priory Park
The Hornsey Club
Swim. Pool
Town Hall
Fitness First
Durnsford Spts. Cen.
Club House
Lauderdale House
Shepherd's Hill Gds.
Stationers Park
Parkland Walk
DURNSFORD RD.
ALEXANDRA PARK RD.
ALBERT RD.
MUSWELL HILL
PRIORY RD.
HIGH STREET
PARK RD.
TOTTENHAM LA.
CROUCH END HILL
HORNSEY LANE
HORNSEY RISE
CROUCH HILL
HORNSEY RD.
HIGH ROAD
WOOD GREEN HIGH RD.
STATION RD.
MAYES RD.
TURNPIKE LA.
ALEXANDRA PALACE WAY
MUSWELL HILL BROADWAY
CRANLEY GARDENS
PRIORY AVENUE
TOTTENHAM LANE
HORNSEY PARK RD.
STROUD GRN. RD.
N22
N10
N8
N19
N11
A1
A103
A105
A109
A504
A1201
B106
B138
B151
B540
B550

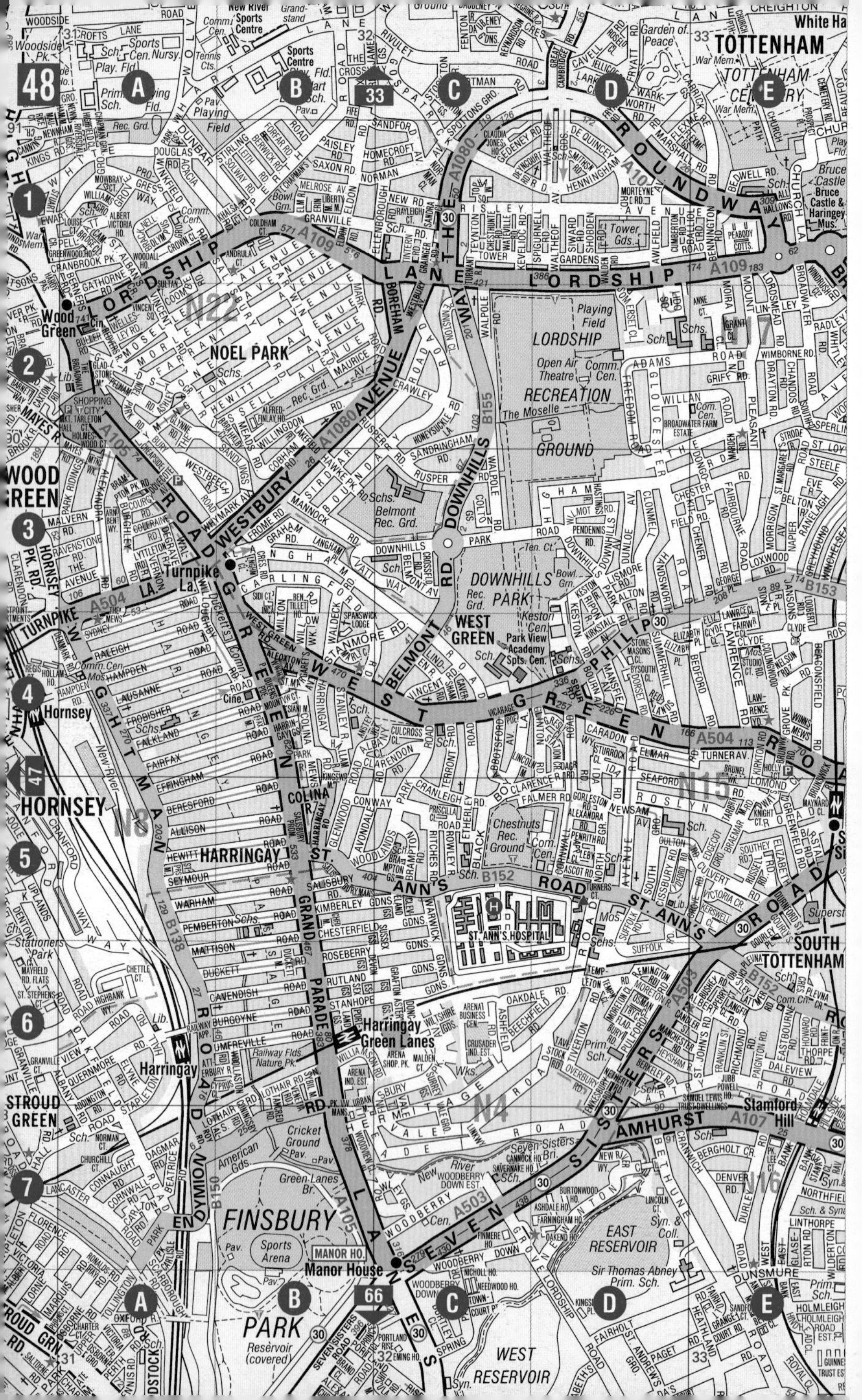
48
33
47
66
TOTTENHAM
TOTTENHAM CEMETERY
NOEL PARK
N22
Wood Green
WOOD GREEN
Shopping City
LORDSHIP LANE
A109
ROUNDWAY
A10
LORDSHIP RECREATION GROUND
Open Air Theatre
The Moselle
Broadwater Farm Estate
WESTBURY AVENUE
A1080
DOWNHILLS WAY
B155
DOWNHILLS PARK
Belmont Rec. Grd.
WEST GREEN
Park View Academy Spts. Cen.
WEST GREEN ROAD
A504
PHILIP LANE
N15
N17
N8
HORNSEY
Hornsey
Turnpike La.
TURNPIKE LANE
A105
GREEN LANES
WIGHTMAN ROAD
HARRINGAY
Harringay
Harringay Green Lanes
GRAND PARADE
ST. ANN'S ROAD
B152
ST. ANN'S HOSPITAL
Chestnuts Rec. Ground
COLINA
SOUTH TOTTENHAM
SEVEN SISTERS ROAD
A503
AMHURST PARK
A107
Stamford Hill
N16
N4
FINSBURY PARK
Sports Arena
Manor House
Cricket Ground
American Gds.
EAST RESERVOIR
WEST RESERVOIR
Reservoir (covered)
STROUD GREEN
Stationers Park
Railway Flds. Nature Pk.
Sir Thomas Abney Prim. Sch.
Garden of Peace
Bruce Castle & Haringey Mus.
New River Sports Centre
Woodside Pk.

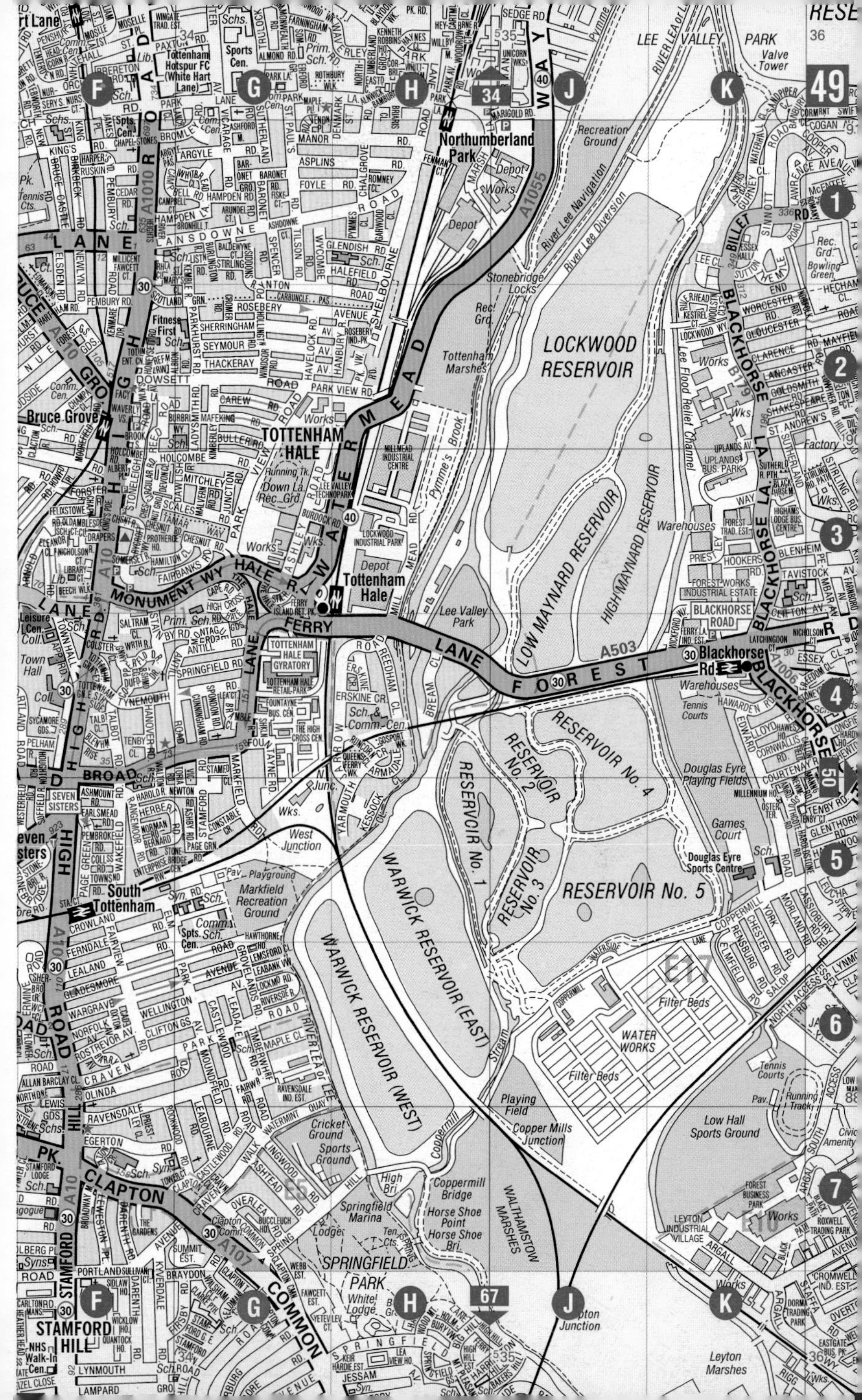

LEE VALLEY PARK
Valve Tower
Recreation Ground
Northumberland Park
Depot
Works
A1055
River Lee Navigation
River Lee Diversion
Stonebridge Locks
Rec. Grd.
Tottenham Marshes
LOCKWOOD RESERVOIR
Lee Flood Relief Channel
Pymme's Brook
MILLMEAD INDUSTRIAL CENTRE
LEE VALLEY TECHNOPARK
LOCKWOOD INDUSTRIAL PARK
TOTTENHAM HALE
Tottenham Hale
Tottenham Hotspur FC (White Hart Lane)
Bruce Grove
Fitness First
Running Tk.
Down La. Rec. Grd.
LOW MAYNARD RESERVOIR
HIGH MAYNARD RESERVOIR
Lee Valley Park
UPLANDS BUS. PARK
Warehouses
FOREST TRAD. EST.
FOREST WORKS INDUSTRIAL ESTATE
BLACKHORSE ROAD
Blackhorse Rd
A503
FOREST
LANE
FERRY LANE
TOTTENHAM HALE GYRATORY
TOTTENHAM HALE RETAIL PARK
FOUNTAYNE BUS. CEN.
THE HIGH CROSS CEN.
Sch. & Comm. Cen.
RESERVOIR No. 1
RESERVOIR No. 2
RESERVOIR No. 3
RESERVOIR No. 4
RESERVOIR No. 5
Douglas Eyre Playing Fields
Games Court
Douglas Eyre Sports Centre
Tennis Courts
SEVEN SISTERS
Seven Sisters
West Junction
South Tottenham
Playground
Markfield Recreation Ground
WARWICK RESERVOIR (WEST)
WARWICK RESERVOIR (EAST)
E17
Filter Beds
WATER WORKS
Stream
Playing Field
Copper Mills Junction
Cricket Ground
Sports Ground
Coppermill Bridge
Horse Shoe Point
Horse Shoe Bri.
WALTHAMSTOW MARSHES
Springfield Marina
Lodge
SPRINGFIELD PARK
White Lodge
Low Hall Sports Ground
Running Track
FOREST BUSINESS PARK
LEYTON INDUSTRIAL VILLAGE
E10
E5
ROXWELL TRADING PARK
CROMWELL IND. EST.
Clapton Junction
Leyton Marshes
STAMFORD HILL
HIGH ROAD
STAMFORD HILL
CLAPTON COMMON
A107
A10
A1010
HIGH ROAD
MONUMENT WY
HALE R.
WATERMEAD WAY
BLACKHORSE LA.
BLACKHORSE ROAD
BROAD LANE
LANE
34
67
50
F G H J K
1 2 3 4 5 6 7

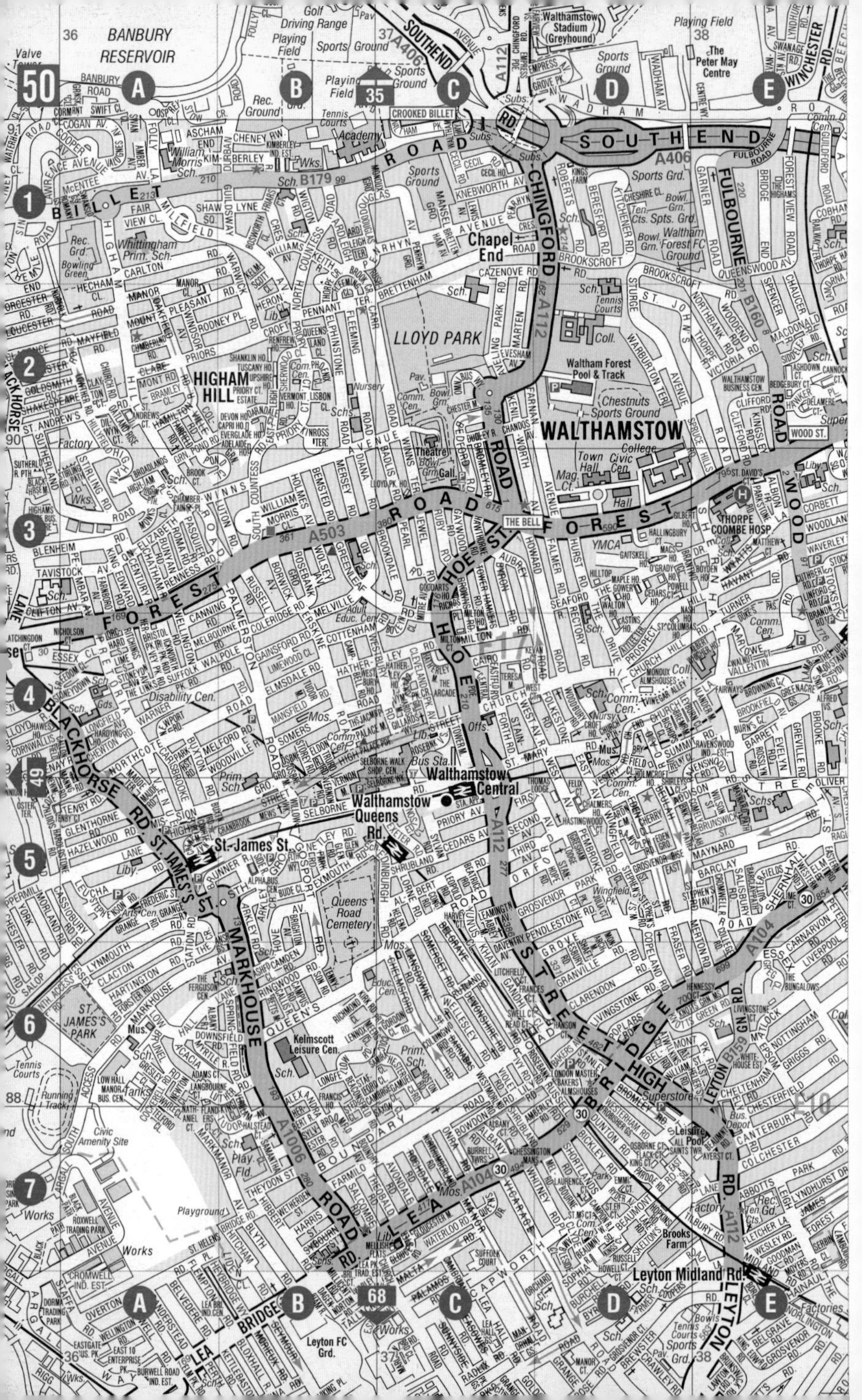

50
35
49
68
A
B
C
D
E
1
2
3
4
5
6
7
36
37
38
90
88
BANBURY RESERVOIR
Valve Tower
Golf Driving Range
Playing Field
Sports Ground
Playing Field
Sports Ground
Walthamstow Stadium (Greyhound)
The Peter May Centre
SOUTHEND
A406
A112
CHINGFORD RD.
WINCHESTER RD.
BANBURY ROAD
SWIFT CL.
Rec. Ground
Tennis Courts
CROOKED BILLET
Academy
WADHAM AV.
WADHAM
SOUTHEND
FULBOURNE ROAD
GUILDFORD ROAD
BILLET ROAD
B179
ASCHAM END
CHENEY RW.
KIMBERLEY
William Morris Sch.
KIMBERLEY IND. EST.
Wks.
Sports Ground
CECIL RD.
KNEBWORTH AV.
CHINGFORD
ROBERTS RD.
KINGS FARM
BERESFORD RD.
KITCHENER RD.
CHESHIRE CL.
Sports Grd.
Bowl. Grn.
Waltham Forest FC Ground
FULBOURNE
FOREST VIEW ROAD
BRIDGE END
Chapel End
HIGHAM HILL
Whittingham Prim. Sch.
MILLFIELD
CARLTON RD.
HECHAM CL.
MANOR
MOUNT PLEASANT RD.
RODNEY PL.
PENRHYN AV.
BRETTENHAM
CAZENOVE RD.
BROOKSCROFT
ST. JOHN'S
QUEENSWOOD AV.
B160
LLOYD PARK
ELPHINSTONE
FLEMING
AVELING PARK RD.
MARTEN RD.
Waltham Forest Pool & Track
Chestnuts Sports Ground
WALTHAMSTOW
Town Hall
Civic Cen.
College
Mag. Ct.
WALTHAMSTOW BUSINESS CEN.
WOOD ST.
ST. DAVID'S CT.
THORPE COOMBE HOSP.
FOREST ROAD
A503
THE BELL
Theatre
Bowl. Grn.
Gall.
SOUTH COUNTESS RD.
WILLIAM MORRIS CL.
HOLMES AV.
BEMSTED RD.
MERSEY
DIANA
BADLIS RD.
JEWEL
PEARL
RUBY
GAYWOOD
BROOKDALE
ROSEBANK
WOLSEY AV.
HOE ST.
YMCA
FOREST
HILLTOP
BLENHEIM
TAVISTOCK AV.
CLIFTON AV.
NICHOLSON CT.
ESSEX CL.
FOREST ROAD
CANNING
MELBOURNE
COLERIDGE RD.
COTTENHAM
GAINSFORD RD.
LIMEWOOD CL.
ELMSDALE RD.
MANSFIELD RD.
Adult Educ. Cen.
HOE
E17
Disability Cen.
BLACKHORSE RD.
WARNER
MELFORD RD.
WOODVILLE RD.
CHURCH HILL
PROSPECT HILL
Comm. Cen.
Monoux Almshouses
VINEGAR ALLEY
Coll.
BROOKFIELD
GREENACRE
BARRETT
EVELYN
BROOKE
GREVILLE RD.
The Arcade
HIGH STREET
HIGH PALACE HO.
SELBORNE WALK SHOP. CEN.
Bus Sta.
Walthamstow Central
Walthamstow Queens Rd.
ST. MARY RD.
Mus.
ST. JAMES'S ST.
St. James St.
Liby.
Prim. Sch.
SELBORNE RD.
CRANBROOK MEWS
GLENTHORNE
HAZELWOOD RD.
TENBY RD.
MARKHOUSE RD.
A112
Queens Road Cemetery
SHRUBLAND RD.
EDINBURGH
EXMOUTH RD.
GROVE RD.
ORFORD RD.
GROSVENOR PARK
Wingfield Pk.
PENDLESTONE RD.
MAYNARD
BARCLAY
SHERNHALL ST.
OLIVER
CARNARVON
LIVERPOOL
A104
LYNMOUTH
CLACTON RD.
HARTINGTON
MARKHOUSE
ST. JAMES'S PARK
Tennis Courts
Running Track
Kelmscott Leisure Cen.
QUEEN'S ROAD
BELGRAVE
SOMERSET RD.
WELLESLEY
DEVONSHIRE RD.
GRANVILLE
CLARENDON
LIVINGSTONE RD.
HIGH ST.
BAKERS ALMSHOUSES
LONDON MASTER BAKERS ALMSHOUSES
Superstore
Leisure Pool
Bus Depot
LEYTON GN. RD.
B159
NOTTINGHAM
CHELTENHAM
CHESTERFIELD
CANTERBURY
COLCHESTER
PARK
ABBOTTS
E10
BOUNDARY RD.
LEA BRIDGE RD.
A1006
A104
BURRELL TWRS.
CHESSINGTON MANS.
Civic Amenity Site
ROXWELL TRADING PARK
Works
Playground
CROMWELL IND. EST.
DORMA TRADING PARK
EASTGATE BUS. PK.
EAST 10 ENTERPRISE PK.
BURWELL ROAD IND. EST.
LEA BRIDGE RD.
Leyton FC Grd.
Works
Brooks Farm
Leyton Midland Rd.
LEYTON RD.
Factory
Bowls
Tennis Courts
Sports Grd.
Factories
BELGRAVE
GROSVENOR
SUNNYSIDE
CAPWORTH
VICARAGE

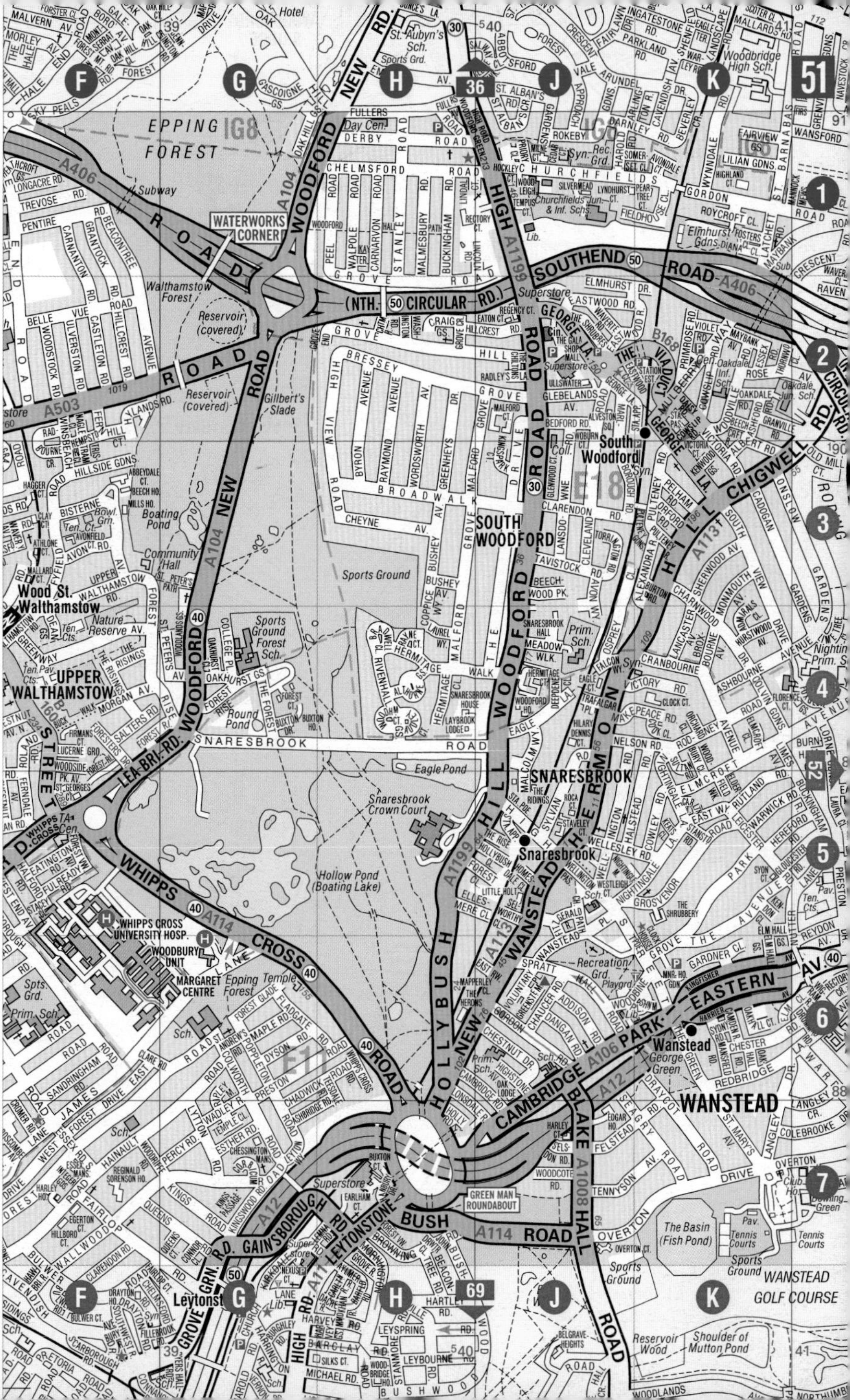
51
36
69
52
F
G
H
J
K
1
2
3
4
5
6
7
EPPING FOREST
IG8
E18
E11
A406
A104
A503
A1199
A113
A114
A106
A12
A1008
A112
B160
B168
NORTH CIRCULAR RD.
SOUTHEND ROAD
WOODFORD NEW ROAD
WATERWORKS CORNER
Walthamstow Forest
Reservoir (covered)
Reservoir (Covered)
Gilbert's Slade
Boating Pond
Community Hall
Nature Reserve
Wood St. Walthamstow
UPPER WALTHAMSTOW
Sports Ground Forest Sch.
Round Pond
SNARESBROOK ROAD
Eagle Pond
Snaresbrook Crown Court
Hollow Pond (Boating Lake)
WHIPPS CROSS ROAD
WHIPPS CROSS UNIVERSITY HOSP.
WOODBURY UNIT
MARGARET CENTRE
Epping Forest
Sports Ground
SOUTH WOODFORD
South Woodford
Churchfields Jun. & Inf. Schs.
Woodbridge High Sch.
GEORGE LA.
THE GALA SHOP. MALL
Superstore
CHIGWELL ROAD
SNARESBROOK
Snaresbrook
HIGH ROAD WOODFORD
HOLLYBUSH HILL
NEW WANSTEAD
HERMON HILL
Recreation Grd.
EASTERN AV.
PARK
Wanstead
George Green
WANSTEAD
CAMBRIDGE PARK
BLAKE HALL ROAD
GREEN MAN ROUNDABOUT
BUSH ROAD
LEYTONSTONE
GAINSBOROUGH RD.
Leytonstone
The Basin (Fish Pond)
Tennis Courts
Sports Ground
WANSTEAD GOLF COURSE
Reservoir Wood
Shoulder of Mutton Pond
BELGRAVE HEIGHTS
Oakdale Inf. Sch.
Oakdale Jun. Sch.
St. Aubyn's Sch.
Hotel

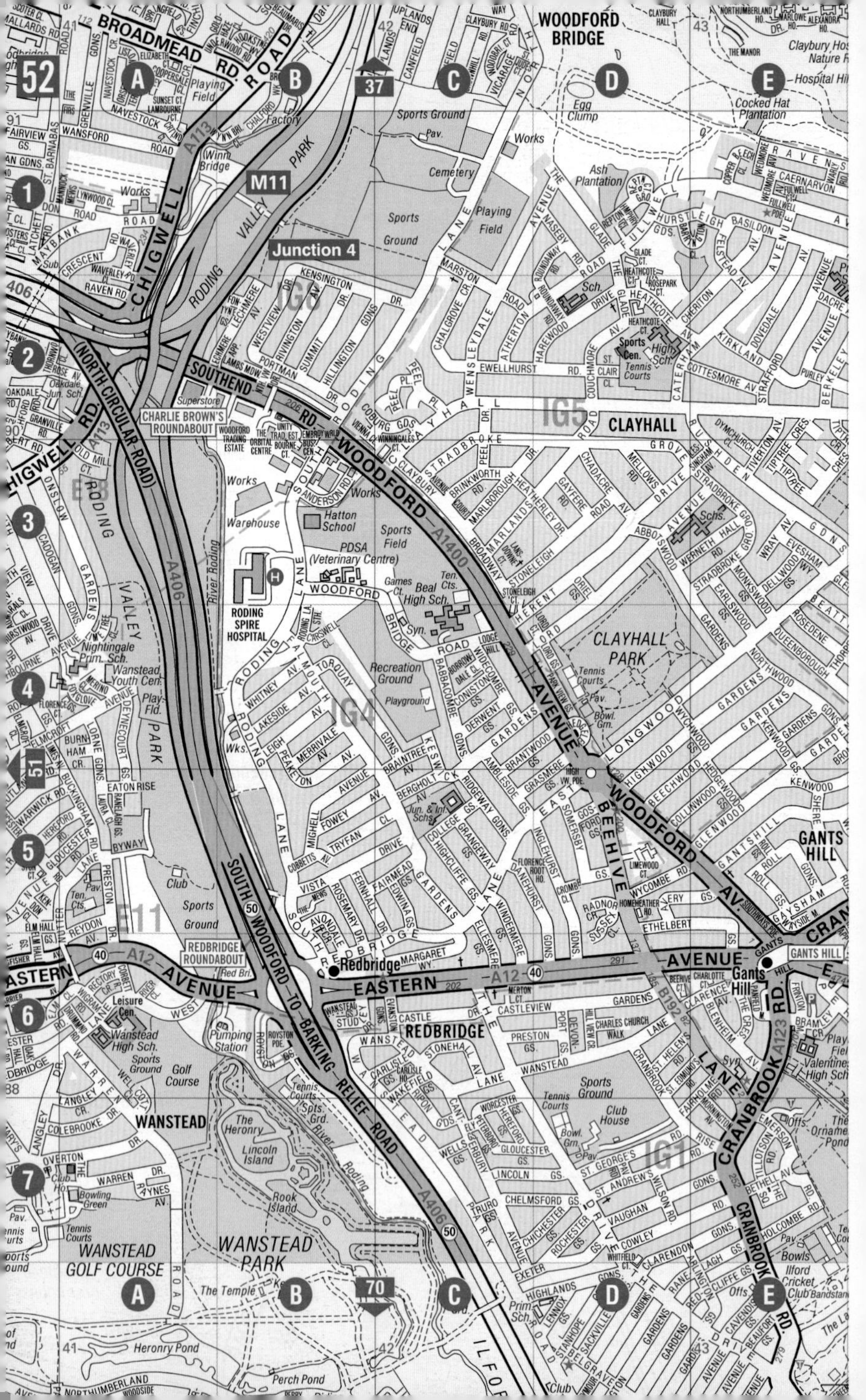

52
A
B
C
D
E
1
2
3
4
5
6
7
37
51
70
WOODFORD BRIDGE
BROADMEAD RD.
ROAD
CHIGWELL
M11
Junction 4
RODING VALLEY PARK
Sports Ground
Pav.
Cemetery
Sports Ground
Playing Field
Works
Egg Clump
Ash Plantation
Cocked Hat Plantation
Claybury Hos Nature R
Hospital Hill
THE MANOR
CLAYBURY HALL
Playing Field
Factory
Winn Bridge
WANSFORD ROAD
FAIRVIEW GS.
LYNWOOD CL.
Works
CRESCENT
RAVEN RD.
406
(NORTH CIRCULAR ROAD)
A406
A113
CHIGWELL RD.
SOUTHEND RD
Superstore
CHARLIE BROWN'S ROUNDABOUT
WOODFORD TRADING ESTATE
THE ORBITAL CENTRE
KENSINGTON DR.
IG8
IG6
IG5
IG4
IG1
E18
E11
PORTMAN DR.
RODING LANE
CLAYHALL AV.
CLAYHALL
WOODFORD AVENUE
A1400
Works
Warehouse
Hatton School
Sports Field
PDSA (Veterinary Centre)
WOODFORD BRIDGE ROAD
Beal High Sch.
RODING SPIRE HOSPITAL
River Roding
Recreation Ground
Playground
CLAYHALL PARK
Tennis Courts
Bowl. Grn.
Sports Cen.
High Sch.
Tennis Courts
Sch.
LONGWOOD GARDENS
GANTS HILL
Nightingale Prim. Sch.
Wanstead Youth Cen.
Play. Fld.
VALLEY
PARK
Club
Sports Ground
REDBRIDGE ROUNDABOUT
Red Bri.
EASTERN AVENUE
A12
40
SOUTH WOODFORD TO BARKING RELIEF ROAD
50
Redbridge
REDBRIDGE
A123
CRANBROOK RD.
BEEHIVE LANE
B192
Gants Hill
Leisure Cen.
Wanstead High Sch.
Sports Ground
Golf Course
Pumping Station
The Heronry
Lincoln Island
Rook Island
River Roding
WANSTEAD
WANSTEAD PARK
WANSTEAD GOLF COURSE
Bowling Green
Tennis Courts
The Temple
Heronry Pond
Perch Pond
Sports Ground
Club House
Tennis Courts
Valentines High Sch.
Ilford Cricket Club
Prim. Sch.
NORTHUMBERLAND
41
42
43
ILFORD

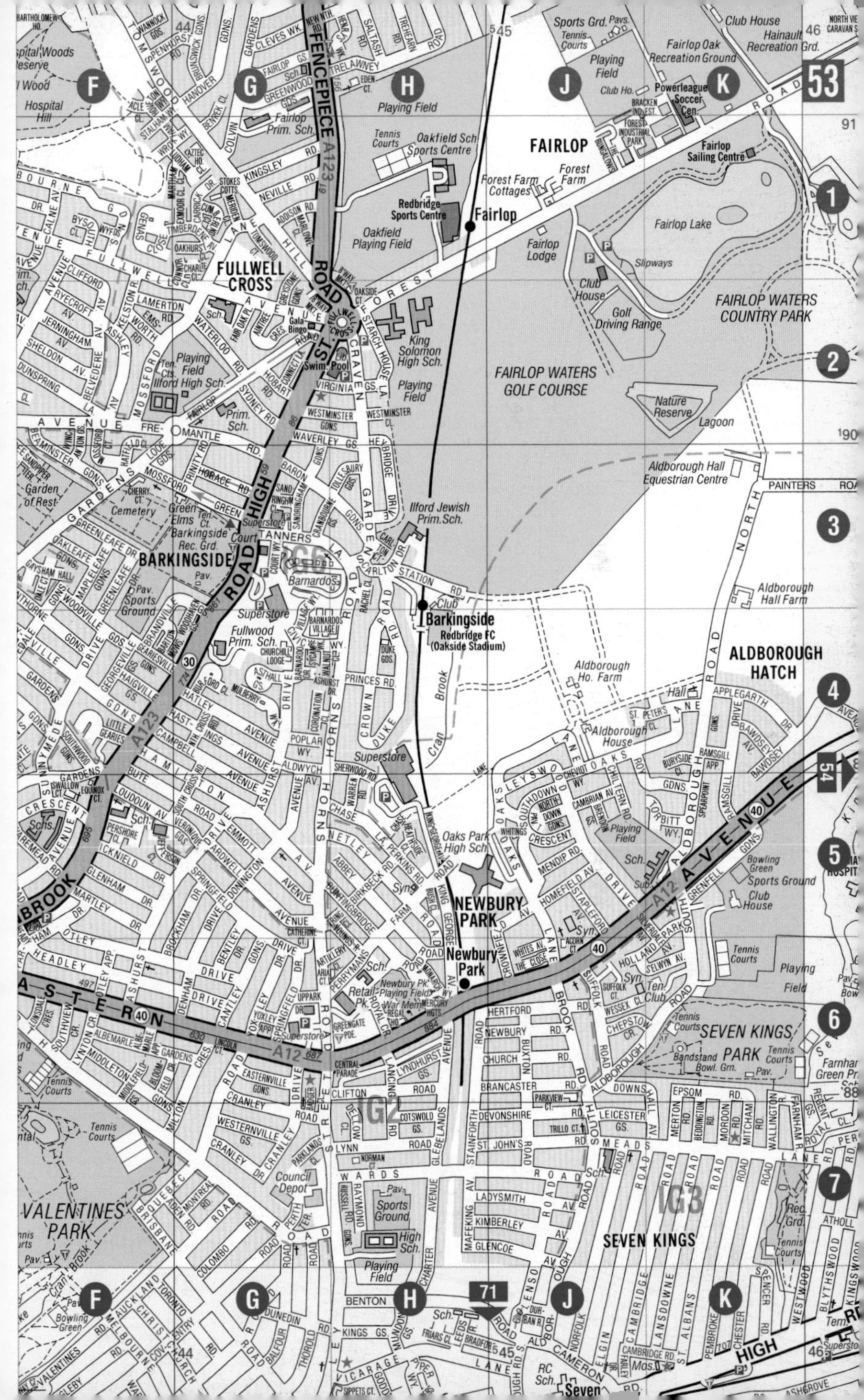
53
FULLWELL CROSS
BARKINGSIDE
FAIRLOP
ALDBOROUGH HATCH
NEWBURY PARK
SEVEN KINGS
VALENTINES PARK
SEVEN KINGS PARK
FAIRLOP WATERS COUNTRY PARK
FAIRLOP WATERS GOLF COURSE
Fairlop Lake
Fairlop Oak Recreation Ground
Hainault Recreation Grd.
Fairlop Sailing Centre
Powerleague Soccer Cen.
Redbridge Sports Centre
Oakfield Sch. Sports Centre
Oakfield Playing Field
King Solomon High Sch.
Ilford Jewish Prim.Sch.
Barkingside
Redbridge FC (Oakside Stadium)
Aldborough Hall Equestrian Centre
Aldborough Hall Farm
Aldborough Ho. Farm
Aldborough House
Oaks Park High Sch.
Newbury Park
Fairlop
Hospital Hill
Cemetery
Garden of Rest
Barnardos
Fullwood Prim. Sch.
Ilford High Sch.
Fairlop Prim. Sch.
Golf Driving Range
Nature Reserve
Lagoon
Slipways
Club House
Fairlop Lodge
Forest Farm
Forest Farm Cottages
Council Depot
Sports Ground
FENCEPIECE ROAD A123
HIGH ROAD
FOREST ROAD
FULLWELL AVENUE
EASTERN AVENUE A12
HORNS ROAD
NORTH ROAD
ALDBOROUGH ROAD NORTH
TANNERS LA.
STATION RD.
CRAVEN GARDENS
WESTMINSTER GDNS.
HORACE RD.
MOSSFORD GREEN
HAMILTON AVENUE
HATLEY AVENUE
CAMPBELL AVENUE
DONINGTON AVENUE
ASHURST DRIVE
BENTLEY DR.
CANTLEY GDNS.
HEADLEY DRIVE
GLENHAM DR.
MARTLEY DR.
OTLEY DR.
WARDS ROAD
BENTON RD.
ST. JOHN'S ROAD
MEADS LANE
EPSOM RD.
HIGH RD.
KINGS GS.
VICARAGE LANE
CAMERON RD.
54
71
F
G
H
J
K
1
2
3
4
5
6
7
44
45
46
91
90
88
IG2
IG3
IG6
A12
40
30

54
Hainault Rec. Grd.
NORTH VIEW CARAVAN SITE
FOREST ROAD
HAINAULT ROAD
Seven Kings Water
WHALEBONE LANE
A1112
A B C D E
1 2 3 4 5 6 7
46 47 48
91 90 88
Fairlop Sailing Centre
FAIRLOP WATERS COUNTRY PARK
FAIRLOP WATERS
IG6
Farm Cottages
Hainault Works
Hainault Farm
Marks Gate
Furze Cottage
Furze House Farm
FURZE FM. CL.
ROAD
KINGSTON HILL AV.
BEANSLAND GRO.
PAINTERS ROAD
IG2
Aldborough Hall Farm
ALDBOROUGH HATCH
Red House Farm
Hainault House
BILLET ROAD
Willow Farm
Playing Field
Little Heath Sch.
Sports Ground
RM6
REYNOLDS CT.
DANBURY CL.
BILLET CL.
NEWHOUSE AV.
ROSE HATCH AV.
TANTONY GRO.
Rec. Grd.
Jun. Sch.
Comm. Cen.
Lib.
Infant Sch.
Chadwell Heath Cemetery
BARDFIELD
FAV. PADNALL CT.
PADNALL
ARNEWAYS AV.
LONGHAYES AV.
HARVEY HO.
COLIN POND CT.
NASH RD.
HOPE CL.
CAVALIER GR.
GREGORY RD.
ACOTT CL.
WOODRUSH WY.
LAKE RD.
FEWS LODGE
HUTCHINSON CT.
CRABTREE AV.
ROLES GRO.
LAWN FARM GRO.
THATCHES GRO.
BAGLEYS SPRING
RAMS GRO.
SHEEPCOTES RD.
SHEEPCOTES LANE
HATCH GRO.
HIGHVIEW HO.
NORTH
ST. JAMES GS.
EASTERN AVENUE
A12
50
EASTERN AV. W.
53
40
BAWDSEY AV.
Nursery
North Residence
KING GEORGE HOSPITAL
South Residence
CHADWELL HEATH LANE
LT. HEATH
FRESHWELL AV.
CHAFFORD WAY
INVERCLYDE GDS.
FIRST AV.
NEWTON IND. EST.
SHEPHERDS
WARREN TER.
MELBOURNE GS.
ROCHFORD AV.
ONGAR CL.
ROSEWOOD CT.
TENDRING WY.
DRIVE
Redbridge College
Grove Prim. Sch.
Ethel Davis Sch.
LITTLE HEATH
GOODMAYES HOSPITAL
Sports Ground
Club House
Playing Field
Pav.
Bowls
Tennis Courts
IG3
Brookside
Farnham Green Prim. Sch.
SECOND AV.
HAVERING GARDENS
TOLWORTH GDNS.
PORTLAND GDNS.
HATHAWAY GS.
ADELAIDE GDNS.
GENEVA GDNS.
PEMBERTON GDNS.
LANSBURY AV.
NORBURY GS.
CHADVILLE GDNS.
EAST PARK CL.
NORTH ROAD
THE CLOSE
KELLY WY.
CAVENDISH
HAINAULT
Playgrd.
ST. CHAD'S PARK
BLACKBUSH AV.
CANON AV.
BISHOPS AV.
Sch.
GLANDFORD
NORWICH
HEVINGHAM
GRESHAM
LEXDEN DR.
ABERCORN GDNS.
JOYDON DR.
LANGHAM DR.
The Chadwell Cen.
BLACKSMITHS CL.
Playing Field
QUARLES PK.
PRIESTLEY GDNS.
GALSWORTHY AV.
MANNIN RD.
CHRISTIE GDNS.
FLORA GDNS.
CONWAY GDNS.
JUNIPER CT.
BARLEYFIELDS CL.
Sch.
FLORENCE GDNS.
ROXY AV.
PRIMROSE AV.
DOUGLAS RD.
ECCLESTON CRES.
Prim. Sch.
Play. Fld.
THACKERAY DR.
Rec. Grd.
Bowl. Grn.
HAWKRIDGE CL.
JARROW RD.
HALL RD.
MANOR RD.
PERCIVAL GS.
Playground
SOUTH RD.
ALEXANDRA RD.
MILL LA.
WILLOW RD.
Bowl. Grns.
Pav.
CHADWELL HEATH
EDWARD RD.
LEE AV.
BEACONSFIELD RD.
HIGH ROAD
A118
GROVE FARM RETAIL PK.
HICKMAN RD.
ASTON M.
Mecca Bingo
BACK LANE
ERIC RD.
CECIL RD.
KENNETH RD.
HEATH
EUSTACE RD.
JUNCTION RD.
WOODLANDS AV.
MERTEN RD.
BURLINGTON
MIRRAVALE TRADING EST.
Works
RM8
SELINAS LA.
Warehouse
Chadwell Heath
SPRING CL.
FRESHWATER ROAD
LYMINGTON
CHADWELL HEATH INDUSTRIAL PARK
Playing Field
KEMP RD.
CLARIDGE
Works
BARLEY LANE
B177
PERCY ROAD
ROYAL CL.
REGENT GS.
WALLINGTON RD.
FARNHAM RD.
Rec. Grd.
Tennis Courts
ATHOLL RD.
BLYTHSWOOD RD.
KINGSWOOD RD.
WELLWOOD RD.
EASTWOOD RD.
WESTWOOD
SPENCER RD.
Superstore
GOODMAYES
Goodmayes
GOODMAYES RETAIL PARK
72
Superstore
RAVENINGS PARADE
FENMAN GS.
KINFAUNS ROAD
ASHGROVE
KILDOWAN
Play. Field
Mayfield Sch. Coll.
CROSS RD.
MILTON CT.
RAILWAY ST.
GIBSON CL.
COULSON CL.
OVERTON DR.
BELFAIRS DR.
BIRCHDALE GDNS.
MANSTED GDNS.
MONTPELIER GDNS.
ESSEX RD.
Sch.
STATION RD.
BARON RD.
CLARENCE RD.
BRADY CT.
BURNSIDE
ARMY
PALMER
STRONG
889 968 1221 153 97 101 149 150

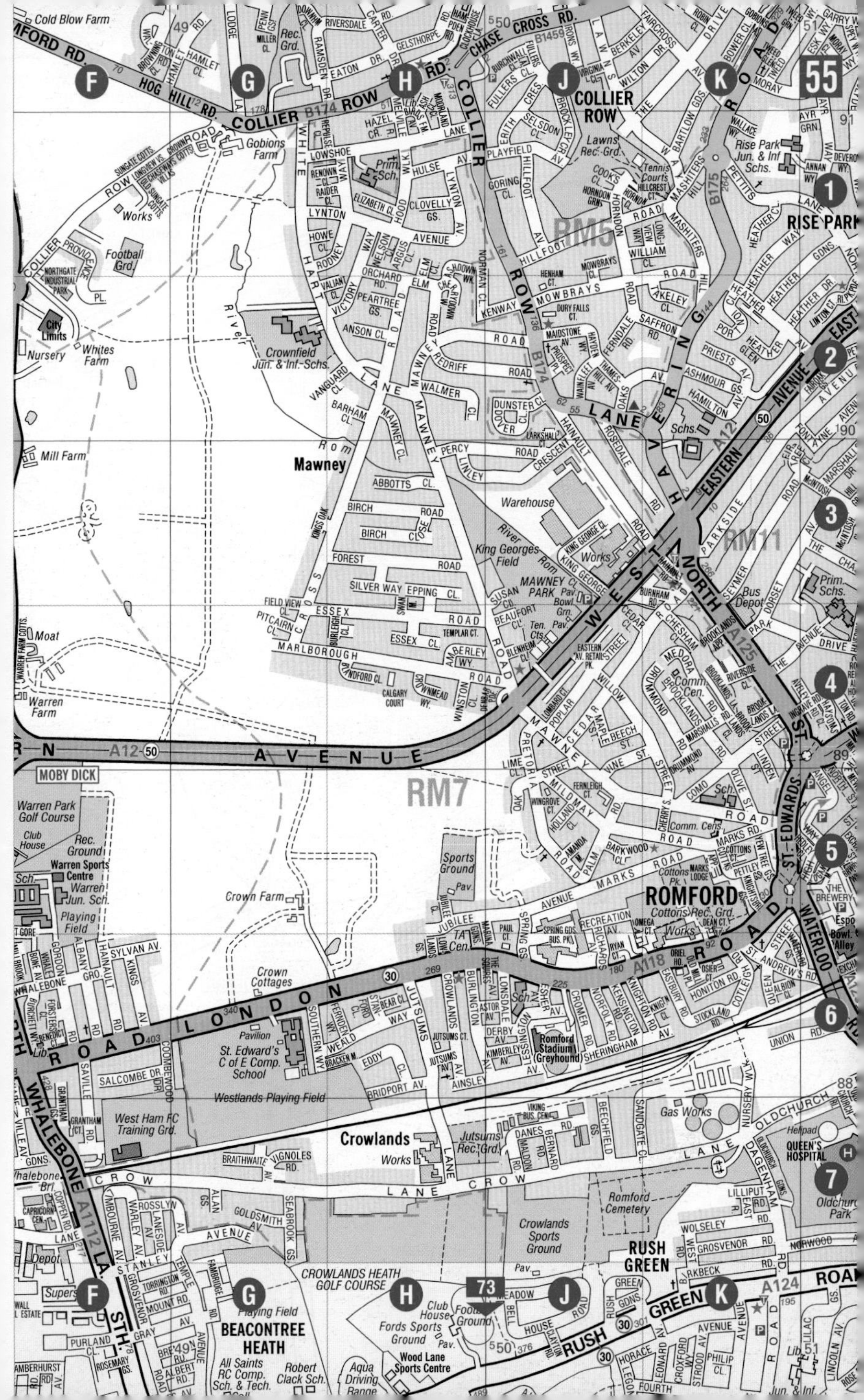
55
Cold Blow Farm
ROMFORD RD.
HOG HILL RD.
COLLIER ROW RD.
CHASE CROSS RD.
COLLIER ROW
Lawns Rec. Grd.
Rise Park Jun. & Inf. Schs.
RISE PARK
Gobions Farm
COLLIER ROW LANE
WHITE HART LANE
Prim. Sch.
Works
Football Grd.
NORTHGATE INDUSTRIAL PARK
City Limits
Nursery
Whites Farm
Crownfield Jun. & Inf. Schs.
River Rom
RM5
MAWNEY ROAD
Mawney
Mill Farm
Moat
Warren Farm
Warehouse
King Georges Field
MAWNEY PARK
WEST
NORTH STREET
EASTERN AVENUE
A12
HAVERING ROAD
B174
B175
RM11
Bus Depot
Prim. Schs.
Comm. Cen.
Sch.
Warren Park Golf Course
Club House
Rec. Ground
Warren Sports Centre
Warren Jun. Sch.
Playing Field
MOBY DICK
A12 AVENUE
RM7
Sports Ground
Crown Farm
Crown Cottages
ROMFORD
Cottons Rec. Grd.
Cottons Pk.
Works
ST. EDWARDS WAY
WATERLOO RD.
THE BREWERY
Bowl. Alley
A118
ROAD LONDON
Pavilion
St. Edward's C of E Comp. School
Westlands Playing Field
West Ham FC Training Grd.
Romford Stadium (Greyhound)
Gas Works
Crowlands
Jutsums Rec. Grd.
Works
QUEEN'S HOSPITAL
Helipad
Oldchurch Park
OLDCHURCH RD.
CROW LANE
WHALEBONE LA. NTH.
A1112
Whalebone Bri.
Romford Cemetery
Crowlands Sports Ground
RUSH GREEN
RUSH GREEN ROAD
A124
CROWLANDS HEATH GOLF COURSE
Club House
Football Ground
Fords Sports Ground
Wood Lane Sports Centre
Aqua Driving Range
Playing Field
BEACONTREE HEATH
All Saints RC Comp. Sch. & Tech.
Robert Clack Sch.
Depot
Supers
73
F
G
H
J
K
1
2
3
4
5
6
7

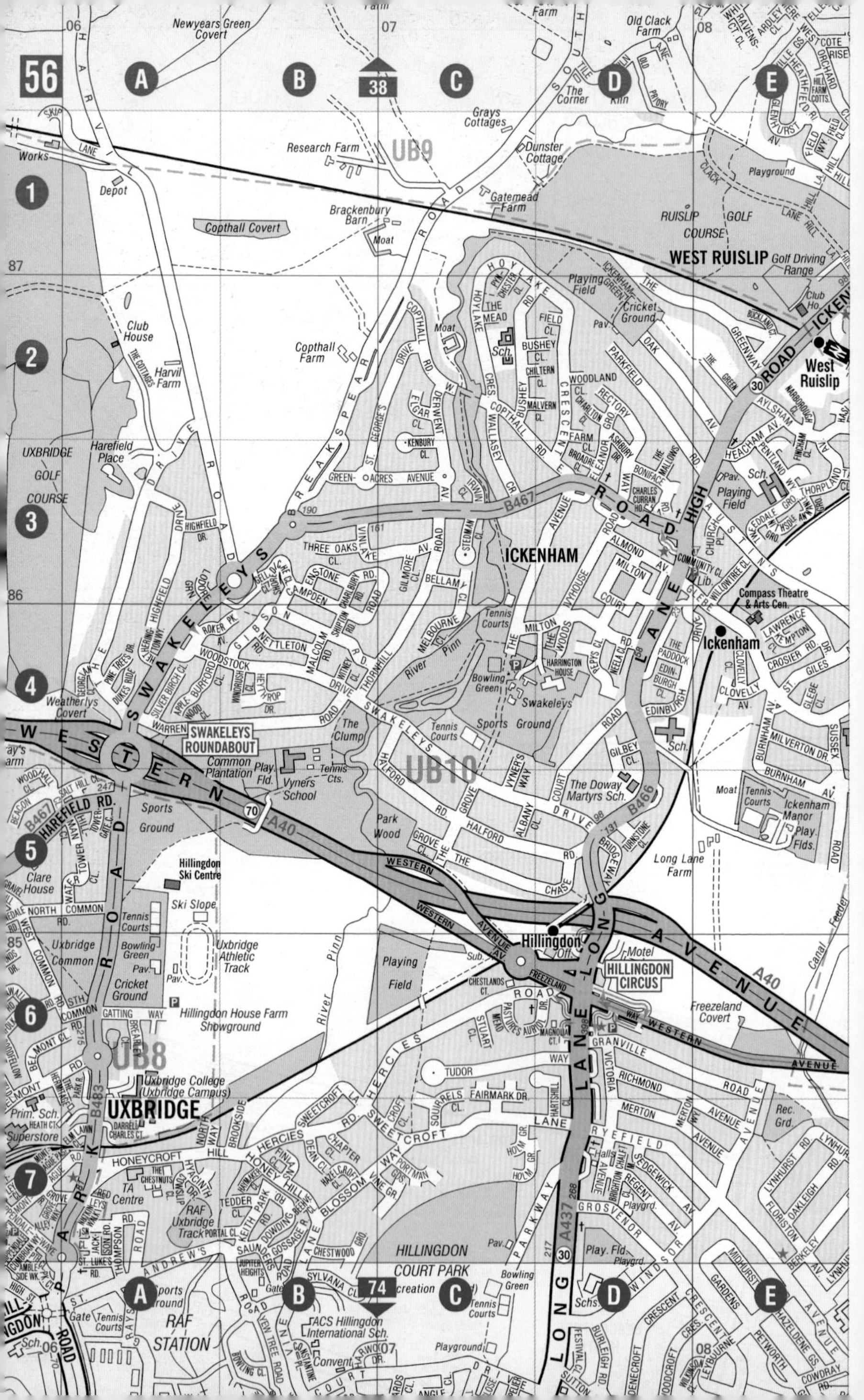
Newyears Green Covert
Old Clack Farm
38
74
UB9
UB10
UB8
Research Farm
Grays Cottages
Dunster Cottage
Gatemead Farm
Brackenbury Barn
Moat
Copthall Covert
Depot
Works
Club House
Harvil Farm
Harefield Place
UXBRIDGE GOLF COURSE
RUISLIP GOLF COURSE
WEST RUISLIP
Golf Driving Range
West Ruislip
Copthall Farm
ICKENHAM
Ickenham
Compass Theatre & Arts Cen.
Playing Field
Cricket Ground
Tennis Courts
Bowling Green
Swakeleys Sports Ground
SWAKELEYS ROUNDABOUT
Common Plantation
Vyners School
The Clump
Park Wood
The Doway Martyrs Sch.
Ickenham Manor
Long Lane Farm
Weatherlys Covert
Clare House
Sports Ground
Hillingdon Ski Centre
Ski Slope
Uxbridge Athletic Track
Uxbridge Common
Cricket Ground
Hillingdon House Farm Showground
Hillingdon
HILLINGDON CIRCUS
Motel
Freezeland Covert
Uxbridge College (Uxbridge Campus)
UXBRIDGE
Superstore
Prim. Sch.
TA Centre
RAF Uxbridge Track
HILLINGDON COURT PARK
RAF STATION
ACS Hillingdon International Sch.
Convent
Rec. Grd.
WESTERN AVENUE
A40
B467
B466
B483
A437
SWAKELEYS ROAD
HIGH ROAD
LONG LANE
HARVIL ROAD
BREAKSPEAR ROAD
PARK ROAD
HAREFIELD RD.
SOUTH ROAD

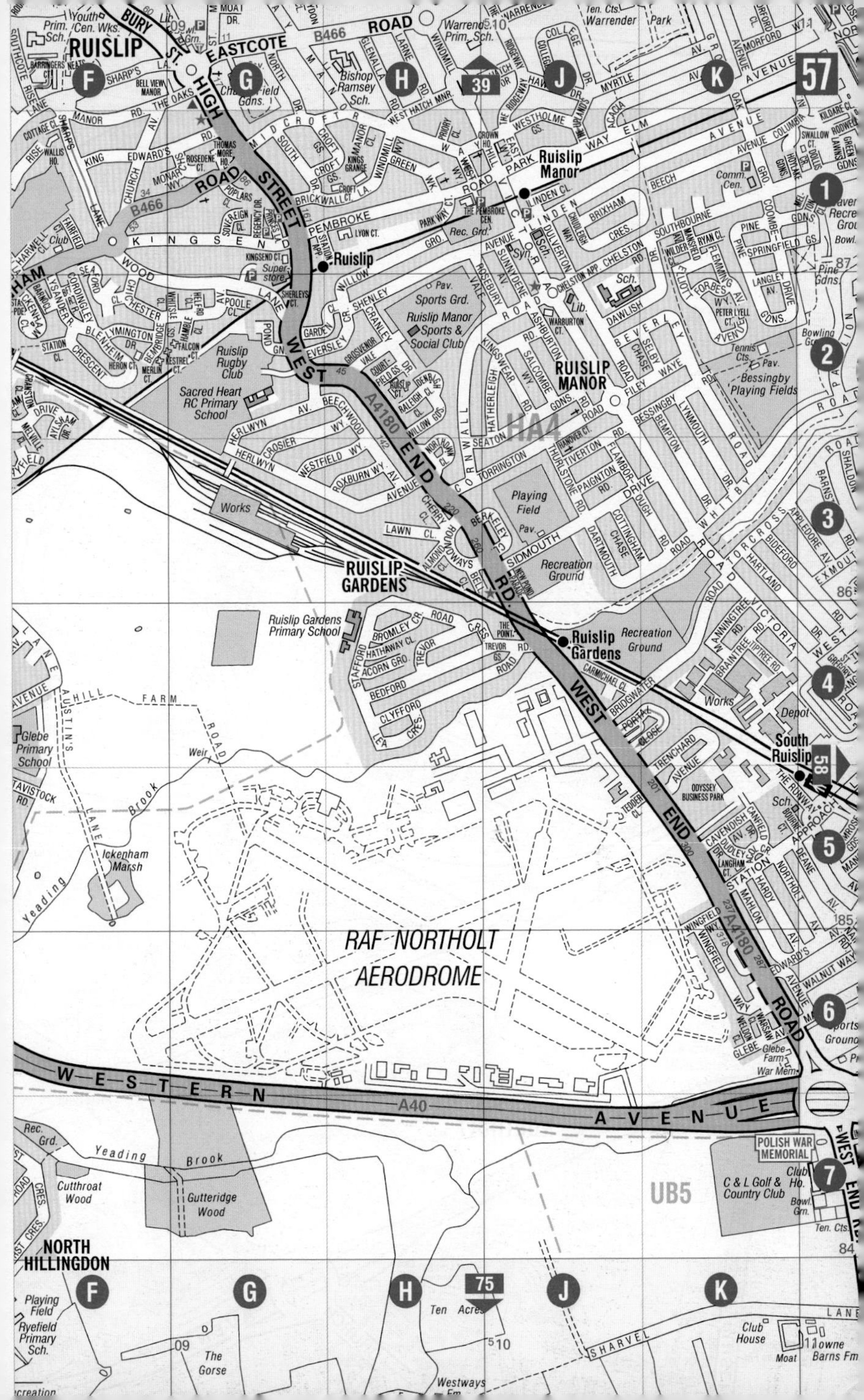
RUISLIP
Youth Cen. Wks.
Prim. Sch.
BURY ST.
HIGH STREET
EASTCOTE ROAD
B466
Warrender Prim. Sch.
Ten. Cts.
Warrender Park
Bishop Ramsey Sch.
39
COLLEGE DR.
MYRTLE AV.
MORFORD WY.
ELM AVENUE
OAK AVENUE
COLUMBIA AV.
SHARP'S LA.
BELL VIEW MANOR
THE OAKS
Chapel-field Gdns.
MANOR RD.
MIDCROFT
WEST HATCH MNR.
PRIORY CL.
WESTHOLME GS.
THE UPLANDS
ACACIA AV.
KING EDWARD'S RD.
THOMAS MORE HO.
ROSEDENE CT.
MONARCH WY.
CHURCH AV.
KINGS GRANGE
WINDMILL WY.
GREEN WK.
PARK WAY
Ruislip Manor
CROWN HO.
EAST WY.
BEECH AV.
Comm. Cen.
SWALLOW CT.
KILDARE CL.
RODWELL GDNS.
LAWNS
WALLIS HO.
POPLARS CL.
SOVEREIGN CL.
REGENCY DR.
BRICKWALL LA.
PEMBROKE RD.
THE PEMBROKE CEN.
LYON CT.
Rec. Grd.
LINDEN CL.
DULVERTON RD.
BRIXHAM CRES.
SOUTHBOURNE AV.
MANSFIELD AV.
RYAN CL.
PINE GDNS.
SPRINGFIELD GS.
COOMBE DR.
Bowl.
Pine Gdns.
87
KINGSEND
Club
FAIRFIELD RD.
Ruislip
STATION APP.
Super-store
KINGSEND CT.
WOOD LANE
POOLE CL.
SHERLEYS CT.
WILLOW GRO.
Syn.
SUNNYDENE AV.
Sch.
CHELSTON RD.
CHELSTON APP.
WILDER CL.
ELLIOTT AV.
FLEMMING AV.
FORBES WY.
PETER LYELL CT.
LANGLEY AV.
DRIVE
Lib.
Pav.
Sports Grd.
Ruislip Manor Sports & Social Club
ROSEBURY VALE
ASHBURTON RD.
WARBURTON CT.
DAWLISH DR.
BEVERLEY RD.
Bowling Grn.
Tennis Cts.
Pav.
Bessingby Playing Fields
CHESTER CL.
HELFORD CL.
HAMBLE CL.
TALCON CT.
KESTREL CT.
MERLIN CT.
HERON CT.
BLENHEIM CRESCENT
LYMINGTON DR.
BEMBRIDGE
STATION CL.
Ruislip Rugby Club
Sacred Heart RC Primary School
POND GN.
GARDEN CL.
EVERSLEY CR.
SHENLEY AV.
CRANLEY DR.
GROSVENOR VALE
COURTFIELD GS.
RUISLIP CL.
RALEIGH CL.
DENBIGH CL.
WILLOW GDS.
KINGSWEAR RD.
SALCOMBE WY.
RUISLIP MANOR
SELBY CHASE
FILEY WAYE
BESSINGBY RD.
BEMPTON DR.
LYNMOUTH RD.
WEST END
A4180
HA4
HERLWYN AV.
BEECHWOOD AV.
CROSIER WY.
WESTFIELD WY.
ROXBURN WY.
AVENUE
NORTHOLT CL.
CORNWALL RD.
HATHERLEIGH RD.
SEATON GDNS.
HANOVER CT.
TIVERTON RD.
FLAMBOROUGH RD.
HURLSTONE RD.
PAIGNTON RD.
TORRINGTON RD.
Playing Field
Pav.
DRIVE
WHITBY RD.
SHALDON
BARNSTAPLE
APPLEDORE AV.
BIDEFORD RD.
HARTLAND DR.
EXMOUTH
TORCROSS RD.
86
DRYLAWN CL.
Works
LAWN CL.
CHERRY CL.
ALMOND CL.
ROUNDWAYS
BERKELEY CL.
BELL
SIDMOUTH DR.
DARTMOUTH RD.
COTTINGHAM CHASE
Recreation Ground
RUISLIP GARDENS
NEW POND PARADE
RD.
THE POINT
Ruislip Gardens
Recreation Ground
MANNINGTREE RD.
VICTORIA RD.
WEST RD.
Ruislip Gardens Primary School
BROMLEY CR.
HATHAWAY CL.
TREVOR CRES.
ACORN GRO.
TREVOR GS.
BEDFORD RD.
CLYFFORD RD.
LEA CRES.
STAFFORD RD.
CARMICHAEL CL.
BRIDGWATER RD.
BRAINTREE RD.
TIPTREE RD.
Works
Depot
South Ruislip
58
PORTAL CLOSE
TRENCHARD AVENUE
ODYSSEY BUSINESS PARK
THE RUNWAY
Sch.
BOURNE CT.
APPROACH
CAVENDISH AV.
DUDLEY DR.
CANFIELD DR.
ACOL CR.
LANGHAM CT.
STATION
NORTHOLT AV.
HARDY AV.
MAHLON AV.
DEANE AV.
TEDDER CL.
AVENUE
HILL FARM ROAD
AUSTIN'S LANE
Glebe Primary School
TAVISTOCK RD.
Weir
Brook
Ickenham Marsh
Yeading
RAF NORTHOLT AERODROME
WINGFIELD WY.
WINGFIELD WAY
A4180
ROAD
EDWARD'S AV.
WALNUT WAY
185
Sports Ground
WELDON CL.
WARSAW CL.
GLEBE
Glebe Farm War Mem.
WESTERN AVENUE
A40
Rec. Grd.
Yeading Brook
POLISH WAR MEMORIAL
WEST END RD.
Club Ho.
C & L Golf & Country Club
Bowl. Grn.
Ten. Cts.
UB5
Cutthroat Wood
Gutteridge Wood
84
NORTH HILLINGDON
Playing Field
Ryefield Primary Sch.
75
Ten Acres
The Gorse
09
10
SHARVEL LANE
Club House
Moat
Towne Barns Fm
Westways Fm
Recreation
F
G
H
J
K
1
2
3
4
5
6
7

Eastcote
Roxbourne Park
Rayners Lane
RAYNERS LANE
ALEXANDRA AV.
IMPERIAL DR.
Rayners La. Junc.
Sports Ground
Cavendish Recreation Ground
Bowl. Grn.
Ten. Cts.
Pine Gdns.
Bowling Green
Bessingby Playing Fields
Miniature Railway
Yeading Brook
Roxbourne First & Mid. Schs.
Recreation Ground
Newton Farm First & Mid. Sch.
Newton Park West
Tennis Courts
The Roxbourne
Alexandra Sch.
Newton Ecology Park
Tennis Cts.
Club
Football Grd.
Field End Jun. & Inf. Schs.
Playground
High Sch.
HA4
SOUTH RUISLIP
Rec. Grd.
Deane Park
Tennis Courts
Learning Cen.
Deanesfield Prim. Sch.
Queensmead Sch.
Playing Fields
Queensmead Sports Centre
Superstore
Depot
CHANCERYGATE BUS. CEN.
VICTORIA RETAIL PARK
Warehouses
South Ruislip
Superstore
Harrow Borough FC (Earlsmead Stadium)
Sch.
Solid Waste Transfer Station
VICTORIA WAY
NORTHOLT PARK
Play Centre
Play Fld.
Northolt High Sch.
Bourne Primary School
Rec. Grd.
Sports Ground
POLISH WAR MEMORIAL
Priors Fm.
Glebe Farm
War Mem.
Lord Halsbury Memorial Playing Flds.
Willow Tree Prim. Sch.
WESTERN AVENUE
A40
NORTHOLT
Islip Manor Park
Comm. Cen.
Bowl. Grn.
Playground
UB5
Northolt Swimarama
Northolt
MANDEVILLE ROAD
A312
A4180
A4090
LONDON GOLF COURSE
Sports Ground
Tennis Courts
Club Ho.
Northolt Prim. Sch.
John Chilton Sch.
West London Academy
Leis. Cen.
Youth Cen.
TARGET ROUNDABOUT
CHURCH RD.
Comm. Cen.
Belvue Park
Moat
Health Club
Driving Range
Sch.
Golf Club
Towne Barns Fm.
Lime Tree Park
Playing Fields
40
57
76
A
B
C
D
E
1
2
3
4
5
6
7
84
85
86
87
11
12
13

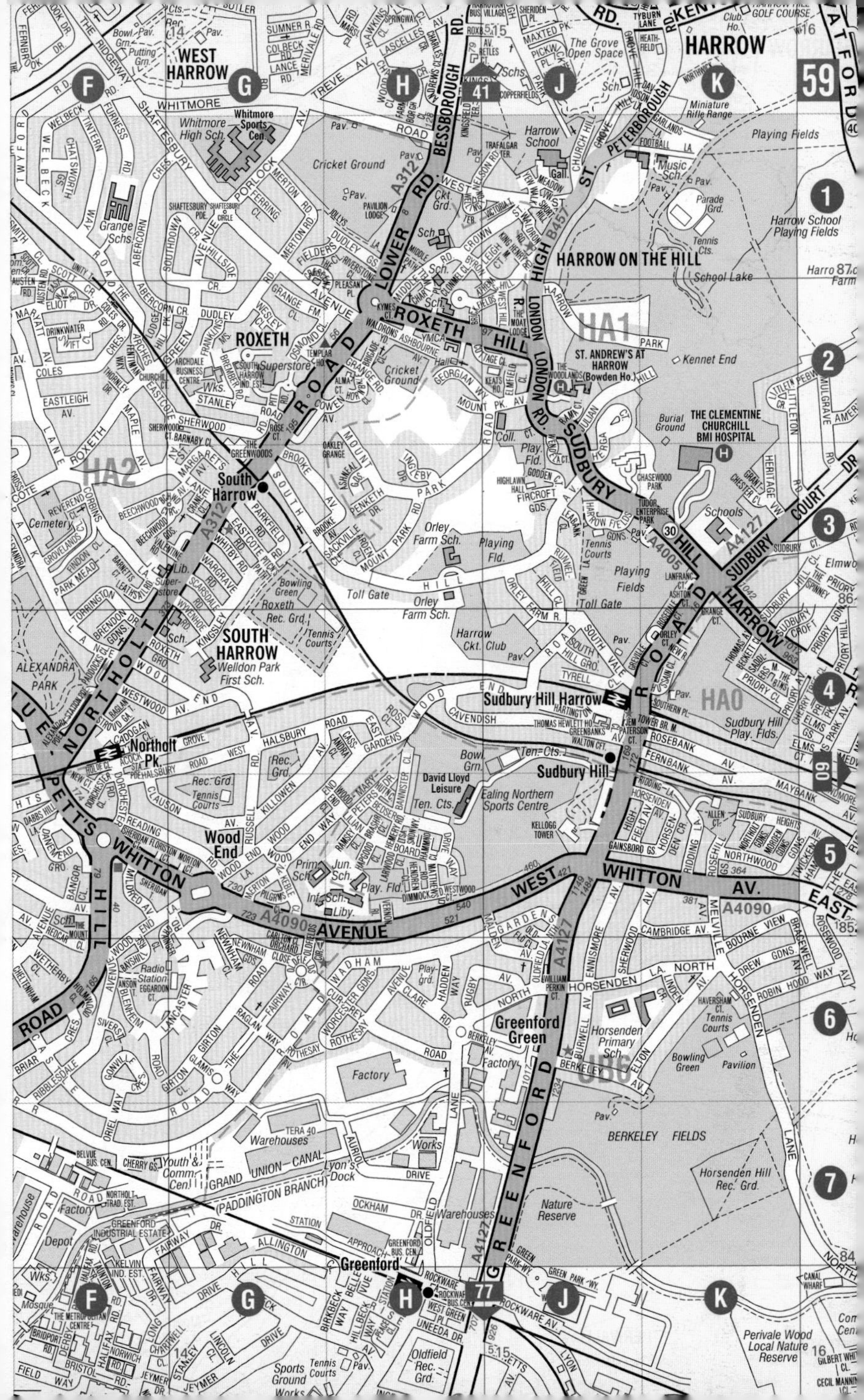
59
F
G
H
J
K
1
2
3
4
5
6
7
41
77
60
WEST HARROW
HARROW
HARROW ON THE HILL
ROXETH
SOUTH HARROW
HA1
HA2
HA0
UB6
Wood End
Greenford Green
Greenford
Northolt Pk.
South Harrow
Sudbury Hill Harrow
Sudbury Hill
Whitmore High Sch.
Whitmore Sports Cen.
Grange Schs.
Cricket Ground
Harrow School
Music Sch.
Parade Grd.
Harrow School Playing Fields
Playing Fields
Miniature Rifle Range
School Lake
The Grove Open Space
ST. ANDREW'S AT HARROW (Bowden Ho.)
Kennet End
THE CLEMENTINE CHURCHILL BMI HOSPITAL
Burial Ground
Orley Farm Sch.
Playing Fld.
Toll Gate
Harrow Ckt. Club
Roxeth Rec. Grd.
Welldon Park First Sch.
Cemetery
ALEXANDRA PARK
David Lloyd Leisure
Ealing Northern Sports Centre
KELLOGG TOWER
Horsenden Primary Sch.
BERKELEY FIELDS
Horsenden Hill Rec. Grd.
Nature Reserve
Factory
Warehouses
Works
GRAND UNION CANAL
(PADDINGTON BRANCH)
Lyon's Dock
Youth & Comm. Cen.
GREENFORD INDUSTRIAL ESTATE
KELVIN IND. EST.
Mosque
Oldfield Rec. Grd.
Perivale Wood Local Nature Reserve
Sudbury Hill Play. Flds.
LOWER RD.
BESSBOROUGH RD.
ROXETH HILL
LONDON RD.
HIGH ST.
SUDBURY HILL
SUDBURY COURT DR.
NORTHOLT ROAD
WHITTON AVENUE
WEST WHITTON AV.
EAST
GREENFORD ROAD
A312
A4127
A4005
A4090
B457

HARROW
60
42
59
78
A
B
C
D
E
1
2
3
4
5
6
7
HA1
HA0
UB6
NORTHWICK PARK HOSPITAL
ST. MARK'S HOSP.
Sports Centre
Playing Fields
NORTHWICK PARK
Northwick Park Playgolf
Club Ho.
Harrow School Playing Fields
Harrow School Farm
John Billam Playing Fields
Preston Road
PRESTON
Tennis Courts
Pav.
Playground
Preston Park Recreation Ground
Byron Ct. Prim. Sch.
South Kenton
NORTH WEMBLEY
Train. Cen.
EAST LANE BUSINESS PARK
WEMBLEY COMMERCIAL CENTRE
Sports Grd.
Rec. Grd.
Play. Fld. Wembley High Tech. Coll.
North Wembley
EAST LANE
A4088
Elmwood Pk.
Vale Farm Sports Ground
East Lane Pavilion Rugby Football Grd.
Vale Farm Sports Centre
Tennis Courts
Pavilion
Wembley FC (Vale Farm)
East La. Theatre Club
Wembley Manor Jun. & Inf. Sch.
KING EDWARD VII PARK
Bowl. Grns.
Prim. Sch.
HARROW ROAD
A4005
WATFORD ROAD
A404
SUDBURY COURT DRIVE
A4127
Butler's Grn.
SUDBURY
Maybank Open Space
Sudbury & Harrow Road
BARHAM PARK
Library
HARROW RD.
HIGH ROAD
NHS Walk-In Centre
Wembley Central
WHITTON AVENUE EAST
A4090
Sudbury Town
BRIDGEWATER ROAD
Horsenden Wood
Club House
HORSENDEN HILL GOLF COURSE
Horsenden Hill
SUDBURY GOLF COURSE
A4089
EALING ROAD
Alperton Cemetery
Playground
One Tree Hill Rec. Grd.
Hindu Tem.
Alperton Sch.
Spts. Cen.
Alperton
Bus Garage
Club
GRAND UNION CANAL (PADDINGTON BRANCH)
Horsenden Farm
Moat
CANAL WHARF
Comm. Centre
PERIVALE
Lib.
Perivale Wood Local Nat. Reserve
Govt. Training Cen.
Wks.
PHOENIX TRAD. EST.
ABERCORN COMMERCIAL CEN.
GREENPARK

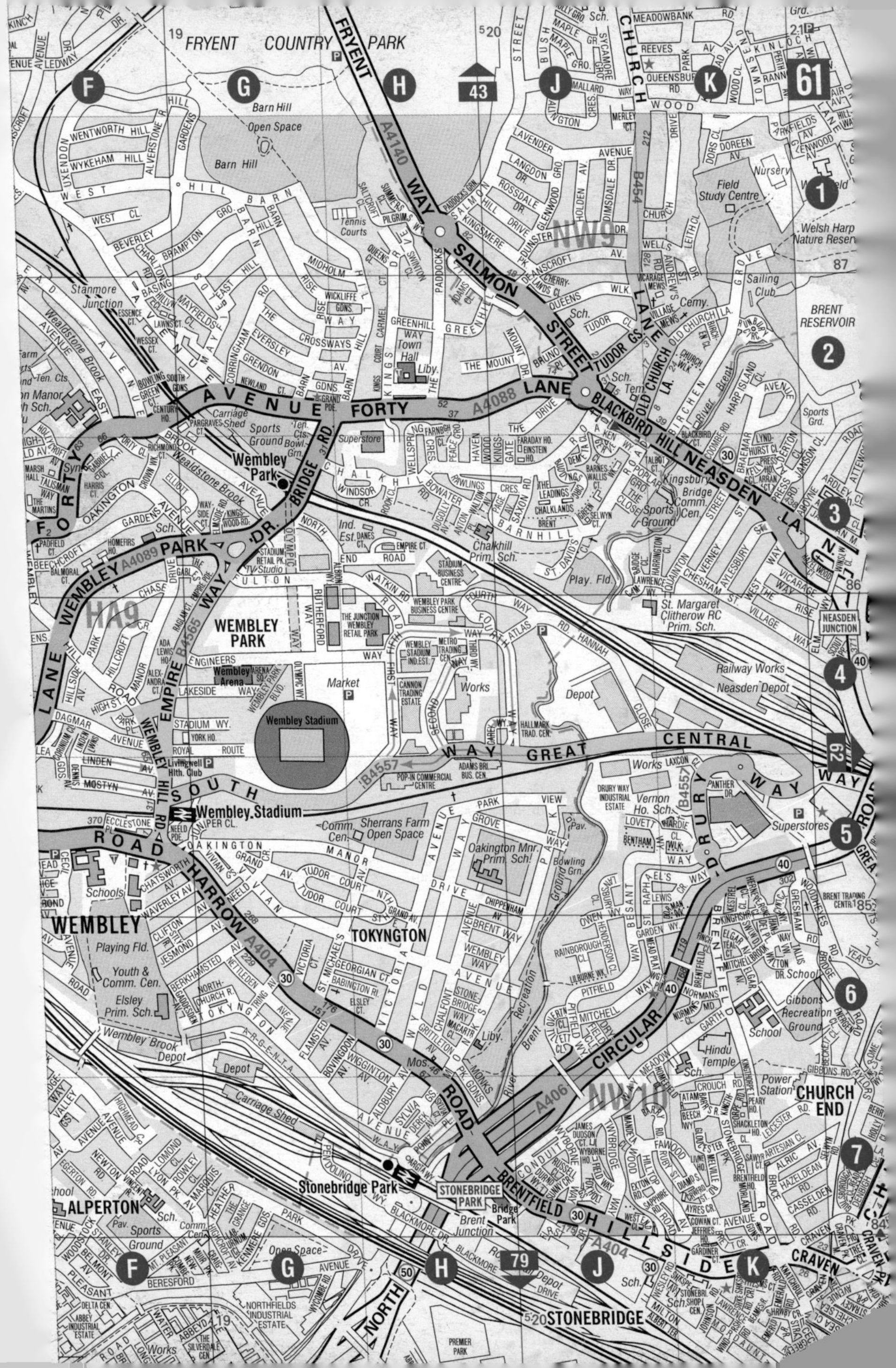
61
43
62
79
FRYENT COUNTRY PARK
Barn Hill Open Space
Barn Hill
FRYENT WAY
A4140
SALMON STREET
NW9
Field Study Centre
Welsh Harp Nature Reserve
Sailing Club
BRENT RESERVOIR
FORTY AVENUE
FORTY LANE
A4088
BLACKBIRD HILL
NEASDEN LA.
OLD CHURCH LA.
CHURCH LANE
B454
Kingsbury Bridge Comm. Cen.
Sports Ground
Town Hall
Liby.
Superstore
Stanmore Junction
Wealdstone Brook
Wembley Park
WEMBLEY PARK
BRIDGE RD.
PARK DR.
WEMBLEY PARK
A4089
EMPIRE WAY
B4565
HA9
Chalkhill Prim. Sch.
THE JUNCTION WEMBLEY RETAIL PARK
Wembley Arena
Market
Wembley Stadium
Works
Depot
Railway Works
Neasden Depot
NEASDEN JUNCTION
St. Margaret Clitherow RC Prim. Sch.
Play. Fld.
GREAT CENTRAL WAY
B4557
DRURY WAY
Superstores
SOUTH WAY
Wembley Stadium
Livingwell Hlth. Club
HARROW ROAD
A404
Oakington Mnr. Prim. Sch.
Sherrans Farm Open Space
Bowling Grn.
TOKYNGTON
WEMBLEY
Playing Fld.
Youth & Comm. Cen.
Elsley Prim. Sch.
Wembley Brook Depot
Carriage Shed
Depot
NORTH CIRCULAR ROAD
A406
NW10
Brent Recreation Ground
Hindu Temple
Gibbons Recreation Ground
School
Power Station
CHURCH END
Stonebridge Park
STONEBRIDGE PARK
Bridge Park
Brent Junction
BRENTFIELD
HILLSIDE
ALPERTON
Sports Ground
Open Space
NORTHFIELDS INDUSTRIAL ESTATE
STONEBRIDGE
CRAVEN PK.
PREMIER PARK

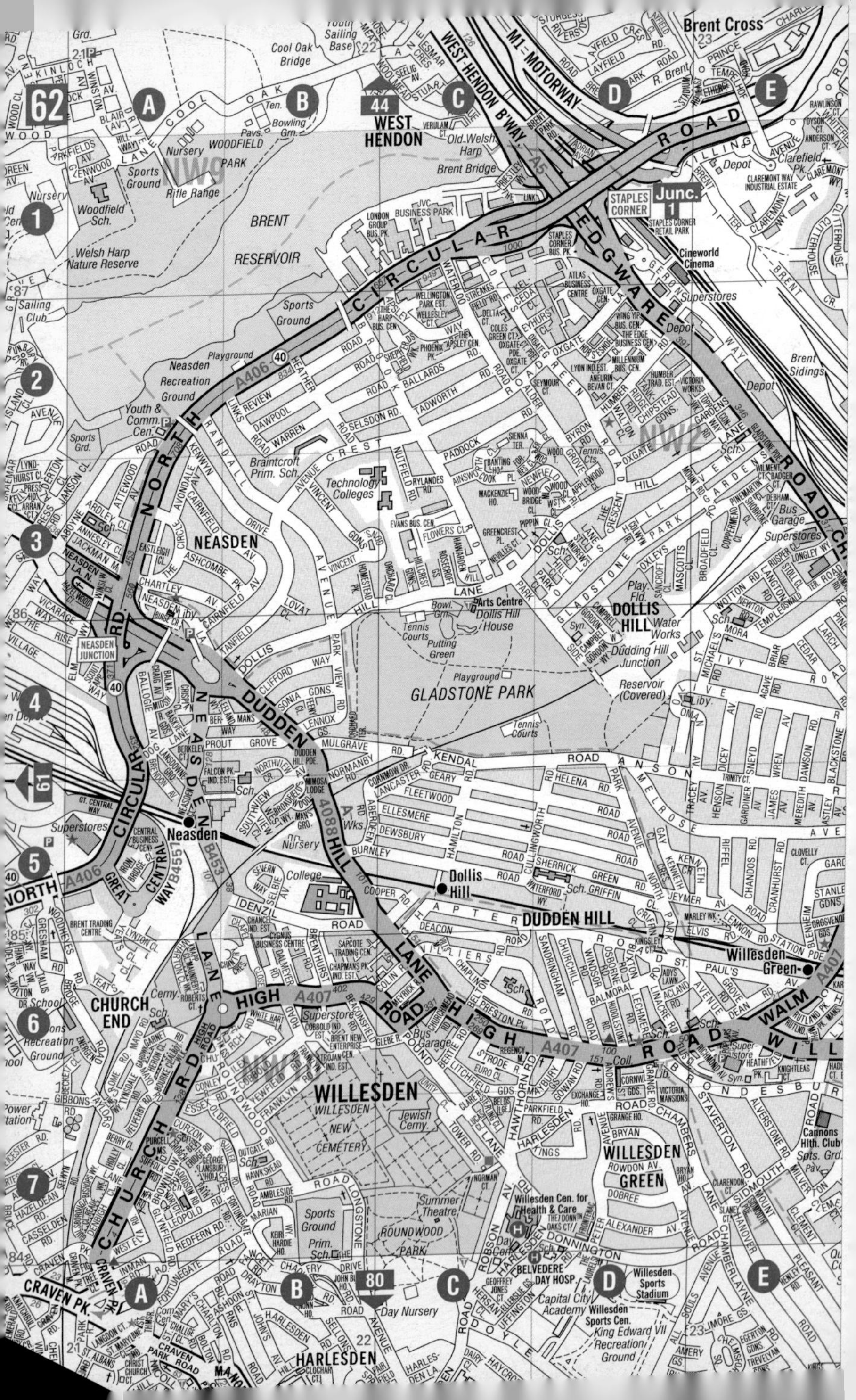
62
44
80
61
A
B
C
D
E
1
2
3
4
5
6
7
Brent Cross
M1 MOTORWAY
WEST HENDON B'WAY
WEST HENDON
Cool Oak Bridge
Youth Sailing Base
COOL OAK LANE
Old Welsh Harp
Brent Bridge
Nursery
WOODFIELD PARK
Sports Ground
Rifle Range
Woodfield Sch.
NW9
BRENT RESERVOIR
Welsh Harp Nature Reserve
Sailing Club
Sports Ground
Neasden Recreation Ground
Playground
Youth & Comm. Cen.
STAPLES CORNER
Junc. 1
STAPLES CORNER RETAIL PARK
Cineworld Cinema
Superstores
Depot
Brent Sidings
Clarefield Pk.
CLAREMONT WAY INDUSTRIAL ESTATE
CIRCULAR ROAD
NORTH CIRCULAR
EDGWARE ROAD
A406
A5
A407
A4088
B4557
B453
NW2
NW10
NEASDEN
NEASDEN JUNCTION
Neasden
Braintcroft Prim. Sch.
Technology Colleges
DOLLIS HILL
Dollis Hill House
Arts Centre
Tennis Courts
Putting Green
Playground
GLADSTONE PARK
Water Works
Dudding Hill Junction
Reservoir (Covered)
DUDDEN HILL LANE
DUDDEN HILL
Dollis Hill
College
Nursery
Superstores
CHURCH END
Recreation Ground
CHURCH ROAD
HIGH ROAD
WILLESDEN
WILLESDEN NEW CEMETERY
Jewish Cemy.
Willesden Green
WILLESDEN GREEN
Bus Garage
Willesden Cen. for Health & Care
BELVEDERE DAY HOSP
Capital City Academy
Willesden Sports Stadium
Willesden Sports Cen.
King Edward VII Recreation Ground
Summer Theatre
ROUNDWOOD PARK
Sports Ground
Prim. Sch.
Day Nursery
HARLESDEN
CRAVEN PK.
Cannons Hlth. Club
GLADSTONE PARK GARDENS
OXGATE LANE
Bus Garage
Superstores

63
45
81
64
F
G
H
J
K
1
2
3
4
5
6
7
HAMPSTEAD
HEATH
Bunkers Hill
GOLDERS GREEN
Golders Green
NW11
NORTH END ROAD
A502
FINCHLEY ROAD
A598
HENDON WAY
A41
Clitterhouse Recreation Ground
Hendon FC (Claremont Rd.)
Tennis Courts
Superstores
Sports Cen.
Basing Hill Park
Synagogue
Childs Hill Park
CHILD'S HILL
GOLDERS HILL PARK
Leg of Mutton Pond
West Heath
The Hill
Jack Straws Castle
WEST HEATH ROAD
PLATT'S LANE
NW3
CRICKLEWOOD
Cricklewood
CRICKLEWOOD LANE
A407
HOCROFT AV.
CRICKLEWOOD BROADWAY
A5
CHICHELE RD.
SHOOT UP HILL
Sports Ground
Pavilion
Hampstead School
Hampstead Cemetery
Fortune Green
FORTUNE GREEN RD.
B510
A41
REDINGTON RD.
FROGNAL
Camden Arts Cen.
Finchley Rd. & Frognal
WEST HAMPSTEAD
West Hampstead Thameslink
West Hampstead
WEST END LANE
Kilburn
KILBURN HIGH RD.
Brondesbury
BRONDESBURY
BRONDESBURY PARK
Brondesbury Park
WILLESDEN LANE
A4003
IVERSON RD.
B520
MILL LANE
The Hope Cen.
Mosque
Hindu Temple
Kilburn Grange Park
Games Ct.
SOUTH HAMPSTEAD
ABBEY ROAD
B509
BELSIZE ROAD
Willesden Lane Cemetery
Fitness First
Playing Field
Superstore
Bingo Hall
Bingo
Coll.
Univ.
Res. (cov.)
Hosp.

64
46
63
82
HAMPSTEAD HEATH
HIGHGATE
HAMPSTEAD
VALE OF HEALTH
North End
PARLIAMENT HILL
GOSPEL OAK
Gospel Oak
SOUTH HAMPSTEAD
PRIMROSE HILL
Kenwood House
KEN WOOD
Highgate Ponds
Hampstead Ponds
Ladies Bathing Pond
Parliament Hill Fields
Parliament Hill Fields Athletics Track
William Ellis School
Parliament Hill School
THE ROYAL FREE HOSPITAL
Swiss Cottage
Finchley Rd. & Frognal
Finchley Rd.
Belsize Pk.
Chalk Farm
Hampstead Heath
Hampstead
Sigmund Freud Statue
Camden Arts Cen.
Keats Ho.
Burgh Ho.
Jack Straws Castle
West Heath
Sandy Heath
East Heath
Mount Tyndal
Turners Wood
The Spaniards
Open Air Stage
Caen Wood Towers Farm
Sports Ground
NW11
NW3
NW6
N6
SPANIARDS ROAD
NORTH END
HAVERSTOCK HILL
ROSSLYN HILL
FITZJOHN'S AVENUE
FINCHLEY ROAD
ADELAIDE ROAD
MALDEN ROAD
CHALK FARM
B519
B518
B511
B509
B517
A502
A41

65
F
G
H
J
K
1
2
3
4
5
6
7
47
83
99
HIGHGATE
HORNSEY
ARCHWAY
Crouch Hill
HORNSEY RISE
N19
Archway
HOLLOWAY
Upper Holloway
UPPER HOLLOWAY
DARTMOUTH PARK
Highgate Mental Health Centre
WHITTINGTON HOSPITAL
HIGHGATE CEMETERY
WATERLOW PARK
Lauderdale House
Middlesex Uni.
JUNCTION RD.
Tufnell Pk.
TUFNELL PARK
BRECKNOCK ROAD
CAMDEN RD.
HOLLOWAY ROAD
NAG'S HEAD
SEVEN SISTERS
HMP HOLLOWAY
Holloway Rd.
LOWER HOLLOWAY
KENTISH TOWN
Kentish Town
Caledonian Rd.
CALEDONIAN RD.
HMP PENTONVILLE
BARNSBURY
Caledonian Rd. and Barnsbury
CAMDEN TOWN
Camden Town
Camden Rd.
YORK WAY
Islington Ten. Cen.
Odeon Cinema
Sobell Leisure Cen.
High Speed 1

FINSBURY
PARK
Reservoir (covered)
Sports Arena
Manor House
MANOR HO.
48
FINSBURY PARK
Rowans Complex
Finsbury Park
SEVEN SISTERS RD.
GREEN LANES
STROUD GREEN RD.
BLACKSTOCK RD.
BROWNSWOOD PARK
BROWNSWOOD RD.
WEST RESERVOIR
West Reservoir Centre
The Castle Climbing Cen.
EAST RESERVOIR
Sir Thomas Abney Prim. Sch.
LORDSHIP PARK
MANOR RD.
ABNEY PARK CEMETERY
STOKE NEWINGTON
STOKE NEWINGTON CHURCH ST.
CLISSOLD PARK
Clissold Ho.
Council Offices
Tennis Courts
Bowl. Grn.
Paddling Pool
Clissold Leisure Cen.
N4
N16
N5
N7
N1
Isledon Village
Gillespie Local Park
Arsenal
Highbury Stadium
Ashburton Grove
Arsenal FC (Emirates Stadium)
Drayton Park
HOLLOWAY RD.
HORNSEY RD.
TOLLINGTON RD.
ISLEDON RD.
Sobell Leisure Cen.
University
HIGHBURY
HIGHBURY PARK
HIGHBURY GROVE
HIGHBURY FIELDS
Highbury Pool
Highbury & Islington
HIGHBURY CNR.
Canonbury
CANONBURY
CANONBURY RD.
ST. PAUL'S RD.
BALLS POND RD.
NEWINGTON GRN. RD.
ALBION RD.
MILDMAY
Dalston Kingsland
KINGSLAND
ESSEX RD.
Essex Rd.
UPPER ST.
LIVERPOOL RD.
BARNSBURY
City Farm
Paradise Park
ISLINGTON
NEW NTH. RD.
DE BEAUVOIR TOWN
Kingsland Basin
84
65
A
B
C
D
E
1
2
3
4
5
6
7

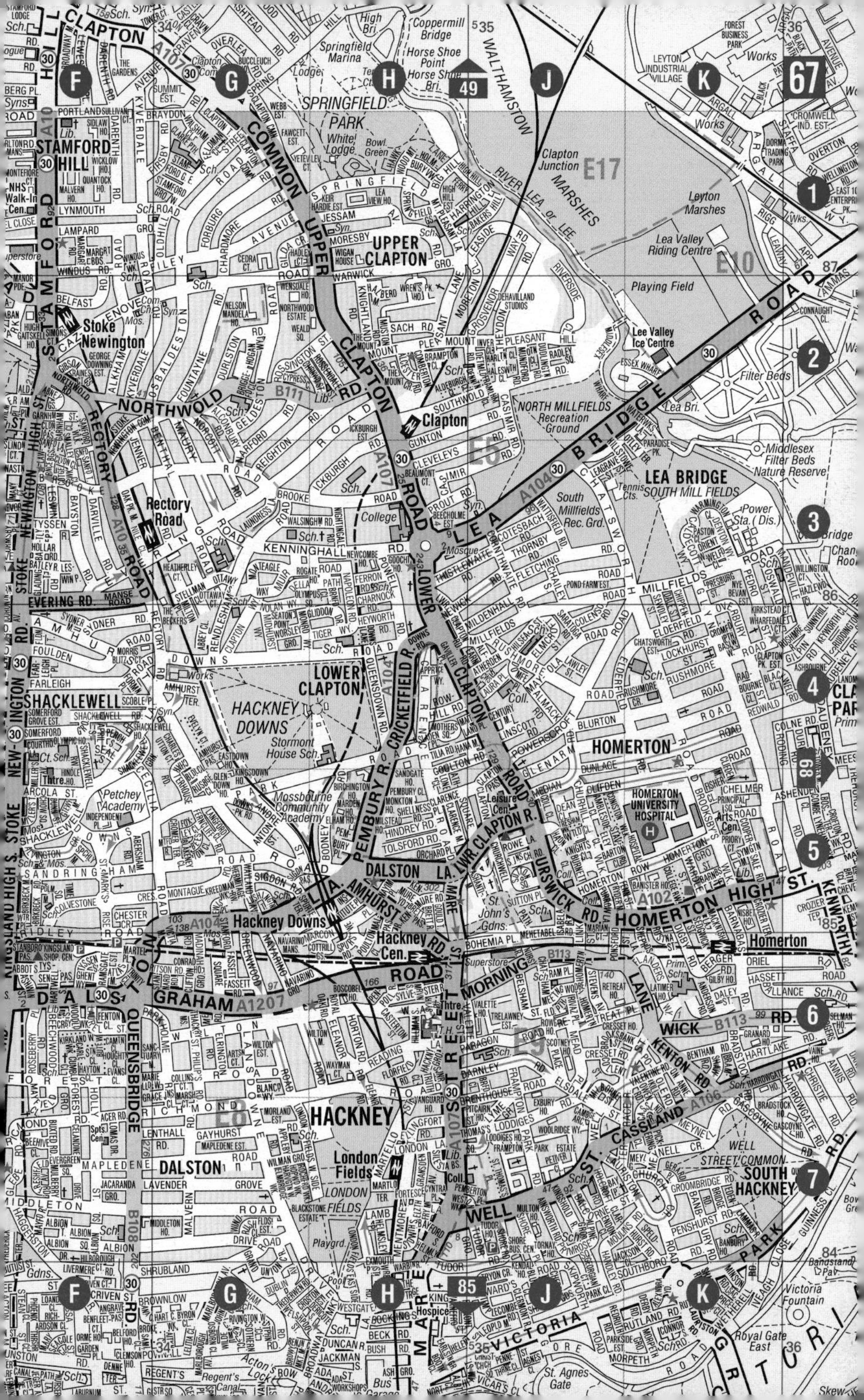

67
49
68
85
CLAPTON
STAMFORD HILL
Stoke Newington
UPPER CLAPTON
SPRINGFIELD PARK
Springfield Marina
Coppermill Bridge
Horse Shoe Point
WALTHAMSTOW
Clapton Junction
MARSHES
E17
RIVER LEA or LEE
Leyton Marshes
Lea Valley Riding Centre
E10
Playing Field
Lee Valley Ice Centre
Filter Beds
Lea Bri.
Middlesex Filter Beds Nature Reserve
LEA BRIDGE ROAD
NORTH MILLFIELDS Recreation Ground
LEA BRIDGE
SOUTH MILL FIELDS
South Millfields Rec. Grd.
Power Sta. (Dis.)
LEYTON INDUSTRIAL VILLAGE
FOREST BUSINESS PARK
NORTHWOLD ROAD
UPPER CLAPTON ROAD
CLAPTON ROAD
LOWER CLAPTON ROAD
E5
Clapton
Rectory Road
STOKE NEWINGTON HIGH ST.
STOKE NEWINGTON ROAD
SHACKLEWELL
Petchey Academy
HACKNEY DOWNS
LOWER CLAPTON
Stormont House Sch.
Mossbourne Community Academy
Hackney Downs
Hackney Cen.
HOMERTON
HOMERTON UNIVERSITY HOSPITAL
HOMERTON HIGH ST.
Homerton
DALSTON LA.
AMHURST RD.
GRAHAM ROAD
DALSTON
KINGSLAND HIGH ST.
QUEENSBRIDGE RD.
HACKNEY
E8
E9
MARE STREET
London Fields
LONDON FIELDS
WELL ST.
CASSLAND RD.
SOUTH HACKNEY
WELL STREET COMMON
VICTORIA PARK
WICK RD.
Victoria Fountain
Royal Gate East
Hospice
St. Agnes Gate
Regent's Canal
Acton's Lock

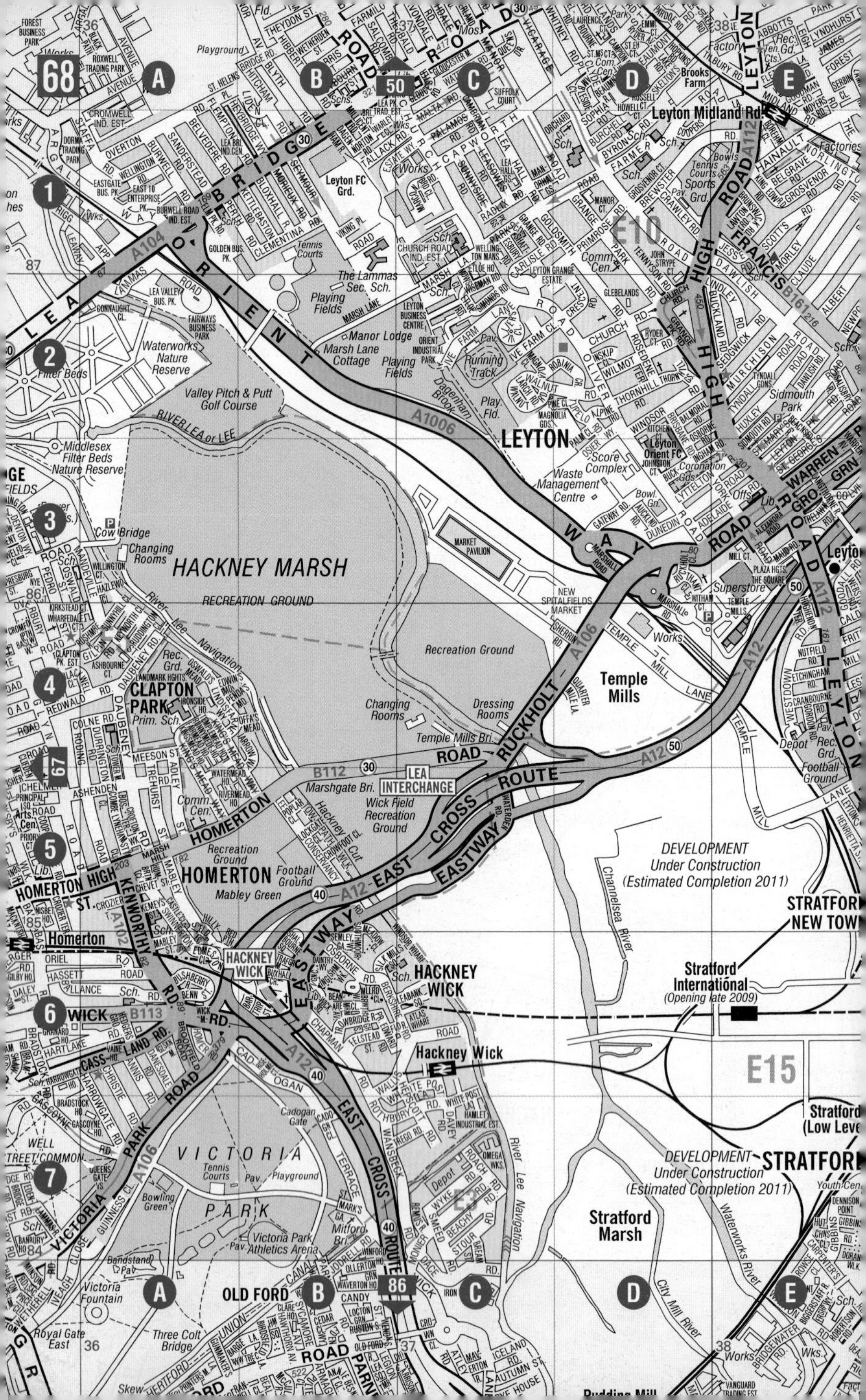
68
50
86
67
A
B
C
D
E
1
2
3
4
5
6
7
LEYTON
HACKNEY MARSH
RECREATION GROUND
HOMERTON
CLAPTON PARK
HACKNEY WICK
VICTORIA PARK
OLD FORD
E10
E15
E3
Temple Mills
Stratford Marsh
STRATFORD NEW TOWN
STRATFORD
Stratford International
(Opening late 2009)
Stratford (Low Level)
Leyton Midland Rd.
Hackney Wick
Homerton
DEVELOPMENT
Under Construction
(Estimated Completion 2011)
LEA INTERCHANGE
Marshgate Bri.
Wick Field Recreation Ground
Hackney Cut
Temple Mills Bri.
Changing Rooms
Dressing Rooms
Recreation Ground
Mabley Green
Football Ground
Waterworks Nature Reserve
Filter Beds
Valley Pitch & Putt Golf Course
RIVER LEA or LEE
Middlesex Filter Beds Nature Reserve
Cow Bridge
River Lee Navigation
Channelsea River
Waterworks River
City Mill River
The Lammas Sec. Sch.
Playing Fields
Manor Lodge
Marsh Lane Cottage
Leyton FC Grd.
Tennis Courts
Running Track
Score Complex
Waste Management Centre
MARKET PAVILION
NEW SPITALFIELDS MARKET
Superstore
Leyton Orient FC
Coronation Gdns.
Sidmouth Park
Brooks Farm
Sports Grd.
Comm. Cen.
Victoria Park Athletics Arena
Victoria Fountain
Royal Gate East
Three Colt Bridge
Cadogan Gate
Bowling Green
Bandstand
Mitford Bri.
Skew Bri.
Playground
LEA BRIDGE ROAD
ORIENT WAY
A1006
A104
A106
A12
A102
A112
B112
B113
B161
HIGH ROAD LEYTON
CHURCH ROAD
RUCKHOLT ROAD
EAST CROSS ROUTE
EASTWAY
HOMERTON ROAD
HOMERTON HIGH ST.
KENWORTHY RD.
WICK RD.
CASS LAND RD.
VICTORIA PARK ROAD
WICK ROAD
TEMPLE MILL LANE
MARSH LANE
OLIVER ROAD
FRANCIS ROAD
WARREN ROAD
GROSVENOR RD.
NORLINGTON RD.
CAPWORTH ST.
CHURCH ROAD IND. EST.
LEYTON BUSINESS CENTRE
ORIENT INDUSTRIAL PARK
LEA VALLEY BUS. PK.
FAIRWAYS BUSINESS PARK
GOLDEN BUS. PK.
BURWELL ROAD IND. EST.
EAST 10 ENTERPRISE PK.
EASTGATE BUS. PK.
CROMWELL IND. EST.
ROXWELL TRADING PARK
FOREST BUSINESS PARK
HAMLET INDUSTRIAL EST.
Leyton
Arts Cen.
Lib.
Works
Depot
30
40
50
36
37
38
84
85
86
87

69
F
G
H
J
K
1
2
3
4
5
6
7
GREEN MAN ROUNDABOUT
BUSH RD.
51
40
41
WANSTEAD GOLF COURSE
Bush Wood
Reservoir Wood
Shoulder of Mutton Pond
Sports Ground
Leytonstone
Leytonstone High Rd.
LEYTONSTONE
E11
E12
Playing Field
Horse Ride
WANSTEAD FLATS
ALDERSBROOK ROAD
A116
A114
A12
A11
A106
A112
A118
B161
B164
B165
HARROW ROAD
DAMES ROAD
LAKE HOUSE ROAD
WOODFORD ROAD
CENTRE ROAD
BLAKE HALL ROAD
LEYTONSTONE RD.
HIGH ROAD
GROVE GREEN
CATHALL
CANN HALL ROAD
St. Patrick's RC Cemetery
Cann Hall
Cemetery
West Ham Cemetery
Wanstead Park
70
Forest Gate
FOREST GATE
E7
CHOBHAM RD.
ROAD ANGEL LA.
Maryland
WATER LANE
ROMFORD ROAD
UPTON LANE
WOODGRANGE RD.
GREEN STREET
Stratford
BROADWAY
WEST HAM LA.
GREAT EASTERN
HIGH ST.
VICARAGE LA.
WEST HAM PARK
Football Ground
Netball Court
Football Pitch
Tennis Courts
PORTWAY
87
PLASHET
UPTON
UPTON ROAD
Upton Park
WEST HAM
NEW PLAISTOW R.
Jubilee

70
52
69
88
A
B
C
D
E
1
2
3
4
5
6
7
WANSTEAD PARK
WANSTEAD GOLF COURSE
The Temple
Keepers Lodge
Heronry Pond
Perch Pond
Rook Island
E11
Riding Sch.
Aldersbrook Prim. Sch.
ALDERSBROOK
WANSTEAD FLATS
CITY OF LONDON CEMETERY
City of London Crematorium
Lodge
SOUTH WOODFORD TO BARKING RELIEF ROAD
ILFORD GOLF COURSE
River Roding
Alders Brook
CRANBROOK
Cranbrook Coll.
Ilford Cricket Club
NHS Walk-In Cen.
Ilford
MANOR PARK
THE MANOR PARK CEMETERY
Manor Park Crem.
Manor Park
E12
E7
ROMFORD ROAD
Woodgrange Park
Woodgrange Park Cemetery
War Mem.
LITTLE ILFORD
Little Ilford Park
NORTH CIRCULAR
PLASHET
Jewish Cemetery
PLASHET PARK
Bowling Green
Tennis Courts
The Shrewsbury Cen.
HIGH STREET NORTH
East Ham
E6
WALLEND
Sports Ground
Gasholder
Running Track
Playing Field
UPTON PARK
Upton Park
PLASHET RD.
GREEN STREET
KATHERINE ROAD
BARKING
Acad. of Mus.
Priory Pk.
Bingo
RON LEIGHTON WY.
FOREST DRIVE
A116
A118
A117
A406
A123
B165
B167
B109

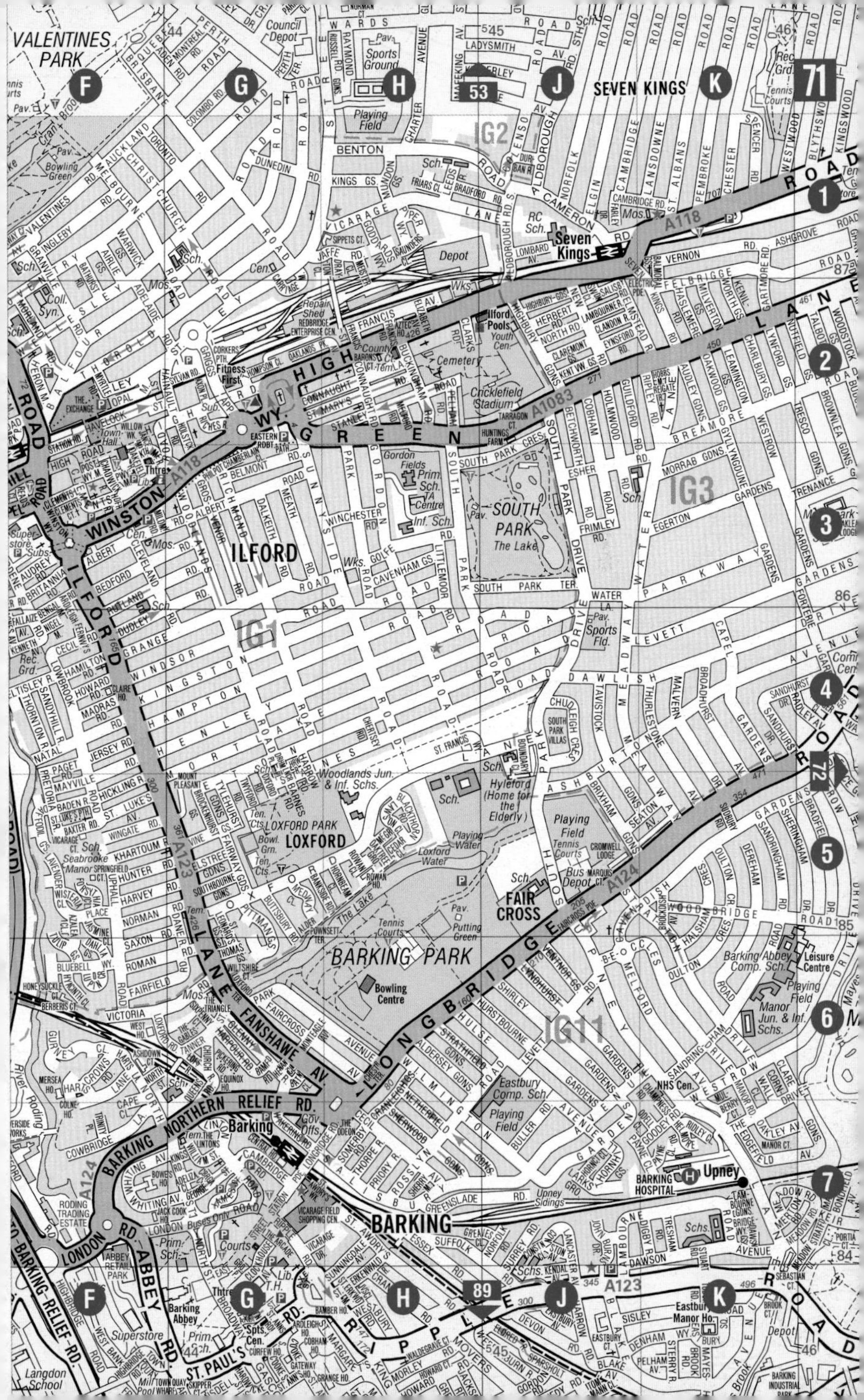

VALENTINES PARK
F
G
H
J
K
71
53
SEVEN KINGS
Seven Kings
IG2
IG3
IG1
IG11
ILFORD
LOXFORD
SOUTH PARK
The Lake
BARKING PARK
FAIR CROSS
BARKING
Barking
Upney
BARKING HOSPITAL
Barking Abbey
72
89
1
2
3
4
5
6
7
A118
A1083
A123
A124
HIGH ROAD
ILFORD LANE
FANSHAWE AV.
LONGBRIDGE ROAD
BARKING NORTHERN RELIEF RD.
RIPPLE ROAD
GREEN LANE
WINSTON WY.
Sports Ground
Playing Field
Depot
Cemetery
Cricklefield Stadium
Ilford Pools
Town Hall
Loxford Water
Bowling Centre
Eastbury Comp. Sch.
Barking Abbey Comp. Sch.
Leisure Centre
Langdon School
Superstore
VICARAGE FIELD SHOPPING CEN.
RODING TRADING ESTATE
ABBEY RETAIL PARK
Upney Sidings
Hyleford (Home for the Elderly)

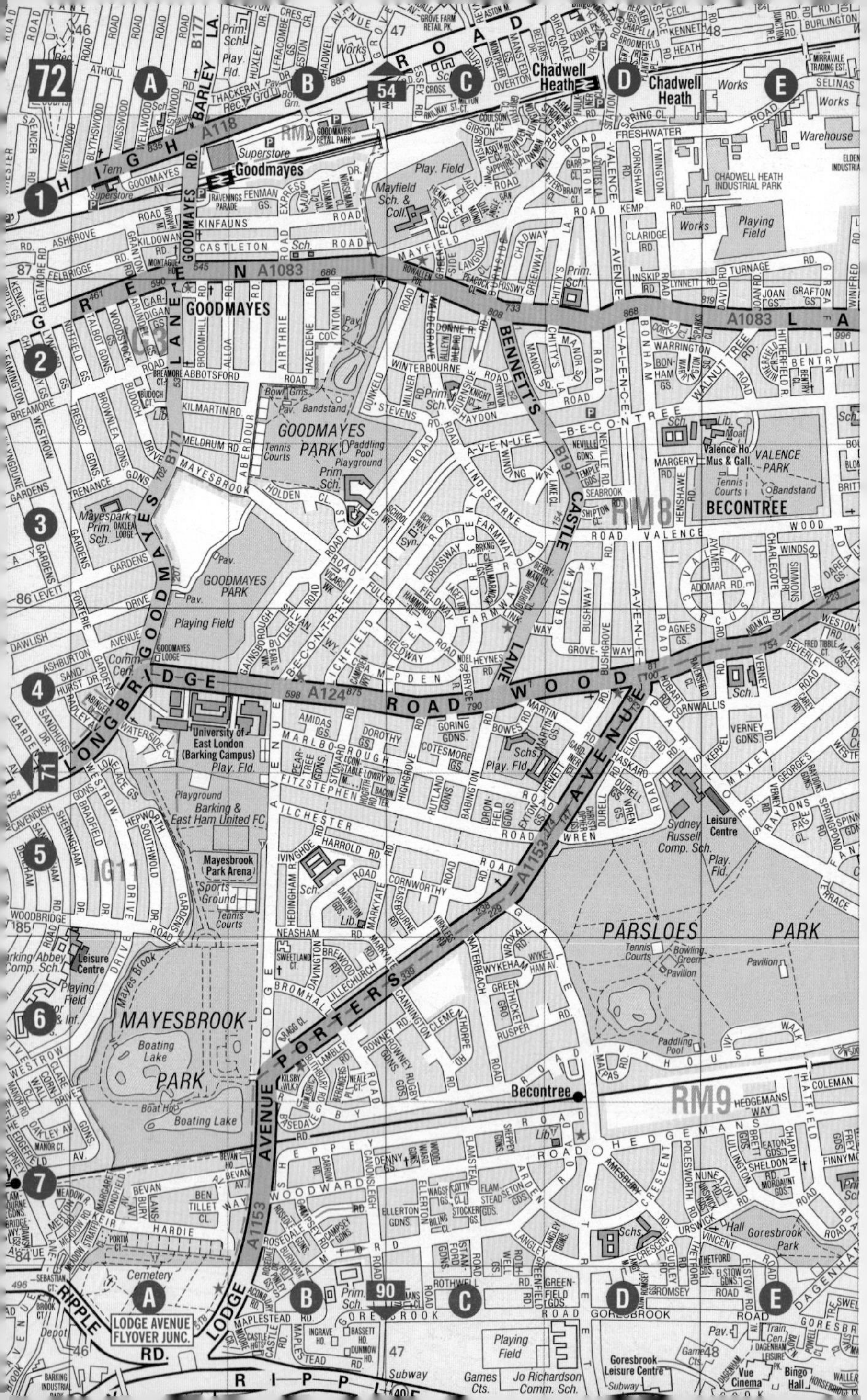
72
A
B
C
D
E
1
2
3
4
5
6
7
54
71
90
Chadwell Heath
Goodmayes
GOODMAYES
Superstore
GOODMAYES RETAIL PARK
GROVE FARM RETAIL PK.
CHADWELL HEATH INDUSTRIAL PARK
MIRRAVALE TRADING EST.
Mayfield Sch. & Coll.
Play. Field
Playing Field
Warehouse
Works
HIGH ROAD
A118
A1083
GREEN LANE
GOODMAYES LANE
B177
BARLEY LA.
BENNETT'S CASTLE LANE
B191
RM6
RM8
RM9
IG3
IG11
GOODMAYES PARK
Paddling Pool
Playground
Prim. Sch.
Bandstand
Tennis Courts
Valence Ho. Mus & Gall.
VALENCE PARK
BECONTREE
BECONTREE AVENUE
VALENCE AVENUE
LONGBRIDGE ROAD
A124
WOOD LANE
University of East London (Barking Campus)
Barking & East Ham United FC
Mayesbrook Park Arena
Sports Ground
MAYESBROOK PARK
Boating Lake
Mayes Brook
Leisure Centre
Barking Abbey Comp. Sch.
Sydney Russell Comp. Sch.
PARSLOES PARK
Pavilion
Bowling Green
Paddling Pool
PORTERS AVENUE
A1153
LODGE AVENUE
Becontree
HEDGEMANS ROAD
GORESBROOK ROAD
Goresbrook Park
Cemetery
LODGE AVENUE FLYOVER JUNC.
RIPPLE RD.
BARKING INDUSTRIAL PARK
Goresbrook Leisure Centre
Jo Richardson Comm. Sch.
Games Cts.
Subway
DAGENHAM LEISURE PK.
Vue Cinema
Bingo Hall

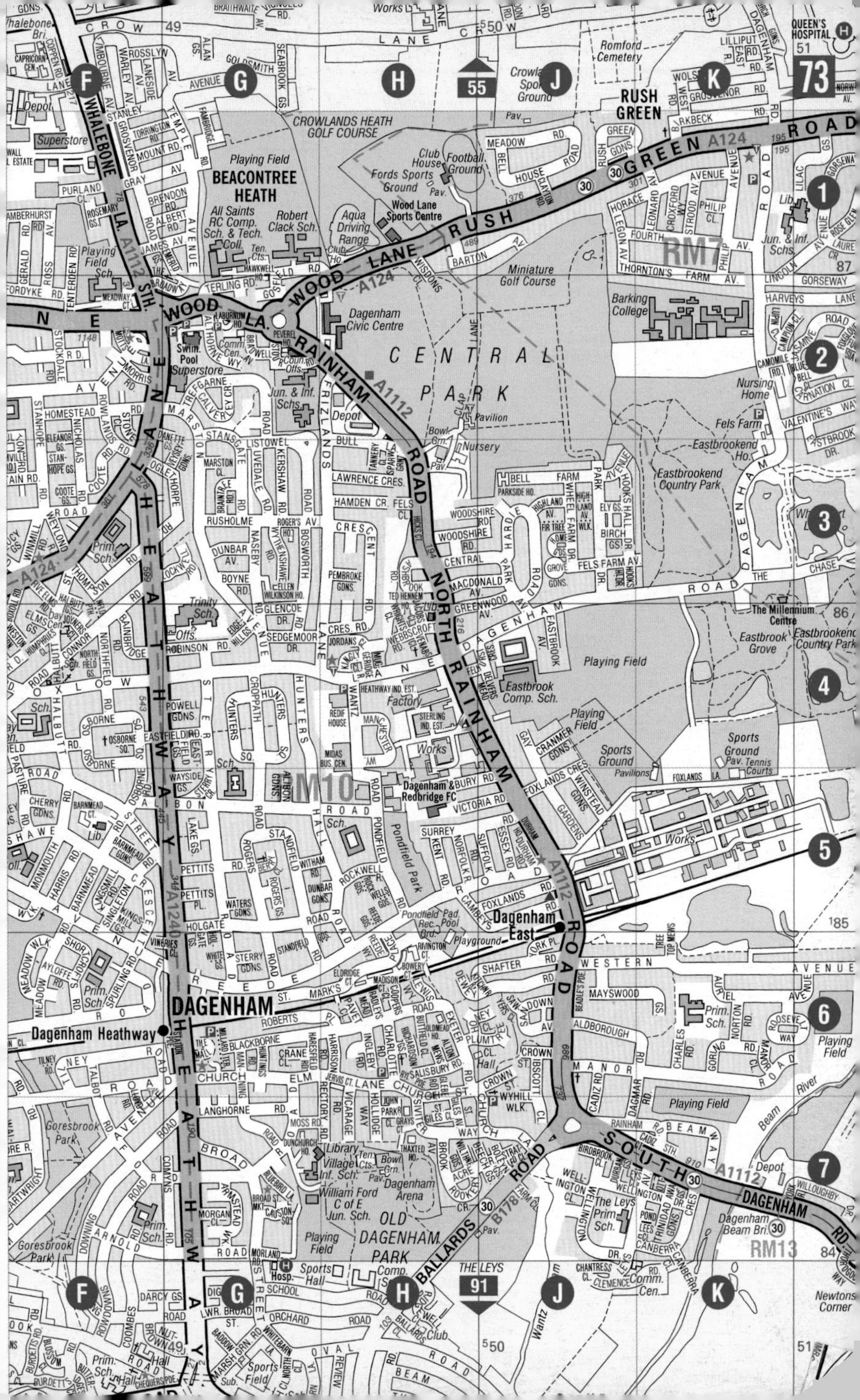
73
55
91
THE LEYS
RUSH GREEN
BEACONTREE HEATH
DAGENHAM
OLD DAGENHAM PARK
CENTRAL PARK
RM7
RM10
RM13
Queen's Hospital
Romford Cemetery
Crowlands Heath Golf Course
Crowlands Sports Ground
Fords Sports Ground
Football Ground
Club House
Wood Lane Sports Centre
Aqua Driving Range
Robert Clack Sch.
All Saints RC Comp. Sch. & Tech. Coll.
Playing Field
Dagenham Civic Centre
Swim. Pool
Superstore
Miniature Golf Course
Barking College
Nursing Home
Fels Farm
Eastbrookend Ho.
Eastbrookend Country Park
The Millennium Centre
Eastbrook Grove
Eastbrook Comp. Sch.
Trinity Sch.
Sports Ground
Pavilions
Tennis Courts
Dagenham & Redbridge FC
Pondfield Park
Dagenham East
Dagenham Heathway
Goresbrook Park
Village Inf. Sch.
William Ford C of E Jun. Sch.
Dagenham Arena
Dagenham Beam Bri.
Newtons Corner
Beam River
Works
Depot
Playground
WOOD LANE
RUSH GREEN ROAD
RAINHAM ROAD NORTH
RAINHAM ROAD SOUTH
HEATHWAY
WHALEBONE LA.
BALLARDS ROAD
DAGENHAM RD.
A124
A1112
A1240
B178
CROW LANE
F
G
H
J
K
1
2
3
4
5
6
7
49
50
51
84
85
86
87

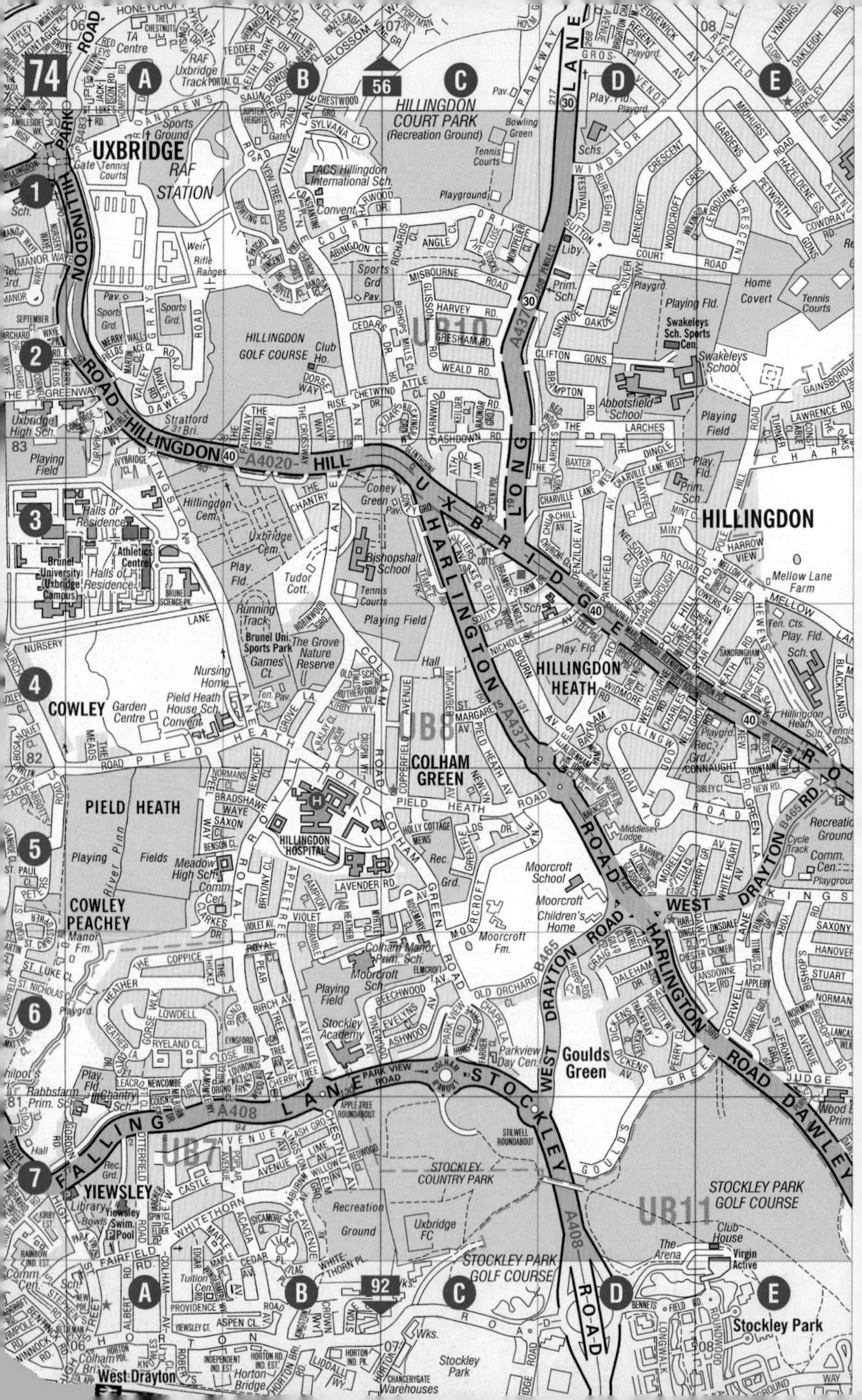
74
56
92
A
B
C
D
E
1
2
3
4
5
6
7
UXBRIDGE
RAF STATION
HILLINGDON COURT PARK (Recreation Ground)
HILLINGDON GOLF COURSE
UB10
UB8
UB7
UB11
HILLINGDON
HILLINGDON HEATH
COLHAM GREEN
COWLEY
PIELD HEATH
COWLEY PEACHEY
YIEWSLEY
Goulds Green
Stockley Park
West Drayton
STOCKLEY COUNTRY PARK
STOCKLEY PARK GOLF COURSE
HILLINGDON HOSPITAL
Brunel University (Uxbridge Campus)
Halls of Residence
Athletics Centre
BRUNEL SCIENCE PK.
Brunel Uni. Sports Park
Running Track
Hillingdon Cem.
Uxbridge Cem.
Bishopshalt School
The Grove Nature Reserve
Swakeleys School
Abbotsfield School
Moorcroft School
Moorcroft Children's Home
Stockley Academy
Uxbridge High Sch.
Meadow High Sch.
Pield Heath House Sch. Convent
TACS Hillingdon International Sch.
Colham Manor Prim. Sch.
Rabbsfarm Prim. Sch.
Yiewsley Swim. Pool
Uxbridge FC
Virgin Active
The Arena
Playing Fields
Recreation Ground
HILLINGDON ROAD
HILLINGDON HILL
A4020
UXBRIDGE ROAD
LONG LANE
A437
HARLINGTON ROAD
FALLING LANE
STOCKLEY ROAD
A408
WEST DRAYTON ROAD
B465
DAWLEY ROAD
PIELD HEATH ROAD
ROYAL LANE
COLHAM GREEN ROAD
KINGSTON LANE
HORTON ROAD
COURT DRIVE
CHARVILLE LANE
COLHAM R'ABOUT
STILWELL ROUNDABOUT
APPLE TREE ROUNDABOUT
Horton Bridge
CHANCERYGATE Warehouses

75
57
93
76
F
G
H
J
K
1
2
3
4
5
6
7
NORTH HILLINGDON
Cutthroat Wood
Gutteridge Wood
Yeading Brook
C & L Golf & Country Club
Club Ho.
WEST END RD.
Ten Acres
SHARVEL LANE
Club House
Moat
Barns Fm.
The Gorse
Recreation Ground
Westways Fm.
Lane Covert
Playing Field
Ryefield Primary Sch.
Rugby Ground
Hare Plantation
Playground
UB5
West London Shooting Grounds
Children's Cen.
Comm. Cen.
Charville Prim. Sch.
Canal Feeder
Hedgewood School
Grosvenor Playing Field
LANSBURY DRIVE
KINGSHILL DRIVE
Hayes Shrub
Hayes Park
Home Farm
HAYES END
The Paddocks Farm
Hostel
Nursery
UB4
Grange Park Jun. & Inf. Schs.
Belmore Playing Fields
YEADING
Comm. Cen.
Belmore Prim. Sch.
Barnhill High Sch.
Playing Fields
Prim. Sch.
UXBRIDGE ROAD
A4020
WOOD END GREEN
Rosedale Park
Hayes Manor Spts. Cen.
The Hayes Manor Sch. Playing Fld.
UB3
Hayes Stadium & Sports Cen.
WOOD END
The Beck Theatre
Norman Leddy Mem. Gds.
Cricket Grd.
Barra Hall
Open Air Theatre
Town Hall Park
Mecca Bingo
Yeading Schs.
HAYES
Hayes & Yeading FC
Uxbridge Coll. (Hayes Comm. Campus)
LOMBARDY RETAIL PARK
OSSIE GARVIN ROUNDABOUT
PARKWAY
A312
A437
Works
BMX Track
Lake Farm Country Park
Minet Jun. & Inf. Schs.
Hillingdon Cycling Circuit
THE SQUARE

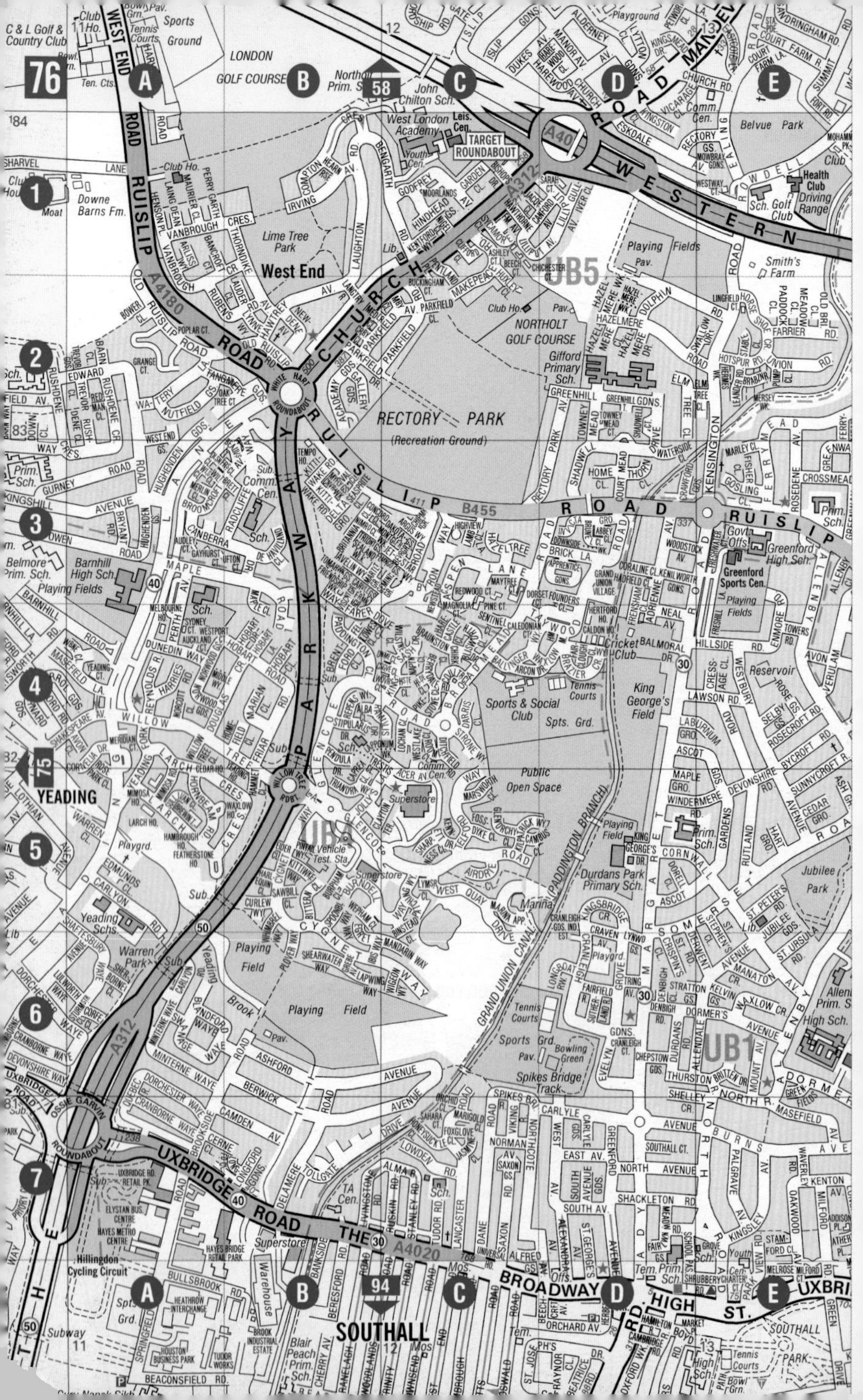

LONDON GOLF COURSE
West End
Lime Tree Park
NORTHOLT GOLF COURSE
RECTORY PARK
(Recreation Ground)
UB5
UB4
UB1
YEADING
SOUTHALL
WESTERN
A40
A312
A4180
A4020
B455
RUISLIP ROAD
CHURCH ROAD
PARKWAY
UXBRIDGE ROAD
THE BROADWAY
HIGH ST.
WEST END ROAD
TARGET ROUNDABOUT
WHITE HART ROUNDABOUT
WILLOW TREE RDBT.
OSSIE GARVIN ROUNDABOUT
GRAND UNION CANAL (PADDINGTON BRANCH)
King George's Field
Public Open Space
Sports & Social Club
Durdans Park Primary Sch.
Gifford Primary Sch.
Greenford High Sch.
Greenford Sports Cen.
Barnhill High Sch.
Belmore Prim. Sch.
Yeading Schs.
Warren Park
Playing Field
Belvue Park
Jubilee Park
Smith's Farm
Downe Barns Fm.
West London Academy
Hillingdon Cycling Circuit
Spikes Bridge Track
Marina
Superstore
C & L Golf & Country Club
Sports Ground
58
75
94

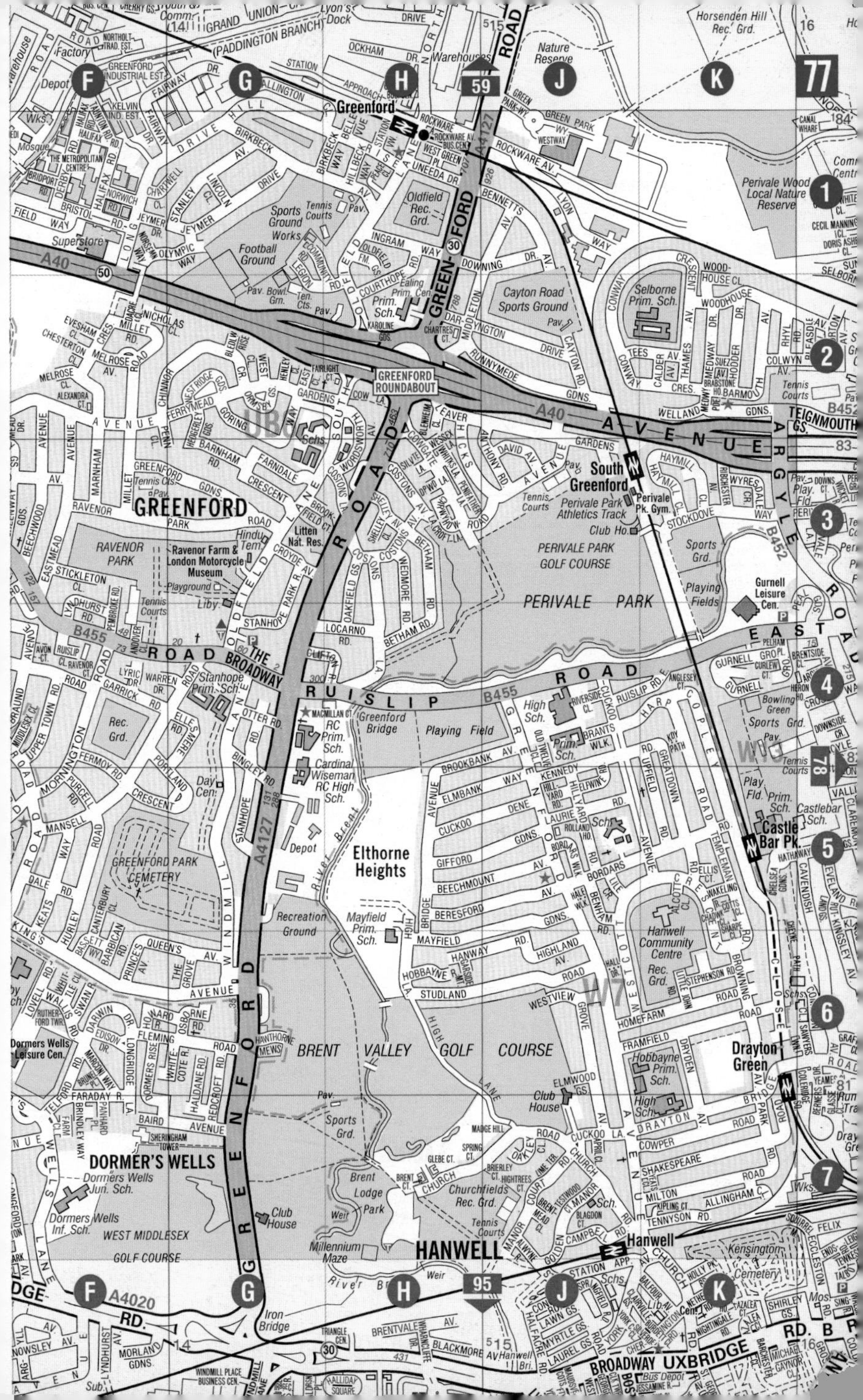
77
59
95
78
F
G
H
J
K
1
2
3
4
5
6
7
GREENFORD
DORMER'S WELLS
HANWELL
Elthorne Heights
Drayton Green
Greenford
South Greenford
Castle Bar Pk.
Hanwell
GRAND UNION CANAL (PADDINGTON BRANCH)
Lyon's Dock
Horsenden Hill Rec. Grd.
Nature Reserve
Perivale Wood Local Nature Reserve
GREENFORD INDUSTRIAL EST.
KELVIN IND. EST.
THE METROPOLITAN CENTRE
Superstore
Mosque
Factory
Depot
Wks.
Warehouses
A40
A4127
A4020
B455
B452
GREENFORD ROUNDABOUT
GREENFORD ROAD
WESTERN AVENUE
RUISLIP ROAD
RUISLIP ROAD EAST
ARGYLE ROAD
UXBRIDGE RD.
BROADWAY
ROCKWARE AV.
OLDFIELD LANE
Oldfield Rec. Grd.
Sports Ground Works
Football Ground
Cayton Road Sports Ground
Selborne Prim. Sch.
Ealing Prim. Cen.
Prim. Sch.
Litten Nat. Res.
Ravenor Farm & London Motorcycle Museum
RAVENOR PARK
Hindu Tem.
Liby.
Playground
Stanhope Prim. Sch.
Rec. Grd.
Day Cen.
GREENFORD PARK CEMETERY
Recreation Ground
Greenford Bridge
Playing Field
RC Prim. Sch.
Cardinal Wiseman RC High Sch.
Mayfield Prim. Sch.
PERIVALE PARK GOLF COURSE
PERIVALE PARK
Perivale Park Athletics Track
Perivale Pk. Gym.
Club Ho.
Sports Grd.
Playing Fields
Gurnell Leisure Cen.
Bowling Green
Sports Grd.
High Sch.
Castlebar Sch.
Hanwell Community Centre
BRENT VALLEY GOLF COURSE
Club House
Sports Grd.
Brent Lodge Park
Millennium Maze
Churchfields Rec. Grd.
Hobbayne Prim. Sch.
High Sch.
Dormers Wells Leisure Cen.
Dormers Wells Jun. Sch.
Dormers Wells Inf. Sch.
WEST MIDDLESEX GOLF COURSE
Kensington Cemetery
River Brent
Iron Bridge
Weir
UB6
W7
W13
WINDMILL PLACE BUSINESS CEN.
Bus Depot

Horsenden Hill
Horsenden Farm
GRAND UNION CANAL
(PADDINGTON BRANCH)
60
Alperton Cemetery
BRIDGEWATER ROAD
A4005
Alperton
EALING ROAD
ALPERTON
PERIVALE
Perivale Wood Local Nature Reserve
PERIVALE INDUSTRIAL PARK
Perivale
Schools
Metropolitan Police Traffic Unit
Alperton Sports Grd.
HA0
UB6
WESTERN AVENUE
A40
ALPERTON LANE
HANGER LANE
Hanger La.
MANHATTAN BUSINESS PARK
Club House
EALING GOLF COURSE
Perivale Bri. Playing Fields
Gurnell Leisure Cen.
RUISLIP RD. EAST
Pitshanger Park
Football Ground
Brentham Club
BRUNSWICK ROAD
GOLF COURSE
Hanger Hill
ARGYLE ROAD
SCOTCH COMMON
KENT GDS.
PITSHANGER LANE
77
Castlebar Sch.
Cleveland Park
CASTLEBAR HILL
CASTLEBAR ROAD
W5
EALING CYGNET HOSP.
Cricket Ground
Ealing Abbey
W13
Ealing Coll.
HAVEN GRN.
Ealing Squash & Fitness Club
Ealing Broadway
Drayton Green
WEST EALING
EALING
West Ealing
THE MALL
UXBRIDGE ROAD
A4020
The Questors Theatre
Pitshanger Manor Mus.
Ealing & West London Coll.
WALPOLE PARK
Ealing Studios
96
BROADWAY
NORTHFIELD
HIGH ST.
EALING GRN

Stonebridge Park
STONEBRIDGE PARK
Brent Junction
61
STONEBRIDGE
Stonebridge Rec. Grd.
HILLSIDE
CRAVEN PK.
Royal Mail Depot
Open Space
NORTHFIELDS INDUSTRIAL ESTATE
NORTH CIRCULAR ROAD
A406
50
PARK ROYAL JUNCTION
PREMIER PARK
NW10
TOWNSEND INDUSTRIAL ESTATE
Harlesden
Lower Place
GRAND UNION CANAL (Paddington Branch)
OLIVER BUSINESS PARK
Power Station
ROYAL LONDON INDUSTRIAL ESTATE
Twyford Abbey
CENTRAL MIDDLESEX HOSPITAL
PARK ROYAL
ACTON LANE
B4492
Playing Field
FROGMORE INDUSTRIAL ESTATE
Brewery
Offices
CORONATION
WESTERN AVENUE
Hypermkt.
PARK ROYAL
Sports Grd.
NORTH ACTON
Cemetery
North Acton
80
82
Hanger Hill
Park Royal
Bowl. Alley
Cinema
A40
GYPSY CORNER
NORTH ACTON PLAYING FIELDS
West Acton
WESTERN AVENUE
Sports Ground
Nth. Ealing
W3
Acton Main Line
HORN LANE
A4000
Japanese Sch. London
EAST ACTON
Ealing Common
ACTON
Twyford Spts. Cen.
97
HIGH STREET
Acton Central
ACTON PARK
GUNNERSBURY AV.
HANGER LANE
A406
The Park Club
Football Pitch
Cricket Grd.
F
G
H
J
K
1
2
3
4
5
6
7
19
20
21

80
WILLESDEN GREEN
HARLESDEN
NW10
Kensal Rise
Kensal Green
COLLEGE PARK
KENSAL GREEN CEMETERY
ST. MARY'S RC CEMETERY
West London Crematorium
Grand Union Canal
Willesden Junction
Harlesden
Willesden Sports Stadium
Willesden Sports Cen.
King Edward VII Recreation Ground
Capital City Academy
Willesden Cen. for Health & Care
BELVEDERE DAY HOSP.
ROUNDWOOD PARK
Day Nursery
HARROW ROAD
SCRUBS LANE
OLD OAK LANE
OLD OAK ROAD
VICTORIA ROAD
TUBBS RD.
HIGH STREET
Freightliner Depot
Power Station
Superstore
Old Oak Sidings
Engine Shed
Carriage Shed
Old Oak Common Sidings
North Pole International Depot
West London Junc.
Mitre Bridge
OLD OAK COMMON
WORMWOOD SCRUBS PARK
Little Wormwood Scrubs Rec. Grd.
Wormwood Scrubs Pony Cen.
Linford Christie Stadium
HAMMERSMITH HOSP., QUEEN CHARLOTTE'S & CHELSEA HOSP.
Burlington Danes Academy
HMP WORMWOOD SCRUBS
W12
East Acton
W3
EAST ACTON
WESTERN AVENUE
WESTWAY
WHITE CITY
White City
Wood La.
BBC Television Cen.
The King Fahad Academy
Wormholt Park
Phoenix High Sch.
The Park Club
Shepherd's Bush Mkt.
Acton Central
ACTON PARK
A40
A219
A404
A4000
B412
B451
62
79
98
A B C D E
1 2 3 4 5 6 7
21 22 23

81
BRONDESBURY
WILLESDEN
KILBURN
Brondesbury Park
BRONDESBURY PARK
Willesden Lane Cemetery
QUEENS PARK
KENSAL RISE
Queens Park
Kilburn High Road
Kilburn Park
KENSAL GREEN
WEST KILBURN
Paddington Rec. Grd.
Maida Vale
MAIDA VALE
MAIDA HILL
KENSAL TOWN
HARROW ROAD
Paddington Bowl. & Spts. Club
BBC Studios
WESTBOURNE GREEN
Westbourne Park
Royal Oak
ST. CHARLES HOSPITAL
Carmelite Monastery
NORTH KENSINGTON
WESTWAY
Ladbroke Grove
Latimer Rd.
NOTTING HILL
BAYSWATER
Bayswater
Queensway
Notting Hill Gate
Holland Park
KENSINGTON GARDENS
The Orangery
NW6
W9
W10
W11
W2
A5
A40
A404
B413
B450
63
82
99
F
G
H
J
K
1
2
3
4
5
6
7

82
A
B
C
D
E
1
2
3
4
5
6
7
64
4
5
81
10
100
NW3
NW8
W9
W2
PRIMROSE HILL
REGENT'S PARK
London Zoo
The Hub
Winfield House
London Central Mosque
Open Air Theatre
QUEEN MARY'S GARDENS
Boating Lake
Regent's College
MARYLEBONE
Baker St.
Madame Tussaud's
Middlesex CC Club
Lord's Cricket Ground
ST. JOHN'S WOOD
St. John's Wood
Maida Vale
MAIDA VALE
Warwick Av.
Little Venice
Royal Oak
PADDINGTON
Paddington
ST. MARY'S HOSP
Paddington Basin
Edgware Rd.
LISSON GROVE
MARYLEBONE FLYOVER
WESTWAY
BAYSWATER
Bayswater
Queensway
Lancaster Gate
Marble Arch
St. George's Field
HYDE PARK
Speakers' Corner
Reformers Tree
The Lookout Education Cen.
Rangers Lodge
Peter Pan Statue
Speke's Monument
KENSINGTON GARDENS
The Fountains
Temple Lodge
MAYFAIR
Roosevelt Mem.
Wallace Collection
Chalk Farm
Swiss Cottage
South Hampstead
Cecil Sharp Ho.
Gloucester Gate
Running Track
Reservoir (covered)
Barrow Hill
Tennis Courts
Clarence Gate
WELLINGTON RD.
PRINCE ALBERT RD.
ABBEY ROAD
FINCHLEY ROAD
EDGWARE RD.
BAYSWATER RD.
PARK LANE
OXFORD ST.
SEYMOUR
MARYLEBONE RD.
BAKER ST.
SUSSEX GDNS.
PRAED ST.
A5
A40
A41
A404
A4202
A5205
B507
B509
B525

CAMDEN TOWN
Camden Town
BRITANNIA JUNC.
Camden Rd.
KENTISH TOWN RD.
CAMDEN HIGH ST.
PARKWAY
DELANCEY ST.
ALBANY ST.
REGENT'S PARK
Regent's Park
Mornington Cres.
HAMPSTEAD RD.
EVERSHOLT ST.
PANCRAS WAY
ST. PANCRAS HOSPITAL
Ryl. Veterinary Coll.
The Granary Complex & Goods Yard
Visitor Cen.
GOODS WAY
MIDLAND RD.
PANCRAS RD.
KING'S CROSS
ST. PANCRAS INTERNATIONAL
SOMERS TOWN
British Library
EUSTON
EUSTON RD.
Euston Sq.
EUSTON UNDERPASS
YORK WAY
A5200
COPENHAGEN ST.
CALEDONIAN RD.
WHARFDALE R.
PENTONVILLE
PENTONVILLE RD.
GRAY'S INN RD.
KING'S CROSS RD.
FARRINGDON RD.
CLERKENWELL
ST. PANCRAS
Coram's Fields
GUILFORD ST.
BLOOMSBURY
Russell Sq.
SOUTHAMPTON ROW
THEOBALDS RD.
British Museum
Univ. of London
University College
GOWER ST.
Warren St.
TOTTENHAM COURT RD.
Goodge St.
Gt. Portland St.
PORTLAND PL.
GT. PORTLAND ST.
BEDFORD SQ.
MONTAGUE PL.
Holborn
HIGH HOLBORN
HOLBORN
KINGSWAY
Chancery La.
Law Courts
NEW OXFORD ST.
Tottenham Ct. R.
CHARING CROSS RD.
Oxford Circus
REGENT ST.
NEW BOND ST.
CONDUIT ST.
SOHO
SHAFTESBURY AV.
Leicester Sq.
Piccadilly Circus
PICCADILLY
Green Park
ST. JAMES'S ST.
PALL MALL
Covent Gdn.
Opera Ho.
STRAND
ALDWYCH
FLEET ST.
Temple
Somerset Ho.
EMBANKMENT
VICTORIA EMBANKMENT
Cleopatra's Needle
Embankment
Charing Cross
CHARING CROSS
National Gallery
Nelson's Col.
Admiralty Arch
THE MALL
NORTHUMBERLAND AV.
WHITEHALL
WATERLOO BRI.
RIVER THAMES
Festival Pier
Royal Festival Hall
National Theatre
The London Television Centre
F G H J K
1 2 3 4 5 6 7
65
6
7
84
101

84
A
B
C
D
E
66
1
2
3
4
5
6
7
ISLINGTON
Essex Rd.
DE BEAUVOIR TOWN
Angel
PENTONVILLE RD.
7
8
9
FINSBURY
HOXTON
SHOREDITCH
CLERKENWELL
83
Old Street
ST. LUKE'S
Farringdon
Barbican
Moorgate
LIVERPOOL ST.
City Thameslink
St. Paul's
CITY
Bank
Mansion Ho.
Monument
Temple
VICTORIA EMB.
BLACKFRIARS
RIVER THAMES
SOUTHWARK
CANNON STREET
LONDON BRIDGE HOSP
102
National Theatre
Royal Festival Hall
Tate Modern
Charterhouse
Arts Centre
BARBICAN
Shoreditch Park
Britannia Centre
Barnard Park
Regent's Canal
City Road Basin
Lloyd's Bdg.
Law Courts
Bankside Pier
Blackfriars Millennium Pier
Millennium Bridge

85
DALSTON
London Fields
SOUTH HACKNEY
HAGGERSTON
Haggerston
Regent's Canal
Acton's Lock
VICTORIA PARK
St. Agnes Gate
Gore Gate
Bonner Hall Bri.
Crown Gate West
Royal Gate East
Victoria Fountain
Skew Bridge
Cambridge Heath
BETHNAL GREEN
Bethnal Green
Bethnal Grn.
GLOBE TOWN
MILE END
MILE END HOSPITAL
Queen Mary University of London
Stepney Green
STEPNEY
RATCLIFF
SPITALFIELDS
Old Spitalfields Mkt.
Whitechapel
ROYAL LONDON HOSP.
WHITECHAPEL
Aldgate East
Aldgate
Tower Hill
Tower Gateway
The Tower of London
St. Katharine Docks
St. Katharine's Pier
Tower Bridge Wharf
Butlers Wharf Pier
Shadwell
SHADWELL
Shadwell Basin
King Edward Mem. Park
Shadwell Dock Stairs
Pelican Stairs
New Crane Stairs
Wapping
RIVER THAMES
ROTHERHITHE TUNNEL
Globe Stairs
John Orwell Sports Cen.
Fisher Athletic FC
VICTORIA PARK RD.
GROVE RD.
OLD FORD RD.
ROMAN RD.
MILE END RD.
WHITECHAPEL RD.
COMMERCIAL RD.
COMMERCIAL ST.
CAMBRIDGE HEATH RD.
MARE ST.
QUEENSBRIDGE RD.
HACKNEY RD.
BETHNAL GREEN RD.
CABLE ST.
THE HIGHWAY
EAST SMITHFIELD
NEW RD.
CANNON ST. RD.
SEWARDSTONE RD.
GLOBE RD.
A107
A1208
A1209
A1205
A11
A13
A1202
A1203
B108
B118
B135
B127
B126
B134
B140
E8
E9
E2
E1
67
9
15
103
86
F
G
H
J
K
1
2
3
4
5
6
7

SOUTH HACKNEY
86
STRATFORD
Stratford Marsh
68
VICTORIA PARK
OLD FORD
DEVELOPMENT Under Construction Estimated Completion 2011
Pudding Mill Lane
BOW INTERCHANGE
BLACKWALL
BOW ROAD
Bow Church
Bow Rd.
MILE END PARK
MILE END HOSPITAL
Queen Mary University of London
Mile End
ST. CLEMENT'S HOSPITAL
TOWER HAMLETS CEMETERY
BROMLEY
Bromley-by-Bow
Devons Rd.
BOW COMMON
Mile End Park Leisure Centre
Mile End Stadium
Ragged Sch. Mus.
85
RATCLIFF
LIMEHOUSE
Limehouse
Limehouse Basin
Westferry
POPLAR
Poplar
All Saints
Langdon Pk.
RIVER THAMES
West India Quay
Canary Wharf
Billingsgate Fish Market
104
The Mus. in Docklands
Canary Wharf Pier
Hilton Docklands Pier
BLACKWALL BASIN
SALTER
ROTHERHITHE
EAST INDIA DOCK RD.
NORTHERN APPROACH

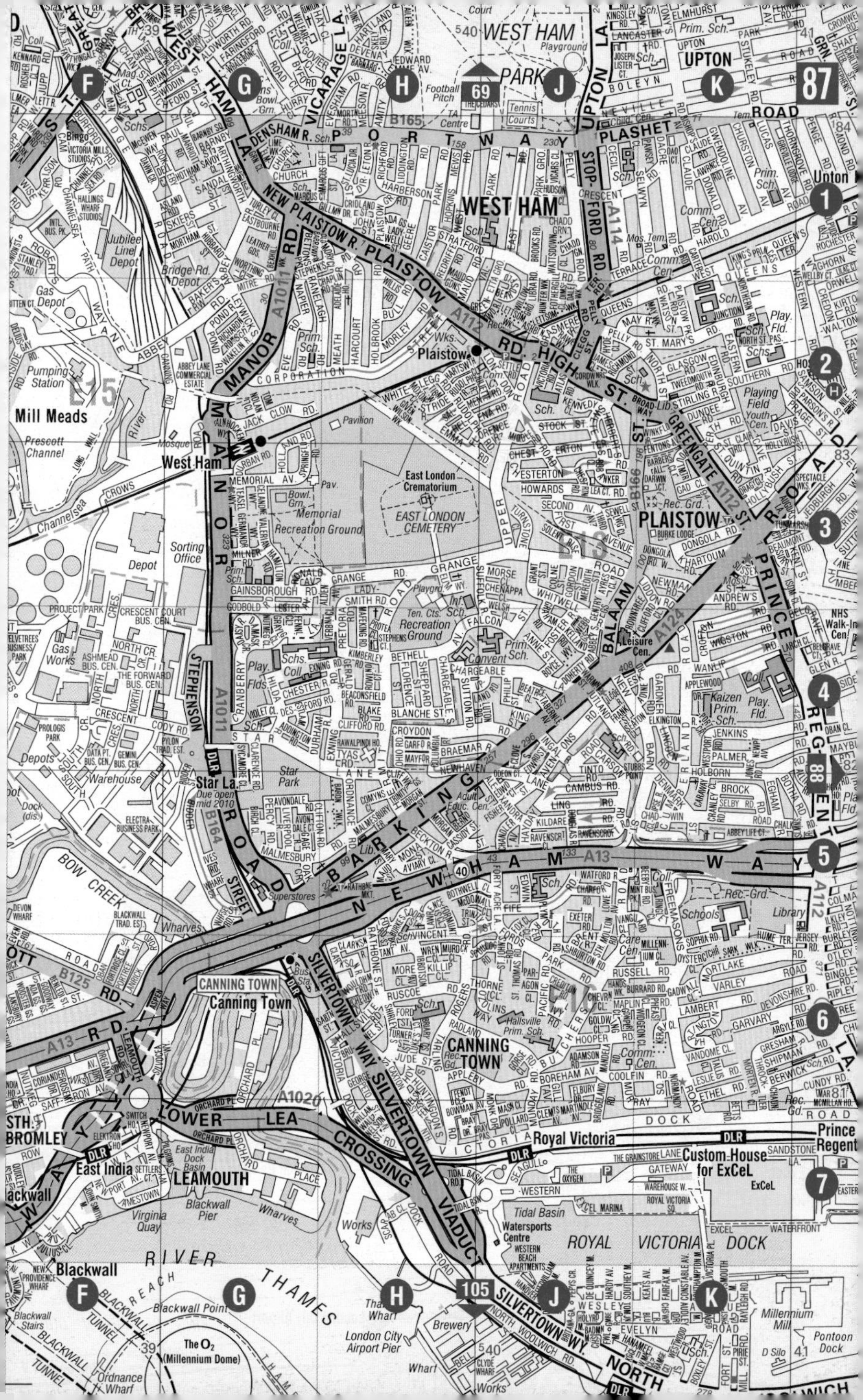

87
WEST HAM
PARK
69
UPTON
PLASHET
PORTWAY
WEST HAM
NEW PLAISTOW RD.
PLAISTOW RD.
HIGH ST.
Plaistow
MANOR RD.
A1011
A112
A114
A124
A13
B165
B166
B164
B125
A1020
E15
E13
Mill Meads
Prescott Channel
Channelsea
Jubilee Line Depot
Bridge Rd. Depot
Gas Depot
Pumping Station
ABBEY LANE COMMERCIAL ESTATE
West Ham
East London Crematorium
EAST LONDON CEMETERY
Memorial Recreation Ground
Sorting Office
Depot
PROJECT PARK
CRESCENT COURT BUS. CEN.
Gas Works
ASHMEAD BUS. CEN.
THE FORWARD BUS. CEN.
PROLOGIS PARK
Depots
Warehouse
ELECTRA BUSINESS PARK
Star La.
Due open mid 2010
Star Park
Recreation Ground
Convent
PLAISTOW
Leisure Cen.
BALAAM ST.
GREENGATE ST.
PRINCE REGENT LA.
88
NHS Walk-in Cen.
Kaizen Prim. Sch.
BARKING RD.
NEWHAM WAY
BOW CREEK
BLACKWALL TRAD. EST.
DEVON WHARF
Wharves
Superstores
CANNING TOWN
Canning Town
SILVERTOWN WAY
Hallsville Prim. Sch.
CANNING TOWN
LOWER LEA CROSSING
STH. BROMLEY
East India
LEAMOUTH
East India Dock Basin
Virginia Quay
Blackwall Pier
Blackwall
RIVER THAMES
BLACKWALL REACH
Blackwall Point
BLACKWALL TUNNEL
The O2 (Millennium Dome)
Ordnance Wharf
Blackwall Stairs
NEW PROVIDENCE WHARF
Royal Victoria
Custom House for ExCeL
ExCeL
Prince Regent
Tidal Basin
Watersports Centre
WESTERN BEACH APARTMENTS
ROYAL VICTORIA DOCK
SILVERTOWN VIADUCT
105
SILVERTOWN WY.
NORTH WOOLWICH RD.
Thames Wharf
London City Airport Pier
Brewery
Millennium Mill
Pontoon Dock
D Silo
Works
Wharf
F G H J K
1 2 3 4 5 6 7

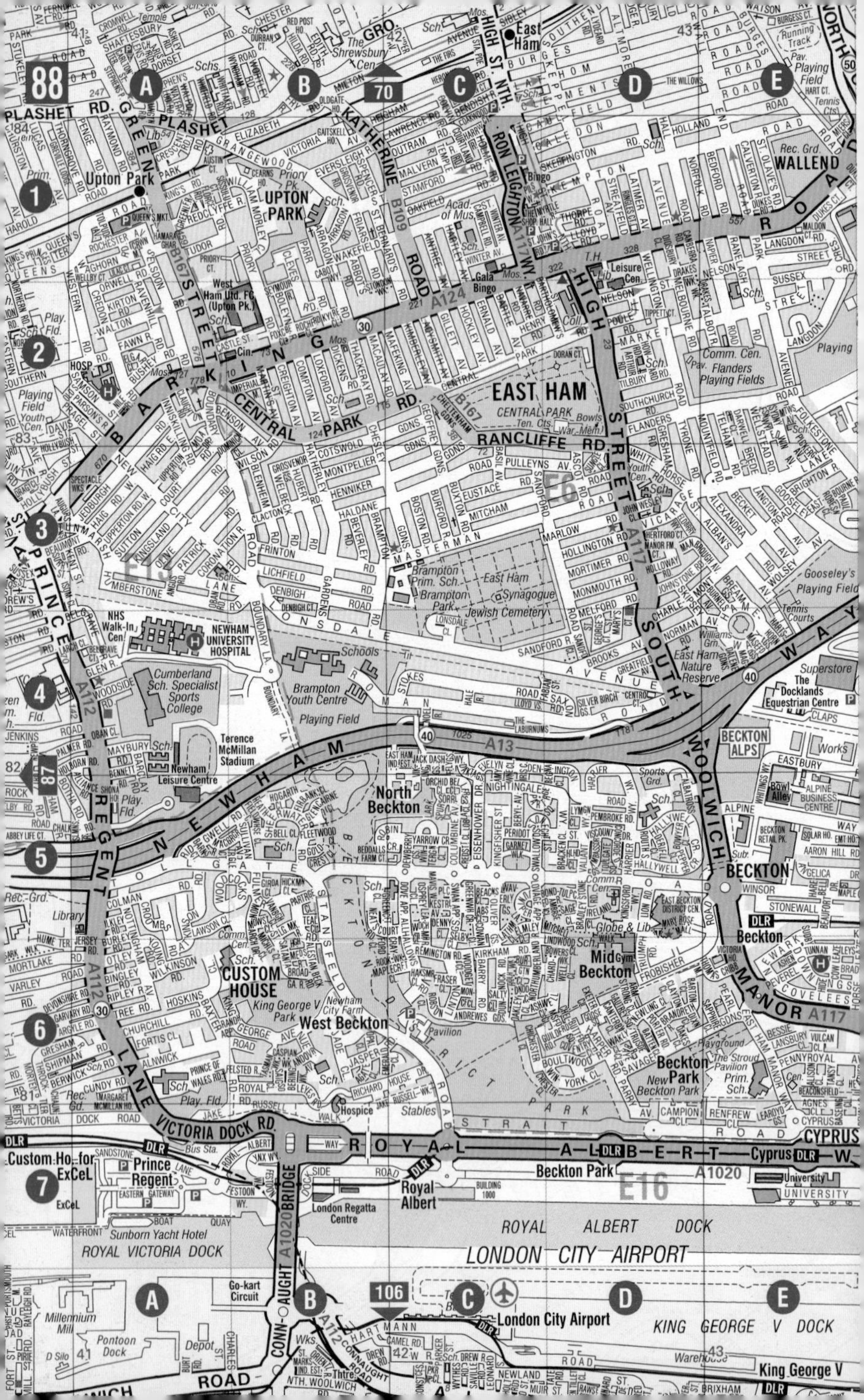

A
B
C
D
E
1
2
3
4
5
6
7
70
87
106
Upton Park
UPTON PARK
East Ham
EAST HAM
WALLEND
BECKTON
Beckton
North Beckton
Mid Beckton
West Beckton
CUSTOM HOUSE
CYPRUS
E6
E13
E16
PLASHET RD.
GREEN STREET
BARKING ROAD
CENTRAL PARK RD.
HIGH STREET NTH.
HIGH STREET SOUTH
KATHERINE ROAD
RANCLIFFE RD.
NEWHAM WAY
PRINCE REGENT LANE
VICTORIA DOCK RD.
ROYAL ALBERT WAY
WOOLWICH MANOR WAY
TOLLGATE ROAD
CONNAUGHT BRIDGE
West Ham Utd. FC (Upton Pk.)
NEWHAM UNIVERSITY HOSPITAL
NHS Walk-in Cen.
Cumberland Sch. Specialist Sports College
Terence McMillan Stadium
Newham Leisure Centre
Brampton Youth Centre
East Ham Synagogue Jewish Cemetery
East Ham Nature Reserve
The Docklands Equestrian Centre
BECKTON ALPS
Gooseley's Playing Field
Flanders Playing Fields
King George V Park
Newham City Farm
Beckton Park
New Beckton Park
Custom Ho. for ExCeL
Prince Regent
Royal Albert
Beckton Park
Cyprus
University
London Regatta Centre
Sunborn Yacht Hotel
ROYAL VICTORIA DOCK
ROYAL ALBERT DOCK
LONDON CITY AIRPORT
London City Airport
KING GEORGE V DOCK
King George V
Millennium Mill
Pontoon Dock
Go-kart Circuit

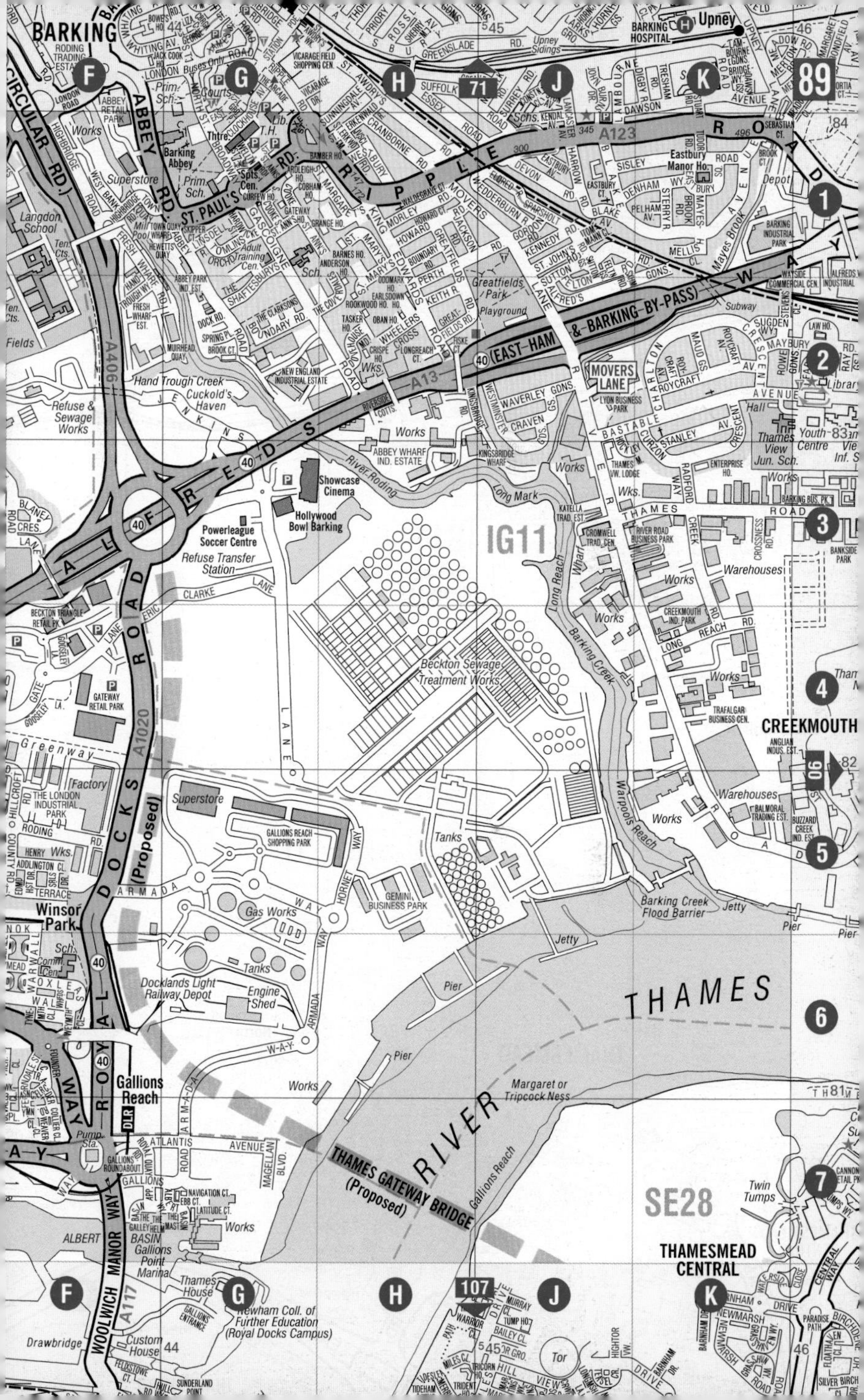
BARKING
Upney
BARKING HOSPITAL
RODING TRADING ESTATE
VICARAGE FIELD SHOPPING CEN.
Barking Abbey
Superstore
Langdon School
RIPPLE ROAD
A123
Eastbury Manor Ho.
BARKING INDUSTRIAL PARK
ST. PAUL'S RD.
ABBEY RD.
CIRCULAR RD.
A406
EAST HAM & BARKING BY-PASS
A13
ALFREDS WAY
Greatfields Park
Playground
MOVERS LANE
LYON BUSINESS PARK
NEW ENGLAND INDUSTRIAL ESTATE
ABBEY WHARF IND. ESTATE
KINGSBRIDGE WHARF
River Roding
Showcase Cinema
Hollywood Bowl Barking
Powerleague Soccer Centre
Refuse Transfer Station
Refuse & Sewage Works
Hand Trough Creek
Cuckold's Haven
IG11
THAMES ROAD
RIVER ROAD BUSINESS PARK
CREEKMOUTH IND. PARK
Warehouses
Beckton Sewage Treatment Works
TRAFALGAR BUSINESS CEN.
CREEKMOUTH
ANGLIAN INDUS. EST.
BALMORAL TRADING EST.
BUZZARD CREEK IND. EST.
Barking Creek
Long Reach
Warpools Reach
Barking Creek Flood Barrier
Jetty
Pier
BECKTON TRIANGLE RETAIL PK.
GATEWAY RETAIL PARK
Greenway
THE LONDON INDUSTRIAL PARK
DOCKS ROAD
A1020
(Proposed)
ROYAL DOCKS ROAD
GALLIONS REACH SHOPPING PARK
Superstore
GEMINI BUSINESS PARK
Tanks
Gas Works
Docklands Light Railway Depot
Engine Shed
Winsor Park
Gallions Reach
DLR
GALLIONS ROUNDABOUT
ATLANTIS AVENUE
THAMES
RIVER
Margaret or Tripcock Ness
THAMES GATEWAY BRIDGE (Proposed)
Gallions Reach
SE28
Twin Tumps
THAMESMEAD CENTRAL
WOOLWICH MANOR WAY
A117
Gallions Point Marina
Thames House
Newham Coll. of Further Education (Royal Docks Campus)
Custom House
Drawbridge
Tor
F
G
H
J
K
1
2
3
4
5
6
7
44
45
46
71
90
107

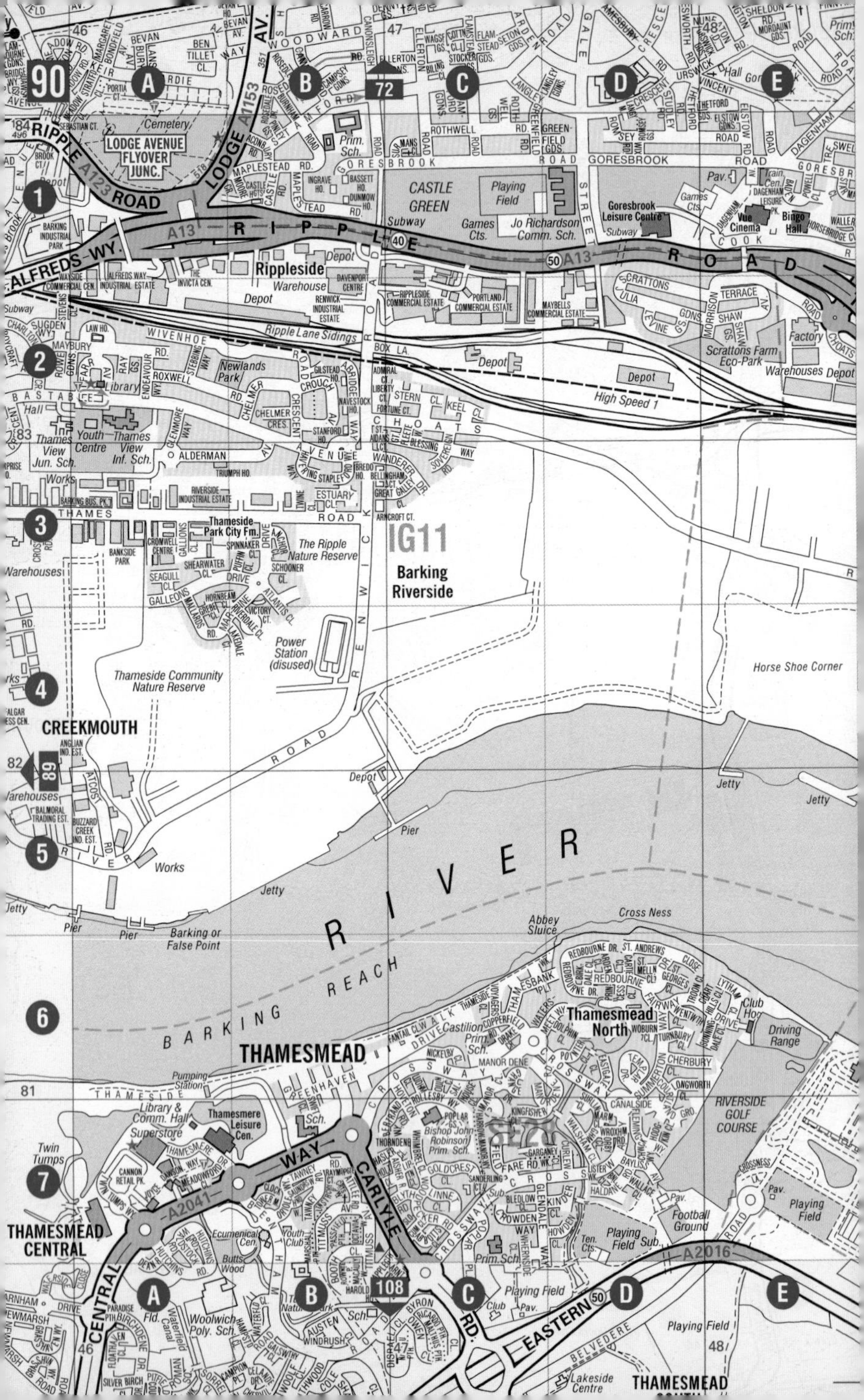

90
72
108
68
A
B
C
D
E
1
2
3
4
5
6
7
LODGE AVENUE FLYOVER JUNC.
RIPPLE ROAD
A123
A13
A1153
LODGE AV.
RIPPLE ROAD
ALFREDS WY.
CASTLE GREEN
Playing Field
Jo Richardson Comm. Sch.
Goresbrook Leisure Centre
Vue Cinema
Bingo Hall
GORESBROOK ROAD
Rippleside
Depot
Warehouse
Ripple Lane Sidings
High Speed 1
Scrattons Farm Eco-Park
Newlands Park
Library
Youth Centre
Thames View Inf. Sch.
Thames View Jun. Sch.
THAMES ROAD
CHOATS ROAD
RENWICK ROAD
IG11
Barking Riverside
Thameside Park City Fm.
The Ripple Nature Reserve
Power Station (disused)
Thameside Community Nature Reserve
CREEKMOUTH
Horse Shoe Corner
Jetty
Pier
Works
RIVER
BARKING REACH
Barking or False Point
Abbey Sluice
Cross Ness
THAMESMEAD
Thamesmead North
Thamesmere Leisure Cen.
Library & Comm. Hall
Superstore
Twin Tumps
THAMESMEAD CENTRAL
A2041
CARLYLE WAY
RIVERSIDE GOLF COURSE
Driving Range
Football Ground
Playing Field
A2016
EASTERN WAY
Woolwich Poly. Sch.
Bishop John Robinson Prim. Sch.
Lakeside Centre
THAMESMEAD SOUTH

F
G
H
J
K
1
2
3
4
5
6
7
49
50
51
73
109
Goresbrook Park
Prim. Sch.
Village Inf. Sch.
William Ford C of E Jun. Sch.
Dagenham Arena
Old Dagenham Pk.
Playing Field
Sports Hall
Comp. Sch.
Hosp.
THE LEYS
The Leys Prim. Sch.
Comm. Cen.
DAGENHAM
Dagenham Beam Bri.
Newtons Corner
Wantz Stream
Beam River
Beam Valley Country Park
RM10
RIPPLE ROAD
NEW ROAD
HEATHWAY
A1240
A1306
B178
BALLARDS
Superstore
GORESBROOK INTERCHANGE
Works
Dagenham Dock
Sports Field
Bowl. Alley
Club
Beam Prim. Sch.
Play. Fld.
Adventure Playgrd.
Playing Field
SOUTH HORNCHURCH
Prim. Sch.
Beam Bri.
RM9
A13
THAMES
BREACH LA.
THAMES GATEWAY PARK
Dagenham Breach
Motor Works
Power Station
Industrial Estate
Depot
Oil Storage Depot
Jetty
Thunderer Jetty
Dock
Landing Stage
Pontoon
FORD INDUSTRIAL PARK
Works
Beam River
HORNCHURCH MARSHES
Car Compound
Car Compound
GATEWAY
RM13
Rainham Steel Mills
Thames Gateway College (CEME)
BASEPOINT BUSINESS CENTRE
Timber Yard
Rainham Creek
Wks.
Old Man's Head
Depot
Frog Island
Jetty
Hornchurch Shoot
THAMES
The Crossness Engines Museum
SEWAGE WORKS
DA18
DA17
Jetty
BURTS WHARF
Warehouses
Works
Lighthouse
Warehouse
Jenningtree Point
BELVEDERE IND. EST.
Works
Wharf

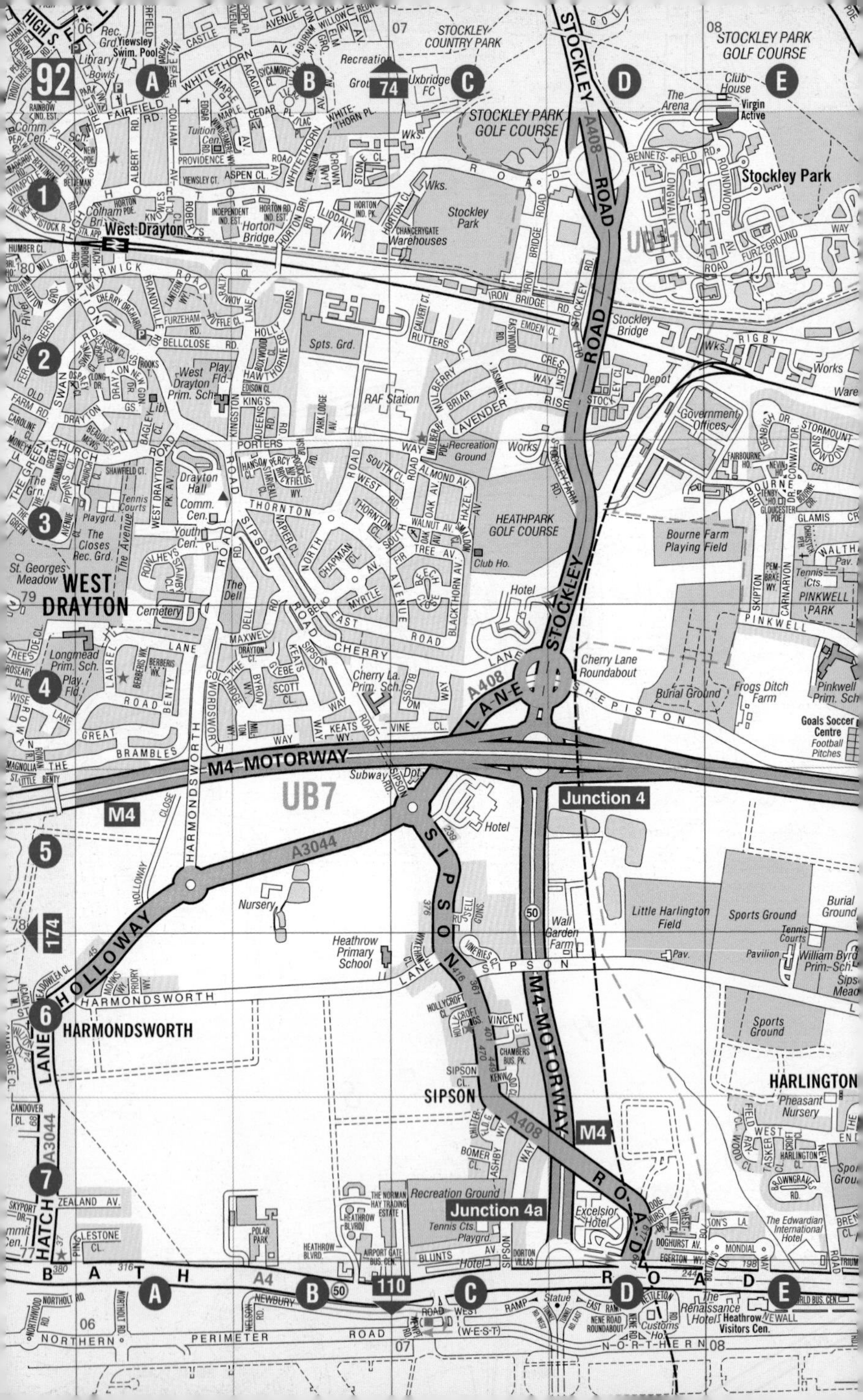

92
74
110
174
A
B
C
D
E
1
2
3
4
5
6
7
06
07
08
77
78
79
80
STOCKLEY COUNTRY PARK
STOCKLEY PARK GOLF COURSE
Stockley Park
Club House
The Arena
Virgin Active
Uxbridge FC
Recreation Ground
Yiewsley Swim. Pool
Library
Bowls
WHITETHORN AV.
FAIRFIELD RD.
HORTON ROAD
HORTON BRIDGE
West Drayton
Colham Bri.
Horton Bridge
INDEPENDENT IND. EST.
HORTON RD. IND. EST.
HORTON IND. PK.
CHANCERYGATE Warehouses
IRON BRIDGE RD.
BENNETS FIELD RD.
LONGWALK
ROUNDWOOD AV.
FURZEGROUND WAY
UB11
Stockley Bridge
RIGBY
Works
Depot
Government Offices
STOCKLEY ROAD
A408
Spts. Grd.
RAF Station
West Drayton Prim. Sch.
Play. Fld.
Lib.
Drayton Hall
Comm. Cen.
Youth Cen.
Tennis Courts
Playgrd.
The Closes Rec. Grd.
St. Georges Meadow
WEST DRAYTON
Cemetery
The Dell
Longmead Prim. Sch.
THORNTON
SIPSON ROAD
CHERRY LANE
Recreation Ground
HEATHPARK GOLF COURSE
Club Ho.
Hotel
Cherry Lane Roundabout
SHEPISTON
Burial Ground
Frogs Ditch Farm
Bourne Farm Playing Field
PINKWELL PARK
Pinkwell Prim. Sch.
Goals Soccer Centre
Football Pitches
Cherry La. Prim. Sch.
M4 MOTORWAY
M4
UB7
Junction 4
Subway
A3044
HOLLOWAY
HARMONDSWORTH
Nursery
Heathrow Primary School
SIPSON LANE
Wall Garden Farm
Little Harlington Field
Sports Ground
Pav.
Pavilion
William Byrd Prim. Sch.
Burial Ground
HARMONDSWORTH
HATCH LANE
SIPSON
HARLINGTON
Pheasant Nursery
Recreation Ground
Junction 4a
Tennis Cts.
THE NORMAN HAY TRADING ESTATE
POLAR PARK
AIRPORT GATE BUS. CEN.
Excelsior Hotel
The Edwardian International Hotel
The Renaissance Hotel
Heathrow Visitors Cen.
Statue
Customs Ho.
NENE ROAD ROUNDABOUT
BATH ROAD
A4
NORTHERN PERIMETER ROAD

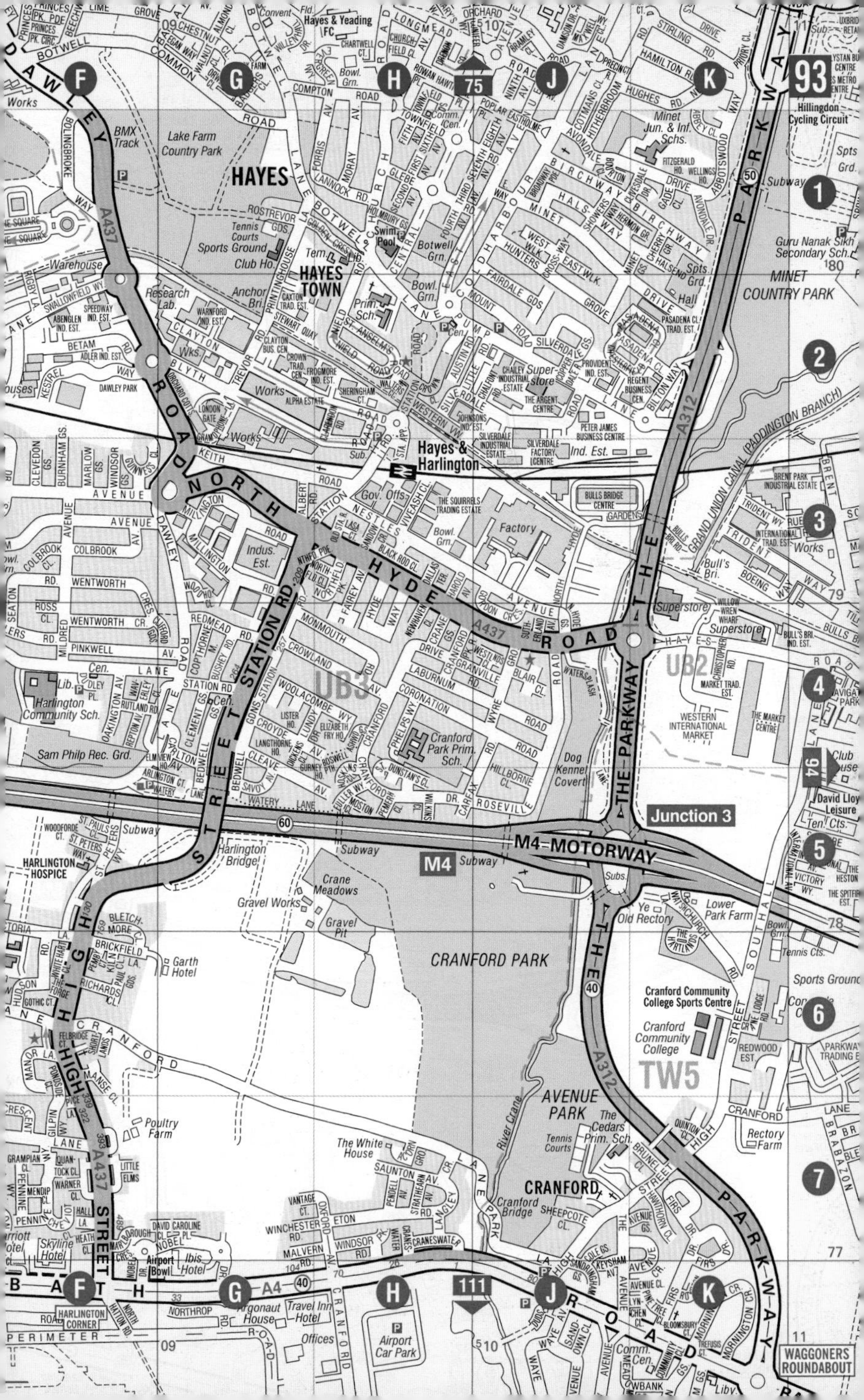
93
75
94
111
F
G
H
J
K
1
2
3
4
5
6
7
HAYES
HAYES TOWN
Hayes & Yeading FC
Lake Farm Country Park
BMX Track
Sports Ground
Tennis Courts
Club Ho.
Research Lab.
Anchor Bri.
Swim Pool
Botwell Grn.
Prim. Sch.
Hayes & Harlington
Hillingdon Cycling Circuit
Minet Jun. & Inf. Schs.
Guru Nanak Sikh Secondary Sch.
MINET COUNTRY PARK
GRAND UNION CANAL (PADDINGTON BRANCH)
UB3
UB2
TW5
Harlington Community Sch.
Sam Philp Rec. Grd.
Cranford Park Prim. Sch.
Dog Kennel Covert
WESTERN INTERNATIONAL MARKET
Junction 3
M4 MOTORWAY
M4
Harlington Bridge
HARLINGTON HOSPICE
Crane Meadows
Gravel Works
Gravel Pit
CRANFORD PARK
Garth Hotel
Poultry Farm
The White House
AVENUE PARK
The Cedars Prim. Sch.
CRANFORD
Cranford Bridge
Cranford Community College Sports Centre
Cranford Community College
Rectory Farm
Lower Park Farm
Ye Old Rectory
Skyline Hotel
Airport Bowl
Ibis Hotel
Argonaut House
Travel Inn Hotel
Offices
Airport Car Park
HARLINGTON CORNER
WAGGONERS ROUNDABOUT
BATH ROAD
A4
A437
A312
THE PARKWAY
DAWLEY ROAD
NORTH HYDE ROAD
STATION RD.
HIGH STREET
PERIMETER ROAD
09
510
11
77
78
79
180

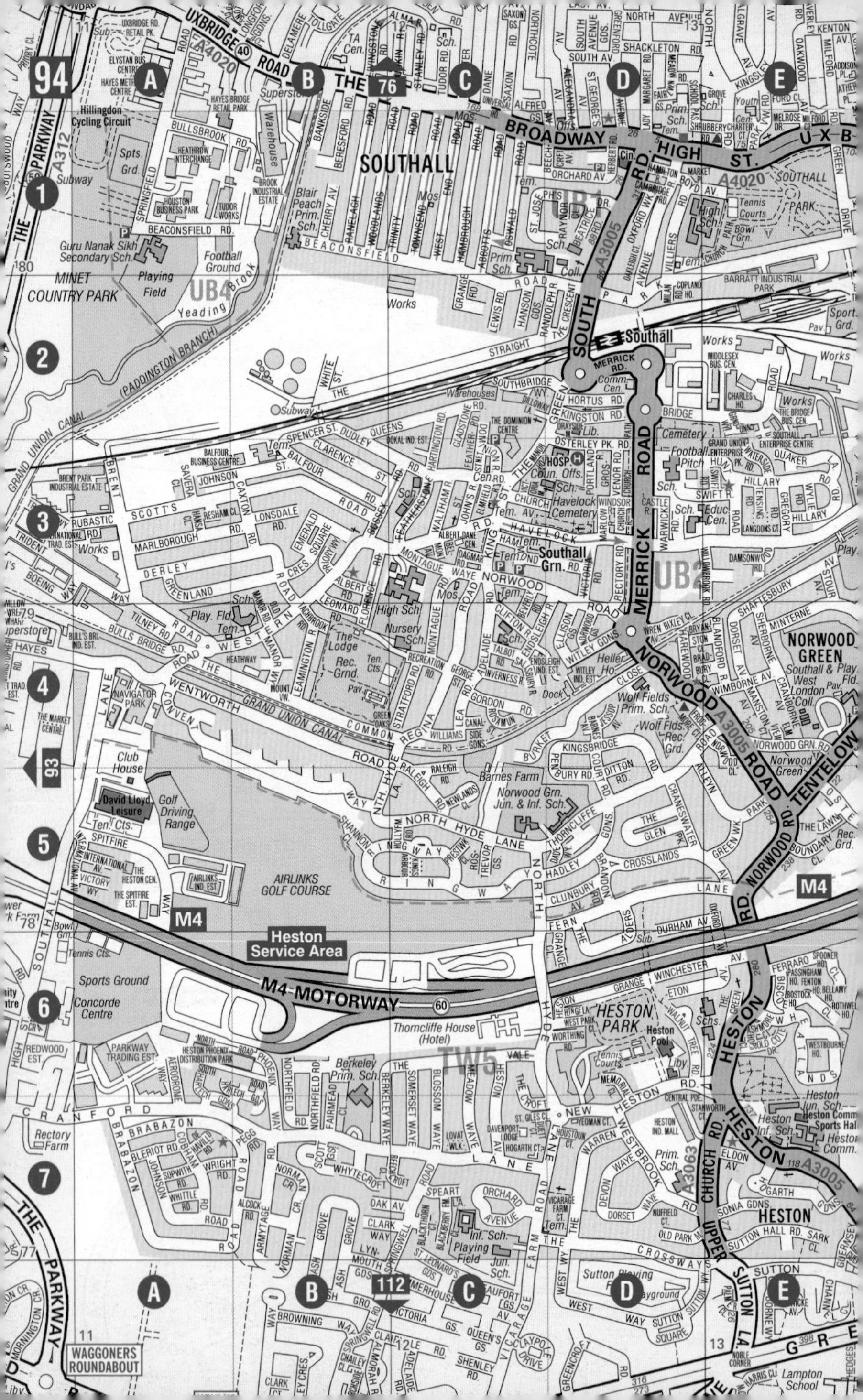
94
76
93
112
A
B
C
D
E
1
2
3
4
5
6
7
SOUTHALL
UXBRIDGE ROAD
A4020
THE BROADWAY
HIGH ST.
SOUTH RD.
A3005
MERRICK ROAD
NORWOOD ROAD
TENTELOW LA.
HESTON RD.
CHURCH RD.
UPPER SUTTON LA.
THE PARKWAY
A312
SOUTHALL LANE
NORTH HYDE LANE
NTH. HYDE LA.
RINGWAY
CRANFORD LANE
PARKWAY TRADING EST.
HESTON PHOENIX DISTRIBUTION PARK
Southall
UB1
UB2
UB4
TW5
Hillingdon Cycling Circuit
MINET COUNTRY PARK
Guru Nanak Sikh Secondary Sch.
Football Ground
Playing Field
Yeading Brook
GRAND UNION CANAL
(PADDINGTON BRANCH)
THE STRAIGHT
Blair Peach Prim. Sch.
BEACONSFIELD RD.
HAYES BRIDGE RETAIL PARK
UXBRIDGE RD. RETAIL PK.
ELYSTAN BUS CENTRE
HAYES METRO CENTRE
HEATHROW INTERCHANGE
HOUSTON BUSINESS PARK
TUDOR WORKS
BROOK INDUSTRIAL ESTATE
Warehouse
Superstore
Works
SOUTHALL PARK
Tennis Courts
Bowl Grn.
High Sch.
BARRATT INDUSTRIAL PARK
Sports Grd.
Cemetery
Havelock Cemetery
Football Pitch
MIDDLESEX BUS. CEN.
THE BRIDGE BUS. CEN.
GRAND UNION ENTERPRISE PK.
THE DOMINION CENTRE
HOSP
Coun. Offs.
Southall Grn.
NORWOOD GREEN
Southall & Play. Fld.
West London Coll.
Norwood Green
Wolf Fields Prim. Sch.
Wolf Flds. Rec. Grd.
Barnes Farm
Norwood Grn. Jun. & Inf. Sch.
The Lodge Rec. Grnd.
High Sch.
Nursery Sch.
Heller Ho.
BRENT PARK INDUSTRIAL ESTATE
RUBASTIC RD
INTERNATIONAL TRAD. EST.
BALFOUR BUSINESS CENTRE
NAVIGATOR PARK
THE MARKET CENTRE
Club House
David Lloyd Leisure
Golf Driving Range
AIRLINKS GOLF COURSE
THE HESTON CEN.
THE SPITFIRE EST.
FAIRLINKS IND. EST.
M4
Heston Service Area
M4-MOTORWAY
60
Sports Ground
Concorde Centre
Thorncliffe House (Hotel)
HESTON PARK
Heston Pool
Liby.
Tennis Courts
Berkeley Prim. Sch.
HESTON IND. MALL
Prim. Sch.
A3063
Heston Jun. Sch.
Heston Inf. Sch.
Heston Comm. Sports Hall
HESTON
Rectory Farm
Inf. Sch.
Playing Field
Jun. Sch.
Sutton Playing Fields
Playground
Lampton School
WAGGONERS ROUNDABOUT
11
12
13
180
79
78
77

DORMER'S WELLS
WEST MIDDLESEX GOLF COURSE
Hanwell
HANWELL
95
77
96
113
OSTERLEY PARK
M4 MOTORWAY
WYKE GREEN GOLF COURSE
TW7
W7
OSTERLEY
SPRING GROVE
EALING HOSP.
ST. BERNARD'S HOSPITAL
Hanwell Locks
Glade Lane Canalside Park
Osterley Sports Club
Warren Farm Sports Centre
Osterley Park House
Elthorne Park
Kensington Cemetery
City of Westminster Cemetery
GREAT WESTERN INDUSTRIAL PARK
UXBRIDGE ROAD
BOSTON RD.
WINDMILL LANE
SYON LANE
GREAT WEST ROAD
JERSEY ROAD

96
78
95
114
A
B
C
D
E
1
2
3
4
5
6
7
West Ealing
EALING
WEST EALING
HANWELL
Westminster Cemetery
Kensington Cemetery
Oaklands Primary Sch.
UXBRIDGE ROAD
BROADWAY
NORTHFIELD AVENUE
Walpole Park
Pitshanger Manor Mus.
Ealing & West London Coll.
Ealing Studios
The Questors Theatre
Thames Valley Uni.
Lammas Park
W13
W5
Grange Primary School
South Ealing
Northfields
Northfields Depot
Blondin Pk. Sports Ground
Elthorne Park
Elthorne Sports Cen.
Evershed Spts. Grnd.
Boston Manor
Boston Manor Playing Field
Boston Manor House
Boston Manor Park
BOSTON MANOR ROAD
BOSTON ROAD
M4 MOTORWAY
Junc. 2
Gunnersbury RC Sch.
Reynard Mills Trading Estate
Little Ealing
South Ealing Cemetery
Claypond Hosp.
SOUTH EALING ROAD
POPES LA.
Grand Union Canal
Gallows Bridge
Clitheroe's Lock
River Brent
TW7
TW8
Brentford
BRENTFORD
Brentford FC (Griffin Pk.)
BRENTFORD END
GREAT WEST ROAD
HIGH STREET
Watermans Arts Centre
Old Brentford
Brentford Gate
KEW GARDENS
ROYAL BOTANIC GARDENS
Syon Lane
SYON PARK
Syon Ho.
Syon Garden Centre
London Butterfly House
Busch Corner
LONDON ROAD
Gillette Cnr.
Centaurs Business Park
Superstore
West Cross Centre
Brentside Executive Centre
Brentford Business Centre

F
G
H
J
K
97
79
98
115
1
2
3
4
5
6
7
EAST ACTON
ACTON
Ealing Common
Acton Central
ACTON PARK
THE VALE
A4020
HIGH ST.
STEYNE RD.
HORN LA.
GUNNERSBURY LANE
GUNNERSBURY AVENUE
A406
A4000
W3
SOUTH ACTON
Acton Town
South Acton
ACTON GREEN
SOUTHFIELD
Southfields Rec. Grd.
BEDFORD PARK
THE AVENUE
SOUTH PARADE
Chiswick Pk.
Chiswick Common
GUNNERSBURY
Esporta Health & Fitness
GUNNERSBURY PARK
Gunnersbury Park Mus.
Boating Lake
Miniature Golf Course
PARK
Kensington Cemetery
Kew East Junc.
M4
M4 MOTORWAY
CHISWICK HIGH RD.
A315
Gunnersbury
HEATHFIELD TER.
TURNHAM GREEN
W4
Junc.1
GT. WEST RD.
CEDARS RD.
ELLESMERE RD.
A4
A3000
Kew Bridge
Brentford Fountain Leis. Cen.
WELLESLEY
KEW BRIDGE
A205
KEW RD.
Steam Mus.
Strand on the Green
Oliver's Island
CHISWICK
Chiswick House
Cricket Ground
Temple
KEW
Kew Green
Botanical Library
Main Gate
Kew Gardens Gallery
Orangery
Princess of Wales Conservatory
Plants & People Exhibition
Palm House
The Pond
Rose Garden
Visitor Cen.
Victoria Ga.
Temple of Bellona
TW9
MORTLAKE
A307
The National Archives
Chiswick
BURLINGTON
Sports Hall
ALEXANDRA AV.
A316
Chiswick Cemetery
GROVE PARK
Sports Ground
Kew Gds.
GT. CHERTSEY RD.

98
80
97
116
A
B
C
D
E
1
2
3
4
5
6
7
EAST ACTON
White City
White City
Wood Lane
(Open 2008)
BBC Television Centre
QPR FC
Wormholt Park
The King Fahad Academy
Recreation Ground
Sports Ground
The Park Club
Sports
Cricket Ground
Football Pitch
Leisure Cen.
THE VALE ESTATE
Comm. Cen.
Maples Sch.
ACTON PARK
THE VALE
A4020
UXBRIDGE ROAD
Shepherd's Bush
Westfield (Open Late 2008)
Shepherd's Bush Thtre.
Goldhawk Rd.
W12
W6
W4
SW13
Wendell Park
Cathnor Park
Ravenscourt Park
Adventure Playground
SEVEN STARS CORNER
B408
A402
GOLDHAWK RD.
PADDENSWICK RD.
ASKEW RD.
BEDFORD PARK
THE AVENUE
B491
BATH RD.
B409
STH. PDE.
Turnham Green
Stamford Brook
Ravenscourt Park
GLENTHORNE ROAD
KING ST.
CHISWICK HIGH RD.
A315
CHISWICK LA.
A316
Bus Depot
Chiswick Common
Hammersmith
Lyric Theatre
Town Hall
GREAT WEST ROAD
A4
HAMMERSMITH FLYOVER
Apollo
Furnival Gdns.
Hammersmith Pier
Homefield Recreation Ground
TURNHAM GREEN
HOGARTH LA.
HOGARTH RBT.
Brewery
Chiswick Lodge
Chiswick Eyot
RIVER THAMES
St. Pauls School
Play. Flds.
Tennis Courts
Playing Field
Riverside Studios
HAMMERSMITH BRIDGE
CASTELNAU
A306
Castelnau
LONSDALE ROAD
B350
Swedish Sch.
Church Wharf
Corney Reach
Chiswick Pier
Lifeboat Sta.
Lonsdale Road Reservoir Bird Sanctuary
The Harrodian Sch.
Rec. Grd.
Prim. Sch.
LONDON WETLAND CENTRE
Peter Scott Visitor Centre
Barn Elms
CHISWICK
Chiswick House
Temple
Chiswick Ho. Grds.
BURLINGTON LA.
A316
Pool
Bowling Green
Riverside Recreation Ground
Sports Ground
Bandstand
Pavilion
Small Profits
Riverside Health
Blakes Wharves
Eternit Wharf
Stevenage Wharves
Day Cen.

NOTTING HILL
81
Notting Hill Gate
KENSINGTON GARDENS
The Orangery
Round Pond
Kensington Palace
Holland Park
HOLLAND PARK
King George VI Memorial Youth Hostel
Holland Ho.
Theatre
Cricket Field
Commonwealth Inst.
KENSINGTON
High St. Kensington
Shepherd's Bush
Kensington Olympia
Olympia
HOLLAND ROAD
HOLLAND PARK AVENUE
KENSINGTON HIGH STREET
KENSINGTON RD.
CHURCH ST.
Brook Green
HAMMERSMITH
WEST KENSINGTON
FLYOVER
TALGARTH ROAD
West Kensington
Barons Court
Hammersmith Cemetery
The Queen's Club
CHARING CROSS HOSP.
Gloucester Rd.
CROMWELL ROAD
SOUTH KENSINGTON
100
EARL'S COURT
Earl's Court
Earls Court Exhibition Building
BROMPTON
OLD BROMPTON ROAD
West Brompton
WEST BROMPTON
Brompton Cemetery
LILLIE ROAD
DAWES ROAD
NORTH END ROAD
Fulham Pools
Fulham Cemetery
Chelsea FC (Stamford Bridge)
Fulham Broadway
FULHAM ROAD
WALHAM GREEN
KING'S ROAD
FULHAM
117
Parsons
SANDS END
Gas Works

A
B
C
D
E
82
1
2
3
4
5
6
7
KENSINGTON GARDENS
HYDE PARK
W2
Lancaster Gate
BAYSWATER RD
Marlborough Gate
The Fountains
Lancaster Gate
Porchester Ter. Gate
Black Lion Gate
Speke's Monument
Peter Pan Statue
The Long Water
Temple Lodge
Round Pond
The Orangery
Kensington Palace
Bandstand
Serpentine Gallery
Princess of Wales Memorial Fountain
Cafeteria
THE SERPENTINE
Fishermans Keep
Nannies Lawn
The Holocaust Mem. Gdn.
Rose Garden
Queen Elizabeth Gate
ROTTEN ROW
Albert Memorial
Palace Gate
Queen's Gate
Alexandra Gate
Prince of Wales Gate
SOUTH CARRIAGE DRIVE
(Closed Midnight - 5am) New Ride
SCOTCH HOUSE
Hyde Park Corner
Nursery
The Lookout Education Cen.
Rangers Lodge
Reformers Tree
Entrance to Underground Car Park
Refreshment Kiosk
Speakers' Corner
Victoria Gate
Clarendon Gate
Albion Gate
Stanhope Place Gate
MAYFAIR
Roosevelt Mem.
PARK LANE
A4202
10
KENSINGTON ROAD
KENSINGTON GORE
A315
KNIGHTSBRIDGE
Knightsbridge
Royal Albert Hall
Ryl. Coll. of Music
Imperial Coll.
Science Museum
Natural History Mus.
Victoria & Albert Museum
Brompton Oratory
Harrods
BROMPTON
BROMPTON ROAD
CROMWELL RD.
A4
THURLOE PL.
Gloucester Rd.
Sth. Kensington
SOUTH KENSINGTON
16
99
BROMPTON RD
A3218
OLD BROMPTON RD
The Royal Marsden Hosp.
Royal Brompton Hosp.
CHELSEA
SYDNEY ST
B304
KINGS RD
A308
A3217
SLOANE ST
A3216
Sloane Square
Saatchi Gallery
Burton's Court
Royal Hospital Chelsea
Ranelagh Gardens
CHELSEA BRIDGE RD
BELGRAVE SQ.
EATON PL.
B310
B319
PONT ST.
PIMLICO RD.
Chelsea Barracks
ROYAL HOSPITAL RD
CHELSEA EMBANKMENT
17
THAMES
RIVER
CHELSEA REACH
Cadogan Pier
Pier
CHEYNE WALK
OAKLEY ST
16
Chelsea & Westminster Hosp.
WEST BROMPTON
REDCLIFFE GDNS
FULHAM RD
EDITH GRO.
A3220
A3212
A3031
ALBERT BRIDGE
ALBERT BRIDGE ROAD
BATTERSEA BRI. RD.
BATTERSEA PARK
Peace Pagoda
Children's Zoo
British Genius Site
The Pump Ho. Gallery
Boating Lake
CARRIAGE DRIVE NORTH
CENTRAL AVENUE
SW11
Cremorne Gardens
Chelsea Wharf
Cremorne Wharf
Chelsea Creek
Gas Works
SANDS END
BATTERSEA
118
WESTBRIDGE
Old Swan Wharf
Wharves
Bascule Bri.
PRINCE OF WALES DR.

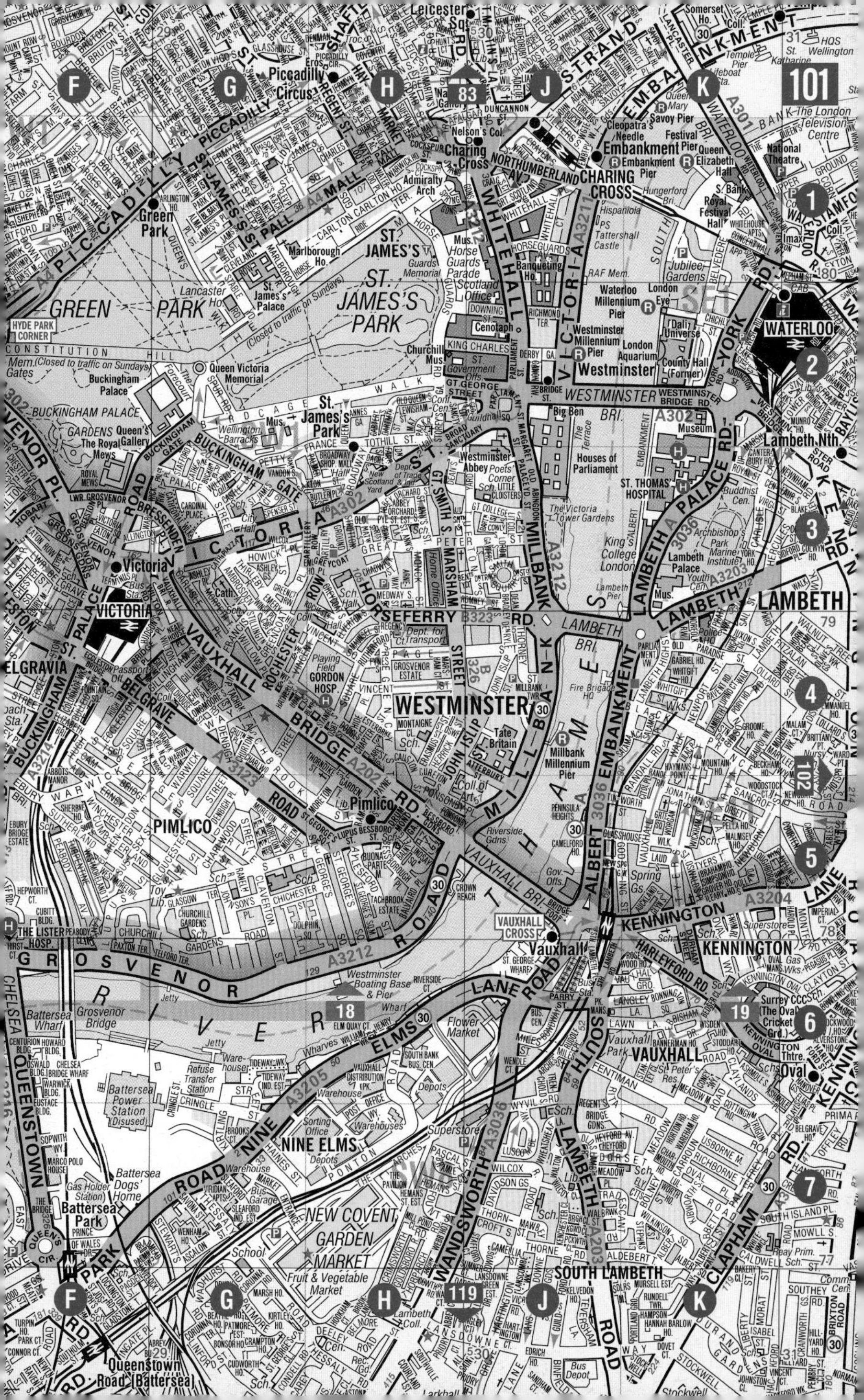
101
F
G
H
J
K
83
Piccadilly Circus
Leicester Sq.
Charing Cross
Nelson's Col.
Admiralty Arch
Embankment
Cleopatra's Needle
Somerset Ho.
Queen Mary
Savoy Pier
Festival Pier
Queen Elizabeth Hall
Embankment Pier
Hungerford Bri.
National Theatre
The London Television Centre
Royal Festival Hall
Imax
Waterloo
Green Park
St. James's Palace
Marlborough Ho.
St. James's Park
Green Park
Hyde Park Corner
Constitution Hill
Buckingham Palace
Queen Victoria Memorial
Buckingham Palace Gardens
Queen's Gallery
The Royal Mews
Wellington Barracks
Horse Guards Parade
Banqueting Ho.
Scotland Office
Cenotaph
Churchill Mus.
Whitehall
Westminster
London Eye
London Aquarium
County Hall (Former)
Dali Universe
Jubilee Gardens
Waterloo Millennium Pier
Westminster Millennium Pier
Big Ben
Houses of Parliament
Westminster Abbey
St. Thomas' Hospital
Museum
Lambeth Nth.
Lambeth Palace
Archbishop's Park
The Victoria Tower Gardens
King's College London
Lambeth Pier
Lambeth
Victoria
Victoria Coach Sta.
Belgravia
Home Office
Dept. for Transport
Gordon Hosp.
Westminster
Tate Britain
Millbank Millennium Pier
Pimlico
Vauxhall Bridge Rd.
Riverside Gdns.
Vauxhall Cross
Vauxhall
Kennington
Surrey CCC (The Oval) Cricket Grd.
Oval
Vauxhall Park
Spring Gs.
River Thames
Grosvenor Road
Chelsea Bridge
Grosvenor Bridge
Westminster Boating Base & Pier
18
19
102
Battersea Power Station (Disused)
Nine Elms
New Covent Garden Market
Fruit & Vegetable Market
Flower Market
Battersea Park
Battersea Dogs' Home
Queenstown Road (Battersea)
South Lambeth
Wandsworth Road
Clapham Road
119
1
2
3
4
5
6
7

EMBANKMENT
UNDERPASS
RIVER THAMES
BLACKFRIARS
Millennium Bridge
84
Blackfriars Millennium Pier
HMS President
HQS Wellington
Bankside Pier
CANNON STREET
LOWER THAMES ST.
BYWARD ST.
The London Television Centre
National Theatre
Tate Modern
SOUTHWARK
Golden Hinde
Vinopolis
LONDON BRIDGE HOSP
London Bri. City Pier
HMS Belfast
Tower Millennium Pier
The Scoop
LONDON BRI.
TOOLEY
STAMFORD ST.
SOUTHWARK ST.
UNION ST.
THE BOROUGH
GUY'S HOSP.
Waterloo East
Southwark
WATERLOO
THE CUT
WATERLOO RD.
BLACKFRIARS RD.
SOUTHWARK BRIDGE RD.
BOROUGH HIGH ST.
Borough
LONG LA.
BERMONDSEY ST.
14
15
Lambeth Nth.
WESTMINSTER BRI. RD.
ST. GEORGE'S CIRCUS
BOROUGH RD.
LONDON RD.
NEWINGTON CAUSEWAY
HARPER RD.
GREAT DOVER ST.
TOWER BRIDGE RD.
LAMBETH RD.
Imperial War Mus.
Geraldine Mary Harmsworth Park
ST. GEORGE'S RD.
NEWINGTON
Elephant & Castle
NEW KENT RD.
BRICKLAYER'S ARMS
LAMBETH
KENNINGTON RD.
WALWORTH RD.
19
101
KENNINGTON LANE
Kennington
WALWORTH
KENNINGTON PARK RD.
Faraday Gdns.
KENNINGTON
Surrey CCC (The Oval Cricket Grd.)
Oval
KENNINGTON OVAL
Kennington Park
ALBANY RD.
BURGESS PARK
Burgess Park
Burgess Pk. Kart Track
CAMBERWELL RD.
CAMBERWELL NEW RD.
SOUTHAMPTON WAY
CLAPHAM RD.
BRIXTON RD.
120
CAMBERWELL GREEN
Leisure Cen.
PECKHAM
CAMBERWELL CHURCH STREET
St. Gabriel's Manor
MYATTS FIELDS
A B C D E
1 2 3 4 5 6 7

103
85
15
104
121
F
G
H
J
K
1
2
3
4
5
6
7
Tower Hill
Gateway
SHADWELL
THE HIGHWAY
EAST SMITHFIELD
The Tower of London
St. Katharine Docks
St. Katharine's Pier
Tower Bridge Wharf
King Edward Mem. Park
Shadwell Basin
Shadwell Dock Stairs
THAMES
Wapping
WAPPING
WAPPING HIGH ST.
John Orwell Sports Cen.
Wapping Old Stairs
Wapping New Stairs
New Crane Stairs
Pelican Stairs
Bellamy's Wharf
ROTHERHITHE TUNNEL
RIVER
UPPER POOL
LOWER POOL
Cherry Garden Pier
Cumberland Wharf
BERMONDSEY
Bermondsey
JAMAICA ROAD
BRUNEL RD.
TUNNEL APP.
SALTER RD.
Rotherhithe
Canada Water
ROTHERHITHE
Printing Works
Superstores
Surrey Quays Shopping Centre
Bowl. Alley & Gala Bingo
Odeon Cinema
Leisure Cen.
SOUTHWARK PARK
Cafe Gallery
Southwark Pk. Sports Cen. Track
Sports Complex
LOWER RD
REDRIFF RD
Surrey Quays
PLOUGH WY
GREENLAND DOCK
Ecological Park
Mun. Offices
Bermondsey Spa
Harris Academy
SOUTHWARK PARK RD.
RAYMOUTH RD
Tower Bridge Bus. Complex
DUNTON RD.
ROLLS ROAD
Paterson Pk.
CATLIN ST.
ROTHERHITHE NEW RD.
South Bermondsey
Lewisham Lions Cen.
Millwall FC (The Den)
Waste Transfer Station
STOCKHOLM RD.
SURREY CANAL ROAD
OLD KENT ROAD
TRAFALGAR AV.
Burgess Pk.
Superstore
CANAL BRIDGE
South Eastern Gas Works
Civic Cen.
Mus.
Rec. Grd.
Mosque
PECKHAM PARK RD.
PECKHAM HILL ST.
SE15
SE16
SE14
Brimmington Pk.
NEW CROSS RD.
NEW CROSS GATE
New Cross Gate
Bus Garage
Eckington Gdns.
Hatcham Gdns.
PECKHAM HIGH ST.
QUEEN'S ROAD
Queens Rd. (Peckham)
Leisure Cen.
SANFORD ST.
TRUNDLEYS ROAD
EVELYN ST.

POPLAR
Poplar
West India Quay
Canary Wharf
Billingsgate Fish Market
WEST INDIA DOCKS
BLACKWALL BASIN
Heron Quays
South Quay
ISLE OF DOGS
Crossharbour
MILLWALL
MILLWALL OUTER DOCK
CUBITT TOWN
Mudchute Farm
MUDCHUTE PARK
Mudchute
Island Gds.
MILLWALL PARK
Docklands Sailing Cen.
Masthouse Terrace Pier
Greenwich Pier
Cutty Sark for Maritime Greenwich
DEPTFORD
Deptford
Deptford Bri.
Greenwich
New Cross
New Cross Gate
NEW CROSS
NEW CROSS GATE
Goldsmiths' College
SE8
CONVOY'S WHARF
DEPTFORD PARK
Pepys Park
RIVER THAMES
LIMEHOUSE REACH
GREENWICH REACH
Hilton Docklands Pier
Canary Wharf Pier
Greenland Pier
SALTER ROAD
REDRIFF ROAD
PLOUGH WAY
EVELYN ST.
DEPTFORD CHURCH ST.
CREEK ROAD
WESTFERRY ROAD
MANCHESTER ROAD
PRESTON'S ROAD
NEW CROSS RD.
GREENWICH HIGH RD.
BLACKHEATH HILL
BLACKHEATH RD.
A1261
A1206
A200
A2
A206
B205
B206
B207
B208
B209
Sports Cen.
Ecological Park
Stave Hill
Russia Dock Woodland
Surrey Docks Farm
Printing Works
Bowl. Alley & Gala Bingo
Watersports Cen.
Greenland Lock
South Dock
Playground
86
103
122

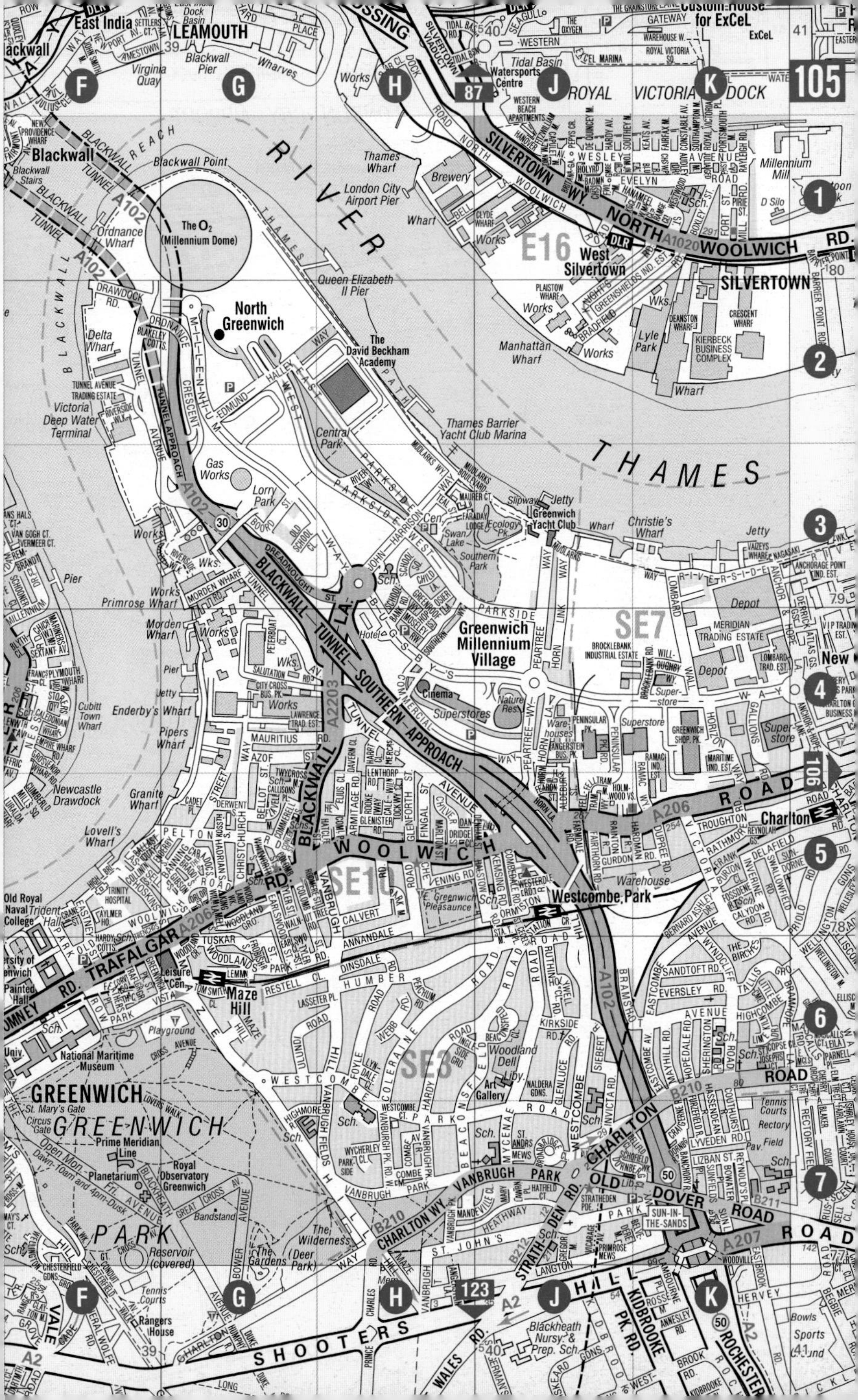
East India
LEAMOUTH
Blackwall
Virginia Quay
Blackwall Pier
Wharves
Custom House for ExCeL
ExCeL
Tidal Basin
Watersports Centre
ROYAL VICTORIA DOCK
87
F
G
H
J
K
1
2
3
4
5
6
7
BLACKWALL REACH
Blackwall Point
RIVER
THAMES
The O2 (Millennium Dome)
Blackwall Tunnel
Ordnance Wharf
A102
Thames Wharf
London City Airport Pier
Brewery
Wharf
Works
E16
West Silvertown
SILVERTOWN WY.
NORTH WOOLWICH RD.
A1020
SILVERTOWN
Millennium Mill
Queen Elizabeth II Pier
North Greenwich
The David Beckham Academy
Delta Wharf
Victoria Deep Water Terminal
TUNNEL AVENUE TRADING ESTATE
Central Park
Manhattan Wharf
Lyle Park
Thames Barrier Yacht Club Marina
Gas Works
Lorry Park
Greenwich Yacht Club
Christie's Wharf
Jetty
Ecology Pk.
Southern Park
Greenwich Millennium Village
SE7
Pier
Primrose Wharf
Morden Wharf
Cinema
Superstores
Nature Res.
Enderby's Wharf
Pipers Wharf
Cubitt Town Wharf
Granite Wharf
Newcastle Drawdock
Lovell's Wharf
BLACKWALL TUNNEL SOUTHERN APPROACH
A2203
WOOLWICH ROAD
A206
SE10
Charlton
106
Westcombe Park
Old Royal Naval College
Trident Hall
TRAFALGAR RD.
E. Greenwich Pleasaunce
Maze Hill
Leisure Cen.
National Maritime Museum
GREENWICH
GREENWICH PARK
SE3
Woodland Dell
Art Gallery
Playground
Prime Meridian Line
Royal Observatory Greenwich
Planetarium
Bandstand
Reservoir (covered)
The Wilderness (Deer Park)
The Gardens
Rangers House
Tennis Courts
CHARLTON WY.
VANBRUGH PARK
OLD DOVER ROAD
CHARLTON ROAD
B210
A207
SHOOTERS HILL
123
A2
Blackheath Nursy. & Prep. Sch.
KIDBROOKE PK. RD.
ROCHESTER WAY
Bowls
Sports Ground
Rectory Field

106
Prince Regent
ExCeL
Royal Albert
Beckton Park
University
London Regatta Centre
88
ROYAL ALBERT DOCK
ROYAL VICTORIA DOCK
LONDON CITY AIRPORT
Terminal Building
London City Airport
KING GEORGE V DOCK
King George V
E16
Go-kart Circuit
Millennium Mill
Pontoon Dock
Depot
NORTH WOOLWICH RD.
CONNAUGHT BRIDGE
A1020
Pontoon Dock
SILVERTOWN
Thames Barrier Park
THAMES ROAD IND. EST.
THAMESIDE INDUSTRIAL ESTATE
Sugar Refinery
FACTORY ROAD
ALBERT RD.
A112
STANDARD INDUSTRIAL ESTATE
Old Sta. Mus.
Victoria
NORTH WOOLWICH
PIER RD.
A117
North Woolwich Pier
WOOLWICH REACH
THAMES FLOOD BARRIER
RIVER
WOOLWICH FREE FERRY
Subway
Barrier Gardens Pier
Thames Barrier Visitors Cen.
Waterfront Leisure Cen.
WOOLWICH HIGH ST.
Gala Bingo
ANCHORAGE POINT IND. EST.
V I P TRADING EST.
New Charlton
WOOLWICH ROAD
A206
WOOLWICH CHURCH ST.
Woolwich Dockyard
WOOLWICH
JOHN WILSON ST.
Super-store
105
Charlton
Charlton Athletic FC (The Valley)
MARYON PARK
MARYON WILSON PARK
LITTLE HEATH
HILL REACH
ARTILLERY PL.
B210
Gun Park
Royal Artillery Barracks
Repository Woods
Rifle Range
Playground
Barrack Field
GRAND DEPOT RD.
A205
SE7
CHARLTON
Charlton House
Library
CHARLTON PARK RD.
CHARLTON PARK
Charlton School
Cricket Ground
CHARLTON CEMETERY
CHARLTON ROAD
QUEEN ELIZABETH HOSPITAL
Sports Ground
Hornfair Park
Charlton Lido
WOOLWICH COMMON
Playing Field
Old Royal Military Academy
SHOOTERS HILL ROAD
A207
124
Recreation Ground
Bowls
Reservoir (covered)
Shooters Hill Post 16 Campus
ACADEMY RD.
A
B
C
D
E
1
2
3
4
5
6
7

F
G
H
J
K
89
107
108
125
THAMESMEAD CENTRAL
THAMESMEAD
(Proposed)
Tor
THAMES
GALLIONS REACH
Gallions Point
Gallions Point Marina
Thames House
Newham Coll. of Further Education (Royal Docks Campus)
Custom House
Drawbridge
ALBERT
WOOLWICH MANOR WAY
A117
GALLIONS ROUNDABOUT
Royal Victoria Gardens
Hoba Wharf
THAMESMEAD WEST
Gallions Park
Gallions Lake
Broadwater
Broadwater Green
Royal Arsenal Woolwich Pier
Firepower (The Royal Artillery Mus.)
Greenwich Heritage Cen.
Royal Arsenal West
Royal Brass Foundry
British Liby.
WESTERN WAY
A2016
PLUMSTEAD MARSHES
Thamesmead South West
SE28
HMP BELMARSH
Crown Ct. & Magistrates Ct.
WEST THAMESMEAD BUSINESS PK
WEST THAMESMEAD BUSINESS PARK
Southern Outflow Sewers
Comm. Cen.
Works
Bus. Depot
Recreation Ground
Bowling Green
BERESFORD ST.
A206
PLUMSTEAD RD.
PETTMAN CRES.
Woolwich Arsenal
Plumstead
PLUMSTEAD HIGH STREET
Plumstead Gdns.
PLUMSTEAD
WINN'S COMMON
PLUMSTEAD COMMON
SE18
Plumstead Common
SHREWSBURY PARK
SHOOTERS HILL GOLF COURSE
Clothworkers Wood
Club House
Woolwich Cemetery
Rockliffe Gds.
Playing Field
Play. Field
Tennis Courts
East Wickham Open Space
WICKHAM LANE
A209
BLEAK HILL LANE
Bleak Hill
Willow Dene School
1
2
3
4
5
6
7
44
45
46
76
77
78
79
80

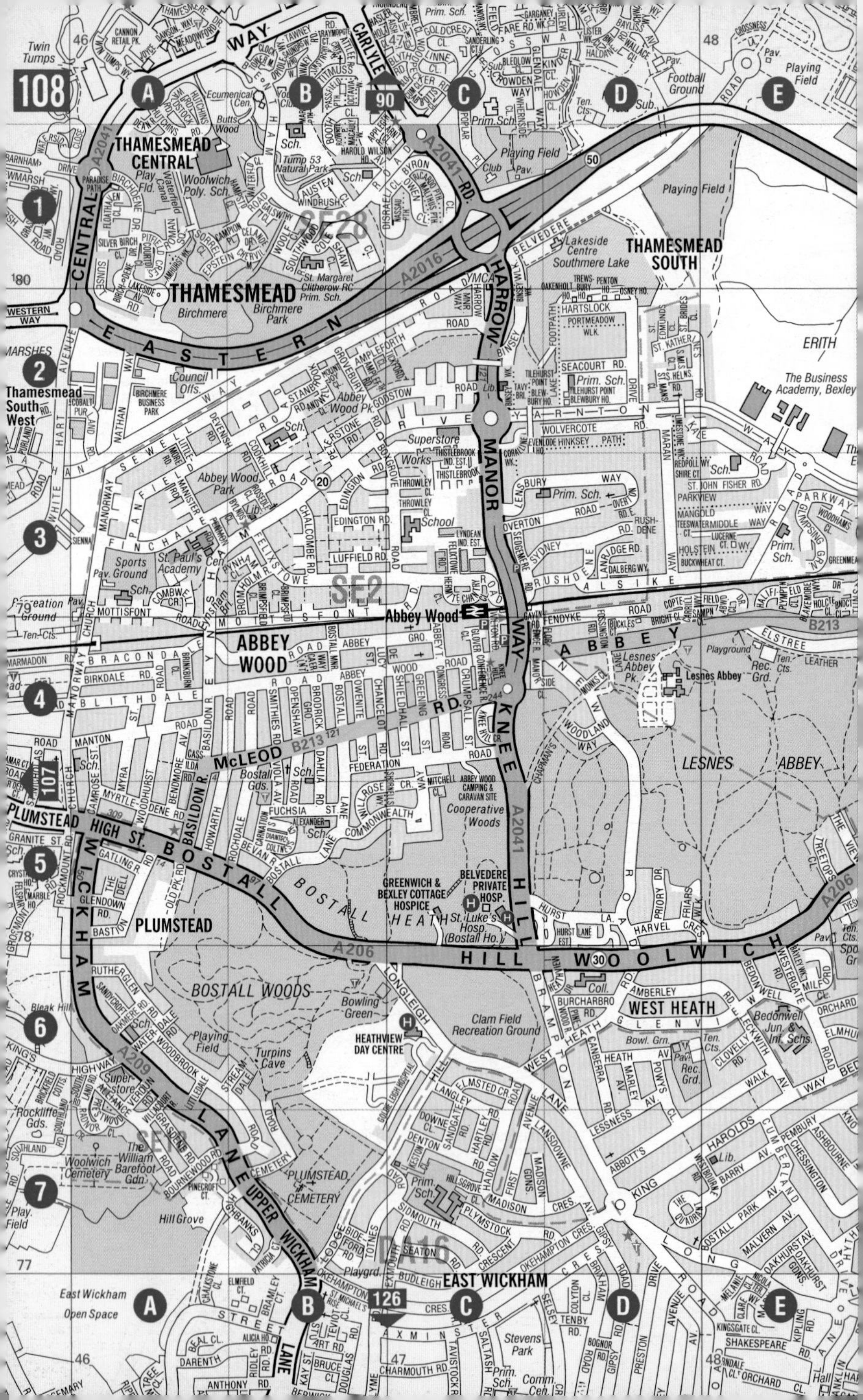
108
90
107
126
A
B
C
D
E
1
2
3
4
5
6
7
46
47
48
80
79
78
77
THAMESMEAD CENTRAL
THAMESMEAD
THAMESMEAD SOUTH
Thamesmead South West
SE28
SE2
SE18
DA16
ABBEY WOOD
Abbey Wood
PLUMSTEAD
WEST HEATH
EAST WICKHAM
ERITH
Twin Tumps
Ecumenical Cen.
Butts Wood
Woolwich Poly. Sch.
Tump 53 Natural Park
Birchmere
Birchmere Park
St. Margaret Clitherow RC Prim. Sch.
Lakeside Centre
Southmere Lake
Playing Field
Football Ground
The Business Academy, Bexley
Council Offs.
Birchmere Business Park
Abbey Wood Pk.
Abbey Wood Park
Superstore
Works
Sports Ground
St. Paul's Academy
Recreation Ground
LESNES ABBEY
Lesnes Abbey
Lesnes Abbey Pk.
Cooperative Woods
Abbey Wood Camping & Caravan Site
Greenwich & Bexley Cottage Hospice
Belvedere Private Hosp.
St. Luke's Hosp. (Bostall Ho.)
BOSTALL HEATH
BOSTALL WOODS
Bowling Green
Turpins Cave
Heathview Day Centre
Clam Field Recreation Ground
Bedonwell Jun. & Inf. Schs.
Plumstead Cemetery
Woolwich Cemetery
The William Barefoot Gdn.
Rockliffe Gds.
Hill Grove
East Wickham Open Space
Stevens Park
EASTERN WAY
HARROW MANOR WAY
KNEE HILL
WOOLWICH ROAD
BOSTALL HILL
PLUMSTEAD HIGH ST.
WICKHAM LANE
UPPER WICKHAM LANE
McLEOD RD.
ABBEY ROAD
YARNTON WAY
CARLYLE
A2041
A2016
A206
A209
B213

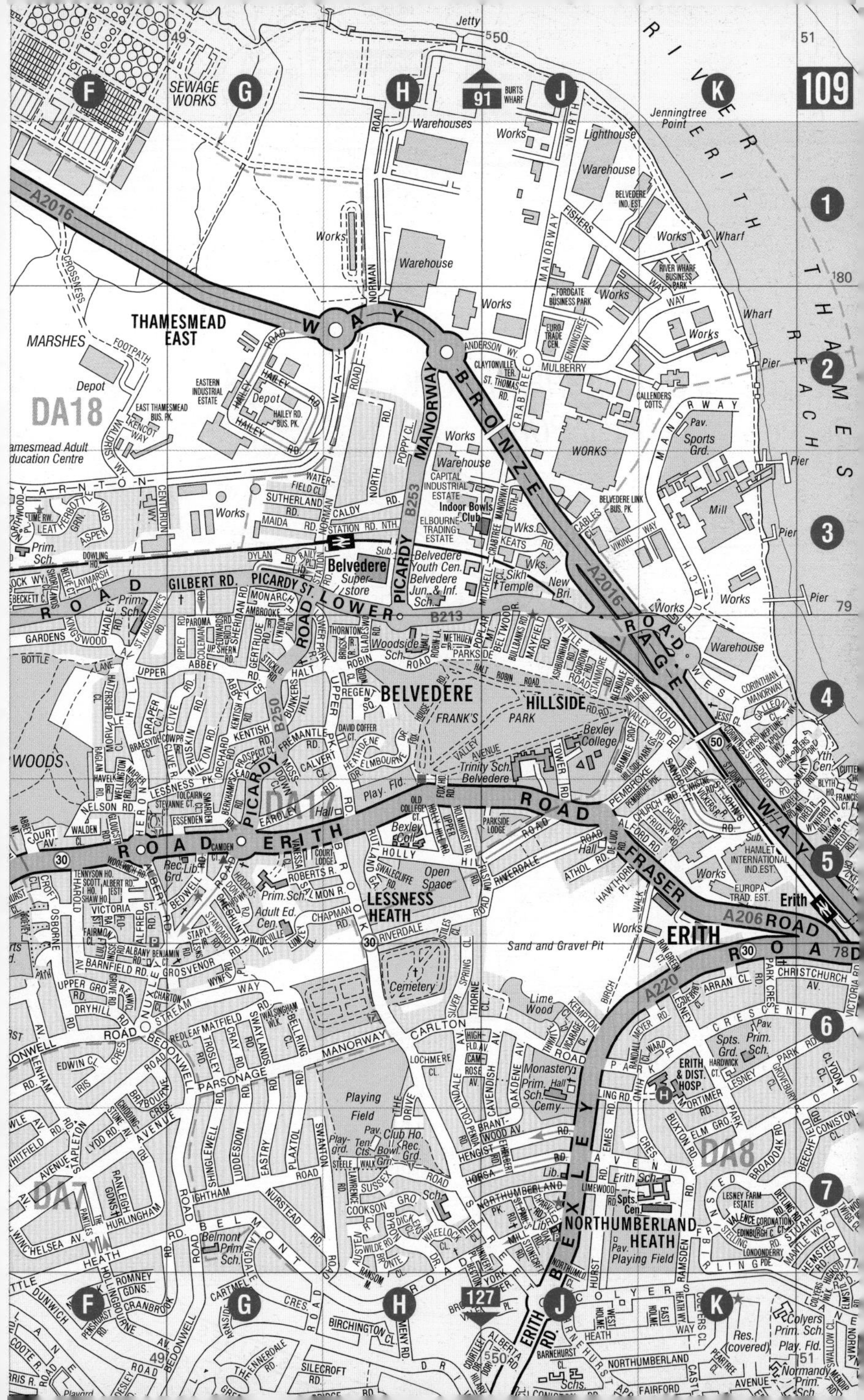
SEWAGE WORKS
Jetty
BURTS WHARF
91
Warehouses
Works
Lighthouse
Warehouse
Jenningtree Point
RIVER THAMES
ERITH REACH
BELVEDERE IND. EST.
Wharf
RIVER WHARF BUSINESS PARK
FORDGATE BUSINESS PARK
EURO TRADE CEN.
THAMESMEAD EAST
MARSHES
Depot
DA18
EASTERN INDUSTRIAL ESTATE
EAST THAMESMEAD BUS. PK.
HAILEY RD. BUS. PK.
Thamesmead Adult Education Centre
A2016
WAY
BRONZE
MANORWAY
CLAYTONVILLE TER.
MULBERRY
CALLENDERS COTTS.
Pier
Sports Grd.
Pav.
WORKS
Mill
CAPITAL INDUSTRIAL ESTATE
Indoor Bowls Club
ELBOURNE TRADING ESTATE
BELVEDERE LINK BUS. PK.
Belvedere
Superstore
Belvedere Youth Cen.
Belvedere Jun. & Inf. Sch.
Sikh Temple
New Bri.
GILBERT RD.
PICARDY ST.
LOWER
B213
B253
Woodside Sch.
BELVEDERE
HILLSIDE
FRANK'S PARK
Bexley College
Trinity Sch. Belvedere
Play. Fld.
Hall
DA17
ERITH ROAD
B250
LESSNESS HEATH
Open Space
Bexley Coll.
Prim. Sch.
Adult Ed. Cen.
Rec. Grd.
HAMLET INTERNATIONAL IND. EST.
EUROPA TRAD. EST.
Erith
ERITH
FRASER ROAD
A206
Sand and Gravel Pit
Cemetery
Lime Wood
A220
ERITH & DIST. HOSP.
Spts. Grd.
Prim. Sch.
Monastery Prim. Sch.
Playing Field
Club Ho.
Rec. Grd.
Erith Sch.
Spts. Cen.
NORTHUMBERLAND HEATH
Playing Field
DA8
DA7
Belmont Prim. Sch.
BEXLEY
LESNEY FARM ESTATE
Res. (covered)
Colyers Prim. Sch.
Normandy Prim. Sch.
Schs.
127
F
G
H
J
K
1
2
3
4
5
6
7
49
50
51
77
78
79
80

110
92
174
128
06
07
08
A
B
C
D
E
1
2
3
4
5
6
7
Junction 4a
HATCH LA.
ZEALAND AV.
PINGLESTONE CL.
POLAR PARK
THE NORMAN HAY TRADING EST.
HEATHROW BLVRD.
AIRPORT GATE BUS. CEN.
Rec. Grd.
Tennis Cts.
BLUNTS AV.
Hotel
SIPSON WAY
DORTON VILLAS
BOMER CL.
ASHBY WAY
M4
SIPSON RD.
Excelsior Hotel
DOGHURST DR.
DOGHURST AV.
EGERTON WY.
HARLINGTON CL.
BROWNGRAVE RD.
TON'S LA
MONDIAL WAY
The Edwardian International Hotel
Sports Ground
BATH A4 ROAD
NORTHOLT RD.
NORTHWOOD RD.
NELSON RD.
NEWBURY ROAD WEST
NORTHERN PERIMETER ROAD (W-E-S-T)
RAMP
Statue
EAST RAMP
NENE ROAD ROUNDABOUT
NENE RD.
NETTLETON RD.
Customs Ho.
The Renaissance Hotel
Heathrow Visitors Cen.
NEWALL RD.
WORLD BUS. CEN.
N-O-R-T-H-E-R-N
Compass Base
LONDON-HEATHROW AIRPORT
D'Albiac House
Vehicle Tunnel
TERMINAL 1
TERMINAL 2
TERMINAL 3
TERMINAL 4
Heathrow Cen.
Bus Sta.
CONTROL TOWER
Control Twr.
Heathrow Terminals 1,2&3
Queen's Building
COURTNEY RD.
CAMBORNE RD.
INNER RING
CROYDON RD.
CONWAY R.
CLIFTON WAY
Airside Road Tunnel
Heathrow Express Rail Link
Cargo Tunnel
TW6
175
SHOREHAM ROAD WEST
SHOREHAM ROAD EAST
SANDRINGHAM RD.
Cargo Terminal
SHOLTO RD.
EAST RD.
TUNNEL LINK RD.
SOUTHAMPTON RD.
STANSTED RD.
SEALAND RD.
SHORT R.
STIRLING RD.
SOUTHERN PERIMETER ROAD
Heathrow Terminal 4
STARLIGHT WY.
SKY VAN
Hilton Hotel
SHREWSBY-SWANSEA RD.
Warehouses
UNITAIR CEN.
HM Customs & Excise
Heathrow Corporate Cen.
Factory
Works
SCYLLA RD.
Longford River
SANCTUARY RD.
BEACON RD.
WEST BEDFONT
CLEVELAND PK.
CARGO POINT
COURT FARM INDUSTRIAL EST.
SPROGGIT IND. EST.
BLACKBURN TRAD. EST.
THE CAMGATE CENTRE
CRANE RD.
DUDLEY PL.
CLAY LA.
BROOK CL.
STANWELL ROAD
BEDFONT ROAD
Stanwell Fields C of E Prim. Sch.
STANWELL
TW19
Tennis Cts.
Recreation Ground
Pav.
Depot
Ashford Town FC
Westview Cotts
Sports Ground
Works
CLOCKHOUSE ROUNDABOUT
GREAT WEST ROAD A30
STAINES ROAD
CLOCKHOUSE LANE
Warehouse
Nursery
Playing Field
Homers Farm
CORDELIA RD.
CAMBRIA GDS.
CANOPUS WAY
CRANFORD CL.
HADRIAN WAY
LONGFORD AV.
HILLINGDON AV.
OSBORNE AV.
RAVENSBOURNE AV.
CHICHESTER CT.
HOLYWELL WAY
KINGSWAY
CLYDE RD.
ENSIGN WAY
VISCOUNT RD.
NIGHTINGALES
SHORT LANE
FALCON DR.
EVEREST RD.
COMET RD.
WESTLAND CL.
VIEW ROAD
DRIVE
VICARAGE CT.
ST. MARY'S
SAFFRON CT.
SPINNEY

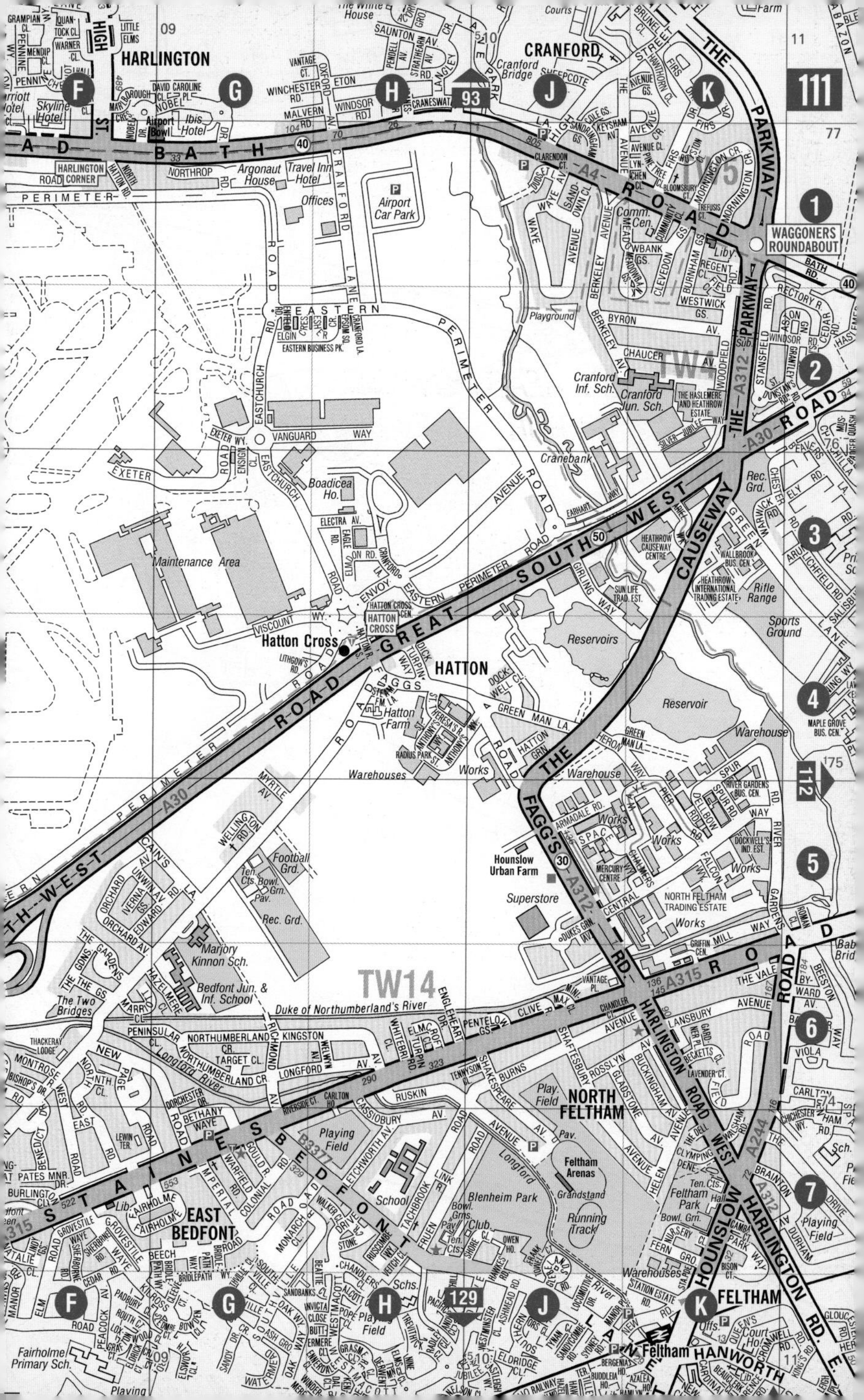
111
HARLINGTON
CRANFORD
Cranford Bridge
HATTON
NORTH FELTHAM
EAST BEDFONT
FELTHAM
HANWORTH
TW5
TW4
TW14
WAGGONERS ROUNDABOUT
HARLINGTON CORNER
HATTON CROSS
Hatton Cross
Skyline Hotel
Ibis Hotel
Airport Bowl
Argonaut House
Travel Inn Hotel
Offices
Airport Car Park
EASTERN BUSINESS PK.
Maintenance Area
Boadicea Ho.
Playground
Cranford Inf. Sch.
Cranford Jun. Sch.
THE HASLEMERE AND HEATHROW ESTATE
Cranebank
HEATHROW CAUSEWAY CENTRE
WALLBROOK BUS. CEN.
HEATHROW INTERNATIONAL TRADING ESTATE
SUN LIFE TRAD. EST.
Rifle Range
Sports Ground
Reservoirs
Reservoir
Warehouse
MAPLE GROVE BUS. CEN.
Hatton Farm
RADIUS PARK
Warehouses
Works
Hounslow Urban Farm
Superstore
RIVER GARDENS BUS. CEN.
DOCKWELL'S IND. EST.
NORTH FELTHAM TRADING ESTATE
MERCURY CENTRE
Football Grd.
Rec. Grd.
Marjory Kinnon Sch.
Bedfont Jun. & Inf. School
The Two Bridges
Duke of Northumberland's River
Longford River
Playing Field
School
Blenheim Park
Feltham Arenas
Grandstand
Running Track
Feltham Park
Fairholme Primary Sch.
GREAT SOUTH WEST ROAD
BATH ROAD
THE PARKWAY
THE CAUSEWAY
FAGG'S RD.
STAINES RD.
BEDFONT LANE
HARLINGTON ROAD WEST
HOUNSLOW ROAD
HARLINGTON RD. E.
PERIMETER ROAD
EASTERN PERIMETER ROAD
A4
A30
A312
A315
A244
B3377
93
112
129
175

94
111
130
A
B
C
D
E
1
2
3
4
5
6
7
WAGGONERS ROUNDABOUT
HENLYS ROUNDABOUT
THE PARKWAY
A312
BATH RD.
A4
GREAT WEST ROAD
GT. SOUTH WEST RD.
A30
A3006
A3063
A315
A314
A244
SUTTON LANE
WELLINGTON RD. NTH.
WELLINGTON ROAD SOUTH
STAINES RD.
HANWORTH ROAD
HOUNSLOW RD.
HARLINGTON ROAD EAST
NELSON ROAD
HESTON
TW5
TW4
TW14
TW13
Hounslow West
HOUNSLOW WEST
Beaversfield Park
Cavalry Barracks
Playing Field
Sutton Playing Field
Lampton School
LAMPTON PARK
Lampton Sports Cen.
Civic Centre
Sports Ground
Rifle Range
Warehouse
PROLOGIS PARK
CENTRAL PARK ESTATE
Heath Nurseries
HOUNSLOW HEATH GOLF COURSE
HOUNSLOW HEATH NATURE RESERVE
NORTH FELTHAM
Baber Bridge
Weir
River Crane
The Heathland School
Mosque
St. Mark's Cath. Sch.
Gala Bingo
Hounslow Cemy.
HEATHROW GATEWAY
MILL FARM BUS. PK.
South West Middlesex Crematorium
De Brome Building
Bridge Farm Nursery
Cemetery
Heathfield Jun. & Inf. Schs.

F
G
H
J
K
1
2
3
4
5
6
7
95
114
131
Osterley
GREAT WEST ROAD
Playing Field
Pavilion
Indian Gymkhana Club
Spts. Grd.
Campion Ho.
Crown Court
Play Fld.
Sch.
Hall
Wood Lane Cen.
Sports Grd.
SPRING GROVE
LAMPTON
SPRING GROVE RD.
B363
A4
A3005
West Thames College
Isleworth
LONDON ROAD
A315
Research Laboratory
Gov. Offices
Hounslow East
Alexandra Jun. & Inf. Schs.
Bus Depot
Mecca Bingo
WOODLANDS
Playing Field
Hounslow Central
Hounslow Manor Sch.
Sports Hall
Bowling Green
HIGH STREET
Prim. Sch.
Depot
Lib.
TREATY CENTRE
Inwood Park
Tennis Courts
Comm. Cen.
HOUNSLOW
TW3
TW7
ISLEWORTH
CLOCK TOWER IND. EST.
Isleworth Rec. Cen.
REDLEES PARK
A310
WORTON HALL INDUSTRIAL ESTATE
VICTORY BUSINESS CENTRE
Works
West Middlesex Drainage Works
Hounslow
Maswell Park
B361
A314
Queen's Bri.
Superstore
Duke of Northumberland's River
The Museum of Rugby
Twickenham Rugby Union Football Grd.
TWICKENHAM TRADING ESTATE
LONDON RD. ROUNDABOUT
CHERTSEY ROAD
A316
WHITTON RD. R'BOUT
Hall
Murray Park
Royal Military Sch. of Music (Kneller Hall)
Sports Ground
Playing Field
Chase Bridge
KNELLER ROAD
WHITTON ROAD
Richmond upon Thames College
Harlequins RUFC & Club
Harlequins RLFC (The Twickenham Stoop)
TW2
TW1
Play. Fld.
Playing Field
WHITTON
Whitton
TWICKENHAM
Depot
Kneller Gdns.
Pav.
Twickenham Cemetery
Sports Ground
HOSPITAL BRIDGE RD.
B358
LONDON ROAD
TWICKENHAM ROAD

114
A
B
C
D
E
1
2
3
4
5
6
7
96
113
132
Old Brentford
Brentford Gate
Marina
Syon Lane
SYON PARK
London Butterfly House
Syon Garden Centre
Syon House
TW8
DUKE OF NORTHUMBERLAND ESTATE
Syon Park Sch.
Busch Corner
LONDON ROAD
TWICKENHAM RD.
WEST MIDDLESEX UNIVERSITY HOSP.
RIVER THAMES
Syon Reach
Isleworth Ferry Gate (Closed)
ROYAL BOTANIC GARDENS
Syon Vista
The Lake
Arboretum
Evolution House
Temperate House
Water Lily Pond
Cedar Vista
Conservation Area
Queen Charlotte's Cottage
King's Steps Gate
Japanese Gateway & Landscape
Pagoda
OLD DEER PARK
ROYAL MID-SURREY GOLF COURSE
King's Observatory
Richmond Athletic Ground
Club Ho.
Rugby Grd.
Grand Stand
Tennis Courts
Pools on the Park
Old Deer Park Recreation Ground
Obelisk
London Welsh RUFC
Cricket Grd.
Old Isleworth
Isleworth Ait Nature Reserve
Nazareth Ho.
ISLEWORTH
REDLEES PARK
SOUTH ST.
ST. JOHN'S RD.
RICHMOND RD.
ST. MARGARETS RD.
Richmond Lock
TWICKENHAM ROAD
A316
RICHMOND
Richmond Green
Richmond
LOWER
SHEEN RD.
PARADISE RD.
ST. MARGARETS
Pleasure Gdns.
THE AVENUE
ST. MARGARETS R'BOUT
LONDON RD. ROUNDABOUT
CHERTSEY
Cole Park
Moor Mead Gd.
St. Margarets
Corporation Island
RICHMOND ROAD
CROWN RD.
PETERSHAM ROAD
RICHMOND HILL
Terrace Gardens
Terrace Fld.
Royal Star & Garter Home
Petersham Common
MARBLE HILL PARK
Marble Hill House
Glover's Island
Petersham Meadows
Petersham Farm
Buccleuch Gdns.
Orleans Ho. Gallery
Orleans Gdns.
Foot Ferry
Twickenham
TWICKENHAM
Theatre
Baths
Playing Field
Petersham Gate
The German Sch., London
Sports Grd.
A310
A3004
A305
A307
B321
B363
B454
A315

KEW
Princess of Wales Conservatory
Seven Sisters
Palm House
The Pond
Rose Garden
Visitor Centre
Victoria Ga.
Temple of Bellona
Berberis Dell
Marianne North Gallery
The National Archives
KEW RIVERSIDE PARK
Kew Gds.
Chiswick
BURLINGTON
Sports Hall
Cemetery
97
W4
GROVE PARK
University of Westminster Sports Ground
Yacht Basin
Stadium
Sports Ground
Westminster Boathouse
Riverside Lands
Playing Fields
Riverside & Raquets Club
DUKE'S MEADOWS
DUKE'S MEADOW GOLF COURSE
Driving Range
Boat Houses
RIVER
THAMES
A316
A205
A307
B353
A3003
A305
B351
Refuse Dpt.
Mortlake Crematorium
Hammersmith Cemetery
FULHAM (NORTH SHEEN) CEMETERY
CHALKER'S CORNER
Playing Field
Rec. Ground
NORTH SHEEN
MORTLAKE
Brewery
Pav. Sports Ground
The Green
Mortlake
MANOR CIRCUS
Superstore
North Sheen
Holy Trinity C of E Prim. Sch.
RICHMOND
UPPER
LOWER
MORTLAKE RD.
SANDYCOMBE
MANOR
CHERTSEY
GREAT
CHISWICK
CLIFFORD
EAST SHEEN
SW14
TW9
Day Cen.
Sheen Mt Prim. Sch.
Pesthouse Common
Christ's Sch.
East Sheen Cemetery
SHEEN COMMON
Football Ground
Bowling Green
Tennis Courts
Ranger's Gdn.
Teck Plantation
Sheen Wood
East Sheen Gate
Adam's Pond
Horse Ride
Palewell Common
Palewell Fields
Playing Fields
Pitch and Putt Course
116
Richmond Cemetery
Bog Gate
The Bog
Riding Ring
RICHMOND PARK
King's House Sch.
Cambrian Gate
Bishop's Pond
TW10
Conduit Wood
Holly Lodge
Sheen Cross Wood
(Open during daylight hours only)
Polo Field
Playing Field
Barn Wood Pond
Richmond Gate
SAWYER'S HILL
Saw Pit Plantation
Roehampton Gate
Kidney Wood
Jubilee Plantation
Queen's Ride
133
Duchess' Wood
Deer Pen
White Lodge Plantation
Queen Mother's Copse
The Royal Ballet School
SIDMOUTH WOOD
King Henry VIII Mound
Pen Ponds
Victory Plantation
1
2
3
4
5
6
7
F
G
H
J
K
19
20
21
74
75
76
77

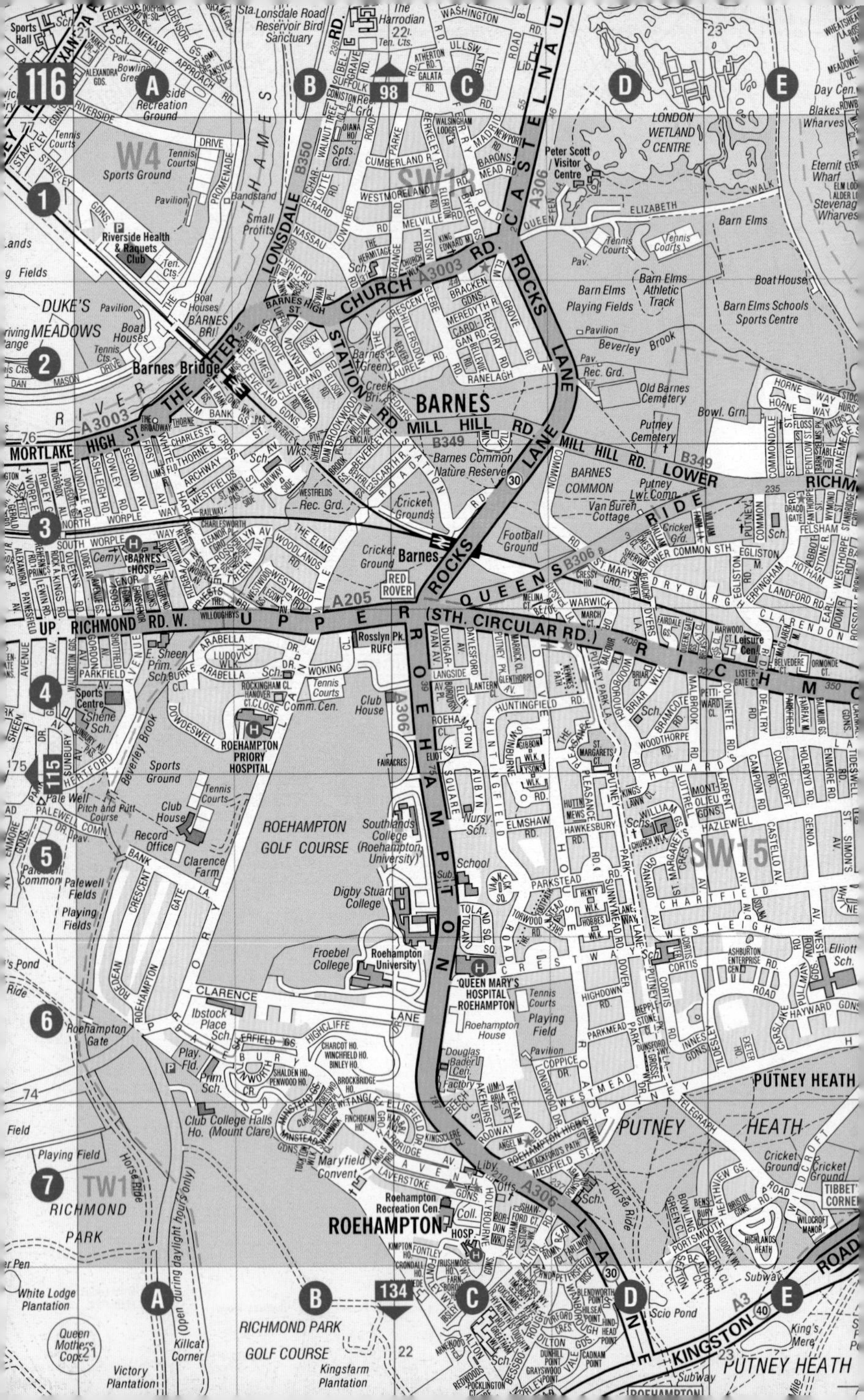

A
B
C
D
E
1
2
3
4
5
6
7
98
115
134
W4
SW13
SW15
TW1
Lonsdale Road Reservoir Bird Sanctuary
The Harrodian
Riverside Recreation Ground
Sports Ground
Riverside Health & Raquets Club
DUKE'S MEADOWS
Barnes Bridge
RIVER THAMES
MORTLAKE
HIGH ST.
A3003
LONSDALE RD.
B350
CHURCH RD.
CASTELNAU
A306
ROCKS LANE
LONDON WETLAND CENTRE
Peter Scott Visitor Centre
Barn Elms
Barn Elms Playing Fields
Barn Elms Athletic Track
Boat House
Barn Elms Schools Sports Centre
Beverley Brook
Old Barnes Cemetery
Putney Cemetery
BARNES
MILL HILL RD.
B349
Barnes Common Nature Reserve
BARNES COMMON
Putney Lwr. Comn.
Van Buren Cottage
LOWER RICHMOND
QUEENS RIDE
B306
Football Ground
Cricket Ground
Barnes
RED ROVER
A205
UP. RICHMOND RD. W.
UPPER RICHMOND RD.
(STH. CIRCULAR RD.)
Rosslyn Pk. RUFC
Barnes Hosp.
Sports Centre
Shene Sch.
E. Sheen Prim. Sch.
ROEHAMPTON PRIORY HOSPITAL
Sports Ground
Pale Well Pitch and Putt Course
Palewell Common
Palewell Fields Playing Fields
Record Office
Clarence Farm
ROEHAMPTON GOLF COURSE
Southlands College (Roehampton University)
Digby Stuart College
Froebel College
Roehampton University
ROEHAMPTON LANE
QUEEN MARY'S HOSPITAL ROEHAMPTON
Roehampton House
Playing Field
Douglas Bader Cen.
Ibstock Place Sch.
Roehampton Gate
Maryfield Convent
Roehampton Recreation Cen.
ROEHAMPTON
PUTNEY HEATH
PUTNEY
HEATH
TELEGRAPH RD.
KINGSTON RD.
A3
Scio Pond
King's Mere
Highlands Heath
Wildcroft Manor
TIBBET'S CORNER
RICHMOND PARK
Horse Ride
(Open during daylight hours only)
White Lodge Plantation
Queen Mothers Copse
Killcat Corner
Victory Plantation
RICHMOND PARK GOLF COURSE
Kingsfarm Plantation
Elliott Sch.
Leisure Cen.
Day Cen.
Blakes Wharves
Eternit Wharf
Stevenage Wharves

FULHAM
Fulham FC (Craven Cottage)
Fulham Palace
Moat Garden
Bishop's Park
Putney Pier
Putney Bri.
WALHAM GREEN
Eel Brook Common
Parsons Grn.
PARSONS GRN.
SANDS END
SW6
HURLINGHAM PARK
Hurlingham Stadium
Hurlingham
The Hurlingham Club
SOUTH PARK
RIVER THAMES
Wandsworth Park
PUTNEY
Putney
WANDSWORTH
East Putney
Wandsworth Town
WANDSWORTH GYRATORY
WEST HILL
SW18
King George's Park
SOUTHFIELDS
Southfields
Earlsfield
ROYAL HOSP FOR NEURO DISABILITY
Broadway
FULHAM BROADWAY
Wandle Rec. Cen
Mecca Bingo
99
118
135
F
G
H
J
K
1
2
3
4
5
6
7
24
25
26

BATTERSEA PARK
The Pump Ho. Gallery
Boating Lake
General Games Ground
Cremorne Gardens
Chelsea Wharf
Cremorne Wharf
Chelsea Creek
Gas Works
SANDS END
Chelsea Harbour Pier
Bascule Bri.
RIVER THAMES
BATTERSEA REACH
Lensbury Wharf
Shell Wharf
WESTON LONDON HELIPORT
Fulham Wharf
Warehouse
Superstore
Leisure Cen.
BATTERSEA
CLAPHAM JUNCTION
Falcon Park
Open Space
York Gdns.
WANDSWORTH BRI.
Wandsworth Town
Spencer Park
Emanuel School
Tennis Courts
Bowling Green
Cricket Ground
HMP WANDSWORTH
WANDSWORTH COMMON
Wandsworth Common
WANDSWORTH CEMETERY
EARLSFIELD
Earlsfield
Beatrix Potter Prim. Sch.
BALHAM
Balham
St. Mary's Cemy.
Rec. Grd.
Playground
CLAPHAM COMMON NORTH SIDE
CLAPHAM COMN. W. SIDE
BATTERSEA BRIDGE RD.
ALBERT BRIDGE RD.
BATTERSEA PARK RD.
LATCHMERE RD.
FALCON RD.
LAVENDER HILL
ST. JOHN'S HILL
BATTERSEA RISE
NORTHCOTE ROAD
BOLINGBROKE GRO.
NIGHTINGALE LA.
TRINITY RD.
WANDSWORTH COMMON
YORK ROAD
EAST HILL
WANDSWORTH RD.
GARRATT LANE
EARLSFIELD RD.
SPENCER PARK
WINDMILL RD.
ELSPETH R.
PRINCE OF WALES DR.
A3220
A3205
A3036
A3207
A3031
A217
A214
A205
A3
B305
B229
B234
B237
SW11
SW18
SW12
100
117
136
A B C D E
1 2 3 4 5 6 7

119
F
G
H
J
K
101
137
120
1
2
3
4
5
6
7
Battersea Park
NEW COVENT GARDEN MARKET
Fruit & Vegetable Market
SOUTH LAMBETH
Queenstown Road (Battersea)
Larkhall Park
SW8
Stockwell
Angell Town
Heathbrook Park
Wandsworth Rd.
STOCKWELL
Clapham High St.
SW9
LAMBETH HOSPITAL
Clapham North
CLAPHAM
Clapham Comn.
CLAPHAM COMMON
COMMON NORTH SIDE
LONG RD.
A3
CLAPHAM COMMON
Long Pond
Lambeth Academy
SW4
BRIXTON
Mount Pond
Eagle Pond
CLAPHAM PARK
SW2
Windmill Gdns.
Sports Ground
HMP BRIXTON
Clapham Sth.
CAVENDISH RD.
POYNDERS RD.
A205
ATKINS RD.
STREATHAM PL.
CHRISTCHURCH RD.
BRIXTON HILL
STREATHAM
BALHAM
ACRE LANE
A2217
QUEENSTOWN RD.
WANDSWORTH RD.
CLAPHAM RD.
STOCKWELL RD.
SOUTH LAMBETH RD.
BEDFORD RD.
A3036
A203
A23
A24
B221
B224
A3216
A3205
A204
B303

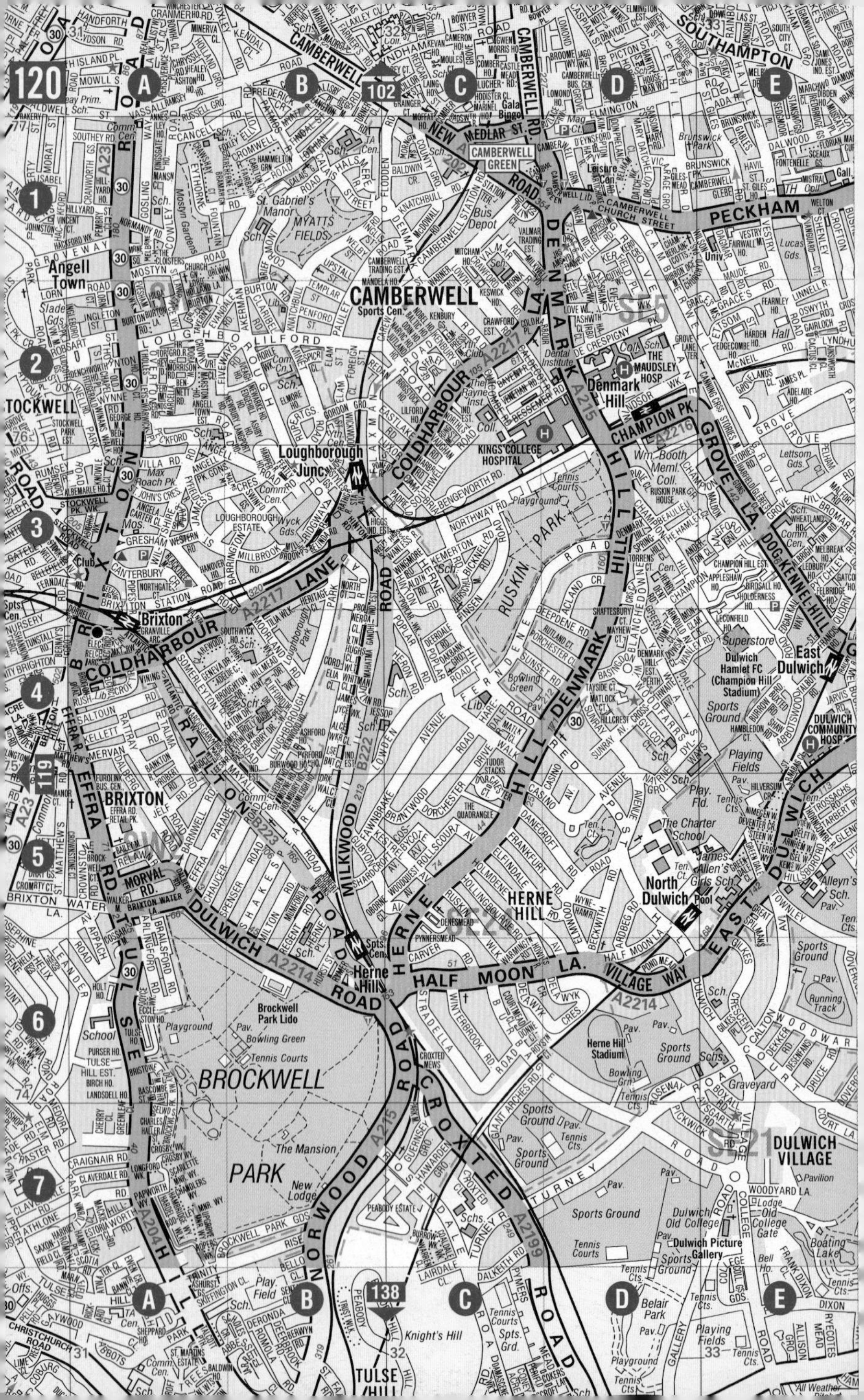
A
B
C
D
E
1
2
3
4
5
6
7
102
119
138
CAMBERWELL
CAMBERWELL GREEN
CAMBERWELL RD.
NEW MEDLAR ST.
CAMBERWELL CHURCH STREET
PECKHAM
SOUTHAMPTON
Angell Town
STOCKWELL
BRIXTON
Brixton
COLDHARBOUR
COLDHARBOUR LANE
LOUGHBOROUGH
Loughborough Junc.
LOUGHBOROUGH ESTATE
MYATTS FIELDS
St. Gabriel's Manor
Sports Cen.
SE5
DENMARK HILL
Denmark Hill
KINGS COLLEGE HOSPITAL
THE MAUDSLEY HOSP.
CHAMPION PK.
Wm. Booth Meml. Coll.
RUSKIN PARK
FERNDENE ROAD
MILKWOOD ROAD
HERNE HILL
Herne Hill
DULWICH ROAD
HALF MOON LA.
VILLAGE WAY
North Dulwich
East Dulwich
DOG KENNEL HILL
GROVE LA.
Dulwich Hamlet FC (Champion Hill Stadium)
DULWICH COMMUNITY HOSP.
EAST DULWICH GROVE
The Charter School
James Allen's Girls Sch.
Herne Hill Stadium
BROCKWELL PARK
Brockwell Park Lido
The Mansion
New Lodge
NORWOOD ROAD
CROXTED ROAD
TURNEY ROAD
DULWICH VILLAGE
SE21
Dulwich Old College
Dulwich Picture Gallery
Belair Park
Knight's Hill
TULSE HILL
EFFRA RD.
BRIXTON WATER LA.
TULSE HILL
RAILTON RD.
Alleyn's Sch.
Boating Lake

121
103
139
122
F
G
H
J
K
1
2
3
4
5
6
7
PECKHAM
PECKHAM HIGH ST.
QUEEN'S ROAD
A202
Queens Rd. (Peckham)
NEW CROSS GATE
NEW CROSS
Peckham Rye
Leisure Cen.
SE15
SE14
Telegraph Hill Park
Nunhead
NUNHEAD
NUNHEAD CEMETERY
Reservoirs (covered)
BROCKLEY
EVELINA ROAD
NUNHEAD LA.
EAST DULWICH ROAD
EAST DULWICH
PECKHAM RYE COMMON
PECKHAM RYE PARK
Warwick Gardens
Goose Grn.
Harris Girls Academy East Dulwich
AQUARIUS GOLF COURSE
Water Works
Newlands
Honor Oak Crematorium
Camberwell New Cemetery
Recreation Pav. Ground
ONE TREE HILL
HONOR OAK
Honor Oak Park
HONOR OAK ROAD
FOREST HILL ROAD
RYE LANE
BARRY ROAD
LORDSHIP LANE
SE22
SE23
Camberwell Old Cemetery
DULWICH PARK
Court La. Gate
Horse Ride
Aviary
Queen Mary's Gate
DULWICH COMMON
THE GROVE
Horniman Gardens
Horniman Museum
FOREST HILL
STANSTEAD RD.
BROCKLEY RI.
GROVE VALE
A2216
B238
B219
A2214
B2142
B218

122
New Cross Gate
New Cross
NEW CROSS
NEW CROSS GATE
Goldsmiths College
Deptford Bri.
DEPTFORD BROADWAY
BROOKMILL ROAD
BLACKHEATH RD.
GREENWICH HIGH RD.
LEWISHAM WAY
LEWISHAM RD.
ST. JOHNS
St. Johns
Elverson Rd.
LOAMPIT HILL
LOAMPIT VALE
THURSTON RD.
Lewisham
LEWISHAM
LEWISHAM HIGH STREET
Lewisham College
DRAKEFELL RD.
Brockley
BROCKLEY
BROCKLEY ROAD
MALPAS RD.
HILLY FIELDS
Cricket Ground
Prendergast School
ADELAIDE AV.
LADYWELL RD.
Ladywell
LADYWELL
LEWISHAM UNIVERSITY HOSPITAL
Ladywell Cemetery
Brockley Cemetery
Crofton Park
Crofton Pk.
Honor Oak Crematorium
Honor Oak Pk.
HONOR OAK PARK
STONDON PARK
Crofton Leisure Centre
Ladywell Arena (Running Track)
Ladywell Fields
Lewisham Park
Blythe Hill Fields
Blythe Hill
Catford Bridge
Catford
CATFORD
CATFORD GYRATORY
RUSHEY GRN.
BROWNHILL RD.
STANSTEAD ROAD
Powerleague Soccer Centre
St. Dunstans Coll.
104
121
140

123
Planetarium
Royal Observatory Greenwich
GREENWICH PARK
Reservoir (covered)
The Gardens
The Wilderness (Deer Park)
Tennis Courts
Rangers House
Bandstand
VANBRUGH PARK
OLD DOVER ROAD
SUN-IN-THE-SANDS
ROCHESTER WAY RELIEF ROAD
SHOOTERS HILL ROAD
BLACKHEATH
Blackheath Vale
PRINCE CHARLES RD.
PRINCE OF WALES RD.
Hollyhedge Ho.
Blackheath Nursy. & Prep. Sch.
KIDBROOKE PARK RD.
Morden College (Almshouses)
SE3
BLACKHEATH
Blackheath
Concert Halls
College
Playing Field
Academy
LEE HIGH ROAD
BELMONT HILL
LEE TERRACE
Sports Grd.
Sports Ground
Warehouse
Thomas Tallis Sch.
Superstore
Kidbrooke
BLACKHEATH PARK
Sports Ground
David Lloyd Leis.
Golf Driving Range
Quaggy River
Sports Grounds
Euro Cen.
LEE GRN.
Manor House Gdns.
Manor Park
Roan School Playing Fields
SUTCLIFFE PARK
Sutcliffe Pk. Athletics Track
ELTHAM ROAD
A20
SIDCUP ROAD
Brindishe Prim. Sch.
LEE
BURNT ASH RD.
Horn Park
Hither Green
HITHER GREEN
Depot
CHILTONIAN IND. EST.
Colfes Sch.
Colfes Leisure Cen.
Lee
SE12
WESTHORNE AVENUE
A205
BURNT ASH HILL
BARING ROAD
ST. MILDREDS ROAD
Horn Park Prim. Sch.
Comm. Cen.
Horn Park
Warehouse
Green Sidings
141
105
124
F
G
H
J
K
1
2
3
4
5
6
7

124
106
123
142
A
B
C
D
E
1
2
3
4
5
6
7
SHOOTERS HILL ROAD
A207
WOOLWICH COMMON
ACADEMY ROAD
A205
Old Royal Military Academy
Hornfair Park
Bowling Green
Recreation Ground
Reservoir (covered)
Shooters Hill Post 16 Campus
Royal Herbert Pavilions
ROCHESTER WAY RELIEF ROAD
ROCHESTER WAY
A2
WRICKLEMARSH ROAD
Bowls Sports Ground
SE3
Kidbrooke School
Playing Fields
KIDBROOKE
Sam Montague Boys Club
Sports Ground
CEMETERY
ELTHAM COMMON
Memorial Hospital
Severndroog Castle
CASTLE WOOD
Rose Cottage
JACK WOOD
WELL HALL ROAD
Well Hall Roundabout
Kidbrooke
Kidbrooke Grn. Nature Res.
Thomas Tallis Sch.
Meadowside Leis. Cen.
SUTCLIFFE PARK
Harrow Meadow
Sutcliffe Park Athletics Track
Rec. Ground
ELTHAM PARK
SE9
Eltham
Tudor Barn
WESTHORNE AVENUE
ELTHAM ROAD
A210
ELTHAM HILL
ELTHAM HIGH STREET
Yorkshire Grey
Eltham Green Sch.
Playing Field
Moatbridge Sch.
ELTHAM
Eltham Coll.
Queenscroft Park
Eltham Hill Sch.
Swim. Pool
Supermarket
Eltham Palace
Institute of Army Education
Community Centre
SIDCUP ROAD
A20
SE12
Horn Park Prim. Sch.
COURT ROAD
A208
ROYAL BLACKHEATH GOLF COURSE
Club House
Bowling Green
Superstore
Comp. Sch.
FOOTSCRAY ROAD
MOTTINGHAM ROAD
A2212
Hadlow Coll. (Mottingham Centre)
Mottingham Farm
Mottingham
Bird Sanctuary
The Tarn
BRITTAIN CT.
SHRUBSALL CL.
AVENUE

SHREWSBURY PARK
SHOOTERS HILL
Eaglesfield Rec. Grd.
SHOOTERS HILL GOLF COURSE
Club House
Clothworkers Wood
Willow Dene School
Playing Field
East Wickham Open Space
Woodlands Farm
Garden Centre
Council Offices
SHOOTERS HILL ROAD
A207
BELLEGROVE ROAD
Welling
Jackwood Ho.
Oxleas Meadows
OXLEAS WOOD
Eastcote Prim. Sch.
WELLING WAY
Falconwood Field
MONTROSE AVENUE
DA16
Playing Field
SHEPHERDLEAS WOOD
ELTHAM PARK NORTH
Falconwood
A2
ROCHESTER WAY
FALCONWOOD
Prim. Sch.
Coll.
Playing Field
Comm. Cen.
Eltham Cemetery
Eltham Crematorium
EAST ROCHESTER WAY
ELTHAM PARK SOUTH
ELTHAM WARREN GOLF COURSE
Crown Woods School
Nature Study Centre
BEXLEY ROAD
BLACKFEN ROAD
A210
University of Greenwich (Avery Hill Campus)
AVERY HILL
AVERY HILL PARK
Alderwood Prim. Sch.
Parish Wood
Days Lane Prim. Sch.
BLACKFEN
Hollyoak Wood Park
DA15
Sports Ground
All Weather Pitches
Halls of Residence
Sparrow's Farm Leisure Cen.
River Shuttle
AVERY HILL RD. B2214
HALFWAY STREET
Willersley Pk.
A211
Lamorbey
Marlborough Sch.
107
126
143
F G H J K
1 2 3 4 5 6 7
44 45 46
77 76 74 175

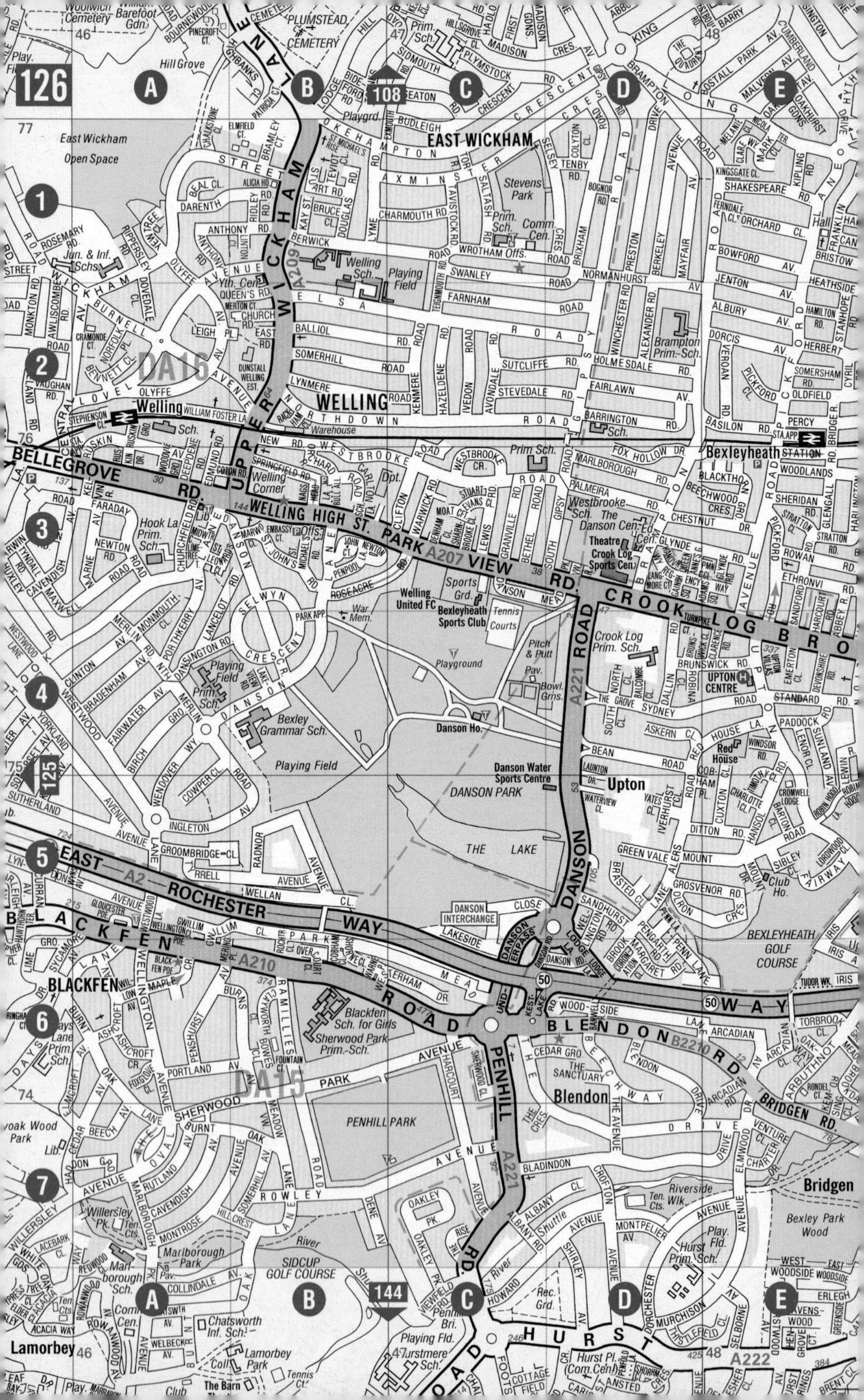

A
B
C
D
E
1
2
3
4
5
6
7
108
125
144
East Wickham Open Space
EAST WICKHAM
Stevens Park
WELLING
Welling
DA16
DA15
UPPER WICKHAM LANE
A209
BELLEGROVE RD.
WELLING HIGH ST.
PARK VIEW RD.
A207
CROOK LOG
Bexleyheath
Bexleyheath STATION
BRAMPTON ROAD
Brampton Prim. Sch.
NORTHDOWN ROAD
Welling Corner
Welling United FC
Bexleyheath Sports Club
Sports Grd.
Tennis Courts
Pitch & Putt
Playground
Danson Ho.
DANSON PARK
THE LAKE
Danson Water Sports Centre
DANSON ROAD
A221
Upton
UPTON CENTRE
Red House
Crook Log Prim. Sch.
Crook Log Sports Cen.
Bexley Grammar Sch.
Playing Field
EAST ROCHESTER WAY
A2
BLACKFEN ROAD
A210
BLACKFEN
DANSON INTERCHANGE
BLENDON RD.
B2210
Blendon
BEXLEYHEATH GOLF COURSE
BRIDGEN RD.
Bridgen
Bexley Park Wood
PENHILL RD.
PENHILL PARK
Blackfen Sch. for Girls
Sherwood Park Prim. Sch.
Marlborough Park
Marlborough Sch.
Willersley Pk.
SIDCUP GOLF COURSE
River Shuttle
Riverside Wlk.
Hurst Prim. Sch.
HURST ROAD
A222
Lamorbey
Lamorbey Park
Chatsworth Inf. Sch.
The Barn
Penhill Bri.
Rec. Grd.
Hurst Pl. (Com. Cen.)
Plumstead Cemetery
Woolwich Cemetery
Hill Grove
Hook La. Prim. Sch.
Westbrooke Sch.
The Danson Cen.
Welling Sch.
Warehouse

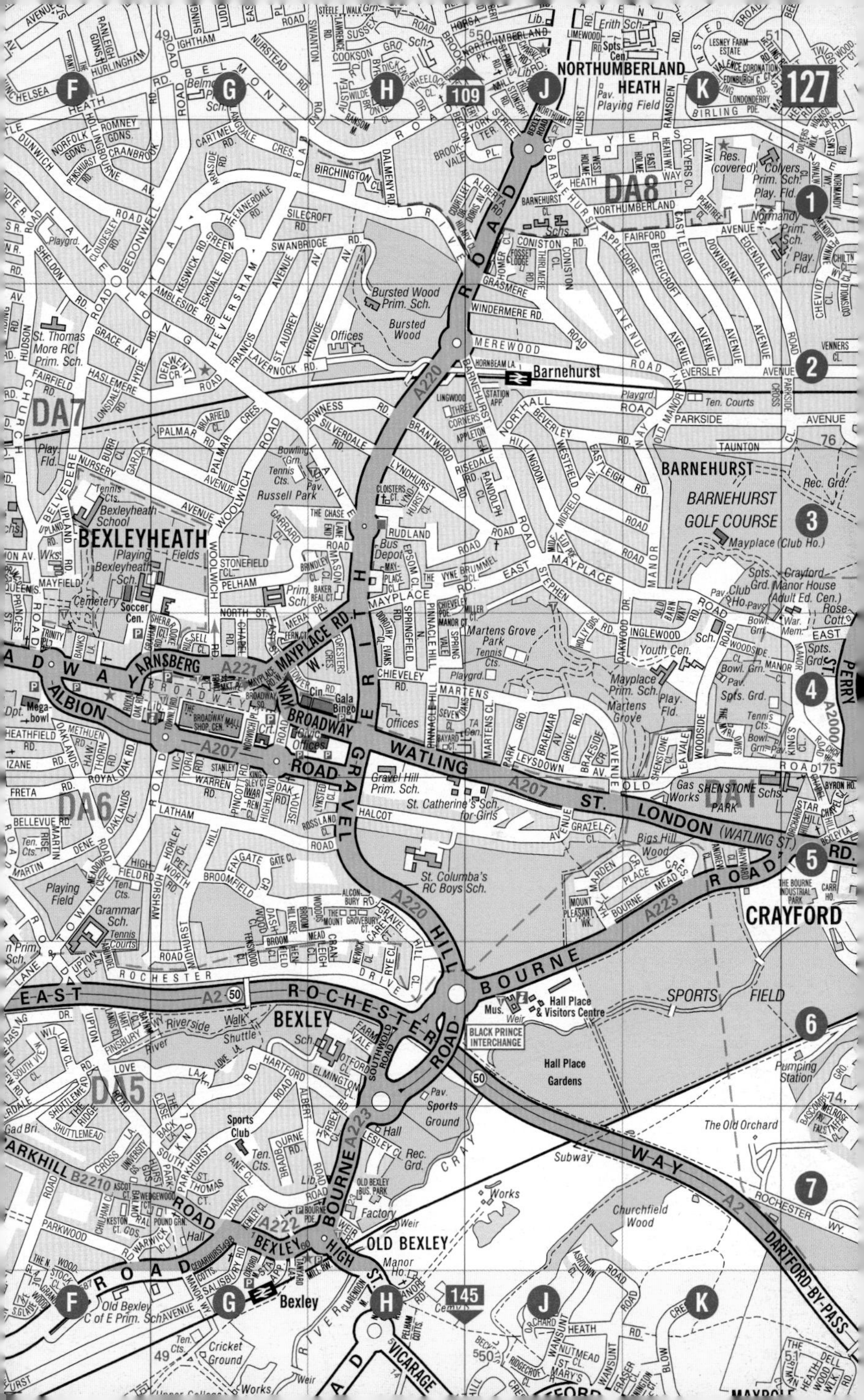

127
109
145
NORTHUMBERLAND HEATH
BARNEHURST
BARNEHURST GOLF COURSE
BEXLEYHEATH
BEXLEY
OLD BEXLEY
CRAYFORD
DA1
DA5
DA6
DA7
DA8
Barnehurst
Bexley
BROADWAY
WATLING ST.
LONDON RD.
MAYPLACE RD.
BARNEHURST ROAD
GRAVEL HILL
BOURNE ROAD
BOURNE WAY
HIGH ST.
BEXLEY ROAD
EAST ROCHESTER WAY
ROCHESTER WAY
DARTFORD-BY-PASS
ALBION ROAD
ARNSBERG WAY
LONG LANE
BELMONT ROAD
COLYERS LANE
NORTHUMBERLAND AV.
MAYPLACE
A2
A207
A220
A221
A222
A223
A2000
B2210
Bursted Wood
Bursted Wood Prim. Sch.
Russell Park
Martens Grove Park
Martens Grove
Mayplace Prim. Sch.
Bexleyheath School
Grammar Sch.
Gravel Hill Prim. Sch.
St. Catherine's Sch. for Girls
St. Columba's RC Boys Sch.
St. Thomas More RC Prim. Sch.
Civic Offices
Bus Depot
Gala Bingo
Hall Place & Visitors Centre
Hall Place Gardens
BLACK PRINCE INTERCHANGE
SPORTS FIELD
Churchfield Wood
Bigs Hill Wood
SHENSTONE PARK
Crayford Manor House (Adult Ed. Cen.)
Mayplace (Club Ho.)
Old Bexley C of E Prim. Sch.
Cricket Ground
Riverside Walk
Pumping Station
The Old Orchard
Subway
F
G
H
J
K
1
2
3
4
5
6
7

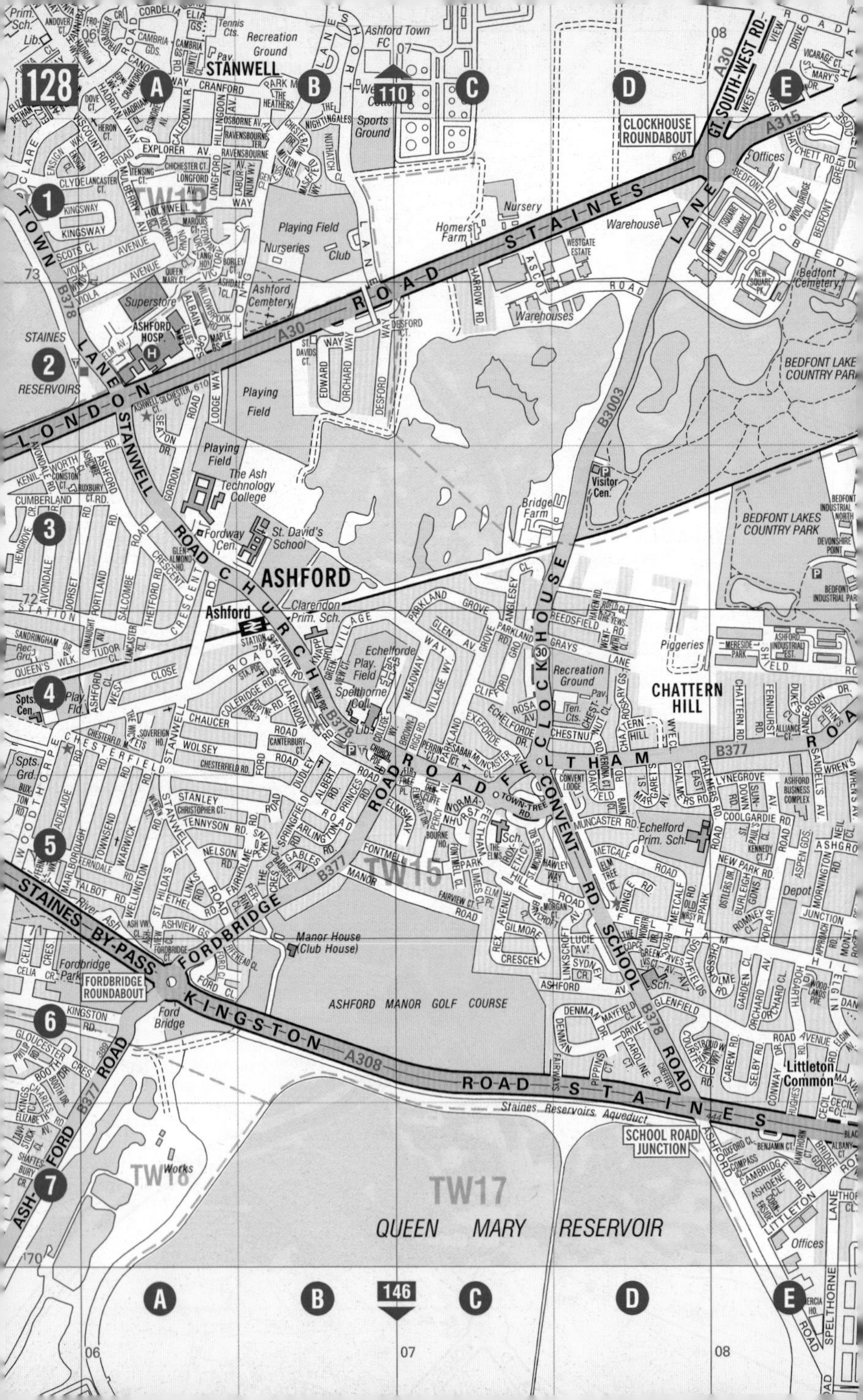

128
110
146
A
B
C
D
E
1
2
3
4
5
6
7
06
07
08
73
72
71
170
STANWELL
ASHFORD
CHATTERN HILL
Littleton Common
TW19
TW15
TW18
TW17
QUEEN MARY RESERVOIR
STAINES RESERVOIRS
Staines Reservoirs Aqueduct
ASHFORD MANOR GOLF COURSE
Manor House (Club House)
CLOCKHOUSE ROUNDABOUT
FORDBRIDGE ROUNDABOUT
SCHOOL ROAD JUNCTION
BEDFONT LAKES COUNTRY PARK
Bedfont Cemetery
Ashford Cemetery
Ashford Town FC
Sports Ground
Recreation Ground
Tennis Cts.
Playing Field
Nurseries
Club
Nursery
Homers Farm
Warehouse
Warehouses
WESTGATE ESTATE
Offices
Superstore
ASHFORD HOSP.
Playing Field
The Ash Technology College
St. David's School
Fordway Cen.
Clarendon Prim. Sch.
Ashford
Echelforde Play. Field
Spelthorne Coll.
Lib.
Recreation Ground
Visitor Cen.
Bridge Farm
Piggeries
BEDFONT INDUSTRIAL NORTH
DEVONSHIRE POINT
BEDFONT INDUSTRIAL PARK
ASHFORD INDUSTRIAL EST.
MERESIDE PARK
ASHFORD BUSINESS COMPLEX
Echelford Prim. Sch.
Depot
Fordbridge Park
Ford Bridge
Works
Spts. Cen.
Spts. Grd.
Rec. Grd.
LONDON ROAD
STAINES ROAD
A30
A315
B378
B3003
B377
A308
GT. SOUTH-WEST RD.
STANWELL RD.
CHURCH ROAD
CLOCKHOUSE LANE
FELTHAM ROAD
CONVENT RD.
SCHOOL ROAD
KINGSTON ROAD
STAINES BY-PASS
FORDBRIDGE RD.
ASHFORD ROAD
WOODTHORPE RD.
CHESTERFIELD RD.
STATION RD.
VILLAGE WAY
PARKLAND GROVE
GRAYS LANE
CHATTERN HILL
MUNCASTER RD.
ECHELFORDE DR.
TOWN LANE
KINGSWAY
EXPLORER AV.
CRANFORD AV.
LONGFORD AV.
DESFORD WAY
EDWARD WAY
ORCHARD WAY
GILMORE CRESCENT
DENMAN DR.
GLENFIELD RD.
SPELTHORNE LANE
LITTLETON LANE

129
111
130
147
F
G
H
J
K
1
2
3
4
5
6
7
EAST BEDFONT
Fairholme Primary Sch.
Playing Field
TW14
BEDFONT
Blenheim Pk.
School
Feltham Arenas
Grandstand
Running Track
Feltham Park
Warehouses
Feltham
HANWORTH RD.
HARLINGTON ROAD
HOUNSLOW
B3377
A312
Gala Bingo
Bowl Alley
Cineworld
LEISURE WEST
FELTHAM
Ordnance Depot
Sports Ground
Works
Superstore
Grosvenor Park
Edward Pauling Prim. Sch.
Vineyard Nurseries
BEDFONT TRADING ESTATE
HM Young Offenders Institution Feltham
LOWER FELTHAM
Feltham Hill Jun. & Inf. Schs.
Cemetery
HIGH STREET
A244
ASHFORD ROAD
B377
Rec. Grd.
Warehouse
CHERTSEY ROAD
SNAKEY LANE
Croft Farm
TW13
Garden Centre
Rugby Football Ground
Club Ho.
FELTHAMHILL
Playing Field
Kenyngton Manor Prim. Sch.
Sports Ground
Laboratories
Spelthorne Jun. & Inf. Schs.
Offices
ASHFORD COMMON
SUNBURY COMMON
King George's Fld.
Warehouse
Depot
Stables
Kempton Park
KEMPTON PARK RACECOURSE
Grandstand
Junc.1
A316
HANWORTH RD.
COUNTRY WAY
M3 MOTORWAY
SUNBURY CROSS
STAINES ROAD
A308
Sunbury
WEST
Club Ho.
Sports Ground
Pumping Station
Filter Beds
Superstore
M3
Sunbury Manor Sch.
Playing Field
Virgin Active
St. Paul's Catholic
Adult Edu. Cen.
Sports Grd.
Staines Reserv
Filter Beds
TW16

130
112
129
148
A
B
C
D
E
1
2
3
4
5
6
7
FELTHAM
HARLINGTON ROAD EAST
HANWORTH RD.
UXBRIDGE ROAD
A312
A314
A316
A305
HANWORTH ROAD
HOUNSLOW ROAD
HAMPTON RD. WEST
HAMPTON RD. EAST
GREAT CHERTSEY
TWICKENHAM RD.
COUNTRY WAY
APEX CORNER
South West Middlesex Crematorium
De Brome Building
Playing Field
Feltham Community College
Gala Bingo
Bowl. Alley
Cineworld
LEISURE WEST
FELTHAM BUSINESS COMPLEX
Tennis Courts
Feltham Airparcs Leisure Centre
Mount Corner
Hanworth Park House
HANWORTH PARK
HANWORTH
Rectory Meadow
Hounslow Cemy.
HEATHROW GATEWAY
MILL FARM BUS. PK.
Cemetery
Recreation Grd.
Heathfield Jun. & Inf. Schs.
Nature Reserve
HANWORTH TRAD. EST.
AIR LINKS IND. EST.
HAMPTON FARM IND. EST.
APEX RETAIL PK.
The Racquets & Fitness Spa
TWICKENHAM GOLF CO
Superstore
Longford River
TW13
TW12
TW4
TW16
Rec. Grd.
Hampton Comm. Coll.
Hampton Spts. Cen.
Hospice
Sports Hall
Lindon Bennett Sch.
Play. Fld.
Reservoir
Staines Reservoirs Aqueduct
Filter Beds
Works
Dairy
Sports Ground
Hatherop Park
Half Moon Covert
Stables
Grandstand
KEMPTON PARK RACECOURSE
Football Ground
Hydes Field
Portlane Bridge
St. Mary's Lodge
KEMPTON PK.
KINGSWAY BUS. PK.
STAINES RD. EAST
12
13
70
71
72
73

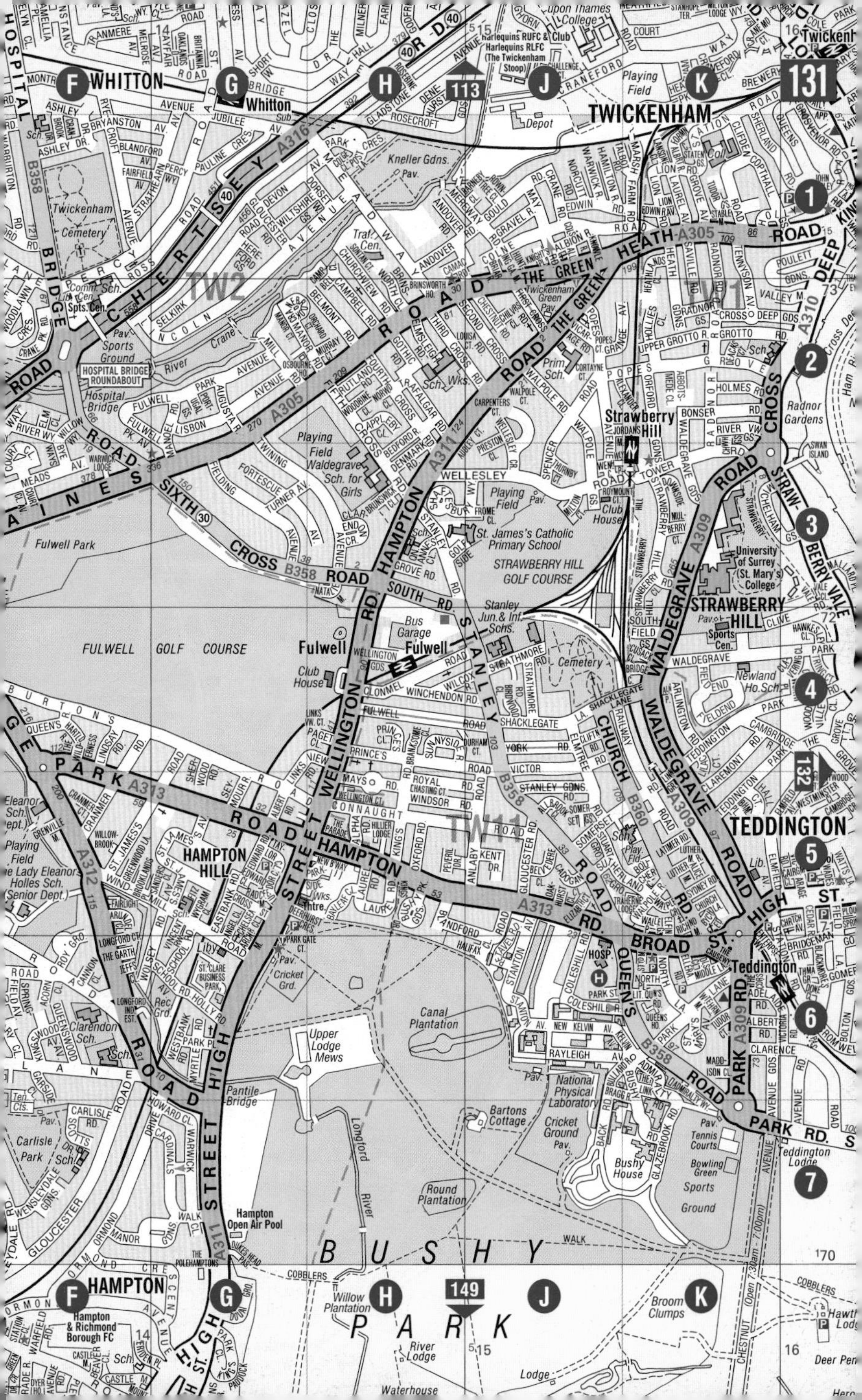

WHITTON
Whitton
113
131
132
149
TWICKENHAM
TW2
TW1
TW11
Twickenham Cemetery
Harlequins RUFC & Club
Harlequins RLFC
(The Twickenham Stoop)
Kneller Gdns.
Playing Field
Depot
CHERTSEY ROAD
A316
HEATH ROAD
A305
THE GREEN
Twickenham Green
HOSPITAL BRIDGE ROUNDABOUT
Hospital Bridge
Pav. Sports Ground
River Crane
Spts. Cen.
Comm. Sch.
STAINES ROAD
SIXTH CROSS ROAD
B358
Fulwell Park
FULWELL GOLF COURSE
Fulwell
Club House
Bus Garage
HAMPTON ROAD
A311
Playing Field
Waldegrave Sch. for Girls
St. James's Catholic Primary School
STRAWBERRY HILL GOLF COURSE
Stanley Jun.& Inf. Schs.
Strawberry Hill
Radnor Gardens
CROSS DEEP
A310
STRAWBERRY VALE
University of Surrey (St. Mary's) College
STRAWBERRY HILL
Sports Cen.
Newland Ho.Sch.
WALDEGRAVE ROAD
A309
Cemetery
CHURCH ROAD
B360
STANLEY ROAD
TEDDINGTON
Teddington
HIGH ST.
BROAD ST.
PARK ROAD
A313
HAMPTON HILL
WELLINGTON ROAD
HIGH STREET
QUEEN'S ROAD
HOSP.
Cricket Grd.
Upper Lodge Mews
Canal Plantation
National Physical Laboratory
Bartons Cottage
Cricket Ground
Bushy House
Tennis Courts
Bowling Green
Sports Ground
Teddington Lodge
Round Plantation
Longford River
Hampton Open Air Pool
Pantile Bridge
Clarendon Sch.
Carlisle Park
Playing Field
Lady Eleanor Holles Sch. (Senior Dept.)
A312
HAMPTON
Hampton & Richmond Borough FC
BUSHY PARK
Willow Plantation
Broom Clumps
River Lodge
Waterhouse
Lodge
CHESTNUT AVENUE (Open 7:30am - 7:00pm)
COBBLERS WALK
F
G
H
J
K
1
2
3
4
5
6
7
14
15
16
170

132
114
131
150
A
B
C
D
E
1
2
3
4
5
6
7
TWICKENHAM
Twickenham
TW1
TW10
TW11
PETERSHAM
STRAWBERRY HILL
TEDDINGTON
Teddington
HAM
KINGSTON UPON THAMES
HAMPTON WICK
Hampton Wick
BUSHY PARK
RIVER THAMES
MARBLE HILL PARK
Marble Hill House
Orleans Ho. Gallery
Orleans Gdns.
Glover's Island
Petersham Meadows
Petersham Farm
Royal Star & Garter Home
Petersham Common
Petersham Gate
PETERSHAM PARK
SUDBROOK PARK
Sudbrook Park (Club Ho.)
The Wilderness
RICHMOND GOLF COURSE
Ham House
Polo Ground
The German Sch. London
The Russell Sch. (Juniors)
The Russell Sch. (Infants)
Strathmore Sch.
The Copse
Ham Riverside Lands
Ham Lands Nature Reserve
Radnor Gardens
Swan Island
Eel Pie Island
Thames Eyot
Miniature Rifle Range
Playing Field
Ham Fields
Thames Young Mariners Base
Ham Green
Grey Court School
Convent
The Cassel Hosp.
Meadlands Prim. Sch.
University of Surrey (St. Mary's) College
Teddington Lock
Teddington Weir
Teddington Studios
Lensbury Club
Sports Ground
Ham Riverside Lands
Rec. Gd.
Arts Cen.
Pool
Athletic Ground
Collis Prim. Sch.
YMCA Sports Grd.
Trowlock Island
Foot Ferry
Sports Cen.
Recreation Ground
Steven's Eyot
The Avenue Centre
St. George's Industrial Estate
The Tiffin Girls' Sch.
Tiffins Girls Comm. Spts. Cen.
Fern Hill Prim. Sch.
Canbury Gdns.
Fitness Club
Teddington Lodge
Warren Plantation
Hawthorn Lodge
Half Moon Plantation
Deer Pen
Leg-of-Mutton Pond
Thatched Cottage
A310
A305
A307
A313
B352
B353
B358
HEATH RD.
CROSS DEEP
STRAWBERRY VALE
TWICKENHAM RD.
MANOR R.
KINGSTON ROAD
HIGH STREET
PARK RD.
SANDY LANE
PETERSHAM ROAD
UPPER HAM RD.
RICHMOND ROAD
HAM COMMON
HAM GATE
RIVERSIDE DRIVE
DUKES AVENUE
BROOM ROAD
LOWER HAM ROAD
UP. TEDDINGTON RD.
WALDEGRAVE RD.
SANDY LA.

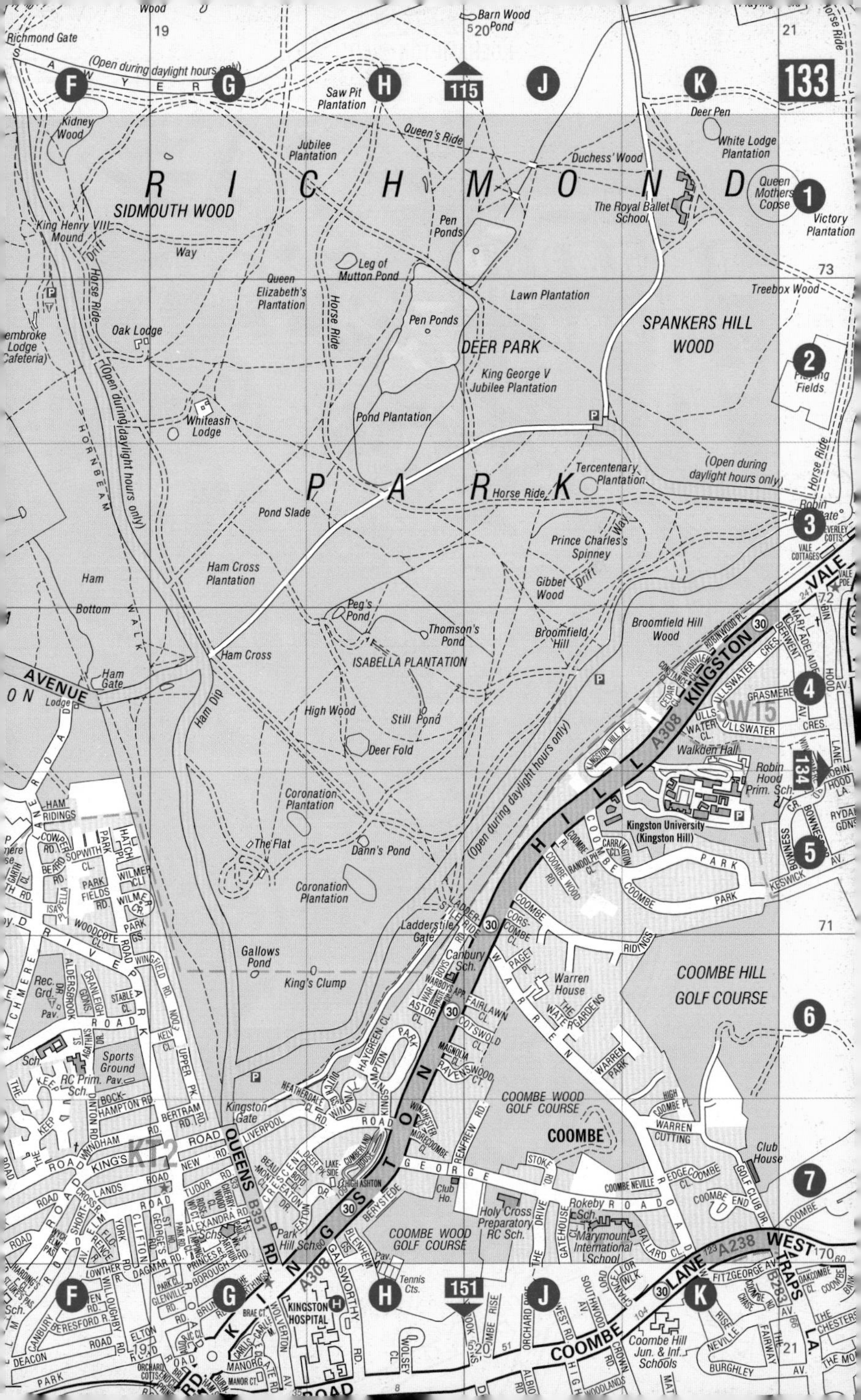

133
115
151
134
F
G
H
J
K
1
2
3
4
5
6
7
19
20
21
73
72
71
170
RICHMOND PARK
Richmond Gate
SAWYER'S HILL
(Open during daylight hours only)
Barn Wood Pond
Kidney Wood
Saw Pit Plantation
Queen's Ride
Deer Pen
White Lodge Plantation
Duchess' Wood
Jubilee Plantation
Queen Mothers Copse
Victory Plantation
The Royal Ballet School
SIDMOUTH WOOD
King Henry VIII Mound
Way
Drift
Horse Ride
Pen Ponds
Leg of Mutton Pond
Queen Elizabeth's Plantation
Lawn Plantation
Treebox Wood
SPANKERS HILL WOOD
Pembroke Lodge (Cafeteria)
Oak Lodge
DEER PARK
King George V Jubilee Plantation
Playing Fields
Whiteash Lodge
HORNBEAM WALK
Pond Plantation
Tercentenary Plantation
Pond Slade
Robin Hood Gate
Prince Charles's Spinney
BEVERLEY COTTS.
VALE COTTAGES
Ham Cross Plantation
Gibbet Wood
Ham Bottom
Peg's Pond
Thomson's Pond
Broomfield Hill
Broomfield Hill Wood
Ham Cross
ISABELLA PLANTATION
HAM GATE AVENUE
Ham Gate
Lodge
Ham Dip
High Wood
Still Pond
Deer Fold
KINGSTON HILL
A308
SW15
ULLSWATER CRES.
Walkden Hall
Robin Hood Prim. Sch.
Kingston University (Kingston Hill)
Coronation Plantation
The Flat
Dann's Pond
COOMBE PARK
KESWICK AV.
Ladderstile Gate
LADDERSTILE RIDE
Gallows Pond
King's Clump
Canbury Sch.
Warren House
The Water Gardens
COOMBE HILL GOLF COURSE
Sports Ground
RC Prim. Sch.
Rec. Grd.
KT2
COOMBE WOOD GOLF COURSE
COOMBE
WARREN CUTTING
Club House
Kingston Gate
QUEENS RD.
B351
GEORGE RD.
Holy Cross Preparatory RC Sch.
Rokeby Sch.
Marymount International School
Park Hill Sch.
COOMBE WOOD GOLF COURSE
KINGSTON HOSPITAL
Tennis Cts.
COOMBE LANE WEST
A238
B283
TRAPS LA.
Coombe Hill Jun. & Inf. Schools
ROAD

ROEHAMPTON
116
RICHMOND PARK
RICHMOND PARK GOLF COURSE
White Lodge Plantation
Queen Mothers Copse
Killcat Corner
Victory Plantation
Kingsfarm Plantation
Treebox Wood
Playing Fields
Beverley Brook
Horse Ride
(Open during daylight hours only)
Robin Hood Gate
Beverley Bridge
SW15
Chohole Gate
Silver Hill
STAG LANE
Hyde Park Nursery
ROEHAMPTON LANE
KINGSTON ROAD
ROEHAMPTON VALE
KINGSTON VALE
A3
A308
A306
Scio Pond
King's Mere
PUTNEY HEATH
Jerry's Hill
Stag Ride
Inner Park Ride
Ladies Mile
Putney Vale Crematorium
PUTNEY VALE CEMETERY
Superstore
Newlands Hall
PUTNEY VALE
Kingston University (Roehampton Vale Centre)
Memorial Gardens
War Memorial
ROBIN HOOD
Wimbledon Windmill Museum
Queen's Mere
Club House
Manor Cottage
WINDMILL ROAD
Silent Pools
Stag Bog
WIMBLEDON COMMON
Gravelly Ride
Horse Exercise Ring
Gravelly Hill
Horse Exercise Area
WIMBLEDON COMMON & LONDON SCOTTISH GOLF COURSE
White Cottage
Thatched Cottage
ROBIN HOOD WAY (KINGSTON BY-PASS)
133
Robin Hood Prim. Sch.
ROBIN HOOD ROAD
Farm Bog
Farm Ravine
Caesar's Camp
Club House
Warren Farm
Fishpond Wood
Mill Corner
ROYAL WIMBLEDON GOLF COURSE
Shadwell Wood
The Warren
Cannizaro House
Cannizaro Park
Lady Jane's Wood
WEST SIDE COMMON
COOMBE HILL GOLF COURSE
Club House
KT2
COOMBE LANE WEST
A238
NEW VICTORIA HOSPITAL
COOMBE LANE
152
SW20
The Rowans Sch.
The Wolfson Rehabilitation Cen.
COPSE HILL
Sports Grd.
Tennis Courts
WOODHAYES RD.
COTTENHAM PARK ROAD
B281
DURHAM RD.
Holland Gdns.
Cottenham Park
COTTENHAM PARK
Wimbledon

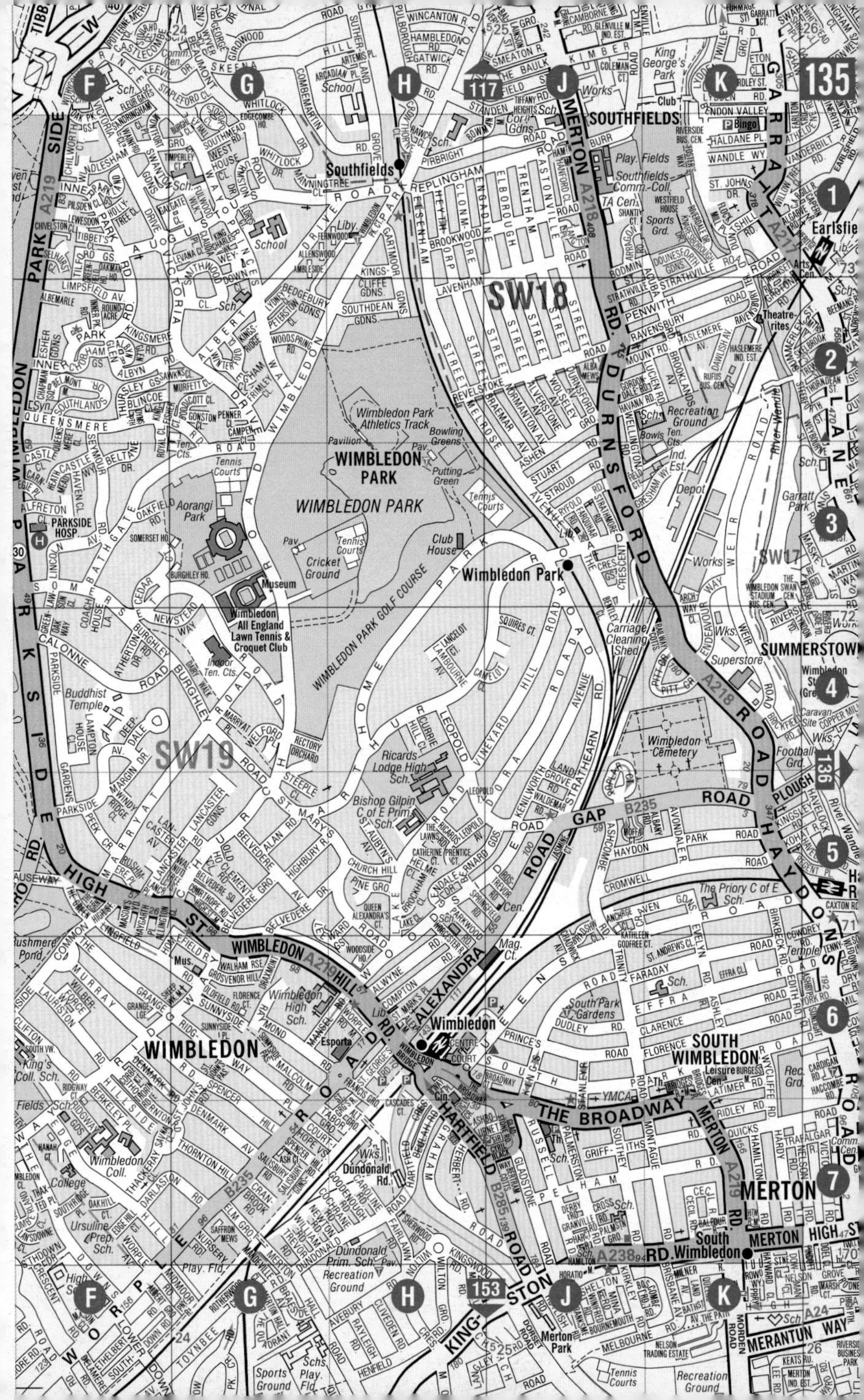
135
117
136
153
F
G
H
J
K
1
2
3
4
5
6
7
SW18
SW19
SW17
SOUTHFIELDS
Southfields
EARLSFIELD
WIMBLEDON PARK
Wimbledon Park
Wimbledon Park Athletics Track
Wimbledon Park Golf Course
Wimbledon All England Lawn Tennis & Croquet Club
Museum
Aorangi Park
Cricket Ground
Club House
Bowling Greens
Putting Green
Tennis Courts
Pavilion
Wimbledon Cemetery
Carriage Cleaning Shed
Superstore
SUMMERSTOWN
Football Grd.
Caravan Site
Recreation Ground
Ind. Est.
Depot
Works
Play. Fields
Southfields Comm.-Coll.
Sports Grd.
King George's Park
Garratt Park
River Wandle
Theatre-rites
Ricards Lodge High Sch.
Bishop Gilpin C of E Prim. Sch.
The Priory C of E Sch.
Buddhist Temple
PARKSIDE HOSP.
Rushmere Pond
WIMBLEDON
Wimbledon
Wimbledon High Sch.
Wimbledon Coll.
King's Coll. Sch.
Ursuline Prep. Sch.
College
Esporta
Mus.
Centre Court
Cin.
YMCA
SOUTH WIMBLEDON
South Wimbledon
South Park Gardens
Leisure Cen.
Rec. Grd.
MERTON
Merton Park
Dundonald Rd.
Dundonald Prim. Sch.
Recreation Ground
Sports Ground
Schs. Play. Fld.
Tennis Courts
NELSON TRADING ESTATE
MERTON IND. EST.
PARK SIDE
A219
A218
A217
B235
B285
A238
A24
HIGH ST.
WIMBLEDON HILL RD.
ALEXANDRA RD.
THE BROADWAY
HARTFIELD ROAD
MERTON RD.
DURNSFORD RD.
MERTON HIGH ST.
MERANTUN WAY
HAYDONS ROAD
PLOUGH LANE
GARRATT LANE
KINGSTON ROAD
WORPLE ROAD
ARTHUR ROAD
HOME PARK ROAD
CHURCH ROAD
GAP ROAD
QUEENS ROAD
PRINCES WAY
AUGUSTUS ROAD
WIMBLEDON PARK ROAD
WIMBLEDON PARK SIDE
VICTORIA DRIVE
SOMERSET ROAD
BURGHLEY ROAD
CALONNE ROAD
MARRYAT ROAD
RIDGWAY
LOWER DOWNS ROAD
REVELSTOKE RD.
REPLINGHAM RD.
KIMBER RD.
WEIR ROAD
STRATHEARN RD.
HAYDON PARK ROAD
CROMWELL ROAD
SOUTH PARK ROAD
FAIRLAWN ROAD
CLIFTON ROAD
WIMBLEDON STADIUM BUS. CEN.

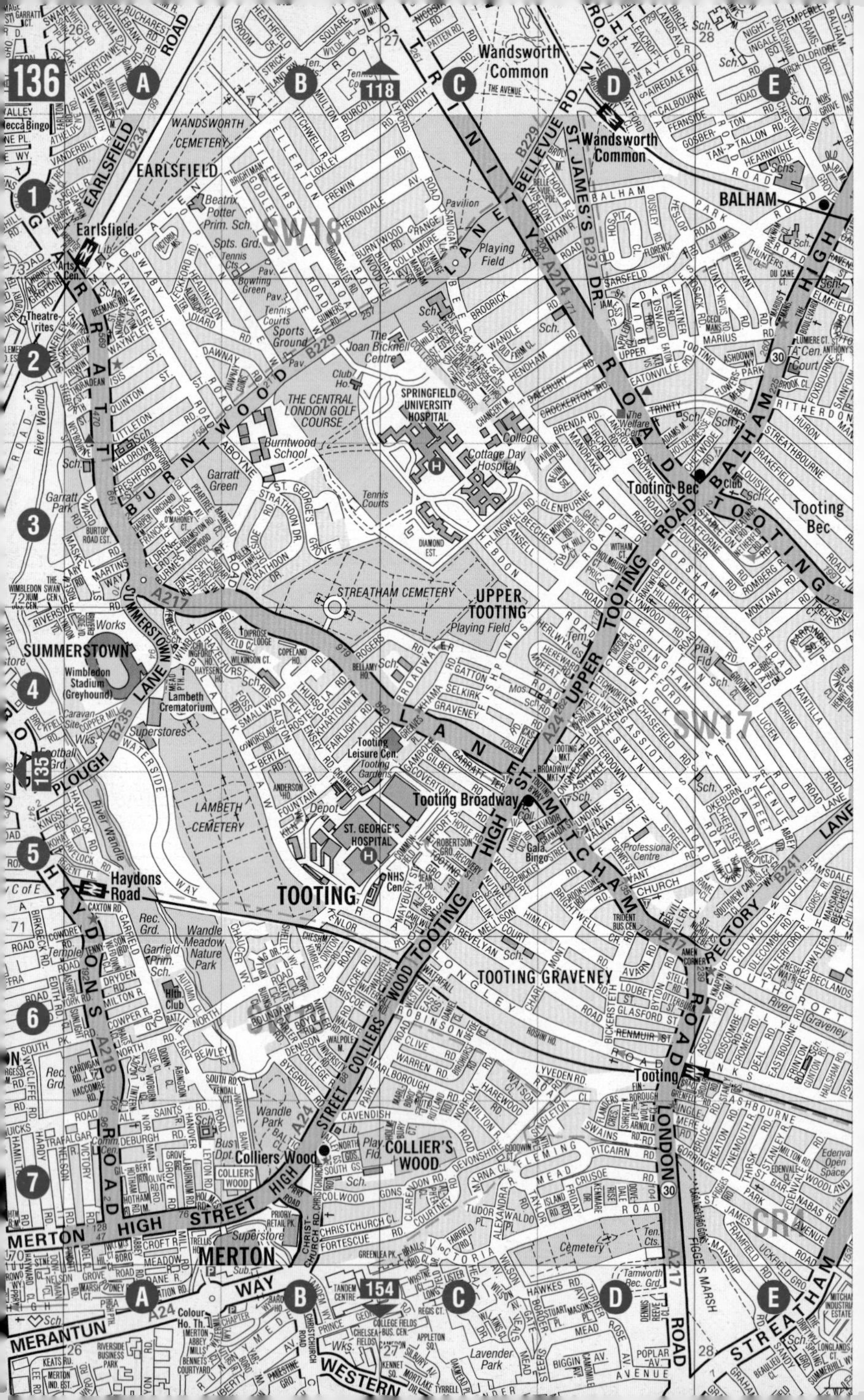
136
118
154
135
Wandsworth Common
EARLSFIELD
Earlsfield
WANDSWORTH CEMETERY
SW18
SW17
BALHAM
THE CENTRAL LONDON GOLF COURSE
SPRINGFIELD UNIVERSITY HOSPITAL
STREATHAM CEMETERY
UPPER TOOTING
Tooting Bec
SUMMERSTOWN
Wimbledon Stadium (Greyhound)
Lambeth Crematorium
LAMBETH CEMETERY
Haydons Road
Tooting Broadway
ST. GEORGE'S HOSPITAL
TOOTING
TOOTING GRAVENEY
Tooting
Colliers Wood
COLLIER'S WOOD
MERTON
MERTON HIGH STREET
BURNTWOOD LANE
TRINITY ROAD
UPPER TOOTING ROAD
TOOTING HIGH ST.
MITCHAM ROAD
LONDON ROAD
GARRATT LANE
PLOUGH LANE
HAYDONS ROAD
BALHAM HIGH ROAD
STREATHAM
Lavender Park
Wandle Meadow Nature Park
Garratt Green
Garratt Park

F
G
H
J
K
119
155
138
1
2
3
4
5
6
7
SW12
SW2
SW16
Balham
STREATHAM HILL
Streatham Hill
STREATHAM
Streatham
STREATHAM PARK
FURZEDOWN
STREATHAM VALE
Streatham Common
STREATHAM COMMON
NORBURY
Norbury
Lonesome
TOOTING BEC COMMON
Tooting Graveney Common
Tooting Bec Lido
Football Pitch
Woodfield Rec. Grd.
Athletic Ground
Leisure Cen.
Riva Bingo
Megabowl
Odeon Cin.
Secondary School
Superstore
Leis. Cen. Ice Arena
Karting Track
Paddling Pool
The Rookery
Sports Ground
School Playing Fields
Streatham Vale Park
Beecholme Prim. Sch.
Fish Pond
Nature Gdn.
Bus Depot
BEDFORD ROAD
CHRISTCHURCH ROAD
BRIXTON HILL
STREATHAM HILL
STREATHAM HIGH ROAD
BEC ROAD
TOOTING BEC ROAD
BEC HILL
GARRAD'S RD.
MITCHAM ROAD
MITCHAM LANE
STREATHAM COMMON NORTH
GREYHOUND LA.
GREEN LANE
LONDON ROAD
CHURCH LANE
STREATHAM VALE
KINGS AV.
THORNTON AV.
ATKINS RD.
EMMANUEL RD.
STERNHOLD AV.
A23
A24
A205
A214
A216
B221
B242
B272
B273

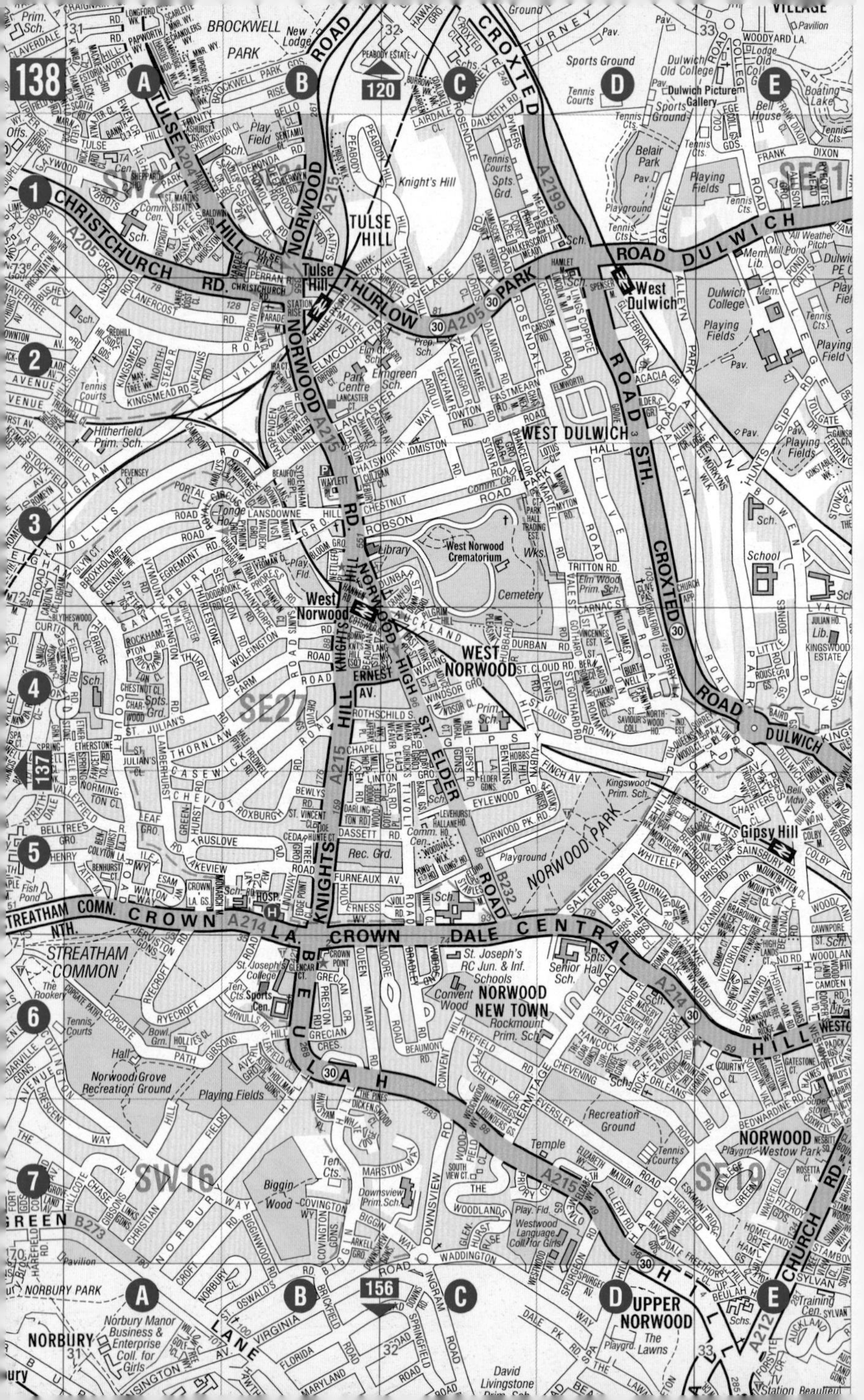
138
120
137
156
A
B
C
D
E
1
2
3
4
5
6
7
BROCKWELL PARK
New Lodge
Sports Ground
Dulwich Old College
Dulwich Picture Gallery
Belair Park
Playing Fields
Boating Lake
Bell House
Knight's Hill
TULSE HILL
Tulse Hill
CHRISTCHURCH RD.
THURLOW PARK ROAD
DULWICH
West Dulwich
WEST DULWICH
Dulwich College
Playing Fields
NORWOOD ROAD
CROXTED ROAD
SW2
SE21
SE27
SE19
SW16
West Norwood Crematorium
Cemetery
West Norwood
WEST NORWOOD
KNIGHTS HILL
NORWOOD HIGH ST.
ELDER ROAD
GIPSY HILL
Gipsy Hill
NORWOOD PARK
Kingswood Estate
DULWICH WOOD
Rec. Grd.
STREATHAM COMN. NTH.
CROWN LA.
CROWN DALE
CENTRAL HILL
STREATHAM COMMON
The Rookery
Norwood Grove Recreation Ground
Playing Fields
BEULAH HILL
NORWOOD NEW TOWN
Convent Wood
St. Joseph's RC Jun. & Inf. Schools
Rockmount Prim. Sch.
Recreation Ground
Biggin Wood
Downsview Prim. Sch.
Westwood Language Coll. for Girls
NORWOOD
Westow Park
CHURCH RD.
UPPER NORWOOD
The Lawns
NORBURY
NORBURY PARK
Norbury Manor Business & Enterprise Coll. for Girls
David Livingstone Prim. Sch.
Training Cen.
A205
A204
A215
A2199
A214
A212
B232
B273

139
F
G
H
J
K
1
2
3
4
5
6
7
121
140
157
DULWICH PARK
COMMON
LORDSHIP LA.
THE GROVE
LONDON ROAD
Horniman Gardens
Horniman Museum
SE23
Forest Hill
FOREST HILL
PERRY RISE
DEVONSHIRE RD.
WALDRAM PK. RD.
STANSTEAD RD.
DULWICH & SYDENHAM HILL GOLF COURSE
DULWICH
Dulwich Wood
Sydenham Hill
SYDENHAM HILL
DARTMOUTH RD.
KIRKDALE
UPPER SYDENHAM
Sydenham Wells Park
SE26
Mayow Park
LOWER SYDENHAM
DACRES ESTATE
SYDENHAM ROAD
Sydenham
WESTWOOD HILL
CRYSTAL PALACE PARK
CRYSTAL PALACE PARK RD.
Crystal Palace National Sports Centre
Crystal Palace Athletics Stadium
CRYSTAL PALACE
Crystal Palace Museum
Crystal Palace
SYDENHAM
St. Christopher's Hospice
Penge East
NEWLANDS PARK
PARISH LANE
Alexandra Rec. Grd.
Alexandra Jun. Sch.
HIGH ST.
Penge West
ANERLEY HILL
ANERLEY ROAD
Anerley
PENGE
SE20
CROYDON ROAD
Kent House
City Technology Coll.
James Dixon Prim. Sch.
Orchard Lodge (Remand Centre)

140
A
B
C
D
E
1
2
3
4
5
6
7
36
37
38
70
71
72
73
122
139
158
Blythe Hill
Catford Bridge
Catford
CATFORD RD.
CATFORD GYRATORY
BROWNHILL ROAD
RINGSTEAD RD.
MELBOURNE MS.
CARSWELL RD.
REDFERN RD.
BOWNESS RD.
JUTLAND RD.
ENGLEHEART RD.
SANGLEY ROAD
CULVERLEY ROAD
WINDSOR MEWS
HARRIS LODGE
SHORNDEAN ST.
CATFORD
PENERLEY RD.
THE PRIORY APARTMENTS
BARGERY ROAD
INCHMERY ROAD
ARRAN ROAD
NEWQUAY ROAD
CRANTOCK ROAD
CALLANDER ROAD
DANEBY RD.
BELLINGHAM ROAD
CONISBOROUGH CRES.
SE6
SE23
SE26
BR3
DUNCOMBE HILL
AGNEW RD.
WHATMAN RD.
LOWTHER HILL
BROCKLEY RI.
BROCKLEY PARK
Tennis Court
AUSTIN CL.
OWENS WAY
RAVENSBOURNE PK.
BOURNVILLE RD.
WESTDOWN RD.
CASSLEE RD.
ACUTE RD.
BLYTHE HILL
BLYTHE CL.
St. Dunstans Coll.
Pav.
Prim. Sch.
ST. GERMAN'S PL.
WINDSOR MS.
STANSTEAD ROAD
A205
A212
A21
A2218
A2015
B218
B227
Council Offs.
Lib.
RUSHEY GRN.
PLASSY RD.
Powerleague Soccer Centre
Private Banks Sports Ground
CANADIAN AV.
MAPLE CT.
Comm. Cen.
COLFE RD.
CRANSTON RD.
KILMORIE RD.
ELSINORE RD.
HURSTBOURNE RD.
FERMOR RD.
NORTHWOOD RD.
CARHOLME RD.
BLYTHE VALE
RATHFERN RD.
PATTENDEN RD.
BECHFIELD RD.
VINEYARD CL.
THE VINERIES
MARLER RD.
LOXTON RD.
VANCOUVER ROAD
CATFORD HILL
River Ravensbourne
River Pool
Wks.
Warehouse
BARMESTON RD.
CHARSLEY RD.
AITKEN RD.
CATFORD TRADING ESTATE
Bus Garage
Syn.
SUNDERLAND RD.
CIBBER RD.
VESTRIS RD.
TRILBY RD.
COMO RD.
SHIPMAN RD.
NORMANTON ST.
SIDDONS RD.
HAWKESFIELD RD.
WOOLSTONE RD.
TICEHURST RD.
HOUSTON RD.
Sports Ground
Sports Grd.
RIVERVIEW WALK
WATER CL.
EXBURY RD.
Tennis Cts.
RUTLAND WK.
RUTLAND PK.
CASTLANDS R.
DATCHET RD.
CLOWDERS R.
Cricket Grd./Club Ho.
Play Park
Play Park
GHENT ST.
KNAPMILL RD.
KNAPMILL WY.
BROOKEHOWSE RD.
GRANGEMILL WAY
GRANGEMILL RD.
FORDMILL RD.
ATHELNEY ST.
BROADMEAD
Bellingham
BELLINGHAM TRAD. EST.
FRANTHORNE WAY
RANDISBOURNE GDNS.
ALLERFORD RD.
PASSFIELDS
WOODHAM
DANESWOOD AV.
CARSTAIRS RD.
BOSBURY RD.
Catford Girls' School
PERRY VALE
PERRY RISE
PERRY HILL
PEARFIELD RD.
WYNELL RD.
ALLENBY RD.
GARLIES RD.
WINSFORD RD.
SELWORTHY RD.
PRIESTFIELD RD.
SILVER BIRCH CL.
Gasholder Station
Meml.
Playing Fields
SWALLANDS RD.
BELLINGHAM GREEN
BELLINGHAM
Playing Field
DURNFORD HO.
DUNSTER HO.
TA Cen.
FALKLAND HO.
WHITEFOOT LANE
Sch.
Bowl. Grn.
HOLLAND DR.
QUEENSWOOD RD.
Schs.
FRENE RD.
FAIRWYN RD.
CHAMPION RD.
DILLWYN CL.
ADAMSRILL RD.
BELL GREEN
Superstore
BELL GRN.
SOUTHEND LA.
STANTON WAY
MOREMEAD
OTTERDEN ST.
FIRHILL RD.
RANDLESDOWN RD.
COWDEN ST.
ALFRED AV.
SWALLANDS RD.
OVERDOWN RD.
ARNULF ST.
FARMSTEAD RD.
WATERMEAD RD.
LWR. SYDENHAM
SYDENHAM RD.
SOUTHEND LANE
ADOLF ST.
KING ALFRED AV.
Super-store
BERKSHIRE HO.
Southend Park
Tennis Cts.
Club Sports Grd.
Weir
BRUNNER HO.
MARRIETT HO.
WATERER HO.
BOURBON HO.
Home Park
Lib. Hall
Leis. Cen.
Sports Ground
Lwr. Sydenham
MEADOWVIEW RD.
WINCHFIELD RD.
LUSHINGTON RD.
THURBARN RD.
DUNFIELD RD.
Beckenham Hill
BRANGBOURNE RD.
FAIRLAWN PK.
HILLMORE GRO.
BRYDEN CL.
KANGLEY BUS. CEN.
ABBEY TRADING ESTATE
ORCHARD BUS. CEN.
LWR. SYDENHAM IND. EST.
GARDNER IND. EST.
Worsley Bri.
Bank Cottage
Sports Ground
Secondary School
Recreation Gr
Lodge
KENT HOUSE RD.
WOODBASTWICK RD.
Playing Field
Alexandra Jun. Sch.
Cricket Grd.
KANGLEY BR. RD.
THE METRO BUS. CEN.
BECKENHAM BUSINESS CENTRE
GATEWAY BUS. CEN.
Athletic Grd.
The Cottage
Athletic Ground
Stumpshill Wood
Ash Plantation
BECKENHAM HILL RD.
BRAESIDE RD.
Playing Field
Tennis Courts
NEW BECKENHAM
Bowling Grn.
Sports Ground
GRANGE WOOD
Athletic Ground
Tennis Cts.
Sports Ground
Play. Fld.
STUMPS HILL LA.
Beckenham Place Club House
Putting Grn.
BECKENHAM PLACE PARK
GOLF COURSE
The Cottage
Club
Summerhouse Wood
THURSTON HO.
New Beckenham
The Park
LENNARD RD.
Sch.
Spts. Grd.
CATOR PARK
Sports Grd.
SOUTHEND ROAD
BRACKLEY RD.
COPERS COPE RD.
ABBEY PK.
PLACE PARK
Cricket Grd.
St. Mary's Cath. Prim. School
Westgate Lodge
FOXGROVE RD.
FOXGROVE AV.
THE HEIGHTS
EVENING HILL
Kent House
Beckenham Road
BECKENHAM RD.
BRIDGE RD.
BLAKENEY AV.
RECTORY RD.
Beckenham Junc.
ALBEMARLE RD.
BECKENHAM
THE WILLOWS
WAYLANDS
OAKLANDS
RALEIGH CT.
GLENHURST
FORSYTH SHADES
EMBASSY GDNS.
CHURCH

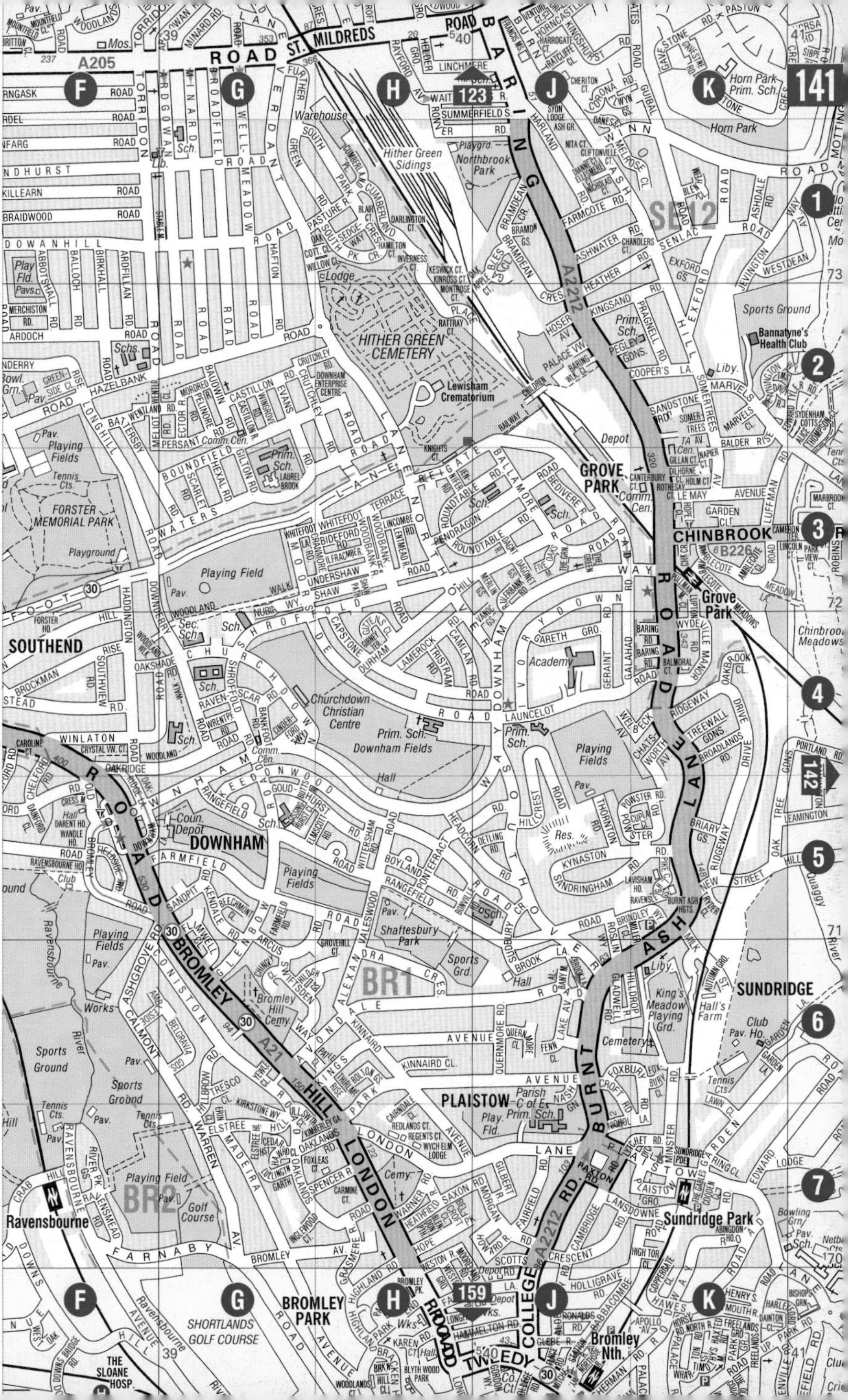
A205
ROAD
ST. MILDREDS
123
F
G
H
J
K
Horn Park
Horn Park Prim. Sch.
SE12
Hither Green Sidings
Northbrook Park
HITHER GREEN CEMETERY
Lewisham Crematorium
A2212
BARING ROAD
Sports Ground
Bannatyne's Health Club
GROVE PARK
CHINBROOK ROAD
B226
Grove Park
Chinbrook Meadows
FORSTER MEMORIAL PARK
Playing Field
SOUTHEND
Academy
Churchdown Christian Centre
Prim. Sch. Downham Fields
DOWNHAM
Playing Fields
Shaftesbury Park
BR1
Sports Grd.
Bromley Hill Cemy.
King's Meadow Playing Grd.
Hall's Farm
SUNDRIDGE
BURNT ASH LANE
BROMLEY ROAD
A21
LONDON ROAD
PLAISTOW
Parish C of E Prim. Sch.
142
Sports Ground
Playing Field
Golf Course
BR2
Ravensbourne
Sundridge Park
Cemy.
BROMLEY PARK
159
COLLEGE RD.
Bromley Nth.
SHORTLANDS GOLF COURSE
THE SLOANE HOSP.
1
2
3
4
5
6
7

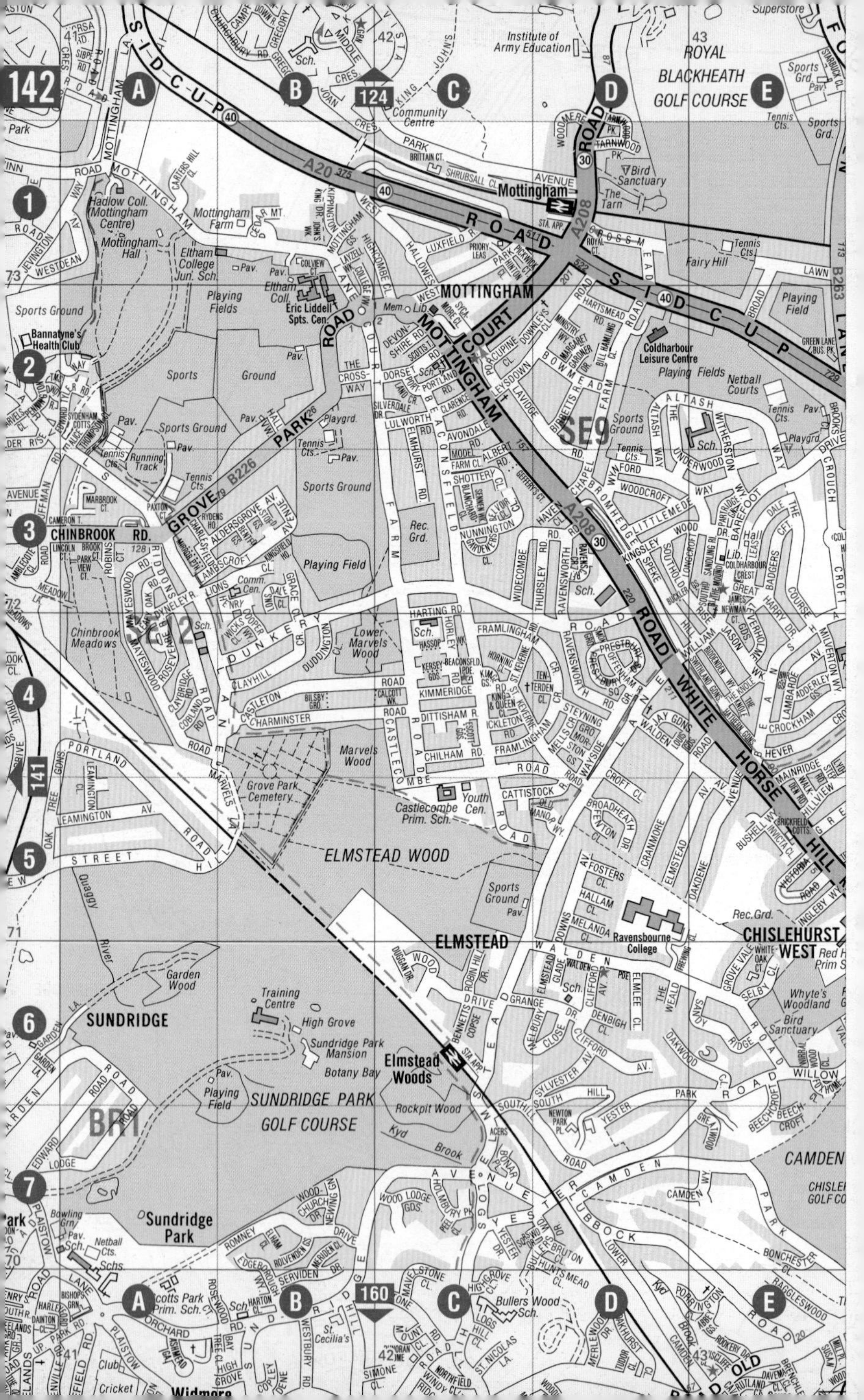
142
124
141
160
A
B
C
D
E
1
2
3
4
5
6
7
Institute of Army Education
ROYAL BLACKHEATH GOLF COURSE
Superstore
Community Centre
SIDCUP ROAD
A20
A208
B226
B263
Mottingham
MOTTINGHAM
MOTTINGHAM ROAD
MOTTINGHAM LANE
Hadlow Coll. (Mottingham Centre)
Mottingham Hall
Mottingham Farm
Eltham College Jun. Sch.
Eltham Coll.
Eric Liddell Spts. Cen.
Playing Fields
Sports Ground
Bannatyne's Health Club
Bird Sanctuary
The Tarn
Fairy Hill
Playing Field
Coldharbour Leisure Centre
Netball Courts
SE9
SE12
GROVE PARK ROAD
CHINBROOK RD.
COURT ROAD
WHITE HORSE ROAD
WHITE HORSE HILL
Chinbrook Meadows
Running Track
Rec. Grd.
Playing Field
Lower Marvels Wood
Marvels Wood
Grove Park Cemetery
Castlecombe Prim. Sch.
Youth Cen.
ELMSTEAD WOOD
ELMSTEAD
Ravensbourne College
CHISLEHURST WEST
Whyte's Woodland
SUNDRIDGE
Garden Wood
Training Centre
High Grove
Sundridge Park Mansion
Botany Bay
Elmstead Woods
SUNDRIDGE PARK GOLF COURSE
Rockpit Wood
Kyd Brook
Quaggy River
BR1
Sundridge Park
Scotts Park Prim. Sch.
Bullers Wood Sch.
CAMDEN
Widmore

143
125
161
144
F
G
H
J
K
1
2
3
4
5
6
7
Sports Ground
Sparrow's Farm Leisure Cen.
Playing Fields
Lamorbey
DA15
New Eltham
NEW ELTHAM
FIVEWAYS
St. Olave's Prep. School
Cricket Ground
Old Farm Park
Playground King George's Rec. Grd.
LONGLANDS
World Of Golf) at Sidcup
Flamingo Park Sports Grd.
Pitch & Putt Course
SIDCUP
DA14
Ashen Grove
Kemnal Manor
Edgebury Prim. Sch.
Foxbury
Esporta Health & Fitness
Beavers Wood
Chislehurst Cemetery
Hoblands Wood
Playing Field
Old Elthamians Sports Club
Beaverwood Sch. for Girls
Athletic Ground
Darul Uloom London Islamic Sch.
Garden Centre
FROGNAL CORNER
St. Mary & St. Joseph's Catholic Sch.
Sixth Form Coll.
Bank's Shaw
Square Clump
Bushy Clump
SCADBURY PARK (Nature Reserve)
Farringtons & Stratford House
Icehouse Wood
PARK WOOD
Moat
Archway
BR7
Selwood
Mead Rd. Inf. Sch.
CHISLEHURST
CHISLEHURST COMMON
War Mem.
SIDCUP BY-PASS
MAIN ROAD
SIDCUP ROAD
CRAY ROAD
HALFWAY STREET
PERRY STREET
BROMLEY LANE
BROMLEY RD.
HIGH ST.
A20
A211
A222
A208
B263
B264
B2214

144
126
143
A
B
C
D
E
1
2
3
4
5
6
7
Lamorbey
HALFWAY
Sidcup
SIDCUP
Albany Park
Bridgen
DA14
BR7
BR5
SIDCUP GOLF COURSE
Chatsworth Inf. Sch.
Lamorbey Park
The Barn Theatre
The Glade
Chislehurst & Sidcup Grammar Sch.
Abbeyhill Park
King George's Rec. Grd.
Hurstmere Sch.
Hurst Prim. Sch.
Bexley Park Wood
Hurst Pl. (Com. Cen.)
Rutland Shaw
Sidcup Cemy.
Birkbeck Prim. Sch.
WARING PARK
Cleeve Pk. Sch.
Royal Park Prim. Sch.
The Alders
North Cray Woods
Five Arch Bri.
FOOTS CRAY MEADOWS
Foots Cray Place
Dower House
David Lloyd Leisure
Cray Youth & Community Centre
St. Peter Chanel RC Prim. Sch.
Warehouse
FIVE ARCHES BUSINESS PARK
SIDCUP TECHNOLOGY CENTRE
Sidcup Place
Sidcup Place Park
QUEEN MARY'S HOSPITAL
FROGNAL CORNER
Orchard Prim. Sch.
Football Grd.
FOOTS CRAY
Spring Shaw
Black Clump
Bank's Shaw
Little Wood
SCADBURY PARK (Nature Reserve)
Irish Plantation
Kemnal Tech. College
CRITTALLS CORNER
Superstore
RUXLEY
Ruxley Corner
RUXLEY WOOD
Midfield Prim. Sch.
The Meadow School
ST. PAUL'S CRAY
Grays Farm Cottages
CRAYFIELDS BUSINESS PARK
Dragons Health Club
Bromley Ski Centre
RUXLEY (PUBLIC) GOLF COURSE
CRAY VALLEY GOLF COURSE
HURST ROAD
A222
A221
A211
A2001
A224
A223
A20
B2214
B2173
STATION ROAD
MAIN RD.
HIGH ST.
SIDCUP HILL
MAIDSTONE RD.
EDGINGTON WY.
SEVENOAKS WY.
SIDCUP BY-PASS
NORTH CRAY ROAD
CHISLEHURST RD.
PENHILL RD.
BEXLEY LANE
RECTORY LANE
FOOTS CRAY LANE
LONGMEAD DRIVE
FARADAY AVENUE
MIDFIELD WAY

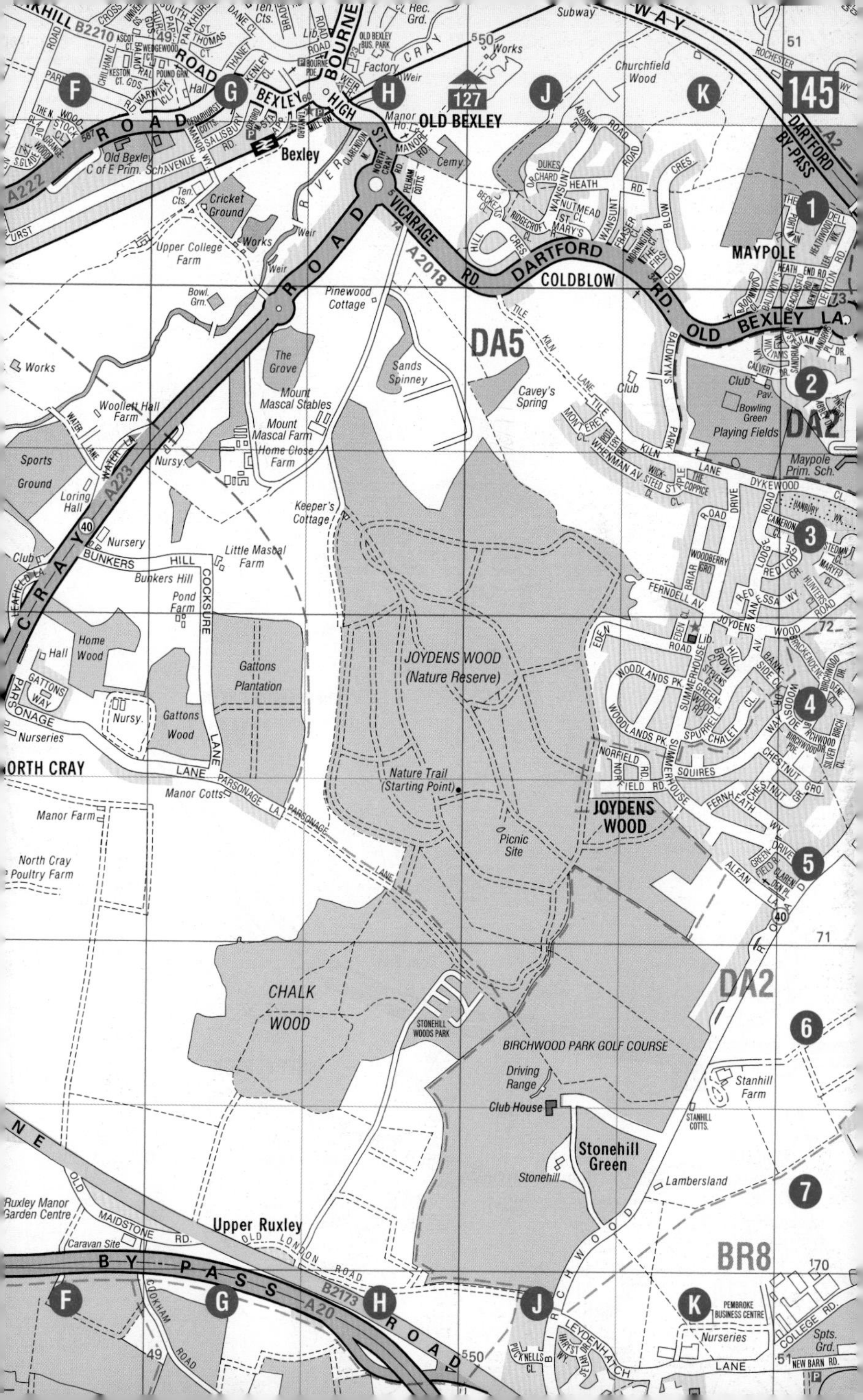

145
127
OLD BEXLEY
Bexley
Old Bexley C of E Prim. Sch.
BEXLEY HIGH ST.
BOURNE ROAD
Cricket Ground
Works
Weir
Upper College Farm
Churchfield Wood
Factory
Manor Ho.
Cemy.
VICARAGE RD.
DARTFORD RD.
COLDBLOW
OLD BEXLEY LA.
DARTFORD BY-PASS
A2
A2018
A222
A223
MAYPOLE
Maypole Prim. Sch.
DA5
DA2
BR8
Bowl. Grn.
Pinewood Cottage
The Grove
Sands Spinney
Mount Mascal Stables
Mount Mascal Farm
Home Close Farm
Woollett Hall Farm
Sports Ground
Loring Hall
Nursery
Nursy.
Keeper's Cottage
Cavey's Spring
TILE KILN LANE
Club
Bowling Green
Playing Fields
BALDWYN'S PARK
BUNKERS HILL
Bunkers Hill
Little Mascal Farm
Pond Farm
COCKSURE LANE
CRAY ROAD
Home Wood
Hall
Gattons Plantation
Gattons Wood
JOYDENS WOOD (Nature Reserve)
Nature Trail (Starting Point)
Picnic Site
JOYDENS WOOD
PARSONAGE LANE
NORTH CRAY
Nurseries
Manor Cotts.
Manor Farm
North Cray Poultry Farm
CHALK WOOD
STONEHILL WOODS PARK
BIRCHWOOD PARK GOLF COURSE
Driving Range
Club House
Stonehill Green
Stonehill
Stanhill Farm
STANHILL COTTS.
Lambersland
Ruxley Manor Garden Centre
MAIDSTONE RD.
Caravan Site
Upper Ruxley
OLD LONDON ROAD
BY PASS ROAD
A20
B2173
B2210
COOKHAM ROAD
BIRCHWOOD ROAD
LEYDENHATCH LANE
PEMBROKE BUSINESS CENTRE
Nurseries
COLLEGE RD.
Spts. Grd.
NEW BARN RD.
WOODLANDS PK
SUMMERHOUSE DRIVE
JOYDENS WOOD ROAD
FERNDELL AV
DYKEWOOD CL.
Lib.
550
51
71
72
73
170
49

128
A
B
C
D
E
1
2
3
4
5
6
7
06
07
08
70
69
68
67
QUEEN MARY RESERVOIR
Works
ASHFORD RD.
Pumping Station
Round Copse
TW18
TW17
KT16
KT13
LALEHAM STUDIOS
Shepperton Film Studios
LITTLETON
Littleton Fm.
Play. Fld.
The Green
NEW ROAD
ROAD
CHARLTON ROAD
CHARLTON LANE
River Ash
Laleham Nurseries
Nurseries
Squire's Bridge
SHEPPERTON RD.
B376
LALEHAM ROAD
SHEPPERTON GREEN
Rec. Grd.
Staines Road Farm
Nurseries
Saxon Prim. Sch.
Gravel Pit
Pool End
Playing Field
M3 MOTORWAY
M3
SHEPPERTON
Shepperton
HIGH ST.
GREEN
CHERTSEY ROAD
B375
RENFREE WAY
RUSSELL
Halliford Mere Lake
Cemetery
War Close
Cricket Ground
Las Palmas Estate
Lords Bri.
Riversleigh Farm
Mead Farm
DUMSEY EYOT
RIVER THAMES
The Range
DOCKETT EDDY LANE
FERRY LANE
Desborough Sailing Club
DESBOROUGH
Chertsey Meads
DOCKETT MOORINGS
DOCKETT EDDY
Driving Range
SUNBURY GO
CHARLTO
Manor Farm
SPELTHORNE ROAD
QUEEN MARY RD.
30
Offices
MERCIA HO.
SHEPPERTON BUSINESS PK.
STATION RD.
STATION APP.
Prim. Sch.
Lib.
Play. Fld.
Halliford Sch.
Works
ISLA

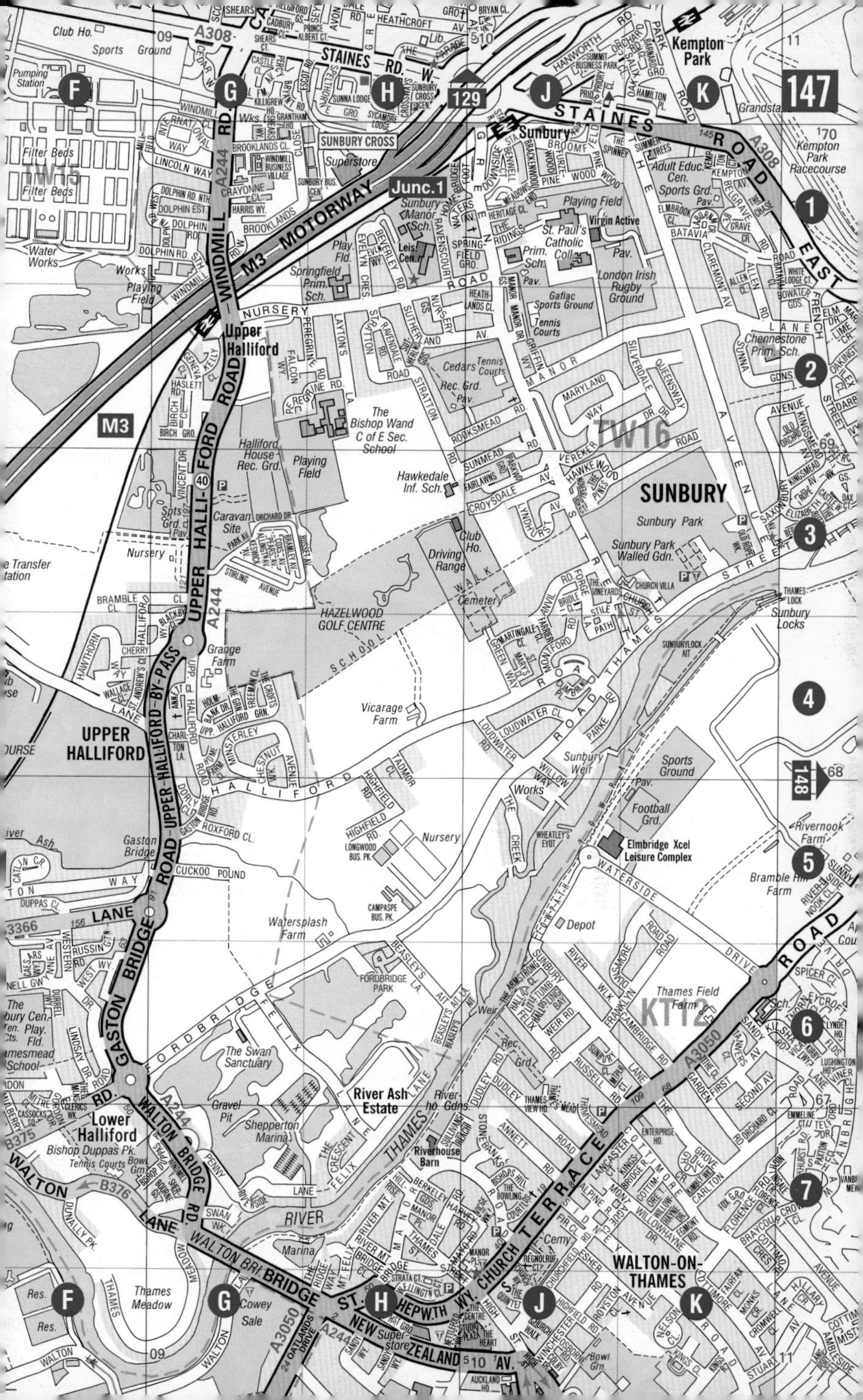

147
129
148
Kempton Park
Kempton Park Racecourse
Sunbury
SUNBURY
Sunbury Cross
Sunbury Park
Sunbury Locks
Upper Halliford
UPPER HALLIFORD
Lower Halliford
WALTON-ON-THAMES
STAINES RD. W.
STAINES ROAD
M3 MOTORWAY
Junc. 1
M3
A308
A244
A3050
B375
B376
WINDMILL RD.
UPPER HALLIFORD ROAD
UPPER HALLIFORD BY-PASS
GASTON BRIDGE ROAD
WALTON BRIDGE RD.
NURSERY ROAD
MANOR LANE
FRENCH STREET
GREEN STREET
THE AVENUE
THAMES STREET
CHURCH STREET
SCHOOL WALK
HALLIFORD ROAD
FORDBRIDGE ROAD
NEW ZEALAND AV.
CHURCH TERRACE
HEPWORTH WY.
BRIDGE ST.
WATERSIDE DRIVE
WALTON LANE
RIVER THAMES
TW15
TW16
KT12
Filter Beds
Water Works
Hazelwood Golf Centre
The Bishop Wand C of E Sec. School
London Irish Rugby Ground
St. Paul's Catholic Coll.
Sunbury Manor Sch.
Springfield Prim. Sch.
Chennestone Prim. Sch.
Hawkedale Inf. Sch.
Sunbury Park Walled Gdn.
Elmbridge Xcel Leisure Complex
Thames Field Farm
River Ash Estate
The Swan Sanctuary
Shepperton Marina
Riverhouse Barn
Thames Meadow
Cowey Sale
Gravel Pit
Vicarage Farm
Watersplash Farm
Sunbury Weir
Cemetery
Sports Ground
Football Grd.
Bishop Duppas Pk.

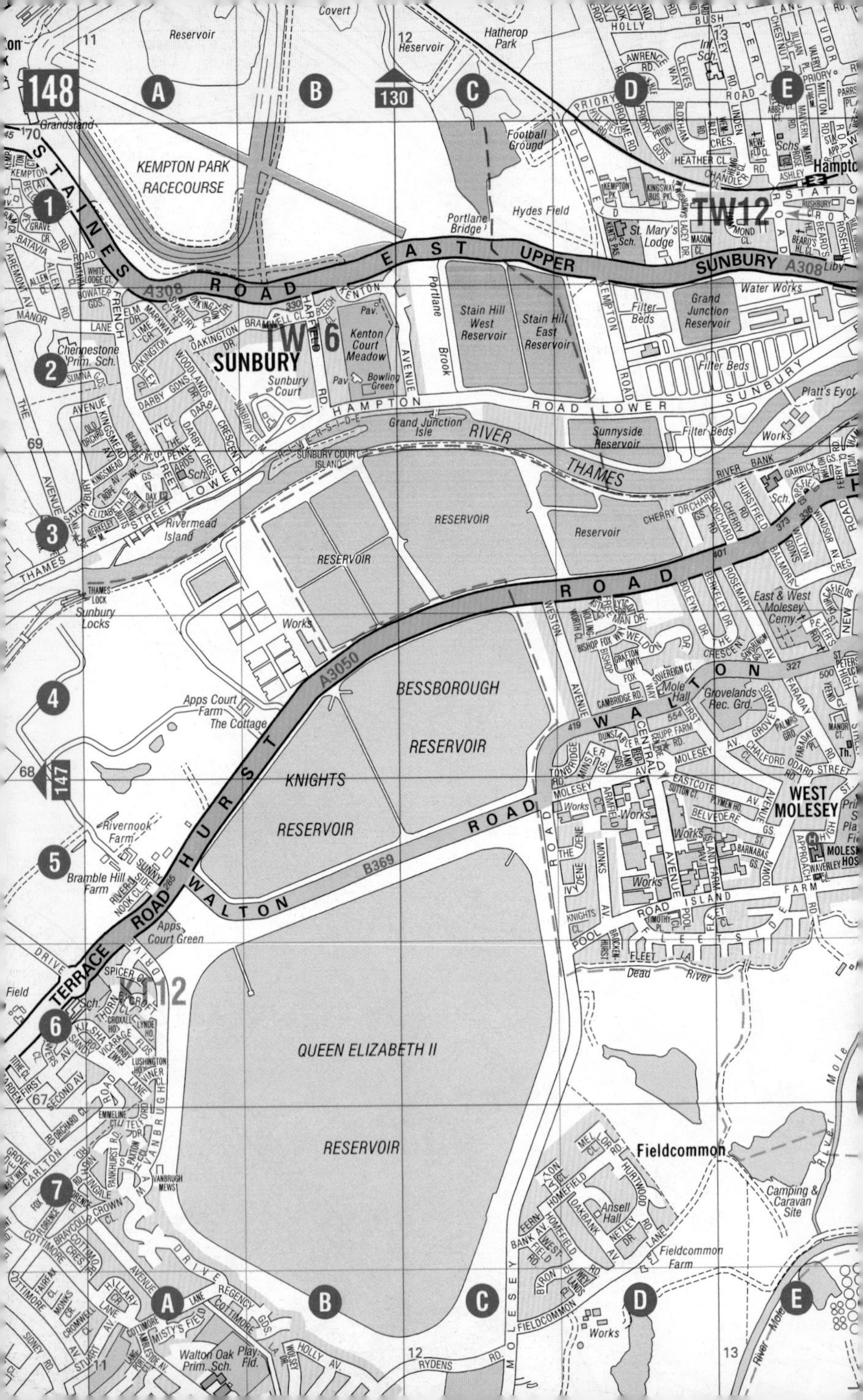
148
130
147
A
B
C
D
E
1
2
3
4
5
6
7
Reservoir
Covert
Hatherop Park
Grandstand
KEMPTON PARK RACECOURSE
Football Ground
Hydes Field
Portlane Bridge
TW12
Hampton
St. Mary's Sch.
St. Mary's Lodge
Inf. Sch.
Schs
EAST UPPER SUNBURY ROAD
A308
STAINES ROAD
Water Works
Grand Junction Reservoir
Filter Beds
Stain Hill West Reservoir
Stain Hill East Reservoir
Portlane Brook
Kenton Court Meadow
Pav.
Bowling Green
TW16
SUNBURY
Sunbury Court
Chennestone Prim. Sch.
HAMPTON ROAD
LOWER SUNBURY ROAD
Platt's Eyot
Grand Junction Isle
RIVER THAMES
Sunnyside Reservoir
Works
SUNBURY COURT ISLAND
RIVERSIDE
LOWER THAMES STREET
Rivermead Island
Thames Lock
Sunbury Locks
RESERVOIR
Reservoir
WALTON ROAD
A3050
East & West Molesey Cemy.
BESSBOROUGH RESERVOIR
KNIGHTS RESERVOIR
Apps Court Farm
The Cottage
Rivernook Farm
Bramble Hill Farm
HURST ROAD
TERRACE ROAD
Apps Court Green
WALTON ROAD
B369
Mole Hall
Grovelands Rec. Grd.
WEST MOLESEY
ISLAND FARM ROAD
FLEETSIDE
Dead River
KT12
Field
QUEEN ELIZABETH II RESERVOIR
Fieldcommon
Ansell Hall
Fieldcommon Farm
Camping & Caravan Site
River Mole
MOLESEY ROAD
FIELDCOMMON LANE
Walton Oak Prim. Sch.
Play. Fld.
RYDENS RD.
HOLLY AV.
COTTIMORE LANE
11
12
13
67
68
69
70

149
131
150
HAMPTON
Hampton & Richmond Borough FC
Hampton Open Air Pool
BUSHY PARK
TW11
Willow Plantation
Round Plantation
Bushy House
Bowling Green
Sports Ground
Teddington Lodge
Broom Clumps
River Lodge
Lodge
Waterhouse Woodland Garden
Waterhouse Pond
Fisher's Pond
White Lodge
Red Brick Bridge
Deer Pen
Diana Fountain
Heron Pond
CHESTNUT AVENUE
COBBLERS WALK
HIGH STREET
CHURCH ST.
THAMES ST.
HAMPTON COURT ROAD
A308
A311
A3050
A309
B369
B3379
B364
A307
Filter Beds
Foot Ferry
Garrick's Ait
Garrick's Lawn
St. Alban's Lodge
Hurst Park Open Space
HURST PARK
Hurst Park
Terrace Gardens
Taggs Island
Cricket Ground
Ash Island
Hampton Court House
Hampton Court Gate
Hampton Court Green
ROYAL MEWS
HAMPTON COURT
Maze
Hampton Court Gardens
Hampton Court Palace
Privy Garden
North Canal
South Canal
Cigarette Island Park
Hampton Court
EAST MOLESEY
Hurst Pool
Molesey Hurst Rec. Grd.
The Pav. Sports & Fitness Club
Vine Hall
Play. Fld.
School
Lib.
Molesey FC Grd.
KT8
Prim. Sch.
Ditton Field
Albany Reach
Pavilion Terrace
THAMES DITTON
Thames Ditton Island
Sports Ground
Rec. Grd.
Grist Memorial Sports Ground
Tennis Courts
Tanners Bridge
Nielson Playing Field
Sports Ground
Molesey Pony Farm
ISLAND BARN RESERVOIR
Imber Court Trading Estate
Imber Court
Football Grd.
Recreation Grd.
RIVER EMBER
KT10
KT7
Esher College
Playing Field
Thames Ditton
Thames Ditton Jun. Sch.
Giggshill
Giggs Hill Grn.
WESTON GREEN
Weston Green
Cranmere Primary School
Water Pollution Control Works
Golf Course
ESHER LANE
EMBER LANE
EMBER COURT RD.
STATION RD.
HAMPTON COURT WAY
BRIDGE ROAD
MOLESEY ROAD
WALTON ROAD
THE DRIVE

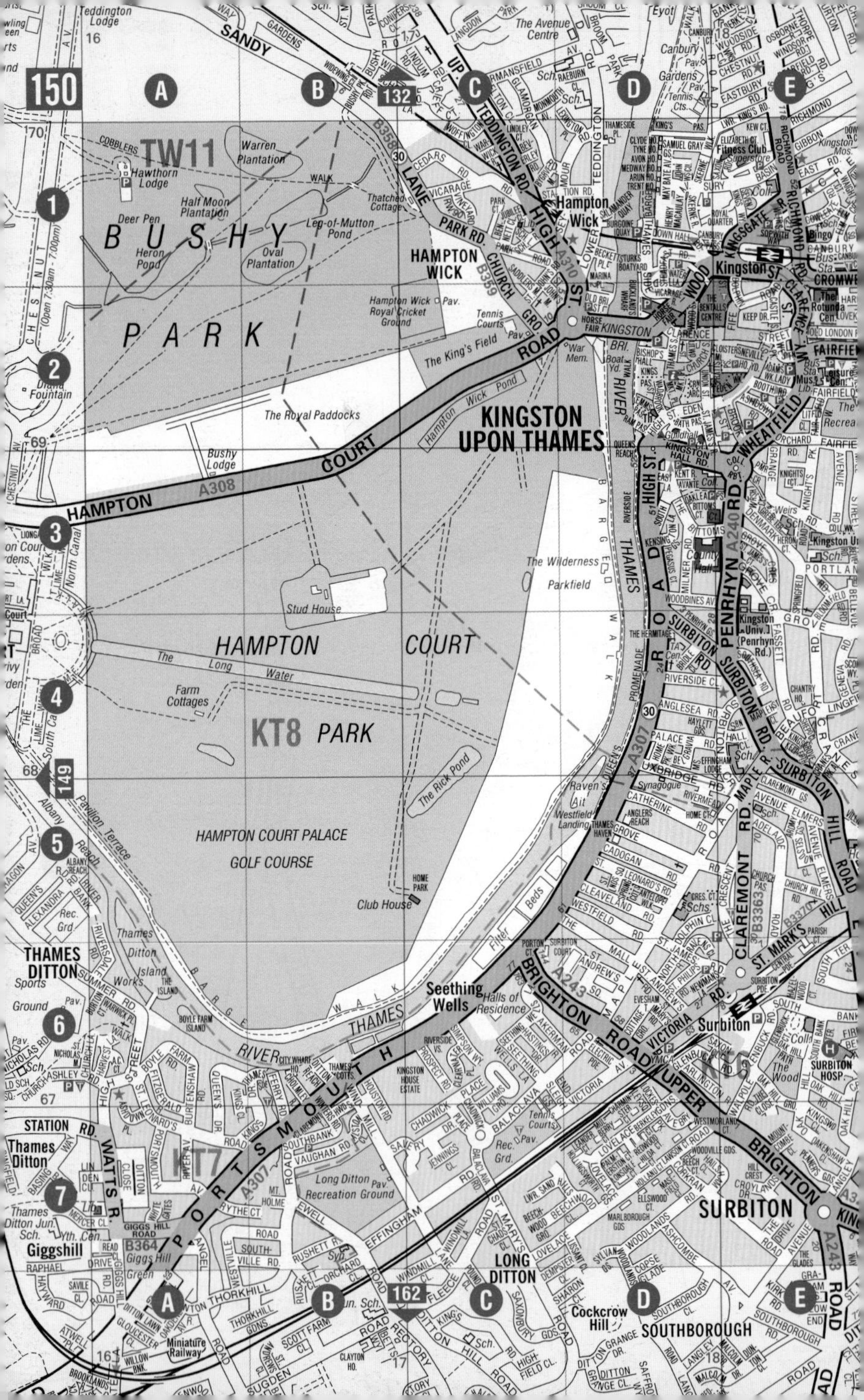
TW11
BUSHY PARK
Teddington Lodge
Hawthorn Lodge
Warren Plantation
Half Moon Plantation
Deer Pen
Heron Pond
Oval Plantation
Leg-of-Mutton Pond
Thatched Cottage
Diana Fountain
CHESTNUT AV.
(Open 7:30am - 7:00pm)
HAMPTON WICK
Hampton Wick
Hampton Wick Royal Cricket Ground
The King's Field
The Royal Paddocks
Hampton Wick Pond
Bushy Lodge
HAMPTON COURT ROAD
A308
KINGSTON UPON THAMES
Kingston
TEDDINGTON RD.
HIGH ST.
A310
B358
B359
SANDY LANE
PARK RD.
CHURCH GRO.
KINGSTON BRI.
Stud House
HAMPTON COURT
The Long Water
Farm Cottages
KT8
PARK
The Rick Pond
HAMPTON COURT PALACE GOLF COURSE
Club House
HOME PARK
The Wilderness
Parkfield
THAMES
BARGE WALK
RIVER THAMES
Raven's Ait
Westfield Landing
QUEEN'S PROMENADE
PORTSMOUTH ROAD
A307
Seething Wells
Halls of Residence
Filter Beds
Thames Ditton Island
Boyle Farm Island
Pavilion Terrace
Albany Reach
North Canal
THAMES DITTON
Thames Ditton
Sports Ground
STATION RD.
WATTS R.
HIGH STREET
KT7
Giggshill
Giggs Hill Green
B364
Miniature Railway
Long Ditton Recreation Ground
LONG DITTON
Cockcrow Hill
SOUTHBOROUGH
SURBITON
Surbiton
BRIGHTON ROAD
A243
VICTORIA RD.
UPPER BRIGHTON ROAD
CLAREMONT RD.
B3363
ST. MARK'S HILL
B3370
SURBITON HILL ROAD
SURBITON RD.
PENRHYN RD.
A240
County Hall
Kingston Univ. (Penrhyn Rd.)
SURBITON HOSP.
WOOD ST.
KINGSGATE RD.
RICHMOND ROAD
CLARENCE ST.
The Bentalls Centre
The Rotunda Cen.
Fitness Club
Canbury Gardens
The Avenue Centre
Kingston Hall Rd.
Guildhall
The Wood
Rec. Grd.
Tennis Courts
Synagogue
A
B
C
D
E
1
2
3
4
5
6
7
132
149
162
16
17
18
69
68
67
70
163

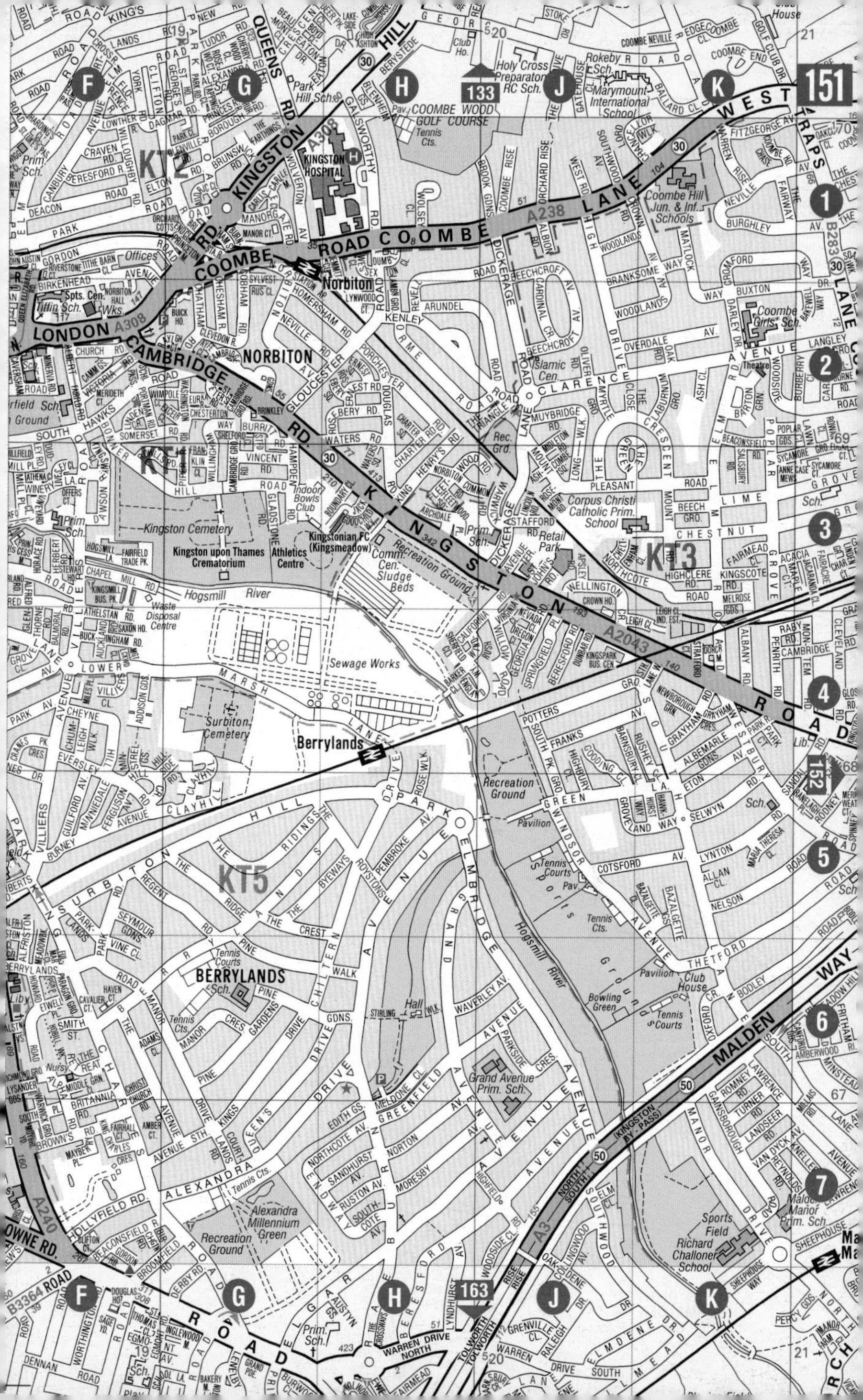

151
152
133
163
F
G
H
J
K
1
2
3
4
5
6
7
KT2
KT1
KT3
KT5
KINGSTON HOSPITAL
Norbiton
NORBITON
COOMBE WOOD GOLF COURSE
Holy Cross Preparatory RC Sch.
Marymount International School
Coombe Hill Jun. & Inf. Schools
Coombe Girls' Sch.
Kingston Cemetery
Kingston upon Thames Crematorium
Athletics Centre
Kingstonian FC (Kingsmeadow)
Recreation Ground
Sludge Beds
Hogsmill River
Waste Disposal Centre
Sewage Works
Surbiton Cemetery
Berrylands
BERRYLANDS
Corpus Christi Catholic Prim. School
Retail Park
Islamic Cen.
Grand Avenue Prim. Sch.
Alexandra Millennium Green
Richard Challoner School
Malden Manor Prim. Sch.
Sports Field
Bowling Green
KINGSTON HILL
QUEENS RD.
COOMBE LANE WEST
COOMBE ROAD
LONDON ROAD
CAMBRIDGE RD.
KINGSTON ROAD
MALDEN WAY
KINGSTON BY-PASS
EWELL ROAD
A308
A238
A2043
A3
A240
B3364
B283

152
134
151
164
A
B
C
D
E
1
2
3
4
5
6
7
COOMBE LA. WEST
COOMBE LANE
COOMBE FLYOVER
NEW VICTORIA HOSPITAL
KT2
COPSE HILL
The Wolfson Rehabilitation Cen.
The Rowans Sch.
Play. Fld.
Sports Grd.
Tennis Courts
Playing Field
St. Matthew's C of E Prim. Sch.
COTTENHAM PARK
COTTENHAM PARK ROAD
Cottenham Park
Holland Gdns.
DURHAM ROAD
B281
COOMBE
A238
CAMBRIDGE
RICHMOND
PARKFIELDS
WORPLE RD.
Raynes Park
Wimbledon College Playing Fields
Tennis Courts Sports Ground
Civil Service Sports Ground
Raynes Park Sports Ground
Tennis Courts
Bowling Green
BEVERLEY
A3
(KINGSTON BY-PASS)
50
MALDEN
GOLF
COURSE
Coombe Brook
Beverley Brook
Club House
Sports Ground
Club Ho.
Coombe Girls' Sch.
COOMBE LANE
B283
TRAPS
THE FAIRWAY
BURGHLEY
CROMFORD
BUXTON
LANGLEY
THE MOAT
THE CHESTERS
AVENUE
ALRIC
GROVE
CHESTNUT
LIME
Sch.
New Malden
DUKES
HOWARD
MALDEN HILL
THE MOUNT
BEVERLEY PARK
Golf Driving Range
Emanuel School Playing Field
Blagdon House
Tennis Courts
Sports Ground
RAINBOW IND. EST.
Superstore
Wks.
Sports Cen.
Raynes Pk. High Sch.
Superstore
BUSHEY
WEST BARNES ROAD
B282
A298
Alliance Sports Ground
Tennis Courts
RECTORY CL.
CHURCH WLK.
GRAND DRIVE
PRINCE GE... PLAYING
Football Grd.
RAYNES PARK
Spts. Grd.
B279
HEATH
GREENWAY
CROSSWAY
ELM CL.
NEW MALDEN
Comm. Cen.
The Malden Cen.
The Crescent
B282
BURLINGTON
SHANNON CORNER
SHANNON CNR. RETAIL PK.
Superstore
KINGSTON RD.
HIGH ST.
MALDEN RD.
A2043
FOUNTAIN ROUNDABOUT
Lib.
Sch.
KT3
WEST BARNES
Motspur Pk.
Pavilion
Sports Ground
St. John Fisher RC Prim. Sch.
Coombe Boys Sch.
MALDEN JUNC.
BY-PASS
MALDEN (KINGSTON
Study Sch.
University of London Athletic Ground
Running Track
WEST BARNES LA.
Sports Ground
Tennis Cts.
Old Blues Rugby Football Grd.
Club
Nursery
North East Surrey Crematorium
Bowling Green
Putting Green
The Sir Joseph Hood Memorial Playing Fields
MORDEN CEMETERY
BBC Sports Ground
MOTSPUR PARK
Gas Works
Beverley Brook
Playing Fields
Merton & Sutton Joint Cemetery
Green Lane Prim. Sch.
Refuse Destructor
Mayflower Park
KT4
ASM Ten. Cen.
MANOR PARK
Hall
Bowling Green
MALDEN
MOTSPUR
BRAMSHAW RISE
AMBERWOOD
MINSTEAD WY.
Malden Manor Prim. Sch.
Malden Manor
OLD MALDEN
B284
CHURCH
Malden Green
Worcester Park
Sports Grd.
Tennis Courts
MALDEN ROAD

153
135
154
165
F
G
H
J
K
1
2
3
4
5
6
7
SW20
SW19
MERTON
MERTON PARK
MORDEN
MORDEN PARK
BUSHEY MEAD
ROSEHILL
Wimbledon Chase
South Merton
Merton Park
Morden
Morden South
St. Helier
Morden Rd.
Sth. Wimbledon
MERTON HIGH ST.
KINGSTON ROAD
A238
MORDEN ROAD
A24
DORSET ROAD
B285
MARTIN WAY
B286
LONDON ROAD
CENTRAL ROAD
A239
EPSOM ROAD
STONECOT HILL
SUTTON COMMON ROAD
B279
TUDOR DRIVE
LOWER MORDEN LANE
GREEN LANE
B278
HILL CROSS
MORDEN HALL RD.
A297
ST. HELIER AVENUE
ROSE HILL
B2230
REIGATE AV.
A217
WORPLE ROAD
B235
CANNON HILL LANE
CANNON HILL COMMON
(Recreation Ground)
Cannon Hill
Messines Playing Field
Joseph Hood Recreation Ground
Raynes Park Playing Fields
David Lloyd Leisure & Lloyds Lanes Raynes Park
Nelson Hosp.
John Innes Park
Rutlish Sch.
Mostyn Gardens
Poplar Prim. Sch.
Morden Park School Sports Centre
School Playing Fields
Merton College
Morden Park Pool
Morden Hall
River Wandle
Recreation Ground
Risley Sports Ground
King George's Field
Aragon Prim. Sch.
Hatfield Prim. Sch.
THE WOODSTOCK
ROSE HILL ROUNDABOUT
Glenthorne High Sch.
Rosehill Recreation Ground
Civic Cen.
Depot
Mosque
Scout Hall
Cherry Wood

MERTON
MITCHAM
ST. HELIER
ROSEHILL
BEDDINGTON CORNER
SW19
SM4
SM5
CR4
MERANTUN WAY
WESTERN ROAD
LONDON ROAD
STREATHAM ROAD
MORDEN ROAD
MORDEN HALL ROAD
ST. HELIER AVENUE
BISHOPSFORD ROAD
CARSHALTON ROAD
CRICKET GRN.
CRANMER RD.
COMMONSIDE WEST
COMMONSIDE EAST
CENTRAL ROAD
REIGATE AV.
A24
A217
A236
A239
A297
A237
A216
B278
B2230
MORDEN HALL PARK
Morden Hall
Morden Cottage
Morden Lodge
Phipps Bridge
Belgrave Wlk.
Ravensbury Park
River Wandle
Lavender Park
Deen City Farm
Superstore
Colour Ho. Th.
Tandem Centre
Mitcham
Mitcham Junction
Beehive Bridge
Blue Houses Bridge
Cranmer Bri.
Willow Lane Bri.
The Canons Leisure Centre & Lib.
Running Track
Sports Ground
Cricket Green
Watermeads
Tooting & Mitcham United FC (Imperial Fields)
Poulter Park
Bennett's Hole
Bishopsford House
Bishopsford Comm. Sch.
Moreton Green
Open Space
Playing Fields
Playing Field
Nature Reserves
Mill Green
Sutton Arena Leisure Centre
St. Helier Open Space
St. Helier Hospital
Greenshaw Wood
ROSE HILL ROUNDABOUT
GOLF C
Club House
Cemetery
Tamworth Rec. Grd.
FIGGE'S MARSH
MITCHAM INDUSTRIAL ESTATE
136
153
166
A B C D E
1 2 3 4 5 6 7

STREATHAM VALE
Streatham Vale Park
Lonesome
Beecholme Prim. Sch.
Lonesome Prim. Sch.
St Mark's C of E Academy
South London Crematorium
Streatham Park Cemetery
Jewish Cemetery
Sports Ground
Playing Field
School Playing Fields
Sports Ground
Powerleague Soccer Centre
Stanford Prim. Sch.
SW16
NORBURY
Norbury
NORBURY PARK
Hermitage Bridge
Norbury Hall Sports Grd.
Cannons Health Club
Harris Academy Merton
William Morris Primary Sch.
Garden Prim. Sch.
Donnelly Green
Sherwood Park Sch.
MITCHAM COMMON
Mitcham Common
Playing Fields
CR7
Gonville Prim. Sch.
Croydon Athletic FC Grd.
Croydon Crematorium
CROYDON CEMETERY
The Archbishop Lanfranc Sch.
CR0
Beddington Lane
Traq Motor Racing
Hundred Acre Bridge
Irrigation Bridge
Therapia Lane
Ikea Ampere Way
LOMBARD ROUNDABOUT
Bus Depot
PIONEERS INDUSTRIAL PARK
BEDDINGTON TRADING ESTATE
Beddington Sewage Treatment Works
Superstores
LONDON ROAD
MITCHAM ROAD
BEDDINGTON LANE
WINDMILL RD.
ROWAN RD.
MANOR RD.
THORNTON ROAD
PURLEY WAY
A23
A236
B272
B273
137
156
167
F
G
H
J
K
1
2
3
4
5
6
7

156
A
B
C
D
E
1
2
3
4
5
6
7
138
155
168
NORBURY
NORBURY PARK
Norbury Manor Business & Enterprise Coll. for Girls
Kensington Avenue Prim. School
UPPER NORWOOD
The Lawns
David Livingstone Prim. Sch.
BEAULAH
Westwood Language Coll. for Girls
Downsview Prim. Sch.
Biggin Wood
Norbury Hall
Sports Grd.
Cannons Health Club
SW16
Sports Ground
Comm. Cen.
RC Prim. Sch.
PARCHMORE
Rec. Ground
Thornton Heath
THORNTON HEATH
Spurgeon's College
Grangewood Park
Coun. Offs.
Cypress Inf. Sch.
Beaulieu Heights
Crystal Palace FC (Selhurst Park)
WHITEHORSE
CR7
Ecclesbourne Jun. & Inf. Schs.
Queen's Rd. Cemy.
MAYDAY UNIVERSITY HOSP.
THORNTON HEATH POND
Gala Bingo
BRIGSTOCK
Selhurst
SELHURST
St. Chad's Cat. Prim. Sch.
Heavers Farm Centre
Norbury Brook
Works
Lupin Bri.
Gloucester Rd Junc.
Cottage Bri.
Cottage Junc.
BROAD GREEN
Canterbury Rec. Grd.
MITCHAM
PURLEY
WINDMILL
ST. JAMES'S
NORTHCOTE
West Croydon
CROYDON
ADDISCOMBE
LOWER
Comm. Cen.
High Sch.
Super store
Gym
Bus Sta.
A23
A212
A213
A215
A222
A235
A236
B266
B273

157
139
158
169
Anerley
ANERLEY
PENGE
SOUTH NORWOOD
WOODSIDE
Birkbeck
Elmers End
ELMERS END
Kent House
Avenue Road
Harrington Rd.
Norwood Junc.
Bromley Junction
Woodside
Blackhorse La.
Addiscombe
Shirley Oaks
SOUTH NORWOOD COUNTRY PARK
SE19
SE20
SE25
BR3
CR0
Harris City Technology Coll.
Orchard Lodge (Remand Centre)
James Dixon Prim. Sch.
Orchard School Sports Centre
South Norwood Lake
Athletic Grounds
Betts Park
Beckenham Crematorium
Croydon Sports Arena
Croydon FC Grd.
Ryelands Prim. Sch.
Croydon Golf Driving Range
South Norwood Country Park Visitors Cen.
Pitch & Putt Course
Ashburton Playing Fields
Ashburton Learning Village & Comm. Sch.
SHIRLEY OAKS BMI HOSPITAL
Monks Orchard Prim. Sch.
Recreation Ground
A214
A213
A215
A222
A234
B243
CROYDON RD.
ANERLEY ROAD
ELMERS END ROAD
PORTLAND RD.
HIGH ST.
PENGE RD.
LONG LANE
SPRING LANE
WOODSIDE GREEN
ADDISCOMBE ROAD
SHIRLEY ROAD
LWR. ADDISCOMBE RD.
BECKENHAM RD.
HIGH ST.

158
140
157
170
A
B
C
D
E
1
2
3
4
5
6
7
36
37
38
CATOR PARK
Kent House
Beckenham Road
Beckenham Junc.
Clock Ho.
BECKENHAM
BR3
CR0
ELMERS END
EDEN PARK
PARK LANGLEY
UPPER ELMERS END
MONKS ORCHARD
LANGLEY
WEST WICKHAM
West Wickham
Eden Park
BECKENHAM HOSPITAL
Recreation Ground
Kelsey Park
Elgood Playing Field
Kelsey Park Sports College
Crease Park
Langley Court (Research Labs)
Langley Park Schools
Sports Centre
LANGLEY PARK GOLF COURSE
The Rookery
Crouch Oak Wood
Cold Shaw
High Broom Wood
THE BETHLEM ROYAL HOSPITAL
Edenham High Sch.
Amida Leisure Cen.
Unicorn Prim. Sch.
Oak Lodge Prim. Sch.
Blake Recreation Ground
Parkfields Recreation Ground
Nurses' Home
Caravan Park
Glade Wood
West Wickham Leisure Ce
BECKENHAM ROAD
HIGH STREET
HIGH ROAD
CROYDON ROAD
UPPER ELMERS END ROAD
ELMERS END ROAD
SOUTH EDEN PARK RD.
BECKENHAM RD.
LINKS WAY
PARK LANGLEY
HAYES ROAD
BROMLEY ROAD
MANOR RD.
SOUTHEND ROAD
RECTORY ROAD
WICKHAM ROAD
A234
A2015
A222
A214
B230
A214

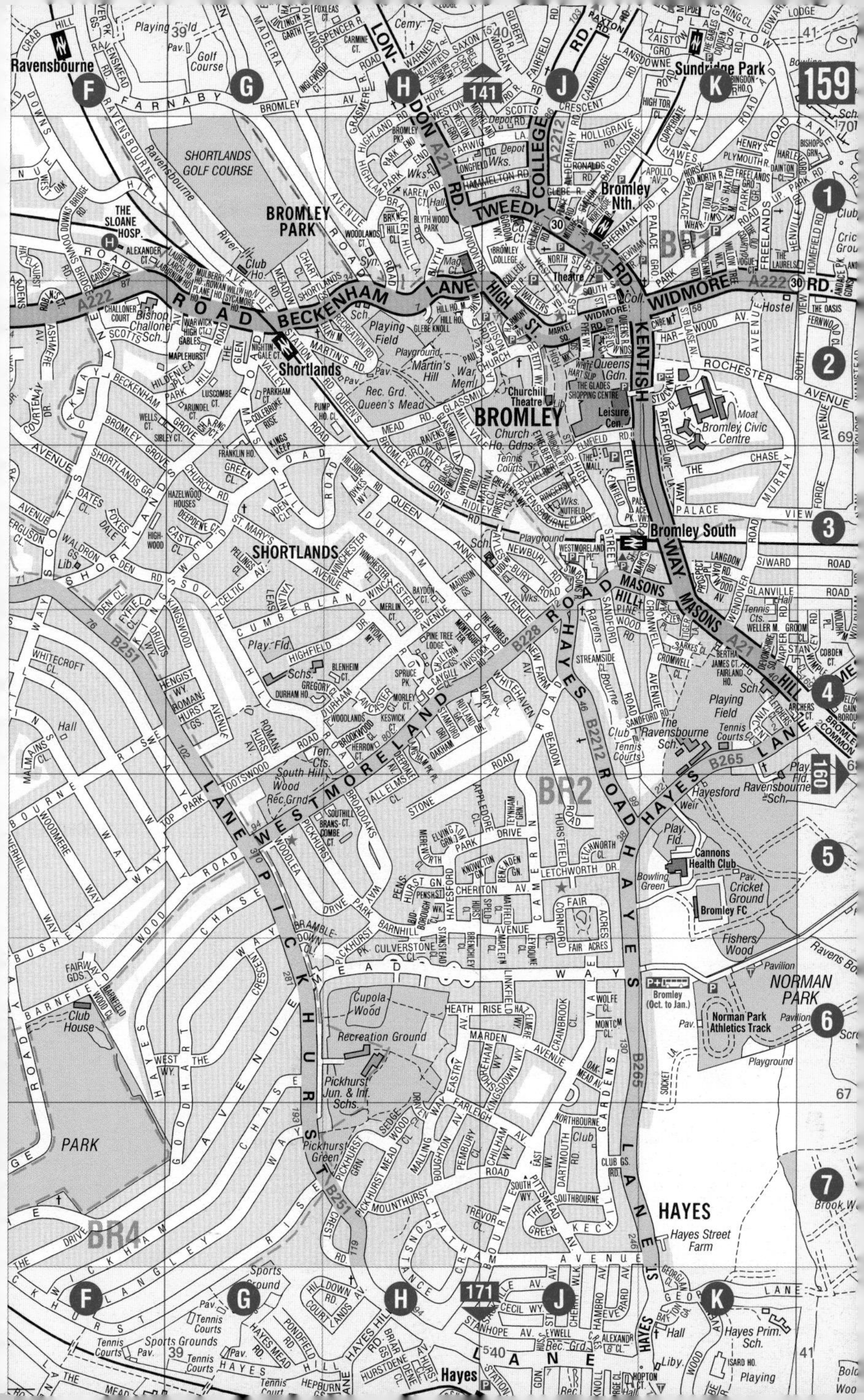
159
141
171
160
Ravensbourne
Sundridge Park
Bromley Nth.
Shortlands
Bromley South
Hayes
SHORTLANDS GOLF COURSE
BROMLEY PARK
THE SLOANE HOSP.
Bishop Challoner Sch.
BROMLEY
SHORTLANDS
HAYES
NORMAN PARK
Norman Park Athletics Track
Cannons Health Club
Bromley FC
Bromley Civic Centre
Churchill Theatre
Queens Gdn.
THE GLADES SHOPPING CENTRE
Leisure Cen.
Martin's Hill
Rec. Grd. Queen's Mead
South Hill Wood
Cupola Wood
Recreation Ground
Pickhurst Jun. & Inf. Schs.
Pickhurst Green
Hayes Street Farm
Hayes Prim. Sch.
The Ravensbourne Sch.
Fishers Wood
Sports Grounds
Club House
PARK
BR1
BR2
BR4
A21
A222
A2212
B228
B2212
B265
B251
WIDMORE RD.
BECKENHAM LANE
TWEEDY RD.
KENTISH WAY
MASONS HILL
WESTMORELAND ROAD
HAYES ROAD
HAYES LANE
PICKHURST LANE
WEST WICKHAM
BARNFIELD
F
G
H
J
K
1
2
3
4
5
6
7

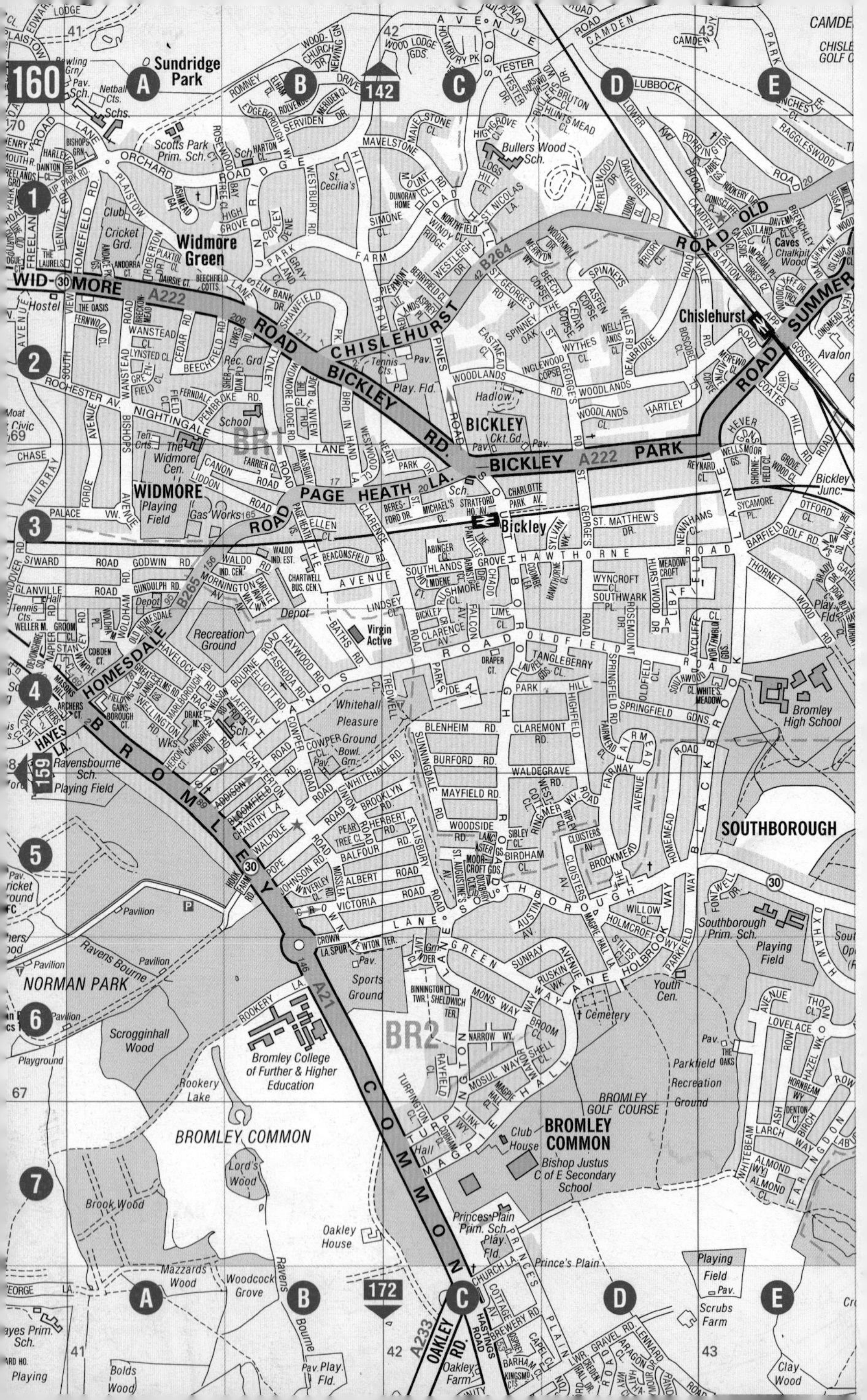
Sundridge Park
Widmore Green
WIDMORE
BICKLEY
Chislehurst
SOUTHBOROUGH
BROMLEY COMMON
NORMAN PARK
BR1
BR2
A
B
C
D
E
1
2
3
4
5
6
7
41
42
43
170
67
142
172
159
30
A222
A21
A233
B264
B265
WIDMORE ROAD
CHISLEHURST ROAD
BICKLEY RD.
BICKLEY PARK
OLD ROAD
SUMMER HILL
PAGE HEATH LA.
HOMESDALE ROAD
BROMLEY COMMON
HAYES LA.
OAKLEY RD.
HASTINGS ROAD
PLAISTOW LANE
SUNDRIDGE AVENUE
FARM LANE
LOGS HILL
CAMDEN PARK ROAD
LUBBOCK ROAD
SOUTHBOROUGH LANE
BLACKBROOK LANE
OLDFIELD ROAD
HAWTHORNE ROAD
SOUTHBOROUGH ROAD
TURPINGTON LANE
MAGPIE HALL LANE
CROWN LANE
PRINCES PLAIN
Scotts Park Prim. Sch.
Bullers Wood Sch.
St. Cecilia's
Tennis Cts.
Play. Fld.
Rec. Grd.
School
The Widmore Cen.
Playing Field
Gas Works
Recreation Ground
Virgin Active
Whitehall Pleasure Ground
Bowl. Grn.
Ravensbourne Sch. Playing Field
Bromley High School
Southborough Prim. Sch.
Playing Field
Youth Cen.
Cemetery
Sports Ground
Bromley College of Further & Higher Education
Scrogginhall Wood
Rookery Lake
Lord's Wood
Brook Wood
Mazzards Wood
Woodcock Grove
Oakley House
Princes Plain Prim. Sch.
Prince's Plain
Club House
Bishop Justus C of E Secondary School
BROMLEY GOLF COURSE
Parkfield Recreation Ground
Scrubs Farm
Clay Wood
Oakley Farm
Bolds Wood
Hayes Prim. Sch.
Chalkpit Wood
Caves
Avalon
Bickley Junc.
Hadlow
Ckt. Gd.
Cricket Grd.
Hostel
Depot
Pavilion
Ravens Bourne
Playground

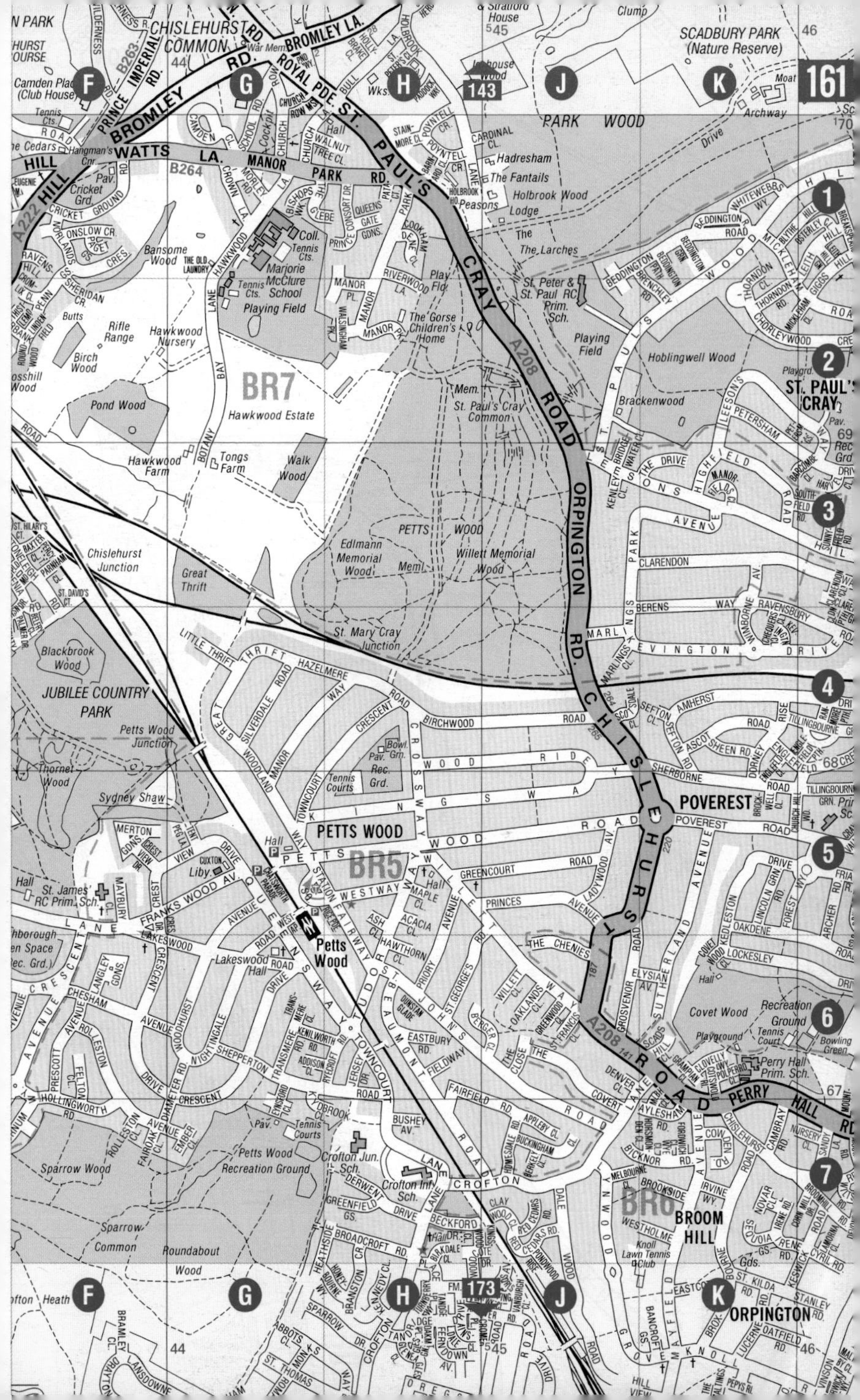
CHISLEHURST COMMON
SCADBURY PARK
(Nature Reserve)
Moat
Archway
PARK WOOD
Drive
Camden Place
(Club House)
BROMLEY RD.
BROMLEY LA.
ROYAL PDE.
PRINCE IMPERIAL RD.
B263
WATTS LA.
MANOR PARK RD.
B264
A222
HILL
Hangman's Cnr.
Cricket Grd.
CRICKET GROUND
Bansome Wood
THE OLD LAUNDRY
Coll.
Tennis Cts.
Marjorie McClure School
Playing Field
Rifle Range
Butts
Hawkwood Nursery
Birch Wood
Pond Wood
BR7
Hawkwood Estate
Hawkwood Farm
Tongs Farm
Walk Wood
BOTANY BAY LANE
HAWKWOOD
ST. PAUL'S CRAY ROAD
A208
Hadresham
The Fantails
Holbrook Wood
Peasons
Lodge
The Larches
St. Peter & St. Paul RC Prim. Sch.
Playing Field
The Gorse Children's Home
Mem.
St. Paul's Cray Common
Hoblingwell Wood
Brackenwood
ST. PAUL'S CRAY
Playgrd.
Pav.
Rec Grd
ORPINGTON RD.
PETTS WOOD
Edlmann Memorial Wood
Meml
Willett Memorial Wood
Chislehurst Junction
Great Thrift
St. Mary Cray Junction
Blackbrook Wood
JUBILEE COUNTRY PARK
Petts Wood Junction
Thornet Wood
Sydney Shaw
CHISLEHURST
BIRCHWOOD ROAD
WOOD RIDE
KINGSWAY
PETTS WOOD
BR5
Bowl. Grn.
Pav. Rec. Grd.
Tennis Courts
POVEREST
POVEREST ROAD
SHERBORNE ROAD
CLARENDON
BERENS WAY
RAVENSBURY
KEVINGTON DRIVE
MARLINGS
Hall
Liby.
St. James' RC Prim. Sch.
Petts Wood
Lakeswood Hall
FRANKS WOOD AV.
QUEENSWAY
TUDOR WAY
TOWNCOURT
ST. JOHN'S RD.
CHESHAM AVENUE
CRESCENT
NIGHTINGALE
SHEPPERTON
DRIVE
HOLLINGWORTH
Sparrow Wood
Petts Wood Recreation Ground
Tennis Courts
Crofton Jun. Sch.
Crofton Inf. Sch.
CROFTON LANE
Sparrow Common
Roundabout Wood
Covet Wood
Recreation Ground
Playground
Tennis Court
Bowling Green
Perry Hall Prim. Sch.
PERRY HALL RD.
A208
BR6
BROOM HILL
Knoll Lawn Tennis Club
ORPINGTON
143
173
F
G
H
J
K
1
2
3
4
5
6
7
44
45
46
67
68
69
70

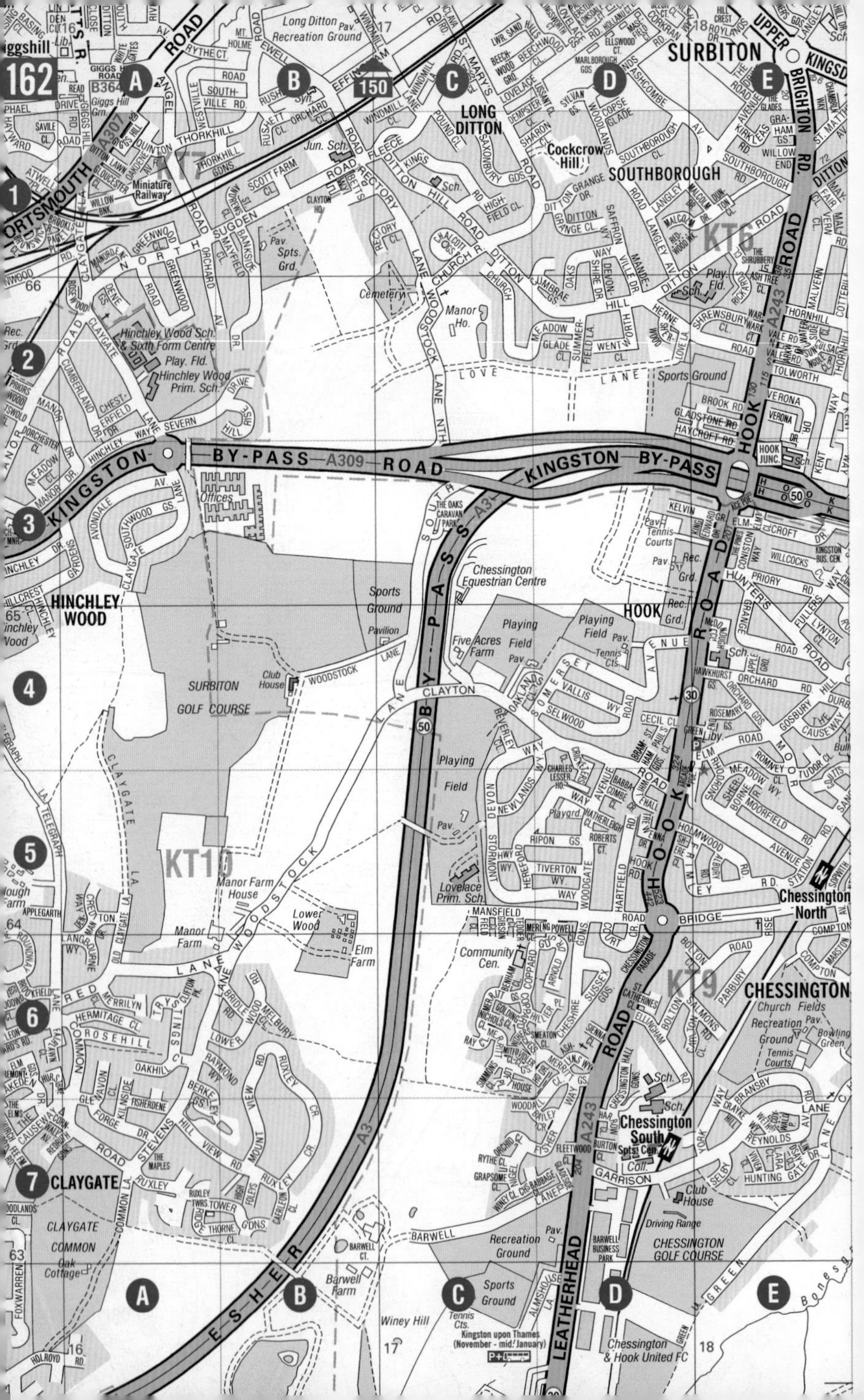

162
150
SURBITON
LONG DITTON
Long Ditton Recreation Ground
Cockcrow Hill
SOUTHBOROUGH
KT6
KT7
Giggs Hill Grn.
Miniature Railway
PORTSMOUTH ROAD
A307
B364
Hinchley Wood Sch. & Sixth Form Centre
Hinchley Wood Prim. Sch.
Play. Fld.
Pav. Spts. Grd.
Cemetery
Manor Ho.
Sports Ground
KINGSTON BY-PASS
A309
ROAD
A3
Offices
HINCHLEY WOOD
The Oaks Caravan Park
Chessington Equestrian Centre
Sports Ground
Pavilion
SURBITON GOLF COURSE
Club House
Five Acres Farm
Playing Field
HOOK
HOOK ROAD
A243
Hook Junc.
Kingston Bus. Cen.
Playing Field
Lovelace Prim. Sch.
KT10
Manor Farm House
Manor Farm
Lower Wood
Elm Farm
Community Cen.
KT9
Chessington North
CHESSINGTON
Church Fields Recreation Ground
Bowling Green
Tennis Courts
Chessington South
Spts. Cen.
Coll.
Club House
Driving Range
CHESSINGTON GOLF COURSE
CLAYGATE
CLAYGATE COMMON
Oak Cottage
ESHER ROAD
Barwell Farm
Recreation Ground
Sports Ground
Winey Hill
LEATHERHEAD ROAD
Kingston upon Thames (November - mid January)
Chessington & Hook United FC
Barwell Business Park
A
B
C
D
E
1
2
3
4
5
6
7
16
17
18
63
64
65
66

163
151
164
F
G
H
J
K
1
2
3
4
5
6
7
19
20
21
65
64
63
66
ALEXANDRA
Tennis Cts.
Alexandra Millennium Green
Recreation Ground
KING CHARLES ROAD
BEACONSFIELD R.
B3364 ROAD
A240
ROAD
WORTHINGTON RD.
DENNAN ROAD
TOLWORTH
TOLWORTH HOSP.
Sch.
Play. Fld.
RAVENSCAR RD.
PARK ROAD
TANKERTON RD.
HAMILTON
LARGEWOOD
ADYWOOD RD.
SELBOURNE
RAVENSWOOD AVENUE
CRANBORNE
PRINCES AVENUE
WARREN DRIVE NORTH
WARREN DRIVE SOUTH
Prim. Sch.
FAIRMEAD
TOLWORTH BROADWAY
TOLWORTH TWR.
Lib.
Bowl. Alley
A3
KINGSTON ROAD
TOLWORTH JUNCTION
Tolworth
Government Offices
RISE (KINGSTON-BY-PASS)
Tolworth Rec. Cen.
Playing Field
RED LION BUS. PARK
SWALLOW PARK
KT5
KNOLLMEAD
ALPINE AV.
Community Centre
Knollmead Prim. Sch.
Sports Ground
Pav.
Bowl. Grn. Ten. Ct.
Tennis Courts
Sports Ground
Playing Field
Tennis Courts
Nursery
Maori Sports Ground
RIVERHILL MOBILE HOME PARK
KT4
Riverhill
Cricket Ground
Sports Ground
Hogsmill River
MALDEN LANE
CHURCH RD.
Malden Manor
Richard Challoner School
Sports
Linden Br. Schoo
WORCESTER PARK RD.
OLD
B284
A240 ROAD
King George's Field Playing Field
Pav. Bowling Green
Corinthian Casuals FC Club Grd.
King George's Field
HOOK RISE SOUTH IND. PARK
ARGENT CT.
KING GEORGE'S INDUSTRIAL EST.
Works
DAVIS ROAD
LANE
JUBILEE WAY
Tolworth Court Bridge
CHESSINGTON TRADE PK.
CHESSINGTON PARK
Depot
Buckland Inf. Sch.
MOUNT RD.
CHANTRY RD.
Moor Lane Jun. Sch.
Playing Field
MOOR LANE
Hogsmill River
Youth Cen.
Comm. Cen.
Riverview C of E Prim. Sch.
Play. Fld.
Dragons Hlth. Club
Sports Ground
Pav.
RUXLEY LANE
West Ewell Inf. Sch.
Epsom & Ewell High Sch.
Playing Field
Playing Field
Weir
Pack Horse Bri.
Play. Gnd.
King George's Field
The Harriers Cen.
Running Track
KT19
Tennis Cts. Playing Field
Jun. Sch.
WEST EWELL
CHESSINGTON ROAD
B2200
CHESSINGTON RD.
Butcher's Grove
Castle Hill
HORTON COUNTRY PARK
HORTON PARK COUNTRY CLUB (PUBLIC) GOLF COURSE
Club Ho.
Driving Range
Hook Road Arena
Gt. Wood
St. Ebba's Farm Cottage
Cemetery
HOOK ROAD
B284
HORTON LANE
Playing Field
ST. EBBA'S
ROAD
Rec. Grd.

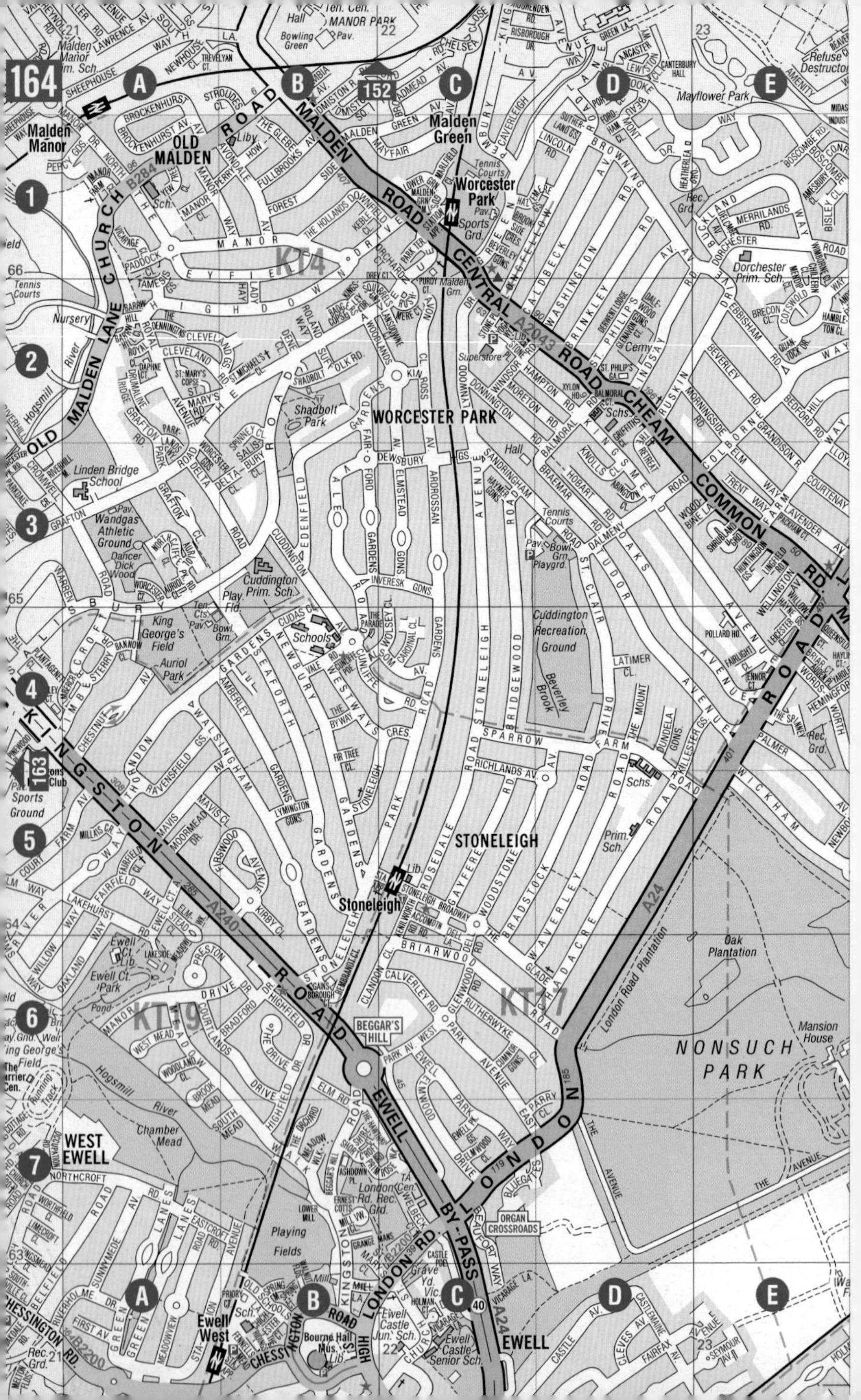

152
163
A
B
C
D
E
1
2
3
4
5
6
7
21
22
23
66
65
64
63
Malden Manor
OLD MALDEN
Malden Green
Worcester Park
WORCESTER PARK
KT4
STONELEIGH
Stoneleigh
KT17
KT19
WEST EWELL
Ewell West
EWELL
NONSUCH PARK
Mansion House
Oak Plantation
London Road Plantation
Mayflower Park
Refuse Destructor
MALDEN ROAD
CENTRAL ROAD
CHEAM COMMON RD.
A2043
OLD MALDEN LANE
CHURCH ROAD
B284
KINGSTON ROAD
A240
LONDON ROAD
A24
EWELL BY-PASS
BEGGAR'S HILL
ORGAN CROSSROADS
Hogsmill River
Beverley Brook
Cuddington Recreation Ground
Cuddington Prim. Sch.
King George's Field
Auriol Park
Shadbolt Park
Linden Bridge School
Wandgas Athletic Ground
Dancer Dick Wood
Dorchester Prim. Sch.
Ewell Ct. Park
Chamber Mead
Playing Fields
London Rd. Rec. Grd.
Bourne Hall Mus.
Ewell Castle Jun. Sch.
Ewell Castle Senior Sch.
Tennis Courts
Sports Grd.
Superstore
Cemy.
Schs.
Prim. Sch.
Rec. Grd.
Hall

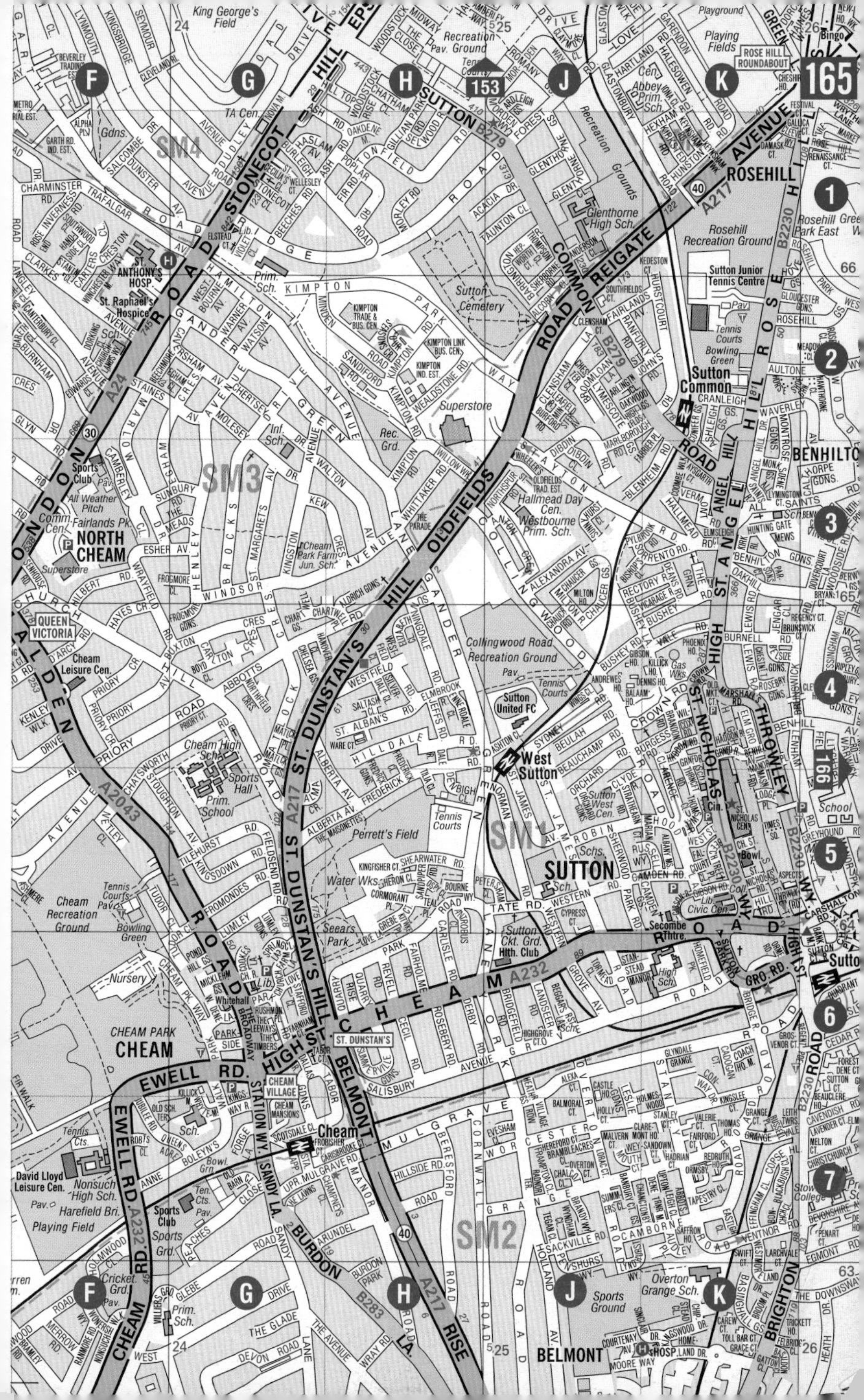
165
153
166
F
G
H
J
K
1
2
3
4
5
6
7
24
25
26
SM4
SM3
SM1
SM2
NORTH CHEAM
CHEAM
SUTTON
BELMONT
ROSEHILL
BENHILTON
CHEAM PARK
STONECOT HILL
LONDON ROAD
A24
MALDEN ROAD
A2043
ST. DUNSTAN'S HILL
A217
OLDFIELDS ROAD
REIGATE AVENUE
SUTTON COMMON ROAD
B279
CHEAM ROAD
A232
HIGH ST.
EWELL RD.
BELMONT RISE
BURDON LA.
B283
BRIGHTON ROAD
B2230
ANGEL HILL
ST. NICHOLAS WAY
THROWLEY WAY
GANDER GREEN LANE
COLLINGWOOD ROAD
KIMPTON PARK WAY
MULGRAVE ROAD
GRANGE ROAD
CORNWALL ROAD
WORCESTER ROAD
SALISBURY AVENUE
QUEEN VICTORIA
ROSE HILL ROUNDABOUT
ST. DUNSTAN'S
Sutton Common
West Sutton
Cheam
Sutton Cemetery
Recreation Grounds
Rosehill Recreation Ground
Sutton Junior Tennis Centre
Glenthorne High Sch.
St. Anthony's Hosp.
St. Raphael's Hospice
Superstore
Collingwood Road Recreation Ground
Sutton United FC
Perrett's Field
Water Wks.
Cheam High Sch.
Cheam Leisure Cen.
Cheam Recreation Ground
Nursery
David Lloyd Leisure Cen.
Nonsuch High Sch.
Overton Grange Sch.
Sports Ground
Cheam Village
Secombe Thtre.
Civic Cen.
Sutton Ckt. Grd. Hlth. Club
Kimpton Trade & Bus. Cen.
Kimpton Link Bus. Cen.
Kimpton Ind. Est.
Hallmead Day Cen.
Westbourne Prim. Sch.
King George's Field
Recreation Pav. Ground
Playing Fields
Bingo

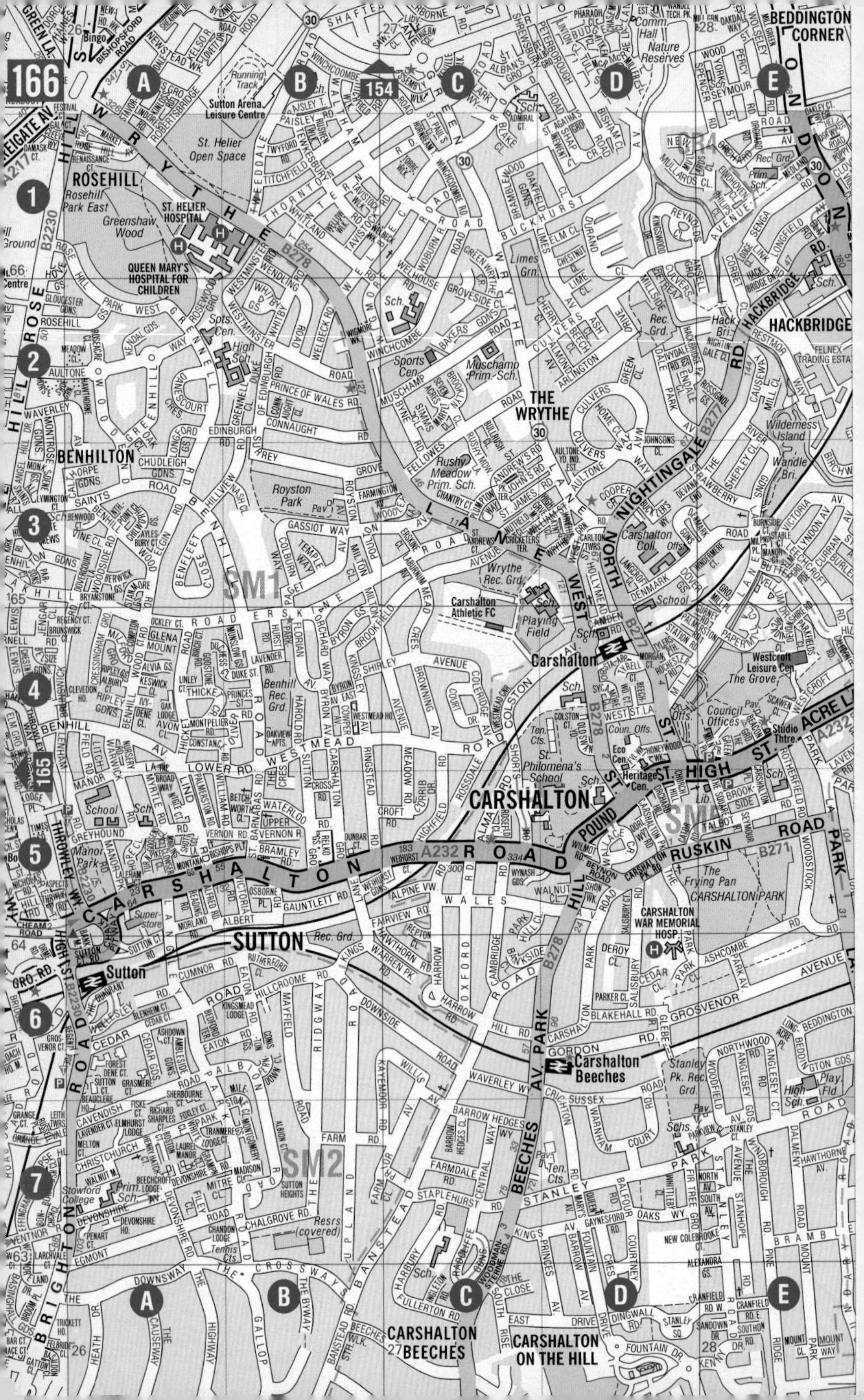
154
165
A
B
C
D
E
1
2
3
4
5
6
7
BEDDINGTON CORNER
ROSEHILL
Rosehill Park East
Greenshaw Wood
St. Helier Open Space
Sutton Arena Leisure Centre
ST. HELIER HOSPITAL
QUEEN MARY'S HOSPITAL FOR CHILDREN
BENHILTON
SM1
Royston Park
THE WRYTHE
Muschamp Prim. Sch.
Rushy Meadow Prim. Sch.
Wrythe Rec. Grd.
Carshalton Athletic FC
Carshalton Coll.
HACKBRIDGE
Wilderness Island
Wandle Bri.
Westcroft Leisure Cen.
The Grove
Council Offices
Studio Thtre.
Carshalton
CARSHALTON
St. Philomena's School
Benhill Rec. Grd.
Manor Park
SUTTON
Sutton
The Frying Pan
CARSHALTON PARK
CARSHALTON WAR MEMORIAL HOSP.
Carshalton Beeches
Stanley Pk. Rec. Grd.
SM2
Sutton Heights
Resrs (covered)
Stowford College
CARSHALTON BEECHES
CARSHALTON ON THE HILL
WRYTHE LANE
CARSHALTON ROAD
NIGHTINGALE RD.
WEST ST.
HIGH ST.
RUSKIN ROAD
BRIGHTON ROAD
BEECHES AV.
A232
B278
B277
B2230
B271
A217

167
168
155
F
G
H
J
K
1
2
3
4
5
6
7
29
30
31
63
Hackbridge
Irrigation Bridge
Mile Road Bridge
MILE ROAD
Beddington Sewage Treatment Works
Factory
Works
PROLOGIS PARK
Bus Depot
ASHWORTH ESTATE
PIONEERS INDUSTRIAL PARK
BEDDINGTON TRADING ESTATE
VALLEY LEISURE PARK
Superstores
Vue Cinema
Megabowl Croydon
Ikea Ampere Way
LOMBARD ROUNDABOUT
Waddon Marsh
Superstore
Warehouse
CR0
THE ORION CENTRE
Electricity Switching Station
BEDDINGTON
WADDON
Waddon Ponds
Waddon
BEDDINGTON PARK
River Wandle
Tennis Courts
Sports Ground
Pavilions
Carew Manor & Dovecote
Carew Manor Sch.
The Grange
Boating Lake
Manor Gdn.
Grammar Sch.
CROYDON ROAD
A232
A237
A23
B272
B271
LONDON RD.
BEDDINGTON LANE
PLOUGH LANE
MANOR ROAD
WOODCOTE ROAD
STAFFORD ROAD
PURLEY WAY
SM6
Bandonhill
Bandon Hill Cemetery
Retail Park
FIVEWAYS CORNER
Playing Field
WALLINGTON
Wallington
Mellows Park
SOUTH BEDDINGTON
Foresters Prim. Sch.
Powerleague Soccer Cen.
Wilson's Sch.
CROYDON AIRPORT IND. EST.
Esporta Health & Racquets Club
Visitor Cen.
Roundshaw
Roundshaw Park (Playing Fields)
Phoenix Cen.
Amy Johnson Prim. Sch.
Roundshaw Park
Nature Reserve
Sports Ground
FORESTERS DRIVE
SANDY LA.
STANLEY PK. RD.
BOUNDARY RD.

168
156
167
A
B
C
D
E
1
2
3
4
5
6
7
CROYDON
West Croydon
East Croydon
South Croydon
SOUTH CROYDON
Sanderstead
WADDON
Waddon
Waddon Marsh
WANDLE PARK
Wandle Park
Warehouses
Centrale
Reeves Cnr.
Church St.
George St.
Wellesley Rd.
Lebanon Rd.
FIVEWAYS CORNER
Duppas Hill
Sports Ground
Recreation Ground
Playing Fields
Whitgift Sch.
HALING PARK
HALING GROVE
PURLEY WAY
PLAYING FIELDS
Roundshaw Park (Playing Fields)
Nature Reserve
Russell Hill Resr. (covered)
Croydon Rec. Grd.
Fairfield Halls
Coombe Cliff (CETS)
Park Hill
CR0
CR2
MITCHAM ROAD
ROMAN WAY
OLD TOWN
DUPPAS HILL RD.
DENNING AV.
WARHAM ROAD
BRIGHTON ROAD
SOUTH END
SELSDON ROAD
PURLEY WAY
COOMBE ROAD
PARK LANE
WELLESLEY ROAD
LOWER ADDISCOMBE ROAD
CHERRY ORCHARD ROAD
FLYOVER
ST. JAMES'S ROAD
A23
A212
A213
A222
A232
A235
A236
B243
B269
B271
B274
B275

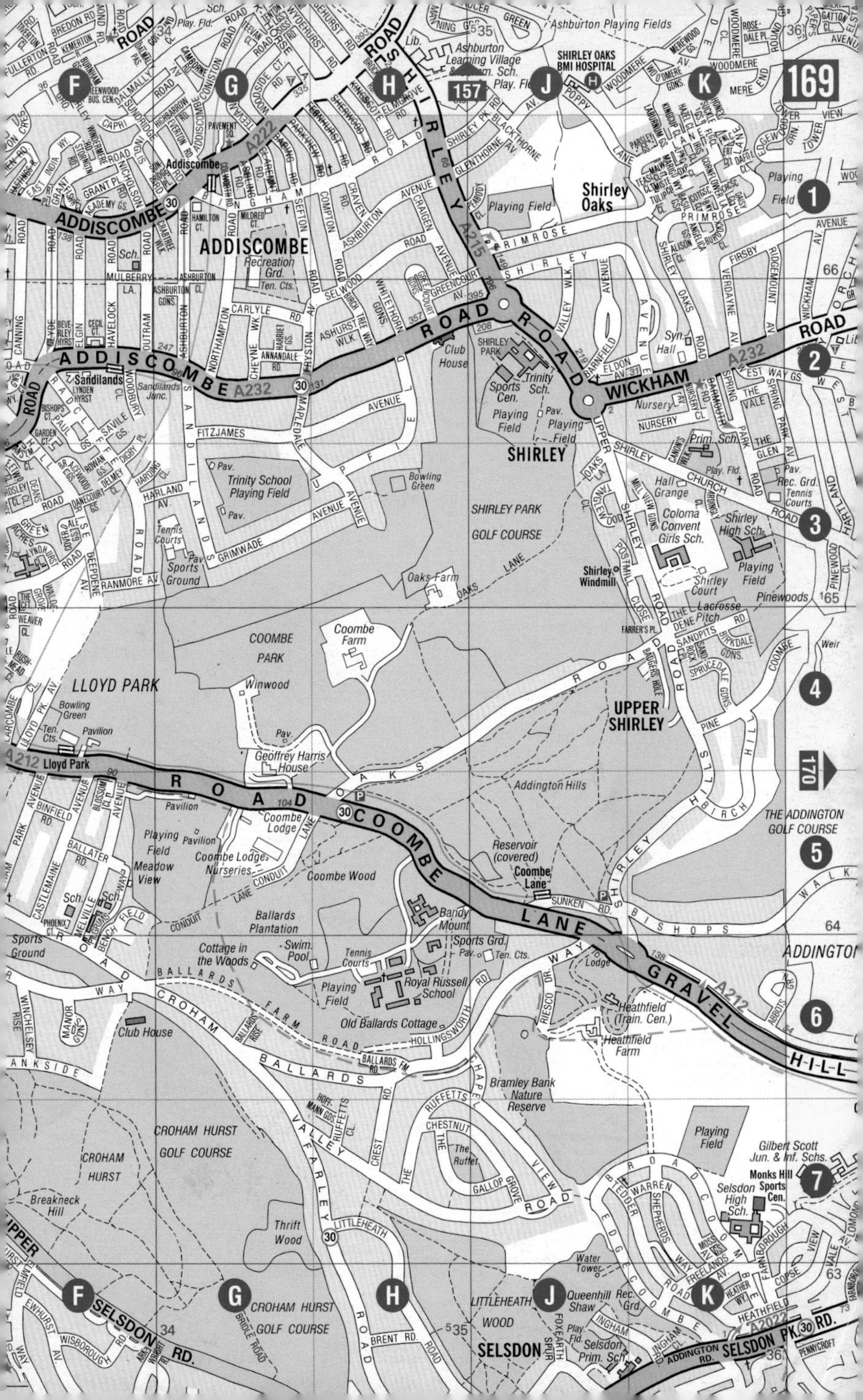
F
G
H
J
K
1
2
3
4
5
6
7
157
170
ADDISCOMBE
ADDISCOMBE ROAD
A222
A232
A215
A212
A2022
Addiscombe
SHIRLEY ROAD
WICKHAM ROAD
Shirley Oaks
SHIRLEY OAKS BMI HOSPITAL
Ashburton Playing Fields
Ashburton Learning Village
Lib.
Recreation Grd.
Ten. Cts.
Sandilands
Sandilands Junc.
Trinity School Playing Field
Trinity Sch.
Sports Cen.
Playing Field
SHIRLEY
SHIRLEY PARK GOLF COURSE
Club House
Bowling Green
Oaks Farm
Shirley Windmill
Coloma Convent Girls Sch.
Shirley High Sch.
Shirley Court
Lacrosse Pitch
Pinewoods
Weir
UPPER SHIRLEY
Addington Hills
THE ADDINGTON GOLF COURSE
ADDINGTON
COOMBE PARK
Coombe Farm
Winwood
LLOYD PARK
Lloyd Park
Pavilion
Geoffrey Harris House
OAKS ROAD
COOMBE ROAD
Coombe Lodge
Coombe Lodge Nurseries
Coombe Wood
Reservoir (covered)
Coombe Lane
COOMBE LANE
GRAVEL HILL
Bandy Mount
Sports Grd.
Ballards Plantation
Cottage in the Woods
Swim. Pool
Tennis Courts
Royal Russell School
Old Ballards Cottage
Heathfield (Train. Cen.)
Heathfield Farm
Bramley Bank Nature Reserve
Sports Ground
Club House
CROHAM ROAD
CROHAM HURST GOLF COURSE
CROHAM HURST
Breakneck Hill
Thrift Wood
LITTLEHEATH WOOD
Queenhill Shaw
Water Tower
SELSDON
Selsdon Prim. Sch.
Selsdon High Sch.
Monks Hill Sports Cen.
Gilbert Scott Jun. & Inf. Schs.
SELSDON RD.
SELSDON PK. RD.
ADDINGTON RD.
FARLEY ROAD
BROADCOOMBE
EDGECOOMBE
BISHOPS WALK
Meadow View

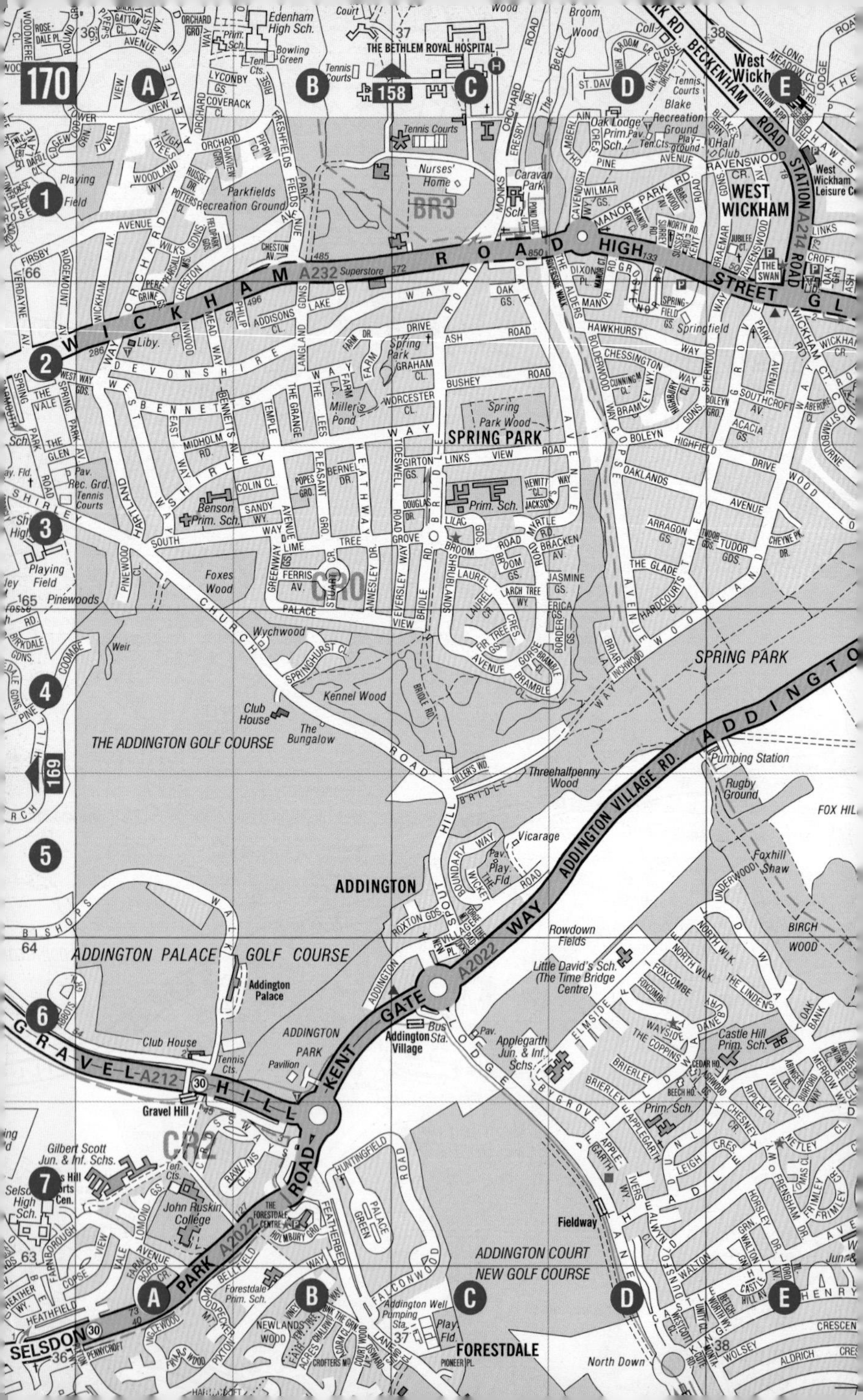
170
A
B
C
D
E
1
2
3
4
5
6
7
158
169
THE BETHLEM ROYAL HOSPITAL
Edenham High Sch.
Bowling Green
Tennis Courts
Nurses' Home
BR3
Caravan Park
Broom Wood
Oak Lodge Prim. Sch.
Blake Recreation Ground
West Wickham
WEST WICKHAM
BECKENHAM ROAD
STATION ROAD A214
HIGH STREET
West Wickham Leisure Ce
THE SWAN
Parkfields Recreation Ground
Playing Field
WICKHAM ROAD A232
Superstore
Liby.
Spring Park
Miller's Pond
Spring Park Wood
SPRING PARK
DEVONSHIRE WAY
SHIRLEY WAY
BENNETTS WAY
Benson Prim. Sch.
Prim. Sch.
Springfield
Foxes Wood
CRO
SHIRLEY CHURCH ROAD
Wychwood
Kennel Wood
Club House
The Bungalow
THE ADDINGTON GOLF COURSE
SPRING PARK
ADDINGTON VILLAGE RD.
Pumping Station
Rugby Ground
Threehalfpenny Wood
Vicarage
Foxhill Shaw
FOX HIL
ADDINGTON
ADDINGTON PALACE GOLF COURSE
Addington Palace
Rowdown Fields
Little David's Sch. (The Time Bridge Centre)
BIRCH WOOD
Castle Hill Prim. Sch.
Applegarth Jun. & Inf. Schs.
Prim. Sch.
ADDINGTON PARK
Pavilion
Club House
Addington Village
Bus Sta.
KENT GATE WAY A2022
GRAVEL HILL A212
Gravel Hill
CR2
Gilbert Scott Jun. & Inf. Schs.
John Ruskin College
Selsdon High Sch.
PARK WAY A2022
Forestdale Prim. Sch.
Addington Well Pumping Sta.
Play. Fld.
ADDINGTON COURT NEW GOLF COURSE
Fieldway
FORESTDALE
SELSDON
North Down
ADDINGTON PALACE
FIELDWAY
LODGE LANE
KING HENRY'S DRIVE
36
37
38
63
64
65
66
30

HAYES
Hayes Farm
Hayes Prim. Sch.
Playing Field
Bolds Wood
Brook Wood
Hayes
HAYES LANE
BASTON ROAD
B251
B265
A232
A2022
BR2
BR4
Hawes Down Jun.& Inf. Schs.
Glebe Sch.
Youth Cen.
Sports Ground
Sports Grounds
Tennis Courts
Pickhurst
Hayes Hill
Hayes Lane
The Mead
Station App.
Ridgeway
Warren Road
Bourne Way
Coney Hill
Addington Rd.
Croydon Road
West Wickham Common
Hayes Grove Priory Hosp.
The Hayes Grove Priory Hosp.
Hayes Sch.
Baston School
Play. Fld.
Hayes Court
HAYES COMMON
Baston Manor Rd.
Baston Manor
Five Elms Road
Gorsewood
Hast Hill
Keston Court Riding School
Miry Grove
Fox Lane
Heritage Hill
Jackass Lane
Fox Hill Nursery
CONEY HALL
Coney Hall Rec. Grd.
Recreation Ground
Lodge
Wickham Court Sch.
All Saints Catholic School
Sparrow's Den Playing Fields
Bowling Green
Sports Ground
War Mem.
Thtre.
Sylvan Way
Kingsway
Gates Green Road
School
Playing Field
Rouse Farm
Arlington Orchard
Wickham Court Farm
The Cottages
The Bungalows
Well Wood
Cooper's Wood
Long Shaw
Elm Farm
Elm Farm Lane
NASH
Nash
Nash Farm
North Pole Farm
North Pole Lane
Fuller's Wood
James's Wood
Waytes
Five Oaks
Baldwin Shaw
Bradmanshill Wood
Castlehill Ruffs
Electricity Sub Station
Rushfield Shaw
Broomfieldbank Shaw
Nash Road
Metropolitan Police Dog Training Establishment
NEW ADDINGTON
Rowdown Wood
Milchder
159
172
F G H J K
1 2 3 4 5 6 7
66 65 64 63
39 540 41

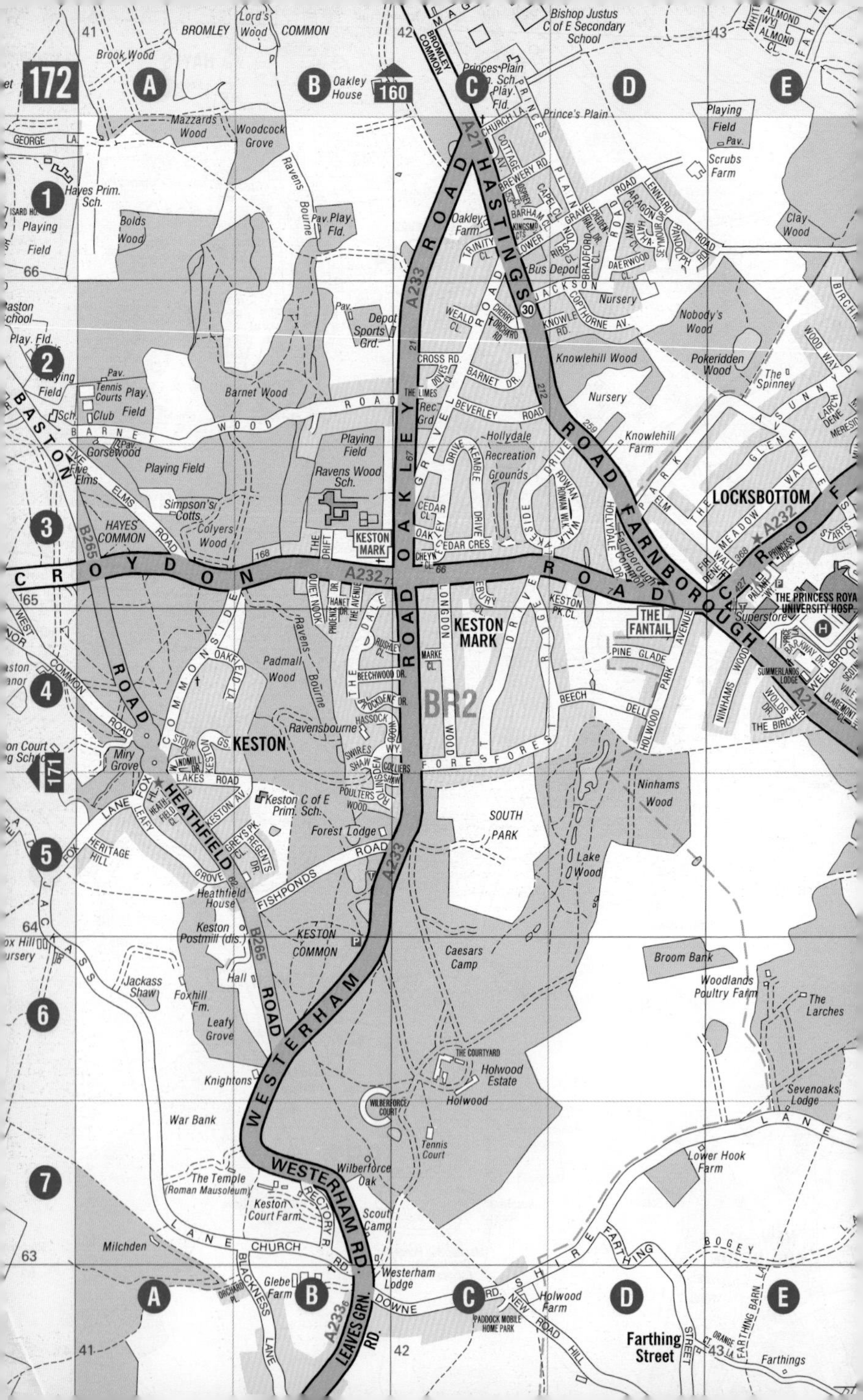
160
171
A
B
C
D
E
1
2
3
4
5
6
7
41
42
43
66
165
64
63
BROMLEY COMMON
Lord's Wood
Brook Wood
Oakley House
BROMLEY COMMON
Bishop Justus C of E Secondary School
Princes Plain Sch.
Play. Fld.
Prince's Plain
Playing Field
Pav.
Scrubs Farm
Mazzards Wood
Woodcock Grove
GEORGE LA.
Hayes Prim. Sch.
Playing Field
Ravens Bourne
Pav. Play. Fld.
Bolds Wood
Oakley Farm
Clay Wood
CHURCH LA.
BREWERY RD.
PRINCES PLAIN
CAPEL CT.
GRAVEL ROAD
LENNARD ROAD
ARAGON CL.
SEYMOUR DR.
TRINITY CL.
LOWER
Bus Depot
BRADFORD CL.
DAERWOOD
JACKSON
Nursery
Nobody's Wood
Baston School
Play. Fld.
Pav.
Tennis Courts
Club
Play. Field
Sch.
Depot Sports Grd.
WEALD CL.
CHERRY ORCHARD RD.
KNOWLE RD.
COPTHORNE AV.
Knowlehill Wood
Pokeridden Wood
The Spinney
WOOD WAY
BASTON
BARNET WOOD ROAD
Barnet Wood
CROSS RD.
BARNET DR.
THE LIMES
Rec. Grd.
BEVERLEY ROAD
Nursery
Knowlehill Farm
Hollydale Recreation Grounds
KEMBLE DRIVE
ROWAN WALK
LAKESIDE DRIVE
Gorsewood
FIVE ELMS
Five Elms
Playing Field
Playing Field
Ravens Wood Sch.
SUNNYDALE
GLENDALE WAY
LARCH DENE
Simpson's Cotts.
Colyers Wood
HAYES COMMON
ELMS ROAD
B265
THE DRIFT
KESTON MARK
OAKLEY ROAD
CEDAR CL.
CEDAR CRES.
CHEYNE CL.
HOLLYDALE DR.
Farnborough Common
FARNBOROUGH ROAD
A21
LOCKSBOTTOM
MEADOW
ELM
FIR DENE
WALK
PRINCESS PDE.
A232
CROYDON ROAD
A232
A233
HASTINGS ROAD
QUIET NOOK
THANET DR.
PHOENIX DR.
THE AVENUE
THE DALE
EBURY CL.
LONGDON WOOD
KESTON PK.CL.
THE FANTAIL
AVENUE
Superstore
THE PRINCESS ROYAL UNIVERSITY HOSP.
WEST COMMON ROAD
Padmall Wood
Ravens Bourne
RUSHLEY CL.
THE BEECHWOOD DR.
BROCKDENE DR.
KESTON MARK
MARKET CL.
PINE GLADE
NINHAMS WOOD
SUMMERLANDS LODGE
WELLBROOK
BR2
OAKFIELD LA.
COMMONSIDE
Ravensbourne
HASSOCK WOOD
BEECH DELL
HOLWOOD PARK
WOLDS DR.
THE BIRCHES
Miry Grove
STOUR CL.
KESTON
Court School
SWIRES SHAW
COLLIERS SHAW
LINSDEN
FORESTDALE
FOREST RIDGE
Ninhams Wood
WINDMILL DR.
LAKES ROAD
KESTON AV.
FOX HL.
HEATHFIELD
LEAFY
LANE
Keston C of E Prim. Sch.
POULTERS WOOD
Forest Lodge
SOUTH PARK
FOX
HERITAGE HILL
GROVE
GREYS PK. CL.
REGENTS DR.
FISHPONDS ROAD
Lake Wood
Heathfield House
Keston Postmill (dis.)
KESTON COMMON
Fox Hill Nursery
Caesars Camp
Broom Bank
JACKASS
Jackass Shaw
Hall
Foxhill Fm.
Leafy Grove
B265 ROAD
WESTERHAM ROAD
Woodlands Poultry Farm
The Larches
THE COURTYARD
Holwood Estate
Holwood
Knightons
War Bank
WILBERFORCE COURT
Tennis Court
Sevenoaks Lodge
LANE
The Temple (Roman Mausoleum)
Keston Court Farm
RECTORY R.
WESTERHAM RD.
Wilberforce Oak
Scout Camp
Lower Hook Farm
Milchden
LANE CHURCH RD.
SHIRE
FARTHING
BOGEY
ORCHARD PL.
BLACKNESS LANE
Glebe Farm
Westerham Lodge
DOWNE RD.
NEW ROAD HILL
Holwood Farm
PADDOCK MOBILE HOME PARK
A233
LEAVES GRN. RD.
Farthing Street
STREET
ORANGE CT. LA.
FARTHING BARN LA.
Farthings

Sparrow Wood
Petts Wood Recreation Ground
Crofton Jun. Sch.
Crofton Inf. Sch.
161
F
G
H
J
K
Sparrow Common
Roundabout Wood
Crofton Heath
BROOM HILL
Knoll Lawn Tennis Club
BR5
ORPINGTON
Gumping Common
CROFTON
Orpington
Civic Halls
Villa
A232
CROFTON ROAD
STATION ROAD
SPUR RD.
1
2
3
4
5
6
7
Hall
Darrick Wood Swimming Pool
Darrick Wood School
Darrick Wood Sports Cen.
Darrick Wood
Darrick Wood Jun. & Inf. Schs.
Tennis Courts
Farnborough Pav.
Recreation Ground
Newstead Wood
Play. Fld
Newstead Wood Sch. for Girls
Playing Field
Tubbenden Jun. & Inf. Schools
Rec. Grd.
Prim. Sch.
Ontario Centre
A223
SEVENOAKS ROAD
HOSPICE
ORPINGTON HOSPITAL
Bassetts Cen.
The Green
FARNBOROUGH COMMON
CHERRYCOT HILL
A21
Scouts Hall
HIGH STREET FARNBOROUGH
B2158
Club Sports Ground
Pav.
Farnborough Prim. Sch.
The Manse
BR6
FARNBOROUGH
Mill Hill
Church Field Plantation
Play. Fld.
Glentrammon Rec. Grd.
Pav.
Ramus Wood
GREEN STREET GREEN
Cocksett Plantation
Cocksett Hill
The Lodge
High Elms Nature Cen.
Woodpiece
SHIRE LANE
North End Farm
HIGH ELMS COUNTRY PARK
Whitelands Wood
Playgrd.
Club House
North End Farm Cotts.
Blacklands
High Elms Clockhouse
The Rookery
HIGH ELMS GOLF COURSE
Rec. Grd.
Chelsfield Hall
Rounds Wood
SEVENOAKS ROAD
HIGH ST.
WAY
44
45
46
63
64
65
66

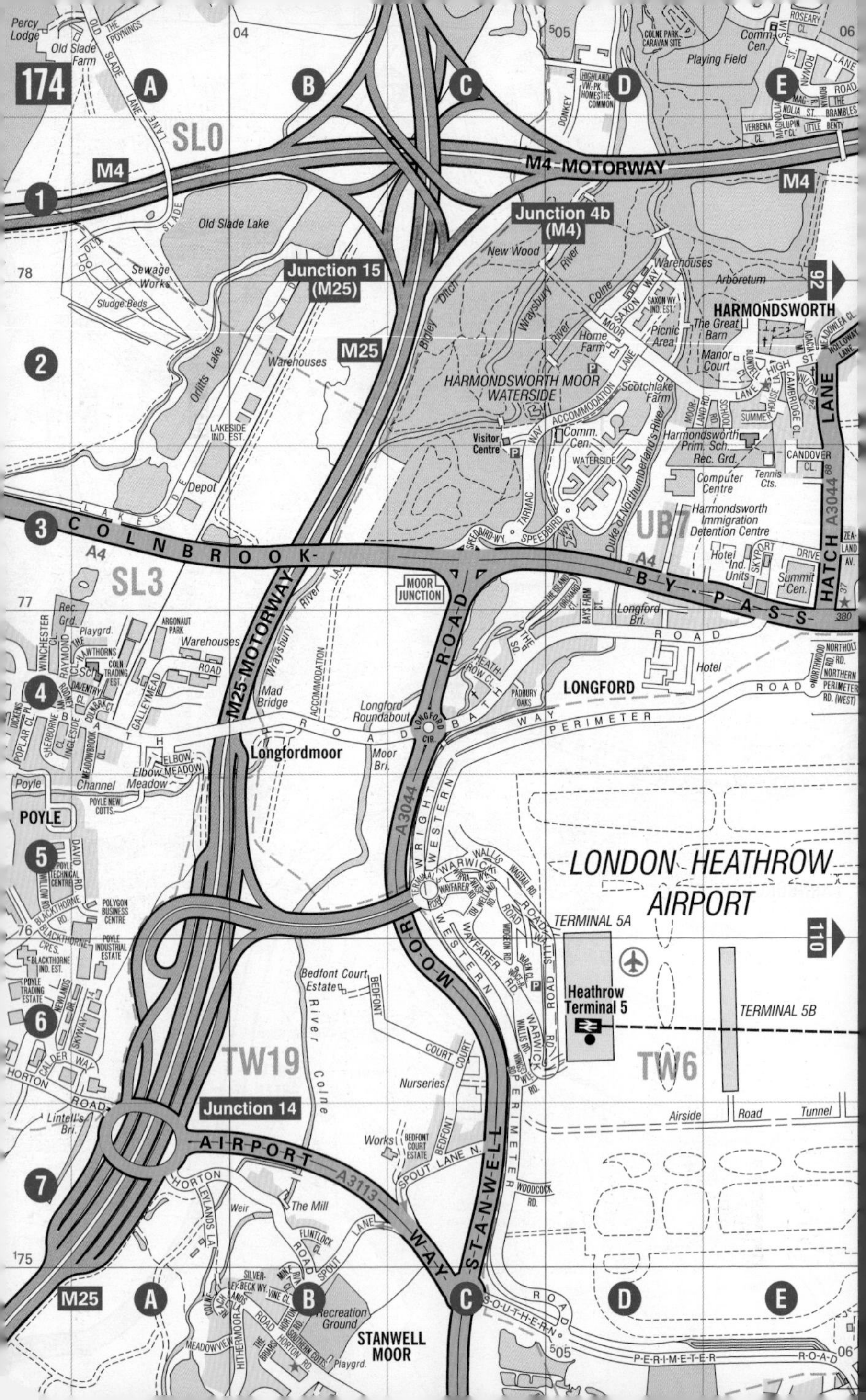
174
92
110
M4 MOTORWAY
M25 MOTORWAY
Junction 4b (M4)
Junction 15 (M25)
Junction 14
COLNBROOK BY-PASS
A4
A3044
A3113
AIRPORT WAY
STANWELL MOOR ROAD
BATH ROAD
PERIMETER ROAD
SOUTHERN PERIMETER ROAD
WESTERN PERIMETER ROAD
NORTHERN PERIMETER RD. (WEST)
HATCH LANE
SL0
SL3
UB7
TW19
TW6
Percy Lodge
Old Slade Farm
Old Slade Lake
Sewage Works
Sludge Beds
Orlitts Lake
Warehouses
LAKESIDE IND. EST.
Depot
New Wood
Bigley Ditch
Wraysbury River
River Colne
HARMONDSWORTH MOOR WATERSIDE
Visitor Centre
Comm. Cen.
WATERSIDE
Home Farm
Picnic Area
The Great Barn
Manor Court
Scotchlake Farm
Duke of Northumberland's River
HARMONDSWORTH
Arboretum
Playing Field
COLNE PARK CARAVAN SITE
Harmondsworth Prim. Sch.
Rec. Grd.
Computer Centre
Tennis Cts.
Harmondsworth Immigration Detention Centre
Hotel
Ind. Units
Summit Cen.
MOOR JUNCTION
Longford Bri.
Hotel
LONGFORD
Longford Roundabout
LONGFORD CIR.
Longfordmoor
Mad Bridge
Moor Bri.
POYLE
Poyle Channel
Elbow Meadow
POYLE NEW COTTS.
POYLE TECHNICAL CENTRE
POLYGON BUSINESS CENTRE
POYLE INDUSTRIAL ESTATE
BLACKTHORNE IND. EST.
POYLE TRADING ESTATE
ARGONAUT PARK
COLN TRADING EST.
Rec. Grd.
Playgrd.
LONDON HEATHROW AIRPORT
TERMINAL 5A
TERMINAL 5B
Heathrow Terminal 5
Airside Road Tunnel
Bedfont Court Estate
BEDFONT COURT ESTATE
Nurseries
Works
Lintell's Bri.
The Mill
Weir
Recreation Ground
STANWELL MOOR
Playgrd.
HORTON ROAD
SPOUT LANE
SPOUT LANE N.
WOODCOCK RD.
CALDER WAY
SKYWAY
TARMAC WAY
SPEEDBIRD WY.
SAXON WAY
MOOR LANE
ACCOMMODATION LANE
HIGH ST.
CANDOVER CL.
SKYPORT DRIVE
WARWICK ROAD
WAYFARER RD.
WALLIS RD.
M4
M25
A B C D E
1 2 3 4 5 6 7
04 05 06
78 77 76 75

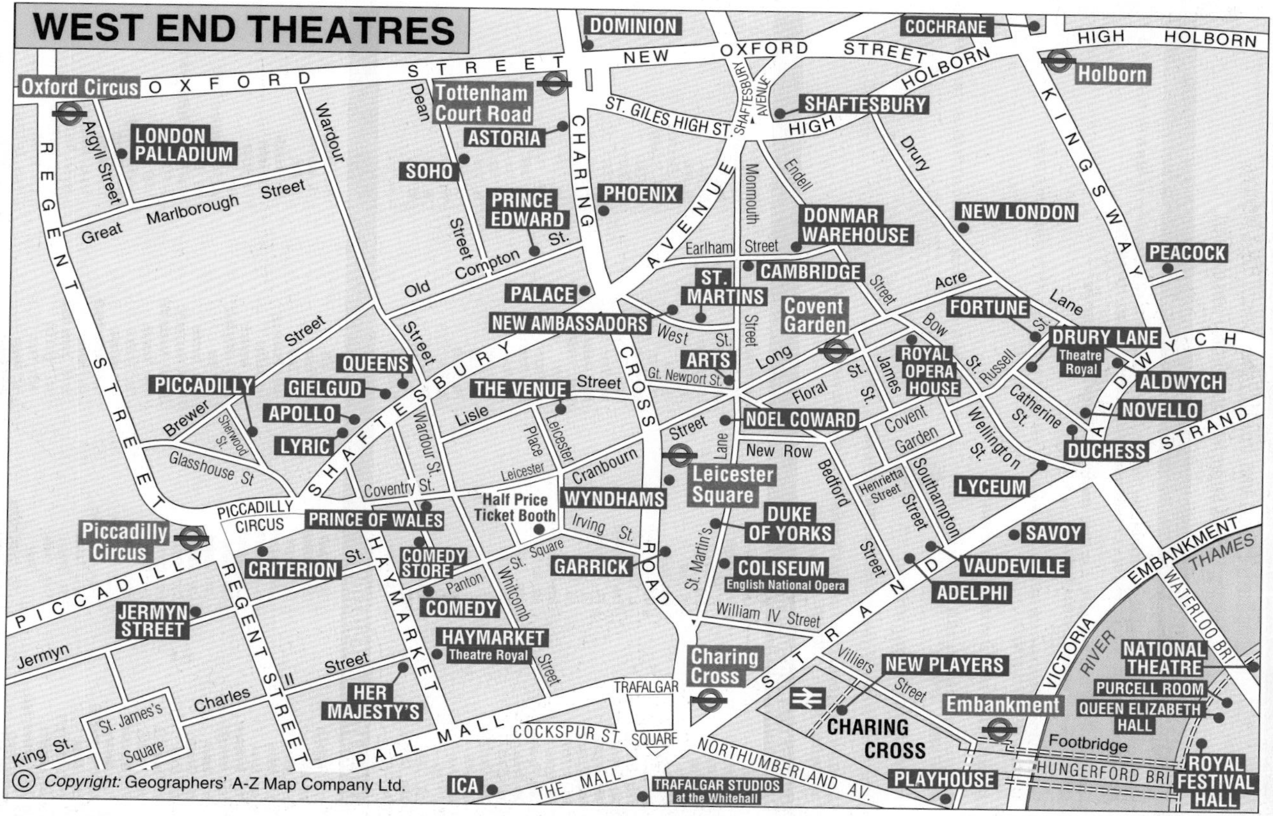
WEST END THEATRES
DOMINION
COCHRANE
Holborn
Oxford Circus
Tottenham Court Road
LONDON PALLADIUM
ASTORIA
SHAFTESBURY
SOHO
PRINCE EDWARD
PHOENIX
DONMAR WAREHOUSE
NEW LONDON
PEACOCK
CAMBRIDGE
ST. MARTINS
PALACE
NEW AMBASSADORS
Covent Garden
FORTUNE
DRURY LANE
Theatre Royal
ARTS
ROYAL OPERA HOUSE
ALDWYCH
QUEENS
PICCADILLY
GIELGUD
THE VENUE
APOLLO
LYRIC
NOEL COWARD
NOVELLO
DUCHESS
Leicester Square
WYNDHAMS
LYCEUM
Half Price Ticket Booth
Piccadilly Circus
PRINCE OF WALES
DUKE OF YORKS
SAVOY
COMEDY STORE
GARRICK
COLISEUM
English National Opera
VAUDEVILLE
CRITERION
ADELPHI
COMEDY
JERMYN STREET
HAYMARKET
Theatre Royal
NATIONAL THEATRE
Charing Cross
NEW PLAYERS
PURCELL ROOM
HER MAJESTY'S
Embankment
QUEEN ELIZABETH HALL
CHARING CROSS
ROYAL FESTIVAL HALL
PLAYHOUSE
ICA
TRAFALGAR STUDIOS at the Whitehall
OXFORD STREET
NEW OXFORD STREET
HIGH HOLBORN
KINGSWAY
REGENT STREET
CHARING CROSS ROAD
SHAFTESBURY AVENUE
ST. GILES HIGH ST.
ALDWYCH
STRAND
PICCADILLY
HAYMARKET
PALL MALL
COCKSPUR ST.
TRAFALGAR SQUARE
NORTHUMBERLAND AV.
THE MALL
VICTORIA EMBANKMENT
RIVER THAMES
WATERLOO BRI
HUNGERFORD BRI
Footbridge
PICCADILLY CIRCUS
Argyll Street
Great Marlborough Street
Wardour Street
Dean Street
Old Compton Street
Earlham Street
Monmouth Street
Endell Street
Drury Lane
Long Acre
Bow St.
Russell St.
Catherine St.
Wellington St.
West St.
Gt. Newport St.
Floral St.
James St.
Covent Garden
Lisle Street
Leicester Place
Leicester Street
Cranbourn Street
New Row
Bedford Street
Henrietta Street
Southampton Street
Brewer Street
Sherwood St.
Glasshouse St
Wardour St.
Coventry St.
Irving St.
St. Martin's Lane
Leicester Square
Whitcomb Street
Panton St.
William IV Street
Villiers Street
Jermyn Street
Charles II Street
King St.
St. James's Square
© Copyright: Geographers' A-Z Map Company Ltd.

INDEX

Including Streets, Places & Areas, Industrial Estates, Selected Flats & Walkways, Junction Names & Service Areas and Selected Places of Interest.

HOW TO USE THIS INDEX

1. Each street name is followed by its Postcode District (or, if outside the London Postcodes, by its Locality Abbreviation(s)) and then by its map reference; e.g. **Abbey Av.** HA0: Wemb . . . . 2E **78** is in the HA0 Postcode District and the Wembley Locality and is to be found in square 2E on page **78**. The page number being shown in bold type.

2. A strict alphabetical order is followed in which Av., Rd., St., etc. (though abbreviated) are read in full and as part of the street name; e.g. **Alder M.** appears after **Aldermary Rd.** but before **Aldermoor Rd.**

3. Streets and a selection of flats and walkways too small to be shown on the maps, appear in the index with the thoroughfare to which it is connected shown in brackets; e.g. **Abady Ho.** *SW1 . . . . 3D **18** (off Page St.)*

4. Addresses that are in more than one part are referred to as not continuous.

5. Places and areas are shown in the index in **BLUE TYPE** and the map reference is to the actual map square in which the town centre or area is located and not to the place name shown on the map; e.g. **ABBEY WOOD 4C 108**

6. An example of a selected place of interest is **Barnet Mus.** 4B **20**

7. Junction names and Service Areas are shown in the index in **BOLD CAPITAL TYPE**; e.g. **ALDGATE 6F 85**

8. Map references for entries that appear on large scale pages **4-19** are shown first, with small scale map references shown in brackets; e.g. **Abbey Orchard St.** SW1 . . . . 1C **18** (3H **101**)

GENERAL ABBREVIATIONS

All. : Alley
App. : Approach
Arc. : Arcade
Av. : Avenue
Bk. : Back
Blvd. : Boulevard
Bri. : Bridge
B'way. : Broadway
Bldg. : Building
Bldgs. : Buildings
Bungs. : Bungalows
Bus. : Business
Cvn. : Caravan
C'way. : Causeway
Cen. : Centre
Chu. : Church
Chyd. : Churchyard
Circ. : Circle
Cir. : Circus
Cl. : Close
Coll. : College
Comn. : Common
Cnr. : Corner
Cott. : Cottage
Cotts. : Cottages
Ct. : Court
Cres. : Crescent
Cft. : Croft
Dpt. : Depot
Dr. : Drive
E. : East
Emb. : Embankment
Ent. : Enterprise
Est. : Estate
Fld. : Field
Flds. : Fields
Gdn. : Garden
Gdns. : Gardens
Gth. : Garth
Ga. : Gate
Gt. : Great
Grn. : Green
Gro. : Grove
Hgts. : Heights
Ho. : House
Ho's. : Houses
Ind. : Industrial
Info. : Information
Intl. : International
Junc. : Junction
La. : Lane
Lit. : Little
Lwr. : Lower
Mnr. : Manor
Mans. : Mansions
Mkt. : Market
Mdw. : Meadow
Mdws. : Meadows
M. : Mews
Mt. : Mount
Mus. : Museum
Nth. : North
No. : Number
Pal. : Palace
Pde. : Parade
Pk. : Park
Pas. : Passage
Pav. : Pavilion
Pl. : Place
Pct. : Precinct
Prom. : Promenade
Quad. : Quadrant
Ri. : Rise
Rd. : Road
Rdbt. : Roundabout
Shop. : Shopping
Sth. : South
Sq. : Square
Sta. : Station
St. : Street
Ter. : Terrace
Twr. : Tower
Trad. : Trading
Up. : Upper
Va. : Vale
Vw. : View
Vs. : Villas
Vis. : Visitors
Wlk. : Walk
W. : West
Yd. : Yard

LOCALITY ABBREVIATIONS

Addtn : **Addington**
Ark : **Arkley**
Ashf : **Ashford**
Bark : **Barking**
Barn : **Barnet**
Beck : **Beckenham**
Bedd : **Beddington**
Bedf : **Bedfont**
Belv : **Belvedere**
Bexl : **Bexley**
Bex : **Bexleyheath**
Bford : **Brentford**
Brim : **Brimsdown**
Brom : **Bromley**
Buck H : **Buckhurst Hill**
Bush : **Bushey**
B Hea : **Bushy Heath**
Cars : **Carshalton**
Chad H : **Chadwell Heath**
Cheam : **Cheam**
Chels : **Chelsfield**
Chert : **Chertsey**
Chess : **Chessington**
Chig : **Chigwell**
Chst : **Chislehurst**
Clay : **Claygate**
Cockf : **Cockfosters**
Col R : **Collier Row**
Coln : **Colnbrook**
Cowl : **Cowley**
Cran : **Cranford**
Cray : **Crayford**
C'don : **Croydon**
Dag : **Dagenham**
Dart : **Dartford**
Downe : **Downe**
E Barn : **East Barnet**
E Mos : **East Molesey**
Eastc : **Eastcote**
Edg : **Edgware**
E'tree : **Elstree**
Enf : **Enfield**
Enf H : **Enfield Highway**
Enf L : **Enfield Lock**
Enf W : **Enfield Wash**
Eps : **Epsom**
Erith : **Erith**
Esh : **Esher**
Ewe : **Ewell**
Farnb : **Farnborough**
Felt : **Feltham**
G'frd : **Greenford**
Had W : **Hadley Wood**
Ham : **Ham**
Hamp : **Hampton**
Ham H : **Hampton Hill**
Ham W : **Hampton Wick**
Hanw : **Hanworth**
Hare : **Harefield**
Harl : **Harlington**
Harm : **Harmondsworth**
Harr : **Harrow**
Hrw W : **Harrow Weald**
Hat E : **Hatch End**
Hayes : **Hayes**
Hest : **Heston**
Hext : **Hextable**
Hil : **Hillingdon**
Hin W : **Hinchley Wood**
Houn : **Hounslow**
Ick : **Ickenham**
Ilf : **Ilford**
Isle : **Isleworth**
Kent : **Kenton**
Kes : **Keston**
Kew : **Kew**
King T : **Kingston Upon Thames**
Lale : **Laleham**
H'row A : **London Heathrow Airport**
Lford : **Longford**
Lough : **Loughton**
Mawney : **Mawney**
Mitc : **Mitcham**
Mord : **Morden**
New Ad : **New Addington**
New Bar : **New Barnet**
N Mald : **New Malden**
N'olt : **Northolt**
Nwood : **Northwood**
Orp : **Orpington**
Pet W : **Petts Wood**
Pinn : **Pinner**

Pond E : Ponders End
Poyle : Poyle
Prat B : Pratts Bottom
Purl : Purley
Rain : Rainham
Rich P : Richings Park
Rich : Richmond
Rom : Romford
Ruis : Ruislip
Rush G : Rush Green
St M Cry : St Mary Cray
St P : St Pauls Cray
Sande : Sanderstead
Sels : Selsdon
Shep : Shepperton
Sidc : Sidcup
Sip : Sipson
S'hall : Southall
S Croy : South Croydon
Staines : Staines
Stan : Stanmore
Stanw : Stanwell
Stan M : Stanwell Moor
Stock P : Stockley Park
Sun : Sunbury
Surb : Surbiton
Sutt : Sutton
Swan : Swanley
Tedd : Teddington
T Ditt : Thames Ditton
Thor H : Thornton Heath
Twick : Twickenham
Uxb : Uxbridge
Wadd : Waddon
Wall : Wallington
Walt T : Walton-on-Thames
W'stone : Wealdstone
Well : Welling
Wemb : Wembley
W Dray : West Drayton
W Mole : West Molesey
W W'ck : West Wickham
Weyb : Weybridge
Whitt : Whitton
Wfd G : Woodford Green
Wor Pk : Worcester Park
Yead : Yeading
Yiew : Yiewsley

198 Gallery ... 6B 120
(off Railton Rd.)

A

Aaron Hill Rd. E6 ... 5E 88
Abady Ho. *SW1* ... *3D 18*
(off Page St.)
Abberley M. SW4 ... 3F 119
Abbess Cl. E6 ... 5C 88
SW2 ... 1B 138
Abbeville M. SW4 ... 4H 119
Abbeville Rd. N8 ... 5H 47
SW4 ... 6G 119
Abbey Av. HA0: Wemb ... 2E 78
Abbey Bus. Cen. SW8 ... 1G 119
Abbey Cl. E5 ... 4G 67
HA5: Pinn ... 3K 39
SW8 ... 1H 119
UB3: Hayes ... 1K 93
UB5: N'olt ... 3D 76
Abbey Ct. *NW8* ... *2A 82*
(off Abbey Rd.)
SE17 ... *5C 102*
(off Macleod St.)
TW12: Hamp ... 7E 130
Abbey Cres. DA17: Belv ... 4G 109
Abbeydale Ct. E17 ... 3F 51
Abbeydale Rd. HA0: Wemb ... 1F 79
Abbey Dr. DA2: Dart ... 2K 145
SW17 ... 5E 136
Abbey Est. NW8 ... 1K 81
Abbeyfield Cl. CR4: Mitc ... 2C 154
Abbeyfield Est. SE16 ... 4J 103
Abbeyfield Rd. SE16 ... 4J 103
(not continuous)
Abbeyfields Cl. NW10 ... 2G 79
Abbey Gdns. BR7: Chst ... 1E 160
NW8 ... 2A 82
SE16 ... 4G 103
W6 ... 6G 99
Abbey Gro. SE2 ... 4B 108
Abbeyhill Rd. DA15: Sidc ... 2C 144
Abbey Ho. *E15* ... *2G 87*
(off Baker's Row)
NW8 ... 1A 4
Abbey Ind. Est. CR4: Mitc ... 5D 154
HA0: Wemb ... 1F 79
Abbey La. BR3: Beck ... 7C 140
E15 ... 2E 86
Abbey La. Commercial Est.
E15 ... 2G 87
Abbey Life Ct. E16 ... 5K 87
Abbey Lodge NW8 ... 2D 4
Abbey M. E17 ... 5C 50
TW7: Isle ... 1B 114
Abbey Mt. DA17: Belv ... 5F 109
Abbey Orchard St. SW1 ... 1C 18 (3H 101)
Abbey Orchard St. Est.
SW1 ... 1D 18 (3H 101)
(not continuous)
Abbey Pde. *SW19* ... *7A 136*
(off Merton High St.)
W5 ... 3F 79
Abbey Pk. BR3: Beck ... 7C 140
Abbey Pk. Ind. Est. IG11: Bark ... 2G 89
Abbey Retail Pk. IG11: Bark ... 7F 71
Abbey Rd. CR0: C'don ... 3B 168
DA7: Bex ... 4E 126
DA17: Belv ... 4D 108
E15 ... 2F 87
EN1: Enf ... 5K 23
IG2: Ilf ... 5H 53
IG11: Bark ... 1F 89
NW6 ... 7K 63
NW8 ... 1A 4 (7K 63)
NW10 ... 1H 79
SE2 ... 4D 108
SW19 ... 7A 136
Abbey Sports Cen. ... 1G 89
Abbey St. E13 ... 4J 87
SE1 ... 7H 15 (3F 103)
Abbey Ter. SE2 ... 4C 108
Abbey Trad. Est. SE26 ... 5B 140
Abbey Vw. NW7 ... 3G 29
Abbey Wlk. KT8: W Mole ... 3F 149
Abbey Wharf Ind. Est.
IG11: Bark ... 3H 89
ABBEY WOOD ... 4C 108
Abbey Wood Camping & Cvn. Site
SE2 ... 4C 108
Abbey Wood Rd. SE2 ... 4B 108
Abbot Cl. HA4: Ruis ... 3B 58
Abbot Ct. *SW8* ... *7J 101*
(off Hartington Rd.)
Abbot Ho. *E14* ... *7D 86*
(off Smythe St.)
Abbotsbury *NW1* ... *7H 65*
(off Camley St.)
Abbotsbury Cl. E15 ... 2E 86
W14 ... 2G 99
Abbotsbury Gdns.
HA5: Eastc ... 7A 40
Abbotsbury Ho. W14 ... 2G 99
Abbotsbury M. SE15 ... 3J 121
Abbotsbury Rd.
BR2: Hayes ... 2H 171
SM4: Mord ... 5K 153
W14 ... 2G 99
Abbots Cl. BR5: Farnb ... 1G 173
Abbots Ct. *W8* ... *2K 99*
(off Thackeray St.)
Abbots Dr. HA2: Harr ... 2E 58
Abbotsford Av. N15 ... 4C 48
Abbotsford Gdns.
IG8: Wfd G ... 7D 36
Abbotsford Rd. IG3: Ilf ... 2A 72
Abbots Gdns. N2 ... 4B 46
Abbots Grn. CR0: Addtn ... 6K 169
Abbotshade Rd. SE16 ... 1K 103
Abbotshall Av. N14 ... 3B 32
Abbotshall Rd. SE6 ... 1F 141
Abbot's Ho. *W14* ... *3H 99*
(off St Mary Abbots Ter.)
Abbots La. SE1 ... 5H 15 (1E 102)
Abbotsleigh Cl. SM2: Sutt ... 7K 165
Abbotsleigh Rd.
SW16 ... 4G 137
Abbots Mnr. SW1 ... 5J 17 (4F 101)
Abbots Mead TW10: Ham ... 4D 132
Abbotsmede Cl.
TW1: Twick ... 2K 131
Abbots Pk. SW2 ... 1A 138
Abbot's Pl. NW6 ... 1K 81
Abbots Rd. E6 ... 1B 88
HA8: Edg ... 7D 28
Abbots Ter. N8 ... 6J 47
Abbotstone Rd. SW15 ... 3E 116
Abbot St. E8 ... 6F 67
Abbots Wlk. W8 ... 3K 99
Abbots Way BR3: Beck ... 5A 158
Abbotswell Rd. SE4 ... 5B 122
Abbotswood Cl. DA17: Belv ... 3E 108
Abbotswood Gdns.
IG5: Ilf ... 3D 52
Abbotswood Rd. SE22 ... 4E 120
SW16 ... 3H 137
Abbotswood Way UB3: Hayes ... 1K 93
Abbott Av. SW20 ... 1F 153
Abbott Cl. TW12: Hamp ... 6C 130
UB5: N'olt ... 6D 58
Abbott Rd. E14 ... 5E 86
(not continuous)
Abbotts Cl. N1 ... 6C 66
RM7: Mawney ... 3H 55
SE28 ... 7C 90
UB8: Cowl ... 5A 74
Abbotts Cres. E4 ... 4A 36
EN2: Enf ... 2G 23
Abbotts Dr. HA0: Wemb ... 2B 60
Abbotts Ho. *SW1* ... *6C 18*
(off Aylesford St.)
Abbotts Pk. Rd.
E10 ... 7E 50
Abbotts Rd. CR4: Mitc ... 4G 155
(not continuous)
EN5: New Bar ... 4E 20
SM3: Cheam ... 4G 165
UB1: S'hall ... 1C 94
Abbott's Wlk. DA7: Bex ... 7D 108
Abbott's Wharf *E14* ... *6C 86*
(off Stainsby Pl.)
Abchor Ho. *SW1* ... *5J 17*
(off Warwick Way)
Abchurch La. EC4 ... 2F 15 (7D 84)
(not continuous)
Abchurch Yd. EC4 ... 2E 14 (7D 84)
Abdale Rd. W12 ... 1D 98
Abel Ho. *SE11* ... *7K 19*
(off Kennington Rd.)
Abenglen Ind. Est.
UB3: Hayes ... 2F 93
Aberavon Rd. E3 ... 3A 86
Abercairn Rd. SW16 ... 7G 137
Aberconway Rd. SM4: Mord ... 4K 153
Abercorn Cl. NW7 ... 7B 30
NW8 ... 3A 82
Abercorn Commercial Cen.
HA0: Wemb ... 1D 78
Abercorn Cotts. *NW8* ... *3A 82*
(off Abercorn Pl.)
Abercorn Cres. HA2: Harr ... 1F 59
Abercorn Gdns. HA3: Kent ... 7D 42
RM6: Chad H ... 6B 54
Abercorn Gro. HA4: Ruis ... 4F 39
Abercorn Mans. *NW8* ... *2A 82*
(off Abercorn Pl.)
Abercorn M. TW10: Rich ... 4F 115
Abercorn Pl. NW8 ... 3A 82
Abercorn Rd. HA7: Stan ... 7H 27
NW7 ... 7B 30
Abercorn Wlk. NW8 ... 3A 82
Abercorn Way SE1 ... 5G 103
Abercrombie Dr.
EN1: Enf ... 1B 24
Abercrombie St. SW11 ... 2C 118
Aberdale Ct. *SE16* ... *2K 103*
(off Garter Way)
Aberdare Cl. BR4: W W'ck ... 2E 170
Aberdare Gdns. NW6 ... 7K 63
NW7 ... 7A 30
Aberdare Rd. EN3: Pond E ... 4D 24
Aberdeen Cotts. HA7: Stan ... 7H 27
Aberdeen Ct. *W9* ... *4A 4*
(off Maida Va.)
Aberdeen La. N5 ... 5C 66
Aberdeen Mans.
WC1 ... *3E 6*
(off Kenton St.)
Aberdeen Pde. *N18* ... *5C 34*
(off Montagu Rd.)
Aberdeen Pk. N5 ... 5C 66
Aberdeen Pl. NW8 ... 4A 4 (4B 82)
Aberdeen Rd. CR0: C'don ... 4C 168
HA3: W'stone ... 2K 41
N5 ... 4C 66
N18 ... 5B 34
(not continuous)
NW10 ... 5B 62
Aberdeen Sq. E14 ... 1B 104
Aberdeen Ter. SE3 ... 2F 123
Aberdeen Wharf *E1* ... *1H 103*
(off Wapping High St.)
Aberdour Rd. IG3: Ilf ... 3B 72
Aberdour St. SE1 ... 4E 102
Aberfeldy Ho. SE5 ... 7B 102
(not continuous)
Aberfeldy St. E14 ... 5E 86
(not continuous)
Aberford Gdns. SE18 ... 1C 124
Aberfoyle Rd. SW16 ... 6H 137
(not continuous)
Abergeldie Rd. SE12 ... 6K 123
Abernethy Rd. SE13 ... 4G 123
Abersham Rd. E8 ... 5F 67
Abery St. SE18 ... 4J 107
Ability Towers *EC1* ... *1C 8*
(off Macclesfield Rd.)
Abingdon *W14* ... *4H 99*
(off Kensington Village)
Abingdon Cl. KT4: Wor Pk ... 3D 164
NW1 ... 6H 65
SE1 ... *4F 103*
(off Bushwood Dr.)
SW19 ... 6A 136
UB10: Hil ... 1B 74

Abingdon Ct. *W8* 3J **99**
(off Abingdon Vs.)
Abingdon Gdns. W8 3J **99**
Abingdon Ho. BR1: Brom 7K **141**
E2 3J **9**
(off Boundary St.)
Abingdon Lodge
BR2: Brom 2H **159**
(off Beckenham La.)
W8 3J **99**
Abingdon Mans. *W8* 3J **99**
(off Pater St.)
Abingdon Rd. N3 2A **46**
SW16 2J **155**
W8 3J **99**
Abingdon St. SW1 1E **18** (3J **101**)
Abingdon Vs. W8 3J **99**
Abinger Cl. BR1: Brom 3C **160**
CR0: New Ad 6E **170**
IG11: Bark 4A **72**
SM6: Wall 5J **167**
Abinger Ct. *SM6: Wall* 5J **167**
(off Abinger Cl.)
W5 7C **78**
Abinger Gdns. TW7: Isle 3J **113**
Abinger Gro. SE8 6B **104**
Abinger Ho. *SE1* 7E **14**
(off Gt. Dover St.)
Abinger M. W9 4J **81**
Abinger Rd. W4 3A **98**
Ablett St. SE16 5J **103**
Abney Gdns. N16 2F **67**
Abney Pk. Ter. *N16* 2F **67**
(off Cazenov Rd.)
Aborfield NW5 5G **65**
Aboyne Dr. SW20 2C **152**
Aboyne Rd. NW10 3A **62**
SW17 3B **136**
Abraham Fisher Ho.
E12 5E **70**
Abridge Way IG11: Bark 2B **90**
Abyssinia Cl. SW11 4C **118**
Abyssinia Ct. N8 5K **47**
Abyssinia Rd. SW11 4C **118**
Acacia Av. HA4: Ruis 1J **57**
HA9: Wemb 5E **60**
N17 7J **33**
TW8: Bford 7B **96**
TW17: Shep 5C **146**
UB3: Hayes 6H **75**
UB7: Yiew 7B **74**
Acacia Bus. Cen. E11 3G **69**
Acacia Cl. BR5: Pet W 5H **161**
HA7: Stan 6D **26**
SE8 4A **104**
SE20 2G **157**
Acacia Ct. HA1: Harr 5F **41**
Acacia Dr. SM3: Sutt 1H **165**
Acacia Gdns. BR4: W W'ck 2E **170**
NW8 2B **82**
Acacia Gro. KT3: N Mald 3K **151**
SE21 2D **138**
Acacia Ho. *N22* 1A **48**
(off Douglas Rd.)
Acacia M. UB7: Harm 2E **174**
Acacia Pl. NW8 2B **82**
Acacia Rd. BR3: Beck 3B **158**
CR4: Mitc 2E **154**
E11 2G **69**
E17 6A **50**
EN2: Enf 1J **23**
N22 1A **48**
NW8 2B **82**
SW16 1J **155**
TW12: Hamp 6E **130**
W3 7J **79**
Acacias, The EN4: E Barn 5G **21**
Acacia Wlk. *SW10* 7A **100**
(off Tadema Rd.)
Acacia Way DA15: Sidc 1K **143**
Academy Apartments *E8* 5H **67**
(off Dalston La.)
E8 5H **67**
(off Institute Pl.)
Academy Bldgs. *N1* 1G **9**
(off Fanshaw St.)
Academy Ct. *E2* 3J **85**
(off Kirkwall Pl.)
Academy Gdns. CR0: C'don 1F **169**
UB5: N'olt 2B **76**
W8 2J **99**
Academy Ho. *E3* 5D **86**
(off Violet Rd.)
Academy Pl. SE18 1D **124**
Academy Rd. SE18 1D **124**
Acanthus Dr. SE1 5G **103**
Acanthus Rd. SW11 3E **118**
Accommodation La.
UB7: Harm 2D **174**
UB7: Lford 4B **174**
Accommodation Rd. KT17: Ewe 5C **164**
NW11 1H **63**
AC Court KT7: T Ditt 6A **150**
Ace Pde. KT9: Chess 3E **162**
Acer Av. UB4: Yead 5C **76**
Acer Ct. *EN3: Enf H* 3F **25**
(off Enstone Rd.)
Acer Rd. E8 7F **67**
Acers BR7: Chst 7C **142**
Acfold Rd. SW6 1K **117**
Achilles Cl. SE1 5G **103**
Achilles Ho. *E2* 2H **85**
(off Old Bethnal Grn. Rd.)
Achilles Rd. NW6 5J **63**
Achilles Statue 5H **11** (1E **100**)
Achilles St. SE14 7A **104**
Achilles Way W1 5H **11** (1E **100**)
Acklam Rd. W10 5G **81**
(not continuous)
Acklington Dr. NW9 1A **44**
Ackmar Rd. SW6 1J **117**
Ackroyd Dr. E3 5B **86**
Ackroyd Rd. SE23 7K **121**
Acland Cl. SE18 7H **107**
Acland Cres. SE5 3D **120**
Acland Ho. SW9 1K **119**
Acland Rd. NW2 6D **62**
Acle Cl. IG6: Ilf 1F **53**
Acme Ho. E14 5E **86**
Acock Gro. UB5: N'olt 4F **59**
Acol Ct. NW6 7J **63**
Acol Cres. HA4: Ruis 5K **57**
Acol Rd. NW6 7J **63**
Aconbury Rd. RM9: Dag 1B **90**
Acorn Cl. BR7: Chst 5G **143**
E4 5J **35**
EN2: Enf 1G **23**
HA7: Stan 7G **27**
TW12: Hamp 6F **131**
Acorn Ct. E6 7C **70**
IG2: Ilf 6J **53**
Acorn Gdns. SE19 1F **157**
W3 5K **79**
Acorn Gro. HA4: Ruis 4H **57**
UB3: Harl 7H **93**
Acorn Pde. SE15 7H **103**
Acorn Production Cen. N7 7J **65**
Acorn Wlk. SE16 1A **104**
Acorn Way BR3: Beck 5E **158**
BR6: Farnb 4F **173**
SE23 3K **139**
Acqua Ho. TW9: Kew 7H **97**
Acre Dr. SE22 4G **121**
Acrefield Ho. *NW4* 4F **45**
(off Belle Vue Est.)
Acre La. SM5: Cars 4E **166**
SM6: Wall 4E **166**
SW2 4J **119**
Acre Path *UB5: N'olt* 6C **58**
(off Arnold Rd.)
Acre Rd. KT2: King T 1E **150**
RM10: Dag 7H **73**
SW19 6B **136**
Acre Way HA6: Nwood 1H **39**
Acris St. SW18 5A **118**
Acropolis Ho. *KT1: King T* 3F **151**
(off Winery La.)
ACTON 1J **97**
Acton Central Ind. Est.
W3 1H **97**
Acton Cl. N9 2B **34**
ACTON GREEN 3J **97**
Acton Hill M. W3 1H **97**
Acton Ho. *E8* 1F **85**
(off Lee St.)
W3 6J **79**
Acton La. NW10 3J **79**
W3 2J **97**
Acton M. E8 1F **85**
Acton Pk. Est. W3 2K **97**
Acton Sports Club 4G **97**
Acton St. WC1 2G **7** (3K **83**)
Acton Swimming Baths 1J **97**
(off Salisbury St.)
Acton Va. Ind. Pk. W3 2B **98**
Acuba Rd. SW18 2K **135**
Acworth Cl. N9 7D **24**
Acworth Ho. *SE18* 6F **107**
(off Barnfield Rd.)
Ada Cl. N11 3J **31**
Ada Ct. *N1* 1C **84**
(off Packington St.)
W9 2A **4** (3A **82**)
Ada Gdns. E14 6F **87**
E15 1H **87**
Ada Ho. *E2* 1G **85**
(off Ada Pl.)
Adair Cl. SE25 3H **157**
Adair Ho. SW3 7D **16**
Adair Rd. W10 4G **81**
Adair Twr. *W10* 4G **81**
(off Appleford Rd.)
Ada Kennedy Ct. *SE10* 7E **104**
(off Greenwich Sth. St.)
Ada Lewis Ho. HA9: Wemb 4F **61**
Adam & Eve Ct. W1 7B **6**
Adam & Eve M. W8 3J **99**
Adam Cl. SE6 4B **140**
Adam Ct. *SE11* 4B **102**
(off Opal St.)
SW7 4A **100**
(off Gloucester Rd.)
Adam Rd. E4 6G **35**
Adams Bri. Bus. Cen. HA9: Wemb 5H **61**
Adams Cl. KT5: Surb 6F **151**
N3 7D **30**
NW9 2H **61**
Adams Ct. E17 6A **50**
EC2 7F **9** (6E **84**)
Adams Gdns. Est. SE16 2J **103**
Adams Ho. *E14* 6F **87**
(off Aberfeldy St.)
Adams M. N22 7E **32**
SW17 2D **136**
Adamson Ct. N2 3C **46**
Adamson Rd. E16 6J **87**
NW3 7B **64**
Adamson Way BR3: Beck 5E **158**
Adams Pl. *E14* 1D **104**
(off The Nth. Colonnade)
N7 5K **65**
Adams Quarter TW8: Bford 6C **96**
Adamsrill Cl. EN1: Enf 6J **23**
Adamsrill Rd. SE26 4K **139**
Adams Rd. BR3: Beck 5A **158**
N17 2D **48**
Adam's Row W1 3H **11** (7E **82**)
Adams Sq. DA6: Bex 3E **126**
Adam St. WC2 3F **13** (7J **83**)
Adams Wlk. KT1: King T 2E **150**
Adams Way CR0: C'don 6F **157**
SE25 5H **157**
Adam Wlk. SW6 7E **98**
Ada Pl. E2 1G **85**
Adare Wlk. SW16 3K **137**
Ada Rd. HA0: Wemb 3D **60**
SE5 7E **102**
Adastral Ho. *WC1* 5G **7**
(off Harpur St.)
Ada St. E8 1H **85**
Ada Workshops E8 1H **85**
Adcock Wlk. BR6: Orp 4K **173**
Adderley Gdns. SE9 4E **142**
Adderley Gro. SW11 5E **118**
Adderley Rd. HA3: W'stone 1K **41**
Adderley St. E14 6E **86**
Addey Ho. SE8 7B **104**
ADDINGTON 5C **170**
Addington Ct. SW14 3K **115**
Addington Dr. N12 6G **31**
Addington Gro. SE26 4A **140**
Addington Ho. *SW9* 2K **119**
(off Stockwell Rd.)
Addington Palace 6B **170**
Addington Rd. BR4: W W'ck 4E **170**
CR0: C'don 1A **168**
CR2: Sande, Sels 7K **169**
E3 3C **86**
E16 4G **87**
N4 6A **48**
Addington Sq. SE5 6D **102**
Addington St. SE1 7H **13** (2K **101**)
Addington Village Rd.
CR0: Addtn 6B **170**
(not continuous)
Addis Cl. EN3: Enf H 1E **24**
ADDISCOMBE 1G **169**
Addiscombe Av. CR0: C'don 1G **169**
Addiscombe Cl. HA3: Kent 5C **42**
Addiscombe Ct. Rd.
CR0: C'don 1E **168**
Addiscombe Gro.
CR0: C'don 2E **168**
Addiscombe Rd. CR0: C'don 2D **168**
(not continuous)
Addis Ho. *E1* 5J **85**
(off Lindley St.)
Addisland Ct. *W14* 2G **99**
(off Holland Vs. Rd.)
Addison Av. N14 6A **22**
TW3: Houn 1G **113**
W11 1G **99**
Addison Bri. Pl. W14 4H **99**
Addison Cl. BR5: Pet W 6G **161**
HA6: Nwood 1J **39**
Addison Ct. *NW6* 1J **81**
(off Brondesbury Rd.)
Addison Cres. W14 3G **99**
(not continuous)
Addison Dr. SE12 5K **123**
Addison Gdns. KT5: Surb 4F **151**
W14 3F **99**
Addison Gro. W4 3A **98**
Addison Ho. NW8 1A **4**
Addison Pk. Mans. *W14* 3F **99**
(off Richmond Way)
Addison Pl. SE25 4G **157**
UB1: S'hall 7E **76**
W11 1G **99**
Addison Rd. BR2: Brom 5A **160**
E11 6J **51**
E17 5D **50**
EN3: Enf H 1D **24**
IG6: Ilf 1G **53**
SE25 4G **157**
TW11: Tedd 6B **132**
W14 2G **99**
Addisons Cl. CR0: C'don 2B **170**
Addison Ter. *W4* 4J **97**
(off Chiswick Rd.)

Addison Way HA6: Nwood 1H 39
NW11 4H 45
UB3: Hayes 6J 75
Addle Hill EC4 1B 14 (6B 84)
Addlestone Ho. W10 5E 80
(off Sutton Way)
Addle St. EC2 7D 8 (6C 84)
Addy Ho. SE16 4J 103
Adecroft Way KT8: W Mole 3G 149
Adela Av. KT3: N Mald 5D 152
Adela Ho. W6 5E 98
(off Queen Caroline St.)
Adelaide Av. SE4 4B 122
Adelaide Cl. EN1: Enf 1K 23
HA7: Stan 4F 27
SW9 4A 120
Adelaide Ct. BR3: Beck 7B 140
NW8 1A 4
W7 2K 95
Adelaide Gdns. RM6: Chad H 5E 54
Adelaide Gro. W12 1C 98
Adelaide Ho. E15 2H 87
E17 2B 50
SE5 2E 120
W11 6H 81
(off Portobello Rd.)
Adelaide Rd. BR7: Chst 5F 143
E10 3D 68
IG1: Ilf 2F 71
KT6: Surb 5E 150
NW3 7B 64
SW18 5J 117
TW5: Hest 1C 112
TW9: Rich 4F 115
TW11: Tedd 6K 131
TW15: Ashf 5A 128
UB2: S'hall 4C 94
W13 1A 96
Adelaide St. WC2 3E 12 (7J 83)
Adelaide Ter. TW8: Bford 5D 96
Adela St. W10 4G 81
Adelina Gro. E1 5J 85
Adelina M. SW12 1H 137
Adelina Yd. E1 5J 85
(off Adelina Gro.)
Adeline Pl. WC1 6D 6 (5H 83)
Adeliza Cl. IG11: Bark 7G 71
Adelphi Ct. E8 7F 67
(off Celandine Dr.)
SE16 2K 103
(off Garter Way)
W4 6K 97
Adelphi Cres. UB4: Hayes 3G 75
Adelphi Ter. WC2 3F 13 (7J 83)
Adelphi Theatre 3F 13
(off Strand)
Adelphi Way UB4: Hayes 3H 75
Adeney Cl. W6 6F 99
Aden Gro. N16 4D 66
Aden Ho. E1 5K 85
(off Duckett St.)
Adenmore Rd. SE6 7C 122
Aden Rd. EN3: Brim 4F 25
IG1: Ilf 7G 53
Aden Ter. N16 4D 66
Adeyfield Ho. EC1 2F 9
(off Cranwood St.)
Adie Rd. W6 3E 98
Adine Rd. E13 4K 87
Adler Ind. Est. UB3: Hayes 2F 93
Adler St. E1 6G 85
Adley St. E5 5A 68
Adlington Cl. N18 5J 33
Admaston Rd. SE18 7G 107
Admiral Ct. IG11: Bark 2B 90
SM5: Cars 1C 166
SW10 1A 118
(off Admiral Sq.)
W1 6G 5
(off Blandford St.)
Admiral Ho. SW1 3B 18
(off Willow Pl.)
TW11: Tedd 4A 132
Admiral Hyson Ind. Est. SE16 5H 103
Admiral M. W10 4F 81
Admiral Pl. SE16 1A 104
Admirals Cl. E18 4K 51
Admirals Ct. E6 6F 89
(off Trader Rd.)
SE1 5J 15
(off Horselydown La.)
Admiral Seymour Rd. SE9 4D 124
Admiral's Ga. SE10 1D 122
Admiral Sq. SW10 1A 118
Admiral St. SE8 2C 122
Admirals Wlk. NW3 3A 64
Admirals Way E14 2C 104
Admiralty Arch 4D 12 (1H 101)
Admiralty Cl. SE8 7C 104
UB7: W Dray 2A 92
Admiralty Rd. TW11: Tedd 6K 131
Admiralty Way TW11: Tedd 6K 131
Admiral Wlk. W9 5J 81
Adolf St. SE6 4D 140
Adolphus Rd. N4 2B 66
Adolphus St. SE8 7B 104
Adomar Rd. RM8: Dag 3D 72
Adpar St. W2 5A 4 (5B 82)
Adrian Av. NW2 1D 62
Adrian Boult Ho. E2 3H 85
(off Mansford St.)
Adrian Cl. EN5: Barn 6A 20
Adrian Ho. N1 1K 83
(off Barnsbury Est.)
SW8 7J 101
(off Wyvil Rd.)
Adrian M. SW10 6K 99
Adriatic Apartments E16 7J 87
(off Western Gateway)
Adriatic Bldg. E14 7A 86
(off Horseferry Rd.)
Adriatic Ho. E1 4K 85
(off Ernest St.)
Adrienne Av. UB1: S'hall 4D 76
Adron Ho. SE16 4J 103
(off Millender Wlk.)
Adstock Ho. N1 7B 66
(off The Sutton Est.)
Advance Rd. SE27 4C 138
Adventure Kingdom 2K 159
(off Stockwell Cl.)
Adventurers Ct. E14 7F 87
(off Newport Av.)
Advent Way N18 5D 34
Adys Lawn NW2 6D 62
Ady's Rd. SE15 3F 121
Aegean Apartments E16 7J 87
(off Western Gateway)
Aegon Ho. E14 3D 104
(off Lanark Sq.)
Aerodrome Rd. NW4 2B 44
NW9 2B 44
Aerodrome Way TW5: Hest 6A 94
Aeroville NW9 2A 44
Affleck St. N1 1G 7 (2K 83)
Afghan Rd. SW11 2C 118
Afsil Ho. EC1 6K 7
(off Viaduct Bldgs.)
Aftab Ter. E1 4H 85
(off Tent St.)
Agamemnon Rd. NW6 4H 63
Agar Cl. KT6: Surb 2F 163
Agar Gro. NW1 7G 65
Agar Gro. Est. NW1 7H 65
Agar Ho. KT1: King T 3E 150
(off Denmark Rd.)
Agar Pl. NW1 7G 65
Agar St. WC2 3E 12 (7J 83)
Agate Cl. E16 6B 88
Agate Rd. W6 3E 98
Agatha Cl. E1 1H 103
Agaton Path SE9 2G 143
Agaton Rd. SE9 2G 143
Agave Rd. NW2 4E 62
Agdon St. EC1 3A 8 (4B 84)
Agincourt Rd. NW3 4D 64
Agnes Av. IG1: Ilf 4E 70
Agnes Cl. E6 7E 88
Agnesfield Cl. N12 6H 31
Agnes Gdns. RM8: Dag 4D 72
Agnes Ho. W11 7F 81
(off St Ann's Rd.)
Agnes Rd. W3 1B 98
Agnes St. E14 6B 86
Agnew Rd. SE23 7K 121
Agricola Pl. EN1: Enf 5A 24
Aidan Cl. RM8: Dag 4E 72
Aigburth Mans. SW9 7A 102
(off Mowll St.)
Ailantus Ct. HA8: Edg 5A 28
Aileen Wlk. E15 7H 69
Ailsa Av. TW1: Twick 5A 114
Ailsa Ho. E16 7E 88
(off University Way)
Ailsa Rd. TW1: Twick 5B 114
Ailsa St. E14 5E 86
Ailsa Wlk. E14 2C 104
(off Cassilis Rd.)
Ainger M. NW3 7D 64
(off Ainger Rd.)
Ainger Rd. NW3 7D 64
Ainsdale NW1 1A 6
(off Harrington St.)
Ainsdale Cl. BR6: Orp 1H 173
Ainsdale Cres. HA5: Pinn 3E 40
Ainsdale Dr. SE1 5G 103
Ainsdale Rd. W5 4D 78
Ainsley Av. RM7: Rom 6H 55
Ainsley Cl. N9 1K 33
Ainsley St. E2 3H 85
Ainslie Ct. HA0: Wemb 2E 78
Ainslie Wlk. SW12 7F 119
Ainslie Wood Cres. E4 5J 35
Ainslie Wood Gdns. E4 4J 35
Ainslie Wood Nature Reserve 5J 35
Ainslie Wood Rd. E4 5H 35
Ainsty Est. SE16 2K 103
Ainsty St. SE16 2J 103
Ainsworth Cl. NW2 3C 62
SE15 2E 120
Ainsworth Ho. NW8 1K 81
(off Ainsworth Way)
W10 3G 81
(off Kilburn La.)
Ainsworth Rd. CR0: C'don 1B 168
E9 7J 67
Ainsworth Way NW8 1A 82
Aintree Av. E6 1C 88
Aintree Cl. UB8: Hil 6D 74
Aintree Cres. IG6: Ilf 2G 53
Aintree Est. SW6 7G 99
(off Aintree St.)
Aintree Rd. UB6: G'frd 2B 78
Aintree St. SW6 7G 99
Airbourne Ho. SM6: Wall 4G 167
(off Maldon Rd.)
Air Call Bus. Cen. NW9 3K 43
Aird Ho. SE1 3C 102
(off Rockingham St.)
Airdrie Cl. N1 7K 65
UB4: Yead 5C 76
Airedale Av. W4 4B 98
Airedale Av. Sth. W4 5B 98
Airedale Rd. SW12 7D 118
W5 3C 96
Airlie Gdns. IG1: Ilf 1F 71
W8 1J 99
Air Links Ind. Est. TW13: Hanw 3C 130
Airlinks Ind. Est. TW5: Cran 5A 94
Air Pk. Way TW13: Felt 2K 129
Airport Bowl 1G 111
Airport Ga. Bus. Cen.
UB7: Sip 7B 92
Airport Way TW19: Stan M 7A 174
Air St. W1 3B 12 (7G 83)
Airthrie Rd. IG3: Ilf 2B 72
Aisgill Av. W14 5H 99
(not continuous)
Aisher Rd. SE28 7C 90
Aislibie Rd. SE12 4G 123
Aiten Pl. W6 4C 98
Aithan Ho. E14 6B 86
(off Copenhagen Pl.)
Aitken Cl. CR4: Mitc 7D 154
E8 1G 85
Aitken Rd. SE6 2D 140
Aitman Dr. W4 5G 97
Aits Vw. KT8: W Mole 3F 149
Ajax Av. NW9 3A 44
Ajax Ho. E2 2H 85
(off Old Bethnal Grn. Rd.)
Ajax Rd. NW6 4H 63
Akabusi Cl. CR0: C'don 6G 157
Akbar Ho. E14 4D 104
(off Cahir St.)
Akehurst St. SW15 6C 116
Akenside Rd. NW3 5B 64
Akerman Rd. KT6: Surb 6C 150
SW9 2B 120
Akintaro Ho. SE8 6B 104
(off Alverton St.)
Alabama St. SE18 7H 107
Alacross Rd. W5 2C 96
Alamaro Lodge SE10 3H 105
Alandale Dr. HA5: Pinn 1K 39
Aland Ct. SE16 3A 104
Alander M. E17 4E 50
Alan Dr. EN5: Barn 6B 20
Alan Gdns. RM7: Rush G 7G 55
Alan Hocken Way E15 2G 87
Alan Preece Ct. NW6 7F 63
Alan Rd. SW19 5G 135
Alanthus Cl. SE12 6J 123
Alaska Apartments
E16 7J 87
(off Western Gateway)
Alaska Bldg. SE10 1D 122
(off Deal's Gateway)
Alaska Bldgs. SE1 3E 102
Alaska St. SE1 5J 13 (1A 102)
Alastor Ho. E14 3E 104
(off Strattondale Ho.)
Alba Cl. UB4: Yead 4B 76
Albacore Cres. SE13 6D 122
Alba Gdns. NW11 6G 45
Albain Cres. TW15: Ashf 2A 128
Alba M. SW18 2J 135
Alban Highwalk EC2 7D 8
(not continuous)
Albany N12 6E 30
W1 3A 12 (7G 83)
Albany, The IG8: Wfd G 4C 36
Albany Cl. DA5: Bexl 7C 126
N15 4B 48
SW14 4H 115
UB10: Ick 5C 56
Albany Ct. E4 6H 25
(Chelwood Cl.)
E4 5G 35
(Westward Rd.)
E10 7C 50
HA8: Edg 1K 43
NW8 1A 4
(off Abbey Rd.)
NW10 3D 80
(off Trenmar Gdns.)
TW15: Ashf 7E 128
Albany Courtyard W1 3B 12 (7G 83)
Albany Cres. HA8: Edg 7B 28
Albany Mans. SW11 7C 100

Albany M. BR1: Brom 6J 141
KT2: King T 6D 132
N1 7A 66
SE5 6C 102
SM1: Sutt 5K 165
Albany Pde. TW8: Bford 6E 96
Albany Pk. Av. EN3: Enf W 1D 24
Albany Pk. Rd. KT2: King T 6D 132
Albany Pas. TW10: Rich 5E 114
Albany Pl. TW8: Bford 6D 96
Albany Reach KT7: T Ditt 5K 149
Albany Rd. BR7: Chst 5F 143
DA5: Bexl 7C 126
DA17: Belv 6F 109
E10 7C 50
E12 4B 70
E17 6A 50
KT3: N Mald 4K 151
N4 6A 48
N18 5D 34
RM6: Chad H 6F 55
SE5 6D 102
SW19 5K 135
TW8: Bford 6D 96
TW10: Rich 5F 115
W13 7B 78
Albany St. NW1 1K 5 (2F 83)
Albany Ter. NW1 4K 5
TW10: Rich 5F 115
(off Albany Pas.)
Albany Vw. IG9: Buck H 1D 36
Alba Pl. W11 6H 81
Albatross NW9 2B 44
Albatross Cl. E6 5D 88
Albatross St. SE18 7J 107
Albatross Way SE16 2K 103
Albemarle SW19 2F 135
Albemarle App. IG2: Ilf 6F 53
Albemarle Av. TW2: Whitt 1D 130
Albemarle Gdns. IG2: Ilf 6F 53
KT3: N Mald 4K 151
Albemarle Ho. SE8 4B 104
(off Foreshore)
SW9 3A 120
Albemarle Pk. BR3: Beck 1D 158
HA7: Stan 5H 27
Albemarle Rd. BR3: Beck 1D 158
EN4: E Barn 7H 21
Albemarle St. W1 3K 11 (7F 83)
Albemarle Way EC1 4A 8 (4B 84)
Alberon Gdns. NW11 4H 45
Alberta Av. SM1: Sutt 4G 165
Alberta Est. SE17 5B 102
(off Alberta St.)
Alberta Ho. E14 1E 104
(off Gaselee St.)
Alberta Rd. DA8: Erith 1J 127
EN1: Enf 6A 24
Alberta St. SE17 5B 102
Albert Av. E4 4H 35
SW8 7K 101
Albert Barnes Ho. SE1 3C 102
(off New Kent Rd.)
Albert Basin Way E16 7G 89
Albert Bigg Point E15 2E 86
(off Godfrey St.)
Albert Bri. SW11 7D 16 (6C 100)
Albert Bri. Rd. SW11 7C 100
Albert Carr Gdns. SW16 5J 137
Albert Cl. E9 1H 85
N22 1H 47
Albert Cotts. E1 5G 85
(off Deal St.)
Albert Ct. E7 4J 69
SW7 7A 10 (3B 100)
Albert Ct. Ga. SW1 7E 10
(off Knightsbridge)
Albert Cres. E4 4H 35
Albert Dane Cen. UB2: S'hall 3C 94
Albert Dr. SW19 2G 135
Albert Emb. SE1 1G 19 (3K 101)
(Lambeth Pal. Rd.)
SE1 6F 19 (5J 101)
(Vauxhall Bri.)
Albert Gdns. E1 6K 85
Albert Ga. SW1 6F 11 (2D 100)
Albert Gray Ho. SW10 7B 100
(off Worlds End Est.)
Albert Gro. SW20 1F 153
Albert Hall Mans.
SW7 7A 10 (2B 100)
(not continuous)
Albert Ho. E18 3K 51
(off Albert Rd.)
SE28 3G 107
Albert Mans. CR0: C'don 1D 168
(off Lansdowne Rd.)
Albert Memorial 7A 10 (2B 100)
Albert M. E14 7A 86
(off Northey St.)
N4 1K 65
SE4 4A 122
W8 3A 100
Albert Pal. Mans. SW11 1F 119
(off Lurline Gdns.)
Albert Pl. N3 1J 45
N17 3F 49
W8 3K 99
Albert Rd. BR2: Brom 5B 160
CR4: Mitc 3D 154
DA5: Bexl 6G 127
DA17: Belv 5F 109
E10 2E 68
E16 1C 106
E17 5C 50
E18 3K 51
EN4: E Barn 4F 21
HA2: Harr 3G 41
IG1: Ilf 3F 71
IG9: Buck H 2G 37
KT1: King T 2F 151
KT3: N Mald 4B 152
N4 1K 65
N15 6E 48
N22 1G 47
NW4 4F 45
NW6 2H 81
NW7 5G 29
RM8: Dag 1G 73
SE9 3C 142
SE20 6K 139
SE25 4G 157
SM1: Sutt 5B 166
TW1: Twick 1K 131
TW3: Houn 4E 112
TW10: Rich 5E 114
TW11: Tedd 6K 131
TW12: Ham H 5G 131
TW15: Ashf 5B 128
UB2: S'hall 3B 94
UB3: Hayes 3G 93
UB7: Yiew 1A 92
W5 4B 78
Albert Rd. Cen. NW6 2H 81
(off Albert Rd.)
Albert Rd. Est. DA17: Belv 5F 109
Alberts Ct. NW1 3D 4
Albert Sleet Ct. N9 3C 34
(off Colthurst Dr.)
Albert Sq. E15 5G 69
SW8 7K 101
Albert Starr Ho. SE8 4K 103
(off Bush Rd.)
Albert St. N12 5F 31
NW1 1F 83
Albert Studios SW11 1D 118
Albert Ter.
IG9: Buck H 2H 37
NW1 1E 82
NW10 1J 79
Albert Ter. W5 4B 78
W6 5C 98
(off Beavor La.)
Albert Ter. M. NW1 1E 82
Albert Victoria Ho. N22 1A 48
Albert Wlk. E16 2E 106
Albert Way SE15 7H 103
Albert Westcott Ho. SE17 5B 102
Albert Whicher Ho. E17 4E 50
Albert Yd. SE19 6E 138
Albery Ct. E8 7F 67
(off Middleton Rd.)
Albion Av. N10 1E 46
SW8 2H 119
Albion Bldgs. N1 2J 83
(off Albion Yd.)
Albion Cl. RM7: Rom 6K 55
W2 2D 10 (7C 82)
Albion Ct. SM2: Sutt 7B 166
W6 4D 98
(off Albion Pl.)
Albion Dr. E8 7F 67
Albion Est. SE16 2K 103
Albion Gdns. W6 4D 98
Albion Ga. W2 2D 10
(not continuous)
Albion Gro. N16 4E 66
Albion Ho. E16 1F 107
(off Church St.)
SE8 7C 104
(off Watsons St.)
Albion M. N1 1A 84
NW6 7H 63
W2 2D 10 (7C 82)
W6 4D 98
Albion Pde. N16 4D 66
Albion Pl. EC1 5A 8 (5B 84)
EC2 6F 9 (5D 84)
SE25 3G 157
W6 4D 98
Albion Riverside Bldg. SW11 7C 100
Albion Rd. DA6: Bex 4F 127
E17 3E 50
KT2: King T 1J 151
N16 4D 66
N17 2G 49
SM2: Sutt 6B 166
TW2: Twick 1J 131
TW3: Houn 4E 112
UB3: Hayes 6G 75
Albion Sq. E8 7F 67
(not continuous)
Albion St. CR0: C'don 1B 168
SE16 2J 103
W2 1D 10 (6C 82)
Albion Ter. E4 4J 25
E8 7F 67
Albion Vs. Rd. SE26 3J 139
Albion Wlk. N1 1F 7
(off York Way)
Albion Way EC1 6C 8 (5C 84)
HA9: Wemb 3G 61
SE13 4E 122
Albion Yd. E1 5H 85
N1 2J 83
Albon Ho. SW18 6K 117
(off Neville Gill Cl.)
Albrighton Rd. SE22 3E 120
Albuhera Cl. EN2: Enf 1F 23
Albury Av. DA7: Bex 2E 126
TW7: Isle 7K 95
Albury Cl. TW12: Hamp 6F 131
Albury Ct. CR2: S Croy 4C 168
(off Tanfield Rd.)
CR4: Mitc 2B 154
SE8 6C 104
(off Albury St.)
SM1: Sutt 4A 166
UB5: Yead 3A 76
(off Canberra Dr.)
Albury Dr. HA5: Pinn 1A 40 & 1C 40
Albury Ho. SE1 7B 14
(off Boyfield St.)
Albury M. E12 2A 70
Albury Rd. KT9: Chess 5E 162
Albury St. SE8 6C 104
Albyfield BR1: Brom 4D 160
Albyn Rd. SE8 1C 122
Alcester Ct. SM6: Wall 4F 167
Alcester Cres. E5 2H 67
Alcester Rd. SM6: Wall 4F 167
Alcock Cl. SM6: Wall 7H 167
Alcock Rd. TW5: Hest 7B 94
Alconbury DA6: Bex 5H 127
Alconbury Rd. E5 2G 67
Alcorn Cl. SM3: Sutt 2J 165
Alcott Cl. TW14: Felt 1H 129
W7 5K 77
Alcuin Ct. HA7: Stan 7H 27
Aldam Pl. N16 2F 67
Aldborough Ct. IG2: Ilf 5K 53
(off Aldborough Rd. Nth.)
ALDBOROUGH HATCH 4K 53
Aldborough Rd. RM10: Dag 6J 73
Aldborough Rd. Nth. IG2: Ilf 5K 53
Aldborough Rd. Sth. IG3: Ilf 1J 71
Aldbourne Rd. W12 1B 98
(not continuous)
Aldbridge St. SE17 5E 102
Aldburgh M. W1 7H 5 (6E 82)
(not continuous)
Aldbury Av. HA9: Wemb 7H 61
Aldbury Ho. SW3 5C 16
(off Cale St.)
Aldbury M. N9 7J 23
Aldebert Ter. SW8 7J 101
Aldeburgh Cl. E5 2H 67
Aldeburgh Pl. IG8: Wfd G 4D 36
SE10 4J 105
(off Aldeburgh St.)
Aldeburgh St. SE10 5J 105
Alden Av. E15 3H 87
Alden Ct. CR0: C'don 3E 168
Aldenham Dr. UB8: Hil 4D 74
Aldenham Ho. NW1 1B 6
(off Aldenham St.)
Aldenham St. NW1 1C 6 (2G 83)
Alden Ho. E8 1H 85
(off Duncan Rd.)
Aldensley Rd. W6 3D 98
Alderbrook Rd. SW12 6F 119
Alderbury Rd. SW13 6C 98
Alder Cl. SE15 6F 103
Alder Gro. NW2 2C 62
Aldergrove Gdns. TW3: Houn 2C 112
Alder Ho. NW3 6D 64
SE4 3C 122
SE15 6F 103
(off Alder Cl.)
Alder Lodge SW6 1E 116
Alderman Av. IG11: Bark 3A 90
Aldermanbury EC2 7D 8 (6C 84)
Aldermanbury Sq. EC2 6D 8 (5C 84)
Alderman Judge Mall
KT1: King T 2E 150
(off Eden St.)
Aldermans Hill N13 4D 32
Aldermans Wlk. EC2 6G 9 (5E 84)
Aldermary Rd. BR1: Brom 1J 159
Alder M. N19 2G 65
Aldermoor Rd. SE6 3B 140
Alderney Av. TW5: Hest, Isle 7F 95
Alderney Ct. SE10 6F 105
(off Trafalgar Rd.)
Alderney Gdns. UB5: N'olt 7D 58
Alderney Ho. EN3: Enf W 1E 24
N1 6C 66
(off Arran Wlk.)
Alderney M. SE1 3D 102
Alderney Rd. E1 4K 85

Alderney St. SW1 4K 17 (4F 101)
Alder Rd. DA14: Sidc 3K 143
SW14 3K 115
Alders, The BR4: W W'ck 1D 170
N21 6F 23
SW16 4G 137
TW5: Hest 6D 94
TW13: Hanw 4C 130
Alders Av. IG8: Wfd G 6B 36
ALDERSBROOK 2K 69
Aldersbrook Av. EN1: Enf 2K 23
Aldersbrook Dr. KT2: King T 6F 133
Aldersbrook La. E12 3D 70
Aldersbrook Rd. E11 2K 69
E12 2K 69
Alders Cl. E11 2K 69
HA8: Edg 5D 28
W5 3D 96
Aldersey Gdns. IG11: Bark 6H 71
Aldersford Cl. SE4 5K 121
Aldersgate Ct. *EC1* *6C 8*
(off Bartholomew Cl.)
Aldersgate St. EC1 5C 8 (5C 84)
Alders Gro. KT8: E Mos 5H 149
Aldersgrove Av. SE9 3B 142
Aldershot Rd. NW6 1H 81
Aldershot Ter. SE18 7E 106
Aldersmead Av.
CR0: C'don 6K 157
Aldersmead Rd. BR3: Beck 7A 140
Alderson Pl. UB2: S'hall 1G 95
Alderson St. W10 4G 81
Alders Rd. HA8: Edg 5D 28
Alderton Cl. NW10 3K 61
Alderton Ct. *KT8: W Mole* *4D 148*
(off Walton Rd.)
Alderton Cres. NW4 5D 44
Alderton Rd. CR0: C'don 7F 157
SE24 3C 120
Alderton Way NW4 5D 44
Alderville Rd. SW6 2H 117
Alder Wlk. IG1: Ilf 5G 71
Alderwick Ct. *N7* *6K 65*
(off Cornelia St.)
Alderwick Dr. TW3: Houn 3H 113
Alderwood M. EN4: Had W 1F 21
Alderwood Rd. SE9 6H 125
Aldford Ho. *W1* *4G 11*
(off Park St.)
Aldford St. W1 4H 11 (1E 100)
ALDGATE 6F 85
Aldgate EC3 1J 15 (6E 84)
Aldgate Av. E1 7J 9 (6F 85)
Aldgate Barrs E1 7K 9
Aldgate High St. EC3 1J 15 (6F 85)
Aldgate Triangle *E1* *6G 85*
(off Coke St.)
Aldham Ho. *SE14* *2B 122*
(off Malpas Rd.)
Aldine Ct. *W12* *2E 98*
(off Aldine St.)
Aldine Pl. W12 2E 98
Aldine St. W12 2E 98
Aldington Cl. RM8: Dag 1C 72
Aldington Ct. *E8* *7G 67*
(off London Flds. W. Side)
Aldington Rd. SE18 3B 106
Aldis M. SW17 5C 136
Aldis St. SW17 5C 136
Aldred Rd. NW6 5J 63
Aldren Rd. SW17 3A 136
Aldrich Cres. CR0: New Ad 7E 170
Aldriche Way E4 6K 35
Aldrich Gdns. SM3: Cheam 3H 165
Aldrich Ter. SW18 2A 136
Aldrick Ho. *N1* *1K 83*
(off Barnsbury Est.)
Aldridge Av. HA4: Ruis 5K 39
HA7: Stan 1E 42
HA8: Edg 3C 28
Aldridge Ct. *W11* *5H 81*
(off Aldridge Rd. Vs.)
Aldridge Ri. KT3: N Mald 7A 152
Aldridge Rd. Vs. W11 5H 81
Aldridge Wlk. N14 7D 22
Aldrington Rd. SW16 5G 137
Aldsworth Cl. W9 4K 81
Aldwick Cl. SE9 3H 143
Aldwick Rd. CR0: Bedd 3K 167
Aldworth Gro. SE13 6E 122
Aldworth Rd. E15 7G 69
Aldwych WC2 2G 13 (6K 83)
Aldwych Av. IG6: Ilf 4G 53
Aldwych Ct. *E8* *7F 67*
(off Middleton Rd.)
Aldwych Theatre *1G 13*
(off Aldwych)
Aldwyn Ho. *SW8* *7J 101*
(off Davidson Gdns.)
Alers Rd. DA6: Bex 5D 126
Alesia Cl. N22 7D 32
Alestan Beck Rd. E16 6B 88
Alexa Ct. SM2: Sutt 6J 165
W8 4J 99
Alexander Av. NW10 7D 62
Alexander Cl. BR2: Hayes 1J 171
DA15: Sidc 6J 125
EN4: E Barn 4G 21
TW2: Twick 2J 131
UB2: S'hall 1G 95
Alexander Ct. BR3: Beck 1F 159
HA7: Stan 3F 43
Alexander Evans M. SE23 2K 139
Alexander Fleming Laboratory Mus.
7B 4 (6B 82)
Alexander Ho. *E14* *3C 104*
(off Tiller Rd.)
KT2: King T *1E 150*
(off Seven Kings Way)
Alexander M. SW16 5G 137
W2 6K 81
Alexander Pl. SW7 3C 16 (4C 100)
Alexander Rd. BR7: Chst 6F 143
DA7: Bex 2D 126
N19 3J 65
Alexander Sq. SW3 3C 16 (4C 100)
Alexander St. W2 6J 81
Alexander Studios *SW11* *4B 118*
(off Haydon Way)
Alexander Ter. SE2 5B 108
Alexandra Av. HA2: Harr 1D 58
N22 1H 47
SM1: Sutt 3J 165
SW11 1E 118
UB1: S'hall 7D 76
W4 7K 97
Alexandra Cl. HA2: Harr 3E 58
SE8 6B 104
TW15: Ashf 7F 129
Alexandra Cotts. SE14 1B 122
Alexandra Ct. HA9: Wemb 4F 61
N14 5B 22
SW7 1A 16
TW3: Houn 2F 113
TW15: Ashf 6F 129
UB6: G'frd 2F 77
W2 *7K 81*
(off Moscow Rd.)
W9 *4A 82*
(off Maida Va.)
Alexandra Cres.
BR1: Brom 6H 141
Alexandra Dr. KT5: Surb 7G 151
SE19 5E 138
Alexandra Gdns. N10 4F 47
SM5: Cars 7E 166
TW3: Houn 2F 113
W4 7A 98
Alexandra Gro. N4 1B 66
N12 5E 30
Alexandra Ho. *E16* *1K 105*
(off Wesley Av.)
IG8: Wfd G 7K 37
W6 *5E 98*
(off Queen Caroline St.)
Alexandra Mans. *SW3* *7A 16*
(off King's Rd.)
Alexandra M. N2 3D 46
SW19 6H 135
Alexandra National Ho. N4 1B 66
Alexandra Palace 2H 47
Alexandra Pal. Way N22 4G 47
Alexandra Pde. HA2: Harr 4F 59
Alexandra Pk. Rd. N10 2F 47
N22 1G 47
Alexandra Pl. CR0: C'don 1E 168
NW8 1A 82
SE25 5D 156
Alexandra Rd. CR0: C'don 1E 168
CR4: Mitc 7C 136
E6 3E 88
E10 3E 68
E17 6B 50
E18 3K 51
EN3: Pond E 4E 24
KT2: King T 7G 133
KT7: T Ditt 5K 149
N8 3A 48
N9 7C 24
N10 7A 32
N15 5D 48
NW4 4F 45
NW8 1A 82
RM6: Chad H 6E 54
SE26 6K 139
SW14 3K 115
SW19 6H 135
TW1: Twick 6C 114
TW3: Houn 2F 113
TW8: Bford 6D 96
TW9: Kew 2F 115
TW15: Ashf 7F 129
W4 2K 97
Alexandra Rd. Ind. Est.
EN3: Pond E 4E 24
Alexandra Sq. SM4: Mord 5J 153
Alexandra St. E16 5J 87
SE14 7A 104
Alexandra Ter. *E14* *5D 104*
(off Westferry Rd.)
Alexandra Wlk. SE19 5E 138
Alexandra Wharf *E2* *1H 85*
(off Darwen Pl.)
Alexandra Yd. E9 1K 85
Alexandria Apartments *SE17* *4E 102*
(off Townsend St.)
Alexandria Rd. W13 7A 78
Alexis St. SE16 4G 103
Alfan La. DA2: Dart 5K 145
Alfearn Rd. E5 4J 67
Alford Ct. *N1* *1D 8*
(off Shepherdess Wlk.)
Alford Grn. CR0: New Ad 6F 171
Alford Ho. N6 6G 47
Alford Pl. N1 1D 8 (2C 84)
Alford Rd. DA8: Erith 5J 109
Alfoxton Av. N15 4B 48
Alfreda St. SW11 1F 119
Alfred Cl. W4 4K 97
Alfred Dickens Ho. *E16* *6H 87*
(off Hallsville Rd.)
Alfred Finlay Ho. N22 2B 48
Alfred Gdns. UB1: S'hall 7C 76
Alfred Ho. *E9* *5A 68*
(off Homerton Rd.)
E12 *7C 70*
(off Tennyson Av.)
Alfred M. W1 5C 6 (5H 83)
Alfred Nunn Ho. NW10 1B 80
Alfred Pl. WC1 5C 6 (5H 83)
Alfred Prior Ho. E12 4E 70
Alfred Rd. DA17: Belv 5F 109
E15 5H 69
IG9: Buck H 2G 37
KT1: King T 3E 150
SE25 5G 157
SM1: Sutt 5A 166
TW13: Felt 2A 130
W2 5J 81
W3 1J 97
Alfred Salter Ho. *SE1* *4F 103*
(off Fort Rd.)
Alfred's Gdns. IG11: Bark 2J 89
Alfred St. E3 3B 86
Alfreds Way IG11: Bark 3F 89
Alfreds Way Ind. Est. IG11: Bark 1A 90
Alfred Vs. E17 4E 50
Alfreton Cl. SW19 3F 135
Alfriston KT5: Surb 6F 151
Alfriston Av. CR0: C'don 7J 155
HA2: Harr 6E 40
Alfriston Cl. KT5: Surb 5F 151
Alfriston Rd. SW11 5D 118
Algar Cl. HA7: Stan 5E 26
TW7: Isle 3A 114
Algar Ho. SE1 7A 14
Algar Rd. TW7: Isle 3A 114
Algarve Rd. SW18 1K 135
Algernon Rd. NW4 6C 44
NW6 1J 81
SE13 4D 122
Algiers Rd. SE13 4C 122
Alibon Gdns. RM10: Dag 5G 73
Alibon Rd. RM9: Dag 5F 73
RM10: Dag 5G 73
Alice Cl. *EN5: New Bar* *4F 21*
(off Station App.)
Alice Gilliatt Ct. *W14* *6H 99*
(off Star Rd.)
Alice La. E3 1B 86
Alice M. TW11: Tedd 5K 131
Alice Owen Technology Cen. *EC1* *1A 8*
(off Goswell Rd.)
Alice Shepherd Ho. *E14* *2E 104*
(off Manchester Rd.)
Alice St. SE1 3E 102
(not continuous)
Alice Thompson Cl. SE12 2A 142
Alice Walker Cl. SE24 4B 120
Alice Way TW3: Houn 4F 113
Alicia Av. HA3: Kent 4B 42
Alicia Cl. HA3: Kent 4C 42
Alicia Gdns. HA3: Kent 4B 42
Alicia Ho. DA16: Well 1B 126
Alie St. E1 1K 15 (6F 85)
Alington Cres. NW9 7J 43
Alington Gro. SM6: Wall 7G 167
Alison Cl. CR0: C'don 1K 169
E6 6E 88
HA5: Eastc 6K 39
Alison Ct. SE1 5G 103
Aliwal M. SW11 4C 118
Aliwal Rd. SW11 4C 118
Alkerden Rd. W4 5A 98
Alkham Rd. N16 2F 67
Allan Barclay Cl. N15 6F 49
Allan Cl. KT3: N Mald 5K 151
Allandale Av. N3 3G 45
Allanson Ct. *E10* *2C 68*
(off Leyton Grange Est.)
Allan Way W3 5J 79
Allard Cres. WD23: B Hea 1B 26
Allard Gdns. SW4 5H 119
Allard Ho. *NW9* *2B 44*
(off Boulevard Dr.)
Allardyce St. SW4 4K 119
Allbrook Cl. TW11: Tedd 5J 131
Allcott Ho. *W12* *6D 80*
(off Du Cane Rd.)
Allcroft Rd. NW5 5E 64

Allder Way CR2: S Croy 7B 168
Allenby Cl. UB6: G'frd 3E 76
Allenby Rd. SE23 . . . . 3A 140
SE28 . . . . 3G 107
UB1: S'hall 3E 76
Allen Cl. CR4: Mitc 1F 155
TW16: Sun 1K 147
Allen Ct. *E17* *6C 50*
(off Yunus Khan Cl.)
UB6: G'frd 5K 59
Allendale Av. UB1: S'hall 6E 76
Allendale Cl. SE5 . . . . 2D 120
SE26 . . . . 5K 139
Allendale Rd. UB6: G'frd 6B 60
Allen Edwards Dr. SW8 . . . . 1J 119
Allenford Ho. *SW15* *6B 116*
(off Tunworth Cres.)
Allen Ho. *W8* *3J 99*
(off Allen St.)
Allen Mans. *W8* *3J 99*
(off Allen St.)
Allen Rd. BR3: Beck 2K 157
CR0: C'don 1A 168
E3 . . . . 2B 86
N16 . . . . 4E 66
TW16: Sun 1K 147
Allensbury Pl. NW1 . . . . 7H 65
Allens Rd. EN3: Pond E 5D 24
Allen St. W8 . . . . 3J 99
Allenswood SW19 . . . . 1G 135
Allenswood Rd. SE9 . . . . 3C 124
Allerford Ct. HA2: Harr 5G 41
Allerford Rd. SE6 . . . . 3D 140
Allerton Ho. *N1* *1E 8*
(off Provost Est.)
Allerton Rd. N16 . . . . 2C 66
Allerton St. N1 . . . . 1E 8 (3D 84)
Allerton Wlk. N7 . . . . 2K 65
Allestree Rd. SW6 . . . . 7G 99
Alleyn Cres. SE21 . . . . 2D 138
Alleyndale Rd.
RM8: Dag 2C 72
Alleyn Ho. *SE1* *3D 102*
(off Burbage Cl.)
Alleyn Pk. SE21 . . . . 2D 138
UB2: S'hall 5E 94
Alleyn Rd. SE21 . . . . 3D 138
Alley Way UB8: Uxb 7A 56
Allfarthing La. SW18 . . . . 6K 117
Allgood Cl. SM4: Mord 6F 153
Allgood St. E2 . . . . 1K 9 (2F 85)
Allhallows La. EC4 . . . . 3E 14 (7D 84)
All Hallows Rd. N17 . . . . 1E 48
Allhallows Rd. E6 . . . . 5C 88
Alliance Cl. HA0: Wemb 4D 60
TW4: Houn 5D 112
Alliance Ct. TW15: Ashf 4E 128
W3 . . . . 5H 79
Alliance Rd. E13 . . . . 5A 88
SE18 . . . . 6A 108
W3 . . . . 4H 79
Allied Ct. *N1* *7E 66*
(off Enfield Rd.)
Allied Ind. Est. W3 . . . . 2A 98
Allied Way W3 . . . . 2A 98
Allingham Cl. W7 . . . . 7K 77
Allingham M. *N1* *2C 84*
(off Allingham St.)
Allingham St. N1 . . . . 2C 84
Allington Av. N17 . . . . 6K 33
TW17: Shep 3G 147
Allington Cl. SW19 . . . . 5F 135
UB6: G'frd 7G 59
Allington Ct. *CR0: C'don* *6J 157*
(off Chart Cl.)
EN3: Pond E 5E 24
(not continuous)
SW1 . . . . *2K 17*
(off Allington St.)
SW8 . . . . 2G 119
Allington Rd. BR6: Orp 2H 173
HA2: Harr 5G 41
NW4 . . . . 5D 44
W10 . . . . 3G 81
Allington St.
SW1 . . . . 2K 17 (3F 101)
Allison Cl. SE10 . . . . 1E 122
Allison Gro. SE21 . . . . 1E 138
Allison Rd. N8 . . . . 5A 48
W3 . . . . 6J 79
Alliston Ho. *E2* *2K 9*
(off Gibraltar Wlk.)
Allitsen Rd. NW8 . . . . 2C 82
(not continuous)
All Nations Ho. *E8* *7H 67*
(off Martello St.)
Allnutt Way SW4 . . . . 5H 119
Alloa Rd. IG3: Ilf 2A 72
SE8 . . . . 5K 103
Allom Ho. *W11* *7G 81*
(off Clarendon Rd.)
Allonby Dr. HA4: Ruis 7D 38
Allonby Gdns. HA9: Wemb 1C 60
Allonby Ho. *E14* *5A 86*
(off Aston St.)
Allotment Way NW2 . . . . 3F 63
Alloway Rd. E3 . . . . 3A 86
Allport Ho. *SE5* *3D 120*
(off Denmark Hill)
Allport M. *E1* *4J 85*
(off Hayfield Pas.)
All Saints Cl. N9 . . . . 2B 34
SW8 . . . . 1J 119
All Saints Ct. *E1* *7J 85*
(off Johnson St.)
SW11 . . . . *7F 101*
(off Prince of Wales Dr.)
TW5: Hest *1B 112*
(off Springwell Rd.)
All Saints Dr. SE3 . . . . 2G 123
(not continuous)
All Saints Ho. *W11* *5H 81*
(off All Saints Rd.)
All Saints M. HA3: Hrw W 6D 26
All Saints Pas. SW18 . . . . 5J 117
All Saints Rd. SM1: Sutt 3K 165
SW19 . . . . 7A 136
(not continuous)
W3 . . . . 3J 97
W11 . . . . 5H 81
All Saints St. N1 . . . . 2K 83
All Saints Twr. E10 . . . . 7D 50
Allsop Pl. NW1 . . . . 4F 5 (4D 82)
All Souls Av. NW10 . . . . 2D 80
All Souls' Pl. W1 . . . . 6K 5 (5F 83)
Allum Way N20 . . . . 1F 31
Alluvium Ct. *SE1* *7G 15*
(off Long La.)
Allwood Cl. SE26 . . . . 4K 139
Alma Av. E4 . . . . 7K 35
Alma Birk Ho. NW6 . . . . 7G 63
Almack Rd. E5 . . . . 4J 67
Alma Cl. N10 . . . . 1F 47
Alma Ct. HA2: Harr 2H 59
Alma Cres. SM1: Sutt 5G 165
Alma Gro. SE1 . . . . 4F 103
Alma Ho. N9 . . . . 4B 34
TW8: Bford 6E 96
Alma Pl. CR7: Thor H 5A 156
NW10 . . . . 3D 80
SE19 . . . . 7F 139
Alma Rd. DA14: Sidc 3A 144
EN3: Pond E 5F 25
KT10: Esh 7J 149
N10 . . . . 7A 32
SM5: Cars 5C 166
SW18 . . . . 4A 118
UB1: S'hall 7C 76
Alma Rd. Ind. Est. EN3: Pond E 4E 24
Alma Row HA3: Hrw W 1H 41
Alma Sq. NW8 . . . . 2A 82
Alma St. E15 . . . . 6F 69
NW5 . . . . 6F 65
Alma Ter. *E3* *1B 86*
(off Beale Rd.)
SW18 . . . . 7B 118
W8 . . . . 3J 99
Almeida St. N1 . . . . 1B 84
Almeida Theatre *1B 84*
(off Almeida St.)
Almeric Rd. SW11 . . . . 4D 118
Almer Rd. SW20 . . . . 7C 134
Almington St. N4 . . . . 1K 65
Almond Av. SM5: Cars 2D 166
UB7: W Dray 3C 92
UB10: Ick 3D 56
W5 . . . . 3D 96
Almond Cl. BR2: Brom 7E 160
HA4: Ruis 3H 57
SE15 . . . . 2G 121
TW13: Felt 1J 129
TW17: Shep 2E 146
UB3: Hayes 7G 75
Almond Gro. TW8: Bford 7B 96
Almond Rd. N17 . . . . 7B 34
SE16 . . . . 4H 103
Almonds Av. IG9: Buck H 2D 36
Almond Way BR2: Brom 7E 160
CR4: Mitc 5H 155
HA2: Harr 2F 41
Almorah Rd. N1 . . . . 7D 66
TW5: Hest 1B 112
Almshouse La. KT9: Chess 7C 162
Alnmouth Ct. *UB1: S'hall* *6G 77*
(off Fleming Rd.)
Alnwick N17 . . . . 7C 34
Alnwick Gro. SM4: Mord 4K 153
Alnwick Rd. E16 . . . . 6A 88
SE12 . . . . 6K 123
ALPERTON 2E 78
Alperton Community School Sports Cen.
. . . . 1D 78
Alperton La. HA0: Wemb 3C 78
UB6: G'frd 3C 78
Alperton St. W10 . . . . 4H 81
Alphabet Gdns. SM5: Cars 6B 154
Alphabet Sq. E3 . . . . 5C 86
Alpha Bus. Cen. E17 . . . . 5B 50
Alpha Cl. NW1 . . . . 2D 4 (4C 82)
Alpha Est. UB3: Hayes 2G 93
Alphage Highwalk *EC2* *5C 84*
(off Wood St.)
Alpha Gro. E14 . . . . 2C 104
Alpha Ho. NW6 . . . . 2J 81
NW8 . . . . 4D 4
SW4 . . . . 4K 119
Alpha Pl. NW6 . . . . 2J 81
SM4: Mord 1F 165
SW3 . . . . 7D 16 (6C 100)
Alpha Rd. CR0: C'don 1E 168
E4 . . . . 3H 35
EN3: Pond E 4F 25
KT5: Surb 6F 151
N18 . . . . 6B 34
SE14 . . . . 1B 122
TW11: Tedd 5H 131
UB10: Hil 4D 74
Alpha St. SE15 . . . . 2G 121
Alphea Cl. SW19 . . . . 7C 136
Alpine Av. KT5: Surb 2J 163
Alpine Bus. Cen. E6 . . . . 5E 88
Alpine Cl. CR0: C'don 3E 168
Alpine Copse BR1: Brom 2E 160
Alpine Gro. E9 . . . . 7J 67
Alpine Rd. E10 . . . . 2D 68
KT12: Walt T 7J 147
SE16 . . . . 5K 103
Alpine Vw. SM5: Cars 5C 166
Alpine Wlk. HA7: Stan 2D 26
Alpine Way E6 . . . . 5E 88
Alric Av. KT3: N Mald 3A 152
NW10 . . . . 7K 61
Alroy Rd. N4 . . . . 7A 48
Alsace Rd. SE17 . . . . 5E 102
Alscot Rd. SE1 . . . . 4F 103
(not continuous)
Alscot Rd. Ind. Est. SE1 . . . . 3F 103
Alscot Way SE1 . . . . 4F 103
Alsike Rd. DA18: Erith 3D 108
SE2 . . . . 3D 108
Alsom Av. KT4: Wor Pk 4C 164
Alston Cl. KT6: Surb 7B 150
Alston Rd. EN5: Barn 3B 20
N18 . . . . 5C 34
SW17 . . . . 4B 136
Alston Works EN5: Barn 2B 20
Altair Cl. N17 . . . . 6A 34
Altash Way SE9 . . . . 2D 142
Altenburg Av. W13 . . . . 3B 96
Altenburg Gdns. SW11 . . . . 4D 118
Alt Gro. SW19 . . . . 7H 135
Altham Ct. HA2: Harr 1F 41
Altham Rd. HA5: Pinn 1C 40
Althea St. SW6 . . . . 2K 117
Althorne Gdns. E18 . . . . 4H 51
Althorne Way RM10: Dag 2G 73
Althorp Cl. EN5: Ark 1H 29
Althorpe M. SW11 . . . . 1B 118
Althorpe Rd. HA1: Harr 5G 41
Althorp Rd. SW17 . . . . 1D 136
Altima Ct. SE22 . . . . 4G 121
Altior Ct. N6 . . . . 6G 47
Altmore Av. E6 . . . . 7D 70
Alton Av. HA7: Stan 7E 26
Alton Cl. DA5: Bexl 1E 144
TW7: Isle 2K 113
Alton Gdns. BR3: Beck 7C 140
TW2: Whitt 7H 113
Alton Rd. CR0: Wadd 3A 168
N17 . . . . 3D 48
SW15 . . . . 1C 134
TW9: Rich 4E 114
Alton St. E14 . . . . 5D 86
Altyre Cl. BR3: Beck 5B 158
Altyre Rd. CR0: C'don 2D 168
Altyre Way BR3: Beck 5B 158
Aluna Ct. SE15 . . . . 3J 121
Alvanley Gdns. NW6 . . . . 5K 63
Alverstone Av. EN4: E Barn 7H 21
SW19 . . . . 2J 135
Alverstone Gdns. SE9 . . . . 1G 143
Alverstone Ho. SE11 . . . . 7J 19 (6A 102)
Alverstone Rd. E12 . . . . 4E 70
HA9: Wemb 1F 61
KT3: N Mald 4B 152
NW2 . . . . 7E 62
Alverston Gdns. SE25 . . . . 5E 156
Alverton St. SE8 . . . . 5B 104
(not continuous)
Alveston Av. HA3: Kent 3B 42
Alveston Sq. E18 . . . . 2J 51
Alvey St. SE17 . . . . 5E 102
Alvia Gdns. SM1: Sutt 4A 166
Alvington Cres. E8 . . . . 5F 67
Alway Av. KT19: Ewe 5K 163
Alwold Cres. SE12 . . . . 6K 123
Alwyn Av. W4 . . . . 5K 97
Alwyn Cl. CR0: New Ad 7D 170
Alwyne La. N1 . . . . 7B 66
Alwyne Pl. N1 . . . . 6C 66
Alwyne Rd. N1 . . . . 7C 66
SW19 . . . . 6H 135
W7 . . . . 7J 77
Alwyne Sq. N1 . . . . 6C 66
Alwyne Vs. N1 . . . . 7B 66
Alwyn Gdns. NW4 . . . . 4C 44
W3 . . . . 6H 79
Alyth Gdns. NW11 . . . . 6J 45
Alzette Ho. *E2* *2K 85*
(off Mace St.)

Amadeus Ho. BR1: Brom 3K 159
(off Elmfield Rd.)
Amalgamated Dr. TW8: Bford 6B 96
Amanda Ct. TW15: Ashf 2B 128
(off Edward Way)
Amanda M. RM7: Rom 5J 55
Amar Ct. SE18 . . . . . 4K 107
Amar Deep Ct. SE18 . . . . . 5K 107
Amazon Bldg. N8 . . . . . 4K 47
Amazon St. E1 . . . . . 6G 85
Ambassador Cl.
TW3: Houn 2C 112
Ambassador Gdns. E6 . . . . . 5D 88
Ambassadors Ct. E8 . . . . . 7F 67
(off Holly St.)
SW1 . . . . . 5B 12
Ambassador Sq. E14 . . . . . 4D 104
Amber Av. E17 . . . . . 1A 50
Amber Ct. CR0: C'don 1E 168
KT5: Surb 7F 151
Amberden Av. N3 . . . . . 3J 45
Ambergate St. SE17 . . . . . 5B 102
Amber Gro. NW2 . . . . . 1F 63
Amberley Cl. BR6: Chels 5K 173
HA5: Pinn 3D 40
Amberley Ct. BR3: Beck 7B 140
DA14: Sidc 5C 144
Amberley Gdns. EN1: Enf 7K 23
KT19: Ewe 4B 164
Amberley Gro. CR0: C'don 7F 157
SE26 . . . . . 5H 139
Amberley Rd. E10 . . . . . 7C 50
EN1: Enf 7A 24
IG9: Buck H 1F 37
N13 . . . . . 2E 32
SE2 . . . . . 6D 108
W9 . . . . . 5J 81
Amberley Way
RM7: Mawney 4H 55
SM4: Mord 7H 153
TW4: Houn 5A 112
UB10: Uxb 2A 74
Amber M. N22 . . . . . 3A 48
(off High Rd.)
Amberside Cl. TW7: Isle 6H 113
Amber Wharf E2 . . . . . 1F 85
(off Nursery La.)
Amberwood Cl. SM6: Wall 5J 167
Amberwood Ri. KT3: N Mald 6A 152
Amblecote Cl. SE12 . . . . . 3K 141
Amblecote Mdws. SE12 . . . . . 3K 141
Amblecote Rd. SE12 . . . . . 3K 141
Ambler Rd. N4 . . . . . 3B 66
Ambleside BR1: Brom 6F 141
NW1 . . . . . 1K 5
SW19 . . . . . 1G 135
Ambleside Av. BR3: Beck 5A 158
KT12: Walt T 7A 148
SW16 . . . . . 4H 137
Ambleside Cl. E9 . . . . . 5J 67
E10 . . . . . 7D 50
N17 . . . . . 3F 49
Ambleside Cres. EN3: Enf H 3E 24
Ambleside Dr. TW14: Felt 1H 129
Ambleside Gdns.
HA9: Wemb 1D 60
IG4: Ilf 4C 52
SM2: Sutt 6A 166
SW16 . . . . . 5H 137
Ambleside Point SE15 . . . . . 7J 103
(off Tustin Est.)
Ambleside Rd. DA7: Bex 2G 127
NW10 . . . . . 7B 62
Ambleside Wlk. UB8: Uxb 1A 74
(off Cumbrian Way)
Ambrooke Rd. DA17: Belv 3G 109
Ambrosden Av. SW1 . . . . . 2B 18 (3G 101)
Ambrose Av. NW11 . . . . . 7G 45
Ambrose Cl. BR6: Orp 3K 173
E6 . . . . . 5D 88
Ambrose Ho. E14 . . . . . 5C 86
(off Selsey St.)
Ambrose M. SW11 . . . . . 2D 118
Ambrose St. SE16 . . . . . 4H 103
Ambrose Wlk. E3 . . . . . 2C 86
AMC Bus. Cen. NW10 . . . . . 3H 79
Amelia Cl. W3 . . . . . 1H 97
Amelia Ho. TW9: Kew 7H 97
W6 . . . . . 5E 98
(off Queen Caroline St.)
Amelia St. SE17 . . . . . 5C 102
Amen Cnr. EC4 . . . . . 1B 14 (6B 84)
SW17 . . . . . 6D 136
Amen Ct. EC4 . . . . . 1B 14 (6B 84)
Amenity Way SM4: Mord 7E 152
American International University of
London, The 6E 114
America Sq. EC3 . . . . . 2J 15 (7F 85)
America St. SE1 . . . . . 5C 14 (1C 102)
Amerland Rd. SW18 . . . . . 5H 117
Amersham Av. N18 . . . . . 6J 33
Amersham Gro. SE14 . . . . . 7B 104
Amersham Rd. CR0: C'don 6C 156
SE14 . . . . . 1B 122
Amersham Va. SE14 . . . . . 7B 104
Amery Gdns. NW10 . . . . . 1E 80
Amery Ho. SE17 . . . . . 5E 102
(off Kinglake St.)
Amery Rd. HA1: Harr 2A 60
Amesbury Av. SW2 . . . . . 2J 137
Amesbury Cl. KT4: Wor Pk 1E 164
Amesbury Ct. EN2: Enf 2F 23
Amesbury Dr. E4 . . . . . 6J 25
Amesbury Rd. BR1: Brom 3B 160
RM9: Dag 7D 72
TW13: Felt 2B 130
Amesbury Twr. SW8 . . . . . 2G 119
Ames Cotts. E14 . . . . . 5A 86
(off Maroon St.)
Ames Ho. E2 . . . . . 2K 85
(off Mace St.)
Amethyst Cl. N11 . . . . . 7C 32
Amethyst Ct. BR6: Chels 5J 173
(off Farnborough Hill)
EN3: Enf H 3F 25
(off Enstone Rd.)
Amethyst Rd. E15 . . . . . 4F 69
AMF Bowling
Lewisham 3E 122
Amherst Av. W13 . . . . . 6C 78
Amherst Dr. BR5: St M Cry 4K 161
Amherst Gdns. W13 . . . . . 6C 78
(off Amherst Rd.)
Amherst Ho. SE16 . . . . . 2K 103
(off Wolfe Cres.)
Amherst Rd. W13 . . . . . 6C 78
Amhurst Gdns. TW7: Isle 2A 114
Amhurst Pde. N16 . . . . . 7F 49
(off Amhurst Pk.)
Amhurst Pk. N16 . . . . . 7D 48
Amhurst Pas. E8 . . . . . 4G 67
Amhurst Rd. E8 . . . . . 5H 67
N16 . . . . . 4F 67
Amhurst Ter. E8 . . . . . 4G 67
Amhurst Wlk. SE28 . . . . . 1A 108
Amias Ho. EC1 . . . . . 3C 8
(off Central St.)
Amida Leisure Cen. 5B 158
Amidas Gdns. RM8: Dag 4B 72
Amiel St. E1 . . . . . 4J 85
Amies St. SW11 . . . . . 3D 118
Amigo Ho. SE1 . . . . . 1K 19
(off Morley St.)
Amina Way SE16 . . . . . 3G 103
Amiot Ho. NW9 . . . . . 2B 44
(off Heritage Av.)
Amis Av. KT19: Ewe 6H 163
Amisha Ct. SE1 . . . . . 3F 103
(off Spa Rd.)
Amity Gro. SW20 . . . . . 1D 152
Amity Rd. E15 . . . . . 7H 69
Ammanford Grn. NW9 . . . . . 6A 44
Ammonite Ho. E15 . . . . . 7H 69
Amner Rd. SW11 . . . . . 6E 118
Amor Rd. W6 . . . . . 3E 98
Amory Ho. N1 . . . . . 1K 83
(off Barnsbury Est.)
Amott Rd. SE15 . . . . . 3G 121
Amoy Pl. E14 . . . . . 7C 86
(not continuous)
Ampere Way CR0: Wadd 7J 155
Ampleforth Rd. SE2 . . . . . 2B 108
Ampthill Est. NW1 . . . . . 1B 6 (2G 83)
Ampthill Sq. NW1 . . . . . 1B 6 (2G 83)
Ampton Pl. WC1 . . . . . 2G 7 (3K 83)
Ampton St. WC1 . . . . . 2G 7 (3K 83)
Amroth Cl. SE23 . . . . . 1H 139
Amroth Grn. NW9 . . . . . 6A 44
Amstel Ct. SE15 . . . . . 7F 103
Amsterdam Rd. E14 . . . . . 3E 104
Amundsen Ct. E14 . . . . . 5C 104
(off Napier Av.)
Amundsen Ho. NW10 . . . . . 7K 61
(off Stonebridge Pk.)
Amwell Cl. EN2: Enf 5J 23
Amwell Ct. Est. N4 . . . . . 2C 66
Amwell St. EC1 . . . . . 1J 7 (3A 84)
Amyand Cotts. TW1: Twick 6B 114
Amyand La. TW1: Twick 7B 114
Amyand Pk. Gdns.
TW1: Twick 7B 114
Amyand Pk. Rd. TW1: Twick 7A 114
Amy Cl. SM6: Wall 7J 167
Amy Johnson Ct. HA8: Edg 2H 43
Amyruth Rd. SE4 . . . . . 5C 122
Amy Warne Cl. E6 . . . . . 4C 88
Anatola Rd. N19 . . . . . 2G 65
Ancaster Cres. KT3: N Mald 6C 152
Ancaster M. BR3: Beck 3K 157
Ancaster Rd. BR3: Beck 3K 157
Ancaster St. SE18 . . . . . 7J 107
Anchor SW18 . . . . . 4K 117
Anchorage Cl. SW19 . . . . . 5J 135
Anchorage Ho. E14 . . . . . 7F 87
(off Clove Cres.)
Anchorage Point E14 . . . . . 2B 104
(off Cuba St.)
Anchorage Point Ind. Est.
SE7 . . . . . 3A 106
Anchor & Hope La. SE7 . . . . . 3K 105
Anchor Brewhouse SE1 . . . . . 5J 15 (1F 103)
Anchor Bus. Cen.
CR0: Bedd 3J 167
Anchor Cl. IG11: Bark 3B 90
Anchor Ct. EN1: Enf 5K 23
SW1 . . . . . 4C 18
(off Vauxhall Bri. Rd.)
Anchor Ho. E16 . . . . . 5H 87
(off Barking Rd.)
E16 . . . . . 6A 88
(off Prince Regent La.)
EC1 . . . . . 3C 8
(off Old St.)
SW10 . . . . . 6B 100
(off Cremorne Est.)
Anchor M. N1 . . . . . 6E 66
SW12 . . . . . 6F 119
Anchor Retail Pk. E1 . . . . . 4J 85
Anchor Rd. E12 . . . . . 2B 70
Anchor St. SE16 . . . . . 4H 103
Anchor Ter. E1 . . . . . 4J 85
Anchor Wharf E3 . . . . . 5D 86
(off Yeo St.)
Anchor Yd. EC1 . . . . . 3D 8 (4C 84)
Ancill Cl. W6 . . . . . 6G 99
Ancona Rd. NW10 . . . . . 2C 80
SE18 . . . . . 5H 107
Andace Pk. Gdns.
BR1: Brom 2A 160
Andalus Rd. SW9 . . . . . 3J 119
Andaman Ho. E1 . . . . . 5A 86
(off Duckett St.)
Ander Cl. HA0: Wemb 4D 60
Anderson Cl. N21 . . . . . 5E 22
SM3: Sutt 1J 165
W3 . . . . . 6K 79
Anderson Ct. NW2 . . . . . 1E 62
Anderson Dr. TW15: Ashf 4E 128
Anderson Hgts. SW16 . . . . . 2K 155
Anderson Ho. E14 . . . . . 7E 86
(off Woolmore St.)
IG11: Bark 1H 89
SW17 . . . . . 5B 136
W12 . . . . . 6D 80
(off Du Cane Rd.)
Anderson Pl. TW3: Houn 4F 113
Anderson Rd. E9 . . . . . 6K 67
IG8: Wfd G 3B 52
Anderson Sq. N1 . . . . . 1B 84
(off Gaskin St.)
Anderson St. SW3 . . . . . 5E 16 (5D 100)
Anderson Way DA17: Belv 2H 109
Anderton Cl. SE5 . . . . . 3D 120
Anderton Ct. N22 . . . . . 2H 47
Andora Ct. NW6 . . . . . 7G 63
(off Brondesbury Pk.)
Andorra Ct. BR1: Brom 1A 160
Andover Av. E16 . . . . . 6B 88
Andover Cl. TW14: Felt 1H 129
UB6: G'frd 4F 77
Andover Ct. TW19: Stanw 7A 110
Andover Pl. NW6 . . . . . 2K 81
Andover Rd. BR6: Orp 1H 173
N7 . . . . . 2K 65
TW2: Twick 1H 131
Andoversford Ct. SE15 . . . . . 6E 102
(off Bibury Cl.)
Andover Ter. W6 . . . . . 4D 98
(off Raynham Rd.)
Andreck Ct. BR3: Beck 2E 158
(off Crescent Rd.)
Andre St. E8 . . . . . 5G 67
Andrew Borde St. WC2 . . . . . 7D 6 (6H 83)
Andrew Cl. DA1: Cray 5K 127
Andrew Ct. SE23 . . . . . 2K 139
Andrewes Gdns. E6 . . . . . 6C 88
Andrewes Highwalk EC2 . . . . . 6D 8
Andrewes Ho. EC2 . . . . . 6D 8
SM1: Sutt 4J 165
Andrew Pl. SW8 . . . . . 7H 101
Andrew Reed Ho. SW18 . . . . . 7G 117
(off Linstead Way)
Andrews Cl. HA1: Harr 7H 41
IG9: Buck H 2F 37
KT4: Wor Pk 2E 164
Andrews Crosse WC2 . . . . . 1J 13
Andrews Ho. CR2: S Croy 6C 168
NW3 . . . . . 7D 64
(off Fellows Rd.)
Andrews Pl. DA2: Dart 2K 145
SE9 . . . . . 6F 125
Andrew's Rd. E8 . . . . . 1H 85
Andrew St. E14 . . . . . 6E 86
Andrews Wlk. SE17 . . . . . 6B 102
Andringham Lodge BR1: Brom 1K 159
(off Palace Gro.)
Andrula Ct. N22 . . . . . 1B 48
Andwell Cl. SE2 . . . . . 2B 108
ANERLEY 2H 157
Anerley Gro. SE19 . . . . . 7F 139
Anerley Hill SE19 . . . . . 6F 139
Anerley Pk. SE20 . . . . . 7G 139
Anerley Pk. Rd. SE20 . . . . . 7H 139
Anerley Rd. SE19 . . . . . 7G 139
SE20 . . . . . 7G 139
Anerley Sta. Rd. SE20 . . . . . 1H 157
Anerley Va. SE19 . . . . . 7F 139
Aneurin Bevan Ct. NW2 . . . . . 2D 62
Aneurin Bevan Ho. N11 . . . . . 7C 32
Anfield Cl. SW12 . . . . . 7G 119

ANGEL 2A 84
Angela Carter Cl. SW9 3A 120
Angela Davies Ind. Est. SE24 4B 120
Angel All. E1 7K 9
Angel Cen., The N1 1K 7
Angel Cl. N18 5A 34
TW12: Ham H 5G 131
Angel Cnr. Pde. N18 4B 34
Angel Ct. EC2 7F 9 (6D 84)
SW1 5B 12 (1G 101)
ANGEL EDMONTON JUNC. 5B 34
Angelfield TW3: Houn 4F 113
Angel Ga. EC1 1B 8 (3B 84)
(not continuous)
Angel Hill SM1: Sutt 3K 165
(not continuous)
Angel Hill Dr. SM1: Sutt 3K 165
Angelica Cl. UB7: Yiew 6A 74
Angelica Dr. E6 5E 88
Angelica Gdns. CR0: C'don 1K 169
Angelina Ho. *SE15* *1G 121*
(off Goldsmith Rd.)
Angelis Apartments *N1* *1B 8*
(off Graham St.)
Angel La. E15 6F 69
UB3: Hayes 5F 75
Angell Pk. Gdns. SW9 3A 120
Angell Rd. SW9 3A 120
ANGELL TOWN 1A 120
Angell Town Est. SW9 2A 120
Angel M. E1 7H 85
N1 2A 84
SW15 7C 116
Angelo M. SW16 3K 155
Angel Pas. EC4 3E 14 (7D 84)
Angel Pl. N18 4B 34
SE1 6E 14 (2D 102)
Angel Rd. HA1: Harr 6J 41
KT7: T Ditt 7A 150
N18 5B 34
Angel Rd. Works N18 5D 34
Angel Sq. EC1 2B 84
Angel St. EC1 7C 8 (6C 84)
Angel Wlk. W6 4E 98
Angel Way RM1: Rom 5K 55
Angel Yd. N6 1E 64
Angerstein Bus. Pk. SE10 4J 105
Angerstein La. SE3 1H 123
Anglebury *W2* *6J 81*
(off Talbot Rd.)
Angle Cl. UB10: Hil 1C 74
Angle Grn. RM8: Dag 1C 72
Anglers, The *KT1: King T* *3D 150*
(off High St.)
Anglers Cl. TW10: Ham 4C 132
Angler's La. NW5 6F 65
Anglers Reach KT6: Surb 5D 150
Anglesea Av. SE18 4F 107
Anglesea Ho. *KT1: King T* *4D 150*
(off Anglesea Rd.)
Anglesea M. SE18 4F 107
Anglesea Rd. KT1: King T 4D 150
SE18 4F 107
Anglesea Ter. W6 3D 98
Anglesey Cl. TW15: Ashf 3C 128
Anglesey Ct. W7 4K 77
Anglesey Ct. Rd. SM5: Cars 6E 166
Anglesey Gdns. SM5: Cars 6E 166
Anglesey Ho. *E14* *6C 86*
(off Lindfield St.)
Anglesey Rd. EN3: Pond E 4C 24
Anglesmede Cres.
HA5: Pinn 3E 40
Anglesmede Way HA5: Pinn 3E 40
Angles Rd. SW16 4J 137
Anglia Cl. N17 7C 34
Anglia Ct. *RM8: Dag* *1D 72*
(off Spring Cl.)
Anglia Ho. *E14* *6A 86*
(off Salmon La.)
Anglian Ind. Est. IG11: Bark 4K 89
Anglian Rd. E11 3F 69
Anglia Wlk. *E6* *1E 88*
(off Napier Rd.)
Anglo Rd. E3 2B 86
Angrave Ct. *E8* *1F 85*
(off Scriven St.)
Angrave Pas. E8 1F 85
Angus Cl. KT9: Chess 5G 163
Angus Dr. HA4: Ruis 4A 58
Angus Gdns. NW9 1K 43
Angus Ho. SW2 7H 119
Angus Rd. E13 3A 88
Angus St. SE14 7A 104
Anhalt Rd. SW11 7C 100
Ankerdine Cres. SE18 7F 107
Anlaby Rd. TW11: Tedd 5J 131
Anley Rd. W14 2F 99
Anmersh Gro. HA7: Stan 1D 42
Annabel Cl. E14 6D 86
Anna Cl. E8 1F 85
Annandale Gro. UB10: Ick 3E 56
Annandale Rd. CR0: C'don 2G 169
DA15: Sidc 7J 125
SE10 6H 105
W4 5A 98
Anna Neagle Cl. E7 4J 69
Annan Way RM1: Rom 1K 55
Anne Boleyn Ct. SE9 6G 125
Anne Boleyn's Wlk.
KT2: King T 5E 132
SM3: Cheam 7F 165
Anne Case M. KT3: N Mald 3K 151
Anne Compton M. SE12 7H 123
Anne Goodman Ho. *E1* *6J 85*
(off Jubilee St.)
Anne of Cleeves Ct. SE9 6H 125
Annes Ct. NW1 3D 4
Annesley Av. NW9 3K 43
Annesley Cl. NW10 3A 62
Annesley Dr. CR0: C'don 3B 170
Annesley Ho. SW9 1A 120
Annesley Rd. SE3 1K 123
Annesley Wlk. N19 2G 65
Annesmere Gdns. SE3 3B 124
Anne St. E13 4J 87
Anne Sutherland Ho.
BR3: Beck 7A 140
Annett Cl. TW17: Shep 4G 147
Annette Cl. HA3: W'stone 2J 41
Annette Cres. N1 7C 66
Annette Rd. N7 3K 65
(not continuous)
Annett Rd. KT12: Walt T 7J 147
Anne Way KT8: W Mole 4F 149
Annie Besant Cl. E3 1B 86
Annie Taylor Ho. *E12* *4E 70*
(off Walton Rd.)
Anning St. EC2 3H 9 (4E 84)
Annington Rd. N2 3D 46
Annis Rd. E9 6A 68
Ann La. SW10 6B 100
Ann Moss Way SE16 3J 103
Ann's Cl. SW1 7F 11
Ann's Pl. E1 6J 9
Ann St. SE18 5G 107
(not continuous)
Ann Stroud Ct. SE12 5J 123
Annsworthy Av.
CR7: Thor H 3D 156
Annsworthy Cres. SE25 2D 156
Ansar Gdns. E17 5B 50
Ansdell Rd. SE15 2J 121
Ansdell St. W8 3K 99
Ansdell Ter. W8 3K 99
Ansell Gro. SM5: Cars 1E 166
Ansell Ho. *E1* *5J 85*
(off Mile End Rd.)
Ansell Rd. SW17 3C 136
Anselm Cl. CR0: C'don 3F 169
Anselm Rd. HA5: Hat E 1D 40
SW6 6J 99
Ansford Rd.
BR1: Brom 5E 140
Ansleigh Pl. W11 7F 81
Anson Cl. RM7: Mawney 2H 55
Anson Ho. *E1* *4A 86*
(off Shandy St.)
SW1 *7A 18*
(off Churchill Gdns.)
Anson Pl. SE28 2H 107
Anson Rd. N7 4G 65
NW2 4D 62
Anson Ter. UB5: N'olt 6F 59
Anstey Ct. W3 2H 97
Anstey Ho. *E9* *1J 85*
(off Templecombe Rd.)
Anstey Rd. SE15 3G 121
Anstey Wlk. N15 4B 48
Anstice Cl. W4 7A 98
Anstridge Path SE9 6H 125
Anstridge Rd. SE9 6H 125
Antelope Rd. SE18 3D 106
Antelope Wlk.
KT6: Surb 5D 150
Antenor Ho. *E2* *2H 85*
(off Old Bethnal Grn. Rd.)
Anthony Cl. NW7 4F 29
Anthony Cope Ct. *N1* *1F 9*
(off Chart St.)
Anthony Ho. *NW8* *4C 4*
(off Ashbridge St.)
Anthony Rd. DA16: Well 1A 126
SE25 6G 157
UB6: G'frd 3J 77
Anthony St. E1 6H 85
Anthony Way N18 6E 34
Antigua Wlk. SE19 5D 138
Antilles Bay E14 2E 104
Antill Rd. E3 3A 86
N15 4G 49
Antill Ter. E1 6K 85
Antlers Hill E4 5J 25
Anton Cres. SM1: Sutt 3J 165
Antoneys Cl. HA5: Pinn 2B 40
Antonine Hgts. SE1 7G 15
Anton Pl. HA9: Wemb 3H 61
Anton St. E8 5G 67
Antony Ho. *SE14* *7K 103*
(off Barlborough St.)
SE16 *4J 103*
(off Raymouth Rd.)
Antrim Gro. NW3 6D 64
Antrim Ho. *E3* *1B 86*
(off Birdsfield La.)
Antrim Rd. NW3 6D 64
Antrobus Cl. SM1: Sutt 5H 165
Antrobus Rd. W4 4J 97
Anvil Cl. SW16 7G 137
Anvil Rd. TW16: Sun 3J 147
Anworth Cl. IG8: Wfd G 6E 36
AOP Gallery *3G 9*
(off Leonard St.)
Apeldoorn Dr. SM6: Wall 7J 167
Apex Cl. BR3: Beck 1D 158
APEX CORNER
Feltham 3D 130
Mill Hill 4F 29
Apex Ct. W13 7A 78
Apex Ind. Est. NW10 4B 80
Apex Pde. *NW7* *4E 28*
(off Selvage La.)
Apex Retail Pk.
TW13: Hanw 3D 130
Aphrodite Ct. *E14* *4C 104*
(off Homer Dr.)
Aplin Way TW7: Isle 1J 113
Apollo Av. BR1: Brom 1K 159
Apollo Bldg. E14 4C 104
Apollo Bus. Cen. SE8 5K 103
Apollo Ct. *E1* *7G 85*
(off Thomas More St.)
SW9 *1A 120*
(off Southey Rd.)
Apollo Ho. *E2* *2H 85*
(off St Jude's Rd.)
N6 7D 46
SW10 *7B 100*
(off Milman's St.)
Apollo Pl. E11 3G 69
SW10 7B 100
Apollo Theatre
Soho *2C 12*
(off Shaftesbury Av.)
Victoria *2A 18*
(off Wilton Rd.)
Apollo Way DA8: Erith 4K 109
SE28 3H 107
Apollo West End Cinema *3C 12*
(off Regent St.)
Apostle Way CR7: Thor H 2B 156
Apothecary St. EC4 1A 14 (6B 84)
Appach Rd. SW2 5A 120
Apple Blossom Ct. *SW8* *7H 101*
(off Pascal St.)
Appleby Cl. BR5: Pet W 7J 161
E4 6K 35
N15 5D 48
TW2: Twick 2H 131
UB8: Hil 6E 74
Appleby Ct. *W3* *2J 97*
(off Newport Rd.)
Appleby Gdns. TW14: Felt 1H 129
Appleby Rd. E8 7G 67
E16 6H 87
Appleby St. E2 2F 85
Appledore Av. DA7: Bex 1J 127
HA4: Ruis 3K 57
Appledore Cl. BR2: Brom 5H 159
HA8: Edg 1G 43
SW17 2D 136
Appledore Cres. DA14: Sidc 3J 143
Appledore Way NW7 7A 30
Appleford Ho. *W10* *4G 81*
(off Bosworth Rd.)
Appleford Rd. W10 4G 81
Apple Gth. TW8: Bford 4D 96
Applegarth CR0: New Ad 7D 170
(not continuous)
KT10: Clay 5A 162
Applegarth Dr.
IG2: Ilf 4K 53
Applegarth Ho. SE1 6B 14
SE15 *7G 103*
(off Bird in Bush Rd.)
Applegarth Rd. SE28 1B 108
W14 3F 99
Apple Gro. EN1: Enf 3K 23
KT9: Chess 4E 162
Apple Mkt. *KT1: King T* *2D 150*
(off Market Pl.)
Apple Rd. E11 3G 69
Appleshaw Ho. SE5 3E 120
Appleton Cl. DA7: Bex 2J 127
Appleton Gdns.
KT3: N Mald 6C 152
Appleton Rd. SE9 3C 124
Appleton Sq. CR4: Mitc 1C 154
Appletree Av. UB8: Hil 5B 74
Appletree Cl. SE20 1H 157
Appletree Gdns. EN4: E Barn 4H 21
Apple Tree Rdbt. UB7: Yiew 7B 74
Apple Tree Yd. SW1 4B 12 (1G 101)
Applewood Cl. N20 1H 31
NW2 3D 62
UB10: Ick 4A 56
Applewood Dr. E13 4K 87
Appold St. EC2 5G 9 (5E 84)
Apprentice Gdns. UB5: N'olt 3D 76
Apprentice Way E5 4H 67

Approach, The BR6: Orp . . . 2K 173
EN1: Enf . . . 2C 24
NW4 . . . 5F 45
W3 . . . 6K 79
Approach Cl. N16 . . . 4E 66
Approach Rd. E2 . . . 2J 85
EN4: E Barn . . . 4G 21
HA8: Edg . . . 6B 28
KT8: W Mole . . . 5E 148
SW20 . . . 2E 152
TW15: Ashf . . . 6E 128
Aprey Gdns. NW4 . . . 4E 44
April Cl. BR6: Chels . . . 5K 173
TW13: Felt . . . 3J 129
W7 . . . 7J 77
April Ct. *E2* . . . *2G 85*
(off Teale St.)
April Glen SE23 . . . 3K 139
April St. E8 . . . 4F 67
Apsley Cen., The NW2 . . . 2C 62
Apsley Cl. HA2: Harr . . . 5G 41
Apsley House . . . 6H 11
Apsley Ho. *E1* . . . *5J 85*
(off Stepney Way)
NW8 . . . *2B 82*
(off Finchley Rd.)
TW4: Houn . . . 4D 112
Apsley Rd. KT3: N Mald . . . 3J 151
SE25 . . . 4H 157
Apsley Way NW2 . . . 2C 62
W1 . . . 6H 11 (2E 100)
(not continuous)
Aquarius TW1: Twick . . . 1B 132
Aquarius Bus. Pk. *NW2* . . . *1C 62*
(off Priestley Way)
Aquila St. NW8 . . . 2B 82
Aquinas St. SE1 . . . 5K 13 (1A 102)
Arabella Ct. *NW8* . . . *2A 82*
(off Marlborough Pl.)
Arabella Dr. SW15 . . . 4A 116
Arabia Cl. E4 . . . 7K 25
Arabian Ho. *E1* . . . *4A 86*
(off Ernest St.)
Arabin Rd. SE4 . . . 4A 122
Arado Ho. *NW9* . . . *2B 44*
(off Boulevard Dr.)
Aragon Av. KT7: T Ditt . . . 5K 149
Aragon Cl. BR2: Brom . . . 1D 172
EN2: Enf . . . 1E 22
TW16: Sun . . . 6H 129
Aragon Ct. KT8: E Mos . . . 4G 149
Aragon Dr. HA4: Ruis . . . 1B 58
Aragon Ho. *E16* . . . *1J 105*
(off Capulet M.)
Aragon Pl. SM4: Mord . . . 7G 153
Aragon Rd. KT2: King T . . . 5E 132
SM4: Mord . . . 6F 153
Aragon Twr. SE8 . . . 4B 104
Aral Ho. *E1* . . . *4K 85*
(off Ernest St.)
Arandora Cres. RM6: Chad H . . . 7B 54
Aran Dr. HA7: Stan . . . 4H 27
Aran Lodge *NW6* . . . *7J 63*
(off Woodchurch Rd.)
Arapiles Ho. *E14* . . . *6F 87*
(off Blair St.)
Arbery Rd. E3 . . . 3A 86
Arbon Ct. *N1* . . . *1C 84*
(off Linton St.)
Arbor Cl. BR3: Beck . . . 2D 158
Arbor Ct. N16 . . . 2D 66
Arboretum Ct. *N1* . . . *6D 66*
(off Dove Rd.)
Arborfield Cl. SW2 . . . 1K 137
Arborfield Ho. *E14* . . . *7C 86*
(off E. India Dock Rd.)
Arbor Rd. E4 . . . 3A 36
Arbour Ho. *E1* . . . *6K 85*
(off Arbour Sq.)
Arbour Rd. EN3: Pond E . . . 3E 24
Arbour Sq. E1 . . . 6K 85
Arbroath Rd. SE9 . . . 3C 124
Arbury Ter. SE26 . . . 3G 139
Arbuthnot La. DA5: Bexl . . . 6E 126
Arbuthnot Rd. SE14 . . . 2K 121
Arbutus St. E8 . . . 1F 85
Arcade CR0: C'don . . . 2C 168
Arcade, The *CR0: C'don* . . . *3C 168*
(off High St.)
E17 . . . 4C 50
EC2 . . . 6G 9
IG11: Bark . . . 7G 71
N7 . . . *4J 65*
(off Macready Pl.)
SE9 . . . *6E 124*
(off High St.)
Arcade Chambers SE9 . . . 6E 124
Arcade Pde. KT9: Chess . . . 5D 162
Arcadia Av. N3 . . . 2J 45
Arcadia Cen., The W5 . . . 7D 78
Arcadia Cl. SM5: Cars . . . 4E 166
Arcadia Ct. E1 . . . 7J 9
Arcadian Av. DA5: Bexl . . . 6E 126
Arcadian Cl. DA5: Bexl . . . 6E 126
Arcadian Gdns. N22 . . . 7E 32
Arcadian Pl. SW18 . . . 7H 117
Arcadian Rd. DA5: Bexl . . . 6E 126
Arcadia St. E14 . . . 6C 86
Archangel St. SE16 . . . 2K 103
Archbishop Lanfranc School Sports Cen. . . . 6J 155
Archbishop's Pl. SW2 . . . 7K 119
Archdale Bus. Cen. HA2: Harr . . . 2G 59
Archdale Ct. W12 . . . 1D 98
Archdale Ho. *SE1* . . . *7G 15*
(off Long La.)
Archdale Pl. KT3: N Mald . . . 3H 151
Archdale Rd. SE22 . . . 5F 121
Archel Rd. W14 . . . 6H 99
Archer Apartments *N1* . . . *2E 84*
(off Fern Cl.)
Archer Cl. KT2: King T . . . 7E 132
Archer Ho. *N1* . . . *1E 84*
(off Whitmore Est.)
SE14 . . . 1A 122
SW11 . . . 1B 118
W11 . . . *7H 81*
(off Westbourne Gro.)
W13 . . . *1B 96*
(off Sherwood Cl.)
Archer M. TW12: Ham H . . . 6G 131
Archer Rd. BR5: St M Cry . . . 5K 161
SE25 . . . 4H 157
Archers Ct. BR2: Brom . . . 4K 159
CR2: S Croy . . . *5C 168*
(off Nottingham Rd.)
Archers Dr. EN3: Enf H . . . 2D 24
Archers Lodge *SE16* . . . *5G 103*
(off Culloden Cl.)
Archer Sq. SE14 . . . 6A 104
Archer St. W1 . . . 2C 12 (7H 83)
Archer Ter. UB7: Yiew . . . 7A 74
Archery Cl. HA3: W'stone . . . 3K 41
W2 . . . 1D 10 (6C 82)
Archery Flds. Ho. *WC1* . . . *3A 84*
(off Wharton St.)
Archery Rd. SE9 . . . 5D 124
Archery Steps W2 . . . 2D 10
Arches SW8 . . . 6J 101
Arches, The HA2: Harr . . . 2F 59
NW1 . . . 7F 65
SW8 . . . 7H 101
WC2 . . . *4F 13*
(off Villiers St.)
Arches Bus. Cen., The *UB2: S'hall* . . . *2D 94*
(off Merrick Rd.)
Arches Leisure Cen. . . . 6G 105
Archgate Bus. Cen. N12 . . . 5F 31
Archibald M. W1 . . . 3J 11 (7F 83)
Archibald Rd. N7 . . . 4H 65
Archibald St. E3 . . . 3C 86
Archie St. SE1 . . . 7H 15 (2E 102)
Arch St. SE1 . . . 3C 102
ARCHWAY . . . 2G 65
Archway Bus. Cen. N19 . . . 3H 65
Archway Cl. N19 . . . 2G 65
SM6: Bedd . . . 3H 167
SW19 . . . 3K 135
W10 . . . 5F 81
Archway Leisure Cen. . . . 2G 65
Archway Mall N19 . . . 2G 65
Archway M. *SW15* . . . *4G 117*
(off Putney Bri. Rd.)
Archway Rd. N6 . . . 6E 46
N19 . . . 6E 46
Archway St. SW13 . . . 3A 116
Arcola St. E8 . . . 5F 67
Arcola Theatre . . . 5F 67
Arcon Dr. UB5: N'olt . . . 4C 76
Arcon Ter. N9 . . . 7B 24
Arctic Ho. *NW9* . . . *2B 44*
(off Heritage Av.)
Arctic St. NW5 . . . 5F 65
Arcus Rd. BR1: Brom . . . 6G 141
Ardbeg Rd. SE24 . . . 5D 120
Arden Cl. HA1: Harr . . . 3H 59
SE28 . . . 6D 90
Arden Ct. Gdns. N2 . . . 6B 46
Arden Cres. E14 . . . 4C 104
RM9: Dag . . . 7C 72
Arden Est. N1 . . . 2E 84
Arden Grange N12 . . . 4F 31
Arden Gro. BR6: Farnb . . . 4F 173
Arden Ho. N1 . . . 1G 9
SE11 . . . 4G 19
SW9 . . . *2J 119*
(off Grantham Rd.)
Arden M. E17 . . . 5D 50
Arden Mhor HA5: Eastc . . . 4K 39
Arden Rd. N3 . . . 3H 45
W13 . . . 7C 78
Ardent Cl. SE25 . . . 3E 156
Ardent Ho. *E3* . . . *2A 86*
(off Roman Rd.)
Ardfern Av. SW16 . . . 3A 156
Ardfillan Rd. SE6 . . . 1F 141
Ardgowan Rd. SE6 . . . 7G 123
Ardilaun Rd. N5 . . . 4C 66
Ardingly Cl. CR0: C'don . . . 3K 169
Ardleigh Ct. *BR1: Brom* . . . *7H 141*
(off London Rd.)
Ardleigh Gdns.
SM3: Sutt . . . 7J 153
Ardleigh Ho. IG11: Bark . . . 1G 89
Ardleigh M. IG1: Ilf . . . 3F 71
Ardleigh Rd. E17 . . . 1B 50
N1 . . . 6E 66
Ardleigh Ter. E17 . . . 1B 50
Ardley Cl. HA4: Ruis . . . 7E 38
NW10 . . . 3A 62
SE6 . . . 3A 140
Ardlui Rd. SE27 . . . 2C 138
Ardmay Gdns. KT6: Surb . . . 5E 150
Ardmere Rd. SE13 . . . 6F 123
Ardmore La. IG9: Buck H . . . 1E 36
Ardmore Pl. IG9: Buck H . . . 1E 36
Ardoch Rd. SE6 . . . 2F 141
Ardra Rd. N9 . . . 3E 34
Ardrossan Gdns. KT4: Wor Pk . . . 3C 164
Ardshiel Cl. SW15 . . . 3F 117
Ardwell Av. IG6: Ilf . . . 5G 53
Ardwell Rd. SW2 . . . 2J 137
Ardwick Rd. NW2 . . . 4J 63
Arena, The EN3: Enf L . . . 1G 25
Arena Bus. Cen. N4 . . . 6C 48
Arena Ind. Est. N4 . . . 6B 48
Arena Shop. Pk. N4 . . . 6C 48
Arena Sq. HA9: Wemb . . . 4G 61
Ares Ct. *E14* . . . *4C 104*
(off Homer Dr.)
Arethusa Ho. *E14* . . . *4C 104*
(off Cahir St.)
Argali Ho. *DA18: Erith* . . . *3E 108*
(off Kale Rd.)
Argall Av. E10 . . . 7K 49
Argall Way E10 . . . 1K 67
Argenta Way HA9: Wemb . . . 6G 61
NW10 . . . 7H 61
Argent Cen., The UB3: Hayes . . . 2J 93
Argent Ct. KT6: Surb . . . 3G 163
Argo Bus. Cen. *NW6* . . . *3J 81*
(off Kilburn Pk. Rd.)
Argonaut Pk. SL3: Poyle . . . 4A 174
Argon M. SW6 . . . 7J 99
Argon Rd. N18 . . . 5D 34
Argos Ct. *SW9* . . . *1A 120*
(off Caldwell St.)
Argos Ho. *E2* . . . *2H 85*
(off Old Bethnal Grn. Rd.)
Argosy Ho. SE8 . . . 4A 104
Argosy La. TW19: Stanw . . . 7A 110
Argus Cl. RM7: Mawney . . . 1H 55
Argus Way UB5: N'olt . . . 3C 76
Argyle Av. TW3: Houn . . . 6E 112
(not continuous)
Argyle Cl. W13 . . . 4A 78
Argyle Ho. E14 . . . 3E 104
Argyle Pas. N17 . . . 1F 49
Argyle Pl. W6 . . . 4D 98
Argyle Rd. E1 . . . 4K 85
E15 . . . 4G 69
E16 . . . 6K 87
EN5: Barn . . . 4A 20
HA2: Harr . . . 6F 41
IG1: Ilf . . . 2E 70
N12 . . . 5E 30
N17 . . . 1G 49
N18 . . . 4B 34
TW3: Houn . . . 5F 113
UB6: G'frd . . . 3K 77
W13 . . . 5A 78
Argyle Sq. WC1 . . . 1F 7 (3J 83)
Argyle St. WC1 . . . 1E 6 (3J 83)
Argyle Wlk. WC1 . . . 2F 7 (3J 83)
Argyle Way SE16 . . . 5G 103
Argyll Av. UB1: S'hall . . . 1F 95
Argyll Cl. SW9 . . . 3K 119
Argyll Gdns. HA8: Edg . . . 2H 43
Argyll Mans. SW3 . . . 7B 16 (6B 100)
W14 . . . *4G 99*
(off Hammersmith Rd.)
Argyll Rd. SE18 . . . 3G 107
W8 . . . 2J 99
Argyll St. W1 . . . 1A 12 (6G 83)
Aria Ct. IG2: Ilf . . . 6G 53
Arica Ho. *SE16* . . . *3H 103*
(off Slippers Pl.)
Arica Rd. SE4 . . . 4A 122
Ariel Ct. SE11 . . . 4K 19 (4B 102)
Ariel Rd. NW6 . . . 6J 63
Ariel Way TW4: Houn . . . 3K 111
W12 . . . 1E 98
Aristotle Rd. SW4 . . . 3H 119
Arizona Bldg. *SE10* . . . *1D 122*
(off Deal's Gateway)
Ark, The *W6* . . . *5F 99*
(off Talgarth Rd.)
Arkell Gro. SE19 . . . 7B 138
Arkindale Rd. SE6 . . . 3E 140
Arklay Cl. UB8: Hil . . . 4B 74
Arkley Cres. E17 . . . 5B 50
Arkley Rd. E17 . . . 5B 50
Arklow Ho. SE17 . . . 6D 102
Arklow M. KT6: Surb . . . 2E 162
Arklow Rd. SE14 . . . 6B 104
Arklow Rd. Trad. Est. SE14 . . . 6A 104
Arkwright Ho. *SW2* . . . *7J 119*
(off Streatham Pl.)
Arkwright Rd. CR2: Sande . . . 7F 169
NW3 . . . 5A 64

Arlesey Cl. SW15 5G 117
Arlesford Rd. SW9 3J 119
Arlidge Ho. *EC1* *5K 7*
(off Kirby St.)
Arlingford Rd. SW2 5A 120
Arlington N12 3D 30
Arlington Av. N1 1C 84
(not continuous)
Arlington Bldg. E3 2C 86
Arlington Cl. DA15: Sidc 7J 125
SE13 5F 123
SM1: Sutt 2J 165
TW1: Twick 6C 114
Arlington Ct. UB3: Harl 5G 93
W3 *2H 97*
(off Mill Hill Rd.)
Arlington Dr. HA4: Ruis 6F 39
SM5: Cars 2D 166
Arlington Gdns. IG1: Ilf 1E 70
W4 5J 97
Arlington Grn. NW7 7A 30
Arlington Ho. *EC1* *1K 7*
(off Arlington Way)
SE8 *6B 104*
(off Evelyn St.)
SW1 4A 12 (1G 101)
TW9: Kew 7H 97
W12 *1D 98*
(off Tunis Rd.)
Arlington Lodge SW2 4K 119
Arlington Pk. Mans. *W4* *5J 97*
(off Sutton La. Nth.)
Arlington Pas. TW11: Tedd 4K 131
Arlington Pl. SE10 7E 104
Arlington Rd. IG8: Wfd G 1J 51
KT6: Surb 6D 150
N14 2A 32
NW1 1F 83
TW1: Twick 6C 114
TW10: Ham 2D 132
TW11: Tedd 4K 131
TW15: Ashf 5B 128
W13 6B 78
Arlington Sq. N1 1C 84
Arlington St. SW1 4A 12 (1G 101)
Arlington Way EC1 1K 7 (3A 84)
Arliss Ho. HA1: Harr 5K 41
Arliss Way UB5: N'olt 1A 76
Arlow Rd. N21 1F 33
Armada Ct. SE8 6C 104
Armadale Cl. N17 4H 49
Armadale Rd. SW6 7J 99
TW14: Felt 5J 111
Armada St. SE8 6C 104
Armada Way E6 5F 89
Armagh Rd. E3 1B 86
Armfield Cl. KT8: W Mole 5D 148
Armfield Cres.
CR4: Mitc 2D 154
Armfield Rd. EN2: Enf 1J 23
Arminger Rd. W12 1D 98
Armistice Gdns. SE25 3G 157
Armitage Ho. *NW1* *5D 4*
(off Lisson Gro.)
Armitage Rd. NW11 1G 63
SE10 5H 105
Armour Cl. N7 6K 65
Armoury Rd. SE8 2D 122
Armoury Way SW18 5J 117
Armsby Ho. *E1* *5J 85*
(off Stepney Way)
Armstead Wlk. RM10: Dag 7G 73
Armstrong Av. IG8: Wfd G 6B 36
Armstrong Cl.
BR1: Brom 3C 160
E6 6D 88
HA5: Eastc 6J 39
KT12: Walt T 6J 147
RM8: Dag 7D 54
Armstrong Cres. EN4: Cockf 3G 21
Armstrong Rd. SE18 3G 107
SW7 2A 16 (3B 100)
TW13: Hanw 5C 130
W3 1B 98
Armstrong Way UB2: S'hall 2F 95
Armytage Rd. TW5: Hest 7B 94
Arnal Cres. SW18 7G 117
Arncliffe NW6 2K 81
Arncliffe Cl. N11 6K 31
Arncroft Ct. IG11: Bark 3B 90
Arndale Wlk. SW18 5K 117
Arne Gro. BR6: Orp 3K 173
Arne Ho. SE11 5G 19
Arne St. WC2 1F 13 (6J 83)
Arnett Sq. E4 6G 35
Arne Wlk. SE3 4H 123
Arneways Av.
RM6: Chad H 3D 54
Arneway St. SW1 2D 18 (3H 101)
Arnewood Cl. SW15 1C 134
Arneys La. CR4: Mitc 6E 154
Arngask Rd. SE6 7F 123
Arnhem Pl. E14 3C 104
Arnhem Way SE22 5E 120
Arnhem Wharf E14 3B 104
Arnison Rd. KT8: E Mos 4H 149
Arnold Bennett Way N8 3A 48
Arnold Cir. E2 2J 9 (3F 85)
Arnold Cl. HA3: Kent 7F 43
Arnold Ct. N22 7D 32
Arnold Cres. TW7: Isle 5H 113
Arnold Dr. KT9: Chess 6D 162
Arnold Est. SE1 7K 15 (2F 103)
Arnold Gdns. N13 5G 33
Arnold Ho. *SE3* *7A 106*
(off Shooters Hill Rd.)
SE17 *5B 102*
(off Doddington Gro.)
Arnold Mans. *W14* *6H 99*
(off Queen's Club Gdns.)
Arnold Rd. E3 3C 86
N15 3F 49
RM9: Dag 7F 73
SW17 7D 136
UB5: N'olt 6B 58
Arnold Ter. HA7: Stan 5E 26
Arnos Gro. N14 4C 32
Arnos Gro. Ct. *N11* *5B 32*
(off Palmer's Rd.)
Arnos Rd. N11 5B 32
Arnos Swimming Pool 5C 32
Arnot Ho. *SE5* *7C 102*
(off Comber Gro.)
Arnott Cl. SE28 1C 108
W4 4K 97
Arnould Av. SE5 4D 120
Arnsberg Way DA6: Bex 4G 127
DA7: Bex 4G 127
Arnside Gdns. HA9: Wemb 1D 60
Arnside Ho. *SE17* *6D 102*
(off Arnside St.)
Arnside Rd. DA7: Bex 1G 127
Arnside St. SE17 6D 102
Arnulf St. SE6 4D 140
Arnulls Rd. SW16 6B 138
Arodene Rd. SW2 6K 119
Arosa Rd. TW1: Twick 6D 114
(not continuous)
Arpley Sq. *SE20* *7J 139*
(off High St.)
Arragon Gdns. BR4: W W'ck 3D 170
SW16 7J 137
Arragon Rd. E6 1B 88
SW18 1J 135
TW1: Twick 7A 114
Arran Cl. DA8: Erith 6K 109
SM6: Wall 4F 167
Arran Ct. NW9 2B 44
NW10 3K 61
Arran Dr. E12 1B 70
Arran Ho. *E14* *1E 104*
(off Raleana Rd.)
Arran M. W5 1F 97
Arran Rd. SE6 2D 140
Arran Wlk. N1 7C 66
Arras Av. SM4: Mord 5A 154
Arrol Ho. SE1 3C 102
Arrol Rd. BR3: Beck 3J 157
Arrow Ct. *SW5* *4J 99*
(off W. Cromwell Rd.)
Arrow Ho. *N1* *1E 84*
(off Wilmer Gdns.)
Arrow Rd. E3 3D 86
Arrowscout Wlk. *UB5: N'olt* *3C 76*
(off Argus Way)
Arrows Ho. *SE15* *7J 103*
(off Clifton Way)
Arrowsmith Ho. SE11 5G 19
Arsenal FC 4A 66
Arsenal Rd. SE9 2D 124
Arsenal Way SE18 3G 107
Arta Ho. *E1* *6J 85*
(off Devonport St.)
Artemis Ct. *E14* *4C 104*
(off Homer Dr.)
Artemis Pl. SW18 7H 117
Arterberry Rd. SW20 7E 134
Artesian Cl. NW10 7K 61
Artesian Gro.
EN5: New Bar 4F 21
Artesian Ho. *SE1* *3F 103*
(off Grange Rd.)
Artesian Rd. W2 6J 81
Artesian Wlk. E11 3G 69
Arthingworth St. E15 1G 87
Arthur Ct. *CR0: C'don* *3E 168*
(off Fairfield Path)
SW11 1E 118
W2 *6K 81*
(off Queensway)
W10 *6F 81*
(off Silchester Rd.)
Arthur Deakin Ho. *E1* *5K 9*
(off Hunton St.)
Arthurdon Rd. SE4 5C 122
Arthur Gro. SE18 4G 107
Arthur Henderson Ho. *SW6* *2H 117*
(off Fulham Rd.)
Arthur Horsley Wlk. *E7* *5H 69*
(off Twr. Hamlets Rd.)
Arthur Ho. *N1* *1E 84*
(off New Era Est.)
Arthur Newton Ho. *SW11* *3B 118*
(off Winstanley Est.)
Arthur Rd. E6 2D 88
KT2: King T 7G 133
KT3: N Mald 5D 152
N7 4K 65
N9 2A 34
RM6: Chad H 6C 54
SW19 5H 135
Arthur St. EC4 2F 15 (7D 84)
Arthur Wade Ho. *E2* *3F 85*
(off Baroness Rd.)
Artichoke Hill E1 7H 85
Artichoke M. *SE5* *1D 120*
(off Artichoke Pl.)
Artichoke Pl. SE5 1D 120
Artillery Cl. IG2: Ilf 6G 53
Artillery Ho. E15 6G 69
SE18 *5E 106*
(off Connaught M.)
Artillery La. E1 6H 9 (5E 84)
W12 6C 80
Artillery Pas. E1 6J 9
Artillery Pl. HA3: Hrw W 7B 26
SE18 5D 106
SW1 2C 18 (3H 101)
Artillery Row
SW1 2C 18 (3G 101)
Artillery Sq. *SE18* *3F 107*
(off No 1 St.)
Artington Cl. BR6: Farnb 4G 173
Artisan Cl. E6 6F 89
Artisan Ct. E8 6G 67
Artisan M. *NW10* *3F 81*
(off Warfield Rd.)
Artisan Quarter *NW10* *3F 81*
(off Wellington Rd.)
Artizan St. E1 7J 9
Arts Depot 5F 31
Arts Theatre *2E 12*
(off Gt. Newport St.)
Arun Ct. SE25 5G 157
Arundale *KT1: King T* *4D 150*
(off Anglesea Rd.)
Arundel Av. SM4: Mord 4H 153
Arundel Bldgs. *SE1* *3E 102*
(off Swan Mead)
Arundel Cl. CR0: Wadd 3B 168
DA5: Bexl 6F 127
E15 4G 69
SW11 5C 118
TW12: Ham H 5F 131
Arundel Ct. BR2: Brom 2G 159
HA2: Harr 4E 58
N12 6H 31
N17 1G 49
SE16 *5H 103*
(off Verney Rd.)
SW3 *5D 16*
(off Jubilee Pl.)
SW13 *6D 98*
(off Arundel Ter.)
W11 *7H 81*
(off Arundel Gdns.)
Arundel Dr. HA2: Harr 4D 58
IG8: Wfd G 7D 36
Arundel Gdns. HA8: Edg 7E 28
IG3: Ilf 2A 72
N21 1F 33
W11 7H 81
Arundel Gt. Ct.
WC2 2H 13 (7K 83)
Arundel Gro. N16 5E 66
Arundel Ho. *CR0: C'don* *5D 168*
(off Heathfield Rd.)
W3 *2H 97*
(off Park Rd. Nth.)
Arundel Mans. *SW6* *1H 117*
(off Kelvedon Rd.)
Arundel Pl. N1 6A 66
Arundel Rd. CR0: C'don 6D 156
EN4: Cockf 3H 21
KT1: King T 2H 151
SM2: Cheam, Sutt 7H 165
TW4: Houn 3A 112
Arundel Sq. N7 6A 66
Arundel St. WC2 2H 13 (7K 83)
Arundel Ter. SW13 6D 98
Arun Ho. KT2: King T 1D 150
Arvon Rd. N5 5A 66
(not continuous)
Asa Ct. UB3: Harl 3H 93
Asbridge Ct. *W6* *3D 98*
(off Dalling Rd.)
Ascalon Ho. *SW8* *7G 101*
(off Thessaly Rd.)
Ascalon St. SW8 7G 101
Ascent Ho. *NW9* *2C 44*
(off Boulevard Dr.)
Ascham Dr. E4 7J 35
Ascham End E17 1A 50
Ascham St. NW5 5G 65
Aschurch Rd. CR0: C'don 7F 157
Ascot Cl. UB5: N'olt 5E 58
Ascot Ct. DA5: Bexl 7F 127
NW8 2A 4
Ascot Gdns.
UB1: S'hall 4D 76

Ascot Ho. NW1 . . . 1K 5
W9 . . . 4J 81
(off Harrow Rd.)
Ascot Lodge NW6 . . . 1K 81
Ascot Pl. HA7: Stan . . . 5H 27
Ascot Rd. BR5: St M Cry . . . 4K 161
E6 . . . 3D 88
N15 . . . 5D 48
N18 . . . 4B 34
SW17 . . . 6E 136
TW14: Bedf . . . 1C 128
Ascott Av. W5 . . . 2E 96
Ascott Cl. HA5: Eastc . . . 4J 39
Ashanti M. E8 . . . 5J 67
Ashbee Ho. E2 . . . 3J 85
(off Portman Pl.)
Ashbourne Av. DA7: Bex . . . 7E 108
E18 . . . 4K 51
HA2: Harr . . . 2H 59
N20 . . . 2J 31
NW11 . . . 5H 45
Ashbourne Cl. N12 . . . 4E 30
W5 . . . 5G 79
Ashbourne Ct. E5 . . . 4A 68
N12 . . . 4E 30
(off Ashbourne Cl.)
Ashbourne Gro. NW7 . . . 5E 28
SE22 . . . 4F 121
W4 . . . 5A 98
Ashbourne Pde. NW11 . . . 4H 45
W5 . . . 4F 79
Ashbourne Ri. BR6: Orp . . . 4J 173
Ashbourne Rd. CR4: Mitc . . . 7E 136
W5 . . . 4F 79
Ashbourne Ter. SW19 . . . 7H 135
Ashbourne Way NW11 . . . 4H 45
Ashbridge Rd. E11 . . . 7G 51
Ashbridge St. NW8 . . . 4C 4 (4C 82)
Ashbrook HA8: Edg . . . 6A 28
Ashbrook Rd. N19 . . . 1H 65
RM10: Dag . . . 3H 73
Ashburn Gdns. SW7 . . . 4A 100
Ashburnham Av. HA1: Harr . . . 6K 41
Ashburnham Cl. N2 . . . 3B 46
Ashburnham Ct. BR3: Beck . . . 2E 158
Ashburnham Gdns.
HA1: Harr . . . 6K 41
Ashburnham Gro. SE10 . . . 7D 104
Ashburnham Mans. SW10 . . . 7A 100
(off Ashburnham Rd.)
Ashburnham Pl. SE10 . . . 7D 104
Ashburnham Retreat SE10 . . . 7D 104
Ashburnham Rd. DA17: Belv . . . 4J 109
NW10 . . . 3E 80
SW10 . . . 7A 100
TW10: Ham . . . 3B 132
Ashburnham Twr. SW10 . . . 7B 100
(off Worlds End Est.)
Ashburn Pl. SW7 . . . 4A 100
Ashburton Av. CR0: C'don . . . 1H 169
IG3: Ilf . . . 5J 71
Ashburton Cl. CR0: C'don . . . 1G 169
Ashburton Ent. Cen.
SW15 . . . 6E 116
Ashburton Gdns.
CR0: C'don . . . 2G 169
Ashburton Ho. W9 . . . 4H 81
(off Fernhead Rd.)
Ashburton Memorial Homes
CR0: C'don . . . 7H 157
Ashburton Rd. CR0: C'don . . . 2G 169
E16 . . . 6J 87
HA4: Ruis . . . 2J 57
Ashburton Ter. E13 . . . 2J 87
Ashburton Triangle N7 . . . 4A 66
Ashbury Dr. UB10: Ick . . . 3D 56
Ashbury Gdns. RM6: Chad H . . . 5D 54
Ashbury Pl. SW19 . . . 6A 136
Ashbury Rd. SW11 . . . 3D 118
Ashby Av. KT9: Chess . . . 6G 163
Ashby Ct. NW8 . . . 3B 4
(off Pollitt Dr.)
Ashby Gro. N1 . . . 7C 66
(not continuous)
Ashby Ho. N1 . . . 7C 66
(off Essex Rd.)
SW9 . . . 2B 120
UB5: N'olt . . . 4D 76
Ashby M. SE4 . . . 2B 122
SW2 . . . 5J 119
(off Prague Pl.)
Ashby Rd. N15 . . . 5G 49
SE4 . . . 2B 122
Ashby St. EC1 . . . 2B 8 (3B 84)
Ashby Wlk. CR0: C'don . . . 6C 156
Ashby Way UB7: Sip . . . 7C 92
Ashchurch Gro. W12 . . . 3C 98
Ashchurch Pk. Vs. W12 . . . 3C 98
Ashchurch Ter. W12 . . . 3C 98
Ash Cl. BR5: Pet W . . . 5H 161
DA14: Sidc . . . 3B 144
HA7: Stan . . . 6F 27
HA8: Edg . . . 4D 28
KT3: N Mald . . . 2K 151
RM5: Col R . . . 1H 55
SE20 . . . 2J 157
SM5: Cars . . . 2D 166
UB9: Hare . . . 1A 38
Ashcombe Av. KT6: Surb . . . 7D 150
Ashcombe Cl. TW15: Ashf . . . 3A 128
Ashcombe Gdns. HA8: Edg . . . 4B 28
Ashcombe Ho. EN3: Pond E . . . 3E 24
Ashcombe Pk. NW2 . . . 3A 62
Ashcombe Rd. SM5: Cars . . . 6E 166
SW19 . . . 5J 135
Ashcombe Sq. KT3: N Mald . . . 3J 151
Ashcombe St. SW6 . . . 2K 117
Ash Ct. KT19: Ewe . . . 4J 163
SW19 . . . 7G 135
Ashcroft HA5: Hat E . . . 6A 26
N14 . . . 2C 32
Ashcroft Av. DA15: Sidc . . . 6A 126
Ashcroft Ct. N20 . . . 2G 31
Ashcroft Cres. DA15: Sidc . . . 6A 126
Ashcroft Ho. SW8 . . . 1G 119
(off Wadhurst Rd.)
Ashcroft Rd. KT9: Chess . . . 3F 163
Ashcroft Sq. W6 . . . 4E 98
Ashcroft Theatre . . . 3D 168
(in Fairfield Halls)
Ashdale Cl. TW2: Whitt . . . 7G 113
TW19: Stanw . . . 2A 128
Ashdale Gro. HA7: Stan . . . 6E 26
Ashdale Ho. N4 . . . 7D 48
Ashdale Rd. SE12 . . . 1K 141
Ashdale Way TW2: Whitt . . . 7F 113
Ashdene HA5: Pinn . . . 3A 40
SE15 . . . 7H 103
Ashdene Cl. TW15: Ashf . . . 7E 128
Ashdon Cl. IG8: Wfd G . . . 6E 36
Ashdon Rd. NW10 . . . 1B 80
Ashdown W13 . . . 5B 78
(off Clivedon Ct.)
Ashdown Cl. BR3: Beck . . . 2D 158
DA5: Bexl . . . 7J 127
Ashdown Ct. E17 . . . 2E 50
IG11: Bark . . . 6F 71
SM2: Sutt . . . 6A 166
Ashdown Cres. NW5 . . . 5E 64
Ashdowne Ct. N17 . . . 1G 49
Ashdown Ho. SW1 . . . 2B 18
Ashdown Pl. KT7: T Ditt . . . 7A 150
KT17: Ewe . . . 7B 164
Ashdown Rd. EN3: Enf H . . . 2D 24
KT1: King T . . . 2E 150
UB10: Hil . . . 2C 74
Ashdown Wlk. E14 . . . 4C 104
(off Copeland Dr.)
RM7: Mawney . . . 1H 55
Ashdown Way SW17 . . . 2E 136
Ashe Ho. TW1: Twick . . . 6D 114
Ashen E6 . . . 6E 88
Ashenden SE17 . . . 4C 102
(off Deacon Way)
Ashenden Rd. E5 . . . 5A 68
Ashen Gro. SW19 . . . 3J 135
Ashentree Ct. EC4 . . . 1K 13
Asher Loftus Way N11 . . . 6J 31
Asher Way E1 . . . 7G 85
Ashfield Av. TW13: Felt . . . 1K 129
WD23: Bush . . . 1B 26
Ashfield Cl. BR3: Beck . . . 7C 140
TW10: Ham . . . 1E 132
Ashfield Ct. SW9 . . . 2J 119
(off Clapham Rd.)
Ashfield Ho. W14 . . . 5H 99
(off W. Cromwell Rd.)
Ashfield La. BR7: Chst . . . 6F 143
(not continuous)
Ashfield Pde. N14 . . . 1C 32
Ashfield Rd. N4 . . . 6C 48
N14 . . . 3B 32
W3 . . . 1B 98
Ashfield St. E1 . . . 5H 85
Ashfield Yd. E1 . . . 5J 85
ASHFORD . . . 4B 128
Ashford Av. N8 . . . 4J 47
TW15: Ashf . . . 6D 128
UB4: Yead . . . 6B 76
Ashford Bus. Complex TW15: Ashf . . . 5E 128
Ashford Cl. E17 . . . 6B 50
TW15: Ashf . . . 4A 128
ASHFORD COMMON . . . 7F 129
Ashford Ct. HA8: Edg . . . 3C 28
NW2 . . . 4F 63
Ashford Cres. EN3: Enf H . . . 2D 24
TW15: Ashf . . . 3A 128
Ashford Ho. SE8 . . . 6B 104
SW9 . . . 4B 120
Ashford Ind. Est. TW15: Ashf . . . 4E 128
Ashford M. N17 . . . 1G 49
Ashford Pas. NW2 . . . 4F 63
Ashford Rd. E6 . . . 7E 70
E18 . . . 2K 51
NW2 . . . 4F 63
TW13: Felt . . . 4F 129
TW15: Ashf . . . 7E 128
TW18: Lale, Staines . . . 7A 128
Ashford Sports Cen. . . . 4A 128
Ashford St. N1 . . . 1G 9 (3E 84)
Ash Gro. BR4: W W'ck . . . 2E 170
E8 . . . 1H 85
(not continuous)
EN1: Enf . . . 7K 23
HA0: Wemb . . . 4A 60
N10 . . . 4F 47
N13 . . . 3H 33
NW2 . . . 4F 63
SE12 . . . 1J 141
SE20 . . . 2J 157
TW5: Hest . . . 1B 112
TW14: Felt . . . 1G 129
UB1: S'hall . . . 5E 76
UB3: Hayes . . . 7F 75
UB7: Yiew . . . 7B 74
UB9: Hare . . . 1A 38
W5 . . . 2E 96
Ashgrove Ct. W9 . . . 5J 81
(off Elmfield Way)
Ashgrove Ho. SW1 . . . 5D 18
(off Lindsay Sq.)
Ashgrove Rd. BR1: Brom . . . 6F 141
IG3: Ilf . . . 1K 71
TW15: Ashf . . . 5E 128
Ash Hill Cl. WD23: Bush . . . 1A 26
Ash Hill Dr. HA5: Pinn . . . 3A 40
Ash Ho. E14 . . . 2E 104
(off E. Ferry Rd.)
SE1 . . . 4F 103
(off Longfield Est.)
Ash Ho. TW15: Ashf . . . 4B 128
(off Station Rd.)
W10 . . . 4G 81
(off Heather Wlk.)
Ashingdon Cl. E4 . . . 3K 35
Ashington Ho. E1 . . . 4H 85
(off Barnsley St.)
Ashington Rd. SW6 . . . 2H 117
Ashlake Rd. SW16 . . . 4J 137
Ashland Pl. W1 . . . 5G 5 (5E 82)
Ashlar Pl. SE18 . . . 4F 107
Ashleigh Commercial Est. SE7 . . . 3A 106
Ashleigh Ct. N14 . . . 7B 22
W5 . . . 4D 96
(off Murray Rd.)
Ashleigh Gdns. SM1: Sutt . . . 2K 165
Ashleigh Point SE23 . . . 3K 139
Ashleigh Rd. SE20 . . . 3H 157
SW14 . . . 3A 116
Ashley Av. IG6: Ilf . . . 2F 53
SM4: Mord . . . 5J 153
Ashley Cl. HA5: Pinn . . . 2K 39
NW4 . . . 2E 44
Ashley Ct. EN5: New Bar . . . 5F 21
NW4 . . . 2E 44
NW9 . . . 2B 44
(off Guilfoyle)
SW1 . . . 2A 18
(off Morpeth Ter.)
UB5: N'olt . . . 1C 76
Ashley Cres. N22 . . . 2A 48
SW11 . . . 3E 118
Ashley Dr. TW2: Whitt . . . 7F 113
TW7: Isle . . . 6J 95
Ashley Gdns. BR6: Orp . . . 5J 173
HA9: Wemb . . . 2E 60
N13 . . . 4H 33
SW1 . . . 2B 18 (3G 101)
(not continuous)
TW10: Ham . . . 2D 132
Ashley La. CR0: Wadd . . . 4B 168
NW4 . . . 7K 29
Ashley Pl. SW1 . . . 2A 18 (3G 101)
(not continuous)
Ashley Rd. CR7: Thor H . . . 4K 155
E4 . . . 6H 35
E7 . . . 7A 70
EN3: Enf H . . . 2D 24
KT7: T Ditt . . . 6K 149
N17 . . . 3G 49
N19 . . . 1J 65
SW19 . . . 6K 135
TW9: Rich . . . 3E 114
TW12: Hamp . . . 1E 148
Ashley Wlk. NW7 . . . 7A 30
Ashling Rd. CR0: C'don . . . 1G 169
Ashlin Rd. E15 . . . 4F 69
Ash Lodge TW16: Sun . . . 7H 129
(off Forest Dr.)
Ashlone Rd. SW15 . . . 3E 116
Ashlyns Way KT9: Chess . . . 6D 162
Ashmead N14 . . . 5B 22
Ashmead Bus. Cen. E16 . . . 4F 87
Ashmead Ga. BR1: Brom . . . 1A 160
Ashmead Ho. E9 . . . 5A 68
(off Homerton Rd.)
Ashmead M. SE8 . . . 2C 122
Ashmead Rd. SE8 . . . 2C 122
TW14: Felt . . . 1J 129
Ashmere Av. BR3: Beck . . . 2F 159
Ashmere Cl.
SM3: Cheam . . . 5F 165
Ashmere Gro. SW2 . . . 4J 119
Ash M. NW5 . . . 5G 65
Ashmill St. NW1 . . . 5C 4 (5C 82)
Ashmole Pl. SW8 . . . 6K 101
Ashmole St. SW8 . . . 6K 101
Ashmore NW1 . . . 7H 65
(off Agar Gro.)
Ashmore Cl. SE15 . . . 7F 103

Ashmore Ct. N11 6J 31
TW5: Hest 6E 94
Ashmore Gro. DA16: Well 3H 125
Ashmore Ho. *W14* *3G 99*
(off Russell Rd.)
Ashmore Rd. W9 2H 81
Ashmount Est. N19 7H 47
Ashmount Rd. N15 5F 49
N19 7G 47
Ashmount Ter. W5 4D 96
Ashmour Gdns. RM1: Rom 2K 55
Ashneal Gdns. HA1: Harr 3H 59
Ashness Gdns. UB6: G'frd 6B 60
Ashness Rd. SW11 5D 118
Ashpark Ho. *E14* *6B 86*
(off Norbiton Rd.)
Ashridge Cl. HA3: Kent 6C 42
Ashridge Ct. N14 5B 22
UB1: S'hall *6G 77*
(off Redcroft Rd.)
Ashridge Cres. SE18 7G 107
Ashridge Gdns. HA5: Pinn 4C 40
N13 5C 32
Ashridge Way SM4: Mord 3H 153
TW16: Sun 6J 129
Ash Rd. BR6: Chels 7K 173
CR0: C'don 2C 170
E15 5G 69
SM3: Sutt 7G 153
TW17: Shep 4C 146
Ash Row BR2: Brom 7E 160
Ashtead Rd. E5 7G 49
Ashton Cl. SM1: Sutt 4J 165
Ashton Ct. E4 3B 36
HA1: Harr 3K 59
Ashton Gdns. RM6: Chad H 6E 54
TW4: Houn 4D 112
Ashton Hgts. SE23 1J 139
Ashton Ho. SW9 7A 102
Ashton Rd. E15 5F 69
Ashton St. E14 7E 86
Ashtree Av. CR4: Mitc 2B 154
Ash Tree Cl. CR0: C'don 6A 158
KT6: Surb 2E 162
Ashtree Cl. BR6: Farnb 4F 173
Ash Tree Ct. *TW15: Ashf* *5D 128*
(off Feltham Hill Rd.)
Ash Tree Dell NW9 5J 43
Ash Tree Ho. *SE5* *7C 102*
(off Pitman St.)
Ash Tree Way CR0: C'don 5K 157
Ashurst Cl. SE20 1H 157
Ashurst Dr. IG2: Ilf 6F 53
IG6: Ilf 5G 53
(Hamilton Av.)
IG6: Ilf 4G 53
(Horns Rd.)
TW17: Shep 5A 146
Ashurst Gdns. SW2 1A 138
Ashurst Rd. EN4: Cockf 5J 21
N12 5H 31
Ashurst Wlk. CR0: C'don 2H 169
Ashvale Rd. SW17 5D 136
Ash Vw. Cl. TW15: Ashf 5A 128
Ashview Gdns. TW15: Ashf 5A 128
Ashville Rd. E11 2F 69
Ash Wlk. HA0: Wemb 4C 60
Ashwater Rd. SE12 1J 141
Ashway Cen., The KT2: King T 1E 150
Ashwell Cl. E6 6C 88
Ashwell Ct. TW15: Ashf 2A 128
Ashwin St. E8 6F 67
Ashwood Av. UB8: Hil 6C 74
Ashwood Gdns. CR0: New Ad 6E 170
UB3: Harl 4H 93
Ashwood Ho. *NW4* *4E 44*
(off Harmony Way)
Ashwood Rd. E4 3A 36
Ashworth Cl. SE5 2D 120
Ashworth Est. CR0: Bedd 1J 167
Ashworth Mans. *W9* *3K 81*
(off Elgin Av.)
Ashworth Rd. W9 3K 81
Aske Ho. N1 1G 9
Asker Ho. N7 4J 65
Askern Cl. DA6: Bex 4D 126
Aske St. N1 1G 9 (3E 84)
Askew Cres. W12 2B 98
Askew Est. *W12* *1B 98*
(off Uxbridge Rd.)
Askew Rd. W12 2B 98
Askham Ct. W12 1C 98
Askham Rd. W12 1C 98
Askill Dr. SW15 5G 117
Askwith Rd. RM13: Rain 3K 91
Asland Rd. E15 1G 87
Aslett St. SW18 7K 117
Asman Ho. *N1* *2B 84*
(off Colebrooke Rd.)
Asmara Rd. NW2 5G 63
Asmuns Hill NW11 5J 45
Asmuns Pl. NW11 5H 45
Asolando Dr. SE17 4C 102
Aspect Ct. *E14* *2E 104*
(off Manchester Rd.)
SW6 2A 118
Aspects SM1: Sutt 5K 165
Aspen Cl. N19 2G 65
UB7: Yiew 1B 92
W5 2F 97
Aspen Copse BR1: Brom 2D 160
Aspen Dr. HA0: Wemb 3A 60
Aspen Gdns. CR4: Mitc 5E 154
TW15: Ashf 5E 128
W6 5D 98
Aspen Grn. DA18: Erith 3F 109
Aspen Gro. HA5: Eastc 3H 39
Aspen Ho. DA15: Sidc 2A 144
SE15 *6J 103*
(off Sharratt St.)
Aspen La. UB5: N'olt 3C 76
Aspenlea Rd. W6 6F 99
Aspen Lodge *W8* *3K 99*
(off Abbots Wlk.)
Aspen Way E14 7D 86
TW13: Felt 3K 129
Aspern Gro. NW3 5C 64
Aspinall Rd. SE4 3K 121
(not continuous)
Aspinden Rd. SE16 4H 103
Aspire National Training Cen. 2G 27
Aspley Rd. SW18 5K 117
Asplins Rd. N17 1G 49
Asprey M. BR3: Beck 5B 158
Asprey Pl. BR1: Brom 2C 160
Asquith Cl. RM8: Dag 1C 72
Asquith Ho. *SW1* *2D 18*
(off Monck St.)
Assam St. *E1* *6G 85*
(off White Church La.)
Assata M. N1 6B 66
Assembly Pas. E1 5J 85
Assembly Wlk.
SM5: Cars 7C 154
Ass Ho. La. HA3: Hrw W 4A 26
Astall Cl. HA3: Hrw W 1J 41
Astbury Bus. Pk.
SE15 1J 121
Astbury Ho. SE11 2J 19
Astbury Rd. SE15 1J 121
Astell Ho. *SW3* *5D 16*
(off Astell St.)
Astell St. SW3 5D 16 (5C 100)
Aste St. E14 2E 104
Astey's Row N1 7C 66
Asthall Gdns. IG6: Ilf 4G 53
Astins Ho. E17 4D 50
Astleham Rd. TW17: Shep 3A 146
Astle St. SW11 2E 118
Astley Av. NW2 5E 62
Astley Ho. *SE1* *5F 103*
(off Rowcross St.)
SW13 *6D 98*
(off Wyatt Dr.)
W2 *5J 81*
(off Alfred Rd.)
Aston Av. HA3: Kent 7C 42
Aston Cl. DA14: Sidc 3A 144
Aston Ct. IG8: Wfd G 6D 36
Aston Grn. TW4: Cran 2A 112
Aston Ho. SW8 1H 119
W11 *7H 81*
(off Westbourne Gro.)
Aston M. RM6: Chad H 7C 54
Aston Pl. SW16 6B 138
Aston Rd. SW20 2E 152
W5 6D 78
Aston St. E14 5A 86
Aston Ter. SW12 6F 119
Astonville St. SW18 1J 135
Aston Webb Ho. SE1 5H 15
Astor Av. RM7: Rom 6J 55
Astor Cl. KT2: King T 6H 133
Astor Ct. *E16* *6A 88*
(off Ripley Rd.)
SW6 *7A 100*
(off Maynard Cl.)
Astoria, The *7D 6*
(off Sutton Row)
Astoria Ct. *E8* *7F 67*
(off Queensbridge Rd.)
Astoria Ho. *NW9* *2B 44*
(off Boulevard Dr.)
Astoria Mans. SW16 3J 137
Astoria Wlk. SW9 3A 120
Astra Ho. *SE14* *6B 104*
(off Arklow Rd.)
Astral Ho. *E1* *6H 9*
(off Middlesex Rd.)
Astrid Ho. TW13: Felt 2A 130
Astrop M. W6 3E 98
Astrop Ter. W6 2E 98
Astwood M. SW7 4A 100
Asylum Rd. SE15 7H 103
Atalanta St. SW6 7F 99
Atbara Rd. TW11: Tedd 6B 132
Atcham Rd. TW3: Houn 4G 113
Atcost Rd. IG11: Bark 5A 90
Atcraft Cen. HA0: Wemb 1E 78
Atheldene Rd. SW18 1K 135
Athelney St. SE6 3C 140
Athelstane Gro. E3 2B 86
Athelstane M. N4 1A 66
Athelstan Gdns. NW6 7G 63
Athelstan Ho. *KT1: King T* *4F 151*
(off Athelstan Rd.)
Athelstan Rd. KT1: King T 4F 151
Athelstone Rd. HA3: W'stone 2H 41
Athena Cl. HA2: Harr 2H 59
KT1: King T 3F 151
Athena Ct. *SE1* *7G 15*
(off City Wlk.)
Athenaeum Ct. N5 4C 66
Athenaeum Pl. N10 3F 47
Athenaeum Rd. N20 1F 31
Athena Pl. HA6: Nwood 1H 39
Athene Pl. *EC4* *7K 7*
(off St Andrew St.)
Athenia Ho. *E14* *6F 87*
(off Blair St.)
Athenlay Rd. SE15 5K 121
Athens Gdns. *W9* *4J 81*
(off Harrow Rd.)
Atherden Rd. E5 4J 67
Atherfold Rd. SW9 3J 119
Atherley Way TW4: Houn 7D 112
Atherstone Ct. *W2* *5K 81*
(off Delamere Ter.)
Atherstone M. SW7 4A 100
Atherton Dr. SW19 4F 135
Atherton Hgts. HA0: Wemb 7C 60
Atherton Leisure Cen. 6H 69
Atherton M. E7 6H 69
Atherton Pl. HA2: Harr 3H 41
UB1: S'hall 7E 76
Atherton Rd. E7 6H 69
IG5: Ilf 2C 52
SW13 7C 98
Atherton St. SW11 2C 118
Athlone Cl. E5 5H 67
Athlone Ct. E17 3F 51
Athlone Ho. *E1* *6J 85*
(off Sidney St.)
Athlone Rd. SW2 7K 119
Athlone St. NW5 6E 64
Athlon Ind. Est. HA0: Wemb 1D 78
Athlon Rd. HA0: Wemb 2D 78
Athol Cl. HA5: Pinn 1K 39
Athole Gdns. EN1: Enf 5K 23
Athol Gdns. HA5: Pinn 1K 39
Atholl Ho. *W9* *3A 82*
(off Maida Va.)
Atholl Rd. IG3: Ilf 7A 54
Athol Rd. DA8: Erith 5J 109
Athol Sq. E14 6E 86
Athol Way UB10: Hil 3C 74
Atkin Bldg. *WC1* *5H 7*
(off Raymond Bldgs.)
Atkins Dr. BR4: W W'ck 2F 171
Atkins Lodge *W8* *2J 99*
(off Thornwood Gdns.)
Atkinson Cl. BR6: Chels 5K 173
Atkinson Ct. *E10* *7D 50*
(off Kings Cl.)
Atkinson Ho. *E2* *2G 85*
(off Pritchards Rd.)
E13 *4H 87*
(off Sutton Rd.)
SE17 *4D 102*
(off Catesby St.)
SW11 *1E 118*
(off Austin Rd.)
Atkinson Rd. E16 5A 88
Atkins Rd. E10 6D 50
SW12 7G 119
Atlanta Bldg. *SE10* *1D 122*
(off Deal's Gateway)
Atlanta Ct. CR7: Thor H 3C 156
Atlanta Ho. *SE16* *3A 104*
(off Brunswick Quay)
Atlantic Apartments *E16* *7J 87*
(off Seagull La.)
Atlantic Ct. *E14* *7F 87*
(off Jamestown Way)
Atlantic Ho. *E1* *5A 86*
(off Harford St.)
NW9 *2B 44*
(off Boulevard Dr.)
Atlantic Rd. SW9 4A 120
Atlantic Wharf E1 7K 85
Atlantis Av. E16 7G 89
Atlantis Cl. IG11: Bark 3B 90
Atlas Bus. Cen. NW2 1D 62
Atlas Cres. HA8: Edg 2C 28
Atlas Gdns. SE7 4A 106
Atlas M. E8 6F 67
N7 6K 65
Atlas Rd. E13 2J 87
HA9: Wemb 4J 61
N11 7K 31
NW10 3A 80
Atlas Wharf E9 6C 68
Atley Rd. E3 1C 86
Atlip Rd. HA0: Wemb 1E 78
Atney Rd. SW15 4G 117
Atrium, The IG9: Buck H 2G 37
Atrium Apartments *N1* *1D 84*
(off Felton St.)
Atterbury Rd. N4 6A 48
Atterbury St. SW1 4D 18 (4J 101)

Attewood Av. NW10 . . . 3A 62
Attewood Rd. UB5: N'olt . . . 6C 58
Attfield Cl. N20 . . . 2G 31
Attfield Ct. KT1: King T . . . 2F 151
(off Albert Rd.)
Attilburgh Ho. SE1 . . . 7J 15
(off St Saviour's Est.)
Attleborough Ct. SE23 . . . 2G 139
Attle Cl. UB10: Hil . . . 2C 74
Attlee Cl. CR7: Thor H . . . 5C 156
UB4: Yead . . . 3K 75
Attlee Rd. SE28 . . . 7B 90
UB4: Yead . . . 3J 75
Attlee Ter. E17 . . . 4D 50
Attneave St. WC1 . . . 2J 7 (3A 84)
Atunbi Ct. NW1 . . . 7G 65
(off Farrier St.)
Atwater Cl. SW2 . . . 1A 138
Atwell Cl. E10 . . . 6D 50
Atwell Pl. KT7: T Ditt . . . 7K 149
Atwell Rd. SE15 . . . 2G 121
Atwood Av. TW9: Kew . . . 2G 115
Atwood Ho. W14 . . . 4H 99
(off Beckford Cl.)
Atwood Rd. W6 . . . 4D 98
Atwoods All. TW9: Kew . . . 1G 115
Aubert Ct. N5 . . . 4B 66
Aubert Pk. N5 . . . 4B 66
Aubert Rd. N5 . . . 4B 66
Aubrey Beardsley Ho. SW1 . . . 4B 18
(off Vauxhall Bri. Rd.)
Aubrey Mans. NW1 . . . 5C 4
(off Lisson St.)
Aubrey Moore Point E15 . . . 2E 86
(off Abbey La.)
Aubrey Pl. NW8 . . . 2A 82
Aubrey Rd. E17 . . . 3C 50
N8 . . . 5J 47
W8 . . . 1H 99
Aubrey Wlk. W8 . . . 1H 99
Auburn Cl. SE14 . . . 7A 104
Aubyn Hill SE27 . . . 4C 138
Aubyn Sq. SW15 . . . 5C 116
Auckland Cl. SE19 . . . 1F 157
Auckland Ct. UB4: Yead . . . 4A 76
Auckland Gdns. SE19 . . . 1E 156
Auckland Hill SE27 . . . 4C 138
Auckland Ho. W12 . . . 7D 80
(off White City Est.)
Auckland Ri. SE19 . . . 1E 156
Auckland Rd. E10 . . . 3D 68
IG1: Ilf . . . 1F 71
KT1: King T . . . 4F 151
SE19 . . . 1F 157
SW11 . . . 4C 118
Auckland St.
SE11 . . . 6G 19 (5K 101)
Audax NW9 . . . 2B 44
Auden Pl. NW1 . . . 1E 82
SM3: Cheam . . . 4E 164
Audleigh Pl. IG7: Chig . . . 6K 37
Audley Cl. N10 . . . 7A 32
SW11 . . . 3E 118
Audley Ct. E18 . . . 4H 51
HA5: Pinn . . . 2A 40
TW2: Twick . . . 3H 131
UB5: Yead . . . 3A 76
Audley Dr. E16 . . . 1K 105
Audley Gdns. IG3: Ilf . . . 2K 71
Audley Pl. SM2: Sutt . . . 7K 165
Audley Rd. EN2: Enf . . . 2G 23
NW4 . . . 5C 44
TW10: Rich . . . 5F 115
W5 . . . 5F 79
Audley Sq. W1 . . . 4H 11 (1E 100)
Audrey Cl. BR3: Beck . . . 6D 158
Audrey Gdns. HA0: Wemb . . . 2B 60
Audrey Rd. IG1: Ilf . . . 3F 71
Audrey St. E2 . . . 2G 85
Audric Cl. KT2: King T . . . 1G 151
Augurs La. E13 . . . 3K 87
Augusta Cl. KT8: W Mole . . . 3D 148
Augusta Rd. TW2: Twick . . . 2G 131
Augusta St. E14 . . . 6D 86
Augustine Rd. HA3: Hrw W . . . 1F 41
W14 . . . 3F 99
Augustus Cl. HA7: Stan . . . 3J 27
TW8: Bford . . . 7C 96
W12 . . . 2D 98
Augustus Ct. SE1 . . . 4E 102
(off Old Kent Rd.)
SW16 . . . 2H 137
TW13: Hanw . . . 4D 130
Augustus Ho. NW1 . . . 1A 6
(off Augustus St.)
Augustus La. BR6: Orp . . . 2K 173
Augustus Rd. SW19 . . . 1F 135
Augustus St. NW1 . . . 1K 5 (2F 83)
Aultone Way SM1: Sutt . . . 2K 165
SM5: Cars . . . 3D 166
Aultone Yd. Ind. Est.
SM5: Cars . . . 3D 166
Aulton Pl. SE11 . . . 6K 19 (5A 102)
Aura Ct. SE15 . . . 4H 121
Aura Ho. TW9: Kew . . . 1H 115
Aurelia Gdns. CR0: C'don . . . 5K 155
Aurelia Rd. CR0: C'don . . . 6J 155
Auriel Av. RM10: Dag . . . 6K 73
Auriga M. N1 . . . 5D 66
Auriol Cl. KT4: Wor Pk . . . 3A 164
Auriol Dr. UB6: G'frd . . . 7H 59
UB10: Hil . . . 6C 56
Auriol Ho. W12 . . . 1D 98
(off Ellerslie Rd.)
Auriol Mans. W14 . . . 4G 99
(off Edith Rd.)
Auriol Pk. Rd. KT4: Wor Pk . . . 3A 164
Auriol Rd. W14 . . . 4G 99
Aurora Bldg. E14 . . . 1E 104
(off Blackwall Way)
Aurora Ho. E14 . . . 6D 86
(off Kerbey St.)
Austell Gdns. NW7 . . . 3F 29
Austell Hgts. NW7 . . . 3F 29
(off Austell Gdns.)
Austen Apartments SE20 . . . 2H 157
Austen Cl. SE28 . . . 1B 108
Austen Ho. NW6 . . . 3J 81
(off Cambridge Rd.)
Austen Rd. DA8: Erith . . . 7H 109
HA2: Harr . . . 2F 59
Austin Av. BR2: Brom . . . 5C 160
Austin Cl. SE23 . . . 7A 122
TW1: Twick . . . 5C 114
Austin Ct. E6 . . . 1A 88
EN1: Enf . . . 5K 23
SE15 . . . 3G 121
(off Philip Wlk.)
Austin Friars EC2 . . . 7F 9 (6D 84)
(not continuous)
Austin Friars Pas. EC2 . . . 7F 9
Austin Friars Sq. EC2 . . . 7F 9
(off Austin Friars)
Austin Ho. SE14 . . . 7B 104
(off Achilles St.)
Austin Rd. SW11 . . . 1E 118
UB3: Hayes . . . 2H 93
Austin's La. HA4: Ruis . . . 4F 57
UB10: Ick . . . 3E 56
Austin St. E2 . . . 2J 9 (3F 85)
Austin Ter. SE1 . . . 1K 19
(off Morley St.)
Austral Cl. DA15: Sidc . . . 3K 143
Australian War Memorial . . . 6H 11
(off Duke of Wellington Pl.)
Australia Rd. W12 . . . 7D 80
Austral St. SE11 . . . 3K 19 (4B 102)
Austyn Gdns.
KT5: Surb . . . 1H 163
Austyns Pl. KT17: Ewe . . . 7C 164
Autumn Cl. EN1: Enf . . . 1B 24
SW19 . . . 6A 136
Autumn Gro. BR1: Brom . . . 6K 141
Autumn Lodge CR0: C'don . . . 4E 168
(off South Pk. Hill Rd.)
Autumn St. E3 . . . 1C 86
Avalon Cl. EN2: Enf . . . 2F 23
SW20 . . . 2G 153
W13 . . . 5A 78
Avalon Rd. SW6 . . . 1K 117
W13 . . . 4A 78
Avante KT1: King T . . . 3D 150
Avard Gdns. BR6: Farnb . . . 4G 173
Avarn Rd. SW17 . . . 6D 136
Avebury Ct. N1 . . . 1D 84
(off Imber St.)
Avebury Pk. KT6: Surb . . . 7D 150
Avebury Rd. BR6: Orp . . . 3H 173
E11 . . . 1F 69
SW19 . . . 1H 153
Avebury St. N1 . . . 1D 84
Aveley Mans. IG11: Bark . . . 7F 71
(off Whiting Av.)
Aveley Rd. RM1: Rom . . . 4K 55
Aveline St. SE11 . . . 5H 19 (5A 102)
Aveling Pk. Rd. E17 . . . 2C 50
Ave Maria La. EC4 . . . 1B 14 (6B 84)
Avenell Mans. N5 . . . 4B 66
Avenell Rd. N5 . . . 3B 66
Avenfield Ho. W1 . . . 2F 11
(off Park La.)
Avening Rd. SW18 . . . 7J 117
Avening Ter. SW18 . . . 7J 117
Avenons Rd. E13 . . . 4J 87
Avenue, The BR1: Brom . . . 3B 160
BR2: Kes . . . 4B 172
BR3: Beck . . . 1D 158
(not continuous)
BR4: W W'ck . . . 7E 158
BR5: St P . . . 7B 144
BR6: Orp . . . 2K 173
CR0: C'don . . . 3E 168
DA5: Bexl . . . 7D 126
E4 . . . 6A 36
E11 . . . 6K 51
EN5: Barn . . . 3B 20
HA3: Hrw W . . . 1K 41
HA5: Pinn . . . 6D 40
HA9: Wemb . . . 1E 60
IG9: Buck H . . . 2F 37
KT4: Wor Pk . . . 2B 164
KT5: Surb . . . 6F 151
KT17: Ewe . . . 7D 164
N3 . . . 2J 45
N8 . . . 3A 48
N10 . . . 2G 47
N11 . . . 5A 32
N17 . . . 3D 48
NW6 . . . 1F 81
RM1: Rom . . . 4K 55
SE10 . . . 7F 105
SM2: Cheam . . . 7G 165
SM3: Cheam . . . 7E 164
SM5: Cars . . . 7E 166
SW4 . . . 4E 118
SW18 . . . 7C 118
TW1: Twick . . . 5B 114
TW3: Houn . . . 5F 113
TW5: Cran . . . 7J 93
TW9: Kew . . . 2F 115
TW12: Hamp . . . 6D 130
TW16: Sun . . . 1K 147
UB10: Ick . . . 4C 56
W4 . . . 3A 98
W13 . . . 6B 78
Avenue Cl. N14 . . . 6B 22
NW8 . . . 1C 82
(not continuous)
TW5: Cran . . . 1K 111
UB7: W Dray . . . 3A 92
Avenue Ct. IG5: Ilf . . . 3C 52
N14 . . . 6B 22
NW2 . . . 3H 63
SW3 . . . 4E 16
(off Draycott Av.)
Avenue Cres. TW5: Cran . . . 1K 111
W3 . . . 2H 97
Avenue Elmers KT6: Surb . . . 5E 150
Avenue Gdns. SE25 . . . 2G 157
SW14 . . . 3A 116
TW5: Cran . . . 7K 93
TW11: Tedd . . . 7K 131
W3 . . . 2H 97
Avenue Ho. NW6 . . . 7G 63
(off The Avenue)
NW8 . . . 2C 82
(off Allitsen Rd.)
NW10 . . . 2D 80
(off All Souls Av.)
Avenue Ind. Est. E4 . . . 6H 35
Avenue Lodge NW8 . . . 7B 64
(off Avenue Rd.)
Avenue Mans. NW3 . . . 5K 63
(off Finchley Rd.)
Avenue M. N10 . . . 3F 47
Avenue Pde. N21 . . . 7J 23
TW16: Sun . . . 3K 147
Avenue Pk. Rd. SE27 . . . 2B 138
Avenue Rd. BR3: Beck . . . 2K 157
DA7: Bex . . . 3E 126
DA8: Erith . . . 7J 109
DA17: Belv, Erith . . . 4J 109
E7 . . . 4K 69
HA5: Pinn . . . 3C 40
IG8: Wfd G . . . 6F 37
KT1: King T . . . 3E 150
KT3: N Mald . . . 4A 152
N6 . . . 7G 47
N12 . . . 4F 31
N14 . . . 7B 22
N15 . . . 5D 48
NW3 . . . 7B 64
NW8 . . . 7B 64
NW10 . . . 2B 80
RM6: Chad H . . . 7B 54
SE20 . . . 1J 157
SE25 . . . 2F 157
SM6: Wall . . . 7G 167
SW16 . . . 2H 155
SW20 . . . 2D 152
TW7: Isle . . . 1K 113
TW8: Bford . . . 5C 96
TW11: Tedd . . . 7A 132
TW12: Hamp . . . 1F 149
TW13: Felt . . . 3H 129
UB1: S'hall . . . 1D 94
W3 . . . 2H 97
Avenue Sth. KT5: Surb . . . 7G 151
Avenue Ter. KT3: N Mald . . . 3J 151
Averil Gro. SW16 . . . 6B 138
Averill St. W6 . . . 6F 99
Avern Gdns. KT8: W Mole . . . 4F 149
Avern Rd. KT8: W Mole . . . 4F 149
Avery Farm Row SW1 . . . 4J 17 (4E 100)
Avery Gdns. IG2: Ilf . . . 5D 52
AVERY HILL . . . 6H 125
Avery Hill Rd. SE9 . . . 6H 125
Avery Row W1 . . . 2J 11 (7F 83)
Aviary Cl. E16 . . . 5H 87
Aviation Sq. NW9 . . . 2C 44
Aviemore Cl. BR3: Beck . . . 5B 158
Aviemore Way
BR3: Beck . . . 5A 158
Avignon Rd. SE4 . . . 3K 121
Avingdor Ct. W3 . . . 1J 97
(off Horn La.)
Avington Ct. SE1 . . . 4E 102
(off Old Kent Rd.)
Avington Gro. SE20 . . . 7J 139
Avion Cres. NW9 . . . 1C 44

Avis Sq. E1 6K 85
Avoca Rd. SW17 4E 136
Avocet Cl. SE1 5G 103
Avocet M. SE28 3H 107
Avon Cl. KT4: Wor Pk 2C 164
SM1: Sutt 4A 166
UB4: Yead 4A 76
Avon Ct. E4 1K 35
IG9: Buck H 1E 36
N12 5E 30
SW15 5G 117
UB6: G'frd 4F 77
W9 5J 81
(off Elmfield Way)
Avondale Av. EN4: E Barn 1J 31
KT4: Wor Pk 1B 164
KT10: Hin W 3A 162
N12 5E 30
NW2 3A 62
Avondale Ct. E11 1G 69
E16 5G 87
E18 1K 51
SM2: Sutt 7A 166
(off Brighton Rd.)
Avondale Cres. EN3: Enf H 3F 25
IG4: Ilf 5B 52
Avondale Dr. UB3: Hayes 1J 93
Avondale Gdns.
TW4: Houn 5D 112
Avondale Ho. *SE1* 5G 103
(off Avondale Sq.)
Avondale Pk. Gdns. W11 7G 81
Avondale Pk. Rd. W11 7G 81
Avondale Pavement SE1 5G 103
Avondale Ri. SE15 3F 121
Avondale Rd. BR1: Brom 6G 141
CR2: S Croy 6C 168
DA16: Well 2C 126
E16 5G 87
E17 7C 50
HA3: W'stone 3K 41
N3 1A 46
N13 2F 33
N15 5B 48
SE9 2C 142
SW14 3A 116
SW19 5K 135
TW15: Ashf 3A 128
Avondale Sq. SE1 5G 103
Avonfield Ct. E17 3F 51
Avon Ho. KT2: King T 1D 150
W8 3J 99
(off Allen St.)
W14 4H 99
(off Kensington Village)
Avonhurst Ho. NW2 7G 63
Avonley Rd. SE14 7J 103
Avon M. HA5: Hat E 1D 40
Avonmore Gdns. W14 4H 99
Avonmore Mans. *W14* 4G 99
(off Avonmore Rd.)
Avonmore Pl. W14 4G 99
Avonmore Rd. W14 4G 99
Avonmouth St. SE1 7C 14 (3C 102)
Avon Path CR2: S Croy 6C 168
Avon Pl. SE1 7D 14 (2C 102)
Avon Rd. E17 3F 51
SE4 3C 122
TW16: Sun 7H 129
UB6: G'frd 4E 76
Avonstowe Cl. BR6: Farnb 3G 173
Avon Way E18 3J 51
Avonwick Rd. TW3: Houn 2F 113
Avril Way E4 5K 35
Avro Ho. *NW9* 2B 44
(off Boulevard Dr.)
SW8 7F 101
(off Havelock Ter.)
Avro Way SM6: Wall 7J 167
Awlfield Av. N17 1D 48
Awliscombe Rd. DA16: Well 2K 125
Axe St. IG11: Bark 1G 89
(not continuous)
Axholme Av. HA8: Edg 1G 43
Axiom Apartments *BR2: Brom* 4K 159
(off Masons Hill)
Axis Ct. *SE10* 6G 105
(off Woodland Cres.)
SE16 2G 103
(off East La.)
Axminster Cres. DA16: Well 1C 126
Axminster Rd. N7 3J 65
Axon Pl. IG1: Ilf 2G 71
Aybrook St. W1 6G 5 (5E 82)
Aycliffe Cl. BR1: Brom 4D 160
Aycliffe Ho. *SE17* 6D 102
(off Portland St.)
Aycliffe Rd. W12 1C 98
Ayerst Ct. E10 7E 50
Aylands Cl. HA9: Wemb 2E 60
Aylesbury Cl. E7 6H 69
Aylesbury Ct. SM1: Sutt 3A 166
Aylesbury Ho. *SE15* 6G 103
(off Friary Est.)
Aylesbury Rd. BR2: Brom 3J 159
SE17 5D 102
Aylesbury St. EC1 4A 8 (4B 84)
NW10 3K 61
Aylesford Av. BR3: Beck 5A 158
Aylesford Ho. *SE1* 7F 15
(off Long La.)
Aylesford St. SW1 5C 18 (5H 101)
Aylesham Cen., The SE15 1G 121
Aylesham Cl. NW7 7H 29
Aylesham Rd. BR6: Orp 7K 161
Ayles Rd. UB4: Yead 3K 75
Aylestone Av. NW6 7F 63
Aylett Rd. SE25 4H 157
TW7: Isle 2J 113
Ayley Cft. EN1: Enf 5B 24
Ayliffe Cl. KT1: King T 2G 151
Aylmer Cl. HA7: Stan 4F 27
Aylmer Ct. N2 5D 46
Aylmer Dr. HA7: Stan 4F 27
Aylmer Ho. SE10 5F 105
Aylmer Pde. N2 5D 46
Aylmer Rd. E11 1H 69
N2 5C 46
RM8: Dag 3E 72
W12 2B 98
Ayloffe Rd. RM9: Dag 6F 73
Aylsham Dr. UB10: Ick 2E 56
Aylton Est. SE16 2J 103
Aylward Rd. SE23 2K 139
SW20 2H 153
Aylward School Sports Cen. 4J 33
Aylwards Ri. HA7: Stan 4F 27
Aylward St. E1 6J 85
(Jamaica St.)
E1 6J 85
(Jubilee St.)
Aylwin Est. SE1 3E 102
Aynhoe Mans. *W14* 4F 99
(off Aynhoe Rd.)
Aynhoe Rd. W14 4F 99
Aynscombe Path SW14 2J 115
Ayr Ct. W3 5G 79
Ayres Cl. E13 3J 87
Ayres Cres. NW10 7K 61
Ayres St. SE1 6D 14 (2C 102)
Ayr Grn. RM1: Rom 1K 55
Ayrsome Rd. N16 3E 66
Ayrton Gould Ho. *E2* 3K 85
(off Roman Rd.)
Ayrton Rd. SW7 1A 16 (3B 100)
Ayr Way RM1: Rom 1K 55
Aysgarth Ct. SM1: Sutt 3K 165
Aysgarth Rd. SE21 7E 120
Ayshford Ho. *E2* 3H 85
(off Viaduct St.)
Ayston Ho. *SE16* 4K 103
(off Plough Way)
Aytoun Pl. SW9 2K 119
Aytoun Rd. SW9 2K 119
Azalea Cl. IG1: Ilf 5F 71
W7 1K 95
Azalea Ct. IG8: Wfd G 6B 36
W7 1K 95
Azalea Ho. *SE14* 7B 104
(off Achilles St.)
TW13: Felt 1K 129
Azalea Wlk. HA5: Eastc 5K 39
Azania M. NW5 6F 65
Azenby Rd. SE15 2F 121
Azof St. SE10 4G 105
Azov Ho. *E1* 4A 86
(off Commodore St.)
Aztec Ho. IG1: Ilf 2H 71
IG6: Ilf 1G 53
Azura Ct. *E15* 1E 86
(off Warton Rd.)
Azure Ho. *E2* 3G 85
(off Buckfast St.)

B

Baalbec Rd. N5 5B 66
Babbacombe Cl. KT9: Chess 5D 162
Babbacombe Gdns. IG4: Ilf 4C 52
Babbacombe Rd. BR1: Brom 1J 159
Baber Bri. Cvn. Site
TW14: Felt 5A 112
Baber Dr. TW14: Felt 6A 112
Babington Ct. WC1 5G 7
Babington Ho. *SE1* 6D 14
(off Disney St.)
Babington Ri. HA9: Wemb 6G 61
Babington Rd. NW4 4D 44
RM8: Dag 5C 72
SW16 5H 137
Babmaes St.
SW1 3C 12 (7H 83)
Bacchus Wlk. *N1* 2E 84
(off Regan Way)
Bache's St. N1 1F 9 (3D 84)
Back All. EC3 1H 15
Bk. Church La. E1 6G 85
Back Hill EC1 4K 7 (4A 84)
Backhouse Pl. SE17 4E 102
Back La. DA5: Bexl 7G 127
HA8: Edg 1J 43
IG9: Buck H 2G 37
N8 5J 47
NW3 4A 64
RM6: Chad H 7D 54
TW8: Bford 6D 96
TW10: Ham 3C 132
Backley Gdns. SE25 6G 157
Back Pas. *EC1* 5B 8
(off Long La.)
Back Rd. DA14: Sidc 4A 144
TW11: Tedd 7J 131
Bacon Gro. SE1 3F 103
Bacon La. HA8: Edg 1G 43
NW9 4H 43
(not continuous)
Bacon's College Sports Cen. 1A 104
Bacons La. N6 1E 64
Bacon St. E1 3K 9 (4F 85)
E2 3K 9 (4F 85)
Bacon Ter. RM8: Dag 5B 72
Bacton NW5 5E 64
Bacton St. E2 3J 85
Baddeley Ho.
KT8: W Mole 5E 148
(off Down St.)
Baddesley Ho. SE11 5H 19
Baddow Cl. IG8: Wfd G 6F 37
RM10: Dag 1G 91
Baddow Wlk. *N1* 1C 84
(off New North Rd.)
Baden Pl. SE1 6E 14 (2D 102)
Baden Powell Cl. KT6: Surb 2F 163
RM9: Dag 1E 90
Baden Powell Ho. *DA17: Belv* 3G 109
(off Ambrooke Rd.)
SW7 2A 16
Baden Rd. IG1: Ilf 5F 71
N8 4H 47
Badger Cl. IG2: Ilf 6G 53
TW4: Houn 3A 112
TW13: Felt 3K 129
Badger Ct. NW2 3E 62
Badgers Cl. EN2: Enf 3G 23
HA1: Harr 6H 41
TW15: Ashf 5B 128
UB3: Hayes 7G 75
Badgers Copse BR6: Orp 2K 173
KT4: Wor Pk 2B 164
Badgers Cft. N20 7B 20
SE9 3E 142
Badgers Hole CR0: C'don 4K 169
Badgers Wlk. KT3: N Mald 2A 152
Badlis Rd. E17 3C 50
Badma Cl. N9 3D 34
Badminton Cl. HA1: Harr 4J 41
UB5: N'olt 6E 58
Badminton M. E16 1J 105
Badminton Rd. SW12 6E 118
Badric Ct. SW11 2B 118
Badsworth Rd. SE5 1C 120
Baffin Way E14 1E 104
Bafton Ga. BR2: Hayes 1K 171
Bagley Cl. UB7: W Dray 2A 92
Bagley's La. SW6 1K 117
Bagleys Spring RM6: Chad H 4E 54
Bagnigge Ho. *WC1* 2J 7
(off Margery St.)
Bagshot Ct. SE18 1E 124
Bagshot Ho. NW1 1K 5
Bagshot Rd. EN1: Enf 7A 24
Bagshot St. SE17 5E 102
Baildon *E2* 2J 85
(off Cyprus St.)
Baildon St. SE8 7B 104
Bailey Cl. E4 4K 35
N11 7C 32
SE28 1J 107
Bailey Cotts. *E14* 5A 86
(off Maroon St.)
Bailey Cres. KT9: Chess 7D 162
Bailey Ho. *SW10* 7K 99
(off Coleridge Gdns.)
Bailey M. SW2 5A 120
W4 6H 97
(off Hervert Gdns.)
Bailey Pl. SE26 6K 139
Baillies Wlk. W5 2D 96
Bainbridge Cl. TW10: Ham 5E 132
Bainbridge Rd. RM9: Dag 4F 73
Bainbridge St. WC1 7D 6 (6H 83)
Baines Cl. CR2: S Croy 5D 168
Baird Av. UB1: S'hall 7F 77
Baird Cl. E10 1C 68
NW9 6J 43
Baird Gdns. SE19 4E 138
Baird Ho. *W12* 7D 80
(off White City Est.)
Baird Memorial Cotts. *N14* 2C 32
(off Balaams La.)
Baird Rd. EN1: Enf 3C 24
Baird St. EC1 3D 8 (4C 84)
Bairny Wood App. IG8: Wfd G 6E 36
Baizdon Rd. SE3 2G 123
Bakehouse M. TW12: Hamp 7E 130
Baker Beal Ct. DA7: Bex 3H 127
Baker Ho. W7 1K 95
WC1 4F 7
(off Colonnade)

Baker La. CR4: Mitc 2E 154
Baker Pas. NW10 1A 80
Baker Rd. NW10 1A 80
SE18 7C 106
Bakers Av. E17 6D 50
Bakers Ct. SE25 3E 156
Bakers End SW20 2G 153
Baker's Fld. N7 4J 65
Bakers Gdns. SM5: Cars 2C 166
Bakers Hall Ct. EC3 3G 15
Bakers Hill E5 1J 67
EN5: New Bar 2E 20
Bakers Ho. *W5* 7D 78
(off The Grove)
Bakers La. N6 6D 46
Bakers M. BR6: Chels 6K 173
W1 7G 5 (6E 82)
Bakers Pas. *NW3* 4A 64
(off Heath St.)
Baker's Rents E2 2J 9 (3F 85)
Baker's Row E15 2G 87
EC1 4J 7 (4A 84)
BAKER STREET 5D 82
Baker St. EN1: Enf 3J 23
NW1 4F 5 (4D 82)
W1 5F 5 (4D 82)
Baker's Yd. EC1 4J 7
Bakery Cl. SW9 7K 101
Bakery M. KT6: Surb 1G 163
Bakery Path *HA8: Edg* 6C 28
(off St Margaret's Rd.)
Bakery Pl. SW11 4D 118
Bakewell Way KT3: N Mald 2A 152
Balaam Ho. SM1: Sutt 4J 165
Balaam Leisure Cen. 4J 87
Balaams La. N14 2C 32
Balaam St. E13 4J 87
Balaclava Rd. KT6: Surb 7C 150
SE1 4F 103
Bala Grn. *NW9* 6A 44
(off Ruthin Cl.)
Balcaskie Rd. SE9 5D 124
Balchen Rd. SE3 2B 124
Balchier Rd. SE22 6H 121
Balcombe Cl. DA6: Bex 4D 126
Balcombe Ho. *NW1* 3E 4
(off Taunton Pl.)
Balcombe St. NW1 3E 4 (4D 82)
Balcon Ct. W5 6F 79
Balcorne St. E9 7J 67
Balder Ri. SE12 2K 141
Balderton Flats *W1* 1H 11
(off Balderton St.)
Balderton St. W1 1H 11 (6E 82)
Baldewyne Ct. N17 1G 49
Baldock St. E3 2D 86
Baldrey Ho. *SE10* 5H 105
(off Blackwall La.)
Baldry Gdns. SW16 6J 137
Baldwin Cres. SE5 1C 120
Baldwin Gdns. TW3: Houn 1G 113
Baldwin Ho. SW2 1A 138
Baldwin Rd. SW11 6E 118
Baldwins Gdns. EC1 5J 7 (5A 84)
Baldwin St. EC1 2E 8 (3D 84)
Baldwin Ter. N1 2C 84
Baldwyn Gdns. W3 7K 79
Baldwyn's Pk. DA5: Bexl 2K 145
Baldwyn's Rd. DA5: Bexl 2K 145
Balearic Apartments *E16* 7J 87
(off Western Gateway)
Bale Rd. E1 5A 86
Bales Ter. N9 3A 34
Balfern Gro. W4 5A 98
Balfern St. SW11 2C 118
Balfe St. N1 2J 83
Balfour Av. W7 1K 95
Balfour Bus. Cen.
UB2: S'hall 3A 94
Balfour Gro. N20 3J 31
Balfour Ho. *W10* 5F 81
(off St Charles Sq.)
Balfour M. N9 3B 34
W1 4H 11 (1E 100)
Balfour Pl. SW15 4D 116
W1 3H 11 (7E 82)
Balfour Rd. BR2: Brom 5B 160
HA1: Harr 5H 41
IG1: Ilf 2F 71
N5 4C 66
SE25 5G 157
SM5: Cars 7D 166
SW19 7K 135
TW3: Houn 3F 113
UB2: S'hall 3B 94
W3 5J 79
W13 2A 96
Balfour St. SE17 4D 102
Balfour Ter. N3 2K 45
Balfron Twr. E14 6E 86
Balgonie Rd. E4 1A 36
Balgowan Cl. KT3: N Mald 5A 152
Balgowan Rd. BR3: Beck 3A 158
Balgowan St. SE18 4K 107
BALHAM 1E 136
Balham Continental Mkt. *SW12* 1F 137
(off Shipka Rd.)
Balham Gro. SW12 7E 118
Balham High Rd. SW12 3E 136
SW17 3E 136
Balham Hill SW12 7F 119
Balham Leisure Cen. 2F 137
Balham New Rd. SW12 7F 119
Balham Pk. Rd. SW12 1D 136
Balham Rd. N9 2B 34
Balham Sta. Rd. SW12 1F 137
Balin Ho. *SE1* 6E 14
(off Long La.)
Balkan Wlk. E1 7H 85
Balladier Wlk. E14 5D 86
Ballamore Rd. BR1: Brom 3J 141
Ballance Rd. E9 6K 67
Ballantine St. SW18 4A 118
Ballantrae Ho. NW2 4H 63
Ballard Cl. KT2: King T 7K 133
Ballard Ho. *SE10* 6D 104
(off Thames St.)
Ballards Cl. RM10: Dag 1H 91
Ballards Farm Rd. CR0: C'don 6G 169
CR2: C'don, S Croy 6G 169
Ballards La. N3 1J 45
N12 1J 45
Ballards M. HA8: Edg 6B 28
Ballards Ri. CR2: Sels 6G 169
Ballards Rd. NW2 2C 62
RM10: Dag 2H 91
Ballards Way CR0: C'don 6G 169
CR2: Sels 6G 169
Ballast Quay SE10 5F 105
Ballater Rd. CR2: S Croy 5F 169
SW2 4J 119
Ball Ct. *EC3* 1F 15
(off Cornhill)
Balletica Apartments *WC2* 1F 13
(off Long Acre)
Ball Ho. *NW9* 3B 44
(off Aerodrome Rd.)
Ballina St. SE23 7K 121
Ballin Ct. *E14* 2E 104
(off Stewart St.)
Ballingdon Rd. SW11 6E 118
Ballinger Way UB5: N'olt 4C 76
Balliol Av. E4 4B 36
Balliol Rd. DA16: Well 2B 126
N17 1E 48
W10 6E 80
Balloch Rd. SE6 1F 141
Ballogie Av. NW10 4A 62
Ballow Cl. SE5 7E 102
Balls Pond Pl. N1 6D 66
Balls Pond Rd. N1 6D 66
Balmain Cl. W5 1D 96
Balmain Ct. TW3: Houn 1F 113
Balmain Lodge *KT5: Surb* 4E 150
(off Cranes Pk. Av.)
Balman Ho. *SE16* 4K 103
(off Rotherhithe New Rd.)
Balmer Rd. E3 2B 86
Balmes Rd. N1 1D 84
Balmoral Apartments *W2* 6C 4
(off Praed St.)
Balmoral Av. BR3: Beck 4A 158
N11 6K 31
Balmoral Cl. SW15 6F 117
Balmoral Ct. *BR3: Beck* 1E 158
(off The Avenue)
HA9: Wemb 3F 61
KT4: Wor Pk 2D 164
NW8 2B 82
(off Queen's Ter.)
SE12 4K 141
SE16 1K 103
(off King & Queen Wharf)
SE17 5D 102
(off Lytham St.)
SE27 4C 138
SM2: Sutt 7J 165
Balmoral Cres. KT8: W Mole 3E 148
Balmoral Dr. UB1: S'hall 4D 76
UB4: Hayes 4G 75
Balmoral Gdns. DA5: Bexl 7F 127
IG3: Ilf 1K 71
W13 3A 96
Balmoral Gro. N7 6K 65
Balmoral Ho. *E14* 3D 104
(off Lanark Sq.)
E16 1K 105
(off Keats Av.)
W14 4G 99
(off Windsor Way)
Balmoral M. W12 3B 98
Balmoral Rd. E7 4A 70
E10 2D 68
HA2: Harr 4E 58
KT1: King T 4F 151
KT4: Wor Pk 3D 164
NW2 6D 62
Balmoral Trad. Est. IG11: Bark 5K 89
Balmore Cl. E14 6E 86
Balmore Cres. EN4: Cockf 5K 21
Balmore St. N19 2F 65
Balmuir Gdns. SW15 4E 116
Balnacraig Av. NW10 4A 62
Balniel Ga.
SW1 5D 18 (5H 101)
Balsam Ho. *E14* 7D 86
(off E. India Dock Rd.)
Baltic Apartments *E16* 7J 87
(off Western Gateway)
Baltic Cen., The TW8: Bford 5D 96
Baltic Cl. SW19 7B 136
Baltic Ct. SE16 2K 103
Baltic Ho. SE5 2C 120
Baltic Pl. N1 1E 84
Baltic St. E. EC1 4C 8 (4C 84)
Baltic St. W. EC1 4C 8 (4C 84)
Baltimore Ct. *SW1* 4C 18
(off Chapter St.)
Baltimore Ho. SE11 5J 19
SW18 4A 118
Baltimore Pl. DA16: Well 2K 125
Balvaird Pl. SW1 6D 18 (5H 101)
Balvernie Gro. SW18 7H 117
Balvernie M. SW18 7J 117
Bamber Ho. IG11: Bark 1H 89
Bamber Rd. SE15 1F 121
Bamborough Gdns.
W12 2E 98
Bamburgh N17 7C 34
Bamford Av. HA0: Wemb 1F 79
Bamford Rd. BR1: Brom 5E 140
IG11: Bark 6G 71
Bampfylde Cl. SM6: Wall 3G 167
Bampton Ct. W5 6D 78
Bampton Dr. NW7 7H 29
Bampton Rd. SE23 3K 139
Banavie Gdns. BR3: Beck 1E 158
Banbury Cl. EN2: Enf 1G 23
Banbury Ct. SM2: Sutt 7J 165
WC2 2E 12
Banbury Ho. E9 7K 67
Banbury Rd. E9 7K 67
E17 7E 34
Banbury St. SW11 2C 118
Banbury Wlk. *UB5: N'olt* 2E 76
(off Brabazon Rd.)
Banchory Rd. SE3 7K 105
Bancroft Av. IG9: Buck H 2D 36
N2 5C 46
Bancroft Cl. TW15: Ashf 5C 128
Bancroft Ct. *SW8* 7J 101
(off Allen Edwards Dr.)
UB5: N'olt 1A 76
Bancroft Gdns. BR6: Orp 1K 173
HA3: Hrw W 1G 41
Bancroft Ho. *E1* 4J 85
(off Cephas St.)
Bancroft Rd. E1 3J 85
HA3: Hrw W 2G 41
Bandon Cl. UB10: Uxb 2B 74
BANDONHILL 5H 167
Bandon Ri. SM6: Wall 5H 167
Banfield Rd. SE15 3H 121
Banfor Ct. SM6: Wall 5G 167
Bangalore St. SW15 3E 116
Bangor Cl. UB5: N'olt 5F 59
Banim St. W6 4D 98
Banister Ho. E9 5K 67
SW8 1G 119
(off Wadhurst Rd.)
W10 3G 81
(off Bruckner St.)
Banister M. NW6 7K 63
Banister Rd. W10 3F 81
Bank, The N6 1F 65
Bank Av. CR4: Mitc 2B 154
Bank Bldgs. *E4* 6A 36
(off The Avenue)
Bank End SE1 4D 14 (1C 102)
Bankfoot Rd. BR1: Brom 4G 141
Bankhurst Rd. SE6 7B 122
Bank La. KT2: King T 7E 132
SW15 5A 116
Bank M. SM1: Sutt 6A 166
Bank of England 1E 14 (6D 84)
Bank of England Mus. 1F 15
Banks Ho. *SE1* 3C 102
(off Rockingham St.)
Banksian Wlk. TW7: Isle 1J 113
Banksia Rd. N18 5E 34
Bankside CR2: S Croy 6F 169
EN2: Enf 1G 23
SE1 3C 14 (7C 84)
(not continuous)
UB1: S'hall 1B 94
Bankside Av. SE13 3E 122
UB5: Yead 2J 75
Bankside Cl. DA5: Bexl 4K 145
SM5: Cars 6C 166
TW7: Isle 4K 113
Bankside Dr. KT7: T Ditt 1B 162
Bankside Gallery 3B 14 (7B 84)
Bankside Pk. IG11: Bark 3A 90
Bankside Rd. IG1: Ilf 5G 71
Bankside Way SE19 6E 138
Banks La. DA6: Bex 4F 127
Bank St. E14 1D 104
Banks Way E12 4E 70
Bankton Rd. SW2 4A 120
Bankwell Rd. SE13 4G 123

Bannatyne's Health Club
Chingford . . . 6H 35
Grove Park . . . 2K 141
Banner Ct. SE16 . . . 4J 103
(off Rotherhithe New Rd.)
Bannerman Ho. SW8 . . . 7G 19 (6K 101)
Banner St. EC1 . . . 4D 8 (4C 84)
Banning St. SE10 . . . 5G 105
Bannister Cl. SW2 . . . 1A 138
UB6: G'frd . . . 5H 59
Bannister Ho. HA3: W'stone . . . 3J 41
(off Headstone Dr.)
SE14 . . . 6K 103
(off John Williams Cl.)
Bannockburn Rd. SE18 . . . 4J 107
Bannow Cl. KT19: Ewe . . . 4A 164
Banqueting House . . . 5E 12 (1J 101)
Banstead Ct. W12 . . . 7B 80
Banstead Gdns. N9 . . . 3K 33
Banstead Rd. SM5: Cars . . . 7B 166
Banstead Rd. Sth.
SM2: Sutt . . . 7B 166
Banstead St. SE15 . . . 3J 121
Banstead Way SM6: Wall . . . 5J 167
Banstock Rd. HA8: Edg . . . 6C 28
Bantam Ho. NW9 . . . 2B 44
(off Heritage Av.)
Banting Dr. N21 . . . 5E 22
Banting Ho. NW2 . . . 3C 62
Bantock Ho. W10 . . . 3G 81
(off Third Av.)
Banton Cl. EN1: Enf . . . 2C 24
Bantry Ho. E1 . . . 4K 85
(off Ernest St.)
Bantry St. SE5 . . . 7D 102
Banwell Rd. DA5: Bexl . . . 6D 126
Banyard Rd. SE16 . . . 3H 103
Baptist Gdns. NW5 . . . 6E 64
Barandon Rd. W11 . . . 7F 81
(off Grenfell Rd.)
Barandon Wlk. W11 . . . 7F 81
Barbanel Ho. E1 . . . 4J 85
(off Cephas St.)
Barbara Brosnan Ct. NW8 . . . 1A 4 (2B 82)
Barbara Castle Cl. SW6 . . . 6H 99
Barbara Cl. TW17: Shep . . . 5D 146
Barbara Hucklesby Cl. N22 . . . 2B 48
Barbauld Rd. N16 . . . 3E 66
Barber Beaumont Ho. E1 . . . 3K 85
(off Bancroft Rd.)
Barber Cl. N21 . . . 7F 23
Barbers All. E13 . . . 3K 87
Barbers Rd. E15 . . . 2D 86
Barbican EC2 . . . 5D 8
Barbican Arts Cen. . . . 5D 8 (5C 84)
Barbican Cinema . . . 5D 8
(in Barbican Arts Cen.)
Barbican Rd. UB6: G'frd . . . 6F 77
Barbican Theatre . . . 5D 8
(in Barbican Arts Cen.)
Barbican Trade Cen. EC1 . . . 5D 8
(off Beech St.)
Barb M. W6 . . . 3E 98
Barbon All. EC2 . . . 7H 9
(off Houndsditch)
Barbon Cl. WC1 . . . 5F 7 (5K 83)
Barbot Cl. N9 . . . 3B 34
Barchard St. SW18 . . . 5K 117
Barchester Cl. W7 . . . 1K 95
Barchester Rd. HA3: Hrw W . . . 2H 41
Barchester St. E14 . . . 5D 86
Barclay Cl. SW6 . . . 7J 99
Barclay Ho. E9 . . . 7J 67
(off Well St.)
Barclay Oval IG8: Wfd G . . . 4D 36
Barclay Path E17 . . . 5E 50
Barclay Rd. CR0: C'don . . . 3D 168
E11 . . . 1H 69
(not continuous)
E13 . . . 4A 88
Barclay Rd. E17 . . . 5E 50
N18 . . . 6J 33
SW6 . . . 7J 99
Barcombe Av. SW2 . . . 2J 137
Barcombe Cl. BR5: St P . . . 3K 161
Bardell Ho. SE1 . . . 7K 15
(off Parkers Row)
Barden St. SE18 . . . 7J 107
Bardfield Av. RM6: Chad H . . . 3D 54
Bardney Rd. SM4: Mord . . . 4K 153
Bardolph Rd. N7 . . . 4J 65
TW9: Rich . . . 3F 115
Bard Rd. W10 . . . 7F 81
Bardsey Pl. E1 . . . 4J 85
(off Mile End Rd.)
Bardsey Wlk. N1 . . . 6C 66
(off Douglas Rd. Nth.)
Bardsley Cl. CR0: C'don . . . 3F 169
Bardsley Ho. SE10 . . . 6E 104
(off Bardsley La.)
Bardsley La. SE10 . . . 6E 104
Barents Ho. E1 . . . 4K 85
(off White Horse La.)
Barfett St. W10 . . . 4H 81
Barfield Av. N20 . . . 2J 31
Barfield Rd. BR1: Brom . . . 3E 160
E11 . . . 1H 69
Barfleur La. SE8 . . . 4B 104
Barford Cl. NW4 . . . 2C 44
Barford St. N1 . . . 1A 84
Barforth Rd. SE15 . . . 3H 121
Barfreston Way SE20 . . . 1H 157
Bargate Cl.
KT3: N Mald . . . 7C 152
SE18 . . . 5K 107
Barge Ho. Rd. E16 . . . 2F 107
Barge Ho. St. SE1 . . . 4K 13 (1A 102)
Barge La. E3 . . . 1A 86
Bargery Rd. SE6 . . . 1D 140
Barge Wlk. KT1: Ham W . . . 3D 150
KT8: E Mos . . . 3H 149
(Hampton Ct. Cres.)
KT8: E Mos . . . 6A 150
(The Island)
Bargrove Cl. SE20 . . . 7G 139
Bargrove Cres. SE6 . . . 2B 140
Barham Cl. BR2: Brom . . . 1C 172
BR7: Chst . . . 5F 143
HA0: Wemb . . . 6B 60
RM7: Mawney . . . 2H 55
Barham Ct. CR2: S Croy . . . 4C 168
(off Barham Rd.)
Barham Ho. SE17 . . . 5E 102
(off Kinglake Est.)
Barham Rd. BR7: Chst . . . 5F 143
CR2: S Croy . . . 4C 168
SW20 . . . 7C 134
Baring Cl. SE12 . . . 2J 141
Baring Ct. N1 . . . 1D 84
(off Baring St.)
Baring Ho. E14 . . . 6C 86
(off Canton St.)
Baring Rd. CR0: C'don . . . 1G 169
EN4: Cockf . . . 4G 21
SE12 . . . 7J 123
Baring St. N1 . . . 1D 84
Barker Cl. HA6: Nwood . . . 1H 39
KT3: N Mald . . . 4H 151
TW9: Kew . . . 2H 115
Barker Dr. NW1 . . . 7G 65
Barker Ho. SE17 . . . 4E 102
(off Congreve St.)
Barker M. SW4 . . . 4F 119
Barkers Arc. W8 . . . 2K 99
Barker St. SW10 . . . 6A 100
Barker Wlk. SW16 . . . 3H 137
Barkham Rd. N17 . . . 7J 33
Barkham Ter. SE1 . . . 1K 19
BARKING . . . 7G 71
Barking Abbey . . . 1G 89
Barking Abbey School Leisure Cen. . . . 6A 72
Barking Bus. Pk. IG11: Bark . . . 3K 89
Barking Ind. Pk. IG11: Bark . . . 1K 89
Barking Northern Relief Rd.
IG11: Bark . . . 7F 71
BARKING RIVERSIDE . . . 3C 90
Barking Rd. E6 . . . 2A 88
E13 . . . 5H 87
E16 . . . 5H 87
BARKINGSIDE . . . 3G 53
Bark Pl. W2 . . . 7K 81
Barkston Gdns. SW5 . . . 4K 99
Barkway Ct. N4 . . . 2C 66
Barkway Dr. BR6: Farnb . . . 4E 172
Barkwith Ho. SE14 . . . 6K 103
(off Cold Blow La.)
Barkwood Cl. RM7: Rom . . . 5J 55
Barkworth Rd. SE16 . . . 5H 103
Barlborough St. SE14 . . . 7K 103
Barlby Gdns. W10 . . . 4F 81
Barlby Rd. W10 . . . 5E 80
Barley Cl. HA0: Wemb . . . 4D 60
Barleycorn Way E14 . . . 7B 86
(not continuous)
Barleyfields Cl. RM6: Chad H . . . 6B 54
Barley La. IG3: Ilf . . . 7A 54
RM6: Chad H . . . 7A 54
Barley Mow Pas. EC1 . . . 5B 8
W4 . . . 5K 97
Barley Mow Way TW17: Shep . . . 4C 146
Barley Shotts Bus. Pk.
W10 . . . 5H 81
Barling NW1 . . . 6F 65
(off Castlehaven Rd.)
Barlings Ho. SE4 . . . 4K 121
(off Frendsbury Rd.)
Barlow Cl. SM6: Wall . . . 6J 167
Barlow Dr. SE18 . . . 1C 124
Barlow Ho. N1 . . . 1E 8
(off Provost Est.)
SE16 . . . 4H 103
(off Rennie Est.)
W11 . . . 7G 81
(off Walmer Rd.)
Barlow Pl. W1 . . . 3K 11 (7F 83)
Barlow Rd. NW6 . . . 6H 63
TW12: Hamp . . . 7E 130
W3 . . . 1H 97
Barlow St. SE17 . . . 4D 102
Barlow Way RM13: Rain . . . 5K 91
Barmeston Rd. SE6 . . . 2D 140
Barmor Cl. HA2: Harr . . . 2F 41
Barmouth Av. UB6: G'frd . . . 2K 77
Barmouth Rd. CR0: C'don . . . 2K 169
SW18 . . . 6A 118
Barnabas Ct. EN2: Enf . . . 4F 23
Barnabas Ho. EC1 . . . 2C 8
Barnabas Rd. E9 . . . 5K 67
Barnaby Cl. HA2: Harr . . . 2G 59
Barnaby Ct. NW9 . . . 3A 44
SE16 . . . 2G 103
(off Scott Lidgett Cres.)
Barnaby Pl. SW7 . . . 4A 16
Barnaby Way IG7: Chig . . . 3K 37
Barnard Cl. BR7: Chst . . . 1H 161
SE18 . . . 4E 106
SM6: Wall . . . 7H 167
TW16: Sun . . . 7K 129
Barnard Gdns. KT3: N Mald . . . 4C 152
UB4: Yead . . . 4K 75
Barnard Gro. E15 . . . 7H 69
Barnard Hill N10 . . . 1F 47
Barnard Ho. E2 . . . 3H 85
(off Ellsworth St.)
Barnard Lodge EN5: New Bar . . . 4F 21
W9 . . . 5J 81
(off Admiral Wlk.)
Barnard M. SW11 . . . 4C 118
Barnardo Dr. IG6: Ilf . . . 4G 53
Barnardo Gdns. E1 . . . 7K 85
Barnardo St. E1 . . . 6K 85
Barnardos Village IG6: Ilf . . . 4G 53
Barnard Rd. CR4: Mitc . . . 3E 154
EN1: Enf . . . 2C 24
SW11 . . . 4C 118
Barnards Ho. SE16 . . . 2B 104
(off Wyatt Cl.)
Barnard's Inn EC1 . . . 6J 7
Barnbrough NW1 . . . 1G 83
(off Camden St.)
Barnby Sq. E15 . . . 1G 87
Barnby St. E15 . . . 1G 87
NW1 . . . 1B 6 (2G 83)
Barn Cl. NW5 . . . 5H 65
(off Torriano Av.)
TW15: Ashf . . . 5D 128
UB5: Yead . . . 2A 76
Barn Cres. HA7: Stan . . . 6H 27
Barncroft Cl. UB8: Hil . . . 5D 74
Barneby Cl. TW2: Twick . . . 1J 131
BARNEHURST . . . 3J 127
Barnehurst Av. DA7: Bex . . . 1J 127
DA8: Erith . . . 1J 127
Barnehurst Cl. DA8: Erith . . . 1J 127
Barnehurst Rd. DA7: Bex . . . 2J 127
Barn Elms Athletic Track . . . 1D 116
Barn Elms Pk. SW15 . . . 3E 116
BARNES . . . 2B 116
Barnes All. TW12: Hamp . . . 2G 149
Barnes Av. SW13 . . . 7C 98
UB2: S'hall . . . 4D 94
Barnes Cl. E12 . . . 4B 70
Barnes Common Nature Reserve
. . . 3C 116
Barnes Ct. CR7: Thor H . . . 3C 156
E16 . . . 5A 88
EN5: New Bar . . . 4E 20
IG8: Buck H, Wfd G . . . 5G 37
N1 . . . 7A 66
Barnes End KT3: N Mald . . . 5C 152
Barnes High St. SW13 . . . 2B 116
Barnes Ho. E2 . . . 2J 85
(off Wadeson St.)
IG11: Bark . . . 1H 89
NW1 . . . 7G 65
(off Camden Rd.)
SE14 . . . 6K 103
(off John Williams Cl.)
Barnes Pikle W5 . . . 7D 78
Barnes Rd. IG1: Ilf . . . 5G 71
N18 . . . 4D 34
Barnes St. E14 . . . 6A 86
Barnes Ter. SE8 . . . 5B 104
Barnes Wallis Ct. HA9: Wemb . . . 3J 61
BARNET . . . 3B 20
Barnet Burnt Oak Leisure Cen. . . . 1K 43
Barnet Bus. Cen. EN5: Barn . . . 3B 20
Barnet By-Pass NW7 . . . 6G 29
Barnet Copthall Stadium . . . 7K 29
Barnet Dr. BR2: Brom . . . 2C 172
Barnet FC . . . 5D 20
Barnet Ga. La. EN5: Ark . . . 1H 29
Barnet Gro. E2 . . . 1K 9 (3G 85)
Barnet Hill EN5: Barn . . . 4C 20
Barnet Ho. N20 . . . 2F 31
Barnet La. EN5: Barn . . . 1C 30
N20: Barn . . . 1C 30
Barnet Mus. . . . 4B 20
Barnet Trad. Est. EN5: Barn . . . 3C 20
Barnetts Ct. HA2: Harr . . . 3F 59
Barnett St. E1 . . . 6H 85
BARNET VALE . . . 5E 20
Barnet Way NW7 . . . 3E 28
Barnet Wood Rd. BR2: Brom . . . 2A 172
Barney Cl. SE7 . . . 5A 106
Barn Fld. NW3 . . . 5D 64
Barnfield KT3: N Mald . . . 6A 152
Barnfield Av. CR0: C'don . . . 2J 169
CR4: Mitc . . . 4F 155
KT2: King T . . . 4D 132

Barnfield Cl. N4 7J 47
SW17 3B 136
Barnfield Gdns. KT2: King T 4E 132
SE18 6F 107
Barnfield Pl. E14 4C 104
Barnfield Rd. CR2: Sande 7E 168
DA17: Belv 6F 109
HA8: Edg 1J 43
SE18 6F 107
(not continuous)
W5 4C 78
Barnfield Wood Cl. BR3: Beck 6F 159
Barnfield Wood Rd. BR3: Beck 6F 159
Barnham Dr. SE28 1K 107
(not continuous)
Barnham Rd. UB6: G'frd 3G 77
Barnham St. SE1 6H 15 (2E 102)
Barn Hill HA9: Wemb 1G 61
Barnhill HA5: Eastc 5A 40
Barnhill Av. BR2: Brom 5H 159
Barnhill La. UB4: Yead 3K 75
Barnhill Rd. HA9: Wemb 3J 61
UB4: Yead 3K 75
Barningham Way NW9 6K 43
Barnlea Cl. TW13: Hanw 2C 130
Barnmead Ct. RM9: Dag 5F 73
Barnmead Gdns.
RM9: Dag 5F 73
Barnmead Rd. BR3: Beck 1K 157
RM9: Dag 5F 73
Barn M. HA2: Harr 3E 58
Barn Ri. HA9: Wemb 1G 61
BARNSBURY 7K 65
Barnsbury Cl. KT3: N Mald 4J 151
Barnsbury Cres. KT5: Surb 1J 163
Barnsbury Est. N1 1K 83
(not continuous)
Barnsbury Gro. N7 7K 65
Barnsbury Ho. SW4 6H 119
Barnsbury La. KT5: Surb 2H 163
Barnsbury Pk. N1 7A 66
Barnsbury Rd. N1 2A 84
Barnsbury Sq. N1 7A 66
Barnsbury St. N1 7A 66
Barnsbury Ter. N1 7K 65
Barnscroft SW20 3D 152
Barnsdale Av. E14 4D 104
Barnsdale Rd. W9 4H 81
Barnsley St. E1 4H 85
Barnstable La. SE13 4E 122
Barnstaple Ho. *SE10* 7D 104
(off Devonshire Dr.)
SE12 5H 123
(off Taunton Rd.)
Barnstaple Rd. HA4: Ruis 3A 58
Barnston Wlk. *N1* 1C 84
(off Popham St.)
Barn St. N16 2E 66
Barn Theatre, The
Bexley 1A 144
West Molesey 4E 148
Barn Way HA9: Wemb 1G 61
Barnwell Ho. *SE5* 1E 120
(off St Giles Rd.)
Barnwell Rd. SW2 5A 120
Barnwood Cl. HA4: Ruis 2F 57
N20 1C 30
W9 4K 81
Baron Cl. N11 5K 31
Baroness Rd. E2 1K 9 (3F 85)
Baronet Gro. N17 1G 49
Baronet Rd. N17 1G 49
Baron Gdns. IG6: Ilf 3G 53
Baron Gro. CR4: Mitc 4C 154
Baron Ho. SW19 1B 154
Baron Rd. RM8: Dag 1D 72
Barons, The
TW1: Twick 6B 114
Baronsclere Ct. N6 7G 47
BARONS COURT 5G 99
Barons Ct. IG1: Ilf 2H 71
NW9 6K 43
SM6: Bedd 3H 167
Baron's Ct. Rd. W14 5G 99
Barons Court Theatre 5G 99
(off Comeragh Rd.)
Baronsfield Rd. TW1: Twick 6B 114
Barons Ga. EN4: E Barn 6H 21
W4 3J 97
Barons Keep W14 5G 99
Barons Mead HA1: Harr 4J 41
Baronsmead Rd. SW13 1C 116
Baronsmede W5 2F 97
Baronsmere Ct. EN5: Barn 4B 20
Baronsmere Rd. N2 4C 46
Baron's Pl. SE1 7K 13 (2A 102)
Baron St. N1 2A 84
Baron's Wlk. CR0: C'don 6A 158
Baron Wlk. CR4: Mitc 4C 154
E16 5H 87
Baroque Ct. TW3: Houn 3G 113
Barque M. SE8 6C 104
Barrack Rd. TW4: Houn 4B 112
Barracks La. EN5: Barn 3B 20
Barra Hall Cir. UB3: Hayes 7G 75
Barra Hall Rd. UB3: Hayes 7G 75
Barratt Av. N22 2K 47
Barratt Ho. *N1* 7B 66
(off Sable St.)
Barratt Ind. Pk. E3 4E 86
UB1: S'hall 2E 94
Barratt Way HA3: W'stone 2H 41
Barrenger Rd. N10 1D 46
Barret Ho. NW6 1J 81
SW9 3K 119
(off Benedict Rd.)
Barrett Ho. *SE17* 5C 102
(off Browning St.)
Barrett Rd. E17 4E 50
Barrett's Grn. Rd. NW10 3J 79
Barrett's Gro. N16 5E 66
Barrett St. W1 1H 11 (6E 82)
Barrhill Rd. SW2 2J 137
Barrie Ct. *EN5: New Bar* 5F 21
(off Lyonsdown Rd.)
Barriedale SE14 2A 122
Barrie Est. W2 2A 10 (7B 82)
Barrie Ho. *NW8* 1C 82
(off St Edmund's Ter.)
W2 7A 82
(off Lancaster Ga.)
Barrier App. SE7 3B 106
Barrier Point Rd. E16 1A 106
Barringers Ct. HA4: Ruis 7F 39
Barringer Sq. SW17 4E 136
Barrington Cl. IG5: Ilf 1D 52
NW5 5E 64
Barrington Ct. N10 2E 46
SW4 2J 119
W3 2H 97
(off Cheltenham Pl.)
Barrington Rd. DA7: Bex 2D 126
E12 6E 70
N8 5H 47
SM3: Sutt 2J 165
SW9 3B 120
Barrington Vs. SE18 1E 124
Barrington Wlk. SE19 6E 138
Barrow Av. SM5: Cars 7D 166
Barrow Cl. N21 3G 33
Barrow Ct. *SE6* 1H 141
(off Cumberland Pl.)
Barrowdene Cl. HA5: Pinn 2C 40
Barrowell Grn. N21 2G 33
Barrowfield Cl. N9 3C 34
Barrowgate Rd. W4 5J 97
Barrow Hedges Cl. SM5: Cars 7C 166
Barrow Hedges Way SM5: Cars 7C 166
Barrow Hill KT4: Wor Pk 2A 164
Barrow Hill Cl. KT4: Wor Pk 2A 164
Barrow Hill Est. *NW8* 2C 82
(off Barrow Hill Rd.)
Barrow Hill Rd. NW8 1C 4 (2C 82)
Barrow Point Av. HA5: Pinn 2C 40
Barrow Point La. HA5: Pinn 2C 40
Barrow Rd. CR0: Wadd 5A 168
SW16 6H 137
Barrow Store Ct. *SE1* 7G 15
(off Decima St.)
Barrow Wlk. TW8: Bford 6C 96
Barrs Rd. NW10 7K 61
Barry Av. DA7: Bex 7E 108
N15 6F 49
Barry Cl. BR6: Orp 3J 173
Barrydene N20 1G 31
Barry Ho. *SE16* 4H 103
(off Rennie Est.)
Barry Rd. E6 6C 88
NW10 7J 61
SE22 6G 121
Barset Rd. SE15 3J 121
(not continuous)
Barson Cl. SE20 7J 139
Barston Rd. SE27 3C 138
Barstow Cres. SW2 1K 137
Barter St. WC1 6F 7 (5J 83)
Barters Wlk. HA5: Pinn 3C 40
Barth M. SE18 4J 107
Bartholomew Cl. EC1 6B 8 (5C 84)
(not continuous)
SW18 4A 118
Bartholomew Ct. *E14* 7F 87
(off Newport Av.)
EC1 3D 8
(off Old St.)
HA8: Edg 7J 27
Bartholomew Ho. IG8: Wfd G 7K 37
Bartholomew La. EC2 1F 15 (6D 84)
Bartholomew Pl. EC1 6C 8
Bartholomew Rd. NW5 6G 65
Bartholomew Sq. E1 4H 85
EC1 3D 8 (4C 84)
Bartholomew St. SE1 3D 102
Bartholomew Vs. NW5 6G 65
Barth Rd. SE18 4J 107
(not continuous)
Bartle Av. E6 2C 88
Bartle Rd. W11 6G 81
Bartlett Cl. E14 6C 86
Bartlett Ct. EC4 7K 7 (6A 84)
Bartlett Ho's. *RM10: Dag* 7H 73
(off Vicarage Rd.)
Bartletts Pas. *EC4* 7K 7
(off Fetter La.)
Bartlett St. CR2: S Croy 5D 168
Bartlow Gdns. RM5: Col R 1K 55
Bartok Ho. *W11* 1H 99
(off Lansdowne Wlk.)
Barton Av. RM7: Rush G 1H 73
Barton Cl. DA6: Bex 5E 126
E6 6D 88
E9 5J 67
NW4 5C 44
SE15 3H 121
TW17: Shep 6D 146
Barton Ct. *W14* 5G 99
(off Baron's Ct. Rd.)
Barton Grn. KT3: N Mald 2K 151
Barton Green Theatre 2K 151
Barton Ho. *N1* 7B 66
(off Sable St.)
SW6 3K 117
(off Wandsworth Bri. Rd.)
Barton Mdws. IG6: Ilf 4F 53
Barton Rd. DA14: Sidc 6E 144
W14 5G 99
Barton St. SW1 1E 18 (3J 101)
Bartonway *NW8* 1B 82
(off Queen's Ter.)
Bartram Cl. UB8: Hil 4D 74
Bartram Rd. SE4 5A 122
Bartrams La. EN4: Had W 1F 21
Bartrip St. E9 6B 68
Barts Cl. BR3: Beck 5C 158
Barville Cl. SE4 4A 122
Barwell Bus. Pk. KT9: Chess 7D 162
Barwell Ct. KT9: Chess 7B 162
Barwell Ho. *E2* 4G 85
(off Menotti St.)
Barwell La. KT9: Chess 7C 162
Barwick Dr. UB8: Hil 5D 74
Barwick Ho. *W3* 2J 97
(off Strafford Rd.)
Barwick Rd. E7 4K 69
Barwood Av. BR4: W W'ck 1D 170
Bascombe Gro. DA1: Bexl, Cray 7K 127
Bascombe St. SW2 6A 120
Basden Gro. TW13: Hanw 2E 130
Basden Ho. TW13: Hanw 2E 130
Basedale Rd. RM9: Dag 7B 72
Baseing Cl. E6 7E 88
Baseline Bus. Studios *W11* 7F 81
(off Barandon Wlk.)
Basepoint Bus. Cen. RM13: Rain 4K 91
Basevi Way SE8 6D 104
Bashley Rd. NW10 4K 79
Basil Av. E6 3C 88
Basildene Rd. TW4: Houn 3B 112
Basildon Av. IG5: Ilf 1E 52
Basildon Cl. SM2: Sutt 7K 165
Basildon Ct. *W1* 5H 5
(off Devonshire Rd.)
Basildon Rd. SE2 5A 108
Basil Gdns. CR0: C'don 1K 169
SE27 5C 138
Basil Ho. *SW8* 7J 101
(off Wyvil Rd.)
Basil Mans. *SW3* 7E 10
(off Basil St.)
Basilon Rd. DA7: Bex 2E 126
Basil Spence Ho. N22 1K 47
Basil St. SW3 1E 16 (3D 100)
Basin App. E14 6A 86
E16 7F 89
Basing Cl. KT7: T Ditt 7K 149
Basing Ct. SE15 1F 121
Basingdon Way SE5 4D 120
Basing Dr. DA5: Bexl 6F 127
Basingfield Rd. KT7: T Ditt 7K 149
Basinghall Av. EC2 7E 8 (6D 84)
Basinghall Gdns. SM2: Sutt 7K 165
Basinghall St. EC2 7E 8 (6D 84)
Basing Hill HA9: Wemb 2F 61
NW11 1H 63
Basing Ho. *IG11: Bark* 1H 89
(off St Margarets)
Basing Ho. Yd. E2 1H 9
Basing Pl. E2 1H 9 (3E 84)
Basing St. W11 6H 81
Basing Way KT7: T Ditt 7K 149
N3 3J 45
Basire St. N1 1C 84
Baskerville Gdns. NW10 4A 62
Baskerville Rd. SW18 7C 118
Basket Gdns. SE9 5C 124
Baslow Cl. HA3: Hrw W 1H 41
Baslow Wlk. E5 4K 67
Basnett Rd. SW11 3E 118
Basque Ct. *SE16* 2K 103
(off Garter Way)
Bassano St. SE22 5F 121
Bassant Rd. SE18 6K 107
Bassein Pk. Rd. W12 2B 98
Bassett Gdns. TW7: Isle 7G 95
Bassett Ho. RM9: Dag 1B 90
Bassett Rd. E7 4B 70
W10 6F 81
Bassett's Cl. BR6: Farnb 4F 173
Bassett St. NW5 6E 64
Bassett's Way BR6: Farnb 4F 173

Bassett Way UB6: G'frd 6F 77
Bassingbourn Ho. N1 ....7A 66
(off The Sutton Est.)
Bassingham Rd. HA0: Wemb 6D 60
SW18 ....7A 118
Bassishaw Highwalk EC2 ....6E 8
Basswood Cl. SE15 ....3H 121
Bastable Av. IG11: Bark 2J 89
Basterfield Ho. EC1 ....4C 8
(off Golden La. Est.)
Bastion Highwalk EC2 ....6C 8
Bastion Ho. EC2 ....6D 8
(off London Wall)
Bastion Rd. SE2 ....5A 108
Baston Mnr. Rd.
BR2: Hayes, Kes 3K 171
Baston Rd. BR2: Hayes 2K 171
Bastwick St. EC1 ....3C 8 (4C 84)
Basuto Rd. SW6 ....1J 117
Batavia Cl. TW16: Sun 1K 147
Batavia Ho. SE14 ....7A 104
(off Batavia Rd.)
Batavia M. SE14 ....7A 104
Batavia Rd. SE14 ....7A 104
TW16: Sun 1K 147
Batchelor St. N1 ....1A 84
Bateman Cl. IG11: Bark 6G 71
Bateman Ho. SE17 ....6B 102
(off Otto St.)
Bateman Rd. E4 ....6H 35
Bateman's Bldgs. W1 ....1C 12
Bateman's Row EC2 ....3H 9 (4E 84)
Bateman St. W1 ....1C 12 (6H 83)
Bates Cres. CR0: Wadd 5A 168
SW16 ....7G 137
Bateson St. SE18 ....4J 107
Bates Point E13 ....1J 87
(off Pelly Rd.)
Bate St. E14 ....7B 86
Bath Cl. SE15 ....7H 103
Bath Ct. EC1 ....4J 7
SE26 ....3G 139
(off Droitwich Cl.)
Bathgate Rd. SW19 ....3F 135
Bath Gro. E2 ....2G 85
(off Horatio St.)
Bath Ho. E2 ....4G 85
(off Ramsey St.)
SE1 ....3C 102
(off Bath Ter.)
Bath Ho. Rd. CR0: Bedd 1J 167
Bath Pas. KT1: King T 2D 150
Bath Pl. EC2 ....2G 9 (3E 84)
EN5: Barn 3C 20
W6 ....5E 98
(off Peabody Est.)
Bath Rd. E7 ....6B 70
N9 ....2C 34
RM6: Chad H 6E 54
TW3: Houn 2B 112
TW4: Houn 2B 112
TW5: Cran 1G 111
TW6: H'row A 1G 111
UB3: Harl 1G 111
UB7: Harm, Sip 1A 110
UB7: Lford 4C 174
W4 ....4A 98
Baths Rd. BR2: Brom 4B 160
Bath St. EC1 ....2D 8 (3C 84)
Bath Ter. SE1 ....3C 102
Bathurst Av. SW19 ....1K 153
Bathurst Gdns. NW10 ....2D 80
Bathurst Ho. W12 ....7D 80
(off White City Est.)
Bathurst M. W2 ....2B 10 (6B 82)
Bathurst Rd. IG1: Ilf 1F 71
Bathurst St. W2 ....2B 10 (7B 82)
Bathway SE18 ....4E 106
Batley Cl. CR4: Mitc 7D 154
Batley Pl. N16 ....3F 67
Batley Rd. EN2: Enf 1H 23
N16 ....3F 67
Batman Cl. W12 ....1D 98
Batoum Gdns. W6 ....3E 98
Batson Ho. E1 ....6G 85
(off Fairclough St.)
Batson St. W12 ....2C 98
Batsworth Rd. CR4: Mitc 3B 154
Battenberg Wlk. SE19 ....6E 138
Batten Cl. E6 ....6D 88
Batten Cotts. E14 ....5A 86
(off Maroon St.)
Batten Ho. SW4 ....5G 119
W10 ....3G 81
(off Third Av.)
Batten St. SW11 ....3C 118
Battersby Rd. SE6 ....2F 141
BATTERSEA 1E 118
Battersea Bri. SW11 ....7B 100
Battersea Bri. Rd. SW11 ....7C 100
Battersea Bus. Cen. SW11 ....3E 118
Battersea Church Rd. SW11 ....1B 118
Battersea High St. SW11 ....1B 118
(not continuous)
Battersea Pk. 7D 100
Battersea Pk. Children's Zoo 7E 100
Battersea Pk. Equestrian Cen. 2C 118
Battersea Pk. Rd. SW8 ....1E 118
SW11 ....2C 118
Battersea Ri. SW11 ....5C 118
Battersea Sports Cen. 3B 118
Battersea Sq. SW11 ....1B 118
Battery Rd. SE28 ....2J 107
Battilion Ho. NW9 ....2B 44
(off Heritage Av.)
Battishill St. N1 ....7B 66
Battlebridge Ct. N1 ....2J 83
(off Wharfdale Rd.)
Battle Bri. La. SE1 ....5G 15 (1E 102)
Battle Cl. SW19 ....6A 136
Battledean Rd. N5 ....5B 66
Battle Ho. SE15 ....6G 103
(off Haymerle Rd.)
Battle Rd. DA8: Erith 4J 109
DA17: Belv, Erith 4J 109
Batty St. E1 ....6G 85
Batwa Ho. SE16 ....5H 103
Baudwin Rd. SE6 ....2G 141
Baugh Rd. DA14: Sidc 5C 144
Baulk, The SW18 ....7J 117
Bavant Rd. SW16 ....2J 155
Bavaria Rd. N19 ....2J 65
(not continuous)
Bavdene M. NW4 ....4D 44
(off The Burroughs)
Bavent Rd. SE5 ....2C 120
Bawdale Rd. SE22 ....5F 121
Bawdsey Av. IG2: Ilf 4K 53
Bawtree Rd. SE14 ....7A 104
Bawtry Rd. N20 ....3J 31
Baxendale N20 ....2F 31
Baxendale St. E2 ....3G 85
Baxter Cl. BR1: Brom 3F 161
UB2: S'hall 3F 95
UB10: Hil 3D 74
Baxter Rd. E16 ....6A 88
IG1: Ilf 5F 71
N1 ....6D 66
N18 ....4C 34
Bayard Ct. DA6: Bex 4H 127
Bay Ct. E1 ....4K 85
(off Frimley Way)
W5 ....3E 96
Baycroft Cl. HA5: Eastc 3A 40
Baydon Ct. BR2: Brom 3H 159
Bayer Ho. EC1 ....4C 8
(off Golden La. Est.)
Bayes Cl. SE26 ....5J 139
Bayes Ct. NW3 ....7D 64
(off Primrose Hill Rd.)
Bayfield Ho. SE4 ....4K 121
(off Coston Wlk.)
Bayfield Rd. SE9 ....4B 124
Bayford M. E8 ....7H 67
(off Bayford St.)
Bayford Rd. NW10 ....3F 81
Bayford St. E8 ....7H 67
Bayford St. Bus. Cen. E8 ....7H 67
(off Sidworth St.)
Baygrove M. KT1: Ham W 1C 150
Bayham Pl. NW1 ....1G 83
Bayham Rd. SM4: Mord 4K 153
W4 ....3K 97
W13 ....7B 78
Bayham St. NW1 ....1G 83
Bayhurst Wood Country Pk. 5B 38
Bayleaf Cl. TW12: Ham H 5H 131
Bayley St. WC1 ....6C 6 (5H 83)
Bayley Wlk. SE2 ....6E 108
Baylis M. TW1: Twick 7A 114
Baylis Rd. SE1 ....7J 13 (2A 102)
Bayliss Av. SE28 ....7D 90
Bayliss Cl. N21 ....5D 22
Bayne Cl. E6 ....6D 88
Baynes Cl. EN1: Enf 1B 24
Baynes M. NW3 ....6B 64
Baynes St. NW1 ....7G 65
Baynham Cl. DA5: Bexl 6F 127
Bayonne Rd. W6 ....6G 99
Bays Ct. HA8: Edg 5C 28
Bays Farm Ct. UB7: Lford 4D 174
Bayshill Ri. UB5: N'olt 6F 59
Bayston Rd. N16 ....3F 67
BAYSWATER 7A 82
Bayswater Rd. W2 ....3A 10 (7K 81)
Baythorne St. E3 ....5B 86
Bayton Ct. E8 ....7G 67
(off Lansdowne Dr.)
Bay Tree Cl. BR1: Brom 1B 160
Baytree Cl. DA15: Sidc 1K 143
Baytree Ct. SW2 ....4K 119
Baytree Ho. E4 ....7J 25
Baytree M. SE17 ....4D 102
Baytree Rd. SW2 ....4K 119
Bazalgette Cl. KT3: N Mald 5K 151
Bazalgette Gdns.
KT3: N Mald 5K 151
Bazalgette Ho. NW8 ....3B 4
(off Orchardson St.)
Bazeley Ho. SE1 ....7A 14
(off Library St.)
Bazely St. E14 ....7E 86
Bazile Rd. N21 ....6F 23
BBC Broadcasting House 6K 5 (5F 83)
BBC Maida Vale Studios 4K 81
(off Delaware Rd.)
BBC Television Cen. 7E 80
BBC Worldwide 6E 80
(off Wood La.)
Beacham Cl. SE7 ....5B 106
Beachborough Rd. BR1: Brom 4E 140
Beachcroft Rd. E11 ....3G 69
Beachcroft Way N19 ....1H 65
Beach Gro. TW13: Hanw 2E 130
Beach Ho. SW5 ....5J 99
(off Philbeach Gdns.)
TW13: Hanw 2E 130
Beachy Rd. E3 ....7C 68
Beacon Bingo Hall 4F 63
Beacon Cl. UB8: Uxb 5A 56
Beacon Ga. SE14 ....3K 121
Beacon Gro. SM5: Cars 4E 166
Beacon Hill N7 ....5J 65
Beacon Ho. E14 ....5D 104
(off Burrells Wharf Sq.)
SE5 ....7E 102
(off Southampton Way)
Beacon Pl. CR0: Bedd 3J 167
Beacon Rd. SE13 ....6F 123
TW6: H'row A 6C 110
Beacons Cl. E6 ....5C 88
Beaconsfield WC1 ....5K 83
(off Red Lion St.)
Beaconsfield Cl. N11 ....5K 31
SE3 ....6J 105
W4 ....5J 97
Beaconsfield Pde. SE9 ....4C 142
Beaconsfield Rd.
BR1: Brom 3B 160
CR0: C'don 6D 156
DA5: Bexl 2K 145
E10 ....2E 68
E16 ....4H 87
E17 ....6B 50
KT3: N Mald 2K 151
KT5: Surb 7F 151
N9 ....3B 34
N11 ....3K 31
N15 ....4E 48
NW10 ....6B 62
SE3 ....7H 105
SE9 ....2C 142
SE17 ....5D 102
TW1: Twick 6B 114
UB1: S'hall 1B 94
UB4: Yead 1A 94
W4 ....3K 97
W5 ....2C 96
Beaconsfield Ter. RM6: Chad H 6D 54
Beaconsfield Ter. Rd. W14 ....3G 99
Beaconsfield Wlk. E6 ....6E 88
SW6 ....1H 117
Beacontree Av. E17 ....1F 51
BEACONTREE HEATH 1G 73
Beacontree Rd. E11 ....1H 69
Beadle's Pde. RM10: Dag 6J 73
Beadlow Cl. SM5: Cars 6B 154
Beadman Pl. SE27 ....4B 138
Beadman St. SE27 ....4B 138
Beadnell Rd. SE23 ....1K 139
Beadon Rd. BR2: Brom 4J 159
W6 ....4E 98
Beaford Gro. SW20 ....3G 153
Beagle Cl. TW13: Felt 4K 129
Beak St. W1 ....2B 12 (7G 83)
Beal Cl. DA16: Well 1A 126
Beale Cl. N13 ....5G 33
Beale Pl. E3 ....2B 86
Beale Rd. E3 ....1B 86
Beal Rd. IG1: Ilf 2E 70
Beam Av. RM10: Dag 1H 91
Beames Rd. NW10 ....1K 79
Beaminster Gdns. IG6: Ilf 2F 53
Beaminster Ho. SW8 ....7K 101
(off Dorset Rd.)
Beamish Dr. WD23: B Hea 1B 26
Beamish Ho. SE16 ....4H 103
(off Rennie Est.)
Beamish Rd. N9 ....1B 34
Beam Vs. RM9: Dag 2J 91
Beamway RM10: Dag 7K 73
Beanacre Cl. E9 ....6B 68
Bean Rd. DA6: Bex 4D 126
Beanshaw SE9 ....4E 142
Beansland Gro. RM6: Chad H 2E 54
Bear All. EC4 ....7A 8 (6B 84)
Bear Cl. RM7: Rom 6H 55
Beardell St. SE19 ....6F 139
Beardow Gro. N14 ....6B 22
Beard Rd. KT2: King T 5F 133
Beardsfield E13 ....2J 87
Beard's Hill TW12: Hamp 1E 148
Beard's Hill Cl.
TW12: Hamp 1E 148
Beardsley Ter. RM8: Dag 5B 72
(off Fitzstephen Rd.)
Beardsley Way W3 ....2K 97
Beard's Rd. TW15: Ashf 6G 129
Bearfield Rd.
KT2: King T 7E 132

Bear Gdns. SE1 . . . . . 4C **14** (1C **102**)
Bear La. SE1 . . . . . 4B **14** (1B **102**)
Bear Rd. TW13: Hanw 4B **130**
Bearstead Ri. SE4 . . . . . 5B **122**
Bearsted Ter. BR3: Beck 1C **158**
Bear St. WC2 . . . . . 2D **12** (7H **83**)
Beasley's Ait TW16: Sun 6H **147**
Beasley's Ait La.
TW16: Sun 6H **147**
Beaton Cl. SE15 . . . . . 1F **121**
Beatrice Av. HA9: Wemb 5E **60**
SW16 . . . . . 3K **155**
Beatrice Cl. E13 . . . . . 4J **87**
HA5: Eastc 4J **39**
Beatrice Ct. IG9: Buck H 2G **37**
Beatrice Ho. *W6* *5E **98***
(off Queen Caroline St.)
Beatrice Pl. W8 . . . . . 3K **99**
Beatrice Rd. E17 . . . . . 5C **50**
N4 . . . . . 7A **48**
N9 . . . . . 7D **24**
SE1 . . . . . 4G **103**
TW10: Rich 5F **115**
UB1: S'hall 1D **94**
Beatrix Ho. *SW5* *5K **99***
(off Old Brompton Rd.)
Beatson Wlk. SE16 . . . . . 1A **104**
(not continuous)
Beattie Cl. TW14: Felt 7H **111**
Beattie Ho. SW8 . . . . . 1G **119**
Beattock Ri. N10 . . . . . 4F **47**
Beatty Ho. *E14* *2C **104***
(off Admirals Way)
NW1 . . . . . *3A **6***
(off Drummond St.)
SW1 . . . . . *6B **18***
(off Dolphin Sq.)
Beatty Rd. HA7: Stan 6H **27**
N16 . . . . . 4E **66**
Beatty St. NW1 . . . . . 2G **83**
Beattyville Gdns. IG6: Ilf 4E **52**
Beauchamp Cl. W4 . . . . . 3J **97**
Beauchamp Ct. *EN5: Barn* *4C **20***
(off Victors Way)
HA7: Stan 5H **27**
Beauchamp Pl. SW3 . . . . . 1D **16** (3C **100**)
Beauchamp Rd. E7 . . . . . 7K **69**
KT8: W Mole, E Mos 5F **149**
SE19 . . . . . 1D **156**
SM1: Sutt 4J **165**
SW11 . . . . . 4C **118**
TW1: Twick 7A **114**
Beauchamp St. EC1 . . . . . 6J **7** (5A **84**)
Beauchamp Ter. SW15 . . . . . 3D **116**
Beauclerc Ct. TW16: Sun 2A **148**
Beauclerc Rd. W6 . . . . . 3D **98**
Beauclere Ho. SM2: Sutt 6A **166**
Beauclerk Cl. TW13: Felt 1K **129**
Beauclerk Ho. SW16 . . . . . 3J **137**
Beaudesert M.
UB7: W Dray 2A **92**
Beaufort E6 . . . . . 5E **88**
Beaufort Av. HA3: Kent 4A **42**
Beaufort Cl. E4 . . . . . 6J **35**
RM7: Mawney 4J **55**
SW15 . . . . . 7D **116**
W5 . . . . . 5F **79**
Beaufort Ct. *E14* *2C **104***
(off Admirals Way)
EN5: New Bar 5F **21**
N11 . . . . . *5A **32***
(off The Limes Av.)
SW6 . . . . . 6J **99**
TW10: Ham 4C **132**
Beaufort Dr. NW11 . . . . . 4J **45**
Beaufort Gdns. IG1: Ilf 1E **70**
NW4 . . . . . 6E **44**
SW3 . . . . . 1D **16** (3C **100**)
SW16 . . . . . 7K **137**
TW5: Hest 1C **112**
Beaufort Ho. *E16* *1K **105***
(off Fairfax M.)
SW1 . . . . . *6C **18***
(off Aylesford St.)
SW1 . . . . . *5K **17***
(off Sutherland Row)
SW3 . . . . . *7B **16***
(off Beaufort St.)
Beaufort Mans. SW3 . . . . . 7B **16** (6B **100**)
Beaufort M. SW6 . . . . . 6H **99**
BEAUFORT PARK 2B **44**
Beaufort Pk. NW11 . . . . . 4J **45**
Beaufort Rd. HA4: Ruis 2F **57**
KT1: King T 4E **150**
TW1: Twick 7C **114**
TW10: Ham 4C **132**
W5 . . . . . 5F **79**
Beaufort St. SW3 . . . . . 7A **16** (6B **100**)
Beaufort Ter. *E14* *5E **104***
(off Ferry St.)
Beaufort Way KT17: Ewe 7C **164**
Beaufoy Ho. SE27 . . . . . 3B **138**
SW8 . . . . . *7K **101***
(off Rita Rd.)
Beaufoy Rd. N17 . . . . . 7K **33**
Beaufoy Wlk. SE11 . . . . . 4H **19** (4K **101**)
Beaulieu Av. E16 . . . . . 1K **105**
SE26 . . . . . 4H **139**
Beaulieu Cl. CR4: Mitc 1E **154**
NW9 . . . . . 4A **44**
SE5 . . . . . 3D **120**
TW1: Twick 6D **114**
TW4: Houn 5D **112**
Beaulieu Ct. W5 . . . . . 5E **78**
Beaulieu Dr. HA5: Pinn 6B **40**
Beaulieu Gdns. N21 . . . . . 7H **23**
Beaulieu Lodge *E14* *3F **105***
(off Schooner Cl.)
Beaulieu Pl. W4 . . . . . 3J **97**
Beaumanor Gdns. SE9 . . . . . 4E **142**
Beaumanor Mans. *W2* *7K **81***
(off Queensway)
Beaumaris Dr. IG8: Wfd G 7G **37**
Beaumaris Grn. NW9 . . . . . 6A **44**
Beaumaris Twr. *W3* *2H **97***
(off Park Rd. Nth.)
Beaumont *W14* *4H **99***
(off Kensington Village)
Beaumont Av. HA0: Wemb 5C **60**
HA2: Harr 6F **41**
TW9: Rich 3F **115**
W14 . . . . . 5H **99**
Beaumont Bldgs. *WC2* *1F **13***
(off Martlett Ct.)
Beaumont Cl. KT2: King T 7G **133**
Beaumont Ct. E1 . . . . . 3A **86**
E5 . . . . . 3H **67**
HA0: Wemb 5C **60**
NW1 . . . . . 1H **83**
NW9 . . . . . *2B **44***
(off Cherry Cl.)
W1 . . . . . *5H **5***
(off Beaumont St.)
W4 . . . . . 5J **97**
Beaumont Cres. W14 . . . . . 5H **99**
Beaumont Dr. KT4: Wor Pk 7D **152**
TW15: Ashf 5F **129**
Beaumont Gdns.
NW3 . . . . . 3J **63**
Beaumont Gro. E1 . . . . . 4K **85**
Beaumont Ho. *E10* *7D **50***
(off Skelton's La.)
E15 . . . . . *1H **87***
(off John St.)
W9 . . . . . *3H **81***
(off Fernhead Rd.)
Beaumont Lodge *E8* *6G **67***
(off Greenwood Rd.)
Beaumont M. HA5: Pinn 3C **40**
W1 . . . . . 5H **5** (5E **82**)
Beaumont Pl. EN5: Barn 1C **20**
TW7: Isle 5K **113**
W1 . . . . . 3B **6** (4G **83**)
Beaumont Ri. N19 . . . . . 1H **65**
Beaumont Rd. BR5: Pet W 6H **161**
E10 . . . . . 7D **50**
(not continuous)
E13 . . . . . 3K **87**
SE19 . . . . . 6C **138**
SW19 . . . . . 7G **117**
W4 . . . . . 3J **97**
Beaumont Sq. E1 . . . . . 5K **85**
Beaumont St. W1 . . . . . 5H **5** (5E **82**)
Beaumont Ter. *SE13* *7G **123***
(off Wellmeadow Rd.)
Beaumont Wlk. NW3 . . . . . 7D **64**
Beauvais Ter. UB5: Yead 3B **76**
Beauvale *NW1* *7E **64***
(off Ferdinand St.)
Beauval Rd. SE22 . . . . . 6F **121**
Beaux Arts Bldg., The N7 . . . . . 3J **65**
Beaverbank Rd. SE9 . . . . . 1H **143**
Beaver Cl. SE20 . . . . . 7G **139**
SM4: Mord 7E **152**
TW12: Hamp 1F **149**
Beaver Ct. BR3: Beck 7D **140**
Beaver Gro. UB5: N'olt 3C **76**
Beavers Cres. TW4: Houn 4A **112**
Beavers La. TW4: Houn 2A **112**
(not continuous)
Beavers La. Campsite TW4: Houn 4B **112**
Beavers Lodge DA14: Sidc 4K **143**
Beaverwood Rd. BR7: Chst 5J **143**
Beavor Gro. *W6* *5C **98***
(off Beavor La.)
Beavor La. W6 . . . . . 5C **98**
Bebbington Rd. SE18 . . . . . 4J **107**
Beblets Cl. BR6: Chels 5K **173**
Beccles Dr. IG11: Bark 6J **71**
Beccles St. E14 . . . . . 6B **86**
Bec Cl. HA4: Ruis 3B **58**
Bechervaise Ct. *E10* *1D **68***
(off Leyton Grange Est.)
Bechtel Ho. *W6* *4F **99***
(off Hammersmith Rd.)
Beck Cl. SE13 . . . . . 1D **122**
Beck Ct. BR3: Beck 3K **157**
BECKENHAM 1C **158**
Beckenham Bus. Cen.
BR3: Beck 6A **140**
Beckenham Crematorium
BR3: Beck 3J **157**
Beckenham Gdns. N9 . . . . . 3K **33**
Beckenham Gro. BR2: Brom 2F **159**
Beckenham Hill Est. BR3: Beck 5D **140**
Beckenham Hill Rd.
BR3: Beck 6D **140**
SE6 . . . . . 6D **140**
Beckenham La. BR2: Brom 2G **159**
Beckenham Pl. Pk. BR3: Beck 7D **140**
Beckenham Rd. BR3: Beck 1K **157**
BR4: W W'ck 7D **158**
Beckenham Theatre Cen., The 2D **158**
Beckers, The N16 . . . . . 4G **67**
Becket Av. E6 . . . . . 3E **88**
Becket Cl. SE25 . . . . . 6G **157**
SW19 . . . . . *1K **153***
(off High Path)
Becket Fold HA1: Harr 5K **41**
Becket Ho. *E16* *1K **105***
(off Constable Av.)
SE1 . . . . . 7E **14**
Becket Rd. N18 . . . . . 4D **34**
Becket St. SE1 . . . . . 7E **14** (3D **102**)
Beckett Cl. DA17: Belv 3F **109**
NW10 . . . . . 6A **62**
SW16 . . . . . 2H **137**
Beckett Ho. *E1* *5J **85***
(off Jubilee St.)
SW9 . . . . . 2J **119**
Becketts Cl. BR6: Orp 3K **173**
DA5: Bexl 1J **145**
TW14: Felt 6K **111**
Becketts Ho. IG1: Ilf 3E **70**
Becketts Pl. KT1: Ham W 1D **150**
Beckett Wlk. BR3: Beck 6A **140**
Beckfoot *NW1* *1B **6***
(off Ampthill Est.)
Beckford Cl. W14 . . . . . 4H **99**
Beckford Dr. BR5: Orp 7H **161**
Beckford Ho. N16 . . . . . 5E **66**
Beckford Pl. SE17 . . . . . 5C **102**
Beckford Rd. CR0: C'don 6F **157**
Beckham Ho.
SE11 . . . . . 4H **19** (4K **101**)
Beckhaven Ho. *SE11* *4A **102***
(off Gilbert Rd.)
Beck Ho. *N18* *5C **34***
(off Upton Rd.)
Beck La. BR3: Beck 3K **157**
Becklow Gdns. *W12* *2C **98***
(off Becklow Rd.)
Becklow M. *W12* *2C **98***
(off Becklow Rd.)
Becklow Rd. W12 . . . . . 2B **98**
(not continuous)
Beck River Pk. BR3: Beck 1C **158**
Beck Rd. CR4: Mitc 6D **154**
E8 . . . . . 1H **85**
Becks Rd. DA14: Sidc 3A **144**
Beck Theatre, The 6H **75**
BECKTON 5E **88**
BECKTON ALPS 4D **88**
BECKTON PARK 6D **88**
Beckton Retail Pk. E6 . . . . . 5E **88**
Beckton Rd. E16 . . . . . 5H **87**
Beckton Triangle Retail Pk. E6 . . . . . 4F **89**
Beck Way BR3: Beck 3B **158**
Beckway Rd. SW16 . . . . . 2H **155**
Beckway St. SE17 . . . . . 4E **102**
(not continuous)
Beckwith Ho. *E2* *2H **85***
(off Wadeson St.)
Beckwith Rd. SE24 . . . . . 5D **120**
Beclands Rd. SW17 . . . . . 6E **136**
Becmead Av. HA3: Kent 5B **42**
SW16 . . . . . 4H **137**
Becondale Rd. SE19 . . . . . 5E **138**
BECONTREE 4D **72**
Becontree Av. RM8: Dag 4B **72**
Becquerel Ct. *SE10* *3H **105***
(off West Parkside)
Bective Pl. SW15 . . . . . 4H **117**
Bective Rd. E7 . . . . . 4J **69**
SW15 . . . . . 4H **117**
Becton Pl. DA8: Erith 7H **109**
Bedale Rd. EN2: Enf 1H **23**
Bedale St. SE1 . . . . . 5E **14** (1D **102**)
Beddalls Farm Ct. E6 . . . . . 5B **88**
BEDDINGTON 4J **167**
BEDDINGTON CORNER 7E **154**
Beddington Cross CR0: Bedd 7H **155**
Beddington Farm Rd. CR0: Bedd 7J **155**
Beddington Gdns. SM5: Cars 6E **166**
SM6: Wall 6E **166**
Beddington Grn. BR5: St P 1K **161**
Beddington Gro. SM6: Wall 5H **167**
Beddington La. CR0: C'don 5G **155**
Beddington Pk. 2F **167**
Beddington Pk. Cotts. SM6: Bedd 3H **167**
Beddington Path BR5: St P 1K **161**
Beddington Rd. BR5: St P 2J **161**
IG3: Ilf 7K **53**
Beddington Ter. CR0: C'don 7K **155**
Beddington Trad. Est. CR0: Bedd 1J **167**
Bede Cl. HA5: Pinn 1B **40**
Bedefield WC1 . . . . . 2F **7** (3J **83**)
Bede Ho. *SE4* *1B **122***
(off Clare Rd.)
Bedens Rd. DA14: Sidc 6E **144**

Bede Rd. RM6: Chad H 6C 54
Bedevere Rd. N9 3B 34
Bedfont Cl. CR4: Mitc 2E 154
TW14: Bedf 6E 110
Bedfont Ct. TW19: Stan M 6B 174
Bedfont Ct. Est. TW19: Stan M 7C 174
Bedfont Grn. Cl. TW14: Bedf 1E 128
Bedfont Ind. Pk. TW15: Ashf 3E 128
Bedfont Ind. Pk. Nth. TW15: Ashf 3E 128
Bedfont Lakes Country Pk. 2E 128
Bedfont Lakes Country Pk. Vis. Cen. 3D 128
Bedfont La. TW13: Felt 7G 111
TW14: Felt 7G 111
Bedfont Rd. TW13: Felt 1E 128
TW14: Bedf 1E 128
TW19: Stanw 6A 110
Bedfont Trad. Est. TW14: Bedf 2F 129
Bedford Av. EN5: Barn 5C 20
UB4: Yead 6K 75
WC1 6D 6 (5H 83)
Bedfordbury WC2 2E 12 (7J 83) (not continuous)
Bedford Cl. N10 7K 31
W4 6A 98
Bedford Cnr. *W4* *4A 98* (off South Pde.)
Bedford Ct. *CR0: C'don* *1C 168* (off Tavistock Rd.)
WC2 3E 12 (7J 83) (not continuous)
Bedford Ct. Mans. WC1 6D 6
Bedford Gdns. W8 1J 99
Bedford Gdns. Ho. *W8* *1J 99* (off Bedford Gdns.)
Bedford Hill SW12 1F 137
SW16 1F 137
Bedford Ho. *SW4* *4J 119* (off Solon New Rd. Est.)
Bedford M. N2 3C 46
SE6 2D 140
BEDFORD PARK 3K 97
Bedford Pk. CR0: C'don 1C 168
Bedford Pk. Cnr. W4 4A 98
Bedford Pk. Mans. W4 4K 97
Bedford Pas. *SW6* *7G 99* (off Dawes Rd.)
W1 5B 6 (5G 83)
Bedford Pl. CR0: C'don 1D 168
WC1 5E 6 (5J 83)
Bedford Rd. DA15: Sidc 3J 143
E6 1E 88
E17 2C 50
E18 2J 51
HA1: Harr 6G 41
HA4: Ruis 4H 57
IG1: Ilf 3F 71
KT4: Wor Pk 2E 164
N2 3C 46
N8 6H 47
N9 7C 24
N15 4E 48
N22 2J 47
NW7 2F 29
SW4 4J 119
TW2: Twick 3H 131
W4 3K 97
W13 7B 78
Bedford Row WC1 5H 7 (5K 83)
Bedford Sq. WC1 6D 6 (5H 83)
Bedford St. WC2 2E 12 (7J 83)
Bedford Ter. SM2: Sutt 6A 166
SW2 5J 119
Bedford Way WC1 4D 6 (4H 83)
Bedgebury Ct. E17 2E 50
Bedgebury Gdns. SW19 2G 135
Bedgebury Rd. SE9 4B 124
Bedivere Rd. BR1: Brom 3J 141
Bedlam M. SE11 3J 19
Bedlow Way CR0: Bedd 4K 167
Bedmond Ho. *SW3* *5C 16* (off Cale St.)
Bedonwell Rd.
DA7: Belv, Bex, Erith 6F 109
DA17: Belv 6E 108
SE2 6E 108
Bedser Cl. CR7: Thor H 3C 156
SE11 7H 19 (6K 101)
Bedser Dr. UB6: G'frd 5H 59
Bedster Gdns. KT8: W Mole 2F 149
Bedwardine Rd. SE19 7E 138
Bedwell Ct. *RM6: Chad H* *7D 54* (off Broomfield Rd.)
Bedwell Gdns. UB3: Harl 5G 93 (not continuous)
Bedwell Ho. SW9 2A 120
Bedwell Rd. DA17: Belv 5G 109
N17 1E 48
Beeby Rd. E16 5K 87
Beech Av. DA15: Sidc 7A 126
HA4: Ruis 1K 57
IG9: Buck H 2E 36
N20 1H 31
TW8: Bford 7B 96
W3 1A 98
Beech Cl. N9 6B 24
SE8 6C 104
SM5: Cars 2D 166
SW15 7C 116
SW19 6E 134
TW15: Ashf 5F 129
TW16: Sun 2B 148
UB7: W Dray 3C 92
Beech Copse BR1: Brom 1D 160
CR2: S Croy 5E 168
Beech Ct. *BR1: Brom* *1H 159* (off Blyth Rd.)
BR3: Beck 7B 140
IG1: Ilf *3E 70* (off Riverdene Rd.)
KT6: Surb 7D 150
UB5: N'olt 1C 76
W9 *5J 81* (off Elmfield Way)
Beech Cres. Ct. N5 4B 66
Beechcroft BR7: Chst 7E 142
Beechcroft Av. DA7: Bex 1K 127
HA2: Harr 7E 40
KT3: N Mald 1J 151
NW11 7H 45
UB1: S'hall 1D 94
Beechcroft Cl. BR6: Orp 4H 173
SW16 5K 137
TW5: Hest 7C 94
Beechcroft Ct. N12 4E 30
NW11 *7H 45* (off Beechcroft Av.)
Beechcroft Gdns. HA9: Wemb 3F 61
Beechcroft Ho. W5 5E 78
Beechcroft Lodge SM2: Sutt 7A 166
Beechcroft Rd. BR6: Orp 4H 173
E18 2K 51
KT9: Chess 3F 163
SW14 3J 115
SW17 2C 136
Beechdale N21 2E 32
Beechdale Rd. SW2 6K 119
Beech Dell BR2: Kes 4D 172
Beechdene *SE15* *1H 121* (off Carlton Gro.)
Beech Dr. N2 2D 46
Beechen Cliff Way TW7: Isle 2K 113
Beechen Gro. HA5: Pinn 3D 40
Beechen Pl. SE23 2K 139
Beeches, The *CR2: S Croy* *5D 168* (off Blunt Rd.)
E12 7C 70
TW3: Houn 1F 113
Beeches Av. SM5: Cars 7C 166
Beeches Cl. SE20 1J 157
Beeches Rd. SM3: Sutt 1G 165
SW17 3C 136
Beeches Wlk. SM5: Cars 7B 166
Beechey Ho. *E1* *1H 103* (off Watts St.)
Beechfield Cotts. BR1: Brom 1A 160
Beechfield Ct. *CR2: S Croy* *4C 168* (off Bramley Hill)
Beechfield Gdns. RM7: Rush G 7J 55
Beechfield Rd. BR1: Brom 2A 160
DA8: Erith 7K 109
N4 6C 48
SE6 1B 140
Beech Gdns. *EC2* *5C 8* (off Beech St.)
RM10: Dag 7J 73
W5 2E 96
Beech Gro. CR4: Mitc 5H 155 (not continuous)
KT3: N Mald 3K 151
Beech Hall Cres. E4 7A 36
Beech Hall Rd. E4 7K 35
Beech Haven Ct. *DA1: Cray* *5K 127* (off London Rd.)
Beech Hill EN4: Had W 1G 21
Beech Hill Av. EN4: Had W 1F 21
Beechhill Rd. SE9 5E 124
Beech Ho. CR0: New Ad 6D 170
E17 3F 51
SE16 *2J 103* (off Ainsty Est.)
Beech Ho. Rd. CR0: C'don 3D 168
Beech La. IG9: Buck H 2E 36
Beech Lawns N12 5G 31
Beechmont Cl. BR1: Brom 5G 141
Beechmore Gdns.
SM3: Cheam 2F 165
Beechmore Rd. SW11 1D 118
Beechmount Av. W7 5H 77
Beecholme N12 5E 30
Beecholme Av. CR4: Mitc 1F 155
Beecholme Est. E5 3H 67
Beech Rd. N11 6D 32
SW16 2J 155
TW14: Bedf 7G 111
Beechrow TW10: Ham 4E 132
Beech St. EC2 5C 8 (5C 84)
RM7: Rom 4J 55
Beech Tree Cl. HA7: Stan 5H 27
N1 7A 66
Beech Tree Glade E4 1C 36
Beech Tree Pl.
SM1: Sutt 5K 165
Beechvale Cl. N12 5H 31
Beech Wlk. N17 3F 49
NW7 6F 29
Beech Way NW10 7K 61
TW2: Twick 3E 130
Beechway DA5: Bexl 6D 126
Beechwood Av. BR6: Chels 5J 173
CR7: Thor H 4B 156
HA2: Harr 3F 59
HA4: Ruis 2H 57
N3 3H 45
TW9: Kew 1G 115
TW16: Sun 6J 129
UB3: Hayes 7F 75
UB6: G'frd 3F 77
UB8: Hil 6C 74
Beechwood Circ. HA2: Harr 3F 59
Beechwood Cl. KT6: Surb 7C 150
N2 *4D 46* (off Western Rd.)
NW7 5F 29
Beechwood Ct. SM5: Cars 4D 166
TW16: Sun 6J 129
W4 6K 97
Beechwood Cres. DA7: Bex 3D 126
Beechwood Dr. BR2: Kes 4B 172
IG8: Wfd G 5C 36
Beechwood Gdns. HA2: Harr 3F 59
IG5: Ilf 5D 52
NW10 3F 79
Beechwood Gro. KT6: Surb 7C 150
W3 7A 80
Beechwood Hall N3 3H 45
Beechwood Ho. *E2* *2G 85* (off Teale St.)
Beechwood M. N9 2B 34
Beechwood Pk. E18 3J 51
Beechwood Ri. BR7: Chst 4F 143
Beechwood Rd. CR2: Sande 7E 168
E8 6F 67
N8 4H 47
Beechwoods Ct. SE19 5F 139
Beechworth NW6 7G 63
Beechworth Cl. NW3 2J 63
Beecroft La. SE4 5A 122
Beecroft M. SE4 5A 122
Beecroft Rd. SE4 5A 122
Beehive Cl. E8 7F 67
UB10: Uxb 7B 56
Beehive Ct. IG1: Ilf 6D 52
Beehive La. IG1: Ilf 5D 52
IG4: Ilf 5D 52
Beehive Pl. SW9 3A 120
Beeken Dene BR6: Farnb 4G 173
Beeleigh Rd. SM4: Mord 4K 153
Beemans Row SW18 2A 136
Bee Pas. *EC3* *1G 15* (off Lime St.)
Beeston Cl. E8 5G 67
Beeston Ho. *SE1* *3D 102* (off Burbage Cl.)
Beeston Pl. SW1 1K 17 (3F 101)
Beeston Rd. EN4: E Barn 6G 21
Beeston Way TW14: Felt 6A 112
Beethoven St. W10 3G 81
Beeton Cl. HA5: Hat E 1E 40
Begbie Rd. SE3 1A 124
BEGGAR'S HILL 6B 164
Beggar's Hill KT17: Ewe 7B 164
Beggars Roost La.
SM1: Sutt 6J 165
Begonia Cl. E6 5D 88
Begonia Pl. TW12: Hamp 6E 130
Begonia Wlk. W12 6B 80
Beira St. SW12 7F 119
Bejun Ct. EN5: New Bar 4F 21
Bekesbourne St. E14 6A 86
Belcroft Cl. BR1: Brom 7H 141
Beldanes Lodge NW10 7C 62
Beldham Gdns. KT8: W Mole 2F 149
Belfairs Dr. RM6: Chad H 7C 54
Belfast Rd. N16 2F 67
SE25 4H 157
Belfield Rd. KT19: Ewe 7K 163
Belfont Wlk. N7 4J 65 (not continuous)
Belford Gro. SE18 4E 106
Belford Ho. E8 1F 85
Belfort Rd. SE15 2J 121
Belfry Cl. BR1: Brom 4F 161
SE16 5H 103
Belfry Rd. E12 2B 70
Belgrade Rd. N16 4E 66
TW12: Hamp 1F 149
Belgrave Cl. N14 5B 22
NW7 5E 28
W3 2H 97
Belgrave Ct. *E2* *2H 85* (off Temple St.)
E13 4A 88
E14 *7B 86* (off Westferry Cir.)
SW8 *7G 101* (off Ascalon St.)
W4 5J 97
Belgrave Cres.
TW16: Sun 1K 147

Belgrave Gdns. HA7: Stan 5H 27
N14 5C 22
NW8 1K 81
Belgrave Hgts. E11 1J 69
Belgrave Ho. SW9 7A 102
Belgrave Mans. NW8 1K 81
(off Belgrave Gdns.)
Belgrave M. Nth. SW1 7G 11 (2E 100)
Belgrave M. Sth. SW1 1H 17 (3E 100)
Belgrave M. W. SW1 1G 17 (3E 100)
Belgrave Pl. SW1 1H 17 (3E 100)
Belgrave Rd. CR4: Mitc 3B 154
E10 1E 68
E11 2J 69
E13 4A 88
E17 5C 50
IG1: Ilf 1D 70
SE25 4F 157
SW1 4K 17 (4F 101)
SW13 7B 98
TW4: Houn 3D 112
TW16: Sun 1K 147
Belgrave Sq. SW1 1G 17 (3E 100)
Belgrave St. E1 5K 85
Belgrave Ter. IG8: Wfd G 3D 36
Belgrave Wlk. CR4: Mitc 3B 154
Belgrave Yd. SW1 2J 17
BELGRAVIA 2H 17 (3E 100)
Belgravia Cl. EN5: Barn 3C 20
Belgravia Ct. SW1 2J 17
Belgravia Gdns. BR1: Brom 6G 141
Belgravia Ho. SW1 1G 17
(off Halkin Pl.)
SW4 6H 119
Belgravia M. KT1: King T 4D 150
Belgravia Workshops N19 2J 65
(off Marlborough Rd.)
Belgrove St. WC1 1F 7 (3J 83)
Belham Wlk. SE5 1D 120
Belinda Rd. SW9 3B 120
Belitha Vs. N1 7K 65
BELL, THE 3C 50
Bella Best Ho. SW1 5K 17
(off Westmoreland Ter.)
W1 6H 83
(off Westmoreland Ter.)
Bellamy Cl. E14 2C 104
HA8: Edg 2D 28
UB10: Ick 3C 56
W14 5H 99
Bellamy Ct. HA7: Stan 1B 42
Bellamy Dr. HA7: Stan 1B 42
Bellamy Ho. SW17 4B 136
TW5: Hest 6E 94
Bellamy Rd. E4 6J 35
EN2: Enf 2J 23
Bellamy's Ct. SE16 1K 103
(off Abbotshade Rd.)
Bellamy St. SW12 7F 119
Bel La. TW13: Hanw 3C 130
Bellasis Av. SW2 2J 137
Bell Av. UB7: W Dray 4B 92
Bell Cl. HA4: Ruis 3H 57
HA5: Pinn 2A 40
Bellclose Rd. UB7: W Dray 2A 92
Bell Ct. NW4 4E 44
Bell Dr. SW18 7G 117
Bellefields Rd. SW9 3K 119
Bellegrove Cl. DA16: Well 2K 125
Bellegrove Pde. DA16: Well 3K 125
Bellegrove Rd. DA16: Well 2H 125
Bellenden Rd. SE15 1F 121
Bellenden Rd. Retail Pk. SE15 1G 121
Bellermine Cl. SE28 1K 107
Bellestaines Pleasaunce E4 2H 35
Belleville Rd. SW11 5C 118
Belle Vue UB6: G'frd 1H 77
Belle Vue Est. NW4 4F 45
Belle Vue La. WD23: B Hea 1C 26
Bellevue M. N11 5K 31
Bellevue Pde. SW17 1D 136
Belle Vue Pk. CR7: Thor H 3C 156
Bellevue Pl. E1 4J 85
Belle Vue Rd. E17 2F 51
NW4 4E 44
Bellevue Rd. DA6: Bex 5F 127
KT1: King T 3E 150
(not continuous)
N11 4K 31
SW13 2C 116
SW17 1C 136
W13 4B 78
Bellew St. SW17 3A 136
Bell Farm Av. RM10: Dag 3J 73
Bellfield CR0: Sels 7A 170
Bellfield Av. HA3: Hrw W 6C 26
Bellfield Cl. SE3 7J 105
Bellflower Cl. E6 5C 88
Bell Gdns. E10 1C 68
(off Church Rd.)
Bellgate M. NW5 4F 65
BELL GREEN 4A 140
Bell Grn. SE26 4B 140
Bell Grn. La. SE26 5B 140
Bellhaven E15 6F 69
Bell Hill CR0: C'don 2C 168
Bell Ho. HA9: Wemb 3E 60
SE10 6E 104
(off Haddo St.)
Bellhouse Cotts. UB3: Hayes 7G 75
Bell Ho. Rd. RM7: Rush G 1J 73
Bellina M. NW5 4F 65
Bell Ind. Est. W4 4J 97
BELLINGHAM 3C 140
Bellingham N17 7C 34
(off Park La.)
Bellingham Ct. IG11: Bark 3B 90
Bellingham Grn. SE6 3C 140
Bellingham Rd. SE6 3D 140
Bellingham Trad. Est. SE6 3D 140
Bell Inn Yd. EC3 1F 15 (6D 84)
Bell Junc. TW3: Houn 3F 113
Bell La. E1 6J 9 (5F 85)
E16 1H 105
EN3: Enf H, Enf W 1E 24
HA9: Wemb 2D 60
NW4 4F 45
TW1: Twick 1A 132
Bellmaker Ct. E3 5C 86
Bell Mdw. SE19 5E 138
Bell Moor NW3 3A 64
(off E. Heath Rd.)
Bello Cl. SE24 7B 120
Bellot Gdns. SE10 5G 105
(off Bellot St.)
Bellot St. SE10 5G 105
Bellring Cl. DA17: Belv 6G 109
Bell Rd. EN1: Enf 1J 23
KT8: E Mos 5H 149
TW3: Houn 3F 113
Bells All. SW6 2J 117
Bells Hill EN5: Barn 5A 20
Bellsize Ct. NW3 5B 64
Bell St. NW1 5C 4 (5C 82)
SE18 1C 124
Belltrees Gro. SW16 5K 137
Bell Vw. Mnr. HA4: Ruis 7F 39
Bell Water Ga. SE18 3E 106
Bell Wharf La. EC4 3D 14 (7C 84)
Bellwood Rd. SE15 4K 121
Bell Yd. WC2 1J 13 (6A 84)
Bell Yd. M. SE1 7H 15 (2E 102)
Belmarsh Rd. SE28 2J 107
BELMONT
HA3 2A 42
SM2 7J 165
Belmont Av. DA16: Well 2J 125
EN4: Cockf 5J 21
HA0: Wemb 1F 79
KT3: N Mald 5C 152
Belmont Av. N9 1B 34
N13 5E 32
N17 3C 48
UB2: S'hall 3C 94
Belmont Circ. HA3: Kent 1B 42
Belmont Cl. E4 5A 36
EN4: Cockf 4J 21
IG8: Wfd G 4E 36
N20 1E 30
SW4 3G 119
UB8: Uxb 6A 56
Belmont Ct. N5 4C 66
NW11 5H 45
Belmont Gro. SE13 3F 123
W4 4K 97
Belmont Hall Ct. SE13 3F 123
Belmont Hill SE13 3E 122
Belmont La. BR7: Chst 5G 143
(not continuous)
HA7: Stan 1C 42
Belmont Lodge
HA3: Hrw W 7C 26
Belmont M. SW19 2F 135
Belmont Pde. BR7: Chst 5G 143
NW11 5H 45
Belmont Pk. SE13 4F 123
Belmont Pk. Cl. SE13 4G 123
Belmont Pk. Rd. E10 6D 50
Belmont Ri. SM2: Sutt 6H 165
Belmont Rd. BR3: Beck 2A 158
BR7: Chst 5F 143
DA8: Erith 7G 109
HA3: W'stone 3K 41
IG1: Ilf 3G 71
N15 4C 48
N17 4C 48
SE25 5H 157
SM6: Wall 5F 167
SW4 3G 119
TW2: Twick 2H 131
UB8: Uxb 7A 56
W4 4K 97
Belmont St. NW1 7E 64
Belmont Ter. W4 4K 97
Belmore Av. UB4: Hayes 6J 75
Belmore Ho. N7 5H 65
Belmore La. N7 5H 65
Belmore St. SW8 1H 119
Beloe Cl. SW15 4C 116
Belsham St. E9 6J 67
Belsize Av. N13 6E 32
NW3 6B 64
W13 3B 96
Belsize Ct. Garages NW3 5B 64
(off Belsize La.)
Belsize Cres. NW3 5B 64
Belsize Gdns. SM1: Sutt 4K 165
Belsize Gro. NW3 6C 64
Belsize La. NW3 6B 64
Belsize M. NW3 6B 64
Belsize Pk. NW3 6B 64
Belsize Pk. Gdns. NW3 6B 64
Belsize Pk. M. NW3 6B 64
Belsize Pl. NW3 5B 64
Belsize Rd. HA3: Hrw W 7C 26
NW6 1K 81
Belsize Sq. NW3 6B 64
Belsize Ter. NW3 6B 64
Belson Rd. SE18 4D 106
Beltane Dr. SW19 3F 135
Belthorn Cres. SW12 7G 119
Belton Rd. DA14: Sidc 4A 144
E7 7K 69
E11 4G 69
N17 3E 48
NW2 6C 62
Belton Way E3 5C 86
Beltran Rd. SW6 2K 117
Beltwood Rd. DA17: Belv 4J 109
BELVEDERE 3G 109
Belvedere, The SW10 1A 118
(off Chelsea Harbour)
Belvedere Av. IG5: Ilf 2F 53
SW19 5G 135
Belvedere Bldgs. SE1 7B 14 (2B 102)
Belvedere Cl. TW11: Tedd 5J 131
Belvedere Ct. DA17: Belv 3F 109
N1 1E 84
(off De Beauvoir Cres.)
N2 5B 46
NW2 6F 63
(off Willesden La.)
SW15 4E 116
Belvedere Dr. SW19 5G 135
Belvedere Gdns. KT8: W Mole 5D 148
Belvedere Gro. SW19 5G 135
Belvedere Ind. Est. DA17: Belv 1J 109
Belvedere Link Bus. Pk.
DA8: Erith 3J 109
Belvedere M. SE3 7K 105
SE15 3J 121
Belvedere Pl. SE1 7B 14 (2B 102)
SW2 4K 119
Belvedere Rd. DA7: Bex 3F 127
E10 1A 68
SE1 6H 13 (1K 101)
SE2 1C 108
SE19 7F 139
W7 3K 95
Belvedere Sq. SW19 5G 135
Belvedere Strand NW9 2B 44
Belvedere Way HA3: Kent 6E 42
Belvoir Cl. SE9 3C 142
Belvoir Ho. SW1 4G 101
Belvoir Rd. SE22 7G 121
Belvue Bus. Cen. UB5: N'olt 7F 59
Belvue Cl. UB5: N'olt 7E 58
Belvue Rd. UB5: N'olt 7E 58
Bembridge Cl. NW6 7G 63
Bembridge Gdns. HA4: Ruis 2F 57
Bembridge Ho. KT2: King T 2G 151
(off Coombe Rd.)
SE8 4B 104
(off Longshore)
SW18 6K 117
(off Iron Mill Rd.)
Bemersyde Point E13 3K 87
(off Dongola Rd. W.)
Bemerton Est. N1 7J 65
Bemerton St. N1 1K 83
Bemish Rd. SW15 3F 117
Bempton Dr. HA4: Ruis 2K 57
Bemsted Rd. E17 3B 50
Benares Rd. SE18 4K 107
Benbow Ct. W6 3E 98
(off Benbow Rd.)
Benbow Ho. SE8 6C 104
(off Benbow St.)
Benbow Rd. W6 3D 98
Benbow St. SE8 6C 104
Benbury Cl. BR1: Brom 5E 140
Bence Ho. SE8 4A 104
(off Rainsborough Av.)
Bench, The TW10: Ham 3C 132
Bench Fld. CR2: S Croy 6F 169
Bencroft Rd. SW16 7G 137
Bencurtis Pk. BR4: W W'ck 3F 171
Bendall Ho. NW1 5D 4
(off Bell St.)
Bendall M. NW1 5D 4
Bendemeer Rd. SW15 3F 117
Benden Ho. SE13 5E 122
(off Monument Gdns.)
Bendish Point SE28 2G 107
Bendish Rd. E6 7C 70
Bendmore Av. SE2 5A 108
Bendon Valley SW18 7K 117
Benedict Cl. BR6: Orp 3J 173
DA17: Belv 3E 108
Benedict Ct. RM6: Chad H 6F 55

Benedict Dr. TW14: Bedf . . . 7F 111
Benedict Rd. CR4: Mitc . . . 3B 154
SW9 . . . 3K 119
Benedict Way N2 . . . 3A 46
Benedict Wharf CR4: Mitc . . . 3C 154
Benenden Grn. BR2: Brom . . . 5J 159
Benenden Ho. *SE17* . . . *5E 102*
(off Mina Rd.)
Benett Gdns. SW16 . . . 2J 155
Ben Ezra Ct. *SE17* . . . *4C 102*
(off Asolando Dr.)
Benfleet Cl. SM1: Sutt . . . 3A 166
Benfleet Ct. E8 . . . 1F 85
Benfleet Way N11 . . . 2K 31
Bengal Ct. *EC3* . . . *1F 15*
(off Birchin La.)
Bengal Ho. *E1* . . . *5K 85*
(off Duckett St.)
Bengal Rd. IG1: Ilf . . . 4F 71
Bengarth Dr. HA3: Hrw W . . . 2H 41
Bengarth Rd. UB5: N'olt . . . 1C 76
Bengeo Gdns. RM6: Chad H . . . 6C 54
Bengeworth Rd. HA1: Harr . . . 2A 60
SE5 . . . 3C 120
Ben Hale Cl. HA7: Stan . . . 5G 27
Benham Cl. KT9: Chess . . . 6C 162
SW11 . . . 3B 118
Benham Gdns. TW4: Houn . . . 5D 112
Benham Ho. *SW10* . . . *7K 99*
(off Coleridge Gdns.)
Benham Rd. W7 . . . 5J 77
Benham's Pl. NW3 . . . 4A 64
Benhill Av. SM1: Sutt . . . 4K 165
(not continuous)
Benhill Rd. SE5 . . . 7D 102
SM1: Sutt . . . 3A 166
Benhill Wood Rd. SM1: Sutt . . . 3A 166
BENHILTON . . . 2K 165
Benhilton Gdns.
SM1: Sutt . . . 3K 165
Benhurst Ct. SW16 . . . 5A 138
Benhurst La. SW16 . . . 5A 138
Benin Ho. *WC1* . . . *5K 83*
(off Procter St.)
Benin St. SE13 . . . 7F 123
Benjafield Cl. N18 . . . 4C 34
Benjamin Cl. E8 . . . 1G 85
Benjamin Ct. DA17: Belv . . . 6F 109
TW15: Ashf . . . 7E 128
Benjamin Franklin House . . . *4E 12*
(off Craven St.)
Benjamin M. SW12 . . . 7G 119
Benjamin St. EC1 . . . 5A 8 (5B 84)
Ben Jonson Ct. N1 . . . 2E 84
Ben Jonson Ho. EC2 . . . 5D 8
Ben Jonson Pl. EC2 . . . 5D 8
Ben Jonson Rd. E1 . . . 5K 85
Benledi St. E14 . . . 6F 87
Benlow Works *UB3: Hayes* . . . *2H 93*
(off Silverdale Rd.)
Bennelong Cl. W12 . . . 7D 80
Bennerley Rd. SW11 . . . 5C 118
Bennets Courtyard SW19 . . . 1A 154
Bennets Fld. Rd. UB11: Stock P . . . 1D 92
Bennet's Hill EC4 . . . 2B 14 (7C 84)
Bennets Lodge EN2: Enf . . . 3G 23
Bennet St. SW1 . . . 4A 12 (1G 101)
Bennett Cl. DA16: Well . . . 2A 126
HA6: Nwood . . . 1H 39
KT1: Ham W . . . 1C 150
TW4: Houn . . . 5C 112
Bennett Ct. N7 . . . 3K 65
Bennett Gro. SE13 . . . 1D 122
Bennett Ho. *SW1* . . . *3D 18*
(off Page St.)
Bennett Pk. SE3 . . . 3H 123
Bennett Rd. E13 . . . 4A 88
N16 . . . 4E 66
RM6: Chad H . . . 6E 54
SW9 . . . 2A 120
Bennetts Av. CR0: C'don . . . 2A 170
UB6: G'frd . . . 1J 77
Bennett's Castle La. RM8: Dag . . . 2C 72
Bennetts Cl. CR4: Mitc . . . 1F 155
N17 . . . 6A 34
Bennetts Copse BR7: Chst . . . 6C 142
Bennett St. W4 . . . 6A 98
Bennetts Way CR0: C'don . . . 2A 170
Bennett's Yd. SW1 . . . 2D 18 (3H 101)
Benningholme Rd. HA8: Edg . . . 6F 29
Bennington Rd. IG8: Wfd G . . . 7B 36
N17 . . . 1E 48
Benn's All. TW12: Hamp . . . 2F 149
Benn St. E9 . . . 6A 68
Benns Wlk. *TW9: Rich* . . . *4E 114*
(off Michelsdale Dr.)
Benrek Cl. IG6: Ilf . . . 1G 53
Bensbury Cl. SW15 . . . 7D 116
Bensham Cl. CR7: Thor H . . . 4C 156
Bensham Gro. CR7: Thor H . . . 2C 156
Bensham La. CR0: C'don . . . 7B 156
CR7: Thor H . . . 5B 156
Bensham Mnr. Rd. CR7: Thor H . . . 4C 156
Bensham Mnr. Rd. Pas.
CR7: Thor H . . . 4C 156
Bensley Cl. N11 . . . 5J 31
Ben Smith Way SE16 . . . 3G 103
Benson Av. E6 . . . 2A 88
Benson Cl. TW3: Houn . . . 4E 112
UB8: Hil . . . 5A 74
Benson Ho. *E2* . . . *3J 9*
(off Ligonier St.)
SE1 . . . *5K 13*
(off Hatfields)
Benson Quay E1 . . . 7J 85
Benson Rd. CR0: Wadd . . . 3A 168
SE23 . . . 1J 139
Bentalls Cen., The KT1: King T . . . 2D 150
Bentfield Gdns. SE9 . . . 3B 142
Bentfield Ho. *NW9* . . . *3B 44*
(off Heritage Way)
Benthal Rd. N16 . . . 2G 67
Bentham Ct. *N1* . . . *7C 66*
(off Ecclesbourne Rd.)
Bentham Hall *WC1* . . . *3H 83*
(off Cartwright Gdns.)
Bentham Ho. *SE1* . . . *3D 102*
(off Falmouth Rd.)
Bentham Rd. E9 . . . 6K 67
SE28 . . . 7B 90
Bentham Wlk. NW10 . . . 5J 61
Ben Tillet Cl. E16 . . . 1D 106
IG11: Bark . . . 7A 72
Ben Tillet Ho. N15 . . . 3B 48
Bentinck Cl. NW8 . . . 2C 82
Bentinck Ho. *SW1* . . . *2D 18*
(off Monck St.)
W12 . . . *7D 80*
(off White City Est.)
Bentinck Mans. *W1* . . . *7H 5*
(off Bentinck St.)
Bentinck M. W1 . . . 7H 5 (6E 82)
Bentinck Rd. UB7: Yiew . . . 1A 92
Bentinck St. W1 . . . 7H 5 (6E 82)
Bentley Cl. SW19 . . . 3J 135
Bentley Ct. *SE13* . . . *4E 122*
(off Whitburn Rd.)
Bentley Dr. IG2: Ilf . . . 6G 53
NW2 . . . 3H 63
Bentley Ho. *SE5* . . . *1E 120*
(off Peckham Rd.)
Bentley Lodge WD23: B Hea . . . 2D 26
Bentley M. EN1: Enf . . . 6J 23
Bentley Rd. N1 . . . 6E 66
Bentley Way HA7: Stan . . . 5F 27
IG8: Buck H, Wfd G . . . 2D 36
Benton Rd. IG1: Ilf . . . 1H 71
Bentons La. SE27 . . . 4C 138
Benton's Ri. SE27 . . . 5D 138
Bentry Cl. RM8: Dag . . . 2E 72
Bentry Rd. RM8: Dag . . . 2E 72
Bentworth Ct. *E2* . . . *3K 9*
(off Granby St.)
Bentworth Rd. W12 . . . 6D 80
Benville Ho. *SW8* . . . *7K 101*
(off Oval Pl.)
Benwell Ct. TW16: Sun . . . 1J 147
Benwell Rd. N7 . . . 4A 66
Benwick Cl. SE16 . . . 4H 103
Benwood Ct. SM1: Sutt . . . 3A 166
Benworth St. E3 . . . 3B 86
Benyon Ct. *N1* . . . *1E 84*
(off De Beauvoir Est.)
Benyon Ho. *EC1* . . . *1K 7*
(off Myddelton Pas.)
Benyon Rd. N1 . . . 1D 84
Benyon Wharf *E8* . . . *1E 84*
(off Kingsland Rd.)
Berberis Ct. IG1: Ilf . . . 6F 71
Berberis Ho. *E3* . . . *5C 86*
(off Gale St.)
TW13: Felt . . . 2J 129
Berberis Wlk. UB7: W Dray . . . 4A 92
Berber Pde. SE18 . . . 1C 124
Berber Pl. E14 . . . 7C 86
Berber Rd. SW11 . . . 5D 118
Berberry Cl. HA8: Edg . . . 4D 28
Bercta Rd. SE9 . . . 2G 143
Berengers Pl. RM9: Dag . . . 6B 72
Berenger Twr. *SW10* . . . *7B 100*
(off Worlds End Est.)
Berenger Wlk. *SW10* . . . *7B 100*
(off Worlds End Est.)
Berens Ct. DA14: Sidc . . . 4K 143
Berens Rd. NW10 . . . 3F 81
Berens Way BR7: Chst . . . 3K 161
Beresford Av.
HA0: Wemb . . . 1F 79
KT5: Surb . . . 1H 163
N20 . . . 2J 31
TW1: Twick . . . 6C 114
W7 . . . 5H 77
Beresford Dr. BR1: Brom . . . 3C 160
IG8: Wfd G . . . 4F 37
Beresford Gdns. EN1: Enf . . . 4K 23
RM6: Chad H . . . 5E 54
TW4: Houn . . . 5D 112
Beresford Rd. E4 . . . 1B 36
E17 . . . 1D 50
HA1: Harr . . . 5H 41
KT2: King T . . . 1F 151
KT3: N Mald . . . 4J 151
N2 . . . 3C 46
N5 . . . 5D 66
N8 . . . 5A 48
SM2: Sutt . . . 7H 165
UB1: S'hall . . . 1B 94
Beresford Sq. SE18 . . . 4F 107
Beresford St. SE18 . . . 3F 107
Beresford Ter. N5 . . . 5C 66
Berestede Rd. W6 . . . 5B 98
Bere St. E1 . . . 7K 85
Bergen Ho. *SE5* . . . *2C 120*
(off Carew St.)
Bergenia Ho.
TW13: Felt . . . 1K 129
Bergen Sq. SE16 . . . 3A 104
Berger Cl. BR5: Pet W . . . 6H 161
Berger Rd. E9 . . . 6K 67
Berghem M. W14 . . . 3F 99
Bergholt Av. IG4: Ilf . . . 5C 52
Bergholt Cres. N16 . . . 7E 48
Bergholt M. NW1 . . . 7H 65
Berglen Ct. E14 . . . 6A 86
Bering Sq. E14 . . . 5C 104
Bering Wlk. E16 . . . 6B 88
Berisford M. SW18 . . . 6A 118
Berkeley Av. DA7: Bex . . . 1D 126
IG5: Ilf . . . 2E 52
RM5: Col R . . . 1J 55
Berkeley Av. TW4: Cran . . . 1J 111
UB6: G'frd . . . 6H 59
(not continuous)
Berkeley Cl. BR5: Pet W . . . 7J 161
HA4: Ruis . . . 3J 57
KT2: King T . . . 7E 132
Berkeley Ct. *CR0: C'don* . . . *4D 168*
(off Coombe Rd.)
KT6: Surb . . . 7D 150
N3 . . . 1K 45
N14 . . . 6B 22
NW1 . . . 4F 5
NW10 . . . 4A 62
NW11 . . . *7H 45*
(off Ravenscroft Av.)
SM6: Wall . . . 3G 167
W5 . . . *7C 78*
(off Gordon Rd.)
Berkeley Cres. EN4: E Barn . . . 5G 21
Berkeley Dr. KT8: W Mole . . . 3D 148
Berkeley Gdns.
KT10: Clay . . . 6A 162
KT12: Walt T . . . 7H 147
N21 . . . 7J 23
W8 . . . 1J 99
Berkeley Ho. *SE8* . . . *5B 104*
(off Grove St.)
TW8: Bford . . . *6D 96*
(off Albany Rd.)
Berkeley M. TW16: Sun . . . 3A 148
W1 . . . 1F 11 (6D 82)
Berkeley Pl. SW19 . . . 6F 135
Berkeley Rd. E12 . . . 5C 70
N8 . . . 5H 47
N15 . . . 6D 48
NW9 . . . 4G 43
SW13 . . . 1C 116
UB10: Hil . . . 7E 56
Berkeleys, The SE25 . . . 4G 157
Berkeley Sq. W1 . . . 3K 11 (7F 83)
Berkeley St. W1 . . . 3K 11 (7F 83)
Berkeley Twr. *E14* . . . *1B 104*
(off Westferry Cir.)
Berkeley Wlk. *N7* . . . *2K 65*
(off Durham Rd.)
Berkeley Waye TW5: Hest . . . 6B 94
Berkhampstead Rd. DA17: Belv . . . 5G 109
Berkhamsted Av. HA9: Wemb . . . 6F 61
Berkley Cl. *TW2: Twick* . . . *3J 131*
(off Wellesley Rd.)
Berkley Gro. NW1 . . . 7E 64
Berkley Rd. NW1 . . . 7D 64
Berkshire Ct. *W7* . . . *4K 77*
(off Copley Cl.)
Berkshire Gdns. N13 . . . 6F 33
N18 . . . 5C 34
Berkshire Ho. SE6 . . . 4C 140
Berkshire Rd. E9 . . . 6B 68
Berkshire Sq. CR4: Mitc . . . 4J 155
Berkshire Way CR4: Mitc . . . 4J 155
Bermans Way NW10 . . . 4A 62
BERMONDSEY . . . 7K 15 (2G 103)
Bermondsey Exchange *SE1* . . . *7H 15*
(off Bermondsey St.)
Bermondsey Sq. SE1 . . . 7H 15 (3E 102)
Bermondsey St. SE1 . . . 5G 15 (1E 102)
Bermondsey Trad. Est. SE16 . . . 5J 103
Bermondsey Wall E. SE16 . . . 2G 103
Bermondsey Wall W. SE16 . . . 2G 103
Bernal Cl. SE28 . . . 7D 90
Bernard Angell Ho. *SE10* . . . *6F 105*
(off Trafalgar Rd.)
Bernard Ashley Dr. SE7 . . . 5K 105
Bernard Av. W13 . . . 3B 96
Bernard Cassidy St. E16 . . . 5H 87
Bernard Gdns. SW19 . . . 5H 135
Bernard Hegarty Lodge *E8* . . . *7G 67*
(off Lansdowne Dr.)
Bernard Ho. *E1* . . . *5F 85*
(off Toynbee St.)

Bernard Mans. *WC1* 4E 6
(off Bernard St.)
Bernard Rd. N15 5F 49
RM7: Rush G 7J 55
SM6: Wall 4F 167
Bernard Shaw Ct. *NW1* 7G 65
(off St Pancras Way)
Bernard Shaw Ho. *NW10* 1K 79
(off Knatchbull Rd.)
Bernard St. WC1 4E 6 (4J 83)
Bernard Sunley Ho. *SW9* 7A 102
(off Sth. Island Pl.)
Bernays Cl. HA7: Stan 6H 27
Bernays Gro. SW9 4K 119
Bernel Dr. CR0: C'don 3B 170
Berne Rd. CR7: Thor H 5C 156
Berners Dr. W13 7A 78
Berners Ho. *N1* 2A 84
(off Barnsbury Est.)
Berners M. W1 6B 6 (5G 83)
Berners Pl. W1 7B 6 (6G 83)
Berners Rd. N1 1B 84
N22 1A 48
Berners St. W1 6B 6 (5G 83)
Berner Ter. *E1* 6G 85
(off Fairclough St.)
Berney Ho. BR3: Beck 5A 158
Berney Rd. CR0: C'don 7D 156
Bernhardt Cres. NW8 3C 4 (4C 82)
Bernhart Cl. HA8: Edg 7D 28
Bernville Way HA3: Kent 5F 43
Bernwell Rd. E4 3B 36
Berridge Grn. HA8: Edg 7B 28
Berridge M. NW6 5J 63
Berridge Rd. SE19 5D 138
Berriman Rd. N7 3K 65
Berrington Ho. *W2* 7J 81
(off Herrington Rd.)
Berriton Rd. HA2: Harr 1D 58
Berrybank Cl. E4 2K 35
Berry Cl. N21 1G 33
NW10 7A 62
RM10: Dag 5G 73
Berry Cotts. *E14* 6A 86
(off Maroon St.)
Berry Ct. TW4: Houn 5D 112
Berrydale Rd. UB4: Yead 4C 76
Berryfield Cl. BR1: Brom 1C 160
E17 4D 50
Berryfield Rd. SE17 5B 102
Berry Hill HA7: Stan 4J 27
Berryhill SE9 4F 125
Berryhill Gdns. SE9 4F 125
Berry Ho. *E1* 4H 85
(off Headlam St.)
SW11 2D 118
(off Culvert Rd.)
BERRYLANDS 6G 151
Berrylands KT5: Surb 6F 151
SW20 3E 152
Berrylands Rd. KT5: Surb 6F 151
Berry La. SE21 4D 138
Berryman Cl. RM8: Dag 3C 72
Berryman's La. SE26 4K 139
Berrymead Gdns. W3 1J 97
Berrymede Rd. W4 3K 97
Berry Pl. EC1 2B 8 (3B 84)
Berry St. EC1 3B 8 (4B 84)
Berry Way W5 3E 96
Bertal Rd. SW17 4B 136
Bertha Hollamby Ct.
DA14: Sidc 5C 144
(off Sidcup Hill)
Bertha James Ct. BR2: Brom 4K 159
Berthons Gdns. *E17* 5F 51
(off Wood St.)
Berthon St. SE8 7C 104
Bertie Rd. NW10 6C 62
SE26 6K 139
Bertram Cotts. SW19 7J 135
Bertram Rd. EN1: Enf 4B 24
KT2: King T 7G 133
NW4 6C 44
Bertram St. N19 2F 65
Bertrand Ho. *SW16* 3J 137
(off Leigham Av.)
Bertrand St. SE13 3D 122
Bertrand Way SE28 7B 90
Bert Rd. CR7: Thor H 5C 156
Bert Way EN1: Enf 4A 24
Berwick Av. UB4: Yead 6B 76
Berwick Cl. HA7: Stan 6E 26
TW2: Whitt 1E 130
Berwick Ct. SE1 7D 14
Berwick Cres. DA15: Sidc 7J 125
Berwick Gdns. SM1: Sutt 3A 166
Berwick Ho. N2 2B 46
Berwick Rd. DA16: Well 1B 126
E16 6K 87
N22 1B 48
Berwick St. W1 7B 6 (6G 83)
Berwick Way BR6: Orp 1K 173
Berwyn Av. TW3: Houn 1F 113
Berwyn Rd. SE24 1B 138
TW10: Rich 4H 115
Beryl Av. E6 5C 88
Beryl Ho. *SE18* 5K 107
(off Spinel Cl.)
Beryl Rd. W6 5F 99
Berystede KT2: King T 7H 133
Besant Cl. NW2 3G 63
Besant Ct. N1 5D 66
SE28 1B 108
(off Titmuss Av.)
Besant Ho. *NW8* 1A 82
(off Boundary Rd.)
Besant Pl. SE22 4F 121
Besant Rd. NW2 4G 63
Besant Wlk. N7 2K 65
Besant Way NW10 5J 61
Besford Ho. *E2* 2G 85
(off Pritchard's Rd.)
Besley St. SW16 6G 137
Bessant Dr. TW9: Kew 1G 115
Bessborough Gdns. SW1 5D 18 (5H 101)
Bessborough Pl. SW1 5D 18 (5H 101)
Bessborough Rd. HA1: Harr 1H 59
SW15 1C 134
Bessborough St. SW1 5C 18 (5H 101)
Bessemer Ct. *NW1* 7G 65
(off Rochester Sq.)
Bessemer Pk. Ind. Est.
SE24 4B 120
Bessemer Rd. SE5 2C 120
Bessie Lansbury Cl. E6 6E 88
Bessingby Rd. HA4: Ruis 2K 57
Bessingham Wlk. *SE4* 4K 121
(off Aldersford Cl.)
Besson St. SE14 1J 121
Bessy St. E2 3J 85
Bestwood St. SE8 4K 103
Beswick M. NW6 6K 63
Betam Rd. UB3: Hayes 2F 93
Beta Pl. SW4 4K 119
Betchworth Cl. SM1: Sutt 5B 166
Betchworth Rd. IG3: Ilf 2J 71
Betchworth Way
CR0: New Ad 7E 170
Bethal Est. SE1 5H 15
Betham Rd. UB6: G'frd 3H 77
Bethany Waye
TW14: Bedf 7G 111
Bethecar Rd. HA1: Harr 5J 41
Bethel Cl. NW4 5F 45
Bethell Av. E16 4H 87
IG1: Ilf 7E 52
Bethel Rd. DA16: Well 3C 126
Bethersden Cl. BR3: Beck 7B 140
Bethersden Ho. *SE17* 5E 102
(off Kinglake Est.)
Bethlehem Ho. *E14* 7B 86
(off Limehouse C'way.)
BETHNAL GREEN 3H 85
Bethnal Green Cen. for
Sports & Performing Arts 3F 85
Bethnal Green Mus. of Childhood 3J 85
Bethnal Grn. Rd. E1 3J 9 (4F 85)
E2 3J 9 (4F 85)
Bethune Av. N11 4J 31
Bethune Cl. N16 1E 66
Bethune Rd. N16 7D 48
NW10 4K 79
Bethwin Rd. SE5 7B 102
Betjeman Cl. HA5: Pinn 4E 40
Betjeman Ct. UB7: Yiew 1A 92
Betony Cl. CR0: C'don 1K 169
Betoyne Av. E4 4B 36
Betsham Ho. *SE1* 6E 14
(off Newcomen St.)
Betstyle Cir. N11 4A 32
Betstyle Ho. N10 7K 31
Betstyle Rd. N11 4A 32
Betterton Dr. DA14: Sidc 2E 144
Betterton Ho. *WC2* 1F 13
(off Betterton St.)
Betterton Rd. RM13: Rain 3K 91
Betterton St. WC2 1E 12 (6J 83)
Bettons Pk. E15 1G 87
Bettridge Rd. SW6 2H 117
Betts Cl. BR3: Beck 2A 158
Betts Ho. *E1* 7H 85
(off Betts St.)
Betts M. E17 6B 50
Betts Rd. E16 7K 87
Betts St. E1 7H 85
Betts Way KT6: Surb 1B 162
SE20 1H 157
Betty Brooks Ho. E11 3F 69
Betty May Gray Ho. *E14* 4E 104
(off Pier St.)
Beulah Av. CR7: Thor H 2C 156
Beulah Cl. HA8: Edg 3C 28
Beulah Cres. CR7: Thor H 2C 156
Beulah Gro. CR0: C'don 6C 156
Beulah Hill SE19 6B 138
Beulah Path E17 5E 50
Beulah Rd. CR7: Thor H 3C 156
E17 5D 50
SM1: Sutt 4J 165
SW19 7H 135
Bevan Av. IG11: Bark 7A 72
Bevan Ct. CR0: Wadd 5A 168
E3 2C 86
(off Tredegar Rd.)
Bevan Ho. IG11: Bark 7B 72
N1 1E 84
(off New Era Est.)
TW1: Twick 6D 114
WC1 5F 7
(off Boswell St.)
Bevan Rd. EN4: Cockf 4J 21
SE2 5B 108
Bevan St. N1 1C 84
Bev Callender Cl. SW8 3F 119
Bevenden St. N1 1F 9 (3D 84)
Bevercote Wlk. *DA17: Belv* 6F 109
(off Osborne Rd.)
Beveree Stadium 1F 149
Beveridge Ct. *SE28* 7B 90
(off Saunders Way)
Beveridge Rd. NW10 7A 62
Beverley Av. DA15: Sidc 7K 125
SW20 1B 152
TW4: Houn 4D 112
Beverley Cl. EN1: Enf 4K 23
KT9: Chess 4C 162
N21 1H 33
SW11 4B 118
SW13 2C 116
Beverley Cotts. SW15 3A 134
Beverley Ct. HA2: Harr 3H 41
HA3: Kent 4C 42
N2 4D 46
(off Western Rd.)
N14 7B 22
NW6 7A 64
(off Fairfax Rd.)
SE4 3B 122
(not continuous)
TW4: Houn 4D 112
W4 5J 97
Beverley Cres. IG8: Wfd G 1K 51
Beverley Dr. HA8: Edg 3G 43
Beverley Gdns. HA7: Stan 1A 42
HA9: Wemb 1F 61
KT4: Wor Pk 1C 164
NW11 7G 45
SW13 3B 116
Beverley Ho. *BR1: Brom* 5F 141
(off Brangbourne Rd.)
Beverley Hyrst CR0: C'don 2F 169
Beverley La. KT2: King T 7A 134
SW15 3B 134
Beverley M. E4 6A 36
Beverley Path SW13 2B 116
Beverley Rd. BR2: Brom 2C 172
CR4: Mitc 4H 155
DA7: Bex 2J 127
E4 6A 36
E6 3B 88
HA4: Ruis 2J 57
KT1: Ham W 1C 150
KT3: N Mald 4C 152
KT4: Wor Pk 2E 164
RM9: Dag 4E 72
SE20 2H 157
SW13 3B 116
TW16: Sun 1H 147
UB2: S'hall 4C 94
W4 5B 98
Beverley Trad. Est. SM4: Mord 7F 153
Beverley Way KT3: N Mald 1B 152
SW20 1B 152
Beversbrook Rd. N19 3H 65
Beverstone Rd. CR7: Thor H 4A 156
SW2 5K 119
Beverston M. W1 6E 4
Bevill Allen Cl. SW17 5D 136
Bevill Cl. SE25 3G 157
Bevin Cl. SE16 1A 104
Bevin Ct. WC1 1H 7 (3K 83)
Bevington Path SE1 7J 15
Bevington Rd. BR3: Beck 2D 158
W10 5G 81
Bevington St. SE16 2G 103
Bevin Ho. *E2* 3J 85
(off Butler St.)
Bevin Rd. UB4: Yead 3J 75
Bevin Sq. SW17 3D 136
Bevin Way WC1 1J 7 (2A 84)
Bevis Marks EC3 7H 9 (6E 84)
Bewcastle Gdns. EN2: Enf 4D 22
Bew Ct. SE22 7G 121
Bewdley St. N1 7A 66
Bewick M. SE15 7H 103
Bewick St. SW8 2F 119
Bewley Ho. *E1* 7H 85
(off Bewley St.)
Bewley St. E1 7J 85
SW19 6A 136
Bewlys Rd. SE27 5B 138
Bexhill Cl. TW13: Felt 2C 130
Bexhill Rd. N11 5C 32
SE4 6B 122
SW14 3J 115
Bexhill Wlk. E15 1G 87
BEXLEY 7G 127
Bexley Gdns. N9 3J 33
RM6: Chad H 5B 54
BEXLEYHEATH 4F 127

Bexleyheath Sports Club . . . 3C 126
Bexley High St. DA5: Bexl . . . 7G 127
Bexley Ho. SE4 . . . 4A 122
Bexley La. DA1: Cray . . . 5K 127
DA14: Sidc . . . 4C 144
Bexley Lawn Tennis & Squash Club . . . 7G 127
Bexley Mus. . . . 6J 127
Bexley Music & Dance Cen. . . . 4A 144
(off Station Rd.)
Bexley Rd. DA8: Erith . . . 7J 109
SE9 . . . 5F 125
Beynon Rd. SM5: Cars . . . 5D 166
BFI Southbank . . . 4H 13
Bianca Ho. N1 . . . 1G 9
(off Arden Est.)
Bianca Rd. SE15 . . . 6G 103
Bibsworth Rd. N3 . . . 2H 45
Bibury Cl. SE15 . . . 6E 102
(not continuous)
Bicester Rd. TW9: Rich . . . 3G 115
Bickels Yd. SE1 . . . 2E 102
Bickenhall Mans. W1 . . . 5F 5
(not continuous)
Bickenhall St. W1 . . . 5F 5 (5D 82)
Bickersteth Rd. SW17 . . . 6D 136
Bickerton Rd. N19 . . . 2G 65
BICKLEY . . . 3C 160
Bickley Cres. BR1: Brom . . . 4C 160
Bickley Pk. Rd. BR1: Brom . . . 3C 160
Bickley Rd. BR1: Brom . . . 2B 160
E10 . . . 7D 50
Bickley St. SW17 . . . 5C 136
Bicknell Ho. E1 . . . 6G 85
(off Ellen St.)
Bicknell Rd. SE5 . . . 3C 120
Bicknoller Rd. EN1: Enf . . . 1K 23
Bicknor Rd. BR6: Orp . . . 7J 161
Bidborough Cl. BR2: Brom . . . 5H 159
Bidborough St. WC1 . . . 2E 6 (3J 83)
Biddenden Way SE9 . . . 4E 142
Biddenham Ho. SE16 . . . 4K 103
(off Plough Way)
Bidder St. E16 . . . 5G 87
(not continuous)
Biddesden Ho. SW3 . . . 4E 16
(off Cadogan St.)
Biddestone Rd. N7 . . . 4K 65
Biddulph Ho. SE18 . . . 4D 106
Biddulph Mans. W9 . . . 3K 81
(off Elgin Av.)
Biddulph Rd. W9 . . . 3K 81
Bideford Av. UB6: G'frd . . . 2B 78
Bideford Cl. HA8: Edg . . . 1G 43
TW13: Hanw . . . 3D 130
Bideford Gdns. EN1: Enf . . . 7K 23
Bideford Rd. BR1: Brom . . . 3H 141
DA16: Well . . . 7B 108
EN3: Enf L . . . 1G 25
HA4: Ruis . . . 3K 57
Bidwell Gdns. N11 . . . 7B 32
Bidwell St. SE15 . . . 1H 121
Big Ben . . . 7F 13 (2J 101)
Bigbury Cl. N17 . . . 7J 33
Biggerstaff Rd. E15 . . . 1E 86
Biggerstaff St. N4 . . . 2A 66
Biggin Av. CR4: Mitc . . . 1D 154
Biggin Hill SE19 . . . 1B 156
Biggin Hill Cl. KT2: King T . . . 5C 132
Biggin Way SE19 . . . 7B 138
Bigginwood Rd. SW16 . . . 7B 138
Biggs Row SW15 . . . 3F 117
Big Hill E5 . . . 1H 67
Bigland St. E1 . . . 6H 85
Bignell Rd. SE18 . . . 5F 107
Bignold Rd. E7 . . . 4J 69
Bigwood Ct. NW11 . . . 5K 45
Bigwood Rd. NW11 . . . 5K 45
Bilberry Ho. E3 . . . 5C 86
(off Watts Gro.)
Billet Cl. RM6: Chad H . . . 3D 54
Billet Rd. E17 . . . 1K 49
RM6: Chad H . . . 3B 54
Billets Hart Cl. W7 . . . 2J 95
Bill Hamling Cl. SE9 . . . 2D 142
Billing Cl. RM9: Dag . . . 7C 72
Billingford Cl. SE4 . . . 4K 121
Billing Ho. E1 . . . 6K 85
(off Bower St.)
Billingley NW1 . . . 1G 83
(off Pratt St.)
Billing Pl. SW10 . . . 7K 99
Billing Rd. SW10 . . . 7K 99
Billingsgate Fish Market . . . 1D 104
Billing St. SW10 . . . 7K 99
Billington M. W3 . . . 1H 97
(off High St.)
Billington Rd. SE14 . . . 7K 103
Billinton Hill CR0: C'don . . . 2D 168
Billiter Sq. EC3 . . . 1H 15
Billiter St. EC3 . . . 1H 15 (6E 84)
Bill Nicholson Way N17 . . . 7A 34
(off High Rd.)
Billockby Cl. KT9: Chess . . . 6F 163
Billson St. E14 . . . 4E 104
Bilsby Gro. SE9 . . . 4B 142
Bilsby Lodge HA9: Wemb . . . 3J 61
(off Chalklands)
Bilton Cen., The UB6: G'frd . . . 1B 78
Bilton Rd. UB6: G'frd . . . 1A 78
Bilton Towers W1 . . . 1F 11
(off Gt. Cumberland Pl.)
Bilton Way EN3: Enf L . . . 1F 25
UB3: Hayes . . . 2K 93
Bina Gdns. SW5 . . . 4A 100
Binbrook Ho. W10 . . . 5E 80
(off Sutton Way)
Bincote Rd. EN2: Enf . . . 3E 22
Binden Rd. W12 . . . 3B 98
Bindon Grn. SM4: Mord . . . 4K 153
Binfield Rd. CR2: S Croy . . . 5F 169
SW4 . . . 1J 119
Bingfield St. N1 . . . 1J 83
(not continuous)
Bingham Ct. N1 . . . 7B 66
(off Halton Rd.)
Bingham Pl. W1 . . . 5G 5 (5E 82)
Bingham Point SE18 . . . 4F 107
(off Wilmount St.)
Bingham Rd. CR0: C'don . . . 1G 169
Bingham St. N1 . . . 6D 66
Bingley Rd. E16 . . . 6A 88
TW16: Sun . . . 7J 129
UB6: G'frd . . . 4G 77
Binley Ho. SW15 . . . 6B 116
Binney St. W1 . . . 1H 11 (6E 82)
Binnie Ct. SE10 . . . 7D 104
(off Greenwich High Rd.)
Binnie Ho. SE1 . . . 3C 102
(off Bath Ter.)
Binnington Twr. BR2: Brom . . . 6C 160
Binns Rd. W4 . . . 5A 98
Binns Ter. W4 . . . 5A 98
Binsey Wlk. SE2 . . . 2C 108
(not continuous)
Binstead Cl. UB4: Yead . . . 5C 76
Binyon Cres. HA7: Stan . . . 5E 26
Birbetts Rd. SE9 . . . 2D 142
Bircham Path SE4 . . . 4K 121
(off Aldersford Cl.)
Birchanger Rd. SE25 . . . 5G 157
Birch Av. N13 . . . 3H 33
UB7: Yiew . . . 6B 74
Birch Cl. E16 . . . 5G 87
IG9: Buck H . . . 3G 37
N19 . . . 2G 65
RM7: Mawney . . . 3H 55
SE15 . . . 2G 121
TW3: Houn . . . 2H 113
TW8: Bford . . . 7B 96
Birch Cl. TW11: Tedd . . . 5A 132
TW17: Shep . . . 2G 147
Birch Ct. N12 . . . 4E 30
RM6: Chad H . . . 6C 54
SM1: Sutt . . . 4A 166
SM6: Wall . . . 4F 167
Birch Cres. UB10: Uxb . . . 1B 74
Birchdale Gdns. RM6: Chad H . . . 7D 54
Birchdale Rd. E7 . . . 5A 70
Birchdene Dr. SE28 . . . 1A 108
Birchen Cl. NW9 . . . 2K 61
Birchend Cl. CR2: S Croy . . . 6D 168
Birchen Gro. NW9 . . . 2K 61
Birches, The BR2: Brom . . . 4H 159
(off Durham Rd.)
BR6: Farnb . . . 4E 172
E12 . . . 4C 70
N21 . . . 6E 22
SE7 . . . 6K 105
TW4: Houn . . . 7D 112
Birches Cl. CR4: Mitc . . . 3D 154
HA5: Pinn . . . 5C 40
Birchfield Ct. KT12: Walt T . . . 7K 147
(off Grove Cres.)
Birchfield Ho. E14 . . . 7C 86
(off Birchfield St.)
Birchfield St. E14 . . . 7C 86
Birch Gdns. RM10: Dag . . . 3J 73
Birch Grn. NW9 . . . 7F 29
Birch Gro. DA16: Well . . . 4A 126
E11 . . . 4G 69
SE12 . . . 7H 123
TW17: Shep . . . 2G 147
W3 . . . 1G 97
Birchgrove Ho. TW9: Kew . . . 7H 97
Birch Hill CR0: C'don . . . 5K 169
Birch Ho. N22 . . . 1A 48
(off Acacia Rd.)
SE14 . . . 1B 122
SW2 . . . 6A 120
(off Tulse Hill)
W10 . . . 4G 81
(off Droop St.)
Birchington Cl. DA7: Bex . . . 1H 127
Birchington Ct. NW6 . . . 1K 81
(off West End La.)
Birchington Ho. E5 . . . 5H 67
Birchington Rd. KT5: Surb . . . 7F 151
N8 . . . 6H 47
NW6 . . . 1J 81
Birchin La. EC3 . . . 1F 15 (6D 84)
Birchlands Av. SW12 . . . 7D 118
Birchmead BR6: Farnb . . . 2E 172
Birchmead Av. HA5: Pinn . . . 4A 40
Birchmere Bus. Pk. SE28 . . . 2A 108
Birchmere Lodge SE16 . . . 5H 103
(off Sherwood Gdns.)
Birchmere Row SE3 . . . 2H 123
Birchmore Hall N5 . . . 3C 66
Birchmore Wlk. N5 . . . 3C 66
Birch Pk. HA3: Hrw W . . . 7B 26
Birch Rd. RM7: Mawney . . . 3H 55
TW13: Hanw . . . 5B 130
Birch Row BR2: Brom . . . 7E 160
Birch Tree Av.
BR4: W W'ck . . . 5H 171
Birch Tree Way CR0: C'don . . . 2H 169
Birch Va. Ct. NW8 . . . 3B 4
(off Pollitt Dr.)
Birchville Ct. WD23: B Hea . . . 1D 26
Birch Wlk. CR4: Mitc . . . 1F 155
DA8: Erith . . . 6J 109
Birchway UB3: Hayes . . . 1J 93
Birchwood Av. BR3: Beck . . . 4B 158
DA14: Sidc . . . 2B 144
N10 . . . 3E 46
SM6: Wall . . . 3E 166
Birchwood Cl. SM4: Mord . . . 4K 153
Birchwood Ct. HA8: Edg . . . 2J 43
N13 . . . 5G 33
Birchwood Dr. DA2: Dart . . . 4K 145
NW3 . . . 3K 63
Birchwood Gro. TW12: Hamp . . . 6E 130
Birchwood Pde. DA2: Dart . . . 4K 145
Birchwood Rd. BR5: Pet W . . . 4H 161
BR8: Swan . . . 7J 145
DA2: Dart . . . 7J 145
SW17 . . . 5F 137
Birdbrook Cl. RM10: Dag . . . 7J 73
Birdbrook Ho. N1 . . . 7C 66
(off Popham Rd.)
Birdbrook Rd. SE3 . . . 3A 124
Birdcage Wlk. SW1 . . . 7A 12 (2G 101)
Birdham Cl. BR1: Brom . . . 5C 160
Birdhurst Av. CR2: S Croy . . . 4D 168
Birdhurst Ct. SM6: Wall . . . 7G 167
(off Woodcote Av.)
Birdhurst Gdns. CR2: S Croy . . . 4D 168
Birdhurst Ri. CR2: S Croy . . . 5E 168
Birdhurst Rd. CR2: S Croy . . . 5E 168
SW18 . . . 5A 118
SW19 . . . 6C 136
Bird in Bush BMX Track . . . 7H 103
(off Bird in Bush Rd.)
Bird in Bush Rd. SE15 . . . 7G 103
Bird in Hand La. BR1: Brom . . . 2B 160
Bird-in-Hand Pas. SE23 . . . 2J 139
Bird in Hand Path CR0: C'don . . . 7D 156
(off Sydenham Rd.)
Bird in Hand Yd. NW3 . . . 4A 64
(off Holly Bush Va.)
NW3 . . . 4A 64
(Perrin's Ct.)
Birdsall Ho. SE5 . . . 3E 120
Birds Farm Av. RM5: Col R . . . 1H 55
Birdsfield La. E3 . . . 1B 86
Bird St. W1 . . . 1H 11 (6E 82)
Bird Wlk. TW2: Whitt . . . 1D 130
Birdwood Cl. TW11: Tedd . . . 4J 131
Birkbeck Av. UB6: G'frd . . . 1G 77
W3 . . . 7J 79
Birkbeck College . . . 5D 6 (5H 83)
Birkbeck Ct. W3 . . . 1K 97
Birkbeck Gdns. IG8: Wfd G . . . 2D 36
Birkbeck Gro. W3 . . . 2K 97
Birkbeck Hill SE21 . . . 1B 138
Birkbeck M. E8 . . . 5F 67
W3 . . . 1K 97
Birkbeck Pl. SE21 . . . 2C 138
Birkbeck Rd. BR3: Beck . . . 2J 157
DA14: Sidc . . . 3A 144
E8 . . . 5F 67
EN2: Enf . . . 1J 23
IG2: Ilf . . . 5H 53
N8 . . . 4J 47
N12 . . . 5F 31
N17 . . . 1F 49
NW7 . . . 5G 29
RM7: Rush G . . . 1K 73
SW19 . . . 5K 135
W3 . . . 1K 97
W5 . . . 4C 96
Birkbeck St. E2 . . . 3H 85
Birkbeck Way UB6: G'frd . . . 1H 77
Birkdale Av. HA5: Pinn . . . 3E 40
Birkdale Cl. BR6: Orp . . . 7H 161
SE16 . . . 5H 103
SE28 . . . 6D 90
Birkdale Ct. UB1: S'hall . . . 6G 77
(off Redcroft Rd.)
Birkdale Gdns. CR0: C'don . . . 4K 169
Birkdale Rd. SE2 . . . 4A 108
W5 . . . 4E 78
Birkenhead Av. KT2: King T . . . 2F 151
Birkenhead St. WC1 . . . 1F 7 (3J 83)
Birkhall Rd. SE6 . . . 1F 141
Birkwood Cl. SW12 . . . 7H 119
Birley Lodge NW8 . . . 2B 82
(off Acacia Rd.)
Birley Rd. N20 . . . 2F 31

Birley St. SW11 2E 118
Birling Rd. DA8: Erith 7K 109
Birnam Rd. N4 2K 65
Birnbeck Ct. EN5: Barn 4A 20
NW11 5H 45
Birrell Ho. SW9 2K 119
(off Stockwell Rd.)
Birse Cres. NW10 3A 62
Birstall Rd. N15 5E 48
Biscay Ho. E1 4K 85
(off Mile End Rd.)
Biscayne Av. E14 1F 105
Biscay Rd. W6 5F 99
Biscoe Cl. TW5: Hest 6E 94
Biscoe Way SE13 3F 123
Biscott Ho. E3 4D 86
Bisenden Rd. CR0: C'don 2E 168
Bisham Cl. SM5: Cars 1D 166
Bisham Gdns. N6 1E 64
Bishop Butt Cl. BR6: Orp 3K 173
Bishop Ct. TW9: Rich 3E 114
Bishop Duppas Pk.
TW17: Shep 7G 147
Bishop Fox Way KT8: W Mole 4D 148
Bishopgate Chu. Yd. EC2 7G 9 (5E 84)
Bishop Hall UB8: Cowl 3A 74
(off Kingston La.)
Bishop Ken Rd. HA3: W'stone 2K 41
Bishop King's Rd. W14 4G 99
Bishop Ramsey C of E School Sports Hall 7J 39
(off Highgrove Way)
Bishop Rd. N14 7A 22
Bishops Av. BR1: Brom 2A 160
E13 1K 87
RM6: Chad H 6C 54
SW6 2F 117
Bishops Av., The N2 7B 46
Bishop's Bri. Rd. W2 6A 4 (6K 81)
Bishops Cl. E17 4D 50
EN1: Enf 2C 24
EN5: Barn 6A 20
N19 3G 65
SE9 2G 143
SM1: Sutt 3J 165
TW10: Ham 3D 132
UB10: Hil 2C 74
W4 5J 97
Bishops Ct. CR0: C'don 2F 169
EC4 7A 8
HA0: Wemb 4B 60
W2 6K 81
(off Bishop's Bri. Rd.)
WC2 7J 7
Bishopsdale Ho. NW6 1J 81
(off Kilburn Va.)
Bishops Dr. TW14: Bedf 6F 111
UB5: N'olt 1C 76
Bishopsford Rd. SM4: Mord 7A 154
Bishopsgate EC2 1G 15 (6E 84)
Bishopsgate Arc. EC2 6H 9
Bishopsgate Institute & Libraries 6H 9
(off Bishopsgate)
Bishops Grn. BR1: Brom 1A 160
Bishops Gro. N2 6C 46
TW12: Hamp 4D 130
Bishops Gro. Cvn. Site
TW12: Hamp 4E 130
Bishop's Hall KT1: King T 2D 150
Bishops Hill KT12: Walt T 7J 147
Bishops Ho. SW8 7J 101
(off Sth. Lambeth Rd.)
Bishop's Mans. SW6 2F 117
(not continuous)
Bishops Mead SE5 7C 102
(off Camberwell Rd.)
Bishops Pk. Rd. SW6 2F 117
SW16 1J 155
Bishops Pl. SM1: Sutt 5A 166
Bishops Rd. CR0: C'don 7B 156
N6 6E 46
SW6 1G 117
SW11 7C 100
UB3: Hayes 6E 74
W7 2J 95
Bishops Sq. E1 5H 9 (5E 84)
Bishop's Ter. SE11 3K 19 (4A 102)
Bishopsthorpe Rd. SE26 4K 139
Bishop St. N1 1C 84
Bishops Vw. Ct. N10 4F 47
Bishops Wlk. BR7: Chst 1G 161
CR0: Addtn 5K 169
HA5: Pinn 3C 40
Bishops Way E2 2H 85
NW10 7A 62
Bishops Wood Almshouses E5 4H 67
(off Lwr. Clapton Rd.)
Bishopswood Rd. N6 7D 46
Bishop Wilfred Wood Cl. SE15 2G 121
Bishop Wilfred Wood Ct. E13 2A 88
(off Pragel St.)
Bisley Cl. KT4: Wor Pk 1E 164
Bison Ct. TW14: Felt 7K 111
Bispham Rd. NW10 3F 79
Bissextile Ho. SE13 2D 122
Bisson Rd. E15 2E 86
Bisterne Av. E17 3F 51
Bittacy Bus. Cen. NW7 6B 30
Bittacy Cl. NW7 6A 30
Bittacy Ct. NW7 7B 30
Bittacy Hill NW7 6A 30
Bittacy Pk. Av. NW7 5A 30
Bittacy Ri. NW7 7K 29
Bittacy Rd. NW7 6A 30
Bittern Cl. UB4: Yead 5B 76
Bittern Ct. NW9 2A 44
SE8 6C 104
Bittern Ho. SE1 7C 14
(off Gt. Suffolk St.)
Bittern Pl. N22 2K 47
Bittern St. SE1 7C 14 (2C 102)
Bittoms, The KT1: King T 3D 150
(not continuous)
Bittoms Ct. KT1: King T 3D 150
Bixley Cl. UB2: S'hall 4D 94
Blackall St. EC2 3G 9 (4E 84)
Blackberry Cl. TW17: Shep 4G 147
Blackberry Ct. HA9: Wemb 7E 42
Blackberry Farm Cl. TW5: Hest 7C 94
Blackberry Fld. BR5: St P 7A 144
Blackbird Ct. NW9 3K 61
Blackbird Hill NW9 2J 61
Blackbird Yd. E2 1K 9 (3F 85)
Blackborne Rd. RM10: Dag 6G 73
Black Boy La. N15 5C 48
Blackbrook La. BR1: Brom 5D 160
BR2: Brom 5E 160
Black Bull Yd. EC1 5K 7
(off Hatton Wall)
Blackburn NW9 2B 44
Blackburne's M. W1 2G 11 (7E 82)
Blackburn Rd. NW6 6K 63
Blackburn Trad. Est.
TW19: Stanw 6B 110
Blackburn Way TW4: Houn 5C 112
Blackbush Av. RM6: Chad H 5D 54
Blackbush Cl. SM2: Sutt 7K 165
Blackdown Cl. N2 2A 46
Blackdown Ter. SE18 1D 124
Blackett St. SW15 3F 117
Black Fan Cl. EN2: Enf 1H 23
BLACKFEN 7A 126
Blackfen Pde. DA15: Sidc 6A 126
Blackfen Rd. DA15: Sidc 5J 125
Blackford Cl. CR2: S Croy 7B 168
Blackford's Path SW15 7C 116
Blackfriars Bri. EC4 2A 14 (7B 84)
SE1 7B 84
Blackfriars Ct. EC4 2A 14
Black Friars La. EC4 2A 14 (6B 84)
(not continuous)
Blackfriars Pas. EC4 2A 14 (7B 84)
Blackfriars Rd. SE1 4A 14 (2B 102)
Blackfriars Underpass EC4 2A 14 (7A 84)
Black Gates HA5: Pinn 3D 40
BLACKHEATH 2H 123
Blackheath Av. SE10 7F 105
Blackheath Bus. Est. SE10 1E 122
(off Blackheath Hill)
Blackheath Concert Halls 3H 123
Blackheath Gro. SE3 2H 123
Blackheath Hill SE10 1E 122
BLACKHEATH PARK 3J 123
Blackheath Pk. SE3 3H 123
Blackheath Ri. SE13 2E 122
(not continuous)
Blackheath Rd. SE10 1D 122
BLACKHEATH VALE 2H 123
Blackheath Va. SE3 2G 123
Blackheath Village SE3 2H 123
Black Horse Ct. SE1 3D 102
Blackhorse La. CR0: C'don 7G 157
E17 2K 49
Blackhorse M. E17 3K 49
Black Horse Pde. HA5: Eastc 5K 39
BLACKHORSE ROAD 4K 49
Blackhorse Rd.
DA14: Sidc 4A 144
E17 4K 49
SE8 6A 104
Blacklands Dr. UB4: Hayes 4E 74
Blacklands Rd. SE6 4E 140
Blacklands Ter. SW3 4E 16 (4D 100)
Black Lion La. W6 4C 98
Black Lion M. W6 4C 98
Blackmans Yd. E2 3K 9
(off Cheshire St.)
Blackmore Av. UB1: S'hall 1H 95
Blackmore Dr. NW10 7H 61
Blackmore Ho. N1 1K 83
(off Barnsbury Est.)
Blackmore Rd. IG9: Buck H 1H 37
Blackmore's Gro. TW11: Tedd 6A 132
Blackmore Twr. W3 3J 97
(off Stanley Rd.)
Blackness La. BR2: Kes 7B 172
Black Path E10 7A 50
Blackpool Gdns. UB4: Hayes 4G 75
Blackpool Rd. SE15 2H 121
BLACK PRINCE INTERCHANGE 6H 127
Black Prince Rd. SE1 4G 19 (4K 101)
SE11 4G 19 (4K 101)
Black Rod Cl. UB3: Hayes 3H 93
Blackshaw Rd. SW17 4A 136
Blacksmiths Cl. RM6: Chad H 6C 54
Blacksmiths Ho. E17 4C 50
(off Gillards M.)
Blacks Rd. W6 5E 98
Blackstock M. N4 2B 66
Blackstock Rd. N4 2B 66
N5 2B 66
Blackstone Est. E8 7G 67
Blackstone Ho. SW1 6A 18
(off Churchill Gdns.)
Blackstone Rd. NW2 5E 62
Black Swan Yd. SE1 6H 15 (2E 102)
Blackthorn Av. UB7: W Dray 4C 92
Blackthorn Ct. E15 4F 69
(off Hall Rd.)
TW5: Hest 7C 94
Blackthorne Av. CR0: C'don 1J 169
Blackthorne Ct. SE15 7F 103
(off Cator St.)
TW15: Ashf 7E 128
UB1: S'hall 1F 95
(off Dormer's Wells La.)
Blackthorne Cres. SL3: Poyle 5A 174
Blackthorne Dr. E4 4A 36
Blackthorne Ind. Est. SL3: Poyle 6A 174
Blackthorne Rd. SL3: Poyle 5A 174
Blackthorn Gro. DA7: Bex 3E 126
Blackthorn Rd. IG1: Ilf 5H 71
Blackthorn St. E3 4C 86
Blacktree M. SW9 3A 120
BLACKWALL 1E 104
Blackwall La. SE10 5G 105
Blackwall Trad. Est. E14 5F 87
Blackwall Tunnel E14 1F 105
(not continuous)
SE10 1F 105
Blackwall Tunnel App. E14 6E 86
Blackwall Tunnel Northern App.
E3 2D 86
E14 2C 86
Blackwall Tunnel Southern App.
SE10 3G 105
Blackwall Way E14 1E 104
Blackwater Cl. E7 4H 69
RM13: Rain 5K 91
Blackwater Ho. NW8 5B 4
(off Church St.)
Blackwater St. SE22 5F 121
Blackwell Cl. E5 4K 67
HA3: Hrw W 7C 26
Blackwell Gdns. HA8: Edg 4B 28
Blackwell Ho. SW4 6H 119
Blackwood Av. N18 5E 34
Blackwood Ho. E1 4H 85
(off Collingwood St.)
Blackwood St. SE17 5D 102
Blade M. SW15 4H 117
Bladen Ho. E1 6K 85
(off Dunelm St.)
Blades Ct. SW15 4H 117
W6 5D 98
(off Lower Mall)
Blades Ho. SE11 7J 19
(off Kennington Oval)
Bladindon Dr. DA5: Bexl 7C 126
Bladon Ct. SW16 6J 137
Bladon Gdns. HA2: Harr 6F 41
Blagdens Cl. N14 2C 32
Blagdens La. N14 2B 32
Blagdon Ct. W7 7J 77
Blagdon Rd.
KT3: N Mald 4B 152
(not continuous)
SE13 6D 122
Blagdon Wlk.
TW11: Tedd 6C 132
Blagrove Rd. W10 5G 81
Blair Av. NW9 7A 44
Blair Cl. DA15: Sidc 5J 125
N1 6C 66
UB3: Harl 4J 93
Blair Ct. BR3: Beck 1D 158
NW8 1B 82
SE6 1H 141
Blairderry Rd. SW2 2J 137
Blairgowrie Ct. E14 6F 87
(off Blair St.)
Blair Ho. SW9 2K 119
Blair St. E14 6E 86
Blake Av. IG11: Bark 1J 89
Blake Bldg. N8 3K 47
Blake Cl. DA16: Well 1J 125
SM5: Cars 1C 166
UB4: Hayes 2F 75
Blake Ct. N21 5E 22
NW6 3J 81
(off Malvern Rd.)
SE16 5H 103
(off Stubbs Dr.)
Blakeden Dr.
KT10: Clay 6A 162
Blake Gdns. SW6 1K 117
Blake Hall Cres. E11 1J 69
Blake Hall Rd. E11 7J 51
Blakehall Rd. SM5: Cars 6D 166

Blake Ho. *E14* *2C 104*
(off Admirals Way)
SE1 1J **19** (3A **102**)
SE8 *6C 104*
(off New King St.)
Blakeley Cotts. SE10 2F **105**
Blake M. TW9: Kew 1G **115**
Blakemore Gdns. SW13 6D **98**
Blakemore Rd. CR7: Thor H 5K **155**
SW16 3J **137**
Blakemore Way DA17: Belv 3E **108**
Blakeney Av. BR3: Beck 1B **158**
Blakeney Cl. E8 5G **67**
N20 1F **31**
NW1 7H **65**
Blakeney Rd. BR3: Beck 7B **140**
Blakenham Rd. SW17 4D **136**
Blaker Ct. SE7 7A **106**
(not continuous)
Blake Rd. CR0: C'don 2E **168**
CR4: Mitc 3C **154**
E16 4H **87**
N11 7B **32**
Blaker Rd. E15 2E **86**
Blakes Av. KT3: N Mald 5B **152**
Blakes Cl. W10 5E **80**
Blake's Grn. BR4: W W'ck 1E **170**
Blakes La. KT3: N Mald 5B **152**
Blakesley Av. W5 6C **78**
Blakesley Wlk. SW20 2H **153**
Blake's Rd. SE15 7E **102**
Blakes Ter. KT3: N Mald 5C **152**
Blakesware Gdns. N9 7J **23**
Blakewood Cl. TW13: Hanw 4A **130**
Blakewood Ct. *SE20* *7H 139*
(off Anerley Pk.)
Blanchard Cl. SE9 3C **142**
Blanchard Ho. *TW1: Twick* *6D 114*
(off Clevedon Rd.)
Blanchard Way E8 6G **67**
Blanch Cl. SE15 7J **103**
Blanchedowne SE5 4D **120**
Blanche St. E16 4H **87**
Blanchland Rd. SM4: Mord 5K **153**
Blandfield Rd. SW12 7E **118**
Blandford Av. BR3: Beck 2A **158**
TW2: Whitt 1F **131**
Blandford Cl. CR0: Bedd 3J **167**
N2 4A **46**
RM7: Mawney 4H **55**
Blandford Ct. *N1* *7E 66*
(off St Peter's Way)
NW6 7F **63**
Blandford Cres. E4 7K **25**
Blandford Ho. *SW8* *7K 101*
(off Richborne Ter.)
Blandford Rd. BR3: Beck 2J **157**
TW11: Tedd 5H **131**
UB2: S'hall 4E **94**
W4 3A **98**
W5 2D **96**
Blandford Sq. NW1 4D **4** (4C **82**)
Blandford St. W1 7F **5** (6D **82**)
Blandford Waye
UB4: Yead 6A **76**
Bland Ho. SE11 5H **19**
Bland St. SE9 4B **124**
Blaney Cres. E6 3F **89**
Blanmerle Rd. SE9 1F **143**
Blann Cl. SE9 6B **124**
Blantyre St. SW10 7B **100**
Blantyre Twr. *SW10* *7B 100*
(off Blantyre St.)
Blantyre Wlk. *SW10* *7B 100*
(off Worlds End Est.)
Blashford *NW3* *7D 64*
(off Adelaide Rd.)
Blashford St. SE13 7F **123**
Blasker Wlk. E14 5D **104**
Blawith Rd. HA1: Harr 4J **41**
Blaxland Ho. *W12* *7D 80*
(off White City Est.)
Blaydon Cl. HA4: Ruis 7G **39**
N17 7C **34**
Blaydon Ct. UB5: N'olt 6E **58**
Blaydon Wlk. N17 7C **34**
Blazer Ct. NW8 2B **4**
Bleak Hill La. SE18 6K **107**
Blean Gro. SE20 7J **139**
Bleasdale Av. UB6: G'frd 2A **78**
Blechynden Ho. *W10* *6F 81*
(off Kingsdown Cl.)
Blechynden St. W10 7F **81**
Bledlow Cl. NW8 4B **4** (4B **82**)
SE28 7C **90**
Bledlow Ri. UB6: G'frd 2G **77**
Bleeding Heart Yd. EC1 6K **7**
Blegborough Rd. SW16 6G **137**
Blemundsbury *WC1* *5G 7*
(off Dombey St.)
BLENDON **6D 126**
Blendon Dr. DA5: Bexl 6D **126**
Blendon Path BR1: Brom 7H **141**
Blendon Rd. DA5: Bexl 6D **126**
Blendon Row *SE17* *4D 102*
(off Townley St.)
Blendon Ter. SE18 5G **107**
Blendworth Point SW15 1D **134**
Blenheim Av. IG2: Ilf 6E **52**
Blenheim Bus. Cen. *CR4: Mitc* *2D 154*
(off London Rd.)
Blenheim Cl. N21 1H **33**
RM7: Mawney 4J **55**
SE12 1K **141**
SM6: Wall 7G **167**
SW20 3E **152**
UB6: G'frd 2H **77**
Blenheim Ct. BR2: Brom 4H **159**
DA14: Sidc 3H **143**
HA3: Kent 6A **42**
IG8: Wfd G 7E **36**
N19 2J **65**
SE16 *1K 103*
(off King & Queen Wharf)
SM2: Sutt 6A **166**
Blenheim Cres. CR2: S Croy 7C **168**
HA4: Ruis 2F **57**
W11 7G **81**
Blenheim Dr. DA16: Well 1K **125**
Blenheim Gdns. HA9: Wemb 3E **60**
KT2: King T 7H **133**
NW2 6E **62**
SM6: Wall 6G **167**
SW2 6K **119**
Blenheim Gro. SE15 2G **121**
Blenheim Ho. *E16* *1K 105*
(off Constable Av.)
SE18 3G **107**
SW3 *6D 16*
(off Kings Rd.)
TW3: Houn 3E **112**
Blenheim Pde. UB10: Hil 4D **74**
Blenheim Pk. Rd. CR2: S Croy 7C **168**
Blenheim Pas. NW8 2A **82**
(not continuous)
Blenheim Pl. TW11: Tedd 5K **131**
Blenheim Ri. N15 4F **49**
Blenheim Rd. BR1: Brom 4C **160**
DA15: Sidc 1C **144**
E6 3B **88**
E15 4G **69**
E17 3K **49**
EN5: Barn 3A **20**
HA2: Harr 6F **41**
NW8 2A **82**
SE20 7J **139**
SM1: Sutt 3J **165**
SW20 3E **152**
UB5: N'olt 6F **59**
W4 3A **98**
Blenheim Shop. Cen. SE20 7J **139**
Blenheim St. W1 1J **11** (6F **83**)
Blenheim Ter. NW8 2A **82**
Blenheim Way TW7: Isle 1A **114**
Blenkarne Rd. SW11 6D **118**
Bleriot *NW9* *2B 44*
(off Belvedere Strand)
Bleriot Rd. TW5: Hest 7A **94**
Blessbury Rd. HA8: Edg 1J **43**
Blessington Cl. SE13 3F **123**
Blessington Rd. SE13 3F **123**
Blessing Way IG11: Bark 3C **90**
Bletchingley Cl. CR7: Thor H 4B **156**
Bletchley Ct. N1 1E **8**
Bletchley St. N1 1D **8** (2D **84**)
Bletchmore Cl. UB3: Harl 5F **93**
Bletsoe Wlk. N1 2C **84**
Blewbury Ho. SE2 2C **108**
(Tavy Bri.)
SE2 2D **108**
(Tilehurst Point)
Blick Ho. *SE16* *3J 103*
(off Neptune St.)
Blincoe Cl. SW19 2F **135**
Bliss Cres. SE13 2D **122**
Blissett St. SE10 1E **122**
Bliss Ho. EN1: Enf 1B **24**
Bliss M. W10 3G **81**
Blisworth Cl. UB4: Yead 4C **76**
Blisworth Ho. *E2* *1G 85*
(off Whiston Rd.)
Blithbury Rd. RM9: Dag 6B **72**
Blithdale Rd. SE2 4A **108**
Blithfield St. W8 3K **99**
Blockley Rd. HA0: Wemb 2B **60**
Block Wharf *E14* *2C 104*
(off Cuba St.)
Bloemfontein Av. W12 1D **98**
Bloemfontein Rd. W12 7D **80**
Bloemfontein Way W12 1D **98**
Blomfield Ct. *W9* *3A 4*
(off Maida Va.)
Blomfield Mans. *W12* *1E 98*
(off Stanlake Rd.)
Blomfield Rd. W9 4A **4** (5K **81**)
Blomfield St. EC2 6F **9** (5D **84**)
Blomfield Vs. W2 5K **81**
Blomville Rd. RM8: Dag 3E **72**
Blondell Cl. UB7: Harm 2E **174**
Blondel St. SW11 2E **118**
Blondin Av. W5 4C **96**
Blondin St. E3 2C **86**
Bloomburg St. SW1 4B **18** (4H **101**)
Bloomfield Ct. *E10* *3D 68*
(off Brisbane Rd.)
N6 6E **46**
Bloomfield Cres. IG2: Ilf 6F **53**
Bloomfield Ho. *E1* *5G 85*
(off Old Montague St.)
Bloomfield Pl. W1 2K **11**
Bloomfield Rd. BR2: Brom 5B **160**
KT1: King T 4E **150**
N6 6E **46**
SE18 6F **107**
Bloomfield Ter. SW1 5H **17** (5E **100**)
Bloom Gro. SE27 3B **138**
Bloomhall Rd. SE19 5D **138**
Bloom Pk. Rd. SW6 7H **99**
BLOOMSBURY **5E 6 (5J 83)**
Bloomsbury Cl. NW7 7H **29**
W5 7F **79**
Bloomsbury Ct. HA5: Pinn 3D **40**
TW5: Cran 1K **111**
WC1 6F **7**
Bloomsbury Ho. SW4 6H **119**
Bloomsbury Mans. *BR1: Brom* *1K 159*
(off Widmore Rd.)
Bloomsbury M. IG8: Wfd G 6H **37**
Bloomsbury Pl. SW18 5A **118**
WC1 5F **7** (5J **83**)
Bloomsbury Sq. WC1 6F **7** (5J **83**)
Bloomsbury St. WC1 6D **6** (5H **83**)
Bloomsbury Theatre 3C **6**
Bloomsbury Way WC1 6E **6** (5J **83**)
Blore Cl. SW8 1H **119**
Blore Ct. W1 1C **12**
Blore Ho. *SW10* *7K 99*
(off Coleridge Gdns.)
Blossom Cl. CR2: S Croy 5F **169**
RM9: Dag 1F **91**
W5 2E **96**
Blossom La. EN2: Enf 1H **23**
Blossom St. E1 4H **9** (4E **84**)
Blossom Way UB7: W Dray 4C **92**
UB10: Hil 7B **56**
Blossom Waye TW5: Hest 6C **94**
Blount St. E14 6A **86**
Bloxam Gdns. SE9 5C **124**
Bloxhall Rd. E10 1B **68**
Bloxham Cres. TW12: Hamp 7D **130**
Bloxworth Cl. SM6: Wall 3G **167**
Blucher Rd. SE5 7C **102**
Blue Anchor All. TW9: Rich 4E **114**
Blue Anchor La. SE16 4G **103**
Blue Anchor Yd. E1 2K **15** (7G **85**)
Blue Ball Yd. SW1 5A **12** (1G **101**)
Bluebell Av. E12 5B **70**
Blue Bell Cl. UB5: N'olt 6D **58**
Bluebell Cl. BR6: Farnb 2G **173**
E9 1J **85**
RM7: Rush G 2K **73**
SE26 4F **139**
SM6: Wall 1F **167**
Bluebell Way IG1: Ilf 6F **71**
Blueberry Cl. IG8: Wfd G 6D **36**
Bluebird La. RM10: Dag 7G **73**
Bluebird Way SE28 2H **107**
Blue Bldg. *SE10* *5H 105*
(off Glenforth St.)
Blue Ct. *N1* *1D 84*
(off Sherborne St.)
Blue Elephant Theatre *7C 102*
(off Bethwin Rd.)
Bluefield Cl. TW12: Hamp 5E **130**
Bluegate M. E1 7H **85**
Bluegates KT17: Ewe 7C **164**
Bluehouse Rd. E4 2B **36**
Blue Lion Pl. SE1 7G **15** (3E **102**)
Blueprint Apartments
SW12 *7F 119*
(off Balham Gro.)
Blue Riband Ind. Est.
CR0: C'don 2B **168**
Blue Water SW18 4K **117**
Blundell Cl. E8 5G **67**
Blundell Rd. HA8: Edg 1K **43**
Blundell St. N7 7J **65**
Blunden Cl. RM8: Dag 1C **72**
Blunt Rd. CR2: S Croy 5D **168**
Blunts Av. UB7: Sip 7C **92**
Blunts Rd. SE9 5E **124**
Blurton Rd. E5 4J **67**
Blydon Ct. *N21* *5E 22*
(off Chaseville Pk. Rd.)
Blyth Cl. E14 4F **105**
TW1: Twick 6K **113**
Blyth Ct. *BR1: Brom* *1H 159*
(off Blyth Rd.)
Blythe Cl. SE6 7B **122**
BLYTHE HILL 7B **122**
Blythe Hill BR5: St P 1K **161**
SE6 7B **122**
Blythe Hill La. SE6 7B **122**
Blythe Hill Pl. SE23 7A **122**
Blythe Ho. SE11 7J **19** (6A **102**)
Blythe M. W14 3F **99**
Blythendale Ho. *E2* *2G 85*
(off Mansford St.)
Blythe Rd. W14 3F **99**
(not continuous)

Blythe St. E2 3H 85
Blytheswood Pl. SW16 4K 137
Blythe Va. SE6 1B 140
Blyth Hill Pl. *SE23* 7A 122
(off Brockley Pk.)
Blyth Ho. DA8: Erith 5K 109
Blyth Rd. BR1: Brom 1H 159
E17 7B 50
SE28 7C 90
UB3: Hayes 2G 93
Blyth's Wharf E14 7A 86
Blythswood Rd. IG3: Ilf 1A 72
Blyth Wood Pk.
BR1: Brom 1H 159
Blythwood Rd. HA5: Pinn 1B 40
N4 7J 47
Boades M. NW3 4B 64
Boadicea St. N1 1K 83
Boakes Cl. NW9 4J 43
Boardman Av. E4 5J 25
Boardman Cl. EN5: Barn 5B 20
Boardwalk Pl. E14 1E 104
Boarhound *NW9* 2B 44
(off Further Acre)
Boarley Ho. *SE17* 4E 102
(off Massinger St.)
Boars Head Yd. TW8: Bford 7D 96
Boatemah Wlk. *SW9* 2A 120
(off Peckford Pl.)
Boathouse Cen., The *W10* 4F 81
(off Canal Cl.)
Boathouse Wlk. SE15 7F 103
(not continuous)
Boat Lifter Way SE16 4A 104
Boat Quay E16 7A 88
Bob Anker Cl. E13 3J 87
Bobbin Cl. SW4 3G 119
Bobby Moore Way N10 7J 31
Bob Hope Theatre, The 6D 124
Bob Marley Way SE24 4A 120
Bockhampton Rd. KT2: King T 7F 133
Bocking St. E8 1H 85
Boddicott Cl. SW19 2G 135
Boddington Gdns. W3 2G 97
Boddington Ho. *SE14* 1J 121
(off Pomeroy St.)
SW13 6D 98
(off Wyatt Dr.)
Bodeney Ho. *SE5* 1E 120
(off Peckham Rd.)
Boden Ho. *E1* 5K 9
(off Woodseer St.)
Bodiam Cl. EN1: Enf 2K 23
Bodiam Rd. SW16 7H 137
Bodiam Way NW10 3F 79
Bodicea M. TW4: Houn 6D 112
Bodington Ct. W12 2F 99
Bodley Cl. KT3: N Mald 5A 152
Bodley Mnr. Way SW2 7A 120
Bodley Rd. KT3: N Mald 6K 151
Bodmin *NW9* 2B 44
(off Further Acre)
Bodmin Cl. HA2: Harr 3D 58
Bodmin Gro. SM4: Mord 5K 153
Bodmin St. SW18 1J 135
Bodnant Gdns. SW20 3C 152
Bodney Rd. E8 5H 67
Boeing Way UB2: S'hall 3K 93
Boevey Path DA17: Belv 5F 109
Bogart Ct. *E14* 7C 86
(off Premiere Pl.)
Bogey La. BR6: Downe 7E 172
Bognor Rd. DA16: Well 1D 126
Bohemia Pl. E8 6J 67
Bohn Rd. E1 5A 86
Bohun Gro. EN4: E Barn 6H 21
Boileau Pde. *W5* 6F 79
(off Boileau Rd.)
Boileau Rd. SW13 7C 98
W5 6F 79
Boisseau Ho. *E1* 5J 85
(off Stepney Way)
Bolden St. SE8 2D 122
Boldero Pl. NW8 4C 4
Bolderwood Way BR4: W W'ck 2D 170
Boldmere Rd. HA5: Eastc 7A 40
Boleyn Av. EN1: Enf 1C 24
Boleyn Cl. E17 4C 50
Boleyn Ct. IG9: Buck H 1D 36
KT8: E Mos 4H 149
(off Bridge Rd.)
Boleyn Dr. HA4: Ruis 2B 58
KT8: W Mole 3D 148
Boleyn Gdns. BR4: W W'ck 2D 170
RM10: Dag 7J 73
Boleyn Gro. BR4: W W'ck 2E 170
Boleyn Ho. *E16* 1J 105
(off Southey M.)
Boleyn Rd. E6 2B 88
E7 7J 69
N16 5E 66
Boleyn Way EN5: New Bar 3F 21
Bolina Rd. SE16 5J 103
Bolingbroke Gro. SW11 4C 118
Bolingbroke Rd. W14 3F 99
Bolingbroke Wlk. SW11 1B 118
Bolingbroke Way UB3: Hayes 1F 93
Bolliger Ct. NW10 4J 79
Bollo Bri. Rd. W3 3H 97
Bollo Ct. *W3* 3J 97
(off Bollo Bri. Rd.)
Bollo La. W3 2H 97
W4 4J 97
Bolney Ga. SW7 7C 10 (2C 100)
Bolney St. SW8 7K 101
Bolney Way TW13: Hanw 3C 130
Bolsover St. W1 4K 5 (4F 83)
Bolstead Rd. CR4: Mitc 1F 155
Bolster Gro. N22 7C 32
Bolt Ct. EC4 1K 13
Boltmore Cl. NW4 3F 45
Bolton Cl. KT9: Chess 6D 162
SE20 2G 157
Bolton Cres. SE5 7B 102
Bolton Dr. SM4: Mord 7A 154
Bolton Gdns. BR1: Brom 6H 141
NW10 2F 81
SW5 5K 99
TW11: Tedd 6A 132
Bolton Gdns. M. SW10 5A 100
Bolton Ho. *SE10* 5G 105
(off Trafalgar Rd.)
Bolton Pl. *NW8* 1K 81
(off Bolton Rd.)
Bolton Rd. E15 6H 69
HA1: Harr 4G 41
KT9: Chess 6D 162
N18 5A 34
NW8 1K 81
NW10 1A 80
W4 7J 97
Boltons, The HA0: Wemb 4K 59
IG8: Wfd G 4D 36
SW10 5A 100
Boltons Ct. *SW5* 5K 99
(off Old Brompton Rd.)
Bolton's La. UB3: Harl 1E 110
(not continuous)
Boltons Pl. SW5 5A 100
Bolton St. W1 4K 11 (1F 101)
Bolton Studios SW10 5A 100
Bolton Wlk. *N7* 2K 65
(off Durham Rd.)
Bombay Ct. *SE16* 2J 103
(off St Marychurch St.)
Bombay St. SE16 4H 103
Bomer Cl. UB7: Sip 7C 92
Bomore Rd. W11 7G 81
Bonar Pl. BR7: Chst 7C 142
Bonar Rd. SE15 7G 103
Bonchester Cl. BR7: Chst 7E 142
Bonchurch Cl. SM2: Sutt 7K 165
Bonchurch Rd. W10 5G 81
W13 1B 96
Bond Cl. UB7: Yiew 6B 74
Bond Ct. EC4 2E 14 (7D 84)
Bondfield Av. UB4: Yead 3J 75
Bondfield Rd. E6 5D 88
Bond Gdns. SM6: Wall 4G 167
Bond Ho. *NW6* 2H 81
(off Rupert Rd.)
SE14 7A 104
(off Goodwood Rd.)
Bonding Yd. Wlk. SE16 3A 104
Bond Rd. CR4: Mitc 2C 154
KT6: Surb 2F 163
Bond St. E15 5G 69
W4 4K 97
W5 7D 78
Bondway SW8 7F 19 (6J 101)
Boneta Rd. SE18 3D 106
Bonfield Rd. SE13 4E 122
Bonham Gdns. RM8: Dag 2D 72
Bonham Ho. *W11* 1H 99
(off Boyne Ter. M.)
Bonham Rd. RM8: Dag 2D 72
SW2 5K 119
Bonheur Rd. W4 2K 97
Bonhill St. EC2 4F 9 (4D 84)
Boniface Gdns. HA3: Hrw W 7A 26
Boniface Rd. UB10: Ick 3D 56
Boniface Wlk. HA3: Hrw W 7A 26
Bonington Ho. EN1: Enf 5B 24
Bonita M. SE4 3K 121
Bon Marche Ter. M. *SE27* 4E 138
(off Gypsy Rd.)
Bonner Hill Rd. KT1: King T 2F 151
(not continuous)
Bonner Rd. E2 2J 85
Bonnersfield Cl. HA1: Harr 6K 41
Bonnersfield La. HA1: Harr 6K 41
(not continuous)
Bonner St. E2 2J 85
Bonneville Gdns. SW4 6G 119
Bonnington Ct. *UB5: N'olt* 2B 76
(off Gallery Gdns.)
Bonnington Ho. N1 2K 83
Bonnington Sq. SW8 7G 19 (6K 101)
Bonny St. NW1 7G 65
Bonser Rd. TW1: Twick 2K 131
Bonsor Ho. SW8 1G 119
Bonsor St. SE5 7E 102
Bonville Gdns. NW4 4D 44
Bonville Rd. BR1: Brom 5H 141
Bookbinders Cott. Homes N20 3J 31
Booker Cl. E14 5B 86
Booker Rd. N18 5B 34
Bookham Ct. CR4: Mitc 3B 154
Boone Ct. N9 3D 34
Boones Rd. SE13 4G 123
Boone St. SE13 4G 123
Boord St. SE10 3G 105
Boothby Ct. E4 3K 35
Boothby Rd. N19 2H 65
Booth Cl. E9 1H 85
SE28 1B 108
Booth Dr. TW18: Staines 6A 128
Booth Ho. *TW8: Bford* 7C 96
(off High St.)
Booth La. EC4 2C 14
Boothman Ho. HA3: Kent 3D 42
Booth Rd. CR0: C'don 2B 168
NW9 2K 43
Booth's Pl. W1 6B 6 (5G 83)
Boot Pde. *HA8: Edg* 6B 28
(off High St.)
Boot St. N1 2G 9 (3E 84)
Bordars Rd. W7 5J 77
Bordars Wlk. W7 5J 77
Borden Av. EN1: Enf 6J 23
Border Cres. SE26 5H 139
Border Gdns. CR0: C'don 4D 170
Bordergate CR4: Mitc 1C 154
Border Rd. SE26 5H 139
Bordesley Rd. SM4: Mord 5K 153
Bordeston Ct. *TW8: Bford* 7C 96
(off The Ham)
Bordon Wlk. SW15 7C 116
Boreas Wlk. N1 1B 8
Boreham Av. E16 6J 87
Boreham Cl. E11 1E 68
Boreham Rd. N22 2C 48
Boreman Ho. *SE10* 6E 104
(off Thames St.)
Borgard Rd. SE18 4D 106
Borkwood Pk. BR6: Orp 4K 173
Borkwood Way BR6: Orp 4J 173
Borland Rd. SE15 4J 121
TW11: Tedd 7B 132
Borley Ct. TW19: Stanw 1A 128
Borneo St. SW15 3E 116
BOROUGH, THE 7D 14 (2D 102)
Borough High St. SE1 7D 14 (2C 102)
Borough Hill CR0: Wadd 3B 168
Borough Mkt. SE1 5E 14
Borough Rd. CR4: Mitc 2C 154
E18 3J 51
KT2: King T 1G 151
SE1 7B 14 (3B 102)
TW7: Isle 1J 113
Borough Rd. Hall *UB8: Cowl* 3A 74
(off Kingston La.)
Borough Sq. SE1 7C 14
Borrett Cl. SE17 5C 102
Borrodaile Rd. SW18 6K 117
Borrowdale *NW1* 2A 6
(off Robert St.)
Borrowdale Av. HA3: W'stone 2A 42
Borrowdale Cl. IG4: Ilf 4C 52
Borrowdale Ct. EN2: Enf 1H 23
Borthwick M. E15 4G 69
Borthwick Rd. E15 4G 69
NW9 6B 44
Borthwick St. SE8 5C 104
Borwick Av. E17 3B 50
Bosanquet Cl. UB8: Cowl 4A 74
Bosbury Rd. SE6 3E 140
Boscastle Rd. NW5 3F 65
Boscobel Cl. BR1: Brom 2D 160
Boscobel Ho. E8 6H 67
Boscobel Pl. SW1 3H 17 (4E 100)
Boscobel St. NW8 4B 4 (4B 82)
Bosco Cl. BR6: Orp 4K 173
Boscombe Av. E10 7F 51
Boscombe Cir. NW9 1K 43
Boscombe Cl. E5 5A 68
Boscombe Gdns. SW16 6J 137
Boscombe Ho. *CR0: C'don* 1D 168
(off Sydenham Rd.)
Boscombe Rd. KT4: Wor Pk 1E 164
SW17 6E 136
SW19 1K 153
W12 1C 98
Bose Cl. N3 1G 45
Bosgrove E4 2K 35
Boss Ho. *SE1* 6J 15
(off Boss St.)
Boss St. SE1 6J 15 (2F 103)
Bostall Hill SE2 5A 108
Bostall La. SE2 4B 108
Bostall Mnr. Way SE2 4B 108
Bostall Pk. Av. DA7: Bex 7E 108
Bostall Rd. BR5: St P 7B 144
Bostock Ho. TW5: Hest 6E 94
Boston Bus. Pk. W7 3J 95
Boston Ct. SE25 4F 157
SM2: Sutt 7A 166
Boston Gdns. TW8: Bford 4A 96
W4 6A 98
W7 4A 96

Boston Gro. HA4: Ruis 6E 38
Boston Ho. *SW5* *4K 99*
(off Collingham Rd.)
BOSTON MANOR 4A 96
Boston Manor House 5B 96
Boston Mnr. Rd. TW8: Bford 4B 96
Boston Pde. W7 .... 3A 96
Boston Pk. Rd. TW8: Bford 5C 96
Boston Pl. NW1 .... 4E 4 (4D 82)
Boston Rd. CR0: C'don 6K 155
E6 .... 3C 88
E17 .... 6C 50
HA8: Edg 7D 28
W7 .... 1J 95
Bostonthorpe Rd. W7 .... 2J 95
Boston Va. W7 .... 4A 96
Bosun Cl. E14 .... 2C 104
Boswell Ct. *KT2: King T* *1F 151*
(off Clifton Rd.)
W14 .... *3F 99*
(off Blythe Rd.)
WC1 .... 5F 7 (5J 83)
Boswell Ho. *WC1* *5F 7*
(off Boswell St.)
Boswell Path UB3: Harl 4H 93
Boswell Rd. CR7: Thor H 4C 156
Boswell St. WC1 .... 5F 7 (5J 83)
Boswood Ct. TW3: Houn 3D 112
Bosworth Cl. E17 .... 1B 50
Bosworth Ho. *W10* *4G 81*
(off Bosworth Rd.)
Bosworth Rd. EN5: New Bar 3D 20
N11 .... 6C 32
RM10: Dag 3G 73
W10 .... 4G 81
Botany Bay La. BR7: Chst 3G 161
Botany Cl. EN4: E Barn 4H 21
Boteley Cl. E4 .... 2A 36
Botham Cl. HA8: Edg 7D 28
Botha Rd. E13 .... 5K 87
Bothwell Cl. E16 .... 5H 87
Bothwell St. W6 .... 6F 99
Botolph All. EC3 .... 2G 15
Botolph La. EC3 .... 3G 15 (7E 84)
Botsford Rd. SW20 .... 2G 153
Botts M. W2 .... 6J 81
Botwell Comn. Rd.
UB3: Hayes 7F 75
Botwell Cres. UB3: Hayes 6G 75
Botwell La. UB3: Hayes 7G 75
Boucher Cl. TW11: Tedd 5K 131
Bouchier Ho. N2 .... 2B 46
Boughton Av. BR2: Hayes 7H 159
Boughton Ho. *SE1* *6E 14*
(off Tennis St.)
Boughton Rd. SE28 .... 3J 107
Boulcott St. E1 .... 6K 85
Boulevard, The IG8: Wfd G 6K 37
SW6 .... 1A 118
SW17 .... 2E 136
SW18 .... 4K 117
Boulevard Dr. NW9 .... 2B 44
Boulogne Ho. *SE1* *7J 15*
(off St Saviour's Est.)
Boulogne Rd. CR0: C'don 6C 156
Boulter Cl. BR1: Brom 3E 160
Boulter Ho. *SE14* *1J 121*
(off Kender St.)
Boulton Ho. TW8: Bford 5E 96
Boulton Rd. RM8: Dag 2E 72
Boultwood Rd. E6 .... 6D 88
Bounces La. N9 .... 2C 34
Bounces Rd. N9 .... 2C 34
Boundaries Rd. SW12 .... 2D 136
TW13: Felt 1A 130
Boundary Av. E17 .... 7B 50
Boundary Bus. Ct. CR4: Mitc 3B 154
Boundary Cl. EN5: Barn 1C 20
IG3: Ilf 4J 71
KT1: King T 3H 151
Boundary Cl. SE20 .... 2G 157
UB2: S'hall 5E 94
Boundary Ct. *N18* *6A 34*
(off Snells Pk.)
Boundary Ho. SE5 .... 7C 102
W11 .... *1F 99*
(off Queensdale Cres.)
Boundary La. E13 .... 3B 88
SE17 .... 6C 102
Boundary Pas. E1 .... 3J 9 (4F 85)
Boundary Rd. DA15: Sidc 5J 125
E13 .... 2A 88
E17 .... 7B 50
HA5: Eastc 7B 40
HA9: Wemb 3E 60
IG11: Bark 2G 89
(Gascoigne Rd.)
IG11: Bark 1H 89
(King Edwards Rd.)
N2 .... 1B 46
N9 .... 6D 24
N22 .... 3B 48
NW8 .... 1K 81
SM5: Cars 6F 167
SM6: Wall 6F 167
SW19 .... 6B 136
Boundary Row SE1 .... 6A 14 (2B 102)
Boundary St. E2 .... 2J 9 (3F 85)
Boundary Way
CR0: Addtn 5C 170
Boundfield Rd. SE6 .... 3G 141
BOUNDS GREEN 6C 32
Bounds Grn. Ct. *N11* *6C 32*
(off Bounds Grn. Rd.)
Bounds Grn. Ind. Est. N11 .... 6B 32
Bounds Grn. Rd. N11 .... 6B 32
N22 .... 6B 32
Bourbon Ho. SE6 .... 5E 140
Bourchier St. W1 .... 2C 12 (7H 83)
(not continuous)
Bourdon Pl. W1 .... 2K 11
Bourdon Rd. SE20 .... 2J 157
Bourdon St. W1 .... 3J 11 (7F 83)
Bourke Cl. NW10 .... 6A 62
SW4 .... 6J 119
Bourlet Cl. W1 .... 6A 6 (5G 83)
Bourn Av. EN4: E Barn 5G 21
N15 .... 4D 48
UB8: Hil 4C 74
Bournbrook Rd. SE3 .... 3B 124
Bourne, The N14 .... 1C 32
Bourne Av. HA4: Ruis 5A 58
N14 .... 2D 32
UB3: Harl 3E 92
Bourne Cir. UB3: Harl 3E 92
Bourne Cl. TW7: Isle 3J 113
Bourne Ct. HA4: Ruis 5K 57
IG8: Wfd G 3B 52
W4 .... 6J 97
Bourne Dr. CR4: Mitc 2B 154
Bourne Est. EC1 .... 5J 7 (5A 84)
Bourne Gdns. E4 .... 4J 35
Bourne Hall Mus. 7B 164
Bourne Hill N13 .... 2D 32
Bourne Hill Cl. N13 .... 2E 32
Bourne Ho. IG9: Buck H 3G 37
TW15: Ashf 5C 128
Bourne Ind. Pk., The
DA1: Cray 5K 127
Bourne Mead DA5: Bexl 5K 127
Bournemead Av. UB5: Yead 2J 75
Bournemead Cl. UB5: Yead 3J 75
Bournemead Way
UB5: Yead 2K 75
Bourne M. W1 .... 1H 11 (6E 82)
Bournemouth Cl. SE15 .... 2G 121
Bournemouth Rd. SE15 .... 2G 121
SW19 .... 1J 153
Bourne Pde. DA5: Bexl 7H 127
Bourne Pl. W4 .... 5K 97
Bourne Rd. BR2: Brom 4B 160
DA1: Cray 6J 127
DA5: Bexl, Dart 7H 127
E7 .... 3H 69
N8 .... 6J 47
Bournes Ho. *N15* *6E 48*
(off Chisley Rd.)
Bourneside Cres. N14 .... 1C 32
Bourneside Gdns. SE6 .... 5E 140
Bourne St. CR0: C'don 2B 168
SW1 .... 4G 17 (4E 100)
Bourne Ter. W2 .... 5K 81
Bourne Va. BR2: Hayes 1H 171
Bournevale Rd. SW16 .... 4J 137
Bourne Vw. UB6: G'frd 6K 59
Bourne Way BR2: Hayes 2H 171
KT19: Ewe 4J 163
SM1: Sutt 5H 165
Bournewood Rd. SE18 .... 7A 108
Bournville Rd. SE6 .... 7C 122
Bournwell Cl. EN4: Cockf 3J 21
Bourton Cl. UB3: Hayes 1J 93
Bousfield Rd. SE14 .... 2K 121
Boutflower Rd. SW11 .... 4C 118
Boutique Hall SE13 .... 4E 122
Bouton Pl. *N1* *7B 66*
(off Waterloo Ter.)
Bouverie Gdns. HA3: Kent 6D 42
Bouverie M. N16 .... 2E 66
Bouverie Pl. W2 .... 7B 4 (6B 82)
Bouverie Rd. HA1: Harr 6G 41
N16 .... 1E 66
Bouverie St. EC4 .... 1K 13 (6A 84)
Bouvier Rd. EN3: Enf W 1D 24
Boveney Rd. SE23 .... 7K 121
Bovill Rd. SE23 .... 7K 121
Bovingdon Av. HA9: Wemb 6G 61
Bovingdon Cl. N19 .... 2G 65
Bovingdon La. NW9 .... 1A 44
Bovingdon Rd. SW6 .... 1K 117
Bovingdon Sq. CR4: Mitc 4J 155
Bovril Ct. *SW6* *7K 99*
(off Fulham Rd.)
BOW 3B 86
Bowater Cl. NW9 .... 5K 43
SW2 .... 6J 119
Bowater Gdns. TW16: Sun 2A 148
Bowater Ho. *EC1* *4C 8*
(off Golden La. Est.)
SW1 .... 6F 11
Bowater Pl. SE3 .... 7K 105
Bowater Rd. HA9: Wemb 3H 61
SE18 .... 3B 106
Bow Bri. Est. E3 .... 3D 86
Bow Brook, The *E2* *2K 85*
(off Mace St.)
Bow Chyd. EC4 .... 1D 14
BOW COMMON 5C 86
Bow Comn. La. E3 .... 4B 86
Bowden Cl. TW14: Bedf 1G 129
Bowden St. SE11 .... 6K 19 (5A 102)
Bowditch SE8 .... 4B 104
Bowdon Rd. E17 .... 7C 50
Bowen Dr. SE21 .... 3E 138
Bowen Rd. HA1: Harr 7G 41
Bowen St. E14 .... 6D 86
Bower Av. SE10 .... 1G 123
Bower Cl. RM5: Col R 1K 55
UB5: N'olt 2A 76
Bower Ct. *E4* *1K 35*
(off The Ridgeway)
Bowerdean St. SW6 .... 1K 117
Bower Ho. *SE14* *1K 121*
(off Besson St.)
Bowerman Av. SE14 .... 6A 104
Bowerman Ct. *N19* *2H 65*
(off St John's Way)
Bower St. E1 .... 6K 85
Bowers Wlk. E6 .... 6D 88
Bowery Ct. RM10: Dag 6H 73
Bowes Cl. DA15: Sidc 6B 126
Bowe's Ho. IG11: Bark 7F 71
Bowes-Lyon Hall *E16* *1J 105*
(off Wesley Av., not continuous)
BOWES PARK 6D 32
Bowes Rd. N11 .... 5B 32
N13 .... 5B 32
RM8: Dag 4C 72
W3 .... 7A 80
Bowfell Rd. W6 .... 6E 98
Bowford Av. DA7: Bex 1E 126
Bowhill Cl. SW9 .... 7A 102
Bowie Cl. SW4 .... 7H 119
BOW INTERCHANGE 2D 86
Bowland Rd. IG8: Wfd G 6F 37
SW4 .... 4H 119
Bowland Yd. SW1 .... 7F 11
Bow La. EC4 .... 1D 14 (6C 84)
N12 .... 7F 31
SM4: Mord 6G 153
Bowl Ct. EC2 .... 4H 9 (4E 84)
Bowles Ct. N12 .... 7H 31
Bowles Rd. SE1 .... 6G 103
Bowley Cl. SE19 .... 6F 139
Bowley Ho. SE16 .... 3G 103
Bowley La. SE19 .... 5F 139
Bowling, The KT12: Walt T 7J 147
Bowling Cl. UB10: Uxb 1B 74
Bowling Grn. Cl. SW15 .... 7D 116
Bowling Grn. Ct. HA9: Wemb 2F 61
Bowling Grn. Ho. *SW10* *7B 100*
(off Riley St.)
Bowling Grn. La. EC1 .... 3K 7 (4A 84)
Bowling Grn. Pl. SE1 .... 6E 14 (2D 102)
Bowling Grn. Row SE18 .... 3D 106
Bowling Grn. St. SE11 .... 7J 19 (6A 102)
Bowling Grn. Wlk. N1 .... 1G 9 (3E 84)
Bow Locks E3 .... 4E 86
Bowls Cl. HA7: Stan 5G 27
Bowman Av. E16 .... 7H 87
Bowman M. SW18 .... 1H 135
Bowman's Bldgs. *NW1* *5C 4*
(off Penfold Pl.)
Bowmans Cl. W13 .... 1B 96
Bowmans Lea SE23 .... 7J 121
Bowmans Mdw. SM6: Wall 3F 167
Bowman's M. E1 .... 7G 85
N7 .... 3J 65
Bowman's Pl. N7 .... 3J 65
Bowman Trad. Est. NW9 .... 3G 43
Bowmead SE9 .... 2D 142
Bowmore Wlk. NW1 .... 7H 65
Bowness Cl. *E8* *6F 67*
(off Beechwood Rd.)
Bowness Cres. SW15 .... 5A 134
Bowness Dr. TW4: Houn 4C 112
Bowness Ho. *SE15* *7J 103*
(off Hillbeck Cl.)
Bowness Rd. DA7: Bex 2H 127
SE6 .... 7D 122
Bowood Rd. EN3: Enf H 2E 24
SW11 .... 5E 118
Bow Rd. E3 .... 3B 86
Bowrons Av. HA0: Wemb 7D 60
Bowry Ho. *E14* *5B 86*
(off Wallwood St.)
Bowsley Ct. TW13: Felt 2J 129
Bowsprit Point *E14* *3C 104*
(off Westferry Rd.)
Bow St. E15 .... 5G 69
WC2 .... 1F 13 (6J 83)
Bow Triangle Bus. Cen. E3 .... 4C 86
Bowyer Cl. E6 .... 5D 88
Bowyer Ho. *N1* *1E 84*
(off Mill Row)
Bowyer Pl. SE5 .... 7C 102
Bowyer St. SE5 .... 7C 102
Boxall Rd. SE21 .... 6E 120
Boxelder Cl. HA8: Edg 5D 28
Boxgrove Rd. SE2 .... 3C 108

Box La. IG11: Bark 2B 90
Boxley Rd. SM4: Mord 4A 154
Boxley St. E16 1K 105
Boxmoor Ho. *E2 1G 85*
(off Whiston Rd.)
W11 1F 99
(off Queensdale Cres.)
Boxmoor Rd. HA3: Kent 4B 42
Boxoll Rd. RM9: Dag 4F 73
Boxted Cl. IG9: Buck H 1H 37
Box Tree Ho. SE8 6A 104
Boxtree La. HA3: Hrw W 1G 41
Boxtree Rd. HA3: Hrw W 7C 26
Boxwood Cl. UB7: W Dray 2B 92
Boxworth Cl. N12 5G 31
Boxworth Gro. N1 1K 83
Boyard Rd. SE18 5F 107
Boyce Ho. SW16 5G 137
W10 3H 81
(off Bruckner St.)
Boyce Way E13 4J 87
Boycroft Av. NW9 6J 43
Boyd Av. UB1: S'hall 1D 94
Boyd Cl. KT2: King T 7G 133
Boydell Ct. NW8 7B 64
(not continuous)
Boyden Ho. E17 3E 50
Boyd Rd. SW19 6B 136
Boyd St. E1 6G 85
Boyfield St. SE1 7B 14 (2B 102)
Boyland Rd. BR1: Brom 5H 141
Boyle Av. HA7: Stan 6F 27
Boyle Cl. UB10: Uxb 2B 74
Boyle Farm Island
KT7: T Ditt 6A 150
Boyle Farm Rd. KT7: T Ditt 6A 150
Boyle St. W1 2A 12 (7G 83)
Boyne Av. NW4 4F 45
Boyne Rd. RM10: Dag 3G 73
SE13 3E 122
Boyne Ter. M. W11 1H 99
Boyseland Ct. HA8: Edg 2D 28
Boyson Rd. SE17 6C 102
(not continuous)
Boyson Wlk. SE17 6D 102
Boyton Cl. E1 4J 85
N8 3J 47
Boyton Ho. *NW8 2B 82*
(off Wellington Rd.)
Boyton Rd. N8 3J 47
Brabant Ct. EC3 2G 15
Brabant Rd. N22 2K 47
Brabazon Av. SM6: Wall 7J 167
Brabazon Rd. TW5: Hest 7A 94
UB5: N'olt 2E 76
Brabazon St. E14 6D 86
Brabner Ho. *E2 1K 9*
(off Wellington Row)
Brabourne Cl. SE19 5E 138
Brabourne Cres. DA7: Bex 6F 109
Brabourne Hgts. NW7 3F 29
Brabourne Ri. BR3: Beck 5E 158
Brabourn Gro. SE15 2J 121
Brabrook Ct. SM6: Wall 4F 167
Brabstone Ho. UB6: G'frd 2K 77
Bracer Ho. *N1 2E 84*
(off Whitmore Est.)
Bracewell Av. UB6: G'frd 5K 59
Bracewell Rd. W10 5E 80
Bracewood Gdns. CR0: C'don 3F 169
Bracey M. N4 2J 65
Bracey St. N4 2J 65
Bracken, The E4 2K 35
Bracken Av. CR0: C'don 3C 170
SW12 6E 118
Brackenbridge Dr.
HA4: Ruis 3B 58
Brackenbury *N4 1A 66*
(off Osborne Rd.)
Brackenbury Gdns. W6 3D 98
Brackenbury Rd. N2 3A 46
W6 3D 98
Bracken Cl. E6 5D 88
TW2: Whitt 7E 112
TW16: Sun 6H 129
Brackendale N21 2E 32
Brackendale Cl. TW3: Houn 1F 113
Brackendene DA2: Dart 4K 145
Bracken End TW7: Isle 5H 113
Brackenfield Cl. E5 3H 67
Bracken Gdns. SW13 2C 116
Brackenhill HA4: Ruis 4C 58
Bracken Hill Cl. BR1: Brom 1H 159
Bracken Hill La. BR1: Brom 1H 159
Bracken Ho. *E3 5C 86*
(off Devons Rd.)
Bracken Ind. Est. IG6: Ilf 1J 53
Bracken M. E4 1K 35
RM7: Rom 6H 55
Brackens BR3: Beck 7C 140
Brackens, The EN1: Enf 7K 23
Brackenwood TW16: Sun 1J 147
Brackenwood Lodge *EN5: New Bar 4D 20*
(off Prospect Rd.)
Brackley Av. SE15 3J 121
Brackley Cl. SM6: Wall 7J 167
Brackley Ct. *NW8 3B 4*
(off Pollitt Dr.)
Brackley Rd. BR3: Beck 7B 140
W4 5A 98
Brackley Sq. IG8: Wfd G 7G 37
Brackley St. EC1 5D 8 (4C 84)
Brackley Ter. W4 5A 98
Bracklyn Ct. N1 2D 84
(not continuous)
Bracklyn St. N1 2D 84
Bracknell Cl. N22 1A 48
Bracknell Gdns. NW3 4K 63
Bracknell Ga. NW3 5K 63
Bracknell Way NW3 4K 63
Bracondale Rd. SE2 4A 108
Bradbeer Ho. *E2 3J 85*
(off Cornwall Av.)
Bradbourne Rd. DA5: Bexl 7G 127
Bradbourne St. SW6 2J 117
Bradbury Cl. UB2: S'hall 4D 94
Bradbury M. *N16 5E 66*
(off Bradbury St.)
Bradbury St. N16 5E 66
Bradby Ho. *NW8 2K 81*
(off Hamilton Ter.)
Braddock Cl. TW7: Isle 2K 113
Braddon Ct. EN5: Barn 3B 20
Braddon Rd. TW9: Rich 3F 115
Braddyll St. SE10 5G 105
Bradenham *SE17 6D 102*
(off Bradenham Cl.)
Bradenham Av. DA16: Well 4A 126
Bradenham Cl. SE17 6D 102
Bradenham Rd. HA3: Kent 4B 42
UB4: Hayes 3G 75
Braden St. W9 4K 81
Bradfield Ct. *NW1 7F 65*
(off Hawley Rd.)
Bradfield Dr. IG11: Bark 5A 72
Bradfield Ho. IG8: Wfd G 6K 37
Bradfield Rd. E16 2J 105
HA4: Ruis 5C 58
Bradford Cl. BR2: Brom 1D 172
N17 6A 34
SE26 4H 139
Bradford Dr. KT19: Ewe 6B 164
Bradford Ho. *W14 3F 99*
(off Spring Va. Ter.)
Bradford Rd. IG1: Ilf 1H 71
W3 2A 98
Bradgate Rd. SE6 6D 122
Brading Cres. E11 2K 69
Brading Rd. CR0: C'don 6K 155
SW2 7K 119
Brading Ter. W12 3C 98
Bradiston Rd. W9 3H 81
Bradley Cl. N7 6J 65
Bradley Gdns. W13 6B 78
Bradley Ho. IG8: Wfd G 7D 36
SE16 4J 103
(off Raymouth Rd.)
Bradley M. SW17 1D 136
Bradley Rd. N22 2K 47
SE19 6C 138
Bradley's Cl. N1 2A 84
Bradley Stone Rd. E6 5D 88
Bradman Row HA8: Edg 7D 28
Bradmead SW8 7F 101
Bradmore Ct. *EN3: Enf H 3F 25*
(off Enstone Rd.)
Bradmore Pk. Rd. W6 4D 98
Bradon *NW9 2B 44*
(off Further Acre)
Brad Rd. NW7 6A 30
Bradshaw Cl. SW19 6J 135
Bradshaw Cotts. *E14 6A 86*
(off Repton St.)
Bradshaw Dr. NW7 7A 30
Bradshawe Waye UB8: Hil 5B 74
Bradshaws Cl. SE25 3G 157
Bradstock Ho. E9 7K 67
Bradstock Rd. E9 6K 67
KT17: Ewe 5C 164
Brad St. SE1 5K 13 (1A 102)
Bradwell Av. RM10: Dag 2G 73
Bradwell Cl. E18 4H 51
Bradwell Ho. *NW6 1K 81*
(off Mortimer Cres.)
Bradwell M. N18 4B 34
Bradwell Rd. IG9: Buck H 1H 37
Brady Ct. RM8: Dag 1D 72
Brady Dr. BR1: Brom 3E 160
Brady Ho. *SW8 1G 119*
(off Corunna Rd.)
Bradymead E6 6E 88
Brady St. E1 4H 85
Braeburn Ct. EN4: E Barn 4G 21
Brae Ct. KT2: King T 1G 151
Braemar SW15 6F 117
Braemar Av. CR2: S Croy 7C 168
CR7: Thor H 3A 156
DA7: Bex 4J 127
HA0: Wemb 7D 60
N22 1J 47
NW10 3K 61
SW19 2J 135
Braemar Cl. *SE16 5H 103*
(off Masters Dr.)
Braemar Ct. SE6 1H 141
Braemar Gdns. BR4: W W'ck 1E 170
DA15: Sidc 3H 143
NW9 1K 43
Braemar Ho. *W9 3A 82*
(off Maida Va.)
Braemar Mans. *SW7 3K 99*
(off Cornwall Gdns.)
Braemar Rd. E13 4H 87
KT4: Wor Pk 3D 164
N15 5E 48
TW8: Bford 6D 96
Braeside BR3: Beck 5C 140
Braeside Av. SW19 1G 153
Braeside Cres. DA7: Bex 4J 127
Braeside Rd. SW16 7G 137
Braes St. N1 7B 66
Braesyde Cl. DA17: Belv 4F 109
Brafferton Rd. CR0: C'don 4C 168
Braganza St. SE17 5B 102
Bragg Cl. RM8: Dag 6B 72
Bragg Rd. TW11: Tedd 6J 131
Braham Ho. SE11 6H 19 (5K 101)
Braham St. E1 1K 15 (6F 85)
Braid Av. W3 6A 80
Braid Cl. TW13: Hanw 2D 130
Braid Ho. *SE10 1E 122*
(off Blackheath Hill)
Braidwood Pas. *EC1 5C 8*
(off Aldersgate St.)
Braidwood Rd. SE6 1F 141
Braidwood St. SE1 5G 15 (1E 102)
Brailsford Cl. CR4: Mitc 7C 136
Brailsford Rd. SW2 5A 120
Brainton Av. TW14: Felt 7K 111
Braintree Av. IG4: Ilf 4C 52
Braintree Ho. *E1 4J 85*
(off Malcolm Rd.)
Braintree Rd. HA4: Ruis 4K 57
RM10: Dag 3G 73
Braintree St. E2 3J 85
Braithwaite Av. RM7: Rush G 7G 55
Braithwaite Gdns. HA7: Stan 1C 42
Braithwaite Ho. *EC1 3E 8*
(off Bunhill Row)
Braithwaite Rd. EN3: Brim 3G 25
Braithwaite Twr. W2 5B 4
Bramah Grn. SW9 1A 120
Bramah Tea & Coffee Mus.
5D 14 (1C 102)
Bramalea Cl. N6 6E 46
Bramall Cl. E15 5H 69
Bramall Ct. *N7 5K 65*
(off George's Rd.)
Bramber WC1 2E 6
Bramber Ct. TW8: Bford 4E 96
W14 6H 99
(off North End Rd.)
Bramber Ho. *KT2: King T 1E 150*
(off Seven Kings Way)
Bramber Rd. N12 5H 31
W14 6H 99
Brambleacres Cl. SM2: Sutt 7J 165
Bramblebury Rd. SE18 5G 107
Bramble Cl. BR3: Beck 5E 158
CR0: C'don 4C 170
HA7: Stan 7J 27
N15 4G 49
TW17: Shep 3F 147
UB8: Hil 6B 74
Bramble Cft. DA8: Erith 4J 109
Brambledown Cl. BR4: W W'ck 5G 159
Brambledown Rd. CR2: Sande 7E 168
SM5: Cars 7E 166
SM6: Wall 7E 166
Bramble Gdns. W12 7B 80
Bramble Ho. *E3 5C 86*
(off Devons Rd.)
Bramble La. TW12: Hamp 6D 130
Brambles, The *SW19 5H 135*
(off Woodside)
UB7: W Dray 1E 174
Brambles Cl. TW7: Isle 7B 96
Brambles Farm Dr. UB10: Hil 3C 74
Bramblewood Cl. SM5: Cars 1C 166
Brambling Ct. *SE8 6B 104*
(off Abinger Gro.)
Bramblings, The E4 4A 36
Bramcote Av. CR4: Mitc 4D 154
Bramcote Ct. *CR4: Mitc 4D 154*
(off Bramcote Av.)
Bramcote Gro. SE16 5J 103
Bramcote Rd. SW15 4D 116
Bramdean Cres. SE12 1J 141
Bramdean Gdns. SE12 1J 141
Bramerton *NW6 7F 63*
(off Willesden La.)
Bramerton Rd. BR3: Beck 3B 158
Bramerton St. SW3 7C 16 (6C 100)
Bramfield Ct. *N4 2C 66*
(off Queens Dr.)
Bramfield Rd. SW11 6C 118
Bramford Ct. N14 2C 32
Bramford Rd. SW18 4A 118
Bramham Gdns. KT9: Chess 4D 162
SW5 5K 99

Bramhope La. SE7 6K 105
Bramlands Cl. SW11 3C 118
Bramley Av. TW17: Shep 3G 147
Bramley Bank Nature Reserve 6J 169
Bramley Cl. BR6: Farnb 1F 173
CR2: S Croy 5C 168
E17 2A 50
HA5: Eastc 3H 39
IG8: Wfd G 7F 37
N14 5A 22
TW2: Whitt 6G 113
UB3: Hayes 7J 75
Bramley Ct. CR4: Mitc 2B 154
DA16: Well 1B 126
E4 1K 35
(off The Ridgeway)
EN4: E Barn 4H 21
UB1: S'hall 7G 77
(off Haldane Rd.)
Bramley Cres. IG2: Ilf 6E 52
SW8 7H 101
Bramley Hill CR2: S Croy 5B 168
Bramley Ho. SW15 6B 116
(off Tunworth Cres.)
TW4: Houn 4D 112
W10 6F 81
Bramleyhyrst CR2: S Croy 5C 168
(off Bramley Hill)
Bramley Lodge HA0: Wemb 4D 60
Bramley Pde. N14 4C 22
Bramley Rd. N14 5A 22
SM1: Sutt 5B 166
SM2: Cheam 7F 165
W5 3C 96
W10 6F 81
(not continuous)
Bramley Sports Ground 5K 21
Bramley Way BR4: W W'ck 2D 170
TW4: Houn 5D 112
Brampton WC1 6G 7
(off Red Lion Sq.)
Brampton Cl. E5 2H 67
Brampton Ct. NW4 4D 44
RM7: Rush G 6K 55
(off Union Rd.)
Brampton Gdns. N15 5C 48
Brampton Gro. HA3: Kent 4A 42
HA9: Wemb 1G 61
NW4 4D 44
Brampton La. NW4 4E 44
Brampton Pk. Rd. N8 3A 48
Brampton Rd. CR0: C'don 7F 157
DA7: Bex 3D 126
E6 3B 88
N15 5C 48
NW9 4G 43
SE2 6C 108
UB10: Hil 2D 74
Bramshaw Ri. KT3: N Mald 6A 152
Bramshaw Rd. E9 6K 67
Bramshill Gdns. NW5 3F 65
Bramshill Rd. NW10 2B 80
Bramshot Av. SE7 6J 105
Bramshurst NW8 1K 81
(off Abbey Rd.)
Bramston Rd. NW10 2C 80
SW17 3A 136
Bramwell Cl. TW16: Sun 2B 148
Bramwell Ho. SE1 3C 102
SW1 6A 18
(off Churchill Gdns.)
Bramwell M. N1 1K 83
Brancaster Dr. NW7 7H 29
Brancaster Ho. E1 3K 85
(off Moody St.)
Brancaster Rd. E12 4D 70
IG2: Ilf 6J 53
SW16 3J 137
Brancepeth Gdns. IG9: Buck H 2D 36
Branch Hill NW3 3A 64
Branch Hill Ho. NW3 3K 63
Branch Pl. N1 1D 84
Branch Rd. E14 7A 86
Branch St. SE15 7E 102
Brancker Rd. HA3: Kent 3D 42
Brancroft Way EN3: Brim 1F 25
Brand Cl. N4 1B 66
Brandesbury Sq. IG8: Wfd G 7K 37
Brandlehow Rd. SW15 4H 117
Brandon Est. SE17 6B 102
Brandon Ho. BR3: Beck 5D 140
(off Beckenham Hill Rd.)
Brandon Mans. W14 6G 99
(off Queen's Club Gdns.)
Brandon M. EC2 6E 8
SE17 4C 102
Brandon Rd. E17 4E 50
N7 7J 65
SM1: Sutt 4K 165
UB2: S'hall 5D 94
Brandon St. SE17 4C 102
(not continuous)
Brandram M. SE13 4G 123
(off Brandram Rd.)
Brandram Rd. SE13 3G 123
Brandrams Wharf SE16 2J 103
Brandreth Ct. HA1: Harr 6K 41
Brandreth Rd. E6 6D 88
SW17 2F 137
Brandries, The SM6: Bedd 3H 167
Brands Ho. NW6 1H 81
(off Lincoln M.)
Brand St. SE10 7E 104
Brandville Gdns. IG6: Ilf 4F 53
Brandville Rd. UB7: W Dray 2A 92
Brandy Way SM2: Sutt 7J 165
Brangbourne Rd. BR1: Brom 5E 140
Brangton Rd. SE11 6H 19 (5K 101)
Brangwyn Ct. W14 3G 99
(off Blythe Rd.)
Brangwyn Cres. SW19 1A 154
Branham Ho. SE18 5F 107
Branksea St. SW6 7G 99
Branksome Av. N18 6A 34
Branksome Cl. TW11: Tedd 4H 131
Branksome Ho. SW8 7K 101
(off Meadow Rd.)
Branksome Rd. SW2 5J 119
SW19 1J 153
Branksome Way HA3: Kent 6F 43
KT3: N Mald 1J 151
Branksone Ct. N2 3A 46
Bransby Rd. KT9: Chess 6E 162
Branscombe NW1 1G 83
(off Plender St.)
Branscombe Ct. BR2: Brom 5H 159
Branscombe Gdns. N21 7F 23
Branscombe St. SE13 3D 122
Bransdale Cl. NW6 1J 81
Bransgrove Rd. HA8: Edg 1F 43
Branston Cres. BR5: Pet W 1H 173
Branstone Rd. TW9: Kew 1F 115
Brants Wlk. W7 4J 77
Brantwood Av. DA8: Erith 7J 109
TW7: Isle 4A 114
Brantwood Cl. E17 3D 50
Brantwood Gdns. EN2: Enf 4D 22
IG4: Ilf 4C 52
Brantwood Ho. SE5 7C 102
(off Wyndam Est.)
Brantwood Rd. CR2: S Croy 7C 168
DA7: Bex 2H 127
N17 6B 34
SE24 5C 120
Branxholme Ct. BR1: Brom 1H 159
(off Highland Rd.)
Brasenose Dr. SW13 6E 98
Brasher Cl. UB6: G'frd 5H 59
Brassett Point E15 1G 87
(off Abbey Rd.)
Brassey Cl. TW14: Felt 1J 129
Brassey Ho. E14 4D 104
(off Cahir St.)
Brassey Rd. NW6 6H 63
Brassey Sq. SW11 3E 118
Brassie Av. W3 6A 80
Brass Talley All. SE16 2K 103
Brasted Cl. BR6: Orp 2K 173
DA6: Bex 5D 126
SE26 4J 139
Brasted Lodge BR3: Beck 7C 140
Brathay NW1 1B 6
(off Ampthill Est.)
Brathway Rd. SW18 7J 117
Bratley St. E1 4G 85
Bratten Ct. CR0: C'don 6D 156
Braund Av. UB6: G'frd 4F 77
Braundton Av. DA15: Sidc 1K 143
Braunston Dr. UB4: Yead 4C 76
Bravington Cl.
TW17: Shep 5B 146
Bravington Pl. W9 4H 81
Bravington Rd. W9 2H 81
Bravingtons Wlk. N1 1F 7
(off York Way)
Brawne Ho. SE17 6B 102
(off Brandon Est.)
Braxfield Rd. SE4 4A 122
Braxted Pk. SW16 6K 137
Bray NW3 7C 64
Brayards Rd. SE15 2H 121
Brayards Rd. Est. SE15 2J 121
(off Brayards Rd.)
Braybourne Dr. TW7: Isle 7K 95
Braybrooke Gdns. SE19 7E 138
Braybrook St. W12 5B 80
Brayburne Av. SW4 2G 119
Bray Ct. SW16 5J 137
Braycourt Av.
KT12: Walt T 7K 147
Bray Cres. SE16 2K 103
Braydon Rd. N16 1G 67
Bray Dr. E16 7H 87
Brayfield Ter. N1 7A 66
Brayford Sq. E1 6J 85
Bray Pas. E16 7J 87
Bray Pl. SW3 4E 16 (4D 100)
Bray Rd. NW7 6A 30
Brayton Gdns. EN2: Enf 4C 22
Braywood Rd. SE9 4H 125
Brazier Cres. UB5: N'olt 4D 76
Brazil Cl. CR0: Bedd 7J 155
Breach La. RM9: Dag 3G 91
Bread St. EC4 1D 14 (6C 84)
(not continuous)
Breakspear Crematorium
HA4: Ruis 5E 38
Breakspear M. UB9: Hare 3A 38
Breakspear Rd. HA4: Ruis 7D 38
Breakspear Rd. Nth. UB9: Hare 3A 38
Breakspear Rd. Sth. UB9: Hare 3B 56
UB10: Ick 3B 56
Breakspears Dr. BR5: St P 1K 161
Breakspears M. SE4 2B 122
Breakspears Rd. SE4 4B 122
Breakwell Ct. W10 4G 81
(off Wornington Rd.)
Bream Cl. N17 4H 49
Bream Gdns. E6 3E 88
Breamore Cl. SW15 1C 134
Breamore Ct. IG3: Ilf 2A 72
Breamore Ho. SE15 7G 103
(off Friary Est.)
Breamore Rd. IG3: Ilf 2K 71
Bream's Bldgs. EC4 7J 7 (6A 84)
Bream St. E3 7C 68
Breamwater Gdns. TW10: Ham 3B 132
Brearley Cl. HA8: Edg 7D 28
UB8: Uxb 6A 56
Breasley Cl. SW15 4D 116
Breasy Pl. NW4 4D 44
(off Burroughs Gdns.)
Brechin Pl. SW7 4A 100
Brecknock Rd. N7 5H 65
N19 4G 65
Brecknock Rd. Est. N19 4G 65
Breckonmead BR1: Brom 2A 160
Brecon Cl. CR4: Mitc 3J 155
KT4: Wor Pk 2E 164
Brecon Grn. NW9 6A 44
Brecon Ho. W2 6A 82
(off Hallfield Est.)
Brecon M. N7 5H 65
Brecon Rd. EN3: Pond E 4D 24
W6 6G 99
Brede Cl. E6 3E 88
Bredel Ho. E14 5C 86
(off St Paul's Way)
Bredgar SE13 5D 122
Bredgar Rd. N19 2G 65
Bredhurst Cl. SE20 6J 139
Bredinghurst SE22 7G 121
Bredin Ho. SW10 7K 99
(off Coleridge Gdns.)
Bredo Ho. IG11: Bark 3B 90
Bredon Rd. CR0: C'don 7F 157
Breer St. SW6 3K 117
Breezers Ct. E1 7G 85
(off The Highway)
Breezer's Hill E1 7G 85
Brember Rd. HA2: Harr 2G 59
Bremer M. E17 4D 50
Bremner Rd. SW7 1A 16 (3A 100)
Brenchley Cl. BR2: Brom 6H 159
BR7: Chst 1E 160
Brenchley Gdns. SE23 6J 121
Brenchley Rd. BR5: St P 2K 161
Brenda Rd. SW17 2D 136
Brende Gdns. KT8: W Mole 4F 149
Brendon Av. NW10 4A 62
Brendon Cl. UB3: Harl 7E 92
Brendon Ct. UB2: S'hall 4F 95
Brendon Gdns. HA2: Harr 4F 59
IG2: Ilf 5J 53
Brendon Gro. N2 2A 46
Brendon Rd. RM8: Dag 1F 73
SE9 2H 143
Brendon St. W1 7D 4 (6C 82)
Brendon Vs. N21 1H 33
Brendon Way EN1: Enf 7K 23
Brenley Cl. CR4: Mitc 3E 154
Brenley Gdns. SE9 4B 124
Brenley Ho. SE1 6E 14
(off Tennis St.)
Brennand Ct. N19 3G 65
Brent Cl. DA5: Bexl 1E 144
Brentcot Cl. W13 4B 78
Brent Ct. NW11 7F 45
W7 7H 77
Brent Cres. NW10 2F 79
BRENT CROSS 7E 44
Brent Cross Fly-Over NW2 7F 45
NW4 7F 45
Brent Cross Gdns. NW4 6F 45
BRENT CROSS INTERCHANGE 6E 44
Brent Cross Shop. Cen. NW4 7E 44
Brentfield NW10 7H 61
Brentfield Cl. NW10 6K 61
Brentfield Gdns. NW2 7F 45
Brentfield Ho. NW10 7K 61
Brentfield Rd. NW10 6K 61
BRENTFORD 6D 96
Brentford Bus. Cen.
TW8: Bford 7C 96
Brentford Cl. UB4: Yead 4B 76
BRENTFORD END 7B 96
Brentford FC 6D 96
Brentford Fountain Leisure Cen. 5G 97
Brentford Ho. TW1: Twick 7B 114
Brentford Musical Mus. 6F 97

Brent Grn. NW4 ... 5E **44**
Brent Grn. Wlk. HA9: Wemb ... 3J **61**
Brentham Club ... 3C **78**
Brentham Way W5 ... 4D **78**
Brent Ho. *E9* ... *6J* **67**
(off Brenthouse Rd.)
Brenthouse Rd. E9 ... 7J **67**
Brenthurst Rd. NW10 ... 6B **62**
Brent Lea TW8: Bford ... 7C **96**
Brentmead Cl. W7 ... 7J **77**
Brentmead Gdns. NW10 ... 2F **79**
Brentmead Pl. NW11 ... 6F **45**
Brent Mus. ... *6D* **62**
(within Library)
Brent New Ent. Cen. NW10 ... 6B **62**
Brenton St. E14 ... 6A **86**
Brent Pk. Ind. Est. UB2: S'hall ... 3K **93**
Brent Pk. Rd. NW4 ... 7D **44**
NW9 ... 7D **44**
Brent Pl. EN5: Barn ... 5C **20**
Brent Rd. CR2: Sels ... 7H **169**
E16 ... 6J **87**
SE18 ... 7F **107**
TW8: Bford ... 6C **96**
UB2: S'hall ... 3A **94**
Brent Side TW8: Bford ... 6C **96**
Brentside Cl. W13 ... 4A **78**
Brentside Executive Cen.
TW8: Bford ... 6B **96**
Brent St. NW4 ... 4E **44**
Brent Ter. NW2 ... 1E **62**
(not continuous)
Brent Trad. Cen. NW10 ... 5A **62**
Brentvale Av. HA0: Wemb ... 1F **79**
UB1: S'hall ... 1H **95**
Brent Vw. Rd. NW9 ... 6C **44**
Brentwaters Bus. Pk. TW8: Bford ... 7C **96**
Brent Way HA9: Wemb ... 6H **61**
N3 ... 6D **30**
TW8: Bford ... 7D **96**
Brentwick Gdns. TW8: Bford ... 4E **96**
Brentwood Cl. SE9 ... 1G **143**
Brentwood Ho. *SE18* ... *7B* **106**
(off Portway Gdns.)
Brentwood Lodge *NW4* ... *5F* **45**
(off Holmdale Gdns.)
Brereton Rd. N17 ... 7A **34**
Bressay Dr. NW7 ... 7H **29**
Bressenden Pl. SW1 ... 1K **17** (3F **101**)
Bressey Av. EN1: Enf ... 1B **24**
Bressey Gro. E18 ... 2H **51**
Breton Highwalk *EC1* ... *5D* **8**
(off Golden La.)
Breton Ho. EC2 ... 5D **8**
SE1 ... *7J* **15**
(off St Saviour's Est.)
Brett Cl. N16 ... 2E **66**
UB5: Yead ... 3B **76**
Brett Ct. N9 ... 2D **34**
Brett Cres. NW10 ... 1K **79**
Brettell St. SE17 ... 5D **102**
Brettenham Av. E17 ... 1C **50**
Brettenham Rd. E17 ... 2C **50**
N18 ... 4B **34**
Brett Gdns. RM9: Dag ... 7E **72**
Brett Ho. Cl. SW15 ... 7F **117**
Brettinghurst *SE1* ... *5G* **103**
(off Avondale Sq.)
Brett Pas. E8 ... 5H **67**
Brett Rd. E8 ... 5H **67**
Brewer's Grn. SW1 ... 1C **18**
Brewer's Hall Gdn. *EC2* ... *6D* **8**
(off London Wall)
Brewers La. TW9: Rich ... 5D **114**
Brewer St. W1 ... 2B **12** (7G **83**)
Brewery, The EC2 ... 5E **8** (5C **84**)
RM1: Rom ... 5K **55**
Brewery Cl. HA0: Wemb ... 5A **60**
Brewery Ind. Est., The *N1* ... *1D* **8**
(off Wenlock Rd.)
Brewery La. TW1: Twick ... 7K **113**
Brewery M. Cen. TW7: Isle ... 3A **114**
Brewery Rd. BR2: Brom ... 1C **172**
N7 ... 7J **65**
SE18 ... 5H **107**
Brewery Sq. EC1 ... 3A **8** (4B **84**)
SE1 ... 5J **15**
Brewery Wlk. RM1: Rom ... 5K **55**
Brewhouse La. E1 ... 1H **103**
SW15 ... 3G **117**
Brewhouse Rd. SE18 ... 4D **106**
Brewhouse Wlk. SE16 ... 1A **104**
Brewhouse Yd. EC1 ... 3A **8** (4B **84**)
Brewin Ter. UB4: Yead ... 5A **76**
Brewood Rd. RM8: Dag ... 6B **72**
Brewster Gdns. W10 ... 5E **80**
Brewster Ho. *E14* ... *7B* **86**
(off Three Colt St.)
SE1 ... *4F* **103**
(off Dunton Rd.)
Brewster Rd. E10 ... 1D **68**
Brian Rd. RM6: Chad H ... 5C **54**
Briant Ho. SE1 ... 2J **19**
Briants Cl. HA5: Pinn ... 2D **40**
Briant St. SE14 ... 1K **121**
Briar Av. SW16 ... 7K **137**
Briarbank Rd. W13 ... 6A **78**
Briar Cl. IG9: Buck H ... 2G **37**
N2 ... 3K **45**
N13 ... 3H **33**
TW7: Isle ... 5K **113**
TW12: Hamp ... 5D **130**
Briar Ct. SM3: Cheam ... 4E **164**
SW15 ... 4D **116**
Briar Cres. UB5: N'olt ... 6F **59**
Briardale HA8: Edg ... 4E **28**
Briardale Gdns. NW3 ... 3J **63**
Briarfield Av. N3 ... 3K **45**
(not continuous)
Briarfield Cl. DA7: Bex ... 2G **127**
Briar Gdns. BR2: Hayes ... 1H **171**
Briaris Cl. N17 ... 7C **34**
Briar La. CR0: Addtn ... 4D **170**
Briar Rd. DA5: Bexl ... 3K **145**
HA3: Kent ... 5C **42**
NW2 ... 4E **62**
SW16 ... 3J **155**
TW2: Twick ... 1J **131**
TW17: Shep ... 5B **146**
Briars, The TW19: Stan M ... 7B **174**
WD23: B Hea ... 1D **26**
Briarswood Way BR6: Chels ... 5K **173**
Briar Wlk. HA8: Edg ... 7D **28**
SW15 ... 4D **116**
W10 ... 4G **81**
Briar Way UB7: W Dray ... 2C **92**
Briarwood Cl. NW9 ... 6J **43**
TW13: Felt ... 4G **129**
Briarwood Ct. *KT4: Wor Pk* ... *1C* **164**
(off The Avenue)
Briarwood Dr. HA6: Nwood ... 2J **39**
Briarwood Rd. KT17: Ewe ... 6C **164**
SW4 ... 5H **119**
Briary Cl. NW3 ... 7C **64**
Briary Ct. DA14: Sidc ... 5B **144**
E16 ... 6H **87**
Briary Gdns. BR1: Brom ... 5K **141**
Briary Gro. HA8: Edg ... 2H **43**
Briary La. N9 ... 3A **34**
Briary Lodge BR3: Beck ... 1E **158**
Brickbarn Cl. *SW10* ... *7A* **100**
(off King's Barn)
Brick Ct. EC4 ... 1J **13** (6A **84**)
Brickett Cl. HA4: Ruis ... 5E **38**
Brick Farm Cl. TW9: Kew ... 1H **115**
Brickfield Cl. E9 ... 6J **67**
TW8: Bford ... 7C **96**
Brickfield Cotts. BR7: Chst ... 5E **142**
SE18 ... 6K **107**
Brickfield Farm Gdns. BR6: Farnb ... 4G **173**
Brickfield La. UB3: Harl ... 6F **93**
Brickfield Rd. CR7: Thor H ... 1B **156**
SW19 ... 4K **135**
Brickfields HA2: Harr ... 2H **59**
(not continuous)
Brickfields Way UB7: W Dray ... 3B **92**
Brick La. E1 ... 3K **9** (4F **85**)
E2 ... 2K **9** (3F **85**)
EN1: Enf ... 2C **24**
EN3: Enf H ... 2C **24**
HA7: Stan ... 7J **27**
UB5: N'olt ... 3D **76**
Brick Lane Music Hall ... 1B **106**
BRICKLAYER'S ARMS ... 4D **102**
Bricklayers Arms Bus. Cen.
SE1 ... 4E **102**
Brick St. W1 ... 5J **11** (1F **101**)
Brickwall La. HA4: Ruis ... 1G **57**
Brickwood Cl. SE26 ... 3H **139**
Brickwood Rd. CR0: C'don ... 2E **168**
Brideale Cl. SE15 ... 6F **103**
Bride Ct. EC4 ... 1A **14**
Bride La. EC4 ... 1A **14** (6B **84**)
Bridel M. *N1* ... *1B* **84**
(off Colebrook Row)
Brides Pl. *N1* ... *7E* **66**
(off De Beauvoir Rd.)
Bride St. N7 ... 6K **65**
Bridewain St. SE1 ... 7J **15** (3F **103**)
Bridewell Pl. E1 ... 1H **103**
EC4 ... 1A **14** (6B **84**)
Bridford M. W1 ... 5K **5** (5F **83**)
Bridge, The HA3: W'stone ... 4K **41**
SW8 ... 7F **101**
Bridge App. NW1 ... 7E **64**
Bridge Av. W6 ... 4E **98**
W7 ... 5H **77**
Bridge Av. Mans. *W6* ... *5E* **98**
(off Bridge Av.)
Bridge Bus. Cen., The UB2: S'hall ... 2E **94**
Bridge Cl. EN1: Enf ... 2C **24**
KT12: Walt T ... 7H **147**
TW11: Tedd ... 4K **131**
W10 ... 6F **81**
Bridge Ct. E10 ... 1B **68**
E14 ... *7F* **87**
(off Newport Av.)
KT12: Walt T ... *7H* **147**
(off Bridge St.)
Bridge Dr. N13 ... 4E **32**
Bridge End E17 ... 1E **50**
Bridge End Cl. KT2: King T ... 1G **151**
Bridgefield Rd. SM1: Sutt ... 6J **165**
Bridgefoot SE1 ... 6F **19** (5J **101**)
TW16: Sun ... 1H **147**
Bridge Gdns. KT8: E Mos ... 4H **149**
N16 ... 4D **66**
TW15: Ashf ... 7E **128**
Bridge Ga. N21 ... 7H **23**
Bridge Ho. *E9* ... *6K* **67**
(off Shepherds La.)
NW3 ... *7E* **64**
(off Adelaide Rd.)
NW10 ... *2F* **81**
(off Chamberlayne Rd.)
SE4 ... 4B **122**
SM2: Sutt ... *6K* **165**
(off Bridge Rd.)
SW1 ... *5J* **17**
(off Ebury Bri.)
UB7: W Dray ... 1A **92**
W2 ... 6A **4**
Bridgehouse Ct. *SE1* ... *7A* **14**
(off Blackfriars Rd.)
Bridge Ho. Quay E14 ... 1E **104**
Bridgeland Rd. E16 ... 7J **87**
Bridgelands Cl. BR3: Beck ... 7B **140**
Bridge La. NW11 ... 4G **45**
SW11 ... 1C **118**
Bridge Leisure Cen., The ... 4B **140**
Bridgeman Ho. *E9* ... *7J* **67**
(off Frampton Pk. Rd.)
Bridgeman Rd. N1 ... 7K **65**
TW11: Tedd ... 6A **132**
Bridgeman St. NW8 ... 2C **82**
Bridge Mdws. SE14 ... 6K **103**
BRIDGEN ... 7E **126**
Bridgend Rd. SW18 ... 4A **118**
Bridgenhall Rd. EN1: Enf ... 1A **24**
Bridgen Ho. *E1* ... *6H* **85**
(off Nelson St.)
Bridgen Rd. DA5: Bexl ... 7E **126**
Bridge Pde. *N21* ... *7H* **23**
(off Ridge Av.)
Bridge Pk. ... 7H **61**
Bridgepark SW18 ... 5J **117**
Bridge Pl. CR0: C'don ... 1D **168**
SW1 ... 3K **17** (4F **101**)
Bridgepoint Lofts E7 ... 7A **70**
Bridgepoint Pl. *N6* ... *1G* **65**
(off Hornsey La.)
Bridgeport Pl. E1 ... 1G **103**
Bridge Rd. BR3: Beck ... 7B **140**
DA7: Bex ... 2E **126**
E6 ... 7D **70**
E15 ... 7F **69**
E17 ... 7B **50**
HA9: Wemb ... 3G **61**
KT8: E Mos ... 4H **149**
KT9: Chess ... 5E **162**
N9 ... 3B **34**
N22 ... 1J **47**
NW10 ... 6A **62**
SM2: Sutt ... 6K **165**
SM6: Wall ... 5F **167**
TW1: Twick ... 6B **114**
TW3: Houn, Isle ... 3H **113**
TW7: Isle ... 3H **113**
UB2: S'hall ... 2D **94**
Bridge Row CR0: C'don ... 1D **168**
Bridges Ct. SW11 ... 3B **118**
(not continuous)
Bridges Ho. *SE5* ... *7D* **102**
(off Elmington Est.)
Bridgeside Lodge *N1* ... *2C* **84**
(off Wharf Rd.)
Bridges La. CR0: Bedd ... 4J **167**
Bridges Pl. SW6 ... 1H **117**
Bridges Rd. HA7: Stan ... 5E **26**
SW19 ... 6K **135**
Bridges Rd. M. SW19 ... 6K **135**
Bridge St. HA5: Pinn ... 3C **40**
KT12: Walt T ... 7G **147**
SW1 ... 7E **12** (2J **101**)
TW9: Rich ... 6D **114**
W4 ... 4K **97**
Bridge Ter. E15 ... 7F **69**
Bridgetown Cl. SE19 ... 5E **138**
Bridge Vw. W6 ... 5E **98**
Bridge Vw. Ct. *SE1* ... *3E* **102**
(off Grange Rd.)
Bridge Wlk. *IG1: Ilf* ... *2F* **71**
(in The Exchange)
Bridgewalk Hgts. *SE1* ... *6F* **15**
(off Weston St.)
Bridgewater Cl. BR7: Chst ... 3J **161**
Bridgewater Gdns. HA8: Edg ... 2F **43**
Bridgewater Highwalk EC2 ... 5C **8**
Bridgewater Rd. E15 ... 1E **86**
HA0: Wemb ... 6C **60**
Bridgewater Sq. EC2 ... 5C **8** (5C **84**)
Bridgewater St. EC2 ... 5C **8** (5C **84**)
Bridge Way N11 ... 3B **32**
NW11 ... 5H **45**
TW2: Whitt ... 7G **113**
UB10: Ick ... 5D **56**
Bridgeway HA0: Wemb ... 7E **60**
IG11: Bark ... 7K **71**
Bridgeway St. NW1 ... 2G **83**
Bridge Wharf E2 ... 2K **85**

Bridge Wharf Rd. TW7: Isle 3B 114
Bridgewood Cl. SE20 7H 139
Bridgewood Rd. KT4: Wor Pk 4C 164
SW16 7H 137
Bridge Yd. SE1 4F 15 (1D 102)
Bridgford St. SW18 3A 136
Bridgman Rd. W4 3J 97
Bridgnorth Ho. *SE15* *6G 103*
(off Friary Est.)
Bridgwater Ho. *W2* *6A 82*
(off Hallfield Est.)
Bridgwater Rd. HA4: Ruis 4J 57
Bridle Cl. KT1: King T 4D 150
KT19: Ewe 5K 163
TW16: Sun 3J 147
Bridle La. TW1: Twick 6B 114
W1 2B 12 (7G 83)
Bridle M. EN5: Barn 4C 20
Bridle Path CR0: Bedd 3J 167
(not continuous)
Bridle Path, The IG8: Wfd G 7B 36
Bridlepath Way TW14: Bedf 7G 111
Bridle Rd. CR0: C'don 3C 170
(not continuous)
CR2: Sande 7G 169
HA5: Eastc 6K 39
KT10: Clay 6B 162
Bridle Way BR6: Farnb 4G 173
CR0: C'don 5C 170
Bridleway, The
SM6: Wall 5G 167
Bridlington Rd. N9 7C 24
Bridport *SE17* *5D 102*
(off Cadiz St.)
Bridport Av. RM7: Rom 6H 55
Bridport Ho. *N1* *1D 84*
(off Bridport Pl.)
N18 *5A 34*
(off Gilpin Cres.)
Bridport Pl. N1 1D 84
(not continuous)
Bridport Rd.
CR7: Thor H 3A 156
N18 5K 33
UB6: G'frd 1F 77
Bridstow Pl. W2 6J 81
Brief St. SE5 1B 120
Brierfield *NW1* *1G 83*
(off Arlington Rd.)
Brierley CR0: New Ad 6D 170
(not continuous)
Brierley Av. N9 1D 34
Brierley Cl. SE25 4G 157
Brierley Ct. W7 7J 77
Brierley Rd. E11 4F 69
SW12 2G 137
Brierly Gdns. E2 2J 85
Brigade Cl. HA2: Harr 2H 59
Brigade St. *SE3* *2H 123*
(off Tranquil Va.)
Brigadier Av. EN2: Enf 1H 23
Brigadier Hill
EN2: Enf 1H 23
Brigadier Ho. *NW9* *2B 44*
(off Heritage Av.)
Briggeford Cl. E5 2G 67
Briggs Cl. CR4: Mitc 1F 155
Briggs Ho. *E2* *1K 9*
(off Chambord St.)
Bright Cl. DA17: Belv 4D 108
Brightfield Rd. SE12 5G 123
Brightling Rd. SE4 6B 122
Brightlingsea Pl. E14 7B 86
Brightman Rd. SW18 1B 136
Brighton Av. E17 5B 50
Brighton Bldgs. *SE1* *3E 102*
(off Tower Bri. Rd.)
Brighton Cl. UB10: Hil 7D 56
Brighton Dr. UB5: N'olt 6E 58
Brighton Gro. SE14 1A 122
Brighton Rd. CR2: S Croy 5C 168
E6 3E 88
(not continuous)
KT6: Surb 6C 150
N2 2A 46
N16 4E 66
SM2: Sutt 7K 165
Brighton Ter. SW9 4K 119
Brightside, The EN3: Enf H 1E 24
Brightside Rd. SE13 6F 123
Bright St. E14 6D 86
Brightwell Cl. CR0: C'don 1A 168
Brightwell Cres. SW17 5D 136
Brightwen Gro. HA7: Stan 2F 27
Brig M. SE8 6C 104
Brigstock Ho. SE5 2C 120
Brigstock Rd. CR7: Thor H 5A 156
DA17: Belv 4H 109
Brill Pl. NW1 1D 6 (2H 83)
Brim Hill N2 4A 46
Brimpsfield Cl. SE2 3B 108
(not continuous)
BRIMSDOWN 2G 25
Brimsdown Av. EN3: Enf H 2F 25
Brimsdown Ho. E3 4D 86
Brimsdown Ind. Est.
EN3: Brim 1G 25
(Lockfield Av.)
EN3: Brim 2G 25
(Stockingswater La.)
Brimsdown Sports & Social Club *2E 24*
Brimstone Ho. *E15* *7G 69*
(off Victoria St.)
Brindle Ga. DA15: Sidc 1J 143
Brindley Cl. DA7: Bex 3H 127
HA0: Wemb 1D 78
Brindley Ho. *W2* *5J 81*
(off Alfred Rd.)
Brindley St. SE14 1B 122
Brindley Way BR1: Brom 5J 141
UB1: S'hall 7F 77
Brindwood Rd. E4 3G 35
Brinkburn Cl. HA8: Edg 3H 43
SE2 4A 108
Brinkburn Gdns. HA8: Edg 3G 43
Brinkley KT1: King T 2G 151
Brinkley Rd. KT4: Wor Pk 2D 164
Brinklow Cres. SE18 7F 107
Brinklow Ho. *W2* *5K 81*
(off Torquay St.)
Brinkworth Rd. IG5: Ilf 3C 52
Brinkworth Way E9 6B 68
Brinsdale Rd. NW4 3F 45
Brinsley Ho. *E1* *6J 85*
(off Tarling St.)
Brinsley Rd. HA3: Hrw W 2H 41
Brinsley St. E1 6H 85
Brinsworth Cl. TW2: Twick 1H 131
Brinsworth Ho. TW2: Twick 2H 131
Brinton Wlk. SE1 5A 14
Brion Pl. E14 5E 86
Brisbane Av. SW19 1K 153
Brisbane Ho. *W12* *7D 80*
(off White City Est.)
Brisbane Rd. E10 2D 68
IG1: Ilf 7F 53
W13 2A 96
Brisbane Road Stadium 3D 68
Brisbane St. SE5 7D 102
Briscoe Cl. E11 2H 69
Briscoe Rd. SW19 6B 136
Briset Rd. SE9 3B 124
Briset St. EC1 5A 8 (5B 84)
Briset Way N7 2K 65
Bristol Cl. SM6: Wall 7J 167
TW4: Houn 7E 112
TW19: Stanw 6A 110
Bristol Ct. TW19: Stanw 6A 110
Bristol Gdns. SW15 7E 116
W9 4K 81
Bristol Ho. *IG11: Bark* *7A 72*
(off Margaret Bondfield Av.)
SE11 2J 19
SW1 *5G 17*
(off Lwr. Sloane St.)
WC1 *5F 7*
(off Southampton Row)
Bristol M. W9 4K 81
Bristol Pk. Rd. E17 4A 50
Bristol Rd. E7 6A 70
SM4: Mord 5A 154
UB6: G'frd 1F 77
Briston Gro. N8 6J 47
Briston M. NW7 7H 29
Bristow Ct. *E8* *1H 85*
(off Triangle Rd.)
Bristowe Cl. SW2 6A 120
Bristow Rd. CR0: Bedd 4J 167
DA7: Bex 1E 126
SE19 5E 138
TW3: Houn 3G 113
Britain & London Vis. Cen. *4C 12*
(off Regent St.)
Britain at War Experience 5G 15
Britannia Bri. *E14* *6B 86*
(off Commercial Rd.)
Britannia Bldg. *N1* *1E 8*
(off Ebenezer St.)
Britannia Bus. Cen. NW2 4F 63
Britannia Cl. SW4 4H 119
UB5: N'olt 3B 76
Britannia Ct. *KT2: King T* *1D 150*
(off Skerne Wlk.)
UB7: W Dray 3A 92
Britannia Ga. E16 1J 105
BRITANNIA JUNC. 1F 83
Britannia La. TW2: Whitt 7G 113
Britannia Leisure Cen. 1D 84
Britannia Rd. E14 4C 104
IG1: Ilf 3F 71
KT5: Surb 7F 151
N12 3F 31
SW6 7K 99
(not continuous)
Britannia Row N1 1B 84
Britannia St. WC1 1G 7 (3K 83)
Britannia Wlk. N1 1E 8 (2D 84)
(not continuous)
Britannia Way NW10 4H 79
SW6 *7K 99*
(off Britannia Rd.)
TW19: Stanw 7A 110
Britannic Highwalk *EC2* *6E 8*
(off Moor La.)
British Genius Site 7E 100
British Gro. W4 5B 98
British Gro. Pas. W4 5B 98
British Gro. Sth. *W4* *5B 98*
(off British Gro. Pas.)
British Legion Rd. E4 2C 36
British Library 1D 6 (3H 83)
British Mus. 6D 6 (5J 83)
British St. E3 3B 86
British Telecom Cen. EC1 7C 8
British Wharf Ind. Est. SE14 5K 103
Britley Ho. *E14* *6B 86*
(off Copenhagen Pl.)
Brittain Ct. SE9 1C 142
Brittain Rd. RM8: Dag 3E 72
Brittany Ho. EN2: Enf 1H 23
Brittany Point SE11 4J 19 (4A 102)
Britten Cl. NW11 1K 63
Britten Ct. E15 2F 87
Brittenden Cl. BR6: Chels 6K 173
Brittenden Pde. BR6: Chels 6K 173
Britten Dr. UB1: S'hall 6E 76
Britten Ho. *SW3* *5D 16*
(off Britten St.)
Britten St. SW3 6C 16 (5C 100)
Britton Cl. SE6 7F 123
Britton St. EC1 4A 8 (4B 84)
Brixham Cres. HA4: Ruis 1J 57
Brixham Gdns. IG3: Ilf 5J 71
Brixham Rd. DA16: Well 1D 126
Brixham St. E16 1E 106
BRIXTON 4K 119
Brixton Academy *3A 120*
(off Brixton Rd.)
Brixton Hill SW2 7J 119
Brixton Hill Ct. SW2 5K 119
Brixton Hill Pl. SW2 7J 119
Brixton Oval SW2 4A 120
Brixton Recreation Cen. *3A 120*
(off Brixton Sta. Rd.)
Brixton Rd. SE11 7J 19 (6A 102)
SW9 4A 120
Brixton Sta. Rd. SW9 3A 120
Brixton Water La. SW2 5K 119
Broadacre Cl. UB10: Ick 3D 56
Broadbent Cl. N6 1F 65
Broadbent St. W1 2J 11 (7F 83)
Broadberry Ct. N18 6C 34
Broadbridge Cl. SE3 7J 105
Broad Comn. Est. *N16* *1G 67*
(off Osbaldeston Rd.)
Broadcoombe CR2: Sels 7J 169
Broad Ct. WC2 1F 13 (6J 83)
Broadcroft Av. HA7: Stan 2D 42
Broadcroft Rd. BR5: Pet W 7H 161
Broadeaves Cl. CR2: S Croy 5E 168
Broadfield NW6 6K 63
Broadfield Cl. CR0: Wadd 2K 167
NW2 3E 62
Broadfield Ct. *HA2: Harr* *1F 41*
(off Broadfields)
WD23: B Hea 2D 26
Broadfield La. NW1 7J 65
Broadfield Pde. *HA8: Edg* *3C 28*
(off Glengall Rd.)
Broadfield Rd. SE6 7G 123
Broadfields HA2: Harr 2F 41
KT8: E Mos 6J 149
Broadfields Av. HA8: Edg 4C 28
N21 6F 23
Broadfields Hgts. HA8: Edg 4C 28
Broadfield Sq. EN1: Enf 2C 24
Broadfields Way NW10 5B 62
Broadfield Way IG9: Buck H 3F 37
Broadford Ho. *E1* *4A 86*
(off Commodore St.)
Broadgate EC2 6F 9
Broadgate Circ. EC2 5G 9 (5E 84)
Broadgate Ice Rink 6G 9
Broadgate Rd. E16 6B 88
Broadgates Av. EN4: Had W 1E 20
Broadgates Ct. *SE11* *6K 19*
(off Cleaver St.)
Broadgates Rd. SW18 1B 136
BROAD GREEN 7B 156
Broad Grn. Av. CR0: C'don 7B 156
Broadhead Strand NW9 1B 44
Broadheath Dr. BR7: Chst 5D 142
Broadhinton Rd. SW4 3F 119
Broadhurst Av. HA8: Edg 4C 28
IG3: Ilf 4K 71
Broadhurst Cl. NW6 6A 64
TW10: Rich 5F 115
Broadhurst Gdns. HA4: Ruis 2A 58
NW6 6K 63
Broadlands E17 3A 50
TW13: Hanw 3E 130
Broadlands Av. EN3: Enf H 3C 24
SW16 2J 137
TW17: Shep 6E 146
Broadlands Cl. EN3: Enf H 3D 24
N6 7E 46
SW16 2J 137
Broadlands Ct. *TW9: Kew* *7G 97*
(off Kew Gdns. Rd.)
Broadlands Lodge N6 7D 46

Broadlands Rd. BR1: Brom 4K 141
N6 ....7D 46
Broadlands Way KT3: N Mald 6B 152
Broad La. EC2 ....5G 9 (5E 84)
N8 ....5K 47
N15 ....4F 49
TW12: Hamp 7D 130
Broad Lawn SE9 ....2E 142
Broadlawns Ct. HA3: Hrw W 1K 41
Broadley St. NW8 ....5B 4 (5B 82)
Broadley Ter. NW1 ....4D 4 (4C 82)
Broadmayne *SE17* *5D 102*
(*off Portland St.*)
Broadmead SE6 ....3C 140
W14 ....4G 99
Broadmead Av. KT4: Wor Pk 7C 152
Broadmead Cen. *IG8: Wfd G* *7F 37*
(*off Navestock Cres.*)
Broadmead Cl. HA5: Hat E 1C 40
TW12: Hamp 6E 130
Broadmead Ct. IG8: Wfd G 6D 36
Broadmead Rd. IG8: Wfd G 6D 36
(not continuous)
UB4: Yead 4C 76
UB5: N'olt 4C 76
Broad Oak IG8: Wfd G 5E 36
TW16: Sun 6H 129
Broad Oak Cl. E4 ....5H 35
Broadoak Ct. *SW9* *3A 120*
(*off Gresham Rd.*)
Broadoak Ho. *NW6* *1K 81*
(*off Mortimer Cres.*)
Broadoak Rd. DA8: Erith 7K 109
Broadoaks KT6: Surb 2H 163
Broadoaks Way BR2: Brom 5H 159
Broad Sanctuary SW1 ....7D 12 (2H 101)
Broadstone *NW1* *7H 65*
(*off Agar Gro.*)
Broadstone Ho. *SW8* *7K 101*
(*off Dorset Rd.*)
Broadstone Pl. W1 ....6G 5 (5E 82)
Broad St. RM10: Dag 7G 73
TW11: Tedd 6K 131
Broad St. Av. EC2 ....6G 9 (5E 84)
Broad St. Mkt. RM10: Dag 7G 73
Broad St. Pl. EC2 ....6F 9
Broadview NW9 ....6G 43
Broadview Rd. SW16 ....7H 137
Broad Wlk. N21 ....2E 32
NW1 ....1H 5 (1E 82)
SE3 ....2A 124
TW5: Hest 1B 112
TW9: Kew 7F 97
W1 ....3F 11 (7D 82)
Broad Wlk., The KT8: E Mos 4K 149
W8 ....1K 99
Broadwalk E18 ....3H 51
HA2: Harr 5E 40
Broadwalk, The HA6: Nwood 2E 38
Broadwalk Ct. *W8* *1J 99*
(*off Palace Gdns. Ter.*)
Broadwalk Ho. EC2 ....5G 9 (4E 84)
SW7 ....*2A 100*
(*off Hyde Pk. Ga.*)
Broad Wlk. La. NW11 ....7H 45
Broadwalk Shop. Cen. HA8: Edg 6C 28
Broadwall SE1 ....4K 13 (1A 102)
Broadwater Farm Est. N17 ....2D 48
Broadwater Gdns. BR6: Farnb 4F 173
Broadwater Rd. N17 ....1E 48
SE28 ....3H 107
SW17 ....4C 136
Broadway DA6: Bex 4E 126
(not continuous)
E13 ....2K 87
E15 ....7F 69
IG11: Bark 1G 89
SW1 ....7C 12 (3H 101)
W7 ....1J 95
W13 ....1A 96
Broadway, The CR0: Bedd 4J 167
E4 ....6A 36
HA3: W'stone 2J 41
HA6: Nwood 2J 39
HA7: Stan 5H 27
HA9: Wemb 3E 60
IG8: Wfd G 6E 36
KT7: T Ditt 7J 149
N8 ....6J 47
N9 ....3B 34
N11 ....5J 31
N14 ....*1C 32*
(*off Southgate Cir.*)
N22 ....2A 48
NW7 ....5F 29
RM8: Dag 1F 73
SM1: Sutt 5A 166
SM3: Cheam 6G 165
SW13 ....2A 116
SW19 ....6H 135
UB1: S'hall 7B 76
UB6: G'frd 4G 77
W3 ....*2G 97*
(*off Ridgeway Dr.*)
W5 ....7D 78
Broadway Arc. *W6* *4E 98*
(*off Hammersmith B'way.*)
Broadway Av. CR0: C'don 5D 156
TW1: Twick 6B 114
Broadway Cen., The W6 ....4E 98
Broadway Chambers *W6* *4E 98*
(*off Hammersmith B'way.*)
Broadway Cl. IG8: Wfd G 6E 36
Broadway Ct. BR3: Beck 3E 158
SW19 ....6J 135
Broadway Gdns. CR4: Mitc 4C 154
IG8: Wfd G 6E 36
Broadway Ho. *BR1: Brom* *5F 141*
(*off Bromley Rd.*)
E8 ....*1H 85*
(*off Ada St.*)
Broadway Mans. *SW6* *7J 99*
(*off Fulham Rd.*)
Broadway Mkt. E8 ....1H 85
IG6: Ilf 1H 53
(Forest Rd.)
IG6: Ilf 2G 53
(Greystone Gdns.)
SW17 ....4D 136
Broadway Mkt. M. E8 ....1G 85
Broadway M. E5 ....7F 49
N13 ....5E 32
N21 ....1G 33
Broadway Pde. E4 ....6K 35
HA2: Harr 5F 41
N8 ....6J 47
UB3: Hayes 1J 93
Broadway Pl. SW19 ....6H 135
Broadway Retail Pk. NW2 ....4F 63
Broadway Shop. Cen. DA6: Bex 4G 127
Broadway Shop. Mall
SW1 ....1C 18 (3H 101)
Broadway Sq. DA6: Bex 4G 127
Broadway Theatre, The
Barking 1G 89
Catford 7D 122
Broadway Wlk. E14 ....2C 104
Broadwell Ct. *TW5: Hest* *1B 112*
(*off Springwell Rd.*)
Broadwell Pde. *NW6* *6K 63*
(*off Broadhurst Gdns.*)
Broadwick St. W1 ....2B 12 (7G 83)
Broadwood Av. HA4: Ruis 6F 39
Broadwood Ter. W8 ....4H 99
Broad Yd. EC1 ....4A 8 (4B 84)
Brocas Cl. NW3 ....7C 64
Brockbridge Ho. SW15 ....6B 116
Brockdene Dr. BR2: Kes 4B 172
Brockdish Av. IG11: Bark 5K 71
Brockenhurst KT8: W Mole 5D 148
Brockenhurst Av. KT4: Wor Pk 1A 164
Brockenhurst Gdns. IG1: Ilf 5G 71
NW7 ....5F 29
Brockenhurst M. N18 ....4B 34
Brockenhurst Rd. CR0: C'don 7H 157
Brockenhurst Way SW16 ....2H 155
Brocket Ho. SW8 ....2H 119
Brockham Cl. SW19 ....5H 135
Brockham Cres. CR0: New Ad 7F 171
Brockham Dr. IG2: Ilf 6F 53
SW2 ....7K 119
Brockham Ho. *NW1* *1G 83*
(*off Bayham Pl.*)
SW2 ....*7K 119*
(*off Brockham Dr.*)
Brockham St. SE1 ....7D 14 (3C 102)
Brockhurst Cl. HA7: Stan 6E 26
Brockill Cres. SE4 ....4A 122
Brocklebank Ho. *E16* *1E 106*
(*off Glenister St.*)
Brocklebank Ind. Est. SE7 ....4J 105
Brocklebank Rd. SE7 ....4K 105
SW18 ....7A 118
Brocklehurst St. SE14 ....7K 103
Brocklesby Rd. SE25 ....4H 157
BROCKLEY 4K 121
Brockley Av. HA7: Stan 3K 27
Brockley Cl. HA7: Stan 4K 27
Brockley Cres. RM5: Col R 1J 55
Brockley Cross SE4 ....3A 122
Brockley Cross Bus. Cen. SE4 ....3A 122
Brockley Footpath SE4 ....5A 122
(not continuous)
SE15 ....4J 121
Brockley Gdns. SE4 ....2B 122
Brockley Gro. SE4 ....5B 122
Brockley Hall Rd. SE4 ....5A 122
Brockley Hill HA7: Stan 1H 27
Brockley Jack Theatre 5A 122
Brockley M. SE4 ....5A 122
Brockley Pk. SE23 ....7A 122
Brockley Ri. SE23 ....1A 140
Brockley Rd. SE4 ....3B 122
Brockleyside HA7: Stan 4K 27
Brockley Vw. SE23 ....7A 122
Brockley Way SE4 ....5K 121
Brockman Ri. BR1: Brom 4F 141
Brockmer Ho. *E1* *7H 85*
(*off Crowder St.*)
Brock Pl. E3 ....4D 86
Brock Rd. E13 ....5K 87
Brocks Dr. SM3: Cheam 3G 165
Brockshot Cl. TW8: Bford 5D 96
Brock St. SE15 ....3J 121
Brockway Cl. E11 ....2G 69
Brockweir *E2* *2J 85*
(*off Cyprus St.*)
Brockwell Av. BR3: Beck 5D 158
Brockwell Cl. BR5: St M Cry 5K 161
Brockwell Ct. SW2 ....5A 120
Brockwell Ho. *SE11* *7H 19*
(*off Vauxhall St.*)
Brockwell Pk. 6B 120
Brockwell Pk. Gdns. SE24 ....7A 120
Brockwell Pk. Lido 6B 120
Brockwell Pk. Row SW2 ....7A 120
Brodia Rd. N16 ....3E 66
Brodie Ho. *SE1* *5F 103*
(*off Cooper's Rd.*)
Brodie Rd. E4 ....1K 35
EN2: Enf 1H 23
Brodie St. SE1 ....5F 103
Brodlove La. E1 ....7K 85
Brodrick Gro. SE2 ....4B 108
Brodrick Rd. SW17 ....2C 136
Brody Ho. *E1* *5F 85*
(*off Strype St.*)
Brograve Gdns. BR3: Beck 2D 158
Broken Wharf EC4 ....2C 14 (7C 84)
Brokesley St. E3 ....3B 86
Broke Wlk. E8 ....1F 85
Bromar Rd. SE5 ....3E 120
Bromefield HA7: Stan 1C 42
Bromell's Rd. SW4 ....4G 119
Brome Rd. SE9 ....3D 124
Bromfelde Rd. SW4 ....3H 119
Bromfelde Wlk. SW4 ....2H 119
Bromfield St. N1 ....1A 84
Bromhall Rd. RM8: Dag 6B 72
Bromhead Rd. *E1* *6J 85*
(*off Jubilee St.*)
Bromhead St. E1 ....6J 85
Bromhedge SE9 ....3D 142
Bromholm Rd. SE2 ....3B 108
Bromleigh Ct. SE23 ....2G 139
Bromleigh Ho. *SE1* *7J 15*
(*off St Saviour's Est.*)
BROMLEY
BR1 ....2J 159
E3 ....3D 86
Bromley Av. BR1: Brom 7G 141
Bromley Coll. BR1: Brom 1J 159
BROMLEY COMMON 1C 172
Bromley Comn. BR2: Brom 4A 160
Bromley Cres. BR2: Brom 3H 159
HA4: Ruis 4H 57
Bromley FC 5K 159
Bromley Gdns. BR2: Brom 3H 159
Bromley Gro. BR2: Brom 2F 159
Bromley Hall Rd. E14 ....5E 86
Bromley High St. E3 ....3D 86
Bromley Hill BR1: Brom 6G 141
Bromley Ho. *BR1: Brom* *1J 159*
(*off North St.*)
Bromley Ind. Cen.
BR1: Brom 3B 160
Bromley La. BR7: Chst 7G 143
BROMLEY PARK 1G 159
Bromley Pk. BR1: Brom 1H 159
Bromley Pl. W1 ....5A 6 (5G 83)
Bromley Rd. BR1: Brom 1D 140
BR2: Brom 2D 158
BR3: Beck 1D 158
BR7: Chst 1F 161
E10 ....6D 50
E17 ....3C 50
N17 ....1F 49
N18 ....3J 33
SE6 ....1D 140
Bromley Ski Cen. 7E 144
Bromley St. E1 ....5K 85
BROMPTON 2D 16 (3C 100)
Brompton Arc. SW3 ....7E 10
Brompton Cl. SE20 ....2G 157
TW4: Houn 5D 112
Brompton Cotts. *SW10* *6A 100*
(*off Hollywood Rd.*)
Brompton Gro. N2 ....4C 46
Brompton Oratory 2C 16 (3C 100)
Brompton Pk. Cres. SW6 ....6K 99
Brompton Pl. SW3 ....1D 16 (3C 100)
Brompton Rd. SW1 ....3C 16 (4C 100)
SW3 ....3C 16 (4C 100)
Brompton Sq.
SW3 ....1C 16 (3C 100)
Brompton Ter. SE18 ....1D 124
Brompton Vs. *SW6* *6J 99*
(*off Lillie Rd.*)
Bromwich Av. N6 ....2E 64
Bromyard Av. W3 ....7A 80
Bromyard Ho. *SE15* *7H 103*
(*off Commercial Way*)
Bromyard Leisure Cen. 1A 98
Bron Ct. NW6 ....1J 81
BRONDESBURY 7H 63
Brondesbury Ct. NW2 ....6F 63
Brondesbury M. NW6 ....7J 63
BRONDESBURY PARK 1E 80
Brondesbury Pk. NW2 ....6E 62
NW6 ....6D 62

Brondesbury Pk. Mans. NW6 . . . . 1G 81
(off Salusbury Rd.)
Brondesbury Rd. NW6 . . . . 2H 81
Brondesbury Vs. NW6 . . . . 2H 81
Bronhill Ter. N17 . . . . 1G 49
Bronsart Rd. SW6 . . . . 7G 99
Bronson Rd. SW20 . . . . 2F 153
Bronte Cl. DA8: Erith 7H 109
E7 . . . . 4J 69
IG2: Ilf 4E 52
Bronte Ct. W3 . . . . 2G 97
W14 . . . . 3F 99
(off Girdler's Rd.)
Bronte Ho. N16 . . . . 5E 66
NW6 . . . . 3J 81
SW4 . . . . 7G 119
Bronti Cl. SE17 . . . . 5C 102
Bronwen Ct. NW8 . . . . 2A 4
(off Grove End Rd.)
Bronze Age Way DA8: Erith 2H 109
DA17: Belv 2H 109
Bronze St. SE8 . . . . 7C 104
Brook Av. HA8: Edg 6C 28
HA9: Wemb 3G 61
RM10: Dag 7H 73
Brookbank Av. W7 . . . . 5H 77
Brookbank Rd. SE13 . . . . 3C 122
Brook Cl. HA4: Ruis 7G 39
NW7 . . . . 7B 30
SW17 . . . . 2E 136
SW20 . . . . 3D 152
TW19: Stanw 7B 110
W3 . . . . 1G 97
Brook Ct. BR3: Beck 1B 158
E11 . . . . 3G 69
E17 . . . . 3A 50
HA8: Edg 5C 28
IG11: Bark 2G 89
(Abbey Rd.)
IG11: Bark 1K 89
(Ripple Av.)
SE12 . . . . 3A 142
Brook Cres. E4 . . . . 4H 35
N9 . . . . 4C 34
Brookdale N11 . . . . 4B 32
Brookdale Rd. DA5: Bexl 6E 126
E17 . . . . 3C 50
SE6 . . . . 6D 122
(not continuous)
Brookdales NW11 . . . . 4G 45
Brookdene Rd. SE18 . . . . 4J 107
Brook Dr. HA1: Harr 4G 41
HA4: Ruis 7G 39
SE11 . . . . 3A 102
Brooke Av. HA2: Harr 3G 59
Brooke Cl. WD23: Bush 1B 26
Brooke Ct. W10 . . . . 2G 81
(off Kilburn La.)
Brooke Ho. SE14 . . . . 1A 122
WD23: Bush 1B 26
Brookehowse Rd. SE6 . . . . 2C 140
Brookend Rd. DA15: Sidc 1J 143
Brooke Rd. E5 . . . . 3G 67
E17 . . . . 4E 50
N16 . . . . 3F 67
Brooke's Ct. EC1 . . . . 6J 7 (5A 84)
Brooke's Mkt. EC1 . . . . 5J 7
Brooke St. EC1 . . . . 6J 7 (5A 84)
Brooke Way WD23: Bush 1B 26
Brookfield N6 . . . . 3E 64
Brookfield Av. E17 . . . . 4E 50
NW7 . . . . 6J 29
SM1: Sutt 4B 166
W5 . . . . 4D 78
Brookfield Cl. NW7 . . . . 6J 29
Brookfield Ct. N12 . . . . 4E 30
UB6: G'frd 3G 77
Brookfield Cres. HA3: Kent 5E 42
NW7 . . . . 6J 29
Brookfield Gdns. KT10: Clay 6A 162
Brookfield Pk. NW5 . . . . 3F 65
Brookfield Path IG8: Wfd G 6B 36
Brookfield Rd. E9 . . . . 6A 68
N9 . . . . 3B 34
W4 . . . . 2K 97
Brookfields EN3: Pond E 4E 24
Brookfields Av. CR4: Mitc 5C 154
Brook Gdns. E4 . . . . 4J 35
KT2: King T 1J 151
SW13 . . . . 3B 116
Brook Ga. W1 . . . . 3F 11 (7D 82)
BROOK GREEN 4F 99
Brook Grn. W6 . . . . 3F 99
Brook Grn. Flats W14 . . . . 3F 99
(off Dunsany Rd.)
Brookhill Cl. EN4: E Barn 5H 21
SE18 . . . . 5F 107
Brookhill Rd. EN4: E Barn 5H 21
SE18 . . . . 6F 107
Brook Ho. W6 . . . . 4E 98
(off Shepherd's Bush Rd.)
Brookhouse Gdns. E4 . . . . 4B 36
Brook Ho's. NW1 . . . . 2G 83
(off Cranleigh St.)
Brook Ind. Est. UB4: Yead 1B 94
Brooking Cl. RM8: Dag 3C 72
Brooking Rd. E7 . . . . 5J 69
Brookland Cl. NW11 . . . . 4J 45
Brookland Gth. NW11 . . . . 4J 45
Brookland Hill NW11 . . . . 4K 45
Brookland Ri. NW11 . . . . 4J 45
Brooklands, The TW7: Isle 1H 113
Brooklands App. RM1: Rom 4K 55
Brooklands Av. DA15: Sidc 2H 143
SW19 . . . . 2K 135
Brooklands Cl. RM7: Rom 4K 55
TW16: Sun 1G 147
Brooklands Ct. CR4: Mitc 2B 154
KT1: King T 4D 150
(off Surbiton Rd.)
N21 . . . . 5J 23
NW6 . . . . 7H 63
Brooklands Dr. UB6: G'frd 1C 78
Brooklands La. RM7: Rom 4K 55
(not continuous)
Brooklands Pk. SE3 . . . . 3J 123
Brooklands Pas. SW8 . . . . 1H 119
Brooklands Pl. TW12: Ham H 5F 131
Brooklands Rd. KT7: T Ditt 1A 162
RM7: Rom 4K 55
Brook La. BR1: Brom 6J 141
DA5: Bexl, Bex 6D 126
SE3 . . . . 2K 123
Brook La. Bus. Cen. TW8: Bford 5D 96
Brook La. Nth. TW8: Bford 5D 96
(not continuous)
Brooklea Cl. NW9 . . . . 1A 44
Brook Lodge NW11 . . . . 5F 45
(off Nth. Circular Rd.)
RM7: Rom 4K 55
(off Medora Rd.)
Brooklyn SE20 . . . . 7G 139
Brooklyn Av. SE25 . . . . 4H 157
Brooklyn Cl. SM5: Cars 2C 166
Brooklyn Ct. W12 . . . . 1E 98
(off Frithville Gdns.)
Brooklyn Gro. SE25 . . . . 4H 157
Brooklyn Pas. W12 . . . . 2E 98
(off Lime Gro.)
Brooklyn Rd. BR2: Brom 5B 160
SE25 . . . . 4H 157
Brookmarsh Ind. Est. SE10 . . . . 7D 104
Brook Mead KT19: Ewe 6A 164
Brookmead CR0: Bedd 6G 155
Brookmead Av. BR1: Brom 5D 160
Brookmead Ind. Est.
CR0: Bedd 6G 155
Brook Mdw. N12 . . . . 3E 30
Brook Mdw. Cl. IG8: Wfd G 6B 36
Brookmead Rd. CR0: C'don 6G 155
Brook M. WC2 . . . . 1D 12
Brook M. Nth. W2 . . . . 2A 10 (7A 82)
Brookmill Rd. SE8 . . . . 1C 122
Brook Pde. IG7: Chig 3K 37
Brook Pk. Cl. N21 . . . . 5G 23
Brook Pl. EN5: Barn 5D 20
Brook Ri. IG7: Chig 3K 37
Brook Rd. CR7: Thor H 4C 156
IG2: Ilf 6J 53
IG9: Buck H, Wfd G 2D 36
KT6: Surb 2E 162
N2 . . . . 7H 31
N8 . . . . 4J 47
N22 . . . . 3K 47
NW2 . . . . 2B 62
TW1: Twick 6A 114
Brook Rd. Sth. TW8: Bford 6D 96
Brooks Av. E6 . . . . 4D 88
Brooksbank Ho. E9 . . . . 6J 67
(off Brooksbank St.)
Brooksbank St. E9 . . . . 6J 67
Brooksby Ho. N1 . . . . 7A 66
(off Liverpool Rd.)
Brooksby M. N1 . . . . 7A 66
Brooksby St. N1 . . . . 7A 66
Brooksby's Wlk. E9 . . . . 5K 67
Brooks Cl. SE9 . . . . 2E 142
Brooks Ct. SW8 . . . . 7G 101
Brookscroft E17 . . . . 3D 50
(off Forest Rd.)
Brookscroft Rd. E17 . . . . 1D 50
(not continuous)
Brooks Farm 7D 50
Brookshill HA3: Hrw W 5C 26
Brookshill Av. HA3: Hrw W 5C 26
Brookshill Dr. HA3: Hrw W 5C 26
Brookshill Ga. HA3: Hrw W 5C 26
Brookside BR6: Orp 7K 161
EN4: E Barn 6H 21
N21 . . . . 6E 22
SM5: Cars 5E 166
UB10: Uxb 7B 56
Brookside Cl. EN5: Barn 6B 20
HA2: Harr 4C 58
HA3: Kent 5D 42
TW13: Felt 3J 129
Brookside Cres.
KT4: Wor Pk 1C 164
Brookside Rd. N9 . . . . 4C 34
(not continuous)
N19 . . . . 2G 65
NW11 . . . . 6G 45
UB4: Yead 7A 76
Brookside Sth. EN4: E Barn 7K 21
Brookside Wlk. N12 . . . . 6D 30
NW11 . . . . 4G 45
Brookside Way CR0: C'don 6K 157
Brooks La. W4 . . . . 6G 97
Brooks Lodge N1 . . . . 2E 84
(off Hoxton St.)
Brook's M. W1 . . . . 2J 11 (7F 83)
Brook Sq. SE18 . . . . 1C 124
Brooks Rd. E13 . . . . 1J 87
W4 . . . . 5G 97
Brook St. DA8: Erith 5H 109
DA17: Belv, Erith 5H 109
KT1: King T 2E 150
N17 . . . . 2F 49
W1 . . . . 2J 11 (7F 83)
W2 . . . . 2B 10 (7B 82)
Brooksville Av. NW6 . . . . 1G 81
Brooks Wlk. N3 . . . . 3G 45
Brookvale DA8: Erith 1H 127
Brookview Ct. EN1: Enf 5K 23
Brookview Rd. SW16 . . . . 5G 137
Brookville Rd. SW6 . . . . 7H 99
Brook Wlk. HA8: Edg 6E 28
N2 . . . . 1B 46
Brook Way IG7: Chig 3K 37
Brookway SE3 . . . . 3J 123
Brookwood Av. SW13 . . . . 2B 116
Brookwood Cl. BR2: Brom 4H 159
Brookwood Ho. SE1 . . . . 7B 14
(off Webber St.)
Brookwood Rd. SW18 . . . . 1H 135
TW3: Houn 2F 113
Broom Cl. BR2: Brom 6C 160
TW11: Tedd 7D 132
Broomcroft Av. UB5: Yead 3A 76
Broome Rd. TW12: Hamp 7D 130
Broome Way SE5 . . . . 7D 102
Broomfield E17 . . . . 7B 50
NW1 . . . . 7E 64
(off Ferdinand St.)
TW16: Sun 1J 147
Broomfield Av. N13 . . . . 5E 32
Broomfield Ct. SE16 . . . . 3G 103
(off Ben Smith Way)
Broomfield Ho. HA7: Stan 3F 27
(off Stanmore Hill)
SE17 . . . . 4E 102
(off Massinger St.)
Broomfield La. N13 . . . . 4D 32
Broomfield Pl. W13 . . . . 1B 96
Broomfield Rd. BR3: Beck 3A 158
DA6: Bex 5G 127
KT5: Surb 1F 163
N13 . . . . 5D 32
RM6: Chad H 7D 54
TW9: Kew 1F 115
TW11: Tedd 6C 132
W13 . . . . 1B 96
Broomfield St. E14 . . . . 5C 86
Broom Gdns. CR0: C'don 3C 170
Broomgrove Gdns. HA8: Edg 1G 43
Broomgrove Rd. SW9 . . . . 2K 119
Broomhall Rd. CR2: Sande 7D 168
BROOM HILL 7K 161
Broomhill Ct. IG8: Wfd G 6D 36
Broom Hill Ri. DA6: Bex 5G 127
Broomhill Rd. BR6: Orp 7K 161
IG3: Ilf 2A 72
IG8: Wfd G 6D 36
(not continuous)
SW18 . . . . 5J 117
Broomhill Wlk. IG8: Wfd G 6C 36
Broomhouse La. SW6 . . . . 2J 117
(not continuous)
Broomhouse Rd. SW6 . . . . 2J 117
Broomleigh BR1: Brom 1J 159
(off Tweedy Rd.)
Broomloan La. SM1: Sutt 2J 165
Broom Lock TW11: Tedd 6C 132
Broom Mead DA6: Bex 6G 127
Broom Pk. TW11: Tedd 7D 132
Broom Rd. CR0: C'don 3C 170
TW11: Tedd 5B 132
Broomsleigh Bus. Pk. SE26 . . . . 5B 140
Broomsleigh St. NW6 . . . . 5H 63
Broom Water TW11: Tedd 6C 132
Broom Water W. TW11: Tedd 5C 132
Broomwood Cl. CR0: C'don 5K 157
DA5: Bexl 2K 145
Broomwood Rd. SW11 . . . . 6D 118
Broseley Gro. SE26 . . . . 5A 140
Broster Gdns. SE25 . . . . 3F 157
Brougham Rd. E8 . . . . 1G 85
W3 . . . . 6J 79
Brougham St. SW11 . . . . 2D 118
Brough Cl. KT2: King T 5D 132
SW8 . . . . 7J 101
Broughton Av. N3 . . . . 3G 45
TW10: Ham 3B 132
Broughton Ct. W13 . . . . 7B 78
Broughton Dr. SW9 . . . . 4A 120
Broughton Gdns. N6 . . . . 6G 47
Broughton Rd. BR6: Orp 2H 173
CR7: Thor H 6A 156
SW6 . . . . 2K 117
W13 . . . . 7B 78

Broughton St. SW8 . . . 2E 118
Broughton St. Ind. Est. SW11 . . . 2E 118
Brouncker Rd. W3 . . . 2J 97
Browells La. TW13: Felt . . . 2K 129
(not continuous)
Brown Bear Ct. TW13: Hanw . . . 4B 130
Brown Cl. SM6: Wall . . . 7J 167
Browne Ho. SE8 . . . 7C 104
(off Deptford Church St.)
Brownfield Area E14 . . . 6D 86
Brownfield St. E14 . . . 6D 86
Browngraves Rd. UB3: Harl . . . 7E 92
Brown Hart Gdns. W1 . . . 2H 11 (7E 82)
Brownhill Rd. SE6 . . . 7D 122
Browning Av. KT4: Wor Pk . . . 1D 164
SM1: Sutt . . . 4C 166
W7 . . . 6K 77
Browning Cl. DA16: Well . . . 1J 125
E17 . . . 4E 50
RM5: Col R . . . 1F 55
TW12: Hamp . . . 4D 130
W9 . . . 4A 4 (4A 82)
Browning Ct. W14 . . . 6H 99
(off Turneville Rd.)
Browning Ho. N16 . . . 4E 66
(off Shakspeare Wlk.)
SE14 . . . 1A 122
(off Loring Rd.)
W12 . . . 6E 80
(off Wood La.)
Browning M. W1 . . . 6H 5 (5F 83)
Browning Rd. E11 . . . 7H 51
E12 . . . 5D 70
EN2: Enf . . . 1J 23
Browning St. SE17 . . . 5C 102
Browning Way TW5: Hest . . . 1B 112
Brownlea Gdns. IG3: Ilf . . . 2A 72
Brownlow Cl. EN4: E Barn . . . 5G 21
Brownlow Ct. N2 . . . 5A 46
N11 . . . 6D 32
(off Brownlow Rd.)
Brownlow Ho. SE16 . . . 2G 103
(off George Row)
Brownlow M. WC1 . . . 4H 7 (4K 83)
Brownlow Rd. CR0: C'don . . . 4E 168
E7 . . . 4J 69
E8 . . . 1F 85
N3 . . . 7E 30
N11 . . . 6D 32
NW10 . . . 7A 62
W13 . . . 1A 96
Brownlow St. WC1 . . . 6H 7 (5K 83)
Brownrigg Rd. TW15: Ashf . . . 4C 128
Browns Arc. W1 . . . 3B 12
(off Regent St.)
Brown's Bldgs. EC3 . . . 1H 15 (6E 84)
Brownsea Wlk. NW7 . . . 6A 30
Browns La. NW5 . . . 5F 65
Brownspring Dr. SE9 . . . 4F 143
Browns Rd. E17 . . . 3C 50
KT5: Surb . . . 7F 151
Brown St. W1 . . . 7E 4 (6D 82)
Brownswell Rd. N2 . . . 2B 46
BROWNSWOOD PARK . . . 2B 66
Brownswood Rd. N4 . . . 3B 66
Broxash Rd. SW11 . . . 6E 118
Broxbourne Av. E18 . . . 4K 51
Broxbourne Gdns. BR6: Orp . . . 7K 161
Broxbourne Rd. BR6: Orp . . . 1K 173
E7 . . . 3J 69
Broxholme Cl. SE25 . . . 4D 156
Broxholme Ho. SW6 . . . 1K 117
(off Harwood Rd.)
Broxholm Rd. SE27 . . . 3A 138
Broxted Rd. SE6 . . . 2B 140
Broxwood Way NW8 . . . 1C 82
Bruce Av. TW17: Shep . . . 6E 146
Bruce Castle . . . 1E 48
Bruce Castle Ct. N17 . . . 1F 49
(off Lordship La.)
Bruce Castle Rd. N17 . . . 1F 49
Bruce Cl. DA16: Well . . . 1B 126
W10 . . . 5F 81
Bruce Ct. DA15: Sidc . . . 4K 143
Bruce Gdns. N20 . . . 3J 31
Bruce Gro. N17 . . . 1E 48
Bruce Hall M. SW17 . . . 4E 136
Bruce Ho. W10 . . . 5F 81
Bruce Rd. CR4: Mitc . . . 7E 136
E3 . . . 3D 86
EN5: Barn . . . 3B 20
HA3: W'stone . . . 2J 41
NW10 . . . 7K 61
SE25 . . . 4D 156
Bruckner St. W10 . . . 3G 81
Brudenell Rd. SW17 . . . 3D 136
Bruffs Mdw. UB5: N'olt . . . 6C 58
Bruford Ct. SE8 . . . 6C 104
Bruges Pl. NW1 . . . 7G 65
(off Randolph St.)
Brumfield Rd.
KT19: Ewe . . . 5J 163
Brummel Cl. DA7: Bex . . . 3J 127
Brune Ho. E1 . . . 6J 9
Brunei Gallery . . . 5D 6 (5H 83)
Brunel Cl. SE19 . . . 6F 139
TW5: Cran . . . 7K 93
UB5: N'olt . . . 3D 76
Brunel Ct. SE16 . . . 2J 103
(off Canon Beck Rd.)
Brunel Engine House Mus. . . . 2J 103
Brunel Est. W2 . . . 5J 81
Brunel Ho. E14 . . . 5D 104
(off Ship Yd.)
Brunel M. W10 . . . 3F 81
(off Kilburn La.)
Brunel Pl. UB1: S'hall . . . 6F 77
Brunel Rd. E17 . . . 6A 50
IG8: Wfd G . . . 5J 37
SE16 . . . 2J 103
W3 . . . 5A 80
Brunel Science Pk. UB8: Cowl . . . 3A 74
Brunel St. E16 . . . 6H 87
Brunel University
Uxbridge Campus . . . 3A 74
Brunel University Indoor Athletics Cen.
. . . 3A 74
Brunel University Sports Pk. . . . 4B 74
Brunel Wlk. N15 . . . 4E 48
SW10 . . . 7B 100
(off Cheyne Rd.)
TW2: Whitt . . . 7E 112
Brune St. E1 . . . 6J 9 (5F 85)
Brunlees Ho. SE1 . . . 3C 102
(off Bath Ter.)
Brunner Cl. NW11 . . . 5K 45
Brunner Ho. SE6 . . . 4E 140
Brunner Rd. E17 . . . 5A 50
W5 . . . 4D 78
Bruno Pl. NW9 . . . 2J 61
Brunswick Av. N11 . . . 3K 31
(not continuous)
Brunswick Cen. WC1 . . . 3E 6 (4J 83)
Brunswick Cl. DA6: Bex . . . 4D 126
HA5: Pinn . . . 6C 40
KT7: T Ditt . . . 1A 162
TW2: Twick . . . 3H 131
Brunswick Cl. Est.
EC1 . . . 2A 8 (3B 84)
Brunswick Ct. EC1 . . . 2A 8
(off Tompion St.)
EN4: E Barn . . . 5G 21
SE1 . . . 7H 15 (2E 102)
SM1: Sutt . . . 4K 165
SW1 . . . 4D 18
(off Regency St.)
Brunswick Cres. N11 . . . 3K 31
Brunswick Fitness Cen. . . . 1C 32
Brunswick Flats W11 . . . 6J 81
(off Westbourne Gro.)
Brunswick Gdns. IG6: Ilf . . . 1G 53
W5 . . . 4E 78
W8 . . . 1J 99
Brunswick Gro. N11 . . . 3K 31
Brunswick Ho. E2 . . . 2F 85
(off Thurtle Rd.)
N3 . . . 1H 45
SE16 . . . 3A 104
(off Brunswick Quay)
Brunswick Ind. Pk. N11 . . . 4A 32
Brunswick Mans. WC1 . . . 3F 7
(off Handel St.)
Brunswick M. SW16 . . . 6H 137
W1 . . . 7F 5 (6D 82)
BRUNSWICK PARK . . . 3J 31
Brunswick Pk. SE5 . . . 1E 120
Brunswick Pk. Gdns.
N11 . . . 2K 31
Brunswick Pk. Rd. N11 . . . 2K 31
Brunswick Pl. N1 . . . 2F 9 (3D 84)
NW1 . . . 4H 5 (4E 82)
(not continuous)
SE19 . . . 7G 139
Brunswick Quay SE16 . . . 3K 103
Brunswick Rd. DA6: Bex . . . 4D 126
E10 . . . 1E 68
E14 . . . 6E 86
EN3: Enf L . . . 1H 25
KT2: King T . . . 1G 151
N15 . . . 4E 48
(not continuous)
SM1: Sutt . . . 4K 165
W5 . . . 4D 78
Brunswick Sq. N17 . . . 6A 34
WC1 . . . 3F 7 (4J 83)
Brunswick St. E17 . . . 5E 50
Brunswick Ter. BR3: Beck . . . 1D 158
Brunswick Vs. SE5 . . . 1E 120
Brunswick Way N11 . . . 4A 32
Brunton Pl. E14 . . . 6A 86
Brushfield St. E1 . . . 5H 9 (5E 84)
Brushwood Cl. E14 . . . 5D 86
Brussels Rd. SW11 . . . 4B 118
Bruton Cl. BR7: Chst . . . 7D 142
Bruton La. W1 . . . 3K 11 (7F 83)
Bruton Pl. W1 . . . 3K 11 (7F 83)
Bruton Rd. SM4: Mord . . . 4A 154
Bruton St. W1 . . . 3K 11 (7F 83)
Bruton Way W13 . . . 5A 78
Brutus Ct. SE11 . . . 4B 102
(off Kennington La.)
Bryan Av. NW10 . . . 7D 62
Bryan Cl. TW16: Sun . . . 7J 129
Bryan Ho. NW10 . . . 7D 62
SE16 . . . 2B 104
Bryan Rd. SE16 . . . 2B 104
Bryan's All. SW6 . . . 2K 117
Bryanston Av. TW2: Whitt . . . 1F 131
Bryanston Cl. UB2: S'hall . . . 4D 94
Bryanston Ct. W1 . . . 7E 4
Bryanstone Ct. SM1: Sutt . . . 3A 166
Bryanstone Rd. N8 . . . 5H 47
Bryanston Mans. W1 . . . 5E 4
(off York St.)
Bryanston M. E. W1 . . . 6E 4 (5D 82)
Bryanston M. W. W1 . . . 6E 4 (5D 82)
Bryanston Pl. W1 . . . 6E 4 (5D 82)
Bryanston Sq. W1 . . . 6E 4 (6D 82)
Bryanston St. W1 . . . 1E 10 (6D 82)
Bryant Cl. EN5: Barn . . . 5C 20
Bryant Ct. E2 . . . 2F 85
(off Whiston Rd., not continuous)
W3 . . . 1K 97
Bryant Rd. UB5: Yead . . . 3A 76
Bryant St. E15 . . . 7F 69
Bryantwood Rd. N7 . . . 5A 66
Brycedale Cres. N14 . . . 4C 32
Bryce Ho. SE14 . . . 6K 103
(off John Williams Cl.)
Bryce Rd. RM8: Dag . . . 4C 72
Brydale Ho. SE16 . . . 4K 103
(off Rotherhithe New Rd.)
Bryden Cl. SE26 . . . 5A 140
Brydges Pl. WC2 . . . 3E 12 (7J 83)
Brydges Rd. E15 . . . 5F 69
Brydon Wlk. N1 . . . 1J 83
Bryer Ct. EC2 . . . 5C 8
Bryett Rd. N7 . . . 3J 65
Bryher Ct. SE11 . . . 5J 19
Brymay Cl. E3 . . . 2C 86
Brynmaer Rd. SW11 . . . 1D 118
Bryn-y-mawr Rd. EN1: Enf . . . 4A 24
Bryony Cl. UB8: Hil . . . 5B 74
Bryony Rd. W12 . . . 7C 80
Bryony Way TW16: Sun . . . 6J 129
Buccleugh Ho. E5 . . . 7G 49
Buchanan Cl. N21 . . . 5E 22
Buchanan Ct. SE16 . . . 4K 103
(off Worgan St.)
Buchanan Gdns. NW10 . . . 2D 80
Buchan Ho. W3 . . . 2H 97
(off Hanbury Rd.)
Buchan Rd. SE15 . . . 3J 121
Bucharest Rd. SW18 . . . 7A 118
Buckden Cl. N2 . . . 4D 46
SE12 . . . 6J 123
Buckfast Ct. W13 . . . 7A 78
(off Romsey Rd.)
Buckfast Ho. N14 . . . 5B 22
Buckfast Rd. SM4: Mord . . . 4K 153
Buckfast St. E2 . . . 3G 85
Buck Hill Wlk. W2 . . . 3B 10 (7B 82)
Buckhold Rd. SW18 . . . 6J 117
Buckhurst Av. SM5: Cars . . . 1C 166
Buckhurst Ct. IG9: Buck H . . . 2G 37
(off Albert Rd.)
IG9: Buck H . . . 1G 37
(Roding La.)
BUCKHURST HILL . . . 2F 37
Buckhurst Hill Ho. IG9: Buck H . . . 2E 36
Buckhurst Ho. N7 . . . 5H 65
Buckhurst St. E1 . . . 4H 85
Buckhurst Way IG9: Buck H . . . 4G 37
Buckingham Arc. WC2 . . . 3E 12
Buckingham Av. CR7: Thor H . . . 1A 156
DA16: Well . . . 4J 125
KT8: W Mole . . . 2F 149
N20 . . . 7F 21
TW14: Felt . . . 6K 111
UB6: G'frd . . . 1A 78
Buckingham Chambers SW1 . . . 3B 18
(off Greencoat Pl.)
Buckingham Cl. BR5: Pet W . . . 7J 161
EN1: Enf . . . 2K 23
TW12: Hamp . . . 5D 130
W5 . . . 5C 78
Buckingham Ct. NW4 . . . 3C 44
UB5: N'olt . . . 2C 76
W7 . . . 4K 77
(off Copley Cl.)
W11 . . . 7J 81
(off Kensington Pk.)
Buckingham Dr. BR7: Chst . . . 4G 143
Buckingham Gdns.
CR7: Thor H . . . 2A 156
HA8: Edg . . . 7K 27
KT8: W Mole . . . 2F 149
Buckingham Ga. SW1 . . . 1A 18 (3G 101)
Buckingham Gro. UB10: Hil . . . 2C 74
Buckingham La. SE23 . . . 7A 122
Buckingham Mans. NW6 . . . 5K 63
(off West End La.)
Buckingham M. N1 . . . 6E 66
NW10 . . . 2B 80
SW1 . . . 1A 18
Buckingham Palace . . . 7K 11 (2F 101)
Buckingham Pal. Rd. SW1 . . . 4J 17 (4F 101)
Buckingham Pde.
HA7: Stan . . . 5H 27
Buckingham Pl. SW1 . . . 1A 18 (3G 101)

Buckingham Rd. CR4: Mitc 4J 155
E10 3D 68
E11 5A 52
E15 5H 69
E18 1H 51
HA1: Harr 5H 41
HA8: Edg 7A 28
IG1: Ilf 2H 71
KT1: King T 4F 151
N1 6E 66
N22 1J 47
NW10 2B 80
TW10: Ham 2D 132
TW12: Hamp 4D 130
Buckingham St. WC2 4F 13 (7J 83)
Buckingham Way SM6: Wall 7G 167
Buckland Cl. NW7 4H 29
Buckland Ct. *N1* *2E 84*
(off St John's Est.)
UB10: Ick 2E 56
Buckland Cres. NW3 7B 64
Buckland Ho. *SW1* *5F 101*
(off Abbots Mnr.)
Buckland Ri. HA5: Pinn 1A 40
Buckland Rd. BR6: Orp 4J 173
E10 2E 68
KT9: Chess 5F 163
Bucklands Rd. TW11: Tedd 6C 132
Buckland St. N1 2D 84
Buckland's Wharf KT1: King T 2D 150
Buckland Wlk. SM4: Mord 4A 154
W3 2J 97
Buckland Way KT4: Wor Pk 1E 164
Buck La. NW9 5K 43
Bucklebury *NW1* *3A 6*
(off Stanhope St.)
Buckleigh Av. SW20 3G 153
Buckleigh Rd. SW16 6H 137
Buckleigh Way SE19 7F 139
Buckler Gdns. SE9 3D 142
Bucklers All. SW6 6H 99
(not continuous)
Bucklersbury EC4 1E 14 (6D 84)
Bucklersbury Pas. EC2 6D 84
Buckler's Way SM5: Cars 3D 166
Buckles Ct. DA17: Belv 4D 108
Buckle St. E1 7K 9 (6F 85)
Buckley Cl. SE23 7H 121
Buckley Ct. NW6 7H 63
Buckley Ho. *W14* *2G 99*
(off Holland Pk. Av.)
Buckley Rd. NW6 7H 63
Buckmaster Cl. *SW9* *3A 120*
(off Stockwell Pk. Rd.)
Buckmaster Ho. N7 4K 65
Buckmaster Rd. SW11 4C 118
Bucknall St. WC2 7D 6 (6J 83)
Bucknall Way BR3: Beck 4D 158
Bucknell Cl. SW2 4K 119
Buckner Rd. SW2 4K 119
Bucknill Ho. *SW1* *5J 17*
(off Ebury Bri. Rd.)
Buckrell Rd. E4 2A 36
Buckridge Ho. *EC1* *5J 7*
(off Portpool La.)
Buckshead Ho. *W2* *5J 81*
(off Gt. Western Rd.)
Buckstone Cl. SE23 6J 121
Buckstone Rd. N18 5B 34
Buck St. NW1 7F 65
Buckters Rents SE16 1A 104
Buckthorne Rd. SE4 5A 122
Buckthorn Ho. *DA15: Sidc* *3K 143*
(off Longlands Rd.)
Buck Wlk. E17 4F 51
Buckwheat Ct. DA18: Erith 3D 108
Budd Cl. N12 4E 30
Buddings Circ. HA9: Wemb 3J 61
Buddleia Ho. TW13: Felt 1J 129
Budd's All. TW1: Twick 5C 114
Bude Cl. E17 5B 50
Budge La. CR4: Mitc 7D 154
Budge Row EC4 2E 14 (7D 84)
Budge's Wlk. W2 3A 10
Budleigh Cres. DA16: Well 1C 126
Budleigh Ho. *SE15* *7G 103*
(off Bird in Bush Rd.)
Budoch Ct. IG3: Ilf 2A 72
Budoch Dr. IG3: Ilf 2A 72
Buer Rd. SW6 2G 117
Bugsby's Way SE7 4H 105
SE10 4H 105
Buick Ho. KT1: King T 2G 151
Building 50 SE18 3G 107
Building 1000 E16 7C 88
Bulbarrow *NW8* *1K 81*
(off Abbey Rd.)
Bulganak Rd. CR7: Thor H 4C 156
Bulinga St. SW1 4E 18
Bullace Row SE5 1D 120
Bull All. DA16: Well 3B 126
Bullard Rd. TW11: Tedd 6J 131
Bullard's Pl. E2 3K 85
Bullbanks Rd. DA17: Belv 4J 109
Bulleid Way SW1 4K 17 (4F 101)
Bullen Ho. *E1* *4H 85*
(off Collingwood St.)
Bullen St. SW11 2C 118
Buller Cl. SE15 7G 103
Buller Rd. CR7: Thor H 2D 156
IG11: Bark 7J 71
N17 2G 49
N22 2A 48
NW10 3F 81
Bullers Cl. DA14: Sidc 5E 144
Bullers Wood Dr. BR7: Chst 7D 142
Bullescroft Rd. HA8: Edg 3B 28
Bullingham Mans. *W8* *2J 99*
(off Pitt St.)
Bull Inn Ct. WC2 3F 13
Bullivant St. E14 7E 86
Bull La. BR7: Chst 7H 143
N18 5K 33
RM10: Dag 3H 73
Bull Rd. E15 2H 87
Bullrush Cl. CR0: C'don 6E 156
SM5: Cars 2C 166
Bull's All. SW14 2K 115
Bulls Bri. Cen. UB3: Hayes 3J 93
Bull's Bri. Ind. Est.
UB2: S'hall 4A 94
Bulls Bri. Rd. UB2: S'hall 4A 94
UB3: Hayes 3K 93
Bullsbrook Rd. UB4: Yead 1A 94
Bulls Gdns. SW3 3D 16 (4C 100)
(not continuous)
Bulls Head Pas. EC3 1G 15
Bull Yd. SE15 1G 121
Bulmer Gdns. HA3: Kent 7D 42
Bulmer M. W11 7J 81
Bulmer Pl. W11 1J 99
Bulow Est. *SW6* *1K 117*
(off Pearscroft Rd.)
Bulrington Cnr. *NW1* *7G 65*
(off Camden Rd.)
Bulstrode Av. TW3: Houn 2D 112
Bulstrode Gdns. TW3: Houn 3E 112
Bulstrode Pl. W1 6H 5 (5E 82)
Bulstrode Rd. TW3: Houn 3E 112
Bulstrode St. W1 7H 5 (6E 82)
Bulwer Ct. E11 1F 69
Bulwer Ct. Rd. E11 1F 69
Bulwer Gdns. EN5: New Bar 4F 21
Bulwer Rd. E11 7F 51
EN5: New Bar 4E 20
N18 4K 33
Bulwer St. W12 1E 98
Bunbury Ho. *SE15* *7G 103*
(off Fenham Rd.)
Bunce's La. IG8: Wfd G 7C 36
Bungalow Rd. SE25 4E 156
Bungalows, The E10 6E 50
IG6: Ilf 1J 53
SM6: Wall 5F 167
SW16 7F 137
Bunhill Row EC1 3E 8 (4D 84)
Bunhouse Pl. SW1 5H 17 (5E 100)
Bunkers Hill DA14: Sidc 3F 145
DA17: Belv 4G 109
NW11 7A 46
Bunning Way N7 7J 65
Bunns La. NW7 6F 29
(not continuous)
Bunsen Ho. *E3* *2A 86*
(off Grove Rd.)
Bunsen St. E3 2A 86
Buntingbridge Rd. IG2: Ilf 5H 53
Bunting Cl. CR4: Mitc 5D 154
N9 1E 34
Bunting Ct. NW9 2A 44
Bunton St. SE18 3E 106
Bunyan Ct. EC2 5C 8
Bunyan Rd. E17 3A 50
Buonaparte M. SW1 5C 18 (5H 101)
Burbage Cl. SE1 3D 102
UB3: Hayes 6F 75
Burbage Ho. *N1* *1D 84*
(off Poole St.)
SE14 *6K 103*
(off Samuel Cl.)
Burbage Rd. SE21 6C 120
SE24 6C 120
Burberry Cl. KT3: N Mald 2A 152
Burbidge Rd. TW17: Shep 4C 146
Burbridge Way N17 2G 49
Burcham St. E14 6D 86
Burcharbro Rd. SE2 6D 108
Burchell Ct. WD23: Bush 1B 26
Burchell Ho. *SE11* *5H 19*
(off Jonathan St.)
Burchell Rd. E10 1D 68
SE15 1H 121
Burcher Gale Gro. SE15 7F 103
Burchetts Way TW17: Shep 6D 146
Burchett Way RM6: Chad H 6F 55
Burchwall Cl. RM5: Col R 1J 55
Burcote Rd. SW18 7B 118
Burden Cl. TW8: Bford 5C 96
Burden Ho. *SW8* *7J 101*
(off Thorncroft St.)
Burdenshott Av.
TW10: Rich 4H 115
Burden Way E11 2K 69
Burder Cl. N1 6E 66
Burder Rd. N1 6E 66
Burdett Av. SW20 1C 152
Burdett Cl. DA14: Sidc 5E 144
W7 1K 95
Burdett M. NW3 6B 64
W2 6K 81
Burdett Rd. CR0: C'don 6D 156
E3 4A 86
E14 4A 86
TW9: Rich 2F 115
Burdetts Rd. RM9: Dag 1F 91
Burdock Cl. CR0: C'don 1K 169
Burdock Rd. N17 3G 49
Burdon La. SM2: Cheam 7G 165
Burdon Pk. SM2: Cheam 7H 165
Bure Ct. EN5: New Bar 5E 20
Burfield Cl. SW17 4B 136
Burford Cl. IG6: Ilf 4G 53
RM8: Dag 3C 72
UB10: Ick 4A 56
Burford Gdns. N13 3E 32
Burford Ho. TW8: Bford 5D 96
Burford Rd. BR1: Brom 4C 160
E6 3C 88
E15 1F 87
KT4: Wor Pk 7B 152
Burford Rd. SE6 2B 140
SM1: Sutt 2J 165
TW8: Bford 5E 96
Burford Wlk. SW6 7A 100
Burford Way CR0: New Ad 6E 170
Burford Wharf Apartments
E15 *1F 87*
(off Cam Rd.)
Burge Rd. E7 4B 70
Burges Gro. SW13 7D 98
Burges Rd. E6 7C 70
Burgess Av. NW9 6K 43
Burgess Bus. Pk. SE5 7D 102
Burgess Cl. TW13: Hanw 4C 130
Burgess Ct. E6 7E 70
UB1: S'hall *6F 77*
(off Fleming Rd.)
Burgess Hill NW2 4J 63
Burgess Ho. *SE5* *7C 102*
(off Bethwin Rd.)
Burgess M. SW19 6K 135
Burgess Pk. Kart Track 6D 102
Burgess Rd. E6 7E 70
E15 4G 69
SM1: Sutt 4K 165
Burgess St. E14 5C 86
Burge St. SE1 3D 102
Burgh House 4B 64
Burghill Rd. SE26 4A 140
Burghley Av. KT3: N Mald 1K 151
Burghley Hall Cl. SW19 1G 135
Burghley Ho. SW19 3G 135
Burghley Pl. CR4: Mitc 5D 154
Burghley Rd. E11 1G 69
N8 3A 48
NW5 4F 65
SW19 4F 135
Burghley Twr. W3 7B 80
Burgh St. N1 2B 84
Burgoine Quay
KT1: Ham W 1D 150
Burgon St. EC4 1B 14 (6B 84)
Burgos Cl. CR0: Wadd 6A 168
Burgos Gro. SE10 1D 122
Burgoyne Rd. N4 6B 48
SE25 4F 157
SW9 3K 119
TW16: Sun 6H 129
Burgundy Ho. *EN2: Enf* *1H 23*
(off Bedale Rd.)
Burham Cl. SE20 7J 139
Burhill Gro. HA5: Pinn 2C 40
Burke Cl. SW15 4A 116
Burke Lodge E13 3K 87
Burke St. E16 5H 87
(not continuous)
Burket Cl. UB2: S'hall 4C 94
Burland Rd. SW11 5D 118
Burleigh Av. DA15: Sidc 5K 125
SM6: Wall 3E 166
Burleigh Cl. RM7: Mawney 4H 55
Burleigh Gdns. N14 1B 32
TW15: Ashf 5E 128
Burleigh Ho. SW3 7B 16
W10 *5G 81*
(off St Charles Sq.)
Burleigh Pde. N14 1C 32
Burleigh Pl. SW15 5F 117
Burleigh Rd. EN1: Enf 4K 23
SM3: Sutt 1G 165
UB10: Hil 1D 74
Burleigh St. WC2 2G 13 (7K 83)
Burleigh Wlk. SE6 1E 140
Burleigh Way EN2: Enf 3J 23
Burley Cl. E4 5H 35
SW16 2H 155
Burley Ho. *E1* *6K 85*
(off Chudleigh St.)
Burley Rd. E16 6A 88
Burlington Arc. W1 3A 12 (7G 83)

Burlington Av. RM7: Rom 6H 55
TW9: Kew 1G 115
Burlington Cl. BR6: Farnb 2F 173
E6 6C 88
HA5: Eastc 3K 39
TW14: Bedf 7F 111
W9 4J 81
Burlington Gdns. RM6: Chad H 7E 54
SW6 2G 117
W1 3A 12 (7G 83)
W3 1J 97
W4 5J 97
Burlington La. W4 7J 97
Burlington M. SW15 5H 117
W3 1J 97
Burlington Pl. IG8: Wfd G 3E 36
SW6 2G 117
Burlington Ri. EN4: E Barn 1H 31
Burlington Rd.
CR7: Thor H 2C 156
EN2: Enf 1J 23
KT3: N Mald 4B 152
N10 3E 46
N17 1G 49
SW6 2G 117
TW7: Isle 1H 113
W4 5J 97
Burma M. N16 4D 66
Burma Rd. N16 4D 66
Burmarsh NW5 6E 64
Burmarsh Ct. SE20 1J 157
Burma Ter. SE19 5E 138
Burmester Rd. SW17 3A 136
Burnaby Cres. W4 6J 97
Burnaby Gdns. W4 6H 97
Burnaby St. SW10 7A 100
Burnand Ho. *W14* *3F 99*
(off Redan St.)
Burnard Pl. N7 5K 65
Burnbrae Cl. N12 6E 30
Burnbury Rd. SW12 1G 137
Burncroft Av. EN3: Enf H 2D 24
Burndell Way UB4: Yead 5B 76
Burne Jones Ho. W14 4G 99
Burnell Av. DA16: Well 2A 126
TW10: Ham 5C 132
Burnell Gdns. HA7: Stan 2D 42
Burnell Rd. SM1: Sutt 4K 165
Burnell Wlk. *SE1* *5F 103*
(off Abingdon Cl.)
Burnels Av. E6 3E 88
Burness Cl. N7 6K 65
Burne St. NW1 5C 4 (5C 82)
Burnett Cl. E9 5J 67
Burnett Ho. *SE13* *2E 122*
(off Lewisham Hill)
Burnett Rd. IG6: Ilf 7K 37
Burney Av. KT5: Surb 5F 151
Burney St. SE10 7E 104
Burnfoot Av. SW6 1G 117
Burnham NW3 7C 64
Burnham Av. UB10: Ick 4E 56
Burnham Cl. EN1: Enf 1K 23
HA3: W'stone 4A 42
NW7 7H 29
SE1 4F 103
Burnham Ct. *NW4* *4E 44*
(off Brent St.)
NW6 *7A 64*
(off Fairhazel Gdns.)
W2 *7K 81*
(off Moscow Rd.)
Burnham Cres. E11 4A 52
Burnham Dr. KT4: Wor Pk 2F 165
Burnham Est. *E2* *3J 85*
(off Burnham St.)
Burnham Gdns.
CR0: C'don 7F 157
TW4: Cran 1K 111
UB3: Harl 3F 93
Burnham Rd. DA14: Sidc 2E 144
E4 5G 35
RM7: Rom 3K 55
RM9: Dag 7B 72
SM4: Mord 4K 153
Burnham St. E2 3J 85
KT2: King T 1G 151
Burnham Way SE26 5B 140
W13 4B 96
Burnhill Cl. SE15 7H 103
Burnhill Rd. BR3: Beck 2C 158
Burnley Rd. NW10 5B 62
SW9 2K 119
Burnsall St. SW3 6D 16 (5C 100)
Burns Av. DA15: Sidc 6B 126
RM6: Chad H 7C 54
TW14: Felt 6J 111
UB1: S'hall 7E 76
Burns Cl. DA16: Well 1K 125
E17 4E 50
SW19 6B 136
UB4: Hayes 5H 75
Burns Ho. *E2* *3J 85*
(off Cornwall Av.)
SE17 *5B 102*
(off Doddington Gro.)
Burnside Av. E4 6G 35
Burnside Cl. EN5: New Bar 3D 20
SE16 1K 103
TW1: Twick 6A 114
Burnside Ct. SM5: Cars 3E 166
Burnside Cres. HA0: Wemb 1D 78
Burnside Rd. RM8: Dag 2C 72
Burns Rd. HA0: Wemb 2E 78
NW10 1B 80
SW11 2D 118
W13 2B 96
Burns Way TW5: Hest 2B 112
Burnt Ash Hgts. BR1: Brom 5K 141
Burnt Ash Hill SE12 6H 123
Burnt Ash La. BR1: Brom 7J 141
Burnt Ash Rd. SE12 5H 123
Burnthwaite Rd. SW6 7H 99
BURNT OAK 2J 43
Burnt Oak HA8: Edg 7B 28
Burnt Oak B'way. HA8: Edg 7B 28
Burnt Oak Flds. HA8: Edg 1J 43
Burnt Oak La. DA15: Sidc 6A 126
Burntwood Cl. SW18 1C 136
Burntwood Grange Rd. SW18 1B 136
Burntwood La. SW17 3A 136
Burntwood Vw. SE19 5F 139
Buross St. E1 6H 85
Burpham Cl. UB4: Yead 5B 76
Burrage Ct. *SE16* *4K 103*
(off Worgan St.)
Burrage Gro. SE18 4G 107
Burrage Pl. SE18 5F 107
Burrage Rd. SE18 6G 107
Burrard Ho. *E2* *2J 85*
(off Bishop's Way)
Burrard Rd. E16 6K 87
NW6 5J 63
Burr Cl. DA7: Bex 3F 127
E1 4K 15 (1G 103)
Burrell Cl. CR0: C'don 6A 158
HA8: Edg 2C 28
Burrell Row BR3: Beck 2C 158
Burrell St. SE1 4A 14 (1B 102)
Burrells Wharf Sq. E14 5D 104
Burrell Towers E10 7C 50
Burrhill Ct. *SE16* *3K 103*
(off Worgan St.)
Burritt Rd. KT1: King T 2G 151
Burroughs, The NW4 4D 44
Burroughs Club, The 4D 44
Burroughs Cotts. *E14* *5A 86*
(off Halley St.)
Burroughs Gdns. NW4 4D 44
Burroughs Pde. NW4 4D 44
Burrow Ho. *SW9* *2A 120*
(off Stockwell Pk. Rd.)
Burrow Rd. SE22 4E 120
Burrows M. SE1 6A 14 (2B 102)
Burrows Rd. NW10 3E 80
Burrow Wlk. SE21 7C 120
Burr Rd. SW18 1J 135
Bursar St. SE1 5G 15 (1E 102)
Bursdon Cl. DA15: Sidc 2K 143
Bursland Rd. EN3: Pond E 4E 24
Burslem St. E1 6G 85
Burstock Rd. SW15 4G 117
Burston Rd. SW15 5F 117
Burston Vs. *SW15* *5F 117*
(off St John's Av.)
Burstow Rd. SW20 1G 153
Burtenshaw Rd. KT7: T Ditt 7A 150
Burtley Cl. N4 1C 66
Burton Bank *N1* *7D 66*
(off Yeate St.)
Burton Cl. CR7: Thor H 3D 156
KT9: Chess 7D 162
Burton Ct. KT7: T Ditt 6A 150
SE20 2J 157
SW3 *5F 17*
(off Franklin's Row)
Burton Gdns. TW5: Hest 1D 112
Burton Gro. SE17 5D 102
Burtonhole Cl. NW7 4A 30
Burtonhole La. N12 4B 30
NW7 5K 29
Burton Ho. *SE16* *2H 103*
(off Cherry Gdn. St.)
Burton La. SW9 2A 120
(not continuous)
Burton M. SW1 4H 17 (4E 100)
Burton Pl. WC1 2D 6 (3H 83)
Burton Rd. E18 3K 51
KT2: King T 7E 132
NW6 7H 63
SW9 2B 120
(Akerman Rd.)
SW9 2A 120
(Evesham Wlk.)
Burton's Rd. TW12: Ham H 4F 131
Burton St. WC1 2D 6 (3H 83)
Burtonwood Ho. N4 7D 48
Burtop Rd. Est. SW17 3A 136
Burt Rd. E16 1A 106
Burts Wharf DA17: Belv 7J 91
Burtt Ho. *N1* *1G 9*
(off Aske St.)
Burtwell La. SE27 4D 138
Burwash Ho. *SE1* *7F 15*
(off Kipling Est.)
Burwash Rd. SE18 5H 107
Burwell *KT1: King T* *2G 151*
(off Excelsior Rd.)
Burwell Av. UB6: G'frd 6J 59
Burwell Cl. E1 6H 85
Burwell Rd. E10 1A 68
Burwell Rd. Ind. Est.
E10 1A 68
Burwell Wlk. E3 4C 86
Burwood Av.
BR2: Hayes 2K 171
HA5: Eastc 5K 39
Burwood Cl. KT6: Surb 1G 163
Burwood Ho. SW9 4B 120
Burwood Pl. EN4: Had W 1F 21
W2 7D 4 (6C 82)
Bury Av. HA4: Ruis 6E 38
UB4: Hayes 2G 75
Bury Cl. SE16 1K 103
Bury Ct. EC3 7H 9 (6E 84)
Buryfield Ct. *SE8* *4K 103*
(off Lower Rd.)
Bury Gro. SM4: Mord 5K 153
Bury Hall Vs. N9 7A 24
Bury Pl. WC1 6E 6 (5J 83)
Bury Rd. E4 1B 36
N22 2A 48
RM10: Dag 5H 73
Buryside Cl. IG2: Ilf 4K 53
Bury St. EC3 1H 15 (6E 84)
HA4: Ruis 5E 38
N9 7A 24
SW1 4B 12 (1G 101)
Bury St. W. N9 7J 23
Bury Wlk. SW3 4C 16 (4C 100)
Busbridge Ho. *E14* *5C 86*
(off Brabazon St.)
Busby Ho. SW16 4G 137
Busby M. NW5 6H 65
Busby Pl. NW5 6H 65
Busch Cl. TW7: Isle 1B 114
Bushbaby Cl. SE1 3E 102
Bushberry Rd. E9 6A 68
Bush Cl. IG2: Ilf 5H 53
Bush Cotts. SW18 5J 117
Bush Ct. N14 1C 32
W12 2F 99
Bushell Cl. SW2 2K 137
Bushell Grn. WD23: B Hea 2C 26
Bushell St. E1 1G 103
Bushell Way BR7: Chst 5E 142
BUSHEY 1C 26
Bushey Av. BR5: Pet W 7H 161
E18 3H 51
Bushey Cl. E4 3K 35
UB10: Ick 2C 56
Bushey Ct. SW20 3D 152
Bushey Down SW12 2F 137
BUSHEY HEATH 1C 26
Bushey Hill Rd. SE5 1E 120
Bushey La. SM1: Sutt 4J 165
BUSHEY MEAD 2F 153
Bushey Rd. CR0: C'don 2C 170
E13 2A 88
N15 6E 48
SM1: Sutt 4J 165
SW20 3D 152
UB3: Harl 4G 93
UB10: Ick 2C 56
Bushey Way BR3: Beck 6F 159
Bush Fair Ct. N14 6A 22
Bushfield Cl. HA8: Edg 2C 28
Bushfield Cres. HA8: Edg 2C 28
Bush Gro. HA7: Stan 1D 42
NW9 7J 43
Bushgrove Rd. RM8: Dag 4D 72
Bush Hill N21 7H 23
Bush Hill Pde. EN1: Enf 7J 23
N9 7J 23
BUSH HILL PARK 6A 24
Bush Hill Rd. HA3: Kent 6F 43
N21 6J 23
Bush Ind. Est. N19 3G 65
NW10 4K 79
Bush La. EC4 2E 14 (7D 84)
Bushmead Cl. N15 4F 49
Bushmoor Cres. SE18 7F 107
Bushnell Rd. SW17 2F 137
Bush Rd. E8 1H 85
E11 7H 51
IG9: Buck H 4G 37
SE8 *4K 103*
(off Rotherhithe New Rd.)
TW9: Kew 6F 97
TW17: Shep 5B 146
Bush Theatre 2E 98
Bushway RM8: Dag 4D 72
Bushwood E11 1H 69
Bushwood Dr. SE1 4F 103
Bushwood Rd.
TW9: Kew 6G 97
Bushy Ct. *KT1: Ham W* *1C 150*
(off Up. Teddington Rd.)
Bushy Lees DA15: Sidc 6K 125
Bushy Pk. Gdns. TW11: Tedd 5H 131

Bushy Pk. Rd. TW11: Tedd 7B 132
(not continuous)
Bushy Rd. TW11: Tedd 6K 131
Business Design Cen. *N1* *1A 84*
(off Upper St.)
Business Village, The SW18 5J 117
Buspace Studios *W10* *4G 81*
(off Conlan St.)
Butcher Row E1 7K 85
E14 7K 85
Butchers Rd. E16 6J 87
Bute Av. TW10: Ham 2E 132
Bute Ct. SM6: Wall 5G 167
Bute Gdns. SM6: Wall 5G 167
TW10: Ham 1E 132
W6 4F 99
Bute Gdns. W. SM6: Wall 5G 167
Bute M. NW11 5A 46
Bute Rd. CR0: C'don 1A 168
IG6: Ilf 5F 53
SM6: Wall 4G 167
Bute St. SW7 3A 16 (4B 100)
Bute Wlk. N1 6D 66
Butfield Ho. *E9* *6J 67*
(off Stevens Av.)
Butler Av. HA1: Harr 7H 41
Butler Cl. HA8: Edg 2H 43
Butler Ct. HA0: Wemb 4A 60
RM8: Dag *2G 73*
(off Gosfield Rd.)
Butler Ho. *E2* *3J 85*
(off Bacton St.)
E14 *6B 86*
(off Burdett St.)
SW9 *1B 120*
(off Lothian Rd.)
Butler Pl. SW1 1C 18 (3H 101)
Butler Rd. HA1: Harr 7G 41
NW10 7B 62
RM8: Dag 4B 72
Butlers & Colonial Wharf *SE1* *6K 15*
(off Shad Thames)
Butlers Cl. TW3: Houn 3D 112
Butlers Dr. E4 1K 25
Butler St. E2 3J 85
UB10: Hil 4D 74
Butlers Wharf SE1 1F 103
Butlers Wharf W. *SE1* *5J 15*
(off Shad Thames)
Butley Ct. *E3* *2A 86*
(off Ford St.)
Buttercup Cl. UB5: N'olt 6D 58
Butterfield Cl. N17 6H 33
SE16 2H 103
TW1: Twick 6K 113
Butterfields E17 5E 50
Butterfield Sq. E6 6D 88
Butterfly La. SE9 6F 125
Butterfly Wlk. *SE5* *1D 120*
(off Denmark Hill)
Butter Hill SM5: Cars 3E 166
SM6: Wall 3E 166
Butteridges Cl. RM9: Dag 1F 91
Buttermere *NW1* *1K 5*
(off Augustus St.)
Buttermere Cl. E15 4F 69
SE1 4F 103
SM4: Mord 6F 153
TW14: Felt 1H 129
Buttermere Ct. *NW8* *1B 82*
(off Boundary Rd.)
Buttermere Dr. SW15 5G 117
Buttermere Wlk. E8 6F 67
Butterwick W6 4F 99
Butterworth Gdns. IG8: Wfd G 6D 36
Butterworth Ter. *SE17* *5C 102*
(off Sutherland Wlk.)
Buttesland St. N1 1F 9 (3D 84)
Buttfield Cl. RM10: Dag 6H 73
Buttmarsh Cl. SE18 5F 107
Butts, The TW8: Bford 6C 96
TW16: Sun 3A 148
Buttsbury Rd. IG1: Ilf 5G 71
Butts Cotts TW13: Hanw 3C 130
Butts Cres. TW13: Hanw 3E 130
Buttsmead HA6: Nwood 1E 38
Butts Piece UB5: Yead 2K 75
Butts Rd. BR1: Brom 5G 141
Buxhall Cres. E9 6B 68
Buxted Rd. E8 7F 67
N12 5H 31
SE22 4E 120
Buxton Cl. IG8: Wfd G 6G 37
N9 2D 34
Buxton Ct. E11 7H 51
N1 1D 8
Buxton Cres. SM3: Cheam 4G 165
Buxton Dr. E11 4G 51
KT3: N Mald 2K 151
Buxton Gdns. W3 7H 79
Buxton Ho. E11 4G 51
Buxton M. SW4 2H 119
Buxton Rd. CR7: Thor H 5B 156
DA8: Erith 7K 109
E4 1A 36
E6 3C 88
E15 5G 69
E17 4A 50
(not continuous)
IG2: Ilf 6J 53
N19 1H 65
NW2 6D 62
SW14 3A 116
TW15: Ashf 5A 128
Buxton St. E1 4K 9 (4F 85)
Buzzard Creek Ind. Est.
IG11: Bark 5A 90
Byam St. SW6 2A 118
Byards Ct. *SE16* *4K 103*
(off Worgan St.)
Byards Cft. SW16 1H 155
Byatt Wlk. TW12: Hamp 6C 130
Bychurch End TW11: Tedd 5K 131
Bycroft Rd. UB1: S'hall 4E 76
Bycroft St. SE20 7K 139
Bycullah Av. EN2: Enf 3G 23
Bycullah Rd. EN2: Enf 2G 23
Bye, The W3 6A 80
Byegrove Rd. SW19 6B 136
Byelands Cl. SE16 1K 103
Bye Way, The HA3: W'stone 1J 41
Byeway, The SW14 3J 115
Byeways TW2: Twick 3F 131
Byeways, The KT5: Surb 5G 151
Byfeld Gdns. SW13 1C 116
Byfield Cl. SE16 2B 104
Byfield Rd. TW7: Isle 3A 114
Byford Cl. E15 7G 69
Byford Ho. EN5: Barn 4A 20
Bygrove CR0: New Ad 6D 170
Bygrove St. E14 6D 86
(not continuous)
Byland Cl. N21 7E 22
SM4: Mord 7A 154
Bylands Cl. SE2 3B 108
Byne Rd. SE26 6J 139
SM5: Cars 2C 166
Bynes Rd. CR2: S Croy 7D 168
Byng Pl. WC1 4D 6 (4H 83)
Byng Rd. EN5: Barn 2A 20
Byng St. E14 2C 104
Bynon Av. DA7: Bex 3F 127
Byre Rd. N14 6A 22
Byrne Rd. SW12 1F 137
Byron Av. E12 6C 70
E18 3H 51
KT3: N Mald 5C 152
NW9 4H 43
SM1: Sutt 4B 166
TW4: Cran 2J 111
Byron Av. E. SM1: Sutt 4B 166
Byron Cl. E8 1G 85
KT12: Walt T 7C 148
SE20 3H 157
SE26 4A 140
SE28 1C 108
SW16 6J 137
TW12: Hamp 4D 130
Byron Ct. *E11* *4K 51*
(off Makepeace Rd.)
EN2: Enf 2G 23
HA1: Harr 6J 41
NW6 *7A 64*
(off Fairfax Rd.)
SE22 1G 139
SW3 *4D 16*
(off Elystan St.)
W7 *4A 96*
(off Boston Rd.)
W9 *4J 81*
(off Lanhill Rd.)
WC1 *3G 7*
(off Mecklenburgh Sq.)
Byron Dr. DA8: Erith 7H 109
N2 6B 46
Byron Gdns. SM1: Sutt 4B 166
Byron Hill Rd. HA2: Harr 1H 59
Byron Ho. DA1: Cray 5K 127
Byron M. NW3 4C 64
W9 4J 81
Byron Pde. UB10: Hil 4E 74
Byron Rd. E10 1D 68
E17 3C 50
HA0: Wemb 2C 60
HA1: Harr 6J 41
HA3: W'stone 2K 41
NW2 2D 62
NW7 5H 29
W5 1F 97
Byron St. E14 6E 86
Byron Ter. N9 6D 24
Byron Way UB4: Hayes 4H 75
UB5: N'olt 3C 76
UB7: W Dray 4B 92
Bysouth Cl. IG5: Ilf 1F 53
N15 4D 48
Bythorn St. SW9 3K 119
Byton Rd. SW17 6D 136
Byward Av. TW14: Felt 6A 112
Byward St. EC3 3H 15 (7E 84)
Bywater Ho. SE18 3C 106
Bywater Pl. SE16 1A 104
Bywater St. SW3 5E 16 (5D 100)
Byway E11 5A 52
Byway, The KT19: Ewe 4B 164
SM2: Sutt 7B 166
Bywell Pl. W1 6A 6
Bywood Av. CR0: C'don 6J 157
Byworth Wlk. N19 1J 65

C

Cabbell St. NW1 6C 4 (5C 82)
Cabinet Way E4 6G 35
Cable Ho. *WC1* *1J 7*
(off Gt. Percy St.)
Cable Pl. SE10 1E 122
Cables Cl. DA17: Belv 3J 109
Cable St. E1 7G 85
Cable Trade Pk. SE7 4A 106
Cabot Ct. *SE16* *4K 103*
(off Worgan St.)
Cabot Sq. E14 1C 104
Cabot Way E6 1B 88
Cabul Rd. SW11 2C 118
Caci Ho. *W14* *4H 99*
(off Kensington Village)
Cactus Cl. SE15 2E 120
Cactus Wlk. W12 6B 80
Cadbury Cl. TW7: Isle 1A 114
TW16: Sun 7G 129
Cadbury Rd. TW16: Sun 7G 129
Cadbury Way SE16 3F 103
Caddington Cl. EN4: E Barn 5H 21
Caddington Rd. NW2 3G 63
Caddis Cl. HA7: Stan 7E 26
Cadell Cl. E2 1K 9 (2F 85)
Cade Rd. SE10 1F 123
Cader Rd. SW18 6A 118
Cadet Dr. SE1 4F 103
Cadet Pl. SE10 5G 105
Cadiz Ct. RM10: Dag 7K 73
Cadiz Rd. RM10: Dag 7J 73
Cadiz St. SE17 5C 102
Cadley Ter. SE23 2J 139
Cadman Cl. SW9 7B 102
Cadman Ct. *W4* *5H 97*
(off Chaseley Dr.)
Cadmer Cl. KT3: N Mald 4A 152
Cadmore Ho. *N1* *7B 66*
(off The Sutton Est.)
Cadmus Cl. SW4 3H 119
Cadmus Ct. *SW9* *1A 120*
(off Southey Rd.)
Cadnam Lodge *E14* *3E 104*
(off Schooner Cl.)
Cadnam Point SW15 1D 134
Cadogan Cl. BR3: Beck 1F 159
E9 7B 68
HA2: Harr 4F 59
TW11: Tedd 5J 131
Cadogan Ct. SM2: Sutt 6K 165
SW3 *4E 16*
(off Draycott Av.)
Cadogan Ct. Gdns. *SW1* *3G 17*
(off D'Oyley St.)
Cadogan Gdns. E18 3K 51
N3 1K 45
N21 5F 23
SW3 3F 17 (4D 100)
Cadogan Ga. SW1 3F 17 (4D 100)
Cadogan Hall *3G 17*
(off Sloane Ter.)
Cadogan Ho. IG8: Wfd G 7K 37
SW3 7B 16
Cadogan La. SW1 2G 17 (3E 100)
Cadogan Mans. *SW3* *4F 17*
(off Cadogan Gdns.)
Cadogan Pl. SW1 1F 17 (3D 100)
Cadogan Rd. KT6: Surb 5D 150
SE18 3G 107
Cadogan Sq. SW1 2E 16 (3D 100)
Cadogan St. SW3 4E 16 (4D 100)
Cadogan Ter. E9 6B 68
Cadoxton Av. N15 6F 49
Cadwallon Rd. SE9 2F 143
Caedmon Rd. N7 4K 65
Caerleon Cl. DA14: Sidc 5C 144
KT10: Clay 7B 162
Caerleon Ter. SE2 4B 108
Caernafon Ho. HA7: Stan 5F 27
Caernarvon Cl. CR4: Mitc 3J 155
Caernarvon Dr. IG5: Ilf 1E 52
Caernarvon Ho. *E16* *1K 105*
(off Audley Dr.)
W2 *6A 82*
(off Hallfield Est.)
Caesar Ct. *E2* *2K 85*
(off Palmer's Rd.)
Caesars Wlk. CR4: Mitc 5D 154
Caesars Way TW17: Shep 6F 147
Cafe Gallery 3J 103
Cahill St. EC1 4D 8 (4C 84)
Cahir St. E14 4D 104
Cain Ct. *W5* *5C 78*
(off Castlebar M.)
Caine Ho. *W3* *2H 97*
(off Hanbury Rd.)
Cain's La. TW14: Felt 5G 111

Caird St. W10 .... 3G 81
Cairn Av. W5 .... 1D 96
Cairncross M. *N8* *6J 47*
(off Felix Av.)
Cairndale Cl. BR1: Brom 7H 141
Cairnfield Av. NW2 .... 3A 62
Cairngorm Cl. TW11: Tedd 5A 132
Cairns Av. IG8: Wfd G 6H 37
Cairns M. SE18 .... 1C 124
Cairns Rd. SW11 .... 5C 118
Cairn Way HA7: Stan 6E 26
Cairo New Rd. CR0: C'don 2B 168
Cairo Rd. E17 .... 4C 50
Caister Ho. N7 .... 6K 65
Caistor Ho. *E15* *1H 87*
(off Caistor Pk. Rd.)
Caistor M. SW12 .... 7F 119
Caistor Pk. Rd. E15 .... 1H 87
Caistor Rd. SW12 .... 7F 119
Caithness Gdns. DA15: Sidc 6K 125
Caithness Ho. *N1* *1K 83*
(off Twyford St.)
Caithness Rd. CR4: Mitc 7F 137
W14 .... 3F 99
Calabria Rd. N5 .... 6B 66
Calais Ga. SE5 .... 1B 120
Calais St. SE5 .... 1B 120
Calbourne Rd. SW12 .... 7D 118
Calcott Ct. *W14* *3G 99*
(off Blythe Rd.)
Calcott Wlk. SE9 .... 4C 142
Calcraft Ho. *E2* *2J 85*
(off Bonner Rd.)
Caldbeck Av. KT4: Wor Pk 2C 164
Caldecote *KT1: King T* *2G 151*
(off Excelsior Cl.)
Caldecote Gdns. WD23: Bush 1D 26
CALDECOTE HILL 1E 26
Caldecot Rd. SE5 .... 2C 120
Caldecott Way E5 .... 3K 67
Calder Av. UB6: G'frd 2K 77
Calder Cl. EN1: Enf 3K 23
Calder Ct. SE16 .... 1B 104
Calder Gdns. HA8: Edg 3G 43
Calderon Ho. *NW8* *2C 82*
(off Townshend Est.)
Calderon Pl. W10 .... 5E 80
Calderon Rd. E11 .... 4E 68
Calder Rd. SM4: Mord 5A 154
Caldervale Rd. SW4 .... 5H 119
Calder Way SL3: Poyle 6A 174
Calderwood St. SE18 .... 4E 106
(not continuous)
Caldew Ct. NW7 .... 7H 29
Caldew St. SE5 .... 7D 102
Caldicot Grn. NW9 .... 6A 44
Caldon Ho. UB5: N'olt 4D 76
Caldwell Ho. *SW13* *7E 98*
(off Trinity Chu. Rd.)
Caldwell St. SW9 .... 7K 101
Caldy Rd. DA17: Belv 3H 109
Caldy Wlk. N1 .... 7C 66
Caleb St. SE1 .... 6C 14 (2C 102)
Caledonia Ct. *IG11: Bark* *2C 90*
(off Keel Cl.)
Caledonia Ho. *E14* *6A 86*
(off Salmon La.)
Caledonian Cl. IG3: Ilf 1B 72
Caledonian Ct. UB5: N'olt 4C 76
Caledonian Rd. N1 .... 1F 7 (2J 83)
N7 .... 4K 65
Caledonian Sq. NW1 .... 6H 65
Caledonian Wharf E14 .... 4F 105
Caledonia Rd.
TW19: Stanw 1A 128
Caledonia St. N1 .... 1F 7 (2J 83)
Caledon Rd. E6 .... 1D 88
SM6: Wall 4E 166
Cale St. SW3 .... 5C 16 (5C 100)
Caletock Way SE10 .... 5H 105
Calgarth *NW1* *1B 6*
(off Ampthill Est.)
Calgary Ct. RM7: Mawney 4H 55
SE16 .... *2J 103*
(off Canada Est.)
Caliban Twr. *N1* *2E 84*
(off Arden Est.)
Calico Ho. *EC4* *1D 14*
(off Well Ct.)
Calico Row SW11 .... 3A 118
Calidore Cl. SW2 .... 6K 119
California Bldg. *SE10* *1D 122*
(off Deal's Gateway)
California La. WD23: B Hea 1C 26
California Pl. *WD23: B Hea* *1C 26*
(off High Rd.)
California Rd. KT3: N Mald 4H 151
Callaby Ter. N1 .... 6D 66
Callaghan Cl. SE13 .... 4G 123
Callahan Cotts. *E1* *5J 85*
(off Lindley St.)
Callander Rd. SE6 .... 2D 140
Callanders, The WD23: B Hea 1D 26
Callard Av. N13 .... 4G 33
Callcott Ct. NW6 .... 7H 63
Callcott Rd. NW6 .... 7H 63
Callcott St. W8 .... 1J 99
Callendar Rd. SW7 .... 1A 16 (3B 100)
Callender Ct. *CR0: C'don* *6C 156*
(off Harry Cl.)
Callenders Cotts. DA17: Belv 2K 109
Callingham Cl. E14 .... 5B 86
Callis Farm Cl. TW19: Stanw 6A 110
Callisons Pl. SE10 .... 5G 105
Callis Rd. E17 .... 6B 50
Callonfield E17 .... 4K 49
Callow St. SW3 .... 7A 16 (6B 100)
Cally Swimming Pool 1K 83
Calmington Rd. SE5 .... 6E 102
Calmont Rd. BR1: Brom 6F 141
Calne Av. IG5: Ilf 1F 53
Calonne Rd. SW19 .... 4F 135
Calshot Ho. *N1* *2K 83*
(off Calshot St.)
Calshot Rd. TW6: H'row A 2C 110
(not continuous)
Calshot St. N1 .... 1G 7 (2K 83)
Calshot Way EN2: Enf 3G 23
TW6: H'row A 2C 110
(not continuous)
Calstock *NW1* *1G 83*
(off Royal Coll. St.)
Calstock Ho. SE11 .... 5K 19
Calthorpe Gdns. HA8: Edg 5K 27
(not continuous)
SM1: Sutt 3A 166
Calthorpe St. WC1 .... 3H 7 (4K 83)
Calton Av. SE21 .... 6E 120
Calton Rd. EN5: New Bar 6F 21
Calverley Cl. BR3: Beck 6D 140
Calverley Ct. KT19: Ewe 4K 163
Calverley Cres. RM10: Dag 2G 73
Calverley Gdns. HA3: Kent 7D 42
Calverley Gro. N19 .... 1H 65
Calverley Rd. KT17: Ewe 6C 164
Calvert Av. E2 .... 2H 9 (3E 84)
Calvert Cl. DA14: Sidc 6E 144
DA17: Belv 4G 109
Calvert Ct. TW9: Rich 4F 115
Calvert Dr. DA2: Dart 2K 145
Calvert Ho. *W12* *7D 80*
(off White City Est.)
Calverton *SE5* *6E 102*
(off Albany Rd.)
Calverton Rd. E6 .... 1E 88
Calvert Rd. EN5: Barn 2A 20
SE10 .... 5H 105
Calvert's Bldgs. SE1 .... 5E 14 (1D 102)
Calvert St. NW1 .... 1E 82
Calvin St. E1 .... 4J 9 (4F 85)
Calydon Rd. SE7 .... 5K 105
Calypso Cres. SE15 .... 7F 103
Calypso Way SE16 .... 3B 104
Camac Rd. TW2: Twick 1H 131
Camarthen Grn. NW9 .... 5A 44
Cambalt Rd. SW15 .... 5F 117
Cambay Ho. *E1* *4A 86*
(off Harford St.)
Camber Ho. SE15 .... 6J 103
Camberley Av. EN1: Enf 4K 23
SW20 .... 2D 152
Camberley Cl. SM3: Cheam 3F 165
Camberley Ho. NW1 .... 1K 5
Camberley Rd.
TW6: H'row A 3C 110
Cambert Way SE3 .... 4K 123
CAMBERWELL 1D 120
Camberwell Bus. Cen. SE5 .... 7D 102
Camberwell Chu. St. SE5 .... 1D 120
Camberwell Glebe SE5 .... 1E 120
CAMBERWELL GREEN 1D 120
Camberwell Grn. SE5 .... 1D 120
Camberwell Gro. SE5 .... 1D 120
Camberwell Leisure Cen. 1D 120
Camberwell New Rd. SE5 .... 6A 102
Camberwell Pl. SE5 .... 1C 120
Camberwell Rd. SE5 .... 6C 102
Camberwell Sta. Rd. SE5 .... 1C 120
Camberwell Trad. Est. SE5 .... 1B 120
Cambeys Rd. RM10: Dag 5H 73
Camborne Av. W13 .... 2B 96
Camborne Cl. TW6: H'row A 3C 110
Camborne Cres.
TW6: H'row A 3C 110
Camborne M. SW18 .... 7J 117
Camborne Rd.
CR0: C'don 7G 157
DA14: Sidc 3C 144
DA16: Well 2K 125
SM2: Sutt 7J 165
SM4: Mord 5F 153
SW18 .... 7J 117
TW6: H'row A 3C 110
Camborne Way TW5: Hest 1E 112
TW6: H'row A 3C 110
Cambourne Av. N9 .... 7E 24
Cambourne M. W11 .... 6G 81
Cambourne Wlk.
TW10: Rich 6D 114
Cambrai Ct. N13 .... 3D 32
Cambray Rd. BR6: Orp 7K 161
SW12 .... 1G 137
Cambria Cl. DA15: Sidc 1H 143
TW3: Houn 4E 112
Cambria Ct. TW14: Felt 7K 111
Cambria Gdns. TW19: Stanw 7A 110
(not continuous)
Cambria Ho. *E14* *6A 86*
(off Salmon La.)
SE26 .... *4G 139*
(off High Level Dr.)
Cambrian Av. IG2: Ilf 5J 53
Cambrian Cl. SE27 .... 3B 138
Cambrian Grn. *NW9* *5A 44*
(off Snowden Dr.)
Cambrian Rd. E10 .... 7C 50
TW10: Rich 6F 115
Cambria Rd. SE5 .... 3C 120
Cambria St. SW6 .... 7K 99
Cambridge Arc. *E9* *7J 67*
(off Elsdale St.)
Cambridge Av. DA16: Well 4K 125
KT3: N Mald 3A 152
(not continuous)
NW6 .... 2J 81
NW10 .... 3E 80
UB6: G'frd 5K 59
Cambridge Barracks Rd.
SE18 .... 4D 106
Cambridge Cir. WC2 .... 1D 12 (6H 83)
Cambridge Cl. E17 .... 6B 50
EN4: E Barn 1K 31
N22 .... 1A 48
NW10 .... 3J 61
SW20 .... 1D 152
TW4: Houn 4C 112
UB7: Harm 2E 174
Cambridge Cotts. TW9: Kew 6G 97
Cambridge Ct. *E2* *2H 85*
(off Cambridge Heath Rd.)
N16 .... *7E 48*
(off Amhurst Pk.)
NW6 .... 2J 81
W2 .... *6C 4*
(off Edgware Rd.)
W6 .... *4E 98*
(off Shepherd's Bush Rd.)
Cambridge Cres. E2 .... 2H 85
TW11: Tedd 5A 132
Cambridge Dr. HA4: Ruis 2A 58
SE12 .... 5J 123
Cambridge Gdns. EN1: Enf 2B 24
KT1: King T 2G 151
N10 .... 1E 46
N17 .... 7J 33
N21 .... 7J 23
NW6 .... 2J 81
W10 .... 6F 81
Cambridge Ga. NW1 .... 3J 5 (4F 83)
Cambridge Ga. M. NW1 .... 3K 5 (4F 83)
Cambridge Grn. SE9 .... 1F 143
Cambridge Gro. SE20 .... 1H 157
W6 .... 4D 98
Cambridge Gro. Rd. KT1: King T 3G 151
(not continuous)
Cambridge Heath Rd. E1 .... 5H 85
E2 .... 5H 85
Cambridge Ho. *W6* *4D 98*
(off Cambridge Gro.)
W13 .... 6A 78
Cambridge Pde. EN1: Enf 1B 24
Cambridge Pk. E11 .... 7J 51
TW1: Twick 6C 114
Cambridge Pk. Ct. TW1: Twick 7D 114
Cambridge Pk. Rd. *E11* *7J 51*
(off Lonsdale Rd.)
Cambridge Pl. W8 .... 2K 99
Cambridge Rd. BR1: Brom 7J 141
CR4: Mitc 3G 155
DA14: Sidc 4J 143
E4 .... 1A 36
E11 .... 6H 51
HA2: Harr 5E 40
IG3: Ilf 1J 71
IG11: Bark 7G 71
KT1: King T 2F 151
KT3: N Mald 4K 151
KT8: W Mole 4D 148
KT12: Walt T 6K 147
NW6 .... 2J 81
(not continuous)
SE20 .... 3H 157
SM5: Cars 6C 166
SW11 .... 1D 118
SW13 .... 2B 116
SW20 .... 1C 152
TW1: Twick 6D 114
TW4: Houn 4C 112
TW9: Kew 7G 97
TW11: Tedd 4K 131
TW12: Hamp 7D 130
TW15: Ashf 7E 128
UB1: S'hall 1D 94
W7 .... 2K 95
Cambridge Rd. Nth. W4 .... 5H 97
Cambridge Rd. Sth.
W4 .... 5H 97
Cambridge Row SE18 .... 5F 107
Cambridge Sq. W2 .... 7C 4 (6C 82)
Cambridge St. SW1 .... 4K 17 (4F 101)

Cambridge Ter. N9 . . . 7K 23
NW1 . . . 2J 5 (3F 83)
Cambridge Ter. M. NW1 . . . 2K 5 (3F 83)
Cambridge Theatre . . . 1E 12
(off Earlham St.)
Cambridge Yd. W7 . . . 2K 95
Cambstone Cl. N11 . . . 2K 31
Cambus Cl. UB4: Yead . . . 5C 76
Cambus Rd. E16 . . . 5J 87
Cam Ct. SE15 . . . 6F 103
Camdale Rd. SE18 . . . 7K 107
Camden Arts Cen. . . . 5K 63
Camden Av. TW13: Felt . . . 1A 130
UB4: Yead . . . 7B 76
Camden Cl. BR7: Chst . . . 1G 161
Camden Ct. DA17: Belv . . . 5G 109
NW1 . . . 7G 65
(off Rousden St.)
Camden Gdns.
CR7: Thor H . . . 3B 156
NW1 . . . 7F 65
SM1: Sutt . . . 5K 165
Camden Gro. BR7: Chst . . . 6F 143
Camden High St. NW1 . . . 7F 65
Camden Hill Rd. SE19 . . . 6E 138
Camden Ho. SE8 . . . 5B 104
Camdenhurst St. E14 . . . 6A 86
Camden La. N7 . . . 5H 65
Camden Lock Market . . . 7F 65
(off Camden Lock Pl.)
Camden Lock Pl. NW1 . . . 7F 65
Camden Market . . . 1F 83
(off Dewsbury Ter.)
Camden Markets . . . 7F 65
(off Camden Lock Pl.)
Camden M. NW1 . . . 7G 65
Camden Pk. Rd. BR7: Chst . . . 7D 142
NW1 . . . 6H 65
Camden Pas. N1 . . . 1B 84
Camden Peoples Theatre . . . 3A 6
(off Hampstead Rd.)
Camden Rd. DA5: Bexl . . . 1E 144
E11 . . . 6K 51
E17 . . . 6B 50
N7 . . . 4J 65
NW1 . . . 7G 65
SM1: Sutt . . . 5K 165
SM5: Cars . . . 4D 166
Camden Row HA5: Pinn . . . 3A 40
SE3 . . . 2G 123
Camden Sq. NW1 . . . 7H 65
(not continuous)
SE15 . . . 1F 121
Camden St. NW1 . . . 7G 65
Camden Studios NW1 . . . 1G 83
(off Camden St.)
Camden Ter. NW1 . . . 6H 65
CAMDEN TOWN . . . 1F 83
Camden Wlk. N1 . . . 1B 84
Camden Way BR7: Chst . . . 7D 142
CR7: Thor H . . . 3B 156
Cameford Ct. SW2 . . . 7J 119
Camelford NW1 . . . 1G 83
(off Royal Coll. St.)
Camelford Ct. W11 . . . 6G 81
Camelford Ho. SE1 . . . 5F 19 (5J 101)
Camelford Wlk. W11 . . . 6G 81
Camel Gro. KT2: King T . . . 5D 132
Camellia Ho. SE8 . . . 7B 104
(off Idonia St.)
TW13: Felt . . . 1J 129
(off Tilley Rd.)
Camellia Pl. TW2: Whitt . . . 7F 113
Camellia St. SW8 . . . 7J 101
(not continuous)
Camelot Cl. SE28 . . . 2H 107
SW19 . . . 4H 135
Camelot Ho. NW1 . . . 6H 65
Camel Rd. E16 . . . 1C 106
Camera Pl. SW10 . . . 7A 16 (6B 100)
Cameret Ct. W11 . . . 2F 99
(off Holland Rd.)
Cameron Cl. DA5: Bexl . . . 3K 145
N18 . . . 4C 34
N20 . . . 2G 31
Cameron Ho. NW8 . . . 2C 82
(off St John's Wood Ter.)
SE5 . . . 7C 102
Cameron Pl. E1 . . . 6H 85
SW16 . . . 2A 138
Cameron Rd. BR2: Brom . . . 5J 159
CR0: C'don . . . 6B 156
IG3: Ilf . . . 1J 71
SE6 . . . 2B 140
Cameron Sq. CR4: Mitc . . . 1C 154
Cameron Ter. SE12 . . . 3K 141
Camerton Cl. E8 . . . 6F 67
Camgate Cen., The
TW19: Stanw . . . 6B 110
Camgate Mans. SE5 . . . 6C 102
(off Camberwell Rd.)
Camilla Cl. TW16: Sun . . . 6H 129
Camilla Rd. SE16 . . . 4H 103
Camille Cl. SE25 . . . 3G 157
Camlan Rd. BR1: Brom . . . 4H 141
Camlet St. E2 . . . 3J 9 (4F 85)
Camlet Way EN4: Barn, Had W . . . 2D 20
Camley St. NW1 . . . 7H 65
Camley Street Natural Pk. Vis. Cen.
. . . 2H 83
Camm Gdns. KT1: King T . . . 2F 151
KT7: T Ditt . . . 7K 149
Camomile Av. CR4: Mitc . . . 1D 154
Camomile Rd. RM7: Rush G . . . 2K 73
Camomile St. EC3 . . . 7H 9 (6E 84)
Camomile Way UB7: Yiew . . . 6A 74
Campana Rd. SW6 . . . 1J 117
Campania Bldg. E1 . . . 7K 85
(off Jardine Rd.)
Campaspe Bus. Pk. TW16: Sun . . . 5H 147
Campbell Av. IG6: Ilf . . . 4F 53
Campbell Cl. HA4: Ruis . . . 6J 39
SE18 . . . 1E 124
SW16 . . . 4H 137
TW2: Twick . . . 1H 131
Campbell Ct. N17 . . . 1F 49
NW9 . . . 6J 43
SE22 . . . 1G 139
SW7 . . . 3A 100
(off Gloucester Rd.)
Campbell Cft. HA8: Edg . . . 5B 28
Campbell Gordon Way NW2 . . . 4D 62
Campbell Ho. SW1 . . . 6A 18
(off Churchill Gdns.)
W2 . . . 4A 4
(off Hall Pl.)
W12 . . . 7D 80
(off White City Est.)
Campbell Rd. CR0: C'don . . . 7B 156
E3 . . . 3C 86
E6 . . . 1C 88
E15 . . . 4H 69
E17 . . . 4B 50
KT8: E Mos . . . 3J 149
N17 . . . 1F 49
TW2: Twick . . . 2H 131
W7 . . . 7J 77
Campbell Wlk. N1 . . . 1J 83
(off Outram Pl.)
Campdale Rd. N7 . . . 3H 65
Campden Cres. HA0: Wemb . . . 3B 60
RM8: Dag . . . 4B 72
Campden Gro. W8 . . . 2J 99
Campden Hill W8 . . . 2J 99
Campden Hill Ct. W8 . . . 2J 99
Campden Hill Gdns. W8 . . . 1J 99
Campden Hill Ga. W8 . . . 2J 99
Campden Hill Mans. W8 . . . 1J 99
(off Edge St.)
Campden Hill Pl. W11 . . . 1H 99
Campden Hill Rd. W8 . . . 1J 99
Campden Hill Sq. W8 . . . 1H 99
Campden Hill Towers W11 . . . 1J 99
Campden Ho. NW6 . . . 7B 64
(off Harben Rd.)
W8 . . . 1J 99
(off Sheffield Ter.)
Campden Ho. Cl. W8 . . . 2J 99
Campden Ho's. W8 . . . 1J 99
Campden Ho. Ter. W8 . . . 1J 99
(off Kensington Chu. St.)
Campden Mans. W8 . . . 1J 99
(off Kensington Chu. St.)
Campden Rd. CR2: S Croy . . . 5E 168
UB10: Ick . . . 3B 56
Campden St. W8 . . . 1J 99
Campden Way RM8: Dag . . . 4B 72
Campe Ho. N10 . . . 7K 31
Campen Cl. SW19 . . . 2G 135
Camperdown St. E1 . . . 1K 15 (6F 85)
Campfield Rd. SE9 . . . 7B 124
Campion Cl. CR0: C'don . . . 4E 168
E6 . . . 7D 88
HA3: Kent . . . 6F 43
RM7: Rush G . . . 2K 73
UB8: Hil . . . 5B 74
Campion Ct. HA0: Wemb . . . 2E 78
Campion Gdns. IG8: Wfd G . . . 5D 36
Campion Pl. SE28 . . . 1A 108
Campion Rd. SW15 . . . 4E 116
TW7: Isle . . . 1K 113
Campion Ter. NW2 . . . 3F 63
Campion Way HA8: Edg . . . 4D 28
Camplin Rd. HA3: Kent . . . 5E 42
Camplin St. SE14 . . . 7K 103
Camp Rd. SW19 . . . 5D 134
(not continuous)
Campsbourne, The N8 . . . 4J 47
Campsbourne Ho. N8 . . . 4J 47
(off Pembroke Rd.)
Campsbourne Rd. N8 . . . 3J 47
(not continuous)
Campsey Gdns. RM9: Dag . . . 7B 72
Campsey Rd. RM9: Dag . . . 7B 72
Campsfield Ho. N8 . . . 3J 47
(off Campsfield Rd.)
Campsfield Rd. N8 . . . 3J 47
Campshill Pl. SE13 . . . 5E 122
Campshill Rd. SE13 . . . 5E 122
Campus Rd. E17 . . . 6B 50
Campus Way NW4 . . . 3D 44
Camp Vw. SW19 . . . 5D 134
Cam Rd. E15 . . . 1F 87
Camrose Av. DA8: Erith . . . 6H 109
HA8: Edg . . . 2F 43
TW13: Felt . . . 4A 130
Camrose Cl. CR0: C'don . . . 7A 158
SM4: Mord . . . 4J 153
Camrose St. SE2 . . . 5A 108
Canada Av. N18 . . . 6H 33
Canada Cres. W3 . . . 5J 79
Canada Est. SE16 . . . 3J 103
Canada Gdns. SE13 . . . 5E 122
Canada Ho. SE16 . . . 3A 104
(off Brunswick Quay)
Canada Memorial . . . 6A 12
(off Green Pk.)
Canada Pl. E14 . . . 1D 104
(off Up. Bank St.)
Canada Rd. W3 . . . 5J 79
Canada Sq. E14 . . . 1D 104
Canada St. SE16 . . . 2K 103
Canada Way W12 . . . 7D 80
Canada Wharf SE16 . . . 1B 104
Canadian Av. SE6 . . . 1D 140
Canal App. SE8 . . . 5A 104
Canal Blvd. NW1 . . . 6H 65
CANAL BRIDGE . . . 6G 103
Canal Bldg. N1 . . . 2C 84
(off Shepherdess Wlk.)
Canal Cl. E1 . . . 4A 86
W10 . . . 4F 81
Canal Gro. SE15 . . . 6H 103
Canal Market . . . 7F 65
(off Castlehaven Rd.)
Canal Path E2 . . . 1F 85
Canalside SE28 . . . 7D 90
Canalside Activity Cen. . . . 4F 81
Canalside Gdns. UB2: S'hall . . . 4C 94
Canal Side Studios NW1 . . . 1H 83
(off St Pancras Way)
Canal St. SE5 . . . 6D 102
Canal Wlk. CR0: C'don . . . 6E 156
N1 . . . 1D 84
NW10 . . . 7J 61
(off Westend Cl.)
SE26 . . . 5J 139
Canal Way W10 . . . 4F 81
Canal Wharf UB6: G'frd . . . 1A 78
Canberra Cl. NW4 . . . 3C 44
RM10: Dag . . . 1K 91
Canberra Cres. RM10: Dag . . . 7K 73
Canberra Dr. UB5: Yead . . . 3A 76
Canberra Rd. DA7: Bex . . . 6D 108
E6 . . . 1D 88
SE7 . . . 6A 106
TW6: H'row A . . . 3C 110
W13 . . . 1A 96
Canbury Av. KT2: King T . . . 1F 151
Canbury Bus. Cen.
KT2: King T . . . 1E 150
Canbury Bus. Pk. KT2: King T . . . 1E 150
(off Canbury Pk. Rd.)
Canbury Ct. KT2: King T . . . 7D 132
Canbury M. SE26 . . . 3G 139
Canbury Pk. Rd.
KT2: King T . . . 1E 150
Canbury Pas. KT2: King T . . . 1D 150
Cancell Rd. SW9 . . . 1A 120
Candahar Rd. SW11 . . . 2C 118
Candida Ct. NW1 . . . 7F 65
Candid Ho. NW10 . . . 3D 80
(off Trenmar Gdns.)
Candle Gro. SE15 . . . 3H 121
Candlelight Ct. E15 . . . 6H 69
(off Romford Rd.)
Candler M. TW1: Twick . . . 7A 114
Candler St. N15 . . . 6D 48
Candover Cl. UB7: Harm . . . 3E 174
Candover St. W1 . . . 6A 6 (5G 83)
Candy St. E3 . . . 1B 86
Caney M. NW2 . . . 2F 63
Canfield Dr. HA4: Ruis . . . 5K 57
Canfield Gdns. NW6 . . . 7K 63
Canfield Ho. N15 . . . 6E 48
(off Albert Rd.)
Canfield Pl. NW6 . . . 6A 64
Canfield Rd. IG8: Wfd G . . . 7H 37
Canford Av. UB5: N'olt . . . 1D 76
Canford Cl. EN2: Enf . . . 2F 23
Canford Gdns.
KT3: N Mald . . . 6A 152
Canford Pl. TW11: Tedd . . . 6C 132
Canford Rd. SW11 . . . 5E 118
Canham Rd. SE25 . . . 3E 156
W3 . . . 2A 98
Canmore Gdns. SW16 . . . 7G 137
CANN HALL . . . 4G 69
Cann Hall Rd. E11 . . . 4G 69
Cann Ho. W14 . . . 3G 99
(off Russell Rd.)
Canning Cres. N22 . . . 1K 47
Canning Cross SE5 . . . 2E 120
Canning Ho. W12 . . . 7D 80
(off Australia Rd.)
Canning Pas. W8 . . . 3A 100
(not continuous)
Canning Pl. W8 . . . 3A 100
Canning Pl. M. W8 . . . 3A 100
(off Canning Pl.)

Canning Rd. CR0: C'don 2F 169
E15 2G 87
E17 4A 50
HA3: W'stone 3J 41
N5 3B 66
Cannington Rd. RM9: Dag 6C 72
CANNING TOWN 6H 87
CANNING TOWN 5G 87
Cannizaro Rd. SW19 6E 134
Cannock Ct. E17 2E 50
Cannock Ho. N4 7C 48
Cannonbury Av. HA5: Pinn 6B 40
Cannon Cl. SW20 3E 152
TW12: Hamp 6F 131
Cannon Ct. EC1 3B 8
(off Brewhouse Yd.)
Cannon Dr. E14 7C 86
Cannon Hill N14 3D 32
NW6 5J 63
Cannon Hill La. SW20 5F 153
Cannon Hill M. N14 3D 32
Cannon Ho. SE11 4H 19
Cannon La. HA5: Pinn 5C 40
NW3 3B 64
Cannon Pl. NW3 3B 64
SE7 5C 106
Cannon Retail Pk. SE28 7A 90
Cannon Rd. DA7: Bex 1E 126
N14 3D 32
Cannons Health Club
Bromley 5K 159
Cannon Street 3E 14
Fulham 1F 117
Norbury 2K 155
Sutton 6J 165
Twickenham 7J 113
Willesden Green 7E 62
Cannon St. EC4 1C 14 (6C 84)
Cannon St. Rd. E1 6H 85
Cannon Trad. Est. HA9: Wemb 4H 61
Cannon Way KT8: W Mole 4E 148
Cannon Wharf Bus. Cen. SE8 4A 104
Cannon Workshops E14 7C 86
(off Cannon Dr.)
Canon All. EC4 1C 14
(off Queen's Head Pas.)
Canon Av. RM6: Chad H 5C 54
Canon Beck Rd. SE16 2J 103
Canonbie Rd. SE23 7J 121
CANONBURY 6C 66
Canonbury Bus. Cen. N1 1C 84
Canonbury Cotts. EN1: Enf 1K 23
Canonbury Ct. N1 7B 66
(off Hawes St.)
Canonbury Cres. N1 7C 66
Canonbury Gro. N1 7C 66
Canonbury Hgts. N1 6D 66
(off Dove Rd.)
Canonbury La. N1 7B 66
Canonbury Pk. Nth. N1 6C 66
Canonbury Pk. Sth. N1 6C 66
Canonbury Pl. N1 6B 66
(not continuous)
Canonbury Rd. EN1: Enf 1K 23
N1 6B 66
Canonbury Sq. N1 7B 66
Canonbury St. N1 7C 66
Canonbury Vs. N1 7B 66
Canon Mohan Cl. N14 6K 21
Canon Rd. BR1: Brom 3A 160
Canon Row SW1 7E 12 (2J 101)
(not continuous)
Canons Cl. HA8: Edg 6A 28
N2 7B 46
Canons Cnr. HA8: Edg 4K 27
Canons Ct. E15 4G 69
HA8: Edg 6A 28
Canons Dr. HA8: Edg 6K 27
Canonsleigh Rd. RM9: Dag 7B 72
Canons Leisure Cen., The 4D 154
CANONS PARK 7J 27
Canons Pk. HA7: Stan 6J 27
Canons Pk. Cl. HA8: Edg 7K 27
Canon St. N1 1C 84
Canon's Wlk. CR0: C'don 3K 169
Canopus Way TW19: Stanw 7A 110
Canrobert St. E2 2H 85
Cantelowes Rd. NW1 6H 65
(not continuous)
Canterbury Av. DA15: Sidc 2B 144
IG1: Ilf 7C 52
Canterbury Cl. BR3: Beck 1D 158
E6 6D 88
KT4: Wor Pk 2F 165
SE5 2C 120
(off Lilford Rd.)
UB6: G'frd 5F 77
Canterbury Ct. CR2: S Croy 7C 168
(off St Augustines Av.)
NW6 2J 81
(off Canterbury Rd.)
NW9 2A 44
SE5 7A 102
SE12 3K 141
TW15: Ashf 4B 128
Canterbury Cres. SW9 3A 120
Canterbury Gro. SE27 4A 138
Canterbury Hall KT4: Wor Pk 7D 152
WC1 3J 83
(off Cartwright Gdns.)
Canterbury Ho. CR0: C'don 1D 168
(off Sydenham Rd.)
IG11: Bark 7A 72
(off Margaret Bondfield Av.)
SE1 1H 19 (3K 101)
Canterbury Ind. Pk. SE15 6J 103
Canterbury Pl. SE17 5B 102
Canterbury Rd. CR0: C'don 7K 155
E10 7E 50
HA1: Harr 5F 41
HA2: Harr 5F 41
NW6 2H 81
(not continuous)
SM4: Mord 7K 153
TW13: Hanw 2C 130
Canterbury Ter. NW6 2J 81
Cantium Retail Pk. SE1 6G 103
Cantley Gdns. IG2: Ilf 6G 53
SE19 1F 157
Cantley Rd. W7 3A 96
Canton St. E14 6C 86
Cantrell Rd. E3 4B 86
Cantwell Rd. SE18 7F 107
Canute Gdns. SE16 4K 103
Canvey St. SE1 4C 14 (1C 102)
Cape Cl. IG11: Bark 7F 71
Cape Henry Ct. E14 7F 87
(off Jamestown Way)
Cape Ho. E8 6F 67
(off Dalston La.)
Capel Av. SM6: Wall 5K 167
Capel Cl. BR2: Brom 1C 172
N20 3F 31
Capel Ct. EC2 1F 15
(off Bartholomew La.)
SE20 1J 157
Capel Cres. HA7: Stan 2F 27
Capel Gdns. HA5: Pinn 4D 40
IG3: Bark, Ilf 4K 71
Capel Ho. E9 7J 67
(off Loddiges Rd.)
Capel Rd. E7 4K 69
E12 4K 69
EN4: E Barn 6H 21
Capener's Cl. SW1 7F 11
Capern Rd. SW18 1A 136
Cape Rd. N17 3G 49
Cape Yd. E1 7G 85
Capital Bus. Cen. CR2: S Croy 7D 168
HA0: Wemb 2D 78
Capital E. Apartments E16 7J 87
(off Western Gateway)
Capital Ind. Est. CR4: Mitc 5D 154
DA17: Belv 3H 109
Capital Interchange Way
TW8: Bford 5G 97
Capital Wharf E1 1G 103
Capitol Ind. Pk. NW9 3J 43
Capitol Way NW9 3J 43
Capland Ho. NW8 3B 4
(off Capland St.)
Capland St. NW8 3B 4 (4B 82)
Caple Ho. SW10 7A 100
(off King's Rd.)
Caple Rd. NW10 2B 80
Capper St. WC1 4B 6 (4G 83)
Caprea Cl. UB4: Yead 5B 76
Capricorn Cen. RM8: Dag 7F 55
Capri Ho. E17 2B 50
Capri Rd. CR0: C'don 1F 169
Capstan Cl. RM6: Chad H 6B 54
Capstan Ct. E1 7J 85
(off Wapping Wall)
Capstan Ho. E14 7F 87
(off Clove Cres.)
E14 4E 104
(off Stebondale St.)
Capstan Ride EN2: Enf 2F 23
Capstan Rd. SE8 4B 104
Capstan Sq. E14 2E 104
Capstan Way SE16 1A 104
Capstone Rd. BR1: Brom 4H 141
Capthorne Av. HA2: Harr 1C 58
Capuchin Cl. HA7: Stan 6G 27
Capulet M. E16 1J 105
Capworth St. E10 1C 68
Caradoc Cl. W2 6J 81
Caradoc Evans Cl. N11 5A 32
(off Springfield Rd.)
Caradoc St. SE10 5G 105
Caradon Cl. E11 1G 69
Caradon Way N15 4D 48
Cara Ho. N1 7A 66
(off Liverpool Rd.)
Caranday Vs. W11 1F 99
(off Norland Rd.)
Caravel Cl. E14 3C 104
Caravelle Gdns. UB5: N'olt 3B 76
Caravel M. SE8 6C 104
Caraway Apartments SE1 6K 15
(off Cayenne Ct.)
Caraway Cl. E13 5K 87
Caraway Hgts. E14 7E 86
(off Poplar High St.)
Caraway Pl. SM6: Wall 3F 167
Carberry Rd. SE19 6E 138
Carbery Av. W3 2F 97
Carbis Cl. E4 1A 36
Carbis Rd. E14 6B 86
Carbrooke Ho. E9 1J 85
(off Templecombe Rd.)
Carbuncle Pas. N17 2G 49
Carburton St. W1 5K 5 (5F 83)
Cardale St. E14 2E 104
Cardamon Bldg. SE1 5K 15
(off Shad Thames)
Carden Rd. SE15 3H 121
Cardiff Ho. SE15 6G 103
(off Friary Est.)
Cardiff Rd. EN3: Pond E 4C 24
W7 3A 96
Cardiff St. SE18 7J 107
Cardigan Ct. W7 4K 77
(off Copley Cl.)
Cardigan Gdns. IG3: Ilf 2A 72
Cardigan Pl. SE3 2F 123
Cardigan Rd. E3 2B 86
SW13 2C 116
SW19 6A 136
TW10: Rich 6E 114
Cardigan St.
SE11 5J 19 (5A 102)
Cardigan Wlk. N1 7C 66
(off Ashby Gro.)
Cardinal Av. KT2: King T 5E 132
SM4: Mord 6G 153
Cardinal Bourne St. SE1 3D 102
Cardinal Cap All. SE1 1C 102
Cardinal Cl. BR7: Chst 1H 161
HA8: Edg 7D 28
KT4: Wor Pk 4C 164
SM4: Mord 6G 153
Cardinal Ct. E1 7G 85
(off Thomas More St.)
Cardinal Cres. KT3: N Mald 2J 151
Cardinal Hinsley Cl. NW10 2C 80
Cardinal Mans. SW1 3A 18
(off Carlisle Pl.)
Cardinal Pl. SW1 1A 18 (3G 101)
SW15 4F 117
Cardinal Rd. HA4: Ruis 1B 58
TW13: Felt 1K 129
Cardinals Wlk. TW12: Hamp 7G 131
TW16: Sun 6G 129
Cardinals Way N19 1H 65
Cardinal Wlk. SW1 2A 18
Cardinal Way HA3: W'stone 3J 41
Cardine M. SE15 7H 103
Cardington Sq. TW4: Houn 4B 112
Cardington St. NW1 1B 6 (3G 83)
Cardinham Rd. BR6: Chels 4K 173
Cardozo Rd. N7 5J 65
Cardrew Av. N12 5G 31
Cardrew Cl. N12 5H 31
Cardrew Ct. N12 5G 31
Cardross Ho. W6 3D 98
(off Cardross St.)
Cardross St. W6 3D 98
Cardwell Rd. N7 4J 65
Cardwell Ter. N7 4J 65
(off Cardwell Rd.)
Career Ct. SE16 2K 103
(off Christopher Cl.)
Carew Cl. N7 2K 65
Carew Ct. RM6: Chad H 6B 54
(off Quarles Pk. Rd.)
SE14 6K 103
(off Samuel Cl.)
SM2: Sutt 7K 165
Carew Manor & Dovecote 3G 167
Carew Mnr. Cotts. SM6: Bedd 3H 167
Carew Rd. CR4: Mitc 2E 154
CR7: Thor H 4B 156
N17 2G 49
SM6: Wall 6G 167
TW15: Ashf 6E 128
W13 2C 96
Carew St. SE5 2C 120
Carey Ct. DA6: Bex 5H 127
SE5 7C 102
Carey Gdns. SW8 1G 119
Carey La. EC2 7C 8 (6C 84)
Carey Mans. SW1 3C 18
(off Rutherford St.)
Carey Pl. SW1 4C 18 (4H 101)
Carey Rd. RM9: Dag 4E 72
Carey St. WC2 1H 13 (6K 83)
Carey Way HA9: Wemb 4H 61
Carfax Pl. SW4 4H 119
Carfax Rd. UB3: Harl 5H 93
Carfree Cl. N1 7A 66
Cargill Rd. SW18 1K 135
Cargo Point TW19: Stanw 6B 110
Cargreen Pl. SE25 4F 157
Cargreen Rd. SE25 4F 157
Cargrey Ho. HA7: Stan 5H 27
Carholme Rd. SE23 1B 140
Carillon Ct. W5 7D 78
Carinthia Ct. SE16 4A 104
(off Plough Way)

Carisbrook N10 2F 47
Carisbrook Cl. EN1: Enf 1A 24
Carisbrooke Av. DA5: Bexl 1D 144
Carisbrooke Cl. HA7: Stan 2D 42
TW4: Houn 7C 112
Carisbrooke Ct. SM2: Cheam 7H 165
UB5: N'olt 1D 76
(off Eskdale Av.)
W1 6H 5
(off Weymouth St.)
W3 2J 97
(off Brouncker Rd.)
Carisbrooke Gdns. SE15 7F 103
Carisbrooke Ho. *KT2: King T 1E 150*
(off Seven Kings Way)
TW10: Rich 5G 115
Carisbrooke Rd.
BR2: Brom 4A 160
CR4: Mitc 4H 155
E17 4A 50
Carker's La. NW5 5F 65
Carleton Av. SM6: Wall 7H 167
Carleton Cl. KT10: Esh 7H 149
Carleton Gdns. N19 5G 65
Carleton Rd. N7 5H 65
Carleton Vs. NW5 5G 65
Carlile Cl. E3 2B 86
Carlile Ho. *SE1 3D 102*
(off Tabard St.)
Carlina Gdns. IG8: Wfd G 5E 36
Carlingford Gdns. CR4: Mitc 7D 136
Carlingford Rd. N15 3B 48
NW3 4B 64
SM4: Mord 6F 153
Carlisle Av. EC3 1J 15 (6F 85)
W3 6A 80
Carlisle Cl. HA5: Pinn 7C 40
KT2: King T 1G 151
Carlisle Gdns. HA3: Kent 7D 42
IG1: Ilf 6C 52
Carlisle Ho. IG1: Ilf 6C 52
Carlisle La. SE1 2H 19 (3K 101)
Carlisle Mans. *SW1 3A 18*
(off Carlisle Pl.)
Carlisle M. KT2: King T 1G 151
Carlisle Pl. N11 4A 32
SW1 2A 18 (3G 101)
Carlisle Rd. E10 1C 68
N4 7A 48
NW6 1G 81
NW9 3J 43
SM1: Sutt 6H 165
TW12: Hamp 7F 131
Carlisle St. W1 1C 12 (6H 83)
Carlisle Wlk. E8 6F 67
Carlisle Way SW17 5E 136
Carlos Pl. W1 3H 11 (7E 82)
Carlow St. NW1 2G 83
Carlson Ct. SW15 4H 117
Carlton Av. CR2: S Croy 7E 168
HA3: Kent 5B 42
N14 5C 22
TW14: Felt 6A 112
UB3: Harl 4G 93
Carlton Av. E. HA9: Wemb 2D 60
Carlton Av. W. HA0: Wemb 2B 60
Carlton Cl. HA8: Edg 5B 28
KT9: Chess 6D 162
NW3 2J 63
UB5: N'olt 5G 59
Carlton Ct. IG6: Ilf 3H 53
N3 7D 30
SE20 1H 157
SW9 1B 120
UB8: Cowl 5A 74
W9 2K 81
(off Maida Va.)
Carlton Cres. SM3: Cheam 4G 165
Carlton Dr. IG6: Ilf 3H 53
SW15 5F 117
Carlton Gdns. SW1 5C 12 (1H 101)
W5 6C 78
Carlton Grn. DA14: Sidc 4K 143
Carlton Gro. SE15 1H 121
Carlton Hill NW8 2K 81
Carlton Ho. *NW6 2J 81*
(off Canterbury Ter., not continuous)
SE16 2K 103
(off Wolfe Cres.)
TW3: Houn 6E 112
TW14: Felt 6H 111
Carlton Ho. Ter. SW1 5C 12 (1H 101)
Carlton Lodge *N4 7A 48*
(off Carlton Rd.)
Carlton Mans. N16 1F 67
NW6 7J 63
(off West End La.)
W9 3K 81
W14 2G 99
(off Holland Pk. Gdns.)
Carlton M. *NW6 5J 63*
(off West Cotts.)
Carlton Pde. HA9: Wemb 2E 60
Carlton Pk. Av. SW20 2F 153
Carlton Rd. CR2: S Croy 6D 168
DA8: Erith 6H 109
DA14: Sidc 5K 143
DA16: Well 3B 126
E11 1H 69
E12 4B 70
E17 1A 50
KT3: N Mald 2A 152
KT12: Walt T 7K 147
N4 7A 48
N11 5K 31
SW14 3J 115
TW16: Sun 7H 129
W4 2K 97
W5 7C 78
Carlton Sq. E1 4K 85
(not continuous)
Carlton St. SW1 3C 12 (7H 83)
Carlton Ter. E7 7A 70
E11 5K 51
(not continuous)
N18 3J 33
SE26 3J 139
Carlton Twr. Pl. SW1 3D 100
Carlton Towers SM5: Cars 3D 166
Carlton Va. NW6 2H 81
Carlton Vs. SW15 5G 117
Carlton Works, The
SE15 7H 103
(off Asylum Rd.)
Carlwell St. SW17 5C 136
Carlyle Av. BR1: Brom 3B 160
UB1: S'hall 7D 76
Carlyle Cl. KT8: W Mole 2F 149
N2 6A 46
Carlyle Ct. *SW6 1K 117*
(off Imperial Rd.)
SW10 1A 118
(off Chelsea Harbour Dr.)
Carlyle Gdns. UB1: S'hall 7D 76
Carlyle Ho. *KT8: W Mole 5E 148*
(off Down St.)
N16 3E 66
SE5 7C 102
(off Bethwin Rd.)
SW3 7B 16
(off Old Church St.)
Carlyle Mans. *SW3 7C 16*
(off Cheyne Wlk.)
W8 1J 99
(off Kensington Mall)
Carlyle M. E1 4K 85
Carlyle Pl. SW15 4F 117
Carlyle Rd. CR0: C'don 2G 169
E12 4C 70
NW10 1K 79
Carlyle Rd. SE28 7B 90
W5 4C 96
Carlyle's House 7C 16
Carlyle Sq. SW3 6B 16 (5B 100)
Carlyon Av. HA2: Harr 4D 58
Carlyon Cl. HA0: Wemb 1E 78
Carlyon Rd. HA0: Wemb 2E 78
UB4: Yead 5A 76
(not continuous)
Carlys Cl. BR3: Beck 2K 157
Carmalt Gdns. SW15 4E 116
Carmarthen Ct. *W7 4K 77*
(off Copley Cl.)
Carmarthen Pl. SE1 6G 15 (2E 102)
Carmel Cl. TW9: Rich 2H 115
Carmel Ct. HA9: Wemb 2H 61
W8 2K 99
(off Holland St.)
Carmelite Cl. HA3: Hrw W 1G 41
Carmelite Rd. HA3: Hrw W 1G 41
Carmelite St. EC4 2K 13 (7A 84)
Carmelite Wlk.
HA3: Hrw W 1G 41
Carmelite Way HA3: Hrw W 2G 41
Carmel Lodge *SW6 6J 99*
(off Lillie Rd.)
Carmen St. E14 6D 86
Carmichael Cl. HA4: Ruis 4J 57
SW11 3B 118
Carmichael Ct. *SW13 2B 116*
(off Grove Rd.)
Carmichael Ho. *E14 7E 86*
(off Poplar High St.)
Carmichael M. SW18 7B 118
Carmichael Rd. SE25 5F 157
Carmine Ct. BR1: Brom 7H 141
Carminia Rd. SW17 2F 137
Carnaby St. W1 1A 12 (6G 83)
Carnac St. SE27 4D 138
Carnanton Rd. E17 1F 51
Carnarvon Av. EN1: Enf 3A 24
Carnarvon Dr. UB3: Harl 3E 92
Carnarvon Rd. E10 5E 50
E15 6H 69
E18 1H 51
EN5: Barn 3B 20
Carnation Cl. RM7: Rush G 2K 73
Carnation St. SE2 5B 108
Carnbrook M. SE3 3B 124
Carnbrook Rd. SE3 3B 124
Carnecke Gdns. SE9 5C 124
Carnegie Cl. KT6: Surb 2F 163
Carnegie Pl. SW19 3F 135
Carnegie Rd. HA1: Harr 7K 41
Carnegie St. N1 1K 83
Carnforth Cl. KT19: Ewe 6H 163
Carnforth Rd. SW16 7H 137
(not continuous)
Carnie Lodge SW17 3F 137
Carnival Ho. *SE1 6K 15*
(off Gainsford St.)
Carnoustie Cl. SE28 6D 90
Carnoustie Dr. N1 7K 65
(not continuous)
Carnwath Rd. SW6 3J 117
Caroe Ct. N9 1C 34
Carol Cl. NW4 4F 45
Carole Ho. *NW1 1D 82*
(off Regent's Pk. Rd.)
Carolina Cl. E15 5G 69
Carolina Rd. CR7: Thor H 2B 156
Caroline Cl. CR0: C'don 4E 168
N10 2F 47
SW16 3K 137
TW7: Isle 7H 95
UB7: W Dray 2A 92
W2 7K 81
Caroline Ct. HA7: Stan 6F 27
SE6 4F 141
TW15: Ashf 6D 128
Caroline Gdns. E2 1H 9 (3E 84)
SE15 7H 103
Caroline Ho. *W2 7K 81*
(off Bayswater Rd.)
W6 5E 98
(off Queen Caroline St.)
Caroline Pl. SW11 2E 118
UB3: Harl 7G 93
W2 7K 81
Caroline Pl. M. W2 7K 81
Caroline Rd. SW19 7H 135
Caroline St. E1 6K 85
Caroline Ter.
SW1 4G 17 (4E 100)
Caroline Wlk. *W6 6G 99*
(off Lillie Rd.)
Carol St. NW1 1G 83
Caronia Ct. *SE16 4A 104*
(off Plough Way)
Carpenter Gdns. N21 2G 33
Carpenter Ho. *E14 5C 86*
(off Burgess St.)
NW11 6A 46
Carpenters Arms Path SE9 6D 124
Carpenters Cl. EN5: New Bar 6E 20
Carpenters Ct. *NW1 1G 83*
(off Pratt St.)
TW2: Twick 2J 131
Carpenters M. N7 5J 65
Carpenters Pl. SW4 4H 119
Carpenter's Rd. E15 7E 68
Carpenter St. W1 3J 11 (7F 83)
Carradale Ho. *E14 6E 86*
(off St Leonard's Rd.)
Carrara Cl. SE24 4A 120
SW9 4B 120
Carrara M. *E8 6G 67*
(off Dalston La.)
Carrara Wharf SW6 3G 117
Carr Cl. HA7: Stan 6F 27
Carre M. *SE5 1B 120*
(off Calais St.)
Carr Gro. SE18 4C 106
Carr Ho. DA1: Cray 5K 127
Carriage Dr. E. SW11 7E 100
Carriage Dr. Nth. SW11 7H 17 (6E 100)
(Carriage Dr. E.)
SW11 7D 100
(The Parade)
Carriage Dr. Sth. SW11 1D 118
(not continuous)
Carriage Dr. W. SW11 7D 100
Carriage M. IG1: Ilf 2G 71
Carriage Pl. N16 3D 66
SW16 5G 137
Carriage St. SE18 3F 107
Carrick Cl. TW7: Isle 3A 114
Carrick Dr. IG6: Ilf 1G 53
Carrick Gdns. N17 7K 33
Carrick Ho. *N7 6K 65*
(off Caledonian Rd.)
SE11 5K 19 (5A 102)
Carrick M. SE8 6C 104
Carrill Way DA17: Belv 3D 108
Carrington Av. TW3: Houn 5F 113
Carrington Cl. CR0: C'don 7A 158
KT2: King T 5J 133
Carrington Ct. *SW11 4C 118*
(off Barnard Rd.)
Carrington Gdns. E7 4J 69
Carrington Ho. *W1 5J 11*
(off Carrington St.)
Carrington Rd. TW10: Rich 4G 115
Carrington Sq.
HA3: Hrw W 6B 26
Carrington St. W1 5J 11 (1F 101)
Carrock Ct. *RM7: Rush G 6K 55*
(off Union Rd.)
Carrol Cl. NW5 4F 65
Carroll Cl. E15 5H 69

Carroll Ct. *W3* 3H 97
(off Osborne Rd.)
Carroll Ho. *W2* 2A 10
(off Craven Ter.)
Carronade Ct. N7 5K 65
Carronade Pl. SE28 3H 107
Carron Cl. E14 6D 86
Carroun Rd. SW8 7K 101
Carroway La. UB6: G'frd 3H 77
Carrow Rd. RM9: Dag 7B 72
Carr Rd. E17 2B 50
UB5: N'olt 6E 58
Carrs La. N21 5H 23
Carr St. E14 5A 86
CARSHALTON 4E 166
Carshalton Athletic FC 3C 166
CARSHALTON BEECHES 7C 166
Carshalton Gro. SM1: Sutt 4B 166
CARSHALTON ON THE HILL 7E 166
Carshalton Pk. Rd.
SM5: Cars 5D 166
Carshalton Pl. SM5: Cars 5E 166
Carshalton Rd. CR4: Mitc 4E 154
SM1: Sutt 5A 166
SM5: Cars 5A 166
Carslake Rd. SW15 6E 116
Carson Rd. E16 4J 87
EN4: Cockf 4J 21
SE21 2D 138
Carstairs Rd. SE6 3E 140
Carston Cl. SE12 5H 123
Carswell Cl. IG4: Ilf 4B 52
Carswell Rd. SE6 7E 122
Carter Cl. NW9 6K 43
SM6: Wall 7H 167
Carter Ct. EC4 1A 14
Carter Dr. RM5: Col R 1H 55
Carteret Ho. *W12* 7D 80
(off White City Est.)
Carteret St. SW1 7C 12 (2H 101)
Carteret Way SE8 4A 104
Carterhatch La. EN1: Enf 1A 24
Carterhatch Rd. EN3: Enf H 1D 24
Carter Ho. E1 6J 9
Carter La. EC4 1B 14 (6B 84)
Carter Pl. SE17 5C 102
Carter Rd. E13 1K 87
SW19 6B 136
Carters Cl. KT4: Wor Pk 2F 165
NW5 5H 65
(off Torriano Av.)
Carters Hill Cl. SE9 1A 142
Carters La. SE23 2A 140
Carter St. SE17 6C 102
Carter's Yd. SW18 5J 117
Carthew Rd. W6 3D 98
Carthew Vs. W6 3D 98
Carthusian St. EC1 5C 8 (5C 84)
Cartier Circ. E14 1D 104
Carting La. WC2 3F 13 (7J 83)
Cart La. E4 1B 36
Cartmel *NW1* 1A 6
(off Hampstead Rd.)
Cartmel Cl. N17 7C 34
Cartmel Ct. UB5: N'olt 6C 58
Cartmel Gdns. SM4: Mord 5A 154
Cartmel Rd. DA7: Bex 1G 127
Carton Ho. *SE16* 3G 103
(off Marine St.)
W11 7F 81
(off St Ann's Rd.)
Cartoon Mus. 6E 6
(off Lit. Russell St.)
Cartridge Pl. SE18 3F 107
Cartwright Gdns. WC1 2E 6 (3J 83)
Cartwright Ho. *SE1* 3C 102
(off County St.)
Cartwright Rd. RM9: Dag 7F 73
Cartwright St. E1 2K 15 (7F 85)
Cartwright Way SW13 7D 98
Carvel Ho. *E14* 5E 104
(off Manchester Rd.)
Carver Cl. W4 3J 97
Carver Rd. SE24 6C 120
Carville Cres. TW8: Bford 4E 96
Cary Rd. E11 4G 69
Carysfort Rd. N8 5H 47
N16 3D 66
Casby Ho. *SE16* 3G 103
(off Marine St.)
Cascade Av. N10 4G 47
Cascade Cl. IG9: Buck H 2G 37
Cascade Rd. IG9: Buck H 2G 37
Cascades Ct. SW19 7H 135
Cascades Twr. E14 1B 104
Casel Ct. *HA7: Stan* 2F 27
(off Brightwen Gro.)
Casella Rd. SE14 7K 103
Casewick Rd. SE27 5A 138
Casey Cl. NW8 2C 4 (3C 82)
Casimir Rd. E5 2J 67
Casino Av. SE24 5C 120
Caspian Ho. *E1* 5K 85
(off Shandy St.)
Caspian St. SE5 7D 102
Caspian Wlk. E16 6B 88
Cassandra Cl. UB5: N'olt 4H 59
Casselden Rd. NW10 7K 61
Cassell Ho. *SW9* 2J 119
(off Stockwell Gdns. Est.)
Cassidy Rd. SW6 7J 99
(not continuous)
Cassilda Rd. SE2 4A 108
Cassilis Rd. E14 2C 104
TW1: Twick 5B 114
Cassiobury Av. TW14: Felt 7H 111
Cassiobury Rd. E17 5A 50
Cassland Rd. CR7: Thor H 4D 156
E9 7K 67
Casslee Rd. SE6 7B 122
Cassocks Sq. TW17: Shep 7F 147
Casson Ho. *E1* 5K 9
(off Hanbury St.)
Casson St. E1 5G 85
Castalia Sq. E14 2E 104
Castellain Mans. *W9* 4K 81
(off Castellain Rd., not continuous)
Castellain Rd. W9 4K 81
Castellane Cl. HA7: Stan 7E 26
Castell Ho. SE8 7C 104
Castello Av. SW15 5E 116
CASTELNAU 6D 98
Castelnau SW13 1C 116
Castelnau Gdns. SW13 6D 98
Castelnau Mans. *SW13* 6D 98
(off Castelnau, not continuous)
Castelnau Row SW13 6D 98
Casterbridge *NW6* 1K 81
(off Abbey Rd.)
W11 6H 81
(off Dartmouth Cl.)
Casterbridge Rd. SE3 3J 123
Casterton St. E8 6H 67
Castile Rd. SE18 4E 106
Castillon Rd. SE6 2G 141
Castlands Rd. SE6 2B 140
Castleacre *W2* 1C 10
(off Hyde Pk. Cres.)
Castle Av. E4 5A 36
KT17: Ewe 7D 164
UB7: Yiew 7A 74
Castlebar Ct. W5 5C 78
Castlebar Hill W5 5C 78
Castlebar M. W5 5C 78
Castlebar Pk. W5 5B 78
Castlebar Rd. W5 5C 78
Castle Baynard St. EC4 2B 14 (7B 84)
Castlebrook Ct. SE11 4B 102
Castle Bus. Cen. *TW12: Hamp* 1F 149
(off Castle M.)
Castle Climbing Cen., The 2C 66
Castle Cl. BR2: Brom 3G 159
E9 5A 68
SW19 3F 135
TW16: Sun 7G 129
W3 2H 97
Castlecombe Dr. SW19 7F 117
Castlecombe Rd. SE9 4C 142
Castle Ct. *EC3* 1F 15
(off Birchin La.)
SE26 4A 140
Castleden Ho. *NW3* 7B 64
(off Hilgrove Rd.)
Castledine Rd. SE20 7H 139
Castle Dr. IG4: Ilf 6C 52
Castleford Av. SE9 1F 143
Castleford Cl. N17 6A 34
Castleford Ct. *NW8* 3B 4
(off Henderson Dr.)
Castlegate TW9: Rich 3F 115
Castlehaven Rd. NW1 7F 65
Castle Hgts. RM9: Dag 1B 90
Castle Hill Av. CR0: New Ad 7D 170
Castle Hill Pde. *W13* 7B 78
(off The Avenue)
Castle Ho. *SE1* 4C 102
(off Walworth Rd.)
SM2: Sutt 6J 165
SW8 7J 101
(off Sth. Lambeth Rd.)
Castle Ind. Est. SE17 4C 102
Castle La. SW1 1B 18 (3G 101)
Castleleigh Ct. EN2: Enf 5J 23
Castlemaine SW11 2D 118
Castlemaine Av. CR2: S Croy 5F 169
KT17: Ewe 7D 164
Castlemain St. E1 5H 85
Castle Mead SE5 7C 102
Castle M. N12 5F 31
NW1 6F 65
SW17 4C 136
TW12: Hamp 1F 149
(not continuous)
Castle Pde. KT17: Ewe 7C 164
Castle Pl. NW1 6F 65
W4 4A 98
Castle Point *E13* 2A 88
(off Boundary Rd.)
Castlereagh Ho. HA7: Stan 6G 27
Castlereagh St. W1 7E 4 (6D 82)
Castle Rd. EN3: Enf H 1F 25
N12 5F 31
NW1 6F 65
RM9: Dag 1B 90
TW7: Isle 2K 113
UB2: S'hall 3D 94
UB5: N'olt 6F 59
Castle Row W4 5K 97
Castle St. E6 2A 88
KT1: King T 2E 150
Castleton Av. DA7: Bex 1K 127
HA9: Wemb 4E 60
Castleton Cl. CR0: C'don 6A 158
Castleton Gdns. HA9: Wemb 3E 60
Castleton Ho. *E14* 4E 104
(off Pier St.)
Castleton Rd. CR4: Mitc 4H 155
(not continuous)
E17 2F 51
HA4: Ruis 1B 58
IG3: Ilf 1A 72
SE9 4B 142
Castletown Rd. W14 5G 99
Castleview Cl. N4 2C 66
Castleview Gdns. IG1: Ilf 6C 52
Castle Wlk. TW16: Sun 3A 148
Castle Way SW19 3F 135
TW13: Hanw 4A 130
Castle Wharf *E14* 7G 87
(off Orchard Pl.)
Castlewood Dr. SE9 2D 124
Castlewood Rd. EN4: Cockf 3G 21
N15 6G 49
N16 6G 49
Castle Yd. N6 7E 46
SE1 4B 14 (1B 102)
TW10: Rich 5D 114
Castor La. E14 7D 86
Catalina Rd. TW6: H'row A 2D 110
Catalpa Ct. SE13 6F 123
Caterham Av. IG5: Ilf 2D 52
Caterham Rd. SE13 3F 123
Catesby Ho. *E9* 7J 67
(off Frampton Pk. Rd.)
Catesby St. SE17 4D 102
CATFORD 7D 122
Catford Art Gallery 7D 122
Catford B'way. SE6 7D 122
CATFORD GYRATORY 7D 122
Catford Hill SE6 1B 140
Catford Island SE6 7D 122
Catford M. SE6 7D 122
Catford Rd. SE6 7C 122
Catford Trad. Est. SE6 2D 140
Cathall Leisure Cen. 2G 69
Cathall Rd. E11 2F 69
Cathay Ho. SE16 2H 103
Cathay St. SE16 2H 103
Cathay Wlk. *UB5: N'olt* 2E 76
(off Brabazon Rd.)
Cathcart Dr. BR6: Orp 2J 173
Cathcart Hill N19 3G 65
Cathcart Rd. SW10 6K 99
Cathcart St. NW5 6F 65
Cathedral Lodge *EC1* 5C 8
(off Aldersgate St.)
Cathedral Mans. *SW1* 3A 18
(off Vauxhall Bri. Rd.)
Cathedral Piazza SW1 2A 18 (3G 101)
Cathedral St. SE1 4E 14 (1D 102)
Cathedral Wlk. SW1 1A 18
Catherall Rd. N5 3C 66
Catherine Cl. NW4 4D 44
Catherine Ct. IG2: Ilf 5G 53
N14 5B 22
SW3 7A 16
(off Callow St.)
SW19 5H 135
Catherine Dr. TW9: Rich 4E 114
TW16: Sun 6H 129
Catherine Gdns. TW3: Houn 4H 113
Catherine Griffiths Ct. *EC1* 3K 7
(off Northampton Rd.)
Catherine Gro. SE10 1D 122
Catherine Ho. *N1* 1E 84
(off Whitmore Est.)
Catherine Howard Ct. SE9 6H 125
Catherine of Aragon Ct. SE9 6G 125
Catherine Parr Ct. SE9 6H 125
Catherine Pl. HA1: Harr 5K 41
SW1 1A 18 (3G 101)
Catherine Rd. KT6: Surb 5D 150
Catherine St. WC2 2G 13 (7K 83)
Catherine Wheel All.
E1 6H 9 (5E 84)
Catherine Wheel Rd.
TW8: Bford 7D 96
Catherine Wheel Yd. SW1 5A 12
Catherwood Ct. N1 1E 8
Cat Hill EN4: E Barn 6H 21
Cathles Rd. SW12 6F 119
Cathnor Rd. W12 2D 98
Catlin Cres. TW17: Shep 5F 147
Catling Cl. SE23 3J 139
Catlin's La. HA5: Eastc 3K 39
Catlin St. SE16 5G 103
Cator La. BR3: Beck 1B 158
Cato Rd. SW4 3H 119
Cator Rd. SE26 6K 139
SM5: Cars 5D 166

Cator St. SE15 7F 103
(Commercial Way)
SE15 6F 103
(Ebley Cl.)
Cato St. W1 6D 4 (5C 82)
Catsey La. WD23: Bush 1B 26
Catsey Woods
WD23: Bush 1B 26
Catterick Cl. N11 6K 31
Cattistock Rd.
SE9 5C 142
Cattley Cl. EN5: Barn 4B 20
Catton St. WC1 6G 7 (5K 83)
Caudwell Ter. SW18 6B 118
Caughley Ho. SE11 2J 19
Caulfield Ct. *NW1* 7G 65
(off Baynes St.)
Caulfield Rd. E6 1C 88
SE15 2H 121
Causeway, The
KT9: Chess 4E 162
KT10: Clay 7A 162
N2 4C 46
SM2: Sutt 7A 166
SM5: Cars 3E 166
SW18 5K 117
(not continuous)
SW19 5E 134
TW4: Houn 4J 111
TW11: Tedd 6K 131
TW14: Felt, Houn 4J 111
Causeyware Rd. N9 7D 24
Causton Cotts. *E14* 6A 86
(off Galsworthy Av.)
Causton Ho. SE5 6C 102
Causton Rd. N6 7F 47
Causton Sq. RM10: Dag 7G 73
Causton St. SW1 4D 18 (4H 101)
Cautley Av. SW4 5G 119
Cavalier Cl. RM6: Chad H 4D 54
Cavalier Ct. KT5: Surb 6F 151
Cavalier Gdns. UB3: Hayes 6F 75
Cavalry Cres. TW4: Houn 4B 112
Cavalry Gdns. SW15 5H 117
Cavan Pl. HA5: Hat E 1D 40
Cavaye Ho. *SW10* 7A 16
(off Cavaye Pl.)
Cavaye Pl. SW10 6A 16 (5A 100)
Cavell Dr. EN2: Enf 2F 23
Cavell Ho. *N1* 1E 84
(off Colville Est.)
Cavell Rd. N17 7J 33
Cavell St. E1 5H 85
Cavendish Av.
DA8: Erith 6J 109
DA15: Sidc 7A 126
DA16: Well 3K 125
HA1: Harr 4H 59
HA4: Ruis 5K 57
IG8: Wfd G 1K 51
KT3: N Mald 5C 152
N3 2J 45
NW8 1B 4 (2B 82)
W13 5A 78
Cavendish Cl. N18 5C 34
NW6 6H 63
NW8 1B 4 (3B 82)
TW16: Sun 6H 129
UB4: Hayes 5G 75
Cavendish Ct. EC3 7H 9
SE6 1D 140
(off Bromley Rd.)
SM6: Wall 6F 167
TW16: Sun 6H 129
Cavendish Dr. E11 1F 69
HA8: Edg 6A 28
Cavendish Gdns. IG1: Ilf 1E 70
IG11: Bark 5J 71
RM6: Chad H 5E 54
SW4 6G 119
Cavendish Ho. *NW8* 1B 4
(off Wellington Rd.)
SW1 2D 18
(off Monck St.)
Cavendish Mans. *EC1* 4J 7
(off Rosebery Av.)
NW6 5J 63
Cavendish M. Nth. W1 5K 5 (5F 83)
Cavendish M. Sth. W1 6K 5 (5F 83)
Cavendish Pde. *SW4* 6F 119
(off Clapham Comn. Sth. Side)
TW4: Houn 2C 112
Cavendish Pl. NW2 6F 63
SW4 5H 119
W1 7K 5 (6F 83)
Cavendish Rd. CR0: C'don 1B 168
E4 6K 35
EN5: Barn 3A 20
KT3: N Mald 4B 152
N4 6B 48
N18 5C 34
NW6 7G 63
SM2: Sutt 7A 166
SW12 6F 119
SW19 7B 136
TW16: Sun 6H 129
W4 1J 115
Cavendish Sq. W1 7K 5 (6F 83)
Cavendish St. N1 2D 84
Cavendish Ter. E3 3B 86
TW13: Felt 2J 129
Cavendish Way BR4: W W'ck 1D 170
Cavenham Gdns. IG1: Ilf 3H 71
Caverleigh Way KT4: Wor Pk 1C 164
Cave Rd. E13 3K 87
TW10: Ham 4C 132
Caversham Av. N13 3F 33
SM3: Cheam 2G 165
Caversham Ct. *N11* 3K 31
(off Brunswick Pk. Rd.)
Caversham Ho. *KT1: King T* 2E 150
(off Lady Booth Rd.)
N15 4C 48
(off Caversham Rd.)
SE15 6G 103
(off Haymerle Rd.)
Caversham Rd. KT1: King T 2F 151
N15 4C 48
NW5 6G 65
Caversham St. SW3 7E 16 (6D 100)
Caverswall St. W12 6E 80
Caveside Cl. BR7: Chst 1E 160
Cavour Ho. *SE17* 5B 102
(off Alberta Est.)
Cawdor Cres. W7 4A 96
Cawnpore St. SE19 5E 138
Caxton Ct. SW11 2C 118
Caxton Gro. E3 3C 86
Caxton Hall *SW1* 3H 101
(off Caxton St.)
Caxton M. TW8: Bford 6D 96
Caxton Pl. IG1: Ilf 3E 70
Caxton Rd. N22 2K 47
SW19 5A 136
UB2: S'hall 3B 94
W12 2F 99
Caxton St. SW1 1C 18 (3G 101)
Caxton St. Nth. E16 6H 87
Caxton Trad. Est.
UB3: Hayes 2G 93
Caxton Wlk. WC2 1D 12 (6H 83)
Cayenne Ct. SE1 5K 15 (2F 103)
Caygill Cl. BR2: Brom 4H 159
Cayley Rd. UB2: S'hall 3F 95
Cayton Pl. EC1 2E 8
Cayton Rd. UB6: G'frd 2J 77
Cayton St. EC1 2E 8 (3D 84)
Cazenove Rd. E17 1C 50
N16 2F 67
Cearns Ho. E6 1B 88
Cecil Av. EN1: Enf 4A 24
HA9: Wemb 5F 61
IG11: Bark 7H 71
Cecil Cl. KT9: Chess 4D 162
TW15: Ashf 7E 128
W5 5D 78
Cecil Ct. CR0: C'don 2F 169
EN2: Enf 4J 23
EN5: Barn 3A 20
NW6 7K 63
SW10 6A 100
(off Fawcett St.)
WC2 3E 12 (7J 83)
Cecile Pk. N8 6J 47
Cecil Ho. E17 1C 50
Cecilia Cl. N2 3A 46
Cecilia Rd. E8 5F 67
Cecil Manning Cl. UB6: G'frd 1A 78
Cecil Pk. HA5: Pinn 4C 40
Cecil Pl. CR4: Mitc 5D 154
Cecil Rhodes Ho. *NW1* 2H 83
(off Goldington St.)
Cecil Rd. CR0: C'don 6J 155
E11 3H 69
E13 1J 87
E17 1C 50
EN2: Enf 3H 23
HA3: W'stone 3J 41
IG1: Ilf 4F 71
N10 2F 47
N14 1B 32
NW9 3A 44
NW10 1A 80
RM6: Chad H 7D 54
SM1: Sutt 6H 165
SW19 7K 135
TW3: Houn 2G 113
TW15: Ashf 7E 128
W3 5J 79
Cecil Rosen Ct. HA0: Wemb 3B 60
Cecil Sharp House 1E 82
Cecil Way BR2: Hayes 1J 171
Cedar Av. DA15: Sidc 7A 126
EN3: Enf H 2D 24
EN4: E Barn 7H 21
HA4: Ruis 5A 58
RM6: Chad H 5E 54
TW2: Whitt 6F 113
UB3: Hayes 6J 75
UB7: Yiew 7B 74
Cedar Cl. BR2: Brom 3C 172
E3 1B 86
IG1: Ilf 5H 71
IG9: Buck H 2G 37
KT8: E Mos 4J 149
RM7: Rom 4J 55
SE21 1C 138
SM5: Cars 6D 166
SW15 4K 133
Cedar Copse BR1: Brom 2D 160
Cedar Ct. E18: Wfd G 1J 51
N1 7C 66
N10 2E 46
N11 5B 32
N20 1G 31
SE1 7G 15
(off Royal Oak Yd.)
SE7 6A 106
SM2: Sutt 6A 166
SW19 3F 135
TW8: Bford 6C 96
Cedar Cres. BR2: Brom 3C 172
Cedarcroft Rd. KT9: Chess 4F 163
Cedar Dr. HA5: Hat E 6A 26
N2 4C 46
Cedar Gdns. SM2: Sutt 6A 166
Cedar Grange EN1: Enf 5K 23
Cedar Gro. DA5: Bexl 6D 126
UB1: S'hall 5E 76
W5 3E 96
Cedar Hgts. NW2 6H 63
TW10: Ham 1E 132
Cedar Ho. *E2* 2H 85
(off Mowlem St.)
E14 2E 104
(off Manchester Rd.)
N22 1A 48
(off Acacia Rd.)
SE14 1K 121
SE16 2K 103
(off Woodland Cres.)
SW6 2A 118
TW9: Kew 1H 115
TW16: Sun 7H 129
(off Spelthorne Gro.)
UB4: Yead 4A 76
W8 3K 99
(off Marloes Rd.)
Cedarhurst BR1: Brom 7G 141
Cedarhurst Cotts. DA5: Bexl 7G 127
Cedarhurst Dr. SE9 5A 124
Cedarland Ter. SW20 7D 134
Cedar Lawn Av. EN5: Barn 5B 20
Cedar Mt. SE9 1B 142
Cedarne Rd. SW6 7K 99
Cedar Pk. Gdns. RM6: Chad H 7D 54
Cedar Pk. Rd. EN2: Enf 1H 23
Cedar Pl. SE7 5A 106
Cedar Ri. N14 7K 21
Cedar Rd. BR1: Brom 2A 160
CR0: C'don 2D 168
EN2: Enf 1G 23
KT8: E Mos 4J 149
N17 1F 49
NW2 4E 62
RM7: Rom 4J 55
SM2: Sutt 6A 166
TW4: Cran 2A 112
TW11: Tedd 5A 132
TW14: Bedf 1F 129
Cedars, The E15 7H 69
IG9: Buck H 1D 36
SM6: Wall 4G 167
TW11: Tedd 6K 131
W13 6C 78
Cedars Av. CR4: Mitc 4E 154
E17 5C 50
Cedars Cl. NW4 3F 45
SE13 3F 123
Cedars Ct. N9 2K 33
Cedars Dr. UB10: Hil 2B 74
Cedars Ho. E17 3D 50
Cedars M. SW4 4F 119
(not continuous)
Cedars Rd. BR3: Beck 2A 158
CR0: Bedd 3J 167
E15 6G 69
KT1: Ham W 1C 150
N9 2B 34
N21 2G 33
SM4: Mord 4J 153
SW4 3F 119
SW13 2C 116
W4 5J 97
Cedar Ter. TW9: Rich 4E 114
Cedar Tree Gro. SE27 5B 138
Cedar Vw. *KT1: King T* 3D 150
(off Milner Rd.)
Cedarville Gdns. SW16 6K 137
Cedar Way NW1 7H 65
TW16: Sun 7G 129
Cedar Way Ind. Est. NW1 7H 65
Cedra Ct. N16 1G 67
Cedric Rd. SE9 3G 143
Celadon Cl. EN3: Enf H 3F 25
Celandine Cl. E14 5C 86
Celandine Ct. E4 3J 35
Celandine Dr. E8 7F 67
SE28 1B 108
Celandine Gro. N14 5B 22

Celandine Way E15 3G **87**
Celbridge M. W2 5K **81**
Celestial Gdns. SE13 4F **123**
Celia Cres. TW15: Ashf 6A **128**
Celia Ho. *N1* *2E **84***
(off Arden Est.)
Celia Rd. N19 4G **65**
Celtic Av. BR2: Brom 3G **159**
Celtic St. E14 5D **86**
Cemetery La. SE7 6C **106**
TW17: Shep 7D **146**
Cemetery Rd. E7 5H **69**
N17 7K **33**
SE2 7B **108**
Cenacle Cl. NW3 3J **63**
Cenotaph 6E **12** (2J **101**)
Centaur Ct. TW8: Bford 5E **96**
Centaurs Bus. Pk. TW7: Isle 6A **96**
Centaur St. SE1 1H **19** (3K **101**)
Centenary Rd. EN3: Brim 4G **25**
Centenary Trad. Est. EN3: Brim 3G **25**
Centennial Av. WD6: E'tree 1H **27**
Centennial Ct. WD6: E'tree 1H **27**
Centennial Pk. WD6: E'tree 1H **27**
Central Av. DA16: Well 2K **125**
E11 2F **69**
E12 3B **70**
EN1: Enf 2C **24**
HA5: Pinn 6D **40**
KT8: W Mole 4D **148**
N2 2B **46**
(Oak La.)
N2 4K **45**
(Rosemary Av.)
N9 3K **33**
SM6: Wall 5J **167**
SW11 7D **100**
TW3: Houn 4G **113**
UB3: Hayes 1H **93**
Central Bus. Cen. NW10 5A **62**
Central Church Sports Club *2K **139***
(off Normanton St.)
Central Cir. NW4 5D **44**
Centrale Shop. Cen.
CR0: C'don 2C **168**
Central Gallery *IG1: Ilf* *2F **71***
(in The Exchange)
Central Gdns. SM4: Mord 5K **153**
Central Hill SE19 5C **138**
Central Ho. E15 2D **86**
IG11: Bark 7G **71**
Central Mall *SW18* *6K **117***
(off South Mall)
Central Mans. *NW4* *5D **44***
(off Watford Way)
Central Markets (Smithfield) 6A **8**
Central Pde. DA15: Sidc 3A **144**
E17 4C **50**
EN3: Enf H 2D **24**
HA1: Harr 5K **41**
IG2: Ilf 6H **53**
KT6: Surb 6E **150**
KT8: W Mole 4D **148**
SE20 *7K **139***
(off High St.)
TW5: Hest 7D **94**
TW14: Felt 7A **112**
UB6: G'frd 3A **78**
W3 2H **97**
Central Pk. Av.
RM10: Dag 3H **73**
Central Pk. Est. TW4: Houn 5B **112**
Central Pk. Rd. E6 2B **88**
Central Pl. SE25 5G **157**
Central Rd. HA0: Wemb 5B **60**
KT4: Wor Pk 1C **164**
SM4: Mord 6J **153**
Central St Martins College of Art & Design
6G **7**
Central School Path SW14 3J **115**
Central Sq. *HA9: Wemb* *5E **60***
(off Sevenex Pde.)
NW11 6K **45**
Central St. EC1 1C **8** (3C **84**)
Central Ter. BR3: Beck 3K **157**
Central Way NW10 3J **79**
SE28 1A **108**
SM5: Cars 7C **166**
TW14: Felt 5J **111**
Central Wharf *E14* *6C **86***
(off Thomas Rd.)
Centre, The KT12: Walt T 7J **147**
TW3: Houn 3F **113**
TW13: Felt 1K **129**
Centre Av. N2 2C **46**
NW10 3E **80**
W3 1K **97**
Centre Comn. Rd. BR7: Chst 6G **143**
Centre Ct. Shop. Cen. SW19 6H **135**
Centre Dr. E7 4A **70**
Centre for the Magic Arts, The *3B **6***
(off Stephenson Way)
Centre Hgts. *NW3* *7B **64***
(off Finchley Rd.)
Centre Point SE1 5G **103**
Centrepoint WC2 7D **6**
Centre Point Ho. *WC2* *7D **6***
(off St Giles High St.)
Centre Rd. E7 2J **69**
E11 2J **69**
RM10: Dag 2H **91**
Centre Sq. *SW18* *5J **117***
(off Buckhold Rd.)
Centre St. E2 2H **85**
Centre Way E17 7K **35**
N9 2D **34**
Centreway Apartments *IG1: Ilf* *2G **71***
(off Axon Pl.)
Centric Cl. NW1 1E **82**
Centrillion Point *CR0: C'don* *4C **168***
(off Mason's Av.)
Centro Ct. E6 4D **88**
Centurian Sq. SE18 1C **124**
Centurion Bldg. SW8 7J **17** (6F **101**)
Centurion Cl. N7 7K **65**
Centurion Ct. SE18 4E **106**
SM6: Wall 2F **167**
Centurion La. E3 1B **86**
Centurion Way DA18: Erith 3F **109**
Century Cl. NW4 5F **45**
Century Ho. HA9: Wemb 2F **61**
SW15 4F **117**
Century M. E5 4J **67**
Century Plaza *HA8: Edg* *6B **28***
(off Station Rd.)
Century Rd. E17 3A **50**
Century Yd. SE23 2J **139**
(not continuous)
Cephas Av. E1 4J **85**
Cephas Ho. *E1* *4J **85***
(off Doveton St.)
Cephas St. E1 4J **85**
Ceres Rd. SE18 4K **107**
Cerise Rd. SE15 1G **121**
Cerne Cl. UB4: Yead 7A **76**
Cerne Rd. SM4: Mord 6A **154**
Cerney M. W2 2A **10** (7B **82**)
Cervantes Ct. W2 6K **81**
Cester St. E2 1G **85**
Ceylon Rd. W14 3F **99**
Ceylon Wharf Apartments *SE16* *2J **103***
(off St Marychurch St.)
Chabot Dr. SE15 3H **121**
Chadacre Av. IG5: Ilf 3D **52**
Chadacre Ct. *E15* *1J **87***
(off Vicars Cl.)
Chadacre Ho. *SW9* *4B **120***
(off Loughborough Pk.)
Chadacre Rd. KT17: Ewe 6D **164**
Chadbourn St. E14 5D **86**
Chadbury Ct. NW7 1C **44**
Chad Cres. N9 3D **34**
Chadd Dr. BR1: Brom 3C **160**
Chadd Grn. E13 1J **87**
(not continuous)
Chadston Ho. *N1* *7B **66***
(off Halton Rd.)
Chadswell *WC1* *2F **7***
(off Cromer St.)
Chadview Ct. RM6: Chad H 7D **54**
Chadville Gdns. RM6: Chad H 5D **54**
Chadway RM8: Dag 1C **72**
Chadwell Av. RM6: Chad H 7B **54**
CHADWELL HEATH 7D **54**
Chadwell Heath Ind. Pk.
RM8: Dag 1E **72**
Chadwell Heath La.
RM6: Chad H 4B **54**
Chadwell Ho. *SE17* *5D **102***
(off Inville Rd.)
Chadwell La. N8 3K **47**
Chadwell St. EC1 1K **7** (3A **84**)
Chadwick Av. E4 4A **36**
N21 5E **22**
SW19 6J **135**
Chadwick Cl. SW15 7B **116**
TW11: Tedd 6A **132**
W7 5K **77**
Chadwick M. W4 6H **97**
Chadwick Pl. KT6: Surb 7C **150**
Chadwick Rd. E11 6G **51**
IG1: Ilf 3F **71**
NW10 1B **80**
SE15 2F **121**
Chadwick St. SW1 2C **18** (3H **101**)
Chadwick Way SE28 7D **90**
Chadwin Rd. E13 5K **87**
Chadworth Ho. *EC1* *2C **8***
(off Lever St.)
N4 1C **66**
Chaffinch Av. CR0: C'don 6K **157**
Chaffinch Bus. Pk. BR3: Beck 4K **157**
Chaffinch Cl. CR0: C'don 5K **157**
KT6: Surb 3G **163**
N9 1E **34**
Chaffinch Rd. BR3: Beck 1A **158**
Chafford Way RM6: Chad H 4C **54**
Chagford St. NW1 4E **4** (4D **82**)
Chailey Av. EN1: Enf 2A **24**
Chailey Cl. TW5: Hest 1B **112**
Chailey Ind. Est. UB3: Hayes 2J **93**
Chailey St. E5 3J **67**
Chalbury Wlk. N1 2K **83**
Chalcombe Rd. SE2 3B **108**
Chalcot Cl. SM2: Sutt 7J **165**
Chalcot Cres. NW1 1D **82**
Chalcot Gdns. NW3 6D **64**
Chalcot M. SW16 3J **137**
Chalcot Rd. NW1 7E **64**
Chalcot Sq. NW1 7E **64**
(not continuous)
Chalcott Gdns. KT6: Surb 1C **162**
Chalcroft Rd. SE13 5G **123**
Chaldon Ct. SE19 1D **156**
Chaldon Path CR7: Thor H 4B **156**
Chaldon Rd. SW6 7G **99**
Chale Rd. SW2 6J **119**
Chalet Cl. DA5: Bexl 4K **145**
Chalet Ct. CR7: Thor H 5C **156**
Chalet Est. NW7 4H **29**
Chalfont Av. HA9: Wemb 6H **61**
Chalfont Ct. *HA1: Harr* *6K **41***
(off Northwick Pk. Rd.)
NW1 *4F **5***
(off Baker St.)
NW9 3B **44**
Chalfont Grn. N9 3K **33**
Chalfont Ho. *SE16* *3H **103***
(off Keetons Rd.)
Chalfont M. UB10: Hil 7D **56**
Chalfont Rd. N9 3K **33**
SE25 3F **157**
UB3: Hayes 2J **93**
Chalfont Wlk. HA5: Pinn 2A **40**
Chalfont Way W13 3B **96**
Chalford *NW6* *6A **64***
(off Finchley Rd.)
Chalford Cl. KT8: W Mole 4E **148**
Chalford Rd. SE21 4D **138**
Chalford Wlk. IG8: Wfd G 1B **52**
Chalgrove Av. SM4: Mord 5J **153**
Chalgrove Cres. IG5: Ilf 2C **52**
Chalgrove Gdns. N3 3G **45**
Chalgrove Rd. N17 1H **49**
SM2: Sutt 7B **166**
Chalice Cl. SM6: Wall 6H **167**
Chalice Ct. N2 4C **46**
Chalkenden Cl. SE20 7H **139**
CHALKER'S CORNER 3H **115**
CHALK FARM 7E **64**
Chalk Farm *NW3* *7E **64***
(off Adelaide Rd.)
Chalk Farm Rd. NW1 7E **64**
Chalk Hill Rd. W6 4F **99**
Chalkhill Rd. HA9: Wemb 3H **61**
Chalklands HA9: Wemb 3J **61**
Chalk La. EN4: Cockf 3J **21**
Chalkley Cl. CR4: Mitc 2D **154**
Chalkmill Dr. EN1: Enf 3C **24**
Chalk Pit Way SM1: Sutt 5A **166**
Chalk Rd. E13 5K **87**
Chalkstone Cl. DA16: Well 1A **126**
Chalkwell Ho. *E1* *6K **85***
(off Pitsea St.)
Chalkwell Pk. Av. EN1: Enf 4K **23**
Challenge Cl. NW10 1A **80**
Challenge Ct. TW2: Twick 7J **113**
Challenger Ho. *E14* *7A **86***
(off Victory Pl.)
Challenge Rd. TW15: Ashf 3F **129**
Challice Way SW2 1K **137**
Challin St. SE20 1J **157**
Challis Rd. TW8: Bford 5D **96**
Challoner Cl. N2 2B **46**
Challoner Ct. BR2: Brom 2F **159**
W14 *5H **99***
(off Challoner St.)
Challoner Cres. W14 5H **99**
Challoner Mans. *W14* *5H **99***
(off Challoner St.)
Challoners Cl. KT8: E Mos 4H **149**
Challoner St. W14 5H **99**
Chalmers Ho. E17 5D **50**
Chalmers Rd. TW15: Ashf 5D **128**
Chalmers Rd. E. TW15: Ashf 4D **128**
Chalmers Wlk. *SE17* *6B **102***
(off Hillingdon St.)
Chalmers Way TW14: Felt 5K **111**
Chaloner Ct. SE1 6E **14**
Chalsey Rd. SE4 4B **122**
Chalton Dr. N2 6B **46**
Chalton Ho. *NW1* *1C **6***
(off Chalton St.)
Chalton St. NW1 1C **6** (2G **83**)
(not continuous)
Chamberlain Cl. IG1: Ilf 3G **71**
SE28 3H **107**
Chamberlain Cotts. SE5 1D **120**
Chamberlain Cres. BR4: W W'ck 1D **170**
Chamberlain Gdns. TW3: Houn 1G **113**
Chamberlain Ho. *E1* *7J **85***
(off Cable St.)
NW1 1D **6**
SE1 *7J **13***
(off Westminster Bri. Rd.)
Chamberlain La. HA5: Eastc 4J **39**
Chamberlain Pl. E17 3A **50**
Chamberlain Rd. N2 2A **46**
W13 2A **96**
Chamberlain St. NW1 7D **64**

Chamberlain Wlk. TW13: Hanw 4C 130
(off Swift Rd.)
Chamberlain Way HA5: Eastc 3K 39
KT6: Surb 7E 150
Chamberlayne Av. HA9: Wemb 3E 60
Chamberlayne Mans. NW10 . . . . . 3F 81
(off Chamberlayne Rd.)
Chamberlayne Rd. NW10 . . . . . 1E 80
Chamberlens Garages W6 . . . . . 4D 98
(off Dalling Rd.)
Chambers, The SW10 . . . . . 1A 118
(off Chelsea Harbour Dr.)
Chambers Bus. Pk. UB7: Sip 6C 92
Chambers Gdns. N2 . . . . . 1B 46
Chambers La. NW10 . . . . . 7D 62
Chambers Pl. CR2: S Croy 7D 168
Chambers Rd. N7 . . . . . 4J 65
Chambers St. SE16 . . . . . 2G 103
Chamber St. E1 . . . . . 2K 15 (7F 85)
Chambers Wlk. HA7: Stan 5G 27
Chambers Wharf SE16 . . . . . 2G 103
Chambon Pl. W6 . . . . . 4C 98
Chambord St. E2 . . . . . 2K 9 (3F 85)
Chamomile Ct. E17 . . . . . 6C 50
(off Yunus Khan Cl.)
Champa Cl. N17 . . . . . 2F 49
Champion Cres. SE26 . . . . . 4A 140
Champion Gro. SE5 . . . . . 3D 120
Champion Hill SE5 . . . . . 3D 120
Champion Hill Est. SE5 . . . . . 3E 120
Champion Hill Stadium 4E 120
Champion Pk. SE5 . . . . . 2D 120
Champion Rd. SE26 . . . . . 4A 140
Champions Way NW4 . . . . . 1D 44
Champlain Ho. W12 . . . . . 7D 80
(off White City Est.)
Champness Cl. SE27 . . . . . 4D 138
Champness Rd. IG11: Bark 6K 71
Champneys Cl. SM2: Cheam 7H 165
Chancel Ind. Est. NW10 . . . . . 5B 62
Chancellor Gdns. CR2: S Croy 7B 168
Chancellor Gro. SE21 . . . . . 2C 138
Chancellor Ho. E1 . . . . . 1H 103
(off Green Bank)
SW7 . . . . . 3A 100
(off Hyde Pk. Ga.)
Chancellor Pas. E14 . . . . . 1C 104
Chancellor Pl. NW9 . . . . . 2B 44
Chancellors Ct. WC1 . . . . . 5G 7
Chancellor's Rd. W6 . . . . . 5E 98
Chancellor's St. W6 . . . . . 5E 98
Chancellors Wharf W6 . . . . . 5E 98
Chancelot Rd. SE2 . . . . . 4B 108
Chancel St. SE1 . . . . . 5A 14 (1B 102)
Chancery Bldgs. E1 . . . . . 7H 85
(off Lowood St.)
Chancerygate UB7: Yiew 1C 92
Chancerygate Bus. Cen.
HA4: Ruis 4C 58
Chancery La. BR3: Beck 2D 158
WC2 . . . . . 6H 7 (6A 84)
Chancery M. SW17 . . . . . 2C 136
Chance St. E1 . . . . . 3J 9 (4F 85)
E2 . . . . . 3J 9 (4F 85)
Chanctonbury Cl. SE9 . . . . . 3F 143
Chanctonbury Gdns. SM2: Sutt 7K 165
Chanctonbury Way N12 . . . . . 4C 30
Chandaria Ct. CR0: C'don 2C 168
(off Church Rd.)
Chandler Av. E16 . . . . . 5J 87
Chandler Cl. TW12: Hamp 1E 148
Chandler Ct. TW14: Felt 6J 111
Chandler Ho. NW6 . . . . . 1H 81
(off Willesden La.)
WC1 . . . . . 4F 7
(off Colonnade)
Chandlers Cl. KT8: W Mole 5F 149
TW14: Felt 7H 111
Chandlers Ct. SE12 . . . . . 1K 141
Chandlers Dr. DA8: Erith 4K 109
Chandlers M. E14 . . . . . 2C 104
Chandler St. E1 . . . . . 1H 103
Chandlers Way SW2 . . . . . 7A 120
Chandler Way SE15 . . . . . 6E 102
Chandlery, The SE1 . . . . . 1K 19
(off Gerridge St.)
Chandlery Ho. E1 . . . . . 6G 85
(off Gower's Wlk.)
Chandon Lodge SM2: Sutt 7A 166
Chandos Av. E17 . . . . . 2C 50
N14 . . . . . 3B 32
N20 . . . . . 1F 31
W5 . . . . . 4C 96
Chandos Cl. IG9: Buck H 2E 36
Chandos Ct. HA7: Stan 6G 27
HA8: Edg 7A 28
N14 . . . . . 2C 32
Chandos Cres. HA8: Edg 7A 28
Chandos Pde. HA8: Edg 7A 28
Chandos Pl. WC2 . . . . . 3E 12 (7J 83)
Chandos Rd. E15 . . . . . 5F 69
HA1: Harr 5G 41
HA5: Eastc 7B 40
N2 . . . . . 2B 46
N17 . . . . . 2E 48
NW2 . . . . . 5E 62
NW10 . . . . . 4A 80
Chandos St. W1 . . . . . 6K 5 (5F 83)
Chandos Way NW11 . . . . . 1K 63
Change All. EC3 . . . . . 1F 15 (6D 84)
Channel 4 TV 3H 101
(off Horseferry Rd.)
Channel Cl. TW5: Hest 1E 112
Channel Ga. Rd. NW10 . . . . . 3A 80
Channel Ho. E14 . . . . . 5A 86
(off Aston St.)
Channel Islands Est. N1 . . . . . 6C 66
(off Guernsey Rd.)
Channelsea Path E15 . . . . . 1F 87
Channelsea Rd. E15 . . . . . 1F 87
Channon Ct. KT6: Surb 5E 150
(off Maple Rd)
Chanticleer Ct. SE1 . . . . . 5F 103
(off Rolls Rd.)
Chantress Cl. RM10: Dag 1J 91
Chantrey Ho. SW1 . . . . . 3J 17
Chantrey Rd. SW9 . . . . . 3K 119
Chantry, The E4 . . . . . 1K 35
UB8: Hil 3B 74
Chantry Cl. DA14: Sidc 5E 144
EN2: Enf 1H 23
HA3: Kent 5F 43
SE2 . . . . . 3C 108
TW16: Sun 7J 129
UB7: Yiew 7A 74
W9 . . . . . 4J 81
Chantry Ct. SM5: Cars 3C 166
Chantry Cres. NW10 . . . . . 6B 62
Chantry Ho.
KT1: King T 4E 150
RM13: Rain 2K 91
Chantry La. BR2: Brom 5B 160
Chantry Pl. HA3: Hrw W 1F 41
Chantry Rd. HA3: Hrw W 1F 41
KT9: Chess 5F 163
Chantry Sq. W8 . . . . . 3K 99
Chantry St. N1 . . . . . 1B 84
Chantry Way
CR4: Mitc 3B 154
RM13: Rain 2K 91
Chant Sq. E15 . . . . . 7F 69
Chant St. E15 . . . . . 7F 69
Chapel Av. E12 . . . . . 3B 70
Chapel Cl. DA1: Cray 5K 127
NW10 . . . . . 5B 62
Chapel Ct. N2 . . . . . 3C 46
SE1 . . . . . 6E 14 (2D 102)
UB3: Hayes 7H 75
CHAPEL END 1D 50
Chapel Farm Rd. SE9 . . . . . 3D 142
Chapel Hill DA1: Cray 5K 127
N2 . . . . . 2C 46
Chapel Ho. St. E14 . . . . . 5D 104
Chapelier Ho. SW18 . . . . . 4J 117
Chapel La. HA5: Pinn 3B 40
RM6: Chad H 7D 54
UB8: Hil 6C 74
Chapel Mkt. N1 . . . . . 2A 84
Chapel M. IG8: Wfd G 6K 37
Chapel Mill Rd. KT1: King T 3F 151
Chapelmount Rd. IG8: Wfd G 6J 37
Chapel of St John the Evangelist 3J 15
(in The Tower of London)
Chapel of St Peter & St Paul 6F 105
(in Old Royal Naval College)
Chapel Path E11 . . . . . 6K 51
(off Woodbine Pl.)
Chapel Pl. EC2 . . . . . 2G 9 (3E 84)
N1 . . . . . 2A 84
N17 . . . . . 7A 34
W1 . . . . . 1J 11 (6F 83)
Chapel Rd. DA7: Bex 4G 127
IG1: Ilf 3E 70
SE27 . . . . . 4B 138
TW1: Twick 7B 114
TW3: Houn 3F 113
W13 . . . . . 1B 96
Chapel Side W2 . . . . . 7K 81
Chapel Stones N17 . . . . . 1F 49
Chapel St. EN2: Enf 3H 23
NW1 . . . . . 6C 4 (5C 82)
SW1 . . . . . 1H 17 (3E 100)
Chapel Vw. CR2: Sels 6J 169
Chapel Wlk. CR0: C'don 2C 168
NW4 . . . . . 4D 44
(not continuous)
Chapel Way N7 . . . . . 3K 65
Chapel Yd. SW18 . . . . . 5K 117
(off Wandsworth High St.)
Chaplin Cl. HA0: Wemb 6D 60
SE1 . . . . . 6K 13 (2A 102)
Chaplin Cres. TW16: Sun 6G 129
Chaplin Ho. DA14: Sidc 4A 144
(off Sidcup High St.)
Chaplin Rd. E15 . . . . . 2H 87
HA0: Wemb 6C 60
N17 . . . . . 3F 49
NW2 . . . . . 6C 62
RM9: Dag 7E 72
Chaplin Sq. N12 . . . . . 7G 31
Chapman Cl.
UB7: W Dray 3B 92
Chapman Cres. HA3: Kent 6E 42
Chapman Grn. N22 . . . . . 1A 48
Chapman Ho. E1 . . . . . 6H 85
(off Bigland St.)
Chapman Pl. N4 . . . . . 2B 66
Chapman Rd. CR0: C'don 1A 168
DA17: Belv 5G 109
E9 . . . . . 6B 68
Chapman's La. SE2: Belv 4C 108
Chapmans Pk. Ind. Est. NW10 . . . . . 6B 62
Chapman Sq. SW19 . . . . . 2F 135
Chapman's Ter. N22 . . . . . 1B 48
Chapman St. E1 . . . . . 7H 85
Chapone Pl. W1 . . . . . 1C 12 (6H 83)
Chapter Chambers SW1 . . . . . 4C 18
(off Chapter St.)
Chapter Cl. UB10: Hil 7B 56
W4 . . . . . 3J 97
Chapter House 1C 14
Chapter Rd. NW2 . . . . . 5C 62
SE17 . . . . . 5B 102
Chapter St. SW1 . . . . . 4C 18 (4H 101)
Chapter Way SW19 . . . . . 1B 154
TW12: Hamp 4E 130
Chara Pl. W4 . . . . . 6K 97
Charcot Ho. SW15 . . . . . 6B 116
Charcroft Ct. W14 . . . . . 2F 99
(off Minford Gdns.)
Charcroft Gdns. EN3: Pond E 4E 24
Chardin Ho. SW9 . . . . . 1A 120
(off Gosling Way)
Chardin Rd. W4 . . . . . 4A 98
Chardmore Rd. N16 . . . . . 1G 67
Chard Rd. TW6: H'row A 2D 110
Chardwell Cl. E6 . . . . . 6D 88
Charecroft Way W12 . . . . . 2F 99
Charfield Ct. W9 . . . . . 4K 81
(off Shirland Rd.)
Charford Rd. E16 . . . . . 5J 87
Chargeable La. E13 . . . . . 4H 87
Chargeable St. E16 . . . . . 4H 87
Chargrove Cl. SE16 . . . . . 2K 103
Charing Cl. BR6: Orp 4K 173
Charing Ct. BR2: Brom 2G 159
Charing Cross SW1 . . . . . 4E 12
Charing Cross Rd. WC2 . . . . . 7D 6 (6H 83)
Charing Cross Sports Club 6F 99
Charing Cross Underground Shop. Cen.
WC2 . . . . . 3E 12
Charing Ho. SE1 . . . . . 6K 13
(off Windmill Wlk.)
Chariot Cl. E3 . . . . . 1C 86
Charlbert Ct. NW8 . . . . . 2C 82
(off Charlbert St.)
Charlbert St. NW8 . . . . . 2C 82
Charlbury Av. HA7: Stan 5J 27
Charlbury Gdns. IG3: Ilf 2K 71
Charlbury Gro. W5 . . . . . 6C 78
Charlbury Rd. UB10: Ick 3B 56
Charldane Rd. SE9 . . . . . 3F 143
Charlecote Gro. SE26 . . . . . 3H 139
Charlecote Rd. RM8: Dag 3E 72
Charlemont Rd. E6 . . . . . 4D 88
Charles II Pl. SW3 . . . . . 6E 16 (5D 100)
Charles II St. SW1 . . . . . 4C 12 (1H 101)
Charles Allen Ho. EC1 . . . . . 3A 84
(off Amwell St.)
Charles Auffray Ho. E1 . . . . . 5J 85
(off Smithy St.)
Charles Babbage Cl. KT9: Chess 7C 162
Charles Barry Cl. SW4 . . . . . 3G 119
Charles Bradlaugh Ho. N17 . . . . . 7C 34
(off Haynes Cl.)
Charles Chu. Wlk. IG1: Ilf 6D 52
Charles Cl. DA14: Sidc 4B 144
Charles Cobb Gdns. CR0: Wadd 5A 168
Charles Coveney Rd. SE15 . . . . . 1F 121
Charles Cres. HA1: Harr 7H 41
(not continuous)
Charles Curran Ho. UB10: Ick 3D 56
Charles Darwin Ho. E2 . . . . . 3H 85
(off Canrobert St.)
Charles Dickens Ho. E2 . . . . . 3G 85
(off Mansford St.)
Charle Sevright Dr. NW7 . . . . . 5A 30
Charlesfield SE9 . . . . . 3A 142
Charles Flemwell M. E16 . . . . . 1J 105
Charles Gardner Ct. N1 . . . . . 1F 9
(off Haberdasher St.)
Charles Grinling Wlk.
SE18 . . . . . 4E 106
Charles Gro. N14 . . . . . 1B 32
Charles Haller St. SW2 . . . . . 7A 120
Charles Harrod Ct. SW13 . . . . . 6E 98
(off Somerville Av.)
Charles Hocking Ho. W3 . . . . . 2J 97
(off Bollo Bri. Rd.)
Charles House 4H 99
(off Kensington High St.)
Charles Ho. N17 . . . . . 7A 34
(off Love La.)
UB2: S'hall 2E 94
Charles Lamb Ct. N1 . . . . . 2B 84
(off Gerrard Rd.)
Charles La. NW8 . . . . . 2C 82
Charles Lesser Ho. KT9: Chess 5D 162
Charles Mackenzie Ho. SE16 . . . . . 4G 103
(off Linsey St.)

Charlesmere Gdns. SE28 2J 107
(off Thames Reach)
Charles Nex M. SE21 2C 138
Charles Pl. NW1 2B 6 (3G 83)
Charles Rd. E7 7A 70
RM6: Chad H 6D 54
RM10: Dag 6K 73
SW19 1J 153
TW18: Staines 6A 128
W13 6A 78
Charles Rowan Ho. WC1 2J 7
(off Margery St.)
Charles Simmons Ho. WC1 2J 7
(off Margery St.)
Charles Sq. N1 2F 9 (3D 84)
Charles Sq. Est. N1 2F 9
Charles St. CR0: C'don 3C 168
E16 1A 106
EN1: Enf 5A 24
SW13 2A 116
TW3: Houn 2D 112
UB10: Hil 4D 74
W1 4J 11 (1F 101)
Charleston Cl. TW13: Felt 3J 129
Charleston St. SE17 4C 102
Charles Townsend Ho. EC1 3A 8
(off Skinner St.)
Charles Uton Ct. E8 4G 67
Charles Whincup Rd. E16 1K 105
Charlesworth Ho. E14 6B 86
(off Dod St.)
Charlesworth Pl. SW13 3A 116
Charleville Cir. SE26 5G 139
Charleville Ct. W14 5H 99
(off Charleville Rd.)
Charleville Mans. W14 5G 99
(off Charleville Rd., not continuous)
Charleville M. TW7: Isle 4B 114
Charleville Rd. W14 5G 99
CHARLIE BROWN'S RDBT. 2A 52
Charlie Chaplin Wlk. SE1 5H 13
Charlieville Rd. DA8: Erith 7J 109
Charlmont Rd. SW17 6C 136
Charlotte Cl. DA6: Bex 5E 126
IG6: Ilf 1G 53
Charlotte Ct. IG2: Ilf 6E 52
N8 6H 47
SE1 4E 102
(off Old Kent Rd.)
W6 4C 98
(off Invermead Cl.)
Charlotte Despard Av. SW11 1E 118
Charlotte Ho. E16 1K 105
(off Fairfax M.)
W6 5E 98
(off Queen Caroline St.)
Charlotte M. W1 5B 6 (5G 83)
W10 6F 81
W14 4G 99
Charlotte Pk. Av. BR1: Brom 3C 160
Charlotte Pl. NW9 5J 43
SW1 4A 18 (4G 101)
W1 6B 6 (5G 83)
Charlotte Rd. EC2 2G 9 (3E 84)
RM10: Dag 6H 73
SM6: Wall 6G 167
SW13 1B 116
Charlotte Row SW4 3G 119
Charlotte Sq. TW10: Rich 6F 115
Charlotte St. W1 5B 6 (5G 83)
Charlotte Ter. N1 1K 83
Charlow Cl. SW6 2A 118
CHARLTON
SE7 7B 106
TW17 3E 146
Charlton Athletic FC 5A 106
Charlton Chu. La. SE7 5A 106
Charlton Cl. UB10: Ick 2D 56
Charlton Ct. E2 1F 85
NW5 5H 65
Charlton Cres. IG11: Bark 2K 89
Charlton Dene SE7 7A 106
Charlton Ga. Bus. Pk. SE7 4A 106
Charlton House 6B 106
Charlton Ho. TW8: Bford 6E 96
Charlton King's Rd. NW5 5H 65
Charlton La. SE7 4B 106
TW17: Shep 3E 146
(not continuous)
Charlton Lido 7B 106
Charlton Pk. La. SE7 7B 106
Charlton Pk. Rd. SE7 6B 106
Charlton Pl. N1 2B 84
Charlton Rd. HA3: Kent 4D 42
HA9: Wemb 1F 61
N9 1E 34
NW10 1A 80
SE3 7J 105
SE7 7J 105
TW17: Shep 3E 146
Charlton Way SE3 1G 123
Charlwood CR0: Sels 7B 170
Charlwood Cl. HA3: Hrw W 6D 26
Charlwood Ho. SW1 4C 18
(off Vauxhall Bri. Rd.)
TW9: Kew 7H 97
Charlwood Ho's. WC1 2F 7
(off Midhope St.)
Charlwood Pl. SW1 4B 18 (4G 101)
Charlwood Rd. SW15 4F 117
Charlwood St. SW1 6A 18 (5G 101)
(not continuous)
Charlwood Ter. SW15 4F 117
Charmans Ho. SW8 7J 101
(off Wandsworth Rd.)
Charmian Av. HA7: Stan 3D 42
Charmian Ho. N1 1G 9
(off Arden Est.)
Charminster Av. SW19 2J 153
Charminster Ct. KT6: Surb 7D 150
Charminster Rd. KT4: Wor Pk 1F 165
SE9 4B 142
Charmouth Ct. TW10: Rich 5F 115
Charmouth Ho. SW8 7K 101
Charmouth Rd. DA16: Well 1C 126
Charnock Ho. W12 7D 80
(off White City Est.)
Charnock Rd. E5 3H 67
Charnwood Av. SW19 2J 153
Charnwood Cl. KT3: N Mald 4A 152
Charnwood Dr. E18 3K 51
Charnwood Gdns. E14 4C 104
Charnwood Pl. N20 3F 31
Charnwood Rd. SE25 5D 156
UB10: Hil 2C 74
Charnwood St. E5 2H 67
Charrington Bowl 2H 163
Charrington Rd. CR0: C'don 2C 168
Charrington St. NW1 2H 83
Charsley Rd. SE6 2D 140
Chart Cl. BR2: Brom 1G 159
CR0: C'don 6J 157
CR4: Mitc 4D 154
Charter Av. IG2: Ilf 1H 71
Charter Ct. KT3: N Mald 3A 152
N4 1A 66
N22 1H 47
UB1: S'hall 1E 94
Charter Cres. TW4: Houn 4C 112
Charter Dr. DA5: Bexl 7E 126
Charterhouse 4B 8
Charter Ho. SM2: Sutt 6K 165
(off Mulgrave Rd.)
WC2 1F 13
(off Crown Ct.)
Charterhouse Av. HA0: Wemb 4C 60
Charterhouse Bldgs. EC1 4B 8 (4C 84)
Charterhouse M. EC1 5B 8 (5B 84)
Charterhouse Rd. BR6: Chels 3K 173
E8 4G 67
Charterhouse Sq. EC1 5B 8 (5B 84)
Charterhouse St. EC1 6K 7 (5A 84)
Charteris Community Sports Cen. 1J 81
Charteris Rd. IG8: Wfd G 7E 36
N4 1A 66
NW6 1H 81
Charter Quay KT1: King T 2D 150
(off Wadbrook St.)
Charter Rd. KT1: King T 3H 151
Charter Rd., The IG8: Wfd G 6B 36
Charters Cl. SE19 5E 138
Charter Sq. KT1: King T 2H 151
Charter Way N3 4H 45
N14 6B 22
Chartes Ho. SE1 7H 15
(off Stevens St.)
Chartfield Av. SW15 5D 116
Chartfield Sq. SW15 5F 117
Chartham Ct. SW9 3A 120
(off Canterbury Cres.)
Chartham Gro. SE27 3B 138
Chartham Ho. SE1 7F 15
(off Weston St.)
Chartham Rd. SE25 3H 157
Chart Hills Cl. SE28 6E 90
Chart Ho. CR4: Mitc 2D 154
E14 5D 104
(off Burrells Wharf Sq.)
Chartley Av. HA7: Stan 6E 26
NW2 3A 62
Charton Cl. DA17: Belv 6F 109
Chartres Ct. UB6: G'frd 2H 77
Chartridge SE17 6D 102
(off Westmoreland Rd.)
Chart St. N1 1F 9 (3D 84)
Chartwell Bus. Cen.
BR1: Brom 3B 160
Chartwell Cl. CR0: C'don 1D 168
SE9 2H 143
UB6: G'frd 1F 77
Chartwell Ct. EN5: Barn 4B 20
IG8: Wfd G 7C 36
UB3: Hayes 7H 75
Chartwell Dr. BR6: Farnb 5H 173
Chartwell Gdns. SM3: Cheam 4G 165
Chartwell Ho. W11 1H 99
(off Ladbroke Rd.)
Chartwell Lodge BR3: Beck 7C 140
Chartwell Pl. HA2: Harr 2H 59
SM3: Cheam 4G 165
Chartwell Way SE20 1H 157
Charville Ct. HA1: Harr 6K 41
Charville La. UB4: Hayes 3E 74
Charville La. W. UB10: Hil 3D 74
(not continuous)
Charwood SW16 4A 138
Chase, The BR1: Brom 3K 159
DA7: Bex 3H 127
E12 4B 70
HA5: Eastc 6A 40
HA5: Pinn 4D 40
HA7: Stan 6F 27
HA8: Edg 1H 43
RM1: Rom 3K 55
RM6: Chad H 6E 54
RM7: Rush G 3K 73
(not continuous)
SM6: Wall 5J 167
SW4 3F 119
SW16 7K 137
SW20 1G 153
TW16: Sun 1K 147
UB10: Ick 5C 56
Chase Bank Ct. N14 6B 22
(off Avenue Rd.)
Chase Cen., The NW10 3K 79
Chase Ct. SW3 2E 16
(off Beaufort Gdns.)
SW20 2G 153
TW7: Isle 2A 114
Chase Ct. Gdns. EN2: Enf 3H 23
Chase Cross Rd. RM5: Col R 1J 55
Chasefield Rd. SW17 4D 136
Chase Gdns. E4 4H 35
TW2: Whitt 7H 113
Chase Grn. EN2: Enf 3H 23
Chase Grn. Av. EN2: Enf 2G 23
Chase Hill EN2: Enf 3H 23
Chase La. IG2: Ilf 5H 53
IG6: Ilf 5H 53
(not continuous)
Chaseley Dr. W4 5H 97
Chaseley St. E14 6A 86
Chasemore Cl. CR4: Mitc 7D 154
Chasemore Gdns. CR0: Wadd 5A 168
Chasemore Ho. SW6 7G 99
(off Williams Cl.)
Chase Ridings EN2: Enf 2F 23
Chase Rd. N14 5B 22
NW10 4K 79
Chase Rd. Trad. Est. NW10 4K 79
CHASE SIDE 1J 23
Chase Side EN2: Enf 3H 23
N14 6K 21
Chase Side Av. EN2: Enf 2H 23
Chaseside Av. SW20 1G 153
Chase Side Cres. EN2: Enf 1H 23
Chase Side Ind. Est. N14 7C 22
Chase Side Pl. EN2: Enf 2H 23
Chaseville Pde. N21 5E 22
Chaseville Pk. Rd. N21 5D 22
Chase Way N14 2A 32
Chaseways Vs. RM5: Col R 1F 55
Chasewood Av. EN2: Enf 2G 23
Chasewood Ct. NW7 5E 28
Chasewood Pk. HA1: Harr 3K 59
Chaston Pl. NW5 5E 64
(off Grafton Ter.)
Chater Ho. E2 3K 85
(off Roman Rd.)
Chatfield Rd. CR0: C'don 1B 168
SW11 3A 118
Chatham Av. BR2: Hayes 7H 159
Chatham Cl. NW11 5J 45
SE18 3F 107
SM3: Sutt 7H 153
Chatham Ho. SM6: Wall 5F 167
(off Melbourne Rd.)
Chatham Pl. E9 6J 67
Chatham Rd. E17 3A 50
E18 2H 51
KT1: King T 2G 151
SW11 6D 118
Chatham St. SE17 4D 102
Chatsfield Pl. W5 6E 78
Chats Palace Arts Cen. 5K 67
Chatsworth Av. BR1: Brom 4K 141
DA15: Sidc 1A 144
HA9: Wemb 5F 61
NW4 2E 44
SW20 1G 153
Chatsworth Cl. BR4: W W'ck 2H 171
NW4 2E 44
W4 6J 97
Chatsworth Ct. HA7: Stan 5H 27
SW16 3K 155
W8 4J 99
(off Pembroke Rd.)
Chatsworth Cres. TW3: Houn 4H 113
Chatsworth Dr. EN1: Enf 7B 24
Chatsworth Est. E5 4K 67
Chatsworth Gdns. HA2: Harr 1F 59
KT3: N Mald 5B 152
W3 1H 97
Chatsworth Ho. BR2: Brom 4J 159
(off Westmoreland Rd.)
E16 1K 105
(off Wesley Av.)
Chatsworth Lodge W4 5K 97
(off Bourne Pl.)

Chatsworth Pde. BR5: Pet W 5G 161
Chatsworth Pl. CR4: Mitc 3D 154
TW11: Tedd 4A 132
Chatsworth Ri. W5 ....4F 79
Chatsworth Rd. CR0: C'don 4D 168
E5 ....3J 67
E15 ....5H 69
NW2 ....6E 62
SM3: Cheam 5F 165
UB4: Yead 4K 75
W4 ....6J 97
W5 ....4F 79
Chatsworth Way SE27 ....3B 138
CHATTERN HILL 4D 128
Chattern Hill TW15: Ashf 4D 128
Chattern Rd. TW15: Ashf 4E 128
Chatterton Ct. TW9: Kew 2F 115
Chatterton M. *N4* *3B 66*
(off Chatterton Rd.)
Chatterton Rd. BR2: Brom 4B 160
N4 ....3B 66
Chatto Rd. SW11 ....5D 118
Chaucer Av. TW4: Cran 2K 111
TW9: Rich 3G 115
UB4: Hayes 5J 75
Chaucer Cl. N11 ....5B 32
Chaucer Ct. EN5: New Bar 5E 20
N16 ....4E 66
Chaucer Dr. SE1 ....4F 103
Chaucer Gdns. SM1: Sutt 3J 165
(not continuous)
Chaucer Grn. CR0: C'don 7H 157
Chaucer Ho. EN5: Barn 4A 20
SM1: Sutt 3J 165
(off Chaucer Gdns.)
SW1 ....6A 18
(off Churchill Gdns.)
Chaucer Mans. *W14* *6G 99*
(off Queen's Club Gdns.)
Chaucer Rd. DA15: Sidc 1C 144
DA16: Well 1J 125
E7 ....6J 69
E11 ....6J 51
E17 ....2E 50
SE24 ....5A 120
SM1: Sutt 4J 165
TW15: Ashf 4A 128
W3 ....1J 97
Chaucer Theatre *7K 9*
(off Colchester St.)
Chaucer Way SW19 ....5B 136
Chaulden Ho. *EC1* *2F 9*
(off Cranwood St.)
Chauncey Cl. N9 ....3B 34
Chaundrye Cl. SE9 ....6D 124
Chauntler Cl. E16 ....6K 87
Chaville Ct. N11 ....4K 31
Chaville Way N3 ....1J 45
Cheadle Ct. *NW8* *3B 4*
(off Henderson Dr.)
Cheadle Ho. *E14* *6B 86*
(off Copenhagen Pl.)
CHEAM 6G 165
Cheam Comn. Rd. KT4: Wor Pk 2D 164
Cheam Leisure Cen. 4F 165
Cheam Mans. SM3: Cheam 7G 165
Cheam Pk. Way SM3: Cheam 6G 165
Cheam Rd. SM1: Sutt 6H 165
Cheam Sports Club 7F 165
Cheam St. SE15 ....3J 121
CHEAM VILLAGE 6G 165
Cheapside EC2 ....1D 14 (6C 84)
N13 ....4J 33
N22 ....3A 48
Chearsley *SE17* *4C 102*
(off Deacon Way)
Cheddar Cl. N11 ....6J 31
Cheddar Waye UB4: Yead 6K 75
Cheddington Ho. *E2* *1G 85*
(off Whiston Rd.)
Cheddington Rd. N18 ....3K 33
Chedworth Cl. E16 ....6H 87
Chedworth Ho. *N15* *4D 48*
(off West Grn. Rd.)
Cheeseman Cl. TW12: Hamp 6C 130
Cheesemans Ter. W14 ....5H 99
(not continuous)
Cheethams Rd. E12 ....3C 70
Cheffery Ct. TW15: Ashf 6D 128
Cheldon Av. NW7 ....7A 30
Chelford Rd. BR1: Brom 5F 141
Chelmer Cres. IG11: Bark 2B 90
Chelmer Rd. E9 ....5K 67
Chelmsford Cl. E6 ....6D 88
W6 ....6F 99
Chelmsford Ct. *N14* *7C 22*
(off Chelmsford Rd.)
Chelmsford Gdns. IG1: Ilf 7C 52
Chelmsford Ho. *N7* *4K 65*
(off Holloway Rd.)
Chelmsford Rd. E11 ....1F 69
E17 ....6C 50
E18 ....1H 51
N14 ....7B 22
Chelmsford Sq. NW10 ....1E 80
Chelmsine Ct. HA4: Ruis 5E 38
CHELSEA 6D 16 (5C 100)
Chelsea Barracks 5H 17 (5E 100)
Chelsea Bri. SW1 ....7J 17 (6F 101)
SW8 ....7J 17 (6F 101)
Chelsea Bri. Rd. SW1 ......5G 17 (5E 100)
Chelsea Bri. Wharf
SW8 ....6F 101
Chelsea Cinema 6D 16 (5C 100)
Chelsea Cloisters SW3 .....4D 16 (4C 100)
Chelsea Cl. HA8: Edg 2G 43
KT4: Wor Pk 7C 152
NW10 ....1K 79
TW12: Ham H 5G 131
Chelsea College of Art & Design
.......................6C 16 (5C 100)
Chelsea Ct. *BR1: Brom* *3C 160*
(off Holmdene Ct.)
SW3 ....7G 17
(off Embankment Gdns.)
Chelsea Cres. NW2 ....6H 63
SW10 ....1A 118
Chelsea Emb. SW3 ....7D 16 (6C 100)
Chelsea Farm Ho. Studios
SW10 ....6B 100
(off Cremorne Est.)
Chelsea FC 7K 99
Chelsea Flds. SW19 ....1B 154
Chelsea Gdns. SM3: Cheam 4G 165
SW1 ....6H 17 (5E 100)
W13 ....5K 77
Chelsea Ga. SW1 ....6H 17
Chelsea Harbour SW10 ....1A 118
Chelsea Harbour Design Cen.
SW10 ....1A 118
(off Chelsea Harbour Dr.)
Chelsea Harbour Dr. SW10 ....1A 118
Chelsea Lodge *SW3* *7F 17*
(off Tite St.)
Chelsea Mnr. Ct. SW3 .....7D 16 (6C 100)
Chelsea Mnr. Gdns. SW3 ...6D 16 (5C 100)
Chelsea Mnr. St. SW3 ......6D 16 (5C 100)
Chelsea Mnr. Studios *SW3* *6D 16*
(off Flood St.)
Chelsea Pk. Gdns. SW3 .....7A 16 (6B 100)
Chelsea Physic Garden 7E 16 (6D 100)
Chelsea Reach Twr. *SW10* *7B 100*
(off Worlds End Est.)
Chelsea Sports Cen. 6D 16 (5C 100)
Chelsea Sq. SW3 ....5B 16 (5B 100)
Chelsea Studios *SW6* *7K 99*
(off Fulham Rd.)
Chelsea Towers SW3 ....7D 16
Chelsea Village *SW6* *7K 99*
(off Fulham Rd.)
Chelsea Vista SW6 ....1A 118
Chelsea Wharf *SW10* *7B 100*
(off Lots Rd.)
Chelsfield Av. N9 ....7E 24
Chelsfield Gdns. SE26 ....3J 139
Chelsfield Grn. N9 ....7E 24
(not continuous)
Chelsfield Ho. *SE17* *4E 102*
(off Massinger St.)
Chelsham Rd. CR2: S Croy 7D 168
SW4 ....3H 119
Chelsiter Ct. DA14: Sidc 4K 143
Chelston App. HA4: Ruis 2J 57
Chelston Rd. HA4: Ruis 1J 57
Chelsworth Dr. SE18 ....6H 107
Cheltenham Av.
TW1: Twick 7A 114
Cheltenham Cl. KT3: N Mald 3J 151
UB5: N'olt 6F 59
Cheltenham Ct. *HA7: Stan* *5H 27*
(off Marsh La.)
Cheltenham Gdns. E6 ....2C 88
Cheltenham Ho.
IG8: Wfd G 6K 37
Cheltenham Pl. HA3: Kent 4E 42
W3 ....1H 97
Cheltenham Rd. BR6: Chels 3K 173
E10 ....6E 50
SE15 ....4J 121
Cheltenham Ter. SW3 ......5F 17 (5D 100)
Chelverton Rd. SW15 ....4F 117
Chelwood N20 ....2G 31
Chelwood Cl. E4 ....6J 25
Chelwood Gdns. TW9: Kew 2G 115
Chelwood Gdns. Pas. TW9: Kew 2G 115
Chelwood Ho. *W2* *1B 10*
(off Gloucester Sq.)
Chelwood Wlk. SE4 ....4A 122
Chenappa Cl. E13 ....3J 87
Chenduit Way HA7: Stan 5E 26
Cheney Ct. SE23 ....1K 139
Cheney Row E17 ....1B 50
Cheneys Rd. E11 ....3G 69
Cheney St. HA5: Eastc 4A 40
Chenies, The BR6: Pet W 6J 161
NW1 ....2H 83
(off Pancras Rd.)
Chenies Ho. *W2* *7K 81*
(off Moscow Rd.)
W4 ....7B 98
(off Corney Reach Way)
Chenies M. WC1 ....4C 6 (4H 83)
Chenies Pl. NW1 ....2H 83
Chenies St. WC1 ....5C 6 (5H 83)
Cheniston Gdns. W8 ....3K 99
Chepstow Cl. SW15 ....5G 117
Chepstow Cnr. *W2* *6J 81*
(off Chepstow Pl.)
Chepstow Ct. *W11* *7J 81*
(off Chepstow Vs.)
Chepstow Cres. IG3: Ilf 6J 53
W11 ....7J 81
Chepstow Gdns. UB1: S'hall 6D 76
Chepstow Hall *UB8: Cowl* *3A 74*
(off Kingston La.)
Chepstow Pl. W2 ....6J 81
Chepstow Ri. CR0: C'don 3E 168
Chepstow Rd. CR0: C'don 3E 168
W2 ....6J 81
W7 ....3A 96
Chepstow Vs. W11 ....7H 81
Chequers IG9: Buck H 1E 36
Chequers, The HA5: Pinn 3B 40
Chequers Cl. BR5: St P 4K 161
NW9 ....3A 44
Chequers Ct. *EC1* *4D 8*
(off Chequer St.)
Chequers Ho. *NW8* *3C 4*
(off Jerome Cres.)
Chequers La. RM9: Dag 4F 91
Chequers Pde. N13 ....5H 33
RM9: Dag 1F 91
SE9 ....6D 124
(off Eltham High St.)
Chequer St. EC1 ....4D 8 (4C 84)
(not continuous)
Chequers Way N13 ....5G 33
Cherbury Cl. SE28 ....6D 90
Cherbury Ct. *N1* *2D 84*
(off St John's Est.)
Cherbury St. N1 ....2D 84
Cherchefelle M. HA7: Stan 5G 27
Cherimoya Gdns. KT8: W Mole 3F 149
Cherington Rd. W7 ....1J 95
Cheriton Av. BR2: Brom 5H 159
IG5: Ilf 2D 52
Cheriton Cl. EN4: Cockf 3J 21
W5 ....5C 78
Cheriton Ct. SE12 ....7J 123
Cheriton Dr. SE18 ....7H 107
Cheriton Sq. SW17 ....2E 136
Cherry Av. UB1: S'hall 1B 94
Cherry Blossom Cl. N13 ....5G 33
Cherry Cl. E17 ....5D 50
HA4: Ruis 3H 57
NW9 ....2A 44
SM4: Mord 4G 153
SM5: Cars 2D 166
SW2 ....7A 120
W5 ....3D 96
Cherrycot Hill BR6: Farnb 4G 173
Cherrycot Ri. BR6: Farnb 4G 173
Cherry Ct. HA5: Pinn 2B 40
IG6: Ilf 3F 53
W3 ....1A 98
Cherry Cres. TW8: Bford 7B 96
Cherrydown Av. E4 ....3G 35
Cherrydown Cl. E4 ....3H 35
Cherrydown Rd. DA14: Sidc 2D 144
Cherrydown Wlk. RM7: Mawney 2H 55
Cherry Gdn. Ho. *SE16* *2H 103*
(off Cherry Gdn. St.)
Cherry Gdns. RM9: Dag 5F 73
UB5: N'olt 7F 59
Cherry Gdn. St. SE16 ....2H 103
Cherry Gth. TW8: Bford 5D 96
Cherry Gro. UB3: Hayes 1K 93
UB8: Hil 5D 74
Cherry Hill EN5: New Bar 6E 20
HA3: Hrw W 6E 26
Cherry Hill Gdns. CR0: Wadd 4K 167
Cherrylands Cl. NW9 ....2J 61
Cherry La. UB7: W Dray 4B 92
Cherry Laurel Wlk. SW2 ....6K 119
Cherry Orchard SE7 ....6A 106
UB7: W Dray 2A 92
Cherry Orchard Gdns.
CR0: C'don 1D 168
KT8: W Mole 3D 148
Cherry Orchard Rd.
BR2: Brom 2C 172
CR0: C'don 2D 168
KT8: W Mole 3E 148
Cherry Rd. EN3: Enf W 1D 24
Cherry St. RM7: Rom 5K 55
Cherry Tree Av. UB7: Yiew 6B 74
Cherry Tree Cl. E9 ....1J 85
HA0: Wemb 4A 60
Cherry Tree Ct. *NW1* *7G 65*
(off Camden Rd.)
NW9 ....4J 43
SE7 ....6A 106
Cherry Tree Dr. SW16 ....3J 137
Cherry Tree Hill N2 ....5C 46
Cherry Tree Ho. N22 ....7D 32
Cherry Tree Ri. IG9: Buck H 4F 37
Cherry Tree Rd. E15 ....5G 69
N2 ....4D 46
Cherry Tree Ter. *SE1* *7H 15*
(off Whites Grounds)

Cherry Tree Wlk. BR3: Beck 4B 158
BR4: W W'ck 4H 171
EC1 4D 8 (4C 84)
Cherry Tree Way HA7: Stan 6G 27
Cherry Wlk. BR2: Hayes 1J 171
Cherry Way KT19: Ewe 6K 163
TW17: Shep 4F 147
Cherrywood Cl. E3 3A 86
KT2: King T 7G 133
Cherrywood Ct. TW11: Tedd 5A 132
Cherrywood Dr. SW15 5F 117
Cherrywood La. SM4: Mord 4G 153
Cherry Wood Way W5 5G 79
Chertsey Bri. Rd. KT16: Chert 7A 146
Chertsey Ct. SW14 3H 115
Chertsey Dr. SM3: Cheam 2G 165
CHERTSEY MEADS 7A 146
Chertsey Rd. E11 2F 69
IG1: Ilf 4H 71
TW1: Twick 6K 113
TW2: Twick 2F 131
TW13: Felt 3G 129
TW15: Ashf 7F 129
TW16: Sun 7F 129
TW17: Shep 7A 146
Chertsey St. SW17 5E 136
Chervil Cl. TW13: Felt 3J 129
Chervil M. SE28 1B 108
Cherwell Ct. KT19: Ewe 4J 163
Cherwell Ho. NW8 4B 4
Cherwell Way HA4: Ruis 6E 38
Cheryls Cl. SW6 1K 117
Cheseman St. SE26 3H 139
Chesfield Rd. KT2: King T 7E 132
Chesham Av. BR5: Pet W 6F 161
Chesham Cl. RM7: Rom 4K 55
SW1 2G 17
Chesham Cres. SE20 1J 157
Chesham Flats *W1* *2H 11*
(off Brown Hart Gdns.)
Chesham M. SW1 1G 17
Chesham Pl. SW1 2G 17 (3E 100)
(not continuous)
Chesham Rd. KT1: King T 2G 151
SE20 2J 157
SW19 5B 136
Chesham St. NW10 3K 61
SW1 2G 17 (3E 100)
Chesham Ter. W13 2B 96
Cheshire Cl. CR4: Mitc 3J 155
E17 1D 50
SE4 2B 122
Cheshire Ct. *EC4* *1K 13*
(off Fleet St.)
Cheshire Gdns. KT9: Chess 6D 162
Cheshire Ho. N18 4C 34
SM4: Mord 7K 153
Cheshire Rd. N22 7E 32
Cheshire St. E2 3K 9 (4F 85)
Cheshir Ho. NW4 4E 44
Chesholm Rd. N16 3E 66
Cheshunt Ho. *NW6* *1K 81*
(off Mortimer Cres.)
Cheshunt Rd. DA17: Belv 5G 109
E7 6K 69
Chesil Ct. E2 2J 85
SW3 7D 16 (6C 100)
Chesilton Rd. SW6 1H 117
Chesil Way UB4: Hayes 3H 75
Chesley Gdns. E6 2B 88
Chesney Ct. *W9* *4J 81*
(off Shirland Rd.)
Chesney Cres. CR0: New Ad 7E 170
Chesney Ho. *SE13* *4F 123*
(off Mercator Rd.)
Chesney St. SW11 1E 118
Chesnut Gro. N17 3F 49
Chesnut Rd. N17 3F 49
(not continuous)
Chesnut Row N3 7D 30
Chessell Cl. CR7: Thor H 4B 156
Chessholme Ct. *TW16: Sun* *7G 129*
(off Scotts Av.)
Chessholme Rd. TW15: Ashf 6E 128
Chessing Ct. *N2* *3D 46*
(off Fortis Grn.)
CHESSINGTON 5F 163
Chessington Av. DA7: Bex 7E 108
N3 3G 45
Chessington Cl. KT19: Ewe 6J 163
Chessington Ct. HA5: Pinn 4D 40
N3 *3H 45*
(off Charter Way)
Chessington Hall Gdns.
KT9: Chess 7D 162
Chessington Hill Pk.
KT9: Chess 5G 163
Chessington Ho. SW8 2H 119
Chessington Lodge N3 3H 45
Chessington Mans. E10 7C 50
E11 7G 51
Chessington Pde. KT9: Chess 6D 162
Chessington Pk. KT9: Chess 4G 163
Chessington Rd. KT17: Ewe 7B 164
KT19: Ewe 6G 163
Chessington Sports Cen. 7D 162
Chessington Trade Pk.
KT9: Chess 4G 163
Chessington Way BR4: W W'ck 2D 170
Chesson Rd. W14 6H 99
Chesswood Way HA5: Pinn 2B 40
Chestbrook Ct. *EN1: Enf* *5K 23*
(off Forsyth Pl.)
Chester Av. TW2: Whitt 1D 130
TW10: Rich 6F 115
Chester Cl. SM1: Sutt 2J 165
SW1 7J 11 (2F 101)
SW13 3D 116
TW10: Rich 6F 115
TW15: Ashf 5F 129
UB8: Hil 6D 74
Chester Cl. Nth. NW1 1K 5 (3F 83)
Chester Cl. Sth. NW1 2K 5 (3F 83)
Chester Cotts. SW1 4G 17
Chester Ct. *BR2: Brom* *4H 159*
(off Durham Rd.)
NW1 1K 5 (3F 83)
(not continuous)
SE5 *7D 102*
(off Lomond Gro.)
SE8 5K 103
W6 *4F 99*
(off Wolverton Gdns.)
Chester Cres. E8 5F 67
Chester Dr. HA2: Harr 6D 40
Chesterfield Cl. SE13 2F 123
Chesterfield Ct. *KT5: Surb* *5E 150*
(off Cranes Pk.)
Chesterfield Dr. KT10: Hin W 2A 162
Chesterfield Flats *EN5: Barn* *5A 20*
(off Bells Hill)
Chesterfield Gdns. N4 5B 48
SE10 1F 123
W1 4J 11 (1F 101)
Chesterfield Gro. SE22 5F 121
Chesterfield Hill W1 4J 11 (1F 101)
Chesterfield Ho. *W1* *4H 11*
(off Chesterfield Gdns.)
Chesterfield Lodge *N21* *7E 22*
(off Church Hill)
Chesterfield M. N4 5B 48
TW15: Ashf 4A 128
Chesterfield Rd. E10 6E 50
EN5: Barn 5A 20
KT19: Ewe 7K 163
N3 6D 30
TW15: Ashf 4A 128
W4 6J 97
Chesterfield St. W1 4J 11 (1F 101)
Chesterfield Wlk. SE10 1F 123
Chesterfield Way SE15 7J 103
UB3: Hayes 2J 93
Chesterford Gdns. NW3 4K 63
Chesterford Ho. *SE18* *1B 124*
(off Tellson Av.)
Chesterford Rd. E12 5D 70
Chester Gdns. EN3: Pond E 6C 24
SM4: Mord 6A 154
W13 6B 78
Chester Ga. NW1 2J 5 (3F 83)
Chester Ho. N10 2F 47
SE8 6B 104
SW1 *3J 17*
(off Eccleston Pl.)
SW9 *7A 102*
(off Brixton Rd.)
Chesterman Ct. *W4* *7A 98*
(off Corney Reach Way)
Chester M. E17 2C 50
SW1 1J 17 (3F 101)
Chester Pl. NW1 1J 5 (3F 83)
Chester Rd. DA15: Sidc 5J 125
(not continuous)
E7 7B 70
E11 6K 51
E16 4G 87
E17 5K 49
HA6: Nwood 1H 39
IG3: Ilf 1K 71
IG7: Chig 3K 37
N9 1C 34
N17 3D 48
N19 2F 65
NW1 2H 5 (3E 82)
SW19 6E 134
TW4: Houn 3K 111
TW6: H'row A 3C 110
Chester Row SW1 4G 17 (4E 100)
Chesters, The KT3: N Mald 1A 152
Chester Sq. SW1 3H 17 (4E 100)
Chester Sq. M. SW1 2J 17
Chester St. E2 4G 85
SW1 1H 17 (3E 100)
Chester Ter. IG11: Bark 6H 71
NW1 1J 5 (3F 83)
(not continuous)
Chesterton Cl. SW18 5J 117
UB6: G'frd 2F 77
Chesterton Ct. *W3* *3H 97*
(off Bollo Bri. Rd.)
W5 5D 78
Chesterton Dr. TW19: Stanw 1B 128
Chesterton Ho. *CR0: C'don* *4D 168*
(off Heathfield Rd.)
SW11 *3B 118*
(off Ingrave St.)
W10 *5G 81*
(off Portobello Rd.)
Chesterton Rd. E13 3J 87
W10 5F 81
Chesterton Sq. W8 4J 99
Chesterton Ter. E13 3J 87
KT1: King T 2G 151
Chester Way SE11 4K 19 (4A 102)
Chesthunte Rd. N17 1C 48
Chestlands Ct. UB10: Hil 6C 56
Chestnut All. SW6 6H 99
Chestnut Av.
BR4: W W'ck 5G 171
E7 4K 69
E12 2C 70
HA0: Wemb 5B 60
HA6: Nwood 2H 39
HA8: Edg 6K 27
IG9: Buck H 3G 37
KT8: E Mos 3K 149
KT10: Esh 7H 149
KT19: Ewe 4A 164
N8 5J 47
SW14 3K 115
Chestnut Av. TW8: Bford 4D 96
TW11: Tedd 2K 149
TW12: Hamp 7E 130
UB7: Yiew 7B 74
Chestnut Av. Nth. E17 4F 51
Chestnut Av. Sth. E17 5E 50
Chestnut Cl. BR6: Chels 5K 173
DA15: Sidc 1A 144
IG9: Buck H 3G 37
N14 5B 22
N16 2D 66
SE6 5E 140
SE14 1B 122
SM5: Cars 1D 166
SW16 4A 138
TW15: Ashf 4D 128
TW16: Sun 6H 129
UB3: Hayes 7G 75
UB7: Harl, Sip 7D 92
Chestnut Ct. *CR2: S Croy* *4C 168*
(off Bramley Hill)
N8 5J 47
SW6 6H 99
TW13: Hanw 5B 130
W8 *3K 99*
(off Abbots Wlk.)
Chestnut Dr. DA7: Bex 3D 126
E11 6J 51
HA3: Hrw W 7E 26
HA5: Pinn 6B 40
Chestnut Gro. CR2: Sels 7H 169
CR4: Mitc 5H 155
DA2: Dart 4K 145
EN4: E Barn 5J 21
HA0: Wemb 5B 60
KT3: N Mald 3K 151
SE20 7H 139
SW12 7E 118
TW7: Isle 4A 114
W5 3D 96
Chestnut Ho. *W4* *4A 98*
(off The Orchard)
Chestnut La. N20 1B 30
Chestnut Pl. SE26 4F 139
Chestnut Ri. SE18 6H 107
WD23: Bush 1A 26
Chestnut Rd. KT2: King T 7E 132
SE27 3B 138
SW20 2F 153
TW2: Twick 2J 131
TW15: Ashf 4D 128
Chestnuts, The HA5: Hat E 1D 40
N5 *4C 66*
(off Highbury Grange)
UB10: Uxb 7A 56
Chestnut Ter. SM1: Sutt 4K 165
Chestnut Wlk. IG8: Wfd G 5D 36
TW17: Shep 4G 147
Chestnut Way TW13: Felt 3K 129
Cheston Av. CR0: C'don 2A 170
Chestwood Gro. UB10: Hil 7B 56
Chettle Cl. *SE1* *3D 102*
(off Spurgeon St.)
Chettle Ct. N8 6A 48
Chetwode Ho. NW8 3C 4
Chetwode Rd. SW17 3D 136
Chetwood Wlk. *E6* *5C 88*
(off Greenwich Cres.)
Chetwynd Av. EN4: E Barn 1J 31
Chetwynd Dr. UB10: Hil 2B 74
Chetwynd Rd. NW5 4F 65
Chetwynd Vs. *NW5* *4F 65*
(off Chetwynd Rd.)
Chevalier Cl. HA7: Stan 4K 27
Cheval Pl. SW7 1D 16 (3C 100)
Cheval St. E14 3C 104
Cheveney Wlk. BR2: Brom 3J 159
Chevening Rd. NW6 2F 81
SE10 5H 105
SE19 6D 138

Chevenings, The DA14: Sidc 3C 144
Cheverell Ho. E2 . . . . 2G 85
(off Pritchard's Rd.)
Cheverton Rd. N19 . . . . 1H 65
Chevet St. E9 . . . . 5A 68
Chevington NW2 . . . . 6H 63
Cheviot N17 . . . . 7C 34
(off Northumberland Gro.)
Cheviot Cl. DA7: Bex 2K 127
EN1: Enf 2J 23
UB3: Harl 7F 93
Cheviot Ct. SE14 . . . . 6J 103
(off Avonley Rd.)
UB2: S'hall 4F 95
Cheviot Gdns. NW2 . . . . 2F 63
SE27 . . . . 4B 138
Cheviot Ga. NW2 . . . . 2G 63
Cheviot Ho. E1 . . . . 6H 85
(off Commercial Rd.)
Cheviot Rd. SE27 . . . . 5A 138
Cheviot Way IG2: Ilf 4J 53
Chevron Cl. E16 . . . . 6J 87
Chevy Rd. UB2: S'hall 2G 95
Chewton Rd. E17 . . . . 4A 50
Cheylesmore Ho. SW1 . . . . 5J 17
(off Ebury Bri. Rd.)
Cheyne Av. E18 . . . . 3H 51
TW2: Whitt 1D 130
Cheyne Cl. BR2: Brom 3C 172
NW4 . . . . 5E 44
Cheyne Ct. SW3 . . . . 7E 16 (6D 100)
Cheyne Gdns. SW3 . . . . 7D 16 (6C 100)
Cheyne Hill KT5: Surb 4F 151
Cheyne M. SW3 . . . . 7D 16 (6C 100)
Cheyne Pk. Dr. BR4: W W'ck 3E 170
Cheyne Path W7 . . . . 5K 77
Cheyne Pl. SW3 . . . . 7E 16 (6D 100)
Cheyne Rd. TW15: Ashf 7F 129
Cheyne Row SW3 . . . . 7C 16 (6C 100)
Cheyne Wlk. CR0: C'don 2G 169
N21 . . . . 5G 23
NW4 . . . . 6E 44
SW3 . . . . 7C 16 (7B 100)
(not continuous)
SW10 . . . . 7B 100
Cheyneys Av. HA8: Edg 6J 27
Chichele Gdns. CR0: C'don 4E 168
Chichele Ho. HA8: Edg 4A 28
Chichele Rd. NW2 . . . . 5F 63
Chicheley Gdns. HA3: Hrw W 7B 26
(not continuous)
Chicheley Rd. HA3: Hrw W 7B 26
Chicheley St. SE1 . . . . 6H 13 (2K 101)
Chichester Av. HA4: Ruis 2F 57
Chichester Cl. E6 . . . . 6C 88
SE3 . . . . 7A 106
TW12: Hamp 6D 130
Chichester Ct. HA7: Stan 3E 42
HA8: Edg 6B 28
(off Whitchurch La.)
KT17: Ewe 7B 164
NW1 . . . . 7G 65
(off Royal Coll. St.)
TW19: Stanw 1A 128
UB5: N'olt 1D 76
Chichester Gdns. IG1: Ilf 7C 52
Chichester Ho. NW6 . . . . 2J 81
SW9 . . . . 7A 102
(off Brixton Rd.)
Chichester M. SE27 . . . . 4A 138
Chichester Rents WC2 . . . . 7J 7
Chichester Rd. CR0: C'don 3E 168
E11 . . . . 3G 69
N9 . . . . 1B 34
NW6 . . . . 2J 81
W2 . . . . 5K 81
Chichester St. SW1 . . . . 6B 18 (5G 101)
Chichester Way E14 . . . . 4F 105
TW14: Felt 7A 112
Chicken Shed Theatre 5K 21
Chicksand Ho. E1 . . . . 5K 9
(off Chicksand St.)
Chicksand St. E1 . . . . 6K 9 (5F 85)
(not continuous)
Chiddingfold N12 . . . . 3D 30
Chiddingstone SE13 . . . . 5E 122
Chiddingstone Av. DA7: Bex 7F 109
Chiddingstone St. SW6 . . . . 2J 117
Chieveley Pde. DA7: Bex 4H 127
(off Chieveley Rd.)
DA7: Bex 3H 127
(Mayplace Rd. E.)
Chieveley Rd. DA7: Bex 4H 127
Chignell Pl. W13 . . . . 1A 96
CHIGWELL 3K 37
Chigwell Hill E1 . . . . 7H 85
Chigwell Hurst Ct.
HA5: Pinn 3B 40
Chigwell Pk. IG7: Chig 4K 37
Chigwell Pk. Dr. IG7: Chig 4K 37
Chigwell Ri. IG7: Chig 2K 37
Chigwell Rd. E18 . . . . 3K 51
IG8: Wfd G 2A 52
Chilcombe Ho. SW15 . . . . 7C 116
(off Fontley Way)
Chilcot Cl. E14 . . . . 6D 86
Chilcott Cl. HA0: Wemb 4C 60
Childebert Rd. SW17 . . . . 2F 137
Childeric Rd. SE14 . . . . 7A 104
Childerley KT1: King T 3G 151
(off Burritt Rd.)
Childerley St. SW6 . . . . 1G 117
Childers, The IG8: Wfd G 5J 37
Childers St. SE8 . . . . 6A 104
Child La. SE10 . . . . 3H 105
Children's Discovery Cen. 7F 69
Childs Ct. UB3: Hayes 7J 75
CHILD'S HILL 3J 63
Childs Hill Wlk. NW2 . . . . 3H 63
(off Cricklewood La.)
Child's La. SE19 . . . . 6E 138
Child's M. SW5 . . . . 4J 99
(off Child's Pl.)
Child's Pl. SW5 . . . . 4J 99
Child's St. SW5 . . . . 4J 99
Child's Wlk. SW5 . . . . 4J 99
(off Child's St.)
Childs Way NW11 . . . . 5H 45
Chilham Cl. DA5: Bexl 7F 127
UB6: G'frd 2A 78
Chilham Ho. SE1 . . . . 3D 102
SE15 . . . . 6J 103
Chilham Rd. SE9 . . . . 4C 142
Chilham Way BR2: Hayes 7J 159
Chilianwallan Memorial 7G 17 (6E 100)
Chillerton Rd. SW17 . . . . 5E 136
Chillingford Ho. SW17 . . . . 4A 136
Chillington Dr. SW11 . . . . 4B 118
Chillingworth Gdns.
TW1: Twick 3K 131
Chillingworth Rd. N7 . . . . 5A 66
Chilmark Gdns. KT3: N Mald 6C 152
Chilmark Rd. SW16 . . . . 2H 155
Chiltern Av. TW2: Whitt 1E 130
Chiltern Cl. CR0: C'don 3E 168
DA7: Bex 1K 127
KT4: Wor Pk 1E 164
UB10: Ick 2C 56
Chiltern Ct. EN5: New Bar 5F 21
HA1: Harr 5H 41
N10 . . . . 2E 46
NW1 . . . . 4F 5
(off Baker St.)
SE14 . . . . 7J 103
(off Avonley Rd.)
UB8: Hil 4D 74
Chiltern Dene EN2: Enf 4E 22
Chiltern Dr. KT5: Surb 6G 151
Chiltern Gdns. BR2: Brom 4H 159
NW2 . . . . 3F 63
Chiltern Ho. N9 . . . . 3B 34
SE17 . . . . 6D 102
(off Portland Wlk.)
W5 . . . . 5E 78
W10 . . . . 5G 81
(off Telford Rd.)
Chiltern Rd. E3 . . . . 4C 86
HA5: Eastc 5A 40
IG2: Ilf 5J 53
Chilterns, The BR1: Brom 2K 159
(off Murray Av.)
Chiltern St. W1 . . . . 5G 5 (5E 82)
Chiltern Way IG8: Wfd G 3D 36
Chilthorne Cl. SE6 . . . . 7B 122
Chilton Av. W5 . . . . 4D 96
Chilton Ct. N22 . . . . 7D 32
(off Truro Rd.)
Chilton Gro. SE8 . . . . 4K 103
Chiltonian Ind. Est. SE12 . . . . 6H 123
Chilton Rd. HA8: Edg 6B 28
TW9: Rich 3G 115
Chiltons, The E18 . . . . 2J 51
Chilton St. E2 . . . . 3K 9 (4F 85)
Chilvers Cl. TW2: Twick 2J 131
Chilver St. SE10 . . . . 5H 105
Chilworth Ct. SW19 . . . . 1F 135
Chilworth Gdns. SM1: Sutt 3A 166
Chilworth M. W2 . . . . 1A 10 (6B 82)
Chilworth St. W2 . . . . 1A 10 (6A 82)
Chimes Av. N13 . . . . 5F 33
Chimney Ct. E1 . . . . 1H 103
(off Brewhouse La.)
China Ct. E1 . . . . 1H 103
(off Asher Way)
China Hall M. SE16 . . . . 3J 103
China M. SW2 . . . . 7K 119
China Wlk. SE11 . . . . 2J 19 (4K 101)
China Wharf SE1 . . . . 6K 15 (2G 103)
Chinbrook Cres. SE12 . . . . 3K 141
Chinbrook Rd. SE12 . . . . 3K 141
Chinchilla Dr. TW4: Houn 2A 112
Chine, The HA0: Wemb 5B 60
N10 . . . . 4G 47
N21 . . . . 6G 23
Ching Ct. WC2 . . . . 1E 12
(off Monmouth St.)
Chingdale Rd. E4 . . . . 3B 36
CHINGFORD 1K 35
Chingford Av. E4 . . . . 3H 35
CHINGFORD GREEN 7K 25
CHINGFORD HATCH 4A 36
Chingford Ind. Cen. E4 . . . . 5F 35
Chingford La. IG8: Wfd G 4B 36
CHINGFORD MOUNT 4H 35
Chingford Mt. Rd. E4 . . . . 4H 35
Chingford Rd. E4 . . . . 6H 35
E17 . . . . 1D 50
Chingley Cl. BR1: Brom 6G 141
Ching Way E4 . . . . 6G 35
(not continuous)
Chinnery Cl. EN1: Enf 1A 24
Chinnock's Wharf E14 . . . . 7A 86
(off Narrow St.)
Chinnor Cres. UB6: G'frd 2F 77
Chipka St. E14 . . . . 2E 104
(not continuous)
Chipley St. SE14 . . . . 6A 104
Chipmunk Gro. UB5: N'olt 3C 76
Chippendale All. UB8: Uxb 7A 56
Chippendale Ho. SW1 . . . . 6K 17
(off Churchill Gdns.)
Chippendale St. E5 . . . . 3K 67
Chippendale Waye UB8: Uxb 7A 56
Chippenham KT1: King T 2F 151
(off Excelsior Cl.)
Chippenham Av. HA9: Wemb 5H 61
Chippenham Cl. HA5: Eastc 4H 39
Chippenham Gdns. NW6 . . . . 3J 81
Chippenham M. W9 . . . . 4J 81
Chippenham Rd. W9 . . . . 4J 81
Chipperfield Ho. SW3 . . . . 5C 16
(off Cale St.)
Chipperfield Rd. BR5: St P 7A 144
(not continuous)
CHIPPING BARNET 4B 20
Chipping Cl. EN5: Barn 3B 20
Chipstead Av. CR7: Thor H 4B 156
Chipstead Cl. SE19 . . . . 7F 139
SM2: Sutt 7K 165
Chipstead Gdns. NW2 . . . . 2D 62
Chipstead St. SW6 . . . . 1J 117
Chip St. SW4 . . . . 3H 119
Chirk Cl. UB4: Yead 4C 76
Chisenhale Rd. E3 . . . . 2A 86
Chisholm Ct. W6 . . . . 5C 98
Chisholm Rd. CR0: C'don 2E 168
TW10: Rich 6F 115
Chisledon Wlk. E9 . . . . 6B 68
(off Osborne Rd.)
CHISLEHURST 6F 143
Chislehurst Av. N12 . . . . 7F 31
Chislehurst Caves 1E 160
Chislehurst Rd. BR1: Brom 2B 160
BR5: Pet W 4J 161
BR6: Orp, Pet W, St M Cry 4J 161
BR7: Chst 2B 160
DA14: Sidc 5A 144
TW10: Rich 5E 114
CHISLEHURST WEST 5E 142
Chislet Cl. BR3: Beck 7C 140
Chisley Rd. N15 . . . . 6E 48
Chiswell Sq. SE3 . . . . 2K 123
Chiswell St. EC1 . . . . 5E 8 (5C 84)
SE5 . . . . 7D 102
(off Edmund St.)
CHISWICK 5K 97
Chiswick Bri. W4 . . . . 2J 115
Chiswick Cl. CR0: Bedd 3K 167
Chiswick Comn. Rd. W4 . . . . 4K 97
Chiswick Community Sports Hall 7K 97
Chiswick Ct. HA5: Pinn 3D 40
W4 . . . . 4H 97
Chiswick High Rd. TW8: Bford 5G 97
(not continuous)
Chiswick House 6A 98
Chiswick La. W4 . . . . 5A 98
Chiswick La. Sth. W4 . . . . 6B 98
Chiswick Mall W4 . . . . 6B 98
W6 . . . . 5C 98
Chiswick Pk. W4 . . . . 4H 97
Chiswick Plaza W4 . . . . 6J 97
Chiswick Quay W4 . . . . 1J 115
Chiswick Rd. N9 . . . . 2B 34
W4 . . . . 4J 97
CHISWICK RDBT. 5G 97
Chiswick Sq. W4 . . . . 6A 98
Chiswick Staithe W4 . . . . 1J 115
Chiswick Ter. W4 . . . . 4J 97
(off Chiswick Rd.)
Chiswick Village W4 . . . . 6G 97
Chiswick Wharf W4 . . . . 6B 98
Chitterfield Ga. UB7: Sip 7C 92
Chitty's La. RM8: Dag 2D 72
Chitty St. W1 . . . . 5B 6 (5G 83)
Chivalry Rd. SW11 . . . . 5C 118
Chivelston SW19 . . . . 1F 135
Chivenor Gro. KT2: King T 5D 132
Chivers Rd. E4 . . . . 3J 35
Choats Mnr. Way
RM9: Dag 2E 90
Choats Rd. IG11: Bark 2C 90
RM9: Bark, Dag 2C 90
Chobham Gdns. SW19 . . . . 2F 135
Chobham Rd. E15 . . . . 5F 69
Chocolate Studios N1 . . . . 1E 8
(off Shepherdess Pl.)
Choice Vw. IG1: Ilf 2G 71
(off Axon Pl.)
Cholmeley Cres. N6 . . . . 7F 47
Cholmeley Lodge N6 . . . . 1F 65

Cholmeley Pk. N6 . . . 1F **65**
Cholmeley Gdns. NW6 . . . 5J **63**
Cholmeley Rd. KT7: T Ditt . . . 6B **150**
Cholmeley Ter. *KT7: T Ditt . . . 7B **150***
(off Portsmouth Rd.)
Cholmeley Vs. *KT7: T Ditt . . . 6B **150***
(off Portsmouth Rd.)
Cholmondeley Av. NW10 . . . 2C **80**
Cholmondeley Wlk. TW9: Rich . . . 5C **114**
(not continuous)
Choppin's Ct. E1 . . . 1H **103**
Chopwell Cl. E15 . . . 7F **69**
Chorleywood Cres. BR5: St P . . . 2K **161**
Choumert Gro. SE15 . . . 2G **121**
Choumert M. SE15 . . . 2G **121**
Choumert Rd. SE15 . . . 3F **121**
Choumert Sq. SE15 . . . 2G **121**
Chow Sq. E8 . . . 5F **67**
Chrisp Ho. *SE10 . . . 6G **105***
(off Maze Hill)
Chrisp St. E14 . . . 5D **86**
(not continuous)
Christabel Cl. TW7: Isle . . . 3J **113**
Christchurch Av. DA8: Erith . . . 6K **109**
HA0: Wemb . . . 6E **60**
HA3: Kent, W'stone . . . 4K **41**
N12 . . . 6F **31**
NW6 . . . 1F **81**
TW11: Tedd . . . 5A **132**
Christchurch Cl. EN2: Enf . . . 2H **23**
N12 . . . 7G **31**
SW19 . . . 7B **136**
Christ Chu. Ct. NW10 . . . 1A **80**
Christchurch Ct. *EC4 . . . 7B **8***
(off Warwick La.)
*UB4: Yead . . . 4A **76***
(off Dunedin Way)
Christchurch Flats TW9: Rich . . . 3E **114**
Christchurch Gdns. HA3: W'stone . . . 4A **42**
Christchurch Grn. HA0: Wemb . . . 6E **60**
Christchurch Hill NW3 . . . 3B **64**
Christchurch Ho. *SW2 . . . 1K **137***
(off Christchurch Rd.)
Christchurch La. EN5: Barn . . . 2B **20**
Christchurch Lodge
EN4: Cockf . . . 4J **21**
Christchurch Pk. SM2: Sutt . . . 7A **166**
Christchurch Pas. EN5: Barn . . . 2B **20**
NW3 . . . 3A **64**
Christchurch Path UB3: Harl . . . 3E **92**
Christchurch Pl. SW8 . . . 2H **119**
Christ Chu. Rd. BR3: Beck . . . 2C **158**
SW14 . . . 5H **115**
Christchurch Rd. DA15: Sidc . . . 4K **143**
IG1: Ilf . . . 1F **71**
KT5: Surb . . . 6F **151**
N8 . . . 6J **47**
SW2 . . . 1K **137**
SW19 . . . 7B **136**
Christ Church Sports Cen. . . . *5G **31***
(off Hilton Av.)
Christchurch Sq. E9 . . . 1J **85**
Christchurch St. SW3 . . . 7E **16** (6D **100**)
Christchurch Ter. SW3 . . . 7E **16**
Christchurch Way SE10 . . . 5G **105**
Christian Ct. SE16 . . . 1B **104**
Christian Flds. SW16 . . . 7A **138**
Christian Pl. *E1 . . . 6G **85***
(off Burslem St.)
Christian St. E1 . . . 6G **85**
Christie Ct. N19 . . . 2J **65**
Christie Dr. CR0: C'don . . . 5G **157**
Christie Gdns. RM6: Chad H . . . 6B **54**
Christie Ho. *SE10 . . . 5H **105***
(off Blackwall La.)
Christie Rd. E9 . . . 6A **68**
Christina Sq. N4 . . . 1B **66**
Christina St. EC2 . . . 3G **9** (4E **84**)
Christine Worsley Cl. N21 . . . 1G **33**
Christopher Av. W7 . . . 3A **96**
Christopher Cl.
DA15: Sidc . . . 5K **125**
SE16 . . . 2K **103**
Christopher Ct. TW15: Ashf . . . 5A **128**
Christopher Gdns. RM9: Dag . . . 5D **72**
Christopher Ho. *DA15: Sidc . . . 2A **144***
(off Station Rd.)
Christopher Pl. NW1 . . . 1D **6** (3H **83**)
Christopher Rd. UB2: S'hall . . . 4K **93**
Christophers M. W11 . . . 1G **99**
Christopher St. EC2 . . . 4F **9** (4D **84**)
Chryssell Rd. SW9 . . . 7A **102**
Chubworthy St. SE14 . . . 6A **104**
Chudleigh DA14: Sidc . . . 4B **144**
Chudleigh Cres. IG3: Ilf . . . 4J **71**
Chudleigh Gdns. SM1: Sutt . . . 3A **166**
Chudleigh Rd. NW6 . . . 7F **63**
SE4 . . . 5B **122**
TW2: Twick . . . 6J **113**
(not continuous)
Chudleigh St. E1 . . . 6K **85**
Chudleigh Way HA4: Ruis . . . 1J **57**
Chulsa Rd. SE26 . . . 5H **139**
Chumleigh Gdns. *SE5 . . . 6E **102***
(off Chumleigh St.)
Chumleigh St. SE5 . . . 6E **102**
Chumleigh Wlk. KT5: Surb . . . 4F **151**
Church All. CR0: C'don . . . 1A **168**
Church App. SE21 . . . 3D **138**
Church Av. BR3: Beck . . . 1C **158**
DA14: Sidc . . . 5A **144**
E4 . . . 6A **36**
(not continuous)
E12 . . . 3B **70**
HA4: Ruis . . . 1F **57**
HA5: Pinn . . . 6C **40**
N2 . . . 2B **46**
NW1 . . . 6F **65**
SW14 . . . 3K **115**
UB2: S'hall . . . 3C **94**
UB5: N'olt . . . 7D **58**
Churchbank *E17 . . . 4C **50***
(off Teresa M.)
Churchbury Cl. EN1: Enf . . . 2K **23**
Churchbury La. EN1: Enf . . . 3J **23**
Churchbury Rd. EN1: Enf . . . 2K **23**
SE9 . . . 7B **124**
Church Cloisters EC3 . . . 3G **15**
Church Cl. HA6: Nwood . . . 1H **39**
HA8: Edg . . . 5D **28**
N20 . . . 3H **31**
TW3: Houn . . . 2C **112**
UB4: Hayes . . . 5F **75**
UB7: W Dray . . . 3A **92**
W8 . . . 2K **99**
Church Ct. *SE16 . . . 2B **104***
(off Rotherhithe St.)
TW9: Rich . . . 5D **114**
Church Cres. E9 . . . 7K **67**
N3 . . . 1H **45**
N10 . . . 4F **47**
N20 . . . 3H **31**
Churchcroft Cl. SW12 . . . 7E **118**
Churchdown BR1: Brom . . . 4G **141**
Church Dr. BR4: W W'ck . . . 3G **171**
HA2: Harr . . . 6E **40**
NW9 . . . 1K **61**
Church Elm La. RM10: Dag . . . 6G **73**
CHURCH END
N3 . . . 1H **45**
NW10 . . . 7A **62**
Church End E17 . . . 4D **50**
NW4 . . . 3D **44**
Church Entry EC4 . . . 1B **14**
Church Est. Almshouses
*TW9: Rich . . . 4F **115***
(off Sheen Rd.)
Church Farm House Mus. . . . 3D **44**
Church Farm La. SM3: Cheam . . . 6G **165**
Church Farm Pool . . . 7J **21**
Churchfield Av. N12 . . . 6G **31**
Churchfield Cl. HA2: Harr . . . 4G **41**
UB3: Hayes . . . 7H **75**
Churchfield Ho. *W2 . . . 4B **82***
(off Hall Pl.)
Churchfield Mans. *SW6 . . . 2H **117***
(off New Kings Rd.)
Churchfield Pl. TW17: Shep . . . 7D **146**
Churchfield Rd.
DA16: Well . . . 3A **126**
KT12: Walt T . . . 7J **147**
W3 . . . 1J **97**
W7 . . . 2J **95**
W13 . . . 1B **96**
Churchfields E18 . . . 1J **51**
KT8: W Mole . . . 3E **148**
SE10 . . . 6E **104**
Churchfields Av. TW13: Hanw . . . 3D **130**
Churchfields Rd. BR3: Beck . . . 2K **157**
Churchfield Way N12 . . . 6F **31**
Church Gdns. HA0: Wemb . . . 4A **60**
W5 . . . 2D **96**
Church Gth. *N19 . . . 2H **65***
(off St John's Gro.)
Church Ga. SW6 . . . 3G **117**
Church Grn. SW9 . . . 1A **120**
UB3: Hayes . . . 6H **75**
Church Gro. KT1: Ham W . . . 1C **150**
SE13 . . . 5D **122**
Church Hill DA1: Cray . . . 4K **127**
E17 . . . 4C **50**
HA1: Harr . . . 1J **59**
N21 . . . 7E **22**
SE18 . . . 3D **106**
SM5: Cars . . . 5D **166**
SW19 . . . 5H **135**
Church Hill Rd. E17 . . . 4D **50**
EN4: E Barn . . . 6H **21**
KT6: Surb . . . 5E **150**
SM3: Cheam . . . 3F **165**
Church Hill Wood
BR5: St M Cry . . . 5K **161**
Church Ho. *EC1 . . . 3B **8***
(off Compton St.)
*SW1 . . . 1D **18***
(off Gt. Smith St.)
Church Hyde SE18 . . . 6J **107**
Churchill Av. HA3: Kent . . . 6B **42**
UB10: Hil . . . 3D **74**
Churchill Cl. TW14: Felt . . . 1H **129**
UB10: Hil . . . 3D **74**
Churchill Ct. BR6: Farnb . . . 5G **173**
HA2: Harr . . . 2F **59**
(Eastcote Av.)
HA2: Harr . . . 5F **41**
(Station Rd.)
HA5: Hat E . . . 1C **40**
N4 . . . 7A **48**
N9 . . . 1K **33**
UB5: N'olt . . . 5E **58**
W5 . . . 4F **79**
Churchill Gdns. SW1 . . . 6A **18**
(not continuous)
W3 . . . 6G **79**
Churchill Gdns. Rd.
SW1 . . . 6K **17** (5F **101**)
Churchill Lodge IG6: Ilf . . . 4G **53**
Churchill Mus. (Cabinet War Rooms)
. . . 6D **12** (2H **101**)
Churchill Pl. E14 . . . 1D **104**
HA1: Harr . . . 4J **41**
Churchill Rd. CR2: S Croy . . . 7C **168**
E16 . . . 6A **88**
HA8: Edg . . . 6A **28**
NW2 . . . 6D **62**
NW5 . . . 4F **65**
Churchills M. IG8: Wfd G . . . 6C **36**
Churchill Ter. E4 . . . 4H **35**
Churchill Theatre & Library . . . 2J **159**
Churchill Wlk. E9 . . . 5J **67**
Churchill Way BR1: Brom . . . 2J **159**
TW16: Sun . . . 5J **129**
Churchlands Way KT4: Wor Pk . . . 2F **165**
Church La. BR2: Brom . . . 1C **172**
BR7: Chst . . . 1G **161**
E11 . . . 1G **69**
E17 . . . 4D **50**
EN1: Enf . . . 3J **23**
HA3: W'stone . . . 1K **41**
HA5: Pinn . . . 3C **40**
KT7: T Ditt . . . 6K **149**
KT9: Chess . . . 6F **163**
N2 . . . 3B **46**
N8 . . . 4K **47**
N9 . . . 2B **34**
N17 . . . 1E **48**
NW9 . . . 6J **43**
RM10: Dag . . . 7J **73**
SM6: Bedd . . . 3H **167**
(not continuous)
SW17 . . . 5D **136**
SW19 . . . 1H **153**
TW1: Twick . . . 1A **132**
TW10: Ham . . . 1E **132**
TW11: Tedd . . . 5K **131**
UB3: Hayes . . . 6G **75**
W5 . . . 2C **96**
Churchley Rd. SE26 . . . 4H **139**
Church Manorway DA8: Erith . . . 4K **109**
SE2 . . . 5A **108**
Church Mead *SE5 . . . 7C **102***
(off Camberwell Rd.)
Churchmead Cl. EN4: E Barn . . . 6H **21**
Church Mdw. KT6: Surb . . . 2C **162**
Churchmead Rd. NW10 . . . 6C **62**
Churchmore Rd. SW16 . . . 1G **155**
Church Mt. N2 . . . 5B **46**
Church Paddock Ct.
SM6: Bedd . . . 3H **167**
Church Pde. TW15: Ashf . . . 4B **128**
Church Pas. *EC2 . . . 7D **8***
(off Guildhall Yd.)
EN5: Barn . . . 3B **20**
KT6: Surb . . . 5E **150**
TW1: Twick . . . 1B **132**
Church Path CR0: C'don . . . 2C **168**
CR4: Mitc . . . 3C **154**
(not continuous)
E11 . . . 5J **51**
E17 . . . 4D **50**
N5 . . . 5B **66**
*N8 . . . 5K **47***
(off Tottenham La.)
N12 . . . 3F **31**
(Woodside La.)
N12 . . . 4F **31**
(Woodside Pk. Rd.)
N17 . . . 7K **33**
NW10 . . . 7A **62**
SW14 . . . 3K **115**
(not continuous)
SW19 . . . 2H **153**
(not continuous)
UB1: S'hall . . . 1E **94**
UB2: S'hall . . . 3D **94**
(not continuous)
W3 . . . 2J **97**
(not continuous)
Church Pl. CR4: Mitc . . . 3C **154**
SW1 . . . 3B **12** (7G **83**)
UB10: Ick . . . 3E **56**
W5 . . . 2D **96**
Church Ri. KT9: Chess . . . 6F **163**
SE23 . . . 2K **139**
Church Rd. BR2: Brom . . . 2J **159**
(Glassmill La.)
BR2: Brom . . . 3G **159**
(Shortlands Rd.)
BR2: Kes . . . 7B **172**
BR6: Farnb . . . 5G **173**

Church Rd. CR0: C'don 3C 168
(not continuous)
CR4: Mitc 1B 154
DA7: Bex 2F 127
DA8: Erith 5K 109
DA14: Sidc 4A 144
DA16: Well 2B 126
E10 1C 68
E12 5C 70
E17 2A 50
EN3: Pond E 6D 24
HA6: Nwood 1H 39
HA7: Stan 5G 27
IG2: Ilf 6J 53
IG9: Buck H 1E 36
IG11: Bark 6G 71
KT1: King T 2F 151
KT4: Wor Pk 1A 164
KT6: Surb 1C 162
KT8: E Mos 4H 149
KT10: Clay 7A 162
KT19: Ewe 7K 163
N1 6C 66
N6 6E 46
N17 1E 48
(not continuous)
NW4 4D 44
NW10 7A 62
SE19 1E 156
SM3: Cheam 6G 165
SM6: Bedd 3H 167
SW13 2B 116
SW19 5G 135
(High St. Wimbledon)
SW19 1B 154
(Western Rd.)
TW5: Cran 5K 93
TW5: Hest 7E 94
TW7: Isle 1H 113
TW9: Rich 4E 114
TW10: Ham 4D 132
TW10: Rich 5E 114
TW11: Tedd 4J 131
TW13: Hanw 5B 130
TW15: Ashf 3B 128
TW17: Shep 7D 146
UB2: S'hall 3D 94
UB3: Hayes 1H 93
UB5: N'olt 2B 76
UB7: W Dray 3A 92
UB8: Cowl 4A 74
W3 1J 97
W7 7H 77
Church Rd. Almshouses *E10* 2D 68
(off Church Rd.)
Church Rd. Ind. Est. E10 1C 68
Church Rd. Nth. N2 2B 46
Church Rd. Sth. N2 2B 46
Church Row BR7: Chst 1G 161
NW3 4A 64
SW6 7K 99
(off Park Rd.)
Church Row M. BR7: Chst 7G 143
Church Sq. TW17: Shep 7D 146
Church St.
CR0: C'don 3B 168
E15 1G 87
E16 1F 107
EN2: Enf 3H 23
KT1: King T 2D 150
KT12: Walt T 7J 147
KT17: Ewe 7C 164
N9 7J 23
NW8 5B 4 (5B 82)
RM10: Dag 6H 73
SM1: Sutt 5K 165
TW1: Twick 1A 132
TW7: Isle 3B 114
TW12: Hamp 1G 149
TW16: Sun 3K 147
Church St. W2 5B 4 (5B 82)
W4 6B 98
Church St. Est. NW8 4B 4 (4B 82)
Church St. Nth. E15 1G 87
Church St. Pas. *E15* 1G 87
(off Church St.)
Church Stretton Rd. TW3: Houn 5G 113
Church Ter. NW4 3D 44
SE13 3G 123
TW10: Rich 5D 114
Church Va. N2 3D 46
SE23 2K 139
Church Vw. TW10: Rich 5E 114
Churchview Rd. TW2: Twick 1H 131
Church Villa TW16: Sun 3K 147
Church Wlk. EN2: Enf 3J 23
KT7: T Ditt 6K 149
KT12: Walt T 7J 147
(not continuous)
N6 3E 64
N16 3D 66
(not continuous)
NW2 3H 63
NW4 3E 44
NW9 2K 61
SW13 1C 116
SW15 5D 116
SW16 2G 155
SW20 3E 152
TW8: Bford 6C 96
(not continuous)
TW9: Rich 5D 114
UB3: Hayes 6G 75
Churchward Ho. *SE17* 6B 102
(off Lorrimore Sq.)
W14 5H 99
(off Ivatt Pl.)
Church Way EN4: Cockf 4J 21
HA8: Edg 6B 28
N20 3H 31
Churchway NW1 1D 6 (3H 83)
(not continuous)
Churchwell Path E9 5J 67
Churchwood Gdns. IG8: Wfd G 4D 36
Churchyard Pas. SE5 2D 120
Churchyard Row SE11 4B 102
Church Yd. Wlk. *W2* 5A 4
(off St Mary's Sq.)
Churnfield N4 2A 66
Churston Av. E13 1K 87
Churston Cl. SW2 1A 138
Churston Dr. SM4: Mord 5F 153
Churston Gdns. N11 6B 32
Churston Mans. WC1 4H 7
Churton Pl. SW1 4B 18 (4G 101)
Churton St. SW1 4B 18 (4G 101)
Chusan Pl. E14 6B 86
Chute Ho. *SW9* 2A 120
(off Stockwell Pk. Rd.)
Chuter Ede Ho. *SW6* 6H 99
(off North End Rd.)
Chyngton Cl. DA15: Sidc 3K 143
Cibber Rd. SE23 2K 139
Cicada Rd. SW18 6A 118
Cicely Ho. *NW8* 2B 82
(off Cochrane St.)
Cicely Rd. SE15 1G 121
Cinderella Path NW11 1K 63
Cinderford Way BR1: Brom 4G 141
Cine Lumiere 3A 16
(off Queensberry Pl.)
Cineworld Cinema
Bexleyheath 4H 127
Chelsea, Fulham Rd. 5A 100
Chelsea, King's Rd. 6B 100
Enfield 4B 24
Feltham 2K 129
Hammersmith 4D 98
Haymarket 3C 12
(off Haymarket)
Cineworld Cinema
Ilford 3F 71
(off Winston Way)
Shaftesbury Av. 7H 83
(off Shaftesbury Av.)
Staples Corner 1D 62
Wandsworth 5K 117
West India Quay 7C 86
Wood Green 2A 48
(in Wood Green Shop. City)
Cinnabar Wharf Central *E1* 1G 103
(off Wapping High St.)
Cinnabar Wharf E. *E1* 1G 103
(off Wapping High St.)
Cinnabar Wharf W. *E1* 1G 103
(off Wapping High St.)
Cinnamon Cl. CR0: C'don 7J 155
SE15 7F 103
Cinnamon Row SW11 3A 118
Cinnamon St. E1 1H 103
Cinnamon Wharf *SE1* 6K 15
(off Shad Thames)
Cintra Pk. SE19 7F 139
Circa Apartments NW1 7E 64
Circle, The NW2 3A 62
NW7 6E 28
SE1 6J 15
(off Queen Elizabeth St.)
Circle Gdns. SW19 2J 153
Circuits, The HA5: Pinn 4A 40
Circular Rd. N2 2B 46
N17 3F 49
Circular Way SE18 6D 106
(not continuous)
Circus Lodge NW8 1A 4
Circus M. W1 5E 4
Circus Pl. EC2 6F 9 (5D 84)
Circus Rd. NW8 1A 4 (3B 82)
Circus St. SE10 7E 104
Cirencester St. W2 5K 81
Cirrus Cl. SM6: Wall 7J 167
Cissbury Ho. SE26 3G 139
Cissbury Ring Nth. N12 5C 30
Cissbury Ring Sth. N12 5C 30
Cissbury Rd. N15 5D 48
Citadel Pl. SE11 5G 19 (5K 101)
Citizen Ho. N7 4A 66
Citizen Rd. N7 4A 66
Citrus Ho. *SE8* 5B 104
(off Alverton St.)
City Apartments *E1* 7K 9
(off White Church La.)
City Bus. Cen. SE16 3J 103
City Central Est. *EC1* 2C 8
(off Seward St.)
City Ct. CR0: C'don 7B 156
City Cross Bus. Pk. SE10 4G 105
City Forum EC1 1C 8 (3C 84)
City Gdn. Row N1 1C 8 (2B 84)
City Ga. Ho. *IG2: Ilf* 6E 52
(off Eastern Av.)
City Harbour *E14* 3D 104
(off Selsdon Way)
City Hgts. *SE1* 5H 15
(off Weavers La.)
City Limits
Collier Row 2F 55
Croydon 6A 168
(off Purley Way)
CITY OF LONDON 1E 14 (6D 84)
City of London Almshouses SW9 4K 119
City of London Crematorium E12 3C 70
City of London Point *N7* 6H 65
(off York Way)
City of Westminster College 2C 12 (7G 83)
City Pav. *EC1* 5A 8
(off Britton St.)
City Pl. Ho. *EC2* 5D 84
(off London Wall)
Citypoint EC2 5E 8
City Rd. EC1 1A 8 (2B 84)
City Tower *EC2* 6E 8
(off Basinghall St.)
City University 2A 8 (3B 84)
City University Saddlers Sports Cen., The 3B 8 (4B 84)
City Vw. *IG1: Ilf* 2G 71
(off Axon Pl.)
Cityview SE7 6A 106
City Vw. Apartments *N1* 7C 66
(off Essex Rd.)
City Vw. Ct. SE22 7G 121
City Wlk. SE1 7G 15 (2E 102)
City Wlk. Apartments *EC1* 2C 8
(off Seward St.)
City Wharf Ho. KT7: T Ditt 6B 150
Civic Way HA4: Ruis 5B 58
IG6: Ilf 4G 53
Clabon M. SW1 2E 16 (3D 100)
Clack La. HA4: Ruis 1E 56
Clack St. SE16 2J 103
Clacton Rd. E6 3B 88
E17 6A 50
N17 2F 49
Claigmar Gdns. N3 1K 45
Claire Ct. HA5: Hat E 1D 40
N12 3F 31
NW2 6G 63
WD23: B Hea 1C 26
Claire Gdns. HA7: Stan 5H 27
Claire Ho. IG1: Ilf 4F 71
Claire Pl. E14 3C 104
Clairvale Rd. TW5: Hest 1B 112
Clairview Rd. SW16 5F 137
Clairville Gdns. W7 1J 95
Clairville Point *SE23* 3K 139
(off Dacres Rd.)
Clamp Hill HA7: Stan 4C 26
Clancarty Rd. SW6 2J 117
Clandeboye Ho. *E15* 1H 87
(off John St.)
Clandon Cl. KT17: Ewe 6B 164
W3 2H 97
Clandon Gdns. N3 3J 45
Clandon Ho. *SE1* 7B 14
(off Webber St.)
Clandon Rd. IG3: Ilf 2J 71
Clandon St. SE8 2C 122
Clandon Ter. SW20 2F 153
Clanricarde Gdns. W2 7J 81
CLAPHAM 4G 119
CLAPHAM COMMON 4H 119
Clapham Comn. Nth. Side SW4 4D 118
Clapham Comn. Sth. Side SW4 6F 119
Clapham Comn. W. Side SW4 4D 118
(not continuous)
Clapham Cres. SW4 4H 119
Clapham High St. SW4 4H 119
CLAPHAM JUNCTION 3C 118
Clapham Junc. App. SW11 3C 118
Clapham Leisure Cen. 3H 119
Clapham Mnr. Ct. SW4 3G 119
Clapham Mnr. St. SW4 3G 119
CLAPHAM PARK 7H 119
Clapham Pk. Est. SW4 6H 119
Clapham Pk. Rd. SW4 4G 119
Clapham Pk. Ter. *SW2* 5J 119
(off Kings Av.)
Clapham Picturehouse 4G 119
Clapham Rd. SW9 3J 119
Clapham Rd. Est. SW4 3J 119
Clap La. RM10: Dag, Rush G 2H 73
Claps Ga. La. E6 4E 88
Clapton Comn. E5 7F 49
(not continuous)
CLAPTON PARK 4K 67
Clapton Pk. Est. E5 4K 67
Clapton Pas. E5 5J 67
Clapton Sq. E5 5J 67
Clapton Ter. N16 1G 67

Clapton Way E5 ....4G 67
Clara Grant Ho. E14 ....3C 104
(off Mellish St.)
Clara Nehab Ho. NW11 ....5H 45
(off Leeside Cres.)
Clara Pl. SE18 ....4E 106
Clare Cl. N2 ....3A 46
Clare Cnr. SE9 ....7F 125
Clare Ct. W11 ....7G 81
(off Clarendon Rd.)
WC1 ....2F 7
(off Judd St.)
Claredale Ho. E2 ....2H 85
(off Claredale St.)
Claredale St. E2 ....2G 85
Clare Gdns. E7 ....4J 69
IG11: Bark 6K 71
W11 ....6G 81
Clare Ho. E3 ....1B 86
E16 ....7E 88
(off University Way)
HA8: Edg 2J 43
(off Burnt Oak B'way.)
SE1 ....5F 103
(off Cooper's Rd.)
Clare La. N1 ....7C 66
Clare Lawn Av. SW14 ....5J 115
Clare Mkt. WC2 ....1H 13 (6K 83)
Clare M. SW6 ....7K 99
Claremont TW17: Shep 6D 146
(off Laleham Rd.)
Claremont Av. HA3: Kent 5E 42
KT3: N Mald 5C 152
TW16: Sun 1K 147
Claremont Cl. BR6: Farnb 4E 172
E16 ....1E 106
N1 ....1K 7 (2A 84)
SW2 ....1J 137
Claremont Ct. W2 ....6K 81
(off Queensway)
W9 ....2H 81
(off Claremont Rd.)
Claremont Dr.
TW17: Shep 6D 146
Claremont Gdns. IG3: Ilf 2J 71
KT6: Surb 5E 150
Claremont Gro. IG8: Wfd G 6F 37
W4 ....7A 98
Claremont Ho. SM2: Sutt 7K 165
Claremont Pk. N3 ....1G 45
Claremont Pl. KT10: Clay 6A 162
Claremont Road 2F 63
Claremont Rd. BR1: Brom 4C 160
CR0: C'don 1G 169
E7 ....5K 69
E11 ....3F 69
E17 ....2A 50
HA3: W'stone 2J 41
KT6: Surb 5E 150
N6 ....7G 47
NW2 ....7F 45
TW1: Twick 7B 114
TW11: Tedd 5K 131
W9 ....2G 81
W13 ....5A 78
Claremont Sq. N1 ....1J 7 (2A 84)
Claremont St. E16 ....2E 106
N18 ....6B 34
SE10 ....6D 104
Claremont Ter. KT7: T Ditt 7B 150
Claremont Vs. SE5 ....7D 102
(off Southampton Way)
Claremont Way NW2 ....1E 62
(not continuous)
Claremont Way Ind. Est.
NW2 ....1E 62
Clarence Av. BR1: Brom 4C 160
IG2: Ilf 6E 52
KT3: N Mald 2J 151
SW4 ....7H 119
Clarence Cl. EN4: E Barn 5G 21
WD23: B Hea 1E 26
Clarence Ct. NW7 ....5F 29
W6 ....4D 98
(off Cambridge Gro.)
Clarence Cres. DA14: Sidc 3B 144
SW4 ....6H 119
Clarence Gdns. NW1 ....2K 5 (3F 83)
Clarence Ga. IG8: Ilf, Wfd G 6K 37
Clarence Ga. Gdns. NW1 ....4F 5
(off Glentworth St.)
Clarence House 6B 12
Clarence Ho. SE17 ....6C 102
(off Merrow St.)
Clarence La. SW15 ....6A 116
Clarence M. E5 ....5H 67
SE16 ....1K 103
SW12 ....7F 119
Clarence Pl. E5 ....5H 67
Clarence Rd. BR1: Brom 3B 160
CR0: C'don 7D 156
DA6: Bex 4E 126
DA14: Sidc 3B 144
E5 ....4H 67
E12 ....4A 70
E16 ....4G 87
E17 ....2K 49
EN3: Pond E 5C 24
N15 ....5C 48
N22 ....7D 32
NW6 ....7H 63
SE8 ....6D 104
SE9 ....2C 142
SM1: Sutt 5K 165
SM6: Wall 5F 167
SW19 ....6K 135
TW9: Kew 1F 115
TW11: Tedd 6K 131
W4 ....5G 97
Clarence St. KT1: King T 2D 150
(not continuous)
TW9: Rich 4E 114
UB2: S'hall 3B 94
Clarence Ter. NW1 ....3F 5 (4D 82)
TW3: Houn 4F 113
Clarence Wlk. SW4 ....2J 119
Clarence Way NW1 ....7F 65
Clarenden Pl. DA2: Dart 5K 145
Clarendon Cl. BR5: St P 3K 161
E9 ....7J 67
W2 ....2C 10 (7C 82)
Clarendon Ct. BR3: Beck 1D 158
(off Blair Ct.)
NW2 ....7E 62
NW11 ....4H 45
TW5: Cran 1J 111
TW9: Kew 1F 115
Clarendon Cres. TW2: Twick 3H 131
Clarendon Cross W11 ....7G 81
Clarendon Dr. SW15 ....4E 116
Clarendon Flats W1 ....1H 11
(off Balderton St.)
Clarendon Gdns.
HA9: Wemb 3D 60
IG1: Ilf 7D 52
NW4 ....3C 44
W9 ....4A 82
Clarendon Grn. BR5: St P 4K 161
Clarendon Gro. CR4: Mitc 3D 154
NW1 ....1C 6 (3H 83)
Clarendon Ho. NW1 ....1B 6
(off Werrington St.)
W2 ....2C 10
(off Strathearn Pl.)
Clarendon Lodge W11 ....7G 81
(off Clarendon Rd.)
Clarendon M. DA5: Bexl 1H 145
W2 ....2C 10 (7C 82)
Clarendon Path BR5: St P 4K 161
(not continuous)
Clarendon Pl.
W2 ....2C 10 (7C 82)
Clarendon Ri. SE13 ....4E 122
Clarendon Rd. CR0: C'don 2B 168
E11 ....1F 69
E17 ....6D 50
E18 ....3J 51
HA1: Harr 6J 41
N8 ....3K 47
N15 ....4C 48
N18 ....6B 34
N22 ....2K 47
SM6: Wall 6G 167
SW19 ....7C 136
TW15: Ashf 4B 128
UB3: Hayes 2H 93
W5 ....3E 78
W11 ....7G 81
Clarendon St. SW1 ....5K 17 (5F 101)
Clarendon Ter. W9 ....3A 4 (4A 82)
Clarendon Wlk. W11 ....6G 81
Clarendon Way BR5: St P 3K 161
BR7: Chst 3K 161
N21 ....6H 23
Clarens St. SE6 ....2B 140
Clare Pl. SW15 ....7B 116
Clare Point NW2 ....1F 63
(off Whitefield Av.)
Clare Rd. E11 ....6F 51
NW10 ....7C 62
SE14 ....1B 122
TW4: Houn 3D 112
TW19: Stanw 1A 128
UB6: G'frd 6H 59
Clare St. E2 ....2H 85
Claret Gdns. SE25 ....3E 156
Clareville Ct. SW7 ....4A 16
(off Clareville St.)
Clareville Gro. SW7 ....4A 16 (4A 100)
Clareville Gro. M. SW7 ....4A 16 (4A 100)
Clareville Rd. BR5: Farnb 2G 173
Clareville St. SW7 ....4A 16 (4A 100)
Clare Way DA7: Bex 1E 126
Clarewood Ct. W1 ....6E 4
(off Seymour Pl.)
Clarewood Wlk. SW9 ....4A 120
Clarges M. W1 ....4J 11 (1F 101)
Clarges St. W1 ....4K 11 (1F 101)
Claribel Rd. SW9 ....2B 120
Clarice Way SM6: Wall 7J 167
Claridge Ct. SW6 ....2H 117
Claridge Rd. RM8: Dag 1D 72
Clarinet Ct. HA8: Edg 7C 28
Clarion Ho. E3 ....2A 86
(off Roman Rd.)
SW1 ....5B 18
(off Moreton Pl.)
W1 ....1C 12
(off St Anne's Ct.)
Clarissa Ho. E14 ....6D 86
(off Cordela St.)
Clarissa Rd.
RM6: Chad H 7D 54
Clarissa St. E8 ....1F 85
Clarke Cl. CR0: C'don 6C 156
Clarke Mans. IG11: Bark 7K 71
(off Upney La.)
Clarke M. N9 ....3C 34
Clarke Path N16 ....1G 67
Clarkes Av. KT4: Wor Pk 1F 165
Clarkes Dr. UB8: Hil 5A 74
Clarke's M. W1 ....5H 5 (5E 82)
Clark Ho. SW10 ....7A 100
(off Coleridge Gdns.)
Clarks Mead WD23: Bush 1B 26
Clarkson Rd. E16 ....6H 87
Clarkson Row NW1 ....2G 83
(off Mornington Ter.)
Clarksons, The IG11: Bark 2G 89
Clarkson St. E2 ....3H 85
Clarks Rd. IG1: Ilf 2H 71
Clark St. E1 ....5H 85
Clark Way TW5: Hest 7B 94
Classic Mans. E9 ....7H 67
(off Wells St.)
Classon Cl. UB7: W Dray 2A 92
Claude Rd. E10 ....2E 68
E13 ....1K 87
SE15 ....2H 121
Claude St. E14 ....4C 104
Claudia Jones Ho. N17 ....1C 48
Claudia Jones Way SW2 ....6J 119
Claudia Pl. SW19 ....1G 135
Claudius Cl. HA7: Stan 3J 27
Claughton Rd. E13 ....2A 88
Clauson Av. UB5: N'olt 5F 59
Clavell St. SE10 ....6E 104
Claverdale Rd. SW2 ....7K 119
Clavering Av. SW13 ....6D 98
Clavering Cl. TW1: Twick 4A 132
Clavering Ho. SE13 ....4F 123
(off Blessington Rd.)
Clavering Ind. Est. N9 ....2D 34
(off Montagu Rd.)
Clavering Rd. E12 ....1B 70
Claverley Gro. N3 ....1K 45
Claverley Vs. N3 ....7E 30
Claverton St. SW1 ....6B 18 (5G 101)
Clave St. E1 ....1J 103
Claxton Gro. W6 ....5F 99
Claxton Path SE4 ....4K 121
(off Coston Wlk.)
Clay Av. CR4: Mitc 2F 155
Claybank Gro. SE13 ....3D 122
Claybourne M. SE19 ....7E 138
Claybridge Rd. SE12 ....4A 142
Claybrook Cl. N2 ....3B 46
Claybrook Rd. W6 ....6F 99
Claybury B'way. IG5: Ilf 3C 52
Claybury Hill IG8: Wfd G 7J 37
Claybury Rd. IG8: Wfd G 7H 37
Clay Ct. E17 ....3F 51
SE1 ....7G 15
(off Long La.)
Claydon SE17 ....4C 102
(off Deacon Way)
Claydon Dr. CR0: Bedd 4J 167
Claydon Ho. NW4 ....2F 45
(off Holders Hill Rd.)
Claydown M. SE18 ....5E 106
Clay Farm Rd. SE9 ....2G 143
CLAYGATE 7A 162
Claygate Cres. CR0: New Ad 6E 170
Claygate La. KT7: T Ditt 1A 162
KT10: Clay, Hin W 2A 162
Claygate Rd. W13 ....3B 96
CLAYHALL 3C 52
Clayhall Av. IG5: Ilf 3C 52
Clay Hill EN2: Enf 1K 23
Clayhill KT5: Surb 5G 151
Clayhill Cres. SE9 ....4B 142
Claylands Pl. SW8 ....7A 102
Claylands Rd. SW8 ....7H 19 (6K 101)
Clay La. HA8: Edg 2B 28
TW19: Stanw 7B 110
WD23: B Hea 1D 26
Claymill Ho. SE18 ....5G 107
Claymore Cl. SM4: Mord 7J 153
Claypole Ct. E17 ....5C 50
(off Yunus Khan Cl.)
Claypole Dr. TW5: Hest 1C 112
Claypole Rd. E15 ....2E 86
Clayponds Av. TW8: Bford 4D 96
Clayponds Gdns. W5 ....4D 96
(not continuous)
Clayponds La. TW8: Bford 5E 96
(not continuous)
Clay St. W1 ....6F 5 (5D 82)
Clayton Av. HA0: Wemb 7E 60
Clayton Bus. Cen. UB3: Hayes 2G 93

Clayton Cl. E6 6D **88**
Clayton Ct. E17 2A **50**
Clayton Cres. N1 1J **83**
TW8: Bford 5D **96**
Clayton Dr. SE8 5A **104**
Clayton Fld. NW9 7F **29**
Clayton Ho. *E9* *7J* ***67***
(off Frampton Pk. Rd.)
KT7: T Ditt 1B **162**
SW13 *7E* ***98***
(off Trinity Church Rd.)
Clayton M. SE10 1F **123**
Clayton Rd. KT9: Chess 4C **162**
RM7: Rush G 1J **73**
SE15 1G **121**
TW7: Isle 3J **113**
UB3: Hayes 2G **93**
Clayton St. SE11 7J **19** (6A **102**)
Clayton Ter. UB4: Yead 5C **76**
Claytonville Ter. DA17: Belv 2J **109**
Clay Wood Cl. BR6: Orp 7J **161**
Clayworth Cl. DA15: Sidc 6B **126**
Cleanthus Cl. SE18 1F **125**
Cleanthus Rd. SE18 2F **125**
(not continuous)
Clearbrook Way E1 6J **85**
Clearwater Pl. KT6: Surb 6C **150**
Clearwater Ter. W11 2F **99**
Clearwater Yd. *NW1* *1F* ***83***
(off Inverness St.)
Clearwell Dr. W9 4K **81**
Cleave Av. BR6: Chels 6J **173**
UB3: Harl 4G **93**
Cleaveland Rd. KT6: Surb 5D **150**
Cleaverholme Cl. SE25 6H **157**
Cleaver Ho. *NW3* *7D* ***64***
(off Adelaide Rd.)
Cleaver Sq. SE11 6K **19** (5A **102**)
Cleaver St. SE11 5K **19** (5A **102**)
Cleaves Almshouses
KT2: King T *2E* ***150***
(off London Rd.)
Cleeve Ct. TW14: Bedf 1G **129**
Cleeve Hill SE23 1H **139**
Cleeve Ho. E2 2H **9**
Cleeve Pk. Gdns. DA14: Sidc 2B **144**
Cleeve Way SM1: Sutt 1K **165**
SW15 7B **116**
Cleeve Workshops *E2* *2H* ***9***
(off Boundary Rd.)
Clegg Ho. SE3 4K **123**
SE16 *3J* ***103***
(off Moodkee St.)
Clegg St. E1 1H **103**
E13 2J **87**
Cleland Ho. *E2* *2J* ***85***
(off Sewardstone Rd.)
Clematis Gdns. IG8: Wfd G 5D **36**
Clematis St. W12 7C **80**
Clem Attlee Ct. SW6 6H **99**
Clem Attlee Pde. *SW6* *6H* ***99***
(off North End Rd.)
Clemence Rd. RM10: Dag 1J **91**
Clemence St. E14 5B **86**
Clement Av. SW4 4H **119**
Clement Cl. NW6 7E **62**
W4 4K **97**
Clement Gdns. UB3: Harl 4G **93**
Clementhorpe Rd. RM9: Dag 6C **72**
Clement Ho. SE8 4A **104**
W10 *5E* ***80***
(off Dalgarno Gdns.)
Clementina Rd. E10 1B **68**
Clementine Cl. W13 2B **96**
Clementine Wlk.
IG8: Wfd G 7D **36**
Clement Rd. BR3: Beck 2K **157**
SW19 5G **135**
Clement's Av. E16 7J **87**
Clements Cl. N12 4E **30**
Clements Ct. IG1: Ilf 3F **71**
TW4: Houn 4B **112**
Clement's Inn WC2 1H **13** (6K **83**)
Clement's Inn Pas. WC2 1H **13**
Clements La. EC4 2F **15** (7D **84**)
IG1: Ilf 3F **71**
Clements Pl. TW8: Bford 5D **96**
Clements Rd. E6 7C **70**
IG1: Ilf 3F **71**
SE16 3G **103**
Clemson Ho. E8 1F **85**
Clendon Way SE18 4H **107**
Clennam St. SE1 6D **14** (2C **102**)
Clensham Ct. SM1: Sutt 2J **165**
Clensham La. SM1: Sutt 2J **165**
Clenston M. W1 7E **4** (6D **82**)
Cleopatra Cl. HA7: Stan 3J **27**
Cleopatra's Needle 4G **13** (1J **101**)
Clephane Rd. N1 6C **66**
Clephane Rd. Nth. N1 6C **66**
Clephane Rd. Sth. N1 6D **66**
Clere Pl. EC2 3F **9** (4D **84**)
Clere St. EC2 3F **9** (4D **84**)
Clerics Wlk. TW17: Shep 7F **147**
CLERKENWELL 3J **7** (4A **84**)
Clerkenwell Cl. EC1 3K **7** (4A **84**)
(not continuous)
Clerkenwell Grn. EC1 4K **7** (4A **84**)
Clerkenwell Rd. EC1 4J **7** (4A **84**)
Clerk's Pl. EC2 7G **9** (6E **84**)
Clermont Rd. E9 1J **85**
Clevedon Cl. N16 3F **67**
Clevedon Ct. CR2: S Croy 5E **168**
Clevedon Gdns. TW5: Cran 1K **111**
UB3: Harl 3F **93**
Clevedon Ho. SM1: Sutt 4A **166**
Clevedon Mans. NW5 4E **64**
Clevedon Pas. N16 2F **67**
Clevedon Rd. KT1: King T 2G **151**
SE20 1K **157**
TW1: Twick 6D **114**
(not continuous)
Cleve Ho. NW6 7K **63**
Cleveland Av. SW20 2H **153**
TW12: Hamp 7D **130**
W4 4B **98**
Cleveland Ct. W13 5B **78**
Cleveland Gdns. KT4: Wor Pk 2A **164**
N4 5C **48**
NW2 2F **63**
SW13 2B **116**
W2 6A **82**
Cleveland Gro. E1 4J **85**
Cleveland Ho. *N2* *2B* ***46***
(off The Grange)
Cleveland Mans. *NW6* *7H* ***63***
(off Willesden La.)
SW9 *7A* ***102***
(off Mowll St.)
W9 4J **81**
Cleveland M. W1 5A **6** (5G **83**)
Cleveland Pk. TW19: Stanw 6A **110**
Cleveland Pk. Av. E17 4C **50**
Cleveland Pk. Cres. E17 4C **50**
Cleveland Pl. SW1 4B **12** (1G **101**)
Cleveland Ri. SM4: Mord 7F **153**
Cleveland Rd. DA16: Well 2K **125**
E18 3J **51**
IG1: Ilf 3F **71**
KT3: N Mald 4A **152**
KT4: Wor Pk 2A **164**
N1 7D **66**
N9 7C **24**
SW13 2B **116**
TW7: Isle 4A **114**
W4 3J **97**
W13 5A **78**
Cleveland Row SW1 5A **12** (1G **101**)
Cleveland Sq. W2 6A **82**
Cleveland St. W1 4K **5** (4F **83**)
Cleveland Ter. W2 6A **82**
Cleveland Way E1 4J **85**
Cleveley Cl. SE7 4B **106**
Cleveley Cres. W5 2E **78**
Cleveleys Rd. E5 3H **67**
Cleverly Est. W12 1C **98**
Cleve Rd. DA14: Sidc 3D **144**
NW6 7J **63**
Cleves Av. KT17: Ewe 7D **164**
Cleves Ho. *E16* *1J* ***105***
(off Southey M.)
Cleves Rd. E6 1B **88**
TW10: Ham 3C **132**
Cleves Wlk. IG6: Ilf 1G **53**
Cleves Way
HA4: Ruis 1B **58**
TW12: Hamp 7D **130**
TW16: Sun 6H **129**
Clewer Ct. *E10* *1C* ***68***
(off Leyton Grange Est.)
Clewer Cres. HA3: Hrw W 1H **41**
Clewer Ho. *SE2* *2D* ***108***
(off Wolvercote Rd.)
Cley Ho. SE4 4K **121**
Clichy Est. E1 5J **85**
Clichy Ho. *E1* *5J* ***85***
(off Stepney Way)
Clifden M. E9 5K **67**
Clifden Rd. E5 5J **67**
TW1: Twick 1K **131**
TW8: Bford 6D **96**
Cliffe Ho. *SE10* *5H* ***105***
(off Blackwall La.)
Cliffe Rd. CR2: S Croy 5D **168**
Cliffe Wlk. *SM1: Sutt* *5A* ***166***
(off Greyhound Rd.)
Clifford Av. BR7: Chst 6D **142**
IG5: Ilf 1F **53**
SM6: Wall 4G **167**
SW14 3H **115**
(not continuous)
Clifford Cl. UB5: N'olt 1C **76**
Clifford Ct. *W2* *5K* ***81***
(off Westbourne Pk. Vs.)
Clifford Dr. SW9 4B **120**
Clifford Gdns. NW10 2E **80**
UB3: Harl 4G **93**
Clifford Gro. TW15: Ashf 4C **128**
Clifford Haigh Ho. SW6 7F **99**
Clifford Ho. *BR3: Beck* *6D* ***140***
(off Calverley Cl.)
W14 *4H* ***99***
(off Edith Vs.)
Clifford Rd. E16 4H **87**
E17 2E **50**
EN5: New Bar 3E **20**
HA0: Wemb 7D **60**
N1 1E **84**
N9 6D **24**
SE25 4G **157**
TW4: Houn 3B **112**
TW10: Ham 2D **132**
Clifford's Inn Pas.
EC4 1J **13** (6A **84**)
Clifford St. W1 3A **12** (7G **83**)
Clifford Way NW10 4B **62**
Cliff Rd. NW1 6H **65**
Cliffsend Ho. *SW9* *1A* ***120***
(off Cowley Rd.)
Cliff Ter. SE8 2C **122**
Cliffview Rd. SE13 3C **122**
Cliff Vs. NW1 6H **65**
Cliff Wlk. E16 5H **87**
Clifton Av. E17 3K **49**
HA7: Stan 2B **42**
HA9: Wemb 6F **61**
N3 1H **45**
TW13: Felt 3A **130**
W12 1B **98**
Clifton Cl. BR6: Farnb 5G **173**
Clifton Ct. BR3: Beck 1D **158**
IG8: Wfd G 6D **36**
KT5: Surb 7F **151**
N4 2A **66**
NW8 3A **4**
SE15 7H **103**
TW19: Stanw 6A **110**
Clifton Cres. SE15 7H **103**
Clifton Est. SE15 1H **121**
Clifton Gdns. EN2: Enf 4D **22**
N15 6F **49**
NW11 6H **45**
UB10: Hil 2D **74**
W4 4K **97**
(not continuous)
W9 4A **82**
Clifton Ga. SW10 6A **100**
Clifton Gro. E8 6G **67**
Clifton Hall *UB8: Cowl* *3A* ***74***
(off Kingston La.)
Clifton Hill NW8 2K **81**
Clifton Ho. *E2* *3J* ***9***
(off Club Row)
E11 2G **69**
Clifton M. SE25 4E **156**
Clifton Pde. TW13: Felt 3A **130**
Clifton Pk. Av. SW20 2E **152**
Clifton Pl. SE16 2J **103**
SW10 *6A* ***100***
(off Hollywood Rd.)
W2 1B **10** (6B **82**)
Clifton Ri. SE14 7A **104**
(not continuous)
Clifton Rd. DA14: Sidc 4J **143**
DA16: Well 3C **126**
E7 6B **70**
E16 5G **87**
HA3: Kent 4F **43**
IG2: Ilf 6H **53**
KT2: King T 7F **133**
N1 6C **66**
N3 1A **46**
N8 6H **47**
N22 1G **47**
NW10 2C **80**
SE25 4E **156**
SM6: Wall 5F **167**
SW19 6F **135**
TW7: Isle 2J **113**
TW11: Tedd 4J **131**
UB2: S'hall 4C **94**
UB6: G'frd 4G **77**
W9 3A **4** (4A **82**)
Clifton St. EC2 4G **9** (4E **84**)
Clifton Ter. N4 2A **66**
Clifton Vs. W9 5A **82**
Cliftonville Ct.
SE12 1J **141**
Clifton Wlk. *W6* *4D* ***98***
(off King St.)
Clifton Way HA0: Wemb 1E **78**
SE15 7H **103**
TW6: H'row A 3C **110**
Climsland Ho. SE1 4K **13** (1A **102**)
Clinch Ct. *E16* *5J* ***87***
(off Plymouth Rd.)
Cline Rd. N11 6B **32**
Clinger Ct. *N1* *1E* ***84***
(off Hobbs Pl. Est.)
Clink Prison Mus. 4E **14**
Clink St. SE1 4D **14** (1D **102**)
Clink Wharf *SE1* *4E* ***14***
(off Clink St.)
Clinton Av. DA16: Well 4A **126**
KT8: E Mos 4G **149**
Clinton Ho. *KT6: Surb* *7D* ***150***
(off Lovelace Gdns)
Clinton Rd. E3 3A **86**
E7 4J **69**
N15 4D **48**

Clipper Apartments SE10 ....6E 104
(off Welland St.)
Clipper Cl. SE16 ....2K 103
Clipper Ho. E14 ....5E 104
(off Manchester Rd.)
Clipper Way SE13 ....4E 122
Clippesby Cl. KT9: Chess 6F 163
Clipstone M. W1 ....5A 6 (5G 83)
Clipstone Rd. TW3: Houn 3E 112
Clipstone St. W1 ....5K 5 (5F 83)
Clissold Cl. N2 ....3D 46
Clissold Ct. N4 ....2C 66
Clissold Cres. N16 ....3D 66
Clissold Leisure Cen. 3D 66
Clissold Rd. N16 ....3D 66
Clitheroe Av. HA2: Harr 1E 58
Clitheroe Rd. SW9 ....2J 119
Clitherow Av. W7 ....3A 96
Clitherow Ct. TW8: Bford 5C 96
Clitherow Pas. TW8: Bford 5C 96
Clitherow Rd. TW8: Bford 5B 96
Clitterhouse Cres. NW2 ....1E 62
Clitterhouse Rd. NW2 ....1E 62
Clive Av. N18 ....6B 34
Clive Ct. W9 ....4A 82
Cliveden Cl. N12 ....4F 31
Cliveden Ho. E16 ....1J 105
(off Fitzwilliam M.)
SW1 ....3G 17
(off Cliveden Pl.)
Cliveden Pl. SW1 ....3G 17 (4E 100)
TW17: Shep 6E 146
Cliveden Rd. SW19 ....1H 153
Clivedon Ct. W13 ....5B 78
Clivedon Rd. E4 ....5B 36
Clive Ho. SE10 ....6E 104
(off Haddo St.)
Clive Lloyd Ho. N15 ....5C 48
(off Woodlands Pk. Rd.)
Clive Lodge NW4 ....6F 45
Clive Pas. SE21 ....3D 138
Clive Rd. DA17: Belv 4G 109
EN1: Enf 4B 24
SE21 ....3D 138
SW19 ....6C 136
TW1: Twick 4K 131
TW14: Felt 6J 111
Clivesdale Dr. UB3: Hayes 1K 93
Clive Way EN1: Enf 4B 24
Cloak La. EC4 ....2D 14 (7C 84)
Clochar Ct. NW10 ....1B 80
Clock Ct. E11 ....4K 51
Clock End Bri. N5 ....4A 66
(off Drayton Pk.)
Clock Ho. E3 ....3E 86
E17 ....4F 51
(off Wood St.)
Clockhouse, The SW19 ....3E 134
Clockhouse Av. IG11: Bark 1G 89
Clockhouse Cl. SW19 ....2E 134
Clockhouse Ct. BR3: Beck 2A 158
CLOCKHOUSE JUNC. 5E 32
Clockhouse La.
RM5: Col R 1H 55
TW14: Bedf 4C 128
TW15: Ashf 4C 128
Clock Ho. Pde. E11 ....6K 51
Clockhouse Pde. N13 ....5F 33
Clockhouse Pl. SW15 ....6G 117
Clock Ho. Rd. BR3: Beck 3A 158
CLOCKHOUSE RDBT. 1D 128
Clock Mus., The 7D 8
Clock Pde. EN2: Enf 5J 23
Clock Pl. SE1 ....4B 102
(off Newington Butts)
Clock Twr. Ind. Est. TW7: Isle 3K 113
Clock Twr. M. N1 ....1C 84
SE28 ....7B 90
W7 ....1J 95
Clock Twr. Rd. TW7: Isle 3K 113
Cloister Cl. TW11: Tedd 5B 132
Cloister Gdns. HA8: Edg 5D 28
SE25 ....6H 157
Cloister Rd. NW2 ....3H 63
W3 ....5J 79
Cloisters, The 1E 18
Cloisters, The E1 ....4J 9
SW9 ....1A 120
TW7: Isle 3A 114
(off Pulteney Cl.)
Cloisters Av. BR2: Brom 5D 160
Cloisters Bus. Cen. SW8 ....7F 101
(off Battersea Pk. Rd.)
Cloisters Ct. DA7: Bex 3H 127
Cloisters Mall KT1: King T 2E 150
Clonard Way HA5: Hat E 6A 26
Clonbrock Rd. N16 ....4E 66
Cloncurry St. SW6 ....2F 117
Clonmel Cl. HA2: Harr 2H 59
Clonmell Rd. N17 ....3D 48
Clonmel Rd. SW6 ....7H 99
TW11: Tedd 4H 131
Clonmore St. SW18 ....1H 135
Cloonmore Av. BR6: Chels 4K 173
Clorane Gdns. NW3 ....3J 63
Close, The BR3: Beck 4A 158
BR5: Pet W 6J 161
CR4: Mitc 4D 154
DA5: Bexl 6G 127
DA14: Sidc 4B 144
E4 ....7K 35
EN4: E Barn 6J 21
HA0: Wemb 6E 60
HA3: Hrw W 2G 41
HA5: Eastc 7A 40
HA5: Pinn 7D 40
HA9: Wemb 3J 61
IG2: Ilf 6J 53
KT3: N Mald 2J 151
KT6: Surb 6E 150
N10 ....2F 47
N14 ....2C 32
N20 ....2C 30
RM6: Chad H 6E 54
SE3 ....2F 123
SE25 ....6G 157
SM3: Sutt 7H 153
SM5: Cars 7C 166
TW7: Isle 2H 113
TW9: Rich 3H 115
UB10: Hil 1C 74
Cloth Ct. EC1 ....6B 8
Cloth Fair EC1 ....6B 8 (5B 84)
Clothier St. E1 ....7H 9 (6E 84)
Cloth St. EC1 ....5C 8 (5C 84)
Clothworkers Rd. SE18 ....7H 107
Cloudesdale Rd. SW17 ....2F 137
Cloudesley Mans. N1 ....1A 84
(off Cloudesley Pl.)
Cloudesley Pl. N1 ....1A 84
Cloudesley Rd. DA7: Bex 1F 127
N1 ....1A 84
(not continuous)
Cloudesley Sq. N1 ....1A 84
Cloudesley St. N1 ....1A 84
Clouston Cl. SM6: Wall 5J 167
Clova Rd. E7 ....6H 69
Clove Cres. E14 ....7E 86
Clove Hitch Quay
SW11 ....3A 118
Clovelly Av. NW9 ....4B 44
UB10: Ick 4E 56
Clovelly Cl. HA5: Eastc 3K 39
UB10: Ick 4E 56
Clovelly Ct. NW2 ....5E 62
Clovelly Gdns. EN1: Enf 7K 23
RM7: Mawney 1H 55
SE19 ....1F 157
Clovelly Ho. W2 ....6A 82
(off Hallfield Est.)
Clovelly Rd. DA7: Bex 6E 108
N8 ....4H 47
TW3: Houn 2E 112
W4 ....2K 97
W5 ....2C 96
Clovelly Way BR6: St M Cry 6K 161
E1 ....6J 85
HA2: Harr 2D 58
Clover Cl. E11 ....2F 69
Cloverdale Ct. SM6: Wall 6F 167
Cloverdale Gdns. DA15: Sidc 6K 125
Clover M. SW3 ....7F 17 (6D 100)
Clover Way SM6: Wall 1E 166
Clove St. E13 ....4J 87
Clowders Rd. SE6 ....3B 140
Clowser Cl. SM1: Sutt 5A 166
Cloysters Grn. E1 ....1G 103
Cloyster Wood HA8: Edg 7J 27
Club Gdns. Rd. BR2: Hayes 7J 159
Club Row E1 ....3J 9 (4F 85)
E2 ....3J 9 (4F 85)
Clumps, The TW15: Ashf 4F 129
Clunbury Av. UB2: S'hall 5D 94
Clunbury St. N1 ....2D 84
Clunie Ho. SW1 ....1F 17
(off Pavillion Rd.)
Cluny Est. SE1 ....7G 15 (3E 102)
Cluny M. SW5 ....4J 99
Cluny Pl. SE1 ....7G 15 (3E 102)
Cluse Ct. N1 ....2C 84
(off St Peters St., not continuous)
Clutton St. E14 ....5D 86
Clydach Rd. EN1: Enf 4A 24
Clyde Cir. N15 ....4E 48
Clyde Ct. NW1 ....2H 83
(off Hampden Cl.)
Clyde Flats SW6 ....7H 99
(off Rhylston Rd.)
Clyde Ho. KT2: King T 1D 150
Clyde Pl. E10 ....7D 50
Clyde Rd. CR0: C'don 2F 169
N15 ....4E 48
N22 ....1H 47
SM1: Sutt 5J 165
SM6: Wall 6G 167
TW19: Stanw 1A 128
Clydesdale EN3: Pond E 4E 24
Clydesdale Av. HA7: Stan 3D 42
Clydesdale Cl. TW7: Isle 3K 113
Clydesdale Ct. N20 ....1G 31
Clydesdale Gdns. TW10: Rich 4H 115
Clydesdale Ho. DA18: Erith 2E 108
(off Kale Rd.)
W11 ....6H 81
(off Clydesdale Rd.)
Clydesdale Rd. W11 ....6H 81
Clyde St. SE8 ....6B 104
Clyde Ter. SE23 ....2J 139
Clyde Va. SE23 ....2J 139
Clyde Way RM1: Rom 1K 55
Clyde Wharf E16 ....1J 105
Clydon Cl. DA8: Erith 6K 109
Clyfford Rd. HA4: Ruis 4H 57
Clymping Dene TW14: Felt 7K 111
Clynes Ho. E2 ....3K 85
(off Knottisford St.)
RM10: Dag 3G 73
(off Uvedale Rd.)
Clyston St. SW8 ....2G 119
Coach & Horses Yd. W1 ....2K 11 (7G 83)
Coach Ho. La. N5 ....4B 66
SW19 ....4F 135
Coach Ho. M. SE1 ....7G 15
(off Long La.)
SE23 ....6K 121
SM2: Sutt 6K 165
Coachhouse M. SE20 ....7H 139
Coach Ho. Yd. NW3 ....4A 64
(off Heath St.)
SW18 ....4K 117
Coachmaker M. SW4 ....3J 119
(off Fenwick Pl.)
Coach Yd. M. N19 ....1J 65
Coaldale Wlk. SE21 ....7C 120
Coalecroft Rd. SW15 ....4E 116
Coal Port Cl. BR6: Chels 6K 173
Coalport Ho. SE11 ....2J 19
Coatbridge Ho. N1 ....7K 65
(off Carnoustie Dr.)
Coates Av. SW18 ....6C 118
Coates Cl. CR7: Thor H 3C 156
Coates Hill Rd. BR1: Brom 2E 160
Coate St. E2 ....2G 85
Coates Wlk. TW8: Bford 6E 96
Cobalt SE28 ....2A 108
Cobalt Sq. SW8 ....7G 19
Cobbett Rd. SE9 ....3C 124
TW2: Whitt 1E 130
Cobbetts Av. IG4: Ilf 5B 52
Cobbett St. SW8 ....7K 101
Cobble La. N1 ....7B 66
Cobble M. N5 ....3C 66
Cobblers Wlk. KT1: Ham W 1A 150
KT8: E Mos 1A 150
TW11: Tedd 1A 150
TW12: Hamp, Tedd 1G 149
(not continuous)
Cobblestone Pl. CR0: C'don 1C 168
Cobbold Ct. SW1 ....3C 18
(off Elverton St.)
Cobbold Ind. Est. NW10 ....6B 62
Cobbold M. W12 ....2B 98
Cobbold Rd. E11 ....3H 69
NW10 ....6B 62
W12 ....2A 98
Cobb's Ct. EC4 ....1B 14
Cobb's Hall SW6 ....6F 99
(off Fulham Pal. Rd.)
Cobb's Rd. TW4: Houn 4D 112
Cobbsthorpe Vs. SE26 ....4K 139
Cobb St. E1 ....6J 9 (5F 85)
Cobden Bldgs. WC1 ....1G 7
(off Weston Rd.)
Cobden Ct. BR2: Brom 4A 160
Cobden Ho. E2 ....3G 85
(off Nelson Gdns.)
NW1 ....2G 83
(off Arlington Rd.)
Cobden M. SE26 ....5H 139
Cobden Rd. BR6: Farnb 4H 173
E11 ....3G 69
SE25 ....5G 157
Cobham Av. KT3: N Mald 5C 152
Cobham Cl. BR2: Brom 7C 160
DA15: Sidc 6B 126
EN1: Enf 3B 24
HA8: Edg 2H 43
SM6: Wall 6J 167
SW11 ....6C 118
Cobham Ct. CR4: Mitc 2B 154
Cobham Ho. IG11: Bark 1G 89
(not continuous)
Cobham M. NW1 ....7H 65
Cobham Pl. DA6: Bex 5D 126
Cobham Rd. E17 ....1E 50
IG3: Ilf 2J 71
KT1: King T 2G 151
N22 ....3B 48
TW5: Hest 7A 94
Cobland Rd. SE12 ....4A 142
Coborn Rd. E3 ....2B 86
Coborn St. E3 ....3B 86
Cobourg Rd. SE5 ....6F 103
Cobourg St. NW1 ....2B 6 (3G 83)
Coburg Cl. SW1 ....3B 18 (4G 101)
Coburg Cres. SW2 ....1K 137
Coburg Dwellings E1 ....6J 85
(off Hardinge St.)
Coburg Gdns. IG5: Ilf 2B 52
Coburg Rd. N22 ....3K 47

Cochrane Cl. NW8 1B 4
Cochrane Ct. E10 1C 68
(off Leyton Grange Est.)
Cochrane Ho. E14 2C 104
(off Admirals Way)
Cochrane M. NW8 2B 82
Cochrane Rd. SW19 7G 135
Cochrane St. NW8 1B 4 (2B 82)
Cochrane Theatre 6F 7
(off Southampton Row)
Cockburn Ho. SW1 6D 18
(off Aylesford St.)
COCKCROW HILL 1D 162
Cockerell Rd. E17 7A 50
COCKFOSTERS 4K 21
Cockfosters Pde. EN4: Cockf 4K 21
Cockfosters Rd.
EN4: Cockf, Had W 1H 21
Cock Hill E1 6H 9 (5E 84)
Cock La. EC1 6A 8 (5B 84)
Cockpit Steps SW1 7C 12
Cockpit Theatre 4C 4
(off Gateforth St.)
Cockpit Yd. WC1 5H 7 (5K 83)
Cocks Cres. KT3: N Mald 4B 152
Cocksett Av. BR6: Chels 6J 173
Cockspur Ct. SW1 4D 12 (1H 101)
Cockspur St. SW1 4D 12 (1H 101)
Cocksure La. DA14: Sidc 3G 145
Coda Cen., The SW6 7G 99
Code St. E1 4K 9 (4F 85)
Codicote Ho. SE8 4K 103
(off Chilton Gro.)
Codicote Ter. N4 2C 66
Codling Cl. E1 1G 103
Codling Way HA0: Wemb 4D 60
Codrington Ct. E1 4H 85
SE16 7A 86
Codrington Hill SE23 7A 122
Codrington M. W11 6G 81
Cody Cl. HA3: Kent 3D 42
SM6: Wall 7H 167
Cody Rd. E16 4F 87
Coe Av. SE25 6G 157
Coe's All. EN5: Barn 4B 20
Coffey St. SE8 7C 104
Cogan Av. E17 1A 50
Coin St. SE1 4J 13 (1A 102)
(not continuous)
Coity Rd. NW5 6E 64
Cokers La. SE21 1D 138
Coke St. E1 6G 85
Colas M. NW6 1J 81
Colbalt Cl. BR3: Beck 4K 157
Colbeck M. SW7 4K 99
Colbeck Rd. HA1: Harr 7G 41
Colberg Pl. N16 7F 49
Colborne Ho. E14 7C 86
(off E. India Dock Rd.)
Colborne Way KT4: Wor Pk 3E 164
Colbrook Av. UB3: Harl 3F 93
Colbrook Cl. UB3: Harl 3F 93
Colburn Way SM1: Sutt 3B 166
Colby M. SE19 5E 138
Colby Rd. KT12: Walt T 7J 147
SE19 5E 138
Colchester Av. E12 4D 70
Colchester Dr. HA5: Pinn 5B 40
Colchester Rd. E10 7E 50
E17 6C 50
HA6: Nwood 2J 39
HA8: Edg 7D 28
Colchester St. E1 7K 9 (6F 85)
Coldbath Sq. EC1 3J 7 (4A 84)
Coldbath St. SE13 1D 122
COLDBLOW 1J 145
Cold Blow Cres. DA5: Bexl 1K 145
Cold Blow La. SE14 7K 103
(not continuous)
Cold Blows CR4: Mitc 3D 154
Coldershaw Rd. W13 1A 96
Coldfall Av. N10 2E 46
Coldham Ct. N22 1B 48
Coldharbour E14 2E 104
Coldharbour Crest SE9 3E 142
Coldharbour Ind. Est. SE5 2C 120
Coldharbour La. SE5 3C 120
SW9 4A 120
UB3: Hayes 1J 93
Coldharbour Leisure Cen. 2D 142
Coldharbour Pl. SE5 2C 120
Coldharbour Rd. CR0: Wadd 5A 168
Coldharbour Way CR0: Wadd 5A 168
Coldstream Gdns. SW18 6H 117
Colebeck M. N1 6B 66
Colebert Av. E1 4J 85
Colebert Ho. E1 4J 85
(off Colebert Av.)
Colebrook Cl. NW7 6A 30
SW15 7F 117
Colebrook Ct. SW3 4D 16
(off Makins St.)
Colebrooke Av. W13 6B 78
Colebrooke Ct. DA14: Sidc 3B 144
Colebrooke Dr. E11 7A 52
Colebrooke Pl. N1 1B 84
Colebrooke Ri. BR2: Brom 2G 159
Colebrooke Row N1 2B 84
Colebrook Ho. E14 6D 86
(off Ellesmere St.)
Colebrook Rd. SW16 1J 155
Colebrook Way N11 5A 32
Coleby Path SE5 7D 102
Colechurch Ho. SE1 5G 103
(off Avondale Sq.)
Cole Cl. SE28 1B 108
Cole Ct. TW1: Twick 7A 114
Coledale Dr. HA7: Stan 1C 42
Coleford Rd. SW18 5A 118
Cole Gdns. TW5: Cran 7J 93
Colegrave Rd. E15 5F 69
Colegrove Rd. SE15 6F 103
Coleherne Ct. SW5 5K 99
Coleherne Mans. SW5 5K 99
(off Old Brompton Rd.)
Coleherne M. SW10 5K 99
Coleherne Rd. SW10 5K 99
Colehill Gdns. SW6 2G 117
Colehill La. SW6 1G 117
Cole Ho. SE1 7K 13
(off Baylis Rd.)
Coleman Cl. SE25 2G 157
Coleman Ct. SW18 7J 117
Coleman Flds. N1 1C 84
Coleman Mans. N8 7J 47
Coleman Rd. DA17: Belv 4G 109
RM9: Dag 6E 72
SE5 7E 102
Colemans Heath SE9 3E 142
Coleman St. EC2 7E 8 (6D 84)
Coleman St. Bldgs. EC2 7E 8
Colenso Dr. NW7 7H 29
Colenso Rd. E5 4J 67
IG2: Ilf 1J 71
COLE PARK 6A 114
Cole Pk. Gdns. TW1: Twick 5A 114
Cole Pk. Rd. TW1: Twick 6A 114
Cole Pk. Vw. TW1: Twick 6A 114
Colepits Wood Rd. SE9 5H 125
Coleraine Rd. N8 3A 48
SE3 6H 105
Coleridge Av. E12 6C 70
SM1: Sutt 4C 166
Coleridge Cl. SW8 2F 119
Coleridge Ct. EN5: New Bar 5E 20
(off Station Rd.)
SW1 3C 18
(off Fynes St.)
W14 3F 99
(off Blythe Rd.)
Coleridge Cres. SL3: Poyle 4A 174
Coleridge Gdns. NW6 7A 64
SW10 7K 99
Coleridge Ho. SE17 5C 102
(off Browning St.)
SW1 6B 18
(off Churchill Gdns.)
Coleridge La. N8 6J 47
Coleridge Rd. CR0: C'don 7J 157
E17 4B 50
N4 2A 66
N8 6H 47
N12 5F 31
TW15: Ashf 4A 128
Coleridge Sq. SW10 7A 100
(off Coleridge Gdns.)
W13 6A 78
Coleridge Wlk. NW11 4J 45
Coleridge Way UB4: Hayes 6J 75
UB7: W Dray 4A 92
Cole Rd. TW1: Twick 6A 114
Colesburg Rd. BR3: Beck 3B 158
Coles Cres. HA2: Harr 2F 59
Coles Grn. WD23: B Hea 1B 26
Coles Grn. Ct. NW2 2C 62
Coles Grn. Rd. NW2 1C 62
Coleshill Flats SW1 4H 17
Coleshill Rd. TW11: Tedd 6J 131
Colestown St. SW11 2C 118
Cole St. SE1 7D 14 (2C 102)
Colesworth Ho. HA8: Edg 2J 43
(off Burnt Oak B'way.)
Colet Cl. N13 6G 33
Colet Ct. W6 4F 99
(off Hammersmith Rd.)
Colet Flats E1 6A 86
(off Troon St.)
Colet Gdns. W14 4F 99
Colet Ho. SE17 5B 102
(off Doddington Gro.)
Colette Ct. SE16 2K 103
(off Eleanor Cl.)
Coley St. WC1 4H 7 (4K 83)
Colfe & Hatcliffe Glebe SE13 5D 122
(off Lewisham High St.)
Colfe Rd. SE23 1A 140
Colfes Leisure Cen. 6J 123
Colham Av. UB7: Yiew 1A 92
COLHAM GREEN 5C 74
Colham Grn. Rd. UB8: Hil 5C 74
Colham Mill Rd. UB7: W Dray 2A 92
Colham Rd. UB8: Hil 4B 74
Colham Rdbt. UB8: Hil 6C 74
Colina M. N15 4B 48
Colina Rd. N15 5B 48
Colin Cl. BR4: W W'ck 3H 171
CR0: C'don 3B 170
NW9 4A 44
Colin Ct. SE6 7B 122
Colin Cres. NW9 4B 44
COLINDALE 3K 43
Colindale Av. NW9 3K 43
Colindale Bus. Pk. NW9 3J 43
Colindeep Gdns. NW4 4C 44
Colindeep La. NW4 3A 44
NW9 3A 44
Colin Dr. NW9 5B 44
Colinette Rd. SW15 4E 116
Colin Gdns. NW9 4B 44
Colin Pde. NW9 4A 44
Colin Pk. Rd. NW9 4A 44
Colin Pond Ct. RM6: Chad H 4D 54
Colin Rd. NW10 6C 62
Colinsdale N1 1B 84
(off Camden Wlk.)
Colinton Rd. IG3: Ilf 2B 72
Colin Winter Ho. E1 4J 85
(off Nicholas Rd.)
Coliseum Theatre 3E 12
(off St Martin's La.)
Coliston Pas. SW18 7J 117
(off Coliston Rd.)
Coliston Rd. SW18 7J 117
Collamore Av. SW18 1C 136
Collapit Cl. HA1: Harr 6F 41
Collard Pl. NW1 7F 65
Collards Almshouses E17 5E 50
(off Maynard Rd.)
Collection Pl. NW8 1K 81
(off Bolton Pl.)
College App. SE10 6E 104
College Av. HA3: Hrw W 1J 41
College Cl. E9 5J 67
HA3: Hrw W 7D 26
N18 5A 34
TW2: Twick 1H 131
College Ct. EN3: Pond E 5D 24
NW3 6B 64
(off College Cres.)
SW3 6F 17
W5 7E 78
W6 5E 98
(off Queen Caroline St.)
College Cres. NW3 6A 64
College Cross N1 7A 66
College Dr. HA4: Ruis 7J 39
KT7: T Ditt 7J 149
College E. E1 6K 9 (5F 85)
College Flds. Bus. Cen. SW19 1C 154
College Gdns. E4 7J 25
EN2: Enf 1J 23
IG4: Ilf 5C 52
KT3: N Mald 5B 152
N18 5A 34
SE21 1E 138
SW17 2C 136
(not continuous)
College Grn. SE19 7E 138
College Gro. NW1 1G 83
College Hill EC4 2D 14 (7C 84)
College Hill Rd. HA3: Hrw W 7D 26
College La. NW5 4F 65
College Mans. NW6 1G 81
(off Winchester Av.)
College M. N1 7A 66
(off College Cross, not continuous)
SW1 1E 18
SW18 5K 117
College of Arms 2C 14
College Pde. NW6 1G 81
COLLEGE PARK 3D 80
College Pk. Cl. SE13 4F 123
College Pk. Rd. N17 6A 34
College Pl. E17 4G 51
NW1 1G 83
SW10 7A 100
College Point E15 6H 69
College Rd. BR1: Brom 1J 159
BR8: Hext 7K 145
CR0: C'don 2D 168
E17 5E 50
EN2: Enf 2J 23
HA1: Harr 6J 41
HA3: Hrw W 1J 41
HA9: Wemb 1D 60
N17 6A 34
N21 2F 33
NW10 2E 80
SE19 5F 139
SE21 7E 120
SW19 6B 136
TW7: Isle 1K 113
W13 6B 78
College Rdbt. KT1: King T 3E 150
College Row E9 5K 67
College Slip BR1: Brom 1J 159
College St. EC4 2D 14 (7C 84)
College Ter. E3 3B 86
N3 2H 45
College Vw. SE9 1B 142

College Wlk. KT1: King T . . . 3E 150
College Way TW15: Ashf . . . 4B 128
UB3: Hayes . . . 7J 75
College Yd. NW5 . . . 4F 65
Collent St. E9 . . . 6J 67
Collerston Ho. *SE10* . . . *5H 105*
(off Armitage Rd.)
Colless Rd. N15 . . . 5F 49
Collett Rd. SE16 . . . 3G 103
Collett Way UB2: S'hall . . . 2F 95
Collier Cl. E6 . . . 7F 89
KT19: Ewe . . . 6G 163
Collier Dr. HA8: Edg . . . 2G 43
COLLIER ROW . . . 1H 55
Collier Row La. RM5: Col R . . . 1H 55
Collier Row Rd. RM5: Col R . . . 1F 55
Colliers Ct. *CR0: C'don* . . . *4D 168*
(off St Peter's Rd.)
Colliers Shaw BR2: Kes . . . 5B 172
Collier St. N1 . . . 2K 83
Colliers Water La. CR7: Thor H . . . 5A 156
COLLIERS WOOD . . . 7B 136
COLLIERS WOOD . . . 7B 136
Colliers Wood SW19 . . . 6B 136
Collindale Av. DA8: Erith . . . 7H 109
DA15: Sidc . . . 1A 144
Collingbourne Rd. W12 . . . 1D 98
Collingham Gdns. SW5 . . . 4K 99
Collingham Pl. SW5 . . . 4K 99
Collingham Rd. SW5 . . . 4K 99
Collings Cl. N22 . . . 6E 32
Collington St. SE10 . . . 5F 105
Collingtree Rd. SE26 . . . 4J 139
Collingwood Av. KT5: Surb . . . 1J 163
N10 . . . 3E 46
Collingwood Cl. SE20 . . . 1H 157
TW2: Whitt . . . 7E 112
Collingwood Ct. EN5: New Bar . . . 5E 20
W5 . . . 5F 79
Collingwood Ho. *E1* . . . *4H 85*
(off Darling Row)
SE16 . . . *2H 103*
(off Cherry Gdn. St.)
SW1 . . . *6C 18*
(off Dolphin Sq.)
W1 . . . *5A 6*
(off Clipstone St.)
Collingwood Rd. CR4: Mitc . . . 3C 154
E17 . . . 6C 50
N15 . . . 4E 48
SM1: Sutt . . . 3J 165
UB8: Hil . . . 4D 74
Collingwood St. E1 . . . 4H 85
Collins Av. HA7: Stan . . . 2E 42
Collins Ct. E8 . . . 6G 67
Collins Dr. HA4: Ruis . . . 2A 58
Collins Ho. *E14* . . . *7E 86*
(off Newby Pl.)
E15 . . . *1H 87*
(off John St.)
SE10 . . . *5H 105*
(off Armitage Rd.)
Collinson Ct. *SE1* . . . *7C 14*
(off Gt. Suffolk St.)
Collinson Ho. *SE15* . . . *7G 103*
(off Peckham Pk. Rd.)
Collinson St. SE1 . . . 7C 14 (2C 102)
Collinson Wlk. SE1 . . . 7C 14 (2C 102)
Collins Path TW12: Hamp . . . 6D 130
Collins Rd. N5 . . . 4C 66
Collins Sq. SE3 . . . 2H 123
Collins St. SE3 . . . 2G 123
(not continuous)
Collin's Yd. N1 . . . 1B 84
Collinwood Av. EN3: Enf H . . . 3D 24
Collinwood Gdns. IG5: Ilf . . . 5D 52
Collis All. TW2: Twick . . . 1J 131
Collison Pl. N16 . . . 1E 66
Coll's Rd. SE15 . . . 1J 121
Collyer Av. CR0: Bedd . . . 4J 167
Collyer Pl. SE15 . . . 1G 121
Collyer Rd. CR0: Bedd . . . 4J 167
Colman Ct. HA7: Stan . . . 6G 27
N12 . . . 6F 31
Colman Pde. EN1: Enf . . . 3K 23
Colman Rd. E16 . . . 5A 88
Colmans Wharf *E14* . . . *5D 86*
(off Morris Rd.)
Colmar Cl. E1 . . . 4K 85
Colmer Pl. HA3: Hrw W . . . 7C 26
Colmer Rd. SW16 . . . 1J 155
Colmore M. SE15 . . . 1H 121
Colmore Rd. EN3: Pond E . . . 4D 24
Colnbrook By-Pass SL3: Coln . . . 3A 174
UB7: Harm . . . 3A 174
Colnbrook Ct. SL3: Poyle . . . 4A 174
Colnbrook St. SE1 . . . 3B 102
Colne Ct. KT19: Ewe . . . 4J 163
W7 . . . *6H 77*
(off High La.)
Colnedale Rd. UB8: Uxb . . . 5A 56
Colne Ho. IG11: Bark . . . 7F 71
NW8 . . . *4B 4*
(off Penfold St.)
Colne Pk. Cvn. Site UB7: W Dray . . . 1D 174
Colne Reach TW19: Stan M . . . 7A 174
Colne Rd. E5 . . . 4A 68
N21 . . . 7J 23
TW1: Twick . . . 1J 131
TW2: Twick . . . 1J 131
Colne St. E13 . . . 3J 87
COLNEY HATCH . . . 6J 31
Colney Hatch La. N10 . . . 6J 31
N11 . . . 6J 31
Coln Trad. Est. SL3: Poyle . . . 4A 174
Cologne Rd. SW11 . . . 4B 118
Coloma Ct. BR4: W W'ck . . . 4G 171
Colombo Rd. IG1: Ilf . . . 1G 71
Colombo St. SE1 . . . 5A 14 (1B 102)
Colombo Street Sports & Community Cen.
. . . 5A 14
Colomb St. SE10 . . . 5G 105
Colonel's Wlk. EN2: Enf . . . 3G 23
Colonial Av. TW2: Whitt . . . 6G 113
Colonial Ct. N7 . . . 3K 65
Colonial Dr. W4 . . . 4J 97
Colonial Rd. TW14: Felt . . . 7G 111
Colonnade WC1 . . . 4F 7 (4J 83)
Colonnade, The SE8 . . . 4B 104
Colonnades, The CR0: Wadd . . . 6A 168
W2 . . . 6K 81
Colonnade Wlk. SW1 . . . 4J 17 (4F 101)
Colony M. *N1* . . . *5D 66*
(off Mildmay Gro. Nth.)
Colorado Apartments *N8* . . . *3K 47*
(off Gt. Amwell La.)
Colorado Bldg. *SE10* . . . *1D 122*
(off Deal's Gateway)
Colosseum Ter. NW1 . . . 2K 5
Colour Ct. SW1 . . . 5B 12
Colour Ho. *SE1* . . . *7H 15*
(off Bell Yd M.)
Colour House Theatre . . . 1A 154
Colroy Ct. NW11 . . . 5G 45
Colson Rd. CR0: C'don . . . 2E 168
Colson Way SW16 . . . 4G 137
Colstead Ho. *E1* . . . *6H 85*
(off Watney Mkt.)
Colsterworth Rd. N15 . . . 4F 49
(not continuous)
Colston Av. SM5: Cars . . . 4C 166
Colston Ct. SM5: Cars . . . 4D 166
Colston Rd. E7 . . . 6B 70
SW14 . . . 4J 115
Coltash Ct. *EC1* . . . *3D 8*
(off Whitecross St.)
Colthurst Cres. N4 . . . 2B 66
Colthurst Dr. N9 . . . 3C 34
Coltman Ho. *SE10* . . . *6E 104*
(off Welland St.)
Coltman St. E14 . . . 5A 86
Coltness Cres. SE2 . . . 5B 108
Colton Gdns. N17 . . . 3C 48
Colton Rd. HA1: Harr . . . 5J 41
Coltsfoot Dr. UB7: Yiew . . . 6A 74
Columbas Dr. NW3 . . . 1B 64
Columbia Av. HA4: Ruis . . . 1K 57
HA8: Edg . . . 1H 43
KT4: Wor Pk . . . 7B 152
Columbia Point *SE16* . . . *3J 103*
(off Surrey Quays Rd.)
Columbia Rd. E2 . . . 1J 9 (3F 85)
E13 . . . 4H 87
Columbia Road Flower Market
(Sundays only) . . . *1K 9*
(off Columbia Rd.)
Columbia Sq. SW14 . . . 4J 115
Columbia Wharf EN3: Pond E . . . 6F 25
Columbine Av. CR2: S Croy . . . 7B 168
E6 . . . 5C 88
Columbine Way SE13 . . . 2E 122
Columbus Ct. *SE16* . . . *1J 103*
(off Rotherhithe St.)
Columbus Ct. Yd. E14 . . . 1C 104
Columbus Gdns. HA6: Nwood . . . 1J 39
Colva Wlk. N19 . . . 2F 65
Colverson Ho. *E1* . . . *5J 85*
(off Lindley St.)
Colvestone Cres. E8 . . . 5F 67
Colview Ct. SE9 . . . 1B 142
Colville Est. N1 . . . 1E 84
Colville Est. W. E2 . . . 2K 9
Colville Gdns. W11 . . . 6H 81
(not continuous)
Colville Ho. *E2* . . . *2J 85*
(off Waterloo Gdns.)
Colville Ho's. W11 . . . 6H 81
Colville M. W11 . . . 6H 81
Colville Pl. W1 . . . 6B 6 (5G 83)
Colville Rd. E11 . . . 3E 68
E17 . . . 2A 50
N9 . . . 1C 34
W3 . . . 3H 97
W11 . . . 6H 81
Colville Sq. W11 . . . 6H 81
Colville Ter. W11 . . . 6H 81
Colvin Cl. SE26 . . . 5J 139
Colvin Gdns. E4 . . . 3K 35
E11 . . . 4K 51
IG6: Ilf . . . 1G 53
Colvin Rd. CR7: Thor H . . . 5A 156
E6 . . . 7C 70
Colwall Gdns. IG8: Wfd G . . . 5D 36
Colwell Rd. SE22 . . . 5F 121
Colwick Cl. N6 . . . 7H 47
Colwith Rd. W6 . . . 6E 98
Colwood Gdns. SW19 . . . 7B 136
Colworth Gro. SE17 . . . 4C 102
Colworth Rd. CR0: C'don . . . 1G 169
E11 . . . 6G 51
Colwyn Av. UB6: G'frd . . . 2K 77
Colwyn Cl. SW16 . . . 5G 137
Colwyn Cres. TW3: Houn . . . 1G 113
Colwyn Grn. *NW9* . . . *6A 44*
(off Snowdon Dr.)
Colwyn Ho. SE1 . . . 2J 19 (3A 102)
Colwyn Rd. NW2 . . . 3D 62
Colyer Cl. N1 . . . 2K 83
SE9 . . . 2F 143
Colyers Cl. DA8: Erith . . . 1K 127
Colyers La. DA8: Erith . . . 1J 127
Colyers Wlk. DA8: Erith . . . 1K 127
Colyton Cl. DA16: Well . . . 1D 126
HA0: Wemb . . . 6C 60
Colyton La. SW16 . . . 5A 138
Colyton Rd. SE22 . . . 5H 121
Colyton Way N18 . . . 5B 34
Combe, The NW1 . . . 2K 5 (3F 83)
Combe Av. SE3 . . . 7H 105
Combedale Rd. SE10 . . . 5J 105
Combe Dene *BR2: Brom* . . . *4H 159*
(off Cumberland Rd.)
Combe Ho. *W2* . . . *5J 81*
(off Gt. Western Rd.)
Combemartin Rd. SW18 . . . 7G 117
Combe M. SE3 . . . 7H 105
Comber Cl. NW2 . . . 3D 62
Comber Gro. SE5 . . . 7C 102
Comber Ho. SE5 . . . 7C 102
Combermere Rd. SM4: Mord . . . 6K 153
SW9 . . . 3K 119
Comberton *KT1: King T* . . . *2G 151*
(off Eureka Rd.)
Comberton Rd. E5 . . . 2H 67
Combeside SE18 . . . 7K 107
Combwell Cres. SE2 . . . 3A 108
Comedy Store . . . *3C 12*
(off Oxendon St.)
Comedy Theatre . . . *3C 12*
(off Panton St.)
Comely Bank Rd. E17 . . . 5E 50
Comeragh M. W14 . . . 5G 99
Comeragh Rd. W14 . . . 5G 99
Comer Cres. *UB2: S'hall* . . . *1G 95*
(off Windmill Av.)
Comerell Pl. SE10 . . . 5H 105
Comerford Rd. SE4 . . . 4A 122
Comer Ho. EN5: New Bar . . . 4F 21
Comet Cl. E12 . . . 4B 70
Comet Pl. SE8 . . . 7C 104
(not continuous)
Comet Rd. TW19: Stanw . . . 7A 110
Comet St. SE8 . . . 7C 104
Comfort St. SE15 . . . 6E 102
Commerce Pk. CR0: Wadd . . . 2K 167
Commerce Rd. N22 . . . 1K 47
TW8: Bford . . . 6C 96
Commerce Way CR0: Wadd . . . 2K 167
Commercial Dock Path *SE16* . . . *3B 104*
(off Gulliver St.)
Commercial Rd. E1 . . . 7K 9 (6G 85)
E14 . . . 6G 85
N18 . . . 5K 33
Commercial Rd. Ind. Est.
N18 . . . 6A 34
Commercial St. E1 . . . 4J 9 (4F 85)
Commercial Way NW10 . . . 2H 79
SE10 . . . 4H 105
SE15 . . . 7F 103
Commerell St. SE10 . . . 5G 105
Commodity Quay
E1 . . . 3K 15 (7F 85)
Commodore Ct. *SE8* . . . *1C 122*
(off Albyn Rd.)
Commodore Ho. *E14* . . . *7E 86*
(off Poplar High St.)
SW18 . . . 3A 118
Commodore Sq. SW10 . . . 1A 118
Commodore St. E1 . . . 4A 86
Common, The E15 . . . 6G 69
HA7: Stan . . . 2D 26
UB2: S'hall . . . 4A 94
UB7: W Dray . . . 1D 174
W5 . . . 7E 78
(not continuous)
Commondale SW15 . . . 3E 116
Commonfield La. SW17 . . . 5C 136
Common La. KT10: Clay . . . 7A 162
Common Mile Cl. SW4 . . . 5H 119
Common Rd. HA7: Stan . . . 4C 26
KT10: Clay . . . 6A 162
SW13 . . . 3D 116
Commonside BR2: Kes . . . 4A 172
Commonside E. CR4: Mitc . . . 3E 154
(not continuous)
Commonside W. CR4: Mitc . . . 3D 154
Commonwealth Av. UB3: Hayes . . . 6F 75
W12 . . . 7D 80
(not continuous)
Commonwealth Conference Cen. . . . 5B 12

Commonwealth Hall WC1 3J 83
(off Cartwright Gdns.)
Commonwealth Institute 3H 99
Commonwealth Rd. N17 7B 34
Commonwealth Way SE2 5B 108
Community Cl. TW5: Cran 1K 111
UB10: Ick 3D 56
Community La. N7 5H 65
Community Rd. E15 5F 69
UB6: G'frd 1G 77
Como Rd. SE23 2A 140
Como St. RM7: Rom 5K 55
Compass Cl. HA8: Edg 4A 28
TW15: Ashf 7E 128
Compass Ct. SE1 5J 15
(off Shad Thames)
Compass Hill TW10: Rich 6D 114
Compass Ho. SW18 4K 117
Compass La. BR1: Brom 1J 159
(off North St.)
Compass Point E14 7B 86
(off Grenade St.)
Compass Theatre & Arts Cen. 3E 56
Compayne Gdns. NW6 7K 63
Compayne Mans. NW6 6K 63
(off Fairhazel Gdns.)
Compter Pas. EC2 1D 14
Compton Av. E6 2B 88
HA0: Wemb 4C 60
N1 6B 66
N6 7C 46
Compton Cl. E3 5C 86
HA8: Edg 7D 28
NW1 2K 5
NW11 3F 63
SE15 7G 103
W13 6A 78
Compton Ct. SE19 6E 138
SM1: Sutt 4A 166
Compton Cres. KT9: Chess 5E 162
N17 7H 33
UB5: N'olt 1B 76
W4 6J 97
Compton Ho. SW11 1C 118
Compton Leisure Cen., The 1C 76
Compton Pas. EC1 3B 8 (4B 84)
Compton Pl. WC1 3E 6 (4J 83)
Compton Ri. HA5: Pinn 5C 40
Compton Rd. CR0: C'don 1H 169
N1 6B 66
N21 1F 33
NW10 3F 81
SW19 6H 135
UB3: Hayes 7G 75
Compton Sports Cen. 6H 31
Compton St. EC1 3A 8 (4B 84)
Compton Ter. N1 6B 66
N21 1F 33
Comreddy Cl. EN2: Enf 1G 23
Comus Ho. SE17 4E 102
(off Comus Pl.)
Comus Pl. SE17 4E 102
Comyn Rd. SW11 4C 118
Comyns, The WD23: B Hea 1B 26
Comyns Cl. E16 5H 87
Comyns Rd. RM9: Dag 7G 73
Conant Ho. SE11 7K 19
(off St Agnes Pl.)
Conant M. E1 7G 85
Concanon Rd. SW2 4K 119
Concert Hall App. SE1 5H 13 (1K 101)
Concord Bus. Cen.
W3 4H 79
Concord Cl. UB5: N'olt 3B 76
Concord Ct. KT1: King T 3F 151
(off Winery La.)
Concorde Cl. TW3: Houn 2F 113
UB10: Uxb 2A 74
Concorde Dr. E6 5D 88
Concorde Way SE16 4K 103
Concord Ho. KT3: N Mald 3A 152
N17 7A 34
(off Park La.)
Concordia Wharf E14 1E 104
(off Coldharbour)
Concord Rd. EN3: Pond E 5D 24
W3 4H 79
Concord Ter. HA2: Harr 2F 59
(off Coles Cres.)
Concourse, The N9 2B 34
(in Edmonton Grn. Shop. Cen.)
NW9 1A 44
Condell Rd. SW8 1G 119
Conder St. E14 6A 86
Condor Path UB5: N'olt 2E 76
(off Union Rd.)
Condover Cres. SE18 7F 107
Condray Pl. SW11 7C 100
Conduit Av. SE10 1F 123
Conduit Ct. WC2 2E 12
Conduit La. CR0: C'don 5G 169
CR2: S Croy 5G 169
EN3: Pond E 6F 25
N18 5D 34
Conduit M. SE18 5F 107
W2 1A 10 (6B 82)
Conduit Pas. W2 1A 10
Conduit Pl. W2 1A 10 (6B 82)
Conduit Rd. SE18 5F 107
Conduit St. W1 2K 11 (7F 83)
Conduit Way NW10 7J 61
Conewood St. N5 3B 66
Coney Acre SE21 1C 138
Coney Burrows E4 2B 36
Coney Gro. UB8: Hil 3C 74
Coneygrove Path UB5: N'olt 6C 58
(off Arnold Rd.)
CONEY HALL 3G 171
Coney Hall Pde. BR4: W W'ck 3G 171
Coney Hill Rd. BR4: W W'ck 2G 171
Coney Way SW8 6K 101
Conference Cl. E4 2K 35
Conference Rd. SE2 4C 108
Congers Ho. SE8 7C 104
Congleton Gro. SE18 5G 107
Congo Dr. N9 3D 34
Congo Rd. SE18 5H 107
Congress Rd. SE2 4C 108
Congreve Ho. N16 5E 66
Congreve Rd. SE9 3D 124
Congreve St. SE17 4E 102
Congreve Wlk. E16 5B 88
(off Fulmer Rd.)
Conical Cnr. EN2: Enf 2H 23
Conifer Cl. BR6: Orp 4H 173
Conifer Ct. TW15: Ashf 5B 128
(off The Crescent)
Conifer Gdns. EN1: Enf 6K 23
SM1: Sutt 2K 165
SW16 3J 137
Conifer Ho. SE4 4B 122
(off Brockley Rd.)
Conifers Cl. TW11: Tedd 7B 132
Conifer Way HA0: Wemb 3C 60
UB3: Hayes 7J 75
Coniffe Ct. SE9 5F 125
Coniger Rd. SW6 2J 117
Coningham Ct. SW10 7A 100
(off King's Rd.)
Coningham M. W12 1C 98
Coningham Rd. W12 2D 98
Coningsby Av. NW9 2A 44
Coningsby Cotts. W5 2D 96
Coningsby Ct. CR4: Mitc 2E 154
Coningsby Gdns. E4 6J 35
Coningsby Rd. CR2: S Croy 7C 168
N4 7B 48
W5 2D 96
Conington Rd. SE13 2D 122
Conisbee Ct. N14 5B 22
Conisborough Cres. SE6 3E 140
Conisbrough NW1 1G 83
(off Bayham St.)
Coniscliffe Cl. BR7: Chst 1E 160
Coniscliffe Rd. N13 3H 33
Coniston NW1 1A 6
(off Harrington St.)
Coniston Av. DA16: Well 3J 125
IG11: Bark 7J 71
UB6: G'frd 3B 78
Coniston Cl. DA7: Bex 1J 127
DA8: Erith 7K 109
IG11: Bark 7J 71
N20 3F 31
SW13 7B 98
SW20 6F 153
W4 7J 97
Coniston Ct. NW7 7B 30
(off Langstone Way)
SE16 2K 103
(off Eleanor Cl.)
SM6: Wall 4F 167
TW15: Ashf 3A 128
W2 1D 10
(off Kendal St.)
Conistone Way N7 7J 65
Coniston Gdns. HA5: Eastc 4J 39
HA9: Wemb 1C 60
IG4: Ilf 4C 52
N9 1D 34
NW9 5K 43
SM2: Sutt 6B 166
Coniston Ho. E3 4B 86
(off Southern Gro.)
SE5 7C 102
(off Wyndham Rd.)
Coniston Rd. BR1: Brom 6G 141
CR0: C'don 7G 157
DA7: Bex 1J 127
N10 2F 47
N17 6B 34
TW2: Whitt 6F 113
Coniston Wlk. E9 5J 67
Coniston Way KT9: Chess 3E 162
Conlan St. W10 4G 81
Conley Rd. NW10 6A 62
Conley St. SE10 5G 105
Connaught Av. E4 7K 25 & 1A 36
EN1: Enf 2K 23
EN4: E Barn 1J 31
SW14 3J 115
TW4: Houn 4C 112
TW15: Ashf 4A 128
Connaught Bri. E16 1B 106
Connaught Bus. Cen.
CR0: Wadd 6K 167
CR4: Mitc 5D 154
NW9 5B 44
Connaught Cl. E10 2A 68
EN1: Enf 2K 23
SM1: Sutt 2B 166
UB8: Hil 4E 74
W2 1D 10
Connaught Ct. E17 4D 50
(off Orford Rd.)
W2 1E 10
(off Connaught Ct.)
Connaught Dr. NW11 4J 45
Connaught Gdns. N10 5F 47
N13 4G 33
SM4: Mord 4A 154
Connaught Hall WC1 4H 83
(off Gordon Sq.)
Connaught Hgts. UB10: Hil 4E 74
(off Uxbridge Rd.)
Connaught Ho. NW10 3D 80
(off Trenmar Gdns.)
W1 3J 11
(off Davies St.)
Connaught La. IG1: Ilf 2G 71
Connaught Lodge N4 7A 48
(off Connaught Rd.)
Connaught M. NW3 4C 64
SE11 3K 19
(off Walcot Sq.)
SE18 5E 106
SW6 1G 117
Connaught Pl. W2 2E 10 (7D 82)
Connaught Rd. E4 1B 36
E11 1F 69
E16 1B 106
E17 5C 50
EN5: Barn 6A 20
HA3: W'stone 1K 41
IG1: Ilf 2H 71
KT3: N Mald 4A 152
N4 7A 48
NW10 1A 80
SE18 5E 106
SM1: Sutt 2B 166
TW10: Rich 5F 115
TW11: Tedd 5H 131
W13 7B 78
Connaught Rdbt. E16 7B 88
(off Victoria Dock Rd.)
Connaught Sq. W2 1D 10 (6D 82)
Connaught St. W2 1D 10 (6C 82)
Connaught Way N13 4G 33
Connect La. IG6: Ilf 2G 53
Connell Ct. SE14 6K 103
(off Myers La.)
Connell Cres. W5 4F 79
Connington Cres. E4 3A 36
Connolly Ct. RM7: Rush G 6K 55
(off Union Rd.)
Connor Cl. E11 7G 51
IG6: Ilf 1G 53
Connor Ct. SW11 1F 119
Connor Rd. RM9: Dag 4F 73
Connor St. E9 1K 85
Conolly Dell W7 1J 95
(off Conolly Rd.)
Conolly Rd. W7 1J 95
Conrad Dr. KT4: Wor Pk 1E 164
Conrad Ho. E8 6G 67
E14 7A 86
(off Victory Pl.)
E16 1K 105
(off Wesley Av.)
N16 5E 66
(off Matthias Rd.)
SW8 7J 101
(off Wyvil Rd.)
Conrad Twr. W3 3H 97
Consfield Av. KT3: N Mald 4C 152
Consort Ct. W8 3K 99
(off Wright's La.)
Consort Ho. E14 5D 104
(off St Davids Sq.)
W2 7K 81
(off Queensway)
Consort Lodge NW8 1D 82
(off Prince Albert Rd.)
Consort M. TW7: Isle 5H 113
Consort Rd. SE15 1H 121
Cons St. SE1 6K 13 (2A 102)
Constable Av. E16 1K 105
Constable Cl. N11 5J 31
NW11 6K 45
UB4: Hayes 2E 74
Constable Ct. SE16 5H 103
(off Stubbs Dr.)
W4 5H 97
(off Chaseley Dr.)
Constable Cres. N15 5G 49
Constable Gdns. HA8: Edg 1G 43
TW7: Isle 5H 113
Constable Ho. NW3 7D 64
UB5: N'olt 2B 76
(off Gallery Gdns.)

Constable Ho's. *E14* 2C **104**
(*off Cassilis Rd.*)
Constable M. BR1: Brom 2K **159**
RM8: Dag 4B **72**
Constable Wlk. SE21 . . . . . 3E **138**
Constance Allen Ho. *W10* 6F **81**
(*off Bridge Cl.*)
Constance Cl. SW15 . . . . . 4K **133**
Constance Cres. BR2: Hayes 7H **159**
Constance Rd.
CR0: C'don 7B **156**
EN1: Enf 6K **23**
SM1: Sutt 4A **166**
TW2: Whitt 7F **113**
Constance St. E16 . . . . . 1C **106**
Constant Ho. *E14* 7D **86**
(*off Harrow La.*)
Constantine Ct. *E1* 6G **85**
(*off Fairclough St.*)
Constantine Pl. UB10: Hil 1B **74**
Constantine Rd. NW3 . . . . . 4C **64**
Constitution Hill SW1 . . . . . 6J **11** (2F **101**)
Constitution Ri. SE18 . . . . . 1E **124**
Consul Av. RM9: Dag, Rain 3J **91**
RM13: Rain 3J **91**
Content St. SE17 . . . . . 4D **102**
Contessa Cl. BR6: Farnb 5J **173**
Control Twr. Rd. TW6: H'row A 3C **110**
Convair Wlk. UB5: N'olt 3B **76**
Convent Cl. BR3: Beck 7E **140**
Convent Gdns. W5 . . . . . 4C **96**
W11 . . . . . 6G **81**
Convent Hill SE19 . . . . . 6C **138**
Convent Lodge TW15: Ashf 5D **128**
Convent Rd. TW15: Ashf 5C **128**
Convent Way UB2: S'hall 4A **94**
Conway Cl. BR3: Beck 1A **158**
HA7: Stan 6F **27**
Conway Cres. RM6: Chad H 6C **54**
UB6: G'frd 2J **77**
Conway Dr. SM2: Sutt 6K **165**
TW15: Ashf 6E **128**
UB3: Harl 3E **92**
Conway Gdns. CR4: Mitc 4J **155**
EN2: Enf 1K **23**
HA9: Wemb 7C **42**
Conway Gro. W3 . . . . . 5K **79**
Conway Ho. *E14* 4C **104**
(*off Cahir St.*)
E17 . . . . . 5A **50**
(*off Mission Gro.*)
SW3 . . . . . 6F **17**
(*off Ormonde Ga.*)
Conway M. W1 . . . . . 4A **6**
Conway Rd. N14 . . . . . 3D **32**
N15 . . . . . 5B **48**
NW2 . . . . . 2E **62**
SE18 . . . . . 4H **107**
SW20 . . . . . 1E **152**
TW4: Houn 7D **112**
TW6: H'row A 3D **110**
TW13: Hanw 5B **130**
Conway St. W1 . . . . . 4A **6** (4G **83**)
(not continuous)
Conway Wlk. TW12: Hamp 6D **130**
Conybeare NW3 . . . . . 7C **64**
Conyers Cl. IG8: Wfd G 6B **36**
Conyer's Rd. SW16 . . . . . 5H **137**
Conyer St. E3 . . . . . 2A **86**
Cooden Cl. BR1: Brom 7K **141**
Cook Ct. *SE8* 5A **104**
(*off Evelyn St.*)
SE16 . . . . . 1J **103**
(*off Rotherhithe St.*)
Cookes Cl. E11 . . . . . 2H **69**
Cookes La. SM3: Cheam 6G **165**
Cooke St. IG11: Bark 1G **89**
Cookham Cl. UB2: S'hall 3F **95**
Cookham Cres. SE16 . . . . . 2K **103**
Cookham Dene Cl. BR7: Chst 1H **161**
Cookham Ho. *E2* 3J **9**
(*off Montclare St.*)
Cookham Rd. BR8: Swan 7G **145**
Cookhill Rd. SE2 . . . . . 2B **108**
Cook Rd. RM9: Dag 1E **90**
Cook's Cl. RM5: Col R 1J **55**
Cooks Hole Rd. EN2: Enf 1H **23**
Cookson Gro. DA8: Erith 7H **109**
Cooks Rd. E15 . . . . . 2D **86**
SE17 . . . . . 6B **102**
Coolfin Rd. E16 . . . . . 6J **87**
Coolgardie Av. E4 . . . . . 5A **36**
IG7: Chig 3K **37**
Coolgardie Rd. TW15: Ashf 5E **128**
Coolhurst Rd. N8 . . . . . 6H **47**
Cool Oak La. NW9 . . . . . 7A **44**
Coomassie Rd. W9 . . . . . 4H **81**
COOMBE 7K **133**
Coombe Av. CR0: C'don 4E **168**
Coombe Bank KT2: King T 1A **152**
Coombe Cl. HA8: Edg 2F **43**
TW3: Houn 4E **112**
Coombe Cnr. N21 . . . . . 1G **33**
Coombe Ct. *CR0: C'don* 4D **168**
(*off St Peter's Rd.*)
Coombe Cres. TW12: Hamp 7D **130**
Coombe Dr. HA4: Ruis 1K **57**
Coombe End KT2: King T 7K **133**
Coombefield Cl. KT3: N Mald 5A **152**
Coombe Gdns. KT3: N Mald 4B **152**
SW20 . . . . . 2C **152**
Coombe Hill Glade KT2: King T 7A **134**
Coombe Hill Rd. KT2: King T 7A **134**
Coombe Ho. E4 . . . . . 6G **35**
N7 . . . . . 5H **65**
Coombe Ho. Chase KT3: N Mald 1K **151**
Coombehurst Cl. EN4: Cockf 2J **21**
COOMBE LANE 1B **152**
Coombe La. CR0: C'don 5H **169**
SW20 . . . . . 1B **152**
Coombe La. Flyover SW20 . . . . . 1B **152**
Coombe La. W. KT2: King T 1H **151**
Coombe Lea BR1: Brom 3C **160**
Coombe Lodge SE7 . . . . . 6A **106**
Coombe Neville KT2: King T 7K **133**
Coombe Pk. KT2: King T 5J **133**
Coombe Pl. KT2: King T 5J **133**
Coomber Ho. *SW6* 3K **117**
(*off Wandsworth Bri. Rd.*)
Coombe Ridings KT2: King T 5J **133**
Coombe Ri. KT2: King T 1J **151**
Coombe Rd. CR0: C'don 4D **168**
KT2: King T 1G **151**
KT3: N Mald 2A **152**
N22 . . . . . 2A **48**
NW10 . . . . . 3K **61**
SE26 . . . . . 4H **139**
TW12: Hamp 6D **130**
W4 . . . . . 5A **98**
W13 . . . . . 3B **96**
Coomber Way CR0: Bedd 7H **155**
Coombes Rd. RM9: Dag 1F **91**
Coombe Wlk. SM1: Sutt 3K **165**
Coombewood Dr. RM6: Chad H 6F **55**
Coombe Wood Rd. KT2: King T 5J **133**
Coombrook Ct. *SE16* 2A **104**
(*off Elgar St.*)
Coombs St. N1 . . . . . 1B **8** (2B **84**)
Coomer M. SW6 . . . . . 6H **99**
Coomer Pl. SW6 . . . . . 6H **99**
Coomer Rd. SW6 . . . . . 6H **99**
Cooms Wlk. HA8: Edg 1J **43**
Coope Ct. *RM7: Rush G* 6K **55**
(*off Union Rd.*)
Cooperage, The *SE1* 6J **15**
(*off Gainsford St.*)
Cooperage Cl. N17 . . . . . 6A **34**
Co Operative Ho. SE15 . . . . . 3G **121**
Cooper Av. E17 . . . . . 1A **50**
Cooper Cl. SE1 . . . . . 7K **13** (2A **102**)
Cooper Ct. SE18 . . . . . 6F **107**
Cooper Cres. SM5: Cars 3D **166**
Cooper Ho. *NW8* 4A **4**
(*off Lyons Pl.*)
TW4: Houn 3D **112**
Cooper Rd. CR0: Wadd 4B **168**
NW4 . . . . . 6F **45**
NW10 . . . . . 5C **62**
Coopersale Cl. IG8: Wfd G 7F **37**
Coopersale Rd. E9 . . . . . 5K **67**
Coopers Cl. E1 . . . . . 4J **85**
RM10: Dag 6H **73**
Coopers Ct. *E3* 4B **86**
(*off Eric St.*)
TW7: Isle 2K **113**
(*off Woodlands Rd.*)
W3 . . . . . 1J **97**
(*off Church Rd.*)
Coopers La. E10 . . . . . 1D **68**
NW1 . . . . . 2H **83**
(not continuous)
SE12 . . . . . 2K **141**
Coopers Lodge *SE1* 6J **15**
(*off Tooley St.*)
Coopers M. BR3: Beck 2C **158**
Cooper's Rd. SE1 . . . . . 5F **103**
Coopers Row EC3 . . . . . 2J **15** (7F **85**)
Cooper St. E16 . . . . . 5H **87**
Coopers Wlk. E15 . . . . . 5G **69**
Coopers Yd. *N1* 7B **66**
(*off Upper St.*)
SE19 . . . . . 6E **138**
Coote Gdns. RM8: Dag 3F **73**
Coote Rd. DA7: Bex 1F **127**
RM8: Dag 3F **73**
Cope Ho. EC1 . . . . . 2D **8**
Copeland Dr. E14 . . . . . 4C **104**
Copeland Ho. SE11 . . . . . 2H **19**
SW17 . . . . . 4B **136**
Copeland Rd. E17 . . . . . 6D **50**
SE15 . . . . . 2G **121**
Copeman Cl. SE26 . . . . . 5J **139**
Copenhagen Gdns. W4 . . . . . 2K **97**
Copenhagen Ho. *N1* 1K **83**
(*off Barnsbury Est.*)
Copenhagen Pl. E14 . . . . . 6B **86**
(not continuous)
Copenhagen St. N1 . . . . . 1J **83**
Cope Pl. W8 . . . . . 3J **99**
Copers Cope Rd. BR3: Beck 7B **140**
Cope St. SE16 . . . . . 4K **103**
Copford Cl. IG8: Wfd G 6H **37**
Copford Wlk. *N1* 1C **84**
(*off Popham St.*)
Copgate Path SW16 . . . . . 6K **137**
Copinger Wlk. HA8: Edg 1H **43**
Copland Av. HA0: Wemb 5D **60**
Copland Cl. HA0: Wemb 5C **60**
Copland Ho. UB1: S'hall 2D **94**
Copland M. HA0: Wemb 6E **60**
Copland Rd. HA0: Wemb 6E **60**
Copleston M. SE15 . . . . . 2F **121**
Copleston Pas. SE5 . . . . . 2F **121**
Copleston Rd. SE15 . . . . . 3F **121**
Copley Cl. SE17 . . . . . 6C **102**
W7 . . . . . 4K **77**
Copley Dene BR1: Brom 1B **160**
Copley Pk. SW16 . . . . . 6K **137**
Copley Rd. HA7: Stan 5H **27**
Copley St. E1 . . . . . 5K **85**
Coppard Gdns. KT9: Chess 6C **162**
Coppelia Rd. SE3 . . . . . 4H **123**
Coppen Rd. RM8: Dag 7F **55**
Copperas St. SE8 . . . . . 6D **104**
Copper Beech Cl. IG5: Ilf 1E **52**
Copperbeech Cl. NW3 . . . . . 5B **64**
Copper Beeches Ct. TW7: Isle 1H **113**
Copper Cl. N17 . . . . . 7C **34**
SE19 . . . . . 7F **139**
Copperdale Rd. UB3: Hayes 2J **93**
Copperfield Av. UB8: Hil 5C **74**
Copperfield Dr. N15 . . . . . 4F **49**
Copperfield Ho. *SE1* 7K **15**
(*off Wolseley St.*)
W1 . . . . . 5H **5**
(*off Marylebone High St.*)
W11 . . . . . 1F **99**
(*off St Ann's Rd.*)
Copperfield M. N18 . . . . . 4K **33**
Copperfield Rd. E3 . . . . . 4A **86**
SE28 . . . . . 6C **90**
Copperfields BR3: Beck 1E **158**
HA1: Harr 7J **41**
Copperfields Ct. W3 . . . . . 2G **97**
Copperfield St. SE1 . . . . . 6B **14** (2B **102**)
Copperfield Way
BR7: Chst 6G **143**
HA5: Pinn 4D **40**
Coppergate Cl. BR1: Brom 1K **159**
Coppermead Cl. NW2 . . . . . 3E **62**
Copper Mill Dr. TW7: Isle 2K **113**
Copper Mill La. SW17 . . . . . 4A **136**
Coppermill La. E17 . . . . . 6J **49**
Copper Row SE1 . . . . . 5J **15**
Copperworks, The *N1* 2J **83**
(*off Railway St.*)
Coppetts Cen. N12 . . . . . 7J **31**
Coppetts Cl. N12 . . . . . 7H **31**
Coppetts Rd. N10 . . . . . 7J **31**
Coppice, The DA5: Bexl 3K **145**
EN2: Enf 4G **23**
EN5: New Bar 6E **20**
(*off Great Nth. Rd.*)
TW15: Ashf 6D **128**
UB7: Yiew 6A **74**
Coppice Cl. BR3: Beck 4D **158**
HA4: Ruis 6F **39**
HA7: Stan 6E **26**
SW20 . . . . . 3E **152**
Coppice Dr. SW15 . . . . . 6D **116**
Coppice Wlk. N20 . . . . . 3D **30**
Coppice Way E18 . . . . . 4H **51**
Coppies Gro. N11 . . . . . 4A **32**
Copping Cl. CR0: C'don 4E **168**
Coppins, The CR0: New Ad 6D **170**
HA3: Hrw W 6D **26**
Coppock Cl. SW11 . . . . . 2C **118**
Coppsfield KT8: W Mole 3E **148**
Copse, The E4 . . . . . 1C **36**
N2 . . . . . 3D **46**
Copse Av. BR4: W W'ck 2D **170**
Copse Cl. HA6: Nwood 2E **38**
SE7 . . . . . 6K **105**
Copse Glade KT6: Surb 7D **150**
COPSE HILL 7D **134**
Copse Hill SM2: Sutt 7K **165**
SW20 . . . . . 1C **152**
Copse Vw. CR2: Sels 7K **169**
Copsewood Cl. DA15: Sidc 6J **125**
Copse Wood Way HA6: Nwood 1D **38**
Coptain Ho. SW18 . . . . . 4J **117**
Coptefield Dr. DA17: Belv 3D **108**
Copthall Av. EC2 . . . . . 7F **9** (6D **84**)
(not continuous)
Copthall Bldgs. EC2 . . . . . 7F **9**
Copthall Cl. EC2 . . . . . 7E **8** (6D **84**)
Copthall Dr. NW7 . . . . . 7H **29**
Copthall Gdns. NW7 . . . . . 7H **29**
TW1: Twick 1K **131**
Copthall Rd. E. UB10: Ick 2C **56**
Copthall Rd. W.
UB10: Ick 2C **56**
Copthall Swimming Pool 7J **29**
Copthorne Av. BR2: Brom 2D **172**
SW12 . . . . . 7H **119**
Copthorne Chase TW15: Ashf 4B **128**
Copthorne Cl. TW17: Shep 6E **146**
Copthorne M. UB3: Harl 4G **93**
Coptic St. WC1 . . . . . 6E **6** (5J **83**)
Copwood Cl. N12 . . . . . 4G **31**

Coral Apartments E16 7J 87 (off Western Gateway)
Coral Cl. RM6: Chad H 3D 54
Coral Ho. E1 4A 86 (off Harford St.)
Coraline Cl. UB1: S'hall 3D 76
Coralline Wlk. SE2 3C 108
Coral Row SW11 3A 118
Coral St. SE1 7K 13 (2A 102)
Coram Ho. W4 5A 98 (off Wood St.)
WC1 3E 6
Coram Mans. WC1 4K 83 (off Millman St.)
Coram St. WC1 4E 6 (4J 83)
Coran Cl. N9 7E 24
Corban Rd. TW3: Houn 3E 112
Corbar Cl. EN4: Had W 1G 21
Corbden Cl. SE15 1F 121
Corbet Cl. SM6: Wall 1E 166
Corbet Ct. EC3 1F 15 (6D 84)
Corbet Ho. N1 2A 84 (off Barnsbury Est.)
SE5 7C 102 (off Wyndham Rd.)
Corbet Pl. E1 5J 9 (5F 85)
Corbett Ct. SE26 4B 140
Corbett Gro. N22 7D 32
Corbett Ho. SW10 6A 100 (off Cathcart Rd.)
Corbett Rd. E11 6A 52
E17 3E 50
Corbetts La. SE16 4J 103 (not continuous)
Corbetts Pas. SE16 4J 103 (off Corbetts La.)
Corbetts Wharf SE16 2H 103 (off Bermondsey Wall E.)
Corbicum E11 7G 51
Corbidge Ct. SE8 6D 104 (off Glaisher St.)
Corbiere Ct. SW19 6F 135
Corbiere Ho. N1 1D 84 (off De Beauvoir Est.)
Corbins La. HA2: Harr 3F 59
Corbridge N17 7C 34
Corbridge Cres. E2 2H 85
Corby Cres. EN2: Enf 4D 22
Corbylands Rd. DA15: Sidc 7J 125
Corbyn St. N4 1J 65
Corby Rd. NW10 2K 79
Corby Way E3 4C 86
Cordelia Cl. SE24 4B 120
Cordelia Gdns. TW19: Stanw 7A 110
Cordelia Ho. N1 2E 84 (off Arden Est.)
Cordelia Rd. TW19: Stanw 7A 110
Cordelia St. E14 6D 86
Cordell Ho. N15 5F 49 (off Newton Rd.)
Cordingley Rd. HA4: Ruis 2F 57
Cording St. E14 5D 86
Cordwainers Ct. E9 7J 67 (off St Thomas's Sq.)
Cordwainers Wlk. E13 2J 87
Cord Way E14 3C 104
Cordwell Rd. SE13 5G 123
Corefield Cl. N11 2K 31
Corelli Ct. SW5 4J 99 (off W. Cromwell Rd.)
Corelli Rd. SE3 2C 124
Corfe Av. HA2: Harr 4E 58
Corfe Cl. TW4: Houn 1C 130
UB4: Yead 6A 76
Corfe Ho. SW8 7K 101 (off Dorset Rd.)
Corfe Twr. W3 2H 97
Corfield Rd. N21 5E 22
Corfield St. E2 3H 85
Corfton Lodge W5 5E 78
Corfton Rd. W5 6E 78
Coriander Av. E14 6F 87
Coriander Ct. SE1 6K 15 (off Gainsford St.)
Cories Cl. RM8: Dag 2D 72
Corinium Cl. HA9: Wemb 4F 61
Corinne Rd. N19 4G 65
Corinthian Manorway DA8: Erith 4K 109
Corinthian Rd. DA8: Erith 4K 109
Corinthian Way TW19: Stanw 7A 110
Corkers Path IG1: Ilf 2G 71
Corker Wlk. N7 2K 65
Corkran Rd. KT6: Surb 7D 150
Corkscrew Hill BR4: W W'ck 2E 170
Cork Sq. E1 1H 103
Cork St. W1 3A 12 (7G 83)
Cork St. M. W1 3A 12
Cork Tree Ho. SE27 5B 138 (off Lakeview Rd.)
Cork Tree Retail Pk. E4 5F 35
Cork Tree Way E4 5F 35
Corlett St. NW1 5C 4 (5C 82)
Cormont Rd. SE5 1B 120
Cormorant Cl. E17 7F 35
Cormorant Ct. SE8 6B 104 (off Pilot Cl.)
Cormorant Ho. EN3: Pond E 5E 24
Cormorant Lodge E1 1G 103 (off Thomas More St.)
Cormorant Pl. SM1: Sutt 5H 165
Cormorant Rd. E7 5H 69
Cornbury Ho. SE8 6B 104 (off Evelyn St.)
Cornbury Rd. HA8: Edg 7J 27
Cornel Ho. DA15: Sidc 3A 144
Cornelia Dr. UB4: Yead 4A 76
Cornelia Ho. TW1: Twick 6D 114 (off Denton Rd.)
Cornelia St. N7 6K 65
Cornell Bldg. E1 6G 85 (off Coke St.)
Cornell Cl. DA14: Sidc 6E 144
Cornell Ct. EN3: Enf H 3F 25
Cornell Ho. HA2: Harr 3D 58
Corner, The W5 1E 96
Cornercroft SM3: Cheam 5F 165 (off Wickham Av.)
Corner Fielde SW2 1K 137
Corner Grn. SE3 2J 123
Corner Ho. St. WC2 4E 12
Corner Mead NW9 7G 29
Cornerside TW15: Ashf 7E 128
Cornerstone Ho. CR0: C'don 7C 156
Corney Reach Way W4 7A 98
Corney Rd. W4 6A 98
Cornfield Cl. UB8: Uxb 2A 74
Cornflower La. CR0: C'don 1K 169
Cornflower Ter. SE22 6H 121
Cornford Cl. BR2: Brom 5J 159
Cornford Gro. SW12 2F 137
Cornhill EC3 1F 15 (6D 84)
Cornick Ho. SE16 3H 103 (off Slippers Pl.)
Cornish Ct. N9 7C 24
Cornish Gro. SE20 1H 157
Cornish Ho. SE17 6B 102 (off Brandon Est.)
TW8: Bford 5F 97
Corn Mill Dr. BR6: Orp 7K 161
Cornmill La. SE13 3E 122
Cornmow Dr. NW10 5B 62
Cornshaw Rd. RM8: Dag 1D 72
Cornthwaite Rd. E5 3J 67
Cornwall Av. DA16: Well 3J 125
E2 3J 85
KT10: Clay 7A 162
N3 7D 30
N22 1J 47
UB1: S'hall 5D 76
Cornwall Cl. IG11: Bark 6K 71
Cornwall Ct. HA5: Hat E 1D 40
W7 4K 77 (off Copley Cl.)
Cornwall Cres. W11 6G 81
Cornwall Dr. BR5: St P 7C 144
Cornwall Gdns. NW10 6D 62
SE25 4F 157
SW7 3K 99
Cornwall Gdns. Wlk. SW7 3K 99
Cornwall Gro. W4 5A 98
Cornwall Ho. SW7 3K 99 (off Cornwall Gdns.)
Cornwallis Av. N9 2C 34
SE9 2H 143
Cornwallis Ct. SW8 1J 119 (off Lansdowne Grn.)
Cornwallis Gro. N9 2C 34
Cornwallis Ho. SE16 2H 103 (off Cherry Gdn. St.)
W12 7D 80 (off India Way)
Cornwallis Rd. E17 4K 49
N9 2C 34
N19 2J 65
RM9: Dag 4D 72
SE18 3G 107
Cornwallis Sq. N19 2J 65
Cornwallis Wlk. SE9 3D 124
Cornwall Mans. SW10 7A 100 (off Cremorne Rd.)
W8 2K 99 (off Kensington Ct.)
W14 3F 99 (off Blythe Rd.)
Cornwall M. Sth. SW7 3A 100
Cornwall M. W. SW7 3K 99
Cornwall Rd. CR0: C'don 2B 168
HA1: Harr 6G 41
HA4: Ruis 3H 57
HA5: Hat E 1D 40
N4 7A 48
N15 5D 48
N18 5B 34
SE1 4J 13 (1A 102)
SM2: Sutt 7H 165
TW1: Twick 7A 114
UB8: Uxb 6A 56
Cornwall Sq. SE11 5K 19
Cornwall St. E1 7H 85
Cornwall Ter. NW1 4F 5 (4D 82)
Cornwall Ter. M. NW1 4F 5
Corn Way E11 3F 69
Cornwell Cres. E7 4A 70
Cornwood Cl. N2 5B 46
Cornwood Dr. E1 6J 85
Cornworthy Rd. RM8: Dag 5C 72
Corona Bldg. E14 1E 104 (off Blackwall Way)
Corona Rd. SE12 7J 123
Coronation Av. N16 4F 67
Coronation Cl. DA5: Bexl 6D 126
IG6: Ilf 4G 53
Coronation Ct. DA8: Erith 7K 109
E15 6H 69
KT1: King T 4E 150 (off Surbiton Rd.)
W10 5E 80 (off Brewster Gdns.)
Coronation Rd. E13 3A 88
NW10 4G 79
UB3: Harl 4H 93
Coronation Vs. NW10 4H 79
Coronation Wlk. TW2: Whitt 1E 130
Coroners' Court 1H 83 (off Camley St.)
Coronet Cinema 1J 99 (off Notting Hill Ga.)
Coronet Pde. HA0: Wemb 6E 60
Coronet St. N1 2G 9 (3E 84)
Coronet Theatre 3C 102 (off New Kent Rd.)
Corporate Dr. TW13: Felt 3K 129
Corporate Ho. HA3: Hrw W 1H 41
Corporation Av. TW4: Houn 4C 112
Corporation Row EC1 3K 7 (4A 84)
Corporation St. E15 2G 87
N7 5J 65
Corrance Rd. SW2 4J 119
Corri Av. N14 4C 32
Corrib Ct. N13 3E 32
Corrib Dr. SM1: Sutt 5C 166
Corrigan Cl. NW4 3E 44
Corringham Ct. NW11 7J 45
Corringham Ho. E1 6K 85 (off Pitsea St.)
Corringham Rd. HA9: Wemb 2G 61
NW11 7J 45
Corringway NW11 7K 45
W5 4G 79
Corris Grn. NW9 5A 44
Corry Dr. SW9 4B 120
Corry Ho. E14 7D 86 (off Wade's Pl.)
Corsair Cl. TW19: Stanw 7A 110
Corsair Rd. TW19: Stanw 7A 110
Corscombe Cl. KT2: King T 5J 133
Corsehill St. SW16 6G 137
Corsham St. N1 2F 9 (3D 84)
Corsica St. N5 6B 66
Corsley Way E9 6B 68 (off Osborne Rd.)
Cortayne Ct. TW2: Twick 2J 131
Cortayne Rd. SW6 2H 117
Cortis Rd. SW15 6D 116
Cortis Ter. SW15 6D 116
Corunna Rd. SW8 1G 119
Corunna Ter. SW8 1G 119
Corvette Sq. SE10 6F 105
Corwell Gdns. UB8: Hil 6E 74
Corwell La. UB8: Hil 6E 74 (not continuous)
Coryton Path W9 4H 81 (off Ashmore Rd.)
Cosbycote Av. SE24 5C 120
Cosdach Av. SM6: Wall 7H 167
Cosedge Cres. CR0: Wadd 5A 168
Cosgrove Cl. N21 2H 33
UB4: Yead 4C 76
Cosgrove Ho. E2 1G 85 (off Whiston Rd.)
Cosmo Pl. WC1 5F 7 (5J 83)
Cosmur Cl. W12 3B 98
Cossall Wlk. SE15 2H 121
Cossar M. SW2 5A 120
Cosser St. SE1 1J 19 (3A 102)
Costa St. SE15 2G 121
Costons Av. UB6: G'frd 3H 77
Costons La. UB6: G'frd 3H 77 (not continuous)
Coston Wlk. SE4 4K 121
Cosway Mans. NW1 5D 4 (off Shroton St.)
Cosway St. NW1 5D 4 (5C 82)
Cotall St. E14 5C 86
Coteford Cl. HA5: Eastc 5J 39
Coteford St. SW17 4D 136
Cotelands CR0: C'don 3E 168
Cotesbach Rd. E5 3J 67
Cotes Ho. NW8 4C 4 (off Broadley St.)
Cotesmore Gdns. RM8: Dag 4C 72
Cotford Rd. CR7: Thor H 4C 156
Cotham St. SE17 4C 102
Cotherstone Rd. SW2 1K 137
Cotleigh Av. DA5: Bexl 2D 144
Cotleigh Rd. NW6 7J 63
RM7: Rom 6K 55
Cotman Cl. NW11 6A 46
SW15 6F 117

Cotman Gdns. HA8: Edg 2G 43
Cotman Ho. *NW8* *2C 82*
(off Townshend Est.)
UB5: N'olt *2B 76*
(off Academy Gdns.)
Cotman M. *RM8: Dag* *5C 72*
(off Highgrove Rd.)
Cotmans Cl. UB3: Hayes 1J 93
Coton Rd. DA16: Well 3A 126
Cotsford Av. KT3: N Mald 5J 151
Cotswold Cl. DA7: Bex 2K 127
KT2: King T 6J 133
KT10: Hin W 2A 162
N11 4K 31
Cotswold Ct. EC1 3C 8
UB6: G'frd *2K 77*
(off Hodder Dr.)
Cotswold Gdns. E6 3B 88
IG2: Ilf 7H 53
NW2 2F 63
Cotswold Ga. NW2 1G 63
Cotswold Grn. EN2: Enf 4E 22
Cotswold M. SW11 1B 118
Cotswold Ri. BR6: St M Cry 6K 161
Cotswold Rd. TW12: Hamp 5E 130
Cotswold St. SE27 4B 138
Cotswold Way EN2: Enf 3E 22
KT4: Wor Pk 2E 164
Cottage Av. BR2: Brom 1C 172
Cottage Cl. *E1* *4J 85*
(off Hayfield Pas.)
HA2: Harr 2H 59
HA4: Ruis 1F 57
Cottage Fld. Cl. DA14: Sidc 1C 144
Cottage Grn. SE5 7D 102
Cottage Gro. KT6: Surb 6D 150
SW9 3J 119
Cottage Pl. SW3 1C 16 (3C 100)
Cottage Rd. KT19: Ewe 7K 163
N7 5K 65
Cottages, The UB10: Ick 2A 56
Cottage St. E14 7D 86
Cottage Wlk. N16 3F 67
Cottenham Dr. NW9 3B 44
SW20 7D 134
Cottenham Pde. SW20 2D 152
COTTENHAM PARK 1D 152
Cottenham Pk. Rd. SW20 1C 152
(not continuous)
Cottenham Pl. SW20 7D 134
Cottenham Rd. E17 4B 50
Cotterill Rd. KT6: Surb 2E 162
Cottesbrook St. SE14 7A 104
Cottesloe Ho. NW8 3C 4
Cottesloe M. *SE1* *1K 19*
(off Emery St.)
Cottesloe Theatre *4H 13*
(in National Theatre)
Cottesmore Av. IG5: Ilf 2E 52
Cottesmore Ct. *W8* *3K 99*
(off Stanford Rd.)
Cottesmore Gdns. W8 3K 99
Cottimore Av. KT12: Walt T 7K 147
Cottimore Cres. KT12: Walt T 7K 147
Cottimore La. KT12: Walt T 7K 147
(not continuous)
Cottimore Ter. KT12: Walt T 7K 147
Cottingham Chase HA4: Ruis 3J 57
Cottingham Rd. SE20 7K 139
SW8 7K 101
Cottington Rd. TW13: Hanw 4B 130
Cottington St. SE11 5K 19 (5A 102)
Cottle Way *SE16* *2H 103*
(off Paradise St.)
Cotton Av. W3 6K 79
Cotton Cl. E11 2G 69
RM9: Dag 7C 72
Cottongrass Cl. CR0: C'don 1K 169
Cotton Hill BR1: Brom 4E 140
Cotton Ho. SW2 7J 119
Cotton Row SW11 3A 118
Cottons App. RM7: Rom 5K 55
Cottons Cen. SE1 4G 15 (1E 102)
Cottons Ct. RM7: Rom 5K 55
Cotton's Gdns. E2 1H 9 (3E 84)
Cottons La. SE1 4F 15 (1D 102)
Cotton St. E14 7E 86
Cottrell Ct. *SE10* *4H 105*
(off Hop St.)
Cottrill Gdns. E8 6H 67
Cotts Cl. W7 5K 77
Couchmore Av. IG5: Ilf 2D 52
Coulgate St. SE4 3A 122
Coulson Cl. RM8: Dag 1C 72
Coulson St. SW3 5E 16 (5D 100)
Coulter Cl. UB4: Yead 4C 76
Coulter Rd. W6 3D 98
Coulthurst Ct. *SW16* *7J 137*
(off Heybridge Av.)
Councillor St. SE5 7C 102
Counter Ct. *SE1* *5E 14*
(off Borough High St.)
Counters Ct. *W14* *3G 99*
(off Holland Rd.)
Counter St. SE1 5G 15 (1E 102)
Countess Rd. NW5 5G 65
Countisbury Av. EN1: Enf 7A 24
Country Way TW13: Hanw 6K 129
County Ga. EN5: New Bar 6E 20
SE9 3G 143
County Gro. SE5 1C 120
County Hall Apartments SE1 6G 13
County Hall (Former) 7G 13 (2K 101)
County Pde. TW8: Bford 7D 96
County Rd. CR7: Thor H 2B 156
E6 5F 89
County St. SE1 3C 102
Coupland Pl. SE18 5G 107
Courcy Rd. N8 3A 48
Courier Rd. RM9: Dag 4J 91
Courland Gro. SW8 1H 119
Courland St. SW8 1H 119
Course, The SE9 3E 142
Court, The HA4: Ruis 4C 58
Courtauld Cl. SE28 1A 108
Courtauld Ho. *E2* *1G 85*
(off Goldsmiths Row)
Courtauld Institute of Art Gallery 2G 13
Courtauld Rd. N19 1J 65
Court Av. DA17: Belv 5F 109
Court Cl. HA3: Kent 3E 42
NW8 *7B 64*
(off Boydell Ct., not continuous)
SM6: Wall 7H 167
TW2: Twick 3F 131
Court Cl. Av. TW2: Twick 3F 131
Court Cres. KT9: Chess 5D 162
Court Downs Rd. BR3: Beck 2D 158
Court Dr. CR0: Wadd 4K 167
HA7: Stan 4K 27
SM1: Sutt 4C 166
UB10: Hil 1B 74
Courtenay Av. HA3: Hrw W 7B 26
N6 7C 46
SM2: Sutt 7J 165
Courtenay Dr. BR3: Beck 2F 159
Courtenay Gdns. HA3: Hrw W 2G 41
Courtenay M. E17 5A 50
Courtenay Pl. E17 5A 50
Courtenay Rd. E11 3H 69
E17 4K 49
HA9: Wemb 3D 60
KT4: Wor Pk 3E 164
SE20 6K 139
Courtenay Sq. SE11 6J 19 (5A 102)
Courtenay St. SE11 5J 19 (5A 102)
Courtens M. HA7: Stan 7H 27
Court Farm Av. KT19: Ewe 5K 163
Court Farm Ind. Est.
TW19: Stanw 6B 110
Court Farm La. UB5: N'olt 7E 58
Court Farm Rd. SE9 2B 142
UB5: N'olt 7E 58
Courtfield W5 5C 78
Courtfield Av. HA1: Harr 5K 41
Courtfield Cres. HA1: Harr 5K 41
Courtfield Gdns. HA4: Ruis 2H 57
SW5 4K 99
W13 6A 78
Courtfield Ho. *EC1* *5J 7*
(off Baldwins Gdns.)
Courtfield M. SW5 4A 100
Courtfield Ri. BR4: W W'ck 3F 171
Courtfield Rd. SW7 4A 100
TW15: Ashf 6D 128
Court Gdns. N7 6A 66
(not continuous)
Courtgate Cl. NW7 6G 29
Courthill Rd. SE13 4E 122
Courthope Ho. *SE16* *3J 103*
(off Lower Rd.)
SW8 *7J 101*
(off Hartington Rd.)
Courthope Rd. NW3 4D 64
SW19 5G 135
UB6: G'frd 2H 77
Courthope Vs. SW19 7G 135
Court Ho. Gdns. N3 6D 30
Courthouse La. E8 4F 67
Court House Rd. N12 6E 30
Courtland Av. E4 2C 36
IG1: Ilf 2D 70
NW7 3E 28
SW16 7K 137
Courtland Cl. IG8: Wfd G 1A 52
Courtland Gro. SE28 6D 90
Courtland Rd. E6 1C 88
Courtlands KT12: Walt T 7J 147
TW10: Rich 5G 115
Courtlands Av. BR2: Hayes 1G 171
SE12 5K 123
TW9: Kew 2H 115
TW12: Hamp 6D 130
Courtlands Cl. HA4: Ruis 7H 39
Courtlands Dr. KT19: Ewe 6A 164
Courtlands Rd.
KT5: Surb 7G 151
Court La. SE21 6E 120
Court La. Gdns. SE21 7E 120
Courtleet Dr. DA8: Erith 1H 127
Courtleigh NW11 5H 45
Courtleigh Gdns. NW11 4G 45
Court Lodge DA17: Belv 5G 109
SW1 *4G 17*
(off Sloane Sq.)
Courtman Rd. N17 7H 33
Court Mead UB5: N'olt 3D 76
Courtmead Cl. SE24 6C 120
Courtnell St. W2 6J 81
Courtney Cl. SE19 6E 138
Courtney Ct. N7 5A 66
Courtney Cres. SM5: Cars 7D 166
Courtney Ho. *NW4* *3E 44*
(off Mulberry Cl.)
W14 *3G 99*
(off Russell Rd.)
Courtney Pl. CR0: Wadd 3A 168
Courtney Rd. CR0: Wadd 3A 168
N7 5A 66
SW19 7C 136
TW6: H'row A 3C 110
Courtney Way TW6: H'row A 2C 110
Court Pde. HA0: Wemb 3B 60
(not continuous)
Courtrai Rd. SE23 6A 122
Court Rd. SE9 6D 124
SE25 2F 157
UB2: S'hall 4D 94
UB10: Ick 5D 56
Court Royal SW15 5G 117
Courtside N8 6H 47
SE26 3H 139
Court St. BR1: Brom 2J 159
E1 5H 85
Courtville Ho. *W10* *3G 81*
(off Third Av.)
Court Way IG6: Ilf 3G 53
IG8: Wfd G 5F 37
NW9 4A 44
TW2: Twick 7K 113
W3 5J 79
Court Wood La. CR0: Sels 7B 170
Court Yd. SE9 6D 124
Courtyard, The BR2: Kes 6C 172
EC3 *1F 15*
(in Royal Exchange)
N1 7K 65
NW1 7E 64
SW3 *7B 16*
(off Waldron M.)
Courtyard Ho. SW6 2A 118
Courtyard M. BR5: St P 7A 144
Courtyard Theatre 3E 84
Cousin La. EC4 3E 14 (7D 84)
Cousins Cl. UB7: Yiew 7A 74
Couthurst Rd. SE3 6K 105
Coutts Av. KT9: Chess 5E 162
Coutt's Cres. NW5 3E 64
Couzens Ho. *E3* *5B 86*
(off Weatherley Cl.)
Coval Gdns. SW14 4H 115
Coval La. SW14 4H 115
Coval Pas. SW14 4J 115
Coval Rd. SW14 4H 115
Covelees Wall E6 6E 88
Covell Ct. *EN2: Enf* *1E 22*
(off The Ridgeway)
SE8 7C 104
COVENT GARDEN 2F 13 (7J 83)
Covent Garden 2F 13 (7J 83)
Covent Gdn. WC2 2F 13 (7J 83)
Coventry Cl. E6 6D 88
NW6 2J 81
Coventry Cross E3 4E 86
Coventry Hall SW16 5J 137
Coventry Rd. E1 4H 85
E2 4H 85
IG1: Ilf 2F 71
SE25 4G 157
Coventry St. W1 3C 12 (7H 83)
Coverack Cl. CR0: C'don 7A 158
N14 6B 22
Coverdale Cl. HA7: Stan 5G 27
Coverdale Gdns.
CR0: C'don 3F 169
Coverdale Rd. N11 6K 31
NW2 7F 63
W12 2D 98
Coverdales, The IG11: Bark 2H 89
Coverley Cl. E1 5G 85
Coverley Point SE11 4G 19
Covert, The BR6: Pet W 6J 161
HA6: Nwood 1E 38
SE19 *7F 139*
(off Fox Hill)
Coverton Rd. SW17 5C 136
Covert Way EN4: Had W 2F 21
Covet Wood Cl.
BR5: St M Cry 6K 161
Covey Cl. SW19 2K 153
Covington Gdns. SW16 7B 138
Covington Way SW16 6K 137
(not continuous)
Cowan Cl. E6 5C 88
Cowan Ct. NW10 7K 61
Cowbridge La. IG11: Bark 7F 71
Cowbridge Rd. HA3: Kent 4F 43
Cowcross St. EC1 5A 8 (5B 84)
Cowdenbeath Path N1 1K 83
Cowden Rd. BR6: Orp 7K 161

Cowden St. SE6 . . . 4C 140
Cowdray Rd. UB10: Hil . . . 1E 74
Cowdrey Cl. EN1: Enf . . . 2K 23
Cowdrey Rd. SW19 . . . 5K 135
Cowen Av. HA2: Harr . . . 2H 59
Cowgate Rd. UB6: G'frd . . . 3H 77
Cowick Rd. SW17 . . . 4D 136
Cowings Mead UB5: N'olt . . . 6C 58
Cowland Av. EN3: Pond E . . . 4D 24
Cow La. UB6: G'frd . . . 2H 77
Cow Leaze E6 . . . 6E 88
Cowleaze Rd. KT2: King T . . . 1E 150
COWLEY . . . 4A 74
Cowley La. E11 . . . 3G 69
COWLEY PEACHEY . . . 6A 74
Cowley Pl. NW4 . . . 5E 44
Cowley Rd. E11 . . . 5K 51
IG1: Ilf . . . 7D 52
SW9 . . . 1A 120
(not continuous)
SW14 . . . 3A 116
W3 . . . 1B 98
Cowley St. SW1 . . . 1E 18 (3J 101)
Cowling Cl. W11 . . . 1G 99
Cowper Av. E6 . . . 7C 70
SM1: Sutt . . . 4B 166
Cowper Cl. BR2: Brom . . . 4B 160
DA16: Well . . . 5A 126
Cowper Gdns. N14 . . . 6A 22
SM6: Wall . . . 6G 167
Cowper Ho. *SE17* . . . *5C 102*
(off Browning St.)
SW1 . . . *6C 18*
(off Aylesford St.)
Cowper Rd. BR2: Brom . . . 4B 160
DA17: Belv . . . 4G 109
KT2: King T . . . 5F 133
N14 . . . 1A 32
N16 . . . 5E 66
N18 . . . 5B 34
SW19 . . . 6A 136
W3 . . . 1K 97
W7 . . . 7K 77
Cowper's Ct. *EC3* . . . *1F 15*
(off Birchin La.)
Cowper St. EC2 . . . 3F 9 (4D 84)
Cowper Ter. W10 . . . 5F 81
Cowslip Cl. UB10: Uxb . . . 7A 56
Cowslip Rd. E18 . . . 2K 51
Cowthorpe Rd. SW8 . . . 1H 119
Cox Ct. EN4: E Barn . . . 4H 21
Coxe Pl. HA3: W'stone . . . 4A 42
Cox Ho. *W6* . . . *6G 99*
(off Field Rd.)
Cox La. KT9: Chess . . . 4F 163
KT19: Ewe . . . 5H 163
(not continuous)
Coxmount Rd. SE7 . . . 5B 106
Coxs Av. TW17: Shep . . . 3G 147
Coxson Way SE1 . . . 7J 15 (2F 103)
Cox's Wlk. SE21 . . . 1G 139
Coxwell Rd. SE18 . . . 5H 107
SE19 . . . 7E 138
Coxwold Path KT9: Chess . . . 7E 162
Crabbs Cft. Cl. BR6: Farnb . . . 5G 173
Crab Hill BR3: Beck . . . 7F 141
Crabtree Av. HA0: Wemb . . . 2E 78
RM6: Chad H . . . 4D 54
Crabtree Cl. E2 . . . 2F 85
Crabtree Ct. EN5: New Bar . . . 4E 20
Crabtree Hall *SW6* . . . *7E 98*
(off Crabtree La.)
Crabtree La. SW6 . . . 7E 98
(not continuous)
Crabtree Manorway Nth.
DA17: Belv, Erith . . . 2J 109
Crabtree Manorway Sth. DA17: Belv . . . 3J 109
Crabtree Wlk. CR0: C'don . . . 1G 169
SE15 . . . *1F 121*
(off Peckham Rd.)
Crace St. NW1 . . . 1C 6 (3H 83)
Craddock Rd. EN1: Enf . . . 3A 24
Craddock St. NW5 . . . 6E 64
Cradley Rd. SE9 . . . 1H 143
Crafts Council & Gallery . . . 2A 84
Cragie Ho. *SE1* . . . *4F 103*
(off Balaclava Rd.)
Craig Dr. UB8: Hil . . . 6D 74
Craigen Av. CR0: C'don . . . 1H 169
Craigerne Rd. SE3 . . . 7K 105
Craig Gdns. E18 . . . 2H 51
Craigholm SE18 . . . 2E 124
Craig Ho. TW10: Ham . . . 4D 132
Craigmore Ct. HA6: Nwood . . . 1G 39
Craigmuir Pk. HA0: Wemb . . . 1F 79
Craignair Rd. SW2 . . . 7A 120
Craignish Av. SW16 . . . 2K 155
Craig Pk. Rd. N18 . . . 4C 34
Craig Rd. TW10: Ham . . . 4C 132
Craig's Ct. SW1 . . . 4E 12 (1J 101)
Craigton Rd. SE9 . . . 4D 124
Craigweil Cl. HA7: Stan . . . 5J 27
Craigweil Dr. HA7: Stan . . . 5J 27
Craigwell Av. TW13: Felt . . . 3J 129
Craik Ct. *NW6* . . . *2H 81*
(off Carlton Va.)
Crail Row SE17 . . . 4D 102
Crales Ho. SE18 . . . 3C 106
Cramer St. W1 . . . 6H 5 (5E 82)
Crammond Cl. W6 . . . 6G 99
Cramond Ct. TW14: Bedf . . . 1G 129
Cramonde Ct. DA16: Well . . . 2A 126
Crampton Ho. SW8 . . . 1G 119
Crampton Rd. SE20 . . . 6J 139
Crampton St. SE17 . . . 4C 102
Cranberry Cl. UB5: N'olt . . . 2B 76
Cranberry Ent. Pk.
N17 . . . *7A 34*
(off White Hart La.)
Cranberry La. E16 . . . 4G 87
Cranborne Av. KT6: Surb . . . 3G 163
UB2: S'hall . . . 4E 94
Cranborne Rd. IG11: Bark . . . 1H 89
Cranborne Waye UB4: Yead . . . 6K 75
(not continuous)
Cranbourn All. *WC2* . . . *2D 12*
(off Cranbourn St.)
Cranbourne *NW1* . . . *7H 65*
(off Agar Gro.)
Cranbourne Av. E11 . . . 4K 51
Cranbourne Cl. SW16 . . . 3J 155
Cranbourne Ct. *SW11* . . . *7C 100*
(off Albert Bri. Rd.)
Cranbourne Dr. HA5: Pinn . . . 5B 40
Cranbourne Gdns.
IG6: Ilf . . . 3G 53
NW11 . . . 5G 45
Cranbourne Pas. SE16 . . . 2H 103
Cranbourne Rd. E12 . . . 5C 70
E15 . . . 4E 68
HA6: Nwood . . . 3H 39
N10 . . . 2F 47
Cranbourn Ho. *SE16* . . . *2H 103*
(off Marigold St.)
Cranbourn St. WC2 . . . 2D 12 (7H 83)
CRANBROOK . . . 1D 70
Cranbrook *NW1* . . . *1G 83*
(off Camden St.)
Cranbrook Cl. BR2: Hayes . . . 6J 159
Cranbrook Ct. TW8: Bford . . . 6C 96
Cranbrook Dr. KT10: Esh . . . 7G 149
TW2: Whitt . . . 1F 131
Cranbrook Est. E2 . . . 2K 85
Cranbrook La. N11 . . . 4A 32
Cranbrook M. E17 . . . 5B 50
Cranbrook Pk. N22 . . . 1A 48
Cranbrook Ri. IG1: Ilf . . . 6D 52
Cranbrook Rd. CR7: Thor H . . . 2C 156
DA7: Bex . . . 1F 127
EN4: E Barn . . . 6G 21
Cranbrook Rd. IG1: Ilf . . . 7E 52
IG2: Ilf . . . 5E 52
IG6: Ilf . . . 5E 52
SE8 . . . 1C 122
SW19 . . . 7G 135
TW4: Houn . . . 4D 112
W4 . . . 5A 98
Cranbrook St. E2 . . . 2K 85
Cranbury Rd. SW6 . . . 2K 117
Crandley Ct. SE8 . . . 4A 104
Crane Av. TW7: Isle . . . 5A 114
W3 . . . 7J 79
Cranebank M. TW1: Twick . . . 4A 114
Cranebrook TW2: Twick . . . 2G 131
Crane Cl. HA2: Harr . . . 3G 59
RM10: Dag . . . 6G 73
Crane Ct. EC4 . . . 6A 84
KT19: Ewe . . . 4J 163
Craneford Cl. TW2: Twick . . . 7K 113
Craneford Way TW2: Twick . . . 7J 113
Crane Gdns. UB3: Harl . . . 4H 93
Crane Gro. N7 . . . 6A 66
Crane Ho. *E3* . . . *2A 86*
(off Roman Rd.)
SE15 . . . 1F 121
TW13: Hanw . . . 3E 130
Crane Lodge Rd. TW5: Cran . . . 6K 93
Crane Mead Ct. TW1: Twick . . . 7K 113
Crane Pk. Island Nature Reserve . . . 2D 130
Crane Pk. Rd. TW2: Whitt . . . 2F 131
Crane Rd. TW2: Twick . . . 1J 131
TW19: Stanw . . . 6C 110
Cranesbill Cl. NW9 . . . 3K 43
Cranes Dr. KT5: Surb . . . 4E 150
Cranes Pk. KT5: Surb . . . 4E 150
Cranes Pk. Av. KT5: Surb . . . 4E 150
Cranes Pk. Cres. KT5: Surb . . . 4F 151
Crane St. SE10 . . . 5F 105
SE15 . . . 1F 121
Craneswater UB3: Harl . . . 7H 93
Craneswater Pk.
UB2: S'hall . . . 5D 94
Crane Way TW2: Whitt . . . 7G 113
Cranfield Cl. SE27 . . . 3C 138
Cranfield Ct. W1 . . . 6D 4
Cranfield Dr. NW9 . . . 7F 29
Cranfield Ho. WC1 . . . 5E 6
Cranfield Rd. SE4 . . . 3B 122
Cranfield Rd. E. SM5: Cars . . . 7E 166
Cranfield Rd. W. SM5: Cars . . . 7D 166
Cranfield Row SE1 . . . 1K 19
CRANFORD . . . 1J 111
Cranford Av. N13 . . . 5D 32
TW19: Stanw . . . 7A 110
Cranford Cl. SW20 . . . 7D 134
TW19: Stanw . . . 7A 110
Cranford Community College Sports Cen.
. . . 6K 93
Cranford Cotts. *E1* . . . *7K 85*
(off Cranford St.)
Cranford Dr. UB3: Harl . . . 4H 93
Cranford La. TW5: Cran, Hest . . . 7K 93
TW6: H'row A . . . 1H 111
(Bath Rd., not continuous)
TW6: H'row A . . . 3H 111
(Elmdon Rd.)
UB3: Cran, Harl . . . 6F 93
Cranford Pk. Rd.
UB3: Harl . . . 4H 93
Cranford St. E1 . . . 7K 85
Cranford Way N8 . . . 4K 47
Cranhurst Rd. NW2 . . . 5E 62
Cranleigh *W11* . . . *1H 99*
(off Ladbroke Rd.)
Cranleigh Cl. BR6: Chels . . . 3K 173
DA5: Bexl . . . 6H 127
SE20 . . . 2H 157
Cranleigh Ct. CR4: Mitc . . . 3B 154
TW9: Rich . . . 3G 115
UB1: S'hall . . . 6D 76
Cranleigh Gdns. HA3: Kent . . . 5E 42
IG11: ark . . . 7H 71
KT2: King T . . . 6F 133
N21 . . . 5F 23
SE25 . . . 3E 156
SM1: Sutt . . . 2K 165
UB1: S'hall . . . 6D 76
Cranleigh Gdns. Ind. Est.
UB1: S'hall . . . 5D 76
Cranleigh Ho's. *NW1* . . . *2G 83*
(off Cranleigh St.)
Cranleigh M. SW11 . . . 2C 118
Cranleigh Rd. N15 . . . 5C 48
SW19 . . . 3J 153
TW13: Felt . . . 4H 129
Cranleigh St. NW1 . . . 2G 83
Cranley Dene Ct. N10 . . . 4F 47
Cranley Dr. HA4: Ruis . . . 2H 57
IG2: Ilf . . . 7G 53
CRANLEY GARDENS . . . 4F 47
Cranley Gdns. N10 . . . 4F 47
N13 . . . 3E 32
SM6: Wall . . . 7G 167
SW7 . . . 5A 16 (5A 100)
Cranley M. SW7 . . . 5A 16 (5A 100)
Cranley Pde. *SE9* . . . *4C 142*
(off Beaconsfield Rd.)
Cranley Pl. SW7 . . . 4A 16 (4B 100)
Cranley Rd. E13 . . . 5K 87
IG2: Ilf . . . 6G 53
Cranmer Av. W13 . . . 3B 96
Cranmer Cl. HA4: Ruis . . . 1B 58
HA7: Stan . . . 7H 27
SM4: Mord . . . 6F 153
Cranmer Ct. N3 . . . 2G 45
SW3 . . . 4D 16 (4C 100)
SW4 . . . 3H 119
TW12: Ham H . . . 5F 131
Cranmere Ct. EN2: Enf . . . 2F 23
SE5 . . . 1C 120
Cranmer Farm Cl. CR4: Mitc . . . 4D 154
Cranmer Gdns. RM10: Dag . . . 4J 73
Cranmer Ho. *SW9* . . . *7A 102*
(off Brixton Rd.)
SW11 . . . *1C 118*
(off Surrey La. Est.)
Cranmer Rd. CR0: C'don . . . 3B 168
CR4: Mitc . . . 4D 154
E7 . . . 4K 69
HA8: Edg . . . 3C 28
KT2: King T . . . 5E 132
SW9 . . . 7A 102
TW12: Ham H . . . 5F 131
UB3: Hayes . . . 6F 75
Cranmer Ter. SW17 . . . 5B 136
Cranmore Av. TW7: Isle . . . 7G 95
Cranmore Rd. BR1: Brom . . . 3H 141
BR7: Chst . . . 5D 142
Cranmore Way N10 . . . 4G 47
Cranston Cl. TW3: Houn . . . 2C 112
UB10: Ick . . . 2F 57
Cranston Est. N1 . . . 2D 84
Cranston Gdns. E4 . . . 6J 35
Cranston Rd. SE23 . . . 1A 140
Cranswick Rd. SE16 . . . 5H 103
Crantock Rd. SE6 . . . 2D 140
Cranwell Cl. E3 . . . 4D 86
Cranwell Gro. TW17: Shep . . . 4B 146
Cranwell Rd. TW6: H'row A . . . 2D 110
Cranwich Av. N21 . . . 7J 23
Cranwich Rd. N16 . . . 7D 48
Cranwood Ct. EC1 . . . 2F 9
Cranwood St. EC1 . . . 2E 8 (3D 84)
Cranworth Cres. E4 . . . 1A 36
Cranworth Gdns. SW9 . . . 1A 120
Craster Rd. SW2 . . . 7K 119
Crathie Rd. SE12 . . . 6K 123
Cravan Av. TW13: Felt . . . 2J 129
Craven Av. UB1: S'hall . . . 5D 76
W5 . . . 7C 78

Craven Cl. N16 7G 49
UB4: Hayes 6J 75
Craven Cottage 2F 117
Craven Ct. NW10 1A 80
RM6: Chad H 6E 54
Craven Gdns. IG6: Ilf 2H 53
IG11: Bark 2J 89
SW19 5J 135
Craven Hill W2 7A 82
Craven Hill Gdns. W2 7A 82
(not continuous)
Craven Hill M. W2 7A 82
Craven Ho. *N2* *2B 46*
(off High Rd. E. Finchley)
Craven Lodge *W2* *7A 82*
(off Craven Hill)
Craven M. SW11 3E 118
Craven Pk. NW10 1K 79
Craven Pk. M. NW10 7A 62
Craven Pk. Rd. N15 6F 49
NW10 1A 80
Craven Pas. *WC2* *4E 12*
(off Craven St.)
Craven Rd. CR0: C'don 1H 169
KT2: King T 1F 151
NW10 1K 79
W2 1A 10 (7A 82)
W5 7C 78
Craven St. WC2 4E 12 (1J 101)
Craven Ter. W2 2A 10 (7A 82)
Craven Wlk. N16 7G 49
Crawford Av. HA0: Wemb 5D 60
Crawford Bldgs. *W1* *6D 4*
(off Homer St.)
Crawford Cl. TW7: Isle 2J 113
Crawford Est. SE5 2C 120
Crawford Gdns. N13 3G 33
UB5: N'olt 3D 76
Crawford Mans. *W1* *6D 4*
(off Crawford St.)
Crawford M. W1 6E 4 (5D 82)
Crawford Pas. EC1 4K 7 (4A 84)
Crawford Pl. W1 7D 4 (6C 82)
Crawford Point *E16* *6H 87*
(off Wouldham Rd.)
Crawford Rd. SE5 1C 120
Crawford St. NW10 7K 61
W1 6E 4 (5C 82)
Crawley Rd. E10 1D 68
EN1: Enf 7K 23
N22 2C 48
Crawshay Ct. SW9 1A 120
Crawthew Gro. SE22 4F 121
Craybrooke Rd. DA14: Sidc 4B 144
Craybury End SE9 2G 143
Crayfields Bus. Pk. BR5: St P 7C 144
CRAYFORD 5K 127
Crayford Cl. E6 6C 88
Crayford Ho. *SE1* *7F 15*
(off Long La.)
Crayford Rd. N7 4H 65
Cray Ho. *NW8* *5B 4*
(off Penfold St.)
Crayke Hill KT9: Chess 7E 162
Crayle Ho. *EC1* *3B 8*
(off Malta St.)
Crayleigh Ter. DA14: Sidc 6C 144
Crayonne Cl. TW16: Sun 1G 147
Cray Rd. DA14: Sidc 6C 144
DA17: Belv 6G 109
Cray Valley Rd. BR5: St M Cry 5K 161
Crealock Gro. IG8: Wfd G 5C 36
Crealock St. SW18 6K 117
Creasy Est. SE1 3E 102
Creative Ho. *SW8* *7F 101*
(off Princes of Wales Dr.)
Crebor St. SE22 6G 121
Credenhall Dr. BR2: Brom 1D 172
Credenhill Ho. SE15 7H 103
Credenhill St. SW16 6G 137
Crediton Hgts. *NW10* *1F 81*
(off Okehampton Rd.)
Crediton Hill NW6 5K 63
Crediton Rd. E16 6J 87
NW10 1F 81
Crediton Way KT10: Clay 5A 162
Credon Rd. E13 2A 88
SE16 5H 103
Creechurch La. EC3 1H 15 (6E 84)
(not continuous)
Creechurch Pl. EC3 1H 15
Creed Ct. E1 3A 86
EC4 1B 14
Creed La. EC4 1B 14 (6B 84)
Creek, The TW16: Sun 5J 147
Creek Cotts. *KT8: E Mos* *4J 149*
(off Creek Rd.)
Creek Ho. *W14* *3G 99*
(off Russell Rd.)
CREEKMOUTH 4K 89
Creekmouth Ind. Pk. IG11: Bark 4K 89
Creek Rd. IG11: Bark 3K 89
KT8: E Mos 4J 149
SE8 6C 104
SE10 6C 104
Creekside SE8 7D 104
Creekside Foyer *SE8* *6D 104*
(off Stowage)
Creek Way RM13: Rain 5K 91
Creeland Gro. SE6 1B 140
Crefeld Cl. W6 6G 99
Creffield Rd. W3 7F 79
W5 7F 79
Creighton Av. E6 2B 88
N2 3C 46
N10 3C 46
Creighton Cl. W12 7C 80
Creighton Rd. N17 7K 33
NW6 2F 81
W5 3D 96
Cremer Bus. Cen. *E2* *1J 9*
(off Cremer St.)
Cremer Ho. *SE8* *7C 104*
(off Deptford Chu. St.)
Cremer St. E2 1J 9 (2F 85)
Cremorne Est. SW10 6B 100
(not continuous)
Cremorne Rd. SW10 7A 100
Creon Ct. *SW9* *7A 102*
(off Caldwell St.)
Crescent EC3 2J 15 (7F 85)
Crescent, The BR3: Beck 1C 158
BR4: W W'ck 6G 159
CR0: C'don 5D 156
DA5: Bexl 7C 126
DA14: Sidc 4K 143
E17 6A 50
EN5: New Bar 2E 20
HA0: Wemb 2B 60
HA2: Harr 1G 59
IG2: Ilf 6E 52
KT3: N Mald 3J 151
KT6: Surb 5E 150
KT8: W Mole 4E 148
N9 2C 34
N11 4J 31
NW2 3D 62
SM1: Sutt 5B 166
SW13 2B 116
SW19 3J 135
TW15: Ashf 5B 128
TW17: Shep 7H 147
UB1: S'hall 2D 94
UB3: Harl 7E 92
W3 6A 80
Crescent Arc. *SE10* *6E 104*
(off Creek Rd.)
Crescent Ct. KT6: Surb 5D 150
SW4 *5H 119*
(off Park Hill)
Crescent Ct. Bus. Cen. E16 4F 87
Crescent Dr. BR5: Pet W 5F 161
Crescent E. EN4: Had W 1F 21
Crescent Gdns. HA4: Ruis 7K 39
SW19 3J 135
Crescent Gro. CR4: Mitc 4C 154
SW4 4G 119
Crescent Ho. *EC1* *4C 8*
(off Golden La. Est.)
SE13 2D 122
Crescent La. SW4 4G 119
Crescent Mans. *W11* *7G 81*
(off Elgin Cres.)
Crescent M. N22 1J 47
Crescent Pde. UB10: Hil 3C 74
Crescent Pl. SW3 3D 16 (4C 100)
Crescent Ri. EN4: E Barn 5H 21
N3 1H 45
N22 1H 47
Crescent Rd. BR1: Brom 7J 141
BR3: Beck 2D 158
DA15: Sidc 3K 143
E4 1B 36
E6 1A 88
E10 2D 68
E13 1J 87
E18 1A 52
EN2: Enf 4G 23
EN4: E Barn 4G 21
KT2: King T 7G 133
N3 1H 45
N8 6H 47
N9 1B 34
N11 4J 31
N15 3B 48
N22 1H 47
RM10: Dag 3H 73
SE18 5F 107
SW20 1F 153
TW17: Shep 5E 146
Crescent Row EC1 4C 8 (4C 84)
Crescent Stables SW15 5G 117
Crescent St. N1 7K 65
Crescent Way BR6: Orp 5J 173
N12 6H 31
SE4 3C 122
SW16 6K 137
Crescent W. EN4: Had W 1F 21
Crescent Wharf E16 2K 105
Crescent Wood Rd. SE26 3G 139
Cresford Rd. SW6 1K 117
Crespigny Rd. NW4 6D 44
Cressage Cl. UB1: S'hall 4E 76
Cressage Ho. *TW8: Bford* *6E 96*
(off Ealing Rd.)
Cressal Ho. *E14* *3C 104*
(off Tiller Rd.)
Cresset Ho. E9 6J 67
Cresset Rd. E9 6J 67
Cresset St. SW4 3H 119
Cressfield Cl. NW5 5E 64
Cressida Rd. N19 1G 65
Cressingham Gro. SM1: Sutt 4A 166
Cressingham Rd. HA8: Edg 6E 28
SE13 3E 122
Cressington Cl. N16 5E 66
Cress M. BR1: Brom 5F 141
Cresswell NW9 2B 44
Cresswell Gdns. SW5 5A 100
Cresswell Ho. HA9: Wemb 3E 60
TW19: Stanw *6A 110*
(off Douglas Rd.)
Cresswell Pk. SE3 3H 123
Cresswell Pl. SW10 5A 100
Cresswell Rd. SE25 4G 157
TW1: Twick 6D 114
TW13: Hanw 3C 130
Cresswell Way N21 7F 23
Cressy Ct. E1 5J 85
W6 3D 98
Cressy Ho. SW15 3D 116
Cressy Ho's. *E1* *5J 85*
(off Hannibal Rd.)
Cressy Pl. E1 5J 85
Cressy Rd. NW3 5D 64
Crest, The KT5: Surb 5G 151
N13 4F 33
NW4 5E 44
Cresta Ct. W5 4F 79
Cresta Ho. *NW3* *7B 64*
(off Finchley Rd.)
Crestbrook Av. N13 3G 33
Crestbrook Pl. *N13* *3G 33*
(off Green Lanes)
Crest Ct. NW4 5E 44
Crest Dr. EN3: Enf W 1D 24
Crestfield St. WC1 1F 7 (3J 83)
Crest Gdns. HA4: Ruis 3A 58
Creston Way KT4: Wor Pk 1F 165
Crest Rd. BR2: Hayes 7H 159
CR2: Sels 7H 169
NW2 2B 62
Crest Vw. HA5: Pinn 4B 40
Crest Vw. Dr. BR5: Pet W 5F 161
Crestway SW15 6C 116
Crestwood Way TW4: Houn 5C 112
Creswell Dr. BR3: Beck 5D 158
Creswick Ct. W3 7H 79
Creswick Rd. W3 7H 79
Creswick Wlk. E3 3C 86
NW11 4H 45
Creton St. SE18 3E 106
Crewdson Rd. SW9 7A 102
Crewe Pl. NW10 3B 80
Crewkerne Ct. *SW11* *1B 118*
(off Bolingbroke Wlk.)
Crews St. E14 4C 104
Crewys Rd. NW2 2H 63
SE15 2H 121
Crichton Av. SM6: Bedd 5H 167
Crichton Ho. DA14: Sidc 6D 144
Crichton Rd. SM5: Cars 6D 166
Crichton St. SW8 2G 119
Crick Ct. *IG11: Bark* *2G 89*
(off Spring Pl.)
Cricketers Arms Rd. EN2: Enf 2H 23
Cricketers Cl. DA8: Erith 5K 109
KT9: Chess 4D 162
N14 7B 22
Cricketers Ct. *SE11* *4B 102*
(off Kennington La.)
Cricketers M. SW18 5K 117
Cricketers Ter. SM5: Cars 3C 166
Cricketers Wlk. SE26 5J 139
Cricketfield Rd. E5 4H 67
Cricket Grn. CR4: Mitc 3D 154
Cricket Ground Rd. BR7: Chst 1F 161
Cricket La. BR3: Beck 6A 140
Cricklade Av. SW2 2J 137
CRICKLEWOOD 3G 63
Cricklewood B'way. NW2 3E 62
Cricklewood La. NW2 4F 63
Cridland St. E15 1H 87
Crieff Ct. TW11: Tedd 7C 132
Crieff Rd. SW18 6A 118
Criffel Av. SW2 2H 137
Crimscott St. SE1 3E 102
Crimsworth Rd. SW8 1H 119
Crinan St. N1 2J 83
Cringle St. SW8 7G 101
Cripplegate St. EC2 5D 8 (5C 84)
Cripps Grn. UB4: Yead 4K 75
Crispe Ho. IG11: Bark 2H 89
N1 *1K 83*
(off Barnsbury Est.)
Crispen Rd. TW13: Hanw 4C 130
Crispian Cl. NW10 4A 62
Crispin Cl. CR0: Bedd 2J 167
Crispin Ct. *SE17* *4E 102*
(off Freemantle St.)

Crispin Cres. CR0: Bedd ... 3H 167
Crispin Lodge N11 ... 5J 31
Crispin Pl. E1 ... 5J 9 (5F 85)
Crispin Rd. HA8: Edg ... 6D 28
Crispin St. E1 ... 6J 9 (5F 85)
Crispin Way UB8: Hil ... 4B 74
Crisp Rd. W6 ... 5E 98
Cristowe Rd. SW6 ... 2H 117
Criterion Bldgs. *KT7: T Ditt* ... *7B 150*
(off Portsmouth Rd.)
Criterion Ct. *E8* ... *7F 67*
(off Middleton Rd.)
Criterion M. N19 ... 2H 65
Criterion Theatre ... *3C 12*
(off Piccadilly Cir.)
CRITTALLS CORNER ... 7C 144
Crockerton Rd. SW17 ... 2D 136
Crockham Way SE9 ... 4E 142
Crocus Cl. CR0: C'don ... 1K 169
Crocus Fld. EN5: Barn ... 6C 20
Croft, The CR0: C'don ... 3F 169
E4 ... 2B 36
EN5: Barn ... 4B 20
HA0: Wemb ... 5C 60
HA4: Ruis ... 4A 58
HA5: Pinn ... 7D 40
HA8: Edg ... 7C 28
NW10 ... 2B 80
TW5: Hest ... 6C 94
W5 ... 5E 78
Croft Av. BR4: W W'ck ... 1E 170
Croft Cl. BR7: Chst ... 5D 142
DA17: Belv ... 5F 109
NW7 ... 3F 29
UB3: Harl ... 7E 92
UB10: Hil ... 7C 56
Croft Ct. HA4: Ruis ... 1H 57
SE13 ... 6E 122
Croftdown Rd. NW5 ... 3E 64
Croft End Cl. KT9: Chess ... 3F 163
Crofters Cl. TW7: Isle ... 5H 113
Crofters Ct. *SE8* ... *4A 104*
(off Croft St.)
Crofters Mead CR0: Sels ... 7B 170
Crofters Way NW1 ... 1H 83
Croft Gdns. HA4: Ruis ... 1G 57
W7 ... 2A 96
Croft Ho. E17 ... 4D 50
W10 ... *3G 81*
(off Third Av.)
Croft Lodge Cl. IG8: Wfd G ... 6E 36
Croft M. N12 ... 3F 31
CROFTON ... 2H 173
Crofton Av. BR6: Farnb ... 2G 173
DA5: Bexl ... 7D 126
W4 ... 7J 97
Croftongate Way SE4 ... 5A 122
Crofton Gro. E4 ... 4A 36
Crofton Ho. *SW1* ... *5K 17*
(off Sutherland St.)
SW3 ... *7C 16*
(off Old Church St.)
Crofton La.
BR5: Farnb, Orp, Pet W ... 2H 173
BR6: Pet W ... 7H 161
Crofton Leisure Cen. ... 6C 122
CROFTON PARK ... 5B 122
Crofton Pk. Rd. SE4 ... 6B 122
Crofton Rd.
BR6: Farnb, Orp ... 3E 172
E13 ... 4K 87
SE5 ... 1E 120
Crofton Roman Villa ... 2J 173
Crofton Ter. E5 ... 5A 68
TW9: Rich ... 4F 115
Crofton Way EN2: Enf ... 2F 23
EN5: New Bar ... 6E 20
Croft Rd. BR1: Brom ... 6J 141
EN3: Enf H ... 1F 25
SM1: Sutt ... 5C 166
Croft Rd. SW16 ... 1A 156
SW19 ... 7A 136
Crofts, The TW17: Shep ... 4G 147
Crofts Ho. *E2* ... *2G 85*
(off Teale St.)
Croftside, The SE25 ... 3G 157
Crofts La. N22 ... 7F 33
Crofts Rd. HA1: Harr ... 6A 42
Crofts St. E1 ... 3K 15 (7G 85)
Crofts Vs. HA1: Harr ... 6A 42
Croft Way DA15: Sidc ... 3J 143
Croftway NW3 ... 4J 63
TW10: Ham ... 3B 132
Crogsland Rd. NW1 ... 7E 64
Croham Cl. CR2: S Croy ... 7E 168
Croham Mnr. Rd. CR2: S Croy ... 7E 168
Croham Mt. CR2: S Croy ... 7E 168
Croham Pk. Av. CR2: S Croy ... 5E 168
Croham Rd. CR2: S Croy ... 5D 168
Croham Valley Rd. CR2: Sels ... 6G 169
Croindene Rd. SW16 ... 1J 155
Crokesley Ho. *HA8: Edg* ... *2J 43*
(off Burnt Oak B'way.)
Cromartie Rd. N19 ... 7H 47
Cromarty Ct. SW2 ... 5K 119
Cromarty Ho. *E1* ... *5A 86*
(off Ben Jonson Rd.)
Cromarty Rd. HA8: Edg ... 2C 28
Cromberdale Ct. *N17* ... *1G 49*
(off Spencer Rd.)
Crombie Cl. IG4: Ilf ... 5D 52
Crombie M. SW11 ... 2C 118
Crombie Rd. DA15: Sidc ... 1H 143
Crome Ho. *UB5: N'olt* ... *2C 76*
(off Parkfield Dr.)
Cromer Cl. UB8: Hil ... 6E 74
Cromerhyde SM4: Mord ... 5K 153
Crome Rd. NW10 ... 6A 62
Cromer Pl. BR6: Orp ... 1J 173
Cromer Rd. E10 ... 7F 51
EN5: New Bar ... 4F 21
IG8: Wfd G ... 4D 36
N17 ... 2G 49
RM6: Chad H ... 6E 54
RM7: Rom ... 6J 55
SE25 ... 3H 157
SW17 ... 6E 136
TW6: H'row A ... 2C 110
Cromer St. WC1 ... 2E 6 (3J 83)
Cromer Ter. E8 ... 5G 67
RM6: Chad H ... 5B 54
Cromer Vs. Rd. SW18 ... 6H 117
Cromford Cl. BR6: Orp ... 3J 173
Cromford Path E5 ... 4K 67
Cromford Rd. SW18 ... 5J 117
Cromford Way KT3: N Mald ... 1K 151
Cromlix Cl. BR7: Chst ... 2F 161
Crompton Ct.
SW3 ... 3C 16 (4C 100)
Crompton Ho. *SE1* ... *3C 102*
(off County St.)
W2 ... *4A 4*
(off Hall Pl.)
Crompton Pl. EN3: Enf L ... 1H 25
Crompton St. W2 ... 4A 4 (4B 82)
Cromwell Av. BR2: Brom ... 4K 159
KT3: N Mald ... 5B 152
N6 ... 1F 65
W6 ... 5D 98
Cromwell Cen. IG11: Bark ... 3A 90
NW10 ... 3K 79
Cromwell Cen., The *RM8: Dag* ... *7F 55*
(off Whalebone La. Sth.)
Cromwell Cl. BR2: Brom ... 4K 159
E1 ... 1G 103
KT12: Walt T ... 7K 147
N2 ... 4B 46
W3 ... 1J 97
(not continuous)
Cromwell Ct. EN3: Pond E ... 5E 24
Cromwell Cres. SW5 ... 4J 99
Cromwell Gdns. SW7 ... 2B 16 (3B 100)
Cromwell Gro. W6 ... 3E 98
Cromwell Highwalk EC2 ... 5D 8
Cromwell Ho. CR0: C'don ... 3B 168
SW11 ... *1E 118*
(off Charlotte Despard Av.)
Cromwell Ind. Est. E10 ... 1A 68
Cromwell Lodge DA6: Bex ... 5E 126
E1 ... *4J 85*
(off Cleveland Gro.)
IG11: Bark ... 5J 71
Cromwell Mans. *SW5* ... *4J 99*
(off Cromwell Rd.)
Cromwell M. SW7 ... 3B 16 (4B 100)
Cromwell Pl. *EC2* ... *5D 8*
(off Beech St.)
N6 ... 1F 65
SW7 ... 3B 16 (4B 100)
SW14 ... 3J 115
Cromwell Rd. BR3: Beck ... 2A 158
CR0: C'don ... 7D 156
E7 ... 7A 70
E17 ... 5E 50
HA0: Wemb ... 2E 78
KT2: King T ... 1E 150
KT4: Wor Pk ... 3K 163
N3 ... 1A 46
N10 ... 7K 31
(not continuous)
SW5 ... 4J 99
SW7 ... 3A 16 (4J 99)
SW9 ... 1B 120
SW19 ... 5J 135
TW3: Houn ... 4E 112
TW11: Tedd ... 6A 132
TW13: Felt ... 1K 129
UB3: Hayes ... 6F 75
Cromwell St. TW3: Houn ... 4E 112
Cromwell Twr. EC2 ... 5D 8
Cromwell Trad. Cen. IG11: Bark ... 3J 89
Crondace Rd. SW6 ... 1J 117
Crondall Ct. N1 ... 1F 9
Crondall Ho. SW15 ... 7C 116
Crondall St. N1 ... 1F 9 (2D 84)
Crone Ct. *NW6* ... *2H 81*
(off Denmark Rd.)
Cronin St. SE15 ... 7F 103
CROOKED BILLET ... 7H 35
Crooked Billet SW19 ... 6E 134
Crooked Billet Yd. E2 ... 1H 9
Crooked Usage N3 ... 3G 45
Crooke Rd. SE8 ... 5A 104
Crookham Rd. SW6 ... 1H 117
Crook Log DA6: Bex ... 3D 126
Crook Log Sports Cen. ... 3D 126
Crookston Rd. SE9 ... 3E 124
Croombs Rd. E16 ... 5A 88
Croom's Hill SE10 ... 7E 104
Croom's Hill Gro. SE10 ... 7E 104
Cropley Ct. *N1* ... *2D 84*
(off Cropley St., not continuous)
Cropley St. N1 ... 1E 8 (2D 84)
Croppath Rd. RM10: Dag ... 4G 73
Cropthorne Ct. W9 ... 3A 82
Crosbie NW9 ... 2B 44
Crosbie Ho. *E17* ... *3E 50*
(off Prospect Hill)
Crosby Cl. TW13: Hanw ... 3C 130
Crosby Ct. SE1 ... 6E 14 (2D 102)
Crosby Ho. E7 ... 6J 69
E14 ... *3E 104*
(off Manchester Rd.)
Crosby Rd. E7 ... 6J 69
RM10: Dag ... 2H 91
Crosby Row SE1 ... 7E 14 (2D 102)
Crosby Sq. EC3 ... 1G 15 (6E 84)
Crosby Wlk. E8 ... 6F 67
SW2 ... 7A 120
Crosby Way SW2 ... 7A 120
Crosier Cl. SE3 ... 1C 124
Crosier Rd. UB10: Ick ... 4E 56
Crosier Way HA4: Ruis ... 3G 57
Crosland Pl. SW11 ... 3E 118
Cross Av. SE10 ... 6F 105
Crossbow Ho. *N1* ... *1E 84*
(off Whitmore Est.)
W13 ... *1B 96*
(off Sherwood Cl.)
Crossbrook Rd. SE3 ... 2C 124
Cross Cl. SE15 ... 2H 121
Cross Ct. *SE28* ... *7B 90*
(off Titmuss Av.)
Cross Deep TW1: Twick ... 2K 131
Cross Deep Gdns. TW1: Twick ... 2K 131
Crossfield Ct. *W10* ... *6F 81*
(off Cambridge Gdns.)
Crossfield Ho. *W11* ... *7G 81*
(off Mary Pl.)
Crossfield Rd. N17 ... 3C 48
NW3 ... 6B 64
Crossfield St. SE8 ... 7C 104
(not continuous)
Crossford St. SW9 ... 2K 119
Cross Ga. HA8: Edg ... 3B 28
Crossgate UB6: G'frd ... 6B 60
Cross Keys Cl. *N9* ... *2B 34*
(off Lacey Cl.)
W1 ... 6H 5 (5E 82)
Cross Keys Sq. *EC1* ... *6C 8*
(off Little Britain)
Cross Lances Rd. TW3: Houn ... 4F 113
Crossland Rd. CR7: Thor H ... 6B 156
Crosslands Av. UB2: S'hall ... 5D 94
W5 ... 1F 97
Crosslands Rd. KT19: Ewe ... 6K 163
Cross La. DA5: Bexl ... 7F 127
EC3 ... 3G 15 (7E 84)
(not continuous)
N8 ... 3K 47
(not continuous)
Crossleigh Ct. *SE14* ... *7B 104*
(off New Cross Rd.)
Crosslet St. SE17 ... 4D 102
Crosslet Va. SE10 ... 1D 122
Crossley St. N7 ... 6A 66
Crossmead SE9 ... 1D 142
Crossmead Av. UB6: G'frd ... 3E 76
Crossmount Ho. *SE5* ... *7C 102*
(off Bowyer St.)
Crossness Engines Mus., The ... 6F 91
Crossness Footpath DA18: Erith ... 1F 109
Crossness La. SE2 ... 7E 90
Crossness Rd. IG11: Bark ... 3K 89
Cross Rd. BR2: Brom ... 2C 172
CR0: C'don ... 1D 168
DA14: Sidc ... 4B 144
E4 ... 1A 36
EN1: Enf ... 4K 23
HA1: Harr ... 4H 41
HA2: Harr ... 3F 59
HA3: W'stone ... 2A 42
IG8: Wfd G ... 6J 37
KT2: King T ... 7F 133
N11 ... 5A 32
N22 ... 7F 33
RM6: Chad H ... 7C 54
RM7: Mawney ... 4G 55
SE5 ... 2E 120
SM1: Sutt ... 5B 166
SW19 ... 7J 135
TW13: Hanw ... 4C 130
Cross St. N1 ... 1B 84
N18 ... 5B 34
SE5 ... 3D 120
SW13 ... 2A 116
TW12: Ham H ... 5G 131
Crossthwaite Av. SE5 ... 4D 120
Crosstrees Ho. *E14* ... *3C 104*
(off Cassilis Rd.)

Crosswall EC3 .... 2J 15 (7F 85)
Cross Way IG8: Wfd G 4F 37
Cross Way, The
HA3: W'stone 2J 41
Crossway BR5: Pet W 4H 161
EN1: Enf 7K 23
HA4: Ruis 4A 58
HA5: Pinn 2K 39
N12 .... 6G 31
N16 .... 5E 66
NW9 .... 4B 44
RM8: Dag 3C 72
SE28 .... 6B 90
SW20 .... 4E 152
UB3: Hayes 1J 93
W13 .... 4A 78
Crossway, The N22 .... 7G 33
SE9 .... 2B 142
UB10: Hil 2B 74
Crossway Ct. SE4 .... 2A 122
Crossway Pde. N22 .... 7G 33
(off The Crossway)
Crossways CR2: Sels 7A 170
N21 .... 6H 23
SM2: Sutt 7B 166
TW16: Sun 7H 129
Crossways, The HA9: Wemb 2G 61
KT5: Surb 1H 163
TW5: Hest 7D 94
Crossways Rd. BR3: Beck 4C 158
CR4: Mitc 3F 155
Crossways Ter. E5 .... 4J 67
Crosswell Cl. TW17: Shep 2E 146
Croston St. E8 .... 1G 85
Crothall Cl. N13 .... 3E 32
Crouch Av. IG11: Bark 2B 90
Crouch Cl. BR3: Beck 6C 140
Crouch Cft. SE9 .... 3E 142
CROUCH END 7H 47
Crouch End Hill N8 .... 7H 47
Crouch Hall Ct. N19 .... 1J 65
Crouch Hall Rd. N8 .... 6H 47
Crouch Hill N4 .... 6J 47
N8 .... 6J 47
Crouch Hill Recreation Cen. 7J 47
Crouchman's Cl. SE26 .... 3F 139
Crouch Rd. NW10 .... 7K 61
Crowborough Rd. SW17 .... 6E 136
Crowden Way SE28 .... 7C 90
Crowder Cl. N12 .... 1A 46
Crowder St. E1 .... 7H 85
Crowfield Ho. N5 .... 4C 66
Crowfoot Cl. E9 .... 5B 68
SE28 .... 1J 107
Crowhurst Cl. SW9 .... 2A 120
Crowhurst Ho. SW9 .... 2K 119
(off Aytoun Rd.)
Crowland Av. UB3: Harl 4G 93
Crowland Gdns. N14 .... 7D 22
Crowland Ho. NW8 .... 1A 82
(off Springfield Rd.)
Crowland Rd. CR7: Thor H 4D 156
N15 .... 5F 49
CROWLANDS 7H 55
Crowlands Av. RM7: Rom 6H 55
Crowland Ter. N1 .... 7D 66
Crowland Wlk.
SM4: Mord 6K 153
Crow La. RM7: Rush G 7F 55
Crowley Cres. CR0: Wadd 5A 168
Crowline Wlk. N1 .... 6C 66
Crowmarsh Gdns. SE23 .... 7J 121
Crown All. SE9 .... 6D 124
Crown Arc. KT1: King T 2D 150
Crownbourne Ct. SM1: Sutt 4K 165
(off St Nicholas Way)
Crown Bldgs. E4 .... 1A 36
(off Richmond Rd.)
E4 .... 1K 35
(Woodland Rd.)
Crown Cl. E3 .... 1C 86
KT12: Walt T 7A 148
N22 .... 1A 48
NW6 .... 6K 63
NW7 .... 2G 29
UB3: Hayes 2H 93
Crown Cl. Bus. Cen. E3 .... 1C 86
(off Crown Cl.)
Crown Cotts. RM5: Col R 1G 55
Crown Ct. EC2 .... 1D 14
N10 .... 7K 31
NW8 .... 2D 4
(off Park Rd.)
SE12 .... 6K 123
WC2 .... 1F 13 (6J 83)
Crown Dale SE19 .... 6B 138
Crowndale Ct. NW1 .... 2H 83
(off Crowndale Rd.)
Crowndale Rd. NW1 .... 2G 83
Crownfield Av. IG2: Ilf 6J 53
Crownfield Rd. E15 .... 4F 69
Crowngate Ho. E3 .... 2B 86
(off Hereford Rd.)
Crown Hill CR0: C'don 2C 168
Crown Hill Rd. NW10 .... 1B 80
Crownhill Rd. IG8: Wfd G 7H 37
Crown Ho. HA4: Ruis 1J 57
KT3: N Mald 3J 151
NW10 .... 2G 79
Crown La. BR2: Brom 5B 160
BR7: Chst 1G 161
N14 .... 1B 32
SM4: Mord 4J 153
SW16 .... 5A 138
Crown La. Gdns. SW16 .... 5A 138
Crown La. Spur
BR2: Brom 6B 160
Crown Lodge SW3 .... 4D 16
Crownmead Way RM7: Mawney 4H 55
Crown M. E1 .... 5K 85
(off White Horse La.)
E13 .... 1A 88
W6 .... 4C 98
Crown Office Row EC4 .... 2J 13 (7A 84)
Crown Pde. N14 .... 1B 32
SM4: Mord 3J 153
Crown Pas. KT1: King T 2D 150
(off Church St.)
SW1 .... 5B 12 (1G 101)
Crown Pl. EC2 .... 5G 9 (5E 84)
(not continuous)
NW5 .... 6F 65
SE16 .... 5H 103
Crown Point SE19 .... 6B 138
Crown Point Pde. SE19 .... 6B 138
(off Crown Dale)
Crown Reach SW1 .... 6D 18 (5H 101)
Crown Rd. EN1: Enf 3B 24
HA4: Ruis 5B 58
IG6: Ilf 4H 53
KT3: N Mald 1J 151
N10 .... 7K 31
SM1: Sutt 4K 165
SM4: Mord 4K 153
TW1: Twick 6B 114
Crownstone Ct. SW2 .... 5A 120
Crownstone Rd. SW2 .... 5A 120
Crown St. HA2: Harr 1H 59
RM10: Dag 6J 73
(not continuous)
SE5 .... 7C 102
W3 .... 1H 97
Crown Ter. N14 .... 1C 32
(off Crown La.)
TW9: Rich 4F 115
Crown Trad. Cen.
UB3: Hayes 2G 93
Crowntree Cl. TW7: Isle 6K 95
Crown Wlk. HA9: Wemb 3F 61
Crown Way UB7: Yiew 1B 92
Crown Wharf E14 .... 1E 104
(off Coldharbour)
SE8 .... 5B 104
(off Grove St.)
Crown Woods SE18 .... 2F 125
Crown Woods Way SE9 .... 5H 125
Crown Yd. TW3: Houn 3G 113
Crowshott Av. HA7: Stan 2C 42
Crows Rd. E15 .... 3F 87
IG11: Bark 6F 71
Crowther Av. TW8: Bford 4E 96
Crowther Cl. SW6 .... 6H 99
(off Bucklers All.)
Crowther Rd. SE25 .... 5G 157
Crowthorne Cl. SW18 .... 7H 117
Crowthorne Rd. W10 .... 6F 81
Croxall Ho. KT12: Walt T 6A 148
Croxden Cl. HA8: Edg 3G 43
Croxden Wlk. SM4: Mord 6A 154
Croxford Gdns. N22 .... 7G 33
Croxford Way RM7: Rush G 1K 73
Croxley Grn. BR5: St P 7B 144
Croxley Rd. W9 .... 3H 81
Croxted Cl. SE21 .... 7C 120
Croxted M. SE24 .... 6C 120
Croxted Rd. SE21 .... 7C 120
SE24 .... 7C 120
Croxteth Ho. SW8 .... 2H 119
Croyde Av. UB3: Harl 4G 93
UB6: G'frd 3G 77
Croyde Cl. DA15: Sidc 7H 125
CROYDON 3C 168
Croydon N17 .... 2D 48
(off Gloucester Rd.)
Croydon Airport Ind. Est.
CR0: Wadd 6K 167
Croydon Airport Vis. Cen. 6A 168
Croydon Clocktower 3C 168
(off Katherine St.)
Croydon Crematorium CR0: C'don 5K 155
Croydon Flyover, The
CR0: C'don 4B 168
Croydon Gro. CR0: C'don 1B 168
Croydon Ho. SE1 .... 6K 13
(off Wootton St.)
Croydon Rd. BR2: Hayes, Kes 3A 172
BR2: Kes 3A 172
BR3: Beck 4K 157
BR4: Hayes, W W'ck 3G 171
CR0: Bedd, Wadd 4F 167
CR0: C'don 4E 154
CR4: Mitc 4E 154
E13 .... 4H 87
SE20 .... 2H 157
SM6: Wall, Bedd 4F 167
TW6: H'row A 2D 110
Croydon Rd. Ind. Est. BR3: Beck 4K 157
Croydon Sports Arena 5J 157
Croyland Rd. N9 .... 1B 34
Croylands Dr. KT6: Surb 7E 150
Croysdale Av. TW16: Sun 3J 147
Crozier Ho. SE3 .... 3K 123
SW8 .... 7K 101
(off Wilkinson St.)
Crozier Ter. E9 .... 5K 67
(not continuous)
Crucible Cl. RM6: Chad H 6B 54
Crucifix La. SE1 .... 6H 15 (2E 102)
Cruden Ho. SE17 .... 6B 102
(off Brandon Est.)
Cruden St. N1 .... 1B 84
Cruikshank Ho. NW8 .... 2C 82
(off Townshend Rd.)
Cruikshank Rd. E15 .... 4G 69
Cruikshank St. WC1 .... 1J 7 (3A 84)
Crummock Gdns. NW9 .... 5A 44
Crumpsall St. SE2 .... 4C 108
Crundale Av. NW9 .... 5G 43
Crunden Rd. CR2: S Croy 7D 168
Crusader Gdns. CR0: C'don 3E 168
Crusader Ind. Est. N4 .... 6C 48
Crusoe M. N16 .... 2D 66
Crusoe Rd. CR4: Mitc 7D 136
DA8: Erith 5K 109
Crutched Friars EC3 .... 2H 15 (7E 84)
Crutchley Rd. SE6 .... 2G 141
Crystal Ct. SE19 .... 5F 139
(off College Rd.)
Crystal Ho. SE18 .... 5K 107
CRYSTAL PALACE 6F 139
Crystal Palace Athletics Stadium 6G 139
Crystal Palace FC 4E 156
Crystal Palace Indoor Bowling Club
.... 1H 157
Crystal Palace Mus. 6F 139
Crystal Palace National Sports Cen.
.... 6G 139
Crystal Pal. Pde. SE19 .... 6F 139
Crystal Pal. Pk. Rd. SE26 .... 5G 139
Crystal Pal. Rd. SE22 .... 6F 121
Crystal Pal. Sta. Rd. SE19 .... 6G 139
Crystal Ter. SE19 .... 6D 138
Crystal Vw. Ct. BR1: Brom 4F 141
Crystal Way HA1: Harr 5K 41
RM8: Dag 1C 72
Crystal Wharf N1 .... 2B 84
Cuba Dr. EN3: Enf H 2D 24
Cuba St. E14 .... 2C 104
Cube Ho. SE16 .... 3F 103
Cubitt Bldg. SW1 .... 7J 17 (5F 101)
Cubitt Ho. SW4 .... 6G 119
Cubitt Sq. UB2: S'hall 1G 95
Cubitt Steps E14 .... 1C 104
Cubitt St. WC1 .... 2H 7 (3K 83)
Cubitt's Yd. WC2 .... 2F 13
Cubitt Ter. SW4 .... 3G 119
CUBITT TOWN 4E 104
Cuckoo Av. W7 .... 4J 77
Cuckoo Dene W7 .... 5H 77
Cuckoo Hall La. N9 .... 7D 24
Cuckoo Hall Rd. N9 .... 7D 24
Cuckoo Hill HA5: Eastc 3A 40
Cuckoo Hill Dr. HA5: Pinn 3A 40
Cuckoo Hill Rd. HA5: Pinn 4A 40
Cuckoo La. W7 .... 7J 77
Cuckoo Pound TW17: Shep 5G 147
Cudas Cl. KT19: Ewe 4B 164
Cuddington SE17 .... 4C 102
(off Deacon Way)
Cuddington Av. KT4: Wor Pk 3B 164
Cudham La. Nth. BR6: Downe 7J 173
Cudham St. SE6 .... 7E 122
Cudworth Ho. SW8 .... 1G 119
Cudworth St. E1 .... 4H 85
Cuff Cres. SE9 .... 6B 124
Cuffley Ho. W10 .... 5E 80
(off Sutton Way)
Cuff Point E2 .... 1J 9
(off Columbia Rd.)
Culand Ho. SE17 .... 4E 102
(off Congreve St.)
Culford Gdns. SW3 .... 4F 17 (4D 100)
Culford Gro. N1 .... 6E 66
Culford Mans. SW3 .... 4F 17
(off Culford Gdns.)
Culford M. N1 .... 6E 66
Culford Rd. N1 .... 7E 66
Culford Ter. N1 .... 6E 66
(off Balls Pond Rd.)
Culgaith Gdns. EN2: Enf 4D 22
Culham Ho. E2 .... 2J 9
(off Palissy St.)
W2 .... 5J 81
(off Gt. Western Rd.)
Cullen Way NW10 .... 4J 79
Culling Rd. SE16 .... 3J 103
Cullington Cl. HA3: W'stone 4A 42
Cullingworth Rd. NW10 .... 5C 62
Culloden Cl. SE16 .... 5G 103
Culloden Rd. EN2: Enf 2G 23

Cullum St. EC3 ... 2G 15 (7E 84)
Cullum Welch Ct. N1 ... 1F 9
(off Haberdasher St.)
Cullum Welch Ho. EC1 ... 4C 8
(off Golden La. Est.)
Culmington Pde. W13 ... 1C 96
(off Uxbridge Rd.)
Culmington Rd. CR2: S Croy ... 7C 168
W13 ... 1C 96
Culmore Rd. SE15 ... 7H 103
Culmstock Rd. SW11 ... 5E 118
Culpepper Cl. N18 ... 5C 34
Culpepper Ct. SE11 ... 3J 19
Culross Bldgs. NW1 ... 2J 83
(off Battle Bri. Rd.)
Culross Cl. N15 ... 4C 48
Culross Ho. W10 ... 6F 81
(off Bridge Cl.)
Culross St. W1 ... 3G 11 (7E 82)
Culsac Rd. KT6: Surb ... 2E 162
Culverden Rd. SW12 ... 2G 137
Culver Gro. HA7: Stan ... 2C 42
Culverhouse WC1 ... 6G 7
(off Red Lion Sq.)
Culverhouse Gdns. SW16 ... 3K 137
Culverlands Cl. HA7: Stan ... 4G 27
Culverley Rd. SE6 ... 1D 140
Culvers Av. SM5: Cars ... 2D 166
Culvers Retreat SM5: Cars ... 1D 166
Culverstone Cl. BR2: Brom ... 6H 159
Culvers Way SM5: Cars ... 2D 166
Culvert Pl. SW11 ... 2E 118
Culvert Rd. N15 ... 5E 48
(off Lydford Rd.)
N15 ... 5E 48
(Oulton Rd.)
SW11 ... 2D 118
Culworth Ho. NW8 ... 2C 82
(off Allitsen Rd.)
Culworth St. NW8 ... 2C 82
Culzean Cl. SE27 ... 3B 138
Cumberland Av. DA16: Well ... 3J 125
NW10 ... 3H 79
Cumberland Bus. Pk. NW10 ... 3H 79
Cumberland Cl. E8 ... 6F 67
IG6: Ilf ... 1G 53
SW20 ... 7F 135
TW1: Twick ... 6B 114
Cumberland Ct. CR0: C'don ... 1D 168
DA16: Well ... 2J 125
HA1: Harr ... 3J 41
(off Princes Dr.)
SW1 ... 5K 17
(off Cumberland St.)
W1 ... 1F 11
(off Gt. Cumberland Pl.)
Cumberland Cres. W14 ... 4G 99
(not continuous)
Cumberland Dr. DA7: Bex ... 7E 108
KT9: Chess ... 3E 162
KT10: Hin W ... 2A 162
Cumberland Gdns. NW4 ... 2G 45
WC1 ... 1J 7 (3A 84)
Cumberland Ga. W1 ... 2E 10 (7D 82)
Cumberland Ho. E16 ... 1J 105
(off Wesley Av.)
KT2: King T ... 7H 133
N9 ... 1D 34
(off Cumberland Rd.)
SE28 ... 2G 107
W8 ... 2K 99
(off Kensington Ct.)
Cumberland Mans. W1 ... 7E 4
Cumberland Mkt. NW1 ... 1K 5 (3F 83)
Cumberland M. SE11 ... 6K 19 (5A 102)
Cumberland Mills Sq.
E14 ... 5F 105
Cumberland Pk. W3 ... 7J 79
Cumberland Pk. Ind. Est.
NW10 ... 3C 80
Cumberland Pl. NW1 ... 1J 5 (3F 83)
SE6 ... 1H 141
TW16: Sun ... 4J 147
Cumberland Rd. BR2: Brom ... 4G 159
E12 ... 4B 70
E13 ... 5K 87
E17 ... 2A 50
HA1: Harr ... 5F 41
HA7: Stan ... 3F 43
N9 ... 1D 34
N22 ... 2K 47
SE25 ... 6H 157
SW13 ... 1B 116
TW9: Kew ... 7G 97
TW15: Ashf ... 3A 128
W3 ... 7J 79
W7 ... 2K 95
Cumberland St. SW1 ... 5K 17 (5F 101)
Cumberland Ter. NW1 ... 1J 5 (2F 83)
Cumberland Ter. M. NW1 ... 1J 5
(not continuous)
Cumberland Vs. W3 ... 7J 79
(off Cumberland Rd.)
Cumberland Wharf SE16 ... 2J 103
(off Rotherhithe St.)
Cumberlow Av. SE25 ... 3F 157
Cumbernauld Gdns. TW16: Sun ... 5H 129
Cumberton Rd. N17 ... 1D 48
Cumbrae Gdns. KT6: Surb ... 2D 162
Cumbrian Gdns. NW2 ... 2F 63
Cumbrian Way UB8: Uxb ... 7A 56
Cuming Mus. ... 4C 102
(off Walworth Rd.)
Cumming St. N1 ... 1H 7 (2K 83)
Cumnor Cl. SW9 ... 2K 119
(off Robsart St.)
Cumnor Gdns. KT17: Ewe ... 6C 164
Cumnor Rd. SM2: Sutt ... 6A 166
Cunard Ct. HA7: Stan ... 2F 27
(off Brightwen Gro.)
Cunard Cres. N21 ... 6J 23
Cunard Pl. EC3 ... 1H 15 (6E 84)
Cunard Rd. NW10 ... 3K 79
Cunard Wlk. SE16 ... 4K 103
Cundy Rd. E16 ... 6A 88
Cundy St. SW1 ... 4H 17 (4E 100)
Cunliffe Pde. KT19: Ewe ... 4B 164
Cunliffe Rd. KT19: Ewe ... 4B 164
Cunliffe St. SW16 ... 6G 137
Cunningham Cl. BR4: W W'ck ... 2D 170
RM6: Chad H ... 5C 54
Cunningham Ct. E10 ... 3D 68
(off Oliver Rd.)
W9 ... 4A 4
(off Blomfield Rd.)
Cunningham Ho. SE5 ... 7D 102
(off Elmington Est.)
Cunningham Pk.
HA1: Harr ... 5G 41
Cunningham Pl. NW8 ... 3A 4 (4B 82)
Cunningham Rd.
N15 ... 4G 49
Cunnington St. W4 ... 3J 97
Cupar Rd. SW11 ... 1E 118
Cupola Cl. BR1: Brom ... 5K 141
Cureton St. SW1 ... 4D 18 (4H 101)
Curfew Ho. IG11: Bark ... 1G 89
Curie Ct. HA1: Harr ... 7B 42
Curie Gdns. NW9 ... 2A 44
Curlew Cl. SE28 ... 7D 90
Curlew Ct. KT6: Surb ... 3G 163
W13 ... 4K 77
Curlew Ho. EN3: Pond E ... 5E 24
SE4 ... 4A 122
(off St Norbert Rd.)
SE15 ... 1F 121
Curlew St. SE1 ... 6K 15 (2F 103)
Curlew Way UB4: Yead ... 5B 76
Curness St. SE13 ... 4E 122
Curnick's La. SE27 ... 4C 138
Curran Av. DA15: Sidc ... 5K 125
SM6: Wall ... 3E 166
Curran Ho. SW3 ... 4C 16
(off Lucan Pl.)
Currey Rd. UB6: G'frd ... 6H 59
Curricle St. W3 ... 1A 98
Currie Hill Cl. SW19 ... 4H 135
Currie Ho. E14 ... 6F 87
(off Abbott Rd.)
Curry Ri. NW7 ... 6A 30
Cursitor St. EC4 ... 7J 7 (6A 84)
Curtain Pl. EC2 ... 3H 9 (3E 84)
Curtain Rd. EC2 ... 2H 9 (4E 84)
Curthwaite Gdns. EN2: Enf ... 4C 22
Curtis Dr. W3 ... 6K 79
Curtis Fld. Rd. SW16 ... 4K 137
Curtis Ho. N11 ... 5B 32
(off Ladderswood Way)
SE17 ... 5D 102
(off Morecambe St.)
Curtis La. HA0: Wemb ... 5E 60
Curtis Rd. KT19: Ewe ... 4J 163
TW4: Houn ... 7D 112
Curtis St. SE1 ... 4F 103
Curtis Way SE1 ... 4F 103
SE28 ... 7B 90
Curtlington Ho. HA8: Edg ... 2J 43
(off Burnt Oak B'way.)
Curve, The W12 ... 7C 80
Curwen Av. E7 ... 4K 69
Curwen Rd. W12 ... 2C 98
Curzon Av. EN3: Pond E ... 5E 24
HA7: Stan ... 1A 42
Curzon Cinema
Mayfair ... 5J 11
(off Curzon St.)
Soho ... 2D 12
(off Shaftesbury Av.)
Curzon Cl. BR6: Orp ... 4H 173
Curzon Ct. SW6 ... 1A 118
(off Imperial Rd.)
Curzon Cres. IG11: Bark ... 2K 89
NW10 ... 7A 62
Curzon Ga. W1 ... 5H 11 (1E 100)
Curzon Pl. HA5: Eastc ... 5A 40
Curzon Rd. CR7: Thor H ... 6A 156
N10 ... 2F 47
W5 ... 4B 78
Curzon Sq. W1 ... 5H 11 (1E 100)
Curzon St. W1 ... 5H 11 (1E 100)
Cusack Cl. TW1: Twick ... 4K 131
Custance Ho. N1 ... 1E 8
(off Provost Est.)
Custance St. N1 ... 1E 8 (3D 84)
CUSTOM HOUSE ... 6A 88
Custom Ho. EC3 ... 3G 15 (7E 84)
Custom Ho. Reach SE16 ... 2B 104
Custom Ho. Wlk. EC3 ... 3G 15 (7E 84)
Cut, The SE1 ... 6K 13 (2A 102)
Cutbush Ho. N7 ... 5H 65
Cutcombe Rd. SE5 ... 2C 120
Cuthberga Cl. IG11: Bark ... 7G 71
Cuthbert Gdns. SE25 ... 3E 156
Cuthbert Harrowing Ho. EC1 ... 4C 8
(off Golden La. Est.)
Cuthbert Ho. W2 ... 5A 4
(off Hall Pl.)
Cuthbert Rd. CR0: C'don ... 2B 168
E17 ... 3E 50
N18 ... 5B 34
Cuthbert St. W2 ... 5A 4 (5B 82)
Cuthill Wlk. SE5 ... 1D 120
Cutlers Gdns. EC2 ... 6H 9
Cutlers Gdns. Arc. EC2 ... 6E 84
(off Devonshire Sq.)
Cutlers Sq. E14 ... 4C 104
Cutler St. E1 ... 7H 9 (6E 84)
Cutter Ho. DA8: Erith ... 4K 109
Cutthroat All. TW10: Ham ... 2C 132
Cutty Sark ... 6E 104
Cutty Sark Gdns. SE10 ... 6E 104
(off King William Wlk.)
Cuxton BR5: Pet W ... 5G 161
Cuxton Cl. DA6: Bex ... 5E 126
Cuxton Ho. SE17 ... 5E 102
(off Mina Rd.)
Cyclamen Cl. TW12: Hamp ... 6E 130
Cyclamen Way KT19: Ewe ... 5J 163
Cyclops M. E14 ... 4C 104
Cygnet Av. TW14: Felt ... 7A 112
Cygnet Cl. NW10 ... 5K 61
Cygnet Ho. SW3 ... 6D 16
(off King's Rd.)
Cygnet Ho. Nth. E14 ... 6D 86
(off Chrisp St.)
Cygnet Ho. Sth. E14 ... 6D 86
(off Chrisp St.)
Cygnets, The TW13: Hanw ... 4C 130
Cygnet St. E1 ... 3K 9 (4F 85)
Cygnet Way UB4: Yead ... 5B 76
Cygnus Bus. Cen. NW10 ... 5B 62
Cymbeline Ct. HA1: Harr ... 6K 41
(off Gayton Rd.)
Cynthia St. N1 ... 1H 7 (2K 83)
Cyntra Pl. E8 ... 7H 67
Cypress Av. TW2: Whitt ... 7G 113
Cypress Cl. E5 ... 2G 67
Cypress Ct. SM1: Sutt ... 5J 165
Cypress Gdns. SE4 ... 5A 122
Cypress Ho. SE14 ... 1K 121
SE16 ... 2K 103
(off Woodland Cres.)
Cypress Pl. W1 ... 4B 6 (4G 83)
Cypress Rd. HA3: Hrw W ... 2H 41
SE25 ... 2E 156
Cypress Tree Cl. DA15: Sidc ... 1K 143
CYPRUS ... 7E 88
Cyprus Av. N3 ... 2G 45
Cyprus Cl. N4 ... 6B 48
Cyprus Gdns. N3 ... 2G 45
Cyprus Pl. E2 ... 2J 85
E6 ... 7E 88
Cyprus Rd. N3 ... 2H 45
N9 ... 2A 34
Cyprus St. E2 ... 2J 85
(not continuous)
Cyrena Rd. SE22 ... 6F 121
Cyril Lodge DA14: Sidc ... 4A 144
Cyril Mans. SW11 ... 1D 118
Cyril Rd. BR6: Orp ... 7K 161
DA7: Bex ... 2E 126
Cyrus Ho. EC1 ... 3B 8
Cyrus St. EC1 ... 3B 8
Czar St. SE8 ... 6C 104

D

Dabbs Hill La. UB5: N'olt ... 6D 58
(not continuous)
Dabbs La. EC1 ... 4K 7
(off Farringdon Rd.)
Dabin Cres. SE10 ... 1E 122
Dacca St. SE8 ... 6B 104
Dace Rd. E3 ... 1C 86
Dacre Av. IG5: Ilf ... 2E 52
Dacre Cl. UB6: G'frd ... 2F 77
Dacre Gdns. SE13 ... 4G 123
Dacre Ho. SW3 ... 7B 16
Dacre Pk. SE13 ... 3G 123
Dacre Pl. SE13 ... 3G 123
Dacre Rd. CR0: C'don ... 7J 155
E11 ... 1H 69
E13 ... 1K 87
Dacres Est. SE23 ... 3K 139
Dacres Ho. SW4 ... 3F 119
Dacres Rd. SE23 ... 2K 139
Dacre St. SW1 ... 1C 18 (3H 101)
Dade Way UB2: S'hall ... 5D 94
Daerwood Cl. BR2: Brom ... 1D 172

Daffodil Cl. CR0: C'don 1K 169
Daffodil Gdns. IG1: Ilf 5F 71
Daffodil Pl. TW12: Hamp 6E 130
Daffodil St. W12 7B 80
Dafforne Rd. SW17 3E 136
Da Gama Pl. E14 5C 104
DAGENHAM 6G 73
Dagenham & Redbridge FC 5H 73
Dagenham Av. RM9: Dag 1E 90
(not continuous)
Dagenham Leisure Pk. RM9: Dag 1E 90
Dagenham Rd. E10 1B 68
RM7: Rush G 7K 55
RM10: Dag, Rush G 4J 73
RM13: Rain 7K 73
Dagenham Swimming Pool 2G 73
Dagmar Av. HA9: Wemb 4F 61
Dagmar Ct. E14 3E 104
Dagmar Gdns. NW10 2F 81
Dagmar M. UB2: S'hall 3C 94
(off Dagmar Rd.)
Dagmar Pas. N1 1B 84
(off Cross St.)
Dagmar Rd. KT2: King T 1F 151
N4 7A 48
N15 4D 48
N22 1H 47
RM10: Dag 7J 73
SE5 1E 120
SE25 5E 156
UB2: S'hall 3C 94
Dagmar Ter. N1 1B 84
Dagnall Pk. SE25 6E 156
Dagnall Rd. SE25 5E 156
Dagnall St. SW11 2D 118
Dagnan Rd. SW12 7F 119
Dagobert Ho. E1 5J 85
(off Smithy St.)
Dagonet Gdns. BR1: Brom 3J 141
Dagonet Rd. BR1: Brom 3J 141
Dahlia Gdns. CR4: Mitc 4H 155
IG1: Ilf 6F 71
Dahlia Rd. SE2 4B 108
Dahomey Rd. SW16 6G 137
Daimler Way SM6: Wall 7J 167
Dain Ct. W8 4J 99
(off Lexham Gdns.)
Daines Cl. E12 3D 70
Dainford Cl. BR1: Brom 5F 141
Dainton Cl. BR1: Brom 1K 159
Dainton Ho. W2 5J 81
(off Gt. Western Rd.)
Daintry Cl. HA3: W'stone 4A 42
Daintry Way E9 6B 68
Dairsie Ct. BR1: Brom 1A 160
Dairsie Rd. SE9 3E 124
Dairy Cl. BR1: Brom 7K 141
CR7: Thor H 2C 156
NW10 1C 80
Dairy La. SE18 4D 106
Dairyman Cl. NW2 3F 63
Dairy M. N2 4C 46
SW9 3J 119
Dairy Wlk. SW19 4G 135
Daisy Cl. CR0: C'don 1K 169
Daisy Dobbings Wlk. N19 7J 47
(off Jessie Blythe La.)
Daisy La. SW6 3J 117
Daisy Rd. E16 4G 87
E18 2K 51
Dakin Pl. E1 5A 86
Dakota Bldg. SE10 1D 122
(off Deal's Gateway)
Dakota Cl. SM6: Wall 7K 167
Dakota Gdns. E6 4C 88
UB5: N'olt 3C 76
Dalberg Rd. SW2 4A 120
(not continuous)
Dalberg Way SE2 3D 108
Dalby Rd. SW18 4A 118
Dalbys Cres. N17 6K 33
Dalby St. NW5 6F 65
Dalcross Rd. TW4: Houn 2C 112
Dale, The BR2: Kes 4B 172
Dale Av. HA8: Edg 1F 43
TW4: Houn 3C 112
Dalebury Rd. SW17 2D 136
Dale Cl. EN5: New Bar 6E 20
HA5: Pinn 1K 39
SE3 3J 123
Dale Ct. EN2: Enf 1H 23
KT2: King T 7F 133
(off York Rd.)
Dale Dr. UB4: Hayes 4H 75
Dalefield IG9: Buck H 1F 37
(off Roebuck La.)
Dale Gdns. IG8: Wfd G 4E 36
Dale Grn. Rd. N11 3A 32
Dale Gro. N12 5F 31
Daleham Dr. UB8: Hil 6D 74
Daleham Gdns. NW3 5B 64
Daleham M. NW3 6B 64
Dalehead NW1 1A 6
(off Hampstead Rd.)
Dale Ho. N1 1E 84
(off New Era Est.)
NW8 1A 82
(off Boundary Rd.)
SE4 4A 122
Dale Lodge N6 6G 47
Dalemain M. E16 1J 105
Dale Pk. Av. SM5: Cars 2D 166
Dale Pk. Rd. SE19 1C 156
Dale Rd. KT12: Walt T 7H 147
NW5 5E 64
SE17 6B 102
SM1: Sutt 4H 165
TW16: Sun 7H 129
UB6: G'frd 5F 77
Dale Row W11 6G 81
Daleside Rd. KT19: Ewe 6K 163
SW16 5F 137
Dale St. W4 5A 98
Dale Vw. Av. E4 2K 35
Dale Vw. Cres. E4 2K 35
Dale Vw. Gdns. E4 3A 36
Daleview Rd. N15 6E 48
Dalewood Gdns.
KT4: Wor Pk 2D 164
Dale Wood Rd. BR6: Orp 7J 161
Daley Ho. W12 6D 80
Daley St. E9 6K 67
Daley Thompson Way SW8 2F 119
Dalgarno Gdns. W10 5E 80
Dalgarno Way W10 4E 80
Dalgleish St. E14 6A 86
Daling Way E3 1A 86
Dali Universe 6G 13 (2K 101)
Dalkeith Ct. SW1 3D 18
(off Vincent St.)
Dalkeith Gro. HA7: Stan 5J 27
Dalkeith Ho. SW9 1B 120
(off Lothian Rd.)
Dalkeith Rd. IG1: Ilf 3G 71
SE21 1C 138
Dallas Rd. NW4 7C 44
SE26 3H 139
SM3: Cheam 6G 165
W5 5F 79
Dallas Ter. UB3: Harl 3H 93
Dallega Cl. UB3: Hayes 7F 75
Dallinger Rd. SE12 6H 123
Dalling Rd. W6 4D 98
Dallington Sq. EC1 3B 8
(off Dallington St.)
Dallington St. EC1 3B 8 (4B 84)
Dallin Rd. DA6: Bex 4D 126
SE18 7F 107
Dalmain Rd. SE23 1K 139
Dalmally Rd. CR0: C'don 7F 157
Dalmany Pas. CR0: C'don 7F 157
Dalmeny Av. N7 4H 65
SW16 2A 156
Dalmeny Cl. HA0: Wemb 6C 60
Dalmeny Cres. TW3: Houn 4H 113
Dalmeny Rd. DA8: Erith 1H 127
EN5: New Bar 6F 21
KT4: Wor Pk 3D 164
N7 3H 65
(not continuous)
SM5: Cars 7E 166
Dalmeyer Rd. NW10 6B 62
Dalmore Rd. SE21 2C 138
Dalo Lodge E3 5C 86
(off Gale St.)
Dalrymple Cl. N14 7C 22
Dalrymple Rd. SE4 4A 122
DALSTON 6F 67
Dalston Gdns. HA7: Stan 1E 42
Dalston La. E8 6F 67
Dalton Av. CR4: Mitc 2C 154
Dalton Cl. BR6: Orp 3J 173
UB4: Hayes 4F 75
Dalton Ho. HA7: Stan 5F 27
SE14 6K 103
(off John Williams Cl.)
SW1 5J 17
(off Ebury Bri. Rd.)
Dalton Rd. HA3: W'stone 2H 41
Dalton St. SE27 2B 138
Dalwood St. SE5 1E 120
Daly Dr. BR1: Brom 3E 160
Dalyell Rd. SW9 3K 119
Damascene Wlk. SE21 1C 138
Damask Ct. SM1: Sutt 1K 165
Damask Cres. E16 4G 87
Damer Ter. SW10 7A 100
Dames Rd. E7 3J 69
Dame St. N1 2C 84
Damien Ct. E1 6H 85
(off Damien St.)
Damien St. E1 6H 85
Damon Cl. DA14: Sidc 3B 144
Damory Ho. SE16 4H 103
(off Abbeyfield Est.)
Damson Dr. UB3: Hayes 7J 75
Damsonwood Rd. UB2: S'hall 3E 94
Danbrook Rd. SW16 1J 155
Danbury Cl. RM6: Chad H 3D 54
Danbury Mans. IG11: Bark 7F 71
(off Whiting Av.)
Danbury M. SM6: Wall 4F 167
Danbury St. N1 2B 84
Danbury Way IG8: Wfd G 6F 37
Danby Ct. EN2: Enf 3H 23
Danby Ho. E9 7J 67
(off Frampton Pk. Rd.)
W10 3G 81
(off Bruckner St.)
Danby St. SE15 3F 121
Dancer Rd. SW6 1H 117
TW9: Rich 3G 115
Dando Cres. SE3 3K 123
Dandridge Cl. SE10 5H 105
Dandridge Ho. E1 5J 9
(off Lamb St.)
Danebury CR0: New Ad 6E 170
Danebury Av. SW15 6A 116
(not continuous)
Daneby Rd. SE6 3D 140
Dane Cl. BR6: Farnb 5H 173
DA5: Bexl 7G 127
Danecourt Gdns. CR0: C'don 3F 169
Danecroft Rd. SE24 5C 120
Danehill Wlk. DA14: Sidc 3A 144
Danehurst TW8: Bford 7C 96
Danehurst Gdns. IG4: Ilf 5C 52
Danehurst St. SW6 1G 117
Daneland EN4: E Barn 6J 21
Danemead Gro. UB5: N'olt 5F 59
Danemere St. SW15 3E 116
Dane Pl. E3 2A 86
Dane Rd. IG1: Ilf 5G 71
N18 3D 34
SW19 1A 154
TW15: Ashf 6E 128
UB1: S'hall 7C 76
W13 1C 96
Danesbury Rd. TW13: Felt 1K 129
Danescombe SE12 1J 141
Danes Ct. HA9: Wemb 3H 61
NW8 1D 82
(off St Edmund's Ter.)
Danescourt Cres. SM1: Sutt 2A 166
Danescroft NW4 5F 45
Danescroft Av. NW4 5F 45
Danescroft Gdns. NW4 5F 45
Danesdale Rd. E9 6A 68
Danesfield SE5 6E 102
(off Albany Rd.)
Danes Ga. HA1: Harr 3J 41
Danes Ho. W10 5E 80
(off Sutton Way)
Danes Rd. RM7: Rush G 7J 55
Dane St. WC1 6G 7 (5K 83)
Daneswood Av. SE6 3E 140
Danethorpe Rd. HA0: Wemb 6D 60
Danetree Cl. KT19: Ewe 7J 163
Danetree Rd. KT19: Ewe 7J 163
Danette Gdns. RM10: Dag 2G 73
Daneville Rd. SE5 1D 120
Dangan Rd. E11 6J 51
Daniel Bolt Cl. E14 5D 86
Daniel Cl. N18 4D 34
SW17 6C 136
TW4: Houn 7D 112
Daniel Ct. NW9 1A 44
Daniel Gdns. SE15 7F 103
Daniell Ho. N1 2D 84
(off Cranston Est.)
Daniell Way CR0: Wadd 1J 167
Daniel Pl. NW4 7D 44
Daniel Rd. W5 7F 79
Daniels Rd. SE15 3J 121
Danleigh Ct. N14 7C 22
Dan Leno Wlk. SW6 7K 99
Dan Mason Dr. W4 2J 115
Dansey Pl. W1 2C 12
Dansington Rd. DA16: Well 4A 126
Danson Cres. DA16: Well 3B 126
Danson House 4C 126
DANSON INTERCHANGE 5D 126
Danson La. DA16: Well 4B 126
Danson Mead DA16: Well 3C 126
Danson Pk. 5C 126
Danson Rd. DA5: Bexl, Bex 6C 126
DA6: Bex 5D 126
SE17 5B 102
Danson Underpass DA15: Sidc 6C 126
Danson Water Sports Cen. 4C 126
Dante Pl. SE11 4B 102
Dante Rd. SE11 4B 102
Danube Apartments N8 3K 47
(off Gt. Amwell La.)
Danube Ct. SE15 7F 103
(off Daniel Gdns.)
Danube St. SW3 5D 16 (5C 100)
Danvers Ho. E1 6G 85
(off Christian St.)
Danvers Rd. N8 4H 47
Danvers St. SW3 7B 16 (6B 100)
Dao Ct. E13 1K 87
Da Palma Ct. SW6 6J 99
(off Anselm Rd.)
Daphne Ct. KT4: Wor Pk 2A 164
Daphne Gdns. E4 3K 35
Daphne Ho. N22 1A 48
(off Acacia Rd.)
Daphne St. SW18 6A 118
Daplyn St. E1 5K 9 (5G 85)

D'Arblay St. W1 1B 12 (6G 83)
Darby Cres. TW16: Sun 2A 148
Darby Gdns. TW16: Sun 2A 148
Darcy Av. SM6: Wall 4G 167
Darcy Cl. N20 2G 31
D'Arcy Dr. HA3: Kent 4D 42
Darcy Gdns. HA3: Kent 4D 42
RM9: Dag 1F 91
Darcy Ho. E8 1H 85
(off London Flds. E. Side)
D'Arcy Pl. BR2: Brom 4J 159
Darcy Rd. SM3: Cheam 4F 165
SW16 2J 155
TW7: Isle 1A 114
Dare Gdns. RM8: Dag 3E 72
Darell Rd. TW9: Rich 3G 115
Darent Ho. BR1: Brom 5F 141
NW8 5B 4
(off Church St. Est.)
Darenth Rd. DA16: Well 1A 126
N16 7F 49
Darfield NW1 1G 83
(off Bayham St.)
Darfield Rd. SE4 5B 122
Darfield Way W10 6F 81
Darfur St. SW15 3F 117
Dargate Cl. SE19 7F 139
Darien Ho. E1 5K 85
(off Shandy St.)
Darien Rd. SW11 3B 118
Daring Ho. E3 2A 86
(off Roman Rd.)
Dark Ho. Wlk. EC3 3F 15 (7D 84)
Darland Lake Nature Reserve 3B 30
Darlands Dr. EN5: Barn 5A 20
Darlan Rd. SW6 7H 99
Darlaston Rd. SW19 7F 135
Darley Cl. CR0: C'don 6A 158
Darley Dr. KT3: N Mald 2K 151
Darley Gdns. SM4: Mord 6A 154
Darley Ho. SE11 6G 19
Darley Rd. N9 1A 34
SW11 6D 118
Darling Ho. TW1: Twick 6D 114
Darling Rd. SE4 3C 122
Darling Row E1 4H 85
Darlington Ct. SE6 1H 141
Darlington Ho. SW8 7H 101
(off Hemans St.)
Darlington Rd. SE27 5B 138
Darmaine Cl. CR2: S Croy 7C 168
Darnall Ho. SE10 1E 122
(off Royal Hill)
Darnaway Pl. E14 5E 86
(off Aberfeldy St.)
Darnay Ho. SE16 7K 15 (3G 103)
Darndale Cl. E17 2B 50
Darnley Ho. E14 6A 86
(off Camdenhurst St.)
Darnley Rd. E9 6J 67
IG8: Wfd G 1J 51
Darnley Ter. W11 1F 99
Darrell Charles Ct. UB8: Uxb 7A 56
Darrell Rd. SE22 5G 121
Darren Cl. N4 7K 47
Darren Ct. N7 4J 65
Darrick Wood Rd. BR6: Orp 2H 173
Darrick Wood Sports Cen. 3G 173
Darrick Wood Swimming Pool 3G 173
Darris Cl. UB4: Yead 4C 76
Darsley Dr. SW8 1H 119
Dartford Av. N9 6D 24
Dartford By-Pass DA5: Bexl, Dart 7K 127
Dartford Gdns. RM6: Chad H 5B 54
Dartford Ho. SE1 4F 103
(off Longfield Est.)
Dartford Rd. DA5: Bexl 1J 145
Dartford St. SE17 6C 102
Dartington NW1 1G 83
(off Plender St.)
Dartington Ho. SW8 2H 119
(off Union Gro.)
W2 5K 81
(off Senior St.)
Dartle Ct. SE16 2G 103
(off Scott Lidgett Cres.)
Dartmoor Wlk. E14 4C 104
(off Charnwood Gdns.)
Dartmouth Cl. W11 6H 81
Dartmouth Ct. SE10 1E 122
Dartmouth Gro. SE10 1E 122
Dartmouth Hill SE10 1E 122
Dartmouth Ho.
KT2: King T 1E 150
(off Seven Kings Way)
SE10 1D 122
(off Catherine Gro.)
DARTMOUTH PARK 3F 65
Dartmouth Pk. Av. NW5 3F 65
Dartmouth Pk. Hill N19 1F 65
NW5 1F 65
Dartmouth Pk. Rd. NW5 4F 65
Dartmouth Pl. SE23 2J 139
W4 6A 98
Dartmouth Rd. BR2: Hayes 7J 159
HA4: Ruis 3J 57
NW2 6F 63
NW4 6C 44
SE23 3H 139
SE26 3H 139
Dartmouth Row SE10 2E 122
Dartmouth St. SW1 7D 12 (2H 101)
Dartmouth Ter. SE10 1F 123
Dartnell Rd. CR0: C'don 7F 157
Darton Ct. W3 1J 97
Dartrey Twr. SW10 7A 100
(off Worlds End Est.)
Dartrey Wlk. SW10 7A 100
Dart St. W10 3G 81
Darvell Ho. SE17 5D 102
(off Inville Rd.)
Darville Rd. N16 3F 67
Darwell Cl. E6 2E 88
Darwen Pl. E2 2H 85
Darwin Cl. BR6: Farnb 5H 173
N11 3A 32
Darwin Ct. E13 3K 87
NW1 1F 83
(not continuous)
SE17 4D 102
(off Barlow St.)
Darwin Dr. UB1: S'hall 6F 77
Darwin Ho. SW1 7A 18
Darwin Rd. DA16: Well 3K 125
N22 1B 48
W5 5C 96
Darwin St. SE17 4D 102
Darwood Ct. NW6 7A 64
(off Belsize Rd.)
Daryngton Dr. UB6: G'frd 2H 77
Daryngton Ho. SE1 7F 15
(off Manciple St.)
SW8 7J 101
(off Hartington Rd.)
Dashwood Cl. DA6: Bex 5G 127
Dashwood Rd. N8 6K 47
Dassett Rd. SE27 5B 138
Data Point Bus. Cen. E16 4F 87
Datchelor Pl. SE5 1D 120
Datchet Ho. NW1 1K 5
(off Augustus St.)
Datchet Rd. SE6 2B 140
Datchworth Ct. EN1: Enf 5K 23
Datchworth Ho. N1 7B 66
(off The Sutton Est.)
Date St. SE17 5D 102
Daubeney Gdns. N17 7H 33
Daubeney Pl.
TW12: Hamp 1G 149
(off High St.)
Daubeney Rd. E5 4A 68
N17 7H 33
Daubeney Twr. SE8 5B 104
(off Bowditch)
Dault Rd. SW18 6A 118
Dauncey Ho. SE1 7A 14
Davema Cl. BR7: Chst 1E 160
Davenant Rd. CR0: C'don 4B 168
N19 2H 65
Davenant St. E1 5G 85
Davenport Cen. IG11: Bark 1B 90
Davenport Cl.
TW11: Tedd 6A 132
Davenport Ct. CR0: C'don 7B 156
Davenport Ho. SE11 3J 19
(off Walnut Tree Wlk.)
Davenport Lodge TW5: Hest 7C 94
Davenport Rd. DA14: Sidc 2E 144
SE6 6D 122
Daventer Dr. HA7: Stan 7E 26
Daventry Av. E17 6C 50
Daventry Cl. SL3: Poyle 4A 174
Daventry St. NW1 5C 4 (5C 82)
Daver Ct. SW3 5D 16 (5C 100)
W5 4D 78
Davern Cl. SE10 4H 105
Davey Cl. N7 6K 65
N13 5E 32
Davey Rd. E9 7C 68
Davey's Ct. WC2 2E 12
Davey St. SE15 6F 103
David Av. UB6: G'frd 3J 77
David Beckham Academy, The 2H 105
David Cl. UB3: Harl 7G 93
David Coffer Ct. DA17: Belv 4H 109
David Ct. N20 3F 31
Davidge Ho. SE1 7K 13
(off Coral St.)
Davidge St. SE1 7A 14 (2B 102)
David Hewitt Ho. E3 5D 86
(off Watts Gro.)
David Ho. DA15: Sidc 3A 144
SW8 7J 101
(off Wyvil Rd.)
David Lean Cinema 3C 168
(in Croydon Clocktower)
David Lee Point E15 1G 87
(off Leather Gdns.)
David Lloyd Leisure
Barnet 7G 31
Cheam 7F 165
Ealing 5H 59
Enfield 2B 24
Epping Forest 1J 37
Fulham Broadway 7J 99
(within Fulham Broadway Shop. Cen.)
Hounslow 5A 94
Kidbrooke 4K 123
Kingston upon Thames 2E 150
(in The Rotunda Cen.)
Merton 3F 153
Sidcup 5C 144
South Kensington 4K 99
David M. W1 5F 5 (5D 82)
David Rd. RM8: Dag 2E 72
SL3: Poyle 5A 174
David's Ct. UB1: S'hall 6G 77
(off Whitecote Rd.)
Davidson Gdns. SW8 7J 101
Davidson La. HA1: Harr 7K 41
Davidson Rd. CR0: C'don 1E 168
Davidson Terraces
E7 5K 69
(off Claremont Rd., not continuous)
David's Rd. SE23 1J 139
David St. E15 6F 69
David Twigg Cl. KT2: King T 1E 150
Davies Cl. CR0: C'don 6G 157
Davies La. E11 2G 69
Davies M. W1 2J 11 (7F 83)
Davies St. W1 1J 11 (6F 83)
Davies Wlk. TW7: Isle 1H 113
Da Vinci Ct. SE16 5H 103
(off Rossetti Rd.)
Davington Gdns. RM8: Dag 5B 72
Davington Rd. RM8: Dag 6B 72
Davinia Cl. IG8: Wfd G 6J 37
Davis Ho. W12 7D 80
(off White City Est.)
Davis Rd. KT9: Chess 4G 163
W3 1B 98
Davis St. E13 2K 87
Davisville Rd. W12 2C 98
Davmor Ct. TW8: Bford 5C 96
Dawes Av. TW7: Isle 5A 114
Dawes Ho. SE17 4D 102
(off Orb St.)
Dawes Rd. SW6 7G 99
UB10: Uxb 2A 74
Dawes St. SE17 5D 102
Dawley Av. UB8: Hil 5E 74
Dawley Pde. UB3: Hayes 7E 74
Dawley Pk. UB3: Hayes 2F 93
Dawley Rd. UB3: Harl, Hayes 7E 74
Dawlish Av. N13 4D 32
SW18 2K 135
UB6: G'frd 2A 78
Dawlish Dr. HA4: Ruis 2J 57
HA5: Pinn 5C 40
IG3: Ilf 4J 71
Dawlish Rd. E10 1E 68
N17 3G 49
NW2 6F 63
Dawnay Gdns. SW18 2B 136
Dawnay Rd. SW18 2A 136
Dawn Cl. TW4: Houn 3C 112
Dawn Cres. E15 1F 87
Dawpool Rd. NW2 2B 62
Daws Hill E4 2K 25
Daws La. NW7 5G 29
Dawson Av. IG11: Bark 7J 71
Dawson Cl. SE18 4G 107
UB3: Hayes 5F 75
Dawson Gdns. IG11: Bark 7K 71
Dawson Ho. E2 3J 85
(off Sceptre Rd.)
Dawson Pl. W2 7J 81
Dawson Rd. KT1: King T 3F 151
NW2 5E 62
Dawson St. E2 1K 9 (2F 85)
Dawson Ter. N9 7D 24
Dax Ct. TW16: Sun 3A 148
Daybrook Rd. SW19 2K 153
Day Ho. SE5 7C 102
(off Bethwin Rd.)
Daylesford Av. SW15 4C 116
Daymer Gdns. HA5: Eastc 4K 39
Daynor Ho. NW6 1J 81
(off Quex Ho.)
Daysbrook Rd. SW2 1K 137
Days La. DA15: Sidc 7J 125
Dayton Gro. SE15 1J 121
Deaconess Ct. N15 4F 49
(off Tottenham Grn. E.)
Deacon Est., The E4 6G 35
Deacon Ho. SE11 4H 19
(off Black Prince Rd.)
Deacon M. N1 7D 66
Deacon Rd. KT2: King T 1F 151
NW2 5C 62
Deacons Cl. HA5: Pinn 2K 39
Deacons Ct. TW1: Twick 2K 131
Deacons Leas BR6: Orp 4H 173
Deacon's Ri. N2 5B 46
Deacons Ter. N1 6C 66
(off Harecourt Rd.)
Deacons Wlk.
TW12: Hamp 4E 130
Deacon Way IG8: Wfd G 7J 37
SE17 4C 102

Deal Ct. NW9 2B 44
(off Hazel Cl.)
UB1: S'hall 6G 77
(off Haldane Rd.)
Deal Ho. SE15 6K 103
(off Lovelinch La.)
SE17 5E 102
(off Mina Rd.)
Deal M. W5 4D 96
Deal Porters Wlk. SE16 2K 103
Deal Porters Way SE16 3J 103
Deal Rd. SW17 6E 136
Deal's Gateway SE10 1C 122
Deal St. E1 5G 85
Dealtry Rd. SW15 4E 116
Deal Wlk. SW9 7A 102
Dean Abbott Ho. SW1 3C 18
(off Vincent St.)
Dean Bradley St. SW1 2E 18 (3J 101)
Dean Cl. E9 5J 67
SE16 1K 103
UB10: Hil 7B 56
Dean Ct. HA0: Wemb 3B 60
HA8: Edg 6C 28
RM7: Rom 5K 55
SW8 7J 101
(off Thorncroft St.)
W3 6K 79
Deancross St. E1 6J 85
Dean Dr. HA7: Stan 2E 42
Deane Av. HA4: Ruis 5A 58
Deane Ct. HA6: Nwood 1G 39
Deane Cft. Rd. HA5: Eastc 6A 40
Deanery Cl. N2 4C 46
Deanery M. W1 4H 11
Deanery Rd. E15 6G 69
Deanery St.
W1 4H 11 (1E 100)
Deane Way HA4: Ruis 6K 39
Dean Farrar St. SW1 1D 18 (3H 101)
Deanfield Gdns. CR0: C'don 4D 168
Dean Gdns. E17 4F 51
Deanhill Ct. SW14 4H 115
Deanhill Rd. SW14 4H 115
Dean Ho. E1 6J 85
(off Tarling St.)
SE14 7A 104
(off New Cross Rd.)
Dean Rd. CR0: C'don 4D 168
NW2 6E 62
SE28 1A 108
TW3: Houn 5F 113
TW12: Hamp 5E 130
Dean Ryle St. SW1 3E 18 (4J 101)
Deansbrook Cl. HA8: Edg 7D 28
Deansbrook Rd. HA8: Edg 7C 28
Dean's Bldgs. SE17 4D 102
Deans Cl. CR0: C'don 3F 169
HA8: Edg 6D 28
W4 6H 97
Dean's Ct. EC4 1B 14 (6B 84)
Deanscroft Av. NW9 1J 61
Deans Dr. HA8: Edg 5E 28
N13 6G 33
Deans Ga. Cl. SE23 3K 139
Deanshanger Ho. SE8 4K 103
(off Chilton Gro.)
Deans La. HA8: Edg 6D 28
W4 6H 97
(off Deans Cl.)
Dean's M. W1 7K 5 (6F 83)
Deans Rd. SM1: Sutt 3K 165
W7 1K 95
Dean Stanley St. SW1 2E 18 (3J 101)
Deanston Wharf E16 2K 105
Dean St. E7 5J 69
W1 7C 6 (6H 83)
Deans Way HA8: Edg 5D 28
Deansway N2 4B 46
N9 3K 33
Deanswood N11 6C 32
Dean's Yd. SW1 1D 18 (3H 101)
Dean Trench St. SW1 2E 18 (3J 101)
Dean Wlk. HA8: Edg 6D 28
Dean Way UB2: S'hall 2F 95
Dearne Cl. HA7: Stan 5F 27
Dearn Gdns. CR4: Mitc 3C 154
Dearsley Ho. RM13: Rain 2K 91
Dearsley Rd. EN1: Enf 3B 24
Deason St. E15 1E 86
Deauville Ct. SE16 2K 103
(off Eleanor Cl.)
SW4 6G 119
De Barowe M. N5 4B 66
Debdale Ho. E2 1G 85
(off Whiston Rd.)
Debden N17 2D 48
(off Gloucester Rd.)
Debden Cl. IG8: Wfd G 7G 37
KT2: King T 5D 132
NW9 1A 44
De Beauvoir Ct. N1 7D 66
(off Northchurch Rd.)
De Beauvoir Cres. N1 1E 84
De Beauvoir Est. N1 1E 84
De Beauvoir Pl. N1 6E 66
De Beauvoir Rd. N1 1E 84
De Beauvoir Sq. N1 7E 66
DE BEAUVOIR TOWN 1E 84
Debenham Ct. E8 1G 85
(off Pownall Rd.)
Debham Ct. NW2 3E 62
Debnams Rd. SE16 4J 103
De Bohun Av. N14 6A 22
Deborah Cl. TW7: Isle 1J 113
Deborah Ct. E18 3K 51
(off Victoria Rd.)
Deborah Cres. HA4: Ruis 7F 39
Deborah Lodge HA8: Edg 1H 43
Debrabant Cl. DA8: Erith 6K 109
De Brome Rd. TW13: Felt 1A 130
De Bruin Ct. E14 5E 104
(off Ferry St.)
Deburgh Rd. SW19 7A 136
Debussy NW9 2B 44
Decima St. SE1 7G 15 (3E 102)
Decimus Cl. CR7: Thor H 4D 156
Deck Cl. SE16 1K 103
Decoy Av. NW11 5G 45
De Crespigny Pk. SE5 2D 120
Dee Ct. W7 6H 77
(off Hobbayne Rd.)
Dee Ho. KT2: King T 1D 150
(off May Bate Av.)
Deeley Rd. SW8 1H 119
Deena Cl. W3 6F 79
Deen City Farm 2A 154
Deepdale SW19 4F 135
Deepdale Av. BR2: Brom 4H 159
Deepdale Cl. N11 6K 31
Deepdale Ct. CR0: C'don 4D 168
(off Birdhurst Av.)
Deep Dene W5 4F 79
Deepdene Av. CR0: C'don 3F 169
Deepdene Cl. E11 4J 51
Deepdene Ct. BR2: Brom 3G 159
N21 6G 23
Deepdene Gdns. SW2 7K 119
Deepdene Point SE23 3K 139
Deepdene Rd. DA16: Well 3A 126
SE5 4D 120
Deepwell Cl. TW7: Isle 1A 114
Deepwood La. UB6: G'frd 3H 77
Deerbrook Rd. SE24 1B 138
Deerdale Rd. SE24 4C 120
Deerfield Cl. NW9 5B 44
Deerfield Cotts. NW9 5B 44
Deerhurst Cl. TW13: Felt 4K 129
Deerhurst Cres.
TW12: Ham H 5G 131
Deerhurst Ho. SE15 6G 103
(off Haymerle Rd.)
Deerhurst Rd. NW2 6F 63
SW16 5K 137
Deerings Dr. HA5: Eastc 5J 39
Deerleap Gro. E4 5J 25
Dee Rd. TW9: Rich 4F 115
Deer Pk. Cl. KT2: King T 7H 133
Deer Pk. Gdns. CR4: Mitc 4B 154
Deer Pk. Rd. SW19 2K 153
Deer Pk. Way BR4: W W'ck 2H 171
Deeside Rd. SW17 3B 136
Dee St. E14 6E 86
Defence Cl. SE28 1J 107
Defiance Wlk. SE18 3D 106
Defiant NW9 2B 44
(off Further Acre)
Defiant Way SM6: Wall 7J 167
Defoe Av. TW9: Kew 7G 97
Defoe Cl. SE16 2B 104
SW17 6C 136
Defoe Ho. EC2 5D 8
Defoe Pl. EC2 5C 8
(off Beech St.)
SW17 4D 136
Defoe Rd. N16 3E 66
De Frene Rd. SE26 4K 139
Degema Rd. BR7: Chst 5F 143
Dehar Cres. NW9 7B 44
De Haviland Dr. SE18 6F 107
De Haviland Rd. HA8: Edg 2G 43
De Havilland Cl. UB5: Yead 3B 76
De Havilland Rd. HA8: Edg 2G 43
TW5: Hest 7A 94
Dehavilland Studios E5 2J 67
De Havilland Way TW19: Stanw 6A 110
Dekker Ho. SE5 7D 102
(off Elmington Est.)
Dekker Rd. SE21 6E 120
Delacourt Rd. SE3 7K 105
Delafield Ho. E1 6G 85
(off Christian St.)
Delafield Rd. SE7 5K 105
Delaford Rd. SE16 5H 103
Delaford St. SW6 7G 99
Delamare Cres. CR0: C'don 6J 157
Delamere Ct. E17 2E 50
Delamere Gdns. NW7 6E 28
Delamere Rd. SW20 1F 153
UB4: Yead 7B 76
W5 2E 96
Delamere St. W2 5K 81
Delamere Ter. W2 5K 81
Delancey Pas. NW1 1F 83
(off Delancey St.)
Delancey St. NW1 1F 83
Delancey Studios
NW1 1F 83
Delany Ho. SE10 6E 104
(off Thames St.)
Delarch Ho. SE1 7A 14
De Laune St. SE17 6K 19 (5B 102)
Delaware Mans. W9 4K 81
(off Delaware Rd.)
Delaware Rd. W9 4K 81
Delawyk Cres. SE24 6C 120
Delcombe Av. KT4: Wor Pk 1E 164
Delderfield Ho. RM1: Rom 2K 55
(off Portnoi Cl.)
Delfina Studio Trust 6G 15
(off Bermondsey St.)
Delft Ho. KT2: King T 7F 133
(off Acre Rd.)
Delft Way SE22 5E 120
Delhi Rd. EN1: Enf 7A 24
Delhi St. N1 1J 83
Delia St. SW18 7K 117
Delisle Rd. SE28 2J 107
(not continuous)
Delius Gro. E15 2F 87
Dell, The DA5: Bexl 1K 145
HA0: Wemb 5B 60
HA5: Pinn 2B 40
IG8: Wfd G 3E 36
SE2 5A 108
SE19 1F 157
TW8: Bford 6C 96
TW14: Felt 7K 111
Della Path E5 3G 67
Dellbow Rd. TW14: Felt 5K 111
Dell Cl. E15 1F 87
IG8: Wfd G 3E 36
SM6: Wall 4G 167
Dell Farm Rd. HA4: Ruis 5F 39
Dellfield Cl. BR3: Beck 1E 158
Dell La. KT17: Ewe 5C 164
Dellors Cl. EN5: Barn 5A 20
Dellow Cl. IG2: Ilf 7H 53
Dellow Ho. E1 7H 85
(off Dellow St.)
Dellow St. E1 7H 85
Dell Rd. KT17: Ewe 6C 164
UB7: W Dray 4B 92
Dells Cl. E4 7J 25
TW11: Tedd 6K 131
Dell's M. SW1 4B 18
Dell Wlk. KT3: N Mald 2A 152
Dell Way W13 6C 78
Dellwood Gdns. IG5: Ilf 3E 52
Delmare Cl. SW9 4K 119
Delme Cres. SE3 2K 123
Delmerend Ho. SW3 5C 16
(off Cale St.)
Delmey Cl. CR0: C'don 3F 169
Deloraine Ho. SE8 1C 122
Delorme St. W6 6F 99
Delroy Ct. N20 7F 21
Delta Bldg. E14 6E 86
(off Ashton St.)
Delta Cen. HA0: Wemb 1F 79
Delta Cl. KT4: Wor Pk 3B 164
Delta Ct. NW2 2C 62
Delta Gro. UB5: N'olt 3B 76
Delta Pk. SW18 4K 117
Delta Pk. Ind. Est. EN3: Brim 3G 25
Delta Point CR0: C'don 1C 168
(off Wellesley Rd.)
E2 3G 85
(off Delta St.)
Delta Rd. KT4: Wor Pk 3A 164
Delta St. E2 3G 85
De Luci Rd. DA8: Erith 5J 109
De Lucy St. SE2 4B 108
Delvan Cl. SE18 7E 106
Delvers Mead RM10: Dag 4J 73
Delverton Ho. SE17 5B 102
(off Delverton Rd.)
Delverton Rd. SE17 5B 102
Delvino Rd. SW6 1J 117
Demesne Rd. SM6: Wall 4H 167
Demeta Cl. HA9: Wemb 3J 61
De Montfort Pde. SW16 3J 137
De Montfort Rd. SW16 3J 137
De Morgan Cen., The 5J 117
De Morgan Rd. SW6 3K 117
Dempster Cl. KT6: Surb 1C 162
Dempster Rd. SW18 5A 118
Den, The 5J 103
Denbar Pde. RM7: Rom 4J 55
Denberry Dr. DA14: Sidc 3B 144
Denbigh Cl. BR7: Chst 6D 142
HA4: Ruis 2H 57
NW10 7A 62
SM1: Sutt 5H 165
UB1: S'hall 6D 76
W11 7H 81
Denbigh Ct. E6 3B 88
W7 5K 77
(off Copley Cl.)
Denbigh Dr. UB3: Harl 2E 92

Denbigh Gdns. TW10: Rich 5F 115
Denbigh Ho. SW1 1F 17
(off Hans Pl.)
W11 7H 81
(off Westbourne Gro.)
Denbigh M. SW1 4A 18
Denbigh Pl. SW1 5A 18 (5G 101)
Denbigh Rd. E6 3B 88
TW3: Houn 2F 113
UB1: S'hall 6D 76
W11 7H 81
W13 7B 78
Denbigh St. SW1 4A 18 (4G 101)
(not continuous)
Denbigh Ter. W11 7H 81
Denbridge Rd. BR1: Brom 2D 160
Denby Ct. SE11 3H 19
Dence Ho. E2 2K 9
(off Turin St.)
Denchworth Ho. SW9 2A 120
Dencliffe TW15: Ashf 5C 128
Den Cl. BR3: Beck 3F 159
Dencora Cen., The EN3: Brim 3F 25
Dene, The CR0: C'don 4K 169
HA9: Wemb 4E 60
KT8: W Mole 5D 148
W13 5B 78
Dene Av. DA15: Sidc 7B 126
TW3: Houn 3D 112
Dene Cl. BR2: Hayes 1H 171
DA2: Dart 4K 145
KT4: Wor Pk 2B 164
SE4 3A 122
Dene Ct. CR2: S Croy 5C 168
(off Warham Rd.)
W5 5C 78
Denecroft Cres. UB10: Hil 1D 74
Dene Gdns. HA7: Stan 5H 27
KT7: T Ditt 2A 162
Dene Ho. N14 7C 22
Denehurst Gdns. IG8: Wfd G 4E 36
NW4 6E 44
TW2: Twick 7H 113
TW10: Rich 4G 115
W3 1H 97
Dene Rd. IG9: Buck H 1G 37
N11 1J 31
Denesmead SE24 5C 120
Denewood EN5: New Bar 5F 21
Denewood Rd. N6 6D 46
Denford St. SE10 5H 105
(off Glenforth St.)
Dengie Wlk. N1 1C 84
(off Basire St.)
Denham Cl. DA16: Well 3C 126
Denham Ct. NW6 7A 64
(off Fairfax Rd.)
SE26 3H 139
(off Kirkdale)
UB1: S'hall 7G 77
(off Baird Av.)
Denham Cres. CR4: Mitc 4D 154
Denham Dr. IG2: Ilf 6G 53
Denham Ho. W12 7D 80
(off White City Est.)
Denham Rd. N20 3J 31
TW14: Felt 7A 112
Denham St. SE10 5J 105
Denham Way IG11: Bark 1J 89
Denholme Rd. W9 3H 81
Denison Cl. N2 3A 46
Denison Ho. E14 6C 86
(off Farrance St.)
Denison Rd. SW19 6B 136
TW13: Felt 4H 129
W5 4C 78
Deniston Av. DA5: Bexl 1E 144
Denis Way SW4 3H 119
Denland Ho. SW8 7K 101
(off Dorset Rd.)
Denleigh Gdns. KT7: T Ditt 6J 149
N21 1F 33
Denman Dr. KT10: Clay 5A 162
NW11 5J 45
TW15: Ashf 6D 128
Denman Dr. Nth. NW11 5J 45
Denman Dr. Sth. NW11 5J 45
Denman Ho. N16 2E 66
Denman Pl. W1 2C 12
Denman Rd. SE15 1F 121
Denman St. W1 3C 12 (7H 83)
Denmark Av. SW19 7G 135
Denmark Ct. SM4: Mord 6J 153
Denmark Gdns. SM5: Cars 3D 166
Denmark Gro. N1 2A 84
DENMARK HILL 3C 120
Denmark Hill SE5 1D 120
Denmark Hill Dr. NW9 3C 44
Denmark Hill Est. SE5 4D 120
Denmark Ho. SE7 4C 106
Denmark Mans. SE5 2C 120
(off Coldharbour La.)
Denmark Path SE25 5H 157
Denmark Pl. E3 3C 86
WC2 7D 6 (6H 83)
Denmark Rd. BR1: Brom 1K 159
KT1: King T 3E 150
N8 4A 48
NW6 2H 81
(not continuous)
SE5 1C 120
SE25 5G 157
SM5: Cars 3D 166
SW19 6F 135
TW2: Twick 3H 131
W13 7B 78
Denmark St. E11 3G 69
E13 5K 87
N17 1H 49
WC2 7D 6 (6H 83)
Denmark Ter. N2 3D 46
Denmark Wlk. SE27 4C 138
Denmead Ho. SW15 6B 116
(off Highcliffe Dr.)
Denmead Rd. CR0: C'don 1B 168
Denmore Ct. SM6: Wall 5F 167
Dennan Rd. KT6: Surb 1F 163
Dennard Way BR6: Farnb 4F 173
Denner Rd. E4 2H 35
Denne Ter. E8 1F 85
Dennett Rd. CR0: C'don 1A 168
Dennett's Rd. SE14 1J 121
Denning Av. CR0: Wadd 4A 168
Denning Cl. NW8 1A 4 (3A 82)
TW12: Hamp 5D 130
Denning M. SW12 6E 118
Denning Point E1 7K 9
(off Commercial St.)
Denning Rd. NW3 4B 64
Dennington Cl. E5 2J 67
Dennington Pk. Rd. NW6 6J 63
Denningtons, The KT4: Wor Pk 2A 164
Dennis Av. HA9: Wemb 5F 61
Dennis Cl. TW15: Ashf 7F 129
Dennis Gdns. HA7: Stan 5H 27
Dennis Ho. SM1: Sutt 4K 165
Dennis La. HA7: Stan 3G 27
Dennison Point E15 7E 68
Dennis Pde. N14 1C 32
Dennis Pk. Cres. SW20 1G 153
Dennis Reeve Cl. CR4: Mitc 1D 154
Dennis Rd. KT8: E Mos 4G 149
Denny Cl. E6 5C 88
Denny Cres. SE11 5K 19 (5A 102)
Denny Gdns. RM9: Dag 7B 72
Denny Rd. N9 1C 34
Denny St. SE11 5K 19 (5A 102)
Den Rd. BR2: Brom 3F 159
Densham Ho. NW8 1B 4
(off Cochrane St.)
Densham Rd. E15 1G 87
Densole Cl. BR3: Beck 1A 158
Denstone Ho. SE15 6G 103
(off Haymerle Rd.)
Densworth Gro. N9 2D 34
Dent Ho. SE17 4E 102
(off Tatum St.)
Denton NW1 6E 64
Denton Ct. BR2: Brom 7E 160
Denton Ho. N1 7B 66
(off Halton Rd.)
Denton Rd. DA5: Bexl 2K 145
DA16: Well 7C 108
N8 5K 47
N18 4K 33
TW1: Twick 6D 114
Denton St. SW18 6K 117
Denton Ter. DA5: Bexl 2K 145
Denton Way E5 3K 67
Dents Rd. SW11 6D 118
Denver Cl. BR6: Pet W 6J 161
Denver Rd. N16 7E 48
Denwood SE23 3K 139
Denyer St. SW3 4D 16 (4C 100)
Denys Ho. EC1 5J 7
(off Bourne Est.)
Denziloe Av. UB10: Hil 3D 74
Denzil Rd. NW10 5B 62
Deodar Rd. SW15 4G 117
Deodora Cl. N20 3H 31
Department for Transport 3G 101
(off Warwick Row)
Department for Transport SW1 1A 18
Depot App. NW2 4F 63
Depot Rd. TW3: Houn 3H 113
W12 7E 80
Depot St. SE5 6D 102
DEPTFORD 7C 104
Deptford Bri. SE8 1C 122
Deptford B'way. SE8 1C 122
Deptford Bus. Pk. SE15 6J 103
Deptford Chu. St. SE8 6C 104
Deptford Creek Bri. SE8 6D 104
(off Creek Rd.)
Deptford Ferry Rd. E14 4C 104
Deptford Grn. SE8 6C 104
Deptford High St. SE8 6C 104
Deptford Pk. Bus. Cen. SE8 5A 104
Deptford Strand SE8 4B 104
Deptford Trad. Est. SE8 5A 104
Deptford Wharf SE8 4B 104
De Quincey Ho. SW1 6A 18
(off Lupus St.)
De Quincey M. E16 1J 105
De Quincey Rd. N17 1D 48
Derby Av. HA3: Hrw W 1H 41
N12 5F 31
RM7: Rom 6J 55
Derby Ga. SW1 6E 12 (2J 101)
(not continuous)
Derby Hill SE23 2J 139
Derby Hill Cres. SE23 2J 139
Derby Ho. HA5: Pinn 2B 40
SE11 3J 19
Derby Lodge N3 2H 45
WC1 1G 7
(off Britannia St.)
Derby Rd. CR0: C'don 1B 168
E7 7B 70
E9 1K 85
E18 1H 51
EN3: Pond E 5C 24
KT5: Surb 1G 163
N18 5D 34
SM1: Sutt 6H 165
SW14 4H 115
SW19 7J 135
TW3: Houn 4F 113
UB6: G'frd 1F 77
Derby Rd. Ind. Est. TW3: Houn 4F 113
Derbyshire St. E2 3G 85
(not continuous)
Derby St. W1 5H 11 (1E 100)
Dereham Ho. SE4 4K 121
(off Frendsbury Rd.)
Dereham Pl. EC2 2H 9 (3E 84)
Dereham Rd. IG11: Bark 5K 71
Derek Av. HA9: Wemb 7H 61
KT19: Ewe 6G 163
SM6: Wall 4F 167
Derek Cl. KT19: Ewe 5H 163
Derek Walcott Cl.
SE24 5B 120
Dericote St. E8 1H 85
Deri Dene Cl. TW19: Stanw 6A 110
Derifall Cl. E6 5D 88
Dering Pl. CR0: C'don 4C 168
Dering Rd. CR0: C'don 4C 168
Dering St. W1 1K 11 (6F 83)
Dering Yd. W1 1K 11 (6F 83)
Derinton Rd. SW17 4D 136
Derley Rd. UB2: S'hall 3A 94
Dermody Gdns. SE13 5F 123
Dermody Rd. SE13 5F 123
Deronda Rd. SE24 1B 138
Deroy Cl. SM5: Cars 6D 166
Derrick Gdns. SE7 3A 106
Derrick Rd. BR3: Beck 3B 158
Derrycombe Ho. W2 5J 81
(off Gt. Western Rd.)
Derry Ho. NW8 4B 4
(off Church St. Est.)
Derry Rd. CR0: Bedd 3J 167
Derry St. W8 2K 99
Dersingham Av. E12 4D 70
Dersingham Rd. NW2 3G 63
Derwent NW1 2A 6
(off Robert St.)
Derwent Av. EN4: E Barn 1J 31
N18 5J 33
NW7 6E 28
NW9 5A 44
SW15 4A 134
UB10: Ick 2C 56
Derwent Cl. TW14: Felt 1H 129
Derwent Ct. SE16 2K 103
(off Eleanor Cl.)
Derwent Cres. DA7: Bex 2G 127
HA7: Stan 2C 42
N20 3F 31
Derwent Dr. BR5: Pet W 7H 161
UB4: Hayes 5G 75
Derwent Gdns. HA9: Wemb 7C 42
IG4: Ilf 4C 52
Derwent Gro. SE22 4F 121
Derwent Ho. E3 4B 86
(off Southern Gro.)
KT2: King T 1D 150
(off May Bate Av.)
SE20 2H 157
(off Derwent Rd.)
SW7 3A 16
(off Cromwell Rd.)
Derwent Lodge KT4: Wor Pk 2D 164
TW7: Isle 2H 113
Derwent Ri. NW9 6A 44
Derwent Rd. N13 4E 32
SE20 2G 157
SW20 6F 153
TW2: Whitt 6F 113
UB1: S'hall 6D 76
W5 3C 96
Derwent St. SE10 5G 105
Derwent Wlk. SM6: Wall 7F 167
Derwentwater Rd. W3 1J 97
Derwent Yd. W5 3C 96
(off Derwent Rd.)
De Salis Rd. UB10: Hil 4E 74
Desborough Cl. TW17: Shep 7C 146
W2 5K 81

Desborough Ho. *W14* 6H 99
(off North End Rd.)
Desborough Sailing Club 7D 146
Desborough St. *W2* 5K 81
(off Cirencester St.)
Desenfans Rd. SE21 6E 120
Desford Ct. TW15: Ashf 2C 128
Desford Rd. E16 4G 87
Desford Way TW15: Ashf 2B 128
Design Mus. 6K 15 (2F 103)
Desmond Ho. EN4: E Barn 6H 21
Desmond St. SE14 6A 104
Desmond Tutu Dr.
SE23 1B 140
Despard Rd. N19 1G 65
Desvignes Dr. SE13 6F 123
Dethick Ct. E3 1A 86
Detling Ho. *SE17* 4E 102
(off Congreve St.)
Detling Rd. BR1: Brom 5J 141
DA8: Erith 7K 109
Detmold Rd. E5 2J 67
Devalls Cl. E6 7F 89
Devana End SM5: Cars 3D 166
Devas Rd. SW20 1E 152
Devas St. E3 4D 86
Devenay Rd. E15 7H 69
Devenish Rd. SE2 2A 108
Deventer Cres. SE22 5E 120
Deveraux Cl.
BR3: Beck 5E 158
De Vere Cl. SM6: Wall 7J 167
De Vere Cotts. *W8* 3A 100
(off De Vere Gdns.)
De Vere Gdns. IG1: Ilf 2D 70
W8 2A 100
Deverell St. SE1 3D 102
De Vere M. *W8* 3A 100
(off De Vere Gdns.)
Devereux Ct. WC2 1J 13
Devereux La. SW13 7D 98
Devereux Rd. SW11 6D 118
Deveron Way RM1: Rom 1K 55
Devey Cl. KT2: King T 7B 134
Devitt Ho. *E14* 7D 86
(off Wade's Pl.)
Devizes St. N1 1D 84
Devon Av. TW2: Twick 1G 131
Devon Cl. IG9: Buck H 2E 36
N17 3F 49
UB6: G'frd 1C 78
Devon Ct. TW12: Hamp 7E 130
W7 5K 77
(off Copley Cl.)
Devoncroft Gdns.
TW1: Twick 7A 114
Devon Gdns. N4 6B 48
Devon Ho. E17 2B 50
N1 2B 84
(off Upper St.)
Devonhurst Pl. W4 5K 97
Devonia Gdns. N18 6H 33
Devonia Rd. N1 2B 84
Devon Mans. *HA3: Kent* 5C 42
(off Woodcock Hill)
SE1 6J 15
(off Tooley St.)
Devon Pde. HA3: Kent 5C 42
Devonport W2 1C 10 (6C 82)
Devonport Gdns. IG1: Ilf 6D 52
Devonport Ho. *W2* 5J 81
(off Gt. Western Rd.)
Devonport M. W12 2D 98
Devonport Rd. W12 1D 98
(not continuous)
Devonport St. E1 6K 85
Devon Ri. N2 4B 46
Devon Rd. IG11: Bark 1J 89
SM2: Cheam 7G 165
Devons Est. E3 3D 86
Devonshire Av. SM2: Sutt 7A 166
Devonshire Cl. E15 4G 69
N13 3F 33
W1 5J 5 (5F 83)
Devonshire Ct. *E1* 3J 85
(off Bancroft Rd.)
HA5: Hat E 1D 40
(off Devonshire Rd.)
N18 6H 33
WC1 5F 7
(off Boswell St.)
Devonshire Cres. NW7 7A 30
Devonshire Dr. KT6: Surb 1D 162
SE10 7D 104
Devonshire Gdns. N17 6H 33
N21 7H 23
W4 7J 97
Devonshire Gro. SE15 6H 103
Devonshire Hall *E9* 6J 67
(off Frampton Pk. Rd.)
Devonshire Hill La.
N17 6G 33
(not continuous)
Devonshire Ho. *E14* 4C 104
(off Westferry Rd.)
IG8: Wfd G 7K 37
NW6 6H 63
(off Kilburn High Rd.)
SE1 3C 102
(off Bath Ter.)
SM2: Sutt 7A 166
SW1 5D 18
(off Lindsay Sq.)
Devonshire Ho. Bus. Cen.
BR2: Brom 4K 159
(off Devonshire Sq.)
Devonshire M. N13 4F 33
SW10 7A 16
(off Park Wlk.)
W4 5A 98
Devonshire M. Nth. W1 5J 5 (5F 83)
Devonshire M. Sth. W1 5J 5 (5F 83)
Devonshire M. W. W1 4H 5 (4E 82)
Devonshire Pas. W4 5A 98
Devonshire Pl. NW2 3J 63
W1 4H 5 (4E 82)
W8 3K 99
Devonshire Pl. M. W1 4H 5 (5E 82)
Devonshire Point TW15: Ashf 3E 128
Devonshire Rd. BR6: Orp 7K 161
CR0: C'don 7D 156
DA6: Bex 4E 126
E16 6K 87
E17 6C 50
HA1: Harr 6H 41
HA5: Eastc 6A 40
HA5: Hat E 1D 40
IG2: Ilf 7H 53
N9 1D 34
N13 4E 32
N17 6H 33
NW7 7A 30
SE9 2C 142
SE23 1J 139
SM2: Sutt 7A 166
SM5: Cars 4E 166
SW19 7C 136
TW13: Hanw 3C 130
UB1: S'hall 5E 76
W4 5A 98
W5 3C 96
Devonshire Road Nature Reserve 7K 121
Devonshire Row EC2 6H 9 (5E 84)
Devonshire Row M.
W1 4K 5
Devonshire Sq. BR2: Brom 4K 159
EC2 6H 9 (6E 84)
Devonshire St. W1 5H 5 (5E 82)
W4 5A 98
Devonshire Ter. W2 6A 82
Devonshire Way
CR0: C'don 2A 170
UB4: Yead 6K 75
Devons Rd. E3 3D 86
Devon St. SE15 6H 103
Devon Way KT9: Chess 5C 162
KT19: Ewe 5H 163
UB10: Hil 2B 74
Devon Waye TW5: Hest 7D 94
Devon Wharf E14 5E 86
De Walden Ho. *NW8* 2C 82
(off Allitsen Rd.)
De Walden St. W1 6H 5 (5E 82)
Dewar St. SE15 3G 121
Dewberry Gdns. E6 5C 88
Dewberry St. E14 5E 86
Dewey La. *SW2* 6A 120
(off Tulse Hill)
Dewey Rd. N1 2A 84
RM10: Dag 6H 73
Dewey St. SW17 5D 136
Dewhurst Rd. W14 3F 99
Dewsbury Cl. HA5: Pinn 6C 40
Dewsbury Ct. W4 4J 97
Dewsbury Gdns. KT4: Wor Pk 3C 164
Dewsbury Rd. NW10 5C 62
Dewsbury Ter. NW1 1F 83
Dexter Ho. *DA18: Erith* 3E 108
(off Kale Rd.)
Dexter Rd. EN5: Barn 6A 20
Deyncourt Rd. N17 1C 48
Deynecourt Gdns. E11 4A 52
D'Eynsford Rd. SE5 1D 120
Dhonau Ho. *SE1* 4F 103
(off Longfield Est.)
Diadem Ct. W1 7C 6
Dial Wlk., The *W8* 2K 99
(off The Broad Wlk.)
Diameter Rd. BR5: Pet W 7F 161
Diamond Cl. RM8: Dag 1C 72
Diamond Est. SW17 3C 136
Diamond Ho. *E3* 2A 86
(off Roman Rd.)
Diamond Rd. HA4: Ruis 4B 58
Diamond St. NW10 7K 61
SE15 7E 102
Diamond Ter. SE10 1E 122
Diamond Way SE8 6C 104
Diana Cl. DA14: Sidc 2E 144
E18 1K 51
SE8 6B 104
Diana Gdns. KT6: Surb 2F 163
Diana Ho. SW13 1B 116
Diana, Princess of Wales Memorial Walk
1A 100
(in Kensington Gdns.)
Diana Rd. E17 3B 50
Dianne Ct. SE12 1J 141
Dianne Way EN4: E Barn 4H 21
Dianthus Cl. SE2 5B 108
Dibden Ho. SE5 7E 102
Dibden St. N1 1C 84
Dibdin Cl. SM1: Sutt 3J 165
Dibdin Ho. W9 2K 81
Dibdin Rd. SM1: Sutt 3J 165
Dicey Av. NW2 4E 62
Dickens Av. N3 1A 46
UB8: Hil 6D 74
Dickens Cl. DA8: Erith 7H 109
TW10: Ham 2E 132
UB3: Harl 4G 93
Dickens Ct. *E11* 4J 51
(off Makepeace Rd.)
Dickens Dr. BR7: Chst 6G 143
Dickens Est. SE1 2G 103
SE16 3G 103
Dickens' House 4G 7
Dickens Ho. *NW6* 3J 81
(off Malvern Rd.)
NW8 3B 4
Dickens Ho. *SE17* 5B 102
(off Doddington Gro.)
WC1 3E 6
Dickens La. N18 5K 33
Dickens M. *EC1* 5A 8
(off Turnmill St.)
Dickenson Cl. N9 1B 34
Dickenson Ho. N8 6K 47
Dickenson Rd. N8 7J 47
TW13: Hanw 5A 130
Dickensons La. SE25 5G 157
(not continuous)
Dickensons Pl. SE25 6G 157
Dickens Pl. SL3: Poyle 4A 174
Dickens Ri. IG7: Chig 3K 37
Dickens Rd. E6 2B 88
Dickens Sq. SE1 7D 14 (3C 102)
Dickens St. SW8 2F 119
Dickenswood Cl. SE19 7B 138
Dickerage La. KT3: N Mald 3J 151
Dickerage Rd. KT1: King T 1J 151
KT3: N Mald 1J 151
Dickinson Ct. *EC1* 3B 8
(off Brewhouse Yd.)
Dicksee Ho. *NW8* 4A 4
(off Lyons Pl.)
Dickson Fold HA5: Pinn 4B 40
Dickson Ho. *E1* 6H 85
(off Philpot St.)
Dickson Rd. SE9 3C 124
Dick Turpin Way TW14: Felt 4H 111
Didsbury Cl. E6 1D 88
Dieppe Cl. W14 5H 99
Digby Bus. Cen. *E9* 6K 67
(off Digby Rd.)
Digby Cres. N4 2C 66
Digby Gdns. RM10: Dag 1G 91
Digby Mans. *W6* 5D 98
(off Hammersmith Bri. Rd.)
Digby Pl. CR0: C'don 3F 169
Digby Rd. E9 6K 67
IG11: Bark 7K 71
Digby St. E2 3J 85
Diggon St. E1 5K 85
Dighton Ct. SE5 6C 102
Dighton Rd. SW18 5A 118
Dignum St. N1 2A 84
Digswell St. N7 6A 66
Dilhorne Cl. SE12 3K 141
Dilke St. SW3 7F 17 (6D 100)
Dilloway La. UB2: S'hall 2C 94
Dillwyn Cl. SE26 4A 140
Dilston Cl. UB5: Yead 3A 76
Dilston Gro. SE16 4J 103
Dilton Gdns. SW15 1C 134
Dilwyn Ct. E17 2A 50
Dimes Pl. W6 4D 98
Dimmock Dr. UB6: G'frd 5H 59
Dimond Cl. E7 4J 69
Dimsdale Dr. EN1: Enf 7B 24
NW9 1J 61
Dimsdale Wlk. E13 2J 87
Dimson Cres. E3 3C 86
Dinerman Ct. NW8 1A 82
Dingle, The UB10: Hil 3D 74
Dingle Gdns. E14 7C 86
Dingle Rd. TW15: Ashf 5D 128
Dingles Ct. HA5: Pinn 1B 40
Dingley La. SW16 2H 137
Dingley Pl. EC1 1D 8 (3C 84)
Dingley Rd. EC1 2C 8 (3C 84)
Dingwall Av. CR0: C'don 2C 168
Dingwall Gdns. NW11 6J 45
Dingwall Rd. CR0: C'don 1D 168
SM5: Cars 7D 166
SW18 7A 118
Dinmont Est. E2 2G 85
Dinmont Ho. *E2* 2G 85
(off Pritchard's Rd.)
Dinmont St. E2 2H 85

Dinmore Ho. *E9* ... *1J 85*
(off Templecombe Rd.)
Dinnington Ho. *E1* ... *4H 85*
(off Coventry Rd.)
Dinsdale Gdns. EN5: New Bar ... 5E 20
SE25 ... 5E 156
Dinsdale Rd. SE3 ... 6H 105
Dinsmore Rd. SW12 ... 7F 119
Dinton Ho. *NW8* ... *3D 4*
(off Lilestone St.)
Dinton Rd. KT2: King T ... 7F 133
SW19 ... 6B 136
Diploma Av. N2 ... 4C 46
Diploma Ct. N2 ... 4C 46
Diprose Lodge SW17 ... 4B 136
Dirleton Rd. E15 ... 1H 87
Disbrowe Rd. W6 ... 6G 99
Discovery Bus. Pk. *SE16* ... *3G 103*
(off St James's Rd.)
Discovery Ho. *E14* ... *7E 86*
(off Newby Pl.)
Discovery Wlk. E1 ... 1H 103
Dishforth La. NW9 ... 7F 29
Disley Ct. *UB1: S'hall* ... *6F 77*
(off Howard Rd.)
Disney Pl. SE1 ... 6D 14 (2C 102)
Disney St. SE1 ... 6D 14 (2C 102)
Dison Cl. EN3: Enf H ... 1E 24
Disraeli Cl. SE28 ... 1C 108
W4 ... 3K 97
Disraeli Gdns. SW15 ... 4H 117
Disraeli Rd. E7 ... 6J 69
NW10 ... 2K 79
SW15 ... 4G 117
W5 ... 1D 96
Diss St. E2 ... 1J 9 (3F 85)
Distaff La. EC4 ... 2C 14 (7C 84)
Distillery La. W6 ... 5E 98
Distillery Rd. W6 ... 5E 98
Distillery Wlk. TW8: Bford ... 6E 96
Distin St. SE11 ... 4J 19 (4A 102)
District Rd. HA0: Wemb ... 5B 60
Ditch All. SE13 ... 1D 122
Ditchburn St. E14 ... 7E 86
Ditchfield Rd. UB4: Yead ... 4C 76
Ditchley Ct. *W7* ... *5K 77*
(off Templeman Rd.)
Dittisham Rd. SE9 ... 4C 142
Ditton Cl. KT7: T Ditt ... 7A 150
Dittoncroft Cl. CR0: C'don ... 4E 168
Ditton Grange Cl. KT6: Surb ... 1D 162
Ditton Grange Dr. KT6: Surb ... 1D 162
Ditton Hill KT6: Surb ... 1C 162
Ditton Hill Rd. KT6: Surb ... 1C 162
Ditton Lawn KT7: T Ditt ... 1A 162
Ditton Pl. SE20 ... 1H 157
Ditton Reach KT7: T Ditt ... 6B 150
Ditton Rd. DA6: Bex ... 5D 126
KT6: Surb ... 2D 162
UB2: S'hall ... 5D 94
Divisional Rd. E12 ... 2B 70
Divis Way *SW15* ... *6D 116*
(off Dover Pk. Dr.)
Dixon Clark Ct. N1 ... 6B 66
Dixon Cl. E6 ... 6D 88
Dixon Ho. *W10* ... *6F 81*
(off Darfield Way)
Dixon Pl. BR4: W W'ck ... 1D 170
Dixon Rd. SE14 ... 1A 122
SE25 ... 3E 156
Dixon's All. SE16 ... 2H 103
Dobbin Cl. HA3: Kent ... 2A 42
Dobell Rd. SE9 ... 5D 124
Dobree Av. NW10 ... 7D 62
Dobson Cl. NW6 ... 7B 64
Dobson Ho. *SE14* ... *6K 103*
(off John Williams Cl.)
Doby Ct. EC4 ... 2D 14
Dock Cotts. *E1* ... *7J 85*
(off The Highway)
Dockers Tanner Rd. E14 ... 3C 104
Dockett Eddy KT16: Chert ... 7A 146
Dockett Eddy La. TW17: Shep ... 7B 146
Dockett Moorings KT16: Chert ... 7A 146
Dockhead SE1 ... 7K 15 (2F 103)
Dockhead Wharf *SE1* ... *7K 15*
(off Shad Thames)
Dock Hill Av. SE16 ... 1K 103
Docklands Equestrian Cen., The ... 4E 88
Docklands Sailing Cen. ... 3C 104
Dockland St. E16 ... 1E 106
(not continuous)
Dockley Rd. SE16 ... 3G 103
Dockley Rd. Ind. Est. *SE16* ... *3G 103*
(off Dockley Rd.)
Dock Offices *SE16* ... *3J 103*
(off Surrey Quays Rd.)
Dock Rd. E16 ... 7H 87
IG11: Bark ... 2G 89
TW8: Bford ... 7D 96
Dockside Rd. E16 ... 7B 88
Dock St. E1 ... 7G 85
Dockwell Cl. TW14: Felt ... 4J 111
Dockwell's Ind. Est.
TW14: Felt ... 5K 111
Doctor Johnson Av. SW17 ... 3F 137
Doctors Cl. SE26 ... 5J 139
Docwra's Bldgs. N1 ... 6E 66
Dodbrooke Rd. SE27 ... 3A 138
Dodd Ho. *SE16* ... *4H 103*
(off Rennie Est.)
Doddington Gro. SE17 ... 6B 102
Doddington Pl. SE17 ... 6B 102
Dodsley Pl. N9 ... 3D 34
Dodson St. SE1 ... 7K 13 (2A 102)
Dod St. E14 ... 6B 86
Doebury Wlk. *SE18* ... *6A 108*
(off Prestwood Cl.)
Doel Cl. SW19 ... 7A 136
Dog & Duck Yd. WC1 ... 5H 7
Doggett Rd. SE6 ... 7C 122
Doggetts Ct. EN4: E Barn ... 5H 21
Doghurst Av. UB3: Harl ... 7D 92
Doghurst Dr. UB7: Sip ... 7D 92
Dog Kennel Hill SE22 ... 3E 120
Dog Kennel Hill Est. *SE22* ... *3E 120*
(off Albrighton Rd.)
Dog La. NW10 ... 4A 62
Doherty Rd. E13 ... 4J 87
Dokal Ind. Est.
B2: S'hall ... 3C 94
Dolben Ct. *SW1* ... *4D 18*
(off Montaigne Cl.)
Dolben St. SE1 ... 5A 14 (1B 102)
(not continuous)
Dolby Rd. SW6 ... 2H 117
Dolland Ho. SE11 ... 6H 19
Dolland St. SE11 ... 6H 19 (5K 101)
Dollar Bay Ct. *E14* ... *2E 104*
(off Lawn Ho. Cl.)
Dollary Pde. *KT1: King T* ... *3H 151*
(off Kingston Rd.)
Dolliffe Cl. CR4: Mitc ... 2C 154
Dollis Av. N3 ... 1H 45
Dollis Brook Wlk. EN5: Barn ... 6B 20
Dollis Cres. HA4: Ruis ... 1A 58
Dolliscroft NW7 ... 7B 30
DOLLIS HILL ... 2D 62
Dollis Hill Av. NW2 ... 3D 62
Dollis Hill La. NW2 ... 4B 62
Dollis M. N3 ... 1J 45
Dollis Pk. N3 ... 1H 45
Dollis Rd. N3 ... 7B 30
NW7 ... 7B 30
Dollis Valley Dr. EN5: Barn ... 6C 20
Dollis Valley Way
EN5: Barn ... 6C 20
Dolman Cl. N3 ... 2A 46
Dolman Rd. W4 ... 4K 97
Dolman St. SW4 ... 4K 119
Dolphin Cl. KT6: Surb ... 5D 150
SE16 ... 2K 103
SE28 ... 6D 90
Dolphin Ct. NW11 ... 6G 45
Dolphin Est. TW16: Sun ... 1G 147
Dolphin Ho. SW18 ... 4K 117
Dolphin La. E14 ... 7D 86
Dolphin Rd. TW16: Sun ... 1G 147
UB5: N'olt ... 2D 76
Dolphin Rd. Nth. TW16: Sun ... 1G 147
Dolphin Rd. Sth. TW16: Sun ... 1F 147
Dolphin Rd. W. TW16: Sun ... 1G 147
Dolphin Sq. SW1 ... 6B 18 (5G 101)
W4 ... 7A 98
Dolphin St. KT1: King T ... 2E 150
Dolphin Twr. *SE8* ... *6B 104*
(off Abinger Gro.)
Dombey Ho. *SE1* ... *7K 15*
(off Wolseley St.)
W11 ... *1F 99*
(off St Ann's Rd.)
Dombey St. WC1 ... 5G 7 (5K 83)
(not continuous)
Domecq Ho. *EC1* ... *3B 8*
(off Dallington St.)
Dome Hill Pk. SE26 ... 4F 139
Domelton Ho. *SW18* ... *6K 117*
(off Iron Mill Rd.)
Domett Cl. SE5 ... 4D 120
Domfe Pl. E5 ... 4J 67
Domingo St. EC1 ... 3C 8 (4C 84)
Dominica Cl. E13 ... 2B 88
Dominion Bus. Pk. N9 ... 2E 34
Dominion Cen., The
UB2: S'hall ... 2C 94
Dominion Cl. TW3: Houn ... 2H 113
Dominion Ct. *E8* ... *7F 67*
(off Middleton Rd.)
Dominion Ho. *E14* ... *5D 104*
(off St Davids Sq.)
Dominion Ind. Est. *UB2: S'hall* ... *2C 94*
(off Feather Rd.)
Dominion Pde. HA1: Harr ... 5K 41
Dominion Rd. CR0: C'don ... 7F 157
UB2: S'hall ... 2C 94
Dominion St. EC2 ... 5F 9 (5D 84)
Dominion Theatre ... *7D 6*
(off Tottenham Ct. Rd.)
Domonic Dr. SE9 ... 4F 143
Domville Cl. N20 ... 2G 31
Domville Ct. *SE17* ... *5E 102*
(off Bagshott St.)
Donald Dr. RM6: Chad H ... 5C 54
Donald Hunter Ho. *E7* ... *5K 69*
(off Woodgrange Rd.)
Donald Rd. CR0: C'don ... 7A 156
E13 ... 1K 87
Donaldson Rd. NW6 ... 1H 81
SE18 ... 1E 124
Donald Woods Gdns. KT5: Surb ... 2H 163
Donato Dr. SE15 ... 6E 102
Doncaster Dr. UB5: N'olt ... 5D 58
Doncaster Gdns. N4 ... 6C 48
UB5: N'olt ... 5D 58
Doncaster Rd. N9 ... 7C 24
Donegal Ho. *E1* ... *4H 85*
(off Cambridge Heath Rd.)
Donegal St. N1 ... 2K 83
Doneraile Ho. *SW1* ... *5J 17*
(off Ebury Bri. Rd.)
Doneraile St. SW6 ... 2F 117
Dongola Rd. E1 ... 5A 86
E13 ... 3K 87
N17 ... 3E 48
Dongola Rd. W. E13 ... 3K 87
Don Gratton Ho. *E1* ... *5G 85*
(off Old Montague St.)
Donington Av. IG2: Ilf ... 5G 53
IG6: Ilf ... 5G 53
Donkey All. SE22 ... 7G 121
Donkey La. EN1: Enf ... 2B 24
UB7: W Dray ... 1D 174
Donkin Ho. *SE16* ... *4H 103*
(off Rennie Est.)
Donmar Warehouse Theatre ... *1E 12*
(off Earlham St.)
Donnatt's Rd. SE14 ... 1B 122
Donne Ct. SE24 ... 6C 120
Donnefield Av. HA8: Edg ... 7K 27
Donne Ho. *E14* ... *6C 86*
(off Dod St.)
SE14 ... *6K 103*
(off Samuel Cl.)
Donnelly Ct. *SW6* ... *7G 99*
(off Dawes Rd.)
Donne Pl. CR4: Mitc ... 4F 155
SW3 ... 3D 16 (4C 100)
Donne Rd. RM8: Dag ... 2C 72
Donnington Ct. *NW1* ... *7F 65*
(off Castlehaven Rd.)
NW10 ... *7D 62*
(off Donnington Rd.)
Donnington Mans. *NW10* ... *1E 80*
(off Donnington Rd.)
Donnington Rd. HA3: Kent ... 5D 42
KT4: Wor Pk ... 2C 164
NW10 ... 7D 62
Donnybrook Rd. SW16 ... 7G 137
Donoghue Bus. Pk. NW2 ... 3F 63
Donoghue Cotts. *E14* ... *5A 86*
(off Galsworthy Av.)
Donovan Av. N10 ... 2F 47
Donovan Ct. *SW10* ... *6A 16*
(off Drayton Gdns.)
Donovan Ho. *E1* ... *7J 85*
(off Cable St.)
Donovan Pl. N21 ... 5E 22
Don Phelan Cl. SE5 ... 1D 120
Doone Cl. TW11: Tedd ... 6A 132
Doon St. SE1 ... 5J 13 (1A 102)
Dora Ho. *E14* ... *6B 86*
(off Rhodeswell Rd.)
W11 ... *7F 81*
(off St Ann's Rd.)
Doral Way SM5: Cars ... 5D 166
Doran Ct. E6 ... 2D 88
Dorando Cl. W12 ... 7D 80
Doran Gro. SE18 ... 7J 107
Doran Mnr. *N2* ... *5D 46*
(off Great Nth. Rd.)
Doran Wlk. E15 ... 7E 68
Dora Rd. SW19 ... 5J 135
Dora St. E14 ... 6B 86
Dora Way SW9 ... 2A 120
Dorchester Av.
DA5: Bexl ... 1D 144
HA2: Harr ... 6G 41
N13 ... 4H 33
Dorchester Cl. BR5: St P ... 7B 144
KT10: Hin W ... 2A 162
UB5: N'olt ... 5F 59
Dorchester Ct. *E18* ... *1H 51*
(off Buckingham Rd.)
N1 ... *7E 66*
(off Englefield Rd.)
N10 ... 3F 47
N14 ... 7A 22
NW2 ... 3F 63
SE24 ... 5C 120
SW1 ... *2F 17*
(off Pavillion Rd.)
Dorchester Dr. SE24 ... 5C 120
TW14: Bedf ... 6G 111
Dorchester Gdns. E4 ... 4H 35
NW11 ... 4J 45
Dorchester Gro. W4 ... 5A 98
Dorchester Ho. TW9: Kew ... 7H 97
Dorchester M.
KT3: N Mald ... 4K 151
TW1: Twick ... 6C 114

Dorchester Rd. KT4: Wor Pk 1E **164**
SM4: Mord 7K **153**
UB5: N'olt 5F **59**
Dorchester Ter. *NW2* *3F* ***63***
(off Needham Ter.)
Dorchester Way HA3: Kent 6F **43**
Dorchester Waye UB4: Yead 6A **76**
(Quebec Rd.)
UB4: Yead 6K **75**
(Wimborne Av.)
Dorcis Av. DA7: Bex 2E **126**
Dordrecht Rd. W3 . . . . .1A **98**
Dore Av. E12 . . . . .5E **70**
Doreen Av. NW9 . . . . .1K **61**
Doreen Capstan Ho. *E11* *3G* ***69***
(off Apollo Pl.)
Dore Gdns. SM4: Mord 7K **153**
Dorell Cl. UB1: S'hall 5D **76**
Dorey Ho. *TW8: Bford* *7C* ***96***
(off High St.)
Doria Rd. SW6 . . . . .2H **117**
Doric Ho. *E2* *2K* ***85***
(off Mace St.)
Doric Way NW1 . . . . .1C **6** (3H **83**)
Dorie M. N12 . . . . .4E **30**
Dorien Rd. SW20 . . . . .2F **153**
Doris Ashby Cl. UB6: G'frd 1A **78**
Doris Av. DA8: Erith 1J **127**
Doris Emmerton Ct. SW11 . . . . .4A **118**
Doris Rd. E7 . . . . .7J **69**
TW15: Ashf 6F **129**
Dorking Cl. KT4: Wor Pk 2F **165**
SE8 . . . . .6B **104**
Dorking Ct. *N17* *1G* ***49***
(off Hampden La.)
Dorking Ho. SE1 . . . . .3D **102**
Dorlcote Rd. SW18 . . . . .7C **118**
Dorly Cl. TW17: Shep 5G **147**
Dorman Pl. N9 .2B **34**
Dormans Cl. HA6: Nwood 1F **39**
Dorman Wlk. NW10 . . . . .5K **61**
Dorman Way NW8 . . . . .1B **82**
Dorma Trad. Pk. E10 . . . . .1K **67**
Dormay St. SW18 . . . . .5K **117**
Dormer Cl. E15 . . . . .6H **69**
EN5: Barn 5A **20**
Dormer's Av. UB1: S'hall 6E **76**
Dormers Ri. UB1: S'hall 6F **77**
DORMER'S WELLS 6E **76**
Dormer's Wells La. UB1: S'hall 6E **76**
Dormers Wells Leisure Cen. 6F **77**
Dormstone Ho. *SE17* *4E* ***102***
(off Congreve St.)
Dormywood HA4: Ruis 5H **39**
Dornberg Cl. SE3 . . . . .7J **105**
Dornberg Rd. SE3 . . . . .7K **105**
Dorncliffe Rd. SW6 . . . . .2G **117**
Dorney NW3 . . . . .7C **64**
Dorney Ri. BR5: St M Cry 4K **161**
Dorney Way TW4: Houn 5C **112**
Dornfell St. NW6 . . . . .5H **63**
Dornton Rd. CR2: S Croy 6D **168**
SW12 .2F **137**
Dorothy Av. HA0: Wemb 7E **60**
Dorothy Evans Cl. DA7: Bex 4H **127**
Dorothy Gdns. RM8: Dag 4B **72**
Dorothy Pettingell Ho.
SM1: Sutt *3K* ***165***
(off Angel Hill)
Dorothy Rd. SW11 . . . . .3D **118**
Dorrell Pl. SW9 . . . . .3A **120**
Dorrien Wlk. SW16 . . . . .2H **137**
Dorrington Ct. SE25 . . . . .2E **156**
Dorrington St. EC1 . . . . .5J **7** (5A **84**)
Dorrington Way BR3: Beck 5E **158**
Dorrit Ho. *W11* *1F* ***99***
(off St Ann's Rd.)
Dorrit M. N18 .5K **33**
Dorrit St. SE1 . . . . .6D **14** (2C **102**)
Dorrit Way BR7: Chst 6G **143**
Dorryn Ct. SE26 . . . . .5K **139**
Dors Cl. NW9 . . . . .1K **61**
Dorset Av. DA16: Well 4K **125**
RM1: Rom 4K **55**
UB2: S'hall 4E **94**
UB4: Hayes 3G **75**
Dorset Bldgs. EC4 . . . . .1A **14** (6B **84**)
Dorset Cl. NW1 . . . . .5E **4** (5D **82**)
UB4: Hayes 3G **75**
Dorset Ct. HA6: Nwood 1H **39**
N1 . . . .*7E* ***66***
(off Hertford Rd.)
UB5: N'olt 3C **76**
W7 . . . .*5K* ***77***
(off Copley Cl.)
Dorset Dr. HA8: Edg 6A **28**
Dorset Gdns. CR4: Mitc 4K **155**
Dorset Ho. *NW1* *5F* ***5***
(off Gloucester Pl.)
Dorset Mans. *SW6* *6F* ***99***
(off Lille Rd.)
Dorset M. N3 . . . . .1J **45**
SW1 . . . . .1J **17** (3F **101**)
Dorset Pl. E15 .6F **69**
Dorset Ri. EC4 . . . . .1A **14** (6B **84**)
Dorset Rd. BR3: Beck 3K **157**
CR4: Mitc 2C **154**
E7 . . . . .7A **70**
HA1: Harr 6G **41**
N15 . . . . .4D **48**
N22 . . . . .1J **47**
SE9 . . . . .2C **142**
SW8 . . . . .7J **101**
SW19 .1J **153**
TW15: Ashf 3A **128**
W5 . . . . .3C **96**
Dorset Sq. NW1 . . . . .4E **4** (4D **82**)
Dorset St. W1 . . . . .6F **5** (5D **82**)
Dorset Way TW2: Twick 1H **131**
UB10: Hil 2B **74**
Dorset Waye TW5: Hest 7D **94**
Dorset Wharf *W6* *7E* ***98***
(off Rainville Rd.)
Dorton Cl. SE15 . . . . .7E **102**
Dorton Vs. UB7: Sip 7C **92**
Dorville Cres. W6 . . . . .3D **98**
Dorville Rd. SE12 . . . . .5H **123**
Dothill Rd. SE18 . . . . .7G **107**
Douai Gro. TW12: Hamp 1G **149**
Doughty Ct. *E1* *1H* ***103***
(off Prusom St.)
Doughty Ho. *SW10* *6A* ***100***
(off Netherton Gro.)
Doughty M. WC1 . . . . .4G **7** (4K **83**)
Doughty St. WC1 . . . . .3G **7** (4K **83**)
Douglas Av. E17 . . . . .1B **50**
HA0: Wemb 7E **60**
KT3: N Mald 4D **152**
Douglas Cl. HA7: Stan 5F **27**
IG6: Ilf .7K **37**
SM6: Wall 6J **167**
Douglas Ct. *KT1: King T* *4E* ***150***
(off Geneva Rd.)
N3 . . . . .2K **45**
NW6 . . . .*7J* ***63***
(off Quex Rd.)
Douglas Cres. UB4: Yead 4A **76**
Douglas Dr. CR0: C'don 3C **170**
Douglas Est. *N1* *6C* ***66***
(off Oransay Rd.)
Douglas Eyre Sports Cen. 5K **49**
Douglas Ho. KT6: Surb 1F **163**
Douglas Johnstone Ho. *SW6* *6H* ***99***
(off Clem Attlee Ct.)
Douglas Mans. TW3: Houn 3F **113**
Douglas M. NW2 . . . . .3G **63**
Douglas Path *E14* *5E* ***104***
(off Manchester Rd.)
Douglas Pl. *SW1* *4C* ***18***
(off Douglas St.)
Douglas Rd. DA16: Well 1B **126**
E4 . . . . .1B **36**
E16 . . . . .5J **87**
IG3: Ilf 7A **54**
KT1: King T 2H **151**
KT6: Surb 2F **163**
N1 . . . . .7C **66**
N22 . . . . .1A **48**
NW6 . . . . .1H **81**
TW3: Houn 3F **113**
TW19: Stanw 6A **110**
Douglas Rd. Nth. N1 . . . . .6C **66**
Douglas Rd. Sth. N1 . . . . .6C **66**
Douglas Robinson Ct. *SW16* *7J* ***137***
(off Streatham High Rd.)
Douglas Sq. SM4: Mord 6J **153**
Douglas St. SW1 . . . . .4C **18** (4H **101**)
Douglas Ter. E17 . . . . .1B **50**
Douglas Waite Ho. NW6 . . . . .7J **63**
Douglas Way SE8 . . . . .7B **104**
(Stanley St.)
SE8 . . . . .7C **104**
(Watsons St.)
Doulton Ho. SE11 . . . . .2H **19**
Doulton M. NW6 . . . . .6K **63**
Dounesforth Gdns. SW18 . . . . .1K **135**
Douro Pl. W8 .3K **99**
Douro St. E3 . . . . .2C **86**
Douthwaite Sq. E1 . . . . .1G **103**
Dove App. E6 . . . . .5C **88**
Dove Cl. NW7 .7G **29**
SM6: Wall 7K **167**
UB5: N'olt 4B **76**
Dove Commercial Cen. NW5 . . . . .5G **65**
Dovecot Cl. HA5: Eastc 5A **40**
Dovecote Av. N22 . . . . .3A **48**
Dovecote Gdns. SW14 . . . . .3K **115**
Dove Ct. EC2 . . . . .1E **14**
Dovedale Av. HA3: Kent 6C **42**
IG5: Ilf .2E **52**
Dovedale Bus. Est. *SE15* *2G* ***121***
(off Blenheim Gro.)
Dovedale Cl. DA16: Well 2A **126**
Dovedale Ri. CR4: Mitc 7D **136**
Dovedale Rd. SE22 . . . . .5H **121**
Dovedon Cl. N14 . . . . .2D **32**
Dovehouse Ct. *UB5: N'olt* *3B* ***76***
(off Delta Gro.)
Dove Ho. Gdns. E4 . . . . .2H **35**
Dovehouse Mead IG11: Bark 2H **89**
Dovehouse St.
SW3 . . . . .5B **16** (5B **100**)
Dove M. SW5 . . . . .4A **100**
Dove Pk. HA5: Hat E 1E **40**
Dover Cl. NW2 .2F **63**
RM5: Col R 2J **55**
Dover Ct. *EC1* *3A* ***8***
(off St John St.)
Dovercourt Av. CR7: Thor H 5A **156**
Dovercourt Est. N1 . . . . .6D **66**
Dovercourt Gdns.
HA7: Stan 5K **27**
Dovercourt La. SM1: Sutt 3A **166**
Dovercourt Rd. SE22 . . . . .6E **120**
Doverfield Rd. SW2 . . . . .7J **119**
Dover Flats SE1 . . . . .4E **102**
Dover Gdns. SM5: Cars 3D **166**
Dover Ho. N18 .5A **34**
SE15 . . . . .6J **103**
Dover Ho. Rd. SW15 . . . . .4C **116**
Doveridge Gdns. N13 . . . . .4G **33**
Dove Rd. N1 . . . . .6D **66**
Dove Row E2 . . . . .1G **85**
Dover Pk. Dr. SW15 . . . . .6D **116**
Dover Patrol SE3 . . . . .2K **123**
Dover Rd. E12 .2A **70**
N9 . . . . .2D **34**
RM6: Chad H 6E **54**
SE19 . . . . .6D **138**
Dover St. W1 . . . . .3K **11** (7F **83**)
Dover Ter. *TW9: Rich* *2F* ***115***
(off Sandycombe Rd.)
Dover Yd. W1 . . . . .4A **12**
Doves Cl. BR2: Brom 2C **172**
Doves Yd. N1 . . . . .1A **84**
Dovet Ct. SW9 .1K **119**
Doveton Ho. *E1* *4J* ***85***
(off Doveton St.)
Doveton Rd. CR2: S Croy 5D **168**
Doveton St. E1 .4J **85**
Dove Wlk. SW1 . . . . .5G **17** (5E **100**)
Dovey Lodge *N1* *7A* ***66***
(off Bewdley St.)
Dowanhill Rd. SE6 . . . . .1F **141**
Dowd Cl. N11 . . . . .2K **31**
Dowdeswell Cl. SW15 . . . . .4A **116**
Dowding Ho. *N6* *7E* ***46***
(off Hillcrest)
Dowding Pl. HA7: Stan 6F **27**
Dowding Rd. UB10: Uxb 7B **56**
Dowdney Cl. NW5 . . . . .5G **65**
Dowe Ho. SE3 .3G **123**
Dower Av. SM6: Wall 7F **167**
Dowes Ho. SW16 . . . . .3J **137**
Dowgate Hill EC4 . . . . .2E **14** (7D **84**)
Dowland St. W10 . . . . .3G **81**
Dowlas St. SE5 . . . . .7E **102**
Dowler Ct. KT2: King T 1E **150**
Dowler Ho. *E1* *6G* ***85***
(off Burslem St.)
Dowlerville Rd. BR6: Chels 6K **173**
Dowling Ho. DA17: Belv 3F **109**
Dowman Cl. SW19 . . . . .7K **135**
Downage NW4 .3E **44**
(not continuous)
Downalong WD23: B Hea 1C **26**
Downbank Av. DA7: Bex 1K **127**
Down Barns Rd. HA4: Ruis 3B **58**
Downbury M. SW18 . . . . .5J **117**
Down Cl. UB5: Yead 2K **75**
Downderry Rd. BR1: Brom 3F **141**
Downe Cl. DA16: Well 7C **108**
Down End SE18 . . . . .7F **107**
Downend Ct. *SE15* *6E* ***102***
(off Bibury Cl.)
Downe Rd. BR2: Kes 7B **172**
CR4: Mitc 2D **154**
Downer's Cott. SW4 . . . . .4G **119**
Downesbury *NW3* *6D* ***64***
(off Steele's Rd.)
Downes Cl. TW1: Twick 6B **114**
Downes Ct. N21 . . . . .1F **33**
Downes Ho. *CR0: Wadd* *4B* ***168***
(off Violet La.)
Downe Ter. TW10: Rich 6E **114**
Downey Ho. *E1* *4K* ***85***
(off Globe Rd.)
Downfield KT4: Wor Pk 1B **164**
Downfield Cl. W9 . . . . .4K **81**
Down Hall Rd. KT2: King T 1D **150**
DOWNHAM 5F **141**
Downham Cl. RM5: Col R 1G **55**
Downham Ct. *N1* *7D* ***66***
(off Downham Rd.)
Downham Ent. Cen. SE6 . . . . .2H **141**
Downham La. BR1: Brom 5F **141**
Downham Rd. N1 . . . . .7D **66**
Downham Way BR1: Brom 5F **141**
Downhills Av. N17 . . . . .3D **48**
Downhills Pk. Rd. N17 . . . . .3C **48**
Downhills Way N17 . . . . .3C **48**
Downhurst Av. NW7 . . . . .5E **28**
Downhurst Ct. NW4 . . . . .3E **44**
Downing Cl. HA2: Harr 3G **41**
Downing Dr. UB6: G'frd 1H **77**
Downing Ho. *W10* *6F* ***81***
(off Cambridge Gdns.)
Downing Rd. RM9: Dag 7F **73**
Downings E6 . . . . .6E **88**
Downing St. SW1 . . . . .6E **12** (2J **101**)

Downland Cl. N20 1F 31
Downland Ct. E11 2G 69
Downleys Cl. SE9 2C 142
Downman Rd. SE9 3C 124
Down Pl. W6 4D 98
Down Rd. TW11: Tedd 6B 132
Downs, The SW20 7F 135
Downs Av. BR7: Chst 5D 142
HA5: Pinn 6C 40
Downsbridge Rd. BR3: Beck 1F 159
Downs Ct. UB6: G'frd 3A 78
Downs Ct. Pde. E8 5H 67
(off Amhurst Rd.)
Downsell Rd. E15 4E 68
Downsfield Rd. E17 6A 50
Downshall Av. IG3: Ilf 6J 53
Downs Hill BR3: Beck 7F 141
Downshire Hill NW3 4B 64
Downside TW1: Twick 3K 131
TW16: Sun 1J 147
Downside Cl. SW19 6A 136
Downside Cres. NW3 5C 64
W13 4A 78
Downside Rd. SM2: Sutt 6B 166
Downside Wlk. TW8: Bford 6D 96
(off Windmill Rd.)
UB5: N'olt 3D 76
Downs La. E5 4H 67
Downs Pk. Rd. E5 5F 67
E8 5F 67
Downs Rd. BR3: Beck 2D 158
(not continuous)
CR7: Thor H 1C 156
E5 4G 67
EN1: Enf 4K 23
Down St. KT8: W Mole 5E 148
W1 5J 11 (1F 101)
Down St. M. W1 5J 11 (1F 101)
Downs Vw. TW7: Isle 1K 113
Downsview Gdns. SE19 7B 138
Downsview Rd. SE19 7C 138
Downsway BR6: Orp 5J 173
Downsway, The SM2: Sutt 7A 166
Downton Av. SW2 2J 137
Downtown Rd. SE16 2A 104
Down Way UB5: Yead 3K 75
Dowrey St. N1 1A 84
Dowsett Rd. N17 2F 49
Dowson Cl. SE5 4D 120
Dowson Ho. E1 6K 85
(off Bower St.)
Doyce St. SE1 6C 14 (2C 102)
Doyle Gdns. NW10 1C 80
Doyle Ho. SW13 7E 98
(off Trinity Chu. Rd.)
Doyle Rd. SE25 4G 157
D'Oyley St. SW1 3G 17 (4E 100)
Doynton St. N19 2F 65
Draco Ga. SW15 3E 116
Draco St. SE17 6C 102
Dragonfly Cl. E13 3K 87
Dragon Rd. SE15 6E 102
Dragons Health Club
Epsom 4K 163
Northolt 1E 76
Northwood Hills 2H 39
Purley 7A 168
St Paul's Cray 7D 144
Dragon Yd. WC1 7F 7 (6J 83)
Dragoon Rd. SE8 5B 104
Dragor Rd. NW10 4J 79
Drake Cl. SE16 2K 103
Drake Ct. KT5: Surb 4E 150
(off Cranes Pk. Av.)
SE1 7D 14
(off Swan St.)
SE19 5F 139
W12 2E 98
(off Scott's Rd.)
Drake Cres. SE28 6C 90
Drakefell Rd. SE4 3A 122
SE14 2K 121
Drakefield Rd. SW17 3E 136
Drake Hall E16 1K 105
(off Wesley Av.)
Drake Ho. E1 5J 85
(off Stepney Way)
E14 7A 86
(off Victory Pl.)
SW1 7C 18
(off Dolphin Sq.)
Drakeland Ho. W9 4H 81
(off Fernhead Rd.)
Drakeley Ct. N5 4B 66
Drake M. BR2: Brom 4A 160
Drake Rd. CR0: C'don 7K 155
CR4: Mitc 6E 154
HA2: Harr 2D 58
KT9: Chess 5G 163
SE4 3C 122
Drakes Ct. SE23 1J 139
Drakes Courtyard NW6 7H 63
Drakes Dr. HA6: Nwood 1D 38
Drake St. EN2: Enf 1J 23
WC1 6G 7 (5K 83)
Drakes Wlk. E6 1D 88
Drakewood Rd. SW16 7H 137
Draper Cl. DA17: Belv 4F 109
TW7: Isle 2H 113
Draper Ct. BR1: Brom 4C 160
Draper Ho. SE1 4B 102
(off Elephant & Castle)
Draper Pl. N1 1B 84
(off Dagmar Ter.)
Drapers Cott. Homes NW7 4G 29
(not continuous)
Draper's Ct. SW11 1E 118
(off Battersea Pk. Rd.)
Drapers Gdns. EC2 7F 9 (6D 84)
Drapers Rd. E15 4F 69
EN2: Enf 2G 23
N17 3F 49
Drappers Way SE16 4G 103
Draven Cl. BR2: Hayes 7H 159
Drawdock Rd. SE10 2F 105
Drawell Cl. SE18 5J 107
Drax Av. SW20 7C 134
Draxmont SW19 6G 135
Draycot Rd. E11 6K 51
KT6: Surb 1G 163
Draycott Av. HA3: Kent 6B 42
SW3 3D 16 (4C 100)
Draycott Cl. HA3: Kent 6B 42
NW2 3F 63
SE5 7D 102
(not continuous)
Draycott M. SW6 2H 117
(off Laurel Bank Gdns.)
Draycott Pl. SW3 4E 16 (4D 100)
Draycott Ter. SW3 4F 17 (4D 100)
Drayford Cl. W9 4H 81
Dray Gdns. SW2 5K 119
Draymans M. SE15 2F 121
Draymans Way TW7: Isle 3K 113
Drayside M. UB2: S'hall 2D 94
Drayson M. W8 2J 99
Drayton Av. BR6: Farnb 1F 173
W13 7A 78
Drayton Bri. Rd. W7 7K 77
W13 7K 77
Drayton Cl. IG1: Ilf 1H 71
TW4: Houn 5D 112
Drayton Ct. UB7: W Dray 4B 92
Drayton Gdns. N21 7G 23
SW10 6A 16 (5A 100)
UB7: W Dray 2A 92
W13 7A 78
Drayton Grn. W13 7A 78
Drayton Grn. Rd. W13 7B 78
Drayton Gro. W13 7A 78
Drayton Ho. E11 1F 69
SE5 7D 102
(off Elmington Rd.)
Drayton Pk. N5 4A 66
Drayton Pk. M. N5 5A 66
Drayton Rd. CR0: C'don 2B 168
E11 1F 69
N17 2E 48
NW10 1B 80
W13 7A 78
Drayton Waye HA3: Kent 6B 42
Dreadnought Cl. SW19 1A 154
(off Nelson Gro. Rd.)
SW19 2B 154
(Brangwyn Cres.)
Dreadnought St. SE10 3G 105
Drenon Sq. UB3: Hayes 7H 75
Dresden Cl. NW6 6K 63
Dresden Ho. SE11 3H 19
SW11 2E 118
(off Dagnall St.)
Dresden Rd. N19 1G 65
Dressington Av. SE4 6C 122
Drew Av. NW7 6B 30
Drewery Ct. SE3 3G 123
Drewett Ho. E1 6G 85
(off Christian St.)
Drew Gdns. UB6: G'frd 6K 59
Drew Ho. SW16 3J 137
Drewitts Ct. KT12: Walt T 7H 147
Drew Rd. E16 1B 106
(not continuous)
Drewstead La. SW16 2H 137
Drewstead Rd. SW16 2H 137
Drey Ct. KT4: Wor Pk 1B 164
Driffield Ct. NW9 1A 44
(off Pageant Av.)
Driffield Rd. E3 2A 86
Drift, The BR2: Brom 3B 172
Driftway, The CR4: Mitc 1E 154
Drill Hall Arts Cen. 5C 6
(off Chenies St.)
Drinkwater Ho. SE5 7D 102
(off Picton St.)
Drinkwater Rd. HA2: Harr 2F 59
Drive, The BR3: Beck 2C 158
BR4: W W'ck 7F 159
BR6: Orp 2K 173
BR7: Chst 3K 161
CR7: Thor H 4D 156
DA5: Bexl 6C 126
DA8: Erith 7H 109
DA14: Sidc 3B 144
E4 1A 36
E17 3D 50
E18 4J 51
EN2: Enf 1J 23
EN5: Barn 3B 20
EN5: New Bar 6F 21
HA2: Harr 7E 40
HA6: Nwood 2G 39
HA8: Edg 5B 28
HA9: Wemb 2J 61
IG1: Ilf 6C 52
IG9: Buck H 1F 37
IG11: Bark 7K 71
KT2: King T 7J 133
KT6: Surb 7E 150
KT10: Esh 7G 149
KT19: Ewe 6B 164
N3 7D 30
N6 5D 46
N7 6K 65
(not continuous)
N11 6B 32
NW10 1B 80
NW11 7G 45
RM5: Col R 1K 55
SM4: Mord 5A 154
SW6 2G 117
Drive, The SW20 7E 134
TW3: Houn 2H 113
TW7: Isle 2H 113
TW14: Felt 7A 112
TW15: Ashf 7F 129
UB10: Ick 4A 56
W3 6J 79
Drive Ct. HA8: Edg 5B 28
Drive Mans. SW6 2G 117
(off Fulham Rd.)
Driveway, The E17 6D 50
(off Hoe St.)
Dr Johnson's House 1K 13
(off Pemberton Row)
Droitwich Cl. SE26 3G 139
Dromey Gdns. HA3: Hrw W 7E 26
Dromore Rd. SW15 6G 117
Dronfield Gdns. RM8: Dag 5C 72
Dron Ho. E1 5J 85
(off Adelina Gro.)
Droop St. W10 3F 81
Drovers Ct. KT1: King T 2E 150
(off Fairfield E.)
Drovers Pl. SE15 7J 103
Drovers Rd. CR2: S Croy 5D 168
Druce Rd. SE21 6E 120
Druid St. SE1 6H 15 (2E 102)
(not continuous)
Druids Way BR2: Brom 4F 159
Drumaline Ridge KT4: Wor Pk 2A 164
Drummond Av. RM7: Rom 4K 55
Drummond Ct. N12 7H 31
Drummond Cres. NW1 1C 6 (3H 83)
Drummond Dr. HA7: Stan 7E 26
Drummond Ga. SW1 5D 18 (5H 101)
Drummond Ho. E2 2G 85
(off Goldsmiths Row)
N2 2A 46
(off Font Hills)
Drummond Pl. TW1: Twick 7B 114
Drummond Rd. CR0: C'don 2C 168
(not continuous)
E11 6A 52
RM7: Rom 4K 55
SE16 3H 103
Drummonds, The IG9: Buck H 2E 36
Drummonds Pl. TW9: Rich 4E 114
Drummond St. NW1 3A 6 (4G 83)
Drum St. E1 7K 9 (6F 85)
Drury Cres. CR0: Wadd 2A 168
Drury Ho. SW8 1G 119
Drury La. WC2 7F 7 (6J 83)
Drury Lane Theatre Royal 1F 13
(off Drury La.)
Drury Rd. HA1: Harr 7G 41
Drury Way NW10 5K 61
Drury Way Ind. Est. NW10 5J 61
Dryad St. SW15 3F 117
Dryburgh Gdns. NW9 3G 43
Dryburgh Ho. SW1 5K 17
(off Abbots Mnr.)
Dryburgh Rd. SW15 3D 116
Dryden Av. W7 6K 77
Dryden Cl. SW4 5H 119
Dryden Ct. SE11 4K 19 (4B 102)
Dryden Mans. W14 6G 99
(off Queen's Club Gdns.)
Dryden Rd. DA16: Well 1K 125
EN1: Enf 6K 23
HA3: W'stone 1K 41
SW19 6A 136
Dryden St. WC2 1F 13 (6J 83)
Dryfield Cl. NW10 6J 61
Dryfield Rd. HA8: Edg 6D 28
Dryfield Wlk. SE8 6C 104
Dryhill Rd. DA17: Belv 6F 109
Dryland Av. BR6: Orp 4K 173
Drylands Rd. N8 6J 47
Drysdale Av. E4 7J 25
Drysdale Cl. HA6: Nwood 1G 39

Drysdale Dwellings *E8* ... *5F 67*
(off Dunn St.)
Drysdale Ho. *N1* ... *3E 84*
(off Drysdale Pl.)
Drysdale Pl. N1 ... 1H **9** (3E **84**)
Drysdale St. N1 ... 1H **9** (3E **84**)
Dublin Av. E8 ... 1G **85**
Dublin Ct. *HA2: Harr* ... *2H 59*
(off Northolt Rd.)
Du Burstow Ter. W7 ... 2J **95**
Ducal St. E2 ... 2K **9** (3F **85**)
Du Cane Cl. W12 ... 6E **80**
Du Cane Ct. SW17 ... 1E **136**
Du Cane Rd. W12 ... 6B **80**
Ducavel Ho. SW2 ... 1K **137**
Duchess Cl. N11 ... 5A **32**
SM1: Sutt ... 4A **166**
Duchess Gro. IG9: Buck H ... 2E **36**
Duchess M. W1 ... 6K **5** (5F **83**)
Duchess of Bedford Ho. *W8* ... *2J 99*
(off Duchess of Bedford's Wlk.)
Duchess of Bedford's Wlk.
W8 ... 2J **99**
Duchess St. W1 ... 6K **5** (5F **83**)
Duchess Theatre ... *2G 13*
(off Catherine St.)
Duchy Rd. EN4: Had W ... 1G **21**
Duchy St. SE1 ... 4K **13** (1A **102**)
(not continuous)
Ducie St. SW4 ... 4K **119**
Duckett M. N4 ... 6B **48**
Duckett Rd. N4 ... 6A **48**
Duckett St. E1 ... 4K **85**
Duck La. W1 ... 1C **12**
Duck Lees La. EN3: Pond E ... 4F **25**
Duck's Hill Rd. HA4: Ruis ... 1D **38**
HA6: Nwood ... 1D **38**
DUCKS ISLAND ... **6A 20**
Ducks Wlk. TW1: Twick ... 5C **114**
Du Cros Dr. HA7: Stan ... 6J **27**
Du Cros Rd. W3 ... 1A **98**
DUDDEN HILL ... **5D 62**
Dudden Hill La. NW10 ... 4B **62**
Dudden Hill Pde. NW10 ... 4B **62**
Duddington Cl. SE9 ... 4B **142**
Dudley Av. HA3: Kent ... 3C **42**
Dudley Ct. NW11 ... 4H **45**
W1 ... *1E 10*
(off Up. Berkeley St.)
WC2 ... 7E **6** (6J **83**)
Dudley Dr. HA4: Ruis ... 5K **57**
SM4: Mord ... 1G **165**
Dudley Gdns. HA2: Harr ... 1H **59**
W13 ... 2B **96**
Dudley Ho. *W2* ... *6A 4*
(off Nth. Wharf Rd.)
Dudley M. SW2 ... 6A **120**
Dudley Pl. TW19: Stanw ... 6B **110**
UB3: Harl ... 4F **93**
Dudley Rd. E17 ... 2C **50**
HA2: Harr ... 2G **59**
IG1: Ilf ... 4F **71**
KT1: King T ... 3F **151**
KT12: Walt T ... 6J **147**
N3 ... 2K **45**
NW6 ... 2G **81**
SW19 ... 6J **135**
TW9: Rich ... 2F **115**
TW14: Bedf ... 1E **128**
TW15: Ashf ... 5B **128**
UB2: S'hall ... 2B **94**
Dudley St. W2 ... 6A **4** (5B **82**)
Dudlington Rd. E5 ... 2J **67**
Dudmaston M. SW3 ... 5B **16**
Dudrich Cl. N11 ... 6J **31**
Dudrich M. EN2: Enf ... 1F **23**
SE22 ... 5F **121**
Dudsbury Rd. DA14: Sidc ... 6B **144**
Dudset La. TW5: Cran ... 1J **111**
Duett Ct. TW5: Hest ... 7C **94**
Duffell Ho. SE11 ... 6H **19**
Dufferin Av. EC1 ... 4E **8**
Dufferin Ct. *EC1* ... *4E 8*
(off Dufferin St.)
Dufferin St. EC1 ... 4D **8** (4C **84**)
Duffield Cl. HA1: Harr ... 5K **41**
Duffield Dr. N15 ... 4F **49**
Duff St. E14 ... 6D **86**
Dufour's Pl. W1 ... 1B **12** (6G **83**)
Dugard Way SE11 ... 4B **102**
Duggan Dr. BR7: Chst ... 6C **142**
Dugolly Av. HA9: Wemb ... 3H **61**
Duke Gdns. IG6: Ilf ... 4H **53**
Duke Humphrey Rd. SE3 ... 1G **123**
Duke of Cambridge Cl.
TW2: Whitt ... 6H **113**
Duke of Edinburgh Rd. SM1: Sutt ... 2B **166**
Duke of Wellington Av. SE18 ... 3F **107**
Duke of Wellington Pl.
SW1 ... 6H **11** (2E **100**)
Duke of York Column (Memorial) ... 5C **12**
Duke of Yorks Sq. SW3 ... 4F **17** (5D **100**)
Duke of York's Theatre ... *3E 12*
(off St Martin's La.)
Duke of York St. SW1 ... 4B **12** (1G **101**)
Duke Rd. IG6: Ilf ... 4H **53**
W4 ... 5K **97**
Dukes Av. HA1: Harr ... 4J **41**
HA2: Harr ... 6D **40**
HA8: Edg ... 6A **28**
KT2: King T ... 4C **132**
KT3: N Mald ... 3A **152**
N3 ... 1K **45**
N10 ... 3F **47**
TW4: Houn ... 4C **112**
TW10: Ham ... 4C **132**
UB5: N'olt ... 7C **58**
W4 ... 5K **97**
Dukes Cl. TW12: Hamp ... 5D **130**
TW15: Ashf ... 4E **128**
Dukes Ct. E6 ... 1E **88**
(not continuous)
SE13 ... 2E **122**
SW14 ... 2K **115**
W2 ... *7K 81*
(off Moscow Rd.)
Dukes Ga. W4 ... 4J **97**
Dukes Grn. Av. TW14: Felt ... 5J **111**
Dukes Head Pas. TW12: Hamp ... 7G **131**
Duke's Head Yd. N6 ... 1F **65**
Duke Shore Wharf E14 ... 7B **86**
Duke's Ho. *SW1* ... *3D 18*
(off Vincent St.)
Dukes La. W8 ... 2K **99**
Duke's La. Chambers
W8 ... *2K 99*
(off Dukes La.)
Duke's La. Mans. *W8* ... *2K 99*
(off Dukes La.)
Dukes Lodge *W8* ... *1H 99*
(off Holland Wlk.)
Dukes M. N10 ... 3F **47**
W1 ... 7H **5**
Dukes Orchard DA5: Bexl ... 1J **145**
Duke's Pas. E17 ... 4E **50**
Duke's Pl. EC3 ... 1H **15** (6E **84**)
Dukes Point *N6* ... *1F 65*
(off Dukes Head Yd.)
Dukes Ride UB10: Ick ... 4A **56**
Dukes Rd. E6 ... 1E **88**
W3 ... 4G **79**
WC1 ... 2D **6** (3H **83**)
Dukesthorpe Rd. SE26 ... 4K **139**
Duke St. SM1: Sutt ... 4B **166**
SW1 ... 4B **12** (1G **101**)
TW9: Rich ... 4D **114**
W1 ... 7H **5** (6E **82**)
Duke St. Hill SE1 ... 4F **15** (1D **102**)
Duke St. Mans. *W1* ... *1H 11*
(off Duke St.)
Dukes Way BR4: W W'ck ... 3G **171**
Duke's Yd. W1 ... 2H **11** (7E **82**)
Dulas St. N4 ... 1K **65**
Dulford St. W11 ... 7G **81**
Dulka Rd. SW11 ... 5D **118**
Dulverton *NW1* ... *1G 83*
(off Royal College St.)
Dulverton Mans. WC1 ... 4H **7**
Dulverton Rd. HA4: Ruis ... 1J **57**
SE9 ... 2G **143**
DULWICH ... **2E 138**
Dulwich Bus. Cen. SE23 ... 1K **139**
Dulwich Comn. SE21 ... 1E **138**
SE22 ... 1E **138**
Dulwich Hamlet FC ... 4E **120**
Dulwich Lawn Cl. SE22 ... 5F **121**
Dulwich Leisure Cen. ... 4G **121**
Dulwich Oaks, The SE21 ... 3F **139**
Dulwich Picture Gallery ... 7D **120**
Dulwich Ri. Gdns. SE22 ... 5F **121**
Dulwich Rd. SE24 ... 5A **120**
Dulwich Upper Wood Nature Pk. ... 5F **139**
DULWICH VILLAGE ... **7E 120**
Dulwich Village SE21 ... 6D **120**
Dulwich Wood Av. SE19 ... 4E **138**
Dulwich Wood Pk. SE19 ... 4E **138**
Dumain Ct. *SE11* ... *4B 102*
(off Opal St.)
Dumbarton Ct. SW2 ... 6J **119**
Dumbarton Rd. SW2 ... 6J **119**
Dumbleton Cl. KT1: King T ... 1H **151**
Dumbreck Rd. SE9 ... 4D **124**
Dumont Rd. N16 ... 3E **66**
Dumpton Pl. NW1 ... 7E **64**
Dumsey Eyot KT16: Chert ... 7A **146**
Dunally Pk. TW17: Shep ... 7F **147**
Dunbar Av. BR3: Beck ... 4A **158**
RM10: Dag ... 3G **73**
SW16 ... 2A **156**
Dunbar Cl. UB4: Hayes ... 6K **75**
Dunbar Ct. *BR2: Brom* ... *3H 159*
(off Durham Rd.)
SM1: Sutt ... 5B **166**
Dunbar Gdns. RM10: Dag ... 5G **73**
Dunbar Rd. E7 ... 6J **69**
KT3: N Mald ... 4J **151**
N22 ... 1A **48**
Dunbar St. SE27 ... 3C **138**
Dunbar Wharf *E14* ... *7B 86*
(off Narrow St.)
Dunblane Cl. HA8: Edg ... 2C **28**
Dunblane Rd. SE9 ... 3C **124**
Dunboe Pl. TW17: Shep ... 7E **146**
Dunboyne Rd. NW3 ... 5D **64**
Dunbridge Ho. *SW15* ... *6B 116*
(off Highcliffe Dr.)
Dunbridge St. E2 ... 4G **85**
Duncan Cl. EN5: New Bar ... 4F **21**
Duncan Ct. *E14* ... *5E 86*
(off Teviot St.)
N21 ... 1G **33**
Duncan Gro. W3 ... 6A **80**
Duncan Ho. *NW3* ... *7D 64*
(off Fellows Rd.)
SW1 ... *6B 18*
(off Dolphin Sq.)
Duncannon Ho. *SW1* ... *6D 18*
(off Lindsay Sq.)
Duncannon St. WC2 ... 3E **12** (7J **83**)
Duncan Rd. E8 ... 1H **85**
TW9: Rich ... 4E **114**
Duncan St. N1 ... 2B **84**
Duncan Ter. N1 ... 2B **84**
(not continuous)
Dunch St. E1 ... 6H **85**
Dunchurch Ho. RM10: Dag ... 7G **73**
Duncombe Hill SE23 ... 7A **122**
Duncombe Rd. N19 ... 1H **65**
Duncrievie Rd. SE13 ... 6F **123**
Duncroft SE18 ... 7J **107**
Dundalk Ho. *E1* ... *6J 85*
(off Clark St.)
Dundalk Rd. SE4 ... 3A **122**
Dundas Gdns. KT8: W Mole ... 3F **149**
Dundas Ho. *E2* ... *2J 85*
(off Bishop's Way)
Dundas Rd. SE15 ... 2J **121**
Dundee Ct. *E1* ... *1H 103*
(off Wapping High St.)
SE1 ... *7G 15*
(off Long La.)
Dundee Ho. *W9* ... *3A 82*
(off Maida Va.)
Dundee Rd. E13 ... 2K **87**
SE25 ... 5H **157**
Dundee St. E1 ... 1H **103**
Dundee Way EN3: Brim ... 3F **25**
Dundee Wharf E14 ... 7B **86**
Dundela Gdns. KT4: Wor Pk ... 4D **164**
Dundonald Cl. E6 ... 6C **88**
Dundonald Ho. *E14* ... *2D 104*
(off Admirals Way)
Dundonald Rd. NW10 ... 1F **81**
SW19 ... 7G **135**
(not continuous)
Dundry Ho. SE26 ... 3G **139**
Dunedin Ho. *E16* ... *1D 106*
(off Manwood St.)
Dunedin Rd. E10 ... 3D **68**
IG1: Ilf ... 1G **71**
Dunedin Way UB4: Yead ... 4A **76**
Dunelm Gro. SE27 ... 3C **138**
Dunelm St. E1 ... 6K **85**
Dunfield Gdns. SE6 ... 5D **140**
Dunfield Rd. SE6 ... 5D **140**
(not continuous)
Dunford Ct. HA5: Hat E ... 1D **40**
Dunford Rd. N7 ... 4K **65**
Dungarvan Av. SW15 ... 4C **116**
Dunheved Cl. CR7: Thor H ... 6A **156**
Dunheved Rd. Nth. CR7: Thor H ... 6A **156**
Dunheved Rd. Sth. CR7: Thor H ... 6A **156**
Dunheved Rd. W. CR7: Thor H ... 6A **156**
Dunhill Point SW15 ... 1C **134**
Dunholme Grn. N9 ... 3A **34**
Dunholme La. N9 ... 3A **34**
Dunholme Rd. N9 ... 3A **34**
Dunkeld Ho. *E14* ... *6F 87*
(off Abbott Rd.)
Dunkeld Rd. RM8: Dag ... 2B **72**
SE25 ... 4D **156**
Dunkery Rd. SE9 ... 4B **142**
Dunkirk St. SE27 ... 4C **138**
Dunlace Rd. E5 ... 4J **67**
Dunleary Cl. TW4: Houn ... 7D **112**
Dunley Dr. CR0: New Ad ... 7D **170**
Dunlin Ho. *SE16* ... *4K 103*
(off Tawny Way)
Dunloe Av. N17 ... 3D **48**
Dunloe Ct. E2 ... 2F **85**
Dunloe Pas. *E2* ... *2F 85*
(off Dunloe St.)
Dunloe St. E2 ... 2F **85**
Dunlop Pl. SE16 ... 3F **103**
Dunmore Point *E2* ... *2J 9*
(off Gascoigne Pl.)
Dunmore Rd. NW6 ... 1G **81**
SW20 ... 1E **152**
Dunmow Cl. RM6: Chad H ... 5C **54**
TW13: Hanw ... 3C **130**
Dunmow Ho. RM9: Dag ... 1B **90**
SE11 ... *5H 19*
(off Newburn St.)
Dunmow Rd. E15 ... 4F **69**
Dunmow Wlk. *N1* ... *1C 84*
(off Popham St.)
Dunnage Cres. SE16 ... 4A **104**
(not continuous)
Dunnico Ho. *SE17* ... *5E 102*
(off East St.)

Dunn Mead NW9 . . . . . 7G **29**
Dunnock Cl. N9 . . . . . 1E **34**
Dunnock Rd. E6 . . . . . 6C **88**
Dunn's Pas. WC1 . . . . . 7F **7**
Dunn St. E8 . . . . . 5F **67**
Dunollie Pl. NW5 . . . . . 5G **65**
Dunollie Rd. NW5 . . . . . 5G **65**
Dunoon Gdns. SE23 . . . . . 7K **121**
Dunoon Ho. *N1* *1K* ***83***
(off Bemerton Est.)
Dunoon Rd. SE23 . . . . . 7J **121**
Dunoran Home BR1: Brom 1C **160**
Dunraven Dr. EN2: Enf 2F **23**
Dunraven Rd. W12 . . . . . 1C **98**
Dunraven St. W1 . . . . . 2F **11** (7D **82**)
Dunsany Rd. W14 . . . . . 3F **99**
Dunsfold Cl. *SM2: Sutt* *7K* ***165***
(off Blackbush Cl.)
Dunsfold Way CR0: New Ad 7D **170**
Dunsford Way SW15 . . . . . 6D **116**
Dunsmore Cl. UB4: Yead 4C **76**
Dunsmore Rd.
KT12: Walt T 6K **147**
Dunsmure Rd. N16 . . . . . 1E **66**
Dunspring La. IG5: Ilf 2F **53**
Dunstable M. W1 . . . . . 5H **5** (5E **82**)
Dunstable Rd. KT8: W Mole 4D **148**
TW9: Rich 4E **114**
Dunstall Rd. SW20 . . . . . 6D **134**
Dunstall Way KT8: W Mole 3F **149**
Dunstall Welling Est.
DA16: Well 2B **126**
Dunstan Cl. N2 . . . . . 3A **46**
Dunstan Glade BR5: Pet W 6H **161**
Dunstan Ho's. *E1* *5J* ***85***
(off Stepney Grn.)
Dunstan Rd. NW11 . . . . . 1H **63**
Dunstan's Gro. SE22 . . . . . 6H **121**
Dunstan's Rd. SE22 . . . . . 7G **121**
Dunster Av. SM4: Mord 1F **165**
Dunster Cl. EN5: Barn 4A **20**
RM5: Col R 2J **55**
Dunster Ct. EC3 . . . . . 2H **15** (7E **84**)
Dunster Dr. NW9 . . . . . 1J **61**
Dunster Gdns. NW6 . . . . . 7H **63**
Dunster Ho. SE6 . . . . . 3E **140**
Dunsterville Way SE1 . . . . . 7F **15** (2D **102**)
Dunster Way HA2: Harr 3C **58**
SM6: Wall 1E **166**
Dunston Rd. E8 . . . . . 1F **85**
SW11 . . . . . 2E **118**
Dunston St. E8 . . . . . 1E **84**
Dunton Cl. KT6: Surb 1E **162**
Dunton Ct. SE23 . . . . . 2H **139**
Dunton Rd. E10 . . . . . 7D **50**
RM1: Rom 4K **55**
SE1 . . . . . 5F **103**
Duntshill Rd. SW18 . . . . . 1K **135**
Dunvegan Cl. KT8: W Mole 4F **149**
Dunvegan Rd. SE9 . . . . . 4D **124**
Dunwich Ct. *RM6: Chad H* *5B* ***54***
(off Glandford Way)
Dunwich Rd. DA7: Bex 1F **127**
Dunworth M. W11 . . . . . 6H **81**
Duplex Ride SW1 . . . . . 7F **11** (2D **100**)
Dupont Rd. SW20 . . . . . 2F **153**
Duppas Av. CR0: Wadd 4B **168**
Duppas Cl. TW17: Shep 5F **147**
Duppas Ct. *CR0: C'don* *3B* ***168***
(off Duppas Hill Ter.)
Duppas Hill La. CR0: C'don 4B **168**
Duppas Hill Rd. CR0: Wadd 4A **168**
Duppas Hill Ter. CR0: C'don 3B **168**
Duppas Rd. CR0: Wadd 3A **168**
Dupree Rd. SE7 . . . . . 5K **105**
Duraden Cl. BR3: Beck 7D **140**
Durand Cl. SM5: Cars 1D **166**
Durand Gdns. SW9 . . . . . 1K **119**
Durands Wlk. SE16 . . . . . 2B **104**
Durand Way NW10 . . . . . 7J **61**
Durants Pk. Av. EN3: Pond E 4E **24**
Durants Rd. EN3: Pond E 4D **24**
Durant St. E2 . . . . . 2G **85**
Durban Ct. E7 . . . . . 7B **70**
Durban Gdns. RM10: Dag 7J **73**
Durban Ho. *W12* *7D* ***80***
(off White City Est.)
Durban Rd. BR3: Beck 2B **158**
E15 . . . . . 3G **87**
E17 . . . . . 1B **50**
IG2: Ilf 1J **71**
N17 . . . . . 6K **33**
SE27 . . . . . 4C **138**
Durbin Rd. KT9: Chess 4E **162**
Durdan Cotts. *UB1: S'hall* *6D* ***76***
(off Denbigh Rd.)
Durdans Ho. *NW1* *7F* ***65***
(off Farrier St.)
Durdans Rd. UB1: S'hall 6D **76**
Durell Gdns. RM9: Dag 5D **72**
Durell Ho. *SE16* *2K* ***103***
(off Wolfe Cres.)
Durell Rd. RM9: Dag 5D **72**
Durfey Pl. SE5 . . . . . 7D **102**
Durford Cres. SW15 . . . . . 1D **134**
Durham Av. BR2: Brom 4H **159**
IG8: Buck H, Wfd G 5G **37**
TW5: Hest 5D **94**
Durham Cl. SW20 . . . . . 2D **152**
Durham Ct. *NW6* *2J* ***81***
(off Kilburn Pk. Rd.)
TW11: Tedd 4J **131**
Durham Hill BR1: Brom 4H **141**
Durham Ho. BR2: Brom 4G **159**
IG11: Bark *7A* ***72***
(off Margaret Bondfield Av.)
NW8 . . . . . *2D* ***4***
(off Lorne Cl.)
RM10: Dag 5J **73**
Durham Ho. St. WC2 . . . . . 3F **13**
Durham Pl. IG1: Ilf 4G **71**
SW3 . . . . . 6E **16** (5D **100**)
Durham Ri. SE18 . . . . . 5G **107**
Durham Rd. BR2: Brom 3H **159**
DA14: Sidc 5B **144**
E12 . . . . . 4B **70**
E16 . . . . . 4G **87**
HA1: Harr 5F **41**
N2 . . . . . 3C **46**
N7 . . . . . 2K **65**
N9 . . . . . 2B **34**
RM10: Dag 5J **73**
SW20 . . . . . 1D **152**
TW14: Felt 7A **112**
W5 . . . . . 3D **96**
Durham Row E1 . . . . . 5K **85**
Durham St. SE11 . . . . . 6G **19** (5K **101**)
Durham Ter. W2 . . . . . 6K **81**
Durham Wharf Dr. TW8: Bford 7C **96**
Durham Yd. E2 . . . . . 3H **85**
Durley Av. HA5: Pinn 7C **40**
Durley Rd. N16 . . . . . 7E **48**
Durlston Rd. E5 . . . . . 2G **67**
KT2: King T 6E **132**
Durnford Ho. SE6 . . . . . 3E **140**
Durnford St. N15 . . . . . 5E **48**
SE10 . . . . . 6E **104**
Durning Rd. SE19 . . . . . 5D **138**
Durnsford Av. SW19 . . . . . 2J **135**
Durnsford Ct. *EN3: Enf H* *3F* ***25***
(off Enstone Rd.)
Durnsford Rd. N11 . . . . . 1H **47**
SW19 . . . . . 2J **135**
Durnsford Sports Cen. 1G **47**
Durrant Ct. HA3: Hrw W 2J **41**
Durrant Ho. *EC1* *5D* ***84***
(off Chiswell St.)
Durrant Way BR6: Farnb 5H **173**
Durrell Rd. SW6 . . . . . 1H **117**
Durrell Way TW17: Shep 6F **147**
Durrels Ho. *W14* *4H* ***99***
(off Warwick Gdns.)
Durrington Av. SW20 . . . . . 7E **134**
Durrington Pk. Rd. SW20 . . . . . 1E **152**
Durrington Rd. E5 . . . . . 4A **68**
Durrington Twr. SW8 . . . . . 2G **119**
Durrisdeer Ho. *NW2* *4H* ***63***
(off Lyndale)
Dursley Cl. SE3 . . . . . 2A **124**
Dursley Gdns. SE3 . . . . . 1B **124**
Dursley Rd. SE3 . . . . . 2A **124**
Durward Ho. *W8* *2K* ***99***
(off Kensington Ct.)
Durward St. E1 . . . . . 5H **85**
Durweston M. W1 . . . . . 5F **5**
Durweston St. W1 . . . . . 6F **5** (5D **82**)
Dury Falls Ct. RM5: Col R 2J **55**
Dury Rd. EN5: Barn 1C **20**
Dutch Barn Cl. TW19: Stanw 6A **110**
Dutch Gdns. KT2: King T 6H **133**
Dutch Yd. SW18 . . . . . 5J **117**
Dutton St. SE10 . . . . . 1E **122**
Duval Ho. *N19* *2H* ***65***
(off Ashbrook Rd.)
Duxberry Av. TW13: Felt 3A **130**
Duxberry Cl. BR2: Brom 5C **160**
Duxford Ho. *SE2* *2D* ***108***
(off Wolvercote Rd.)
Dye Ho. La. E3 . . . . . 1C **86**
Dyer Ho. TW12: Hamp 1F **149**
Dyer's Bldgs. EC1 . . . . . 6J **7** (5A **84**)
Dyers Hall Rd. E11 . . . . . 1G **69**
Dyers Hill Rd. E11 . . . . . 2F **69**
Dyers La. SW15 . . . . . 4D **116**
Dykes Way BR2: Brom 3H **159**
Dykewood Cl. DA5: Bexl 3K **145**
Dylan Rd. DA17: Belv 3G **109**
SE24 . . . . . 4B **120**
Dylways SE5 . . . . . 4D **120**
Dymchurch Cl. BR6: Orp 4J **173**
IG5: Ilf 2E **52**
Dymes Path SW19 . . . . . 2F **135**
Dymock St. SW6 . . . . . 3K **117**
Dyneley Rd. SE12 . . . . . 3A **142**
Dyne Rd. NW6 . . . . . 7G **63**
Dynevor Rd. N16 . . . . . 3E **66**
TW10: Rich 5E **114**
Dynham Rd. NW6 . . . . . 7J **63**
Dyott St. WC1 . . . . . 7D **6** (6H **83**)
Dysart Av. KT2: King T 5C **132**
Dysart St. EC2 . . . . . 4G **9** (4D **84**)
Dyson Ct. HA0: Wemb 4A **60**
NW2 . . . . . 1E **62**
Dyson Ho. *SE10* *5H* ***105***
(off Blackwall La.)
Dyson Rd. E11 . . . . . 6G **51**
E15 . . . . . 6H **69**
Dysons Rd. N18 . . . . . 5C **34**

E

Eade Rd. N4 . . . . . 7C **48**
Eagans Cl. N2 . . . . . 3B **46**
Eagle Av. RM6: Chad H 6E **54**
Eagle Cl. EN3: Pond E 4D **24**
SE16 . . . . . 5J **103**
SM6: Wall 6J **167**
Eagle Ct. E11 . . . . . 4J **51**
EC1 . . . . . 5A **8** (5B **84**)
Eagle Dr. NW9 . . . . . 2A **44**
Eagle Dwellings *EC1* *1D* ***8***
(off City Rd.)
Eagle Hgts. SW11 . . . . . 3C **118**
Eagle Hill SE19 . . . . . 6D **138**
Eagle Ho. *E1* *4H* ***85***
(off Headlam St.)
N1 . . . . . *2D* ***84***
(off Eagle Wharf Rd.)
Eagle Ho. M. SW4 . . . . . 5G **119**
Eagle La. E11 . . . . . 4J **51**
Eagle Lodge NW11 . . . . . 7H **45**
Eagle Mans. *N16* *5F* ***67***
(off Salcombe Rd.)
Eagle M. N1 . . . . . 6E **66**
Eagle Pl. SW1 . . . . . 3B **12**
SW7 . . . . . 5A **100**
Eagle Rd. HA0: Wemb 7D **60**
TW6: H'row A 3H **111**
Eaglesfield Rd. SE18 . . . . . 1F **125**
Eagle St. WC1 . . . . . 6G **7** (5K **83**)
Eagle Ter. IG8: Wfd G 7E **36**
Eagle Trad. Est. CR4: Mitc 6D **154**
Eagle Wharf Ct. *SE1* *5J* ***15***
(off Lafone St.)
Eagle Wharf E. *E14* *7A* ***86***
(off Narrow St.)
Eagle Wharf Rd. N1 . . . . . 2C **84**
Eagle Wharf W. *E14* *7A* ***86***
(off Narrow St.)
Eagle Works E. E1 . . . . . 4K **9**
Eagle Works W. E1 . . . . . 4J **9** (4F **85**)
Eagling Cl. E3 . . . . . 3C **86**
Ealdham Sq. SE9 . . . . . 4A **124**
EALING 7D **78**
Ealing B'way. Cen. W5 . . . . . 7D **78**
EALING COMMON 7F **79**
Ealing Grn. W5 . . . . . 1D **96**
Ealing Pk. Gdns. W5 . . . . . 4C **96**
Ealing Pk. Mans. *W5* *3D* ***96***
(off Sth. Ealing Rd.)
Ealing Rd. HA0: Wemb 6E **60**
TW8: Bford 4D **96**
UB5: N'olt 1E **76**
Ealing Rd. Trad. Est. TW8: Bford 5D **96**
Ealing Squash & Fitness Club 6E **78**
Ealing Studios 1D **96**
Ealing Village W5 . . . . . 6E **78**
Eamont Cl. HA4: Ruis 7D **38**
Eamont Ct. *NW8* *2C* ***82***
(off Eamont St.)
Eamont St. NW8 . . . . . 2C **82**
Eardley Cres. SW5 . . . . . 5J **99**
Eardley Point *SE18* *4F* ***107***
(off Wilmount St.)
Eardley Rd. DA17: Belv 5G **109**
SW16 . . . . . 5G **137**
Earhart Way TW6: Cran, H'row A 3J **111**
Earl Cl. N11 . . . . . 5A **32**
Earldom Rd. SW15 . . . . . 4E **116**
Earle Gdns. KT2: King T 7E **132**
Earle Ho. *SW1* *4D* ***18***
(off Montaigne Cl.)
Earlham Ct. E11 . . . . . 7H **51**
Earlham Gro. E7 . . . . . 5H **69**
N22 . . . . . 7E **32**
Earlham St. WC2 . . . . . 1D **12** (6J **83**)
Earl Ho. *NW1* *4D* ***4***
(off Lisson Gro.)
Earlom Ho. *WC1* *2J* ***7***
(off Margery St.)
Earl Ri. SE18 . . . . . 5H **107**
Earl Rd. SW14 . . . . . 4J **115**
EARL'S COURT 4K **99**
Earls Court Exhibition Building 5J **99**
Earl's Ct. Gdns. SW5 . . . . . 4K **99**
Earls Ct. Rd. SW5 . . . . . 3J **99**
W8 . . . . . 3J **99**
Earl's Ct. Sq. SW5 . . . . . 5K **99**
Earls Cres. HA1: Harr 4J **41**
Earlsdown Ho. IG11: Bark 2H **89**
Earlsferry Way N1 . . . . . 7J **65**
(not continuous)
EARLSFIELD 1A **136**
Earlsfield Ho. *KT2: King T* *1D* ***150***
(off Skerne Rd.)
Earlsfield Rd. SW18 . . . . . 1A **136**
Earlshall Rd. SE9 . . . . . 4D **124**
Earls Ho. TW9: Kew 7H **97**
Earlsmead HA2: Harr 4D **58**

Earlsmead Rd. N15 5F 49
NW10 3E 80
Earlsmead Stadium 4D 58
Earls Ter. W8 3H 99
Earlsthorpe M. SW12 6E 118
Earlsthorpe Rd. SE26 4K 139
Earlstoke St. EC1 1A 8 (3B 84)
Earlston Gro. E9 1H 85
Earl St. EC2 5G 9 (5D 84)
(not continuous)
Earls Wlk. RM8: Dag 4B 72
W8 3J 99
Earls Way BR6: Orp 2K 173
Earlswood Av. CR7: Thor H 5A 156
Earlswood Cl. SE10 6G 105
Earlswood Gdns. IG5: Ilf 3E 52
Earlswood St. SE10 5G 105
Early M. NW1 1F 83
Earnshaw St. WC2 7D 6 (6H 83)
Earsby St. W14 4G 99
(not continuous)
Easby Cres. SM4: Mord 6K 153
Easebourne Rd. RM8: Dag 5C 72
Easedale Ho. TW7: Isle 5K 113
Eashing Point *SW15* *1D 134*
(off Wanborough Dr.)
Easleys M. W1 7H 5 (6E 82)
East 10 Ent. Pk. E10 1A 68
EAST ACTON 7B 80
E. Acton Arc. W3 6A 80
E. Acton Ct. W3 7A 80
E. Acton La. W3 1A 98
E. Arbour St. E1 6K 85
East Av. E12 7C 70
E17 4D 50
N2 4K 45
SM6: Wall 5K 167
UB1: S'hall 7D 76
UB3: Hayes 1H 93
East Bank N16 7E 48
Eastbank Rd. TW12: Ham H 5G 131
EAST BARNET 6H 21
E. Barnet Rd. EN4: E Barn 4G 21
E. Beckton District Cen. E6 5D 88
EAST BEDFONT 7G 111
East Block *SE1* *6H 13*
(off York Rd.)
E. Boundary Rd. E12 3D 70
Eastbourne Av. W3 6K 79
Eastbourne Gdns. SW14 3J 115
Eastbourne M. W2 7A 4 (6A 82)
Eastbourne Rd. E6 3E 88
(not continuous)
E15 1G 87
N15 6E 48
SW17 6E 136
TW8: Bford 5C 96
TW13: Felt 2B 130
W4 6J 97
Eastbourne Ter.
W2 7A 4 (6A 82)
Eastbournia Av. N9 3C 34
Eastbrook Av. N9 7D 24
RM10: Dag 4J 73
Eastbrook Dr. RM7: Rush G 3K 73
Eastbrookend Country Pk. 4K 73
Eastbrook Rd. SE3 1K 123
Eastbury Av. EN1: Enf 1A 24
IG11: Bark 1J 89
Eastbury Ct. *EN5: New Bar* *5F 21*
(off Lyonsdown Rd.)
IG11: Bark 1J 89
Eastbury Gro. W4 5A 98
Eastbury Manor House 1K 89
Eastbury Rd. BR5: Pet W 6H 161
E6 4E 88
KT2: King T 7E 132
RM7: Rom 6K 55
Eastbury Sq. IG11: Bark 1K 89
Eastbury Ter. E1 4K 85
Eastcastle St. W1 7A 6 (6G 83)
Eastcheap EC3 2G 15 (7E 84)
E. Churchfield Rd. W3 1K 97
Eastchurch Rd. TW6: H'row A 2G 111
East Cl. EN4: Cockf 4K 21
UB6: G'frd 2G 77
W5 4G 79
Eastcombe Av. SE7 6K 105
EASTCOTE 7K 39
Eastcote BR6: Orp 1K 173
Eastcote Av. HA2: Harr 2F 59
KT8: W Mole 5D 148
UB6: G'frd 5A 60
Eastcote Hockey & Badminton Club 6H 39
Eastcote Ind. Est. HA4: Ruis 7A 40
Eastcote La. HA2: Harr 4C 58
UB5: N'olt 5D 58
(not continuous)
Eastcote La. Nth. UB5: N'olt 6D 58
Eastcote Pl. HA5: Eastc 6K 39
Eastcote Rd. DA16: Well 2H 125
HA2: Harr 3G 59
HA4: Ruis 7G 39
HA5: Pinn 5B 40
Eastcote St. SW9 2K 119
Eastcote Vw. HA5: Pinn 4A 40
EASTCOTE VILLAGE 5K 39
East Ct. HA0: Wemb 2C 60
East Cres. EN1: Enf 5A 24
N11 4J 31
Eastcroft Rd. KT19: Ewe 7A 164
E. Cross Route E3 7B 68
E9 5B 68
(Crowfoot Cl.)
E9 7B 68
(Wansbeck Rd.)
E15 5B 68
Eastdown Ct. SE13 4F 123
Eastdown Ho. E8 4G 67
Eastdown Pk. SE13 4F 123
East Dr. SM5: Cars 7C 166
E. Duck Lees La. EN3: Pond E 4F 25
EAST DULWICH 4F 121
E. Dulwich Gro. SE22 5E 120
E. Dulwich Rd. SE22 4F 121
(not continuous)
East End Farm HA5: Pinn 3D 40
East End Rd. N2 3K 45
N3 2J 45
East End Way HA5: Pinn 3C 40
East Entrance RM10: Dag 2H 91
Eastern Av. E11 6K 51
HA5: Pinn 7B 40
IG2: Ilf 6F 53
IG4: Ilf 6C 52
RM6: Chad H 4A 54
Eastern Av. E. RM1: Rom 3K 55
Eastern Av. Retail Pk.
RM7: Rom 4J 55
Eastern Av. W. RM6: Chad H 4E 54
RM7: Chad H, Mawney, Rom 4A 54
Eastern Bus. Pk. TW6: H'row A 2G 111
Eastern Gateway E16 7A 88
Eastern Ho. *E2* *3H 85*
(off Bethnal Grn. Rd.)
Eastern Ind. Est. DA18: Erith 2G 109
Eastern Perimeter Rd.
TW6: H'row A 2H 111
Eastern Quay Apartments *E16* *1K 105*
(off Portsmouth M.)
Eastern Rd. E13 2K 87
E17 5E 50
N2 3D 46
N22 1J 47
SE4 4C 122
Eastern Rdbt. IG1: Ilf 2G 71
Easternville Gdns. IG2: Ilf 6G 53
Eastern Way DA17: Belv 2A 108
SE2: Belv, Erith 2A 108
SE28 2A 108
E. Ferry Rd. E14 4D 104
Eastfield Gdns. RM10: Dag 4G 73
Eastfield Rd. E17 4C 50
EN3: Enf W 1E 24
N8 3J 47
RM10: Dag 4G 73
Eastfields HA5: Eastc 5A 40
Eastfields Av. SW18 4J 117
Eastfields Rd. CR4: Mitc 2E 154
W3 5J 79
Eastfield St. E14 5A 86
EAST FINCHLEY 4C 46
East Gdns. SW17 6C 136
Eastgate Bus. Pk. E10 1A 68
Eastgate Cl. SE28 6D 90
Eastglade HA5: Pinn 3D 40
EAST HAM 2D 88
E. Ham & Barking By-Pass
IG11: Bark 2J 89
Eastham Cl. EN5: Barn 5B 20
E. Ham Ind. Est. E6 4C 88
East Ham Leisure Cen. 1D 88
E. Ham Mnr. Way E6 6E 88
East Ham Nature Reserve 4D 88
E. Harding St. EC4 7K 7 (6A 84)
E. Heath Rd. NW3 3A 64
East Hill HA9: Wemb 2G 61
SW18 5K 117
Eastholm NW11 4K 45
East Holme DA8: Erith 1K 127
Eastholme UB3: Hayes 1J 93
E. India Bldgs. *E14* *7C 86*
(off Saltwell St.)
E. India Ct. *SE16* *2J 103*
(off St Marychurch St.)
E. India Dock Ho. E14 6E 86
E. India Dock Rd. E14 6C 86
E. India Way CR0: C'don 1F 169
Eastlake Ho. NW8 4B 4
Eastlake Rd. SE5 2C 120
Eastlands Cres. SE21 6F 121
East La. HA0: Wemb 3B 60
HA9: Wemb 3B 60
KT1: King T 3D 150
SE16 2G 103
(Chambers St.)
SE16 2G 103
(Scott Lidgett Cres.)
East La. Bus. Pk. HA9: Wemb 2D 60
Eastlea M. E16 4G 87
Eastleigh Av. HA2: Harr 2F 59
Eastleigh Cl. NW2 3A 62
SM2: Sutt 7K 165
Eastleigh Rd. DA7: Bex 3J 127
E17 2B 50
Eastleigh Wlk. SW15 7C 116
Eastleigh Way TW14: Felt 1J 129
East Lodge *E16* *1J 105*
(off Wesley Av.)
E. London Crematorium E13 3H 87
East London Gymnastic Cen. 6D 88
Eastman Ho. SW4 6G 119
Eastman Rd. W3 2K 97
East Mascalls SE7 6A 106
East Mead HA4: Ruis 3B 58
Eastmead Av. UB6: G'frd 3F 77
Eastmead Cl. BR1: Brom 2C 160
Eastmearn Rd. SE21 2C 138
EAST MOLESEY 4H 149
Eastmoor Pl. SE7 3B 106
Eastmoor St. SE7 3B 106
East Mt. St. E1 5H 85
(not continuous)
Eastney Rd. CR0: C'don 1B 168
Eastney St. SE10 5F 105
Eastnor Rd. SE9 1G 143
Easton St. WC1 3J 7 (4A 84)
East Pk. Cl. RM6: Chad H 5D 54
East Parkside SE10 2G 105
East Pas. EC1 5C 8
East Pl. SE27 4C 138
East Point SE1 5G 103
E. Pole Cotts. N14 4C 22
E. Poultry Av. EC1 6A 8 (5B 84)
East Ramp TW6: H'row A 1D 110
East Rd. DA16: Well 2B 126
E15 1J 87
EN3: Enf W 1D 24
EN4: E Barn 1K 31
HA1: Harr 7B 42
HA8: Edg 1H 43
KT2: King T 1E 150
N1 2E 8 (3D 84)
N2 1C 46
RM6: Chad H 5E 54
RM7: Rush G 7K 55
SW3 6G 17 (5E 100)
SW19 6A 136
TW14: Bedf 7F 111
UB7: W Dray 4B 92
E. Rochester Way DA5: Bexl 6F 127
DA15: Bexl, Sidc 4J 125
East Row E11 6J 51
W10 4G 81
Eastry Av. BR2: Hayes 6H 159
Eastry Ho. *SW8* *7J 101*
(off Hartington Rd.)
Eastry Rd. DA8: Erith 7G 109
EAST SHEEN 4J 115
E. Sheen Av. SW14 5K 115
Eastside Rd. NW11 4H 45
East Smithfield E1 3K 15 (7F 85)
East Sq. E10 7D 50
East St. BR1: Brom 2J 159
DA7: Bex 4G 127
IG11: Bark 1G 89
SE17 5C 102
(not continuous)
TW8: Bford 7C 96
E. Surrey Gro. SE15 7F 103
E. Tenter St. E1 1K 15 (6F 85)
East Ter. DA15: Sidc 1J 143
E. Thamesmead Bus. Pk.
DA18: Erith 2F 109
East Towers HA5: Pinn 5B 40
East Va. W3 1B 98
East Vw. E4 5K 35
EN5: Barn 2C 20
Eastview Av. SE18 7J 107
Eastville Av. NW11 6H 45
East Wlk. EN4: E Barn 7K 21
UB3: Hayes 1J 93
East Way BR2: Hayes 7J 159
CR0: C'don 2A 170
E11 5K 51
HA4: Ruis 1J 57
UB3: Hayes 1J 93
Eastway E9 6B 68
(not continuous)
SM4: Mord 5F 153
SM6: Wall 4G 167
Eastway Cres. HA2: Harr 2F 59
Eastwell Cl. BR3: Beck 7A 140
Eastwell Ho. SE1 7F 15
EAST WICKHAM 1C 126
Eastwood Cl. E18 2J 51
N7 5A 66
N17 7C 34
Eastwood Rd. E18 2J 51
IG3: Ilf 1A 72
N10 2E 46
UB7: W Dray 2C 92
East Woodside
DA5: Bexl 7E 126
Eastwood St. SW16 6G 137
Eatington Rd. E10 5F 51
Eaton Cl. HA7: Stan 4G 27
SW1 4G 17 (4E 100)
Eaton Ct. E18 2J 51
HA8: Edg 4B 28

Eaton Dr. KT2: King T .7G 133
RM5: Col R .1H 55
SW9 .4B 120
Eaton Gdns. RM9: Dag .7E 72
Eaton Ga. SW1 .3G 17 (4E 100)
Eaton Ho. *E14* .*7B 86*
(off Westferry Cir.)
SW11 .1B 118
Eaton La. SW1 .2K 17 (3F 101)
Eaton Mans. *SW1* .*4G 17*
(off Bourne St.)
Eaton M. Nth. SW1 .3G 17 (4E 100)
Eaton M. Sth. SW1 .3H 17 (4E 100)
Eaton M. W. SW1 .3H 17 (4E 100)
Eaton Pk. Rd. N13 .2F 33
Eaton Pl. SW1 .2G 17 (4E 100)
Eaton Ri. E11 .5A 52
W5 .5D 78
Eaton Rd. DA14: Sidc .2D 144
EN1: Enf .4K 23
NW4 .5E 44
SM2: Sutt .6B 166
TW3: Houn .4H 113
Eaton Row SW1 .2J 17 (3F 101)
Eatons Mead E4 .2H 35
Eaton Sq. SW1 .3G 17 (4E 100)
Eaton Ter. E3 .3A 86
SW1 .3G 17 (4E 100)
Eaton Ter. M. SW1 .3G 17
Eatonville Rd. SW17 .2D 136
Eatonville Vs. SW17 .2D 136
Ebb Ct. E16 .7G 89
Ebbett Ct. W3 .5K 79
Ebbisham Dr. SW8 .7G 19 (6K 101)
Ebbisham Rd. KT4: Wor Pk .2E 164
Ebbsfleet Rd. NW2 .5G 63
Ebdon Way SE3 .3K 123
Ebenezer Ho. SE11 .4K 19 (4B 102)
Ebenezer Mussel Ho. *E2* .*2J 85*
(off Patriot Sq.)
Ebenezer St. N1 .1E 8 (3D 84)
Ebenezer Wlk. SW16 .1G 155
Ebley Cl. SE15 .6F 103
Ebner St. SW18 .5K 117
Ebony Ho. *E2* .*3G 85*
(off Buckfast St.)
Ebor Cotts. SW15 .3A 134
Ebor St. E1 .3J 9 (4F 85)
Ebrington Rd. HA3: Kent .6D 42
Ebsworth St. SE23 .7K 121
Eburne Rd. N7 .3J 65
Ebury Bri. SW1 .5J 17 (5F 101)
Ebury Bri. Est. SW1 .5J 17 (5F 101)
Ebury Bri. Rd. SW1 .6H 17 (5E 100)
Ebury Cl. BR2: Kes .3C 172
Ebury M. SE27 .3B 138
SW1 .3J 17 (4F 101)
Ebury M. E. SW1 .2J 17 (3F 101)
Ebury Sq. SW1 .4H 17 (4E 100)
Ebury St. SW1 .4H 17 (4E 100)
Ecclesbourne Cl. N13 .5F 33
Ecclesbourne Gdns. N13 .5F 33
Ecclesbourne Rd. CR7: Thor H .5C 156
N1 .7C 66
Eccleshill *BR2: Brom* .*4H 159*
(off Durham Rd.)
Eccles Rd. SW11 .4D 118
Eccleston Bri. SW1 .3K 17 (4F 101)
Eccleston Cl. BR6: Orp .1H 173
EN4: Cockf .4J 21
Eccleston Cres. RM6: Chad H .7B 54
Ecclestone Ct. HA9: Wemb .5E 60
Ecclestone M. HA9: Wemb .5E 60
Ecclestone Pl. HA9: Wemb .5F 61
Eccleston Ho. SW2 .6A 120
Eccleston M. SW1 .2H 17 (3E 100)
Eccleston Pl. SW1 .3J 17 (4F 101)
Eccleston Rd. W13 .7A 78
Eccleston Sq. SW1 .4K 17 (4F 101)
Eccleston Sq. M. SW1 .4A 18 (4F 101)
Eccleston St. SW1 .2J 17 (3F 101)
Echelforde Dr. TW15: Ashf .4C 128
Echo Hgts. E4 .1J 35
Eckford St. N1 .2A 84
Eckington Ho. *N15* .*6D 48*
(off Fladbury Rd.)
Eckstein Rd. SW11 .4C 118
Eclipse Ho. *N22* .*2K 47*
(off Station Rd.)
Eclipse Rd. E13 .5K 87
Ecology Cen. and Arts Pavilion .3A 86
Ector Rd. SE6 .2G 141
Edam Ct. DA15: Sidc .3A 144
Edans Ct. W12 .2B 98
Edar Ho. CR0: New Ad .6D 170
Edbrooke Rd. W9 .4J 81
Eddington Cl. CR0: New Ad .6E 170
Eddisbury Ho. SE26 .3G 139
Eddiscombe Rd. SW6 .2H 117
Eddy Cl. RM7: Rom .6H 55
Eddystone Rd. SE4 .5A 122
Eddystone Twr. SE8 .5A 104
Eddystone Wlk. TW19: Stanw .7A 110
Ede Cl. TW3: Houn .3D 112
Edenbridge Cl. *SE16* .*5H 103*
(off Masters Dr.)
Edenbridge Rd. E9 .7K 67
EN1: Enf .6K 23
Eden Cl. DA5: Bexl .4K 145
HA0: Wemb .1D 78
NW3 .2J 63
W8 .3J 99
Eden Ct. IG6: Ilf .1H 53
Edencourt Rd. SW16 .6F 137
Edendale W3 .7H 79
Edendale Rd. DA7: Bex .1K 127
Edenfield Gdns. KT4: Wor Pk .3B 164
Eden Gro. E17 .5D 50
N7 .5K 65
Edenham Way W10 .4H 81
Eden Ho. *NW8* .*4C 4*
(off Church St.)
Edenhurst Av. SW6 .3H 117
Eden Lodge NW6 .7F 63
Eden M. SW17 .3A 136
EDEN PARK .5C 158
Eden Pk. Av. BR3: Beck .4A 158
(not continuous)
Eden Rd. BR3: Beck .4A 158
CR0: C'don .4D 168
DA5: Bexl .4J 145
E17 .5D 50
SE27 .4B 138
Edensor Gdns. W4 .7A 98
Edensor Rd. W4 .7A 98
Eden St. KT1: King T .2D 150
Edenvale Cl. CR4: Mitc .7E 136
Edenvale Rd. CR4: Mitc .7E 136
Edenvale St. SW6 .2A 118
Eden Wlk. KT1: King T .2E 150
Eden Way BR3: Beck .5B 158
E3 .1B 86
Ederline Av. SW16 .3K 155
Edgar Ct. KT3: N Mald .2A 152
Edgar Ho. *E9* .*5A 68*
(off Homerton Rd.)
E11 .7J 51
SW8 .*7J 101*
(off Wyvil Rd.)
Edgar Kail Way SE22 .4E 120
Edgarley Ter. SW6 .1G 117
Edgar Rd. E3 .3D 86
RM6: Chad H .7D 54
TW4: Houn .7D 112
UB7: Yiew .7A 74
Edgar Wallace Cl. SE15 .7E 102
Edgar Wright Ct. *SW6* .*7H 99*
(off Dawes Rd.)
Edgcott Ho. *W10* .*5E 80*
(off Sutton Way)
Edgeborough Way
BR1: Brom .7B 142
Edgebury BR7: Chst .4F 143
Edgebury Wlk. BR7: Chst .4G 143
Edge Bus. Cen., The NW2 .2D 62
Edgecombe Ho. SE5 .2E 120
SW19 .1G 135
Edgecoombe CR2: Sels .7J 169
Edgecoombe Cl. KT2: King T .7K 133
Edgecote Cl. W3 .1J 97
Edgecot Gro. N15 .5E 48
Edgefield Av. IG11: Bark .7K 71
Edgefield Ct. *IG11: Bark* .*7K 71*
(off Edgefield Av.)
Edge Hill SE18 .6F 107
SW19 .7F 135
Edge Hill Av. N3 .4J 45
Edge Hill Ct. DA14: Sidc .4K 143
SW19 .7F 135
Edgehill Gdns. RM10: Dag .4G 73
Edgehill Ho. SW9 .2B 120
Edgehill Rd. BR7: Chst .3G 143
CR4: Mitc .1F 155
W13 .5C 78
Edgeley La. SW4 .3H 119
Edgeley Rd. SW4 .3H 119
Edgel St. SW18 .4K 117
Edge Point Cl. SE27 .5B 138
Edge St. W8 .1J 99
Edgewood Dr. BR6: Chels .5K 173
Edgewood Grn. CR0: C'don .1K 169
Edgeworth Av. NW4 .5C 44
Edgeworth Cl. NW4 .5C 44
Edgeworth Ct.
EN4: Cockf .*4H 21*
(off Fordham Rd.)
Edgeworth Cres. NW4 .5C 44
Edgeworth Ho. *NW8* .*1A 82*
(off Boundary Rd.)
Edgeworth Rd. EN4: Cockf .4H 21
SE9 .4A 124
Edgington Rd. SW16 .6H 137
Edgington Way DA14: Sidc .7C 144
Edgson Ho. *SW1* .*5J 17*
(off Ebury Bri. Rd.)
EDGWARE .6B 28
EDGWARE BURY .1A 28
Edgwarebury Gdns. HA8: Edg .5B 28
Edgwarebury La. HA8: Edg .1A 28
WD6: E'tree .1A 28
Edgware Ct. HA8: Edg .6B 28
Edgware Rd. NW2 .1D 62
NW9 .2J 43
W2 .4A 4 (4B 82)
Edgware Town & Wealdstone FC
(Edgware Football Ground) .7B 28
Edgware Way HA8: Edg .4A 28
NW7 .4A 28
WD6: Edg, E'tree .1J 27
Edinburgh Cl. E2 .2J 85
HA5: Pinn .7B 40
UB10: Ick .4D 56
Edinburgh Ct. DA8: Erith .7K 109
KT1: King T .*3E 150*
(off Watersplash Cl.)
SE16 .*1K 103*
(off Rotherhithe St.)
SW20 .5F 153
Edinburgh Dr. UB10: Ick .4D 56
Edinburgh Ga. SW1 .6E 10 (2D 100)
Edinburgh Ho. NW4 .3E 44
W9 .*3K 81*
(off Maida Va.)
Edinburgh Rd. E13 .2K 87
E17 .5C 50
(not continuous)
N18 .5B 34
SM1: Sutt .2A 166
W7 .2K 95
Edington NW5 .6E 64
Edington Rd. EN3: Enf H .2D 24
SE2 .3B 108
Edison Bldg. E14 .2C 104
Edison Cl. E17 .5C 50
UB7: W Dray .2B 92
Edison Ct. *SE10* .*3H 105*
(off Schoolbank Rd.)
Edison Dr. HA9: Wemb .3E 60
UB1: S'hall .6F 77
Edison Gro. SE18 .7K 107
Edison Ho. *HA9: Wemb* .*3J 61*
(off Barnhill Rd.)
SE1 .*4D 102*
(off New Kent Rd.)
Edison Rd. BR2: Brom .2J 159
DA16: Well .1K 125
EN3: Brim .2G 25
N8 .6H 47
Edis St. NW1 .1E 82
Editha Mans. *SW10* .*6A 100*
(off Edith Gro.)
Edith Brinson Ho. *E14* .*6F 87*
(off Oban St.)
Edith Cavell Cl. N19 .7J 47
Edith Cavell Way SE18 .1C 124
Edith Gdns. KT5: Surb .7H 151
Edith Gro. SW10 .6A 100
Edith Ho. *W6* .*5E 98*
(off Queen Caroline St.)
Edithna St. SW9 .3J 119
Edith Neville Cotts. *NW1* .*1C 6*
(off Drummond Cres.)
Edith Ramsay Ho. *E1* .*5A 86*
(off Duckett St.)
Edith Rd. E6 .7B 70
E15 .5F 69
N11 .7C 32
RM6: Chad H .7D 54
SE25 .5D 156
SW19 .6K 135
W14 .4G 99
Edith Row SW6 .1K 117
Edith St. E2 .2G 85
Edith Summerskill Ho. *SW6* .*7H 99*
(off Clem Attlee Est.)
Edith Ter. SW10 .7A 100
Edith Vs. W14 .4H 99
Edith Yd. SW10 .7A 100
Edmansons Cl. N17 .1F 49
Edmeston Cl. E9 .6A 68
Edmond Ct. SE14 .1J 121
Edmonscote W13 .5A 78
EDMONTON .3B 34
Edmonton Ct. *SE16* .*3J 103*
(off Canada Est.)
Edmonton Grn. Shop. Cen. N9 .2B 34
Edmonton Leisure Cen. .3B 34
Edmund Gro. TW13: Hanw .2D 130
Edmund Halley Way SE10 .2G 105
Edmund Ho. SE17 .6B 102
Edmund Hurst Dr. E6 .5F 89
Edmund Rd. CR4: Mitc .3C 154
DA16: Well .3A 126
Edmundsbury Ct. Est. SW9 .4K 119
Edmunds Cl. UB4: Yead .5A 76
Edmund St. SE5 .7D 102
Edmunds Wlk. N2 .4C 46
Ednam Ho. *SE15* .*6G 103*
(off Haymerle Rd.)
Edna Rd. SW20 .2F 153
Edna St. SW11 .1C 118
Edred Ho. *E9* .*4A 68*
(off Lindisfarne Way)
Edrich Ho. SW4 .1J 119
Edric Ho. *SW1* .*3D 18*
(off Page St.)
Edrick Rd. HA8: Edg .6D 28
Edrick Wlk. HA8: Edg .6D 28
Edric Rd. SE14 .7K 103
Edridge Rd. CR0: C'don .3C 168

Edward VII Mans. *NW10* ... *3F 81*
(off Chamberlayne Rd.)
Edward Alderton Theatre ... 3D 126
Edward Av. E4 ... 6J 35
SM4: Mord ... 5B 154
Edward Bond Ho. *WC1* ... *2F 7*
(off Cromer St.)
Edward Clifford Ho. *SE17* ... *4D 102*
(off Elsted St.)
Edward Cl. N9 ... 7A 24
NW2 ... 4F 63
TW12: Ham H ... 5G 131
Edward Ct. E16 ... 5J 87
Edward Dodd Ct. *N1* ... *1F 9*
(off Chart St.)
Edward Edward's Ho. SE1 ... 5A 14
Edwardes Pl. W8 ... 3H 99
Edwardes Sq. W8 ... 3H 99
Edward Gro. EN4: E Barn ... 5G 21
Edward Ho. SE11 ... 5H 19
W2 ... *4A 4*
(off Hall Pl.)
Edward Kennedy Ho. *W10* ... *4G 81*
(off Wornington Rd.)
Edward Mann Cl. *E1* ... *6K 85*
(off Caroline St.)
Edward M. NW1 ... 1K 5 (3F 83)
Edward Pl. SE8 ... 6B 104
Edward Rd. BR1: Brom ... 7K 141
BR7: Chst ... 5F 143
CR0: C'don ... 7E 156
E17 ... 4K 49
EN4: E Barn ... 5G 21
HA2: Harr ... 3G 41
RM6: Chad H ... 6E 54
SE20 ... 7K 139
TW12: Ham H ... 5G 131
TW14: Felt ... 5F 111
UB5: Yead ... 2A 76
Edward Robinson Ho. *SE14* ... *7K 103*
(off Reaston St.)
Edward's Av. HA4: Ruis ... 6K 57
Edwards Cl. KT4: Wor Pk ... 2F 165
Edward's Cotts. N1 ... 6B 66
Edwards Ct. *CR0: C'don* ... *4E 168*
(off South Pk. Hill Rd.)
Edwards Dr. N11 ... 7C 32
Edward's La. N16 ... 2E 66
Edwards Mans. *IG11: Bark* ... *7K 71*
(off Upney La.)
Edwards M. N1 ... 7A 66
W1 ... 1G 11 (6E 82)
Edward Sq. N1 ... 1K 83
SE16 ... 1A 104
Edwards Rd. DA17: Belv ... 4G 109
Edward St. E16 ... 4J 87
(not continuous)
SE8 ... 6B 104
SE14 ... 7A 104
Edwards Yd. HA0: Wemb ... 1E 78
Edward Temme Av. E15 ... 7H 69
Edward Tyler Rd. SE12 ... 2A 142
Edward Way TW15: Ashf ... 2B 128
Edwina Gdns. IG4: Ilf ... 5C 52
Edwin Arnold Ct. DA14: Sidc ... 4K 143
Edwin Av. E6 ... 2E 88
(not continuous)
Edwin Cl. DA7: Bex ... 6F 109
Edwin Ho. SE15 ... 7G 103
Edwin Pl. *CR0: C'don* ... *1E 168*
(off Leslie Gro.)
Edwin Rd. HA8: Edg ... 6E 28
TW1: Twick ... 1K 131
TW2: Twick ... 1J 131
Edwin's Mead E9 ... 4A 68
Edwin Stray Ho. TW13: Hanw ... 2E 130
Edwin St. E1 ... 4J 85
E16 ... 5J 87
Edwin Ware Ct. HA5: Pinn ... 2A 40
Edwyn Cl. EN5: Barn ... 6A 20
Edwyn Ho. *SW18* ... *6K 117*
(off Neville Gill Cl.)
Eel Brook Cl. SW6 ... 1K 117
Eel Pie Island TW1: Twick ... 1A 132
Effie Pl. SW6 ... 7J 99
Effie Rd. SW6 ... 7J 99
Effingham Cl. SM2: Sutt ... 7K 165
Effingham Lodge
KT1: King T ... 4D 150
Effingham Rd. CR0: C'don ... 7K 155
KT6: Surb ... 7B 150
N8 ... 5A 48
SE12 ... 5G 123
Effort St. SW17 ... 5C 136
Effra Cl. SW19 ... 6K 135
Effra Ct. *SW2* ... *5K 119*
(off Brixton Hill)
Effra Pde. SW2 ... 5A 120
Effra Rd. SW2 ... 4A 120
SW19 ... 6K 135
Effra Rd. Retail Pk. SW2 ... 5A 120
Egan Way UB3: Hayes ... 7G 75
Egbert St. NW1 ... 1E 82
Egbury Ho. *SW15* ... *6B 116*
(off Tangley Gro.)
Egeremont Rd. SE13 ... 2D 122
Egerton Cl. HA5: Eastc ... 4J 39
Egerton Ct. E11 ... 7F 51
Egerton Cres. SW3 ... 3D 16 (4C 100)
Egerton Dr. SE10 ... 1D 122
Egerton Gdns. IG3: Ilf ... 3K 71
NW4 ... 4D 44
NW10 ... 1E 80
SW3 ... 2C 16 (4C 100)
W13 ... 6B 78
Egerton Gdns. M. SW3 ... 2D 16 (3C 100)
Egerton Pl. SW3 ... 2D 16 (3C 100)
Egerton Rd. HA0: Wemb ... 7F 61
KT3: N Mald ... 4B 152
N16 ... 7F 49
SE25 ... 3E 156
TW2: Twick ... 7J 113
Egerton Ter. SW3 ... 2D 16 (3C 100)
Egerton Way UB3: Harl ... 7D 92
Eggardon Ct. UB5: N'olt ... 6F 59
Egham Cl. SM3: Cheam ... 2G 165
SW19 ... 2G 135
Egham Cres. SM3: Cheam ... 3G 165
Egham Rd. E13 ... 5K 87
Eglantine Rd. SW18 ... 5A 118
Egleston Rd. SM4: Mord ... 6K 153
Eglington Ct. SE17 ... 6C 102
Eglington Rd. E4 ... 7K 25
Eglinton Hill SE18 ... 6F 107
Eglinton Rd. SE18 ... 6E 106
Egliston M. SW15 ... 3E 116
Egliston Rd. SW15 ... 3E 116
Eglon M. NW1 ... 7D 64
Egmont Av. KT6: Surb ... 1F 163
Egmont Ct. KT12: Walt T ... 7K 147
Egmont Rd. KT3: N Mald ... 4B 152
KT6: Surb ... 1F 163
KT12: Walt T ... 7K 147
SM2: Sutt ... 7A 166
Egmont St. SE14 ... 7K 103
Egremont Ho. *SE13* ... *2D 122*
(off Russett Way)
Egremont Rd. SE27 ... 3A 138
Egret Ho. *SE16* ... *4K 103*
(off Tawny Way)
Egret Way UB4: Yead ... 5B 76
Eider Cl. E7 ... 5H 69
UB4: Yead ... 5B 76
Eider Ct. *SE8* ... *6B 104*
(off Pilot Cl.)
Eighteenth Rd. CR4: Mitc ... 4J 155
Eighth Av. E12 ... 4D 70
UB3: Hayes ... 1J 93
Eileen Rd. SE25 ... 5D 156
Eindhoven Cl. SM5: Cars ... 1E 166
Einstein Ho. HA9: Wemb ... 3J 61
Eisenhower Dr. E6 ... 5C 88
Elaine Gro. NW5 ... 5E 64
Elam Cl. SE5 ... 2B 120
Elam St. SE5 ... 2B 120
Elan Ct. E1 ... 5H 85
Eland Ho. *SW1* ... *1A 18*
(off Bressenden Pl.)
Eland Pl. CR0: Wadd ... 3B 168
Eland Rd. CR0: Wadd ... 3B 168
SW11 ... 3D 118
Elba Pl. SE17 ... 4C 102
Elberon Av. CR0: Bedd ... 6G 155
Elbe St. SW6 ... 2A 118
Elborough Rd. SE25 ... 5G 157
Elborough St. SW18 ... 1J 135
Elbourne Ct. *SE16* ... *3K 103*
(off Worgan St.)
Elbourne Trad. Est. DA17: Belv ... 3H 109
Elbourn Ho. *SW3* ... *5C 16*
(off Cale St.)
Elbow Mdw. SL3: Poyle ... 4A 174
Elbury Dr. E16 ... 6J 87
Elcho St. SW11 ... 7C 100
Elcot Av. SE15 ... 7H 103
Elden Ho. *SW3* ... *3C 16*
(off Sloane Av.)
Eldenwall Ind. Est. RM8: Dag ... 1E 72
Elder Av. N8 ... 5J 47
Elderberry Gro. SE27 ... 4C 138
Elderberry Rd. W5 ... 2E 96
Elderberry Way E6 ... 3D 88
Elder Cl. DA15: Sidc ... 1K 143
N20 ... 2E 30
UB7: Yiew ... 7A 74
Elder Ct. WD23: B Hea ... 2D 26
Elderfield Ho. E14 ... 7C 86
Elderfield Pl. SW17 ... 4F 137
Elderfield Rd. E5 ... 4K 67
Elderfield Wlk. E11 ... 5K 51
Elderflower Way E15 ... 7G 69
Elder Gdns. SE27 ... 5C 138
Elder Oak Cl. SE20 ... 1H 157
Elder Oak Ct. *SE20* ... *1H 157*
(off Anerley Ct.)
Elder Rd. SE27 ... 5C 138
Elderslie Cl. BR3: Beck ... 5C 158
Elderslie Rd. SE9 ... 5E 124
Elder St. E1 ... 5J 9 (4F 85)
(not continuous)
Elderton Rd. SE26 ... 4A 140
Eldertree Pl. CR4: Mitc ... 1G 155
Eldertree Way CR4: Mitc ... 1G 155
Elder Wlk. *N1* ... *1B 84*
(off Popham St.)
SE13 ... 3E 122
Elderwood Pl. SE27 ... 5C 138
Eldon Av. CR0: C'don ... 2J 169
TW5: Hest ... 7E 94
Eldon Ct. NW6 ... 1J 81
Eldon Gro. NW3 ... 5B 64
Eldon Pk. SE25 ... 4H 157
Eldon Rd. E17 ... 4B 50
N9 ... 1D 34
N22 ... 1B 48
W8 ... 3K 99
Eldon St. EC2 ... 6F 9 (5D 84)
Eldon Way NW10 ... 3H 79
Eldred Rd. IG11: Bark ... 1J 89
Eldrick Ct. TW14: Bedf ... 1F 129
Eldridge Cl. TW14: Felt ... 1J 129
Eldridge Ct. RM10: Dag ... 6H 73
SE16 ... 3G 103
Eleanor Cl. N15 ... 3F 49
SE16 ... 2K 103
Eleanor Ct. *E2* ... *1G 85*
(off Whiston Rd.)
Eleanor Cres. NW7 ... 5A 30
Eleanor Gdns. EN5: Barn ... 5A 20
RM8: Dag ... 2F 73
Eleanor Gro. SW13 ... 3A 116
UB10: Ick ... 3D 56
Eleanor Ho. *W6* ... *5E 98*
(off Queen Caroline St.)
Eleanor Rathbone Ho. *N6* ... *7H 47*
(off Avenue Rd.)
Eleanor Rd. E8 ... 6H 67
E15 ... 6H 69
N11 ... 6D 32
Eleanor's Station
Ruislip Lido Railway ... 3G 39
Eleanor St. E3 ... 3C 86
Eleanor Wlk. SE18 ... 4C 106
Electra Av. TW6: H'row A ... 3H 111
Electra Bus. Pk. E16 ... 5F 87
Electric Av. SW9 ... 4A 120
Electric La. SW9 ... 4A 120
(not continuous)
Electric Pde. *E18* ... *2J 51*
(off George La.)
IG3: Ilf ... 2J 71
KT6: Surb ... 6D 150
Elektron Ho. E14 ... 7F 87
ELEPHANT & CASTLE ... 3B 102
Elephant & Castle SE1 ... 4B 102
Elephant & Castle Superbowl ... *4C 102*
(within Shopping Cen.)
Elephant La. SE16 ... 2J 103
Elephant Rd. SE17 ... 4C 102
Elers Rd. UB3: Harl ... 4F 93
W13 ... 2C 96
Eley Rd. N18 ... 4D 34
Eley Rd. Retail Pk. N18 ... 5D 34
Eleys Est. N18 ... 3E 34
(not continuous)
Elfindale Rd. SE24 ... 5C 120
Elfin Gro. TW11: Tedd ... 5K 131
Elford Cl. SE3 ... 4K 123
Elford M. SW4 ... 5G 119
Elfort Rd. N5 ... 4A 66
Elfrida Cres. SE6 ... 4C 140
Elf Row E1 ... 7J 85
Elfwine Rd. W7 ... 5J 77
Elgal Cl. BR6: Farnb ... 5F 173
Elgar *N8* ... *3J 47*
(off Boyton Cl.)
Elgar Av. KT5: Surb ... 1G 163
NW10 ... 6K 61
(not continuous)
SW16 ... 3J 155
W5 ... 2E 96
Elgar Cl. E13 ... 2A 88
IG9: Buck H ... 2G 37
SE8 ... 7C 104
UB10: Ick ... 2C 56
Elgar Ct. *W14* ... *3G 99*
(off Blythe Rd.)
Elgar Ho. *NW6* ... *7A 64*
(off Fairfax Rd.)
SW1 ... *6K 17*
(off Churchill Gdns.)
Elgar St. SE16 ... 3A 104
Elgin Av. HA3: Kent ... 2B 42
TW15: Ashf ... 6E 128
W9 ... 4H 81
W12 ... 2C 98
Elgin Cl. W12 ... 2D 98
Elgin Ct. *CR2: S Croy* ... *4C 168*
(off Bramley Hill)
W9 ... 4K 81
Elgin Cres. TW6: H'row A ... 2G 111
W11 ... 7G 81
Elgin Dr. HA6: Nwood ... 1G 39
Elgin Est. *W9* ... *4J 81*
(off Elgin Av.)
Elgin Ho. *E14* ... *6D 86*
(off Ricardo St.)
Elgin Mans. W9 ... 3K 81
Elgin M. W11 ... 6G 81
Elgin M. Nth. W9 ... 3K 81

Elgin M. Sth. W9 3K 81
Elgin Rd. CR0: C'don 2F 169
IG3: Ilf 1J 71
N22 2G 47
SM1: Sutt 3A 166
SM6: Wall 6G 167
Elgood Cl. W11 7G 81
Elgood Ho. NW8 2B 82
(off Wellington Rd.)
SE1 2D 102
(off Nebraska St.)
Elham Cl. BR1: Brom 7B 142
Elham Ho. E5 5H 67
Elia M. N1 1A 8 (2B 84)
Elias Pl. SW8 6A 102
Elia St. N1 1B 8 (2B 84)
Elibank Rd. SE9 4D 124
Elim Est. SE1 7G 15 (3E 102)
Elim St. SE1 7G 15 (3D 102)
(not continuous)
Elim Way E13 3H 87
Eliot Bank SE23 2H 139
Eliot Cotts. SE3 2G 123
Eliot Ct. SW18 6K 117
Eliot Dr. HA2: Harr 2F 59
Eliot Gdns. SW15 4C 116
Eliot Hill SE13 2E 122
Eliot M. NW8 2A 82
Eliot Pk. SE13 2E 122
Eliot Pl. SE3 2G 123
Eliot Rd. RM9: Dag 4D 72
Eliot Va. SE3 2F 123
Elis David Almshouses
CR0: C'don 3B 168
Elizabethan Cl. TW19: Stanw 7A 110
Elizabethan Way TW19: Stanw 7A 110
Elizabeth Av. EN2: Enf 3G 23
IG1: Ilf 2H 71
N1 1C 84
TW18: Staines 7A 128
Elizabeth Barnes Ct. SW6 2K 117
(off Marinefield Rd.)
Elizabeth Blackwell Ho. N22 1A 48
(off Progress Way)
Elizabeth Blount Ct. E14 6A 86
(off Carr St.)
Elizabeth Bri. SW1 4J 17 (4F 101)
Elizabeth Cl. E14 6D 86
EN5: Barn 3A 20
RM7: Mawney 1H 55
SM1: Sutt 4H 165
W9 4A 82
Elizabeth Clyde Cl. N15 4E 48
Elizabeth Cotts. TW9: Kew 1F 115
Elizabeth Ct. BR1: Brom 1H 159
(off Highland Rd.)
CR0: C'don 3E 168
(off The Avenue)
E4 5G 35
IG8: Wfd G 7F 37
KT2: King T 1E 150
NW1 3D 4
SW1 2D 18
SW10 6B 100
(off Milman's St.)
TW11: Tedd 5J 131
TW16: Sun 3A 148
(off Elizabeth Gdns.)
Elizabeth Fry Ho.
UB3: Harl 4H 93
Elizabeth Fry M. E8 7H 67
Elizabeth Fry Pl. SE18 1C 124
Elizabeth Gdns.
HA7: Stan 6H 27
TW7: Isle 4A 114
TW16: Sun 3A 148
W3 1B 98
Elizabeth Garrett Anderson Ho.
DA17: Belv 3G 109
(off Ambrook Rd.)
Elizabeth Ho. SE11 4K 19
(off Reedworth St.)
SM3: Cheam 6G 165
(off Park La.)
W6 5E 98
(off Queen Caroline St.)
Elizabeth Ind. Est. SE14 6K 103
Elizabeth M. HA1: Harr 6J 41
NW3 6C 64
Elizabeth Newcomen Ho. SE1 6E 14
(off Newcomen St.)
Elizabeth Pl. N15 4D 48
Elizabeth Ride N9 7C 24
Elizabeth Rd. E6 1B 88
N15 5E 48
Elizabeth Sq. SE16 7A 86
(off Sovereign Cres.)
Elizabeth St. SW1 3H 17 (4E 100)
Elizabeth Ter. SE9 6D 124
Elizabeth Way SE19 7D 138
TW13: Hanw 4A 130
Elkanette M. N20 2F 31
Elkington Point SE11 4J 19
Elkington Rd. E13 4K 87
Elkstone Rd. W10 5H 81
Ella Cl. BR3: Beck 2C 158
Ellacott M. SW16 2H 137
Ellaline Rd. W6 6F 99
Ella M. NW3 4D 64
Ellanby Cres. N18 4C 34
Elland Ho. E14 6B 86
(off Copenhagen Pl.)
Elland Rd. SE15 4J 121
Ella Rd. N8 7J 47
Ellement Cl. HA5: Pinn 5B 40
Ellena Ct. N14 3D 32
(off Conway Rd.)
Ellenborough Ho. W12 7D 80
(off White City Est.)
Ellenborough Pl. SW15 4C 116
Ellenborough Rd. DA14: Sidc 5D 144
N22 1C 48
Ellenbridge Way CR2: Sande 7E 168
Ellen Cl. BR1: Brom 3B 160
Ellen Ct. E4 1K 35
(off The Ridgeway)
N9 2D 34
Ellen St. E1 6G 85
Ellen Terry Ct. NW1 7F 65
(off Farrier St.)
Ellen Webb Dr.
HA3: W'stone 3J 41
Ellen Wilkinson Ho. E2 3K 85
(off Usk St.)
RM10: Dag 3G 73
SW6 6H 99
(off Clem Attlee Ct.)
Elleray Rd. TW11: Tedd 6K 131
Ellerby St. SW6 1F 117
Ellerdale Cl. NW3 4A 64
Ellerdale Rd. NW3 5A 64
Ellerdale St. SE13 4D 122
Ellerdine Rd. TW3: Houn 4G 113
Ellerker Gdns. TW10: Rich 6E 114
Ellerman Av. TW2: Whitt 1D 130
Ellerslie Gdns. NW10 1C 80
Ellerslie Rd. W12 1D 98
Ellerslie Sq. Ind. Est. SW2 5J 119
Ellerton Gdns. RM9: Dag 7C 72
Ellerton Lodge N3 2J 45
Ellerton Rd. KT6: Surb 2F 163
RM9: Dag 7C 72
SW13 1C 116
SW18 1B 136
SW20 7C 134
Ellery Ho. SE17 4D 102
Ellery Rd. SE19 7D 138
Ellery St. SE15 2H 121
Ellesmere Av. BR3: Beck 2D 158
NW7 3E 28
Ellesmere Cl. E11 5H 51
HA4: Ruis 7E 38
Ellesmere Ct. SE12 1J 141
W4 5K 97
Ellesmere Gdns. IG4: Ilf 5C 52
Ellesmere Gro. EN5: Barn 5C 20
Ellesmere Ho. SW10 6A 100
(off Fulham Rd.)
Ellesmere Mans. NW6 6A 64
(off Canfield Gdns.)
Ellesmere Rd. E3 2A 86
NW10 5C 62
TW1: Twick 6C 114
UB6: G'frd 4G 77
W4 6J 97
Ellesmere St. E14 6D 86
Ellies M. TW15: Ashf 2A 128
Ellingfort Rd. E8 7H 67
Ellingham Rd. E15 4F 69
KT9: Chess 6D 162
W12 2C 98
Ellington Ct. N14 2C 32
Ellington Ho. SE1 3C 102
Ellington Rd. N10 4F 47
TW3: Houn 2F 113
TW13: Felt 4H 129
Ellington St. N7 6A 66
Elliot Cl. E15 7G 69
Elliot Ct. IG8: Wfd G 6G 37
Elliot Ho. W1 6D 4
(off Cato St.)
Elliot Rd. NW4 6D 44
Elliott Av. HA4: Ruis 2K 57
Elliott Cl. HA9: Wemb 3F 61
Elliott Gdns. TW17: Shep 4C 146
Elliott Rd. BR2: Brom 4B 160
CR7: Thor H 4B 156
HA7: Stan 6F 27
SW9 1B 120
W4 4A 98
Elliott's Pl. N1 1B 84
Elliott Sq. NW3 7C 64
Elliotts Row SE11 4B 102
Ellis Cl. HA8: Edg 6F 29
NW10 6D 62
SE9 2G 143
Elliscombe Mt. SE7 6A 106
Elliscombe Rd. SE7 6A 106
Ellis Ct. W7 5K 77
Ellisfield Dr. SW15 7C 116
Ellis Franklin Ct. NW8 2A 82
(off Abbey Rd.)
Ellis Ho. SE17 5D 102
(off Brandon St.)
Ellison Gdns. UB2: S'hall 4D 94
Ellison Ho. SE13 2D 122
(off Lewisham Rd.)
Ellison Rd. DA15: Sidc 1H 143
SW13 2B 116
SW16 7H 137
Ellis Rd. CR4: Mitc 6D 154
UB2: S'hall 1G 95
Ellis St. SW1 3F 17 (4E 100)
Elliston Ho. SE18 4E 106
(off Wellington St.)
Ellora Rd. SW16 5H 137
Ellswood Ct. KT6: Surb 7D 150
Ellsworth St. E2 3H 85
Ellwood Ct. W9 4K 81
(off Clearwell Dr.)
Elmar Rd. N15 4D 48
Elm Av. HA4: Ruis 1J 57
TW19: Stanw 2A 128
W5 1E 96
Elmbank N14 7D 22
Elmbank Av. EN5: Barn 4A 20
Elm Bank Dr. BR1: Brom 2B 160
Elm Bank Gdns. SW13 2A 116
Elmbank Way W7 5H 77
Elmbourne Dr. DA17: Belv 4H 109
Elmbourne Rd. SW17 3F 137
Elmbridge Av. KT5: Surb 5H 151
Elmbridge Cl. HA4: Ruis 6J 39
Elmbridge Dr. HA4: Ruis 5H 39
Elmbridge Wlk. E8 7G 67
Elmbridge Xcel Leisure Complex 5K 147
Elmbrook Cl. TW16: Sun 1K 147
Elmbrook Gdns. SE9 4C 124
Elmbrook Rd. SM1: Sutt 4H 165
Elm Cl. CR2: S Croy 6E 168
E11 6K 51
HA2: Harr 6F 41
IG9: Buck H 2G 37
KT5: Surb 7J 151
N19 2G 65
NW4 5F 45
RM7: Mawney 1H 55
SM5: Cars 1D 166
SW20 4E 152
TW2: Twick 2F 131
UB3: Hayes 6J 75
Elmcote HA5: Pinn 2B 40
Elm Cotts. CR4: Mitc 2D 154
Elm Ct. CR4: Mitc 2D 154
EC4 1J 13
EN4: E Barn 7H 21
KT8: W Mole 4F 149
SE1 7G 15
(off Royal Oak Yd.)
SE13 3F 123
TW16: Sun 7H 129
(off Grangewood Dr.)
W9 5J 81
(off Admiral Wlk.)
Elmcourt Rd. SE27 2B 138
Elm Cres. KT2: King T 1E 150
W5 1E 96
Elmcroft N6 7G 47
Elmcroft Av. DA15: Sidc 7K 125
E11 5K 51
N9 6C 24
NW11 7H 45
Elmcroft Cl. E11 4K 51
KT9: Chess 3E 162
N8 5K 47
TW14: Felt 6H 111
W5 6D 78
Elmcroft Cres. HA2: Harr 3E 40
NW11 7G 45
Elmcroft Dr. KT9: Chess 3E 162
TW15: Ashf 5C 128
Elmcroft Gdns. NW9 4G 43
Elmcroft St. E5 4J 67
Elmcroft Ter. UB8: Hil 6C 74
Elmdale Rd. N13 5E 32
Elmdene KT5: Surb 1J 163
Elmdene Cl. BR3: Beck 6B 158
Elmdene Rd. SE18 5F 107
Elmdon Rd. TW4: Houn 2B 112
TW6: H'row A 3H 111
Elm Dr. HA2: Harr 6F 41
TW16: Sun 2A 148
Elmer Cl. EN2: Enf 3E 22
Elmer Gdns. HA8: Edg 7C 28
TW7: Isle 3H 113
Elmer Ho. NW1 5C 4
(off Penfold St.)
Elmer Rd. SE6 7E 122
Elmers Dr. TW11: Tedd 6B 132
ELMERS END 4K 157
Elmers End Rd.
BR3: Beck 2J 157
SE20 2J 157
Elmerside Rd. BR3: Beck 4A 158
Elmers Lodge BR3: Beck 4K 157
Elmers Rd. SE25 7G 157
Elmfield Av. CR4: Mitc 1E 154
N8 5J 47
TW11: Tedd 5K 131
Elmfield Cl. HA1: Harr 2J 59

Elmfield Ct. DA16: Well 1B 126
Elmfield Ho. *N2* *2B 46*
(*off The Grange*)
NW8 .....*2K 81*
(*off Carlton Hill*)
W9 .....*4J 81*
(*off Goldney Rd.*)
Elmfield Pk. BR1: Brom 3J 159
Elmfield Rd. BR1: Brom 2J 159
E4 .....2K 35
E17 .....6K 49
N2 .....3B 46
SW17 .....2E 136
UB2: S'hall 3C 94
Elmfield Way CR2: Sande 7F 169
W9 .....5J 81
Elm Friars Wlk. NW1 .....7H 65
Elm Gdns. CR4: Mitc 4H 155
KT10: Clay 6A 162
N2 .....3A 46
Elmgate Av. TW13: Felt 3K 129
Elmgate Gdns. HA8: Edg 5D 28
Elm Grn. W3 .....6A 80
Elmgreen Cl. E15 .....1G 87
Elm Gro. BR6: Orp 1K 173
DA8: Erith 7K 109
HA2: Harr 7E 40
IG8: Wfd G 5C 36
KT2: King T 1E 150
N8 .....6J 47
NW2 .....4F 63
SE15 .....2F 121
SM1: Sutt 4K 165
SW19 .....7G 135
UB7: Yiew 7B 74
Elmgrove Cres. HA1: Harr 5K 41
Elmgrove Gdns. HA1: Harr 5A 42
Elm Gro. Pde. SM6: Wall 3E 166
Elm Gro. Rd. SW13 .....1C 116
W5 .....2E 96
Elmgrove Rd. CR0: C'don 7H 157
HA1: Harr 5K 41
HA3: W'stone 5A 42
Elm Hall Gdns. E11 .....5K 51
(not continuous)
Elm Ho. *E14* *2E 104*
(*off E. Ferry Rd.*)
KT2: King T *7F 133*
(*off Elm Rd.*)
W10 .....*4G 81*
(*off Briar Wlk.*)
Elmhurst DA17: Belv 6E 108
Elmhurst Av. CR4: Mitc 7F 137
N2 .....3B 46
Elmhurst Ct. CR0: C'don 4D 168
Elmhurst Dr. E18 .....2J 51
Elmhurst Lodge SM2: Sutt 7A 166
Elmhurst Mans. SW4 .....3H 119
Elmhurst Rd. E7 .....7K 69
N17 .....2F 49
SE9 .....2C 142
Elmhurst St. SW4 .....3H 119
Elmington Cl. DA5: Bexl 6H 127
Elmington Est. SE5 .....7D 102
Elmington Rd. SE5 .....7D 102
Elmira St. SE13 .....3D 122
Elm La. SE6 .....2B 140
Elm Lawn Cl. UB8: Uxb 7A 56
Elmlea Dr. UB3: Hayes 5G 75
Elm Lea Trad. Est. N17 .....6C 34
Elmlee Cl. BR7: Chst 6D 142
Elmley Cl. E6 .....5C 88
Elmley St. SE18 .....5H 107
(not continuous)
Elm Lodge SW6 .....1E 116
Elmore Cl. HA0: Wemb 2E 78
Elmore Ho. SW9 .....2B 120
Elmore Rd. E11 .....3E 68
EN3: Enf W 1E 24
Elmore St. N1 .....7C 66
Elm Pde. DA14: Sidc 4A 144
Elm Pk. HA7: Stan 5G 27
SW2 .....6K 119
Elm Pk. Av. N15 .....5F 49
Elm Pk. Chambers *SW10* *6A 16*
(*off Fulham Rd.*)
Elm Pk. Ct. HA5: Pinn 2A 40
Elm Pk. Gdns. NW4 .....5F 45
SW10 .....6A 16 (5B 100)
Elm Pk. Ho. SW10 .....6A 16 (5B 100)
Elm Pk. La. SW3 .....6A 16 (5B 100)
Elm Pk. Mans. SW10 .....7A 16
Elm Pk. Rd. E10 .....1A 68
HA5: Pinn 2A 40
N3 .....7C 30
N21 .....7H 23
SE25 .....3F 157
SW3 .....7A 16 (6B 100)
Elm Pas. EN5: Barn 4C 20
Elm Pl. SW7 .....5A 16 (5B 100)
TW15: Ashf 5C 128
Elm Quay Ct. SW8 .....7C 18 (6H 101)
Elm Rd. BR3: Beck 2B 158
BR6: Chels 7K 173
CR7: Thor H 4D 156
DA14: Sidc 4A 144
E7 .....6H 69
E11 .....2F 69
E17 .....5E 50
EN5: Barn 4C 20
HA9: Wemb 5E 60
KT2: King T 1F 151
KT3: N Mald 2K 151
KT9: Chess 4E 162
KT17: Ewe 6B 164
N22 .....1B 48
RM7: Mawney 2H 55
SM6: Wall 1E 166
SW14 .....3J 115
TW14: Bedf 1F 129
Elm Rd. W. SM3: Sutt 7H 153
Elm Row NW3 .....3A 64
Elms, The *CR0: C'don* *1C 168*
(*off Tavistock Rd.*)
E12 .....6B 70
KT10: Clay 7A 162
SW13 .....3B 116
TW15: Ashf 5C 128
Elms Av. N10 .....3F 47
NW4 .....5F 45
Elmscott Gdns. N21 .....6H 23
Elmscott Rd. BR1: Brom 5G 141
Elms Ct. HA0: Wemb 4A 60
Elms Cres. SW4 .....6G 119
Elmsdale Rd. E17 .....4B 50
Elms Gdns. HA0: Wemb 4A 60
RM9: Dag 4F 73
Elmshaw Rd. SW15 .....5C 116
Elmshurst Cres. N2 .....4B 46
Elmside CR0: New Ad 6D 170
Elmside Rd. HA9: Wemb 3G 61
Elms La. HA0: Wemb 3A 60
Elmsleigh Av. HA3: Kent 4B 42
Elmsleigh Ct. SM1: Sutt 3K 165
Elmsleigh Ho. *TW2: Twick* *2H 131*
(*off Staines Rd.*)
Elmsleigh Rd. TW2: Twick 2H 131
Elmslie Cl. IG8: Wfd G 6J 37
Elmslie Point *E3* *5B 86*
(*off Leopold St.*)
Elms M. W2 .....2A 10 (7B 82)
Elms Pk. Av. HA0: Wemb 4A 60
Elms Rd. HA3: Hrw W 7D 26
SW4 .....5G 119
ELMSTEAD 6D 142
Elmstead Av. BR7: Chst 5D 142
HA9: Wemb 1E 60
Elmstead Cl. KT19: Ewe 5A 164
N20 .....2D 30
Elmstead Gdns. KT4: Wor Pk 3C 164
Elmstead Glade BR7: Chst 6D 142
Elmstead La. BR7: Chst 7C 142
Elmstead Rd. DA8: Erith 1K 127
IG3: Ilf 2J 71
Elmsted Cres. DA16: Well 6C 108
Elmstone Rd. SW6 .....1J 117
Elm St. WC1 .....4H 7 (4K 83)
Elmsway TW15: Ashf 5C 128
Elmsworth Av. TW3: Houn 2F 113
Elm Ter. HA3: Hrw W 1H 41
NW2 .....3J 63
NW3 .....4C 64
SE9 .....6E 124
Elm Terrace Fitness Cen. 6E 124
Elmton Ct. *NW8* *3A 4*
(*off Cunningham Pl.*)
Elm Tree Av. KT10: Esh 7H 149
Elm Tree Cl. NW8 .....1A 4 (3B 82)
TW15: Ashf 5D 128
UB5: N'olt 2D 76
Elm Tree Ct. NW8 .....1A 4
SE7 .....6A 106
Elm Tree Rd. NW8 .....1A 4 (3B 82)
Elmtree Rd. TW11: Tedd 4J 131
Elm Vw. Ct. UB2: S'hall 4E 94
Elm Vw. Ho. UB3: Harl 4F 93
Elm Wlk. BR6: Farnb 3D 172
NW3 .....2J 63
SW20 .....4E 152
Elm Way KT4: Wor Pk 3E 164
KT19: Ewe 5K 163
N11 .....6K 31
NW10 .....4A 62
Elmwood Av. HA3: Kent 5A 42
N13 .....5D 32
TW13: Felt 2J 129
Elmwood Cl. KT17: Ewe 7C 164
SM6: Wall 2F 167
Elmwood Ct. *E10* *1C 68*
(*off Goldsmith Rd.*)
HA0: Wemb 3A 60
SW11 .....1F 119
Elmwood Cres. NW9 .....4J 43
Elmwood Dr. DA5: Bexl 7E 126
KT17: Ewe 6C 164
Elmwood Gdns. W7 .....6J 77
Elmwood Ho. *NW10* *2D 80*
(*off All Souls Av.*)
Elmwood Rd. CR0: C'don 7B 156
CR4: Mitc 3D 154
SE24 .....5D 120
W4 .....6J 97
Elmworth Gro. SE21 .....2D 138
Elnathan M. W9 .....4K 81
Elphinstone Ct. SW16 .....6J 137
Elphinstone Rd. E17 .....2B 50
Elphinstone St. N5 .....4B 66
Elrington Rd. E8 .....6G 67
IG8: Wfd G 5D 36
Elsa Cotts. *E14* *5A 86*
(*off Halley St.*)
Elsa Ct. BR3: Beck 1B 158
Elsa Rd. DA16: Well 2B 126
Elsa St. E1 .....5A 86
Elsdale St. E9 .....6J 67
Elsden M. E2 .....2J 85
Elsden Rd. N17 .....1F 49
Elsenham Rd. E12 .....5E 70
Elsenham St. SW18 .....1H 135
Elsham Rd. E11 .....3G 69
W14 .....2G 99
Elsham Ter. *W14* *3G 99*
(*off Elsham Rd.*)
Elsiedene Rd. N21 .....7H 23
Elsie La. Ct. *W2* *5J 81*
(*off Westbourne Pk. Vs.*)
Elsiemaud Rd. SE4 .....5B 122
Elsie Rd. SE22 .....4F 121
Elsinore Av. TW19: Stanw 7A 110
Elsinore Gdns. NW2 .....3G 63
Elsinore Ho. *N1* *1A 84*
(*off Denmark Gro.*)
SE5 .....*2C 120*
(*off Denmark Rd.*)
SE7 .....4C 106
W6 .....*5F 99*
(*off Fulham Pal. Rd.*)
Elsinore Rd. SE23 .....1A 140
Elsinore Way TW9: Rich 3H 115
Elsley Ct. HA9: Wemb 6H 61
Elsley Rd. SW11 .....3D 118
Elspeth Rd. HA0: Wemb 5E 60
SW11 .....4D 118
Elsrick Av. SM4: Mord 5J 153
Elstan Way CR0: C'don 7A 158
Elstead Ct. SM3: Sutt 1G 165
Elstead Ho. *SW2* *7K 119*
(*off Redlands Way*)
Elsted St. SE17 .....4D 102
Elstow Cl. HA4: Ruis 7B 40
SE9 .....5D 124
(not continuous)
Elstow Gdns. RM9: Dag 1E 90
Elstow Grange NW6 .....7F 63
Elstow Rd. RM9: Dag 1E 90
Elstree Gdns. DA17: Belv 4E 108
IG1: Ilf 5G 71
N9 .....1C 34
Elstree Hill BR1: Brom 7G 141
Elstree Hill Sth. WD6: E'tree 1H 27
Elstree Rd. WD23: B Hea 1C 26
Elswick Rd. SE13 .....2D 122
Elswick St. SW6 .....2A 118
Elsworth Cl. TW14: Bedf 1G 129
Elsworthy KT7: T Ditt 6J 149
Elsworthy Ct. *NW3* *7D 64*
(*off Primrose Hill Rd.*)
Elsworthy Ri. NW3 .....7C 64
Elsworthy Rd. NW3 .....1C 82
Elsworthy Ter. NW3 .....7C 64
Elsynge Rd. SW18 .....5B 118
ELTHAM 6D 124
Eltham Crematorium SE9 .....4H 125
Eltham Grn. SE9 .....5B 124
Eltham Grn. Rd. SE9 .....4A 124
Eltham High St. SE9 .....6D 124
Eltham Hill SE9 .....5B 124
Eltham Palace 7C 124
Eltham Pal. Rd. SE9 .....6A 124
ELTHAM PARK 4E 124
Eltham Pk. Gdns. SE9 .....4E 124
Eltham Pools 6C 124
Eltham Rd. SE9 .....5H 123
SE12 .....5H 123
Elthiron Rd. SW6 .....1J 117
Elthorne Av. W7 .....2K 95
Elthorne Ct. TW13: Felt 1A 130
ELTHORNE HEIGHTS 5J 77
Elthorne Pk. Rd. W7 .....2K 95
Elthorne Rd. N19 .....2H 65
NW9 .....7K 43
Elthorne Sports Cen. 3K 95
Elthorne Way NW9 .....6K 43
Elthruda Rd. SE13 .....6F 123
Eltisley Rd. IG1: Ilf 4F 71
Elton Av. EN5: Barn 5C 20
HA0: Wemb 5B 60
UB6: G'frd 6J 59
Elton Cl. KT1: Ham W 7C 132
Elton Ho. *E3* *1B 86*
(*off Candy St.*)
Elton Pl. N16 .....5E 66
Elton Rd. KT2: King T 1F 151
Eltringham St. SW18 .....4A 118
Eluna Apartments *E1* *7H 85*
(*off Wapping La.*)
Elvaston M. SW7 .....2A 16 (3A 100)
Elvaston Pl. SW7 .....2A 16 (3A 100)
Elveden Ho. SE24 .....5B 120
Elveden Pl. NW10 .....2G 79

Elveden Rd. NW10 2G 79
Elvedon Rd. TW13: Felt 3H 129
Elvendon Rd. N13 6D 32
Elver Gdns. E2 3G 85
Elverson Rd. SE8 2D 122
Elverton St. SW1 3C 18 (4H 101)
Elvington Grn. BR2: Brom 5H 159
Elvington La. NW9 1A 44
Elvino Rd. SE26 5A 140
Elvis Rd. NW2 6E 62
Elwill Way BR3: Beck 4E 158
Elwin St. E2 1K 9 (3G 85)
Elwood Cl. EN5: New Bar 4F 21
Elwood St. N5 3B 66
Elworth Ho. *SW8* *7K 101*
(off Oval Pl.)
Elwyn Gdns. SE12 7J 123
Ely Cl. KT3: N Mald 2B 152
Ely Cotts. SW8 7K 101
Ely Ct. EC1 6K 7
NW6 *2J 81*
(off Chichester Rd.)
Ely Gdns. IG1: Ilf 7C 52
RM10: Dag 3J 73
Ely Ho. *SE15* *7G 103*
(off Friary Est.)
Elyne Rd. N4 6A 48
Ely Pl. EC1 6K 7 (5A 84)
IG8: Wfd G 6K 37
Ely Rd. CR0: C'don 5D 156
E10 6E 50
TW4: Houn 3A 112
Elysian Av. BR5: St M Cry 6K 161
Elysian Pl. CR2: S Croy 7C 168
Elysium Pl. *SW6* *2H 117*
(off Elysium St.)
Elysium St. SW6 2H 117
Elystan Bus. Cen. UB4: Yead 7A 76
Elystan Cl. SM6: Wall 7G 167
Elystan Pl. SW3 5D 16 (5C 100)
Elystan St. SW3 4C 16 (4C 100)
Elystan Wlk. N1 1A 84
Emanuel Av. W3 6J 79
Emanuel Dr. TW12: Hamp 5D 130
Emanuel Ho. SW1 2C 18 (3H 101)
Embankment SW15 2F 117
(not continuous)
Embankment, The TW1: Twick 1A 132
Embankment Gdns. SW3 7F 17 (6D 100)
Embankment Pl. WC2 4F 13 (1J 101)
Embassy Ct. DA14: Sidc 3B 144
DA16: Well 3B 126
N11 *6C 32*
(off Bounds Grn. Rd.)
NW8 1B 4
SM6: Wall 6F 167
W5 7F 79
Embassy Gdns. BR3: Beck 1B 158
Embassy Ho. NW6 7K 63
Embassy Lodge *N3* *2H 45*
(off Cyprus Rd.)
Embassy Theatre
Central School of Speech & Drama
7B 64
(off College Cres.)
Emba St. SE16 2G 103
Ember Cl. BR5: Pet W 7G 161
Ember Ct. NW9 2B 44
Embercourt Rd. KT7: T Ditt 6J 149
Ember Farm Av. KT8: E Mos 6H 149
Ember Farm Way KT8: E Mos 6H 149
Ember Gdns. KT7: T Ditt 7J 149
Ember La. KT8: E Mos 7H 149
KT10: Esh 7H 149
Emberton *SE5* *6E 102*
(off Albany Rd.)
Emberton Ct. *EC1* *2A 8*
(off Tompion St.)
Embleton Rd. SE13 4D 122
Embleton Wlk. TW12: Hamp 5D 130
Embroidery Bus. Cen. *IG8: Wfd G* *2B 52*
(off Southend Rd.)
Embroidery World Bus. Cen.
IG8: Wfd G 2B 52
Embry Cl. HA7: Stan 4F 27
Embry Dr. HA7: Stan 6F 27
Embry Way HA7: Stan 5F 27
Emden Cl. UB7: W Dray 2C 92
Emden St. SW6 1K 117
Emerald Cl. E16 6B 88
Emerald Gdns. RM8: Dag 1G 73
Emerald Rd. NW10 1K 79
(not continuous)
Emerald Sq. UB2: S'hall 3B 94
Emerald St. WC1 5G 7 (5K 83)
Emerson Apartments N8 3K 47
Emerson Gdns. HA3: Kent 6F 43
Emerson Rd. IG1: Ilf 7E 52
Emerson St. SE1 4C 14 (1C 102)
Emerton Cl. DA6: Bex 4E 126
Emery Hill St. SW1 2B 18 (3G 101)
Emery St. SE1 1K 19 (3A 102)
Emery Theatre *6D 86*
(off Annabel Cl.)
Emes Rd. DA8: Erith 7J 109
Emilia Cl. EN3: Pond E 5C 24
Emily Ct. *SE1* *7C 14*
(off Sudrey St.)
Emily Ho. *W10* *4G 81*
(off Kensal Rd.)
Emily St. *E16* *6H 87*
(off Jude St.)
Emirates Stadium 4A 66
Emlyn Gdns. W12 2A 98
Emlyn Rd. W12 2A 98
Emmanuel Ct. E10 7D 50
Emmanuel Ho. SE11 4J 19 (4A 102)
Emmanuel Rd. HA6: Nwood 1H 39
SW12 1G 137
Emma Rd. E13 2H 87
Emma St. E2 2H 85
Emmaus Way IG7: Chig 5K 37
Emmeline Ct. KT12: Walt T 7A 148
Emminster *NW6* *1K 81*
(off Abbey Rd.)
Emmott Av. IG6: Ilf 5G 53
Emmott Cl. E1 4A 86
NW11 6A 46
Emms Pas. KT1: King T 2D 150
Emperor's Ga. SW7 3A 100
Empingham Ho. *SE8* *4K 103*
(off Chilton Ho.)
Empire Av. N18 5H 33
Empire Cinema
Leicester Sq. *2D 12*
(off Leicester Sq.)
Empire Ct. HA9: Wemb 3H 61
Empire Ho. SW7 2C 16
Empire Pde. HA9: Wemb 3G 61
N18 6J 33
Empire Rd. UB6: G'frd 1B 78
Empire Sq. N7 3J 65
SE20 *7K 139*
(off High St.)
Empire Sq. Sth. SE1 7E 14
Empire Sq. W. SE1 7E 14
Empire Way HA9: Wemb 4F 61
Empire Wharf *E3* *1A 86*
(off Old Ford Rd.)
Empire Wharf Rd. E14 4F 105
Empress App. SW6 5J 99
Empress Av. E4 7J 35
E12 2A 70
IG1: Ilf 2D 70
IG8: Wfd G 7C 36
Empress Dr. BR7: Chst 6F 143
Empress M. SE5 2C 120
Empress Pde. E4 7H 35
Empress Pl. SW6 5J 99
Empress State Bldg. SW6 5J 99
Empress St. SE17 6C 102
Empson St. E3 4D 86
Emsworth Cl. N9 1D 34
Emsworth Ct. SW16 3J 137
Emsworth Rd. IG6: Ilf 2F 53
Emsworth St. SW2 2K 137
EMT Ho. E6 5E 88
Emu Rd. SW8 2F 119
Ena Rd. SW16 3J 155
Enbrook St. W10 3G 81
Enclave, The SW13 2B 116
Enclave Ct. *EC1* *3B 8*
(off Dallington St.)
Endale Cl. SM5: Cars 2D 166
Endeavour Way CR0: Bedd 7J 155
IG11: Bark 2A 90
SW19 4K 135
Endell St. WC2 7E 6 (6J 83)
Enderby St. SE10 5F 105
Enderley Cl. HA3: Hrw W 2J 41
Enderley Rd. HA3: Hrw W 1J 41
Endersleigh Gdns. NW4 4C 44
Endlebury Rd. E4 2K 35
Endlesham Rd. SW12 7E 118
Endsleigh Ct. WC1 3D 6
Endsleigh Gdns. IG1: Ilf 2D 70
KT6: Surb 6C 150
WC1 3C 6 (4H 83)
Endsleigh Ind. Est.
UB2: S'hall 4C 94
Endsleigh Pl. WC1 3D 6 (4H 83)
Endsleigh Rd. UB2: S'hall 4C 94
W13 7A 78
Endsleigh St. WC1 3D 6 (4H 83)
Endway KT5: Surb 7H 151
Endwell Rd. SE4 2A 122
Endymion Rd. N4 7A 48
SW2 6K 119
Energen Cl. NW10 6A 62
Energize Fitness Club *5G 99*
(in Hammersmith & West London College)
ENFIELD 3J 23
Enfield Bus. Cen. EN3: Enf H 2D 24
Enfield Cloisters *N1* *1G 9*
(off Fanshaw St.)
Enfield College Sports Cen. 3D 24
ENFIELD HIGHWAY 3D 24
Enfield Ho. *SW9* *2J 119*
(off Stockwell Rd.)
ENFIELD ISLAND VILLAGE 1H 25
ENFIELD LOCK 1H 25
Enfield Lock EN3: Enf L 1H 25
Enfield Retail Pk. EN1: Enf 3C 24
Enfield Rd. EN2: Enf 4C 22
N1 7E 66
TW6: H'row A 2G 111
TW8: Bford 5D 96
W3 2H 97
ENFIELD TOWN 3J 23
Enfield Wlk. TW8: Bford 5D 96
ENFIELD WASH 1F 25
Enford St. W1 5E 4 (5D 82)
Engadine Cl. CR0: C'don 3F 169
Engadine St. SW18 1H 135
Engate St. SE13 4E 122
Engel Pk. NW7 6K 29
Engine Ct. *SW1* *5B 12*
(off Ambassador's Ct.)
Engineer Cl. SE18 6E 106
Engineers Way HA9: Wemb 4G 61
England's La. NW3 6D 64
England Way KT3: N Mald 4H 151
Englefield *NW1* *2A 6*
(off Clarence Gdns.)
Englefield Cl. BR5: St M Cry 5K 161
CR0: C'don 6C 156
EN2: Enf 2F 23
Englefield Cres. BR5: St M Cry 4K 161
Englefield Path BR5: St M Cry 4K 161
Englefield Rd. N1 7D 66
Engleheart Dr. TW14: Felt 6H 111
Engleheart Rd. SE6 7D 122
Englewood Rd. SW12 6F 119
English Grounds SE1 5G 15 (1E 102)
English St. E3 4B 86
Enid St. SE16 7K 15 (3F 103)
Enmore Av. SE25 5G 157
Enmore Gdns. SW14 5K 115
Enmore Rd. SE25 5G 157
SW15 4E 116
UB1: S'hall 4E 76
Ennerdale *NW1* *1A 6*
(off Varndell St.)
Ennerdale Av. HA7: Stan 3C 42
Ennerdale Cl. SM1: Sutt 4H 165
TW14: Felt 1H 129
Ennerdale Ct. *E11* *7J 51*
(off Cambridge Rd.)
Ennerdale Dr. NW9 5A 44
Ennerdale Gdns. HA9: Wemb 1C 60
Ennerdale Ho. E3 4B 86
Ennerdale Rd. DA7: Bex 1G 127
TW9: Rich 2F 115
Ennersdale Rd. SE13 5F 123
Ennis Ho. *E14* *6D 86*
(off Vesey Path)
Ennismore Av. UB6: G'frd 6J 59
W4 4B 98
Ennismore Gdns. KT7: T Ditt 6J 149
SW7 7C 10 (2C 100)
Ennismore Gdns. M.
SW7 1C 16 (3C 100)
Ennismore M. SW7 7C 10 (3C 100)
Ennismore St. SW7 1C 16 (3C 100)
Ennis Rd. N4 1A 66
SE18 6G 107
Ennor Ct. SM3: Cheam 4E 164
Ensbury Ho. *SW8* *7K 101*
(off Carroun Rd.)
Ensign Cl. TW6: H'row A 3G 111
TW19: Stanw 1A 128
Ensign Dr. N13 3H 33
Ensign Ho. *E14* *2C 104*
(off Admirals Way)
SW18 3A 118
Ensign Ind. Cen. *E1* *7G 85*
(off Ensign St.)
Ensign St. E1 7G 85
Ensign Way SM6: Wall 7J 167
TW19: Stanw 1A 128
Enslin Rd. SE9 6E 124
Ensor M. SW7 5A 16 (5B 100)
Enstone Rd. EN3: Enf H 3F 25
UB10: Ick 3B 56
Enterprise Bus. Pk. E14 2D 104
Enterprise Cen., The *BR3: Beck* *5A 140*
(off Cricket La.)
Enterprise Cl. CR0: C'don 1A 168
Enterprise Ho. E4 7K 25
E9 *7J 67*
(off Tudor Gro.)
E14 *5D 104*
(off St Davids Sq.)
IG11: Bark 3K 89
KT12: Walt T 7K 147
Enterprise Ind. Est. SE16 5J 103
Enterprise Row N15 5F 49
Enterprise Trad. Est. UB2: S'hall 2F 95
Enterprise Way NW10 3B 80
SW18 4J 117
TW11: Tedd 6K 131
Enterprize Way SE8 4B 104
Envoy Av. TW6: H'row A 3H 111
Epcot M. NW10 3F 81
Epirus M. SW6 7J 99
Epirus Rd. SW6 7H 99
Epping Cl. E14 4C 104
RM7: Mawney 3H 55
Epping Glade E4 6K 25
Epping New Rd. IG9: Buck H 2E 36

Epping Pl. N1 6A 66
Epping Way E4 6J 25
Epple Rd. SW6 1H 117
Epsom Cl. DA7: Bex 3H 127
UB5: N'olt 5D 58
Epsom Rd. CR0: Wadd 4A 168
E10 6E 50
IG3: Ilf 6K 53
SM3: Sutt 7H 153
SM4: Mord 7H 153
Epsom Sq. TW6: H'row A 2H 111
Epstein Rd. SE28 1A 108
Epworth Rd. TW7: Isle 7B 96
Epworth St. EC2 4F 9 (4D 84)
Equana Apartments SE8 5A 104
(off Evelyn St.)
Equinox Ct. IG2: Ilf 5F 53
Equinox Ho. IG11: Bark 6G 71
Equity M. W5 1D 96
Equity Sq. E2 2K 9
(off Shacklewell St.)
Erasmus St. SW1 4D 18 (4H 101)
Erconwald St. W12 6B 80
Erebus Dr. SE28 3G 107
Eresby Dr. BR3: Beck 1C 170
Eresby Ho. SW7 7D 10
(off Rutland Ga.)
Eresby Pl. NW6 7J 63
Erica Gdns. CR0: C'don 3D 170
Erica Ho. N22 1A 48
(off Acacia Rd.)
SE4 3B 122
Erica St. W12 7C 80
Eric Clarke La. IG11: Bark 4F 89
Eric Cl. E7 4J 69
Ericcson Cl. SW18 5J 117
Eric Fletcher Ct. N1 7C 66
(off Essex Rd.)
Eric Liddell Sports Cen. 2B 142
Eric Rd. E7 4J 69
NW10 6B 62
RM6: Chad H 7D 54
Eric Shipman Ter. E13 4J 87
(off Balaam St.)
Ericson Ho. SE13 4F 123
(off Blessington Rd.)
Eric St. E3 4B 86
(not continuous)
Eric Wilkins Ho. SE1 5G 103
(off Old Kent Rd.)
Eridge Rd. W4 3K 97
Erin Cl. BR1: Brom 7G 141
IG3: Ilf 6A 54
Erindale SE18 6H 107
Erindale Ter. SE18 6H 107
Erin M. N22 1B 48
ERITH 5K 109
Erith Cres. RM5: Col R 1J 55
Erith Rd. DA7: Bex 4H 127
DA8: Erith 5G 109
DA17: Belv, Erith 5G 109
Erith School Community Sports Cen. 7K 109
Erlanger Rd. SE14 1K 121
Erlesmere Gdns. W13 3A 96
Erlich Cotts. E1 5J 85
(off Sidney St.)
Ermine Cl. TW4: Houn 2A 112
Ermine Ho. N17 7A 34
(off Moselle St.)
Ermine M. E2 1F 85
Ermine Rd. N15 6F 49
SE13 4D 122
Ermine Side EN1: Enf 5B 24
Ermington Rd. SE9 2G 143
Ernald Av. E6 2C 88
Erncroft Way TW1: Twick 6K 113
Ernest Av. SE27 4B 138
Ernest Cl. BR3: Beck 5C 158
Ernest Cotts. KT17: Ewe 7B 164
Ernest Gdns. W4 6H 97
Ernest Gro. BR3: Beck 5B 158
Ernest Harriss Ho. W9 4J 81
(off Elgin Av.)
Ernest Rd. KT1: King T 2H 151
Ernest Sq. KT1: King T 2H 151
Ernest St. E1 4K 85
Ernle Rd. SW20 7D 134
Ernshaw Pl. SW15 5G 117
Eros 3C 12 (7H 83)
Eros Ho. Shops SE6 7D 122
(off Brownhill Rd.)
Erpingham Rd. SW15 3E 116
Erridge Rd. SW19 2J 153
Errington Rd. W9 4H 81
Errol Gdns. KT3: N Mald 4C 152
UB4: Yead 4K 75
Errol St. EC1 4D 8 (4C 84)
Erskine Cl. SM1: Sutt 3C 166
Erskine Cres. N17 4H 49
Erskine Hill NW11 4J 45
Erskine Ho. SW1 6A 18
(off Churchill Gdns.)
Erskine M. NW3 7D 64
(off Erskine Rd.)
Erskine Rd. E17 4B 50
NW3 7D 64
SM1: Sutt 4B 166
Erwood Rd. SE7 5C 106
Esam Way SW16 5A 138
Escot Rd. TW16: Sun 7G 129
Escott Gdns. SE9 4C 142
Escreet Gro. SE18 4E 106
Esher Av. KT12: Walt T 7J 147
RM7: Rom 6J 55
SM3: Cheam 3F 165
Esher By-Pass KT9: Chess 7B 162
KT10: Clay 7B 162
Esher Cl. DA5: Bexl 1E 144
Esher Cres. TW6: H'row A 2H 111
Esher Gdns. SW19 2F 135
Esher M. CR4: Mitc 3E 154
Esher Rd. IG3: Ilf 3J 71
KT8: E Mos 6H 149
Eskdale NW1 1A 6
(off Stanhope St.)
Eskdale Av. UB5: N'olt 1D 76
Eskdale Cl. HA9: Wemb 2D 60
Eskdale Rd. DA7: Bex 2G 127
Eskmont Ridge SE19 7D 138
Esk Rd. E13 4J 87
Esk Way RM1: Rom 1K 55
Esmar Cres. NW9 7C 44
Esmeralda Rd. SE1 4G 103
Esmond Ct. W8 3K 99
(off Thackeray St.)
Esmond Gdns. W4 4K 97
Esmond Rd. NW6 1H 81
W4 4K 97
Esmond St. SW15 4G 117
Esparto St. SW18 7K 117
Esporta Health & Fitness
Chislehurst 5J 143
Enfield 4J 23
Finchley Rd. 6A 64
(in O2 Cen.)
Gunnersbury 4H 97
Ilford 3F 71
(off Winston Way)
Islington 1B 84
Kingston upon Thames 1E 150
New Southgate 5K 31
Repton Park 7K 37
Romford 5K 55
Wandsworth 4K 117
Wimbledon 6H 135
Esporta Health & Racquets Club
Purley 6K 167
Esprit Ct. E1 6J 9
(off Brune St.)
Essan Ho. W5 5B 78
Essence Ct. HA9: Wemb 2F 61
Essenden Rd. CR2: S Croy 7E 168
DA17: Belv 5G 109
Essendine Mans. W9 3J 81
Essendine Rd. W9 3J 81
Essex Av. TW7: Isle 3J 113
Essex Cl. E17 4A 50
HA4: Ruis 1B 58
RM7: Mawney 4H 55
SM4: Mord 7F 153
Essex Ct. EC4 1J 13
SW13 2B 116
W6 3E 98
(off Hammersmith Gro.)
Essex Gdns. N4 6B 48
Essex Gro. SE19 6D 138
Essex Hall E17 1K 49
Essex Ho. E14 6D 86
(off Giraud St.)
Essex Mans. E11 7F 51
Essex Pk. N3 6E 30
Essex Pk. M. W3 1A 98
Essex Pl. W4 4J 97
(not continuous)
Essex Pl. Sq. W4 4K 97
Essex Rd. E4 1B 36
E10 6E 50
E12 5C 70
E17 6A 50
E18 2K 51
EN2: Enf 4J 23
IG11: Bark 7H 71
N1 1B 84
NW10 7A 62
RM6: Chad H 7C 54
RM7: Mawney 4H 55
RM10: Dag 5J 73
W3 7J 79
W4 4K 97
(not continuous)
Essex Rd. Sth. E11 7F 51
Essex St. E7 5J 69
WC2 1J 13 (6A 84)
Essex Twr. SE20 1H 157
(off Jasmine Gro.)
Essex Vs. W8 2J 99
Essex Wharf E5 2K 67
Essian St. E1 5A 86
Essoldo Way HA8: Edg 3F 43
Estate Way E10 1B 68
Estcourt Rd. SE25 6H 157
SW6 7H 99
Estella Av. KT3: N Mald 4D 152
Estella Ho. W11 7F 81
(off St Ann's Rd.)
Estelle Rd. NW3 4D 64
Esterbrooke St. SW1 4C 18 (4H 101)
Este Rd. SW11 3C 118
Esther Cl. N21 7F 23
Esther Rd. E11 7G 51
Estoria Cl. SW2 7A 120
Estorick Collection of Modern Italian Art 6B 66
Estreham Rd. SW16 6H 137
Estridge Cl. TW3: Houn 4E 112
Estuary Cl. IG11: Bark 3B 90
Eswyn Rd. SW17 4D 136
Etal Ho. N1 7B 66
(off The Sutton Est.)
Etcetera Theatre 7F 65
(off Camden High St.)
Etchingham Ct. N3 7E 30
Etchingham Pk. Rd. N3 7E 30
Etchingham Rd. E15 4E 68
Eternit Wlk. SW6 1E 116
Etfield Gro. DA14: Sidc 5B 144
Ethelbert Cl. BR1: Brom 2J 159
Ethelbert Ct. BR1: Brom 3J 159
(off Ethelbert Rd.)
Ethelbert Gdns. IG2: Ilf 5D 52
Ethelbert Rd. BR1: Brom 3J 159
DA8: Erith 7J 109
SW20 1F 153
Ethelbert St. SW12 1F 137
Ethel Brooks Ho. SE18 6F 107
Ethelburga St. SW11 1C 118
Ethelburga Twr. SW11 1C 118
(off Maskelyne Cl.)
Etheldene Av. N10 4G 47
Ethelden Rd. W12 1D 98
Ethel Rd. E16 6K 87
TW15: Ashf 5A 128
Ethel St. SE17 4C 102
Etheridge Rd. NW4 7E 44
(not continuous)
Etherley Rd. N15 5C 48
Etherow St. SE22 7G 121
Etherstone Grn. SW16 4A 138
Etherstone Rd. SW16 4A 138
Ethnard Rd. SE15 6H 103
Ethronvi Rd. DA7: Bex 3E 126
Etloe Ho. E10 1C 68
Etloe Rd. E10 2C 68
Eton Av. EN4: E Barn 6H 21
HA0: Wemb 4B 60
KT3: N Mald 5K 151
N12 7F 31
NW3 7B 64
TW5: Hest 6D 94
Eton Cl. SW18 7K 117
Eton Coll. Rd. NW3 6D 64
Eton Ct. HA0: Wemb 4C 60
NW3 7B 64
Eton Garages NW3 6C 64
Eton Gro. NW9 3G 43
SE13 3G 123
Eton Hall NW3 6D 64
Eton Ho. N5 4B 66
(off Leigh Rd.)
Eton Mnr. Ct. E10 2C 68
(off Leyton Grange Est.)
Eton Pl. NW3 7E 64
Eton Ri. NW3 6D 64
Eton Rd. IG1: Ilf 4G 71
NW3 7D 64
UB3: Harl 7H 93
Eton St. TW9: Rich 5E 114
Eton Vs. NW3 6D 64
Etta St. SE8 6A 104
Ettrick St. E14 6E 86
(not continuous)
Etwell Pl. KT5: Surb 6F 151
Euesden Cl. N9 3C 34
Eugene Cotter Ho. SE17 4D 102
(off Tatum St.)
Eugenia Rd. SE16 4J 103
Eugenie M. BR7: Chst 1F 161
Eureka Rd. KT1: King T 2G 151
Euro Cl. NW10 6C 62
Eurolink Bus. Cen. SW2 5A 120
Europa Pl. EC1 2C 8 (3C 84)
Europa Trad. Est. DA8: Erith 5K 109
European Bus. Cen.
NW9 3J 43
(not continuous)
Europe Rd. SE18 3D 106
Euro Trade Cen. DA17: Belv 2J 109
Eustace Bldg. SW8 6F 101
Eustace Ho. SE11 3G 19
Eustace Pl. SE18 4D 106
Eustace Rd. E6 3C 88
RM6: Chad H 7D 54
SW6 7J 99
Euston Cen. NW1 3A 6 (4G 83)
(not continuous)
Euston Gro. NW1 2C 6
(off Euston Sq.)
Euston Rd. CR0: C'don 1A 168
NW1 4A 6 (4F 83)

Euston Sq. NW1 3A 6
(off Euston Twr.)
NW1 2C 6 (3H 83)
(Melton St., not continuous)
Euston Sta. Colonnade
NW1 2C 6 (3H 83)
Euston St. NW1 2B 6 (3G 83)
Euston Twr. NW1 3A 6 (4G 83)
EUSTON UNDERPASS 4G 83
Evandale Rd. SW9 2A 120
Evangelist Ho. EC4 1A 14
(off Black Friars La.)
Evangelist Rd. NW5 4F 65
Evans Bus. Cen. NW2 3C 62
Evans Cl. E8 6F 67
Evans Gro. TW13: Hanw 2E 130
Evans Ho. SW8 7H 101
(off Wandsworth Rd.)
TW13: Hanw 2E 130
W12 7D 80
(off White City Est.)
Evans Rd. SE6 2G 141
Evanston Av. E4 7K 35
Evanston Gdns. IG4: Ilf 6C 52
Eva Rd. RM6: Chad H 7C 54
Evedon Ho. N1 1E 84
(off New Era Est.)
Evelina Mans. SE5 7D 102
Evelina Rd. SE15 3J 121
SE20 7J 139
Eveline Rd. CR4: Mitc 1D 154
Evelyn Av. HA4: Ruis 7G 39
NW9 4K 43
Evelyn Cl. TW2: Whitt 7F 113
Evelyn Ct. E8 4G 67
N1 1E 8
(off Evelyn Wlk.)
Evelyn Cres. TW16: Sun 1H 147
Evelyn Denington Ct. N1 7B 66
(off The Sutton Est.)
Evelyn Denington Rd. E6 4C 88
Evelyn Dr. HA5: Pinn 1B 40
Evelyn Fox Ct. W10 5E 80
Evelyn Gdns. SW7 6A 16 (5A 100)
TW9: Rich 4E 114
Evelyn Gro. UB1: S'hall 6D 76
W5 1F 97
Evelyn Ho. SE14 1A 122
(off Loring Rd.)
W8 2K 99
(off Hornton Pl.)
W12 2B 98
(off Cobbold Rd.)
Evelyn Lowe Est. SE16 3G 103
Evelyn Mans. SW1 2A 18
(off Carlisle Pl.)
W14 6G 99
(off Queen's Club Gdns.)
Evelyn Rd. E16 1J 105
E17 4E 50
EN4: Cockf 4J 21
SW19 5K 135
TW9: Rich 3E 114
TW10: Ham 3C 132
W4 3K 97
Evelyns Cl. UB8: Hil 6C 74
Evelyn St. SE8 4A 104
Evelyn Ter. TW9: Rich 3E 114
Evelyn Wlk. N1 1E 8 (2D 84)
Evelyn Way SM6: Bedd 4H 167
TW16: Sun 1H 147
Evelyn Yd. W1 7C 6 (6H 83)
Evening Hill BR3: Beck 7E 140
Evenlode Ho. SE2 2C 108
Evenwood Cl. SW15 5G 117
Everard Av. BR2: Hayes 1J 171
Everard Ct. N13 3E 32
Everard Ho. E1 6G 85
(off Boyd St.)
Everard Way HA9: Wemb 3E 60
Everatt Cl. SW18 6H 117
Everdon Rd. SW13 6C 98
Everest Pl. E14 5E 86
Everest Rd. SE9 5D 124
TW19: Stanw 7A 110
Everett Cl. HA5: Eastc 3H 39
WD23: B Hea 1D 26
Everett Ho. SE17 5D 102
(off East St.)
Everett Wlk. DA17: Belv 5F 109
(off Osborne Rd.)
Everglade Ho. E17 2B 50
Everglade Strand NW9 1B 44
Evergreen Apartments
IG8: Wfd G 1H 51
(off High Rd. Woodford Grn.)
Evergreen Cl. SE20 7J 139
Evergreen Sq. E8 7F 67
Evergreen Way
UB3: Hayes 7H 75
Everilda St. N1 1K 83
Evering Rd. E5 3F 67
N16 3F 67
Everington Rd. N10 2D 46
Everington St. W6 6F 99
(not continuous)
Everitt Rd. NW10 3K 79
Everleigh St. N4 1K 65
Eve Rd. E11 4G 69
E15 2G 87
N17 3E 48
TW7: Isle 4A 114
Eversfield Gdns. NW7 6F 29
Eversfield Rd. TW9: Kew 2F 115
Evershed Wlk. W4 3J 97
Eversholt Ct. EN5: New Bar 5F 21
Eversholt St.
NW1 1B 6 (2G 83)
Evershot Rd. N4 1K 65
Eversleigh Ct. N3 7D 30
Eversleigh Rd. E6 1B 88
EN5: New Bar 5F 21
N3 7C 30
SW11 3D 118
Eversley Av. DA7: Bex 2K 127
HA9: Wemb 2G 61
Eversley Cl. N21 6E 22
Eversley Cres. HA4: Ruis 2G 57
N21 6F 23
TW7: Isle 1H 113
Eversley Ho. E2 2K 9
(off Gossett St.)
Eversley Mt. N21 6E 22
Eversley Pk. SW19 6D 134
Eversley Pk. Rd. N21 6E 22
Eversley Rd. KT5: Surb 4F 151
SE7 6K 105
SE19 7D 138
Eversley Way
CR0: C'don 4C 170
Everthorpe Rd. SE15 3F 121
Everton Bldgs.
NW1 2A 6 (3G 83)
Everton Ct. HA7: Stan 3E 42
(off Honeypot La.)
Everton Dr. HA7: Stan 3E 42
Everton Rd. CR0: C'don 1G 169
Evesham Av. E17 2C 50
Evesham Cl. SM2: Sutt 7J 165
UB6: G'frd 2F 77
Evesham Ct. TW10: Rich 6F 115
W13 1A 96
(off Tewkesbury Rd.)
Evesham Grn. SM4: Mord 6K 153
Evesham Ho. E2 2J 85
(off Old Ford Rd.)
NW8 1A 82
(off Abbey Rd.)
SW1 5F 101
(off Sutherland Row)
Evesham Rd. E15 7H 69
N11 5B 32
SM4: Mord 6K 153
Evesham St. W11 7F 81
Evesham Ter. KT6: Surb 6D 150
Evesham Wlk. SE5 2D 120
SW9 2A 120
Evesham Way IG5: Ilf 3E 52
SW11 3E 118
Evry Rd. DA14: Sidc 6C 144
Ewald Rd. SW6 2H 117
Ewanrigg Ter. IG8: Wfd G 5F 37
Ewart Gro. N22 1K 47
Ewart Pl. E3 2B 86
Ewart Rd. SE23 7K 121
Ewe Cl. N7 6J 65
EWELL 7C 164
Ewell By-Pass KT17: Ewe 7C 164
Ewell Ct. Av. KT19: Ewe 5A 164
Ewellhurst Rd. IG5: Ilf 2C 52
Ewell Pk. Gdns. KT17: Ewe 7C 164
Ewell Pk. Way KT17: Ewe 6C 164
Ewell Rd. KT6: Surb 6E 150
(Surbiton Hill Rd.)
KT6: Surb 7B 150
(Thornhill Rd.)
SM3: Cheam 6F 165
Ewelme Rd. SE23 1J 139
Ewen Cres. SW2 7A 120
Ewen Henderson Ct. SE14 7A 104
(off Goodwood Rd.)
Ewen Ho. N1 1K 83
(off Barnsbury Est.)
Ewer St. SE1 5C 14 (1C 102)
Ewhurst Av. CR2: Sande 7F 169
Ewhurst Cl. E1 5J 85
Ewhurst Ct. CR4: Mitc 3B 154
Ewhurst Rd. SE4 6B 122
Exbury Ho. E9 7J 67
SW1 5C 18
(off Rampayne St.)
Exbury Rd. SE6 2C 140
ExCeL 7K 87
Excel Ct. WC2 3D 12
Excel Marina E16 7J 87
Excelsior Cl. KT1: King T 2G 151
Excelsior Gdns. SE13 2E 122
Excelsior Ind. Est. SE15 6J 103
Excel Waterfront E16 7K 87
Exchange, The IG1: Ilf 2F 71
Exchange Apartments
BR2: Brom 4K 159
(off Sparkes Cl.)
Exchange Arc. EC2 5H 9 (5E 84)
Exchange Bldg. E1 4J 9
(off Commercial St.)
Exchange Cl. N11 2K 31
Exchange Ct. WC2 3F 13 (7J 83)
Exchange Ho. EC2 5H 9
NW10 7D 62
SW1 4C 18
(off Vauxhall Bri. Rd.)
Exchange Mans. NW11 7H 45
Exchange Pl. EC2 5G 9 (5E 84)
Exchange Sq. EC2 5G 9 (5E 84)
Exchange St. EC1 2C 8 (3C 84)
RM1: Rom 5K 55 & 6K 55
Exchange Wlk.
HA5: Pinn 7C 40
Exeforde Av. TW15: Ashf 4C 128
Exeter Cl. E6 6D 88
Exeter Ct. KT6: Surb 5E 150
(off Maple Rd.)
NW6 2J 81
(off Cambridge Rd.)
Exeter Gdns. IG1: Ilf 1C 70
Exeter Ho. IG11: Bark 7A 72
(off Margaret Bondfield Av.)
N1 1E 84
(off New Era Est.)
Exeter Ho. SE15 6G 103
(off Friary Est.)
SW15 6E 116
TW13: Hanw 2D 130
(off Watermill Way)
W2 6A 82
(off Hallfield Est.)
Exeter Mans. NW2 6G 63
Exeter M. NW6 6K 63
SW6 7J 99
Exeter Rd. CR0: C'don 7E 156
DA16: Well 2K 125
E16 5J 87
E17 5C 50
EN3: Pond E 3E 24
HA2: Harr 2C 58
N9 2D 34
N14 1A 32
NW2 5G 63
RM10: Dag 6H 73
TW6: H'row A 3F 111
TW13: Hanw 3D 130
Exeter St. WC2 2F 13 (7J 83)
Exeter Way SE14 7B 104
TW6: H'row A 2G 111
Exford Gdns. SE12 1K 141
Exford Rd. SE12 2K 141
Exhibition Cl. W12 7E 80
Exhibition Rd. SW7 7B 10 (2B 100)
Exit Rd. N2 2B 46
Exmoor Cl. IG6: Ilf 1G 53
Exmoor Ho. E3 2A 86
(off Gernon Rd.)
Exmoor St. W10 4F 81
Exmouth Ho. E14 4D 104
(off Cahir St.)
EC1 3J 7
(off Pine St.)
Exmouth Mkt. EC1 3J 7 (4A 84)
Exmouth M. NW1 2B 6 (3G 83)
Exmouth Pl. E8 7H 67
Exmouth Rd. DA16: Well 1C 126
E17 5B 50
HA4: Ruis 3A 58
UB4: Hayes 3G 75
Exmouth St. E1 6J 85
Exning Rd. E16 4H 87
Exonbury NW8 1K 81
(off Abbey Rd.)
Exon St. SE17 5E 102
Explorer Av. TW19: Stanw 1A 128
Explorers Ct. E14 7F 87
(off Newport Av.)
Export Ho. SE1 7H 15
(off Tower Bri. Rd.)
Express Dr. IG3: Ilf 1B 72
Express Newspapers SE1 4A 14
(off Blackfriars Rd.)
Exton Gdns. RM8: Dag 5C 72
Exton Rd. NW10 7J 61
Exton St. SE1 5J 13 (1A 102)
Eyebright Cl. CR0: C'don 1K 169
Eyhurst Cl. NW2 2C 62
Eylewood Rd. SE27 5C 138
Eynella Rd. SE22 7F 121
Eynham Rd. W12 6E 80
Eynsford Cl. BR5: Pet W 7G 161
Eynsford Cres. DA5: Bexl 1C 144
Eynsford Ho. SE1 7E 14
(off Crosby Row)
SE15 6J 103
SE17 4E 102
(off East St.)
Eynsford Rd. IG3: Ilf 2J 71
Eynsford Ter. UB7: Yiew 6B 74
Eynsham Dr. SE2 4A 108
Eynswood Dr. DA14: Sidc 5B 144
Eyot Gdns. W6 5B 98
Eyot Grn. W4 5B 98
Eyre Ct. NW8 2B 82

Eyre St. Hill EC1 . . . . . 4J 7 (4A 84)
Eysham Ct. EN5: New Bar 5E 20
Eythorne Rd. SW9 . . . . . 1A 120
Ezra St. E2 . . . . . 1K 9 (3F 85)

F

F1 City Go-Kart Circuit 1B 106
Faber Gdns. NW4 . . . . . 5C 44
Fabian Rd. SW6 . . . . . 7H 99
Fabian St. E6 . . . . . 4D 88
Facade, The SE23 . . . . . 2J 139
Factory La. CR0: C'don 1A 168
N17 . . . . . 2F 49
Factory Rd. E16 . . . . . 1B 106
Factory Yd. W7 . . . . . 1J 95
Faggs Rd. TW14: Felt 4H 111
Fairacre HA5: Eastc 4J 39
KT3: N Mald 3A 152
Fairacre Ct. HA6: Nwood 1G 39
Fair Acres BR2: Brom 5J 159
CR0: Sels 7B 170
Fairacres HA4: Ruis 7H 39
SW15 . . . . . 4B 116
Fairbairn Grn. SW9 . . . . . 1B 120
Fairbank Av. BR6: Farnb 2F 173
Fairbank Est. N1 . . . . . 1F 9 (2D 84)
Fairbanks Rd. N17 . . . . . 3F 49
Fairbourne Ho. UB3: Harl 3E 92
Fairbourne Rd. N17 . . . . . 3E 48
Fairbriar Residence SW7 . . . . . 4A 100
(off Cromwell Rd.)
Fairbridge Rd. N19 . . . . . 2H 65
Fairbrook Cl. N13 . . . . . 5F 33
Fairbrook Rd. N13 . . . . . 6F 33
Fairburn Ct. SW15 . . . . . 5G 117
Fairburn Ho. W14 . . . . . 5H 99
(off Ivatt Pl.)
Fairby Ho. SE1 . . . . . 4F 103
(off Longfield Est.)
Fairby Rd. SE12 . . . . . 5K 123
Faircharm Trad. Est. SE8 . . . . . 7D 104
Fairchild Cl. SW11 . . . . . 2B 118
Fairchild Ho. E9 . . . . . 7J 67
(off Frampton Pk. Rd.)
N1 . . . . . 1G 9
(off Fanshaw St.)
N3 . . . . . 1J 45
Fairchild Pl. EC2 . . . . . 4H 9
Fairchild St. EC2 . . . . . 3H 9 (4E 84)
Fair Cl. WD23: Bush 1A 26
Fairclough Cl. UB5: N'olt 4D 76
Fairclough St. E1 . . . . . 6G 85
Faircroft Ct. TW11: Tedd 6A 132
FAIR CROSS 5J 71
Faircross Av. IG11: Bark 6G 71
RM5: Col R 1K 55
Faircross Pde. IG11: Bark 5J 71
Fairdale Gdns. SW15 . . . . . 4D 116
UB3: Hayes 2J 93
Fairey Av. UB3: Harl 4H 93
Fairfax Av. KT17: Ewe 7D 164
Fairfax Cl. KT12: Walt T 7K 147
Fairfax Ct. NW6 . . . . . 7A 64
(off Fairfax Rd.)
Fairfax Gdns. SE3 . . . . . 1A 124
Fairfax Ho. KT1: King T 3F 151
(off Livesey Cl.)
Fairfax Mans. NW6 . . . . . 6A 64
(off Finchley Rd.)
Fairfax M. E16 . . . . . 1K 105
N8 . . . . . 4B 48
SW15 . . . . . 4E 116
Fairfax Pl. NW6 . . . . . 7A 64
W14 . . . . . 3G 99
Fairfax Rd. N8 . . . . . 4A 48
NW6 . . . . . 7A 64
TW11: Tedd 6A 132
W4 . . . . . 3A 98
Fairfax Way N10 . . . . . 7K 31
Fairfield E1 . . . . . 5J 85
(off Redman's Rd.)
KT1: King T 2F 151
N20 . . . . . 7G 21
NW1 . . . . . 1G 83
(off Arlington Rd.)
Fairfield Av. HA4: Ruis 7E 38
HA8: Edg 6C 28
NW4 . . . . . 6D 44
TW2: Whitt 1F 131
Fairfield Cl. CR4: Mitc 7C 136
DA15: Sidc 6K 125
EN3: Pond E 4E 24
KT19: Ewe 5A 164
N12 . . . . . 4F 31
Fairfield Ct. HA4: Ruis 1F 57
HA6: Nwood 2J 39
NW10 . . . . . 1C 80
Fairfield Cres. HA8: Edg 6C 28
Fairfield Dr. HA2: Harr 3G 41
SW18 . . . . . 5K 117
UB6: G'frd 1C 78
Fairfield E. KT1: King T 2E 150
Fairfield Gdns. N8 . . . . . 5J 47
Fairfield Gro. SE7 . . . . . 6B 106
Fairfield Halls 3D 168
Fairfield Nth. KT1: King T 2E 150
Fairfield Path CR0: C'don 3D 168
Fairfield Pl. KT1: King T 3E 150
Fairfield Rd. BR1: Brom 7J 141
BR3: Beck 2C 158
BR5: Pet W 6H 161
CR0: C'don 3D 168
DA7: Bex 2F 127
E3 . . . . . 2C 86
E17 . . . . . 2A 50
IG1: Ilf 6F 71
IG8: Wfd G 6D 36
KT1: King T 2E 150
(not continuous)
N8 . . . . . 5J 47
N18 . . . . . 4B 34
UB1: S'hall 6D 76
UB7: Yiew 7A 74
UB8: Uxb 6A 56
Fairfields Cl. NW9 . . . . . 5J 43
Fairfields Cres. NW9 . . . . . 4J 43
Fairfield Sth. KT1: King T 2E 150
Fairfields Rd. TW3: Houn 3G 113
Fairfield St. SW18 . . . . . 5K 117
Fairfield Trade Pk. KT1: King T 3F 151
Fairfield Way EN5: Barn 5D 20
KT19: Ewe 5A 164
Fairfield W. KT1: King T 2E 150
Fairfoot Rd. E3 . . . . . 4C 86
Fairford SE6 . . . . . 1C 140
Fairford Av. CR0: C'don 5K 157
DA7: Bex 1K 127
Fairford Cl. CR0: C'don 5A 158
Fairford Ct. SM2: Sutt 7K 165
Fairford Gdns.
KT4: Wor Pk 2B 164
Fairford Ho. SE11 . . . . . 4K 19 (4A 102)
Fairgreen EN4: Cockf 3J 21
Fairgreen Ct. EN4: Cockf 3J 21
Fairgreen E. EN4: Cockf 3J 21
Fairgreen Rd.
CR7: Thor H 5B 156
Fairhall Ct. KT5: Surb 7F 151
Fairhaven Av. CR0: C'don 6K 157
Fairhaven Ct. CR2: S Croy 5C 168
(off Warham Rd.)
Fairhazel Gdns. NW6 . . . . . 6K 63
Fairhazel Mans. NW6 . . . . . 7A 64
(off Fairhazel Gdns.)
Fairholme TW14: Bedf 7F 111
Fairholme Cl. N3 . . . . . 4G 45
Fairholme Cres. UB4: Hayes 4H 75
Fairholme Gdns. N3 . . . . . 3G 45
Fairholme Rd.
CR0: C'don 7A 156
HA1: Harr 5K 41
IG1: Ilf 7D 52
SM1: Sutt 6H 165
TW15: Ashf 5A 128
W14 . . . . . 5G 99
Fairholt Cl. N16 . . . . . 1E 66
Fairholt Rd. N16 . . . . . 1D 66
Fairholt St. SW7 . . . . . 1D 16 (3C 100)
Fairland Ho. BR2: Brom 4K 159
Fairland Rd. E15 . . . . . 6H 69
Fairlands Av. CR7: Thor H 4K 155
IG9: Buck H 2D 36
SM1: Sutt 2J 165
Fairlands Ct. SE9 . . . . . 6E 124
Fairlawn SE7 . . . . . 7A 106
Fairlawn Av. DA7: Bex 2D 126
N2 . . . . . 4C 46
W4 . . . . . 4J 97
Fair Lawn Cl. KT10: Clay 6A 162
Fairlawn Cl. KT2: King T 6J 133
N14 . . . . . 6B 22
TW13: Hanw 4D 130
Fairlawn Ct. SE7 . . . . . 7A 106
(not continuous)
W4 . . . . . 4J 97
Fairlawn Dr. IG8: Wfd G 7D 36
Fairlawnes SM6: Wall 5F 167
Fairlawn Gdns. UB1: S'hall 7D 76
Fairlawn Gro. W4 . . . . . 4J 97
Fairlawn Mans. SE14 . . . . . 1K 121
Fairlawn Pk. SE26 . . . . . 5A 140
Fairlawn Rd. SW19 . . . . . 7H 135
Fairlawns HA5: Pinn 2B 40
TW1: Twick 6C 114
TW16: Sun 3J 147
Fairlead Ho. E14 . . . . . 3C 104
(off Alpha Gro.)
Fairlea Pl. W5 . . . . . 4C 78
Fairlie Gdns. SE23 . . . . . 7J 121
Fairlight TW12: Ham H 5F 131
Fairlight Av. E4 . . . . . 2A 36
IG8: Wfd G 6D 36
NW10 . . . . . 2A 80
Fairlight Cl. E4 . . . . . 2A 36
KT4: Wor Pk 4E 164
Fairlight Ct. NW10 . . . . . 2A 80
UB6: G'frd 2G 77
Fairlight Rd. SW17 . . . . . 4B 136
Fairline Ct. BR3: Beck 2E 158
FAIRLOP 1J 53
Fairlop Ct. E11 . . . . . 1F 69
Fairlop Gdns. IG6: Ilf 1G 53
Fairlop Rd. E11 . . . . . 7F 51
IG6: Ilf 2G 53
Fairlop Sailing Cen. 1K 53
Fairlop Waters Country Pk. 1K 53
Fairlop Waters Country Pk. Nature Reserve 2K 53
Fairmark Dr. UB10: Hil 6C 56
Fairmead BR1: Brom 4D 160
KT5: Surb 1H 163
Fairmead Cl. BR1: Brom 4D 160
KT3: N Mald 3K 151
TW5: Hest 7B 94
Fairmead Ct. TW9: Rich 2H 115
Fairmead Cres. HA8: Edg 3D 28
Fairmead Gdns. IG4: Ilf 5C 52
Fairmead Ho. E9 . . . . . 4A 68
Fairmead Rd. CR0: C'don 7K 155
N19 . . . . . 3H 65
Fairmile Av. SW16 . . . . . 5H 137
Fairmile Ho. TW11: Tedd 4A 132
Fairmont Av. E14 . . . . . 1F 105
Fairmont Cl. DA17: Belv 5F 109
Fairmount Rd. SW2 . . . . . 6K 119
Fairoak Cl. BR5: Pet W 7F 161
Fairoak Dr. SE9 . . . . . 5H 125
Fairoak Gdns. RM1: Rom 2K 55
Fair Oak Pl. IG6: Ilf 2G 53
Fairseat Cl. WD23: B Hea 2D 26
Fairstead Lodge IG8: Wfd G 6D 36
(off Snakes La.)
Fairstead Wlk. N1 . . . . . 1C 84
(off Popham St.)
Fair St. SE1 . . . . . 6H 15 (2E 102)
TW3: Houn 3G 113
Fairthorne Vs. SE7 . . . . . 5J 105
(off Felltram Way)
Fairthorn Rd. SE7 . . . . . 5J 105
Fairview HA4: Ruis 4A 58
Fairview Av. HA0: Wemb 6D 60
Fairview Cl. E17 . . . . . 1A 50
SE26 . . . . . 5A 140
Fairview Ct. NW4 . . . . . 2F 45
TW15: Ashf 5C 128
Fairview Cres. HA2: Harr 1E 58
Fairview Dr. BR6: Orp 4H 173
TW17: Shep 5B 146
Fairview Est. NW10 . . . . . 3J 79
Fairview Gdns. IG8: Wfd G 1K 51
Fairview Ho. SW2 . . . . . 7K 119
Fairview Ind. Pk.
RM13: Rain 5K 91
Fairview Pl. SW2 . . . . . 7K 119
Fairview Rd. EN2: Enf 1F 23
N15 . . . . . 5F 49
SM1: Sutt 5B 166
SW16 . . . . . 1K 155
Fairview Vs. E4 . . . . . 7J 35
Fairview Way HA8: Edg 4B 28
Fairwall Ho. SE5 . . . . . 1E 120
Fairwater Av. DA16: Well 4A 126
Fairwater Ho. TW11: Tedd 4A 132
Fair Way IG8: Wfd G 5F 37
Fairway BR5: Pet W 5H 161
DA6: Bex 5E 126
SW20 . . . . . 3E 152
Fairway, The BR1: Brom 5D 160
EN5: New Bar 6E 20
HA0: Wemb 3B 60
HA4: Ruis 4A 58
KT3: N Mald 1K 151
KT8: W Mole 3F 149
N13 . . . . . 3H 33
N14 . . . . . 6A 22
NW7 . . . . . 3E 28
UB5: N'olt 6G 59
UB10: Hil 2B 74
W3 . . . . . 6A 80
Fairway Av. NW9 . . . . . 3H 43
Fairway Cl. CR0: C'don 5A 158
KT19: Ewe 4J 163
NW11 . . . . . 7A 46
TW4: Houn 5A 112
(Green La.)
TW4: Houn 5B 112
(Staines Rd.)
Fairway Ct. EN5: New Bar 6E 20
NW7 . . . . . 3E 28
SE16 . . . . . 2K 103
(off Christopher Cl.)
Fairway Dr. SE28 . . . . . 6D 90
UB6: G'frd 7F 59
Fairway Gdns. BR3: Beck 6F 159
IG1: Ilf 5G 71
Fairways E17 . . . . . 4E 50
HA7: Stan 2E 42
TW7: Isle 1H 113
TW11: Tedd 7D 132
TW15: Ashf 6D 128
Fairways Bus. Pk. E10 . . . . . 2A 68
Fairway Trad. Est.
TW4: Houn 5A 112
Fairweather Cl. N15 . . . . . 4E 48
Fairweather Ct. N13 . . . . . 4E 32
Fairweather Ho. N7 . . . . . 4J 65
Fairweather Rd. N16 . . . . . 6G 49
Fairwyn Rd. SE26 . . . . . 4A 140

Fakenham Cl. NW7 7H 29
UB5: N'olt 6E 58
Fakruddin St. E1 4G 85
Falcon WC1 5F 7
(off Old Gloucester St.)
Falcon Av. BR1: Brom 4C 160
Falconberg Ct. W1 7D 6 (6H 83)
Falconberg M. W1 7D 6 (6H 83)
Falcon Cl. HA6: Nwood 1G 39
W4 6J 97
Falcon Ct. E18 3K 51
(off Albert Rd.)
EC4 1K 13 (6A 84)
EN5: New Bar 4F 21
HA4: Ruis 2G 57
N1 1B 8
(off City Gdn. Row)
Falcon Cres. EN3: Pond E 5E 24
Falcon Dr. TW19: Stanw 6A 110
Falconer Ct. N17 7H 33
(off Compton Cres.)
Falconer Wlk. N7 2K 65
Falconet Ct. E1 1H 103
(off Wapping High St.)
Falcon Gro. SW11 3C 118
Falcon Highwalk EC2 6C 8
Falcon Ho. E14 5D 104
(off St Davids Sq.)
NW6 1K 81
(off Springfield Wlk.)
SW5 5K 99
(off Old Brompton Rd.)
Falcon La. SW11 3C 118
Falcon Lodge W9 5J 81
(off Admiral Wlk.)
Falcon Pk. Ind. Est. NW10 4A 62
Falcon Point SE1 3B 14 (7B 84)
Falcon Rd. EN3: Pond E 5E 24
SW11 2C 118
TW12: Hamp 7D 130
Falconry Ct. KT1: King T 3E 150
(off Fairfield Sth.)
Falcon St. E13 4H 87
Falcon Ter. SW11 3C 118
Falcon Way E11 4J 51
E14 4D 104
HA3: Kent 5E 42
NW9 2A 44
TW14: Felt 5K 111
TW16: Sun 2G 147
Falcon Wharf SW11 2B 118
FALCONWOOD 4K 125
FALCONWOOD 4H 125
Falconwood Av. DA16: Well 2H 125
Falconwood Ct. SE3 2H 123
(off Montpelier Row)
Falconwood Pde. DA16: Well 4J 125
Falconwood Rd. CR0: Sels 7B 170
Falcourt Cl. SM1: Sutt 5K 165
Falkirk Ct. SE16 1K 103
(off Rotherhithe St.)
Falkirk Ho. W9 2K 81
(off Maida Va.)
Falkirk St. N1 1H 9 (2E 84)
Falkland Av. N3 7D 30
N11 4A 32
Falkland Ho. SE6 4E 140
W8 3K 99
W14 5H 99
(off Edith Vs.)
Falkland Pk. Av. SE25 3E 156
Falkland Pl. NW5 5G 65
Falkland Rd. EN5: Barn 2B 20
N8 4A 48
NW5 5G 65
Fallaize Av. IG1: Ilf 4F 71
Falling La. UB7: Yiew 7A 74
Falloden Way NW11 4J 45
Fallodon Ho. W11 5H 81
(off Tavistock Cres.)
FALLOW CORNER 7F 31
Fallow Ct. SE16 5G 103
(off Argyle Way)
Fallow Ct. Av. N12 7F 31
Fallowfield HA7: Stan 4F 27
Fallowfield Ct. HA7: Stan 3F 27
Fallowfields Dr. N12 6H 31
Fallowhurst Path N3 7F 31
Fallows Cl. N2 2B 46
Fallsbrook Rd. SW16 6F 137
Falman Cl. N9 1B 34
Falmer Rd. E17 3D 50
EN1: Enf 4K 23
N15 5C 48
Falmouth Av. E4 5A 36
Falmouth Cl. N22 7E 32
SE12 5H 123
Falmouth Gdns. IG4: Ilf 4B 52
Falmouth Ho. HA5: Hat E 1D 40
KT2: King T 1D 150
(off Skerne Rd.)
SE11 5K 19
(off Seaton Cl.)
W2 2C 10
(off Clarendon Pl.)
Falmouth Rd. SE1 7E 14 (3C 102)
Falmouth St. E15 5F 69
Falmouth Way E17 5B 50
Falstaff Bldg. E1 7H 85
(off Cannon St. Rd.)
Falstaff Cl. DA1: Cray 7K 127
Falstaff Ct. SE11 4B 102
(off Opal St.)
Falstaff Ho. N1 1G 9
(off Arden Est.)
Falstaff M. TW12: Ham H 5H 131
(off Parkside)
Fambridge Cl. SE26 4B 140
Fambridge Ct. RM7: Rom 5K 55
(off Marks Rd.)
Fambridge Rd. RM8: Dag 1G 73
Fane St. W14 6H 99
Fan Mus., The 7E 104
Fann St. EC1 4C 8 (4C 84)
EC2 4C 8 (4C 84)
(not continuous)
Fanshawe Av. IG11: Bark 6G 71
Fanshawe Cres. RM9: Dag 5E 72
Fanshawe Rd. TW10: Ham 4C 132
Fanshaw St. N1 1G 9 (3E 84)
FANTAIL, THE 3D 172
Fantail Cl. SE28 6C 90
Fanthorpe St. SW15 3E 116
Faraday Av. DA14: Sidc 2A 144
Faraday Cl. N7 6K 65
Faraday Hall UB8: Cowl 3A 74
(off Kingston La.)
Faraday Ho. E14 7B 86
(off Brightlingsea Pl.)
HA9: Wemb 3J 61
SE1 7E 14
(off Cole St.)
W10 5G 81
(off Wornington Rd.)
Faraday Lodge SE10 3H 105
Faraday Mans. W14 6G 99
(off Queen's Club Gdns.)
Faraday Mus. 3A 12 (7G 83)
Faraday Pl. KT8: W Mole 4E 148
Faraday Rd. DA16: Well 3A 126
E15 6H 69
KT8: W Mole 4E 148
SW19 6J 135
UB1: S'hall 7F 77
W3 7J 79
W10 5G 81
Faraday Way CR0: Wadd 1K 167
SE18 3B 106
Fareham Rd. TW14: Felt 7A 112
Fareham St. W1 7C 6 (6H 83)
Farewell Pl. CR4: Mitc 1C 154
Faringdon Av. BR2: Brom 7E 160
Faringford Rd. E15 7G 69
Farjeon Ho. NW6 7B 64
(off Hilgrove Rd.)
Farjeon Rd. SE3 1B 124
Farleigh Av. BR2: Hayes 7H 159
Farleigh Ct. CR2: S Croy 5C 168
Farleigh Ho. N1 7B 66
(off Halton Rd.)
Farleigh Pl. N16 4F 67
Farleigh Rd. N16 4F 67
Farley Ct. NW1 4G 5
(off Allsop Pl.)
W14 3H 99
Farley Dr. IG3: Ilf 1J 71
Farley Ho. SE26 3H 139
Farley Pl. SE25 4G 157
Farley Rd. CR2: Sels 7H 169
SE6 7D 122
Farlington Pl. SW15 7D 116
Farlow Rd. SW15 3F 117
Farlton Rd. SW18 1K 135
Farman Gro. UB5: N'olt 3B 76
Farman Ter. HA3: Kent 4D 42
Farm Av. HA0: Wemb 6C 60
HA2: Harr 7D 40
NW2 3G 63
SW16 4J 137
Farmborough Cl. HA1: Harr 7H 41
Farm Cl. BR4: W W'ck 3H 171
IG9: Buck H 3F 37
RM10: Dag 7J 73
SM2: Sutt 7B 166
SW6 7J 99
TW17: Shep 7C 146
UB1: S'hall 7F 77
UB10: Ick 2D 56
Farmcote Rd. SE12 1J 141
Farm Ct. NW4 3C 44
Farmdale Rd. SE10 5J 105
SM5: Cars 7C 166
Farm Dr. CR0: C'don 2B 170
Farm End HA6: Nwood 1D 38
Farmer Rd. E10 1D 68
Farmer's Rd. SE5 7B 102
Farmer St. W8 1J 99
Farmfield Rd. BR1: Brom 5G 141
Farm Ho. Ct. NW7 7H 29
Farmhouse Rd. SW16 7G 137
Farmilo Rd. E17 7B 50
Farmington Av. SM1: Sutt 3B 166
Farmlands EN2: Enf 1F 23
HA5: Eastc 4J 39
Farmlands, The UB5: N'olt 6D 58
Farmland Wlk. BR7: Chst 5F 143
Farm La. CR0: C'don 2B 170
N14 7K 21
SW6 6J 99
(not continuous)
Farm La. Trad. Est. SW6 6J 99
Farmleigh N14 7B 22
Farmleigh Ho. SW9 5B 120
Farm M. CR4: Mitc 2F 155
Farm Pl. W8 1J 99
Farm Rd. E12 2C 70
HA8: Edg 6C 28
N21 1H 33
NW10 1K 79
SM2: Sutt 7B 166
SM4: Mord 5K 153
TW4: Houn 1C 130
Farmstead Ct. SM6: Wall 5F 167
(off Melbourne Rd.)
Farmstead Rd.
HA3: Hrw W 1H 41
SE6 4D 140
Farm St. W1 3J 11 (7F 83)
Farm Va. DA5: Bexl 6H 127
Farm Wlk. NW11 5H 45
Farm Way IG9: Buck H 4F 37
KT4: Wor Pk 3E 164
Farmway RM8: Dag 3C 72
Farnaby Ho. W10 3H 81
(off Bruckner St.)
Farnaby Rd. BR1: Brom 7F 141
BR2: Brom 7F 141
SE9 4A 124
Farnan Av. E17 2C 50
Farnan Rd. SW16 5J 137
FARNBOROUGH 5G 173
Farnborough Av. CR2: Sels 7K 169
E17 3A 50
Farnborough Cl. HA9: Wemb 2H 61
Farnborough Comn. BR6: Farnb 3D 172
Farnborough Cres. BR2: Hayes 1H 171
CR2: Sels 7A 170
Farnborough Hill BR6: Chels, Farnb 5H 173
Farnborough Ho. SW15 1C 134
Farnborough Way
BR6: Chels, Farnb 5G 173
Farncombe St. SE16 2G 103
Farndale Av. N13 2G 33
Farndale Ct. SE18 7C 106
Farndale Cres. UB6: G'frd 3G 77
Farndale Ho. NW6 1K 81
(off Kilburn Va.)
Farnell M. SW5 5K 99
Farnell Pl. W3 7H 79
Farnell Rd. TW7: Isle 3H 113
Farnham Cl. N20 7F 21
Farnham Ct. SM3: Cheam 6G 165
UB1: S'hall 7G 77
(off Redcroft Rd.)
Farnham Gdns. SW20 2D 152
Farnham Ho. NW1 4D 4
SE1 5C 14
(off Union St.)
Farnham Pl. SE1 5B 14 (1B 102)
Farnham Rd. DA16: Well 2C 126
IG3: Ilf 7K 53
Farnham Royal SE11 6H 19 (5K 101)
Farningham Ct. SW16 7H 137
Farningham Ho. N4 7D 48
Farningham Rd. N17 7B 34
Farnley Ho. SW8 2H 119
Farnley Rd. E4 1B 36
SE25 4D 156
Farnsworth Ct. SE10 3H 105
(off West Parkside)
Farnworth Ho. E14 4F 105
(off Manchester Rd.)
Faro Cl. BR1: Brom 2E 160
Faroe Rd. W14 3F 99
Farorna Wlk. EN2: Enf 1F 23
Farquhar Rd. SE19 5F 139
SW19 3J 135
Farquharson Rd. CR0: C'don 1C 168
Farrance Rd. RM6: Chad H 6E 54
Farrance St. E14 6C 86
Farrans Ct. HA3: Kent 7B 42
Farrant Av. N22 2A 48
Farrant Cl. BR6: Chels 7K 173
Farr Av. IG11: Bark 2A 90
Farrell Ho. E1 6J 85
(off Ronald St.)
Farren Rd. SE23 2A 140
Farrer Ct. TW1: Twick 7D 114
Farrer Ho. SE8 7C 104
Farrer M. N8 4G 47
Farrer Rd. HA3: Kent 5E 42
N8 4G 47
Farrer's Pl. CR0: C'don 4K 169
Farrier Cl. BR1: Brom 3B 160
TW16: Sun 4J 147
UB8: Hil 6C 74
Farrier Pl. SM1: Sutt 3K 165
Farrier Rd. UB5: N'olt 2E 76
Farriers Ho. EC1 4D 8
(off Errol St.)

Farriers M. SE15 ... 3J 121
Farrier St. NW1 ... 7F 65
Farrier Wlk. SW10 ... 6A 100
Farringdon Ho. TW9: Kew ... 7H 97
Farringdon La. EC1 ... 4K 7 (4A 84)
Farringdon Rd. EC1 ... 3J 7 (4A 84)
Farringdon St. EC4 ... 6A 8 (5B 84)
Farrington Pl. BR7: Chst ... 7H 143
Farrins Rents SE16 ... 1A 104
Farrow La. SE14 ... 7J 103
Farrow Pl. SE16 ... 3A 104
Farr Rd. EN2: Enf ... 1J 23
Farthingale Wlk. E15 ... 7F 69
Farthing All. SE1 ... 7K 15 (2G 103)
Farthing Barn La. BR6: Downe ... 7E 172
Farthing Ct. NW7 ... 7B 30
Farthing Flds. E1 ... 1H 103
Farthings, The KT2: King T ... 1G 151
Farthings Cl. E4 ... 3B 36
HA5: Eastc ... 6K 39
FARTHING STREET ... 7D 172
Farthing St. BR6: Downe ... 7D 172
Farwell Rd. DA14: Sidc ... 4B 144
Farwig La. BR1: Brom ... 1H 159
Fashion & Textile Mus. ... 6H 15 (2E 102)
Fashion St. E1 ... 6K 9 (5F 85)
Fashoda Rd. BR2: Brom ... 4B 160
Fassett Rd. E8 ... 6G 67
KT1: King T ... 4E 150
Fassett Sq. E8 ... 6G 67
Fauconberg Ct. *W4* ... *6J 97*
(off Fauconberg Rd.)
Fauconberg Rd. W4 ... 6J 97
Faulkner Cl. RM8: Dag ... 7D 54
Faulkners All. EC1 ... 5A 8 (5B 84)
Faulkner St. SE14 ... 1J 121
Fauna Cl. HA7: Stan ... 4J 27
RM6: Chad H ... 6C 54
Faunce Ho. *SE17* ... *6B 102*
(off Doddington Gro.)
Faunce St. SE17 ... 5B 102
Favart Rd. SW6 ... 1J 117
Faversham Av. E4 ... 1B 36
EN1: Enf ... 6J 23
Faversham Ho. *NW1* ... *1G 83*
(off Bayham Pl.)
SE17 ... *5E 102*
(off Kinglake St.)
Faversham Rd. BR3: Beck ... 2B 158
SE6 ... 7B 122
SM4: Mord ... 6K 153
Fawcett Cl. SW11 ... 2B 118
SW16 ... 5A 138
Fawcett Ct. *SW10* ... *6A 100*
(off Fawcett St.)
Fawcett Est. E5 ... 1G 67
Fawcett Rd. CR0: C'don ... 3C 168
NW10 ... 7B 62
Fawcett St. SW10 ... 6A 100
Fawe Pk. M. SW15 ... 4H 117
Fawe Pk. Rd. SW15 ... 4H 117
Fawe St. E14 ... 5D 86
Fawkham Ho. *SE1* ... *4F 103*
(off Longfield Est.)
Fawley Lodge *E14* ... *4F 105*
(off Millennium Dr.)
Fawley Rd. NW6 ... 5K 63
Fawnbrake Av. SE24 ... 5B 120
Fawn Rd. E13 ... 2A 88
Fawns Mnr. Cl. TW14: Bedf ... 1E 128
Fawns Mnr. Rd. TW14: Bedf ... 1F 129
Fawood Av. NW10 ... 7J 61
Faygate Cres. DA6: Bex ... 5G 127
Faygate Rd. SW2 ... 2K 137
Fayland Av. SW16 ... 5G 137
Fazeley Ct. *W9* ... *5J 81*
(off Elmfield Way)
Fearnley Cres. TW12: Hamp ... 5C 130
Fearnley Ho. SE5 ... 2E 120
Fearon St. SE10 ... 5J 105
Featherbed La. CR0: Sels ... 7B 170
Feathers Pl. SE10 ... 6F 105
Featherstone Av. SE23 ... 2H 139
Featherstone Ho. UB4: Yead ... 5A 76
Featherstone Ind. Est. *UB2: S'hall* ... *3C 94*
(off Feather Rd.)
Featherstone Rd. NW7 ... 6J 29
UB2: S'hall ... 3C 94
Featherstone St. EC1 ... 3E 8 (4D 84)
Featherstone Ter. UB2: S'hall ... 3C 94
Featley Rd. SW9 ... 3B 120
Federal Rd. UB6: G'frd ... 1C 78
Federation Rd. SE2 ... 4B 108
Fee Farm Rd. KT10: Clay ... 7A 162
Feeny Cl. NW10 ... 4B 62
Felbridge Av. HA7: Stan ... 1A 42
Felbridge Cl. SM2: Sutt ... 7K 165
SW16 ... 4A 138
Felbridge Ct. *TW13: Felt* ... *1K 129*
(off High St.)
UB3: Harl ... 6F 93
Felbridge Ho. SE22 ... 3E 120
Felbrigge Rd. IG3: Ilf ... 2K 71
Felday Rd. SE13 ... 6D 122
Felden Cl. HA5: Hat E ... 1C 40
Felden St. SW6 ... 1H 117
Feldman Cl. N16 ... 1G 67
Feldspar Ct. *EN3: Enf H* ... *3F 25*
(off Enstone Rd.)
Felgate M. W6 ... 4D 98
Felhampton Rd. SE9 ... 2F 143
Felhurst Cres. RM10: Dag ... 4H 73
Feline Ct. EN4: E Barn ... 6H 21
Felix Av. N8 ... 6J 47
Felix Ct. E17 ... 5D 50
Felix Ho. *E16* ... *7E 88*
(off University Way)
Felix La. TW17: Shep ... 6G 147
Felix Mnr. BR7: Chst ... 6J 143
Felix Neubergh Ho. EN1: Enf ... 4K 23
Felix Pl. *SW2* ... *5A 120*
(off Talma Rd.)
Felix Rd. KT12: Walt T ... 6J 147
W13 ... 7A 78
Felixstowe Ct. E16 ... 1F 107
Felixstowe Rd. N9 ... 3B 34
N17 ... 3F 49
NW10 ... 3D 80
SE2 ... 3B 108
Felix St. E2 ... 2H 85
Fellbrigg Rd. SE22 ... 5F 121
Fellbrigg St. E1 ... 4H 85
Fellbrook TW10: Ham ... 3B 132
Fellmongers Path SE1 ... 7J 15
Fellmongers Yd. *CR0: C'don* ... *3C 168*
(off Surrey St.)
Fellowes Cl. UB4: Yead ... 4B 76
Fellowes Rd. SM5: Cars ... 3C 166
Fellows Ct. E2 ... 1J 9 (2F 85)
(not continuous)
Fellows Rd. NW3 ... 7B 64
Fell Rd. CR0: C'don ... 3C 168
(not continuous)
Felltram M. SE7 ... 5J 105
Felltram Way SE7 ... 5J 105
Fell Wlk. HA8: Edg ... 1J 43
Felmersham Cl. SW4 ... 4J 119
Felmingham Rd. SE20 ... 2J 157
Felnex Trad. Est. NW10 ... 2K 79
SM6: Wall ... 2E 166
Felsberg Rd. SW2 ... 6J 119
Fels Cl. RM10: Dag ... 3H 73
Fels Farm Av. RM10: Dag ... 3J 73
Felsham M. *SW15* ... *3F 117*
(off Felsham Rd.)
Felsham Rd. SW15 ... 3E 116
Felspar Cl. SE18 ... 5K 107
Felstead Av. IG5: Ilf ... 1E 52
Felstead Cl. N13 ... 5F 33
Felstead Gdns. E14 ... 5E 104
Felstead Rd. E9 ... 6B 68
E11 ... 7J 51
Felstead St. E9 ... 6B 68
Felstead Wharf E14 ... 5E 104
Felsted Rd. E16 ... 6B 88
FELTHAM ... 1K 129
Feltham Airparcs Leisure Cen. ... 2B 130
Feltham Arenas ... 7J 111
Feltham Av. KT8: E Mos ... 4J 149
Felthambrook Ind. Est.
TW13: Felt ... 3K 129
Felthambrook Way
TW13: Felt ... 3K 129
Feltham Bus. Complex
TW13: Felt ... 2K 129
Feltham Corporate Cen.
TW13: Felt ... 3K 129
FELTHAMHILL ... 5H 129
Feltham Hill Rd. TW15: Ashf ... 5C 128
Feltham Rd. CR4: Mitc ... 2D 154
TW15: Ashf ... 4C 128
Felton Cl. BR5: Pet W ... 6F 161
Felton Gdns. IG11: Bark ... 1J 89
Felton Ho. *N1* ... *1D 84*
(off Branch Pl.)
SE3 ... 4K 123
Felton Lea DA14: Sidc ... 5K 143
Felton Rd. IG11: Bark ... 2J 89
W13 ... 2C 96
Felton St. N1 ... 1D 84
Fencepiece Rd. IG6: Chig, Ilf ... 1G 53
Fenchurch Av. EC3 ... 1G 15 (6E 84)
Fenchurch Bldgs. EC3 ... 1H 15 (6E 84)
Fenchurch Ho. *EC3* ... *1J 15*
(off Minories)
Fenchurch Pl. EC3 ... 2H 15 (6E 84)
Fenchurch St. EC3 ... 2G 15 (7E 84)
Fen Ct. EC3 ... 2G 15 (6E 84)
Fendall Rd. KT19: Ewe ... 5J 163
Fendall St. SE1 ... 3E 102
(not continuous)
Fendt Cl. E16 ... 6H 87
Fendyke Rd. DA17: Belv ... 4D 108
Fenelon Pl. W14 ... 4H 99
Fen Gro. DA15: Sidc ... 5K 125
Fenham Rd. SE15 ... 7G 103
Fen La. SW13 ... 1D 116
Fenman Ct. N17 ... 1H 49
Fenman Gdns. IG3: Ilf ... 1B 72
Fenn Cl. BR1: Brom ... 6J 141
Fennel Apartments *SE1* ... *5J 15*
(off Cayenne Ct.)
Fennel Cl. CR0: C'don ... 1K 169
E16 ... 4G 87
Fennells Mead KT17: Ewe ... 7B 164
Fennell St. SE18 ... 6E 106
Fenner Cl. SE16 ... 4H 103
Fenner Ho. *E1* ... *1H 103*
(off Watts St.)
Fenner Sq. SW11 ... 3B 118
Fenn Ho. TW7: Isle ... 1B 114
Fenning St. SE1 ... 6G 15 (2E 102)
Fenn St. E9 ... 5K 67
Fenstanton *N4* ... *1K 65*
(off Marquis Rd.)
Fenstanton Av. N12 ... 6G 31
Fen St. E16 ... 7H 87
Fenswood Cl. DA5: Bexl ... 6G 127
Fentiman Rd. SW8 ... 7F 19 (6J 101)
Fentiman Way HA2: Harr ... 2F 59
Fenton Cl. BR7: Chst ... 5D 142
E8 ... 6F 67
SW9 ... 2K 119
Fenton House ... *4A 64*
(off Windmill Hill)
Fenton Ho. SE14 ... 7A 104
TW5: Hest ... 6E 94
Fenton Rd. N17 ... 7H 33
Fentons Av. E13 ... 3K 87
Fenton St. E1 ... 6H 85
Fenwick Cl. SE18 ... 6E 106
Fenwick Gro. SE15 ... 3G 121
Fenwick Pl. CR2: S Croy ... 7B 168
SW9 ... 3J 119
Fenwick Rd. SE15 ... 3G 121
Ferby Ct. *DA14: Sidc* ... *4K 143*
(off Main Rd.)
SE9 ... *3H 143*
(off Main Rd.)
Ferdinand Ho. *NW1* ... *7E 64*
(off Ferdinand Pl.)
Ferdinand Pl. NW1 ... 7E 64
Ferdinand St. NW1 ... 7E 64
Ferguson Av. KT5: Surb ... 5F 151
Ferguson Cen., The
E17 ... 6A 50
Ferguson Cl. BR2: Brom ... 3F 159
E14 ... 4C 104
Ferguson Dr. W3 ... 6K 79
Ferguson Ho. SE10 ... 1E 122
Fergus Rd. N5 ... 5B 66
Fermain Ct. E. *N1* ... *1E 84*
(off De Beauvoir Est.)
Fermain Ct. Nth. *N1* ... *1E 84*
(off De Beauvoir Est.)
Fermain Ct. W. *N1* ... *1E 84*
(off De Beauvoir Est.)
Ferme Pk. Rd. N4 ... 5J 47
N8 ... 5J 47
Fermor Rd. SE23 ... 1A 140
Fermoy Ho. *W9* ... *4H 81*
(off Fermoy Rd.)
Fermoy Rd. UB6: G'frd ... 4F 77
W9 ... 4H 81
Fern Av. CR4: Mitc ... 4H 155
Fernbank IG9: Buck H ... 1E 36
Fernbank Av. HA0: Wemb ... 4K 59
KT12: Walt T ... 7C 148
Fernbank M. SW12 ... 6G 119
Fernbrook Av. DA15: Sidc ... 5J 125
Fernbrook Cres. *SE13* ... *6G 123*
(off Leahurst Rd.)
Fernbrook Dr. HA2: Harr ... 7F 41
Fernbrook Rd. SE13 ... 5G 123
Ferncliff Rd. E8 ... 5G 67
Fern Cl. N1 ... 2E 84
Fern Ct. DA7: Bex ... 4G 127
SE14 ... 2K 121
Ferncroft Av. HA4: Ruis ... 2A 58
N12 ... 6J 31
NW3 ... 3J 63
Ferndale BR1: Brom ... 2A 160
Ferndale Av. E17 ... 5F 51
TW4: Houn ... 3C 112
Ferndale Cl. DA7: Bex ... 1E 126
Ferndale Community Sports Cen. ... 3K 119
Ferndale Rd. E7 ... 7K 69
E11 ... 2G 69
N15 ... 6F 49
RM5: Col R ... 2J 55
SE25 ... 5H 157
SW4 ... 4J 119
SW9 ... 4J 119
TW15: Ashf ... 5A 128
Ferndale St. E6 ... 7F 89
Ferndale Ter. HA1: Harr ... 4K 41
Ferndale Way
BR6: Farnb ... 5H 173
Ferndell Av. DA5: Bexl ... 3K 145
Fern Dene W13 ... 5B 78
Ferndene Rd. SE24 ... 4C 120
Fernden Way RM7: Rom ... 6H 55
Ferndown HA6: Nwood ... 2J 39
NW1 ... *7H 65*
(off Camley St.)
Ferndown Av. BR6: Orp ... 1H 173
Ferndown Cl. HA5: Pinn ... 1C 40
SM2: Sutt ... 6B 166
Ferndown Ct. *UB1: S'hall* ... *6G 77*
(off Haldane Rd.)

Ferndown Lodge E14 . . . 3E 104
(off Manchester Rd.)
Ferndown Rd. SE9 . . . 7B 124
Ferney Meade Way TW7: Isle . . . 2A 114
Ferney Rd. EN4: E Barn . . . 7K 21
Fern Gro. TW14: Felt . . . 7K 111
Fernhall Dr. IG4: Ilf . . . 5B 52
Fernham Rd. CR7: Thor H . . . 3C 156
Fernhead Rd. W9 . . . 3H 81
Fernheath Way DA2: Dart . . . 5K 145
Fernhill Ct. E17 . . . 2F 51
Fernhill Gdns. KT2: King T . . . 5D 132
Fern Hill Pl. BR6: Farnb . . . 5G 173
Fernhill St. E16 . . . 1D 106
Fernholme Rd. SE15 . . . 5K 121
Fernhurst Gdns. HA8: Edg . . . 6B 28
Fernhurst Rd. CR0: C'don . . . 7H 157
SW6 . . . 1G 117
TW15: Ashf . . . 4E 128
Fern La. TW5: Hest . . . 5D 94
Fernlea Rd. CR4: Mitc . . . 2E 154
SW12 . . . 1F 137
Fernleigh Cl. CR0: Wadd . . . 4A 168
W9 . . . 3H 81
Fernleigh Ct. HA2: Harr . . . 2F 41
HA9: Wemb . . . 2E 60
RM7: Rom . . . 5J 55
Fernleigh Rd. N21 . . . 2F 33
Fernley Cl. HA5: Eastc . . . 4J 39
Fernsbury St. WC1 . . . 2J 7 (3A 84)
Fernshaw Cl. SW10 . . . 6A 100
Fernshaw Mans. SW10 . . . 6A 100
(off Fernshaw Rd.)
Fernshaw Rd. SW10 . . . 6A 100
Fernside IG9: Buck H . . . 1E 36
NW11 . . . 2J 63
Fernside Av. NW7 . . . 3E 28
TW13: Felt . . . 4K 129
Fernside Ct. NW4 . . . 2F 45
(off Holders Hill Rd.)
Fernside Rd. SW12 . . . 1D 136
Ferns Rd. E15 . . . 6H 69
Fern St. E3 . . . 4C 86
Fernthorpe Rd. SW16 . . . 6G 137
Ferntower Rd. N5 . . . 5D 66
Fern Wlk. SE16 . . . 5G 103
TW15: Ashf . . . 5A 128
Fernways IG1: Ilf . . . 4F 71
Fernwood SW19 . . . 1H 135
Fernwood Av.
HA0: Wemb . . . 6C 60
SW16 . . . 4H 137
Fernwood Cl. BR1: Brom . . . 2A 160
Fernwood Ct. N14 . . . 7B 22
Fernwood Cres. N20 . . . 3J 31
Ferranti Cl. SE18 . . . 3B 106
Ferraro Cl. TW5: Hest . . . 6E 94
Ferrers Av. SM6: Bedd . . . 4H 167
UB7: W Dray . . . 2A 92
Ferrers Rd. SW16 . . . 5H 137
Ferrestone Rd. N8 . . . 4K 47
Ferrey M. SW9 . . . 2A 120
Ferriby Cl. N1 . . . 7A 66
Ferrier Ind. Est. SW18 . . . 4K 117
(off Ferrier St.)
Ferrier Point E16 . . . 5J 87
(off Forty Acre La.)
Ferrier St. SW18 . . . 4K 117
Ferring Cl. HA2: Harr . . . 1G 59
Ferrings SE21 . . . 3E 138
Ferris Av. CR0: C'don . . . 3B 170
Ferris Rd. SE22 . . . 4G 121
Ferron Rd. E5 . . . 3H 67
Ferry App. SE18 . . . 3E 106
Ferrybridge Ho. SE11 . . . 2H 19
Ferrydale Lodge NW4 . . . 4E 44
(off Parson St.)
Ferry Ho. E5 . . . 1H 67
(off Harrington Hill)
Ferry Island Retail Pk. N17 . . . 3G 49
Ferry La. N17 . . . 4G 49
SW13 . . . 6B 98
TW8: Bford . . . 6E 96
TW9: Kew . . . 6F 97
TW17: Shep . . . 7C 146
Ferry La. Ind. Est. E17 . . . 4K 49
Ferryman's Quay SW6 . . . 2A 118
Ferrymead Av. UB6: G'frd . . . 3E 76
Ferrymead Dr. UB6: G'frd . . . 2E 76
Ferrymead Gdns. UB6: G'frd . . . 2G 77
Ferrymoor TW10: Ham . . . 3B 132
Ferry Pl. SE18 . . . 3E 106
Ferry Quays TW8: Bford . . . 7D 96
(off Point Wharf La.)
TW8: Bford . . . 6E 96
(Ferry La.)
Ferry Rd. KT7: T Ditt . . . 6B 150
KT8: W Mole . . . 3E 148
SW13 . . . 7C 98
TW1: Twick . . . 1B 132
TW11: Tedd . . . 5B 132
Ferry Sq. TW8: Bford . . . 7E 96
Ferry St. E14 . . . 5E 104
Ferry Wharf TW8: Bford . . . 7E 96
Festing Rd. SW15 . . . 3F 117
Festival Cl. DA5: Bexl . . . 1D 144
UB10: Hil . . . 1D 74
Festival Ct. E8 . . . 7F 67
(off Holly St.)
SM1: Sutt . . . 7K 153
Festival Wlk. SM5: Cars . . . 4D 166
Festoon Way E16 . . . 7B 88
Fetherton Ct. IG11: Bark . . . 2G 89
(off Spring Pl.)
Fetter La. EC4 . . . 1K 13 (6A 84)
(not continuous)
Fettes Ho. NW8 . . . 2B 82
(off Wellington Rd.)
Fews Lodge RM6: Chad H . . . 4D 54
Ffinch St. SE8 . . . 7C 104
Fidgeon Cl. BR1: Brom . . . 3E 160
Field Cl. BR1: Brom . . . 2A 160
E4 . . . 6J 35
HA4: Ruis . . . 1E 56
IG9: Buck H . . . 3F 37
KT8: W Mole . . . 5F 149
KT9: Chess . . . 5C 162
NW2 . . . 2C 62
TW4: Cran . . . 1K 111
UB3: Harl . . . 7E 92
UB10: Ick . . . 2D 56
FIELDCOMMON . . . 7D 148
Fieldcommon La. KT12: Walt T . . . 7C 148
Field Ct. SW19 . . . 3J 135
WC1 . . . 6H 7 (5K 83)
Field End HA4: Ruis . . . 6A 58
UB5: N'olt . . . 6B 58
Fieldend TW1: Twick . . . 4K 131
Field End Rd. HA4: Ruis . . . 1B 58
HA5: Eastc . . . 5K 39
Fieldend Rd. SW16 . . . 1G 155
Fielders Cl. EN1: Enf . . . 4K 23
HA2: Harr . . . 1G 59
Fieldfare Rd. SE28 . . . 7C 90
Fieldgate La. CR4: Mitc . . . 2C 154
Fieldgate Mans. E1 . . . 5G 85
(off Fieldgate St., not continuous)
Fieldgate St. E1 . . . 5G 85
Field Ho. NW6 . . . 3F 81
(off Harvist Rd.)
Fieldhouse Cl. E18 . . . 1J 51
Fieldhouse Rd. SW12 . . . 1G 137
Fielding Av. TW2: Twick . . . 3G 131
Fielding Ct. WC2 . . . 1E 12
(off Tower St.)
Fielding Ho. NW6 . . . 3J 81
NW8 . . . 1A 82
(off Ainsworth Way)
W4 . . . 6A 98
(off Devonshire Rd.)
Fielding La. BR2: Brom . . . 4A 160
Fielding M. SW13 . . . 6D 98
Fielding Rd. W4 . . . 3K 97
W14 . . . 3F 99
Fieldings, The SE23 . . . 1J 139
Fielding St. SE17 . . . 6C 102
Fielding Ter. W5 . . . 7F 79
Fielding Wlk. W13 . . . 3B 96
Field La. TW8: Bford . . . 7C 96
TW11: Tedd . . . 5A 132
Field Mead NW7 . . . 7F 29
NW9 . . . 7G 29
Fieldpark Gdns. CR0: C'don . . . 1A 170
Field Pl. KT3: N Mald . . . 6B 152
Field Point E7 . . . 4J 69
Field Rd. E7 . . . 4H 69
N17 . . . 3D 48
TW14: Felt . . . 6K 111
W6 . . . 5G 99
Fieldsend Rd. SM3: Cheam . . . 5G 165
Fields Est. E8 . . . 7G 67
Fieldside Cl. BR6: Farnb . . . 4G 173
Fieldside Rd. BR1: Brom . . . 5F 141
Fields Pk. Cres. RM6: Chad H . . . 5D 54
Field St. WC1 . . . 1G 7 (3K 83)
Fieldsway Ho. N5 . . . 5A 66
Field Vw. TW13: Felt . . . 4F 129
Fieldview SW18 . . . 1B 136
Field Vw. Cl. RM7: Mawney . . . 3G 55
Fieldview Cotts. N14 . . . 2C 32
(off Balaams La.)
Field Way HA4: Ruis . . . 1E 56
NW10 . . . 7J 61
UB6: G'frd . . . 1F 77
Fieldway BR5: Pet W . . . 6H 161
CR0: New Ad . . . 7D 170
RM8: Dag . . . 3C 72
Fieldway Cres. N5 . . . 5A 66
Fiennes Cl. RM8: Dag . . . 1C 72
Fifehead Cl. TW15: Ashf . . . 6A 128
Fife Rd. E16 . . . 5J 87
KT1: King T . . . 2E 150
(not continuous)
N22 . . . 7G 33
SW14 . . . 5J 115
Fife Ter. N1 . . . 2K 83
Fifield Path SE23 . . . 3K 139
Fifth Av. E12 . . . 4D 70
UB3: Hayes . . . 1H 93
W10 . . . 3G 81
Fifth Cross Rd. TW2: Twick . . . 2H 131
Fifth Way HA9: Wemb . . . 4H 61
Figges Rd. CR4: Mitc . . . 7E 136
Fig Tree Cl. NW10 . . . 1A 80
Figure Ct. SW3 . . . 6F 17
Filanco Ct. W7 . . . 1K 95
(off Uxbridge Rd.)
Filby Rd. KT9: Chess . . . 6F 163
Filey Av. N16 . . . 1G 67
Filey Cl. SM2: Sutt . . . 7A 166
Filey Waye HA4: Ruis . . . 2J 57
Filigree Ct. SE16 . . . 1B 104
Fillebrook Av. EN1: Enf . . . 2K 23
Fillebrook Rd. E11 . . . 1F 69
Filmer Chambers SW6 . . . 1G 117
(off Filmer Rd.)
Filmer M. SW6 . . . 1H 117
Filmer Rd. SW6 . . . 1G 117
Filston Rd. DA8: Erith . . . 5J 109
Filton Cl. NW9 . . . 1A 44
Filton Ct. SE14 . . . 7J 103
(off Farrow La.)
Finborough Ho. SW10 . . . 6A 100
(off Finborough Rd.)
Finborough Rd. SW10 . . . 5K 99
SW17 . . . 6D 136
Finborough Theatre, The . . . 6K 99
(off Finborough Rd.)
Finchale Rd. SE2 . . . 3A 108
Fincham Cl. UB10: Ick . . . 3E 56
Finch Av. SE27 . . . 4D 138
Finch Cl. EN5: Barn . . . 5D 20
NW10 . . . 6K 61
Finch Ct. DA14: Sidc . . . 3B 144
Finchdean Ho. SW15 . . . 7B 116
Finch Dr. TW14: Felt . . . 7B 112
Finch Gdns. E4 . . . 5H 35
Finch Ho. SE8 . . . 7D 104
(off Bronze St.)
Finchingfield Av. IG8: Wfd G . . . 7F 37
Finch La. EC3 . . . 1F 15 (6D 84)
FINCHLEY . . . 1J 45
Finchley Ct. N3 . . . 6E 30
Finchley Ind. Est. N12 . . . 4F 31
Finchley La. NW4 . . . 4E 44
Finchley Lido . . . 7G 31
Finchley Pk. N12 . . . 4F 31
Finchley Pl. NW8 . . . 2B 82
Finchley Rd. NW2 . . . 1J 63
NW3 . . . 1J 63
NW8 . . . 1B 82
NW11 . . . 4H 45
Finchley Way N3 . . . 7D 30
Finch Lodge W9 . . . 5J 81
(off Admiral Wlk.)
Finch M. SE15 . . . 1F 121
Finch's Ct. E14 . . . 7D 86
Finden Rd. E7 . . . 5A 70
Findhorn Av. UB4: Yead . . . 5K 75
Findhorn St. E14 . . . 6E 86
Findon Cl. HA2: Harr . . . 3F 59
SW18 . . . 6J 117
Findon Rd. N9 . . . 1C 34
W12 . . . 2C 98
Fine Bush La. UB9: Hare . . . 6D 38
Fingal St. SE10 . . . 5H 105
Fingest Ho. NW8 . . . 3C 4
(off Lilestone St.)
Finians Cl. UB10: Uxb . . . 7B 56
Finland Rd. SE4 . . . 3A 122
Finland St. SE16 . . . 3A 104
Finlays Cl. KT9: Chess . . . 5G 163
Finlay St. SW6 . . . 1F 117
Finmere Ho. N4 . . . 7C 48
Finnemore Ho. N1 . . . 1C 84
(off Britannia Row)
Finney La. TW7: Isle . . . 1A 114
Finn Ho. N1 . . . 1F 9
(off Bevenden St.)
Finnis St. E2 . . . 3H 85
Finnymore Rd. RM9: Dag . . . 7E 72
FINSBURY . . . 3C 8 (3A 84)
Finsbury Av. EC2 . . . 6F 9 (5D 84)
(not continuous)
Finsbury Av. Sq. EC2 . . . 5G 9
Finsbury Cir. EC2 . . . 6F 9 (5D 84)
Finsbury Cotts. N22 . . . 7D 32
Finsbury Est. EC1 . . . 2K 7 (3A 84)
Finsbury Ho. N22 . . . 1J 47
Finsbury Leisure Cen. . . . 3C 8 (3C 84)
Finsbury Mkt. EC2 . . . 4G 9 (4E 84)
(not continuous)
FINSBURY PARK . . . 1A 66
Finsbury Pk. Av. N4 . . . 6C 48
Finsbury Pk. Rd. N4 . . . 2B 66
(not continuous)
Finsbury Pavement EC2 . . . 5F 9 (5D 84)
Finsbury Rd. N22 . . . 7E 32
(not continuous)
Finsbury Sq. EC2 . . . 4F 9 (4D 84)
Finsbury St. EC2 . . . 5E 8 (5D 84)
Finsbury Way DA5: Bexl . . . 6F 127
Finsen Rd. SE5 . . . 4C 120
Finstock Rd. W10 . . . 6F 81
Finucane Ct. TW9: Rich . . . 3F 115
(off Lwr. Mortlake Rd.)
Finucane Ri.
WD23: B Hea . . . 2B 26
Finwhale Ho. E14 . . . 3D 104
(off Glengall Gro.)

Fiona Ct. EN2: Enf .3G 23
NW6 .2J 81
Firbank Cl. E16 .5B 88
EN2: Enf .4H 23
Firbank Rd. SE15 .2H 121
Fir Cl. KT12: Walt T .7J 147
Fircroft Gdns. HA1: Harr .3J 59
Fircroft Rd. KT9: Chess .4F 163
SW17 .2D 136
Fir Dene BR6: Farnb .3D 172
Firdene KT5: Surb .1J 163
Fire Bell All. KT6: Surb .6E 150
Firecrest Dr. NW3 .3K 63
Firefly Gdns. E6 .4C 88
Firemans Flats N22 .7D 32
Firepower (The Royal Artillery Mus.) .3F 107
Fire Sta. All. EN5: Barn .3B 20
Fire Sta. M. BR3: Beck .1C 158
Firethorn Cl. HA8: Edg .4D 28
Fir Gro. KT3: N Mald .6B 152
Fir Gro. Rd. SW9 .2A 120
Firhill Rd. SE6 .4C 140
Fir Ho. W10 .4G 81
(off Droop St.)
Firle Ho. W10 .5E 80
(off Sutton Way)
Firmans Ct. E17 .4F 51
Fir Rd. SM3: Sutt .1H 165
TW13: Hanw .5B 130
Firs, The DA5: Bexl .1K 145
DA15: Sidc .2K 143
E6 .7C 70
HA8: Edg .4E 28
(off Stoneyfields La.)
IG8: Wfd G .7F 37
N20 .1G 31
SE26 .5H 139
(Border Rd.)
SE26 .5J 139
(Waverley Ct.)
W5 .5D 78
Firs Av. N10 .3E 46
N11 .6J 31
SW14 .4J 115
Firsby Av. CR0: C'don .1K 169
Firsby Rd. N16 .1G 67
Firs Cl. CR4: Mitc .2F 155
N10 .4E 46
SE23 .7A 122
Firscroft N13 .3H 33
Firs Dr. TW5: Cran .7K 93
Firs Ho. N22 .1A 48
(off Acacia Rd.)
Firside Gro. DA15: Sidc .1K 143
Firs La. N13 .3H 33
N21 .7H 23
Firs Pk. Av. N21 .1J 33
Firs Pk. Gdns. N21 .1H 33
First Av. DA7: Bex .7C 108
E12 .4C 70
E13 .3J 87
E17 .5C 50
EN1: Enf .5A 24
HA9: Wemb .2D 60
KT8: W Mole .4D 148
KT12: Walt T .6K 147
KT19: Ewe .7A 164
N18 .4D 34
NW4 .4E 44
RM6: Chad H .5C 54
RM10: Dag .2H 91
SW14 .3A 116
UB3: Hayes .1H 93
W3 .1B 98
W10 .4H 81
First Cl. KT8: W Mole .3G 149
First Cross Rd. TW2: Twick .2J 131
First Dr. NW10 .7J 61
First St. SW3 .3D 16 (4C 100)
First Way HA9: Wemb .4H 61
Firstway SW20 .2E 152
Firs Wlk. IG8: Wfd G .5D 36
Firswood Av. KT19: Ewe .5A 164
Firth Gdns. SW6 .1G 117
Firth Ho. E2 .3G 85
(off Turin St.)
Fir Tree Av. UB7: W Dray .3C 92
Firtree Av. CR4: Mitc .2E 154
Fir Tree Cl. BR6: Chels .5K 173
KT19: Ewe .4B 164
RM1: Rom .3K 55
W5 .6E 78
Firtree Cl. SW16 .5G 137
Fir Tree Gdns. CR0: C'don .4C 170
Fir Tree Gro. SM5: Cars .7D 166
Fir Tree Ho. SE14 .7J 103
(off Avonley Rd.)
Fir Tree Pl. TW15: Ashf .5C 128
Fir Tree Rd. TW4: Houn .4C 112
Fir Trees Cl. SE16 .1A 104
Fir Tree Wlk. EN1: Enf .3J 23
RM10: Dag .3J 73
Fir Wlk. SM3: Cheam .6F 165
Fisher Athletic FC .1K 103
Fisher Cl. CR0: C'don .1F 169
E9 .5K 67
UB6: G'frd .3E 76
Fisher Ho. E1 .7J 85
(off Cable St.)
N1 .1A 84
(off Barnsbury Est.)
Fisherman Cl. TW10: Ham .4B 132
Fishermans Dr. SE16 .2K 103
Fisherman's Pl. W4 .6B 98
Fishermans Wlk. E14 .1C 104
SE28 .2J 107
Fisher Rd. HA3: W'stone .2K 41
Fisher's Cl. SW16 .3H 137
Fishers Ct. SE14 .1K 121
Fishersdene KT10: Clay .7A 162
Fisher's La. W4 .4K 97
Fisher St. E16 .5J 87
WC1 .6G 7 (5K 83)
Fishers Way DA17: Belv .1J 109
Fisherton St. NW8 .4A 4 (4B 82)
Fishguard Way E16 .1F 107
Fishmongers Hall Wharf
EC4 .3E 14
Fishponds Rd. BR2: Kes .5B 172
SW17 .4C 136
Fish St. Hill EC3 .3F 15 (7D 84)
Fish Wharf EC3 .3F 15 (7D 84)
Fisk Cl. TW16: Sun .6H 129
Fiske Ct. IG11: Bark .2H 89
N17 .1G 49
SM2: Sutt .7A 166
Fitness First Health Club
Alperton .1E 78
America Sq. .2J 15
Bloomsbury .4E 6
Brixton .3A 120
Camden .1F 83
Chalk Farm .7E 64
(off Chalk Farm Rd.)
Chancery Lane .6K 7
Clapham Junction .3C 118
(off Lavender Hill)
Covent Garden .3F 13
(off Bedford St.)
Crouch End .6J 47
Croydon .1B 168
Embankment .4F 13
(off Embankment Pl.)
Fetter La. .1K 13
(off Fetter La.)
Gt. Marlborough St. .1A 12
Gracechurch St. .2G 15
(off Gracechurch St.)
Hammersmith .4E 98
Fitness First Health Club
High Holborn .6G 7
(off High Holborn)
Islington .1A 8 (2B 84)
Kilburn .1H 81
Kingly St. .2A 12
Kingsbury .5G 43
Lewisham .3E 122
London Bridge .5F 15
(off London Bri.)
London Victoria .2K 17
Mitcham .2D 154
North Finchley .5F 31
Old Street .3E 8
(off Bunhill Row)
Paternoster Sq. .7B 8
Pinner .3B 40
Queen Victoria St. .2C 14
(off Queen Victoria St.)
South Kensington .3A 16
(off Harrington Rd.)
Tooting Bec .3E 136
Tottenham .2F 49
Walworth Rd. .5C 102
Westminster .1A 18
Woolwich .3F 107
Fitrooms .6H 99
Fitzalan Rd. N3 .3G 45
Fitzalan St. SE11 .3H 19 (4A 102)
Fitzgeorge Av. KT3: N Mald .1K 151
W14 .4G 99
Fitzgerald Av. SW14 .3A 116
Fitzgerald Ct. E10 .1D 68
(off Leyton Grange Est.)
Fitzgerald Ho. E14 .6D 86
(off E. India Dock Rd.)
SW9 .2A 120
UB3: Hayes .1K 93
Fitzgerald Rd. E11 .5J 51
KT7: T Ditt .6A 150
SW14 .3K 115
Fitzhardinge Ho. W1 .7G 5
(off Portman Sq.)
Fitzhardinge St. W1 .7G 5 (6E 82)
Fitzherbert Wlk. UB1: S'hall .2H 95
Fitzhugh Gro. SW18 .6B 118
Fitzjames Av. CR0: C'don .2G 169
W14 .4G 99
Fitzjohn Av. EN5: Barn .5B 20
Fitzjohn's Av. NW3 .4A 64
Fitzmaurice Ho. SE16 .4H 103
(off Rennie Est.)
Fitzmaurice Pl. W1 .4K 11 (1F 101)
Fitzneal St. W12 .6B 80
FITZROVIA .5K 5
Fitzroy Cl. N6 .1D 64
Fitzroy Ct. CR0: C'don .7D 156
N6 .6G 47
W1 .4B 6
Fitzroy Cres. W4 .7K 97
Fitzroy Gdns. SE19 .7E 138
Fitzroy Ho. E14 .5B 86
(off Wallwood St.)
SE1 .5F 103
(off Cooper's Rd.)
Fitzroy M. W1 .4A 6
Fitzroy Pk. N6 .1D 64
Fitzroy Rd. NW1 .1E 82
Fitzroy Sq. W1 .4A 6 (4G 83)
Fitzroy St. W1 .4A 6 (4G 83)
(not continuous)
Fitzroy Yd. NW1 .1E 82
Fitzsimmons Ct. NW10 .1K 79
Fitzstephen Rd. RM8: Dag .5B 72
Fitzwarren Gdns. N19 .1G 65
Fitzwilliam Av. TW9: Rich .2F 115
Fitzwilliam Cl. N20 .1K 31
Fitzwilliam Hgts. SE23 .2J 139
Fitzwilliam Ho. TW9: Rich .4D 114
Fitzwilliam M. E16 .1J 105
Fitzwilliam Rd. SW4 .3G 119
Fitzwygram Cl. TW12: Ham H .5G 131
Five Acre NW9 .2B 44
Fiveacre Cl. CR7: Thor H .6A 156
Five Arches Bus. Pk.
DA14: Sidc .5D 144
Five Bell All. E14 .6B 86
(off Three Colt St.)
Five Elms Rd. BR2: Hayes .3K 171
RM9: Dag .3F 73
Five Oaks M. BR1: Brom .3J 141
Fives Ct. SE11 .3B 102
FIVEWAYS .2F 143
Five Ways Bus. Cen. TW13: Felt .3K 129
FIVEWAYS CORNER
Croydon .4A 168
Hendon .1C 44
Fiveways Rd. SW9 .2A 120
Flack Ct. E10 .7D 50
Fladbury Rd. N15 .6D 48
Fladgate Rd. E11 .6G 51
Flag Cl. CR0: C'don .1K 169
Flagon Ct. CR0: C'don .4C 168
(off St Andrew's Rd.)
Flag Wlk. HA5: Eastc .6J 39
Flambard Rd. HA1: Harr .6A 42
Flamborough Ho. SE15 .1G 121
(off Clayton Rd.)
Flamborough Rd. HA4: Ruis .3J 57
Flamborough St. E14 .6A 86
Flamborough Wlk. E14 .6A 86
(off Flamborough St.)
Flamingo Ct. SE8 .7C 104
(off Hamilton St.)
Flamingo Gdns. UB5: N'olt .3C 76
Flamstead Gdns. RM9: Dag .7C 72
Flamstead Ho. SW3 .5C 16
(off Cale St.)
Flamstead Rd. RM9: Dag .7C 72
Flamsted Av. HA9: Wemb .6G 61
Flamsteed Rd. SE7 .5C 106
Flanchford Rd. W12 .3B 98
Flanders Ct. E17 .7A 50
Flanders Cres. SW17 .7D 136
Flanders Mans. W4 .4B 98
Flanders Rd. E6 .2D 88
W4 .4A 98
Flanders Way E9 .6K 67
(not continuous)
Flandrian Cl. EN3: Enf L .1J 25
Flank St. E1 .7G 85
Flansham Ho. E14 .6B 86
(off Clemence St.)
Flask Wlk. NW3 .4A 64
Flatford Ho. SE6 .4E 140
Flather Cl. SW16 .5G 137
Flat Iron Sq. SE1 .5D 14
(off Union St.)
Flatiron Yd. SE1 .5D 14
(off Union St.)
Flavell M. SE10 .5G 105
Flaxen Cl. E4 .3J 35
Flaxen Rd. E4 .3J 35
Flaxley Ho. SW1 .5F 101
(off Abbots Mnr.)
Flaxley Rd. SM4: Mord .7K 153
Flaxman Ct. DA17: Belv .5G 109
(off Hoddesdon Rd.)
W1 .1C 12
WC1 .2D 6
(off Flaxman Ter.)
Flaxman Ho. SE1 .3B 102
(off London Rd.)
W4 .5A 98
(off Devonshire St.)
Flaxman Rd. SE5 .3B 120
Flaxman Sports Cen. .2C 120
Flaxman Ter. WC1 .2D 6 (3H 83)
Flaxton Rd. SE18 .1H 125
Flecker Cl. HA7: Stan .5E 26

Flecker Ho. SE5 . . . . 7D 102
(off Lomond Gro.)
Fleece Dr. N9 . . . . 4B 34
Fleece Rd. KT6: Surb 1C 162
Fleece Wlk. N7 . . . . 6J 65
Fleeming Cl. E17 . . . . 2B 50
Fleeming Rd. E17 . . . . 2B 50
Fleetbank Ho. EC4 . . . . 1K 13
(off Salisbury Sq.)
Fleet Bldg. EC4 . . . . 7A 8
Fleet Cl. HA4: Ruis 6E 38
KT8: W Mole 5D 148
Fleetfield WC1 . . . . 1F 7
(off Birkenhead St.)
Fleet Ho. E14 . . . . 7A 86
(off Victory Pl.)
Fleet La. KT8: W Mole 6D 148
Fleet Pl. EC4 . . . . 7A 8 (6B 84)
(not continuous)
Fleet Rd. NW3 . . . . 5C 64
Fleetside KT8: W Mole 5D 148
Fleet Sq. WC1 . . . . 2H 7 (3K 83)
Fleet St. EC4 . . . . 1J 13 (6A 84)
Fleet St. Hill E1 . . . . 4G 85
Fleetway WC1 . . . . 1F 7
(off Birkenhead St.)
Fleetway W. Bus. Pk. UB6: G'frd 2B 78
Fleetwood Cl. CR0: C'don 3F 169
E16 . . . . 5B 88
KT9: Chess 7D 162
Fleetwood Ct. E6 . . . . 5D 88
(off Evelyn Dennington Rd.)
TW19: Stanw 6A 110
(off Douglas Rd.)
Fleetwood Rd. KT1: King T 3H 151
NW10 . . . . 5C 62
Fleetwood Sq. KT1: King T 3H 151
Fleetwood St. N16 . . . . 2E 66
Fleming N8 . . . . 3J 47
(off Boyton Cl.)
Fleming Cl. W9 . . . . 4J 81
Fleming Ct. CR0: Wadd 5A 168
W2 . . . . 5A 4
Fleming Dr. N21 . . . . 5E 22
Fleming Ho. HA9: Wemb 3J 61
(off Barnhill Rd.)
N4 . . . . 1C 66
SE16 . . . . 2G 103
(off George Row)
Fleming Lodge W9 . . . . 5J 81
(off Admiral Wlk.)
Fleming Mead CR4: Mitc 7C 136
Fleming Rd. SE17 . . . . 6B 102
UB1: S'hall 6F 77
Fleming Wlk. NW9 . . . . 3A 44
Fleming Way SE28 . . . . 7D 90
TW7: Isle 4K 113
Flemming Av. HA4: Ruis 1K 57
Flemming Cl. SW10 . . . . 7A 16
(off Park Wlk.)
Flempton Rd. E10 . . . . 1A 68
Fletcher Bldgs. WC2 . . . . 1F 13
(off Martlett Ct.)
Fletcher Cl. E6 . . . . 6F 89
Fletcher Ho. SE15 . . . . 7J 103
(off Clifton Way)
Fletcher La. E10 . . . . 7E 50
Fletcher Path SE8 . . . . 7C 104
Fletcher Rd. W4 . . . . 3J 97
Fletchers Cl. BR2: Brom 4K 159
Fletcher St. E1 . . . . 7G 85
Fletching Rd. E5 . . . . 3J 67
SE7 . . . . 6A 106
Fletton Rd. N11 . . . . 7D 32
Fleur-de-Lis St. E1 . . . . 4H 9 (4F 85)
Fleur Gates SW19 . . . . 7F 117
Flexmere Gdns. N17 . . . . 1D 48
Flexmere Rd. N17 . . . . 1D 48
Flight App. NW9 . . . . 2B 44
Flimwell Cl. BR1: Brom 5G 141
Flinders Ho. E1 . . . . 1H 103
(off Green Bank)
Flint Cl. BR6: Chels 6K 173
CR0: C'don 6K 155
E15 . . . . 7H 69
Flintlock Cl.
TW19: Stan M 7B 174
Flintmill Cres. SE3 . . . . 2C 124
(not continuous)
Flinton St. SE17 . . . . 5E 102
Flint St. SE17 . . . . 4D 102
Flitcroft St. WC2 . . . . 1D 12 (6H 83)
Flitton Ho. N1 . . . . 7B 66
(off The Sutton Est.)
Floathaven Cl. SE28 . . . . 1A 108
Flock Mill Pl. SW18 . . . . 1K 135
Flockton St. SE16 . . . . 2G 103
Flodden Rd. SE5 . . . . 1C 120
Flood La. TW1: Twick 1A 132
Flood Pas. SE18 . . . . 3C 106
Flood St. SW3 . . . . 6D 16 (5C 100)
Flood Wlk. SW3 . . . . 7D 16 (6C 100)
Flora Cl. E14 . . . . 6D 86
HA7: Stan 3K 27
Flora Gdns. RM6: Chad H 6C 54
W6 . . . . 4D 98
(off Albion Gdns.)
Floral Pl. N1 . . . . 5D 66
Floral St. WC2 . . . . 2E 12 (7J 83)
Flora St. DA17: Belv 5F 109
Florence Av. EN2: Enf 3H 23
SM4: Mord 5A 154
Florence Cantwell Wlk.
N19 . . . . 7J 47
(off Jessie Blythe La.)
Florence Cl. KT12: Walt T 7K 147
Florence Ct. E11 . . . . 4K 51
N1 . . . . 7B 66
(off Florence St.)
SW19 . . . . 6G 135
W9 . . . . 3A 82
(off Maida Va.)
Florence Dr. EN2: Enf 3H 23
Florence Elson Cl. E12 . . . . 4E 70
Florence Gdns. RM6: Chad H 7C 54
W4 . . . . 6J 97
Florence Ho. KT2: King T 7F 133
(off Florence Rd)
SE16 . . . . 5H 103
(off Rotherhithe New Rd.)
W11 . . . . 7F 81
(off St Ann's Rd.)
Florence Mans. NW4 . . . . 5D 44
(off Vivian Av.)
Florence Nightingale Mus. 7G 13 (2K 101)
Florence Rd. BR1: Brom 1J 159
BR3: Beck 2A 158
CR2: Sande 7D 168
E6 . . . . 1A 88
E13 . . . . 2J 87
KT2: King T 7F 133
KT12: Walt T 7K 147
N4 . . . . 7K 47
(not continuous)
SE2 . . . . 4C 108
SE14 . . . . 1B 122
SW19 . . . . 6K 135
TW13: Felt 1K 129
UB2: S'hall 4B 94
W4 . . . . 3K 97
W5 . . . . 7E 78
Florence Root Ho. IG4: Ilf 5C 52
Florence St. E16 . . . . 4H 87
N1 . . . . 7B 66
NW4 . . . . 4E 44
Florence Ter. SE14 . . . . 1B 122
SW15 . . . . 3A 134
Florence Way SW12 . . . . 1D 136
Flores Ho. E1 . . . . 5K 85
(off Shandy St.)
Florey Lodge W9 . . . . 5J 81
(off Admiral Wlk.)
Florey Sq. N21 . . . . 5E 22
Florfield Pas. E8 . . . . 6H 67
(off Florfield Rd.)
Florfield Rd. E8 . . . . 6H 67
Florian SE5 . . . . 1E 120
Florian Av. SM1: Sutt 4B 166
Florian Rd. SW15 . . . . 4G 117
Florida Cl. WD23: B Hea 2C 26
Florida Ct. BR2: Brom 4H 159
(off Westmoreland Rd.)
Florida Rd. CR7: Thor H 1B 156
Florida St. E2 . . . . 3G 85
Florin Ct. EC1 . . . . 5C 8
N18 . . . . 4K 33
SE1 . . . . 7J 15
(off Tanner St.)
Floris Pl. SW4 . . . . 3G 119
Floriston Av. UB10: Hil 7E 56
Floriston Cl. HA7: Stan 1B 42
Floriston Ct. UB5: N'olt 5F 59
Floriston Gdns. HA7: Stan 1B 42
Florys Ct. SW19 . . . . 1G 135
Floss St. SW15 . . . . 2E 116
Flower & Dean Wlk.
E1 . . . . 6K 9 (5F 85)
Flower La. NW7 . . . . 5G 29
Flower M. NW11 . . . . 6G 45
Flowerpot Cl. N15 . . . . 6F 49
Flowers Cl. NW2 . . . . 3C 62
Flowersmead SW17 . . . . 2E 136
Flowers M. N19 . . . . 2G 65
Flower Wlk., The SW7 . . . . 6A 10 (2A 100)
Floyd Rd. SE7 . . . . 5A 106
Floyer Cl. TW10: Rich 5F 115
Fludyer St. SE13 . . . . 4G 123
Flynn Ct. E14 . . . . 7C 86
(off Garford St.)
Foley Ho. E1 . . . . 6J 85
(off Tarling St.)
Foley St. W1 . . . . 6A 6 (5G 83)
Folgate St. E1 . . . . 5H 9 (5E 84)
(not continuous)
Foliot Ho. N1 . . . . 2K 83
(off Priory Grn. Est.)
Foliot St. W12 . . . . 6B 80
Folkestone Ct. UB5: N'olt 5F 59
(off Newmarket Av.)
Folkestone Rd. E6 . . . . 2E 88
E17 . . . . 4D 50
N18 . . . . 4B 34
Folkingham La. NW9 . . . . 1K 43
Folkington Cnr. N12 . . . . 5C 30
Folkstone Ho. SE17 . . . . 5E 102
(off Upnor Way)
Folland NW9 . . . . 2B 44
(off Hundred Acre)
Follett Ho. SW10 . . . . 7B 100
(off Worlds End Est.)
Follett St. E14 . . . . 6E 86
Follingham Ct. N1 . . . . 1H 9
(off Drysdale Pl.)
Folly La. E4 . . . . 6G 35
E17 . . . . 1A 50
Folly M. W11 . . . . 6H 81
Folly Wall E14 . . . . 2E 104
Fonda Ct. E14 . . . . 7C 86
(off Premiere Pl.)
Fontaine Rd. SW16 . . . . 7K 137
Fontarabia Rd. SW11 . . . . 4E 118
Fontayne Av.
RM1: Rom 2K 55
Fontenelle Gdns. SE5 . . . . 1E 120
Fontenoy Ho. SE11 . . . . 4B 102
(off Kennington La.)
Fontenoy Rd. SW12 . . . . 2F 137
Fonteyne Gdns.
IG8: Wfd G 2B 52
Fonthill Cl. SE20 . . . . 2G 157
Fonthill Ho. SW1 . . . . 5F 101
(off Sutherland St.)
W14 . . . . 3G 99
(off Russell Rd.)
Fonthill M. N4 . . . . 2K 65
Fonthill Rd. N4 . . . . 1K 65
Font Hills N2 . . . . 2A 46
Fontley Way SW15 . . . . 7C 116
Fontmell Cl. TW15: Ashf 5C 128
Fontmell Pk. TW15: Ashf 5B 128
(not continuous)
Fontwell Cl. HA3: Hrw W 7D 26
UB5: N'olt 6E 58
Fontwell Dr. BR2: Brom 5E 160
Football La. HA1: Harr 1K 59
Footpath, The SW15 . . . . 6C 116
FOOTS CRAY 6C 144
Foots Cray High St. DA14: Sidc 6C 144
Foots Cray La. DA14: Sidc 1C 144
Footscray Rd. SE9 . . . . 6E 124
Forber Ho. E2 . . . . 3J 85
(off Cornwall Av.)
Forbes Cl. NW2 . . . . 3C 62
Forbes Ho. W4 . . . . 5G 97
(off Stonehill Rd.)
Forbes St. E1 . . . . 6G 85
Forbes Way HA4: Ruis 2K 57
Forburg Rd. N16 . . . . 1G 67
Fordbridge Ct. TW15: Ashf 6A 128
Fordbridge Pk. TW16: Sun 6H 147
Fordbridge Rd. TW15: Ashf 6A 128
TW16: Sun 6G 147
TW17: Shep 6G 147
FORDBRIDGE RDBT. 6A 128
Ford Cl. CR7: Thor H 5B 156
E3 . . . . 2A 86
HA1: Harr 7H 41
TW15: Ashf 6A 128
TW17: Shep 4C 146
Forde Av. BR1: Brom 3A 160
Fordel Rd. SE6 . . . . 1E 140
Ford End IG8: Wfd G 6E 36
Fordgate Bus. Pk. DA17: Belv 2J 109
Fordham KT1: King T 2G 151
(off Excelsior Cl.)
Fordham Cl. EN4: Cockf 3H 21
KT4: Wor Pk 1D 164
Fordham Ho. SE14 . . . . 7A 104
(off Angus St.)
Fordham Rd. EN4: Cockf 3G 21
Fordham St. E1 . . . . 6G 85
Fordhook Av. W5 . . . . 1F 97
Ford Ho. EN5: New Bar 5E 20
Fordie Ho. SW1 . . . . 2F 17
(off Sloane St.)
Ford Ind. Pk. RM9: Dag 4H 91
Fordingley Rd. W9 . . . . 3H 81
Fordington Ho. SE26 . . . . 3G 139
Fordington Rd. N6 . . . . 5D 46
Fordmill Rd. SE6 . . . . 2C 140
Ford Rd. E3 . . . . 2B 86
RM9: Dag 7F 73
TW15: Ashf 4B 128
Fords Gro. N21 . . . . 1H 33
Fords Pk. Rd. E16 . . . . 5J 87
Ford Sq. E1 . . . . 5H 85
Ford St. E3 . . . . 1A 86
E16 . . . . 6H 87
Fordview Ind. Est. RM13: Rain 3K 91
Fordwich Cl. BR6: Orp 7K 161
Fordwych Rd. NW2 . . . . 4G 63
Fordyce Rd. SE13 . . . . 6E 122
Fordyke Rd. RM8: Dag 2F 73
Foreign St. SE5 . . . . 2B 120
Foreland Ct. NW4 . . . . 1F 45
Foreland Ho. W11 . . . . 7G 81
(off Walmer Rd.)
Foreland St. SE18 . . . . 4H 107
Foreman Ct. TW1: Twick 1K 131
Foreshore SE8 . . . . 4B 104

Forest, The E11 ... 4G **51**
Forest App. E4 ... 1B **36**
IG8: Wfd G ... 7D **36**
Forest Av. E4 ... 1B **36**
IG7: Chig ... 5K **37**
Forest Bus. Pk. E10 ... 7K **49**
Forest Cl. BR7: Chst ... 1E **160**
E11 ... 5J **51**
IG8: Wfd G ... 3E **36**
N10 ... 1F **47**
NW6 ... 7G **63**
Forest Ct. E4 ... 1C **36**
E11 ... 4G **51**
N12 ... 5E **30**
Forest Cft. SE23 ... 2H **139**
FORESTDALE ... **7B 170**
Forestdale N14 ... 4C **32**
Forestdale Cen., The CR0: Sels ... 7B **170**
Forest Dene Ct. SM2: Sutt ... 6A **166**
Forest Dr. BR2: Kes ... 4C **172**
E12 ... 3B **70**
IG8: Wfd G ... 7A **36**
TW16: Sun ... 7H **129**
Forest Dr. E. E11 ... 7F **51**
Forest Dr. W. E11 ... 7E **50**
Forest Edge IG9: Buck H ... 4F **37**
Forester Ho. *E14* ... *7A* ***86***
(off Victory Pl.)
Forester Rd. SE15 ... 3H **121**
Foresters Cl. SM6: Wall ... 7H **167**
Foresters Cres. DA7: Bex ... 4H **127**
Foresters Dr. E17 ... 4F **51**
SM6: Wall ... 7H **167**
Forest Gdns. N17 ... 2F **49**
FOREST GATE ... **5J 69**
Forest Ga. NW9 ... 4A **44**
Forest Ga. Retreat *E7* ... *5J* ***69***
(off Odessa Rd.)
Forest Glade E4 ... 4B **36**
E11 ... 6G **51**
Forest Gro. E8 ... 6F **67**
Forest Hgts. IG9: Buck H ... 2D **36**
FOREST HILL ... **2J 139**
Forest Hill Bus. Cen. *SE23* ... *2J* ***139***
(off Clyde Va.)
Forest Hill Ind. Est. SE23 ... 2J **139**
Forest Hill Pool ... 2J 139
Forest Hill Rd. SE22 ... 5H **121**
SE23 ... 5H **121**
Forestholme Cl. SE23 ... 2J **139**
Forest Ind. Pk. IG6: Ilf ... 1J **53**
Forest La. E7 ... 5G **69**
E15 ... 5G **69**
IG7: Chig ... 5K **37**
Forest Lodge *SE23* ... *3J* ***139***
(off Dartmouth Rd.)
Forest Mt. Rd. IG8: Wfd G ... 7A **36**
Forest Point *E7* ... *5K* ***69***
(off Windsor Rd.)
Fore St. EC2 ... 6D **8** (5C **84**)
HA5: Eastc ... 4H **39**
N9 ... 4B **34**
N18 ... 6A **34**
Fore St. Av. EC2 ... 6E **8** (5D **84**)
Forest Ridge BR2: Kes ... 4C **172**
BR3: Beck ... 3C **158**
Forest Ri. E17 ... 3F **51**
(not continuous)
Forest Rd. E7 ... 4J **69**
E8 ... 6F **67**
E11 ... 7F **51**
E17 ... 3D **50**
IG6: Chig, Ilf ... 2H **53**
IG8: Wfd G ... 3D **36**
N9 ... 1C **34**
N17 ... 4J **49**
RM7: Mawney ... 3H **55**
SM3: Sutt ... 1J **165**
TW9: Kew ... 7G **97**
TW13: Felt ... 2A **130**
Forest Side E4 ... 1C **36**
E7 ... 4K **69**
IG9: Buck H ... 1F **37**
KT4: Wor Pk ... 1B **164**
Forest St. E7 ... 5J **69**
Forest Ter. IG7: Chig ... 5K **37**
Forest Trad. Est. E17 ... 3K **49**
Forest Vw. E4 ... 7K **25** & 1B **36**
E11 ... 7H **51**
Forest Vw. Av. E10 ... 5F **51**
Forest Vw. Rd. E12 ... 4C **70**
E17 ... 1E **50**
Forest Wlk. N10 ... 1F **47**
Forest Way BR5: St M Cry ... 5K **161**
DA15: Sidc ... 7H **125**
IG8: Wfd G ... 4E **36**
N19 ... 2G **65**
Forest Works Ind. Est. E17 ... 3K **49**
Forfar Rd. N22 ... 1B **48**
SW11 ... 1E **118**
Forge, The UB3: Harl ... 6F **93**
Forge Cl. BR2: Hayes ... 1J **171**
Forge Cotts. W5 ... 1D **96**
Forge Dr. KT10: Clay ... 7A **162**
Forge La. HA6: Nwood ... 1G **39**
SM3: Cheam ... 7G **165**
TW10: Ham ... 1E **132**
TW13: Hanw ... 5C **130**
TW16: Sun ... 3J **147**
Forge M. CR0: Addtn ... 5C **170**
Forge Pl. NW1 ... 6E **64**
Forges Rd. E12 ... 2B **70**
Forman Pl. N16 ... 4F **67**
Formation, The *E16* ... *2F* ***107***
(off Woolwich Mnr. Way)
Formby Av. HA7: Stan ... 3C **42**
Formby Ct. *N7* ... *5A* ***66***
(off Morgan Rd.)
Formosa Ho. *E1* ... *4A* ***86***
(off Ernest St.)
Formosa St. W9 ... 4K **81**
Formunt Cl. E16 ... 5H **87**
Forres Gdns. NW11 ... 6J **45**
Forrester Path SE26 ... 4J **139**
Forrest Gdns. SW16 ... 3K **155**
Forris Av. UB3: Hayes ... 1H **93**
Forset Ct. *W2* ... *7D* ***4***
(off Edgware Rd.)
Forset St. W1 ... 7D **4** (6C **82**)
(not continuous)
Forstal Cl. BR2: Brom ... 3J **159**
Forster Cl. IG8 ... 7A **36**
Forster Ho. BR1: Brom ... 4F **141**
Forster Rd. BR3: Beck ... 3A **158**
E17 ... 6A **50**
N17 ... 3F **49**
SW2 ... 7J **119**
Forsters Cl. RM6: Chad H ... 6F **55**
Forsters Way UB4: Yead ... 6K **75**
Forston St. N1 ... 2C **84**
Forsyte Cres. SE19 ... 1E **156**
Forsyte Ho. SW3 ... 6D **16**
Forsythe Shades Ct. BR3: Beck ... 1E **158**
Forsyth Gdns. SE17 ... 6B **102**
Forsyth Ho. *E9* ... *7J* ***67***
(off Frampton Pk. Rd.)
SW1 ... *5B* ***18***
(off Tachbrook St.)
Forsythia Cl. IG1: Ilf ... 5F **71**
Forsyth Pl. EN1: Enf ... 5K **23**
Forterie Gdns. IG3: Bark, Ilf ... 3A **72**
Fortescue Av. E8 ... 7H **67**
TW2: Twick ... 3G **131**
Fortescue Rd. HA8: Edg ... 1K **43**
SW19 ... 7B **136**
Fortess Gro. NW5 ... 5G **65**
Fortess Rd. NW5 ... 5F **65**
Fortess Wlk. NW5 ... 5F **65**
Fortess Yd. NW5 ... 4F **65**
Forthbridge Rd. SW11 ... 4E **118**
Fortis Cl. E16 ... 6A **88**
Fortis Ct. N10 ... 3E **46**
FORTIS GREEN ... **4D 46**
Fortis Grn. N2 ... 4C **46**
N10 ... 4C **46**
Fortis Grn. Av. N2 ... 3D **46**
Fortis Grn. Rd. N10 ... 3E **46**
Fortismere Av. N10 ... 3E **46**
Fortnam Rd. N19 ... 2H **65**
Fortnum's Acre HA7: Stan ... 6E **26**
Fort Rd. SE1 ... 4F **103**
UB5: N'olt ... 7E **58**
Fortrose Cl. E14 ... 6F **87**
Fortrose Gdns. SW2 ... 1J **137**
Fort St. E1 ... 6H **9** (5E **84**)
E16 ... 1K **105**
Fortuna Cl. N7 ... 6K **65**
Fortune Ct. *E8* ... *7F* ***67***
(off Queensbridge Rd.)
IG11: Bark ... 2C **90**
Fortunegate Rd. NW10 ... 1A **80**
FORTUNE GREEN ... **5J 63**
Fortune Grn. Rd. NW6 ... 4J **63**
Fortune Ho. *EC1* ... *4D* ***8***
(off Fortune St.)
SE11 ... 4J **19**
Fortune Pl. SE1 ... 5F **103**
Fortunes Mead UB5: N'olt ... 6C **58**
Fortune St. EC1 ... 4D **8** (4C **84**)
Fortune Theatre ... *1F 13*
(off Russell St.)
Fortune Wlk. *SE28* ... *3H* ***107***
(off Broadwater Rd.)
Fortune Way NW10 ... 3C **80**
Forty Acre La. E16 ... 5J **87**
Forty Av. HA9: Wemb ... 3F **61**
Forty Cl. HA9: Wemb ... 3F **61**
Forty Footpath SW14 ... 3J **115**
Forty Foot Way SE9 ... 7G **125**
FORTY HILL ... **1A 24**
Forty Hill EN2: Enf ... 1K **23**
Forty La. HA9: Wemb ... 2H **61**
Forum, The KT8: W Mole ... 4F **149**
Forum Cl. E3 ... 1C **86**
Forum Magnum Sq. *SE1* ... *6H* ***13***
(off York Rd.)
Forumside HA8: Edg ... 6B **28**
Forum Way HA8: Edg ... 6B **28**
Forval Cl. CR4: Mitc ... 5D **154**
Forward Bus. Cen., The E16 ... 4F **87**
Forward Dr. HA3: W'stone ... 4K **41**
Fosbrooke Ho. *SW8* ... *7J* ***101***
(off Davidson Gdns.)
Fosbury M. W2 ... 7K **81**
Foscote Ct. *W9* ... *4J* ***81***
(off Foscote M.)
Foscote M. W9 ... 4J **81**
Foscote Rd. NW4 ... 6D **44**
Foskett Ho. *N2* ... *2B* ***46***
(off The Grange)
Foskett Rd. SW6 ... 2H **117**
Foss Av. CR0: Wadd ... 5A **168**
Fossdene Rd. SE7 ... 5K **105**
Fossdyke Cl. UB4: Yead ... 5C **76**
Fosset Lodge DA7: Bex ... 1J **127**
Fosse Way W13 ... 5A **78**
Foss Ho. *NW8* ... *2K* ***81***
(off Carlton Hill)
Fossil Ct. *SE1* ... *7G* ***15***
(off Long La.)
Fossil Rd. SE13 ... 3C **122**
Fossington Rd.
DA17: Belv ... 4D **108**
Foss Rd. SW17 ... 4B **136**
Fossway RM8: Dag ... 2C **72**
Foster Ct. *E16* ... *7H* ***87***
(off Tarling Rd.)
NW1 ... *7G* ***65***
(off Royal College St.)
NW4 ... 4E **44**
Foster Ho. SE14 ... 1B **122**
Foster La. EC2 ... 7C **8** (6C **84**)
Foster Rd. E13 ... 4J **87**
W3 ... 7A **80**
W4 ... 5K **97**
Fosters Cl. BR7: Chst ... 5D **142**
E18 ... 1K **51**
Foster St. NW4 ... 4E **44**
Foster's Way SW18 ... 1K **135**
Foster Wlk. NW4 ... 4E **44**
Fothergill Cl. E13 ... 2J **87**
Fothergill Dr. N21 ... 5D **22**
Fotheringham Rd. EN1: Enf ... 4A **24**
(not continuous)
Foubert's Pl. W1 ... 1A **12** (6G **83**)
Foulden Rd. N16 ... 4F **67**
Foulden Ter. N16 ... 4F **67**
Foulis Ter. SW7 ... 5B **16** (5B **100**)
Foulser Rd. SW17 ... 3D **136**
Foulsham Rd. CR7: Thor H ... 3C **156**
Founder Cl. E6 ... 6F **89**
Founders Cl. UB5: N'olt ... 3D **76**
Founders Ct. EC2 ... 7E **8**
Founders Gdns. SE19 ... 7C **138**
Founders Ho. *SW1* ... *6C* ***18***
(off Aylesford St.)
Foundling Ct. *WC1* ... *3E* ***6***
(off Brunswick Cen.)
Foundling Mus., The ... 3F 7
Foundry Cl. SE16 ... 1A **104**
Foundry Ho. *E14* ... *5D* ***86***
(off Morris Rd.)
Foundry M. NW1 ... 3B **6**
TW3: Houn ... 4F **113**
Foundry Pl. *E1* ... *5J* ***85***
(off Redman's Rd.)
SW18 ... 7K **117**
Fountain Cl. UB8: Hil ... 5E **74**
Fountain Ct. DA15: Sidc ... 6B **126**
EC4 ... 2J **13** (7A **84**)
SE23 ... 2K **139**
SW1 ... *4J* ***17***
(off Buckingham Pal. Rd.)
W11 ... *2F* ***99***
(off Clearwater Ter.)
Fountain Dr. SE19 ... 4F **139**
SM5: Cars ... 7D **166**
Fountain Grn. Sq. SE16 ... 2G **103**
Fountain Ho. CR4: Mitc ... 2D **154**
NW6 ... 7G **63**
SE16 ... *2G* ***103***
(off Bermondsey Wall E.)
SW6 ... 2A **118**
W1 ... *4G* ***11***
(off Park St.)
Fountain M. *N5* ... *4C* ***66***
(off Highbury Grange)
NW3 ... 6D **64**
Fountain Pl. SW9 ... 1A **120**
Fountain Rd. CR7: Thor H ... 3C **156**
SW17 ... 5B **136**
Fountain Rdbt. KT3: N Mald ... 4A **152**
Fountains, The *N3* ... *7E* ***30***
(off Ballards La.)
Fountains Av. TW13: Hanw ... 3D **130**
Fountains Cl. TW13: Hanw ... 2D **130**
(not continuous)
Fountains Cres. N14 ... 7D **22**
Fountain Sq. SW1 ... 3K **17** (4F **101**)
Fountayne Bus. Cen. N15 ... 4G **49**
Fountayne Rd. N15 ... 4G **49**
N16 ... 2G **67**
Fount St. SW8 ... 7H **101**
Four Acres N12 ... 3E **30**
Fouracres EN3: Enf H ... 1F **25**
Fourland Wlk. HA8: Edg ... 6D **28**
Fournier St. E1 ... 5J **9** (5F **85**)
Fourscore Mans. *E8* ... *7G* ***67***
(off Shrubland Rd.)
Four Seasons Cl. E3 ... 2C **86**

Four Seasons Cres. SM3: Sutt 2H 165
Four Sq. Ct. TW3: Houn 6E 112
Fourth Av. E12 4D 70
RM7: Rush G 1K 73
UB3: Hayes 1H 93
W10 4G 81
Fourth Cross Rd. TW2: Twick 2H 131
Fourth Way HA9: Wemb 4H 61
Four Wents, The E4 1A 36
Fovant Ct. SW8 2G 119
Fowey Av. IG4: Ilf 5B 52
Fowey Cl. E1 1H 103
Fowey Ho. SE11 5K 19
Fowler Cl. SW11 3B 118
Fowler Ho. *N15* *5D 48*
(off South Gro.)
Fowler Rd. CR4: Mitc 2E 154
E7 4J 69
N1 1B 84
Fowlers Cl. DA14: Sidc 5E 144
Fowlers M. *N19* *2G 65*
(off Holloway Rd.)
Fowler's Wlk. W5 4D 78
Fownes St. SW11 3C 118
Fox & Knot St. EC1 5B 8
Foxberry Rd. SE4 3A 122
Foxborough Gdns. SE4 5C 122
Foxbourne Rd. SW17 2E 136
Foxbury Av. BR7: Chst 6H 143
Foxbury Cl. BR1: Brom 6K 141
Foxbury Rd. BR1: Brom 6J 141
Fox Cl. BR6: Chels 5K 173
E1 4J 85
E16 5J 87
Foxcombe CR0: New Ad 6D 170
(not continuous)
Foxcombe Cl. E6 2B 88
Foxcombe Rd. SW15 1C 134
Foxcote SE5 5E 102
Foxcroft *WC1* *1H 7*
(off Penton Ri.)
Foxcroft Rd. SE18 1F 125
Foxearth Spur CR2: Sels 7J 169
Foxes Dale BR2: Brom 3F 159
SE3 3J 123
Foxfield *NW1* *1F 83*
(off Arlington Rd.)
Foxfield Rd. BR6: Orp 2H 173
Foxglove Cl. DA15: Sidc 6A 126
N9 1D 34
UB1: S'hall 7C 76
Foxglove Ct. HA0: Wemb 2E 78
Foxglove Gdns. E11 4A 52
Foxglove La. KT9: Chess 4G 163
Foxglove Path *SE28* *1J 107*
(off Martins Pl.)
Foxglove Rd. RM7: Rush G 2K 73
Foxglove St. W12 7B 80
Foxglove Way SM6: Wall 1F 167
Fox Gro. KT12: Walt T 7K 147
Foxgrove N14 3D 32
Foxgrove Av. BR3: Beck 7D 140
Foxgrove Rd. BR3: Beck 7D 140
Foxham Rd. N19 3H 65
Fox Hill BR2: Kes 5A 172
SE19 7F 139
Fox Hill Gdns. SE19 7F 139
Foxhole Rd. SE9 5C 124
Fox Hollow Cl. SE18 5J 107
Fox Hollow Dr. DA7: Bex 3D 126
Foxholt Gdns. NW10 7J 61
Foxhome Cl. BR7: Chst 6E 142
Fox Ho. Rd. DA17: Belv 5H 109
(not continuous)
Foxlands Cres. RM10: Dag 5J 73
Foxlands La. RM10: Dag 5K 73
Foxlands Rd. RM10: Dag 5J 73
Fox La. BR2: Kes 5K 171
N13 2E 32
W5 4E 78
Foxleas Ct. BR1: Brom 7G 141
Foxlees HA0: Wemb 4A 60
Foxley Cl. E8 5G 67
Foxley Ct. SM2: Sutt 7A 166
Foxley Rd. CR7: Thor H 4B 156
SW9 7A 102
Foxley Sq. SW9 1B 120
Foxmead Cl. EN2: Enf 3E 22
Foxmore St. SW11 1D 118
Fox Rd. E16 5H 87
Fox's Path CR4: Mitc 2C 154
Fox's Yd. *E2* *4F 85*
(off Rhoda St.)
Foxton Gro. CR4: Mitc 2B 154
Foxton Ho. *E16* *2E 106*
(off Albert Rd.)
Foxwarren KT10: Clay 7A 162
Foxwell M. SE4 3A 122
Foxwell St. SE4 3A 122
Foxwood Cl. NW7 4F 29
TW13: Felt 3K 129
Foxwood Grn. Cl. EN1: Enf 6K 23
Foxwood Rd. SE3 4H 123
Foyle Rd. N17 1G 49
SE3 6H 105
Framfield Cl. N12 3D 30
Framfield Ct. *EN1: Enf* *6K 23*
(off Queen Annes Gdns.)
Framfield Rd. CR4: Mitc 7E 136
N5 5B 66
W7 6J 77
Framlingham Cl. E5 2J 67
Framlingham Ct. *RM6: Chad H* *5B 54*
(off Norwich Cres.)
Framlingham Cres. SE9 4C 142
Frampton *NW1* *7H 65*
(off Wrotham Rd.)
Frampton Cl. SM2: Sutt 7J 165
Frampton Ct. *W3* *2J 97*
(off Avenue Rd.)
Frampton Ho. *NW8* *4B 4*
(off Frampton St.)
Frampton Pk. Est. E9 7J 67
Frampton Pk. Rd. E9 6J 67
Frampton Rd. TW4: Houn 5C 112
Frampton St. NW8 4B 4 (4B 82)
Francemary Rd. SE4 5C 122
Frances Ct. E17 6C 50
SE25 3G 157
Frances Rd. E4 6H 35
Frances St. SE18 3D 106
Franche Ct. Rd. SW17 3A 136
Francis & Dick James Ct. NW7 7B 30
Francis Av. DA7: Bex 2G 127
IG1: Ilf 2H 71
TW13: Felt 3J 129
Francis Barber Cl. SW16 5K 137
Francis Bentley M. SW4 3G 119
Franciscan Rd. SW17 5D 136
Francis Chichester Way
SW11 1E 118
Francis Cl. E14 4F 105
KT19: Ewe 4K 163
TW17: Shep 4C 146
Francis Ct. DA8: Erith 5K 109
EC1 5A 8
KT5: Surb *4E 150*
(off Cranes Pk. Av.)
NW7 *5G 29*
(off Watford Way)
SE14 *6K 103*
(off Myers La.)
Francis Gro. SW19 6H 135
(not continuous)
Francis Ho. E17 6B 50
N1 *1E 84*
(off Colville Est.)
SW10 *7K 99*
(off Coleridge Gdns.)
Francis M. SE12 7J 123
Francis Rd. CR0: C'don 7B 156
E10 1E 68
HA1: Harr 5A 42
HA5: Eastc 5A 40
IG1: Ilf 2H 71
N2 4D 46
SM6: Wall 6G 167
TW4: Houn 2B 112
UB6: G'frd 2B 78
Francis St. E15 5G 69
IG1: Ilf 2H 71
SW1 3A 18 (4G 101)
Francis Ter. N19 3G 65
Francis Wlk. N1 1K 83
Francklyn Gdns. HA8: Edg 3B 28
Franconia Rd. SW4 5H 119
Frank Bailey Wlk. E12 5E 70
Frank Beswick Ho. *SW6* *6H 99*
(off Clem Attlee Ct.)
Frank Burton Cl. SE7 5K 105
Frank Dixon Cl. SE21 7E 120
Frank Dixon Way SE21 1E 138
Frankfurt Rd. SE24 5C 120
Frank Godley Ct. DA14: Sidc 5B 144
Frankham Ho. *SE8* *7C 104*
(off Frankham St.)
Frankham St. SE8 7C 104
Frank Ho. *SW8* *7J 101*
(off Wyvil Rd.)
Frankland Cl. IG8: Wfd G 5F 37
SE16 3H 103
Frankland Rd. E4 5H 35
SW7 2A 16 (3B 100)
Franklin Bldg. E14 2C 104
Franklin Cl. KT1: King T 3G 151
N20 7F 21
SE13 1D 122
SE27 3B 138
Franklin Cotts. HA7: Stan 4G 27
Franklin Cres. CR4: Mitc 4G 155
Franklin Ho. BR2: Brom 3G 159
E1 *1H 103*
(off Watts St.)
E14 *6F 87*
(off E. India Dock Rd.)
NW9 6B 44
Franklin Ind. Est. *SE20* *1J 157*
(off Franklin Rd.)
Franklin Pas. SE9 3C 124
Franklin Pl. SE13 1D 122
Franklin Rd. DA7: Bex 1E 126
SE20 7J 139
Franklins M. HA2: Harr 2G 59
Franklin Sq. W14 5H 99
Franklin's Row SW3 5F 17 (5D 100)
Franklin St. E3 3D 86
N15 6E 48
Franklin Way CR0: Wadd 7J 155
Franklyn Rd. KT12: Walt T 6J 147
NW10 6B 62
Franks Av. KT3: N Mald 4J 151
Frank Soskice Ho. *SW6* *6H 99*
(off Clem Attlee Ct.)
Frank St. E13 4J 87
Franks Wood Av. BR5: Pet W 5F 161
Frankswood Av. UB7: Yiew 6B 74
Frank Towell Ct. TW14: Felt 7J 111
Frank Welsh Ct. HA5: Eastc 4A 40
Frank Whymark Ho. *SE16* *2J 103*
(off Rupack St.)
Franlaw Cres. N13 4H 33
Fransfield Gro. SE26 3H 139
Frans Hals Ct. E14 3F 105
Franshams *WD23: B Hea* *2D 26*
(off Hartsbourne Rd.)
Frant Cl. SE20 7J 139
Franthorne Way SE6 2D 140
Frant Rd. CR7: Thor H 5B 156
Fraser Cl. DA5: Bexl 1J 145
E6 6C 88
Fraser Ct. *E14* *5E 104*
(off Ferry St.)
SE1 7D 14
SW11 *1C 118*
(off Surrey La. Est.)
Fraser Ho. TW8: Bford 5F 97
Fraser Rd. DA8: Erith 5K 109
E17 5D 50
N9 3C 34
UB6: G'frd 1B 78
Fraser St. W4 5A 98
Frating Cres. IG8: Wfd G 6E 36
Frazer Av. HA4: Ruis 5A 58
Frazier St. SE1 7J 13 (2A 102)
Frean St. SE16 3G 103
Frearson Ho. *WC1* *1H 7*
(off Penton Ri.)
Freda Corbet Cl. SE15 7G 103
Frederica Rd. E4 1A 36
Frederica St. N7 7K 65
Frederick Charrington Ho. *E1* *4J 85*
(off Wickford St.)
Frederick Cl. SM1: Sutt 4H 165
W2 2D 10 (7D 82)
Frederick Ct. *SW3* *4F 17*
(off Duke of York Sq.)
Frederick Cres. EN3: Enf H 2D 24
SW9 7B 102
Frederick Dobson Ho. *W11* *7G 81*
(off Cowling Cl.)
Frederick Gdns. CR0: C'don 6B 156
SM1: Sutt 5H 165
Frederick Ho. *SE18* *4C 106*
(off Pett St.)
Frederick Pl. SE18 5F 107
Frederick Rd. RM13: Rain 2K 91
SE17 6B 102
SM1: Sutt 5H 165
Fredericks Pl. EC2 1E 14 (6D 84)
N12 4F 31
Frederick Sq. *SE16* *7A 86*
(off Sovereign Cres.)
Frederick's Row EC1 1A 8 (3B 84)
Frederick St. WC1 2G 7 (3K 83)
Frederick Ter. E8 7F 67
Frederick Vs. *W7* *1J 95*
(off Lwr. Boston Rd.)
Frederic M. SW1 7F 11
Frederic St. E17 5A 50
Fredora Av. UB4: Hayes 4H 75
Fred Styles Ho. SE7 6A 106
Fred Tibble Ct. RM9: Dag 4E 72
Fred White Wlk. N7 6J 65
Freedom Cl. E17 4A 50
Freedom Rd. N17 2D 48
Freedom St. SW11 2D 118
Freegrove Rd. N7 5J 65
(not continuous)
Freeland Ct. DA15: Sidc 3A 144
Freeland Pk. NW4 2G 45
Freeland Rd. W5 7F 79
Freelands Av. CR2: Sels 7K 169
Freelands Gro. BR1: Brom 1K 159
Freelands Rd. BR1: Brom 1K 159
Freeling Ho. *NW8* *1B 82*
(off Dorman Way)
Freeling St. N1 7K 65
(Carnoustie Dr.)
N1 7J 65
(Pembroke St.)
Freeman Cl. TW17: Shep 4G 147
UB5: N'olt 7C 58
Freeman Ct. SW16 2J 155
Freeman Dr. KT8: W Mole 3D 148
Freeman Rd. SM4: Mord 5B 154
Freemans La. UB3: Hayes 7G 75
Freemantle Av. EN3: Pond E 5E 24
Freemantle St. SE17 5E 102
Freemasons Pl. *CR0: C'don* *1E 168*
(off Freemasons Rd.)

Freemasons Rd. CR0: C'don 1E 168
E16 5K 87
Freesia Cl. BR6: Chels 5K 173
Freethorpe Cl. SE19 7D 138
Free Trade Wharf E1 7K 85
Freezeland Way UB10: Hil 6D 56
Freke Rd. SW11 3E 118
Fremantle Ho. *E1* 4H 85
(off Somerford St.)
Fremantle Rd. DA17: Belv 4G 109
IG6: Ilf 2F 53
Fremont St. E9 1H 85
(not continuous)
French Horn Yd. WC1 6G 7
French Ordinary Ct. EC3 2H 15
French Pl. E1 2H 9 (3E 84)
French St. TW16: Sun 2A 148
Frendsbury Rd. SE4 4A 122
Frensham Cl. UB1: S'hall 4D 76
Frensham Ct. SW19 3B 154
Frensham Dr. CR0: New Ad 7E 170
SW15 3B 134
(not continuous)
Frensham Rd. SE9 2H 143
Frensham St. SE15 6G 103
Frere St. SW11 2C 118
Fresham Ho. *BR2: Brom* 3H 159
(off Durham Rd.)
Freshfield Av. E8 7F 67
Freshfield Cl. SE13 4F 123
Freshfield Dr. N14 7A 22
Freshfields CR0: C'don 1B 170
Freshford St. SW18 3A 136
Freshill La. UB1: S'hall 4E 76
Freshwater Cl. SW17 6E 136
Freshwater Ct. UB1: S'hall 3E 76
W1 6D 4
(off Crawford St.)
Freshwater Rd. RM8: Dag 1D 72
SW17 6E 136
Freshwell Av. RM6: Chad H 4C 54
Fresh Wharf Est. IG11: Bark 2F 89
Fresh Wharf Rd. IG11: Bark 1F 89
Freshwood Cl. BR3: Beck 1D 158
Freshwood Way SM6: Wall 7F 167
Freston Gdns. EN4: Cockf 5K 21
Freston Pk. N3 2H 45
Freston Rd. W10 7F 81
W11 7F 81
Freswick Ho. *SE8* 4K 103
(off Chilton Gro.)
Freta Rd. DA6: Bex 5F 127
Freud Mus., The 6B 64
Frewell Ho. *EC1* 5J 7
(off Bourne Est.)
Frewing Cl. BR7: Chst 6D 142
Frewin Rd. SW18 1B 136
Friar M. SE27 3B 138
Friar Rd. BR5: St M Cry 5K 161
UB4: Yead 4B 76
Friars Av. N20 3H 31
SW15 3B 134
Friars Cl. E4 3K 35
IG1: Ilf 1H 71
SE1 5B 14
UB5: Yead 3B 76
Friars Ct. E17 1B 50
SM6: Wall 4F 167
Friars Gdns. W3 6K 79
Friars Ga. Cl. IG8: Wfd G 4D 36
Friars La. TW9: Rich 5D 114
Friars Mead E14 3E 104
Friars M. SE9 5E 124
Friars Pl. La. W3 7K 79
Friars Rd. E6 1B 88
Friars Stile Pl. TW10: Rich 6E 114
Friars Stile Rd. TW10: Rich 6E 114
Friar St. EC4 1B 14 (6B 84)
Friars Wlk. N14 7A 22
SE2 5D 108

Friars Way W3 6K 79
Friars Wood CR0: Sels 7A 170
Friary Cl. N12 5H 31
Friary Ct. SW1 5B 12
Friary Est. SE15 6G 103
(not continuous)
Friary La. IG8: Wfd G 4D 36
Friary Pk. Ct. W3 6J 79
Friary Rd. N12 4G 31
SE15 7G 103
W3 6J 79
Friary Way N12 4H 31
FRIDAY HILL 2B 36
Friday Hill E4 2B 36
Friday Hill E. E4 3B 36
(not continuous)
Friday Hill W. E4 2B 36
Friday Rd. CR4: Mitc 7D 136
DA8: Erith 5K 109
Friday St. EC4 2C 14 (7C 84)
Frideswide Pl. NW5 5G 65
Freightliners City Farm 6A 66
Friendly Pl. SE13 1D 122
Friendly St. SE8 2C 122
Friendly St. M. SE8 2C 122
Friendship Ho. *SE1* 7B 14
(off Belvedere Pl.)
Friendship Wlk. UB5: N'olt 3B 76
Friendship Way E15 1E 86
Friends Rd. CR0: C'don 3D 168
Friend St. EC1 1A 8 (3B 84)
FRIERN BARNET 5J 31
Friern Barnet La. N11 2G 31
N20 2G 31
Friern Barnet Rd. N11 5J 31
Friern Barnet School Sports Cen. 5J 31
(off Hemington Av.)
Friern Bri. Retail Pk. N11 6A 32
Friern Ct. N20 3G 31
Friern Mt. Dr. N20 7F 21
Friern Pk. N12 5F 31
Friern Rd. SE22 7G 121
Friern Watch Av. N12 4F 31
Frigate Ho. *E14* 4E 104
(off Stebondale St.)
Frigate M. SE8 6C 104
Frimley Av. SM6: Wall 5J 167
Frimley Cl. CR0: New Ad 7E 170
SW19 2G 135
Frimley Ct. DA14: Sidc 5C 144
Frimley Cres.
CR0: New Ad 7E 170
Frimley Gdns. CR4: Mitc 3C 154
Frimley Rd. IG3: Ilf 3J 71
KT9: Chess 5D 162
Frimley St. *E1* 4K 85
(off Frimley Way)
Frimley Way E1 4K 85
Fringewood Cl. HA6: Nwood 1D 38
Frinstead Ho. *W10* 7F 81
(off Freston Rd.)
Frinsted Rd. DA8: Erith 7K 109
Frinton Ct. *W13* 5B 78
(off Hardwick Grn.)
Frinton Dr. IG8: Wfd G 7A 36
Frinton M. IG2: Ilf 6E 52
Frinton Rd. DA14: Sidc 2E 144
E6 3B 88
N15 6E 48
SW17 6E 136
Friston St. SW6 2K 117
Friswell Pl. DA6: Bex 4G 127
Fritham Cl. KT3: N Mald 6A 152
Frith Ct. NW7 7B 30
Frith Ho. *NW8* 4B 4
(off Frampton St.)
Frith La. NW7 7B 30
Frith Rd. CR0: C'don 2C 168
E11 4E 68
Frith St. W1 1C 12 (6H 83)

Frithville Ct. *W12* 1E 98
(off Frithville Gdns.)
Frithville Gdns. W12 1E 98
Frizlands La. RM10: Dag 2H 73
Frobisher Cl. HA5: Pinn 7B 40
Frobisher Ct. NW9 2A 44
SE8 5A 104
(off Evelyn St.)
SE10 6F 105
(off Old Woolwich Rd.)
SE23 2H 139
SM3: Cheam 7G 165
W12 2E 98
(off Lime Gro.)
Frobisher Cres. *EC2* 5D 8
(off Beech St.)
TW19: Stanw 7A 110
Frobisher Gdns. E10 7D 50
TW19: Stanw 7A 110
Frobisher Ho. *E1* 1H 103
(off Watts St.)
SW1 7C 18
(off Dolphin Sq.)
Frobisher M. EN2: Enf 4J 23
Frobisher Pas. E14 1C 104
Frobisher Pl. Pioneer Cen. SE15 1J 121
Frobisher Rd. E6 6D 88
N8 4A 48
Frobisher St. SE10 6G 105
Frog La. RM13: Rain 6K 91
Frogley Rd. SE22 4F 121
Frogmore SW18 5J 117
Frogmore Av. UB4: Hayes 4G 75
Frogmore Cl. SM3: Cheam 3F 165
Frogmore Ct. UB2: S'hall 4D 94
Frogmore Gdns. SM3: Cheam 4G 165
UB4: Hayes 4G 75
Frogmore Ind. Est. N5 5C 66
NW10 3J 79
UB3: Hayes 2G 93
Frognal NW3 4A 64
Frognal Av. DA14: Sidc 5A 144
HA1: Harr 4K 41
Frognal Cl. NW3 5A 64
FROGNAL CORNER 6K 143
Frognal Ct. NW3 6A 64
Frognal Gdns. NW3 4A 64
Frognal La. NW3 5K 63
Frognal Pde. NW3 6A 64
Frognal Pl. DA14: Sidc 6A 144
Frognal Ri. NW3 3A 64
Frognal Way NW3 4A 64
Froissart Rd. SE9 5B 124
Frome Ho. SE15 4H 121
Frome Rd. N22 3B 48
Frome St. N1 2C 84
Fromondes Rd. SM3: Cheam 5G 165
Frontenac NW10 7D 62
Frontier Works N17 6K 33
Frostic Wlk. E1 6K 9 (5G 85)
Froude St. SW8 2F 119
Fruen Rd. TW14: Felt 7H 111
Fruiterers Pas. *EC4* 3D 14
(off Queen St. Pl.)
Fryatt Rd. N17 7J 33
(not continuous)
Fryday Gro. M. *SW12* 7G 119
(off Weir Rd.)
Fryent Cl. NW9 6G 43
Fryent Country Pk. 7G 43
Fryent Cres. NW9 6A 44
Fryent Flds. NW9 6A 44
Fryent Gro. NW9 6A 44
Fryent Way NW9 5G 43
Fry Ho. E6 7A 70
Frying Pan All. E1 6J 9
Fry Rd. E6 7B 70
NW10 1B 80
Fryston Av. CR0: C'don 2G 169
Fuchsia Cl. RM7: Rush G 2K 73

Fuchsia St. SE2 5B 108
Fulbeck Dr. NW9 1A 44
Fulbeck Ho. *N7* 6K 65
(off Sutterton St.)
Fulbeck Rd. N19 4G 65
Fulbeck Wlk. HA8: Edg 2C 28
Fulbeck Way HA2: Harr 2G 41
Fulbourn *KT1: King T* 2G 151
(off Eureka Rd.)
Fulbourne Rd. E17 1E 50
Fulbourne St. E1 5H 85
Fulbrook M. N19 4G 65
Fulcher Ho. *N1* 1E 84
(off Colville Est.)
SE8 5B 104
Fulford Ho. KT19: Ewe 7K 163
Fulford Rd. KT19: Ewe 7K 163
Fulford St. SE16 2H 103
FULHAM 2G 117
FULHAM BROADWAY 7J 99
Fulham B'way. SW6 7J 99
Fulham Broadway Shop. Cen.
SW6 7J 99
Fulham Bus. Exchange
SW6 1A 118
(off The Boulevard)
Fulham Cl. UB10: Hil 4E 74
Fulham Ct. SW6 1J 117
(not continuous)
Fulham FC 1F 117
Fulham High St. SW6 2G 117
Fulham Palace 2G 117
Fulham Pal. Rd. SW6 5E 98
W6 5E 98
Fulham Pk. Gdns. SW6 2H 117
Fulham Pk. Rd. SW6 2H 117
Fulham Pools 6G 99
Fulham Rd. SW3 7A 16 (7K 99)
SW6 2G 117
(Fulham High St.)
SW6 7K 99
(King's Rd.)
SW10 7A 16 (7K 99)
Fullbrooks Av. KT4: Wor Pk 1B 164
Fuller Cl. BR6: Chels 5K 173
E2 3K 9
WD23: Bush 1C 26
Fuller Rd. RM8: Dag 3B 72
Fullers Av. IG8: Wfd G 7C 36
KT6: Surb 2F 163
Fullers Cl. RM5: Col R 1J 55
Fuller's Griffin Brewery & Vis. Cen. 6B 98
Fullers La. RM5: Col R 1J 55
Fullers Rd. E18 7C 36
Fuller St. NW4 4E 44
Fullers Way Nth. KT6: Surb 3F 163
Fullers Way Sth. KT9: Chess 4E 162
Fuller's Wood CR0: C'don 5C 170
Fullerton Ct. TW11: Tedd 6A 132
Fullerton Rd. CR0: C'don 7F 157
SM5: Cars 7C 166
SW18 5K 117
Fuller Way UB3: Harl 5H 93
Fullwell Av. IG5: Ilf 1D 52
IG6: Ilf 1F 53
FULLWELL CROSS 1G 53
Fullwell Cross IG6: Ilf 2H 53
Fullwell Cross Swimming Pool & Recreation Cen. 2H 53
Fullwell Pde. IG5: Ilf 1E 52
Fullwood's M. N1 1F 9 (3D 84)
Fulmar Cl. KT5: Surb 6F 151
Fulmar Ho. *SE16* 4K 103
(off Tawny Way)
Fulmead St. SW6 1K 117
Fulmer Cl. TW12: Hamp 5C 130
Fulmer Ho. *NW8* 4D 4
(off Mallory St.)
Fulmer Rd. E16 5B 88
Fulmer Way W13 3B 96

Fulneck *E1* ... *5J 85*
(off Mile End Rd.)
Fulready Rd. E10 ... 5F 51
Fulstone Cl.
TW4: Houn ... 4D 112
Fulthorp Rd. SE3 ... 2H 123
Fulton M. W2 ... 7A 82
Fulton Rd. HA9: Wemb ... 3G 61
FULWELL ... 4H 131
Fulwell Ct. IG5: Ilf ... 1E 52
UB1: S'hall ... *7G 77*
(off Baird Av.)
Fulwell Pk. Av. TW2: Twick ... 2F 131
Fulwell Rd. TW11: Tedd ... 4H 131
Fulwood Av.
HA0: Wemb ... 2F 79
Fulwood Cl. UB3: Hayes ... 6H 75
Fulwood Ct. HA3: Kent ... 6A 42
Fulwood Gdns.
TW1: Twick ... 6K 113
Fulwood Pl. WC1 ... 6H 7 (5K 83)
Fulwood Wlk. SW19 ... 1G 135
Funland ... *2C 12*
(in Trocadero Cen.)
Furber St. W6 ... 3D 98
Furham Fld. HA5: Hat E ... 7A 26
Furley Ho. *SE15* ... *7G 103*
(off Peckham Pk. Rd.)
Furley Rd. SE15 ... 7G 103
Furlong Cl. SM6: Wall ... 1F 167
Furlong Path *UB5: N'olt* ... *6C 58*
(off Cowings Mead)
Furlong Rd. N7 ... 6A 66
Furmage St. SW18 ... 7K 117
Furneaux Av. SE27 ... 5B 138
Furness Ho. *SW1* ... *5J 17*
(off Abbots Mnr.)
Furness Rd. HA2: Harr ... 7F 41
NW10 ... 2C 80
SM4: Mord ... 6K 153
SW6 ... 2K 117
Furnival Mans. *W1* ... *6A 6*
(off Wells St.)
Furnival St. EC4 ... 7J 7 (6A 84)
Furrow La. E9 ... 5J 67
Fursby Av. N3 ... 6D 30
Fursecroft W1 ... 7E 4
Further Acre NW9 ... 2B 44
Furtherfield Cl.
CR0: C'don ... 6A 156
Further Grn. Rd. SE6 ... 7G 123
FURZEDOWN ... 5F 137
Furzedown Dr. SW17 ... 5F 137
Furzedown Rd. SW17 ... 5F 137
Furze Farm Cl. RM6: Chad H ... 2E 54
Furzefield Cl. BR7: Chst ... 6F 143
Furzefield Rd. SE3 ... 6K 105
Furzeground Way
UB11: Stock P ... 1E 92
Furzeham Rd. UB7: W Dray ... 2A 92
Furze Rd. CR7: Thor H ... 3C 156
Furze St. E3 ... 5C 86
Furzewood TW16: Sun ... 1J 147
Fusion Health & Leisure Cen. ... 4B 102
Future Fitness Health Club ... *2A 48*
(in Wood Green Shop. City)
Fye Foot La. *EC4* ... *2C 14*
(off Queen Victoria St.)
Fyfe Way BR1: Brom ... 2J 159
Fyfield *N4* ... *2A 66*
(off Six Acres Est.)
Fyfield Cl. BR2: Brom ... 4F 159
Fyfield Ct. E7 ... 6J 69
Fyfield Ho. *E6* ... *1C 88*
(off Ron Leighton Way)
Fyfield Rd. E17 ... 3F 51
EN1: Enf ... 3K 23
IG8: Wfd G ... 7F 37
SW9 ... 3A 120
Fynes St. SW1 ... 3C 18 (4H 101)

G

Gable Cl. HA5: Hat E ... 1E 40
Gable Ct. SE26 ... 4H 139
Gables, The BR1: Brom ... 7K 141
HA9: Wemb ... 3G 61
IG11: Bark ... 6G 71
N10 ... *3E 46*
(off Fortis Grn.)
Gables Av. TW15: Ashf ... 5B 128
Gables Cl. SE5 ... 1E 120
SE12 ... 1J 141
Gables Lodge EN4: Had W ... 1F 21
Gabriel Cl. TW13: Hanw ... 4C 130
Gabriel Ho. *N1* ... *1B 84*
(off Islington Grn.)
SE11 ... 3G 19 (4K 101)
Gabrielle Cl. HA9: Wemb ... 3F 61
Gabrielle Ct. NW3 ... 6B 64
Gabriel M. NW2 ... 2H 63
Gabriel St. SE23 ... 7K 121
Gabriels Wharf
SE1 ... 4J 13 (1A 102)
Gad Cl. E13 ... 3K 87
Gaddesden Av.
HA9: Wemb ... 6F 61
Gaddesden Ho. *EC1* ... *2F 9*
(off Cranwood St.)
Gadebridge Ho. *SW3* ... *5C 16*
(off Cale St.)
Gade Cl. UB3: Hayes ... 1K 93
Gadesden Rd. KT19: Ewe ... 6J 163
(not continuous)
Gadsbury Cl. NW9 ... 6B 44
Gadsden Ho. *W10* ... *4G 81*
(off Hazlewood Cres.)
Gadwall Cl. E16 ... 6K 87
Gadwall Way SE28 ... 2H 107
Gage Brown Ho. *W10* ... *6F 81*
(off Bridge Cl.)
Gage Rd. E16 ... 5G 87
Gage St. WC1 ... 5F 7 (5J 83)
Gainford Ho. *E2* ... *3H 85*
(off Ellsworth St.)
Gainford St. N1 ... 1A 84
Gainsboro Gdns. UB6: G'frd ... 5J 59
Gainsborough Av. *E12* ... *6E 70*
(off Barrington Rd.)
E12 ... 5E 70
(Church Rd.)
Gainsborough Cl. BR3: Beck ... 7C 140
KT10: Esh ... 7J 149
Gainsborough Ct. BR2: Brom ... 4A 160
KT19: Ewe ... 6B 164
N12 ... 5E 30
SE16 ... *5H 103*
(off Stubbs Dr.)
SE21 ... 2E 138
W4 ... *5H 97*
(off Chaseley Dr.)
W12 ... 2E 98
Gainsborough Gdns. HA8: Edg ... 2F 43
NW3 ... 3B 64
NW11 ... 7H 45
TW7: Isle ... 5H 113
Gainsborough Ho. *E14* ... *2C 104*
(off Cassilis Rd.)
E14 ... *7A 86*
(off Victory Pl.)
EN1: Enf ... 5B 24
RM8: Dag ... *4B 72*
(off Earl's Wlk.)
SW1 ... *4D 18*
(off Erasmus St.)
Gainsborough Lodge *HA1: Harr* ... *5K 41*
(off Hindes Rd.)
Gainsborough Mans. *W14* ... *6G 99*
(off Queen's Club Gdns.)
Gainsborough M. SE26 ... 3H 139
Gainsborough Rd. E11 ... 7G 51
E15 ... 3G 87
IG8: Wfd G ... 6H 37
KT3: N Mald ... 6K 151
N12 ... 5E 30
RM8: Dag ... 4B 72
TW9: Rich ... 2F 115
UB4: Hayes ... 2E 74
W4 ... 4B 98
Gainsborough Sq. DA6: Bex ... 3D 126
Gainsborough St. E9 ... 6B 68
Gainsborough Studios E. *N1* ... *1D 84*
(off Poole St.)
Gainsborough Studios Nth. *N1* ... *1D 84*
(off Poole St.)
Gainsborough Studios Sth. *N1* ... *1D 84*
(off Poole St.)
Gainsborough Studios W. *N1* ... *1D 84*
(off Poole St.)
Gainsborough Ter. *SM2: Sutt* ... *7H 165*
(off Belmont Ri.)
Gainsborough Twr. *UB5: N'olt* ... *2B 76*
(off Academy Gdns.)
Gainsfield Ct. E11 ... 3G 69
Gainsford Rd. E17 ... 4B 50
Gainsford St. SE1 ... 6J 15 (2F 103)
Gairloch Ho. *NW1* ... *7H 65*
(off Stratford Vs.)
Gairloch Rd. SE5 ... 2E 120
Gaisford St. NW5 ... 6G 65
Gaitskell Ct. SW11 ... 2C 118
Gaitskell Ho. E6 ... 1B 88
E17 ... 3D 50
SE17 ... *6E 102*
(off Villa St.)
Gaitskell Rd. SE9 ... 1G 143
Gaitskell Way *SE1* ... *6C 14*
(off Weller St.)
Gala Bingo
Acton ... *1K 97*
(off High St.)
Bexleyheath ... 4H 127
Camberwell ... 7C 102
Crystal Palace ... 6F 139
Enfield ... 4B 24
Feltham ... 2K 129
Fullwell Cross ... 2G 53
Greenhill ... 5K 41
Hounslow ... 4E 112
Kingston upon Thames ... 1E 150
Stratford ... 1F 87
Surrey Quays ... 3K 103
Thornton Heath ... 5A 156
Tooting ... 5C 136
Upton Pk. ... 1C 88
Woolwich ... 3E 106
Galahad Rd. BR1: Brom ... 4J 141
N9 ... 3B 34
Galata Rd. SW13 ... 7C 98
Galatea Sq. SE15 ... 3H 121
Galaxy Bldg. *E14* ... *4C 104*
(off Crews St.)
Galaxy Ho. *EC2* ... *3F 9*
(off Leonard St.)
Galba Ct. TW8: Bford ... 7D 96
Galbraith St. E14 ... 3E 104
Galdana Av. EN5: New Bar ... 3F 21
Galeborough Av.
IG8: Wfd G ... 7A 36
Gale Cl. CR4: Mitc ... 3B 154
TW12: Hamp ... 6C 130
Gale Ct. BR2: Brom ... 2G 159
Galena Arches *W6* ... *4D 98*
(off Galena Rd.)
Galena Ho. *SE18* ... *5K 107*
(off Grosmont Rd.)
Galena Rd. W6 ... 4D 98
Galen Pl. WC1 ... 6F 7 (5J 83)
Galesbury Rd. SW18 ... 6A 118
Gales Gdns. E2 ... 3H 85
Gale St. E3 ... 5C 86
RM9: Dag ... 5C 72
Gales Way IG8: Wfd G ... 7H 37
Galgate Cl. SW19 ... 1F 135
Gallants Farm Rd.
EN4: E Barn ... 7H 21
Galleon Cl. DA8: Erith ... 4K 109
SE16 ... 2K 103
Galleon Ho. *E14* ... *4E 104*
(off Glengarnock Av.)
Galleons Dr. IG11: Bark ... 3A 90
Galleria Ct. SE15 ... 6F 103
Galleria Shop. Mall, The E18 ... 2J 51
Gallery Ct. *SE1* ... *7E 14*
(off Pilgrimage St.)
SW10 ... *6A 100*
(off Gunter Gro.)
Gallery Gdns. UB5: N'olt ... 2B 76
Gallery Rd. SE21 ... 1D 138
Galley, The E16 ... 7F 89
Galleymead Rd. SL3: Poyle ... 4A 174
Galleywall Rd. SE16 ... 4H 103
Galleywall Rd. Trad. Est. *SE16* ... *4H 103*
(off Galleywall Rd.)
Galleywood Ho. *W10* ... *5E 80*
(off Sutton Way)
Galliard Cl. N9 ... 6D 24
Galliard Ct. N9 ... 6B 24
Galliard Rd. N9 ... 1B 34
Gallia Rd. N5 ... 5B 66
Gallica Ct. SM1: Sutt ... 1K 165
Gallions Cl. IG11: Bark ... 3A 90
Gallions Entrance E16 ... 1G 107
Gallions Reach Shop. Pk.
E6 ... 5G 89
Gallions Rd. E16 ... 7F 89
SE7 ... 4K 105
(not continuous)
Gallions Rdbt. E16 ... 7F 89
Gallions Vw. Rd. SE28 ... 2J 107
Gallon Cl. SE7 ... 4A 106
Gallop, The CR2: Sels ... 7H 169
SM2: Sutt ... 7B 166
Gallosson Rd. SE18 ... 4J 107
Galloway Path CR0: C'don ... 4D 168
Galloway Rd. W12 ... 1C 98
Gallus Cl. N21 ... 6E 22
Gallus Sq. SE3 ... 3K 123
Galpins Rd. CR7: Thor H ... 5J 155
Galsworthy Av. E14 ... 6A 86
RM6: Chad H ... 7B 54
Galsworthy Cl. NW2 ... 4G 63
SE28 ... 1B 108
Galsworthy Ct. *W3* ... *3H 97*
(off Bollo Bri. Rd.)
Galsworthy Cres. SE3 ... 1A 124
Galsworthy Ho. *W11* ... *6G 81*
(off Elgin Cres.)
Galsworthy Rd. KT2: King T ... 7H 133
NW2 ... 4G 63
Galsworthy Ter. N16 ... 3E 66
Galton St. W10 ... 3G 81
Galva Cl. EN4: Cockf ... 4K 21
Galvani Way CR0: Wadd ... 1K 167
Galveston Ho. *E1* ... *4A 86*
(off Harford St.)
Galveston Rd. SW15 ... 5H 117
Galway Cl. *SE16* ... *5H 103*
(off Masters Dr.)
Galway Ho. *E1* ... *5K 85*
(off White Horse La.)
EC1 ... 2D 8
Galway St. EC1 ... 2D 8 (3C 84)
Galy NW9 ... 2B 44
Gambetta St. SW8 ... 2F 119
Gambia St. SE1 ... 5B 14 (1B 102)
Gambier Ho. *EC1* ... *2D 8*
(off Mora St.)
Gambole Rd. SW17 ... 4C 136
Games Rd. EN4: Cockf ... 3H 21

Gamlen Rd. SW15 ....4F 117
Gamuel Cl. E17 ....6C 50
Gander Grn. Cres. TW12: Hamp 1E 148
Gander Grn. La. SM1: Sutt 3H 165
SM3: Cheam 2G 165
Gandhi Cl. E17 ....6C 50
Gandolfi St. SE15 ....6E 102
Ganley Ct. *SW11* *3B 118*
(off Winstanley Est.)
Ganton St. W1 ....2A 12 (7G 83)
GANTS HILL 6E 52
GANTS HILL 6E 52
Gants Hill IG2: Ilf 6E 52
Gantshill Cres. IG2: Ilf 5E 52
Gap Rd. SW19 ....5J 135
Garage Rd. W3 ....6G 79
Garbett Ho. *SE17* *6B 102*
(off Doddington Gro.)
Garbutt Pl. W1 ....5H 5 (5E 82)
Garden Av. CR4: Mitc 7F 137
DA7: Bex 3F 127
Garden City HA8: Edg 6B 28
Garden Cl. E4 ....5H 35
HA4: Ruis 2G 57
SE12 ....3K 141
SM6: Wall 5J 167
SW15 ....7E 116
TW12: Hamp 5D 130
TW15: Ashf 6E 128
UB5: N'olt 1C 76
Garden Ct. CR0: C'don 2F 169
EC4 ....2J 13
HA7: Stan 5H 27
N12 ....5E 30
NW8 ....*1A 4*
(off Garden Rd.)
TW9: Kew 1F 115
TW12: Hamp 5D 130
W4 ....3J 97
W11 ....*7G 81*
(off Clarendon Rd.)
Gardener Gro. TW13: Hanw 2D 130
Gardeners Cl. N11 ....2K 31
SE9 ....3C 142
Gardeners Rd. CR0: C'don 1B 168
Garden Ho. *N2* *2B 46*
(off The Grange)
SW7 ....*3K 99*
(off Cornwall Gdns.)
Garden Ho., The *W6* *6F 99*
(off Bothwell St.)
Gardenia Rd. BR1: Brom 3E 160
EN1: Enf 6K 23
Gardenia Way IG8: Wfd G 6D 36
Garden La. BR1: Brom 6K 141
SW2 ....1K 137
Garden M. W2 ....7J 81
Garden Pl. E8 ....1F 85
Garden Rd. BR1: Brom 7K 141
KT12: Walt T 6K 147
NW8 ....1A 4 (3A 82)
SE20 ....1J 157
TW9: Rich 3G 115
Garden Row SE1 ....3B 102
Garden Royal SW15 ....6F 117
Gardens, The BR3: Beck 1E 158
E5 ....7F 49
HA1: Harr 6G 41
HA5: Pinn 6D 40
N8 ....4J 47
(not continuous)
SE22 ....4G 121
TW14: Felt 5F 111
Garden St. E1 ....5K 85
Gardens Way E12 ....3C 70
Garden Ter. SW1 ....5C 18 (5H 101)
SW7 ....7D 10
Garden Vw. E7 ....4A 70
Garden Wlk. BR3: Beck 1B 158
EC2 ....2G 9 (3E 84)
Garden Way NW10 ....6J 61
Gardiner Av. NW2 ....5E 62
Gardiner Cl. EN3: Pond E 6E 24
RM8: Dag 4D 72
Gardiner Ct. CR2: S Croy 6C 168
NW10 ....1K 79
Gardiner Ho. SW11 ....1C 118
Gardner Cl. E11 ....6K 51
Gardner Ct. *EC1* *3A 8*
(off Brewery Sq.)
N5 ....4C 66
Gardner Ho. TW13: Hanw 2D 130
UB1: S'hall *7B 76*
(off The Broadway)
Gardner Ind. Est. SE26 ....5B 140
Gardner Pl. TW14: Felt 6K 111
Gardner Rd. E13 ....4K 87
Gardners La. EC4 ....2C 14 (7C 84)
Gardnor Rd. NW3 ....4B 64
Gard St. EC1 ....1B 8 (3B 84)
Garendon Gdns. SM4: Mord 7K 153
Garendon Rd. SM4: Mord 7K 153
Garenne Ct. E4 ....1K 35
Gareth Cl. KT4: Wor Pk 2F 165
Gareth Ct. SW16 ....3H 137
Gareth Dr. N9 ....2B 34
Gareth Gro. BR1: Brom 4J 141
Garfield *EN2: Enf* *5J 23*
(off Private Rd.)
Garfield Ct. *NW6* *7G 63*
(off Willesden La.)
Garfield M. SW11 ....3E 118
Garfield Rd. E4 ....1A 36
E13 ....4H 87
EN3: Pond E 4D 24
SW11 ....3E 118
SW19 ....5A 136
TW1: Twick 1A 132
Garford St. E14 ....7C 86
Garganey Ct. *NW10* *6K 61*
(off Elgar Av.)
Garganey Wlk. SE28 ....7C 90
Garibaldi St. SE18 ....4J 107
Garland Ct. *E14* *7C 86*
(off Premiere Pl.)
SE17 ....*4C 102*
(off Wansey St.)
Garland Dr. TW3: Houn 2G 113
Garland Ho. *KT2: King T* *1E 150*
(off Seven Kings Way)
Garland Rd. HA7: Stan 1E 42
SE18 ....7H 107
Garlands Ct. *CR0: C'don* *4D 168*
(off Chatsworth Rd.)
Garlands Ho. *NW8* *2A 82*
(off Carlton Hill)
Garlands La. HA1: Harr 1K 59
Garlick Hill EC4 ....2D 14 (7C 84)
Garlies Rd. SE23 ....3A 140
Garlinge Rd. NW2 ....6H 63
Garman Cl. N18 ....5J 33
Garman Rd. N17 ....7C 34
(not continuous)
Garnault M. EC1 ....2K 7
Garnault Pl. EC1 ....2K 7 (3A 84)
Garnault Rd. EN1: Enf 1A 24
Garner Cl. RM8: Dag 1D 72
Garner Ct. *TW19: Stanw* *6A 110*
(off Jeppesen Ct.)
Garner Rd. E17 ....1E 50
Garner St. E2 ....2G 85
Garnet Ho. *E1* *1J 103*
(off Garnet St.)
Garnet Rd. CR7: Thor H 4C 156
NW10 ....6A 62
Garnet St. E1 ....7J 85
Garnett Cl. SE9 ....3D 124
Garnett Rd. NW3 ....5D 64
Garnett Way *E17* *1A 50*
(off Swansland Gdns.)
Garnet Wlk. E6 ....5C 88
Garnham Cl. N16 ....2F 67
Garnham St. N16 ....2F 67
Garnies Cl. SE15 ....7F 103
Garrad's Rd. SW16 ....3H 137
Garrard Cl. BR7: Chst 5F 143
DA7: Bex 3G 127
Garrard Wlk. NW10 ....6A 62
Garratt Cl. CR0: Bedd 4J 167
Garratt Ct. SW18 ....7K 117
Garratt La. SW17 ....6K 117
SW18 ....6K 117
Garratt Rd. HA8: Edg 7B 28
Garratts Rd.
WD23: Bush 1B 26
Garratt Ter. SW17 ....4C 136
Garraway Ct. *SW13* *7E 98*
(off Wyatt Dr.)
Garrett Cl. W3 ....5K 79
Garrett Ho. *SE1* *6A 14*
(off Burrows M.)
W12 ....*6D 80*
(off Du Cane Rd.)
Garrett St. EC1 ....3D 8 (4C 84)
Garrick Av. NW11 ....6G 45
Garrick Cl. SW18 ....4A 118
TW9: Rich 5D 114
W5 ....4E 78
Garrick Ct. *E8* *7F 67*
(off Jacaranda Gro.)
HA8: Edg 4A 28
Garrick Cres. CR0: C'don 2E 168
Garrick Dr. NW4 ....2E 44
SE28 ....3H 107
Garrick Gdns. KT8: W Mole 3E 148
Garrick Ho. *KT1: King T* *4E 150*
(off Surbiton Rd.)
W1 ....5J 11
W4 ....6A 98
Garrick Ind. Est. NW9 ....5B 44
Garrick Pk. NW4 ....2F 45
Garrick Rd. NW9 ....6B 44
TW9: Rich 2G 115
UB6: G'frd 4F 77
Garricks Ho. *KT1: King T* *2D 150*
(off Wadbrook St.)
Garrick St. WC2 ....2E 12 (7J 83)
Garrick Theatre *3E 12*
(off Charing Cross Rd.)
Garrick Way NW4 ....4F 45
Garrick Yd. WC2 ....2E 12
Garrison Cl. SE18 ....7E 106
TW4: Houn 5D 112
Garrison La. KT9: Chess 7D 162
Garrison Rd. E3 ....1C 86
Garrowsfield EN5: Barn 6C 20
Garry Way RM1: Rom 1K 55
Garsdale Cl. N11 ....6K 31
Garsdale Ter. *W14* *5H 99*
(off Aisgill Av.)
Garside Cl. SE28 ....3H 107
TW12: Hamp 6F 131
Garsington M. SE4 ....3B 122
Garson Ho. *W2* *2A 10*
(off Gloucester Ter.)
Garston Ho. *N1* *7B 66*
(off The Sutton Est.)
Garter Way SE16 ....2K 103
Garth, The HA3: Kent 6F 43
TW12: Ham H 6F 131
Garth Cl. HA4: Ruis 1B 58
KT2: King T 5F 133
SM4: Mord 7F 153
Garth Ct. *HA1: Harr* *6K 41*
(off Northwick Pk. Rd.)
W4 ....5K 97
Garth Ho. NW2 ....2H 63
Garth M. W5 ....4E 78
Garthorne Rd. SE23 ....7K 121
Garthorne Road Nature Reserve 7K 121
Garth Rd. KT2: King T 5F 133
NW2 ....2H 63
SM4: Mord 6E 152
W4 ....5K 97
Garth Rd. Ind. Est. SM4: Mord 1F 165
Garthside TW10: Ham 5E 132
Garthway N12 ....6H 31
Gartmoor Gdns. SW19 ....1H 135
Gartmore Rd. IG3: Ilf 2K 71
Garton Pl. SW18 ....6A 118
Gartons Cl. EN3: Pond E 4D 24
Gartons Way SW11 ....3A 118
Garvary Rd. E16 ....6K 87
Garway Rd. W2 ....6K 81
Garwood Cl. N17 ....1H 49
Gascoigne Gdns. IG8: Wfd G 7B 36
Gascoigne Pl. E2 ....1J 9 (3F 85)
(not continuous)
Gascoigne Rd. CR0: New Ad 7F 171
IG11: Bark 1G 89
Gascony Av. NW6 ....7J 63
Gascoyne Ho. E9 ....7A 68
Gascoyne Rd. E9 ....7K 67
Gaselee St. *E14* *1E 104*
(off Baffin Way)
Gaskarth Rd. HA8: Edg 1J 43
SW12 ....6F 119
Gaskell Rd. N6 ....6D 46
Gaskell St. SW4 ....2J 119
Gaskin St. N1 ....1B 84
Gaspar Cl. SW5 ....4K 99
Gaspar M. SW5 ....4K 99
Gassiot Rd. SW17 ....4D 136
Gassiot Way SM1: Sutt 3B 166
Gasson Ho. *SE14* *6K 103*
(off John Williams Cl.)
Gastein Rd. W6 ....6F 99
Gastigny Ho. EC1 ....2D 8
Gaston Bell Cl. TW9: Rich 3F 115
Gaston Bri. Rd. TW17: Shep 6F 147
Gaston Rd. CR4: Mitc 3E 154
Gaston Way TW17: Shep 5F 147
Gataker Ho. *SE16* *3H 103*
(off Slippers Pl.)
Gataker St. SE16 ....3H 103
Gatcombe Ct. BR3: Beck 7C 140
Gatcombe Ho. SE22 ....3E 120
Gatcombe M. W5 ....7F 79
Gatcombe Rd. E16 ....1J 105
N19 ....3H 65
Gatcombe Way EN4: Cockf 3J 21
Gateacre Ct. DA14: Sidc 4B 144
Gate Cen., The TW8: Bford 7A 96
Gate Cinema *1J 99*
(off Notting Hill Ga.)
Gateforth St. NW8 ....4C 4 (4C 82)
Gate Hill Ct. *W11* *1H 99*
(off Ladbroke Ter.)
Gate Ho. *N1* *7D 66*
(off Ufton Rd.)
Gatehouse Cl. KT2: King T 7J 133
Gatehouse Sq. SE1 ....4D 14
Gatehouse Theatre 1E 64
Gateley Ho. *SE4* *4K 121*
(off Coston Wlk.)
Gateley Rd. SW9 ....3K 119
Gate Lodge *W9* *5J 81*
(off Admiral Wlk.)
Gate M. SW7 ....7D 10
Gater Dr. EN2: Enf 1J 23
Gates NW9 ....2B 44
Gatesborough St. EC2 ....3G 9 (4E 84)
Gates Ct. SE17 ....5C 102
Gatesden WC1 ....2G 7 (3J 83)
Gates Grn. Rd. BR2: Kes 3H 171
BR4: W W'ck 3H 171
Gateside Rd. SW17 ....3D 136
Gatestone Ct. SE19 ....6E 138
Gatestone Rd. SE19 ....6E 138
Gate St. WC2 ....7G 7 (6K 83)

Gate Theatre, The 1J 99
(off Pembridge Rd.)
Gateway SE17 6C 102
Gateway Arc. N1 2B 84
(off Upper St.)
Gateway Bus. Cen. BR3: Beck 6A 140
SE28 3H 107
Gateway Ct. IG2: Ilf 6E 52
(off Parham Dr.)
Gateway Ho. IG11: Bark 1G 89
Gateway Ind. Est. NW10 3B 80
Gateway M. E8 5F 67
Gateway Retail Pk. E6 4F 89
Gateway Rd. E10 3D 68
Gateways KT6: Surb 5E 150
(off Surbiton Hill Rd.)
Gateways, The SW3 4D 16
TW9: Rich 4D 114
(off Park La.)
Gateways Ct. SM6: Wall 5F 167
Gatfield Gro. TW13: Hanw 2E 130
Gatfield Ho. TW13: Hanw 2D 130
Gathorne Rd. N22 2A 48
Gathorne St. E2 2K 85
Gatley Av. KT19: Ewe 5H 163
Gatliff Cl. SW1 6H 17
Gatliff Rd. SW1 6J 17 (5F 101)
(not continuous)
Gatling Rd. SE2 5A 108
Gatonby St. SE15 1F 121
Gatting Cl. HA8: Edg 7D 28
Gatting Way UB8: Uxb 6A 56
Gattis Wharf N1 2J 83
(off New Wharf Rd.)
Gatton Cl. SM2: Sutt 7K 165
Gatton Rd. SW17 4C 136
Gattons Way DA14: Sidc 4F 145
Gatward Cl. N21 6G 23
Gatward Grn. N9 2A 34
Gatwick Ho. E14 6B 86
(off Clemence St.)
Gatwick Rd. SW18 7H 117
Gauden Cl. SW4 3H 119
Gauden Rd. SW4 2H 119
Gaugin Ct. SE16 5H 103
(off Stubbs Dr.)
Gaumont Ter. W12 2E 98
(off Lime Gro.)
Gauntlet NW9 2B 44
(off Five Acre)
Gauntlet Cl. UB5: N'olt 7C 58
Gauntlett Ct. HA0: Wemb 5B 60
Gauntlett Rd. SM1: Sutt 5B 166
Gaunt St. SE1 3C 102
Gautrey Rd. SE15 2J 121
Gautrey Sq. E6 6D 88
Gavel St. SE17 4D 102
Gaverick M. E14 4C 104
Gavestone Cres. SE12 7K 123
Gavestone Rd. SE12 7K 123
Gaviller Pl. E5 4H 67
Gavina Cl. SM4: Mord 5C 154
Gavin Ho. SE18 4J 107
Gawain Wlk. N9 3B 34
Gawber St. E2 3J 85
Gawsworth Cl. E15 5H 69
Gawthorne Av. NW7 5B 30
Gawthorne Ct. E3 2C 86
Gay Cl. NW2 5D 62
Gaydon Ho. W2 5K 81
(off Bourne Ter.)
Gaydon La. NW9 1A 44
Gayfere Rd. IG5: Ilf 3D 52
KT17: Ewe 5C 164
Gayfere St. SW1 2E 18 (3J 101)
Gayford Rd. W12 2B 98
Gay Gdns. RM10: Dag 4J 73
Gay Ho. N16 5E 66
Gayhurst SE17 6D 102
(off Hopwood Rd.)
Gayhurst Ct. UB5: Yead 3A 76
Gayhurst Ho. NW8 3C 4
(off Mallory St.)
Gayhurst Rd. E8 7G 67
Gaylor Rd. UB5: N'olt 5D 58
Gaymead NW8 1K 81
(off Abbey Rd.)
Gaynesford Rd. SE23 2K 139
SM5: Cars 7D 166
Gaynes Hill Rd. IG8: Wfd G 6H 37
Gay Rd. E15 2F 87
Gaysham Av. IG2: Ilf 5E 52
Gaysham Hall IG5: Ilf 3F 53
Gaysley Ho. SE11 4J 19
Gay St. SW15 3F 117
Gayton Ct. HA1: Harr 6K 41
Gayton Cres. NW3 4B 64
Gayton Rd. HA1: Harr 6K 41
NW3 4B 64
SE2 3C 108
Gayville Rd. SW11 6D 118
Gaywood Cl. SW2 1K 137
Gaywood Rd. E17 3C 50
Gaywood St. SE1 3B 102
Gaza St. SE17 5B 102
Gaze Ho. E14 6F 87
(off Blair St.)
Gazelle Ho. E15 6G 69
Gean Ct. E11 4F 69
Geariesville Gdns. IG6: Ilf 4F 53
Gearing Cl. SW17 4E 136
Geary Rd. NW10 5C 62
Geary St. N7 5K 65
Geddes Pl. DA7: Bex 4G 127
(off Arnsberg Way)
Gedeney Rd. N17 1C 48
Gedling Pl. SE1 7K 15 (3F 103)
Geere Rd. E15 1H 87
Gees Ct. W1 1H 11 (6E 82)
Gee St. EC1 3C 8 (4C 84)
Geffery's Ct. SE9 3C 142
Geffrye Ct. N1 2E 84
Geffrye Est. N1 2E 84
Geffrye Mus. 1J 9
Geffrye St. E2 1J 9 (2F 85)
Geldart Rd. SE15 7H 103
Geldeston Rd. E5 2G 67
Gellatly Rd. SE14 2J 121
Gell Cl. UB10: Ick 3B 56
Gelsthorpe Rd. RM5: Col R 1H 55
Gemini Bus. Cen. E16 4F 87
Gemini Bus. Est. SE14 5K 103
Gemini Bus. Pk. E6 5H 89
Gemini Ct. E1 7G 85
(off Vaughan Way)
Gemini Gro. UB5: N'olt 3C 76
Genas Cl. IG6: Ilf 1F 53
General Gordon Pl. SE18 4F 107
General Wolfe Rd. SE10 1F 123
Genesis Bus. Pk. NW10 2H 79
Genesis Cl. TW19: Stanw 1B 128
Genesta Rd. SE18 6F 107
Geneva Cl. TW17: Shep 2G 147
Geneva Ct. NW9 5B 44
Geneva Dr. SW9 4A 120
Geneva Gdns. RM6: Chad H 5E 54
Geneva Rd. CR7: Thor H 5C 156
KT1: King T 4E 150
Genever Cl. E4 5H 35
Genista Rd. N18 5C 34
Genoa Av. SW15 5E 116
Genoa Ho. E1 4K 85
(off Ernest St.)
Genoa Rd. SE20 1J 157
Genotin Rd. EN1: Enf 3J 23
Genotin Ter. EN1: Enf 4J 23
Gentlemans Row EN2: Enf 3H 23
Gentry Gdns. E13 4J 87
Geoffrey Bower Sports Cen. 2D 52
Geoffrey Cl. SE5 2C 120
Geoffrey Ct. SE4 2B 122
Geoffrey Gdns. E6 2C 88
Geoffrey Ho. SE1 7F 15
(off Pardoner St.)
Geoffrey Jones Ct. NW10 1C 80
Geoffrey Rd. SE4 3B 122
George V Av. HA5: Pinn 2D 40
George V Cl. HA5: Pinn 3E 40
George V Way UB6: G'frd 1B 78
George Beard Rd. SE8 4B 104
George Belt Ho. E2 3K 85
(off Smart St.)
George Comberton Wlk. E12 5E 70
George Ct. WC2 3F 13
George Cres. N10 7K 31
George Davies Lodge IG6: Ilf 5G 53
(off Veronique Gdns.)
George Downing Est. N16 2F 67
George Eliot Ho. SW1 4B 18
(off Vauxhall Bri. Rd.)
George Elliot Ho. SE17 5C 102
(off Crampton St.)
George Elliston Ho. SE1 5G 103
(off Old Kent Rd.)
George Eyre Ho. NW8 2B 82
(off Cochrane St.)
George Furness Ho. NW10 6D 62
(off Grange Rd.)
George Gange Way HA3: W'stone 3J 41
George Gillett Ct. EC1 3D 8
George Gro. Rd. SE20 1G 157
George Hudson Twr. E15 2D 86
(off High St.)
George Inn Yd. SE1 5E 14 (1D 102)
George La. BR2: Hayes 1K 171
E18 2J 51
(not continuous)
SE13 6D 122
George Lansbury Ho. N22 1A 48
(off Progress Way)
NW10 7A 62
George Lindgren Ho. SW6 7H 99
(off Clem Attlee Ct.)
George Loveless Ho. E2 1K 9
(off Diss St.)
George Lowe Ct. W2 5K 81
(off Bourne Ter.)
George Mathers Rd. SE11 4B 102
George M. EN2: Enf 3J 23
NW1 2B 6
SW9 2A 120
George Padmore Ho. E8 1G 85
(off Brougham Rd.)
George Peabody Ct. NW1 5C 4
(off Burne St.)
George Pl. N17 3E 48
George Potter Ho. SW11 2B 118
(off George Potter Way)
George Potter Way SW11 2B 118
George Rd. E4 6H 35
KT2: King T 7H 133
(not continuous)
KT3: N Mald 4B 152
George Row SE16 2G 103
George Sq. SW19 3J 153
George's Rd. N7 5K 65
George's Sq. SW6 6H 99
(off North End Rd.)
George St. CR0: C'don 2C 168
E16 6H 87
(not continuous)
IG11: Bark 7G 71
TW3: Houn 2D 112
TW9: Rich 5D 114
UB2: S'hall 4C 94
W1 7E 4 (6D 82)
W7 1J 95
George Tingle Ho. SE1 3F 103
(off Grange Wlk.)
Georgetown Cl. SE19 5E 138
Georgette Pl. SE10 7E 104
Georgeville Gdns. IG6: Ilf 4F 53
George Walter Ct. SE16 4J 103
(off Millender Wlk.)
George Wyver Cl. SW19 7G 117
George Yd. EC3 1F 15 (6D 84)
W1 2H 11 (7E 82)
Georgiana St. NW1 1G 83
Georgian Cl. BR2: Hayes 1K 171
HA7: Stan 7F 27
UB10: Ick 4A 56
Georgian Ct. CR0: C'don 1D 168
(off Cross Rd.)
E9 1J 85
EN5: New Bar 4F 21
HA9: Wemb 6G 61
N3 1H 45
NW4 5D 44
SW16 4J 137
Georgian Ho. E16 1J 105
(off Capulet M.)
Georgian Way HA1: Harr 2H 59
Georgia Rd. CR7: Thor H 1B 156
KT3: N Mald 4J 151
Georgina Gdns. E2 1K 9 (3F 85)
Geraint Rd. BR1: Brom 4J 141
Geraldine Rd. SW18 5A 118
W4 6G 97
Geraldine St. SE11 2K 19 (3B 102)
Gerald M. SW1 3H 17
Gerald Rd. E16 4H 87
RM8: Dag 2F 73
SW1 3H 17 (4E 100)
Gerard Av. TW4: Houn 7E 112
Gerard Gdns. RM13: Rain 2K 91
Gerard Pl. E9 7K 67
Gerard Rd. HA1: Harr 6A 42
SW13 1B 116
Gerards Cl. SE16 5J 103
Gerda Rd. SE9 2G 143
Germander Way E15 3G 87
Gernigan Ho. SW18 6B 118
Gernon Rd. E3 2A 86
Geron Way NW2 1D 62
Gerrard Gdns. HA5: Eastc 5J 39
Gerrard Ho. SE14 7J 103
(off Briant St.)
Gerrard Pl. W1 2D 12 (7H 83)
Gerrard Rd. N1 2B 84
Gerrards Cl. N14 5B 22
Gerrards Ct. W5 3D 96
Gerrard St. W1 2D 12 (7H 83)
Gerridge Ct. SE1 1K 19
(off Gerridge St.)
Gerridge St. SE1 1K 19 (3A 102)
Gerry Raffles Sq. E15 7F 69
Gertrude Rd. DA17: Belv 4G 109
Gertrude St. SW10 7A 16 (6A 100)
Gervase Cl. HA9: Wemb 3J 61
Gervase Rd. HA8: Edg 1J 43
Gervase St. SE15 7H 103
Gervis Ct. TW7: Isle 7G 95
Ghent St. SE6 2C 140
Ghent Way E8 6F 67
Giant Arches Rd. SE24 7C 120
Giant Tree Hill WD23: B Hea 1C 26
Gibbfield Cl. RM6: Chad H 3E 54
Gibbings Ho. SE1 7B 14
(off King James St.)
Gibbins Rd. E15 7E 68
Gibbon Ho. NW8 4B 4
(off Fisherton St.)
Gibbon Rd. KT2: King T 1E 150
SE15 2J 121
W3 7A 80
Gibbons M. NW11 5H 45
Gibbon's Rents SE1 5G 15
Gibbons Rd. NW10 6A 62
Gibbon Wlk. SW15 4C 116
Gibbs Av. SE19 5D 138

Gibbs Cl. SE19 . . . . . 6D 138
Gibbs Grn. HA8: Edg 4D 28
W14 . . . . . 5H 99
(not continuous)
Gibbs Ho. *BR1: Brom* *1H 159*
(off Longfield)
Gibb's Rd. N18 . . . . . 4D 34
Gibbs Sq. SE19 . . . . . 5D 138
Gibney Ter. BR1: Brom 4H 141
Gibraltar Wlk. E2 . . . . . 2K 9
Gibson Bus. Cen., The
N17 . . . . . 7A 34
Gibson Cl. E1 . . . . . 4J 85
KT9: Chess 5C 162
N21 . . . . . 6F 23
TW7: Isle 3J 113
Gibson Gdns. N16 . . . . . 2F 67
Gibson Ho. SM1: Sutt 4J 165
Gibson M. TW1: Twick 6C 114
Gibson Rd. RM8: Dag 1C 72
SE11 . . . . . 4H 19 (4K 101)
SM1: Sutt 5K 165
UB10: Ick 4B 56
Gibsons Hill SW16 . . . . . 7A 138
(not continuous)
Gibson Sq. N1 . . . . . 1A 84
Gibson St. SE10 . . . . . 5G 105
Gideon Cl. DA17: Belv 4H 109
Gideon M. W5 . . . . . 2D 96
Gideon Rd. SW11 . . . . . 3E 118
Gielgud Theatre *2C 12*
(off Shaftesbury Av.)
Giesbach Rd. N19 . . . . . 2H 65
Giffard Rd. N18 . . . . . 6K 33
Giffen Sq. Mkt. *SE8* *7C 104*
(off Giffen St.)
Giffin St. SE8 . . . . . 7C 104
Gifford Gdns. W7 . . . . . 5H 77
Gifford Ho. *SE10* *5F 105*
(off Eastney St.)
SW1 . . . . . *6A 18*
(off Churchill Gdns.)
Gifford St. N1 . . . . . 7J 65
Gift La. E15 . . . . . 1G 87
GIGGSHILL 7A 150
Giggs Hill BR5: St P 2K 161
Giggs Hill Gdns.
KT7: T Ditt 1A 162
Giggs Hill Rd. KT7: T Ditt 7A 150
Gilbert Bri. *EC2* *5D 8*
(off Gilbert Ho.)
Gilbert Cl. SE18 . . . . . 1D 124
SW19 . . . . . *1K 153*
(off High Path)
Gilbert Ct. *W5* *6F 79*
(off Green Va.)
Gilbert Gro. HA8: Edg 1K 43
Gilbert Ho. *E2* *3K 85*
(off Usk St.)
E17 . . . . . 3D 50
EC2 . . . . . 5D 8
SE8 . . . . . 6C 104
SW1 . . . . . *6K 17*
(off Churchill Gdns.)
SW8 . . . . . *7J 101*
(off Wyvil Rd.)
SW13 . . . . . *7D 98*
(off Trinity Chu. Rd.)
Gilbert Pl. WC1 . . . . . 6E 6 (5J 83)
Gilbert Rd. BR1: Brom 7J 141
DA17: Belv 3G 109
HA5: Pinn 4B 40
SE11 . . . . . 4K 19 (4A 102)
SW19 . . . . . 7A 136
UB9: Hare 2A 38
Gilbert Scott SW18 . . . . . 6G 117
Gilbert Sheldon Ho. *W2* *5B 4*
(off Edgware Rd.)
Gilbertson Ho. *E14* *3C 104*
(off Mellish St.)
Gilbert St. E15 . . . . . 4G 69
TW3: Houn 3G 113
W1 . . . . . 1H 11 (6E 82)
Gilbert Way CR0: Wadd 2K 167
Gilbert White Cl. UB6: G'frd 1A 78
Gilbey Cl. UB10: Ick 4D 56
Gilbey Ho. NW1 . . . . . 7F 65
Gilbey Rd. SW17 . . . . . 4C 136
Gilbeys Yd. NW1 . . . . . 7E 64
Gilbourne Rd. SE18 . . . . . 6K 107
Gilby Ho. E9 . . . . . 6K 67
Gilda Av. EN3: Pond E 5F 25
Gilda Ct. NW7 . . . . . 1C 44
Gilda Cres. N16 . . . . . 1G 67
Gildea Cl. HA5: Hat E 1E 40
Gildea St. W1 . . . . . 6K 5 (5F 83)
Gilden Cres. NW5 . . . . . 5E 64
Gildersome St. SE18 . . . . . 6E 106
Gilders Rd. KT9: Chess 7F 163
Giles Coppice SE19 . . . . . 4F 139
Giles Ho. SE16 . . . . . 7K 15
W11 . . . . . *6J 81*
(off Westbourne Gro.)
Gilesmead SE5 . . . . . 1D 120
Gilfrid Cl. UB8: Hil 6D 74
Gilkes Cres. SE21 . . . . . 6E 120
Gilkes Pl. SE21 . . . . . 6E 120
Gillam Ho. *SE16* *4J 103*
(off Silwood St.)
Gillan Ct. SE12 . . . . . 3K 141
Gillan Grn. WD23: B Hea 2B 26
Gillards M. E17 . . . . . 4C 50
Gillards Way E17 . . . . . 4C 50
Gill Av. E16 . . . . . 6J 87
Gillender St. E3 . . . . . 4E 86
E14 . . . . . 4E 86
Gillespie Rd. N5 . . . . . 3A 66
Gillett Av. E6 . . . . . 2C 88
GILLETTE CORNER 7A 96
Gillett Ho. *N8* *3J 47*
(off Campsfield Rd.)
Gillett Pl. N16 . . . . . 5E 66
Gillett Rd. CR7: Thor H 4D 156
Gillett St. N16 . . . . . 5E 66
Gillfoot *NW1* *1A 6*
(off Hampstead Rd.)
Gillham Ter. N17 . . . . . 6B 34
Gillian Ho. HA3: Hrw W 6D 26
Gillian Pk. Rd. SM3: Sutt 1H 165
Gillian St. SE13 . . . . . 5D 122
Gillies Ho. *NW6* *7B 64*
(off Hilgrove Rd.)
Gillies St. NW5 . . . . . 5E 64
Gilling Ct. NW3 . . . . . 6C 64
Gillingham M. SW1 . . . . . 3A 18 (4G 101)
Gillingham Rd. NW2 . . . . . 3G 63
Gillingham Row SW1 . . . . . 3A 18 (4G 101)
Gillingham St. SW1 . . . . . 3A 18 (4G 101)
Gillings Ct. *EN5: Barn* *4B 20*
(off Wood St.)
Gillison Wlk. SE16 . . . . . 3H 103
Gillman Dr. E15 . . . . . 1H 87
Gillman Ho. *E2* *2G 85*
(off Pritchard's Rd.)
Gillray Ho. *SW10* *6B 100*
(off Ann La.)
Gill St. E14 . . . . . 6B 86
Gillum Cl. EN4: E Barn 1J 31
Gilmore Cl. UB10: Ick 3C 56
Gilmore Ct. N11 . . . . . 5J 31
Gilmore Cres. TW15: Ashf 5C 128
Gilmore Rd. SE13 . . . . . 4F 123
Gilpin Av. SW14 . . . . . 4K 115
Gilpin Cl. CR4: Mitc 2C 154
W2 . . . . . *5A 4*
(off Porteus Rd.)
Gilpin Cres. N18 . . . . . 5A 34
TW2: Whitt 7F 113
Gilpin Rd. E5 . . . . . 4A 68
Gilpin Way UB3: Harl 7F 93
Gilray Ho. *W2* *2A 10*
(off Gloucester Ter.)
Gilsland Rd. CR7: Thor H 4D 156
Gilstead Ho. IG11: Bark 2B 90
Gilstead Rd. SW6 . . . . . 2K 117
Gilston Rd. SW10 . . . . . 7A 16 (5A 100)
Gilton Rd. SE6 . . . . . 3G 141
Giltspur St. EC1 . . . . . 7B 8 (6B 84)
Gilwell Cl. E4 . . . . . 4J 25
Gilwell La. E4 . . . . . 4J 25
(not continuous)
GILWELL PARK 4K 25
Gilwell Pk. E4 . . . . . 3K 25
Ginger Apartments *SE1* *6K 15*
(off Cayenne Ct.)
Ginsburg Yd. NW3 . . . . . 4A 64
Gippeswyck Cl. HA5: Pinn 1B 40
Gipsy Hill SE19 . . . . . 4E 138
Gipsy La. SW15 . . . . . 3D 116
Gipsy Moth IV 6E 104
Gipsy Rd. DA16: Well 7D 108
SE27 . . . . . 4C 138
Gipsy Rd. Gdns. SE27 . . . . . 4C 138
Giralda Cl. E16 . . . . . 5B 88
Giraud St. E14 . . . . . 6D 86
Girdler's Rd. W14 . . . . . 4F 99
Girdlestone Wlk. N19 . . . . . 2G 65
Girdwood Rd. SW18 . . . . . 7G 117
Girling Ho. *N1* *1E 84*
(off Colville Est.)
Girling Way TW14: Felt 3J 111
Gironde Rd. SW6 . . . . . 7H 99
Girtin Ho. *UB5: N'olt* *2B 76*
(off Academy Gdns.)
Girton Av. NW9 . . . . . 3G 43
Girton Cl. UB5: N'olt 6G 59
Girton Gdns. CR0: C'don 3C 170
Girton Rd. SE26 . . . . . 5K 139
UB5: N'olt 6G 59
Girton Vs. W10 . . . . . 6F 81
Gisbourne Cl. SM6: Bedd 3H 167
Gisburn Ho. *SE15* *6G 103*
(off Friary Est.)
Gisburn Rd. N8 . . . . . 4K 47
Gissing Wlk. N1 . . . . . 7A 66
Gittens Cl. BR1: Brom 4H 141
Given Wilson Wlk. E13 . . . . . 2H 87
Glacier Way HA0: Wemb 2D 78
Gladbeck Way EN2: Enf 4G 23
Gladding Rd. E12 . . . . . 4B 70
Glade, The BR1: Brom 2B 160
BR4: W W'ck 3D 170
CR0: C'don 5K 157
EN2: Enf 3F 23
IG5: Ilf 1D 52
IG8: Wfd G 3E 36
KT17: Ewe 6C 164
N12 . . . . . 3G 31
N21 . . . . . 6E 22
SE7 . . . . . 7A 106
SM2: Cheam 7G 165
W12 . . . . . *2D 98*
(off Coningham Rd.)
Glade Cl. KT6: Surb 2D 162
Glade Ct. IG5: Ilf 1D 52
Glade Gdns. CR0: C'don 7A 158
Glade La. UB2: S'hall 2F 95
Glade Rd. E12 . . . . . 3D 70
Glades, The KT6: Surb 7E 150
Gladeside CR0: C'don 6K 157
N21 . . . . . 6E 22
Gladeside Cl. KT9: Chess 7D 162
Gladesmore Community School &
Sports Cen. 5G 49
Gladesmore Rd. N15 . . . . . 6F 49
Glades Pl. BR1: Brom 2J 159
Glades Shop. Cen., The BR1: Brom . . . 2J 159
Gladeswood Rd. DA17: Belv 4H 109
Gladiator St. SE23 . . . . . 7A 122
Glading Ter. N16 . . . . . 3F 67
Gladioli Cl. TW12: Hamp 6E 130
Gladsdale Dr. HA5: Eastc 4J 39
Gladsmuir Rd. EN5: Barn 2B 20
N19 . . . . . 1G 65
Gladstone Av. E12 . . . . . 7C 70
N22 . . . . . 2A 48
TW2: Twick 1H 131
TW14: Felt 6J 111
Gladstone Ct. *NW6* *7A 64*
(off Fairfax Rd.)
SW1 . . . . . *4D 18*
(off Regency St.)
Gladstone Ct. Bus. Cen. *SW8* *1F 119*
(off Pagden St.)
Gladstone Gdns. TW3: Houn 1G 113
Gladstone Ho. CR4: Mitc 2D 154
E14 . . . . . *6C 86*
(off E. India Dock Rd.)
Gladstone M. N22 . . . . . 2A 48
NW6 . . . . . 7H 63
SE20 . . . . . 7J 139
Gladstone Pde. NW2 . . . . . 2E 62
Gladstone Pk. Gdns. NW2 . . . . . 3D 62
Gladstone Pl. E3 . . . . . 2B 86
EN5: Barn 4A 20
KT8: E Mos 5J 149
Gladstone Rd. BR6: Farnb 5G 173
CR0: C'don 7D 156
IG9: Buck H 1F 37
KT1: King T 3G 151
KT6: Surb 2D 162
SW19 . . . . . 7J 135
UB2: S'hall 2C 94
W4 . . . . . 3K 97
Gladstone St. SE1 . . . . . 3B 102
Gladstone Ter. *SE27* *5C 138*
(off Bentons La.)
SW8 . . . . . 1F 119
Gladstone Way HA3: W'stone 3J 41
Gladwell Rd. BR1: Brom 6J 141
N8 . . . . . 6K 47
Gladwin Ho. *NW1* *1B 6*
(off Werrington St.)
Gladwyn Rd. SW15 . . . . . 3F 117
Gladys Dimson Ho. E7 . . . . . 5H 69
Gladys Rd. NW6 . . . . . 7J 63
Glaisher St. SE8 . . . . . 6C 104
Glamis Ct. W3 . . . . . 2H 97
Glamis Cres. UB3: Harl 3E 92
Glamis Pl. E1 . . . . . 7J 85
Glamis Rd. E1 . . . . . 7J 85
Glamis Way UB5: N'olt 6G 59
Glamorgan Cl. CR4: Mitc 3J 155
Glamorgan Ct. *W7* *5K 77*
(off Copley Cl.)
Glamorgan Rd. KT1: Ham W 7C 132
Glandford Way RM6: Chad H 5B 54
Glanfield Rd. BR3: Beck 4B 158
Glanleam Rd. HA7: Stan 4J 27
Glanville M. HA7: Stan 5F 27
Glanville Rd. BR2: Brom 3K 159
SW2 . . . . . 5J 119
Glasbrook Av.
TW2: Whitt 1D 130
Glasbrook Rd. SE9 . . . . . 7B 124
Glaserton Rd. N16 . . . . . 7E 48
Glasford St. SW17 . . . . . 6D 136
Glasfryn Ct. *HA2: Harr* *2H 59*
(off Roxeth Hill)
Glasfryn Ho. *HA2: Harr* *2H 59*
(off Roxeth Hill)
Glasgow Ho. *W9* *2K 81*
(off Maida Va.)
Glasgow Rd. E13 . . . . . 2K 87
N18 . . . . . 5C 34
Glasgow Ter.
SW1 . . . . . 6A 18 (5G 101)
Glasier Ct. E15 . . . . . 7G 69
Glaskin M. E9 . . . . . 6A 68
Glass Art Gallery, The 7G 15 (2E 102)

Glass Bldg., The *NW1* 1F 83
(off Jamestown Rd.)
Glasse Cl. W13 7A 78
Glasshill St. SE1 6B 14 (2B 102)
Glass Ho. *WC2* 1E 12
(off Shaftesbury Av.)
Glass Ho., The *SE1* 7G 15
(off Royal Oak Yd.)
Glasshouse Cl. UB8: Hil 5D 74
Glasshouse Flds. E1 7K 85
(not continuous)
Glasshouse St. W1 3B 12 (7G 83)
Glasshouse Wlk. SE11 5F 19 (5J 101)
Glasshouse Yd. EC1 4C 8 (4C 84)
Glasslyn Rd. N8 5H 47
Glassmill La. BR2: Brom 2H 159
(not continuous)
Glass St. E2 4H 85
Glassworks Studios *E2* 1H 9
(off Basing Pl.)
Glass Yd. SE18 3E 106
Glastonbury Av. IG8: Wfd G 7G 37
Glastonbury Ct. *SE14* 7J 103
(off Farrow La.)
W13 1A 96
(off Talbot Rd.)
Glastonbury Ho. *SE12* 5H 123
(off Wantage Rd.)
SW1 5J 17
(off Abbots Mnr.)
Glastonbury Pl. E1 6J 85
Glastonbury Rd. N9 1B 34
SM4: Mord 7J 153
Glastonbury St. NW6 5H 63
Glaston Ct. *W5* 1D 96
(off Grange Rd.)
Glaucus St. E3 5D 86
Glazbury Rd. W14 4G 99
Glazebrook Cl. SE21 2D 138
Glazebrook Rd. TW11: Tedd 7K 131
Glebe, The BR7: Chst 1G 161
KT4: Wor Pk 1B 164
SE3 3G 123
SW16 4H 137
UB7: W Dray 4B 92
Glebe Av. CR4: Mitc 2C 154
EN2: Enf 3G 23
HA3: Kent 4E 42
HA4: Ruis 6K 57
IG8: Wfd G 6D 36
UB10: Ick 3E 56
Glebe Cl. UB10: Ick 4E 56
W4 5A 98
Glebe Cotts. *TW13: Hanw* 3E 130
(off Twickenham Rd.)
Glebe Ct. CR4: Mitc 3D 154
HA7: Stan 5H 27
N13 3F 33
SE3 3G 123
W5 1D 96
W7 7H 77
Glebe Cres. HA3: Kent 3E 42
NW4 4E 44
Glebe Gdns. KT3: N Mald 7A 152
Glebe Ho. *SE16* 3H 103
(off Slippers Pl.)
Glebe Ho. Dr. BR2: Hayes 1K 171
Glebe Hyrst SE19 4E 138
Glebe Knoll BR2: Brom 2H 159
Glebeland Gdns. TW17: Shep 6E 146
Glebelands E10 2D 68
KT8: W Mole 5F 149
Glebelands Av. E18 2J 51
IG2: Ilf 7H 53
Glebelands Cl. N12 1B 46
SE5 3E 120
Glebelands Local Nature Reserve 6J 31
Glebelands Rd. TW14: Felt 1J 129
Glebe La. HA3: Kent 4E 42
Glebe Path CR4: Mitc 3D 154
Glebe Pl. SW3 7C 16 (6C 100)
Glebe Rd. BR1: Brom 1J 159
E8 7F 67
HA7: Stan 5H 27
N3 1A 46
N8 4K 47
NW10 6C 62
RM10: Dag 6H 73
SM2: Cheam 7G 165
SM5: Cars 6D 166
SW13 2C 116
UB3: Hayes 1H 93
Glebe Side TW1: Twick 6K 113
Glebe Sq. CR4: Mitc 3D 154
Glebe St. W4 5A 98
Glebe Ter. E3 3D 86
W4 5A 98
Glebe Way BR4: W W'ck 2E 170
IG8: Wfd G 5F 37
TW13: Hanw 3E 130
Gledhow Gdns. SW5 4A 100
Gledstanes Rd. W14 5G 99
Gledwood Av. UB4: Hayes 5H 75
Gledwood Cres. UB4: Hayes 5H 75
Gledwood Dr. UB4: Hayes 5H 75
Gledwood Gdns. UB4: Hayes 5H 75
Gleed Av. WD23: B Hea 2C 26
Gleeson Dr. BR6: Chels 5K 173
Glegg Pl. SW15 4F 117
Glen, The BR2: Brom 2G 159
BR6: Farnb 3D 172
CR0: C'don 3K 169
EN2: Enf 4G 23
HA5: Eastc 5K 39
HA5: Pinn 7C 40
HA9: Wemb 4E 60
UB2: S'hall 5D 94
Glenaffric Av. E14 4E 104
Glen Albyn Rd. SW19 2F 135
Glenallan Ho. *W14* 4H 99
(off North End Cres.)
Glenalla Rd. HA4: Ruis 7H 39
Glenalmond Ho. TW15: Ashf 3A 128
Glenalmond Rd. HA3: Kent 4E 42
Glenalvon Way SE18 4C 106
Glena Mt. SM1: Sutt 4A 166
Glenarm Rd. E5 4J 67
Glen Av. TW15: Ashf 4C 128
Glenavon Cl. KT10: Clay 6A 162
Glenavon Ct. KT4: Wor Pk 2D 164
Glenavon Lodge
BR3: Beck 7C 140
Glenavon Rd. E15 7G 69
Glenbarr Cl. SE9 3F 125
Glenbow Rd. BR1: Brom 6G 141
Glenbrook Nth. EN2: Enf 4E 22
Glenbrook Rd. NW6 5J 63
Glenbrook Sth. EN2: Enf 4E 22
Glenbuck Ct. KT6: Surb 6E 150
Glenbuck Rd. KT6: Surb 6D 150
Glenburnie Rd. SW17 3D 136
Glencairn Dr. W5 4C 78
Glencairne Cl. E16 5B 88
Glencairn Rd. SW16 1J 155
Glencar Ct. SE19 6B 138
Glen Cl. TW17: Shep 4C 146
Glencoe Av. IG2: Ilf 7H 53
Glencoe Dr. RM10: Dag 4G 73
Glencoe Mans. *SW9* 7A 102
(off Mowll St.)
Glencoe Rd. UB4: Yead 5B 76
Glen Ct. DA15: Sidc 4A 144
Glen Cres. IG8: Wfd G 6E 36
Glendale Av. HA8: Edg 4A 28
N22 7F 33
RM6: Chad H 7C 54
Glendale Cl. SE9 3E 124
Glendale Dr. SW19 5H 135
Glendale Gdns. HA9: Wemb 1D 60
Glendale M. BR3: Beck 1D 158
Glendale Rd. DA8: Erith 4J 109
Glendale Way SE28 7C 90
Glendall St. SW9 4K 119
Glendarvon St. SW15 3F 117
Glendevon Cl. HA8: Edg 3C 28
Glendish Rd. N17 1H 49
Glendor Gdns. NW7 4E 28
Glendower Gdns. SW14 3K 115
Glendower Pl. SW7 3A 16 (4B 100)
Glendower Rd. E4 1A 36
SW14 3K 115
Glendown Ho. E8 5G 67
Glendown Rd. SE2 5A 108
Glendun Ct. W3 7A 80
Glendun Rd. W3 7A 80
Gleneagle M. SW16 5H 137
Gleneagle Rd. SW16 5H 137
Gleneagles HA7: Stan 7G 27
W13 5B 78
(off Malvern Way)
Gleneagles Cl. BR6: Orp 1H 173
SE16 5H 103
Gleneagles Grn. BR6: Orp 1H 173
Gleneagles Twr. *UB1: S'hall* 6G 77
(off Fleming Rd.)
Gleneldon M. SW16 4J 137
Gleneldon Rd. SW16 4J 137
Glenelg Rd. SW2 5J 119
Glenesk Rd. SE9 3E 124
Glenfarg Rd. SE6 1E 140
Glenfield Cres. HA4: Ruis 7F 39
Glenfield Rd. SW12 1G 137
TW15: Ashf 6D 128
W13 2B 96
Glenfield Ter. W13 2B 96
Glenfinlas Way SE5 7B 102
Glenforth St. SE10 5H 105
Glengall Gro. E14 3D 104
Glengall Pas. *NW6* 1J 81
(off Priory Pk. Rd.)
Glengall Rd. DA7: Bex 3E 126
HA8: Edg 3C 28
IG8: Wfd G 6D 36
NW6 1H 81
SE15 5F 103
Glengall Ter. SE15 6F 103
Glen Gdns. CR0: Wadd 3A 168
Glengarnock Av. E14 4E 104
Glengarriff Mans. *SW9* 7A 102
(off Sth. Island Pl.)
Glengarry Rd. SE22 5E 120
Glenham Dr. IG2: Ilf 5F 53
Glenhead Cl. SE9 3F 125
Glenhill Cl. N3 2J 45
Glen Ho. *E16* 1E 106
(off Storey St.)
Glenhouse Rd. SE9 5E 124
Glenhurst BR3: Beck 1E 158
Glenhurst Av. DA5: Bexl 1F 145
HA4: Ruis 7E 38
NW5 4E 64
Glenhurst Ct. SE19 5F 139
Glenhurst Ri. SE19 7C 138
Glenhurst Rd. N12 5G 31
TW8: Bford 6C 96
Glenilla Rd. NW3 6C 64
Glenister Ho. *UB3: Hayes* 1K 93
(off Avondale Dr.)
Glenister Pk. Rd. SW16 7H 137
Glenister Rd. SE10 5H 105
Glenister St. E16 1E 106
Glenkerry Ho. *E14* 6E 86
(off Burcham St.)
Glenlea Rd. SE9 5D 124
Glenloch Rd. EN3: Enf H 2D 24
NW3 6C 64
Glenluce Rd. SE3 6J 105
Glenlyon Rd. SE9 5E 124
Glenmead IG9: Buck H 1F 37
Glenmere Av. NW7 7H 29
Glen M. E17 5B 50
Glenmill TW12: Hamp 5D 130
Glenmore Lawns W13 6A 78
Glenmore Lodge BR3: Beck 1D 158
Glenmore Pde. HA0: Wemb 1E 78
Glenmore Rd. DA16: Well 7K 107
NW3 6C 64
Glenmore Way IG11: Bark 2A 90
Glenmount Path SE18 5G 107
Glennie Ct. SE22 1G 139
Glennie Ho. *SE10* 1E 122
(off Blackheath Hill)
Glennie Rd. SE27 3A 138
Glenny Rd. IG11: Bark 6G 71
Glenorchy Cl. UB4: Yead 5C 76
Glenpark Ct. W13 7A 78
Glenparke Rd. E7 6K 69
(not continuous)
Glenridding *NW1* 1B 6
(off Ampthill Est.)
Glen Ri. IG8: Wfd G 6E 36
Glen Rd. E13 4A 88
E17 5B 50
KT9: Chess 4F 163
Glen Rd. End SM6: Wall 7F 167
Glenrosa St. SW6 2A 118
Glenrose Ct. DA14: Sidc 5B 144
SE1 7G 15
(off Long La.)
Glenroy St. W12 6E 80
Glensdale Rd. SE4 3B 122
Glenshaw Mans. *SW9* 7A 102
(off Brixton Rd.)
Glenshiel Rd. SE9 5E 124
Glentanner Way SW17 3B 136
Glen Ter. *E14* 2E 104
(off Manchester Rd.)
Glentham Gdns. SW13 6D 98
Glentham Rd. SW13 6C 98
Glenthorne Av. CR0: C'don 1H 169
Glenthorne Cl. SM3: Sutt 1J 165
UB10: Hil 3C 74
Glenthorne Gdns. IG6: Ilf 3E 52
SM3: Sutt 1J 165
Glenthorne M. W6 4D 98
Glenthorne Rd. E17 5A 50
KT1: King T 4F 151
N11 5J 31
W6 4D 98
Glenthorpe Av. SW15 4C 116
Glenthorpe Rd.
SM4: Mord 5F 153
Glenton Rd. SE13 4G 123
Glentrammon Av. BR6: Chels 6K 173
Glentrammon Cl. BR6: Chels 5K 173
Glentrammon Gdns.
BR6: Chels 6K 173
Glentrammon Rd. BR6: Chels 6K 173
Glentworth St. NW1 4F 5 (4D 82)
Glenure Rd. SE9 5E 124
Glenvern Ct. *TW7: Isle* 2A 114
(off White Lodge Cl.)
Glenview SE2 6D 108
Glenview Rd. BR1: Brom 2B 160
Glenville Av. EN2: Enf 1H 23
Glenville Gro. SE8 7B 104
Glenville M. SW18 7K 117
Glenville M. Ind. Est. SW18 7J 117
Glenville Rd. KT2: King T 1G 151
Glen Wlk. TW7: Isle 5H 113
(not continuous)
Glenwood Av. NW9 1A 62
Glenwood Cl. HA1: Harr 5K 41
Glenwood Ct. DA14: Sidc 4A 144
E18 3J 51
Glenwood Gdns. IG2: Ilf 5E 52
Glenwood Gro. NW9 1J 61
Glenwood Rd. KT17: Ewe 6C 164
N15 5B 48
NW7 3F 29

Glenwood Rd. SE6 .... 1B **140**
TW3: Houn 3H **113**
Glenwood Way CR0: C'don 6K **157**
Glenworth Av. E14 .... 4F **105**
Gliddon Dr. E5 .... 4H **67**
Gliddon Rd. W14 .... 4G **99**
Glimpsing Grn. DA18: Erith 3E **108**
Glisson Rd. UB10: Hil 2C **74**
Global App. E3 .... 2E **86**
Globe, The SE1 .... 7E **14** (2C **102**)
Globe Pond Rd. SE16 .... 1A **104**
Globe Rd. E1 .... 3J **85**
E2 .... 3J **85**
E15 .... 5H **69**
IG8: Wfd G 6F **37**
Globe Rope Wlk. *E14* *4D* **104**
(off E. Ferry Rd.)
Globe St. SE1 .... 7E **14** (3D **102**)
Globe Ter. E2 .... 3J **85**
GLOBE TOWN 3K **85**
Globe Town Mkt. E2 .... 3K **85**
Globe Vw. *EC4* *2C* **14**
(off High Timber St.)
Globe Wharf SE16 .... 7K **85**
Globe Yd. W1 .... 1J **11**
Glossop Rd. CR2: Sande 7D **168**
Gloster Rd. KT3: N Mald 4A **152**
Gloucester *W14* *4H* **99**
(off Mornington Av.)
Gloucester Arc. SW7 .... 4A **100**
Gloucester Av. DA15: Sidc 2J **143**
DA16: Well 4K **125**
NW1 .... 7E **64**
Gloucester Cir. SE10 .... 7E **104**
Gloucester Cl. KT7: T Ditt 1A **162**
NW10 .... 7K **61**
Gloucester Ct. CR4: Mitc 5J **155**
EC3 .... 3H **15** (7E **84**)
HA1: Harr 3J **41**
NW11 .... *7H* **45**
(off Golders Grn. Rd.)
SE1 .... *7D* **14**
(off Swan St.)
SE22 .... 1G **139**
TW9: Kew 7G **97**
W7 .... *5K* **77**
(off Copley Cl.)
Gloucester Cres. NW1 .... 1F **83**
TW18: Staines 6A **128**
Gloucester Dr. N4 .... 2B **66**
NW11 .... 4J **45**
Gloucester Gdns. EN4: Cockf 4K **21**
IG1: Ilf 7C **52**
NW11 .... 7H **45**
SM1: Sutt 2K **165**
W2 .... 6A **82**
Gloucester Ga. NW1 .... 2F **83**
(not continuous)
Gloucester Ga. M. NW1 .... 2F **83**
Gloucester Gro. HA8: Edg 1K **43**
Gloucester Ho. *E16* *1J* **105**
(off Gatcombe Rd.)
NW6 .... *2J* **81**
(off Cambridge Rd.)
SW9 .... 7A **102**
TW10: Rich 5G **115**
Gloucester M. E10 .... 7C **50**
W2 .... 1A **10** (6A **82**)
Gloucester M. W. W2 .... 6A **82**
Gloucester Pde. DA15: Sidc 5A **126**
UB3: Harl 3E **92**
Gloucester Pk. Apartments SW7 .... 4A **100**
Gloucester Pl. NW1 .... 4E **4** (4D **82**)
W1 .... 4E **4** (4D **82**)
Gloucester Pl. M. W1 .... 6F **5** (5D **82**)
Gloucester Rd. CR0: C'don 1D **168**
DA17: Belv 5F **109**
E10 .... 7C **50**
E11 .... 5K **51**
E12 .... 3D **70**
Gloucester Rd. E17 .... 2K **49**
EN2: Enf 1H **23**
EN5: New Bar 5E **20**
HA1: Harr 5F **41**
KT1: King T 2G **151**
N17 .... 2D **48**
N18 .... 5A **34**
SW7 .... 4A **16** (3A **100**)
TW2: Twick 1G **131**
TW4: Houn 4C **112**
TW9: Kew 7G **97**
TW11: Tedd 5J **131**
TW12: Hamp 7F **131**
TW13: Felt 1A **130**
W3 .... 2J **97**
W5 .... 2C **96**
Gloucester Sq. E2 .... 1G **85**
W2 .... 1B **10** (6B **82**)
Gloucester St. SW1 .... 6A **18** (5G **101**)
Gloucester Ter. *N14* *1C* **32**
(off Crown La.)
W2 .... 1A **10** (6K **81**)
Gloucester Wlk. W8 .... 2J **99**
Gloucester Way EC1 .... 2K **7** (3A **84**)
Glover Cl. SE2 .... 4C **108**
Glover Dr. N18 .... 6D **34**
Glover Ho. *NW6* *7A* **64**
(off Harben Rd.)
SE15 .... 4H **121**
Glover Rd. HA5: Pinn 6B **40**
Glovers Gro. HA4: Ruis 7D **38**
Gloxinia Wlk. TW12: Hamp 6E **130**
Glycena Rd. SW11 .... 3D **118**
Glyn Av. EN4: E Barn 4G **21**
Glyn Cl. SE25 .... 2E **156**
Glyn Ct. HA7: Stan 6G **27**
SW16 .... 3A **138**
Glyndale Grange SM2: Sutt 6K **165**
Glyndebourne Ct. *UB5: Yead* *3A* **76**
(off Canberra Dr.)
Glyndebourne Pk. BR6: Farnb 2F **173**
Glynde M. SW3 .... 2D **16**
Glynde Reach WC1 .... 2F **7**
Glynde Rd. DA7: Bex 3D **126**
Glynde St. SE4 .... 6B **122**
Glyndon Rd. SE18 .... 4G **107**
(not continuous)
Glyn Dr. DA14: Sidc 4B **144**
Glynfield Rd. NW10 .... 7A **62**
Glyn Mans. *W14* *4G* **99**
(off Hammersmith Rd.)
Glynne Rd. N22 .... 2A **48**
Glyn Rd. E5 .... 3K **67**
EN3: Pond E 4D **24**
KT4: Wor Pk 2F **165**
Glyn St. SE11 .... 6G **19** (5K **101**)
Glynswood Pl. HA6: Nwood 1D **38**
Glynwood Ct. SE23 .... 2J **139**
Goals Soccer Cen.
Bexleyheath 3F **127**
Hayes 4E **92**
Goater's All. *SW6* *7H* **99**
(off Dawes Rd.)
Goat Ho. Bri. SE25 .... 3G **157**
Goat La. EN1: Enf 1A **24**
Goat Rd. CR4: Cars, Mitc 7D **154**
Goat Wharf TW8: Bford 6E **96**
Gobions Av. RM5: Col R 1K **55**
Godalming Av. SM6: Wall 5J **167**
Godalming Rd. E14 .... 5D **86**
Godbold Rd. E15 .... 4G **87**
Goddard Cl. TW17: Shep 3B **146**
Goddard Ct. HA3: Kent 2A **42**
Goddard Pl. N19 .... 3G **65**
Goddard Rd. BR3: Beck 4K **157**
Goddards Way IG1: Ilf 1H **71**
Goddarts Ho. E17 .... 3C **50**
Goddington La. BR6: Chels 3K **173**
Godfree Ct. *SE1* *6E* **14**
(off Long La.)
Godfrey Av. TW2: Whitt 7H **113**
UB5: N'olt 1C **76**
Godfrey Hill SE18 .... 4C **106**
Godfrey Ho. EC1 .... 2E **8**
Godfrey Rd. SE18 .... 4D **106**
Godfrey St. E15 .... 2E **86**
SW3 .... 5D **16** (5C **100**)
Godfrey Way TW4: Houn 7C **112**
Goding St. SE11 .... 5F **19** (5J **101**)
Godley Cl. SE14 .... 1J **121**
Godley Rd. SW18 .... 1B **136**
Godliman St. EC4 .... 1B **14** (6B **84**)
Godman Rd. SE15 .... 2H **121**
Godolphin Cl. N13 .... 6G **33**
Godolphin Ho. *NW3* *7C* **64**
(off Fellows Rd.)
Godolphin Pl. W3 .... 7K **79**
Godolphin Rd. W12 .... 1D **98**
(not continuous)
Godric Cres. CR0: New Ad 7F **171**
Godson Rd. CR0: Wadd 3A **168**
Godstone Ho. *SE1* *7F* **15**
(off Pardoner St.)
Godstone Rd. SM1: Sutt 4A **166**
TW1: Twick 6B **114**
Godstow Rd. SE2 .... 2B **108**
Godwin Cl. E4 .... 1K **25**
KT19: Ewe 6J **163**
N1 .... 2C **84**
Godwin Ct. *NW1* *2G* **83**
(off Chalton St.)
Godwin Ho. *E2* *2F* **85**
(off Thurtle Rd.)
NW6 .... *2K* **81**
(off Tollgate Gdns., not continuous)
Godwin Rd. BR2: Brom 3A **160**
E7 .... 4K **69**
Goffers Rd. SE3 .... 1G **123**
Goffs Rd. TW15: Ashf 6F **129**
Goidel Cl. SM6: Bedd 4H **167**
Golborne Gdns. W10 .... 4G **81**
Golborne Ho. *W10* *4G* **81**
(off Adair Rd.)
Golborne M. W10 .... 5G **81**
Golborne Rd. W10 .... 5G **81**
Golda Cl. EN5: Barn 6A **20**
Golda Ct. N3 .... 2H **45**
Goldbeaters Gro. HA8: Edg 6F **29**
Goldbeaters Ho. *W1* *1D* **12**
(off Manette St.)
Goldcliff Cl. SM4: Mord 7J **153**
Goldcrest Cl. E16 .... 5B **88**
SE28 .... 7C **90**
Goldcrest M. W5 .... 5D **78**
Goldcrest Way CR0: New Ad 7F **171**
WD23: Bush 1B **26**
Golden Bus. Pk. E10 .... 1A **68**
Golden Ct. EN4: E Barn 4H **21**
TW7: Isle 2H **113**
TW9: Rich 5D **114**
Golden Cres. UB3: Hayes 1H **93**
Golden Cross M. *W11* *6H* **81**
(off Portobello Rd.)
Golden Hinde 4E **14** (1D **102**)
Golden Hind Pl. *SE8* *4B* **104**
(off Grove St.)
Golden Jubilee Bridges, The *1K* **101**
(off Belvedere Rd.)
Golden La. EC1 .... 3C **8** (4C **84**)
Golden La. Est. EC1 .... 4C **8** (4C **84**)
Golden Lane Leisure Cen. 4C **8**
Golden Mnr. W7 .... 7J **77**
Golden M. SE20 .... 1J **157**
Golden Pde. *E17* *3E* **50**
(off Wood St.)
Golden Plover Cl. E16 .... 6J **87**
Golden Sq. W1 .... 2B **12** (7G **83**)
Golden Yd. *NW3* *4A* **64**
(off Holly Mt.)
Golders Cl. HA8: Edg 5C **28**
Golders Ct. NW11 .... 7H **45**
Golders Gdns. NW11 .... 7G **45**
GOLDERS GREEN 6G **45**
Golders Grn. Crematorium
NW11 .... 7J **45**
Golders Grn. Cres. NW11 .... 7H **45**
Golders Grn. Rd. NW11 .... 6G **45**
Goldersiea NW11 .... 1J **63**
Golders Mnr. Dr. NW11 .... 6F **45**
Golders Pk. Cl. NW11 .... 1J **63**
Golders Ri. NW4 .... 5F **45**
Golders Way NW11 .... 7H **45**
Golderton *NW4* *4D* **44**
(off Prince of Wales Cl.)
Goldfinch Rd. SE28 .... 3H **107**
Goldhawk Ind. Est. W6 .... 3D **98**
Goldhawk M. W12 .... 2D **98**
Goldhawk Rd. W6 .... 4B **98**
W12 .... 4B **98**
Goldhaze Cl. IG8: Wfd G 7F **37**
Gold Hill HA8: Edg 6E **28**
Goldhurst Mans. *NW6* *6A* **64**
(off Goldhurst Ter.)
Goldhurst Ter. NW6 .... 7K **63**
Goldie Ho. N19 .... 7H **47**
Goldie Leigh Hospital SE2 .... 7B **108**
Golding Cl. KT9: Chess 6C **162**
Golding Ct. IG1: Ilf 3E **70**
Golding St. E1 .... 6G **85**
Golding Ter. E1 .... 6G **85**
SW11 .... 2E **118**
Goldington Bldgs. *NW1* *1H* **83**
(off Royal College St.)
Goldington Cres. NW1 .... 2H **83**
Goldington St. NW1 .... 2H **83**
Gold La. HA8: Edg 6E **28**
Goldman Cl. E2 .... 3K **9** (4G **85**)
Goldmark Ho. SE3 .... 3K **123**
Goldney Rd. W9 .... 4J **81**
Goldrill Dr. N11 .... 2K **31**
Goldsboro' Rd. SW8 .... 1H **119**
Goldsborough Cres. E4 .... 2J **35**
Goldsborough Ho. *E14* *5D* **104**
(off St Davids Sq.)
Goldsdown Cl. EN3: Enf H 2F **25**
Goldsdown Rd. EN3: Enf H 2E **24**
Goldsmid St. SE18 .... 5J **107**
Goldsmith Av. E12 .... 6C **70**
NW9 .... 5A **44**
RM7: Rush G 7G **55**
W3 .... 7K **79**
Goldsmith Cl. HA2: Harr 1E **58**
Goldsmith Ct. *WC2* *7F* **7**
(off Stukeley St.)
Goldsmith La. NW9 .... 4H **43**
Goldsmith Rd. E10 .... 1C **68**
E17 .... 2K **49**
N11 .... 5J **31**
SE15 .... 1G **121**
W3 .... 1K **97**
Goldsmith's Bldgs. W3 .... 1K **97**
Goldsmiths Cl. W3 .... 1K **97**
Goldsmiths College 1A **122**
Goldsmith's Pl. *NW6* *1K* **81**
(off Springfield La.)
Goldsmith's Row E2 .... 2G **85**
Goldsmith's Sq. E2 .... 2G **85**
Goldsmith St. EC2 .... 7D **8** (6C **84**)
Goldsworthy Gdns.
SE16 .... 5J **103**
Goldthorpe *NW1* *1G* **83**
(off Camden St.)
Goldwell Ho. SE22 .... 3E **120**
Goldwell Rd. CR7: Thor H 4K **155**
Goldwin Cl. SE14 .... 1J **121**
Goldwing Cl. E16 .... 6J **87**
Golf Cl. CR7: Thor H 1A **156**
HA7: Stan 7H **27**
Golf Club Dr. KT2: King T 7K **133**
Golfe Rd. IG1: Ilf 3H **71**

Golf Rd. BR1: Brom 3E **160**
W5 6F **79**
Golf Side TW2: Twick 3H **131**
Golfside Cl. KT3: N Mald 2A **152**
N20 3H **31**
Gollogly Ter. SE7 5A **106**
Gomer Gdns. TW11: Tedd 6A **132**
Gomer Pl. TW11: Tedd 6A **132**
Gomm Rd. SE16 3J **103**
Gomshall Av. SM6: Wall 5J **167**
Gondar Gdns. NW6 5H **63**
Gonson St. SE8 6D **104**
Gonston Cl. SW19 2G **135**
Gonville Cres. UB5: N'olt 6F **59**
Gonville Rd. CR7: Thor H 5K **155**
Gonville St. SW6 3G **117**
Gooch Ho. E5 3H **67**
EC1 *5J* ***7***
(off Portpool La.)
Goodall Ho. SE4 4K **121**
Goodall Rd. E11 3E **68**
Gooden Ct. HA1: Harr 3J **59**
Goodenough Rd. SW19 7H **135**
Goodey Rd. IG11: Bark 7K **71**
Goodfaith Ho. *E14* *7D* ***86***
(off Simpson's Rd.)
Goodge Pl. W1 6B **6** (5G **83**)
Goodge St. W1 6B **6** (5G **83**)
Goodhall Cl. HA7: Stan 6F **27**
Goodhall St. NW10 3B **80**
(not continuous)
Goodhart Pl. E14 7A **86**
Goodhart Way BR4: W W'ck 7G **159**
Goodhew Rd. CR0: C'don 6G **157**
Goodhope Ho. *E14* *7D* ***86***
(off Poplar High St.)
Gooding Cl. KT3: N Mald 4J **151**
Goodinge Cl. N7 6J **65**
Gooding Ho. SE7 5A **106**
Goodman Ct. CR0: C'don 6B **156**
Goodman Cres. SW2 2J **137**
Goodman Rd. E10 7E **50**
Goodmans Ct. E1 2J **15** (7F **85**)
HA0: Wemb 4D **60**
Goodman's Stile E1 6G **85**
Goodmans Yd. E1 2J **15** (7F **85**)
GOODMAYES 2A **72**
Goodmayes Av. IG3: Ilf 1A **72**
Goodmayes La. IG3: Ilf 4A **72**
Goodmayes Retail Pk.
RM6: Chad H 1B **72**
Goodmayes Rd. IG3: Ilf 1A **72**
Goodrich Ct. W10 6F **81**
Goodrich Ho. *E2* *2J* ***85***
(off Sewardstone Rd.)
Goodrich Rd. SE22 6F **121**
Goodson Rd. NW10 7A **62**
Goodson St. N1 2A **84**
Goodspeed Ho. *E14* *7D* ***86***
(off Simpson's Rd.)
Goods Way NW1 2J **83**
Goodway Gdns. E14 6F **87**
Goodwill Ho. *E14* *7D* ***86***
(off Simpson's Rd.)
Goodwin Cl. CR4: Mitc 3B **154**
SE16 3F **103**
Goodwin Ct. EN4: E Barn 6H **21**
N8 *3J* ***47***
(off Campsbourne Rd.)
SW19 7C **136**
Goodwin Dr. DA14: Sidc 3D **144**
Goodwin Gdns. CR0: Wadd 6B **168**
Goodwin Ho. N9 1D **34**
Goodwin Rd. CR0: Wadd 5B **168**
N9 1E **34**
W12 2C **98**
Goodwins Ct. WC2 2E **12** (7J **83**)
Goodwin St. N4 2A **66**
Goodwood Cl. HA7: Stan 5H **27**
SM4: Mord 4J **153**
Goodwood Ct. *W1* *5K* ***5***
(off Devonshire St.)
Goodwood Dr. UB5: N'olt 6E **58**
Goodwood Ho. *SE14* *7A* ***104***
(off Goodwood Rd.)
Goodwood Pde. BR3: Beck 4A **158**
Goodwood Rd. SE14 7A **104**
Goodwyn Av. NW7 5F **29**
Goodwyns Va. N10 1E **46**
Goodyear Ho. *N2* *2B* ***46***
(off The Grange)
Goodyear Pl. SE5 6C **102**
Goodyer Ho. *SW1* *5C* ***18***
(off Tachbrook St.)
Goodyers Gdns. NW4 5F **45**
Goosander Way SE28 3H **107**
Gooseacre La. HA3: Kent 5D **42**
Goose Grn. Trad. Est. SE22 4F **121**
Gooseley La. E6 4F **89**
(Claps Ga. La.)
E6 3E **88**
(Vicarage La.)
Goosens Cl. SM1: Sutt 5A **166**
Goose Sq. E6 6D **88**
Gophir La. EC4 2E **14** (7D **84**)
Gopsall St. N1 1D **84**
Gordon Av. E4 6B **36**
HA7: Stan 7E **26**
SW14 4A **116**
TW1: Twick 5A **114**
Gordonbrock Rd. SE4 5C **122**
Gordon Cl. E17 6C **50**
N19 1G **65**
Gordon Cotts. *W8* *2K* ***99***
(off Dukes La.)
Gordon Ct. HA8: Edg 5A **28**
Gordon Cres. CR0: C'don 1E **168**
UB3: Hayes 4J **93**
Gordondale Rd. SW19 2J **135**
Gordon Dr. TW17: Shep 7F **147**
Gordon Gdns. HA8: Edg 2H **43**
Gordon Gro. SE5 2B **120**
Gordon Hall *UB8: Cowl* *3A* ***74***
(off Kingston La.)
Gordon Hill EN2: Enf 1H **23**
Gordon Ho. *E1* *7J* ***85***
(off Glamis Rd.)
SW1 *2B* ***18***
(off Greencoat Pl.)
W5 3E **78**
Gordon Ho. Rd. NW5 4E **64**
Gordon Mans. *W14* *3F* ***99***
(off Addison Gdns.)
WC1 *4C* ***6***
(off Torrington Pl.)
Gordon Pl. W8 2J **99**
Gordon Rd. BR3: Beck 3B **158**
DA15: Sidc 5J **125**
DA17: Belv 4J **109**
E4 1B **36**
E11 6J **51**
E15 4E **68**
E18 1K **51**
EN2: Enf 1H **23**
HA3: W'stone 3J **41**
IG1: Ilf 3H **71**
IG11: Bark 1J **89**
KT2: King T 1F **151**
KT5: Surb 7F **151**
N3 7C **30**
N9 2C **34**
N11 7C **32**
RM6: Chad H 6F **55**
SE15 2H **121**
SM5: Cars 6D **166**
TW3: Houn 4G **113**
TW9: Rich 2F **115**
TW15: Ashf 3A **128**
TW17: Shep 6F **147**
UB2: S'hall 4C **94**
Gordon Rd. UB7: Yiew 7A **74**
W4 6H **97**
W5 7B **78**
W13 7B **78**
Gordon Sq. WC1 3C **6** (4H **83**)
Gordon St. E13 3J **87**
WC1 3C **6** (4H **83**)
Gordon Way BR1: Brom 1J **159**
EN5: Barn 4C **20**
Gore Ct. NW9 5G **43**
Gorefield Ho. *NW6* *2J* ***81***
(off Gorefield Pl.)
Gorefield Pl. NW6 2J **81**
Gore Rd. E9 1J **85**
SW20 2E **152**
GORESBROOK INTERCHANGE 2F **91**
Goresbrook Leisure Cen. 1D **90**
Goresbrook Rd. RM9: Dag 1B **90**
Gore St. SW7 3A **100**
Gorham Ho. *SE16* *2K* ***103***
(off Wolfe Cres.)
Gorham Pl. W11 7G **81**
Goring Cl. RM5: Col R 1J **55**
Goring Gdns. RM8: Dag 4C **72**
Goring Rd. N11 6D **32**
RM10: Dag 6K **73**
Goring St. EC3 7H **9**
Goring Way UB6: G'frd 2G **77**
Gorleston Rd. N15 5D **48**
Gorleston St. W14 4G **99**
(not continuous)
Gorman Rd. SE18 4D **106**
Gorringe Pk. Av.
CR4: Mitc 7D **136**
Gorse Cl. E16 6J **87**
Gorsefield Ho. *E14* *7C* ***86***
(off E. India Dock Rd.)
Gorse Ri. SW17 5E **136**
Gorse Rd. CR0: C'don 4C **170**
Gorse Wlk. UB7: Yiew 6A **74**
Gorseway RM7: Rush G 1K **73** & 2K **73**
Gorst Rd. NW10 4J **79**
SW11 6D **118**
Gorsuch Pl. E2 1J **9** (3F **85**)
Gorsuch St. E2 1J **9** (2F **85**)
Gosberton Rd. SW12 1D **136**
Gosbury Hill KT9: Chess 4E **162**
Gosfield Rd. RM8: Dag 2G **73**
Gosfield St. W1 6A **6** (5G **83**)
Gosford Gdns. IG4: Ilf 5D **52**
Goshawk Gdns.
UB4: Hayes 3G **75**
Goslett Yd. WC2 1D **12** (6H **83**)
Gosling Cl. UB6: G'frd 3E **76**
Gosling Ho. *E1* *7J* ***85***
(off Sutton St.)
Gosling Way SW9 1A **120**
Gospatrick Rd. N17 7H **33**
GOSPEL OAK 4E **64**
Gosport Rd. E17 5B **50**
Gosport Wlk. N17 4H **49**
Gossage Rd. SE18 5H **107**
UB10: Uxb 7B **56**
Gosset St. E2 1K **9** (3F **85**)
Gosshill Rd. BR7: Chst 2E **160**
Gossington Cl. BR7: Chst 4F **143**
Gosterwood St. SE8 6A **104**
Gostling Rd. TW2: Whitt 1E **130**
Goston Gdns.
CR7: Thor H 3A **156**
Goswell Pl. EC1 2B **8**
Goswell Rd. EC1 1A **8** (2B **84**)
Gothic Cotts. *EN2: Enf* *2H* ***23***
(off Chase Grn. Av.)
Gothic Ct. *SE5* *7C* ***102***
(off Wyndham Rd.)
UB3: Harl 6F **93**
Gothic Rd. TW2: Twick 2H **131**
Gottfried M. NW5 4G **65**
Goudhurst Rd. BR1: Brom 5G **141**
Gough Ho. *KT1: King T* *2E* ***150***
(off Eden St.)
N1 *1B* ***84***
(off Windsor St.)
Gough Rd. E15 4H **69**
EN1: Enf 2C **24**
Gough Sq. EC4 1K **13** (6A **84**)
Gough St. WC1 3H **7** (4K **83**)
Gough Wlk. E14 6C **86**
Goulden Ho. SW11 2C **118**
Goulden Ho. App. SW11 2C **118**
Goulding Gdns. CR7: Thor H 2B **156**
Gouldman Ho. *E1* *4J* ***85***
(off Wyllen Cl.)
Gould Rd. TW2: Twick 1J **131**
TW14: Felt 7G **111**
GOULDS GREEN 5D **74**
Gould's Grn. UB8: Hil 7D **74**
Gould Ter. E8 5H **67**
Goulston St. E1 7J **9** (6F **85**)
Goulton Rd. E5 4H **67**
Gourley Pl. N15 5E **48**
Gourley St. N15 5E **48**
Gourock Rd. SE9 5E **124**
Govan St. E2 1G **85**
Gover Ct. SW4 2J **119**
Govett Av. TW17: Shep 5E **146**
Govier Cl. E15 7G **69**
Gowan Av. SW6 1G **117**
Gowan Ho. *E2* *2K* ***9***
(off Chambord St.)
Gowan Rd. NW10 6D **62**
Gower Cl. SW4 6G **119**
Gower Ct. WC1 3C **6** (4H **83**)
Gower Ho. E17 3D **50**
SE17 *5C* ***102***
(off Morecambe St.)
Gower M. WC1 6D **6** (5H **83**)
Gower M. Mans. *WC1* *5D* ***6***
(off Gower M.)
Gower Pl. WC1 3B **6** (4H **83**)
Gower Rd. E7 6J **69**
TW7: Isle 6K **95**
Gower St. WC1 3B **6** (4G **83**)
Gower's Wlk. E1 6G **85**
Gowland Pl. BR3: Beck 2B **158**
Gowlett Rd. SE15 3G **121**
Gowlland Cl. CR0: C'don 7G **157**
Gowrie Rd. SW11 3E **118**
Graburn Way KT8: E Mos 3H **149**
Grace Av. DA7: Bex 2F **127**
Grace Bus. Cen. CR4: Mitc 6D **154**
Gracechurch St. EC3 2F **15** (7D **84**)
Grace Cl. HA8: Edg 7D **28**
SE9 3B **142**
Grace Ct. *CR0: C'don* *3B* ***168***
(off Waddon Rd.)
SM2: Sutt 7K **165**
Gracedale Rd. SW16 5F **137**
Gracefield Gdns. SW16 3J **137**
Gracehill *E1* *5J* ***85***
(off Hannibal Rd.)
Grace Ho. SE11 7H **19**
Grace Jones Cl. E8 6G **67**
Grace M. *SE20* *2J* ***157***
(off Marlow Rd.)
Grace Path SE26 4J **139**
Grace Pl. E3 3D **86**
Grace Rd. CR0: C'don 6C **156**
Graces All. E1 7G **85**
Graces M. NW8 2A **82**
SE5 2D **120**
Grace's Rd. SE5 2E **120**
Grace St. E3 3D **86**
Gradient, The SE26 4G **139**
Graduate Pl. SE1 7F **15**
Graeme Rd. EN1: Enf 2J **23**
Graemesdyke Av. SW14 3H **115**
Grafton Chambers *NW1* *3H* ***83***
(off Churchway)

Grafton Cl. KT4: Wor Pk 3A 164
TW4: Houn 1C 130
W13 6A 78
Grafton Ct. TW14: Bedf 1F 129
Grafton Cres. NW1 6F 65
Grafton Gdns. N4 6C 48
RM8: Dag 2E 72
Grafton Ho. SE8 5B 104
Grafton M. W1 4A 6 (4G 83)
Grafton Pk. Rd. KT4: Wor Pk 2A 164
Grafton Pl. NW1 2D 6 (3H 83)
Grafton Rd. CR0: C'don 1A 168
EN2: Enf 3E 22
HA1: Harr 5G 41
KT3: N Mald 3A 152
KT4: Wor Pk 3K 163
NW5 5E 64
RM8: Dag 2E 72
W3 7J 79
Graftons, The NW2 3J 63
Grafton Sq. SW4 3G 119
Grafton St. W1 3K 11 (7F 83)
Grafton Ter. NW5 5D 64
Grafton Way KT8: W Mole 4D 148
W1 4A 6 (4G 83)
WC1 4A 6 (4G 83)
Grafton Yd. NW5 6F 65
Graham Av. CR4: Mitc 1E 154
W13 2B 96
Graham Cl. CR0: C'don 2C 170
Graham Ct. *SE14* *6K 103*
(off Myers La.)
UB5: N'olt 5D 58
GRAHAME PARK 1B 44
Grahame Pk. Est. NW9 1A 44
Grahame Pk. Way NW7 7G 29
NW9 2B 44
Grahame Twr. *W3* *3H 97*
(off Hanbury Rd.)
Grahame White Ho. HA3: Kent 3D 42
Graham Gdns. KT6: Surb 1E 162
Graham Ho. *N9* *1D 34*
(off Cumberland Rd.)
Graham Lodge NW4 6D 44
Graham Mans. *IG11: Bark* *7A 72*
(off Lansbury Av.)
Graham Rd. CR4: Mitc 1E 154
DA6: Bex 4F 127
E8 6G 67
E13 4J 87
HA3: W'stone 3J 41
N15 3B 48
NW4 6D 44
SW19 7H 135
TW12: Ham H 4E 130
W4 3K 97
Graham St. N1 1B 8 (2B 84)
Graham Ter. *DA15: Sidc* *6B 126*
(off Westerham Dr.)
SW1 4G 17 (4E 100)
Grainger Cl. UB5: N'olt 5F 59
Grainger Ct. SE5 7C 102
Grainger Rd. N22 1C 48
TW7: Isle 2K 113
Grainstore, The E16 7J 87
Gramer Cl. E11 2F 69
Gramophone La. UB3: Hayes 2G 93
Grampian Cl. BR6: St M Cry 6K 161
SM2: Sutt 7A 166
UB3: Harl 7F 93
Grampian Gdns. NW2 1G 63
Grampians, The *W6* *2F 99*
(off Shepherd's Bush Rd.)
Gramsci Way SE6 3D 140
Granada St. SW17 5D 136
Granard Av. SW15 5D 116
Granard Bus. Cen. NW7 6F 29
Granard Ho. E9 6K 67
Granard Rd. SW12 7D 118
Granary Cl. N9 7D 24
Granary Complex, The & Goods Yard 1J 83
Granary Mans. SE28 2G 107
Granary Rd. E1 4H 85
Granary Sq. N1 6A 66
Granary St. NW1 1H 83
Granby Pl. *SE1* *7J 13*
(off Lower Marsh)
Granby Rd. SE9 2D 124
Granby St. E2 3K 9 (4G 85)
(not continuous)
Granby Ter. NW1 1A 6 (2G 83)
Grand Arc. N12 5F 31
Grand Av. EC1 5B 8 (5B 84)
(not continuous)
HA9: Wemb 5G 61
KT5: Surb 5H 151
N10 4E 46
Grand Av. E. HA9: Wemb 5H 61
Grand Dpt. Rd. SE18 5E 106
Grand Dr. SW20 2E 152
UB2: S'hall 2G 95
Granden Rd. SW16 2J 155
Grandfield Ct. W4 6K 97
Grandison Rd. KT4: Wor Pk 2E 164
SW11 5D 118
Grand Junc. Wharf N1 2C 84
Grand Pde. HA9: Wemb 2G 61
KT6: Surb 1G 163
N4 5B 48
SW14 *4J 115*
(off Up. Richmond Rd. W.)
Grand Pde. M. SW15 5G 117
Grand Union W2 6B 4
Grand Union Cen. *W10* *4F 81*
(off West Row)
Grand Union Cl. W9 5J 81
Grand Union Cres. E8 1G 85
Grand Union Ent. Pk. UB2: S'hall 3E 94
Grand Union Hgts. HA0: Wemb 1D 78
Grand Union Ind. Est. NW10 2H 79
Grand Union Village UB5: N'olt 3D 76
Grand Union Wlk. *NW1* *7F 65*
(off Kentish Town Rd.)
Grand Union Way UB2: S'hall 2E 94
Grand Vitesse Ind. Cen. *SE1* *5B 14*
(off Dolben St.)
Grand Wlk. E1 4A 86
Granfield St. SW11 1B 118
Grange, The CR0: C'don 2B 170
E17 *5A 50*
(off Grange Rd.)
HA0: Wemb 7G 61
KT3: N Mald 5B 152
KT4: Wor Pk 4K 163
N2 2B 46
N20 1F 31
(Grangeview Rd.)
N20 1G 31
(Oxford Gdns.)
SE1 3F 103
SW19 6F 135
W3 2H 97
W4 5H 97
W13 5C 78
W14 4H 99
Grange Av. EN4: E Barn 1H 31
HA7: Stan 2B 42
IG8: Wfd G 6D 36
N12 5F 31
N20 7B 20
SE25 2E 156
TW2: Twick 2J 131
Grangecliffe Gdns. SE25 2E 156
Grange Cl. DA15: Sidc 3A 144
HA8: Edg 5D 28
IG8: Wfd G 7D 36
KT8: W Mole 4F 149
TW5: Hest 6D 94
UB3: Hayes 5G 75
Grange Ct. HA0: Wemb 4K 59
HA5: Pinn 3C 40
NW10 *3A 62*
(off Neasden La.)
SM2: Sutt 7K 165
SM6: Wall 3F 167
TW17: Shep 4C 146
UB5: N'olt 2A 76
WC2 1H 13 (6K 83)
Grangecourt Rd. N16 1E 66
Grange Cres. SE28 6C 90
Grangedale Cl. HA6: Nwood 1G 39
Grange Dr. BR7: Chst 6C 142
Grange Farm Cl. HA2: Harr 2G 59
Grangefield *NW1* *7H 65*
(off Marquis Rd.)
Grange Gdns. HA5: Pinn 3C 40
N14 1C 32
NW3 3K 63
SE25 2E 156
Grange Gro. N1 6C 66
Grange Hill HA8: Edg 5D 28
SE25 2E 156
Grangehill Pl. SE9 3D 124
Grangehill Rd. SE9 4D 124
Grange Ho. IG11: Bark 1H 89
NW10 7D 62
SE1 3F 103
Grange La. SE21 2F 139
Grange Lodge SW19 6F 135
Grange Mans. KT17: Ewe 7B 164
Grange M. N21 6G 23
TW13: Felt 4J 129
Grangemill Rd. SE6 3C 140
Grangemill Way SE6 2C 140
GRANGE PARK 6G 23
Grange Pk. W5 1E 96
Grange Pk. Av. N21 6H 23
Grange Pk. Pl. SW20 7D 134
Grange Pk. Rd. CR7: Thor H 4D 156
E10 1D 68
Grange Pl. NW6 7J 63
Grange Rd. BR6: Orp 2H 173
CR2: S Croy 7C 168
CR7: Thor H 4D 156
E10 1C 68
E13 3H 87
E17 5A 50
(not continuous)
HA1: Harr 5A 42
HA2: Harr 2H 59
HA8: Edg 6E 28
IG1: Ilf 4F 71
KT1: King T 3E 150
KT8: W Mole 4F 149
KT9: Chess 4E 162
N6 6E 46
N17 6B 34
N18 6B 34
NW10 6D 62
SE1 3E 102
SE19 4D 156
SE25 4D 156
SM2: Sutt 7J 165
SW13 1C 116
UB1: S'hall 2C 94
UB3: Hayes 6G 75
W4 5H 97
W5 1D 96
Grange St. N1 1D 84
Grange Va. SM2: Sutt 7K 165
Grangeview Rd. N20 1F 31
Grange Wlk. SE1 3E 102
Grange Wlk. M. *SE1* *3E 102*
(off Grange Wlk.)
Grange Way IG8: Wfd G 4F 37
N12 4E 30
NW6 7J 63
Grangeway, The N21 6G 23
Grangeway Gdns. IG4: Ilf 5C 52
Grangewood DA5: Bexl 1F 145
Grangewood Cl. HA5: Eastc 5J 39
Grangewood Dr. TW16: Sun 7H 129
Grangewood La. BR3: Beck 6B 140
Grangewood St. E6 1B 88
Grangewood Ter. SE25 2D 156
Grange Yd. SE1 3F 103
Granham Gdns. N9 2A 34
Granite Apartments E15 6F 69
Granite St. SE18 5K 107
Granleigh Rd. E11 2G 69
Gransden Av. E8 7H 67
Gransden Ho. SE8 5B 104
Gransden Rd. W12 2B 98
Grantbridge St. N1 2B 84
Grantchester *KT1: King T* *2G 151*
(off St Peters Rd.)
Grantchester Cl. HA1: Harr 3K 59
Grant Cl. N14 7B 22
N17 2E 48
TW17: Shep 6D 146
Grant Ct. *E4* *1K 35*
(off The Ridgeway)
NW9 *2B 44*
(off Hazel Cl.)
Grantham Cl. HA8: Edg 3K 27
Grantham Ct. KT2: King T 5D 132
RM6: Chad H 7F 55
SE16 *2K 103*
(off Eleanor Cl.)
Grantham Gdns.
RM6: Chad H 6F 55
Grantham Ho. *SE15* *6G 103*
(off Friary Est.)
TW16: Sun 7G 129
Grantham Pl. W1 5J 11 (1F 101)
Grantham Rd. E12 4E 70
SW9 2J 119
W4 7A 98
Grantley Ho. *SE14* *6K 103*
(off Myers La.)
Grantley Rd. TW4: Cran 2A 112
Grantley St. E1 3K 85
Grant Mus. of Zoology & Comparative Anatomy 4C 6
Grantock Rd. E17 1F 51
Granton Rd. DA14: Sidc 6C 144
IG3: Ilf 1A 72
SW16 1G 155
Grant Pl. CR0: C'don 1F 169
Grant Rd. CR0: C'don 1F 169
HA3: W'stone 3K 41
SW11 4B 118
Grants Cl. NW7 7K 29
Grants Quay Wharf EC3 3F 15 (7D 84)
Grant St. E13 3J 87
N1 2A 84
Grant Ter. *N16* *7G 49*
(off Castlewood Rd.)
Grantully Rd. W9 3K 81
Grant Way TW7: Isle 6A 96
Granville Arc. SW9 4A 120
Granville Av. N9 3D 34
TW3: Houn 5E 112
TW13: Felt 2J 129
Granville Cl.
CR0: C'don 2E 168
Granville Ct. N1 1E 84
N4 6K 47
SE14 *7A 104*
(off Nynehead St.)
Granville Gdns. SW16 1K 155
W5 1F 97
Granville Gro. SE13 3E 122
Granville Ho. *E14* *6C 86*
(off E. India Dock Rd.)
Granville Mans. *W12* *2E 98*
(off Shepherd's Bush Grn.)
Granville M. DA14: Sidc 4A 144
Granville Pk. SE13 3E 122

Granville Pl. HA5: Pinn 3B **40**
N12 7F **31**
SW6 7K **99**
W1 1G **11** (6E **82**)
Granville Point NW2 2H **63**
Granville Rd. DA14: Sidc 4A **144**
DA16: Well 3C **126**
E17 6D **50**
E18 2K **51**
EN5: Barn 4A **20**
IG1: Ilf 1F **71**
N4 6K **47**
N12 7F **31**
N13 6E **32**
N22 1B **48**
NW2 2H **63**
NW6 2J **81**
(not continuous)
SW18 7H **117**
SW19 7J **135**
UB3: Harl 4H **93**
UB10: Hil 6D **56**
Granville Sq. SE15 7E **102**
WC1 2H **7** (3K **83**)
Granville St. WC1 2H **7** (3K **83**)
Granwood Ct. TW7: Isle 1J **113**
Grape St. WC2 7E **6** (6J **83**)
Graphite Sq. SE11 5G **19** (5K **101**)
Grapsome Cl. KT9: Chess 7C **162**
Grasdene Rd. SE18 7A **108**
Grasgarth Cl. W3 7J **79**
Grasmere *NW1* *2K* ***5***
(off Osnaburgh St.)
Grasmere Av. BR6: Farnb 3F **173**
HA4: Ruis 7E **38**
HA9: Wemb 7C **42**
SW15 4K **133**
SW19 3J **153**
TW3: Houn 6F **113**
W3 7K **79**
Grasmere Cl. TW14: Felt 1H **129**
Grasmere Ct. N22 6E **32**
SE26 5G **139**
SM2: Sutt 6A **166**
SW13 *6C* ***98***
(off Verdun Rd.)
Grasmere Gdns. BR6: Farnb 3F **173**
HA3: W'stone 2A **42**
IG4: Ilf 5D **52**
Grasmere Point *SE15* *7J* ***103***
(off Old Kent Rd.)
Grasmere Rd. BR1: Brom 1H **159**
BR6: Farnb 3F **173**
DA7: Bex 2J **127**
E13 2J **87**
N10 1F **47**
N17 6B **34**
SE25 6H **157**
SW16 5K **137**
Grasshaven Way SE28 1K **107**
(not continuous)
Grassington Cl. N11 6K **31**
Grassington Rd. DA14: Sidc 4A **144**
Grassmount SE23 2H **139**
Grass Pk. N3 1H **45**
Grass Way SM6: Wall 4G **167**
Grasvenor Av. EN5: Barn 5D **20**
Gratton Rd. W14 3G **99**
Gratton Ter. NW2 3F **63**
Gravel Hill CR0: Addtn 6K **169**
DA6: Bex 4H **127**
N3 2H **45**
UB8: Uxb 5A **56**
Gravel Hill Cl. DA6: Bex 5H **127**
Gravel La. E1 7J **9** (6F **85**)
Gravel Pit La. SE9 5F **125**
Gravel Pit Way BR6: Orp 2K **173**
Gravel Rd. BR2: Brom 3C **172**
TW2: Twick 1J **131**
Gravelwood Cl. BR7: Chst 3G **143**
Gravely Ho. *SE8* *4A* ***104***
(off Chilton Gro.)
Gravenel Gdns. *SW17* *5C* ***136***
(off Nutwell St.)
Graveney Gro. SE20 7J **139**
Graveney Rd. SW17 4C **136**
Gravesend Rd. W12 7C **80**
Gray Av. RM8: Dag 1F **73**
Grayham Cres. KT3: N Mald 4K **151**
Grayham Rd. KT3: N Mald 4K **151**
Gray Ho. *SE17* *5C* ***102***
(off King & Queen St.)
Grayland Cl. BR1: Brom 1B **160**
Grayling Cl. E16 4G **87**
Grayling Ct. *W5* *1D* ***96***
(off Grange Rd.)
Grayling Rd. N16 2D **66**
Grayling Sq. *E2* *3G* ***85***
(off Nelson Gdns.)
Grays Ct. RM10: Dag 7H **73**
Grayscroft Rd. SW16 7H **137**
Grays Farm Production Village
BR5: St P 7B **144**
Grays Farm Rd. BR5: St P 7B **144**
Grayshott Rd. SW11 2E **118**
Gray's Inn 5H **7** (5K **83**)
Gray's Inn Bldgs. *EC1* *4J* ***7***
(off Rosebery Av.)
Gray's Inn Pl. WC1 6H **7** (5K **83**)
Gray's Inn Rd. WC1 1F **7** (3J **83**)
Gray's Inn Sq. WC1 5J **7** (5K **83**)
Grays La. TW15: Ashf 4D **128**
Grayson Ho. EC1 2D **8**
Grays Rd. UB10: Uxb 2A **74**
Grays Ter. E7 6A **70**
Gray St. SE1 7K **13** (2A **102**)
Grayswood Gdns. SW20 2D **152**
Grayswood Point SW15 1C **134**
Gray's Yd. W1 1H **11**
Graywood Ct. N12 7F **31**
Grazebrook Rd. N16 2D **66**
Grazeley Cl. DA6: Bex 5J **127**
Grazeley Ct. SE19 5E **138**
Gt. Acre Ct. SW4 4H **119**
Gt. Amwell La. N8 3K **47**
Gt. Arthur Ho. *EC1* *4C* ***8***
(off Golden La. Est.)
Gt. Bell All. EC2 7E **8** (6D **84**)
Great Benty UB7: W Dray 4A **92**
Great Brownings SE21 4F **139**
Gt. Bushey Dr. N20 1E **30**
Gt. Cambridge Ind. Est.
EN1: Enf 5C **24**
GREAT CAMBRIDGE JUNC. 4J **33**
Gt. Cambridge Rd. EN1: Enf 4J **33**
N9 4J **33**
N17 5J **33**
N18 4J **33**
Gt. Castle St. W1 7K **5** (6F **83**)
Gt. Central Av. HA4: Ruis 5A **58**
Gt. Central St. NW1 5E **4** (5D **82**)
Gt. Central Way HA9: Wemb 4J **61**
NW10 4J **61**
Gt. Chapel St. W1 7C **6** (6H **83**)
Gt. Chart St. SW11 4B **118**
Gt. Chertsey Rd. TW2: Twick 2F **131**
TW13: Hanw, Twick 3D **130**
W4 1J **115**
Gt. Church La. W6 4F **99**
Gt. College St. SW1 1E **18** (3J **101**)
Great Cft. *WC1* *2F* ***7***
(off Cromer St.)
Gt. Cross Av. SE10 7F **105**
(not continuous)
Gt. Cumberland M. W1 1E **10** (6D **82**)
Gt. Cumberland Pl. W1 7E **4** (6D **82**)
Gt. Dover St. SE1 7D **14** (2C **102**)
Greatdown Rd. W7 4K **77**
Gt. Eastern Ent. Cen. E14 2D **104**
Gt. Eastern Rd. E15 7F **69**
Gt. Eastern St. EC2 2G **9** (3E **84**)
Gt. Eastern Wlk. EC2 6H **9**
Gt. Eastern Wharf SW11 7C **100**
Gt. Elms Rd. BR2: Brom 4A **160**
Great Fld. NW9 1A **44**
Greatfield NW5 5G **65**
Greatfield Av. E6 4D **88**
Greatfield Cl. N19 4G **65**
SE4 4C **122**
Greatfields Dr. UB8: Hil 5C **74**
Greatfields Rd. IG11: Bark 1H **89**
Gt. Fleete Way IG11: Bark 2C **90**
Gt. Galley Cl. IG11: Bark 3B **90**
Gt. Gatton Cl. CR0: C'don 7A **158**
Gt. George St. SW1 7D **12** (2H **101**)
Gt. Guildford Bus. Sq.
SE1 5C **14** (1C **102**)
Gt. Guildford St. SE1 4C **14** (1C **102**)
Great Hall 6F **17** (5D **100**)
Great Hall *SW11* *1E* ***118***
(off Battersea Pk. Rd.)
Greatham Wlk. SW15 1C **134**
Gt. Harry Dr. SE9 3E **142**
Gt. James St. WC1 5G **7** (5K **83**)
Gt. Marlborough St. W1 1A **12** (6G **83**)
Gt. Maze Pond SE1 6F **15** (2D **102**)
Gt. Newport St. WC2 2E **12** (7J **83**)
Gt. New St. *EC4* *7K* ***7***
(off W. Harding St.)
Great Nth. Leisure Pk. N12 7G **31**
Great Nth. Rd. EN5: Barn 2C **20**
EN5: New Bar 5D **20**
N2 5C **46**
N6 5C **46**
Great Nth. Way NW4 2D **44**
Greatorex Ho. *E1* *5G* ***85***
(off Greatorex St.)
Greatorex St. E1 5G **85**
Gt. Ormond St. WC1 5F **7** (5J **83**)
Gt. Owl Rd. IG7: Chig 3K **37**
Gt. Percy St. WC1 1H **7** (3K **83**)
Gt. Peter St. SW1 2C **18** (3H **101**)
Gt. Portland St. W1 4K **5** (4F **83**)
Gt. Pulteney St. W1 2B **12** (7G **83**)
Gt. Queen St. WC2 1F **13** (6J **83**)
Gt. Russell Mans. *WC1* *6E* ***6***
(off Gt. Russell St.)
Gt. Russell St. WC1 7D **6** (6H **83**)
Great St Helen's EC3 7G **9** (6E **84**)
Gt. St Thomas Apostle
EC4 2D **14** (7C **84**)
Gt. Scotland Yd. SW1 5E **12** (1J **101**)
Gt. Smith St. SW1 1D **18** (3H **101**)
Great Sth. W. Rd. TW4: Houn 4H **111**
TW14: Bedf, Felt 7E **110**
Great Spilmans SE22 5E **120**
Great Strand NW9 1B **44**
Gt. Suffolk St. SE1 5B **14** (1B **102**)
Gt. Sutton St. EC1 4B **8** (4B **84**)
Gt. Swan All. EC2 7E **8** (6D **84**)
(not continuous)
Great Thrift BR5: Pet W 4G **161**
Gt. Titchfield St. W1 4K **5** (4F **83**)
Gt. Tower St. EC3 2G **15** (7E **84**)
Gt. Trinity La. EC4 2D **14** (7C **84**)
Great Turnstile WC1 6H **7** (5K **83**)
Gt. Turnstile Ho. *WC1* *6H* ***7***
(off Great Turnstile)
Gt. Western Ind. Pk. UB2: S'hall 2F **95**
Gt. Western Rd. W9 5H **81**
W11 5H **81**
Gt. West Rd. TW5: Hest 2B **112**
TW7: Bford, Isle 2B **112**
TW8: Bford 2B **112**
W4 5B **98**
(Cedars Rd.)
W4 5H **97**
(Harvard Rd.)
W6 5B **98**
Gt. West Trad. Est. TW8: Bford 6B **96**
Gt. Winchester St. EC2 7F **9** (6D **84**)
Gt. Windmill St. W1 2C **12** (7H **83**)
Greatwood BR7: Chst 7E **142**
Great Yd. SE1 6H **15**
Greaves Cl. IG11: Bark 7H **71**
Greaves Cotts. E14 5A **86**
Greaves Pl. SW17 4C **136**
Greaves Twr. *SW10* *7A* ***100***
(off Worlds End Est.)
Grebe Av. UB4: Yead 6B **76**
Grebe Cl. E7 5H **69**
E17 7F **35**
IG11: Bark 4A **90**
Grebe Ct. *E14* *2E* ***104***
(off River Barge Cl.)
SE8 *6B* ***104***
(off Dorking Cl.)
SM1: Sutt 5H **165**
Grebe Ter. KT1: King T 3E **150**
Grecian Cres. SE19 6B **138**
Greek Ct. W1 1D **12** (6H **83**)
Greek St. W1 1D **12** (6H **83**)
Green, The BR1: Brom 3J **141**
(not continuous)
BR2: Hayes 7J **159**
BR5: St P 7B **144**
CR0: Sels 7B **170**
DA7: Bex 1G **127**
DA14: Sidc 4A **144**
DA16: Well 4J **125**
E4 1K **35**
E11 6K **51**
E15 6G **69**
HA0: Wemb 2A **60**
IG8: Wfd G 5D **36**
IG9: Buck H 1E **36**
KT3: N Mald 3K **151**
N9 2B **34**
N14 2C **32**
N17 6H **33**
N21 7F **23**
SM1: Sutt 3K **165**
SM4: Mord 4G **153**
SM5: Cars 4E **166**
SW19 5F **135**
TW2: Twick 1J **131**
TW5: Hest 6E **94**
TW9: Rich 5D **114**
TW13: Felt 2K **129**
TW17: Shep 4G **147**
UB2: S'hall 3C **94**
UB7: W Dray 3A **92**
UB10: Ick 2E **56**
W3 6A **80**
W5 7D **78**
Greenacre Cl. EN5: Barn 1C **20**
UB5: N'olt 5D **58**
Greenacre Gdns. E17 4E **50**
Greenacre Pl. SM6: Wall 2F **167**
Green Acres CR0: C'don 3F **169**
Greenacres DA14: Sidc 4A **144**
N3 2H **45**
SE9 6E **124**
WD23: B Hea 2C **26**
Greenacres Av. UB10: Ick 3B **56**
Greenacres Cl.
BR6: Farnb 4G **173**
Greenacres Dr. HA7: Stan 6G **27**
Greenacre Sq. SE16 2K **103**
Greenacre Wlk. N14 3C **32**
Green Arbour Ct. *EC1* *7A* ***8***
(off Old Bailey)
Green Av. NW7 4E **28**
W13 3B **96**
Greenaway Av. N18 6E **34**
Greenaway Gdns. NW3 4K **63**
Greenaway Ho. *NW8* *1A* ***82***
(off Boundary Rd.)
WC1 *2J* ***7***
(off Fernsbury St.)

Greenaway Ter.
TW19: Stanw 1A 128
(off Victory Cl.)
Green Bank E1 . . . . .1H 103
Greenbank N12 . . . . .4E 30
Greenbank Av. HA0: Wemb 5A 60
Green Bank Cl. E4 . . . . .2K 35
Greenbank Cres. NW4 . . . . .4G 45
Greenbank Lodge BR7: Chst 2E 160
(off Forest Cl.)
Greenbanks HA1: Harr 4J 59
Greenbay Rd. SE7 . . . . .7B 106
Greenberry St. NW8 . . . . .1C 4 (2C 82)
Greenbrook Av. EN4: Had W 1F 21
Green Cl. BR2: Brom 3G 159
NW9 . . . . .6J 43
NW11 . . . . .7A 46
SM5: Cars 2D 166
TW13: Hanw 5C 130
Greencoat Mans. SW1 . . . . .2B 18
(off Greencoat Row)
Greencoat Pl. SW1 . . . . .3B 18 (4G 101)
Greencoat Row SW1 . . . . .2B 18 (3G 101)
Green Ct. TW16: Sun 6H 129
Greencourt Av. CR0: C'don 2H 169
HA8: Edg .1H 43
Greencourt Gdns.
CR0: C'don 1H 169
Greencourt Ho. E1 . . . . .4K 85
(off Mile End Rd.)
Greencourt Rd. BR5: Pet W 5H 161
Greencrest Pl. NW2 . . . . .3C 62
Greencroft HA8: Edg 5D 28
Greencroft Av. HA4: Ruis 2A 58
Greencroft Cl. E6 . . . . .5B 88
Greencroft Gdns. EN1: Enf 3K 23
NW6 . . . . .7K 63
Greencroft Rd. TW5: Hest 1D 112
Green Dale SE5 . . . . .4D 120
SE22 . . . . .5E 120
Greendale NW7 . . . . .4F 29
Green Dale Cl. SE22 . . . . .5E 120
Green Dragon Ct. SE1 . . . . .4E 14
Green Dragon Ho. WC2 . . . . .7F 7
(off Dragon Yd.)
Green Dragon La. N21 . . . . .6F 23
TW8: Bford 5E 96
Green Dragon Yd. E1 . . . . .6K 9 (5G 85)
Green Dr. UB1: S'hall 1E 94
Greene Ct. SE14 . . . . .6K 103
(off Samuel Cl.)
Greene Ho. SE1 . . . . .3D 102
(off Burbage Cl.)
Green End KT9: Chess 4E 162
N21 . . . . .2G 33
Greenend Rd. W4 . . . . .2A 98
Greener Ct. CR0: C'don 6B 156
(off Goodman Ct.)
Greener Ho. SW4 . . . . .3H 119
Green Farm Cl. BR6: Chels 6K 173
Greenfell Mans. SE8 . . . . .6D 104
Greenfield Av. KT5: Surb 7H 151
Greenfield Dr. BR1: Brom 2A 160
N2 . . . . .4D 46
Greenfield Gdns. BR5: Pet W 7H 161
NW2 . . . . .2G 63
RM9: Dag .1D 90
Greenfield Ho. SW19 . . . . .1F 135
Greenfield Rd. DA2: Dart 5K 145
E1 . . . . .5G 85
N15 . . . . .5E 48
RM9: Dag .7C 72
Greenfields UB1: S'hall 6E 76
Greenfield Way HA2: Harr 3F 41
GREENFORD 3E 76
Greenford Av. UB1: S'hall 7D 76
W7 . . . . .4J 77
Greenford Bus. Cen. UB6: G'frd 7H 59
Greenford Gdns. UB6: G'frd 3F 77
GREENFORD GREEN 6J 59
Greenford Ind. Est. UB6: G'frd 7F 59
Greenford Rd. HA1: Harr 7J 59
SM1: Sutt 4K 165
(not continuous)
UB1: S'hall 1G 95
UB6: G'frd 7G 77
GREENFORD RDBT. 2H 77
Greenford Sports Cen. 3E 76
Green Gdns. BR6: Farnb 5G 173
Greengate UB6: G'frd 6B 60
Greengate Lodge E13 . . . . .2K 87
(off Hollybush St.)
Greengate Pde. IG2: Ilf 6H 53
Greengate St. E13 . . . . .2K 87
Greenhalgh Wlk. N2 . . . . .4A 46
Greenham Cl. SE1 . . . . .7J 13 (2A 102)
Greenham Cres. E4 . . . . .6G 35
Greenham Ho. E9 . . . . .1J 85
(off Templecombe Rd.)
TW7: Isle 3H 113
Greenham Rd. N10 . . . . .2E 46
Greenhaven Dr. SE28 . . . . .6B 90
Greenheath Bus. Cen. E2 . . . . .4H 85
(off Three Colts La.)
Green Hedges TW1: Twick 5C 114
Greenheys Cl. HA6: Nwood 1G 39
Greenheys Dr. E18 . . . . .3H 51
GREENHILL 5J 41
Green Hill SE18 . . . . .5D 106
Greenhill HA9: Wemb 2H 61
IG9: Buck H 1F 37
NW3 . . . . .4B 64
SM1: Sutt 2A 166
Greenhill Ct. EN5: New Bar 5E 20
SE18 . . . . .5D 106
Greenhill Gdns. UB5: N'olt 2D 76
Greenhill Gro. E12 . . . . .4C 70
Greenhill Pde. EN5: New Bar 5E 20
Greenhill Pk. EN5: New Bar 5E 20
NW10 . . . . .1A 80
Greenhill Rd. HA1: Harr 6J 41
NW10 . . . . .1A 80
Greenhill's Rents EC1 . . . . .5A 8 (5B 84)
Greenhills Ter. N1 . . . . .6D 66
Greenhill Ter. SE18 . . . . .5D 106
UB5: N'olt .2D 76
Greenhill Way HA1: Harr 6J 41
HA9: Wemb 2H 61
Greenhithe Cl. DA15: Sidc 7J 125
Greenholm Rd. SE9 . . . . .5F 125
Green Hundred Rd. SE15 . . . . .6G 103
Greenhurst Rd. SE27 . . . . .5A 138
Greening St. SE2 . . . . .4C 108
Greenland Cres. UB2: S'hall 3A 94
Greenland Ho. E1 . . . . .4A 86
(off Ernest St.)
Greenland M. SE8 . . . . .5K 103
Greenland Pl. NW1 . . . . .1F 83
Greenland Quay SE16 . . . . .4K 103
Greenland Rd. EN5: Barn 6A 20
NW1 . . . . .1G 83
Greenlands KT19: Ewe 5H 163
Greenlands La. NW4 . . . . .1D 44
Greenland St. NW1 . . . . .1F 83
Greenland Way CR0: Bedd 7H 155
Green La. BR7: Chst 4F 143
CR7: Thor H 7K 137
HA1: Harr .3J 59
HA7: Stan .4G 27
HA8: Edg .4A 28
IG1: Ilf 2H 71
IG3: Ilf 2H 71
KT3: N Mald 5J 151
KT4: Wor Pk 1C 164
KT8: W Mole 5F 149
KT9: Chess 7D 162
NW4 . . . . .4F 45
RM8: Dag .2H 71
SE9 . . . . .1F 143
SE20 . . . . .7K 139
Green La. SM4: Mord 6J 153
(Central Rd.)
SM4: Mord 7E 152
(Lwr. Morden La.)
SW16 . . . . .7K 137
TW4: Houn 3K 111
TW13: Hanw 5C 130
TW16: Sun 7H 129
TW17: Shep 6E 146
UB8: Hil 5E 74
W7 . . . . .2J 95
Green La. Bus. Pk. SE9 . . . . .2E 142
Green La. Cotts. HA7: Stan 4G 27
Green La. Gdns. CR7: Thor H 2C 156
Green Lanes KT19: Ewe 7A 164
(not continuous)
N4 . . . . .1C 66
N8 . . . . .3B 48
N13 . . . . .6E 32
N15 . . . . .3B 48
N16 . . . . .1C 66
N21 . . . . .3F 33
Greenlaw Ct. W5 . . . . .6D 78
(off Mount Pk. Rd.)
Greenlaw Gdns. KT3: N Mald 7B 152
Green Lawn La. TW8: Bford 4D 96
Green Lawns HA4: Ruis 1A 58
Greenlawns N12 . . . . .6E 30
Greenlawns, The SE18 . . . . .4F 107
(off Vincent Rd.)
Greenlaw St. SE18 . . . . .3E 106
Green Leaf Av. SM6: Bedd 4H 167
Greenleaf Cl. SW2 . . . . .7A 120
Greenleafe Dr. IG6: Ilf 3F 53
Greenleaf Rd. E6 . . . . .1A 88
E17 . . . . .3B 50
Greenleaf Way HA3: W'stone 3K 41
Greenlea Pk. SW19 . . . . .7B 136
Green Leas KT1: King T 3E 150
(off Mill St.)
TW16: Sun 6H 129
Green Leas Cl. TW16: Sun 6H 129
Greenleaves Ct. TW15: Ashf 6D 128
Green Link Wlk. TW9: Kew 1H 115
Green Man Gdns. W13 . . . . .7A 78
Green Man La. TW14: Felt 4J 111
(not continuous)
W13 . . . . .7A 78
Green Man Pas. W13 . . . . .7B 78
(not continuous)
GREEN MAN RDBT. 7H 51
Greenman St. N1 . . . . .7C 66
Greenmead DA18: Erith 3E 108
Greenmead Cl. SE25 . . . . .5G 157
Green Moor Link N21 . . . . .7G 23
Greenmoor Rd. EN3: Enf H 2D 24
Greenoak Pl. EN4: Cockf 2J 21
Green Oaks UB2: S'hall 4B 94
Greenoak Way SW19 . . . . .4F 135
Greenock Rd. SW16 . . . . .1H 155
W3 . . . . .3H 97
Greeno Cres. TW17: Shep 5C 146
Green Pde. TW3: Houn 5F 113
Green Pk. 5K 11 (2F 101)
Greenpark Ct. HA0: Wemb 7C 60
Green Pk. Way UB6: G'frd 7J 59
(not continuous)
Green Point E15 . . . . .6G 69
Green Pond Cl. E17 . . . . .3B 50
Green Pond Rd. E17 . . . . .3A 50
Green Rd. N14 .6A 22
N20 . . . . .3F 31
Green Rd. Nth. EN3: Pond E 4F 25
Greenroof Way SE10 . . . . .3H 105
(off School Bank Rd.)
Green's Ct. W1 . . . . .2C 12
W11 . . . . .1H 99
(off Lansdowne M.)
Green's End SE18 . . . . .4F 107
Greenshank Cl. E17 . . . . .7F 35
Greens Health & Fitness
Chingford .4K 35
Purley 6A 168
Greenshields Ind. Est. E16 . . . . .2J 105
Green Side RM8: Dag 1C 72
Greenside DA5: Bexl 1E 144
Greenside Cl. N20 . . . . .2G 31
SE6 . . . . .2F 141
Greenside Rd. CR0: C'don 7A 156
W12 . . . . .3C 98
Greenslade Rd. IG11: Bark 7H 71
Greenstead Av. IG8: Wfd G 7F 37
Greenstead Cl. IG8: Wfd G 6F 37
Greenstead Gdns. IG8: Wfd G 6F 37
SW15 . . . . .5D 116
Greensted Rd. IG10: Lough 1H 37
Greenstone M. E11 . . . . .6J 51
Green St. E7 . . . . .6K 69
E13 . . . . .6K 69
EN3: Brim, Enf H 2D 24
TW16: Sun 1J 147
W1 . . . . .2G 11 (7E 82)
GREEN STREET GREEN 6K 173
Greenstreet Hill SE14 . . . . .2K 121
Green Ter. EC1 . . . . .2K 7 (3A 84)
Green Va. DA6: Bex 5D 126
W5 . . . . .6F 79
Greenvale Rd. SE9 . . . . .4D 124
Green Verges HA7: Stan 7J 27
Green Vw. KT9: Chess 7F 163
Greenview Av. BR3: Beck 6A 158
CR0: C'don 6A 158
Greenview Cl. W3 . . . . .1A 98
Greenview Ct. TW15: Ashf 4B 128
Green Wlk. HA4: Ruis 1H 57
IG8: Wfd G 6H 37
IG10: Lough 1H 37
NW4 . . . . .5F 45
SE1 . . . . .3E 102
TW12: Hamp 6D 130
UB2: S'hall 5E 94
Green Wlk., The E4 . . . . .1A 36
Green Way BR2: Brom 6C 160
IG8: Wfd G 5F 37
SE9 . . . . .5B 124
SM6: Wall 4G 167
TW16: Sun 4J 147
Green Way, The HA5: Pinn 6D 40
Greenway BR7: Chst 5E 142
HA3: Kent .5E 42
HA5: Pinn .2K 39
N14 . . . . .2D 32
N20 . . . . .2D 30
RM8: Dag .2C 72
SW20 . . . . .4E 152
UB4: Yead .3J 75
Greenway, The
HA3: W'stone 1J 41
NW9 . . . . .2K 43
TW4: Houn 4D 112
UB8: Uxb .2A 74
UB10: Ick .2D 56
Greenway Av. E17 . . . . .4F 51
Greenway Cl. N4 . . . . .2C 66
N11 . . . . .6K 31
N15 . . . . .4F 49
N20 . . . . .2D 30
NW9 . . . . .2K 43
Greenway Ct. IG1: Ilf 1E 70
Greenway Gdns. CR0: C'don 3B 170
HA3: W'stone 2J 41
NW9 . . . . .2K 43
UB6: G'frd 3E 76
Greenways BR3: Beck 3C 158
Greenways, The TW1: Twick 6A 114
Greenwell St. W1 . . . . .4K 5 (4F 83)
GREENWICH 7E 104
Greenwich Bus. Pk. SE10 . . . . .7D 104
Greenwich Chu. St. SE10 . . . . .6E 104
Greenwich Cinema 7E 104

Greenwich Commercial Cen.
SE10 7D 104
Greenwich Ct. *E1* *6H 85*
(off Cavell St.)
SE13 6F 123
Greenwich Cres. E6 5C 88
Greenwich Gateway Vis. Cen. 6E 104
Greenwich Hgts. SE18 7C 106
Greenwich Heritage Cen. 3F 107
Greenwich High Rd. SE10 1D 122
Greenwich Ind. Est. SE10 7D 104
Greenwich Mkt. SE10 6E 104
GREENWICH MILLENNIUM VILLAGE
3H 105
Greenwich Pk. 7F 105
Greenwich Pk. St. SE10 6F 105
Greenwich Quay SE8 6D 104
Greenwich Shop. Pk. SE7 4K 105
Greenwich Sth. St. SE10 1D 122
Greenwich Theatre 7E 104
Greenwich Vw. Pl. E14 3D 104
Greenwich Yacht Club 3J 105
Greenwood Av. EN3: Enf H 2F 25
RM10: Dag 4H 73
Greenwood Bus. Cen.
CR0: C'don 7F 157
Greenwood Cl. BR5: Pet W 6J 161
DA15: Sidc 2A 144
KT7: T Ditt 1A 162
SM4: Mord 4G 153
WD23: B Hea 1D 26
Greenwood Dr. E4 5A 36
Greenwood Gdns. IG6: Ilf 1G 53
N13 3G 33
Greenwood Ho. N22 1A 48
SE4 4K 121
WC1 *3A 84*
(off Wilmington Sq.)
Greenwood La. TW12: Ham H 5F 131
Greenwood Mans. *IG11: Bark* *7A 72*
(off Lansbury Av.)
Greenwood Pk. KT2: King T 7A 134
Greenwood Pl. NW5 5F 65
Greenwood Rd.
CR0: C'don 7B 156
CR4: Mitc 3H 155
DA5: Bexl 4K 145
E8 6G 67
E13 2H 87
KT7: T Ditt 1A 162
TW7: Isle 3K 113
Greenwoods, The HA2: Harr 3G 59
Greenwood Ter. NW10 1K 79
Greenwood Theatre 2D 102
Green Wrythe Cres. SM5: Cars 1C 166
Green Wrythe La. SM5: Cars 6B 154
Green Yd. WC1 3H 7 (4K 83)
Green Yd., The EC3 1G 15
Greer Rd. HA3: Hrw W 1G 41
Greet Ho. SE1 7K 13
Greet St. SE1 5K 13 (1A 102)
Greg Cl. E10 6E 50
Gregor M. SE3 7J 105
Gregory Cl. BR2: Brom 4G 159
Gregory Cres. SE9 7B 124
Gregory Pl. W8 2K 99
Gregory Rd. RM6: Chad H 4D 54
UB2: S'hall 3E 94
Greig Cl. N8 5J 47
Greig Ter. SE17 6B 102
Grenaby Av. CR0: C'don 7D 156
Grenaby Rd. CR0: C'don 7D 156
Grenada Ho. *E14* *7B 86*
(off Limehouse C'way.)
Grenada Rd. SE7 7A 106
Grenade St. E14 7B 86
Grenadier St. E16 1E 106
Grena Gdns. TW9: Rich 4F 115
Grenard Cl. SE15 7G 103
Grena Rd. TW9: Rich 4F 115
Grendon Gdns. HA9: Wemb 2G 61
Grendon Ho. *E9* *7J 67*
(off Shore Pl.)
N1 *2K 83*
(off Calshot St.)
Grendon Lodge HA8: Edg 2D 28
Grendon St. NW8 3C 4 (4C 82)
Grenfell Ct. NW7 6J 29
Grenfell Gdns. HA3: Kent 7E 42
IG3: Ilf 5K 53
Grenfell Ho. SE5 7C 102
Grenfell Rd. CR4: Mitc 6D 136
W11 7F 81
Grenfell Twr. W11 7F 81
Grenfell Wlk. W11 7F 81
Grenier Apartments SE15 7H 103
Grennell Cl. SM1: Sutt 2B 166
Grennell Rd. SM1: Sutt 2A 166
Grenoble Gdns. N13 6F 33
Grenville Cl. KT5: Surb 1J 163
N3 1G 45
Grenville Ct. W13 5B 78
Grenville Gdns. IG8: Wfd G 1A 52
Grenville Ho. *E3* *2A 86*
(off Arbery Rd.)
SE8 *6C 104*
(off New King St.)
SW1 *7C 18*
(off Dolphin Sq.)
Grenville M. N19 1J 65
SW7 4A 100
TW12: Ham H 5F 131
Grenville Pl. NW7 5E 28
SW7 3A 100
Grenville Rd. N19 1J 65
Grenville St. WC1 4F 7 (4J 83)
Gresham Av. N20 4J 31
Gresham Cl. DA5: Bexl 6E 126
EN2: Enf 3H 23
Gresham Dr. RM6: Chad H 5B 54
Gresham Gdns. NW11 1G 63
Gresham Lodge E17 5D 50
Gresham Pl. N19 2H 65
Gresham Rd. BR3: Beck 2A 158
E6 2D 88
E16 6K 87
HA8: Edg 6A 28
NW10 5K 61
SE25 4G 157
SW9 3A 120
TW3: Houn 1G 113
TW12: Hamp 6E 130
UB10: Hil 2C 74
Gresham St. EC2 7C 8 (6C 84)
Gresham Way SW19 3K 135
Gresham Way Ind. Est. *SW19* *3K 135*
(off Gresham Way)
Gresley Cl. E17 6A 50
N15 4D 48
Gresley Rd. N19 1G 65
Gressenhall Rd. SW18 6H 117
Gresse St. W1 6C 6 (6H 83)
Gresswell Cl. DA14: Sidc 3A 144
Greswell St. SW6 1F 117
Gretton Ho. *E2* *3J 85*
(off Globe Rd.)
Gretton Rd. N17 7A 34
Greville Cl. TW1: Twick 7B 114
Greville Ct. *E5* *3H 67*
(off Napoleon Rd.)
HA1: Harr 4J 59
Greville Hall NW6 2K 81
Greville Ho. *SW1* *1G 17*
(off Halkin Arc.)
Greville Lodge E13 1K 87
HA8: Edg *4C 28*
(off Broadhurst Av.)
N12 5E 30
Greville M. *NW6* *1K 81*
(off Greville Rd.)
Greville Pl. NW6 2K 81
Greville Rd. E17 4E 50
NW6 2K 81
TW10: Rich 6F 115
Greville St. EC1 6J 7 (5A 84)
(not continuous)
Grey Cl. NW11 6A 46
Greycoat Gdns. *SW1* *2C 18*
(off Greycoat St.)
Greycoat Pl. SW1 2C 18 (3H 101)
Greycoat St. SW1 2C 18 (3H 101)
Greycot Rd. BR3: Beck 5C 140
Grey Eagle St. E1 4K 9 (4F 85)
Greyfell Cl. HA7: Stan 5G 27
Greyfriars *SE26* *3G 139*
(off Wells Pk. Rd.)
Greyfriars Pas. EC1 7B 8 (6B 84)
Greyhound Ct. WC2 2H 13 (7K 83)
Greyhound Hill NW4 3C 44
Greyhound La. SW16 6H 137
Greyhound Mans. *W6* *6G 99*
(off Greyhound Rd.)
Greyhound Rd. N17 3E 48
NW10 3D 80
SM1: Sutt 5A 166
W6 6F 99
W14 6F 99
Greyhound Ter. SW16 1G 155
Grey Ho. *W12* *7D 80*
(off White City Est.)
Greyladies Gdns. SE10 2E 122
Greys Pk. Cl. BR2: Kes 5B 172
Greystead Rd. SE23 7J 121
Greystoke Av. HA5: Pinn 3E 40
Greystoke Ct. W5 4E 78
Greystoke Dr. HA4: Ruis 6D 38
Greystoke Gdns. EN2: Enf 4C 22
W5 4E 78
Greystoke Ho. *SE15* *6G 103*
(off Peckham Pk. Rd.)
W5 4E 78
Greystoke Lodge *W5* *4F 79*
(off Hanger La.)
Greystoke Pk. Ter. W5 3D 78
Greystoke Pl. EC4 7J 7 (6A 84)
Greystone Gdns.
HA3: Kent 6C 42
IG6: Ilf 2G 53
Greystone Path *E11* *7H 51*
(off Mornington Rd.)
Greyswood Av. N18 6E 34
Greyswood St. SW16 6F 137
Grey Turner Ho. W12 6C 80
Grierson Ho. SW16 4G 137
Grierson Rd. SE23 7K 121
Griffin Cen. TW14: Felt 5K 111
Griffin Cen., The
KT1: King T *2D 150*
(off Market Pl.)
Griffin Cl. NW10 5D 62
Griffin Ct. TW8: Bford 6E 96
W4 5B 98
Griffin Ho. *E14* *6D 86*
(off Ricardo St.)
N1 *1E 84*
(off New Era Est.)
W6 *4F 99*
(off Hammersmith Rd.)
Griffin Mnr. Way SE28 3H 107
Griffin Pk. 6D 96
Griffin Rd. N17 2E 48
SE18 5H 107
Griffins Cl. N21 7J 23
Griffin Way TW16: Sun 2J 147
Griffith Cl. RM8: Dag 7C 54
Griffiths Cl. KT4: Wor Pk 2D 164
Griffiths Rd. SW19 7J 135
Griggs App. IG1: Ilf 2G 71
Griggs Ct. *SE1* *3E 102*
(off Grigg's Pl.)
Grigg's Pl. SE1 3E 102
Griggs Rd. E10 6E 50
Grilse Cl. N9 4C 34
Grimaldi Ho. *N1* *2K 83*
(off Calshot St.)
Grimsby Gro. E16 2F 107
Grimsby St. E2 4K 9 (4F 85)
Grimsdyke Rd. HA5: Hat E 1D 40
Grimsel Path SE5 7B 102
Grimshaw Cl. N6 7E 46
Grimston Rd. SW6 2H 117
Grimthorpe Ho. EC1 3A 8
Grimwade Av. CR0: C'don 3G 169
Grimwade Cl. SE15 3J 121
Grimwood Rd. TW1: Twick 7K 113
Grindall Cl. CR0: Wadd 4B 168
Grindall Ho. *E1* *4H 85*
(off Darling Row)
Grindal St. SE1 7J 13 (2A 102)
Grindleford Av. N11 2K 31
Grindley Gdns. CR0: C'don 6F 157
Grindley Ho. *E3* *5B 86*
(off Leopold St.)
Grinling Pl. SE8 6C 104
Grinstead Rd. SE8 5A 104
Grisedale *NW1* *1A 6*
(off Cumberland Mkt.)
Grittleton Av. HA9: Wemb 6H 61
Grittleton Rd. W9 4J 81
Grizedale Ter. SE23 2H 139
Grocer's Hall Ct. EC2 1E 14 (6D 84)
Grocer's Hall Gdns. EC2 1E 14
Grogan Cl. TW12: Hamp 6D 130
Groombridge Cl. DA16: Well 5A 126
Groombridge Ho. *SE17* *5E 102*
(off Upnor Way)
Groombridge Rd. E9 7K 67
Groom Cl. BR2: Brom 4K 159
Groom Cres. SW18 7B 118
Groome Ho. SE11 4H 19 (4K 101)
Groomfield Cl. SW17 4E 136
Groom Pl. SW1 1H 17 (3E 100)
Grooms Dr. HA5: Eastc 5J 39
Grosmont Rd. SE18 5K 107
Grosse Way SW15 6D 116
Grosvenor Av. HA2: Harr 6F 41
N5 5C 66
SM5: Cars 6D 166
SW14 3A 116
TW10: Rich 5E 114
UB4: Hayes 2H 75
Grosvenor Cotts. SW1 3G 17 (4E 100)
Grosvenor Ct. E10 1D 68
N14 7B 22
NW6 1F 81
NW7 *5E 28*
(off Hale La.)
SE5 6C 102
SM2: Sutt 6K 165
SM4: Mord 4J 153
TW11: Tedd 6A 132
W3 1G 97
W5 *7E 78*
(off The Grove)
W14 *3F 99*
(off Irving Rd.)
Grosvenor Ct. Mans. *W2* *1E 10*
(off Edgware Rd.)
Grosvenor Cres. NW9 4G 43
SW1 7H 11 (2E 100)
UB10: Hil 7D 56
Grosvenor Cres. M. SW1 7G 11 (2E 100)
Grosvenor Est. SW1 3D 18 (4H 101)
Grosvenor Gdns. E6 3B 88
IG8: Wfd G 6D 36
KT2: King T 6D 132
N10 3G 47
N14 4C 22
NW2 6E 62
NW11 6H 45

Grosvenor Gdns. SM6: Wall 7G 167
SW1 ....1J 17 (3F 101)
SW14 ....3A 116
Grosvenor Gdns. M. E. SW1 ....1K 17
Grosvenor Gdns. M. Nth. SW1 ....2J 17
Grosvenor Gdns. M. Sth. SW1 ....2K 17
Grosvenor Ga. W1 ....3G 11 (7E 82)
Grosvenor Hill SW19 ....6G 135
W1 ....2J 11 (7F 83)
Grosvenor Hill Ct. *W1* *2J 11*
(off Bourdon St.)
Grosvenor Ho. SM1: Sutt 5K 165
Grosvenor Pde. *W5* *1G 97*
(off Uxbridge Rd.)
Grosvenor Pk. SE5 ....7C 102
Grosvenor Pk. Rd. E17 ....5C 50
Grosvenor Pl. SW1 ....7H 11 (2E 100)
Grosvenor Ri. E. E17 ....5D 50
Grosvenor Rd.
BR4: W W'ck 1D 170
BR5: St M Cry 6J 161
DA6: Bex 5D 126
DA17: Belv 6G 109
E6 ....1B 88
E7 ....6K 69
E10 ....1E 68
E11 ....5K 51
IG1: Ilf 3G 71
N3 ....7C 30
N9 ....1C 34
N10 ....1F 47
RM7: Rush G 7K 55
RM8: Dag 1F 73
SE25 ....4F 157
SM6: Wall 6F 167
SW1 ....7J 17 (6F 101)
TW1: Twick 1A 132
TW3: Houn 3D 112
TW8: Bford 6D 96
TW10: Rich 5E 114
UB2: S'hall 3D 94
W4 ....5H 97
W7 ....1A 96
Grosvenor Sq. W1 ....2H 11 (7E 82)
Grosvenor St. W1 ....2J 11 (7F 83)
Grosvenor Studios *SW1* *3G 17*
(off Eaton Ter.)
Grosvenor Ter. SE5 ....7C 102
Grosvenor Va. HA4: Ruis 2H 57
Grosvenor Way E5 ....2J 67
Grosvenor Wharf Rd. E14 ....4F 105
Grotes Bldgs. SE3 ....2G 123
Grote's Pl. SE3 ....2G 123
Groton Rd. SW18 ....2K 135
Grotto Ct. SE1 ....6B 14 (2B 102)
Grotto Pas. W1 ....5H 5 (5E 82)
Grotto Rd. TW1: Twick 2K 131
GROVE, THE 1G 139
Grove, The BR4: W W'ck 3D 170
DA6: Bex 4D 126
DA14: Sidc 5E 144
E15 ....6G 69
EN2: Enf 2F 23
HA8: Edg 4C 28
KT12: Walt T 7K 147
N3 ....1J 45
N4 ....7K 47
N6 ....1E 64
N8 ....5H 47
N13 ....4F 33
(not continuous)
N14 ....5B 22
NW9 ....5K 43
NW11 ....7G 45
TW1: Twick 6B 114
TW7: Isle 1J 113
TW11: Tedd 4A 132
UB6: G'frd 6G 77
UB10: Ick 5C 56
W5 ....1D 96
Grove Av. HA5: Pinn 4C 40
N3 ....7D 30
N10 ....2G 47
SM1: Sutt 6J 165
TW1: Twick 1K 131
W7 ....6J 77
Grovebury Cl. DA8: Erith 6K 109
Grovebury Ct. DA6: Bex 5H 127
N14 ....7C 22
Grovebury Rd. SE2 ....2B 108
Grove Cl. BR2: Hayes 2J 171
KT1: King T 4F 151
N14 ....7B 22
SE23 ....1A 140
TW13: Hanw 4C 130
UB10: Ick 5C 56
Grove Cotts. SW3 ....7D 16
W4 ....6A 98
Grove Ct. *EN5: Barn* *3C 20*
(off Hadley Ridge)
KT1: King T *3E 150*
(off Grove Cres.)
KT8: E Mos 4H 149
NW8 ....1A 4
SW10 ....*6A 16*
(off Drayton Gdns.)
TW3: Houn 4E 112
W5 ....1E 96
Grove Cres. E18 ....2H 51
KT1: King T 3E 150
KT12: Walt T 7K 147
NW9 ....4J 43
TW13: Hanw 4C 130
Grove Cres. Rd. E15 ....6F 69
Grovedale Rd. N19 ....2H 65
Grove Dwellings E1 ....5J 85
Grove End E18 ....2H 51
NW5 ....4F 65
Grove End Gdns. NW8 ....2B 82
Grove End Ho. NW8 ....2A 4
Grove End La. KT10: Esh 7H 149
Grove End Rd. NW8 ....1A 4 (2B 82)
Grove Farm Retail Pk. RM6: Chad H 7C 54
Grovefield *N11* *4A 32*
(off Coppies Gro.)
Grove Footpath KT5: Surb 4E 150
Grove Gdns. EN3: Enf W 1E 24
NW4 ....5C 44
NW8 ....2D 4 (3C 82)
RM10: Dag 3J 73
TW10: Rich 6F 115
TW11: Tedd 4A 132
Grove Grn. Rd. E11 ....3E 68
Grove Hall Ct. NW8 ....1A 4 (3A 82)
Grove Hill E18 ....2H 51
HA1: Harr 7J 41
Grovehill Ct. BR1: Brom 6H 141
Grove Hill Rd. HA1: Harr 7K 41
SE5 ....3E 120
Grove Ho. N3 ....3F 45
SW3 ....*7D 16*
(off Chelsea Mnr. St.)
Grove Ho. Rd. N8 ....4J 47
Groveland Av. SW16 ....7K 137
Groveland Ct. EC4 ....1D 14
Groveland Rd. BR3: Beck 3B 158
Grovelands *KT1: King T* *4D 150*
(off Palace Rd.)
KT8: W Mole 4E 148
Grovelands Cl. HA2: Harr 3F 59
SE5 ....2E 120
Grovelands Ct. N14 ....7C 22
Grovelands Rd. BR5: St P 7A 144
N13 ....4E 32
N15 ....6G 49
Groveland Way KT3: N Mald 5J 151
Grove La. KT1: King T 4E 150
SE5 ....1D 120
UB8: Hil 4B 74
Grove La. Ter. SE5 ....2D 120
Groveley Rd. TW13: Felt 5H 129
TW16: Sun 5H 129
Grove Mans. *W6* *2E 98*
(off Hammersmith Gro.)
Grove Mkt. Pl. SE9 ....6D 124
Grove M. W6 ....3E 98
Grove Mill Pl. SM5: Cars 3E 166
Grove Nature Reserve, The 4B 74
GROVE PARK
BR1 ....3K 141
W4 ....1J 115
Grove Pk. E11 ....6K 51
NW9 ....4J 43
SE5 ....2E 120
Grove Pk. Av. E4 ....7J 35
Grove Pk. Bri. W4 ....7J 97
Grove Pk. Gdns. W4 ....7H 97
Grove Pk. Ind. Est. NW9 ....3K 43
Grove Pk. M. W4 ....7J 97
Grove Pk. Rd. N15 ....4E 48
SE9 ....3A 142
W4 ....7H 97
Grove Pk. Ter. W4 ....7H 97
(not continuous)
Grove Pas. E2 ....2H 85
Grove Pl. IG11: Bark 7G 71
NW3 ....3B 64
SW12 ....7F 119
W3 ....1J 97
Grover Ct. SE13 ....2D 122
Grover Ho. SE11 ....6H 19 (5K 101)
Grove Rd. CR4: Mitc 3E 154
(not continuous)
CR7: Thor H 4A 156
DA7: Bex 4J 127
DA17: Belv 6F 109
E3 ....1K 85
E4 ....4K 35
E11 ....7H 51
E17 ....6D 50
E18 ....2H 51
EN4: Cockf 3H 21
HA5: Pinn 5D 40
HA8: Edg 6B 28
KT6: Surb 5D 150
KT8: E Mos 4H 149
N11 ....5A 32
N12 ....5G 31
N15 ....5E 48
NW2 ....6E 62
RM6: Chad H 7B 54
SM1: Sutt 6J 165
SW13 ....2B 116
SW19 ....7A 136
TW2: Twick 3H 131
TW3: Houn 4E 112
TW7: Isle 1J 113
TW8: Bford 5C 96
TW10: Rich 6F 115
TW17: Shep 6E 146
UB8: Uxb 7A 56
W3 ....1J 97
W5 ....7D 78
Groveside Cl. SM5: Cars 2C 166
W3 ....5G 79
Groveside Ct. SW11 ....2B 118
Groveside Rd. E4 ....2B 36
Grovestile Waye TW14: Bedf 7F 111
Grove St. N18 ....5A 34
SE8 ....4B 104
Grove Ter. NW5 ....3F 65
TW11: Tedd 4A 132
UB1: S'hall 7E 76
Grove Ter. M. NW5 ....3F 65
Grove Va. BR7: Chst 6E 142
SE22 ....4F 121
Grove Vs. E14 ....7D 86
Grove Way HA9: Wemb 5H 61
KT10: Esh 7G 149
UB8: Uxb 7A 56
Groveway RM8: Dag 4D 72
SW9 ....1K 119
Grovewood TW9: Kew 1G 115
Grove Wood Cl. BR1: Brom 3E 160
Grovewood Pl. IG8: Wfd G 6J 37
Grummant Rd. SE15 ....1F 121
Grundy St. E14 ....6D 86
Gruneisen Rd. N3 ....7E 30
Guardian Ct. SE12 ....5G 123
Guards Memorial 5D 12 (1H 101)
Guards' Mus. 7B 12 (2G 101)
Gubyon Av. SE24 ....5B 120
Guerin Sq. E3 ....3B 86
Guernsey Cl. TW5: Hest 7E 94
Guernsey Gro. SE24 ....7C 120
Guernsey Ho. *EN3: Enf W* *1E 24*
(off Eastfield Rd.)
N1 ....*6C 66*
(off Douglas Rd. Nth.)
Guernsey Rd. E11 ....1F 69
Guibal Rd. SE12 ....7K 123
Guildersfield Rd. SW16 ....7J 137
Guildford Av. TW13: Felt 2H 129
Guildford Ct. *SW8* *7J 101*
(off Guildford Rd.)
Guildford Gro. SE10 ....1D 122
Guildford Rd. CR0: C'don 6D 156
E6 ....6D 88
E17 ....1E 50
IG3: Ilf 2J 71
SW8 ....1J 119
Guildford Way SM6: Wall 5J 167
Guildhall
City 7E 8
Westminster 7E 12
Guildhall Art Gallery *7E 8*
(off Aldermanbury)
Guildhall Bldgs. EC2 ....7E 8
Guildhall Library 7D 8
Guildhall Offices EC2 ....7D 8
Guildhall Yd. EC2 ....7D 8 (6C 84)
Guildhouse St. SW1 ....3A 18 (4G 101)
Guildown Av. N12 ....4E 30
Guild Rd. SE7 ....6B 106
Guildsway E17 ....1B 50
Guilford Av. KT5: Surb 5F 151
Guilford Pl. WC1 ....4G 7 (4K 83)
Guilford St. WC1 ....4E 6 (4J 83)
Guilfoyle NW9 ....2B 44
Guillemot Ct. *SE8* *6B 104*
(off Alexandra Cl.)
Guillemot Pl. N22 ....2K 47
Guilsborough Cl. NW10 ....7A 62
Guinea Ct. *E1* *7G 85*
(off Royal Mint St.)
Guinness Cl. E9 ....7A 68
UB3: Harl 3F 93
Guinness Ct. CR0: C'don 2F 169
E1 ....1J 15
EC1 ....2D 8
NW8 ....1C 82
SE1 ....6G 15
SW3 ....4E 16 (4D 100)
Guinness Sq. SE1 ....4E 102
Guinness Trust SW3 ....4D 100
Guinness Trust Bldgs. SE11 ....5B 102
W6 ....*5F 99*
(off Fulham Pal. Rd.)
Guinness Trust Est. *E15* *1H 87*
(off John St.)
N16 ....1E 66
Guion Rd. SW6 ....2H 117
Gulland Wlk. *N1* *6C 66*
(off Church Rd.)
Gulliver Cl. UB5: N'olt 1D 76
Gulliver Rd. DA15: Sidc 2H 143
Gulliver's Ho. EC1 ....4C 8
Gulliver St. SE16 ....3A 104
Gulston Wlk. SW3 ....4F 17
Gumleigh Rd. W5 ....4C 96

Gumley Gdns. TW7: Isle 3A 114
Gumping Rd. BR5: Farnb 2G 173
Gundulph Rd. BR2: Brom 3A 160
Gun Ho. *E1* *1H 103*
(off Wapping High St.)
Gunmaker's La. E3 ....1A 86
E9 ....1A 86
Gunnell Cl. CR0: C'don 6F 157
SE25 ....*6G 157*
(off Backley Gdns.)
SE26 ....4G 139
Gunner La. SE18 ....5E 106
GUNNERSBURY 5H 97
Gunnersbury Av. W4 ....1F 97
W5 ....1F 97
Gunnersbury Cl. W4 ....5H 97
Gunnersbury Ct. W3 ....2H 97
Gunnersbury Cres. W3 ....2G 97
Gunnersbury Dr. W5 ....2F 97
Gunnersbury Gdns. W3 ....2G 97
Gunnersbury La. W3 ....3G 97
Gunnersbury Mnr. W5 ....1F 97
Gunnersbury M. W4 ....5H 97
GUNNERSBURY PARK 3G 97
Gunnersbury Pk. Mus. 3G 97
Gunnersbury Triangle Nature Reserve
....4J 97
Gunners Gro. E4 ....3K 35
Gunners Rd. SW18 ....2B 136
Gunnery Ter. SE18 ....3G 107
Gunning St. SE18 ....4J 107
Gunpowder Sq. *EC4* *7K 7*
(off Gough Sq., not continuous)
Gunstor Rd. N16 ....4E 66
Gun St. E1 ....6J 9 (5F 85)
Gunter Gro. HA8: Edg 1K 43
SW10 ....6A 100
Gunter Hall Studios *SW10* *6A 100*
(off Gunter Gro.)
Gunterstone Rd. W14 ....4G 99
Gunthorpe St. E1 ....6K 9 (5F 85)
Gunton Rd. E5 ....3H 67
SW17 ....6E 136
Gunwhale Cl. SE16 ....1K 103
Gun Wharf *E1* *1J 103*
(off Wapping High St.)
Gun Wharf Bus. Cen. *E3* *1A 86*
(off Old Ford Rd.)
Gurdon Ho. *E14* *6C 86*
(off Dod St.)
Gurdon Rd. SE7 ....5J 105
Gurnard Cl. UB7: Yiew 7A 74
Gurnell Gro. W13 ....4K 77
Gurnell Leisure Cen. 3K 77
Gurney Cl. E15 ....5G 69
E17 ....1K 49
IG11: Bark 6F 71
Gurney Cres. CR0: C'don 1K 167
Gurney Dr. N2 ....4A 46
Gurney Ho. *E2* *2G 85*
(off Goldsmiths Row)
UB3: Harl 5G 93
Gurney Rd. E15 ....5G 69
SM5: Cars 4E 166
SW6 ....3A 118
UB5: Yead 3K 75
Guthrie Ct. SE1 ....7K 13
Guthrie St. SW3 ....5C 16 (5B 100)
Gutter La. EC2 ....7C 8 (6C 84)
Guyatt Gdns. CR4: Mitc 2E 154
Guy Barnett Gro. SE3 ....3J 123
Guy Rd. SM6: Bedd 3H 167
Guyscliff Rd. SE13 ....5E 122
Guys Retreat
IG9: Buck H 1F 37
Guy St. SE1 ....6F 15 (2D 102)
Gwalior Ho. N14 ....6B 22
Gwalior Rd. SW15 ....4F 117
Gwendolen Av. SW15 ....4F 117
Gwendolen Cl. SW15 ....5F 117
Gwendolen Ho. *TW19: Stanw* *1A 128*
(off Yeoman Dr.)
Gwendoline Av. E13 ....1K 87
Gwendwr Rd. W14 ....5G 99
Gweneth Cotts. HA8: Edg 6B 28
Gwen Morris Ho. SE5 ....7C 102
Gwent Ct. *SE16* *1K 103*
(off Rotherhithe St.)
Gwillim Cl. DA15: Sidc 5A 126
Gwilym Maries Ho. *E2* *3H 85*
(off Blythe St.)
Gwydor Rd. BR3: Beck 3K 157
Gwydyr Rd. BR2: Brom 3H 159
Gwyn Cl. SW6 ....7A 100
Gwynne Av. CR0: C'don 7K 157
Gwynne Cl. W4 ....6B 98
Gwynne Ho. *E1* *5H 85*
(off Turner St.)
SW1 ....*5G 17*
(off Lwr. Sloane St.)
WC1 ....*2J 7*
(off Lloyd Baker St.)
Gwynne Pk. Av. IG8: Wfd G 6J 37
Gwynne Pl. WC1 ....2H 7 (3K 83)
Gwynne Rd. SW11 ....2B 118
Gylcote Cl. SE5 ....4D 120
Gyles Pk. HA7: Stan 1C 42
Gyllyngdune Gdns. IG3: Ilf 2K 71
GYPSY CORNER 5K 79

H

Haarlem Rd. W14 ....3F 99
Haberdasher Est. N1 ....1F 9 (3D 84)
Haberdasher Pl. N1 ....1F 9 (3D 84)
Haberdashers Ct. SE14 ....3K 121
Haberdasher St. N1 ....1F 9 (3D 84)
Habitat Cl. SE15 ....2H 121
Habitat Sq. *SE10* *3H 105*
(off Teal St.)
Haccombe Rd. SW19 ....6A 136
HACKBRIDGE 1E 166
Hackbridge Grn. SM6: Wall 2E 166
Hackbridge Pk. Gdns. SM5: Cars 2D 166
Hackbridge Rd. SM6: Wall 2E 166
Hackford Rd. SW9 ....1K 119
Hackford Wlk. SW9 ....1K 119
Hackington Cres. BR3: Beck 6C 140
HACKNEY 6H 67
Hackney City Farm 2G 85
Hackney Empire Theatre 6H 67
Hackney Gro. E8 ....6H 67
Hackney Rd. E2 ....2J 9 (3F 85)
HACKNEY WICK 6B 68
HACKNEY WICK 6A 68
Hacon Sq. *E8* *7H 67*
(off Mare St.)
Hadar Cl. N20 ....1D 30
Hadden Rd. SE28 ....3J 107
Hadden Way UB6: G'frd 6H 59
Haddington Rd. BR1: Brom 3F 141
Haddo Ho. *SE10* *6D 104*
(off Haddo St.)
Haddon Cl. EN1: Enf 6B 24
KT3: N Mald 5B 152
Haddon Ct. NW4 ....3E 44
W3 ....7B 80
Haddonfield SE8 ....4K 103
Haddon Gro. DA15: Sidc 7K 125
Haddon Hall St. *SE1* *3D 102*
(off Rephidim St.)
Haddon Rd. SM1: Sutt 4K 165
(not continuous)
Haddo St. SE10 ....6D 104
Haden Ct. N4 ....2A 66
Haden La. N11 ....4B 32
Hadfield Cl. UB1: S'hall 3D 76
Hadfield Ho. *E1* *6G 85*
(off Ellen St.)
Hadleigh Cl. E1 ....4J 85
SW20 ....2H 153
Hadleigh Ct. E4 ....1B 36
NW2 ....6E 62
Hadleigh Ho. *E1* *4J 85*
(off Hadleigh Cl.)
Hadleigh Lodge *IG8: Wfd G* *6D 36*
(off Snakes La.)
Hadleigh Rd. N9 ....7C 24
Hadleigh St. E2 ....3J 85
Hadleigh Wlk. E6 ....6C 88
HADLEY 3C 20
Hadley Cl. N21 ....6F 23
Hadley Comn. EN5: Barn, New Bar 2D 20
Hadley Ct. EN5: New Bar 3E 20
N16 ....1G 67
SL3: Poyle *4A 174*
(off Coleridge Cres.)
Hadley Gdns. UB2: S'hall 5D 94
W4 ....5K 97
Hadley Grn. EN5: Barn 2C 20
Hadley Grn. Rd. EN5: Barn 2C 20
Hadley Grn. W. EN5: Barn 2C 20
Hadley Gro. EN5: Barn 2B 20
Hadley Highstone EN5: Barn 1C 20
Hadley M. EN5: Barn 3C 20
Hadley Pde. *EN5: Barn* *3B 20*
(off High St.)
Hadley Ridge EN5: Barn 3C 20
Hadley Rd. CR4: Mitc 4H 155
DA17: Belv 4F 109
EN2: Enf 1A 22
EN4: Had W 1K 21
EN5: New Bar 2E 20
Hadley St. NW1 ....6F 65
(not continuous)
Hadley Way N21 ....6F 23
HADLEY WOOD 1F 21
Hadley Wood Lawn Tennis Club 1F 21
Hadley Wood Nature Reserve 2F 21
Hadley Wood Rd. EN4: Cockf 2F 21
EN5: Cockf, New Bar 2F 21
Hadlow Ho. *SE17* *5E 102*
(off Kinglake Est.)
Hadlow Pl. SE19 ....7G 139
Hadlow Rd. DA14: Sidc 4A 144
DA16: Well 7C 108
Hadrian Cl. *E3* *1C 86*
(off Garrison Rd.)
TW19: Stanw 7A 110
Hadrian Ct. SM2: Sutt 7K 165
Hadrian Est. E2 ....2G 85
Hadrian M. N7 ....7K 65
Hadrians Ride EN1: Enf 5A 24
Hadrian St. SE10 ....5G 105
Hadrian Way TW19: Stanw 7A 110
(not continuous)
Hadstock Ho. *NW1* *1D 6*
(off Ossulston St.)
Hadyn Pk. Ct. *W12* *2C 98*
(off Curwen Rd.)
Hadyn Pk. Rd. W12 ....2C 98
Hafer Rd. SW11 ....4D 118
Hafton Rd. SE6 ....1G 141
Haggard Rd. TW1: Twick 7B 114
Hagger Ct. E17 ....3F 51
HAGGERSTON 7F 67
Haggerston Rd. E8 ....7F 67
Haggerston Studios *E8* *1F 85*
(off Kingsland Rd.)
Hague St. E2 ....3G 85
Ha Ha Rd. SE18 ....6D 106
Haig Ho. *E2* *1K 9*
(off Shipton St.)
Haig Pl. SM4: Mord 6J 153
Haig Rd. HA7: Stan 5H 27
UB8: Hil 5D 74
Haig Rd. E. E13 ....3A 88
Haig Rd. W. E13 ....3A 88
Haigville Gdns. IG6: Ilf 4F 53
Hailes Cl. SW19 ....6A 136
Haileybury Av. EN1: Enf 6A 24
Hailey Rd. DA18: Erith 2G 109
Hailey Rd. Bus. Pk. DA18: Erith 2G 109
Hailing M. *BR2: Brom* *3K 159*
(off Wendover Rd.)
Hailsham Av. SW2 ....2K 137
Hailsham Cl. KT6: Surb 7D 150
Hailsham Dr. HA1: Harr 3H 41
Hailsham Ho. *NW8* *4C 4*
(off Salisbury St.)
Hailsham Rd. SW17 ....6E 136
Hailsham Ter. N18 ....5J 33
Haimo Rd. SE9 ....5B 124
Hainault Ct. E17 ....4F 51
Hainault Gore RM6: Chad H 5E 54
Hainault Rd. E11 ....1E 68
RM5: Col R, Rom 2J 55
RM6: Chad H 1B 54
(Forest Rd.)
RM6: Chad H 6F 55
(High Rd.)
Hainault St. IG1: Ilf 2G 71
SE9 ....1F 143
Haines Cl. N1 ....7E 66
Haines St. SW8 ....7G 101
Haines Wlk. SM4: Mord 7K 153
Hainford Cl. SE4 ....4K 121
Haining Cl. W4 ....5G 97
Hainthorpe Rd. SE27 ....3B 138
Hainton Cl. E1 ....6H 85
Halberd M. E5 ....2H 67
Halbutt Gdns. RM9: Dag 3F 73
Halbutt St. RM9: Dag 4F 73
Halcomb St. N1 ....1E 84
Halcot Av. DA6: Bex 5H 127
Halcrow St. E1 ....5H 85
Halcyon *EN1: Enf* *5K 23*
(off Private Rd.)
Halcyon Wharf *E1* *1G 103*
(off Hermitage Wall)
Haldane Cl. N10 ....7A 32
Haldane Pl. SW18 ....1K 135
Haldane Rd. E6 ....3B 88
SE28 ....7D 90
SW6 ....7H 99
UB1: S'hall 7G 77
Haldan Rd. E4 ....6K 35
Haldon Rd. SW18 ....6H 117
HALE, THE 5D 28
Hale, The E4 ....7A 36
N17 ....3G 49
(not continuous)
Hale Cl. BR6: Farnb 4G 173
E4 ....3K 35
HA8: Edg 5D 28
Hale Ct. HA8: Edg 5D 28
Hale Dr. NW7 ....6D 28
HALE END 6B 36
Hale End Cl. HA4: Ruis 6J 39
Hale End Rd. E4 ....6A 36
E17 ....1E 50
IG8: Wfd G 7A 36
Halefield Rd. N17 ....1H 49
Hale Gdns. N17 ....4G 49
W3 ....1G 97
Hale Gro. Gdns. NW7 ....5F 29
Hale Ho. *SW1* *5D 18*
(off Lindsay Sq.)
Hale La. HA8: Edg 5C 28
NW7 ....5E 28
Hale Path SE27 ....4B 138
Hale Rd. E6 ....4C 88
N17 ....3G 49
Halesowen Rd. SM4: Mord 7K 153
Hales Prior *N1* *1G 7*
(off Calshot St.)
Hales St. SE8 ....7C 104
Hale St. E14 ....7D 86
Halesworth Cl. E5 ....2J 67

Halesworth Rd. SE13 3D 122
Hale Wlk. W7 5J 77
Haley Rd. NW4 6E 44
Half Acre HA7: Stan 5H 27
TW8: Bford 6D 96
Half Acre Rd. W7 1J 95
Half Moon Ct. EC1 6C 8
Half Moon Cres. N1 2K 83
(not continuous)
Half Moon La. SE24 6C 120
Half Moon Pas. E1 1K 15 (6F 85)
(not continuous)
Half Moon St. W1 4K 11 (1F 101)
Halford Cl. HA8: Edg 2H 43
Halford Rd. E10 5F 51
SW6 6J 99
TW10: Rich 5E 114
UB10: Ick 4C 56
Halfway St. DA15: Sidc 7H 125
Haliburton Rd. TW1: Twick 5A 114
Haliday Ho. *N1* *6D 66*
(off Mildmay St.)
Haliday Wlk. N1 6D 66
Halidon Cl. E9 5J 67
Halifax NW9 2B 44
Halifax Cl. TW11: Tedd 6J 131
Halifax Rd. EN2: Enf 2H 23
UB6: G'frd 1F 77
Halifax St. SE26 3H 139
Halifield Dr. DA17: Belv 3E 108
Haling Down Pas. CR8: Purl 7C 168
(not continuous)
Haling Gro. CR2: S Croy 7C 168
Haling Pk. Gdns. CR2: S Croy 6B 168
Haling Pk. Rd. CR2: S Croy 5B 168
Haling Rd. CR2: S Croy 6D 168
Haliwell Ho. *NW6* *1K 81*
(off Mortimer Cres.)
Halkett Ho. *E2* *1J 85*
(off Waterloo Gdns.)
Halkin Arc. SW1 1F 17 (3D 100)
Halkin M. SW1 1G 17 (3E 100)
Halkin Pl. SW1 1G 17 (3E 100)
Halkin St. SW1 7H 11 (2E 100)
Hall, The SE3 3J 123
Hallam Cl. BR7: Chst 5D 142
Hallam Ct. *W1* *5K 5*
(off Hallam St.)
Hallam Gdns. HA5: Hat E 1C 40
Hallam Ho. *SW1* *6B 18*
(off Churchill Gdns.)
Hallam M. W1 5K 5 (5F 83)
Hallam Rd. N15 4B 48
SW13 3D 116
Hallam St. W1 4K 5 (4F 83)
Hallane Ho. SE27 5C 138
Hall Cl. W5 5E 78
Hall Ct. TW11: Tedd 5K 131
Hall Dr. SE26 5J 139
W7 6J 77
Halley Gdns. SE13 4F 123
Halley Ho. *E2* *2G 85*
(off Pritchards Rd.)
SE10 *5H 105*
(off Armitage Rd.)
Halley Rd. E7 6A 70
E12 6A 70
Halley St. E14 5A 86
Hall Farm Cl. HA7: Stan 4G 27
Hall Farm Dr. TW2: Whitt 7H 113
Hallfield Est. W2 6A 82
(not continuous)
Hall Gdns. E4 4G 35
Hall Ga. NW8 1A 4 (3B 82)
Halliards, The KT12: Walt T 6J 147
Halliday Sq. UB2: S'hall 1H 95
Halliford Cl. TW17: Shep 4F 147
Halliford Rd. TW16: Sun 5G 147
TW17: Shep 5G 147
Halliford St. N1 7C 66
Hallingbury Ct. E17 3D 50
Halling Ho. *SE1* *7F 15*
(off Long La.)
Hallings Wharf Studios E15 1F 87
Halliwell Ct. SE22 5G 121
Halliwell Rd. SW2 6K 119
Halliwick Ct. Pde. *N12* *6J 31*
(off Woodhouse Rd.)
Halliwick Rd. N10 1E 46
Hall La. E4 5F 35
NW4 1C 44
UB3: Harl 7F 93
HALL LANE JUNC. 5E 34
Hallmark Trad. Cen.
HA9: Wemb 4J 61
Hallmead Rd. SM1: Sutt 3K 165
Hall Oak Wlk. NW6 6H 63
Hallowell Av. CR0: Bedd 4J 167
Hallowell Cl. CR4: Mitc 3E 154
Hallowell Rd. HA6: Nwood 1G 39
Hallowfield Way CR4: Mitc 3B 154
Hallows Gro. TW16: Sun 5H 129
Hall Pl. W2 4A 4 (4B 82)
(not continuous)
Hall Place & Vis. Cen. 6J 127
Hall Pl. Cres. DA5: Bexl 5J 127
Hall Place Gdns. 6J 127
Hall Rd. E6 1D 88
E15 4F 69
NW8 1A 4 (3A 82)
RM6: Chad H 6C 54
SM6: Wall 7F 167
TW7: Isle 5H 113
Hallside Rd. EN1: Enf 1A 24
Hall St. EC1 1B 8 (3B 84)
N12 5F 31
Hallsville Rd. E16 6H 87
Hallswelle Pde. NW11 5H 45
Hallswelle Rd. NW11 5H 45
Hall Twr. W2 5B 4
Hall Vw. SE9 2B 142
Hallywell Cres. E6 5D 88
Halons Rd. SE9 7E 124
Halpin Pl. SE17 4D 102
Halsbrook Rd. SE3 3A 124
Halsbury Cl. HA7: Stan 4G 27
Halsbury Ct. HA7: Stan 5G 27
Halsbury Ho. *N7* *4K 65*
(off Biddestone Rd.)
Halsbury Rd. W12 1D 98
Halsbury Rd. E. UB5: N'olt 4G 59
Halsbury Rd. W.
UB5: N'olt 5F 59
Halsend UB3: Hayes 1K 93
Halsey Ho. *WC1* *5K 83*
(off Dane St.)
Halsey M. SW3 3E 16 (4D 100)
Halsey St. SW3 3E 16 (4D 100)
Halsham Cres. IG11: Bark 5K 71
Halsmere Rd. SE5 1B 120
Halstead Cl. CR0: C'don 3C 168
Halstead Ct. E17 7B 50
N1 *1F 9*
(off Murray Gro.)
Halstead Gdns. N21 1J 33
Halstead Rd. E11 5J 51
EN1: Enf 4K 23
N21 1H 33
Halston Cl. SW11 6D 118
Halstow Rd. NW10 3F 81
SE10 5J 105
Halsway UB3: Hayes 1J 93
Halton Cl. N11 6J 31
Halton Cross St. N1 1B 84
Halton Ho. *N1* *7B 66*
(off Halton Rd.)
Halton Mans. N1 7B 66
Halton Pl. N1 1C 84
Halton Rd. N1 7B 66
Halt Robin La. DA17: Belv 4H 109
Halt Robin Rd. DA17: Belv 4G 109
(not continuous)
Halyard Ho. E14 3E 104
HAM 3C 132
Ham, The TW8: Bford 7C 96
Hamara Ghar E13 1A 88
Hambalt Rd. SW4 5G 119
Hamble Cl. HA4: Ruis 2G 57
Hambledon *SE17* *6D 102*
(off Villa St.)
Hambledon Cl. UB8: Hil 4D 74
Hambledon Ct. SE22 4E 120
W5 7E 78
Hambledon Gdns. SE25 3F 157
Hambledon Pl. SE21 1E 138
Hambledon Rd. SW18 7H 117
Hambledown Rd.
DA15: Sidc 7H 125
Hamblehyrst BR3: Beck 2D 158
Hamble St. SW6 3K 117
Hambleton Cl. KT4: Wor Pk 2E 164
Hamble Wlk. *UB5: N'olt* *2E 76*
(off Brabazon Rd.)
Hambley Ho. *SE16* *4H 103*
(off Camilla Rd.)
Hamblin Ho. *UB1: S'hall* *7C 76*
(off The Broadway)
Hambridge Way SW2 7A 120
Hambro Av. BR2: Hayes 1J 171
Hambrook Rd. SE25 3H 157
Hambro Rd. SW16 6H 137
Hambrough Ho.
UB4: Yead 5A 76
Hambrough Rd. UB1: S'hall 1C 94
Ham Cl. TW10: Ham 3C 132
(not continuous)
Ham Comn. TW10: Ham 3D 132
Ham Ct. NW9 2A 44
Ham Cft. Cl. TW13: Felt 3J 129
Hamden Cres. RM10: Dag 3H 73
Hamel Cl. HA3: Kent 4D 42
Hame Way E6 4E 88
Ham Farm Rd. TW10: Ham 4D 132
Hamfrith Rd. E15 6H 69
Ham Ga. Av. TW10: Ham 3D 132
Ham House 1C 132
Hamilton Av. IG6: Ilf 4F 53
KT6: Surb 2G 163
N9 7B 24
RM1: Rom 2K 55
SM3: Cheam 2G 165
Hamilton Bldgs. EC2 4H 9
Hamilton Cl. EN4: Cockf 4H 21
HA7: Stan 2D 26
N17 3F 49
NW8 2A 4 (3B 82)
SE16 2A 104
TW11: Tedd 6B 132
TW13: Felt 5H 129
Hamilton Ct. CR0: C'don 1G 169
SE6 1H 141
SW15 3G 117
W5 7E 78
W9 *3A 82*
(off Maida Va.)
Hamilton Cres. HA2: Harr 3D 58
N13 4F 33
TW3: Houn 5F 113
Hamilton Gdns. NW8 1A 4 (3A 82)
Hamilton Hall *NW8* *2A 82*
(off Hamilton Ter.)
Hamilton Ho. *E14* *5D 104*
(off St Davids Sq.)
E14 *7B 86*
(off Victory Pl.)
NW8 1A 4
W4 6A 98
W8 *2K 99*
(off Vicarage Ga.)
Hamilton La. N5 4B 66
Hamilton Lodge *E1* *4J 85*
(off Cleveland Gro.)
Hamilton M. SW18 1J 135
SW19 7J 135
W1 6J 11 (2F 101)
Hamilton Pde. TW13: Felt 4H 129
Hamilton Pk. N5 4B 66
Hamilton Pk. W. N5 4B 66
Hamilton Pl. N19 3H 65
TW16: Sun 7K 129
W1 5H 11 (1E 100)
Hamilton Rd. CR7: Thor H 3D 156
DA7: Bex 2E 126
DA15: Sidc 4A 144
E15 3G 87
E17 2A 50
EN4: Cockf 4H 21
HA1: Harr 5J 41
IG1: Ilf 4F 71
N2 3A 46
N9 7B 24
NW10 5C 62
NW11 7F 45
SE27 4D 138
SW19 7K 135
TW2: Twick 1J 131
TW8: Bford 6D 96
TW13: Felt 4H 129
UB1: S'hall 1D 94
UB3: Hayes 7K 75
W4 2A 98
W5 7E 78
Hamilton Rd. Ind. Est. *SE27* *4D 138*
(off Hamilton Rd.)
Hamilton Rd. M. SW19 7K 135
Hamilton Sq. N12 6G 31
SE1 6F 15 (2D 102)
Hamilton St. SE8 6C 104
Hamilton Ter. NW8 2A 4 (2K 81)
Hamilton Way N3 6D 30
N13 4G 33
SM6: Wall 7H 167
Ham Lands Nature Reserve 2A 132
Hamlea Cl. SE12 5J 123
Hamlet, The SE5 3D 120
Hamlet Cl. RM5: Col R 1G 55
SE13 4G 123
Hamlet Ct. EN1: Enf 5K 23
SE11 *5B 102*
(off Opal St.)
W6 4C 98
Hamlet Gdns. W6 4C 98
Hamlet Ind. Est. E9 7C 68
Hamlet Intl. Ind. Est. DA8: Erith 5K 109
Hamlet M. SE21 1D 138
Hamlet Rd. RM5: Col R 1G 55
SE19 7F 139
Hamlet Sq. NW2 3G 63
Hamlets Way E3 4B 86
Hamlet Way SE1 6F 15 (2D 102)
Hamlin Cres. HA5: Eastc 5A 40
Hamlyn Cl. HA8: Edg 3K 27
Hamlyn Gdns. SE19 7E 138
Hamlyn Ho. TW13: Felt 1K 129
Hammelton Ct. *BR1: Brom* *1H 159*
(off London Rd.)
Hammelton Grn. SW9 1B 120
Hammelton Rd. BR1: Brom 1H 159
Hammerfield Ho. *SW3* *5D 16*
(off Cale St.)
Hammers La. NW7 5H 29
Hammersley Ho. *SE14* *7J 103*
(off Pomeroy St.)
HAMMERSMITH 4E 98
Hammersmith Apollo 5E 98
Hammersmith Bri. SW13 6D 98
W6 6D 98
Hammersmith Bri. Rd. W6 5E 98
HAMMERSMITH BROADWAY 4E 98
Hammersmith B'way. W6 4E 98

Hammersmith Fitness & Squash Cen. . . . 4F 99
(off Chalk Hill Rd.)
HAMMERSMITH FLYOVER . . . 5E 98
Hammersmith Flyover W6 . . . 5E 98
Hammersmith Gro. W6 . . . 2E 98
Hammersmith Ind. Est. W6 . . . 6E 98
Hammersmith Rd. W6 . . . 4F 99
W14 . . . 4F 99
Hammersmith Ter. W6 . . . 5C 98
Hammet Cl. UB4: Yead . . . 5B 76
Hammett St. EC3 . . . 2J 15 (7F 85)
Hammond Av. CR4: Mitc . . . 2F 155
Hammond Cl. EN5: Barn . . . 5B 20
TW12: Hamp . . . 1E 148
UB6: G'frd . . . 5H 59
Hammond Ct. E10 . . . 2D 68
(off Crescent Rd.)
E17 . . . 5A 50
(off Maude Rd.)
Hammond Ho. E14 . . . 3C 104
(off Tiller Rd.)
SE14 . . . 7J 103
(off Lubbock St.)
Hammond Lodge W9 . . . 5J 81
(off Admiral Wlk.)
Hammond Rd. EN1: Enf . . . 2C 24
UB2: S'hall . . . 3C 94
Hammonds Cl. RM8: Dag . . . 3C 72
Hammond St. NW5 . . . 6G 65
Hammond Way SE28 . . . 7B 90
Hamond Cl. CR2: S Croy . . . 7B 168
Hamonde Cl. HA8: Edg . . . 2C 28
Hamond Sq. N1 . . . 2E 84
Ham Pk. Rd. E7 . . . 7H 69
E15 . . . 7H 69
Hampden Av. BR3: Beck . . . 2A 158
Hampden Cl. NW1 . . . 2H 83
Hampden Ct. N10 . . . 7K 31
Hampden Gurney St. W1 . . . 1E 10 (6D 82)
Hampden Ho. SW9 . . . 2A 120
Hampden La. N17 . . . 1F 49
Hampden Rd. BR3: Beck . . . 2A 158
HA3: Hrw W . . . 1G 41
KT1: King T . . . 3G 151
N8 . . . 4A 48
N10 . . . 7K 31
N17 . . . 1G 49
N19 . . . 2H 65
RM5: Col R . . . 1H 55
Hampden Sq. N14 . . . 1A 32
Hampden Way N14 . . . 1A 32
Hampshire Cl. N18 . . . 5C 34
Hampshire Hog La. W6 . . . 5D 98
Hampshire Rd. N22 . . . 7E 32
Hampshire St. NW5 . . . 6H 65
Hampson Way SW8 . . . 1K 119
HAMPSTEAD . . . 4B 64
Hampstead Av. IG8: Wfd G . . . 7K 37
Hampstead Cl. SE28 . . . 1B 108
Hampstead Gdns. NW11 . . . 6J 45
RM6: Chad H . . . 5B 54
HAMPSTEAD GARDEN SUBURB . . . 5A 46
Hampstead Ga. NW3 . . . 5A 64
Hampstead Grn. NW3 . . . 5C 64
Hampstead Gro. NW3 . . . 3A 64
Hampstead Heath . . . 2B 64
Hampstead Heath Info. Cen. . . . 4E 64
(off Lissenden Gdns.)
Hampstead Hgts. N2 . . . 3A 46
Hampstead High St. NW3 . . . 4B 64
Hampstead Hill Gdns. NW3 . . . 4B 64
Hampstead Ho. NW1 . . . 3G 83
(off William Rd.)
Hampstead La. N6 . . . 1B 64
NW3 . . . 1B 64
Hampstead Lodge NW1 . . . 5C 4
(off Bell St.)
Hampstead Mus. . . . 4B 64
(in Burgh House)
Hampstead Rd. NW1 . . . 1A 6 (2G 83)
Hampstead Sq. NW3 . . . 3A 64
Hampstead Theatre . . . 7B 64
Hampstead Wlk. E3 . . . 1B 86
Hampstead Way NW11 . . . 5H 45
Hampstead W. NW6 . . . 6J 63
HAMPTON . . . 1F 149
Hampton & Richmond Borough FC . . . 1F 149
Hampton Cl. N11 . . . 5A 32
NW6 . . . 3J 81
SW20 . . . 7E 134
HAMPTON COURT . . . 4J 149
Hampton Court . . . 2J 149
HAMPTON COURT . . . 3J 149
Hampton Ct. N1 . . . 6B 66
N22 . . . 1G 47
SE16 . . . 7K 85
(off King & Queen Wharf)
Hampton Ct. Av. KT8: E Mos . . . 6H 149
Hampton Ct. Bri. KT8: E Mos . . . 4J 149
Hampton Ct. Cres. KT8: E Mos . . . 3H 149
Hampton Ct. Est. KT7: T Ditt . . . 4J 149
Hampton Ct. M. KT8: E Mos . . . 4J 149
(off Feltham Av.)
Hampton Court Palace . . . 4K 149
Hampton Ct. Pde. KT8: E Mos . . . 4J 149
Hampton Ct. Rd. KT1: Ham W . . . 3K 149
KT8: E Mos . . . 3K 149
TW12: Hamp . . . 2G 149
Hampton Ct. Way KT7: T Ditt . . . 7J 149
KT8: E Mos . . . 7J 149
Hampton Farm Ind. Est.
TW13: Hanw . . . 3C 130
HAMPTON HILL . . . 5G 131
Hampton Hill Bus. Pk.
TW12: Ham H . . . 5G 131
(off High St.)
Hampton Hill Playhouse Theatre . . . 5G 131
Hampton Ho. DA7: Bex . . . 2H 127
(off Erith Rd.)
SW8 . . . 7G 101
(off Ascalon St.)
Hampton La. TW13: Hanw . . . 4C 130
Hampton M. NW10 . . . 3K 79
Hampton Open Air Pool . . . 7G 131
Hampton Ri. HA3: Kent . . . 6E 42
Hampton Rd. CR0: C'don . . . 6C 156
E4 . . . 5G 35
E7 . . . 5K 69
E11 . . . 1F 69
IG1: Ilf . . . 4G 71
KT4: Wor Pk . . . 2C 164
TW2: Twick . . . 3H 131
TW11: Tedd . . . 5H 131
TW12: Ham H . . . 5H 131
Hampton Rd. E. TW13: Ham H . . . 4D 130
Hampton Rd. Ind. Pk.
CR0: C'don . . . 6C 156
Hampton Rd. W. TW13: Hanw . . . 3C 130
Hampton Sport, Arts & Fitness Cen. . . . 5E 130
Hampton St. SE17 . . . 4B 102
HAMPTON WICK . . . 1C 150
Hampton Youth Project (Sports Hall) . . . 6D 130
Ham Ridings
TW10: Ham . . . 5F 133
Hamshades Cl. DA15: Sidc . . . 3K 143
Hamston Ho. W8 . . . 3K 99
(off Kensington Ct. Pl.)
Ham St. TW10: Ham . . . 1B 132
Ham Vw. CR0: C'don . . . 6A 158
Ham Yd. W1 . . . 2C 12 (7H 83)
Hanah Ct. SW19 . . . 7F 135
Hanameel St. E16 . . . 1J 105
Hana M. E5 . . . 4H 67
Hanbury Cl. NW4 . . . 3E 44
Hanbury Ct. HA1: Harr . . . 6K 41
Hanbury Dr. E11 . . . 7H 51
N21 . . . 5E 22
Hanbury Ho. E1 . . . 5G 85
(off Hanbury St.)
SW8 . . . 7J 101
(off Regent's Bri. Gdns.)
Hanbury M. N1 . . . 1C 84
Hanbury Rd. N17 . . . 2H 49
W3 . . . 2H 97
Hanbury St. E1 . . . 5K 9 (5F 85)
Hanbury Wlk. DA5: Bexl . . . 3K 145
Hancock Nunn Ho. NW3 . . . 6D 64
(off Fellows Rd.)
Hancock Rd. E3 . . . 3E 86
SE19 . . . 6D 138
Handa Wlk. N1 . . . 6D 66
Hand Ct. WC1 . . . 6H 7 (5K 83)
Handcroft Rd. CR0: C'don . . . 7B 156
Handel Bus. Cen. SW8 . . . 7E 18 (6J 101)
Handel Cl. HA8: Edg . . . 6A 28
Handel House Mus. . . . 2J 11
(off Brook St.)
Handel Mans. SW13 . . . 7E 98
WC1 . . . 3F 7
(off Handel St.)
Handel Pde. HA8: Edg . . . 7B 28
(off Whitchurch La.)
Handel Pl. NW10 . . . 6K 61
Handel St. WC1 . . . 3E 6 (4J 83)
Handel Way HA8: Edg . . . 7B 28
Handen Rd. SE12 . . . 5G 123
Handforth Rd. IG1: Ilf . . . 3F 71
SW9 . . . 7A 102
Handley Gro. NW2 . . . 3F 63
Handley Page Rd. SM6: Wall . . . 7K 167
Handley Rd. E9 . . . 7J 67
Handowe Cl. NW4 . . . 4C 44
Handside Cl. KT4: Wor Pk . . . 1F 165
Hands Wlk. E16 . . . 6J 87
Handsworth Av. E4 . . . 6A 36
Handsworth Rd. N17 . . . 3D 48
Handtrough Way IG11: Bark . . . 2F 89
Hanford Cl. SW18 . . . 1J 135
Hanford Row SW19 . . . 6E 134
Hanger Ct. W5 . . . 4F 79
Hanger Grn. W5 . . . 4G 79
HANGER HILL . . . 4F 79
HANGER LANE . . . 3E 78
Hanger La. W5 . . . 2E 78
Hanger Va. La. W5 . . . 6F 79
(not continuous)
Hanger Vw. Way W3 . . . 6G 79
Hanging Sword All. EC4 . . . 1K 13
Hankey Ho. SE1 . . . 7F 15
(off Manciple St.)
Hankey Pl. SE1 . . . 7F 15 (2D 102)
Hankins La. NW7 . . . 2F 29
Hanley Gdns. N4 . . . 1K 65
Hanley Pl. BR3: Beck . . . 7C 140
Hanley Rd. N4 . . . 1J 65
Hanmer Wlk. N7 . . . 2K 65
Hannah Barlow Ho. SW8 . . . 1K 119
Hannah Cl. BR3: Beck . . . 3E 158
NW10 . . . 4J 61
Hannah Mary Way SE1 . . . 4G 103
Hannah M. SM6: Wall . . . 7G 167
Hannay La. N8 . . . 7H 47
Hannay Wlk. SW16 . . . 2H 137
Hannell Rd. SW6 . . . 7G 99
Hannen Rd. SE27 . . . 3B 138
Hannibal Rd. E1 . . . 5J 85
TW19: Stanw . . . 7A 110
Hannibal Way
CR0: Wadd . . . 5K 167
Hannington Rd. SW4 . . . 3F 119
Hanover Av. E16 . . . 1J 105
TW13: Felt . . . 1J 129
Hanover Circ. UB3: Hayes . . . 6E 74
Hanover Cl. SM3: Cheam . . . 4G 165
TW9: Kew . . . 7G 97
Hanover Ct. HA4: Ruis . . . 3J 57
NW9 . . . 3A 44
Hanover Ct. SE19 . . . 7G 139
(off Anerley Rd.)
SW15 . . . 4B 116
W12 . . . 1C 98
(off Uxbridge Rd.)
Hanover Dr. BR7: Chst . . . 4G 143
Hanover Flats W1 . . . 2H 11
(off Binney St.)
Hanover Gdns. IG6: Ilf . . . 1G 53
SE11 . . . 6A 102
Hanover Ga. NW1 . . . 2D 4 (3C 82)
Hanover Ga. Mans. NW1 . . . 3D 4
Hanover Ho. E14 . . . 1B 104
(off Westferry Cir.)
NW8 . . . 1C 4
SW9 . . . 3A 120
Hanover Mans. SW2 . . . 5A 120
(off Barnwell Rd.)
Hanover Mead NW11 . . . 5G 45
Hanover Pk. SE15 . . . 1G 121
Hanover Pl. E3 . . . 3B 86
WC2 . . . 1F 13 (6J 83)
Hanover Rd. N15 . . . 4F 49
NW10 . . . 7E 62
SW19 . . . 7A 136
Hanover Sq. W1 . . . 1K 11 (6F 83)
Hanover Steps W2 . . . 1D 10
Hanover St. CR0: C'don . . . 3B 168
W1 . . . 1K 11 (6F 83)
Hanover Ter. NW1 . . . 2E 4 (3C 82)
TW7: Isle . . . 1A 114
Hanover Ter. M. NW1 . . . 2D 4 (3C 82)
Hanover Trad. Est. N7 . . . 5J 65
Hanover Way DA6: Bex . . . 3D 126
Hanover W. Ind. Est. NW10 . . . 3K 79
Hanover Yd. N1 . . . 2C 84
(off Noel Rd.)
Hansa Cl. UB2: S'hall . . . 3A 94
Hansard M. W14 . . . 2F 99
Hansart Way EN2: Enf . . . 1F 23
Hanscomb M. SW4 . . . 4G 119
Hans Ct. SW3 . . . 1E 16
Hans Cres. SW1 . . . 1E 16 (3D 100)
Hanselin Cl. HA7: Stan . . . 5E 26
Hansen Dr. N21 . . . 5E 22
Hanshaw Dr. HA8: Edg . . . 1K 43
Hansler Ct. SW19 . . . 1G 135
(off Princes Way)
Hansler Gro. KT8: E Mos . . . 4H 149
Hansler Rd. SE22 . . . 5F 121
Hansol Rd. DA6: Bex . . . 5E 126
Hansom Ter. BR1: Brom . . . 1K 159
(off Freelands Gro.)
Hanson Cl. BR3: Beck . . . 6D 140
SW12 . . . 7F 119
SW14 . . . 3J 115
UB7: W Dray . . . 3B 92
Hanson Ct. E17 . . . 6D 50
Hanson Gdns. UB1: S'hall . . . 2C 94
Hanson St. W1 . . . 5A 6 (5G 83)
Hans Pl. SW1 . . . 1F 17 (3D 100)
Hans Rd. SW3 . . . 1E 16 (3D 100)
Hans St. SW1 . . . 2F 17 (3D 100)
Hanway Pl. W1 . . . 7C 6 (6H 83)
Hanway Rd. W7 . . . 6H 77
Hanway St. W1 . . . 7C 6 (6H 83)
HANWELL . . . 1K 95
Hanwell Fitness Cen. . . . 1K 95
Hanwell Ho. W2 . . . 5J 81
(off Gt. Western Rd.)
HANWORTH . . . 4B 130
Hanworth Ho. SE5 . . . 7B 102
(not continuous)
Hanworth Rd. TW3: Houn . . . 1C 130
TW4: Houn . . . 1C 130
TW12: Hamp . . . 4D 130
TW13: Felt . . . 1K 129
TW16: Sun . . . 7J 129
(not continuous)
Hanworth Ter. TW3: Houn . . . 4F 113

Hanworth Trad. Est.
TW13: Hanw 3C 130
Hapgood Cl. UB6: G'frd 5H 59
Harad's Pl. E1 7G 85
Harben Pde. *NW3* *7A 64*
(off Finchley Rd.)
Harben Rd. NW6 7A 64
Harberson Rd. E15 1H 87
SW12 1F 137
Harberton Rd. N19 1G 65
Harbet Rd. E4 5F 35
N18 5F 35
W2 6B 4 (5B 82)
Harbex Cl. DA5: Bexl 7H 127
Harbinger Rd. E14 4D 104
Harbledown Ho. *SE1* *7E 14*
(off Manciple St.)
Harbledown Rd. SW6 1J 117
Harbord Cl. SE5 2D 120
Harbord Ho. *SE16* *4K 103*
(off Cope St.)
Harbord St. SW6 1F 117
Harborough Av. DA15: Sidc 7J 125
Harborough Rd. SW16 4K 137
Harbour Av. SW10 1A 118
Harbour Club Leisure Cen., The 2A 118
Harbour Club Notting Hill 5J 81
Harbour Exchange Sq. E14 2D 104
Harbour Quay E14 1E 104
Harbour Reach SW6 1A 118
Harbour Rd. SE5 3C 120
Harbour Yd. SW10 1A 118
Harbridge Av. SW15 7B 116
Harbury Rd. SM5: Cars 7C 166
Harbut Rd. SW11 4B 118
(not continuous)
Harcombe Rd. N16 3E 66
Harcourt Av. DA15: Sidc 6C 126
E12 4D 70
HA8: Edg 3D 28
SM6: Wall 4F 167
Harcourt Bldgs. EC4 2J 13
Harcourt Cl. TW7: Isle 3A 114
Harcourt Fld. SM6: Wall 4F 167
Harcourt Ho. *W1* *7J 5*
(off Cavendish Sq.)
Harcourt Lodge SM6: Wall 4F 167
Harcourt Rd. CR7: Thor H 6K 155
DA6: Bex 4E 126
E15 2H 87
N22 1H 47
SE4 3B 122
SM6: Wall 4F 167
SW19 7J 135
Harcourt St. W1 6D 4 (5C 82)
Harcourt Ter. SW10 5K 99
Hardcastle Cl. CR0: C'don 6G 157
Hardcastle Ho. *SE14* *1A 122*
(off Loring Rd.)
Hardcourts Cl. BR4: W W'ck 3D 170
Hardel Ri. SW2 1B 138
Hardel Wlk. SW2 7A 120
Harden Ct. SE7 4C 106
Harden Ho. SE5 2E 120
Harden's Manorway SE7 3B 106
(not continuous)
Harders Rd. SE15 2H 121
Hardess St. SE24 3C 120
Hardie Cl. NW10 5K 61
Hardie Rd. RM10: Dag 3J 73
Harding Cl. CR0: C'don 3F 169
SE17 6C 102
Hardinge Cl. UB8: Hil 5D 74
Hardinge Cres. SE18 3G 107
Hardinge La. E1 6J 85
(not continuous)
Hardinge Rd. N18 6K 33
NW10 1D 80
Hardinge St. E1 7J 85
(not continuous)
Harding Ho. *SW13* *6D 98*
(off Wyatt Dr.)
UB3: Hayes 6K 75
Harding Rd. DA7: Bex 2F 127
Harding's Cl. KT2: King T 1F 151
Hardings La. SE20 6K 139
Hardington *NW1* *7E 64*
(off Belmont St.)
Hardman Rd. KT2: King T 2E 150
SE7 5K 105
Hardwick Cl. HA7: Stan 5H 27
Hardwick Ct. DA8: Erith 6K 109
Hardwicke Av. TW5: Hest 1E 112
Hardwicke M. WC1 2H 7
Hardwicke Rd. N13 6D 32
TW10: Ham 4C 132
W4 4K 97
Hardwicke St. IG11: Bark 1G 89
Hardwick Grn. W13 5B 78
Hardwick Ho. *NW8* *3D 4*
(off Lilestone St.)
Hardwick Pl. SW16 7G 137
Hardwick St. EC1 2K 7 (3A 84)
Hardwicks Way SW18 5J 117
Hardwidge St. SE1 6G 15 (2E 102)
Hardy Av. E16 1J 105
HA4: Ruis 5K 57
Hardy Cl. EN5: Barn 6B 20
HA5: Pinn 7B 40
SE16 2K 103
Hardy Cotts. SE10 6F 105
Hardy Ho. SW4 7G 119
SW18 7K 117
Hardying Ho. E17 4A 50
Hardy Pas. N22 1K 47
Hardy Rd. E4 6G 35
SE3 7H 105
SW19 7K 135
Hardy's M. KT8: E Mos 4J 149
Hardy Way EN2: Enf 1F 23
Hare & Billet Rd. SE3 1F 123
Harebell Dr. E6 5E 88
Harecastle Cl. UB4: Yead 4C 76
Hare Ct. EC4 1J 13 (6A 84)
Harecourt Rd. N1 6C 66
Haredale Ho. *SE16* *2G 103*
(off East La.)
Haredale Rd. SE24 4C 120
Haredon Cl. SE23 7K 121
HAREFIELD 1A 38
Harefield Cl. EN2: Enf 1F 23
Harefield Grn. NW7 6K 29
Harefield M. SE4 3B 122
Harefield Rd. DA14: Sidc 2D 144
N8 5H 47
SE4 3B 122
SW16 7K 137
UB8: Uxb 5A 56
Hare Marsh E2 4G 85
Hare Pl. *EC4* *1K 13*
(off Pleydell St.)
Hare Row E2 2H 85
Haresfield Rd. RM10: Dag 6G 73
Hare St. SE18 3E 106
Hare Wlk. N1 2E 84
(not continuous)
Harewood Av. NW1 4D 4 (4C 82)
UB5: N'olt 7D 58
Harewood Cl. UB5: N'olt 7D 58
Harewood Dr. IG5: Ilf 2D 52
Harewood Pl. W1 1K 11 (6F 83)
Harewood Rd. CR2: S Croy 6E 168
SW19 6C 136
TW7: Isle 7K 95
Harewood Row NW1 5D 4 (5C 82)
Harewood Ter. UB2: S'hall 4D 94
Harfield Gdns. SE5 3E 120
Harfield Rd. TW16: Sun 2B 148
Harfleur Ct. *SE11* *4B 102*
(off Opal St.)
Harford Cl. E4 7J 25
Harford Ho. *SE5* *6C 102*
(off Bethwin Rd.)
W11 5H 81
Harford M. N19 3H 65
Harford Rd. E4 7J 25
Harford St. E1 4A 86
Harford Wlk. N2 4B 46
Harfst Way BR8: Swan 7J 145
Hargood Cl. HA3: Kent 6E 42
Hargood Rd. SE3 1A 124
Hargrave Mans. N19 2H 65
Hargrave Pk. N19 2G 65
Hargrave Pl. N7 5H 65
Hargrave Rd. N19 2G 65
Hargraves Ho. *W12* *7D 80*
(off White City Est.)
Hargwyne St. SW9 3K 119
Haringey Mus. 1E 48
Haringey Pk. N8 6J 47
Haringey Pas. N8 4A 48
Haringey Rd. N8 4J 47
Harington Ter. N9 3J 33
N18 3J 33
Harkett Cl. HA3: W'stone 2K 41
Harkett Ct. HA3: W'stone 2K 41
Harkness Ct. *SM1: Sutt* *1K 165*
(off Cleeve Way)
Harkness Ho. *E1* *6G 85*
(off Christian St.)
Harland Av. CR0: C'don 3F 169
DA15: Sidc 3H 143
Harland Cl. SW19 3K 153
Harland Rd. SE12 1J 141
Harlands Gro. BR6: Farnb 4F 173
Harlech Gdns. HA5: Pinn 7B 40
TW5: Hest 6A 94
Harlech Rd. N14 3D 32
Harlech Twr. W3 2J 97
Harlequin Av. TW8: Bford 6A 96
Harlequin Cl. TW7: Isle 5J 113
UB4: Yead 5B 76
Harlequin Ct. *E1* *7G 85*
(off Thomas More St.)
NW10 *6K 61*
(off Mitchellbrook Way)
W5 7C 78
Harlequin Ho. *DA18: Erith* *3E 108*
(off Kale Rd.)
Harlequin Rd. TW11: Tedd 7B 132
Harlequins RLFC 7J 113
Harlequins RUFC 7J 113
Harlescott Rd. SE15 4K 121
HARLESDEN 2B 80
Harlesden Gdns. NW10 1B 80
Harlesden La. NW10 1C 80
Harlesden Plaza NW10 2B 80
Harlesden Rd. NW10 1C 80
Harleston Cl. E5 2J 67
Harley Cl. HA0: Wemb 6D 60
Harley Ct. E11 7J 51
HA1: Harr 4H 41
N20 3F 31
Harley Cres. HA1: Harr 4H 41
Harleyford BR1: Brom 1K 159
Harleyford Ct. SE11 7G 19
Harleyford Mnr. *W3* *1J 97*
(off Edgecote Cl.)
Harleyford Rd. SE11 7G 19 (6K 101)
Harleyford St. SE11 7J 19 (6A 102)
Harley Gdns. BR6: Orp 4J 173
SW10 5A 100
Harley Gro. E3 3B 86
Harley Ho. E11 7F 51
NW1 4H 5
Harley Pl. W1 6J 5 (5F 83)
Harley Rd. HA1: Harr 4H 41
NW3 7B 64
NW10 2A 80
Harley St. W1 4J 5 (4F 83)
Harley Vs. NW10 2A 80
Harling Ct. SW11 2D 118
Harlinger St. SE18 3C 106
HARLINGTON 6F 93
Harlington Cl. UB3: Harl 7E 92
HARLINGTON CORNER 1F 111
Harlington Rd. DA7: Bex 3E 126
UB8: Hil 3C 74
Harlington Rd. E. TW13: Felt 7K 111
TW14: Felt 7K 111
Harlington Rd. W. TW14: Felt 6K 111
Harlington Sports Cen., The *4F 93*
(off Pinkwell La.)
Harlowe Ho. *E8* *1F 85*
(off Clarissa St.)
Harlow Mans. *IG11: Bark* *7F 71*
(off Whiting Av.)
Harlow Rd. N13 3J 33
Harlyn Dr. HA5: Eastc 3K 39
Harlynwood *SE5* *7C 102*
(off Wyndham Rd.)
Harman Av. IG8: Wfd G 6C 36
Harman Cl. E4 4A 36
NW2 3G 63
SE1 5G 103
Harman Dr. DA15: Sidc 6K 125
NW2 3G 63
Harman Rd. EN1: Enf 5A 24
HARMONDSWORTH 2E 174
Harmondsworth La. UB7: Harm, Sip 6A 92
Harmondsworth Moor Waterside 2C 174
Harmondsworth Moor Waterside Vis. Cen. 2C 174
Harmondsworth Rd.
UB7: W Dray 5A 92
Harmon Ho. SE8 4B 104
Harmont Ho. *W1* *6J 5*
(off Harley St.)
Harmony Cl. NW11 5G 45
SM6: Wall 7J 167
Harmony Pl. SE1 5F 103
Harmony Way BR1: Brom 2J 159
NW4 4E 44
Harmood Gro. NW1 7F 65
Harmood Ho. *NW1* *7F 65*
(off Harmood St.)
Harmood Pl. NW1 7F 65
Harmood St. NW1 6F 65
Harmsworth M. SE11 2K 19 (3A 102)
Harmsworth St. SE17 6K 19 (5B 102)
Harmsworth Way N20 1C 30
Harold Av. DA17: Belv 5F 109
UB3: Hayes 3H 93
Harold Ct. *SE16* *2K 103*
(off Christopher Cl.)
Harold Est. SE1 3E 102
Harold Gibbons Ct. SE7 6A 106
Harold Ho. *E2* *2K 85*
(off Mace St.)
Harold Laski Ho. *EC1* *2B 8*
(off Percival St.)
Harold Maddison Ho.
SE17 *5B 102*
(off Penton Pl.)
Harold Pl. SE11 6J 19 (5A 102)
Harold Rd. E4 4K 35
E11 1G 69
E13 1K 87
IG8: Wfd G 1J 51
N8 5K 47
N15 5F 49
NW10 3K 79
SE19 7D 138
SM1: Sutt 4B 166
Haroldstone Rd. E17 5K 49
Harold Wilson Ho.
SE28 1B 108
SW6 *6H 99*
(off Clem Attlee Ct.)
Harp All. EC4 7A 8 (6B 84)

Harp Bus. Cen., The NW2 2C 62
Harpenden Rd. E12 2A 70
SE27 3B 138
Harpenmead Point NW2 2H 63
Harper Cl. N14 5B 22
Harper Ho. SW9 3B 120
Harper M. SW17 3A 136
Harper Rd. E6 6D 88
SE1 7C 14 (3C 102)
Harpers Yd. N17 1F 49
TW7: Isle 2J 113
(off Rennels Way)
Harp Island Cl. NW10 2K 61
Harp La. EC3 3G 15 (7E 84)
Harpley Sq. E1 4K 85
Harpour Rd. IG11: Bark 6G 71
Harp Rd. W7 4K 77
Harpsden St. SW11 1E 118
Harpur M. WC1 5G 7 (5K 83)
Harpur St. WC1 5G 7 (5K 83)
Harraden Rd. SE3 1A 124
Harrier Av. E11 6K 51
Harrier Cen., The 6K 163
Harrier Ct. TW4: Houn 3C 112
Harrier M. SE28 2H 107
Harrier Rd. NW9 2A 44
Harriers Cl. W5 7E 78
Harrier Way E6 5D 88
Harries Rd. UB4: Yead 4A 76
Harriet Cl. E8 1G 85
Harriet Gdns. CR0: C'don 2G 169
Harriet Ho. SW6 7K 99
(off Wandon Rd.)
Harriet St. SW1 7F 11 (2D 100)
Harriet Tubman Cl. SW2 7K 119
Harriet Wlk. SW1 7F 11 (2D 100)
Harriet Way WD23: Bush 1C 26
HARRINGAY 5B 48
Harringay Gdns. N8 4B 48
Harringay Rd. N15 5B 48
(not continuous)
Harrington Cl. CR0: Bedd 2J 167
NW10 3K 61
Harrington Ct. CR0: C'don 2D 168
SW7 3B 16
(off Harrington Rd.)
W10 3H 81
Harrington Gdns. SW7 4K 99
Harrington Hill E5 1H 67
Harrington Ho. NW1 1A 6
(off Harrington St.)
UB10: Ick 4D 56
Harrington Rd. E11 1G 69
SE25 4G 157
SW7 3A 16 (4B 100)
Harrington Sq. NW1 2G 83
Harrington St.
NW1 1A 6 (2G 83)
(not continuous)
Harrington Way SE18 3B 106
Harriott Cl. SE10 4H 105
Harriott Ho. E1 5J 85
(off Jamaica St.)
Harris Bldgs. E1 6G 85
(off Burslem St.)
Harris Cl. EN2: Enf 1G 23
TW3: Houn 1E 112
Harris Ct. HA9: Wemb 3F 61
Harris Ho. SW9 3A 120
(off St James's Cres.)
Harris Lodge SE6 1E 140
Harrison Cl. N20 1H 31
Harrison Dr. BR1: Brom 4E 160
Harrison Ho. SE17 5D 102
(off Brandon St.)
Harrison Rd. RM10: Dag 6H 73
Harrisons Ct. SE14 6K 103
(off Myers La.)
Harrison's Ri. CR0: Wadd 3B 168
Harrison St. WC1 2F 7 (3J 83)
Harrison Way TW17: Shep 5D 146
Harris Rd. DA7: Bex 1E 126
RM9: Dag 5F 73
Harris St. E17 7B 50
SE5 7D 102
Harris Way TW16: Sun 1G 147
Harrods 1E 16 (3D 100)
Harrogate Ct. N11 6K 31
SE12 7J 123
SE26 3G 139
(off Droitwich Cl.)
Harrold Ho. NW3 7B 64
Harrold Rd. RM8: Dag 5B 72
Harrovian Bus. Village HA1: Harr 7J 41
HARROW 6J 41
Harrow Av. EN1: Enf 6A 24
Harroway Rd. SW11 2B 118
Harrow Borough FC 4D 58
Harrowby Ho. W1 6D 82
(off Harrowby St.)
Harrowby St. W1 7D 4 (6C 82)
Harrow Cl. KT9: Chess 7D 162
Harrow Club Sports Cen. 7F 81
Harrowdene Cl. HA0: Wemb 4D 60
Harrowdene Gdns. TW11: Tedd 6A 132
Harrowdene Rd. HA0: Wemb 3D 60
Harrow Dr. N9 1A 34
Harrowes Meade HA8: Edg 3B 28
Harrow Flds. Gdns. HA1: Harr 3J 59
Harrowgate Ho. E9 6K 67
Harrowgate Rd. E9 6A 68
Harrow Grn. E11 3G 69
Harrow High School Sports Cen. 6A 42
Harrow La. E14 7D 86
Harrow Leisure Cen. 3K 41
Harrow Lodge NW8 3A 4
(off Northwick Ter.)
Harrow Mnr. Way SE2 1C 108
SE28 7C 90
Harrow Mus. & Heritage Cen. 3G 41
HARROW ON THE HILL 1J 59
Harrow Pk. HA1: Harr 2J 59
Harrow Pl. E1 7H 9 (6E 84)
Harrow Rd. E6 1C 88
E11 3G 69
HA0: Wemb 4K 59
HA9: Wemb 5G 61
IG1: Ilf 4G 71
IG11: Bark 1J 89
NW10 3D 80
SM5: Cars 6C 166
TW14: Bedf 2C 128
W2 6A 4 (5A 82)
(not continuous)
W9 4F 81
W10 4G 81
Harrow Rd. Bri. W2 5A 82
Harrow Safari Cinema 5K 41
Harrow St. NW1 5D 4
Harrow Vw. HA1: Harr 2G 41
HA2: Harr 2G 41
UB3: Hayes 6J 75
UB10: Hil 3E 74
Harrow Vw. Rd. W5 4B 78
Harrow Way TW17: Shep 2E 146
HARROW WEALD 1J 41
Harrow Weald Lawn Tennis Club 1J 41
Harrow Weald Pk. HA3: Hrw W 6C 26
Harry Cl. CR0: C'don 6C 156
Harry Hinkins Ho. SE17 5C 102
(off Bronti Cl.)
Harry Lambourn Ho. SE15 7H 103
(off Gervase St.)
Hartcliff Ct. W7 2K 95
Hart Ct. E6 7E 70
Harte Rd. TW3: Houn 2D 112
Hartfield Av. UB5: Yead 2K 75
Hartfield Cres. BR4: W W'ck 3J 171
SW19 7H 135
Hartfield Gro. SE20 1J 157
Hartfield Ho. UB5: Yead 2K 75
(off Hartfield Av.)
Hartfield Rd. BR4: W W'ck 4J 171
KT9: Chess 5D 162
SW19 7H 135
Hartfield Ter. E3 2C 86
Hartford Av. HA3: Kent 3A 42
Hartford Rd. DA5: Bexl 6G 127
KT19: Ewe 6H 163
Hart Gro. UB1: S'hall 5E 76
W5 1G 97
Hart Gro. Ct. W5 1G 97
Hartham Cl. N7 5J 65
TW7: Isle 1A 114
Hartham Rd. N7 5J 65
N17 2F 49
TW7: Isle 1K 113
Harting Rd. SE9 3C 142
Hartington Cl. BR6: Farnb 5G 173
HA1: Harr 4J 59
Hartington Ct. SW8 1J 119
W4 7H 97
Hartington Ho. SW1 5D 18
(off Drummond Ga.)
Hartington Rd. E16 6K 87
E17 6A 50
SW8 1J 119
TW1: Twick 7B 114
UB2: S'hall 3C 94
W4 7H 97
W13 7B 78
Hartismere Rd. SW6 7H 99
Hartlake Rd. E9 6K 67
Hartland NW1 1G 83
(off Royal College St.)
Hartland Cl. HA8: Edg 2B 28
N21 6H 23
Hartland Ct. N11 5J 31
(off Hartland Rd.)
Hartland Dr. HA4: Ruis 3K 57
HA8: Edg 2B 28
Hartland Rd. E15 7H 69
N11 5J 31
NW1 7F 65
NW6 2H 81
SM4: Mord 7J 153
TW7: Isle 3A 114
TW12: Ham H 4F 131
Hartlands, The TW5: Cran 6K 93
Hartlands Cl. DA5: Bexl 6F 127
Hartland Way CR0: C'don 3A 170
SM4: Mord 7H 153
Hartlepool Ct. E16 1F 107
(off Fishguard Way)
Hartley Av. E6 1C 88
NW7 5G 29
Hartley Cl. BR1: Brom 2D 160
NW7 5G 29
Hartley Ho. SE1 4F 103
(off Longfield Est.)
Hartley Rd. CR0: C'don 7C 156
DA16: Well 7C 108
E11 1H 69
Hartley St. E2 3J 85
(not continuous)
Hart Lodge EN5: Barn 3B 20
Hartmann Rd. E16 1B 106
Hartnoll St. N7 5K 65
Harton Cl. BR1: Brom 1B 160
Harton Rd. N9 2C 34
Harton St. SE8 1C 122
Hartop Point SW6 7G 99
(off Pellant Rd.)
Hartsbourne Av. WD23: B Hea 2B 26
Hartsbourne Cl. WD23: B Hea 2C 26
Hartsbourne Ct. UB1: S'hall 6G 77
(off Fleming Rd.)
Hartsbourne Pk. WD23: B Hea 2D 26
Hartsbourne Rd. WD23: B Hea 2C 26
Harts Gro. IG8: Wfd G 5D 36
Hartshill Cl. UB10: Hil 7D 56
Hartshorn All. EC3 1H 15
Hartshorn Gdns. E6 4E 88
Harts La. IG11: Bark 6F 71
SE14 1A 122
Hartslock Dr. SE2 2D 108
Hartsmead Rd. SE9 2D 142
Hart St. EC3 2H 15 (7E 84)
Hartsway EN3: Pond E 4D 24
Hartswood Gdns. W12 3B 98
Hartswood Grn. WD23: B Hea 2C 26
Hartswood Rd. W12 2B 98
Hartsworth Cl. E13 2H 87
Hartville Rd. SE18 4J 107
Hartwell Cl. SW2 1K 137
Hartwell Dr. E4 6K 35
Hartwell Ho. SE7 5K 105
(off Troughton Rd.)
Hartwell St. E8 6F 67
Harvard Ct. NW6 5K 63
Harvard Hill W4 6H 97
Harvard Ho. SE17 6B 102
(off Doddington Gro.)
Harvard La. W4 5J 97
Harvard Rd. SE13 5E 122
TW7: Isle 1J 113
W4 5H 97
Harvel Cl. BR5: St P 3K 161
Harvel Cres. SE2 5D 108
Harvest Bank Rd. BR4: W W'ck 3H 171
Harvest Ct. TW17: Shep 4C 146
Harvesters Cl. TW7: Isle 5H 113
Harvest La. KT7: T Ditt 6A 150
Harvest Rd. TW13: Felt 4J 129
Harvey Ct. E17 5C 50
Harvey Dr. TW12: Hamp 1F 149
Harvey Gdns. E11 1H 69
SE7 5A 106
Harvey Ho. E1 4H 85
(off Brady St.)
N1 1D 84
(off Colville Est.)
RM6: Chad H 4D 54
SW1 6D 18
(off Aylesford St.)
TW8: Bford 5E 96
Harvey Lodge W9 5J 81
(off Admiral Wlk.)
Harvey M. N8 5K 47
(off Harvey Rd.)
Harvey Point E16 5J 87
(off Fife Rd.)
Harvey Rd. E11 1G 69
IG1: Ilf 5F 71
KT12: Walt T 7H 147
N8 5K 47
SE5 1D 120
(not continuous)
TW4: Houn 7D 112
UB5: N'olt 7A 58
UB10: Hil 2C 74
Harvey's Bldgs. WC2 3F 13 (7J 83)
Harveys La. RM7: Rush G 2K 73
Harvey St. N1 1D 84
Harvill Rd. DA14: Sidc 5E 144
Harvil Rd. UB9: Hare 6A 38
UB10: Ick 5A 38
Harvington Wlk. E8 7G 67
Harvist Est. N7 4A 66
Harvist Rd. NW6 2F 81
Harwell Cl. HA4: Ruis 1F 57
Harwell Pas. N2 4D 46
Harwood Av. BR1: Brom 2K 159
CR4: Mitc 3C 154
Harwood Cl. HA0: Wemb 4D 60
N12 6H 31
Harwood Ct. N1 1D 84
(off Colville Est.)
SW15 4E 116
Harwood Dr. UB10: Hil 1B 74

Harwood M. SW6 7J 99
Harwood Point SE16 2B 104
Harwood Rd. SW6 7J 99
Harwoods Yd. N21 7F 23
Harwood Ter. SW6 1K 117
Haselbury Rd. N9 4K 33
N18 4K 33
Haseley End SE23 7J 121
Haselrigge Rd. SW4 4H 119
Haseltine Rd. SE26 4B 140
Haselwood Dr. EN2: Enf 4G 23
Haskard Rd. RM9: Dag 4D 72
Hasker St. SW3 3D 16 (4C 100)
Haslam Av. SM3: Sutt 1G 165
Haslam Cl. N1 7A 66
UB10: Ick 2E 56
Haslam Ct. N11 4A 32
Haslam Ho. N1 7C 66
(off Canonbury Rd.)
Haslam St. SE15 7F 103
Haslemere and Heathrow Est., The
TW4: Cran 2K 111
Haslemere Av. CR4: Mitc 2B 154
EN4: E Barn 1J 31
NW4 6F 45
SW18 2K 135
TW5: Cran 2A 112
W7 3A 96
W13 3A 96
Haslemere Bus. Cen. EN1: Enf 4C 24
Haslemere Cl. SM6: Wall 5J 167
TW12: Hamp 5D 130
Haslemere Gdns. N3 3H 45
Haslemere Ind. Est. SW18 2K 135
Haslemere Rd. CR7: Thor H 5B 156
DA7: Bex 2F 127
IG3: Ilf 2K 71
N8 7H 47
N21 2G 33
Hasler Cl. SE28 7B 90
Haslers Wharf E3 1A 86
(off Old Ford Rd.)
Haslett Rd. TW17: Shep 2G 147
Hasluck Gdns. EN5: New Bar 6E 20
Hassard St. E2 1K 9 (2F 85)
Hassendean Rd. SE3 6K 105
Hassett Rd. E9 6K 67
Hassocks Cl. SE26 3H 139
Hassocks Rd. SW16 1H 155
Hassock Wood BR2: Kes 4B 172
Hassop Rd. NW2 4F 63
Hassop Wlk. SE9 4C 142
Hasted Rd. SE7 5B 106
Haste Hill Station
Ruislip Lido Railway 3G 39
Hastings Av. IG6: Ilf 4G 53
Hastings Cl. EN5: New Bar 4F 21
HA0: Wemb 4C 60
SE15 7G 103
Hastings Ct. TW11: Tedd 5H 131
Hastings Dr. KT6: Surb 6C 150
Hastings Ho. EN3: Enf H 2D 24
SE18 4D 106
(off Mulgrave Rd.)
W12 7D 80
(off White City Est.)
W13 7B 78
WC1 2E 6
(off Hastings St.)
Hastings Rd. BR2: Brom 1C 172
CR0: C'don 1F 169
N11 5B 32
N17 3D 48
W13 7B 78
Hastings St. SE18 3G 107
WC1 2E 6 (3J 83)
Hastingwood Ct. E17 5D 50
Hastingwood Trad. Est. N18 6E 34
Hastoe Cl. UB4: Yead 4C 76
Hasty Cl. CR4: Mitc 1F 155
Hat & Mitre Ct. EC1 4B 8
Hatch, The EN3: Enf H 1E 24
Hatcham M. Bus. Cen. SE14 1K 121
(off Hatcham Pk. Rd.)
Hatcham Pk. M. SE14 1K 121
Hatcham Pk. Rd. SE14 1K 121
Hatcham Rd. SE15 6J 103
Hatchard Rd. N19 2H 65
Hatchcroft NW4 3D 44
HATCH END 7A 26
Hatch End Lawn Tennis Club 6A 26
Hatch End Swimming Pool 1E 40
Hatchers M. SE1 7H 15
Hatchett Rd. TW14: Bedf 1E 128
Hatchfield Ho. N15 6E 48
(off Albert Rd.)
Hatch Gro. RM6: Chad H 4E 54
Hatch La. E4 4A 36
(not continuous)
UB7: Harm 3E 174
Hatch Pl. KT2: King T 5F 133
Hatch Rd. SW16 2J 155
Hatch Side IG7: Chig 5K 37
Hatchwood Cl. IG8: Wfd G 4C 36
Hatcliffe Almshouses SE10 5G 105
(off Tuskar St.)
Hatcliffe Cl. SE3 3H 123
Hatcliffe St. SE10 5H 105
Hatfeild Mead SM4: Mord 5J 153
Hatfield Cl. CR4: Mitc 4B 154
IG6: Ilf 3F 53
SE14 7K 103
Hatfield Ct. SE3 7J 105
UB5: Yead 3A 76
(off Canberra Dr.)
Hatfield Ho. EC1 4C 8
Hatfield Rd. E15 5G 69
RM9: Dag 6E 72
W4 2K 97
W13 1A 96
Hatfields SE1 1A 102
Hathaway Cl. BR2: Brom 1D 172
HA4: Ruis 4H 57
HA7: Stan 5F 27
Hathaway Cres. E12 6D 70
Hathaway Gdns. RM6: Chad H 5D 54
W13 5A 78
Hathaway Ho. N1 1G 9 (2E 84)
Hathaway Rd. CR0: C'don 7B 156
Hatherleigh Cl.
EN4: Had W 1E 20
KT9: Chess 5D 162
NW7 6A 30
SM4: Mord 4J 153
Hatherleigh Rd. HA4: Ruis 2J 57
Hatherley Ct. W2 6K 81
(off Hatherley Gro.)
Hatherley Cres. DA14: Sidc 2A 144
Hatherley Gdns. E6 3B 88
N8 6J 47
Hatherley Gro. W2 6K 81
Hatherley Ho. E17 4C 50
Hatherley M. E17 4C 50
Hatherley Rd. DA14: Sidc 4A 144
E17 4B 50
TW9: Kew 1F 115
Hatherley St. SW1 4B 18 (4G 101)
Hathern Gdns. SE9 4E 142
Hatherop Rd. TW12: Hamp 7D 130
Hathersage Ct. N1 5D 66
Hathorne Cl. SE15 2H 121
Hathway St. SE15 2K 121
Hathway Ter. SE14 2K 121
(off Hathway St.)
Hatley Av. IG6: Ilf 4G 53
Hatley Cl. N11 5J 31
Hatley Rd. N4 2K 65
Hatteraick St. SE16 2J 103
Hattersfield Cl. DA17: Belv 4F 109
HATTON 4H 111
Hatton Cl. SE18 7H 107
HATTON CROSS 4H 111
Hatton Cross Cen.
TW6: H'row A 3H 111
Hatton Gdn. EC1 5K 7 (5A 84)
Hatton Gdns. CR4: Mitc 5D 154
Hatton Grn. TW14: Felt 4J 111
Hatton Gro. UB7: W Dray 2A 92
Hatton Ho. KT1: King T 2F 151
(off Victoria Rd.)
Hatton Pl. EC1 5K 7 (5A 84)
Hatton Rd. CR0: C'don 1A 168
TW14: Bedf, Felt 7E 110
Hatton Rd. Sth. TW14: Felt 4H 111
Hatton Row NW8 4B 4
Hatton St. NW8 4B 4 (4B 82)
Hatton Wall EC1 5K 7 (5A 84)
Haughmond N12 4E 30
Haunch of Venison Yd. W1 1J 11 (6F 83)
Hauteville Ct. Gdns. W6 3B 98
(off South Side)
Havana Rd. SW19 2J 135
Havannah St. E14 2C 104
Havant Rd. E17 3E 50
Havelock Cl. W12 7D 80
Havelock Ct. UB2: S'hall 3D 94
(off Havelock Rd.)
Havelock Ho. SE1 4F 103
(off Fort Rd.)
SE23 1J 139
Havelock Pl. HA1: Harr 6J 41
Havelock Rd. BR2: Brom 4A 160
CR0: C'don 2F 169
DA17: Belv 4F 109
HA3: W'stone 3J 41
N17 2G 49
SW19 5A 136
UB2: S'hall 3C 94
Havelock St. IG1: Ilf 2F 71
N1 1J 83
Havelock Ter. SW8 1F 119
Havelock Ter. Arches SW8 1F 119
(off Havelock Ter.)
Havelock Wlk. SE23 1J 139
Haven, The N14 6A 22
TW9: Rich 3G 115
TW16: Sun 7J 129
Haven Cl. DA14: Sidc 6C 144
SE9 3D 142
SW19 3F 135
UB4: Hayes 4G 75
Haven Ct. BR3: Beck 2E 158
KT5: Surb 6F 151
Haven Grn. W5 6D 78
Haven Grn. Ct. W5 6D 78
Havenhurst Ri. EN2: Enf 2F 23
Haven La. W5 6E 78
Haven Lodge EN1: Enf 6K 23
(off Village Rd.)
SE18 4F 107
(off Vincent Rd.)
Haven M. E3 5B 86
N1 7A 66
Haven Pl. W5 7D 78
Havenpool NW8 1K 81
(off Abbey Rd.)
Haven Rd. TW15: Ashf 4D 128
Haven St. NW1 7F 65
Haven Wood HA9: Wemb 3H 61
Haverfield Gdns. TW9: Kew 7G 97
Haverfield Rd. E3 3A 86
Haverford Way HA8: Edg 1F 43
Haverhill Rd. E4 1K 35
SW12 1G 137
Havering NW1 7F 65
(off Castlehaven Rd.)
Havering Dr. RM1: Rom 4K 55
Havering Gdns. RM6: Chad H 5C 54
Havering Rd. RM1: Rom 3K 55
Havering St. E1 6K 85
Havering Way IG11: Bark 3B 90
Haversham Cl. TW1: Twick 6D 114
Haversham Ct. UB6: G'frd 6K 59
Haversham Pl. N6 2D 64
Haverstock Hill NW3 5C 64
Haverstock Pl. N1 1B 8
(off Haverstock St.)
Haverstock Rd. NW5 5E 64
Haverstock St. N1 1B 8 (2B 84)
Haverthwaite Rd. BR6: Orp 2H 173
Havilland Ct. HA8: Edg 4A 28
Havil St. SE5 7E 102
Havingham Dr. RM6: Chad H 5C 54
Havisham Ho. SE16 2G 103
Havisham Pl. SE19 7B 138
Hawarden Gro. SE24 7C 120
Hawarden Hill NW2 3C 62
Hawarden Rd. E17 4K 49
Hawbridge Rd. E11 1F 69
Hawes Ho. E17 4K 49
Hawes La. BR4: W W'ck 1E 170
Hawes Rd. BR1: Brom 1K 159
(not continuous)
N18 6C 34
Hawes St. N1 7B 66
Haweswater Ho. TW7: Isle 5K 113
Hawgood St. E3 5C 86
Hawkdene E4 6J 25
Hawke Ct. UB4: Yead 4A 76
(off Perth Av.)
Hawke Ho. E1 4K 85
(off Ernest St.)
Hawke Pk. Rd. N22 3B 48
Hawke Pl. SE16 2K 103
Hawker NW9 1B 44
(off Everglade Strand)
Hawker Ct. KT1: King T 2F 151
(off Church Rd.)
Hawke Rd. SE19 6D 138
Hawker Pl. E17 2E 50
Hawker Rd. CR0: Wadd 6A 168
Hawkesbury Rd. SW15 5D 116
Hawkesfield Rd. SE23 2A 140
Hawkesley Cl. TW1: Twick 4A 132
Hawkes Rd. CR4: Mitc 1D 154
TW14: Felt 7J 111
Hawkesworth Cl. HA6: Nwood 1G 39
Hawke Twr. SE14 6A 104
Hawkewood Rd. TW16: Sun 3J 147
Hawkfield Ct. TW7: Isle 2J 113
Hawkhurst Gdns.
KT9: Chess 4E 162
Hawkhurst Rd. SW16 1H 155
Hawkhurst Way BR4: W W'ck 2D 170
KT3: N Mald 5K 151
Hawkinge N17 2D 48
(off Gloucester Rd.)
Hawkins Cl. HA1: Harr 7H 41
NW7 5E 28
Hawkins Ct. SE18 4C 106
Hawkins Ho. SE8 6C 104
(off New King St.)
SW1 7B 18
(off Dolphin Sq.)
Hawkins Rd. TW11: Tedd 6B 132
Hawkins Ter. SE7 5C 106
Hawkins Way SE6 5C 140
Hawkley Gdns. SE27 2B 138
Hawkridge Cl. RM6: Chad H 6C 54
Hawksbrook La. BR3: Beck 6D 158
(not continuous)
Hawkshaw Cl. SW2 7J 119
Hawkshead NW1 1A 6
Hawkshead Cl.
BR1: Brom 7G 141
Hawkshead Rd. NW10 7B 62
W4 2A 98
Hawkslade Rd. SE15 5K 121
Hawksley Rd. N16 3E 66
Hawks M. SE10 7E 104

Hawksmoor Cl. E6 6C 88
SE18 5J 107
Hawksmoor M. E1 7H 85
Hawksmoor Pl. *E2* *3K 9*
(off Cheshire St.)
Hawksmoor St. W6 6F 99
Hawksmouth E4 7K 25
Hawks Pas. *KT1: King T* *2F 151*
(off Minerva Rd.)
Hawks Rd. KT1: King T 2F 151
Hawkstone Rd. SE16 4J 103
Hawkwell Ct. E4 3K 35
Hawkwell Ho. RM8: Dag 1G 73
Hawkwell Wlk. *N1* *1C 84*
(off Maldon Cl.)
Hawkwood Cres. E4 6J 25
Hawkwood La. BR7: Chst 1G 161
Hawkwood Mt. E5 1H 67
Hawlands Dr. HA5: Pinn 7C 40
Hawley Cl. TW12: Hamp 6D 130
Hawley Cres. NW1 7F 65
Hawley M. NW1 7F 65
Hawley Rd. N18 5E 34
NW1 7F 65
(not continuous)
Hawley St. NW1 7F 65
Hawley Way TW15: Ashf 5C 128
Hawstead Rd. SE6 6D 122
Hawsted IG9: Buck H 1E 36
Hawthorn Av. CR7: Thor H 1B 156
E3 1B 86
N13 5D 32
Hawthorn Cen. HA1: Harr 5K 41
Hawthorn Cl. BR5: Pet W 6H 161
TW5: Cran 7K 93
TW12: Hamp 5E 130
Hawthorn Cotts. *DA16: Well* *3A 126*
(off Hook La.)
Hawthorn Ct. *HA5: Pinn* *2A 40*
(off Rickmansworth Rd.)
TW9: Kew 1H 115
TW15: Ashf 7E 128
Hawthorn Cres. SW17 5E 136
Hawthornden Cl. N12 6H 31
Hawthorndene Cl. BR2: Hayes 2H 171
Hawthorndene Rd. BR2: Hayes 2H 171
Hawthorn Dr. BR4: W W'ck 4G 171
HA2: Harr 6E 40
Hawthorne Av. CR4: Mitc 2B 154
HA3: Kent 6A 42
HA4: Ruis 6K 39
SM5: Cars 7E 166
Hawthorne Cl. BR1: Brom 3D 160
N1 6E 66
SM1: Sutt 2A 166
Hawthorne Ct. HA6: Nwood 2J 39
W5 1E 96
Hawthorne Cres. UB7: W Dray 2B 92
Hawthorne Farm Av. UB5: N'olt 1C 76
Hawthorne Gro. NW9 7J 43
Hawthorne Ho. N15 5G 49
SW1 *6B 18*
(off Churchill Gdns.)
Hawthorne M. UB6: G'frd 6G 77
Hawthorne Pl. UB3: Hayes 7H 75
Hawthorne Rd. BR1: Brom 3C 160
E17 3C 50
Hawthorne Way N9 2A 34
Hawthorn Gdns. W5 3D 96
Hawthorn Gro. EN2: Enf 1J 23
SE20 7H 139
Hawthorn Hatch TW8: Bford 7B 96
Hawthorn M. NW7 1G 45
Hawthorn Pl. DA8: Erith 5J 109
Hawthorn Rd. DA6: Bex 4F 127
IG9: Buck H 4G 37
N8 3H 47
N18 6A 34
NW10 7C 62
SM1: Sutt 6C 166
Hawthorn Rd. SM6: Wall 7F 167
TW8: Bford 7B 96
TW13: Felt 1J 129
Hawthorns *CR2: S Croy* *4B 168*
(off Bramley Hill)
IG8: Wfd G 3D 36
Hawthorns, The KT17: Ewe 7B 164
SL3: Poyle 4A 174
Hawthorn Ter. DA15: Sidc 5K 125
N19 *1H 65*
(off Calverley Gro.)
Hawthorn Wlk. W10 4G 81
Hawthorn Way TW17: Shep 4F 147
Hawtrey Av. UB5: N'olt 2B 76
Hawtrey Dr. HA4: Ruis 7J 39
Hawtrey Rd. NW3 7C 64
Haxted Rd. BR1: Brom 1K 159
Hay Cl. E15 7G 69
Haycroft Gdns. NW10 1C 80
Haycroft Rd. KT6: Surb 2D 162
SW2 5J 119
Hay Currie St. E14 6D 86
Hayday Rd. E16 5J 87
(not continuous)
Hayden Ct. TW13: Felt 4G 129
Hayden Piper Ho. *SW3* *7E 16*
(off Caversham St.)
Haydens M. W3 6J 79
Hayden's Pl. W11 6H 81
Hayden Way RM5: Col R 2J 55
Haydock Av. UB5: N'olt 6E 58
Haydock Grn. UB5: N'olt 6E 58
Haydock Grn. Flats *UB5: N'olt* *6E 58*
(off Haydock Grn.)
Haydon Cl. EN1: Enf 6K 23
NW9 4J 43
Haydon Ct. NW9 4J 43
Haydon Dr. HA5: Eastc 4J 39
Haydon Pk. Rd. SW19 5J 135
Haydon Rd. RM8: Dag 2C 72
Haydons Rd. SW19 5K 135
Haydon St. EC3 2J 15 (7F 85)
Haydon Wlk. E1 1K 15 (6F 85)
Haydon Way SW11 4B 118
HAYES
BR2 1J 171
UB3 6G 75
Hayes & Yeading FC (Church Road) 7H 75
Hayes Bri. Retail Pk. UB4: Yead 7A 76
Hayes Chase BR4: W W'ck 6F 159
Hayes Cl. BR2: Hayes 2J 171
Hayes Ct. *SE5* *7C 102*
(off Camberwell New Rd.)
SW2 1J 137
Hayes Cres. NW11 5H 45
SM3: Cheam 4F 165
HAYES END 4F 75
Hayes End Cl. UB4: Hayes 4F 75
Hayes End Dr. UB4: Hayes 4F 75
Hayes End Rd. UB4: Hayes 4F 75
Hayesens Ho. SW17 4A 136
Hayesford Pk. Dr.
BR2: Brom 5H 159
Hayes Gdn. BR2: Hayes 2J 171
Hayes Gro. SE22 3F 121
Hayes Hill BR2: Hayes 1G 171
Hayes Hill Rd. BR2: Hayes 1H 171
Hayes La. BR2: Brom, Hayes 5K 159
BR3: Beck 3E 158
Hayes Manor Sports Cen. 6F 75
Hayes Mead Rd. BR2: Hayes 1G 171
Hayes Metro Cen. UB4: Yead 7A 76
Hayes Pl. NW1 4D 4 (4C 82)
Hayes Rd. BR2: Brom 4J 159
UB2: S'hall 4K 93
Hayes Stadium & Sports Cen. 6F 75
Hayes St. BR2: Hayes 1K 171
Hayes Swimming Pool 1H 93
HAYES TOWN 2H 93
Hayes Way BR3: Beck 4E 158
Hayes Wood Av. BR2: Hayes 1K 171
Hayfield Pas. E1 4J 85
Hayfield Yd. E1 4J 85
Haygarth Pl. SW19 5F 135
Haygreen Cl. KT2: King T 6H 133
Hay Hill W1 3K 11 (7F 83)
Hayhurst Ct. *N1* *1B 84*
(off Dibden St.)
Hayland Cl. NW9 4K 43
Hay La. NW9 4J 43
Hayles Bldgs. *SE11* *4B 102*
(off Elliotts Row)
Hayles St. SE11 4B 102
Haylett Gdns. KT1: King T 4D 150
Hayling Av. TW13: Felt 3J 129
Hayling Cl. N16 5E 66
Hayling Ct. SM3: Cheam 4E 164
Haymaker Cl. UB10: Uxb 7B 56
Hayman Cres. UB4: Hayes 2F 75
Haymans Point SE11 5G 19 (4K 101)
Hayman St. N1 7B 66
Haymarket SW1 3C 12 (7H 83)
Haymarket Arc. SW1 3C 12
Haymarket Ct. *E8* *7F 67*
(off Jacaranda Gro.)
Haymarket Theatre Royal *3D 12*
(off Haymarket)
Haymer Gdns. KT4: Wor Pk 3C 164
Haymerle Ho. *SE15* *6G 103*
(off Haymerle Rd.)
Haymerle Rd. SE15 6G 103
Haymill Cl. UB6: G'frd 3K 77
Hayne Ho. *W11* *1G 99*
(off Penzance Pl.)
Hayne Rd. BR3: Beck 2B 158
Haynes Cl. N11 3K 31
N17 7C 34
SE3 3G 123
Haynes Dr. N9 3C 34
Haynes La. SE19 6E 138
Haynes Rd. HA0: Wemb 7E 60
Hayne St. EC1 5B 8 (5B 84)
Haynt Wlk. SW20 3G 153
Hay's Ct. *SE16* *2J 103*
(off Rotherhithe St.)
Hay's Galleria SE1 4G 15 (1E 102)
Hays La. SE1 4G 15 (1E 102)
Haysleigh Gdns. SE20 2G 157
Hay's M. W1 4J 11 (1F 101)
Haysoms Cl. RM1: Rom 4K 55
Haystall Cl. UB4: Hayes 2G 75
Hay St. E2 1G 85
Hayter Ct. E11 2K 69
Hayter Rd. SW2 5J 119
Hayton Cl. E8 6F 67
Hayward Cl. DA1: Cray 5K 127
SW19 7K 135
Hayward Ct. *SW4* *2J 119*
(off Clapham Rd.)
Hayward Gallery 5H 13
Hayward Gdns. SW15 6E 116
Hayward Ho. *N1* *2A 84*
(off Penton St.)
Hayward Rd. KT7: T Ditt 7K 149
N20 2F 31
Haywards Cl. RM6: Chad H 5B 54
Hayward's Pl. EC1 3A 8 (4B 84)
Haywards Yd. *SE4* *5B 122*
(off Lindal Rd.)
Haywood Cl. HA5: Pinn 2B 40
Haywood Lodge *N11* *6D 32*
(off Oak La.)
Haywood Ri. BR6: Orp 5J 173
Haywood Rd. BR2: Brom 4B 160
Hazel Av. UB7: W Dray 3C 92
Hazel Bank SE25 2E 156
Hazelbank KT5: Surb 1J 163
Hazelbank Rd. SE6 2F 141
Hazelbourne Rd. SW12 6F 119
Hazelbury Cl. SW19 2J 153
Hazelbury Grn. N9 3K 33
Hazelbury La. N9 3K 33
Hazel Cl. CR0: C'don 7K 157
CR4: Mitc 4H 155
N13 3J 33
N19 2G 65
NW9 2A 44
TW2: Whitt 7G 113
TW8: Bford 7B 96
Hazel Ct. W5 7E 78
Hazel Cres. RM5: Col R 1H 55
Hazelcroft HA5: Hat E 6A 26
Hazelcroft Cl. UB10: Hil 7B 56
Hazeldean Rd. NW10 7K 61
Hazeldene Dr. HA5: Pinn 3A 40
Hazeldene Gdns. UB10: Hil 1E 74
Hazeldene Rd. DA16: Well 2C 126
IG3: Ilf 2B 72
Hazeldon Rd. SE4 5A 122
Hazeleigh Gdns. IG8: Wfd G 5H 37
Hazel Gdns. HA8: Edg 4C 28
Hazelgreen Cl. N21 1G 33
Hazel Gro. BR6: Farnb 2F 173
EN1: Enf 6B 24
HA0: Wemb 1E 78
RM6: Chad H 3E 54
SE26 4K 139
TW13: Felt 1J 129
Hazelhurst BR3: Beck 1F 159
Hazelhurst Ct. *SE6* *5E 140*
(off Beckenham Hill Rd.)
Hazelhurst Rd. SW17 4A 136
Hazel La. IG6: Ilf 6K 37
TW10: Ham 2E 132
Hazellville Rd. N19 7H 47
Hazelmere Cl. TW14: Felt 6G 111
UB5: N'olt 2D 76
Hazelmere Ct. SW2 1K 137
Hazelmere Dr. UB5: N'olt 2D 76
Hazelmere Rd. BR5: Pet W 4G 161
NW6 1H 81
UB5: N'olt 2D 76
Hazelmere Wlk. UB5: N'olt 2D 76
(not continuous)
Hazelmere Way BR2: Hayes 6J 159
Hazel M. *N22* *3A 48*
(off High Rd.)
Hazel Rd. E15 5G 69
NW10 3D 80
(not continuous)
Hazeltree La. UB5: N'olt 3C 76
Hazel Wlk. BR2: Brom 6E 160
Hazel Way E4 6G 35
SE1 4F 103
Hazelwood Av. SM4: Mord 4K 153
Hazelwood Cl. HA2: Harr 4F 41
W5 2E 96
Hazelwood Ct. KT6: Surb 6E 150
N13 *4F 33*
(off Hazelwood La.)
NW10 3A 62
Hazelwood Cres. N13 4F 33
Hazelwood Dr. HA5: Pinn 2K 39
Hazelwood Ho. SE8 4A 104
Hazelwood Ho's. BR2: Brom 3G 159
Hazelwood La. N13 4F 33
Hazelwood Lawn Tennis & Squash Club 7H 23
Hazelwood Rd. E17 5A 50
EN1: Enf 6A 24
Hazlebury Rd. SW6 2K 117
Hazledean Rd. CR0: C'don 2D 168
Hazledene Rd. W4 6J 97
Hazlemere Gdns. KT4: Wor Pk 1C 164
Hazlewell Rd. SW15 5E 116
Hazlewood Cl. E5 3A 68
Hazlewood Cres. W10 4G 81
Hazlewood M. SW9 3J 119
Hazlewood Twr. *W10* *4G 81*
(off Golborne Gdns.)

Hazlitt Cl. TW13: Hanw 4C 130
Hazlitt M. W14 3G 99
Hazlitt Rd. W14 3G 99
Heacham Av. UB10: Ick 3E 56
Headbourne Ho.
SE1 7F 15 (3D 102)
Headcorn Pl. CR7: Thor H 4K 155
Headcorn Rd. BR1: Brom 5H 141
CR7: Thor H 4K 155
N17 7A 34
Headfort Pl. SW1 7H 11 (2E 100)
Headington Ct. *CR0: C'don* *4C 168*
(off Tanfield Rd.)
Headington Rd. SW18 2A 136
Headlam Rd. SW4 6H 119
(not continuous)
Headlam St. E1 4H 85
Headley App. IG2: Ilf 5F 53
Headley Av. SM6: Wall 5K 167
Headley Cl. KT19: Ewe 6G 163
Headley Ct. SE26 5J 139
Headley Dr. CR0: New Ad 7D 170
IG2: Ilf 6F 53
Head's M. W11 6J 81
HEADSTONE 3H 41
Headstone Dr. HA1: Harr 3H 41
HA3: W'stone 3H 41
Headstone Gdns. HA2: Harr 4G 41
Headstone La. HA2: Harr 4E 40
HA3: Hrw W 7A 26
Headstone Pde. HA1: Harr 4H 41
Headstone Rd. HA1: Harr 5J 41
Head St. E1 6K 85
(not continuous)
Headway Cl. TW10: Ham 4C 132
Heald St. SE14 1C 122
Healey Ho. SW9 7A 102
Healey St. NW1 6F 65
Healy Dr. BR6: Orp 4K 173
Hearne Rd. W4 6G 97
Hearn Ri. UB5: N'olt 1B 76
Hearn's Bldgs. SE17 4D 102
Hearnshaw St. E14 6A 86
Hearn St. EC2 4H 9 (4E 84)
Hearnville Rd. SW12 1E 136
Heart, The KT12: Walt T 7J 147
Heath, The W7 1J 95
Heatham Pk. TW2: Twick 7K 113
Heath Av. DA7: Bex 6D 108
Heathbourne Rd. HA7: Stan 2D 26
WD23: B Hea 1D 26
Heath Brow NW3 3A 64
Heath Bus. Cen. TW3: Houn 4G 113
Heath Cl. CR2: S Croy 6B 168
NW11 7K 45
UB3: Harl 7F 93
W5 4F 79
Heathcock Ct. *WC2* *3F 13*
(off Exchange Ct.)
Heathcote Av. IG5: Ilf 2D 52
Heathcote Ct. IG5: Ilf 1D 52
(Glade Ct.)
IG5: Ilf 2D 52
(Heathcote Av.)
Heathcote Gro. E4 3K 35
Heathcote Rd. TW1: Twick 6B 114
Heathcote St. WC1 3G 7 (4K 83)
Heath Ct. *CR0: C'don* *4D 168*
(off Heathfield Rd.)
SE9 1G 143
TW4: Houn 4D 112
UB8: Uxb 7A 56
Heath Cft. NW11 1K 63
Heathcroft W5 4F 79
Heathcroft Av. TW16: Sun 7H 129
Heathcroft Gdns. E17 1F 51
Heathdale Av. TW4: Houn 3C 112
Heathdene Dr. DA17: Belv 4H 109
Heathdene Rd. SM6: Wall 7F 167
SW16 7K 137
Heath Dr. NW3 4K 63
SM2: Sutt 7A 166
SW20 4E 152
Heathedge SE26 2H 139
Heath End Rd. DA5: Bexl 1K 145
Heather Av. RM1: Rom 2K 55
Heatherbank BR7: Chst 2E 160
SE9 2D 124
Heather Cl. E6 6E 88
N7 3K 65
RM1: Rom 1K 55
SE13 7F 123
SW8 3F 119
TW7: Isle 5H 113
TW12: Hamp 1D 148
UB8: Hil 5B 74
Heather Ct. DA14: Sidc 6D 144
Heatherdale Cl. KT2: King T 6G 133
Heatherdene Cl. CR4: Mitc 4B 154
N12 7F 31
Heather Dr. EN2: Enf 2G 23
RM1: Rom 2K 55
Heatherfold Way HA5: Eastc 3H 39
Heather Gdns. NW11 6G 45
RM1: Rom 2K 55
SM2: Sutt 6J 165
Heather Glen RM1: Rom 2K 55
Heather Ho. *E14* *6E 86*
(off Dee St.)
Heatherlands TW16: Sun 6J 129
Heather La. UB7: Yiew 6A 74
Heatherlea Gro. KT4: Wor Pk 1D 164
Heatherley Ct. E5 3G 67
Heatherley Dr. IG5: Ilf 3C 52
Heather Pk. Dr. HA0: Wemb 7G 61
Heather Pk. Pde. *HA0: Wemb* *7F 61*
(off Heather Pk. Dr.)
Heather Rd. E4 6G 35
NW2 2B 62
SE12 2J 141
Heathers, The TW19: Stanw 7B 110
Heatherset Gdns. SW16 7K 137
Heatherside Rd. DA14: Sidc 3C 144
KT19: Ewe 7K 163
Heatherton Ter. N3 2K 45
Heather Wlk. HA8: Edg 5C 28
TW2: Whitt *7E 112*
(off Stephenson Rd.)
W10 4G 81
Heather Way CR2: Sels 7K 169
HA7: Stan 6E 26
RM1: Rom 2K 55
Heatherwood Cl. E12 2A 70
Heatherwood Dr. UB4: Hayes 2F 75
Heathfield BR7: Chst 6G 143
E4 3K 35
HA1: Harr 7K 41
Heathfield Av. SW18 7B 118
Heathfield Cl. BR2: Kes 5A 172
E16 5B 88
Heathfield Ct. SE20 7J 139
W4 5K 97
Heathfield Dr. CR4: Mitc 1C 154
Heathfield Gdns. CR0: C'don 4D 168
NW11 6F 45
SE3 *2G 123*
(off Baizdon Rd.)
SW18 6B 118
W4 5J 97
Heathfield Ho. SE3 2G 123
Heathfield Nth. TW2: Twick 7J 113
Heathfield Pk. NW2 6E 62
Heathfield Pk. Dr. RM6: Chad H 5B 54
Heathfield Ri. HA4: Ruis 7E 38
Heathfield Rd. BR1: Brom 7H 141
BR2: Kes 5A 172
CR0: C'don 4D 168
DA6: Bex 4F 127
SW18 6A 118
W3 2H 97
Heathfields Ct. TW4: Houn 5C 112
Heathfield Sth. TW2: Twick 7K 113
Heathfield Sq. SW18 7B 118
Heathfield St. *W11* *7G 81*
(off Portland Rd.)
Heathfield Ter. SE18 6J 107
W4 5J 97
Heathfield Va. CR2: Sels 7K 169
Heath Gdns. TW1: Twick 1K 131
Heathgate NW11 6K 45
Heathgate Pl. NW3 5D 64
Heath Gro. SE20 7J 139
TW16: Sun 7H 129
Heath Ho. DA15: Sidc 4K 143
Heath Hurst Rd. NW3 4C 64
Heathland Rd. N16 1E 66
Heathlands Cl. TW1: Twick 2K 131
TW16: Sun 2J 147
Heathlands Way
TW4: Houn 5C 112
Heath La. SE3 2F 123
(not continuous)
Heathlee Rd. SE3 4H 123
Heathley End BR7: Chst 6G 143
Heath Lodge WD23: B Hea 1D 26
Heathmans Rd. SW6 1H 117
Heath Mead SW19 3F 135
Heath Pk. Dr. BR1: Brom 3C 160
Heath Pas. NW3 2K 63
Heathpool Ct. E1 4H 85
Heath Ri. BR2: Hayes 6H 159
SW15 6F 117
Heath Rd. CR7: Thor H 3C 156
DA5: Bexl 1J 145
HA1: Harr 7G 41
RM6: Chad H 7D 54
SW8 2F 119
TW1: Twick 1K 131
TW2: Twick 1K 131
TW3: Houn, Isle 4F 113
UB10: Hil 4E 74
HEATHROW AIRPORT 3C 110
Heathrow Blvd. UB7: Sip 7B 92
(not continuous)
Heathrow C'way. Cen.
TW4: Houn 3K 111
Heathrow Cl. UB7: Lford 4C 174
Heathrow Gateway TW4: Houn 7C 112
Heathrow Interchange UB4: Yead 1A 94
Heathrow Intl. Trad. Est.
TW4: Houn 3K 111
Heathrow Vis. Cen. 1E 110
Heath Royal SW15 6F 117
Heaths Cl. EN1: Enf 2K 23
Heath Side NW3 4B 64
Heathside BR5: Pet W 1G 173
NW11 1J 63
SE13 2E 122
TW4: Houn 7D 112
Heathside Av. DA7: Bex 1E 126
Heathside Cl. IG2: Ilf 5H 53
Heathstan Rd. W12 6C 80
Heath St. NW3 3A 64
Heathurst Rd. CR2: Sande 7E 168
Heath Vw. N2 4A 46
Heathview NW5 4E 64
Heath Vw. Cl. N2 4A 46
Heathview Dr. SE2 6D 108
Heathview Gdns. SW15 7E 116
Heathview Rd. CR7: Thor H 4A 156
Heath Vs. NW3 3B 64
SE18 5K 107
Heathville Rd. N19 7J 47
Heathwall St. SW11 3D 118
HEATHWAY 1G 91
Heath Way DA8: Erith 1J 127
IG8: Wfd G 5F 37
Heathway CR0: C'don 3B 170
RM9: Dag 3F 73
RM10: Dag 3F 73
Heathway SE3 7J 105
UB2: S'hall 4B 94
Heathway Ct. NW3 2J 63
Heathway Ind. Est.
RM10: Dag 4H 73
Heathwood Gdns. SE7 4C 106
Heathwood Point SE23 3K 139
Heathwood Wlk. DA5: Bexl 1K 145
Heaton Cl. E4 3K 35
Heaton Ho. *SW10* *6A 100*
(off Seymour Wlk.)
Heaton Rd. CR4: Mitc 7E 136
SE15 2H 121
Heaven Tree Cl. N1 6C 66
Heaver Rd. SW11 3B 118
Heavitree Cl. SE18 5H 107
Heavitree Rd. SE18 5H 107
(not continuous)
Hebden Ct. E2 1F 85
Hebden Ter. N17 6K 33
Hebdon Rd. SW17 3C 136
Heber Mans. *W14* *6G 99*
(off Queen's Club Gdns.)
Heber Rd. NW2 5F 63
SE22 6F 121
Hebron Rd. W6 3E 98
Hecham Cl. E17 2A 50
Heckfield Pl. SW6 7J 99
Heckford Ho. *E14* *6D 86*
(off Grundy St.)
Heckford St. E1 7K 85
Hector *NW9* *1B 44*
(off Five Acre)
Hector Ct. *SW9* *7A 102*
(off Caldwell St.)
Hector Ho. *E2* *2H 85*
(off Old Bethnal Grn. Rd.)
Hector St. SE18 4J 107
Heddington Gro. N7 5K 65
Heddon Cl. TW7: Isle 4A 114
Heddon Ct. Av. EN4: Cockf 5J 21
Heddon Ct. Pde. EN4: Cockf 5K 21
Heddon Rd. EN4: Cockf 5J 21
Heddon St. W1 2A 12 (7G 83)
Hedgegate Ct. *W11* *6H 81*
(off Powis Ter.)
Hedge Hill EN2: Enf 1G 23
Hedge La. N13 3G 33
Hedgeley IG4: Ilf 4D 52
Hedgemans Rd. RM9: Dag 7D 72
Hedgemans Way RM9: Dag 6E 72
Hedgerley Gdns. UB6: G'frd 2G 77
Hedgerow Ct. *E6* *1D 88*
(off Nelson St.)
Hedgers Gro. E9 6A 68
Hedger St. SE11 4B 102
Hedge Wlk. SE6 5D 140
Hedgewood Gdns. IG5: Ilf 5E 52
Hedgley M. SE12 5H 123
Hedgley St. SE12 5H 123
Hedingham Cl. N1 7C 66
Hedingham Ho.
KT2: King T *1E 150*
(off Seven Kings Way)
Hedingham Rd.
RM8: Dag 5B 72
Hedley Ct. RM1: Rom 5K 55
Hedley Ho. *E14* *3E 104*
(off Stewart St.)
Hedley Rd. TW2: Whitt 7E 112
Hedley Row N5 5D 66
Hedsor Ho. *E2* *3J 9*
(off Ligonier St.)
Heenan Cl. IG11: Bark 6G 71
Heene Rd. EN2: Enf 1J 23
Hega Ho. *E14* *5E 86*
(off Ullin St.)
Heidegger Cres. SW13 7D 98
Heigham Rd. E6 7C 70
Heighton Gdns. CR0: Wadd 5B 168

Heights, The BR3: Beck 7E 140
(not continuous)
SE7 5A 106
UB5: N'olt 5D 58
Heights Cl. SW20 7D 134
Heiron St. SE17 6B 102
Helby Rd. SW4 6H 119
Heldar Ct. SE1 7F 15 (2D 102)
Helder Gro. SE12 7H 123
Helder St. CR2: S Croy 6D 168
Heldmann Cl. TW3: Houn 4H 113
Helegan Cl. BR6: Chels 4K 173
Helena Ct. W5 5D 78
Helena Pl. E9 1H 85
Helena Rd. E13 2H 87
E17 5C 50
NW10 5D 62
W5 5D 78
Helena Sq. SE16 7A 86
(off Sovereign Cres.)
Helen Av. TW14: Felt 7K 111
Helen Cl. KT8: W Mole 4F 149
N2 3A 46
Helen Gladstone Ho. SE1 6A 14
(off Surrey Row)
Helen Ho. E2 2H 85
(off Old Bethnal Grn. Rd.)
Helen Mackay Ho. E14 6F 87
(off Blair St.)
Helen Peele Cotts. SE16 3J 103
(off Lower Rd.)
Helenslea Av. NW11 1J 63
Helen's Pl. E2 3J 85
Helen St. SE18 4F 107
Helen Taylor Ho. SE16 3G 103
(off Evelyn Lowe Est.)
Helford Cl. HA4: Ruis 2G 57
Helgiford Gdns. TW16: Sun 7G 129
Helios Rd. SM6: Wall 1E 166
Heliport Ind. Est. SW11 2B 118
Helix Ct. W11 1F 99
(off Swanscombe Rd.)
Helix Gdns. SW2 6K 119
Helix Rd. SW2 6K 119
Hellings St. E1 1G 103
Helm, The E16 7F 89
Helme Cl. SW19 5H 135
Helmet Row EC1 2D 8 (4C 84)
Helmore Rd. IG11: Bark 7K 71
Helmsdale Cl. UB4: Yead 4C 76
Helmsdale Ho. NW6 2K 81
(off Carlton Va.)
Helmsdale Rd. SW16 1H 155
Helmsley Pl. E8 7H 67
Helmsley St. E8 7H 67
Helperby Rd. NW10 7A 62
Helsby Ct. NW8 3A 4
(off Pollitt Dr.)
Helsinki Sq. SE16 3A 104
Helston NW1 1G 83
(off Camden St.)
Helston Cl. HA5: Hat E 1D 40
Helston Ct. N15 5E 48
(off Culvert Rd.)
Helston Ho. SE11 5K 19
(off Kennings Way)
Helvetia St. SE6 2B 140
Helwys Ct. E4 6J 35
Hemans St. SW8 7H 101
Hemans St. Est. SW8 7H 101
Hemberton Rd. SW9 3J 119
Hemery Rd. UB6: G'frd 5H 59
Hemingford Cl. N12 5G 31
Hemingford Rd. N1 1K 83
SM3: Cheam 4E 164
Heming Rd. HA8: Edg 7C 28
Hemington Av. N11 5J 31
Hemingway Cl. NW5 4E 64
Hemlock Rd. W12 7B 80
(not continuous)
Hemmen La. UB3: Hayes 6H 75
Hemming Cl. TW12: Hamp 1E 148
Hemmings Cl. DA14: Sidc 2B 144
Hemmings Mead KT19: Ewe 6J 163
Hemming St. E1 4G 85
Hempstead Cl. IG9: Buck H 2D 36
Hempstead Rd. E17 3F 51
Hemp Wlk. SE17 4D 102
Hemsby Rd. KT9: Chess 6F 163
Hemstal Rd. NW6 7J 63
Hemsted Rd. DA8: Erith 7K 109
Hemswell Dr. NW9 1A 44
Hemsworth Ct. N1 2E 84
Hemsworth St. N1 2E 84
Hemus Pl. SW3 6D 16 (5C 100)
Hen & Chicken Ct. EC4 1J 13
(off Fleet St.)
Hen & Chickens Theatre 6B 66
(off St Paul's Rd.)
Henchman St. W12 6B 80
Hendale Av. NW4 3D 44
Henderson Cl. NW10 6J 61
Henderson Ct. N12 4E 30
NW3 5B 64
(off Fitzjohn's Av.)
SE14 6K 103
(off Myers La.)
Henderson Dr. NW8 3A 4 (4B 82)
Henderson Ho. RM10: Dag 3G 73
(off Kershaw Rd.)
Henderson Rd. CR0: C'don 6D 156
E7 6A 70
N9 1C 34
SW18 7C 118
UB4: Yead 3J 75
Hendfield Ct. SM6: Wall 6F 167
Hendham Rd. SW17 2C 136
HENDON 4E 44
Hendon Av. N3 1G 45
Hendon Crematorium NW4 1F 45
Hendon FC 1F 63
Hendon Hall Ct. NW4 3F 45
Hendon Ho. NW4 5F 45
Hendon La. N3 3G 45
Hendon Lodge NW4 3D 44
Hendon Pk. Mans. NW4 5E 44
Hendon Pk. Row NW11 6H 45
Hendon Rd. N9 2B 34
Hendon Way NW2 7F 45
NW4 6D 44
Hendon Wood La. NW7 1G 29
Hendon Youth Sports Cen. 7F 45
Hendre Ho. SE1 4E 102
(off Old Kent Rd.)
Hendren Cl. UB6: G'frd 5H 59
Hendre Rd. SE1 4E 102
Hendrick Av. SW12 7D 118
Heneage La. EC3 1H 15 (6E 84)
Heneage Pl. EC3 1H 15 (6E 84)
Heneage St. E1 5K 9 (5F 85)
Henera's Ct. BR1: Brom 3E 160
(off Brady Dr.)
Henfield Cl. DA5: Bexl 6G 127
N19 1G 65
Henfield Rd. SW19 1H 153
Hengelo Gdns. CR4: Mitc 4B 154
Hengist Rd. DA8: Erith 7H 109
SE12 7K 123
Hengist Way BR2: Brom 4G 159
Hengrave Rd. SE23 6J 121
Hengrove Ct. DA5: Bexl 1E 144
Hengrove Cres. TW15: Ashf 3A 128
Henham Ct. RM5: Col R 1J 55
Henley Av. SM3: Cheam 3G 165
Henley Cl. SE16 2J 103
(off St Marychurch St.)
TW7: Isle 1K 113
UB6: G'frd 2G 77
Henley Ct. N14 7B 22
NW2 6F 63
Henley Dr. KT2: King T 7B 134
SE1 4F 103
Henley Gdns. HA5: Eastc 3K 39
RM6: Chad H 5E 54
Henley Ho. E2 3K 9
(off Swanfield St.)
Henley Prior N1 1G 7
(off Affleck St.)
Henley Rd. E16 2D 106
IG1: Ilf 4G 71
N18 4K 33
NW10 1E 80
Henley St. SW11 2E 118
Henley Way TW13: Hanw 5B 130
Henlow Pl. TW10: Ham 2D 132
HENLYS CORNER 4H 45
HENLYS RDBT. 2A 112
Hennel Cl. SE23 3J 139
Hennessy Ct. E10 6E 50
Hennessy Rd. N9 2D 34
Henniker Gdns. E6 3B 88
Henniker M. SW3 7A 16 (6B 100)
Henniker Point E15 5G 69
(off Leytonstone Rd.)
Henniker Rd. E15 5F 69
Henningham Rd. N17 1D 48
Henning St. SW11 1C 118
Henrietta Cl. SE8 6C 104
Henrietta Ct. TW1: Twick 7C 114
(off Richmond Rd.)
Henrietta Ho. N15 6E 48
(off St Ann's Rd.)
W6 5E 98
(off Queen Caroline St.)
Henrietta M. WC1 3F 7 (4J 83)
Henrietta Pl. W1 1J 11 (6F 83)
Henrietta St. E15 5E 68
WC2 2F 13 (7J 83)
Henriques St. E1 6G 85
Henry Addlington Cl. E6 5F 89
Henry Cl. EN2: Enf 1K 23
Henry Cooper Way SE9 3B 142
Henry Darlot Dr. NW7 5A 30
Henry Dent Rd. SE5 3D 120
Henry Dickens Ct. W11 7F 81
Henry Doulton Dr. SW17 4E 136
Henry Hatch Ct. SM2: Sutt 7A 166
Henry Ho. SE1 5J 13 (1A 102)
SW8 7J 101
(off Wyvil Rd.)
Henry Jackson Rd. SW15 3F 117
Henry Macaulay Av. KT2: King T 1D 150
Henry Peters Dr. TW11: Tedd 5J 131
(off Somerset Gdns.)
Henry Purcell Ho. E16 1K 105
(off Evelyn Rd.)
Henry Rd. E6 2C 88
EN4: E Barn 5G 21
N4 1C 66
Henrys Av. IG8: Wfd G 5C 36
Henryson Rd. SE4 5C 122
Henry St. BR1: Brom 1K 159
Henry's Wlk. IG6: Ilf 1H 53
Henry Tate M. SW16 5K 137
Henry Tudor Ct. SE9 7G 125
Henry Wise Ho. SW1 4B 18
(off Vauxhall Bri. Rd.)
Hensford Gdns. SE26 4H 139
Henshall St. N1 6D 66
Henshawe Rd. RM8: Dag 3D 72
Henshaw St. SE17 4D 102
Henslowe Rd. SE22 5G 121
Henslow Ho. SE15 7G 103
(off Peckham Pk. Rd.)
Henson Av. NW2 5E 62
Henson Cl. BR6: Farnb 2F 173
Henson Path HA3: Kent 3D 42
Henson Pl. UB5: N'olt 1A 76
Henstridge Pl. NW8 1C 82
Henty Cl. SW11 7C 100
Henty Wlk. SW15 5D 116
Henville Rd. BR1: Brom 1K 159
Henwick Rd. SE9 3B 124
Henwood Side IG8: Wfd G 6J 37
Hepburn Gdns. BR2: Hayes 1G 171
Hepburn M. SW11 5D 118
Hepple Cl. TW7: Isle 2B 114
Hepplestone Cl. SW15 6D 116
Hepscott Rd. E9 6C 68
Hepworth Ct. N1 1B 84
(off Gaskin St.)
NW3 5C 64
SM3: Sutt 1J 165
SW1 6J 17
Hepworth Gdns. IG11: Bark 5A 72
Hepworth Rd. SW16 7J 137
Hepworth Way KT12: Walt T 7H 147
Heracles NW9 1B 44
(off Five Acre)
Hera Ct. E14 4C 104
(off Homer Dr.)
Herald Gdns. SM6: Wall 2F 167
Herald's Pl. SE11 3K 19
Herald St. E2 4H 85
Herbal Hill EC1 4K 7 (4A 84)
Herbal Hill Gdns. EC1 4K 7
(off Herbal Hill)
Herbal Pl. EC1 4K 7
Herbert Cres. SW1 1F 17 (3D 100)
Herbert Gdns. NW10 2D 80
RM6: Chad H 7D 54
W4 6H 97
Herbert Ho. E1 7J 9
(off Old Castle St.)
Herbert M. SW2 6A 120
Herbert Morrison Ho. SW6 6H 99
(off Clem Attlee Ct.)
Herbert Pl. SE18 6F 107
Herbert Rd. BR2: Brom 5B 160
DA7: Bex 2E 126
E12 4C 70
E17 7B 50
IG3: Ilf 2J 71
KT1: King T 3F 151
N11 7D 32
N15 5F 49
NW9 6C 44
SE18 7E 106
(not continuous)
SW19 7H 135
(not continuous)
UB1: S'hall 1D 94
Herbert St. E13 2J 87
NW5 6E 64
Herbrand Est. WC1 3E 6 (4J 83)
Herbrand St. WC1 3E 6 (4J 83)
Hercies Rd. UB10: Hil 7B 56
Hercules Ct. SE14 6A 104
Hercules Pl. N7 3J 65
(not continuous)
Hercules Rd. SE1 2H 19 (3K 101)
Hercules St. N7 3J 65
Hercules Wharf E14 7G 87
(off Orchard Pl.)
Hercules Yd. N7 3J 65
Hereford Av. EN4: E Barn 1J 31
Hereford Bldgs. SW3 7B 16
(off Old Church St.)
Hereford Ct. HA1: Harr 4J 41
SM2: Sutt 7J 165
W7 5K 77
(off Copley Cl.)
Hereford Gdns. HA5: Pinn 5C 40
IG1: Ilf 7C 52
SE13 5G 123
TW2: Twick 1G 131
Hereford Ho. N18 5C 34
(off Cavendish Cl.)
NW6 2J 81
(off Carlton Va.)

Hereford Ho. SW3 1D 16
(off Ovington Gdns.)
SW10 7K 99
(off Fulham Rd.)
Hereford M. W2 6J 81
Hereford Pl. SE14 7B 104
Hereford Retreat SE15 7G 103
Hereford Rd. E3 2B 86
E11 5K 51
TW13: Felt 1A 130
W2 6J 81
W3 7H 79
W5 3C 96
Hereford Sq. SW7 4A 100
Hereford St. E2 4G 85
Hereford Way KT9: Chess 5C 162
Herent Dr. IG5: Ilf 4C 52
Hereward Gdns. N13 5F 33
Hereward Rd. SW17 4D 136
Herga Ct. HA1: Harr 3J 59
Herga Rd. HA3: W'stone 4K 41
Heriot Av. E4 2H 35
Heriot Rd. NW4 5E 44
Heriots Cl. HA7: Stan 4F 27
Heritage Av. NW9 3B 44
Heritage Cl. SW9 3B 120
TW16: Sun 1J 147
Heritage Ct. SE8 5K 103
(off Trundley's Rd.)
Heritage Hill BR2: Kes 5A 172
Heritage Pl. SW18 1A 136
Heritage Vw. HA1: Harr 3K 59
Herlwyn Av. HA4: Ruis 2G 57
Herlwyn Gdns. SW17 4D 136
Her Majesty's Theatre 4C 12
(off Haymarket)
Herm Cl. TW7: Isle 7G 95
Hermes Cl. W9 4J 81
Hermes Ct. SW2 6K 119
SW9 1A 120
(off Southey Rd.)
Hermes St. N1 1J 7 (2A 84)
Hermes Wlk. UB5: N'olt 2E 76
Hermes Way SM6: Wall 7H 167
Herm Ho. EN3: Enf W 1E 24
N1 6C 66
Hermiston Av. N8 5J 47
Hermitage, The KT1: King T 4D 150
SE13 2E 122
SE23 1J 139
SW13 1B 116
TW10: Rich 5E 114
TW13: Felt 3H 129
UB8: Uxb 6A 56
Hermitage Cl. E18 4H 51
EN2: Enf 2G 23
KT10: Clay 6A 162
SE2 3C 108
TW17: Shep 4C 146
Hermitage Ct. E1 1G 103
(off Knighten St.)
E18 4J 51
NW2 3J 63
Hermitage Gdns. NW2 3J 63
SE19 7C 138
Hermitage Grn. SW16 1J 155
Hermitage Ho. N1 2B 84
(off Gerrard Rd.)
Hermitage La. CR0: C'don 7G 157
N18 5J 33
NW2 3J 63
SE25 6G 157
(not continuous)
SW16 7K 137
Hermitage Path SW16 1J 155
Hermitage Rd. N4 7B 48
N15 7B 48
SE19 7C 138
Hermitage Row E8 5G 67
Hermitage St. W2 6A 4 (5B 82)
Hermitage Vs. SW6 6J 99
(off Lillie Rd.)
Hermitage Wlk. E18 4H 51
Hermitage Wall E1 1G 103
Hermitage Waterside E1 1G 103
(off Thomas More St.)
Hermitage Way HA7: Stan 1A 42
Hermit Pl. NW6 1K 81
Hermit Rd. E16 5H 87
Hermit St. EC1 1A 8 (3B 84)
Hermon Gro. UB3: Hayes 1J 93
Hermon Hill E11 5J 51
E18 5J 51
Herndon Rd. SW18 5A 118
Herne Cl. NW10 5K 61
UB3: Hayes 6H 75
Herne Ct. WD23: Bush 1B 26
HERNE HILL 5C 120
Herne Hill SE24 6C 120
Herne Hill Ho. SE24 6B 120
(off Railton Rd.)
Herne Hill Rd. SE24 3C 120
Herne Hill Stadium 6D 120
Herne M. N18 4B 34
Herne Pl. SE24 5B 120
Herne Rd. KT6: Surb 2D 162
Heron Cl. E17 2B 50
IG9: Buck H 1D 36
NW10 6A 62
SM1: Sutt 5H 165
Heron Ct. BR2: Brom 4A 160
E14 3E 104
(off New Union Cl.)
HA4: Ruis 2F 57
KT1: King T 3E 150
NW9 2A 44
TW19: Stanw 1A 128
Heron Cres. DA14: Sidc 3J 143
Herondale Av. SW18 1B 136
Heron Dr. N4 2C 66
Herongate N1 1C 84
(off Ridgewell Cl.)
Herongate Cl. EN1: Enf 2A 24
Herongate Rd. E12 2A 70
Heron Hill DA17: Belv 5F 109
Heron Ho. DA14: Sidc 3B 144
E6 7C 70
NW8 1C 4
(off Newcourt St.)
SW11 7C 100
(off Searles Cl.)
W13 4A 78
Heron Ind. Est. E15 2D 86
Heron Mead EN3: Enf L 1H 25
Heron M. IG1: Ilf 2F 71
Heron Pl. SE16 1A 104
W1 7H 5
(off Thayer St.)
Heron Quay E14 1C 104
Heron Rd. CR0: C'don 2E 168
SE24 4C 120
TW1: Twick 4A 114
Herons, The E11 6H 51
Heronsforde W13 6C 78
Heronsgate HA8: Edg 5B 28
Heron's Lea N6 6D 46
Heronslea Dr. HA7: Stan 5K 27
Heron's Pl. TW7: Isle 3B 114
Heron Sq. TW9: Rich 5D 114
Herons Ri. EN4: E Barn 4H 21
Heron Trad. Est. W3 5H 79
Heron Vw. TW8: Bford 7C 96
(off Commerce Rd.)
Heron Way IG8: Wfd G 4F 37
TW14: Felt 4J 111
Herrick Ho. N16 4D 66
(off Howard Rd.)
SE5 7D 102
(off Elmington Est.)
Herrick Rd. N5 3C 66
Herrick St.
SW1 4D 18 (4H 101)
Herries St. W10 2G 81
Herringham Rd. SE7 3A 106
Herron Ct. BR2: Brom 4H 159
Hersant Cl. NW10 1C 80
Herschell M. SE5 3C 120
Herschell Rd. SE23 7A 122
Hersham Cl. SW15 7C 116
Hershell Ct. SW14 4H 115
Hertford Av. SW14 5K 115
Hertford Cl. EN4: Cockf 3F 21
Hertford Ct. E6 3D 88
N13 3F 33
Hertford Ho. UB5: N'olt 4D 76
Hertford Pl. W1 4B 6 (4G 83)
Hertford Rd. EN3: Enf H, Enf W 3D 24
EN4: Cockf 3F 21
IG2: Ilf 6J 53
IG11: Bark 7E 70
N1 1E 84
(not continuous)
N2 3C 46
N9 2C 34
Hertford St. W1 5J 11 (1F 101)
Hertford Wlk. DA17: Belv 5G 109
Hertford Way CR4: Mitc 4J 155
Hertslet Rd. N7 3K 65
Hertsmere Ho. E14 7C 86
(off Hertsmere Rd.)
Hertsmere Rd. E14 1C 104
Hertswood Ct. EN5: Barn 4B 20
Hervey Cl. N3 1J 45
Hervey Pk. Rd. E17 4A 50
Hervey Rd. SE3 1K 123
Hervey Way N3 1J 45
Hesa Rd. UB3: Hayes 6J 75
Hesewall Cl. SW4 2G 119
Hesketh Pl. W11 7G 81
Hesketh Rd. E7 3J 69
Heslop Rd. SW12 1D 136
Hesper M. SW5 4K 99
Hesperus Cres. E14 4D 104
Hessel Rd. W13 2A 96
Hessel St. E1 6H 85
Hestercombe Av. SW6 2G 117
Hesterman Way CR0: Wadd 1K 167
Hester Rd. N18 5B 34
SW11 7C 100
Hester Ter. TW9: Rich 3G 115
Hestia Ho. SE1 7G 15
HESTON 7E 94
Heston Av. TW5: Hest 6C 94
Heston Cen., The TW5: Cran 5A 94
Heston Community Sports Hall 7E 94
Heston Grange TW5: Hest 6D 94
Heston Grange La. TW5: Hest 6D 94
Heston Ho. SE8 1C 122
Heston Ind. Mall TW5: Hest 7D 94
Heston Phoenix Distribution Pk.
TW5: Hest 6A 94
Heston Pool 6D 94
Heston Rd. TW5: Hest 6E 94
HESTON SERVICE AREA 6B 94
Heston St. SE14 1C 122
Hetherington Rd. SW4 4J 119
TW17: Shep 2E 146
Hetherington Way UB10: Ick 4A 56
Hethpool Ho. W2 4A 4
Hetley Gdns. SE19 7F 139
Hetley Rd. W12 1D 98
Heton Gdns. NW4 4D 44
Hevelius Cl. SE10 5H 105
Hever Cft. SE9 4E 142
Hever Gdns. BR1: Brom 2E 160
Heverham Rd. SE18 4J 107
Hever Ho. SE15 6K 103
(off Lovelinch Cl.)
Heversham Ho. SE15 6J 103
Heversham Rd. DA7: Bex 2G 127
Hewens Rd. UB4: Hil 4E 74
UB10: Hil 4E 74
Hewer St. W10 5F 81
Hewett Cl. HA7: Stan 4G 27
Hewett Rd. RM8: Dag 5D 72
Hewetts Quay IG11: Bark 1F 89
Hewett St. EC2 4H 9 (4E 84)
Hewish Rd. N18 4K 33
Hewison St. E3 2B 86
Hewitt Av. N22 2B 48
Hewitt Cl. CR0: C'don 3C 170
Hewitt Rd. N8 5A 48
Hewlett Ho. SW8 7F 101
(off Havelock Ter.)
Hewlett Rd. E3 2A 86
Hexagon, The N6 1D 64
Hexal Rd. SE6 3G 141
Hexham Gdns. TW7: Isle 7A 96
Hexham Rd. EN5: New Bar 4E 20
SE27 2C 138
SM4: Mord 1K 165
Heybourne Rd. N17 7C 34
Heybridge NW1 6F 65
(off Lewis St.)
Heybridge Av. SW16 7J 137
Heybridge Dr. IG6: Ilf 2H 53
Heybridge Way E10 7A 50
Heydon Ho. SE14 1J 121
(off Kender St.)
Heyford Av. SW8 7J 101
SW20 3H 153
Heyford Rd. CR4: Mitc 2C 154
Heyford Ter. SW8 7J 101
Heygate St. SE17 4C 102
Heylyn Sq. E3 3B 86
Heynes Rd. RM8: Dag 4C 72
Heysham La. NW3 3K 63
Heysham Rd. N15 6D 48
Heythorp St. SW18 1H 135
Heythrop Dr. UB10: Ick 4B 56
Heywood Av. NW9 1A 44
Heywood Ct. HA7: Stan 5H 27
Heywood Ho. SE14 6K 103
(off Myers La.)
Heyworth Rd. E5 4H 67
E15 5H 69
Hibbert Ho. E14 3C 104
(off Tiller Rd.)
Hibbert Rd. E17 7B 50
HA3: W'stone 2K 41
Hibbert St. SW11 3B 118
Hibernia Gdns. TW3: Houn 4E 112
Hibernia Point SE2 2D 108
(off Wolvercote Rd.)
Hibernia Rd. TW3: Houn 4E 112
Hibiscus Cl. HA8: Edg 4D 28
Hichisson Rd. SE15 5J 121
Hickes Ho. NW6 7B 64
Hickey's Almshouses
TW9: Rich 4F 115
Hickin Cl. SE7 4B 106
Hickin St. E14 3E 104
Hickleton NW1 1G 83
(off Camden St.)
Hickling Ho. SE16 3H 103
(off Slippers Pl.)
Hickling Rd. IG1: Ilf 5F 71
Hickman Av. E4 6K 35
Hickman Cl. E16 5B 88
Hickman Rd. RM6: Chad H 7C 54
Hickmore Wlk. SW4 3H 119
Hickory Cl. N9 7B 24
Hicks Av. UB6: G'frd 3H 77
Hicks Bolton Ho. NW6 2H 81
(off Denmark Ho.)
Hicks Cl. SW11 3C 118
Hicks Ct. RM10: Dag 3H 73
Hicks St. SE8 5A 104
Hidcote Gdns. SW20 3D 152
Hidden Cl. KT8: W Mole 4G 149

Hide E6 . . . 6E **88**
Hide Pl. SW1 . . . 4C **18** (4H **101**)
Hider Ct. SE3 . . . 7A **106**
Hide Rd. HA1: Harr . . . 4G **41**
Hides St. N7 . . . 6K **65**
Hide Twr. *SW1* . . . *4C 18*
(*off Regency St.*)
Higgins Ho. *N1* . . . *1E 84*
(*off Colville Est.*)
Higginson Ho. *NW3* . . . *7D 64*
(*off Fellows Rd.*)
Higgins Wlk. *TW12: Hamp* . . . *6C 130*
(*off Abbott Cl.*)
Higgs Ind. Est. SE24 . . . 3B **120**
High Acres EN2: Enf . . . 3G **23**
HIGHAM HILL . . . **2A 50**
Higham Hill Rd. E17 . . . 1A **50**
Higham M. UB5: N'olt . . . 4D **76**
Higham Path E17 . . . 3A **50**
Higham Pl. E17 . . . 3A **50**
Higham Rd. IG8: Wfd G . . . 6D **36**
N17 . . . 3D **48**
Highams, The E17 . . . 1E **50**
Highams Ct. E4 . . . 3A **36**
Highams Lodge Bus. Cen. E17 . . . 3K **49**
HIGHAMS PARK . . . **6A 36**
Highams Pk. Ind. Est. E4 . . . 6K **35**
Higham Sta. Av. E4 . . . 6H **35**
Higham St. E17 . . . 3A **50**
High Ashton KT2: King T . . . 7H **133**
Highbanks Cl. DA16: Well . . . 7B **108**
Highbanks Rd. HA5: Hat E . . . 6A **26**
Highbank Way N8 . . . 6A **48**
HIGH BARNET . . . **2A 20**
Highbarrow Rd. CR0: C'don . . . 1G **169**
High Beech CR2: S Croy . . . 7E **168**
N21 . . . 6E **22**
High Beeches DA14: Sidc . . . 5E **144**
High Birch Ct. *EN4: E Barn* . . . *4H 21*
(*off Park Rd.*)
High Bri. SE10 . . . 5F **105**
Highbridge Ct. *SE14* . . . *7J 103*
(*off Farrow La.*)
Highbridge Rd. IG11: Bark . . . 1F **89**
High Bri. Wharf *SE10* . . . *5F 105*
(*off High Bri.*)
Highbrook Rd. SE3 . . . 3B **124**
High Broom Cres. BR4: W W'ck . . . 7D **158**
HIGHBURY . . . **4B 66**
Highbury Av. CR7: Thor H . . . 2A **156**
Highbury Cl. BR4: W W'ck . . . 2D **170**
KT3: N Mald . . . 4J **151**
HIGHBURY CORNER . . . **6B 66**
Highbury Cres. N5 . . . 5B **66**
Highbury Est. N5 . . . 5C **66**
Highbury Gdns. IG3: Ilf . . . 2J **71**
Highbury Grange N5 . . . 4C **66**
Highbury Gro. N5 . . . 5B **66**
Highbury Gro. Ct. N5 . . . 6C **66**
Highbury Hill N5 . . . 3A **66**
Highbury Mans. *N1* . . . *7B 66*
(*off Upper St.*)
Highbury New Pk. N5 . . . 5C **66**
Highbury Pk. N5 . . . 3B **66**
(not continuous)
Highbury Pk. M. N5 . . . 4C **66**
Highbury Pl. N5 . . . 6B **66**
Highbury Pool . . . 6B **66**
Highbury Quad. N5 . . . 3C **66**
Highbury Rd. SW19 . . . 5G **135**
Highbury Sq. N14 . . . 1B **32**
Highbury Stadium . . . 3B **66**
Highbury Sta. Rd. N1 . . . 6A **66**
Highbury Ter. N5 . . . 5B **66**
Highbury Ter. M. N5 . . . 5B **66**
High Cedar Dr. SW20 . . . 7E **134**
Highclere Rd. KT3: N Mald . . . 3K **151**
Highclere St. SE26 . . . 4A **140**
Highcliffe *W13* . . . *5B 78*
(*off Clivedon Ct.*)
Highcliffe Dr. SW15 . . . 6B **116**
Highcliffe Gdns. IG4: Ilf . . . 5C **52**
Highcombe SE7 . . . 6K **105**
Highcombe Cl. SE9 . . . 1B **142**
High Coombe Pl. KT2: King T . . . 6K **133**
Highcroft NW9 . . . 5A **44**
Highcroft Av. HA0: Wemb . . . 7G **61**
Highcroft Est. N19 . . . 7J **47**
Highcroft Gdns. NW11 . . . 6H **45**
Highcroft Rd. N19 . . . 7J **47**
High Cross Cen., The N15 . . . 4G **49**
High Cross Rd. N17 . . . 3G **49**
Highcross Way SW15 . . . 1C **134**
Highdaun Dr. SW16 . . . 4K **155**
Highdown KT4: Wor Pk . . . 2A **164**
Highdown Rd. SW15 . . . 6D **116**
High Dr. KT3: N Mald . . . 1J **151**
High Elms IG8: Wfd G . . . 5D **36**
High Elms Country Pk. . . . 7H **173**
High Elms Nature Cen. . . . 7H **173**
High Elms Rd. BR6: Downe . . . 7G **173**
Highfield WD23: B Hea . . . 2D **26**
Highfield Av. BR6: Chels . . . 5K **173**
DA8: Erith . . . 6H **109**
HA5: Pinn . . . 5D **40**
HA9: Wemb . . . 3F **61**
NW9 . . . 5J **43**
NW11 . . . 7F **45**
UB6: G'frd . . . 5J **59**
Highfield Cl. HA6: Nwood . . . 1G **39**
KT6: Surb . . . 1C **162**
N22 . . . 1A **48**
NW9 . . . 5J **43**
SE13 . . . 6F **123**
Highfield Ct. N14 . . . 6B **22**
NW11 . . . 6G **45**
Highfield Cres. HA6: Nwood . . . 1G **39**
Highfield Dr. BR2: Brom . . . 4G **159**
BR4: W W'ck . . . 2D **170**
KT19: Ewe . . . 6B **164**
UB10: Ick . . . 4A **56**
Highfield Gdns. NW11 . . . 6G **45**
Highfield Hill SE19 . . . 7D **138**
Highfield M. *NW6* . . . *7K 63*
(*off Compayne Gdns.*)
Highfield Rd. BR1: Brom . . . 4D **160**
BR7: Chst . . . 3K **161**
DA6: Bex . . . 5F **127**
HA6: Nwood . . . 1G **39**
IG8: Wfd G . . . 7H **37**
KT5: Surb . . . 7J **151**
KT12: Walt T . . . 7J **147**
N21 . . . 2G **33**
NW11 . . . 6G **45**
SM1: Sutt . . . 5C **166**
TW7: Isle . . . 1K **113**
TW13: Felt . . . *1J 129*
(*off Railway Ter.*)
TW13: Felt . . . 2J **129**
(Tiley Rd.)
TW16: Sun . . . 5H **147**
W3 . . . 5H **79**
Highfields SM1: Sutt . . . 2J **165**
Highfields Gro. N6 . . . 1D **64**
High Foleys KT10: Clay . . . 7B **162**
High Gables BR2: Brom . . . 2G **159**
HIGHGATE . . . **6E 46**
Highgate Av. N6 . . . 7F **47**
Highgate Cemetery N6 . . . 1E **64**
Highgate Cl. N6 . . . 7E **46**
Highgate Edge N2 . . . 5C **46**
Highgate Hgts. N6 . . . 6G **47**
Highgate High St. N6 . . . 1E **64**
Highgate Hill N6 . . . 1F **65**
N19 . . . 1F **65**
Highgate Ho. SE26 . . . 3G **139**
Highgate Rd. NW5 . . . 3E **64**
Highgate Spinney N8 . . . 6H **47**
Highgate Wlk. SE23 . . . 2J **139**
Highgate W. Hill N6 . . . 1E **64**
Highgate Wood School Sports Cen. . . . 5G **47**
High Gro. BR1: Brom . . . 1B **160**
SE18 . . . 7H **107**
Highgrove Cl. BR7: Chst . . . 1C **160**
N11 . . . 5K **31**
Highgrove Ct. BR3: Beck . . . 7C **140**
SM1: Sutt . . . 6J **165**
Highgrove M. SM5: Cars . . . 3D **166**
Highgrove Rd. RM8: Dag . . . 5C **72**
Highgrove Swimming Pool . . . 6J **39**
Highgrove Way HA4: Ruis . . . 6J **39**
High Hill Est. E5 . . . 1H **67**
High Hill Ferry E5 . . . 1H **67**
High Holborn WC1 . . . 7E **6** (6J **83**)
Highland Av. RM10: Dag . . . 3J **73**
(not continuous)
W7 . . . 6J **77**
Highland Cotts. SM6: Wall . . . 4G **167**
Highland Ct. E18 . . . 1K **51**
Highland Cft. BR3: Beck . . . 5D **140**
Highland Dr. WD23: Bush . . . 1A **26**
Highland Pk. TW13: Felt . . . 4H **129**
Highland Rd. BR1: Brom . . . 1H **159**
BR2: Brom . . . 1H **159**
DA6: Bex . . . 5G **127**
HA6: Nwood . . . 2H **39**
SE19 . . . 6E **138**
Highlands N20 . . . 2G **31**
Highlands, The
EN5: New Bar . . . 4D **20**
HA8: Edg . . . 2H **43**
Highlands Av. N21 . . . 5E **22**
W3 . . . 7J **79**
Highlands Cl. N4 . . . 7J **47**
TW3: Houn . . . 1F **113**
Highlands Ct. SE19 . . . 6E **138**
Highlands Gdns. IG1: Ilf . . . 1D **70**
Highlands Heath SW15 . . . 7E **116**
Highlands Rd. EN5: New Bar . . . 5D **20**
HIGHLANDS VILLAGE . . . **5E 22**
Highland Ter. *SE13* . . . *3D 122*
(*off Algernon Rd.*)
Highland Vw. Pk. Homes
UB7: W Dray . . . 1D **174**
High La. W7 . . . 5H **77**
Highlawn Hall HA1: Harr . . . 3J **59**
Highlea Cl. NW9 . . . 7F **29**
High Level Dr. SE26 . . . 4G **139**
Highlever Rd. W10 . . . 5E **80**
High Mead BR4: W W'ck . . . 2F **171**
HA1: Harr . . . 5J **41**
Highmead *N18* . . . *5B 34*
(*off Alpha Rd.*)
SE18 . . . 7K **107**
Highmead Cres. HA0: Wemb . . . 7F **61**
High Mdw. Cl. HA5: Eastc . . . 4A **40**
High Mdw. Cres. NW9 . . . 5K **43**
High Meads Rd. E16 . . . 6B **88**
Highmore Rd. SE3 . . . 7G **105**
High Mt. NW4 . . . 6C **44**
High Oaks EN2: Enf . . . 1E **22**
High Pde., The SW16 . . . 3J **137**
High Pk. Av. TW9: Kew . . . 1G **115**
High Pk. Rd. TW9: Kew . . . 1G **115**
High Path SW19 . . . 1K **153**
High Point N6 . . . 7E **46**
SE9 . . . 3F **143**
High Ridge N10 . . . 1F **47**
Highridge Pl. *EN2: Enf* . . . *1E 22*
(*off Oak Av.*)
High Rd. E18 . . . 1J **51**
HA0: Wemb . . . 5D **60**
HA3: Hrw W . . . 7D **26**
HA5: Eastc . . . 6J **39**
HA9: Wemb . . . 5D **60**
IG1: Ilf . . . 3F **71**
(not continuous)
IG3: Chad H, Ilf . . . 2G **71**
IG7: Chig . . . 5K **37**
IG9: Buck H . . . 2E **36**
High Rd. N11 . . . 5A **32**
N15 . . . 4F **49**
N17 . . . 2F **49**
N22 . . . 1K **47**
NW10 . . . 6A **62**
RM6: Chad H . . . 7D **54**
UB4: Hayes . . . 5G **75**
UB10: Ick . . . 3E **56**
WD23: B Hea . . . 1C **26**
High Rd. E. Finchley N2 . . . 1B **46**
High Rd. Leyton E10 . . . 6D **50**
E15 . . . 2D **68**
High Rd. Leytonstone E11 . . . 4G **69**
E15 . . . 4G **69**
High Rd. Nth. Finchley N12 . . . 3F **31**
High Rd. Whetstone N20 . . . 7F **21**
High Rd. Woodford Grn. E18 . . . 1J **51**
IG8: Wfd G . . . 6C **36**
High Sheldon N6 . . . 6D **46**
Highshore Rd. SE15 . . . 2F **121**
(not continuous)
Highstead Cres. DA8: Erith . . . 1K **127**
Highstone Av. E11 . . . 6J **51**
Highstone Ct. *E11* . . . *6H 51*
(*off New Wanstead*)
Highstone Mans. *NW1* . . . *7G 65*
(*off Camden Rd.*)
High St. BR1: Brom . . . 2J **159**
BR3: Beck . . . 2C **158**
BR4: W W'ck . . . 1D **170**
BR6: Chels . . . 7K **173**
BR6: Farnb . . . 5F **173**
BR6: Orp . . . 2K **173**
BR7: Chst . . . 6F **143**
CR0: C'don . . . 3C **168**
(not continuous)
E11 . . . 5J **51**
E13 . . . 2J **87**
E15 . . . 2E **86**
E17 . . . 5A **50**
EN3: Pond E . . . 6D **24**
EN5: Barn . . . 3B **20**
HA1: Harr . . . 1J **59**
HA3: W'stone . . . 2J **41**
(not continuous)
HA4: Ruis . . . 7G **39**
HA5: Pinn . . . 3C **40**
HA6: Nwood . . . 1H **39**
HA8: Edg . . . 6B **28**
HA9: Wemb . . . 4F **61**
IG6: Ilf . . . 3G **53**
KT1: Ham W . . . 1C **150**
KT1: King T . . . 3D **150**
KT3: N Mald . . . 4A **152**
KT7: T Ditt . . . 6A **150**
KT8: W Mole . . . 4E **148**
KT12: Walt T . . . 7J **147**
KT17: Ewe . . . 7B **164**
N8 . . . 4J **47**
N14 . . . 1C **32**
NW7 . . . 5J **29**
RM1: Rom . . . 5K **55**
SE20 . . . 6J **139**
SE25 . . . 4F **157**
SM1: Sutt . . . 4K **165**
SM3: Cheam . . . 6G **165**
SM5: Cars . . . 5E **166**
SW19 . . . 5F **135**
TW2: Whitt . . . 7G **113**
TW3: Houn . . . 3F **113**
(not continuous)
TW5: Cran . . . 1J **111**
TW8: Bford . . . 7C **96**
TW11: Tedd . . . 5K **131**
TW12: Hamp, Ham H . . . 1G **149**
TW13: Felt . . . 3H **129**
TW17: Shep . . . 6D **146**
TW19: Stanw . . . 6A **110**
UB1: S'hall . . . 1D **94**
UB3: Harl . . . 6F **93**

High St. UB7: Harm 2E 174
UB7: Yiew 7A 74
UB8: Uxb 1A 74
W3 1H 97
W5 1D 96
High St. Colliers Wood SW19 7B 136
High St. Harlesden NW10 2B 80
High St. M. SW19 5G 135
High St. Nth. E6 5C 70
E12 5C 70
High St. Sth. E6 2D 88
High Timber St. EC4 2C 14 (7C 84)
High Tor Cl. BR1: Brom 7K 141
High Tor Vw. SE28 1J 107
High Trees CR0: C'don 1A 170
EN4: E Barn 5H 21
N20 3F 31
SW2 1A 138
Hightrees Ct. W7 7J 77
Hightrees Ho. SW12 6E 118
High Vw. HA5: Pinn 4A 40
Highview N6 6G 47
NW7 3E 28
UB5: N'olt 3C 76
Highview Av. HA8: Edg 4D 28
SM6: Wall 5K 167
High Vw. Cl. SE19 2F 157
High Vw. Ct. HA3: Hrw W 7D 26
Highview Gdns. HA8: Edg 4D 28
N3 3G 45
N11 5B 32
Highview Ho. RM6: Chad H 4E 54
Highview Lodge *EN2: Enf* 3G 23
(off The Ridgeway)
High Vw. Pde. IG4: Ilf 5D 52
High Vw. Rd. DA14: Sidc 4B 144
E18 2H 51
N2 1D 46
SE19 6D 138
Highview Rd. W13 5A 78
Highway, The E1 7G 85
HA7: Stan 1K 41
SM2: Sutt 7A 166
Highway Bus. Pk., The *E1* 7K 85
(off Heckford St.)
Highway Trad. Cen., The *E1* 7K 85
(off Heckford St.)
Highwood BR2: Brom 3F 159
Highwood Av. N12 4F 31
Highwood Cl. BR6: Farnb 2G 173
Highwood Ct. EN5: New Bar 5D 20
N12 3F 31
SE22 1G 139
Highwood Dr. BR6: Farnb 2G 173
Highwood Gdns. IG5: Ilf 5D 52
Highwood Gro. NW7 5E 28
HIGHWOOD HILL 3G 29
Highwood Hill NW7 2G 29
Highwood Rd. N19 3J 65
High Worple HA2: Harr 7D 40
Highworth Rd. N11 6C 32
Highworth St. NW1 5D 4
Hi-Gloss Cen. SE8 5A 104
Hilary Av. CR4: Mitc 3E 154
Hilary Cl. DA8: Erith 1H 127
SW6 7K 99
Hilary Dennis Ct. E11 4J 51
Hilary Rd. W12 6B 80
(not continuous)
Hilberry Ct. WD23: Bush 1A 26
Hilbert Rd. SM3: Cheam 3F 165
Hilborough Cl. SW19 7A 136
Hilborough Ct. E8 7F 67
Hilborough Way BR6: Farnb 5H 173
Hilda Ct. KT6: Surb 7D 150
Hilda Lockert Wlk. *SW9* 2B 120
(off Loughborough Rd.)
Hilda Rd. E6 7B 70
E16 4G 87
(not continuous)
Hilda Ter. SW9 2A 120
Hilda Va. Cl. BR6: Farnb 4F 173
Hilda Va. Rd. BR6: Farnb 4E 172
Hildenborough Gdns.
BR1: Brom 6G 141
Hildenborough Ho. *BR3: Beck* 7B 140
(off Bethersden Cl.)
Hildenlea Pl. BR2: Brom 2F 159
Hilderley Ho. *KT1: King T* 3F 151
(off Winery La.)
Hildreth St. SW12 1F 137
Hildreth St. M. SW12 1F 137
Hildyard Rd. SW6 6J 99
Hiley Rd. NW10 3E 80
Hilgrove Rd. NW6 7A 64
Hiliary Gdns. HA7: Stan 2C 42
Hillary *N8* 3J 47
(off Boyton Cl.)
Hillary Ct. *TW19: Stanw* 1A 128
(off Explorer Av.)
W12 2E 98
(off Titmuss St.)
Hillary Cres. KT12: Walt T 7A 148
Hillary Dr. TW7: Isle 5K 113
Hillary Ri. EN5: New Bar 4D 20
Hillary Rd. UB2: S'hall 3E 94
Hillbeck Cl. SE15 7J 103
(not continuous)
Hillbeck Way UB6: G'frd 1H 77
Hillborne Cl. UB3: Harl 5J 93
Hillboro Ct. E11 7F 51
Hillbrook Rd. SW17 3D 136
Hill Brow BR1: Brom 1B 160
Hillbrow KT3: N Mald 3B 152
Hill Brow Cl. DA5: Bexl 4K 145
Hillbrow Rd. BR1: Brom 7G 141
Hillbury Av. HA3: Kent 5B 42
Hillbury Rd. SW17 3F 137
Hill Cl. BR7: Chst 5F 143
HA1: Harr 3J 59
HA7: Stan 4G 27
NW2 3D 62
NW11 6J 45
Hillcote Av. SW16 7A 138
Hill Ct. EN4: E Barn 4H 21
UB5: N'olt 5E 58
W5 4F 79
Hillcourt Av. N12 6E 30
Hillcourt Est. N16 1D 66
Hillcourt Rd. SE22 6H 121
Hill Cres. DA5: Bexl 1J 145
HA1: Harr 5A 42
KT4: Wor Pk 2E 164
KT5: Surb 5F 151
N20 2E 30
Hill Crest DA15: Sidc 7A 126
KT6: Surb 7E 150
Hillcrest N6 7E 46
N21 7F 23
SE24 4D 120
W11 7H 81
(off St John's Gdns.)
Hillcrest Av. HA5: Pinn 4B 40
HA8: Edg 4C 28
NW11 5H 45
Hillcrest Cl. BR3: Beck 6B 158
SE26 4G 139
Hillcrest Ct. RM5: Col R 1K 55
SM2: Sutt 6B 166
(off Eaton Rd.)
Hill Crest Gdns. NW2 3C 62
Hillcrest Gdns. KT10: Hin W 3A 162
N3 4G 45
Hillcrest Rd. BR1: Brom 5J 141
BR6: Chels 2K 173
E17 2F 51
E18 2H 51
W3 1H 97
W5 5E 78
Hillcrest Vw. BR3: Beck 6B 158
Hillcroft Av. HA5: Pinn 6D 40
Hillcroft Cres. HA4: Ruis 3B 58
HA9: Wemb 4F 61
W5 6D 78
Hillcroft Rd. E6 5F 89
Hillcroome Rd. SM2: Sutt 6B 166
Hillcross Av. SM4: Mord 6F 153
Hilldale Rd. SM1: Sutt 4H 165
Hilldown Ct. SW16 7J 137
Hilldown Rd. BR2: Hayes 1G 171
SW16 7J 137
Hill Dr. NW9 1J 61
SW16 3K 155
Hilldrop Cres. N7 5H 65
Hilldrop Est. N7 5H 65
(not continuous)
Hilldrop La. N7 5H 65
Hilldrop Rd. BR1: Brom 6K 141
N7 5H 65
Hill End BR6: Orp 2K 173
Hillend SE18 1E 124
Hillersden Ho. *SW1* 5J 17
(off Ebury Bri. Rd.)
Hillersdon Av. HA8: Edg 5A 28
SW13 2C 116
Hillery Cl. SE17 4D 102
Hill Farm Cotts. HA4: Ruis 7E 38
Hill Farm Rd. UB10: Ick 4F 57
W10 5E 80
Hillfield Av. HA0: Wemb 7E 60
N8 5J 47
NW9 5A 44
SM4: Mord 6C 154
Hillfield Cl. HA2: Harr 4G 41
Hillfield Ct. NW3 5C 64
Hillfield Ho. N5 5C 66
Hillfield M. N8 4K 47
Hillfield Pk. N10 4F 47
N21 2F 33
Hillfield Pk. M. N10 4F 47
Hill Fld. Rd. TW12: Hamp 7D 130
Hillfield Rd. NW6 5H 63
Hillfoot Av. RM5: Col R 1J 55
Hillfoot Rd. RM5: Col R 1J 55
Hillgate Pl. SW12 7F 119
W8 1J 99
Hillgate St. W8 1J 99
Hillgate Wlk. N6 6G 47
Hill Gro. RM1: Rom 3K 55
TW13: Hanw 2D 130
Hill Ho. BR2: Brom 2H 159
E5 1H 67
(off Harrington Hill)
SE28 1H 107
Hill Ho. Av. HA7: Stan 7E 26
Hill Ho. Cl. N21 7F 23
Hill Ho. Dr. TW12: Hamp 1E 148
Hill Ho. M. BR2: Brom 2H 159
Hill Ho. Rd. SW16 5K 137
Hilliard Ho. *E1* 1H 103
(off Prusom St.)
Hilliard Rd. HA6: Nwood 1H 39
Hilliards Ct. E1 1J 103
Hillier Cl. EN5: New Bar 6E 20
Hillier Gdns. CR0: Wadd 5A 168
Hillier Ho. *NW1* 7H 65
(off Camden Sq.)
Hillier Lodge TW11: Tedd 5H 131
Hillier Pl. KT9: Chess 6D 162
Hillier Rd. SW11 6D 118
Hilliers Av. UB8: Hil 3C 74
Hilliers La. CR0: Bedd 3J 167
HILLINGDON 3C 74
Hillingdon Athletic Club 5F 39
Hillingdon Av. TW19: Stanw 1A 128
HILLINGDON CIRCUS 6D 56
Hillingdon Ct. HA3: Kent 4D 42
Hillingdon Cycling Circuit 1A 94
HILLINGDON HEATH 4D 74
Hillingdon Hill UB10: Hil 2A 74
Hillingdon Rd. DA7: Bex 2J 127
UB8: Uxb 1A 74
UB10: Uxb 1A 74
Hillingdon Ski Cen. 5A 56
Hillingdon St. SE17 6B 102
Hillington Gdns. IG8: Wfd G 2B 52
Hill La. HA4: Ruis 1E 56
Hillman Cl. UB8: Uxb 5A 56
Hillman Dr. W10 4E 80
Hillman St. E8 6H 67
Hillmarton Rd. N7 5J 65
Hillmarton Ter. *N7* 5J 65
(off Hillmarton Rd.)
Hillmead Dr. SW9 4B 120
Hillmore Ct. *SE13* 3F 123
(off Belmont Hill)
Hillmore Gro. SE26 5A 140
Hill Path SW16 5K 137
Hillreach SE18 5D 106
Hill Ri. HA4: Ruis 1E 56
KT10: Hin W 2B 162
N9 6C 24
NW11 4K 45
SE23 1H 139
TW10: Rich 5D 114
UB6: G'frd 7G 59
Hillrise KT12: Walt T 7H 147
Hillrise Mans. *N19* 7J 47
(off Warltersville Rd.)
Hillrise Rd. N19 7J 47
Hill Rd. CR4: Mitc 1F 155
HA0: Wemb 3B 60
HA1: Harr 5A 42
HA5: Pinn 5C 40
N10 1D 46
NW8 2A 82
SM1: Sutt 5K 165
SM5: Cars 6C 166
Hillsboro' Rd. SE22 5E 120
Hillsborough Ct. *NW6* 1K 81
(off Mortimer Cres.)
Hillsgrove Cl. DA16: Well 7C 108
HILLSIDE 4J 109
Hillside DA8: Erith 4J 109
EN5: New Bar 5F 21
N8 6H 47
NW5 3E 64
NW9 4K 43
NW10 7J 61
SE10 7F 105
(off Crooms Hill)
SW19 6F 135
Hillside Av. HA9: Wemb 4F 61
IG8: Wfd G 6F 37
N11 6J 31
Hillside Cl. IG8: Wfd G 5F 37
NW8 2K 81
SM4: Mord 4G 153
Hillside Cres. HA2: Harr 1G 59
HA6: Nwood 1J 39
Hillside Dr. HA8: Edg 6B 28
Hillside Gdns. E17 3F 51
EN5: Barn 4B 20
HA3: Kent 7E 42
HA6: Nwood 1J 39
HA8: Edg 4A 28
N6 6F 47
N11 6B 32
SM6: Wall 7G 167
SW2 2A 138
Hillside Gro. N14 7C 22
NW7 7H 29
Hillside Ho. *CR0: Wadd* 4B 168
(off Violet La.)
Hillside La. BR2: Hayes 2H 171
(not continuous)
Hillside Mans.
EN5: Barn 4C 20
Hillside Pas. SW16 2K 137
Hillside Ri. HA6: Nwood 1J 39

Hillside Rd. BR2: Brom . . . 3H 159
CR0: Wadd . . . 5B 168
HA5: Pinn . . . 1K 39
HA6: Nwood . . . 1J 39
KT5: Surb . . . 4F 151
N15 . . . 7E 48
SM2: Sutt . . . 7H 165
SW2 . . . 2K 137
UB1: S'hall . . . 4E 76
W5 . . . 5E 78
Hills La. HA6: Nwood . . . 1G 39
Hillsleigh Rd. W8 . . . 1H 99
Hills M. W5 . . . 7E 78
Hills Pl. W1 . . . 1A 12 (6G 83)
Hills Rd. IG9: Buck H . . . 1E 36
Hillstowe St. E5 . . . 3J 67
Hill St. TW9: Rich . . . 5D 114
W1 . . . 4H 11 (1E 100)
Hill Top SM3: Sutt . . . 7H 153
SM4: Mord . . . 6J 153
Hilltop E17 . . . 3D 50
NW11 . . . 4K 45
Hilltop Av. NW10 . . . 7J 61
Hill Top Ct. IG8: Wfd G . . . 6J 37
Hilltop Ct. NW8 . . . 7A 64
(off Alexandra Rd.)
Hilltop Gdns. BR6: Orp . . . 2J 173
NW4 . . . 2D 44
Hilltop Ho. N6 . . . 7H 47
Hilltop Rd. NW6 . . . 7J 63
Hill Top Vw. IG8: Wfd G . . . 6J 37
Hilltop Way HA7: Stan . . . 3F 27
Hill Vw. NW3 . . . 1D 82
(off Ainger Rd.)
Hillview SW20 . . . 7D 134
Hillview Av. HA3: Kent . . . 5E 42
Hillview Cl. HA9: Wemb . . . 2F 61
Hill Vw. Cres. BR6: Orp . . . 1J 173
IG1: Ilf . . . 6D 52
Hill Vw. Dr. DA16: Well . . . 2J 125
SE28 . . . 1J 107
Hill Vw. Gdns. NW9 . . . 5K 43
Hillview Gdns. HA2: Harr . . . 3E 40
NW4 . . . 4F 45
Hill Vw. Rd. BR6: Orp . . . 1K 173
KT10: Clay . . . 7A 162
TW1: Twick . . . 6A 114
Hillview Rd. BR7: Chst . . . 5E 142
HA5: Hat E . . . 1D 40
NW7 . . . 4A 30
SM1: Sutt . . . 3A 166
Hillway N6 . . . 2E 64
NW9 . . . 1A 62
Hill-Wood Ho. NW1 . . . 1B 6
(off Polygon Rd.)
Hillworth BR3: Beck . . . 2D 158
Hillworth Rd. SW2 . . . 7A 120
Hillyard Ho. SW9 . . . 1A 120
Hillyard Rd. W7 . . . 5J 77
Hillyard St. SW9 . . . 1A 120
Hillyfield E17 . . . 2A 50
Hillyfield Cl. E9 . . . 5A 68
Hilly Flds. Cres. SE4 . . . 3C 122
SE13 . . . 3C 122
Hilsea Point SW15 . . . 1D 134
Hilsea St. E5 . . . 4J 67
Hilton Av. N12 . . . 5G 31
Hilton Ho. SE4 . . . 4K 121
Hilton's Wharf SE10 . . . 6D 104
(off Norman Rd.)
Hilversum Cres. SE22 . . . 5E 120
Himalaya Palace Cinema . . . 1D 94
Himley Rd. SW17 . . . 5C 136
Hinchinbrook Ho. NW6 . . . 1K 81
(off Mortimer Cres.)
Hinchley Cl. KT10: Hin W . . . 4A 162
Hinchley Dr. KT10: Hin W . . . 3A 162
Hinchley Mnr. KT10: Hin W . . . 3A 162
Hinchley Way KT10: Hin W . . . 3A 162
HINCHLEY WOOD . . . 3A 162
Hinckley Rd. SE15 . . . 4G 121
Hind Ct. EC4 . . . 1K 13 (6A 84)
Hind Cres. DA8: Erith . . . 6K 109
Hinde Ho. W1 . . . 7H 5
(off Hinde St.)
Hinde M. W1 . . . 7H 5
Hindes Rd. HA1: Harr . . . 5H 41
Hinde St. W1 . . . 7H 5 (6E 82)
Hind Gro. E14 . . . 6C 86
Hindhead Cl. N16 . . . 1E 66
UB8: Hil . . . 5D 74
Hindhead Gdns. UB5: N'olt . . . 1C 76
Hindhead Point SW15 . . . 1D 134
Hindhead Way SM6: Wall . . . 5J 167
Hind Ho. N7 . . . 4A 66
SE14 . . . 6K 103
(off Myers La.)
Hindle Ho. E8 . . . 5F 67
Hindlip Ho. SW8 . . . 1H 119
Hindmans Rd. SE22 . . . 5G 121
Hindmans Way RM9: Dag . . . 4F 91
Hindmarsh Cl. E1 . . . 7G 85
Hindon Ct. SW1 . . . 3A 18
Hindrey Rd. E5 . . . 5H 67
Hindsley's Pl. SE23 . . . 2J 139
Hinkler Rd. HA3: Kent . . . 3D 42
Hinksey Path SE2 . . . 2D 108
Hinstock NW6 . . . 1K 81
(off Belsize Rd.)
Hinstock Rd. SE18 . . . 6G 107
Hinton Av. TW4: Houn . . . 4B 112
Hinton Cl. SE9 . . . 1C 142
Hinton Ct. E10 . . . 2D 68
(off Leyton Grange Est.)
Hinton Ho. W5 . . . 6C 78
Hinton Rd. N18 . . . 4K 33
SE24 . . . 3B 120
SM6: Wall . . . 6G 167
Hippisley Ct. TW7: Isle . . . 3K 113
Hippodrome M. W11 . . . 7G 81
Hippodrome Pl. W11 . . . 7G 81
Hiroshima Prom. SE7 . . . 3A 106
Hirst Ct. SW1 . . . 7J 17
Hirst Cres. HA9: Wemb . . . 3E 60
Hitcham Rd. E17 . . . 7B 50
Hitchcock Cl. TW17: Shep . . . 3B 146
Hitchin Sq. E3 . . . 2A 86
Hithe Gro. SE16 . . . 3J 103
Hitherbroom Rd. UB3: Hayes . . . 1J 93
Hither Farm Rd. SE3 . . . 3A 124
Hitherfield Rd. RM8: Dag . . . 2E 72
SW16 . . . 2K 137
HITHER GREEN . . . 6G 123
Hither Grn. La. SE13 . . . 5E 122
Hithermoor Rd. TW19: Stan M . . . 7B 174
Hitherwell Dr. HA3: Hrw W . . . 1H 41
Hitherwood Dr. SE19 . . . 4F 139
Hive Cl. WD23: B Hea . . . 2C 26
Hive Rd. WD23: B Hea . . . 2C 26
(not continuous)
HMP Brixton SW2 . . . 6J 119
HMP Holloway N7 . . . 4J 65
HMP Pentonville N7 . . . 6K 65
HMP Wandsworth SW18 . . . 7B 118
HMP Wormwood Scrubs W12 . . . 6C 80
HMS Belfast . . . 4H 15 (1E 102)
HM Young Offenders Institution Feltham
TW13: Felt . . . 3F 129
Hoadly Ho. SE1 . . . 5C 14
(off Union St.)
Hoadly Rd. SW16 . . . 3H 137
Hobart Cl. N20 . . . 2H 31
UB4: Yead . . . 4B 76
Hobart Ct. CR2: S Croy . . . 5D 168
(off South Pk. Hill Rd.)
Hobart Dr. UB4: Yead . . . 4B 76
Hobart Gdns. CR7: Thor H . . . 3D 156
Hobart La. UB4: Yead . . . 4B 76
Hobart Pl. SW1 . . . 1J 17 (3F 101)
TW10: Rich . . . 7F 115
Hobart Rd. IG6: Ilf . . . 2G 53
KT4: Wor Pk . . . 3D 164
RM9: Dag . . . 4D 72
UB4: Yead . . . 4B 76
Hobbayne Rd. W7 . . . 6H 77
Hobbes Wlk. SW15 . . . 5D 116
Hobbs Ct. SE1 . . . 6K 15
(off Mill St.)
Hobbs Grn. N2 . . . 3A 46
Hobbs M. IG3: Ilf . . . 2K 71
Hobbs Pl. N1 . . . 1E 84
Hobbs Pl. Est. N1 . . . 2E 84
(off Hobbs Pl.)
Hobbs Rd. SE27 . . . 4C 138
Hobby St. EN3: Pond E . . . 5E 24
Hobday St. E14 . . . 6D 86
Hobill Wlk. KT5: Surb . . . 6F 151
Hoblands End BR7: Chst . . . 6J 143
Hobson's Pl. E1 . . . 5G 85
Hobury St. SW10 . . . 7A 16 (6A 100)
Hocker St. E2 . . . 2J 9 (3F 85)
Hockett Cl. SE8 . . . 4A 104
Hockington Ct. EN5: New Bar . . . 4E 20
Hockley Av. E6 . . . 2C 88
Hockley Ct. E18 . . . 1J 51
Hockley M. IG11: Bark . . . 3J 89
Hockliffe Ho. W10 . . . 5E 80
(off Sutton Way)
Hockney Ct. SE16 . . . 5H 103
(off Rossetti Rd.)
Hocroft Av. NW2 . . . 3H 63
Hocroft Ct. NW2 . . . 3H 63
Hocroft Rd. NW2 . . . 3H 63
Hocroft Wlk. NW2 . . . 3H 63
Hodder Dr. UB6: G'frd . . . 2K 77
Hoddesdon Rd. DA17: Belv . . . 5G 109
Hodes Row NW3 . . . 4E 64
Hodford Rd. NW11 . . . 1H 63
Hodgkin Cl. SE28 . . . 7D 90
Hodgkins M. HA7: Stan . . . 5G 27
Hodister Cl. SE5 . . . 7C 102
Hodnet Gro. SE16 . . . 4K 103
Hodson Cl. HA2: Harr . . . 3D 58
Hoecroft Ct. EN3: Enf W . . . 1D 24
(off Hoe La.)
Hoe La. EN1: Enf . . . 1B 24
EN3: Enf W . . . 1C 24
Hoe St. E17 . . . 4C 50
Hoever Ho. SE6 . . . 4E 140
Hoffmann Gdns. CR2: Sels . . . 7H 169
Hoffman Sq. N1 . . . 1F 9
Hofland Rd. W14 . . . 3G 99
Hogan M. W2 . . . 5A 4 (5A 82)
Hogan Way E5 . . . 2G 67
Hogarth Av. TW15: Ashf . . . 6E 128
Hogarth Bus. Pk. W4 . . . 6A 98
Hogarth Cl. E16 . . . 5B 88
W5 . . . 5E 78
Hogarth Ct. E1 . . . 6G 85
(off Batty St.)
EC3 . . . 2H 15 (6E 84)
NW1 . . . 7G 65
(off St Pancras Way)
SE19 . . . 4F 139
TW5: Hest . . . 7C 94
Hogarth Cres. CR0: C'don . . . 7C 156
SW19 . . . 1B 154
Hogarth Gdns. TW5: Hest . . . 7E 94
Hogarth Hill NW11 . . . 4H 45
Hogarth Ho. SW1 . . . 4D 18
(off Erasmus St.)
UB5: N'olt . . . 2B 76
(off Gallery Gdns.)
Hogarth Ind. Est. NW10 . . . 4C 80
Hogarth La. W4 . . . 6A 98
Hogarth Pl. SW5 . . . 4K 99
(off Hogarth Rd.)
Hogarth Rd. HA8: Edg . . . 2G 43
RM8: Dag . . . 5B 72
SW5 . . . 4K 99
HOGARTH RDBT. . . . 6A 98
Hogarth's House . . . 6A 98
(off Hogarth La.)
Hogarth Ter. W4 . . . 6A 98
Hogarth Way TW12: Hamp . . . 1G 149
Hog Hill Rd. RM5: Col R . . . 1F 55
Hogshead Pas. E1 . . . 7H 85
(off Reunion Row)
Hogsmill Ho. KT1: King T . . . 3F 151
(off Vineyard Cl.)
Hogsmill La. KT1: King T . . . 3F 151
Hogsmill Wlk. KT1: King T . . . 3E 150
(off Penrhyn Rd.)
Hogsmill Way KT19: Ewe . . . 5J 163
Holbeach Cl. NW9 . . . 1A 44
Holbeach Gdns. DA15: Sidc . . . 6J 125
Holbeach M. SW12 . . . 1F 137
Holbeach Rd. SE6 . . . 7C 122
Holbeck Row SE15 . . . 7G 103
Holbein Ho. SW1 . . . 5G 17
(off Holbein M.)
Holbein M. SW1 . . . 5G 17 (5E 100)
Holbein Pl. SW1 . . . 4G 17 (4E 100)
Holbein Ter. RM8: Dag . . . 4C 72
(off Marlborough Rd.)
Holberton Gdns. NW10 . . . 3D 80
HOLBORN . . . 6G 7 (5K 83)
Holborn WC1 . . . 5K 83
Holborn Cir EC1 . . . 6K 7 (5A 84)
Holborn Pl. WC1 . . . 6G 7
Holborn Rd. E13 . . . 4K 87
Holborn Viaduct EC1 . . . 6K 7 (5A 84)
Holborn Way CR4: Mitc . . . 2D 154
Holbrook Cl. EN1: Enf . . . 1A 24
N19 . . . 1F 65
Holbrooke Ct. N7 . . . 3J 65
Holbrooke Pl. TW10: Rich . . . 5D 114
Holbrook Ho. BR7: Chst . . . 1H 161
Holbrook La. BR7: Chst . . . 7H 143
Holbrook Rd. E15 . . . 2H 87
Holbrook Way BR2: Brom . . . 6D 160
Holburne Cl. SE3 . . . 1A 124
Holburne Gdns. SE3 . . . 1B 124
Holburne Rd. SE3 . . . 1A 124
Holcombe Hill NW7 . . . 3H 29
Holcombe Ho. SW9 . . . 3J 119
(off Landor Rd.)
Holcombe Pl. SE4 . . . 3A 122
(off St Asaph Rd.)
Holcombe Rd. IG1: Ilf . . . 7E 52
N17 . . . 3F 49
(not continuous)
Holcombe St. W6 . . . 4D 98
Holcote Cl. DA17: Belv . . . 3E 108
Holcroft Ct. W1 . . . 5A 6
Holcroft Ho. SW11 . . . 3B 118
Holcroft Rd. E9 . . . 7J 67
Holden Av. N12 . . . 5E 30
NW9 . . . 1J 61
Holdenby Rd. SE4 . . . 5A 122
Holden Cl. RM8: Dag . . . 3B 72
Holden Ho. N1 . . . 1C 84
(off Prebend St.)
SE8 . . . 7C 104
Holdenhurst Av. N12 . . . 7F 31
Holden Rd. N12 . . . 5E 30
Holden St. SW11 . . . 2E 118
Holder Cl. N3 . . . 7E 30
Holdernesse Cl.
TW7: Isle . . . 1A 114
Holdernesse Rd. SW17 . . . 3D 136
Holderness Ho. SE5 . . . 3E 120
Holderness Way SE27 . . . 5B 138
HOLDERS HILL . . . 2F 45
Holder's Hill Av. NW4 . . . 2F 45
Holders Hill Cir. NW7 . . . 7B 30
Holders Hill Cres. NW4 . . . 2F 45
Holders Hill Dr. NW4 . . . 3F 45
Holder's Hill Gdns. NW4 . . . 2G 45
Holders Hill Pde. NW7 . . . 1G 45

Holders Hill Rd. NW4 ... 2F 45
NW7 ... 2F 45
Holford Ho. *SE16* ... *4H 103*
(off Camilla Rd.)
WC1 ... *1H 7*
(off Gt. Percy St.)
Holford M. WC1 ... 1J 7
Holford Pl. WC1 ... 1H 7 (3K 83)
Holford Rd. NW3 ... 3A 64
Holford St. WC1 ... 1J 7 (3K 83)
Holford Yd. *WC1* ... *1J 7*
(off Cruikshank St.)
Holgate Av. SW11 ... 3B 118
Holgate Gdns. RM10: Dag ... 6G 73
Holgate Rd. RM10: Dag ... 5G 73
Holgate St. SE7 ... 3B 106
Hollam Ho. N8 ... 4K 47
Holland Av. SM2: Sutt ... 7J 165
SW20 ... 1B 152
Holland Cl. BR2: Hayes ... 2H 171
EN5: New Bar ... 7G 21
HA7: Stan ... 5G 27
RM7: Rom ... 5J 55
Holland Ct. *E17* ... *4E 50*
(off Evelyn Rd.)
KT6: Surb ... 7D 150
NW7 ... 6H 29
Holland Dr. SE23 ... 3A 140
Holland Dwellings *WC2* ... *7F 7*
(off Newton St.)
Holland Gdns. TW8: Bford ... 6F 97
W14 ... 3G 99
Holland Gro. SW9 ... 7A 102
Holland Ho. E4 ... 4K 35
NW10 ... *2D 80*
(off Holland Rd.)
HOLLAND PARK ... 1H 99
Holland Pk. ... 2H 99
Holland Pk. W11 ... 1G 99
Holland Pk. Av. IG3: Ilf ... 6J 53
W11 ... 2G 99
Holland Pk. Ct. *W14* ... *2G 99*
(off Holland Pk. Gdns.)
Holland Pk. Gdns. W14 ... 2G 99
Holland Pk. Mans. *W14* ... *1G 99*
(off Holland Pk. Gdns.)
Holland Pk. M. W11 ... 1G 99
Holland Pk. Rd. W14 ... 3H 99
HOLLAND PARK RDBT. ... 2F 99
Holland Pk. Ter. *W11* ... *1G 99*
(off Portland Rd.)
Holland Pk. Theatre (Open Air) ... 2H 99
Holland Pas. *N1* ... *1C 84*
(off Basire St.)
Holland Pl. *W8* ... *2K 99*
(off Kensington Chu. St.)
Holland Pl. Chambers *W8* ... *2K 99*
(off Holland Pl.)
Holland Ri. Ho. *SW9* ... *7K 101*
(off Clapham Rd.)
Holland Rd. E6 ... 1D 88
E15 ... 3G 87
HA0: Wemb ... 6D 60
NW10 ... 1C 80
SE25 ... 5G 157
W14 ... 2F 99
Hollands, The KT4: Wor Pk ... 1B 164
TW13: Hanw ... 4B 130
Holland St.
SE1 ... 4B 14 (1B 102)
W8 ... 2J 99
Holland Vs. Rd. W14 ... 2G 99
Holland Wlk. HA7: Stan ... 5F 27
N19 ... 1H 65
W8 ... 1H 99
Holland Way BR2: Hayes ... 2H 171
Hollar Rd. N16 ... 3F 67
Hollen St. W1 ... 7C 6 (6H 83)
Holles Cl. TW12: Hamp ... 6E 130
Holles Ho. SW9 ... 2A 120
Holles St. W1 ... 7K 5 (6F 83)
Holley Rd. W3 ... 2A 98
Hollick Wood Av. N12 ... 6J 31
Holliday Sq. *SW11* ... *3B 118*
(off Fowler Cl.)
Hollidge Way RM10: Dag ... 7H 73
Hollies, The *E11* ... *5J 51*
(off New Wanstead)
HA3: W'stone ... 4A 42
N20 ... 1G 31
Hollies Av. DA15: Sidc ... 2K 143
Hollies Cl. SW16 ... 6A 138
TW1: Twick ... 2K 131
Hollies End NW7 ... 5J 29
Hollies Rd. W5 ... 4C 96
Hollies Way SW12 ... 7E 118
Holligrave Rd. BR1: Brom ... 1J 159
Hollingbourne Av.
DA7: Bex ... 1F 127
Hollingbourne Gdns. W13 ... 5B 78
Hollingbourne Rd. SE24 ... 5C 120
Hollingsworth Ct.
KT6: Surb ... 7D 150
Hollingsworth Rd.
CR0: C'don ... 6H 169
Hollington Ct. BR7: Chst ... 6F 143
Hollington Cres.
KT3: N Mald ... 6B 152
Hollington Rd. E6 ... 3D 88
N17 ... 2G 49
Hollingworth Cl. KT8: W Mole ... 4D 148
Hollingworth Rd. BR5: Pet W ... 6F 161
Hollins Ho. N7 ... 4J 65
Hollisfield *WC1* ... *2F 7*
(off Cromer St.)
Hollman Gdns. SW16 ... 6B 138
Hollow, The IG8: Wfd G ... 4C 36
HOLLOWAY ... 3J 65
Holloway Cl. UB7: Harm ... 5A 92
Holloway Ho. *NW2* ... *3E 62*
(off Stoll Cl.)
Holloway La. UB7: Harm, W Dray ... 2E 174
Holloway Rd. E6 ... 3D 88
E11 ... 3F 69
N7 ... 4K 65
N19 ... 2H 65
Holloway St. TW3: Houn ... 3F 113
Hollowfield Wlk. UB5: N'olt ... 6C 58
Hollows, The TW8: Bford ... 6F 97
Holly Av. HA7: Stan ... 2E 42
KT12: Walt T ... 7B 148
Hollybank Cl. TW12: Hamp ... 5E 130
Hollyberry La. NW3 ... 4A 64
Hollybrake Cl. BR7: Chst ... 7H 143
Hollybush Cl. E11 ... 5J 51
HA3: Hrw W ... 1J 41
Hollybush Gdns. E2 ... 3H 85
Hollybush Hill E11 ... 6H 51
NW3 ... 4A 64
Hollybush Ho. E2 ... 3H 85
Holly Bush La. TW12: Hamp ... 7D 130
Hollybush Pl. E2 ... 3H 85
Hollybush Rd. KT2: King T ... 5E 132
Hollybush Steps *NW3* ... *4A 64*
(off Holly Mt.)
Hollybush St. E13 ... 3K 87
Holly Bush Va. NW3 ... 4A 64
Hollybush Wlk. SW9 ... 4B 120
Holly Cl. BR3: Beck ... 4E 158
IG9: Buck H ... 3G 37
NW10 ... 7A 62
SM6: Wall ... 7F 167
TW13: Hanw ... 5C 130
Holly Cott. M. UB8: Hil ... 5C 74
Holly Ct. *DA14: Sidc* ... *4B 144*
(off Sidcup Hill)
N15 ... 4E 48
SM2: Sutt ... 7J 165
Holly Cres. BR3: Beck ... 5B 158
IG8: Wfd G ... 7A 36
Hollycroft Av. HA9: Wemb ... 2F 61
NW3 ... 3J 63
Hollycroft Cl. CR2: S Croy ... 5E 168
UB7: Sip ... 6C 92
Hollycroft Gdns. UB7: Sip ... 6C 92
Hollydale Cl. UB5: N'olt ... 4F 59
Hollydale Dr. BR2: Brom ... 3D 172
Hollydale Rd. SE15 ... 1J 121
Hollydene *BR2: Brom* ... *1H 159*
(off Beckenham La.)
SE13 ... 6F 123
SE15 ... 1H 121
Hollydown Way E11 ... 3F 69
Holly Dr. E4 ... 7J 25
Holly Farm Rd. UB2: S'hall ... 5C 94
Hollyfield Av. N11 ... 5J 31
Hollyfield Rd. KT5: Surb ... 7F 151
Holly Gdns. DA7: Bex ... 4J 127
UB7: W Dray ... 2B 92
Holly Gro. HA5: Pinn ... 1C 40
NW9 ... 7J 43
SE15 ... 2F 121
Hollygrove WD23: Bush ... 1C 26
Hollygrove Cl. TW3: Houn ... 4D 112
Holly Hedge Ter. SE13 ... 5F 123
Holly Hill N21 ... 6E 22
NW3 ... 4A 64
Holly Hill Rd. DA8: Erith ... 5H 109
DA17: Belv, Erith ... 5H 109
Holly Ho. TW8: Bford ... 6C 96
W10 ... *4G 81*
(off Hawthorn Wlk.)
Holly Lodge HA1: Harr ... 5H 41
W8 ... *2J 99*
(off Thornwood Gdns.)
Holly Lodge Gdns. N6 ... 2E 64
Holly Lodge Mans. N6 ... 2E 64
Hollymead SM5: Cars ... 3D 166
Holly M. SW10 ... 6A 16 (5A 100)
Holly Mt. NW3 ... 4A 64
Hollymount Cl. SE10 ... 1E 122
Holly Pk. N3 ... 3H 45
N4 ... 7J 47
(not continuous)
Holly Pk. Est. N4 ... 7K 47
Holly Pk. Gdns. N3 ... 3J 45
Holly Pk. Rd. N11 ... 5K 31
W7 ... 1K 95
Holly Pl. *NW3* ... *4A 64*
(off Holly Berry La.)
Holly Rd. E11 ... 7H 51
TW1: Twick ... 1K 131
TW3: Houn ... 4F 113
TW12: Ham H ... 6G 131
W4 ... 4K 97
Holly St. E8 ... 7F 67
Holly Ter. N6 ... 1E 64
N20 ... 2F 31
Holly Tree Cl. SW19 ... 1F 135
Holly Tree Ho. *SE4* ... *3B 122*
(off Brockley Rd.)
Hollytree Pde. *DA14: Sidc* ... *6C 144*
(off Sidcup Hill)
Holly Vw. Cl. NW4 ... 6C 44
Holly Village N6 ... 2F 65
Holly Vs. *W6* ... *3D 98*
(off Wellesley Av.)
Holly Wlk. EN2: Enf ... 3H 23
NW3 ... 4A 64
Holly Way CR4: Mitc ... 4H 155
Hollywood Bowl
Barking ... 3G 89
Finchley ... 7G 31
Surrey Quays ... 3K 103
Hollywood Ct. *SW10* ... *6A 100*
(off Hollywood Ct.)
W5 ... 7F 79
Hollywood Gdns.
UB4: Yead ... 6K 75
Hollywood M. SW10 ... 6A 100
Hollywood Rd. E4 ... 5F 35
SW10 ... 6A 100
Hollywood Way IG8: Wfd G ... 7A 36
Holman Ct. KT17: Ewe ... 7C 164
Holman Ho. *E2* ... *3K 85*
(off Roman Rd.)
Holman Hunt Ho. *W6* ... *5G 99*
(off Field Rd.)
Holman Rd. KT19: Ewe ... 5J 163
SW11 ... 2B 118
Holmbank Dr. TW17: Shep ... 4G 147
Holmbridge Gdns. EN3: Pond E ... 4E 24
Holmbrook *NW1* ... *2G 83*
(off Eversholt St.)
Holmbrook Dr. NW4 ... 5F 45
Holmbury Ct. CR2: S Croy ... 5E 168
SW17 ... 3D 136
SW19 ... 7C 136
Holmbury Gdns. UB3: Hayes ... 1H 93
Holmbury Gro. CR0: Sels ... 7B 170
Holmbury Ho. SE24 ... 5B 120
Holmbury Mnr.
DA14: Sidc ... 4A 144
Holmbury Pk. BR1: Brom ... 7C 142
Holmbury Vw. E5 ... 1H 67
Holmbush Rd. SW15 ... 6G 117
Holmcote Gdns. N5 ... 5C 66
Holm Ct. SE12 ... 3K 141
Holmcroft Ho. E17 ... 4D 50
Holmcroft Way BR2: Brom ... 5D 160
Holmdale Gdns. NW4 ... 5F 45
Holmdale Rd. BR7: Chst ... 5G 143
NW6 ... 5J 63
Holmdale Ter. N15 ... 7E 48
Holmdene N12 ... 5E 30
Holmdene Av. HA2: Harr ... 3F 41
NW7 ... 6H 29
SE24 ... 5C 120
Holmdene Cl. BR3: Beck ... 2E 158
Holmdene Ct. BR1: Brom ... 3C 160
Holmead Rd. SW6 ... 7K 99
Holmebury Cl. WD23: B Hea ... 2D 26
Holme Ct. TW7: Isle ... 3A 114
Holmefield Ho. *W10* ... *4G 81*
(off Hazlewood Cres.)
Holme Ho. *SE15* ... *7H 103*
(off Studholme St.)
Holme Lacey Rd. SE12 ... 6H 123
Holme Rd. E6 ... 1C 88
Holmes Av. E17 ... 3B 50
NW7 ... 5B 30
Holmes Cl. SE22 ... 4G 121
Holmesdale Av. SW14 ... 3H 115
Holmesdale Cl. SE25 ... 3F 157
Holmesdale Ho. *NW6* ... *1J 81*
(off Kilburn Va.)
Holmesdale Rd. CR0: C'don ... 5D 156
DA7: Bex ... 2D 126
N6 ... 7F 47
SE25 ... 5D 156
TW9: Kew ... 1F 115
TW11: Tedd ... 7C 132
Holmesley Rd. SE23 ... 6A 122
Holmes Pl. SW10 ... 6A 100
Holmes Place Health Club
Barbican ... *5C 8*
(off Aldersgate St.)
Croydon ... *3C 168*
Hammersmith ... *4F 99*
(off Hammersmith Rd.)
St Luke's ... *4E 8*
Holmes Rd. NW5 ... 5F 65
SW19 ... 7A 136
TW1: Twick ... 2K 131
Holmes Ter. SE1 ... 6J 13
Holmeswood SM2: Sutt ... 6K 165
Holmeswood Ct. N22 ... 2A 48
Holme Way HA7: Stan ... 6E 26
Holmewood Gdns.
SW2 ... 7K 119

Holmewood Rd. SE25 .... 3E 156
SW2 .... 7J 119
Holmfield Av. NW4 .... 5F 45
Holmfield Ct. NW3 .... 5C 64
Holm Gro. UB10: Hil 7C 56
Holmhurst SE13 .... 6F 123
Holmhurst Rd. DA17: Belv 5H 109
Holmlea Ct. CR0: C'don 4D 168
(off Chatsworth Rd.)
Holmleigh Ct. EN3: Pond E 4D 24
Holmleigh Rd. N16 .... 1E 66
Holmleigh Rd. Est. N16 .... 1E 66
Holm Oak Cl. SW15 .... 6H 117
Holm Oak M. SW4 .... 5J 119
Holmoaks Ho. BR3: Beck 2E 158
Holmsdale Ho. E14 .... 7D 86
(off Poplar High St.)
N11 .... 4A 32
(off Coppies Gro.)
Holmshaw Cl. SE26 .... 4A 140
Holmside Rd. SW12 .... 6E 118
Holmsley Cl. KT3: N Mald 6B 152
Holmsley Ho. SW15 .... 7B 116
(off Tangley Gro.)
Holmstall Av. HA8: Edg 3J 43
Holmstall Pde. HA8: Edg 2J 43
Holm Wlk. SE3 .... 2J 123
Holmwood Cl. HA2: Harr 3G 41
SM2: Cheam 7F 165
UB5: N'olt 6F 59
Holmwood Gdns. N3 .... 2J 45
SM6: Wall 6F 167
Holmwood Gro. NW7 .... 5E 28
Holmwood Rd. IG3: Ilf 2J 71
KT9: Chess 5D 162
SM2: Cheam 7E 164
Holmwood Vs. SE7 .... 5J 105
Holne Chase N2 .... 6A 46
SM4: Mord 6H 153
Holness Rd. E15 .... 6H 69
Holocaust Memorial Garden, The 6F 11
Holroyd Rd. KT10: Clay 7A 162
SW15 .... 4E 116
Holst Ct. SE1 .... 1J 19
(off Westminster Bri. Rd.)
Holstein Way DA18: Erith 3D 108
Holst Mans. SW13 .... 6E 98
Holstock Rd. IG1: Ilf 2G 71
Holsworth Cl. HA2: Harr 5G 41
Holsworthy Sq. WC1 .... 4H 7
Holsworthy Way KT9: Chess 5C 162
Holt, The SM4: Mord 4J 153
SM6: Wall 4G 167
Holt Cl. N10 .... 4E 46
SE28 .... 7B 90
Holt Ct. SE10 .... 6E 104
(off Horseferry Pl.)
Holt Ho. SW2 .... 6A 120
Holton St. E1 .... 4K 85
Holt Rd. E16 .... 1C 106
HA0: Wemb 3B 60
Holtwhite Av. EN2: Enf 2H 23
Holtwhite's Hill EN2: Enf 1G 23
Holwell Pl. HA5: Pinn 4C 40
Holwood Pk. Av. BR6: Farnb 4D 172
Holwood Pl. SW4 .... 4H 119
Holybourne Av. SW15 .... 7C 116
Holyhead Cl. E3 .... 3C 86
E6 .... 5D 88
Holyhead Ct. KT1: King T 4D 150
(off Anglesea Rd.)
Holyoake Ct. SE16 .... 2B 104
Holyoake Ho. W5 .... 4C 78
Holyoake Wlk. N2 .... 3A 46
W5 .... 4C 78
Holyoak Rd. SE11 .... 4B 102
Holyport Rd. SW6 .... 7F 99
Holyrood Av. HA2: Harr 4C 58
Holyrood Ct. NW1 .... 1F 83
(off Gloucester Av.)
Holyrood Gdns. HA8: Edg 3H 43
Holyrood M. E16 .... 1J 105
(off Badminton M.)
Holyrood Rd. EN5: New Bar 6F 21
Holyrood St. SE1 .... 5G 15 (1E 102)
Holywell Cen. EC2 .... 3G 9
(off Phipp St.)
Holywell Cl. BR6: Chels 4K 173
SE3 .... 6J 105
SE16 .... 5H 103
TW19: Stanw 1A 128
Holywell La. EC2 .... 3H 9 (4E 84)
Holywell Row EC2 .... 4G 9 (4E 84)
Holywell Way
TW19: Stanw 1A 128
Homan Ct. N12 .... 4G 31
Homebush Ho. E4 .... 7J 25
Homecedars Ho. WD23: B Hea 1C 26
Home Cl. SM5: Cars 2D 166
UB5: N'olt 3D 76
Home Ct. KT6: Surb 5D 150
Homecroft Rd. N22 .... 1C 48
SE26 .... 5J 139
Home Farm Cl. KT7: T Ditt 7K 149
TW17: Shep 4G 147
Homefarm Rd. W7 .... 6J 77
Home Fld. EN5: Barn 5C 20
Homefield SM4: Mord 4J 153
Homefield Av. IG2: Ilf 5J 53
Homefield Cl. NW10 .... 6J 61
UB4: Yead 4B 76
Homefield Gdns. CR4: Mitc 2A 154
N2 .... 3B 46
Homefield Ho. SE23 .... 3K 139
Homefield M. BR3: Beck 1C 158
Homefield Pk. SM1: Sutt 6K 165
Homefield Rd. BR1: Brom 1A 160
HA0: Wemb 4A 60
HA8: Edg 6E 28
KT12: Walt T 7C 148
SW19 .... 6F 135
W4 .... 5B 98
Homefield St. N1 .... 1G 9 (2E 84)
Homefirs Ho. HA9: Wemb 3F 61
Home Gdns. RM10: Dag 3J 73
Homeheather Ho. IG4: Ilf 5D 52
Homeland Dr. SM2: Sutt 7K 165
Homelands Dr. SE19 .... 7E 138
Home Lea BR6: Chels 5K 173
Homeleigh Ct. SW16 .... 3J 137
Homeleigh Rd. SE15 .... 5K 121
Home Mead HA7: Stan 1C 42
Homemead Rd. BR2: Brom 5D 160
CR0: C'don 6G 155
Home Pk. KT8: E Mos 5C 150
Home Pk. Ct. KT1: King T 4D 150
(off Palace Rd.)
Home Pk. Pde. KT1: Ham W 2D 150
(off High St.)
Home Pk. Rd. SW19 .... 4H 135
Home Pk. Ter. KT1: Ham W 2D 150
(off Hampton Ct. Rd.)
Home Pk. Wlk.
KT1: King T 4D 150
Homer Cl. DA7: Bex 1J 127
Homer Dr. E14 .... 4C 104
Home Rd. SW11 .... 2C 118
Homer Rd. CR0: C'don 6K 157
E9 .... 6A 68
Homer Row W1 .... 6D 4 (5C 82)
Homersham Rd.
KT1: King T 2G 151
Homer St. W1 .... 6D 4 (5C 82)
HOMERTON 5K 67
Homerton Gro. E9 .... 5K 67
Homerton High St. E9 .... 5K 67
Homerton Rd. E9 .... 5A 68
Homerton Row E9 .... 5J 67
Homerton Ter. E9 .... 6J 67
(not continuous)
Homesdale Cl. E11 .... 5J 51
Homesdale Rd. BR1: Brom 4A 160
BR2: Brom 4A 160
BR5: Pet W 7J 161
Homesfield NW11 .... 5J 45
Homestall Rd. SE22 .... 5J 121
Homestead Ct. EN5: New Bar 5D 20
Homestead Paddock N14 .... 5A 22
Homestead Pk. NW2 .... 3B 62
Homestead Rd. RM8: Dag 2F 73
SW6 .... 7H 99
Homesteads, The N11 .... 4A 32
Homewalk Ho. SE26 .... 4H 139
Homewaters Av. TW16: Sun 1H 147
Homewillow Cl. N21 .... 6G 23
Homewood Cl. TW12: Hamp 6D 130
Homewood Cres. BR7: Chst 6J 143
Homewoods SW12 .... 7G 119
Homildon Ho. SE26 .... 3G 139
Honduras St. EC1 .... 3C 8 (4C 84)
Honeybourne Rd. NW6 .... 5K 63
Honeybourne Way
BR5: Pet W 1H 173
Honeybrook Rd. SW12 .... 7G 119
Honey Cl. RM10: Dag 6H 73
Honeycroft Hill UB10: Uxb 7A 56
Honeyden Rd. DA14: Sidc 6E 144
Honey Hill UB10: Uxb 7B 56
Honey La. EC2 .... 1D 14
Honey La. Ho. SW10 .... 6K 99
(off Finborough Rd.)
Honeyman Cl. NW6 .... 7F 63
Honeymead N8 .... 3J 47
(off Campsfield Rd.)
Honeypot Bus. Cen. HA7: Stan 1E 42
Honeypot Cl. NW9 .... 4F 43
Honeypot La. HA7: Stan 7J 27
NW9 .... 1D 42
Honeysett Rd. N17 .... 2F 49
Honeysuckle Cl. UB1: S'hall 7C 76
Honeysuckle Ct. IG1: Ilf 6F 71
IG9: Buck H 3G 37
Honeysuckle Gdns. CR0: C'don 7K 157
Honeysuckle La. N22 .... 2C 48
Honeywell Rd. SW11 .... 6D 118
Honeywood Heritage Cen. 5D 166
Honeywood Rd. NW10 .... 2B 80
TW7: Isle 4A 114
Honeywood Wlk. SM5: Cars 4D 166
Honister Cl. HA7: Stan 1B 42
Honister Gdns. HA7: Stan 7G 27
Honister Pl. HA7: Stan 1B 42
Honiton Gdns. NW7 .... 7A 30
SE15 .... 2J 121
(off Gibbon Rd.)
Honiton Ho. EN3: Pond E 3E 24
Honiton Rd. DA16: Well 2K 125
NW6 .... 2H 81
RM7: Rom 6K 55
Honley Rd. SE6 .... 7D 122
Honnor Gdns. TW7: Isle 2H 113
HONOR OAK 6J 121
Honor Oak Crematorium
SE23 .... 5K 121
HONOR OAK PARK 7A 122
Honor Oak Pk. SE23 .... 6J 121
Honor Oak Ri. SE23 .... 6J 121
Honor Oak Rd. SE23 .... 1J 139
Hood Av. N14 .... 6A 22
SW14 .... 5J 115
Hood Cl. CR0: C'don 1B 168
Hoodcote Gdns. N21 .... 7G 23
Hood Ct. EC4 .... 1K 13
Hood Ho. SE5 .... 7D 102
(off Elmington Est.)
SW1 .... 6C 18
(off Dolphin Sq.)
Hood Point SE16 .... 2B 104
(off Rotherhithe St.)
Hood Rd. SW20 .... 7B 134
Hood Wlk. RM7: Mawney 1H 55
HOOK 5E 162
Hook, The EN5: New Bar 6G 21
Hooke Ho. E3 .... 2A 86
(off Gernon Rd.)
Hookers Rd. E17 .... 3K 49
Hook Farm Rd. BR2: Brom 5B 160
Hookham Ct. SW8 .... 1H 119
Hooking Grn. HA2: Harr 5F 41
HOOK JUNC. 3E 162
Hook La. DA16: Well 4K 125
Hook Ri. Nth. KT6: Surb 3E 162
Hook Ri. Sth. KT6: Surb 3E 162
Hook Ri. Sth. Ind. Pk.
KT6: Surb 3F 163
Hook Rd. KT6: Surb 2E 162
KT9: Chess 5D 162
KT19: Eps, Ewe 7J 163
Hooks Cl. SE15 .... 1H 121
Hooks Hall Dr. RM10: Dag 3J 73
Hookstone Way IG8: Wfd G 7G 37
Hook Wlk. HA8: Edg 6D 28
Hool Cl. NW9 .... 5J 43
Hooper Dr. UB8: Hil 5D 74
Hooper Rd. E16 .... 6J 87
Hooper's Ct. SW3 .... 7E 10 (2D 100)
Hoopers M. W3 .... 1J 97
WD23: Bush 1A 26
Hooper Sq. E1 .... 6G 85
(off Hooper St.)
Hooper St. E1 .... 6G 85
Hoop La. NW11 .... 7H 45
(not continuous)
Hope Cl. IG8: Wfd G 6F 37
N1 .... 6C 66
RM6: Chad H 4D 54
SE12 .... 3K 141
SM1: Sutt 5A 166
TW8: Bford 5E 96
Hope Ct. NW10 .... 3F 81
(off Chamberlayne Rd.)
SE1 .... 5G 103
(off Avocet Cl.)
Hopedale Rd. SE7 .... 6K 105
Hopefield Av. NW6 .... 2G 81
Hope Gdns. W3 .... 2H 97
Hope Ho. CR0: C'don 4E 168
(off Steep Hill)
Hope La. SE9 .... 2F 143
Hope Pk. BR1: Brom 7H 141
Hopes Cl. TW5: Hest 6E 94
Hope Sq. EC2 .... 6G 9
Hope St. SW11 .... 3B 118
Hopetown St. E1 .... 6K 9 (5F 85)
Hopewell St. SE5 .... 7D 102
Hopewell Yd. SE5 .... 7D 102
(off Hopewell St.)
Hope Wharf SE16 .... 2J 103
Hop Gdns. WC2 .... 3E 12 (7J 83)
Hopgood St. W12 .... 1E 98
Hopkins Cl. N10 .... 7K 31
Hopkins Ho. E14 .... 6C 86
(off Canton St.)
Hopkins M. E15 .... 1H 87
Hopkinsons Pl. NW1 .... 1E 82
Hopkins Rd. E10 .... 7D 50
Hopkins St. W1 .... 1B 12 (6G 83)
Hoppers Rd. N13 .... 2F 33
N21 .... 2F 33
Hoppett Rd. E4 .... 2B 36
Hopping La. N1 .... 6B 66
Hoppingwood Av.
KT3: N Mald 3A 152
Hoppner Rd. UB4: Hayes 2F 75
Hop St. SE10 .... 4H 105
Hopton Ct. BR2: Hayes 1K 171
Hopton Gdns. KT3: N Mald 6C 152
Hopton Rd. SE18 .... 3F 107
SW16 .... 5J 137
Hopton's Gdns. SE1 .... 4B 14

Hopton St. SE1 3A 14 (7B 84)
Hoptree Cl. N12 5E 30
Hopwood Cl. SW17 3A 136
Hopwood Rd. SE17 6D 102
Hopwood Wlk. E8 7G 67
Horace Av. RM7: Rush G 1J 73
Horace Rd. E7 4K 69
IG6: Ilf 3G 53
KT1: King T 3F 151
Horatio Ct. SE16 1J 103
(off Rotherhithe St.)
Horatio Ho. E2 2F 85
(off Horatio St.)
W6 5F 99
(off Fulham Pal. Rd.)
Horatio Pl. E14 1E 104
(off Preston's Rd.)
SW19 1J 153
Horatio St. E2 2F 85
Horatius Way CR0: Wadd 5K 167
Horbury Cres. W11 7J 81
Horbury M. W11 7H 81
Horder Rd. SW6 1G 117
Hordle Prom. E. SE15 7F 103
Hordle Prom. Sth. SE15 7F 103
(off Quarley Way)
Horizon Bldg. E14 7C 86
(off Hertsmere Rd.)
Horizon Bus. Cen. N9 2E 34
(off Goodwin Rd.)
Horizon Ct. SM2: Cheam 7G 165
(off Up. Mulgrave Rd.)
Horizon Way SE7 4K 105
Horle Wlk. SE5 2B 120
Horley Cl. DA6: Bex 5G 127
Horley Rd. SE9 4C 142
Hormead Rd. W9 4H 81
Hornbeam Cl. IG1: Ilf 5H 71
IG9: Buck H 3G 37
IG11: Bark 3A 90
NW7 3G 29
SE11 3J 19 (4A 102)
UB5: N'olt 5D 58
Hornbeam Cres. TW8: Bford 7B 96
Hornbeam Gdns. KT3: N Mald 6C 152
Hornbeam Gro. E4 3B 36
Hornbeam Ho. IG9: Buck H 3H 37
Hornbeam La. DA7: Bex 2J 127
Hornbeam Rd. IG9: Buck H 3G 37
UB4: Yead 5A 76
Hornbeam Sq. E3 1B 86
Hornbeams Ri. N11 6K 31
Hornbeam Ter. SM5: Cars 1C 166
Hornbeam Wlk. TW10: Rich 2F 133
Hornbeam Way
BR2: Brom 6E 160
Hornblower Cl. SE16 3A 104
Hornbuckle Cl. HA2: Harr 2H 59
Hornby Cl. NW3 7B 64
Hornby Ho. SE11 7J 19
Horncastle Cl. SE12 7J 123
Horncastle Rd. SE12 7J 123
Hornchurch N17 2D 48
(off Gloucester Rd.)
Hornchurch Cl.
KT2: King T 4D 132
Horndean Cl. SW15 1C 134
Horndon Cl. RM5: Col R 1J 55
Horndon Grn. RM5: Col R 1J 55
Horndon Rd. RM5: Col R 1J 55
Horner Ho. N1 1E 84
(off Whitmore Est.)
Horner La. CR4: Mitc 2B 154
Horne Rd. TW17: Shep 4C 146
Hornet Way E6 5H 89
Horne Way SW15 2E 116
Hornfair Rd. SE7 6A 106
Horniman Dr. SE23 1H 139
Horniman Mus. 1H 139
Horning Cl. SE9 4C 142
Horn La. IG8: Wfd G 6D 36
SE10 5J 105
(not continuous)
W3 7J 79
(not continuous)
Horn Link Way SE10 4J 105
HORN PARK 5K 123
Horn Pk. Cl. SE12 5K 123
Hornpark La. SE12 5K 123
Hornscroft Cl. IG11: Bark 7J 71
Horns End Pl. HA5: Eastc 4A 40
HORNSEY 4J 47
Hornsey N8 4J 47
Hornsey Club, The 5H 47
Hornsey La. N6 1F 65
Hornsey La. Est. N19 7H 47
Hornsey La. Gdns. N6 7G 47
Hornsey Pk. Rd. N8 3K 47
Hornsey Ri. N19 7H 47
Hornsey Ri. Gdns. N19 7H 47
Hornsey Rd. N7 1J 65
N19 1J 65
Hornsey St. N7 5K 65
HORNSEY VALE 5K 47
Hornshay St. SE15 6J 103
Horns Rd. IG2: Ilf 5G 53
IG6: Ilf 4H 53
Hornton Ct. W8 2J 99
(off Kensington High St.)
Hornton Pl. W8 2K 99
Hornton St. W8 2J 99
Horsa Rd. DA8: Erith 7H 109
SE12 7A 124
Horse & Dolphin Yd. W1 2D 12
Horsebridge Cl. RM9: Dag 1E 90
Horsecroft Rd. HA8: Edg 7E 28
Horse Fair KT1: King T 2D 150
Horseferry Pl. SE10 6E 104
Horseferry Rd. E14 7A 86
SW1 2C 18 (3H 101)
Horseferry Rd. Est. SW1 2C 18
Horseguards Av. SW1 5E 12 (1J 101)
Horse Guards Parade 5E 12 (1H 101)
Horse Guards Rd. SW1 5D 12 (1H 101)
Horse Leaze E6 6E 88
Horsell Rd. BR5: St P 7B 144
N5 5A 66
(not continuous)
Horselydown La. SE1 6J 15 (2F 103)
Horselydown Mans. SE1 6J 15
(off Lafone St.)
Horsemongers M. SE1 7D 14
Horsenden Av. UB6: G'frd 5K 59
Horsenden Cres. UB6: G'frd 5K 59
Horsenden La. Nth. UB6: G'frd 6J 59
Horsenden La. Sth. UB6: G'frd 1A 78
Horse Ride SW1 5C 12 (1G 101)
Horseshoe Cl. E14 5E 104
NW2 2D 62
Horseshoe Ct. EC1 3B 8
(off Brewhouse Yd.)
Horse Shoe Cres.
UB5: N'olt 2E 76
Horseshoe Dr. UB8: Hil 6C 74
Horse Shoe Grn. SM1: Sutt 2K 165
Horseshoe La. EN2: Enf 3H 23
N20 1A 30
Horseshoe M. SW2 4J 119
Horseshoe Wharf SE1 4E 14
(off Clink St.)
Horse Yd. N1 1B 84
(off Essex Rd.)
Horsfeld Gdns. SE9 5C 124
Horsfeld Rd. SE9 5B 124
Horsfield Ho. N1 7C 66
(off Northampton St.)
Horsford Rd. SW2 5K 119
Horsham Av. N12 5H 31
Horsham Ct. N17 1G 49
(off Lansdowne Rd.)
Horsham Rd. DA6: Bex 5G 127
TW14: Bedf 6E 110
Horsley Dr. CR0: New Ad 7E 170
KT2: King T 5D 132
Horsley Rd. BR1: Brom 1K 159
E4 2K 35
Horsley St. SE17 6D 102
Horsman Ho. SE5 6C 102
(off Bethwin Rd.)
Horsman St. SE5 6C 102
Horsmonden Cl. BR6: Orp 7K 161
Horsmonden Rd. SE4 5B 122
Hortensia Ho. SW10 7A 100
(off Gunter Gro.)
Hortensia Rd. SW10 7A 100
Horticultural Pl. W4 5K 97
Horton Av. NW2 4G 63
Horton Bri. Rd. UB7: Yiew 1B 92
Horton Cl. UB7: Yiew 1C 92
Horton Ho. SE15 6J 103
SW8 7K 101
W6 5G 99
(off Field Rd.)
Horton Ind. Pk. UB7: Yiew 1B 92
Horton La. KT19: Eps 7H 163
Horton Pde. UB7: Yiew 1A 92
Horton Rd. E8 6H 67
SL3: Poyle 6A 174
TW19: Stan M 7A 174
UB7: Yiew 1A 92
UB11: Yiew 1A 92
Horton Rd. Ind. Est. UB7: Yiew 1B 92
Horton St. SE13 3D 122
Horton Way CR0: C'don 5K 157
Hortus Rd. E4 2K 35
UB2: S'hall 2D 94
Horwood Ho. E2 3H 85
(off Pott St.)
NW8 3D 4
(off Paveley St.)
Hosack Rd. SW17 2E 136
Hoser Av. SE12 2J 141
Hosier La. EC1 6A 8 (5B 84)
Hoskins Cl. E16 6A 88
UB3: Harl 5H 93
Hoskins St. SE10 5F 105
Hospital Bri. Rd.
TW2: Twick, Whitt 7F 113
HOSPITAL BRIDGE RDBT. 2F 131
Hospital Rd. E9 5K 67
TW3: Houn 3E 112
Hospital Way SE13 7F 123
Hotham Cl. KT8: W Mole 3E 148
Hotham Rd. SW15 3E 116
SW19 7A 136
Hotham Rd. M. SW19 7A 136
Hotham St. E15 1G 87
Hothfield Pl. SE16 3J 103
Hotspur Ind. Est. N17 6C 34
Hotspur Rd. UB5: N'olt 2E 76
Hotspur St. SE11 5J 19 (4A 102)
Houblon Rd. TW10: Rich 5E 114
Houghton Cl. E8 6F 67
TW12: Hamp 6C 130
Houghton Rd. N15 4F 49
Houghton Sq. SW9 2J 119
(off Clapham Rd.)
Houghton St.
WC2 1H 13 (6K 83)
(not continuous)
Houlder Cres. CR0: Wadd 6B 168
Houndsden Rd. N21 6E 22
Houndsditch EC3 7H 9 (6E 84)
Houndsfield Rd. N9 7C 24
HOUNSLOW 3F 113
Hounslow and District Indoor Bowls Club 2D 112
(off Sutton La.)
Hounslow Av. TW3: Houn 5F 113
Hounslow Bus. Pk. TW3: Houn 4E 112
Hounslow Cen. TW3: Houn 3F 113
Hounslow Gdns. TW3: Houn 5F 113
Hounslow Heath Nature Reserve 6B 112
Hounslow Manor Sports Hall 2G 113
Hounslow Rd. TW2: Whitt 6F 113
TW13: Hanw 4B 130
TW14: Felt 1K 129
Hounslow Urban Farm 5J 111
HOUNSLOW WEST 2C 112
Household Cavalry Mus., The 5D 12 (1H 101)
Houseman Way SE5 7D 102
Houses of Parliament 1F 19 (3J 101)
Houston Bus. Pk. UB4: Yead 1A 94
Houston Pl. KT10: Esh 7H 149
Houston Rd. KT6: Surb 6B 150
SE23 2A 140
Houstoun Ct. TW5: Hest 7D 94
Hove Av. E17 5B 50
Hoveden Rd. NW2 5G 63
Hove Gdns. SM1: Sutt 1K 165
Hove St. SE15 7J 103
(off Culmore Rd.)
Hoveton Rd. SE28 6C 90
Hoveton Way IG6: Ilf 1F 53
Howard Av. DA5: Bexl 1C 144
Howard Bldg. SW8 7J 17 (6F 101)
Howard Cl. N11 2K 31
NW2 4G 63
TW12: Hamp 7G 131
TW16: Sun 6H 129
W3 6H 79
WD23: B Hea 1D 26
Howard Ct. IG11: Bark 1H 89
Howard Ho. E16 1K 105
(off Wesley Av.)
SE8 6B 104
(off Evelyn St.)
SW1 6B 18
(off Dolphin Sq.)
SW9 3B 120
(off Barrington Rd.)
W1 4K 5
(off Cleveland St.)
Howard M. N5 4B 66
Howard Rd. BR1: Brom 7J 141
E6 2D 88
E11 3G 69
E17 3C 50
IG1: Ilf 4F 71
IG11: Bark 1H 89
KT3: N Mald 3A 152
KT5: Surb 6F 151
N15 6E 48
N16 4D 66
NW2 4F 63
SE20 1J 157
SE25 5G 157
TW7: Isle 3K 113
UB1: S'hall 6F 77
Howards Cl. HA5: Pinn 2K 39
Howards Crest Cl.
BR3: Beck 2E 158
Howard's La. SW15 4D 116
Howards Rd. E13 3J 87
Howard St. KT7: T Ditt 7B 150
Howard Wlk. N2 4A 46
Howard Way EN5: Barn 5A 20
Howarth Rd. SE2 5A 108
Howberry Cl. HA8: Edg 6J 27
Howberry Rd. CR7: Thor H 1D 156
HA7: Stan 6J 27
HA8: Edg 6J 27
Howbury Rd. SE15 3J 121
Howcroft Cres. N3 7D 30
Howcroft La. UB6: G'frd 3H 77
Howden Cl. SE28 7D 90
Howden Rd. SE25 2F 157
Howden St. SE15 3G 121
Howe Cl. RM7: Mawney 1G 55

Howell Cl. RM6: Chad H 5D 54
Howell Ct. E10 7D 50
Howell Wlk. SE1 4B 102
Howerd Way SE18 1C 124
(not continuous)
Howes Cl. N3 3J 45
Howeth Ct. N11 6J 31
(off Ribblesdale Av.)
Howfield Pl. N17 3F 49
Howgate Rd. SW14 3K 115
Howick Pl. SW1 2B 18 (3G 101)
Howie St. SW11 7C 100
Howitt Cl. N16 4E 66
NW3 6C 64
Howitt Rd. NW3 6C 64
Howland Est. SE16 3J 103
Howland Ho. SW16 3J 137
Howland M. E. W1 5B 6 (5G 83)
Howland St. W1 5A 6 (5G 83)
Howland Way SE16 2A 104
Howletts La. HA4: Ruis 5E 38
Howlett's Rd. SE24 6C 120
Howley Pl. W2 5A 4 (5A 82)
Howley Rd. CR0: C'don 3B 168
Howsman Rd. SW13 6C 98
Howson Rd. SE4 4A 122
Howson Ter. TW10: Rich 6E 114
How's St. E2 2F 85
Howton Pl. WD23: B Hea 1C 26
HOXTON 2E 84
Hoxton Hall Theatre 2E 84
(off Hoxton St.)
Hoxton Mkt. N1 2G 9
Hoxton Sq. N1 2G 9 (3E 84)
Hoxton St. N1 2H 9 (1E 84)
Hoylake Cres. UB10: Ick 2C 56
Hoylake Gdns. CR4: Mitc 3G 155
HA4: Ruis 1K 57
Hoylake Rd. W3 6A 80
Hoyland Cl. SE15 7H 103
Hoyle Rd. SW17 5C 136
Hoy St. E16 6H 87
HQS Wellington 3J 13
Hub, The 1F 5 (2D 82)
Hubbard Ct. IG10: Lough 1H 37
Hubbard Dr. KT9: Chess 6D 162
Hubbard Rd. SE27 4C 138
Hubbards Cl. UB8: Hil 6D 74
Hubbard St. E15 1G 87
Huberd Ho. SE1 7F 15
(off Manciple St.)
Hubert Cl. SW19 1A 154
(off Nelson Gro. Rd.)
Hubert Gro. SW9 3J 119
Hubert Ho. NW8 4C 4
(off Ashbridge St.)
Hubert Rd. E6 3B 88
Hucknall Ct. NW8 3A 4
(off Cunningham Pl.)
Huddart St. E3 5B 86
(not continuous)
Huddleston Cl. E2 2J 85
Huddlestone Rd. E7 4H 69
NW2 6D 62
Huddleston Rd. N7 3G 65
Hudson NW9 1B 44
(off Near Acre)
Hudson Apartments N8 3K 47
Hudson Bldg. E1 6K 9
(off Chicksand St.)
Hudson Cl. E15 1J 87
W12 7D 80
Hudson Ct. E14 5C 104
(off Maritime Quay)
Hudson Gdns. BR6: Chels 6K 173
Hudson Ho. SW10 7A 100
(off Hortensia Rd.)
W11 6G 81
(off Ladbroke Gro.)
Hudson Pl. SE18 5G 107
Hudson Rd. DA7: Bex 2F 127
UB3: Harl 6F 93
Hudson's Pl. SW1 3A 18 (4F 101)
Hudson Way N9 3D 34
NW2 3F 63
Huggin Ct. EC4 2D 14
Huggin Hill EC4 2D 14 (7C 84)
Huggins Pl. SW2 1K 137
Hughan Rd. E15 5F 69
Hugh Astor Ct. SE1 7B 14
(off Keyworth St.)
Hugh Clark Ho. W13 1A 96
(off Singapore Rd.)
Hugh Cubitt Ho. N1 2K 83
(off Collier St.)
Hugh Dalton Av. SW6 6H 99
Hughenden Av. HA3: Kent 5B 42
Hughenden Gdns. UB5: Yead 3A 76
(not continuous)
Hughenden Ho. NW8 3C 4
Hughenden Rd. KT4: Wor Pk 7C 152
Hughendon EN5: New Bar 4E 20
Hughendon Ter. E15 4E 68
Hughes Cl. N12 5F 31
Hughes Ct. N7 5H 65
Hughes Hall WC1 3J 83
(off Cartwright Gdns.)
Hughes Ho. E2 3J 85
(off Sceptre Ho.)
SE8 6C 104
(off Benbow St.)
SE17 4B 102
(off Peacock St.)
Hughes Mans. E1 4G 85
Hughes Parry Hall WC1 3J 83
(off Cartwright Gdns.)
Hughes Rd. TW15: Ashf 6E 128
UB3: Hayes 7K 75
Hughes Ter. E16 5H 87
(off Clarkson Rd.)
SW9 3B 120
(off Styles Gdns.)
Hughes Wlk. CR0: C'don 7C 156
Hugh Gaitskell Cl. SW6 6H 99
Hugh Gaitskell Ho. N16 2F 67
Hugh Herland Ho. KT1: King T 3E 150
Hugh M. SW1 4K 17 (4F 101)
Hugh Platt Ho. E2 2H 85
(off Patriot Sq.)
Hugh St. SW1 4K 17 (4F 101)
Hugo Ho. SW1 1F 17
(off Sloane St.)
Hugon Rd. SW6 3K 117
Hugo Rd. N19 4G 65
Huguenot Pl. E1 5K 9 (5F 85)
SW18 5A 118
Huguenot Sq. SE15 3H 121
Hullbridge M. N1 1D 84
Hull Cl. SE16 2K 103
Hull Pl. E16 1G 107
Hull St. EC1 2C 8 (3C 84)
Hulme Pl. SE1 7D 14 (2C 102)
Hulse Av. IG11: Bark 6H 71
RM7: Mawney 1H 55
Humber Cl. UB7: W Dray 1A 92
Humber Ct. W7 6H 77
(off Hobbayne Rd.)
Humber Dr. W10 4F 81
Humber Rd. NW2 2D 62
SE3 6H 105
Humberstone Rd. E13 3A 88
Humberton Cl. E9 5A 68
Humber Trad. Est. NW2 2D 62
Humbolt Rd. W6 6G 99
Hume Ct. N1 7B 66
(off Hawes St.)
Hume Ho. W11 1F 99
(off Queensdale Cres.)
Humes Av. W7 3J 95
Hume Ter. E16 5K 87
Hume Way HA4: Ruis 6J 39
Humphrey Cl. IG5: Ilf 1D 52
Humphrey St. SE1 5F 103
Humphries Cl. RM9: Dag 4F 73
Hundred Acre NW9 2B 44
Hungerdown E4 1K 35
Hungerford Ho. SW1 7B 18
(off Churchill Gdns.)
Hungerford La. WC2 4F 13
(not continuous)
Hungerford Rd. N7 6H 65
Hungerford St. E1 6H 85
Hunsdon Cl. RM9: Dag 6E 72
Hunsdon Rd. SE14 7K 103
Hunslett St. E2 3J 85
Hunstanton Ho. NW1 5D 4
(off Cosway St.)
Hunston Rd. SM4: Mord 1K 165
Hunt Cl. W11 1F 99
Hunt Ct. N14 7A 22
RM7: Rush G 6K 55
(off Union Rd.)
UB5: N'olt 2B 76
(off Gallery Gdns.)
Hunter Cl. SE1 3D 102
SM6: Wall 7J 167
Hunter Ho. SE1 7B 14
(off King James St.)
SW5 5J 99
(off Old Brompton Rd.)
SW8 7H 101
(off Fount St.)
TW13: Felt 1J 129
(off Lemon Gro.)
WC1 3F 7
(off Hunter St.)
Hunterian Mus., The 7H 7
(off Portugal St.)
Hunter Lodge W9 5J 81
(off Admiral Wlk.)
Hunter Rd. CR7: Thor H 3D 156
IG1: Ilf 5F 71
SW20 1E 152
Hunters Cl. DA5: Bexl 3K 145
SW12 1E 136
Hunters Ct. TW9: Rich 5D 114
Hunters Gro. BR6: Farnb 4G 173
HA3: Kent 4C 42
UB3: Hayes 1J 93
Hunters Hall Rd. RM10: Dag 4G 73
Hunters Hill HA4: Ruis 3A 58
Hunters Mdw. SE19 4E 138
Hunter's Rd. KT9: Chess 3E 162
Hunters Sq. RM10: Dag 4G 73
Hunter St. WC1 3F 7 (4J 83)
Hunters Way CR0: C'don 4E 168
EN2: Enf 1F 23
Hunter Wlk. E13 2J 87
Huntingdon Cl. CR4: Mitc 3J 155
UB5: N'olt 6E 58
Huntingdon Gdns.
KT4: Wor Pk 3E 164
W4 7J 97
Huntingdon Rd. N2 3C 46
N9 2D 34
Huntingdon St. E16 6H 87
N1 7K 65
Huntingfield CR0: Sels 7B 170
Huntingfield Rd. SW15 4C 116
Hunting Ga. Cl. EN2: Enf 3F 23
Hunting Ga. Dr. KT9: Chess 7E 162
Hunting Ga. M. SM1: Sutt 3K 165
TW2: Twick 1J 131
Huntings Farm IG1: Ilf 2J 71
Huntings Rd. RM10: Dag 6G 73
Huntley Cl. TW19: Stanw 7A 110
Huntley St. WC1 4B 6 (4G 83)
Huntley Way SW20 2C 152
Huntly Dr. N3 6D 30
Huntly Rd. SE25 4E 156
Hunton St. E1 4K 9 (5G 85)
Hunt Rd. UB2: S'hall 3E 94
Hunt's Cl. SE3 2J 123
Hunt's Ct. WC2 3D 12 (7H 83)
Hunts La. E15 2E 86
Huntsmans Cl. TW13: Felt 4K 129
Huntsman St. SE17 4E 102
Hunts Mead EN3: Enf H 3E 24
Huntsmead Cl. BR7: Chst 7D 142
Huntsmoor Rd. KT19: Ewe 5K 163
Huntspill St. SW17 3A 136
Hunts Slip Rd. SE21 3E 138
Huntsworth M. NW1 3E 4 (4D 82)
Hurdwick Ho. NW1 2G 83
(off Harrington Sq.)
Hurdwick Pl. NW1 2G 83
(off Hampstead Rd.)
Hurleston Ho. SE8 5B 104
Hurley Ct. W5 6C 78
Hurley Cres. SE16 2K 103
Hurley Ho.
SE11 4K 19 (4B 102)
Hurley Rd. UB6: G'frd 6F 77
HURLINGHAM 3K 117
Hurlingham Bus. Pk. SW6 3J 117
Hurlingham Club, The 3J 117
Hurlingham Ct. SW6 3H 117
Hurlingham Gdns. SW6 3H 117
Hurlingham Retail Pk. SW6 3K 117
Hurlingham Rd. DA7: Bex 7F 109
SW6 2H 117
Hurlingham Sq. SW6 3J 117
Hurlingham Stadium 3H 117
Hurlock St. N5 3B 66
Hurlstone Rd. SE25 5E 156
Hurn Ct. TW4: Houn 2B 112
Hurn Ct. Rd. TW4: Houn 2B 112
Huron Cl. BR6: Chels 6J 173
Huron Rd. SW17 2E 136
Huron University 1B 16 (3B 100)
Hurren Cl. SE3 3G 123
Hurricane Rd. SM6: Wall 7J 167
Hurricane Trad. Cen. NW9 1C 44
Hurry Cl. E15 7G 69
Hurst Av. E4 4H 35
N6 6G 47
Hurstbourne KT10: Clay 6A 162
Hurstbourne Gdns. IG11: Bark 6J 71
Hurstbourne Ho. SW15 6B 116
(off Tangley Gro.)
Hurstbourne Rd. SE23 1A 140
Hurst Cl. BR2: Hayes 1H 171
E4 3H 35
KT9: Chess 5G 163
NW11 6K 45
UB5: N'olt 6D 58
Hurstcombe IG9: Buck H 2D 36
Hurst Ct. DA15: Sidc 2A 144
E6 5B 88
(off Tollgate Rd.)
IG8: Wfd G 6E 36
(off Snakes La.)
Hurstcourt Rd. SM1: Sutt 2K 165
Hurstdene Av. BR2: Hayes 1H 171
Hurstdene Gdns. N15 7E 48
Hurstfield BR2: Brom 5J 159
Hurstfield Cres. UB4: Hayes 4G 75
Hurstfield Rd. KT8: W Mole 3E 148
Hurst Gro. KT12: Walt T 7H 147
Hurst Ho. WC1 1H 7
(off Penton Ri.)
Hurst La. KT8: E Mos 4G 149
SE2 5D 108
Hurst La. Est. SE2 5D 108
Hurstleigh Gdns. IG5: Ilf 1D 52
Hurstmead Ct. HA8: Edg 4C 28
HURST PARK 2G 149
Hurst Pl. HA6: Nwood 1D 38
Hurst Pool 3F 149
Hurst Ri. EN5: New Bar 3D 20

Hurst Rd. CR0: C'don 5D **168**
DA5: Bexl 1D **144**
DA8: Erith 1J **127**
DA15: Bexl, Sidc 2A **144**
E17 .... 3D **50**
IG9: Buck H 1G **37**
KT8: W Mole, E Mos 3F **149**
KT12: Walt T 5A **148**
N21 .... 1F **33**
Hurst Springs DA5: Bexl 1E **144**
Hurst St. SE24 .... 6B **120**
Hurstview Grange CR2: S Croy 7B **168**
Hurst Vw. Rd. CR2: S Croy 7E **168**
Hurst Way CR2: S Croy 6E **168**
Hurstway Rd. W11 .... 7F **81**
Hurstway Wlk. W11 .... 7F **81**
Hurstwood Av. DA5: Bexl 1E **144**
E18 .... 4K **51**
Hurstwood Ct. N12 .... 6H **31**
NW11 .... *4H 45*
(off Finchley Rd.)
Hurstwood Dr. BR1: Brom 3D **160**
Hurstwood Rd. NW11 .... 4G **45**
Hurtwood Rd. KT12: Walt T 7D **148**
Husborne Ho. *SE8* *4A 104*
(off Chilton Gro.)
Huson Cl. NW3 .... 7C **64**
Hussain Cl. HA1: Harr 4K **59**
Hussars Cl. TW4: Houn 3C **112**
Husseywell Cres. BR2: Hayes 1J **171**
Hutchings St. E14 .... 2C **104**
Hutchings Wlk. NW11 .... 4K **45**
Hutchings Wharf *E14* *2C 104*
(off Hutchings St.)
Hutchins Cl. E15 .... 7E **68**
Hutchinson Ct. RM6: Chad H 4D **54**
Hutchinson Ho. NW3 .... 7D **64**
SE14 .... 7J **103**
Hutchinson Ter. HA9: Wemb 3D **60**
Hutchins Rd. SE28 .... 7A **90**
Hutton Cl. IG8: Wfd G 6E **36**
UB6: G'frd 5H **59**
Hutton Ct. *N4* *1K 65*
(off Victoria Rd.)
N9 .... *7D 24*
(off Tramway Av.)
W5 .... 5B **78**
Hutton Gdns. HA3: Hrw W 7B **26**
Hutton Gro. N12 .... 5E **30**
Hutton La. HA3: Hrw W 7B **26**
Hutton M. SW15 .... 5D **116**
Hutton Row HA8: Edg 7D **28**
Hutton St. EC4 .... 2K **13** (6B **84**)
Hutton Wlk. HA3: Hrw W 7B **26**
Huxbear St. SE4 .... 5B **122**
Huxley Cl. UB5: N'olt 2C **76**
UB8: Cowl 4A **74**
Huxley Dr. RM6: Chad H 7B **54**
Huxley Gdns. NW10 .... 3F **79**
Huxley Ho. *NW8* *4B 4*
(off Fisherton St.)
Huxley Pde. N18 .... 5J **33**
Huxley Pl. N13 .... 3G **33**
Huxley Rd. DA16: Well 3K **125**
E10 .... 2E **68**
N18 .... 4J **33**
Huxley Sayze N18 .... 5J **33**
Huxley Sth. N18 .... 5J **33**
Huxley St. W10 .... 3G **81**
Hyacinth Cl. IG1: Ilf 6F **71**
TW12: Hamp 6E **130**
Hyacinth Dr. UB10: Uxb 7A **56**
Hyacinth Rd. SW15 .... 1C **134**
HYDE, THE **5B 44**
Hyde, The NW9 .... 4A **44**
(not continuous)
Hyde Cl. E13 .... 2J **87**
EN5: Barn 3C **20**
TW15: Ashf 6G **129**
Hyde Ct. N20 .... 3G **31**
Hyde Cres. NW9 .... 5A **44**
Hyde Est. Rd. NW9 .... 5B **44**
Hyde Farm M. SW12 .... 1H **137**
Hydefield Cl. N21 .... 1J **33**
Hydefield Ct. N9 .... 2K **33**
Hyde Ho. TW3: Houn 3G **113**
W13 .... *1A 96*
(off Singapore Rd.)
Hyde Ind. Est., The NW9 .... 5B **44**
Hyde La. SW11 .... 1C **118**
Hyde Pk. .... **4D 10 (1C 100)**
Hyde Pk. Av. N21 .... 2H **33**
Hyde Pk. Barracks **7D 10**
HYDE PARK CORNER **2F 101**
Hyde Pk. Cnr. W1 .... 6H **11** (2E **100**)
Hyde Pk. Cres. W2 .... 1C **10** (6C **82**)
Hyde Pk. Gdns. N21 .... 1H **33**
W2 .... 2B **10** (7B **82**)
Hyde Pk. Gdns. M. W2 .... 2B **10** (7B **82**)
Hyde Pk. Ga. SW7 .... 2A **100**
(not continuous)
Hyde Pk. Ga. M. SW7 .... 2A **100**
Hyde Pk. Mans. *NW1* *6C 4*
(off Cabbell St., not continuous)
Hyde Pk. Pl. W2 .... 2D **10** (7C **82**)
Hyde Pk. Sq. W2 .... 1C **10** (6C **82**)
Hyde Pk. Sq. M. W2 .... 1C **10**
Hyde Pk. St. W2 .... 1C **10** (6C **82**)
Hyde Pk. Towers W2 .... 7A **82**
Hyderabad Way E15 .... 7G **69**
Hyde Rd. DA7: Bex 2F **127**
N1 .... 1E **84**
TW10: Rich 5F **115**
Hydeside Gdns. N9 .... 2A **34**
Hyde's Pl. N1 .... 7B **66**
Hyde St. SE8 .... 6C **104**
Hyde Ter. TW15: Ashf 6G **129**
Hydethorpe Av. N9 .... 2A **34**
Hydethorpe Rd. SW12 .... 1G **137**
Hyde Va. SE10 .... 7E **104**
Hyde Wlk. SM4: Mord 7J **153**
Hyde Way N9 .... 2A **34**
UB3: Harl 4H **93**
Hydon Ct. N11 .... 5J **31**
Hydra Bldg., The EC1 .... 2K **7**
Hylands Rd. E17 .... 2F **51**
Hylton St. SE18 .... 4K **107**
Hyndewood SE23 .... 3K **139**
Hyndman Ho. *RM10: Dag* *3G 73*
(off Kershaw Rd.)
Hyndman St. SE15 .... 6H **103**
Hynton Rd. RM8: Dag 2C **72**
Hyperion Ho. *E3* *2A 86*
(off Arbery Rd.)
SW2 .... 6K **119**
Hyrstdene CR2: S Croy 4B **168**
Hyson Rd. SE16 .... 5H **103**
Hythe Av. DA7: Bex 7E **108**
Hythe Cl. N18 .... 4B **34**
Hythe Ho. *SE16* *2J 103*
(off Swan Rd.)
W6 .... *4E 98*
(off Shepherd's Bush Rd.)
Hythe Rd. CR7: Thor H 2D **156**
NW10 .... 3B **80**
Hythe Rd. Ind. Est. NW10 .... 3C **80**

I

Ian Bowater Ct. *N1* *1F 9*
(off East Rd.)
Ian Ct. SE23 .... 2J **139**
Ian Sq. EN3: Enf H 1E **24**
Ibberton Ho. *SW8* *7K 101*
(off Meadow Rd.)
W14 .... *3G 99*
(off Russell Rd.)
Ibbotson Av. E16 .... 6H **87**
Ibbott St. E1 .... 4J **85**
Iberia Ho. N19 .... 7H **47**
Iberian Av. SM6: Bedd 4H **167**
Ibex Ho. *E15* *5G 69*
(off Forest La.)
Ibis Ct. *SE8* *6B 104*
(off Edward Pl.)
Ibis La. W4 .... 1J **115**
Ibis Way UB4: Yead 6B **76**
Ibrox Ct. IG9: Buck H 2F **37**
Ibscott Cl. RM10: Dag 6J **73**
Ibsley Gdns. SW15 .... 1C **134**
Ibsley Way EN4: Cockf 5H **21**
ICA Cinema **4D 12**
(off Carlton Ho. Ter.)
ICA Theatre **4D 12**
(off Carlton Ho. Ter.)
Iceland Rd. E3 .... 1C **86**
Iceland Wharf SE8 .... 4A **104**
Iceni Ct. IG9: Buck H 1E **36**
Ice Wharf N1 .... 2J **83**
Ice Wharf Marina *N1* *2J 83*
(off New Wharf Rd.)
Ice Works, The *NW1* *7F 65*
(off Jamestown Rd.)
Ickburgh Est. E5 .... 2H **67**
Ickburgh Rd. E5 .... 3H **67**
ICKENHAM **3D 56**
Ickenham Cl. HA4: Ruis 2F **57**
Ickenham Grn. UB10: Ick 1D **56**
Ickenham Rd. HA4: Ruis 2E **56**
Ickleton Rd. SE9 .... 4C **142**
Icknield Dr. IG2: Ilf 5F **53**
Icknield Ho. *SW3* *5D 16*
(off Cale St.)
Ickworth Pk. Rd. E17 .... 4A **50**
Icon Apartments *SE1* *7G 15*
(off Cluny Pl.)
Icona Point *E15* *1E 86*
(off Warton Rd.)
Idaho Bldg. *SE10* *1D 122*
(off Deal's Gateway)
Ida Rd. N15 .... 4D **48**
Ida St. E14 .... 6E **86**
(not continuous)
Iden Cl. BR2: Brom 3G **159**
Idlecombe Rd. SW17 .... 6E **136**
Idmiston Rd. E15 .... 4H **69**
KT4: Wor Pk 7B **152**
SE27 .... 3C **138**
Idmiston Sq. KT4: Wor Pk 7B **152**
Idol La. EC3 .... 3G **15** (7E **84**)
Idonia St. SE8 .... 7C **104**
Iffley Cl. UB8: Uxb 7A **56**
Iffley Rd. W6 .... 3D **98**
Ifield Ho. *SE17* *5E 102*
(off Madron St.)
Ifield Rd. SW10 .... 6K **99**
Ifor Evans Pl. E1 .... 4K **85**
Ightham Ho. *BR3: Beck* *7B 140*
(off Bethersden Cl.)
SE17 .... *4E 102*
(off Beckway St.)
Ightham Rd. DA8: Erith 7G **109**
Ikon Ho. *E1* *7J 85*
(off Devonport St.)
Ilbert St. W10 .... 3F **81**
Ilchester Gdns. W2 .... 7K **81**
Ilchester Mans. *W8* *3J 99*
(off Abingdon Rd.)
Ilchester Pl. W14 .... 3H **99**
Ilchester Rd. RM8: Dag 5B **72**
Ildersly Gro. SE21 .... 2D **138**
Ilderton Rd. SE15 .... 5J **103**
SE16 .... 5J **103**
Ilderton Wharf *SE15* *6J 103*
(off Rollins St.)
Ilex Cl. TW16: Sun 2A **148**
Ilex Rd. NW10 .... 6B **62**
Ilex Way SW16 .... 5A **138**
ILFORD **3F 71**
Ilford Hill IG1: Ilf 3E **70**
Ilford Ho. *N1* *6D 66*
(off Dove Rd.)
Ilford La. IG1: Bark, Ilf 3F **71**
Ilford Pools **2J 71**
Ilfracombe Flats *SE1* *6D 14*
(off Marshalsea Rd.)
Ilfracombe Gdns. RM6: Chad H 7B **54**
Ilfracombe Rd. BR1: Brom 3H **141**
Iliffe St. SE17 .... 5B **102**
Iliffe Yd. *SE17* *5B 102*
(off Crampton St.)
Ilkeston Ct. *E5* *4K 67*
(off Overbury St.)
Ilkley Cl. SE19 .... 6D **138**
Ilkley Rd. E16 .... 5A **88**
Illingworth Cl. CR4: Mitc 3B **154**
Illingworth Way EN1: Enf 5K **23**
Ilmington Rd. HA3: Kent 6D **42**
Ilminster Gdns. SW11 .... 4C **118**
Ilsley Ct. SW8 .... 2G **119**
Imani Mans. SW11 .... 2B **118**
IMAX National Film Theatre .... **5J 13 (1A 102)**
Imber Cl. N14 .... 7B **22**
Imber Ct. Trad. Est. KT8: E Mos 6H **149**
Imber Cross KT7: T Ditt 6K **149**
Imber Gro. KT10: Esh 7H **149**
Imber Pk. Rd. KT10: Esh 7H **149**
Imber St. N1 .... 1D **84**
Impact Bus. Pk. UB6: G'frd 2B **78**
Impact Ct. SE20 .... 2H **157**
Imperial Av. N16 .... 4E **66**
Imperial Cl. HA2: Harr 6E **40**
Imperial College of Science, Technology & Medicine .... **1A 16 (3B 100)**
Imperial Coll. Rd. SW7 .... 2A **16** (3B **100**)
Imperial Ct. HA2: Harr 7E **40**
N6 .... 6G **47**
N20 .... 3F **31**
NW8 .... *2C 82*
(off Prince Albert Rd.)
SE11 .... 6J **19** (5A **102**)
Imperial Cres. SW6 .... 2A **118**
Imperial Dr. HA2: Harr 7E **40**
Imperial Gdns. CR4: Mitc 3F **155**
Imperial Ho. *E3* *3A 86*
(off Grove Rd.)
E14 .... *7B 86*
(off Victory Pl.)
Imperial M. E6 .... 2B **88**
Imperial Pl. BR7: Chst 1E **160**
Imperial Rd. N22 .... 7D **32**
SW6 .... 1K **117**
TW14: Felt 7G **111**
Imperial Sq. SW6 .... 1K **117**
Imperial St. E3 .... 3E **86**
Imperial War Mus. .... **2K 19 (3A 102)**
Imperial Way BR7: Chst 3G **143**
CR0: Wadd 6K **167**
HA3: Kent 6E **42**
Imperial Wharf *E2* *2H 85*
(off Darwen Pl.)
SW6 .... 2A **118**
Imre Cl. W12 .... 1D **98**
Inca Dr. SE9 .... 7F **125**
Inca Ter. N15 .... 3B **48**
Inchmery Rd. SE6 .... 2D **140**
Inchwood CR0: Addtn 4D **170**
Independence Ho. *SW19* *1B 154*
(off Chapter Way)
Independent Ind. Est. UB7: Yiew 1A **92**
Independent Pl. E8 .... 5F **67**
Independents Rd. SE3 .... 3H **123**
Inderwick Rd. N8 .... 5K **47**
Indescon Ct. E14 .... 2D **104**
India Gdns. UB5: N'olt 7A **58**
Indiana Bldg. *SE10* *1C 122*
(off Deal's Gateway)

India Pl. WC2 2G 13
India St. EC3 1J 15 (6F 85)
India Way W12 7D 80
Indigo M. E14 7E 86
N16 3D 66
Indus Ct. *SE15* *7F 103*
(*off Amstel Ct.*)
Indus Rd. SE7 7A 106
Infirmary Ct. SW3 7F 17
Inforum M. SE15 7G 103
Ingal Rd. E13 4J 87
Ingate Pl. SW8 1F 119
Ingatestone Rd. E12 1A 70
IG8: Wfd G 7E 36
SE25 4H 157
Ingelow Ho. *W8* *2K 99*
(*off Holland St.*)
Ingelow Rd. SW8 2F 119
Ingersoll Rd. EN3: Enf W 1D 24
W12 1D 98
Ingestre Pl. W1 1B 12 (6G 83)
Ingestre Rd. E7 4J 69
NW5 4F 65
Ingham Cl. CR2: Sels 7K 169
Ingham Rd. CR2: Sels 7J 169
NW6 4J 63
Inglebert St. EC1 1J 7 (3A 84)
Ingleborough St. SW9 2A 120
Ingleby Dr. HA1: Harr 3H 59
Ingleby Rd. IG1: Ilf 1F 71
N7 3J 65
RM10: Dag 6H 73
Ingleby Way BR7: Chst 5E 142
SM6: Wall 7H 167
Ingle Cl. HA5: Pinn 3C 40
Ingledew Rd. SE18 5H 107
Inglefield Sq. *E1* *1H 103*
(*off Prusom St.*)
Inglehurst Gdns. IG4: Ilf 5D 52
Inglemere Rd. CR4: Mitc 7D 136
SE23 3K 139
Ingle M. EC1 1J 7 (3A 84)
Inglesham Wlk. E9 6B 68
Ingleside SL3: Poyle 4A 174
Ingleside Cl. BR3: Beck 7C 140
Ingleside Gro. SE3 6H 105
Inglethorpe St. SW6 1F 117
Ingleton Av. DA16: Well 5A 126
Ingleton Rd. N18 6B 34
SM5: Cars 7C 166
Ingleton St. SW9 2A 120
Ingleway N12 6G 31
Inglewood BR7: Chst 6H 143
CR0: Sels 7A 170
Inglewood Cl. E14 4C 104
Inglewood Copse BR1: Brom 2C 160
Inglewood Ct. BR1: Brom 7G 141
Inglewood M. KT6: Surb 1G 163
Inglewood Rd. DA7: Bex 4K 127
NW6 5J 63
Inglis Rd. CR0: C'don 1F 169
W5 7F 79
Inglis St. SE5 1B 120
Ingoldisthorpe Gro. SE15 6F 103
Ingram Av. NW11 7A 46
Ingram Cl. HA7: Stan 5H 27
SE11 3H 19 (4K 101)
Ingram Ho. E3 1A 86
Ingram Rd. CR7: Thor H 1C 156
N2 4C 46
Ingram Way UB6: G'frd 1H 77
Ingrave Ho. RM9: Dag 1B 90
Ingrave Rd. RM1: Rom 4K 55
Ingrave St. SW11 3B 118
Ingrebourne Ct. E4 3J 35
Ingrebourne Ho.
BR1: Brom *5F 141*
(*off Brangbourne Rd.*)
NW8 *5B 4*
(*off Broadley St.*)
Ingress St. W4 5A 98
Inigo Jones Rd. SE7 7C 106
Inigo Pl. WC2 2E 12
Inkerman Rd. NW5 6F 65
Inkerman Ter. *W8* *3J 99*
(*off Allen St.*)
Inks Grn. E4 5K 35
Inkster Ho. SW11 3C 118
Inkwell Cl. N12 3F 31
Ink Works Ct. *SE1* *2E 102*
(*off Bell Yd. M.*)
Inman Rd. NW10 1A 80
SW18 7A 118
Inmans Row IG8: Wfd G 4D 36
Inner Circ. NW1 2G 5 (3E 82)
Inner Ct. SW3 7C 16 (6C 100)
Innered Ct. *CR0: C'don* *6C 156*
(*off Harry Cl.*)
Inner Pk. Rd. SW19 1F 135
Inner Ring E. TW6: H'row A 3D 110
Inner Ring W. TW6: H'row A 3C 110
Inner Temple La. EC4 1J 13
Innes Cl. SW20 2G 153
Innes Gdns. SW15 6D 116
Innes Yd. CR0: C'don 3C 168
Innis Ho. *SE17* *5E 102*
(*off East St.*)
Inniskilling Rd. E13 2A 88
Innis St. SE15 7E 102
Innova Ct. CR0: C'don 1E 168
Innovation Cen., The *E14* *2E 104*
(*off Marsh Wall*)
Innovation Cl. HA0: Wemb 1E 78
Inns of Court & City Yeomanry Mus. *6H 7*
(*off Chancery La.*)
Inskip Cl. E10 2D 68
Inskip Rd. RM8: Dag 1D 72
Institute of Archaeology 4H 83
Institute of Classical Studies 4H 83
Institute of Contemporary Arts 4D 12
Institute of Latin Studies 4H 83
Institute Pl. E8 5H 67
Integer Gdns. E11 7F 51
Interface Ho. *TW3: Houn* *3E 112*
(*off Staines Rd.*)
International Av. TW5: Cran 5A 94
International Bus. Pk. E15 1F 87
International Ho. *E1* *3K 15*
(*off St Katharine's Way*)
International Trad. Est.
UB2: S'hall 3K 93
International Way TW16: Sun 1G 147
Inverary Pl. SE18 6H 107
Inver Cl. E5 2J 67
Inverclyde Gdns. RM6: Chad H 4C 54
(not continuous)
Inver Ct. W2 6K 81
W6 3C 98
Inveresk Gdns. KT4: Wor Pk 3C 164
Inverforth Cl. NW3 2A 64
Inverforth Rd. N11 5A 32
Invergarry Ho. *NW6* *2K 81*
(*off Carlton Va.*)
Inverine Rd. SE7 5K 105
Invermead Cl. W6 3C 98
Invermore Pl. SE18 4G 107
Inverness Av. EN1: Enf 1K 23
Inverness Ct. SE6 1H 141
Inverness Gdns. W8 1K 99
Inverness M. E16 1G 107
W2 7K 81
Inverness Pl. W2 7K 81
Inverness Rd. KT4: Wor Pk 1F 165
N18 5C 34
TW3: Houn 4D 112
UB2: S'hall 4C 94
Inverness St. NW1 1F 83
Inverness Ter. W2 6K 81
Inverton Rd. SE15 4K 121
Invicta Cen., The IG11: Bark 1A 90
Invicta Cl. BR7: Chst 5E 142
TW14: Felt 1H 129
Invicta Gro. UB5: N'olt 3D 76
Invicta Pde. DA14: Sidc 4B 144
Invicta Plaza SE1 4A 14 (1B 102)
Invicta Rd. SE3 7J 105
Invicta Sq. E3 5C 86
Inville Rd. SE17 5D 102
(not continuous)
Inville Wlk. SE17 5D 102
Inwen Ct. SE8 5A 104
Inwood Av. TW3: Houn 3G 113
Inwood Bus. Pk. TW3: Houn 4F 113
Inwood Cl. CR0: C'don 2A 170
Inwood Ct. *NW1* *7G 65*
(*off Rochester Sq.*)
Inwood Rd. TW3: Houn 4F 113
Inworth St. SW11 2C 118
Inworth Wlk. *N1* *1C 84*
(*off Popham St.*)
IO Centre SE18 3G 107
(not continuous)
Iona Cl. SE6 7C 122
SM4: Mord 7K 153
Ion Ct. E2 2G 85
Ionian Bldg. E14 7A 86
Ionian Ho. *E1* *4K 85*
(*off Duckett St.*)
Ion Sq. E2 2G 85
Ipsden Bldgs. SE1 5K 13
Ipswich Ho. SE4 5K 121
Ipswich Rd. SW17 6E 136
Ira Ct. SE27 2B 138
Ireland Cl. E6 5D 88
Ireland Pl. N22 7D 32
Ireland Yd. EC4 1B 14 (6B 84)
Irene M. *W7* *1K 95*
(*off Uxbridge Rd.*)
Irene Rd. BR6: Orp 7K 161
SW6 1J 117
Ireton Cl. N10 7K 31
Ireton St. E3 4C 86
Iris Av. DA5: Bexl 5E 126
Iris Cl. CR0: C'don 1K 169
E6 5C 88
KT6: Surb 7F 151
Iris Ct. *SE14* *1J 121*
(*off Briant St.*)
Iris Cres. DA7: Bex 6F 109
Iris Rd. KT19: Ewe 5H 163
Iris Wlk. HA8: Edg 4D 28
Iris Way E4 6G 35
Irkdale Av. EN1: Enf 1A 24
Iron Bri. Cl. NW10 5A 62
Ironbridge Cl. UB2: S'hall 1G 95
Iron Bri. Ho. NW1 7D 64
Iron Bri. Rd. UB7: W Dray 2C 92
UB11: W Dray, Yiew 2C 92
Iron Mill Pl. SW18 6K 117
Iron Mill Rd. SW18 6K 117
Ironmonger La. EC2 1D 14 (6C 84)
Ironmonger Pas. *EC1* *2D 8*
(*off Ironmonger Row*)
Ironmonger Row EC1 2D 8 (3C 84)
Ironmonger Row Baths 2D 8
Ironmongers Pl. E14 4C 104
Ironside Cl. SE16 2K 103
Ironside Ho. E9 4A 68
Irons Way RM5: Col R 1J 55
Iron Works E3 1C 86
Ironworks, The *N1* *2J 83*
(*off Albion Wlk.*)
Irvine Av. HA3: Kent 3A 42
Irvine Cl. E14 5D 86
N20 2H 31
Irvine Ct. *W1* *4B 6*
(*off Whitfield St.*)
Irvine Ho. *N7* *6K 65*
(*off Caledonian Rd.*)
Irvine Way BR6: Orp 7K 161
Irving Av. UB5: N'olt 1B 76
Irving Gro. SW9 2K 119
Irving Ho. *SE17* *5B 102*
(*off Doddington Gro.*)
Irving Mans. *W14* *6G 99*
(*off Queen's Club Gdns.*)
Irving M. N1 6C 66
Irving Rd. W14 3F 99
Irving St. WC2 3D 12 (7H 83)
Irving Way NW9 5C 44
Irwell Ct. *W7* *6H 77*
(*off Hobbayne Rd.*)
Irwell Est. SE16 3J 103
Irwin Av. SE18 7J 107
Irwin Cl. UB10: Ick 3C 56
Irwin Gdns. NW10 1D 80
Isaac Way *SE1* *6D 14*
(*off Lant St.*)
Isabel Hill Cl. TW12: Hamp 2F 149
Isabella Cl. N14 7B 22
Isabella Dr. BR6: Farnb 4G 173
Isabella Ho. SE11 5K 19
W6 *5E 98*
(*off Queen Caroline St.*)
Isabella Pl. KT2: King T 5F 133
Isabella Rd. E9 5J 67
Isabella St. SE1 5A 14 (1B 102)
Isabel St. SW9 1K 119
Isambard M. E14 3E 104
Isambard Pl. SE16 1J 103
Isard Ho. BR2: Hayes 1K 171
Isel Way SE22 5E 120
Isham Rd. SW16 2J 155
Isis Cl. HA4: Ruis 6E 38
SW15 4E 116
Isis Ct. W4 7H 97
Isis Ho. N18 6A 34
NW8 *4B 4*
(*off Church St. Est.*)
Isis St. SW18 2A 136
Island, The KT7: T Ditt 6A 150
UB7: Lford 3D 174
Island Apartments N1 1C 84
Island Farm Av. KT8: W Mole 5D 148
Island Farm Rd. KT8: W Mole 5D 148
Island Ho. E15 3E 86
Island Rd. CR4: Mitc 7D 136
SE16 4K 103
Island Row E14 6B 86
Isla Rd. SE18 6G 107
Islay Gdns. TW4: Houn 5B 112
Islay Wlk. *N1* *6C 66*
(*off Douglas Rd. Sth.*)
Isleden Ho. *N1* *1C 84*
(*off Prebend St.*)
Isledon Rd. N7 3A 66
ISLEDON VILLAGE 3A 66
Islehurst Cl. BR7: Chst 1E 160
ISLEWORTH 3A 114
Isleworth Ait Nature Reserve 3B 114
Isleworth Bus. Complex
TW7: Isle 2K 113
Isleworth Prom. TW1: Twick 4B 114
Isleworth Recreation Cen. 4K 113
Isley Ct. SW8 2G 119
ISLINGTON 7B 66
Islington Bus. Cen. *N1* *1C 84*
(*off Coleman Flds.*)
Islington Crematorium
N2 1D 46
Islington Grn. N1 1B 84
Islington High St. N1 2A 84
(not continuous)
Islington Mus. 7B 66
Islington Pk. M. N1 7B 66
Islington Pk. St. N1 7A 66
Islington Pl. N1 1A 84
Islington Tennis Cen. 6J 65
Islip Gdns. HA8: Edg 7E 28
UB5: N'olt 7C 58

Islip Mnr. Rd. UB5: N'olt 7C 58
Islip St. NW5 .... 5G 65
Ismailia Rd. E7 .... 7K 69
Isobel Ho. HA1: Harr 5K 41
Isom Cl. E13 .... 3K 87
Issigonis Ho. W3 .... 1B 98
(off Cowley Rd.)
Itaska Cotts. WD23: B Hea 1D 26
Ivanhoe Cl. UB8: Cowl 5A 74
Ivanhoe Dr. HA3: Kent 3A 42
Ivanhoe Ho. E3 .... 2A 86
(off Grove Rd.)
Ivanhoe Rd. SE5 .... 3F 121
TW4: Houn 3B 112
Ivatt Pl. W14 .... 5H 99
Ivatt Way N17 .... 3B 48
Iveagh Av. NW10 .... 2G 79
Iveagh Cl. E9 .... 1K 85
HA6: Nwood 1D 38
NW10 .... 2G 79
Iveagh Ct. BR3: Beck 3E 158
E1 .... 1J 15
Iveagh Ho. SW9 .... 2B 120
SW10 .... 7A 100
(off King's Rd.)
Iveagh Ter. NW10 .... 2G 79
(off Iveagh Av.)
Ivedon Rd. DA16: Well 2C 126
Ive Farm Cl. E10 .... 2C 68
Ive Farm La. E10 .... 2C 68
Iveley Rd. SW4 .... 2G 119
Ivere Dr. EN5: New Bar 6E 20
Iver Ho. N1 .... 1E 84
(off New Era Est.)
Iverhurst Cl. DA6: Bex 5D 126
Iverna Ct. W8 .... 3J 99
Iverna Gdns. TW14: Felt 5F 111
W8 .... 3J 99
Iverson Rd. NW6 .... 6H 63
Ivers Way CR0: New Ad 7D 170
Ives Rd. E16 .... 5G 87
Ives St. SW3 .... 3D 16 (4C 100)
Ivestor Ter. SE23 .... 7J 121
Ivimey St. E2 .... 3G 85
Ivinghoe Cl. EN1: Enf 1K 23
Ivinghoe Ho. N7 .... 5H 65
Ivinghoe Rd. RM8: Dag 5B 72
Ivor Ct. N8 .... 6J 47
NW1 .... 3E 4
(off Gloucester Pl.)
Ivor Gro. SE9 .... 1F 143
Ivories, The N1 .... 7C 66
(off Northampton St.)
Ivor Pl. NW1 .... 4E 4 (4D 82)
Ivor St. NW1 .... 7G 65
Ivory Ct. TW13: Felt 1J 129
Ivorydown BR1: Brom 4J 141
Ivory Ho. E1 .... 3K 15 (1F 103)
Ivory Pl. W11 .... 7G 81
(off Treadgold St.)
Ivory Sq. SW11 .... 3A 118
Ivybridge Cl. TW1: Twick 7A 114
UB8: Uxb 3A 74
Ivybridge Ct. BR7: Chst 1E 160
(off Old Hill)
NW1 .... 7F 65
(off Lewis St.)
Ivybridge La. WC2 .... 3F 13 (7J 83)
Ivy Bri. Retail Pk.
TW7: Isle 5K 113
Ivychurch Cl. SE20 .... 7J 139
Ivychurch La. SE17 .... 5F 103
Ivy Cl. HA2: Harr 4D 58
HA5: Eastc 7A 40
TW16: Sun 2A 148
Ivy Cotts. E14 .... 7E 86
UB10: Hil 3C 74
Ivy Ct. SE16 .... 5G 103
(off Argyle Way)
Ivy Cres. W4 .... 4J 97
Ivydale Rd. SE15 .... 3K 121
SM5: Cars 2D 166
Ivyday Gro. SW16 .... 3K 137
Ivydene KT8: W Mole 5D 148
Ivydene Cl. SM1: Sutt 4A 166
Ivy Gdns. CR4: Mitc 3H 155
N8 .... 6J 47
Ivyhouse Rd. RM9: Dag 6D 72
UB10: Ick 3D 56
Ivy La. TW4: Houn 4D 112
Ivy Lodge W11 .... 1J 99
(off Notting Hill Ga.)
Ivymount Rd. SE27 .... 3A 138
Ivy Rd. E16 .... 6J 87
E17 .... 6C 50
KT6: Surb 1G 163
N14 .... 7B 22
NW2 .... 4E 62
SE4 .... 4B 122
SW17 .... 5C 136
TW3: Houn 4F 113
Ivy St. N1 .... 2E 84
Ivy Wlk. HA6: Nwood 1G 39
RM9: Dag 6E 72
Ixworth Pl. SW3 .... 5C 16 (5C 100)
Izane Rd. DA6: Bex 4F 127

J

Jacana Ct. E1 .... 3K 15
(off Star Pl.)
Jacaranda Cl. KT3: N Mald 3A 152
Jacaranda Gro. E8 .... 7F 67
Jackass La. BR2: Kes 5K 171
Jack Barnett Way N22 .... 2K 47
Jack Clow Rd. E15 .... 2G 87
Jack Cook Ho. IG11: Bark 7F 71
Jack Cornwell St. E12 .... 4E 70
Jack Dash Way E6 .... 4C 88
Jackets La. HA6: Nwood 1D 38
Jack Goodchild Way
KT1: King T 3H 151
Jacklin Grn. IG8: Wfd G 4D 36
Jackman Ho. E1 .... 1H 103
(off Watts St.)
Jackman M. NW10 .... 3A 62
Jackman St. E8 .... 1H 85
Jackson Cl. E9 .... 7J 67
UB10: Uxb 7A 56
Jackson Ct. E7 .... 6K 69
Jackson Ho. N11 .... 5B 32
Jackson Rd. BR2: Brom 2D 172
EN4: E Barn 6H 21
IG11: Bark 1H 89
N7 .... 4K 65
UB10: Uxb 7A 56
Jacksons La. N6 .... 7E 46
Jacksons Lane Theatre 6F 47
(off Archway Rd.)
Jacksons Pl. CR0: C'don 1D 168
Jackson St. SE18 .... 6E 106
Jackson's Way CR0: C'don 3C 170
Jackson Way UB2: S'hall 2F 95
Jacks Pl. E1 .... 5J 9
(off Corbet Pl.)
Jack Walker Ct. N5 .... 4B 66
Jacob Ho. DA18: Erith 2D 108
(off Kale Rd.)
Jacobin Lodge N7 .... 5J 65
Jacob Mans. E1 .... 6H 85
(off Commercial Rd.)
Jacob M. HA7: Stan 2F 27
Jacobs Cl. RM10: Dag 4H 73
Jacobs Ho. E13 .... 3A 88
(off New City Rd.)
Jacob St. SE1 .... 6K 15 (2G 103)
Jacob's Well M. W1 .... 6H 5 (5E 82)
Jacotts Ho. W10 .... 4E 80
(off Sutton Way)
Jacqueline Cl. UB5: N'olt 1C 76
Jacqueline Creft Ter. N6 .... 6E 46
(off Grange Rd.)
Jacqueline Ho. NW1 .... 1D 82
(off Regent's Pk. Rd.)
Jacqueline Vs. E17 .... 5E 50
(off Shernhall St.)
Jade Cl. E16 .... 6B 88
NW2 .... 7F 45
RM8: Dag 1C 72
Jade Ter. NW6 .... 7A 64
Jaffe Rd. IG1: Ilf 1H 71
Jaffray Pl. SE27 .... 4B 138
Jaffray Rd. BR2: Brom 4B 160
Jaggard Way SW12 .... 7D 118
Jagger Ho. SW11 .... 1D 118
(off Rosenau Rd.)
Jago Cl. SE18 .... 6G 107
Jago Wlk. SE5 .... 7D 102
Jake Russell Wlk. E16 .... 7A 88
Jamaica Rd. CR7: Thor H 6B 156
SE1 .... 7K 15 (2F 103)
SE16 .... 7K 15 (2F 103)
Jamaica St. E1 .... 6J 85
James Allens School Swimming Pool
.... 5E 120
James Anderson Ct. E2 .... 2E 84
(off Kingsland Rd.)
James Av. NW2 .... 5E 62
RM8: Dag 1F 73
James Bedford Cl. HA5: Pinn 2A 40
James Boswell Cl. SW16 .... 4K 137
James Brine Ho. E2 .... 1K 9
(off Ravenscroft St.)
James Campbell Ho. E2 .... 2J 85
(off Old Ford Rd.)
James Clavell Sq. SE18 .... 3F 107
(off Cartridge St.)
James Cl. E13 .... 2J 87
NW11 .... 6G 45
James Collins Cl. W9 .... 4H 81
James Ct. HA6: Nwood 1H 39
N1 .... 1C 84
(off Raynor Pl.)
NW9 .... 2A 44
UB5: N'olt 2C 76
(off Church Rd.)
James Docherty Ho. E2 .... 2H 85
(off Patriot Sq.)
James Dudson Ct. NW10 .... 7J 61
James Est. CR4: Mitc 2D 154
James Gdns. N22 .... 7G 33
James Hammett Ho. E2 .... 1K 9
(off Ravenscroft St.)
James Hill Ho. W10 .... 4G 81
(off Kensal Rd.)
James Ho. E1 .... 4A 86
(off Solebay St.)
SE16 .... 2K 103
(off Wolfe Cres.)
SW8 .... 7J 101
(off Wheatsheaf La.)
James Joyce Wlk. SE24 .... 4B 120
James La. E10 .... 7E 50
E11 .... 7F 51
James Lind Ho. SE8 .... 4B 104
(off Grove St.)
James Middleton Ho. E2 .... 3H 85
(off Middleton St.)
James Newman Ct. SE9 .... 3E 142
Jameson Cl. W3 .... 2J 97
Jameson Ct. E2 .... 2J 85
(off Russia La.)
Jameson Ho. SE11 .... 5G 19
(off Glasshouse Wlk.)
Jameson Lodge N6 .... 6G 47
Jameson St. W8 .... 1J 99
James Pl. N17 .... 1F 49
James's Cotts. TW9: Kew 7G 97
James Stewart Ho. NW6 .... 7H 63
James St. EN1: Enf 5A 24
IG11: Bark 7G 71
TW3: Houn 3H 113
W1 .... 1H 11 (6E 82)
WC2 .... 1F 13 (7J 83)
James Stroud Ho. SE17 .... 5C 102
(off Walworth Pl.)
James Ter. SW14 .... 3K 115
(off Church Path)
James Terry Ct.
CR2: S Croy 5C 168
(off Warham Rd.)
Jamestown Rd. NW1 .... 1F 83
Jamestown Way E14 .... 7F 87
James Yd. E4 .... 6A 36
Jam Factory, The SE1 .... 3E 102
(off Green Wlk.)
SE1 .... 3E 102
(off Rothsay St.)
Jamieson Ho. TW4: Houn 6D 112
Jamilah Ho. E16 .... 7E 88
(off University Way)
Jamuna Cl. E14 .... 5A 86
Jane Austen Hall E16 .... 1K 105
(off Wesley Av.)
Jane Austen Ho. SW1 .... 6A 18
(off Churchill Gdns.)
Jane Seymour Ct. SE9 .... 7H 125
Jane St. E1 .... 6H 85
Janet St. E14 .... 3C 104
Janeway Pl. SE16 .... 2H 103
Janeway St. SE16 .... 2G 103
Janice M. IG1: Ilf 2F 71
Jansen Wlk. SW11 .... 3B 118
Janson Cl. E15 .... 5G 69
NW10 .... 3A 62
Janson Rd. E15 .... 5G 69
Jansons Rd. N15 .... 3E 48
Japan Cres. N4 .... 1K 65
Japan Rd. RM6: Chad H 6D 54
Jardine Rd. E1 .... 7K 85
Jarman Ho. E1 .... 5J 85
(off Jubilee St.)
SE16 .... 4K 103
(off Hawkstone Rd.)
Jarrett Cl. SW2 .... 1B 138
Jarrow Cl. SM4: Mord 5K 153
Jarrow Rd. N17 .... 4H 49
RM6: Chad H 6C 54
SE16 .... 4J 103
Jarrow Way E9 .... 4B 68
Jarvis Cl. EN5: Barn 5A 20
IG11: Bark 1H 89
Jarvis Rd. CR2: S Croy 6D 168
SE22 .... 4E 120
Jashoda Ho. SE18 .... 5E 106
(off Connaught M.)
Jasmin Cl. HA6: Nwood 1H 39
Jasmin Ct. SE12 .... 6J 123
Jasmine Cl. BR6: Farnb 2F 173
IG1: Ilf 5F 71
UB1: S'hall 7C 76
Jasmine Ct. SW19 .... 5J 135
Jasmine Gdns. CR0: C'don 3D 170
HA2: Harr 2E 58
Jasmine Gro. SE20 .... 1H 157
Jasmine Rd.
RM7: Rush G 2K 73
Jasmine Sq. E3 .... 1B 86
(off Hawthorn Av.)
Jasmine Ter. UB7: W Dray 2C 92
Jasmine Way KT8: E Mos 4J 149
Jasmin Lodge SE16 .... 5H 103
(off Sherwood Gdns.)
Jasmin Rd. KT19: Ewe 5H 163
Jason Ct. SW9 .... 1A 120
(off Southey Rd.)
W1 .... 7H 5
Jason Wlk. SE9 .... 4E 142
Jasper Cl. EN3: Enf W 1D 24

Jasper Pas. SE19 . . . 6F 139
Jasper Rd. E16 . . . 6B 88
SE19 . . . 5F 139
Jasper Wlk. N1 . . . 3D 84
Java Wharf *SE1* . . . *6K 15*
(off Shad Thames)
Javelin Ct. *HA7: Stan* . . . *5G 27*
(off William Dr.)
Javelin Way UB5: N'olt . . . 3B 76
Jaycroft EN2: Enf . . . 1F 23
Jay Gdns. BR7: Chst . . . 4D 142
Jay M. SW7 . . . 7A 10 (2A 100)
Jazzfern Ter. HA0: Wemb . . . 5A 60
Jean Batten Cl. SM6: Wall . . . 7K 167
Jean Darling Ho. *SW10* . . . *6B 100*
(off Milman's St.)
Jean Ho. SW17 . . . 5C 136
Jean Pardies Ho. *E1* . . . *5J 85*
(off Jubilee St.)
Jebb Av. SW2 . . . 6J 119
(not continuous)
Jebb St. E3 . . . 2C 86
Jedburgh Rd. E13 . . . 3A 88
Jedburgh St. SW11 . . . 4E 118
Jeddo M. W12 . . . 2B 98
Jeddo Rd. W12 . . . 2B 98
Jefferson Bldg. E14 . . . 2C 104
Jefferson Cl. IG2: Ilf . . . 5F 53
W13 . . . 3B 96
Jefferson Wlk. SE18 . . . 6E 106
Jeffrey Row SE12 . . . 5K 123
Jeffrey's Pl. NW1 . . . 7G 65
Jeffreys Rd. EN3: Brim . . . 4F 25
SW4 . . . 2J 119
Jeffrey's St. NW1 . . . 7G 65
Jeffreys Walk SW4 . . . 2J 119
Jeffries Ho. NW10 . . . 7K 61
Jeffs Cl. TW12: Hamp . . . 6F 131
Jeffs Rd. SM1: Sutt . . . 4H 165
Jeger Av. E2 . . . 1F 85
Jeken Rd. SE9 . . . 4A 124
Jelf Rd. SW2 . . . 5A 120
Jelico Point *SE16* . . . *2B 104*
(off Rotherhithe St.)
Jellicoe Gdns. HA7: Stan . . . 6E 26
Jellicoe Ho. *E2* . . . *2G 85*
(off Ropley St.)
NW1 . . . 4F 83
Jellicoe Rd. E13 . . . 4J 87
N17 . . . 7J 33
Jemmett Cl. KT2: King T . . . 1H 151
Jemotts Ct. *SE14* . . . *6K 103*
(off Myers La.)
Jem Paterson Ct. HA1: Harr . . . 4J 59
Jengar Cl. SM1: Sutt . . . 4K 165
Jenkins La. IG11: Bark . . . 2G 89
Jenkinson Ho. *E2* . . . *3K 85*
(off Usk St.)
Jenkins Rd. E13 . . . 4K 87
Jenner Av. W3 . . . 5K 79
Jenner Cl. DA14: Sidc . . . 4A 144
Jenner Ho. *SE3* . . . *6G 105*
(off Restell Cl.)
WC1 . . . *3F 7*
(off Hunter St.)
Jenner Pl. SW13 . . . 6D 98
Jenner Rd. N16 . . . 3F 67
Jennett Rd. CR0: Wadd . . . 3A 168
Jennifer Ho. *SE11* . . . *4K 19*
(off Reedworth St.)
Jennifer Rd. BR1: Brom . . . 3H 141
Jenningsbury Ho. *SW3* . . . *5D 16*
(off Cale St.)
Jennings Cl. KT6: Surb . . . 7C 150
Jennings Ho. *SE10* . . . *5F 105*
(off Old Woolwich Rd.)
Jennings Rd. SE22 . . . 6F 121
Jennings Way EN5: Barn . . . 3A 20
Jenningtree Way DA17: Belv . . . 2J 109
Jenny Hammond Cl. E11 . . . 3H 69
Jenson Way SE19 . . . 7F 139
Jenton Av. DA7: Bex . . . 1E 126
Jephson Ct. SW4 . . . 2J 119
Jephson Ho. *SE17* . . . *6B 102*
(off Doddington Gro.)
Jephson Rd. E7 . . . 7A 70
Jephson St. SE5 . . . 1D 120
Jephtha Rd. SW18 . . . 6J 117
Jeppos La. CR4: Mitc . . . 4D 154
Jepson Ho. *SW6* . . . *1K 117*
(off Pearscroft Rd.)
Jerdan Ho. *SW6* . . . *7J 99*
(off North End Rd.)
Jerdan Pl. SW6 . . . 7J 99
Jeremiah St. E14 . . . 6D 86
Jeremy Bentham Ho. *E2* . . . *3G 85*
(off Mansford St.)
Jeremy's Grn. N18 . . . 4C 34
Jermyn St. SW1 . . . 4A 12 (1G 101)
Jermyn Street Theatre . . . 3C 12
(off Jermyn St.)
Jerningham Av. IG5: Ilf . . . 2F 53
Jerningham Ct. SE14 . . . 1A 122
Jerningham Rd. SE14 . . . 2A 122
Jerome Cres. NW8 . . . 3C 4 (4C 82)
Jerome Ho. *KT1: Ham W* . . . *2D 150*
(off Old Bri. St.)
NW1 . . . *5D 4*
(off Lisson Gro.)
SW7 . . . *3A 16*
(off Glendower Pl.)
Jerome Pl. *KT1: King T* . . . *2D 150*
(off Wadbrook St.)
Jerome St. E1 . . . 5J 9 (4F 85)
Jerome Twr. W3 . . . 2H 97
Jerrard St. SE13 . . . 3D 122
Jerrold St. N1 . . . 1H 9 (2E 84)
Jersey Av. HA7: Stan . . . 2B 42
Jersey Dr. BR5: Pet W . . . 6H 161
Jersey Ho. *EN3: Enf W* . . . *1E 24*
(off Eastfield Rd.)
N1 . . . 6C 66
Jersey Rd. E11 . . . 1F 69
E16 . . . 6A 88
IG1: Ilf . . . 4F 71
N1 . . . 6C 66
SW17 . . . 6F 137
TW3: Houn . . . 1F 113
TW5: Hest . . . 1F 113
TW7: Isle . . . 7H 95
W7 . . . 2A 96
Jersey St. E2 . . . 3H 85
Jerusalem Pas. EC1 . . . 4A 8 (4B 84)
Jervis Bay Ho. *E14* . . . *6F 87*
(off Blair St.)
Jervis Ct. RM10: Dag . . . 6H 73
SE10 . . . *1E 122*
(off Blissett St.)
W1 . . . 1K 11
Jervis Rd. SW6 . . . 6H 99
Jerviston Gdns. SW16 . . . 6A 138
Jerwood Space Art Gallery . . . 6C 14
Jesmond Av. HA9: Wemb . . . 6F 61
Jesmond Cl. CR4: Mitc . . . 3F 155
Jesmond Rd. CR0: C'don . . . 7F 157
Jesmond Way HA7: Stan . . . 5K 27
Jessam Av. E5 . . . 1H 67
Jessamine Rd. W7 . . . 1K 95
Jessel Ho. *SW1* . . . *3D 18*
(off Page St.)
WC1 . . . *2E 6*
(off Judd St.)
Jessel Mans. *W14* . . . *6G 99*
(off Queen's Club Gdns.)
Jesse Rd. E10 . . . 1E 68
Jessett Cl. DA8: Erith . . . 4K 109
Jessica Rd. SW18 . . . 6A 118
Jessie Blythe La. N19 . . . 7J 47
Jessie Duffett Ho. *SE5* . . . *7C 102*
(off Pitman St.)
Jessie Wood Ct. *SW9* . . . *7A 102*
(off Caldwell St.)
Jessiman Ter. TW17: Shep . . . 5C 146
Jesson Ho. *SE17* . . . *4D 102*
(off Orb St.)
Jessop Av. UB2: S'hall . . . 4D 94
Jessop Ct. N1 . . . 2B 84
Jessop Ho. *W4* . . . *4K 97*
(off Kirton Cl.)
Jessop Rd. SE24 . . . 4B 120
Jessop Sq. E14 . . . 1C 104
Jessops Way CR0: Bedd, Mitc . . . 6G 155
Jessup Cl. SE18 . . . 4G 107
Jetstar Way UB5: N'olt . . . 3C 76
Jevington Way SE12 . . . 1K 141
Jevons Ho. *NW8* . . . *7B 64*
(off Hilgrove Rd.)
Jewel Rd. E17 . . . 3C 50
Jewel Tower . . . 1E 18
(off College M.)
Jewish Mus.
Camden Town . . . 1F 83
Finchley . . . 2K 45
Jewry St. EC3 . . . 1J 15 (6F 85)
Jew's Row SW18 . . . 4K 117
Jews' Wlk. SE26 . . . 4H 139
Jeymer Av. NW2 . . . 5D 62
Jeymer Dr. UB6: G'frd . . . 1F 77
(not continuous)
Jeypore Pas. SW18 . . . 6A 118
Jeypore Rd. SW18 . . . 7A 118
Jigger Mast Ho. SE18 . . . 3E 106
Jillian Cl. TW12: Hamp . . . 7E 130
Jim Bradley Cl. SE18 . . . 4E 106
Jim Griffiths Ho. *SW6* . . . *6H 99*
(off Clem Attlee Ct.)
Joan Cres. SE9 . . . 7B 124
Joan Gdns. RM8: Dag . . . 2E 72
Joanna Ho. *W6* . . . *5E 98*
(off Queen Caroline St.)
Joan Rd. RM8: Dag . . . 2E 72
Joan St. SE1 . . . 5A 14 (1B 102)
Jocelin Ho. *N1* . . . *1K 83*
(off Barnsbury Est.)
Jocelyn Rd. TW9: Rich . . . 3E 114
Jocelyn St. SE15 . . . 1G 121
Jockey's Flds. WC1 . . . 5H 7 (5K 83)
Jodane St. SE8 . . . 4B 104
Jodrell Cl. TW7: Isle . . . 1A 114
Jodrell Rd. E3 . . . 1B 86
Joe Hunte Ct. SE27 . . . 5B 138
Joel St. HA5: Eastc . . . 3J 39
HA6: Nwood . . . 2J 39
Johanna St. SE1 . . . 7J 13 (2A 102)
John Adams Ct. N9 . . . 2A 34
John Adam St. WC2 . . . 3F 13 (7J 83)
John Aird Ct. W2 . . . 5A 4
(not continuous)
John Archer Way SW18 . . . 6B 118
John Ashby Cl. SW2 . . . 6J 119
John Austin Cl.
KT2: King T . . . 1F 151
John Baird Ct. SE26 . . . 4J 139
John Barker Ct. NW6 . . . 7G 63
John Barnes Wlk. E15 . . . 6H 69
John Betts' Ho. W12 . . . 3B 98
John Bradshaw Rd. N14 . . . 1C 32
John Brent Ho. *SE8* . . . *4K 103*
(off Bush Rd.)
John Buck Ho. NW10 . . . 1B 80
John Burns Dr. IG11: Bark . . . 7J 71
John Campbell Rd. N16 . . . 5E 66
John Carpenter St. EC4 . . . 2A 14 (7B 84)
John Cartwright Ho.
E2 . . . *3H 85*
(off Old Bethnal Grn. Rd.)
John Drinkwater Cl. E11 . . . 7H 51
John Fearon Wlk. *W10* . . . *3G 81*
(off Dart St.)
John Felton Rd. SE16 . . . 2G 103
John Fielden Ho. *E2* . . . *3H 85*
(off Canrobert St.)
John Fisher St. E1 . . . 2K 15 (7G 85)
John Goddard Way TW13: Felt . . . 2K 129
John Gooch Dr. EN2: Enf . . . 1G 23
John Harrison Way SE10 . . . 3H 105
John Horner M. N1 . . . 2C 84
John Islip St. SW1 . . . 5D 18 (4H 101)
John Kaye Ct. TW17: Shep . . . 5C 146
John Keats Ho. N22 . . . 7E 32
John Keats Lodge EN2: Enf . . . 1J 23
John Kennedy Ct. *N1* . . . *6D 66*
(off Newington Grn. Rd.)
John Kennedy Ho. *SE16* . . . *4K 103*
(off Rotherhithe Old Rd.)
John Kirk Ho. *E6* . . . *6E 88*
(off Pearl Cl.)
John Knight Lodge SW6 . . . 7J 99
John Lamb Ct. HA3: W'stone . . . 1J 41
John McDonald Ho. *E14* . . . *3E 104*
(off Glengall Gro.)
John McKenna Wlk. SE16 . . . 3G 103
John Masefield Ho. *N15* . . . *6D 48*
(off Fladbury Rd.)
John Maurice Cl. SE17 . . . 4D 102
John Newton Ct. DA16: Well . . . 3B 126
John Orwell Sports Cen. . . . 1H 103
John Owen Sports Cen., The . . . 1A 26
John Parker Cl. RM10: Dag . . . 7H 73
John Parker Sq. SW11 . . . 3B 118
John Parry Ct. *N1* . . . *2E 84*
(off Hare Wlk.)
John Penn Ho. *SE14* . . . *7B 104*
(off Amersham Va.)
John Penn St. SE13 . . . 1D 122
John Penry Ho. *SE1* . . . *5G 103*
(off Marlborough Gro.)
John Perrin Pl. HA3: Kent . . . 7E 42
John Prince's St. W1 . . . 7K 5 (6F 83)
John Pritchard Ho. *E1* . . . *4G 85*
(off Buxton St.)
John Ratcliffe Ho. *NW6* . . . *3J 81*
(off Chippenham Gdns.)
John Rennie Wlk. E1 . . . 7H 85
John Roll Way SE16 . . . 3G 103
John Ruskin St. SE5 . . . 7B 102
John's Av. NW4 . . . 4E 44
John's Cl. TW15: Ashf . . . 4E 128
John Scurr Ho. *E14* . . . *6A 86*
(off Ratcliffe La.)
John Silkin La. SE8 . . . 5K 103
John's La. SM4: Mord . . . 5A 154
John's M. WC1 . . . 4H 7 (4K 83)
John Smith Av. SW6 . . . 7H 99
John Smith M. E14 . . . 7F 87
Johnson Cl. E8 . . . 1G 85
Johnson Ho. *E2* . . . *3G 85*
(off Roberta St.)
NW1 . . . *2G 83*
(off Cranleigh St.)
NW3 . . . *7D 64*
(off Adelaide Rd.)
SW1 . . . *4H 17*
(off Cundy St.)
SW8 . . . *7H 101*
(off Wandsworth Rd.)
W8 . . . *2J 99*
(off Campden Hill)
Johnson Lodge *W9* . . . *5J 81*
(off Admiral Wlk.)
Johnson Mans. *W14* . . . *6G 99*
(off Queen's Club Gdns.)
Johnson Rd. BR2: Brom . . . 5B 160
CR0: C'don . . . 7D 156
NW10 . . . 1K 79
TW5: Hest . . . 7A 94
Johnsons Cl. SM5: Cars . . . 2D 166
Johnson's Ct. EC4 . . . 6A 84
Johnsons Dr. TW12: Hamp . . . 1G 149
Johnsons Ind. Est. UB3: Hayes . . . 2H 93

Johnson's Pl. SW1 ....6A 18 (5G 101)
Johnson St. E1 ....7J 85
UB2: S'hall 3A 94
Johnsons Way NW10 ....4H 79
John Spencer Sq. N1 ....6B 66
John's Pl. E1 ....6H 85
John's Ter. CR0: C'don 1E 168
Johnston Cl. SW9 ....1K 119
Johnston Ct. E10 ....3D 68
Johnstone Ho. SE13 ....3F 123
(off Belmont Hill)
Johnstone Rd. E6 ....3D 88
Johnston Rd. IG8: Wfd G 6D 36
Johnston Ter. NW2 ....3F 63
John Strachey Ho. SW6 ....6H 99
(off Clem Attlee Ct.)
John St. E15 ....1H 87
EN1: Enf 5A 24
SE25 ....4G 157
TW3: Houn 2C 112
WC1 ....4H 7 (4K 83)
John Strype Ct. E10 ....1D 68
John Trundle Ct. EC2 ....5C 8
John Trundle Highwalk EC2 ....5C 8
(off Beech St.)
John Tucker Ho. E14 ....3C 104
(off Mellish St.)
John Watkin Cl. KT19: Eps 7H 163
John Wesley Cl. E6 ....3D 88
John Wesley Ct. TW1: Twick 1A 132
John Wesley Highwalk EC2 ....6C 8
(off Barbican)
John Wheatley Ho. SW6 ....6H 99
(off Clem Attlee Ct.)
John Williams Cl. KT2: King T 1D 150
SE14 ....6K 103
John Wilson St. SE18 ....3E 106
John Woolley Cl. SE13 ....4G 123
Joiners Arms Yd. SE5 ....1D 120
Joiners Pl. N5 ....4D 66
Joiner St. SE1 ....5F 15 (1D 102)
Joiners Yd. N1 ....1F 7
(off Caledonia St.)
Joint Rd. N2 ....1C 46
Jollys La. HA2: Harr 1H 59
UB4: Yead 5B 76
Jonathan St. SE11 ....5G 19 (5K 101)
Jones Ho. E14 ....6F 87
(off Blair St.)
Jones M. SW15 ....4G 117
Jones Rd. E13 ....4K 87
Jones St. W1 ....3J 11 (7F 83)
Jones Wlk. TW10: Rich 6F 115
Jonquil Gdns. TW12: Hamp 6E 130
Jonson Cl. CR4: Mitc 4F 155
UB4: Hayes 5J 75
Jonson Ho. SE1 ....3D 102
(off Burbage Cl.)
Jordan Cl. HA2: Harr 3D 58
Jordan Ct. SW15 ....4F 117
Jordan Ho. N1 ....1D 84
(off Colville Est.)
SE4 ....4K 121
(off St Norbert Rd.)
Jordan Rd. UB6: G'frd 1B 78
Jordans Cl. RM10: Dag 4H 73
TW7: Isle 1J 113
Jordans Ho. NW8 ....3C 4
(off Capland St.)
Jordans M. TW2: Twick 2J 131
Joscoyne Ho. E1 ....6H 85
(off Philpot St.)
Joseph Av. W3 ....6K 79
Joseph Conrad Ho. SW1 ....4B 18
(off Tachbrook St.)
Joseph Ct. N16 ....6E 48
(off Amhurst Pk.)
Joseph Hardcastle Cl.
SE14 ....7K 103
Josephine Av. SW2 ....5K 119
Joseph Irwin Ho. E14 ....7B 86
(off Gill St.)
Joseph Lister Ct. E7 ....7J 69
Joseph Powell Cl. SW12 ....6G 119
Joseph Priestley Ho.
E2 ....3H 85
(off Canrobert St.)
Joseph Ray Rd. E11 ....2G 69
Joseph St. E3 ....4B 86
Joseph Trotter Cl. EC1 ....2K 7
Joshua Cl. CR2: S Croy 7B 168
N10 ....7A 32
Joshua St. E14 ....6E 86
Joslings Cl. W12 ....7C 80
Joslyn Cl. EN3: Enf L 1H 25
Josseline Ct. E3 ....2A 86
(off Ford St.)
Joubert Mans. SW3 ....5D 16
(off Jubilee Pl.)
Joubert St. SW11 ....2D 118
Jowett St. SE15 ....7F 103
Jowitt Ho. E2 ....3K 85
(off Morpeth St.)
Joyce Av. N18 ....5A 34
Joyce Butler Ho. N22 ....1K 47
Joyce Dawson Way SE28 ....7A 90
Joyce Latimore Ct. N9 ....3C 34
(off Colthurst Dr.)
Joyce Page Cl. SE7 ....6B 106
Joyce Wlk. SW2 ....6A 120
JOYDENS WOOD 4K 145
Joydens Wood (Nature Reserve) 4H 145
Joydens Wood Rd. DA5: Bexl 4K 145
Joydon Dr. RM6: Chad H 6B 54
Joyners Cl. RM9: Dag 4F 73
Joystone Ct. EN4: E Barn 4H 21
(off Park Rd.)
Jubb Powell Ho. N15 ....6E 48
Jubilee, The SE10 ....7D 104
Jubilee Av. E4 ....6K 35
RM7: Rom 5H 55
TW2: Whitt 1G 131
Jubilee Bldgs. NW8 ....1B 82
Jubilee Cl. HA5: Pinn 2A 40
KT1: Ham W 1C 150
NW9 ....6K 43
NW10 ....2A 80
RM7: Rom 5H 55
Jubilee Country Pk. 4F 161
Jubilee Ct. BR4: W W'ck 1E 170
HA3: Kent 7E 42
N10 ....3E 46
TW3: Houn 3F 113
(off Bristow Rd.)
Jubilee Cres. E14 ....3E 104
N9 ....1B 34
Jubilee Dr. HA4: Ruis 4B 58
Jubilee Gdns. UB1: S'hall 5E 76
Jubilee Hall Sports Cen. 2F 13
(off The Piazza)
Jubilee Ho. HA7: Stan 5J 27
SE11 ....4K 19
(off Reedworth St.)
WC1 ....3G 7
Jubilee La. W5 ....6E 78
Jubilee Mans. E1 ....6J 85
(off Jubilee St.)
Jubilee Mkt. IG8: Wfd G 6F 37
WC2 ....2F 13
Jubilee Pde. IG8: Wfd G 6F 37
Jubilee Pl. SW3 ....5D 16 (5C 100)
Jubilee Pl. Shop. Mall
E14 ....1D 104
(off Bank St.)
Jubilee Rd. SM3: Cheam 7F 165
UB6: G'frd 1B 78
Jubilee Sports Cen. & Baths 3H 81
Jubilee St. E1 ....6J 85
Jubilee Vs. KT10: Esh 7H 149
Jubilee Walkway SE1 ....3B 14 (7B 84)
Jubilee Way DA14: Sidc 2A 144
KT9: Chess 4G 163
SW19 ....1K 153
TW14: Felt 1J 129
Jubilee Yd. SE1 ....6J 15
Judd Apartments N8 ....3K 47
(off Gt. Amwell La.)
Judd St. WC1 ....2E 6 (3J 83)
Jude St. E16 ....6H 87
Judge Heath La. UB3: Hayes 6E 74
Judges Wlk. NW3 ....3A 64
Juer St. SW11 ....7C 100
Jules Thorn Av. EN1: Enf 4B 24
Julia Ct. E17 ....5D 50
Julia Gdns. IG11: Bark 2D 90
Julia Garfield M. E16 ....1K 105
(not continuous)
Juliana Cl. N2 ....2A 46
Julian Av. W3 ....7H 79
Julian Cl. EN5: New Bar 3E 20
Julian Ct. NW1 ....7G 65
(off Rochester Sq.)
Julian Hill HA1: Harr 2J 59
Julian Ho. SE21 ....4E 138
Julian Pl. E14 ....5D 104
Julian Taylor Path SE23 ....2H 139
Julia St. NW5 ....4E 64
Julien Rd. W5 ....3C 96
Juliet Ho. N1 ....2E 84
(off Arden Est.)
Juliette Rd. E13 ....2J 87
Julius Caesar Way HA7: Stan 3J 27
Julius Ho. E14 ....6F 87
(off E. India Dock Rd.)
Julius Nyerere Cl. N1 ....1K 83
(off Copenhagen St.)
Junction App. SE13 ....3E 122
SW11 ....3C 118
Junction Av. NW10 ....4E 80
Junction M. W2 ....7C 4 (6C 82)
Junction Pl. W2 ....7B 4
Junction Rd. CR2: S Croy 5D 168
E13 ....2K 87
HA1: Harr 6J 41
N9 ....1B 34
N17 ....3G 49
N19 ....4G 65
TW8: Bford 4C 96
TW15: Ashf 5E 128
W5 ....4C 96
Junction Rd. E. RM6: Chad H 7E 54
Junction Rd. W. RM6: Chad H 7E 54
Junction Wembley Retail Pk., The
HA9: Wemb 4H 61
Juniper Cl. EN5: Barn 5A 20
HA9: Wemb 5G 61
KT9: Chess 5F 163
Juniper Ct. HA3: Hrw W 1K 41
HA6: Nwood 1J 39
KT8: W Mole 4F 149
RM6: Chad H 6B 54
TW3: Houn 4F 113
(off Grove Rd.)
W8 ....3K 99
(off St Mary's Pl.)
Juniper Cres. NW1 ....7E 64
Juniper Dr. SW18 ....4A 118
Juniper Gdns. SW16 ....1G 155
TW16: Sun 6H 129
Juniper Ho. SE14 ....7J 103
TW9: Kew 1H 115
W10 ....4G 81
(off Fourth Av.)
Juniper La. E6 ....5C 88
Juniper Rd. IG1: Ilf 3E 70
Juniper St. E1 ....7J 85
Juniper Way UB3: Hayes 7F 75
Juno Ct. SW9 ....7A 102
(off Caldwell St.)
Juno Way SE14 ....6K 103
Juno Way Ind. Est. SE14 ....6K 103
Jupiter Ct. SW9 ....7A 102
(off Caldwell St.)
UB5: N'olt 3B 76
(off Seasprite Cl.)
Jupiter Hgts. UB10: Uxb 1B 74
Jupiter Ho. E14 ....5D 104
(off St Davids Sq.)
Jupiter Way N7 ....6K 65
Jupp Rd. E15 ....7F 69
Jupp Rd. W. E15 ....1F 87
Jura Ho. SE16 ....4K 103
(off Plough Way)
Jurston Ct. SE1 ....7K 13
Justice Wlk. SW3 ....7C 16 (6C 100)
Justin Cl. TW8: Bford 7D 96
Justines Pl. E2 ....3K 85
Justin Pl. N22 ....7E 32
Justin Plaza CR4: Mitc 4C 154
Justin Rd. E4 ....6G 35
Jute La. EN3: Brim 2F 25
Jutland Cl. N19 ....1J 65
Jutland Ho. SE5 ....2C 120
SE18 ....4C 106
(off Prospect Vale)
Jutland Rd. E13 ....4J 87
SE6 ....7E 122
Jutsums Av. RM7: Rom 6H 55
Jutsums Ct. RM7: Rom 6H 55
Jutsums La.
RM7: Rom, Rush G 6H 55
Juxon Cl. HA3: Hrw W 1F 41
Juxon Ho. EC4 ....1B 14
(off St Paul's Chyd.)
Juxon St. SE11 ....3H 19 (4K 101)
JVC Bus. Pk. NW2 ....1C 62

K

Kaduna Cl. HA5: Eastc 5J 39
Kale Rd. DA18: Erith 2D 108
Kambala Rd. SW11 ....3B 118
Kangley Bri. Rd. SE26 ....6B 140
Kangley Bus. Cen. SE26 ....5B 140
Kaplan Dr. N21 ....5E 22
Kapuvar Cl. SE15 ....2G 121
Karanjia Ct. NW2 ....6E 62
Kara Way NW2 ....4F 63
Karen Ct. BR1: Brom 1H 159
Karen Ter. E11 ....2H 69
Karenza Ct. HA9: Wemb 7C 42
Kariba Cl. N9 ....3D 34
Karma Way HA2: Harr 1E 58
Karoline Gdns. UB6: G'frd 2H 77
Kashgar Rd. SE18 ....4K 107
Kashmir Rd. SE7 ....7B 106
Kassala Rd. SW11 ....1D 118
Katella Trad. Est. IG11: Bark 3J 89
Katharine Ho. CR0: C'don 3C 168
(off Katharine St.)
Katharine St. CR0: C'don 3C 168
Katherine Cl. SE16 ....1K 103
Katherine Ct. SE23 ....1H 139
Katherine Gdns. SE9 ....4B 124
Katherine Ho. W10 ....4G 81
(off Portobello Rd.)
Katherine Rd. E6 ....5A 70
E7 ....5A 70
TW1: Twick 1A 132
Katherine Sq. W11 ....1G 99
Kathleen Av. HA0: Wemb 7E 60
W3 ....5J 79
Kathleen Godfree Ct. SW19 ....6J 135
Kathleen Rd. SW11 ....3D 118
Kayemoor Rd. SM2: Sutt 6B 166
Kay Rd. SW9 ....2J 119
Kay St. DA16: Well 1B 126
E2 ....2G 85
E15 ....7F 69

Kay Ter. E18 ....1H **51**
Kean Ho. SE17 ....6B **102**
TW1: Twick *6D* ***114***
(off Arosa Rd.)
Kean St. WC2 ....1G **13** (6K **83**)
Keatley Grn. E4 ....6G **35**
Keats Av. E16 ....1K **105**
Keats Cl. E11 ....5K **51**
EN3: Pond E 5E **24**
NW3 ....4C **64**
SE1 ....4F **103**
SW19 ....6B **136**
UB4: Hayes 5J **75**
Keats Est. *N16* *2F* ***67***
(off Kyverdale Rd.)
Keats Gro. NW3 ....4C **64**
Keats House 4C 64
Keats Ho. *E2* *3J* ***85***
(off Roman Rd.)
HA2: Harr 2J **59**
SE5 ....*7C* ***102***
(off Elmington Est.)
SW1 ....*7B* ***18***
(off Churchill Gdns.)
Keats Pde. *N9* *2B* ***34***
(off Church St.)
Keats Pl. *EC2* *6E* ***8***
(off Moorfields)
Keats Rd. DA16: Well 1J **125**
DA17: Belv 3J **109**
Keats Way CR0: C'don 6J **157**
UB6: G'frd 5F **77**
UB7: W Dray 4B **92**
Kebbell Ter. *E7* *5K* ***69***
(off Claremont Rd.)
Keble Cl. KT4: Wor Pk 1B **164**
UB5: N'olt 5G **59**
Keble Pl. SW13 ....6D **98**
Keble St. SW17 ....4A **136**
Kechill Gdns. BR2: Hayes 7J **159**
Kedeston Ct. SM1: Sutt 1K **165**
Kedge Ho. *E14* *3C* ***104***
(off Tiller Rd.)
Kedleston Dr. BR5: St M Cry 6K **161**
Kedleston Wlk. E2 ....3H **85**
Kedyngton Ho. *HA8: Edg* *2J* ***43***
(off Burnt Oak B'way.)
Keeble Cl. SE18 ....6F **107**
Keedonwood Rd.
BR1: Brom 5G **141**
Keel Cl. IG11: Bark 2C **90**
SE16 ....1K **103**
Keel Ct. *E14* *7F* ***87***
(off Newport Av.)
Keeley Rd. CR0: C'don 2C **168**
Keeley St. WC2 ....1G **13** (6K **83**)
Keeling Ho. *E2* *2H* ***85***
(off Claredale St.)
Keeling Rd. SE9 ....5B **124**
Keelson Ho. *E14* *3C* ***104***
(off Mellish St.)
Keely Cl. EN4: E Barn 5H **21**
Keemor Cl. SE18 ....7E **106**
Keens Cl. SW16 ....5H **137**
Keens Rd. CR0: C'don 4C **168**
Keen's Yd. N1 ....6B **66**
Keep, The KT2: King T 6F **133**
SE3 ....2J **123**
Keepers Ct. *CR2: S Croy* *5C* ***168***
(off Warham Rd.)
Keepers M. TW11: Tedd 6C **132**
Keepier Wharf *E14* *7K* ***85***
(off Narrow St.)
Keeton's Rd. SE16 ....3H **103**
(not continuous)
Keevil Dr. SW19 ....7F **117**
Keighley Cl. N7 ....5J **65**
Keightley Dr. SE9 ....1G **143**
Keilder Cl. UB10: Hil 2C **74**
Keildon Rd. SW11 ....4D **118**
Keiller Ho. *E16* *1D* ***106***
(off Kennard St.)
Keir, The SW19 ....5E **134**
Keir Hardie Ct. NW10 ....7B **62**
Keir Hardie Est. E5 ....1H **67**
Keir Hardie Ho. N19 ....7H **47**
W6 ....*6F* ***99***
(off Fulham Pal. Rd.)
Keir Hardie Way IG11: Bark 7A **72**
UB4: Yead 3J **75**
Keith Connor Cl. SW8 ....3F **119**
Keith Gro. W12 ....2C **98**
Keith Ho. *NW6* *2K* ***81***
(off Carlton Va.)
SW8 ....*7J* ***101***
(off Wheatsheaf La.)
Keith Pk. Rd. UB10: Uxb 7B **56**
Keith Rd. E17 ....1B **50**
IG11: Bark 2H **89**
UB3: Hayes 3G **93**
Kelbrook Rd. SE3 ....2C **124**
Kelby Ho. *N7* *6K* ***65***
(off Sutterton St.)
Kelby Path SE9 ....3F **143**
Kelceda Cl. NW2 ....2C **62**
Kelf Gro. UB3: Hayes 6H **75**
Kelfield Ct. W10 ....6F **81**
Kelfield Gdns. W10 ....6E **80**
Kelfield M. W10 ....6F **81**
Kelland Cl. N8 ....5H **47**
Kelland Rd. E13 ....4J **87**
Kellaway Rd. SE3 ....2B **124**
Keller Cres. E12 ....4B **70**
Kellerton Rd. SE13 ....5G **123**
Kellet Ho's. *WC1* *2F* ***7***
(off Tankerton St.)
Kellett Ho. *N1* *1E* ***84***
(off Colville Est.)
Kellett Rd. SW2 ....4A **120**
Kelling Gdns. CR0: C'don 7B **156**
Kellino St. SW17 ....4D **136**
Kellner Rd. SE28 ....3K **107**
Kellogg Twr. UB6: G'frd 5J **59**
Kellow Ho. *SE1* *6E* ***14***
(off Tennis St.)
Kell St. SE1 ....7B **14** (3B **102**)
Kelly Av. SE15 ....7F **103**
Kelly Cl. NW10 ....3K **61**
TW17: Shep 2G **147**
Kelly Ct. *E14* *7C* ***86***
(off Garford St.)
Kelly M. W9 ....4H **81**
Kelly Rd. NW7 ....6B **30**
Kelly St. NW1 ....6F **65**
Kelly Way RM6: Chad H 5E **54**
Kelman Cl. SW4 ....2H **119**
Kelmore Gro. SE22 ....4G **121**
Kelmscott Cl. E17 ....1B **50**
Kelmscott Gdns. W12 ....3C **98**
Kelmscott Leisure Cen. 6B 50
Kelmscott Rd. SW11 ....5C **118**
Kelross Pas. N5 ....4C **66**
Kelross Rd. N5 ....4C **66**
Kelsall Cl. SE3 ....2K **123**
Kelsey Ga. BR3: Beck 2D **158**
Kelsey La. BR3: Beck 2C **158**
Kelsey Pk. Av. BR3: Beck 2D **158**
(not continuous)
Kelsey Pk. Rd. BR3: Beck 2C **158**
Kelsey Sq. BR3: Beck 2C **158**
Kelsey St. E2 ....4G **85**
Kelsey Way BR3: Beck 3C **158**
Kelson Ho. E14 ....3E **104**
Kelso Pl. W8 ....3K **99**
Kelso Rd. SM5: Cars 7A **154**
Kelston Rd. IG6: Ilf 2F **53**
Kelvedon Cl. KT2: King T 6G **133**
Kelvedon Ho. SW8 ....1J **119**
Kelvedon Rd. SW6 ....7H **99**
Kelvedon Way IG8: Wfd G 6J **37**
Kelvin Av. N13 ....6E **32**
TW11: Tedd 6J **131**
Kelvinbrook KT8: W Mole 3F **149**
Kelvin Cl. KT19: Ewe 6G **163**
Kelvin Ct. SE20 ....1H **157**
TW7: Isle 2J **113**
W11 ....7J **81**
Kelvin Cres. HA3: Hrw W 7D **26**
Kelvin Dr. TW1: Twick 6B **114**
Kelvin Gdns. CR0: Wadd 7J **155**
UB1: S'hall 6E **76**
Kelvin Gro. KT9: Chess 3D **162**
SE26 ....3H **139**
Kelvington Cl. CR0: C'don 7A **158**
Kelvington Rd. SE15 ....5K **121**
Kelvin Ind. Est. UB6: G'frd 7F **59**
Kelvin Pde. BR6: Orp 1J **173**
Kelvin Rd. DA16: Well 3A **126**
N5 ....4C **66**
Kember St. N1 ....7K **65**
Kemble Dr. BR2: Brom 3C **172**
Kemble Ho. *SW9* *3B* ***120***
(off Barrington Rd.)
Kemble Rd. CR0: Wadd 3B **168**
N17 ....1G **49**
SE23 ....1K **139**
Kemble St. WC2 ....1G **13** (6K **83**)
Kemerton Rd. BR3: Beck 2D **158**
CR0: C'don 7F **157**
SE5 ....3C **120**
Kemeys St. E9 ....5A **68**
Kemnal Rd. BR7: Chst 4H **143**
(not continuous)
Kemp *NW9* *1B* ***44***
(off The Concourse)
Kemp Ct. *SW8* *7J* ***101***
(off Hartington Rd.)
Kempe Ho. *SE1* *3D* ***102***
(off Burbage Cl.)
Kempe Rd. NW6 ....2F **81**
Kemp Gdns. CR0: C'don 6C **156**
Kemp Ho. *E2* *2K* ***85***
(off Sewardstone Rd.)
E6 ....6E **70**
W1 ....*2C* ***12***
(off Berwick St.)
Kempis Way SE22 ....5E **120**
Kemplay Rd. NW3 ....4B **64**
Kemp Rd. RM8: Dag 1D **72**
Kemps Ct. *W1* *1B* ***12***
(off Hopkins St.)
Kemps Dr. E14 ....7C **86**
HA6: Nwood 1H **39**
Kempsford Gdns. SW5 ....5J **99**
Kempsford Rd. SE11 ....4K **19** (4A **102**)
(not continuous)
Kemps Gdns. SE13 ....5E **122**
Kempshott Rd. SW16 ....7H **137**
Kempson Rd. SW6 ....1J **117**
Kempthorne Rd. SE8 ....4B **104**
Kempton Av. TW16: Sun 1K **147**
UB5: N'olt 6E **58**
Kempton Cl. DA8: Erith 6J **109**
UB10: Ick 4E **56**
Kempton Ct. E1 ....5H **85**
TW16: Sun 1K **147**
Kempton Ho. *N1* *1E* ***84***
(off Hoxton St.)
Kempton Pk. TW12: Hamp 1D **148**
Kempton Pk. Racecourse 7A 130
Kempton Rd. E6 ....1D **88**
TW12: Hamp 2D **148**
(not continuous)
Kempton Wlk. CR0: C'don 6A **158**
Kempt St. SE18 ....6E **106**
Kemsing Cl. BR2: Hayes 2H **171**
CR7: Thor H 4C **156**
DA5: Bexl 7E **126**
Kemsing Ho. *SE1* *7F* ***15***
(off Long La.)
Kemsing Rd. SE10 ....5J **105**
Kemsley SE13 ....5D **122**
Kemsley Ct. W13 ....1C **96**
Kenbrook Ho. NW5 ....5G **65**
W14 ....3H **99**
Kenbury Cl. UB10: Ick 3C **56**
Kenbury Gdns. SE5 ....2C **120**
Kenbury Mans. *SE5* *2C* ***120***
(off Kenbury St.)
Kenbury St. SE5 ....2C **120**
Kenchester Cl. SW8 ....7J **101**
Kencot Way DA18: Erith 2F **109**
Kendal *NW1* *1K* ***5***
(off Augustus St.)
Kendal Av. IG11: Bark 1J **89**
N18 ....4J **33**
W3 ....4G **79**
(not continuous)
Kendal Cl. IG8: Wfd G 2C **36**
N20 ....2H **31**
SW9 ....7B **102**
TW14: Felt 1H **129**
UB4: Hayes 2G **75**
Kendal Ct. W3 ....5G **79**
Kendale Rd. BR1: Brom 5G **141**
Kendal Gdns. N18 ....4J **33**
SM1: Sutt 2A **166**
Kendal Ho. E9 ....1J **85**
N1 ....*2K* ***83***
(off Priory Grn. Est.)
SE20 ....*2G* ***157***
(off Derwent Rd.)
Kendall Av. BR3: Beck 2A **158**
CR2: Sande 7D **168**
Kendall Ct. DA15: Sidc 3A **144**
SW19 ....6B **136**
Kendall Lodge *BR1: Brom* *1K* ***159***
(off Willow Tree Wlk.)
Kendall Pl. W1 ....6G **5** (5E **82**)
Kendall Rd. BR3: Beck 2A **158**
SE18 ....1C **124**
TW7: Isle 2A **114**
Kendalmere Cl. N10 ....1F **47**
Kendal Pde. N18 ....4J **33**
Kendal Pl. SW15 ....5H **117**
Kendal Rd. NW10 ....4C **62**
Kendal Steps W2 ....1D **10**
Kendal St. W2 ....1D **10** (6C **82**)
Kender Est. *SE14* *1J* ***121***
(off Queen's Rd.)
Kender St. SE14 ....7J **103**
Kendoa Rd. SW4 ....4H **119**
Kendon Cl. E11 ....5K **51**
Kendra Hall Rd. CR2: S Croy 7B **168**
Kendrey Gdns. TW2: Whitt 7J **113**
Kendrick Ct. *SE15* *1H* ***121***
(off Woods Rd.)
Kendrick M. SW7 ....3A **16** (4B **100**)
Kendrick Pl. SW7 ....4A **16** (4B **100**)
Kenelm Cl. HA1: Harr 3A **60**
Kenerne Dr. EN5: Barn 5B **20**
Kenilford Rd. SW12 ....7F **119**
Kenilworth Av. E17 ....2C **50**
HA2: Harr 4D **58**
SW19 ....5J **135**
Kenilworth Ct. *SW15* *3G* ***117***
(off Lwr. Richmond Rd.)
Kenilworth Cres. EN1: Enf 1K **23**
Kenilworth Gdns. IG3: Ilf 2K **71**
SE18 ....2F **125**
UB1: S'hall 3D **76**
UB4: Hayes 5H **75**
Kenilworth Rd. BR5: Pet W 6G **161**
E3 ....2A **86**
HA8: Edg 3D **28**
KT17: Ewe 5C **164**
NW6 ....1H **81**
SE20 ....1K **157**
TW15: Ashf 3A **128**
W5 ....1E **96**

Kenley N17 ... 2D 48
(off Gloucester Rd.)
Kenley Av. NW9 ... 1A 44
Kenley Cl. BR7: Chst ... 3J 161
DA5: Bexl ... 7G 127
EN4: E Barn ... 4H 21
Kenley Gdns. CR7: Thor H ... 4B 156
Kenley Rd. KT1: King T ... 2H 151
SW19 ... 2J 153
TW1: Twick ... 6B 114
Kenley Wlk. SM3: Cheam ... 4F 165
W11 ... 7G 81
Kenlor Rd. SW17 ... 5B 136
Kenmare Dr. CR4: Mitc ... 7D 136
N17 ... 2F 49
Kenmare Gdns. N13 ... 4H 33
Kenmare Rd. CR7: Thor H ... 6A 156
Kenmere Gdns. HA0: Wemb ... 1G 79
Kenmere Rd. DA16: Well ... 2C 126
Kenmont Gdns. NW10 ... 3D 80
Kenmore Av.
HA3: Kent, W'stone ... 4A 42
Kenmore Cl. TW9: Kew ... 7G 97
Kenmore Ct. NW6 ... 7K 63
(off Acol Rd.)
Kenmore Cres.
UB4: Hayes ... 3H 75
Kenmore Gdns. HA8: Edg ... 2H 43
Kenmore Rd. HA3: Kent ... 3D 42
Kenmure Rd. E8 ... 5H 67
Kenmure Yd. E8 ... 5H 67
Kennacraig Cl. E16 ... 1J 105
Kennard Ho. SW11 ... 2E 118
Kennard Rd. E15 ... 7F 69
N11 ... 5J 31
Kennard St. E16 ... 1D 106
SW11 ... 1E 118
Kennedy Av. EN3: Pond E ... 6D 24
Kennedy Cl. BR5: Pet W ... 1H 173
CR4: Mitc ... 1E 154
E13 ... 2J 87
Kennedy Ct. TW15: Ashf ... 5E 128
WD23: B Hea ... 2C 26
Kennedy Cox Ho. E16 ... 5H 87
(off Burke St.)
Kennedy Ho. SE11 ... 5G 19
(off Vauxhall Wlk.)
Kennedy Path W7 ... 4K 77
Kennedy Rd. IG11: Bark ... 1J 89
W7 ... 5J 77
Kennedy Wlk. SE17 ... 4D 102
(off Elsted St.)
Kennet Cl. SW11 ... 4B 118
Kennet Ct. W9 ... 5J 81
(off Elmfield Way)
Kenneth Av. IG1: Ilf ... 4F 71
Kenneth Campbell Ho.
NW8 ... 3B 4
(off Orchardson St.)
Kenneth Chambers Ct.
IG8: Wfd G ... 6H 37
Kenneth Ct. SE11 ... 3K 19 (4A 102)
Kenneth Cres. NW2 ... 5D 62
Kenneth Gdns. HA7: Stan ... 6F 27
Kenneth More Rd. IG1: Ilf ... 3F 71
Kenneth More Theatre ... 3F 71
Kennet Ho. NW8 ... 4B 4
(off Church St. Est.)
Kenneth Rd. RM6: Chad H ... 7D 54
Kenneth Robbins Ho. N17 ... 7C 34
Kenneth Younger Ho. SW6 ... 6H 99
(off Clem Attlee Ct.)
Kennet Rd. TW7: Isle ... 3K 113
W9 ... 4H 81
Kennet Sq. CR4: Mitc ... 1C 154
Kennet St. E1 ... 1G 103
Kennett Ct. W4 ... 7H 97
Kennett Dr. UB4: Yead ... 5C 76
Kennett Wharf La. EC4 ... 3D 14
KENNINGHALL JUNC. ... 5D 34
Kenninghall Rd. E5 ... 3G 67
N18 ... 5D 34
Kenning Ho. N1 ... 1E 84
(off Colville Est.)
Kenning St. SE16 ... 2J 103
Kennings Way SE11 ... 5K 19 (5A 102)
KENNINGTON ... 7K 19 (6A 102)
Kennington Grn. SE11 ... 6J 19 (5A 102)
Kennington La. SE11 ... 6G 19 (5K 101)
KENNINGTON OVAL ... 6A 102
Kennington Oval SE11 ... 7H 19 (6K 101)
Kennington Pal. Ct. SE11 ... 5J 19
Kennington Pk. Gdns.
SE11 ... 7K 19 (6B 102)
Kennington Pk. Ho. SE11 ... 6K 19
Kennington Pk. Pl.
SE11 ... 7K 19 (6A 102)
Kennington Pk. Rd. SE11 ... 7K 19 (6A 102)
Kennington Rd. SE1 ... 1J 19 (3A 102)
SE11 ... 1J 19 (3A 102)
Kennistoun Ho. NW5 ... 5G 65
Kennoldes SE21 ... 2D 138
(off Croxted Rd.)
Kenny Dr. SM5: Cars ... 7E 166
Kennyland Ct. NW4 ... 6D 44
(off Hendon Way)
Kenny Rd. NW7 ... 6B 30
Kenrick Pl. W1 ... 6G 5 (5E 82)
KENSAL GREEN ... 3E 80
Kensal Ho. W10 ... 4F 81
(off Ladbroke Gro.)
KENSAL RISE ... 2F 81
Kensal Rd. W10 ... 4G 81
KENSAL TOWN ... 4G 81
Kensal Wharf W10 ... 4F 81
KENSINGTON ... 2K 99
Kensington Arc. W8 ... 2K 99
(off Kensington High St.)
Kensington Av. CR7: Thor H ... 1A 156
E12 ... 6C 70
Kensington Cen. W14 ... 4G 99
(not continuous)
Kensington Chu. Ct. W8 ... 2K 99
Kensington Chu. St. W8 ... 1J 99
Kensington Chu. Wlk. W8 ... 2K 99
(not continuous)
Kensington Cl. N11 ... 6K 31
Kensington Ct. SE16 ... 1K 103
(off King & Queen Wharf)
W8 ... 2K 99
Kensington Ct. Gdns. W8 ... 3K 99
(off Kensington Ct. Pl.)
Kensington Ct. Mans. W8 ... 2K 99
(off Kensington Ct.)
Kensington Ct. M. W8 ... 3K 99
(off Kensington Ct. Pl.)
Kensington Ct. Pl. W8 ... 3K 99
Kensington Dr. IG8: Wfd G ... 2B 52
Kensington Gdns. ... 5A 10 (1A 100)
Kensington Gdns. IG1: Ilf ... 1D 70
KT1: King T ... 3D 150
(not continuous)
Kensington Gdns. Sq. W2 ... 6K 81
Kensington Ga. W8 ... 3A 100
Kensington Gore SW7 ... 7A 10 (2A 100)
Kensington Hall Gdns. W14 ... 5H 99
Kensington Hgts. HA1: Harr ... 6K 41
(off Sheepcote Rd.)
W8 ... 1J 99
Kensington High St. W8 ... 3H 99
W14 ... 3H 99
Kensington Ho. IG8: Wfd G ... 7K 37
W8 ... 2K 99
(off Kensington Ct.)
W14 ... 2F 99
Kensington Mall W8 ... 1J 99
Kensington Mans. SW5 ... 5J 99
(off Trebovir Rd., not continuous)
Kensington Palace ... 2K 99
Kensington Pal. Gdns. W8 ... 1K 99
Kensington Pk. Gdns. W11 ... 7H 81
Kensington Pk. M. W11 ... 6H 81
Kensington Pk. Rd. W11 ... 6H 81
Kensington Pl. W8 ... 1J 99
Kensington Rd. RM7: Rom ... 6J 55
SW7 ... 7B 10 (2A 100)
UB5: N'olt ... 3E 76
W8 ... 2A 100
Kensington Sports Cen. ... 7G 81
Kensington Sq. W8 ... 3K 99
Kensington Ter. CR2: S Croy ... 7D 168
Kensington Village W14 ... 4H 99
Kensington W. W14 ... 4G 99
Kensworth Ho. EC1 ... 2F 9
(off Cranwood St.)
Kent Av. DA16: Well ... 5K 125
RM9: Dag ... 4G 91
W13 ... 5B 78
Kent Cl. BR6: Chels ... 6J 173
CR4: Mitc ... 4J 155
Kent Ct. E2 ... 2F 85
NW9 ... 2A 44
Kent Dr. EN4: Cockf ... 4K 21
TW11: Tedd ... 5J 131
Kentford Way UB5: N'olt ... 1C 76
Kent Gdns. HA4: Ruis ... 6J 39
W13 ... 5B 78
Kent Ga. Way CR0: Addtn ... 6B 170
Kent Ho. SE1 ... 5F 103
SW1 ... 5C 18
(off Aylesford St.)
W4 ... 5A 98
(off Devonshire St.)
W8 ... 2K 99
(off Kensington Ct.)
W11 ... 1H 99
(off Boyne Ter. M.)
Kent Ho. App. Rd. BR3: Beck ... 1A 158
Kent Ho. La. BR3: Beck ... 6A 140
Kent Ho. Rd. BR3: Beck ... 1K 157
SE26 ... 5A 140
Kentish Bldgs. SE1 ... 5E 14 (2D 102)
Kentish Rd. DA17: Belv ... 4G 109
KENTISH TOWN ... 5F 65
Kentish Town Forum ... 5F 65
Kentish Town Ind. Est. NW5 ... 5F 65
Kentish Town Rd. NW1 ... 7F 65
NW5 ... 7F 65
Kentish Town Sports Cen. ... 6F 65
Kentish Way BR1: Brom ... 2K 159
BR2: Brom ... 2K 159
Kentlea Rd. SE28 ... 2J 107
Kentmere Ho. SE15 ... 6J 103
Kentmere Mans. W5 ... 4B 78
Kentmere Rd. SE18 ... 4J 107
KENTON ... 5C 42
Kenton Av. HA1: Harr ... 7K 41
TW16: Sun ... 2B 148
UB1: S'hall ... 7E 76
Kenton Ct. HA3: Kent ... 6B 42
SE26 ... 4A 140
(off Adamsrill Rd.)
TW1: Twick ... 6D 114
W14 ... 3H 99
Kentone Ct. SE25 ... 4H 157
Kenton Gdns. HA3: Kent ... 5C 42
Kenton Ho. E1 ... 4J 85
(off Mantus Cl.)
Kenton La.
HA3: Hrw W, Kent, W'stone ... 6E 26
Kenton Pk. Av. HA3: Kent ... 5D 42
Kenton Pk. Cl. HA3: Kent ... 4C 42
Kenton Pk. Cres. HA3: Kent ... 4D 42
Kenton Pk. Mans. HA3: Kent ... 5C 42
(off Kenton Rd.)
Kenton Pk. Pde. HA3: Kent ... 5C 42
Kenton Pk. Rd. HA3: Kent ... 4C 42
Kenton Rd. E9 ... 6K 67
HA1: Harr ... 7K 41
HA3: Kent ... 6A 42
Kenton St. WC1 ... 3E 6 (4J 83)
Kenton Way UB4: Hayes ... 3G 75
Kent Pk. Ind. Est. SE15 ... 6H 103
Kent Pas. NW1 ... 3E 4 (4D 82)
Kent Rd. BR4: W W'ck ... 1D 170
KT1: King T ... 3D 150
KT8: E Mos ... 4G 149
N21 ... 1J 33
RM10: Dag ... 5H 73
TW9: Kew ... 7G 97
W4 ... 3J 97
Kent's Pas. TW12: Hamp ... 1D 148
Kent St. E2 ... 2F 85
E13 ... 3A 88
Kent Ter. NW1 ... 2D 4 (3C 82)
Kent Vw. Gdns. IG3: Ilf ... 2J 71
Kent Wlk. SW9 ... 4B 120
Kent Way KT6: Surb ... 3E 162
Kentwell Cl. SE4 ... 4A 122
Kent Wharf SE8 ... 7D 104
(off Creekside)
Kentwode Grn. SW13 ... 7C 98
Kent Yd. SW7 ... 7D 10 (2C 100)
Kenver Av. N12 ... 6G 31
Kenward Rd. SE9 ... 5A 124
Kenward Way SW11 ... 2E 118
Ken Way HA9: Wemb ... 3J 61
Kenway RM5: Col R ... 2J 55
Kenway Rd. SW5 ... 4K 99
Ken Wilson Ho. E2 ... 2G 85
(off Pritchards Rd.)
Kenwood Av. N14 ... 5C 22
Kenwood Cl. NW3 ... 1B 64
UB7: Sip ... 6C 92
Kenwood Ct. NW9 ... 4J 43
(off Elmwood Cres.)
Kenwood Dr. BR3: Beck ... 3E 158
Kenwood Gdns. E18 ... 3K 51
IG2: Ilf ... 5E 52
IG5: Ilf ... 4E 52
Kenwood House ... 1C 64
Kenwood Ho. SW9 ... 4B 120
Kenwood Rd. N6 ... 6D 46
N9 ... 1B 34
Kenworthy Rd. E9 ... 5A 68
Kenwrick Ho. N1 ... 1K 83
(off Barnsbury Est.)
Kenwyn Dr. NW2 ... 2A 62
Kenwyn Lodge N2 ... 4D 46
Kenwyn Rd. SW4 ... 4H 119
SW20 ... 1E 152
Kenya Rd. SE7 ... 7B 106
Kenyngton Ct. TW16: Sun ... 5J 129
Kenyngton Dr. TW16: Sun ... 5J 129
Kenyngton Pl. HA3: Kent ... 5C 42
Kenyon Ho. SE5 ... 7C 102
(off Camberwell Rd.)
Kenyon Mans. W14 ... 6G 99
(off Queen's Club Gdns.)
Kenyon St. SW6 ... 1F 117
Keogh Rd. E15 ... 6G 69
Kepler Ho. SE10 ... 5H 105
(off Armitage Rd.)
Kepler Rd. SW4 ... 4J 119
Keppel Ho. SE8 ... 5B 104
SW3 ... 4C 16
(off Elystan St.)
Keppel Rd. E6 ... 7D 70
RM9: Dag ... 4E 72
Keppel Row
SE1 ... 5C 14 (1C 102)
Keppel St. WC1 ... 5D 6 (5H 83)
Kerbela St. E2 ... 3K 9 (4G 85)
Kerbey St. E14 ... 6D 86
Kerfield Cres. SE5 ... 1D 120
Kerfield Pl. SE5 ... 1D 120
Kerridge Ct. N1 ... 6E 66
(off Balls Pond Rd.)
Kerrier Ho. SW10 ... 7A 100
(off Stadium St.)

Kerrington Ct. *W10* . . . 4G **81**
(off Wornington Rd.)
W12 . . . 2E **98**
(off Uxbridge Rd.)
Kerrison Pl. W5 . . . 1D **96**
Kerrison Rd. E15 . . . 1F **87**
SW11 . . . 3C **118**
W5 . . . 1D **96**
Kerrison Vs. W5 . . . 1D **96**
Kerry Av. HA7: Stan . . . 4H **27**
Kerry Cl. E16 . . . 6K **87**
N13 . . . 2E **32**
Kerry Ct. HA7: Stan . . . 4J **27**
Kerry Ho. *E1* . . . 6J **85**
(off Sidney St.)
Kerry Path SE14 . . . 6B **104**
Kerry Rd. SE14 . . . 6B **104**
Kersey Gdns. SE9 . . . 4C **142**
Kersfield Ho. SW15 . . . 6F **117**
Kersfield Rd. SW15 . . . 6F **117**
Kershaw Cl. SW18 . . . 6B **118**
Kershaw Rd.
RM10: Dag . . . 3G **73**
Kersley M. SW11 . . . 1D **118**
Kersley Rd. N16 . . . 2E **66**
Kersley St. SW11 . . . 2D **118**
Kerstin Cl. UB3: Hayes . . . 7H **75**
Kerswell Cl. N15 . . . 5E **48**
Kerwick Cl. N7 . . . 7J **65**
Keslake Mans. *NW10* . . . 2F **81**
(off Station Ter.)
Keslake Rd. NW6 . . . 2F **81**
Kessock Cl. N17 . . . 5H **49**
Kestlake Rd. DA5: Bexl . . . 6C **126**
KESTON . . . 5A **172**
Keston Av. BR2: Kes . . . 5A **172**
Keston Cl. DA16: Well . . . 7C **108**
N18 . . . 3J **33**
Keston Ct. DA5: Bexl . . . 7F **127**
KT5: Surb . . . 5F **151**
(off Cranes Pk.)
Keston Gdns. BR2: Kes . . . 4A **172**
Keston Ho. *SE17* . . . 5E **102**
(off Kinglake Est.)
KESTON MARK . . . 4C **172**
KESTON MARK . . . 3C **172**
Keston Pk. Cl. BR2: Kes . . . 3D **172**
Keston Rd. CR7: Thor H . . . 6A **156**
N17 . . . 3D **48**
SE15 . . . 3G **121**
Kestrel Av. E6 . . . 5C **88**
SE24 . . . 5B **120**
Kestrel Cl. KT2: King T . . . 4D **132**
NW9 . . . 2A **44**
NW10 . . . 5K **61**
Kestrel Ct. CR2: S Croy . . . 6C **168**
E17 . . . 2K **49**
HA4: Ruis . . . 2G **57**
SM6: Wall . . . 5G **167**
Kestrel Ho. *EC1* . . . 1C **8**
(off Pickard St.)
EN3: Pond E . . . 5F **25**
Kestrel Pl. SE14 . . . 6A **104**
Kestrel Way
CR0: New Ad . . . 7F **171**
UB3: Hayes . . . 2F **93**
Keswick Av. SW15 . . . 5A **134**
SW19 . . . 2J **153**
TW17: Shep . . . 3G **147**
Keswick B'way. *SW15* . . . 5H **117**
(off Up. Richmond Rd.)
Keswick Cl. SM1: Sutt . . . 4A **166**
Keswick Ct. BR2: Brom . . . 4H **159**
SE6 . . . 1H **141**
SE13 . . . 5D **122**
Keswick Gdns. HA4: Ruis . . . 6F **39**
HA9: Wemb . . . 4E **60**
IG4: Ilf . . . 4C **52**
Keswick Ho. SE5 . . . 2C **120**
Keswick M. W5 . . . 1E **96**
Keswick Rd. BR4: W W'ck . . . 2G **171**
BR6: Orp . . . 1K **173**
DA7: Bex . . . 1G **127**
SW15 . . . 5G **117**
TW2: Whitt . . . 6G **113**
Kettering Ct. CR7: Thor H . . . 4C **156**
Kettering St. SW16 . . . 6G **137**
Kett Gdns. SW2 . . . 5K **119**
Kettlebaston Rd. E10 . . . 1B **68**
Kettleby Ho. *SW9* . . . 3B **120**
(off Barrington Rd.)
Kettlewell Cl. N11 . . . 6K **31**
Ketton Ho. *W10* . . . 4E **80**
(off Sutton Way)
Kevan Ct. E17 . . . 4C **50**
Kevan Ho. SE5 . . . 7C **102**
Kevelioc Rd. N17 . . . 1C **48**
Kevin Cl. TW4: Houn . . . 2B **112**
Kevington Cl. BR5: St P . . . 4K **161**
Kevington Dr. BR5: St P . . . 4K **161**
BR7: Chst . . . 4K **161**
KEW . . . 7G **97**
KEW BRIDGE . . . 5F **97**
Kew Bri. TW8: Bford . . . 6G **97**
TW9: Kew . . . 6G **97**
Kew Bri. Arches TW9: Kew . . . 6G **97**
Kew Bri. Ct. W4 . . . 5G **97**
Kew Bri. Distribution Cen.
TW8: Bford . . . 5F **97**
Kew Bri. Rd. TW8: Bford . . . 6F **97**
Kew Bridge Steam Mus. . . . 5F **97**
Kew Ct. KT2: King T . . . 1E **150**
Kew Cres. SM3: Cheam . . . 3G **165**
Kew Foot Rd. TW9: Rich . . . 4E **114**
Kew Gdns. . . . 7E **96**
Kew Gdns. Plants & People Exhibition . . . 7F **97**
Kew Gdns. Rd. TW9: Kew . . . 7F **97**
Kew Gdns. Vis. Cen. . . . 1F **115**
KEW GREEN . . . 7G **97**
Kew Grn. TW9: Kew . . . 6F **97**
Kew Mdw. Path TW9: Kew . . . 1H **115**
Kew Palace . . . 6F **97**
Kew Retail Pk. TW9: Kew . . . 1H **115**
Kew Riverside Pk. TW9: Kew . . . 7H **97**
Kew Rd. TW9: Kew . . . 6G **97**
TW9: Rich, Kew . . . 4E **114**
Keybridge Ho. *SW8* . . . 7F **19**
(off Miles St.)
Key Cl. E1 . . . 4J **85**
Keyes Ho. *SW1* . . . 6C **18**
(off Dolphin Sq.)
Keyes Rd. NW2 . . . 5F **63**
Keyham Ho. *W2* . . . 5J **81**
(off Westbourne Pk. Rd.)
Key Ho. SE11 . . . 7K **19** (6A **102**)
Keymer Rd. SW2 . . . 2K **137**
Keynes Cl. N2 . . . 4D **46**
Keynes Ct. *SE28* . . . 7B **90**
(off Attlee Rd.)
Keynsham Av. IG8: Wfd G . . . 4B **36**
Keynsham Gdns. SE9 . . . 5C **124**
Keynsham Rd. SE9 . . . 5B **124**
SM4: Mord . . . 1K **165**
Keynsham Wlk. SM4: Mord . . . 1K **165**
Keys Ct. *CR0: C'don* . . . 3D **168**
(off Beech Ho. Rd.)
Keyse Rd. SE1 . . . 3F **103**
Keysham Av.
TW5: Cran . . . 1J **111**
Keystone Cres. N1 . . . 1F **7** (2J **83**)
Keywood Dr.
TW16: Sun . . . 6J **129**
Keyworth Cl. E5 . . . 4A **68**
Keyworth Pl. SE1 . . . 7B **14**
Keyworth St. SE1 . . . 7B **14** (3B **102**)
Kezia M. SE8 . . . 5A **104**
Kezia St. SE8 . . . 5A **104**
Khalsa Ct. N22 . . . 1B **48**
Khama Rd. SW17 . . . 4C **136**
Khartoum Rd. E13 . . . 3K **87**
IG1: Ilf . . . 5F **71**
SW17 . . . 4B **136**
Khyber Rd. SW11 . . . 2C **118**
Kibworth St. SW8 . . . 7K **101**
KIDBROOKE . . . 2K **123**
Kidbrooke Est. SE3 . . . 3A **124**
Kidbrooke Gdns. SE3 . . . 2J **123**
Kidbrooke Green Nature Reserve . . . 3A **124**
Kidbrooke Gro. SE3 . . . 1J **123**
Kidbrooke La. SE9 . . . 4C **124**
Kidbrooke Pk. Cl. SE3 . . . 1K **123**
Kidbrooke Pk. Rd. SE3 . . . 1K **123**
Kidbrooke Way SE3 . . . 2K **123**
Kidderminster Pl. CR0: C'don . . . 1B **168**
Kidderminster Rd. CR0: C'don . . . 1B **168**
Kidderpore Av. NW3 . . . 4J **63**
Kidderpore Gdns. NW3 . . . 4J **63**
Kidd Pl. SE7 . . . 5C **106**
Kierbeck Bus. Complex
E16 . . . 2K **105**
Kiffen St. EC2 . . . 3F **9** (4D **84**)
Kilberry Cl. TW7: Isle . . . 1H **113**
Kilbrennan Ho. *E14* . . . 6E **86**
(off Findhorn St.)
KILBURN . . . 2H **81**
Kilburn Bri. NW6 . . . 1J **81**
Kilburn Ga. NW6 . . . 2K **81**
Kilburn High Rd. NW6 . . . 7H **63**
Kilburn Ho. *NW6* . . . 2H **81**
(off Malvern Pl.)
Kilburn La. W9 . . . 3F **81**
W10 . . . 3F **81**
Kilburn Pk. Rd. NW6 . . . 3J **81**
Kilburn Pl. NW6 . . . 1J **81**
Kilburn Priory NW6 . . . 1K **81**
Kilburns Mill Cl. SM6: Wall . . . 2F **167**
Kilburn Sq. NW6 . . . 1J **81**
Kilburn Va. NW6 . . . 1K **81**
Kilburn Va. Est. *NW6* . . . 1K **81**
(off Kilburn Va.)
Kilby Ct. *SE10* . . . 3H **105**
(off Greenroof Way)
Kildare Cl. HA4: Ruis . . . 1A **58**
Kildare Ct. *W2* . . . 6J **81**
(off Kildare Ter.)
Kildare Gdns. W2 . . . 6J **81**
Kildare Rd. E16 . . . 5J **87**
Kildare Ter. W2 . . . 6J **81**
Kildare Wlk. E14 . . . 6C **86**
Kildoran Rd. SW2 . . . 5J **119**
Kildowan Rd. IG3: Ilf . . . 1A **72**
Kilgour Rd. SE23 . . . 6A **122**
Kilkie St. SW6 . . . 2A **118**
Killarney Rd. SW18 . . . 6A **118**
Killearn Rd. SE6 . . . 1F **141**
Killester Gdns. KT4: Wor Pk . . . 4D **164**
Killick Ho. SM1: Sutt . . . 4K **165**
Killick M. SM3: Cheam . . . 6G **165**
Killick St. N1 . . . 1G **7** (2K **83**)
Killieser Av. SW2 . . . 2J **137**
Killigarth Ct. DA14: Sidc . . . 4A **144**
Killigrew Ho. TW16: Sun . . . 7G **129**
Killip Cl. E16 . . . 6H **87**
Killoran Ho. *E14* . . . 3E **104**
(off Galbraith St.)
Killowen Av. UB5: N'olt . . . 5G **59**
Killowen Rd. E9 . . . 6K **67**
Killyon Rd. SW8 . . . 2G **119**
Killyon Ter. SW8 . . . 2G **119**
Kilmaine Rd. SW6 . . . 7G **99**
Kilmarnock Gdns. RM8: Dag . . . 3C **72**
Kilmarsh Rd. W6 . . . 4E **98**
Kilmartin Av. SW16 . . . 3A **156**
Kilmartin Rd. IG3: Ilf . . . 2A **72**
Kilmington Rd. SW13 . . . 6C **98**
Kilmiston Av. TW17: Shep . . . 6E **146**
Kilmiston Ho. TW17: Shep . . . 6E **146**
Kilmore Ho. *E14* . . . 6D **86**
(off Vesey Path)
Kilmorey Gdns. TW1: Twick . . . 5B **114**
Kilmorey Hall *UB8: Cowl* . . . 3A **74**
(off Kingston La.)
Kilmorey Rd. TW1: Twick . . . 4B **114**
Kilmorie Rd. SE23 . . . 1A **140**
Kilmuir Ho. *SW1* . . . 4H **17**
(off Bury St.)
Kiln Cl. UB3: Harl . . . 6F **93**
Kiln Ct. *E14* . . . 7B **86**
(off Newell St.)
Kilner Ho. *E16* . . . 5K **87**
(off Freemasons Rd.)
SE11 . . . 7J **19**
Kilner St. E14 . . . 5C **86**
Kiln M. SW17 . . . 5B **136**
Kiln Pl. NW5 . . . 5E **64**
Kilnside KT10: Clay . . . 7A **162**
Kilpatrick Way UB4: Yead . . . 5C **76**
Kilravock St. W10 . . . 3G **81**
Kilronan W3 . . . 6K **79**
Kilross Rd. TW14: Bedf . . . 1F **129**
Kilsby Wlk. RM9: Dag . . . 6B **72**
Kilsha Rd. KT12: Walt T . . . 6A **148**
Kimbell Gdns. SW6 . . . 1G **117**
Kimbell Pl. SE3 . . . 4A **124**
Kimber Ct. *SE1* . . . 7G **15**
(off Long La.)
Kimberley Av. E6 . . . 2C **88**
IG2: Ilf . . . 7H **53**
RM7: Rom . . . 6J **55**
SE15 . . . 2H **121**
Kimberley Ct. *NW6* . . . 1G **81**
(off Kimberley Rd.)
Kimberley Dr. DA14: Sidc . . . 2D **144**
Kimberley Gdns. EN1: Enf . . . 3A **24**
N4 . . . 5B **48**
Kimberley Ga. BR1: Brom . . . 7G **141**
Kimberley Ho. *E14* . . . 3E **104**
(off Galbraith St.)
Kimberley Ind. Est. E17 . . . 1B **50**
Kimberley Rd. BR3: Beck . . . 2K **157**
CR0: C'don . . . 6B **156**
E4 . . . 1B **36**
E11 . . . 2F **69**
E16 . . . 4H **87**
E17 . . . 1A **50**
N17 . . . 2G **49**
N18 . . . 6C **34**
NW6 . . . 1G **81**
SW9 . . . 2J **119**
Kimberley Wlk. KT12: Walt T . . . 7K **147**
Kimberley Way E4 . . . 1B **36**
Kimber Rd. SW18 . . . 7J **117**
Kimble Cres. WD23: Bush . . . 1B **26**
Kimble Ho. NW8 . . . 3D **4**
Kimble Rd. SW19 . . . 6B **136**
Kimbolton Cl. SE12 . . . 6H **123**
Kimbolton Ct. *SW3* . . . 4C **16**
(off Fulham Rd.)
Kimbolton Row *SW3* . . . 4C **16**
(off Fulham Rd.)
Kimmeridge Gdns. SE9 . . . 4C **142**
Kimmeridge Rd. SE9 . . . 4C **142**
Kimpton Ho. SW15 . . . 7C **116**
Kimpton Ind. Est. SM3: Sutt . . . 2H **165**
Kimpton Link Bus. Cen.
SM3: Sutt . . . 2H **165**
Kimpton Pk. Way SM1: Sutt . . . 2G **165**
SM3: Sutt . . . 2G **165**
Kimpton Rd. SE5 . . . 1D **120**
SM3: Sutt . . . 2H **165**
Kimpton Trade & Bus. Cen.
SM3: Sutt . . . 2H **165**
Kinburn St. SE16 . . . 2K **103**
Kincaid Rd. SE15 . . . 7H **103**
Kincardine Gdns. *W9* . . . 4J **81**
(off Harrow Rd.)
Kincha Lodge *KT2: King T* . . . 1F **151**
(off Elm Rd.)
Kinch Gro. HA3: Kent . . . 7F **43**

Kinder Cl. SE28 . . . . . 7D 90
Kinder Ho. *N1* *2D 84*
(off Cranston Est.)
Kindersley Ho. *E1* *6G 85*
(off Pinchin St.)
Kinder St. E1 . . . . . 6H 85
Kinderton Cl. N14 . . . . . 1B 32
Kinefold Ho. N7 . . . . . 6J 65
Kinfauns Rd. IG3: Ilf 1A 72
SW2 . . . . . 2A 138
King Alfred Av. SE6 . . . . . 4C 140
(not continuous)
King & Queen Cl. SE9 . . . . . 4C 142
King & Queen St. SE17 . . . . . 5C 102
King & Queen Wharf SE16 . . . . . 7K 85
King Arthur Cl. SE15 . . . . . 7J 103
King Charles I Island WC2 . . . . . 4E 12
King Charles Ct. *SE17* *6B 102*
(off Royal Rd.)
King Charles Cres. KT5: Surb 7F 151
King Charles Ho. *SW6* *7K 99*
(off Wandon Rd.)
King Charles Rd. KT5: Surb 5F 151
King Charles's Ct. *SE10* *6E 104*
(off Park Row)
King Charles St. SW1 . . . . . 6D 12 (2H 101)
King Charles Ter. *E1* *7H 85*
(off Sovereign Cl.)
King Charles Wlk. SW19 . . . . . 1G 135
King Ct. E10 . . . . . 7D 50
Kingcup Cl. CR0: C'don 7K 157
King David La. E1 . . . . . 7J 85
Kingdom St. W2 . . . . . 5A 82
Kingdon Ho. *E14* *3E 104*
(off Galbraith St.)
Kingdon Rd. NW6 . . . . . 6J 63
King Edward III M. SE16 . . . . . 2H 103
King Edward Bldg. *EC1* *7B 8*
(off Newgate St.)
King Edward Ct. HA9: Wemb 5E 60
King Edward Dr. KT9: Chess 3E 162
King Edward Mans. *E8* *1H 85*
(off Mare St.)
King Edward M. SW13 . . . . . 1C 116
King Edward Rd. E10 . . . . . 1E 68
E17 . . . . . 3A 50
EN5: New Bar 4D 20
King Edward's Gdns. W3 . . . . . 1G 97
King Edwards Gro. TW11: Tedd 6B 132
King Edwards Mans. *SW6* *7J 99*
(off Fulham Rd.)
King Edward's Pl. W3 . . . . . 1G 97
King Edwards Rd. E9 . . . . . 1H 85
EN3: Pond E 4E 24
HA4: Ruis 1F 57
IG11: Bark 1H 89
N9 . . . . . 7C 24
King Edward St. EC1 . . . . . 7C 8 (6C 84)
King Edward Wlk. SE1 . . . . . 1K 19 (3A 102)
Kingfield Rd. W5 . . . . . 4D 78
Kingfield St. E14 . . . . . 4E 104
Kingfisher Av. E11 . . . . . 6K 51
Kingfisher Cl.
HA3: Hrw W 7E 26
HA6: Nwood 1D 38
SE28 . . . . . 7C 90
Kingfisher Ct. *E14* *2E 104*
(off River Barge Cl.)
EN2: Enf 1E 22
KT8: E Mos 4J 149
SE1 . . . . . *7D 14*
(off Swan St.)
SM1: Sutt 5H 165
SW19 . . . . . 2F 135
TW3: Houn 5F 113
TW7: Isle 2H 113
Kingfisher Dr. TW10: Ham 4B 132
Kingfisher Ho. SW18 . . . . . 3A 118
W14 . . . . . *3H 99*
(off Melbury Rd.)
Kingfisher Leisure Cen. 2E 150
Kingfisher M. SE13 . . . . . 4C 122
Kingfisher Pl. N22 . . . . . 2K 47
Kingfisher Sq. *SE8* *6B 104*
(off Clyde St.)
Kingfisher St. E6 . . . . . 5C 88
Kingfisher Wlk. NW9 . . . . . 2A 44
Kingfisher Way BR3: Beck 5K 157
NW10 . . . . . 6K 61
King Frederick IX Twr. SE16 . . . . . 3B 104
King Gdns. CR0: Wadd 5B 168
King George IV Ct. *SE17* *5D 102*
(off Dawes St.)
King George VI Av. CR4: Mitc 4D 154
King George VI Memorial 5C 12
King George Av. E16 . . . . . 6A 88
IG2: Ilf 5H 53
King George Cl. RM7: Mawney 3J 55
TW16: Sun 5G 129
King George's Dr. UB1: S'hall 5D 76
King George's Ind. Est.
KT9: Chess 4G 163
King George Sq. TW10: Rich 6F 115
King George's Sailing Club 6H 25
King George St. SE10 . . . . . 7E 104
Kingham Cl. SW18 . . . . . 7A 118
W11 . . . . . 2G 99
King Harolds Way
DA7: Belv, Bex 7D 108
DA17: Belv 7D 108
King Henry M. BR6: Chels 5K 173
HA2: Harr 1J 59
King Henry's Dr. CR0: New Ad 7D 170
King Henry's Reach W6 . . . . . 6E 98
King Henry's Rd. KT1: King T 3H 151
NW3 . . . . . 7C 64
King Henry's Stairs E1 . . . . . 1H 103
King Henry St. N16 . . . . . 5E 66
King Henry's Wlk. N1 . . . . . 6E 66
King Henry Ter. *E1* *7H 85*
(off Sovereign Cl.)
Kinghorn St. EC1 . . . . . 6C 8 (5C 84)
King Ho. W12 . . . . . 6D 80
King James Ct. SE1 . . . . . 7B 14
King James St. SE1 . . . . . 7B 14 (2B 102)
King John Ct. EC2 . . . . . 3H 9 (4E 84)
King John St. E1 . . . . . 5K 85
King John's Wlk. SE9 . . . . . 7C 124
(not continuous)
Kinglake Est. SE17 . . . . . 5E 102
Kinglake St. SE17 . . . . . 5E 102
(not continuous)
Kinglet Cl. E7 . . . . . 6J 69
Kingly Ct. W1 . . . . . 2B 12
Kingly St. W1 . . . . . 1A 12 (6G 83)
Kingsand Rd. SE12 . . . . . 2J 141
Kings Arbour UB2: S'hall 5C 94
King's Arms All. TW8: Bford 6D 96
Kings Arms Ct. E1 . . . . . 5G 85
Kings Arms Yd. EC2 . . . . . 7E 8 (6D 84)
Kingsash Dr. UB4: Yead 4C 76
Kings Av. BR1: Brom 6H 141
IG8: Wfd G 6E 36
IG9: Buck H 2G 37
(Queen's Rd.)
IG9: Buck H 6E 36
(Station Way)
KT3: N Mald 4A 152
N10 . . . . . 3E 46
N21 . . . . . 1G 33
RM6: Chad H 6F 55
SM5: Cars 7C 166
SW4 . . . . . 1H 137
SW12 . . . . . 1H 137
TW3: Houn 1F 113
TW16: Sun 5H 129
UB6: G'frd 5F 77
W5 . . . . . 6D 78
King's Bench St. SE1 . . . . . 6B 14 (2B 102)
King's Bench Wlk. EC4 . . . . . 1K 13 (6A 84)
Kingsbridge Av. W3 . . . . . 2F 97
Kingsbridge Ct. *E14* *3C 104*
(off Dockers Tanner Rd.)
NW1 . . . . . *7F 65*
(off Castlehaven Rd.)
Kingsbridge Cres. UB1: S'hall 5D 76
Kingsbridge Dr. NW7 . . . . . 7A 30
Kingsbridge Rd.
IG11: Bark 2H 89
KT12: Walt T 7K 147
SM4: Mord 6F 153
UB2: S'hall 4D 94
W10 . . . . . 6E 80
Kingsbridge Way UB4: Hayes 3G 75
Kingsbridge Wharf IG11: Bark 3J 89
KINGSBURY 5H 43
Kingsbury Circ. NW9 . . . . . 5G 43
KINGSBURY GREEN 5J 43
Kingsbury Rd. N1 . . . . . 6E 66
NW9 . . . . . 5G 43
Kingsbury Sports Cen. 4H 43
Kingsbury Ter. N1 . . . . . 6E 66
Kingsbury Trad. Est. NW9 . . . . . 6K 43
Kings Chase KT8: E Mos 3G 149
Kings Chase Vw. EN2: Enf 2F 23
Kingsclere Cl. SW15 . . . . . 7C 116
Kingsclere Ct. N12 . . . . . 5H 31
Kingsclere Pl. EN2: Enf 2H 23
Kingscliffe Gdns. SW19 . . . . . 1H 135
Kings Cl. DA1: Cray 4K 127
E10 . . . . . 7D 50
KT7: T Ditt 6A 150
KT12: Walt T 7K 147
NW4 . . . . . 4F 45
TW18: Staines 7A 128
King's Club, The (Sports Cen.) 6E 134
Kings Coll. Ct. NW3 . . . . . 7C 64
King's College London
Dental Institute 2D 120
Hampstead Campus 4J 63
(St Thomas' Campus)
Lambeth Pal. Rd. 2F 19
St Thomas' House 1G 19
Strand Campus 2H 13 (7K 83)
Waterloo Campus 5J 13 (1A 102)
Kings Coll. Rd. HA4: Ruis 6H 39
NW3 . . . . . 7C 64
King's College School of Medicine & Dentistry
. . . . . 2C 120
Kingscote Rd. CR0: C'don 7H 157
KT3: N Mald 3K 151
W4 . . . . . 3K 97
Kingscote St. EC4 . . . . . 2A 14 (7B 84)
Kings Ct. E13 . . . . . 1K 87
HA9: Wemb 2H 61
IG9: Buck H 2G 37
N7 . . . . . *7K 65*
(off Caledonian Rd.)
NW8 . . . . . *1D 82*
(off Prince Albert Rd.)
SE1 . . . . . 6B 14 (2B 102)
W6 . . . . . 4C 98
Kings Ct. M. KT8: E Mos 5H 149
Kings Ct. Nth. SW3 . . . . . 6C 16 (5C 100)
Kingscourt Rd. SW16 . . . . . 3H 137
Kings Ct. Sth. SW3 . . . . . 6C 16
King's Cres. N4 . . . . . 3C 66
Kings Cres. Est. N4 . . . . . 2C 66
Kingscroft SW4 . . . . . 6J 119
Kingscroft Rd. NW2 . . . . . 6H 63
King's Cross Bri. N1 . . . . . 1F 7
King's Cross Rd.
WC1 . . . . . 1G 7 (3K 83)
Kingsdale Gdns. W11 . . . . . 1F 99
Kingsdale Rd. SE18 . . . . . 7K 107
SE20 . . . . . 7K 139
Kingsdown Av.
CR2: S Croy 7C 168
W3 . . . . . 7A 80
W13 . . . . . 2B 96
Kingsdown Cl. *SE16* *5H 103*
(off Masters Dr.)
W10 . . . . . 6F 81
Kingsdowne Rd. KT6: Surb 7E 150
Kingsdown Ho. E8 . . . . . 5G 67
Kingsdown Rd. E11 . . . . . 3G 69
N19 . . . . . 2J 65
SM3: Cheam 5G 165
Kingsdown Way BR2: Hayes 7J 159
Kings Dr. HA8: Edg 4A 28
HA9: Wemb 2H 61
KT5: Surb 7G 151
KT7: T Ditt 7B 150
TW11: Tedd 5H 131
Kingsend HA4: Ruis 1F 57
Kingsend Ct. HA4: Ruis 1G 57
Kings Farm E17 . . . . . 1D 50
Kings Farm Av. TW10: Rich 4G 115
Kingsfield Av. HA2: Harr 4F 41
Kingsfield Ho. SE9 . . . . . 3B 142
Kingsfield Rd. HA1: Harr 7H 41
Kingsfield Ter. HA1: Harr 1H 59
Kingsford St. NW5 . . . . . 5D 64
Kingsford Way E6 . . . . . 5D 88
Kings Gdns. IG1: Ilf 1H 71
NW6 . . . . . 7J 63
Kings Gth. M. SE23 . . . . . 2J 139
Kingsgate HA9: Wemb 3J 61
Kingsgate Av. N3 . . . . . 3J 45
Kingsgate Bus. Cen. *KT2: King T* *1E 150*
(off Kingsgate Rd.)
Kingsgate Cl. DA7: Bex 1E 126
Kingsgate Est. N1 . . . . . 6E 66
Kingsgate Ho. SW9 . . . . . 1A 120
Kingsgate Mans. *WC1* *6G 7*
(off Red Lion Sq.)
Kingsgate Pde. SW1 . . . . . 2B 18
Kingsgate Pl. NW6 . . . . . 7J 63
Kingsgate Rd. KT1: King T 1E 150
KT2: King T 1E 150
NW6 . . . . . 7J 63
Kings Grange HA4: Ruis 1H 57
Kingsground SE9 . . . . . 7B 124
King's Gro. SE15 . . . . . 7H 103
(not continuous)
Kings Hall Leisure Cen. 5J 67
Kingshall M. SE13 . . . . . 3E 122
Kings Hall Rd. BR3: Beck 7A 140
Kings Head Hill E4 . . . . . 7J 25
Kingshead Ho. NW7 . . . . . 4J 29
Kings Head Pas. *SW4* *4H 119*
(off Clapham Pk. Rd.)
Kings Head Theatre *1B 84*
(off Upper St.)
King's Head Yd. SE1 . . . . . 5E 14 (1D 102)
King's Highway SE18 . . . . . 6J 107
Kingshill *SE17* *4C 102*
(off Brandon St.)
Kingshill Av. HA3: Kent 4B 42
KT4: Wor Pk 7C 152
UB4: Hayes 3G 75
UB5: Yead 3G 75
Kingshill Cl. UB4: Hayes 3J 75
Kingshill Ct. EN5: Barn 4B 20
Kingshill Dr. HA3: Kent 2B 42
Kingshold Rd. E9 . . . . . 7J 67
Kingsholm Gdns. SE9 . . . . . 4B 124
Kings Ho. *SW8* *7J 101*
(off Sth. Lambeth Rd.)
SW10 . . . . . *7A 16*
(off King's Rd.)
King's Ho. Studios *SW10* *7A 16*
(off Lamont Rd. Pas.)
Kingshurst Rd. SE12 . . . . . 7J 123
Kingside SE18 . . . . . 3C 106
Kings Keep BR2: Brom 2G 159
KT1: King T 4E 150
SW15 . . . . . 5F 117
KINGSLAND 6E 66
Kingsland NW8 . . . . . 1C 82

Kingsland Grn. E8 .6E 66
Kingsland High St. E8 .6F 67
Kingsland Pas. E8 .6E 66
Kingsland Rd. E2 .2H 9 (3E 84)
E8 .3E 84
E13 .3A 88
Kingsland Shop. Cen. E8 .6F 67
Kings La. SM1: Sutt .6B 166
Kingslawn Cl. SW15 .5D 116
Kingslee Ct. SM2: Sutt .7K 165
Kingsleigh Cl. TW8: Bford .6D 96
Kingsleigh Pl. CR4: Mitc .3D 154
Kingsleigh Wlk. BR2: Brom .4H 159
(off Stamford Dr.)
Kingsley Av. SM1: Sutt .4B 166
TW3: Houn .2G 113
UB1: S'hall .7E 76
W13 .5A 78
Kingsley Cl. N2 .5A 46
RM10: Dag .4H 73
Kingsley Ct. DA6: Bex .4G 127
HA8: Edg .3C 28
KT4: Wor Pk .2B 164
(off The Avenue)
NW2 .6D 62
Kingsley Dr. KT4: Wor Pk .2B 164
Kingsley Flats SE1 .4E 102
(off Old Kent Rd.)
Kingsley Gdns. E4 .5H 35
Kingsley Ho. SW3 .6B 100
(off Beaufort St.)
W14 .4G 99
(off Avonmore Pl.)
Kingsley Mans. W14 .6G 99
(off Greyhound Rd.)
Kingsley M. BR7: Chst .6F 143
E1 .7H 85
W8 .3K 99
Kingsley Pl. N6 .7E 46
Kingsley Rd. BR6: Chels .7K 173
CR0: C'don .1A 168
E7 .7J 69
E17 .2E 50
HA2: Harr .4G 59
HA5: Pinn .4D 40
IG6: Ilf .1G 53
N13 .4F 33
NW6 .1H 81
SW19 .5K 135
TW3: Houn .1F 113
Kingsley St. SW11 .3D 118
Kingsley Way N2 .6A 46
Kingsley Wood Dr. SE9 .3D 142
Kings Lodge N12 .6F 31
Kingslyn Cres. SE19 .1E 156
Kings Mall W6 .4E 98
Kingsman Pde. SE18 .3D 106
Kings Mans. SW3 .7C 16
(off Lawrence St.)
Kingsman St. SE18 .3D 106
Kingsmead EN5: New Bar .4D 20
TW10: Rich .6F 115
Kingsmead Av. CR4: Mitc .3G 155
KT4: Wor Pk .2D 164
KT6: Surb .2G 163
N9 .1C 34
NW9 .7K 43
TW16: Sun .2A 148
Kingsmead Cl.
DA15: Sidc .2A 144
KT19: Ewe .7K 163
TW11: Tedd .6B 132
Kingsmead Cotts. BR2: Brom .1C 172
Kingsmead Ct. N6 .7H 47
Kingsmead Dr. UB5: N'olt .7D 58
Kingsmead Ho. E9 .4A 68
Kingsmead Lodge SM2: Sutt .6B 166
Kingsmeadow .3G 151
Kingsmeadow Athletics Cen. .3G 151
Kingsmead Rd. SW2 .2A 138
King's Mead Way E9 .4A 68
Kingsmere Cl. SW15 .3F 117
Kingsmere Pk. NW9 .1H 61
Kingsmere Pl. N16 .1D 66
Kingsmere Rd. SW19 .2F 135
King's M. SW4 .5J 119
WC1 .4H 7 (4K 83)
Kingsmill NW8 .2B 82
(off Kingsmill Ter.)
Kingsmill Bus. Pk. KT1: King T .3F 151
Kingsmill Gdns. RM9: Dag .5F 73
Kingsmill Ho. SW3 .5D 16
(off Cale St.)
Kingsmill Rd. RM9: Dag .5F 73
Kingsmill Ter. NW8 .2B 82
Kingsnorth Ho. W10 .6F 81
Kingsnympton Pk. KT2: King T .7H 133
Kings Oak RM7: Mawney .3G 55
King's Orchard SE9 .6C 124
King's Paddock TW12: Hamp .1G 149
Kings Pde. HA8: Edg .5B 28
(off Edgwarebury La.)
N17 .3F 49
NW10 .1E 80
SM5: Cars .3D 166
(off Wrythe La.)
W12 .3C 98
Kingspark Bus. Cen. KT3: N Mald .4J 151
Kingspark Ct. E18 .3J 51
Kings Pas. E11 .7G 51
KT1: King T .2D 150
KT2: King T .1D 150
Kings Pl. IG9: Buck H .2F 37
SE1 .7C 14 (2C 102)
W4 .5J 97
King Sq. EC1 .2C 8 (3C 84)
Kings Quarter Apartments N1 .1K 83
(off Copenhagen St.)
King's Quay SW10 .1A 118
(off Chelsea Harbour Dr.)
Kings Reach Twr. SE1 .4A 14
Kings Ride Ga. TW10: Rich .4G 115
Kingsridge SW19 .2G 135
Kings Rd. BR6: Orp .4K 173
CR4: Mitc .3E 154
E4 .1A 36
E6 .1A 88
E11 .7G 51
EN5: Barn .3A 20
HA2: Harr .2D 58
IG11: Bark .7G 71
KT2: King T .7E 132
KT6: Surb .1C 162
KT12: Walt T .7K 147
N17 .1F 49
N18 .5B 34
N22 .1K 47
NW10 .7D 62
SE25 .3G 157
SW3 .6D 16 (2J 117)
SW6 .7K 99
SW10 .7A 16 (7K 99)
SW14 .3K 115
SW19 .6J 135
TW1: Twick .6B 114
TW10: Rich .6F 115
TW11: Tedd .5H 131
TW13: Felt .1A 130
UB7: W Dray .2B 92
W5 .5D 78
Kings Rd. Bungs.
HA2: Harr .4D 58
King's Scholars' Pas.
SW1 .2A 18
King Stairs Cl. SE16 .2H 103
King's Ter. NW1 .1G 83
TW7: Isle .4A 114
Kingsthorpe Rd. SE26 .4K 139
Kingston Av. SM3: Cheam .3G 165
TW14: Felt .6G 111
Kingston Av. UB7: Yiew .7B 74
(Ash Gro.)
UB7: Yiew .1B 92
(Whitethorn Av.)
Kingston Bri. KT1: King T .2D 150
Kingston Bus. Cen. KT9: Chess .3E 162
Kingston By-Pass KT3: N Mald .5A 152
KT6: Surb .3D 162
SW15 .4A 134
SW20 .2C 152
Kingston By-Pass Rd. KT6: Surb .3A 162
KT10: Esh, Hin W .3A 162
Kingston Cl. RM6: Chad H .3E 54
(not continuous)
TW11: Tedd .6B 132
UB5: N'olt .1D 76
Kingston Cres. BR3: Beck .1B 158
Kingston Gdns. CR0: Bedd .3J 167
Kingston Hall Rd. KT1: King T .3D 150
Kingston Hill KT2: King T .1G 151
Kingston Hill Av. RM6: Chad H .3E 54
Kingston Hill Pl. KT2: King T .4J 133
Kingston Ho. KT1: King T .4D 150
(off Surbiton Rd.)
NW1 .1G 83
(off Camden St.)
NW6 .7G 63
Kingston Ho. E. SW7 .7C 10
(off Prince's Ga.)
Kingston Ho. Est. KT6: Surb .6B 150
Kingston Ho. Nth. SW7 .7C 10
(off Prince's Ga.)
Kingston Ho. Sth. SW7 .7C 10
(off Ennismore Gdns.)
Kingstonian FC .3G 151
Kingston La. TW11: Tedd .5A 132
UB7: W Dray .2B 92
UB8: Hil .3A 74
Kingston Lodge KT3: N Mald .4A 152
Kingston Pl. HA3: Hrw W .7E 26
Kingston Rd. EN4: E Barn .5G 21
IG1: Ilf .4F 71
KT1: King T .3H 151
KT3: N Mald .3H 151
KT4: Wor Pk .2H 163
KT5: Surb .2H 163
KT17: Ewe .7B 164
KT19: Ewe .2H 163
N9 .2B 34
SW15 .2C 134
SW19 .2C 134
(Norstead Pl.)
SW19 .2H 153
(Watery La.)
SW20 .2F 153
TW11: Tedd .5B 132
TW15: Ashf .6A 128
UB2: S'hall .2D 94
Kingston Sq. SE19 .5D 138
Kingston Theatre .2D 150
Kingston University
Grange Rd. .3E 150
Kingston Hill .5K 133
Penrhyn Rd. .4E 150
Roehampton Vale Cen. .3B 134
Kingston upon Thames Crematorium
KT1: King T .3G 151
Kingston upon Thames
Library, Art Gallery and Mus.
.2E 150
KINGSTON VALE .4A 134
Kingston Va. SW15 .4K 133
Kingstown St. NW1 .1E 82
(not continuous)
King St. E13 .4J 87
EC2 .1D 14 (6C 84)
N2 .3B 46
N17 .1F 49
SW1 .5B 12 (1G 101)
TW1: Twick .1A 132
King St. TW9: Rich .5D 114
UB2: S'hall .3C 94
W3 .1J 97
W6 .4C 98
WC2 .2E 12 (7J 83)
King St. Cloisters W6 .4D 98
(off Clifton Wlk.)
King St. Pde. TW1: Twick .1A 132
(off King St.)
Kings Wlk. Shop. Cen.
SW3 .5E 16 (5D 100)
Kingswater Pl. SW11 .7C 100
Kings Way CR0: Wadd .5K 167
HA1: Harr .4J 41
IG8: Wfd G .5F 37
Kingsway BR4: W W'ck .3G 171
BR5: Pet W .5H 161
EN3: Pond E .5C 24
HA9: Wemb .4E 60
KT3: N Mald .4E 152
N12 .6F 31
SW14 .3H 115
TW19: Stanw .1A 128
UB3: Hayes .5E 74
WC2 .7G 7 (6K 83)
Kingsway Bus. Pk. TW12: Hamp .1D 148
Kingsway Cres. HA2: Harr .4G 41
Kingsway Est. N18 .6E 34
Kingsway Mans. WC1 .5G 7
(off Red Lion Sq.)
Kingsway Pde. N16 .3D 66
(off Albion Rd.)
Kingsway Pl. EC1 .3K 7
(off Sans Wlk.)
Kingsway Rd. SM3: Cheam .7G 165
Kingswear Rd. HA4: Ruis .2J 57
NW5 .3F 65
Kings Wharf E8 .1E 84
(off Kingsland Rd.)
Kingswood E2 .2J 85
(off Cyprus St.)
Kingswood Av. BR2: Brom .3G 159
CR7: Thor H .5A 156
DA17: Belv .4F 109
NW6 .1G 81
TW3: Houn .1D 112
TW12: Hamp .6F 131
Kingswood Cl. BR6: Orp .7J 161
EN1: Enf .5K 23
KT3: N Mald .6B 152
KT6: Surb .7E 150
N20 .7F 21
SW8 .7J 101
TW15: Ashf .5E 128
Kingswood Ct. E4 .5H 35
NW6 .7J 63
(off West End La.)
SE13 .6F 123
Kingswood Dr. SE19 .4E 138
SM2: Sutt .7K 165
SM5: Cars .1D 166
Kingswood Est. SE21 .4E 138
Kingswood M. N15 .4B 48
Kingswood Pk. N3 .1H 45
Kingswood Pl. SE13 .4G 123
Kingswood Rd. BR2: Brom .4F 159
E11 .7G 51
HA9: Wemb .3G 61
IG3: Ilf .1A 72
SE20 .6J 139
SW2 .6J 119
SW19 .7H 135
W4 .3J 97
Kingswood Ter. W4 .3J 97
Kingswood Way SM6: Wall .5J 167
Kingsworth Cl. BR3: Beck .5A 158
Kingsworthy Cl. KT1: King T .3F 151
Kings Yd. SW15 .3E 116
(off Lwr. Richmond Rd.)
Kingthorpe Rd. NW10 .7K 61

Kingthorpe Ter. NW10 .... 6K 61
Kington Ho. NW6 .... 1K 81
(off Mortimer Cres.)
Kingward Ho. E1 .... 5G 85
(off Hanbury St.)
Kingweston Cl. NW2 .... 3G 63
King William IV Gdns. SE20 .... 6J 139
King William La. SE10 .... 5G 105
King William's Ct. SE10 .... 6F 105
(off Park Row)
King William St. EC4 .... 1F 15 (6D 84)
King William Wlk. SE10 .... 6E 104
(not continuous)
Kingwood Rd. SW6 .... 1G 117
Kinlet Rd. SE18 .... 1G 125
Kinloch Dr. NW9 .... 7K 43
Kinloch St. N7 .... 3K 65
Kinloss Ct. N3 .... 4H 45
Kinloss Gdns. N3 .... 3H 45
Kinloss Rd. SM5: Cars 7A 154
Kinnaird Av. BR1: Brom 6H 141
W4 .... 7J 97
Kinnaird Cl. BR1: Brom 6H 141
Kinnaird Way IG8: Wfd G 6J 37
Kinnear Rd. W12 .... 2B 98
Kinnerton Pl. Nth. SW1 .... 7F 11
Kinnerton Pl. Sth. SW1 .... 7F 11
Kinnerton St. SW1 .... 7G 11 (2E 100)
Kinnerton Yd. SW1 .... 7G 11
Kinnoul Rd. W6 .... 6G 99
Kinross Av. KT4: Wor Pk 2C 164
Kinross Cl. HA3: Kent 5F 43
HA8: Edg 2C 28
TW16: Sun 5H 129
Kinross Ct. BR1: Brom 1H 159
(off Highland Rd.)
SE6 .... 1H 141
Kinross Dr. TW16: Sun 5H 129
Kinross Ho. N1 .... 1K 83
(off Bemerton Est.)
Kinross Ter. E17 .... 2B 50
Kinsale Rd. SE15 .... 3G 121
Kinsella Gdns. SW19 .... 5D 134
Kinsham Ho. E2 .... 4G 85
(off Ramsey St.)
Kintore Way SE1 .... 4F 103
Kintyre Cl. SW16 .... 2K 155
Kintyre Ct. SW2 .... 7J 119
Kintyre Ho. E14 .... 1E 104
(off Coldharbour)
Kinveachy Gdns. SE7 .... 5C 106
Kinver Rd. SE26 .... 4J 139
Kipling Ct. W7 .... 7K 77
Kipling Dr. SW19 .... 6B 136
Kipling Est. SE1 .... 7F 15 (2D 102)
Kipling Ho. E16 .... 1K 105
(off Southampton M.)
SE5 .... 7D 102
(off Elmington Est.)
Kipling Pl. HA7: Stan 6E 26
Kipling Rd. DA7: Bex 1E 126
Kipling St. SE1 .... 7F 15 (2D 102)
Kipling Ter. N9 .... 3J 33
Kipling Twr. W3 .... 3J 97
(off Palmerston Rd.)
Kippington Dr. SE9 .... 1B 142
Kirby Cl. KT19: Ewe 5B 164
Kirby Est. SE16 .... 3H 103
UB7: Yiew 7A 74
Kirby Gro. SE1 .... 6G 15 (2E 102)
Kirby St. EC1 .... 5K 7 (5A 84)
Kirby Way KT12: Walt T 6A 148
UB8: Hil 4B 74
Kirchen Rd. W13 .... 7B 78
Kirkby Cl. N11 .... 6K 31
Kirkdale SE26 .... 2H 139
Kirkdale Cnr. SE26 .... 4J 139
Kirkdale Rd. E11 .... 1G 69
Kirkeby Ho. EC1 .... 5J 7
(off Leather La.)
Kirkfield Cl. W13 .... 1B 96
Kirkham Rd. E6 .... 6C 88
Kirkham St. SE18 .... 6J 107
Kirk Ho. HA9: Wemb 3E 60
Kirkland Av. IG5: Ilf 2E 52
Kirkland Cl. DA15: Sidc 6J 125
Kirkland Dr. EN2: Enf 1H 23
Kirkland Ho. E14 .... 5D 104
(off St Davids Sq.)
E14 .... 5D 104
(off Westferry Rd.)
Kirkland Ter. BR3: Beck 6C 140
Kirkland Wlk. E8 .... 6F 67
Kirk La. SE18 .... 6G 107
Kirkleas Rd. KT6: Surb 1E 162
Kirklees Rd. CR7: Thor H 5A 156
RM8: Dag 5C 72
Kirkley Rd. SW19 .... 1J 153
Kirkman Pl. W1 .... 6C 6
Kirkmichael Rd. E14 .... 6E 86
Kirk Ri. SM1: Sutt 3K 165
Kirk Rd. E17 .... 6B 50
Kirkside Rd. SE3 .... 6J 105
Kirkstall Av. N17 .... 4D 48
Kirkstall Gdns. SW2 .... 1J 137
Kirkstall Ho. SW1 .... 5F 101
(off Sutherland St.)
Kirkstall Rd. SW2 .... 1H 137
Kirkstead Ct. E5 .... 4K 67
Kirksted Rd. SM4: Mord 1K 165
Kirkstone NW1 .... 1A 6
(off Harrington St.)
Kirkstone Way BR1: Brom 7G 141
Kirk St. WC1 .... 4G 7
Kirkton Rd. N15 .... 4E 48
Kirkwall Pl. E2 .... 3J 85
Kirkwood Pl. NW1 .... 7E 64
Kirkwood Rd. SE15 .... 2H 121
Kirn Rd. W13 .... 7B 78
Kirrane Cl. KT3: N Mald 5B 152
Kirtley Ho. SW8 .... 1G 119
Kirtley Rd. SE26 .... 4A 140
Kirtling St. SW8 .... 7G 101
Kirton Cl. W4 .... 4K 97
Kirton Gdns. E2 .... 2K 9 (3F 85)
(not continuous)
Kirton Lodge SW18 .... 6K 117
Kirton Rd. E13 .... 2A 88
Kirton Wlk. HA8: Edg 7D 28
Kirwyn Way SE5 .... 7B 102
Kitcat Ter. E3 .... 3C 86
Kitchen Ct. E10 .... 2D 68
Kitchener Rd. CR7: Thor H 3D 156
E7 .... 6K 69
E17 .... 1D 50
N2 .... 3C 46
N17 .... 3E 48
RM10: Dag 6H 73
Kite Pl. E2 .... 3G 85
(off Lampern Sq.)
Kite Yd. SW11 .... 1D 118
(off Cambridge Rd.)
Kitley Gdns. SE19 .... 1F 157
Kitson Rd. SE5 .... 7D 102
SW13 .... 1C 116
Kittiwake Ct. SE1 .... 7D 14
(off Gt. Dover St.)
SE8 .... 6B 104
(off Abinger Gro.)
Kittiwake Pl. SM1: Sutt 5H 165
Kittiwake Rd. UB5: N'olt 3B 76
Kittiwake Way UB4: Yead 5B 76
Kitto Rd. SE14 .... 2K 121
Kitts End Rd. EN5: Barn 1C 20
Kiver Rd. N19 .... 2H 65
Klea Av. SW4 .... 6G 119
Kleine Wharf N1 .... 1E 84
Klein's Wharf E14 .... 3C 104
(off Westferry Rd.)
Knapdale Cl. SE23 .... 2H 139
Knapmill Rd. SE6 .... 2C 140
Knapmill Way SE6 .... 2D 140
Knapp Cl. NW10 .... 6A 62
Knapp Rd. E3 .... 4C 86
TW15: Ashf 4B 128
Knapton M. SW17 .... 6E 136
Knaresborough Dr. SW18 .... 1K 135
Knaresborough Pl. SW5 .... 4K 99
Knatchbull Rd. NW10 .... 1K 79
SE5 .... 2B 120
Knebworth Av. E17 .... 1C 50
Knebworth Cl. EN5: New Bar 4E 20
Knebworth Ho. SW8 .... 2H 119
Knebworth Rd. N16 .... 4E 66
Knee Hill SE2 .... 4C 108
Kneehill Cres. SE2 .... 4C 108
Kneller Gdns. TW7: Isle 6H 113
Kneller Ho. UB5: N'olt 2B 76
(off Academy Gdns.)
Kneller Rd. KT3: N Mald 7A 152
SE4 .... 4A 122
TW2: Whitt 6G 113
Knevett Ter. TW3: Houn 4E 112
Knight Cl. RM8: Dag 2C 72
Knight Ct. E4 .... 1K 35
(off The Ridgeway)
N15 .... 5E 48
Knighten St. E1 .... 1H 103
Knighthead Point E14 .... 2C 104
Knight Ho. SE17 .... 4E 102
(off Tatum St.)
Knightland Rd. E5 .... 2H 67
Knightleas Ct. NW2 .... 6E 62
Knightleys Ct. E10 .... 1A 68
(off Wellington Rd.)
Knighton Cl. CR2: S Croy 7B 168
IG8: Wfd G 4E 36
RM7: Rom 6K 55
Knighton Dr. IG8: Wfd G 4E 36
Knighton Grn. IG9: Buck H 2E 36
Knighton La. IG9: Buck H 2E 36
Knighton Pk. Rd. SE26 .... 5K 139
Knighton Rd. E7 .... 3J 69
RM7: Rom 6J 55
Knightrider Ct. EC4 .... 2B 14
Knightrider St. EC4 .... 2B 14 (6B 84)
Knights Arc. SW1 .... 7E 10
Knights Av. W5 .... 2E 96
KNIGHTSBRIDGE 7E 10 (2C 100)
Knightsbridge SW1 .... 7D 10 (2D 100)
SW7 .... 7D 10 (2D 100)
Knightsbridge Apartments, The
SW7 .... 7E 10
(off Knightsbridge)
Knightsbridge Ct. SW1 .... 7F 11
Knightsbridge Gdns. RM7: Rom 5K 55
Knightsbridge Grn. SW1 .... 7E 10 (2D 100)
(not continuous)
Knights Cl. E9 .... 5J 67
KT8: W Mole 5D 148
Knightscote Cl. UB9: Hare 2A 38
Knights Ct. BR1: Brom 3H 141
KT1: King T 3E 150
RM6: Chad H 6E 54
(off High Rd.)
WD23: B Hea 1C 26
Knights Hill SE27 .... 5B 138
Knight's Hill Sq. SE27 .... 4B 138
Knights Ho. SW8 .... 7J 101
(off Sth. Lambeth Rd.)
SW10 .... 7A 100
(off Hortensia Rd.)
W14 .... 5H 99
(off Baron's Ct. Rd.)
Knights La. N9 .... 3B 34
Knight's Pk.
KT1: King T 3E 150
Knight's Pl. TW2: Twick 1J 131
Knights Rd. E16 .... 2J 105
HA7: Stan 4H 27
Knight's Wlk. SE11 .... 4K 19 (4B 102)
(not continuous)
Knightswood Cl.
HA8: Edg 2D 28
Knightswood Ct. N6 .... 7H 47
Knightswood Ho. N12 .... 6F 31
Knightwood Cres.
KT3: N Mald 6A 152
Knivet Rd. SW6 .... 6J 99
Knockholt Rd. SE9 .... 5B 124
Knole, The SE9 .... 4E 142
Knole Cl. CR0: C'don 6J 157
Knole Ct. UB5: Yead 3A 76
(off Broomcroft Av.)
Knole Ga. DA15: Sidc 3J 143
Knoll, The BR2: Hayes 2J 171
BR3: Beck 1D 158
W13 .... 5C 78
Knoll Ct. SE19 .... 5F 139
(off Farquhar Rd.)
Knoll Cres. HA6: Nwood 2G 39
(not continuous)
Knoll Dr. N14 .... 7K 21
Knoll Ho. NW8 .... 2A 82
(off Carlton Hill)
Knollmead KT5: Surb 1J 163
Knoll Ri. BR6: Orp 1K 173
Knoll Rd. DA5: Bexl 7G 127
DA14: Sidc 5B 144
SW18 .... 5A 118
Knolls Cl. KT4: Wor Pk 3D 164
Knollys Cl. SW16 .... 3A 138
Knolly's Ho. WC1 .... 3E 6
(off Tavistock Pl.)
Knollys Rd. SW16 .... 3K 137
Knot Ho. SE1 .... 5J 15
(off Brewery Sq.)
Knottisford St. E2 .... 3J 85
Knotts Grn. M. E10 .... 6D 50
Knotts Grn. Rd. E10 .... 6D 50
Knowlden Ho. E1 .... 7J 85
(off Cable St.)
Knowle Av. DA7: Bex 7E 108
Knowle Cl. SW9 .... 3A 120
Knowledge Ct. SW16 .... 3K 155
Knowle Rd. BR2: Brom 2D 172
TW2: Twick 1J 131
Knowles Cl. UB7: Yiew 1A 92
Knowles Ct. HA1: Harr 6K 41
(off Gayton Rd.)
Knowles Hill Cres. SE13 .... 5F 123
Knowles Ho. SW18 .... 6K 117
(off Neville Gill Cl.)
Knowles Wlk. SW4 .... 3G 119
Knowles Wharf NW1 .... 1G 83
(off St Pancras Way)
Knowlton Grn. BR2: Brom 5H 159
Knowlton Ho. SW9 .... 1A 120
(off Cowley Rd.)
Knowsley Av. UB1: S'hall 1F 95
Knowsley Rd. SW11 .... 2D 118
Knox Ct. SW4 .... 2J 119
Knox Rd. E7 .... 6H 69
Knox St. W1 .... 5E 4 (5D 82)
Knoyle Ho. W14 .... 3G 99
(off Russell Rd.)
Knoyle St. SE14 .... 6A 104
Koblenz Ho. N8 .... 3J 47
(off Newland Rd.)
Kohat Rd. SW19 .... 5K 135
Korda Cl. TW17: Shep 3B 146
Kossuth St. SE10 .... 5G 105
Kotree Way SE1 .... 4G 103
Kramer M. SW5 .... 5J 99
Kreedman Wlk. E8 .... 5G 67
Kreisel Wlk. TW9: Kew 6F 97
Kristina Ct. SM2: Sutt 6J 165
(off Overton Rd.)
Krupnik Pl. EC2 .... 2H 9
Kuala Gdns. SW16 .... 1K 155

Kubrick Bus. Est. E7 . . . 4K 69
(off Station App.)
Kuhn Way E7 . . . 5J 69
Kwame Ho. E16 . . . 7F 89
(off University Way)
Kydbrook Cl. BR5: Pet W . . . 7G 161
Kylemore Cl. E6 . . . 2B 88
Kylemore Rd. NW6 . . . 7J 63
Kylestrome Ho. SW1 . . . 4H 17
(off Cundy St.)
Kymberley Rd. HA1: Harr . . . 6J 41
Kymes Ct. HA2: Harr . . . 2H 59
Kynance Gdns. HA7: Stan . . . 1C 42
Kynance M. SW7 . . . 3K 99
Kynance Pl. SW7 . . . 3A 100
Kynaston Av. CR7: Thor H . . . 5C 156
N16 . . . 3F 67
Kynaston Cl. HA3: Hrw W . . . 7C 26
Kynaston Cres. CR7: Thor H . . . 5C 156
Kynaston Rd. BR1: Brom . . . 5J 141
CR7: Thor H . . . 5C 156
EN2: Enf . . . 1J 23
N16 . . . 3E 66
Kynaston Wood HA3: Hrw W . . . 7C 26
Kynnersley Cl. SM5: Cars . . . 3D 166
Kynoch Rd. N18 . . . 4D 34
Kyrle Rd. SW11 . . . 6E 118
Kyverdale Rd. N16 . . . 7F 49

L

Laban Cen. . . . 6D 104
(off Creekside)
Laburnum Av. N9 . . . 2A 34
N17 . . . 7J 33
SM1: Sutt . . . 3C 166
UB7: Yiew . . . 7B 74
Laburnum Cl. E4 . . . 6G 35
HA0: Wemb . . . 1G 79
N11 . . . 6K 31
SE15 . . . 7J 103
Laburnum Ct. E2 . . . 1F 85
HA1: Harr . . . 6F 41
HA7: Stan . . . 4H 27
SE16 . . . 2J 103
(off Albion St.)
Laburnum Cres. TW16: Sun . . . 1K 147
Laburnum Gdns. CR0: C'don . . . 7K 157
N21 . . . 2H 33
Laburnum Gro. HA4: Ruis . . . 6F 39
KT3: N Mald . . . 2K 151
N21 . . . 2H 33
NW9 . . . 7J 43
TW3: Houn . . . 4D 112
UB1: S'hall . . . 4D 76
Laburnum Ho. BR2: Brom . . . 1F 159
RM10: Dag . . . 2G 73
Laburnum Lodge N3 . . . 2H 45
Laburnum Pl. SE9 . . . 5E 124
Laburnum Rd. CR4: Mitc . . . 2E 154
SW19 . . . 7A 136
UB3: Harl . . . 4H 93
Laburnums, The E6 . . . 4C 88
Laburnum St. E2 . . . 1F 85
Laburnum Way BR2: Brom . . . 7E 160
TW19: Stanw . . . 1B 128
La Caye Apartments E14 . . . 4F 105
(off Glenaffric Av.)
Lacebark Cl. DA15: Sidc . . . 7K 125
Lacewing Cl. E13 . . . 3J 87
Lacey Cl. N9 . . . 2B 34
Lacey Dr. HA8: Edg . . . 4A 28
TW12: Hamp . . . 1D 148
Lacey M. E3 . . . 2C 86
Lacine Ct. SE16 . . . 2K 103
(off Christopher Cl.)
Lackington St. EC2 . . . 5F 9 (5D 84)
Lackland Ho. SE1 . . . 5F 103
(off Rowcross St.)
Lacland Ho. SW10 . . . 7B 100
(off Worlds End Est.)
Lacock Cl. SW19 . . . 6A 136
Lacock Ct. W13 . . . 1A 96
Lacon Ho. WC1 . . . 5G 7
(off Theobald's Rd.)
Lacon Rd. SE22 . . . 4G 121
Lacrosse Way SW16 . . . 1H 155
Lacy Dr. RM8: Dag . . . 3C 72
Lacy Hall UB8: Cowl . . . 3A 74
(off Kingston La.)
Lacy Rd. SW15 . . . 4F 117
(not continuous)
Ladas Rd. SE27 . . . 4C 138
Ladbroke Cres. W11 . . . 6G 81
Ladbroke Gdns. W11 . . . 7H 81
Ladbroke Gro. W10 . . . 4F 81
W11 . . . 4F 81
Ladbroke Gro. Ho. W11 . . . 7H 81
(off Ladbroke Gro.)
Ladbroke M. W11 . . . 1G 99
Ladbroke Rd. EN1: Enf . . . 6A 24
W11 . . . 1H 99
Ladbroke Sq. W11 . . . 7H 81
Ladbroke Ter. W11 . . . 7H 81
Ladbroke Wlk. W11 . . . 1H 99
Ladbrook Cl. HA5: Pinn . . . 5D 40
Ladbrooke Cres. DA14: Sidc . . . 3D 144
Ladbrook Rd. SE25 . . . 4D 156
Ladderstile Ride TW10: Rich . . . 5H 133
Ladderswood Way N11 . . . 5B 32
Ladlands SE22 . . . 7G 121
Lady Aylesford Av. HA7: Stan . . . 5F 27
Lady Booth Rd. KT1: King T . . . 2E 150
Ladycroft Gdns. BR6: Farnb . . . 5G 173
Ladycroft Rd. SE13 . . . 3D 122
Ladycroft Wlk. HA7: Stan . . . 1D 42
Ladycroft Way BR6: Farnb . . . 5G 173
Lady Dock Path SE16 . . . 2A 104
Lady Elizabeth Ho. SW14 . . . 3J 115
Ladyfern Ho. E3 . . . 5C 86
(off Gail St.)
Lady Florence Courtyard
SE8 . . . 7C 104
(off Reginald Sq.)
Lady Forsdyke Way KT19: Eps . . . 7G 163
Ladygate Bowls Club . . . 6E 38
(off Ladygate La.)
Ladygate La. HA4: Ruis . . . 6D 38
Lady Harewood Way KT19: Eps . . . 7G 163
Lady Hay KT4: Wor Pk . . . 2B 164
Lady Jane Ct. KT2: King T . . . 2F 151
(off London Rd.)
Lady Margaret Ho. SE17 . . . 6D 102
(off Queen's Row)
Lady Margaret Rd. N19 . . . 5G 65
NW5 . . . 5G 65
UB1: S'hall . . . 7D 76
Lady May Ho. SE5 . . . 7C 102
(off Pitman St.)
Lady Micos Almshouses E1 . . . 6J 85
(off Aylward St.)
Lady Sarah Ho. N11 . . . 6J 31
(off Asher Loftus Way)
Lady Shaw Ct. N13 . . . 2E 32
Ladyship Ter. SE22 . . . 7G 121
Ladysmith Av. E6 . . . 2C 88
IG2: Ilf . . . 7H 53
Ladysmith Cl. NW7 . . . 7H 29
Ladysmith Rd. E16 . . . 3H 87
EN1: Enf . . . 3K 23
(not continuous)
HA3: W'stone . . . 2J 41
N17 . . . 2G 49
N18 . . . 5C 34
SE9 . . . 6E 124
Lady Somerset Rd. NW5 . . . 4F 65
LADYWELL . . . 5D 122
Ladywell Arena . . . 6D 122
Ladywell Cl. SE4 . . . 5C 122
Ladywell Hgts. SE4 . . . 6B 122
Ladywell Leisure Cen. . . . 5E 122
Ladywell Rd. SE4 . . . 5C 122
SE13 . . . 5C 122
Ladywell St. E15 . . . 1H 87
Ladywood Av. BR5: Pet W . . . 5J 161
Ladywood Rd. KT6: Surb . . . 2G 163
LA Fitness
Aldgate . . . 2K 15
(off Portsoken St.)
Bayswater . . . 7K 81
(off Moscow Pl.)
Bloomsbury . . . 5G 7
(off Theobald's Rd.)
Bromley . . . 2J 159
(off East St.)
Edgware . . . 6B 28
Finchley . . . 3K 45
Golders Green . . . 7H 45
Gospel Oak . . . 4F 65
Isleworth . . . 3B 114
(off Swan St.)
Leadenhall . . . 1H 15
(off Leadenhall St.)
Marylebone . . . 5E 4 (5D 82)
Muswell Hill . . . 4F 47
(off Hillfield Pk.)
New Barnet . . . 4G 21
Novello . . . 2G 13
Piccadilly . . . 3C 12
(off Regent St.)
St Pauls . . . 6C 8
(off Little Britain)
South Kensington . . . 3C 16 (4C 100)
Southgate . . . 1C 32
Sydenham . . . 4J 139
Victoria . . . 2A 18
(off Bressenden Pl.)
West India Quay . . . 7C 86
Lafone Av. TW13: Felt . . . 2A 130
Lafone St. SE1 . . . 6J 15 (2F 103)
Lagado M. SE16 . . . 1K 103
Lagare Apartments SE1 . . . 6B 14
(off Surrey Row)
Lagonier Ho. EC1 . . . 2D 8
(off Dingley Rd.)
Laidlaw Dr. N21 . . . 5E 22
Laing Dean UB5: N'olt . . . 1A 76
Laing Ho. SE5 . . . 7C 102
Laings Av. CR4: Mitc . . . 2D 154
Lainlock Pl. TW3: Houn . . . 1F 113
Lainson St. SW18 . . . 7J 117
Lairdale Cl. SE21 . . . 1C 138
Laird Ho. SE5 . . . 7C 102
(off Redcar St.)
Lairs Cl. N7 . . . 5J 65
Lait Ho. BR3: Beck . . . 1D 158
Laitwood Rd. SW12 . . . 1F 137
Lakanal SE5 . . . 1E 120
(off Dalwood St.)
Lake, The WD23: B Hea . . . 1C 26
Lake Av. BR1: Brom . . . 6J 141
Lake Bus. Cen. N17 . . . 7B 34
Lake Cl. RM8: Dag . . . 3D 72
SW19 . . . 5H 135
Lakedale Ct. IG11: Bark . . . 4B 90
Lakedale Rd. SE18 . . . 6J 107
Lake Dr. WD23: B Hea . . . 2C 26
Lake Farm Country Pk. . . . 1G 93
Lakefield Cl. SE20 . . . 7H 139
Lakefield Rd. N22 . . . 2B 48
Lake Footpath SE2 . . . 2D 108
Lake Gdns. RM10: Dag . . . 5G 73
SM6: Wall . . . 3F 167
TW10: Ham . . . 2B 132
Lakehall Gdns. CR7: Thor H . . . 5B 156
Lakehall Rd. CR7: Thor H . . . 5B 156
Lake Ho. SE1 . . . 7C 14
(off Southwark Bri. Rd.)
Lake Ho. Rd. E11 . . . 3J 69
Lakehurst Rd. KT19: Ewe . . . 5A 164
Lakeland Cl. HA3: Hrw W . . . 6C 26
Lakenheath N14 . . . 5B 22
Laker Ct. SW4 . . . 1J 119
Laker Ind. Est. BR3: Beck . . . 5A 140
(off Kent Ho. La.)
Lake Rd. CR0: C'don . . . 2B 170
E10 . . . 7D 50
RM6: Chad H . . . 4D 54
RM9: Dag . . . 3H 91
SW19 . . . 5H 135
Laker Pl. SW15 . . . 6G 117
Lakeside BR3: Beck . . . 3D 158
EN2: Enf . . . 4C 22
KT2: King T . . . 7H 133
KT19: Ewe . . . 6A 164
N3 . . . 2K 45
SM6: Wall . . . 4F 167
W13 . . . 6C 78
Lakeside Av. IG4: Ilf . . . 4B 52
SE28 . . . 1A 108
Lakeside Cl. DA15: Sidc . . . 5C 126
HA4: Ruis . . . 4F 39
SE25 . . . 2G 157
Lakeside Ct. N4 . . . 2C 66
Lakeside Cres. EN4: E Barn . . . 5J 21
Lakeside Dr. BR2: Brom . . . 3C 172
NW10 . . . 3F 79
Lakeside Ind. Est. SL3: Coln . . . 2A 174
Lakeside Rd. N13 . . . 4E 32
SL0: Rich P . . . 3A 174
SL3: Coln, Rich P . . . 3A 174
W14 . . . 3F 99
Lakeside Station
Ruislip Lido Railway . . . 4F 39
Lakeside Ter. EC2 . . . 5D 8
Lakeside Way HA9: Wemb . . . 4G 61
Lakes Rd. BR2: Kes . . . 5A 172
Lakeswood Rd. BR5: Pet W . . . 6F 161
Lake Vw. HA8: Edg . . . 5A 28
Lake Vw. Ct. SW1 . . . 1K 17
(off Bressenden Pl.)
Lake Vw. Est. E3 . . . 2A 86
Lakeview Rd. DA16: Well . . . 4B 126
SE27 . . . 5A 138
Lake Vw. Ter. N18 . . . 4A 34
(off Sweet Briar Wlk.)
Lakis Cl. NW3 . . . 4A 64
Laleham Av. NW7 . . . 3E 28
Laleham Ct. SM1: Sutt . . . 5A 166
Laleham Ho. E2 . . . 3J 9
(off Camlet St.)
Laleham Rd. SE6 . . . 7E 122
TW17: Shep . . . 4B 146
Lalor St. SW6 . . . 2G 117
Lambarde Av. SE9 . . . 4E 142
Lambard Ho. SE10 . . . 7E 104
(off Langdale Rd.)
Lamb Cl. UB5: N'olt . . . 3C 76
Lamb Ct. E14 . . . 7A 86
(off Narrow St.)
Lamberhurst Ho. SE15 . . . 6J 103
Lamberhurst Rd. RM8: Dag . . . 1F 73
SE27 . . . 4A 138
Lambert Av. TW9: Rich . . . 3G 115
Lambert Ct. DA8: Erith . . . 6J 109
(off Park Cres.)
Lambert Jones M. EC2 . . . 5C 8
Lambert Lodge TW8: Bford . . . 5D 96
(off Layton Rd.)
Lambert Rd. E16 . . . 6K 87
N12 . . . 5G 31
SW2 . . . 5J 119
Lambert's Pl. CR0: C'don . . . 1D 168
Lamberts Rd.
KT5: Surb . . . 5E 150
Lambert St. N1 . . . 7A 66
Lambert Wlk. HA9: Wemb . . . 3E 60
Lambert Way N12 . . . 5F 31
LAMBETH . . . 3G 19 (3K 101)

Lambeth Bri. SE1 . . . . . 3F 19 (4J 101)
SW1 . . . . . 3F 19 (4J 101)
Lambeth Crematorium
SW17 . . . . . 4A 136
Lambeth High St. SE1 . . . . . 4G 19 (4K 101)
Lambeth Hill EC4 . . . . . 2C 14 (7C 84)
Lambeth Palace 2G 19 (3K 101)
Lambeth Pal. Rd.
SE1 . . . . . 2G 19 (3K 101)
Lambeth Rd. CR0: C'don 7A 156
SE1 . . . . . 3G 19 (4K 101)
Lambeth Towers SE11 . . . . . 2J 19
Lambeth Wlk. SE11 . . . . . 4H 19 (4K 101)
(not continuous)
Lambfold Ho. N7 . . . . . 6J 65
Lamb Ho. SE5 . . . . . 7C 102
(off Elmington Est.)
SE10 . . . . . 6E 104
(off Haddo St.)
Lambkins M. E17 . . . . . 4E 50
Lamb La. E8 . . . . . 7H 67
Lamble St. NW5 . . . . . 5E 64
Lambley Rd. RM9: Dag 6B 72
Lambolle Pl. NW3 . . . . . 6C 64
Lambolle Rd. NW3 . . . . . 6C 64
Lambourn Cl. CR2: S Croy 7B 168
NW5 . . . . . 4G 65
W7 . . . . . 2K 95
Lambourne Av. SW19 . . . . . 4H 135
Lambourne Ct. IG8: Wfd G 7F 37
Lambourne Gdns. E4 . . . . . 2H 35
EN1: Enf 2A 24
IG11: Bark 7K 71
Lambourne Gro. SE16 . . . . . 4K 103
Lambourne Ho. NW8 . . . . . 5B 4
(off Broadley St.)
Lambourne Pl. SE3 . . . . . 1K 123
Lambourne Rd. E11 . . . . . 7E 50
IG3: Ilf 2J 71
IG11: Bark 7J 71
Lambourn Gro. KT1: King T 2H 151
Lambourn Rd. SW4 . . . . . 3F 119
Lambrook Ho. SE15 . . . . . 1G 121
Lambrook Ter. SW6 . . . . . 1G 117
Lamb's Bldgs. EC1 . . . . . 4E 8 (4D 84)
Lamb's Cl. N9 . . . . . 2B 34
Lamb's Conduit Pas.
WC1 . . . . . 5G 7 (5K 83)
Lamb's Conduit St. WC1 . . . . . 4G 7 (4K 83)
(not continuous)
Lambscroft Av. SE9 . . . . . 3A 142
Lambs Health & Fitness 4E 8
Lambs Mdw. IG8: Wfd G 2B 52
Lamb's M. N1 . . . . . 1B 84
Lamb's Pas. EC1 . . . . . 5E 8 (4D 84)
Lambs Ter. N9 . . . . . 2J 33
Lamb St. E1 . . . . . 5J 9 (5F 85)
Lamb's Wlk. EN2: Enf 2H 23
Lambton M. N19 . . . . . 1J 65
(off Lambton Rd.)
Lambton Pl. W11 . . . . . 7H 81
Lambton Rd. N19 . . . . . 1J 65
SW20 . . . . . 1E 152
Lamb Wlk. SE1 . . . . . 7G 15 (2E 102)
LAMDA 5F 99
(off Talgarth Rd.)
LAMDA Theatre 4J 99
(off Logan Pl.)
Lamerock Rd. BR1: Brom 4H 141
Lamerton Rd. IG6: Ilf 2F 53
Lamerton St. SE8 . . . . . 6C 104
Lamford Cl. N17 . . . . . 7J 33
Lamington St. W6 . . . . . 4D 98
Lamlash St. SE11 . . . . . 4B 102
Lamley Ho. SE10 . . . . . 7D 104
(off Ashburnham Pl.)
Lammas Av. CR4: Mitc 2E 154
Lammas Grn. SE26 . . . . . 3H 139
Lammas Pk. Gdns. W5 . . . . . 1C 96
Lammas Pk. Rd. W5 . . . . . 2D 96
Lammas Rd. E9 . . . . . 7K 67
E10 . . . . . 2A 68
TW10: Ham 4C 132
Lammermoor Rd. SW12 . . . . . 7F 119
Lamont Rd. SW10 . . . . . 7A 16 (6B 100)
Lamont Rd. Pas. SW10 . . . . . 7A 16
LAMORBEY 1K 143
Lamorbey Cl. DA15: Sidc 1K 143
Lamorbey Swimming Cen. 2A 144
Lamorna Cl. BR6: Orp 7K 161
E17 . . . . . 2E 50
Lamorna Gro. HA7: Stan 1D 42
Lampard Gro. N16 . . . . . 1F 67
Lampern Sq. E2 . . . . . 3G 85
Lampeter Cl. NW9 . . . . . 6A 44
Lampeter Sq. W6 . . . . . 6G 99
Lamplighter Cl. E1 . . . . . 4J 85
Lampmead Rd. SE12 . . . . . 5H 123
Lamp Office Ct. WC1 . . . . . 4G 7
Lamport Cl. SE18 . . . . . 4D 106
LAMPTON 1F 113
Lampton Av. TW3: Houn 1F 113
Lampton Ct. TW3: Houn 1F 113
Lampton Ho. Cl. SW19 . . . . . 4F 135
Lampton Pk. Rd. TW3: Houn 2F 113
Lampton Rd. TW3: Houn 2F 113
Lampton Sports Cen. 2E 112
Lanacre Av. NW9 . . . . . 1K 43
Lanain Ct. SE12 . . . . . 7H 123
Lanark Cl. W5 . . . . . 5C 78
Lanark Ct. UB5: N'olt 5E 58
(off Newmarket Av.)
Lanark Ho. SE1 . . . . . 5G 103
(off Old Kent Rd.)
Lanark Mans. W9 . . . . . 4A 82
(off Lanark Rd.)
W12 . . . . . 2E 98
(off Pennard Rd.)
Lanark M. W9 . . . . . 3A 82
Lanark Pl. W9 . . . . . 3A 4 (4A 82)
Lanark Rd. W9 . . . . . 2K 81
Lanark Sq. E14 . . . . . 3D 104
Lanata Wlk. UB4: Yead 4B 76
(off Alba Cl.)
Lanbury Rd. SE15 . . . . . 4K 121
Lancashire Ct. W1 . . . . . 2K 11
Lancaster Av. CR4: Mitc 5J 155
E18 . . . . . 4K 51
EN4: Had W 1F 21
IG11: Bark 7J 71
SE27 . . . . . 2B 138
SW19 . . . . . 5F 135
Lancaster Cl. BR2: Brom 4H 159
KT2: King T 5D 132
N1 . . . . . 7E 66
N17 . . . . . 7B 34
NW9 . . . . . 7G 29
TW15: Ashf 4A 128
TW19: Stanw 6A 110
W2 . . . . . 7K 81
(off St Petersburgh Pl.)
Lancaster Cotts.
TW10: Rich 6E 114
Lancaster Ct.
KT12: Walt T 7J 147
SE27 . . . . . 2B 138
SM2: Sutt 7J 165
(off Mulgrave Rd.)
SW6 . . . . . 7H 99
TW19: Stanw 1A 128
W2 . . . . . 2A 10
(off Lancaster Ga.)
Lancaster Dr. E14 . . . . . 1E 104
NW3 . . . . . 6C 64
Lancaster Gdns. BR1: Brom 5C 160
KT2: King T 5D 132
SW19 . . . . . 5G 135
W13 . . . . . 2B 96
Lancaster Ga. W2 . . . . . 2A 10 (7A 82)
Lancaster Gro. NW3 . . . . . 6B 64
Lancaster Hall E16 . . . . . 1J 105
(off Wesley Av., not continuous)
UB8: Cowl 3A 74
(off Kingston La.)
Lancaster House 6A 12
Lancaster Ho. EN2: Enf 1J 23
Lancaster Lodge W11 . . . . . 6G 81
(off Lancaster Rd.)
Lancaster M. SW18 . . . . . 5K 117
TW10: Rich 6E 114
W2 . . . . . 2A 10 (7A 82)
Lancaster Pk. TW10: Rich 5E 114
Lancaster Pl. IG1: Ilf 5G 71
SW19 . . . . . 5F 135
TW1: Twick 6A 114
TW4: Houn 2A 112
WC2 . . . . . 2G 13 (7K 83)
Lancaster Rd. E7 . . . . . 7J 69
E11 . . . . . 2G 69
E17 . . . . . 2K 49
EN2: Enf 1J 23
EN4: E Barn 5G 21
HA2: Harr 5E 40
N4 . . . . . 7K 47
N11 . . . . . 6C 32
N18 . . . . . 5A 34
NW10 . . . . . 5C 62
SE25 . . . . . 2F 157
SW19 . . . . . 5F 135
UB1: S'hall 7C 76
UB5: N'olt 6G 59
W11 . . . . . 6G 81
Lancaster Rd. Ind. Est.
EN4: E Barn 5G 21
(off Lancaster Rd.)
Lancaster Stables NW3 . . . . . 6C 64
Lancaster St. SE1 . . . . . 7A 14 (2B 102)
Lancaster Ter. W2 . . . . . 2A 10 (7B 82)
Lancaster Wlk. UB3: Hayes 6E 74
W2 . . . . . 3A 10 (1A 100)
Lancaster Way KT4: Wor Pk 7D 152
Lancastrian Rd. SM6: Wall 7J 167
Lancefield Ho. SE15 . . . . . 4H 121
Lancefield St. W10 . . . . . 3H 81
Lancell St. N16 . . . . . 2F 67
Lancelot Av. HA0: Wemb 4D 60
Lancelot Cres. HA0: Wemb 4D 60
Lancelot Gdns. EN4: E Barn 7K 21
Lancelot Pl. SW7 . . . . . 7E 10 (2D 100)
Lancelot Rd. DA16: Well 4A 126
HA0: Wemb 4D 60
Lance Rd. HA1: Harr 7G 41
Lancer Sq. W8 . . . . . 2K 99
(off Kensington Chu. St.)
Lancey Cl. SE7 . . . . . 4C 106
Lanchester Ct. W2 . . . . . 1E 10
(off Seymour St.)
Lanchester Rd. N6 . . . . . 5D 46
Lanchester Way SE14 . . . . . 1J 121
Lancing Gdns. N9 . . . . . 1A 34
Lancing Ho. CR0: C'don 4D 168
(off Coombe Rd.)
Lancing Rd. CR0: C'don 7K 155
IG2: Ilf 6H 53
TW13: Felt 2H 129
W13 . . . . . 7B 78
Lancing St. NW1 . . . . . 2C 6 (3H 83)
Lancresse Ct. N1 . . . . . 1E 84
(off De Beauvoir Est.)
Landale Ho. SE16 . . . . . 3J 103
(off Lower Rd.)
Landau Ct. CR2: S Croy 5C 168
(off Warham Rd.)
Landcroft Rd. SE22 . . . . . 5F 121
Landells Rd. SE22 . . . . . 6F 121
Landford Rd. SW15 . . . . . 3E 116
Landgrove Rd.
SW19 . . . . . 5J 135
Landin Ho. E14 . . . . . 6C 86
(off Thomas Rd.)
Landleys Fld. N7 . . . . . 5H 65
(off Long Mdw.)
Landmann Ho. SE16 . . . . . 4H 103
(off Rennie Est.)
Landmann Way SE14 . . . . . 5K 103
Landmark Arts Cen. 5B 132
Landmark Commercial Cen.
N18 . . . . . 6K 33
Landmark Hgts. E5 . . . . . 4A 68
Landmark Ho. W6 . . . . . 5E 98
(off Hammersmith Bri. Rd.)
Landon Pl. SW1 . . . . . 1E 16 (3D 100)
Landon's Cl. E14 . . . . . 1E 104
Landon Wlk. E14 . . . . . 7D 86
Landon Way TW15: Ashf 6D 128
Landor Ho. SE5 . . . . . 7D 102
(off Elmington Est.)
W2 . . . . . 5J 81
(off Westbourne Pk. Rd.)
Landor Rd. SW9 . . . . . 3J 119
Landor Theatre 3J 119
Landor Wlk. W12 . . . . . 2C 98
Landra Gdns. N21 . . . . . 6G 23
Landrake NW1 . . . . . 1G 83
(off Plender St.)
Landridge Dr. EN1: Enf 1C 24
Landridge Rd. SW6 . . . . . 2H 117
Landrock Rd. N8 . . . . . 6J 47
Landscape Rd. IG8: Wfd G 7E 36
Landsdown Cl. EN5: New Bar 4F 21
Landseer Av. E12 . . . . . 5E 70
Landseer Cl. HA8: Edg 2G 43
SW19 . . . . . 1A 154
Landseer Ct. UB4: Hayes 2F 75
Landseer Ho. NW8 . . . . . 3B 4
(off Frampton St.)
SW1 . . . . . 4D 18
(off Herrick St.)
SW11 . . . . . 1E 118
UB5: N'olt 2B 76
(off Parkfield Dr.)
Landseer Rd. EN1: Enf 5B 24
KT3: N Mald 7K 151
N19 . . . . . 3J 65
(not continuous)
SM1: Sutt 6J 165
Landstead Rd. SE18 . . . . . 7H 107
Landulph Ho. SE11 . . . . . 5K 19
(off Kennings Way)
Landward Ct. W1 . . . . . 7D 4
(off Harrowby St.)
Lane, The NW8 . . . . . 2A 82
SE3 . . . . . 3J 123
Lane App. NW7 . . . . . 5B 30
Lane Cl. NW2 . . . . . 3D 62
Lane End DA7: Bex 3H 127
SW15 . . . . . 6F 117
Lane Gdns. WD23: B Hea 1D 26
Lane M. E12 . . . . . 3D 70
Lanercost Cl. SW2 . . . . . 2A 138
Lanercost Gdns. N14 . . . . . 7D 22
Lanercost Rd. SW2 . . . . . 2A 138
Lanesborough Ct. N1 . . . . . 1G 9
(off Fanshaw St.)
Lanesborough Pl. SW1 . . . . . 6H 11
Laneside BR7: Chst 5F 143
HA8: Edg 5D 28
Laneside Av. RM8: Dag 7F 55
Laneway SW15 . . . . . 5D 116
Laney Ho. EC1 . . . . . 5J 7
(off Leather La.)
Lanfranc Ct. HA1: Harr 3K 59
Lanfranc Rd. E3 . . . . . 2A 86
Lanfrey Pl. W14 . . . . . 5H 99
Langbourne Av. N6 . . . . . 2E 64
Langbourne Ct. E17 . . . . . 6A 50
Langbourne Mans. N6 . . . . . 2E 64
Langbourne Pl. E14 . . . . . 5D 104
Langbourne Way KT10: Clay 6A 162
Langbrook Rd. SE3 . . . . . 3B 124

Langcroft Cl. SM5: Cars 3D 166
Langdale NW1 1A 6
(off Stanhope St.)
Langdale Av. CR4: Mitc 3D 154
Langdale Cl. BR6: Farnb 3F 173
RM8: Dag 1C 72
SE17 6C 102
SW14 4H 115
Langdale Cres. DA7: Bex 7G 109
Langdale Dr. UB4: Hayes 2G 75
Langdale Gdns. UB6: G'frd 3B 78
Langdale Ho. SW1 6A 18
(off Churchill Gdns.)
Langdale Pde. CR4: Mitc 3D 154
Langdale Rd. CR7: Thor H 4A 156
SE10 7E 104
Langdale St. E1 6H 85
Langdon Ct. EC1 1B 8
(off City Rd.)
NW10 1A 80
Langdon Cres. E6 2E 88
Langdon Dr. NW9 1J 61
Langdon Ho. E14 6E 86
Langdon Pk. TW11: Tedd 7C 132
Langdon Pk. Rd. N6 7G 47
Langdon Pl. SW14 3J 115
Langdon Rd. BR2: Brom 3K 159
E6 1E 88
SM4: Mord 5A 154
Langdons Ct. UB2: S'hall 3E 94
Langdon Shaw DA14: Sidc 5K 143
Langdon Wlk. SM4: Mord 5A 154
Langdon Way SE1 4G 103
Langford Cl. E8 5G 67
NW8 2A 82
W3 2H 97
Langford Ct. NW8 2A 82
(off Abbey Rd.)
Langford Cres. EN4: Cockf 4J 21
Langford Grn. SE5 3E 120
Langford Ho. SE8 6C 104
Langford M. N1 7A 66
Langford Pl. DA14: Sidc 3A 144
NW8 2A 82
Langford Rd. EN4: Cockf 4J 21
IG8: Wfd G 6F 37
SW6 2K 117
Langfords IG9: Buck H 2G 37
Langham Cl. N15 3B 48
(off Langham Rd.)
Langham Ct. HA4: Ruis 5K 57
NW4 5F 45
SW20 2E 152
Langham Dr. RM6: Chad H 6B 54
Langham Gdns. HA0: Wemb 2C 60
HA8: Edg 7D 28
N21 5F 23
TW10: Ham 4C 132
W13 7B 78
Langham Ho. Cl. TW10: Ham 4D 132
Langham Mans. SW5 5K 99
(off Earl's Ct. Sq.)
Langham Pk. Pl. BR2: Brom 4H 159
Langham Pl. N15 3B 48
W1 6K 5 (5F 83)
W4 6A 98
Langham Rd. HA8: Edg 6D 28
N15 3B 48
SW20 1E 152
TW11: Tedd 5B 132
Langham St. W1 6K 5 (5F 83)
Langhedge Cl. N18 6A 34
Langhedge La. N18 6A 34
Langhedge La. Ind. Est. N18 6A 34
Langholm Cl. SW12 7H 119
Langholme WD23: Bush 1B 26
Langhorn Dr. TW2: Twick 7J 113
Langhorne Ct. NW8 7B 64
(off Dorman Way)
Langhorne Rd. RM10: Dag 7G 73
Lang Ho. SW8 7J 101
(off Hartington Rd.)
TW19: Stanw 1A 128
Langland Cres. HA7: Stan 2D 42
Langland Dr. HA5: Pinn 1C 40
Langland Gdns. CR0: C'don 2B 170
NW3 5K 63
Langland Ho. SE5 7D 102
(off Edmund St.)
Langler Rd. NW10 2E 80
Langley Av. HA4: Ruis 2K 57
KT4: Wor Pk 1F 165
KT6: Surb 1D 162
Langley Ct. WC2 2E 12 (7J 83)
Langley Cres. E11 7A 52
HA8: Edg 3D 28
RM9: Dag 7C 72
UB3: Harl 7H 93
Langley Dr. E11 7K 51
W3 2H 97
Langley Gdns. BR2: Brom 4A 160
BR5: Pet W 6F 161
RM9: Dag 7D 72
Langley Gro. KT3: N Mald 2A 152
Langley Ho. W2 5J 81
(off Alfred Rd.)
Langley La. SW8 7F 19 (6K 101)
Langley Mans. SW8 7F 19
Langley M. RM9: Dag 7D 72
Langley Pk. NW7 6F 29
Langley Pk. Girls School Sports Cen. 6E 158
Langley Pk. Rd. SM1: Sutt 5A 166
SM2: Sutt 6A 166
Langley Rd. BR3: Beck 4A 158
DA16: Well 6C 108
KT6: Surb 7E 150
SW19 1H 153
TW7: Isle 2K 113
Langley Row EN5: Barn 1C 20
Langley St. WC2 1E 12 (6J 83)
Langley Way BR4: W W'ck 1F 171
Langmead Dr. WD23: B Hea 1D 26
Langmead St. SE27 4B 138
Langmore Ct. DA6: Bex 3D 126
Langmore Ho. E1 6G 85
(off Stutfield St.)
Langport Ct. KT12: Walt T 7A 148
Langport Ho. SW9 2B 120
Langridge M. TW12: Hamp 6D 130
Langroyd Rd. SW17 2D 136
Langside Av. SW15 4C 116
Langside Cres. N14 3C 32
Langstone Way NW7 7A 30
Langston Hughes Cl. SE24 4B 120
Lang St. E1 4J 85
Langthorn Ct. EC2 7E 8 (6D 84)
Langthorne Ct. BR1: Brom 4E 140
Langthorne Ho. UB3: Harl 4G 93
Langthorne Rd. E11 3E 68
Langthorne St. SW6 7F 99
Langton Av. E6 3E 88
N20 7F 21
Langton Cl. WC1 3H 7 (4K 83)
Langton Ho. SE11 3H 19
Langton Pl. SW18 1J 135
Langton Ri. SE23 7H 121
Langton Rd. HA3: Hrw W 7B 26
KT8: W Mole 4G 149
NW2 3E 62
SW9 7B 102
Langton St. SW10 6A 100
Langton Way CR0: C'don 3E 168
SE3 1H 123
Langtry Ho. KT2: King T 1G 151
(off London Rd.)
Langtry Pl. SW6 6J 99
Langtry Rd. NW8 1K 81
UB5: N'olt 2B 76
Langtry Wlk. NW8 1K 81
Langwood Chase
TW11: Tedd 6C 132
Langworth Dr. UB4: Yead 6K 75
Lanhill Rd. W9 4J 81
Lanier Rd. SE13 6F 123
Lanigan Dr. TW3: Houn 5F 113
Lankaster Gdns. N2 1B 46
Lankers Dr. HA2: Harr 6D 40
Lankton Cl. BR3: Beck 1E 158
Lannock Rd. UB3: Hayes 1H 93
Lannoy Point SW6 7G 99
(off Pellant Rd.)
Lannoy Rd. SE9 1G 143
Lanrick Ho. E14 6F 87
(off Lanrick Rd.)
Lanrick Rd. E14 6F 87
Lanridge Rd. SE2 3D 108
Lansbury Av. IG11: Bark 7A 72
N18 5J 33
RM6: Chad H 5E 54
TW14: Felt 6K 111
Lansbury Cl. NW10 5J 61
Lansbury Ct. SE28 7B 90
(off Saunders Way)
Lansbury Dr. UB4: Hayes 2G 75
Lansbury Est. E14 6D 86
Lansbury Gdns. E14 6F 87
Lansbury Rd. EN3: Enf H 1E 24
Lansbury Way N18 5K 33
Lanscombe Wlk. SW8 1J 119
Lansdell Ho. SW2 6A 120
(off Tulse Hill)
Lansdell Rd. CR4: Mitc 2E 154
Lansdowne Av. BR6: Farnb 1F 173
DA7: Bex 7D 108
Lansdowne Cl. KT6: Surb 2H 163
SW20 7F 135
TW1: Twick 1K 131
Lansdowne Ct. IG5: Ilf 3C 52
KT4: Wor Pk 2C 164
W11 7G 81
(off Lansdowne Ri.)
Lansdowne Cres. W11 7G 81
Lansdowne Dr. E8 6G 67
Lansdowne Gdns. SW8 1J 119
Lansdowne Grn. Est. SW8 1J 119
Lansdowne Gro. NW10 4A 62
Lansdowne Hill SE27 3B 138
Lansdowne Ho. W11 1H 99
(off Ladbroke Rd.)
Lansdowne La. SE7 6B 106
Lansdowne M. SE7 5B 106
W11 1H 99
Lansdowne Pl. SE1 3D 102
SE19 7F 139
Lansdowne Ri. W11 7G 81
Lansdowne Rd.
BR1: Brom 7J 141
CR0: C'don 2D 168
E4 2H 35
E11 2H 69
E17 6C 50
E18 3J 51
HA1: Harr 7J 41
HA7: Stan 6H 27
IG3: Ilf 1K 71
KT19: Ewe 7J 163
N3 7D 30
N10 2G 47
N17 1F 49
SW20 7E 134
TW3: Houn 3F 113
UB8: Hil 6E 74
W11 7G 81
Lansdowne Row W1 4K 11 (1F 101)
Lansdowne Ter. WC1 4F 7 (4J 83)
Lansdowne Wlk. W11 1H 99
Lansdowne Way SW8 1H 119
Lansdowne Wood Cl. SE27 3B 138
Lansdowne Workshops SE7 5A 106
Lansdown Rd. DA14: Sidc 3B 144
E7 7A 70
Lansfield Av. N18 4B 34
Lantern SE1 6C 14
(off Lant St.)
Lantern Cl. HA0: Wemb 5D 60
SW15 4C 116
Lantern Pl. BR6: Farnb 4F 173
Lanterns Ct. E14 2D 104
Lantern Way UB7: W Dray 2A 92
Lant Ho. SE1 7C 14
(off Toulmin St.)
Lantry Ct. W3 1H 97
Lant St. SE1 6C 14 (2C 102)
Lanvanor Rd. SE15 2J 121
Lanyard Ho. SE8 4B 104
Lapford Cl. W9 4H 81
Lapponum Wlk. UB4: Yead 4B 76
Lapse Wood Wlk. SE23 1H 139
Lapstone Gdns. HA3: Kent 6C 42
Lapwing Ct. KT6: Surb 3G 163
SE1 7D 14
(off Swan St.)
Lapwing Twr. SE8 6B 104
(off Taylor Cl.)
Lapwing Way UB4: Yead 6B 76
Lapworth N11 4A 32
(off Coppies Gro.)
Lapworth Ct. W2 5K 81
(off Delamere Ter.)
Lara Cl. KT9: Chess 7E 162
SE13 6E 122
Larbert Rd. SW16 7G 137
Larch Av. W3 1A 98
Larch Cl. E13 4K 87
N11 7K 31
N19 2G 65
SE8 6B 104
SW12 2F 137
Larch Ct. SE1 7G 15
(off Royal Oak Yd.)
W9 5J 81
(off Admiral Wlk.)
Larch Cres. KT19: Ewe 6H 163
UB4: Yead 4A 76
Larch Dene BR6: Farnb 2E 172
Larch Dr. W4 5G 97
Larches, The N13 3H 33
UB10: Hil 3D 74
Larches Av. SW14 4K 115
Larch Grn. NW9 1A 44
Larch Gro. DA15: Sidc 1K 143
Larch Ho. BR2: Brom 1G 159
SE16 2J 103
(off Ainsty Est.)
UB4: Yead 5A 76
W10 4G 81
(off Rowan Wlk.)
Larch Rd. E10 2C 68
NW2 4E 62
Larch Tree Way CR0: C'don 3C 170
Larchvale Ct. SM2: Sutt 7K 165
Larch Way BR2: Brom 7E 160
Larchwood Rd. SE9 2F 143
Larcombe Cl. CR0: C'don 4F 169
Larcombe Ct. SM2: Sutt 7K 165
(off Worcester Rd.)
Larcom St. SE17 4C 102
Larden Rd. W3 1A 98
Largewood Av. KT6: Surb 2G 163
Larissa St. SE17 5D 102
Larkbere Rd. SE26 4A 140
Larken Cl. WD23: Bush 1B 26
Larken Dr. WD23: Bush 1B 26
Larkfield Av. HA3: Kent 3B 42
Larkfield Cl. BR2: Hayes 2H 171
Larkfield Rd.
DA14: Sidc 3K 143
TW9: Rich 4E 114
Larkhall La. SW4 2H 119

Larkhall Ri. SW4 .3G 119
(not continuous)
Larkham Cl. TW13: Felt .3G 129
Larkhill Ter. SE18 .7E 106
Lark Row E2 .1J 85
Larksfield Gro. EN1: Enf .1C 24
Larks Gro. IG11: Bark .7J 71
Larkshall Ct. RM7: Mawney .2J 55
Larkshall Cres. E4 .4K 35
Larkshall Rd. E4 .5K 35
Larkspur Cl. E6 .5C 88
HA4: Ruis .7E 38
N17 .7J 33
NW9 .5H 43
Larkspur Gro. HA8: Edg .4D 28
Larkspur Lodge DA14: Sidc .3B 144
Larkspur Way KT19: Ewe .5J 163
Larkswood Ct. E4 .5A 36
Larkswood Leisure Cen. .4K 35
Larkswood Ri. HA5: Eastc .4A 40
Larkswood Rd. E4 .4H 35
Lark Way SM5: Cars .7C 154
Larkway Cl. NW9 .4K 43
Larnaca Ho. *SE1* .*3F 103*
(off Grange Wlk.)
Larnach Rd. W6 .6F 99
Larne Rd. HA4: Ruis .7H 39
Larpent Av. SW15 .5E 116
Larwood Cl. UB6: G'frd .5H 59
Lascelles Av. HA1: Harr .7H 41
Lascelles Cl. E11 .2F 69
Lascelles Ho. NW1 .4D 4
Lascotts Rd. N22 .6E 32
Laseron Ho. *N15* .*4F 49*
(off Tottenham Grn. E.)
Lassa Rd. SE9 .5C 124
Lassell St. SE10 .5F 105
Lasseter Pl. SE3 .6G 105
Latchett Rd. E18 .1K 51
Latchingdon Ct. E17 .4K 49
Latchingdon Gdns. IG8: Wfd G .6H 37
Latchmere Cl. TW10: Ham .5E 132
Latchmere La. KT2: King T .6F 133
TW10: Ham .6F 133
Latchmere Leisure Cen. .2D 118
Latchmere Pas. SW11 .2C 118
Latchmere Rd. KT2: King T .7E 132
SW11 .2D 118
Latchmere St. SW11 .2D 118
Lateward Rd. TW8: Bford .6D 96
Latham Cl. E6 .5C 88
TW1: Twick .7A 114
Latham Ct. *N11* .*6D 32*
(off Brownlow Rd.)
SW5 .*4J 99*
(off W. Cromwell Rd.)
UB5: N'olt .*3B 76*
(off Seasprite Cl.)
Latham Ho. *E1* .*6K 85*
(off Chudleigh St.)
Latham Rd. DA6: Bex .5G 127
TW1: Twick .7K 113
Latham's Way CR0: Wadd .1K 167
Lathkill Cl. EN1: Enf .7B 24
Lathkill Ct. BR3: Beck .1B 158
Lathom Rd. E6 .7C 70
Latimer Av. E6 .1D 88
Latimer Cl. HA5: Pinn .1A 40
KT4: Wor Pk .4D 164
Latimer Ct. *BR2: Brom* .*4H 159*
(off Durham Rd.)
Latimer Gdns. HA5: Pinn .1A 40
Latimer Ho. E9 .6K 67
W11 .*7H 81*
(off Kensington Pk. Rd.)
Latimer Ind. Est. W10 .6E 80
Latimer Pl. W10 .6E 80
Latimer Rd. CR0: C'don .3B 168
E7 .4K 69
EN5: New Bar .3E 20
Latimer Rd. N15 .6E 48
SW19 .6K 135
TW11: Tedd .5K 131
W10 .5E 80
(not continuous)
Latitude Ct. E16 .7G 89
Latitude Ho. *NW1* .*1F 83*
(off Oval Rd.)
Latona Ct. *SW9* .*7A 102*
(off Caldwell St.)
Latona Rd. SE15 .6G 103
La Tourne Gdns. BR6: Farnb .3G 173
Lattimer Pl. W4 .7A 98
Latton Cl. KT12: Walt T .7C 148
Latvia Ct. *SE17* .*5C 102*
(off Sutherland Sq.)
Latymer Ct. W6 .4F 99
Latymer Gdns. N3 .2G 45
Latymer Rd. N9 .1A 34
Latymer Upper School Sports Cen. .5C 98
Latymer Way N9 .2K 33
Laubin Pl. TW1: Twick .4B 114
Lauder Cl. UB5: N'olt .2B 76
Lauder Ct. N14 .7D 22
Lauderdale Dr. TW10: Ham .3D 132
Lauderdale House .1F 65
Lauderdale Ho. *SW9* .*1A 120*
(off Gosling Way)
Lauderdale Mans. *W9* .*3K 81*
(off Lauderdale Rd.)
Lauderdale Pde. W9 .4K 81
Lauderdale Pl. *EC2* .*5C 8*
(off Beech St.)
Lauderdale Rd. W9 .3K 81
Lauderdale Twr. EC2 .5C 8
Laud St. CR0: C'don .3C 168
SE11 .5G 19 (5K 101)
Laugan Wlk. SE17 .5C 102
Laughton Rd. UB5: N'olt .1B 76
Launcelot Rd. BR1: Brom .4J 141
Launcelot St. SE1 .7J 13 (2A 102)
Launceston Gdns.
UB6: G'frd .1C 78
Launceston Pl. W8 .3A 100
Launceston Rd. UB6: G'frd .1C 78
Launch St. E14 .3E 104
Laundress La. N16 .3G 67
Laundry La. N1 .1C 84
Laundry M. SE23 .7A 122
Laundry Rd. W6 .6G 99
Launton Dr. DA6: Bex .4D 126
Laura Cl. E11 .5A 52
EN1: Enf .5K 23
Lauradale Rd. N2 .4D 46
Laura Pl. E5 .4J 67
Laura Ter. N4 .2B 66
Laurel Apartments *SE17* .*4E 102*
(off Townsend St.)
Laurel Av. TW1: Twick .1K 131
Laurel Bank N12 .4F 31
Laurel Bank Gdns.
SW6 .2H 117
Laurel Bank Rd. EN2: Enf .1H 23
Laurel Bank Vs. *W7* .*2J 95*
(off Lwr. Boston Rd.)
Laurelbrook SE6 .3G 141
Laurel Cl. DA14: Sidc .3A 144
N19 .2G 65
SW17 .5C 136
Laurel Ct. *CR2: S Croy* .*4E 168*
(off South Pk. Hill Rd.)
HA0: Wemb .2E 78
Laurel Cres. CR0: C'don .3C 170
RM7: Rush G .1K 73
Laurel Dr. N21 .7F 23
Laurel Gdns. BR1: Brom .4C 160
E4 .7J 25
NW7 .3E 28
TW4: Houn .4C 112
W7 .1J 95
Laurel Gro. SE20 .7H 139
SE26 .4K 139
Laurel Ho. BR2: Brom .1G 159
SE8 .6B 104
Laurel La. UB7: W Dray .4A 92
Laurel Mnr. SM2: Sutt .7A 166
Laurel Pk. HA3: Hrw W .7E 26
Laurel Rd. SW13 .2C 116
SW20 .1D 152
TW12: Ham H .5H 131
Laurels, The BR1: Brom .1K 159
BR2: Brom .4J 159
IG9: Buck H .1F 37
NW10 .1D 80
WD23: B Hea .2D 26
Laurel St. E8 .6F 67
Laurel Vw. N12 .3E 30
Laurel Way E18 .4H 51
N20 .3D 30
Laurence Ct. E10 .7D 50
W11 .*7G 81*
(off Lansdowne Rd.)
Laurence M. W12 .2C 98
Laurence Pountney Hill
EC4 .2E 14 (7D 84)
Laurence Pountney La.
EC4 .2E 14 (7D 84)
Laurie Gro. SE14 .1A 122
Laurie Ho. *SE1* .*3B 102*
(off St George's Rd.)
W8 .*1J 99*
(off Airlie Gdns.)
Laurie Rd. W7 .5J 77
Laurier Rd. CR0: C'don .7F 157
NW5 .3F 65
Laurimel Cl. HA7: Stan .6G 27
Laurino Pl. WD23: B Hea .2B 26
Lauriston Ho. *E9* .*7J 67*
(off Lauriston Rd.)
Lauriston Rd. E9 .7J 67
SW19 .6F 135
Lausanne Rd. N8 .4A 48
SE15 .1J 121
Lavell St. N16 .4D 66
Lavender Av. CR4: Mitc .1C 154
KT4: Wor Pk .3E 164
NW9 .1J 61
Lavender Cl. BR2: Brom .6C 160
E4 .4H 35
SM5: Cars .4F 167
SW3 .7B 16 (6B 100)
Lavender Ct. KT8: W Mole .3F 149
SM2: Sutt .7A 166
TW14: Felt .6K 111
Lavender Gdns. EN2: Enf .1G 23
HA3: Hrw W .6D 26
SW11 .4D 118
Lavender Gro. CR4: Mitc .1C 154
E8 .7G 67
Lavender Hill EN2: Enf .1F 23
SW11 .4C 118
Lavender Ho. *SE16* .*1K 103*
(off Rotherhithe St.)
TW9: Kew .1H 115
Lavender Pl. IG1: Ilf .5F 71
Lavender Pond Nature Pk. .1A 104
Lavender Ri. UB7: W Dray .2C 92
Lavender Rd. CR0: C'don .6K 155
EN2: Enf .1J 23
KT19: Ewe .5H 163
SE16 .1A 104
SM1: Sutt .4B 166
SM5: Cars .4E 166
SW11 .3B 118
UB8: Hil .5B 74
Lavender Sq. E11 .3F 69
Lavender St. E15 .6G 69
Lavender Sweep SW11 .4D 118
Lavender Ter. SW11 .3C 118
Lavender Va. SM6: Wall .6H 167
Lavender Wlk. CR4: Mitc .3E 154
SW11 .4D 118
Lavender Way CR0: C'don .6K 157
Lavendon Ho. *NW8* .*3D 4*
(off Paveley St.)
Lavengro Rd. SE27 .2C 138
Lavenham Rd. SW18 .2H 135
Lavernock Rd. DA7: Bex .2G 127
Lavers Rd. N16 .3E 66
Laverstoke Gdns. SW15 .7B 116
Laverton M. SW5 .4K 99
Laverton Pl. SW5 .4K 99
Lavidge Rd. SE9 .2C 142
Lavina Gro. N1 .2K 83
Lavington Cl. E9 .6B 68
Lavington Rd. CR0: Bedd .3K 167
W13 .1B 96
Lavington St. SE1 .5B 14 (1B 102)
Lavisham Ho. BR1: Brom .5K 141
Lawdons Gdns. CR0: Wadd .4B 168
Lawes Ho. *W10* .*3H 81*
(off Lancefield St.)
Lawford Rd. N1 .7E 66
NW5 .6G 65
W4 .7J 97
Lawfords Wharf *NW1* .*7G 65*
(off Lyme St.)
Law Ho. IG11: Bark .2A 90
Lawless Ho. *E14* .*7E 86*
(off Bazely St.)
Lawless St. E14 .7D 86
Lawley Ho. TW1: Twick .6D 114
Lawley Rd. N14 .7A 22
Lawley St. E5 .4J 67
Lawn, The UB2: S'hall .5E 94
Lawn Cl. BR1: Brom .6K 141
HA4: Ruis .3H 57
KT3: N Mald .2A 152
N9 .7A 24
Lawn Cres. TW9: Kew .2G 115
Lawn Dr. E7 .4B 70
Lawn Farm Gro. RM6: Chad H .4E 54
Lawnfield Ct. *NW6* .*7F 63*
(off Coverdale Rd.)
Lawn Gdns. W7 .1J 95
Lawn Ho. Cl. E14 .2E 104
Lawn La. SW8 .7F 19 (6K 101)
Lawn Rd. BR3: Beck .7B 140
NW3 .5D 64
Lawns, The DA14: Sidc .4B 144
E4 .5H 35
HA5: Hat E .7A 26
SE3 .3H 123
SE19 .1D 156
SL3: Poyle .4A 174
SM2: Cheam .7G 165
SW19 .5H 135
Lawns Ct. HA9: Wemb .2F 61
Lawnside SE3 .4H 123
Lawns Way RM5: Col R .1J 55
Lawnswood EN5: Barn .5B 20
Lawn Ter. SE3 .3G 123
Lawn Va. HA5: Pinn .2C 40
Lawrence Av. E12 .4E 70
E17 .1K 49
KT3: N Mald .6K 151
N13 .4G 33
NW7 .4F 29
NW10 .1K 79
Lawrence Bldgs. N16 .3F 67
Lawrence Campe Cl. N20 .3G 31
Lawrence Cl. E3 .3C 86
N15 .4E 48
W12 .7D 80
Lawrence Ct. N10 .3G 47
N16 .*3F 67*
(off Smalley Rd. Est.)
NW7 .5F 29
W3 .*3J 97*
(off Stanley Rd.)

Lawrence Cres. HA8: Edg 2G 43
RM10: Dag 3H 73
Lawrence Dr. UB10: Ick 4E 56
Lawrence Est. TW4: Houn 4A 112
Lawrence Gdns. NW7 3G 29
Lawrence Hill E4 2H 35
Lawrence Ho. *NW1* *7F 65*
(off Hawley Cres.)
SW1 *4D 18*
(off Cureton St.)
Lawrence La. EC2 7D 8 (6C 84)
Lawrence Mans. *SW1* *5J 17*
(off Sutherland St.)
SW3 *7C 16*
(off Lordship Pl.)
Lawrence Pde. *TW7: Isle* *3B 114*
(off Lower Sq.)
Lawrence Pl. *N1* *1J 83*
(off Brydon Wlk.)
Lawrence Rd. BR4: W W'ck 4J 171
DA8: Erith 7H 109
E6 1C 88
E13 1K 87
HA5: Pinn 6B 40
N15 4E 48
N18 4C 34
(not continuous)
SE25 4F 157
TW4: Houn 4A 112
TW10: Ham 4C 132
TW12: Hamp 7D 130
UB4: Hayes 2E 74
W5 4D 96
Lawrence St. E16 5H 87
NW7 4G 29
SW3 7C 16 (6C 100)
Lawrence Trad. Est. SE10 4G 105
Lawrence Way NW10 3J 61
Lawrence Weaver Cl.
SM4: Mord 6J 153
Lawrence Yd. N15 4E 48
Lawrie Pk. Av. SE26 5H 139
Lawrie Pk. Cres. SE26 5H 139
Lawrie Pk. Gdns. SE26 4H 139
Lawrie Pk. Rd. SE26 6H 139
Laws Cl. SE25 4D 156
Lawson Cl. E16 5A 88
IG1: Ilf 5H 71
SW19 3F 135
Lawson Ct. KT6: Surb 7D 150
N4 *1K 65*
(off Lorne Rd.)
Lawson Gdns. HA5: Eastc 3K 39
Lawson Ho. *SE18* *6E 106*
(off Nightingale Pl.)
W12 *7D 80*
(off White City Est.)
Lawson Rd. EN3: Enf H 1D 24
UB1: S'hall 4E 76
Law St. SE1 3D 102
Lawton Rd. E3 3A 86
(not continuous)
E10 1E 68
EN4: Cockf 3G 21
Laxcon Cl. NW10 5K 61
Laxey Rd. BR6: Chels 6K 173
Laxfield Ct. *E8* *1G 85*
(off Pownall Rd.)
Laxford Ho. *SW1* *4H 17*
(off Cundy St.)
Laxley Cl. SE5 7B 102
Laxton Ct. CR7: Thor H 4C 156
Laxton Pl. NW1 3K 5 (4F 83)
Layard Rd. CR7: Thor H 2D 156
EN1: Enf 1A 24
SE16 4H 103
Layard Sq. SE16 4H 103
Laybourne Ho. *E14* *2C 104*
(off Admirals Way)
Laybrook Lodge E18 4H 51
Laycock St. N1 6A 66
Layer Gdns. W3 7G 79
Layfield Cl. NW4 7D 44
Layfield Cres. NW4 7D 44
Layfield Ho. *SE10* *5J 105*
(off Kemsing Rd.)
Layfield Rd. NW4 7D 44
Layhams Rd. BR2: Kes 3F 171
BR4: W W'ck 4G 171
Laymarsh Cl. DA17: Belv 3F 109
Laymead Cl. UB5: N'olt 6C 58
Laystall Ct. *WC1* *4J 7*
(off Mt. Pleasant)
Laystall St. EC1 4J 7 (4A 84)
Layton Ct. TW8: Bford 5D 96
Layton Cres. CR0: Wadd 5A 168
Layton Pl. TW9: Kew 1G 115
Layton Rd. TW3: Houn 4F 113
TW8: Bford 5D 96
Layton's Bldgs. SE1 6E 14 (2D 102)
Layton's La. TW16: Sun 2H 147
Layzell Wlk. SE9 1B 142
Lazar Wlk. N7 2K 65
Lazenby Ct. WC2 2E 12
Leabank Cl. HA1: Harr 3J 59
Leabank Sq. E9 6C 68
Leabank Vw. N15 6G 49
Lea Bon Ct. *E15* *1H 87*
(off Plaistow Gro.)
Leabourne Rd. N16 7G 49
LEA BRIDGE 3K 67
Lea Bri. Ind. Cen. E10 1A 68
Lea Bri. Rd. E5 3J 67
E10 3J 67
E17 5F 51
Lea Cl. TW2: Whitt 7D 112
Lea Ct. E4 2K 35
E13 3J 87
N15 4G 49
Lea Cres. HA4: Ruis 4H 57
Leacroft Av. SW12 7D 118
Leacroft Cl. N21 2G 33
UB7: Yiew 6A 74
Leadale Av. E4 2H 35
Leadale Rd. N15 6G 49
N16 6G 49
Leadbeaters Cl. N11 5J 31
Leadbetter Ct. *NW10* *7K 61*
(off Melville Rd.)
Leadenhall Mkt. EC3 1G 15 (6E 84)
Leadenhall Pl. EC3 1G 15 (6E 84)
Leadenhall St. EC3 1G 15 (6E 84)
Leadenham Ct. E3 4C 86
Leader Av. E12 5E 70
Leadings, The HA9: Wemb 3J 61
Leaf Cl. HA6: Nwood 1F 39
KT7: T Ditt 5J 149
Leaf Gro. SE27 5A 138
Leaf Ho. *HA1: Harr* *5K 41*
(off Catherine Pl.)
Leafield Cl. SW16 6B 138
Leafield La. DA14: Sidc 3F 145
Leafield Rd. SM1: Sutt 2J 165
SW20 3H 153
Leafy Gro. BR2: Kes 5A 172
Leafy Oak Rd. SE12 4A 142
Leafy Way CR0: C'don 2F 169
Lea Gdns. HA9: Wemb 4F 61
Leagrave St. E5 3J 67
Lea Hall Gdns. E10 1C 68
Lea Hall Rd. E10 1C 68
Leaholme Way HA4: Ruis 6E 38
Lea Ho. *NW8* *4C 4*
(off Salisbury St.)
Leahurst Rd. SE13 5F 123
(not continuous)
LEA INTERCHANGE 5C 68
Leake Ct. SE1 7H 13 (2K 101)
Leake St. SE1 6H 13 (2K 101)
(not continuous)
Lealand Rd. N15 6F 49
Leamington Av. BR1: Brom 5A 142
BR6: Orp 4J 173
E17 5C 50
SM4: Mord 4G 153
Leamington Cl. BR1: Brom 4A 142
E12 5C 70
TW3: Houn 5G 113
Leamington Cres. HA2: Harr 3C 58
Leamington Gdns. IG3: Ilf 2K 71
Leamington Ho. HA8: Edg 5A 28
W11 *5H 81*
(off Leamington Rd. Vs.)
Leamington Pk. W3 5K 79
Leamington Pl. UB4: Hayes 4H 75
Leamington Rd. UB2: S'hall 4B 94
Leamington Rd. Vs. W11 5H 81
Leamore St. W6 4E 98
LEAMOUTH 7G 87
Leamouth Rd. E6 5C 88
E14 6F 87
Leander Ct. *E9* *7K 67*
(off Lauriston Rd.)
KT6: Surb 7D 150
NW9 1A 44
SE8 1C 122
Leander Rd. CR7: Thor H 4K 155
SW2 6K 119
UB5: N'olt 2E 76
Lea Pk. Trad. Est. E10 7B 50
Learner Dr. HA2: Harr 2E 58
Lea Rd. BR3: Beck 2C 158
EN2: Enf 1J 23
UB2: S'hall 4C 94
Learoyd Gdns. E6 7E 88
Leary Ho. SE11 6H 19 (5K 101)
Leas Cl. KT9: Chess 7F 163
Leas Dale SE9 3E 142
Leas Grn. BR7: Chst 6K 143
Leaside Av. N10 3E 46
Leaside Bus. Cen. EN3: Brim 2G 25
Leaside Ct. UB10: Hil 3D 74
Leaside Mans. *N10* *3E 46*
(off Fortis Grn.)
Leaside Rd. E5 1J 67
Leasowes Rd. E10 1C 68
Lea Sq. E3 1B 86
Leatherbottle Grn. DA18: Erith 3F 109
Leather Bottle La. DA17: Belv 4E 108
Leather Cl. CR4: Mitc 2E 154
Leatherdale St. E1 4J 85
(Harpley Sq.)
E1 3K 85
(Portelet Rd.)
Leather Gdns. E15 1G 87
Leatherhead Cl. N16 1F 67
Leatherhead Rd. KT9: Chess 7D 162
Leather La. EC1 5J 7 (5A 84)
(not continuous)
Leathermarket, The SE1 7G 15
Leathermarket Ct.
SE1 7G 15 (2E 102)
Leathermarket St. SE1 7G 15 (2E 102)
Leather Rd. SE16 4K 103
Leathersellers Cl.
EN5: Barn *3B 20*
(off The Avenue)
Leather St. E1 7K 85
Leathsail Rd. HA2: Harr 3F 59
Leathwaite Rd. SW11 4D 118
Leathwell Rd. SE8 2D 122
Lea Va. DA1: Cray 4K 127
Lea Valley Bus. Pk. E10 2A 68
Lea Valley Rd. E4 5F 25
EN3: Pond E 5F 25
Lea Valley Trad. Est. N18 6E 34
Lea Valley Viaduct E4 5E 34
N18 5E 34
Leaveland Cl. BR3: Beck 4C 158
Leaver Gdns. UB6: G'frd 2H 77
Leavesden Rd. HA7: Stan 6F 27
Leaves Grn. Rd. BR2: Kes 7B 172
Lea Vw. Ho. E5 1H 67
Leaway E10 1K 67
Lebanon Av. TW13: Hanw 5B 130
Lebanon Ct. TW1: Twick 7B 114
Lebanon Gdns.
SW18 6J 117
Lebanon Pk. TW1: Twick 7B 114
Lebanon Rd. CR0: C'don 1E 168
SW18 5J 117
Lebrun Sq. SE3 4K 123
Lebus Ho. *NW8* *1C 4*
(off Cochrane St.)
Le Chateau *CR0: C'don* *3D 168*
(off Chatsworth Rd.)
Lechmere App.
IG8: Wfd G 2A 52
Lechmere Av. IG8: Wfd G 2B 52
Lechmere Rd. NW2 6D 62
Leckford Rd. SW18 2A 136
Leckhampton Pl. SW2 7A 120
Leckwith Av. DA7: Bex 6E 108
Lecky St. SW7 5A 16 (5B 100)
Leclair Ho. SE3 3K 123
Leconfield Av. SW13 3B 116
Leconfield Ho. SE5 4E 120
Leconfield Rd. N5 4D 66
Le Cordon Bleu London Culinary
Arts Institute *6H 5*
(off Marylebone La.)
Leda Av. EN3: Enf W 1E 24
Leda Ct. *SW9* *7A 102*
(off Caldwell St.)
Ledam Ho. *EC1* *5J 7*
(off Bourne Est.)
Leda Rd. SE18 3D 106
Ledbury Ho. SE22 3E 120
W11 *6H 81*
(off Colville Rd.)
Ledbury M. Nth. W11 7J 81
Ledbury M. W. W11 7J 81
Ledbury Pl. CR0: C'don 4C 168
Ledbury Rd. CR0: C'don 4D 168
W11 6H 81
Ledbury St. SE15 7G 103
Ledrington Rd. SE19 6G 139
Ledway Dr. HA9: Wemb 7F 43
LEE 6J 123
Lee Av. RM6: Chad H 6E 54
Lee Bri. SE13 3E 122
Leechcroft Av. DA15: Sidc 5K 125
Leechcroft Rd. SM6: Wall 3E 166
Lee Chu. St. SE13 4G 123
Lee Cl. E17 1K 49
EN5: New Bar 4F 21
Lee Conservancy Rd. E9 5B 68
Lee Ct. *SE13* *4F 123*
(off Lee High Rd.)
Leecroft Rd. EN5: Barn 5B 20
Leeds Ct. *EC1* *3A 8*
(off St John St.)
Leeds Rd. IG1: Ilf 1H 71
Leeds St. N18 5B 34
Leefern Rd. W12 2C 98
Leegate SE12 5H 123
LEE GREEN 5H 123
Lee Gro. IG7: Chig 2K 37
Lee High Rd. SE12 3E 122
SE13 3E 122
Leeke St. WC1 1G 7 (3K 83)
Leeland Rd. W13 1A 96
Leeland Ter. W13 1A 96
Leeland Way NW10 4B 62
Lee M. BR3: Beck 3A 158
Leemount Ho. NW4 4F 45
Lee Pk. SE3 4H 123
Lee Pk. Way N9 4E 34
N18 4E 34
Leerdam Dr. E14 3E 104

Lee Rd. EN1: Enf 6B 24
NW7 7A 30
SE3 3H 123
SW19 1K 153
UB6: G'frd 1C 78
Lees, The CR0: C'don 2B 170
Lees Av. HA6: Nwood 1H 39
Lees Ct. *W1* *2G 11*
(off Lees Pl.)
Lees Ho. *SE17* *5D 102*
(off Inville Rd.)
Leeside EN5: Barn 5B 20
Leeside Ct. *SE16* *1K 103*
(off Rotherhithe St.)
Leeside Cres. NW11 6G 45
Leeside Ind. Est. N17 7D 34
Leeside Rd. N17 6C 34
Leeside Works N17 7D 34
Leeson Ho. TW1: Twick 7B 114
Leeson Rd. SE24 4A 120
Leesons Hill BR5: St P 3J 161
BR7: Chst 3J 161
Leeson's Way BR5: St P 2K 161
Lees Pde. UB10: Hil 4D 74
Lees Pl. W1 2G 11 (7E 82)
Lees Rd. UB8: Hil 4D 74
Lee St. E8 1F 85
Lee Ter. SE3 3G 123
SE13 3G 123
Lee Valley Athletic Cen. 1F 35
Lee Valley Ice Cen. 2K 67
Lee Valley Pk.
Haringey 7E 34
Lee Valley Technopark N17 3G 49
Leeve Ho. *W10* *3H 81*
(off Lancefield St.)
Lee Vw. EN2: Enf 1G 23
Leeward Ct. E1 7G 85
Leeward Gdns. SW19 5G 135
Leeward Ho. *N1* *1E 84*
(off New Era Est.)
Leeway SE8 5B 104
Leeway Cl. HA5: Hat E 1D 40
Leeways, The SM3: Cheam 6G 165
Leewood Cl. SE12 6H 123
Lefa Bus. & Ind. Pk. DA14: Sidc 6D 144
Lefevre Wlk. E3 2C 86
Leff Ho. NW6 1G 81
Lefroy Ho. *SE1* *7C 14*
(off Southwark Bri. Rd.)
Lefroy Rd. W12 2B 98
Left Side *N14* *1C 32*
(off Stationе Pde.)
Legard Rd. N5 3B 66
Legatt Rd. SE9 5B 124
Leggatt Rd. E15 2E 86
Legge St. SE13 5E 122
Leghorn Rd. NW10 2B 80
SE18 5H 107
Legion Cl. N1 7A 66
Legion Ct. SM4: Mord 6J 153
Legion Rd. UB6: G'frd 1G 77
Legion Ter. E3 1B 86
Legion Way N12 7H 31
Legon Av. RM7: Rush G 1J 73
Legrace Av. TW4: Houn 2B 112
Leicester Av. CR4: Mitc 4J 155
Leicester Cl. KT4: Wor Pk 4E 164
Leicester Ct. *TW1: Twick* *6D 114*
(off Clevedon Rd.)
W9 *5J 81*
(off Elmfield Way)
WC2 2D 12
Leicester Flds. WC2 3D 12
Leicester Gdns. IG3: Ilf 7J 53
Leicester Ho. *N18* *5C 34*
(off Cavendish Cl.)
SW9 *3B 120*
(off Loughborough Rd.)
Leicester M. N2 3C 46
Leicester Pl. WC2 2D 12 (7H 83)
Leicester Rd. CR0: C'don 7E 156
E11 5K 51
EN5: New Bar 5E 20
N2 3C 46
NW10 7K 61
Leicester Sq. WC2 3D 12 (7H 83)
Leicester St. WC2 2D 12 (7H 83)
Leigh, The KT2: King T 7A 134
Leigham Av. SW16 3J 137
Leigham Cl. SW16 3K 137
Leigham Ct. Rd. SW16 2J 137
Leigham Dr. TW7: Isle 7J 95
Leigham Hall Pde. *SW16* *3J 137*
(off Streatham High Rd.)
Leigham Va. SW2 3K 137
SW16 3K 137
Leigh Av. IG4: Ilf 4B 52
Leigh Cl. KT3: N Mald 4J 151
Leigh Cl. Ind. Est.
KT3: N Mald 4K 151
Leigh Ct. HA2: Harr 1J 59
W14 *4H 99*
(off Avonmore Pl.)
Leigh Cres. CR0: New Ad 7D 170
Leigh Gdns. NW10 2E 80
Leigh Hunt Dr. N14 1C 32
Leigh Orchard Cl. SW16 3K 137
Leigh Pl. DA16: Well 2A 126
EC1 5J 7 (5A 84)
TW13: Felt 1A 130
Leigh Rd. E6 6E 70
E10 7E 50
N5 4B 66
TW3: Houn 4H 113
Leigh St. WC1 2E 6 (3J 83)
Leighton Av. E12 5E 70
HA5: Pinn 3C 40
Leighton Cl. HA8: Edg 2G 43
Leighton Cres. NW5 5G 65
Leighton Gdns. CR0: C'don 1B 168
NW10 2D 80
Leighton Gro. NW5 5G 65
Leighton Ho. *SW1* *4D 18*
(off Herrick St.)
Leighton House Art Gallery & Mus. 3H 99
Leighton Mans. *W14* *6G 99*
(off Greyhound Rd.)
Leighton Pl. NW5 5G 65
Leighton Rd. EN1: Enf 5A 24
HA3: Hrw W 2H 41
NW5 5G 65
W13 2A 96
Leighton St. CR0: C'don 1B 168
Leila Parnell Pl. SE7 6A 106
Leinster Av. SW14 3J 115
Leinster Gdns. W2 6A 82
Leinster M. EN5: Barn 3B 20
W2 7A 82
Leinster Pl. W2 6A 82
Leinster Rd. N10 4F 47
Leinster Sq. W2 6J 81
(not continuous)
Leinster Ter. W2 7A 82
Leisure Way N12 7G 31
Leisure W. TW13: Felt 2K 129
Leitch Ho. *NW8* *7B 64*
(off Hilgrove Rd.)
Leith Cl. NW9 1K 61
Leithcote Gdns. SW16 4K 137
Leithcote Path SW16 3K 137
Leith Hill BR5: St P 1K 161
Leith Hill Grn. BR5: St P 1K 161
Leith Mans. *W9* *3K 81*
(off Grantully Rd.)
Leith Rd. N22 1B 48
Leith Towers SM2: Sutt 7K 165
Leith Yd. *NW6* *1J 81*
(off Quex Rd.)
Lela Av. TW4: Houn 2A 112
Lelitia Cl. E8 1G 85
Lely Ho. *UB5: N'olt* *2B 76*
(off Academy Gdns.)
Leman Pas. E1 1K 15
Leman St. E1 1K 15 (6F 85)
Lemark Cl. HA7: Stan 6H 27
Le May Av. SE12 3K 141
Lemmon Rd. SE10 6G 105
Lemna Rd. E11 7H 51
Le Moal Ho. *E1* *5J 85*
(off Stepney Way)
Lemon Gro. TW13: Felt 1J 129
Lemonwell Dr. SE9 5G 125
Lemsford Cl. N15 6G 49
Lemsford Ct. N4 2C 66
Lemuel St. SW18 6A 118
Lena Cres. N9 2D 34
Lena Gdns. W6 3E 98
Lena Kennedy Cl. E4 6K 35
Lenanton Steps *E14* *2C 104*
(off Manilla St.)
Len Clifton Ho. *SE18* *4D 106*
(off Cambridge Barracks Rd.)
Lendal Ter. SW4 3H 119
Lenelby Rd. KT6: Surb 1G 163
Len Freeman Pl. SW6 6H 99
W6 *4B 98*
(off Goldhawk Rd.)
Lenham Ho. *SE1* *7F 15*
(off Staple St.)
Lenham Rd. CR7: Thor H 2D 156
DA7: Bex 6F 109
SE12 4H 123
SM1: Sutt 4K 165
Lennard Av. BR4: W W'ck 2G 171
Lennard Cl. BR4: W W'ck 2G 171
Lennard Rd. BR2: Brom 1D 172
BR3: Beck 6K 139
CR0: C'don 1C 168
SE20 6K 139
Lennon Rd. NW2 5E 62
Lennox Gdns. CR0: Wadd 4B 168
IG1: Ilf 1D 70
NW10 4B 62
SW1 2E 16 (3D 100)
Lennox Gdns. M. SW1 2E 16 (3D 100)
Lennox Ho. *DA17: Belv* *3G 109*
(off Picardy St.)
TW1: Twick *6D 114*
(off Clevedon Rd.)
Lennox Rd. E17 6B 50
N4 2K 65
Lenor Cl. DA6: Bex 4E 126
Lensbury Av. SW6 2A 118
Lensbury Way SE2 3C 108
Lens Rd. E7 7A 70
Len Taylor Cl. UB4: Hayes 4G 75
Lenthall Ho. *SW1* *6B 18*
(off Churchill Gdns.)
Lenthall Rd. E8 7G 67
Lenthorp Rd. SE10 4H 105
Lentmead Rd. BR1: Brom 3H 141
Lenton Path SE18 6H 107
Lenton Ri. TW9: Rich 3E 114
Lenton St. SE18 4H 107
Len Williams Ct. NW6 2J 81
Leo Ct. TW8: Bford 7D 96
Leof Cres. SE6 5D 140
Leominster Rd. SM4: Mord 6A 154
Leominster Wlk.
SM4: Mord 6A 154
Leonard Av. RM7: Rush G 1K 73
SM4: Mord 5A 154
Leonard Ct. HA3: Hrw W 1J 41
W8 3J 99
WC1 3D 6 (4H 83)
Leonard Pl. N16 4E 66
Leonard Rd. E4 6H 35
E7 4J 69
N9 3A 34
Leonard Rd. SW16 1G 155
UB2: S'hall 3B 94
Leonard Robbins Path *SE28* *7B 90*
(off Tawney Rd.)
Leonard St. E16 1C 106
EC2 3F 9 (4D 84)
Leonora Ho. *W9* *4A 82*
(off Lanark Rd.)
Leontine Cl. SE15 7G 103
Leopards Ct. EC1 5J 7
Leopold Av. SW19 5H 135
Leopold Bldgs. *E2* *1J 9*
(off Columbia Rd.)
Leopold M. E9 1J 85
Leopold Rd. E17 5C 50
N2 3B 46
N18 5C 34
NW10 7A 62
SW19 4H 135
W5 1F 97
Leopold St. E3 5B 86
Leopold Ter. SW19 5H 135
Leopold Wlk. *SE11* *5K 101*
(off Tyers St.)
Leo St. SE15 7H 103
Leo Yd. EC1 4B 8
Leppoc Rd. SW4 5H 119
Leroy St. SE1 4E 102
Lerry Cl. W14 6H 99
Lerwick Ct. EN1: Enf 5K 23
Lescombe Cl. SE23 3A 140
Lescombe Rd. SE23 3A 140
Lesley Cl. DA5: Bexl 7H 127
Lesley Ct. *SW1* *2C 18*
(off Strutton Ground)
Leslie Gdns. SM2: Sutt 6J 165
Leslie Gro. CR0: C'don 1E 168
Leslie Gro. Pl.
CR0: C'don 1E 168
Leslie Ho. *SW8* *7J 101*
(off Wheatsheaf La.)
Leslie Pk. Rd. CR0: C'don 1E 168
Leslie Prince Ct. SE5 7D 102
Leslie Rd. E11 4E 68
E16 6K 87
N2 3B 46
Leslie Smith Sq. SE18 6E 106
Lesnes Abbey 4D 108
Lesney Farm Est. DA8: Erith 7K 109
Lesney Pk. DA8: Erith 6K 109
Lesney Pk. Rd. DA8: Erith 6K 109
Lessar Av. SW4 6G 119
Lessingham Av. IG5: Ilf 3E 52
SW17 4D 136
Lessing St. SE23 7A 122
Lessington Av. RM7: Rom 6J 55
Lessness Av. DA7: Bex 7D 108
LESSNESS HEATH 5H 109
Lessness Pk. DA17: Belv 5F 109
Lessness Rd. DA17: Belv 6G 109
SM4: Mord 6A 154
Lester Av. E15 4G 87
Lestock Cl. *SE25* *3G 157*
(off Manor Rd.)
Leswin Pl. N16 3F 67
Leswin Rd. N16 3F 67
Letchford Gdns. NW10 3C 80
Letchford M. NW10 3C 80
Letchford Ter. HA3: Hrw W 1F 41
Letchmore Ho. *W10* *4E 80*
(off Sutton Way)
Letchworth Av. TW14: Felt 7H 111
Letchworth Cl. BR2: Brom 5J 159
Letchworth Dr. BR2: Brom 5J 159
Letchworth St. SW17 4D 136
Lethbridge Cl. SE13 1E 122
Letterstone Rd. SW6 7H 99
Lettice St. SW6 1H 117
Lett Rd. E15 7F 69
Lettsom St. SE5 2E 120

Lettsom Wlk. E13 . . . . . 2J 87
Leucha Rd. E17 . . . . . 5A 50
Levana Cl. SW19 . . . . . 1G 135
Levant Ho. E1 . . . . . 4K 85
(off Ernest St.)
Levehurst Ho. SE27 . . . . . 5C 138
Levendale Rd. SE23 . . . . . 2A 140
Levenhurst Way SW4 . . . . . 2J 119
Leven Rd. E14 . . . . . 5E 86
Leven Way UB3: Hayes 6G 75
Leverett St. SW3 . . . . . 3D 16 (4C 100)
Leverholme Gdns. SE9 . . . . . 3E 142
Leverington Pl. N1 . . . . . 2F 9 (3D 84)
Leverson St. SW16 . . . . . 6G 137
Leverstock Ho. SW3 . . . . . 5D 16
(off Cale St.)
Lever St. EC1 . . . . . 2B 8 (3B 84)
Leverton Pl. NW5 . . . . . 5G 65
Leverton St. NW5 . . . . . 5G 65
Levett Gdns. IG3: Ilf 4K 71
Levett Rd. IG11: Bark 6J 71
Levine Gdns. IG11: Bark 2D 90
Levison Way N19 . . . . . 1H 65
Levita Ho. NW1 . . . . . 1D 6
(not continuous)
Levyne Ct. EC1 . . . . . 3J 7
(off Pine St.)
Lewes Cl. UB5: N'olt 6E 58
Lewes Ct. CR4: Mitc 3D 154
(off Chatsworth Pl.)
Lewesdon Cl. SW19 . . . . . 1F 135
Lewes Ho. SE1 . . . . . 6H 15
(off Druid St.)
SE15 . . . . . 6G 103
(off Friary Est.)
Lewes Rd. BR1: Brom 2B 160
N12 . . . . . 5H 31
Leweston Pl. N16 . . . . . 7F 49
Lew Evans Ho. SE22 . . . . . 5G 121
Lewey Ho. E3 . . . . . 4B 86
(off Joseph St.)
Lewgars Av. NW9 . . . . . 6J 43
Lewing Cl. BR6: Orp 1J 173
Lewin Rd. DA6: Bex 5E 126
SW14 . . . . . 3K 115
SW16 . . . . . 6H 137
Lewin Ter. TW14: Bedf 7F 111
Lewis Av. E17 . . . . . 1C 50
Lewis Cl. N14 . . . . . 7B 22
Lewis Ct. SE16 . . . . . 5H 103
(off Stubbs Dr.)
Lewis Cres. NW10 . . . . . 5K 61
Lewis Gdns. N2 . . . . . 2B 46
N16 . . . . . 6F 49
Lewis Gro. SE13 . . . . . 4E 122
LEWISHAM 3E 122
Lewisham Bus. Cen. SE14 . . . . . 6K 103
Lewisham Cen. SE13 . . . . . 4E 122
Lewisham Crematorium
SE6 . . . . . 2H 141
Lewisham Hgts. SE23 . . . . . 1J 139
Lewisham High St. SE13 . . . . . 3E 122
(not continuous)
Lewisham Hill SE13 . . . . . 2E 122
Lewisham Lions Cen. 5J 103
Lewisham Model Mkt.
SE13 . . . . . 4E 122
(off Lewisham High St.)
Lewisham Pk. SE13 . . . . . 5E 122
Lewisham Rd. SE13 . . . . . 1D 122
Lewisham St. SW1 . . . . . 7D 12 (2H 101)
Lewisham Way SE4 . . . . . 1B 122
SE14 . . . . . 1B 122
Lewis Ho. E14 . . . . . 1E 104
(off Coldharbour)
Lewis Pl. E8 . . . . . 5G 67
Lewis Rd. CR4: Mitc 2B 154
(not continuous)
DA14: Sidc 3C 144
DA16: Well 3C 126
Lewis Rd. SM1: Sutt 4K 165
TW10: Rich 5D 114
UB1: S'hall 2C 94
Lewis Silkin Ho. SE15 . . . . . 6J 103
(off Lovelinch Cl.)
Lewis Sports and Leisure Cen. 1F 157
Lewis St. NW1 . . . . . 6F 65
(not continuous)
Lewiston Cl. KT4: Wor Pk 7D 152
Lewis Way RM10: Dag 6H 73
Lexden Dr. RM6: Chad H 6B 54
Lexden Rd. CR4: Mitc 4H 155
W3 . . . . . 7H 79
Lexham Gdns. W8 . . . . . 4J 99
Lexham Gdns. M. W8 . . . . . 3K 99
Lexham Ho. IG11: Bark 1H 89
(off St Margarets)
W8 . . . . . 4K 99
(off Lexham Gdns.)
Lexham M. W8 . . . . . 4J 99
Lexham Wlk. W8 . . . . . 3K 99
Lexington Apartments
EC1 . . . . . 3F 9 (4D 84)
Lexington Bldg. E3 . . . . . 2C 86
Lexington Pl. KT1: Ham W 7D 132
Lexington St. W1 . . . . . 2B 12 (7G 83)
Lexington Way EN5: Barn 4A 20
Lexton Gdns. SW12 . . . . . 1H 137
Leyborne Av. W13 . . . . . 2B 96
Leyborne Pk. TW9: Kew 1G 115
Leybourne Cl. BR2: Brom 6J 159
Leybourne Ho. E14 . . . . . 6B 86
(off Dod St.)
SE15 . . . . . 6J 103
Leybourne Rd. E11 . . . . . 1H 69
NW1 . . . . . 7F 65
NW9 . . . . . 5G 43
UB10: Hil 1E 74
Leybourne St. NW1 . . . . . 7F 65
Leybridge Ct. SE12 . . . . . 5J 123
Leyburn Cl. E17 . . . . . 4D 50
Leyburn Gdns. CR0: C'don 2E 168
Leyburn Gro. N18 . . . . . 6B 34
Leyburn Rd. N18 . . . . . 6B 34
Leydenhatch La.
BR8: Dart, Swan 7J 145
Leyden Mans. N19 . . . . . 7J 47
Leyden St. E1 . . . . . 6J 9 (5F 85)
Leydon Cl. SE16 . . . . . 1K 103
Leyes Rd. E16 . . . . . 6B 88
Leyfield KT4: Wor Pk 1A 164
Leyland Av. EN3: Enf H 2F 25
Leyland Gdns. IG8: Wfd G 5F 37
Leyland Ho. E14 . . . . . 7D 86
(off Hale St.)
Leyland Rd. SE12 . . . . . 5J 123
Leylands SW18 . . . . . 6H 117
Leylands La. TW19: Stan M 7A 174
(not continuous)
Leylang Rd. SE14 . . . . . 7K 103
Leys, The HA3: Kent 6F 43
N2 . . . . . 4A 46
Leys Av. RM10: Dag 1J 91
Leys Cl. HA1: Harr 5H 41
RM10: Dag 7J 73
Leys Ct. SW9 . . . . . 2A 120
Leysdown Av. DA7: Bex 4J 127
Leysdown Ho. SE17 . . . . . 5E 102
(off Madron St.)
Leysdown Rd. SE9 . . . . . 2C 142
Leysfield Rd. W12 . . . . . 3C 98
Leys Gdns. EN4: Cockf 5K 21
Leyspring Rd. E11 . . . . . 1H 69
Leys Rd. E. EN3: Enf H 1F 25
Leys Rd. W. EN3: Enf H 1F 25
Leys Sq. N3 . . . . . 1K 45
Ley St. IG1: Ilf 2F 71
IG2: Ilf 2F 71
Leyswood Dr. IG2: Ilf 5J 53
Leythe Rd. W3 . . . . . 2J 97
LEYTON 2E 68
Leyton Bus. Cen. E10 . . . . . 2C 68
Leyton Ct. SE23 . . . . . 1J 139
Leyton FC Ground 1B 68
Leyton Grange Est. E10 . . . . . 1C 68
Leyton Grn. Rd. E10 . . . . . 6E 50
Leyton Grn. Twr. E10 . . . . . 6E 50
(off Leyton Grn. Rd.)
Leyton Grn. Towers E10 . . . . . 6E 50
(off Leyton Grn. Rd.)
Leyton Ind. Village E10 . . . . . 7K 49
Leyton Leisure Lagoon 7D 50
Leyton Orient FC 3D 68
Leyton Pk. Rd. E10 . . . . . 3E 68
Leyton Rd. E15 . . . . . 5E 68
SW19 . . . . . 7A 136
LEYTONSTONE 1G 69
Leytonstone Ho. E11 . . . . . 7H 51
(off Hanbury Dr.)
Leytonstone Rd. E15 . . . . . 5G 69
Leyton Way E11 . . . . . 7G 51
Leywick St. E15 . . . . . 2G 87
Lezayre Rd. BR6: Chels 6K 173
Liardet St. SE14 . . . . . 6A 104
Liberia Rd. N5 . . . . . 6B 66
Liberty Av. SW19 . . . . . 1B 154
Liberty Cl. N18 . . . . . 4A 34
Liberty Ct. IG11: Bark 2B 90
Liberty Ho. E1 . . . . . 7G 85
(off Ensign St.)
Liberty M. N22 . . . . . 1B 48
SW12 . . . . . 6F 119
Liberty Point CR0: C'don 7G 157
(off Blackhorse La.)
Liberty St. SW9 . . . . . 1K 119
Libra Rd. E3 . . . . . 2B 86
E13 . . . . . 2J 87
Library and Lifetime Mus. 3C 168
(off High St.)
Library Ct. N17 . . . . . 3F 49
Library Mans. W12 . . . . . 2E 98
(off Pennard Rd.)
Library Pde. NW10 . . . . . 1A 80
(off Craven Pk. Rd.)
Library Pl. E1 . . . . . 7H 85
Library St. SE1 . . . . . 7A 14 (2B 102)
Library Way TW2: Whitt 7G 113
Libro Ct. E4 . . . . . 4H 35
Lichfield Cl. EN4: Cockf 3J 21
Lichfield Ct. KT6: Surb 5E 150
(off Claremont Rd.)
TW9: Rich 5E 114
Lichfield Gdns. TW9: Rich 4E 114
Lichfield Gro. N3 . . . . . 1J 45
Lichfield Rd. E3 . . . . . 3A 86
E6 . . . . . 3B 88
HA6: Nwood 3J 39
IG8: Wfd G 4B 36
N9 . . . . . 2B 34
NW2 . . . . . 4G 63
RM8: Dag 4B 72
TW4: Houn 3A 112
TW9: Kew 1F 115
Lichfield Ter. TW9: Rich 5E 114
(off Sheen Rd.)
Lichlade Cl. BR6: Orp 4K 173
Lickey Ho. W14 . . . . . 6H 99
(off North End Rd.)
Lidbury Rd. NW7 . . . . . 6B 30
Lidcote Gdns. SW9 . . . . . 2K 119
Liddall Way UB7: Yiew 1B 92
Liddell Cl. HA3: Kent 3D 42
Liddell Gdns. NW10 . . . . . 2E 80
Liddell Rd. NW6 . . . . . 6J 63
Liddiard Ho. W11 . . . . . 7G 81
(off Lansdowne Rd.)
Lidding Rd. HA3: Kent 5D 42
Liddington Rd. E15 . . . . . 1H 87
Liddon Rd. BR1: Brom 3A 160
E13 . . . . . 3K 87
Liden Cl. E17 . . . . . 7B 50
Lidfield Rd. N16 . . . . . 4D 66
Lidgate Rd. SE15 . . . . . 7F 103
Lidiard Rd. SW18 . . . . . 2A 136
Lidlington Pl. NW1 . . . . . 2G 83
Lido Sq. N17 . . . . . 2D 48
Lidyard Rd. N19 . . . . . 1G 65
Liffler Rd. SE18 . . . . . 5J 107
Liffords Pl. SW13 . . . . . 2B 116
Lifford St. SW15 . . . . . 4F 117
Lightcliffe Rd. N13 . . . . . 4F 33
Lighter Cl. SE16 . . . . . 4A 104
Lighterman Ho. E14 . . . . . 7E 86
Lighterman M. E1 . . . . . 6K 85
Lightermans Rd. E14 . . . . . 2C 104
Lightermans Wlk. SW18 . . . . . 4J 117
Lightfoot Rd. N8 . . . . . 5J 47
Light Horse Ct. SW3 . . . . . 6G 17
Lightley Cl. HA0: Wemb 1E 78
Ligonier St. E2 . . . . . 3J 9 (4F 85)
Lilac Cl. E4 . . . . . 6G 35
Lilac Ct. E13 . . . . . 1A 88
TW11: Tedd 4K 131
Lilac Gdns. CR0: C'don 3C 170
RM7: Rush G 1K 73
UB3: Hayes 6G 75
W5 . . . . . 3D 96
Lilac Ho. SE4 . . . . . 3C 122
Lilac M. N22 . . . . . 3A 48
(off High Rd.)
Lilac Pl. SE11 . . . . . 4G 19 (4K 101)
UB7: Yiew 7B 74
Lilac St. W12 . . . . . 7C 80
Lilah M. BR2: Brom 2H 159
Lilburne Gdns. SE9 . . . . . 5C 124
Lilburne Rd. SE9 . . . . . 5C 124
Lilburne Wlk. NW10 . . . . . 6J 61
Lile Cres. W7 . . . . . 5J 77
Lilestone Ho. NW8 . . . . . 3B 4
(off Frampton St.)
Lilestone St. NW8 . . . . . 3C 4 (4C 82)
Lilford Ho. SE5 . . . . . 2C 120
Lilford Rd. SE5 . . . . . 2B 120
Lilian Barker Cl. SE12 . . . . . 5J 123
Lilian Board Way UB6: G'frd 5H 59
Lilian Cl. N16 . . . . . 3E 66
Lilian Gdns. IG8: Wfd G 1K 51
Lilian Rd. SW16 . . . . . 1G 155
Lillechurch Rd. RM8: Dag 6B 72
Lilleshall Rd. SM4: Mord 6B 154
Lilley Cl. E1 . . . . . 1G 103
Lilley La. NW7 . . . . . 5E 28
Lillian Av. W3 . . . . . 2G 97
Lillian Rd. SW13 . . . . . 6C 98
Lillie Bri. Dpt. W14 . . . . . 5H 99
Lillie Mans. SW6 . . . . . 6G 99
(off Lillie Rd.)
Lillie Rd. SW6 . . . . . 6G 99
Lillie Road Fitness Cen. 7F 99
Lillieshall Rd. SW4 . . . . . 3F 119
Lillie Yd. SW6 . . . . . 6J 99
Lillingston Ho. N7 . . . . . 4A 66
Lillington Gdns. Est. SW1 . . . . . 4B 18
Lilliput Av. UB5: N'olt 1C 76
Lilliput Ct. SE12 . . . . . 5K 123
Lilliput Rd. RM7: Rush G 7K 55
Lily Cl. W14 . . . . . 4F 99
(not continuous)
Lily Gdns. HA0: Wemb 2C 78
Lily Nichols Ho. E16 . . . . . 1B 106
(off Connaught Rd.)
Lily Pl. EC1 . . . . . 5K 7 (5A 84)
Lily Rd. E17 . . . . . 6C 50
Lilyville Rd. SW6 . . . . . 1H 117
Limborough Ho. E14 . . . . . 5C 86
(off Thomas Rd.)
Limbourne Av. RM8: Dag 7F 55
Limburg Rd. SW11 . . . . . 4C 118
Lime Av. UB7: Yiew 7B 74
Limeburner La. EC4 . . . . . 1A 14 (6B 84)

Lime Cl. BR1: Brom 4C 160
E1 1G 103
HA3: W'stone 2A 42
HA5: Eastc 3H 39
IG9: Buck H 2G 37
RM7: Rom 4J 55
SM5: Cars 2D 166
Lime Ct. CR4: Mitc 2B 154
E11 2G 69
(off Trinity Cl.)
E17 5E 50
HA1: Harr 6K 41
SE9 2F 143
Lime Cres. TW16: Sun 2A 148
Limecroft Cl. KT19: Ewe 7K 163
Limedene Cl. HA5: Pinn 1B 40
Lime Gro. BR6: Farnb 2F 173
DA15: Sidc 6K 125
E4 6G 35
HA4: Ruis 6K 39
KT3: N Mald 3K 151
N20 1C 30
TW1: Twick 6K 113
UB3: Hayes 7F 75
W12 2E 98
Limeharbour E14 3D 104
LIMEHOUSE 6B 86
Lime Ho. TW9: Kew 1H 115
Limehouse C'way. E14 7B 86
Limehouse Ct. E14 6C 86
Limehouse Cut *E14 5D 86*
(off Morris Rd.)
Limehouse Flds. Est. E14 5A 86
Limehouse Link E14 6A 86
Lime Kiln Dr. SE7 6K 105
Limekiln Pl. SE19 7F 139
Lime Lodge *TW16: Sun 7H 129*
(off Forest Dr.)
Limerick Cl. SW12 7G 119
Lime Rd. TW9: Rich 4F 115
Lime Row DA18: Erith 3F 109
Limerston St. SW10 7A 16 (6A 100)
Limes, The BR2: Brom 2C 172
KT8: W Mole 4F 149
SW18 6J 117
W2 7J 81
Limes Av. CR0: Wadd 3A 168
E11 4K 51
E12 3C 70
N12 4F 31
NW7 6F 29
NW11 7G 45
SE20 7H 139
SM5: Cars 1D 166
SW13 2B 116
Limes Av., The N11 5A 32
Limes Cl. N11 5B 32
TW15: Ashf 5C 128
Limes Ct. *NW6 7G 63*
(off Brondesbury Pk.)
Limesdale Gdns. HA8: Edg 2J 43
Limes Fld. Rd. SW14 3A 116
Limesford Rd. SE15 4K 121
Limes Gdns. SW18 6J 117
Limes Gro. SE13 4E 122
Limes Pl. CR0: C'don 7D 156
Limes Rd. BR3: Beck 2D 158
CR0: C'don 7D 156
Limes Row BR6: Farnb 5F 173
Limestone Wlk. DA18: Erith 2D 108
Lime St. E17 4A 50
EC3 2G 15 (7E 84)
Lime St. Pas. EC3 1G 15 (6E 84)
Limes Wlk. SE15 4J 121
W5 2D 96
Lime Ter. W7 7J 77
Lime Tree Av. KT7: T Ditt 7J 149
KT10: Esh, T Ditt 7H 149
Lime Tree Cl. E18 4A 52
Limetree Cl. SW2 1K 137
Lime Tree Ct. CR2: S Croy 6C 168
E3 5C 86
Lime Tree Gro. CR0: C'don 3B 170
Lime Tree Pl. CR4: Mitc 1F 155
Lime Tree Rd. TW5: Hest 1F 113
Limetree Ter. DA16: Well 3A 126
SE6 1B 140
Lime Tree Wlk. BR4: W W'ck 4H 171
EN2: Enf 1H 23
WD23: B Hea 1D 26
Limetree Wlk. SW17 5E 136
Lime Wlk. E15 1G 87
KT8: E Mos 4K 149
Limewood Cl. BR3: Beck 5E 158
E17 4B 50
W13 6B 78
Limewood Ct. IG4: Ilf 5D 52
Limewood Rd. DA8: Erith 7J 109
Limpsfield Av. CR7: Thor H 5K 155
SW19 2F 135
Linacre Cl. SE15 3H 121
Linacre Ct. W6 5F 99
Linacre Rd. NW2 6D 62
Linale Ho. N1 1E 8
Linberry Wlk. SE8 4B 104
Linchmere Rd. SE12 7H 123
Lincoln Av. N14 3B 32
RM7: Rush G 2K 73
SW19 3F 135
TW2: Twick 2G 131
Lincoln Cl. HA2: Harr 5D 40
SE25 6G 157
UB6: G'frd 1G 77
Lincoln Ct. *CR2: S Croy 5C 168*
(off Warham Rd.)
IG2: Ilf 6G 53
N16 7D 48
SE12 3A 142
Lincoln Cres. EN1: Enf 5K 23
Lincoln Gdns. IG1: Ilf 7C 52
Lincoln Grn. Rd.
BR5: St M Cry 5K 161
Lincoln Ho. SE5 7A 102
SW3 7E 10 (2D 100)
Lincoln M. N15 4C 48
NW6 1H 81
SE21 2D 138
Lincoln Pde. N2 3C 46
Lincoln Rd. CR4: Mitc 5J 155
DA14: Sidc 5B 144
E7 6B 70
E13 4K 87
E18 1J 51
EN1: Enf 4K 23
EN3: Pond E 5B 24
HA0: Wemb 6D 60
HA2: Harr 5D 40
HA6: Nwood 3H 39
KT3: N Mald 3J 151
KT4: Wor Pk 1D 164
N2 3C 46
SE25 3H 157
TW13: Hanw 3D 130
Lincolns, The NW7 3G 29
Lincolns Inn Flds. WC2 7G 7 (6K 83)
Lincoln's Inn Hall 7H 7 (6K 83)
Lincoln St. E11 2G 69
SW3 4E 16 (4D 100)
Lincoln Way EN1: Enf 5C 24
TW16: Sun 1G 147
Lincombe Rd. BR1: Brom 3H 141
Lindal Ct. E18 1H 51
Lindal Cres. EN2: Enf 4D 22
Lindales, The *N17 6B 34*
(off Grasmere Rd.)
Lindal Rd. SE4 5B 122
Lindbergh Rd. SM6: Wall 7J 167
Linden Av. CR7: Thor H 4B 156
EN1: Enf 1B 24
HA4: Ruis 1J 57
Linden Av. HA9: Wemb 5F 61
NW10 2F 81
TW3: Houn 5F 113
Linden Cl. HA4: Ruis 1J 57
HA7: Stan 5G 27
KT7: T Ditt 7K 149
N14 6B 22
Linden Ct. DA14: Sidc 4J 143
SE20 7H 139
(off Anerley Pk.)
W12 1E 98
Linden Cres. IG8: Wfd G 6E 36
KT1: King T 2F 151
UB6: G'frd 6K 59
Lindenfield BR7: Chst 2F 161
Linden Gdns. EN1: Enf 1B 24
W2 7J 81
W4 5A 98
Linden Gro. KT3: N Mald 3A 152
SE15 3H 121
TW11: Tedd 5K 131
Linden Ho. *SE8 6B 104*
(off Abinger Gro.)
TW12: Hamp 6E 130
Linden Lawns HA9: Wemb 4F 61
Linden Lea N2 5A 46
Linden Leas BR4: W W'ck 2F 171
Linden Mans. *N6 1F 65*
(off Hornsey La.)
Linden M. N1 5D 66
W2 7J 81
Linden Pl. CR4: Mitc 4C 154
Linden Rd. N10 4F 47
N11 2J 31
N15 4C 48
TW12: Hamp 7E 130
Lindens, The CR0: New Ad 6E 170
E17 4D 50
(off Prospect Hill)
N12 5G 31
W4 1J 115
Linden St. RM7: Rom 4K 55
Linden Wlk. N19 2G 65
Linden Way N14 6B 22
TW17: Shep 5E 146
Lindeth Cl. HA7: Stan 6G 27
Lindfield Gdns. NW3 5K 63
Lindfield Rd. CR0: C'don 6F 157
W5 4C 78
Lindfield St. E14 6C 86
Lindhill Cl. EN3: Enf H 2E 24
Lindholme Ct. *NW9 1A 44*
(off Pageant Av.)
Lindisfarne Rd. RM8: Dag 3C 72
SW20 7C 134
Lindisfarne Way E9 4A 68
Lindley Ct. KT1: Ham W 1C 150
Lindley Est. SE15 7G 103
Lindley Ho. *E1 5J 85*
(off Lindley St.)
SE15 7G 103
(off Peckham Pk. Rd.)
Lindley Pl. TW9: Kew 1G 115
Lindley Rd. E10 2E 68
Lindley St. E1 5J 85
Lindop Ho. *E1 4A 86*
(off Mile End Rd.)
Lindore Rd. SW11 4D 118
Lindores Rd. SM5: Cars 7A 154
Lindo St. SE15 2J 121
Lind Rd. SM1: Sutt 5A 166
Lindrop St. SW6 2A 118
Lindsay Cl. KT9: Chess 7E 162
TW19: Stanw 5A 110
Lindsay Ct. *CR0: C'don 4D 168*
(off Eden Rd.)
SW11 1B 118
(off Battersea High St.)
Lindsay Dr. HA3: Kent 6E 42
TW17: Shep 6F 147
Lindsay Ho. *SW7 3A 100*
(off Gloucester Rd.)
Lindsay Rd. KT4: Wor Pk 2D 164
TW12: Ham H 4F 131
Lindsay Sq. SW1 5D 18 (5H 101)
Lindsell St. SE10 1E 122
Lindsey Cl. BR1: Brom 3B 160
CR4: Mitc 4J 155
Lindsey Ct. *N13 3F 33*
(off Green Lanes)
Lindsey Gdns. TW14: Bedf 7F 111
Lindsey Ho. W5 4D 96
Lindsey M. N1 7C 66
Lindsey Rd. RM8: Dag 4C 72
Lindsey St. EC1 5B 8 (5B 84)
Lind St. SE8 2C 122
Lindum Rd. TW11: Tedd 7C 132
Lindway SE27 5B 138
Lindwood Cl. E6 6D 88
Linen Ho., The W10 2G 81
Linfield *WC1 2G 7*
(off Sidmouth St.)
Linfield Cl. NW4 3E 44
Linford Christie Stadium 5C 80
Linford Ho. *E2 1G 85*
(off Whiston Rd.)
Linford Rd. E17 3E 50
Linford St. SW8 1G 119
Lingard Ho. *E14 3E 104*
(off Marshfield St.)
Lingards Rd. SE13 4E 122
Lingey Cl. DA15: Sidc 2K 143
Lingfield Av. KT1: King T 4E 150
Lingfield Cl. EN1: Enf 6K 23
HA6: Nwood 1G 39
Lingfield Ct. UB5: N'olt 2E 76
Lingfield Cres. SE9 4H 125
Lingfield Gdns. N9 7C 24
Lingfield Ho. SE1 7B 14
Lingfield Rd. KT4: Wor Pk 3E 164
SW19 5F 135
Lingham Ct. SW9 2J 119
Lingham St. SW9 2J 119
Lingholm Way EN5: Barn 5A 20
Ling Rd. DA8: Erith 6J 109
E16 5J 87
Lingrove Gdns. IG9: Buck H 2E 36
Lings Coppice SE21 2D 138
Lingwell Rd. SW17 3C 136
Lingwood DA7: Bex 2H 127
Lingwood Ct. *N2 3C 46*
(off Norfolk Cl.)
Lingwood Gdns. TW7: Isle 7J 95
Lingwood Rd. E5 7G 49
Linhope St. NW1 3E 4 (4D 82)
Link, The EN3: Enf H 1F 25
HA0: Wemb 1C 60
HA5: Eastc 7A 40
NW2 1C 62
SE9 3E 142
(off William Barefoot Dr.)
TW11: Tedd 6K 131
UB5: N'olt 5D 58
W3 6H 79
Linkenholt Mans. *W6 4B 98*
(off Stamford Brook Av.)
Linkfield BR2: Hayes 6J 159
KT8: W Mole 3F 149
Linkfield Rd. TW7: Isle 2K 113
Link Ho. E3 2D 86
W10 6F 81
(off Kingsdown Cl.)
Link La. SM6: Wall 6H 167
Linklea Cl. NW9 7F 29
Link Rd. E1 2K 15 (7G 85)
E12 2C 70
N11 4K 31
RM9: Dag 2H 91
SM6: Wall 1E 166
TW14: Felt 7H 111

Links, The E17 4A 50
Links Av. SM4: Mord 4J 153
(not continuous)
Linkscroft Av. TW15: Ashf 6D 128
Links Dr. N20 1D 30
Links Gdns. SW16 7A 138
Linkside KT3: N Mald 2A 152
N12 6D 30
Linkside Cl. EN2: Enf 3E 22
Linkside Gdns. EN2: Enf 3E 22
Links Rd. BR4: W W'ck 1E 170
IG8: Wfd G 5D 36
NW2 2B 62
SW17 6E 136
TW15: Ashf 5A 128
W3 6G 79
Links Side EN2: Enf 3E 22
Link St. E9 6J 67
Links Vw. N3 7C 30
Linksview *N2* *5D 46*
(off Great Nth. Rd.)
Links Vw. Cl. HA7: Stan 7F 27
Links Vw. Ct. TW12: Ham H 4H 131
Links Vw. Rd. CR0: C'don 3C 170
TW12: Ham H 5G 131
Links Way BR3: Beck 6C 158
Linksway HA6: Nwood 1E 38
NW4 2F 45
Links Yd. E1 5K 9
Link Way BR2: Brom 7C 160
HA5: Pinn 1B 40
Linkway N4 7C 48
RM8: Dag 4C 72
SW20 3D 152
TW10: Ham 2B 132
Linkway, The EN5: Barn 6E 20
Linkwood Wlk. NW1 7H 65
Linley Ct. SM1: Sutt 4A 166
Linley Cres. RM7: Mawney 3H 55
Linley Rd. N17 2E 48
Linley Sambourne House *3J 99*
(off Stafford Ter.)
Linnell Cl. NW11 6K 45
Linnell Dr. NW11 6K 45
Linnell Ho. *E1* *5J 9*
(off Folgate St.)
NW8 *1A 82*
(off Ainsworth Way)
Linnell Rd. N18 5B 34
SE5 2E 120
Linnet Cl. N9 1E 34
SE28 7C 90
WD23: Bush 1B 26
Linnet M. SW12 7E 118
Linnett Cl. E4 4K 35
Linom Rd. SW4 4J 119
Linscott Rd. E5 4J 67
Linsdell Rd. IG11: Bark 1G 89
Linsey Ct. *E10* *1C 68*
(off Grange Rd.)
Linsey St. SE16 4G 103
(not continuous)
Linslade Cl. HA5: Eastc 3K 39
TW4: Houn 5C 112
Linslade Ho. E2 1G 85
NW8 *3D 4*
(off Paveley St.)
Linslade Rd. BR6: Chels 6K 173
Linstead Hall *SW7* *1B 16*
(off Princes Gdns.)
Linstead St. NW6 7J 63
Linstead Way SW18 7G 117
Linsted Ct. SE9 6J 125
Lintaine Cl. W6 6G 99
Linthorpe Av. HA0: Wemb 6C 60
Linthorpe Rd. EN4: Cockf 3H 21
N16 7E 48
Linton Cl. CR4: Mitc 7D 154
DA16: Well 1B 126
SE7 5A 106
Linton Ct. *NW1* *7G 65*
(off Agar Gro.)
RM1: Rom 2K 55
Linton Gdns. E6 6C 88
Linton Gro. SE27 5B 138
Linton Ho. *E3* *5C 86*
(off St Paul's Way)
Linton Rd. IG11: Bark 7G 71
Lintons, The IG11: Bark 7G 71
Linton St. N1 1C 84
(not continuous)
Lintott Ct. TW19: Stanw 6A 110
Linver Rd. SW6 2J 117
Linwood Cl. SE5 2F 121
Linwood Cres. EN1: Enf 1B 24
Linzee Rd. N8 4J 47
Lion Av. TW1: Twick 1K 131
Lion Cl. SE4 6C 122
TW17: Shep 3A 146
Lion Ct. *E1* *7K 85*
(off The Highway)
N1 *1K 83*
(off Copenhagen St.)
SE1 *5G 15*
(off Magdalen St.)
Lionel Gdns. SE9 5B 124
Lionel Ho. *W10* *5G 81*
(off Portobello Rd.)
Lionel Mans. *W14* *3F 99*
(off Haarlem Rd.)
Lionel M. W10 5G 81
Lionel Rd. SE9 5B 124
Lionel Rd. Nth. TW8: Bford 3E 96
Lionel Rd. Sth. TW8: Bford 5F 97
Liongate Ent. Pk.
CR4: Mitc 4B 154
Lion Ga. Gdns. TW9: Rich 3F 115
Lion Ga. M. SW18 7J 117
Liongate M. KT8: E Mos 3K 149
Lion Head Ct. *CR0: C'don* *4C 168*
(off Southbridge Rd.)
Lion Mills E2 2G 85
Lion Pk. Av. KT9: Chess 4G 163
Lion Rd. CR0: C'don 5C 156
DA6: Bex 4E 126
E6 5D 88
N9 2B 34
TW1: Twick 1K 131
Lions Cl. SE9 3A 142
Lion Way TW8: Bford 7D 96
Lion Wharf Rd. TW7: Isle 3B 114
Lion Yd. SW4 4H 119
Liphook Cres. SE23 7J 121
Lipton Cl. SE28 7C 90
Lipton Rd. E1 6K 85
Lisbon Av. TW2: Twick 2G 131
Lisbon Cl. E17 2B 50
Lisburne Rd. NW3 4D 64
Lisford St. SE15 1F 121
Lisgar Ter. W14 4H 99
Liskeard Cl. BR7: Chst 6G 143
Liskeard Gdns. SE3 1J 123
Liskeard Ho. *SE11* *5K 19*
(off Kennings Way)
Lisle Cl. SW17 4F 137
Lisle Ct. NW2 3G 63
Lisle St. WC2 2D 12 (7H 83)
Lismore *SW19* *5H 135*
(off Woodside)
Lismore Cir. NW5 5E 64
Lismore Cl. TW7: Isle 2A 114
Lismore Ho. SE15 3H 121
Lismore Rd.
CR2: S Croy 6E 168
N17 3D 48
Lismore Wlk. *N1* *6C 66*
(off Clephane Rd. Nth.)
Lissant Cl. KT6: Surb 7D 150
Lisselton Ho. *NW4* *4F 45*
(off Belle Vue Est.)
Lissenden Gdns. NW5 4E 64
(not continuous)
Lissenden Mans. NW5 4E 64
Lisson Grn. Est. *NW8* *3C 4*
(off Tresham Cres.)
LISSON GROVE 5B 4 (5C 82)
Lisson Gro. NW1 3B 4 (4B 82)
NW8 3B 4 (4B 82)
Lisson Ho. *NW1* *5C 4*
(off Lisson St.)
Lisson St. NW1 5C 4 (5C 82)
Lister Cl. CR4: Mitc 1C 154
W3 5K 79
Lister Ct. HA1: Harr 7B 42
N16 2E 66
NW9 2A 44
Lister Gdns. N18 5H 33
Listergate Ct. SW15 4E 116
Lister Ho. E1 5G 85
HA9: Wemb *3J 61*
(off Barnhill Rd.)
SE3 *6G 105*
(off Restell Cl.)
UB3: Harl 4G 93
Lister Lodge *W9* *5J 81*
(off Admiral Wlk.)
Lister Rd. E11 1G 69
Lister Wlk. SE28 7D 90
Liston Rd. N17 1G 49
SW4 3G 119
Liston Way IG8: Wfd G 7F 37
Listowel Cl. SW9 7A 102
Listowel Rd. RM10: Dag 3G 73
Listria Pk. N16 2E 66
Litcham Ho. *E1* *3K 85*
(off Longnor Rd.)
Litchfield Av. E15 6G 69
SM4: Mord 7H 153
Litchfield Ct. E17 6C 50
Litchfield Gdns. NW10 6C 62
Litchfield Rd. SM1: Sutt 4A 166
Litchfield St. WC2 2D 12 (7H 83)
Litchfield Way NW11 5K 45
Lithgow's Rd. TW6: H'row A 4G 111
Lithos Rd. NW3 6K 63
Litten Nature Reserve 3G 77
Little Acre BR3: Beck 3C 158
Lit. Albany St. NW1 2K 5 (3F 83)
(Albany St.)
NW1 3K 5
(Longford St.)
Little Angel Theatre *1B 84*
(off Dagmar Pl.)
Lit. Argyll St. W1 1A 12 (6G 83)
Little Benty UB7: W Dray 1E 174
Little Birches DA15: Sidc 2J 143
Lit. Boltons, The SW5 5K 99
SW10 5K 99
Little Bornes SE21 4E 138
Littlebourne SE13 7G 123
Littlebourne Ho. *SE17* *5E 102*
(off Kinglake St.)
Little Britain EC1 6B 8 (5B 84)
Littlebrook Cl. CR0: C'don 6K 157
Little Brownings SE23 2H 139
Littlebury Rd. SW4 3H 119
Lit. Bury St. N9 1J 33
Lit. Bushey La. WD23: Bush 1C 26
Little Cedars N12 4F 31
Lit. Chelsea Ho. *SW10* *6A 100*
(off Netherton Gro.)
Lit. Chester St. SW1 1J 17 (3F 101)
Little Cloisters SW1 1E 18 (3J 101)
Lit. College La. *EC4* *2E 14*
(off College St.)
Lit. College St. SW1 1E 18 (3J 101)
Littlecombe SE7 6K 105
Littlecombe Cl. SW15 6F 117
Little Comn. HA7: Stan 3F 27
Littlecote Cl. SW19 7G 117
Littlecote Pl.
HA5: Hat E 1C 40
Lit. Cottage Pl. SE10 7D 104
Little Ct. BR4: W W'ck 2G 171
Little Cft. SE9 3E 124
Littledale SE2 6A 108
Lit. Dean's Yd. SW1 1E 18
Little Dimocks SW12 2F 137
Lit. Dorrit Ct. SE1 6D 14 (2C 102)
LITTLE EALING 3D 96
Lit. Ealing La. W5 4C 96
Lit. Edward St. NW1 1K 5 (3F 83)
Little Elms UB3: Harl 7F 93
Lit. Essex St. WC2 2J 13
Lit. Ferry Rd. TW1: Twick 1B 132
Littlefield Cl. KT1: King T 2E 150
N19 4G 65
Littlefield Ho. *KT1: King T* *2E 150*
(off Littlefield Cl.)
Littlefield Rd. HA8: Edg 7D 28
Lit. Friday Rd. E4 2B 36
Little Gearies IG6: Ilf 4F 53
Lit. George St. SW1 7E 12 (2J 101)
Little Grange UB6: G'frd 3A 78
Little Green TW9: Rich 4D 114
Lit. Green St. NW5 4F 65
Littlegrove EN4: E Barn 6H 21
Little Halliards KT12: Walt T 6J 147
LITTLE HEATH 4B 54
Little Heath RM6: Chad H 4B 54
SE7 6C 106
Lit. Heath Rd. DA7: Bex 1F 127
Littleheath Rd. CR2: Sels 7H 169
Little Holt E11 5J 51
LITTLE ILFORD 5D 70
Lit. Ilford La. E12 4D 70
Lit. John Rd. W7 6K 77
Little Larkins EN5: Barn 6B 20
Lit. London Cl. UB8: Hil 5D 74
Lit. London Ct. *SE1* *7K 15*
(off Wolseley St.)
Lit. Marlborough St. W1 1A 12
Littlemede SE9 3D 142
Littlemoor Rd. IG1: Ilf 3H 71
Littlemore Rd. SE2 2A 108
Lit. Moss La. HA5: Pinn 2C 40
Lit. Newport St. WC2 2D 12 (7H 83)
Lit. New St. EC4 7K 7 (6A 84)
Lit. Oaks Cl. TW17: Shep 4B 146
Lit. Orchard Cl. HA5: Pinn 2C 40
Lit. Park Dr. TW13: Felt 2C 130
Lit. Park Gdns. EN2: Enf 3H 23
Lit. Pluckett's Way IG9: Buck H 1G 37
Lit. Portland St. W1 7K 5 (6G 83)
Little Potters WD23: Bush 1C 26
Lit. Queen's Rd. TW11: Tedd 6K 131
Little Redlands BR1: Brom 2C 160
Little Rd. UB3: Hayes 2H 93
Littlers Cl. SW19 1B 154
Lit. Russell St. WC1 6E 6 (5J 83)
Lit. St James's St.
SW1 5A 12 (1G 101)
Lit. St Leonard's SW14 3J 115
Little Sanctuary SW1 7D 12 (2H 101)
Lit. Smith St. SW1 1D 18 (3H 101)
Lit. Somerset St. EC3 1J 15 (6F 85)
LITTLE STANMORE 7A 28
Littlestone Cl.
BR3: Beck 6C 140
Little Strand NW9 2B 44
Little Theatre, The 1J 159
Little Thrift BR5: Pet W 4G 161
Lit. Titchfield St. W1 6A 6 (5G 83)
LITTLETON 3C 146
Littleton Av. E4 1C 36
LITTLETON COMMON 7E 128
Littleton Cres. HA1: Harr 2K 59
Littleton Ho. *SW1* *6A 18*
(off Lupus St.)
Littleton La. TW17: Shep 7A 146

Littleton Rd. HA1: Harr 2K **59**
TW15: Ashf 7E **128**
Littleton St. SW18 . . . . .2A **136**
Lit. Trinity La. EC4 . . . . .2D **14** (7C **84**)
Little Turnstile WC1 . . . . .6G **7** (5K **83**)
Lit. Warkworth Ho. TW7: Isle 2B **114**
Littlewood SE13 . . . . .6E **122**
Littlewood Cl. W13 . . . . .3B **96**
Lit. Wood St. KT1: King T 2D **150**
Livermere Ct. *E8* *1F 85*
(off Queensbridge Rd.)
Livermere Rd. E8 . . . . .1F **85**
Liverpool Gro. SE17 . . . . .5C **102**
Liverpool Rd. CR7: Thor H 3C **156**
E10 . . . . .6E **50**
E16 . . . . .5G **87**
KT2: King T 7G **133**
N1 . . . . .5A **66**
N7 . . . . .5A **66**
W5 . . . . .2D **96**
Liverpool St. EC2 . . . . .6G **9** (5E **84**)
Livesey Cl. KT1: King T 3F **151**
SE28 . . . . .3G **107**
Livesey Mus. for Children 6H **103**
Livesey Pl. SE15 . . . . .6G **103**
Livingstone Ct. E10 . . . . .6E **50**
EN5: Barn *2B 20*
(off Church La.)
HA3: W'stone 3K **41**
TW19: Stanw *1A 128*
(off Explorer Av.)
Livingstone Ho. NW10 . . . . .7K **61**
SE5 . . . .*7C 102*
(off Wyndham Rd.)
Livingstone Lodge *W9* *5J 81*
(off Admiral Wlk.)
Livingstone Mans. *W14* *6G 99*
(off Queen's Club Gdns.)
Livingstone Pl. E14 . . . . .5E **104**
Livingstone Rd. CR7: Thor H 2C **156**
E15 . . . . .1E **86**
E17 . . . . .6D **50**
N13 . . . . .6D **32**
SW11 . . . . .3B **118**
TW3: Houn 4G **113**
UB1: S'hall 7B **76**
LivingWell Health Club
Purley 6A **168**
Wembley 5F **61**
LivingWell Sports Club
Regents Plaza *2K 81*
(off Greville Rd.)
Livonia St. W1 . . . . .1B **12** (6G **83**)
Lizard St. EC1 . . . . .2D **8** (3C **84**)
Lizban St. SE3 . . . . .7K **105**
Lizmans Ter. *W8* *3J 99*
(off Earl's Ct. Rd.)
Llandovery Ho. *E14* *2E 104*
(off Chipka St.)
Llanelly Rd. NW2 . . . . .2H **63**
Llanover Rd. HA9: Wemb 3D **60**
SE18 . . . . .6E **106**
Llanthony Rd. SM4: Mord 5B **154**
Llanvanor Rd. NW2 . . . . .2H **63**
Llewellyn Ct. SE20 . . . . .1J **157**
Llewellyn Mans. *W14* *4G 99*
(off Hammersmith Rd.)
Llewellyn St. SE16 . . . . .2G **103**
Lloyd Av. SW16 . . . . .1J **155**
Lloyd Baker St. WC1 . . . . .2H **7** (3K **83**)
(not continuous)
Lloyd Ct. HA5: Pinn 5B **40**
Lloyd Ho. BR3: Beck 6D **140**
Lloyd M. EN3: Enf L 1H **25**
Lloyd Pk. Av. CR0: C'don 4F **169**
Lloyd Pk. Ho. E17 . . . . .3C **50**
Lloyd Rd. E6 .1D **88**
E17 . . . . .4K **49**
KT4: Wor Pk 3E **164**
RM9: Dag 6F **73**
Lloyd's Av. EC3 . . . . .1H **15** (6E **84**)
Lloyd's Building 1G **15** (6E **84**)
Lloyds Lanes Bowling Alley 2B **24**
Lloyds Lanes Raynes Pk. 3F **153**
Lloyd's Pl. SE3 . . . . .2G **123**
Lloyd Sq. WC1 . . . . .1J **7** (3A **84**)
Lloyd's Row EC1 . . . . .2K **7** (3A **84**)
Lloyd St. WC1 . . . . .1J **7** (3A **84**)
Lloyds Way BR3: Beck 5A **158**
Lloyds Wharf SE1 . . . . .6K **15**
Lloyd Thomas Ct. N22 . . . . .7E **32**
Lloyd Vs. E6 .4C **88**
SE4 . . . . .2C **122**
Loampit Hill SE13 . . . . .2C **122**
LOAMPIT VALE 3E **122**
Loampit Va. SE13 . . . . .3D **122**
Loanda Cl. E8 . . . . .1F **85**
Loats Rd. SW2 . . . . .6J **119**
Lobelia Cl. E6 . . . . .5C **88**
Locarno Ct. SW16 . . . . .5G **137**
Locarno Rd. UB6: G'frd 4H **77**
W3 . . . . .1J **97**
Lochaber Rd. SE13 . . . . .4G **123**
Lochaline St. W6 . . . . .6E **98**
Lochan Cl. UB4: Yead 4C **76**
Lochinvar St. SW12 . . . . .7F **119**
Lochleven Ho. *N2* *2B 46*
(off The Grange)
Lochmere Cl. DA8: Erith 6H **109**
Lochmore Ho. *SW1* *4H 17*
(off Cundy St.)
Lochnagar St. E14 . . . . .5E **86**
Lockbridge Ct. *W9* *5J 81*
(off Woodfield Rd.)
Lock Bldg., The E15 . . . . .2E **86**
Lock Chase SE3 . . . . .3G **123**
Lock Cl. UB2: S'hall 2G **95**
Locke Ho. *SW8* *1G 119*
(off Wadhurst Rd.)
Lockesfield Pl. E14 . . . . .5D **104**
Lockesley Dr. BR5: St M Cry 6K **161**
Lockesley Sq. KT6: Surb 6D **150**
Locket Rd. HA3: W'stone 3J **41**
Locket Rd. M. HA3: W'stone 2J **41**
Lockfield Av. EN3: Brim 2F **25**
Lockgate Cl. E9 . . . . .5B **68**
Lockhart Cl. EN3: Pond E 5C **24**
N7 . . . . .6K **65**
Lockhart St. E3 . . . . .4B **86**
Lockhurst St. E5 . . . . .4K **67**
Lockie Pl. SE25 . . . . .3G **157**
Lockier Wlk. HA9: Wemb 3D **60**
Lockington Rd. SW8 . . . . .1F **119**
Lock Keepers Quay
SE16 . . . .*3K 103*
(off Brunswick Quay)
Lockmead Rd. N15 . . . . .6G **49**
SE13 . . . . .3E **122**
Lock M. *NW5* *6H 65*
(off Northpoint Sq.)
Lock Rd. TW10: Ham 4C **132**
LOCKSBOTTOM 3E **172**
Locksfields *SE17* *4D 102*
(off Catesby St.)
Lockside *E14* *7A 86*
(off Narrow St.)
Locks La. CR4: Mitc 1E **154**
Locksley Est. E14 . . . . .6B **86**
Locksley St. E14 . . . . .5B **86**
Locksmeade Rd.
TW10: Ham 4C **132**
Locksons Cl. E14 . . . . .5D **86**
Lockswood Cl. EN4: Cockf 4J **21**
Lock Vw. Ct. *E14* *7A 86*
(off Narrow St.)
Lockwell Rd. RM10: Dag 3G **73**
Lockwood Cl. SE26 . . . . .4K **139**
Lockwood Ho. SE11 . . . . .7J **19** (6A **102**)
Lockwood Ind. Pk. N17 . . . . .3H **49**
Lockwood Pl. E4 . . . . .6H **35**
Lockwood Sq. SE16 . . . . .3H **103**
Lockwood Way E17 . . . . .2K **49**
KT9: Chess 5G **163**
Lockyer Est. SE1 . . . . .7F **15**
(not continuous)
Lockyer Ho. *SE10* *5H 105*
(off Armitage Rd.)
SW8 . . . .*7H 101*
(off Wandsworth Rd.)
SW15 . . . . .3F **117**
Lockyer M. EN3: Enf L 1J **25**
Lockyer St. SE1 . . . . .7F **15** (2D **102**)
Locomotive Dr. TW14: Felt 1J **129**
Locton Grn. E3 . . . . .1B **86**
Loddiges Ho. E9 . . . . .7J **67**
Loddiges Rd. E9 . . . . .7J **67**
Loddon Ho. *NW8* *4B 4*
(off Church St. Est.)
Loder St. SE15 . . . . .7J **103**
Lodge Av. CR0: Wadd 3A **168**
HA3: Kent 4E **42**
RM8: Dag 6B **72**
RM9: Dag 1A **90**
SW14 . . . . .3A **116**
LODGE AVENUE FLYOVER JUNC. 1A **90**
Lodge Cl. HA8: Edg 6A **28**
N18 . . . . .5H **33**
SM6: Wall 1E **166**
TW7: Isle 1B **114**
Lodge Ct. HA0: Wemb 6E **60**
Lodge Dr. N13 . . . . .4F **33**
Lodge Gdns. BR3: Beck 5B **158**
Lodge Hill IG4: Ilf 4C **52**
SE2: Well 7B **108**
Lodgehill Pk. Cl.
HA2: Harr 2F **59**
Lodge La. CR0: New Ad 6C **170**
DA5: Bexl 6D **126**
N12 . . . . .5F **31**
RM5: Col R 1G **55**
Lodge Pl. SM1: Sutt 5K **165**
Lodge Rd. BR1: Brom 7A **142**
CR0: C'don 6B **156**
NW4 . . . . .4E **44**
NW8 . . . . .2B **4** (3B **82**)
SM6: Wall 5F **167**
Lodge Vs. IG8: Wfd G 6C **36**
Lodge Way TW15: Ashf 2A **128**
TW17: Shep 2E **146**
Lodore Gdns. NW9 . . . . .5A **44**
Lodore Grn. UB10: Ick 3A **56**
Lodore St. E14 . . . . .6E **86**
Loft Ho. Pl. KT9: Chess 6C **162**
Loftie St. SE16 . . . . .2G **103**
Lofting Ho. *N1* *7A 66*
(off Liverpool Rd.)
Lofting Rd. N1 . . . . .7K **65**
Loftus Rd. IG11: Bark 6G **71**
W12 . . . . .1D **98**
Loftus Vs. *W12* *1D 98*
(off Loftus Rd.)
Logan Cl. EN3: Enf H 1E **24**
TW4: Houn 3D **112**
Logan M. RM1: Rom 5K **55**
W8 . . . . .4J **99**
Logan Pl. W8 .4J **99**
Logan Rd. HA9: Wemb 2D **60**
N9 . . . . .2C **34**
Loggetts SE21 . . . . .2E **138**
Logs Hill BR1: Brom 7C **142**
BR7: Chst 7C **142**
Logs Hill Cl. BR7: Chst 1C **160**
Lohmann Ho. SE11 . . . . .7J **19**
Lois Dr. TW17: Shep 5D **146**
Lolesworth Cl. E1 . . . . .6J **9** (5F **85**)
Lolland Ho. SE7 . . . . .4C **106**
Lollard St. SE11 . . . . .3H **19** (4K **101**)
(not continuous)
Loman St. SE1 . . . . .6B **14** (2B **102**)
Lomas Cl. CR0: New Ad 7E **170**
Lomas Dr. E8 .7F **67**
Lomas St. E1 .5G **85**
Lombard Av. EN3: Enf H 1D **24**
IG3: Ilf 1J **71**
Lombard Bus. Pk.
CR0: C'don 7K **155**
SW19 . . . . .2K **153**
Lombard Ct. EC3 . . . . .2F **15** (7D **84**)
RM7: Rom 4J **55**
W3 . . . . .1H **97**
Lombard La. EC4 . . . . .1K **13** (6A **84**)
Lombard Rd. N11 . . . . .5A **32**
SW11 . . . . .2B **118**
SW19 . . . . .2K **153**
LOMBARD RDBT. 7K **155**
Lombard St. EC3 . . . . .1F **15** (6D **84**)
Lombard Trad. Est.
SE7 . . . . .4K **105**
Lombard Wall SE7 . . . . .3K **105**
(not continuous)
Lombardy Cl. IG6: Ilf 7K **37**
Lombardy Pl. W2 . . . . .7K **81**
Lombardy Retail Pk.
UB3: Hayes 7K **75**
Lomond Cl. HA0: Wemb 7F **61**
N15 . . . . .5E **48**
Lomond Gdns. CR2: Sels 7A **170**
Lomond Gro. SE5 . . . . .7D **102**
Lomond Ho. SE5 . . . . .7D **102**
Loncroft Rd. SE5 . . . . .6E **102**
Londesborough Rd. N16 . . . . .4E **66**
Londinium Twr. *E1* *2K 15*
(off W. Tenter St.)
London Aquarium 6G **13** (2K **101**)
London Bri. EC4 . . . . .4F **15** (1D **102**)
SE1 . . . . .4F **15** (1D **102**)
London Bri. St. SE1 . . . . .5F **15** (1D **102**)
London Bri. Wlk. *SE1* *4F 15*
(off Duke St. Hill)
London Business School 3E **4** (4D **82**)
London Butterfly House 1B **114**
London Canal Mus. 2J **83**
LONDON CITY AIRPORT 1C **106**
London City College *5J 13*
(in Schiller International University)
London Coliseum *3E 12*
(off St Martin's La.)
London College of Fashion, The
Hackney 7H **67**
St Luke's 4C **8**
Londonderry Pde. DA8: Erith 7K **109**
London Dungeon 5F **15**
London Eye 6G **13** (2K **101**)
London Flds. E. Side E8 . . . . .7H **67**
London Flds. W. Side E8 . . . . .7G **67**
London Fire Brigade Mus. 2C **102**
London Fruit Exchange
E1 . . . .*6J 9*
(off Brushfield St.)
London Ga. UB3: Hayes 2G **93**
LONDON GATEWAY SERVICE AREA . . .2D **28**
London Group Bus. Pk. NW2 . . . . .1B **62**
London Guildhall University
Coke St. 6G **85**
LONDON-HEATHROW AIRPORT 3C **110**
Terminal 5 . . . . .6D **174**
London Ho. *NW8* *2C 82*
(off Avenue Rd.)
WC1 . . . . .3G **7** (4K **83**)
London Ind. Pk., The E6 . . . . .5F **89**
(not continuous)
London La. BR1: Brom 7H **141**
E8 . . . . .7H **67**
London Master Bakers Almshouses
E10 . . . . .6D **50**
London Metropolitan University
Benwell Rd. 5A **66**
Hornsey St. 5K **65**
Jewry St. *1J 15*
(off Jewry St.)

London Metropolitan University
Minories ... 7F 85
(off Minories)
Moorgate ... 6E 8
Old Castle St. ... 7K 9 (6F 85)
Whitechapel High St. ... 7K 9 (6G 85)
London M. W2 ... 7B 4 (6B 82)
London Motorcycle Mus. ... 3G 77
London Palladium ... 1A 12
(off Argyll St.)
London Regatta Cen. ... 7B 88
London Rd. BR1: Brom ... 7H 141
CR0: C'don ... 7B 156
CR4: Mitc ... 5C 154
(Bishopsford Rd.)
CR4: Mitc ... 7E 154
(Carshalton Rd.)
CR4: Mitc ... 2D 154
(Holborn Way)
CR7: C'don, Thor H ... 1K 155
CR7: Thor H ... 3A 156
DA1: Bexl, Cray ... 5K 127
E13 ... 2J 87
EN2: Enf ... 4J 23
HA1: Harr ... 2J 59
HA7: Stan ... 5H 27
HA9: Wemb ... 5E 60
IG11: Bark ... 7F 71
KT2: King T ... 2F 151
(not continuous)
KT17: Ewe ... 7B 164
RM7: Chad H, Rom ... 6G 55
SE1 ... 7A 14 (3B 102)
SE23 ... 1H 139
SM3: Cheam ... 3F 165
SM4: Mord ... 5J 153
SM6: Wall ... 4F 167
SW16 ... 1K 155
SW17 ... 7D 136
TW1: Twick ... 7A 114
TW3: Houn ... 3G 113
TW7: Bford, Isle ... 2K 113
TW7: Isle, Twick ... 5A 114
TW8: Bford ... 2K 113
TW14: Bedf ... 2A 128
TW15: Ashf ... 2A 128
LONDON ROAD RDBT. ... 6A 114
London School of Economics & Political Science, The ... 1G 13 (6K 83)
London Scottish RUFC ... 3D 114
(off Kew Foot Rd.)
London South Bank University
Borough Rd. ... 7B 14 (3B 102)
Keyworth St. ... 7B 14 (3B 102)
London Rd. ... 7A 14
New Kent Rd. ... 3C 102
(off New Kent Rd.)
London South Bank University Sports Cen. ... 7B 14
(in London South Bank University)
London South Bank University Technopark ... 3B 102
(off London Rd.)
London Stile W4 ... 5G 97
London Stock Exchange ... 7B 8
London St. EC3 ... 2H 15 (7E 84)
W2 ... 7A 4 (6B 82)
London Telecom Tower, The ... 5A 6
London Television Cen., The ... 4J 13 (7A 84)
London Ter. E2 ... 2G 85
London Transport Mus. ... 2F 13 (7J 83)
London Trocadero ... 7H 83
London Underwriting Cen. ... 2H 15
London Wall EC2 ... 6D 8 (5C 84)
London Wall Bldgs. EC2 ... 6F 9
London Welsh RUFC ... 3E 114
London Wetland Cen. ... 1D 116
London Wharf E2 ... 1H 85
(off Wharf Pl.)
London Wildlife Trust Cen. for Wildlife Gardening ... 3F 121
London Zoo ... 2E 82
LONESOME ... 1G 155
Lonesome Cvn. Pk.
CR4: Mitc ... 1F 155
Lonesome Way SW16 ... 1F 155
Long Acre WC2 ... 2E 12 (7J 83)
Long Acre Ct. W13 ... 5A 78
Longacre Pl. SM5: Cars ... 6E 166
Longacre Rd. E17 ... 1F 51
Longbeach Rd. SW11 ... 3D 118
Longberrys NW2 ... 3H 63
Longboat Row UB1: S'hall ... 6D 76
Longbow Ho. EC1 ... 5D 84
(off Chiswell St.)
Longbridge Ho. E16 ... 7F 89
(off University Way)
RM8: Dag ... 4B 72
(off Gainsborough Rd.)
Longbridge Rd. IG11: Bark ... 6H 71
RM8: Dag ... 4A 72
Longbridge Way SE13 ... 5E 122
Longcourt M. E11 ... 4A 52
(off Elmcroft Av.)
Longcroft SE9 ... 3D 142
Longcrofte Rd. HA8: Edg ... 7J 27
Long Deacon Rd. E4 ... 1B 36
LONG DITTON ... 1C 162
Longdon Wood BR2: Kes ... 3C 172
Longdown Rd. SE6 ... 4C 140
Long Dr. HA4: Ruis ... 5A 58
UB6: G'frd ... 1F 77
UB7: W Dray ... 2A 92
W3 ... 6A 80
Long Elmes HA3: Hrw W ... 1F 41
Longfellow Rd. E17 ... 6B 50
KT4: Wor Pk ... 2C 164
Longfellow Way SE1 ... 4F 103
Long Fld. NW9 ... 7F 29
Longfield BR1: Brom ... 1H 159
Longfield Av. E17 ... 4A 50
HA9: Wemb ... 1E 60
NW7 ... 7H 29
SM6: Wall ... 1E 166
W5 ... 7C 78
Longfield Cres. SE26 ... 3J 139
Longfield Dr. CR4: Mitc ... 1C 154
SW14 ... 5H 115
Longfield Est. SE1 ... 4F 103
Longfield Ho. W5 ... 7C 78
Longfield Rd. W5 ... 6C 78
Longfield St. SW18 ... 7J 117
Longfield Wlk. W5 ... 6C 78
LONGFORD ... 4C 174
Longford Av. TW14: Felt ... 6G 111
TW19: Stanw ... 1A 128
UB1: S'hall ... 7F 77
Longford Cir. UB7: Lford ... 4C 174
Longford Cl. TW12: Ham H ... 4E 130
TW13: Hanw ... 3C 130
UB4: Yead ... 7B 76
Longford Ct. E5 ... 4K 67
(off Pedro St.)
KT19: Ewe ... 4J 163
NW4 ... 4F 45
TW12: Ham H ... 6F 131
UB1: S'hall ... 1E 94
(off Uxbridge Rd.)
Longford Gdns. SM1: Sutt ... 3A 166
UB4: Yead ... 7B 76
Longford Ho. BR1: Brom ... 5F 141
(off Brangbourne Rd.)
E1 ... 6J 85
(off Jubilee St.)
TW12: Ham H ... 4E 130
Longford Ind. Est.
TW12: Hamp ... 6F 131
LONGFORDMOOR ... 4B 174
Longford Rd. TW2: Whitt ... 1E 130
Longford St. NW1 ... 3K 5 (4F 83)
Longford Wlk. SW2 ... 7A 120
Longford Way TW19: Stanw ... 1A 128
Longhayes Av. RM6: Chad H ... 4D 54
Longhayes Ct. RM6: Chad H ... 4D 54
Longheath Gdns. CR0: C'don ... 5J 157
Longhedge Ho. SE26 ... 4G 139
(off High Level Dr.)
Long Hedges TW3: Houn ... 2E 112
Longhedge St. SW11 ... 2E 118
Longhill Rd. SE6 ... 2F 141
Longhook Gdns. UB5: Yead ... 2J 75
Longhope Cl. SE15 ... 6E 102
Longhurst Ho. W10 ... 3H 81
(off Lancefield St.)
Longhurst Rd. CR0: C'don ... 6H 157
SE13 ... 5F 123
Longland Ct. SE1 ... 5G 103
Longland Dr. N20 ... 3E 30
LONGLANDS ... 3G 143
Longlands Ct. CR4: Mitc ... 1E 154
DA15: Sidc ... 2K 143
W11 ... 7H 81
Longlands Pk. Cres.
DA15: Sidc ... 3J 143
Longlands Rd. DA15: Sidc ... 3J 143
Long La. CR0: C'don ... 6J 157
DA7: Bex ... 7D 108
EC1 ... 6B 8 (5B 84)
N2 ... 1K 45
N3 ... 1K 45
(not continuous)
SE1 ... 7E 14 (2D 102)
TW19: Stanw ... 2B 128
UB10: Hil, Ick ... 3C 74
Longleat Ho. SW1 ... 5C 18
(off Rampayne St.)
Longleat Rd. EN1: Enf ... 5K 23
Longleat Way TW14: Bedf ... 7F 111
Longleigh Ho. SE5 ... 1E 120
(off Peckham Rd.)
Longleigh La. DA7: Bex ... 6C 108
SE2 ... 6C 108
Long Lents Ho. NW10 ... 1K 79
(off Shrewsbury Cres.)
Longley Av. HA0: Wemb ... 1F 79
Longley Ct. SW8 ... 1J 119
Longley Rd. CR0: C'don ... 7B 156
HA1: Harr ... 5G 41
SW17 ... 6C 136
Long Leys E4 ... 6J 35
Longley St. SE1 ... 4G 103
Longley Way NW2 ... 3E 62
Longman Ho. E2 ... 2K 85
(off Mace St.)
E8 ... 1F 85
(off Haggerston Rd.)
Long Mark Rd. E16 ... 5B 88
Longmarsh La. SE28 ... 1J 107
Long Mead NW9 ... 1B 44
Longmead BR7: Chst ... 2E 160
Longmead Dr. DA14: Sidc ... 2D 144
Longmead Ho. SE27 ... 5C 138
Long Meadow NW5 ... 5H 65
Long Mdw. Cl. BR4: W W'ck ... 7E 158
Longmeadow Rd.
DA15: Sidc ... 1J 143
Longmead Rd. KT7: T Ditt ... 7J 149
SW17 ... 5D 136
UB3: Hayes ... 7H 75
Long Mill SE10 ... 1D 122
(off Greenwich High Rd.)
Longmoore St. SW1 ... 4A 18 (4G 101)
Longmoor Point SW15 ... 1D 134
(off Norley Vale)
Longmore Av. EN4: E Barn ... 6F 21
EN5: New Bar ... 6F 21
Longmore Gdns. Est. SW1 ... 4B 18
Longnor Est. E1 ... 3K 85
Longnor Rd. E1 ... 3K 85
Long Pond Rd. SE3 ... 1G 123
Longreach Ct. IG11: Bark ... 2H 89
Long Reach Rd. IG11: Bark ... 4K 89
Longridge Ho. SE1 ... 3C 102
Longridge La. UB1: S'hall ... 6F 77
Longridge Rd. IG11: Bark ... 7G 71
SW5 ... 4J 99
Long Ridges N2 ... 3E 46
(off Fortis Grn.)
Long Rd. SW4 ... 4F 119
Longs Ct. TW9: Rich ... 4F 115
WC2 ... 3D 12
Longshaw Rd. E4 ... 3A 36
Longshore SE8 ... 4B 104
Longshott Ct. SW5 ... 4J 99
(off W. Cromwell Rd.)
Longstaff Cres. SW18 ... 6J 117
Longstaff Rd. SW18 ... 6J 117
Longstone Av. NW10 ... 7B 62
Longstone Ct. SE1 ... 7E 14
(off Gt. Dover St.)
Longstone Rd. SW17 ... 5F 137
Long St. E2 ... 1J 9 (3F 85)
Longthornton Rd. SW16 ... 2G 155
Longthorpe Ct. W6 ... 4C 98
(off Invermead Cl.)
Longton Av. SE26 ... 4G 139
Longton Gro. SE26 ... 4H 139
Longview Vs. RM5: Col R ... 1F 55
Longview Way RM5: Col R ... 1K 55
Longville Rd. SE11 ... 4B 102
Long Wlk. KT3: N Mald ... 3J 151
SE1 ... 3E 102
SE18 ... 6F 107
SW13 ... 2A 116
Longwalk Rd. UB11: Stock P ... 1D 92
Long Wall E15 ... 3F 87
Longwater Ho. KT1: King T ... 3D 150
(off Portsmouth Rd.)
Longwood Bus. Pk. TW16: Sun ... 5H 147
Longwood Dr. SW15 ... 6C 116
Longwood Gdns. IG5: Ilf ... 4D 52
IG6: Ilf ... 4D 52
Longworth Cl. SE28 ... 6D 90
Long Yd. WC1 ... 4G 7 (4K 83)
Loning, The NW9 ... 4A 44
Lonsdale Av. E6 ... 4B 88
HA9: Wemb ... 5E 60
RM7: Rom ... 6J 55
Lonsdale Cl. E6 ... 4C 88
HA5: Hat E ... 1C 40
HA8: Edg ... 5A 28
SE9 ... 3B 142
UB8: Hil ... 5E 74
Lonsdale Ct. KT6: Surb ... 7D 150
Lonsdale Cres. IG2: Ilf ... 6F 53
Lonsdale Dr. EN2: Enf ... 4C 22
Lonsdale Dr. Nth. EN2: Enf ... 5D 22
Lonsdale Gdns. CR7: Thor H ... 4K 155
Lonsdale Ho. W11 ... 6H 81
(off Lonsdale Rd.)
Lonsdale M. TW9: Kew ... 1G 115
W11 ... 6H 81
(off Lonsdale Rd.)
Lonsdale Pl. N1 ... 7A 66
Lonsdale Rd. DA7: Bex ... 2F 127
E11 ... 6H 51
NW6 ... 1H 81
SE25 ... 4H 157
SW13 ... 1B 116
UB2: S'hall ... 3B 94
W4 ... 4B 98
W11 ... 6H 81
Lonsdale Road Reservoir Bird Sanctuary ... 7B 98
Lonsdale Sq. N1 ... 7A 66
Lonsdale Yd. W11 ... 7J 81
Loobert Rd. N15 ... 3E 48
Looe Gdns. IG6: Ilf ... 3F 53
Loop Rd. BR7: Chst ... 6G 143

Lopen Rd. N18 .4K 33
Lopez Ho. SW9 .3J 119
Lorac Ct. SM2: Sutt .7J 165
Loraine Cl. EN3: Pond E .5D 24
Loraine Cotts. N7 .4K 65
Loraine Ct. BR7: Chst .5F 143
Loraine Ho. SM6: Wall .4F 167
Loraine Rd. N7 .4K 65
W4 .6H 97
Lord Amory Way E14 .2E 104
Lord Av. IG5: Ilf .4D 52
Lord Chancellor Wlk.
KT2: King T .1J 151
Lord Ct. IG5: Ilf .4D 52
Lordell Pl. SW19 .6E 134
Lorden Wlk. E2 .2K 9 (3G 85)
Lord Gdns. IG5: Ilf .4D 52
Lord Hills Bri. W2 .5K 81
Lord Hills Rd. W2 .5K 81
Lord Holland La. SW9 .2A 120
Lord Knyvetts Ct.
TW19: Stanw .6A 110
Lord Napier Pl. W6 .5C 98
Lord Nth. St. SW1 .2E 18 (3J 101)
Lord Roberts M. SW6 .7K 99
Lord Robert's Ter. SE18 .5E 106
Lords Cl. SE21 .2C 138
TW13: Hanw .2C 130
Lord's Cricket Ground .2B 4 (3B 82)
Lordship Gro. N16 .2D 66
Lordship La. N17 .1D 48
N22 .2A 48
SE22 .4F 121
Lordship La. Est. SE21 .7G 121
Lordship Pk. N16 .2C 66
Lordship Pk. M. N16 .2C 66
Lordship Pl. SW3 .7C 16 (6C 100)
Lordship Rd. N16 .1D 66
UB5: N'olt .7C 58
Lordship Ter. N16 .2D 66
Lordsmead Rd. N17 .1E 48
Lord St. E16 .1C 106
Lords Vw. NW8 .2C 4 (3B 82)
Lord Warwick St. SE18 .3D 106
Lordwood Cl. DA6: Bex .5E 126
Loreburn Ho. N7 .4K 65
Lorenzo St. WC1 .1G 7 (3K 83)
Loretto Gdns. HA3: Kent .4E 42
Lorian Cl. N12 .4E 30
Loring Rd. N20 .2H 31
SE14 .1A 122
TW7: Isle .2K 113
Loris Rd. W6 .3E 98
Lorn Ct. SW9 .2A 120
Lorne Av. CR0: C'don .7K 157
Lorne Cl. NW8 .2D 4 (3C 82)
Lorne Gdns. CR0: C'don .7K 157
E11 .4A 52
W11 .2F 99
Lorne Ho. E1 .5A 86
(off Ben Jonson Rd.)
Lorne Rd. E7 .4K 69
E17 .5C 50
HA3: W'stone .2K 41
N4 .1K 65
TW10: Rich .5F 115
Lorne Ter. N3 .2H 45
Lorn Rd. SW9 .2K 119
Lorraine Ct. NW1 .7F 65
Lorraine Pk. HA3: Hrw W .7D 26
Lorrimore Rd. SE17 .6B 102
Lorrimore Sq. SE17 .6B 102
Lorton Ho. NW6 .1J 81
(off Kilburn Va.)
Lothair Rd. W5 .2D 96
Lothair Rd. Nth. N4 .6B 48
Lothair Rd. Sth. N4 .7A 48
Lothbury EC2 .7E 8 (6D 84)
Lothian Av. UB4: Yead .5K 75
Lothian Cl. HA0: Wemb .3A 60
Lothian Rd. SW9 .1B 120
Lothrop St. W10 .3G 81
Lots Rd. SW10 .7A 100
Lotus Cl. SE21 .3D 138
Loubet St. SW17 .6D 136
Loudoun Av. IG6: Ilf .5F 53
Loudoun Rd. NW8 .1A 82
Loudwater Cl. TW16: Sun .4J 147
Loudwater Rd. TW16: Sun .4J 147
Loughborough Est. SW9 .3B 120
Loughborough Pk. SW9 .4B 120
Loughborough Rd. SW9 .2A 120
Loughborough St.
SE11 .5H 19 (5K 101)
Lough Rd. N7 .5K 65
Loughton Way IG9: Buck H .1G 37
Louisa Cl. E9 .1K 85
Louisa Ct. TW2: Twick .2J 131
Louisa Gdns. E1 .4K 85
Louisa St. E1 .4K 85
Louise Aumonier Wlk. N19 .7J 47
(off Jessie Blythe La.)
Louise Bennett Cl. SE24 .4B 120
Louise Ct. N22 .1A 48
Louise De Marillac Ho. E1 .5J 85
(off Smithy St.)
Louise Rd. E15 .6G 69
Louise White Ho. N19 .1H 65
Louis Gdns. BR7: Chst .4D 142
Louis M. N10 .1F 47
Louisville Rd. SW17 .3E 136
Lousada Lodge N14 .6B 22
(off Avenue Rd.)
Louvaine Rd. SW11 .4B 118
Lovage App. E6 .5C 88
Lovat Cl. NW2 .3B 62
Lovat La. EC3 .2G 15 (7E 84)
(not continuous)
Lovatt Cl. HA8: Edg .6C 28
Lovatt Ct. SW12 .1F 137
Lovatt Dr. HA4: Ruis .5J 39
Lovat Wlk. TW5: Hest .7C 94
Loveday Rd. W13 .2B 96
Lovegrove St. SE1 .5G 103
Lovegrove Wlk. E14 .1E 104
Lovekyn Cl. KT2: King T .2E 150
Lovelace Av. BR2: Brom .6E 160
Lovelace Gdns. IG11: Bark .4A 72
KT6: Surb .7D 150
Lovelace Grn. SE9 .3D 124
Lovelace Ho. E8 .1F 85
(off Haggerston Rd.)
W13 .7B 78
Lovelace Rd. EN4: E Barn .7H 21
KT6: Surb .7C 150
SE21 .2C 138
Lovelace Vs. KT7: T Ditt .7B 150
(off Portsmouth Rd.)
Loveland Mans.
IG11: Bark .7K 71
(off Upney La.)
Love La. BR1: Brom .3K 159
(off Elmfield Rd.)
BR1: Brom .3K 159
(Rafford Way)
CR4: Mitc .3C 154
(not continuous)
DA5: Bexl .6F 127
(not continuous)
EC2 .7D 8 (6C 84)
HA5: Pinn .2B 40
IG8: Wfd G .6J 37
KT6: Surb .2C 162
N17 .7A 34
SE18 .4E 106
SE25 .3H 157
(not continuous)
SM1: Sutt .6H 165
SM3: Cheam, Sutt .6G 165
SM4: Mord .7J 153
Lovel Av. DA16: Well .2A 126
Lovelinch Cl. SE15 .6J 103
Lovell Ho. E8 .1G 85
(off Shrubland Rd.)
Lovell Pl. SE16 .3A 104
Lovell Rd. TW10: Ham .3C 132
UB1: S'hall .6F 77
Loveridge M. NW6 .6H 63
Loveridge Rd. NW6 .6H 63
Lovers Wlk. N3 .7D 30
(not continuous)
NW7 .6C 30
SE10 .6F 105
W1 .4G 11 (1E 100)
Lovett Dr. SM5: Cars .7A 154
Lovett Way NW10 .5J 61
Love Wlk. SE5 .2D 120
Lovibonds Av. BR6: Farnb .4F 173
UB7: Yiew .6B 74
Lowbrook Rd. IG1: Ilf .4F 71
Low Cross Wood La. SE21 .3F 139
Lowdell Cl. UB7: Yiew .6A 74
Lowden Rd. N9 .1C 34
SE24 .4B 120
UB1: S'hall .7C 76
Lowder Ho. E1 .1H 103
(off Wapping La.)
Lowe Av. E16 .5J 87
Lowell Ho. SE5 .7C 102
(off Wyndham Est.)
Lowell St. E14 .6A 86
Lowen Rd. RM13: Rain .2K 91
Lwr. Addiscombe Rd.
CR0: C'don .1E 168
Lwr. Addison Gdns. W14 .2G 99
Lwr. Belgrave St. SW1 .2J 17 (3F 101)
Lwr. Boston Rd. W7 .1J 95
Lwr. Broad St. RM10: Dag .1G 91
Lower Camden BR7: Chst .7D 142
Lwr. Church St. CR0: C'don .2B 168
LOWER CLAPTON .4H 67
Lwr. Clapton Rd. E5 .3H 67
Lwr. Clarendon Wlk. W11 .6G 81
(off Clarendon Rd.)
Lower Comn. Sth. SW15 .3D 116
Lwr. Coombe St. CR0: C'don .4C 168
Lwr. Downs Rd. SW20 .1F 153
Lwr. Drayton Pl. CR0: C'don .2B 168
LOWER EDMONTON .2B 34
LOWER FELTHAM .3J 129
Lower Fosters NW4 .5E 44
(off New Brent St.)
Lwr. George St. TW9: Rich .5D 114
Lwr. Gravel Rd. BR2: Brom .1C 172
Lower Grn. Gdns.
KT4: Wor Pk .1C 164
Lower Grn. W. CR4: Mitc .3C 154
Lwr. Grosvenor Pl. SW1 .1K 17 (3F 101)
Lower Gro. Rd. TW10: Rich .6F 115
LOWER HALLIFORD .6F 147
Lwr. Hall La. E4 .5F 35
(not continuous)
Lwr. Hampton Rd. TW16: Sun .3A 148
Lwr. Ham Rd. KT2: King T .5D 132
LOWER HOLLOWAY .5K 65
Lwr. James St. W1 .2B 12 (7G 83)
Lwr. John St. W1 .2B 12 (7G 83)
Lwr. Kenwood Av. EN2: Enf .5D 22
Lwr. King's Rd. KT2: King T .1E 150
Lwr. Lea Crossing E14 .7G 87
E16 .7G 87
Lwr. Maidstone Rd. N11 .6B 32
Lower Mall W6 .5D 98
Lwr. Mardyke Av. RM13: Rain .2J 91
Lower Marsh SE1 .7J 13 (2A 102)
Lwr. Marsh La. KT1: King T .4F 151
(not continuous)
Lwr. Merton Ri. NW3 .7C 64
Lower Mill KT17: Ewe .7B 164
Lwr. Morden La. SM4: Mord .6E 152
Lwr. Mortlake Rd. TW9: Rich .4E 114
Lwr. Park Rd. DA17: Belv .4G 109
N11 .5B 32
Lower Pk. Trad. Est. NW10 .4J 79
LOWER PLACE .2J 79
Lower Pl. Bus. Cen. NW10 .2K 79
(off Steele Rd.)
Lwr. Queen's Rd. IG9: Buck H .2G 37
Lwr. Richmond Rd. SW14 .3G 115
SW15 .3D 116
TW9: Rich .3G 115
Lower Rd. DA8: Erith .3H 109
DA17: Belv .3H 109
HA2: Harr .1H 59
SE1 .6J 13 (2A 102)
SE8 .4K 103
SE16 .2J 103
(not continuous)
SM1: Sutt .4A 166
Lwr. Robert St. WC2 .3F 13
(off Robert St.)
Lwr. Sand Hills KT6: Surb .7C 150
Lwr. Sloane St. SW1 .4G 17 (4E 100)
Lower Sq. TW7: Isle .3B 114
Lower Sq., The SM1: Sutt .5K 165
Lower Strand NW9 .2B 44
Lwr. Sunbury Rd. TW12: Hamp .2D 148
LOWER SYDENHAM .4K 139
Lwr. Sydenham Ind. Est. SE26 .5B 140
Lwr. Teddington Rd.
KT1: Ham W .1D 150
Lower Ter. NW3 .3A 64
SE27 .5B 138
(off Woodcote Pl.)
Lwr. Thames St. EC3 .3F 15 (7D 84)
Lowerwood Ct. W11 .6G 81
(off Westbourne Pk. Rd.)
Lwr. Wood Rd. KT10: Clay .6B 162
Lowestoft Cl. E5 .2J 67
(off Mundford Rd.)
Lowestoft M. E16 .2F 107
Loweswater Cl. HA9: Wemb .2D 60
Loweswater Ho. E3 .4B 86
Lowfield Rd. NW6 .7J 63
W3 .6H 79
Low Hall Cl. E4 .7J 25
Low Hall La. E17 .6A 50
Low Hall Mnr. Bus. Cen. E17 .6A 50
Lowick Rd. HA1: Harr .4J 41
Lowlands Gdns. RM7: Rom .6H 55
Lowlands Rd. HA1: Harr .6J 41
HA5: Eastc .7A 40
Lowman Rd. N7 .4K 65
Lowndes Cl. SW1 .2H 17 (3E 100)
Lowndes Ct. SW1 .1F 17 (3D 100)
W1 .1A 12
Lowndes Lodge SW1 .1F 17
(off Lowndes St.)
Lowndes M. SW16 .2J 137
Lowndes Pl. SW1 .2G 17 (3E 100)
Lowndes Sq. SW1 .7F 11 (2D 100)
Lowndes St. SW1 .1F 17 (3E 100)
Lownds Ct. BR1: Brom .2J 159
Lowood Ct. SE19 .5F 139
(off Farquhar Rd.)
Lowood Ho. E1 .7J 85
(off Bewley St.)
Lowood St. E1 .7H 85
Lowry Cl. DA8: Erith .4K 109
Lowry Ct. SE16 .5H 103
(off Stubbs Dr.)
Lowry Cres. CR4: Mitc .2C 154
Lowry Ho. E14 .2C 104
(off Cassilis Rd.)
N17 .1F 49
(off Pembury Rd.)
Lowry Rd. RM8: Dag .5B 72
Lowshoe La. RM5: Col R .1G 55
Lowswood Cl. HA6: Nwood .1E 38
Lowther Dr. EN2: Enf .4D 22

Lowther Gdns. SW7 1B 16 (2B 100)
Lowther Hill SE23 7A 122
Lowther Ho. *E8* *1F 85*
(*off Clarissa St.*)
SW1 *6B 18*
(*off Churchill Gdns.*)
Lowther Rd. E17 2A 50
HA7: Stan 3F 43
KT2: King T 1F 151
N7 5A 66
SW13 1B 116
Lowth Rd. SE5 1C 120
LOXFORD 5G 71
Loxford Av. E6 2B 88
Loxford La. IG1: Ilf 5G 71
IG3: Ilf 5G 71
Loxford Rd. IG11: Bark 6F 71
Loxford Ter. IG11: Bark 6G 71
Loxham Rd. E4 7J 35
Loxham St. WC1 2F 7 (3J 83)
Loxley Cl. SE26 5K 139
Loxley Ho. HA9: Wemb 3E 60
Loxley Rd. SW18 1B 136
TW12: Hamp 4D 130
Loxton Rd. SE23 1K 139
Loxwood Cl. TW14: Bedf 1F 129
Loxwood Rd. N17 3E 48
LSO St Lukes *3D 8*
(*off St Lukes Cl.*)
Lubbock Ho. *E14* *7D 86*
(*off Poplar High St.*)
Lubbock Rd. BR7: Chst 7D 142
Lubbock St. SE14 7J 103
Lucan Ho. *N1* *1D 84*
(*off Colville Est.*)
Lucan Pl. SW3 4C 16 (4C 100)
Lucan Rd. EN5: Barn 3B 20
Lucas Av. E13 1K 87
HA2: Harr 2E 58
Lucas Cl. NW10 7C 62
Lucas Ct. SE26 5A 140
SW11 1E 118
Lucas Gdns. N2 2A 46
Lucas Ho. *SW10* *7K 99*
(*off Coleridge Gdns.*)
WC1 *3J 83*
(*off Argyle Wlk.*)
Lucas Rd. SE20 6J 139
Lucas Sq. NW11 6J 45
Lucas St. SE8 1C 122
Lucerne Cl. N13 3D 32
Lucerne Ct. DA18: Erith 3E 108
Lucerne Gro. E17 4F 51
Lucerne M. W8 1J 99
Lucerne Rd. BR6: Orp 1K 173
CR7: Thor H 5B 156
N5 4B 66
Lucey Rd. SE16 3G 103
Lucey Way SE16 3G 103
Lucie Av. TW15: Ashf 6D 128
Lucien Rd. SW17 4E 136
SW19 2K 135
Lucinda Ct. EN1: Enf 4K 23
Lucknow St. SE18 7J 107
Lucorn Cl. SE12 6H 123
Luctons Av. IG9: Buck H 1F 37
Lucy Brown Ho. SE1 5D 14
Lucy Cres. W3 5J 79
Lucy Gdns. RM8: Dag 3F 73
Luddesdon Rd. DA8: Erith 7G 109
Ludford Cl. CR0: Wadd 3B 168
Ludgate B'way. EC4 1A 14 (6B 84)
Ludgate Cir. EC4 1A 14 (6B 84)
Ludgate Hill EC4 1A 14 (6B 84)
Ludgate Sq. EC4 1B 14 (6B 84)
Ludham NW5 5D 64
Ludham Cl. IG6: Ilf 1G 53
SE28 6C 90
Ludlow Cl. BR2: Brom 3J 159
HA2: Harr 4D 58
Ludlow Ct. W3 2J 97
Ludlow Rd. TW13: Felt 4J 129
W5 4C 78
Ludlow St. EC1 3C 8 (4C 84)
Ludlow Way N2 4A 46
Ludovick Wlk. SW15 4A 116
Ludwell Ho. *W14* *3G 99*
(*off Russell Rd.*)
Ludwick M. SE14 7A 104
Luffield Rd. SE2 3B 108
Luffman Rd. SE12 3K 141
Lugard Ho. W12 1D 98
Lugard Rd. SE15 2H 121
Lugg App. E12 3E 70
Luke Ho. *E1* *6H 85*
(*off Tillman St.*)
Luke St. EC2 3G 9 (4E 84)
Lukin Cres. E4 3A 36
Lukin St. E1 6J 85
Lullingstone Cl.
BR5: St P 7B 144
Lullingstone Cres. BR5: St P 7A 144
Lullingstone Ho. *SE15* *6J 103*
(*off Lovelinch Cl.*)
Lullingstone La. SE13 6F 123
Lullingstone Rd. DA17: Belv 6F 109
Lullington Gth. BR1: Brom 7G 141
N12 5C 30
Lullington Rd. RM9: Dag 7E 72
SE20 7G 139
Lulot Gdns. N19 2F 65
Lulworth *NW1* *7H 65*
(*off Wrotham Rd.*)
SE17 *5D 102*
(*off Portland St.*)
Lulworth Av. HA9: Wemb 7C 42
TW5: Hest 1F 113
Lulworth Cl. HA2: Harr 3D 58
Lulworth Ct. *N1* *7E 66*
(*off St Peter's Way*)
Lulworth Cres. CR4: Mitc 2C 154
Lulworth Dr. HA5: Pinn 6B 40
Lulworth Gdns. HA2: Harr 2C 58
Lulworth Ho. SW8 7K 101
Lulworth Rd. DA16: Well 2K 125
SE9 2C 142
SE15 2H 121
Lulworth Waye UB4: Yead 6K 75
Lumen Rd. HA9: Wemb 2D 60
Lumiere Bldg., The *E7* *5B 70*
(*off Romford Rd.*)
Lumiere Ct. SW17 2E 136
Lumina Bldgs. *E14* *1E 104*
(*off Prestons Rd.*)
Luminosity Ct. W13 7B 78
Lumley Cl. DA17: Belv 5G 109
Lumley Ct. WC2 3F 13 (7J 83)
Lumley Flats *SW1* *5G 17*
(*off Holbein Pl.*)
Lumley Gdns.
SM3: Cheam 5G 165
Lumley Rd. SM3: Cheam 5G 165
Lumley St. W1 1H 11 (6E 82)
Lumsdon *NW8* *1K 81*
(*off Abbey Rd.*)
Luna Ho. SE16 2G 103
Luna Rd. CR7: Thor H 3C 156
Lund Point E15 1E 86
Lundy Dr. UB3: Harl 4G 93
Lundy Wlk. N1 6C 66
Lunham Rd. SE19 6E 138
Luntley Pl. E1 6K 9
Lupin Cl. CR0: C'don 1K 169
RM7: Rush G 2K 73
SW2 2B 138
UB7: W Dray 1E 174
Lupin Cres. IG1: Ilf 6F 71
Lupino Ct. SE11 3H 19 (4K 101)
Lupin Point SE1 7K 15
Lupton Cl. SE12 3K 141
Lupton St. NW5 4G 65
(not continuous)
Lupus St. SW1 6K 17 (5F 101)
Luralda Wharf E14 5F 105
Lurgan Av. W6 6F 99
Lurline Gdns. SW11 1E 118
Luscombe Ct. BR2: Brom 2G 159
Luscombe Way SW8 7J 101
Lushington Ho. KT12: Walt T 6A 148
Lushington Rd. NW10 2D 80
SE6 4D 140
Lushington Ter. E8 5G 67
Lutea Ho. *SM2: Sutt* *7A 166*
(*off Walnut M.*)
Luther Cl. HA8: Edg 2D 28
Luther King Cl. E17 6B 50
Luther M. TW11: Tedd 5K 131
Luther Rd. TW11: Tedd 5K 131
Luton Ho. *E13* *4J 87*
(*off Luton Rd.*)
Luton Pl. SE10 7E 104
Luton Rd. DA14: Sidc 3C 144
E13 4J 87
E17 3B 50
Luton St. NW8 4B 4 (4B 82)
Lutton Ter. *NW3* *4A 64*
(*off Lakis Cl.*)
Luttrell Av. SW15 5D 116
Lutwyche Rd. SE6 2B 140
Lutyens Ho. *SW1* *6A 18*
(*off Churchill Gdns.*)
Luxborough Ho. *W1* *5G 5*
(*off Luxborough St.*)
Luxborough La. IG7: Chig 3H 37
Luxborough St. W1 5G 5 (5E 82)
Luxborough Twr. W1 5G 5
Luxembourg M. E15 5G 69
Luxemburg Gdns.
W6 4F 99
Luxfield Rd. SE9 1C 142
Luxford St. SE16 4K 103
Luxmore St. SE4 1B 122
Luxor St. SE5 3C 120
Lyall Av. SE21 4E 138
Lyall M. SW1 2G 17 (3E 100)
Lyall M. W. SW1 2G 17 (3E 100)
Lyall St. SW1 2G 17 (3E 100)
Lyal Rd. E3 2A 86
Lycett Pl. W12 2C 98
Lyceum Theatre 2G 13
Lychgate Mnr. HA1: Harr 7J 41
Lych Ga. Wlk.
UB3: Hayes 7H 75
(not continuous)
Lyconby Gdns. CR0: C'don 7A 158
Lydd Cl. DA14: Sidc 3J 143
Lydden Ct. SE9 6J 125
Lydden Gro. SW18 7K 117
Lydden Rd. SW18 7K 117
Lydd Rd. DA7: Bex 7F 109
Lydeard Rd. E6 7D 70
Lyden Ho. *E1* *3K 85*
(*off Westfield Way*)
Lydford *NW1* *1G 83*
(*off Royal College St.*)
Lydford Cl. *N16* *5E 66*
(*off Pellerin Rd.*)
Lydford Rd. N15 5D 48
NW2 6E 62
W9 4H 81
Lydhurst Av. SW2 2K 137
Lydia Ct. *KT1: King T* *3E 150*
(*off Grove Cres.*)
N12 6F 31
Lydney Cl. SW19 2G 135
Lydon Rd. SW4 3G 119
Lydstep Rd.
BR7: Chst 4E 142
Lyford Rd. SW18 7B 118
Lyford St. SE7 4C 106
Lygon Ho. *E2* *1K 9*
(*off Gosset St.*)
SW6 *1G 117*
(*off Fulham Pal. Rd.*)
Lygon Pl. SW1 2J 17 (3F 101)
Lyham Cl. SW2 6J 119
Lyham Rd. SW2 5J 119
Lyle Cl. CR4: Mitc 7E 154
Lyle Ct. SM4: Mord 6B 154
Lyly Ho. *SE1* *3D 102*
(*off Burbage Cl.*)
Lyme Farm Rd. SE12 4J 123
Lyme Gro. E9 7J 67
Lyme Gro. Ho. *E9* *7J 67*
(*off Lyme Gro.*)
Lymer Av. SE19 5F 139
Lyme Rd. DA16: Well 1B 126
Lymescote Gdns.
SM1: Sutt 2J 165
Lyme St. NW1 7G 65
Lyme Ter. NW1 7G 65
Lyminge Cl. DA14: Sidc 4K 143
Lyminge Gdns. SW18 1C 136
Lymington Av. N22 2A 48
Lymington Cl. E6 5D 88
SW16 2H 155
Lymington Ct. SM1: Sutt 3K 165
Lymington Dr. HA4: Ruis 2F 57
Lymington Gdns.
KT19: Ewe 5B 164
Lymington Lodge *E14* *3F 105*
(*off Schooner Cl.*)
Lymington Rd. NW6 6K 63
RM8: Dag 1D 72
Lyminster Cl. UB4: Yead 5C 76
Lympne *N17* *2D 48*
(*off Gloucester Rd.*)
Lympstone Gdns. SE15 7G 103
Lynbridge Gdns. N13 4G 33
Lynbrook Cl. RM13: Rain 2K 91
Lynbrook Gro. SE15 7E 102
Lynch Cl. SE3 2H 123
Lynchen Cl. TW5: Cran 1K 111
Lynch Wlk. *SE8* *6B 104*
(*off Prince St.*)
Lyncott Cres. SW4 4F 119
Lyncourt SE3 2F 123
Lyncroft Av. HA5: Pinn 5C 40
Lyncroft Gdns. NW6 5J 63
TW3: Houn 5G 113
W13 2C 96
Lyncroft Mans. NW6 5J 63
Lyndale KT7: T Ditt 7J 149
NW2 4H 63
Lyndale Av. NW2 3H 63
Lyndale Cl. SE3 6H 105
Lyndean Ind. Est.
SE2 3C 108
Lynde Ho. KT12: Walt T 6A 148
SW4 3H 119
Lynden Hyrst CR0: C'don 2F 169
Lyndhurst Av. HA5: Pinn 1K 39
KT5: Surb 1H 163
N12 6J 31
NW7 6F 29
SW16 2H 155
TW2: Whitt 1D 130
TW16: Sun 3J 147
UB1: S'hall 1F 95
Lyndhurst Cl. BR6: Farnb 4F 173
CR0: C'don 3F 169
DA7: Bex 3H 127
NW10 3K 61
Lyndhurst Ct. E18 1J 51
NW8 *1B 82*
(*off Finchley Rd.*)
SM2: Sutt *7J 165*
(*off Grange Rd.*)
Lyndhurst Dr. E10 7E 50
KT3: N Mald 7A 152

Lyndhurst Gdns. EN1: Enf 4K 23
HA5: Pinn 1K 39
IG2: Ilf 6H 53
IG11: Bark 6J 71
N3 1G 45
NW3 5B 64
Lyndhurst Gro. SE15 2E 120
Lyndhurst Lodge *E14* *4F 105*
(off Millennium Dr.)
Lyndhurst Ri. IG7: Chig 4K 37
Lyndhurst Rd.
CR7: Thor H 4A 156
DA7: Bex 3H 127
E4 7K 35
N18 4B 34
N22 6F 33
NW3 5B 64
UB6: G'frd 4F 77
Lyndhurst Sq. SE15 1F 121
Lyndhurst Ter. NW3 5B 64
Lyndhurst Way SE15 1F 121
SM2: Sutt 7J 165
Lyndon Av. DA15: Sidc 5K 125
SM6: Wall 3E 166
Lyndon Rd. DA17: Belv 4G 109
Lyndon Yd. SW17 4A 136
Lyne Cres. E17 1B 50
Lynegrove Av.
TW15: Ashf 5E 128
Lyneham Dr. NW9 1A 44
Lyneham Wlk. E5 5A 68
HA5: Eastc 3H 39
Lynette Av. SW4 6F 119
Lynford Cl. HA8: Edg 1J 43
Lynford Ct. *CR0: C'don* *4E 168*
(off Coombe Rd.)
Lynford French Ho. *SE17* *5C 102*
(off Penton Pl.)
Lynford Gdns. HA8: Edg 3C 28
IG3: Ilf 2K 71
Lynford Ter. N9 1A 34
Lynhurst Cres. UB10: Hil 7E 56
Lynhurst Rd.
UB10: Hil 7E 56
Lynmere Rd. DA16: Well 2B 126
Lyn M. E3 3B 86
N16 4E 66
Lynmouth Av. EN1: Enf 6A 24
SM4: Mord 6F 153
Lynmouth Dr. HA4: Ruis 2K 57
Lynmouth Gdns.
TW5: Hest 7B 94
UB6: G'frd 1B 78
Lynmouth Rd. E17 6A 50
N2 3D 46
N16 1F 67
UB6: G'frd 1B 78
Lynn Cl. HA3: Hrw W 2H 41
TW15: Ashf 5F 129
Lynne Cl. BR6: Chels 6K 173
SE23 7B 122
Lynne Ct. *CR2: S Croy* *4E 168*
(off Birdhurst Rd.)
NW6 *7K 63*
(off Priory Rd.)
Lynnett Rd. RM8: Dag 2D 72
Lynne Way NW10 7A 62
UB5: N'olt 2B 76
Lynn Ho. *SE15* *6H 103*
(off Friary Est.)
Lynn M. E11 2G 69
Lynn Rd. E11 2G 69
IG2: Ilf 7H 53
SW12 7F 119
Lynn St. EN2: Enf 1J 23
Lynscott Way CR2: S Croy 7B 168
Lynstead Ct. BR3: Beck 2A 158
Lynsted Cl. BR1: Brom 2A 160
DA6: Bex 5H 127
Lynsted Gdns. SE9 4B 124
Lynton Av. N12 4G 31
NW9 4B 44
RM7: Mawney 1G 55
W13 6A 78
Lynton Cl. KT9: Chess 4E 162
NW10 5A 62
TW7: Isle 4K 113
Lynton Cres. IG2: Ilf 6F 53
Lynton Est. SE1 4G 103
Lynton Gdns. EN1: Enf 7K 23
N11 6C 32
Lynton Grange N2 3D 46
Lynton Ho. *IG1: Ilf* *2G 71*
(off Axon Pl.)
W2 *6A 82*
(off Hallfield Est.)
Lynton Mans. *SE1* *1J 19*
(off Kennington Rd.)
Lynton Mead N20 3D 30
Lynton Rd. CR0: C'don 6A 156
E4 5J 35
HA2: Harr 2C 58
KT3: N Mald 5K 151
N8 5H 47
(not continuous)
NW6 2H 81
SE1 4F 103
W3 7G 79
Lynton Ter. W3 6J 79
Lynton Wlk. UB4: Hayes 3G 75
Lynwood Cl. E18 1A 52
HA2: Harr 3C 58
Lynwood Ct. KT1: King T 2H 151
Lynwood Dr. HA6: Nwood 1H 39
KT4: Wor Pk 2C 164
Lynwood Gdns. CR0: Wadd 4K 167
UB1: S'hall 6D 76
Lynwood Gro. BR6: Orp 7J 161
N21 1F 33
Lynwood Rd. KT7: T Ditt 2A 162
SW17 3D 136
W5 3D 78
Lynx Way E16 7B 88
Lyon Bus. Pk. IG11: Bark 2J 89
Lyon Ct. HA4: Ruis 1H 57
Lyon Ho. *NW8* *4C 4*
(off Broadley St.)
Lyon Ind. Est. NW2 2D 62
Lyon Meade HA7: Stan 1C 42
Lyon Pk. Av. HA0: Wemb 6E 60
(not continuous)
Lyon Rd. HA1: Harr 6K 41
SW19 1A 154
LYONSDOWN 5F 21
Lyonsdown Av. EN5: New Bar 6F 21
Lyonsdown Rd. EN5: New Bar 6F 21
Lyons Pl. NW8 4A 4 (4B 82)
Lyon St. N1 7K 65
Lyons Wlk. W14 4G 99
Lyon Way UB6: G'frd 1J 77
Lyoth Rd. BR5: Farnb 2G 173
Lyric Ct. *E8* *7F 67*
(off Holly St.)
Lyric Dr. UB6: G'frd 4F 77
Lyric M. SE26 4J 139
Lyric Rd. SW13 1B 116
Lyric Sq. *W6* *4E 98*
(off King St.)
Lyric Theatre
Hammersmith 4E 98
Westminster *2C 12*
(off Shaftesbury Av.)
Lysander NW9 1B 44
Lysander Gdns. KT6: Surb 6F 151
Lysander Gro. N19 1H 65
Lysander Ho. *E2* *2H 85*
(off Temple St.)
Lysander M. N19 1G 65
Lysander Rd. CR0: Wadd 6K 167
HA4: Ruis 2F 57
Lysander Way BR6: Farnb 3G 173
Lysia Ct. *SW6* *7F 99*
(off Lysia St.)
Lysias Rd. SW12 6F 119
Lysia St. SW6 7F 99
Lysons Wlk. SW15 4C 116
Lytchet Rd. BR1: Brom 7J 141
Lytchet Way EN3: Enf H 1D 24
Lytchgate Cl. CR2: S Croy 7E 168
Lytcott Dr. KT8: W Mole 3D 148
Lytcott Gro. SE22 5E 120
Lytham Cl. SE28 6E 90
Lytham Ct. *UB1: S'hall* *6F 77*
(off Whitecote Rd.)
Lytham Gro. W5 3F 79
Lytham St. SE17 5D 102
Lyttelton Cl. NW3 7C 64
Lyttelton Ct. N2 5A 46
Lyttelton Ho. *E9* *7J 67*
(off Well St.)
Lyttelton Rd. E10 3D 68
N2 5A 46
Lyttelton Theatre *4H 13*
(in National Theatre)
Lyttleton Ct. *UB4: Yead* *4A 76*
(off Dunedin Way)
Lyttleton Rd. N8 3A 48
Lytton Av. EN3: Enf L 1F 25
N13 2F 33
Lytton Cl. N2 6B 46
UB5: N'olt 7D 58
Lytton Gdns. SM6: Bedd 4H 167
Lytton Gro. SW15 5F 117
Lytton Rd. E11 7G 51
EN5: New Bar 4F 21
HA5: Pinn 1C 40
Lytton Strachey Path
SE28 7B 90
Lytton Ter. E12 6D 70
Lyveden Rd. SE3 7K 105
SW17 6D 136

M

Mabbett Ho. *SE18* *6E 106*
(off Nightingale Pl.)
Mabel Evetts Ct. UB3: Hayes 7K 75
Maberley Cres. SE19 7G 139
Maberley Rd. BR3: Beck 3K 157
SE19 1F 157
Mabledon Ct. *WC1* *2D 6*
(off Mabledon Pl.)
Mabledon Pl. WC1 2D 6 (3H 83)
Mablethorpe Rd. SW6 7G 99
Mabley St. E9 5A 68
Mablin Lodge IG9: Buck H 1F 37
McAdam Dr. EN2: Enf 2G 23
Macaret Cl. N20 7E 20
Macarthur Cl. E7 6J 69
HA9: Wemb 6H 61
Macarthur Ter. SE7 6B 106
Macartney Ho. *SE10* *7F 105*
(off Chesterfield Wlk.)
SW9 *1A 120*
(off Gosling Way)
Macaulay Ct. SW4 3F 119
Macaulay Rd. E6 2B 88
SW4 3F 119
Macaulay Sq. SW4 4F 119
Macaulay Way SE28 1B 108
McAuley Cl. SE1 1J 19 (3A 102)
SE9 5F 125
Macauley Ho. *W10* *5G 81*
(off Portobello Rd.)
Macauley M. SE13 2E 122
Macbean St. SE18 3F 107
Macbeth Ho. N1 2E 84
Macbeth St. W6 5D 98
McCall Cl. SW4 2J 119
McCall Cres. SE7 5C 106
McCall Ho. N7 4J 65
McCarthy Rd. TW13: Hanw 5B 130
Macclesfield Ho. *EC1* *2C 8*
(off Central St.)
Macclesfield Rd. EC1 1C 8 (3C 84)
SE25 5J 157
Macclesfield St. W1 2D 12 (7H 83)
McCoid Way SE1 7C 14 (2C 102)
McCrone M. NW3 6B 64
McCullum Rd. E3 1B 86
McDermott Cl. SW11 3C 118
McDermott Rd. SE15 3G 121
Macdonald Av. RM10: Dag 3H 73
Macdonald Ho. *SW11* *2E 118*
(off Dagnall St.)
Macdonald Rd. E7 4J 69
E17 2E 50
(not continuous)
N11 5J 31
N19 2G 65
McDonough Cl. KT9: Chess 4E 162
McDougall Ct. TW9: Rich 2G 115
McDowall Cl. E16 5H 87
McDowall Rd. SE5 1C 120
Macduff Rd. SW11 1E 118
Mace Cl. E1 1H 103
McEntee Av. E17 1A 50
Mace St. E2 2K 85
McEwen Way E15 1F 87
Macey Ho. SW11 1C 118
Macey St. *SE10* *6E 104*
(off Thames St.)
McFadden Ct. *E10* *3D 68*
(off Buckingham Rd.)
Macfarland Gro. SE15 7E 102
Macfarlane La. TW7: Isle 6K 95
Macfarlane Rd. W12 1E 98
Macfarren Pl. NW1 4H 5 (4E 82)
Macfarron Ho. *W10* *3G 81*
(off Parry Rd.)
McGlashon Ho. *E1* *4K 9*
(off Hunton St.)
McGrath Rd. E15 5H 69
McGregor Ct. N1 1H 9
Macgregor Rd. E16 5A 88
McGregor Rd. W11 6H 81
Machell Rd. SE15 3J 121
McIndoe Ct. *N1* *1D 84*
(off Sherborne St.)
McIntosh Cl. RM1: Rom 3K 55
SM6: Wall 7J 167
Macintosh Ho. *W1* *5H 5*
(off Beaumont St.)
McIntosh Ho. *SE16* *4J 103*
(off Millender Wlk.)
McIntosh Rd. RM1: Rom 3K 55
McIntyre Ct. *SE18* *4C 106*
(off Prospect Va.)
Mackay Ho. *W12* *7D 80*
(off White City Est.)
Mackay Rd. SW4 3F 119
McKay Rd. SW20 7D 134
McKellar Cl. WD23: B Hea 2B 26
Mackennal St. NW8 2C 82
Mackenzie Cl. W12 7D 80
Mackenzie Ho. *N8* *4J 47*
(off Pembroke Rd.)
NW2 3C 62
Mackenzie Rd. BR3: Beck 2J 157
N7 6K 65
Mackenzie Wlk. E14 1C 104
McKerrell Rd. SE15 1G 121
Mackeson Rd. NW3 4D 64
Mackie Rd. SW2 7A 120
McKillop Way DA14: Sidc 7C 144
Mackintosh La. E9 5K 67
Macklin St. WC2 7F 7 (6J 83)
Mackonochie Ho. *EC1* *5J 7*
(off Baldwins Gdns.)

Mackrow Wlk. E14 ... 7E 86
Mack's Rd. SE16 ... 4G 103
Mackworth Ho. *NW1* ... *1A 6*
(off Augustus St.)
Mackworth St. NW1 ... 1A 6 (3G 83)
McLaren Ho. *SE1* ... *7A 14*
(off St Georges Cir.)
Maclaren M. SW15 ... 4E 116
Maclean Rd. SE23 ... 6A 122
McLeod Ct. SE22 ... 1G 139
Macleod Rd. N21 ... 5D 22
McLeod Rd. SE2 ... 4B 108
McLeod's M. SW7 ... 4K 99
Macleod St. SE17 ... 5C 102
Maclise Ho. *SW1* ... *4E 18*
(off Marsham St.)
Maclise Rd. W14 ... 3G 99
Macmillan Ct. HA2: Harr ... 1E 58
UB6: G'frd ... 4H 77
Macmillan Ho. *NW8* ... *2D 4*
(off Lorne Cl.)
McMillan Ho. *SE4* ... *3A 122*
(off Arica Rd.)
SE14 ... 1A 122
McMillan St. SE8 ... 6C 104
Macmillan Way SW17 ... 4F 137
McNair Rd. UB2: S'hall ... 3F 95
Macnamara Ho. *SW10* ... *7B 100*
(off Worlds End Est.)
McNeil Rd. SE5 ... 2E 120
McNicol Dr. NW10 ... 2J 79
Macoma Rd. SE18 ... 6H 107
Macoma Ter. SE18 ... 6H 107
Maconochies Rd. E14 ... 5D 104
Macquarie Way E14 ... 4D 104
McRae La. CR4: Mitc ... 7D 154
Macready Ho. *W1* ... *6E 4*
(off Crawford St.)
Macready Pl. N7 ... 4J 65
(not continuous)
Macroom Ho. *W9* ... *3H 81*
(off Macroom Rd.)
Macroom Rd. W9 ... 3H 81
Macs Ho. E17 ... 3D 50
Mac's Pl. EC4 ... 7J 7
Madame Tussaud's ... 4G 5 (4E 82)
Mada Rd. BR6: Farnb ... 3F 173
Maddams St. E3 ... 4D 86
Madderfields Ct. N11 ... 1H 47
Maddison Cl. N2 ... 2A 46
TW11: Tedd ... 6K 131
Maddocks Cl. DA14: Sidc ... 5E 144
Maddocks Ho. *E1* ... *7H 85*
(off Cornwall St.)
Maddock Way SE17 ... 6B 102
Maddox St. W1 ... 2K 11 (7F 83)
Madeira Av. BR1: Brom ... 7G 141
Madeira Gro. IG8: Wfd G ... 6F 37
Madeira Rd. CR4: Mitc ... 4D 154
E11 ... 1F 69
N13 ... 4G 33
SW16 ... 5J 137
Madeleine Cl.
RM6: Chad H ... 6C 54
Madeley Rd. W5 ... 6D 78
Madeline Gro. IG1: Ilf ... 5H 71
Madeline Rd. SE20 ... 7G 139
Madge Gill Way *E6* ... *1C 88*
(off High St. Nth.)
Madge Hill W7 ... 7J 77
Madinah Rd. E8 ... 6G 67
Madison, The *SE1* ... *6E 14*
(off Long La.)
Madison Cl. SM2: Sutt ... 7B 166
Madison Ct. RM10: Dag ... 6H 73
Madison Cres. DA7: Bex ... 7C 108
Madison Gdns. BR2: Brom ... 3H 159
DA7: Bex ... 7C 108
Madison Ho. *E14* ... *7B 86*
(off Victory Pl.)
Madras Pl. N7 ... 6A 66
Madras Rd. IG1: Ilf ... 4F 71
Madrid Rd. SW13 ... 1C 116
Madrigal La. SE5 ... 7B 102
Madron St. SE17 ... 5E 102
Mafeking Av. E6 ... 2C 88
IG2: Ilf ... 7H 53
TW8: Bford ... 6E 96
Mafeking Rd. E16 ... 4H 87
EN1: Enf ... 3A 24
N17 ... 2G 49
Magazine Ga. W2 ... 4D 10 (1C 100)
Magdala Av. N19 ... 2G 65
Magdala Rd. CR2: S Croy ... 7D 168
TW7: Isle ... 3A 114
Magdalene Cl. SE15 ... 2H 121
Magdalene Gdns. E6 ... 4E 88
N20 ... 1J 31
Magdalene Rd. TW17: Shep ... 4B 146
Magdalen Ho. *E16* ... *1K 105*
(off Keats Av.)
Magdalen Pas. E1 ... 2K 15 (7F 85)
Magdalen Rd. SW18 ... 1A 136
Magdalen St. SE1 ... 5G 15 (1E 102)
Magee St. SE11 ... 7J 19 (6A 102)
Magellan Blvd. E16 ... 7G 89
Magellan Ct. *NW10* ... *7K 61*
(off Brentfield Rd.)
Magellan Ho. *E1* ... *4K 85*
(off Ernest St.)
Magellan Pl. E14 ... 4C 104
Magnaville Rd. WD23: B Hea ... 1D 26
Magnet Rd. HA9: Wemb ... 2D 60
Magnin Cl. E8 ... 1G 85
Magnolia Cl. E10 ... 2C 68
KT2: King T ... 6H 133
Magnolia Ct. HA3: Kent ... 7F 43
SM2: Sutt ... *7J 165*
(off Grange Rd.)
SM6: Wall ... 5F 167
TW9: Kew ... 1H 115
TW13: Felt ... *1J 129*
(off Plum Cl.)
UB5: N'olt ... 4C 76
UB10: Hil ... 6D 56
Magnolia Gdns. E10 ... 2C 68
HA8: Edg ... 4D 28
Magnolia Ho. *SE8* ... *6B 104*
(off Evelyn St.)
Magnolia Lodge E4 ... 3J 35
W8 ... *3K 99*
(off St Mary's Ga.)
Magnolia Pl. SW4 ... 5J 119
W5 ... 5D 78
Magnolia Rd. W4 ... 6H 97
Magnolia St.
UB7: W Dray ... 4A 92 & 1E 174
Magnolia Way KT19: Ewe ... 5J 163
Magpie All. EC4 ... 1K 13 (6A 84)
Magpie Cl. E7 ... 5H 69
EN1: Enf ... 1B 24
NW9 ... 2A 44
Magpie Hall Cl. BR2: Brom ... 6C 160
Magpie Hall La. BR2: Brom ... 5D 160
Magpie Hall Rd. WD23: B Hea ... 2D 26
Magpie Pl. SE14 ... 6A 104
Magri Wlk. E1 ... 5J 85
Maguire Dr. TW10: Ham ... 4C 132
Maguire St. SE1 ... 6K 15 (2F 103)
Mahatma Gandhi Ind. Est.
SE24 ... 4B 120
Mahlon Av. HA4: Ruis ... 5K 57
Mahogany Cl. SE16 ... 1A 104
Mahon Cl. EN1: Enf ... 1A 24
Maida Av. E4 ... 7J 25
W2 ... 4A 4 (5A 82)
MAIDA HILL ... 4H 81
Maida Rd. DA17: Belv ... 3G 109
MAIDA VALE ... 4K 81
Maida Va. W9 ... 3A 4 (2K 81)
Maida Way E4 ... 7J 25
Maiden Erlegh Av. DA5: Bexl ... 1E 144
Maiden La. NW1 ... 7H 65
SE1 ... 5D 14 (1C 102)
WC2 ... 3F 13 (7J 83)
Maiden Pl. NW5 ... 3G 65
Maiden Rd. E15 ... 7G 69
Maidenstone Hill SE10 ... 1E 122
Maids of Honour Row
TW9: Rich ... 5D 114
Maidstone Av. RM5: Col R ... 2J 55
Maidstone Bldgs. M.
SE1 ... 5D 14 (1C 102)
Maidstone Ho. *E14* ... *6D 86*
(off Carmen St.)
Maidstone Rd. DA14: Sidc, Swan ... 6D 144
N11 ... 6B 32
Mail Coach Yd. E2 ... 1H 9 (3E 84)
Main Av. EN1: Enf ... 5A 24
Main Dr. HA9: Wemb ... 3D 60
Main Mill *SE10* ... *7D 104*
(off Greenwich High St.)
Mainridge Rd. BR7: Chst ... 4E 142
Main Rd. DA14: Sidc ... 3H 143
Main St. TW13: Hanw ... 5B 130
Mainwaring Ct. CR4: Mitc ... 2E 154
Mais Ho. SE26 ... 2H 139
Maismore St. SE15 ... 6G 103
Maisonettes, The SM1: Sutt ... 5H 165
Maitland Cl. SE10 ... 7D 104
TW4: Houn ... 3D 112
Maitland Ct. *W2* ... *2A 10*
(off Lancaster Ter.)
Maitland Ho. *E2* ... *2J 85*
(off Waterloo Gdns.)
SW1 ... *7A 18*
(off Churchill Gdns.)
Maitland Pk. Est. NW3 ... 6D 64
Maitland Pk. Rd. NW3 ... 6D 64
Maitland Pk. Vs. NW3 ... 6D 64
Maitland Pl. E5 ... 4H 67
Maitland Rd. E15 ... 6H 69
SE26 ... 6K 139
Maitland Yd. W13 ... 1A 96
Maize Row E14 ... 7B 86
Majendie Rd. SE18 ... 5H 107
Majestic Way CR4: Mitc ... 2D 154
Major Cl. SW9 ... 3B 120
Major Rd. E15 ... 5F 69
SE16 ... 3G 103
Makepeace Av. N6 ... 2E 64
Makepeace Mans. N6 ... 2E 64
Makepeace Rd. E11 ... 4J 51
UB5: N'olt ... 2C 76
Makinen Ho. IG9: Buck H ... 1F 37
Makins St. SW3 ... 4D 16 (4C 100)
Malabar Ct. *W12* ... *7D 80*
(off India Way)
Malabar St. E14 ... 2C 104
Malam Ct. SE11 ... 4J 19 (4A 102)
Malam Gdns. E14 ... 7D 86
Malbrook Rd. SW15 ... 4D 116
Malcolm Ct. E7 ... 6H 69
HA7: Stan ... 5H 27
NW4 ... 6C 44
Malcolm Cres. NW4 ... 6C 44
Malcolm Dr. KT6: Surb ... 1E 162
Malcolm Ho. *N1* ... *2E 84*
(off Arden Est.)
Malcolm Pl. E2 ... 4J 85
Malcolm Rd. E1 ... 4J 85
SE20 ... 7J 139
SE25 ... 6G 157
SW19 ... 6G 135
UB10: Ick ... 4B 56
Malcolm Sargent Ho. *E16* ... *1K 105*
(off Evelyn Rd.)
Malcolmson Ho. *SW1* ... *6C 18*
(off Aylesford St.)
Malcolm Way E11 ... 5J 51
Malcoms Way N14 ... 5B 22
Malden Av. SE25 ... 4H 157
UB6: G'frd ... 5J 59
Malden Cen., The ... 4B 152
Malden Ct. KT3: N Mald ... 3D 152
N4 ... 6C 48
Malden Cres. NW1 ... 6E 64
MALDEN GREEN ... 1C 164
Malden Grn. Av. KT4: Wor Pk ... 1B 164
Malden Grn. M. KT4: Wor Pk ... 1C 164
Malden Hill KT3: N Mald ... 3B 152
Malden Hill Gdns.
KT3: N Mald ... 3B 152
MALDEN JUNC. ... 5B 152
Malden Pk. KT3: N Mald ... 6B 152
Malden Pl. NW5 ... 5E 64
Malden Rd. KT3: N Mald ... 5A 152
KT4: Wor Pk ... 5A 152
NW5 ... 5D 64
SM3: Cheam ... 4F 165
Malden Way KT3: N Mald ... 6K 151
Maldon Cl. E15 ... 5G 69
N1 ... 1C 84
SE5 ... 3E 120
Maldon Ct. E6 ... 1E 88
SM6: Wall ... 5G 167
Maldon Rd. N9 ... 3A 34
RM7: Rush G ... 7J 55
SM6: Wall ... 5F 167
W3 ... 7J 79
Maldon Wlk. IG8: Wfd G ... 6F 37
Malet Pl. WC1 ... 4C 6 (4H 83)
Malet St. WC1 ... 4C 6 (4H 83)
Maley Av. SE27 ... 2B 138
Malford Ct. E18 ... 2J 51
Malford Gro. E18 ... 4H 51
Malfort Rd. SE5 ... 3E 120
Malham Cl. N11 ... 6K 31
Malham Rd. SE23 ... 1K 139
Malham Rd. Ind. Est. SE23 ... 1K 139
Malham Ter. *N18* ... *6C 34*
(off Dysons Rd.)
N18 ... 5C 34
(Alston Rd.)
Malibu Ct. SE26 ... 3H 139
Mall, The BR1: Brom ... 3J 159
CR0: C'don ... 2C 168
DA6: Bex ... 4G 127
E15 ... 7F 69
HA3: Kent ... 6F 43
KT6: Surb ... 5D 150
N14 ... 3D 32
RM10: Dag ... 6G 73
SW1 ... 6B 12 (2G 101)
SW14 ... 5J 115
TW8: Bford ... 6D 96
W5 ... 7E 78
Mallams M. SW9 ... 3B 120
Mallard Cl. E9 ... 6B 68
EN5: New Bar ... 6G 21
NW6 ... 2J 81
TW2: Whitt ... 7E 112
W7 ... 2J 95
Mallard Ct. E17 ... 3F 51
Mallard Ho. *NW8* ... *2C 82*
(off Bridgeman St.)
SW6 ... *1A 118*
(off Station Ct.)
Mallard Path *SE28* ... *3H 107*
(off Goosander Way)
Mallard Pl. N22 ... 2K 47
TW1: Twick ... 3A 132
Mallards *E11* ... *7J 51*
(off Blake Hall Rd.)
Mallards Rd. IG8: Wfd G ... 7E 36
IG11: Bark ... 3A 90
Mallard Wlk. BR3: Beck ... 5K 157
DA14: Sidc ... 6C 144
Mallard Way NW9 ... 7J 43
SM6: Wall ... 7G 167

Mall Chambers W8 1J 99
(off Kensington Mall)
Mallet Dr. UB5: N'olt 5D 58
Mallet Rd. SE13 6F 123
Mall Galleries 4D 12
Mall Gallery WC2 1E 12
(in Thomas Neal's Cen.)
Malling SE13 5D 122
Malling Cl. CR0: C'don 6J 157
Malling Gdns. SM4: Mord 6A 154
Malling Way BR2: Hayes 7H 159
Mallinson Rd. CR0: Bedd 3H 167
SW11 5C 118
Mallinson Sports Cen. 7D 46
Mallon Gdns. E1 7K 9
(off Commercial St.)
Mallord St. SW3 7B 16 (6B 100)
Mallory Bldgs. EC1 4A 8
(off St John St.)
Mallory Cl. E14 5D 86
SE4 4A 122
Mallory Gdns. EN4: E Barn 7K 21
Mallory St. NW8 3D 4 (4C 82)
Mallow Cl. CR0: C'don 1K 169
Mallow Mead NW7 7B 30
Mallows, The UB10: Ick 3D 56
Mallow St. EC1 3E 8 (4D 84)
Mall Rd. W6 5D 98
Mall Vs. W6 5D 98
(off Mall Rd.)
Malmains Cl. BR3: Beck 4F 159
Malmains Way BR3: Beck 4E 158
Malmesbury E2 2J 85
(off Cyprus St.)
Malmesbury Cl. HA5: Eastc 4H 39
Malmesbury Rd. E3 3B 86
E16 5G 87
E18 1H 51
SM4: Mord 7A 154
Malmesbury Ter. E16 5H 87
Malmsey Ho. SE11 5H 19 (5K 101)
Malmsmead Ho. E9 5B 68
(off King's Mead Way)
Malory Cl. BR3: Beck 2A 158
Malpas Dr. HA5: Pinn 5B 40
Malpas Rd. E8 5H 67
RM9: Dag 6D 72
SE4 2B 122
Malta Rd. E10 1C 68
Malta St. EC1 3A 8 (4B 84)
Maltby Cl. BR6: Orp 1K 173
Maltby Dr. EN1: Enf 1C 24
Maltby Ho. SE1 3F 103
(off Maltby St.)
Maltby Rd. KT9: Chess 6G 163
Maltby St. SE1 7J 15 (2F 103)
Malthouse Dr. TW13: Hanw 5B 130
W4 6B 98
Malthouse Pas. SW13 2B 116
(off Maltings Cl.)
Malthus Path SE28 1C 108
Malting Ho. E14 7B 86
(off Oak La.)
Maltings W4 5G 97
Maltings, The BR6: Orp 1K 173
Maltings Cl. E3 3E 86
SW13 2B 116
Maltings Lodge W4 6A 98
(off Corney Reach Way)
Maltings M. DA15: Sidc 3A 144
Maltings Pl. SE1 7H 15
SW6 1K 117
Malting Way TW7: Isle 3K 113
Malton M. SE18 6J 107
W10 6G 81
Malton Rd. W10 6G 81
Malton St. SE18 6J 107
Maltravers St.
WC2 2H 13 (7K 83)
Malt St. SE1 6G 103
Malva Cl. SW18 5K 117
Malvern Av. DA7: Bex 7E 108
E4 7A 36
HA2: Harr 3C 58
Malvern Cl. CR4: Mitc 3G 155
KT6: Surb 1E 162
SE20 2G 157
UB10: Ick 2C 56
W10 5H 81
Malvern Ct. SM2: Sutt 7J 165
SW7 3B 16
W12 2C 98
(off Hadyn Pk. Rd.)
Malvern Dr. IG3: Bark, Ilf 4K 71
IG8: Wfd G 5F 37
TW13: Hanw 5B 130
Malvern Gdns. HA3: Kent 4E 42
NW2 2G 63
Malvern Ho. N16 1F 67
Malvern M. NW6 3J 81
Malvern Pl. NW6 3H 81
Malvern Rd. CR7: Thor H 4A 156
E6 1C 88
E8 7G 67
E11 2G 69
KT6: Surb 2E 162
N8 3A 48
N17 3G 49
NW6 2H 81
(not continuous)
TW12: Hamp 7E 130
UB3: Harl 7G 93
Malvern Ter. N1 1A 84
N9 1A 34
Malvern Way W13 5B 78
Malwood Rd. SW12 6F 119
Malyons, The TW17: Shep 6F 147
Malyons Rd. SE13 6D 122
Malyons Ter. SE13 5D 122
Managers St. E14 1E 104
Manatee Pl. SM6: Bedd 3H 167
Manaton Cl. SE15 3H 121
Manaton Cres. UB1: S'hall 6E 76
Manbey Gro. E15 6G 69
Manbey Pk. Rd. E15 6G 69
Manbey Rd. E15 6G 69
Manbey St. E15 6G 69
Manbre Rd. W6 6E 98
Manbrough Av. E6 3D 88
Manchester Ct. E16 6K 87
(off Garvary Rd.)
Manchester Dr. W10 4G 81
Manchester Gro. E14 5E 104
Manchester Ho. SE17 5C 102
Manchester M. W1 6G 5
Manchester Rd. CR7: Thor H 3C 156
E14 5E 104
N15 6D 48
Manchester Sq. W1 7G 5 (6E 82)
Manchester St. W1 6G 5 (5E 82)
Manchester Way RM10: Dag 4H 73
Manchuria Rd. SW11 6E 118
Manciple St. SE1 7E 14 (2D 102)
Mancroft Ct. NW8 1B 82
(off St John's Wood Pk.)
Mandalay Rd. SW4 5G 119
Mandarin Ct. NW10 6K 61
(off Mitchellbrook Way)
SE8 6B 104
Mandarin St. E14 7C 86
Mandarin Way UB4: Yead 6C 76
Mandela Cl. NW10 7J 61
W12 7D 80
Mandela Ho. E2 2J 9
(off Virginia Rd.)
SE5 2B 120
Mandela Rd. E16 6J 87
Mandela St. NW1 1G 83
SW9 7A 102
(not continuous)
Mandela Way SE1 4E 102
Mandel Ho. SW18 4J 117
Manderley W14 3H 99
(off Oakwood La.)
Mandeville Cl. SE3 7H 105
SW20 7G 135
Mandeville Ct. E4 5F 35
Mandeville Dr. KT6: Surb 1D 162
Mandeville Ho. SE1 5F 103
(off Rolls Rd.)
SW4 5G 119
Mandeville M. SW4 4H 119
Mandeville Pl. W1 7H 5 (6E 82)
Mandeville Rd. N14 2A 32
TW7: Isle 2A 114
TW17: Shep 5C 146
UB5: N'olt 7E 58
Mandeville St. E5 3A 68
Mandrake Rd. SW17 3D 136
Mandrake Way E15 7G 69
Mandrell Rd. SW2 5J 119
Manesty Ct. N14 7C 22
(off Ivy Rd.)
Manette St. W1 1D 12 (6H 83)
Manfred Rd. SW15 5H 117
Manger Rd. N7 6J 65
Mangold Way DA18: Erith 3D 108
Manhattan Bldg. E3 2C 86
Manhattan Bus. Pk. W5 3E 78
Manilla Ct. RM6: Chad H 6B 54
(off Quarles Pk. Rd.)
Manilla St. E14 2C 104
Manister Rd. SE2 3A 108
Manitoba Ct. SE16 2J 103
(off Canada Est.)
Manitoba Gdns. BR6: Chels 6K 173
Manley Ct. N16 3F 67
Manley Ho. SE11 5J 19 (4A 102)
Manley St. NW1 1E 82
Mann Cl. CR0: C'don 3C 168
Manneby Prior N1 1H 7
(off Cumming St.)
Manning Ct. SE28 1B 108
(off Titmuss Av.)
Manningford Cl. EC1 1A 8 (3B 84)
Manning Gdns. CR0: C'don 7H 157
HA3: Kent 7D 42
Manning Ho. W11 6G 81
(off Westbourne Pk. Rd.)
Manning Pl. TW10: Rich 6F 115
Manning Rd. E17 5A 50
RM10: Dag 6G 73
Manningtree Cl. SW19 1G 135
Manningtree Rd. HA4: Ruis 4K 57
Manningtree St. E1 6G 85
Mannin Rd. RM6: Chad H 7B 54
Mannock M. E18 1A 52
Mannock Rd. N22 3B 48
Mann's Cl. TW7: Isle 5K 113
Manns Rd. HA8: Edg 6B 28
Manny Shinwell Ho. SW6 6H 99
(off Clem Attlee Ct.)
Manoel Rd. TW2: Twick 3G 131
Manor, The IG8: Wfd G 7K 37
SE23 7J 121
Manor Av. E7 4A 70
SE4 2B 122
TW4: Houn 3B 112
UB5: N'olt 7D 58
Manor Brook SE3 4J 123
MANOR CIRCUS 3G 115
Manor Cl. DA1: Cray 4K 127
E17 1A 50
EN5: Barn 4B 20
HA4: Ruis 1H 57
KT4: Wor Pk 1A 164
NW7 5E 28
NW9 5H 43
RM10: Dag 6K 73
SE28 7C 90
Manor Cotts. HA6: Nwood 1H 39
N2 2A 46
(off Manor Cotts. App.)
Manor Cotts. App. N2 2A 46
Manor Ct. BR4: W W'ck 1D 170
DA7: Bex 4H 127
E4 1B 36
E10 1D 68
HA1: Harr 6K 41
HA9: Wemb 5E 60
IG11: Bark 7K 71
KT2: King T 1G 151
KT8: W Mole 4E 148
N2 5D 46
N14 2C 32
N20 3J 31
(off York Way)
SM5: Cars 3E 166
SW2 5K 119
SW3 6D 16
(off Hemus Pl.)
SW6 1K 117
SW16 3J 137
TW2: Twick 2G 131
W3 4G 97
Manor Ct. Rd. W7 7J 77
Manor Cres. KT5: Surb 6G 151
Manor Dene SE28 6C 90
Manordene Cl. KT7: T Ditt 1A 162
Manordene Rd. SE28 6C 90
Manor Dr. HA9: Wemb 4F 61
KT5: Surb 6F 151
KT10: Hin W 2A 162
KT19: Ewe 6A 164
N14 1A 32
N20 4J 31
NW7 5E 28
TW13: Hanw 5B 130
TW16: Sun 2J 147
Manor Dr., The KT4: Wor Pk 1A 164
Manor Dr. Nth. KT3: N Mald 7K 151
KT4: Wor Pk 1A 164
Manor Est. SE16 4H 103
Mnr. Farm Av. TW17: Shep 6D 146
Mnr. Farm Cl. KT4: Wor Pk 1A 164
Mnr. Farm Ct. E6 3D 88
Mnr. Farm Dr. E4 3B 36
Mnr. Farm Rd. HA0: Wemb 2D 78
SW16 2A 156
Manorfield Cl. N19 4G 65
(off Fulbrook M.)
Manor Flds. SW15 6F 117
Manorfields Cl. BR7: Chst 3K 161
Manor Gdns. CR2: S Croy 6F 169
HA4: Ruis 5A 58
N7 3J 65
SW4 2G 119
(off Larkhall Ri.)
SW20 2H 153
TW9: Rich 4F 115
TW12: Hamp 7F 131
TW16: Sun 1J 147
W3 4G 97
W4 5A 98
Manor Ga. UB5: N'olt 7C 58
Manorgate Rd. KT2: King T 1G 151
Manor Gro. BR3: Beck 2D 158
SE15 6J 103
TW9: Rich 4G 115
Mnr. Hall Av. NW4 2F 45
Mnr. Hall Dr. NW4 2F 45
Manorhall Gdns. E10 1C 68
MANOR HOUSE 7D 48
MANOR HOUSE 7C 48
Manor Ho. NW1 5D 4
(off Lisson Gro.)
UB2: S'hall 3C 94
Manor Ho. Ct. TW17: Shep 7D 146
W9 4A 82
(off Warrington Gdns.)

Manor Ho. Dr. HA6: Nwood 1D **38**
NW6 7F **63**
Manor Ho. Est. HA7: Stan 6G **27**
Manor Ho. Gdn. E11 6K **51**
Manor Ho. Way TW7: Isle 3B **114**
Manor La. SE12 5G **123**
SE13 5G **123**
SM1: Sutt 5A **166**
TW13: Felt 2J **129**
TW16: Sun 2J **147**
UB3: Harl 6F **93**
Manor La. Ter. SE13 4G **123**
Manor Lodge *NW6 6F 63*
(off Willesden La.)
Manor M. *NW6 2J 81*
(off Cambridge Av.)
SE4 2B **122**
Manor Mt. SE23 1J **139**
Manor Pde. HA1: Harr 6K **41**
N16 2F **67**
NW10 2B 80
(off High St. Harlesden)
MANOR PARK 4B **70**
Manor Pk. BR7: Chst 2H **161**
SE13 4F **123**
TW9: Rich 4F **115**
TW13: Felt 2J **129**
Manor Pk. Cl.
BR4: W W'ck 1D **170**
Manor Pk. Crematorium
E7 4A **70**
Manor Pk. Cres. HA8: Edg 6B **28**
Manor Pk. Dr. HA2: Harr 3F **41**
Manor Pk. Gdns. HA8: Edg 5B **28**
Manor Pk. Pde. *SE13 4F 123*
(off Lee High Rd.)
Manor Pk. Rd. BR4: W W'ck 1D **170**
BR7: Chst 1G **161**
E12 4B **70**
(not continuous)
N2 3A **46**
NW10 1B **80**
SM1: Sutt 5A **166**
Manor Pl. BR7: Chst 2H **161**
CR4: Mitc 3G **155**
KT12: Walt T 7H **147**
(not continuous)
SE17 5B **102**
SM1: Sutt 4K **165**
TW14: Felt 1J **129**
Manor Rd. BR3: Beck 2D **158**
BR4: W W'ck 2D **170**
CR4: Mitc 4G **155**
DA1: Cray 4K **127**
DA5: Bexl 1H **145**
DA15: Sidc 3K **143**
E10 7C **50**
E15 2G **87**
E16 2G **87**
E17 2A **50**
EN2: Enf 2H **23**
EN5: Barn 4B **20**
HA1: Harr 6A **42**
HA4: Ruis 1F **57**
IG7: Chig 6J **37**
IG8: Wfd G 6J **37**
IG11: Bark 6K **71**
KT8: E Mos 4H **149**
KT12: Walt T 7H **147**
N16 2D **66**
N17 1G **49**
N22 6D **32**
RM6: Chad H 6D **54**
RM10: Dag 6J **73**
SE25 4G **157**
SM2: Cheam 7H **165**
SM6: Wall 4F **167**
SW20 2H **153**
TW2: Twick 2G **131**
TW9: Rich 4G **115**
Manor Rd. TW11: Tedd 5A **132**
(not continuous)
TW15: Ashf 5B **128**
UB3: Hayes 6J **75**
W13 7A **78**
Manor Rd. Ho. HA1: Harr 6A **42**
Manor Rd. Nth. KT7: T Ditt 3A **162**
KT10: Hin W, T Ditt 3A **162**
SM6: Wall 4F **167**
Manorside EN5: Barn 4B **20**
Manorside Cl. SE2 4C **108**
Manor Sq. RM8: Dag 2C **72**
Manor Va. TW8: Bford 5C **96**
Manor Vw. N3 2K **45**
Manor Way BR2: Brom 6C **160**
BR3: Beck 2C **158**
BR5: Pet W 4G **161**
CR2: S Croy 6E **168**
CR4: Mitc 3G **155**
DA5: Bexl 1G **145**
DA7: Bex 3K **127**
E4 4A **36**
HA2: Harr 4F **41**
HA4: Ruis 7G **39**
IG8: Wfd G 5F **37**
KT4: Wor Pk 1A **164**
NW9 4A **44**
RM13: Rain 4K **91**
SE3 4H **123**
UB2: S'hall 4B **94**
Manor Way, The SM6: Wall 4F **167**
Manorway EN1: Enf 7K **23**
SE7 4B **106**
Mnr. Way Bus. Cen. RM13: Rain 5K **91**
Manor Waye UB8: Uxb 1A **74**
Manpreet Ct. E12 5D **70**
Manresa Rd. SW3 6C **16** (5C **100**)
Mansard Beeches SW17 5E **136**
Mansard Cl. HA5: Pinn 3B **40**
Manse Cl. UB3: Harl 6F **93**
Mansel Gro. E17 1C **50**
Mansell Rd. UB6: G'frd 5F **77**
W3 2K **97**
Mansell St. E1 1K **15** (6F **85**)
Mansel Rd. SW19 6G **135**
Manser Ct. RM13: Rain 3K **91**
Mansergh Cl. SE18 7C **106**
Manse Rd. N16 3F **67**
Manser Rd. RM13: Rain 3K **91**
Mansfield Av. EN4: E Barn 6J **21**
HA4: Ruis 1K **57**
N15 4D **48**
Mansfield Cl. N9 6B **24**
Mansfield Ct. *E2 1F 85*
(off Whiston Rd.)
Mansfield Dr. UB4: Hayes 4G **75**
Mansfield Hgts. N2 5C **46**
Mansfield Hill E4 7J **25**
Mansfield Ho. *N1 1E 84*
(off New Era Est.)
Mansfield M. W1 6J **5** (5F **83**)
Mansfield Pl. CR2: S Croy 6D **168**
NW3 4A **64**
Mansfield Rd. CR2: S Croy 6D **168**
E11 6K **51**
E17 4B **50**
IG1: Ilf 2E **70**
KT9: Chess 5C **162**
NW3 5D **64**
W3 4H **79**
Mansfield St. W1 6J **5** (5F **83**)
Mansford St. E2 2G **85**
Manship Rd. CR4: Mitc 7E **136**
Mansion Cl. SW9 1A **120**
(not continuous)
Mansion Cottage Vis. Info. Cen. 1C **64**
Mansion Gdns. NW3 3K **63**
Mansion House 1E **14** (6D **84**)
Mansion Ho. Pl. EC4 1E **14** (6D **84**)
Mansion Ho. St. EC4 1E **14**
Mansions, The SW5 5K **99**
Manson M. SW7 4A **16** (4B **100**)
Manson Pl. SW7 4A **16** (4B **100**)
Mansted Gdns.
RM6: Chad H 7C **54**
Manston *N17 2D 48*
(off Adams Rd.)
NW1 7G 65
(off Agar Gro.)
Manston Av. UB2: S'hall 4E **94**
Manston Cl. SE20 1J **157**
Manstone Rd. NW2 5G **63**
Manston Gro. KT2: King T 5D **132**
Manston Ho. *W14 3G 99*
(off Russell Rd.)
Manthorp Rd. SE18 5G **107**
Mantilla Rd. SW17 4E **136**
Mantle Ct. *SW18 6K 117*
(off Mapleton Rd.)
Mantle Rd. SE4 3A **122**
Mantlet Cl. SW16 7G **137**
Mantle Way DA8: Erith 7K **109**
E15 7G **69**
Manton Av. W7 2K **95**
Manton Cl. UB3: Hayes 7G **75**
Manton Rd. EN3: Enf L 1H **25**
SE2 4A **108**
Manton Way EN3: Enf L 1J **25**
Mantua St. SW11 3B **118**
Mantus Cl. E1 4J **85**
Mantus Rd. E1 4J **85**
Manuka Cl. W7 1A **96**
Manus Way N20 2F **31**
Manville Gdns. SW17 3F **137**
Manville Rd. SW17 2E **136**
Manwood Rd. SE4 5B **122**
Manwood St. E16 1D **106**
Manygate La.
TW17: Shep 7E **146**
Manygate Mobile Home Est.
TW17: Shep 6F 147
(off Mitre Cl.)
Manygates SW12 2F **137**
Mapesbury Ct. NW2 5G **63**
Mapesbury M. NW4 6C **44**
Mapesbury Rd. NW2 7G **63**
Mapeshill Pl. NW2 6E **62**
Mapes Ho. NW6 7G **63**
Mape St. E2 4H **85**
(not continuous)
Maple Av. E4 5G **35**
HA2: Harr 2F **59**
UB7: Yiew 7A **74**
W3 1A **98**
Maple Cl. BR5: Pet W 5H **161**
CR4: Mitc 1F **155**
HA4: Ruis 6K **39**
IG9: Buck H 3G **37**
N3 6D **30**
N16 6G **49**
SW4 6H **119**
TW12: Hamp 6D **130**
UB4: Yead 3B **76**
Maple Ct. CR0: C'don 4C **168**
(Lwr. Coombe St.)
CR0: C'don 4C 168
(off The Waldrons,)
E6 5E **88**
KT3: N Mald 3K **151**
SE6 1D **140**
TW15: Ashf 7F **129**
Maple Cres. DA15: Sidc 6A **126**
Maplecroft Cl. E6 6B **88**
Mapledale Av.
CR0: C'don 2G **169**
Mapledene BR7: Chst 6G **143**
Mapledene Est. E8 7G **67**
Mapledene Rd. E8 7F **67**
Maple Gdns. HA8: Edg 7F **29**
TW19: Stanw 2A **128**
Maple Gro. NW9 7J **43**
TW8: Bford 7B **96**
UB1: S'hall 5D **76**
W5 3D **96**
Maple Gro. Bus. Cen. TW4: Houn 4A **112**
Maple Ho. E17 3D **50**
KT1: King T 5E 150
(off Maple Rd.)
SE8 7B 104
(off Idonia St.)
TW9: Kew 1H **115**
Maplehurst BR2: Brom 2G **159**
Maplehurst Cl. KT1: King T 4E **150**
Maple Ind. Est. TW13: Felt 3J **129**
Maple Leaf Dr. DA15: Sidc 1K **143**
Mapleleafe Gdns. IG6: Ilf 3F **53**
Maple Leaf Sq. SE16 2K **103**
Maple Lodge *W8 3K 99*
(off Abbots Wlk.)
Maple M. NW6 2K **81**
SW16 5K **137**
Maple Pl. N17 7B **34**
UB7: Yiew 1A **92**
W1 5B **6** (4G **83**)
Maple Rd. E11 6G **51**
KT6: Surb 6D **150**
SE20 1H **157**
UB4: Yead 3A **76**
Maples, The KT1: Ham W 7C **132**
KT10: Clay 7A **162**
Maples Pl. E1 5H **85**
Maplestead Rd. RM9: Dag 1B **90**
SW2 7K **119**
Maple St. E2 2H **85**
RM7: Rom 4J **55**
W1 5A **6** (5G **83**)
Maplethorpe Rd. CR7: Thor H 4A **156**
Mapleton Cl. BR2: Brom 6J **159**
Mapleton Cres. EN3: Enf W 1D **24**
SW18 6K **117**
Mapleton Rd. E4 3K **35**
EN1: Enf 2C **24**
SW18 6J **117**
(not continuous)
Maple Tree M. SE3 1C **124**
Maple Wlk. W10 3F **81**
Maple Way TW13: Felt 3J **129**
Maplin Cl. N21 6E **22**
Maplin Ho. *SE2 2D 108*
(off Wolvercote Rd.)
Maplin Rd. E16 6J **87**
Maplin St. E3 3B **86**
Mapperley Cl. E11 6H **51**
Mapperley Dr. IG8: Wfd G 7B **36**
Marabou Cl. E12 5C **70**
Maran Way DA18: Erith 2D **108**
Marathon Ho. *NW1 5E 4*
(off Marylebone Rd.)
Marathon Way SE28 2K **107**
Marban Rd. W9 3H **81**
Marble Arch 2F **11**
MARBLE ARCH 7D **82**
Marble Arch W1 2E **10** (7D **82**)
Marble Arch Apartments *W1 7E 4*
(off Harrowby St.)
Marble Cl. W3 1H **97**
Marble Dr. NW2 1F **63**
Marble Hill Cl. TW1: Twick 7B **114**
Marble Hill Gdns. TW1: Twick 7B **114**
Marble Hill House 7C **114**
Marble Ho. SE18 5K **107**
W9 4H **81**
Marble Quay E1 4K **15** (1G **103**)
Marbles Ho. *SE5 6C 102*
(off Grosvenor Ter.)
Marbrook Ct. SE12 3A **142**
Marcella Rd. SW9 2A **120**
Marcellina Way BR6: Orp 3J **173**
March *NW9 1B 44*
(off The Concourse)

Marchant Ho. N1 . . . . . 1E 84
(off New Era Est.)
Marchant Rd. E11 . . . . . 2F 69
Marchant St. SE14 . . . . . 6A 104
Marchbank Rd. W14 . . . . . 6H 99
March Ct. SW15 . . . . . 4D 116
Marchmont Gdns. TW10: Rich 5F 115
Marchmont Rd. SM6: Wall 7G 167
TW10: Rich 5F 115
Marchmont St. WC1 . . . . . 3E 6 (4J 83)
March Rd. TW1: Twick 7A 114
Marchside Cl. TW5: Hest 1B 112
Marchwood Cl. SE5 . . . . . 7E 102
Marchwood Cres. W5 . . . . . 6C 78
Marcia Rd. SE1 . . . . . 4E 102
Marcilly Rd. SW18 . . . . . 5B 118
Marcon Ct. E8 . . . . . 5H 67
(off Amhurst Rd.)
Marconi Pl. N11 . . . . . 4A 32
Marconi Rd. E10 . . . . . 1C 68
Marconi Way UB1: S'hall 6F 77
Marcon Pl. E8 . . . . . 6H 67
Marco Polo Ho. SW8 . . . . . 7F 101
Marco Rd. W6 . . . . . 3E 98
Marcourt Lawns W5 . . . . . 4E 78
Marcus Ct. E15 . . . . . 1G 87
Marcus Garvey M. SE22 . . . . . 6H 121
Marcus Garvey Way SE24 . . . . . 4A 120
Marcus St. E15 . . . . . 1H 87
SW18 . . . . . 6K 117
Marcus Ter. SW18 . . . . . 6K 117
Mardale Ct. NW7 . . . . . 7H 29
Mardale Dr. NW9 . . . . . 5K 43
Mardell Rd. CR0: C'don 5K 157
Marden Av. BR2: Hayes 6J 159
Marden Cres. CR0: C'don 6K 155
DA5: Bexl 5J 127
Marden Ho. E8 . . . . . 5H 67
Marden Rd. CR0: C'don 6K 155
N17 . . . . . 2E 48
Marden Sq. SE16 . . . . . 3H 103
Marder Rd. W13 . . . . . 2A 96
Mardyke Cl. RM13: Rain 2J 91
Mardyke Ho. RM13: Rain 2K 91
SE17 . . . . . 4D 102
(off Mason St.)
Marechal Niel Av. DA15: Sidc 3H 143
Marechal Niel Pde. DA14: Sidc 3H 143
(off Main Rd.)
Maresby Ho. E4 . . . . . 2J 35
Maresfield CR0: C'don 3E 168
Maresfield Gdns. NW3 . . . . . 5A 64
Mare St. E8 . . . . . 5H 67
Marfleet Cl. SM5: Cars 2C 166
Margaret Av. E4 . . . . . 6J 25
Margaret Bondfield Av.
IG11: Bark 7A 72
Margaret Bldgs. N16 . . . . . 1F 67
Margaret Ct. EN4: E Barn 4G 21
W1 . . . . . 7A 6
Margaret Gardner Dr. SE9 . . . . . 2D 142
Margaret Herbison Ho. SW6 . . . . . 6H 99
(off Clem Attlee Ct.)
Margaret Ho. W6 . . . . . 5E 98
(off Queen Caroline St.)
Margaret Ingram Cl. SW6 . . . . . 6H 99
Margaret Lockwood Cl.
KT1: King T 4F 151
Margaret McMillan Ho. E16 . . . . . 6A 88
Margaret Rd. DA5: Bexl 6D 126
EN4: E Barn 4G 21
N16 . . . . . 1F 67
Margaret Rutherford Pl. SW12 . . . . . 1G 137
Margaret St. W1 . . . . . 7K 5 (6F 83)
Margaretta Ter. SW3 . . . . . 7C 16 (6C 100)
Margaretting Rd. E12 . . . . . 1A 70
Margaret Way IG4: Ilf 6C 52
Margaret White Ho. NW1 . . . . . 1D 6
(off Chalton St.)
Margate Rd. SW2 . . . . . 5J 119
Margery Fry Ct. N7 . . . . . 3J 65
Margery Pk. Rd. E7 . . . . . 6J 69
Margery Rd. RM8: Dag 3D 72
Margery St. WC1 . . . . . 2J 7 (3A 84)
Margery Ter. E7 . . . . . 6J 69
(off Margery Pk. Rd.)
Margin Dr. SW19 . . . . . 5F 135
Margravine Gdns. W6 . . . . . 5F 99
Margravine Rd. W6 . . . . . 5F 99
Marham Dr. NW9 . . . . . 1A 44
Marham Gdns. SM4: Mord 6A 154
SW18 . . . . . 1C 136
Maria Cl. SE1 . . . . . 4H 103
Maria Ct. SE25 . . . . . 2E 156
Maria Grey Hall
UB8: Cowl 3A 74
(off Kingston La.)
Marian Cl. UB4: Yead 4B 76
Marian Ct. E9 . . . . . 5J 67
SM1: Sutt 5K 165
Marianne North Gallery 2F 115
Marian Pl. E2 . . . . . 2H 85
Marian Rd. SW16 . . . . . 1G 155
Marian St. E2 . . . . . 2H 85
Marian Way NW10 . . . . . 7B 62
Maria Ter. E1 . . . . . 5K 85
Maria Theresa Cl. KT3: N Mald 5K 151
Maribor SE10 . . . . . 7E 104
(off Burney St.)
Maricas Av. HA3: Hrw W 1H 41
Marie Curie SE5 . . . . . 1E 120
Marie Lloyd Gdns. N19 . . . . . 7J 47
Marie Lloyd Ho. N1 . . . . . 1E 8
(off Murray Gro.)
Marie Lloyd Wlk. E8 . . . . . 6F 67
Mariette Way SM6: Wall 7J 167
Marigold All. SE1 . . . . . 3A 14 (7B 84)
Marigold Cl. UB1: S'hall 7C 76
Marigold Rd. N17 . . . . . 7D 34
Marigold St. SE16 . . . . . 2H 103
Marigold Way CR0: C'don 1K 169
Marina App. UB4: Yead 5C 76
Marina Av. KT3: N Mald 5D 152
Marina Cl. BR2: Brom 3J 159
Marina Ct. SW6 . . . . . 2A 118
Marina Dr. DA16: Well 2J 125
Marina Gdns. RM7: Rom 5J 55
Marina One N1 . . . . . 2J 83
(off New Wharf Rd.)
Marina Pl. KT1: Ham W 1D 150
Marina Way TW11: Tedd 7D 132
Marine Ct. E11 . . . . . 2G 69
Marine Dr. IG11: Bark 4A 90
SE18 . . . . . 4D 106
Marinefield Rd. SW6 . . . . . 2K 117
Marinel Ho. SE5 . . . . . 7C 102
Mariner Bus. Cen.
CR0: Wadd 5A 168
Mariner Gdns. TW10: Ham 3C 132
Mariner Rd. E12 . . . . . 4E 70
Mariners Cl. EN4: E Barn 5G 21
Mariners M. E14 . . . . . 4F 105
Marine St. SE16 . . . . . 3G 103
Marine Twr. SE8 . . . . . 6B 104
(off Abinger Gro.)
Marion Av. TW17: Shep 5D 146
Marion Gro. IG8: Wfd G 5B 36
Marion Ho. NW1 . . . . . 1D 82
(off Regent's Pk. Rd.)
Marion M. SE21 . . . . . 3D 138
Marion Rd. CR7: Thor H 5C 156
NW7 . . . . . 5H 29
Marischal Rd. SE13 . . . . . 3F 123
Maritime Ho. SE18 . . . . . 4F 107
Maritime Ind. Est. SE7 . . . . . 4K 105
Maritime Quay E14 . . . . . 5C 104
Maritime St. E3 . . . . . 4B 86
Marius Mans. SW17 . . . . . 2E 136
Marius Rd. SW17 . . . . . 2E 136
Marjorie Gro. SW11 . . . . . 4D 118
Marjorie M. E1 . . . . . 6K 85
Mark Av. E4 . . . . . 6J 25
Mark Cl. DA7: Bex 1E 126
UB1: S'hall 7F 77
Marke Cl. BR2: Kes 4C 172
Market, The SM1: Sutt 1A 166
Market Cen., The UB2: S'hall 4K 93
Market Chambers EN2: Enf 3J 23
(off Church St.)
Market Ct. W1 . . . . . 7A 6
Market Dr. W4 . . . . . 7A 98
Market Entrance SW8 . . . . . 7G 101
Market Est. N7 . . . . . 6J 65
Market Hall N22 . . . . . 2A 48
Market Hill SE18 . . . . . 3E 106
Market La. HA8: Edg 1J 43
W12 . . . . . 2E 98
Market Link RM1: Rom 4K 55
Market M. W1 . . . . . 5J 11 (1F 101)
Market Pde. BR1: Brom 1J 159
(off East St.)
DA14: Sidc 4B 144
E10 . . . . . 6E 50
(off High Rd.)
E17 . . . . . 3B 50
(off Forest Rd.)
N9 . . . . . 2B 34
(off Winchester Rd.)
N16 . . . . . 1G 67
(off Oldhill St.)
SE25 . . . . . 4G 157
TW13: Hanw 3C 130
Market Pav. E10 . . . . . 3C 68
Market Pl. DA6: Bex 4G 127
EN2: Enf 3J 23
KT1: King T 2D 150
N2 . . . . . 3C 46
NW11 . . . . . 4K 45
SE16 . . . . . 4G 103
(not continuous)
TW8: Bford 7C 96
UB1: S'hall 1D 94
W1 . . . . . 7A 6 (6G 83)
W3 . . . . . 1J 97
Market Rd. N7 . . . . . 6J 65
TW9: Rich 3G 115
Market Row SW9 . . . . . 4A 120
Market Sq. BR1: Brom 2J 159
(not continuous)
E14 . . . . . 6D 86
KT1: King T 2D 150
(off Market Pl.)
Market Sq., The N9 . . . . . 2C 34
(off Plevna Rd.)
Market St. E1 . . . . . 5J 9 (5F 85)
E6 . . . . . 2D 88
SE18 . . . . . 4E 106
Market Ter. TW8: Bford 6E 96
(off Albany Rd.)
Market Trad. Est. UB2: S'hall 4K 93
Market Way E14 . . . . . 6D 86
HA0: Wemb 5E 60
Market Yd. M. SE1 . . . . . 7G 15 (2E 102)
Markfield Gdns. E4 . . . . . 7J 25
Markfield Rd. N15 . . . . . 4G 49
Markham Ho. RM10: Dag 3G 73
(off Uvedale Rd.)
Markham Pl. SW3 . . . . . 5E 16 (5D 100)
Markham Sq. SW3 . . . . . 5E 16 (5D 100)
Markham St. SW3 . . . . . 5D 16 (5C 100)
Markhole Cl. TW12: Hamp 7D 130
Mark Ho. E2 . . . . . 2K 85
(off Sewardstone Rd.)
Markhouse Av. E17 . . . . . 6A 50
Markhouse Pas. E17 . . . . . 6B 50
(off Markhouse Rd.)
Markhouse Rd. E17 . . . . . 6B 50
Markland Ho. W10 . . . . . 7F 81
(off Darfield Way)
Mark La. EC3 . . . . . 2H 15 (7E 84)
Mark Lodge EN4: Cockf 4H 21
(off Edgeworth Rd.)
Markmanor Av. E17 . . . . . 7A 50
Mark Rd. N22 . . . . . 2B 48
Marksbury Av. TW9: Rich 3G 115
MARKS GATE 1E 54
Marks Lodge RM7: Rom 5K 55
Mark Sq. EC2 . . . . . 3G 9 (4E 84)
Marks Rd. RM7: Rom 5J 55
(not continuous)
Markstone Ho. SE1 . . . . . 7A 14
(off Lancaster St.)
Mark St. E15 . . . . . 7G 69
EC2 . . . . . 3G 9 (4E 84)
Mark Wade Cl. E12 . . . . . 1B 70
Markway TW16: Sun 2A 148
Markwell Cl. SE26 . . . . . 4H 139
Markyate Ho. W10 . . . . . 4E 80
(off Sutton Way)
Markyate Rd. RM8: Dag 5B 72
Marland Ho. SW1 . . . . . 1F 17
(off Sloane St.)
Marlands Rd. IG5: Ilf 3C 52
Marlborough SW19 . . . . . 1F 135
(off Inner Pk. Rd.)
W9 . . . . . 3A 82
(off Maida Va.)
Marlborough Av. E8 . . . . . 1G 85
(not continuous)
HA4: Ruis 6E 38
HA8: Edg 3C 28
N14 . . . . . 3B 32
Marlborough Cl. BR6: Orp 6K 161
N20 . . . . . 3J 31
SE17 . . . . . 4C 102
SW19 . . . . . 6C 136
Marlborough Ct. CR2: S Croy 4E 168
(off Birdhurst Rd.)
EN1: Enf 5K 23
HA1: Harr 4H 41
HA6: Nwood 1H 39
IG9: Buck H 2F 37
N17 . . . . . 1G 49
(off Kemble Rd.)
SM6: Wall 7G 167
W1 . . . . . 2A 12
W8 . . . . . 4J 99
(off Pembroke Rd.)
Marlborough Cres. UB3: Harl 7F 93
W4 . . . . . 3K 97
Marlborough Dr. IG5: Ilf 3C 52
Marlborough Flats SW3 . . . . . 3D 16
Marlborough Gdns. KT6: Surb 7D 150
N20 . . . . . 3J 31
Marlborough Ga. Ho. W2 . . . . . 2A 10
(off Elms M.)
Marlborough Gro. SE1 . . . . . 5G 103
Marlborough Hill HA1: Harr 4H 41
NW8 . . . . . 2A 82
Marlborough House 5B 12 (1G 101)
Marlborough Ho. E16 . . . . . 1J 105
(off Hardy Av.)
NW1 . . . . . 3K 5
(off Osnaburgh St.)
Marlborough La. SE7 . . . . . 6A 106
Marlborough Lodge NW8 . . . . . 2A 82
(off Marlborough Pl.)
Marlborough Mans. NW6 . . . . . 5K 63
(off Canon Hill)
Marlborough M. SW2 . . . . . 4K 119
Marlborough Pde. HA8: Edg 3C 28
(off Marlborough Av.)
UB10: Hil 4D 74
Marlborough Pk. Av. DA15: Sidc 7A 126
Marlborough Pl. NW8 . . . . . 2A 82
Marlborough Rd. BR2: Brom 4A 160
CR2: S Croy 7C 168
DA7: Bex 3D 126
E4 . . . . . 6J 35
E7 . . . . . 7A 70

Marlborough Rd. E15 4G 69
E18 2J 51
N9 1B 34
N19 2H 65
(not continuous)
N22 7D 32
RM7: Mawney 4G 55
RM8: Dag 4B 72
SE18 3F 107
SM1: Sutt 3J 165
SW1 5B 12 (1G 101)
SW19 6C 136
TW7: Isle 1B 114
TW10: Rich 6F 115
TW12: Hamp 6E 130
TW13: Felt 2B 130
TW15: Ashf 5A 128
UB2: S'hall 3A 94
UB10: Hil 4D 74
W4 5J 97
W5 2D 96
Marlborough St. SW3 4C 16 (4C 100)
Marlborough Yd. N19 2H 65
Marlbury *NW8* *1K 81*
(off Abbey Rd.)
Marler Rd. SE23 1A 140
Marley Av. DA7: Bex 6D 108
Marley Cl. N15 4B 48
UB6: G'frd 3E 76
Marley Ho. *E16* *7F 89*
(off University Way)
W11 *7F 81*
(off St Ann's Rd.)
Marley Wlk. NW2 5E 62
Marlfield Cl. KT4: Wor Pk 1C 164
Marlin Cl. TW16: Sun 6G 129
Marling Ct. TW12: Hamp 6D 130
Marlingdene Cl. TW12: Hamp 6E 130
Marlings Cl. BR7: Chst 4J 161
Marlings Pk. Av. BR7: Chst 4J 161
Marlins Cl. SM1: Sutt 5A 166
Marloes Cl. HA0: Wemb 4D 60
Marloes Rd. W8 3K 99
Marlow Cl. SE20 3H 157
Marlow Ct. N14 7B 22
NW6 7F 63
NW9 3B 44
Marlow Cres. TW1: Twick 6K 113
Marlow Dr. SM3: Cheam 2F 165
Marlowe Bus. Cen. *SE14* *7A 104*
(off Batavia Rd.)
Marlowe Cl. BR7: Chst 6H 143
IG6: Ilf 1G 53
Marlowe Ct. SE19 5F 139
SW3 *4D 16*
(off Petyward)
Marlowe Gdns. SE9 6E 124
Marlowe Ho. IG8: Wfd G 7K 37
KT1: King T *4D 150*
(off Portsmouth Rd.)
Marlowe Path SE8 6C 104
Marlowe Rd. E17 4E 50
Marlowes, The DA1: Cray 4K 127
NW8 1B 82
Marlowe Sq. CR4: Mitc 4G 155
Marlowe Way CR0: Bedd 2J 167
Marlow Gdns. UB3: Harl 3F 93
Marlow Ho. *E2* *2J 9*
(off Calvert Av.)
KT5: Surb *5E 150*
(off Cranes Pk.)
SE1 *7J 15*
(off Abbey St.)
TW11: Tedd 4A 132
W2 *6K 81*
(off Hallfield Est.)
Marlow Rd. E6 3D 88
SE20 3H 157
UB2: S'hall 3D 94
Marlow Way SE16 2K 103
Marlow Workshops *E2* *2J 9*
(off Virginia Rd.)
Marl Rd. SW18 4A 118
Marlton St. SE10 5H 105
Marlwood Cl. DA15: Sidc 2J 143
Marmadon Rd. SE18 4K 107
Marmara Apartments *E16* *7J 87*
(off Western Gateway)
Marmion App. E4 4H 35
Marmion Av. E4 4G 35
Marmion Cl. E4 4G 35
Marmion M. SW11 3E 118
Marmion Rd. SW11 4E 118
Marmont Rd. SE15 1G 121
Marmora Ho. *E1* *5A 86*
(off Ben Jonson Rd.)
Marmora Rd. SE22 6J 121
Marmot Rd. TW4: Houn 3B 112
Marne Av. DA16: Well 3A 126
N11 4A 32
Marnell Way TW4: Houn 3B 112
Marne St. W10 3G 81
Marney Rd. SW11 4E 118
Marnfield Cres. SW2 1A 138
Marnham Av. NW2 4G 63
Marnham Ct. HA0: Wemb 5C 60
Marnham Cres.
UB6: G'frd 3F 77
Marnock Ho. *SE17* *5D 102*
(off Brandon St.)
Marnock Rd. SE4 5B 122
Maroon St. E14 5A 86
Maroons Way SE6 5C 140
Marqueen Ct. *W8* *2K 99*
(off Kensington Chu. St.)
Marqueen Towers SW16 7K 137
Marquess Rd. N1 6D 66
Marquess Rd. Nth. N1 6D 66
Marquess Rd. Sth. N1 6C 66
Marquis Cl. HA0: Wemb 7F 61
Marquis Ct. IG11: Bark 5J 71
KT1: King T *4D 150*
(off Anglesea Rd.)
N4 *1K 65*
(off Marquis Rd.)
TW19: Stanw 1A 128
Marquis Rd. N4 1K 65
N22 6E 32
NW1 6H 65
Marrabon Cl. DA15: Sidc 1A 144
Marrick Cl. SW15 4C 116
Marrick Ho. *NW6* *1K 81*
(off Mortimer Cres.)
Marriett Ho. SE6 4E 140
Marrilyne Av. EN3: Enf L 1G 25
Marriner Ct. *UB3: Hayes* *7G 75*
(off Barra Hall Rd.)
Marriott Cl. TW14: Felt 6F 111
Marriott Rd. E15 1G 87
EN5: Barn 3A 20
N4 1K 65
N10 1D 46
Marriotts Cl. NW9 6B 44
Marryat Cl. TW4: Houn 4D 112
Marryat Ho. *SW1* *6A 18*
(off Churchill Gdns.)
Marryat Pl. SW19 4G 135
Marryat Rd. SW19 5F 135
Marryat Sq. SW6 1G 117
Marsala Rd. SE13 4D 122
Marsden Rd. N9 2C 34
SE15 3F 121
Marsden St. NW5 6E 64
(not continuous)
Marsden Way BR6: Orp 4K 173
Marshall Bldg. *W2* *6A 4*
(off Hermitage St.)
Marshall Cl. HA1: Harr 7H 41
SW18 6A 118
TW4: Houn 5D 112
Marshall Ct. *NW6* *7F 63*
(off Coverdale Rd.)
Marshall Dr. UB4: Hayes 5H 75
Marshall Est. NW7 4H 29
Marshall Ho. *N1* *2D 84*
(off Cranston Est.)
NW6 *2H 81*
(off Albert Rd.)
SE1 *3E 102*
(off Page's Wlk.)
SE17 *5D 102*
(off East St.)
Marshall Path SE28 7B 90
Marshall Rd. E10 3D 68
(not continuous)
N17 1D 48
Marshalls Cl. N11 4A 32
Marshalls Dr. RM1: Rom 3K 55
Marshalls Gro. SE18 4C 106
Marshall's Pl. SE16 3F 103
Marshalls Rd. RM7: Rom 4K 55
SM1: Sutt 4K 165
Marshall St. W1 1B 12 (6G 83)
Marshalsea Rd. SE1 6D 14 (2C 102)
Marsham Cl. BR7: Chst 5F 143
Marsham Ct. SW1 3D 18 (4H 101)
Marsham St. SW1 2D 18 (3H 101)
Marsh Av. CR4: Mitc 2D 154
Marshbrook Cl. SE3 3B 124
Marsh Cen., The *E1* *7K 9*
(off Whitechapel High St.)
Marsh Cl. NW7 3G 29
Marsh Ct. E8 6G 67
SW19 1A 154
Marsh Dr. NW9 6B 44
Marsh Farm Rd. TW2: Twick 1K 131
Marshfield St. E14 3E 104
Marsh Ga. Bus. Cen. E15 1E 86
Marshgate Path SE28 3G 107
Marsh Grn. Rd. RM10: Dag 1G 91
Marsh Hall HA9: Wemb 3F 61
Marsh Hill E9 5A 68
Marsh Ho. *SW1* *6D 18*
(off Aylesford St.)
SW8 1G 119
Marsh La. E10 2B 68
HA7: Stan 5H 27
N17 7C 34
NW7 3F 29
Marsh Rd. HA0: Wemb 3D 78
HA5: Pinn 4C 40
Marshside Cl. N9 1D 34
Marsh St. E14 4D 104
Marsh Wall E14 1C 104
Marsh Way
RM13: Dag, Rain 3K 91
Marshwood Ho. *NW6* *1J 81*
(off Kilburn Va.)
Marsland Cl. SE17 5B 102
Marsom Ho. *N1* *1E 8*
(off Provost Est.)
Marston Av. KT9: Chess 6E 162
RM10: Dag 2G 73
Marston Cl. NW6 7A 64
RM10: Dag 3G 73
Marston Ho. SW9 2A 120
Marston Rd. IG5: Ilf 1C 52
TW11: Tedd 5B 132
Marston Way SE19 7B 138
Marsworth Av. HA5: Pinn 1B 40
Marsworth Cl. UB4: Yead 5C 76
Marsworth Ho. *E2* *1G 85*
(off Whiston Rd.)
Martaban Rd. N16 2F 67
Martara M. SE17 5C 102
Martello St. E8 7H 67
Martello Ter. E8 7H 67
Martell Rd. SE21 3D 138
Martel Pl. E8 6F 67
Marten Rd. E17 2C 50
Martens Av. DA7: Bex 4H 127
Martens Cl. DA7: Bex 4J 127
Martha Ct. E2 2H 85
Martham Cl. IG6: Ilf 1F 53
SE28 7D 90
Martha Rd. E15 6G 69
Martha's Bldgs. EC1 3E 8 (4D 84)
Martha St. E1 6J 85
Marthorne Cres. HA3: Hrw W 2H 41
Martin Bowes Rd. SE9 3D 124
Martinbridge Trad. Est.
EN1: Enf 5B 24
Martin Cl. N9 1E 34
UB10: Uxb 2A 74
Martin Ct. *CR2: S Croy* *5D 168*
(off Birdhurst Rd.)
E14 *2E 104*
(off River Barge Cl.)
Martin Cres. CR0: C'don 1A 168
Martindale SW14 5J 115
Martindale Av. BR6: Chels 5K 173
E16 7J 87
Martindale Ho. *E14* *7D 86*
(off Poplar High St.)
Martin Dale Ind. Est. EN1: Enf 3C 24
Martindale Rd. SW12 7F 119
TW4: Houn 3C 112
Martin Dene DA6: Bex 5F 127
Martin Dr. UB5: N'olt 5D 58
Martineau Dr. TW1: Twick 4B 114
Martineau Est. E1 7J 85
Martineau Ho. *SW1* *6A 18*
(off Churchill Gdns.)
Martineau M. N5 4B 66
Martineau Rd. N5 4B 66
Martingale Cl. TW16: Sun 4J 147
Martingales Cl.
TW10: Ham 3D 132
Martin Gdns. RM8: Dag 4C 72
Martin Gro. SM4: Mord 3J 153
Martin Ho. SE1 3C 102
SW8 *7J 101*
(off Wyvil Rd.)
Martin La. EC4 2F 15 (7D 84)
(not continuous)
Martin Pl. *SE28* *1J 107*
(off Martin St.)
Martin Ri. DA6: Bex 5F 127
Martin Rd. RM8: Dag 4C 72
Martins, The HA9: Wemb 3F 61
SE26 5H 139
Martins Cl. BR4: W W'ck 1F 171
Martin's Mt. EN5: New Bar 4D 20
Martin's Rd. BR2: Brom 2G 159
Martin St. SE28 1J 107
Martins Wlk. N10 1E 46
N22 3A 48
Martin Wlk. *SE28* *1J 107*
(off Martin St.)
Martin Way SM4: Mord 2F 153
SW20 2F 153
Martlesham *N17* *2E 48*
(off Adams Rd.)
Martlesham Wlk. NW9 2A 44
(not continuous)
Martlet Gro. UB5: N'olt 3B 76
Martlett Ct. WC2 1F 13 (6J 83)
Martley Dr. IG2: Ilf 5F 53
Martock Cl. HA3: W'stone 4A 42
Martock Gdns. N11 5J 31
Marton Cl. SE6 3C 140
Marton Rd. N16 2E 66
Martynside NW9 1B 44
Martys Yd. NW3 4B 64
Marvell Av. UB4: Hayes 5J 75
Marvell Ct. *RM6: Chad H* *6B 54*
(off Quarles Pk. Rd.)
Marvell Ho. *SE5* *7D 102*
(off Camberwell Rd.)
Marvels Cl. SE12 2K 141

Marvels La. SE12 2K 141
(not continuous)
Marville Rd. SW6 7H 99
Marvin St. E8 6H 67
Marwell Cl. BR4: W W'ck 2H 171
Marwood Cl. DA16: Well 3B 126
Marwood Dr. NW7 7A 30
Mary Adelaide Cl. SW15 4A 134
Mary Ann Gdns. SE8 6C 104
Maryatt Av. HA2: Harr 2F 59
Mary Bank SE18 4D 106
Mary Bayly Ho. *W11* *1G 99*
(off Wilsham St.)
Mary Cl. HA7: Stan 4F 43
Mary Datchelor Cl. SE5 1D 120
Maryfield Cl. DA5: Bexl 3K 145
Mary Flux Ct. *SW5* *5K 99*
(off Bramham Gdns.)
Mary Grn. NW8 1K 81
Mary Holben Ho. SW16 5G 137
Mary Ho. *W6* *5E 98*
(off Queen Caroline St.)
Mary Jones Ho. *E14* *7C 86*
(off Garford St.)
Maryland Ind. Est. *E15* *5G 69*
(off Maryland Rd.)
Maryland Pk. E15 5G 69
(not continuous)
Maryland Point *E15* *6G 69*
(off The Grove)
Maryland Rd. CR7: Thor H 1B 156
E15 5F 69
N22 6E 32
Maryland Sq. E15 5G 69
Marylands Rd. W9 4J 81
Maryland St. E15 5F 69
Maryland Wlk. *N1* *1C 84*
(off Popham St.)
Maryland Way TW16: Sun 2J 147
Mary Lawrenson Pl. SE3 7J 105
MARYLEBONE 5H 5 (5E 82)
Marylebone Cricket Club 2B 4 (3B 82)
MARYLEBONE FLYOVER 5C 82
Marylebone Fly-Over W2 6B 4 (5B 82)
Marylebone Gdns.
TW9: Rich 4G 115
Marylebone High St. W1 5H 5 (5E 82)
Marylebone La. W1 6H 5 (5E 82)
Marylebone M. W1 6J 5 (5F 83)
Marylebone Pas. W1 7B 6 (6G 83)
Marylebone Rd. NW1 5D 4 (5C 82)
Marylebone St. W1 6H 5 (5E 82)
Marylee Way SE11 4H 19 (4K 101)
Mary Macarthur Ho. *E2* *3K 85*
(off Warley St.)
RM10: Dag *3G 73*
(off Wythenshawe Rd.)
W6 6G 99
Maryon Gro. SE7 4C 106
Maryon Ho. *NW6* *7A 64*
(off Goldhurst Ter.)
Maryon M. NW3 4C 64
Maryon Rd. SE7 4C 106
SE18 4C 106
Mary Peters Dr. UB6: G'frd 5H 59
Mary Pl. W11 7G 81
Mary Rose Cl. TW12: Hamp 1E 148
Mary Rose Mall E6 5D 88
Mary Rose Way N20 1G 31
Marys Ct. NW1 3D 4
Mary Seacole Cl. E8 1F 85
Mary Smith Ct. *SW5* *4J 99*
(off Trebovir Rd.)
Marysmith Ho. *SW1* *5D 18*
(off Cureton St.)
Mary's Ter. TW1: Twick 7A 114
(not continuous)
Mary St. E16 5H 87
N1 1C 84
Mary Ter. NW1 1F 83
Maryville DA16: Well 2K 125
Mary Wallace Theatre 1A 132
Mary Wharrie Ho. *NW3* *7D 64*
(off Fellows Rd.)
Marzell Ho. *W14* *5H 99*
(off North End Rd.)
Marzena Ct. TW3: Houn 6G 113
Masault Ct. *TW9: Rich* *4E 114*
(off Kew Foot Rd.)
Masbro' Rd. W14 3F 99
Mascalls Ct. SE7 6A 106
Mascalls Rd. SE7 6A 106
Mascotte Rd. SW15 4F 117
Mascotts Cl. NW2 3D 62
Masefield Av. HA7: Stan 5E 26
UB1: S'hall 7E 76
Masefield Ct. EN5: New Bar 4F 21
KT6: Surb 7D 150
Masefield Cres. N14 5B 22
Masefield Gdns. E6 4E 88
Masefield Ho. *NW6* *3J 81*
(off Stafford Rd.)
Masefield La. UB4: Yead 4K 75
Masefield Rd. TW12: Hamp 4D 130
Masefield Vw. BR6: Farnb 3G 173
Masefield Way TW19: Stanw 1B 128
Masham Ho. *DA18: Erith* *2D 108*
(off Kale Rd.)
Mashie Rd. W3 6A 80
Mashiters Hill RM1: Rom 1K 55
Maskall Cl. SW2 1A 138
Maskani Wlk. SW16 7G 137
Maskell Rd. SW17 3A 136
Maskelyne Cl. SW11 1C 118
Mason Cl. DA7: Bex 3H 127
E16 7J 87
SE16 5G 103
SW20 1F 153
TW12: Hamp 1D 148
Mason Ho. *E9* *7J 67*
(off Frampton Pk. Rd.)
SE1 *4G 103*
(off Simms Rd.)
Mason Rd. IG8: Wfd G 4B 36
SM1: Sutt 5K 165
Mason's Arms M. W1 1K 11 (6F 83)
Masons Av. CR0: C'don 3C 168
EC2 7E 8 (6D 84)
HA3: W'stone 4K 41
Masons Grn. La. W3 4G 79
W5 4G 79
Masons Hill BR2: Brom 3J 159
SE18 4F 107
Masons Pl. CR4: Mitc 1D 154
EC1 1B 8 (3C 84)
Mason St. SE17 4D 102
Masons Yd. EC1 1B 8 (3B 84)
SW1 4B 12 (1G 101)
SW19 5F 135
Massey Cl. N11 5A 32
Massey Ct. *E6* *1A 88*
(off Florence Rd.)
Massie Rd. E8 6G 67
Massingberd Way SW17 4F 137
Massinger St. SE17 4E 102
Massingham St. E1 4K 85
Masson Av. HA4: Ruis 6A 58
Mast, The E16 7G 89
Mast Ct. *SE16* *4A 104*
(off Boat Lifter Way)
Master Gunners Pl.
SE18 7C 106
Masterman Ho. *SE5* *7D 102*
(off Elmington Est.)
Masterman Rd. E6 3C 88
Masters Cl. SW16 6G 137
Masters Dr. SE16 5H 103
Masters Lodge *E1* *6J 85*
(off Johnson St.)
Masters St. E1 5K 85
Mast Ho. Ter. E14 4C 104
(not continuous)
Mastmaker Ct. E14 2C 104
Mastmaker Rd. E14 2C 104
Mast Quay SE18 3D 106
MASWELL PARK 5G 113
Maswell Pk. Cres.
TW3: Houn 5G 113
Maswell Pk. Rd. TW3: Houn 5F 113
Matcham Ct. *TW1: Twick* *6D 114*
(off Clevedon Rd.)
Matcham Rd. E11 3G 69
Matchless Dr. SE18 7E 106
Matfield Cl. BR2: Brom 5J 159
Matfield Rd. DA17: Belv 6G 109
Matham Gro. SE22 4F 121
Matham Rd. KT8: E Mos 5H 149
Matheson Lang Ho. SE1 7J 13
Matheson Rd. W14 4H 99
Mathews Av. E6 2E 88
Mathews Pk. Av. E15 6H 69
Mathews Yd. WC2 1E 12 (6J 83)
Mathieson Ct. *SE1* *7B 14*
(off King James St.)
Mathison Ho. *SW10* *7A 100*
(off Coleridge Gdns.)
Matilda Cl. SE19 7D 138
Matilda Gdns. E3 2C 86
Matilda Ho. *E1* *1G 103*
(off St Katherine's Way)
Matilda St. N1 1K 83
Matins Pl. SE28 1J 107
Matisse Ct. EC1 3E 8 (4D 84)
Matlock Cl. EN5: Barn 5A 20
SE24 4C 120
Matlock Ct. *NW8* *2A 82*
(off Abbey Rd.)
SE5 4D 120
W11 *7J 81*
(off Kensington Pk. Rd.)
Matlock Cres. SM3: Cheam 4G 165
Matlock Gdns.
SM3: Cheam 4G 165
Matlock Pl. SM3: Cheam 4G 165
Matlock Rd. E10 6E 50
Matlock St. E14 6A 86
Matlock Way KT3: N Mald 1K 151
Maton Ho. *SW6* *7H 99*
(off Estcourt Rd.)
Matrimony Pl. SW4 2G 119
Matson Ct. IG8: Wfd G 7B 36
Matson Ho. SE16 3H 103
Matthew Cl. W10 4F 81
Matthew Ct. CR4: Mitc 5H 155
E17 3E 50
Matthew Parker St. SW1 7D 12 (2H 101)
Matthews Ct. *E17* *1C 50*
(off Chingford Rd.)
Matthews Ho. *E14* *5C 86*
(off Burgess St.)
Matthews Rd. UB6: G'frd 5H 59
Matthews St. SW11 2D 118
Matthews Yd. *CR0: C'don* *3C 168*
(off Surrey St.)
Matthias Apartments *N1* *7D 66*
(off Northchurch Rd.)
Matthias Ct. TW10: Rich 5E 114
Matthias Rd. N16 5E 66
Mattison Rd. N4 6A 48
Mattock La. W5 1B 96
W13 1B 96
Maud Cashmore Way SE18 3D 106
Maude Ho. *E2* *2G 85*
(off Ropley St.)
Maude Rd. E17 5A 50
SE5 1E 120
Maude Ter. E17 5A 50
Maud Gdns. E13 1H 87
IG11: Bark 2K 89
Maudlins Grn. E1 4K 15 (1G 103)
Maud Rd. E10 3E 68
E13 2H 87
Maudslay Rd. SE9 3D 124
Maudsley Ho. TW8: Bford 5E 96
Maud St. E16 5H 87
Maudsville Cotts. W7 1J 95
Maud Wilkes Cl. NW5 5G 65
Maugham Ct. *W3* *3J 97*
(off Palmerston Rd.)
Mauleverer Rd. SW2 5J 119
Maundeby Wlk. NW10 6A 62
Maunder Rd. W7 1K 95
Maunsel St. SW1 3C 18 (4H 101)
Maureen Campbell Ct.
TW17: Shep *5D 146*
(off Harrison Way)
Maureen Ct. BR3: Beck J 157
Maurer Ct. SE10 3H 105
Mauretania Bldg. *E1* *7K 85*
(off Jardine Rd.)
Maurice Av. N22 2B 48
Maurice Bishop Ter. *N6* *6E 46*
(off View Rd.)
Maurice Brown Cl. NW7 5A 30
Maurice Ct. E1 3K 85
N22 1K 47
TW8: Bford 7D 96
Maurice Drummond Ho. *SE10* *1D 122*
(off Catherine Gro.)
Maurice St. W12 6D 80
Maurice Wlk. NW11 4A 46
Maurier Cl. UB5: N'olt 1A 76
Mauritius Rd. SE10 4G 105
Maury Rd. N16 2G 67
Mauveine Gdns.
TW3: Houn 4E 112
Mavelstone Cl. BR1: Brom 1C 160
Mavelstone Rd. BR1: Brom 1B 160
Maverton Rd. E3 1C 86
Mavis Av. KT19: Ewe 5A 164
Mavis Cl. KT19: Ewe 5A 164
Mavis Wlk. *E6* *5C 88*
(off Greenwich Cres.)
Mavor Ho. *N1* *1K 83*
(off Barnsbury Est.)
Mawbey Ho. SE1 5G 103
Mawbey Pl. SE1 5F 103
Mawbey Rd. SE1 5F 103
Mawbey St. SW8 7J 101
Mawdley Ho. SE1 7A 14
MAWNEY 4J 55
Mawney Cl. RM7: Mawney 2H 55
Mawney Rd. RM7: Mawney 2H 55
Mawson Cl. SW20 2G 153
Mawson Ct. *N1* *1D 84*
(off Gopsall St.)
Mawson Ho. *EC1* *5J 7*
(off Baldwins Gdns.)
Mawson La. W4 6B 98
Maxden Ct. SE15 3F 121
Maxey Gdns. RM9: Dag 4E 72
Maxey Rd. RM9: Dag 4E 72
SE18 4G 107
Maxfield Cl. N20 7F 21
Maxilla Wlk. W10 6F 81
Maxim Apartments
BR2: Brom *4K 159*
(off Tiger La.)
Maximfeldt Rd. DA8: Erith 5K 109
Maxim Rd. DA8: Erith 4K 109
N21 6F 23
Maxted Pk. HA1: Harr 7J 41
Maxted Rd. SE15 3F 121
Maxwell Cl. CR0: Wadd 1J 167
UB3: Hayes 7J 75
Maxwell Ct. SE22 1G 139
SW4 5H 119
Maxwell Gdns. BR6: Orp 3K 173
Maxwell Rd. DA16: Well 3K 125
HA6: Nwood 1F 39

Maxwell Rd. SW6 7K 99
TW15: Ashf 6E 128
UB7: W Dray 4B 92
Maxwelton Av. NW7 5E 28
Maxwelton Cl. NW7 5E 28
Maya Angelou Ct. E4 4K 35
Maya Cl. SE15 2H 121
Mayall Cl. EN3: Enf L 1H 25
Mayall Rd. SE24 5B 120
Maya Pl. N11 7C 32
Maya Rd. N2 4A 46
Maybank Av. E18 2K 51
HA0: Wemb 5K 59
Maybank Gdns. HA5: Eastc 5J 39
Maybank Rd. E18 1K 51
May Bate Av. KT2: King T 1D 150
Maybells Commercial Est.
IG11: Bark 2D 90
Mayberry Ct. *BR3: Beck 7B 140*
(off Copers Cope Rd.)
Mayberry Pl. KT5: Surb 7F 151
Maybourne Cl. SE26 6H 139
Maybury Cl. BR5: Pet W 5F 161
EN1: Enf 1C 24
Maybury Ct. *CR2: S Croy 5B 168*
(off Haling Pk. Rd.)
HA1: Harr 6H 41
W1 6H 5
(off Marylebone St.)
Maybury Gdns. NW10 6D 62
Maybury M. N6 7G 47
Maybury Rd. E13 4A 88
IG11: Bark 2K 89
Maybury St. SW17 5C 136
Maychurch Cl. HA7: Stan 7J 27
May Cl. KT9: Chess 6F 163
May Ct. *SW19 1A 154*
(off Pincott Rd.)
Maycroft HA5: Pinn 2K 39
Maycross Av. SM4: Mord 4H 153
Mayday Gdns. SE3 2C 124
Mayday Rd. CR7: Thor H 6B 156
Maydew Ho. *SE16 4J 103*
(off Abbeyfield Est.)
Maydwell Ho. *E14 5C 86*
(off Thomas Rd.)
Mayerne Rd. SE9 5B 124
Mayesbrook Pk. Arena 5A 72
Mayesbrook Rd. IG3: Ilf 3A 72
IG11: Bark 1K 89
RM8: Dag 3A 72
Mayesford Rd. RM6: Chad H 7C 54
Mayes Rd. N22 2K 47
Mayeswood Rd. SE12 4A 142
MAYFAIR 3J 11 (7F 83)
Mayfair Av. DA7: Bex 1D 126
IG1: Ilf 2D 70
KT4: Wor Pk 1C 164
RM6: Chad H 6D 54
TW2: Whitt 7G 113
Mayfair Cl. BR3: Beck 1D 158
KT6: Surb 1E 162
Mayfair Ct. HA8: Edg 5A 28
Mayfair Gdns. IG8: Wfd G 7D 36
N17 6H 33
Mayfair M. *NW1 7D 64*
(off Regents Pk. Rd.)
Mayfair Pl. W1 4K 11 (1F 101)
Mayfair Ter. N14 7C 22
Mayfield DA7: Bex 3F 127
Mayfield Av. BR6: Orp 1K 173
HA3: Kent 5B 42
IG8: Wfd G 6D 36
N12 4F 31
N14 2C 32
W4 4A 98
W13 3B 96
Mayfield Cl. E8 6F 67
KT7: T Ditt 1B 162
SE20 1H 157
Mayfield Cl. SW4 5H 119
TW15: Ashf 6D 128
UB10: Hil 3D 74
Mayfield Cres. CR7: Thor H 4K 155
N9 6C 24
Mayfield Dr. HA5: Pinn 4D 40
Mayfield Gdns. NW4 6F 45
W7 6H 77
Mayfield Ho. *E2 2H 85*
(off Cambridge Heath Rd.)
Mayfield Mans. SW15 5H 117
Mayfield Rd. BR1: Brom 5C 160
CR2: Sande 7D 168
CR7: Thor H 4K 155
DA17: Belv 4J 109
E4 2K 35
E8 7F 67
E13 4H 87
E17 2A 50
EN3: Enf H 2E 24
N8 5K 47
RM8: Dag 1C 72
SM2: Sutt 6B 166
SW19 1H 153
W3 7H 79
W12 2A 98
Mayfield Rd. Flats N8 6K 47
Mayfields HA9: Wemb 2G 61
Mayfields Cl. HA9: Wemb 2G 61
Mayfield Vs. DA14: Sidc 6C 144
Mayflower Cl. HA4: Ruis 6E 38
SE16 4K 103
Mayflower Ho. *IG11: Bark 1H 89*
(off Westbury Rd.)
Mayflower Rd. SW9 3J 119
Mayflower St. SE16 2J 103
Mayfly Cl. HA5: Eastc 7A 40
Mayfly Gdns. UB5: N'olt 3B 76
Mayford NW1 2G 83
(not continuous)
Mayford Cl. BR3: Beck 3K 157
SW12 7D 118
Mayford Rd. SW12 7D 118
May Gdns. HA0: Wemb 3C 78
Maygood Ho. *N1 2K 83*
(off Maygood St.)
Maygood St. N1 2A 84
Maygrove Rd. NW6 6H 63
Mayhew Cl. E4 3H 35
Mayhew Ct. SE5 4D 120
Mayhill Rd. EN5: Barn 6B 20
SE7 6K 105
Mayland Mans. *IG11: Bark 7F 71*
(off Whiting Av.)
Maylands Dr. DA14: Sidc 3D 144
UB8: Uxb 6A 56
Maylands Ho. *SW3 4D 16*
(off Cale St.)
Maylie Ho. *SE16 2H 103*
(off Marigold St.)
Maynard Cl. N15 5E 48
SW6 7K 99
Maynard Path E17 5E 50
Maynard Rd. E17 5E 50
Maynards Quay E1 7J 85
Mayne Ct. SE26 5H 139
Maynooth Gdns.
SM5: Cars 7D 154
Mayo Ct. W13 3B 96
Mayo Ho. *E1 5J 85*
(off Lindley St.)
Mayola Rd. E5 4J 67
Mayo Rd. CR0: C'don 5D 156
KT12: Walt T 7J 147
NW10 6A 62
Mayow Rd. SE23 4K 139
SE26 4K 139
Mayplace Cl. DA7: Bex 3H 127
Mayplace La. SE18 6F 107
(not continuous)
Mayplace Rd. E. DA1: Cray 3J 127
DA7: Bex, Cray 3H 127
Mayplace Rd. W.
DA7: Bex 4G 127
Maypole Ct. *UB2: S'hall 2D 94*
(off Merrick Rd.)
May Rd. E4 6H 35
E13 2J 87
TW2: Twick 1J 131
Mayroyd Av. KT6: Surb 2G 163
May's Bldgs. M. SE10 7E 104
Mays Ct. SE10 7F 105
WC2 3E 12 (7J 83)
Mays Hill Rd. BR2: Brom 2G 159
Mays La. EN5: Ark, Barn 1H 29 & 6A 20
Maysoule Rd. SW11 4B 118
Mays Rd. TW11: Tedd 5H 131
Mayston M. *SE10 5J 105*
(off Ormiston Rd.)
May St. W14 5H 99
(North End Rd.)
W14 5H 99
(Vereker Rd.)
Mayswood Gdns.
RM10: Dag 6J 73
Maythorne Cotts. SE13 5F 123
Mayton St. N7 3K 65
Maytree Cl. HA8: Edg 3D 28
Maytree Ct. CR4: Mitc 3E 154
UB5: N'olt 3C 76
Maytree Gdns. W5 2D 96
May Tree Ho. *SE4 3B 122*
(off Wickham Rd.)
Maytree La. HA7: Stan 7F 27
Maytree Wlk. SW2 2A 138
Mayville Est. N16 5E 66
Mayville Rd. E11 2G 69
(not continuous)
IG1: Ilf 5F 71
May Wlk. E13 2K 87
Mayward Ho. *SE5 1E 120*
(off Peckham Rd.)
Maywood Cl. BR3: Beck 7D 140
May Wynne Ho. *E16 7K 87*
(off Murray Sq.)
Maze Hill SE3 7H 105
SE10 6G 105
Maze Hill Lodge *SE10 6F 105*
(off Park Vista)
Mazenod Av. NW6 7J 63
Maze Rd. TW9: Kew 7G 97
MCC Cricket Mus. & Tours 1A 4 (3B 82)
Mead, The BR3: Beck 1E 158
BR4: W W'ck 1F 171
N2 2A 46
SM6: Wall 6H 167
UB10: Ick 2C 56
W13 5B 78
Meadbank Studios
SW11 7C 100
(off Parkgate Rd.)
Mead Cl. HA3: Hrw W 1H 41
NW1 6E 64
Mead Ct. NW9 5J 43
Mead Cres. E4 4K 35
SM1: Sutt 3C 166
Meadcroft Rd. SE11 7K 19 (6B 102)
(not continuous)
Meade Cl. W4 6G 97
Meader Ct. SE14 7K 103
Mead Fld. HA2: Harr 3D 58
Meadfield HA8: Edg 2C 28
(not continuous)
Meadfield Grn. HA8: Edg 2C 28
Meadfoot Rd. SW16 7G 137
Meadgate Av. IG8: Wfd G 5H 37
Mead Gro. RM6: Chad H 3D 54
Mead Ho. *W11 1H 99*
(off Ladbroke Rd.)
Mead Ho. La. UB4: Hayes 4F 75
Meadhurst Pk. TW16: Sun 6G 129
Meadhurst Sports Club 5H 129
Meadlands Dr.
TW10: Ham 2D 132
Mead Lodge W4 2K 97
Meadow, The BR7: Chst 6G 143
N10 3E 46
Meadow Av. CR0: C'don 6K 157
Meadow Bank N21 6E 22
SE3 3H 123
Meadowbank KT5: Surb 6F 151
NW3 7D 64
Meadowbank Cl. SW6 7E 98
Meadowbank Gdns.
TW5: Cran 1J 111
Meadowbank Rd. NW9 7K 43
Meadowbrook Cl. SL3: Poyle 4A 174
Meadowbrook Ct. TW7: Isle 3J 113
Meadow Cl. BR7: Chst 5F 143
DA6: Bex 5F 127
E4 1J 35
E9 6B 68
EN3: Enf W 1F 25
EN5: Barn 6C 20
HA4: Ruis 6H 39
IG11: Bark 7A 72
KT10: Hin W 3A 162
SE6 5C 140
SM1: Sutt 2A 166
SW20 4E 152
TW4: Houn 6E 112
TW10: Ham 1E 132
UB5: N'olt 2E 76
Meadow Ct. N1 2E 84
TW3: Houn 6F 113
Meadowcourt Rd. SE3 4H 123
Meadowcroft BR1: Brom 3D 160
W4 5G 97
(off Brooks Rd.)
Meadowcroft Cl. N13 2F 33
Meadowcroft Rd. N13 2F 33
Meadow Dr. N10 3F 47
NW4 2E 44
Meadowford Cl. SE28 7A 90
Meadow Gdns. HA8: Edg 6C 28
Meadow Gth. NW10 6J 61
(not continuous)
Meadowgate Cl. NW7 5G 29
Meadow Hill KT3: N Mald 6A 152
Meadow La. SE12 3K 141
Meadowlea Cl. UB7: Harm 2E 174
Meadow M. SW8 6K 101
Meadow Pl. SW8 7J 101
W4 7A 98
Meadow Rd. BR2: Brom 2G 159
HA5: Pinn 4B 40
IG11: Bark 7K 71
RM7: Rush G 1J 73
RM9: Dag 6F 73
SM1: Sutt 4C 166
SW8 7H 19 (7K 101)
SW19 7A 136
TW13: Felt 2C 130
TW15: Ashf 5F 129
UB1: S'hall 7D 76
Meadow Row SE1 3C 102
Meadows Cl. E10 2C 68
Meadows Ct. DA14: Sidc 6B 144
Meadows End TW16: Sun 1J 147
Meadowside SE9 4A 124
TW1: Twick 7D 114
Meadowside Leisure Cen. 4A 124
Meadow Stile CR0: C'don 3C 168
Meadowsweet Cl. E16 5B 88
SW20 4E 152
Meadow Vw. DA15: Sidc 7B 126
HA1: Harr 1J 59
TW19: Stan M 7A 174
Meadow Vw. Rd. CR7: Thor H 5B 156
UB4: Hayes 4F 75

Meadowview Rd.
DA5: Bexl 6E 126
KT19: Ewe 7A 164
SE6 5B 140
Meadow Wlk. E18 4J 51
KT17: Ewe 6A 164
KT19: Ewe 6A 164
(not continuous)
RM9: Dag 6F 73
SM6: Wall 3F 167
Meadow Walks EN5: New Bar 6E 20
Meadow Way BR6: Farnb 3E 172
HA4: Ruis 6K 39
HA9: Wemb 4D 60
KT9: Chess 5E 162
NW9 5K 43
Meadow Way, The
HA3: Hrw W 1J 41
Meadow Waye
TW5: Hest 6C 94
Mead Path SW17 4A 136
Mead Pl. CR0: C'don 1C 168
E9 6J 67
Mead Plat NW10 6J 61
Mead Rd. BR7: Chst 6G 143
HA8: Edg 6B 28
TW10: Ham 3C 132
Mead Row SE1 1J 19 (3A 102)
Meads, The HA8: Edg 6E 28
SM3: Cheam 3G 165
SM4: Mord 5C 154
UB8: Cowl 4A 74
Meads Ct. E15 6H 69
Meadside Cl. BR3: Beck 1A 158
Meads La. IG3: Ilf 7J 53
Meads Rd. EN3: Enf H 1F 25
N22 2B 48
Mead Ter. HA9: Wemb 4D 60
Meadvale Rd. CR0: C'don 7F 157
W5 4B 78
Mead Way BR2: Hayes 6H 159
CR0: C'don 2A 170
HA4: Ruis 6F 39
IG8: Wfd G 5F 37
Meadway BR3: Beck 1E 158
EN5: Barn, New Bar 4D 20
IG3: Bark, Ilf 4J 71
KT5: Surb 1J 163
N14 2C 32
NW11 6J 45
SW20 4E 152
TW2: Twick 1H 131
TW15: Ashf 4C 128
Meadway, The IG9: Buck H 1G 37
SE3 2F 123
Meadway Cl. EN5: Barn 4D 20
HA5: Hat E 6A 26
NW11 6K 45
Meadway Ct. RM8: Dag 2F 73
TW11: Tedd 5C 132
W5 4F 79
Meadway Gdns.
HA4: Ruis 6F 39
Meadway Ga. NW11 6J 45
Meaford Way SE20 7H 139
Meakin Est. SE1 3E 102
Meanley Rd. E12 4C 70
Meard St. W1 1C 12 (6H 83)
(not continuous)
Meath Cres. E2 3K 85
Meath Ho. *SE24* *6B 120*
(off Dulwich Rd.)
Meath Rd. E15 2H 87
IG1: Ilf 3G 71
Meath St. SW11 1F 119
Mecca Bingo
Burnt Oak 2J 43
Camden *1F 83*
(off Arlington Rd.)
Chadwell Heath 7D 54
Mecca Bingo
Croydon *2C 168*
(off Tamworth Rd.)
Dagenham 1E 90
Earlsfield 1K 135
East Ham 1C 88
Fulham Broadway *7J 99*
(off Vanston Pl.)
Hackney 1K 9
Hounslow 2G 113
Islington 7B 66
Kilburn 1J 81
Rosehill 7A 154
Wood Green *2A 48*
(off Lordship La.)
Yeading 6K 75
Mecklenburgh Pl. WC1 3G 7 (4K 83)
Mecklenburgh Sq. WC1 3G 7 (4K 83)
Mecklenburgh St.
WC1 3G 7 (4K 83)
Medburn St. NW1 2H 83
Medcroft Gdns. SW14 4J 115
Medebourne Cl. SE3 3J 123
Mede Ho. *BR1: Brom* *5K 141*
(off Pike Cl.)
Medesenge Way N13 6G 33
Medfield St. SW15 7C 116
Medhurst Cl. E3 2A 86
(not continuous)
Median Rd. E5 5J 67
Medina Gro. N7 3A 66
Medina Rd. N7 3A 66
Medland Cl. SM6: Wall 1E 166
Medland Ho. E14 7A 86
Medlar Cl. UB5: N'olt 2B 76
Medlar Ho. DA15: Sidc 3A 144
Medlar St. SE5 1C 120
Medley Rd. NW6 6J 63
Medora Rd. RM7: Rom 4K 55
SW2 7K 119
Medusa Rd. SE6 6D 122
Medway Bldgs. *E3* *2A 86*
(off Medway Rd.)
Medway Cl. CR0: C'don 6J 157
IG1: Ilf 5G 71
Medway Ct. NW11 6K 45
WC1 *2E 6*
(off Judd St.)
Medway Dr. UB6: G'frd 2K 77
Medway Gdns.
HA0: Wemb 4A 60
Medway Ho. KT2: King T 1D 150
NW8 *4C 4*
(off Penfold St.)
SE1 *7F 15*
(off Hankey Pl.)
Medway M. E3 2A 86
Medway Pde. UB6: G'frd 2K 77
Medway Rd. E3 2A 86
Medway St. SW1 2D 18 (3H 101)
Medwin St. SW4 4K 119
Meerbrook Rd. SE3 3A 124
Meeson Rd. E15 7H 69
Meeson St. E5 4A 68
Meeson's Wharf E15 2E 86
Meeting Fld. Path E9 6J 67
Meeting Ho. All. E1 1H 103
Meeting Ho. La. SE15 1H 121
Megabowl
Acton 4G 79
Bexleyheath 4F 127
Croydon 2K 167
Dagenham 2H 91
Feltham 2K 129
Harrow 5F 41
Kingston upon Thames *2E 150*
(in The Rotunda Cen.)
Streatham Hill 2J 137
Mehetabel Rd. E9 5J 67
Meister Cl. IG1: Ilf 1H 71
Melancholy Wlk.
TW10: Ham 2C 132
Melanda Cl. BR7: Chst 5D 142
Melanie Cl. DA7: Bex 1E 126
Melba Way SE13 1D 122
Melbourne Av. HA5: Pinn 3F 41
N13 6E 32
W13 1A 96
Melbourne Cl. BR6: Orp 7J 161
SE20 7G 139
SM6: Wall 5G 167
UB10: Ick 4C 56
Melbourne Ct. N10 7A 32
W9 *4A 82*
(off Randolph Av.)
Melbourne Gdns. RM6: Chad H 5E 54
Melbourne Gro. SE22 4E 120
Melbourne Ho. UB4: Yead 4A 76
W8 *1J 99*
(off Kensington Pl.)
Melbourne Mans. *W6* *6G 99*
(off Musard Rd.)
Melbourne M. SE6 7E 122
SW9 1A 120
Melbourne Pl. WC2 1H 13 (6K 83)
Melbourne Rd. E6 2D 88
E10 7D 50
E17 4A 50
IG1: Ilf 1F 71
SM6: Wall 5F 167
SW19 1J 153
TW11: Tedd 6C 132
Melbourne Sq. SW9 1A 120
Melbourne Ter. *SW6* *7K 99*
(off Moore Pk. Rd.)
Melbourne Way EN1: Enf 6A 24
Melbray M. SW6 2H 117
Melbreak Ho. SE22 3E 120
Melbury Av. UB2: S'hall 3F 95
Melbury Cl. BR7: Chst 6C 142
KT10: Clay 6B 162
Melbury Ct. W8 3H 99
Melbury Dr. SE5 7E 102
Melbury Gdns. SW20 1D 152
Melbury Ho. *SW8* *7K 101*
(off Richborne Ter.)
Melbury Rd. HA3: Kent 5F 43
W14 3H 99
Melbury Ter. NW1 4D 4 (4C 82)
Melchester *W11* *6H 81*
(off Ledbury Rd.)
Melchester Ho. *N19* *3H 65*
(off Wedmore St.)
Melcombe Ct. *NW1* *5E 4*
(off Melcombe Pl.)
Melcombe Gdns. HA3: Kent 6F 43
Melcombe Ho. *SW8* *7K 101*
(off Dorset Rd.)
Melcombe Pl.
NW1 5E 4 (5D 82)
Melcombe Regis Ct. *W1* *6H 5*
(off Weymouth St.)
Melcombe St. NW1 4F 5 (4D 82)
Meldex Cl. NW7 6K 29
Meldon Cl. SW6 1K 117
Meldone Cl. KT5: Surb 7H 151
Meldrum Rd. IG3: Ilf 2A 72
Melfield Gdns. SE6 4E 140
Melford Av. IG11: Bark 6J 71
Melford Cl. KT9: Chess 5F 163
Melford Ct. *SE1* *3E 102*
(off Fendall St.)
SE22 1G 139
(not continuous)
Melford Pas. SE22 7G 121
Melford Rd. E6 4D 88
E11 2G 69
E17 4A 50
IG1: Ilf 2H 71
SE22 7G 121
Melfort Av. CR7: Thor H 3B 156
Melfort Rd. CR7: Thor H 3B 156
Melgund Rd. N5 5A 66
Melina Cl. UB3: Hayes 5F 75
Melina Ct. SW15 3C 116
Melina Pl. NW8 2A 4 (3B 82)
Melina Rd. W12 2D 98
Melior Ct. N6 6G 47
Melior Pl. SE1 6G 15 (2E 102)
Melior St. SE1 6G 15 (2E 102)
Meliot Rd. SE6 2F 141
Meller Cl. CR0: Bedd 3J 167
Mellifont Cl. SM5: Cars 7B 154
Melling Dr. EN1: Enf 1B 24
Melling St. SE18 6J 107
Mellish Cl. IG11: Bark 1K 89
Mellish Flats E10 7C 50
Mellish Gdns. IG8: Wfd G 5D 36
Mellish Ho. *E1* *6H 85*
(off Varden St.)
Mellish Ind. Est. SE18 3B 106
Mellish St. E14 3C 104
Mellison Rd. SW17 5C 136
Melliss Av. TW9: Kew 1H 115
Mellitus St. W12 5B 80
Mellor Cl. KT12: Walt T 7D 148
Mellow La. E. UB4: Hayes 3E 74
Mellow La. W. UB10: Hil 3E 74
Mellows Rd. IG5: Ilf 3D 52
SM6: Wall 5H 167
Mells Cres. SE9 4D 142
Mell St. SE10 5G 105
Melody La. N5 5C 66
Melody Rd. SW18 5A 118
Melon Pl. W8 2J 99
Melon Rd. E11 3G 69
SE15 1G 121
Melrose Av. CR4: Mitc 7F 137
DA1: Cray 7K 127
N22 1B 48
NW2 5D 62
SW16 3K 155
SW19 2H 135
TW2: Whitt 7F 113
UB6: G'frd 2F 77
Melrose Cl. SE12 1J 141
UB4: Hayes 5J 75
UB6: G'frd 2F 77
Melrose Ct. *W13* *1A 96*
(off Williams Rd.)
Melrose Cres. BR6: Orp 4H 173
Melrose Dr. UB1: S'hall 1E 94
Melrose Gdns. HA8: Edg 3H 43
KT3: N Mald 3K 151
W6 3E 98
Melrose Ho. *E14* *3D 104*
(off Lanark Sq.)
NW6 *3J 81*
(off Carlton Va.)
SW1 *5F 101*
(off Sutherland St.)
Melrose Rd. HA5: Pinn 4D 40
SW13 2B 116
SW18 6H 117
SW19 2J 153
W3 3J 97
Melrose Ter. W6 3E 98
Melrose Tudor *SM6: Wall* *5J 167*
(off Plough La.)
Melsa Rd. SM4: Mord 6A 154
Melthorne Dr. HA4: Ruis 3A 58
Melthorpe Gdns. SE3 1C 124
Melton Cl. HA4: Ruis 1A 58
Melton Ct. SM2: Sutt 7A 166
SW7 3B 16 (4B 100)
Melton St. NW1 2B 6 (3G 83)
Melville Av. CR2: S Croy 5F 169
SW20 7C 134
UB6: G'frd 5K 59
Melville Cl. UB10: Ick 2F 57

Melville Ct. SE8 . . . 4A 104
W4 . . . 5G 97
(off Haining Cl.)
W12 . . . 3D 98
(off Goldhawk Rd.)
Melville Gdns. N13 . . . 5G 33
Melville Ho. EN5: New Bar . . . 5G 21
SE10 . . . 1E 122
Melville Pl. N1 . . . 7C 66
Melville Rd. DA14: Sidc . . . 2C 144
E17 . . . 3B 50
NW10 . . . 7K 61
RM5: Col R . . . 1H 55
SW13 . . . 1C 116
Melville Vs. Rd. W3 . . . 1J 97
Melvin Rd. SE20 . . . 1J 157
Melwood Ho. E1 . . . 6H 85
(off Watney Mkt.)
Melyn Cl. N7 . . . 4G 65
Memel Ct. EC1 . . . 4C 8
Memel St. EC1 . . . 4C 8 (4C 84)
Memess Path SE18 . . . 6E 106
Memorial Av. E12 . . . 2C 70
E15 . . . 3G 87
Memorial Cl. TW5: Hest . . . 6D 94
Menai Pl. E3 . . . 2C 86
(off Blondin St.)
Menard Ct. EC1 . . . 2D 8
(off Galway St.)
Mendham Ho. SE1 . . . 7G 15
(off Cluny Pl.)
Mendip Cl. KT4: Wor Pk . . . 1E 164
SE26 . . . 4J 139
UB3: Harl . . . 7F 93
Mendip Ct. SE14 . . . 6J 103
(off Avonley Rd.)
SW11 . . . 3A 118
Mendip Dr. NW2 . . . 2G 63
Mendip Ho. N9 . . . 2B 34
(off New Rd.)
Mendip Ho's. E2 . . . 3J 85
(off Welwyn St.)
Mendip Rd. DA7: Bex . . . 1K 127
IG2: Ilf . . . 5J 53
SW11 . . . 3A 118
Mendora Rd. SW6 . . . 7G 99
Menelik Rd. NW2 . . . 4G 63
Menier Chocolate Factory
(Theatre and Art Gallery) . . . 5D 14
(off Southwick St.)
Menlo Gdns. SE19 . . . 7D 138
Menlo Lodge N13 . . . 3E 32
(off Crothall Cl.)
Menon Dr. N9 . . . 3C 34
Menotti St. E2 . . . 4G 85
Menteath Ho. E14 . . . 6C 86
(off Dod St.)
Mentmore Cl. HA3: Kent . . . 6C 42
Mentmore Ter. E8 . . . 7H 67
Mentone Mans. SW10 . . . 7K 99
(off Fulham Rd.)
Meon Ct. TW7: Isle . . . 2J 113
Meon Rd. W3 . . . 2J 97
Meopham Rd. CR4: Mitc . . . 1G 155
Mepham Cres. HA3: Hrw W . . . 7B 26
Mepham Gdns.
HA3: Hrw W . . . 7B 26
Mepham St. SE1 . . . 5H 13 (1A 102)
Mera Dr. DA7: Bex . . . 4G 127
Merantun Way SW19 . . . 1K 153
Merbury Cl. SE13 . . . 5E 122
SE28 . . . 1H 107
Merbury Rd. SE28 . . . 1H 107
Mercator Pl. E14 . . . 5C 104
Mercator Rd. SE13 . . . 4F 123
Mercer Bldg. EC2 . . . 3H 9
(off Bateman's Row)
Mercer Cl. KT7: T Ditt . . . 7K 149
Mercer Ho. SW1 . . . 5J 17
(off Ebury Bri. Rd.)
Merceron Ho's. E2 . . . 3J 85
(off Globe Rd.)
Merceron St. E1 . . . 4H 85
Mercer Pl. HA5: Pinn . . . 2A 40
Mercers Cl. SE10 . . . 4H 105
Mercer's Cotts. E1 . . . 6A 86
(off White Horse Rd.)
Mercers M. N19 . . . 3H 65
Mercers Pl. W6 . . . 4F 99
Mercers Rd. N19 . . . 3H 65
(not continuous)
Mercer St. WC2 . . . 1E 12 (6J 83)
Merchant Ct. E1 . . . 1J 103
(off Wapping Wall)
Merchant Ind. Ter. NW10 . . . 4J 79
Merchants Cl. SE25 . . . 4G 157
Merchants Ho. SE10 . . . 5F 105
(off Collington St.)
Merchants Lodge E17 . . . 4C 50
(off Westbury Rd.)
Merchants Row SE10 . . . 5F 105
(off Hoskins St.)
Merchant St. E3 . . . 3B 86
Merchiston Rd. SE6 . . . 2F 141
Merchland Rd. SE9 . . . 1G 143
Mercia Gro. SE13 . . . 4E 122
Mercia Ho. SE5 . . . 2C 120
(off Denmark Rd.)
TW15: Ashf . . . 1E 146
Mercier Rd. SW15 . . . 5G 117
Mercury NW9 . . . 1B 44
(off The Concourse)
Mercury Cen. TW14: Felt . . . 5J 111
Mercury Ct. E14 . . . 4C 104
(off Homer Dr.)
Mercury Hgts. IG2: Ilf . . . 6H 53
Mercury Ho. TW8: Bford . . . 6C 96
(off Glenhurst Rd.)
W5 . . . 4F 79
Mercury Rd. TW8: Bford . . . 6C 96
Mercury Way SE14 . . . 6K 103
Mercy Ter. SE13 . . . 5D 122
Merebank La. CR0: Wadd . . . 5K 167
Mere Cl. BR6: Farnb . . . 2E 172
SW15 . . . 7F 117
Meredith Av. NW2 . . . 5E 62
Meredith Cl. HA5: Pinn . . . 1B 40
Meredith Ho. N16 . . . 5E 66
Meredith M. SE4 . . . 4B 122
Meredith St. E13 . . . 3J 87
EC1 . . . 2A 8 (3B 84)
Meredith Twr. W3 . . . 3H 97
(off Hanbury Rd.)
Meredyth Rd. SW13 . . . 2C 116
Mere End CR0: C'don . . . 7K 157
Mere Rd. TW17: Shep . . . 6D 146
Mereside BR6: Farnb . . . 2E 172
Mereside Pk. TW15: Ashf . . . 4E 128
Meretone Cl. SE4 . . . 4A 122
Mereton Mans. SE8 . . . 1C 122
(off Brookmill Rd.)
Merevale Cres. SM4: Mord . . . 6A 154
Mereway Rd. TW2: Twick . . . 1H 131
Merewood Cl. BR1: Brom . . . 2E 160
Merewood Gdns.
CR0: C'don . . . 7K 157
Merewood Rd. DA7: Bex . . . 2J 127
Mereworth Cl. BR2: Brom . . . 5H 159
Mereworth Dr. SE18 . . . 7F 107
Mereworth Ho. SE15 . . . 6J 103
Merganser Ct. E1 . . . 7G 85
(off Swan Pl.)
SE8 . . . 6B 104
(off Edward St.)
Merganser Gdns. SE28 . . . 3H 107
Meriden Cl. BR1: Brom . . . 7B 142
IG6: Ilf . . . 1G 53
Meriden Ct. SW3 . . . 6C 16
Meriden Ho. N1 . . . 1E 84
(off Wilmer Gdns.)
Merideth Ct. KT1: King T . . . 2F 151
Meridia Ct. E15 . . . 1E 86
(off Biggerstaff Rd.)
Meridiam Ct. UB4: Yead . . . 4A 76
Meridian Cl. NW7 . . . 4E 28
Meridian Ct. SE16 . . . 2G 103
(off Bermondsey Wall W.)
Meridian Ga. E14 . . . 2D 104
Meridian Ho. NW1 . . . 7G 65
(off Baynes St.)
SE10 . . . 4G 105
(off Azof St.)
SE10 . . . 7E 104
(off Royal Hill)
Meridian Pl. E14 . . . 2D 104
Meridian Point SE8 . . . 6D 104
Meridian Rd. SE7 . . . 7B 106
Meridian Sq. E15 . . . 7F 69
Meridian Trad. Est. SE7 . . . 4K 105
Meridian Wlk. N17 . . . 6K 33
Meridian Way EN3: Pond E . . . 7E 24
N9 . . . 4D 34
N18 . . . 5D 34
Merifield Rd. SE9 . . . 4A 124
Merino Cl. E11 . . . 4A 52
Merino Ct. EC1 . . . 2D 8
(off Lever St.)
Merino Pl. DA15: Sidc . . . 6A 126
Merioneth Ct. W7 . . . 5K 77
(off Copley Cl.)
Merivale Rd. HA1: Harr . . . 7G 41
SW15 . . . 4G 117
Merlewood Dr. BR7: Chst . . . 1D 160
Merley Ct. NW9 . . . 1J 61
Merlin NW9 . . . 1B 44
(off The Concourse)
Merlin Cl. CR0: C'don . . . 4E 168
CR4: Mitc . . . 3C 154
SM6: Wall . . . 6K 167
UB5: Yead . . . 3A 76
Merlin Ct. BR2: Brom . . . 3H 159
HA4: Ruis . . . 2F 57
HA7: Stan . . . 5G 27
(off William Dr.)
Merlin Cres. HA8: Edg . . . 1F 43
Merlin Gdns. BR1: Brom . . . 3J 141
Merling Cl. KT9: Chess . . . 5C 162
Merlin Gro. BR3: Beck . . . 4B 158
Merlin Ho. EN3: Pond E . . . 5E 24
Merlin Rd. DA16: Well . . . 4A 126
E12 . . . 2B 70
Merlin Rd. Nth.
DA16: Well . . . 4A 126
Merlins Av. HA2: Harr . . . 3D 58
Merlins Ct. WC1 . . . 2J 7
(off Margery St.)
Merlin St. WC1 . . . 2J 7 (3A 84)
Mermaid Ct. E8 . . . 7F 67
(off Celandine Dr.)
SE1 . . . 6E 14 (2D 102)
SE16 . . . 1B 104
Mermaid Ho. E14 . . . 7E 86
(off Bazely St.)
Mermaid Twr. SE8 . . . 6B 104
(off Abinger Gro.)
Meroe Ct. N16 . . . 2E 66
Merredene St. SW2 . . . 6K 119
Merriam Av. E9 . . . 6B 68
Merriam Cl. E4 . . . 5K 35
Merrick Rd. UB2: S'hall . . . 2D 94
Merrick Sq. SE1 . . . 7E 14 (3D 102)
Merridene N21 . . . 6G 23
Merrielands Cres. RM9: Dag . . . 2F 91
Merrielands Retail Pk.
RM9: Dag . . . 1F 91
Merrilands Rd. KT4: Wor Pk . . . 1E 164
Merrilees Rd. DA15: Sidc . . . 7J 125
Merrilyn Cl. KT10: Clay . . . 6A 162
Merriman Rd. SE3 . . . 1A 124
Merrington Rd. SW6 . . . 6J 99
Merrion Av. HA7: Stan . . . 5J 27
Merritt Gdns. KT9: Chess . . . 6C 162
(not continuous)
Merritt Rd. SE4 . . . 5B 122
Merritt's Bldgs. EC2 . . . 4G 9
Merrivale N14 . . . 6C 22
NW1 . . . 1G 83
(off Camden St.)
Merrivale Av. IG4: Ilf . . . 4B 52
Merrow Bldgs. SE1 . . . 6B 14
(off Rushworth St.)
Merrow Ct. CR4: Mitc . . . 2B 154
Merrow Rd. SM2: Cheam . . . 7F 165
Merrow St. SE17 . . . 5D 102
Merrow Wlk. SE17 . . . 5D 102
Merrow Way CR0: New Ad . . . 6E 170
Merrydown Way BR7: Chst . . . 1C 160
Merryfield SE3 . . . 2H 123
Merryfield Gdns. HA7: Stan . . . 5H 27
Merryfield Ho. SE9 . . . 3A 142
(off Grove Pk. Rd.)
Merryfields UB8: Uxb . . . 2A 74
UB10: Uxb . . . 2A 74
Merryfields Way SE6 . . . 7D 122
MERRY HILL . . . 1A 26
Merryhill Cl. E4 . . . 7J 25
Merry Hill Mt. WD23: Bush . . . 1A 26
Merry Hill Rd. WD23: Bush . . . 1A 26
Merryhills Ct. N14 . . . 5B 22
Merryhills Dr. EN2: Enf . . . 4C 22
Merryweather Ct.
KT3: N Mald . . . 5A 152
N19 . . . 3G 65
Mersea Ho. IG11: Bark . . . 6F 71
Mersey Ct. KT2: King T . . . 1D 150
(off Samuel Gray Gdns.)
Mersey Rd. E17 . . . 3B 50
Mersey Wlk. UB5: N'olt . . . 2E 76
Mersham Dr. NW9 . . . 5G 43
Mersham Pl. CR7: Thor H . . . 2D 156
(off Livingstone Rd.)
SE20 . . . 1H 157
Mersham Rd. CR7: Thor H . . . 3D 156
Merten Rd. RM6: Chad H . . . 7E 54
Merthyr Ter. SW13 . . . 6D 98
MERTON . . . 7A 136
Merton Abbey Mills SW19 . . . 1A 154
Merton Av. UB5: N'olt . . . 5G 59
UB10: Hil . . . 7D 56
W4 . . . 4B 98
Merton Ct. DA16: Well . . . 2B 126
IG1: Ilf . . . 6C 52
Merton Gdns. BR5: Pet W . . . 5F 161
Merton Hall Gdns. SW20 . . . 1G 153
Merton Hall Rd. SW19 . . . 7G 135
Merton High St. SW19 . . . 7K 135
Merton Ind. Pk. SW19 . . . 1K 153
Merton La. N6 . . . 2D 64
Merton Lodge
EN5: New Bar . . . 5F 21
Merton Mans. SW20 . . . 2F 153
MERTON PARK . . . 2J 153
Merton Pk. Pde. SW19 . . . 1H 153
Merton Pl. SW19 . . . 1A 154
(off Nelson Gro. Rd.)
Merton Ri. NW3 . . . 7C 64
Merton Rd. E17 . . . 5E 50
EN2: Enf . . . 1J 23
HA2: Harr . . . 1G 59
IG3: Ilf . . . 7K 53
IG11: Bark . . . 7K 71
SE25 . . . 5F 157
SW18 . . . 6J 117
SW19 . . . 7K 135
Merton Way KT8: W Mole . . . 4F 149
UB10: Hil . . . 7D 56
Mertoun Ter. W1 . . . 7E 4
(off Seymour Pl.)
Merttins Rd. SE4 . . . 5K 121
SE15 . . . 5K 121

Meru Cl. NW5 . . . . 4E 64
Mervan Rd. SW2 . . . . 4A 120
Mervyn Av. SE9 . . . . 3G 143
Mervyn Rd. TW17: Shep 7E 146
W13 . . . . 3A 96
Messaline Av. W3 . . . . 6J 79
Messent Rd. SE9 . . . . 5A 124
Messeter Pl. SE9 . . . . 6E 124
Messina Av. NW6 . . . . 7J 63
Messiter Ho. N1 . . . . 1K 83
(off Barnsbury Est.)
Metcalf Rd. TW15: Ashf 5D 128
Metcalf Wlk. TW13: Hanw 4C 130
Meteor St. SW11 . . . . 4E 118
Meteor Way SM6: Wall 7J 167
Methley St. SE11 . . . . 6K 19 (5A 102)
Methuen Cl. HA8: Edg 7B 28
Methuen Pk. N10 . . . . 3F 47
Methuen Rd. DA6: Bex 4F 127
DA17: Belv 4H 109
HA8: Edg 7B 28
Methwold Rd. W10 . . . . 5F 81
Metro Bus. Cen., The SE26 . . . . 6B 140
Metro Central Hgts. SE1 . . . . 3C 102
(off Newington C'way.)
Metro Ind. Cen. TW7: Isle 2J 113
Metropolis SE11 . . . . 3B 102
(off Oswin St.)
Metropolitan Bus. Cen. N1 . . . . 7E 66
(off Enfield Rd.)
Metropolitan Cen., The
UB6: G'frd 1F 77
Metropolitan Cl. E14 . . . . 5C 86
Metropolitan Club, The 7K 117
Metropolitan Police Norwood Cadet
Training Cen. 1E 156
Metropolitan Sta. Bldgs. W6 . . . . 4E 98
(off Beadon Rd.)
Metropolitan Wharf E1 . . . . 1J 103
Metro Trad. Est. HA9: Wemb 4H 61
Meud Chadburn Pl. SW12 . . . . 6F 119
Mews, The DA14: Sidc 4A 144
IG4: Ilf 5B 52
N1 . . . . 1C 84
N8 . . . . 3A 48
RM1: Rom 4K 55
SE22 . . . . 5G 121
TW1: Twick 6B 114
Mews Pl. IG8: Wfd G 4D 36
Mews St. E1 . . . . 4K 15 (1G 103)
Mexborough NW1 . . . . 1G 83
Mexfield Rd. SW15 . . . . 5H 117
Meyer Grn. EN1: Enf 1B 24
Meyer Rd. DA8: Erith 6K 109
Meymott St. SE1 . . . . 5A 14 (1B 102)
Meynell Cres. E9 . . . . 7K 67
Meynell Gdns. E9 . . . . 7K 67
Meynell Rd. E9 . . . . 7K 67
Meyrick Ho. E14 . . . . 5C 86
(off Burgess St.)
Meyrick Rd. NW10 . . . . 6C 62
SW11 . . . . 3B 118
Miah Ter. E1 . . . . 1G 103
Miall Wlk. SE26 . . . . 4A 140
Micawber Av. UB8: Hil 4C 74
Micawber Ct. N1 . . . . 1D 8
(off Windsor Ter.)
Micawber Ho. SE16 . . . . 2G 103
(off Llewellyn St.)
Micawber St. N1 . . . . 1D 8 (3C 84)
Michael Cliffe Ho. EC1 . . . . 2A 8
Michael Faraday Ho. SE17 . . . . 5E 102
(off Beaconsfield Rd.)
Michael Gaynor Cl. W7 . . . . 1K 95
Michael Haines Ho. SW9 . . . . 7A 102
(off Sth. Island Pl.)
Michael Manley Ind. Est.
SW8 . . . . 2G 119
(off Clyston St.)
Michaelmas Cl. SW20 . . . . 3E 152
Michael Rd. E11 . . . . 1H 69
SE25 . . . . 3E 156
SW6 . . . . 1K 117
Michaels Cl. SE13 . . . . 4G 123
Michael Stewart Ho.
SW6 . . . . 6H 99
(off Clem Attlee Ct.)
Michelangelo Ct. SE16 . . . . 5H 103
(off Stubbs Dr.)
Micheldever Rd. SE12 . . . . 6G 123
Michelham Gdns. TW1: Twick 3K 131
Michelle Ct. BR1: Brom 1H 159
(off Blyth Rd.)
N12 . . . . 5F 31
W3 . . . . 7K 79
Michelsdale Dr. TW9: Rich 4E 114
Michelson Ho. SE11 . . . . 4H 19
Michel's Row TW9: Rich 4E 114
(off Michelsdale Dr.)
Michel Wlk. SE18 . . . . 5F 107
Michigan Av. E12 . . . . 4D 70
Michigan Ho. E14 . . . . 3C 104
Michleham Down N12 . . . . 4C 30
Mickledore NW1 . . . . 1B 6
(off Ampthill Est.)
Mickleham Cl. BR5: St P 2K 161
Mickleham Gdns. SM3: Cheam 6G 165
Mickleham Rd. BR5: St P 1K 161
Mickleham Way CR0: New Ad 7F 171
Micklethwaite Rd. SW6 . . . . 6J 99
Mickleton Ho. W2 . . . . 5J 81
(off Westbourne Pk. Rd.)
Midas Bus. Cen. RM10: Dag 4H 73
Midas Metropolitan Ind. Est.
SM4: Mord 7E 152
MID BECKTON 6D 88
Mid City Lanes
Croydon 6A 168
Midcroft HA4: Ruis 1G 57
Middle Dartrey Wlk. SW10 . . . . 7A 100
(off Dartrey Wlk.)
Middle Dene NW7 . . . . 3E 28
Middlefield NW8 . . . . 1B 82
Middlefielde W13 . . . . 5B 78
Middlefield Gdns. IG2: Ilf 6F 53
Middle Grn. Cl. KT5: Surb 6F 151
Middleham Gdns. N18 . . . . 6B 34
Middleham Rd. N18 . . . . 6B 34
Middle La. N8 . . . . 5J 47
TW11: Tedd 6K 131
Middle La. M. N8 . . . . 5J 47
Middle Mill Halls of Residence
KT1: King T 3F 151
Middle New St. EC4 . . . . 7K 7
(off Pemberton Row)
Middle Pk. Av. SE9 . . . . 6B 124
Middle Path HA2: Harr 1H 59
Middle Rd. E13 . . . . 2J 87
EN4: E Barn 6H 21
HA2: Harr 2H 59
SW16 . . . . 2H 155
Middle Row W10 . . . . 4G 81
Middlesborough Rd. N18 . . . . 6B 34
Middlesex Bus. Cen. UB2: S'hall 2E 94
Middlesex CC Club 1B 4 (3B 82)
Middlesex Cl. UB1: S'hall 4F 77
Middlesex County Cricket School 2K 45
Middlesex Ct. HA1: Harr 5K 41
W4 . . . . 4B 98
Middlesex Filter Beds Nature Reserve
. . . . 3K 67
Middlesex Ho. HA0: Wemb 1D 78
Middlesex Pas. EC1 . . . . 6B 8
Middlesex Pl. E9 . . . . 6J 67
(off Elsdale St.)
Middlesex Rd. CR4: Mitc 5J 155
Middlesex St. E1 . . . . 6H 9 (5E 84)
Middlesex University
Cat Hill Campus 5K 21
Enfield Campus 5C 24
Hendon Campus 4D 44
Quicksilver Place Campus 2J 47
The Archway Campus 1G 65
Trent Pk. Campus 2B 22
Middlesex University Swimming Pool
. . . . 2K 47
Middlesex Wharf E5 . . . . 2J 67
Middle St. CR0: C'don 2C 168
(not continuous)
EC1 . . . . 5C 8 (5C 84)
Middle Temple La. EC4 . . . . 1J 13 (6A 84)
Middleton Av. DA14: Sidc 6B 144
E4 . . . . 4G 35
UB6: G'frd 2H 77
Middleton Cl. E4 . . . . 3G 35
Middleton Dr. HA5: Eastc 3J 39
SE16 . . . . 2K 103
Middleton Gdns. IG2: Ilf 6F 53
Middleton Gro. N7 . . . . 5J 65
Middleton Ho. E8 . . . . 7G 67
SE1 . . . . 3D 102
(off Burbage Cl.)
SW1 . . . . 4D 18
(off Causton St.)
Middleton M. N7 . . . . 5J 65
Middleton Pl. W1 . . . . 6A 6
Middleton Rd. E8 . . . . 7F 67
NW11 . . . . 7J 45
SM4: Mord 6K 153
SM5: Cars 6K 153
UB3: Hayes 5F 75
Middleton St. E2 . . . . 3H 85
Middleton Way SE13 . . . . 4F 123
Middle Way DA18: Erith 3E 108
SW16 . . . . 2H 155
UB4: Yead 4A 76
Middle Way, The HA3: W'stone 2K 41
Middleway NW11 . . . . 5K 45
Middle Yd. SE1 . . . . 4G 15 (1E 102)
Midfield Av. DA7: Bex 3J 127
Midfield Pde. DA7: Bex 3J 127
Midfield Way BR5: St P 7A 144
Midford Ho. NW4 . . . . 4E 44
(off Stratford Rd.)
Midford Pl. W1 . . . . 4B 6 (4G 83)
Midholm HA9: Wemb 1G 61
NW11 . . . . 4K 45
Midholm Cl. NW11 . . . . 4K 45
Midholm Rd. CR0: C'don 2A 170
Midhope Ho. WC1 . . . . 2F 7
(off Midhope St.)
Midhope St. WC1 . . . . 2F 7 (3J 83)
Midhurst SE26 . . . . 6J 139
Midhurst Av. CR0: C'don 7A 156
N10 . . . . 3E 46
Midhurst Gdns. UB10: Hil 1E 74
Midhurst Hill DA6: Bex 6G 127
Midhurst Ho. E14 . . . . 6B 86
(off Salmon La.)
Midhurst Pde. N10 . . . . 3E 46
(off Fortis Grn.)
Midhurst Rd. W13 . . . . 2A 96
Midhurst Way E5 . . . . 4G 67
Midland Pde. NW6 . . . . 6K 63
Midland Pl. E14 . . . . 5E 104
Midland Rd. E10 . . . . 7E 50
NW1 . . . . 1D 6 (2H 83)
Midland Ter. NW2 . . . . 3F 63
NW10 . . . . 4A 80
Midleton Rd. KT3: N Mald 3J 151
Midmoor Rd. SW12 . . . . 1G 137
SW19 . . . . 1F 153
Midship Cl. SE16 . . . . 1K 103
Midship Point E14 . . . . 2C 104
(off The Quarterdeck)
Midstrath Rd. NW10 . . . . 4A 62
Midsummer Av. TW4: Houn 4D 112
Midway SM3: Sutt 7H 153
Midway Ho. EC1 . . . . 1A 8
Midwinter Cl. DA16: Well 3A 126
Midwood Cl. NW2 . . . . 3D 62
Miers Cl. E6 . . . . 1E 88
Mighell Av. IG4: Ilf 5B 52
Milan Ct. N11 . . . . 1H 47
Milan Rd. UB1: S'hall 2D 94
Milborne Gro. SW10 . . . . 6A 16 (5A 100)
Milborne St. E9 . . . . 6J 67
Milborough Cres. SE12 . . . . 6G 123
Milburn Dr. UB7: Yiew 7A 74
Milcote St. SE1 . . . . 7A 14 (2B 102)
Mildenhall Rd. E5 . . . . 4J 67
Mildmay Av. N1 . . . . 6D 66
Mildmay Gro. Nth. N1 . . . . 5D 66
Mildmay Gro. Sth. N1 . . . . 5D 66
Mildmay Pk. N1 . . . . 5D 66
Mildmay Pl. N16 . . . . 5E 66
Mildmay Rd. IG1: Ilf 3F 71
N1 . . . . 5D 66
RM7: Rom 5J 55
Mildmay St. N1 . . . . 6D 66
Mildred Av. UB3: Harl 4F 93
UB5: N'olt 5F 59
Mildred Ct. CR0: C'don 1G 169
Mildred Rd. DA8: Erith 5K 109
Mildrose Ct. NW6 . . . . 3J 81
(off Malvern M.)
Mildura Ct. N8 . . . . 4K 47
MILE END 4B 86
Mile End, The E17 . . . . 1K 49
Mile End Pk. 4A 86
Mile End Pk. Leisure Cen. 5A 86
Mile End Pl. E1 . . . . 4K 85
Mile End Rd. E1 . . . . 5J 85
E3 . . . . 5J 85
Mile End Stadium 5B 86
Mile Rd. SM6: Bedd, Wall 1F 167
(not continuous)
Miles Bldgs. NW1 . . . . 5C 4
(off Penfold Pl.)
Miles Cl. SE28 . . . . 1H 107
Miles Ct. CR0: C'don 2B 168
(off Cuthbert Rd.)
E1 . . . . 6H 85
(off Tillman St.)
Miles Dr. SE28 . . . . 1J 107
Miles Ho. SE10 . . . . 5G 105
(off Tuskar St.)
Miles Lodge HA1: Harr 5H 41
Milespit Hill NW7 . . . . 5J 29
Miles Pl. KT5: Surb 4F 151
NW1 . . . . 5B 4
Miles Rd. CR4: Mitc 3C 154
N8 . . . . 3J 47
Miles St. SW8 . . . . 7E 18 (6J 101)
(not continuous)
Milestone Cl. N9 . . . . 2B 34
SM2: Sutt 6B 166
MILESTONE GREEN 4J 115
Milestone Ho. KT1: King T 3D 150
(off Surbiton Rd.)
Milestone Rd. SE19 . . . . 6F 139
Miles Way N20 . . . . 2H 31
Milfoil St. W12 . . . . 7C 80
Milford Cl. SE2 . . . . 6E 108
Milford Ct. UB1: S'hall 1E 94
Milford Gdns. CR0: C'don 5J 157
HA0: Wemb 4D 60
HA8: Edg 7B 28
Milford Gro. SM1: Sutt 4A 166
Milford La. WC2 . . . . 2H 13 (7A 84)
Milford M. SW16 . . . . 3K 137
Milford Rd. UB1: S'hall 7E 76
W13 . . . . 1B 96
Milford Towers SE6 . . . . 7D 122
Milk St. BR1: Brom 6K 141
E16 . . . . 1F 107
EC2 . . . . 7D 8 (6C 84)
Milkwell Gdns. IG8: Wfd G 7E 36
Milkwell Yd. SE5 . . . . 1C 120

Milkwood Rd. SE24 5B 120
Milk Yd. E1 7J 85
Millais Av. E12 5E 70
Millais Ct. *UB5: N'olt* *2B 76*
(*off Academy Gdns.*)
Millais Cres. KT19: Ewe 5A 164
Millais Gdns. HA8: Edg 2G 43
Millais Ho. *SW1* *4E 18*
(*off Marsham St.*)
Millais Rd. E11 4E 68
EN1: Enf 5A 24
KT3: N Mald 7A 152
Millais Way KT19: Ewe 4J 163
Millard Cl. N16 5E 66
Millard Ter. RM10: Dag 6G 73
Millbank SM6: Wall 5H 167
SW1 2E 18 (3J 101)
Millbank Ct. SW1 3E 18
Millbank Twr. SW1 4E 18 (4J 101)
Millbank Way SE12 5J 123
Millbourne Rd. TW13: Hanw 4C 130
Mill Bri. EN5: Barn 6C 20
Millbrook Av. DA16: Well 4H 125
Millbrook Gdns. RM6: Chad H 6F 55
Millbrook Ho. *SE15* *6G 103*
(*off Peckham Pk. Rd.*)
Millbrook Pas. SW9 3B 120
Millbrook Pl. *NW1* *2G 83*
(*off Hampstead Rd.*)
Millbrook Rd. N9 1C 34
SW9 3B 120
Mill Cl. SM5: Cars 2E 166
Mill Cnr. EN5: Barn 1C 20
Mill Ct. E10 3E 68
SE28 *7B 90*
(*off Titmuss Av.*)
Millcroft Ho. *SE6* *4E 140*
(*off Melfield Gdns.*)
Millender Wlk. *SE16* *4J 103*
(*off New Rotherhithe Rd.*)
Millennium Arena 7E 100
Millennium Bridge 3B 14 (7B 84)
Millennium Bri. Ho. *EC4* *2C 14*
(*off Up. Thames St.*)
Millennium Bus. Cen. NW2 2D 62
Millennium Cen., The 4K 73
Millennium Cl. E16 6K 87
Millennium Dome
The O2 1G 105
Millennium Dr. E14 4F 105
Millennium Ho. E17 5K 49
Millennium Pl. E2 2H 85
Millennium Sq. SE1 6K 15 (2F 103)
Millennium Way SE10 2G 105
Miller Av. EN3: Enf L 1H 25
Miller Cl. BR1: Brom 5K 141
CR4: Mitc 7D 154
HA5: Pinn 2A 40
RM5: Col R 1G 55
Miller Ct. DA7: Bex 3J 127
Miller Rd. CR0: C'don 1K 167
SW19 6B 136
Miller's Av. E8 5F 67
Millers Cl. NW7 4H 29
Millers Ct. *HA0: Wemb* *2E 78*
(*off Vicars Bri. Cl.*)
Millers Grn. Cl. EN2: Enf 3G 23
Millers Mdw. Cl. SE3 4H 123
Miller's Ter. E8 5F 67
Miller St. NW1 2G 83
(not continuous)
Millers Way W6 2E 98
Millers Wharf Ho. *E1* *5K 15*
(*off St Katherine's Way*)
Millers Yd. N3 1K 45
Miller Wlk. SE1 5K 13 (1A 102)
Millet Rd. UB6: G'frd 2F 77
Mill Farm Av. TW16: Sun 7G 129
Mill Farm Bus. Pk.
TW4: Houn 7C 112
Mill Farm Cl. HA5: Pinn 2A 40
Mill Farm Cres.
TW4: Houn 1C 130
Millfield KT1: King T 3F 151
N4 2A 66
TW16: Sun 1F 147
Millfield Av. E17 1A 50
Millfield La. N6 1C 64
(not continuous)
Millfield Pl. N6 2E 64
Millfield Rd. HA8: Edg 2J 43
TW4: Houn 1C 130
Millfields Rd. E5 4J 67
Millfield Theatre 4J 33
Mill Gdns. SE26 3H 139
Mill Grn. CR4: Mitc 7E 154
Mill Grn. Bus. Pk. CR4: Mitc 7E 154
Mill Grn. Rd. CR4: Mitc 7D 154
Millgrove St. SW11 1E 118
Millharbour E14 2D 104
Millhaven Cl. RM6: Chad H 6B 54
MILL HILL 5F 29
Mill Hill SW13 2C 116
MILL HILL CIRCUS 5G 29
Mill Hill Gro. W3 1J 97
Mill Hill Ind. Est. NW7 6G 29
Mill Hill Rd. SW13 2C 116
W3 2H 97
Mill Hill School Leisure Cen. 4H 29
Mill Hill Ter. W3 1H 97
Mill Ho. IG8: Wfd G 5C 36
Millhouse Pl. SE27 4B 138
Millicent Fawcett Ct. N17 1F 49
Millicent Preston Ho. *IG11: Bark* *1H 89*
(*off Ripple Rd.*)
Millicent Rd. E10 1B 68
Milligan St. E14 7B 86
Milliners Ho. *SE1* *7H 15*
(*off Bermondsey St.*)
SW18 4J 117
Milling Rd. HA8: Edg 7E 28
Millington Ho. N16 3D 66
Millington Rd. UB3: Harl 3G 93
Mill La. CR0: Wadd 3K 167
E4 3J 25
IG8: Wfd G 5C 36
KT17: Ewe 7B 164
NW6 5H 63
RM6: Chad H 6E 54
SE18 5E 106
SM5: Cars 4D 166
Mill La. Trad. Est. CR0: Wadd 3K 167
Millman Ct. *WC1* *4G 7*
(*off Millman Ct.*)
Millman M. WC1 4G 7 (4K 83)
Millman Pl. *WC1* *4G 7*
(*off Millman St.*)
Millman St. WC1 4G 7 (4K 83)
Millmark Gro. SE14 2A 122
Millmarsh La. EN3: Brim 2F 25
Millmead Ind. Cen. N17 2H 49
Mill Mead Rd. N17 3H 49
MILL MEADS 2F 87
Mill Pl. BR7: Chst 1E 160
E14 6A 86
KT1: King T 3F 151
Mill Plat TW7: Isle 2A 114
(not continuous)
Mill Plat Av. TW7: Isle 2A 114
Mill Pond Cl. SW8 7H 101
Millpond Est. SE16 2H 103
Millpond Pl. SM5: Cars 3E 166
Mill Ridge HA8: Edg 5A 28
Mill River Trad. Est.
EN3: Pond E 3F 25
Mill Rd. DA8: Erith 7J 109
E16 1K 105
IG1: Ilf 3E 70
SW19 7A 136
TW2: Twick 2G 131
Mill Row DA5: Bexl 1H 145
N1 1E 84
Mills Cl. UB10: Hil 2C 74
Mills Ct. EC2 3G 9
Mills Gro. E14 6E 86
NW4 3F 45
Millshot Cl. SW6 1E 116
Mills Ho. E17 3F 51
SW8 *1G 119*
(*off Thessaly Rd.*)
Millside SM5: Cars 2D 166
Millside Pl. TW7: Isle 2B 114
Millson Cl. N20 2G 31
Mills Row W4 4K 97
Millstone Cl. E15 6F 69
Millstream Cl. N13 5F 33
Millstream Ho. *SE16* *2H 103*
(*off Jamaica Rd.*)
Millstream Rd. SE1 7J 15 (2F 103)
Mill St. KT1: King T 3E 150
SE1 7K 15 (2F 103)
W1 2A 12 (7F 83)
Mill Trad. Est., The
NW10 3J 79
Mill Va. BR2: Brom 2H 159
Mill Vw. Cl. KT17: Ewe 7B 164
Mill Vw. Gdns. CR0: C'don 3K 169
MILLWALL 4D 104
Millwall Dock Rd. E14 3C 104
Millwall FC 5J 103
Millwall Pk. 4E 104
Mill Way TW14: Felt 5K 111
Millway NW7 4F 29
Millway Gdns. UB5: N'olt 6D 58
Millwood Rd. TW3: Houn 5G 113
Millwood St. W10 5G 81
Mill Yd. E1 7G 85
Mill Yd. Ind. Est. HA8: Edg 1H 43
Milman Cl. HA5: Pinn 3B 40
Milman Rd. NW6 2F 81
Milman's Ho. *SW1* *5J 17*
(*off Warwick Way*)
SW10 *6B 100*
(*off Milman's St.*)
Milman's St. SW10 6B 100
Milne Ct. E18 1J 51
Milne Gdns. SE9 5C 124
Milne Ho. *SE18* *4D 106*
(*off Ogilby St.*)
Milner Ct. *SE15* *7F 103*
(*off Colegrove Rd.*)
Milner Dr. TW2: Whitt 7H 113
Milner Pl. N1 1A 84
SM5: Cars 4E 166
Milner Rd. CR7: Thor H 3D 156
E16 3G 87
KT1: King T 3D 150
RM8: Dag 2C 72
SM4: Mord 5B 154
SW19 1K 153
Milner Sq. N1 7B 66
Milner St. SW3 3E 16 (4D 100)
Milner Wlk. SE9 2H 143
Milnthorpe Rd.
W4 6K 97
Milo Gdns. SE22 6F 121
Milo Rd. SE22 6F 121
Milrood Ho. *E1* *5K 85*
(*off Stepney Grn.*)
Milroy Wlk. SE1 4A 14 (1B 102)
Milson Rd. W14 3F 99
Milstead Ho. E5 5H 67
Milton Av.
CR0: C'don 7D 156
E6 7B 70
EN5: Barn 5C 20
N6 7G 47
NW9 3J 43
NW10 1J 79
SM1: Sutt 3B 166
Milton Cl. N2 5A 46
SE1 4F 103
SM1: Sutt 3B 166
UB4: Hayes 6J 75
Milton Ct. E17 4C 50
EC2 5E 8 (5D 84)
RM6: Chad H 7C 54
SE14 6B 104
(not continuous)
Milton Ct. SW18 5J 117
TW2: Twick 3J 131
UB10: Ick 3D 56
Milton Ct. Rd. SE14 6A 104
Milton Ct. Wlk. *EC2* *5E 8*
(*off Silk St.*)
Milton Cres. IG2: Ilf 7F 53
Milton Dr. TW17: Shep 4A 146
Milton Gdn. Est. N16 4D 66
Milton Gdns. TW19: Stanw 1B 128
Milton Gro. N11 5B 32
N16 4D 66
Milton Ho. *E2* *3J 85*
(*off Roman Rd.*)
E17 4C 50
SE5 *7D 102*
(*off Elmington Est.*)
SM1: Sutt 3J 165
Milton Lodge DA14: Sidc 4A 144
TW2: Twick 7K 113
Milton Mans. *W14* *6G 99*
(*off Queen's Club Gdns.*)
Milton Pk. N6 7G 47
Milton Pl. *N7* *5A 66*
(*off Eastwood Cl.*)
Milton Rd. CR0: C'don 7D 156
CR4: Mitc 7E 136
DA16: Well 1K 125
DA17: Belv 4G 109
E17 4C 50
HA1: Harr 4J 41
N6 7G 47
N15 4B 48
NW7 5H 29
NW9 7C 44
SE24 5B 120
SM1: Sutt 3J 165
SM6: Wall 6G 167
SW14 3K 115
SW19 6A 136
TW12: Hamp 7E 130
UB10: Ick 4D 56
W3 1K 97
W7 7K 77
Milton St. EC2 5E 8 (5D 84)
Milton Way UB7: W Dray 4B 92
Milverton Dr. UB10: Ick 4E 56
Milverton Gdns. IG3: Ilf 2K 71
Milverton Ho. SE6 3A 140
Milverton Rd. NW6 7E 62
Milverton St. SE11 6K 19 (5A 102)
Milverton Way SE9 4E 142
Milward St. E1 5H 85
Milward Wlk. SE18 6E 106
Mimosa Ho. UB4: Yead 5A 76
Mimosa Lodge NW10 5B 62
Mimosa Rd. UB4: Yead 5A 76
Mimosa St. SW6 1H 117
Minard Rd. SE6 7G 123
Mina Rd. SE17 5E 102
SW19 1J 153
Minchenden Ct. N14 2C 32
Minchenden Cres. N14 3B 32
Minchin Ho. *E14* *6C 86*
(*off Dod St.*)
Mincing La. EC3 2G 15 (7E 84)
Minden Rd. SE20 1H 157
SM3: Sutt 2G 165
Minehead Rd. HA2: Harr 3E 58
SW16 5K 137
Mineral Cl. EN5: Barn 6A 20

Mineral St. SE18 4J 107
Minera M. SW1 3G 17 (4E 100)
Minerva Cl. DA14: Sidc 3J 143
SW9 7A 102
TW19: Stan M 7B 174
Minerva Lodge N7 6K 65
Minerva Rd. E4 7J 35
KT1: King T 2F 151
NW10 4J 79
Minerva St. E2 2H 85
Minerva Wlk. EC1 7B 8 (6B 84)
Minet Av. NW10 2A 80
Minet Country Pk. 2K 93
Minet Dr. UB3: Hayes 1J 93
Minet Gdns. NW10 2A 80
UB3: Hayes 1K 93
Minet Rd. SW9 2B 120
Minford Gdns. W14 2F 99
Minford Ho. W14 2F 99
(off Minford Gdns.)
Mingard Wlk. N7 2K 65
Ming St. E14 7C 86
Minimax Cl. TW14: Felt 6J 111
Ministry Way SE9 2D 142
Miniver Pl. EC4 2D 14
Mink Ct. TW4: Houn 2A 112
Minniedale KT5: Surb 5F 151
Minnow St. SE17 4E 102
Minnow Wlk. SE17 4E 102
Minories EC3 1J 15 (6F 85)
Minshaw Ct. DA14: Sidc 4K 143
Minshill St. SW8 1H 119
Minshull Pl. BR3: Beck 7C 140
Minson Rd. E9 1K 85
Minstead Gdns. SW15 7B 116
Minstead Way KT3: N Mald 6A 152
Minster Av. SM1: Sutt 2J 165
Minster Ct. EC3 2H 15
W5 4E 78
Minster Dr. CR0: C'don 4E 168
Minster Gdns. KT8: W Mole 4D 148
Minsterley Av.
TW17: Shep 4G 147
Minster Pavement EC3 2H 15
(off Mincing La.)
Minster Rd. BR1: Brom 7K 141
NW2 5G 63
Minster Wlk. N8 4J 47
Minstrel Gdns. KT5: Surb 4F 151
Mint Bus. Pk. E16 5K 87
Mint Cl. UB10: Hil 3D 74
Mintern Cl. N13 3G 33
Minterne Av. UB2: S'hall 4E 94
Minterne Rd. HA3: Kent 5F 43
Minterne Waye UB4: Yead 6A 76
Mintern St. N1 2D 84
Minton Ho. SE11 3J 19
Minton M. NW6 6K 63
Mint Rd. SM6: Wall 4F 167
Mint St. SE1 6C 14 (2C 102)
Mint Wlk. CR0: C'don 3C 168
Mirabel Rd. SW6 7H 99
Miranda Cl. E1 5J 85
Miranda Ct. W3 6F 79
Miranda Ho. N1 1G 9
(off Arden Est.)
Miranda Rd. N19 1G 65
Mirfield St. SE7 4B 106
Miriam Rd. SE18 5J 107
Mirravale Trad. Est. RM8: Dag 7E 54
Mirren Cl. HA2: Harr 4D 58
Mirror Path SE9 3A 142
Misbourne Rd. UB10: Hil 1C 74
Missenden SE17 5D 102
(off Roland Way)
Missenden Cl. TW14: Felt 1H 129
Missenden Gdns. SM4: Mord 6A 154
Missenden Ho. NW8 3C 4
Mission, The E14 6B 86
(off Commercial Rd.)
Mission Gro. E17 5A 50
Mission Pl. SE15 1G 121
Mission Sq. TW8: Bford 6E 96
Missouri Ct. HA5: Eastc 6A 40
Mistletoe Cl. CR0: C'don 1K 169
Mistral SE5 1E 120
Misty's Fld. KT12: Walt T 7A 148
Mitali Pas. E1 6G 85
MITCHAM 3D 154
Mitcham Gdn. Village
CR4: Mitc 5E 154
Mitcham Ho. SE5 1C 120
Mitcham Ind. Est.
CR4: Mitc 1E 154
Mitcham La. SW16 6G 137
Mitcham Pk. CR4: Mitc 4C 154
Mitcham Rd. CR0: C'don 6J 155
E6 3C 88
IG3: Ilf 7K 53
SW17 5D 136
Mitchell NW9 1B 44
(off The Concourse)
Mitchellbrook Way NW10 6K 61
Mitchell Cl. DA17: Belv 3J 109
SE2 4C 108
Mitchell Ho. N1 7B 66
(off College Cross)
W12 7D 80
(off White City Est.)
Mitchell Rd. BR6: Orp 4K 173
N13 5H 33
Mitchell's Pl. SE21 6E 120
(off Aysgarth Rd.)
Mitchell St. EC1 3C 8 (4C 84)
(not continuous)
Mitchell Wlk. E6 5C 88
(off Allhallows Rd.)
E6 5D 88
(Elmley Cl.)
Mitchell Way BR1: Brom 1J 159
NW10 6J 61
Mitchison Rd. N1 6D 66
Mitchley Rd. N17 3G 49
Mitford Bldgs. SW6 7J 99
(off Dawes Rd.)
Mitford Cl. KT9: Chess 6C 162
Mitford Rd. N19 2J 65
Mitre, The E14 7B 86
Mitre Av. E17 3C 50
Mitre Bri. Ind. Pk. W10 4D 80
(not continuous)
Mitre Cl. BR2: Brom 2H 159
SM2: Sutt 7A 166
TW17: Shep 6F 147
Mitre Ct. EC2 7D 8
Mitre Ho. SW3 5E 16
(off King's Rd.)
Mitre Rd. E15 2G 87
SE1 6K 13 (2A 102)
Mitre Sq. EC3 1H 15 (6E 84)
Mitre St. EC3 1H 15 (6E 84)
Mitre Way W10 4D 80
Mitre Yd. SW3 3D 16 (4C 100)
Mizen Ct. E14 2C 104
(off Alpha Gro.)
Mizzen Mast Ho. SE18 3D 106
Moat, The KT3: N Mald 1A 152
Moat Cl. BR6: Chels 6K 173
Moat Ct. DA15: Sidc 3K 143
SE9 6D 124
Moat Cres. N3 3K 45
Moat Cft. DA16: Well 3C 126
Moat Dr. E13 2A 88
HA1: Harr 4G 41
HA4: Ruis 7G 39
Moat Farm Rd. UB5: N'olt 6D 58
Moatfield NW6 7G 63
Moatlands Ho. WC1 2F 7
(off Cromer St.)
Moat La. KT8: E Mos 3K 149
Moat Lodge, The HA2: Harr 2J 59
Moat Pl. SW9 3K 119
W3 6H 79
Moat Side EN3: Pond E 4E 24
TW13: Hanw 4A 130
Moberly Rd. SW4 7H 119
Moberly Sports & Education Cen. 3F 81
(off Chamberlayne Rd.)
Mobil Ct. WC2 1H 13
(off Clement's Inn)
MOBY DICK 4E 54
Mocatta Ho. E1 4H 85
(off Brady St.)
Modbury Gdns. NW5 6E 64
Modder Pl. SW15 4F 117
Model Bldgs. WC1 2H 7
Model Cotts. SW14 4J 115
W13 2B 96
Model Farm Cl. SE9 3C 142
Modern Ct. EC4 7A 8
Modling Ho. E2 2K 85
(off Mace St.)
Moelwyn N7 5H 65
Moelyn M. HA1: Harr 5A 42
Moffat Ct. SW19 5J 135
Moffat Ho. SE5 7C 102
Moffat Rd. CR7: Thor H 2C 156
N13 6D 32
SW17 4D 136
Mogden La. TW7: Isle 5K 113
Mohammedi Pk. UB5: N'olt 1E 76
Mohawk Ho. E3 2A 86
(off Gernon Rd.)
Mohmmad Khan Rd.
E11 1H 69
Moineau NW9 1B 44
(off The Concourse)
Moira Cl. N17 2E 48
Moira Rd. SE9 4D 124
Mokswell Ct. N10 1E 46
Molasses Ho. SW11 3A 118
(off Clove Hitch Quay)
Molasses Row SW11 3A 118
Mole Abbey Gdns.
KT8: W Mole 3F 149
Mole Ct. KT19: Ewe 4J 163
Mole Ho. NW8 4B 4
(off Church St. Est.)
Molember Ct. KT8: E Mos 4J 149
Molember Rd. KT8: E Mos 5J 149
Molescroft SE9 3G 143
Molesey Av. KT8: W Mole 5D 148
Molesey Dr. SM3: Cheam 2G 165
Molesey Pk. Av. KT8: W Mole 5F 149
Molesey Pk. Cl. KT8: E Mos 5G 149
Molesey Pk. Rd.
KT8: W Mole, E Mos 5F 149
Molesey Rd. KT8: W Mole 7C 148
KT12: Walt T, W Mole 7C 148
Molesford Rd. SW6 1J 117
Molesham Cl. KT8: W Mole 3F 149
Molesham Way KT8: W Mole 3F 149
Molesworth Ho. SE17 6B 102
(off Brandon Est.)
Molesworth St. SE13 4E 122
Moliner Ct. BR3: Beck 7C 140
Mollis Ho. E3 5C 86
(off Gale St.)
Mollison Av.
EN3: Brim, Enf L, Enf W, Pond E
4F 25
Mollison Dr. SM6: Wall 7H 167
Mollison Sq. SM6: Wall 7H 167
(off Mollison Dr.)
Mollison Way HA8: Edg 2F 43
Molly Huggins Cl. SW12 7G 119
Molton Ho. N1 1K 83
(off Barnsbury Est.)
Molyneux Dr. SW17 4F 137
Molyneux St. W1 6D 4 (5C 82)
Monarch Cl. BR4: W W'ck 4H 171
TW14: Felt 7G 111
Monarch Ct. N2 5B 46
Monarch Dr. E16 5B 88
Monarch Ho. W8 3J 99
(off Earl's Ct. Rd.)
W8 3J 99
(off Kensington High St.)
Monarch M. E17 6D 50
SW16 5A 138
Monarch Pde. CR4: Mitc 2D 154
Monarch Pl. IG9: Buck H 2F 37
Monarch Point SW6 2A 118
Monarch Rd. DA17: Belv 3G 109
Monarchs Way HA4: Ruis 1F 57
Monarch Way IG2: Ilf 6H 53
Mona Rd. SE15 2J 121
Monastery Gdns. EN2: Enf 2J 23
Mona St. E16 5H 87
Monaveen Gdns. KT8: W Mole 3F 149
Moncks Row SW18 6H 117
Monck St. SW1 2D 18 (3H 101)
Monckton Ct. W14 3H 99
(off Strangways Ter.)
Monclar Rd. SE5 4D 120
Moncorvo Cl. SW7 7C 10 (2C 100)
Moncrieff Cl. E6 6C 88
Moncrieff Pl. SE15 2G 121
Moncrieff St. SE15 2G 121
Monday All. N16 2F 67
(off High St.)
Mondial Way UB3: Harl 7E 92
Monega Rd. E7 6A 70
E12 6A 70
Monet Ct. SE16 5H 103
(off Stubbs Dr.)
Moneyer Ho. N1 1E 8
(off Provost Est.)
Money La. UB7: W Dray 3A 92
Mongers Almshouses E9 7K 67
(off Church Cres.)
Monica Ct. EN1: Enf 5K 23
Monica James Ho. DA14: Sidc 3A 144
Monica Shaw Ct. NW1 1D 6
(off Purchese St., not continuous)
Monier Rd. E3 7C 68
Monivea Rd. BR3: Beck 7B 140
Monk Ct. W12 1C 98
Monk Dr. E16 7J 87
MONKEN HADLEY 2C 20
Monkfrith Av. N14 6A 22
Monkfrith Cl. N14 7A 22
Monkfrith Way N14 7K 21
Monkham's Av. IG8: Wfd G 5E 36
Monkham's Dr. IG8: Wfd G 5E 36
Monkham's La.
IG8: Wfd G 5D 36
IG9: Buck H 3E 36
Monkleigh Rd. SM4: Mord 3G 153
Monk Pas. E16 7J 87
(off Monk Dr.)
Monks Av. EN5: New Bar 6F 21
KT8: W Mole 5D 148
Monks Cl. EN2: Enf 2H 23
HA2: Harr 2E 58
HA4: Ruis 4B 58
SE2 4D 108
Monks Cres. KT12: Walt T 7K 147
Monksdene Gdns.
SM1: Sutt 3K 165
Monks Dr. W3 5G 79
Monks Hill Sports Cen. 7K 169
MONKS ORCHARD 7A 158
Monks Orchard Rd.
BR3: Beck 1C 170
Monks Pk. HA9: Wemb 6H 61
Monks Pk. Gdns.
HA9: Wemb 7H 61
Monks Rd. EN2: Enf 2G 23
Monk St. SE18 4E 106

Monks Way BR3: Beck .6C 158
BR5: Farnb .1G 173
NW11 .4H 45
UB7: Harm .6A 92
Monkswood Gdns.
IG5: Ilf .3E 52
Monkton Ho. E5 .5H 67
SE16 .*2K 103*
(off Wolfe Cres.)
Monkton Rd. DA16: Well .2K 125
Monkton St. SE11 .3K 19 (4A 102)
Monkville Av. NW11 .4H 45
Monkville Pde. NW11 .4H 45
Monkwell Sq. EC2 .6D 8 (5C 84)
Monmouth Av. E18 .3K 51
KT1: Ham W .7C 132
Monmouth Cl. CR4: Mitc .4J 155
DA16: Well .4A 126
W4 .3J 97
Monmouth Ct. *W7* .*5K 77*
(off Copley Cl.)
Monmouth Gro. TW8: Bford .4E 96
Monmouth Pl. *W2* .*6K 81*
(off Monmouth Rd.)
Monmouth Rd. E6 .3D 88
N9 .2C 34
RM9: Dag .5F 73
UB3: Harl .4G 93
W2 .6J 81
Monmouth St. WC2 .1E 12 (6J 83)
Monnery Rd. N19 .3G 65
Monnow Rd. SE1 .5G 103
Mono La. TW13: Felt .2K 129
Monoux Almshouses E17 .4D 50
Monoux Gro. E17 .1C 50
Monroe Cres. EN1: Enf .1C 24
Monroe Dr. SW14 .5H 115
Monroe Ho. *NW8* .*2D 4*
(off Lorne Cl.)
Monro Gdns. HA3: Hrw W .7D 26
Monro Way E5 .4G 67
Monsell Ct. N4 .3B 66
Monsell Rd. N4 .3A 66
Monson Rd. NW10 .2C 80
SE14 .7K 103
Mons Way BR2: Brom .6C 160
Montacute Rd.
CR0: New Ad .7E 170
SE6 .7B 122
SM4: Mord .6B 154
WD23: B Hea .1E 26
Montagu Ct. *W1* .*6F 5*
(off Montagu Sq.)
Montagu Cres. N18 .4C 34
Montague Av. SE4 .4B 122
W7 .1K 95
Montague Cl. EN5: Barn .4C 20
KT12: Walt T .7K 147
SE1 .4E 14 (1D 102)
Montague Ct. DA15: Sidc .3A 144
N7 .*7A 66*
(off St Clements St.)
Montague Gdns. W3 .7G 79
Montague Ho. *E16* .*1K 105*
(off Wesley Av.)
IG3: Ilf .1A 72
N1 .*1E 84*
(off New Era Est.)
Montague Pas. UB8: Uxb .7A 56
Montague Pl. WC1 .5D 6 (5H 83)
Montague Rd. CR0: C'don .1B 168
E8 .5G 67
E11 .2H 69
N8 .5K 47
N15 .4G 49
SW19 .7K 135
TW3: Houn .3F 113
TW10: Rich .6E 114
UB2: S'hall .4C 94
UB8: Uxb .7A 56
Montague Rd. W7 .1K 95
W13 .6B 78
Montague Sq. SE15 .7J 103
Montague St. EC1 .6C 8 (5C 84)
WC1 .5E 6 (5J 83)
Montague Ter. BR2: Brom .4H 159
Montague Walks
HA0: Wemb .1F 79
Montague Waye UB2: S'hall .3C 94
Montagu Gdns. N18 .4C 34
SM6: Wall .4G 167
Montagu Mans. W1 .5F 5 (5D 82)
Montagu M. Nth. W1 .6F 5 (5D 82)
Montagu M. Sth. W1 .7F 5 (6D 82)
Montagu M. W. W1 .7F 5 (6D 82)
Montagu Pl. W1 .6E 4 (5D 82)
Montagu Rd. N9 .4C 34
N18 .5C 34
NW4 .6C 44
Montagu Rd. Ind. Est. N18 .4D 34
Montagu Row W1 .6F 5 (5D 82)
Montagu Sq. W1 .6F 5 (5D 82)
Montagu St. W1 .7F 5 (6D 82)
Montaigne Cl. SW1 .4D 18 (4H 101)
Montalt Rd. IG8: Wfd G .4C 36
Montana Bldg. *SE10* .*1D 122*
(off Deal's Gateway)
Montana Gdns. SE26 .5B 140
SM1: Sutt .5A 166
Montana Rd. SW17 .3E 136
SW20 .1E 152
Montbelle Rd. SE9 .3F 143
Montcalm Cl. BR2: Hayes .6J 159
UB4: Yead .3K 75
Montcalm Ho. E14 .4B 104
Montcalm Rd. SE7 .7B 106
Montclare St. E2 .3J 9 (4F 85)
Monteagle Av. IG11: Bark .6G 71
Monteagle Ct. N1 .2E 84
Monteagle Way E5 .3G 67
SE15 .3H 121
Montefiore Ct. N16 .1F 67
Montefiore St. SW8 .2F 119
Montego Cl. SE24 .4A 120
Montem Rd. KT3: N Mald .4A 152
SE23 .7B 122
Montem St. N4 .1K 65
Montenotte Rd. N8 .5G 47
Monterey Cl. DA5: Bexl .2J 145
NW7 .5F 29
Monterey Studios W10 .2G 81
Montesole Ct. HA5: Pinn .2A 40
Montesquieu Ter. *E16* .*6H 87*
(off Clarkson Rd.)
Montevetro SW11 .1B 118
Montford Pl. SE11 .6J 19 (5A 102)
Montford Rd. TW16: Sun .4J 147
Montfort Ho. *E2* .*3J 85*
(off Victoria Pk. Sq.)
E14 .*3E 104*
(off Galbraith St.)
Montfort Pl. SW19 .1F 135
Montgolfier Wlk. UB5: N'olt .3C 76
Montgomerie M. SE23 .7J 121
Montgomery Cl. CR4: Mitc .4J 155
DA15: Sidc .6K 125
Montgomery Ct. *CR2: S Croy* .*5E 168*
(off Birdhurst Rd.)
W4 .7J 97
Montgomery Gdns. SM2: Sutt .7B 166
Montgomery Ho. *W2* .*6A 4*
(off Harrow Rd.)
Montgomery Lodge *E1* .*4J 85*
(off Cleveland Gro.)
Montgomery Rd. HA8: Edg .6A 28
W4 .4J 97
Montgomery St. E14 .1D 104
Montholme Rd. SW11 .6D 118
Monthope Rd. E1 .6K 9 (5G 85)
Montolieu Gdns. SW15 .5D 116
Montpelier Av. DA5: Bexl .7D 126
W5 .5C 78
Montpelier Cl. UB10: Hil .1C 74
Montpelier Ct. *BR2: Brom* .*4H 159*
(off Westmoreland Rd.)
W5 .5D 78
Montpelier Gdns. E6 .3B 88
RM6: Chad H .7C 54
Montpelier Gro. NW5 .5G 65
Montpelier M. SW7 .1D 16 (3C 100)
Montpelier Pl. E1 .6J 85
SW7 .1D 16 (3C 100)
Montpelier Ri. HA9: Wemb .1D 60
NW11 .7G 45
Montpelier Rd. N3 .1A 46
SE15 .1H 121
SM1: Sutt .4A 166
W5 .5D 78
Montpelier Row SE3 .2H 123
TW1: Twick .7C 114
Montpelier Sq. SW7 .7D 10 (2C 100)
Montpelier St. SW7 .1D 16 (3C 100)
Montpelier Ter. SW7 .7D 10 (2C 100)
Montpelier Va. SE3 .2H 123
Montpelier Wlk. SW7 .1D 16 (3C 100)
Montpelier Way NW11 .7G 45
Montpellier Ct.
KT12: Walt T .6J 147
Montrave Rd. SE20 .6J 139
Montreal Pl. WC2 .2G 13 (7K 83)
Montreal Rd. IG1: Ilf .7G 53
Montrell Rd. SW2 .1J 137
Montrose Av. DA15: Sidc .7A 126
DA16: Well .3H 125
HA8: Edg .2J 43
NW6 .2G 81
TW2: Whitt .7F 113
Montrose Cl. DA16: Well .3K 125
IG8: Wfd G .4D 36
TW15: Ashf .6E 128
Montrose Ct. HA1: Harr .5F 41
NW9 .2J 43
NW11 .4H 45
SE6 .2H 141
SW7 .7B 10 (2B 100)
Montrose Cres. HA0: Wemb .6E 60
N12 .6F 31
Montrose Gdns. CR4: Mitc .2D 154
SM1: Sutt .2K 165
Montrose Ho. E14 .3C 104
SW1 .*7H 11*
(off Montrose Pl.)
Montrose Pl. SW1 .7H 11 (2E 100)
Montrose Rd. HA3: W'stone .2J 41
TW14: Bedf .6F 111
Montrose Wlk. HA7: Stan .6G 27
Montrose Way SE23 .1K 139
Montserrat Av. IG8: Wfd G .7A 36
Montserrat Cl. SE19 .5D 138
Montserrat Rd. SW15 .4G 117
Monument, The .3F 15 (7D 84)
Monument Gdns. SE13 .5E 122
Monument St. EC3 .2F 15 (7D 84)
Monument Way N17 .3F 49
Monza St. E1 .7J 85
Moodkee St. SE16 .3J 103
Moody Rd. SE15 .1F 121
Moody St. E1 .3K 85
Moon Ct. SE12 .4J 123
Moon La. EN5: Barn .3C 20
Moon St. N1 .1B 84
Moorcroft HA8: Edg .1H 43
Moorcroft Gdns.
BR2: Brom .5C 160
Moorcroft La. UB8: Hil .5C 74
Moorcroft Rd. SW16 .3J 137
Moorcroft Way HA5: Pinn .5C 40
Moordown SE18 .7F 107
Moore Cl. CR4: Mitc .2F 155
SW14 .3J 115
Moore Ct. *N1* .*1B 84*
(off Gaskin St.)
Moore Cres. RM9: Dag .1B 90
Moorefield Rd. N17 .2F 49
Moorehead Way SE3 .3J 123
Moore Ho. *E1* .*7J 85*
(off Cable St.)
E2 .*3J 85*
(off Roman Rd.)
E14 .2C 104
N8 .*4J 47*
(off Pembroke Rd.)
SE10 .*5H 105*
(off Armitage Rd.)
Mooreland Rd. BR1: Brom .7H 141
Moore Pk. Ct. *SW6* .*7K 99*
(off Fulham Rd.)
Moore Pk. Rd. SW6 .7J 99
Moore Rd. SE19 .6C 138
Moore St. SW3 .3E 16 (4D 100)
Moore Wlk. E7 .4J 69
Moore Way SM2: Sutt .7J 165
Moorey Cl. E15 .1H 87
Moorfield Av. W5 .4D 78
Moorfield Rd. EN3: Enf H .1D 24
KT9: Chess .5E 162
UB8: Cowl .6A 74
Moorfields EC2 .6E 8 (5D 84)
Moorfields Highwalk *EC2* .*6E 8*
(off Moorfields, not continuous)
Moorgate EC2 .7E 8 (6D 84)
Moorgate Pl. EC2 .7E 8
Moorgreen Ho. EC1 .1A 8
Moorhouse NW9 .1B 44
Moorhouse Rd. HA3: Kent .3D 42
W2 .6J 81
Moorings, The *E16* .*5A 88*
(off Prince Regent La.)
Moorings Ho. TW8: Bford .7C 96
MOOR JUNC. .3C 174
Moorland Cl. RM5: Col R .1H 55
TW2: Whitt .7E 112
Moorland Rd. SW9 .4B 120
UB7: Harm .2D 174
Moorlands UB5: N'olt .1C 76
Moorlands Av. NW7 .6J 29
Moor La. EC2 .6E 8 (5D 84)
(not continuous)
KT9: Chess .4E 162
UB7: Harm .2D 174
Moormead Dr. KT19: Ewe .5A 164
Moor Mead Rd.
TW1: Twick .6A 114
Moor Pk. Gdns. KT2: King T .7A 134
Moor Pl. EC2 .6E 8 (5D 84)
Moorside Rd. BR1: Brom .3G 141
Moor St. W1 .1D 12 (6H 83)
Moot Ct. NW9 .5G 43
Moran Ho. *E1* .*1H 103*
(off Wapping La.)
Morant Pl. N22 .1K 47
Morant St. E14 .7C 86
Mora Rd. NW2 .4E 62
Mora St. EC1 .2D 8 (3C 84)
Morat St. SW9 .1K 119
Moravian Cl. SW10 .7A 16 (6B 100)
Moravian Pl. SW10 .6B 100
Moravian St. E2 .2J 85
Moray Av. UB3: Hayes .1H 93
Moray Cl. HA8: Edg .2C 28
RM1: Rom .1K 55
Moray Ct. *CR2: S Croy* .*5C 168*
(off Warham Rd.)
Moray Ho. *E1* .*4A 86*
(off Harford St.)
Moray M. N7 .2K 65
Moray Rd. N4 .2K 65
Moray Way RM1: Rom .1K 55
Mordaunt Gdns.
RM9: Dag .7E 72

Mordaunt Ho. *NW10* 1K 79
(off Stracey Rd.)
Mordaunt Rd. NW10 1K 79
Mordaunt St. SW9 3K 119
MORDEN 3K 153
Morden Ct. SM4: Mord 4K 153
Morden Ct. Pde.
SM4: Mord 4K 153
Morden Gdns. CR4: Mitc 4B 154
UB6: G'frd 5K 59
Morden Hall Rd. SM4: Mord 3K 153
Morden Hill SE13 2E 122
(not continuous)
Morden Ho. SM4: Mord 4J 153
Morden La. SE13 2E 122
MORDEN PARK 6G 153
Morden Pk. Pool 6H 153
Morden Rd. CR4: Mitc 4A 154
RM6: Chad H 7E 54
SE3 2J 123
SM4: Mord 4A 154
SW19 1K 153
Morden Rd. M. SE3 2J 123
Morden St. SE13 1D 122
Morden Way SM3: Sutt 7J 153
Morden Wharf *SE10* 3G 105
(off Morden Wharf Rd.)
Morden Wharf Rd. SE10 3G 105
Mordern Ho. NW1 3D 4
Mordon Rd. IG3: Ilf 7K 53
Mordred Rd. SE6 2G 141
Morecambe Cl. E1 5K 85
Morecambe Gdns. HA7: Stan 4J 27
Morecambe St. SE17 4C 102
Morecambe Ter. *N18* 4J 33
(off Gt. Cambridge Rd.)
More Cl. E16 6H 87
W14 4F 99
Morecoombe Cl. KT2: King T 7H 133
Moree Way N18 4B 34
Moreland Cotts. *E3* 2C 86
(off Fairfield Rd.)
Moreland Ct. NW2 3J 63
Moreland St. EC1 1B 8 (3B 84)
Moreland Way E4 3J 35
Morella Rd. SW12 7D 118
Morell Cl. EN5: New Bar 3F 21
Morello Av. UB8: Hil 5D 74
More London Pl. SE1 5G 15 (1E 102)
More London Riverside
SE1 5H 15 (1E 102)
Moremead Rd. SE6 4B 140
Morena St. SE6 7D 122
Moresby Av. KT5: Surb 7H 151
Moresby Rd. E5 1H 67
Moresby Wlk. SW8 2G 119
More's Gdn. *SW3* 6B 100
(off Cheyne Wlk.)
Moreton Av. TW7: Isle 1J 113
Moreton Cl. E5 2H 67
N15 6D 48
NW7 6K 29
SW1 5B 18
Moreton Gdns. IG8: Wfd G 5H 37
Moreton Ho. SE16 3H 103
Moreton Pl. SW1 5B 18 (5G 101)
Moreton Rd. CR2: S Croy 5D 168
KT4: Wor Pk 2C 164
N15 6D 48
Moreton St. SW1 5B 18 (5G 101)
Moreton Ter. SW1 5B 18 (5G 101)
Moreton Ter. M. Nth.
SW1 5B 18 (5G 101)
Moreton Ter. M. Sth.
SW1 5B 18 (5G 101)
Moreton Twr. W3 1H 97
Morford Cl. HA4: Ruis 7K 39
Morford Way HA4: Ruis 7K 39
Morgan Av. E17 4F 51
Morgan Cl. RM10: Dag 7G 73
Morgan Ct. SM5: Cars 4D 166
TW15: Ashf 5D 128
Morgan Ho. *SW1* 4B 18
(off Vauxhall Bri. Rd.)
SW8 1G 119
(off Wadhurst Rd.)
Morgan Mans. *N7* 5A 66
(off Morgan Rd.)
Morgan Rd. BR1: Brom 7J 141
N7 5A 66
W10 5H 81
Morgan's La. UB3: Hayes 5F 75
Morgan St. E3 3A 86
E16 5H 87
Morgan Wlk. BR3: Beck 4D 158
Morgan Way IG8: Wfd G 6H 37
Moriatry Cl. N7 4J 65
Moriaty Cl. BR1: Brom 4E 160
Morie St. SW18 5K 117
Morieux Rd. E10 1B 68
Moring Rd. SW17 4E 136
Morkyns Wlk. SE21 3E 138
Morland Av. CR0: C'don 1E 168
Morland Cl. CR4: Mitc 3C 154
NW11 1K 63
TW12: Hamp 5D 130
Morland Ct. *W12* 2D 98
(off Coningham Rd.)
Morland Est. E8 7G 67
Morland Gdns. NW10 7K 61
UB1: S'hall 1F 95
Morland Ho. *NW1* 1B 6
(off Werrington St.)
NW6 1J 81
SW1 3E 18
(off Marsham St.)
W11 6G 81
(off Lancaster Rd.)
Morland M. N1 7A 66
Morland Rd. CR0: C'don 1E 168
E17 5K 49
HA3: Kent 5E 42
IG1: Ilf 2F 71
RM10: Dag 7G 73
SE20 6K 139
SM1: Sutt 5A 166
Morley Av. E4 7A 36
N18 4B 34
N22 2A 48
Morley Cl. BR6: Farnb 2F 173
Morley Ct. BR2: Brom 4H 159
E4 5G 35
Morley Cres. HA4: Ruis 2A 58
HA8: Edg 2D 28
Morley Cres. E. HA7: Stan 2C 42
Morley Cres. W. HA7: Stan 3C 42
Morley Hill EN2: Enf 1J 23
Morley Ho. *SE15* 7F 103
(off Commercial Way)
Morley Rd. BR7: Chst 1G 161
E10 1E 68
E15 2H 87
IG11: Bark 1H 89
RM6: Chad H 5E 54
SE13 4E 122
SM3: Sutt 1H 165
TW1: Twick 6D 114
Morley St. SE1 1K 19 (3A 102)
Morna Rd. SE5 2C 120
Morning La. E9 6J 67
Morningside Rd. KT4: Wor Pk 2E 164
Mornington Av. BR1: Brom 3A 160
IG1: Ilf 7E 52
W14 4H 99
Mornington Av. Mans. *W14* 4H 99
(off Mornington Av.)
Mornington Cl. IG8: Wfd G 4D 36
Mornington Ct. DA5: Bexl 1K 145
NW1 2G 83
(off Mornington Cres.)
Mornington Cres. NW1 2G 83
TW5: Cran 1K 111
Mornington Gro. E3 3C 86
Mornington M. SE5 1C 120
Mornington Pl. NW1 2G 83
SE8 7B 104
(off Mornington Rd.)
Mornington Rd. E4 7K 25
E11 7H 51
(not continuous)
IG8: Wfd G 4C 36
SE8 7B 104
TW15: Ashf 5E 128
UB6: G'frd 5F 77
Mornington Sports & Leisure Cen. 1F 83
(off Arlington Rd.)
Mornington St. NW1 2F 83
Mornington Ter. NW1 1F 83
Mornington Wlk. TW10: Ham 4C 132
Morocco St. SE1 7G 15 (2E 102)
Morocco Wharf *E1* 1H 103
(off Wapping High St.)
Morpeth Gro. E9 1K 85
Morpeth Mans. *SW1* 2A 18
(off Morpeth Ter.)
Morpeth Rd. E9 1K 85
Morpeth St. E2 3J 85
Morpeth Ter. SW1 2A 18 (3G 101)
Morpeth Wlk. N17 7C 34
Morrab Gdns. IG3: Ilf 3K 71
Morrel Ct. *E2* 2G 85
(off Goldsmiths Row)
Morrells Yd. *SE11* 5K 19
(off Cleaver St.)
Morris Av. E12 5D 70
Morris Blitz Ct. N16 4F 67
Morris Cl. BR6: Orp 3J 173
CR0: C'don 5A 158
Morris Ct. E4 3J 35
Morris Gdns. SW18 7J 117
Morris Ho. *E2* 3J 85
(off Roman Rd.)
NW8 4C 4
(off Salisbury St.)
W3 2B 98
Morrish Rd. SW2 7J 119
Morrison Av. E4 6H 35
N17 3E 48
Morrison Bldgs. Nth. *E1* 6G 85
(off Commercial Rd.)
Morrison Ct. *EN5: Barn* 4B 20
(off Manor Way)
N12 7H 31
Morrison Ho. *SW2* 1A 138
(off High Trees)
Morrison Rd. IG11: Bark 2E 90
RM9: Bark, Dag 2E 90
SW9 2A 120
UB4: Yead 3K 75
Morrison St. SW11 3E 118
Morris Pl. N4 2A 66
Morris Rd. E14 5D 86
E15 4G 69
RM8: Dag 2F 73
TW7: Isle 3K 113
Morriss Ho. *SE16* 2H 103
(off Cherry Gdn. St.)
Morris St. E1 6H 85
Morritt Ho. *HA0: Wemb* 5D 60
(off Talbot Rd.)
Morse Cl. E13 3J 87
Morshead Mans. *W9* 3J 81
(off Morshead Rd.)
Morshead Rd. W9 3J 81
Morson Rd. EN3: Pond E 6F 25
Morston Gdns. SE9 4D 142
Mortain Ho. *SE16* 4H 103
(off Roseberry St.)
Morten Cl. SW4 6H 119
Morteyne Rd. N17 1D 48
Mortgramit Sq. SE18 3E 106
Mortham St. E15 1G 87
Mortimer Cl. NW2 2H 63
SW16 2H 137
Mortimer Ct. *NW8* 1A 4
(off Abbey Rd.)
Mortimer Cres. KT4: Wor Pk 3K 163
NW6 1K 81
Mortimer Dr. EN1: Enf 5K 23
Mortimer Est. *NW6* 1K 81
(off Mortimer Pl.)
Mortimer Ho. W11 1F 99
W14 4G 99
(off North End Rd.)
Mortimer Mkt. WC1 4B 6 (4G 83)
Mortimer Pl. NW6 1K 81
Mortimer Rd. CR4: Mitc 1D 154
DA8: Erith 6K 109
E6 3D 88
N1 7E 66
(not continuous)
NW10 3E 80
W13 6C 78
Mortimer Sq. W11 7F 81
Mortimer St. W1 7K 5 (6G 83)
Mortimer Ter. NW5 4F 65
MORTLAKE 3K 115
Mortlake Cl. CR0: Bedd 3J 167
Mortlake Crematorium
TW9: Kew 2H 115
Mortlake Dr. CR4: Mitc 1C 154
Mortlake High St. SW14 3K 115
Mortlake Rd. E16 6K 87
IG1: Ilf 4G 71
TW9: Kew, Rich 7G 97
Mortlake Ter. *TW9: Kew* 7G 97
(off Mortlake Rd.)
Mortlock Cl. SE15 1H 121
Mortlock Ct. E7 4B 70
Morton Cl. SM6: Wall 7K 167
UB8: Hil 4B 74
Morton Ct. UB5: N'olt 5G 59
Morton Cres. N14 4C 32
Morton Gdns. SM6: Wall 5G 167
Morton Ho. SE17 6B 102
Morton M. SW5 4K 99
Morton Pl. SE1 2J 19 (3A 102)
Morton Rd. E15 7H 69
N1 7C 66
SM4: Mord 5B 154
Morton Way N14 3B 32
Morvale Cl. DA17: Belv 4F 109
Morval Rd. SW2 5A 120
Morven Rd. SW17 3D 136
Morville Ho. *SW18* 6B 118
(off Fitzhugh Gro.)
Morville St. E3 2C 86
Morwell St. WC1 6C 6 (5H 83)
Moscow Mans. *SW5* 4J 99
(off Cromwell Rd.)
Moscow Pl. W2 7K 81
Moscow Rd. W2 7J 81
Mosedale *NW1* 2K 5
(off Cumberland Mkt.)
Moseley Row SE10 4H 105
Moselle Av. N22 2A 48
Moselle Cl. N8 3K 47
Moselle Ho. *N17* 7A 34
(off William St.)
Moselle Pl. N17 7A 34
Moselle St. N17 7A 34
Mosque Ter. *E1* 5G 85
(off Fieldgate St.)
Mosque Twr. *E1* 5G 85
(off Fieldgate St.)
E3 2A 86
(off Ford St.)
Mossborough Cl.
N12 6E 30
Mossbury Rd. SW11 3C 118

Moss Cl. E1 5G **85**
HA5: Pinn 2D **40**
N9 1B **34**
Mossdown Cl.
DA17: Belv 4G **109**
Mossford Ct. IG6: Ilf 3F **53**
Mossford Grn. IG6: Ilf 3F **53**
Mossford La. IG6: Ilf 2F **53**
Mossford St. E3 4B **86**
Moss Gdns. CR2: Sels 7K **169**
TW13: Felt 2J **129**
Moss Hall Ct. N12 6E **30**
Moss Hall Cres. N12 6E **30**
Moss Hall Gro. N12 6E **30**
Mossington Gdns.
SE16 4J **103**
Moss La. HA5: Pinn 1C **40**
Mosslea Rd. BR2: Brom 5B **160**
BR6: Farnb 3G **173**
SE20 6J **139**
(not continuous)
Mossop St. SW3 3D **16** (4C **100**)
Moss Rd. RM10: Dag 7G **73**
Mossville Gdns. SM4: Mord 3H **153**
Mosswell Ho. N10 1E **46**
Moston Cl. UB3: Harl 5H **93**
Mostyn Av. HA9: Wemb 5F **61**
Mostyn Gdns. NW10 3F **81**
Mostyn Gro. E3 2C **86**
Mostyn Rd. HA8: Edg 7F **29**
SW9 1A **120**
SW19 1H **153**
Mosul Way BR2: Brom 6C **160**
Motcomb St. SW1 1G **17** (3E **100**)
Moth Cl. SM6: Wall 7J **167**
Mothers Sq. E5 4H **67**
Motley Av. EC2 4G **9**
Motley St. SW8 2G **119**
MOTSPUR PARK 6C **152**
Motspur Pk. KT3: N Mald 6B **152**
MOTTINGHAM 2C **142**
Mottingham Gdns. SE9 1B **142**
Mottingham La. SE9 1A **142**
SE12 1A **142**
Mottingham Rd. N9 6E **24**
SE9 2C **142**
Mottisfont Rd. SE2 3A **108**
Motts La. RM8: Dag 2F **73**
Mott St. E4 1K **25**
Moules Ct. SE5 7C **102**
Moulins Rd. E9 7J **67**
Moulsford Ho. N7 5H **65**
W2 *5J* ***81***
(off Westbourne Pk. Rd.)
Moulton Av. TW3: Houn 2C **112**
Mound, The SE9 3E **142**
Moundfield Rd. N16 6G **49**
Mounsey Ho. *W10* *3G* ***81***
(off Third Av.)
Mount, The *CR2: S Croy* *5C* ***168***
(off Warham Rd.)
DA6: Bex 5H **127**
E5 2H **67**
(not continuous)
HA9: Wemb 2H **61**
KT3: N Mald 3B **152**
KT4: Wor Pk 4D **164**
N20 2F **31**
NW3 3A **64**
UB5: N'olt 5F **59**
W3 1J **97**
W8 *1J* ***99***
(off Bedford Gdns.)
Mountacre Cl. SE26 4F **139**
Mt. Adon Pk. SE22 7G **121**
Mountague Pl. E14 7E **86**
Mountain Ho. SE11 4H **19** (4K **101**)
Mt. Angelus Rd. SW15 7B **116**
Mt. Ararat Rd.
TW10: Rich 5E **114**
Mt. Arlington *BR2: Brom* *2G* ***159***
(off Park Hill Rd.)
Mt. Ash Rd. SE26 3H **139**
Mount Av. E4 3H **35**
UB1: S'hall 6E **76**
W5 5C **78**
Mountbatten Cl. SE18 6J **107**
SE19 5E **138**
Mountbatten Ct. IG9: Buck H 2G **37**
SE16 *1J* ***103***
(off Rotherhithe St.)
Mountbatten Gdns. BR3: Beck 4A **158**
Mountbatten Ho. *N6* *7E* ***46***
(off Hillcrest)
Mountbatten M. SW18 7A **118**
Mountbel Rd. HA7: Stan 1A **42**
Mt. Carmel Chambers *W8* *2J* ***99***
(off Dukes La.)
Mount Cl. BR1: Brom 1C **160**
EN4: Cockf 4K **21**
SM5: Cars 7E **166**
W5 5C **78**
Mountcombe Cl. KT6: Surb 7E **150**
Mount Ct. BR4: W W'ck 2G **171**
SW15 3G **117**
Mt. Culver Av. DA14: Sidc 6D **144**
Mount Dr. DA6: Bex 5E **126**
HA2: Harr 5D **40**
HA9: Wemb 2J **61**
Mountearl Gdns. SW16 3K **137**
Mt. Eaton Ct. *W5* *5C* ***78***
(off Mount Av.)
Mt. Echo Av. E4 2J **35**
Mt. Echo Dr. E4 1J **35**
Mt. Ephraim La. SW16 3H **137**
Mt. Ephraim Rd. SW16 3H **137**
Mount Felix KT12: Walt T 7H **147**
Mountfield Cl. SE6 7F **123**
Mountfield Rd. E6 2E **88**
N3 3H **45**
W5 6D **78**
Mountfield Ter. SE6 7F **123**
Mountford Mans. *SW11* *1E* ***118***
(off Battersea Pk. Rd.)
Mountford Rd. E8 5G **67**
Mountfort Cres. N1 7A **66**
Mountfort Ter. N1 7A **66**
Mount Gdns. SE26 3H **139**
Mount Gro. HA8: Edg 3D **28**
Mountgrove Rd. N5 3B **66**
Mount Holme KT7: T Ditt 7B **150**
Mounthurst Rd. BR2: Hayes 7H **159**
Mountington Pk. Cl. HA3: Kent 6D **42**
Mountjoy Cl. *EC2* *6D* ***8***
(off Barbican)
SE2 2B **108**
Mountjoy Ho. EC2 6C **8**
Mount Lodge N6 6G **47**
Mount M. TW12: Hamp 1F **149**
Mount Mills EC1 2B **8** (3B **84**)
Mt. Nod Rd. SW16 3K **137**
Mt. Olive Ct. W7 2J **95**
Mount Pde. EN4: Cockf 4H **21**
Mount Pk. SM5: Cars 7E **166**
Mount Pk. Av. CR2: S Croy 7B **168**
HA1: Harr 2H **59**
Mount Pk. Cres. W5 6D **78**
Mount Pk. Rd. HA1: Harr 3H **59**
HA5: Eastc 5J **39**
W5 5D **78**
Mount Pl. W3 1H **97**
Mt. Pleasant EN4: Cockf 4H **21**
HA0: Wemb 1E **78**
HA4: Ruis 2A **58**
IG1: Ilf 5G **71**
SE27 4C **138**
WC1 4J **7** (4A **84**)
Mt. Pleasant Cotts. *N14* *7C* ***22***
(off The Wells)
Mt. Pleasant Cres. N4 1K **65**
Mt. Pleasant Hill E5 2H **67**
Mt. Pleasant La. E5 1H **67**
Mt. Pleasant Pl. SE18 4H **107**
Mt. Pleasant Rd. E17 2A **50**
KT3: N Mald 3J **151**
N17 2E **48**
NW10 7E **62**
SE13 6D **122**
W5 4C **78**
Mt. Pleasant Vs. N4 7K **47**
Mt. Pleasant Wlk. DA5: Bexl 5J **127**
Mount Rd. CR4: Mitc 2B **154**
DA6: Bex 5D **126**
EN4: E Barn 5H **21**
KT3: N Mald 3K **151**
KT9: Chess 5F **163**
NW2 3D **62**
NW4 6C **44**
Mount Rd. RM8: Dag 1F **73**
SE19 6D **138**
SW19 2J **135**
TW13: Hanw 3C **130**
UB3: Hayes 2J **93**
Mount Row W1 3J **11** (7F **83**)
Mountsfield Ct. SE13 6F **123**
Mountside HA7: Stan 1K **41**
Mounts Pond Rd. SE3 2F **123**
(not continuous)
Mount Sq., The NW3 3A **64**
Mt. Stewart Av. HA3: Kent 7D **42**
Mount St. W1 3G **11** (7E **82**)
Mount St. M. W1 3J **11** (7F **83**)
Mount Ter. E1 5H **85**
Mount Vernon NW3 4A **64**
Mount Vw. EN2: Enf 1E **22**
NW7 3E **28**
UB2: S'hall 4B **94**
W5 4D **78**
Mountview Cl. NW11 1K **63**
Mountview Ct. N8 4B **48**
Mount Vw. Rd. E4 7K **25**
KT10: Clay 7B **162**
N4 7J **47**
NW9 5K **43**
Mountview Rd. BR6: St M Cry 7K **161**
(not continuous)
Mount Vs. SE27 3B **138**
Mount Way SM5: Cars 7E **166**
Mountwood KT8: W Mole 3F **149**
MOVERS LANE 2J **89**
Movers La. IG11: Bark 1H **89**
Mowat Ct. *KT4: Wor Pk* *2B* ***164***
(off The Avenue)
Mowatt Cl. N19 1H **65**
Mowbray Ct. N22 1A **48**
SE19 7F **139**
Mowbray Gdns. UB5: N'olt 1E **76**
Mowbray Ho. *N2* *2B* ***46***
(off The Grange)
Mowbray Pde. HA8: Edg 4B **28**
Mowbray Rd. EN5: New Bar 5F **21**
HA8: Edg 4B **28**
NW6 7G **63**
SE19 1F **157**
TW10: Ham 3C **132**
Mowbrays Cl. RM5: Col R 1J **55**
Mowbrays Rd. RM5: Col R 2J **55**
Mowlem St. E2 2H **85**
Mowlem Trad. Est. N17 7D **34**
Mowll St. SW9 7A **102**
Moxon Cl. E13 2H **87**
Moxon St. EN5: Barn 3C **20**
W1 6G **5** (5E **82**)
Moye Cl. E2 2G **85**
Moyers Rd. E10 7E **50**
Moylan Rd. W6 6G **99**
Moyle Ho. *SW1* *6B* ***18***
(off Churchill Gdns.)
Moyne Ho. SW9 5B **120**
Moyne Pl. NW10 2G **79**
Moynihan Dr. N21 5D **22**
Moys Cl. CR0: C'don 6J **155**
Moyser Rd. SW16 5F **137**
Mozart St. W10 3H **81**
Mozart Ter. SW1 4H **17** (4E **100**)
Muchelney Rd. SM4: Mord 6A **154**
Mudlarks Blvd. SE10 3H **105**
Mudlarks Way SE7 3J **105**
SE10 3H **105**
(not continuous)
Muggeridge Cl. CR2: S Croy 5D **168**
Muggeridge Rd. RM10: Dag 4H **73**
Muirdown Av. SW14 4K **115**
Muir Dr. SW18 6C **118**
Muirfield W3 6A **80**
Muirfield Cl. SE16 5H **103**
Muirfield Cres. E14 3D **104**
Muirhead Quay IG11: Bark 2G **89**
Muirkirk Rd. SE6 1E **140**
Muir Rd. E5 3G **67**
Muir St. E16 1C **106**
(not continuous)
Mulberry Av. TW19: Stanw 1A **128**
Mulberry Bus. Cen. SE16 2K **103**
Mulberry Cl. E4 2H **35**
EN4: E Barn 4G **21**
N8 5J **47**
NW3 4B **64**
NW4 3E **44**
SE7 6B **106**
SE22 5G **121**
SW3 7B **16** (6B **100**)
SW16 4G **137**
UB5: N'olt 2C **76**
Mulberry Ct. *E11* *4F* ***69***
(off Langthorne Rd.)
EC1 *2B* ***8***
(off Tompion St.)
IG11: Bark 6K **71**
KT6: Surb 7D **150**
N2 *3C* ***46***
(off Bedford Rd.)
SW3 7B **16**
TW1: Twick 3K **131**
Mulberry Cres. TW8: Bford 7B **96**
UB7: W Dray 2C **92**
Mulberry Ho. BR2: Brom 1G **159**
E2 *3J* ***85***
(off Victoria Pk. Sq.)
SE8 6B **104**
Mulberry Housing Co-operative
SE1 4K **13**
Mulberry La. CR0: C'don 1F **169**
Mulberry M. SE14 1B **122**
SM6: Wall 6G **167**
Mulberry Pde. UB7: W Dray 3C **92**
Mulberry Pl. *E14* *7E* ***86***
(off Clove Cres.)
SE9 4B **124**
W6 5C **98**
Mulberry Rd. E8 7F **67**
Mulberry St. E1 6G **85**
Mulberry Tree M. W4 2J **97**
Mulberry Trees TW17: Shep 7F **147**
Mulberry Wlk. SW3 7B **16** (6B **100**)
Mulberry Way DA17: Belv 2J **109**
E18 2K **51**
IG6: Ilf 4G **53**
Mulgrave Ct. *SM2: Sutt* *6K* ***165***
(off Mulgrave Rd.)
Mulgrave Rd. CR0: C'don 3D **168**
HA1: Harr 2A **60**
NW10 4B **62**
SE18 4D **106**
SM2: Sutt 7H **165**
SW6 6H **99**
W5 3D **78**
Mulholland Cl. CR4: Mitc 2F **155**
Mulkern Rd. N19 1H **65**
(not continuous)

Mullards Cl. CR4: Mitc 1D 166
Mullen Twr. WC1 4J 7
(off Mt. Pleasant)
Muller Ho. SE18 5E 106
Muller Rd. SW4 6H 119
Mullet Gdns. E2 3G 85
Mulletsfield WC1 2F 7
(off Cromer St.)
Mullins Path SW14 3K 115
Mullion Cl. HA3: Hrw W 1F 41
Mull Wlk. N1 6C 66
(off Clephane Rd.)
Mulready Ho. SW1 4E 18
(off Marsham St.)
Mulready St. NW8 4C 4 (4C 82)
Multimedia Ho. NW10 4J 79
Multi Way W3 2A 98
Multon Ho. E9 7J 67
Multon Rd. SW18 7B 118
Mulvaney Way SE1 7F 15 (2D 102)
(not continuous)
Mumford Mills SE10 1D 122
(off Greenwich High Rd.)
Mumford Rd. SE24 5B 120
Muncaster Cl. TW15: Ashf 4C 128
Muncaster Rd. SW11 5D 118
TW15: Ashf 5D 128
Muncies M. SE6 2E 140
Mundania Ct. SE22 6H 121
Mundania Rd. SE22 6H 121
Munday Ho. SE1 3D 102
(off Burbage Cl.)
Munday Rd. E16 7J 87
Munden St. W14 4G 99
Mundford Rd. E5 2J 67
Mundon Gdns. IG1: Ilf 1H 71
Mund St. W14 5H 99
Mundy Ho. W10 3G 81
(off Dart St.)
Mundy St. N1 1G 9 (3E 84)
Mungo Pk. Cl. WD23: B Hea 2B 26
Munkenbeck Bldg. W2 6A 4
(off Hermitage St.)
Munnery Way BR6: Farnb 3E 172
Munnings Gdns. TW7: Isle 5H 113
Munnings Ho. E16 1K 105
(off Portsmouth M.)
Munro Dr. N11 6B 32
Munro Ho. SE1 7J 13 (2A 102)
Munro M. W10 5G 81
(not continuous)
Munro Ter. SW10 7B 100
Munslow Gdns. SM1: Sutt 4B 166
Munster Av. TW4: Houn 5C 112
Munster Ct. SW6 2H 117
TW11: Tedd 6C 132
Munster Gdns. N13 4G 33
Munster M. SW6 7G 99
Munster Rd. SW6 7G 99
TW11: Tedd 6B 132
Munster Sq. NW1 2K 5 (3F 83)
Munton Rd. SE17 4C 102
Murchison Av. DA5: Bexl 1D 144
Murchison Ho. W10 5G 81
(off Ladbroke Gro.)
Murchison Rd. E10 2E 68
Murdoch Ho. SE16 3J 103
(off Moodkee St.)
Murdock Cl. E16 6H 87
Murdock St. SE15 6H 103
Murfett Cl. SW19 2G 135
Muriel St. N1 2K 83
(not continuous)
Murillo Rd. SE13 4F 123
Murphy Ho. SE1 7B 14
(off Borough Rd.)
Murphy St. SE1 7J 13 (2A 102)
Murray Av. BR1: Brom 3K 159
TW3: Houn 5F 113
Murray Cl. SE28 1J 107
Murray Ct. HA1: Harr 6K 41
TW2: Twick 2H 131
Murray Cres. HA5: Pinn 1B 40
Murray Gro. N1 1D 8 (2C 84)
Murray Ho. SE18 4D 106
(off Rideout St.)
Murray M. NW1 7H 65
Murray Rd. HA6: Nwood 1G 39
SW19 6F 135
TW10: Ham 2B 132
W5 4C 96
Murray Sq. E16 6J 87
Murray St. NW1 7G 65
Murrays Yd. SE18 4F 107
Murray Ter. NW3 4A 64
W5 4D 96
Mursell Est. SW8 1K 119
Musard Rd. W6 6G 99
Musbury St. E1 6J 85
Muscal W6 6G 99
(off Field Rd.)
Muscatel Pl. SE5 1E 120
Muschamp Rd. SE15 3F 121
SM5: Cars 2C 166
Muscott Ho. E2 1G 85
(off Whiston Rd.)
Muscovy Ho. DA18: Erith 2E 108
(off Kale Rd.)
Muscovy St. EC3 2H 15 (7E 84)
Museum Chambers WC1 6E 6
(off Bury Pl.)
Museum Ho. E2 3J 85
(off Burnham St.)
Mus. in Docklands, The 7C 86
Museum La. SW7 2B 16 (3B 100)
Museum Mans. WC1 6E 6
(off Gt. Russell St.)
Mus. of Brands, Packaging and Advertising 6H 81
(off Colville M.)
Mus. of Classical Archaeology 3C 6
(off Gower Pl.)
Mus. of Domestic Design & Architecture 5K 21
Mus. of Garden History 2G 19 (3K 101)
Mus. of London 6C 8 (5C 84)
Mus. of Richmond 5D 114
Mus. of Rugby, The 6J 113
Mus. of the Order of St John 4A 8
(off St John's La.)
Museum Pas. E2 3J 85
Museum St. WC1 6E 6 (5J 83)
Museum Way W3 2G 97
Musgrave Cl. EN4: Had W 1F 21
Musgrave Ct. SW11 1C 118
Musgrave Cres. SW6 7J 99
Musgrave Rd. TW7: Isle 1K 113
Musgrove Rd. SE14 1K 121
Musjid Rd. SW11 2B 118
Musket Cl. EN4: E Barn 6G 21
Musquash Way
TW4: Houn 2A 112
Muston Rd. E5 2H 67
Mustow Pl. SW6 2H 117
Muswell Av. N10 1F 47
MUSWELL HILL 3F 47
Muswell Hill N10 3F 47
Muswell Hill B'way.
N10 3F 47
Muswell Hill Pl. N10 4F 47
Muswell Hill Rd. N6 6E 46
N10 6E 46
Muswell M. N10 3F 47
Muswell Rd. N10 3F 47
Mutrix Rd. NW6 1J 81
Mutton Pl. NW1 6E 64
Muybridge Rd.
KT3: N Mald 2J 151
Muybridge Yd. KT6: Surb 7F 151
Myatt Rd. SW9 1B 120
Myatts Flds. Sth. SW9 2A 120
(off St Lawrence Way)
Mycenae Rd. SE3 7J 105
Myddelton Av. EN1: Enf 1K 23
Myddelton Cl. EN1: Enf 1A 24
Myddelton Gdns. N21 7H 23
Myddelton Pk. N20 3G 31
Myddelton Pas. EC1 1K 7 (3A 84)
Myddelton Rd. N8 4J 47
(not continuous)
Myddelton Sq. EC1 1K 7 (3A 84)
Myddelton St. EC1 2K 7 (3A 84)
Myddleton Av. N4 2C 66
Myddleton Cl. HA7: Stan 2F 27
Myddleton Ho. N1 1J 7
Myddleton M. N22 7D 32
Myddleton Rd. N22 7D 32
Myers Ho. SE5 7C 102
(off Bethwin Rd.)
Myers La. SE14 6K 103
Myles Ct. SE16 3J 103
(off Neptune St.)
Mylis Cl. SE26 4H 139
Mylius Cl. SE14 7J 103
Mylne Cl. W6 5C 98
Mylne St. EC1 1J 7 (3A 84)
Myra St. SE2 4A 108
Myrdle Ct. E1 6G 85
(off Myrdle St.)
Myrdle St. E1 5G 85
Myrna Cl. SW19 7C 136
Myron Pl. SE13 3E 122
Myrtle Av. HA4: Ruis 7J 39
TW14: Felt 5G 111
Myrtleberry Cl. E8 6F 67
(off Beechwood Rd.)
Myrtle Cl. EN4: E Barn 1J 31
UB7: W Dray 3B 92
UB8: Hil 5B 74
Myrtledene Rd. SE2 5A 108
Myrtle Gdns. W7 1J 95
Myrtle Gro. EN2: Enf 1J 23
KT3: N Mald 2J 151
Myrtle Rd. CR0: C'don 3C 170
E6 1D 88
E17 6A 50
IG1: Ilf 2F 71
N13 3H 33
SM1: Sutt 5A 166
TW3: Houn 2G 113
TW12: Ham H 6G 131
W3 1J 97
Myrtle Wlk. N1 1G 9 (2E 84)
Mysore Rd. SW11 3D 118
Myton Rd. SE21 3D 138
Mytton Ho. SW8 7K 101
(off St Stephens Ter.)

N

N1 Shop. Cen. N1 2A 84
N16 Fitness Cen. 4D 66
Nacton Ct. RM6: Chad H 5C 54
(off Hevingham Dr.)
Nadine Ct. SM6: Wall 7G 167
Nadine St. SE7 5A 106
Nagasaki Wlk. SE7 3K 105
Nagle Cl. E17 2F 51
NAG'S HEAD 3J 65
Nags Head Ct. EC1 4D 8
Nags Head La. DA16: Well 3B 126
Nags Head Rd. EN3: Pond E 4D 24
Nags Head Shop. Cen.
N7 4K 65
Nainby Ho. SE11 4J 19
Nairne Gro. SE24 5D 120
Nairn Rd. HA4: Ruis 6A 58
Nairn St. E14 5E 86
Naldera Gdns. SE3 6J 105
Nallhead Rd. TW13: Hanw 5A 130
Nalton Ho. NW6 7A 64
(off Belsize Rd.)
Namba Roy Cl. SW16 4K 137
Namton Dr. CR7: Thor H 4K 155
Nan Clark's La. NW7 2F 29
Nankin St. E14 6C 86
Nansen Ho. NW10 7K 61
(off Stonebridge Pk.)
Nansen Rd. SW11 3E 118
Nansen Village
N12 4E 30
Nant Ct. NW2 2H 63
Nantes Cl. SW18 4A 118
Nantes Pas. E1 5J 9 (5F 85)
Nant Rd. NW2 2H 63
Nant St. E2 3H 85
Naoroji St. WC1 2J 7 (3A 84)
Napier NW9 1B 44
Napier Av. E14 5C 104
SW6 3H 117
Napier Cl. SE8 7B 104
UB7: W Dray 3B 92
W14 3G 99
Napier Ct. N1 2D 84
(off Cropley St.)
SE12 3K 141
SW6 3H 117
(off Ranelagh Gdns.)
UB4: Yead 4A 76
(off Dunedin Way)
Napier Gro. N1 2C 84
Napier Ho. SE17 6B 102
(off Cooks Rd.)
Napier Lodge TW15: Ashf 6F 129
Napier Pl. W14 3H 99
Napier Rd. BR2: Brom 4K 159
CR2: S Croy 7D 168
DA17: Belv 4F 109
E6 1E 88
E11 4G 69
E15 2G 87
(not continuous)
EN3: Pond E 5E 24
HA0: Wemb 6D 60
N17 3E 48
NW10 3D 80
SE25 4H 157
TW7: Isle 4A 114
TW15: Ashf 7F 129
W14 3H 99
Napier St. SE8 7B 104
(off Napier Cl.)
Napier Ter. N1 7B 66
Napier Wlk. TW15: Ashf 7F 129
Napoleon Rd. E5 3H 67
TW1: Twick 7B 114
Napton Cl. UB4: Yead 4C 76
Narbonne Av. SW4 5G 119
Narborough Cl. UB10: Ick 2E 56
Narborough St. SW6 2K 117
Narcissus Rd. NW6 5J 63
Nardini NW9 1B 44
(off The Concourse)
Naresby Fold HA7: Stan 6H 27
Narford Rd. E5 3G 67
Narrow Boat Cl. SE28 2H 107
Narrow St. E14 7A 86
W3 1H 97
Narrow Way BR2: Brom 6C 160
Narvic Ho. SE5 2C 120
Narwhal Inuit Art Gallery 4K 97
Nascot St. W12 6E 80
Naseby Cl. NW6 7A 64
TW7: Isle 1J 113
Naseby Ct. DA14: Sidc 4K 143
Naseby Rd. IG5: Ilf 1D 52
RM10: Dag 3G 73
SE19 6D 138
NASH 6J 171

Nash Cl. SM1: Sutt 3B 166
Nash Ct. HA3: Kent 6B 42
Nashe Ho. *SE1* *3D 102*
(off Burbage Cl.)
Nash Grn. BR1: Brom 6J 141
Nash Ho. *E14* *2C 104*
(off Alpha Gro.)
E17 . . . . . 3D 50
NW1 . . . . . *2F 83*
(off Park Village E.)
SW1 . . . . . *6K 17*
(off Lupus St.)
Nash La. BR2: Kes 7J 171
Nash Pl. E14 . . . . . 1D 104
Nash Rd. N9 . . . . . 2D 34
RM6: Chad H 4D 54
SE4 . . . . . 4A 122
Nash St. NW1 . . . . . 1K 5 (3F 83)
Nash Way HA3: Kent 6B 42
Nasmyth St. W6 . . . . . 3D 98
Nassau Path SE28 . . . . . 1C 108
Nassau Rd. SW13 . . . . . 1B 116
Nassau St. W1 . . . . . 6A 6 (5G 83)
Nassington Rd. NW3 . . . . . 4D 64
Natalie Cl. TW14: Bedf 7F 111
Natalie M. TW2: Twick 3H 131
Natal Rd. CR7: Thor H 3D 156
IG1: Ilf 4F 71
N11 . . . . . 6D 32
SW16 . . . . . 6H 137
Nathan Ct. *N9* *7D 24*
(off Causeyware Rd.)
Nathan Ho. *SE11* *4K 19*
(off Reedworth St.)
Nathaniel Cl. E1 . . . . . 6K 9 (5F 85)
Nathaniel Ct. E17 . . . . . 7A 50
Nathans Rd. HA0: Wemb 1C 60
Nathan Way SE28 . . . . . 4J 107
National Archives, The 7G 97
National Army Mus. 7F 17 (6D 100)
National Gallery 3D 12 (7H 83)
National Maritime Mus. 6F 105
National Portrait Gallery 3D 12
National Ter. *SE16* *2H 103*
(off Bermondsey Wall E.)
National Theatre 4H 13 (1K 101)
National Walks
TW4: Houn 3D 112
Nation Way E4 . . . . . 1K 35
Natural History Mus.
Knightsbridge 2A 16 (3B 100)
Nautilus Bldg., The *EC1* *1K 7*
(off Myddelton Pas.)
Naval Ho. *E14* *7F 87*
(off Quixley St.)
Naval Row E14 . . . . . 7E 86
Naval Wlk. *BR1: Brom* *2J 159*
(off Mitre Cl.)
Navarino Gro. E8 . . . . . 6G 67
Navarino Mans. E8 . . . . . 6G 67
Navarino Rd. E8 . . . . . 6G 67
Navarre Rd. E6 . . . . . 2C 88
Navarre St. E2 . . . . . 3J 9 (4F 85)
Navenby Wlk. E3 . . . . . 4C 86
Navestock Cl. E4 . . . . . 3K 35
Navestock Cres.
IG8: Wfd G 7F 37
Navestock Ho. IG11: Bark 2B 90
Navigation Ct. E16 . . . . . 7G 89
Navigation Dr.
EN3: Enf L 1H 25
Navigator Dr.
UB2: S'hall 2G 95
Navigator Pk.
UB2: S'hall 4A 94
Navy St. SW4 . . . . . 3H 119
Naxos Bldg. E14 . . . . . 2B 104
Nayim Pl. E8 . . . . . 5H 67
Nayland Ho. SE6 . . . . . 4E 140
Naylor Gro. EN3: Pond E 5E 24
Naylor Ho. *SE17* *4D 102*
(off Flint St.)
W10 . . . . . *3G 81*
(off Dart St.)
Naylor Rd. N20 . . . . . 2F 31
SE15 . . . . . 7H 103
Nazareth Gdns. SE15 . . . . . 2H 121
Nazrul St. E2 . . . . . 1J 9 (3F 85)
Neagle Ho. *NW2* *3E 62*
(off Stoll Cl.)
Neal Av. UB1: S'hall 4D 76
Neal Cl. HA6: Nwood 1J 39
Nealden St. SW9 . . . . . 3K 119
Neale Cl. N2 . . . . . 3A 46
Neale Ct. RM9: Dag 6B 72
Neal St. WC2 . . . . . 1E 12 (6J 83)
Neal's Yd. WC2 . . . . . 1E 12 (6J 83)
Near Acre NW9 . . . . . 1B 44
NEASDEN 3A 62
Neasden Cl. NW10 . . . . . 5A 62
NEASDEN JUNC. 4A 62
Neasden La. NW10 . . . . . 3A 62
Neasden La. Nth. NW10 . . . . . 3K 61
Neasham Rd. RM8: Dag 5B 72
Neate Ho. *SW1* *6B 18*
(off Lupus St.)
Neate St. SE5 . . . . . 6E 102
Neath Gdns. SM4: Mord 6A 154
Neathouse Pl. SW1 . . . . . 3A 18 (4G 101)
Neats Acre HA4: Ruis 7F 39
Neatscourt Rd. E6 . . . . . 5B 88
Nebraska Bldg. *SE10* *1D 122*
(off Deal's Gateway)
Nebraska St. SE1 . . . . . 7E 14 (2D 102)
Neckinger SE16 . . . . . 7K 15 (3F 103)
Neckinger Est. SE16 . . . . . 7K 15 (3F 103)
Neckinger St. SE1 . . . . . 7K 15 (2F 103)
Nectarine Way SE13 . . . . . 2D 122
Needham Ho. SE11 . . . . . 4J 19
Needham Rd. W11 . . . . . 6J 81
Needham Ter. NW2 . . . . . 3F 63
Needleman St. SE16 . . . . . 2K 103
Needwood Ho. N4 . . . . . 1C 66
Neela Cl. UB10: Ick 4D 56
Neeld Cres. HA9: Wemb 5G 61
NW4 . . . . . 5D 44
Neeld Pde. HA9: Wemb 5F 61
Neil Cl. TW15: Ashf 5E 128
Neil Wates Cres. SW2 . . . . . 1A 138
Nelgarde Rd. SE6 . . . . . 7C 122
Nella Rd. W6 . . . . . 6F 99
Nelldale Rd. SE16 . . . . . 4J 103
Nellgrove Rd. UB10: Hil 4D 74
Nell Gwynne Av. TW17: Shep 6F 147
Nell Gwynn Ho. SW3 . . . . . 4D 16 (4C 100)
Nello James Gdns. SE27 . . . . . 4D 138
Nelson Cl. CR0: C'don 1B 168
KT12: Walt T 7K 147
NW6 . . . . . 3J 81
RM7: Mawney 1H 55
TW14: Felt 1H 129
UB10: Hil 3D 74
Nelson Ct. SE1 . . . . . 6B 14 (2B 102)
SE16 . . . . . *1J 103*
(off Brunel Rd.)
Nelson Gdns. E2 . . . . . 3G 85
TW3: Houn 6E 112
Nelson Gro. Rd. SW19 . . . . . 1K 153
Nelson Ho. *SW1* *7B 18*
(off Dolphin Sq.)
Nelson La. UB10: Hil 3D 74
Nelson Mandela Cl.
N10 . . . . . 2E 46
Nelson Mandela Ho.
N16 . . . . . 2G 67
Nelson Mandela Rd.
SE3 . . . . . 3A 124
Nelson Pas. EC1 . . . . . 1D 8 (3C 84)
Nelson Pl. DA14: Sidc 4A 144
N1 . . . . . 1B 8 (2B 84)
Nelson Rd. BR2: Brom 4A 160
DA14: Sidc 4A 144
DA17: Belv 5F 109
E4 . . . . . 6J 35
E11 . . . . . 4J 51
EN3: Pond E 6E 24
HA1: Harr 1H 59
HA7: Stan 6H 27
KT3: N Mald 5K 151
N8 . . . . . 5K 47
N9 . . . . . 2C 34
N15 . . . . . 4E 48
SE10 . . . . . 6E 104
SW19 . . . . . 7K 135
TW2: Whitt 7F 113
TW3: Houn 6E 112
TW6: H'row A 1B 110
TW15: Ashf 5A 128
UB10: Hil 3D 74
Nelson Rd. M. *SW19* *7K 135*
(off Nelson Rd.)
Nelson's Column 4D 12 (1H 101)
Nelson Sq. SE1 . . . . . 6A 14 (2B 102)
Nelson's Row SW4 . . . . . 4H 119
Nelson St. E1 . . . . . 6H 85
E6 . . . . . 2D 88
(not continuous)
E16 . . . . . 7H 87
(not continuous)
Nelsons Yd. *NW1* *2G 83*
(off Mornington Cres.)
Nelson Ter. N1 . . . . . 1B 8 (2B 84)
Nelson Trad. Est. SW19 . . . . . 1K 153
Nelson Wlk. KT19: Eps 7G 163
SE16 . . . . . 1A 104
Nemoure Rd. W3 . . . . . 7J 79
Nene Gdns. TW13: Hanw 3D 130
Nene Rd. TW6: H'row A 1D 110
Nene Rd. Rdbt.
TW6: H'row A 1D 110
Nepaul Rd. SW11 . . . . . 2C 118
Nepean St. SW15 . . . . . 6C 116
Neptune Ct. *E14* *4C 104*
(off Homer Dr.)
Neptune Ho. *SE16* *3J 103*
(off Moodkee St.)
Neptune Rd. HA1: Harr 6H 41
TW6: H'row A 1F 111
Neptune St. SE16 . . . . . 3J 103
Neptune Wlk. DA8: Erith 4K 109
Nero Ct. TW8: Bford 7D 96
Nesbit Rd. SE9 . . . . . 4B 124
Nesbitt Cl. SE3 . . . . . 3G 123
Nesbitts All. EN5: Barn 3C 20
Nesbitt Sq. SE19 . . . . . 7E 138
Nesham Ho. *N1* *1E 84*
(off Hoxton St.)
Nesham St. E1 . . . . . 7G 85
Ness St. SE16 . . . . . 3G 103
Nesta Rd. IG8: Wfd G 6B 36
Nestles Av. UB3: Hayes 3H 93
Nestor Av. N21 . . . . . 6G 23
Nestor Ho. *E2* *2H 85*
(off Old Bethnal Grn. Rd.)
Netheravon Rd. W4 . . . . . 4B 98
W7 . . . . . 1K 95
Netheravon Rd. Sth. W4 . . . . . 5B 98
Netherbury Rd. W5 . . . . . 3D 96
Netherby Gdns. EN2: Enf 4D 22
Netherby Rd. SE23 . . . . . 7J 121
Nether Cl. N3 . . . . . 7D 30
Nethercourt Av. N3 . . . . . 6D 30
Netherfield Gdns. IG11: Bark 6H 71
Netherfield Rd. N12 . . . . . 5E 30
SW17 . . . . . 3E 136
Netherford Rd. SW4 . . . . . 2G 119
Netherhall Gdns. NW3 . . . . . 6A 64
Netherhall Way NW3 . . . . . 5A 64
Netherlands Rd. EN5: New Bar 6G 21
Netherleigh Cl. N6 . . . . . 1F 65
Nether St. N3 . . . . . 1J 45
N12 . . . . . 7D 30
(not continuous)
Netherton Gro. SW10 . . . . . 6A 100
Netherton Rd. N15 . . . . . 6D 48
TW1: Twick 5A 114
Netherwood N2 . . . . . 2B 46
Netherwood Pl. *W14* *3F 99*
(off Netherwood Rd.)
Netherwood Rd. W14 . . . . . 3F 99
Netherwood St. NW6 . . . . . 7H 63
Nethewode Ct. *DA17: Belv* *3H 109*
(off Lower Pk. Rd.)
Netley *SE5* *1E 120*
(off Redbridge Gdns.)
Netley Cl. CR0: New Ad 7E 170
SM3: Cheam 5F 165
Netley Dr. KT12: Walt T 7D 148
Netley Gdns. SM4: Mord 7A 154
Netley Rd. E17 . . . . . 5B 50
IG2: Ilf 5H 53
SM4: Mord 7A 154
TW8: Bford 6E 96
Netley St. NW1 . . . . . 2A 6 (3G 83)
Nettlecombe *NW1* *7H 65*
(off Agar Gro.)
Nettleden Av. HA9: Wemb 6G 61
Nettleden Ho. *SW3* *4D 16*
(off Cale St.)
Nettlefold Pl. SE27 . . . . . 3B 138
Nettlefold Wlk. KT12: Walt T 7H 147
Nettlestead Cl. BR3: Beck 7B 140
Nettleton Ct. *EC2* *6C 8*
(off London Wall)
Nettleton Rd. SE14 . . . . . 1K 121
TW6: H'row A 1D 110
UB10: Ick 4B 56
Nettlewood Rd. SW16 . . . . . 7H 137
Neuchatel Rd. SE6 . . . . . 2B 140
Nevada Cl. KT3: N Mald 4J 151
Nevada St. SE10 . . . . . 6E 104
Nevern Mans. *SW5* *5J 99*
(off Warwick Rd.)
Nevern Pl. SW5 . . . . . 4J 99
Nevern Rd. SW5 . . . . . 4J 99
Nevern Sq. SW5 . . . . . 4J 99
Nevil Ho. *SW9* *2B 120*
(off Loughborough Est.)
Nevill Ct. *SW10* *7A 100*
(off Edith Ter.)
Neville Av. KT3: N Mald 1K 151
Neville Cl. DA15: Sidc 4K 143
E11 . . . . . 3H 69
NW1 . . . . . 2H 83
NW6 . . . . . 2H 81
SE15 . . . . . 1G 121
TW3: Houn 2F 113
W3 . . . . . 2J 97
Neville Ct. NW8 . . . . . 1A 4
Neville Dr. N2 . . . . . 6A 46
Neville Gdns. RM8: Dag 3D 72
Neville Gill Cl. SW18 . . . . . 6J 117
Neville Ho. N11 . . . . . 4K 31
N22 . . . . . *1K 47*
(off Neville Pl.)
NW6 . . . . . *2H 81*
(off Denmark Rd.)
Neville Ho. Yd. KT1: King T 2E 150
Neville Pl. N22 . . . . . 1K 47
Neville Rd. CR0: C'don 7D 156
E7 . . . . . 7J 69
IG6: Ilf 1G 53
KT1: King T 2G 151
NW6 . . . . . 2H 81
RM8: Dag 2D 72
TW10: Ham 3C 132
W5 . . . . . 4D 78
Nevilles Ct. NW2 . . . . . 3C 62
Neville St. SW7 . . . . . 5A 16 (5B 100)
Neville Ter. SW7 . . . . . 5A 16 (5B 100)

Neville Wlk. SM5: Cars 7C 154
Nevill La. EC4 6A 84
(off New Fetter La.)
Nevill Rd. N16 4E 66
Nevin Dr. E4 1J 35
Nevin Ho. UB3: Harl 3E 92
Nevinson Cl. SW18 6B 118
Nevis Rd. SW17 2E 136
Nevitt Ho. N1 2D 84
(off Cranston Est.)
New Acres Rd. SE28 2J 107
(not continuous)
NEW ADDINGTON 7F 171
Newall Ho. SE1 3C 102
(off Bath Ter.)
Newall Rd. TW6: H'row A 1E 110
New Ambassadors Theatre 2D 12
(off West St.)
Newark Cres. NW10 3K 79
Newarke Ho. SW9 2B 120
Newark Knok E6 6E 88
Newark Rd. CR2: S Croy 6D 168
Newark St. E1 5H 85
(not continuous)
Newark Way NW4 4C 44
New Ash Cl. N2 3B 46
New Atlas Wharf E14 3C 104
(off Arnhem Pl.)
New Baltic Wharf SE8 5A 104
(off Evelyn St.)
New Barn Cl. SM6: Wall 6K 167
NEW BARNET 4G 21
New Barn Rd. BR8: Swan 7K 145
New Barns Av. CR4: Mitc 4H 155
(not continuous)
New Barn St. E13 4J 87
New Barns Way IG7: Chig 3K 37
NEW BECKENHAM 6B 140
New Bentham Ct. N1 7C 66
(off Ecclesbourne Rd.)
Newbery Ho. N1 7C 66
(off Northampton St.)
Newbold Cotts. E1 6J 85
Newbolt Av. SM3: Cheam 5E 164
Newbolt Ho. SE17 5D 102
(off Brandon St.)
Newbolt Rd. HA7: Stan 5E 26
New Bond St. W1 1J 11 (6F 83)
Newborough Grn. KT3: N Mald 4K 151
New Brent St. NW4 5E 44
Newbridge Point SE23 3K 139
(off Windrush La.)
New Bri. St. EC4 1A 14 (6B 84)
New Broad St.
EC2 6G 9 (5E 84)
New Broadway TW12: Ham H 5H 131
UB10: Hil 3D 74
W5 7D 78
New Broadway Bldgs. W5 7D 78
Newburgh Rd. W3 1J 97
Newburgh St. W1 1B 12 (6G 83)
New Burlington M. W1 2A 12 (7G 83)
New Burlington Pl. W1 2A 12 (7G 83)
New Burlington St. W1 2A 12 (7G 83)
Newburn Ho. SE11 5H 19
(off Newburn St.)
Newburn St. SE11 5H 19 (5K 101)
Newbury Cl. UB5: N'olt 6D 58
Newbury Ct. DA14: Sidc 4K 143
Newbury Gdns. KT19: Ewe 4B 164
Newbury Ho. N22 1J 47
SW9 2B 120
W2 6K 81
(off Hallfield Est.)
Newbury M. NW5 6E 64
NEWBURY PARK 5H 53
Newbury Rd. BR2: Brom 3J 159
E4 6K 35
IG2: Ilf 6J 53
TW6: H'row A 1B 110
Newbury St. EC1 6C 8 (5C 84)
Newbury Way UB5: N'olt 6C 58
New Bus. Cen., The NW10 3B 80
New Butt La. SE8 7C 104
New Butt La. Nth. SE8 7C 104
(off Hales St.)
Newby NW1 2A 6
(off Robert St.)
Newby Cl. EN1: Enf 2K 23
Newby Ho. E14 7E 86
(off Newby Pl.)
Newby Pl. E14 7E 86
Newby St. SW8 3F 119
New Caledonian Mkt. SE1 7H 15
New Caledonian Wharf
SE16 3B 104
Newcastle Cl. EC4 7A 8 (6B 84)
Newcastle Ct. EC4 2D 14
(off College Hill)
Newcastle Ho. W1 5G 5
(off Luxborough St.)
Newcastle Pl. W2 5B 4 (5B 82)
Newcastle Row EC1 4K 7 (4A 84)
New Cavendish St. W1 6H 5 (5E 82)
New Change EC4 1C 14 (6C 84)
New Chapel Sq. TW13: Felt 1K 129
New Charles St. EC1 1B 8 (3B 84)
NEW CHARLTON 4A 106
New Chiswick Pool 7A 98
New Church Rd. SE5 7C 102
(not continuous)
New City Rd. E13 3A 88
New Cl. SW19 3A 154
TW13: Hanw 5C 130
New Colebrooke Ct. SM5: Cars 7D 166
(off Stanley Rd.)
New College Ct. NW3 6A 64
(off Finchley Rd.)
New College M. N1 7A 66
New College Pde. NW3 6B 64
(off Finchley Rd.)
Newcombe Gdns. SW16 4J 137
TW4: Houn 4D 112
Newcombe Ho. E5 3H 67
Newcombe Pk. HA0: Wemb 1F 79
NW7 5F 29
Newcombe Ri. UB7: Yiew 6A 74
Newcombe St. W8 1J 99
Newcomen Rd. E11 3H 69
SW11 3B 118
Newcomen St. SE1 6E 14 (2D 102)
New Compton St. WC2 1D 12 (6H 83)
New Concordia Wharf
SE1 6K 15 (2G 103)
New Ct. EC4 2J 13
UB5: N'olt 5F 59
Newcourt Ho. E2 3H 85
(off Pott St.)
Newcourt St. NW8 1C 4 (2C 82)
New Covent Garden Market
7D 18 (7H 101)
New Crane Pl. E1 1J 103
New Crane Wharf E1 1J 103
(off New Crane Pl.)
New Cres. Yd. NW10 2B 80
Newcroft Cl. UB8: Hil 5B 74
NEW CROSS 7B 104
NEW CROSS 1B 122
NEW CROSS GATE 1K 121
NEW CROSS GATE 1K 121
New Cross Rd. SE14 7J 103
New Curzon Cinema 4B 48
Newdales Cl. N9 2B 34
Newdene Av. UB5: N'olt 2B 76
Newdigate Ho. E14 6B 86
(off Norbiton Rd.)
Newell St. E14 6B 86
NEW ELTHAM 2G 143
New End NW3 4A 64
New End Sq. NW3 4B 64
New End Theatre
Hampstead 3A 64
New England Ind. Est.
IG11: Bark 2G 89
Newent Cl. SE15 7E 102
SM5: Cars 1D 166
New Era Est. N1 1E 84
(off Phillipp St.)
New Era Ho. N1 1E 84
(off New Era Est.)
New Farm Av. BR2: Brom 4J 159
New Farm La. HA6: Nwood 1G 39
New Fetter La. EC4 7K 7 (6A 84)
Newfield Cl. TW12: Hamp 1E 148
Newfield Ri. NW2 3C 62
New Fieldways EN5: Barn 6C 20
New Forest La. IG7: Chig 6K 37
Newgale Gdns. HA8: Edg 1F 43
New Garden Dr. UB7: W Dray 2A 92
Newgate CR0: C'don 1C 168
Newgate Cl. TW13: Hanw 2C 130
Newgate St. E4 3B 36
(not continuous)
EC1 7B 8 (6B 84)
New Globe Wlk. SE1 4C 14 (1C 102)
New Goulston St. E1 7J 9 (6F 85)
New Grn. Pl. SE19 6E 138
Newham College of Further Education
Stratford Campus 7G 69
Newham Leisure Cen. 4A 88
Newham's Row SE1 7H 15 (3E 102)
Newham Way E6 5A 88
E16 5H 87
Newhaven Cl. UB3: Harl 4H 93
Newhaven Cres. TW15: Ashf 5F 129
Newhaven Gdns. SE9 4B 124
Newhaven La. E16 4H 87
Newhaven Rd. SE25 5D 156
New Heston Rd. TW5: Hest 7D 94
New Hope Ct. NW10 3D 80
(off Harrow Rd.)
New Horizons Ct.
TW8: Bford 6A 96
Newhouse Av. RM6: Chad H 3D 54
Newhouse Cl. KT3: N Mald 7A 152
Newhouse Wlk. SM4: Mord 7A 154
Newick Cl. DA5: Bexl 6H 127
Newick Rd. E5 4H 67
Newing Grn. BR1: Brom 7B 142
NEWINGTON 7C 14 (3C 102)
Newington Barrow Way N7 3K 65
Newington Butts SE1 4B 102
SE11 4B 102
Newington C'way. SE1 7C 14 (3B 102)
Newington Ct. Bus. Cen.
SE1 7C 14
Newington Grn. N1 5D 66
N16 5D 66
Newington Grn. Mans.
N16 5D 66
Newington Grn. Rd. N1 6D 66
Newington Ind. Est. SE17 4C 102
New Inn B'way. EC2 3H 9 (4E 84)
New Inn Pas. WC2 1H 13
New Inn Sq. EC2 3H 9
New Inn St. EC2 3H 9 (4E 84)
New Inn Yd. EC2 3H 9 (4E 84)
New Jubilee Ct.
IG8: Wfd G 7D 36
New Jubilee Wharf E1 1J 103
(off Wapping Wall)
New Kelvin Av.
TW11: Tedd 6J 131
New Kent Rd. SE1 3C 102
New Kings Rd. SW6 2H 117
New King St. SE8 6C 104
Newland Ct. EC1 2E 8
HA9: Wemb 2G 61
Newland Dr. EN1: Enf 1C 24
Newland Gdns. W13 2A 96
Newland Ho. N8 3J 47
(off Newland Rd.)
SE14 6K 103
(off John Williams Cl.)
Newland Rd. N8 3J 47
NEWLANDS
HA8 3K 27
SE23 5K 121
Newlands NW1 1A 6
(off Harrington St.)
Newlands, The KT7: T Ditt 7J 149
SM6: Wall 7G 167
Newlands Av. KT7: T Ditt 7J 149
Newlands Cl. HA0: Wemb 6C 60
HA8: Edg 3K 27
UB2: S'hall 5C 94
Newlands Ct. SE9 6E 124
Newlands Dr. SL3: Poyle 6A 174
Newlands Pk. SE26 6J 139
Newlands Pl. EN5: Barn 5A 20
Newlands Quay E1 7J 85
Newlands Rd.
IG8: Wfd G 2C 36
SW16 2J 155
Newland St. E16 1C 106
Newlands Way KT9: Chess 5C 162
Newlands Wood CR0: Sels 7B 170
Newling Cl. E6 6D 88
New London St. EC3 2H 15
New London Theatre 7F 7
(off Parker St.)
New Lydenburg Commercial Est.
SE7 3A 106
New Lydenburg St. SE7 3A 106
Newlyn NW1 1G 83
(off Plender St.)
Newlyn Cl. BR6: Chels 4K 173
UB8: Hil 5C 74
Newlyn Gdns. HA2: Harr 7D 40
Newlyn Ho. HA5: Hat E 1D 40
Newlyn Rd. DA16: Well 2K 125
EN5: Barn 4C 20
N17 1F 49
NEW MALDEN 4A 152
Newman Ct. BR1: Brom 1J 159
(off North St.)
Newman Ho. SE1 3B 102
Newman Pas. W1 6B 6 (5G 83)
Newman Rd. BR1: Brom 1J 159
CR0: C'don 1K 167
E13 3K 87
E17 5K 49
UB3: Hayes 7K 75
Newman Rd. Ind. Est.
CR0: C'don 7K 155
Newman's Ct. EC3 1F 15
Newmans La. KT6: Surb 6D 150
Newman's Row WC2 6H 7 (5K 83)
Newman St. W1 6B 6 (5G 83)
Newman's Way EN4: Had W 1F 21
Newman Yd. W1 7C 6 (6G 83)
Newmarket Av. UB5: N'olt 5E 58
Newmarket Grn. SE9 7B 124
Newmarsh Rd. SE28 1K 107
Newmill Ho. E3 4E 86
Newminster Rd. SM4: Mord 6A 154
New Mount St. E15 7F 69
Newnes Path SW15 4D 116
Newnham Av. HA4: Ruis 1A 58
Newnham Cl. CR7: Thor H 2C 156
UB5: N'olt 6G 59
Newnham Gdns. UB5: N'olt 6G 59
Newnham Grn. N22 1A 48
(off Highfield Cl.)
Newnham Lodge DA17: Belv 5G 109
(off Erith Rd.)
Newnham M. N22 7F 33
Newnham Rd. N22 1K 47
Newnhams Cl. BR1: Brom 3D 160
Newnham Ter. SE1 1J 19 (3A 102)

Newnham Way HA3: Kent 5E 42
New North Pl. EC2 3G 9 (4E 84)
New North Rd. IG6: Ilf 1G 53
N1 1F 9 (7C 66)
New North St. WC1 5G 7 (5K 83)
Newnton Cl. N4 7D 48
(not continuous)
New Oak Rd. N2 2A 46
New Orleans Wlk. N19 7H 47
New Oxford St. WC1 7D 6 (6H 83)
New Pde. TW15: Ashf 4B 128
UB7: Yiew 1A 92
New Pk. Av. N13 3H 33
New Pk. Cl. UB5: N'olt 6C 58
New Pk. Est. N18 5D 34
New Pk. Ho. N13 4E 32
New Pk. Pde. *SW2* *7J 119*
(off New Pk. Rd.)
New Pk. Rd. SW2 1H 137
TW15: Ashf 5E 128
New Pl. CR0: Addtn 6C 170
New Pl. Sq. SE16 3H 103
New Plaistow Rd. E15 1G 87
New Players Theatre *1J 101*
(off Villiers St.)
New Pond Pde. HA4: Ruis 3J 57
Newport Av. E13 4K 87
E14 7F 87
Newport Ct. WC2 2D 12 (7H 83)
Newport Ho. *E3* *3A 86*
(off Strahan Rd.)
Newport Lodge *EN1: Enf* *5K 23*
(off Village Rd.)
Newport Pl. WC2 2D 12 (7H 83)
Newport Rd. E10 2E 68
E17 4A 50
SW13 1C 116
TW6: H'row A 1C 110
UB4: Hayes 5F 75
W3 2J 97
Newport St. SE11 4G 19 (4K 101)
New Priory Ct. *NW6* *7J 63*
(off Mazenod Av.)
New Providence Wharf E14 1F 105
Newquay Cres. HA2: Harr 2C 58
Newquay Ho. SE11 5J 19 (5A 102)
Newquay Rd. SE6 2D 140
New Quebec St. W1 1F 11 (6D 82)
New Ride SW1 2C 100
SW7 6C 10 (2C 100)
New River Av. N8 3K 47
New River Ct. N5 4C 66
New River Cres. N13 4G 33
New River Head EC1 1K 7 (3A 84)
New River Sports & Recreation Cen. 7G 33
New River Wlk. N1 6C 66
New River Way N4 7D 48
New Rd. CR4: Mitc 1D 166
DA16: Well 2B 126
E1 5H 85
E4 4J 35
E12 2C 70
HA1: Harr 4K 59
IG3: Ilf 2J 71
KT2: King T 7G 133
KT8: W Mole 4E 148
N8 5J 47
N9 2C 34
N17 1F 49
N22 1C 48
NW7 7B 30
RM9: Dag 2G 91
RM10: Dag 2G 91
SE2 4D 108
TW3: Houn 4F 113
TW8: Bford 6D 96
TW10: Ham 4C 132
TW13: Hanw 5C 130
TW14: Bedf 6F 111
New Rd. TW14: Felt 1K 129
TW17: Shep 3C 146
UB3: Harl 7E 92
UB8: Hil 4E 74
New Rd. Hill BR2: Kes 7C 172
BR6: Downe 7C 172
New Rochford St. NW5 5D 64
New Row WC2 2E 12 (7J 83)
Newry Rd. TW1: Twick 5A 114
Newsam Av. N15 5D 48
Newsholme Dr. N21 5E 22
NEW SOUTHGATE 5A 32
New Southgate Crematorium
N11 3A 32
New Southgate Ind. Est.
N11 5B 32
New Spitalfields Mkt. E10 3D 68
New Spring Gdns. Wlk.
SE11 6F 19 (5J 101)
New Sq. TW14: Bedf 1E 128
WC2 7J 7 (6A 84)
New Sq. Pk. TW14: Bedf 1E 128
New Sq. Pas. WC2 7J 7
Newstead Av. BR6: Orp 3H 173
Newstead Cl. N12 6H 31
Newstead Ct. UB5: N'olt 3C 76
Newstead Ho. *N1* *2A 84*
(off Tolpuddle St.)
Newstead Rd. SE12 7H 123
Newstead Wlk. SM5: Cars 7A 154
Newstead Way SW19 4F 135
New St. EC2 6H 9 (5E 84)
New St. Hill BR1: Brom 5K 141
New St. Sq. EC4 7K 7 (6A 84)
(not continuous)
Newton Av. N10 1E 46
W3 2J 97
Newton Cl. E17 6A 50
HA2: Harr 2E 58
Newton Ct. *NW6* *7A 64*
(off Fairfax Rd.)
W8 *2J 99*
(off Kensington Chu. St.)
Newton Gro. W4 4A 98
Newton Ho. *E1* *7H 85*
(off Cornwall St.)
E17 *3D 50*
(off Prospect Hill)
EN3: Enf H 3E 24
NW8 *1K 81*
(off Abbey Rd.)
SE20 7K 139
Newton Ind. Est. RM6: Chad H 4D 54
Newton Mans. *W14* *6G 99*
(off Queen's Club Gdns.)
Newton Pk. Pl. BR7: Chst 7D 142
Newton Pl. E14 4C 104
Newton Point *E16* *6H 87*
(off Clarkson Rd.)
Newton Rd. DA16: Well 3A 126
E15 5F 69
HA0: Wemb 7F 61
HA3: Hrw W 2J 41
N15 5G 49
NW2 4E 62
SW19 7G 135
TW7: Isle 2K 113
W2 6K 81
Newton St. WC2 7F 7 (6J 83)
Newton's Yd. SW18 5J 117
Newton Ter. BR2: Brom 6B 160
Newton Wlk. HA8: Edg 1H 43
Newton Way N18 5H 33
New Twr. Bldgs. E1 1H 103
Newtown St. SW11 1F 119
New Trinity Rd. N2 3B 46
New Turnstile WC1 6G 7
New Union Cl. E14 3E 104
New Union St. EC2 6E 8 (5D 84)
New Wanstead E11 6H 51
New Way Rd. NW9 4A 44
New Wharf Rd. N1 2J 83
NEWYEARS GREEN 7B 38
Newyears Grn. La. UB9: Hare 6A 38
New Zealand Av. KT12: Walt T 7H 147
New Zealand Way W12 7D 80
Nexus Ct. E11 1G 69
Niagara Av. W5 4C 96
Niagra Cl. N1 2C 84
Niagra Ct. *SE16* *3J 103*
(off Canada Est.)
Nibthwaite Rd. HA1: Harr 5J 41
Nice Bus. Pk. SE15 6H 103
Nicholas Cl. UB6: G'frd 2F 77
Nicholas Ct. SE12 1J 141
W4 *6A 98*
(off Corney Reach Way)
Nicholas Gdns. W5 2D 96
Nicholas La. EC4 2F 15 (7D 84)
(not continuous)
Nicholas M. W4 6A 98
Nicholas Pas. EC4 2F 15
Nicholas Rd. CR0: Bedd 4J 167
E1 4J 85
RM8: Dag 2F 73
W11 7F 81
Nicholas Stacey Ho. *SE7* *5K 105*
(off Frank Burton Cl.)
Nicholas Way HA6: Nwood 1E 38
Nicholay Rd. N19 1H 65
(not continuous)
Nichol Cl. N14 1C 32
Nicholes Rd. TW3: Houn 4E 112
Nichol La. BR1: Brom 7J 141
Nicholl Ho. N4 1C 66
Nicholls Av. UB8: Hil 4C 74
Nichollsfield Wlk. N7 5K 65
Nicholls Point *E15* *1J 87*
(off Park Gro.)
Nicholl St. E2 1G 85
Nichols Cl. KT9: Chess 6C 162
N4 *1A 66*
(off Osborne Rd.)
Nichols Ct. E2 2F 85
Nichols Grn. W5 5E 78
Nicholson Ct. E17 4A 50
N17 3F 49
Nicholson Ho. SE17 5D 102
Nicholson M. KT1: King T 4E 150
Nicholson Rd. CR0: C'don 1F 169
Nicholson St. SE1 5A 14 (1B 102)
Nickelby Cl. SE28 6C 90
Nickleby Cl. UB8: Hil 6D 74
Nickleby Ho. *SE16* *7K 15*
(off Parkers Row)
W11 *1F 99*
(off St Ann's Rd.)
Nickols Wlk. SW18 4K 117
Nicola Cl. CR2: S Croy 6C 168
HA3: Hrw W 2H 41
Nicolas Ct. E13 3K 87
Nicola Ter. DA7: Bex 1E 126
Nicol Cl. TW1: Twick 6B 114
Nicoll Ct. N10 7A 32
NW10 1A 80
Nicoll Pl. NW4 6D 44
Nicoll Rd. NW10 1A 80
Nicolson NW9 1A 44
Nicolson Dr. WD23: B Hea 1B 26
Nicosia Rd. SW18 7C 118
Niederwald Rd. SE26 4A 140
Nield Rd. UB3: Hayes 2H 93
Nigel Cl. UB5: N'olt 1C 76
Nigel Ct. N3 7E 30
Nigel Fisher Way
KT9: Chess 7C 162
Nigel Ho. *EC1* *5J 7*
(off Portpool La.)
Nigel M. IG1: Ilf 4F 71
Nigel Playfair Av. W6 4D 98
Nigel Rd. E7 5A 70
SE15 3G 121
Nigeria Rd. SE7 7A 106
Nighthawk NW9 1B 44
Nightingale Av. E4 5B 36
HA1: Harr 7B 42
Nightingale Cl. E4 4A 36
HA5: Eastc 5A 40
SM5: Cars 2E 166
W4 6J 97
Nightingale Ct. BR2: Brom 2G 159
E14 *2E 104*
(off Ovex Cl.)
HA1: Harr 6K 41
N4 *2K 65*
(off Tollington Pk.)
SM1: Sutt 5A 166
SW6 *1K 117*
(off Maltings Pl.)
Nightingale Dr. KT19: Ewe 6H 163
Nightingale Gro. SE13 5F 123
Nightingale Hgts. SE18 6F 107
Nightingale Ho. *E1* *1G 103*
(off Thomas More St.)
E2 *1E 84*
(off Kingsland Rd.)
Nightingale Ho. *SE18* *5E 106*
(off Connaught M.)
W12 *6E 80*
(off Du Cane Rd.)
Nightingale La. BR1: Brom 2A 160
E11 4K 51
N8 4J 47
SW4 7D 118
SW12 7D 118
TW10: Rich 7E 114
Nightingale Lodge *W9* *5J 81*
(off Admiral Wlk.)
Nightingale M. E3 2K 85
E11 5J 51
KT1: King T *3D 150*
(off South La.)
SE11 3K 19 (4B 102)
Nightingale Pl. SE18 6E 106
SW10 7A 16 (6A 100)
Nightingale Rd. BR5: Pet W 6G 161
E5 3H 67
KT8: W Mole 5F 149
KT12: Walt T 7A 148
N1 6C 66
N9 6D 24
N22 1J 47
NW10 2B 80
SM5: Cars 3D 166
TW12: Hamp 5E 130
W7 1K 95
Nightingales, The
TW19: Stanw 1B 128
Nightingale Sq. SW12 7E 118
Nightingale Va. SE18 6E 106
Nightingale Wlk. SW4 6F 119
Nightingale Way E6 5C 88
Nile Cl. N16 3F 67
Nile Dr. N9 2D 34
Nile Path SE18 6E 106
Nile Rd. E13 2A 88
Nile St. N1 1D 8 (3C 84)
Nile Ter. SE15 5F 103
Nimegen Way SE22 5E 120
Nimmo Dr. WD23: B Hea 1C 26
Nimrod NW9 1A 44
Nimrod Cl. UB5: N'olt 3B 76
Nimrod Ho. *E16* *5K 87*
(off Vanguard Cl.)
Nimrod Pas. N1 6E 66
Nimrod Rd. SW16 6F 137
Nina Mackay Cl. E15 1G 87
Nine Acres Cl. E12 5C 70
NINE ELMS 7G 101
Nine Elms Cl. TW14: Felt 1H 129

Nine Elms La. SW8 7C 18 (7G 101)
Nineteenth Rd. CR4: Mitc 4J 155
Ninhams Wood BR6: Farnb 4E 172
Ninth Av. UB3: Hayes 7J 75
Nipponzan Myohoji Peace Pagoda 6D 100
Nirvana Apartments N1 1B 84
(off Islington Grn.)
Nisbet Ho. E9 5K 67
Nisbett Wlk. DA14: Sidc 4A 144
(off Sidcup High St.)
Nita Ct. SE12 1J 141
Nithdale Rd. SE18 7F 107
Nithsdale Gro. UB10: Ick 3E 56
Niton Cl. EN5: Barn 6A 20
Niton Rd. TW9: Rich 3G 115
Niton St. SW6 7F 99
No 1 St. SE18 3F 107
Nobel Dr. UB3: Harl 1F 111
Nobel Ho. SE5 2C 120
Nobel Rd. N18 4D 34
Noble Cnr. TW5: Hest 1E 112
Noble Ct. CR4: Mitc 2B 154
E1 7H 85
(not continuous)
Noblefield Hgts. N2 5C 46
Noble M. N16 3D 66
(off Albion Rd.)
Noble St. EC2 7C 8 (6C 84)
Nocavia Ho. SW6 2A 118
(off Townmead Rd.)
Noel NW9 1A 44
Noel Ct. TW4: Houn 3D 112
Noel Coward Ho. SW1 4B 18
(off Vauxhall Bri. Rd.)
Noel Coward Theatre 2E 12
(off St Martin's La.)
Noel Ho. NW6 7B 64
(off Harben Rd.)
NOEL PARK 2B 48
Noel Pk. Rd. N22 2A 48
Noel Rd. E6 4C 88
N1 2B 84
W3 7G 79
Noel Sq. RM8: Dag 4C 72
Noel St. W1 1B 12 (6G 83)
Noel Ter. DA14: Sidc 4B 144
SE23 2J 139
Noko W10 3F 81
Nolan Way E5 4G 67
Noll Ho. N7 2K 65
(off Tomlins Wlk.)
Nolton Pl. HA8: Edg 1F 43
Nonsuch Ho. SW19 1B 154
Nonsuch Pl. SM3: Cheam 7F 165
(off Ewell Rd.)
Nonsuch Wlk. SM2: Cheam 7F 165
(not continuous)
Nora Gdns. NW4 4F 45
Nora Leverton Ct. NW1 7G 65
(off Randolph St.)
NORBITON 2G 151
Norbiton Av. KT1: King T 1G 151
Norbiton Comn. Rd.
KT1: King T 3H 151
Norbiton Hall KT2: King T 2F 151
Norbiton Ho. NW1 1G 83
(off Camden St.)
Norbiton Rd. E14 6B 86
Norbreck Gdns. NW10 3F 79
Norbreck Pde. NW10 3E 78
Norbroke St. W12 7B 80
Norburn St. W10 5G 81
NORBURY 2K 155
Norbury Av. CR7: Thor H 1K 155
SW16 1K 155
TW3: Houn 4H 113
Norbury Cl. SW16 1A 156
Norbury Ct. Rd. SW16 3J 155
Norbury Cres. SW16 1K 155
Norbury Cross SW16 3J 155
Norbury Gdns. RM6: Chad H 5D 54
Norbury Gro. NW7 3F 29
Norbury Hill SW16 7A 138
Norbury Ri. SW16 3J 155
Norbury Rd. CR7: Thor H 2C 156
E4 5H 35
TW13: Felt 3H 129
Norbury Trad. Est. SW16 2K 155
Norcombe Gdns. HA3: Kent 6C 42
Norcombe Ho. N19 3H 65
(off Wedmore St.)
Norcott Cl. UB4: Yead 4A 76
Norcott Rd. N16 2G 67
Norcroft Gdns. SE22 7G 121
Norcutt Rd. TW2: Twick 1J 131
Nordenfeldt Rd. DA8: Erith 5K 109
Norden Ho. E2 3H 85
(off Pott St.)
Norfield Rd. DA2: Dart 4J 145
Norfolk Av. N13 6G 33
N15 6F 49
Norfolk Cl. EN4: Cockf 4K 21
N2 3C 46
N13 6G 33
TW1: Twick 6B 114
Norfolk Ct. EN5: Barn 4B 20
RM6: Chad H 5B 54
(off Norwich Cres.)
Norfolk Cres. DA15: Sidc 7J 125
W2 7C 4 (6C 82)
Norfolk Gdns. DA7: Bex 1F 127
TW4: Houn 5D 112
Norfolk Ho. BR2: Brom 4H 159
(off Westmoreland Rd.)
EC4 2C 14
SE3 6G 105
(off Restell Cl.)
SE8 1C 122
SE20 1J 157
SW1 3D 18
(off Page St.)
Norfolk Ho. Rd. SW16 3H 137
Norfolk Mans. SW11 1D 118
(off Prince of Wales Dr.)
Norfolk M. W10 5G 81
(off Blagrove Rd.)
Norfolk Pl. DA16: Well 2A 126
W2 7B 4 (6B 82)
(not continuous)
Norfolk Rd. CR7: Thor H 3C 156
E6 1D 88
E17 2K 49
EN3: Pond E 6C 24
EN5: New Bar 3D 20
HA1: Harr 5F 41
IG3: Ilf 1J 71
IG11: Bark 7J 71
NW8 1B 82
NW10 7A 62
RM7: Rom 6J 55
RM10: Dag 5H 73
SW19 7C 136
TW13: Felt 1A 130
UB8: Uxb 6A 56
Norfolk Row SE1 3G 19 (4K 101)
(not continuous)
Norfolk Sq. W2 1B 10 (6B 82)
Norfolk Sq. M. W2 1B 10
Norfolk St. E7 5J 69
Norfolk Ter. W6 5G 99
Norgrove St. SW12 7E 118
Norhyrst Av. SE25 3F 157
Norland Ho. W11 1F 99
(off Queensdale Cres.)
Norland Pl. W11 1G 99
Norland Rd. W11 1F 99
Norlands Cres. BR7: Chst 1F 161
Norland Sq. W11 1G 99
Norland Sq. Mans. W11 1G 99
(off Norland Sq.)
Norley Va. SW15 1C 134
Norlington Rd. E10 1E 68
E11 1E 68
Norman Av. N22 1B 48
TW1: Twick 7C 114
TW13: Hanw 2C 130
UB1: S'hall 7C 76
Norman Butler Ho. W10 4G 81
(off Ladbroke Gro.)
Normanby Cl. SW15 5H 117
Normanby Rd. NW10 4B 62
Norman Cl. BR6: Farnb 3G 173
N22 1C 48
RM5: Col R 1H 55
Norman Ct. IG2: Ilf 7H 53
N3 1J 45
(off Nether St.)
N4 7A 48
NW10 7C 62
W13 1B 96
(off Kirkfield Cl.)
Norman Cres. HA5: Pinn 1A 40
TW5: Hest 7B 94
Normand Gdns. W14 6G 99
(off Greyhound Rd.)
Normand Mans. W14 6G 99
(off Normand M.)
Normand M. W14 6G 99
Normand Rd. W14 6H 99
Normandy Av. EN5: Barn 5C 20
Normandy Cl. SE26 3A 140
Normandy Dr. UB3: Hayes 6E 74
Normandy Ho. E14 2E 104
(off Plevna St.)
EN2: Enf 1H 23
Normandy Rd. SW9 1A 120
Normandy Ter. E16 6K 87
Normandy Way DA8: Erith 1K 127
Norman Gro. E3 2A 86
Norman Hay Trad. Est., The
UB7: Sip 7B 92
Norman Ho. SW8 7J 101
(off Wyvil Rd.)
TW13: Hanw 2D 130
(off Watermill Way)
Normanhurst TW15: Ashf 5C 128
Normanhurst Av. DA7: Bex 1D 126
DA16: Well 1D 126
Normanhurst Dr. TW1: Twick 5A 114
Normanhurst Rd. SW2 2K 137
Norman Pde. DA14: Sidc 2D 144
Norman Pk. Athletics Track 6K 159
Norman Rd. CR7: Thor H 5B 156
DA17: Belv 3H 109
(not continuous)
E6 4D 88
E11 2F 69
IG1: Ilf 5F 71
N15 5F 49
SE10 7D 104
SM1: Sutt 5J 165
SW19 7A 136
TW15: Ashf 6F 129
Normans Cl. NW10 6K 61
UB8: Hil 5B 74
Normansfield Av. TW11: Tedd 7C 132
Normanshire Dr. E4 4H 35
Norman's Mead NW10 6K 61
Norman St. EC1 2D 8 (3C 84)
Normanton Av. SW19 2J 135
Normanton Pk. E4 2B 36
Normanton Rd. CR2: S Croy 5E 168
Normanton St. SE23 2K 139
Norman Way N14 2D 32
W3 5H 79
Normington Cl.
SW16 5A 138
Norrice Lea N2 5B 46
Norris NW9 1B 44
(off The Concourse)
Norris Ho. E9 1J 85
(off Handley Rd.)
N1 1E 84
(off Colville Est.)
SE8 5B 104
(off Grove St.)
Norris St. SW1 3C 12 (7H 83)
Norroy Rd. SW15 4F 117
Norry's Cl. EN4: Cockf 4J 21
Norry's Rd. EN4: Cockf 4J 21
Norseman Cl. IG3: Ilf 1B 72
Norseman Way UB6: G'frd 1F 77
Norstead Pl. SW15 2C 134
Nth. Access Rd. E17 6K 49
North Acre NW9 1A 44
NORTH ACTON 4K 79
Nth. Acton Bus. Pk. W3 5K 79
Nth. Acton Rd. NW10 2K 79
Northall Rd. DA7: Bex 2J 127
Northampton Gro. N1 5D 66
Northampton Pk. N1 6C 66
Northampton Rd.
CR0: C'don 2G 169
EC1 3K 7 (4A 84)
EN3: Pond E 4F 25
Northampton Row EC1 3K 7
Northampton Sq. EC1 2A 8 (3B 84)
Northampton St. N1 7C 66
Northanger Rd. SW16 6J 137
Nth. Audley St. W1 1G 11 (7E 82)
North Av. HA2: Harr 6F 41
N18 4B 34
NW10 3E 80
SM5: Cars 7E 166
TW9: Kew 1G 115
UB1: S'hall 7D 76
UB3: Hayes 7J 75
W13 5B 78
Northaw Ho. W10 4E 80
(off Sutton Way)
North Bank NW8 2C 4 (3C 82)
Nth. Bank Bri. N7 4A 66
Northbank Rd. E17 2E 50
NORTH BECKTON 5C 88
Nth. Birkbeck Rd. E11 3F 69
North Block SE1 6H 13
(off York Rd.)
Northborough Rd. SW16 3H 155
Nth. Boundary Rd. E12 3B 70
Northbourne BR2: Hayes 7J 159
Northbourne Rd. SW4 5H 119
Nth. Branch Av. NW10 3E 80
Northbrook Dr.
HA6: Nwood 1G 39
Northbrook Rd. CR0: C'don 5D 156
EN5: Barn 6B 20
IG1: Ilf 2E 70
N22 7D 32
SE13 5G 123
Northburgh St. EC1 4B 8 (4B 84)
Nth. Carriage Dr. W2 2C 10
NORTH CHEAM 3E 164
North Cheam Sports Club 3F 165
Northchurch SE17 5D 102
(not continuous)
Northchurch Ho. E2 1G 85
(off Whiston Rd.)
Northchurch Rd. HA9: Wemb 6G 61
N1 7D 66
(not continuous)
Northchurch Ter. N1 7E 66
Nth. Circular Rd. E4 6G 35
E18 2A 52
IG1: Ilf 2D 70
IG11: Bark 1F 89
N3 4H 45
N12 2A 46
N13 5F 33
NW2 3A 62
NW4 7E 44

Nth. Circular Rd. NW10 2F **79**
NW11 7E **44**
Northcliffe Cl. KT4: Wor Pk 3A **164**
Northcliffe Dr. N20 1C **30**
North Cl. DA6: Bex 4D **126**
RM10: Dag 1G **91**
SM4: Mord 4G **153**
TW14: Bedf 6F **111**
Nth. Colonnade, The
E14 1C **104**
North Comn. Rd. UB8: Uxb 5A **56**
W5 7E **78**
Northcote HA5: Pinn 2A **40**
Northcote Av. KT5: Surb 7H **151**
TW7: Isle 5A **114**
UB1: S'hall 7C **76**
W5 7E **78**
Northcote M. SW11 4C **118**
Northcote Rd. CR0: C'don 6D **156**
DA14: Sidc 4J **143**
E17 4A **50**
KT3: N Mald 3J **151**
NW10 7A **62**
SW11 5C **118**
TW1: Twick 5A **114**
Northcott Av. N22 1J **47**
Nth. Countess Rd. E17 2B **50**
North Ct. *BR1: Brom* *1K 159*
(off Palace Gro.)
SE24 3B **120**
SW1 *2E 18*
(off Gt. Peter St.)
W1 5B **6** (5G **83**)
NORTH CRAY 5E **144**
Nth. Cray Rd. DA5: Bexl 1H **145**
DA14: Sidc 6E **144**
North Cray Woods 4D **144**
North Cres. E16 4F **87**
N3 2H **45**
WC1 5C **6** (5H **83**)
Northcroft Ct. W12 2C **98**
Northcroft Rd. KT19: Ewe 7A **164**
W13 2B **96**
North Crofts SE23 1H **139**
Northcroft Ter. W13 2B **96**
Nth. Cross Rd. IG6: Ilf 4G **53**
SE22 5F **121**
Northdale Ct. SE25 3F **157**
North Dene NW7 3E **28**
TW3: Houn 1F **113**
Northdene Gdns. N15 6F **49**
Northdown Cl. HA4: Ruis 3H **57**
Northdown Gdns. IG2: Ilf 5J **53**
Northdown Rd. DA16: Well 2B **126**
Northdown St. N1 1G **7** (2J **83**)
North Dr. BR3: Beck 4D **158**
BR6: Orp 4J **173**
HA4: Ruis 7G **39**
SW16 4G **137**
TW3: Houn 2G **113**
North E. Surrey Crematorium
SM4: Mord 6E **152**
NORTH END 2A **64**
North End CR0: C'don 2C **168**
IG9: Buck H 1F **37**
NW3 2A **64**
North End Av. NW3 2A **64**
(not continuous)
North End Cres. W14 4H **99**
North End Ho. W14 4G **99**
North End La. BR6: Downe 7F **173**
North End Pde. *W14* *4G 99*
(off North End Rd.)
North End Rd. HA9: Wemb 3G **61**
NW11 1J **63**
SW6 4G **99**
W14 4G **99**
North End Way NW3 2A **64**
Northern Av. N9 2K **33**
Northernhay Wlk. SM4: Mord 4G **153**
Northern Hgts. *N8* *7H 47*
(off Crescent Rd.)
Northern Perimeter Rd.
TW6: H'row A 1D **110**
Northern Perimeter Rd. (West)
TW6: H'row A 4E **174**
Northern Rd. E13 2K **87**
Northesk Ho. *E1* *4H 85*
(off Tent St.)
Nth. Eyot Gdns. W6 5B **98**
Northey St. E14 7A **86**
NORTH FELTHAM 6K **111**
Nth. Feltham Trad. Est.
TW14: Felt 5K **111**
Northfield Av. HA5: Pinn 4B **40**
W5 1B **96**
W13 1B **96**
Northfield Cl. BR1: Brom 1C **160**
UB3: Harl 3H **93**
Northfield Cres. SM3: Cheam 4G **165**
Northfield Gdns. RM9: Dag 4F **73**
Northfield Ho. SE15 6G **103**
Northfield Ind. Est. NW10 3G **79**
Northfield Pde. UB3: Harl 3G **93**
Northfield Pk. UB3: Harl 3H **93**
Northfield Path
RM9: Dag 4F **73**
Northfield Rd. E6 7D **70**
EN3: Pond E 5C **24**
EN4: Cockf 3H **21**
N16 7E **48**
RM9: Dag 4F **73**
TW5: Hest 6B **94**
W13 2B **96**
NORTHFIELDS 3B **96**
Northfields SW18 4J **117**
Northfields Ind. Est. HA0: Wemb 1G **79**
Northfields Prospect Bus. Cen.
SW18 4J **117**
Northfields Rd. W3 5H **79**
NORTH FINCHLEY 5F **31**
Northfleet Ho. *SE1* *6E 14*
(off Tennis St.)
Northflock St. SE16 2G **103**
Nth. Flower Wlk. W2 3A **10**
North Gdn. E14 1B **104**
North Gdns. SW19 7B **136**
North Ga. NW8 1C **4**
Northgate HA6: Nwood 1E **38**
Northgate Bus. Cen. EN1: Enf 3C **24**
Northgate Ct. SW9 3A **120**
Northgate Dr. NW9 6A **44**
Northgate Ho. *E14* *7C 86*
(off E. India Dock Rd.)
Northgate Ind. Pk. RM5: Col R 1F **55**
North Gates *N12* *1A 46*
(off Bow La.)
Nth. Glade, The DA5: Bexl 7F **127**
Nth. Gower St. NW1 2B **6** (3G **83**)
North Grn. NW9 7F **29**
North Gro. N6 7E **46**
N15 5D **48**
NORTH HARROW 5F **41**
Nth. Hatton Rd. TW6: H'row A 1F **111**
North Hill N6 6D **46**
Nth. Hill Av. N6 6E **46**
NORTH HILLINGDON 7E **56**
North Ho. SE8 5B **104**
Nth. Hyde Gdns. UB3: Harl, Hayes 3J **93**
Nth. Hyde La. TW5: Hest 5C **94**
UB2: S'hall 5B **94**
Nth. Hyde Rd. UB3: Harl 3G **93**
Northiam N12 4D **30**
(not continuous)
WC1 *2F 7*
(off Cromer St.)
Northiam St. E9 1H **85**
Northington St. WC1 4H **7** (4K **83**)
NORTH KENSINGTON 5F **81**
North Kent Indoor Bowls Club 3H **109**
Northlands Av. BR6: Orp 4J **173**
Northlands St. SE5 2C **120**
North La. TW11: Tedd 6K **131**
North Lodge *E16* *1K 105*
(off Wesley Av.)
EN5: New Bar 5F **21**
Nth. Lodge Cl. SW15 5F **117**
Nth. London Bus. Pk. N11 2K **31**
North Mall *N9* *2C 34*
(off Plevna Rd.)
SW18 *5K 117*
(off Buckhold Rd.)
North M. WC1 4H **7** (4K **83**)
North Mt. *N20* *2F 31*
(off High Rd.)
Northolm HA8: Edg 4E **28**
Northolme Gdns. HA8: Edg 1G **43**
Northolme Ri. BR6: Orp 2J **173**
Northolme Rd. N5 4C **66**
NORTHOLT 7E **58**
Northolt *N17* *2E 48*
(off Griffin Rd.)
Northolt Av. HA4: Ruis 5K **57**
Northolt Gdns. UB6: G'frd 5K **59**
Northolt Rd. HA2: Harr 4F **59**
TW6: H'row A 1A **110**
(not continuous)
Northolt Swimarama 6E **58**
Northolt Trad. Est. UB5: N'olt 7F **59**
Northover BR1: Brom 3H **141**
North Pde. HA8: Edg 2G **43**
KT9: Chess 5F **163**
UB1: S'hall *6E 76*
(off North Rd.)
North Pk. SE9 6D **124**
North Pas. SW18 5J **117**
North Pl. CR4: Mitc 7D **136**
TW11: Tedd 6K **131**
North Point N8 5K **47**
Northpoint Cl. SM1: Sutt 3A **166**
Northpoint Sq. NW1 6H **65**
Nth. Pole La. BR2: Kes 6H **171**
Nth. Pole Rd. W10 5E **80**
Northport St. N1 1D **84**
North Ride W2 3C **10** (7C **82**)
North Ri. W2 1D **10** (6C **82**)
North Rd. BR1: Brom 1K **159**
BR4: W W'ck 1D **170**
DA17: Belv 3H **109**
HA1: Harr 7A **42**
HA8: Edg 1H **43**
IG3: Ilf 2J **71**
KT6: Surb 6D **150**
N2 2C **46**
N6 7E **46**
N7 6J **65**
N9 1C **34**
RM6: Chad H 5E **54**
SE18 4J **107**
SW19 6A **136**
TW5: Hest 6A **94**
TW8: Bford 6E **96**
TW9: Kew 1G **115**
TW9: Rich 3G **115**
TW14: Bedf 6F **111**
UB1: S'hall 6E **76**
UB3: Hayes 5F **75**
UB7: W Dray 3B **92**
W5 3D **96**
Northrop Rd. TW6: H'row A 1G **111**
North Row W1 2F **11** (7D **82**)
Nth. Row Bldgs. *W1* *2G 11*
(off North Row)
North Several SE3 2F **123**
NORTH SHEEN 3G **115**
Northside Rd. BR1: Brom 1J **159**
Northside Studios *E8* *1H 85*
(off Andrew's Rd.)
Nth. Side Wandsworth Comn.
SW18 5B **118**
Northspur Rd. SM1: Sutt 3J **165**
North Sq. *N9* *2C 34*
(off Hertford Rd.)
NW11 5J **45**
Northstead Rd. SW2 2A **138**
North St. BR1: Brom 1J **159**
DA7: Bex 4G **127**
E13 2K **87**
IG11: Bark 6F **71**
NW4 5E **44**
RM1: Rom 3K **55**
(not continuous)
SM5: Cars 3D **166**
SW4 3G **119**
TW7: Isle 3A **114**
North St. Pas. E13 2K **87**
Nth. Tenter St. E1 1K **15** (6F **85**)
North Ter. SW3 2C **16** (3C **100**)
WC2 4E **12**
Northumberland All. EC3 1H **15** (6E **84**)
(not continuous)
Northumberland Av.
DA16: Well 4H **125**
E12 1A **70**
EN1: Enf 1C **24**
TW7: Isle 1K **113**
WC2 4E **12** (1J **101**)
Northumberland Cl.
DA8: Erith 7J **109**
TW19: Stanw 6A **110**
Northumberland Cres. TW14: Felt 6G **111**
Northumberland Gdns.
BR1: Brom 4E **160**
CR4: Mitc 5H **155**
N9 3A **34**
TW7: Isle 7A **96**
Northumberland Gro. N17 7C **34**
NORTHUMBERLAND HEATH 7J **109**
Northumberland Ho. IG8: Wfd G 7K **37**
SW1 *4E 12*
(off Northumberland Av.)
Northumberland Pk. DA8: Erith 7J **109**
N17 7A **34**
Northumberland Pk. Ind. Est.
N17 7C **34**
Northumberland Pk. Sports Cen. 7B **34**
Northumberland Pl. TW10: Rich 5D **114**
W2 6J **81**
Northumberland Rd. E6 6C **88**
E17 7C **50**
EN5: New Bar 6F **21**
HA2: Harr 5D **40**
Northumberland St. WC2 4E **12** (1J **101**)
Northumberland Way
DA8: Erith 1J **127**
Northumbria St. E14 6C **86**
Nth. Verbena Gdns. W6 5C **98**
North Vw. HA5: Eastc 7A **40**
SW19 5E **134**
W5 4C **78**
Northview N7 3J **65**
North Vw. Cvn. Site IG6: Ilf 1A **54**
Northview Cres. NW10 4B **62**
North Vw. Dr. IG8: Wfd G 2B **52**
North Vw. Rd. N8 4H **47**
North Vs. NW1 6H **65**
North Wlk. CR0: New Ad 6D **170**
(not continuous)
W2 7K **81**
North Way HA5: Pinn 4B **40**
N9 2E **34**
N11 6B **32**
NW9 3H **43**
UB10: Uxb 7A **56**
Northway NW11 5K **45**
SM4: Mord 3G **153**
SM6: Wall 4G **167**
Northway Cir. NW7 4E **28**
Northway Ct. NW7 4F **29**
Northway Cres. NW7 4E **28**

Northway Gdns. NW11 5K 45
Northway Rd. CR0: C'don 6F 157
SE5 3C 120
Northways Pde. *NW3* *7B 64*
(off College Cres., not continuous)
Northweald La. KT2: King T 5D 132
NORTH WEMBLEY 3D 60
Nth. Western Commercial Cen.
NW1 7J 65
Northwest Pl. N1 2A 84
North Wharf *E14* *1E 104*
(off Coldharbour)
Nth. Wharf Rd. W2 6A 4 (5B 82)
Northwick Av. HA3: Kent 6A 42
Northwick Circ. HA3: Kent 6C 42
Northwick Cl. HA1: Harr 1B 60
NW8 3A 4 (4B 82)
Northwick Ho. NW8 3A 4
Northwick Pk. Rd. HA1: Harr 6K 41
Northwick Rd. HA0: Wemb 1D 78
Northwick Ter. NW8 3A 4 (4B 82)
Northwick Wlk. HA1: Harr 7K 41
Northwold Dr. HA5: Pinn 2A 40
Northwold Rd. E5 2F 67
N16 2F 67
NORTHWOOD 1H 39
Nth. Wood Ct. SE25 3G 157
Northwood Est. E5 2G 67
Northwood FC 2H 39
Northwood Gdns. IG5: Ilf 4E 52
N12 5G 31
UB6: G'frd 5K 59
Northwood Hall N6 7G 47
NORTHWOOD HILLS 2J 39
Northwood Hills Cir. HA6: Nwood 1J 39
Northwood Ho.
KT2: King T *2G 151*
(off Coombe Rd.)
SE27 4D 138
Northwood Pk. 2H 39
Northwood Pl. DA18: Erith 3F 109
Northwood Rd. N6 7F 47
SE23 1B 140
SM5: Cars 6E 166
TW6: H'row A 4E 174
UB9: Hare 1A 38
Northwood Sports Cen. 1J 39
Northwood Way HA6: Nwood 1J 39
SE19 6D 138
UB9: Hare 1A 38
NORTH WOOLWICH 2E 106
North Woolwich Old Station Mus. 2E 106
Nth. Woolwich Rd. E16 1H 105
Nth. Worple Way SW14 3K 115
Norton Av. KT5: Surb 7H 151
Norton Cl. E4 5H 35
EN1: Enf 2C 24
Norton Ct. BR3: Beck 1B 158
Norton Folgate E1 5H 9 (5E 84)
Norton Folgate Ho. *E1* *5J 9*
(off Puma Ct.)
Norton Gdns. SW16 2J 155
Norton Ho. *E1* *6H 85*
(off Bigland St.)
E2 *2K 85*
(off Mace St.)
SW1 *2D 18*
(off Arneway St.)
SW9 *2K 119*
(off Aytoun Rd.)
Norton Rd. E10 1B 68
HA0: Wemb 6D 60
RM10: Dag 6K 73
Norval Rd. HA0: Wemb 2B 60
Norway Ga. SE16 3A 104
Norway Pl. E14 6B 86
Norway St. SE10 6D 104
Norway Wharf *E14* *6B 86*
(off Norway Pl.)
Norwich Cres. RM6: Chad H 5B 54
Norwich Ho. *E14* *6D 86*
(off Cordelia St.)
Norwich M. IG3: Ilf 1A 72
Norwich Pl. DA6: Bex 4G 127
Norwich Rd. CR7: Thor H 3C 156
E7 5J 69
HA6: Nwood 3H 39
RM9: Dag 2G 91
UB6: G'frd 1F 77
Norwich St. EC4 7J 7 (6A 84)
Norwich Wlk. HA8: Edg 7D 28
NORWOOD 6E 138
Norwood Av. HA0: Wemb 1F 79
RM7: Rush G 7K 55
Norwood Cl. NW2 3G 63
TW2: Twick 2H 131
UB2: S'hall 4E 94
Norwood Dr. HA2: Harr 6D 40
Norwood Gdns. UB2: S'hall 4D 94
UB4: Yead 4A 76
NORWOOD GREEN 4D 94
Norwood Grn. Rd.
UB2: S'hall 4E 94
Norwood High St. SE27 3B 138
Norwood Ho. *E14* *7D 86*
(off Poplar High St.)
NORWOOD NEW TOWN 6C 138
Norwood Pk. Rd. SE27 5C 138
Norwood Rd. SE24 1B 138
SE27 2B 138
UB2: S'hall 3C 94
Norwood Ter. UB2: S'hall 4F 95
Nota M. N3 1J 45
Notley St. SE5 7D 102
Notson Rd. SE25 4H 157
Notting Barn Rd. W10 4F 81
Nottingdale Sq. W11 1G 99
Nottingham Av. E16 5A 88
Nottingham Ct. WC2 1E 12 (6J 83)
Nottingham Ho. *WC2* *1E 12*
(off Shorts Gdns.)
Nottingham Pl. W1 4G 5 (5E 82)
Nottingham Rd. CR2: S Croy 4C 168
E10 6E 50
SW17 1D 136
TW7: Isle 2K 113
Nottingham St. W1 5G 5 (5E 82)
Nottingham Ter. NW1 4G 5
NOTTING HILL 7H 81
Notting Hill Ga. W11 1J 99
Nottingwood Ho. *W11* *7G 81*
(off Clarendon Rd.)
Nova Bldg. E14 4C 104
Nova Ct. E. *E14* *1E 104*
(off Yabsley St.)
Nova Ct. W. *E14* *1E 104*
(off Yabsley St.)
Nova M. SM3: Sutt 1G 165
Novar Cl. BR6: Orp 7K 161
Nova Rd. CR0: C'don 1B 168
Novar Rd. SE9 1G 143
Novello St. SW6 1J 117
Nowell Rd. SW13 6C 98
Nower Ct. HA5: Pinn 4D 40
Nower Hill HA5: Pinn 4D 40
Nower Hill School Sports Cen. *4E 40*
(off George V Av.)
Noyna Rd. SW17 3D 136
Nubia Way BR1: Brom 3G 141
Nuding Cl. SE13 3C 122
Nuffield Ct. TW5: Hest 7D 94
Nuffield Lodge N6 6G 47
W9 *5J 81*
(off Admiral Wlk.)
Nugent Rd. N19 1J 65
SE25 3F 157
Nugents Ct. HA5: Pinn 1C 40
Nugent's Pk. HA5: Hat E 1C 40
Nugent Ter. NW8 2A 82
Numa Ct. TW8: Bford 7D 96
No. 10 Bowling Alley 6K 55
Nun Ct. EC2 7E 8
Nuneaton Rd. RM9: Dag 7E 72
NUNHEAD 3H 121
Nunhead Cres. SE15 3H 121
Nunhead Est. SE15 4H 121
Nunhead Grn. SE15 3H 121
Nunhead Gro. SE15 3H 121
Nunhead La. SE15 3H 121
Nunhead Pas. SE15 3G 121
Nunnington Cl. SE9 3C 142
Nunns Rd. EN2: Enf 2H 23
Nupton Dr. EN5: Barn 6A 20
Nurse Cl. HA8: Edg 1J 43
Nursery App. N12 6H 31
Nursery Av. CR0: C'don 2K 169
DA7: Bex 3F 127
N3 2A 46
Nursery Cl. BR6: Orp 7K 161
CR0: C'don 2K 169
EN3: Enf H 1E 24
IG8: Wfd G 5E 36
RM6: Chad H 6D 54
SE4 2B 122
SW15 4F 117
TW14: Felt 7K 111
(not continuous)
Nursery Ct. N17 7A 34
W13 5A 78
Nursery Gdns. BR7: Chst 6F 143
EN3: Enf H 1E 24
TW4: Houn 5D 112
TW12: Hamp 4D 130
TW16: Sun 2H 147
Nursery La. E2 1F 85
E7 6J 69
UB8: Cowl 4A 74
W10 5E 80
Nurserymans Rd. N11 2K 31
Nursery Rd. CR4: Mitc 3C 154
CR7: Thor H 4D 156
E9 6J 67
E12 2C 70
HA5: Pinn 3A 40
N2 1B 46
N14 7B 22
SM1: Sutt 4A 166
SW9 4K 119
SW19 7G 135
(Elm Gro.)
SW19 2K 153
(Parkleigh Rd.)
TW16: Sun 2G 147
Nursery Row EN5: Barn 3B 20
SE17 4D 102
Nursery St. N17 7A 34
Nursery Wlk. NW4 3E 44
RM7: Rush G 7K 55
Nursery Waye UB8: Uxb 1A 74
Nurstead Rd. DA8: Erith 7G 109
Nutbourne St. W10 3G 81
Nutbrook St. SE15 3G 121
Nutbrowne Rd. RM9: Dag 1F 91
Nutcroft Rd. SE15 7H 103
Nutfield Cl. N18 6B 34
SM5: Cars 3C 166
Nutfield Ct. BR1: Brom 3J 159
Nutfield Gdns. IG3: Ilf 2K 71
UB5: Yead 2A 76
Nutfield Pas. *CR7: Thor H* *4B 156*
(off Nutfield Rd.)
Nutfield Rd. CR7: Thor H 4B 156
E15 4E 68
NW2 3C 62
SE22 4F 121
Nutfield Way BR6: Farnb 2F 173
Nutford Pl. W1 7D 4 (6D 82)
Nuthatch Cl. TW19: Stanw 1B 128
Nuthatch Gdns. SE28 2H 107
(not continuous)
Nuthurst Av. SW2 2K 137
Nutkin Wlk. UB8: Uxb 7A 56
Nutley Ter. NW3 6A 64
Nutmead Cl. DA5: Bexl 1J 145
Nutmeg Cl. E16 4G 87
Nutmeg La. E14 6F 87
Nuttall St. N1 2E 84
Nutter La. E11 6A 52
Nutt Gro. HA8: Edg 2J 27
Nutt St. SE15 7F 103
Nutty La. TW17: Shep 3E 146
Nutwell St. SW17 5C 136
Nuxley Rd.
DA17: Belv 6F 109
Nyanza St. SE18 6H 107
Nye Bevan Est. E5 3K 67
Nye Bevan Ho.
SW6 *7H 99*
(off St Thomas's Way)
Nylands Av. TW9: Kew 1G 115
Nymans Gdns. SW20 3D 152
Nynehead St. SE14 7A 104
Nyon Gro. SE6 2B 140
Nyssa Cl. IG8: Wfd G 6J 37
Nyssa Ct. *E15* *3G 87*
(off Teasel Way)
Nyton Cl. N19 1J 65

O

O2, The
(Millennium Dome) 1G 105
O2 Cen. NW3 6A 64
Oak Apple Ct. SE12 1J 141
Oak Av. CR0: C'don 1C 170
EN2: Enf 1E 22
N8 4J 47
N10 7A 32
N17 7J 33
TW5: Hest 7B 94
TW12: Hamp 5C 130
UB7: W Dray 3C 92
UB10: Ick 2D 56
Oak Bank CR0: New Ad 6E 170
Oakbank Av. KT12: Walt T 7D 148
Oakbank Gro. SE24 4C 120
Oakbark Ho. *TW8: Bford* *7C 96*
(off High St.)
Oakbrook Cl. BR1: Brom 4K 141
Oakbury Rd. SW6 2K 117
Oak Cl. N14 7A 22
SM1: Sutt 2A 166
Oakcombe Cl. KT3: N Mald 1A 152
Oak Cott. Cl. SE6 1H 141
Oak Cotts. W7 2J 95
Oak Ct. *SE15* *7F 103*
(off Sumner Rd.)
Oak Cres. E16 5G 87
Oakcroft Bus. Cen.
KT9: Chess 4F 163
Oakcroft Cl. HA5: Pinn 2K 39
Oakcroft Rd. KT9: Chess 4F 163
SE13 2F 123
Oakcroft Vs. KT9: Chess 4F 163
Oakdale N14 1A 32
Oakdale Av. HA3: Kent 5E 42
HA6: Nwood 2J 39
Oakdale Ct. E4 5K 35
Oakdale Gdns. E4 5K 35
Oakdale Rd. E7 7K 69
E11 2F 69
E18 2K 51
KT19: Ewe 7K 163
N4 6C 48
SE15 3J 121
SW16 5J 137
Oakdale Way CR4: Mitc 7E 154
Oakdene SE15 1H 121
W13 5B 78

Oakdene Av. BR7: Chst 5E 142
DA8: Erith 6J 109
KT7: T Ditt 1A 162
Oakdene Cl. HA5: Hat E 1D 40
Oakdene Dr. KT5: Surb 7J 151
Oakdene M. SM3: Sutt 1H 165
Oakdene Pk. N3 7C 30
Oakdene Rd. BR5: St M Cry 5K 161
UB10: Hil 2D 74
Oakden St. SE11 3K 19 (4A 102)
Oake Ct. SW15 5G 117
Oakeford Ho. *W14* *3G 99*
(off Russell Rd.)
Oakend Ho. N4 7D 48
Oakenholt Ho. SE2 1D 108
Oakenshaw Cl.
KT6: Surb 7E 150
Oakes Cl. E6 6D 88
Oakeshott Av. N6 2E 64
Oakey La. SE1 1J 19 (3A 102)
Oakfield E4 5J 35
Oakfield Av. HA3: Kent 3B 42
Oakfield Cen. SE20 7H 139
Oakfield Cl. HA4: Ruis 6H 39
KT3: N Mald 5B 152
Oakfield Ct. N8 7J 47
NW2 7F 45
Oakfield Gdns. BR3: Beck 5D 158
N18 4K 33
SE19 5E 138
(not continuous)
SM5: Cars 1C 166
UB6: G'frd 4H 77
Oakfield Ho. *E3* *5C 86*
(off Gale St.)
Oakfield La. BR2: Kes 4A 172
Oakfield Lodge *IG1: Ilf* *3F 71*
(off Albert Rd.)
Oakfield Rd. CR0: C'don 1C 168
E6 1C 88
E17 2A 50
IG1: Ilf 3F 71
N3 1K 45
N4 6A 48
N14 2D 32
SE20 7H 139
SW19 3F 135
TW15: Ashf 5D 128
Oakfield Rd. Ind. Est. SE20 7H 139
Oakfields Rd. NW11 6G 45
Oakfield St. SW10 6A 100
Oakford Rd. NW5 4G 65
Oak Gdns. CR0: C'don 2C 170
HA8: Edg 2J 43
Oak Glade HA6: Nwood 1D 38
Oak Gro. BR4: W W'ck 1E 170
HA4: Ruis 7K 39
NW2 4G 63
TW16: Sun 7K 129
Oak Gro. Rd. SE20 1J 157
Oakhall Ct. E11 6K 51
Oakhall Dr. TW16: Sun 5H 129
Oak Hall Rd. E11 6K 51
Oakham Cl. EN4: Cockf 3J 21
SE6 2B 140
Oakham Dr. BR2: Brom 4H 159
Oakham Ho. *W10* *4E 80*
(off Sutton Way)
Oakhampton Rd. NW7 7A 30
Oak Hill IG8: Wfd G 7A 36
KT6: Surb 7E 150
Oakhill KT10: Clay 6A 162
Oakhill Av. HA5: Pinn 2C 40
NW3 4K 63
Oak Hill Cl. IG8: Wfd G 7A 36
Oak Hill Ct. IG8: Wfd G 7A 36
Oakhill Ct. SE23 6J 121
SW19 7F 135
Oak Hill Cres. IG8: Wfd G 7A 36
KT6: Surb 7E 150
Oakhill Dr. KT6: Surb 7E 150
Oak Hill Gdns. IG8: Wfd G 1G 51
Oak Hill Gro. KT6: Surb 6E 150
Oak Hill Pk. NW3 4K 63
Oak Hill Pk. M.
NW3 4A 64
Oak Hill Path KT6: Surb 6E 150
Oakhill Pl. SW15 5J 117
Oak Hill Rd. KT6: Surb 6E 150
Oakhill Rd. BR3: Beck 2E 158
BR6: Orp 1K 173
SM1: Sutt 3K 165
SW15 5H 117
SW16 1J 155
Oak Hill Way NW3 4K 63
(not continuous)
Oak Ho. N2 2B 46
TW9: Kew 1H 115
W10 *4G 81*
(off Sycamore Wlk.)
Oakhouse Rd. DA6: Bex 5G 127
Oakhurst Av. DA7: Bex 7E 108
EN4: E Barn 7H 21
Oakhurst Cl. BR7: Chst 1D 160
E17 4G 51
IG6: Ilf 1G 53
TW11: Tedd 5J 131
Oakhurst Ct. *E17* *4G 51*
(off Woodford New Rd.)
Oakhurst Gdns. DA7: Bex 7E 108
E4 1C 36
E17 4G 51
Oakhurst Gro. SE22 4G 121
Oakhurst Rd. KT19: Ewe 6J 163
Oakington Av. HA2: Harr 7E 40
HA9: Wemb 3F 61
UB3: Harl 4F 93
Oakington Cl. TW16: Sun 2A 148
Oakington Ct. EN2: Enf 2G 23
Oakington Dr. TW16: Sun 2A 148
Oakington Mnr. Dr.
HA9: Wemb 5G 61
Oakington Rd. W9 4J 81
Oakington Way N8 7J 47
Oakland Pl. IG9: Buck H 2D 36
Oakland Rd. E15 4F 69
Oaklands BR3: Beck 1D 158
N21 2E 32
W13 5A 78
Oaklands Av. BR4: W W'ck 3D 170
CR7: Thor H 4A 156
DA15: Sidc 7K 125
KT10: Esh 7H 149
N9 6C 24
TW7: Isle 6K 95
Oaklands Cl. BR5: Pet W 6J 161
DA6: Bex 5F 127
HA0: Wemb 5D 60
KT9: Chess 4C 162
Oaklands Ct. HA0: Wemb 5D 60
NW10 *1A 80*
(off Nicoll Rd.)
SE20 *7J 139*
(off Chestnut Gro.)
Oaklands Dr. TW2: Whitt 7G 113
Oaklands Est. SW4 6G 119
Oaklands Gro. W12 1C 98
Oaklands M. *NW2* *4F 63*
(off Oaklands Rd.)
Oaklands Pk. Av. IG1: Ilf 2G 71
Oaklands Pas. *NW2* *4F 63*
(off Oaklands Rd.)
Oaklands Pl. SW4 4G 119
Oaklands Rd. BR1: Brom 7G 141
DA6: Bex 4F 127
N20 7C 20
NW2 4F 63
SW14 3K 115
W7 2K 95
(not continuous)
Oaklands Way SM6: Wall 7H 167
Oakland Way KT19: Ewe 6A 164
Oak La. E14 7B 86
IG8: Wfd G 4C 36
N2 2B 46
N11 6C 32
TW1: Twick 7A 114
TW7: Isle 4J 113
Oakleafe Gdns. IG6: Ilf 3F 53
Oaklea Lodge IG3: Ilf 3A 72
Oaklea Pas. KT1: King T 3D 150
Oakleigh Av. HA8: Edg 2H 43
KT6: Surb 1G 163
N20 2G 31
Oakleigh Cl. N20 3J 31
Oakleigh Ct. EN4: E Barn 6H 21
HA8: Edg 2J 43
N1 1D 8
UB1: S'hall 1D 94
Oakleigh Cres. N20 2H 31
Oakleigh Gdns. BR6: Orp 4J 173
HA8: Edg 5A 28
N20 1F 31
Oakleigh M. N20 1F 31
OAKLEIGH PARK 1F 31
Oakleigh Pk. Av.
BR7: Chst 1E 160
Oakleigh Pk. Lawn Tennis & Squash Club
2G 31
Oakleigh Pk. Nth. N20 1G 31
Oakleigh Pk. Sth. N20 7H 21
Oakleigh Rd. UB10: Hil 7E 56
Oakleigh Rd. Nth. N20 2G 31
Oakleigh Rd. Sth. N11 3K 31
Oakleigh Way CR4: Mitc 1F 155
KT6: Surb 1G 163
Oakley Av. CR0: Bedd 4K 167
IG11: Bark 7K 71
W5 7G 79
Oakley Cl. E4 3K 35
E6 6C 88
TW7: Isle 1H 113
W7 7J 77
Oakley Ct. CR4: Mitc 7E 154
Oakley Cres. EC1 2B 84
Oakley Dr. BR2: Brom 3C 172
SE9 1H 143
SE13 6F 123
Oakley Gdns. N8 5K 47
SW3 7D 16 (6C 100)
Oakley Grange HA1: Harr 2H 59
Oakley Ho. SW1 3F 17
W5 7G 79
Oakley Pk. DA5: Bexl 7C 126
Oakley Pl. SE1 5F 103
Oakley Rd. BR2: Brom 3C 172
HA1: Harr 6J 41
N1 7D 66
SE25 5H 157
Oakley Sq. NW1 2G 83
Oakley St. SW3 7C 16 (6C 100)
Oakley Studios *SW3* *7C 16*
(off Up. Cheyne Row)
Oakley Wlk. W6 6F 99
Oakley Yd. E2 3K 9 (4F 85)
Oak Lodge E11 6J 51
SM1: Sutt 4A 166
TW16: Sun *7H 129*
(off Forest Dr.)
W8 *3K 99*
(off Chantry Sq.)
Oak Lodge Cl. HA7: Stan 5H 27
Oak Lodge Dr. BR4: W W'ck 7D 158
Oaklodge Way NW7 5G 29
Oakman Ho. SW19 1F 135
Oakmead Av. BR2: Hayes 6J 159
Oakmead Ct. HA7: Stan 4H 27
Oakmeade HA5: Hat E 6A 26
Oakmead Gdns. HA8: Edg 4E 28
Oakmead Pl. CR4: Mitc 1C 154
Oakmead Rd. CR0: C'don 6H 155
SW12 1E 136
Oakmede EN5: Barn 4A 20
Oakmere Rd. SE2 6A 108
Oakmont Pl. BR6: Orp 1H 173
Oak Pk. Gdns. SW19 1F 135
Oak Pk. M. N16 3F 67
Oak Pl. SW18 5K 117
Oakridge Dr. N2 3B 46
Oakridge La.
BR1: Brom 5F 141
Oakridge Rd. BR1: Brom 4F 141
Oak Ri. IG9: Buck H 3G 37
Oak Rd. BR6: Chels 7K 173
DA8: Erith 7J 109
KT3: N Mald 2K 151
W5 7D 78
Oak Row SW16 2G 155
Oaks, The BR2: Brom 6E 160
EN2: Enf *3G 23*
(off Byculla Rd.)
HA4: Ruis 7F 39
IG8: Wfd G 7B 36
N12 4E 30
NW6 *7F 63*
(off Brondesbury Pk.)
NW10 7D 62
Oaks, The SE18 5G 107
SM4: Mord 4G 153
UB4: Hayes 2E 74
Oaks Av. KT4: Wor Pk 3D 164
RM5: Col R 2J 55
SE19 5E 138
TW13: Felt 2C 130
Oaks Cvn. Pk., The
KT9: Chess 3C 162
Oaksford Av. SE26 3H 139
Oaks Gro. E4 2B 36
Oakshade Rd. BR1: Brom 4F 141
Oakshaw Rd. SW18 7K 117
Oakshott Ct. NW1 1C 6 (2H 83)
(not continuous)
Oakside Ct. IG6: Ilf 2H 53
Oakside Stadium 4H 53
Oaks La. CR0: C'don 3H 169
IG2: Ilf 5J 53
(not continuous)
Oaks Rd. CR0: C'don 5H 169
TW19: Stanw 5A 110
Oaks Shop. Cen., The W3 1J 97
Oak St. *E14* *2E 104*
(off Stewart St.)
RM7: Rom 5J 55
Oaks Way KT6: Surb 1D 162
SM5: Cars 7D 166
Oakthorpe Ct. N13 5H 33
Oakthorpe Pk. Est. N13 5H 33
Oakthorpe Rd. N13 5F 33
Oaktree Av. N13 3G 33
Oak Tree Cl. HA7: Stan 7H 27
W5 6C 78
Oak Tree Ct. UB5: Yead 2A 76
W3 7H 79
Oak Tree Dell NW9 5J 43
Oak Tree Dr. N20 1E 30
Oak Tree Gdns. BR1: Brom 5K 141
Oaktree Gro. IG1: Ilf 5H 71
Oak Tree Ho. *W9* *4J 81*
(off Shirland Rd.)
Oak Tree Rd. NW8 2B 4 (3C 82)
Oakview Apartments
SM1: Sutt 4B 166
Oakview Gdns. N2 4B 46
Oakview Gro. CR0: C'don 1A 170
Oakview Lodge *NW11* *7H 45*
(off Beechcroft Av.)
Oakview Rd. SE6 5D 140
Oak Village NW5 4E 64
Oak Vs. *NW11* *6H 45*
(off Hendon Pk. Row)

Oak Way CR0: C'don 6K 157
N14 7A 22
SM6: Wall 1E 166
(off Helios Rd.)
TW14: Felt 1G 129
W3 1A 98
Oakway BR2: Brom 2F 159
SW20 4E 152
Oakway Cl. DA5: Bexl 6E 126
Oakways SE9 6F 125
OAKWOOD 4C 22
Oakwood SM6: Wall 7F 167
Oakwood Av. BR2: Brom 3K 159
BR3: Beck 2E 158
CR4: Mitc 2B 154
N14 7C 22
UB1: S'hall 7E 76
Oakwood Bus. Pk. NW10 4K 79
Oakwood Cl. BR7: Chst 6D 142
IG8: Wfd G 6H 37
N14 6B 22
SE13 6F 123
Oakwood Ct. E6 1C 88
HA1: Harr 6H 41
W14 3H 99
Oakwood Cres. N21 6D 22
UB6: G'frd 6A 60
Oakwood Dr. DA7: Bex 4J 127
HA8: Edg 6D 28
SE19 6D 138
Oakwood Gdns. BR6: Farnb 2G 173
IG3: Ilf 2K 71
SM1: Sutt 2J 165
Oakwood Ho. *E9 6J 67*
(off Frampton Pk. Rd.)
Oakwood La. W14 3H 99
Oakwood Lodge *N14 6B 22*
(off Avenue Rd.)
Oakwood Mans. *W14 3H 99*
(off Oakwood Ct.)
Oakwood Pde. EN4: Cockf 4B 22
Oakwood Pk. Rd. N14 7C 22
Oakwood Pl. CR0: C'don 6A 156
Oakwood Rd. BR6: Farnb 2G 173
CR0: C'don 6A 156
HA5: Pinn 2K 39
NW11 4J 45
SW20 1C 152
Oakwood Vw. N14 6C 22
Oakworth Rd. W10 5E 80
Oarsman Pl.
KT8: E Mos 4J 149
Oasis, The BR1: Brom 2A 160
Oasis Sports Cen. 7E 6 (6J 83)
Oast Ct. *E14 7B 86*
(off Newell St.)
Oast Lodge *W4 7A 98*
(off Corney Reach Way)
Oates Cl. BR2: Brom 3F 159
Oatfield Ho. *N15 6E 48*
(off Perry Ct.)
Oatfield Rd. BR6: Orp 1K 173
Oatland Ri. E17 2A 50
Oatlands Dr. KT13: Weyb 7G 147
Oatlands Rd. EN3: Enf H 1D 24
Oat La. EC2 7C 8 (6C 84)
Oatwell Ho. *SW3 4D 16*
(off Cale St.)
Oban Cl. E13 4A 88
Oban Ho. *E14 6F 87*
(off Oban St.)
IG11: Bark 2H 89
Oban Rd. E13 3A 88
SE25 4D 156
Oban St. E14 6F 87
Oberon Ho. *N1 2E 84*
(off Arden Est.)
Oberon Way TW17: Shep 3A 146
Oberstein Rd. SW11 4B 118
Oborne Cl. SE24 5B 120
O'Brien Ho. *E2 3K 85*
(off Roman Rd.)
Observatory Gdns. W8 2J 99
Observatory M. E14 4F 105
Observatory Rd. SW7 2A 16 (3B 100)
SW14 4J 115
Occupation La. SE18 1F 125
W5 4D 96
Occupation Rd. KT19: Ewe 7K 163
SE17 5C 102
W13 2B 96
Ocean Est. E1 5A 86
(Ben Jonson Rd.)
E1 4K 85
(Ernest St.)
Oceanis Apartments *E16 7J 87*
(off Seagull La.)
Ocean Music Venue 6H 67
(off Mare St.)
Ocean St. E1 5K 85
Ocean Wharf E14 2B 104
Ockbrook *E1 5J 85*
(off Hannibal Rd.)
Ockendon M. N1 6D 66
Ockendon Rd. N1 6D 66
Ockham Dr. BR5: St P 7A 144
UB6: G'frd 7H 59
Ockley Ct. DA14: Sidc 3J 143
SM1: Sutt 4A 166
Ockley Rd. CR0: C'don 7K 155
SW16 4J 137
Octagon, The *SW10 7K 99*
(off Coleridge Gdns.)
Octagon Arc. EC2 6G 9 (5E 84)
Octagon Ct. *SE16 1K 103*
(off Rotherhithe St.)
Octavia Cl. CR4: Mitc 5C 154
Octavia Ho. *SW1 2C 18*
(off Medway St.)
W10 4G 81
Octavia M. W9 4H 81
Octavia Rd. TW7: Isle 3J 113
Octavia St. SW11 1C 118
Octavia Way SE28 7B 90
Octavius St. SE8 7C 104
October Pl. NW4 3F 45
Odard Rd. KT8: W Mole 4E 148
Oddmark Rd. IG11: Bark 2H 89
Odelia Ct. *E15 1E 86*
(off Biggerstaff Rd.)
Odell Cl. IG11: Bark 7K 71
Odell Wlk. SE13 3E 122
Odeon, The IG11: Bark 7H 71
Odeon Cinema
Barnet 5D 20
Beckenham 2B 158
Bromley 2J 159
(off High St.)
Camden Town 1F 83
(off Parkway)
Covent Garden 1D 12
(off Shaftesbury Av.)
Edmonton 7E 24
Eltham Park 4C 124
(off Well Hall Rd.)
Greenwich 4H 105
Holloway 3J 65
Kensington 3J 99
Kingston upon Thames 2E 150
(in The Rotunda Cen.)
Leicester Sq. 3D 12
(off Leicester Sq.)
Marble Arch 6D 82
(off Marble Arch)
Muswell Hill 4F 47
Panton St. 3D 12
(off Panton St.)
Putney 3G 117
Richmond, Hill St. 5D 114
Richmond, Red Lion St. 5D 114
Odeon Cinema
South Woodford 2J 51
Streatham 3J 137
Surrey Quays 3K 103
Sutton 5K 165
Swiss Cottage 7B 64
Tottenham Ct. Rd. 6C 6
(off Tottenham Ct. Rd.)
West End 3D 12
(off Leicester Sq.)
Whiteleys 6K 81
Wimbledon 6H 135
Odeon Ct. E16 5J 87
NW10 1A 80
(off St Albans Rd.)
Odeon Pde. *SE9 4C 124*
(off Well Hall Rd.)
UB6: G'frd 6B 60
(off Allendale Rd.)
W3 2G 97
(off Gunnersbury La.)
Odessa Rd. E7 3H 69
NW10 2C 80
Odessa St. SE16 2B 104
Odette Duval Ho. *E1 5J 85*
(off Stepney Way)
Odger St. SW11 2D 118
Odhams Wlk. WC2 1F 13 (6J 83)
Odin Ho. SE5 2C 120
O'Donnell Ct. WC1 3F 7 (4J 83)
Odontological Mus., The 7H 7
(within The Royal College of Surgeons)
O'Driscoll Ho. W12 6D 80
Odyssey Bus. Pk.
HA4: Ruis 5K 57
Offa's Mead E9 4B 68
Offenbach Ho. *E2 2K 85*
(off Mace St.)
Offenham Rd. SE9 4D 142
Offers Ct. KT1: King T 3F 151
Offerton Rd. SW4 3G 119
Offham Ho. *SE17 4E 102*
(off Beckway St.)
Offham Slope N12 5C 30
Offley Pl. TW7: Isle 2H 113
Offley Rd. SW9 7A 102
Offord Cl. N17 6B 34
Offord Rd. N1 7K 65
Offord St. N1 7K 65
Ogden Ho. TW13: Hanw 3C 130
Ogilby St. SE18 4D 106
Ogilvie Ho. *E1 6K 85*
(off Stepney C'way.)
Oglander Rd. SE15 4F 121
Ogle St. W1 5A 6 (5G 83)
Oglethorpe Rd. RM10: Dag 3F 73
O'Gorman Ho. *SW10 7A 100*
(off King's Rd.)
O'Grady Ho. E17 3D 50
Ohio Bldg. *SE10 1D 122*
(off Deal's Gateway)
Ohio Cotts. HA5: Pinn 2A 40
Ohio Rd. E13 4H 87
Oil Mill La. W6 5C 98
Okeburn Rd. SW17 5E 136
Okehampton Cl. N12 5G 31
Okehampton Cres.
DA16: Well 1B 126
Okehampton Rd. NW10 1E 80
Olaf Ct. *W8 2J 99*
(off Kensington Chu. St.)
Olaf St. W11 7F 81
Oldacre M. SW12 7E 118
Old Bailey EC4 1B 14 (6B 84)
Old Bailey
(Central Criminal Court) 7B 8
Old Barge Ho. All. SE1 3K 13
Old Barn Cl. SM2: Cheam 7G 165
Old Barn Way DA7: Bex 3K 127
Old Barracks W8 2K 99
Old Barrack Yd. SW1 7G 11 (2E 100)
(not continuous)
Old Barrowfield E15 1G 87
Old Bellgate Pl. E14 3C 104
Oldberry Rd. HA8: Edg 6E 28
Old Bethnal Grn. Rd. E2 3G 85
OLD BEXLEY 7H 127
Old Bexley Bus. Pk. DA5: Bexl 7H 127
Old Bexley La. DA5: Bexl, Dart 2K 145
Old Billingsgate Mkt. *EC3 3F 15*
(off Lwr. Thames St.)
Old Billingsgate Wlk.
EC3 3G 15 (7E 84)
Old Bond St. W1 3A 12 (7G 83)
Oldborough Rd. HA0: Wemb 3C 60
OLD BRENTFORD 7D 96
Old Brewer's Yd. WC2 1E 12 (6J 83)
Old Brewery M. NW3 4B 64
Old Bridge Cl. UB5: N'olt 2E 76
Old Bridge St. KT1: Ham W 2D 150
Old Broad St. EC2 7F 9 (6D 84)
Old Bromley Rd. BR1: Brom 5F 141
Old Brompton Rd. SW5 5J 99
SW7 4A 16 (5J 99)
Old Bldgs. WC2 7J 7
Old Burlington St. W1 2A 12 (7G 83)
Oldbury Ho. *W2 5K 81*
(off Harrow Rd.)
Oldbury Pl. W1 5H 5 (5E 82)
Oldbury Rd. EN1: Enf 2B 24
Old Canal M. *SE15 5F 103*
(off Trafalgar Av.)
Old Castle St. E1 7J 9 (6F 85)
Old Cavendish St. W1 7J 5 (6F 83)
Old Change Ct. EC4 1C 14
Old Chapel Pl. SW9 2A 120
Old Charlton Rd.
TW17: Shep 5E 146
Old Chelsea M. SW3 7C 16 (6C 100)
Old Chiswick Yd. *W4 6A 98*
(off Pumping Sta. Rd.)
Old Church Ct. N11 5A 32
Oldchurch Gdns. RM7: Rush G 7K 55
Old Church La. HA7: Stan 5G 27
NW9 2K 61
UB6: G'frd 3A 78
Oldchurch Ri. RM7: Rush G 7K 55
Old Church Rd. E1 6K 85
E4 4H 35
Oldchurch Rd. RM7: Rush G 7K 55
Old Church St. SW3 6B 16 (5B 100)
Old Claygate La. KT10: Clay 6A 162
Old Clem Sq. SE18 6E 106
Old Coal Yd. SE28 4H 107
Old College Ct. DA17: Belv 5H 109
Old Compton St. W1 2C 12 (7H 83)
Old Cote Dr. TW5: Hest 6E 94
Old Ct. Ho. *W8 2K 99*
(off Old Ct. Pl.)
Old Ct. Pl. W8 2K 99
Old Courtyard, The BR1: Brom 1K 159
Old Curiosity Shop 7G 7
(off Portsmouth St.)
Old Dairy M. NW5 6F 65
SW12 1E 136
Old Dairy Sq. *N21 7F 23*
(off Wades Hill)
Old Deer Pk. 2C 114
Old Deer Pk. Gdns.
TW9: Rich 3E 114
Old Devonshire Rd. SW12 7F 119
Old Dock Cl. TW9: Kew 6G 97
Old Dover Rd. SE3 7J 105
Oldegate Ho. E6 7B 70
Old Farm Av. DA15: Sidc 1H 143
N14 7B 22
Old Farm Cl. SW17 2C 136
TW4: Houn 4D 112
Old Farm Pas.
TW12: Hamp 1G 149

Old Farm Rd. N2 . . . 1B 46
TW12: Hamp . . . 6D 130
(not continuous)
UB7: W Dray . . . 2A 92
Old Farm Rd. E. DA15: Sidc . . . 2A 144
Old Farm Rd. W. DA15: Sidc . . . 2K 143
Oldfield Cl. BR1: Brom . . . 4D 160
HA7: Stan . . . 5F 27
UB6: G'frd . . . 5J 59
Oldfield Ct. KT5: Surb . . . 4F 151
(off Cranes Pk. Cres.)
Oldfield Farm Gdns.
UB6: G'frd . . . 1H 77
Oldfield Gro. SE16 . . . 4K 103
Oldfield Ho. W4 . . . 5A 98
(off Devonshire Rd.)
Oldfield La. Nth. UB6: G'frd . . . 2H 77
Oldfield La. Sth. UB6: G'frd . . . 4G 77
Oldfield M. N6 . . . 7G 47
Oldfield Rd. BR1: Brom . . . 4D 160
DA7: Bex . . . 2E 126
N16 . . . 3E 66
NW10 . . . 7B 62
SW19 . . . 6G 135
TW12: Hamp . . . 1D 148
W3 . . . 2B 98
Oldfields Cir. UB5: N'olt . . . 6G 59
Oldfields Rd. SM1: Sutt . . . 3H 165
Oldfields Trad. Est.
SM1: Sutt . . . 3J 165
Old Fire Station, The SE18 . . . 7F 107
Old Fish St. Hill EC4 . . . 2C 14
(off Victoria St.)
Old Fleet La. EC4 . . . 7A 8 (6B 84)
Old Fold Cl. EN5: Barn . . . 1C 20
Old Fold La. EN5: Barn . . . 1C 20
Old Fold Vw. EN5: Barn . . . 3A 20
OLD FORD . . . 1C 86
Old Ford Rd. E2 . . . 2J 85
E3 . . . 2A 86
Old Forge Cl. HA7: Stan . . . 4F 27
Old Forge Cres. TW17: Shep . . . 6D 146
Old Forge M. W12 . . . 2D 98
Old Forge Rd. EN1: Enf . . . 1A 24
N19 . . . 2H 65
Old Forge Way DA14: Sidc . . . 4B 144
Old Gloucester St. WC1 . . . 5F 7 (5J 83)
Old Hall Cl. HA5: Pinn . . . 1C 40
Old Hall Dr. HA5: Pinn . . . 1C 40
Oldham Ter. W3 . . . 1J 97
(not continuous)
Old Hatch Mnr. HA4: Ruis . . . 7H 39
Old Hill BR6: Downe . . . 6H 173
BR7: Chst . . . 1E 160
Oldhill St. N16 . . . 1G 67
Old Homesdale Rd.
BR2: Brom . . . 4A 160
Old Hospital Cl. SW12 . . . 1D 136
Old Ho. Cl. SW19 . . . 5G 135
Old Ho. Gdns. TW1: Twick . . . 6C 114
Old Howlett's La. HA4: Ruis . . . 6F 39
OLD ISLEWORTH . . . 3B 114
Old Jamaica Rd. SE16 . . . 7K 15 (3G 103)
Old James St. SE15 . . . 3H 121
Old Jewry EC2 . . . 1E 14 (6D 84)
Old Kenton La. NW9 . . . 5H 43
Old Kent Rd. SE1 . . . 4E 102
SE15 . . . 4E 102
Old Kingston Rd. KT4: Wor Pk . . . 2J 163
Old Laundry, The BR7: Chst . . . 1G 161
Old Lodge Pl. TW1: Twick . . . 6B 114
Old Lodge Way HA7: Stan . . . 5F 27
Old London Rd.
DA14: Sidc, Swan . . . 7G 145
KT2: King T . . . 2E 150
Old Lyonian Sports Club . . . 5G 41
(off Pinner Vw.)
Old Maidstone Rd. DA14: Sidc . . . 7F 145
OLD MALDEN . . . 1A 164
Old Malden La. KT4: Wor Pk . . . 2K 163
Old Manor Ct. NW8 . . . 2A 82
Old Manor Dr. TW7: Isle . . . 6G 113
Old Manor Ho. M. TW17: Shep . . . 3C 146
Old Manor Rd. UB2: S'hall . . . 4B 94
Old Manor Way BR7: Chst . . . 5D 142
DA7: Bex . . . 2K 127
Old Manor Yd. SW5 . . . 4K 99
Old Market Ct. SM1: Sutt . . . 4K 165
Old Market Sq. E2 . . . 1J 9 (3F 85)
Old Marylebone Rd. NW1 . . . 6D 4 (5C 82)
Oldmead Ho. RM10: Dag . . . 6H 73
Old M. HA1: Harr . . . 5J 41
Old Mill Ct. E18 . . . 3A 52
Old Mill Pl. RM7: Rom . . . 6K 55
Old Mill Rd. SE18 . . . 6H 107
Old Mitre Ct. EC4 . . . 1K 13 (6A 84)
Old Montague St. E1 . . . 6K 9 (5G 85)
Old Nichol St. E2 . . . 3J 9 (4F 85)
Old North St. WC1 . . . 5G 7
Old Nursery Ct. E2 . . . 2F 85
(off Dunloe St.)
Old Nursery Pl. TW15: Ashf . . . 5D 128
Old Oak Cl. KT9: Chess . . . 4F 163
OLD OAK COMMON . . . 5A 80
Old Oak Comn. La. NW10 . . . 5A 80
W3 . . . 5A 80
Old Oak La. NW10 . . . 3A 80
Old Oak Rd. W3 . . . 7B 80
Old Orchard TW16: Sun . . . 2A 148
Old Orchard, The NW3 . . . 4D 64
Old Orchard Cl. EN4: Had W . . . 1G 21
UB8: Hil . . . 6C 74
Old Palace La. TW9: Rich . . . 5C 114
Old Palace Rd. CR0: C'don . . . 3B 168
Old Palace Ter. TW9: Rich . . . 5D 114
Old Palace Yd. SW1 . . . 1E 18 (3J 101)
TW9: Rich . . . 5C 114
Old Paradise St. SE11 . . . 3G 19 (4K 101)
Old Park Av. EN2: Enf . . . 5H 23
SW12 . . . 6E 118
Old Park Gro. EN2: Enf . . . 4H 23
Old Park La. W1 . . . 5J 11 (1F 101)
Old Park M. TW5: Hest . . . 7D 94
Old Park Ridings N21 . . . 6G 23
Old Park Rd. EN2: Enf . . . 3G 23
N13 . . . 4E 32
SE2 . . . 5A 108
Old Park Rd. Sth. EN2: Enf . . . 4G 23
Old Park Vw. EN2: Enf . . . 3F 23
Old Pearson St. SE10 . . . 7D 104
Old Perry St. BR7: Chst . . . 6J 143
Old Post Office La. SE3 . . . 3K 123
Old Pound Cl. TW7: Isle . . . 1A 114
Old Priory UB9: Hare . . . 7D 38
Old Pye St. SW1 . . . 1C 18 (3H 101)
Old Pye St. Est. SW1 . . . 2C 18
(off Old Pye St.)
Old Quebec St. W1 . . . 1F 11 (6D 82)
Old Queen St. SW1 . . . 7D 12 (2H 101)
Old Rectory Gdns. HA8: Edg . . . 6B 28
Old Redding HA3: Hrw W . . . 5A 26
Old Red Lion Theatre . . . 2A 84
(off St John St.)
Oldridge Rd. SW12 . . . 7E 118
Old Rd. DA1: Cray . . . 5K 127
EN3: Enf H . . . 1D 24
SE13 . . . 4G 123
Old Rope Wlk. TW16: Sun . . . 3K 147
Old Royal Free Pl. N1 . . . 1A 84
Old Royal Free Sq. N1 . . . 1A 84
Old Royal Naval College . . . 5F 105
Old Ruislip Rd. UB5: N'olt . . . 2A 76
Old School Cl. BR3: Beck . . . 2K 157
SE10 . . . 3G 105
SW19 . . . 2J 153
Old School Ct. N17 . . . 3F 49
Old School Cres. E7 . . . 6J 69
Old School Pl. CR0: Wadd . . . 4A 168
Old School Rd. UB8: Hil . . . 4B 74
Old Schools La. KT17: Ewe . . . 7B 164
Old School Sq. E14 . . . 6C 86
(off Pelling St.)
KT7: T Ditt . . . 6K 149
Old School Ter. SM3: Cheam . . . 7F 165
Old Seacoal La. EC4 . . . 7A 8 (6B 84)
Old Slade La. SL0: Rich P . . . 1A 174
SL3: Coln . . . 1A 174
Old South Cl. HA5: Pinn . . . 1B 40
Old Sth. Lambeth Rd. SW8 . . . 7J 101
Old Speech Room Gallery . . . 1J 59
Old Spitalfields Market . . . 5J 9 (5F 85)
Old Sq. WC2 . . . 7J 7 (6K 83)
Old Stable M. N5 . . . 3C 66
Old Station Gdns. TW11: Tedd . . . 6A 132
(off Victoria Rd.)
Old Station Rd. UB3: Harl . . . 3H 93
Old Station Yd., The E17 . . . 4E 50
Oldstead Rd. BR1: Brom . . . 4E 140
Old Stockley Rd. UB7: W Dray . . . 2D 92
OLD STREET . . . 4D 84
Old St. E13 . . . 2K 87
EC1 . . . 3C 8 (4C 84)
Old Studio Cl. CR0: C'don . . . 7D 156
Old Sungate Cotts.
RM5: Col R . . . 1F 55
Old Sun Wharf E14 . . . 7A 86
(off Narrow St.)
Old Swan Wharf SW11 . . . 1B 118
Old Swan Yd. SM5: Cars . . . 4D 166
Old Theatre Ct. SE1 . . . 4D 14
Old Town CR0: C'don . . . 3B 168
SW4 . . . 3G 119
Old Tramyard SE18 . . . 4J 107
Old Twelve Cl. W7 . . . 4J 77
Old Vic Theatre, The . . . 6K 13
Old Woolwich Rd. SE10 . . . 6F 105
Old York Rd. SW18 . . . 5K 117
Oleander Cl. BR6: Farnb . . . 5H 173
O'Leary Sq. E1 . . . 5J 85
Olga St. E3 . . . 2A 86
Olinda Rd. N16 . . . 6F 49
Oliphant St. W10 . . . 3F 81
Olive Blythe Ho. W10 . . . 4G 81
(off Ladbroke Gro.)
Olive Ct. N1 . . . 1A 84
(off Liverpool Rd.)
Oliver Av. SE25 . . . 3F 157
Oliver Bus. Pk. NW10 . . . 2J 79
Oliver Cl. W4 . . . 6H 97
Oliver Ct. SE18 . . . 4G 107
Oliver Gdns. E6 . . . 5C 88
Oliver Goldsmith Est. SE15 . . . 1G 121
Oliver Gro. SE25 . . . 4F 157
Oliver Ho. SE16 . . . 2G 103
(off George Row)
SW8 . . . 7J 101
(off Wyvil Rd.)
Oliver M. SE15 . . . 2G 121
Olive Rd. E13 . . . 3A 88
NW2 . . . 4E 62
SW19 . . . 7A 136
W5 . . . 3D 96
Oliver Rd. E10 . . . 2D 68
E17 . . . 5E 50
KT3: N Mald . . . 2J 151
NW10 . . . 2J 79
SM1: Sutt . . . 4B 166
Olivers Wharf E1 . . . 1H 103
(off Wapping High St.)
Olivers Yd. EC1 . . . 3F 9 (4D 84)
Olive St. RM7: Rom . . . 5K 55
Olive Tree Ho. SE15 . . . 6J 103
(off Sharratt St.)
Olivette St. SW15 . . . 3F 117
Olive Waite Ho. NW6 . . . 7J 63
Olivia Ct. EN2: Enf . . . 1H 23
(off Chase Side)
Olivia M. HA3: Hrw W . . . 7D 26
Olivier Theatre . . . 4H 13
(in National Theatre)
Ollerton Grn. E3 . . . 1B 86
Ollerton Rd. N11 . . . 5C 32
Olley Cl. SM6: Wall . . . 7J 167
Ollgar Cl. W12 . . . 1B 98
Olliffe St. E14 . . . 3E 104
Olmar St. SE1 . . . 6G 103
Olney Ho. NW8 . . . 3D 4
(off Tresham Cres.)
Olney Rd. SE17 . . . 6B 102
(not continuous)
Olron Cres. DA6: Bex . . . 5D 126
Olven Rd. SE18 . . . 6G 107
Olveston Wlk. SM5: Cars . . . 6B 154
Olwen M. HA5: Pinn . . . 2B 40
Olyffe Av. DA16: Well . . . 1A 126
Olyffe Dr. BR3: Beck . . . 1E 158
Olympia . . . 3G 99
Olympia Ind. Est. N22 . . . 3K 47
Olympia M. W2 . . . 7K 81
Olympian Ct. E14 . . . 4C 104
(off Homer Dr.)
Olympia Way W14 . . . 3G 99
Olympic Ho. N16 . . . 4F 67
Olympic Way
HA9: Wemb . . . 3G 61
UB6: G'frd . . . 1G 77
Olympus Gro. N22 . . . 1A 48
Olympus Sq. E5 . . . 3G 67
O'Mahoney Ct. SW17 . . . 3A 136
Oman Av. NW2 . . . 4E 62
O'Meara St. SE1 . . . 5D 14 (1C 102)
Omega Cl. E14 . . . 3D 104
Omega Ct. RM7: Rom . . . 5K 55
Omega Ho. SW10 . . . 7A 100
(off King's Rd.)
Omega Pl. N1 . . . 1F 7
Omega St. SE14 . . . 1C 122
Omega Works E3 . . . 7C 68
Ommaney Rd. SE14 . . . 1K 121
Omnibus Way E17 . . . 2C 50
Omnium Ct. WC1 . . . 5K 83
(off Princeton St.)
Ondine Rd. SE15 . . . 4F 121
Onega Ga. SE16 . . . 3A 104
O'Neill Ho. NW8 . . . 1B 4
(off Cochrane St.)
O'Neill Path SE18 . . . 6E 106
One Owen St. EC1 . . . 1A 8
(off Goswell St.)
One Tree Cl. SE23 . . . 6J 121
Ongar Cl. RM6: Chad H . . . 5C 54
Ongar Rd. SW6 . . . 6J 99
Onra Rd. E17 . . . 7C 50
Onslow Av. TW10: Rich . . . 5E 114
Onslow Cl. E4 . . . 2K 35
KT7: T Ditt . . . 7J 149
W10 . . . 3H 81
Onslow Ct. SW10 . . . 6A 16
Onslow Cres. BR7: Chst . . . 1F 161
SW7 . . . 4B 16 (4B 100)
Onslow Dr. DA14: Sidc . . . 2D 144
Onslow Gdns. E18 . . . 3K 51
KT7: T Ditt . . . 7J 149
N10 . . . 5F 47
N21 . . . 5F 23
SM6: Wall . . . 6G 167
SW7 . . . 4A 16 (4B 100)
Onslow Ho. KT2: King T . . . 1F 151
(off Acre Rd.)
Onslow M. E. SW7 . . . 4A 16 (4B 100)
Onslow M. W. SW7 . . . 4A 16 (4B 100)
Onslow Pde. N14 . . . 1A 32
Onslow Rd.
CR0: C'don . . . 7K 155
KT3: N Mald . . . 4C 152
TW10: Rich . . . 5E 114
Onslow Sq. SW7 . . . 4B 16 (4B 100)
Onslow St. EC1 . . . 4K 7 (4A 84)
Onslow Way KT7: T Ditt . . . 7J 149
Ontario St. SE1 . . . 3B 102

Ontario Way E14 7C 86
(not continuous)
Onyx M. E15 6H 69
Opal Cl. E16 6B 88
Opal M. IG1: Ilf 2F 71
NW6 1H 81
Opal St. SE11 5K 19 (5B 102)
Open Air Stage 1C 64
Openshaw Rd. SE2 4B 108
Open University, The (Parsifal College) 4J 63
Openview SW18 1A 136
Opera Ct. *N19* *3H 65*
(off Wedmore St.)
Operating Theatre Mus. 5F 15
Ophelia Gdns. NW2 3G 63
Ophelia Ho. *W6* *5F 99*
(off Fulham Pal. Rd.)
Ophir Ter. SE15 1G 121
Opie Ho. *NW8* *2C 82*
(off Townshend Est.)
Opossum Way TW4: Houn 3A 112
Oppenheim Rd. SE13 2E 122
Oppidan Apartments *NW6* *7J 63*
(off Netherwood St.)
Oppidans Rd. NW3 7D 64
Opulens Pl. HA6: Nwood 1D 38
Orange Ct. La. BR6: Downe 7E 172
Orange Gro. E11 3G 69
(not continuous)
Orange Hill Rd. HA8: Edg 7D 28
Orange Pl. SE16 3J 103
Orangery, The TW10: Ham 2C 132
Orangery Gallery, The 2H 99
Orangery La. SE9 5D 124
Orange St. WC2 3D 12 (7H 83)
Orange Tree Ct. *SE5* *7E 102*
(off Havil St.)
Orange Tree Theatre 4E 114
Orange Yd. W1 1D 12
Oransay Rd. N1 6C 66
Oratory La. SW3 5B 16 (5B 100)
Orbain Rd. SW6 7G 99
Orbel St. SW11 1C 118
Orbital Cen., The
IG8: Wfd G 2B 52
Orb St. SE17 4D 102
Orchard, The KT17: Ewe 7B 164
N14 5A 22
N20 1E 30
N21 6J 23
NW11 5J 45
SE3 2F 123
TW3: Houn 2G 113
W4 4K 97
W5 *5D 78*
(off Montpelier Rd.)
Orchard Av. CR0: C'don 2A 170
CR4: Mitc 1E 166
DA17: Belv 6E 108
KT3: N Mald 2A 152
KT7: T Ditt 1A 162
N3 3J 45
N14 6B 22
N20 2G 31
TW5: Hest 7C 94
TW14: Felt 5F 111
TW15: Ashf 6E 128
UB1: S'hall 1D 94
Orchard Bus. Cen. SE26 5B 140
Orchard Cl. DA7: Bex 1E 126
E4 4H 35
E11 4K 51
HA0: Wemb 1E 78
HA4: Ruis 7E 38
HA8: Edg 6K 27
KT7: T Ditt 1B 162
KT12: Walt T 7K 147
KT19: Ewe 6H 163
N1 7C 66
Orchard Cl. NW2 3C 62
SE23 6J 121
SW20 4E 152
TW15: Ashf 6E 128
UB5: N'olt 6G 59
W10 5H 81
WD23: B Hea 1C 26
Orchard Cotts. KT2: King T 1F 151
UB3: Hayes 2G 93
Orchard Ct. E10 1D 68
EN5: New Bar 3E 20
HA8: Edg 5A 28
KT4: Wor Pk 1C 164
KT12: Walt T *7H 147*
(off Bridge St.)
N14 6B 22
SM6: Wall 5F 167
TW2: Twick 2H 131
TW7: Isle 1H 113
UB7: Lford 3D 174
Orchard Cres. EN1: Enf 1A 24
HA8: Edg 5D 28
Orchard Dr. HA8: Edg 5A 28
SE3 2F 123
TW17: Shep 3G 147
Orchard Gdns. KT9: Chess 4E 162
SM1: Sutt 5J 165
Orchard Ga. KT10: Esh 7H 149
NW9 4A 44
UB6: G'frd 6B 60
Orchard Grn. BR6: Orp 2J 173
Orchard Gro. BR6: Orp 2K 173
CR0: C'don 7A 158
HA3: Kent 5F 43
HA8: Edg 1G 43
SE20 7G 139
Orchard Hill DA1: Cray 5K 127
SE13 2D 122
SM5: Cars 5D 166
Orchard Ho. *SE5* *1C 120*
(off County Gro.)
SE16 3J 103
SW6 *7H 99*
(off Varna Rd.)
W1 *7G 5*
(off Fitzhardinge St.)
W12 1C 98
Orchard La. IG8: Wfd G 4F 37
KT8: E Mos 6H 149
SW20 1D 152
Orchardleigh Av. EN3: Enf H 2D 24
Orchard Mead Ho. NW2 2J 63
Orchardmede N21 6J 23
Orchard M. N1 7D 66
N6 7F 47
SW17 3A 136
Orchard Pl. BR2: Kes 7A 172
E5 5H 67
E14 7G 87
(not continuous)
N17 7A 34
Orchard Ri. CR0: C'don 1A 170
HA5: Eastc 3H 39
KT2: King T 1J 151
TW10: Rich 4H 115
Orchard Ri. E. DA15: Sidc 5K 125
Orchard Ri. W. DA15: Sidc 5J 125
Orchard Rd. BR1: Brom 1A 160
BR6: Farnb 5F 173
CR4: Mitc 1E 166
DA14: Sidc 4J 143
DA16: Well 3B 126
DA17: Belv 4G 109
EN3: Pond E 5D 24
EN5: Barn 4C 20
KT1: King T 2E 150
KT9: Chess 4E 162
N6 7F 47
RM7: Mawney 1H 55
RM10: Dag 1G 91
Orchard Rd. SE3 2G 123
SE18 4H 107
SM1: Sutt 5J 165
TW1: Twick 5A 114
TW4: Houn 5D 112
TW8: Bford 6C 96
TW9: Rich 3G 115
TW12: Hamp 7D 130
TW13: Felt 1J 129
TW16: Sun 7K 129
UB3: Hayes 7J 75
Orchardson Ho. NW8 4A 4
Orchardson St. NW8 4A 4 (4B 82)
Orchard Sq. W14 5H 99
Orchard St. E17 4A 50
W1 1G 11 (6E 82)
Orchard Studios *W6* *4F 99*
(off Brook Grn.)
Orchard Ter. EN1: Enf 6B 24
NW10 4B 62
Orchard Vs. DA14: Sidc 6C 144
Orchard Wlk. *KT2: King T* *1G 151*
(off Gordon Rd.)
Orchard Way BR3: Beck 6B 158
CR0: C'don 1A 170
EN1: Enf 3K 23
SM1: Sutt 4B 166
TW15: Ashf 2B 128
Orchard Waye UB8: Uxb 2A 74
Orchard Wharf *E14* *7G 87*
(off Orchard Pl.)
Orchestra Ct. HA8: Edg 7C 28
Orchid Cl. E6 5C 88
KT9: Chess 7C 162
UB1: S'hall 7C 76
Orchid Ct. HA9: Wemb 2E 60
Orchid Gdns. TW3: Houn 4D 112
Orchid Grange N14 7B 22
Orchid Rd. N14 7B 22
Orchid St. W12 7C 80
Orde NW9 1B 44
Orde Hall St. WC1 4G 7 (4K 83)
Ordell Rd. E3 2B 86
Ordnance Cl. TW13: Felt 2J 129
Ordnance Cres. SE10 2F 105
Ordnance Hill NW8 1B 82
Ordnance M. NW8 2B 82
Ordnance Rd. E16 5H 87
SE18 6E 106
Oregano Cl. UB7: Yiew 6A 74
Oregano Dr. E14 6F 87
Oregon Av. E12 4D 70
Oregon Bldg. *SE10* *1D 122*
(off Deal's Gateway)
Oregon Cl. KT3: N Mald 4J 151
Oregon Sq. BR6: Orp 1H 173
Orestes M. NW6 5J 63
Orford Ct. HA7: Stan 6H 27
SE27 2B 138
Orford Gdns. TW1: Twick 2K 131
Orford Rd. E17 5C 50
E18 3K 51
SE6 3D 140
ORGAN CROSSROADS 7C 164
Organ La. E4 2K 35
(not continuous)
Oriana Ho. *E14* *7B 86*
(off Victory Pl.)
Oriel Cl. CR4: Mitc 4H 155
Oriel Ct. CR0: C'don 1D 168
NW3 4A 64
Oriel Dr. SW13 6E 98
Oriel Gdns. IG5: Ilf 3D 52
Oriel Ho. RM7: Rom 6K 55
Oriel Pl. *NW3* *4A 64*
(off Heath St.)
Oriel Rd. E9 6K 67
Oriel Way UB5: N'olt 7F 59
Oriental City NW9 3K 43
Oriental Rd. E16 1B 106
Oriental St. *E14* *7C 86*
(off Pennyfields)
Orient Ho. *SW6* *1A 118*
(off Station Ct.)
Orient Ind. Pk. E10 2C 68
Orient St. SE11 3K 19 (4B 102)
Orient Way E5 3K 67
E10 1A 68
Orient Wharf *E1* *1J 103*
(off Wapping High St.)
Oriole Way SE28 7B 90
Orion *E14* *4C 104*
(off Crews St.)
Orion Bus. Cen. SE14 5K 103
Orion Cen., The CR0: Bedd 2J 167
Orion Ho. *E1* *4H 85*
(off Coventry Rd.)
Orion Rd. N11 7K 31
Orissa Rd. SE18 5J 107
Orkney Ho. *N1* *1K 83*
(off Bemerton Est.)
Orkney St. SW11 2E 118
Orlando Rd. SW4 3G 119
Orleans Ct. TW1: Twick 7B 114
Orleans House Gallery 1B 132
Orleans Pk. School Sports Cen. *7B 114*
(off Richmond Rd.)
Orleans Rd. SE19 6D 138
TW1: Twick 7B 114
Orleston M. N7 6A 66
Orleston Rd. N7 6A 66
Orley Ct. HA1: Harr 4K 59
Orley Farm Rd. HA1: Harr 3J 59
Orlop St. SE10 5G 105
Ormanton Rd. SE26 4G 139
Orme Ct. W2 7K 81
Orme Ct. M. *W2* *7K 81*
(off Orme La.)
Orme Ho. E8 1F 85
Orme La. W2 7K 81
Ormeley Rd. SW12 1F 137
Orme Rd. KT1: King T 2H 151
SM1: Sutt 6K 165
Ormerod Gdns. CR4: Mitc 2E 154
Ormesby Cl. SE28 7D 90
Ormesby Way HA3: Kent 6F 43
Orme Sq. W2 7K 81
Ormiston Gro. W12 1D 98
Ormiston Rd. SE10 5J 105
Ormond Av. TW10: Rich 5D 114
TW12: Hamp 1F 149
Ormond Cl. WC1 5F 7 (5J 83)
Ormond Cres. TW12: Hamp 1F 149
Ormond Dr. TW12: Hamp 7F 131
Ormonde Av. BR6: Farnb 2G 173
Ormonde Ct. *NW8* *1D 82*
(off St Edmund's Cl.)
SW15 4E 116
Ormonde Ga. SW3 6F 17 (5D 100)
Ormonde Mans. *WC1* *5F 7*
(off Southampton Row)
Ormonde Pl. SW1 4G 17 (4E 100)
Ormonde Ri. IG9: Buck H 1F 37
Ormonde Rd. SW14 3J 115
Ormonde Ter. NW8 1D 82
Ormond Ho. N16 2D 66
Ormond M. WC1 4F 7 (4J 83)
Ormond Rd. N19 1J 65
TW10: Rich 5D 114
Ormond Yd. SW1 4B 12 (1G 101)
Ormrod Ct. *W11* *6G 81*
(off Westbourne Pk. Rd.)
Ormsby SM2: Sutt 7K 165
Ormsby Gdns. UB6: G'frd 2G 77
Ormsby Lodge W4 3A 98
Ormsby Pl. N16 3F 67
Ormsby Point *SE18* *4F 107*
(off Vincent Rd.)
Ormsby St. E2 2F 85
Ormside St. SE15 6J 103

Ornan Rd. NW3 5C 64
Orpen Ho. *SW5* *4J 99*
(off Trebovir Rd.)
Orpen Wlk. N16 3E 66
Orpheus St. SE5 1D 120
ORPINGTON 2J 173
Orpington Gdns. N18 3K 33
Orpington Mans. N21 1G 33
Orpington Rd. BR7: Chst 3J 161
N21 1G 33
Orpwood Cl. TW12: Hamp 6D 130
Orsett M. W2 6K 81
(not continuous)
Orsett St. SE11 5H 19 (5K 101)
Orsett Ter. IG8: Wfd G 7F 37
W2 6K 81
Orsman Rd. N1 1E 84
Orton Gro. EN1: Enf 1B 24
Orton St. E1 1G 103
Orville Rd. SW11 2B 118
Orwell Cl. RM13: Rain 5K 91
UB3: Hayes 7G 75
Orwell Ct. *E8* *1G 85*
(off Pownall Rd.)
N5 4C 66
Orwell Rd. E13 2A 88
Osbaldeston Rd. N16 2G 67
Osberton Rd. SE12 5J 123
Osbert St. SW1 4C 18 (4H 101)
Osborn Cl. E8 1G 85
Osborne Av. TW19: Stanw 1A 128
Osborne Cl. BR3: Beck 4A 158
EN4: Cockf 3J 21
TW13: Hanw 5B 130
Osborne Ct. E10 7D 50
W5 5E 78
Osborne Gdns. CR7: Thor H 2C 156
Osborne Gro. E17 4B 50
N4 1A 66
Osborne Ho. *E16* *1J 105*
(off Wesley Av.)
Osborne M. E17 4B 50
Osborne Pl. SM1: Sutt 5B 166
Osborne Rd. CR7: Thor H 2C 156
DA17: Belv 5F 109
E7 5K 69
E9 6B 68
E10 2D 68
EN3: Enf H 2F 25
IG9: Buck H 1E 36
KT2: King T 7E 132
KT12: Walt T 7J 147
N4 1A 66
N13 3F 33
NW2 6D 62
RM9: Dag 5F 73
TW3: Houn 3D 112
UB1: S'hall 6G 77
W3 3H 97
Osborne Sq. RM9: Dag 4F 73
Osborne Ter. *SW17* *5D 136*
(off Church La.)
Osborne Way *KT9: Chess* *5F 163*
(off Bridge Rd.)
Osborn Gdns. NW7 7A 30
Osborn La. SE23 7A 122
Osborn St. E1 6K 9 (5F 85)
Osborn Ter. SE3 4H 123
Osbourne Ct. HA2: Harr 4F 41
Osbourne Ho.
IG8: Wfd G 7K 37
TW2: Twick 2G 131
Oscar Faber Pl. N1 7E 66
Oscar St. SE8 2C 122
(not continuous)
Oseney Cres. NW5 5G 65
Osgood Av. BR6: Chels 5K 173
Osgood Gdns. BR6: Chels 5K 173
OSIDGE 1A 32
Osidge La. N14 1K 31
Osier Ct. *E1* *4K 85*
(off Osier St.)
RM7: Rom 6K 55
TW8: Bford *6E 96*
(off Ealing Rd.)
Osier Cres. N10 1D 46
Osier La. *SE10* *3H 105*
(off School Bank Rd.)
Osier M. W4 6A 98
Osiers Ct. *KT1: King T* *1D 150*
(off Steadfast Rd.)
Osiers Est., The
SW18 4J 117
Osiers Rd. SW18 4J 117
Osier St. E1 4J 85
Osier Way CR4: Mitc 5D 154
E10 3D 68
Oslac Rd. SE6 5D 140
Oslo Ct. *NW8* *2C 82*
(off Prince Albert Rd.)
Oslo Ho. *SE5* *2C 120*
(off Carew St.)
Oslo Sq. SE16 3A 104
Osman Cl. N15 6D 48
Osmani School Sports Cen. 5G 85
Osman Rd. N9 3B 34
W6 3E 98
Osmington Ho. *SW8* *7K 101*
(off Dorset Rd.)
Osmond Cl. HA2: Harr 2G 59
Osmond Gdns.
SM6: Wall 5G 167
Osmund St. W12 5B 80
Osnaburgh St. NW1 4K 5 (4F 83)
(Euston Rd.)
NW1 2K 5
(Robert St.)
Osnaburgh Ter. NW1 3K 5 (4F 83)
Osney Ho. SE2 2D 108
Osney Wlk. SM5: Cars 6B 154
Osprey NW9 1B 44
Osprey Cl. BR2: Brom 1C 172
E6 5C 88
E11 4J 51
E17 7F 35
SM1: Sutt 5H 165
UB7: W Dray 2A 92
Osprey Ct. BR3: Beck 7C 140
E1 *3K 15*
(off Star Pl.)
Osprey Est. SE16 4A 104
Osprey Ho. *E14* *7A 86*
(off Victory Pl.)
Osprey M. EN3: Pond E 5D 24
Ospringe Cl. SE20 7J 139
Ospringe Ct. SE9 6H 125
Ospringe Ho. *SE1* *6K 13*
(off Wootton St.)
Ospringe Rd. NW5 4G 65
Osram Ct. W6 3E 98
Osram Rd. HA9: Wemb 3D 60
Osric Path N1 2E 84
Ossian M. N4 7K 47
Ossian Rd. N4 7K 47
Ossie Garvin Rdbt.
UB4: Yead 7K 75
Ossington Bldgs. W1 5G 5 (5E 82)
Ossington Cl. W2 7J 81
Ossington St. W2 7J 81
Ossory Rd. SE1 6G 103
Ossulston St. NW1 1D 6 (2H 83)
Ossulton Pl. N2 3A 46
Ossulton Way N2 4A 46
Ostade Rd. SW2 7K 119
Ostell Cres.
EN3: Enf L 1H 25
Ostend Pl. SE1 4C 102
Osten M. SW7 3K 99
OSTERLEY 7H 95
Osterley Av. TW7: Isle 7H 95
Osterley Cl. BR5: St P 1K 161
Osterley Ct. TW7: Isle 1H 113
UB5: Yead *3A 76*
(off Canberra Dr.)
Osterley Cres. TW7: Isle 1J 113
Osterley Gdns. CR7: Thor H 2C 156
UB2: S'hall 2G 95
Osterley Ho. *E14* *6D 86*
(off Girauld St.)
Osterley La. TW7: Isle 4G 95
UB2: S'hall 5E 94
(not continuous)
Osterley Lodge *TW7: Isle* *7J 95*
(off Church Rd.)
Osterley Pk. 6G 95
Osterley Pk. House 6G 95
Osterley Pk. Rd. UB2: S'hall 3D 94
Osterley Pk. Vw. Rd.
W7 2J 95
Osterley Rd. N16 4E 66
TW7: Isle 7J 95
Osterley Sports Club 3G 95
Osterley Views UB2: S'hall 1G 95
Oster Ter. E17 5K 49
Ostlers Dr. TW15: Ashf 5E 128
Ostliffe Rd. N13 5H 33
Oswald Bldg. SW8 6F 101
Oswald Rd. UB1: S'hall 1C 94
Oswald's Mead E9 4A 68
Oswald St. E5 3K 67
Oswald Ter. NW2 3E 62
Osward CR0: Sels 7B 170
(not continuous)
Osward Pl. N9 2C 34
Osward Rd. SW17 2D 136
Oswell Ho. *E1* *1H 103*
(off Farthing Flds.)
Oswin St. SE11 4B 102
Oswyth Rd. SE5 2E 120
Otford Cl. BR1: Brom 3E 160
DA5: Bexl 6H 127
SE20 1J 157
Otford Cres. SE4 6B 122
Otford Ho. *SE1* *7F 15*
(off Staple St.)
SE15 *6J 103*
(off Lovelinch Cl.)
Othello Cl. SE11 5K 19 (5B 102)
Otho Ct. TW8: Bford 7D 96
Otis St. E3 3E 86
Otley App. IG2: Ilf 6F 53
Otley Dr. IG2: Ilf 5F 53
Otley Ho. N5 3A 66
Otley Rd. E16 6A 88
Otley Ter. E5 3K 67
Ottawa Gdns. RM10: Dag 7K 73
Ottaway Ct. E5 3G 67
Ottaway St. E5 3G 67
Otterbourne Rd. CR0: C'don 2C 168
E4 3A 36
Otterburn Gdns. TW7: Isle 7A 96
Otterburn Ho. *SE5* *7C 102*
(off Sultan St.)
Otterburn St. SW17 6D 136
Otter Cl. E15 1E 86
Otterden Cl. BR6: Orp 3J 173
Otterden St. SE6 4C 140
Otterfield Rd.
UB7: Yiew 7A 74
Otter Rd. UB6: G'frd 4G 77
Otto Cl. SE26 3H 139
Otto St. SE17 6B 102
Otway Gdns. WD23: Bush 1D 26
Oulton Cl. E5 2J 67
SE28 6C 90
Oulton Cres. IG11: Bark 5K 71
Oulton Rd. N15 5D 48
Ouseley Rd. SW12 1D 136
Outer Circ. NW1 1D 4 & 1J 5 (2C 82)
Outgate Rd. NW10 7B 62
Outram Pl. N1 1J 83
Outram Rd. CR0: C'don 2F 169
E6 1C 88
N22 1H 47
Outwich St. EC3 7H 9
Outwood Ho. *SW2* *7K 119*
(off Deepdene Gdns.)
Oval, The DA15: Sidc 7A 126
E2 2H 85
Oval Ct. HA8: Edg 7D 28
Oval Cricket Ground, The 7H 19 (6K 101)
Oval Ho. *CR0: C'don* *1E 168*
(off Oval Rd.)
Oval House Theatre 7J 19
(off Kennington Oval)
Oval Mans. SE11 7H 19 (6K 101)
Oval Pl. SW8 7K 101
Oval Rd. CR0: C'don 2D 168
NW1 1F 83
Oval Rd. Nth. RM10: Dag 1H 91
Oval Rd. Sth. RM10: Dag 2H 91
Oval Way SE11 6H 19 (5K 101)
Overbrae BR3: Beck 6C 140
Overbrook Wlk. HA8: Edg 7B 28
(not continuous)
Overbury Av. BR3: Beck 3D 158
Overbury Rd. N15 6D 48
Overbury St. E5 4K 67
Overcliff Rd. SE13 3C 122
Overcourt Cl. DA15: Sidc 6B 126
Overdale Av. KT3: N Mald 2J 151
Overdale Rd. W5 3C 96
Overdown Rd. SE6 4C 140
Overhill Rd. SE22 7G 121
Overhill Way BR3: Beck 5F 159
Overlea Rd. E5 7G 49
Overmead DA15: Sidc 7H 125
Oversley Ho. *W2* *5J 81*
(off Alfred Rd.)
Overstand Cl. BR3: Beck 5C 158
Overstone Gdns. CR0: C'don 7B 158
Overstone Ho. *E14* *6C 86*
(off E. India Dock Rd.)
Overstone Rd. W6 3E 98
Overstrand Mans. SW11 1D 118
Overton Cl. NW10 6J 61
TW7: Isle 1K 113
Overton Ct. E11 7J 51
SM2: Sutt 7J 165
Overton Dr. E11 7J 51
RM6: Chad H 7C 54
Overton Ho. *SW15* *7B 116*
(off Tangley Gro.)
Overton Rd. E10 1A 68
N14 5D 22
SE2 3C 108
SM2: Sutt 6J 165
SW9 2A 120
Overton Rd. E. SE2 3D 108
Overton's Yd. CR0: C'don 3C 168
Overy Ho. SE1 7A 14 (2B 102)
Ovesdon Av. HA2: Harr 1D 58
Ovett Cl. SE19 6E 138
Ovex Cl. E14 2E 104
Ovington Ct. *SW3* *2D 16*
(off Brompton Rd.)
Ovington Gdns. SW3 2D 16 (3C 100)
Ovington M. SW3 2D 16
Ovington Sq. SW3 2D 16 (3C 100)
Ovington St. SW3 3D 16 (4C 100)
Owen Cl. CR0: C'don 6D 156
SE28 1C 108
UB5: N'olt 6C 58
UB5: Yead 3K 75
Owen Gdns. IG8: Wfd G 6H 37
Owen Ho. TW1: Twick 7B 114
TW14: Felt 7J 111
Owenite St. SE2 4B 108
Owen Mans. *W14* *6G 99*
(off Queen's Club Gdns.)

Owen Rd. N13 .5H 33
UB4: Yead .3K 75
Owens M. E11 .2G 69
Owen's Row EC1 .1A 8 (3B 84)
Owen St. EC1 .1A 8 (2B 84)
Owens Way SE23 .7A 122
Owen Wlk. SE20 .1G 157
Owen Way NW10 .6J 61
Owgan Cl. SE5 .7D 102
Oxberry Av. SW6 .2G 117
Oxendon St. SW1 .3C 12 (7H 83)
Oxenford St. SE15 .3F 121
Oxenham Ho. *SE8* .6C 104
(off Benbow St.)
Oxenholme *NW1* .1A 6
(off Hampstead Rd.)
Oxenpark Av. HA9: Wemb .7E 42
Oxestall's Rd. SE8 .5A 104
Oxford & Cambridge Mans.
NW1 .6D 4
(off Old Marylebone Rd.)
Oxford Av. N14 .1B 32
NW10 .3D 80
SW20 .2G 153
TW5: Hest .5E 94
UB3: Harl .7H 93
Oxford Cir. W1 .1A 12
Oxford Cir. Av. W1 .1A 12 (6G 83)
Oxford Cl. CR4: Mitc .3G 155
N9 .2C 34
TW15: Ashf .7E 128
Oxford Ct. EC4 .2E 14
TW13: Hanw .4B 130
W3 .6G 79
W4 .5H 97
Oxford Ct. *W7* .5K 77
(off Copley Cl.)
W9 .5J 81
(off Elmfield Way)
Oxford Cres. KT3: N Mald .6K 151
Oxford Dr. HA4: Ruis .2A 58
SE1 .5G 15 (1E 102)
Oxford Gdns. N20 .1G 31
N21 .7H 23
W4 .5G 97
W10 .6E 80
Oxford Ga. W6 .4F 99
Oxford M. DA5: Bexl .7G 127
Oxford Pl. *NW10* .3K 61
(off Press Rd.)
Oxford Rd. DA14: Sidc .5B 144
E15 .6F 69
(not continuous)
EN3: Pond E .5C 24
HA1: Harr .6G 41
HA3: W'stone .3K 41
IG1: Ilf .5G 71
IG8: Wfd G .5G 37
N4 .1A 66
N9 .2C 34
NW6 .2J 81
SE19 .6D 138
SM5: Cars .6C 166
SM6: Wall .5G 167
SW15 .4G 117
TW11: Tedd .5H 131
W5 .7D 78
Oxford Rd. Nth. W4 .5H 97
Oxford Rd. Sth. W4 .5G 97
Oxford Sq. W2 .1D 10 (6C 82)
Oxford St. W1 .1G 11 (6E 82)
Oxford Wlk. UB1: S'hall .1D 94
Oxford Way TW13: Hanw .4B 130
Oxgate Cen. NW2 .2D 62
Oxgate Ct. NW2 .2C 62
Oxgate Ct. Pde. NW2 .2C 62
Oxgate Gdns. NW2 .3D 62
Oxgate La. NW2 .2D 62
Oxgate Pde. NW2 .2C 62
Oxhawth Cres. BR2: Brom .5E 160
Oxhey La. HA5: Hat E .5A 26
Oxleas E6 .6F 89
Oxleas Cl. DA16: Well .2H 125
Oxleay Rd. HA2: Harr .1E 58
Oxleigh Cl. KT3: N Mald .5A 152
Oxley Cl. SE1 .5F 103
Oxleys Rd. NW2 .3D 62
Oxlip Cl. CR0: C'don .1K 169
Oxlow La. RM9: Dag .4F 73
RM10: Dag .4F 73
Oxonian St. SE22 .4F 121
Oxo Tower Wharf
SE1 .3K 13 (7A 84)
Oxted Cl. CR4: Mitc .3B 154
Oxtoby Way SW16 .1H 155
Oxygen, The E16 .7J 87
Oxzygeem Sports Cen. .6B 120
Oystercatcher Cl. E16 .6K 87
Oystergate Wlk. EC4 .3E 14
Oyster Row E1 .6J 85
Oyster Wharf SW11 .2B 118
Ozolins Way E16 .6J 87

P

Pablo Neruda Cl. SE24 .4B 120
Pace Pl. E1 .6H 85
Pacific Cl. TW14: Felt .1H 129
Pacific Ho. *E1* .4K 85
(off Ernest St.)
Pacific Rd. E16 .6J 87
Pacific Wharf SE16 .1K 103
Packenham Ho. *E2* .1K 9
(off Wellington Row)
Packham Ct. KT4: Wor Pk .3E 164
Packington Sq. N1 .1C 84
Packington St. N1 .1B 84
Packmores Rd. SE9 .5H 125
Padbury *SE17* .5E 102
(off Bagshot St.)
Padbury Cl. TW14: Bedf .1F 129
Padbury Ct. E2 .2K 9 (3F 85)
Padbury Ho. *NW8* .3D 4
(off Tresham Cres.)
Padbury Oaks UB7: Lford .4C 174
Padcroft Rd. UB7: Yiew .1A 92
Paddenswick Rd. W6 .3C 98
PADDINGTON .7A 4 (6B 82)
Paddington Bowling & Sports Club .4K 81
Paddington Cl. UB4: Yead .4B 76
Paddington Ct. *W7* .5K 77
(off Copley Cl.)
Paddington Grn. W2 .5A 4 (5B 82)
Paddington St. W1 .5G 5 (5E 82)
Paddock, The N10 .3E 46
NW9 .5G 43
UB10: Ick .4D 56
Paddock Cl. BR6: Farnb .4F 173
KT4: Wor Pk .1A 164
SE3 .2J 123
SE26 .4K 139
UB5: N'olt .2E 76
Paddock Gdns. SE19 .6E 138
Paddock Lodge *EN1: Enf* .5K 23
(off Village Rd.)
Paddock Mobile Home Pk.
BR2: Kes .7C 172
Paddock Pas. *SE19* .6E 138
(off Paddock Gdns.)
Paddock Rd. DA6: Bex .4E 126
HA4: Ruis .3B 58
NW2 .3C 62
Paddocks, The CR0: Addtn .6C 170
EN4: Cockf .3J 21
HA9: Wemb .2H 61
W5 .3D 96
(off Popes La.)
Paddocks Cl. HA2: Harr .4F 59
Paddocks Grn. NW9 .1H 61
Paddock Way BR7: Chst .7H 143
SW15 .7E 116
Padelford La. HA7: Stan .2F 27
Padfield Ct. HA9: Wemb .3F 61
Padfield Rd. SE5 .3C 120
Padley Cl. KT9: Chess .5F 163
Padnall Ct. RM6: Chad H .3D 54
Padnall Rd. RM6: Chad H .3D 54
Padstow Cl. BR6: Chels .4K 173
Padstow Ho. *E14* .7B 86
(off Three Colt St.)
Padstow Rd. EN2: Enf .1G 23
Padstow Wlk. TW14: Felt .1H 129
Padua Rd. SE20 .1J 157
Pagden St. SW8 .1F 119
Pageant Av. NW9 .1K 43
Pageant Cres. SE16 .1A 104
Pageantmaster Ct. EC4 .1A 14
Pageant Wlk. CR0: C'don .3E 168
Page Av. HA9: Wemb .3J 61
Page Cl. HA3: Kent .6F 43
RM9: Dag .5E 72
TW12: Hamp .6C 130
Page Ct. NW7 .7J 29
Page Cres. CR0: Wadd .5B 168
Page Grn. Rd. N15 .5G 49
Page Grn. Ter. N15 .5F 49
Page Heath La. BR1: Brom .3B 160
Page Heath Vs. BR1: Brom .3B 160
Page High *N22* .2A 48
(off Lymington Av.)
Page Ho. *SE10* .6E 104
(off Welland St.)
Pagehurst Rd. CR0: C'don .7H 157
Page Mdw. NW7 .7J 29
Page Rd. TW14: Bedf .6F 111
Pages Hill N10 .2E 46
Pages La. N10 .2E 46
Page St. NW7 .1C 44
SW1 .3D 18 (4H 101)
Page's Wlk. SE1 .4E 102
Pages Yd. W4 .6B 98
Paget Av. SM1: Sutt .3B 166
Paget Cl. TW12: Ham H .4H 131
Paget Gdns. BR7: Chst .1F 161
Paget Ho. *E2* .2J 85
(off Bishop's Way)
Paget La. TW7: Isle .3H 113
Paget Pl. KT2: King T .6J 133
KT7: T Ditt .1A 162
Paget Ri. SE18 .6E 106
Paget Rd. IG1: Ilf .4F 71
N16 .1D 66
UB10: Hil .4E 74
Paget St. EC1 .1A 8 (3B 84)
Paget Ter. SE18 .6F 107
Pagham Ho. *W10* .4E 80
(off Sutton Way)
Pagin Ho. *N15* .5E 48
(off Braemar Rd.)
Pagitts Gro. EN4: Had W .1E 20
Pagnell St. SE14 .7B 104
Pagoda Av. TW9: Rich .3F 115
Pagoda Gdns. SE3 .2F 123
Pagoda Gro. SE27 .2C 138
Paignton Rd. HA4: Ruis .3J 57
N15 .6E 48
Paines Cl. HA5: Pinn .3C 40
Paines La. HA5: Pinn .1C 40
Pain's Cl. CR4: Mitc .2F 155
Painsthorpe Rd. N16 .3E 66
Painswick Ct. *SE15* .7F 103
(off Daniel Gdns.)
Painted Hall
Greenwich .6E 104
Painters M. SE16 .4G 103
Painters Rd. IG2: Ilf .3K 53
Paisley Rd. N22 .1B 48
SM5: Cars .1B 166
Paisley Ter. SM5: Cars .7B 154
Pakeman Ho. *SE1* .6B 14
(off Surrey Row)
Pakeman St. N7 .3K 65
Pakenham Cl. SW12 .1E 136
Pakenham St. WC1 .2H 7 (3K 83)
Pakington Ho. *SW9* .2J 119
(off Stockwell Gdns. Est.)
Palace Av. W8 .2K 99
Palace Bingo Club .4C 102
(within Shopping Cen.)
Palace Ct. *BR1: Brom* .1K 159
(off Palace Gro.)
HA3: Kent .6E 42
NW3 .5K 63
W2 .7K 81
Palace Ct. Gdns. N10 .3G 47
Palace Gdns. IG9: Buck H .1G 37
Palace Gdns. M. W8 .1K 99
Palace Gdns. Shop. Cen.
EN2: Enf .4J 23
Palace Gdns. Ter. W8 .1J 99
Palace Ga. W8 .2A 100
Palace Gates M. *N8* .4J 47
(off The Campsbourne)
Palace Gates Rd. N22 .1H 47
Palace Grn. CR0: Sels .7B 170
W8 .1K 99
Palace Gro. BR1: Brom .1K 159
SE19 .7F 139
Palace Ice Rink, The .2H 47
Palace Mans. *KT1: King T* .4D 150
(off Palace Rd.)
W14 .4G 99
(off Hammersmith Rd.)
Palace M. E17 .4B 50
EN2: Enf .3J 23
SW1 .4H 17
SW6 .7H 99
Palace Pde. E17 .4B 50
Palace Pl. SW1 .1A 18 (3G 101)
Palace Pl. Mans. *W8* .2K 99
(off Kensington Ct.)
Palace Rd. BR1: Brom .1K 159
HA4: Ruis .4C 58
KT1: King T .4D 150
KT8: E Mos .3G 149
N8 .5H 47
(not continuous)
N11 .7D 32
SE19 .7F 139
SW2 .1K 137
Palace Sq. SE19 .7F 139
Palace St. SW1 .1A 18 (3G 101)
Palace Theatre
Soho .1D 12
(off Shaftesbury Av.)
Palace Vw. BR1: Brom .3K 159
(not continuous)
CR0: C'don .4B 170
SE12 .2J 141
Palace Vw. Rd. E4 .5J 35
Palace Wharf *W6* .7E 98
(off Rainville Rd.)
Palamos Rd. E10 .1C 68
Palatine Av. N16 .4E 66
Palatine Rd. N16 .4E 66
Palazzo Apartments *N1* .7E 66
(off Ardleigh Rd.)
Palemead Cl. SW6 .1F 117
Palermo Rd. NW10 .2C 80
Palestine Gro. SW19 .1B 154
Palestra Ho. *SE1* .1B 102
(off Blackfriars Rd.)
Palewell Comn. Dr.
SW14 .5K 115
Palewell Pk. SW14 .5K 115
Palfrey Pl. SW8 .7K 101
Palgrave Av. UB1: S'hall .7E 76
Palgrave Gdns. NW1 .3D 4 (4C 82)

Palgrave Ho. *SE5* 7C 102
(off Wyndham Est.)
TW2: Whitt 7G 113
Palgrave Rd. W12 3B 98
Palissy St. E2 2J 9 (3F 85)
(not continuous)
Palladino Ho. *SW17* 5C 136
(off Laurel Cl.)
Palladium Ct. *E8* 7F 67
(off Queensbridge Rd.)
Pallant Ho. *SE1* 3D 102
(off Tabard St.)
Pallant Way BR6: Farnb 3E 172
Pallett Way SE18 1C 124
Palliser Ct. *W14* 5G 99
(off Palliser Rd.)
Palliser Ho. *E1* 4K 85
(off Ernest St.)
SE10 6F 105
(off Trafalgar Rd.)
Palliser Rd. W14 5G 99
Pall Mall SW1 5B 12 (1G 101)
Pall Mall E. SW1 4D 12 (1H 101)
Pall Mall Pl. SW1 5B 12
Palmar Cres. DA7: Bex 3G 127
Palmar Rd. DA7: Bex 2G 127
Palm Av. DA14: Sidc 6D 144
Palm Cl. E10 3D 68
Palm Ct. *SE15* 7F 103
(off Garnies Cl.)
Palmeira Rd. DA7: Bex 3D 126
Palmer Av. SM3: Cheam 4E 164
Palmer Cl. BR4: W W'ck 3F 171
TW5: Hest 1E 112
UB5: N'olt 6C 58
Palmer Cres. KT1: King T 3E 150
Palmer Dr. BR1: Brom 4F 161
Palmer Gdns. EN5: Barn 5A 20
Palmer Pl. N7 5A 66
Palmer Rd. E13 4K 87
RM8: Dag 1D 72
Palmer's Ct. *N11* 5B 32
(off Palmer's Rd.)
PALMERS GREEN 3F 33
Palmers Gro. KT8: W Mole 4E 148
Palmers La. EN1: Enf 1C 24
EN3: Enf H 1C 24
Palmers Pas. *SW14* 3J 115
(off Palmers Rd.)
Palmers Rd. E2 2K 85
N11 5B 32
SW14 3J 115
SW16 2K 155
Palmerston Cen. HA3: W'stone 3K 41
Palmerston Ct. *E3* 2K 85
(off Old Ford Rd.)
IG9: Buck H 1F 37
KT6: Surb 7D 150
Palmerston Cres. N13 5E 32
SE18 6G 107
Palmerston Gro. SW19 7J 135
Palmerston Ho. *SE1* 7J 13
(off Westminster Bri. Rd.)
W8 1J 99
(off Kensington Pl.)
Palmerston Mans. *W14* 6G 99
(off Queen's Club Gdns.)
Palmerston Rd. BR6: Farnb 4G 173
CR0: C'don 5D 156
E7 6K 69
(not continuous)
E17 3B 50
HA3: W'stone 3J 41
(not continuous)
IG9: Buck H 2E 36
N22 7E 32
NW6 7H 63
(not continuous)
SM1: Sutt 5A 166
SM5: Cars 4D 166
Palmerston Rd. SW14 4J 115
SW19 7J 135
TW2: Twick 6J 113
TW3: Houn 1G 113
W3 3J 97
Palmerston Way SW8 7F 101
Palmer St. SW1 1C 18 (3H 101)
(not continuous)
Palm Gro. W5 3E 96
Palm Rd. RM7: Rom 5J 55
Palm Tree Ho. *SE14* 7K 103
(off Barlborough St.)
Palyn Ho. *EC1* 2D 8
(off Ironmonger Row)
Pamela Ct. N12 6E 30
Pamela Gdns. HA5: Eastc 5K 39
Pamela Ho. *E8* 1F 85
(off Haggerston Rd.)
Pamela Wlk. *E8* 1G 85
(off Marlborough Av.)
Pampisford Rd. CR8: Purl 7B 168
Pams Way KT19: Ewe 5K 163
Panama Ho. *E1* 5K 85
(off Beaumont Sq.)
Pancras La. EC4 1E 14 (6C 84)
Pancras Rd. NW1 1E 6 (2H 83)
Pandian Way NW5 6H 65
Pandora Rd. NW6 6J 63
Panfield M. IG2: Ilf 6E 52
Panfield Rd. SE2 3A 108
Pangbourne *NW1* 2A 6
(off Stanhope St.)
Pangbourne Av. W10 5E 80
Pangbourne Dr. HA7: Stan 5J 27
Panhard Pl. UB1: S'hall 7F 77
Pank Av. EN5: New Bar 5F 21
Pankhurst Av. E16 1K 105
Pankhurst Cl. SE14 7K 103
TW7: Isle 3K 113
Pankhurst Ho. W12 6D 80
Pankhurst Rd. KT12: Walt T 7A 148
Panmuir Rd. SW20 1D 152
Panmure Cl. N5 4B 66
Panmure Ct. *UB1: S'hall* 6G 77
(off Osborne Rd.)
Panmure Rd. SE26 3H 139
Panorama Ct. N6 6G 47
Pansy Gdns. W12 7C 80
Panther Dr. NW10 5K 61
Pantiles, The BR1: Brom 3C 160
DA7: Bex 7F 109
NW11 5H 45
WD23: B Hea 1C 26
Pantiles Cl. N13 5G 33
Panton Cl. CR0: C'don 1B 168
Panton St. SW1 3C 12 (7H 83)
Panyer All. *EC1* 6C 84
(off Newgate St.)
Paper Bldgs. EC4 2K 13
Papermill Cl. SM5: Cars 4E 166
Papillons Wlk. SE3 2J 123
Papworth Gdns. N7 5K 65
Papworth Way SW2 7A 120
Parade, The CR0: C'don 6J 155
KT2: King T 2E 150
(off London Rd.)
KT4: Wor Pk 4B 164
N4 1A 66
SE4 2B 122
(off Up. Brockley Rd.)
SE26 3H 139
(off Wells Pk. Rd.)
SM1: Sutt 3H 165
SM5: Cars 5D 166
(off Beynon Rd.)
SW11 7D 100
TW12: Ham H 5H 131
TW16: Sun 7H 129
UB6: G'frd 5B 60
Parade Mans. NW4 5D 44
Parade M. SE27 2B 138
Paradise Pk. E5 3K 67
Paradise Pas. N7 5A 66
Paradise Path SE28 1A 108
Paradise Pl. SE18 4C 106
Paradise Rd. SW4 2J 119
TW9: Rich 5D 114
Paradise Row E2 3H 85
Paradise St. SE16 2H 103
Paradise Wlk. SW3 7F 17 (6D 100)
Paragon *TW8: Bford* 5C 96
(off Boston Pk. Rd.)
Paragon, The SE3 2H 123
Paragon Cl. E16 6J 87
Paragon Gro. KT5: Surb 6F 151
Paragon M. SE1 4D 102
Paragon Pl. KT5: Surb 6F 151
SE3 2H 123
Paragon Rd. E9 6J 67
Paramount Bldg. *EC1* 3A 8
(off St John St.)
Paramount Ct. WC1 4B 6
Parbury Ri. KT9: Chess 6E 162
Parbury Rd. SE23 6A 122
Parchmore Rd. CR7: Thor H 2B 156
Parchmore Way CR7: Thor H 2B 156
Pardoe Rd. E10 7D 50
Pardoner Ho. *SE1* 3D 102
(off Pardoner St.)
Pardoner St. SE1 7F 15 (3D 102)
(not continuous)
Pardon St. EC1 3B 8 (4B 84)
Parent Shop. Mall *E18* 2J 51
(off Marlborough Rd.)
Parfett St. E1 5G 85
(not continuous)
Parfitt Cl. NW3 1A 64
Parfrey St. W6 6E 98
Pargreaves Ct.
HA9: Wemb 2G 61
Parham Dr. IG2: Ilf 6F 53
Parham Way N10 2G 47
Paris Gdn. SE1 4A 14 (1B 102)
Parish Ct. KT6: Surb 5E 150
Parish Ga. Dr. DA15: Sidc 6J 125
Parish La. SE20 6K 139
Parish M. SE20 7K 139
Paris Ho. *E2* 2H 85
(off Old Bethnal Grn. Rd.)
Parish Wharf Pl. SE18 4C 106
Park, The DA14: Sidc 5A 144
N6 6E 46
NW11 1K 63
SE23 1J 139
SM5: Cars 5D 166
W5 1D 96
Park & Ride
Bromley
(October to January) 6K 159
Kingston-upon-Thames
(November-mid. January) 7C 162
Park App. DA16: Well 4B 126
SE16 3H 103
Park Av. BR1: Brom 6H 141
BR4: W W'ck 2E 170
BR6: Chels 2K 173
BR6: Farnb 3D 172
CR4: Mitc 7F 137
E6 1E 88
E15 6G 69
EN1: Enf 5J 23
HA4: Ruis 6F 39
IG1: Ilf 1E 70
IG8: Wfd G 5E 36
IG11: Bark 6G 71
N3 1K 45
N13 3F 33
N18 4B 34
N22 2J 47
NW2 5D 62
Park Av. NW10 2F 79
(Brent Cres., not continuous)
NW10 5D 62
(Park Av. Nth.)
NW11 1K 63
SM5: Cars 6E 166
SW14 4K 115
TW3: Houn 6F 113
TW17: Shep 3G 147
UB1: S'hall 2D 94
Park Av. E. KT17: Ewe 6C 164
Park Av. M. CR4: Mitc 7F 137
Park Av. Nth. N8 3H 47
NW10 5D 62
Park Av. Rd. N17 7C 34
Park Av. Sth. N8 4H 47
Park Av. W. KT17: Ewe 6C 164
Park Central Bldg. E3 2C 86
Park Chase HA9: Wemb 4F 61
Park Cl. E9 1J 85
HA3: Hrw W 1J 41
KT2: King T 1G 151
N12 3G 31
NW2 3D 62
NW10 3F 79
SM5: Cars 6D 166
SW1 7E 10 (2D 100)
TW3: Houn 5G 113
TW12: Hamp 1G 149
W4 6K 97
W14 3H 99
Park Club, The 1A 98
Park Ct. *CR2: S Croy* 5C 168
(off Warham Rd.)
E4 2K 35
E17 5D 50
HA3: Kent 7E 42
HA9: Wemb 5E 60
KT1: Ham W 1C 150
KT3: N Mald 4K 151
N11 7C 32
N17 7B 34
SE21 3C 138
SE26 6H 139
SM6: Wall 5J 167
SW11 1F 119
UB8: Uxb 1A 74
W6 4C 98
Park Cres. DA8: Erith 6J 109
EN2: Enf 4J 23
HA3: Hrw W 1J 41
N3 7F 31
TW2: Twick 1H 131
W1 4J 5 (4F 83)
Park Cres. M. E. W1 4K 5 (4F 83)
Park Cres. M. W. W1 4J 5 (4F 83)
Park Cres. Rd. DA8: Erith 6K 109
Park Cft. HA8: Edg 1J 43
Parkcroft Rd. SE12 7H 123
Parkdale N11 6C 32
Parkdale Cres. KT4: Wor Pk 3K 163
Parkdale Rd. SE18 5J 107
Park Dr. HA2: Harr 7E 40
HA3: Hrw W 6C 26
N21 6H 23
NW11 1K 63
RM1: Rom 4K 55
RM10: Dag 3J 73
SE7 6C 106
SW14 5K 115
W3 3G 97
Park Dwellings NW3 5D 64
Park E. Bldg. *E3* 2C 86
(off Fairfield Rd.)
Park End BR1: Brom 1H 159
NW3 4C 64
Parker Cl. E16 1C 106
SM5: Cars 6D 166
Parker Ct. *N1* 1C 84
(off Basire St.)

Parker Ho. *E14* 2C 104
(off Admirals Way)
Parker M. WC2 7F 7 (6J 83)
Parke Rd. SW13 1C 116
TW16: Sun 4J 147
Parker Rd. CR0: C'don 4C 168
Parkers Rd. N2 1C 46
Parkers Row SE1 7K 15 (2G 103)
Parker St. E16 1C 106
WC2 7F 7 (6J 83)
Park Farm Cl. HA5: Eastc 5K 39
N2 3A 46
Park Farm Ct. UB3: Hayes 7G 75
Park Farm Rd. BR1: Brom 1B 160
KT2: King T 7E 132
Parkfield TW7: Isle 1J 113
Parkfield Av. HA2: Harr 2G 41
SW14 4A 116
TW13: Felt 3J 129
UB5: N'olt 2B 76
UB10: Hil 3D 74
Parkfield Cl. HA8: Edg 6C 28
UB5: N'olt 2C 76
Parkfield Ct. *SE14* 1B 122
(off Parkfield Rd.)
Parkfield Cres. HA2: Harr 2G 41
HA4: Ruis 2C 58
TW13: Felt 3J 129
Parkfield Dr. UB5: N'olt 2B 76
Parkfield Gdns. HA2: Harr 3F 41
Parkfield Ho. HA2: Harr 1F 41
Parkfield Ind. Est. SW11 2E 118
Parkfield Pde. TW13: Felt 3J 129
Parkfield Rd. HA2: Harr 3G 59
NW10 7D 62
SE14 1B 122
TW13: Felt 3J 129
UB5: N'olt 2C 76
UB10: Ick 2D 56
Parkfields CR0: C'don 1B 170
SW15 4E 116
Parkfields Av. NW9 1K 61
SW20 1D 152
Parkfields Cl. SM5: Cars 4E 166
Parkfields Rd. KT2: King T 5F 133
Parkfield St. N1 2A 84
Parkfield Way BR2: Brom 6D 160
Park Gdns. DA8: Erith 4K 109
E10 1C 68
KT2: King T 5F 133
NW9 3H 43
Park Ga. N2 3B 46
N21 7E 22
SE3 3H 123
W5 5D 78
Parkgate *N1* 1D 84
(off Southgate Rd.)
Parkgate Av. EN4: Had W 1F 21
Parkgate Cl. KT2: King T 6H 133
Park Ga. Ct. TW12: Ham H 6G 131
Parkgate Cres. EN4: Had W 1F 21
Parkgate Gdns. SW14 5K 115
Parkgate M. N6 7G 47
Parkgate Rd. SM6: Wall 5E 166
SW11 7C 100
Park Gates HA2: Harr 4E 58
Park Gro. BR1: Brom 1K 159
DA7: Bex 4J 127
E15 1J 87
HA8: Edg 5A 28
N11 7C 32
Park Gro. Rd. E11 2G 69
Park Hall *SE10* 7F 105
(off Crooms Hill)
Park Hall Rd. SE21 3C 138
Parkhall Rd. N2 4C 46
Park Hall Trad. Est.
SE21 3C 138
Parkham Ct. BR2: Brom 2G 159
Parkham St. SW11 1C 118
Park Hill BR1: Brom 4C 160
SE23 2H 139
SM5: Cars 6C 166
SW4 5H 119
TW10: Rich 6F 115
W5 5D 78
Park Hill Cl. SM5: Cars 5C 166
Park Hill Ct. SW17 3D 136
Park Hill M. CR2: S Croy 5D 168
Park Hill Ri. CR0: C'don 2E 168
Park Hill Rd. BR2: Brom 2G 159
CR0: C'don 2E 168
DA15: Sidc 3J 143
SM6: Wall 7F 167
Parkhill Rd. DA5: Bexl 7F 127
E4 1K 35
NW3 5D 64
Parkhill Wlk. NW3 5D 64
Parkholme Rd. E8 6F 67
Park Ho. *E9* 7J 67
(off Shore Rd.)
N21 7E 22
Park Ho. Gdns. TW1: Twick 5C 114
Park Ho. Pas. N6 7E 46
Parkhouse St. SE5 7D 102
Parkhurst Ct. N7 4J 65
Parkhurst Gdns. DA5: Bexl 7G 127
Parkhurst Rd. DA5: Bexl 7G 127
E12 4E 70
E17 4A 50
N7 4J 65
N11 5K 31
N17 2G 49
N22 6E 32
SM1: Sutt 4B 166
Parkinson Ct. *N1* 2F 9
(off Charles Sq. Est.)
Parkinson Ho. *E9* 7J 67
(off Frampton Pk. Rd.)
SW1 5C 18
(off Tachbrook St.)
Parkland Ct. *E15* 5G 69
(off Maryland Pk.)
W14 2G 99
(off Holland Pk. Av.)
Parkland Gdns. SW19 1F 135
Parkland Gro. TW15: Ashf 3C 128
Parkland Mead BR1: Brom 3F 161
Parkland Rd. IG8: Wfd G 7E 36
N22 2K 47
TW15: Ashf 4C 128
Parklands KT5: Surb 5F 151
N6 7F 47
Parklands Cl. EN4: Had W 1G 21
IG2: Ilf 7G 53
SW14 5J 115
Parklands Ct. TW5: Hest 2B 112
Parklands Dr. N3 3G 45
Parklands Gro. TW7: Isle 1K 113
Parklands Pde. *TW5: Hest* 2B 112
(off Parklands Ct.)
Parklands Rd. SW16 5F 137
Parklands Way KT4: Wor Pk 2A 164
Park La. CR0: C'don 3D 168
E15 1F 87
HA2: Harr 3F 59
HA7: Stan 3F 27
HA9: Wemb 5E 60
N9 3K 33
N17 7A 34
(not continuous)
RM6: Chad H 6D 54
SM3: Cheam 6G 165
SM5: Cars 4E 166
SM6: Wall 5E 166
TW5: Cran 7J 93
TW9: Rich 4D 114
TW11: Tedd 6K 131
UB4: Hayes 5G 75
W1 2F 11 (7D 82)
Park La. Cl. N17 7B 34
Park La. Mans. *CR0: C'don* 3D 168
(off Edridge Rd.)
PARK LANGLEY 4E 158
Parklea Cl. NW9 1A 44
Park Lee Ct. N16 7E 48
Parkleigh Rd. SW19 2K 153
Parkleys TW10: Ham 4D 132
Parkleys Pde. TW10: Ham 4D 132
Park Lodge NW8 7B 64
W14 3H 99
(off Kensington High St.)
Park Lodge Av. UB7: W Dray 2B 92
Park Lofts *SW2* 5J 119
(off Mandrell Rd.)
Park Lorne *NW8* 2D 4
(off Park Rd.)
Park Mnr. *SM2: Sutt* 7A 166
(off Christchurch Pk.)
Park Mans. NW4 5D 44
NW8 2C 82
(off Allitsen Rd.)
SW1 7E 10
(off Knightsbridge)
SW8 7F 19 (6J 101)
SW11 1D 118
(off Prince of Wales Dr.)
Park Mead DA15: Sidc 5B 126
HA2: Harr 3F 59
Parkmead SW15 6D 116
Parkmead Gdns. NW7 6G 29
Park M. BR7: Chst 6F 143
SE10 5H 105
SE24 7C 120
TW19: Stanw 7B 110
W10 2G 81
Parkmore Cl. IG8: Wfd G 4D 36
Park Pde. NW10 2B 80
UB3: Hayes 6G 75
W5 3G 97
Park Pl. *BR1: Brom* 1K 159
(off Park Rd.)
E14 1C 104
HA9: Wemb 4F 61
N1 7D 66
(off Downham Rd.)
SW1 5A 12 (1G 101)
TW12: Ham H 6G 131
W3 4G 97
W5 1D 96
Park Pl. Dr. W3 3G 97
Park Pl. Vs. W2 5A 4 (5A 82)
Park Ridings N8 3A 48
Park Ri. HA3: Hrw W 1J 41
SE23 1A 140
Park Ri. Rd. SE23 1A 140
Park Rd. BR1: Brom 1K 159
BR3: Beck 7B 140
BR7: Chst 6F 143
E6 1A 88
E10 1C 68
E12 1K 69
E15 1J 87
E17 5B 50
EN4: E Barn 4G 21
EN5: Barn 4C 20
HA0: Wemb 6E 60
IG1: Ilf 3H 71
KT1: Ham W 1C 150
KT2: King T 5F 133
KT3: N Mald 4K 151
KT5: Surb 6F 151
KT8: E Mos 4G 149
N2 3B 46
N8 4G 47
N11 7C 32
N14 1C 32
N15 4B 48
N18 4B 34
NW1 2D 4 (3C 82)
Park Rd. NW4 7C 44
NW8 2D 4 (3C 82)
NW9 7K 43
NW10 1A 80
SE25 4E 156
SM3: Cheam 6G 165
SM6: Wall 5F 167
(Clifton Rd.)
SM6: Wall 2F 167
(Elmwood Cl.)
SW19 6B 136
TW1: Twick 6C 114
TW3: Houn 5F 113
TW7: Isle 1B 114
TW10: Rich 6F 115
TW11: Tedd 6K 131
TW12: Ham H 4F 131
TW13: Hanw 4B 130
TW15: Ashf 5D 128
TW16: Sun 7K 129
UB4: Hayes 5G 75
UB8: Uxb 1A 74
W4 7J 97
W7 7K 77
Park Rd. E. UB10: Uxb 2A 74
W3 2H 97
Park Rd. Ho. KT2: King T 7G 133
Park Rd. Nth. W3 2H 97
W4 5K 97
Park Road Swimming Pool 5H 47
Park Row SE10 6F 105
SW2 6A 120
PARK ROYAL 3H 79
PARK ROYAL JUNC. 1G 79
Park Royal Metro Cen. NW10 4H 79
Park Royal Rd. NW10 3J 79
W3 3J 79
Parkshot TW9: Rich 4D 114
Park Side NW2 3C 62
Parkside DA14: Sidc 2B 144
IG9: Buck H 2E 36
N3 1K 45
NW7 6H 29
SE3 7H 105
SM3: Cheam 6G 165
SW1 6F 11
SW19 3F 135
TW12: Ham H 5H 131
UB3: Hayes 7G 75
W3 1A 98
W5 7E 78
Parkside Av. BR1: Brom 4C 160
DA7: Bex 2K 127
RM1: Rom 3K 55
SW19 5F 135
Parkside Bus. Est. SE8 6A 104
(Blackhorse Rd.)
SE8 6A 104
(Rolt St.)
Parkside Cl. SE20 7J 139
Parkside Ct. *E11* 6J 51
(off Wanstead Pl.)
N22 6E 32
Parkside Cres. KT5: Surb 6J 151
N7 3A 66
Parkside Cross DA7: Bex 2K 127
Parkside Dr. HA8: Edg 3B 28
Parkside Est. E9 1J 85
Parkside Gdns. EN4: E Barn 1J 31
SW19 4F 135
Parkside Ho. RM10: Dag 3J 73
Parkside Lodge
DA17: Belv 5J 109
Parkside Rd. DA17: Belv 4H 109
SW11 1E 118
TW3: Houn 5F 113
Parkside Ter. *BR6: Farnb* 3F 173
(off Willow Wlk.)
N18 4J 33
Parkside Way HA2: Harr 4F 41

Park Sth. SW11 1E 118
(off Austin Rd.)
Park Sq. E. NW1 3J 5 (4F 83)
Park Sq. M. NW1 4J 5 (4E 82)
Park Sq. W. NW1 3J 5 (4F 83)
Parkstead Rd. SW15 5C 116
Park Steps W2 2D 10
Parkstone Av. N18 6A 34
Parkstone Rd. E17 3E 50
SE15 2G 121
Park St. CR0: C'don 2C 168
SE1 4C 14 (1C 102)
TW11: Tedd 6J 131
W1 2G 11 (7E 82)
Park Ter. EN3: Enf H 1F 25
KT4: Wor Pk 1C 164
SM5: Cars 3C 166
Parkthorne Cl. HA2: Harr 6F 41
Parkthorne Dr. HA2: Harr 6E 40
Parkthorne Rd. SW12 7H 119
Park Towers W1 5J 11
(off Brick St.)
Park Vw. HA5: Hat E 1D 40
HA9: Wemb 5H 61
KT3: N Mald 3B 152
N5 4C 66
N21 7E 22
RM6: Chad H 6D 54
SE8 5K 103
(off Trundleys Rd.)
UB7: Yiew 7A 74
W3 5J 79
Parkview DA18: Erith 3D 108
UB6: G'frd 3A 78
(off Perivale La.)
Park View Academy Sports Cen. 4C 48
Park Vw. Apartments SE16 3H 103
(off Banyard Rd.)
Parkview Cl. SM5: Cars 7D 166
Park Vw. Ct. N12 4H 31
SE20 1H 157
Parkview Ct. HA3: Hrw W 7D 26
IG2: Ilf 6J 53
SW6 2G 117
SW18 6J 117
Park Vw. Cres. N11 4A 32
Park Vw. Dr. CR4: Mitc 2B 154
Park Vw. Est. E2 2K 85
Park Vw. Gdns. IG4: Ilf 4D 52
N22 1A 48
NW4 5E 44
Park Vw. Ho. E4 5H 35
SE24 6B 120
(off Hurst St.)
Parkview Ho. N9 7C 24
Park Vw. Mans. N4 6B 48
Park Vw. M. SW9 2K 119
Park Vw. Rd. DA16: Well 3C 126
N3 1K 45
N17 3G 49
NW10 4B 62
UB1: S'hall 1E 94
UB8: Hil 6B 74
W5 5E 78
Parkview Rd. CR0: C'don 1G 169
SE9 1F 143
Park Village E. NW1 1K 5 (2F 83)
Park Village W. NW1 2F 83
Park Vs. RM6: Chad H 6D 54
Parkville Rd. SW6 7H 99
Park Vista SE10 6F 105
Park Wlk. EN4: Cockf 3G 21
IG1: Ilf 2F 71
(in The Exchange)
N6 7E 46
SE10 7F 105
SW10 7A 16 (6A 100)
Park Way EN2: Enf 2F 23
HA4: Ruis 1J 57
HA8: Edg 1H 43
Park Way IG8: Wfd G 5F 37
KT8: W Mole 3F 149
N20 4J 31
NW11 5G 45
TW14: Felt 7K 111
W3 3G 97
Parkway DA18: Erith 3E 108
IG3: Ilf 3K 71
N14 2D 32
NW1 1F 83
SW20 4F 153
UB10: Hil 7C 56
Parkway, The TW4: Cran 2K 111
TW5: Cran 5J 93
UB2: S'hall 5J 93
UB3: Hayes 3K 93
UB4: Yead 3K 93
UB5: N'olt 3B 76
Park Way Ct. HA4: Ruis 1H 57
Parkway Trad. Est.
TW5: Hest 6A 94
Park W. W2 7D 4
Park W. Pl. W2 7D 4 (6C 82)
Park Wharf SE8 5A 104
(off Evelyn St.)
Parkwood BR3: Beck 7C 140
N20 3K 31
NW8 1D 82
(off St Edmund's Ter.)
Parkwood Av. KT10: Esh 7G 149
Parkwood Flats N20 3J 31
Parkwood Gro. TW16: Sun 3J 147
Parkwood M. N6 6F 47
Parkwood Rd. DA5: Bexl 7F 127
SW19 5H 135
TW7: Isle 1K 113
Parliament Ct. E1 6H 9
Parliament Hill 3D 64
Parliament Hill NW3 4C 64
Parliament Hill Fields 3E 64
Parliament Hill Lido 4E 64
Parliament Hill Mans. NW5 4E 64
Parliament M. SW14 2J 115
Parliament Sq. SW1 7E 12 (2J 101)
Parliament St. SW1 6E 12 (2J 101)
Parliament Vw. SE1 3G 19 (4K 101)
Parma Cres. SW11 4D 118
Parmiter Ind. Est. E2 2H 85
(off Parmiter St.)
Parmiter St. E2 2H 85
Parmoor Ct. EC1 3C 8
Parndon Ho. IG10: Lough 1H 37
Parnell Cl. HA8: Edg 4C 28
W12 3D 98
Parnell Ho. WC1 6D 6 (5H 83)
Parnell Rd. E3 1B 86
(not continuous)
Parnham Cl. BR1: Brom 3F 161
Parnham St. E14 6A 86
(not continuous)
Parolles Rd. N19 1G 65
Paroma Rd. DA17: Belv 4G 109
Parr Cl. N9 4C 34
N18 4C 34
Parr Ct. N1 2D 84
(off New North Rd.)
TW13: Hanw 4A 130
Parr Ho. E16 1K 105
(off Beaulieu Av.)
Parrington Ho. SW4 6H 119
Parr Rd. E6 1B 88
HA7: Stan 1D 42
Parrs Cl. CR2: Sande 7D 168
Parrs Pl. TW12: Hamp 7E 130
Parr St. N1 2D 84
Parry Av. E6 6D 88
Parry Cl. KT17: Ewe 7D 164
Parry Ho. E1 1H 103
(off Green Bank)
Parry Pl. SE18 4F 107
Parry Rd. SE25 3E 156
W10 3G 81
Parry St. SW8 7F 19 (6J 101)
Parsifal Rd. NW6 5J 63
Parsley Gdns. CR0: C'don 1K 169
Parsloes Av. RM9: Dag 4D 72
Parsonage Cl. UB3: Hayes 6H 75
Parsonage Gdns. EN2: Enf 2H 23
Parsonage La. DA14: Sidc 4F 145
EN1: Enf 2H 23
EN2: Enf 2H 23
Parsonage Manorway DA17: Belv 6G 109
Parsonage St. E14 4E 104
Parsons Cl. SM1: Sutt 3K 165
Parson's Cres. HA8: Edg 3B 28
PARSONS GREEN 2H 117
Parson's Grn. SW6 1J 117
Parson's Grn. La. SW6 1J 117
Parson's Gro. HA8: Edg 3B 28
Parsons Hill SE18 3E 106
(off Powis St.)
Parsons Ho. W2 4A 4
Parsons Lodge NW6 7K 63
(off Priory Rd.)
Parsons Mead CR0: C'don 1B 168
KT8: E Mos 3G 149
Parson's Rd. E13 2A 88
Parson St. NW4 4E 44
Parthenia Rd. SW6 1J 117
Partingdale La.
NW7 5A 30
Partington Cl. N19 1H 65
Partridge Cl. E16 5B 88
EN5: Barn 6A 20
HA7: Stan 4K 27
WD23: Bush 1B 26
Partridge Ct. EC1 3A 8
Partridge Dr. BR6: Farnb 3G 173
Partridge Grn. SE9 3E 142
Partridge Rd. DA14: Sidc 3J 143
TW12: Hamp 6D 130
Partridge Sq. E6 5C 88
Partridge Way N22 1J 47
Pasadena Cl. UB3: Hayes 2J 93
Pasadena Cl. Trad. Est. UB3: Hayes 2K 93
Pascall Ho. SE17 6C 102
(off Draco St.)
Pascal M. SE19 7G 139
Pascal St. SW8 7H 101
Pascoe Rd. SE13 5F 123
Pasley Cl. SE17 5B 102
Pasquier Rd. E17 3A 50
Passage, The TW9: Rich 5E 114
Passey Pl. SE9 6D 124
Passfield Dr. E14 5D 86
Passfield Hall WC1 4H 83
(off Endsleigh Pl.)
Passfield Path SE28 7B 90
Passfields SE6 3D 140
W14 5H 99
(off Star St.)
Passing All. EC1 4B 8
Passingham Ho. TW5: Hest 6E 94
Passmore Edwards Ho. N11 6C 32
Passmore Gdns. N11 6C 32
Passmore House E2 1F 85
(off Kingsland Rd.)
Passmore St. SW1 5G 17 (5E 100)
Pasteur Cl. NW9 2A 44
Pasteur Ct. HA1: Harr 1B 60
Pasteur Gdns. N18 5G 33
Paston Cl. E5 3K 67
SM6: Wall 3G 167
Paston Cres. SE12 7K 123
Pastor Ct. N6 6G 47
Pastor St. SE11 4B 102
Pasture Cl. HA0: Wemb 3B 60
Pasture Rd. HA0: Wemb 2B 60
RM9: Dag 4F 73
SE6 1H 141
Pastures, The N20 1C 30
Pastures Mead UB10: Hil 6C 56
Patcham Ter. SW8 1F 119
Patch Cl. UB10: Uxb 1B 74
Patching Way UB4: Yead 5C 76
Patent Ho. E14 5D 86
(off Morris Rd.)
Paternoster La. EC4 1B 14 (6B 84)
Paternoster Row EC4 1C 14 (6C 84)
Paternoster Sq. EC4 1B 14 (6B 84)
Paterson Ct. EC1 2E 8
Pater St. W8 3J 99
Pates Mnr. Dr. TW14: Bedf 7F 111
Path, The SW19 1K 153
Pathfield Rd. SW16 6H 137
Patience Rd. SW11 2C 118
Patio Cl. SW4 6H 119
Patmore Est. SW8 1G 119
Patmore Ho. N16 5E 66
Patmore St. SW8 1G 119
Patmos Lodge SW9 1B 120
(off Elliott Rd.)
Patmos Rd. SW9 7B 102
Paton Cl. E3 3C 86
Paton Ho. SW9 2K 119
(off Stockwell Rd.)
Paton St. EC1 2C 8 (3C 84)
Patricia Ct. BR7: Chst 1H 161
DA16: Well 7B 108
Patrick Coman Ho. EC1 2A 8
(off St John St.)
Patrick Connolly Gdns. E3 3D 86
Patrick Pas. SW11 2C 118
Patrick Rd. E13 3A 88
Patriot Sq. E2 2H 85
Patrol Pl. SE6 6D 122
Pat Shaw Ho. E1 4K 85
(off Globe Rd.)
Patshull Pl. NW5 6G 65
Patshull Rd. NW5 6G 65
Patten All. TW10: Rich 5D 114
Pattenden Rd. SE6 1B 140
Patten Ho. N4 1C 66
Patten Rd. SW18 7C 118
Patterdale NW1 2K 5
(off Osnaburgh St.)
Patterdale Cl. BR1: Brom 6H 141
Patterdale Rd. SE15 7J 103
Pattern Ho. EC1 3A 8 (4B 84)
Patterson Ct. SE19 7F 139
Patterson Rd. SE19 6F 139
Pattina Wlk. SE16 1A 104
(off Capstan Way)
Pattinson Point E16 5J 87
(off Fife Rd.)
Pattison Ho. E1 6K 85
(off Wellesley St.)
SE1 6D 14
(off Redcross Way)
Pattison Rd. NW2 3J 63
Pattison Wlk. SE18 5G 107
Paul Byrne Ho. N2 3A 46
Paul Cl. E15 7G 69
Paul Ct. N18 4B 34
(off Fairfield Rd.)
RM7: Rom 5J 55
Paul Daisley Ct. NW6 7G 63
(off Christchurch Av.)
Paulet Rd. SE5 2B 120
Paul Gdns. CR0: C'don 2F 169
Paulhan Rd. HA3: Kent 4D 42
Paul Ho. W10 4G 81
(off Ladbroke Gro.)
Paulin Dr. N21 7F 23
Pauline Cres. TW2: Whitt 1G 131
Pauline Ho. E1 5G 85
(off Old Montague St.)
Paul Julius Cl. E14 7F 87
Paul Robeson Cl. E6 3E 88
Paul Robeson Theatre, The 3F 113

Pauls Ho. E3 ....5B 86
(off Timothy Rd.)
Paul St. E15 ....1G 87
EC2 ....4F 9 (4D 84)
Paul's Wlk. EC4 ....2B 14 (7C 84)
Paultons Ho. SW3 ....7B 16
(off King's Rd.)
Paultons Sq. SW3 ....7B 16 (6B 100)
Paultons St. SW3 ....6B 100
Pauntley St. N19 ....1G 65
Pavan Ct. E2 ....3J 85
(off Sceptre Rd.)
Paved Ct. TW9: Rich 5D 114
Paveley Ct. NW7 ....7B 30
(off Langstone Way)
Paveley Dr. SW11 ....7C 100
Paveley Ho. N1 ....2K 83
(off Priory Grn. Est.)
Paveley St. NW8 ....2C 4 (3C 82)
Pavement, The E11 ....1E 68
(off Hainault Rd.)
SW4 ....4G 119
TW7: Isle 3A 114
(off South St.)
W5 ....3E 96
Pavement M. RM6: Chad H 7D 54
Pavement Sq. CR0: C'don 1G 169
Pavet Cl. RM10: Dag 6H 73
Pavilion NW8 ....2B 4 (3B 82)
Pavilion, The SW8 ....7H 101
Pavilion Ct. NW6 ....3J 81
(off Stafford Rd.)
Pavilion La. BR3: Beck 6B 140
Pavilion Leisure Cen., The 2J 159
Pavilion Lodge HA2: Harr 1H 59
Pavilion M. N3 ....3J 45
Pavilion Pde. W12 ....6E 80
(off Wood La.)
Pavilion Rd. IG1: Ilf 7D 52
SW1 ....7F 11 (3D 100)
Pavilion Sports & Fitness Club, The 3G 149
Pavilion Sq. SW17 ....3D 136
Pavilion St. SW1 ....2F 17 (3D 100)
Pavilion Ter. IG2: Ilf 5J 53
W12 ....6E 80
(off Wood La.)
Pavilion Way HA4: Ruis 2A 58
HA8: Edg 7C 28
Pawleyne Cl. SE20 ....7J 139
Pawsey Cl. E13 ....1K 87
Pawsons Rd. CR0: C'don 6C 156
Paxfold HA7: Stan 5J 27
Paxford Rd. HA0: Wemb 2B 60
Paxton Cl. KT12: Walt T 7A 148
TW9: Kew 2F 115
Paxton Ct. CR4: Mitc 2D 154
(off Armfield Cres.)
SE12 ....3A 142
SE26 ....4A 140
(off Adamsrill Rd.)
Paxton Ho. SE17 ....5D 102
(off Morecambe St.)
Paxton Pl. SE27 ....4E 138
Paxton Rd. BR1: Brom 7J 141
N17 ....7A 34
SE23 ....3A 140
W4 ....6A 98
Paxton Ter.
SW1 ....7K 17 (6F 101)
Paymal Ho. E1 ....5J 85
(off Stepney Way)
Payne Cl. IG11: Bark 7J 71
Payne Ho. N1 ....1K 83
(off Barnsbury Est.)
Paynell Ct. SE3 ....3G 123
Payne Rd. E3 ....2D 86
Paynesfield Av. SW14 ....3K 115
Paynesfield Rd.
WD23: B Hea 1E 26
Payne St. SE8 ....7B 104
Paynes Wlk. W6 ....6G 99
Payzes Gdns. IG8: Wfd G 6C 36
Peaberry Ct. NW4 ....3C 44
Peabody Av. SW1 ....5J 17 (5F 101)
Peabody Bldgs. E1 ....2K 15
EC1 ....4D 8
(off Roscoe St.)
SW3 ....7C 16
Peabody Cl. CR0: C'don 1J 169
SE10 ....1D 122
SW1 ....7K 17 (5F 101)
Peabody Cotts. N17 ....1E 48
Peabody Ct. EC1 ....4D 8
(off Roscoe St.)
SE5 ....1D 120
(off Kimpton Rd.)
Peabody Est. E1 ....7K 85
(off Glasmis Pl.)
E2 ....2H 85
(off Minerva St.)
EC1 ....4D 8
(off Dufferin St. not continuous)
EC1 ....4K 7
(off Farringdon La.)
N1 ....1C 84
SE1 ....5K 13 (1A 102)
(Duchy St.)
SE1 ....6D 14
(Marshalsea Rd.)
SE1 ....5C 14 (1C 102)
(Southwark St.)
SE24 ....7B 120
SW1 ....3B 18
SW3 ....7D 16 (6C 100)
SW6 ....6J 99
(off Lillie Rd.)
SW11 ....4C 118
W6 ....5E 98
W10 ....5E 80
Peabody Hill SE21 ....1B 138
Peabody Sq. SE1 ....7A 14 (2B 102)
(not continuous)
Peabody Ter. EC1 ....4K 7
(off Farringdon La.)
Peabody Twr. EC1 ....4D 8
(off Golden La.)
Peabody Trust SE17 ....4D 102
Peabody Yd. N1 ....1C 84
Peace Cl. N14 ....5A 22
SE25 ....4E 156
UB6: G'frd 1H 77
Peace Gro. HA9: Wemb 3H 61
Peace St. SE18 ....6E 106
Peaches Cl. SM2: Cheam 7G 165
Peachey La. UB8: Cowl 5A 74
Peach Gro. E11 ....3F 69
Peach Rd. TW13: Felt 1J 129
W10 ....3F 81
Peach Tree Av. UB7: Yiew 6B 74
Peachum Rd. SE3 ....6H 105
Peachwalk M. E3 ....2K 85
Peachy Cl. HA8: Edg 6B 28
Peacock Av. TW14: Bedf 1F 129
Peacock Cl. E4 ....7G 35
RM8: Dag 1C 72
Peacock Ind. Est. N17 ....7A 34
Peacock St. SE17 ....4B 102
Peacock Theatre 1G 13
(off Portugal St.)
Peacock Wlk. E16 ....6K 87
(off Mortlake Rd.)
N6 ....7F 47
Peacock Yd. SE17 ....5B 102
(off Iliffe St.)
Peak, The SE26 ....3J 139
Peaketon Av. IG4: Ilf 4B 52
Peak Hill SE26 ....4J 139
Peak Hill Av. SE26 ....4J 139
Peak Hill Gdns. SE26 ....4J 139
Peak Ho. N4 ....1C 66
(off Woodberry Down Est.)
Peal Gdns. W13 ....3A 78
Peall Rd. CR0: C'don 6K 155
Peall Rd. Ind. Est. CR0: C'don 6K 155
Pearce Cl. CR4: Mitc 2E 154
Pearcefield Av. SE23 ....1J 139
Pearce Ho. SW1 ....4D 18
(off Causton St.)
Pear Cl. NW9 ....4K 43
SE14 ....7A 104
Pear Ct. SE15 ....7F 103
(off Thruxton Way)
Pearcroft Rd. E11 ....2F 69
Peardon St. SW8 ....2F 119
Peareswood Gdns. HA7: Stan 1D 42
Pearfield Rd. SE23 ....3A 140
Pearl Cl. E6 ....6E 88
NW2 ....7F 45
Pearl Rd. E17 ....3C 50
Pearl St. E1 ....1H 103
Pearmain Cl. TW17: Shep 5D 146
Pearman St. SE1 ....1K 19 (3A 102)
Pear Pl. SE1 ....6J 13 (2A 102)
Pear Rd. E11 ....3F 69
Pears Av. TW17: Shep 3G 147
Pearscroft Ct. SW6 ....1K 117
Pearscroft Rd. SW6 ....1K 117
Pearse St. SE15 ....6E 102
Pearson Cl. EN5: New Bar 3E 20
SE5 ....1C 120
(off Camberwell New Rd.)
Pearson M. SW4 ....3H 119
(off Slievemore Cl.)
Pearson's Av. SE14 ....1C 122
Pearson St. E2 ....2F 85
Pearson Way CR4: Mitc 1E 154
Pears Rd. TW3: Houn 3G 113
Peartree SE26 ....5A 140
Pear Tree Av. UB7: Yiew 6B 74
Peartree Av. SW17 ....3A 136
Pear Tree Cl. BR2: Brom 5B 160
CR4: Mitc 2C 154
E2 ....1F 85
KT9: Chess 5G 163
Peartree Cl. DA8: Erith 1K 127
Pear Tree Ct. E18 ....1K 51
EC1 ....4K 7 (4A 84)
Peartree Gdns.
RM7: Mawney 2H 55
RM8: Dag 4B 72
Pear Tree Ho. SE4 ....3B 122
Peartree La. E1 ....7J 85
Pear Tree Rd. TW15: Ashf 5E 128
Peartree Rd. EN1: Enf 3K 23
Peartrees UB7: Yiew 7A 74
Pear Tree St. EC1 ....3B 8 (4C 84)
Peartree Way SE10 ....4J 105
Peary Ho. NW10 ....7K 61
Peary Pl. E2 ....3J 85
Peas Mead Ter. E4 ....4K 35
Peatfield Cl. DA15: Sidc 3J 143
Pebble Way W3 ....1H 97
(off Steyne Rd.)
Pebworth Rd. HA1: Harr 2A 60
Peckarmans Wood SE26 ....3G 139
Peckett Sq. N5 ....4C 66
Peckford Pl. SW9 ....2A 120
PECKHAM 1G 121
Peckham Gro. SE15 ....7E 102
Peckham High St. SE15 ....1G 121
Peckham Hill St. SE15 ....7G 103
Peckham Pk. Rd. SE15 ....7G 103
Peckham Pulse Health & Leisure Cen. 1G 121
Peckham Rd. SE5 ....1E 120
SE15 ....1E 120
Peckham Rye SE15 ....3G 121
SE22 ....4G 121
Peckham Sq. SE15 ....1G 121
Pecks Yd. E1 ....5J 9
(off Hanbury St.)
Peckwater St. NW5 ....5G 65
Pedlar's Wlk. N7 ....5K 65
Pedley Rd. RM8: Dag 1C 72
Pedley St. E1 ....4K 9 (4F 85)
Pedro St. E5 ....3K 67
Pedworth Gdns. SE16 ....4J 103
Peebles Ct. UB1: S'hall 6G 77
(off Haldane Rd.)
Peebles Ho. NW6 ....2K 81
(off Carlton Va.)
Peek Cres. SW19 ....5F 135
Peel Cl. E4 ....2J 35
N9 ....3B 34
Peel Dr. IG5: Ilf 3C 52
NW9 ....3B 44
Peel Gro. E2 ....2J 85
Peel Pas. W8 ....1J 99
Peel Pl. IG5: Ilf 2C 52
Peel Pct. NW6 ....2J 81
Peel Rd. BR6: Farnb 5G 173
E18 ....1H 51
HA3: W'stone 3K 41
(not continuous)
HA9: Wemb 3D 60
Peel St. W8 ....1J 99
Peel Way UB8: Hil 5A 74
Peerglow Est.
EN3: Pond E 5D 24
Peerless St. EC1 ....2E 8 (3D 84)
Pegamoid Rd. N18 ....3D 34
Pegasus Cl. N16 ....4D 66
Pegasus Ct. KT1: King T 3D 150
N21 ....7H 23
NW10 ....3D 80
(off Trenmar Gdns.)
Pegasus Ct. TW8: Bford 5F 97
W3 ....6J 79
(off Horn La.)
Pegasus Ho. E1 ....4K 85
(off Beaumont Sq.)
Pegasus Pl. SE11 ....7J 19 (6A 102)
SW6 ....1J 117
Pegasus Rd. CR0: Wadd 6A 168
Pegasus Way N11 ....6A 32
Peggotty Way UB8: Hil 6D 74
Pegg Rd. TW5: Hest 7B 94
Pegley Gdns. SE12 ....2J 141
Pegwell St. SE18 ....7J 107
Pekin Cl. E14 ....6C 86
(off Pekin St.)
Pekin St. E14 ....6C 86
Pelabon Ho. TW1: Twick 6D 114
(off Clevedon Rd.)
Peldon Ct. TW9: Rich 4F 115
Peldon Pas. TW10: Rich 4F 115
Peldon Wlk. N1 ....1B 84
(off Popham St.)
Pelham Av. IG11: Bark 1K 89
Pelham Cl. SE5 ....3E 120
Pelham Cotts. DA5: Bexl 1H 145
Pelham Ct. DA14: Sidc 3A 144
SW3 ....4C 16
(off Fulham Rd.)
Pelham Cres. SW7 ....4C 16 (4C 100)
Pelham Ho. SW1 ....2D 18
(off Gt. Peter St.)
W14 ....4H 99
(off Mornington Av.)
Pelham Pl. SW7 ....4C 16 (4C 100)
W13 ....4K 77
Pelham Rd. BR3: Beck 2J 157
DA7: Bex 3G 127
E18 ....3K 51
IG1: Ilf 2H 71
N15 ....4F 49
N22 ....2A 48
SW19 ....7J 135

Pelham St. SW7 . . . 3B 16 (4B 100)
Pelican Est. SE15 . . . 1F 121
Pelican Ho. SE5 . . . 1F 121
SE8 . . . 4B 104
Pelican Pas. E1 . . . 4J 85
Pelican Wlk. SW9 . . . 4B 120
Pelican Wharf *E1* . . . *1J 103*
(off Wapping Wall)
Pelier St. SE17 . . . 6C 102
Pelinore Rd. SE6 . . . 2G 141
Pella Ho. SE11 . . . 5H 19 (5K 101)
Pellant Rd. SW6 . . . 7G 99
Pellatt Gro. N22 . . . 1A 48
Pellatt Rd. HA9: Wemb . . . 2D 60
SE22 . . . 5F 121
Pellerin Rd. N16 . . . 5E 66
Pellew Ho. *E1* . . . *4H 85*
(off Somerford St.)
Pellings Cl. BR2: Brom . . . 3G 159
Pelling St. E14 . . . 6C 86
Pellipar Cl. N13 . . . 3F 33
Pellipar Gdns. SE18 . . . 5D 106
Pellipar Rd. SE18 . . . 5D 106
Pelly Rd. E13 . . . 1J 87
(not continuous)
Pelter St. E2 . . . 1J 9 (3F 85)
Pelton Rd. SE10 . . . 5G 105
Pembar Av. E17 . . . 3A 50
Pemberley Chase
KT19: Ewe . . . 5H 163
Pemberley Cl. KT19: Ewe . . . 5H 163
Pemberley Ho. *KT19: Ewe* . . . *5H 163*
(off Pemberley Chase)
Pember Rd. NW10 . . . 3F 81
Pemberton Ct. *E1* . . . *3K 85*
(off Portelet Rd.)
EN1: Enf . . . 3K 23
Pemberton Gdns. N19 . . . 3G 65
RM6: Chad H . . . 5E 54
Pemberton Ho. *SE26* . . . *4G 139*
(off High Level Dr.)
Pemberton Pl. E8 . . . 7H 67
Pemberton Rd. KT8: E Mos . . . 4G 149
N4 . . . 5A 48
Pemberton Row EC4 . . . 7K 7 (6A 84)
Pemberton Ter. N19 . . . 3G 65
Pembridge Av.
TW2: Whitt . . . 1D 130
Pembridge Cres. W11 . . . 7J 81
Pembridge Gdns. W2 . . . 7J 81
Pembridge M. W11 . . . 7J 81
Pembridge Pl. SW15 . . . 5J 117
W2 . . . 7J 81
Pembridge Rd. W11 . . . 7J 81
Pembridge Sq. W2 . . . 7J 81
Pembridge Studios *W11* . . . *7J 81*
(off Pembridge Vs.)
Pembridge Vs. W2 . . . 7J 81
W11 . . . 7J 81
Pembroke *W14* . . . *4H 99*
(off Mornington Av.)
Pembroke Av. EN1: Enf . . . 1C 24
HA3: Kent . . . 3A 42
HA5: Pinn . . . 1B 58
KT5: Surb . . . 5H 151
N1 . . . 1J 83
Pembroke Bldgs. NW10 . . . 3C 80
Pembroke Bus. Cen.
BR8: Swan . . . 7K 145
Pembroke Cen., The HA4: Ruis . . . 1H 57
Pembroke Cl. SW1 . . . 7H 11 (2E 100)
Pembroke Cotts. *W8* . . . *3J 99*
(off Pembroke Sq.)
Pembroke Ct. *W7* . . . *6K 77*
(off Copley Cl.)
W8 . . . *3J 99*
(off Sth. Edwardes Sq.)
Pembroke Gdns. RM10: Dag . . . 3H 73
W8 . . . 4H 99
Pembroke Gdns. Cl. W8 . . . 3J 99
Pembroke Hall *NW4* . . . *3E 44*
(off Mulberry Cl.)
Pembroke Ho. *SW1* . . . *2G 17*
(off Chesham Ho.)
W2 . . . *6K 81*
(off Hallfield Est.)
W3 . . . *2J 97*
(off Park Rd. E.)
Pembroke Lodge HA7: Stan . . . 6H 27
Pembroke Mans. *NW6* . . . *6A 64*
(off Canfield Gdns.)
Pembroke M. E3 . . . 3A 86
N10 . . . 1E 46
W8 . . . 3J 99
Pembroke Pde. DA8: Erith . . . 5J 109
Pembroke Pl. HA8: Edg . . . 7B 28
TW7: Isle . . . 2J 113
W8 . . . 3J 99
Pembroke Rd. BR1: Brom . . . 2A 160
CR4: Mitc . . . 2E 154
DA8: Erith . . . 5J 109
E6 . . . 5D 88
E17 . . . 5D 50
HA4: Ruis . . . 1G 57
HA9: Wemb . . . 3D 60
IG3: Ilf . . . 1K 71
N8 . . . 4J 47
N10 . . . 1E 46
N13 . . . 3H 33
N15 . . . 5F 49
SE25 . . . 4E 156
UB6: G'frd . . . 4F 77
W8 . . . 4H 99
Pembroke Sq. W8 . . . 3J 99
Pembroke St. N1 . . . 7J 65
(not continuous)
Pembroke Studios W8 . . . 3H 99
Pembroke Ter. *NW8* . . . *1B 82*
(off Queen's Ter.)
Pembroke Vs. TW9: Rich . . . 4D 114
W8 . . . 4J 99
Pembroke Wlk. W8 . . . 4J 99
Pembroke Way
UB3: Harl . . . 3E 92
Pembrook M. SW11 . . . 4B 118
Pembry Cl. SW9 . . . 1A 120
Pembury Av. KT4: Wor Pk . . . 1C 164
Pembury Cl. BR2: Hayes . . . 7H 159
E5 . . . 5H 67
Pembury Ct. UB3: Harl . . . 6F 93
Pembury Cres. DA14: Sidc . . . 2E 144
Pembury Pl. E5 . . . 5H 67
Pembury Rd. DA7: Bex . . . 7E 108
E5 . . . 5H 67
N17 . . . 1F 49
SE25 . . . 4G 157
Pemdevon Rd. CR0: C'don . . . 7A 156
Pemell Cl. E1 . . . 4J 85
Pemell Ho. *E1* . . . *4J 85*
(off Pemell Cl.)
Pemerich Cl. UB3: Harl . . . 5H 93
Pempath Pl. HA9: Wemb . . . 2D 60
Penally Pl. N1 . . . 1D 84
Penang Ho. *E1* . . . *1H 103*
(off Prusom St.)
Penang St. E1 . . . 1H 103
Penard Rd. UB2: S'hall . . . 3F 95
Penart Ct. SM2: Sutt . . . 7A 166
Penarth Cen. SE15 . . . 6J 103
Penarth St. SE15 . . . 6J 103
Penberth Rd. SE6 . . . 2E 140
Penbury Rd. UB2: S'hall . . . 4D 94
Pencombe M. W11 . . . 7H 81
Pencraig Way SE15 . . . 6H 103
Pendall Cl. EN4: E Barn . . . 4H 21
Penda Rd. DA8: Erith . . . 7H 109
Pendarves Rd. SW20 . . . 1E 152
Penda's Mead E9 . . . 4A 68
Pendell Av. UB3: Harl . . . 7H 93
Pendennis Ho. SE8 . . . 4A 104
Pendennis Rd. N17 . . . 3D 48
SW16 . . . 4J 137
Penderel Rd. TW3: Houn . . . 5E 112
Penderry Ri. SE6 . . . 2F 141
Penderyn Way N7 . . . 4H 65
Pendlebury Ct. *KT5: Surb* . . . *4E 150*
(off Cranes Pk.)
Pendle Ct. UB10: Hil . . . 1D 74
Pendle Ho. SE26 . . . 3G 139
Pendle Rd. SW16 . . . 6F 137
Pendlestone Rd. E17 . . . 5D 50
Pendlewood Cl. W5 . . . 5C 78
Pendley Ho. *E2* . . . *1G 85*
(off Whiston Rd.)
Pendolino Way NW10 . . . 7G 61
Pendragon Rd. BR1: Brom . . . 3H 141
Pendragon Wlk. NW9 . . . 6A 44
Pendrell Ho. *WC2* . . . *1D 12*
(off New Compton St.)
Pendrell Rd. SE4 . . . 2A 122
Pendrell St. SE18 . . . 6H 107
Pendula Dr. UB4: Yead . . . 4B 76
Pendulum M. E8 . . . 5F 67
Penerley Rd. SE6 . . . 1D 140
Penfield Lodge *W9* . . . *5J 81*
(off Admiral Wlk.)
Penfields Ho. N7 . . . 6J 65
Penfold Cl. CR0: Wadd . . . 3A 168
Penfold La. DA5: Bexl . . . 2D 144
(Cotleigh Av.)
DA5: Bexl . . . 1D 144
(Stansted Cres.)
Penfold Pl. NW1 . . . 5C 4 (5C 82)
Penfold Rd. N9 . . . 1E 34
Penfold St. NW1 . . . 4B 4 (4B 82)
NW8 . . . 4B 4 (4B 82)
Penford Gdns. SE9 . . . 3B 124
Penford St. SE5 . . . 2B 120
Pengarth Rd. DA5: Bexl . . . 5D 126
PENGE . . . 7J 139
Penge Ho. SW11 . . . 3B 118
Penge La. SE20 . . . 7J 139
Penge Rd. E13 . . . 1A 88
SE20 . . . 3G 157
SE25 . . . 3G 157
Penhale Cl. BR6: Chels . . . 4K 173
Penhall Rd. SE7 . . . 4B 106
Penhill Rd. DA5: Bexl . . . 6C 126
Penhurst Pl. SE1 . . . 1H 19
Penhurst Rd. IG6: Ilf . . . 1F 53
Penifather La. UB6: G'frd . . . 3H 77
Peninsula Apartments *W2* . . . *6C 4*
(off Praed St.)
Peninsula Ct. *E14* . . . *3D 104*
(off E. Ferry Rd.)
Peninsula Hgts. SE1 . . . 5F 19 (5J 101)
Peninsular Cl. TW14: Felt . . . 6F 111
Peninsular Pk. SE7 . . . 4J 105
Peninsular Pk. Rd. SE7 . . . 4J 105
Penistone Rd. SW16 . . . 7J 137
Penketh Dr. HA1: Harr . . . 3H 59
Penley Ct. WC2 . . . 2H 13 (7K 83)
Penmayne Ho. *SE11* . . . *5K 19*
(off Kennings Way)
Penmon Rd. SE2 . . . 3A 108
Pennack Rd. SE15 . . . 6F 103
Penn Almshouses *SE10* . . . *1E 122*
(off Greenwich Sth. St.)
Pennant M. W8 . . . 4K 99
Pennant Ter. E17 . . . 2B 50
Pennard Mans. *W12* . . . *2E 98*
(off Goldhawk Rd.)
Pennard Rd. W12 . . . 2E 98
Pennards, The TW16: Sun . . . 3A 148
Penn Cl. HA3: Kent . . . 4C 42
UB6: G'frd . . . 2F 77
Penn Ct. NW9 . . . 3K 43
Penner Cl. SW19 . . . 2G 135
Penners Gdns. KT6: Surb . . . 7E 150
Pennethorne Cl. E9 . . . 1J 85
Pennethorne Ho. SW11 . . . 3B 118
Pennethorne Rd. SE15 . . . 7H 103
Penn Gdns. BR7: Chst . . . 2F 161
RM5: Col R . . . 1G 55
Penn Ho. *NW8* . . . *4C 4*
(off Mallory St.)
Pennine Dr. NW2 . . . 2F 63
Pennine Ho. *N9* . . . *3B 34*
(off Plevna Rd.)
Pennine La. NW2 . . . 2G 63
Pennine Pde. NW2 . . . 2G 63
Pennine Way DA7: Bex . . . 1K 127
UB3: Harl . . . 7F 93
Pennington Cl. SE27 . . . 4D 138
Pennington Ct. SE16 . . . 1A 104
Pennington Dr. N21 . . . 5D 22
Pennington Lodge
KT5: Surb . . . *5E 150*
(off Cranes Dr.)
Pennington St. E1 . . . 7H 85
Pennington Way SE12 . . . 2K 141
Penniston Cl. N17 . . . 2C 48
Penn La. DA5: Bexl . . . 5D 126
(not continuous)
Penn Rd. N7 . . . 5J 65
Penn St. N1 . . . 1D 84
Pennycroft CR0: Sels . . . 7A 170
Pennyfather La. EN2: Enf . . . 3H 23
Pennyfields E14 . . . 7C 86
(not continuous)
Pennyford Ct. *NW8* . . . *3A 4*
(off St John's Wood Rd.)
Penny La. TW17: Shep . . . 7G 147
Penny M. SW12 . . . 7F 119
Pennymoor Wlk. *W9* . . . *4H 81*
(off Ashmore Rd.)
Penny Rd. NW10 . . . 3H 79
Penny Royal SM6: Wall . . . 6H 167
Pennyroyal Av. E6 . . . 6E 88
Penpoll Rd. E8 . . . 6H 67
Penpool La. DA16: Well . . . 3B 126
Penrhyn Av. E17 . . . 1B 50
Penrhyn Cres. E17 . . . 1C 50
SW14 . . . 4J 115
Penrhyn Gdns. KT1: King T . . . 4D 150
Penrhyn Gro. E17 . . . 1C 50
Penrhyn Rd. KT1: King T . . . 4E 150
Penrith Cl. BR3: Beck . . . 1D 158
SW15 . . . 5G 117
UB8: Uxb . . . 7A 56
Penrith Pl. SE27 . . . 2B 138
Penrith Rd. CR7: Thor H . . . 2C 156
KT3: N Mald . . . 4K 151
N15 . . . 5D 48
Penrith St. SW16 . . . 6G 137
Penrose Gro. SE17 . . . 5C 102
Penrose Ho. N21 . . . 5E 22
SE17 . . . 5C 102
Penrose St. SE17 . . . 5C 102
Penryn Ho. *SE11* . . . *5B 102*
(off Seaton Cl.)
Penryn St. NW1 . . . 2H 83
Penry St. SE1 . . . 4E 102
Pensbury Pl. SW8 . . . 2G 119
Pensbury St. SW8 . . . 2G 119
Pensford Av. TW9: Kew . . . 2G 115
Penshurst NW5 . . . 6E 64
Penshurst Av. DA15: Sidc . . . 6A 126
Penshurst Gdns. HA8: Edg . . . 5C 28
Penshurst Grn. BR2: Brom . . . 5H 159
Penshurst Ho. *SE15* . . . *6J 103*
(off Lovelinch Cl.)
Penshurst Rd. CR7: Thor H . . . 5B 156
DA7: Bex . . . 1F 127
E9 . . . 7K 67
N17 . . . 7A 34
Penshurst Wlk. BR2: Brom . . . 5H 159
Penshurst Way SM2: Sutt . . . 7J 165
Pensilver Cl. EN4: E Barn . . . 4H 21
Penstemon Cl. N3 . . . 6D 30

Penstock Footpath N8 .....3K 47
N22 .....3K 47
Pentagram Yd. W11 .....6J 81
(off Needham Rd.)
Pentavia Retail Pk. NW7 .....7G 29
Pentelow Gdns. TW14: Felt 6J 111
Pentire Rd. E17 .....1F 51
Pentland Av. HA8: Edg 2C 28
TW17: Shep 5C 146
Pentland Cl. N9 .....2D 34
NW11 .....2G 63
Pentland Gdns. SW18 .....6A 118
Pentland Pl. UB5: N'olt 1C 76
Pentland Rd. NW6 .....3J 81
Pentlands Cl. CR4: Mitc 3F 155
Pentland St. SW18 .....6A 118
Pentland Way UB10: Ick 3E 56
Pentlow St. SW15 .....3E 116
Pentlow Way IG9: Buck H 1H 37
Pentney Rd. E4 .....1A 36
SW12 .....1G 137
SW19 .....1G 153
Penton Gro. N1 .....2A 84
Penton Ho. N1 .....2A 84
(off Pentonville Rd.)
SE2 .....1D 108
Penton Pl. SE17 .....5B 102
Penton Ri. WC1 .....1H 7 (3K 83)
Penton St. N1 .....2A 84
PENTONVILLE 2K 83
Pentonville Rd. N1 .....1G 7 (2J 83)
Pentrich Av. EN1: Enf 1B 24
Pentridge St. SE15 .....7F 103
Pentyre Av. N18 .....5J 33
Penwerris Av. TW7: Isle 7G 95
Penwerris Ct. TW5: Hest 7G 95
Penwith Rd. SW18 .....2J 135
Penwood Ct. HA5: Pinn 4D 40
Penwood Ho. SW15 .....6B 116
Penwortham Ct. N22 .....2A 48
(off Mayes Rd.)
Penwortham Rd. SW16 .....6F 137
Penylan Pl. HA8: Edg 7B 28
Penywern Rd. SW5 .....5J 99
Penzance Ho. SE11 .....5K 19
(off Seaton Cl.)
Penzance Pl. W11 .....1G 99
Penzance St. W11 .....1G 99
Peony Ct. IG8: Wfd G 7B 36
SW10 .....7A 16 (6A 100)
Peony Gdns. W12 .....7C 80
Peperfield WC1 .....2G 7
(off Cromer St.)
Pepler Ho. W10 .....4G 81
(off Wornington Rd.)
Pepler M. SE5 .....5F 103
Peploe Rd. NW6 .....2F 81
Peplow Cl. UB7: Yiew 1A 92
Pepper Cl. E6 .....5D 88
Peppercorn Cl. CR7: Thor H 2D 156
Peppermead Sq. SE13 .....5C 122
Peppermint Cl. CR0: C'don 7J 155
Peppermint Pl. E11 .....3G 69
Pepper St. E14 .....3D 104
SE1 .....6C 14 (2C 102)
Peppie Cl. N16 .....2E 66
Pepys Cl. UB10: Ick 4D 56
Pepys Cres. E16 .....1J 105
EN5: Barn 5A 20
Pepys Ho. E2 .....3J 85
(off Kirkwall Pl.)
Pepys Ri. BR6: Orp 1K 173
Pepys Rd. SE14 .....1K 121
SW20 .....1E 152
Pepys St. EC3 .....2H 15 (7E 84)
Perceval Av. NW3 .....5C 64
Perceval Ct. UB5: N'olt 5E 58
Perceval Ho. W5 .....7C 78
Percheron Cl. TW7: Isle 3K 113
Perch St. E8 .....4F 67

Percival Ct. N17 .....7A 34
Percival David Foundation of Chinese Art 3D 6
Percival Gdns. RM6: Chad H 6C 54
Percival Rd. BR6: Farnb 2F 173
EN1: Enf 4A 24
SW14 .....4J 115
TW13: Felt 2H 129
Percival St. EC1 .....3A 8 (4B 84)
Percival Way KT19: Ewe 4K 163
Percy Av. TW15: Ashf 5C 128
Percy Bryant Rd. TW16: Sun 7G 129
Percy Bush Rd. UB7: W Dray 3B 92
Percy Cir. WC1 .....1H 7 (3K 83)
Percy Gdns. EN3: Pond E 5E 24
KT4: Wor Pk 1K 163
TW7: Isle 3A 114
UB4: Hayes 3G 75
Percy Laurie Ho. SW15 .....4F 117
(off Nursery Cl.)
Percy M. W1 .....6C 6
Percy Pas. W1 .....6C 6
Percy Rd. CR4: Mitc 7E 154
DA7: Bex 2E 126
E11 .....7G 51
E16 .....5G 87
IG3: Ilf 7A 54
N12 .....5F 31
N21 .....7H 23
RM7: Mawney 3H 55
SE20 .....1K 157
SE25 .....5G 157
TW2: Whitt 1F 131
TW7: Isle 4A 114
TW12: Hamp 7E 130
W12 .....2C 98
Percy St. W1 .....6C 6 (5H 83)
Percy Ter. BR1: Brom 3F 161
Percy Way TW2: Whitt 1G 131
Percy Yd. WC1 .....1H 7 (3K 83)
Peregrine Cl. NW10 .....5K 61
Peregrine Ct. DA16: Well 1K 125
SE8 .....6C 104
(off Edward St.)
SW16 .....4K 137
Peregrine Gdns. CR0: C'don 2A 170
Peregrine Ho. EC1 .....1B 8
Peregrine Rd. N17 .....7H 33
TW16: Sun 2H 147
Peregrine Way SW19 .....7E 134
Perham Rd. W14 .....5G 99
Peridot St. E6 .....5C 88
Perifield SE21 .....1C 138
Perimeade Rd. UB6: G'frd 2C 78
Periton Rd. SE9 .....4B 124
PERIVALE 1C 78
Perivale Gdns. W13 .....4B 78
Perivale Grange UB6: G'frd 3A 78
Perivale Ind. Pk. UB6: G'frd 2B 78
Perivale La. UB6: G'frd 3A 78
Perivale Lodge UB6: G'frd 3A 78
(off Perivale La.)
Perivale New Bus. Cen.
UB6: G'frd 2C 78
Perivale Pk. Gym 3K 77
Perivale Wood Local Nature Reserve 1K 77
Periwood Cres. UB6: G'frd 1A 78
Perkin Cl. HA0: Wemb 5B 60
TW3: Houn 4E 112
Perkins Ct. TW15: Ashf 5B 128
Perkins Ho. E14 .....5B 86
(off Wallwood St.)
Perkin's Rents SW1 .....2C 18 (3H 101)
Perkins Rd. IG2: Ilf 5H 53
Perkins Sq. SE1 .....4D 14 (1C 102)
Perks Cl. SE3 .....3G 123
Perley Ho. E3 .....5B 86
(off Weatherley Cl.)
Perpins Rd. SE9 .....6J 125

Perran Rd. SW2 .....1B 138
Perran Wlk. TW8: Bford 5E 96
Perren St. NW5 .....6F 65
Perrers Rd. W6 .....4D 98
Perrin Cl. TW15: Ashf 5B 128
Perrin Ct. TW15: Ashf 4C 128
Perring Est. E3 .....5C 86
(off Gale St.)
Perrin Ho. NW6 .....3J 81
Perrin Rd. HA0: Wemb 4B 60
Perrin's Ct. NW3 .....4A 64
Perrin's La. NW3 .....4A 64
Perrin's Wlk. NW3 .....4A 64
Perronet Ho. SE1 .....3B 102
(off Princess St.)
Perrott St. SE18 .....4G 107
Perry Av. W3 .....6K 79
Perry Cl. RM13: Rain 2K 91
UB8: Hil 6D 74
Perry Ct. E14 .....5C 104
(off Maritime Quay)
KT1: King T 2E 150
(off London Rd.)
N15 .....6E 48
Perryfield Way NW9 .....6B 44
TW10: Ham 3B 132
Perry Gdns. N9 .....3J 33
Perry Gth. UB5: N'olt 1A 76
Perry Hall Rd.
BR6: St M Cry 6K 161
Perry Hill SE6 .....3B 140
Perry Ho. RM13: Rain 2K 91
Perry How KT4: Wor Pk 1B 164
Perry Lodge E12 .....1B 70
Perryman Ho. IG11: Bark 1G 89
(off The Shaftesburys)
Perrymans Farm Rd. IG2: Ilf 6H 53
Perry Mead EN2: Enf 2G 23
Perrymead St. SW6 .....1J 117
Perryn Ct. TW1: Twick 6A 114
Perryn Ho. W3 .....7A 80
Perryn Rd. SE16 .....3H 103
W3 .....1K 97
Perry Ri. SE23 .....3A 140
Perry Rd. RM9: Dag 5F 91
Perry's Pl. W1 .....7C 6 (6H 83)
Perry St. BR7: Chst 6H 143
DA1: Cray 4K 127
Perry St. Gdns. BR7: Chst 6J 143
Perry St. Shaw BR7: Chst 7J 143
Perry Va. SE23 .....2J 139
Persant Rd. SE6 .....2G 141
Perseverance Pl. SW9 .....7A 102
TW9: Rich 4E 114
Perseverance Works E2 .....1H 9
(off Kingsland Rd.)
Pershore Cl. IG2: Ilf 5F 53
Pershore Gro. SM5: Cars 6B 154
Pershore Ho. W13 .....1A 96
(off Singapore Rd.)
Pert Cl. N10 .....7A 32
Perth Av. NW9 .....7K 43
UB4: Yead 4A 76
Perth Cl. SE5 .....4D 120
SW20 .....2B 152
UB5: N'olt 5E 58
Perth Ho. N1 .....7K 65
(off Bemerton Est.)
Perth Rd. BR3: Beck 2E 158
E10 .....1A 68
E13 .....2K 87
IG2: Ilf 6E 52
IG11: Bark 2H 89
N4 .....1A 66
N22 .....1B 48
Perth Ter. IG2: Ilf 7G 53
Perwell Av. HA2: Harr 1D 58
Perystreete SE23 .....2J 139
Petavel Rd. TW11: Tedd 6J 131
Peter Av. NW10 .....7D 62

Peter Best Ho. E1 .....6H 85
(off Nelson St.)
Peterboat Cl. SE10 .....4G 105
Peterborough Ct. EC4 .....1K 13 (6A 84)
Peterborough Gdns. IG1: Ilf 7C 52
Peterborough M. SW6 .....2J 117
Peterborough Rd. E10 .....5E 50
HA1: Harr 1J 59
SM5: Cars 6C 154
SW6 .....2J 117
Peterborough Vs. SW6 .....1K 117
Peter Butler Ho. SE1 .....7K 15
(off Wolseley St.)
Peterchurch Ho. SE15 .....6H 103
(off Commercial Way)
Petergate SW11 .....4A 118
Peter Harrison Planetarium 7F 105
Peterhead Ct. UB1: S'hall 6G 77
(off Osborne Rd.)
Peter Heathfield Ho. E15 .....1F 87
(off Wise Rd.)
Peter Hills Ho. SE16 .....4G 103
(off Alexis St.)
Peter Ho. SW8 .....7J 101
(off Luscombe Way)
Peter James Bus. Cen.
UB3: Hayes 2J 93
Peter James Ent. Cen. NW10 .....3J 79
Peter Kennedy Ct. CR0: C'don 6B 158
Peterley Bus. Cen. E2 .....2H 85
Peter Lyell Ct. HA4: Ruis 2K 57
Peter May Cen., The 7K 35
Peter Pan Statue 4A 10 (1B 100)
Peters Cl. DA16: Well 2J 125
HA7: Stan 6J 27
RM8: Dag 1D 72
Peter Scott Vis. Cen., The 1D 116
Peters Ct. W2 .....6K 81
(off Porchester Rd.)
Petersfield Cl. N18 .....5H 33
Petersfield Ri. SW15 .....1D 134
Petersfield Rd. W3 .....2J 97
PETERSHAM 1E 132
Petersham Cl. SM1: Sutt 5J 165
TW10: Ham 2D 132
Petersham Dr. BR5: St P 2K 161
Petersham Gdns. BR5: St P 2K 161
Petersham Ho. SW7 .....3A 16
(off Kendrick M.)
Petersham La. SW7 .....3A 100
Petersham M. SW7 .....3A 100
Petersham Pl. SW7 .....3A 100
Petersham Rd.
TW10: Rich, Ham 6D 114
Petersham Ter. CR0: Bedd 3J 167
(off Richmond Grn.)
Peter's Hill EC4 .....2C 14 (7C 84)
Peter Shore Ct. E1 .....5K 85
(off Beaumont Sq.)
Peter's La. EC1 .....5B 8 (5B 84)
(not continuous)
Peter's Path SE26 .....4H 139
Peterstone Rd. SE2 .....2B 108
Peterstow Cl. SW19 .....2G 135
Peter St. W1 .....2C 12 (7H 83)
Peterwood Pk. CR0: Wadd 2K 167
Peterwood Way
CR0: Wadd 2K 167
Petherton Ct. HA1: Harr 6K 41
(off Gayton Rd.)
NW10 .....1F 81
(off Tiverton Rd.)
Petherton Ho. N4 .....1C 66
(off Woodberry Down Est.)
Petherton Rd. N5 .....5C 66
Petiver Cl. E9 .....7J 67
Petley Rd. W6 .....6F 99
Peto Pl. NW1 .....3K 5 (4F 83)
Peto St. Nth. E16 .....6H 87
Petrie Cl. NW2 .....6G 63

Petrie Ho. SE18 . . . 6E 106
(off Woolwich Comn.)
Petrie Mus. of Egyptian Archaeology . . . 4C 6
Petros Gdns. NW3 . . . 6A 64
Pettacre Cl. SE28 . . . 3G 107
Petticoat La. E1 . . . 6J 9 (5E 84)
Petticoat Lane Market . . . 7J 9
(off Middlesex St.)
Petticoat Sq. E1 . . . 7J 9 (6F 85)
Petticoat Twr. E1 . . . 7J 9
Pettits Cl. RM1: Rom . . . 2K 55
Pettits La. Nth. RM1: Rom . . . 1K 55
Pettits Pl. RM10: Dag . . . 5G 73
Pettits Rd. RM10: Dag . . . 5G 73
Pettiward Cl. SW15 . . . 4E 116
Pettley Gdns. RM7: Rom . . . 5K 55
Pettman Cres. SE28 . . . 3H 107
Pettsgrove Av. HA0: Wemb . . . 5C 60
Pett's Hill UB5: N'olt . . . 5F 59
Petts La. TW17: Shep . . . 4C 146
Pett St. SE18 . . . 4C 106
PETTS WOOD . . . 5G 161
Petts Wood Rd. BR5: Pet W . . . 5G 161
Petty France SW1 . . . 1B 18 (3G 101)
Petty Wales EC3 . . . 3H 15 (7E 84)
Petworth Cl. UB5: N'olt . . . 7D 58
Petworth Gdns. SW20 . . . 3D 152
UB10: Hil . . . 1E 74
Petworth Rd. DA6: Bex . . . 5G 127
N12 . . . 5H 31
Petworth St. SW11 . . . 1C 118
Petyt Pl. SW3 . . . 6C 100
Petyward SW3 . . . 4D 16 (4C 100)
Pevensey Av. EN1: Enf . . . 2K 23
N11 . . . 5C 32
Pevensey Cl. TW7: Isle . . . 7G 95
Pevensey Ct. SW16 . . . 3A 138
W3 . . . 2H 97
Pevensey Ho. E1 . . . 5K 85
(off Ben Jonson Rd.)
Pevensey Rd. E7 . . . 4H 69
SW17 . . . 4B 136
TW13: Felt . . . 1C 130
Peverel E6 . . . 6E 88
Peverel Ho. RM10: Dag . . . 2G 73
Peveret Cl. N11 . . . 5A 32
Peveril Dr. TW11: Tedd . . . 5H 131
Peveril Ho. SE1 . . . 3D 102
(off Rephidim St.)
Pewsey Cl. E4 . . . 5H 35
Peyton Pl. SE10 . . . 7E 104
Pharamond NW2 . . . 6F 63
Pharaoh Cl. CR4: Mitc . . . 7D 154
Pheasant Cl. E16 . . . 6K 87
Pheasantry Ho. SW3 . . . 5D 16
(off Jubilee Pl.)
Phelp St. SE17 . . . 6D 102
Phelps Way UB3: Harl . . . 4H 93
Phene St. SW3 . . . 7D 16 (6C 100)
Philadelphia Ct. SW10 . . . 7A 100
(off Uverdale Rd.)
Philbeach Gdns. SW5 . . . 5J 99
Phil Brown Pl. SW8 . . . 3F 119
(off Wandsworth Rd.)
Philchurch Pl. E1 . . . 6G 85
Philia Ho. NW1 . . . 7G 65
(off Farrier St.)
Philimore Cl. SE18 . . . 5J 107
Philip Av. RM7: Rush G . . . 1K 73
Philip Cl. RM7: Rush G . . . 1K 73
Philip Ct. W2 . . . 5A 4
(off Hall Pl.)
Philip Gdns. CR0: C'don . . . 2B 170
Philip Ho. NW6 . . . 1K 81
(off Mortimer Pl.)
Philip Jones Ct. N4 . . . 1K 65
Philip La. N15 . . . 4D 48
Philip Mole Ho. W9 . . . 4J 81
(off Chippenham Rd.)
Philipot Path SE9 . . . 6D 124
Philippa Gdns. SE9 . . . 5B 124
Philip Rd. TW18: Staines . . . 6A 128
Philips Cl. SM5: Cars . . . 1E 166
Philip Sq. SW8 . . . 2F 119
Philip St. E13 . . . 4J 87
Philip Wlk. SE15 . . . 3G 121
(not continuous)
Phillimore Ct. W8 . . . 2J 99
(off Kensington High St.)
Phillimore Gdns. NW10 . . . 1E 80
W8 . . . 2J 99
Phillimore Gdns. Cl. W8 . . . 3J 99
Phillimore Pl. W8 . . . 2J 99
Phillimore Ter. W8 . . . 3J 99
(off Allen St.)
Phillimore Wlk. W8 . . . 3J 99
Phillipp St. N1 . . . 1E 84
Phillips Ct. HA8: Edg . . . 6B 28
Philpot La. EC3 . . . 2G 15 (7E 84)
Philpot Path
IG1: Ilf . . . 3G 71
Philpots Cl. UB7: Yiew . . . 7A 74
Philpot Sq. SW6 . . . 3K 117
Philpot St. E1 . . . 6H 85
Phineas Pett Rd. SE9 . . . 3C 124
Phipps Bri. Rd.
CR4: Mitc . . . 2A 154
SW19 . . . 2A 154
Phipps Hatch La.
EN2: Enf . . . 1H 23
Phipps Ho. SE7 . . . 5K 105
(off Woolwich Rd.)
W12 . . . 7D 80
(off White City Est.)
Phipp St. EC2 . . . 3G 9 (4E 84)
Phoebeth Rd. SE4 . . . 5C 122
Phoenix Bus. Cen. E3 . . . 5C 86
(off Bow Comn. La.)
Phoenix Cen. . . . 7J 167
Phoenix Cinema
East Finchley . . . 4C 46
Phoenix Cl. BR4: W W'ck . . . 2F 171
E8 . . . 1F 85
E17 . . . 2B 50
Phoenix Ct. CR2: S Croy . . . 5F 169
E1 . . . 4H 85
(off Buckhurst St.)
E4 . . . 3J 35
E14 . . . 4C 104
KT3: N Mald . . . 3B 152
NW1 . . . 1D 6
(off Purchese St.)
SE14 . . . 6A 104
(off Chipley St.)
TW4: Houn . . . 5B 112
TW8: Bford . . . 5E 96
TW13: Felt . . . 4G 129
Phoenix Dr. BR2: Kes . . . 4B 172
Phoenix Ho. SM1: Sutt . . . 4K 165
Phoenix Ind. Est. HA1: Harr . . . 4K 41
Phoenix Lodge Mans. W6 . . . 4F 99
(off Brook Grn.)
Phoenix Pk. NW2 . . . 2C 62
Phoenix Pl. WC1 . . . 3H 7 (4K 83)
Phoenix Rd. NW1 . . . 1C 6 (3H 83)
SE20 . . . 6J 139
Phoenix Sports & Fitness Cen. . . . 7C 80
Phoenix St. WC2 . . . 1D 12 (6H 83)
Phoenix Theatre . . . 1D 12
(off Charing Cross Rd.)
Phoenix Trad. Est. UB6: G'frd . . . 1C 78
Phoenix Trad. Pk. TW8: Bford . . . 5D 96
Phoenix Way TW5: Hest . . . 6B 94
Phoenix Wharf E1 . . . 1H 103
(off Wapping High St.)
Phoenix Wharf Rd. SE1 . . . 7K 15
Phoenix Yd. WC1 . . . 2H 7
Photographers' Gallery . . . 2E 12
(off Gt. Newport St.)
Phyllis Av. KT3: N Mald . . . 5D 152
Phyllis Hodges Ho. NW1 . . . 2H 83
(off Aldenham St.)
Phyllis Ho. CR0: Wadd . . . 4B 168
(off Ashley La.)
Physic Pl. SW3 . . . 7E 16 (6D 100)
Piazza, The UB8: Uxb . . . 7A 56
WC2 . . . 2F 13
(not continuous)
Picardy Ho. EN2: Enf . . . 1H 23
Picardy Manorway DA17: Belv . . . 3H 109
Picardy Rd. DA17: Belv . . . 5G 109
Picardy St. DA17: Belv . . . 3G 109
Piccadilly W1 . . . 5K 11 (1F 101)
Piccadilly Arc. SW1 . . . 4A 12
Piccadilly Circus . . . 3C 12 (7H 83)
Piccadilly Cir. W1 . . . 3C 12 (7H 83)
Piccadilly Ct. N7 . . . 6K 65
(off Caledonian Rd.)
Piccadilly Pl. W1 . . . 3B 12
Piccadilly Theatre . . . 2B 12
(off Denman St.)
Pickard Cl. N14 . . . 1C 32
Pickard St. EC1 . . . 1B 8 (3B 84)
Pickering Av. E6 . . . 2E 88
Pickering Cl. E9 . . . 7K 67
Pickering Gdns. CR0: C'don . . . 6F 157
N11 . . . 6K 31
Pickering Ho. W2 . . . 6A 82
(off Hallfield Est.)
W5 . . . 4C 96
(off Windmill Rd.)
Pickering M. W2 . . . 6K 81
Pickering Pl. SW1 . . . 5B 12
Pickering Rd. IG11: Bark . . . 6G 71
Pickering St. N1 . . . 1B 84
Pickets Cl. WD23: B Hea . . . 1C 26
Pickets St. SW12 . . . 7F 119
Pickett Cft. HA7: Stan . . . 1D 42
Picketts Lock La. N9 . . . 2D 34
Picketts Lock La. Ind. Est. N9 . . . 2F 35
Picketts Ter. SE22 . . . 5G 121
Pickford Cl. DA7: Bex . . . 2E 126
Pickford La. DA7: Bex . . . 2E 126
Pickford Rd. DA7: Bex . . . 3E 126
Pickfords Wharf N1 . . . 2C 84
SE1 . . . 4E 14 (1D 102)
Pickhurst Grn. BR2: Hayes . . . 7H 159
Pickhurst La. BR2: Hayes . . . 5G 159
BR4: W W'ck . . . 5G 159
Pickhurst Mead BR2: Hayes . . . 7H 159
Pickhurst Pk. BR2: Brom . . . 5G 159
Pickhurst Ri. BR4: W W'ck . . . 7E 158
Pickwick Cl. TW4: Houn . . . 5C 112
Pickwick Ct. SE9 . . . 1C 142
Pickwick Ho. SE16 . . . 2G 103
(off George Row)
W11 . . . 1F 99
(off St Ann's Rd.)
Pickwick M. N18 . . . 4K 33
Pickwick Pl. HA1: Harr . . . 7J 41
Pickwick Rd. SE21 . . . 7D 120
Pickwick St. SE1 . . . 7C 14 (2C 102)
Pickwick Way BR7: Chst . . . 6G 143
Pickworth Cl. SW8 . . . 7J 101
Picton Pl. KT6: Surb . . . 1G 163
W1 . . . 1H 11 (6E 82)
Picton St. SE5 . . . 7D 102
Picture Ho. SW16 . . . 2J 137
Pied Bull Ct. WC1 . . . 5J 83
(off Bury Pl.)
Pied Bull Yard N1 . . . 1B 84
(off Theberton St.)
WC1 . . . 6E 6
Piedmont Rd. SE18 . . . 5H 107
(not continuous)
PIELD HEATH . . . 4B 74
Pield Heath Av. UB8: Hil . . . 4C 74
Pield Heath Rd. UB8: Cowl, Hil . . . 4A 74
Pier Head E1 . . . 1H 103
(not continuous)
Pierhead Wharf E1 . . . 1H 103
(off Wapping High St.)
Pier Ho. SW3 . . . 7D 16 (6C 100)
Pieris Ho. TW13: Felt . . . 2J 129
(off High St.)
Piermont Grn. SE22 . . . 5H 121
Piermont Pl. BR1: Brom . . . 2C 160
Piermont Rd. SE22 . . . 5H 121
Pier Pde. E16 . . . 1E 106
(off Pier Rd.)
Pierpoint Bldg. E14 . . . 2B 104
Pierrepoint Rd. W3 . . . 7H 79
Pierrepont Arc. N1 . . . 2B 84
(off Islington High St.)
Pierrepont Row N1 . . . 2B 84
(off Camden Pas.)
Pier Rd. E16 . . . 2D 106
TW14: Felt . . . 5K 111
Pier St. E14 . . . 4E 104
(not continuous)
Pier Ter. SW18 . . . 4K 117
Pier Way SE28 . . . 2G 107
Pietra Lara Bldg. EC1 . . . 3C 8
(off Pear Tree St.)
Pigeon La. TW12: Hamp . . . 4E 130
Piggott Ho. E2 . . . 2K 85
(off Sewardstone Rd.)
Pigott St. E14 . . . 6C 86
Pike Cl. BR1: Brom . . . 5K 141
UB10: Uxb . . . 1B 74
Pikemans Ct. SW5 . . . 4J 99
(off W. Cromwell Rd.)
Pike Rd. NW7 . . . 4E 28
Pike's End HA5: Eastc . . . 4K 39
Pikestone Cl.
UB4: Yead . . . 4C 76
Pikethorne SE23 . . . 2K 139
Pilgrimage St. SE1 . . . 7E 14 (2D 102)
Pilgrim Cl.
SM4: Mord . . . 7K 153
Pilgrim Hill SE27 . . . 4C 138
Pilgrim Ho. SE1 . . . 3D 102
(off Tabard St.)
SE16 . . . 2J 103
(off Brunel Rd.)
Pilgrims Cloisters SE5 . . . 7E 102
(off Sedgmoor Pl.)
Pilgrims Cl. N13 . . . 4E 32
UB5: N'olt . . . 5G 59
Pilgrims Cnr. NW6 . . . 2J 81
(off Chichester Rd.)
Pilgrims Ct. EN1: Enf . . . 2J 23
Pilgrim's La. NW3 . . . 4B 64
Pilgrims M. E14 . . . 7G 87
Pilgrim's Pl. NW3 . . . 4B 64
Pilgrims Ri. EN4: E Barn . . . 5H 21
Pilgrim St. EC4 . . . 1A 14 (6B 84)
Pilgrims Way CR2: S Croy . . . 6F 169
E6 . . . 1C 88
HA9: Wemb . . . 1H 61
N19 . . . 1H 65
Pilkington Rd. BR6: Farnb . . . 3G 173
SE15 . . . 2H 121
Pillions La. UB4: Hayes . . . 4F 75
Pilot Cl. SE8 . . . 6B 104
Pilot Ind. Cen. NW10 . . . 4K 79
Pilsden Cl. SW19 . . . 1F 135
Pilton Est., The
CR0: C'don . . . 2B 168
Pilton Pl. SE17 . . . 5C 102
Pimento Ct. W5 . . . 3D 96
PIMLICO . . . 6B 18 (5G 101)
Pimlico Ho. SW1 . . . 5J 17
(off Ebury Bri. Rd.)
Pimlico Rd. SW1 . . . 5G 17 (5E 100)
Pimlico Wlk. N1 . . . 1G 9
Pinchbeck Rd. BR6: Chels . . . 6K 173
Pinchin & Johnsons Yd. E1 . . . 7G 85
(off Pinchin St.)
Pinchin St. E1 . . . 7G 85

Pincombe Ho. *SE17* 5D 102
(off Orb St.)
Pincott Pl. SE4 3K 121
Pincott Rd. DA6: Bex 5G 127
SW19 7A 136
Pindar St. EC2 5G 9 (5E 84)
Pindock M. W9 4K 81
Pineapple Ct. SW1 1B 18
Pine Av. BR4: W W'ck 1D 170
E15 5F 69
Pine Cl. E10 2D 68
HA7: Stan 4G 27
N14 7B 22
N19 2G 65
SE20 1J 157
Pine Coombe CR0: C'don 4K 169
Pine Ct. N21 5E 22
UB5: N'olt 4C 76
Pinecrest Gdns. BR6: Farnb 4F 173
Pinecroft Ct. DA16: Well 7A 108
Pinecroft Cres. EN5: Barn 4B 20
Pinedene SE15 1H 121
Pinefield Cl. E14 7C 86
Pine Gdns. HA4: Ruis 1K 57
KT5: Surb 6G 151
Pine Glade BR6: Farnb 4D 172
Pine Gro. N4 2J 65
N20 1C 30
SW19 5H 135
Pine Ho. *SE16* 2J 103
(off Ainsty Est.)
W10 4G 81
(off Droop St.)
Pinehurst Ct. *W11* 6H 81
(off Colville Gdns.)
Pinehurst Wlk.
BR6: Orp 1H 173
Pinemartin Cl. NW2 3E 62
Pine M. NW10 2F 81
Pine Pl. UB4: Hayes 4H 75
Pine Ridge SM5: Cars 7E 166
Pineridge Ct. EN5: Barn 4A 20
Pine Rd. N11 2K 31
NW2 4E 62
Pines, The IG8: Wfd G 3D 36
KT9: Chess 3E 162
N14 5B 22
SE19 6B 138
TW16: Sun 3J 147
Pines Rd. BR1: Brom 2C 160
Pine St. EC1 3K 7 (4A 84)
Pine Tree Cl. TW5: Cran 1K 111
Pine Tree Ho. *SE14* 7K 103
(off Reaston St.)
Pine Tree Lodge BR2: Brom 4H 159
Pine Trees Dr. UB10: Ick 4A 56
Pinetree Way SE13 3D 122
Pineview Ct. E4 1K 35
Pine Wlk. KT5: Surb 6G 151
Pine Wood TW16: Sun 1J 147
Pinewood Av. DA15: Sidc 1J 143
HA5: Hat E 6A 26
UB8: Hil 6B 74
Pinewood Cl. BR6: Orp 1H 173
CR0: C'don 3A 170
HA5: Hat E 6A 26
Pinewood Ct. EN2: Enf 3G 23
SW4 6H 119
Pinewood Dr. BR6: Orp 5J 173
Pinewood Gro. W5 6C 78
Pinewood Lodge WD23: B Hea 1C 26
Pinewood Pl. DA2: Dart 2K 145
(not continuous)
KT19: Ewe 4K 163
Pinewood Rd. BR2: Brom 4J 159
SE2 6D 108
TW13: Felt 3K 129
Pinfold Rd. SW16 4J 137
Pinglestone Cl. UB7: Harm 7A 92
Pinkcoat Cl. TW13: Felt 3K 129
Pinkerton Pl. SW16 4H 137
Pinkham Mans. W4 5G 97
Pinkham Way N11 7K 31
Pinkwell Av. UB3: Harl 4F 93
Pinkwell La. UB3: Harl 4E 92
Pinley Gdns. RM9: Dag 1B 90
Pinnace Ho. *E14* 3E 104
(off Manchester Rd.)
Pinnacle Hill DA7: Bex 4H 127
Pinnacle Hill Nth. DA7: Bex 4H 127
Pinnacle Ho. *NW9* 2B 44
(off Heritage Av.)
Pinnacle Pl. HA7: Stan 4G 27
Pinnacle Way *E14* 6A 86
(off Commercial Rd.)
Pinnell Rd. SE9 4B 124
PINNER 4C 40
Pinner Ct. HA5: Pinn 4E 40
NW8 3A 4
PINNER GREEN 2A 40
Pinner Grn. HA5: Pinn 2A 40
Pinner Gro. HA5: Pinn 4C 40
Pinner Hill Farm HA5: Pinn 1K 39
Pinner Hill Rd. HA5: Pinn 1K 39
Pinner Lawn Tennis Club 2D 40
Pinner Pk. 1E 40
Pinner Pk. HA5: Pinn 2E 40
Pinner Pk. Av. HA2: Harr 3F 41
Pinner Pk. Gdns. HA2: Harr 2G 41
Pinner Rd. HA1: Harr 4E 40
HA2: Harr 4E 40
HA5: Pinn 1H 39
(High St.)
HA5: Pinn 4D 40
(Nower Hill)
HA6: Nwood 1H 39
Pinners Pas. *EC2* 7F 9
(off Austin Friars)
Pinner Vw. HA1: Harr 6G 41
HA2: Harr 4G 41
PINNERWOOD PARK 1A 40
Pinn Way HA4: Ruis 7F 39
Pintail Cl. E6 5C 88
Pintail Ct. *SE8* 6B 104
(off Pilot Cl.)
Pintail Rd. IG8: Wfd G 7E 36
Pintail Way UB4: Yead 5B 76
Pinter Ho. *SW9* 2J 119
(off Grantham Rd.)
Pinto Way SE3 4K 123
Pioneer Cl. E14 5D 86
Pioneer Ho. *WC1* 1G 7
(off Britannia St.)
Pioneer Mkt. *IG1: Ilf* 3F 71
(off Winston Way)
Pioneer Pl. CR0: Sels 7C 170
Pioneers Ind. Pk. CR0: Bedd 1J 167
Pioneer St. SE15 1G 121
Pioneer Way W12 6D 80
Piper Building, The SW6 3K 117
Piper Cl. N7 5K 65
Piper Rd. KT1: King T 3G 151
Piper's Gdns. CR0: C'don 7A 158
Pipers Grn. NW9 5J 43
Pipers Grn. La. HA8: Edg 3K 27
(not continuous)
Pipers Ho. *SE10* 5F 105
(off Collington St.)
Piper Way IG1: Ilf 1H 71
Pipewell Rd. SM5: Cars 6C 154
Pippenhall SE9 6F 125
Pippin Cl. CR0: C'don 1B 170
NW2 3C 62
Pippin Ho. *W10* 7F 81
(off Freston Rd.)
Pippins Cl. UB7: W Dray 3A 92
Pippins Ct. TW15: Ashf 6D 128
Piquet Rd. SE20 2J 157
Pirbright Cres. CR0: New Ad 6E 170
Pirbright Rd. SW18 1H 135
Pirie Cl. SE5 3D 120
Pirie St. E16 1K 105
Pitcairn Cl. RM7: Mawney 4G 55
Pitcairn Ho. E9 7J 67
Pitcairn Rd. CR4: Mitc 7D 136
Pitcairn's Path HA2: Harr 3G 59
Pitchford St. E15 7F 69
Pitfield Cres. SE28 1A 108
Pitfield Est. N1 1G 9 (3E 84)
Pitfield St. N1 1G 9 (3E 84)
Pitfield Way EN3: Enf H 1D 24
NW10 6J 61
Pitfold Cl. SE12 6J 123
Pitfold Rd. SE12 6J 123
Pitlake CR0: C'don 2B 168
Pitman Ho. SE8 1C 122
Pitman St. SE5 7C 102
Pitmaston Ho. *SE13* 2E 122
(off Lewisham Rd.)
Pitsea Pl. E1 6K 85
Pitsea St. E1 6K 85
Pitshanger La. W5 4B 78
Pitshanger Manor Mus. 1D 96
Pitt Cres. SW19 4K 135
Pittman Gdns. IG1: Ilf 5G 71
Pitt Rd. BR6: Farnb 4G 173
CR0: C'don 5C 156
CR7: Thor H 5C 156
HA2: Harr 2G 59
Pitt's Head M. W1 5H 11 (1E 100)
Pittsmead Av.
BR2: Hayes 7J 159
Pitt St. W8 2J 99
Pittville Gdns. SE25 3G 157
Pixfield Ct. *BR2: Brom* 2H 159
(off Beckenham La.)
Pixley St. E14 6B 86
Pixton Way CR0: Sels 7A 170
Place, The 2D 6
(off Flaxman Ter.)
Place Farm Av. BR6: Orp 1H 173
Plaisterers Highwalk *EC2* 6C 8
(off Noble St.)
PLAISTOW
BR1 7J 141
E13 2K 87
Plaistow Gro. BR1: Brom 7K 141
E15 1H 87
Plaistow La. BR1: Brom 7J 141
(not continuous)
Plaistow Pk. Rd. E13 2K 87
Plaistow Rd. E15 1H 87
Plaistow Wharf E16 2J 105
Plane Ho. BR2: Brom 2G 159
Plane St. SE26 3H 139
Planetarium
Greenwich 7F 105
Planetree Ct. *W6* 4F 99
(off Brook Grn.)
Plane Tree Cres. TW13: Felt 3K 129
Plane Tree Ho. *SE8* 6A 104
(off Etta St.)
W8 2H 99
(off Duchess of Bedford's Wlk.)
Plane Tree Wlk. N2 3C 46
SE19 6E 138
Plantagenet Cl. KT4: Wor Pk 4K 163
Plantagenet Gdns. RM6: Chad H 7D 54
Plantagenet Ho. *SE18* 3D 106
(off Leda Rd.)
Plantagenet Pl. RM6: Chad H 7D 54
Plantagenet Rd. EN5: New Bar 4F 21
Plantain Gdns. *E11* 3F 69
(off Hollydown Way, not continuous)
Plantain Pl. SE1 6E 14 (2D 102)
Plantation, The SE3 2J 123
Plantation Cl. SW4 5J 119
Plantation La. EC3 2G 15
Plantation Pl. EC3 2G 15
Plantation Wharf SW11 3A 118
Plasel Ct. *E13* 1K 87
(off Pawsey Cl.)
PLASHET 6C 70
Plashet Gro. E6 1A 88
Plashet Rd. E13 1J 87
Plassy Rd. SE6 7D 122
Plate Ho. *E14* 5D 104
(off Burrells Wharf Sq.)
Platina St. EC2 3F 9
Plato Rd. SW2 4J 119
Platt, The SW15 3F 117
Platt Halls NW9 2B 44
Platt's La. NW3 4J 63
Platts Rd. EN3: Enf H 1D 24
Platt St. NW1 2H 83
Plawsfield Rd. BR3: Beck 1K 157
Plaxtol Cl. BR1: Brom 1A 160
Plaxtol Rd. DA8: Erith 7G 109
Plaxton Ct. E11 3H 69
Playfair Ho. *E14* 6C 86
(off Saracen St.)
Playfair Mans. *W14* 6G 99
(off Queen's Club Gdns.)
Playfair St. W6 5E 98
Playfield Av. RM5: Col R 1J 55
Playfield Cres. SE22 5F 121
Playfield Rd. HA8: Edg 2J 43
Playford Rd. N4 2K 65
(not continuous)
Playgreen Way SE6 3C 140
Playground Cl. BR3: Beck 2K 157
Playhouse, The 7H 147
(off Hurst Gro.)
Playhouse Ct. *SE1* 6C 14
(off Southwark Bri. Rd.)
Playhouse Theatre 4F 13
(off Northumberland Av.)
Playhouse Yd. EC4 1A 14 (6B 84)
Playscape Pro Racing Karting Track
5H 137
Plaza Bus. Cen. EN3: Brim 2G 25
Plaza Hgts. E10 3E 68
Plaza Pde. NW6 2K 81
Plaza Shop. Cen., The
W1 7B 6 (6G 83)
Plaza Wlk. NW9 3J 43
Pleasance, The SW15 4D 116
Pleasance Rd. SW15 5D 116
Pleasance Theatre 6J 65
(off Carpenters M.)
Pleasant Gro. CR0: C'don 3B 170
Pleasant Pl. HA2: Harr 2H 59
N1 7B 66
Pleasant Row NW1 1F 83
Pleasant Vw. Pl. BR6: Farnb 5F 173
Pleasant Way HA0: Wemb 2C 78
Plender Ct. *NW1* 1G 83
(off College Pl.)
Plender Pl. *NW1* 1G 83
(off Plender St.)
Plender St. NW1 1G 83
Pleshey Rd. N7 4H 65
Plesman Way SM6: Wall 7J 167
Plessey Bldg. *E14* 6C 86
(off Dod St.)
Plevna Cres. N15 6E 48
Plevna Rd. N9 3B 34
TW12: Hamp 1F 149
Plevna St. E14 3E 104
Pleydell Av. SE19 7F 139
W6 4B 98
Pleydell Ct. *EC4* 1K 13
(off Lombard La.)
Pleydell Est. EC1 2D 8
Pleydell Gdns. *SE19* 6F 139
(off Anerley Hill)
Pleydell St. EC4 1K 13
Plimsoll Cl. E14 6D 86
Plimsoll Rd. N4 3A 66
Plough Ct. EC3 2F 15 (7D 84)

Plough Farm Cl. HA4: Ruis 6F **39**
Plough La. CR8: Purl 7J **167**
SE22 6F **121**
SM6: Bedd 4J **167**
SW17 5K **135**
SW19 5K **135**
TW11: Tedd 5A **132**
Plough La. Cl. SM6: Bedd 5J **167**
Ploughmans Cl. NW1 1H **83**
Ploughmans End TW7: Isle 5H **113**
Ploughmans Wlk. *N2* *2A* ***46***
(off Long La.)
Plough M. SW11 4B **118**
Plough Pl. EC4 7K **7** (6A **84**)
Plough Rd. KT19: Ewe 7K **163**
SW11 3B **118**
Plough St. E1 7K **9** (6F **85**)
Plough Ter. SW11 4B **118**
Plough Way SE16 4K **103**
Plough Yd. EC2 4H **9** (4E **84**)
Plover Ho. *SW9* *7A* ***102***
(off Brixton Rd.)
Plover Way SE16 3A **104**
UB4: Yead 6B **76**
Plowden Bldgs. EC4 2J **13**
Plowman Cl. N18 5J **33**
Plowman Way RM8: Dag 1C **72**
Plumber's Row E1 5G **85**
Plumbridge St. SE10 1E **122**
Plum Cl. TW13: Felt 1J **129**
Plume Ho. *SE10* *6D* ***104***
(off Creek Rd.)
Plum Gth. TW8: Bford 4D **96**
Plum La. SE18 7F **107**
Plummer La. CR4: Mitc 2D **154**
Plummer Rd. SW4 7H **119**
Plumpton Cl. UB5: N'olt 6E **58**
Plumpton Way SM5: Cars 3C **166**
PLUMSTEAD 4J **107**
PLUMSTEAD COMMON 6G **107**
Plumstead Comn. Rd. SE18 6F **107**
Plumstead High St. SE18 4H **107**
Plumstead Leisure Cen. 5K **107**
Plumstead Rd. SE18 4F **107**
Plumtree Cl. RM10: Dag 6H **73**
SM6: Wall 7H **167**
Plumtree Ct. EC4 7A **8** (6B **84**)
Plymen Ho. KT8: W Mole 5E **148**
Plymouth Ct. *KT5: Surb* *4E* ***150***
(off Cranes Pk. Av.)
Plymouth Ho. *IG11: Bark* *7A* ***72***
(off Keir Hardie Way)
SE10 *1D* ***122***
(off Devonshire Dr.)
Plymouth Rd. BR1: Brom 1K **159**
E16 5J **87**
Plymouth Wharf E14 4F **105**
Plympton Av. NW6 7H **63**
Plympton Cl. DA17: Belv 3E **108**
Plympton Pl. NW8 4C **4** (4C **82**)
Plympton Rd. NW6 7H **63**
Plympton St. NW8 4C **4** (4C **82**)
Plymstock Rd. DA16: Well 7C **108**
Pocklington Cl. NW9 2A **44**
W12 *3C* ***98***
(off Ashchurch Pk. Vs.)
Pocklington Ct. SW15 1C **134**
Pocklington Lodge W12 3C **98**
Pocock Av. UB7: W Dray 3B **92**
Pocock St. SE1 6A **14** (2B **102**)
Podmore Rd. SW18 4A **118**
Poets Ct. W3 1J **97**
Poet's Rd. N5 5D **66**
Poets Way HA1: Harr 4J **41**
Point, The *E17* *4C* ***50***
(off Tower M.)
HA4: Ruis 4J **57**
W2 6A **4**
Pointalls Cl. N3 2A **46**
Point Cl. SE10 1E **122**
Pointer Cl. SE28 6D **90**
Pointers Cl. E14 5D **104**
Pointers Cotts. TW10: Ham 2C **132**
Point Hill SE10 7E **104**
Point Pl. HA9: Wemb 7H **61**
Point Pleasant SW18 4J **117**
Point Ter. *E7* *5K* ***69***
(off Claremont Rd.)
Point West SW7 4K **99**
Point Wharf TW8: Bford 7E **96**
Point Wharf La. TW8: Bford 7D **96**
Poland St. W1 1B **12** (6G **83**)
Polar Pk. UB7: Harm 7B **92**
Polebrook Rd. SE3 3A **124**
Pole Cat All. BR2: Hayes 2H **171**
Polecroft La. SE6 2B **140**
Polehamptons, The
TW12: Hamp 7G **131**
Pole Hill Rd. E4 7K **25**
UB10: Hil 4D **74**
Polesden Gdns. SW20 2D **152**
Polesworth Ho. *W2* *5J* ***81***
(off Alfred Rd.)
Polesworth Rd. RM9: Dag 7D **72**
Police Sta. La. WD23: Bush 1A **26**
POLISH WAR MEMORIAL **7A 58**
Polka Theatre for Children 6K **135**
Pollard Cl. E16 7J **87**
N7 4K **65**
Pollard Ho. KT4: Wor Pk 4E **164**
N1 *1G* ***7***
(off Northdown St.)
Pollard Rd. N20 2H **31**
SM4: Mord 5B **154**
Pollard Row E2 3G **85**
Pollards Cres. SW16 3J **155**
Pollards Hill E. SW16 3K **155**
Pollards Hill Nth. SW16 3J **155**
Pollards Hill Sth. SW16 3J **155**
Pollards Hill W. SW16 3K **155**
Pollard St. E2 3G **85**
Pollards Wood Rd. SW16 3J **155**
Pollard Wlk. DA14: Sidc 6C **144**
Pollen St. W1 1A **12** (6G **83**)
Pollitt Dr. NW8 3B **4** (4B **82**)
Pollock Ho. *W10* *4G* ***81***
(off Kensal Rd.)
Pollock's Toy Mus. 5B **6** (5G **83**)
Polperro Cl. BR6: St M Cry 6K **161**
Polperro Ho. *W2* *5J* ***81***
(off Westbourne Pk. Rd.)
Polperro M. SE11 3K **19** (4B **102**)
Polsted Rd. SE6 7B **122**
Polthorne Est. *SE18* *4H* ***107***
(off Polthorne Gro.)
Polthorne Gro. SE18 4G **107**
Polworth Rd. SW16 5J **137**
Polychrome Ct. *SE1* *7A* ***14***
(off Waterloo Rd.)
Polygon, The *NW8* *1B* ***82***
(off Avenue Rd.)
SW4 4G **119**
Polygon Bus. Cen. SL3: Poyle 5A **174**
Polygon Rd. NW1 1C **6** (2H **83**)
Polytechnic St. SE18 4E **106**
Pomell Way E1 7K **9** (6F **85**)
Pomeroy Cl. TW1: Twick 4B **114**
Pomeroy Ho. *E2* *2K* ***85***
(off St James's Av.)
W11 *6G* ***81***
(off Lancaster Rd.)
Pomeroy St. SE14 7J **103**
Pomfret Rd. SE5 3B **120**
Pomoja La. N19 2J **65**
Pomona Ho. *SE8* *4A* ***104***
(off Evelyn St.)
Pond Cl. N12 6H **31**
SE3 2J **123**
Pond Cott. La. BR4: W W'ck 1C **170**
Pond Cotts. SE21 1E **138**
PONDERS END 5D **24**
Ponders End Ind. Est.
EN3: Pond E 5F **25**
Ponder St. N7 7K **65**
Pond Farm Est. E5 3J **67**
Pondfield Ho. SE27 5C **138**
Pondfield Rd. BR2: Hayes 1G **171**
BR6: Farnb 3F **173**
RM10: Dag 5H **73**
Pond Grn. HA4: Ruis 2G **57**
Pond Hill Gdns. SM3: Cheam 6G **165**
Pond Ho. HA7: Stan 6G **27**
SW3 4C **16** (4C **100**)
Pond Lees Cl. RM10: Dag 7K **73**
Pond Mead SE21 6D **120**
Pond Path BR7: Chst 6F **143**
Pond Pl. SW3 4C **16** (4C **100**)
Pond Rd. E15 2G **87**
SE3 2H **123**
Pondside Cl. UB3: Harl 6F **93**
Pond Sq. N6 1E **64**
Pond St. NW3 5C **64**
Pond Way TW11: Tedd 6C **132**
Pondwood Ri. BR6: Orp 7J **161**
Ponler St. E1 6H **85**
Ponsard Rd. NW10 3D **80**
Ponsford St. E9 6J **67**
Ponsonby Ho. *E2* *2J* ***85***
(off Bishop's Way, not continuous)
Ponsonby Pl. SW1 5D **18** (5H **101**)
Ponsonby Rd. SW15 7D **116**
Ponsonby Ter. SW1 5D **18** (5H **101**)
Pontefract Ct. *UB5: N'olt* *5F* ***59***
(off Newmarket Av.)
Pontefract Rd. BR1: Brom 5H **141**
Ponton Rd. SW8 7D **18** (7H **101**)
Pont St. SW1 2E **16** (3D **100**)
Pont St. M. SW1 2E **16** (3D **100**)
Pontypool Pl. SE1 6A **14** (2B **102**)
Pooja Ct. *NW1* *7G* ***65***
(off Agar Gro.)
Pool Cl. BR3: Beck 5C **140**
KT8: W Mole 5D **148**
Pool Ct. SE6 2C **140**
Poole Cl. HA4: Ruis 2G **57**
Poole Ct. *N1* *7E* ***66***
(off St Peter's Way)
TW4: Houn 2C **112**
Poole Ct. Rd. TW4: Houn 2C **112**
Poole Ho. SE11 2H **19**
POOL END 5C **146**
Pool End Cl. TW17: Shep 5C **146**
Poole Rd. E9 6K **67**
KT19: Ewe 6K **163**
Pooles Bldgs. WC1 4J **7**
Pooles Cotts. TW10: Ham 2D **132**
Pooles La. SW10 7A **100**
Pooles Pk. N4 2A **66**
Poole St. N1 1D **84**
Poole Way UB4: Hayes 3G **75**
Pooley Dr. SW14 3J **115**
Pooley Ho. E1 3K **85**
Pool Ho. *NW8* *5C* ***4***
(off Penfold St.)
Poolmans St. SE16 2K **103**
Pool Rd. HA1: Harr 7H **41**
KT8: W Mole 5D **148**
Poolsford Rd. NW9 4A **44**
Pools on the Pk. 4D **114**
Poonah St. E1 6J **85**
Pope Cl. SW19 6B **136**
TW14: Felt 1H **129**
Pope Ho. *SE5* *7D* ***102***
(off Elmington Est.)
SE16 *4H* ***103***
(off Manor Est.)
Pope Rd. BR2: Brom 5B **160**
Popes Av. TW2: Twick 2J **131**
Popes Ct. TW2: Twick 2J **131**
Popes Dr. N3 1J **45**
Popes Gro. CR0: C'don 3B **170**
TW1: Twick 2K **131**
TW2: Twick 2K **131**
Pope's Head All. EC3 1F **15** (6D **84**)
Popes La. W5 3D **96**
Pope's Rd. SW9 3A **120**
Pope St. SE1 7H **15** (2E **102**)
Popham Cl. TW13: Hanw 3D **130**
Popham Gdns. TW9: Rich 3G **115**
Popham Rd. N1 1C **84**
Popham St. N1 1B **84**
(not continuous)
Pop-in Commercial Cen.
HA9: Wemb 5H **61**
Popinjays Row *SM3: Cheam* *5F* ***165***
(off Netley Cl.)
POPLAR 7D **86**
Poplar Av. BR6: Farnb 2F **173**
CR4: Mitc 1D **154**
UB2: S'hall 3F **95**
UB7: Yiew 7B **74**
Poplar Bath St. E14 6D **86**
Poplar Bus. Pk. E14 7E **86**
Poplar Cl. E9 5B **68**
HA5: Pinn 1B **40**
SL3: Poyle 4A **174**
Poplar Ct. SW19 5J **135**
TW1: Twick 6C **114**
UB5: N'olt 2A **76**
Poplar Cres. KT19: Ewe 6J **163**
Poplar Farm Cl. KT19: Ewe 6J **163**
Poplar Gdns. KT3: N Mald 2K **151**
SE28 7C **90**
Poplar Gro. HA9: Wemb 3J **61**
KT3: N Mald 2K **151**
N11 6K **31**
W6 2E **98**
Poplar High St. E14 7D **86**
Poplar Ho. *SE4* *4B* ***122***
(off Wickham Rd.)
SE16 *2K* ***103***
(off Woodland Cres.)
Poplar M. W12 1E **98**
Poplar Mt. DA17: Belv 4H **109**
Poplar Pl. SE28 7C **90**
UB3: Hayes 7J **75**
W2 7K **81**
Poplar Rd. E12 2C **70**
SE24 4C **120**
SM3: Sutt 1H **165**
SW19 2J **153**
TW15: Ashf 5E **128**
Poplar Rd. Sth. SW19 3J **153**
Poplars, The N14 5A **22**
Poplars Av. NW2 6E **62**
Poplars Cl. HA4: Ruis 1G **57**
Poplars Rd. E17 6D **50**
Poplar St. RM7: Rom 4J **55**
Poplar Vw. HA9: Wemb 2D **60**
Poplar Wlk. CR0: C'don 2C **168**
SE24 3C **120**
(not continuous)
Poplar Way IG6: Ilf 4G **53**
TW13: Felt 3J **129**
Poppins Ct. EC4 1A **14** (6B **84**)
Poppleton Rd. E11 6G **51**
Poppy Cl. DA17: Belv 3H **109**
EN5: New Bar 6F **21**
SM6: Wall 1E **166**
UB5: N'olt 6D **58**
Poppy La. CR0: C'don 7J **157**
Porchester Cl. SE5 4C **120**
Porchester Ct. *W2* *7K* ***81***
(off Porchester Gdns.)
Porchester Gdns. W2 7K **81**
Porchester Gdns. M. W2 6K **81**
Porchester Ga. *W2* *7K* ***81***
(off Bayswater Rd.)
Porchester Ho. *E1* *6H* ***85***
(off Philpot St.)

Porchester Leisure Cen. 6K 81
Porchester Mead
BR3: Beck 6D 140
Porchester M. W2 6K 81
Porchester Pl. W2 1D 10 (6C 82)
Porchester Rd.
KT1: King T 2H 151
W2 6K 81
Porchester Sq. W2 6K 81
Porchester Ter. W2 7A 82
Porchester Ter. Nth.
W2 6K 81
Porchester Wlk. *W2* *6K 81*
(off Porchester Ter. Nth.)
Porch Way N20 3J 31
Porcupine Cl. SE9 2C 142
Porden Rd. SW2 4K 119
Porlock Av. HA2: Harr 1G 59
Porlock Ho. SE26 3G 139
Porlock Rd. EN1: Enf 7A 24
Porlock St. SE1 6F 15 (2D 102)
Porrington Cl.
BR7: Chst 1D 160
Porson Ct. SE13 3D 122
Portal Cl. HA4: Ruis 4J 57
(not continuous)
SE27 3A 138
UB10: Uxb 7A 56
Portal Way W3 5K 79
Portbury Cl. SE15 1G 121
Port Cres. E13 4K 87
Portcullis Ho. SW1 7E 12
Portcullis Lodge Rd. EN1: Enf 3J 23
Port E. Apartments *E14* *7C 86*
(off Hertsmere Rd.)
Portelet Ct. *N1* *1E 84*
(off De Beauvoir Est.)
Portelet Rd. E1 3K 85
Porten Ho's. *W14* *3G 99*
(off Porten Rd.)
Porten Rd. W14 3G 99
Porter Rd. E6 6D 88
Porters & Walters Almshouses
N22 *7E 32*
(off Nightingale Rd.)
Porters Av. RM8: Dag 6B 72
RM9: Dag 6B 72
Porters Lodge, The *SW10* *7A 100*
(off Coleridge Gdns.)
Porter Sq. N19 1J 65
Porter St. SE1 4D 14 (1C 102)
W1 5F 5 (5D 82)
Porters Wlk. *E1* *7H 85*
(off Balkan Wlk.)
Porters Way N12 6H 31
UB7: W Dray 3B 92
Porteus Rd. W2 5A 4 (5A 82)
Portgate Cl. W9 4H 81
Porthallow Cl. BR6: Chels 4K 173
Porthcawe Rd.
SE26 4A 140
Porthkerry Av. DA16: Well 4A 126
Port Ho. *E14* *5D 104*
(off Burrells Wharf Sq.)
Portia Ct. IG11: Bark 7A 72
SE11 *5B 102*
(off Opal St.)
Portia Way E3 4B 86
Porticos, The SW3 7A 16
Portinscale Rd. SW15 5G 117
Portishead Ho. *W2* *5J 81*
(off Westbourne Pk. Rd.)
Portland Av. DA15: Sidc 6A 126
KT3: N Mald 7B 152
N16 7F 49
Portland Cl. KT4: Wor Pk 7D 152
RM6: Chad H 5E 54
Portland Commercial Est.
IG11: Bark 2C 90
Portland Cotts. CR0: Bedd 7H 155
Portland Ct. *N1* *7E 66*
(off St Peter's Way)
SE1 *7E 14*
(off Gt. Dover St.)
SE14 *6A 104*
(off Whitcher Cl.)
Portland Cres. HA7: Stan 2D 42
SE9 2C 142
TW13: Felt 4F 129
UB6: G'frd 4F 77
Portland Dr. EN2: Enf 1K 23
Portland Gdns. N4 6B 48
RM6: Chad H 5D 54
Portland Gro. SW8 1K 119
Portland Ho. SW1 1A 18
Portland Mans. *W14* *4H 99*
(off Addison Bri. Pl.)
Portland M. W1 1B 12 (6G 83)
Portland Pl. *SE25* *4G 157*
(off Sth. Norwood Hill)
W1 4J 5 (5F 83)
Portland Ri. N4 1B 66
(not continuous)
Portland Rd. BR1: Brom 4A 142
CR4: Mitc 2C 154
KT1: King T 3E 150
N15 4F 49
SE9 2C 142
SE25 4G 157
TW15: Ashf 3A 128
UB2: S'hall 3D 94
UB4: Hayes 3G 75
W11 7G 81
Portland Sq. E1 1H 103
Portland St. SE17 5D 102
Portland Ter. HA8: Edg 7B 28
TW9: Rich 4D 114
Portland Wlk. SE17 6D 102
Portman Av. SW14 3K 115
Portman Cl. DA5: Bexl 1K 145
DA7: Bex 3E 126
W1 7F 5 (6D 82)
Portman Dr. IG8: Wfd G 2B 52
Portman Gdns. NW9 2K 43
UB10: Hil 7C 56
Portman Ga. NW1 4D 4 (4C 82)
Portman Mans. *W1* *5F 5*
(off Chiltern St.)
Portman M. Sth. W1 1G 11 (6E 82)
Portman Pl. E2 3J 85
Portman Rd. KT1: King T 2F 151
Portman Sq. W1 7G 5 (6E 82)
Portman St. W1 1G 11 (6E 82)
Portman Towers W1 7F 5 (6D 82)
Portmeadow Wlk. SE2 2D 108
Port Meers Cl. E17 6B 50
Portnall Ho. *W9* *3H 81*
(off Portnall Rd.)
Portnall Rd. W9 2H 81
Portnoi Cl. RM1: Rom 2K 55
Portobello Ct. Est. W11 6H 81
Portobello M. W11 7J 81
Portobello Rd. W10 5G 81
W11 6H 81
Portobello Road Market *7H 81*
(off Portobello Rd.)
Porton Ct. KT6: Surb 6C 150
Portpool La. EC1 5J 7 (5A 84)
Portree Cl. N22 7E 32
Portree St. E14 6F 87
Portrush Ct. *UB1: S'hall* *6G 77*
(off Whitecote Rd.)
Portsdown HA8: Edg 5B 28
Portsdown Av. NW11 6H 45
Portsdown M. NW11 6H 45
Portsea Hall *W2* *1D 10*
(off Portsea Pl.)
Portsea M. W2 1D 10
Portsea Pl. W2 1D 10 (6C 82)
Portslade Rd. SW8 2G 119
Portsmouth Av. KT7: T Ditt 7A 150
Portsmouth M. E16 1K 105
Portsmouth Rd.
KT1: King T 7A 150
KT6: Surb 7A 150
KT7: T Ditt 7A 150
KT10: Esh 1A 162
SW15 7D 116
Portsmouth St. WC2 1G 13 (6K 83)
Portsoken St. E1 2J 15 (7F 85)
Portswood Pl. SW15 6B 116
Portugal Gdns. TW2: Twick 2G 131
Portugal St. WC2 1G 13 (6K 83)
Portway E15 1H 87
Portway Gdns. SE18 7B 106
Pory Ho. SE11 4H 19
Poseidon Ct. *E14* *4C 104*
(off Homer Dr.)
Postern, The EC2 6D 8
Postern Grn. EN2: Enf 2F 23
Post La. TW2: Twick 1H 131
Postmasters Lodge
HA5: Pinn 7C 40
Postmill Cl. CR0: C'don 3J 169
Post Office All. *W4* *6H 97*
(off Thames Rd.)
Post Office App. E7 5K 69
Post Office Ct. *EC3* *1F 15*
(off Barbican)
Post Office Way SW8 7H 101
Post Rd. UB2: S'hall 3F 95
Postway M. IG1: Ilf 3F 71
(not continuous)
Potier St. SE1 3D 102
Potter Cl. CR4: Mitc 2F 155
SE15 7E 102
Potteries, The EN5: Barn 5D 20
Potterne Cl. SW19 7F 117
Potters Cl. CR0: C'don 1A 170
Potters Ct. *SM1: Sutt* *6H 165*
(off Rosebery Rd.)
Potters Fld. *EN1: Enf* *4K 23*
(off Lincoln Rd.)
Potters Flds. SE1 5H 15 (1E 102)
Potters Gro. KT3: N Mald 4J 151
Potters Hgts. Cl. HA5: Pinn 1K 39
Potters La. EN5: New Bar 4D 20
SW16 6H 137
Potters Lodge *E14* *5E 104*
(off Manchester Rd.)
Potters Rd. EN5: New Bar 4E 20
SW6 2A 118
Potter St. HA5: Pinn 1K 39
HA6: Nwood 1J 39
Potter St. Hill HA5: Pinn 1K 39
Pottery La. W11 1G 99
Pottery Rd. DA5: Bexl 2J 145
TW8: Bford 6E 96
Pottery St. SE16 2H 103
Pott St. E2 3H 85
Poulett Gdns. TW1: Twick 1A 132
Poulett Rd. E6 2D 88
Poulters Wood BR2: Kes 5B 172
Poulton Av. SM1: Sutt 3B 166
Poulton Cl. E8 6H 67
Poulton Ho. *W3* *5K 79*
(off Victoria Rd.)
Poultry EC2 1E 14 (6D 84)
Pound Cl. BR6: Orp 2H 173
KT6: Surb 1C 162
Pound Ct. Dr. BR6: Orp 2H 173
Pound Farm Cl. KT10: Esh 7G 149
Pound Grn. DA5: Bexl 7G 127
Pound La. NW10 6C 62
Pound Pk. Rd. SE7 4B 106
Pound Pl. SE9 6E 124
Pound St. SM5: Cars 5D 166
Pound Way BR7: Chst 7G 143
Pountney Rd. SW11 3E 118
POVEREST 4K 161
Poverest Rd. BR5: St M Cry 5K 161
Povey Ho. *SE17* *4E 102*
(off Beckway St.)
Powder Mill La. TW2: Whitt 7D 112
Powell Cl. HA8: Edg 6A 28
KT9: Chess 5D 162
SM6: Wall 7J 167
Powell Ct. *CR2: S Croy* *4B 168*
(off Bramley Hill)
E17 3D 50
Powell Gdns. RM10: Dag 4G 73
Powell Ho. *W2* *7B 82*
(off Gloucester Ter.)
Powell Rd. E5 3H 67
IG9: Buck H 1F 37
Powell's Wlk. W4 6A 98
Powergate Bus. Pk. NW10 3K 79
Powerleague Soccer Cen.
Barking 3G 89
Catford 1C 140
Colney Hatch 7K 31
Fairlop 1K 53
Mill Hill 7J 29
Norbury 1J 155
Purley 6K 167
Tottenham 6C 34
Power Rd. W4 4G 97
Powers Ct. TW1: Twick 7D 114
Powerscroft Rd. DA14: Sidc 6C 144
(not continuous)
E5 4J 67
Powis Ct. *W11* *6H 81*
(off Powis Gdns.)
WD23: B Hea *1C 26*
(off Rutherford Way)
Powis Gdns. NW11 7H 45
W11 6H 81
Powis Ho. *WC2* *7F 7*
(off Macklin St.)
Powis M. W11 6H 81
Powis Pl. WC1 4F 7 (4J 83)
Powis Rd. E3 3D 86
Powis Sq. W11 6H 81
(not continuous)
Powis St. SE18 3E 106
Powis Ter. W11 6H 81
Powlesland Ct. *E1* *6A 86*
(off White Horse Rd.)
Powlett Ho. *NW1* *6F 65*
(off Powlett Pl.)
Powlett Pl. NW1 7E 64
Pownall Gdns. TW3: Houn 4F 113
Pownall Rd. E8 1F 85
TW3: Houn 4F 113
Pownsett Ter. IG1: Ilf 5G 71
Powster Rd. BR1: Brom 5J 141
Powys Cl. DA7: Bex 6D 108
Powys Ct. N11 5D 32
Powys La. N13 4D 32
N14 4D 32
POYLE 5A 174
Poyle Ind. Est. SL3: Poyle 6A 174
Poyle New Cotts. SL3: Poyle 5A 174
Poyle Technical Cen.
SL3: Poyle 5A 174
Poyle Trad. Est. SL3: Poyle 6A 174
Poynders Ct. SW4 6G 119
Poynders Gdns. SW4 7G 119
Poynders Rd. SW4 6G 119
Poynings, The SL0: Rich P 1A 174
Poynings Rd. N19 3G 65
Poynings Way N12 5D 30
Poyntell Cres. BR7: Chst 1H 161
Poynter Ct. *UB5: N'olt* *2B 76*
(off Gallery Gdns.)
Poynter Ho. *NW8* *3A 4*
(off Fisherton St.)
W11 *1F 99*
(off Queensdale Cres.)
Poynter Rd. EN1: Enf 5A 24

Poynton Rd. N17 2G 49
Poyntz Rd. SW11 2D 118
Poyser St. E2 2H 85
Praed M. W2 7B 4 (6B 82)
Praed St. W2 1A 10 (6B 82)
Pragel St. E13 2A 88
Pragnell Rd. SE12 2K 141
Prague Pl. SW2 5J 119
Prah Rd. N4 2A 66
Prairie St. SW8 2E 118
Pratt M. NW1 1G 83
Pratts Pas. KT1: King T 2E 150
Pratt St. NW1 1G 83
Pratt Wlk. SE11 3H 19 (4K 101)
Prayle Gro. NW2 1F 63
Preachers Ct. *EC1* *5B 8*
(off Charterhouse Sq.)
Prebend Gdns. W4 4B 98
W6 4B 98
(not continuous)
Prebend Mans. *W4* *4B 98*
(off Chiswick High Rd.)
Prebend St. N1 1C 84
Precinct, The N1 1C 84
Precinct Rd. UB3: Hayes 7J 75
Precincts, The
SM4: Mord 6J 153
Premier Cinema 2G 121
Premier Cnr. W9 2H 81
Premier Ct. EN3: Enf W 1D 24
Premiere Pl. E14 7C 86
Premier Ho. *N1* *7B 66*
(off Waterloo Ter.)
Premier Pk. NW10 1H 79
(not continuous)
Premier Pk. Rd. NW10 2H 79
Premier Pl. SW15 4G 117
Prendergast Rd. SE3 3G 123
Prentice Ct. SW19 5H 135
Prentis Rd. SW16 4H 137
Prentiss Ct. SE7 4B 106
Presburg Rd.
KT3: N Mald 5A 152
Presburg St. E5 3K 67
Prescelly Pl. HA8: Edg 1F 43
Prescot St. E1 2K 15 (7F 85)
Prescott Av. BR5: Pet W 6F 161
Prescott Cl. SW16 7J 137
Prescott Ho. *SE17* *6B 102*
(off Hillingdon St.)
Prescott Pl. SW4 3H 119
Presentation M. SW2 2K 137
Preshaw Cres.
CR4: Mitc 3C 154
President Dr. E1 1H 103
President Ho. EC1 2B 8 (3B 84)
President Quay E1 4K 15
President St. EC1 1C 8
Prespa Cl. N9 2D 34
Press Ct. SE1 5G 103
Press Ho. NW10 3K 61
Press Rd. NW10 3K 61
Prestage Way E14 7E 86
Prestbury Rd. E7 7A 70
Prestbury Sq. SE9 4D 142
Prested Rd. SW11 4C 118
Prestige Way NW4 5E 44
PRESTON 1E 60
Preston Av. E4 6A 36
Preston Cl. SE1 4E 102
TW2: Twick 3J 131
Preston Ct. *DA14: Sidc* *4K 143*
(off The Crescent)
EN5: New Bar 4F 21
Preston Dr. DA7: Bex 1D 126
E11 5A 52
KT19: Ewe 6A 164
Preston Gdns. IG1: Ilf 6C 52
NW10 6B 62
Preston Hill HA3: Kent 7E 42
Preston Ho. *RM10: Dag* *3G 73*
(off Uvedale Rd.)
SE1 *4E 102*
(off Preston Cl.)
SE1 *7J 15*
(off St Saviour's Est.)
Preston Pl. NW2 6C 62
TW10: Rich 5E 114
Preston Rd. E11 6G 51
HA3: Kent 1E 60
HA9: Kent, Wemb 1E 60
SE19 6B 138
SW20 7B 134
TW17: Shep 5C 146
Prestons Rd. BR2: Hayes 3J 171
E14 7E 86
Preston St. E2 2K 85
Preston Waye HA3: Kent 1E 60
Prestwich Ter. SW4 5G 119
Prestwick Cl. UB2: S'hall 5C 94
Prestwick Ct. *UB1: S'hall* *7G 77*
(off Baird Av.)
Prestwood Av. HA3: Kent 4B 42
Prestwood Cl. HA3: Kent 4B 42
SE18 6A 108
Prestwood Gdns. CR0: C'don 7C 156
Prestwood Ho. *SE16* *3H 103*
(off Drummond Rd.)
Prestwood St. N1 1D 8 (2C 84)
Pretoria Av. E17 4A 50
Pretoria Cres. E4 1K 35
Pretoria Rd. E4 1K 35
E11 1F 69
E16 4H 87
IG1: Ilf 5F 71
N17 7A 34
RM7: Rom 4J 55
SW16 6F 137
Pretoria Rd. Nth. N18 6A 34
Prevost Rd. N11 2K 31
Priam Ho. *E2* *2H 85*
(off Old Bethnal Grn. Rd.)
Price Cl. NW7 6B 30
SW17 3D 136
Price Ho. *N1* *1C 84*
(off Britannia Row)
Price Rd. CR0: Wadd 5B 168
Price's Ct. SW11 3B 118
Price's St. SE1 5B 14 (1B 102)
Price's Yd. N1 1K 83
Price Way TW12: Hamp 6C 130
Prichard Ct. N7 6K 65
Pricklers Hill EN5: New Bar 6E 20
Prickley Wood BR2: Hayes 1H 171
Priddy's Yd. CR0: C'don 2C 168
Prideaux Ho. *WC1* *1H 7*
(off Prideaux Pl.)
Prideaux Pl. W3 7K 79
WC1 1H 7 (3K 83)
Prideaux Rd. SW9 3J 119
Pridham Rd. CR7: Thor H 4D 156
Priestfield Rd. SE23 3A 140
Priestlands Pk. Rd.
DA15: Sidc 3K 143
Priestley Cl. N16 7F 49
Priestley Gdns. RM6: Chad H 6B 54
Priestley Ho. *EC1* *3D 8*
(off Old St.)
HA9: Wemb *3J 61*
(off Barnhill Rd.)
Priestley Rd. CR4: Mitc 2E 154
Priestley Way E17 3K 49
NW2 1C 62
Priest Pk. Av. HA2: Harr 2E 58
Priests Av. RM1: Rom 2K 55
Priest's Bri. SW14 3A 116
Priest's Ct. *EC2* *7C 8*
(off Foster La.)
Prima Rd. SW9 7A 102
Prime Meridian Line 7F 105
Primrose Av. EN2: Enf 1J 23
RM6: Chad H 7B 54
Primrose Cl. E3 2C 86
HA2: Harr 3D 58
N3 2K 45
SE6 5E 140
SM6: Wall 7F 155
Primrose Ct. SW12 7H 119
Primrose Gdns. HA4: Ruis 5A 58
NW3 6C 64
WD23: Bush 1A 26
PRIMROSE HILL 1E 82
Primrose Hill EC4 1K 13 (6A 84)
Primrose Hill Ct. NW3 7D 64
Primrose Hill Rd. NW3 7D 64
Primrose Hill Studios NW1 1E 82
Primrose La. CR0: C'don 1J 169
Primrose Mans. SW11 1E 118
Primrose M. *NW1* *7D 64*
(off Sharpleshall St.)
SE3 7J 105
Primrose Pl. TW7: Isle 2K 113
Primrose Rd. E10 1D 68
E18 2K 51
Primrose Sq. E9 7J 67
Primrose St. EC2 5G 9 (5E 84)
Primrose Wlk. KT17: Ewe 7B 164
SE14 7A 104
Primrose Way HA0: Wemb 2D 78
Primula St. W12 6C 80
Prince Albert Ct. *NW8* *1D 82*
(off Prince Albert Rd.)
TW16: Sun 7G 129
Prince Albert Rd. NW1 1C 4 (3C 82)
NW8 1C 4 (3C 82)
Prince Arthur M. NW3 4A 64
Prince Arthur Rd. NW3 5A 64
Prince Charles Cinema 2D 12
Prince Charles Dr. NW4 7E 44
Prince Charles Rd. SE3 2H 123
Prince Charles Way SM6: Wall 3F 167
Prince Consort Dr. BR7: Chst 1H 161
Prince Consort Rd. SW7 1A 16 (3A 100)
Princedale Rd. W11 1G 99
Prince Edward Mans. *W2* *7J 81*
(off Moscow Rd.)
Prince Edward Rd. E9 6B 68
Prince Edward Theatre *1D 12*
(off Old Compton St.)
Prince George Av. N14 5C 22
Prince George Rd. N16 4E 66
Prince George's Av. SW20 2E 152
Prince George's Rd. SW19 1B 154
Prince Henry Rd. SE7 7B 106
Prince Imperial Rd. BR7: Chst 1F 161
SE18 1D 124
Prince John Rd. SE9 5C 124
Princelet St. E1 5K 9 (5F 85)
Prince of Orange Ct. *SE16* *3J 103*
(off Lower Rd.)
Prince of Orange La. SE10 7E 104
Prince of Wales Cl. NW4 4D 44
Prince of Wales Dr. SW8 7F 101
SW11 1C 118
Prince of Wales Mans. SW11 1E 118
Prince of Wales Pas. NW1 2A 6
Prince of Wales Rd. E16 6A 88
NW5 6E 64
SE3 2H 123
SM1: Sutt 2B 166
Prince of Wales Ter. W4 5A 98
W8 2K 99
Prince of Wales Theatre *3C 12*
(off Coventry St.)
Prince Regent Ct. *NW8* *2C 82*
(off Avenue Rd.)
SE16 *7A 86*
(off Edward Sq.)
Prince Regent La. E13 3K 87
E16 3K 87
Prince Regent M. NW1 2A 6
Prince Regent Rd. TW3: Houn 3G 113
Prince Rd. SE25 5E 156
Prince Rupert Rd. SE9 4D 124
Princes Arc. SW1 4B 12
Princes Av. BR5: Pet W 5J 161
IG8: Wfd G 4E 36
KT6: Surb 1G 163
N3 1J 45
N10 3F 47
N13 5F 33
N22 1H 47
NW9 4G 43
SM5: Cars 7D 166
UB6: G'frd 6F 77
W3 3G 97
Princes Cir. WC2 7E 6 (6J 83)
Princes Cl. DA14: Sidc 3D 144
HA8: Edg 5B 28
N4 1B 66
NW9 4G 43
SW4 3G 119
TW11: Tedd 4H 131
Princes Ct. HA9: Wemb 5E 60
SE16 3B 104
SW3 *1E 16*
(off Brompton Rd.)
Princes Ct. Bus. Cen. E1 7H 85
Princes Dr. HA1: Harr 3J 41
Princes Gdns.
SW7 1B 16 (3B 100)
W3 5G 79
W5 4C 78
Prince's Ga. SW7 7B 10 (2B 100)
(not continuous)
Prince's Ga. Ct. SW7 7A 10 (2B 100)
Prince's Ga. M. SW7 1B 16 (3B 100)
Princes Ho. W11 7H 81
Princes La. HA4: Ruis 1G 57
N10 3F 47
Princes M. TW3: Houn 4E 112
W2 7K 81
W6 *5D 98*
(off Down Pl.)
Princes Pde. *NW11* *6G 45*
(off Golders Grn. Rd.)
Princes Pk. Av. NW11 6G 45
UB3: Hayes 7F 75
Princes Pk. Circ. UB3: Hayes 7F 75
Princes Pk. Cl. UB3: Hayes 7F 75
Princes Pk. La. UB3: Hayes 7F 75
Princes Pk. Pde. UB3: Hayes 7F 75
Princes Pl. SW1 4B 12
W11 1G 99
Prince's Plain BR2: Brom 7C 160
Prince's Ri. SE13 2E 122
Princes Riverside Rd. SE16 1K 103
Princes Rd. IG6: Ilf 4H 53
IG9: Buck H 2F 37
KT2: King T 7G 133
N18 4D 34
SE20 6K 139
SW14 3K 115
SW19 6J 135
TW9: Kew 1F 115
TW10: Rich 5F 115
TW11: Tedd 4H 131
TW13: Felt 2H 129
TW15: Ashf 5B 128
W13 1B 96
Princessa Ct. EN2: Enf 5J 23
Princess Alice Ho. W10 4E 80
Princess Alice Way SE28 2H 107
Princess Av. HA9: Wemb 2E 60
Princess Cl. SE28 6D 90
Princess Ct. *KT1: King T* *3F 151*
(off Horace Rd.)
N6 7G 47
NW6 *6K 63*
(off Compayne Gdns.)

Princess Ct. W1 6E 4
(off Bryanston Pl.)
W2 7K 81
(off Queensway)
Princess Cres. N4 2B 66
Princess Louise Cl. W2 5B 4 (5B 82)
Princess Mary Ho. SW1 3D 18
(off Vincent St.)
Princess May Rd. N16 4E 66
Princess M. KT1: King T 3F 151
NW3 5B 64
Princess of Wales Memorial Fountain 6B 10 (2B 100)
Princess Pde. BR6: Farnb 3E 172
RM10: Dag 2G 91
Princess Pk. Mnr. N11 5K 31
Princes Sq. W2 7K 81
(not continuous)
Princess Rd. CR0: C'don 6C 156
NW1 1E 82
NW6 2J 81
Princess St. SE1 3B 102
Princes St. DA7: Bex 3F 127
EC2 1E 14 (6D 84)
N17 6K 33
SM1: Sutt 4B 166
TW9: Rich 4E 114
W1 1K 11 (6F 83)
Princes Ter. E13 1K 87
Prince's Twr. SE16 2J 103
(off Elephant La.)
Prince St. SE8 6B 104
Princes Way BR4: W W'ck 4H 171
CR0: Wadd 5K 167
HA4: Ruis 4C 58
IG9: Buck H 2F 37
SW19 7F 117
W3 3G 97
Prince's Yd. W11 1G 99
Princethorpe Ho. W2 5K 81
(off Woodchester Sq.)
Princethorpe Rd. SE26 4K 139
Princeton Ct. SW15 3F 117
Princeton M. KT2: King T 1G 151
Princeton St. WC1 6G 7 (5K 83)
Prince William Ct. TW15: Ashf 5B 128
(off Princes Rd.)
Principal Cl. N14 1B 32
Principal Sq. E9 5K 67
Pringle Gdns. SW16 4G 137
(not continuous)
Printers Inn Ct. EC4 6A 84
Printers M. E3 1A 86
Printer St. EC4 7K 7 (6A 84)
Printinghouse La. UB3: Hayes 2G 93
Printing Ho. Yd. E2 1H 9 (3E 84)
Printon Ho. E14 5B 86
(off Wallwood St.)
Print Village SE15 2F 121
Printwork Apartments SE1 7G 15
(off Long La.)
Priolo Rd. SE7 5A 106
Prior Av. SM2: Sutt 7C 166
Prior Bolton St. N1 6B 66
Prioress Rd. SE27 3B 138
Prioress St. SE1 3E 102
Prior Rd. IG1: Ilf 3E 70
Priors Cft. E17 2A 50
Priors Farm La. UB5: N'olt 6C 58
Priors Fld. UB5: N'olt 6C 58
Priors Gdns. HA4: Ruis 5A 58
Priors Mead EN1: Enf 1K 23
Prior St. SE10 7E 104
Priors Wood KT10: Hin W 2A 162
Priory, The CR0: Wadd 4A 168
N8 4H 47
SE3 4H 123
Priory Apartments, The SE6 1D 140
Priory Av. BR5: Pet W 6H 161
E4 3G 35
Priory Av. E17 5C 50
HA0: Wemb 4K 59
N8 4H 47
SM3: Cheam 4F 165
W4 4A 98
Priory Cl. BR3: Beck 3A 158
BR7: Chst 1D 160
E4 3G 35
E18 1J 51
HA0: Wemb 4K 59
HA4: Ruis 1H 57
HA7: Stan 3E 26
N3 1H 45
N14 5A 22
N20 1C 30
SW19 1K 153
TW12: Hamp 1D 148
TW16: Sun 7J 129
UB3: Hayes 7K 75
Priory Ct. E6 1A 88
E9 5K 67
E17 2B 50
EC4 1B 14
(off Pilgrim St.)
HA0: Wemb 2E 78
KT1: King T 3E 150
(off Denmark Rd.)
KT17: Ewe 7B 164
SM3: Cheam 4G 165
SW8 1H 119
TW3: Houn 3F 113
WD23: Bush 1B 26
(off Sparrows Herne)
Priory Ct. Est. E17 2B 50
Priory Cres. HA0: Wemb 3A 60
SE19 7C 138
SM3: Cheam 4F 165
Priory Dr. HA7: Stan 3E 26
SE2 5D 108
Priory Fld. Dr. HA8: Edg 4C 28
Priory Gdns. HA0: Wemb 4A 60
N6 6F 47
NW10 3E 78
SE25 4F 157
SW13 3B 116
TW12: Hamp 7D 130
TW15: Ashf 5F 129
W4 4A 98
W5 3E 78
Priory Grange N2 3D 46
(off Fortis Grn.)
Priory Grn. Est. N1 2K 83
Priory Gro. EN5: Barn 5D 20
SW8 1J 119
Priory Hill HA0: Wemb 4A 60
Priory Ho. E1 5J 9
(off Folgate St.)
EC1 3A 8
(off Sans Wlk.)
SW1 5C 18
(off Rampayne St.)
Priory La. KT8: W Mole 4F 149
SW15 6A 116
TW9: Kew 7G 97
Priory Leas SE9 1C 142
Priory Lodge W4 5G 97
(off Kew Bri. Ct.)
Priory Mans. SW10 5A 100
(off Drayton Gdns.)
Priory M. SW8 1J 119
Priory Pk. SE3 3H 123
Priory Pk. Rd. HA0: Wemb 4A 60
NW6 1H 81
Priory Retail Pk. SW19 7B 136
Priory Rd. CR0: C'don 7A 156
E6 1B 88
IG11: Bark 7H 71
KT9: Chess 3E 162
N8 4G 47
NW6 1K 81
Priory Rd. SM3: Cheam 4F 165
SW19 7B 136
TW3: Houn 5G 113
TW9: Kew 6G 97
TW12: Hamp 7D 130
W4 3K 97
Priory St. E3 3D 86
Priory Ter. NW6 1K 81
TW16: Sun 7J 129
Priory Vw. WD23: B Hea 1D 26
Priory Vs. N11 6J 31
(off Colney Hatch La.)
Priory Wlk. SW10 5A 100
Priory Way HA2: Harr 4F 41
UB2: S'hall 3B 94
UB7: Harm 6A 92
Priscilla Cl. N15 5C 48
Pritchard Ho. E2 2H 85
(off Ada Pl.)
Pritchard's Rd. E2 1G 85
Priter Rd. SE16 3G 103
Priter Way SE16 3G 103
Private Rd. EN1: Enf 5J 23
Probert Rd. SW2 5A 120
Probyn Ho. SW1 3D 18
(off Page St.)
Probyn Rd. SW2 2B 138
Procter Ho. SE1 5G 103
(off Avondale Sq.)
SE5 7D 102
(off Picton St.)
Procter St. WC1 6G 7 (5K 83)
Proctor Cl. CR4: Mitc 1E 154
Proctors Cl. TW14: Felt 1J 129
Progress Bus. Pk. CR0: Wadd 2K 167
Progress Cen., The EN3: Pond E 3E 24
Progress Way CR0: Wadd 2K 167
EN1: Enf 5B 24
N22 1A 48
Project Pk. E3 4F 87
Prologis Pk. CR0: Bedd 7H 155
E16 4F 87
TW4: Houn 4A 112
Promenade, The HA8: Edg 5B 28
W4 2A 116
Promenade App. Rd. W4 7A 98
Pronto Trad. Est. UB3: Hayes 5G 75
Prospect Cl. DA17: Belv 4G 109
HA4: Ruis 7B 40
SE26 4H 139
TW3: Houn 1D 112
Prospect Cotts. SW18 4J 117
Prospect Cres. TW2: Whitt 6G 113
Prospect Hill E17 4D 50
Prospect Ho. E17 3E 50
(off Prospect Hill)
N1 2A 84
(off Donegal St.)
SE1 3B 102
(off Gaywood St.)
SW19 1B 154
(off Chapter Way)
W10 6F 81
(off Bridge Cl.)
Prospect Pl. BR2: Brom 3K 159
E1 1J 103
(not continuous)
N2 4B 46
N7 4J 65
N17 7K 33
NW2 3H 63
NW3 4A 64
RM5: Col R 2J 55
SE8 6B 104
(off Evelyn St.)
SW20 7D 134
W4 5K 97
Prospect Quay SW18 4J 117
(off Lightermans Wlk.)
Prospect Ring N2 3B 46
Prospect Rd. EN5: New Bar 4D 20
IG8: Wfd G 6F 37
KT6: Surb 6C 150
NW2 3H 63
Prospect St. SE16 3H 103
Prospect Va. SE18 4C 106
Prospect Wharf E1 7J 85
Prospero Ho. E1 7F 85
(off Portsoken St.)
Prospero Rd. N19 1H 65
Protea Cl. E16 4H 87
Protheroe Ho. N17 3F 49
Prothero Gdns. NW4 5D 44
Prothero Ho. NW10 7K 61
(off Ayres Cres.)
Prothero Rd. SW6 7G 99
Proud Ho. E1 6H 85
(off Amazon St.)
Prout Gro. NW10 4A 62
Prout Rd. E5 3H 67
Provence St. N1 2C 84
Providence Av. HA2: Harr 1E 58
Providence Cl. E9 1K 85
Providence Ct.
W1 2H 11 (7E 82)
Providence La. UB3: Harl 7F 93
Providence Pl. N1 1B 84
RM5: Col R 1F 55
Providence Rd. UB7: Yiew 1A 92
Providence Row N1 1G 7
Providence Row Cl. E2 3H 85
Providence Sq.
SE1 6K 15 (2G 103)
Providence Twr. SE16 2G 103
(off Bermondsey Wall W.)
Providence Yd. E2 1K 9
(off Ezra St.)
Provident Ind. Est. UB3: Hayes 2J 93
Provost Ct. NW3 6D 64
(off Eton Rd.)
Provost Est. N1 1E 8
Provost Rd. NW3 7D 64
Provost St. N1 1E 8 (2D 84)
Prowse Av. WD23: B Hea 1B 26
Prowse Pl. NW1 7G 65
Proyers Path HA1: Harr 7B 42
Prudence La. BR6: Farnb 4E 172
Pruden Cl. N14 2B 32
Prudent Pas. EC2 7D 8
Prusom's Island E1 1J 103
(off Cinnamon St.)
Prusom St. E1 1H 103
Pryors, The NW3 3B 64
Pucknells Cl. BR8: Swan 7J 145
Pudding La. EC3 3F 15 (7D 84)
Pudding Mill La. E15 1D 86
Puddle Dock EC4 2A 14 (7B 84)
(not continuous)
Puffin Cl. BR3: Beck 5K 157
IG11: Bark 3B 90
Pugin Ct. N1 7A 66
(off Liverpool Rd.)
Pulborough Rd. SW18 7H 117
Pulborough Way
TW4: Houn 4A 112
Pulford Rd. N15 6D 48
Pulham Av. N2 4A 46
Pulham Ho. SW8 7K 101
(off Dorset Rd.)
Pullen's Bldgs. SE17 5B 102
(off Iliffe St.)
Puller Rd. EN5: Barn 2B 20
Pulleyns Av. E6 3C 88
Pullman Ct. SW2 1J 137
Pullman Gdns. SW15 6E 116
Pullman M. SE12 3K 141
Pullman Pl. SE9 5C 124
Pulross Rd. SW9 3K 119
Pulse Apartments NW6 5K 63
(off Lymington Rd.)

Pulteney Cl. E3 .... 1B 86
TW7: Isle 3A 114
Pulteney Gdns. E18 .... 3K 51
Pulteney Rd. E18 .... 3K 51
Pulteney Ter. N1 .... 1K 83
(not continuous)
Pulton Ho. SE4 .... 4A 122
(off Turnham Rd.)
Pulton Pl. SW6 .... 7J 99
Puma Ct. E1 .... 5J 9 (5F 85)
Pump All. TW8: Bford 7D 96
Pump Cl. UB5: N'olt 2E 76
Pump Ct. EC4 .... 1J 13 (6A 84)
Pumphandle Path N2 .... 2B 46
(off Oak La.)
Pumphouse, The N8 .... 4K 47
Pump Ho. Cl. BR2: Brom 2G 159
SE16 .... 2J 103
Pumphouse Educational Mus., The 1A 104
Pump House Gallery, The 7E 100
Pump Ho. M. E1 .... 7G 85
(off Hooper St.)
Pump House Steam & Transport Mus. 6A 50
Pumping Ho. E14 .... 7F 87
(off Naval Row)
Pumping Sta. Rd. W4 .... 7A 98
Pump La. SE14 .... 7J 103
UB3: Hayes 2J 93
Pump Pail Nth. CR0: C'don 3C 168
Pump Pail Sth. CR0: C'don 3C 168
Punchard Cres. EN3: Enf L 1J 25
Punderson's Gdns. E2 .... 3H 85
Purbeck Av. KT3: N Mald 6B 152
Purbeck Dr. NW2 .... 2F 63
Purbeck Ho. SW8 .... 7K 101
(off Bolney St.)
Purbrook Est. SE1 .... 7H 15 (2E 102)
Purbrook St. SE1 .... 7H 15 (3E 102)
Purcell Cres. SW6 .... 7F 99
(not continuous)
Purcell Ho. EN1: Enf 1B 24
SW10 .... 6B 100
(off Milman's St.)
Purcell Mans. W14 .... 6G 99
(off Queen's Club Gdns.)
Purcell M. NW10 .... 7A 62
Purcell Rd. UB6: G'frd 5F 77
Purcell Room 4H 13
(off Belvedere Rd.)
Purcells Av. HA8: Edg 5B 28
Purcell St. N1 .... 2E 84
Purchese St. NW1 .... 1D 6 (2H 83)
Purday Ho. W10 .... 3G 81
(off Bruckner St.)
Purdon Ho. SE15 .... 1G 121
(off Peckham High St.)
Purdy Ct. KT4: Wor Pk 2C 164
Purdy St. E3 .... 4D 86
Purelake M. SE13 .... 3F 123
(off Marischal Rd.)
Purkis Cl. UB8: Hayes 7E 74
Purland Cl. RM8: Dag 1F 73
Purland Rd. SE28 .... 2K 107
(not continuous)
Purleigh Av. IG8: Wfd G 6H 37
Purley Av. NW2 .... 2G 63
Purley Cl. IG5: Ilf 2E 52
Purley Pl. N1 .... 7B 66
Purley Rd. CR2: S Croy 7D 168
N9 .... 3K 33
Purley Vw. Ter. CR2: S Croy 7D 168
(off Sanderstead Rd.)
Purley Way CR0: C'don, Wadd 7K 155
Purley Way Cen., The
CR0: Wadd 2A 168
Purley Way Cnr. CR0: C'don 7K 155
Purneys Rd. SE9 .... 4B 124
Purrett Rd. SE18 .... 5K 107

Purser Ho. SW2 .... 6A 120
(off Tulse Hill)
Pursers Cross Rd. SW6 .... 1H 117
(not continuous)
Purse Wardens Cl. W13 .... 1C 96
Pursley Rd. NW7 .... 7J 29
Purves Rd. NW10 .... 3D 80
Purvis Ho. CR0: C'don 7D 156
Pusey Ho. E14 .... 6C 86
(off Saracen St.)
Puteaux Ho. E2 .... 2K 85
(off Mace St.)
PUTNEY 4F 117
Putney Arts Theatre 4F 117
Putney Bri. SW6 .... 3G 117
SW15 .... 3G 117
Putney Bri. App. SW6 .... 3G 117
Putney Bri. Rd. SW15 .... 4G 117
SW18 .... 4G 117
Putney Comn. SW15 .... 3E 116
Putney Exchange Shop. Cen.
SW15 .... 4F 117
Putney Gdns. RM6: Chad H 5B 54
PUTNEY HEATH 6E 116
Putney Heath SW15 .... 7D 116
Putney Heath La. SW15 .... 6F 117
Putney High St. SW15 .... 4F 117
Putney Hill SW15 .... 7F 117
(not continuous)
Putney Leisure Cen. 4E 116
Putney Pk. Av. SW15 .... 4C 116
Putney Pk. La. SW15 .... 4D 116
(not continuous)
PUTNEY VALE 3C 134
Putney Va. Crematorium SW15 .... 2D 134
Putney Wharf SW15 .... 3G 117
Pycroft Way N9 .... 4A 34
Pyecombe Cnr. N12 .... 4C 30
Pylbrook Rd. SM1: Sutt 3J 165
Pylon Trad. Est. E16 .... 4G 87
Pylon Way CR0: Bedd 1J 167
Pym Cl. EN4: E Barn 5G 21
Pymers Mead SE21 .... 1C 138
Pymmes Brook Ho. N10 .... 7K 31
Pymmes Cl. N13 .... 5E 32
N17 .... 1H 49
Pymmes Gdns. Nth. N9 .... 3A 34
Pymmes Gdns. Sth. N9 .... 3A 34
Pymmes Grn. Rd. N11 .... 4A 32
Pymmes Rd. N13 .... 6D 32
Pymms Brook Dr.
EN4: E Barn 4H 21
Pynchester Cl. UB10: Ick 2C 56
Pyne Rd. KT6: Surb 1G 163
Pynfolds SE16 .... 2H 103
Pynham Cl. SE2 .... 3B 108
Pynnacles Cl. HA7: Stan 5G 27
Pynnersmead SE24 .... 5C 120
Pyramid Ct. KT1: King T 2F 151
(off Cambridge Rd.)
Pyramid Ho. TW4: Houn 2C 112
Pyrford Ho. SW9 .... 4B 120
Pyrland Rd. N5 .... 5D 66
TW10: Rich 6F 115
Pyrmont Gro. SE27 .... 3B 138
Pyrmont Rd. W4 .... 6G 97
Pytchley Cres. SE19 .... 6C 138
Pytchley Rd. SE22 .... 3E 120

Q

Q Bldg., The E15 .... 6G 69
(off The Grove)
Quad Ct. SE1 .... 3E 102
(off Grigg's Pl.)
Quadrangle, The E15 .... 6G 69
SE24 .... 5C 120
SW6 .... 7G 99
(Bronsart Rd.)

Quadrangle, The SW6 .... 1A 118
(Thames Av.)
W2 .... 7C 4 (6C 82)
W12 .... 6D 80
(off Du Cane Rd.)
Quadrangle Cl. SE1 .... 4E 102
Quadrangle M. HA7: Stan 7H 27
Quadrant, The DA7: Bex 7D 108
HA2: Harr 3H 41
HA8: Edg 6B 28
NW4 .... 4E 44
SM2: Sutt 6A 166
SW20 .... 1G 153
TW9: Rich 4D 114
W10 .... 3F 81
Quadrant Arc. W1 .... 3B 12
Quadrant Bus. Cen. NW6 .... 1G 81
Quadrant Cl. NW4 .... 5D 44
Quadrant Gro. NW5 .... 5D 64
Quadrant Ho. SE1 .... 4A 14
Quadrant Rd. CR7: Thor H 4B 156
TW9: Rich 4D 114
Quad Rd. HA9: Wemb 3D 60
Quaggy Wlk. SE3 .... 4J 123
Quain Mans. W14 .... 6G 99
(off Queen's Club Gdns.)
Quainton St. NW10 .... 3K 61
Quaker Ct. E1 .... 4J 9
(off Quaker St.)
EC1 .... 3E 8
Quaker La. UB2: S'hall 3E 94
Quakers Course NW9 .... 1B 44
Quakers La. TW7: Isle 7A 96
(not continuous)
Quakers Pl. E7 .... 5B 70
Quaker St. E1 .... 4J 9 (4F 85)
Quakers Wlk. N21 .... 6J 23
Quality Ct. WC2 .... 7J 7
Quantock Cl. UB3: Harl 7F 93
Quantock Dr. KT4: Wor Pk 2E 164
Quantock Gdns. NW2 .... 2F 63
Quantock Ho. N16 .... 1F 67
Quantock M. SE15 .... 2G 121
(off Alpha St.)
Quarles Pk. Rd. RM6: Chad H 6B 54
Quarrendon St. SW6 .... 2J 117
Quarr Rd. SM5: Cars 6B 154
Quarry Pk. Rd. SM1: Sutt 6H 165
Quarry Ri. SM1: Sutt 6H 165
Quarry Rd. SW18 .... 6A 118
Quarterdeck, The E14 .... 2C 104
Quarter Mile La. E10 .... 4D 68
Quastel Ho. SE1 .... 7E 14
(off Long La.)
Quatre Ports E4 .... 5A 36
Quay Ho. E14 .... 2C 104
(off Admirals Way)
Quayside Cotts. E1 .... 1G 103
(off Mews St.)
Quayside Ct. SE16 .... 1K 103
(off Abbotshade Rd.)
Quayside Ho. E14 .... 1B 104
W10 .... 4G 81
Quayside Wlk. KT1: King T 2D 150
(off Wadbrook St.)
Quay Vw. Apartments E14 .... 3C 104
(off Arden Cres.)
Quebec M. W1 .... 1F 11 (6D 82)
Quebec Rd. IG1: Ilf 7F 53
IG2: Ilf 7F 53
UB4: Yead 6A 76
Quebec Way SE16 .... 2K 103
Quebec Way Ind. Est. SE16 .... 2A 104
Quebec Wharf E8 .... 1E 84
(off Kingsland Rd.)
E14 .... 6C 86
Quedgeley Ct. SE15 .... 6F 103
(off Ebley Cl.)
Queen Adelaide Ct. SE20 .... 6J 139
Queen Adelaide Rd. SE20 .... 6J 139

Queen Alexandra Mans. WC1 .... 2E 6
(off Bidborough St.)
Queen Alexandra's Ct.
SW19 .... 5H 135
Queen Anne Av. BR2: Brom 3H 159
Queen Anne Ho. E16 .... 1J 105
(off Hardy Av.)
Queen Anne M. W1 .... 6K 5 (5F 83)
Queen Anne Rd. E9 .... 6K 67
Queen Anne's Cl. TW2: Twick 3H 131
Queen Anne's Ct. SE10 .... 5F 105
(off Park Row)
Queen Anne's Gdns. CR4: Mitc 3D 154
EN1: Enf 6K 23
W4 .... 3A 98
W5 .... 2E 96
Queen Anne's Ga. DA7: Bex 3D 126
SW1 .... 7C 12 (2H 101)
Queen Anne's Gro. EN1: Enf 7J 23
W4 .... 3A 98
W5 .... 2E 96
Queen Anne's Pl. EN1: Enf 6K 23
Queen Anne St. W1 .... 7J 5 (6F 83)
Queen Anne's Wlk. WC1 .... 4F 7
Queen Anne Ter. E1 .... 7H 85
(off Sovereign Cl.)
Queenborough Gdns. BR7: Chst 6H 143
IG2: Ilf 4E 52
Queenbridge Sports & Community Cen. 7F 67
Queen Caroline St. W6 .... 5E 98
(not continuous)
Queen Catherine Ho. SW6 .... 7K 99
(off Wandon Rd.)
Queen Charlotte's Cottage 2D 114
Queen Ct. WC1 .... 4J 83
(off Queen Sq.)
Queen Elizabeth Bldgs. EC4 .... 2J 13
Queen Elizabeth Ct. EN5: Barn 3C 20
Queen Elizabeth Gdns.
SM4: Mord 4J 153
Queen Elizabeth Hall 4H 13 (1K 101)
Queen Elizabeth Ho. SW12 .... 7E 118
Queen Elizabeth II Conference Cen. 7D 12 (2H 101)
Queen Elizabeth Rd. E17 .... 3A 50
KT2: King T 2F 151
Queen Elizabeth's Cl. N16 .... 2D 66
Queen Elizabeth's Coll. SE10 .... 7E 104
Queen Elizabeth's Dr. CR0: New Ad 7F 171
N14 .... 1D 32
Queen Elizabeth's Hunting Lodge 1C 36
Queen Elizabeth Sports Cen. 4C 20
Queen Elizabeth Stadium 2A 24
Queen Elizabeth St. SE1 .... 6H 15 (2E 102)
Queen Elizabeth's Wlk. N16 .... 1D 66
SM6: Bedd 4H 167
(off Croydon Rd.)
SM6: Bedd 4H 167
(Evelyn Way)
Queen Elizabeth Wlk. SW13 .... 1C 116
Queenhithe EC4 .... 2D 14 (7C 84)
Queen Isabella Way EC1 .... 7B 8
(off King Edward St.)
Queen Margaret Flats E2 .... 3H 85
(off St Jude's Rd.)
Queen Margaret's Gro. N1 .... 5E 66
Queen Mary Av. SM4: Mord 5F 153
Queen Mary Cl. KT6: Surb 3G 163
Queen Mary Ct. TW19: Stanw 1A 128
Queen Mary Ho. E16 .... 1K 105
(off Wesley Av.)
Queen Mary Rd. SE19 .... 6B 138
TW17: Shep 2E 146
Queen Mary's Av.
SM5: Cars 7D 166
Queen Marys Bldgs. SW1 .... 3B 18
(off Stillington St.)
Queen Mary's Ct. SE10 .... 6F 105
(off Park Row)

Queen Mary University of London 4K 85
(off Bancroft Rd.)
Queen Mother Sports Cen., The 3A 18
Queen of Denmark Ct. SE16 . . . . .3B 104
Queens Acre SM3: Cheam 7F 165
Queens Av. HA7: Stan 3C 42
IG8: Wfd G 5E 36
N3 . . . . .7F 31
N10 . . . . .3E 46
N20 . . . . .2G 31
N21 . . . . .1G 33
TW13: Hanw 4A 130
UB6: G'frd 6F 77
Queensberry Ho. TW9: Rich 5C 114
Queensberry M. W.
SW7 . . . . .3A 16 (4B 100)
Queensberry Pl. E12 . . . . .5B 70
SW7 . . . . .3A 16 (4B 100)
TW9: Rich 5D 114
(off Retreat Rd.)
Queensberry Way SW7 . . . . . .3A 16 (4B 100)
Queensborough Ct. N3 . . . . .4H 45
(off Tillingbourne Gdns.)
Queensborough M. W2 . . . . .7A 82
Queensborough Pas. W2 . . . . .7A 82
(off Queensborough M.)
Queensborough Studios W2 . . . . .7A 82
(off Queensborough M.)
Queensborough Ter. W2 . . . . .7K 81
Queensbridge Ct. E2 . . . . .1F 85
(off Queensbridge Rd.)
Queensbridge Pk. TW7: Isle 5J 113
Queensbridge Rd. E2 . . . . .6F 67
E8 . . . . .6F 67
QUEENSBURY 3E 42
Queensbury Circ. Pde.HA3: Kent 3E 42
HA7: Stan 3E 42
Queensbury Rd. HA0: Wemb 2F 79
NW9 . . . . .7K 43
Queensbury Sta. Pde. HA8: Edg 3F 43
Queensbury St. N1 . . . . .7C 66
Queen's Chapel of the Savoy, The 3G 13
(off Savoy Hill)
Queen's Cir. SW8 . . . . .7F 101
Queens Cl. HA8: Edg 5B 28
SM6: Wall 5F 167
Queen's Club Gdns. W14 . . . . .6G 99
Queen's Club, The (Tennis Courts) . . .5G 99
Queens Club Ter. W14 . . . . .6H 99
(off Normand Rd.)
Queens Ct. CR2: S Croy 5C 168
(off Warham Rd.)
CR7: Thor H 5A 156
E11 . . . . .7G 51
HA3: Kent 2B 42
IG9: Buck H 2G 37
NW6 . . . . .5K 63
NW8 . . . . .2B 82
(off Queen's Ter.)
NW11 . . . . .5H 45
SE23 . . . . .2J 139
TW10: Rich 6F 115
W2 . . . . .7K 81
(off Queensway)
Queenscourt HA9: Wemb 4E 60
Queen's Cres. NW5 . . . . .6E 64
TW10: Rich 5F 115
Queenscroft Rd. SE9 . . . . .5B 124
Queensdale Cres. W11 . . . . .1F 99
(not continuous)
Queensdale Pl. W11 . . . . .1G 99
Queensdale Rd. W11 . . . . .1F 99
Queensdale Wlk. W11 . . . . .1G 99
Queensdown Rd. E5 . . . . .4H 67
Queens Dr. E10 . . . . .7C 50
KT5: Surb 7G 151
KT7: T Ditt 6A 150
N4 . . . . .2B 66
W3 . . . . .6F 79
W5 . . . . .6F 79
Queen's Elm Pde. SW3 . . . . .5B 16
(off Old Church St.)
Queen's Elm Sq. SW3 . . . . . . .6B 16 (5B 100)
Queens Ferry Wlk. N17 . . . . .4H 49
Queensfield Ct. SM3: Cheam 4E 164
Queen's Gallery 7K 11 (2F 101)
Queen's Gdns. NW4 . . . . .5E 44
RM13: Rain 2K 91
TW5: Hest 1C 112
W2 . . . . .7A 82
W5 . . . . .4C 78
Queen's Ga. SW7 . . . . .1A 16 (2A 100)
Queensgate Ct. N12 . . . . .5E 30
Queens Ga. Gdns. BR7: Chst 1H 161
SW7 . . . . .3A 100
SW15 .4D 116
Queensgate Ho. E3 . . . . .2B 86
(off Hereford Rd.)
Queen's Ga. M. SW7 . . . . .3A 100
Queen's Ga. Pl. SW7 . . . . .3A 100
Queensgate Pl. NW6 . . . . .7J 63
Queen's Ga. Pl. M. SW7 . . . . .2A 16 (3A 100)
Queen's Ga. Ter. SW7 . . . . . . .1A 16 (3A 100)
Queens Ga. Vs. E9 . . . . .7A 68
Queen's Gro. NW8 . . . . .1B 82
Queens Gro. Rd. E4 . . . . .1A 36
Queen's Gro. Studios NW8 . . . . .1B 82
Queen's Head Pas. EC4 . . . . . . .7C 8 (6C 84)
Queen's Head St. N1 . . . . .1B 84
Queen's Head Yd. SE1 . . . . .5E 14
Queen's House, The 6F 105
Queens Ho. SE17 . . . . .6D 102
(off Merrow St.)
SW8 . . . . .7J 101
(off Sth. Lambeth Rd.)
TW11: Tedd 6K 131
W2 . . . . .7K 81
(off Queensway)
Queen's Ice Bowl 7K 81
Queen's Keep TW1: Twick 6C 114
Queensland Av. N18 . . . . .6H 33
SW19 . . . . .1K 153
Queensland Cl. E17 . . . . .2B 50
Queensland Ho. E16 . . . . .1E 106
(off Rymill St.)
Queensland Rd. N7 . . . . .4A 66
Queens La. N10 . . . . .3F 47
Queen's Mans. W6 . . . . .4F 99
(off Brook Grn.)
Queen's Mkt. E13 . . . . .1A 88
Queens Mead HA8: Edg 6A 28
Queensmead NW8 . . . . .1B 82
Queen's Mead Rd. BR2: Brom 2H 159
Queensmead Sports Cen. 4B 58
Queensmere Cl. SW19 . . . . .2F 135
Queensmere Ct. SW13 . . . . .7B 98
Queensmere Rd. SW19 . . . . .2F 135
Queen's M. W2 . . . . .7K 81
Queensmill Rd. SW6 . . . . .7F 99
Queens Pde. N8 . . . . .4B 48
N11 . . . . .5J 31
(off Friern Barnet Rd.)
NW2 . . . . .6E 62
(off Willesden La.)
NW4 . . . . .5E 44
(off Queens Rd.)
W5 . . . . .6F 79
Queen's Pde. Cl. N11 . . . . .5J 31
Queens Pk. Ct. W10 . . . . .3F 81
Queen's Pk. Gdns. TW13: Felt 3H 129
Queen's Pk. Rangers FC (Loftus Road)
. . . . .1D 98
Queens Pk. School Sports Cen. 1F 81
Queens Pas. BR7: Chst 6F 143
Queens Pl. SM4: Mord 4J 153
Queen's Prom.KT1: King T, Surb 4D 150
Queen Sq. WC1 . . . . .4F 7 (4J 83)
Queen Sq. Pl. WC1 . . . . .4F 7
Queen's Quay EC4 . . . . .2C 14
(off Up. Thames St.)
Queens Reach KT1: King T 2D 150
KT8: E Mos 4J 149
Queens Ride SW13 . . . . .3C 116
SW15 .3C 116
Queens Ri. TW10: Rich 6F 115
Queens Rd. BR1: Brom 2J 159
BR3: Beck 2A 158
BR7: Chst 6F 143
CR0: C'don 6B 156
CR4: Mitc 3B 154
DA16: Well 2B 126
E11 . . . . .7F 51
E13 . . . . .1K 87
E17 . . . . .6B 50
EN1: Enf 4K 23
EN5: Barn 3A 20
IG9: Buck H 2E 36
IG11: Bark 6G 71
KT2: King T 7G 133
KT3: N Mald 4B 152
KT7: T Ditt 5K 149
N3 . . . . .1A 46
N9 . . . . .3C 34
N11 . . . . .7D 32
NW4 . . . . .5E 44
SE14 . . . . .1J 121
SE15 . . . . .1H 121
SM4: Mord 4J 153
SM6: Wall 5F 167
SW14 . . . . .3K 115
SW19 . . . . .6H 135
TW1: Twick 1A 132
TW3: Houn 3F 113
TW10: Rich 7F 115
TW11: Tedd 6K 131
TW12: Ham H 4F 131
TW13: Felt 1K 129
UB2: S'hall 2B 94
UB3: Hayes 6G 75
UB7: W Dray 2B 92
W5 . . . . .6E 78
Queens Rd. Est.
EN5: Barn 3A 20
Queens Rd. W. E13 . . . . .2J 87
Queen's Row SE17 . . . . .6D 102
Queens St. TW15: Ashf 4B 128
Queens Ter. E1 . . . . .4J 85
E13 . . . . .1K 87
KT7: T Ditt 6A 150
(off Queens Dr.)
NW8 . . . . .1B 82
TW7: Isle 4A 114
Queen's Ter. Cotts. W7 . . . . .2J 95
Queen's Theatre
Westminster 2C 12
(off Shaftesbury Av.)
Queensthorpe M. SE26 . . . . .4K 139
Queensthorpe Rd. SE26 . . . . .4K 139
Queenstown M.
SW8 . . . . .2F 119
Queenstown Rd.
SW8 . . . . .7J 17 (6F 101)
Queen St. CR0: C'don 4C 168
DA7: Bex 3F 127
EC4 . . . . .2D 14 (7C 84)
(not continuous)
N17 . . . . .6K 33
RM7: Rom 6K 55
W1 . . . . .4J 11 (1F 101)
Queen St. Pl. EC4 . . . . .2D 14 (7C 84)
Queensville Rd.
SW12 .7H 119
Queens Wlk. E4 . . . . .1A 36
HA1: Harr 4J 41
HA4: Ruis 2A 58
N5 . . . . .5B 66
NW9 . . . . .2J 61
SW1 . . . . .5A 12 (1G 101)
TW15: Ashf 4A 128
W5 . . . . .4C 78
Queen's Wlk., The SE1 . . . . . . .3K 13 (7A 84)
(Oxo Tower Wharf)
SE1 . . . . .4F 15 (1E 102)
(Tooley St.)
SE1 . . . . .4H 13 (1K 101)
(Waterloo Rd.)
Queens Wlk. Ter. HA4: Ruis 3A 58
Queens Way NW4 . . . . .5E 44
TW13: Hanw 4A 130
Queensway BR4: W W'ck 3G 171
BR5: Pet W 5G 161
CR0: Wadd 6K 167
EN3: Pond E 4C 24
TW16: Sun 2K 147
W2 . . . . .6K 81
Queensway Bus. Cen. EN3: Pond E 4C 24
Queensway Ind. Est. EN3: Pond E 4D 24
Queenswell Av. N20 . . . . .3H 31
Queens Wharf W6 . . . . .5E 98
Queenswood Av. CR7: Thor H 5A 156
E17 . . . . .1E 50
SM6: Bedd 4H 167
TW3: Houn 2D 112
TW12: Hamp 6F 131
Queenswood Ct. SE27 . . . . .4D 138
SW4 . . . . .5J 119
Queenswood Gdns. E11 . . . . .1K 69
Queenswood Pk. N3 . . . . .2G 45
Queens Wood Rd. N10 . . . . .6F 47
Queenswood Rd. DA15: Sidc 5K 125
SE23 . . . . .3K 139
Queen's Yd. WC1 . . . . .4B 6 (5G 83)
QUEEN VICTORIA 3E 164
Queen Victoria Av. HA0: Wemb 7D 60
Queen Victoria Memorial . . .7A 12 (2G 101)
Queen Victoria Seaman's Rest
E14 . . . . .6D 86
(off E. India Dock Rd.)
Queen Victoria St. EC4 . . . . . . .2A 14 (7B 84)
Queen Victoria Ter. E1 . . . . .7H 85
(off Sovereign Cl.)
Quemerford Rd. N7 . . . . .5K 65
Quendon Ho. W10 . . . . .4E 80
(off Sutton Way)
Quenington Ct. SE15 . . . . .6F 103
Quentin Ho. SE1 . . . . .6A 14
(off Chaplin Cl.)
SE1 . . . . .7K 13
(off Gray St.)
Quentin Pl. SE13 . . . . .3G 123
Quentin Rd. SE13 . . . . .3G 123
Quernmore Cl. BR1: Brom 6J 141
Quernmore Rd. BR1: Brom 6J 141
N4 . . . . .6A 48
Querrin St. SW6 . . . . .2A 118
Quest, The W11 . . . . .7G 81
(off Clarendon Rd.)
Quested Ct. E8 . . . . .5H 67
(off Brett Rd.)
Questors Theatre, The 7C 78
Quex Ct. NW6 . . . . .1K 81
(off West End La.)
Quex M. NW6 . . . . .1J 81
Quex Rd. NW6 . . . . .1J 81
Quiberon Ct. TW16: Sun 3J 147
Quick Rd. W4 . . . . .5A 98
Quicks Rd. SW19 . . . . .7K 135
Quick St. N1 . . . . .2B 84
Quick St. M. N1 . . . . .2B 84
Quickswood NW3 . . . . .7C 64
Quiet Nook BR2: Hayes 3B 172
Quill La. SW15 . . . . .4F 117
Quill St. N4 . . . . .3A 66
W5 . . . . .3E 78
Quilp St. SE1 . . . . .6C 14 (2C 102)
(not continuous)
Quilter St. E2 . . . . .1K 9 (3G 85)
SE18 . . . . .5K 107
Quilting Ct. SE16 . . . . .2K 103
(off Garter Way)

Quince Ho. *SE13* 2D 122
(off Quince Rd.)
Quince Rd. SE13 2D 122
Quinnell Cl. SE18 5K 107
Quinta Dr. EN5: Barn 5A 20
Quintet, The KT12: Walt T 7J 147
Quintin Av. SW20 1H 153
Quintin Cl. HA5: Eastc 4K 39
Quinton Cl. BR3: Beck 3E 158
SM6: Wall 4F 167
TW5: Cran 7K 93
Quinton Ho. *SW8* 7J 101
(off Wyvil Rd.)
Quinton Rd. KT7: T Ditt 1A 162
Quinton St. SW18 2A 136
Quixley St. E14 7F 87
Quorn Rd. SE22 4E 120

R

Rabbit Row W8 1J 99
Rabbits Rd. E12 4C 70
Rabournmead Dr. UB5: N'olt 5C 58
Raby Rd. KT3: N Mald 4K 151
Raby St. E14 6A 86
Raccoon Way TW4: Houn 2A 112
Rachel Cl. IG6: Ilf 3H 53
Racine *SE5* 1E 120
(off Peckham Rd.)
Rackham Cl. DA16: Well 2B 126
Rackham M. SW16 6G 137
Rackstraw Ho. NW3 7D 64
Racquets & Fitness Spa, The 3E 130
Racton Rd. SW6 6J 99
RADA 5C 6
Radbourne Av. W5 4C 96
Radbourne Cl. E5 4K 67
Radbourne Ct. HA3: Kent 6B 42
Radbourne Cres. E17 2F 51
Radbourne Rd. SW12 7G 119
Radcliffe Av. EN2: Enf 1H 23
NW10 2C 80
Radcliffe Gdns. SM5: Cars 7C 166
Radcliffe Ho. *SE16* 4H 103
(off Anchor St.)
Radcliffe M. TW12: Ham H 5G 131
Radcliffe Path SW8 2F 119
Radcliffe Rd. CR0: C'don 2F 169
HA3: W'stone 2A 42
N21 1G 33
SE1 3E 102
Radcliffe Sq. SW15 6F 117
Radcliffe Way UB5: Yead 3B 76
Radcot Point SE23 3K 139
Radcot St. SE11 6K 19 (5A 102)
Raddington Rd. W10 5G 81
Radfield Way DA15: Sidc 7H 125
Radford Ct. *SE15* 7H 103
(off Old Kent Rd.)
Radford Est. NW10 3A 80
Radford Ho. *E14* 5D 86
(off St Leonard's Rd.)
N7 5K 65
Radford Rd. SE13 6E 122
Radford Way IG11: Bark 3K 89
Radipole Rd. SW6 1H 117
Radisson Ct. *SE1* 7G 15
(off Long La.)
Radius Apartments *N1* 1G 7
(off Caledonian Rd.)
Radius Pk. TW14: Felt 4H 111
Radland Rd. E16 6H 87
Radlet Av. SE26 3H 139
Radlett Cl. E7 6H 69
Radlett Pl. NW8 1C 82
Radley Av. IG3: Bark, Ilf 4A 72
Radley Cl. TW14: Felt 1H 129
Radley Ct. SE16 2K 103
Radley Gdns. HA3: Kent 4E 42
Radley Ho. *NW1* 3E 4
(off Gloucester Pl.)
SE2 2D 108
(off Wolvercote Rd.)
Radley M. W8 3J 99
Radley Rd. N17 2E 48
Radley's La. E18 2J 51
Radleys Mead RM10: Dag 6H 73
Radley Sq. E5 2J 67
Radley Ter. *E16* 5H 87
(off Hermit Rd.)
Radlix Rd. E10 1C 68
Radnor Av. DA16: Well 5B 126
HA1: Harr 5J 41
Radnor Cl. BR7: Chst 6J 143
CR4: Mitc 4J 155
Radnor Ct. HA3: Hrw W 1K 41
W7 6K 77
(off Copley Cl.)
Radnor Cres. IG4: Ilf 5D 52
SE18 7A 108
Radnor Gdns. EN1: Enf 1K 23
TW1: Twick 2K 131
Radnor Gro. UB10: Hil 2C 74
Radnor Ho. *EC1* 2D 8
(off Bath St.)
SW16 2K 155
Radnor Lodge *W2* 1B 10
(off Sussex Pl.)
Radnor M. W2 1B 10 (6B 82)
Radnor Pl. W2 1C 10 (6C 82)
Radnor Rd. HA1: Harr 5H 41
NW6 1G 81
SE15 7G 103
TW1: Twick 1K 131
Radnor St. EC1 2D 8 (3C 84)
Radnor Ter. SM2: Sutt 7J 165
W14 4H 99
Radnor Wlk. CR0: C'don 6A 158
E14 4C 104
(off Barnsdale Av.)
SW3 6D 16 (5C 100)
Radnor Way NW10 4H 79
Radstock Av. HA3: Kent 3A 42
Radstock Cl. N11 6K 31
Radstock St. SW11 7C 100
(not continuous)
Radway Ho. *W2* 5J 81
(off Alfred Rd.)
Raeburn Av. KT5: Surb 1H 163
Raeburn Cl. KT1: Ham W 7D 132
NW11 6A 46
Raeburn Ho. *UB5: N'olt* 2B 76
(off Academy Gdns.)
Raeburn Rd. DA15: Sidc 6J 125
HA8: Edg 1G 43
UB4: Hayes 2F 75
Raeburn St. SW2 4J 119
Raffles Ct. HA8: Edg 4A 28
Raffles Ho. NW4 4D 44
Rafford Way BR1: Brom 2K 159
RAF Mus. Hendon 2C 44
RAF NORTHOLT AERODROME 6H 57
Ragged School Mus. 5A 86
Raggleswood BR7: Chst 1E 160
Raglan Cl. TW4: Houn 5D 112
Raglan Ct. CR2: S Croy 5B 168
HA9: Wemb 4F 61
SE12 5J 123
Raglan Rd. BR2: Brom 4A 160
DA17: Belv 4F 109
E17 5E 50
EN1: Enf 7A 24
SE18 5G 107
Raglan St. NW5 6F 65
Raglan Ter. HA2: Harr 4F 59
Raglan Way UB5: N'olt 6G 59
Ragley Cl. W3 2J 97
Ragwort Ct. SE26 5H 139
Raider Cl. RM7: Mawney 1G 55
Railey M. NW5 5G 65
Railshead Rd. TW7: Isle 4B 114
Railton Rd. SE24 4A 120
Railway App. HA3: Harr 4K 41
N4 6A 48
SE1 5F 15 (1D 102)
SM6: Wall 5F 167
TW1: Twick 7A 114
Railway Arches *E2* 1J 9
(off Cremer St.)
E8 7H 67
(off Mentmore Ter.)
W12 2E 98
(off Shepherd's Bush Mkt.)
Railway Av. SE16 2J 103
(not continuous)
Railway Children Wlk.
BR1: Brom 2J 141
SE12 2J 141
Railway Cotts. *E15* 2G 87
(off Baker's Row)
SW19 4K 135
W6 2E 98
(off Sulgrave Rd.)
Railway Gro. SE14 7B 104
Railway M. *E3* 3C 86
(off Wellington Way)
W10 6G 81
Railway Pas. TW11: Tedd 6A 132
Railway Pl. DA17: Belv 3G 109
Railway Ri. SE22 4E 120
Railway Rd. TW11: Tedd 4J 131
Railway Side SW13 3A 116
(not continuous)
Railway St. N1 2J 83
RM6: Chad H 7C 54
Railway Ter. E17 1E 50
SE13 5D 122
TW13: Felt 1J 129
Rainborough Cl. NW10 6J 61
Rainbow Av. E14 5D 104
Rainbow Ct. *SE14* 6A 104
(off Chipley St.)
Rainbow Ind. Est. SW20 2D 152
UB7: Yiew 7A 74
Rainbow Quay SE16 3A 104
Rainbow St. SE5 7E 102
Rainbow Theatre 2A 66
Raine Gdns. IG8: Wfd G 4D 36
Raines Est. Ct. N16 2F 67
Raine St. E1 1H 103
Rainham Cl. SE9 6J 125
SW11 6C 118
Rainham Ho. *NW1* 1G 83
(off Bayham Pl.)
Rainham Rd. NW10 3E 80
Rainham Rd. Nth. RM10: Dag 2G 73
Rainham Rd. Sth. RM10: Dag 4H 73
Rainhill Way E3 3C 86
(not continuous)
Rainsborough Av. SE8 4A 104
Rainsford Cl. HA7: Stan 5H 27
Rainsford Rd. NW10 2H 79
Rainsford St. W2 7C 4 (6C 82)
Rainton Rd. SE7 5J 105
Rainville Rd. W6 6E 98
Raisins Hill HA5: Eastc 3A 40
Raith Av. N14 3C 32
Raleana Rd. E14 1E 104
Raleigh Av. SM6: Bedd 4H 167
UB4: Yead 5K 75
Raleigh Cl. HA4: Ruis 2H 57
HA5: Pinn 7B 40
NW4 5E 44
Raleigh Ct. BR3: Beck 1D 158
SE8 5A 104
(off Evelyn St.)
SE16 1K 103
(off Clarence M.)
SM6: Wall 6F 167
Raleigh Ct. *W12* 2E 98
(off Scott's Rd.)
W13 5B 78
Raleigh Dr. KT5: Surb 1J 163
N20 3H 31
Raleigh Gdns. CR4: Mitc 3D 154
(not continuous)
SW2 6K 119
Raleigh Ho. *BR1: Brom* 1J 159
(off Hammelton Rd.)
E14 2D 104
(off Admirals Way)
SW1 7C 18
(off Dolphin Sq.)
Raleigh M. BR6: Chels 5K 173
N1 1B 84
(off Packington St.)
Raleigh Rd. EN2: Enf 4J 23
N2 2C 46
N8 4A 48
SE20 7K 139
TW9: Rich 3F 115
TW13: Felt 3H 129
UB2: S'hall 5C 94
Raleigh St. N1 1B 84
Raleigh Way N14 1C 32
TW13: Hanw 5A 130
Ralph Brook Ct. *N1* 1F 9
(off Chart St.)
Ralph Ct. *W2* 6K 81
(off Queensway)
Ralph Perring Ct. BR3: Beck 4C 158
Ralston St. SW3 6E 16 (5D 100)
Ramac Ind. Est. SE7 4K 105
Rama Cl. SW16 7J 137
Rama Ct. HA1: Harr 2J 59
Ramac Way SE7 4K 105
Rama La. SE19 7F 139
Ramar Ho. *E1* 5G 85
(off Hanbury St.)
Rambler Cl. SW16 4G 137
Rame Cl. SW17 5E 136
Ramilles Cl. SW2 6J 119
Ramillies Pl. W1 1A 12 (6G 83)
Ramillies Rd. DA15: Sidc 6B 126
NW7 2F 29
W4 4K 97
Ramillies St. W1 1A 12 (6G 83)
Ramones Ter. *CR4: Mitc* 4J 155
(off Yorkshire Rd.)
Rampart St. E1 6H 85
Ram Pas. KT1: King T 2D 150
Rampayne St. SW1 5C 18 (5H 101)
Ram Pl. E9 6J 67
Rampton Cl. E4 3H 35
Ramsay Ho. *NW8* 2C 82
(off Townshend Est.)
Ramsay M. SW3 7C 16 (6C 100)
Ramsay Rd. E7 4G 69
W3 3J 97
Ramscroft Cl. N9 7K 23
Ramsdale Rd. SW17 5E 136
Ramsden Dr. RM5: Col R 1G 55
Ramsden Rd. DA8: Erith 7K 109
N11 5J 31
SW12 6E 118
Ramsey Cl. NW9 6B 44
UB6: G'frd 5H 59
Ramsey Ct. *CR0: C'don* 2B 168
(off Church St.)
Ramsey Ho. SW9 7A 102
Ramsey Rd. CR7: Thor H 6K 155
Ramsey St. E2 4G 85
Ramsey Wlk. *N1* 6D 66
(off Handa Wlk.)
Ramsey Way N14 7B 22
Ramsfort Ho. *SE16* 4H 103
(off Camilla Rd.)
Ramsgate Cl. E16 1K 105
Ramsgate St. E8 6F 67

Ramsgill App. IG2: Ilf 4K 53
Ramsgill Dr. IG2: Ilf 5K 53
Rams Gro. RM6: Chad H 4E 54
Ram St. SW18 5K 117
Ramulis Dr. UB4: Yead 4B 76
Ramuswood Av. BR6: Chels 5J 173
Rancliffe Gdns. SE9 4C 124
Rancliffe Rd. E6 2C 88
Randall Av. NW2 2A 62
Randall Cl. DA8: Erith 6J 109
SW11 1C 118
Randall Ct. NW7 7H 29
Randall Pl. SE10 7E 104
Randall Rd. SE11 4G 19 (5K 101)
Randall Row SE11 4G 19 (4K 101)
Randalls Rents *SE16* 3B 104
(off Gulliver St.)
Randell's Rd. N1 1J 83
Randisbourne Gdns. SE6 3D 140
Randle Rd. TW10: Ham 4C 132
Randlesdown Rd. SE6 4C 140
(not continuous)
Randolph App. E16 6A 88
Randolph Av. W9 4A 4 (2K 81)
Randolph Cl. DA7: Bex 3J 127
KT2: King T 5J 133
Randolph Cres. W9 4A 82
Randolph Gdns. NW6 2K 81
Randolph Gro. RM6: Chad H 5C 54
Randolph M. W9 4A 82
Randolph Rd. BR2: Brom 1D 172
E17 5D 50
UB1: S'hall 2D 94
W9 4A 82
Randolph St. NW1 7G 65
Randon Cl. HA2: Harr 2F 41
Ranelagh Av. SW6 3H 117
SW13 2C 116
Ranelagh Bri. W2 5K 81
Ranelagh Cl. HA8: Edg 4B 28
Ranelagh Cotts. *SW1* 5H 17
(off Ranelagh Gro.)
Ranelagh Dr. HA8: Edg 4B 28
TW1: Twick 4B 114
Ranelagh Gdns. E11 5A 52
IG1: Ilf 1D 70
SW6 3G 117
(not continuous)
W4 7J 97
W6 4B 98
Ranelagh Gdns. Mans. *SW6* 3G 117
(off Ranelagh Gdns.)
Ranelagh Gro. SW1 5H 17 (5E 100)
Ranelagh Ho. *SW3* 5E 16
(off Elystan Pl.)
Ranelagh M. W5 2D 96
Ranelagh Pl. KT3: N Mald 5A 152
Ranelagh Rd. E6 1E 88
E11 4G 69
E15 2G 87
HA0: Wemb 6D 60
N17 3E 48
N22 1K 47
NW10 2B 80
SW1 6B 18 (5G 101)
UB1: S'hall 1B 94
W5 2D 96
Ranfurly Rd. SM1: Sutt 2J 165
Rangbourne Ho. N7 5J 65
Rangefield Rd. BR1: Brom 5G 141
Rangemoor Rd. N15 5F 49
Rangers House 1F 123
Ranger's Rd. E4 1B 36
Rangers Sq. SE10 1F 123
Range Way TW17: Shep 7C 146
Rangeworth Pl. DA15: Sidc 3K 143
Rangoon St. EC3 1J 15
Rankin Cl. NW9 3A 44
Rankine Ho. *SE1* 3C 102
(off Bath Ter.)
Ranleigh Gdns. DA7: Bex 7F 109
Ranmere St. SW12 1F 137
Ranmoor Cl. HA1: Harr 4H 41
Ranmoor Gdns. HA1: Harr 4H 41
Ranmore Av. CR0: C'don 3F 169
Ranmore Path BR5: St M Cry 4K 161
Ranmore Rd. SM2: Cheam 7F 165
Rannoch Cl. HA8: Edg 2C 28
Rannoch Rd. W6 6E 98
Rannock Av. NW9 7K 43
Ransome's Dock Bus. Cen.
SW11 7C 100
Ransom Rd. SE7 4A 106
Ranston St. NW1 5C 4 (5C 82)
Ranulf Rd. NW2 4H 63
Ranwell Cl. E3 1B 86
Ranworth Rd. N9 2D 34
Ranyard Cl. KT9: Chess 3F 163
Raphael Ct. *SE16* 5H 103
(off Stubbs Dr.)
Raphael Dr. KT7: T Ditt 7K 149
Raphael St. SW7 7E 10 (2D 100)
Rapley Ho. *E2* 2K 9
(off Turin St.)
Raquel Ct. *SE1* 6G 15
(off Snowfields)
Rashleigh Ct. SW8 2F 119
Rashleigh Ho. *WC1* 2E 6
(off Thanet St.)
Rasper Rd. N20 2F 31
Rastell Av. SW2 2H 137
RATCLIFF 5A 86
Ratcliffe Cl. SE12 7J 123
Ratcliffe Ct. *SE1* 7D 14
(off Gt. Dover St.)
Ratcliffe Cross St. E1 6K 85
Ratcliffe Ho. *E14* 6A 86
(off Barnes St.)
Ratcliffe La. E14 6A 86
Ratcliffe Orchard E1 7K 85
Ratcliff Rd. E7 5A 70
Rathbone Ho. *E16* 6H 87
(off Rathbone St.)
NW6 1J 81
Rathbone Mkt. E16 5H 87
Rathbone Pl. W1 6C 6 (5H 83)
Rathbone Sq. CR0: C'don 4C 168
Rathbone St. E16 5H 87
W1 6B 6 (5G 83)
Rathcoole Av. N8 5K 47
Rathcoole Gdns. N8 5K 47
Rathfern Rd. SE6 1B 140
Rathgar Av. W13 1B 96
Rathgar Cl. N3 2H 45
Rathgar Rd. SW9 3B 120
Rathmell Dr. SW4 6H 119
Rathmore Rd. SE7 5K 105
Rathnew Ct. *E2* 3K 85
(off Meath Cres.)
Rattray Ct. SE6 2H 141
Rattray Rd. SW2 4A 120
Raul Rd. SE15 2G 121
Raveley St. NW5 4G 65
(not continuous)
Raven Cl. NW9 2A 44
Ravendale Rd. TW16: Sun 2H 147
Ravenet St. SW11 1F 119
(not continuous)
Ravenfield Rd. SW17 3D 136
Ravenhill Rd. E13 2A 88
Raven Ho. *SE16* 4K 103
(off Tawny Way)
Ravenings Pde. IG3: Ilf 1A 72
Ravenna Rd. SW15 5F 117
Ravenor Ct. UB6: G'frd 4F 77
Ravenor Farm 3G 77
Ravenor Pk. Rd. UB6: G'frd 3F 77
Raven Rd. E18 2A 52
Raven Row E1 5H 85
(not continuous)
Ravensbourne Av. BR2: Brom 7F 141
TW19: Stanw 1A 128
Ravensbourne Ct. SE6 7C 122
Ravensbourne Gdns. IG5: Ilf 1E 52
W13 5B 78
Ravensbourne Ho. BR1: Brom 5F 141
NW8 5C 4
(off Broadley St.)
Ravensbourne Mans. *SE8* 6C 104
(off Berthon St.)
Ravensbourne Pk. SE6 7C 122
Ravensbourne Pk. Cres. SE6 7B 122
Ravensbourne Pl. SE13 2D 122
Ravensbourne Rd. BR1: Brom 3J 159
SE6 7B 122
TW1: Twick 6C 114
Ravensbourne Ter. TW19: Stanw 1A 128
Ravensbury Av. SM4: Mord 5A 154
Ravensbury Ct. *CR4: Mitc* 4B 154
(off Ravensbury Gro.)
Ravensbury Gro. CR4: Mitc 4B 154
Ravensbury La. CR4: Mitc 4B 154
Ravensbury Path CR4: Mitc 4B 154
Ravensbury Rd. BR5: St P 3K 161
SW18 2J 135
Ravensbury Ter. SW18 2K 135
Ravenscar *NW1* 1G 83
(off Bayham St.)
Ravenscar Rd. BR1: Brom 4G 141
KT6: Surb 2F 163
Ravens Cl. BR2: Brom 2H 159
EN1: Enf 2K 23
KT6: Surb 6D 150
Ravens Ct. *KT1: King T* 5D 150
(off Uxbridge Rd.)
Ravenscourt TW16: Sun 1H 147
Ravenscourt Av. W6 4C 98
Ravenscourt Cl. HA4: Ruis 7E 38
Ravenscourt Gdns. W6 4C 98
Ravenscourt Pk. EN5: Barn 4A 20
W6 3C 98
Ravenscourt Pk. Mans.
W6 3D 98
(off Paddenswick Rd.)
Ravenscourt Pl. W6 4D 98
Ravenscourt Rd. W6 4D 98
(not continuous)
Ravenscourt Sq. W6 3C 98
Ravenscraig Rd. N11 4B 32
Ravenscroft Av. HA9: Wemb 1E 60
NW11 7H 45
(not continuous)
Ravenscroft Cl. E16 5J 87
Ravenscroft Cotts.
EN5: New Bar 4D 20
Ravenscroft Cres. SE9 3D 142
Ravenscroft Pk. *E2* 3F 85
(off Baroness Rd.)
EN5: Barn 3A 20
Ravenscroft Rd. BR3: Beck 2J 157
E16 5J 87
W4 4J 97
Ravenscroft School Sports Cen. 7C 20
Ravenscroft St. E2 1K 9 (2F 85)
Ravensdale Av. N12 4F 31
Ravensdale Gdns. SE19 7D 138
TW4: Houn 3C 112
Ravensdale Ind. Est. N16 6G 49
Ravensdale Mans. *N8* 6J 47
(off Haringey Pk.)
Ravensdale Rd. N16 7F 49
TW4: Houn 3C 112
Ravensdon St. SE11 6K 19 (5A 102)
Ravensfield Cl. RM9: Dag 4D 72
Ravensfield Gdns. KT19: Ewe 5A 164
Ravenshaw St. NW6 5H 63
Ravenshill BR7: Chst 1F 161
Ravenshurst Av. NW4 4E 44
Ravenside *KT1: King T* 5D 150
(off Portsmouth Rd.)
Ravenside Cl. N18 5E 34
Ravenside Retail Pk. N18 5E 34
Ravenslea Rd. SW12 7D 118
Ravensleigh Gdns. BR1: Brom 5K 141
Ravensmead Rd. BR2: Brom 7F 141
Ravensmede Way W4 4B 98
Ravens M. SE12 5J 123
Ravenstone SE17 5E 102
Ravenstone Rd. N8 3A 48
NW9 6B 44
Ravenstone St. SW12 1E 136
Ravens Way SE12 5J 123
Ravenswood DA5: Bexl 1E 144
Ravenswood Av. BR4: W W'ck 1E 170
KT6: Surb 2F 163
Ravenswood Ct. KT2: King T 6H 133
Ravenswood Cres. BR4: W W'ck 1E 170
HA2: Harr 2D 58
Ravenswood Gdns. TW7: Isle 1J 113
Ravenswood Ind. Est. E17 4E 50
Ravenswood Rd. CR0: Wadd 3B 168
E17 4E 50
SW12 7F 119
Ravensworth Ct. *SW6* 7J 99
(off Fulham Rd.)
Ravensworth Rd. NW10 3D 80
SE9 3D 142
Ravent Rd. SE11 4H 19 (4K 101)
Raven Wharf *SE1* 6J 15
(off Lafone St.)
Ravey St. EC2 3G 9 (4E 84)
Ravine Gro. SE18 6J 107
Rav Pinter Cl. N16 7E 48
Rawalpindi Ho. E16 4H 87
Rawchester Cl. SW18 1H 135
Rawlings Cl. BR3: Beck 5E 158
BR6: Chels 5K 173
Rawlings Cres. HA9: Wemb 3H 61
Rawlings St. SW3 3E 16 (4D 100)
Rawlins Cl. CR2: Sels 7A 170
N3 3G 45
Rawlinson Ct. NW2 7E 44
Rawlinson Ho. *SE13* 4F 123
(off Mercator Rd.)
Rawlinson Point *E16* 5H 87
(off Fox Rd.)
Rawnsley Av. CR4: Mitc 5B 154
Rawreth Wlk. *N1* 1C 84
(off Basire St.)
Rawson St. SW11 1E 118
(not continuous)
Rawsthorne Cl. E16 1D 106
Rawsthorne Ct.
TW4: Houn 4D 112
Rawstone Wlk. E13 2J 87
Rawstorne Pl. EC1 1A 8 (3B 84)
Rawstorne St. EC1 1A 8 (3B 84)
(not continuous)
Raybell Ct. TW7: Isle 2K 113
Rayburne Ct. IG9: Buck H 1F 37
W14 3G 99
Ray Cl. KT9: Chess 6C 162
Raydean Rd. EN5: New Bar 5E 20
Raydons Gdns.
RM9: Dag 4E 72
Raydons Rd. RM9: Dag 5E 72
Raydon St. N19 2F 65
Rayfield Cl. BR2: Brom 6C 160
Rayford Av. SE12 7H 123
Ray Gdns. HA7: Stan 5G 27
IG11: Bark 2A 90
Ray Gunter Ho. *SE17* 5B 102
(off Marsland Cl.)
Ray Ho. *N1* 1E 84
(off Colville Est.)
W10 6F 81
(off Cambridge Gdns.)
Rayleas Cl. SE18 1F 125
Rayleigh Av. TW11: Tedd 6J 131
Rayleigh Cl. N13 3J 33

Rayleigh Ct. KT1: King T 2G **151**
N22 .... 1C **48**
Rayleigh Ri. CR2: S Croy 6E **168**
Rayleigh Rd. E16 .... 1K **105**
IG8: Wfd G 6F **37**
N13 .... 3H **33**
SW19 .... 1H **153**
Ray Lodge Rd. IG8: Wfd G 6F **37**
Ray Massey Way *E6* *1C* ***88***
(off High St. Nth.)
Raymead Av. CR7: Thor H 5A **156**
Raymead Pas. *CR7: Thor H* *5A* ***156***
(off Raymead Av.)
Raymede Towers *W10* *5F* ***81***
(off Treverton St.)
Raymere Gdns. SE18 .... 7H **107**
Raymond Av. E18 .... 3H **51**
W13 .... 3A **96**
Raymond Bldgs. WC1 .... 5H **7** (5K **83**)
Raymond Cl. SE26 .... 5J **139**
SL3: Poyle 4A **174**
Raymond Ct. N10 .... 7A **32**
Raymond Postgate Ct. SE28 .... 7B **90**
Raymond Rd. BR3: Beck 4A **158**
E13 .... 1A **88**
IG2: Ilf 7H **53**
SW19 .... 6G **135**
Raymond Way KT10: Clay 6A **162**
Raymouth Rd. SE16 .... 4H **103**
Raynald Ho. SW16 .... 3J **137**
Rayne Ct. E18 .... 4H **51**
Rayne Ho. SW12 .... 6E **118**
W9 .... *4K* ***81***
(off Delaware Rd.)
Rayner Ct. *W12* *2E* ***98***
(off Bamborough Gdns.)
Rayners Cl. HA0: Wemb 5D **60**
Rayners Cres. UB5: Yead 3K **75**
Rayners Gdns. UB5: Yead 2K **75**
RAYNERS LANE 1D **58**
Rayners La. HA2: Harr 1E **58**
HA5: Harr, Pinn 5D **40**
Rayners Rd. SW15 .... 5G **117**
Rayner Towers *E10* *7C* ***50***
(off Albany Rd.)
Raynes Av. E11 .... 7A **52**
RAYNES PARK 4E **152**
Raynes Pk. Bri. SW20 .... 2E **152**
Raynes Pk. School Sports Cen. 3D **152**
Raynham *W2* *7D* ***4***
(off Norfolk Cres.)
Raynham Av. N18 .... 6B **34**
Raynham Ho. *E1* *4K* ***85***
(off Harpley Sq.)
Raynham Rd. N18 .... 5B **34**
W6 .... 4D **98**
Raynham Ter. N18 .... 5B **34**
Raynor Cl. UB1: S'hall 1D **94**
Raynor Pl. N1 .... 7C **66**
Raynton Cl. HA2: Harr 1C **58**
UB4: Hayes 4H **75**
Raynton Dr. UB4: Hayes 4H **75**
Ray Rd. KT8: W Mole 5F **149**
Rays Av. N18 .... 4D **34**
Rays Rd. BR4: W W'ck 7E **158**
N18 .... 4D **34**
Ray St. EC1 .... 4K **7** (4A **84**)
Ray St. Bri. EC1 .... 4K **7**
Ray Wlk. N7 .... 2K **65**
Raywood Cl. UB3: Harl 7E **92**
Razia M. E12 .... 5D **70**
Reachview Cl. NW1 .... 7G **65**
Read Cl. KT7: T Ditt 7A **150**
Read Ct. E17 .... 6C **50**
Reade Ct. *W3* *3J* ***97***
(off Stanley Rd.)
Reader Ho. *SE5* *1C* ***120***
(off Badsworth Rd.)
Reade Wlk. NW10 .... 7A **62**
Read Ho. SE11 .... 7J **19**
Reading Ho. *SE15* *6G* ***103***
(off Friary Est.)
W2 .... *6A* ***82***
(off Hallfield Est.)
Reading La. E8 .... 6H **67**
Reading Rd. SM1: Sutt 5A **166**
UB5: N'olt 5F **59**
Reading Way NW7 .... 5A **30**
Readman Ct. SE20 .... 1H **157**
Reads Cl. IG1: Ilf 3F **71**
Reapers Cl. NW1 .... 1H **83**
Reapers Way TW7: Isle 5H **113**
Reardon Ct. N21 .... 2G **33**
Reardon Ho. *E1* *1H* ***103***
(off Reardon St.)
Reardon Path E1 .... 1H **103**
(not continuous)
Reardon St. E1 .... 1H **103**
Reaston St. SE14 .... 7K **103**
Rebecca Ct. DA14: Sidc 4B **144**
Reckitt Rd. W4 .... 5A **98**
Record St. SE15 .... 6J **103**
Recovery St. SW17 .... 5C **136**
Recreation Av. RM7: Rom 5J **55**
Recreation Rd. BR2: Brom 2H **159**
DA15: Sidc 3J **143**
SE26 .... 4K **139**
UB2: S'hall 4C **94**
Recreation Way CR4: Mitc 3H **155**
Rector St. N1 .... 1C **84**
Rectory Bus. Cen. DA14: Sidc 4B **144**
Rectory Chambers *SW3* *6C* ***100***
(off Old Church St.)
Rectory Cl. DA14: Sidc 4B **144**
E4 .... 3H **35**
HA7: Stan 5G **27**
KT6: Surb 1C **162**
N3 .... 1H **45**
SW20 .... 3E **152**
TW17: Shep 3C **146**
Rectory Ct. E18 .... 1H **51**
SM6: Wall 4G **167**
TW13: Felt 4A **130**
Rectory Cres. E11 .... 6A **52**
(not continuous)
Rectory Farm Rd. EN2: Enf 1E **22**
(not continuous)
Rectory Fld. Cres. SE7 .... 7A **106**
Rectory Gdns. *BR3: Beck* *1C* ***158***
(off Rectory Rd.)
N8 .... 4J **47**
SW4 .... 3G **119**
UB5: N'olt 1D **76**
Rectory Grn. BR3: Beck 1B **158**
Rectory Gro. CR0: C'don 2B **168**
SW4 .... 3G **119**
TW12: Hamp 4D **130**
Rectory La. DA14: Sidc 4B **144**
HA7: Stan 5G **27**
HA8: Edg 6B **28**
KT6: Surb 1B **162**
SM6: Wall 4G **167**
SW17 .... 6E **136**
Rectory Orchard SW19 .... 4G **135**
Rectory Pk. Av. UB5: N'olt 3D **76**
Rectory Pl. SE18 .... 4E **106**
Rectory Rd. BR2: Kes 7B **172**
BR3: Beck 1C **158**
E12 .... 5D **70**
E17 .... 4D **50**
N16 .... 2F **67**
RM10: Dag 6H **73**
SM1: Sutt 3J **165**
SW13 .... 2C **116**
TW4: Cran 2A **112**
UB2: S'hall 3D **94**
UB3: Hayes 6J **75**
W3 .... 1H **97**
Rectory Sq. E1 .... 5K **85**
Rectory Way UB10: Ick 2D **56**
Reculver Ho. *SE15* *6J* ***103***
(off Lovelinch Cl.)
Reculver M. N18 .... 4B **34**
Reculver Rd. SE16 .... 5K **103**
Red Anchor Cl. SW3 .... 6B **100**
Redan Pl. W2 .... 6K **81**
Redan St. W14 .... 3F **99**
Redan Ter. SE5 .... 2B **120**
Red Barracks Rd. SE18 .... 4D **106**
Redberry Gro. SE26 .... 3J **139**
Redbourne Av. N3 .... 1J **45**
Redbourne Dr. SE28 .... 6D **90**
(not continuous)
Redbourne Ho. *E14* *6B* ***86***
(off Norbiton Rd.)
Redbourn Ho. *W10* *4E* ***80***
(off Sutton Way)
REDBRIDGE 6C **52**
Redbridge Ent. Cen. IG1: Ilf 2G **71**
Redbridge FC 4H **53**
Redbridge Foyer *IG1: Ilf* *2G* ***71***
(off Sylvan Rd.)
Redbridge Gdns. SE5 .... 7E **102**
Redbridge Ho. *E16* *7F* ***89***
(off University Way)
Redbridge La. E. IG4: Ilf 6B **52**
Redbridge La. W. E11 .... 6K **51**
REDBRIDGE RDBT. 6B **52**
Redbridge Sports Cen. 1H **53**
Redburn St. SW3 .... 7E **16** (6D **100**)
Redburn Trad. Est. EN3: Pond E 6E **24**
Redcar Cl. UB5: N'olt 5F **59**
Redcar St. SE5 .... 7C **102**
Redcastle Cl. E1 .... 7J **85**
Red Cedars Rd. BR6: Orp 7J **161**
Redchurch St. E2 .... 3J **9** (4F **85**)
Redcliffe Cl. *SW5* *5K* ***99***
(off Old Brompton Rd.)
Redcliffe Ct. *E5* *3H* ***67***
(off Napoleon Rd.)
Redcliffe Gdns. IG1: Ilf 1E **70**
SW10 .... 5K **99**
W4 .... 7H **97**
Redcliffe M. SW10 .... 5K **99**
Redcliffe Pl. SW10 .... 6A **100**
Redcliffe Rd. SW10 .... 5A **100**
Redcliffe Sq. SW10 .... 5K **99**
Redcliffe St. SW10 .... 6K **99**
Redclose Av. SM4: Mord 5J **153**
Redclyffe Rd. E6 .... 1A **88**
Redclyf Ho. *E1* *4J* ***85***
(off Cephas St.)
Redcourt CR0: C'don 3E **168**
Red Cow La. EC1 .... 3C **8** (4C **84**)
Redcroft Rd. UB1: S'hall 7G **77**
Red Cross Cotts. *SE1* *2C* ***102***
(off Ayres St.)
Redcross Way SE1 .... 6D **14** (2C **102**)
Redding Ho. SE18 .... 3C **106**
Reddings, The NW7 .... 3G **29**
Reddings Cl. NW7 .... 4G **29**
Reddins Rd. SE15 .... 6G **103**
Reddons Rd. BR3: Beck 7A **140**
Redenham Ho. *SW15* *7C* ***116***
(off Ellisfield Dr.)
Rede Pl. W2 .... 6J **81**
Redesdale Gdns. TW7: Isle 7A **96**
Redesdale St. SW3 .... 7D **16** (6C **100**)
Redfern Av. TW4: Houn 7E **112**
Redfern Ho. *E13* *1H* ***87***
(off Redriffe Rd.)
NW8 .... *1B* ***82***
(off Dorman Way)
Redfern Rd. NW10 .... 7A **62**
SE6 .... 7E **122**
Redfield La. SW5 .... 4J **99**
Redfield M. SW5 .... 4K **99**
Redford Av. CR7: Thor H 4K **155**
SM6: Wall 6J **167**
Redford Cl. TW13: Felt 2H **129**
Redford Wlk. *N1* *1C* ***84***
(off Popham St.)
Redgate Dr. BR2: Hayes 2K **171**
Redgate Ter. SW15 .... 6F **117**
Redgrave Cl. CR0: C'don 6F **157**
Redgrave Rd. SW15 .... 3F **117**
Redgrave Ter. *E2* *3G* ***85***
(off Derbyshire St.)
Red Hill BR7: Chst 5F **143**
Redhill Ct. SW2 .... 2A **138**
Redhill Dr. HA8: Edg 2H **43**
Redhill St. NW1 .... 1K **5** (2F **83**)
Red House 4E **126**
Red Ho. La. DA6: Bex 4D **126**
Redhouse Rd. CR0: C'don 6H **155**
Red Ho. Sq. N1 .... 6C **66**
Redif Ho. RM10: Dag 4H **73**
Redington Gdns. NW3 .... 4K **63**
Redington Ho. *N1* *2K* ***83***
(off Priory Grn. Est.)
Redington Rd. NW3 .... 3K **63**
Redknap Ho. TW10: Ham 3C **132**
Redland Gdns. KT8: W Mole 4D **148**
Redlands N15 .... 4D **48**
TW11: Tedd 6A **132**
Redlands, The BR3: Beck 2D **158**
Redlands Ct. BR1: Brom 7H **141**
Redlands Rd. EN3: Enf H 1F **25**
Redlands Way SW2 .... 7K **119**
Red La. KT10: Clay 6A **162**
Redleaf Cl. DA17: Belv 6G **109**
Redleaves Av. TW15: Ashf 6D **128**
Redlees Cl. TW7: Isle 4A **114**
Red Leys UB8: Uxb 7A **56**
Red Lion Bus. Pk. KT6: Surb 3F **163**
Red Lion Cl. *SE17* *6D* ***102***
(off Red Lion Row)
Red Lion Ct. EC4 .... 1K **13** (6A **84**)
SE1 .... 4D **14** (1C **102**)
Red Lion Hill N2 .... 2B **46**
(not continuous)
Red Lion La. SE18 .... 7E **106**
Red Lion Pde. HA5: Pinn 3C **40**
Red Lion Pl. SE18 .... 1E **124**
Red Lion Rd. KT6: Surb 2F **163**
Red Lion Row SE17 .... 6C **102**
Red Lion Sq. SW18 .... 5J **117**
WC1 .... 6G **7** (5K **83**)
Red Lion St. TW9: Rich 5D **114**
WC1 .... 5G **7** (5K **83**)
Red Lion Yd. W1 .... 4H **11**
Red Lodge BR4: W W'ck 1E **170**
Red Lodge Cres. DA5: Bexl 3K **145**
Red Lodge Rd. BR4: W W'ck 1E **170**
DA5: Bexl 3K **145**
Redlynch Ct. *W14* *2G* ***99***
(off Addison Cres.)
Redman Cl. UB5: Yead 2A **76**
Redman Ho. *EC1* *5J* ***7***
(off Bourne Est.)
SE1 .... *7D* ***14***
(off Borough High St.)
Redman's Rd. E1 .... 5J **85**
Redmead La. E1 .... 1G **103**
Redmead Rd. UB3: Harl 4G **93**
Redmill Ho. *E1* *4H* ***85***
(off Headlam St.)
Redmond Ho. *N1* *1K* ***83***
(off Barnsbury Est.)
Redmore Rd. W6 .... 4D **98**
Red Oak Cl. BR6: Farnb 3F **173**
Redo Ho. *E12* *5E* ***70***
(off Dore Av.)
Red Path E9 .... 6A **68**
Red Pl. W1 .... 2G **11** (7E **82**)
Redpoll Way DA18: Erith 3D **108**
Red Post Hill SE21 .... 4D **120**
SE24 .... 4D **120**
Red Post Ho. E6 .... 7B **70**
Redriffe Rd. E13 .... 1H **87**

Redriff Est. SE16 . . . . . 3B 104
Redriff Rd. RM7: Mawney 2H 55
SE16 . . . . . 4K 103
Redroofs Cl. BR3: Beck 1D 158
Redrose Trad. Cen.
EN4: E Barn 5G 21
RED ROVER 4C 116
Redrup Ho. SE14 . . . . . 6K 103
(off John Williams Cl.)
Redruth Cl. N22 . . . . . 7E 32
Redruth Gdns. KT10: Clay 7A 162
Redruth Ho. SM2: Sutt 7K 165
Redruth Rd. E9 . . . . . 1J 85
Redshank Ho. SE1 . . . . . 5F 103
(off Avocet Cl.)
Red Sq. N16 . . . . . 3D 66
Redstart Cl. E6 . . . . . 5C 88
SE14 . . . . . 7A 104
Redstart Mans. IG1: Ilf 3E 70
(off Mill Rd.)
Redston Rd. N8 . . . . . 4H 47
Redvers Rd. N22 . . . . . 2A 48
Redvers St. N1 . . . . . 1H 9 (3E 84)
Redwald Rd. E5 . . . . . 4K 67
Redway Dr. TW2: Whitt 7G 113
Redwing Ct. SE1 . . . . . 7D 14
(off Swan St.)
Redwing M. SE5 . . . . . 2C 120
Redwing Path SE28 . . . . . 2H 107
Redwing Rd. SM6: Wall 7J 167
Redwood Cl. DA15: Sidc 1A 144
E3 . . . . . 2C 86
IG9: Buck H 2E 36
N14 . . . . . 7C 22
SE16 . . . . . 1A 104
UB10: Hil 2D 74
Redwood Ct. KT6: Surb 7D 150
N19 . . . . . 7H 47
NW6 . . . . . 7G 63
UB5: N'olt 3C 76
Redwood Est. TW5: Cran 6K 93
Redwood Gdns. E4 . . . . . 6J 25
Redwood Gro. W5 . . . . . 3B 96
Redwood Mans. W8 . . . . . 3K 99
(off Chantry Sq.)
Redwood M. SW4 . . . . . 3F 119
TW15: Ashf 7F 129
(off Staines Rd. W.)
Redwoods SW15 . . . . . 1C 134
Redwood Wlk. KT6: Surb 1D 162
Redwood Way EN5: Barn 5A 20
Reece M. SW7 . . . . . 3A 16 (4B 100)
Reed Av. BR6: Orp 3J 173
Reed Cl. E16 . . . . . 5J 87
SE12 . . . . . 5J 123
Reede Gdns. RM10: Dag 5H 73
Reede Rd. RM10: Dag 6G 73
Reede Way RM10: Dag 6H 73
Reedham Cl. N17 . . . . . 4H 49
Reedham St. SE15 . . . . . 2G 121
Reedholm Vs. N16 . . . . . 4D 66
Reed Pl. SW4 . . . . . 4H 119
Reed Rd. N17 . . . . . 2F 49
Reedsfield Cl. TW15: Ashf 3D 128
Reedsfield Rd. TW15: Ashf 4D 128
Reed's Pl. NW1 . . . . . 7G 65
Reedworth St. SE11 . . . . . 4K 19 (4A 102)
Reef Ho. E14 . . . . . 3E 104
(off Manchester St.)
Reenglass Rd. HA7: Stan 4J 27
Rees Dr. HA7: Stan 4K 27
Rees Gdns. CR0: C'don 6F 157
Reesland Cl. E12 . . . . . 6E 70
Rees St. N1 . . . . . 1C 84
Reets Farm Cl. NW9 . . . . . 6A 44
Reeves Av. NW9 . . . . . 7K 43
Reeves Cnr. CR0: C'don 2B 168
Reeves Ho. SE1 . . . . . 7J 13
(off Baylis Rd.)
Reeves M. W1 . . . . . 3G 11 (7E 82)
Reeves Rd. E3 . . . . . 4D 86
SE18 . . . . . 6F 107
Reflection, The E16 . . . . . 2F 107
(off Woolwich Mnr. Way)
Reflection Ho. E2 . . . . . 4G 85
(off Cheshire St.)
Reflex Apartments BR2: Brom 4K 159
(off Wheeler Pl.)
Reform Row N17 . . . . . 2F 49
Reform St. SW11 . . . . . 2D 118
Regal Cl. E1 . . . . . 5G 85
W5 . . . . . 5D 78
Regal Ct. CR4: Mitc 3D 154
N18 . . . . . 5A 34
NW6 . . . . . 2H 81
(off Malvern Rd.)
SW6 . . . . . 7J 99
(off Dawes Rd.)
Regal Cres. SM6: Wall 3F 167
Regal Dr. N11 . . . . . 5A 32
Regal Ho. IG2: Ilf 6H 53
Regal Ho., The SW6 . . . . . 2A 118
Regal La. NW1 . . . . . 1E 82
Regal Pl. E3 . . . . . 3B 86
SW6 . . . . . 7K 99
Regal Row SE15 . . . . . 1J 121
Regal Way HA3: Kent 6E 42
Regan Ho. N18 . . . . . 6A 34
Regan Way N1 . . . . . 1G 9 (2E 84)
Regatta Ho. TW11: Tedd 4A 132
Regatta Point E14 . . . . . 2C 104
(off Westferry Rd.)
TW8: Bford 6F 97
Regency Cl. TW12: Hamp 5D 130
W5 . . . . . 6E 78
Regency Ct. E9 . . . . . 1J 85
(off Park Cl.)
E18 . . . . . 2J 51
EN1: Enf 5J 23
SM1: Sutt 4A 166
TW11: Tedd 6B 132
Regency Cres. NW4 . . . . . 2F 45
Regency Dr. HA4: Ruis 1G 57
Regency Gdns. KT12: Walt T 7A 148
Regency Ho. E16 . . . . . 1J 105
(off Pepys Cres.)
N3 . . . . . 2H 45
NW1 . . . . . 3K 5
(off Osnaburgh St.)
SW1 . . . . . 3D 18
(off Regency St.)
SW6 . . . . . 1A 118
Regency Lawn NW5 . . . . . 3F 65
Regency Lodge IG9: Buck H 2G 37
NW3 . . . . . 7B 64
(off Adelaide Rd.)
Regency M. BR3: Beck 7E 140
NW10 . . . . . 6C 62
SW9 . . . . . 7B 102
TW7: Isle 5J 113
Regency Pde. NW3 . . . . . 7B 64
(off Finchley Rd.)
Regency Pl. SW1 . . . . . 3D 18 (4H 101)
Regency St. NW10 . . . . . 4A 80
SW1 . . . . . 3D 18 (4H 101)
Regency Ter. SW7 . . . . . 5A 16
(off Fulham Rd.)
Regency Wlk. CR0: C'don 6B 158
TW10: Rich 5E 114
(off Grosvenor Av.)
TW10: Rich 5E 114
(off The Vineyard)
Regency Way DA6: Bex 3D 126
Regeneration Rd. SE16 . . . . . 4K 103
Regent Av. UB10: Hil 7D 56
Regent Bus. Cen.
UB3: Hayes 2K 93
Regent Cl. HA3: Kent 6E 42
N12 . . . . . 5F 31
TW4: Cran 1K 111
Regent Ct. N3 . . . . . 7E 30
N20 . . . . . 2F 31
NW6 . . . . . 7H 63
(off Cavendish Rd.)
NW8 . . . . . 2C 4
W8 . . . . . 3K 99
(off Wright's La.)
Regent Gdns. IG3: Ilf 7A 54
Regent Ho. W14 . . . . . 4G 99
(off Windsor Way)
Regent Pde. SM2: Sutt 6A 166
Regent Pl. CR0: C'don 1F 169
SW19 . . . . . 5A 136
W1 . . . . . 2B 12 (7G 83)
Regent Rd. KT5: Surb 5F 151
SE24 . . . . . 6B 120
Regents Av. N13 . . . . . 5F 33
Regent's Bri. Gdns. SW8 . . . . . 7J 101
Regents Canal Ho. E14 . . . . . 6A 86
(off Commercial Rd.)
Regents Cl. CR2: S Croy 6E 168
HA8: Edg 4K 27
UB4: Hayes 5H 75
Regents College 3F 5
Regents Ct. BR1: Brom 7H 141
E8 . . . . . 1F 85
(off Pownall Rd.)
HA5: Pinn 2B 40
KT2: King T 1E 150
(off Sopwith Way)
Regents Dr. BR2: Kes 5B 172
IG8: Wfd G 6K 37
Regents Ga. Ho. E14 . . . . . 7A 86
(off Horseferry Rd.)
Regents M. NW8 . . . . . 2A 82
REGENT'S PARK 2K 5 (3F 83)
Regent's Pk. 1F 5 (2D 82)
Regent's Pk. Barracks 1K 5
Regents Pk. Est. NW1 . . . . . 1A 6
Regent's Pk. Gdns. M. NW1 . . . . . 1D 82
Regent's Pk. Ho. NW8 . . . . . 2D 4
(off Park Rd.)
Regent's Pk. Open Air Theatre
. . . . . 2G 5 (3E 82)
Regents Pk. Rd. N3 . . . . . 3H 45
NW1 . . . . . 7D 64
(not continuous)
Regent's Pk. Ter. NW1 . . . . . 1F 83
Regent's Pl. SE3 . . . . . 2J 123
Regents Plaza NW6 . . . . . 2K 81
(off Kilburn High Rd.)
Regent Sq. DA17: Belv 4H 109
E3 . . . . . 3D 86
WC1 . . . . . 2F 7 (3J 83)
Regent's Row E8 . . . . . 1G 85
Regent St. NW10 . . . . . 3F 81
SW1 . . . . . 3C 12 (7H 83)
W1 . . . . . 7K 5 (6F 83)
W4 . . . . . 5G 97
Regents Wharf E2 . . . . . 1H 85
(off Wharf Pl.)
N1 . . . . . 2K 83
Regina Cl. EN5: Barn 3A 20
Regina Ho. SE20 . . . . . 1K 157
Reginald Pl. SE8 . . . . . 7C 104
(off Deptford High St.)
Reginald Rd. E7 . . . . . 7J 69
HA6: Nwood 1H 39
SE8 . . . . . 7C 104
Reginald Sorenson Ho.
E11 . . . . . 7F 51
Reginald Sq. SE8 . . . . . 7C 104
Regina Point SE16 . . . . . 3J 103
Regina Rd. N4 . . . . . 1K 65
SE25 . . . . . 3G 157
UB2: S'hall 4C 94
W13 . . . . . 1A 96
Regina Ter. W13 . . . . . 1B 96
Regis Ct. CR4: Mitc 1C 154
N8 . . . . . 4K 47
Regis Ct. NW1 . . . . . 5E 4
(off Melcombe Pl.)
Regis Ho. W1 . . . . . 5H 5
(off Beaumont St.)
Regis Pl. SW2 . . . . . 4K 119
Regis Rd. NW5 . . . . . 5F 65
Regnart Bldgs. NW1 . . . . . 3B 6
Regnolruf Ct. KT12: Walt T 7J 147
Reid Cl. HA5: Eastc 4J 39
UB3: Hayes 6G 75
Reidhaven Rd. SE18 . . . . . 4J 107
Reigate Av. SM1: Sutt 1J 165
Reigate Rd. BR1: Brom 3H 141
IG3: Ilf 2K 71
Reigate Way SM6: Wall 5J 167
Reighton Rd. E5 . . . . . 3G 67
Reinickendorf Av. SE9 . . . . . 6G 125
Reizel Cl. N16 . . . . . 1F 67
Relay Rd. W12 . . . . . 1E 98
Relf Rd. SE15 . . . . . 3G 121
Reliance Arc. SW9 . . . . . 4A 120
Reliance Sq. EC2 . . . . . 3H 9 (4E 84)
Relko Gdns. SM1: Sutt 5B 166
Relton M. SW7 . . . . . 1D 16 (3C 100)
Rembold Ho. SE10 . . . . . 1E 122
(off Blissett St.)
Rembrandt Cl. E14 . . . . . 3F 105
SW1 . . . . . 4G 17
Rembrandt Ct. KT19: Ewe 6B 164
SE16 . . . . . 5H 103
(off Stubbs Dr.)
Rembrandt Rd. HA8: Edg 2G 43
SE13 . . . . . 4G 123
Remembrance Rd. E7 . . . . . 4B 70
Remington Rd. E6 . . . . . 6C 88
N15 . . . . . 6D 48
Remington St. N1 . . . . . 1B 8 (2B 84)
Remnant St. WC2 . . . . . 7G 7 (6K 83)
Remsted Ho. NW6 . . . . . 1K 81
(off Mortimer Cres.)
Remus Bldg., The EC1 . . . . . 2K 7
(off Hardwick St.)
Remus Rd. E3 . . . . . 7C 68
Renaissance Ct. SM1: Sutt 1A 166
TW3: Houn 3G 113
Renaissance Wlk. SE10 . . . . . 3H 105
(off Teal St.)
Rendle Cl. CR0: C'don 5F 157
Rendle Ho. W10 . . . . . 4G 81
(off Wornington Rd.)
Rendlesham Rd. E5 . . . . . 4G 67
EN2: Enf 1G 23
Renforth St. SE16 . . . . . 3J 103
Renfree Way TW17: Shep 7C 146
Renfrew Cl. E6 . . . . . 7E 88
Renfrew Ct. TW4: Houn 2C 112
Renfrew Ho. E17 . . . . . 2B 50
NW6 . . . . . 2K 81
(off Carlton Va.)
Renfrew Rd. KT2: King T 7H 133
SE11 . . . . . 3K 19 (4B 102)
TW4: Houn 2B 112
Renmuir St. SW17 . . . . . 6D 136
Rennell St. SE13 . . . . . 3E 122
Rennels Way TW7: Isle 2J 113
Renness Rd. E17 . . . . . 3A 50
Rennets Cl. SE9 . . . . . 5J 125
Rennets Wood Rd. SE9 . . . . . 5H 125
Rennie Cotts. E1 . . . . . 4J 85
(off Pemell Cl.)
Rennie Ct. SE1 . . . . . 4A 14
Rennie Est. SE16 . . . . . 4H 103
Rennie Ho. SE1 . . . . . 3C 102
(off Bath Ter.)
Rennie St. SE1 . . . . . 4A 14 (1B 102)
(not continuous)
Renoir Cinema
Brunswick Square 4J 83
Renoir Ct. SE16 . . . . . 5H 103
(off Stubbs Dr.)

Renovation, The *E16* *2F* ***107***
(off Woolwich Mnr. Way)
Renown Cl. CR0: C'don 1B **168**
RM7: Mawney 1G **55**
Rensburg Rd. E17 5K **49**
Renshaw Cl. DA17: Belv 6F **109**
Renters Av. NW4 6E **44**
Renton Cl. SW2 6K **119**
Renwick Ind. Est. IG11: Bark 2B **90**
Renwick Rd. IG11: Bark 4B **90**
Repens Way UB4: Yead 4B **76**
Rephidim St. SE1 3E **102**
Replingham Rd. SW18 1H **135**
Reporton Rd. SW6 7G **99**
Repository Rd. SE18 6D **106**
Repton Av. HA0: Wemb 4C **60**
UB3: Harl 4F **93**
Repton Cl. SM5: Cars 5C **166**
Repton Ct. BR3: Beck 1D **158**
IG5: Ilf 1D **52**
Repton Gro. IG5: Ilf 1D **52**
Repton Ho. *SW1* *4B* ***18***
(off Charlwood St.)
REPTON PARK **7K 37**
Repton Rd. BR6: Chels 3K **173**
HA3: Kent 4F **43**
Repton St. E14 6A **86**
Repulse Cl. RM5: Col R 1G **55**
Reservoir Cl. CR7: Thor H 3D **156**
Reservoir Rd. HA4: Ruis 4F **39**
N14 5B **22**
SE4 2A **122**
Reservoir Studios *E1* *6K* ***85***
(off Cable St.)
Resham Cl. UB2: S'hall 3A **94**
Resolution Wlk. SE18 3D **106**
Resolution Way *SE8* *7C* ***104***
(off Deptford High St.)
Restell Cl. SE3 6G **105**
Restmor Way SM6: Wall 2E **166**
Reston Pl. SW7 2A **100**
Restons Cres. SE9 6H **125**
Restoration Sq. SW11 1B **118**
Restormel Cl. TW3: Houn 5E **112**
Restormel Ho. SE11 4J **19**
Retcar Pl. N19 2F **65**
Retford St. N1 1H **9** (2E **84**)
Retingham Way E4 2J **35**
Retles Ct. HA1: Harr 7J **41**
Retreat, The CR7: Thor H 4D **156**
HA2: Harr 7E **40**
KT4: Wor Pk 2D **164**
KT5: Surb 6F **151**
NW9 5K **43**
SW14 3A **116**
Retreat Cl. HA3: Kent 5C **42**
Retreat Ho. E9 6J **67**
Retreat Pl. E9 6J **67**
Retreat Rd. TW9: Rich 5D **114**
Reubens Ct. *W4* *5H* ***97***
(off Chaseley Dr.)
Reunion Row E1 7H **85**
Reuters Plaza *E14* *1D* ***104***
(off The Sth. Colonnade)
Reveley Sq. SE16 2A **104**
Revell Ri. SE18 6K **107**
Revell Rd. KT1: King T 2H **151**
SM1: Sutt 6H **165**
Revelon Rd. SE4 4A **122**
Revelstoke Rd. SW18 2H **135**
Reventlow Rd. SE9 1G **143**
Reverdy Rd. SE1 4G **103**
Reverend Cl. HA2: Harr 3F **59**
Revesby Rd. SM5: Cars 6B **154**
Review Lodge RM10: Dag 1H **91**
Review Rd. NW2 2B **62**
RM10: Dag 1H **91**
Rewell St. SW6 7A **100**
Rewley Rd. SM5: Cars 6B **154**
Rex Av. TW15: Ashf 6C **128**
Rex Pl. W1 3H **11** (7E **82**)
Reydon Av. E11 5A **52**
Reynard Cl. BR1: Brom 3E **160**
SE4 3A **122**
Reynard Dr. SE19 7F **139**
Reynard Mills Trad. Est.
TW8: Bford 5C **96**
Reynard Pl. SE14 6A **104**
Reynardson Rd. N17 7H **33**
Reynolah Gdns. SE7 5K **105**
Reynolds Av. E12 5E **70**
KT9: Chess 7E **162**
RM6: Chad H 7C **54**
Reynolds Cl. NW11 7K **45**
SM5: Cars 1D **166**
SW19 1B **154**
Reynolds Ct. RM6: Chad H 3D **54**
Reynolds Dr. HA8: Edg 3F **43**
Reynolds Ho. *E2* *2J* ***85***
(off Approach Rd.)
NW8 *2B* ***82***
(off Wellington Rd.)
SW1 *4D* ***18***
(off Erasmus St.)
Reynolds Pl. SE3 7K **105**
TW10: Rich 6F **115**
Reynolds Rd. KT3: N Mald 7K **151**
SE15 4J **121**
UB4: Yead 4A **76**
W4 3J **97**
Reynolds Sports Cen. 2G **97**
Reynolds Way CR0: C'don 4E **168**
Rheidol M. N1 2C **84**
Rheidol Ter. N1 1C **84**
Rheingold Way SM6: Wall 7J **167**
Rhein Ho. *N8* *3J* ***47***
(off Campsfield Rd.)
Rheola Cl. N17 1F **49**
Rhoda St. E2 3K **9** (4F **85**)
Rhodes Av. N22 1G **47**
Rhodes Ho. *N1* *1E* ***8***
(off Provost Est.)
Rhodesia Rd. E11 2F **69**
SW9 2J **119**
Rhodes Moorhouse Ct.
SM4: Mord 6J **153**
Rhodes St. N7 5K **65**
Rhodeswell Rd. E14 5A **86**
(not continuous)
Rhodrons Av. KT9: Chess 5E **162**
Rhondda Gro. E3 3A **86**
Rhyl Rd. UB6: G'frd 2K **77**
Rhyl St. NW5 6E **64**
Rhys Av. N11 7C **32**
Rialto Rd. CR4: Mitc 2E **154**
Ribble Cl. IG8: Wfd G 6F **37**
Ribblesdale Av. N11 6K **31**
UB5: N'olt 6F **59**
Ribblesdale Ho. *NW6* *1J* ***81***
(off Kilburn Va.)
Ribblesdale Rd. N8 4K **47**
SW16 6F **137**
Ribbon Dance M. SE5 1D **120**
Ribchester Av. UB6: G'frd 3K **77**
Ribston Cl. BR2: Brom 1D **172**
Ricardo Path SE28 1C **108**
Ricardo St. E14 6D **86**
Ricards Rd. SW19 5H **135**
Riccall Ct. *NW9* *1A* ***44***
(off Pageant Av.)
Rice Pde. BR5: Pet W 5H **161**
Riceyman Ho. *WC1* *2J* ***7***
(off Lloyd Baker St.)
Richard Anderson Ct. *SE14* *7K* ***103***
(off Monson Rd.)
Richard Burbidge Mans. *SW13* *6E* ***98***
(off Brasenose Dr.)
Richard Burton Ct. *IG9: Buck H* *2F* ***37***
(off Palmerston Rd.)
Richard Cl. SE18 4C **106**
Richard Fell Ho. *E12* *4E* ***70***
(off Walton Rd.)
Richard Ho. *SE16* *4J* ***103***
(off Silwood St.)
Richard Ho. Dr. E16 6B **88**
Richard Neale Ho. *E1* *7H* ***85***
(off Cornwall St.)
Richard Neve Ho. *SE18* *4J* ***107***
(off Plumstead High St.)
Richard Robert Residence, The
E15 *6F* ***69***
(off Salway Rd.)
Richards Av. RM7: Rom 6J **55**
Richards Cl. HA1: Harr 5A **42**
UB3: Harl 6F **93**
UB10: Hil 1C **74**
WD23: Bush 1C **26**
Richards Fld. KT19: Ewe 7K **163**
Richard Sharples Ct. SM2: Sutt 7A **166**
Richardson Cl. E8 1F **85**
Richardson Ct. *SW4* *2J* ***119***
(off Studley Rd.)
Richardson Gdns. RM10: Dag 6H **73**
Richardson Rd. E15 2G **87**
Richardson's M. W1 4A **6**
Richards Pl. E17 3C **50**
SW3 3D **16** (4C **100**)
Richard St. E1 6H **85**
Richbell *WC1* *5F* ***7***
(off Boswell St.)
Richbell Pl. WC1 5G **7** (5K **83**)
Richborne Ter. SW8 7K **101**
Richborough Ho. *SE15* *6J* ***103***
(off Sharratt St.)
Richborough Rd. NW2 4G **63**
Richbourne Ct. *W1* *7D* ***4***
(off Harrowby St.)
Richens Cl. TW3: Houn 2H **113**
Riches Rd. IG1: Ilf 2G **71**
Richfield Rd. WD23: Bush 1B **26**
Richford Ga. W6 3E **98**
Richford Rd. E15 1H **87**
Richford St. W6 2E **98**
Rich Ind. Est. SE1 3E **102**
SE15 6H **103**
Richlands Av. KT17: Ewe 4C **164**
Rich La. SW5 5K **99**
Richman Ho. *SE8* *5B* ***104***
(off Grove St.)
RICHMOND **5D 114**
Richmond University
(The American International
University in London) 3K **99**
Richmond Av. E4 5A **36**
N1 1K **83**
NW10 6E **62**
SW20 1G **153**
TW14: Felt 6G **111**
UB10: Hil 6D **56**
Richmond Bri. TW1: Twick 6D **114**
Richmond Bldgs. W1 1C **12** (6H **83**)
RICHMOND CIRCUS **4E 114**
Richmond Cl. E17 6B **50**
Richmond College
(The American International
University in London) 2K **99**
Richmond Cotts. *W14* *4G* ***99***
(off Hammersmith Rd.)
Richmond Ct. CR4: Mitc 3B **154**
E8 *7H* ***67***
(off Mare St.)
HA9: Wemb 3F **61**
N11 *6K* ***31***
(off Pickering Gdns.)
NW6 *7F* ***63***
(off Willesden La.)
SW1 *7F* ***11***
(off Sloane St.)
W14 *4G* ***99***
(off Hammersmith Rd.)
Richmond Cres. E4 5A **36**
N1 1K **83**
N9 1B **34**
Richmond Cricket Club *3E* ***114***
(off Kew Rd.)
Richmond Dr. IG8: Wfd G 7K **37**
TW17: Shep 6F **147**
Richmond Filmhouse 5D **114**
Richmond Gdns. HA3: Hrw W 7E **26**
NW4 5C **44**
Richmond Grn. CR0: Bedd 3J **167**
Richmond Gro. KT5: Surb 6F **151**
N1 7B **66**
(not continuous)
Richmond Hill TW10: Rich 6E **114**
Richmond Hill Ct. TW10: Rich 6E **114**
Richmond Ho. *NW1* *1K* ***5***
(off Park Village E.)
SE17 *5D* ***102***
(off Portland St.)
Richmond Mans. *SW5* *5K* ***99***
(off Old Brompton Rd.)
TW1: Twick 6D **114**
Richmond M. TW11: Tedd 5K **131**
W1 1C **12** (6H **83**)
Richmond Pde. *TW1: Twick* *6C* ***114***
(off Richmond Rd.)
Richmond Pk. 1G **133**
Richmond Pk. Rd. KT2: King T 1E **150**
SW14 5J **115**
Richmond Pl. SE18 4G **107**
Richmond Rd. CR0: Bedd 3J **167**
CR7: Thor H 3B **156**
E4 1A **36**
E7 5K **69**
(not continuous)
E8 7F **67**
(not continuous)
E11 2F **69**
EN5: New Bar 5E **20**
IG1: Ilf 3G **71**
KT2: King T 5D **132**
N2 2A **46**
N11 6D **32**
N15 6E **48**
SW20 1D **152**
TW1: Twick 7B **114**
TW7: Isle 3A **114**
W5 2E **96**
Richmond RUFC *3D* ***114***
(off Kew Foot Rd.)
Richmond St. E13 2J **87**
Richmond Ter. SW1 6E **12** (2J **101**)
Richmond Theatre 4D **114**
Richmond University 7E **114**
Richmond Way E11 2J **69**
W12 2F **99**
W14 2F **99**
Richmount Gdns. SE3 3J **123**
Rich St. E14 7B **86**
Rickard Cl. NW4 4D **44**
SW2 1A **138**
Rickards Cl. KT6: Surb 2E **162**
Rickett St. SW6 6J **99**
Rickman Ho. *E1* *3J* ***85***
(off Rickman St.)
Rickman St. E1 4J **85**
Rickmansworth Rd. HA5: Pinn 2K **39**
HA6: Nwood 1F **39**
Rick Roberts Way E15 1E **86**
Rickthorne Rd. N19 2J **65**
Rickyard Path SE9 4C **124**
Riddell Ct. *SE5* *5F* ***103***
(off Albany Rd.)
Ridding La. UB6: G'frd 5K **59**
Riddons Rd. SE12 3A **142**
Ride, The EN3: Pond E 3D **24**
TW8: Bford 5B **96**
Rideout St. SE18 4D **106**
Rider Cl. DA15: Sidc 6J **125**

Rideway Dr. W3 .3G 97
Ridgdale St. E3 .2D 86
Ridge, The BR6: Orp .2H 173
DA5: Bexl .7F 127
EN5: Barn .5C 20
KT5: Surb .5G 151
TW2: Whitt .7H 113
Ridge Av. N21 .7H 23
Ridgebrook Rd. SE3 .3B 124
Ridge Cl. NW4 .2F 45
NW9 .4K 43
SE28 .2H 107
Ridge Ct. SE22 .7G 121
Ridge Crest EN2: Enf .1E 22
Ridgecroft Cl. DA5: Bexl .1J 145
Ridge Hill NW11 .1G 63
Ridgemead Cl. N14 .2D 32
Ridgemont Gdns. HA8: Edg .4D 28
Ridgemount Av. CR0: C'don .1K 169
Ridgemount Cl. SE20 .7H 139
Ridgemount Gdns. EN2: Enf .3G 23
Ridge Rd. CR4: Mitc .7F 137
N8 .6K 47
N21 .1H 33
NW2 .3H 63
SM3: Sutt .1G 165
Ridges Yd. CR0: C'don .3B 168
Ridgeview Cl. EN5: Barn .6A 20
Ridgeview Rd. N20 .3E 30
Ridge Way IG8: Wfd G .4F 37
SE19 .6E 138
TW13: Hanw .3C 130
Ridgeway BR2: Hayes .2J 171
TW10: Rich .6E 114
Ridgeway, The CR0: Wadd .3K 167
E4 .2J 35
EN2: Enf .1E 22
HA2: Harr .5D 40
(not continuous)
HA3: Kent .6C 42
HA4: Ruis .7J 39
HA7: Stan .6H 27
KT12: Walt T .7H 147
N3 .7E 30
N11 .4J 31
N14 .2D 32
NW7 .3H 29
NW9 .4K 43
NW11 .7G 45
W3 .3G 97
Ridgeway Av. EN4: E Barn .6J 21
Ridgeway Cres. BR6: Orp .3J 173
Ridgeway Cres. Gdns.
BR6: Orp .2J 173
Ridgeway Dr. BR1: Brom .4K 141
Ridgeway E. DA15: Sidc .5K 125
Ridgeway Gdns. IG4: Ilf .5C 52
N6 .7G 47
Ridgeway Rd. TW7: Isle .7J 95
Ridgeway Rd. Nth. TW7: Isle .6J 95
Ridgeway Wlk. UB5: N'olt .6C 58
(off Cowings Mead)
Ridgeway W. DA15: Sidc .5J 125
Ridgewell Cl. N1 .1C 84
RM10: Dag .1H 91
SE26 .4B 140
Ridgmount Gdns. WC1 .5C 6 (5H 83)
Ridgmount Pl. WC1 .5C 6 (5H 83)
Ridgmount Rd. SW18 .5K 117
Ridgmount St. WC1 .5C 6 (5H 83)
Ridgway SW19 .7E 134
Ridgway, The
SM2: Sutt .7B 166
Ridgway Ct. SW19 .6F 135
Ridgway Gdns. SW19 .7F 135
Ridgway Pl. SW19 .6G 135
Ridgway Rd. SW9 .3B 120
Ridgwell Rd. E16 .5A 88
Riding, The NW11 .7H 45
Riding Ho. St. W1 .6K 5 (5F 83)
Ridings, The E11 .5J 51
EN4: E Barn .7G 21
KT5: Surb .5G 151
KT17: Ewe .7B 164
TW16: Sun .1J 147
W5 .4F 79
Ridings Av. N21 .4G 23
Ridings Cl. N6 .7G 47
Ridler Rd. EN1: Enf .1K 23
Ridley Av. W13 .3B 96
Ridley Cl. IG11: Bark .7K 71
Ridley Ct. SW16 .6J 137
Ridley Ho. SW1 .2D 18
(off Monck St.)
Ridley Rd. BR2: Brom .3H 159
DA16: Well .1B 126
E7 .4A 70
E8 .5F 67
NW10 .2C 80
SW19 .7K 135
Ridsdale Rd. SE20 .1H 157
Riefield Rd. SE9 .4G 125
Riesco Dr. CR0: C'don .6J 169
Riffel Rd. NW2 .5E 62
Rifle Ct. SE11 .7K 19 (6A 102)
Rifle St. E14 .5D 86
Riga Ho. E1 .5K 85
(off Shandy St.)
Riga M. E1 .7K 9
(off Commercial Rd.)
Rigault Rd. SW6 .2G 117
Rigby Cl. CR0: Wadd .3A 168
Rigby La. UB3: Hayes .2E 92
Rigby M. IG1: Ilf .2E 70
Rigden St. E14 .6D 86
Rigeley Rd. NW10 .3C 80
Rigg App. E10 .1K 67
Rigge Pl. SW4 .4H 119
Riggindale Rd. SW16 .5H 137
Riley Ho. SW10 .7B 100
(off Riley St.)
Riley Rd. EN3: Enf W .1D 24
SE1 .7H 15 (3F 103)
Riley St. SW10 .6B 100
Rill Ct. IG11: Bark .2G 89
(off Spring Pl.)
Rill Ho. SE5 .7D 102
(off Harris St.)
Rima Ho. SW3 .7A 16
(off Callow St.)
Rinaldo Rd. SW12 .7F 119
Ring, The SW7 .6B 10 (2B 100)
W2 .2C 10 (7B 82)
Ring Cl. BR1: Brom .7K 141
Ring Ct. SE1 .2B 102
(off The Cut)
Ringcroft St. N7 .5A 66
Ringers Ct. BR1: Brom .3J 159
(off Ringers Rd.)
Ringers Rd. BR1: Brom .3J 159
Ringford Rd. SW18 .5H 117
Ring Ho. E1 .7J 85
(off Sage St.)
Ringles Ct. E6 .1D 88
Ringlet Cl. E16 .5K 87
Ringlewell Cl. EN1: Enf .2C 24
Ringmer Av. SW6 .1G 117
Ringmer Gdns. N19 .2J 65
Ringmer Pl. N21 .5J 23
Ringmer Way BR1: Brom .5C 160
Ringmore Ri. SE23 .7H 121
Ring Rd. W12 .1E 98
Ringsfield Ho. SE17 .5C 102
(off Bronti Cl.)
Ringslade Rd. N22 .2K 47
Ringstead Rd. SE6 .7D 122
SM1: Sutt .4B 166
Ring Way N11 .6B 32
Ringway UB2: S'hall .5B 94
Ringwold Cl. BR3: Beck .7A 140
Ringwood Av. CR0: C'don .7J 155
N2 .2D 46
Ringwood Cl. HA5: Pinn .3A 40
Ringwood Gdns. E14 .4C 104
SW15 .1C 134
Ringwood Rd. E17 .6B 50
Ringwood Way N21 .1G 33
TW12: Ham H .4E 130
Rio Cinema
Dalston .5E 66
(off Kingsland High St.)
Ripley Bldgs. SE1 .6B 14
(off Rushworth St.)
Ripley Cl. BR1: Brom .5D 160
CR0: New Ad .6E 170
Ripley Ct. CR4: Mitc .2B 154
Ripley Gdns. SM1: Sutt .4A 166
(not continuous)
SW14 .3K 115
Ripley Ho. SW1 .7A 18
(off Churchill Gdns.)
Ripley M. E11 .6G 51
Ripley Rd. DA17: Belv .4G 109
E16 .6A 88
EN2: Enf .1H 23
IG3: Ilf .2K 71
TW12: Hamp .7E 130
Ripley Vs. W13 .6C 78
Ripon Cl. UB5: N'olt .5E 58
Ripon Ct. N11 .6K 31
(off Ribblesdale Av.)
Ripon Gdns. IG1: Ilf .6C 52
KT9: Chess .5D 162
Ripon Rd. N9 .7C 24
N17 .3D 48
SE18 .6F 107
Rippersley Rd. DA16: Well .1A 126
Ripple Nature Reserve, The .3B 90
Ripple Rd. IG11: Bark, Dag .7G 71
RM9: Dag .1B 90
RIPPLESIDE .1B 90
Rippleside Commercial Est.
IG11: Bark .2C 90
Ripplevale Gro. N1 .7K 65
Rippolson Rd. SE18 .5K 107
Ripston Rd. TW15: Ashf .5F 129
Risboro' Cl. N10 .3F 47
Risborough SE17 .4C 102
(off Deacon Way)
Risborough Dr. KT4: Wor Pk .7C 152
Risborough Ho. NW8 .3D 4
(off Mallory St.)
Risborough St. SE1 .6B 14 (2B 102)
Risdon Ho. SE16 .2J 103
(off Risdon St.)
Risdon St. SE16 .3J 103
Rise, The DA5: Bexl .7C 126
E11 .5J 51
HA0: Wemb .5A 60
HA8: Edg .5C 28
IG9: Buck H .1G 37
N13 .4F 33
NW7 .6G 29
NW10 .4K 61
UB6: G'frd .5A 60
UB10: Hil .2B 74
Risedale Rd. DA7: Bex .3J 127
Riseholme Ct. E9 .6B 68
Riseldine Rd. SE23 .6A 122
RISE PARK .2K 55
Rise Pk. Pde. RM1: Rom .2K 55
Risinghill St. N1 .2K 83
Risingholme Cl. HA3: Hrw W .1J 41
WD23: Bush .1A 26
Risingholme Rd. HA3: Hrw W .2J 41
Risings, The E17 .4F 51
Rising Sun Ct. EC1 .5B 8
Risley Av. N17 .1C 48
Rita Rd. SW8 .6J 101
Ritches Rd. N15 .5C 48
Ritchie Ho. E14 .6F 87
(off Blair St.)
N19 .1H 65
SE16 .3J 103
(off Howland Est.)
Ritchie Rd. CR0: C'don .6H 157
Ritchie St. N1 .2A 84
Ritchings Av. E17 .4A 50
Ritherdon Rd. SW17 .2E 136
Ritson Ho. N1 .1K 83
(off Barnsbury Est.)
Ritson Rd. E8 .6G 67
Ritter St. SE18 .6E 106
Ritz Pde. W5 .4F 79
Ritzy Picturehouse .4A 120
(off Coldharbour La.)
Riva Bingo .1J 137
Rivaz Pl. E9 .6J 67
Riven Ct. W2 .6K 81
(off Inverness Ter.)
Rivenhall Gdns. E18 .4H 51
River App. HA8: Edg .1J 43
RIVER ASH ESTATE .7H 147
River Av. KT7: T Ditt .7A 150
N13 .3G 33
River Av. Ind. Est. N13 .5F 33
River Bank KT7: T Ditt .5K 149
KT8: E Mos .3J 149
N21 .7H 23
TW12: Hamp .3E 148
Riverbank Rd. BR1: Brom .3J 141
Riverbank Way TW8: Bford .6C 96
River Barge Cl. E14 .2E 104
River Brent Bus. Pk. W7 .3J 95
River Cl. E11 .6A 52
HA4: Ruis .6H 39
UB2: S'hall .2G 95
River Ct. KT6: Surb .5D 150
(off Portsmouth Rd.)
SE1 .3A 14 (7B 84)
TW17: Shep .7E 146
Rivercourt Rd. W6 .4D 98
River Crane Way TW13: Hanw .2D 130
(off Watermill Way)
Riverdale SE13 .4E 122
Riverdale Cl. IG11: Bark .4B 90
Riverdale Ct. N21 .5J 23
Riverdale Dr. SW18 .1K 135
Riverdale Gdns. TW1: Twick .6C 114
Riverdale Rd. DA5: Bexl .7F 127
DA8: Erith .5H 109
SE18 .5K 107
TW1: Twick .6C 114
TW13: Hanw .4C 130
Riverdale Shop. Cen. SE13 .3E 122
Riverdene HA8: Edg .3D 28
Riverdene Rd. IG1: Ilf .3E 70
Riverfleet WC1 .1F 7
(off Birkenhead St.)
Riverford Ho. W2 .5J 81
(off Westbourne Pk. Rd.)
River Front EN1: Enf .3K 23
River Gdns. SM5: Cars .2E 166
TW14: Felt .5K 111
River Gdns. Bus. Cen.TW14: Felt .5K 111
River Gro. Pk. BR3: Beck .1B 158
Riverhead Cl. E17 .2K 49
River Hgts. N17 .1F 49
Riverhill KT4: Wor Pk .2K 163
Riverhill M. KT4: Wor Pk .3K 163
Riverhill Mobile Home Pl.
KT4: Wor Pk .2K 163
Riverholme Dr. KT19: Ewe .7K 163
Riverhope Mans. SE18 .3C 106
River Ho. SE26 .3H 139
Riverhouse Barn .7H 147
River La. TW10: Ham .7D 114
Riverleigh Ct. E4 .5G 35
River Lodge SW1 .7B 18
(off Grosvenor Rd.)

Rivermead KT1: King T 5D **150**
KT8: W Mole 3G **149**
Rivermead Cl. TW11: Tedd 5B **132**
Rivermead Ct. SW6 . . . . 3H **117**
Rivermead Ho. E9 . . . . 5A **68**
TW16: Sun *3A* ***148***
(off Thames St.)
Rivermead Rd. N18 . . . . 6E **34**
River Meads Av. TW2: Twick 3E **130**
River Mt. KT12: Walt T 7H **147**
Rivernook Cl. KT12: Walt T 5A **148**
River Pk. Gdns. BR2: Brom 7F **141**
River Pk. Rd. N22 . . . . 2K **47**
River Pl. N1 . . . . 7C **66**
River Reach TW11: Tedd 5C **132**
River Rd. IG9: Buck H 1H **37**
IG11: Bark 2J **89**
River Rd. Bus. Pk. IG11: Bark 3K **89**
Riversdale Gdns. N22 . . . . 1A **48**
Riversdale Rd. KT7: T Ditt 5A **150**
N5 . . . . 3B **66**
RM5: Col R 1H **55**
Riversfield Rd. EN1: Enf 3K **23**
Rivers Ho. *TW7: Isle* *4B* ***114***
(off Richmond Rd.)
W4 . . . . *5G* ***97***
(off Chiswick High Rd.)
Riverside NW4 . . . . 7D **44**
SE7 . . . . 3K **105**
SW11 . . . . 7C **100**
TW1: Twick 1B **132**
TW9: Rich 5D **114**
TW16: Sun 3B **148**
TW17: Shep 7G **147**
W6 . . . . 6E **98**
WC1 . . . . *1F* ***7***
(off Birkenhead St.)
Riverside, The KT8: E Mos 3H **149**
Riverside Apartments N13 . . . . 5E **32**
Riverside Arts Cen. *3A* ***148***
(off Thames St.)
Riverside Av. KT8: E Mos 5H **149**
Riverside Bus. Cen. SW18 . . . . 1K **135**
Riverside Bus. Pk. SW19 . . . . 1A **154**
Riverside Cl. E5 . . . . 1J **67**
KT1: King T 4D **150**
RM7: Rom 4K **55**
SM6: Wall 3F **167**
W7 . . . . 4J **77**
Riverside Cotts. IG11: Bark 2H **89**
Riverside Ct. E4 . . . . 6H **25**
SE3 . . . . 4H **123**
SW8 . . . . 7D **18** (6H **101**)
TW7: Isle *2K* ***113***
(off Woodlands Rd.)
TW14: Felt 7G **111**
Riverside Dr. CR4: Mitc 5C **154**
NW11 . . . . 6G **45**
TW10: Ham 3B **132**
W4 . . . . 7K **97**
Riverside Gdns. EN2: Enf 2H **23**
HA0: Wemb 2E **78**
N3 . . . . 3G **45**
W6 . . . . 5D **98**
Riverside Health & Raquets Club 1A **116**
Riverside Ho. *N1* *7C* ***66***
(off Canonbury St.)
Riverside Ind. Est. EN3: Pond E 6F **25**
IG11: Bark 3A **90**
Riverside Mans. *E1* *1J* ***103***
(off Milk Yd.)
Riverside M. CR0: Bedd 3J **167**
Riverside Pl. N11 . . . . 3B **32**
TW19: Stanw 6A **110**
Riverside Rd. DA14: Sidc 3E **144**
E15 . . . . 2E **86**
N15 . . . . 6G **49**
SW17 . . . . 4K **135**
TW19: Stanw 5A **110**
(not continuous)
Riverside Studios 5E **98**
Riverside Twr. *SW6* *2A* ***118***
(off The Boulevard)
Riverside Vs. KT6: Surb 6C **150**
Riverside Wlk. BR4: W W'ck 1D **170**
EN5: Barn 6A **20**
(not continuous)
KT1: King T 3D **150**
N12 . . . . 6D **30**
(not continuous)
N20 . . . . 3E **30**
SE10 . . . . 3G **105**
(Morden Wharf Rd.)
SE10 . . . . 2F **105**
(Tunnel Av.)
SW6 . . . . 3G **117**
TW7: Isle 3J **113**
W4 . . . . *6B* ***98***
(off Chiswick Wharf)
Riverside Works IG11: Bark 7F **71**
Riverside Workshops *SE1* *4D* ***14***
(off Park St.)
Riverside Yd. SW17 . . . . 4A **136**
Riverstone Cl. HA2: Harr 1H **59**
Riverstone Ct. KT2: King T 1F **151**
River St. EC1 . . . . 1J **7** (3A **84**)
River Ter. W6 . . . . 5E **98**
WC2 . . . . 3G **13**
River Thames Vis. Cen. *5D* ***114***
(within Mus. of Richmond)
Riverton Cl. W9 . . . . 3H **81**
River Vw. EN2: Enf 3H **23**
Riverview Ct. E14 . . . . 3B **104**
River Vw. Gdns. TW1: Twick 2K **131**
Riverview Gdns. SW13 . . . . 6D **98**
Riverview Gro. W4 . . . . 6H **97**
River Vw. Hgts. *SE16* *2G* ***103***
(off Bermondsey Wall W.)
Riverview Pk. SE6 . . . . 2C **140**
Riverview Rd. KT19: Ewe 4J **163**
W4 . . . . 7H **97**
River Wlk. E4 . . . . 7K **35**
KT12: Walt T 6J **147**
SW6 . . . . 2A **118**
W6 . . . . 7E **98**
River Way KT19: Ewe 5K **163**
SE10 . . . . 3H **105**
TW2: Twick 2F **131**
Riverway N13 . . . . 5F **33**
River Wharf Bus. Pk.
DA17: Belv 1K **109**
Riverwiew Wlk. SE6 . . . . 3B **140**
Riverwood La. BR7: Chst 1H **161**
Rivet Ho. *SE1* *5F* ***103***
(off Cooper's Rd.)
Rivington Av. IG8: Wfd G 2B **52**
Rivington Ct. NW10 . . . . 1C **80**
RM10: Dag 6H **73**
Rivington Cres. NW7 . . . . 7G **29**
Rivington Pl. EC2 . . . . 2H **9** (3E **84**)
Rivington St. EC2 . . . . 2G **9** (3E **84**)
Rivington Wlk. E8 . . . . 1G **85**
Rivulet Rd. N17 . . . . 7H **33**
Rixon Ho. SE18 . . . . 6F **107**
Rixon St. N7 . . . . 3A **66**
Rixsen Rd. E12 . . . . 5C **70**
Roach Rd. E3 . . . . 7C **68**
Roads Pl. N19 . . . . 2J **65**
Roan Ind. Est. *CR4: Mitc* *1D* ***154***
(off Lavender Av.)
Roan St. SE10 . . . . 6E **104**
Robarts Cl. HA5: Eastc 5K **39**
Robbins Hall EN3: Pond E 6E **24**
Robb Rd. HA7: Stan 6F **27**
Robert Adam St. W1 . . . . 7G **5** (6E **82**)
Roberta St. E2 . . . . 3G **85**
Robert Bell Ho. *SE16* *4G* ***103***
(off Rouel Rd.)
Robert Burns Ho. *N17* *7C* ***34***
(off Northumberland Pk.)
Robert Burns M. SE24 . . . . 5B **120**
Robert Cl. *IG11: Bark* *6G* ***71***
(off Tanner St.)
W9 . . . . 4A **4** (4A **82**)
Robert Dashwood Way SE17 . . . . 4C **102**
Robert Gentry Ho. *W14* *5G* ***99***
(off Gledstanes Rd.)
Robert Jones Ho. *SE16* *4G* ***103***
(off Rouel Rd.)
Robert Keen Cl. SE15 . . . . 1G **121**
Robert Lowe Cl. SE14 . . . . 7K **103**
Robert Morton Ho. NW8 . . . . 7A **64**
Roberton Dr. BR1: Brom 1A **160**
Robert Owen Ho. *E2* *3F* ***85***
(off Baroness Rd.)
N22 . . . . *1A* ***48***
(off Progress Way)
SW6 . . . . 1F **117**
Robert Runcie Ct. SW2 . . . . 4K **119**
Roberts All. W5 . . . . 2D **96**
Robertsbridge Rd. SM5: Cars 1A **166**
Roberts Cl. CR7: Thor H 3D **156**
SE9 . . . . 1H **143**
SE16 . . . . 2K **103**
SM3: Cheam 7F **165**
UB7: Yiew 1A **92**
Roberts Ct. KT9: Chess 5D **162**
N1 . . . . *1B* ***84***
(off Essex Rd.)
NW10 . . . . 6A **62**
SE20 . . . . *1J* ***157***
(off Maple Rd.)
Roberts M. BR6: Orp 1K **173**
SW1 . . . . 1G **17** (3E **100**)
Robertson Gro. SW17 . . . . 5C **136**
Robertson Rd. E15 . . . . 1E **86**
Robertson St. SW8 . . . . 3F **119**
Roberts Pl. EC1 . . . . 3K **7** (4A **84**)
RM10: Dag 6G **73**
Roberts Rd. DA17: Belv 5G **109**
E17 . . . . 1D **50**
NW7 . . . . 6B **30**
Robert St. CR0: C'don 3C **168**
E16 . . . . 1F **107**
NW1 . . . . 2K **5** (3F **83**)
SE18 . . . . 5H **107**
(not continuous)
WC2 . . . . 3F **13** (7J **83**)
Robert Sutton Ho. *E1* *6J* ***85***
(off Tarling St.)
Robeson St. E3 . . . . 5B **86**
Robina Cl. DA6: Bex 4D **126**
HA6: Nwood 1H **39**
Robin Cl. NW7 . . . . 3F **29**
RM5: Col R 1K **55**
TW12: Hamp 5C **130**
Robin Ct. E14 . . . . 2E **104**
SE16 . . . . 4G **103**
SM6: Wall 5G **167**
Robin Cres. E6 . . . . 5B **88**
Robin Gro. HA3: Kent 6F **43**
N6 . . . . 2E **64**
TW8: Bford 6C **96**
Robin Hill Dr. BR7: Chst 6C **142**
ROBIN HOOD 3A **134**
Robinhood Cl. CR4: Mitc 3G **155**
Robin Hood Ct. *EC4* *7K* ***7***
(off Shoe La.)
Robin Hood Dr.
HA3: Hrw W 7E **26**
Robin Hood Gdns. *E14* *7E* ***86***
(off Woolmore St., not continuous)
Robin Hood Grn.
BR5: St M Cry 5K **161**
Robin Hood La. DA6: Bex 5E **126**
E14 . . . . 7E **86**
SM1: Sutt 5J **165**
SW15 . . . . 3A **134**
Robinhood La. CR4: Mitc 3G **155**
Robin Hood Rd. SW19 . . . . 5C **134**
Robin Hood Way SW15 . . . . 3A **134**
SW20 . . . . 3A **134**
UB6: G'frd 6K **59**
Robin Ho. *NW8* *2C* ***82***
(off Newcourt St.)
Robin Howard Dance Theatre *2D* ***6***
(in The Place)
Robinia Cl. *SE20* *1G* ***157***
(off Sycamore Gro.)
Robinia Cres. E10 . . . . 2D **68**
Robin La. NW4 . . . . 3F **45**
Robins Ct. BR3: Beck 2F **159**
CR2: S Croy *4E* ***168***
(off Birdhurst Rd.)
SE12 . . . . 3A **142**
Robinscroft M. SE10 . . . . 1E **122**
Robins Gro. BR4: W W'ck 3J **171**
Robinson Cl. E11 . . . . 3G **69**
EN2: Enf 3H **23**
Robinson Ct. CR7: Thor H 6B **156**
N1 . . . . *1B* ***84***
(off St Mary's Path)
TW9: Rich 4F **115**
Robinson Cres. WD23: B Hea 1B **26**
Robinson Ho. *E14* *5C* ***86***
(off Selsey St.)
W10 . . . . *6F* ***81***
(off Bramley Rd.)
Robinson Rd. E2 . . . . 2J **85**
RM10: Dag 4G **73**
SW17 . . . . 6C **136**
Robinson's Cl. W13 . . . . 5A **78**
Robinson St. SW3 . . . . 7E **16** (6D **100**)
Robinwood Gro.
UB8: Hil 4B **74**
Robinwood Pl. SW15 . . . . 4K **133**
Robsart St. SW9 . . . . 2K **119**
Robson Av. NW10 . . . . 7C **62**
Robson Cl. E6 . . . . 6C **88**
EN2: Enf 2G **23**
Robson Rd. SE27 . . . . 3B **138**
Roby Ho. *EC1* *3C* ***8***
(off Mitchell St.)
Roca Ct. E11 . . . . 5J **51**
Rocastle Rd. SE4 . . . . 5A **122**
Roch Av. HA8: Edg 2F **43**
Rochdale Rd. E17 . . . . 7C **50**
SE2 . . . . 5B **108**
Rochdale Way SE8 . . . . 7C **104**
(not continuous)
Roche Ho. *E14* *7B* ***86***
(off Beccles St.)
Rochelle Cl. SW11 . . . . 4B **118**
Rochelle St. E2 . . . . 2J **9** (3F **85**)
(not continuous)
Rochemont Wlk. *E8* *1G* ***85***
(off Pownell Rd.)
Roche Rd. SW16 . . . . 1K **155**
Rochester Av. BR1: Brom 2K **159**
E13 . . . . 1A **88**
TW13: Felt 2H **129**
Rochester Cl. DA15: Sidc 6B **126**
EN1: Enf 1K **23**
SW16 . . . . 7J **137**
Rochester Ct. *E2* *4H* ***85***
(off Wilmot St.)
NW1 . . . . *7G* ***65***
(off Rochester Sq.)
Rochester Dr. DA5: Bexl 6F **127**
HA5: Pinn 5B **40**
Rochester Gdns. CR0: C'don 3E **168**
IG1: Ilf 7D **52**
Rochester Ho. *SE1* *7F* ***15***
(off Manciple St.)
SE15 . . . . *6J* ***103***
(off Sharratt St.)
Rochester M. NW1 . . . . 7G **65**
W5 . . . . 4C **96**
Rochester Pde. TW13: Felt 2J **129**
Rochester Pl. NW1 . . . . 6G **65**

Rochester Rd. HA6: Nwood ... 3H 39
NW1 ... 6G 65
SM5: Cars ... 4D 166
Rochester Row SW1 ... 3B 18 (4G 101)
Rochester Sq. NW1 ... 7G 65
Rochester St. SW1 ... 2C 18 (3H 101)
Rochester Ter. NW1 ... 6G 65
Rochester Wlk. SE1 ... 4E 14 (1D 102)
Rochester Way DA1: Dart ... 7K 127
SE3 ... 1K 123
SE9 ... 2A 124
Rochester Way Relief Rd.
SE3 ... 1K 123
SE9 ... 4A 124
Roche Wlk. SM5: Cars ... 6B 154
Rochford *N17* ... *2E 48*
(off Griffin Rd.)
Rochford Av. RM6: Chad H ... 5C 54
Rochford Cl. E6 ... 2B 88
Rochford Wlk. E8 ... 7G 67
Rochford Way CR0: C'don ... 6J 155
Rochfort Ho. SE8 ... 5B 104
Rock Av. SW14 ... 3K 115
Rockbourne M. SE23 ... 1K 139
Rockbourne Rd. SE23 ... 1K 139
Rock Circus ... *7H 83*
(in Trocadero Cen.)
Rock Cl. CR4: Mitc ... 2B 154
Rockell's Pl. SE22 ... 6H 121
Rockfield Ho. *NW4* ... *4F 45*
(off Belle Vue Est.)
SE10 ... *6E 104*
(off Welland St.)
Rockford Av. UB6: G'frd ... 2A 78
Rock Gdns. RM10: Dag ... 5H 73
Rock Gro. Way SE16 ... 4G 103
(not continuous)
Rockhall Rd. NW2 ... 4F 63
Rockhall Way NW2 ... 3F 63
Rockhampton Cl. SE27 ... 4A 138
Rockhampton Rd. CR2: S Croy ... 6E 168
SE27 ... 4A 138
Rock Hill SE26 ... 4F 139
(not continuous)
Rockingham Cl. SW15 ... 4B 116
Rockingham St. SE1 ... 3C 102
Rockland Rd. SW15 ... 4G 117
Rocklands Dr. HA7: Stan ... 2B 42
Rockley Ct. *W14* ... *2F 99*
(off Rockley Rd.)
Rockley Rd. W14 ... 2F 99
Rockmount Rd. SE18 ... 5K 107
SE19 ... 6D 138
Rocks La. SW13 ... 1C 116
Rock St. N4 ... 2A 66
Rockware Av. UB6: G'frd ... 1H 77
Rockware Av. Bus. Cen.
UB6: G'frd ... 1H 77
Rockwell Gdns. SE19 ... 5E 138
Rockwell Rd. RM10: Dag ... 5H 73
Rockwood Pl. W12 ... 2E 98
Rocliffe St. N1 ... 2B 84
Rocombe Cres. SE23 ... 7J 121
Rocque Ho. *SW6* ... *7H 99*
(off Estcourt Rd.)
Rocque La. SE3 ... 3H 123
Rodale Mans. SW18 ... 6K 117
Rodborough Ct. *W9* ... *4J 81*
(off Hermes Cl.)
Rodborough Rd. NW11 ... 1J 63
Rodd Est. TW17: Shep ... 5E 146
Roden Ct. N6 ... 7H 47
Roden Gdns. CR0: C'don ... 6E 156
Rodenhurst Rd. SW4 ... 6G 119
Roden St. IG1: Ilf ... 3E 70
N7 ... 3K 65
Roden Way *IG1: Ilf* ... *3E 70*
(off Roden St.)
Roderick Ho. *SE16* ... *4J 103*
(off Raymouth Rd.)
Roderick Rd. NW3 ... 4D 64
Rodgers Ho. *SW4* ... *7H 119*
(off Clapham Pk. Est.)
Rodin Ct. *N1* ... *1B 84*
(off Essex Rd.)
Roding Av. IG8: Wfd G ... 6H 37
Roding Ho. *N1* ... *1A 84*
(off Barnsbury Est.)
Roding La. IG7: Chig ... 2K 37
IG9: Buck H ... 1G 37
(not continuous)
Roding La. Nth. IG8: Wfd G ... 6H 37
Roding La. Sth. IG4: Ilf, Wfd G ... 4B 52
(not continuous)
IG8: Wfd G ... 4B 52
Roding M. E1 ... 1G 103
Roding Rd. E5 ... 4K 67
E6 ... 5F 89
Rodings, The IG8: Wfd G ... 6F 37
Rodings Row *EN5: Barn* ... *4B 20*
(off Leecroft Rd.)
Roding Trad. Est. IG11: Bark ... 7F 71
Roding Valley Meadows Nature Reserve
... 1K 37
Roding Vw. IG9: Buck H ... 1G 37
Rodmarton St. W1 ... 6F 5 (5D 82)
Rodmell *WC1* ... *2F 7*
(off Regent Sq.)
Rodmell Cl. UB4: Yead ... 4C 76
Rodmell Slope N12 ... 5C 30
Rodmere St. SE10 ... 5G 105
Rodmill La. SW2 ... 7J 119
Rodney Cl. CR0: C'don ... 1B 168
HA5: Pinn ... 7C 40
KT3: N Mald ... 5A 152
Rodney Ct. EN5: Barn ... 3C 20
W9 ... 3A 4 (4A 82)
Rodney Gdns. BR4: W W'ck ... 4J 171
HA5: Eastc ... 5K 39
Rodney Ho. *E14* ... *4D 104*
(off Cahir St.)
N1 ... *2K 83*
(off Donegal St.)
SW1 ... *6B 18*
(off Dolphin Sq.)
W11 ... *7J 81*
(off Pembridge Cres.)
Rodney Pl. E17 ... 2A 50
SE17 ... 4C 102
SW19 ... 1A 154
Rodney Point *SE16* ... *2B 104*
(off Rotherhithe St.)
Rodney Rd. CR4: Mitc ... 3C 154
E11 ... 4K 51
KT3: N Mald ... 5A 152
SE17 ... 4C 102
(not continuous)
TW2: Whitt ... 6E 112
Rodney St. N1 ... 1H 7 (2K 83)
Rodney Way RM7: Mawney ... 1H 55
SL3: Poyle ... 4A 174
Rodway Rd. BR1: Brom ... 1K 159
SW15 ... 7C 116
Rodwell Cl. HA4: Ruis ... 1A 58
Rodwell Pl. HA8: Edg ... 6B 28
Rodwell Rd. SE22 ... 6F 121
Roe NW9 ... 7G 29
Roebourne Way E16 ... 1E 106
Roebuck Cl. N17 ... 6A 34
TW13: Felt ... 4K 129
Roebuck Hgts. IG9: Buck H ... 1F 37
Roebuck La. IG9: Buck H ... 1F 37
Roebuck Rd. KT9: Chess ... 5G 163
Roedean Av. EN3: Enf H ... 1D 24
Roedean Cl. EN3: Enf H ... 1D 24
Roedean Cres. SW15 ... 6A 116
Roe End NW9 ... 4J 43
ROE GREEN ... 4J 43
Roe Grn. NW9 ... 5J 43
ROEHAMPTON ... 7C 116
Roehampton Cl. SW15 ... 4C 116
Roehampton Dr. BR7: Chst ... 6G 143
Roehampton Ga. SW15 ... 6A 116
Roehampton High St. SW15 ... 7C 116
ROEHAMPTON LANE ... 1D 134
Roehampton La. SW15 ... 4C 116
Roehampton Recreation Cen. ... 7C 116
Roehampton Va. SW15 ... 3B 134
Roe La. NW9 ... 4H 43
Roe Way SM6: Wall ... 6J 167
Roffey St. E14 ... 2E 104
Rogate Ho. E5 ... 3G 67
Roger Bannister Sports Cen., The ... 6B 26
Roger Dowley Ct. E2 ... 2J 85
Roger Harriss Almshouses
E15 ... *1H 87*
(off Gift La.)
Roger Reede's Almshouses
RM1: Rom ... 4K 55
Rogers Ct. *E14* ... *7C 86*
(off Premiere Pl.)
Rogers Est. E2 ... 3J 85
(not continuous)
Rogers Gdns. RM10: Dag ... 5G 73
Rogers Ho. RM10: Dag ... 3G 73
SW1 ... *3D 18*
(off Page St.)
Rogers Rd. E16 ... 6H 87
RM10: Dag ... 5G 73
SW17 ... 4B 136
Rogers Ruff HA6: Nwood ... 1E 38
Roger St. WC1 ... 4H 7 (4K 83)
Rogers Wlk. N12 ... 3E 30
Rohere Ho. EC1 ... 1C 8 (3C 84)
Rojack Rd. SE23 ... 1K 139
Rokeby Gdns. IG8: Wfd G ... 1J 51
Rokeby Ho. *SW12* ... *7F 119*
(off Lochinvar St.)
WC1 ... *4G 7*
(off Millman M.)
Rokeby Pl. SW20 ... 7D 134
Rokeby Rd. HA1: Harr ... 3H 41
SE4 ... 2B 122
Rokeby St. E15 ... 1F 87
Rokell Ho. *BR3: Beck* ... *5D 140*
(off Beckenham Hill Rd.)
Roker Pk. Av. UB10: Ick ... 4A 56
Rokesby Cl. DA16: Well ... 2H 125
Rokesby Pl. HA0: Wemb ... 5D 60
Rokesly Av. N8 ... 5J 47
Roland Gdns. SW7 ... 5A 16 (5A 100)
Roland Ho. *SW7* ... *5A 16*
(off Old Brompton Rd.)
Roland Mans. *SW7* ... *5A 100*
(off Old Brompton Rd.)
Roland M. E1 ... 5K 85
Roland Rd. E17 ... 4F 51
Roland Way KT4: Wor Pk ... 2B 164
SE17 ... 5D 102
SW7 ... 5A 16 (5A 100)
Roles Gro. RM6: Chad H ... 4D 54
Rolfe Cl. EN4: E Barn ... 4H 21
Rolinsden Way BR2: Kes ... 5B 172
Rolland Ho. W7 ... 5J 77
Rollesby Rd. KT9: Chess ... 6G 163
Rollesby Way SE28 ... 6C 90
Rolleston Av. BR5: Pet W ... 6F 161
Rolleston Cl. BR5: Pet W ... 7F 161
Rolleston Rd. CR2: S Croy ... 7D 168
Roll Gdns. IG2: Ilf ... 5E 52
Rollins St. SE15 ... 6J 103
Rollit Cres. TW3: Houn ... 5E 112
Rollit St. N7 ... 5A 66
Rolls Bldgs. EC4 ... 7J 7 (6A 84)
Rollscourt Av. SE24 ... 5C 120
Rolls Pk. Av. E4 ... 5H 35
Rolls Pk. Rd. E4 ... 5J 35
Rolls Pas. EC4 ... 7J 7
Rolls Rd. SE1 ... 5F 103
Rolls Royce Cl. SM6: Wall ... 7J 167
Rolt St. SE8 ... 6A 104
(not continuous)
Rolvenden Gdns. BR1: Brom ... 7B 142
Rolvenden Pl. N17 ... 1G 49
Roman Cl. RM13: Rain ... 2K 91
TW14: Felt ... 5A 112
W3 ... 2H 97
Roman Ct. N7 ... 6K 65
Romanfield Rd. SW2 ... 7K 119
Roman Ho. EC2 ... 6D 8
RM13: Rain ... 2K 91
Romanhurst Av. BR2: Brom ... 4G 159
Romanhurst Gdns. BR2: Brom ... 4G 159
Roman Ind. Est. CR0: C'don ... 7E 156
Roman Ri. SE19 ... 6D 138
Roman Rd. E2 ... 3J 85
E3 ... 1B 86
E6 ... 4B 88
IG1: Ilf ... 6F 71
N10 ... 7A 32
NW2 ... 3E 62
W4 ... 4A 98
Roman Rd. Mkt. *E3* ... *1B 86*
(off Roman Rd.)
Roman Sq. SE28 ... 1A 108
Roman Way CR0: C'don ... 2B 168
EN1: Enf ... 5A 24
N7 ... 6K 65
SE15 ... 7J 103
Roman Way Ind. Est. *N7* ... *7K 65*
(off Roman Way)
Romany Gdns. E17 ... 1A 50
SM3: Sutt ... 7J 153
Romany Ri. BR5: Farnb ... 1G 173
Roma Read Cl. SW15 ... 7D 116
Roma Rd. E17 ... 3A 50
Romayne Ho. SW4 ... 3H 119
Romberg Rd. SW17 ... 3E 136
Romborough Gdns. SE13 ... 5E 122
Romborough Way SE13 ... 5E 122
Romero Cl. SW9 ... 3K 119
Romero Sq. SE3 ... 4A 124
Romeyn Rd. SW16 ... 3K 137
ROMFORD ... 5K 55
Romford Rd. E7 ... 6G 69
E12 ... 5A 70
E15 ... 6G 69
RM5: Col R ... 1E 54
Romford Stadium (Greyhound) ... 6J 55
Romford St. E1 ... 5G 85
Romilly Ho. *W11* ... *7G 81*
(off Wilsham St.)
Romilly Rd. N4 ... 2B 66
Romilly St. W1 ... 2D 12 (7H 83)
Romily Ct. SW6 ... 2H 117
Rommany Rd. SE27 ... 4D 138
(not continuous)
Romney Cl. HA2: Harr ... 7E 40
KT9: Chess ... 4E 162
N17 ... 1H 49
NW11 ... 1A 64
SE14 ... 7J 103
TW15: Ashf ... 5E 128
Romney Ct. NW3 ... 6C 64
W12 ... *2F 99*
(off Shepherd's Bush Grn.)
Romney Dr. BR1: Brom ... 7B 142
HA2: Harr ... 7E 40
Romney Gdns. DA7: Bex ... 1F 127
Romney Ho. *SW1* ... *2E 18*
(off Marsham St.)
Romney M. W1 ... 5G 5 (5E 82)
Romney Pde. UB4: Hayes ... 2F 75
Romney Rd. KT3: N Mald ... 6K 151
SE10 ... 6F 105
UB4: Hayes ... 2F 75
Romney Row *NW2* ... *2F 63*
(off Brent Ter.)
Romney St. SW1 ... 2E 18 (3J 101)
Romola Rd. SE24 ... 1B 138

Romsey Cl. BR6: Farnb 4F 173
Romsey Gdns. RM9: Dag 1D 90
Romsey Rd. RM9: Dag 1D 90
W13 7A 78
Romulus Ct. TW8: Bford 7D 96
Ronald Av. E15 3G 87
Ronald Buckingham Ct. SE16 2J 103
(off Kenning St.)
Ronald Cl. BR3: Beck 4B 158
Ronald Ct. EN5: New Bar 3E 20
Ronald Ho. SE3 4A 124
Ronaldshay N4 7A 48
Ronalds Rd. BR1: Brom 1J 159
N5 5A 66
(not continuous)
Ronaldstone Rd. DA15: Sidc 6J 125
Ronald St. E1 6J 85
Rona Rd. NW3 4E 64
Ronart St. HA3: W'stone 3K 41
Rona Wlk. N1 6D 66
(off Ramsey Wlk.)
Rondel Ct. DA5: Bexl 6E 126
Rondu Rd. NW2 5G 63
Ronelean Rd. KT6: Surb 2F 163
Ron Grn. Ct. DA8: Erith 6K 109
Ron Leighton Way E6 1C 88
Ronnie La. E12 4E 70
Ronver Rd. SE12 1H 141
Rood La. EC3 2G 15 (7E 84)
Roof Ter. Apartments, The EC1 4B 8
(off Gt. Sutton St.)
Rookby Ct. N21 2G 33
Rook Cl. HA9: Wemb 3H 61
Rookeries Cl. TW13: Felt 3K 129
Rookery Cl. NW9 5B 44
Rookery Cres. RM10: Dag 7H 73
Rookery Dr. BR7: Chst 1E 160
Rookery La. BR2: Brom 6B 160
Rookery Rd. SW4 4G 119
Rookery Way NW9 5B 44
Rooke Way SE10 5H 105
Rookfield Av. N10 4G 47
Rookfield Cl. N10 4G 47
Rooksmead Rd. TW16: Sun 2H 147
Rooks Ter. UB7: W Dray 2A 92
Rookstone Rd. SW17 5D 136
Rook Wlk. E6 6B 88
Rookwood Av. KT3: N Mald 4C 152
SM6: Bedd 4H 167
Rookwood Gdns. E4 2C 36
Rookwood Ho. IG11: Bark 2H 89
Rookwood Rd. N16 7F 49
Roosevelt Memorial 2H 11 (7E 82)
Roosevelt Way RM10: Dag 6K 73
Rootes Dr. W10 5F 81
Ropemaker Rd. SE16 2A 104
Ropemaker's Flds. E14 7B 86
Ropemaker St. EC2 5E 8 (5D 84)
Roper La. SE1 7H 15 (2E 102)
Ropers Av. E4 5J 35
Ropers Orchard SW3 6C 100
(off Danvers St.)
Roper St. SE9 5D 124
Ropers Wlk. SW2 7A 120
Roper Way CR4: Mitc 2E 154
Ropery Bus. Pk. SE7 4A 106
Ropery St. E3 4B 86
Rope St. SE16 4A 104
Rope Wlk. TW16: Sun 3A 148
Rope Wlk. Gdns. E1 6G 85
Ropewalk M. E8 7G 67
(off Middleton Rd.)
Rope Yd. Rails SE18 3F 107
Ropley St. E2 2G 85
Rosa Alba M. N5 4C 66
Rosa Av. TW15: Ashf 4C 128
Rosalind Ct. IG11: Bark 7A 72
(off Meadow Rd.)
Rosalind Ho. N1 2E 84
(off Arden Ho.)
Rosaline Rd. SW6 7G 99
Rosaline Ter. SW6 7G 99
(off Rosaline Rd.)
Rosamond St. SE26 3H 139
Rosamund Cl. CR2: S Croy 4D 168
Rosamun St. UB2: S'hall 4C 94
Rosary Cl. TW3: Houn 2C 112
Rosary Gdns. SW7 4A 100
TW15: Ashf 4D 128
Rosaville Rd. SW6 7H 99
Roscoe St. EC1 4D 8 (4C 84)
(not continuous)
Roscoe St. Est. EC1 4D 8 (4C 84)
Roscoff Cl. HA8: Edg 1J 43
Roseacre Cl. SM1: Sutt 2A 166
TW17: Shep 5C 146
W13 5B 78
Roseacre Rd. DA16: Well 3B 126
Rose All. EC2 6H 9
(off Bishopsgate)
SE1 4D 14 (1C 102)
Rose & Crown Ct. EC2 7D 8
Rose & Crown Pas.
TW7: Isle 1A 114
Rose & Crown Yd.
SW1 4B 12 (1G 101)
Roseary Cl. UB7: W Dray 1E 174
Rose Av. CR4: Mitc 1D 154
E18 2K 51
SM4: Mord 5A 154
Rosebank SE20 7H 139
SW6 7E 98
W3 6K 79
Rosebank Av. HA0: Wemb 4K 59
Rose Bank Cl. N12 5H 31
Rosebank Cl. TW11: Tedd 6A 132
Rosebank Gdns. E3 2B 86
W3 6K 79
Rosebank Gro. E17 3B 50
Rosebank Rd. E17 6D 50
W7 2J 95
Rosebank Vs. E17 4C 50
Rosebank Wlk. NW1 7H 65
SE18 4C 106
Rosebank Way W3 6K 79
Rose Bates Dr. NW9 4G 43
Rosebay Ho. E3 5C 86
(off Hawgood St.)
Roseberry Gdns. BR6: Orp 3J 173
N4 6B 48
Roseberry Pl. E8 6F 67
Roseberry St. SE16 4H 103
Rosebery Av. CR7: Thor H 2C 156
DA15: Sidc 7J 125
E12 6C 70
EC1 4J 7 (4A 84)
HA2: Harr 4C 58
KT3: N Mald 2B 152
N17 2G 49
Rosebery Cl. SM4: Mord 6F 153
Rosebery Ct. EC1 4J 7
(off Rosebery Av.)
W1 4J 11
(off Charles St.)
Rosebery Gdns. N8 5J 47
SM1: Sutt 4K 165
W13 6A 78
Rosebery Ho. E2 2J 85
(off Sewardstone Rd.)
Rosebery Ind. Pk. N17 2H 49
Rosebery M. N10 2G 47
Rosebery Rd. KT1: King T 2H 151
N10 2G 47
SM1: Sutt 6H 165
SW2 6J 119
TW3: Houn 5G 113
WD23: Bush 1A 26
Rosebery Sq. EC1 4J 7
KT1: King T 2H 151
Rosebine Av. TW2: Twick 7H 113
Rosebury Rd. SW6 2K 117
Rosebury Sq. IG8: Wfd G 7K 37
Rosebury Va. HA4: Ruis 2J 57
Rose Bush Ct. NW3 5D 64
Rose Ct. E1 6K 9
E8 7F 67
(off Richmond Rd.)
HA0: Wemb 2E 78
(off Vicars Bri. Cl.)
HA2: Harr 2G 59
N1 1B 84
(off Collin's Yd.)
SE16 4K 103
Rosecourt Rd. CR0: C'don 6K 155
Rosecroft N14 2D 32
Rosecroft Av. NW3 3J 63
Rosecroft Gdns. NW2 3C 62
TW2: Twick 1H 131
Rosecroft Rd. UB1: S'hall 4E 76
Rosecroft Wlk. HA0: Wemb 5D 60
HA5: Pinn 5B 40
Rose Dale BR6: Farnb 2F 173
Rosedale Av. UB3: Hayes 5F 75
Rosedale Cl. HA7: Stan 6G 27
SE2 3B 108
W7 2K 95
Rosedale Ct. HA1: Harr 4K 59
N5 4B 66
Rosedale Dr. RM9: Dag 7B 72
Rosedale Gdns. RM9: Dag 7B 72
Rosedale Ho. N16 1D 66
Rosedale Pl. CR0: C'don 7K 157
Rosedale Rd. E7 5A 70
KT17: Ewe 5C 164
RM1: Rom 2J 55
RM9: Dag 7B 72
TW9: Rich 3E 114
Rosedale Ter. W6 3D 98
(off Dalling Rd.)
Rosedene NW6 1F 81
(not continuous)
Rosedene Av. CR0: C'don 7J 155
SM4: Mord 5J 153
SW16 3K 137
UB6: G'frd 3E 76
Rosedene Ct. HA4: Ruis 1G 57
Rosedene Gdns. IG2: Ilf 4E 52
Rosedene Ter. E10 2D 68
Rosedew Rd. W6 6F 99
Rose End KT4: Wor Pk 1F 165
Rosefield Cl. SM5: Cars 5C 166
Rosefield Gdns. E14 7C 86
Roseford Ct. W12 2F 99
(off Shepherd's Bush Grn.)
Rose Gdn. Cl. HA8: Edg 6K 27
Rose Gdns. TW13: Felt 2J 129
UB1: S'hall 4E 76
W5 3D 96
Rosegate Ho. E3 2B 86
(off Hereford Rd.)
Rose Glen NW9 4K 43
RM7: Rush G 1K 73
Rosehart M. W11 6J 81
Rose Hatch Av.
RM6: Chad H 3D 54
Roseheath Rd. TW4: Houn 5D 112
ROSEHILL 7A 154
Rose Hill SM1: Sutt 2K 165
Rosehill KT10: Clay 6A 162
TW12: Hamp 1E 148
Rose Hill Av. SM1: Sutt 1A 166
Rosehill Ct. SM4: Mord 7A 154
(off St Helier Av.)
Rosehill Ct. Pde. SM4: Mord 7A 154
(off St Helier Av.)
Rosehill Gdns. SM1: Sutt 2K 165
UB6: G'frd 5K 59
Rose Hill Pk. W. SM1: Sutt 1A 166
Rosehill Rd. SW18 6A 118
ROSE HILL RDBT. 7A 154
Rose Joan M. NW6 4J 63
Rosekey Ct. SE8 7B 104
(off Baildon St.)
Roseland Cl. N17 7J 33
Rose La. RM6: Chad H 3D 54
Rose Lawn WD23: B Hea 1B 26
Roseleigh Av. N5 4B 66
Roseleigh Cl. TW1: Twick 6D 114
Rosemary Av. EN2: Enf 1K 23
KT8: W Mole 3E 148
N2 4K 45
N3 2K 45
N9 1C 34
TW4: Houn 2B 112
Rosemary Branch Theatre 1D 84
(off Shepperton Rd.)
Rosemary Cl. CR0: C'don 6J 155
UB8: Hil 5C 74
Rosemary Ct. SE8 6B 104
(off Dorking Cl.)
Rosemary Dr. E14 6F 87
IG4: Ilf 5B 52
Rosemary Gdns.
KT9: Chess 4E 162
RM8: Dag 1F 73
SW14 3J 115
Rosemary Ho. N1 1D 84
(off Branch Pl.)
NW10 1D 80
(off Uffington Rd.)
Rosemary La. SW14 3J 115
Rosemary Rd. DA16: Well 1K 125
SE15 7F 103
SW17 3A 136
Rosemary St. N1 1D 84
Rosemead NW9 7B 44
Rosemead Av. CR4: Mitc 3G 155
HA9: Wemb 5E 60
TW13: Felt 2H 129
Rose M. N18 4C 34
Rosemont Av. N12 6F 31
Rosemont Ct. W3 1H 97
(off Rosemont Rd.)
Rosemont Rd. HA0: Wemb 1E 78
KT3: N Mald 3J 151
NW3 6A 64
TW10: Rich 6E 114
W3 7H 79
Rosemoor Ho. W13 1A 96
(off Broadway)
Rosemoor St. SW3 4E 16 (4D 100)
Rosemount SM6: Wall 6G 167
(off Clarendon Rd.)
Rosemount Cl. IG8: Wfd G 6J 37
Rosemount Dr. BR1: Brom 4D 160
Rosemount Point SE23 3K 139
Rosemount Rd. W13 6A 78
Rosenau Cres. SW11 1D 118
Rosenau Rd. SW11 1C 118
Rosendale Rd. SE21 7C 120
SE24 7C 120
Roseneath Av. N21 1G 33
Roseneath Pl. SW16 4K 137
(off Curtis Fld. Rd.)
Roseneath Rd. SW11 6E 118
Roseneath Wlk. EN1: Enf 4K 23
Rosen's Wlk. HA8: Edg 3C 28
Rosenthal Rd. SE6 6D 122
Rosenthorpe Rd. SE15 5K 121
Rose Pk. Cl. UB4: Yead 5A 76
Rosepark Ct. IG5: Ilf 2D 52
Roserton St. E14 2E 104
Rosery, The CR0: C'don 6K 157
Roses, The IG8: Wfd G 7C 36
Rose Sq. SW3 5B 16 (5B 100)
Rose St. EC4 7B 8 (6B 84)
WC2 2E 12 (7J 83)
(not continuous)
Rosethorn Cl. SW12 7H 119
Rose Tree M. IG8: Wfd G 6H 37

Rosetta Cl. SW8 7J 101
(off Kenchester Cl.)
Rosetta Ct. SE19 7E 138
Rosetti Ter. RM8: Dag 4B 72
(off Marlborough Rd.)
Roseveare Rd. SE12 4A 142
Roseville N21 1F 33
(off The Green)
Roseville Av. TW3: Houn 5E 112
Roseville Rd. UB3: Harl 5J 93
Rosevine Rd. SW20 1E 152
Rose Wlk. BR4: W W'ck 2E 170
KT5: Surb 5H 151
Rose Way SE12 5J 123
Roseway HA8: Edg 4D 28
SE21 6D 120
Rosewell Cl. SE20 7H 139
Rosewood KT7: T Ditt 2A 162
Rosewood Av. UB6: G'frd 5A 60
Rosewood Cl. DA14: Sidc 3C 144
Rosewood Ct. BR1: Brom 1A 160
E11 4F 69
KT2: King T 7G 133
RM6: Chad H 5C 54
Rosewood Dr. TW17: Shep 5B 146
Rosewood Gdns. SE13 2E 122
Rosewood Gro. SM1: Sutt 2A 166
Rosewood Ho. SW8 7G 19
Rosewood Sq. W12 6C 80
Rosher Cl. E15 7F 69
Roshni Ho. SW17 6C 136
Rosina St. E9 6K 67
Roskell Rd. SW15 3F 117
Roslin Ho. E1 7K 85
(off Brodlove La.)
Roslin Rd. W3 3H 97
Roslin Way BR1: Brom 5J 141
Roslyn Cl. CR4: Mitc 2B 154
Roslyn Rd. N15 5D 48
Rosmead Rd. W11 7G 81
Rosoman Pl. EC1 3K 7 (4A 84)
Rosoman St. EC1 2K 7 (3A 84)
Rossall Cres. NW10 3F 79
Ross Apartments E16 7J 87
(off Seagull La.)
Ross Av. NW7 5B 30
RM8: Dag 2F 73
Ross Cl. HA3: Hrw W 7B 26
UB3: Harl 4F 93
UB5: N'olt 4H 59
Ross Ct. E5 4H 67
(off Napoleon Rd.)
NW9 3A 44
SW15 7F 117
W13 5B 78
(off Cleveland Rd.)
Rosscourt Mans. SW1 1A 18
(off Buckingham Pal. Rd.)
Rossdale SM1: Sutt 5C 166
Rossdale Dr. N9 6D 24
NW9 1J 61
Rossdale Rd. SW15 4E 116
Rosse Gdns. SE13 6F 123
Rosse M. SE3 1K 123
Rossendale St. E5 2H 67
Rossendale Way NW1 7G 65
Rossetti Ct. WC1 5C 6
(off Ridgmount Pl.)
Rossetti Gdn. Mans. SW3 7E 16
Rossetti Ho. SW1 4D 18
(off Erasmus St.)
Rossetti M. NW8 1B 82
Rossetti Rd. SE16 5H 103
Rossetti Studios SW3 7D 16
(off Flood St.)
Ross Haven Pl. HA6: Nwood 1H 39
Ross Ho. E1 1H 103
(off Prusom St.)
Rossignol Gdns. SM5: Cars 2E 166
Rossindel Rd. TW3: Houn 5E 112
Rossington Cl. EN1: Enf 1C 24
Rossington St. E5 2G 67
Rossiter Flds. EN5: Barn 6B 20
Rossiter Rd. SW12 1F 137
Rossland Cl. DA6: Bex 5H 127
Rosslyn Av. E4 2C 36
EN4: E Barn 6H 21
RM8: Dag 7F 55
SW13 3A 116
TW14: Felt 6J 111
Rosslyn Cl. BR4: W W'ck 3H 171
TW16: Sun 6G 129
UB3: Hayes 5F 75
Rosslyn Cres. HA1: Harr 4K 41
HA9: Wemb 4E 60
Rosslyn Gdns. HA9: Wemb 3E 60
(off Rosslyn Cres.)
Rosslyn Hill NW3 4B 64
Rosslyn Mans. NW6 7A 64
(off Goldhurst Ter.)
Rosslyn M. NW3 4B 64
Rosslyn Pk. M. NW3 5B 64
Rosslyn Pk. RUFC 4B 116
Rosslyn Rd. E17 4E 50
IG11: Bark 7H 71
TW1: Twick 6C 114
Rossmore Cl. EN3: Pond E 4E 24
NW1 4D 4
(off Rossmore Rd.)
Rossmore Ct. NW1 3E 4 (4D 82)
Rossmore Rd. NW1 4D 4 (4C 82)
Ross Pde. SM6: Wall 6F 167
Ross Rd. SE25 3D 156
SM6: Wall 5G 167
TW2: Whitt 1F 131
Ross Way SE9 3C 124
Rosswood Gdns. SM6: Wall 6G 167
Ross Wyld Lodge E17 3C 50
(off Forest Rd.)
Rostella Rd. SW17 4B 136
Rostrevor Av. N15 6F 49
Rostrevor Gdns. UB2: S'hall 5C 94
UB3: Hayes 1G 93
Rostrevor M. SW6 1H 117
Rostrevor Rd. SW6 1H 117
SW19 5J 135
Rotary St. SE1 7A 14 (3B 102)
Rothay NW1 1K 5
(off Albany St.)
Rothbury Cotts. SE10 4G 105
Rothbury Gdns. TW7: Isle 7A 96
Rothbury Hall 4G 105
(off Mauritius Rd.)
Rothbury Rd. E9 7B 68
Rothbury Wlk. N17 7B 34
Rotheley Ho. E9 7J 67
(off Balcorne St.)
Rotherfield Ct. N1 7D 66
(off Rotherfield St.,not continuous)
Rotherfield Rd. SM5: Cars 4E 166
Rotherfield St. N1 7C 66
Rotherham Wlk. SE1 5A 14
Rotherhill Av. SW16 6H 137
ROTHERHITHE 2J 103
Rotherhithe Bus. Est. SE16 4H 103
Rotherhithe New Rd. SE16 5H 103
Rotherhithe Old Rd. SE16 4K 103
Rotherhithe St. SE16 2J 103
Rotherhithe Tunnel SE16 1K 103
Rother Ho. SE15 4H 121
Rotherwick Hill W5 4F 79
Rotherwick Ho. E1 7G 85
(off Thomas More St.)
Rotherwick Rd. NW11 7J 45
Rotherwood Cl. SW20 1G 153
Rotherwood Rd. SW15 3F 117
Rothery St. N1 1B 84
(off St Marys Path)
Rothery Ter. SW9 7B 102
(off Foxley Rd.)
Rothesay Av. SW20 2G 153
TW10: Rich 4H 115
UB6: G'frd 6G 59
(not continuous)
Rothesay Ct. SE6 2H 141
SE11 7J 19
SE12 3K 141
Rothesay Rd. SE25 4D 156
Rothley Ct. NW8 3A 4
(off St John's Wood Rd.)
Rothsay Rd. E7 7A 70
Rothsay St. SE1 3E 102
Rothsay Wlk. E14 4C 104
(off Charnwood Gdns.)
Rothschild Rd. W4 4J 97
Rothschild St. SE27 4B 138
Roth Wlk. N7 2K 65
Rothwell Ct. HA1: Harr 5K 41
Rothwell Gdns. RM9: Dag 7C 72
Rothwell Ho. TW5: Hest 6E 94
Rothwell Rd. RM9: Dag 1C 90
Rothwell St. NW1 1D 82
Rotten Row NW3 1A 64
SW1 6B 10 (2B 100)
SW7 6B 10 (2B 100)
Rotterdam Dr. E14 3E 104
Rotunda, The RM7: Rom 5K 55
(off Yew Tree Gdns.)
Rotunda Cen., The 2E 150
Rouel Rd. SE16 3G 103
(Dockley Rd.)
SE16 4G 103
(Southwark Pk. Rd.)
Rougemont Av. SM4: Mord 6J 153
Roundabout Ho. HA6: Nwood 1J 39
Roundacre SW19 2F 135
Roundaway Rd. IG5: Ilf 1D 52
Roundel Cl. SE4 4B 122
Round Gro. CR0: C'don 7K 157
Roundhay Cl. SE23 2K 139
Roundhedge Way EN2: Enf 1E 22
Round Hill SE26 2J 139
(not continuous)
Roundhill Dr. EN2: Enf 4E 22
Roundhouse, The 7E 64
ROUNDSHAW 7J 167
Roundtable Rd. BR1: Brom 3H 141
Roundtree Rd. HA0: Wemb 5B 60
Roundway, The KT10: Clay 6A 162
N17 1C 48
Roundways HA4: Ruis 3H 57
Roundwood BR7: Chst 2F 161
Roundwood Av. UB11: Stock P 1E 92
Roundwood Cl. HA4: Ruis 7F 39
Roundwood Rd. NW10 6B 62
Rounton Rd. E3 4C 86
Roupell Ho. KT2: King T 7F 133
(off Florence Rd.)
Roupell Rd. SW2 1K 137
Roupell St.
SE1 5K 13 (1A 102)
Rousden St. NW1 7G 65
Rouse Gdns. SE21 4E 138
Rous Rd. IG9: Buck H 1H 37
Routemaster Cl. E13 3K 87
Routh Ct. TW14: Bedf 1F 129
Routh Rd. SW18 7C 118
Routh St. E6 5D 88
Rover Ho. N1 1E 84
(off Mill Row)
Rowallan Rd. SW6 7G 99
Rowallen Pde. RM8: Dag 1C 72
Rowan N10 2F 47
Rowan Av. E4 6G 35
Rowan Cl. HA0: Wemb 3A 60
HA7: Stan 6E 26
IG1: Ilf 5H 71
KT3: N Mald 2A 152
SW16 1G 155
W5 2E 96
Rowan Ct. E13 2K 87
(off High St.)
SE15 7F 103
(off Garnies Cl.)
SW11 6D 118
Rowan Cres. SW16 1G 155
Rowan Dr. NW9 3C 44
Rowan Gdns. CR0: C'don 3F 169
Rowan Ho. BR2: Brom 2G 159
DA14: Sidc 3K 143
IG1: Ilf 5H 71
SE16 2K 103
(off Woodland Cres.)
Rowan Lodge W8 3K 99
(off Chantry Sq.)
Rowan Pl. UB3: Hayes 7H 75
Rowan Rd. DA7: Bex 3E 126
N2 1C 46
SW16 2G 155
TW8: Bford 7B 96
UB7: W Dray 1E 174
W6 4F 99
Rowans, The N13 3G 33
TW16: Sun 5H 129
Rowans Complex 2A 66
Rowan Ter. W6 4F 99
Rowantree Cl. N21 1J 33
Rowantree Rd. EN2: Enf 2G 23
N21 1J 33
Rowan Wlk. BR2: Brom 3D 172
EN5: New Bar 5E 20
N2 5A 46
N19 2G 65
W10 4G 81
Rowan Way RM6: Chad H 3C 54
Rowanwood Av. DA15: Sidc 1A 144
Rowanwood M. EN2: Enf 2G 23
Rowben Cl. N20 1E 30
Rowberry Cl. SW6 7E 98
Rowcross St. SE1 5F 103
Rowdell Rd. UB5: N'olt 1E 76
Rowden Pk. Gdns. E4 7H 35
(off Chingford Rd.)
Rowden Rd. BR3: Beck 1A 158
E4 6J 35
KT19: Ewe 4H 163
Rowditch La. SW11 2E 118
Rowdon Av. NW10 7D 62
Rowdown Cres. CR0: New Ad 7F 171
Rowdowns Rd. RM9: Dag 1F 91
Rowe Gdns. IG11: Bark 2K 89
Rowe Ho. E9 6J 67
Rowe La. E9 5J 67
Rowena Cres. SW11 2C 118
Rowenhurst Mans. NW6 6A 64
(off Canfield Gdns.)
Rowe Wlk. HA2: Harr 3E 58
Rowfant Rd. SW17 1E 136
Rowhill Rd. E5 4H 67
Rowington Cl. W2 5K 81
Rowland Av. HA3: Kent 3C 42
Rowland Ct. E16 4H 87
Rowland Gro. SE26 3H 139
Rowland Hill Almshouses
TW15: Ashf 5C 128
(off Feltham Hill Rd.)
Rowland Hill Av. N17 7H 33
Rowland Hill Ho. SE1 6A 14 (2B 102)
Rowland Hill St. NW3 5C 64
Rowlands Av. HA5: Hat E 5A 26
Rowlands Cl. N6 6E 46
NW7 7H 29
Rowlands Rd. RM8: Dag 2F 73
Rowland Way SW19 1K 153
TW15: Ashf 7F 129
Rowley Av. DA15: Sidc 7B 126
Rowley Cl. HA0: Wemb 7F 61
Rowley Ct. EN1: Enf 5K 23
(off Wellington Rd.)
Rowley Gdns. N4 7C 48

Rowley Ho. SE8 . . . 5C 104
(off Watergate St.)
Rowley Ind. Pk. W3 . . . 3H 97
Rowley Rd. N15 . . . 5C 48
Rowley Way NW8 . . . 1K 81
Rowlheys Pl. UB7: W Dray . . . 3A 92
Rowlls Rd. KT1: King T . . . 3F 151
Rowney Gdns. RM9: Dag . . . 6C 72
Rowney Rd. RM9: Dag . . . 6B 72
Rowntree Clifford Cl. E13 . . . 4J 87
Rowntree Cl. NW6 . . . 6J 63
Rowntree Path SE28 . . . 1B 108
Rowntree Rd. TW2: Twick . . . 1J 131
Rowse Cl. E15 . . . 1E 86
Rowsley Av. NW4 . . . 3E 44
Rowstock Gdns. N7 . . . 5H 65
Rowton Rd. SE18 . . . 7G 107
Roxborough Av. HA1: Harr . . . 7H 41
TW7: Isle . . . 7K 95
Roxborough Hgts. HA1: Harr . . . 6J 41
(off College Rd.)
Roxborough Pk. HA1: Harr . . . 7J 41
Roxborough Rd. HA1: Harr . . . 5H 41
Roxbourne Cl. UB5: N'olt . . . 6B 58
Roxbourne Pk. Miniature Railway . . . 2B 58
Roxburghe Mans. W8 . . . 2K 99
(off Kensington Ct.)
Roxburgh Rd. SE27 . . . 5B 138
Roxburn Way HA4: Ruis . . . 3H 57
Roxby Pl. SW6 . . . 6J 99
ROXETH . . . 2H 59
Roxeth Ct. TW15: Ashf . . . 5C 128
Roxeth Grn. Av. HA2: Harr . . . 3F 59
Roxeth Gro. HA2: Harr . . . 4F 59
Roxeth Hill HA2: Harr . . . 2H 59
Roxford Cl. TW17: Shep . . . 5G 147
Roxley Rd. SE13 . . . 6D 122
Roxton Gdns.
CR0: Addtn . . . 5C 170
Roxwell NW1 . . . 6F 65
(off Hartland Rd.)
Roxwell Rd. IG11: Bark . . . 2A 90
W12 . . . 2C 98
Roxwell Trad. Pk. E10 . . . 7A 50
Roxwell Way IG8: Wfd G . . . 7F 37
Roxy Av. RM6: Chad H . . . 7C 54
Royal Academy of Arts
(Burlington House) . . . 3A 12 (7G 83)
Royal Academy of Music Mus. . . . 4H 5
Royal Air Force Memorial . . . 1J 101
Royal Albert Hall . . . 7A 10 (2B 100)
Royal Albert Rdbt. E16 . . . 7C 88
(off Royal Albert Way)
Royal Albert Way E16 . . . 7B 88
Royal Arc. W1 . . . 3A 12
ROYAL ARSENAL WEST . . . 3F 107
Royal Av. KT4: Wor Pk . . . 2A 164
SW3 . . . 5E 16 (5D 100)
Royal Av. Ho. SW3 . . . 5E 16
(off Royal Av.)
Royal Belgrave Ho. SW1 . . . 4K 17
(off Hugh St.)
Royal Botanic Gdns. . . . 1E 114
Royal Brass Foundry . . . 3F 107
Royal Ceremonial Dress Collection, The
. . . 1K 99
(in Kensington Palace)
Royal Cir. SE27 . . . 3A 138
Royal Cl. BR6: Farnb . . . 4F 173
IG3: Ilf . . . 7A 54
KT4: Wor Pk . . . 2A 164
N16 . . . 1E 66
SE8 . . . 6B 104
SW19 . . . 3F 135
UB8: Hil . . . 6B 74
Royal College of Art . . . 7A 10 (2B 100)
Royal College of Music . . . 1A 16 (3B 100)
Royal College of Obstetricians &
Gynaecologists . . . 3E 4 (4D 82)
Royal College of Physicians . . . 3J 5
Royal College of Surgeons . . . 7H 7
Royal Coll. St. NW1 . . . 7G 65
Royal Connaught Apartments
E16 . . . 1B 106
(off Connaught Rd.)
Royal Ct. EC3 . . . 1F 15
(off Finch La.)
EN1: Enf . . . 6K 23
HA4: Ruis . . . 6J 39
SE9 . . . 1D 142
SE16 . . . 3B 104
Royal Courts of Justice . . . 1H 13
Royal Court Theatre . . . 4G 17
(off Sloane Sq.)
Royal Cres. HA4: Ruis . . . 4C 58
IG2: Ilf . . . 6H 53
W11 . . . 1F 99
Royal Cres. M. W11 . . . 1F 99
Royal Docks Rd. E6 . . . 6F 89
IG11: Bark . . . 6F 89
Royal Dr. N11 . . . 5K 31
Royal Duchess M. SW12 . . . 7F 119
Royale Leisure Pk. W3 . . . 4G 79
Royal Exchange . . . 1F 15 (6D 84)
Royal Exchange Av. EC3 . . . 1F 15
Royal Exchange Bldgs.
EC3 . . . 1F 15
Royal Festival Hall . . . 5H 13 (1K 101)
Royal Fusiliers Mus. . . . 3J 15
(in The Tower of London)
Royal Gdns. W7 . . . 3A 96
Royal Geographical Society . . . 7A 10
Royal Herbert Pavilions
SE18 . . . 1D 124
Royal Hill SE10 . . . 7E 104
Royal Hill Ct. SE10 . . . 7E 104
(off Greenwich High St.)
Royal Hospital Chelsea Mus.
. . . 6G 17 (5E 100)
Royal Hospital Rd. SW3 . . . 7E 16 (6D 100)
Royal La. UB7: Yiew . . . 5B 74
UB8: Hil . . . 5B 74
Royal London Bldgs. SE15 . . . 6H 103
(off Old Kent Rd.)
Royal London Est., The N17 . . . 6C 34
Royal London Ind. Est. NW10 . . . 2K 79
Royal Mews, The . . . 1K 17 (3F 101)
Royal M. KT8: E Mos . . . 3J 149
SW1 . . . 1K 17 (3F 101)
Royal Mid Surrey Golf Course . . . 3D 114
Royal Mint Ct. EC3 . . . 3K 15 (7F 85)
Royal Mint Pl. E1 . . . 2K 15 (7G 85)
Royal Mint St. E1 . . . 2K 15 (7F 85)
Royal Naval Pl. SE14 . . . 7B 104
Royal Oak Ct. N1 . . . 1G 9
(off Pitfield St.)
Royal Oak M. TW11: Tedd . . . 5A 132
Royal Oak Pl. SE22 . . . 6H 121
Royal Oak Rd. DA6: Bex . . . 5F 127
(not continuous)
E8 . . . 6H 67
Royal Oak Yd. SE1 . . . 7G 15 (2E 102)
Royal Observatory Greenwich . . . 7G 105
Royal Opera Arc. SW1 . . . 4C 12 (1H 101)
Royal Opera House . . . 1F 13 (6J 83)
Royal Orchard Cl. SW18 . . . 7G 117
Royal Pde. BR7: Chst . . . 7G 143
RM10: Dag . . . 6H 73
SE3 . . . 2H 123
SW6 . . . 7G 99
TW9: Kew . . . 1G 115
(off Station App.)
W5 . . . 3E 78
Royal Pde. M. BR7: Chst . . . 7G 143
(off Royal Pde.)
SE3 . . . 2H 123
(off Royal Pde.)
Royal Pl. SE10 . . . 7E 104
Royal Quarter KT2: King T . . . 1E 150
Royal Quay Rd. E6 . . . 7F 89
Royal Rd. DA14: Sidc . . . 3D 144
E16 . . . 6B 88
SE17 . . . 6B 102
TW11: Tedd . . . 5H 131
Royal Route HA9: Wemb . . . 4F 61
Royal St. SE1 . . . 1H 19 (3K 101)
Royal Twr. Lodge E1 . . . 3K 15
(off Cartwright St.)
Royalty Mans. W1 . . . 1C 12
(off Meard St.)
Royalty M. W1 . . . 1C 12 (6H 83)
Royalty Studios W11 . . . 6G 81
(off Lancaster Rd.)
Royal Veterinary College
Camden Town . . . 1H 83
Royal Victoria Docks
Watersports Cen. . . . 7J 87
Royal Victoria Patriotic Bldg.
SW18 . . . 6B 118
Royal Victoria Pl. E16 . . . 1K 105
Royal Victoria Sq. E16 . . . 7K 87
Royal Victor Pl. E3 . . . 2K 85
Royal Wlk. SM6: Wall . . . 2F 167
Royal Westminster Lodge SW1 . . . 3C 18
(off Elverton St.)
Roycraft Av. IG11: Bark . . . 2K 89
Roycroft Cl. E18 . . . 1K 51
SW2 . . . 1A 138
Roydene Rd. SE18 . . . 6J 107
Roydon Cl. IG10: Lough . . . 1H 37
SW11 . . . 2D 118
(off Battersea Pk. Rd.)
Roy Gdns. IG2: Ilf . . . 4J 53
Roy Gro. TW12: Hamp . . . 6F 131
Royle Bldg. N1 . . . 2C 84
(off Wenlock Rd.)
Royle Cres. W13 . . . 4A 78
Royley Ho. EC1 . . . 4C 84
(off Whitecross St.)
Roymount Ct. TW2: Twick . . . 3J 131
Roy Rd. HA6: Nwood . . . 1H 39
Roy Sq. E14 . . . 7A 86
Royston Av. E4 . . . 5H 35
SM1: Sutt . . . 3B 166
SM6: Bedd . . . 4H 167
Royston Cl. KT12: Walt T . . . 7J 147
TW5: Cran . . . 1K 111
Royston Ct. E13 . . . 1J 87
(off Stopford Rd.)
SE24 . . . 6C 120
TW9: Kew . . . 1F 115
W8 . . . 1J 99
(off Kensington Chu. St.)
Royston Gdns. IG1: Ilf . . . 6B 52
Royston Ho. N11 . . . 4J 31
SE15 . . . 6H 103
(off Friary Est.)
Royston Pde. IG1: Ilf . . . 6B 52
Royston Pk. Rd. HA5: Hat E . . . 5A 26
Royston Rd. SE20 . . . 1K 157
TW10: Rich . . . 5E 114
Roystons, The KT5: Surb . . . 5H 151
Royston St. E2 . . . 2J 85
Rozel Ct. N1 . . . 1E 84
Rozel Rd. SW4 . . . 3G 119
Rozel Ter. CR0: C'don . . . 2C 168
(off Church Rd.)
RQ33 SW18 . . . 4J 117
Rubastic Rd. UB2: S'hall . . . 3A 94
Rubens Gdns. SE22 . . . 7G 121
(off Lordship La.)
Rubens Pl. SW4 . . . 4J 119
Rubens Rd. UB5: N'olt . . . 2A 76
Rubens St. SE6 . . . 2B 140
Ruby Rd. E17 . . . 3C 50
Ruby St. NW10 . . . 7K 61
SE15 . . . 6H 103
Ruby Triangle SE15 . . . 6H 103
Ruby Way NW9 . . . 1B 44
Ruckholt Cl. E10 . . . 3D 68
Ruckholt Rd. E9 . . . 4C 68
E10 . . . 4C 68
Rucklidge Av. NW10 . . . 2B 80
Rucklidge Pas. NW10 . . . 2B 80
(off Rucklidge Av.)
Rudall Cres. NW3 . . . 4B 64
Rudbeck Ho. SE15 . . . 7G 103
(off Peckham Pk. Rd.)
Ruddington Cl. E5 . . . 4A 68
Ruddock Cl. HA8: Edg . . . 7D 28
Ruddstreet Cl. SE18 . . . 4F 107
Ruddy Way NW7 . . . 6G 29
Rudge Ho. SE16 . . . 3G 103
(off Jamaica Rd.)
Rudgwick Ct. SE18 . . . 4C 106
(off Woodville St., not continuous)
Rudgwick Ter. NW8 . . . 1C 82
Rudland Rd. DA7: Bex . . . 3H 127
Rudloe Rd. SW12 . . . 7G 119
Rudolf Pl. SW8 . . . 7F 19 (6J 101)
Rudolph Rd. E13 . . . 2H 87
NW6 . . . 2J 81
Rudyard Gro. NW7 . . . 6D 28
Ruegg Ho. SE18 . . . 6E 106
(off Woolwich Comn.)
Ruffetts, The CR2: Sels . . . 7H 169
Ruffetts Cl. CR2: Sels . . . 7H 169
Ruffle Cl. UB7: W Dray . . . 2A 92
Rufford Cl. HA3: Kent . . . 6A 42
Rufford St. N1 . . . 1J 83
Rufford St. M. N1 . . . 7J 65
Rufford Twr. W3 . . . 1H 97
Rufforth Ct. NW9 . . . 1A 44
(off Pageant Av.)
Rufus Bus. Cen. SW18 . . . 2K 135
Rufus Cl. HA4: Ruis . . . 3C 58
Rufus Ho. SE1 . . . 7K 15
(off St Saviour's Est.)
Rufus St. N1 . . . 2G 9 (3E 84)
Rugby Av. HA0: Wemb . . . 5B 60
N9 . . . 1A 34
UB6: G'frd . . . 6H 59
Rugby Cl. HA1: Harr . . . 4J 41
Rugby Gdns. RM9: Dag . . . 6C 72
Rugby Mans. W14 . . . 4G 99
(off Bishop King's Rd.)
Rugby Rd. NW9 . . . 4H 43
RM9: Dag . . . 7B 72
TW1: Twick . . . 5J 113
W4 . . . 2A 98
Rugby St. WC1 . . . 4G 7 (4K 83)
Rugg St. E14 . . . 7C 86
Rugless Ho. E14 . . . 2E 104
(off E. Ferry Rd.)
Rugmere NW1 . . . 7E 64
(off Ferdinand St.)
RUISLIP . . . 1G 57
Ruislip Cl. UB6: G'frd . . . 4F 77
RUISLIP COMMON . . . 4E 38
Ruislip Ct. HA4: Ruis . . . 2H 57
RUISLIP GARDENS . . . 3J 57
Ruislip Lido Railway
Eleanor's Station . . . 3G 39
Haste Hill Station . . . 3G 39
Lakeside Station . . . 4F 39
Woody Bay Station . . . 5F 39
Ruislip Local Nature Reserve . . . 3F 39
RUISLIP MANOR . . . 2J 57
Ruislip Rd. UB1: S'hall . . . 2B 76
UB5: N'olt . . . 1A 76
UB6: G'frd . . . 3E 76
Ruislip Rd. E. UB6: G'frd . . . 4H 77
W7 . . . 4J 77
W13 . . . 4H 77
Ruislip St. SW17 . . . 4D 136
Ruislip Woodlands Cen. . . . 4F 39
Rumball Ho. SE5 . . . 7E 102
(off Harris St.)
Rumbold Rd. SW6 . . . 7K 99
Rum Cl. E1 . . . 7J 85

Rumford Ho. *SE1* *3C* **102**
(off Tiverton St.)
Rumney Ct. *UB5: N'olt* *2B* **76**
(off Parkfield Dr.)
Rumsey Cl. TW12: Hamp 6D **130**
Rumsey M. N4 . . . . 3B **66**
Rumsey Rd. SW9 . . . . 3K **119**
Runacres Ct. SE17 . . . . 5C **102**
Runbury Circ. NW9 . . . . 2K **61**
Runcorn Cl. N17 . . . . 4H **49**
Runcorn Pl. W11 . . . . 7G **81**
Rundell Cres. NW4 . . . . 5D **44**
Rundell Twr. SW8 . . . . 1K **119**
Runes Cl. CR4: Mitc 4B **154**
Runnel Ct. *IG11: Bark* *2G* **89**
(off Spring Pl.)
Runnelfield HA1: Harr 3J **59**
Running Horse Yd. TW8: Bford 6E **96**
Runnymede SW19 . . . . 1A **154**
Runnymede Cl. TW2: Whitt 6F **113**
Runnymede Ct. SM6: Wall 6F **167**
SW15 . . . . 1C **134**
Runnymede Cres. SW16 . . . . 1H **155**
Runnymede Gdns. TW2: Whitt 6F **113**
UB6: G'frd 2J **77**
Runnymede Ho. E9 . . . . 4A **68**
Runnymede Rd. TW2: Whitt 6F **113**
Runway NW9 . . . . 2B **44**
Runway, The HA4: Ruis 5K **57**
Rupack St. SE16 . . . . 2J **103**
Rupert Av. HA9: Wemb 5E **60**
Rupert Ct. *KT8: W Mole* *4E* **148**
(off St Peters Rd.)
W1 . . . . 2C **12** (7H **83**)
Rupert Gdns. SW9 . . . . 2B **120**
Rupert Ho.
SE11 . . . . 4K **19** (4A **102**)
SW5 . . . . *4J* **99**
(off Nevern Sq.)
Rupert Rd. N19 . . . . 3H **65**
(not continuous)
NW6 . . . . 2H **81**
W4 . . . . 3A **98**
Rupert St. W1 . . . . 2C **12** (7H **83**)
Rural Way SW16 . . . . 7F **137**
Rusbridge Cl. E8 . . . . 5G **67**
Ruscoe Rd. E16 . . . . 6H **87**
Ruscombe *NW1* *1F* **83**
(off Delancey St.)
Ruscombe Way TW14: Felt 7H **111**
Rush, The *SW20* *1H* **153**
(off Kingston Rd.)
Rusham Rd. SW12 . . . . 6D **118**
Rushbrook Cres. E17 . . . . 1B **50**
Rushbrook Rd. SE9 . . . . 2G **143**
Rushbury Ct. TW12: Hamp 1E **148**
Rush Comn. M. SW2 . . . . 7K **119**
(Cotherstone Rd.)
SW2 . . . . 7J **119**
(New Pk. Rd.)
Rushcroft Rd. E4 . . . . 7J **35**
SW2 . . . . 4A **120**
Rushcutters Ct. *SE16* *4A* **104**
(off Boat Lifter Way)
Rushden Cl. SE19 . . . . 7D **138**
Rushdene SE2 . . . . 3D **108**
(not continuous)
Rushdene Av. EN4: E Barn 7H **21**
Rushdene Cl. UB5: Yead 2A **76**
Rushdene Cres. UB5: Yead 2K **75**
Rushdene Rd. HA5: Eastc 6B **40**
Rushden Gdns. IG5: Ilf 2E **52**
NW7 . . . . 6K **29**
Rushen Wlk. SM5: Cars 1B **166**
Rushett Cl. KT7: T Ditt 1B **162**
Rushett Rd. KT7: T Ditt 7B **150**
Rushey Cl. KT3: N Mald 4K **151**
Rushey Grn. SE6 . . . . 7D **122**
Rushey Hill EN2: Enf 4E **22**
Rushey Mead SE4 . . . . 5C **122**
Rushford Rd. SE4 . . . . 6B **122**
RUSH GREEN 1K **73**
Rush Grn. Gdns. RM7: Rush G 1J **73**
Rush Grn. Rd. RM7: Rush G 1H **73**
Rushgrove Av. NW9 . . . . 5A **44**
Rushgrove Ct. NW9 . . . . 5A **44**
Rushgrove Pde. NW9 . . . . 5A **44**
Rushgrove St. SE18 . . . . 4D **106**
Rush Hill M. *SW11* *3E* **118**
(off Rush Hill Rd.)
Rush Hill Rd. SW11 . . . . 3E **118**
Rushley Cl. BR2: Kes 4B **172**
Rushmead E2 . . . . 3H **85**
TW10: Ham 3B **132**
Rushmead Cl. CR0: C'don 4F **169**
HA8: Edg 2C **28**
Rushmere Ct. KT4: Wor Pk 2C **164**
Rushmere Pl. SW19 . . . . 5F **135**
Rushmon Pl. SM3: Cheam 6G **165**
Rushmon Vs. KT3: N Mald 4B **152**
Rushmoor Cl. HA5: Eastc 4K **39**
Rushmore Cl. BR1: Brom 3C **160**
Rushmore Cres. E5 . . . . 4K **67**
Rushmore Ho. SW15 . . . . 7C **116**
W14 . . . . *3G* **99**
(off Russell Rd.)
Rushmore Rd. E5 . . . . 4J **67**
(not continuous)
Rusholme Av. RM10: Dag 3G **73**
Rusholme Gro. SE19 . . . . 5E **138**
Rusholme Rd. SW15 . . . . 6F **117**
Rushout Av. HA3: Kent 6B **42**
Rushton Ho. SW8 . . . . 2H **119**
Rushton St. N1 . . . . 2D **84**
Rushworth St. SE1 . . . . 6B **14** (2B **102**)
Rushy Mdw. La. SM5: Cars 2C **166**
Ruskin Av. DA16: Well 2A **126**
E12 . . . . 6C **70**
TW9: Kew 7G **97**
TW14: Felt 6H **111**
Ruskin Cl. NW11 . . . . 6K **45**
Ruskin Ct. N21 . . . . 7E **22**
SE5 . . . . *3D* **120**
(off Champion Hill)
Ruskin Dr. BR6: Orp 3J **173**
DA16: Well 3A **126**
KT4: Wor Pk 2D **164**
Ruskin Gdns. HA3: Kent 5F **43**
W5 . . . . 4D **78**
Ruskin Gro. DA16: Well 2A **126**
Ruskin Ho. *CR2: S Croy* *5D* **168**
(off Selsdon Rd.)
SW1 . . . . *4D* **18**
(off Herrick St.)
Ruskin Mans. *W14* *6G* **99**
(off Queen's Club Gdns.)
Ruskin Pde. *CR2: S Croy* *5D* **168**
(off Selsdon Rd.)
Ruskin Pk. Ho. SE5 . . . . 3D **120**
Ruskin Rd. CR0: C'don 2B **168**
DA17: Belv 4G **109**
N17 . . . . 1F **49**
SM5: Cars 5D **166**
TW7: Isle 3K **113**
UB1: S'hall 7C **76**
Ruskin Wlk. BR2: Brom 6D **160**
N9 . . . . 2B **34**
SE24 . . . . 5C **120**
Ruskin Way SW19 . . . . 1B **154**
Rusland Av. BR6: Orp 3H **173**
Rusland Hgts. HA1: Harr 4J **41**
Rusland Pk. Rd. HA1: Harr 4J **41**
Rusper Cl. HA7: Stan 4H **27**
NW2 . . . . 3E **62**
Rusper Ct. *SW9* *2J* **119**
(off Clapham Rd.)
Rusper Rd. N17 . . . . 3C **48**
N22 . . . . 2B **48**
RM9: Dag 6C **72**
Russell Av. N22 . . . . 2A **48**
Russell Chambers *WC1* *6F* **7**
(off Bury Pl.)
Russell Cl. BR3: Beck 3D **158**
DA7: Bex 4G **127**
HA4: Ruis 2A **58**
NW10 . . . . 7J **61**
SE7 . . . . 7A **106**
W4 . . . . 6B **98**
Russell Ct. E10 . . . . 7D **50**
EN5: New Bar 4F **21**
N14 . . . . 6C **22**
SE15 . . . . *2H* **121**
(off Heaton Rd.)
SM6: Wall *5G* **167**
(off Ross Rd.)
SW1 . . . . 5B **12**
SW16 . . . . 5K **137**
WC1 . . . . 4E **6**
Russell Flint Ho. *E16* *1K* **105**
(off Pankhurst Av.)
Russell Gdns. IG2: Ilf 7H **53**
N20 . . . . 2H **31**
NW11 . . . . 6G **45**
TW10: Ham 2C **132**
UB7: Sip 5C **92**
W14 . . . . 3G **99**
Russell Gdns. M. W14 . . . . 2G **99**
Russell Gro. NW7 . . . . 5F **29**
SW9 . . . . 7A **102**
Russell Ho. *E14* *6C* **86**
(off Saracen St.)
SW1 . . . . *5A* **18**
(off Cambridge St.)
Russell Kerr Cl. W4 . . . . 7J **97**
Russell La. N20 . . . . 2H **31**
Russell Lodge E4 . . . . 2K **35**
SE1 . . . . *3D* **102**
(off Spurgeon St.)
Russell Mans. *WC1* *5F* **7**
(off Southampton Row)
Russell Mead
HA3: Hrw W 1K **41**
Russell Pde. *NW11* *6G* **45**
(off Golders Grn. Rd.)
Russell Pl. NW3 . . . . 5C **64**
SE16 . . . . 3A **104**
SM2: Sutt 7K **165**
Russell Rd. CR4: Mitc 3C **154**
E4 . . . . 4G **35**
E10 . . . . 6D **50**
E16 . . . . 6J **87**
E17 . . . . 3B **50**
EN1: Enf 1A **24**
IG9: Buck H 1E **36**
KT12: Walt T 6J **147**
N8 . . . . 6H **47**
N13 . . . . 6E **32**
N15 . . . . 5E **48**
N20 . . . . 2H **31**
NW9 . . . . 6B **44**
SW19 . . . . 7J **135**
TW2: Twick 6K **113**
TW17: Shep 7E **146**
UB5: N'olt 5G **59**
W14 . . . . 3G **99**
Russell's Footpath SW16 . . . . 5J **137**
Russell Sq. WC1 . . . . 4E **6** (5J **83**)
Russell Sq. Mans. *WC1* *5F* **7**
(off Southampton Row)
Russell St. WC2 . . . . 2F **13** (7J **83**)
Russell's Wharf Flats
W10 . . . . 4H **81**
Russell Wlk. TW10: Rich 6F **115**
Russell Way SM1: Sutt 5K **165**
Russell Yd. SW15 . . . . 4G **117**
Russet Av. TW17: Shep 3G **147**
Russet Cl. UB10: Hil 4E **74**
Russet Cres. N7 . . . . 5K **65**
Russet Dr. CR0: C'don 1A **170**
Russets Cl. E4 . . . . 4A **36**
Russett Way SE13 . . . . 2D **122**
Russia Dock Rd. SE16 . . . . 1A **104**
Russia La. E2 . . . . 2J **85**
Russia Row EC2 . . . . 1D **14** (6C **84**)
Russia Wlk. SE16 . . . . 2A **104**
Russington Rd. TW17: Shep 6F **147**
Rusthall Av. W4 . . . . 4K **97**
Rusthall Cl. CR0: C'don 6J **157**
Rustic Av. SW16 . . . . 7F **137**
Rustic Pl. HA0: Wemb 4D **60**
Rustic Wlk. *E16* *6K* **87**
(off Lambert Rd.)
Rustington Wlk. SM4: Mord 7H **153**
Ruston Av. KT5: Surb 7H **151**
Ruston Gdns. N14 . . . . 6K **21**
Ruston M. W11 . . . . 6G **81**
Ruston Rd. SE18 . . . . 3C **106**
Ruston St. E3 . . . . 1B **86**
Rust Sq. SE5 . . . . 7D **102**
Rutford Rd. SW16 . . . . 5J **137**
Ruth Cl. HA7: Stan 4F **43**
Ruth Ct. E3 . . . . 2A **86**
Rutherford Cl. SM2: Sutt 6B **166**
UB8: Hil 4B **74**
Rutherford Ho. *E1* *4H* **85**
(off Brady St.)
HA9: Wemb *3J* **61**
(off Barnhill Rd.)
Rutherford St. SW1 . . . . 3C **18** (4H **101**)
Rutherford Twr. UB1: S'hall 6F **77**
Rutherford Way HA9: Wemb 4G **61**
WD23: B Hea 1C **26**
Rutherglen Rd. SE2 . . . . 6A **108**
Rutherwyke Cl. KT17: Ewe 6C **164**
Ruth Ho. *W10* *4G* **81**
(off Kensal Rd.)
Ruthin Cl. NW9 . . . . 6A **44**
Ruthin Rd. SE3 . . . . 6J **105**
Ruthven St. E9 . . . . 1K **85**
Rutland Av. DA15: Sidc 7A **126**
Rutland Cl. DA5: Bexl 2D **144**
KT9: Chess 6F **163**
SW14 . . . . 3H **115**
SW19 . . . . 7C **136**
Rutland Ct. BR7: Chst 1E **160**
EN3: Pond E 5C **24**
KT1: King T *4D* **150**
(off Palace Rd.)
SE5 . . . . 4D **120**
SE9 . . . . 2G **143**
SW7 . . . . 7D **10**
W3 . . . . 6G **79**
Rutland Dr. SM4: Mord 6H **153**
TW10: Ham 1D **132**
Rutland Gdns. CR0: C'don 4E **168**
N4 . . . . 6B **48**
RM8: Dag 5C **72**
SW7 . . . . 7D **10** (2C **100**)
W13 . . . . 5A **78**
Rutland Gdns. M. SW7 . . . . . . 7D **10** (2C **100**)
Rutland Ga. BR2: Brom 4H **159**
DA17: Belv 5H **109**
SW7 . . . . 7D **10** (2C **100**)
Rutland Ga. M. SW7 . . . . 7C **10**
Rutland Gro. W6 . . . . 5D **98**
Rutland Ho. *UB5: N'olt* *6E* **58**
(off The Farmlands)
W8 . . . . *3K* **99**
(off Marloes Rd.)
Rutland M. NW8 . . . . 1K **81**
Rutland M. E. SW7 . . . . 1C **16**
Rutland M. Sth. SW7 . . . . 1C **16**
Rutland M. W. SW7 . . . . 1C **16**
Rutland Pk. NW2 . . . . 6E **62**
SE6 . . . . 2B **140**
Rutland Pk. Gdns. *NW2* *6E* **62**
(off Rutland Pk.)
Rutland Pk. Mans. NW2 . . . . 6E **62**
Rutland Pl. EC1 . . . . 5B **8** (4B **84**)
WD23: B Hea 1C **26**

Rutland Rd. E7 7B 70
E9 1K 85
E11 5K 51
E17 6C 50
HA1: Harr 6G 41
IG1: Ilf 3F 71
SW19 7C 136
TW2: Twick 2H 131
UB1: S'hall 5E 76
UB3: Harl 4F 93
Rutland St. SW7 1D 16 (3C 100)
Rutland Wlk. SE6 2B 140
Rutley Cl. SE17 6B 102
Rutlish Rd. SW19 1J 153
Rutter Gdns. CR4: Mitc 4A 154
Rutters Cl. UB7: W Dray 2C 92
Rutts, The WD23: B Hea 1C 26
Rutt's Ter. SE14 1K 121
Ruvigny Gdns. SW15 3F 117
Ruxbury Ct. TW15: Ashf 3A 128
RUXLEY 7E 144
Ruxley Cl. DA14: Sidc 6D 144
KT19: Ewe 5H 163
Ruxley Cnr. Ind. Est. DA14: Sidc 6D 144
Ruxley Ct. KT19: Ewe 5J 163
Ruxley Cres. KT10: Clay 6B 162
Ruxley Gdns. TW17: Shep 5E 146
Ruxley La. KT19: Ewe 6H 163
Ruxley M. KT19: Ewe 5H 163
Ruxley Ridge KT10: Clay 7A 162
Ruxley Towers KT10: Clay 7A 162
Ryalls Ct. N20 3J 31
Ryan Cl. HA4: Ruis 1K 57
SE3 4A 124
Ryan Ct. RM7: Rom 6J 55
SW16 7J 137
Ryan Dr. TW8: Bford 6A 96
Ryarsh Cres. BR6: Orp 4J 173
Rycott Path SE22 7G 121
Rycroft Way N17 3F 49
Ryculff Sq. SE3 2H 123
Rydal Cl. NW4 1G 45
Rydal Ct. HA8: Edg 5A 28
HA9: Wemb 7F 43
Rydal Cres. UB6: G'frd 3B 78
Rydal Dr. BR4: W W'ck 2G 171
DA7: Bex 1G 127
Rydal Gdns. HA9: Wemb 1C 60
NW9 5A 44
SW15 5A 134
TW3: Houn 6F 113
Rydal Mt. BR2: Brom 4H 159
Rydal Rd. SW16 4H 137
Rydal Water NW1 2A 6 (3G 83)
Rydal Way EN3: Pond E 6D 24
HA4: Ruis 4A 58
Ryde Ho. *NW6* 1J 81
(off Priory Pk. Rd.)
Rydens Ho. SE9 3A 142
Rydens Rd. KT12: Walt T 7C 148
Ryde Pl. TW1: Twick 6D 114
Ryder Av. E10 7D 50
Ryder Cl. BR1: Brom 5K 141
Ryder Ct. E10 2D 68
SW1 4B 12
Ryder Dr. SE16 5H 103
Ryder Ho. *E1* 4J 85
(off Colebert Av.)
Ryder M. E9 5J 67
Ryder's Ter. NW8 2A 82
Ryder St. SW1 4B 12 (1G 101)
Ryder Yd. SW1 4B 12 (1G 101)
Ryde Va. Rd. SW12 2G 137
Rydon M. SW19 7E 134
Rydons Cl. SE9 3C 124
Rydon St. N1 1C 84
Rydston Cl. N7 7J 65
Rye, The N14 7C 22
Rye Cl. DA5: Bexl 6H 127
Ryecotes Mead SE21 1E 138
Ryecroft Av. IG5: Ilf 2F 53
TW2: Whitt 7F 113
Ryecroft Rd. BR5: Pet W 6H 161
SE13 5E 122
SW16 6A 138
Ryecroft St. SW6 1K 117
Ryedale SE22 6H 121
Ryefield Av. UB10: Hil 7D 56
Ryefield Ct. HA6: Nwood 2J 39
Ryefield Cres. HA6: Nwood 2J 39
Ryefield Pde. *HA6: Nwood* 2J 39
(off Joel St.)
Ryefield Path SW15 1C 134
Ryefield Rd. SE19 6C 138
Rye Hill Pk. SE15 4J 121
Rye Ho. *SE16* 2J 103
(off Swan Rd.)
SW1 5J 17
(off Ebury Bri. Rd.)
Ryeland Cl. UB7: Yiew 6A 74
Ryelands Cres. SE12 6A 124
Rye La. SE15 1G 121
Rye Pas. SE15 3G 121
Rye Rd. SE15 4K 121
Rye Wlk. SW15 5F 117
Rye Way HA8: Edg 6A 28
Ryfold Rd. SW19 3J 135
Ryhope Rd. N11 4A 32
Ryland Cl. TW13: Felt 4H 129
Rylandes Rd. NW2 3C 62
Ryland Rd. NW5 6F 65
Rylett Cres. W12 2B 98
Rylett Rd. W12 2B 98
Rylston Rd. N13 3J 33
SW6 6H 99
Rymer Rd. CR0: C'don 7E 156
Rymer St. SE24 6B 120
Rymill St. E16 1E 106
Rysbrack St. SW3 1E 16 (3D 100)
Rythe Cl. KT9: Chess 7C 162
Rythe Ct. KT7: T Ditt 7A 150

S

Saatchi Gallery 4F 17 (5D 100)
Sabah Ct. TW15: Ashf 4C 128
Sabbarton St. E16 6H 87
Sabella Ct. E3 2B 86
Sabine Rd. SW11 3D 118
Sable Cl. TW4: Houn 3A 112
Sable St. N1 7B 66
Sach Rd. E5 2H 67
Sackville Av. BR2: Hayes 1J 171
Sackville Cl. HA2: Harr 3H 59
Sackville Gdns. IG1: Ilf 1D 70
Sackville Ho. SW16 3J 137
Sackville Rd. SM2: Sutt 7J 165
Sackville St. W1 3B 12 (7G 83)
Saddlebrook Pk. TW16: Sun 7G 129
Saddlers Cl. HA5: Hat E 6A 26
Saddlers M. HA0: Wemb 4K 59
KT1: Ham W 1C 150
SW8 1J 119
Saddlescombe Way N12 5D 30
Saddle Yd. W1 4J 11 (1F 101)
Sadler Cl. CR4: Mitc 2D 154
Sadler Ho. *EC1* 1K 7
(off Spa Grn. Est.)
Sadlers Ride KT8: W Mole 2G 149
Sadler's Wells Theatre 1K 7 (3A 84)
Saffron Av. E14 7F 87
Saffron Cl. CR0: C'don 6J 155
NW11 6H 45
Saffron Ct. *E15* 5G 69
(off Maryland Pk.)
TW14: Bedf 7E 110
Saffron Hill EC1 5K 7 (5A 84)
Saffron Ho. SM2: Sutt 7K 165
TW9: Kew 1H 115
Saffron M. SW19 7G 135
Saffron Rd. RM5: Col R 2K 55
Saffron St. EC1 5K 7 (5A 84)
Saffron Way KT6: Surb 1D 162
Saffron Wharf *SE1* 6K 15
(off Shad Thames)
Sage Cl. E6 5D 88
Sage M. SE22 5F 121
Sage St. E1 7J 85
Sage Way WC1 2G 7
Sage Yd. KT6: Surb 1F 163
Sahara Ct. UB1: S'hall 7C 76
Saigasso Cl. E16 6B 88
Sailacre Ho. *SE10* 5H 105
(off Woolwich Rd.)
Sail Ct. *E14* 7F 87
(off Newport Av.)
Sailmakers Ct. SW6 3A 118
Sail St. SE11 3H 19 (4K 101)
Saimet *NW9* 7G 29
(off Wiggins Mead)
Sainfoin Rd. SW17 2E 136
Sainsbury Rd. SE19 5E 138
Sainsbury Wing 3D 12
(in National Gallery)
St Agatha's Dr. KT2: King T 6F 133
St Agatha's Gro. SM5: Cars 1D 166
St Agnes Cl. E9 1J 85
St Agnes Pl. SE11 7K 19 (6A 102)
St Agnes Well EC1 3F 9
St Aidans Ct. IG11: Bark 2B 90
St Aidan's Rd. SE22 6H 121
W13 2B 96
St Albans Av. E6 3D 88
TW13: Hanw 5B 130
W4 4K 97
St Albans Cl. NW11 1J 63
St Albans Ct. EC2 6D 8
St Alban's Cres. IG8: Wfd G 7D 36
N22 1A 48
St Albans Farm TW4: Houn 5A 112
St Alban's Gdns. TW11: Tedd 5A 132
St Alban's Gro. SM5: Cars 7C 154
W8 3K 99
St Alban's La. NW11 1J 63
St Albans Mans. *W8* 3K 99
(off Kensington Ct. Pl.)
St Alban's Pl. N1 1B 84
St Albans Rd. EN5: Barn 1A 20
IG3: Ilf 1K 71
IG8: Wfd G 7D 36
KT2: King T 6E 132
NW5 3E 64
NW10 1A 80
SM1: Sutt 4H 165
St Alban's St. SW1 3C 12 (7H 83)
St Albans Studios *W8* 3K 99
(off St Albans Gro.)
St Albans Ter. W6 6G 99
St Albans Vs. NW5 3E 64
St Alfege Pas. SE10 6E 104
St Alfege Rd. SE7 6B 106
St Alphage Ct. NW9 3K 43
St Alphage Gdn. EC2 6D 8 (5C 84)
St Alphage Highwalk EC2 6D 8
St Alphage Ho. EC2 6E 8
St Alphage Wlk. HA8: Edg 2J 43
St Alphege Rd. N9 7D 24
St Alphonsus Rd. SW4 4G 119
St Amunds Cl. SE6 4C 140
St Andrew's Av. HA0: Wemb 4A 60
St Andrews Chambers *W1* 6B 6
(off Wells St.)
St Andrews Cl. HA4: Ruis 2B 58
HA7: Stan 2C 42
KT7: T Ditt 1B 162
N12 4F 31
NW2 3D 62
SE16 5H 103
SE28 6D 90
St Andrews Cl. SW19 6K 135
TW7: Isle 1J 113
TW17: Shep 4F 147
St Andrews Ct. E17 2A 50
SM1: Sutt 3C 166
SW18 2A 136
St Andrews Dr. HA7: Stan 1C 42
St Andrew's Gro. N16 1D 66
St Andrew's Hill EC4 2B 14 (7B 84)
(not continuous)
St Andrews Ho. *SE16* 3H 103
(off Southwark Pk. Rd.)
St Andrews Mans. *W1* 6G 5
(off Dorset St.)
W14 6G 99
(off St Andrews Rd.)
St Andrews M. N16 1E 66
SE3 7J 105
SW12 1H 137
St Andrew's Pl.
NW1 3K 5 (4F 83)
St Andrews Rd. CR0: C'don 4C 168
DA14: Sidc 3D 144
E11 6G 51
E12 2C 70
E13 3K 87
E17 2K 49
EN1: Enf 3J 23
IG1: Ilf 7D 52
KT6: Surb 6D 150
N9 7D 24
NW9 1K 61
NW10 6D 62
NW11 6H 45
RM7: Rom 6K 55
SM5: Cars 3C 166
UB10: Uxb 1A 74
W3 7A 80
W7 2J 95
W14 6G 99
St Andrews Sq. KT6: Surb 6D 150
W11 6G 81
St Andrew's Twr. *UB1: S'hall* 7G 77
(off Baird Av.)
St Andrew St. EC1 6K 7 (5A 84)
EC4 6K 7 (5A 84)
St Andrews Way E3 4D 86
St Andrew's Wharf SE1 2F 103
St Anna Rd. EN5: Barn 5A 20
St Anne's Cl. N6 3E 64
St Anne's Ct. BR4: W W'ck 4G 171
NW6 1G 81
W1 1C 12 (6H 83)
St Anne's Flats *NW1* 1C 6
(off Doric Way)
St Anne's Gdns. NW10 3F 79
St Anne's Pas. E14 6B 86
St Anne's Rd. E11 2F 69
HA0: Wemb 5D 60
St Anne's Row E14 6B 86
St Anne's Trad. Est. *E14* 6B 86
(off St Anne's Row)
St Anne St. E14 6B 86
St Ann's IG11: Bark 1G 89
St Ann's Ct. NW4 3D 44
St Ann's Cres. SW18 6K 117
St Ann's Gdns. NW5 6E 64
St Ann's Hill SW18 5K 117
St Ann's Ho. *WC1* 2J 7
(off Margery St.)
St Ann's La. SW1 2D 18 (3H 101)
St Ann's Pk. Rd. SW18 6A 118
St Ann's Pas. SW13 3A 116
St Ann's Rd. HA1: Harr 6J 41
IG11: Bark 1G 89
N9 2A 34
N15 5B 48
SW13 2B 116
W11 7F 81
St Ann's Shop. Cen. HA1: Harr 6J 41

St Ann's St. SW1 1D 18 (3H 101)
St Ann's Ter. NW8 2B 82
St Ann's Vs. W11 1F 99
St Ann's Way CR2: S Croy 6B 168
St Anselms Ct. SW16 5J 137
St Anselm's Pl. W1 2J 11 (7F 83)
St Anselm's Rd. UB3: Hayes 2H 93
St Anthony's Av. IG8: Wfd G 6F 37
St Anthony's Cl. E1 1G 103
SW17 2C 136
St Anthony's Ct. BR6: Farnb 2F 173
SW17 2E 136
St Anthony's Flats *NW1* *2H 83*
(off Aldenham St.)
St Anthony's Way TW14: Felt 4H 111
St Antony's Rd. E7 7K 69
St Arvan's Cl. CR0: C'don 3E 168
St Asaph Rd. SE4 3K 121
St Aubins Ct. N1 1D 84
St Aubyn's Av. SW19 5H 135
TW3: Houn 5E 112
St Aubyn's Cl. BR6: Orp 3K 173
St Aubyn's Gdns. BR6: Orp 2K 173
St Aubyn's Rd. SE19 6F 139
St Audrey Av. DA7: Bex 2G 127
St Augustine's Av.
BR2: Brom 5C 160
CR2: S Croy 6C 168
HA9: Wemb 3E 60
W5 2E 78
St Augustine's Ct. *SE1* *5H 103*
(off Lynton Rd.)
St Augustine's Ho. *NW1* *1C 6*
(off Werrington St.)
St Augustine's Mans. *SW1* *4B 18*
(off Bloomburg St.)
St Augustine's Path N5 4C 66
St Augustine's Rd. DA17: Belv 4F 109
NW1 7H 65
St Austell Cl. HA8: Edg 2F 43
St Austell Rd. SE13 2E 122
St Awdry's Rd. IG11: Bark 7H 71
St Awdry's Wlk. IG11: Bark 7G 71
St Barnabas Cl. BR3: Beck 2E 158
SE22 5E 120
St Barnabas Ct. HA3: Hrw W 1G 41
St Barnabas Gdns.
KT8: W Mole 5E 148
St Barnabas Rd. CR4: Mitc 7E 136
E17 6C 50
IG8: Wfd G 1K 51
SM1: Sutt 5B 166
St Barnabas St. SW1 5H 17 (5E 100)
St Barnabas Ter. E9 5K 67
St Barnabas Vs. SW8 1J 119
St Bartholomew's Cl. SE26 4H 139
St Bartholomew's Ct. *E6* *2C 88*
(off St Bartholomew's Rd.)
St Bartholomew's Hospital Mus. 6B 8
St Bartholomew's Rd. E6 2D 88
St Benedict's Cl. SW17 5E 136
St Benet's Cl. SW17 2C 136
St Benet's Gro. SM5: Cars 7A 154
St Benet's Pl. EC3 2F 15 (7D 84)
St Bernards CR0: C'don 3E 168
St Bernard's Cl. SE27 4D 138
St Bernards Ho. *E14* *3E 104*
(off Galbraith St.)
St Bernard's Rd. E6 1B 88
St Blaise Av. BR1: Brom 2K 159
St Botolph Row EC3 1J 15 (6F 85)
St Botolph St. EC3 7J 9 (6F 85)
St Brelades Ct. N1 1E 84
St Bride's Av. EC4 1A 14
HA8: Edg 1F 43
St Brides Cl. DA18: Erith 2D 108
St Bride's Crypt Mus. *1A 14*
(in St Bride's, off Fleet St.)
St Bride's Pas. EC4 1A 14
St Bride St. EC4 7A 8 (6B 84)
St Catherines Cl. KT9: Chess 6D 162
SW17 2C 136
St Catherines Ct. *TW13: Felt* *1J 129*
(off Orchard Rd.)
W4 3A 98
St Catherine's Dr. SE14 2K 121
St Catherine's Farm Ct.
HA4: Ruis 6E 38
St Catherines M. SW3 3E 16 (4D 100)
St Catherine's Rd. E4 2H 35
HA4: Ruis 6F 39
St Cecelia's Pl. SE3 5J 105
St Cecilia's Cl. SM3: Sutt 1G 165
St Chads Cl. KT6: Surb 7C 150
St Chad's Gdns. RM6: Chad H 7E 54
St Chad's Pl. WC1 1F 7 (3J 83)
St Chad's Rd. RM6: Chad H 7E 54
St Chad's St. WC1 1F 7 (3J 83)
(not continuous)
St Charles Pl. W10 5G 81
St Charles Sq. W10 5F 81
St Christopher Rd. UB8: Cowl 6A 74
St Christopher's Cl. TW7: Isle 1J 113
St Christophers Dr. UB3: Hayes 7K 75
St Christopher's Gdns.
CR7: Thor H 3A 156
St Christopher's Ho. *NW1* *2G 83*
(off Bridgeway St.)
St Christopher's M. SM6: Wall 5G 167
St Christopher's Pl. W1 7H 5 (6E 82)
St Clair Cl. IG5: Ilf 2D 52
St Clair Dr. KT4: Wor Pk 3D 164
St Clair Rd. E13 2K 87
St Clair's Rd. CR0: C'don 2E 168
St Clare Bus. Pk. TW12: Ham H 6G 131
St Clare St. EC3 1J 15 (6F 85)
St Clements Ct. EC4 2F 15
N7 6K 65
SE14 *6K 103*
(off Myers La.)
W11 *7F 81*
(off Stoneleigh St.)
St Clement's Hgts. SE26 3G 139
St Clements Ho. *E1* *6J 9*
(off Leyden St.)
St Clement's La. WC2 1G 13 (6K 83)
St Clements Mans. *SW6* *6F 99*
(off Lillie Rd.)
St Clements St. N7 6A 66
St Clements Yd. SE22 4F 121
St Cloud Rd. SE27 4C 138
St Columbas Ho. E17 4D 50
St Columb's Ho. *W10* *5G 81*
(off Blagrove Rd.)
St Crispin's Cl. NW3 4C 64
UB1: S'hall 6D 76
St Cross St. EC1 5K 7 (5A 84)
St Cuthberts Rd. N13 6F 33
NW2 6H 63
St Cyprian's St. SW17 4D 136
St Daniel Ct. *BR3: Beck* *7C 140*
(off Brackley Rd.)
St Davids Cl. BR4: W W'ck 7D 158
HA9: Wemb 3J 61
SE16 *5H 103*
(off Masters Dr.)
St Davids Ct. BR1: Brom 3F 161
E17 3E 50
TW15: Ashf 2B 128
St David's Dr. HA8: Edg 1F 43
St Davids M. *E3* *3A 86*
(off Morgan St.)
St David's Pl. NW4 7D 44
St Davids Sq. E14 5D 104
St Denis Rd. SE27 4D 138
St Dionis Rd. E12 3C 70
SW6 2H 117
St Domingo Ho. *SE18* *3D 106*
(off Leda Rd.)
St Donatt's Rd. SE14 1B 122
ST DUNSTAN'S 6H 165
St Dunstan's All. EC3 2G 15
St Dunstans Av. W3 7K 79
St Dunstan's Cl. UB3: Harl 5H 93
St Dunstan's Ct. EC4 1K 13 (6A 84)
St Dunstan's Gdns. W3 7K 79
St Dunstans Hill EC3 3G 15 (7E 84)
SM1: Sutt 5G 165
St Dunstan's La. BR3: Beck 6E 158
EC3 3G 15 (7E 84)
St Dunstan's Rd. E7 6K 69
SE25 4F 157
TW4: Cran 2K 111
(not continuous)
TW13: Felt 3H 129
W6 5F 99
W7 2J 95
St Edmund's Av. HA4: Ruis 6F 39
St Edmunds Cl. DA18: Erith 2D 108
NW8 1D 82
SW17 2C 136
St Edmund's Ct. *NW8* *1D 82*
(off St Edmund's Ter.)
St Edmunds Dr. HA7: Stan 1A 42
St Edmund's La. TW2: Whitt 7F 113
St Edmund's Rd. IG1: Ilf 6D 52
N9 7B 24
St Edmunds Sq. SW13 6E 98
St Edmund's Ter. NW8 1C 82
St Edward's Cl. NW11 6J 45
St Edwards Ct. NW11 6J 45
St Edwards Way RM1: Rom 5K 55
St Egberts Way E4 1K 35
St Elizabeth Ct. E10 7D 50
St Elmo Rd. W12 1B 98
(not continuous)
St Elmos Rd. SE16 2A 104
St Erkenwald M. IG11: Bark 1H 89
St Erkenwald Rd. IG11: Bark 1H 89
St Ermin's Hill SW1 1C 18
St Ervan's Rd. W10 5H 81
St Eugene Ct. *NW6* *1G 81*
(off Salusbury Rd.)
St Faith's Cl. EN2: Enf 1H 23
St Faith's Rd. SE21 1B 138
St Fidelis Rd. DA8: Erith 4K 109
St Fillans Rd. SE6 1E 140
St Francis Cl. BR5: Pet W 6J 161
St Francis' Ho. *NW1* *2H 83*
(off Bridgeway St.)
St Francis Pl. SW12 6F 119
St Francis Rd. DA8: Erith 4K 109
SE22 4E 120
St Francis Twr. *E4* *6G 35*
(off Burnside Av.)
St Francis Way IG1: Ilf 4H 71
St Frideswide's M. E14 6E 86
St Gabriel's Cl. E11 2K 69
E14 5D 86
St Gabriels Ct. N11 7C 32
St Gabriels Mnr. *SE5* *1B 120*
(off Cormont Rd.)
St Gabriels Rd. NW2 5F 63
St George's Av. E7 7K 69
N7 4H 65
NW9 4K 43
UB1: S'hall 7D 76
W5 2D 96
St George's Bldgs. *SE1* *3B 102*
(off St George's Rd.)
St George's Cathedral *1K 5*
(off Redhill St.)
St George's Cir. SE1 7A 14 (3B 102)
St Georges Cl. HA0: Wemb 3A 60
NW11 6H 45
SE28 6D 90
SW8 1G 119
St Georges Ct. E6 4D 88
E17 5F 51
EC4 7A 8 (6B 84)
St Georges Ct. *HA3: Kent* *6A 42*
(off Kenton Rd.)
SE1 *3B 102*
(off Garden Row)
SW1 *5A 18*
(off St George's Dr.)
SW3 *3C 16*
(off Brompton Rd.)
SW7 3A 100
SW15 4H 117
St George's Dr. SW1 4K 17 (4F 101)
UB10: Ick 3B 56
ST GEORGE'S FIELD 7C 82
St George's Flds. W2 1D 10 (6C 82)
St George's Gdns. KT6: Surb 2H 163
St George's Gro. SW17 3B 136
St Georges Ho. *NW1* *2H 83*
(off Bridgeway St.)
SW11 *1E 118*
(off Charlotte Despard Av.)
St Georges Ind. Est.
KT2: King T 5D 132
N22 7G 33
St George's La. EC3 2F 15
St George's Mans. *SW1* *5D 18*
(off Causton St.)
St George's M. NW1 7D 64
SE1 1K 19
SE8 4B 104
St Georges Pde. SE6 2B 140
St George's Path *SE4* *4C 122*
(off Adelaide Av.)
St George's Pl. TW1: Twick 1A 132
St George's Pools 7H 85
St George's RC Cathedral 1K 19 (3A 102)
St Georges Rd. BR1: Brom 2D 160
BR3: Beck 1D 158
BR5: Pet W 6H 161
CR4: Mitc 3F 155
DA14: Sidc 6D 144
E7 7K 69
E10 3E 68
EN1: Enf 1A 24
IG1: Ilf 7D 52
KT2: King T 7G 133
N9 3B 34
N13 3E 32
NW11 6H 45
RM9: Dag 5E 72
SE1 1K 19 (3A 102)
SM6: Wall 5F 167
SW19 7H 135
(not continuous)
TW1: Twick 5B 114
TW9: Rich 3F 115
TW13: Hanw 4B 130
W4 2K 97
W7 1K 95
St George's Rd. W. BR1: Brom 1C 160
St George's Shop. & Leisure Cen.
HA1: Harr 6J 41
St Georges Sq. E7 7K 69
E14 7A 86
KT3: N Mald 3A 152
SE8 4B 104
(not continuous)
SW1 5C 18 (5H 101)
St George's Sq. M. SW1 6C 18 (5H 101)
St George's Ter. *E6* *3C 88*
(off Masterman Rd.)
NW1 7D 64
SE15 *7G 103*
(off Peckham Hill St.)
St George's Theatre 4H 65
St George St. W1 1K 11 (7F 83)
St George's Wlk. CR0: C'don 3C 168
St George's Way SE15 6E 102
St George's Wharf *SE1* *6K 15*
(off Shad Thames)
St George Wharf SW8 7E 18 (6J 101)

St Gerards Cl. SW4 .5G 119
St German's Pl. SE3 .1J 123
St German's Rd. SE23 .1A 140
St Giles Av. RM10: Dag .7H 73
UB10: Ick .4E 56
St Giles Cir. W1 .7D 6 (6H 83)
St Giles Cl. BR6: Farnb .5H 173
RM10: Dag .7H 73
TW5: Hest .7C 94
St Giles Ct. WC2 .7E 6
St Giles High St. WC2 .7D 6 (6H 83)
St Giles Ho. EN5: New Bar .4F 21
SE5 .1E 120
St Giles Pas. WC2 .1D 12
St Giles Rd. SE5 .7E 102
St Giles Ter. EC2 .6D 8
(off Barbican)
St Giles Twr. SE5 .1E 120
(off Gables Cl.)
St Gilles Ho. E2 .2K 85
(off Mace St.)
St Gothard Rd. SE27 .4D 138
(not continuous)
St Gregory Cl. HA4: Ruis .4A 58
St Helena Ho. WC1 .2J 7
(off Margery St.)
St Helena Rd. SE16 .4K 103
St Helena St. WC1 .2J 7 (3A 84)
St Helens KT7: T Ditt .7K 149
St Helen's Cres. SW16 .1K 155
St Helen's Gdns. W10 .5F 81
St Helens Pl. E10 .7A 50
EC3 .7G 9 (6E 84)
St Helen's Rd. DA18: Erith .2D 108
IG1: Ilf .6D 52
SW16 .1K 155
W13 .1B 96
ST HELIER .7C 154
St Helier Av. SM4: Mord .7A 154
St Helier Ct. N1 .1E 84
(off De Beauvoir Est.)
SE16 .2K 103
(off Poolmans St.)
St Helier's Av. TW3: Houn .5E 112
St Helier's Rd. E10 .6E 50
St Hilary's Ct. BR1: Brom .3F 161
St Hilda's Av. TW15: Ashf .5A 128
St Hilda's Cl. NW6 .7F 63
SW17 .2C 136
St Hilda's Rd. SW13 .6D 98
St Hilda's Wharf E1 .1J 103
(off Wapping High St.)
St Hubert's Ho. E14 .3C 104
(off Janet St.)
St Hughes Cl. SW17 .2C 136
St Hugh's Rd. SE20 .1H 157
St Ivian Ct. N10 .2E 46
St James SE14 .1A 122
St James Apartments E17 .5A 50
(off High St.)
St James Av. N20 .3H 31
SM1: Sutt .5J 165
W13 .1A 96
St James Cl. EN4: E Barn .4G 21
HA4: Ruis .2A 58
KT3: N Mald .5B 152
N20 .3H 31
SE18 .5G 107
St James Ct. CR0: C'don .7B 156
E2 .3G 85
(off Bethnal Grn. Rd.)
E12 .2A 70
SE3 .1K 123
SW1 .1B 18 (3G 101)
St James Gdns.
HA0: Wemb .7D 60
RM6: Chad H .4B 54
St James Ga. IG9: Buck H .1F 37
St James Gro. SW11 .2D 118
St James Ind. M. SE1 .5G 103
St James Mans. NW6 .7J 63
(off West End La.)
SE1 .1J 19
(off Kennington Rd.)
St James M. E14 .3E 104
E17 .5A 50
(off St James's St.)
St James Residences W1 .2C 12
(off Brewer St.)
St James Rd. CR4: Mitc .7E 136
E15 .5H 69
KT6: Surb .6D 150
N9 .2C 34
SM1: Sutt .5J 165
SM5: Cars .3C 166
ST JAMES'S .4B 12 (1H 101)
St James's SW1 .4B 12 (1G 101)
St James's App. EC2 .4G 9 (4E 84)
St James's Av. BR3: Beck .3A 158
E2 .2J 85
TW12: Ham H .5G 131
St James's Chambers SW1 .4B 12
(off Jermyn St.)
St James's Cl. NW8 .1D 82
(off St James's Ter. M.)
SW17 .2D 136
St James's Cotts. TW9: Rich .5D 114
St James's Ct. HA1: Harr .6A 42
KT1: King T .3E 150
N18 .5B 34
(off Fore St.)
St James's Cres. SW9 .3A 120
St James's Dr. SW17 .1D 136
St James's Gdns. W11 .1G 99
(not continuous)
St James's Ho. SE1 .4G 103
(off Strathnairn St.)
St James's La. N10 .4F 47
St James's Mkt. SW1 .3C 12 (7H 83)
St James's Palace .6B 12 (2G 101)
St James's Pk. .6C 12 (2H 101)
St James's Pk. CR0: C'don .7C 156
St James's Pas. EC3 .1H 15
St James's Pl. SW1 .5A 12 (1G 101)
St James's Rd. CR0: C'don .7B 156
KT1: King T .2D 150
SE1 .6G 103
SE16 .3G 103
TW12: Ham H .5F 131
St James's Sq. SW1 .4B 12 (1G 101)
St James's St. E17 .5A 50
SW1 .4A 12 (1G 101)
St James's Ter. NW8 .1D 82
(off Prince Albert Rd.)
St James's Ter. M. NW8 .1D 82
St James St. W6 .5E 98
St James's Wlk. EC1 .3A 8 (4B 84)
St James Ter. SW12 .1E 136
St James Way DA14: Sidc .5E 144
St Jeromes Gro. UB3: Hayes .6E 74
St Joan's Rd. N9 .2A 34
St John Fisher Rd.
DA18: Erith .3D 108
ST JOHNS .2C 122
St John's Av. N11 .5J 31
NW10 .1B 80
SW15 .5F 117
St Johns Chu. Rd. E9 .5J 67
St Johns Cl. HA9: Wemb .5E 60
N14 .6B 22
N20 .3F 31
(off Rasper Rd.)
SW6 .7J 99
St John's Cotts. SE20 .7J 139
St John's Ct. DA8: Erith .4K 109
E1 .1H 103
(off Scandrett St.)
HA1: Harr .6K 41
HA6: Nwood .1G 39
(off Murray Rd.)
St John's Ct. IG9: Buck H .1E 36
KT1: King T .4E 150
(off Beaufort Rd.)
N4 .2B 66
N5 .4B 66
SE13 .2E 122
TW7: Isle .2K 113
W6 .4D 98
(off Glenthorne Rd.)
St John's Cres. SW9 .3A 120
St Johns Dr. SW18 .1K 135
St John's Est. N1 .2D 84
SE1 .6J 15
St John's Gdns. W11 .7G 81
St John's Gate .4A 8
St John's Gro. N19 .2G 65
SW13 .2B 116
TW9: Rich .4E 114
St John's Hill SW11 .5B 118
St John's Hill Gro. SW11 .4B 118
St Johns Ho. E14 .4E 104
(off Pier St.)
SE17 .6D 102
(off Lytham St.)
St John's La. EC1 .4A 8 (4B 84)
St John's Lodge NW3 .7C 64
(off King Henry's Rd.)
St John's M. KT1: Ham W .2C 150
W11 .6J 81
St Johns Pde. DA14: Sidc .4A 144
(off Sidcup High St.)
W13 .1B 96
St John's Pk. SE3 .7H 105
St John's Pk. Mans. N19 .3G 65
St John's Pas. SW19 .6G 135
St John's Path EC1 .4A 8
St Johns Pathway SE23 .1J 139
St John's Pl. EC1 .4A 8 (4B 84)
St John's Rd. BR5: Pet W .6H 161
CR0: C'don .3B 168
DA8: Erith .5K 109
DA14: Sidc .4B 144
DA16: Well .3B 126
E4 .4J 35
E6 .1C 88
E16 .6J 87
E17 .2D 50
HA1: Harr .6K 41
HA9: Wemb .4D 60
IG2: Ilf .7H 53
IG11: Bark .1J 89
KT1: Ham W .2C 150
KT3: N Mald .3J 151
KT8: E Mos .4H 149
N15 .6E 48
NW11 .6H 45
SE20 .6J 139
SM1: Sutt .2K 165
SM5: Cars .3C 166
SW11 .4C 118
SW19 .7G 135
TW7: Isle .2K 113
TW9: Rich .4E 114
TW13: Hanw .4C 130
UB2: S'hall .3C 94
St John's Sq. EC1 .4A 8 (4B 84)
St John's Ter. E7 .6K 69
SE18 .6G 107
SW15 .3A 134
(off Kingston Va.)
W10 .4F 81
St John St. EC1 .1K 7 (2A 84)
St John's Va. SE8 .2C 122
St John's Vs. N11 .5J 31
(off Friern Barnet Rd.)
N19 .2H 65
W8 .3K 99
(off St Mary's Pl.)
St John's Way N19 .2G 65
ST JOHN'S WOOD .1A 4 (2B 82)
St John's Wood Ct. NW8 .2B 4
St John's Wood High St.
NW8 .1C 4 (2B 82)
St John's Wood Pk. NW8 .1B 82
St John's Wood Rd. NW8 .3A 4 (4B 82)
St John's Wood Ter. NW8 .2B 82
St John's Yd. N17 .7A 34
St Josephs Almshouses W6 .4F 99
(off Brook Grn.)
St Joseph's Cl. BR6: Orp .4K 173
W10 .5G 81
St Joseph's College Sports Cen. .6B 138
St Joseph's Cotts. SW3 .4E 16
(off Cadagon St.)
St Josephs Ct. SE7 .6K 105
St Joseph's Dr. UB1: S'hall .1C 94
St Joseph's Flats NW1 .1C 6
(off Drummond Cres.)
St Joseph's Gro. NW4 .4D 44
St Joseph's Ho. W6 .4F 99
(off Brook Grn.)
St Joseph's Rd. N9 .7C 24
St Joseph's St. SW8 .1F 119
St Joseph's Va. SE3 .3F 123
St Judes Ct. IG8: Wfd G .7H 37
St Jude's Rd. E2 .2H 85
St Jude St. N16 .5E 66
St Julian's Cl. SW16 .4A 138
St Julian's Farm Rd.
SE27 .4A 138
St Julian's Rd. NW6 .1J 81
St Katharine Docks .3K 15
St Katharine's Pct. NW1 .2F 83
St Katharine's Way E1 .4K 15 (1F 103)
(not continuous)
St Katharine's Yacht Haven .1F 103
(off St Katharine's Way)
St Katherine's Rd. DA18: Erith .2D 108
St Katherine's Row EC3 .2H 15
St Katherines Wlk. W11 .1F 99
(off St Ann's Rd.)
St Keverne Rd. SE9 .4C 142
St Kilda Rd. BR6: Orp .1K 173
W13 .1A 96
St Kilda's Rd. HA1: Harr .6J 41
N16 .1D 66
St Kitts Ter. SE19 .5E 138
St Laurence Cl. NW6 .1F 81
St Lawrence Bus. Cen.
TW13: Felt .2K 129
St Lawrence Cl. HA8: Edg .7A 28
St Lawrence Cotts. E14 .1E 104
(off St Lawrence St.)
St Lawrence Ct. N1 .7D 66
St Lawrence Dr. HA5: Eastc .5K 39
St Lawrence Ho. SE1 .7H 15
(off Purbrook St.)
St Lawrence St. E14 .1E 104
St Lawrence Ter. W10 .5G 81
St Lawrence Way SW9 .1A 120
St Leger Ct. NW6 .7F 63
(off Coverdale Rd.)
St Leonard M. N1 .2E 84
(off Hoxton St.)
St Leonard's Av. E4 .6A 36
HA3: Kent .5C 42
St Leonard's Cl. DA16: Well .3A 126
St Leonards Ct. N1 .1F 9
SW14 .3J 115
St Leonard's Gdns. IG1: Ilf .5G 71
TW5: Hest .7C 94
St Leonard's Ri. BR6: Orp .4J 173
St Leonard's Rd.
CR0: Wadd .3B 168
E14 .5D 86
(not continuous)
KT6: Surb .5D 150
KT7: T Ditt .6A 150
KT10: Clay .6A 162
NW10 .4K 79

St Leonard's Rd. SW14 .....3H 115
W13 .....7C 78
(not continuous)
St Leonards Sq. KT6: Surb 5D 150
NW5 .....6E 64
St Leonard's St. E3 .....3D 86
St Leonard's Ter. SW3 .....6E 16 (5D 100)
St Leonard's Wlk. SW16 .....7K 137
St Loo Av. SW3 .....7D 16 (6C 100)
St Loo Ct. *SW3* *7D 16*
(off St Loo Av.)
St Louis Rd. SE27 .....4D 138
St Loy's Rd. N17 .....2E 48
St Lucia Dr. E15 .....1H 87
St Luke Cl. UB8: Cowl 6A 74
ST LUKE'S 3D 8 (4C 84)
St Luke's Av. EN2: Enf 1J 23
IG1: Ilf 5F 71
SW4 .....4H 119
St Luke's Cl. EC1 .....3D 8 (4C 84)
SE25 .....6H 157
St Lukes Ct. *E10* *7D 50*
(off Capworth St.)
W11 .....*6H 81*
(off St Luke's Rd.)
St Luke's Est. EC1 .....2E 8 (3D 84)
St Luke's M. W11 .....6H 81
St Luke's Pas. KT2: King T 1F 151
St Luke's Path IG1: Ilf 5F 71
St Luke's Rd. UB10: Uxb 7A 56
W11 .....5H 81
St Luke's Sq. E16 .....6H 87
St Luke's St. SW3 .....5D 16 (5C 100)
St Luke's Yd. W9 .....2H 81
(not continuous)
St Malo Av. N9 .....3D 34
ST MARGARETS 6B 114
St Margarets IG11: Bark 1H 89
St Margarets Av. DA15: Sidc 3H 143
HA2: Harr 3G 59
N15 .....4B 48
N20 .....1F 31
SM3: Cheam 3G 165
TW15: Ashf 5D 128
UB8: Hil 4C 74
St Margarets Bus. Cen.
TW1: Twick 6B 114
St Margarets Cl. EC2 .....6D 84
St Margarets Ct. HA8: Edg 5C 28
N11 .....4K 31
SE1 .....5D 14 (1C 102)
SW15 .....4D 116
St Margaret's Cres. SW15 .....5D 116
St Margaret's Dr. TW1: Twick 5B 114
St Margaret's Gro. E11 .....3H 69
SE18 .....6G 107
TW1: Twick 6A 114
St Margarets Hall *UB8: Cowl* *3A 74*
(off Kingston La.)
St Margaret's Ho. *NW1* *2H 83*
(off Polygon Rd.)
St Margaret's La. W8 .....3K 99
St Margaret's Pas. SE13 .....3G 123
(not continuous)
St Margarets Path SE18 .....5G 107
St Margarets Rd. E12 .....2A 70
HA4: Ruis 6F 39
HA8: Edg 5C 28
N17 .....3E 48
NW10 .....3E 80
SE4 .....4B 122
(not continuous)
TW1: Twick 6B 114
TW7: Isle 4B 114
W7 .....2J 95
ST MARGARETS RDBT. 6B 114
St Margaret's Ter. SE18 .....5G 107
St Margaret St. SW1 .....7E 12 (2J 101)
St Marks Cl. EN5: New Bar 3E 20
HA1: Harr 7B 42
St Marks Cl. SE10 .....7E 104
SW6 .....1J 117
St Marks Ct. *NW8* *2A 82*
(off Abercorn Pl.)
W7 .....*2J 95*
(off Lwr. Boston Rd.)
St Mark's Cres. NW1 .....1E 82
St Mark's Gro. SW10 .....7K 99
St Mark's Hill KT6: Surb 6E 150
St Marks Ho. *SE17* *6D 102*
(off Lytham St.)
St Marks Ind. Est. E16 .....1B 106
St Mark's Pl. RM10: Dag 6G 73
SW19 .....6H 135
W11 .....6G 81
St Mark's Ri. E8 .....5F 67
St Marks Rd. BR2: Brom 3J 159
CR4: Mitc 2D 154
EN1: Enf 6A 24
SE25 .....4G 157
TW11: Tedd 7B 132
W5 .....1E 96
W7 .....2J 95
W10 .....5F 81
W11 .....*6G 81*
St Mark's Sq. NW1 .....1E 82
St Mark St. E1 .....1K 15 (6F 85)
St Mark's Vs. *N4* *2K 65*
(off Moray Rd.)
St Martin Cl. UB8: Cowl 6A 74
St Martin-in-the-Fields Church *3E 12*
(off St Martin's Pl.)
St Martin's Almshouses NW1 .....1G 83
St Martin's App. HA4: Ruis 7G 39
St Martin's Av. E6 .....2B 88
St Martin's Cl. DA18: Erith 2D 108
EN1: Enf 1C 24
NW1 .....1G 83
St Martins Ct. *EC4* *7C 8*
(off Paternoster Row)
N1 .....*1E 84*
(off De Beauvoir Est.)
WC2 .....2E 12 (7J 83)
St Martins Est. SW2 .....1A 138
St Martin's Ho. *NW1* *3H 83*
(off Polygon Rd.)
St Martin's La. BR3: Beck 5D 158
WC2 .....2E 12 (7J 83)
St Martin's le-Grand EC1 .....7C 8 (6C 84)
St Martin's Pl. WC2 .....3E 12 (7J 83)
St Martin's Rd. N9 .....2C 34
SW9 .....2K 119
St Martin's St. WC2 .....3D 12 (7H 83)
(not continuous)
St Martin's Theatre *2E 12*
(off West St.)
St Martins Way SW17 .....3A 136
St Mary Abbot's Ct. *W14* *3H 99*
(off Warwick Gdns.)
St Mary Abbot's Pl. W8 .....3H 99
St Mary Abbot's Ter. W14 .....3H 99
St Mary at Hill EC3 .....3G 15 (7E 84)
St Mary Av. SM6: Wall 3E 166
St Mary Axe EC3 .....1G 15 (6E 84)
St Marychurch St. SE16 .....2J 103
St Mary Graces Ct. E1 .....3K 15 (7F 85)
St Marylebone Cl. NW10 .....1A 80
St Marylebone Crematorium N2 .....3K 45
St Mary le-Park Ct. *SW11* *7C 100*
(off Parkgate Rd.)
St Mary Newington Cl. *SE17* *5E 102*
(off Surrey Sq.)
St Mary Rd. E17 .....4C 50
St Mary's IG11: Bark 1H 89
St Mary's App. E12 .....5D 70
St Mary's Av. BR2: Brom 3G 159
E11 .....7K 51
N3 .....2G 45
TW11: Tedd 6K 131
St Mary's Av. Central UB2: S'hall 4F 95
St Mary's Av. Nth. UB2: S'hall 4F 95
St Mary's Av. Sth. UB2: S'hall 4F 95
St Mary's Cl. KT9: Chess 7F 163
KT17: Ewe 7B 164
N17 .....1G 49
TW16: Sun 4J 147
St Mary's Copse KT4: Wor Pk 2A 164
St Mary's Ct. E6 .....4D 88
SE7 .....7B 106
SM6: Wall 4G 167
W5 .....2D 96
W6 .....3B 98
St Mary's Cres. NW4 .....3D 44
TW7: Isle 7H 95
UB3: Hayes 7H 75
St Mary's Dr. TW14: Bedf 7E 110
St Mary's Est. *SE16* *2J 103*
(off St Marychurch St.)
St Mary's Flats *NW1* *1C 6*
(off Drummond Cres.)
St Mary's Gdns. SE11 .....3K 19 (4A 102)
St Mary's Ga. W8 .....3K 99
St Mary's Grn. N2 .....2A 46
St Mary's Gro. N1 .....6B 66
SW13 .....3D 116
TW9: Rich 4F 115
W4 .....6H 97
St Mary's Ho. *N1* *1B 84*
(off St Mary's Path)
St Mary's Mans. W2 .....5A 4 (5B 82)
St Marys M. NW6 .....7K 63
TW10: Ham 2C 132
St Mary's Path *E1* *6G 85*
(off Adler St.)
N1 .....1B 84
St Mary's Pl. SE9 .....6D 124
W5 .....2D 96
W8 .....3K 99
St Marys Rd. DA5: Bexl 1J 145
E10 .....3E 68
E13 .....2K 87
EN4: E Barn 7J 21
IG1: Ilf 2G 71
KT4: Wor Pk 2A 164
KT6: Surb 7C 150
(St Chads Cl.)
KT6: Surb 6D 150
(Victoria Rd.)
KT8: E Mos 5H 149
N8 .....4J 47
N9 .....1C 34
(not continuous)
NW10 .....1A 80
NW11 .....7G 45
SE15 .....1J 121
SE25 .....3E 156
SW19 .....5G 135
UB3: Hayes 7H 75
W5 .....2D 96
St Mary's Sq. W2 .....5A 4 (5B 82)
W5 .....2D 96
St Mary's Ter. W2 .....5A 4 (5B 82)
St Mary's Twr. *EC1* *4D 8*
(off Fortune St.)
St Mary St. SE18 .....4D 106
St Mary's University College Sports Cen.
.....4K 131
St Mary's Vw. HA3: Kent 5C 42
St Mary's Wlk. SE11 .....3K 19 (4A 102)
UB3: Hayes 7H 75
St Mary's Way IG7: Chig 5K 37
St Matthew Cl. UB8: Cowl 6A 74
St Matthew's Av. KT6: Surb 1E 162
St Matthews Ct. E10 .....7D 50
N10 .....2E 46
SE1 .....*3C 102*
(off Meadow Row)
TW15: Ashf *4C 128*
(off Feltham Rd.)
St Matthew's Dr. BR1: Brom 3D 160
St Matthews Ho. *SE17* *6D 102*
(off Phelp St.)
St Matthew's Lodge *NW1* *2G 83*
(off Oakley Sq.)
St Matthew's Rd. SW2 .....4K 119
W5 .....1E 96
St Matthew's Row E2 .....3G 85
St Matthew St. SW1 .....2C 18 (3H 101)
St Matthias Cl. NW9 .....5B 44
St Maur Rd. SW6 .....1H 117
St Mellion Cl. SE28 .....6D 90
St Merryn Cl. SE18 .....7H 107
St Merryn Ct. BR3: Beck 7C 140
St Michael's All. EC3 .....1F 15 (6D 84)
St Michael's Av. HA9: Wemb 6G 61
N9 .....7D 24
St Michaels Cl. BR1: Brom 3C 160
DA18: Erith 2D 108
E16 .....5B 88
KT4: Wor Pk 2B 164
N3 .....2H 45
N12 .....5H 31
St Michaels Ct. *CR0: C'don* *1C 168*
(off Station Rd.)
E14 .....*5E 86*
(off St Leonards Rd.)
SE1 .....*7D 14*
(off Trinity St.)
St Michael's Cres. HA5: Pinn 6C 40
St Michael's Flats *NW1* *1C 6*
(off Aldenham St.)
St Michael's Gdns. W10 .....5G 81
St Michaels M. SW1 .....4G 17 (4E 100)
St Michael's Ri. DA16: Well 1B 126
St Michael's Rd. CR0: C'don 1C 168
DA16: Well 3B 126
NW2 .....4E 62
SM6: Wall 6G 167
SW9 .....2K 119
TW15: Ashf 5C 128
St Michael's St. W2 .....7B 4 (6B 82)
St Michaels Ter. *N6* *1E 64*
(off South Gro.)
N22 .....1J 47
St Mildred's Ct. EC2 .....1E 14 (6D 84)
St Mildreds Rd. SE6 .....7G 123
SE12 .....7G 123
St Mirren Ct. EN5: New Bar 5F 21
St Nicholas Cen. SM1: Sutt 5K 165
St Nicholas Cl. UB8: Cowl 6A 74
St Nicholas Ct. *KT1: King T* *4E 150*
(off Surbiton Rd.)
St Nicholas Dr. TW17: Shep 7C 146
St Nicholas' Flats *NW1* *1C 6*
(off Werrington St.)
St Nicholas Glebe SW17 .....5E 136
St Nicholas Ho. *SE8* *6C 104*
(off Deptford Grn.)
SE18 .....*7C 106*
(off Shrapnel Cl.)
St Nicholas M. KT7: T Ditt 6K 149
St Nicholas Rd. KT7: T Ditt 6K 149
SE18 .....5K 107
SM1: Sutt 5K 165
St Nicholas St. SE8 .....1B 122
St Nicholas Way SM1: Sutt 4K 165
St Nicolas La. BR7: Chst 1C 160
St Ninian's Ct. N20 .....3J 31
St Norbert Grn. SE4 .....4A 122
St Norbert Rd. SE4 .....5K 121
St Olaf Ho. SE1 .....4F 15
St Olaf's Rd. SW6 .....7G 99
St Olaf Stairs SE1 .....4F 15
St Olave's Ct. EC2 .....1E 14 (6D 84)
St Olave's Est. SE1 .....6H 15 (2E 102)
St Olave's Gdns. SE11 .....3J 19 (4A 102)
St Olaves Ho. *SE11* *3J 19*
(off Walnut Tree Wlk.)
St Olave's Mans. SE11 .....3J 19

St Olave's Rd. E6 1E 88
St Olave's Ter. SE1 6H 15
St Olaves Wlk. SW16 2G 155
St Olav's Sq. SE16 2J 103
St Onge Pde. EN1: Enf 3J 23
(off Southbury Rd.)
St Oswald's Pl. SE11 6G 19 (5K 101)
St Oswald's Rd. SW16 1B 156
St Oswalds Studios SW6 6J 99
(off Sedlescombe Rd.)
St Oswulf St. SW1 4D 18 (4H 101)
St Owen Ho. SE1 3E 102
(off St Saviour's Est.)
ST PANCRAS 2F 7 (3J 83)
St Pancras Commercial Cen. NW1 1G 83
(off Pratt St.)
St Pancras Ct. N2 2B 46
St Pancras Way NW1 7G 65
St Patrick's Ct. IG8: Wfd G 7B 36
St Paul Cl. UB8: Cowl 5A 74
St Paulinus Ct. DA1: Cray 4K 127
(off Manor Rd.)
St Paul's All. EC4 1B 14
(off St Paul's Chyd.)
St Paul's Arts Cen. 4C 104
(off Westferry Rd.)
St Paul's Av. HA3: Kent 4F 43
NW2 6D 62
SE16 1K 103
St Paul's Bldgs. EC1 3B 8
(off Dallington St.)
St Paul's Cathedral 1B 14 (6C 84)
St Paul's Chyd. EC4 1B 14 (6B 84)
St Pauls Cl. KT9: Chess 4D 162
SE7 5B 106
SM5: Cars 1C 166
TW3: Houn 2C 112
TW15: Ashf 5E 128
UB3: Harl 5F 93
W5 2F 97
St Pauls Ct. SW4 5H 119
TW4: Houn 3C 112
St Pauls Courtyard SE8 7C 104
(off Crossfield St.)
ST PAUL'S CRAY 2K 161
St Paul's Cray Rd. BR7: Chst 1H 161
St Paul's Cres. NW1 7H 65
(not continuous)
St Paul's Dr. E15 5F 69
St Paul's M. NW1 7H 65
St Paul's Pl. N1 6D 66
St Paul's Ri. N13 6G 33
St Paul's Rd. CR7: Thor H 3C 156
DA8: Erith 7J 109
IG11: Bark 1G 89
N1 6B 66
N17 7B 34
TW8: Bford 6D 96
TW9: Rich 3F 115
St Paul's Shrubbery N1 6D 66
St Paul's Sq. BR2: Brom 2H 159
St Paul's Studios W14 5G 99
(off Talgarth Rd.)
St Pauls Ter. SE17 6B 102
St Paul St. N1 1C 84
(not continuous)
St Pauls Vw. Apartments EC1 2J 7
(off Amwell St.)
St Paul's Wlk. KT2: King T 7G 133
St Paul's Way E3 5B 86
N3 7E 30
St Paul's Wood Hill BR5: St P 2J 161
St Peter Claver Ct. BR3: Beck 1D 158
(off Albemarle Rd.)
St Peter's All. EC3 1F 15
(off Cornhill)
St Peters Av. E2 2G 85
E17 4G 51
N2 7H 31
N18 4B 34
St Petersburgh M. W2 7K 81
St Petersburgh Pl. W2 7K 81
St Peter's Cen. E1 1H 103
(off Reardon St.)
St Peter's Chu. Ct. N1 1B 84
(off St Peter's St.)
St Peters Cl. BR7: Chst 7H 143
E2 2G 85
HA4: Ruis 2B 58
IG2: Ilf 4J 53
SW17 2C 136
WD23: B Hea 1C 26
St Peters Ct. KT8: W Mole 4E 148
NW4 5E 44
SE12 5H 123
WC1 2F 7
(off Seaford St.)
St Peter's Gdns. SE27 3A 138
St Peter's Gro. W6 4C 98
St Peters Ho. SE17 6D 102
WC1 2F 7
(off Regent Sq.)
St Peters M. N8 5A 48
St Peter's Path E17 3G 51
St Peters Pl. W9 4K 81
St Peters Rd. CR0: C'don 4D 168
KT1: King T 2G 151
KT8: W Mole 4E 148
N9 1C 34
TW1: Twick 5B 114
UB1: S'hall 5E 76
UB8: Cowl 5A 74
W6 5C 98
St Peter's Sq. E2 2G 85
W6 4B 98
St Peter's St. CR2: S Croy 5D 168
N1 1B 84
St Peter's St. M. N1 2B 84
(off St Peters St.)
St Peter's Ter. SW6 7H 99
St Peter's Vs. W6 4C 98
St Peters Way N1 7E 66
UB3: Harl 5F 93
W5 5D 78
St Peter's Wharf W4 5C 98
St Philip Ho. WC1 2J 7
(off Lloyd Baker St.)
St Philips Av. KT4: Wor Pk 2D 164
N2 7H 31
St Philip's Ga. KT4: Wor Pk 2D 164
St Philip Sq. SW8 2F 119
St Philips Rd. E8 6G 67
KT6: Surb 6D 150
St Philip St. SW8 2F 119
St Philip's Way N1 1C 84
St Quentin Ho. SW18 6B 118
St Quentin Rd. DA16: Well 3K 125
St Quintin Av. W10 5E 80
St Quintin Gdns. W10 5E 80
St Quintin Rd. E13 3K 87
St Raphael's Way NW10 5J 61
St Regis Cl. N10 2F 47
St Regis Hgts. NW3 3K 63
St Richard's Ho. NW1 1C 6
(off Eversholt St.)
St Ronan's Cl. EN4: Had W 1G 21
St Ronan's Cres. IG8: Wfd G 7D 36
St Rule St. SW8 2G 119
St Saviour's Coll. SE27 4D 138
St Saviours Ct. HA1: Harr 5J 41
N22 2H 47
St Saviour's Est. SE1 7J 15 (2F 103)
St Saviour's Rd. CR0: C'don 6B 156
SW2 5K 119
St Saviour's Wharf SE1 6K 15
(off Mill St.)
SE1 6K 15
(off Shad Thames)
Saints Cl. SE27 4B 138
Saints Dr. E7 5B 70
St Silas Pl. NW5 6E 64
St Simon's Av. SW15 5E 116
Saints M. CR4: Mitc 3C 154
St Stephen's Av. E17 5E 50
W12 1D 98
(not continuous)
W13 6B 78
St Stephen's Cl. E17 5D 50
NW8 1C 82
UB1: S'hall 5E 76
St Stephens Ct. EN1: Enf 6K 23
(off Park Av.)
N8 6K 47
W13 6B 78
St Stephen's Cres. CR7: Thor H 3A 156
W2 6J 81
St Stephen's Gdns. SW15 5H 117
TW1: Twick 6C 114
W2 6J 81
(not continuous)
St Stephens Gro. SE13 3E 122
St Stephens Ho. SE17 6D 102
(off Lytham St.)
St Stephen's M. W2 5J 81
St Stephens Pde. E7 7A 70
St Stephen's Pas.
TW1: Twick 6C 114
St Stephen's Rd. E3 1A 86
E6 7A 70
E17 5D 50
EN5: Barn 5A 20
TW3: Houn 6E 112
UB7: Yiew 1A 92
W13 6B 78
St Stephen's Row EC4 1E 14
St Stephen's Ter. SW8 7K 101
St Stephen's Wlk. SW7 4A 100
(off Southwell Gdns.)
St Swithins La. EC4 2E 14 (7D 84)
St Swithun's Rd. SE13 6F 123
St Theresa's Rd. TW14: Felt 4H 111
St Thomas Cl. KT6: Surb 1F 163
St Thomas Ct. DA5: Bexl 7G 127
E10 7D 50
(off Beaumont Rd.)
HA5: Pinn 1C 40
NW1 7G 65
(off Wrotham Rd.)
St Thomas Dr. BR5: Farnb 1G 173
HA5: Pinn 1C 40
St Thomas Gdns. IG1: Ilf 6G 71
St Thomas Ho. E1 6K 85
(off W. Arbour St.)
St Thomas More School Sports Cen.
7F 33
St Thomas Rd. DA17: Belv 2J 109
E16 6J 87
N14 7C 22
W4 6J 97
St Thomas's Gdns. NW5 6E 64
St Thomas's Pl. E9 7J 67
St Thomas's Rd. N4 2A 66
NW10 1A 80
St Thomas's Sq. E9 7J 67
St Thomas St. SE1 5F 15 (1D 102)
St Thomas's Way SW6 7H 99
St Timothys M. BR1: Brom 1K 159
St Ursula Gro. HA5: Pinn 5B 40
St Ursula Rd. UB1: S'hall 6E 76
St Vincent Cl. SE27 5B 138
St Vincent De Paul Ho. E1 5J 85
(off Jubilee St.)
St Vincent Ho. SE1 3F 103
(off St Saviour's Est.)
St Vincent Rd. TW2: Whitt 6G 113
St Vincent's La. NW7 4K 29
St Vincent St. W1 6H 5 (5E 82)
St Wilfrid's Cl. EN4: E Barn 5H 21
St Wilfrid's Rd. EN4: E Barn 5H 21
St Williams Ct. N1 7J 65
St Winefride's Av. E12 5D 70
St Winifred's Rd. TW11: Tedd 6B 132
Sakura Dr. N22 1H 47
Sala Ho. SE3 4K 123
Salamanca Pl. SE1 4G 19 (4K 101)
Salamanca Sq. SE1 4G 19
(off Salamanca Pl.)
Salamanca St. SE1 4F 19 (4K 101)
SE11 4F 19 (4K 101)
Salamander Cl. KT2: King T 5C 132
Salamander Quay KT1: Ham W 1D 150
Salcombe Dr. RM6: Chad H 6F 55
SM4: Mord 1F 165
Salcombe Gdns. NW7 6K 29
Salcombe Rd. E17 7B 50
N16 5E 66
TW15: Ashf 3A 128
Salcombe Vs. TW10: Rich 5E 114
Salcombe Way HA4: Ruis 2J 57
UB4: Hayes 3F 75
Salcott Rd. CR0: Bedd 3J 167
SW11 5C 118
Salehurst Cl. HA3: Kent 5E 42
Salehurst Rd. SE4 6B 122
Salem Pl. CR0: C'don 3C 168
Salem Rd. W2 7K 81
Sale Pl. W2 6C 4 (5C 82)
Sale St. E2 4G 85
Salford Ho. E14 4E 104
(off Seyssel St.)
Salford Rd. SW2 1H 137
Salhouse Cl. SE28 6C 90
Salisbury Av. IG11: Bark 7H 71
N3 3H 45
SM1: Sutt 6H 165
Salisbury Cl. KT4: Wor Pk 3B 164
SE17 4D 102
Salisbury Ct. EC4 1A 14 (6B 84)
EN2: Enf 4J 23
(off London Rd.)
HA8: Edg 4A 28
SE16 3G 103
(off Stork's Rd.)
SM5: Cars 5D 166
UB5: N'olt 5F 59
(off Newmarket Av.)
Salisbury Gdns. IG9: Buck H 2G 37
SW19 7G 135
Salisbury Hall Gdns. E4 6H 35
Salisbury Ho. E14 6D 86
(off Hobday St.)
EC2 6F 9
(off London Wall)
HA7: Stan 6F 27
N1 1B 84
(off St Mary's Path)
SM6: Wall 5F 167
SW1 5D 18
(off Drummond Ga.)
SW9 7A 102
(off Cranmer Rd.)
Salisbury Mans. N15 5B 48
Salisbury M. SW6 7H 99
Salisbury Pas. SW6 7H 99
(off Dawes Rd.)
Salisbury Pavement SW6 7H 99
(off Dawes Rd.)
Salisbury Pl. SW9 7B 102
W1 5E 4 (5D 82)
Salisbury Prom. N8 5B 48
Salisbury Rd. BR2: Brom 5C 160
DA5: Bexl 1G 145
E4 3H 35
E7 6J 69
E10 2E 68
E12 5B 70
E17 5E 50
EN5: Barn 3B 20
HA1: Harr 5H 41
HA5: Eastc 4J 39

Salisbury Rd. IG3: Ilf 2J **71**
KT3: N Mald 3K **151**
KT4: Wor Pk 4K **163**
N4 5B **48**
N22 1B **48**
RM10: Dag 6H **73**
SE25 6G **157**
SM5: Cars 6D **166**
SW19 7G **135**
TW4: Houn 3A **112**
TW6: H'row A 6E **110**
(not continuous)
TW9: Rich 4E **114**
TW13: Felt 1A **130**
UB2: S'hall 4C **94**
W13 2B **96**
Salisbury Sq. EC4 1K **13** (6A **84**)
Salisbury St. NW8 4C **4** (4C **82**)
W3 2J **97**
Salisbury Ter. SE15 3J **121**
Salisbury Wlk. N19 2G **65**
Salix Cl. TW16: Sun 7K **129**
Salix Ct. N3 6D **30**
Salliesfield TW2: Whitt 6H **113**
Sally Murray Cl. E12 4E **70**
Salmen Rd. E13 2H **87**
Salmond Cl. HA7: Stan 6F **27**
Salmon La. E14 6A **86**
Salmon M. NW6 5J **63**
Salmon Rd. DA17: Belv 5G **109**
Salmons Rd. KT9: Chess 6E **162**
N9 1B **34**
Salmon St. E14 6B **86**
NW9 1H **61**
Salomons Rd. E13 5A **88**
Salop Rd. E17 6K **49**
Saltash Cl. SM1: Sutt 4H **165**
Saltash Hall *UB8: Cowl* *3A* ***74***
(off Kingston La.)
Saltash Rd. DA16: Well 1C **126**
IG6: Ilf 1H **53**
Saltcoats Rd. W4 2A **98**
Saltcroft Cl. HA9: Wemb 1H **61**
Saltdene N4 1K **65**
Salter Cl. HA2: Harr 4D **58**
Salterford Rd. SW17 6E **136**
Salter Rd. SE16 1K **103**
Salters Ct. EC4 1D **14**
Salter's Hall Ct. EC4 2E **14**
Salter's Hill SE19 5D **138**
Salters Rd. E17 4F **51**
W10 4F **81**
Salters Row *N1* *6D* ***66***
(off Tilney Gdns.)
Salter St. E14 7B **86**
NW10 3C **80**
Salterton Rd. N7 3K **65**
Salt Hill Cl. UB8: Uxb 5A **56**
Saltley Cl. E6 6C **88**
Saltoun Rd. SW2 4A **120**
Saltram Cl. N15 4F **49**
Saltram Cres. W9 3H **81**
Saltwell St. E14 7C **86**
Saltwood Gro. SE17 5D **102**
Saltwood Ho. *SE15* *6J* ***103***
(off Lovelinch Cl.)
Salusbury Rd. NW6 1G **81**
Salutation Rd. SE10 4G **105**
Salvador SW17 5D **136**
Salvia Gdns. UB6: G'frd 2A **78**
Salvin Rd. SW15 3F **117**
Salway Cl. IG8: Wfd G 7D **36**
Salway Pl. E15 6F **69**
Salway Rd. E15 6F **69**
Samantha Cl. E17 7B **50**
Sam Bartram Cl. SE7 5A **106**
Sambrook Ho. *E1* *5J* ***85***
(off Jubilee St.)
SE11 4J **19**
Sambruck M. SE6 1D **140**
Samels Ct. W6 5C **98**
Samford Ho. *N1* *1A* ***84***
(off Barnsbury Est.)
Samford St. NW8 4C **4** (4B **82**)
Samira Cl. E17 6C **50**
Sam Manners Ho. *SE10* *5G* ***105***
(off Tuskar St.)
Sam March Ho. *E14* *6F* ***87***
(off Blair St.)
Sammi Ct. CR7: Thor H 4C **156**
Samos Rd. SE20 2H **157**
Sampson Av. EN5: Barn 5A **20**
Sampson Cl. DA17: Belv 3D **108**
Sampson Ct. TW17: Shep 5E **146**
Sampson Ho. SE1 4A **14** (1B **102**)
Sampson St. E1 1G **103**
Samsbrooke Ct. EN1: Enf 6K **23**
Samson St. E13 2A **88**
Samuda Est. E14 3E **104**
Samuel Cl. E8 1F **85**
SE14 6K **103**
SE18 4C **106**
Samuel Ct. *N1* *2G* ***9***
(off Pitfield St.)
Samuel Gray Gdns. KT2: King T 1D **150**
Samuel Ho. *E8* *1F* ***85***
(off Clarissa St.)
Samuel Johnson Cl. SW16 4K **137**
Samuel Jones Ind. Est. SE15 7E **102**
Samuel Lewis Bldgs. N1 6A **66**
Samuel Lewis Trust Dwellings
N16 6E **48**
SE5 *1C* ***120***
(off Warner Rd.)
SW3 4C **16** (4C **100**)
SW6 *7J* ***99***
(off Vanston Pl.)
W14 *4H* ***99***
(off Lisgar Ter.)
Samuel Richardson Ho. *W14* *4H* ***99***
(off North End Cres.)
Samuel's Cl. W6 4E **98**
Samuel St. SE15 7F **103**
SE18 4D **106**
Sancroft Cl. NW2 3D **62**
Sancroft Ho. SE11 5H **19**
Sancroft Rd. HA3: W'stone 2K **41**
Sancroft St. SE11 5H **19** (5K **101**)
Sanctuary, The DA5: Bexl 6D **126**
SM4: Mord 6J **153**
SW1 1D **18**
Sanctuary M. E8 6F **67**
Sanctuary Rd. TW6: H'row A 6C **110**
Sanctuary St. SE1 6D **14** (2C **102**)
Sandale Cl. N16 3D **66**
Sandall Cl. W5 4E **78**
Sandall Ho. E3 2A **86**
Sandall Rd. NW5 6G **65**
W5 4E **78**
Sandal Rd. KT3: N Mald 5K **151**
N18 5B **34**
Sandal St. E15 1G **87**
Sandalwood Cl. E1 4A **86**
Sandal Wood Dr. HA4: Ruis 7E **38**
Sandalwood Ho. DA15: Sidc 2K **143**
Sandalwood Mans. *W8* *3K* ***99***
(off Stone Hall Gdns.)
Sandalwood Rd. TW13: Felt 3K **129**
Sandbach Pl. SE18 4G **107**
Sandbanks TW14: Felt 1G **129**
Sandbourne *NW8* *1K* ***81***
(off Abbey Rd.)
W11 *6J* ***81***
(off Dartmouth Cl.)
Sandbourne Av. SW19 2K **153**
Sandbourne Rd. SE4 2A **122**
Sandbrook Cl. NW7 6E **28**
Sandbrook Rd. N16 3E **66**
Sandby Grn. SE9 3C **124**
Sandby Ho. NW6 1J **81**
Sandcliff Rd. DA8: Erith 4K **109**
Sandcroft Cl. N13 6G **33**
Sandell's Av. TW15: Ashf 4E **128**
Sandell St. SE1 6J **13** (2A **102**)
Sanderling Ct. *SE8* *6B* ***104***
(off Abinger Gro.)
SE28 7C **90**
Sanderling Lodge *E1* *3K* ***15***
(off Star Pl.)
Sanders Cl. TW12: Ham H 5G **131**
Sanders Ho. *WC1* *1J* ***7***
(off Gt. Percy St.)
Sanders La. NW7 7K **29**
(Bittacy Ri.)
NW7 7A **30**
(Grants Cl.)
Sanderson Cl. NW5 4F **65**
Sanderson Ho. *SE8* *5B* ***104***
(off Grove St.)
Sanderson Sq. BR1: Brom 3E **160**
Sanderstead Av. NW2 2G **63**
Sanderstead Cl. SW12 7G **119**
Sanderstead Rd.
CR2: Sande, S Croy 7D **168**
E10 1A **68**
Sanders Way N19 1H **65**
Sandfield *WC1* *2F* ***7***
(off Cromer St.)
Sandfield Gdns. CR7: Thor H 3B **156**
Sandfield Pas. CR7: Thor H 3C **156**
Sandfield Pl. CR7: Thor H 3C **156**
Sandfield Rd. CR7: Thor H 3B **156**
Sandford Av. N22 1C **48**
Sandford Cl. E6 4D **88**
Sandford Ct. EN5: New Bar 3E **20**
N16 1E **66**
Sandford Rd. BR2: Brom 3J **159**
DA7: Bex 4E **126**
E6 3C **88**
Sandford Row SE17 5D **102**
Sandford St. SW6 7K **99**
Sandgate Cl. RM7: Rush G 7J **55**
Sandgate Ho. E5 5H **67**
W5 5C **78**
Sandgate La. SW18 1C **136**
Sandgate Rd. DA16: Well 7C **108**
Sandgate St. SE15 6H **103**
Sandgate Trad. Est. *SE15* *6H* ***103***
(off Sandgate St.)
Sandham Ct. SW4 1J **119**
Sandham Point *SE18* *4F* ***107***
(off Vincent Rd.)
Sandhills SM6: Bedd 4H **167**
Sandhills, The *SW10* *7A* ***16***
(off Limerston St.)
Sandhills Mdw. TW17: Shep 7E **146**
Sandhurst Av. HA2: Harr 6F **41**
KT5: Surb 7H **151**
Sandhurst Cl. CR2: Sande 7E **168**
NW9 3G **43**
Sandhurst Ct. SW2 4J **119**
Sandhurst Dr. IG3: Ilf, Bark 4K **71**
Sandhurst Ho. *E1* *5J* ***85***
(off Wolsy St.)
Sandhurst Mkt. *SE6* *1E* ***140***
(off Sandhurst Rd.)
Sandhurst Rd. BR6: Chels 3K **173**
DA5: Bexl 5D **126**
DA15: Sidc 3K **143**
N9 6D **24**
NW9 3G **43**
SE6 1F **141**
Sandhurst Way CR2: Sande 7E **168**
Sandifer Dr. NW2 3F **63**
Sandiford Rd. SM3: Sutt 2H **165**
Sandiland Cres. BR2: Hayes 2H **171**
Sandilands CR0: C'don 2G **169**
Sandilands Rd. SW6 1K **117**
Sandison St. SE15 3G **121**
Sandland St. WC1 6H **7** (5K **83**)
Sandling Ri. SE9 3E **142**
Sandlings, The N22 2A **48**
Sandlings Cl. SE15 2H **121**
Sandmartin Way SM6: Wall 1E **166**
Sandmere Rd. SW4 4J **119**
Sandon Cl. KT10: Esh 7H **149**
Sandow Cres. UB3: Hayes 3H **93**
Sandown Av. RM10: Dag 6J **73**
Sandown Cl. TW5: Cran 1J **111**
Sandown Ct. HA7: Stan 5H **27**
SE26 3H **139**
SM2: Sutt 7K **165**
Sandown Dr. SM5: Cars 7E **166**
Sandown Rd. SE25 5H **157**
Sandown Way UB5: N'olt 6C **58**
Sandpiper Cl. E17 7E **34**
SE16 2B **104**
Sandpiper Ct. *E1* *7G* ***85***
(off Thomas More St.)
E14 *3E* ***104***
(off New Union Cl.)
SE8 *6C* ***104***
(off Edward Pl.)
Sandpiper Rd. SM1: Sutt 5H **165**
Sandpiper Ter. IG5: Ilf 3F **53**
Sandpit Pl. SE7 5C **106**
Sandpit Rd. BR1: Brom 5G **141**
Sandpits Rd. CR0: C'don 4K **169**
TW10: Ham 2D **132**
Sandra Cl. N22 1C **48**
TW3: Houn 5F **113**
Sandra Ct. CR4: Mitc 6D **136**
Sandra Ho. KT8: E Mos 5H **149**
Sandridge Cl. HA1: Harr 4J **41**
Sandridge St. N19 2G **65**
Sandringham Av. SW20 1G **153**
Sandringham Cl. EN1: Enf 2K **23**
IG6: Ilf 3G **53**
SW19 1F **135**
Sandringham Ct. DA15: Sidc 6K **125**
KT2: King T *1E* ***150***
(off Skerne Wlk.)
SE16 *1K* ***103***
(off King & Queen Wharf)
UB10: Hil 4E **74**
W1 *1B* ***12***
(off Dufour's Pl.)
W9 *3A* ***82***
(off Maida Va.)
Sandringham Cres. HA2: Harr 2E **58**
Sandringham Dr. DA2: Dart 2K **145**
DA16: Well 2J **125**
TW15: Ashf 4A **128**
Sandringham Flats *WC2* *2D* ***12***
(off Charing Cross Rd.)
Sandringham Gdns. IG6: Ilf 3G **53**
KT8: W Mole 4E **148**
N8 6J **47**
N12 6G **31**
TW5: Cran 1J **111**
Sandringham Ho. *W14* *4G* ***99***
(off Windsor Way)
Sandringham M. TW12: Hamp 1D **148**
W5 7D **78**
Sandringham Rd. BR1: Brom 5J **141**
CR7: Thor H 5C **156**
E7 5A **70**
E8 5F **67**
E10 6F **51**
IG11: Bark 5K **71**
KT4: Wor Pk 3C **164**
N22 3C **48**
NW2 6D **62**
NW11 7G **45**
TW6: H'row A 5A **110**
UB5: N'olt 7E **58**
Sandrock Pl. CR0: C'don 4K **169**
Sandrock Rd. SE13 3C **122**
SANDS END 1A **118**
Sand's End La. SW6 1K **117**

Sandstone La. E16 7K 87
Sandstone Pl. N19 2F 65
Sandstone Rd. SE12 2K 141
Sands Way IG8: Wfd G 6J 37
Sandtoft Rd. SE7 6K 105
Sandwell Cres. NW6 6J 63
Sandwich Ho. SE16 2J 103
(off Swan Rd.)
WC1 2E 6
(off Sandwich St.)
Sandwich St. WC1 2E 6 (3J 83)
Sandwick Cl. NW7 7H 29
Sandy Bury BR6: Orp 3H 173
Sandycombe Rd.
TW9: Kew, Rich 3F 115
TW14: Felt 1J 129
Sandycoombe Rd. TW1: Twick 6C 114
Sandycroft SE2 6A 108
Sandy Dr. TW14: Felt 1G 129
Sandy Hill Av. SE18 5F 107
Sandy Hill Rd. SE18 4F 107
SM6: Wall 7G 167
Sandyhill Rd. IG1: Ilf 4F 71
Sandy La. BR5: St P 7D 144
BR6: Orp 7K 161
CR4: Mitc 1E 154
(not continuous)
DA14: Sidc 7D 144
HA3: Kent 6F 43
KT1: Ham W 7A 132
KT12: Walt T 6K 147
SM2: Cheam 7G 165
SM6: Wall 6H 167
TW10: Ham 2C 132
TW11: Tedd 7A 132
Sandy La. Nth. SM6: Wall 6H 167
Sandy La. Sth. SM6: Wall 7G 167
Sandymount Av. HA7: Stan 5H 27
Sandy Ridge BR7: Chst 6E 142
Sandy Rd. NW3 2K 63
(not continuous)
NW11 2K 63
Sandys Row E1 6H 9 (5E 84)
Sandy Way CR0: C'don 3B 170
KT12: Walt T 7H 147
Sanford La. N16 3F 67
Sanford St. SE14 6A 104
Sanford Ter. N16 3F 67
Sanford Wlk. N16 2F 67
SE14 6A 104
Sanger Av. KT9: Chess 5E 162
Sangley Rd. SE6 7D 122
SE25 4E 156
Sangora Rd. SW11 4B 118
Sankey Ho. E2 2J 85
(off St James's Av.)
Sansom Rd. E11 2H 69
Sansom St. SE5 1D 120
Sans Wlk. EC1 3K 7 (4A 84)
Santley Ho. SE1 7K 13 (2A 102)
Santley St. SW4 4K 119
Santos Rd. SW18 5J 117
Santway, The HA7: Stan 5D 26
Sapcote Trad. Cen.
NW10 6B 62
Saperton Wlk. SE11 3H 19
Saphora Cl. BR6: Farnb 5H 173
Sapperton Ct. EC1 3C 8
Sapperton Ho. W2 5J 81
(off Westbourne Pk. Rd.)
Sapphire Cl. E6 6E 88
RM8: Dag 1C 72
Sapphire Ct. E1 7G 85
(off Cable St.)
Sapphire Rd. NW10 7J 61
SE8 4A 104
Saracen Cl. CR0: C'don 6D 156
Saracens Head Yd. EC3 1J 15
Saracen St. E14 6C 86
Sarah Ct. UB5: N'olt 1D 76
Sarah Ho. E1 6H 85
(off Commercial Rd.)
Sarah Swift Ho. SE1 6F 15
(off Kipling St.)
Sara La. Ct. N1 2E 84
(off Stanway St.)
Saratoga Rd. E5 4J 67
Sara Turnbull Ho. SE18 4D 106
Sardinia St. WC2 1G 13 (6K 83)
Sarita Cl. HA3: Hrw W 2H 41
Sarjant Path SW19 2F 135
(off Blincoe Cl.)
Sarjeant Ct. BR4: W W'ck 2F 171
(off Bencurtis Pk.)
Sark Cl. TW5: Hest 7E 94
Sark Ho. EN3: Enf W 1E 24
Sark Twr. SE28 2G 107
Sark Wlk. E16 6K 87
Sarnes Ct. N11 4A 32
(off Oakleigh Rd. Sth.)
Sarnesfield Ho. SE15 6H 103
(off Pencraig Way)
Sarnesfield Rd. EN2: Enf 4J 23
Sarratt Ho. W10 5E 80
(off Sutton Way)
Sarre Rd. NW2 5H 63
Sarsen Av. TW3: Houn 2E 112
Sarsfeld Rd. SW12 2D 136
Sarsfield Rd. UB6: G'frd 2B 78
Sartor Rd. SE15 4K 121
Sarum Ho. W11 7H 81
(off Portobello Rd.)
Sarum Ter. E3 4B 86
Sassoon NW9 1B 44
Satanita Cl. E16 6B 88
Satchell Mead NW9 1B 44
Satchwell Rd. E2 2K 9 (3G 85)
Satchwell St. E2 2K 9 (3G 85)
Sattar M. N16 3D 66
Saul Ct. SE15 6F 103
Sauls Grn. E11 3G 69
Saunders Cl. E14 7B 86
(off Limehouse C'way.)
IG1: Ilf 1H 71
Saunders Ho. SE16 2K 103
(off Quebec Way)
Saunders Ness Rd. E14 5E 104
Saunders Rd. SE18 5K 107
UB10: Uxb 7B 56
Saunders St. SE11 3J 19 (4A 102)
Saunders Way SE28 7B 90
Saunderton Rd.
HA0: Wemb 5B 60
Saunton Av. UB3: Harl 7H 93
Saunton Ct. UB1: S'hall 7G 77
(off Haldane Rd.)
Savage Gdns. E6 6D 88
EC3 2H 15 (7E 84)
(not continuous)
Savannah Cl. SE15 7F 103
Savera Cl. UB2: S'hall 3A 94
Savernake Ct.
HA7: Stan 6G 27
Savernake Ho. N4 7C 48
Savernake Rd. N9 6B 24
NW3 4D 64
Savery Dr. KT6: Surb 7B 150
Savile Cl. KT3: N Mald 5A 152
KT7: T Ditt 7K 149
Savile Gdns. CR0: C'don 2F 169
Savile Row W1 2A 12 (7G 83)
Saville Cres.
TW15: Ashf 6F 129
Saville Rd. E16 1C 106
RM6: Chad H 6F 55
TW1: Twick 1K 131
W4 3K 97
Saville Row BR2: Hayes 1H 171
EN3: Enf H 2E 24
Savill Gdns. SW20 3C 152
Savill Ho. E16 1F 107
(off Robert St.)
SW4 6H 119
Savill Row IG8: Wfd G 6C 36
Savin Lodge SM2: Sutt 7A 166
(off Walnut M.)
Savona Cl. SW19 7F 135
Savona Ho. SW8 7G 101
(off Savona St.)
Savona St. SW8 7G 101
Savoy Av. UB3: Harl 5G 93
Savoy Bldgs. WC2 3G 13
SAVOY CIRCUS 7B 80
Savoy Cl. E15 1G 87
HA8: Edg 5B 28
Savoy Ct. NW3 3A 64
SW5 4J 99
(off Cromwell Rd.)
WC2 3F 13 (7K 83)
Savoy Hill WC2 3G 13 (7K 83)
Savoy M. SW9 3J 119
Savoy Pde. EN1: Enf 3K 23
Savoy Pl. WC2 3F 13 (7J 83)
Savoy Row WC2 2G 13
Savoy Steps WC2 3G 13
Savoy St. WC2 3G 13 (7K 83)
Savoy Theatre 3F 13
(off Strand)
Savoy Way WC2 3G 13
Sawbill Cl. UB4: Yead 5B 76
Sawkins Cl. SW19 2G 135
Sawley Rd. W12 1C 98
Sawmill Yd. E3 1A 86
Sawtry Cl. SM5: Cars 7C 154
Sawyer Cl. N9 2B 34
Sawyer Ct. NW10 7K 61
Sawyers Cl. RM10: Dag 6J 73
Sawyer's Hill TW10: Rich 7F 115
Sawyers Lawn W13 6A 78
Sawyer St. SE1 6C 14 (2C 102)
Saxby Rd. SW2 7J 119
Saxham Rd. IG11: Bark 2J 89
Saxlingham Rd. E4 3A 36
Saxon Av. TW13: Hanw 2C 130
Saxonbury Av. TW16: Sun 3K 147
Saxonbury Cl. CR4: Mitc 3B 154
Saxonbury Ct. N7 5J 65
Saxonbury Gdns. KT6: Surb 1C 162
Saxon Bus. Cen. SW19 2A 154
Saxon Cl. E17 7C 50
KT6: Surb 6D 150
UB8: Hil 5B 74
Saxon Dr. W3 6G 79
Saxonfield Cl. SW2 7K 119
Saxon Gdns. UB1: S'hall 7C 76
Saxon Hall W2 7K 81
(off Palace Ct.)
Saxon Ho. E1 6K 9
(off Thrawl St.)
KT1: King T 4F 151
TW13: Hanw 2D 130
Saxon Lodge CR0: C'don 1C 168
(off Tavistock Rd.)
Saxon Rd. BR1: Brom 7H 141
E3 2B 86
E6 4D 88
HA9: Wemb 3J 61
IG1: Ilf 6F 71
KT2: King T 1E 150
N22 1B 48
SE25 5D 156
TW15: Ashf 6F 129
UB1: S'hall 7C 76
Saxon Ter. SE6 2B 140
Saxon Wlk. DA14: Sidc 6C 144
Saxon Way N14 6C 22
UB7: Harm 2D 174
Saxon Way Ind. Est.
UB7: Harm 2D 174
Saxony Pde. UB3: Hayes 5E 74
Saxton Cl. SE13 3F 123
Sayers Ho. N2 2B 46
(off The Grange)
Sayer's Wlk. TW10: Rich 7F 115
Sayesbury La. N18 5B 34
Sayes Ct. SE8 6B 104
Sayes Ct. St. SE8 6B 104
Scadbury Pk. Nature Reserve 7K 143
Scads Hill Cl. BR6: Pet W 6K 161
Scafell NW1 1A 6
(off Stanhope St.)
Scala St. W1 5B 6 (5G 83)
Scales Rd. N17 3F 49
Scampston M. W10 6F 81
Scandrett St. E1 1H 103
Scarab Cl. E16 7H 87
Scarba Wlk. N1 6D 66
(off Marquess Rd.)
Scarborough Rd. E11 1F 69
N4 1A 66
N9 7D 24
TW6: H'row A 6E 110
Scarborough St. E1 1K 15 (6F 85)
Scarbrook Rd. CR0: C'don 3C 168
Scarle Rd. HA0: Wemb 6D 60
Scarlet Rd. SE6 3G 141
Scarlette Mnr. Way
SW2 7A 120
Scarsbrook Rd. SE3 3B 124
Scarsdale Pl. W8 3K 99
Scarsdale Rd. HA2: Harr 3G 59
Scarsdale Studios W8 3J 99
(off Stratford Rd.)
Scarsdale Vs. W8 3J 99
Scarth Rd. SW13 3B 116
Scawen Cl. SM5: Cars 4E 166
Scawen Rd. SE8 5A 104
Scawfell St. E2 2F 85
Sceaux Gdns. SE5 1E 120
Sceptre Ct. E1 3K 15
(off Tower Hill)
Sceptre Ho. E1 4J 85
(off Malcolm Rd.)
Sceptre Rd. E2 3J 85
Sceynes Link N12 4D 30
Schafer Ho. NW1 2A 6 (3G 83)
Schiller International University 5J 13
Schofield Wlk. SE3 7J 105
Scholars Cl. EN5: Barn 4B 20
Scholars Pl. N16 3E 66
Scholars Rd. E4 1A 36
SW12 1G 137
Scholefield Rd. N19 2H 65
Scholey Ho. SW11 3C 118
Schomberg Ho. SW1 3D 18
(off Page St.)
Schonfeld Sq. N16 2D 66
School All. TW1: Twick 1A 132
School App. E2 1H 9
Schoolbank Rd. SE10 3H 105
Schoolbell M. E3 2A 86
School Ho. SE1 4E 102
(off Page's Wlk.)
School Ho. La. E1 7K 85
TW11: Tedd 7B 132
Schoolhouse Yd. SE18 5F 107
School La. DA16: Well 3B 126
HA5: Pinn 4C 40
KT1: Ham W 1C 150
KT6: Surb 1G 163
TW17: Shep 6D 146
WD23: Bush 1A 26
School of Hygiene & Tropical Medicine 5D 6
School Pas. KT1: King T 2F 151
UB1: S'hall 7D 76
School Rd. BR7: Chst 1G 161
E12 4D 70
KT1: Ham W 1C 150
KT8: E Mos 4H 149

School Rd. NW10 ....4K 79
RM10: Dag 1G 91
TW3: Houn 3G 113
TW12: Ham H 6G 131
TW15: Ashf 6D 128
UB7: Harm 2E 174
School Rd. Av. TW12: Ham H 6G 131
SCHOOL ROAD JUNC. 7D 128
School Sq. SE10 ....3H 105
School Wlk. TW16: Sun 4H 147
School Way N12 ....6G 31
RM8: Dag 3C 72
(not continuous)
Schooner Cl. E14 ....3F 105
IG11: Bark 3B 90
SE16 ....2K 103
Schubert Rd. SW15 ....5H 117
Science Mus. 2B 16 (3B 100)
Sclater St. E1 ....3J 9 (4F 85)
Scoble Pl. N16 ....4F 67
Scoles Cres. SW2 ....1B 138
Scoop, The 4H 15 (1E 102)
Scope Way KT1: King T 4E 150
Scoresby St. SE1 ....5A 14 (1B 102)
Scorton Av. UB6: G'frd 2A 78
Scorton Ho. N1 ....2E 84
(off Whitmore Est.)
Scotch Comn. W13 ....5A 78
SCOTCH HOUSE 2D 100
Scoter Cl. IG8: Wfd G 7E 36
Scoter Ct. SE8 ....6B 104
(off Abinger Gro.)
Scot Gro. HA5: Pinn 1B 40
Scotia Bldg. E1 ....7K 85
(off Jardine Rd.)
Scotia Ct. SE16 ....2J 103
(off Canada Est.)
Scotia Rd. SW2 ....7A 120
Scotland Grn. N17 ....2F 49
Scotland Grn. Rd. EN3: Pond E 5E 24
Scotland Grn. Rd. Nth.
EN3: Pond E 4E 24
Scotland Pl. SW1 ....5E 12 (1J 101)
Scotland Rd. IG9: Buck H 1F 37
Scotney Cl. BR6: Farnb 4E 172
Scotney Ho. E9 ....6J 67
Scots Cl. TW19: Stanw 1A 128
Scotsdale Cl. BR5: Pet W 4J 161
SM3: Cheam 7G 165
Scotsdale Rd. SE12 ....5K 123
Scotson Ho. SE11 ....4J 19
Scotswood St. EC1 ....3K 7 (4A 84)
Scotswood Wlk. N17 ....7B 34
Scott Av. SW18 ....6G 117
Scott Cl. KT19: Ewe 5J 163
SW16 ....1K 155
UB7: W Dray 4B 92
Scott Ct. W3 ....2K 97
Scott Cres. HA2: Harr 1F 59
Scott Ellis Gdns. NW8 ....2A 4 (3B 82)
Scottes La. RM8: Dag 1D 72
Scott Farm Cl. KT7: T Ditt 1B 162
Scott Gdns. TW5: Hest 7B 94
Scott Ho. DA17: Belv 5F 109
E13 ....2J 87
(off Queens Rd. W.)
E14 ....2C 104
(off Admirals Way)
N7 ....6K 65
(off Caledonian Rd.)
N18 ....5B 34
(off Woolmer Rd.)
NW8 ....4C 4
(off Broadley St.)
NW10 ....7K 61
(off Stonebridge Pk.)
SE8 ....5B 104
(off Grove St.)
Scott Lidgett Cres. SE16 ....2G 103
Scott Rd. HA8: Edg 2H 43
Scott Russell Pl. E14 ....5D 104
Scotts Av. BR2: Brom 2F 159
TW16: Sun 7G 129
Scotts Ct. W12 ....2E 98
(off Scott's Rd.)
Scotts Dr. TW12: Hamp 7F 131
Scotts Farm Rd. KT19: Ewe 6J 163
Scott's La. BR2: Brom 3F 159
Scotts Pas. SE18 ....4F 107
Scotts Rd. BR1: Brom 7J 141
E10 ....1E 68
UB2: S'hall 3A 94
W12 ....2D 98
Scott's Sufferance Wharf SE1 ....7K 15
Scotts Ter. SE9 ....2C 142
Scott St. E1 ....4H 85
Scotts Way TW16: Sun 7G 129
Scott's Yd. EC4 ....2E 14 (7D 84)
Scott Trimmer Way TW3: Houn 2C 112
Scottwell Dr. NW9 ....5B 44
Scoulding Ho. E14 ....3C 104
(off Mellish St.)
Scoulding Rd. E16 ....6J 87
Scouler St. E14 ....7E 86
Scout App. NW10 ....4A 62
Scout La. SW4 ....3G 119
Scout Way NW7 ....4E 28
Scovell Cres. SE1 ....7C 14
Scovell Rd. SE1 ....7C 14 (2C 102)
Scrattons Ter. IG11: Bark 2D 90
Screen on Baker Street (Cinema) 5F 5
(off Baker St.)
Screen on the Green Cinema 1B 84
(off Upper St.)
Screen on the Hill (Cinema)
Belsize Pk. 5C 64
Scriven Ct. E8 ....1F 85
Scriven St. E8 ....1F 85
Scrooby St. SE6 ....6D 122
Scrope Ho. EC1 ....5J 7
(off Bourne Est.)
Scrubs La. NW10 ....3C 80
W10 ....3C 80
Scrutton Cl. SW12 ....7H 119
Scrutton St. EC2 ....4G 9 (4E 84)
Scudamore La. NW9 ....4J 43
Scutari Rd. SE22 ....5J 121
Scylla Cres. TW6: H'row A 7D 110
(not continuous)
Scylla Rd. SE15 ....3G 121
(not continuous)
TW6: H'row A 6D 110
Seabright St. E2 ....3H 85
Seabrook Dr. BR4: W W'ck 2G 171
Seabrook Gdns. RM7: Rush G 7G 55
Seabrook Rd. RM8: Dag 3D 72
Seaburn Cl. RM13: Rain 2K 91
Seacole Cl. W3 ....6K 79
Sea Containers Ho. SE1 ....3K 13
Seacon Twr. E14 ....2B 104
Seacourt Rd. SE2 ....2D 108
Seafield Rd. N11 ....4C 32
Seaford Cl. HA4: Ruis 1F 57
Seaford Ho. SE16 ....2J 103
(off Swan Rd.)
Seaford Rd. E17 ....3D 50
EN1: Enf 4K 23
N15 ....5D 48
TW6: H'row A 7E 174
W13 ....1B 96
Seaford St. WC1 ....2F 7 (3K 83)
Seaforth Av. KT3: N Mald 5D 152
Seaforth Cres. N5 ....5C 66
Seaforth Gdns.
IG8: Wfd G 5F 37
KT19: Ewe 4B 164
N21 ....7E 22
Seaforth Pl. SW1 ....1B 18
Seager Bldgs. SE8 ....1C 122
Seagrave Cl. E1 ....5K 85
Seagrave Lodge SW6 ....6J 99
(off Seagrave Rd.)
Seagrave Rd. SW6 ....6J 99
Seagry Rd. E11 ....7J 51
Seagull Cl. IG11: Bark 3A 90
Seagull La. E16 ....7J 87
Sealand Rd. TW6: H'row A 6C 110
Sealand Wlk. UB5: N'olt 3B 76
Seal Ho. SE1 ....7F 15
(off Weston St.)
Seal St. E8 ....4F 67
Searles Cl. SW11 ....7C 100
Searles Dr. E6 ....5F 89
Searles Rd. SE1 ....4D 102
Searson Ho. SE17 ....4B 102
(off Canterbury Pl.)
Sears St. SE5 ....7D 102
Seasons Cl. W7 ....1K 95
Seasprite Cl. UB5: N'olt 3B 76
Seaton Av. IG3: Ilf 5K 71
Seaton Cl. E13 ....4J 87
SE11 ....5K 19 (5A 102)
SW15 ....1D 134
TW2: Whitt 6H 113
Seaton Dr. TW15: Ashf 2A 128
Seaton Gdns. HA4: Ruis 3H 57
Seaton Point E5 ....4G 67
Seaton Rd. CR4: Mitc 2C 154
DA16: Well 7C 108
HA0: Wemb 2E 78
TW2: Whitt 6G 113
UB3: Harl 4F 93
Seaton Sq. NW7 ....7A 30
Seaton St. N18 ....5B 34
Seawell Ct. IG11: Bark 2G 89
(off Dock Rd.)
Sebastian Ct. IG11: Bark 1K 89
Sebastian Ho. N1 ....1G 9
(off Hoxton St.)
Sebastian St. EC1 ....2B 8 (3B 84)
Sebastopol Rd. N9 ....4B 34
Sebbon St. N1 ....7B 66
Sebergham Gro. NW7 ....7H 29
Sebert Rd. E7 ....5K 69
Sebright Ho. E2 ....2G 85
(off Coate St.)
Sebright Pas. E2 ....2G 85
Sebright Rd. EN5: Barn 2A 20
Secker Cres. HA3: Hrw W 1G 41
Secker Ho. SW9 ....2B 120
(off Loughborough Est.)
Secker St. SE1 ....5J 13 (1A 102)
Secombe Theatre 5K 165
Second Av. E12 ....4C 70
E13 ....3J 87
E17 ....5C 50
EN1: Enf 5A 24
HA9: Wemb 2D 60
KT12: Walt T 6K 147
N18 ....4D 34
NW4 ....4F 45
RM6: Chad H 5C 54
RM10: Dag 1H 91
SW14 ....3A 116
UB3: Hayes 1H 93
W3 ....1B 98
W10 ....4G 81
Second Cl. KT8: W Mole 4G 149
Second Cross Rd. TW2: Twick 2J 131
Second Way HA9: Wemb 4H 61
Sedan Way SE17 ....5E 102
Sedcombe Cl. DA14: Sidc 4B 144
Sedcote Rd. EN3: Pond E 5D 24
Sedding St. SW1 ....3G 17 (4E 100)
Sedding Studios SW1 ....3G 17
(off Sedding St.)
Seddon Highwalk EC2 ....5C 8
(off Seddon Ho.)
Seddon Ho. EC2 ....5C 8
Seddon Rd. SM4: Mord 5B 154
Seddon St. WC1 ....2H 7 (3K 83)
Sedgebrook Rd. SE3 ....2B 124
Sedgecombe Av. HA3: Kent 5C 42
Sedgefield Ct. UB5: N'olt 5F 59
(off Newmarket Av.)
Sedgeford Rd. W12 ....1B 98
Sedgehill Rd. SE6 ....4C 140
Sedgemere Av. N2 ....3A 46
Sedgemere Rd. SE2 ....3C 108
Sedgemoor Dr. RM10: Dag 4G 73
Sedge Rd. N17 ....7D 34
Sedgeway SE6 ....1H 141
Sedgewick Av. UB10: Hil 7D 56
Sedgewood Cl. BR2: Hayes 7H 159
Sedgmoor Pl. SE5 ....7E 102
Sedgwick Ho. E3 ....5C 86
(off Gale St.)
Sedgwick Rd. E10 ....2E 68
Sedgwick St. E9 ....5K 67
Sedleigh Rd. SW18 ....6H 117
Sedlescombe Rd. SW6 ....6J 99
Sedley Cl. EN1: Enf 1C 24
Sedley Ct. SE26 ....2H 139
Sedley Ho. SE11 ....5H 19
(off Newburn St.)
Sedley Pl. W1 ....1J 11 (6F 83)
Sedum Cl. NW9 ....5H 43
Seeley Dr. SE21 ....4E 138
Seelig Av. NW9 ....7C 44
Seely Rd. SW17 ....6E 136
Seetha Ho. IG1: Ilf 2H 71
(off High Rd.)
Seething La. EC3 ....2H 15 (7E 84)
SEETHING WELLS 6C 150
Seething Wells La. KT6: Surb 6C 150
Sefton Av. HA3: Hrw W 2H 41
NW7 ....5E 28
Sefton Cl. BR5: St M Cry 4K 161
Sefton Ct. EN2: Enf 2G 23
TW3: Houn 1F 113
Sefton Rd. BR5: St M Cry 4K 161
CR0: C'don 1G 169
Sefton St. SW15 ....3E 116
Segal Cl. SE23 ....7A 122
Sekforde St. EC1 ....4A 8 (4B 84)
Sekhon Ter. TW13: Hanw 3E 130
Selah Dr. BR8: Swan 7J 145
Selan Gdns. UB4: Yead 5K 75
Selbie Av. NW10 ....5B 62
Selborne Av. DA5: Bexl 1E 144
E12 ....4E 70
Selborne Gdns. NW4 ....4C 44
UB6: G'frd 1A 78
Selborne Rd. CR0: C'don 3E 168
DA14: Sidc 4B 144
E17 ....5B 50
IG1: Ilf 2E 70
KT3: N Mald 2A 152
N14 ....3D 32
N22 ....1K 47
SE5 ....2D 120
Selborne Wlk. E17 ....5B 50
Selborne Wlk. Shop. Cen.
E17 ....4B 50
Selbourne Av. KT6: Surb 2F 163
Selbourne Ho. SE1 ....7E 14
Selby Cen., The 6K 33
Selby Chase HA4: Ruis 2K 57
Selby Cl. BR7: Chst 6E 142
E6 ....5C 88
KT9: Chess 7E 162
Selby Gdns. UB1: S'hall 4E 76
Selby Grn. SM5: Cars 7C 154
Selby Rd. E11 ....3G 69
E13 ....5K 87
N17 ....7K 33
SE20 ....2G 157
SM5: Cars 7C 154
TW15: Ashf 6E 128
W5 ....4B 78

Selby Sq. W10 3G 81
(off Dowland St.)
Selby St. E1 4G 85
Selcroft Ho. SE10 5H 105
(off Glenister Rd.)
Selden Ho. SE15 2J 121
(off Selden Rd.)
Selden Rd. SE15 2J 121
Selden Wlk. N7 2K 65
Seldon Ho. SW1 6A 18
(off Churchill Gdns.)
SW8 7G 101
(off Stewart's Rd.)
Selfridges 1G 11
SELHURST 6E 156
Selhurst Cl. SW19 1F 135
Selhurst New Rd. SE25 6E 156
Selhurst Pk. 4E 156
Selhurst Pl. SE25: C'don 6E 156
Selhurst Rd. N9 3J 33
SE25 6E 156
Selina Ho. NW8 3B 4
(off Frampton St.)
Selinas La. RM8: Dag 7E 54
Selkirk Ho. N1 1K 83
(off Bingfield St.)
Selkirk Rd. SW17 4C 136
TW2: Twick 2G 131
Sellers Hall Cl. N3 7D 30
Sellincourt Rd. SW17 5C 136
Sellindge Cl.
BR3: Beck 7B 140
Sellons Av. NW10 1B 80
Sellwood Dr. EN5: Barn 5A 20
Selma Ho. W12 6D 80
(off Du Cane Rd.)
Selman Ho. E9 6A 68
SELSDON 7J 169
Selsdon Av. CR2: S Croy 6D 168
Selsdon Cl. KT6: Surb 5E 150
RM5: Col R 1J 55
Selsdon Pk. Rd. CR0: Sels 7K 169
CR2: Sels 7K 169
Selsdon Rd. CR2: S Croy 5D 168
E11 7J 51
E13 1A 88
NW2 2B 62
SE27 3A 138
Selsdon Way E14 3D 104
Selsea Pl. N16 5E 66
Selsey WC1 3J 83
(off Wakefield St.)
Selsey Cres. DA16: Well 1D 126
Selsey St. E14 5C 86
Selvage La. NW7 5E 28
Selway Cl. HA5: Eastc 4K 39
Selway Ho. SW8 1J 119
(off Sth. Lambeth Rd.)
Selwood Pl. SW7 5A 16 (5B 100)
Selwood Rd.
CR0: C'don 2H 169
KT9: Chess 4D 162
SM3: Sutt 1H 165
Selwoods SW2 7A 120
Selwood Ter. SW7 5A 16 (5B 100)
Selworthy Cl. E11 5J 51
Selworthy Rd. SE6 3B 140
Selwyn Av. E4 6K 35
IG3: Ilf 6K 53
TW9: Rich 3E 114
Selwyn Cl. TW4: Houn 4C 112
Selwyn Ct. E17 5C 50
(off Yunus Khan Cl.)
HA8: Edg 7C 28
HA9: Wemb 3J 61
SE3 3H 123
TW10: Rich 5F 115
(off Church Rd.)
Selwyn Cres.
DA16: Well 3B 126
Selwyn Rd. E3 2B 86
E13 1K 87
KT3: N Mald 5K 151
NW10 7K 61
Semley Ga. E9 6B 68
Semley Ho. SW1 4J 17
(off Semley Pl.)
Semley Pl. SW1 4H 17 (4E 100)
Semley Rd. SW16 2J 155
Senate St. SE15 2J 121
Senators Lodge E3 2A 86
(off Roman Rd.)
Senator Wlk. SE28 3H 107
Sendall Ct. SW11 3B 118
(off Winstanley Rd.)
Seneca Rd. CR7: Thor H 4C 156
Sener Ct. CR2: S Croy 6C 168
Senga Rd. SM6: Wall 1E 166
Senhouse Rd. SM3: Cheam 3F 165
Senior St. W2 5K 81
Senlac Rd. SE12 1K 141
Sennen Rd. EN1: Enf 7A 24
Sennen Wlk. SE9 3C 142
Senrab St. E1 6K 85
Sentamu Cl. SE24 1B 138
Sentinel Cl. UB5: N'olt 4C 76
Sentinel Sq. NW4 4E 44
September Ct. UB1: S'hall 1F 95
(off Dormer's Wells La.)
UB8: Uxb 2A 74
September Way HA7: Stan 6G 27
Septimus Pl. EN1: Enf 5B 24
Sequoia Cl. WD23: B Hea 1C 26
Sequoia Gdns. BR6: Orp 7K 161
Sequoia Pk. HA5: Hat E 6A 26
Seraph Ct. EC1 1C 8
(off Moreland St.)
Serbin Cl. E10 7E 50
Serenaders Rd. SW9 2A 120
Sergeant Ind. Est. SW18 6K 117
Serica Ct. SE10 7E 104
Serjeants Inn EC4 1K 13 (6A 84)
Serlby Ct. W14 3H 99
(off Somerset Sq.)
Serle St. WC2 7H 7 (6K 83)
Sermon La. EC4 1C 14
Serpentine, The 1C 100
Serpentine Ct. SE16 2K 103
(off Christopher Cl.)
Serpentine Gallery 6A 10 (2B 100)
Serpentine Rd. W2 5C 10 (1C 100)
Serviden Dr. BR1: Brom 1B 160
Servite Ho. BR3: Beck 1B 158
KT4: Wor Pk 2B 164
(off The Avenue)
N14 5A 22
(off Bramley Rd.)
Servius Ct. TW8: Bford 7D 96
Setchell Rd. SE1 4F 103
Setchell Way SE1 4F 103
Seth St. SE16 2J 103
Seton Gdns. RM9: Dag 7C 72
Settle Point E13 2J 87
(off London Rd.)
Settle Rd. E13 2J 87
Settlers Ct. E14 7F 87
Settles St. E1 5G 85
Settrington Rd. SW6 2K 117
Seven Acres SM5: Cars 2C 166
Seven Dials WC2 1E 12 (6J 83)
Seven Dials Ct. WC2 1E 12
(off Shorts Gdns.)
Sevenex Pde. HA9: Wemb 5E 60
Seven Islands Leisure Cen. 3J 103
SEVEN KINGS 1J 71
Seven Kings Rd. IG3: Ilf 1J 71
Seven Kings Way
KT2: King T 1E 150
Sevenoaks Cl. DA7: Bex 4H 127
Sevenoaks Ct. HA6: Nwood 1E 38
Sevenoaks Rd. BR6: Chels, Orp 5K 173
BR6: Prat B 7K 173
SE4 6A 122
Sevenoaks Way BR5: St P 7C 144
DA14: Sidc 7C 144
Sevenseas Rd. TW6: H'row A 6E 110
SEVEN SISTERS 5F 49
Seven Sisters Rd. N4 2A 66
N7 3K 65
N15 7C 48
Seven Stars Cnr. W6 3C 98
Seven Stars Yd. E1 5K 9
Seventh Av. E12 4D 70
UB3: Hayes 1J 93
Severnake Cl. E14 4C 104
Severn Av. W10 3G 81
Severn Ct. KT2: King T 1D 150
(off John Williams Cl.)
Severn Dr. KT10: Hin W 2A 162
Severn Way NW10 5B 62
Severus Rd. SW11 4C 118
Seville Ho. E1 1G 103
(off Hellings St.)
Seville M. N1 7E 66
Seville St. SW1 7F 11 (2D 100)
Sevington Rd. NW4 6D 44
Sevington St. W9 4K 81
Seward Rd. BR3: Beck 2K 157
W7 2A 96
SEWARDSTONE 1K 25
Sewardstone Gdns. E4 5J 25
Sewardstone Rd. E2 2J 85
E4 7J 25
Seward St. EC1 3B 8 (3B 84)
Sewdley St. E5 3K 67
Sewell Rd. SE2 3A 108
Sewell St. E13 3J 87
Sextant Av. E14 4F 105
Sexton Ct. E14 7F 87
(off Newport Av.)
Sextons Ho. SE10 6E 104
(off Bardsley La.)
Seymer Rd. RM1: Rom 3K 55
Seymour Av. KT17: Ewe 7E 164
N17 2G 49
SM4: Mord 7F 153
Seymour Cl. HA5: Hat E 1D 40
KT8: E Mos 5G 149
Seymour Ct. E4 2C 36
KT1: Ham W 1D 150
(off Seymour Rd.)
N10 2E 46
N21 6E 22
NW2 2D 62
Seymour Dr. BR2: Brom 1D 172
Seymour Gdns. HA4: Ruis 1B 58
IG1: Ilf 1D 70
KT5: Surb 5F 151
SE4 3A 122
TW1: Twick 7B 114
TW13: Hanw 4A 130
Seymour Ho. E16 1J 105
(off De Quincey M.)
NW1 1D 6
(off Churchway)
SM2: Sutt 6K 165
(off Mulgrave Rd.)
WC1 3E 6
(off Tavistock Pl.)
Seymour Leisure Cen. 6E 4 (5D 82)
Seymour M. W1 7G 5 (6E 82)
Seymour Pl. SE25 4H 157
W1 6E 4 (5D 82)
Seymour Rd. CR4: Mitc 7E 154
E4 1J 35
E6 2B 88
E10 1B 68
KT1: Ham W 1D 150
KT8: W Mole, E Mos 5G 149
N3 7E 30
Seymour Rd. N8 5A 48
N9 2C 34
SM5: Cars 5E 166
SW18 7H 117
SW19 3F 135
TW12: Ham H 5G 131
W4 4J 97
Seymour St. SE18 3G 107
W1 1E 10 (6D 82)
W2 1E 10 (6D 82)
Seymour Ter. SE20 1H 157
Seymour Vs. SE20 1H 157
Seymour Wlk. SW10 6A 100
Seymour Way TW16: Sun 7H 129
Seyssel St. E14 4E 104
Shaa Rd. W3 7K 79
Shabana Rd. W12 1D 98
Shacklegate La. TW11: Tedd 4J 131
Shackleton Cl. SE23 2H 139
Shackleton Ct. E14 5C 104
(off Maritime Quay)
TW19: Stanw 6A 110
(off Whitley Cl.)
W12 2D 98
(off Scott's Rd.)
W12 2D 98
(off Titmuss St.)
Shackleton Ho. E1 1J 103
(off Prusom St.)
NW10 7K 61
Shackleton Rd. UB1: S'hall 7D 76
SHACKLEWELL 4F 67
Shacklewell Grn. E8 4F 67
Shacklewell Ho. E8 4F 67
Shacklewell La. E8 5F 67
Shacklewell Rd. N16 4F 67
Shacklewell Row E8 4F 67
Shacklewell St. E2 2K 9 (3F 85)
Shadbolt Av. E4 5F 35
Shadbolt Cl. KT4: Wor Pk 2B 164
Shad Thames SE1 5J 15 (1F 103)
SHADWELL 7H 85
Shadwell Ct. UB5: N'olt 2D 76
Shadwell Dr. UB5: N'olt 3D 76
Shadwell Gdns. E1 7J 85
Shadwell Pierhead E1 7J 85
Shadwell Pl. E1 7J 85
(off Shadwell Gdns.)
Shady Bush Cl. WD23: Bush 1B 26
Shaef Way TW11: Tedd 7A 132
Shafter Rd. RM10: Dag 6J 73
Shaftesbury Av.
EN3: Enf H 2E 24
EN5: New Bar 4F 21
HA2: Harr 1F 59
HA3: Kent 5D 42
TW14: Felt 6J 111
UB2: S'hall 4E 94
W1 3C 12 (7H 83)
WC1 7E 6 (6J 83)
WC2 7E 6 (6J 83)
Shaftesbury Cen. W10 4F 81
(off Barlby Rd.)
Shaftesbury Circ.
HA2: Harr 1G 59
Shaftesbury Ct. E6 6E 88
(off Sapphire Cl.)
N1 2D 84
(off Shaftesbury St.)
SE1 3D 102
(off Alderney M.)
SE5 4D 120
SW6 1K 117
(off Maltings Pl.)
SW16 3H 137
Shaftesbury Cres.
TW18: Staines 7A 128
Shaftesbury Gdns. NW10 4A 80
Shaftesbury Lodge E14 6D 86
(off Upper Nth. St.)

Shaftesbury M. SW4 5G 119
W8 3J 99
(off Stratford Rd.)
Shaftesbury Pde.
HA2: Harr 1G 59
Shaftesbury Pl. *EC2* 6C 8
(off London Wall)
W14 4H 99
(off Warwick Rd.)
Shaftesbury Point *E13* 2J 87
(off High St.)
Shaftesbury Rd.
BR3: Beck 2B 158
E4 1A 36
E7 7A 70
E10 1C 68
E17 6D 50
N18 6K 33
N19 1J 65
SM5: Cars 7B 154
TW9: Rich 3E 114
Shaftesburys, The
IG11: Bark 2G 89
Shaftesbury St. N1 2C 84
(not continuous)
Shaftesbury Theatre 7E 6
(off Shaftesbury Av.)
Shaftesbury Vs. *W8* 3J 99
(off Allen St.)
Shaftesbury Way TW2: Twick 3H 131
Shaftesbury Waye UB4: Yead 5A 76
Shafto M. SW1 2F 17 (3D 100)
Shafton M. E9 1K 85
Shafton Rd. E9 1K 85
Shafts Ct. EC3 1G 15 (6E 84)
Shahjalal Ho. *E2* 2G 85
(off Pritchards Rd.)
Shakespeare Av. N11 5B 32
NW10 1K 79
TW14: Felt 6J 111
UB4: Hayes, Yead 6J 75
(not continuous)
Shakespeare Cl. HA3: Kent 7G 43
Shakespeare Ct. EN5: New Bar 3E 20
HA3: Kent 6F 43
NW6 7A 64
(off Fairfax Rd.)
Shakespeare Cres. E12 6D 70
NW10 1K 79
Shakespeare Dr. HA3: Kent 6F 43
Shakespeare Gdns. N2 4D 46
Shakespeare Ho. *E9* 7J 67
(off Lyme Gro.)
N14 2C 32
Shakespeare Rd. DA7: Bex 1E 126
E17 2K 49
N3 1J 45
NW7 4G 29
NW10 1K 79
SE24 5B 120
W3 1J 97
W7 7K 77
Shakespeare's Globe & Exhibition
4C 14 (1C 102)
Shakespeare Twr. EC2 5D 8
Shakespeare Way TW13: Hanw 4A 130
Shakspeare M. N16 4E 66
Shakspeare Wlk. N16 4E 66
Shalbourne Sq. E9 6B 68
Shalcomb St. SW10 6A 100
Shalden Ho. SW15 6B 116
Shaldon Dr. HA4: Ruis 3A 58
SM4: Mord 5G 153
Shaldon Rd. HA8: Edg 2F 43
Shalfleet Dr. W10 7F 81
Shalford Cl. BR6: Farnb 4G 173
Shalford Ct. *N1* 2B 84
(off Charlton Pl.)
Shalford Ho. SE1 3D 102
Shalimar Gdns. W3 7J 79
Shalimar Rd. W3 7J 79
Shallons Rd. SE9 4F 143
Shalstone Rd. SW14 3H 115
Shalston Vs. KT6: Surb 6F 151
Shamrock Ho. *SE26* 4G 139
(off Talisman Sq.)
Shamrock Rd. CR0: C'don 6K 155
Shamrock St. SW4 3H 119
Shamrock Way N14 1A 32
Shandon Rd. SW4 6G 119
Shand St. SE1 6H 15 (2E 102)
Shandy St. E1 5K 85
Shan Ho. WC1 4G 7
Shanklin Ho. E17 2B 50
Shanklin Rd. N8 5H 47
N15 4G 49
Shannon Cl. NW2 3F 63
UB2: S'hall 5B 94
Shannon Commercial Cen.
KT3: N Mald 4C 152
SHANNON CORNER 4C 152
Shannon Cnr. Retail Pk.
KT3: N Mald 4C 152
Shannon Ct. *CR0: C'don* 1C 168
(off Tavistock Rd.)
N16 3E 66
SE15 7F 103
(off Garnies Cl.)
Shannon Gro. SW9 4K 119
Shannon M. SE3 4H 123
Shannon Pl. NW8 2C 82
Shannon Way BR3: Beck 6D 140
Shanti Ct. SW18 1J 135
Shap Cres. SM5: Cars 1D 166
Shapland Way N13 5E 32
Shap St. E2 2F 85
Shapwick Cl. N11 5J 31
Shardcroft Av. SE24 5B 120
Shardeloes Rd. SE14 2B 122
Shard's Sq. SE15 6G 103
Sharland Cl. CR7: Thor H 6A 156
Sharman Ct. *DA14: Sidc* 4A 144
(off Carlton Rd.)
Sharnbrooke Cl. DA16: Well 3C 126
Sharnbrook Ho. W14 6J 99
Sharon Cl. KT6: Surb 1C 162
Sharon Ct. *CR2: S Croy* 5C 168
(off Warham Rd.)
Sharon Gdns. E9 1J 85
Sharon Rd. EN3: Enf H 2F 25
W4 5K 97
Sharpe Cl. W7 5K 77
Sharp Ho. SW8 3F 119
TW1: Twick 6D 114
Sharpleshall St. NW1 7D 64
Sharpness Cl. UB4: Yead 5C 76
Sharpness Ct. *SE15* 7F 103
(off Daniel Gdns.)
Sharp's La. HA4: Ruis 7F 39
Sharratt St. SE15 6J 103
Sharsted St. SE17 5B 102
Sharvel La. UB5: N'olt 1J 75
Sharwood *WC1* 1H 7
(off Penton Ri.)
Shaver's Pl. SW1 3C 12
Shaw Av. IG11: Bark 2E 90
Shawbrooke Rd. SE9 5A 124
Shawbury Cl. NW9 1A 44
Shawbury Rd. SE22 5F 121
Shaw Cl. SE28 1B 108
WD23: B Hea 2D 26
Shaw Ct. SM4: Mord 7A 154
W3 3J 97
(off All Saints Rd.)
Shaw Cres. E14 6A 86
Shaw Dr. KT12: Walt T 7A 148
Shawfield Ct. UB7: W Dray 3A 92
Shawfield Pk. BR1: Brom 2B 160
Shawfield St. SW3 6D 16 (5C 100)
Shawford Ct. SW15 7C 116
Shawford Rd. KT19: Ewe 6K 163
Shaw Gdns. IG11: Bark 2E 90
Shaw Ho. DA17: Belv 5F 109
E16 1E 106
(off Claremont St.)
Shaw Path BR1: Brom 3H 141
Shaw Rd. BR1: Brom 3H 141
EN3: Enf H 1E 24
SE22 4E 120
Shaws Cotts. SE23 3A 140
Shaws Path *KT1: Ham W* 1C 150
(off Bennett Cl.)
Shaw Sq. E17 1A 50
Shaw Theatre 2D 6 (3H 83)
Shaw Way SM6: Wall 7J 167
Shearing Dr. SM5: Cars 7A 154
Shearling Way N7 6J 65
Shearman Rd. SE3 4H 123
SHEARS, THE 7G 129
Shears Ct. TW16: Sun 7G 129
Shears Way TW16: Sun 1G 147
Shearwater Cl. IG11: Bark 3A 90
Shearwater Ct. *E1* 3K 15
(off Star Pl.)
SE8 6B 104
(off Abinger Gro.)
Shearwater Rd. SM1: Sutt 5H 165
Shearwater Way UB4: Yead 6B 76
Sheath Cotts. *KT7: T Ditt* 6B 150
(off Ferry Rd.)
Sheaveshill Av. NW9 4A 44
Sheaveshill Ct. NW9 4K 43
Sheaveshill Pde. *NW9* 4A 44
(off Sheaveshill Av.)
Sheba Ct. *N17* 6B 34
(off Altair Cl.)
Sheba Pl. E1 4K 9 (4F 85)
Sheen Comn. Dr. TW10: Rich 4G 115
Sheen Ct. TW10: Rich 4G 115
Sheen Ct. Rd. TW10: Rich 4G 115
Sheendale Rd. TW9: Rich 4F 115
Sheenewood SE26 4H 139
Sheen Ga. Gdns. SW14 4J 115
Sheengate Mans. SW14 4K 115
Sheen Gro. N1 1A 84
Sheen La. SW14 5J 115
Sheen Pk. TW9: Rich 4F 115
Sheen Rd. BR5: St M Cry 4K 161
TW9: Rich 5E 114
TW10: Rich 5E 114
Sheen Sports & Fitness Cen. 4A 116
Sheen Way SM6: Wall 5K 167
Sheen Wood SW14 5J 115
Sheepcote Cl. TW5: Cran 7J 93
Sheepcote La. SW11 2D 118
Sheepcote Rd. HA1: Harr 6K 41
Sheepcotes Rd. RM6: Chad H 4E 54
Sheephouse Way KT3: N Mald 1K 163
Sheep La. E8 1H 85
Sheep Wlk. TW17: Shep 7B 146
Sheep Wlk. M. SW19 6F 135
Sheerness M. E16 2F 107
Sheerwater Rd. E16 5B 88
Sheffield Rd.
TW6: H'row A 6E 110
Sheffield Sq. E3 3B 86
Sheffield St. WC2 1G 13 (6K 83)
Sheffield Ter. W8 1J 99
Sheffield Way TW6: H'row A 5F 111
Shelbourne Cl. HA5: Pinn 3D 40
Shelbourne Pl. BR3: Beck 7B 140
Shelbourne Rd. N17 2H 49
Shelburne Dr. TW4: Houn 6E 112
Shelburne Rd. N7 4K 65
Shelbury Cl. DA14: Sidc 3A 144
Shelbury Rd. SE22 5H 121
Sheldon Av. IG5: Ilf 2F 53
N6 7C 46
Sheldon Cl. SE12 5K 123
SE20 1H 157
Sheldon Ct. EN5: New Bar 4E 20
RM7: Rush G 6K 55
(off Union Rd.)
SW8 7J 101
(off Lansdowne Grn.)
Sheldon Ho. *N1* 1E 84
(off Kingsland Rd.)
Sheldon Pl. E2 2G 85
(not continuous)
Sheldon Rd. DA7: Bex 1F 127
N18 4K 33
NW2 4F 63
RM9: Dag 7E 72
Sheldon Sq. W2 6A 4 (5A 82)
Sheldon St. CR0: C'don 3C 168
Sheldrake Cl. E16 1D 106
Sheldrake Ct. *E6* 2C 88
(off St Bartholomew's Rd.)
Sheldrake Ho. *SE16* 4K 103
(off Tawny Way)
Sheldrake Pl. W8 2J 99
Sheldrick Cl. SW19 2B 154
Shelduck Cl. E15 5H 69
Shelduck Ct. *SE8* 6B 104
(off Pilot Cl.)
Sheldwich Ter. BR2: Brom 6C 160
Shelford KT1: King T 2G 151
Shelford Pl. N16 3D 66
Shelford Ri. SE19 7F 139
Shelford Rd. EN5: Barn 6A 20
Shelgate Rd. SW11 5C 118
Shell Cl. BR2: Brom 6C 160
Shellduck Cl. NW9 2A 44
Shelley *N8* 3J 47
(off Boyton Rd.)
Shelley Av. E12 6C 70
UB6: G'frd 3H 77
Shelley Cl. BR6: Orp 3J 173
HA8: Edg 4B 28
SE15 2H 121
UB4: Hayes 5J 75
UB6: G'frd 3H 77
Shelley Ct. *E10* 7D 50
(off Skelton's La.)
E11 4K 51
(off Makepeace Rd.)
N19 1K 65
SW3 7F 17
(off Tite St.)
Shelley Cres. TW5: Hest 1B 112
UB1: S'hall 6D 76
Shelley Dr. DA16: Well 1J 125
Shelley Gdns. HA0: Wemb 2C 60
Shelley Ho. *E2* 3J 85
(off Cornwall Av.)
N16 4E 66
SE17 5C 102
(off Browning St.)
SW1 7B 18
(off Churchill Gdns.)
Shelley Lodge
EN2: Enf 1J 23
Shelley Rd. NW10 1K 79
Shelley Way SW19 5B 136
Shellness Rd. E5 5H 67
Shell Rd. SE13 3D 122
Shellwood Rd. SW11 2D 118
Shelmerdine Cl. E3 5C 86
Shelson Av. TW13: Felt 3H 129
Shelton Rd. SW19 1J 153
Shelton St. WC2 1E 12 (6J 83)
(not continuous)
Shene Ho. *EC1* 5J 7
(off Bourne Est.)
Shenfield Ho. *SE18* 1B 124
(off Portway Gdns.)
Shenfield Rd. IG8: Wfd G 7E 36
Shenfield St. N1 1H 9 (2E 84)
(not continuous)
Shenley Av. HA4: Ruis 2H 57

Shenley Rd. SE5 . . . 1E 120
TW5: Hest . . . 1C 112
Shenstone W13 . . . 1C 96
Shenstone Cl. DA1: Cray . . . 4K 127
Shenstone Ho. SW16 . . . 5G 137
Shepherd Cl. TW13: Hanw . . . 4C 130
Shepherdess Pl. N1 . . . 1D 8 (3C 84)
Shepherdess Wlk. N1 . . . 1D 8 (2C 84)
Shepherd Ho. E14 . . . 6D 86
(off Annabel Cl.)
E16 . . . 7F 89
(off University Way)
Shepherd Mkt. W1 . . . 4J 11 (1F 101)
SHEPHERD'S BUSH . . . 2E 98
Shepherds Bush Empire Theatre . . . 2E 98
Shepherd's Bush Grn. W12 . . . 2E 98
Shepherd's Bush Mkt. W12 . . . 2E 98
(not continuous)
Shepherd's Bush Pl. W12 . . . 2F 99
Shepherd's Bush Rd. W6 . . . 4E 98
Shepherds Cl. BR6: Orp . . . 3K 173
HA7: Stan . . . 5F 27
(not continuous)
N6 . . . 6F 47
RM6: Chad H . . . 5D 54
TW17: Shep . . . 6D 146
W1 . . . 2G 11
(off Lees Pl.)
Shepherds Ct. W12 . . . 2F 99
(off Shepherd's Bush Grn.)
Shepherds Grn. BR7: Chst . . . 7H 143
Shepherd's Hill N6 . . . 6F 47
Shepherds La. E9 . . . 6K 67
Shepherds Leas SE9 . . . 4G 125
Shepherds Ley SE28 . . . 1J 107
Shepherds Path NW3 . . . 5B 64
(off Lyndhurst Rd.)
UB5: N'olt . . . 6C 58
(off Arnold Rd.)
Shepherds Pl. W1 . . . 2G 11 (7E 82)
Shepherd St. W1 . . . 5J 11 (1F 101)
Shepherds Wlk. NW2 . . . 2C 62
NW3 . . . 5B 64
(not continuous)
WD23: B Hea . . . 2C 26
Shepherds Way CR2: Sels . . . 7K 169
Shepiston La. UB3: Harl . . . 4D 92
Shepley Cl. SM5: Cars . . . 3E 166
Sheppard Cl. EN1: Enf . . . 1C 24
KT1: King T . . . 4E 150
Sheppard Dr. SE16 . . . 5H 103
Sheppard Ho. E2 . . . 2G 85
(off Warner Pl.)
SW2 . . . 1A 138
Sheppards Coll. BR1: Brom . . . 1J 159
(off London Rd.)
Sheppard St. E16 . . . 4H 87
SHEPPERTON . . . 6D 146
Shepperton Bus. Pk. TW17: Shep . . . 5E 146
Shepperton Ct. TW17: Shep . . . 6D 146
Shepperton Ct. Dr. TW17: Shep . . . 5D 146
Shepperton Film Studios . . . 3B 146
SHEPPERTON GREEN . . . 4C 146
Shepperton Rd. BR5: Pet W . . . 6G 161
N1 . . . 1C 84
TW18: Lale, Shep . . . 4A 146
Sheppey Gdns. RM9: Dag . . . 7C 72
Sheppey Rd. RM9: Dag . . . 7B 72
Shepton Ho's. E2 . . . 3J 85
(off Welwyn St.)
Sherard Ct. N7 . . . 3J 65
Sherard Ho. E9 . . . 7J 67
(off Frampton Pk. Rd.)
Sherard Rd. SE9 . . . 5C 124
Sheraton Bus. Cen. UB6: G'frd . . . 2B 78
Sheraton Ho. SW1 . . . 7K 17
(off Churchill Gdns.)
Sheraton St. W1 . . . 1C 12 (6H 83)
Sherborne NW1 . . . 7H 65
(off Agar Gro.)
Sherborne Av. EN3: Enf H . . . 2D 24
UB2: S'hall . . . 4E 94
Sherborne Cl. SL3: Poyle . . . 4A 174
UB4: Yead . . . 6A 76
Sherborne Cres. SM5: Cars . . . 7C 154
Sherborne Gdns. NW9 . . . 3G 43
TW17: Shep . . . 7G 147
W13 . . . 5B 78
Sherborne Ho. SW1 . . . 5K 17
(off Winchester St.)
SW8 . . . 7K 101
(off Bolney St.)
Sherborne La. EC4 . . . 2E 14 (7D 84)
Sherborne Rd.
BR5: St M Cry . . . 4K 161
KT9: Chess . . . 5E 162
SM3: Sutt . . . 2J 165
TW14: Bedf . . . 1F 129
(not continuous)
Sherborne St. N1 . . . 1D 84
Sherboro Rd. N15 . . . 6F 49
Sherbourne Ct. SM2: Sutt . . . 6A 166
SW5 . . . 4K 99
(off Cromwell Rd.)
Sherbourne Pl. HA7: Stan . . . 6F 27
Sherbrooke Cl. DA6: Bex . . . 4G 127
Sherbrooke Ho. E2 . . . 2J 85
(off Bonner Rd.)
SW1 . . . 3H 101
(off Monck St.)
Sherbrooke Rd. SW6 . . . 7G 99
Sherbrooke Ter. SW6 . . . 7G 99
(off Sherbrook Rd.)
Sherbrooke Way KT4: Wor Pk . . . 7D 152
Sherbrook Gdns. N21 . . . 7G 23
Shere Cl. KT9: Chess . . . 5D 162
Sheredan Rd. E4 . . . 5A 36
Shere Ho. SE1 . . . 7E 14
Shere Rd. IG2: Ilf . . . 5E 52
Sherfield Cl. KT3: N Mald . . . 4H 151
Sherfield Gdns. SW15 . . . 6B 116
Sheridan Bldgs. WC2 . . . 1F 13
(off Martlett Ct.)
Sheridan Cl. UB10: Hil . . . 4E 74
Sheridan Ct. CR0: C'don . . . 4E 168
(off Coombe Rd.)
HA1: Harr . . . 6H 41
NW6 . . . 7A 64
(off Belsize Rd.)
SW5 . . . 4K 99
(off Barkston Gdns.)
TW4: Houn . . . 5C 112
UB5: N'olt . . . 5F 59
W7 . . . 7K 77
(off Milton Rd.)
Sheridan Cres. BR7: Chst . . . 2F 161
Sheridan Gdns. HA3: Kent . . . 6D 42
Sheridan Ho. E1 . . . 6J 85
(off Tarling St.)
SE11 . . . 4K 19
(off Wincott St.)
Sheridan Lodge BR2: Brom . . . 4A 160
(off Homesdale Rd.)
Sheridan M. E11 . . . 6K 51
Sheridan Pl. BR1: Brom . . . 2B 160
SW13 . . . 3B 116
Sheridan Rd. DA7: Bex . . . 3E 126
DA17: Belv . . . 4G 109
E7 . . . 3H 69
E12 . . . 5C 70
SW19 . . . 1H 153
TW10: Ham . . . 3C 132
Sheridan St. E1 . . . 6H 85
Sheridan Ter. UB5: N'olt . . . 5F 59
Sheridan Wlk. NW11 . . . 6J 45
SM5: Cars . . . 5D 166
Sheridan Way BR3: Beck . . . 1B 158
Sheriden Pl. HA1: Harr . . . 7J 41
TW12: Hamp . . . 1F 149
Sheringham NW8 . . . 1B 82
Sheringham Av. E12 . . . 4D 70
N14 . . . 5C 22
RM7: Rom . . . 6J 55
TW2: Whitt . . . 1D 130
TW13: Felt . . . 3J 129
Sheringham Ct. TW13: Felt . . . 3J 129
(off Sheringham Av.)
UB3: Hayes . . . 2H 93
Sheringham Dr. IG11: Bark . . . 5K 71
Sheringham Ho. NW1 . . . 5C 4
Sheringham Rd. N7 . . . 6K 65
SE20 . . . 3J 157
Sheringham Twr. UB1: S'hall . . . 7F 77
Sherington Av. HA5: Hat E . . . 7A 26
Sherington Rd. SE7 . . . 6K 105
Sherland Rd. TW1: Twick . . . 1K 131
Sherleys Ct. HA4: Ruis . . . 2G 57
Sherlies Av. BR6: Orp . . . 2J 173
Sherlock Ct. NW8 . . . 1B 82
(off Dorman Way)
Sherlock Holmes Mus. . . . 4F 5
Sherlock M. W1 . . . 5G 5 (5E 82)
Sherman Gdns. RM6: Chad H . . . 6C 54
Sherman Ho. E14 . . . 6E 86
(off Dee St.)
Sherman Rd. BR1: Brom . . . 1J 159
Shernhall St. E17 . . . 3E 50
Sherrard Rd. E7 . . . 6A 70
E12 . . . 6A 70
Sherrards Way EN5: Barn . . . 5D 20
Sherren Ho. E1 . . . 4J 85
Sherrick Grn. Rd. NW10 . . . 5D 62
Sherriff Ct. NW6 . . . 6J 63
(off Sherriff Rd.)
Sherriff Rd. NW6 . . . 6J 63
Sherringham Av. N17 . . . 2G 49
Sherrin Rd. E10 . . . 4D 68
Sherrock Gdns. NW4 . . . 4D 44
Sherry M. IG11: Bark . . . 7H 71
Sherston Ct. SE1 . . . 4B 102
(off Newington Butts)
WC1 . . . 2J 7
Sherwin Ho. SE11 . . . 7J 19
Sherwin Rd. SE14 . . . 1K 121
Sherwood KT6: Surb . . . 2D 162
NW6 . . . 7G 63
Sherwood Av. E18 . . . 3K 51
HA4: Ruis . . . 6G 39
SW16 . . . 7H 137
UB4: Yead . . . 4K 75
UB6: G'frd . . . 6J 59
Sherwood Cl. DA5: Bexl . . . 6C 126
E17 . . . 2B 50
SW13 . . . 3D 116
W13 . . . 1B 96
Sherwood Ct. CR2: S Croy . . . 5C 168
(off Nottingham Rd.)
HA2: Harr . . . 2F 59
SW11 . . . 3A 118
W1 . . . 6E 4
(off Bryanston Pl.)
Sherwood Gdns. E14 . . . 4C 104
IG11: Bark . . . 7H 71
SE16 . . . 5G 103
Sherwood Pk. Av. DA15: Sidc . . . 7A 126
Sherwood Pk. Rd. CR4: Mitc . . . 4G 155
SM1: Sutt . . . 5J 165
Sherwood Rd.
CR0: C'don . . . 7H 157
DA16: Well . . . 2J 125
HA2: Harr . . . 2G 59
IG6: Ilf . . . 4H 53
NW4 . . . 3E 44
SW19 . . . 7H 135
TW12: Ham H . . . 5G 131
Sherwood St. N20 . . . 3G 31
W1 . . . 2B 12 (7G 83)
Sherwood Ter. N20 . . . 3G 31
Sherwood Way
BR4: W W'ck . . . 2E 170
Shetland Rd. E3 . . . 2B 86
TW6: H'row A . . . 6E 110
Shield Dr. TW8: Bford . . . 6A 96
Shieldhall St. SE2 . . . 4C 108
Shield Rd. TW15: Ashf . . . 4E 128
Shifford Path SE23 . . . 3K 139
Shillaker Ct. W3 . . . 1B 98
Shillibeer Pl. W1 . . . 6D 4
Shillingford Cl. NW7 . . . 7A 30
Shillingford St. N1 . . . 7B 66
Shilling Pl. W7 . . . 2A 96
Shillingstone Ho. W14 . . . 3G 99
(off Russell Rd.)
Shinfield St. W12 . . . 6E 80
Shinglewell Rd. DA8: Erith . . . 7G 109
Shinners Cl. SE25 . . . 5G 157
Ship All. W4 . . . 6G 97
Ship & Mermaid Row
SE1 . . . 6F 15 (2D 102)
Shipka Rd. SW12 . . . 1F 137
Shiplake Ho. E2 . . . 2J 9
(off Arnold Cir.)
Ship La. SW14 . . . 3J 115
Shipman Rd. E16 . . . 6K 87
SE23 . . . 2K 139
Ship St. SE8 . . . 1C 122
Ship Tavern Pas. EC3 . . . 2G 15 (7E 84)
Shipton Cl. RM8: Dag . . . 3D 72
Shipton Ho. E2 . . . 1K 9
(off Shipton St.)
Shipton Rd. UB10: Ick . . . 4B 56
Shipton St. E2 . . . 1K 9 (2F 85)
Shipwright Rd. SE16 . . . 2A 104
Shipwright Yd. SE1 . . . 5G 15 (1E 102)
Ship Yd. E14 . . . 5D 104
Shirburn Cl. SE23 . . . 7J 121
Shirebrook Rd. SE3 . . . 3B 124
Shire Ct. DA18: Erith . . . 3D 108
KT17: Ewe . . . 7B 164
Shirehall Cl. NW4 . . . 6F 45
Shirehall Gdns. NW4 . . . 6F 45
Shirehall La. NW4 . . . 6F 45
Shirehall Pk. NW4 . . . 5F 45
Shire Horse Way TW7: Isle . . . 3K 113
Shire La. BR2: Kes . . . 7C 172
BR6: Chels, Downe . . . 7F 173
(not continuous)
Shire M. TW2: Whitt . . . 6G 113
Shire Pl. SW18 . . . 7A 118
TW8: Bford . . . 7D 96
Shires, The TW10: Ham . . . 4E 132
Shirland M. W9 . . . 3H 81
Shirland Rd. W9 . . . 3H 81
Shirlbutt St. E14 . . . 7D 86
SHIRLEY . . . 2J 169
Shirley Av. CR0: C'don . . . 1J 169
DA5: Bexl . . . 7D 126
SM1: Sutt . . . 4B 166
Shirley Chu. Rd. CR0: C'don . . . 3K 169
Shirley Cl. TW3: Houn . . . 5G 113
Shirley Ct. SW16 . . . 7J 137
Shirley Cres. BR3: Beck . . . 4A 158
Shirley Dr. TW3: Houn . . . 5G 113
Shirley Gdns. IG11: Bark . . . 6J 71
W7 . . . 1K 95
Shirley Gro. N9 . . . 7D 24
SW11 . . . 3E 118
Shirley Hgts. SM6: Wall . . . 7G 167
Shirley Hills Rd. CR0: C'don . . . 5J 169
Shirley Ho. SE5 . . . 7D 102
(off Picton St.)
Shirley Ho. Dr. SE7 . . . 7A 106
SHIRLEY OAKS . . . 1K 169
Shirley Oaks Rd. CR0: C'don . . . 1K 169
Shirley Pk. CR0: C'don . . . 2J 169
Shirley Pk. Rd. CR0: C'don . . . 1H 169
Shirley Rd. CR0: C'don . . . 7H 157
DA15: Sidc . . . 3J 143
E15 . . . 7G 69
EN2: Enf . . . 3H 23

Shirley Rd. SM6: Wall 7G 167
W4 2K 97
Shirleys Cl. E17 5D 50
Shirley St. E16 6H 87
Shirley Way CR0: C'don 3A 170
Shirley Windmill 3J 169
Shirlock Rd. NW3 4D 64
Shirwell Cl. NW7 7A 30
Shobden Rd. N17 1D 48
Shobroke Cl. NW2 3E 62
Shoebury Rd. E6 7D 70
Shoelands Ct. NW9 3K 43
Shoe La. EC4 7K 7 (6A 84)
Sholto Rd. TW6: H'row A 5B 110
Shona Ho. E13 5A 88
Shooters Av. HA3: Kent 4C 42
SHOOTERS HILL 1E 124
Shooters Hill DA16: Well 1D 124
SE18 1D 124
Shooters Hill Rd. SE3 1F 123
SE10 1F 123
SE18 1F 123
Shooters Rd. EN2: Enf 1G 23
Shoot Up Hill NW2 5G 63
Shopping Hall, The E6 1C 88
Shore Bus. Cen. E9 7J 67
Shore Cl. TW12: Hamp 6C 130
TW14: Felt 7J 111
Shorediche Cl. UB10: Ick 3B 56
SHOREDITCH 1G 9 (3E 84)
Shoreditch Ct. *E8* 7F 67
(off Queensbridge Rd.)
Shoreditch High St. E1 4H 9 (4E 84)
Shoreditch Ho. EC1 2F 9
Shore Gro. TW13: Hanw 2D 130
Shoreham Cl. CR0: C'don 6J 157
DA5: Bexl 1D 144
SW18 5K 117
Shoreham Rd. E. TW6: H'row A 5A 110
Shoreham Rd. W. TW6: H'row A 5A 110
Shoreham Way BR2: Hayes 6J 159
Shore Ho. SW8 3F 119
Shore M. *E9* 7J 67
(off Shore Rd.)
Shore Pl. E9 7J 67
Shore Point IG9: Buck H 2E 36
Shore Rd. E9 7J 67
Shore Way *SW9* 2A 120
(off Crowhurst Cl.)
Shorncliffe Rd. SE1 5F 103
Shorndean St. SE6 1E 140
Shorne Cl. DA15: Sidc 6B 126
Shornefield Cl. BR1: Brom 3E 160
Shornells Way SE2 4C 108
Shorrold's Rd. SW6 7H 99
Shortcroft Rd. KT17: Ewe 7B 164
Shortcrofts Rd. RM9: Dag 6F 73
Shorter St. E1 2K 15 (7F 85)
Shortgate N12 4C 30
Short Hedges TW3: Houn 1E 112
Short Hill HA1: Harr 1J 59
SHORTLANDS 2G 159
Shortlands UB3: Harl 6F 93
W6 4F 99
Shortlands Cl. DA17: Belv 3F 109
N18 3J 33
Shortlands Gdns.
BR2: Brom 2G 159
Shortlands Gro. BR2: Brom 3F 159
Shortlands Rd. BR2: Brom 3F 159
E10 7D 50
KT2: King T 7F 133
Short La. TW19: Stanw 7B 110
Short Path SE18 6F 107
Short Rd. E11 2G 69
TW6: H'row A 6A 110
W4 6A 98
Shorts Cft. NW9 4H 43
Shorts Gdns. WC2 1E 12 (6J 83)
Shorts Rd. SM5: Cars 4C 166
Short St. *NW4* 4E 44
(off Foster St.)
SE1 6K 13 (2A 102)
Short Wall E15 3E 86
Short Way N12 6H 31
SE9 3C 124
TW2: Whitt 7G 113
Shotfield SM6: Wall 6F 167
Shott Cl. SM1: Sutt 5A 166
Shottendane Rd. SW6 1J 117
Shottery Cl. SE9 3C 142
Shottfield Av. SW14 4A 116
Shottsford *W2* 6J 81
(off Talbot Rd.)
Shoulder of Mutton All. E14 7A 86
Shouldham St. W1 6D 4 (5C 82)
Showcase Cinema
Barking 3H 89
Wood Green 2A 48
Showers Way UB3: Hayes 1J 93
Shrapnel Cl. SE18 7C 106
Shrapnel Rd. SE9 3D 124
Shrewsbury Av. HA3: Kent 4E 42
SW14 4J 115
Shrewsbury Cl. KT6: Surb 2E 162
Shrewsbury Ct. EC1 4D 8
Shrewsbury Cres. NW10 1K 79
Shrewsbury Ho. SW3 7C 16
SW8 7H 19
Shrewsbury La. SE18 1F 125
Shrewsbury M. *W2* 5J 81
(off Chepstow Rd.)
Shrewsbury Rd. BR3: Beck 3A 158
E7 5B 70
N11 6B 32
SM5: Cars 6C 154
TW6: H'row A 6E 110
(not continuous)
W2 6J 81
Shrewsbury St. W10 4E 80
Shrewsbury Wlk. TW7: Isle 3A 114
Shrewton Rd. SW17 7D 136
Shroffold Rd. BR1: Brom 4G 141
Shropshire Cl. CR4: Mitc 4J 155
Shropshire Ct. *W7* 6K 77
(off Copley Cl.)
Shropshire Ho. *N18* 5C 34
(off Cavendish Cl.)
Shropshire Pl. WC1 4C 6 (4G 83)
Shropshire Rd. N22 7E 32
Shroton St. NW1 5D 4 (5C 82)
Shrubberies, The E18 2J 51
Shrubbery, The E11 5K 51
KT6: Surb 1E 162
Shrubbery Cl. N1 1C 84
Shrubbery Gdns. N21 7G 23
Shrubbery Rd. N9 3B 34
SW16 4J 137
UB1: S'hall 1D 94
Shrubland Cl. N20 1G 31
Shrubland Gro. KT4: Wor Pk 3E 164
Shrubland Rd. E8 1F 85
E10 7C 50
E17 5C 50
Shrublands Av. CR0: C'don 3C 170
Shrublands Cl. SE26 3J 139
Shrubsall Cl. SE9 1C 142
Shuna Wlk. N1 6D 66
Shurland Av. EN4: E Barn 6G 21
Shurland Gdns. SE15 7F 103
Shurlock Dr. BR6: Farnb 4G 173
Shuters Sq. W14 5H 99
Shuttle Cl. DA15: Sidc 7K 125
Shuttlemead DA5: Bexl 7F 127
Shuttle St. E1 4G 85
Shuttleworth Rd.
SW11 2C 118
Siamese M. N3 1J 45
Siani M. N8 4B 48
Sibella Rd. SW4 2H 119
Sibley Cl. BR1: Brom 5C 160
DA6: Bex 5E 126
Sibley Ct. BR2: Brom 2F 159
UB8: Hil 5E 74
Sibley Gro. E12 7C 70
Sibthorpe Rd. SE12 6K 123
Sibthorp Rd. CR4: Mitc 2D 154
Sibton Rd. SM5: Cars 7C 154
Sicilian Av. WC1 6F 7
Sickle Cnr. RM9: Dag 4H 91
Sidbury St. SW6 1G 117
SIDCUP 4A 144
Sidcup By-Pass
BR5: Sidc, St P, Swan 6A 144
BR7: Chst, Sidc 3H 143
DA14: Sidc 6A 144
Sidcup High St. DA14: Sidc 4A 144
Sidcup Hill DA14: Sidc 4B 144
Sidcup Hill Gdns. DA14: Sidc 5C 144
Sidcup Place 5A 144
Sidcup Pl. DA14: Sidc 5A 144
Sidcup Rd. SE9 1D 142
SE12 6A 124
Sidcup Technical Cen.
DA14: Sidc 5D 144
Siddeley Dr. TW4: Houn 3C 112
Siddeley Rd. E17 2E 50
Siddons La. NW1 4F 5 (4D 82)
Siddons Rd. CR0: Wadd 3A 168
N17 1G 49
SE23 2A 140
Side Rd. E17 5B 50
Sidewood Rd. SE9 1H 143
Sidford Ho. SE1 2H 19
Sidford Pl. SE1 2H 19 (3A 102)
Sidgwick Ho. *SW9* 2K 119
(off Lingham St.)
Sidi Ct. N15 3B 48
Sidings, The E11 1E 68
Sidings M. N7 3A 66
Sidlaw Ho. N16 1F 67
Sidmouth Av. TW7: Isle 2J 113
Sidmouth Dr. HA4: Ruis 3J 57
Sidmouth Ho. *SE15* 7G 103
(off Lympstone Gdns.)
W1 7D 4
(off Cato St.)
Sidmouth Pde. NW2 7E 62
Sidmouth Rd. DA16: Well 7C 108
E10 3E 68
NW2 7E 62
Sidmouth St. WC1 2F 7 (3K 83)
Sidney Av. N13 5E 32
Sidney Boyd Ct. NW6 7J 63
Sidney Elson Way E6 2E 88
Sidney Est. E1 6J 85
(Bromhead St.)
E1 5J 85
(Lindley St.)
Sidney Gdns. TW8: Bford 6D 96
Sidney Godley (VC) Ho. *E2* 3J 85
(off Digby St.)
Sidney Gro. EC1 1A 8 (2B 84)
Sidney Ho. *E2* 2K 85
(off Old Ford Rd.)
Sidney Miller Ct. *W3* 1H 97
(off Crown St.)
Sidney Rd. BR3: Beck 2A 158
E7 3J 69
HA2: Harr 3G 41
KT12: Walt T 7J 147
N22 7E 32
SE25 5G 157
SW9 2K 119
TW1: Twick 6A 114
Sidney Sq. E1 5J 85
Sidney St. E1 5H 85
(not continuous)
Sidney Webb Ho. *SE1* 3D 102
(off Gt. Dover St.)
Sidworth St. E8 7H 67
Siebert Rd. SE3 6J 105
Siege Ho. *E1* 6H 85
(off Sidney St.)
Siemens Rd. SE18 3B 106
Sienna SE28 3A 108
Sienna Cl. KT9: Chess 6D 162
Sienna Ter. NW2 2C 62
Sierra Dr. RM9: Dag 2H 91
Sigdon Pas. E8 5G 67
Sigdon Rd. E8 5G 67
Sigers, The HA5: Eastc 6K 39
Sigmund Freud Statue 6B 64
Signal Ho. *E8* 7H 67
(off Martello Ter.)
Signmakers Yd. *NW1* 1F 83
(off Delancey St.)
Sigrist Sq. KT2: King T 1E 150
Silbury Av. CR4: Mitc 1C 154
Silbury Ho. SE26 3G 139
Silbury St. N1 1E 8 (3D 84)
Silchester Ct. CR7: Thor H 4A 156
TW15: Ashf 2A 128
Silchester Rd. W10 6F 81
Silecroft Rd. DA7: Bex 1G 127
Silesia Bldgs. E8 7H 67
Silex St. SE1 7B 14 (2B 102)
Silk Cl. SE12 5J 123
Silk Ct. *E2* 3G 85
(off Squirries St.)
Silkfield Rd. NW9 5A 44
Silk Ho. NW9 3K 43
Silk Mills Pas. SE13 2D 122
Silk Mills Path SE13 2D 122
(not continuous)
Silk Mills Sq. E9 6B 68
Silks Ct. E11 1H 69
Silkstream Pde. HA8: Edg 1J 43
Silkstream Rd. HA8: Edg 1J 43
Silk St. EC2 5D 8 (5C 84)
Sillitoe Ho. *N1* 1D 84
(off Colville Est.)
Silsoe Ho. NW1 2F 83
Silsoe Rd. N22 2K 47
Silverbeck Way TW19: Stan M 7B 174
Silver Birch Av. E4 5G 35
Silver Birch Cl. DA2: Dart 4K 145
SE6 3B 140
SE28 1A 108
UB10: Ick 4A 56
Silverbirch Cl. N11 6K 31
Silver Birch Gdns. E6 4D 88
Silverbirch Wlk. NW5 6E 64
Silverburn Ho. *SW9* 1B 120
(off Lothian Rd.)
Silvercliffe Gdns. EN4: E Barn 4H 21
Silver Cl. HA3: Hrw W 7C 26
SE14 7A 104
Silver Cres. W4 4H 97
Silverdale EN2: Enf 4D 22
NW1 1A 6
(off Hampstead Rd.)
SE26 4J 139
Silverdale Av. IG2: Ilf 5J 53
Silverdale Cen., The HA0: Wemb 1F 79
Silverdale Cl. SM1: Sutt 4H 165
UB5: N'olt 5D 58
W7 1J 95
Silverdale Ct. EC1 3B 8
Silverdale Dr. SE9 2C 142
TW16: Sun 2K 147
Silverdale Factory Cen.
UB3: Hayes 3J 93
Silverdale Gdns. UB3: Hayes 2J 93
Silverdale Ind. Est.
UB3: Hayes 2J 93
Silverdale Rd. BR5: Pet W 4G 161
DA7: Bex 2H 127
E4 6A 36
UB3: Hayes 2H 93

Silverdene N12 6E 30
(off Thyra Gro.)
Silvergate KT19: Ewe 5J 163
Silverhall St. TW7: Isle 3A 114
Silverholme Cl. HA3: Kent 7E 42
Silver Jubilee Way TW4: Cran 2K 111
Silverland St. E16 1D 106
Silver La. BR4: W W'ck 2F 171
Silverleigh Rd. CR7: Thor H 4K 155
Silvermead E18 1J 51
Silvermere Dr. N18 6E 34
Silvermere Rd. SE6 7D 122
Silver Pl. W1 2B 12 (6G 83)
Silver Rd. SE13 3D 122
W12 7F 81
Silvers IG9: Buck H 1F 37
(off Palmerston Rd.)
Silver Spring Cl. DA8: Erith 6H 109
Silverston Way HA7: Stan 6H 27
Silver St. EN1: Enf 3J 23
N18 4J 33
Silverthorn NW8 1K 81
(off Abbey Rd.)
Silverthorne Loft SE17 6D 102
(off Albany Rd.)
Silverthorne Rd. SW8 2F 119
Silverthorn Gdns. E4 2H 35
Silverton Rd. W6 6F 99
SILVERTOWN 1A 106
Silvertown Viaduct E16 6H 87
Silvertown Way E16 6G 87
(not continuous)
Silvertree La. UB6: G'frd 3H 77
Silver Wlk. SE16 1A 104
Silver Way RM7: Mawney 3H 55
UB10: Hil 2D 74
Silver Wing Ind. Est. CR0: Wadd 6K 167
Silverwood Cl. BR3: Beck 7C 140
CR0: Sels 7B 170
HA6: Nwood 1E 38
Silvester Ho. E1 6H 85
(off Varden St.)
E2 3J 85
(off Sceptre Rd.)
W11 6H 81
(off Basing St.)
Silvester Rd. SE22 5F 121
Silvester St. SE1 7E 14 (2D 102)
Silvocea Way E14 6F 87
Silwood Est. SE16 4J 103
Silwood St. SE16 4J 103
(off Rotherhithe New Rd.)
Simla Ct. N7 7J 65
(off Brewery Rd.)
Simla Ho. SE1 7F 15
(off Kipling Est.)
Simmonds Ct. SW5 4K 99
(off Earl's Ct. Gdns.)
Simmons Cl. KT9: Chess 6C 162
N20 2H 31
Simmons Dr. RM8: Dag 3E 72
Simmons La. E4 2A 36
Simmons Rd. SE18 5F 107
Simmons Way N20 2H 31
Simms Cl. SM5: Cars 2C 166
Simms Gdns. N2 2A 46
Simms Rd. SE1 4G 103
Simnel Rd. SE12 7K 123
Simon Cl. W11 7H 81
Simon Ct. W9 3J 81
(off Saltram Cres.)
Simonds Rd. E10 2C 68
Simone Cl. BR1: Brom 1B 160
Simone Ct. SE26 3J 139
Simon Peter Ct.
EN2: Enf 2G 23
Simons Ct. N16 2F 67
Simons Wlk. E15 5F 69
Simpson Cl. N21 5D 22
Simpson Dr. W3 6K 79
Simpson Ho. NW8 2D 4 (4C 82)
SE11 6G 19 (5K 101)
Simpson Rd. TW4: Houn 6D 112
TW10: Ham 4C 132
Simpsons Rd. BR2: Brom 3J 159
E14 7D 86
Simpson St. SW11 2C 118
Simpson Way KT6: Surb 6C 150
Simrose Ct. SW18 5J 117
Sims Wlk. SE3 4H 123
Sinclair Ct. CR0: C'don 2E 168
Sinclair Dr. SM2: Sutt 7K 165
Sinclair Gdns. W14 2F 99
Sinclair Gro. NW11 6F 45
Sinclair Ho. WC1 2E 6
(off Sandwich St.)
Sinclair Mans. W12 2F 99
(off Richmond Way)
Sinclair Pl. SE4 6C 122
Sinclair Rd. E4 5G 35
W14 2F 99
Sinclare Cl. EN1: Enf 1A 24
Singapore Rd. W13 1A 96
Singer St. EC2 2F 9 (3D 84)
Singleton Cl. CR0: C'don 7C 156
CR4 7D 136
SW17 7D 136
Singleton Rd. RM9: Dag 5F 73
Singleton Scarp N12 5D 30
Sinnott Rd. E17 1K 49
Siobhan Davis Dance Studios 3B 102
(off St George's Rd.)
Sion Ct. TW1: Twick 1B 132
Sion Rd. TW1: Twick 1B 132
Sippets Ct. IG1: Ilf 1H 71
SIPSON 6C 92
Sipson Cl. UB7: Sip 6C 92
Sipson La. UB3: Harl 6C 92
UB7: Sip 6C 92
Sipson Rd. UB7: W Dray, Sip 3B 92
(not continuous)
Sipson Way UB7: Sip 7C 92
Sir Abraham Dawes Cotts.
SW15 4G 117
Sir Alexander Cl. W3 1B 98
Sir Alexander Rd. W3 1B 98
Sir Christopher France Ho. E1 3A 86
Sir Cyril Black Way SW19 7J 135
Sirdar Rd. CR4: Mitc 6E 136
N22 3B 48
W11 7F 81
Sirinham Point SW8 7H 19
Sirius Bldg. E1 7K 85
(off Jardine Rd.)
Sir John Cass Hall E9 7J 67
(off Well St.)
Sir John Kirk Cl. SE5 7C 102
Sir John Lyon Ho. EC4 2C 14
(off High Timber St.)
Sir John Soane's Mus. 7G 7 (6K 83)
Sir Nicholas Garrow Ho. W10 4G 81
(off Kensal Rd.)
Sir Oswald Stoll Foundation, The
SW6 7K 99
(off Fulham Rd.)
Sir Oswald Stoll Mans. SW6 7K 99
(off Fulham Rd.)
Sir William Powell's Almshouses
SW6 2G 117
Sise La. EC4 1E 14 (6D 84)
Siskin Ho. SE16 4K 103
(off Tawny Way)
Sisley Rd. IG11: Bark 1J 89
Sispara Gdns. SW18 6H 117
Sissinghurst Cl. BR1: Brom 5G 141
Sissinghurst Ho. SE15 6J 103
(off Sharratt St.)
Sissinghurst Rd. CR0: C'don 7G 157
Sissulu Ct. E6 1A 88
Sister Mabel's Way SE15 7G 103
Sisters Av. SW11 3D 118
Sistova Rd. SW12 1F 137
Sisulu Pl. SW9 3A 120
Sitarey Ct. W12 1D 98
Sittingbourne Av. EN1: Enf 6J 23
Sitwell Gro. HA7: Stan 5E 26
Siverst Cl. UB5: N'olt 6F 59
Sivill Ho. E2 1K 9
(off Columbia Rd.)
Siviter Way RM10: Dag 7H 73
Siward Rd. BR2: Brom 3K 159
N17 1D 48
SW17 3A 136
Six Acres Est. N4 2K 65
Six Bridges Ind. Est. SE1 5G 103
Sixpenny Ct. IG11: Bark 6G 71
Sixth Av. E12 4D 70
UB3: Hayes 1H 93
W10 3G 81
Sixth Cross Rd. TW2: Twick 3G 131
Skardu Rd. NW2 5G 63
Skeena Hill SW18 7G 117
Skeffington Rd. E6 1D 88
Skeffington St. SE18 3G 107
Skeggs Ho. E14 3E 104
(off Glengall St.)
Skegness Ho. N7 7K 65
(off Sutterton St.)
Skelbrook St. SW18 2A 136
Skelgill Rd. SW15 4H 117
Skelley Rd. E15 7H 69
Skelton Cl. E8 6F 67
Skelton Rd. E7 6J 69
Skelton's La. E10 7D 50
Skelwith Rd. W6 6E 98
Skenfrith Ho. SE15 6H 103
(off Commercial Way)
Skerne Rd. KT2: King T 1D 150
Skerne Wlk. KT2: King T 1D 150
Sketchley Gdns. SE16 5K 103
Sketty Rd. EN1: Enf 3A 24
Skiers St. E15 1G 87
Skiffington Cl. SW2 1A 138
Skillen Lodge HA5: Pinn 1B 40
Skinner Pl. SW1 4G 17
Skinners La. EC4 2D 14 (7C 84)
TW5: Hest 1F 113
Skinner's Row SE10 1D 122
Skinner St. EC1 2A 8 (3A 84)
Skip La. UB9: Hare 1A 56
Skipper Ct. IG11: Bark 1G 89
Skipsea Ho. SW18 6C 118
Skipsey Av. E6 3D 88
Skipton Cl. N11 6K 31
Skipton Dr. UB3: Harl 3E 92
Skipton Ho. SE4 4A 122
Skipwith Ho. EC1 5J 7
(off Bourne Est.)
Skipworth Rd. E9 1J 85
Skua Ct. SE8 6B 104
(off Dorking Cl.)
Skylark Ct. SE1 7D 14
(off Swan St.)
Skyline Ct. CR0: C'don 3D 168
(off Park La.)
SE1 3F 103
Skyline Plaza Bldg. E1 6G 85
(off Commercial Rd.)
Skylines E14 2E 104
Skylines Village E14 2E 104
Sky Peals Rd. IG8: Wfd G 7A 36
Skyport Dr. UB7: Harm 3E 174
Sky Van Cl. TW6: H'row A 5E 110
Skyview Apartments
CR0: C'don 2C 168
(off Park St.)
Skyway SL3: Poyle 6A 174
Slade, The SE18 6J 107
Sladebrook Rd. SE3 3B 124
Slade Ct. EN5: New Bar 3E 20
Sladedale Rd. SE18 5J 107
Slade Ho. TW4: Houn 6D 112
Sladen Pl. E5 4H 67
Slades Cl. EN2: Enf 3F 23
Slades Dr. BR7: Chst 3G 143
Slades Gdns. EN2: Enf 2F 23
Slades Hill EN2: Enf 3F 23
Slades Ri. EN2: Enf 3F 23
Slade Twr. E10 2C 68
(off Leyton Grange Est.)
Slade Wlk. SE17 6B 102
Slade Way CR4: Mitc 1E 154
Slagrove Pl. SE13 5C 122
Slaidburn St. SW10 6A 100
Slaithwaite Rd. SE13 4E 122
Slaney Ct. NW10 7E 62
Slaney Pl. N7 5A 66
Slater Cl. SE18 5E 106
Slatter NW9 7G 29
Slattery Rd. TW13: Felt 1B 130
Sleaford Ind. Est. SW8 7G 101
Sleaford St. SW8 7G 101
Sledmere Ct. TW14: Bedf 1G 129
Sleigh Ho. E2 3J 85
(off Bacton St.)
Slievemore Cl. SW4 3H 119
Sligo Ho. E1 4K 85
(off Beaumont Gro.)
Slindon Ct. N16 3F 67
Slingsby Pl. WC2 2E 12 (7J 83)
Slippers Pl. SE16 3H 103
Slipway Ho. E14 5D 104
(off Burrells Wharf Sq.)
Sloane Av. SW3 4D 16 (4C 100)
Sloane Av. Mans. SW3 4E 16
Sloane Ct. TW7: Isle 1J 113
Sloane Ct. E. SW3 5G 17 (5E 100)
Sloane Ct. W. SW3 5G 17 (5E 100)
Sloane Gdns. BR6: Farnb 3G 173
SW1 4G 17 (4E 100)
Sloane Ga. Mans. SW1 3G 17
(off D'Oyley St.)
Sloane Ho. E9 7J 67
(off Loddiges Rd.)
Sloane M. N8 5J 47
Sloane Sq. SW1 4G 17 (4E 100)
Sloane St. SW1 7F 11 (2D 100)
Sloane Ter. SW1 3G 17 (4E 100)
Sloane Ter. Mans. SW1 3G 17
(off Sloane Ter.)
Sloane Wlk. CR0: C'don 6B 158
Slocum Cl. SE28 7C 90
Slough La. NW9 5J 43
Sly St. E1 6H 85
Smaldon Cl. UB7: W Dray 3C 92
Smallberry Av. TW7: Isle 2K 113
Smallbrook M. W2 1A 10 (6B 82)
Smalley Cl. N16 3F 67
Smalley Rd. Est. N16 3F 67
(off Smalley Cl.)
Smallwood Rd. SW17 4B 136
Smarden Cl. DA17: Belv 5G 109
Smarden Gro. SE9 4D 142
Smart's Pl. N18 5B 34
WC2 7F 7 (6J 83)
Smart St. E2 3K 85
Smead Way SE13 3D 122
Smeaton Cl. KT9: Chess 6D 162
Smeaton Ct. SE1 3C 102
Smeaton Rd. IG8: Wfd G 5J 37
SW18 7J 117
Smeaton St. E1 1H 103
Smedley St. SW4 2H 119
Smeed Rd. E3 7C 68
Smiles Pl. SE13 2E 122
Smith Cl. SE16 1K 103
Smithfield (Central Markets) 6A 8
Smithfield St. EC1 6A 8 (5B 84)
Smith Hill TW8: Bford 6E 96
Smithies Rd. SE2 4B 108

Smith's Ct. W1 2B 12
Smithson Rd. N17 1D 48
Smiths Point E13 1J 87
(off Brooks Rd.)
Smith Sq. SW1 2E 18 (3J 101)
Smith St. KT5: Surb 6F 151
SW3 5E 16 (5D 100)
Smiths Yd. CR0: C'don 3C 168
(off St George's Wlk.)
SW18 2A 136
Smith Ter. SW3 6E 16 (5D 100)
Smithwood Cl. SW19 1G 135
Smithy St. E1 5J 85
Smock Wlk. CR0: C'don 6C 156
Smokehouse Yd. EC1 5B 8
(off St John St.)
Smoothfield Ct. TW3: Houn 4E 112
Smugglers Way SW18 4K 117
Smyrk's Rd. SE17 5E 102
Smyrna Mans. NW6 7J 63
(off Smyrna Rd.)
Smyrna Rd. NW6 7J 63
Smythe St. E14 7D 86
Snag La. BR6: Prat B 7K 173
Snakes La. N14 3A 22
Snakes La. E.
IG8: Buck H, Wfd G 6F 37
Snakes La. W. IG8: Wfd G 5D 36
Snakey La. TW13: Felt 4J 129
SNARESBROOK 5J 51
Snaresbrook Dr. HA7: Stan 4J 27
Snaresbrook Hall E18 4J 51
Snaresbrook Ho. E18 4H 51
Snaresbrook Rd. E11 4G 51
Snarsgate St. W10 5E 80
Sneath Av. NW11 7H 45
Snells Pk. N18 6A 34
Sneyd Rd. NW2 4E 62
Snowberry Cl. E15 4F 69
Snowbury Rd. SW6 2K 117
Snowden Av. UB10: Hil 2D 74
Snowden St. EC2 4G 9 (4E 84)
Snowdon Aviary 1D 82
(in London Zoo)
Snowdon Cres. UB3: Harl 3E 92
Snowdon Dr. NW9 6A 44
Snowdon Rd. TW6: H'row A 6E 110
Snowdown Cl. SE20 1J 157
Snowdrop Cl. TW12: Hamp 6E 130
Snow Hill EC1 6A 8 (5B 84)
Snow Hill Ct. EC1 7B 8 (6B 84)
Snowman Ho. NW6 1K 81
Snowsfields SE1 6F 15 (2D 102)
Snowshill Rd. E12 5C 70
Snowy Fielder Waye TW7: Isle 2B 114
Soames Pl. EN4: Had W 2E 20
Soames St. SE15 3F 121
Soames Wlk. KT3: N Mald 1A 152
Soane Cl. W5 2D 96
Soane Ct. NW1 7G 65
(off St Pancras Way)
Soane Ho. SE17 5D 102
(off Roland Way)
Soaphouse La. TW8: Bford 7E 96
Sobell Leisure Cen. 3K 65
Sobraon Ho. KT2: King T 7F 133
(off Elm Rd.)
Socket La. BR2: Hayes 6K 159
SOHO 1C 12 (6G 83)
Soho Sq. W1 7C 6 (6H 83)
Soho St. W1 7C 6 (6H 83)
Soho Theatre & Writers Cen. 1C 12
(off Dean St.)
Sojourner Truth Cl. E8 6H 67
Solander Gdns. E1 7H 85
(off Cable St.)
E1 7J 85
(The Highway)
Solar Ct. N3 7E 30
Solar Ho. E6 5E 88
Solarium Ct. SE1 4F 103
(off Alscot Rd.)
Soldene Ct. N7 5K 65
(off George's Rd.)
Solebay St. E1 4A 86
Solent Ct. SW16 2K 155
Solent Ho. E1 5A 86
(off Ben Jonson Rd.)
Solent Ri. E13 3J 87
Solent Rd. NW6 5J 63
Soley M. WC1 1J 7 (3A 84)
Solna Av. SW15 5E 116
Solna Rd. N21 1J 33
Solomon Av. N9 4B 34
Solomons Ct. N12 7F 31
Solomon's Pas. SE15 4H 121
Solon New Rd. SW4 4J 119
Solon New Rd. Est. SW4 4J 119
Solon Rd. SW2 4J 119
Solway Cl. E8 6F 67
(off Queensbridge Rd.)
TW4: Houn 3C 112
Solway Ho. E1 4K 85
(off Ernest St.)
Solway Rd. N22 1B 48
SE22 4G 121
Somaford Gro. EN4: E Barn 6G 21
Somali Rd. NW2 5H 63
Sombourne Ho. SW15 7C 116
(off Fontley Way)
Somerby Rd. IG11: Bark 7H 71
Somercoates Cl. EN4: Cockf 3H 21
Somer Ct. SW6 6J 99
(off Anselm Rd.)
Somerfield Rd. N4 2B 66
(not continuous)
Somerfield St. SE16 5K 103
Somerford Cl. HA5: Eastc 4J 39
Somerford Gro. N16 4F 67
N17 7B 34
(not continuous)
Somerford Gro. Est. N16 4F 67
Somerford St. E1 4H 85
Somerford Way SE16 2A 104
Somerhill Av. DA15: Sidc 7B 126
Somerhill Rd. DA16: Well 2B 126
Somerleyton Pas. SW9 4B 120
Somerleyton Rd. SW9 4A 120
Somersby Gdns. IG4: Ilf 5D 52
Somers Cl. NW1 2H 83
Somers Cres. W2 1C 10 (6C 82)
Somerset Av. DA16: Well 5K 125
KT9: Chess 4D 162
SW20 2D 152
Somerset Cl. IG8: Wfd G 1J 51
KT3: N Mald 6A 152
N17 2D 48
Somerset Ct. IG9: Buck H 2F 37
NW1 1C 6 (2H 83)
W7 6K 77
(off Copley Cl.)
Somerset Est. SW11 1B 118
Somerset Gdns. N6 7E 46
N17 7K 33
SE13 2D 122
SW16 3K 155
TW11: Tedd 5J 131
Somerset Hall N17 7K 33
Somerset House 2G 13 (7K 83)
Somerset Ho. SW19 3F 135
Somerset Lodge TW8: Bford 6D 96
Somerset Rd. E17 5C 50
EN5: New Bar 5E 20
HA1: Harr 5G 41
KT1: King T 2F 151
N17 3F 49
N18 5A 34
NW4 4E 44
SW19 3F 135
TW8: Bford 6C 96
Somerset Rd. TW11: Tedd 5J 131
UB1: S'hall 5D 76
W4 3K 97
W13 1B 96
Somerset Sq. W14 2G 99
Somerset Waye TW5: Hest 6C 94
Somersham Rd. DA7: Bex 2E 126
Somers Pl. SW2 7K 119
Somers Rd. E17 4B 50
SW2 6K 119
SOMERS TOWN 1C 6 (2H 83)
Somers Town Community Sports Cen.
2H 83
Somerton Av. TW9: Rich 3H 115
Somerton Ho. WC1 2D 6
Somerton Rd. NW2 3G 63
SE15 4H 121
Somertrees Av. SE12 2K 141
Somervell Rd. HA2: Harr 5D 58
Somerville Av. SW13 6D 98
Somerville Cl. SW9 1K 119
Somerville Point SE16 2B 104
Somerville Rd. RM6: Chad H 6C 54
SE20 7K 139
Sonderburg Rd. N7 2K 65
Sondes St. SE17 6D 102
Songhurst Cl. CR0: C'don 6K 155
Sonia Ct. HA1: Harr 6K 41
HA8: Edg 7A 28
Sonia Gdns. N12 4F 31
NW10 4B 62
TW5: Hest 7E 94
Sonning Gdns. TW12: Hamp 6C 130
Sonning Ho. E2 2J 9
(off Swanfield St.)
Sonning Rd. SE25 6G 157
Sontan Ct. TW2: Twick 1H 131
Soper Cl. E4 5G 35
SE23 1K 139
Soper M. EN3: Enf L 1H 25
Sophia Cl. N7 6K 65
Sophia Ho. W6 5E 98
(off Queen Caroline St.)
Sophia Rd. E10 1D 68
E16 6K 87
Sophia Sq. SE16 7A 86
(off Sovereign Cres.)
Sopwith NW9 7G 29
Sopwith Av. KT9: Chess 5E 162
Sopwith Cl. KT2: King T 5F 133
Sopwith Rd. TW5: Hest 7A 94
Sopwith Way KT2: King T 1E 150
SW8 7J 17 (7F 101)
Sorbus Ct. EN2: Enf 2G 23
Sorensen Ct. E10 2D 68
(off Leyton Grange Est.)
Sorrel Cl. SE28 1A 108
Sorrel Gdns. E6 5C 88
Sorrel La. E14 6F 87
Sorrell Cl. SE14 7A 104
SW9 2A 120
Sorrento Rd. SM1: Sutt 3J 165
Sotheby Rd. N5 3B 66
Sotheran Cl. E8 1G 85
Sotherby Lodge E2 2J 85
(off Sewardstone Rd.)
Sotheron Rd. SW6 7K 99
Soudan Rd. SW11 1D 118
Souldern Rd. W14 3F 99
Sth. Access Rd. E17 7A 50
Southacre W2 1C 10
(off Hyde Pk. Cres.)
Southacre Way HA5: Pinn 1A 40
SOUTH ACTON 2J 97
Sth. Africa Rd. W12 1D 98
SOUTHALL 1D 94
Southall Ct. UB1: S'hall 7D 76
Southall Ent. Cen.
UB2: S'hall 2E 94
SOUTHALL GREEN 3C 94
Southall La. TW5: Cran 6K 93
UB2: S'hall 6K 93
Southall Pl. SE1 7E 14 (2D 102)
Southam Ho. W10 4G 81
(off Southam St.)
Southampton Bldgs. WC2 6J 7 (5A 84)
Southampton Gdns. CR4: Mitc 5J 155
Southampton M. E16 1K 105
Southampton Pl. WC1 6F 7 (5J 83)
Southampton Rd. NW5 5D 64
Southampton Rd. E. TW6: H'row A 6B 110
Southampton Rd. W.
TW6: H'row A 6A 110
(not continuous)
Southampton Row WC1 5F 7 (5J 83)
Southampton St.
WC2 2F 13 (7J 83)
Southampton Way SE5 7D 102
Southam St. W10 4G 81
Sth. Audley St. W1 3H 11 (7E 82)
South Av. E4 7J 25
N2 4K 45
NW10 4E 80
SM5: Cars 7E 166
TW9: Kew 2G 115
UB1: S'hall 7D 76
South Av. Gdns. UB1: S'hall 7D 76
South Bank 4H 13 (1K 101)
South Bank KT6: Surb 6E 150
Southbank KT7: T Ditt 7B 150
Sth. Bank Bus. Cen. SW8 7D 18 (6H 101)
Southbank Bus. Cen. SW11 1D 118
Sth. Bank Ter. KT6: Surb 6E 150
SOUTH BARNET 1K 31
SOUTH BEDDINGTON 6H 167
Sth. Birkbeck Rd. E11 3F 69
Sth. Black Lion La. W6 5C 98
South Block SE1 7G 13
(off Westminster Bri. Rd.)
Sth. Bolton Gdns. SW5 5K 99
SOUTHBOROUGH
BR2 5D 160
KT6 1E 162
Southborough Cl. KT6: Surb 1D 162
Southborough Ho. SE17 5E 102
(off Kinglake Est.)
Southborough La. BR2: Brom 5C 160
Southborough Rd. BR1: Brom 3C 160
E9 1K 85
KT6: Surb 1E 162
Sth. Boundary Rd. E12 3D 70
Southbourne BR2: Hayes 7J 159
Southbourne Av. NW9 2J 43
Southbourne Cl. HA5: Pinn 7C 40
Southbourne Ct. NW9 2J 43
Southbourne Cres. NW4 4G 45
Southbourne Gdns. HA4: Ruis 1K 57
IG1: Ilf 5G 71
SE12 5K 123
Sth. Branch Av. NW10 4E 80
Southbridge Pl. CR0: C'don 4C 168
Southbridge Rd. CR0: C'don 4C 168
Southbridge Way UB2: S'hall 2C 94
SOUTH BROMLEY 7E 86
Southbrook M. SE12 6H 123
Southbrook Rd. SE12 6H 123
SW16 1J 155
Southbury NW8 1A 82
(off Loudoun Rd.)
Southbury Av. EN1: Enf 4B 24
Southbury Leisure Cen. 3B 24
Southbury Rd. EN1: Enf 3K 23
EN3: Pond E 3A 24
Sth. Carriage Dr. SW1 7B 10 (2B 100)
SW7 7B 10 (2B 100)
SOUTH CHINGFORD 5G 35
Southchurch Ct. E6 2D 88
(off High St. Sth.)
Southchurch Rd. E6 2D 88
Sth. Circular Rd. SW15 4C 116

South City Ct. SE15 7E 102
South Cl. DA6: Bex 4D 126
EN5: Barn 3C 20
HA5: Pinn 7D 40
N6 6F 47
RM10: Dag 1G 91
SM4: Mord 6J 153
TW2: Twick 3E 130
UB7: W Dray 3B 92
Sth. Colonnade, The E14 1C 104
Southcombe St. W14 4G 99
South Comn. Rd. UB8: Uxb 6A 56
Southcote Av. KT5: Surb 7H 151
TW13: Felt 2H 129
Southcote Ri. HA4: Ruis 7F 39
Southcote Rd. E17 5K 49
N19 4G 65
SE25 5H 157
Southcott Ho. *W9* *4A 82*
(off Clarendon Gdns.)
Southcott M. NW8 2C 82
Sth. Countess Rd. E17 3B 50
South Cres. E16 4F 87
WC1 6C 6 (5H 83)
Southcroft Av. BR4: W W'ck 2E 170
DA16: Well 3J 125
Southcroft Rd. BR6: Orp 3J 173
SW16 6E 136
SW17 6E 136
Sth. Cross Rd. IG6: Ilf 5G 53
Sth. Croxted Rd. SE21 3D 138
SOUTH CROYDON 5D 168
South Croydon Sports Club 5E 168
Southdean Gdns. SW19 2H 135
South Dene NW7 3E 28
Southdene Ct. N11 3A 32
Southdown Av. W7 3A 96
Southdown Cres. HA2: Harr 1G 59
IG2: Ilf 5J 53
Southdown Dr. SW20 7F 135
Southdown Rd. SM5: Cars 7E 166
SW20 1F 153
South Dr. BR6: Orp 5J 173
E12 3C 70
HA4: Ruis 1G 57
Sth. Ealing Rd. W5 2D 96
Sth. Eastern Av. N9 3A 34
South Eastern University 3K 65
Sth. Eaton Pl. SW1 3H 17 (4E 100)
Sth. Eden Pk. Rd. BR3: Beck 6D 158
Sth. Edwardes Sq. W8 3H 99
SOUTHEND 4F 141
South End CR0: C'don 4C 168
W8 3K 99
South End Cl. NW3 4C 64
Southend Cl. SE9 6F 125
Southend Cres. SE9 6F 125
South End Grn. NW3 4C 64
Southend La. SE6 4B 140
SE26 4B 140
South End Rd. NW3 4C 64
Southend Rd. BR3: Beck 1C 158
E4 5F 35
E6 7D 70
E17 1D 50
E18 1J 51
IG8: Wfd G 2A 52
South End Row W8 3K 99
Southern Av. SE25 3F 157
TW14: Felt 1J 129
Southern Cotts. TW19: Stan M 7B 174
Southerngate Way SE14 7A 104
Southern Gro. E3 3B 86
Southern Perimeter Rd.
TW6: H'row A 5A 110
(Stanwell Moor Rd.)
TW6: H'row A 5E 110
(Swindon Rd.)
TW19: Stanw 6B 110
(not continuous)
Southern Pl. HA0: Wemb 4K 59
Southern Rd. E13 2K 87
N2 4D 46
Southern Row W10 4G 81
Southern St. N1 2K 83
Southern Way RM7: Rom 6G 55
SE10 4H 105
Southernwood Retail Pk. SE1 5F 103
Southerton Rd. W6 4E 98
Sth. Esk Rd. E7 6A 70
Southey Ho. *SE17* *5C 102*
(off Browning St.)
Southey M. E16 1J 105
Southey Rd. N15 5E 48
SW9 1A 120
SW19 7J 135
Southey St. SE20 7K 139
Southfield EN5: Barn 6A 20
Southfield Cl. UB8: Hil 4C 74
Southfield Cotts. W7 2K 95
Southfield Ct. E11 3H 69
Southfield Gdns.
TW1: Twick 4K 131
Southfield Pk. HA2: Harr 4F 41
Southfield Rd. BR7: Chst 3K 161
EN3: Pond E 6C 24
N17 2E 48
W4 2K 97
SOUTHFIELDS 1H 135
Southfields KT8: E Mos 6J 149
NW4 3D 44
Southfields Av. TW15: Ashf 6D 128
Southfields Ct. SM1: Sutt 2J 165
Southfields M. SW18 6J 117
Southfields Pas. SW18 6J 117
Southfields Rd. SW18 6J 117
Southfleet NW5 6E 64
Southfleet Rd. BR6: Orp 3J 173
South Gdns. HA9: Wemb 2G 61
SW19 7B 136
SOUTHGATE 1C 32
Southgate Av. TW13: Felt 4F 129
Southgate Cir. N14 1C 32
Southgate Ct. *N1* *7D 66*
(off Downham Rd.)
Southgate Gro. N1 7D 66
Southgate Leisure Cen. 1C 32
South Ga. Rd. E12 3B 70
Southgate Rd. N1 1D 84
Sth. Gipsy Rd. DA16: Well 3D 126
Sth. Glade, The DA5: Bexl 1F 145
South Grn. NW9 1A 44
South Gro. E17 5B 50
N6 1E 64
N15 5D 48
South Gro. Ho. N6 1E 64
SOUTH HACKNEY 7K 67
SOUTH HAMPSTEAD 7A 64
SOUTH HARROW 3G 59
Sth. Harrow Ind. Est. HA2: Harr 2G 59
South Hill BR7: Chst 6D 142
HA6: Nwood 1G 39
Sth. Hill Av. HA1: Harr 3G 59
HA2: Harr 3G 59
Sth. Hill Gro. HA1: Harr 4J 59
Sth. Hill Pk. NW3 4C 64
Sth. Hill Pk. Gdns. NW3 3C 64
South Hill Rd. BR2: Brom 3G 159
Southholme Cl. SE19 1E 156
SOUTH HORNCHURCH 2K 91
Southill Ct. BR2: Brom 5H 159
Southill La. HA5: Eastc 4K 39
Southill Rd. BR7: Chst 7C 142
Southill St. E14 6D 86
Sth. Island Pl. SW9 7K 101
SOUTH KENSINGTON 4B 100
Sth. Kensington Sta. Arc. *SW7* *3B 16*
(off Pelham St.)
SOUTH LAMBETH 7J 101
Sth. Lambeth Pl. SW8 7F 19 (6J 101)
Sth. Lambeth Rd. SW8 7F 19 (6J 101)
Southland Rd. SE18 7K 107
Southlands Av. BR6: Orp 4H 173
Southlands Dr. SW19 2F 135
Southlands Gro. BR1: Brom 3C 160
Southlands Rd. BR1: Brom 5A 160
BR2: Brom 5A 160
Southland Way TW3: Houn 5H 113
South La. KT1: King T 3D 150
(not continuous)
KT3: N Mald 4K 151
South La. W. KT3: N Mald 4K 151
South Lodge *E16* *1K 105*
(off Audley Dr.)
NW8 1A 4 (2B 82)
SW7 *7D 10*
(off Knightsbridge)
TW2: Whitt 6G 113
Sth. Lodge Av. CR4: Mitc 4J 155
Sth. Lodge Cres. EN2: Enf 4C 22
(not continuous)
Sth. Lodge Dr. N14 4C 22
Sth. London Crematorium
CR4: Mitc 2G 155
South London Gallery 1E 120
South London Theatre *3B 138*
(off Norwood High St.)
South Mall *N9* *3B 34*
(off Plevna Rd.)
SW18 6K 117
South Mead KT19: Ewe 7B 164
NW9 1B 44
Southmead Rd. SW19 1G 135
Sth. Molton La. W1 1J 11 (6F 83)
Sth. Molton Rd. E16 6J 87
Sth. Molton St. W1 1J 11 (6F 83)
Southmoor Way E9 6B 68
South Mt. *N20* *2F 31*
(off High Rd.)
SOUTH NORWOOD 4F 157
South Norwood Country Pk. 4J 157
South Norwood Country Pk. Vis. Cen.
4H 157
Sth. Norwood Hill SE25 1E 156
South Norwood Pools & Fitness Cen.
5H 157
Sth. Oak Rd. SW16 4K 137
Southold Ri. SE9 3D 142
Southolm St. SW11 1F 119
Southover BR1: Brom 5J 141
N12 3D 30
South Pde. HA8: Edg 2G 43
SM6: Wall 6G 167
SW3 5B 16 (5B 100)
W4 4K 97
South Pk. Ct. BR3: Beck 7C 140
South Pk. Cres. IG1: Ilf 3H 71
SE6 1G 141
South Pk. Dr. IG3: Ilf 2J 71
IG11: Bark 5J 71
South Pk. Gro. KT3: N Mald 4J 151
South Pk. Hill Rd.
CR2: S Croy 5D 168
South Pk. M. SW6 3K 117
South Pk. Rd. IG1: Ilf 3H 71
SW19 6J 135
South Pk. Ter. IG1: Ilf 3J 71
South Pk. Vs. IG3: Ilf 4J 71
South Pk. Way
HA4: Ruis 6A 58
South Pl. EC2 5F 9 (5D 84)
EN3: Pond E 5D 24
KT5: Surb 7F 151
South Pl. M. EC2 6F 9 (5D 84)
Southport Rd. SE18 4H 107
Sth. Quay Plaza E14 2D 104
Southridge Pl. SW20 7F 135
South Ri. SM5: Cars 7C 166
W2 2D 10
South Ri. Way SE18 5H 107
South Rd. HA1: Harr 1A 60
HA8: Edg 1H 43
N9 1B 34
South Rd. RM6: Chad H 5C 54
(Chadwell Heath La.)
RM6: Chad H 6E 54
(West Rd.)
SE23 2K 139
SW19 6A 136
TW2: Twick 3H 131
TW5: Hest 6A 94
TW12: Hamp 6C 130
TW13: Hanw 5B 130
UB1: S'hall 2D 94
UB7: W Dray 3C 92
W5 4D 96
South Row SE3 2H 123
SOUTH RUISLIP 4A 58
Southsea Rd. KT1: King T 4E 150
South Sea St. SE16 3B 104
South Side N15 4F 49
W6 3B 98
Southside N7 4H 65
Southside Comn. SW19 6E 134
Southside House 6E 134
Southside Ind. Est. *SW8* *1G 119*
(off Havelock Ter.)
Southside Shop. Cen.
SW18 6K 117
Southspring DA15: Sidc 7H 125
South Sq. NW11 6K 45
WC1 6J 7 (5A 84)
South St. BR1: Brom 2J 159
EN3: Pond E 5D 24
RM13: Rain 2J 91
TW7: Isle 3A 114
W1 4H 11 (1E 100)
Sth. Tenter St. E1 2K 15 (7F 85)
South Ter. KT6: Surb 6E 150
SW7 3C 16 (4C 100)
SOUTH TOTTENHAM 5F 49
South Va. HA1: Harr 4J 59
Southvale SE19 6E 138
Southvale Rd. SE3 2G 123
South Vw. BR1: Brom 2A 160
SW19 6F 135
Southview Av. NW10 5B 62
South Vw. Cl. DA5: Bexl 6F 127
Southview Cl. SW17 5E 136
South Vw. Ct. SE19 7C 138
Southview Cres. IG2: Ilf 6F 53
South Vw. Dr. E18 3K 51
Southview Gdns. SM6: Wall 7G 167
Southview Pde. RM13: Rain 3K 91
South Vw. Rd. HA5: Pinn 1K 39
N8 3H 47
Southview Rd. BR1: Brom 4F 141
South Vs. NW1 6H 65
Southville SW8 1H 119
Southville Cl. KT19: Ewe 7K 163
TW14: Bedf, Felt 1G 129
TW14: Felt 1G 129
Southville Cres. TW14: Felt 1G 129
Southville Rd. KT7: T Ditt 7A 150
TW14: Felt 1G 129
South Wlk. BR4: W W'ck 3G 171
UB3: Hayes 5F 75
SOUTHWARK 5A 14 (1B 102)
Southwark Bri. EC4 7C 84
SE1 3D 14 (7C 84)
Southwark Bri. Bus. Cen. *SE1* *5D 14*
(off Southwark Bri. Rd.)
Southwark Bri. Rd. SE1 3B 102
Southwark Cathedral 4E 14 (1D 102)
Southwark Hall *UB8: Cowl* *3A 74*
(off Kingston La.)
Southwark Pk. Est. SE16 3H 103
Southwark Pk. Rd. SE16 4F 103
Southwark Pk. Sports Cen. Track 4J 103
Southwark Pk. Sports Complex 4J 103

Southwark Pl. BR1: Brom 3D 160
Southwark Playhouse 5C 14
(off Southwark Bri. Rd.)
Southwark St. SE1 . . . . 4A 14 (1B 102)
Southwater Cl. BR3: Beck 7D 140
E14 . . . . 6B 86
South Way BR2: Hayes 7J 159
CR0: C'don 3A 170
HA2: Harr 4E 40
HA9: Wemb 5G 61
N9 . . . . 2D 34
N11 . . . . 6B 32
Southway N20 . . . . 2D 30
NW11 . . . . 6K 45
SM6: Wall 4G 167
SW20 . . . . 5E 152
Southway Cl. W12 . . . . 2D 98
Southways Pde. IG2: Ilf 5E 52
Southwell Av. UB5: N'olt 6E 58
Southwell Gdns. SW7 . . . . 4A 100
Southwell Gro. Rd. E11 . . . . 2G 69
Southwell Ho. SE16 . . . . 4H 103
(off Anchor St.)
Southwell Rd. CR0: C'don 6A 156
HA3: Kent 6D 42
SE5 . . . . 3C 120
Sth. Western Rd. TW1: Twick 6A 114
South W. India Dock Entrance
E14 . . . . 2E 104
South W. Middlesex Crematorium
TW13: Felt 1C 130
Southwest Rd. E11 . . . . 1F 69
Sth. Wharf Rd. W2 . . . . 7A 4 (6B 82)
Southwick M. W2 . . . . 7B 4 (6B 82)
Southwick Pl. W2 . . . . 1C 10 (6C 82)
Southwick St. W2 . . . . 7C 4 (6C 82)
Southwick Yd. W2 . . . . 1C 10
SOUTH WIMBLEDON 6K 135
Southwold Dr. IG11: Bark 5A 72
Southwold Mans.
W9 . . . . 3J 81
(off Widley Rd.)
Southwold Rd. DA5: Bexl 6H 127
E5 . . . . 2H 67
Southwood Av. KT2: King T 1J 151
N6 . . . . 7F 47
Southwood Cl. BR1: Brom 4D 160
KT4: Wor Pk 1F 165
Southwood Ct. EC1 . . . . 2A 8
(off Wynyatt St.)
NW11 . . . . 5K 45
Southwood Dr. KT5: Surb 7J 151
SOUTH WOODFORD 2J 51
Sth. Woodford to Barking Relief Rd.
E11 . . . . 5B 52
E12 . . . . 4E 70
IG1: Ilf 5B 52
IG4: Ilf 5B 52
Southwood Gdns. IG2: Ilf 4F 53
KT10: Hin W 3A 162
Southwood Hall N6 . . . . 6F 47
Southwood Hgts. N6 . . . . 7F 47
Southwood Ho. W11 . . . . 7G 81
(off Avondale Pk. Rd.)
Southwood La. N6 . . . . 7E 46
Southwood Lawn Rd. N6 . . . . 7E 46
Southwood Mans. N6 . . . . 6E 46
(off Southwood La.)
Southwood Pk. N6 . . . . 7E 46
Southwood Rd. SE9 . . . . 2F 143
SE28 . . . . 1B 108
Southwood Smith Ho. E2 . . . . 3H 85
(off Florida St.)
Southwood Smith St. N1 . . . . 1B 84
Sth. Worple Av. SW14 . . . . 3A 116
Sth. Worple Way SW14 . . . . 3K 115
Southwyck Ho. SW9 . . . . 4B 120
Soval Ct. HA6: Nwood 1F 39
Sovereign Bus. Cen.
EN3: Brim 3G 25
Sovereign Cl. E1 . . . . 7H 85
HA4: Ruis 1G 57
W5 . . . . 5C 78
Sovereign Ct. CR2: S Croy 5C 168
(off Warham Rd.)
HA6: Nwood 1J 39
KT8: W Mole 4D 148
TW3: Houn 3E 112
W8 . . . . 3K 99
(off Wright's La.)
Sovereign Cres. SE16 . . . . 7A 86
Sovereign Gro. HA0: Wemb 3D 60
Sovereign Ho. E1 . . . . 4H 85
(off Cambridge Heath Rd.)
SE18 . . . . 3D 106
(off Leda Rd.)
TW15: Ashf 4A 128
Sovereign M. E2 . . . . 2F 85
EN4: Cockf 3J 21
Sovereign Pk. NW10 . . . . 4H 79
Sovereign Pk. Trad. Est. NW10 . . . . . . 4H 79
Sovereign Pl. HA1: Harr 5K 41
Sovereign Rd. IG11: Bark 3C 90
Sowerby Cl. SE9 . . . . 5D 124
Spa at Beckenham, The 1B 158
Space Bus. Pk. NW10 . . . . 3H 79
Space Waye TW14: Felt 5J 111
Spa Cl. SE25 . . . . 1E 156
Spa Ct. SE16 . . . . 3G 103
SW16 . . . . 4K 137
Spafield St. EC1 . . . . 3J 7 (4A 84)
Spa Grn. Est. EC1 . . . . 1K 7 (3B 84)
Spa Hill SE19 . . . . 1D 156
Spalding Cl. HA8 . . . . 7F 29
Spalding Ho. SE4 . . . . 4A 122
Spalding Rd. NW4 . . . . 7E 44
SW17 . . . . 5F 137
Spanby Rd. E3 . . . . 4C 86
Spaniards Cl. NW11 . . . . 1B 64
Spaniards End NW3 . . . . 1A 64
Spaniards Rd. NW3 . . . . 2A 64
Spanish Pl. W1 . . . . 7H 5 (6E 82)
Spanish Rd. SW18 . . . . 5A 118
Spanswick Lodge N15 . . . . 4B 48
Sparkbridge Rd. HA1: Harr 4J 41
Sparkes Cl. BR2: Brom 4K 159
Sparkes Cotts. SW1 . . . . 4G 17
Sparke Ter. E16 . . . . 6H 87
(off Clarkson Rd.)
Sparkford Gdns. N11 . . . . 5K 31
Sparks Cl. RM8: Dag 2D 72
TW12: Hamp 6C 130
W3 . . . . 6K 79
Spa Rd. SE16 . . . . 3F 103
Sparrick's Row SE1 . . . . 6F 15 (2D 102)
Sparrow Cl. TW12: Hamp 6C 130
Sparrow Dr. BR5: Farnb 1G 173
Sparrow Farm Dr. TW14: Felt 7A 112
(not continuous)
Sparrow Farm Rd. KT17: Ewe 4C 164
Sparrow Grn. RM10: Dag 3H 73
Sparrow Ho. E1 . . . . 4J 85
(off Cephas Av.)
Sparrow's Farm Leisure Cen. 7G 125
Sparrows Herne WD23: Bush 1A 26
Sparrows La. SE9 . . . . 7G 125
Sparrows Way WD23: Bush 1B 26
Sparsholt Cl. IG11: Bark 1J 89
(off St John's Rd.)
Sparsholt Rd. IG11: Bark 1J 89
N19 . . . . 1K 65
Spartan Cl. SM6: Wall 7J 167
Sparta St. SE10 . . . . 1E 122
Speakers' Corner 2F 11 (7D 82)
Speakers Ct. CR0: C'don 1D 168
Speakman Ho. SE4 . . . . 3A 122
(off Arica Rd.)
Spearman Ho. E14 . . . . 6C 86
(off Upper Nth. St.)
Spearman St. SE18 . . . . 6E 106
Spear M. SW5 . . . . 4J 99
Spearpoint Gdns. IG2: Ilf 5K 53
Spears Rd. N19 . . . . 1J 65
Speart La. TW5: Hest 7C 94
Spectacle Works E13 . . . . 3A 88
Spectrum Pl. SE17 . . . . 6D 102
(off Lytham St.)
Spectrum Twr. IG1: Ilf 2G 71
(off Hainault St.)
Spedan Cl. NW3 . . . . 3A 64
Speechly M. E8 . . . . 5F 67
Speedbird Way UB7: Harm 3C 174
Speed Highwalk EC2 . . . . 5D 8
(off Silk St.)
Speed Ho. EC2 . . . . 5D 8
Speedway Ind. Est. UB3: Hayes 2F 93
Speedwell Ho. N12 . . . . 4E 30
Speedwell St. SE8 . . . . 7C 104
Speedy Pl. WC1 . . . . 2E 6
Speer Rd. KT7: T Ditt 6K 149
Speirs Cl. KT3: N Mald 6B 152
Speke Hill SE9 . . . . 3D 142
Speke Rd. CR7: Thor H 2D 156
Speke's Monument 4A 10 (1B 100)
Speldhurst Cl. BR2: Brom 5H 159
Speldhurst Rd. E9 . . . . 7K 67
W4 . . . . 3K 97
Spellbrook Wlk. N1 . . . . 1C 84
Spelman Ho. E1 . . . . 6K 9
(off Spelman St.)
Spelman St. E1 . . . . 5K 9 (5G 85)
(not continuous)
Spelthorne Gro. TW16: Sun 7H 129
Spelthorne La. TW15: Ashf 1E 146
Spence Cl. SE16 . . . . 2B 104
Spencer Av. N13 . . . . 6E 32
UB4: Hayes 5J 75
Spencer Cl. BR6: Orp 2J 173
IG8: Wfd G 5F 37
N3 . . . . 2J 45
NW10 . . . . 3F 79
Spencer Ct. BR6: Farnb 5G 173
NW8 . . . . 2A 82
(off Marlborough Pl.)
SW20 . . . . 1D 152
Spencer Courtyard N3 . . . . 2H 45
(off Regents Pk. Rd.)
Spencer Dr. N2 . . . . 6A 46
Spencer Gdns. SE9 . . . . 5D 124
SW14 . . . . 5J 115
Spencer Hill SW19 . . . . 6G 135
Spencer Hill Rd. SW19 . . . . 7G 135
Spencer House 5A 12
Spencer Ho. NW4 . . . . 5D 44
Spencer Mans. W14 . . . . 6G 99
(off Queen's Club Gdns.)
Spencer M. SW8 . . . . 1K 119
(off Sth. Lambeth Rd.)
W6 . . . . 6G 99
SPENCER PARK 5B 118
Spencer Pk. KT8: E Mos 5G 149
SW18 . . . . 5B 118
Spencer Pl. CR0: C'don 7D 156
N1 . . . . 7B 66
Spencer Ri. NW5 . . . . 4F 65
Spencer Rd. BR1: Brom 7H 141
CR2: S Croy 5E 168
CR4: Mitc 3E 154
(Commonside E.)
CR4: Mitc 7E 154
(Wood St.)
E6 . . . . 1B 88
E17 . . . . 2E 50
HA0: Wemb 2C 60
HA3: W'stone 2J 41
IG3: Ilf 1K 71
KT8: E Mos 4G 149
N8 . . . . 5K 47
(not continuous)
N11 . . . . 4A 32
Spencer Rd. N17 . . . . 1G 49
RM13: Rain 3K 91
SW18 . . . . 4B 118
SW20 . . . . 1D 152
TW2: Twick 3J 131
TW7: Isle 1G 113
W3 . . . . 1J 97
W4 . . . . 7J 97
Spencer St. EC1 . . . . 2A 8 (3B 84)
UB2: S'hall 2B 94
Spencer Wlk. NW3 . . . . 4A 64
(off Perrin's Ct.)
NW3 . . . . 4B 64
(Hampstead High St.)
SW15 . . . . 4F 117
Spenlow Ho. SE16 . . . . 3G 103
(off Jamaica Rd.)
Spenser Gro. N16 . . . . 5E 66
Spenser M. SE21 . . . . 2D 138
Spenser Rd. SE24 . . . . 5B 120
Spenser St.
SW1 . . . . 1B 18 (3G 101)
Spens Ho. WC1 . . . . 4G 7
(off Long Yd.)
Spensley Wlk. N16 . . . . 3D 66
Speranza St. SE18 . . . . 5K 107
Sperling Rd. N17 . . . . 2E 48
Spert St. E14 . . . . 7A 86
Speyside N14 . . . . 6B 22
Spey St. E14 . . . . 5E 86
Spey Way RM1: Rom 1K 55
Spezia Rd. NW10 . . . . 2C 80
Sphere, The E16 . . . . 6H 87
(off Hallsville Rd.)
Spice Ct. E1 . . . . 7G 85
Spice Quay Hgts. SE1 . . . . . . 5K 15 (1F 103)
Spicer Cl. KT12: Walt T 6A 148
SW9 . . . . 2B 120
Spicer Ct. EN1: Enf 3K 23
Spice's Yd. CR0: C'don 4C 168
Spigurnell Rd. N17 . . . . 1D 48
Spikes Bri. Rd. UB1: S'hall 6C 76
Spindle Cl. SE18 . . . . 3C 106
Spindlewood Gdns.
CR0: C'don 4E 168
Spindrift Av. E14 . . . . 4C 104
Spinel Cl. SE18 . . . . 5K 107
Spinnaker Cl. IG11: Bark 3B 90
Spinnaker Ct. KT1: Ham W 1D 150
(off Becketts Pl.)
Spinnaker Ho. E14 . . . . 2C 104
(off Byng St.)
Spinnells Rd. HA2: Harr 1D 58
Spinney, The DA14: Sidc 5E 144
EN5: New Bar 2E 20
HA0: Wemb 3A 60
HA7: Stan 4K 27
N21 . . . . 7F 23
SM3: Cheam 4E 164
SW13 . . . . 7D 98
SW16 . . . . 3G 137
TW16: Sun 1J 147
Spinney Cl. BR3: Beck 4D 158
KT3: N Mald 5A 152
KT4: Wor Pk 2B 164
UB7: Yiew 7A 74
Spinney Dr. TW14: Bedf 7E 110
Spinney Gdns. RM9: Dag 5E 72
SE19 . . . . 5F 139
Spinney Oak BR1: Brom 2C 160
Spinneys, The BR1: Brom 2D 160
Spire Ct. BR3: Beck 2D 158
(off Crescent Rd.)
Spire Ho. W2 . . . . 7A 82
(off Lancaster Ga.)
Spires Shop. Cen., The
EN5: Barn 3B 20
Spirit Quay E1 . . . . 1G 103
SPITALFIELDS 5J 9 (5F 85)
Spital Sq. E1 . . . . 5H 9 (5E 84)

Spital St. E1 5K 9 (5G 85)
Spital Yd. E1 5H 9 (5E 84)
Spitfire Bus. Pk. CR0: Wadd 6A 168
Spitfire Est., The TW5: Cran 5A 94
Spitfire Rd. SM6: Wall 7J 167
TW6: H'row A 6E 110
Spitfire Way TW5: Cran 5A 94
Splendour Wlk. SE16 5J 103
(off Verney Rd.)
Spode Ho. SE11 2J 19
Spode Wlk. NW6 5K 63
Spondon Rd. N15 4G 49
Spoonbill Way UB4: Yead 5B 76
Spooner Ho. TW5: Hest 6E 94
Spooners M. W3 1K 97
Spooner Wlk. SM6: Wall 5J 167
Sporle Rd. Ct. SW11 3B 118
Sportsbank St. SE6 7E 122
Sportsman Pl. E2 1G 85
Spottiswood Ct. CR0: C'don 6C 156
(off Harry Cl.)
Spottons Gro. N17 1C 48
Spout Hill CR0: Addtn 5C 170
Spout La. TW19: Stan M 7B 174
Spout La. Nth. TW19: Stan M 7C 174
Spratt Hall Rd. E11 6J 51
Spray La. TW2: Whitt 6J 113
Spray St. SE18 4F 107
Spreighton Rd. KT8: W Mole 4F 149
Spriggs Ho. N1 7B 66
(off Canonbury Rd.)
Sprimont Pl. SW3 5E 16 (5D 100)
Springall St. SE15 7H 103
Springalls Wharf SE16 2G 103
(off Bermondsey Wall W.)
Springbank N21 6E 22
Springbank Rd. SE13 6F 123
Springbank Wlk. NW1 7H 65
Springbourne Ct. BR3: Beck 1E 158
(not continuous)
Spring Bri. M. W5 7D 78
Springbridge Rd. W5 7D 78
Spring Cl. EN5: Barn 5A 20
RM8: Dag 1D 72
Springclose La. SM3: Cheam 6G 165
Spring Cnr. TW13: Felt 3J 129
Spring Cotts. KT6: Surb 5D 150
Spring Ct. KT17: Ewe 7B 164
NW6 6H 63
W7 7H 77
Spring Ct. Rd. EN2: Enf 1F 23
Springcroft Av. N2 4D 46
Springdale M. N16 4D 66
Springdale Rd. N16 4D 66
Spring Dr. HA5: Eastc 6J 39
Springett Ho. SW2 5A 120
(off St Matthews Rd.)
Springfield E5 1H 67
SE25 3G 157
WD23: B Hea 1C 26
Springfield Av. N10 3G 47
SW20 3H 153
TW12: Hamp 6F 131
Springfield Cl. HA7: Stan 3F 27
N12 5E 30
Springfield Ct. IG1: Ilf 5F 71
KT1: King T 3E 150
(off Springfield Rd.)
NW3 7C 64
(off Eton Av.)
SM6: Wall 5F 167
Springfield Dr. IG2: Ilf 5G 53
Springfield Gdns. BR1: Brom 4D 160
BR4: W W'ck 2D 170
E5 1H 67
HA4: Ruis 1K 57
IG8: Wfd G 7F 37
NW9 5K 43
Springfield Gro. SE7 6A 106
TW16: Sun 1H 147
Springfield La. NW6 1K 81
Springfield Mt. NW9 5A 44
Springfield Pde. M. N13 4F 33
Springfield Pl. KT3: N Mald 4J 151
Springfield Ri. SE26 3H 139
Springfield Rd. BR1: Brom 4D 160
CR7: Thor H 1C 156
DA7: Bex 4H 127
DA16: Well 3B 126
E4 1B 36
E6 7D 70
E15 3G 87
E17 6B 50
HA1: Harr 6J 41
KT1: King T 3E 150
N11 5A 32
N15 4G 49
NW8 1A 82
SE26 5H 139
SM6: Wall 5F 167
SW19 5H 135
TW2: Whitt 1E 130
TW11: Tedd 5A 132
TW15: Ashf 5B 128
UB4: Yead 1A 94
W7 1J 95
Springfields EN5: New Bar 5E 20
(off Somerset Rd.)
Springfield Wlk. BR6: Orp 1H 173
(off Place Farm Av.)
NW6 1K 81
Spring Gdns. IG8: Wfd G 7F 37
KT8: W Mole 5F 149
N5 5C 66
RM7: Rom 5J 55
SM6: Wall 5G 167
SW1 4D 12 (1H 101)
(not continuous)
Spring Gdns. Bus. Pk. RM7: Rom 5J 55
SPRING GROVE 1J 113
Spring Gro. CR4: Mitc 1E 154
SE19 7F 139
TW12: Hamp 1F 149
W4 5G 97
Spring Gro. Cres. TW3: Houn 1G 113
Spring Gro. Rd. TW3: Houn, Isle 1F 113
TW7: Isle 1F 113
TW10: Rich 5F 115
Spring Health Leisure Club
Richmond 4D 114
(in Pools on the Pk.)
Spring Hill E5 7G 49
SE26 4J 139
Springhill Cl. SE5 3D 120
Spring Ho. WC1 2J 7
Springhurst Cl. CR0: C'don 4B 170
Spring Lake HA7: Stan 4G 27
Spring La. E5 7H 49
N10 3E 46
SE25 6H 157
Spring M. KT17: Ewe 7B 164
W1 5F 5 (5D 82)
SPRING PARK 3C 170
Spring Pk. Av. CR0: C'don 2K 169
Spring Pk. Dr. N4 1C 66
Springpark Dr. BR3: Beck 3E 158
Spring Pk. Rd. CR0: C'don 2K 169
Spring Pas. SW15 3F 117
Spring Path NW3 5B 64
Spring Pl. IG11: Bark 2G 89
N3 3J 45
NW5 5F 65
Springpond Rd. RM9: Dag 5E 72
Springrice Rd. SE13 6F 123
Spring Rd. TW13: Felt 3H 129
Spring Shaw Rd. BR5: St P 7A 144
Spring St. W2 1A 10 (6B 82)
Spring Ter. TW9: Rich 5E 114
Spring Tide Cl. SE15 1H 121
Spring Va. DA7: Bex 4H 127
Springvale Av. TW8: Bford 5D 96
Spring Va. Ter. W14 3F 99
Spring Villa Pk. HA8: Edg 7B 28
Spring Villa Rd. HA8: Edg 7B 28
Spring Wlk. E1 5G 85
Springwater WC1 5G 7
Springwater Cl. SE18 1E 124
Springway HA1: Harr 7H 41
Springwell Av. NW10 1B 80
Springwell Cl. SW16 4K 137
Springwell Rd. SW16 4A 138
TW4: Houn 2B 112
TW5: Hest 2B 112
Springwood Cl. E3 2C 86
Springwood Ct. CR2: S Croy 4E 168
(off Birdhurst Rd.)
Springwood Cres. HA8: Edg 2C 28
Sproggit Ind. Est. TW19: Stanw 6B 110
Sprowston M. E7 6J 69
Sprowston Rd. E7 5J 69
Spruce Ct. W5 3E 96
Sprucedale Gdns. CR0: C'don 4K 169
Spruce Hills Rd. E17 2E 50
Spruce Ho. SE16 2K 103
(off Woodland Cres.)
Spruce Pk. BR2: Brom 4H 159
Sprules Rd. SE4 2A 122
Spurfield KT8: W Mole 3F 149
Spurgeon Av. SE19 1D 156
Spurgeon Rd. SE19 1D 156
Spurgeon St. SE1 3D 102
Spurling Rd. RM9: Dag 6F 73
SE22 4F 121
Spurrell Av. DA5: Bexl 4K 145
Spur Rd. BR6: Orp 2K 173
HA8: Edg 4K 27
N15 4D 48
SE1 6J 13 (2A 102)
SW1 7A 12 (2G 101)
TW7: Isle 7A 96
TW14: Felt 4K 111
Spurstowe Rd. E8 6H 67
Spurstowe Ter. E8 5G 67
Spurway Pde. IG2: Ilf 5D 52
(off Woodford Av.)
Square, The E10 3E 68
IG1: Ilf 7E 52
IG8: Wfd G 5D 36
SM5: Cars 5E 166
TW9: Rich 5D 114
UB7: Lford 4C 174
UB11: Stock P 1F 93
W6 5E 98
Square of Fame 4G 61
(within Arena Sq.)
Square Rigger Row SW11 3A 118
Squarey St. SW17 3A 136
Squire Gdns. NW8 2A 4
(off Grove End Rd.)
Squires, The RM7: Rom 6J 55
Squire's Bri. Rd.
TW17: Shep 4B 146
Squires Ct. SW4 1J 119
SW19 4J 135
Squires La. N3 2K 45
Squires Mt. NW3 3B 64
Squire's Rd. TW17: Shep 4B 146
Squires Wlk. TW15: Ashf 7F 129
(not continuous)
Squires Way DA2: Dart 4K 145
Squires Wood Dr. BR7: Chst 7C 142
Squirrel Cl. TW4: Houn 3A 112
Squirrel M. W7 7K 77
Squirrels, The HA5: Pinn 3D 40
SE13 3F 123
Squirrels Cl. BR6: Orp 1J 173
N12 4F 31
UB10: Hil 7C 56
Squirrels Ct. KT4: Wor Pk 2B 164
(off The Avenue)
Squirrels Drey BR2: Brom 2G 159
(off Park Hill Rd.)
Squirrels Grn. KT4: Wor Pk 2B 164
Squirrel's La. IG9: Buck H 3G 37
Squirrels Trad. Est., The
UB3: Hayes 3H 93
Squirries St. E2 3G 85
SS Robin 7C 86
Stable Cl. KT2: King T 6F 133
UB5: N'olt 2E 76
Stable Ct. SM6: Wall 3E 166
Stable M. NW5 6F 65
SE6 1G 141
TW1: Twick 1K 131
Stables, The IG9: Buck H 1F 37
Stables End BR6: Farnb 3G 173
Stables Gallery & Arts Cen. 3C 62
Stables Lodge E8 7H 67
(off Mare St.)
Stables Market, The 7F 65
Stables M. SE27 5C 138
Stables Way SE11 5J 19 (5A 102)
Stables Yd. SW18 6J 117
Stable Wlk. N1 2J 83
(off Wharfdale Rd.)
N2 1B 46
Stable Way W10 6E 80
Stable Yd. SW1 6A 12
SW15 3E 116
Stableyard, The SW9 2K 119
Stableyard M. TW11: Tedd 6K 131
Stable Yd. Rd. SW1 6B 12 (2G 101)
(not continuous)
Staburn Ct. HA8: Edg 2J 43
Stacey Av. N18 4D 34
Stacey Cl. E10 5F 51
Stacey St. N7 3A 66
WC2 1D 12 (6H 83)
Stack Ho. SW1 4H 17
(off Cundy St.)
Stackhouse St. SW3 1E 16
Stacy Path SE5 7E 102
Staddon Cl. BR3: Beck 4A 158
Stadium Bus. Cen. HA9: Wemb 3H 61
Stadium Retail Pk. HA9: Wemb 3G 61
Stadium Rd. SE18 7C 106
Stadium Rd. E. NW4 7D 44
Stadium St. SW10 7A 100
Stadium Way HA9: Wemb 4F 61
Staffa Rd. E10 1A 68
Stafford Cl. E17 6B 50
(not continuous)
N14 5B 22
NW6 3J 81
SM3: Cheam 6G 165
Stafford Ct. SW8 7J 101
W7 6K 77
(off Copley Cl.)
W8 3J 99
Stafford Cripps Ho. E2 3J 85
(off Globe Rd.)
SW6 6H 99
(off Clem Attlee Ct.)
Stafford Cross Bus. Pk. CR0: Wadd 5K 167
Stafford Gdns. CR0: Wadd 5K 167
Stafford Ho. SE1 5F 103
(off Cooper's Rd.)
Stafford Mans. SW1 1A 18
(off Stafford Pl.)
SW4 4J 119
SW11 7D 100
(off Albert Bri. Rd.)
W14 3F 99
(off Haarlem Rd.)
Stafford Pl. SW1 1A 18 (3G 101)
TW10: Rich 7F 115
Stafford Rd. CR0: Wadd 4A 168
DA14: Sidc 4J 143
E3 2B 86
E7 7A 70

Stafford Rd. HA3: Hrw W 7B 26
HA4: Ruis 4H 57
KT3: N Mald 3J 151
NW6 3J 81
SM6: Wall 6G 167
Staffordshire St. SE15 1G 121
Stafford St. W1 4A 12 (1G 101)
Stafford Ter. W8 3J 99
Staff St. EC1 2F 9 (3D 84)
Stag Cl. HA8: Edg 2H 43
Stag Ct. KT2: King T 1G 151 (off Coombe Rd.)
STAG LANE 2B 134
Stag La. HA8: Edg 2H 43
IG9: Buck H 2E 36
NW9 2H 43
SW15 3B 134
Stags Way TW7: Isle 6K 95
Stainbank Rd. CR4: Mitc 3F 155
Stainby Cl. UB7: W Dray 3A 92
Stainby Rd. N15 4F 49
Stainer Ho. SE3 4A 124
Stainer St. SE1 5F 15 (1D 102)
Staines Av. SM3: Cheam 2F 165
Staines By-Pass TW15: Ashf 5A 128
Staines Rd. IG1: Ilf 5G 71
TW2: Twick 3E 130
TW3: Houn 7F 111
TW4: Houn 7F 111
TW14: Bedf, Felt 1C 128 (not continuous)
Staines Rd. E. TW16: Sun 7J 129
Staines Rd. W. TW15: Ashf 6D 128
TW16: Sun 6D 128
Staines Wlk. DA14: Sidc 6C 144
Stainford Cl. TW15: Ashf 5F 129
Stainforth Rd. E17 4C 50
IG2: Ilf 7H 53
Staining La. EC2 7D 8 (6C 84)
Stainmore Cl. BR7: Chst 1H 161
Stainsbury St. E2 2J 85
Stainsby Rd. E14 6C 86
Stainton Rd. EN3: Enf H 1D 24
SE6 6F 123
Stalbridge Flats W1 1H 11 (off Lumley St.)
Stalbridge Ho. NW1 1A 6 (off Harrington St.)
Stalbridge St. NW1 5D 4 (5C 82)
Stalham St. SE16 3H 103
Stalham Way IG6: Ilf 1F 53
Stambourne Way BR4: W W'ck 2E 170
SE19 7E 138
Stambourne Woodland Wlk. SE19 7E 138
Stamford Bridge 7K 99
Stamford Bri. Studios SW6 7K 99 (off Wandon Rd.)
Stamford Brook Arches W6 4C 98
Stamford Brook Av. W6 3B 98
Stamford Brook Gdns. W6 3B 98
Stamford Brook Mans. W6 4B 98 (off Goldhawk Rd.)
Stamford Brook Rd. W6 3B 98
Stamford Bldgs. SW8 7J 101 (off Meadow Pl.)
Stamford Cl. HA3: Hrw W 7D 26
N15 4G 49
NW3 3A 64 (off Heath St.)
UB1: S'hall 7E 76
Stamford Cotts. SW10 7K 99 (off Billing St.)
Stamford Ct. HA8: Edg 4A 28
W6 4C 98
Stamford Dr. BR2: Brom 4H 159
Stamford Gdns. RM9: Dag 7C 72
Stamford Ga. SW6 7K 99
Stamford Gro. E. N16 1G 67
Stamford Gro. W. N16 1G 67
STAMFORD HILL 1F 67
Stamford Hill N16 2F 67
Stamford Lodge N16 7F 49
Stamford Rd. E6 1C 88
N1 7E 66
N15 5G 49
RM9: Dag 1B 90
Stamford St. SE1 5J 13 (1A 102)
Stamp Pl. E2 1J 9 (2F 85)
Stanard Cl. N16 7E 48
Stanborough Cl. TW12: Hamp 6D 130
Stanborough Pas. E8 6F 67
Stanborough Rd. TW3: Houn 3H 113
Stanbridge Pl. N21 2G 33
Stanbridge Rd. SW15 3E 116
Stanbrook Rd. SE2 2B 108
Stanbury Ct. NW3 6D 64
Stanbury Rd. SE15 2H 121 (not continuous)
Stancroft NW9 5A 44
Standale Gro. HA4: Ruis 5E 38
Standard Ct. SE6 1D 140
Standard Ind. Est. E16 2D 106
Standard Pl. EC2 2H 9
Standard Rd. DA6: Bex 4E 126
DA17: Belv 5G 109
NW10 4J 79
TW4: Houn 3C 112
Standen Rd. SW18 7H 117
Standfield Gdns. RM10: Dag 6G 73
Standfield Rd. RM10: Dag 5G 73
Standish Ho. SE3 4K 123 (off Elford Cl.)
W6 4C 98 (off St Peter's Gro.)
Standish Rd. W6 4C 98
Standlake Point SE23 3K 139
Stane Cl. SW19 7K 135
Stane Gro. SW4 2J 119
Stanesgate Ho. SE15 7G 103 (off Friary Est.)
Stane Way SE18 7B 106
Stanfield Ho. NW8 3B 4 (off Frampton St.)
UB5: N'olt 2B 76 (off Academy Gdns.)
Stanfield Rd. E3 2A 86
Stanford Cl. HA4: Ruis 6E 38
IG8: Wfd G 5H 37
RM7: Rom 6H 55
TW12: Hamp 6D 130
Stanford Ct. SW6 1K 117
W8 3K 99 (off Cornwall Gdns.)
Stanford Ho. IG11: Bark 2B 90
Stanford M. E8 5G 67
Stanford Pl. SE17 4E 102
Stanford Rd. N11 5J 31
SW16 2H 155
W8 3K 99
Stanford St. SW1 4C 18 (4H 101)
Stanford Way SW16 2H 155
Stangate SE1 1H 19
Stangate Gdns. HA7: Stan 4G 27
Stangate Lodge N21 6E 22
Stanger Rd. SE25 4G 157
Stanhill Cotts. DA2: Dart 7K 145
Stanhope Av. BR2: Hayes 1H 171
HA3: Hrw W 1H 41
N3 3H 45
Stanhope Cl. SE16 2K 103
Stanhope Gdns. IG1: Ilf 1D 70
N4 6B 48
N6 6F 47
NW7 5G 29
RM8: Dag 3F 73
SW7 3A 16 (4A 100)
Stanhope Ga. W1 5H 11 (1E 100)
Stanhope Gro. BR3: Beck 5B 158
Stanhope Ho. N11 4A 32 (off Coppies Gro.)
SE8 7B 104 (off Adolphus St.)
Stanhope M. E. SW7 3A 16 (4A 100)
Stanhope M. Sth. SW7 4A 100
Stanhope M. W. SW7 4A 100
Stanhope Pde. NW1 1A 6 (3G 83)
Stanhope Pk. Rd. UB6: G'frd 4G 77
Stanhope Pl. W2 1E 10 (7D 82)
Stanhope Rd. CR0: C'don 3E 168
DA7: Bex 2E 126
DA15: Sidc 4A 144
E17 5D 50
EN5: Barn 6A 20
N6 6G 47
N12 5F 31
RM8: Dag 2F 73
SM5: Cars 7E 166
UB6: G'frd 5G 77
Stanhope Row W1 5J 11 (1F 101)
Stanhope St. NW1 1A 6 (2G 83)
Stanhope Ter. TW2: Twick 7K 113
W2 2B 10 (7B 82)
Stanier Cl. W14 5H 99
Stanier Ho. SW6 1A 118 (off Station Ct.)
Stanlake M. W12 1E 98
Stanlake Rd. W12 1E 98
Stanlake Vs. W12 1E 98
Stanley Av. BR3: Beck 2E 158
HA0: Wemb 7E 60
IG11: Bark 2K 89
KT3: N Mald 5C 152
RM8: Dag 1F 73
UB6: G'frd 1G 77
Stanley Bri. Studios SW6 7K 99 (off King's Rd.)
Stanley Cl. HA0: Wemb 7E 60
SE9 1G 143
SW8 6K 101
Stanley Cohen Ho. EC1 4C 8 (off Golden La. Est.)
Stanley Ct. SM2: Sutt 7K 165
SM5: Cars 7E 166
W5 5C 78
Stanley Cres. W11 7H 81
Stanleycroft Cl. TW7: Isle 1J 113
Stanley Gdns. CR4: Mitc 6E 136
NW2 5E 62
SM6: Wall 6G 167
W3 2A 98
W11 7H 81
Stanley Gdns. M. W11 7H 81 (off Kensington Pk. Rd.)
Stanley Gdns. Rd. TW11: Tedd 5J 131
Stanley Gro. CR0: C'don 6A 156
SW8 2E 118
Stanley Holloway Ct. E16 6J 87 (off Coolfin Rd.)
Stanley Ho. E14 6C 86 (off Saracen St.)
SW10 7A 100 (off Coleridge Gdns.)
Stanley Mans. SW10 7A 16 (off Park Wlk.)
Stanley M. SW10 7A 100 (off Coleridge Gdns.)
Stanley Pk. Dr. HA0: Wemb 1F 79
Stanley Pk. Rd. SM5: Cars 7C 166
SM6: Wall 6F 167
Stanley Picker Gallery 3E 150 (within Kingston University)
Stanley Rd. BR2: Brom 4K 159
BR6: Orp 1K 173
CR0: C'don 7A 156
CR4: Mitc 7E 136
DA14: Sidc 3A 144
E4 1A 36
E10 6D 50
Stanley Rd. E12 5C 70
E15 1F 87
E18 1H 51
EN1: Enf 3K 23
HA2: Harr 2G 59
HA6: Nwood 1J 39
HA9: Wemb 6F 61
IG1: Ilf 2H 71
N2 3B 46
N9 1A 34
N10 7A 32
N11 6C 32
N15 4B 48
NW9 7C 44
SM2: Sutt 6K 165
SM4: Mord 4J 153
SM5: Cars 7E 166
SW14 4H 115
SW19 6J 135
TW2: Twick 3H 131
TW3: Houn 4G 113
TW11: Tedd 4J 131
TW15: Ashf 5A 128
UB1: S'hall 7C 76
W3 3J 97
Stanley Sq. SM5: Cars 7D 166
Stanley St. SE8 7B 104
Stanley Studios SW10 7A 16 (off Fulham Rd.)
Stanley Ter. DA6: Bex 4G 127
N19 2J 65
Stanliffe Ho. E14 3C 104
Stanmer St. SW11 1C 118
STANMORE 5G 27
Stanmore Gdns. SM1: Sutt 3A 166
TW9: Rich 3F 115
Stanmore Hill HA7: Stan 3F 27
Stanmore Lodge HA7: Stan 4G 27
Stanmore Pl. NW1 1F 83
Stanmore Rd. DA17: Belv 4J 109
E11 1H 69
N15 4B 48
TW9: Rich 3F 115
Stanmore St. N1 1K 83
Stanmore Ter. BR3: Beck 2C 158
Stannard Cotts. E1 4J 85 (off Fox Cl.)
Stannard M. E8 6G 67 (off Stannard Rd.)
Stannard Rd. E8 6G 67
Stannary Pl. SE11 6K 19 (5A 102)
Stannary St. SE11 7K 19 (6A 102)
Stannet Way SM6: Wall 4G 167
Stansbury Sq. W10 3G 81
Stansfeld Ho. SE1 4F 103 (off Longfield Est.)
Stansfeld Rd. E6 5B 88
E16 5B 88
Stansfield Rd. SW9 3K 119
TW4: Cran 2K 111
Stansgate Rd. RM10: Dag 2G 73
Stanstead WC1 3J 83 (off Wakefield St.)
Stanstead Cl. BR2: Brom 5H 159
Stanstead Gro. SE6 1B 140
Stanstead Mnr. SM1: Sutt 6J 165
Stanstead Rd. E11 5K 51
SE6 1A 140
SE23 1K 139
Stansted Cres. DA5: Bexl 1D 144
Stansted Rd. TW6: H'row A 6B 110
Stanswood Gdns. SE5 7E 102
Stanthorpe Cl. SW16 5J 137
Stanthorpe Rd. SW16 5J 137
Stanton Av. TW11: Tedd 6J 131
Stanton Cl. KT4: Wor Pk 1F 165
KT19: Ewe 5H 163
Stanton Ct. CR2: S Croy 5E 168 (off Birdhurst Ri.)

Stanton Ho. *SE10* 6E 104
(off Thames St.)
SE16 2B 104
(off Rotherhithe St.)
Stanton Rd. CR0: C'don 7C 156
SE26 4B 140
SW13 2B 116
SW20 1F 153
Stanton Sq. SE26 4B 140
Stanton Way SE26 4B 140
Stanway Ct. N1 2E 84
(not continuous)
Stanway Gdns. HA8: Edg 5D 28
W3 1G 97
Stanway St. N1 2E 84
STANWELL 6A 110
Stanwell Cl. TW19: Stanw 6A 110
STANWELL MOOR 7B 174
Stanwell Moor Rd.
TW19: Lford, Stan M 7C 174
UB7: Lford 7C 174
Stanwell Rd. TW14: Bedf 7D 110
TW15: Ashf 2A 128
Stanwick Rd. W14 4H 99
Stanworth Ct. TW5: Hest 7D 94
Stanworth St. SE1 7J 15 (3F 103)
Stanyhurst SE23 1A 140
Stapenhill Rd.
HA0: Wemb 3B 60
Staple Cl. DA5: Bexl 3K 145
Staplefield Cl. SW2 1J 137
Stapleford *N17* 2E 48
(off Willan Rd.)
Stapleford Av. IG2: Ilf 5J 53
Stapleford Cl. E4 3K 35
KT1: King T 2G 151
SW19 7G 117
Stapleford Rd. HA0: Wemb 7D 60
Stapleford Way IG11: Bark 3B 90
Staplehurst Rd. SE13 5F 123
SM5: Cars 7C 166
Staple Inn WC1 6J 7
Staple Inn Bldgs. WC1 6J 7 (5A 84)
Staples Cl. SE16 1A 104
STAPLES CORNER 1D 62
Staples Cnr. Bus. Pk. NW2 1D 62
Staples Cnr. Retail Pk. NW2 1D 62
Staples Ho. *E6* 6E 88
(off Savage Gdns.)
Staple St. SE1 7F 15 (2D 102)
Stapleton Gdns. CR0: Wadd 5A 168
Stapleton Hall Rd. N4 1K 65
Stapleton Ho. *E2* 3H 85
(off Ellsworth St.)
Stapleton Rd. BR6: Orp 4K 173
DA7: Bex 7F 109
SW17 3E 136
Stapleton Vs. *N16* 4E 66
(off Wordsworth Rd.)
Stapley Rd. DA17: Belv 5G 109
Stapylton Rd. EN5: Barn 3B 20
Star All. EC3 2H 15
Star & Garter Hill TW10: Rich 1E 132
Starboard Way E14 3C 104
Starbuck Cl. SE9 7E 124
Star Bus. Cen. RM13: Rain 5K 91
Starch Ho. La. IG6: Ilf 2H 53
Star Cl. EN3: Pond E 6D 24
Starcross St. NW1 2B 6 (3G 83)
Starfield Rd. W12 2C 98
Star Hill DA1: Cray 5K 127
Star La. E16 4G 87
Starlight Way TW6: H'row A 5E 110
Starling Cl. CR0: C'don 6A 158
HA5: Pinn 3A 40
IG9: Buck H 1D 36
Starling Ho. *NW8* 2C 82
(off Charlbert St.)
Starling Wlk. TW12: Hamp 5C 130
Starmans Cl. RM9: Dag 1E 90
Star Path *UB5: N'olt* 2E 76
(off Brabazon Rd.)
Star Pl. E1 3K 15 (7G 85)
Star Rd. TW7: Isle 2H 113
UB10: Hil 4E 74
W14 6H 99
Star St. W2 7B 4 (6C 82)
Starts Cl. BR6: Farnb 3E 172
Starts Hill Av. BR6: Farnb 4F 173
Starts Hill Rd. BR6: Farnb 3E 172
Starveall Cl. UB7: W Dray 3B 92
Star Wharf *NW1* 1G 83
(off St Pancras Way)
Star Yd. WC2 7J 7 (6A 84)
State Farm Av. BR6: Farnb 4F 173
Staten Gdns. TW1: Twick 1K 131
Statham Gro. N16 4D 66
N18 5K 33
Statham Ho. *SW8* 1G 119
(off Wadhurst Rd.)
Station App. *BR1: Brom* 3J 159
(off High St.)
BR2: Hayes 1J 171
BR3: Beck 1C 158
BR4: W W'ck 7E 158
BR6: Orp 2K 173
BR7: Chst 6C 142
(Elmstead La.)
BR7: Chst 1E 160
(Vale Rd.)
CR0: C'don 2D 168
(off Dingwall Rd.)
CR2: Sande 7D 168
DA5: Bexl 1G 145
DA7: Bex 2J 127
(Barnehurst Rd.)
DA7: Bex 2E 126
(Pickford La.)
DA16: Well 2A 126
E4 6A 36
E7 4K 69
E11 5J 51
E17 5C 50
(not continuous)
E18 2K 51
EN5: New Bar 4F 21
HA0: Wemb 6B 60
HA1: Harr 7J 41
HA4: Ruis 5K 57
(Mahlon Av.)
HA4: Ruis 1G 57
(Pembroke Rd.)
HA5: Pinn 3C 40
IG8: Wfd G 6E 36
IG9: Buck H 4G 37
KT1: King T 1G 151
KT4: Wor Pk 1C 164
KT17: Ewe 7B 164
KT19: Ewe 5C 164
N11 5A 32
N12 4E 30
NW1 4F 5 (4D 82)
NW10 3B 80
NW11 7F 45
SE3 3K 123
SE9 2G 143
(Bercta Rd.)
SE9 1D 142
(Crossmead)
SE12 6J 123
(off Burnt Ash Hill)
SE26 4J 139
SM2: Cheam 7G 165
SM5: Cars 4D 166
SW6 3G 117
SW14 3J 115
SW16 6H 137
(Estreham Rd.)
SW16 5H 137
(Gleneagle Rd.)
Station App. SW20 2D 152
TW8: Bford 6C 96
(off Sidney Gdns.)
TW9: Kew 1G 115
TW12: Hamp 1E 148
TW15: Ashf 4B 128
TW16: Sun 1J 147
TW17: Shep 5E 146
UB3: Hayes 3H 93
UB6: G'frd 7G 59
UB7: Yiew 1A 92
W7 1J 95
Station App. Nth. DA15: Sidc 2A 144
Station App. Rd. SE1 7H 13 (2A 102)
W4 7J 97
Station Arc. *W1* 4K 5
(off Gt. Portland St.)
Station Av. KT3: N Mald 3A 152
KT19: Ewe 7A 164
SW9 3B 120
TW9: Kew 1G 115
Station Bldgs. *KT1: King T* 2E 150
(off Fife Rd.)
Station Chambers *E6* 7C 70
(off High St. Nth.)
Station Cl. N3 1J 45
N12 4E 30
TW12: Hamp 1F 149
Station Cotts. BR6: Orp 2K 173
Station Ct. N15 5F 49
SW6 1A 118
Station Cres. HA0: Wemb 6B 60
N15 4D 48
SE3 5J 105
TW15: Ashf 3A 128
Stationer's Hall Ct. EC4 1B 14 (6B 84)
Station Est. BR3: Beck 3K 157
E18 2K 51
Station Est. Rd. TW14: Felt 1K 129
Station Garage M. SW16 6H 137
Station Gdns. W4 7J 97
Station Gro. HA0: Wemb 6E 60
Station Hill BR2: Hayes 2J 171
Station Ho. M. N9 4B 34
Station Pde. *DA7: Bex* 2E 126
(off Pickford La.)
DA15: Sidc 2A 144
E6 7C 70
E11 5J 51
E13 1A 88
(off Green St.)
EN4: Cockf 4K 21
HA2: Harr 4F 59
HA3: Kent 2A 42
HA4: Ruis 2F 57
HA8: Edg 7K 27
IG9: Buck H 4G 37
IG11: Bark 7G 71
N14 1C 32
NW2 6E 62
RM9: Dag 6G 73
SM2: Sutt 6A 166
(off High St.)
SW12 1E 136
TW9: Kew 1G 115
TW14: Felt 1K 129
TW15: Ashf 4B 128
UB5: N'olt 7E 58
(Court Farm Rd.)
UB5: N'olt 4F 59
(Halsbury Rd. W.)
W3 6G 79
W4 7J 97
W5 1F 97
Station Pas. E18 2K 51
SE15 1J 121
Station Path *E8* 6H 67
(off Graham Rd.)
SW6 3H 117
Station Pl. N4 2A 66
Station Ri. SE27 2B 138
Station Rd. BR1: Brom 1J 159
BR2: Brom 2G 159
BR4: W W'ck 1E 170
BR6: Orp 2K 173
CR0: C'don 1C 168
DA7: Bex 3E 126
DA15: Sidc 2A 144
DA17: Belv 3G 109
E4 1A 36
E7 4J 69
E12 4C 70
E17 6A 50
EN5: New Bar 5E 20
HA1: Harr 4K 41
HA2: Harr 5F 41
HA8: Edg 6B 28
IG1: Ilf 3F 71
IG6: Ilf 3H 53
KT1: Ham W 1C 150
KT2: King T 1G 151
KT3: N Mald 5D 152
KT7: T Ditt 7K 149
KT9: Chess 5E 162
N3 1J 45
N11 5A 32
N17 3G 49
N19 3G 65
N21 1G 33
N22 2J 47
NW4 6C 44
NW7 6F 29
NW10 2B 80
RM6: Chad H, Dag 7D 54
SE13 3E 122
SE20 6J 139
SE25 4F 157
SM5: Cars 4D 166
SW13 2B 116
SW19 1A 154
TW1: Twick 1K 131
TW3: Houn 4F 113
TW11: Tedd 6A 132
TW12: Hamp 1E 148
TW15: Ashf 4B 128
TW16: Sun 7J 129
TW17: Shep 5E 146
UB3: Harl, Hayes 4G 93
UB7: W Dray 2A 92
W5 6F 79
W7 1J 95
Station Rd. Nth. DA17: Belv 3H 109
Station Sq. BR5: Pet W 5G 161
Station St. E15 7F 69
E16 1F 107
Station Ter. NW10 2F 81
SE5 1C 120
Station Ter. M. SE3 5J 105
Station Vw. UB6: G'frd 1H 77
Station Wlk. *IG1: Ilf* 2F 71
(in The Exchange)
Station Way IG9: Buck H 4F 37
SE15 2G 121
SM3: Cheam 6G 165
Station Yd. TW1: Twick 7A 114
Staton Ct. *E10* 7D 50
(off Kings Cl.)
Staunton Ho. *SE17* 4E 102
(off Tatum St.)
Staunton Rd. KT2: King T 6E 132
Staunton St. SE8 6B 104
Staveley *NW1* 1A 6
(off Varndell St.)
Staveley Cl. E9 5J 67
N7 4J 65
SE15 1H 121
Staveley Ct. E11 5J 51
Staveley Gdns. W4 1K 115
Staveley Rd. TW15: Ashf 6F 129
W4 6J 97

Staverton Rd. NW2 . . . . . 7E 62
Stave Yd. Rd. SE16 . . . . . 1A 104
Stavordale Lodge W14 . . . . . 3H 99
(off Melbury Rd.)
Stavordale Rd. N5 . . . . . 4B 66
SM5: Cars 7A 154
Stayner's Rd. E1 . . . . . 4K 85
Stayton Rd. SM1: Sutt 3J 165
Steadfast Rd. KT1: King T 1D 150
Steadman Ct. EC1 . . . . . 3D 8
(off Old St.)
Steadman Ho. RM10: Dag 3G 73
(off Uvedale Rd.)
Stead St. SE17 . . . . . 4D 102
Steam Farm La.
TW14: Felt 4H 111
Stean St. E8 . . . . . 1F 85
Stebbing Ho. W11 . . . . . 1F 99
(off Queensdale Cres.)
Stebbing Way IG11: Bark 2A 90
Stebondale St. E14 . . . . . 4E 104
Stedham Pl. WC1 . . . . . 7E 6
Stedman Cl. DA5: Bexl 3K 145
UB10: Ick 3C 56
Steedman St. SE17 . . . . . 4C 102
Steeds Rd. N10 . . . . . 1D 46
Steele Ho. E15 . . . . . 2G 87
(off Eve Rd.)
Steele Rd. E11 . . . . . 4G 69
N17 . . . . . 3E 48
NW10 . . . . . 2J 79
TW7: Isle 4A 114
W4 . . . . . 3J 97
Steele's M. Nth. NW3 . . . . . 6D 64
Steele's M. Sth. NW3 . . . . . 6D 64
Steele's Rd. NW3 . . . . . 6D 64
Steele's Studios
NW3 . . . . . 6D 64
Steele Wlk. DA8: Erith 7H 109
Steel's La. E1 . . . . . 6J 85
Steelyard Pas. EC4 . . . . . 3E 14
Steen Way SE22 . . . . . 5E 120
Steep Cl. BR6: Chels 6K 173
Steep Hill CR0: C'don 4E 168
SW16 . . . . . 3H 137
Steeple Cl. SW6 . . . . . 2G 117
SW19 . . . . . 5G 135
Steeple Ct. E1 . . . . . 4H 85
Steeplestone Cl. N18 . . . . . 5H 33
Steeple Wlk. N1 . . . . . 1C 84
(off New Nth. Rd.)
Steerforth St. SW18 . . . . . 2A 136
Steering Cl. N9 . . . . . 1D 34
Steers Mead CR4: Mitc 1D 154
Steers Way SE16 . . . . . 2A 104
Stelfox Ho. WC1 . . . . . 1H 7
(off Penton Ri.)
Stella Cl. UB8: Hil 5D 74
Stellar Ho. N17 . . . . . 6A 34
Stella Rd. SW17 . . . . . 6D 136
Stelling Rd. DA8: Erith 7K 109
Stellman Cl. E5 . . . . . 3G 67
Stembridge Rd. SE20 . . . . . 2H 157
Stephan Cl. E8 . . . . . 1G 85
Stephen Cl. BR6: Orp 3J 173
Stephendale Rd. SW6 . . . . . 3K 117
Stephen Fox Ho. W4 . . . . . 5A 98
(off Chiswick La.)
Stephen M. W1 . . . . . 6C 6 (5H 83)
Stephen Pl. SW4 . . . . . 3G 119
Stephen Rd. DA7: Bex 3J 127
Stephens Ct. E16 . . . . . 4H 87
SE4 . . . . . 3A 122
Stephens Lodge N12 . . . . . 3F 31
(off Woodside La.)
Stephenson Cl. DA16: Well 2A 126
Stephenson Ct.
SM2: Cheam 7G 165
(off Station App.)
Stephenson Ho. SE1 . . . . . 3C 102
Stephenson Rd. E17 . . . . . 5A 50
TW2: Whitt 7E 112
W7 . . . . . 6K 77
Stephenson St. E16 . . . . . 4G 87
NW10 . . . . . 3A 80
Stephenson Way NW1 . . . . . 3B 6 (4G 83)
Stephen's Rd. E15 . . . . . 1G 87
Stephen St. W1 . . . . . 6C 6 (5H 83)
STEPNEY 5K 85
Stepney C'way. E1 . . . . . 6K 85
Stepney City Apartments
E1 . . . . . 5J 85
Stepney Cl. CR4: Mitc 1E 154
Stepney Grn. E1 . . . . . 5J 85
Stepney Grn. Ct. E1 . . . . . 5K 85
(off Stepney Grn.)
Stepney High St. E1 . . . . . 5K 85
Stepney Way E1 . . . . . 5H 85
Sterling Av. HA8: Edg 4A 28
Sterling Cl. NW10 . . . . . 7C 62
Sterling Gdns. SE14 . . . . . 6A 104
Sterling Ho. SE3 . . . . . 4K 123
Sterling Ind. Est. RM10: Dag 4H 73
Sterling Pl. W5 . . . . . 4E 96
Sterling Rd. EN2: Enf 1J 23
Sterling St. SW7 . . . . . 1D 16 (3C 100)
Sterling Way N18 . . . . . 4J 33
Stern Cl. IG11: Bark 2C 90
Sterndale Rd. W14 . . . . . 3F 99
Sterne St. W12 . . . . . 2F 99
Sternhall La. SE15 . . . . . 3G 121
Sternhold Av. SW2 . . . . . 2H 137
Sterry Cres. RM10: Dag 5G 73
Sterry Dr. KT7: T Ditt 6J 149
KT19: Ewe 4A 164
Sterry Gdns. RM10: Dag 6G 73
Sterry Rd. IG11: Bark 1K 89
RM10: Dag 4G 73
Sterry St. SE1 . . . . . 7E 14 (2D 102)
Steucers La. SE23 . . . . . 1A 140
Stevannie Ct. DA17: Belv 5F 109
Steve Biko La. SE6 . . . . . 4C 140
Steve Biko Lodge E13 . . . . . 2J 87
(off London Rd.)
Steve Biko Rd. N7 . . . . . 3A 66
Steve Biko Way TW3: Houn 3E 112
Stevedale Rd. DA16: Well 2C 126
Stevedore St. E1 . . . . . 1H 103
Stevenage Rd. E6 . . . . . 6E 70
SW6 . . . . . 7F 99
Stevens Av. E9 . . . . . 6J 67
Stevens Cl. BR3: Beck 6C 140
DA5: Bexl 4K 145
HA5: Eastc 5A 40
TW12: Hamp 6D 130
Stevens Grn. WD23: B Hea 1B 26
Stevens La. KT10: Clay 7A 162
Stevenson Cl. EN5: New Bar 7G 21
Stevenson Cres. SE16 . . . . . 5G 103
Stevenson Ho. NW8 . . . . . 1A 82
(off Boundary Rd.)
Stevens Rd. RM8: Dag 2C 72
Stevens St. SE1 . . . . . 7H 15 (3E 102)
Steventon Rd. W12 . . . . . 7B 80
Stewards Holte Wlk. N11 . . . . . 4A 32
Steward St. E1 . . . . . 6H 9 (5E 84)
Stewart Av. TW17: Shep 4C 146
Stewart Cl. BR7: Chst 5F 143
NW9 . . . . . 6J 43
TW12: Hamp 6C 130
Stewart Ho. KT1: King T 3F 151
Stewart Quay UB3: Hayes 2G 93
Stewart Rainbird Ho. E12 . . . . . 5E 70
(off Parkhurst Rd.)
Stewart Rd. E15 . . . . . 4F 69
Stewartsby Cl. N18 . . . . . 5H 33
Stewart's Gro. SW3 . . . . . 5B 16 (5B 100)
Stewart's Rd. SW8 . . . . . 7G 101
Stewart St. E14 . . . . . 2E 104
Stew La. EC4 . . . . . 2C 14 (7C 84)
Steyne Ho. W3 . . . . . 1J 97
(off Narrow St.)
Steyne Rd. W3 . . . . . 1H 97
Steyning Gro. SE9 . . . . . 4D 142
Steynings Way N12 . . . . . 5D 30
Steyning Way TW4: Houn 4A 112
Steynton Av. DA5: Bexl 2D 144
Stibbington Ho. NW1 . . . . . 2G 83
(off Cranleigh St.)
Stickland Rd. DA17: Belv 4G 109
Stickleton Cl. UB6: G'frd 3F 77
Stifford Ho. E1 . . . . . 5J 85
(off Stepney Way)
Stilecroft Gdns. HA0: Wemb 3B 60
Stile Hall Gdns. W4 . . . . . 5G 97
Stile Hall Pde. W4 . . . . . 5G 97
Stileman Ho. E3 . . . . . 5B 86
(off Ackroyd Dr.)
Stile Path TW16: Sun 3J 147
Stiles Cl. BR2: Brom 6D 160
DA8: Erith 5H 109
Stillingfleet Rd. SW13 . . . . . 6C 98
Stillington St. SW1 . . . . . 3B 18 (4G 101)
Stillness Rd. SE23 . . . . . 6A 122
Stilwell Dr. UB8: Hil 4B 74
Stilwell Rdbt. UB8: Hil 7C 74
Stipularis Dr. UB4: Yead 4B 76
Stirling Av. HA5: Pinn 1B 58
SM6: Wall 7J 167
TW17: Shep 3G 147
Stirling Cl. DA14: Sidc 4J 143
SW16 . . . . . 1H 155
Stirling Ct. EC1 . . . . . 3A 8
(off St John St.)
W13 . . . . . 7B 78
Stirling Gro. TW3: Houn 2G 113
Stirling Ho. SE18 . . . . . 5F 107
Stirling Rd. E13 . . . . . 2K 87
E17 . . . . . 3A 50
HA3: W'stone 3K 41
N17 . . . . . 1G 49
N22 . . . . . 1B 48
SW9 . . . . . 2J 119
TW2: Whitt 7E 112
TW6: H'row A 6B 110
UB3: Hayes 7K 75
W3 . . . . . 3H 97
Stirling Rd. Path E17 . . . . . 3A 50
Stirling Wlk. KT5: Surb 6H 151
Stirling Way CR0: Bedd 7J 155
Stiven Cres. HA2: Harr 3D 58
Stockbeck NW1 . . . . . 1B 6
(off Ampthill Est.)
Stockbury Rd. CR0: C'don 6J 157
Stockdale Rd. RM8: Dag 2F 73
Stockdove Way UB6: G'frd 3K 77
Stocker Gdns. RM9: Dag 7C 72
Stockfield Rd. SW16 . . . . . 3K 137
Stockford Av. NW7 . . . . . 7A 30
Stockholm Ho. E1 . . . . . 7G 85
(off Swedenborg Gdns.)
Stockholm Rd. SE16 . . . . . 5J 103
Stockholm Way E1 . . . . . 1G 103
Stockhurst Cl. SW15 . . . . . 2E 116
Stockingswater La. EN3: Brim 2G 25
Stockland Rd. RM7: Rom 6K 55
Stockleigh Hall NW8 . . . . . 2C 82
(off Prince Albert Rd.)
Stockley Cl. UB7: W Dray 2D 92
Stockley Country Pk. 7C 74
Stockley Farm Rd.
UB7: W Dray 3D 92
STOCKLEY PARK 1D 92
Stockley Rd. UB7: W Dray 4D 92
UB8: Hil 6C 74
UB11: Stock P 6C 74
Stock Orchard Cres. N7 . . . . . 5K 65
Stock Orchard St. N7 . . . . . 5K 65
Stockport Rd. SW16 . . . . . 1H 155
Stocksfield Rd. E17 . . . . . 3E 50
Stocks Pl. E14 . . . . . 7B 86
UB10: Hil 1C 74
Stock St. E13 . . . . . 2J 87
Stockton Cl. EN5: New Bar 4F 21
Stockton Ct. SW1 . . . . . 2C 18
(off Rochester Row)
Stockton Gdns. N17 . . . . . 7H 33
NW7 . . . . . 3F 29
Stockton Ho. E2 . . . . . 3H 85
(off Ellsworth St.)
HA2: Harr 1E 58
Stockton Rd. N17 . . . . . 7H 33
N18 . . . . . 6B 34
STOCKWELL 2K 119
Stockwell Av. SW9 . . . . . 3K 119
Stockwell Cl. BR1: Brom 2K 159
HA8: Edg 2J 43
Stockwell Gdns. SW9 . . . . . 1K 119
Stockwell Gdns. Est. SW9 . . . . . 2J 119
Stockwell Grn. SW9 . . . . . 2K 119
Stockwell Grn. Ct. SW9 . . . . . 2K 119
Stockwell Hall UB8: Cowl 3A 74
(off Kingston La.)
Stockwell La. SW9 . . . . . 2K 119
Stockwell M. SW9 . . . . . 2K 119
Stockwell Pk. Cres. SW9 . . . . . 2K 119
Stockwell Pk. Est. SW9 . . . . . 2K 119
Stockwell Pk. Rd. SW9 . . . . . 1K 119
Stockwell Pk. Wlk. SW9 . . . . . 3A 120
Stockwell Rd. SW9 . . . . . 2K 119
Stockwell St. SE10 . . . . . 6E 104
Stockwell Ter. SW8 . . . . . 1K 119
Stodart Rd. SE20 . . . . . 1J 157
Stoddart Ho. SW8 . . . . . 7H 19 (6K 101)
Stofield Gdns. SE9 . . . . . 3B 142
Stoford Cl. SW19 . . . . . 7G 117
Stokenchurch St. SW6 . . . . . 1K 117
STOKE NEWINGTON 3F 67
Stoke Newington Chu. St. N16 . . . . . 3D 66
Stoke Newington Comn. N16 . . . . . 2F 67
Stoke Newington High St.
N16 . . . . . 3F 67
Stoke Newington Rd. N16 . . . . . 5F 67
Stoke Pl. NW10 . . . . . 3B 80
Stoke Rd. KT2: King T 7J 133
Stokesby Rd. KT9: Chess 6F 163
Stokes Cotts. IG6: Ilf 1G 53
Stokes Ct. N2 . . . . . 4C 46
Stokesley St. W12 . . . . . 6B 80
Stokes Rd. CR0: C'don 6K 157
E6 . . . . . 4C 88
Stokley Ct. N8 . . . . . 4J 47
Stoll Cl. NW2 . . . . . 3E 62
Stoms Path SE6 . . . . . 5C 140
(off Maroons Way)
Stonard Rd. N13 . . . . . 3F 33
RM8: Dag 5B 72
Stondon Ho. E15 . . . . . 1H 87
(off John St.)
Stondon Pk. SE23 . . . . . 6A 122
Stondon Wlk. E6 . . . . . 2B 88
Stonebanks KT12: Walt T 7J 147
STONEBRIDGE 1K 79
Stonebridge Cen. N15 . . . . . 5F 49
STONEBRIDGE PARK 7H 61
Stonebridge Pk. NW10 . . . . . 7K 61
Stonebridge Rd. N15 . . . . . 5F 49
Stonebridge Shop. Cen.
NW10 . . . . . 1K 79
Stonebridge Way HA9: Wemb 6H 61
Stone Bldgs. WC2 . . . . . 6H 7
Stonechat Sq. E6 . . . . . 5C 88
Stone Cl. RM8: Dag 2F 73
SW4 . . . . . 2G 119
UB7: Yiew 1B 92
Stonecot Cl. SM3: Sutt 1G 165
Stonecot Hill SM3: Sutt 1G 165
Stone Cres. TW14: Felt 7H 111
Stonecroft Rd. DA8: Erith 7J 109
Stonecroft Way CR0: C'don 7J 155

Stonecrop Cl. NW9 .... 3K 43
Stonecutter St. EC4 .... 7A 8 (6B 84)
Stonefield N4 .... 2K 65
Stonefield Cl. DA7: Bex 3G 127
HA4: Ruis 5C 58
Stonefield Mans. *N1* *1A 84*
(off Cloudesley St.)
Stonefield St. N1 .... 1A 84
Stonefield Way HA4: Ruis 4C 58
SE7 .... 7B 106
STONEGROVE 4A 28
Stonegrove HA8: Edg 4K 27
Stone Gro. Ct. HA8: Edg 5A 28
Stonegrove Gdns. HA8: Edg 5K 27
Stone Hall *W8* *3K 99*
(off Stone Hall Gdns.)
Stonehall Av. IG1: Ilf 6C 52
Stone Hall Gdns. W8 .... 3K 99
Stone Hall Pl. W8 .... 3K 99
Stone Hall Rd. N21 .... 7E 22
Stoneham Rd. N11 .... 5B 32
Stonehill Bus. Pk. N18 .... 6F 35
Stonehill Cl. SW14 .... 5K 115
Stonehill Ct. E4 .... 7J 25
STONEHILL GREEN 7J 145
Stone Hill Rd. W4 .... 5G 97
Stonehill Rd. SW14 .... 5J 115
Stonehills Ct. SE21 .... 3E 138
Stonehill Woods Pk. DA14: Sidc 6H 145
Stonehorse Rd. EN3: Pond E 5D 24
Stonehouse *NW1* *1G 83*
(off Plender St.)
Stone Ho. Ct. EC3 .... 6H 9
Stonehouse Ho. *W2* *5J 81*
(off Westbourne Pk. Rd.)
Stone Lake Ind. Pk. SE7 .... 4A 106
Stone Lake Retail Pk. SE7 .... 4A 106
STONELEIGH 5C 164
Stoneleigh Av. EN1: Enf 1C 24
KT4: Wor Pk 4C 164
Stoneleigh B'way. KT17: Ewe 5C 164
Stoneleigh Ct. IG5: Ilf 3C 52
Stoneleigh Cres. KT19: Ewe 5B 164
Stoneleigh M. E3 .... 2A 86
Stoneleigh Pk. Av. CR0: C'don 6K 157
Stoneleigh Pk. Rd. KT19: Ewe 6B 164
Stoneleigh Pl. W11 .... 7F 81
Stoneleigh Rd. BR1: Brom 3F 161
IG5: Ilf 3C 52
N17 .... 3F 49
SM5: Cars 7C 154
Stoneleigh St. W11 .... 7F 81
Stoneleigh Ter. N19 .... 2F 65
Stonell's Rd. SW11 .... 6D 118
Stonemason Ct. *SE1* *7C 14*
(off Borough Rd.)
Stonemasons Cl. N15 .... 4D 48
Stonenest St. N4 .... 1K 65
Stone Pk. Av. BR3: Beck 4C 158
Stone Pl. KT4: Wor Pk 2C 164
Stone Rd. BR2: Brom 5H 159
Stones End St. SE1 .... 7C 14 (2C 102)
Stonewall E6 .... 5E 88
Stonewold Ct. W5 .... 6D 78
Stoney All. SE18 .... 2E 124
Stoneyard La. E14 .... 7D 86
Stoneycroft Cl. SE12 .... 7H 123
Stoneycroft Rd. IG8: Wfd G 6H 37
Stoneydeep TW11: Tedd 4A 132
Stoneydown E17 .... 4A 50
Stoneydown Av. E17 .... 4A 50
Stoneydown Ho. *E17* *4A 50*
(off Blackhorse Rd.)
Stoneyfields Gdns.
HA8: Edg 4D 28
Stoneyfields La. HA8: Edg 5D 28
Stoney La. E1 .... 7H 9 (6F 85)
SE19 .... 6F 139
Stoney St. SE1 .... 4E 14 (1D 102)
Stonhouse St. SW4 .... 4H 119
Stonor Rd. W14 .... 4H 99
Stonycroft Cl. EN3: Enf H 2F 25
Stopes St. SE15 .... 7F 103
Stopford Rd. E13 .... 1J 87
SE17 .... 5B 102
Stopher Ho. *SE1* *7B 14*
(off Webber St.)
Store Rd. E16 .... 2E 106
Storers Quay E14 .... 4F 105
Store St. E15 .... 5F 69
WC1 .... 6C 6 (5H 83)
Storey Ct. NW8 .... 2A 4
Storey Ho. *E14* *7D 86*
(off Cottage St.)
Storey Rd. E17 .... 4B 50
N6 .... 6D 46
Storey's Ga.
SW1 .... 7D 12 (2H 101)
Storey St. E16 .... 1E 106
Stories M. SE5 .... 2E 120
Stories Rd. SE5 .... 3E 120
Stork Rd. E7 .... 6H 69
Storksmead Rd. HA8: Edg 7F 29
Stork's Rd. SE16 .... 3G 103
Stormont Lawn Tennis & Squash Club
.... 5D 46
Stormont Rd. N6 .... 7D 46
SW11 .... 3E 118
Stormont Way KT9: Chess 5C 162
Stormount Dr. UB3: Harl 2E 92
Storrington *WC1* *2F 7*
(off Regent Sq.)
Storrington Rd. CR0: C'don 1F 169
Story St. N1 .... 7K 65
Stothard Ho. *E1* *4J 85*
(off Amiel St.)
Stothard St. E1 .... 4J 85
Stott Cl. SW18 .... 6B 118
Stoughton Av. SM3: Cheam 5F 165
Stoughton Cl. SE11 .... 4H 19 (4K 101)
SW15 .... 1C 134
Stour Av. UB2: S'hall 3E 94
Stourcliffe Cl. W1 .... 1E 10 (6D 82)
Stourcliffe St. W1 .... 1E 10 (6D 82)
Stour Cl. BR2: Kes 4A 172
Stourhead Cl. SW19 .... 7F 117
Stourhead Gdns. SW20 .... 3C 152
Stourhead Ho. *SW1* *5C 18*
(off Tachbrook St.)
Stour Rd. E3 .... 7C 68
RM10: Dag 2G 73
Stourton Av. TW13: Hanw 4D 130
Stowage SE8 .... 6C 104
Stow Cres. E17 .... 7F 35
Stowe Cres. HA4: Ruis 6D 38
Stowe Gdns. N9 .... 1A 34
Stowe Ho. NW11 .... 6A 46
Stowell Ho. *N8* *4J 47*
(off Pembroke Rd.)
Stowe Pl. N15 .... 3E 48
Stowe Rd. W12 .... 2D 98
Stowting Rd. BR6: Orp 4J 173
Stox Mead HA3: Hrw W 1H 41
Stracey Rd. E7 .... 4J 69
NW10 .... 1K 79
Strachan Pl. SW19 .... 6E 134
Stradbroke Dr. IG7: Chig 6K 37
Stradbroke Gro. IG5: Ilf 3C 52
IG9: Buck H 1G 37
Stradbroke Pk. IG7: Chig 6K 37
Stradbroke Rd. N5 .... 4C 66
Stradbrook Cl. HA2: Harr 3D 58
Stradella Rd. SE24 .... 6C 120
Strafford Av. IG5: Ilf 2E 52
Strafford Ho. *SE8* *5B 104*
(off Grove St.)
Strafford Rd. EN5: Barn 3B 20
TW1: Twick 7A 114
TW3: Houn 3D 112
W3 .... 2J 97
Strafford St. E14 .... 2C 104
Strahan Rd. E3 .... 3A 86
Straight, The UB1: S'hall 2B 94
Straightsmouth SE10 .... 7E 104
Strait Rd. E6 .... 7C 88
Strakers Rd. SE15 .... 4H 121
Strale Ho. *N1* *1E 84*
(off Whitmore Est.)
Strand WC2 .... 3F 13 (7J 83)
Strand Ct. SE18 .... 5J 107
Strand Dr. TW9: Kew 7H 97
Strandfield Cl. SE18 .... 5J 107
Strand Ho. SE28 .... 1H 107
Strand La. WC2 .... 2H 13 (7K 83)
STRAND ON THE GREEN 6G 97
Strand on the Grn. W4 .... 6G 97
Strand Pl. N18 .... 4K 33
Strand School App. W4 .... 6G 97
Strand Theatre *2G 13*
(off Aldwych)
Strang Ho. N1 .... 1C 84
Strang Print Room 3C 6
Strangways Ter. W14 .... 3H 99
Stranraer Way N1 .... 7J 65
Strasburg Rd. SW11 .... 1E 118
Strata Ct. KT12: Walt T 7H 147
Stratfield Pk. Cl. N21 .... 7G 23
STRATFORD 7F 69
Stratford Av. UB10: Hil 2B 74
Stratford Cen., The E15 .... 7F 69
Stratford Circus (Performing Arts Cen.)
.... 6F 69
Stratford Cl. IG11: Bark 7A 72
RM10: Dag 7J 73
Stratford Ct. KT3: N Mald 4K 151
Stratford Gro. SW15 .... 4F 117
Stratford Ho. Av.
BR1: Brom 3C 160
STRATFORD MARSH 7D 68
STRATFORD NEW TOWN 5E 68
Stratford Office Village, The
E15 .... *7G 69*
(off Romford Rd.)
Stratford Picture House 6F 69
Stratford Pl. W1 .... 1J 11 (6F 83)
Stratford Rd. CR7: Thor H 4A 156
E13 .... 1H 87
(not continuous)
NW4 .... 4F 45
TW6: H'row A 6D 110
UB2: S'hall 4C 94
UB4: Yead 4K 75
W8 .... 3J 99
Stratford Shop. Cen. *E15* *7F 69*
(off The Stratford Cen.)
Stratford Studios W8 .... 3J 99
Stratford Vs. NW1 .... 7G 65
Stratham Ct. *N19* *3J 65*
(off Alexander Rd.)
Strathan Cl. SW18 .... 6G 117
Strathaven Rd. SE12 .... 6K 123
Strathblaine Rd. SW11 .... 5B 118
Strathbrook Rd. SW16 .... 7K 137
Strathcona Rd.
HA9: Wemb 2D 60
Strathdale SW16 .... 5K 137
Strathdon Dr. SW17 .... 3B 136
Strathearn Av. TW2: Whitt 1F 131
UB3: Harl 7H 93
Strathearn Ho. *W2* *2C 10*
(off Streathern Pl.)
Strathearn Pl. W2 .... 1C 10 (6C 82)
Strathearn Rd. SM1: Sutt 5J 165
SW19 .... 5J 135
Stratheden Pde. SE3 .... 7J 105
Stratheden Rd. SE3 .... 1J 123
Strathfield Gdns. IG11: Bark 6H 71
Strathleven Rd. SW2 .... 5J 119
Strathmore Ct. *NW8* *1C 4*
(off Park Rd.)
Strathmore Gdns. HA8: Edg 2H 43
N3 .... 1K 45
W8 .... 1J 99
Strathmore Rd. CR0: C'don 7D 156
SW19 .... 3J 135
TW11: Tedd 4J 131
Strathnairn St. SE1 .... 4G 103
Strathray Gdns. NW3 .... 6C 64
Strath Ter. SW11 .... 4C 118
Strathville Rd. SW18 .... 2J 135
(not continuous)
Strathyre Av. SW16 .... 3A 156
Stratton Cl. DA7: Bex 3E 126
HA8: Edg 6A 28
SW19 .... 2J 153
TW3: Houn 1E 112
Stratton Ct. *HA5: Hat E* *1D 40*
(off Devonshire Rd.)
N1 .... *7E 66*
(off Hertford Rd.)
Strattondale St. E14 .... 3E 104
Stratton Dr. IG11: Bark 5J 71
Stratton Gdns. UB1: S'hall 6D 76
Stratton Ho. *HA8: Edg* *4A 28*
(off Lacey Dr.)
Stratton Rd. DA7: Bex 3E 126
SW19 .... 2J 153
TW16: Sun 2H 147
Stratton St. W1 .... 4K 11 (1F 101)
Strauss Rd. W4 .... 2K 97
Strawberry Flds. BR6: Farnb 5F 173
STRAWBERRY HILL 3K 131
Strawberry Hill TW1: Twick 3K 131
Strawberry Hill Cl. TW1: Twick 3K 131
Strawberry Hill House *3K 131*
(within St Mary's College)
Strawberry Hill Rd. TW1: Twick 3K 131
Strawberry La. SM5: Cars 3E 166
Strawberry Ter. N10 .... 1D 46
Strawberry Va. N2 .... 1B 46
TW1: Twick 3A 132
(not continuous)
Streakes Fld. Rd. NW2 .... 2C 62
Streamdale SE2 .... 6B 108
Stream La. HA8: Edg 5C 28
Streamline Ct. *SE22* *1G 139*
(off Streamline M.)
Streamline M. SE22 .... 1G 139
Streamside Cl. BR2: Brom 4J 159
N9 .... 1A 34
Stream Way DA17: Belv 6F 109
Streatfeild Av. E6 .... 1D 88
Streatfield Rd. HA3: Kent 3C 42
STREATHAM 5J 137
Streatham Cl. SW16 .... 2J 137
STREATHAM COMMON 6H 137
Streatham Comn. Nth. SW16 .... 5J 137
Streatham Comn. Sth.
SW16 .... 6J 137
Streatham Ct. SW16 .... 3J 137
Streatham High Rd. SW16 .... 4J 137
STREATHAM HILL 2J 137
Streatham Hill SW2 .... 2J 137
Streatham Ice Arena 5H 137
Streatham Leisure Cen. 5H 137
STREATHAM PARK 5G 137
Streatham Pl. SW2 .... 7J 119
Streatham Rd. CR4: Mitc 1E 154
SW16 .... 1E 154
Streatham St. WC1 .... 7E 6 (6J 83)
STREATHAM VALE 7G 137
Streatham Va. SW16 .... 1G 155
Streathbourne Rd. SW17 .... 2E 136
Streatley Pl. NW3 .... 4A 64
Streatley Rd. NW6 .... 7H 63
Streeters La. SM6: Bedd 3H 167
Streetfield M. SE3 .... 3J 123
Streimer Rd. E15 .... 2E 86
Strelley Way W3 .... 7A 80
Stretton Mans. SE8 .... 5C 104

Stretton Rd. CR0: C'don 7E 156
TW10: Ham 2C 132
Strickland Ct. SE15 3G 121
Strickland Ho. *E2* *2K 9*
(off Chambord St.)
Strickland Row SW18 7B 118
Strickland St. SE8 2C 122
Strickland Way BR6: Orp 4K 173
Stride Rd. E13 2H 87
Strimon Cl. N9 2D 34
Stringer Ho. *N1* *1E 84*
(off Whitmore Est.)
Strode Cl. N10 7K 31
Strode Rd. E7 4J 69
N17 2E 48
NW10 6C 62
SW6 7G 99
Strome Ho. *NW6* *2K 81*
(off Carlton Va.)
Strone Rd. E7 6A 70
E12 6A 70
Strone Way UB4: Yead 4C 76
Strongbow Cres. SE9 5D 124
Strongbow Rd. SE9 5D 124
Strongbridge Cl. HA2: Harr 1E 58
Stronsa Rd. W12 2B 98
Strood Av. RM7: Rush G 1K 73
Strood Ho. *SE1* *7F 15*
(off Staple St.)
Stroud Cres. SW15 3C 134
Stroudes Cl. KT4: Wor Pk 7A 152
Stroud Fld. UB5: N'olt 6C 58
Stroud Ga. HA2: Harr 4F 59
STROUD GREEN 7K 47
Stroud Grn. Gdns. CR0: C'don 7J 157
Stroud Grn. Rd. N4 1K 65
Stroud Grn. Way CR0: C'don 7H 157
Stroudley Ho. SW8 1G 119
Stroudley Wlk. E3 3D 86
Stroud Rd. SE25 6G 157
SW19 3J 135
Stroud's Cl. RM6: Chad H 5B 54
Stroud Way TW15: Ashf 6D 128
Strouts Pl. E2 1J 9 (3F 85)
Strudwick Ct. *SW4* *1J 119*
(off Binfield Rd.)
Strutton Ct. *SW1* *2C 18*
(off Strutton Ground)
Strutton Ground SW1 1C 18 (3H 101)
Strype St. E1 6J 9 (5F 85)
Stuart Av. BR2: Hayes 1J 171
HA2: Harr 3D 58
KT12: Walt T 7K 147
NW9 7C 44
W5 2F 97
Stuart Cl. UB10: Hil 6C 56
Stuart Ct. *CR0: C'don* *3B 168*
(off St John's Rd.)
Stuart Cres. CR0: C'don 3B 170
N22 1K 47
UB3: Hayes 6E 74
Stuart Evans Cl.
DA16: Well 3C 126
Stuart Gro. TW11: Tedd 5J 131
Stuart Ho. *E16* *1K 105*
(off Beaulieu Av.)
W14 *4G 99*
(off Windsor Way)
Stuart Mantle Way DA8: Erith 7K 109
Stuart Mill Ho. *N1* *1G 7*
(off Killick St.)
Stuart Pl. CR4: Mitc 1D 154
Stuart Rd. CR7: Thor H 4C 156
DA16: Well 1B 126
EN4: E Barn 7H 21
HA3: W'stone 3K 41
IG11: Bark 7K 71
NW6 3J 81
SE15 4J 121
SW19 3J 135
Stuart Rd. TW10: Ham 2B 132
W3 1J 97
Stuart Twr. *W9* *3A 82*
(off Maida Va.)
Stubbs Cl. NW9 5J 43
Stubbs Ct. *W4* *5H 97*
(off Chaseley Dr.)
Stubbs Dr. SE16 5H 103
Stubbs Ho. *E2* *3K 85*
(off Bonner St.)
SW1 *4D 18*
(off Erasmus St.)
Stubbs M. *RM8: Dag* *4B 72*
(off Marlborough Rd.)
Stubbs Point E13 4J 87
Stubbs Way SW19 1B 154
Stucley Pl. NW1 7F 65
Stucley Rd. TW5: Hest 7G 95
Studdridge St. SW6 2J 117
(not continuous)
Studd St. N1 1B 84
Studholme Ct. NW3 4J 63
Studholme St. SE15 7H 103
Studio Arts & Media Cen., The 1A 158
Studio Ct. N15 4E 48
Studio La. W5 1D 96
Studio M. NW4 4E 44
Studio Pl. SW1 7F 11
Studio Plaza KT12: Walt T 7J 147
Studios, The *W8* *1J 99*
(off Edge St.)
Studios Rd. TW17: Shep 3B 146
Studio Theatre 4E 166
Studland *SE17* *5D 102*
(off Portland St.)
Studland Cl. DA15: Sidc 3K 143
Studland Ho. *E14* *6A 86*
(off Aston St.)
Studland Rd. KT2: King T 6E 132
SE26 5K 139
W7 6H 77
Studland St. W6 4D 98
Studley Av. E4 7A 36
Studley Cl. E5 5A 68
Studley Ct. DA14: Sidc 5B 144
E14 *7F 87*
(off Jamestown Way)
Studley Dr. IG4: Ilf 6B 52
Studley Est. SW4 1J 119
Studley Grange Rd. W7 2J 95
Studley Rd. E7 6K 69
RM9: Dag 7D 72
SW4 1J 119
Stukeley Rd. E7 7K 69
Stukeley St. WC2 7F 7 (6J 83)
Stumps Hill La. BR3: Beck 6C 140
Stunell Ho. *SE14* *6K 103*
(off John Williams Cl.)
Sturdee Ho. *E2* *2G 85*
(off Horatio St.)
Sturdy Ho. *E3* *2A 86*
(off Gernon Rd.)
Sturdy Rd. SE15 2H 121
Sturge Av. E17 2D 50
Sturgeon Rd. SE17 5C 102
Sturges Fld. BR7: Chst 6H 143
Sturgess Av. NW4 7D 44
Sturge St. SE1 6C 14 (2C 102)
Sturmer Way N7 5K 65
Sturminster *NW1* *7H 65*
(off Agar Gro.)
Sturminster Cl. UB4: Yead 6A 76
Sturminster Ho. *SW8* *7K 101*
(off Dorset Rd.)
Sturrock Cl. N15 4D 48
Sturry St. E14 6D 86
Sturt St. N1 1D 8 (2C 84)
Stutfield St. E1 6G 85
Styles Gdns. SW9 3B 120
Styles Ho. SE1 6A 14
Styles Way BR3: Beck 4E 158
Stylus Ho. E1 6J 85
Sudbourne Rd. SW2 5J 119
Sudbrooke Rd. SW12 6D 118
Sudbrook Gdns. TW10: Ham 3D 132
Sudbrook La. TW10: Ham 1E 132
SUDBURY 5B 60
Sudbury E6 5E 88
Sudbury Av. HA0: Wemb 3C 60
Sudbury Cl. RM6: Chad H 5B 54
Sudbury Ct. *SW8* *1H 119*
(off Allen Edwards Dr.)
Sudbury Ct. Dr. HA1: Harr 3K 59
Sudbury Ct. Rd. HA1: Harr 3K 59
Sudbury Cres. BR1: Brom 6J 141
HA0: Wemb 5B 60
Sudbury Cft. HA0: Wemb 4K 59
Sudbury Gdns. CR0: C'don 4E 168
Sudbury Hgts. Av.
UB6: G'frd 5K 59
Sudbury Hill HA1: Harr 2J 59
Sudbury Hill Cl.
HA0: Wemb 4K 59
Sudbury Ho. SW18 5K 117
Sudbury Rd. IG11: Bark 5K 71
Sudeley St. N1 2B 84
Sudlow Rd. SW18 5J 117
Sudrey St. SE1 7C 14 (2C 102)
Suez Av. UB6: G'frd 2K 77
Suez Rd. EN3: Brim 4F 25
SUFFIELD HATCH 4K 35
Suffield Ho. *SE17* *5B 102*
(off Berryfield Rd.)
Suffield Rd. E4 3J 35
N15 5F 49
SE20 2J 157
Suffolk Ct. E10 7C 50
IG3: Ilf 6J 53
RM6: Chad H 6C 54
Suffolk Ho. *CR0: C'don* *2D 168*
(off George St.)
SE20 *1K 157*
(off Croydon Rd.)
Suffolk La. EC4 2E 14 (7D 84)
Suffolk Pk. Rd. E17 4A 50
Suffolk Pl. SW1 4D 12 (1H 101)
Suffolk Rd. DA14: Sidc 6C 144
E13 3J 87
EN3: Pond E 5C 24
HA2: Harr 6D 40
IG3: Ilf 6J 53
IG11: Bark 7H 71
KT4: Wor Pk 2B 164
N15 5D 48
NW10 7A 62
RM10: Dag 5J 73
SE25 4F 157
SW13 7B 98
Suffolk St. E7 4J 69
SW1 3D 12 (7H 83)
Sugar Bakers Ct. EC3 1H 15
Sugar Ho. La. E15 2E 86
Sugar Loaf Wlk. E2 3J 85
Sugar Quay EC3 3H 15
Sugar Quay Wlk. EC3 3H 15 (7E 84)
Sugden Rd. KT7: T Ditt 1B 162
SW11 3E 118
Sugden St. SE5 6D 102
Sugden Way IG11: Bark 2K 89
Sulby Ho. *SE4* *4A 122*
(off Turnham Rd.)
Sulgrave Gdns. W6 2E 98
Sulgrave Rd. W6 3E 98
Sulina Rd. SW2 7J 119
Sulivan Ct. SW6 2J 117
Sulivan Ent. Cen. SW6 3K 117
Sulivan Rd. SW6 3J 117
Sulkin Ho. *E2* *3K 85*
(off Knottisford St.)
Sullivan Av. E16 5B 88
Sullivan Cl. KT8: W Mole 3F 149
SW11 3C 118
UB4: Yead 5A 76
Sullivan Ct. N16 7F 49
SW5 *4J 99*
(off Earls Ct. Rd.)
Sullivan Cres. UB9: Hare 2A 38
Sullivan Ho. *SE11* *4H 19*
(off Vauxhall St.)
SW1 *7K 17*
(off Churchill Gdns.)
Sullivan Rd. SE11 3K 19 (4A 102)
Sullivans Reach KT12: Walt T 7H 147
Sultan Rd. E11 4K 51
Sultan St. BR3: Beck 2K 157
SE5 7C 102
Sultan Ter. N22 2A 48
Sumatra Rd. NW6 5J 63
Sumburgh Rd. SW12 6E 118
Summer Av. KT8: E Mos 5J 149
Summercourt Rd. E1 6J 85
Summer Crossing KT7: T Ditt 5J 149
Summerene Cl. SW16 7G 137
Summerfield *BR1: Brom* *1K 159*
(off Freelands Rd.)
Summerfield Av. NW6 2G 81
Summerfield La. KT6: Surb 2D 162
Summerfield Rd. W5 4B 78
Summerfields Av. N12 6H 31
Summerfield St. SE12 7H 123
Summer Gdns. KT8: E Mos 5J 149
Summer Gro. BR4: W W'ck 2G 171
Summer Hill BR7: Chst 2E 160
Summerhill Cl. BR6: Orp 3J 173
Summerhill Gro. EN1: Enf 6K 23
Summerhill Rd. N15 4D 48
Summerhill Vs. *BR7: Chst* *1E 160*
(off Susan Wood)
Summerhill Way CR4: Mitc 1E 154
Summerhouse Av. TW5: Hest 1C 112
Summerhouse Dr. DA2: Dart 4K 145
DA5: Bexl, Dart 4K 145
Summerhouse La. UB7: Harm 2E 174
Summerhouse Rd. N16 2E 66
Summerland Gdns. N10 3F 47
Summerland Grange N10 3F 47
Summerlands Av. W3 7J 79
Summerlands Lodge BR6: Farnb 4E 172
Summerlee Av. N2 4D 46
Summerlee Gdns. N2 4D 46
Summerley St. SW18 2K 135
Summer Rd. KT7: T Ditt 5J 149
KT8: E Mos 5H 149
(not continuous)
Summersby Rd. N6 6F 47
Summers Cl. HA9: Wemb 1H 61
SM2: Sutt 7J 165
Summerskill Cl. SE15 3H 121
Summerskille Cl. N9 3C 34
Summers La. N12 7G 31
Summers Row N12 6H 31
Summers St. EC1 4J 7 (4A 84)
SUMMERSTOWN 3A 136
Summerstown SW17 3A 136
Summer Theatre 7C 62
Summerton Way SE28 6D 90
Summer Trees TW16: Sun 1K 147
Summerville Gdns.
SM1: Sutt 6H 165
Summerwood Rd. TW7: Isle 5K 113
Summit Av. NW9 5K 43
Summit Bus. Pk. TW16: Sun 7J 129
Summit Cl. HA8: Edg 7B 28
N14 2B 32
NW9 4K 43
Summit Ct. NW2 5G 63
Summit Dr. IG8: Wfd G 2B 52
Summit Est. N16 7G 49
Summit Rd. E17 4D 50
UB5: N'olt 7E 58

Summit Way N14 ... 2A 32
SE19 ... 7E 138
Sumner Av. SE15 ... 1F 121
Sumner Bldgs. SE1 ... 4C 14
Sumner Cl. BR6: Farnb ... 4G 173
Sumner Ct. SW8 ... 7J 101
Sumner Est. SE15 ... 7F 103
Sumner Gdns. CR0: C'don ... 1A 168
Sumner Ho. E3 ... 5D 86
(off Watts Gro.)
Sumner Pl. SW7 ... 4B 16 (4B 100)
Sumner Pl. M. SW7 ... 4B 16 (4B 100)
Sumner Rd. CR0: C'don ... 1A 168
HA1: Harr ... 7G 41
SE15 ... 6F 103
Sumner Rd. Sth.
CR0: C'don ... 1A 168
Sumner St. SE1 ... 4B 14 (1B 102)
Sumpter Cl. NW3 ... 6A 64
Sun All. TW9: Rich ... 4E 114
Sunbeam Cres. W10 ... 4E 80
Sunbeam Rd. NW10 ... 4J 79
SUNBURY ... 3A 148
Sunbury Av. NW7 ... 5E 28
SW14 ... 4K 115
Sunbury Av. Pas. SW14 ... 4A 116
Sunbury Bus. Cen. TW16: Sun ... 1H 147
Sunbury Cl. KT12: Walt T ... 6J 147
SUNBURY COMMON ... 7H 129
Sunbury Ct. EN5: Barn ... 4B 20
Sunbury Ct. Island TW16: Sun ... 3B 148
Sunbury Ct. M. TW16: Sun ... 2B 148
Sunbury Ct. Rd. TW16: Sun ... 2A 148
Sunbury Cres. TW13: Felt ... 4H 129
SUNBURY CROSS ... 7J 129
Sunbury Cross Cen. TW16: Sun ... 7H 129
Sunbury Gdns. NW7 ... 5E 28
Sunbury Ho. E2 ... 2J 9
(off Swanfield St.)
SE14 ... 6K 103
(off Myers La.)
TW16: Sun ... 1G 147
(off Windmill Rd. W.)
Sunbury La. KT12: Walt T ... 6J 147
SW11 ... 1B 118
(not continuous)
Sunbury Leisure Cen. ... 1H 147
Sunburylock Ait KT12: Walt T ... 4K 147
Sunbury Pk. Walled Garden ... 3K 147
Sunbury Rd. SM3: Cheam ... 3F 165
TW13: Felt ... 3H 129
Sunbury St. SE18 ... 3D 106
Sunbury Way TW13: Hanw ... 5A 130
Sunbury Workshops E2 ... 2J 9
(off Swanfield St.)
Sun Ct. EC3 ... 1F 15
Suncroft Pl. SE26 ... 3J 139
Sundeala Cl. TW16: Sun ... 7J 129
(off Hanworth Rd.)
Sunderland Ct. SE22 ... 7G 121
TW19: Stanw ... 6A 110
(off Whitley Cl.)
Sunderland Ho. W2 ... 5J 81
(off Westbourne Pk. Rd.)
Sunderland Mt. SE23 ... 2K 139
Sunderland Point E16 ... 1G 107
Sunderland Rd. SE23 ... 1K 139
W5 ... 3D 96
Sunderland Ter. W2 ... 6K 81
Sunderland Way E12 ... 2B 70
Sundew Av. W12 ... 7C 80
Sundew Cl. W12 ... 7C 80
Sundew Ct. HA0: Wemb ... 2E 78
(off Elmore Cl.)
Sundial Av. SE25 ... 3F 157
Sundial Ct. EC1 ... 5E 8
(off Chiswell St.)
Sundorne Rd. SE7 ... 5A 106
Sundown Rd. TW15: Ashf ... 5E 128
Sundra Wlk. E1 ... 4K 85
SUNDRIDGE ... 6K 141
Sundridge Av. BR1: Brom ... 1B 160
BR7: Chst ... 1B 160
DA16: Well ... 2H 125
Sundridge Ho. E9 ... 7K 67
(off Church Cres.)
Sundridge Pde. BR1: Brom ... 7K 141
SUNDRIDGE PARK ... 7K 141
Sundridge Pl. CR0: C'don ... 1G 169
Sundridge Rd. CR0: C'don ... 7F 157
Sunfields Pl. SE3 ... 7K 105
Sungate Cotts. RM5: Col R ... 1F 55
SUN-IN-THE-SANDS ... 7K 105
Sunken Rd. CR0: C'don ... 5J 169
Sunkist Way SM6: Wall ... 7J 167
Sunland Av. DA6: Bex ... 4E 126
Sun La. SE3 ... 7K 105
Sunleigh Rd. HA0: Wemb ... 1E 78
Sunley Gdns. UB6: G'frd ... 1A 78
Sun Life Trad. Est. TW14: Felt ... 3J 111
Sunlight Cl. SW19 ... 6A 136
Sunlight Sq. E2 ... 3H 85
Sunmead Rd. TW16: Sun ... 3J 147
Sunna Gdns. TW16: Sun ... 2K 147
Sunna Lodge TW16: Sun ... 7H 129
Sunniholme Ct. CR2: S Croy ... 5C 168
(off Warham Rd.)
Sunningdale N14 ... 5C 32
W13 ... 5B 78
(off Hardwick Grn.)
Sunningdale Av. HA4: Ruis ... 1A 58
IG11: Bark ... 1H 89
TW13: Hanw ... 2C 130
W3 ... 7A 80
Sunningdale Cl. E6 ... 3D 88
HA7: Stan ... 6F 27
KT6: Surb ... 2E 162
SE16 ... 5H 103
SE28 ... 6E 90
Sunningdale Ct. TW7: Isle ... 6H 113
(off Whitton Dene)
UB1: S'hall ... 6G 77
(off Fleming Rd.)
Sunningdale Gdns. NW9 ... 5J 43
W8 ... 3J 99
(off Stratford Rd.)
Sunningdale Lodge HA8: Edg ... 5A 28
(off Stonegrove)
Sunningdale Rd. BR1: Brom ... 4C 160
SM1: Sutt ... 3H 165
Sunningfields Cres. NW4 ... 2D 44
Sunningfields Rd. NW4 ... 3D 44
Sunninghill Ct. W3 ... 2J 97
Sunninghill Rd. SE13 ... 2D 122
Sunny Bank SE25 ... 3G 157
Sunny Cres. NW10 ... 7J 61
Sunnycroft Rd. SE25 ... 3G 157
TW3: Houn ... 2F 113
UB1: S'hall ... 5E 76
Sunnydale BR6: Farnb ... 2E 172
Sunnydale Gdns. NW7 ... 6E 28
Sunnydale Rd. SE12 ... 5K 123
Sunnydene Av. E4 ... 5A 36
HA4: Ruis ... 1J 57
Sunnydene Gdns. HA0: Wemb ... 6C 60
Sunnydene St. SE26 ... 4A 140
Sunnyfield NW7 ... 4G 29
Sunnyfield Rd. BR7: Chst ... 3K 161
Sunny Gdns. Pde. NW4 ... 2D 44
Sunny Gdns. Rd. NW4 ... 2D 44
Sunny Hill NW4 ... 3D 44
Sunnyhill Cl. E5 ... 4A 68
Sunnyhill Rd. SW16 ... 4J 137
Sunnyhurst Cl. SM1: Sutt ... 3J 165
Sunnymead Av. CR4: Mitc ... 3H 155
Sunnymead Rd. NW9 ... 7K 43
SW15 ... 5D 116
Sunnymede Av. KT19: Ewe ... 7A 164
Sunnymede Dr. IG2: Ilf ... 5F 53
IG6: Ilf ... 5F 53
Sunny Nook Gdns.
CR2: S Croy ... 6D 168
Sunny Pl. NW4 ... 4E 44
Sunny Rd., The EN3: Enf H ... 1E 24
Sunnyside KT12: Walt T ... 5A 148
NW2 ... 3H 63
SW19 ... 6G 135
Sunnyside Dr. E4 ... 7K 25
Sunnyside Ho's. NW2 ... 3H 63
(off Sunnyside)
Sunnyside Pas. SW19 ... 6G 135
Sunnyside Pl. SW19 ... 6G 135
Sunnyside Rd. E10 ... 1C 68
IG1: Ilf ... 3G 71
N19 ... 7H 47
TW11: Tedd ... 4H 131
W5 ... 1D 96
Sunnyside Rd. E. N9 ... 3B 34
Sunnyside Rd. Nth. N9 ... 3A 34
Sunnyside Rd. Sth. N9 ... 3A 34
Sunnyside Ter. NW9 ... 3K 43
Sunny Vw. NW9 ... 5K 43
Sunny Way N12 ... 7H 31
Sun Pas. SE16 ... 3G 103
(off Old Jamaica Rd.)
Sunray Av. BR2: Brom ... 6C 160
KT5: Surb ... 2H 163
SE24 ... 4D 120
Sunrise Cl. TW13: Hanw ... 3D 130
Sunrise Vw. NW7 ... 6G 29
Sun Rd. W14 ... 5H 99
Sunset Av. E4 ... 1J 35
IG8: Wfd G ... 4C 36
Sunset Ct. IG8: Wfd G ... 7F 37
Sunset Gdns. SE25 ... 2F 157
Sunset Lodge NW10 ... 7E 62
(off Hanover Rd.)
Sunset Rd. SE5 ... 4C 120
SE28 ... 1A 108
SW19 ... 5D 134
Sunset Vw. EN5: Barn ... 2B 20
Sunshine Way CR4: Mitc ... 2D 154
Sun St. EC2 ... 5F 9 (5D 84)
(Finsbury Sq.)
EC2 ... 5E 84
(Primrose St.)
Sun St. Pas. EC2 ... 6G 9 (5E 84)
Sun Wlk. E1 ... 3K 15 (7F 85)
Sunwell Cl. SE15 ... 1H 121
Sun Wharf SE8 ... 7D 104
(off Creekside)
Superior Dr. BR6: Chels ... 6K 173
SURBITON ... 6D 150
Surbiton Ct. KT6: Surb ... 6C 150
Surbiton Cres. KT1: King T ... 4E 150
Surbiton Hall Cl.
KT1: King T ... 4E 150
Surbiton Hill Pk. KT5: Surb ... 5F 151
Surbiton Hill Rd. KT6: Surb ... 4E 150
Surbiton Pde. KT6: Surb ... 6E 150
Surbiton Rd. KT1: King T ... 4D 150
Surlingham Cl. SE28 ... 7D 90
Surma Cl. E1 ... 4H 85
Surmans Cl. RM9: Dag ... 1C 90
Surrendale Pl. W9 ... 4J 81
Surrey Canal Rd. SE14 ... 6J 103
SE15 ... 6J 103
Surrey Cl. N3 ... 3G 45
Surrey County Cricket Club
... 7H 19 (6K 101)
Surrey Cres. W4 ... 5G 97
Surrey Docks Stadium ... 1K 103
Surrey Docks Watersports Cen. ... 3A 104
Surrey Gdns. N4 ... 6C 48
Surrey Gro. SE17 ... 5E 102
SM1: Sutt ... 3B 166
Surrey Ho. SE16 ... 1K 103
(off Rotherhithe St.)
Surrey La. SW11 ... 1C 118
Surrey La. Est. SW11 ... 1C 118
Surrey M. SE27 ... 4E 138
Surrey Mt. SE23 ... 1H 139
Surrey Quays Rd. SE16 ... 3J 103
Surrey Quays Shop. Cen.
SE16 ... 3K 103
Surrey Rd. BR4: W W'ck ... 1D 170
HA1: Harr ... 5G 41
IG11: Bark ... 7J 71
RM10: Dag ... 5H 73
SE15 ... 5K 121
Surrey Row SE1 ... 6A 14 (2B 102)
Surrey Sq. SE17 ... 5E 102
Surrey Steps WC2 ... 2H 13
(off Surrey St.)
Surrey St. CR0: C'don ... 2C 168
E13 ... 3K 87
WC2 ... 2H 13 (7K 83)
Surrey Ter. SE17 ... 5E 102
Surrey Water Rd.
SE16 ... 1K 103
Surridge Ct. SW9 ... 2J 119
(off Clapham Rd.)
Surridge Gdns. SE19 ... 6D 138
Surr St. N7 ... 5J 65
Sury Basin KT2: King T ... 1E 150
Susan Cl. RM7: Mawney ... 3J 55
Susan Constant Ct.
E14 ... 7F 87
(off Newport Av.)
Susan Lawrence Ho. E12 ... 4E 70
(off Walton Rd.)
Susannah St. E14 ... 6D 86
Susan Rd. SE3 ... 2K 123
Susan Wood BR7: Chst ... 1E 160
Sussex Av. TW7: Isle ... 3J 113
Sussex Cl. IG4: Ilf ... 5D 52
KT3: N Mald ... 4A 152
N19 ... 2J 65
TW1: Twick ... 6B 114
Sussex Ct. SE10 ... 6E 104
(off Roan St.)
W2 ... 1A 10
(off Spring St.)
Sussex Cres. UB5: N'olt ... 6E 58
Sussex Gdns. KT9: Chess ... 6D 162
N4 ... 5C 48
N6 ... 5D 46
W2 ... 2A 10 (7B 82)
Sussex Ga. N6 ... 5D 46
Sussex Lodge W2 ... 1B 10
(off Sussex Pl.)
Sussex Mans. SW7 ... 4A 16
WC2 ... 2F 13
(off Maiden La.)
Sussex M. SE6 ... 7C 122
Sussex M. E. W2 ... 1B 10
Sussex M. W. W2 ... 2B 10 (7B 82)
Sussex Pl. KT3: N Mald ... 4A 152
NW1 ... 3E 4 (4D 82)
W2 ... 1B 10 (6B 82)
W6 ... 5E 98
Sussex Ring N12 ... 5D 30
Sussex Rd. BR4: W W'ck ... 1D 170
CR2: S Croy ... 6D 168
CR4: Mitc ... 5J 155
DA8: Erith ... 7H 109
DA14: Sidc ... 5B 144
E6 ... 1E 88
HA1: Harr ... 5G 41
KT3: N Mald ... 4A 152
SM5: Cars ... 6D 166
UB2: S'hall ... 3B 94
UB10: Ick ... 4E 56
Sussex Sq. W2 ... 2B 10 (7B 82)
Sussex St. E13 ... 3K 87
SW1 ... 6K 17 (5F 101)
Sussex Ter. SE20 ... 7J 139
(off Graveney Gro.)
Sussex Way EN4: Cockf ... 5A 22
N7 ... 2J 65

Sussex Way N19 1H **65**
(not continuous)
Sutcliffe Cl. NW11 5K **45**
Sutcliffe Ho. UB3: Hayes 6J **75**
Sutcliffe Pk. Athletics Track 5A **124**
Sutcliffe Rd. DA16: Well 2C **126**
SE18 6J **107**
Sutherland Av.
BR5: St M Cry 6K **161**
DA16: Well 4J **125**
TW16: Sun 2H **147**
UB3: Hayes 4J **93**
W9 4J **81**
W13 6B **78**
Sutherland Cl. EN5: Barn 4B **20**
Sutherland Ct. N16 3D **66**
NW9 5H **43**
W9 *4J* ***81***
(off Marylands Rd.)
Sutherland Dr. SW19 1B **154**
Sutherland Gdns. KT4: Wor Pk 1D **164**
SW14 3A **116**
TW16: Sun 2H **147**
Sutherland Gro. SW18 6G **117**
TW11: Tedd 5J **131**
Sutherland Ho. IG8: Wfd G 7K **37**
W8 3K **99**
Sutherland Pl. W2 6J **81**
Sutherland Rd. CR0: C'don 7A **156**
DA17: Belv 3G **109**
E3 2B **86**
E17 2K **49**
EN3: Pond E 6E **24**
N9 1C **34**
N17 7B **34**
UB1: S'hall 6D **76**
W4 6A **98**
W13 6A **78**
Sutherland Rd. Path
E17 3K **49**
Sutherland Row SW1 5K **17** (5F **101**)
Sutherland Sq. SE17 5C **102**
Sutherland St. SW1 5J **17** (5F **101**)
Sutherland Wlk. SE17 5C **102**
Sutlej Rd. SE7 7A **106**
Sutterton St. N7 6K **65**
SUTTON 5K **165**
Sutton Arena Leisure Cen. 7A **154**
Sutton Cl. BR3: Beck 1D **158**
HA5: Eastc 5J **39**
IG10: Lough 1H **37**
Sutton Comn. Rd. SM1: Sutt 7H **153**
SM3: Sutt 7H **153**
Sutton Ct. KT8: W Mole 5D **148**
SE19 7F **139**
SM2: Sutt 6A **166**
W4 6J **97**
W5 1E **96**
Sutton Ct. Rd. E13 3A **88**
SM1: Sutt 6A **166**
UB10: Hil 1D **74**
W4 7J **97**
Sutton Cres. EN5: Barn 5A **20**
Sutton Dene TW3: Houn 1F **113**
Sutton Ecology Cen. 4D **166**
Sutton Est. EC1 2F **9**
W10 5E **80**
Sutton Est., The N1 7B **66**
SW3 5D **16** (5C **100**)
Sutton Gdns. CR0: C'don 5F **157**
IG11: Bark 1J **89**
Sutton Grn. *IG11: Bark* *1J* ***89***
(off Felton Gdns.)
Sutton Gro. SM1: Sutt 4B **166**
Sutton Hall Rd. TW5: Hest 7E **94**
Sutton Hgts. SM2: Sutt 7B **166**
Sutton Junior Tennis Cen. 1K **165**
Sutton La. *EC1* *4B* ***8***
(off Gt. Sutton St.)
TW3: Houn 3D **112**
Sutton La. Nth. W4 5J **97**
Sutton La. Sth. W4 6J **97**
Sutton Pde. *NW4* *4E* ***44***
(off Church Rd.)
Sutton Pk. Rd. SM1: Sutt 6K **165**
Sutton Pl. E9 5J **67**
Sutton Rd. E13 4H **87**
E17 1K **49**
IG11: Bark 2J **89**
N10 1E **46**
TW5: Hest 1E **112**
Sutton Row W1 7D **6** (6H **83**)
Suttons Bus. Pk.
RM13: Rain 3K **91**
Sutton Sq. E9 5J **67**
TW5: Hest 1D **112**
Sutton St. E1 7J **85**
Sutton Superbowl 5K **165**
Sutton's Way EC1 4D **8** (4C **84**)
Sutton United FC 4J **165**
Sutton Wlk. SE1 5H **13** (1K **101**)
Sutton Way TW5: Hest 1D **112**
W10 4E **80**
Swaby Rd. SW18 1A **136**
Swaffam Ct. RM6: Chad H 6C **54**
Swaffham Way N22 7G **33**
Swaffield Rd. SW18 7K **117**
Swain Cl. SW16 6F **137**
Swain Rd. CR7: Thor H 5C **156**
Swains Cl. UB7: W Dray 2A **92**
Swains La. N6 1E **64**
Swainson Rd. W3 2B **98**
Swains Rd. SW17 7D **136**
Swain St. NW8 3C **4** (4C **82**)
Swakeleys Dr. UB10: Ick 4C **56**
Swakeleys Rd. UB10: Ick 4A **56**
SWAKELEYS RDBT. 4A **56**
Swakeleys School Sports Cen. 2D **74**
Swalecliffe Rd. DA17: Belv 5H **109**
Swaledale Cl. N11 6K **31**
Swallands Rd. SE6 3C **140**
(not continuous)
Swallow Cl. DA8: Erith 1K **127**
SE14 1K **121**
WD23: Bush 1B **26**
Swallow Ct. HA4: Ruis 1A **58**
IG2: Ilf 5F **53**
SE1 *7D* ***14***
(off Swan St.)
SE12 7J **123**
W9 *5J* ***81***
(off Admiral Wlk.)
Swallow Dr. NW10 6K **61**
UB5: N'olt 2E **76**
Swallowfield *NW1* *2K* ***5***
(off Munster Sq.)
Swallowfield Rd. SE7 5K **105**
Swallowfield Way
UB3: Hayes 2F **93**
Swallow Gdns. SW16 5H **137**
Swallow Ho. *NW8* *2C* ***82***
(off Allitsen Rd.)
Swallow Pk. KT6: Surb 3F **163**
Swallow Pas. *W1* *1K* ***11***
(off Swallow Pl.)
Swallow Pl. W1 1K **11** (6F **83**)
Swallow St. E6 5C **88**
W1 3B **12** (7G **83**)
SWAN, THE 2E **170**
Swanage Ct. *N1* *7E* ***66***
(off Hertford Rd.)
Swanage Ho. *SW8* *7K* ***101***
(off Dorset Rd.)
Swanage Rd. E4 7K **35**
SW18 6A **118**
Swanage Waye UB4: Yead 6A **76**
Swan & Pike Rd. EN3: Enf L 1H **25**
Swan App. E6 5C **88**
Swanbourne *SE17* *4C* ***102***
(off Wansey St.)
Swanbourne Ho. *NW8* *3C* ***4***
(off Capland St.)
Swanbridge Rd. DA7: Bex 1G **127**
Swan Cen., The SW17 3K **135**
Swan Cl. CR0: C'don 7E **156**
E17 1A **50**
TW13: Hanw 4C **130**
Swan Ct. *E1* *3K* ***15***
(off Star Pl.)
E14 *6B* ***86***
(off Agnes St.)
SW3 6D **16** (5C **100**)
SW6 *7J* ***99***
(off Fulham Rd.)
TW7: Isle *3B* ***114***
(off Swan St.)
Swandon Way SW18 5K **117**
Swan Dr. NW9 2A **44**
Swanfield St. E2 2J **9** (3F **85**)
Swan Ho. *E15* *7F* ***69***
(off The Broadway)
EN3: Pond E 5D **24**
N1 *7D* ***66***
(off Oakley Rd.)
Swan Island TW1: Twick 3A **132**
Swan La. EC4 3F **15** (7D **84**)
N20 3F **31**
Swanley Ho. *SE17* *5E* ***102***
(off Kinglake Est.)
Swanley Rd. DA16: Well 1C **126**
Swan Mead SE1 3E **102**
Swan M. CR4: Mitc 1D **154**
RM7: Mawney 4H **55**
SW6 1H **117**
SW9 2K **119**
Swann Ct. *TW7: Isle* *3A* ***114***
(off South St.)
Swanne Ho. *SE10* *7E* ***104***
(off Gloucester Cir.)
Swan Pas. E1 3K **15**
Swan Pl. SW13 2B **116**
Swan Rd. SE16 2J **103**
SE18 3B **106**
TW13: Hanw 5C **130**
UB1: S'hall 6F **77**
UB7: W Dray 2A **92**
Swan Sanctuary, The 6G **147**
Swanscombe Ho.
W11 *1F* ***99***
(off St Ann's Rd.)
Swanscombe Point
E16 *5H* ***87***
(off Clarkson Rd.)
Swanscombe Rd. W4 5A **98**
W11 1F **99**
Swansea Ct. *E16* *1F* ***107***
(off Fishguard Way)
Swansea Rd. EN3: Pond E 4D **24**
TW14: Felt 6E **110**
Swansland Gdns. E17 1A **50**
Swan St. SE1 7D **14** (3C **102**)
TW7: Isle 3B **114**
Swanton Gdns. SW19 1F **135**
Swanton Rd. DA8: Erith 7G **109**
Swan Wlk. SW3 7E **16** (6D **100**)
TW17: Shep 7G **147**
Swan Way EN3: Enf H 2E **24**
Swanwick Cl. SW15 7B **116**
Swan Yd. N1 6B **66**
Sward Rd. BR5: St M Cry 6K **161**
Swathling Ho. *SW15* *6B* ***116***
(off Tunworth Cres.)
Swaton Rd. E3 4C **86**
Swaylands Rd. DA17: Belv 6G **109**
Swaythling Cl. N18 4C **34**
Swedeland Ct. EC2 6H **9**
Swedenborg Gdns. E1 7H **85**
Swedenborg Pl. *E1* *7H* ***85***
(off Swedenborg Gdns.)
Sweden Ga. SE16 3A **104**
Swedish Quays SE16 3A **104**
(not continuous)
Sweeney Cres. SE1 7K **15** (2F **103**)
Sweet Briar Grn. N9 3A **34**
Sweet Briar Gro. N9 3A **34**
Sweet Briar Wlk. N18 4A **34**
Sweetcroft La. UB10: Hil 7B **56**
Sweetland Ct. RM8: Dag 6B **72**
Sweetmans Av.
HA5: Pinn 3B **40**
Sweets Way N20 2G **31**
Swell Ct. E17 6C **50**
Swetenham Wlk. SE18 5G **107**
Swete St. E13 2J **87**
Sweyn Pl. SE3 2J **123**
Swift Cen. CR0: Wadd 7K **167**
Swift Cl. E17 7F **35**
HA2: Harr 2F **59**
SE28 7B **90**
UB3: Hayes 6H **75**
Swift Ct. SM2: Sutt 7K **165**
Swift Lodge *W9* *5J* ***81***
(off Admiral Wlk.)
Swift Rd. TW13: Hanw 3C **130**
UB2: S'hall 3E **94**
Swiftsden Way BR1: Brom 6G **141**
Swift St. SW6 1H **117**
Swinbrook Rd. W10 5G **81**
Swinburne Ct. *SE5* *4D* ***120***
(off Basingdon Way)
Swinburne Cres. CR0: C'don 6J **157**
Swinburne Ho. *E2* *3J* ***85***
(off Roman Rd.)
Swinburne Rd. SW15 4C **116**
Swinderby Rd. HA0: Wemb 6E **60**
Swindon Cl. IG3: Ilf 2J **71**
Swindon Rd. TW6: H'row A 5E **110**
Swindon St. W12 1D **98**
Swinfield Cl. TW13: Hanw 3C **130**
Swinford Gdns. SW9 3B **120**
Swingate La. SE18 6J **107**
Swingfield Ho. *E9* *1J* ***85***
(off Templecombe Rd.)
Swinley Ho. *NW1* *1K* ***5***
(off Redhill St.)
Swinnerton St. E9 5A **68**
Swinson Ho. N11 5B **32**
Swinton Cl. HA9: Wemb 1H **61**
Swinton Pl. WC1 1G **7** (3K **83**)
Swinton St. WC1 1G **7** (3K **83**)
Swires Shaw BR2: Kes 4B **172**
Swiss Cen. W1 3C **12**
SWISS COTTAGE 7B **64**
Swiss Cottage Sports Cen. 7B **64**
Swiss Ct. WC2 3D **12**
Swiss Re 7H **9**
Swiss Ter. NW6 7B **64**
Switch Ho. E14 7F **87**
Swithland Gdns. SE9 4E **142**
Swyncombe Av. W5 4B **96**
Swynford Gdns. NW4 4C **44**
Sybil M. N4 6B **48**
Sybil Phoenix Cl. SE8 5K **103**
Sybil Thorndike Casson Ho.
SW5 *5J* ***99***
(off Kramer M.)
Sybourn St. E17 7B **50**
Sycamore Av. DA15: Sidc 6K **125**
E3 1B **86**
UB3: Hayes 7G **75**
W5 3D **96**
Sycamore Cl. CR2: S Croy 5E **168**
E16 4G **87**
EN4: E Barn 6G **21**
HA8: Edg 4D **28**
N9 4B **34**
SE9 2C **142**
SM5: Cars 4D **166**
TW13: Felt 3J **129**
UB5: N'olt 1C **76**

Sycamore Cl. UB7: Yiew 7B **74**
W3 . . . . . 1A **98**
Sycamore Ct. *DA8: Erith* *5K* **109**
(off Sandcliff Rd.)
E7 . . . . . 6J **69**
KT3: N Mald 3A **152**
NW6 . . . . . *1J* **81**
(off Bransdale Cl.)
SE1 . . . . . *7G* **15**
(off Royal Oak Yd.)
TW4: Houn 4C **112**
Sycamore Gdns. CR4: Mitc 2B **154**
N15 . . . . . 4F **49**
W6 . . . . . 2D **98**
Sycamore Gro. KT3: N Mald 3K **151**
NW9 . . . . . 7J **43**
SE6 . . . . . 6E **122**
SE20 . . . . . 1G **157**
Sycamore Hill N11 . . . . . 6K **31**
Sycamore Ho. BR2: Brom 2G **159**
IG9: Buck H 2G **37**
Sycamore Ho. *N2* *2B* **46**
(off The Grange)
SE16 . . . . . *2K* **103**
(off Woodland Cres.)
W6 . . . . . 2D **98**
Sycamore Lodge BR6: Orp 2K **173**
TW16: Sun 7H **129**
W8 . . . . . *3K* **99**
(off Stone Hall Pl.)
Sycamore M. *DA8: Erith* *5K* **109**
(off St John's Rd.)
SW4 . . . . . 3G **119**
Sycamore Pl. BR1: Brom 3E **160**
Sycamore Rd. SW19 . . . . . 6E **134**
Sycamore St. EC1 . . . . . 4C **8** (4C **84**)
Sycamore Wlk. IG6: Ilf 4G **53**
W10 . . . . . 4G **81**
Sycamore Way
CR7: Thor H 5A **156**
TW11: Tedd 6C **132**
Sydcote SE21 . . . . . 1C **138**
SYDENHAM 4J **139**
Sydenham Av. N21 . . . . . 5E **22**
SE26 . . . . . 5H **139**
Sydenham Cotts. SE12 . . . . . 2A **142**
Sydenham Ct. *CR0: C'don* *1D* **168**
(off Sydenham Rd.)
Sydenham Hill SE23 . . . . . 1H **139**
SE26 . . . . . 4F **139**
Sydenham Pk. SE26 . . . . . 3J **139**
Sydenham Pk. Mans. *SE26* *3J* **139**
(off Sydenham Pk.)
Sydenham Pk. Rd. SE26 . . . . . 3J **139**
Sydenham Pl. SE27 . . . . . 3B **138**
Sydenham Ri. SE23 . . . . . 2H **139**
Sydenham Rd. CR0: C'don 1C **168**
SE26 . . . . . 4J **139**
Sydmons Ct. SE23 . . . . . 7J **121**
Sydner M. N16 . . . . . 4F **67**
Sydner Rd. N16 . . . . . 4F **67**
Sydney Chapman Way EN5: Barn 2C **20**
Sydney Cl.
SW3 . . . . . 4B **16** (4B **100**)
Sydney Ct. UB4: Yead 4A **76**
Sydney Cres. TW15: Ashf 6D **128**
Sydney Gro. NW4 . . . . . 5E **44**
Sydney M. SW3 . . . . . 4B **16** (4B **100**)
Sydney Pl. SW7 . . . . . 4B **16** (4B **100**)
Sydney Rd. DA6: Bex 4D **126**
DA14: Sidc 4J **143**
E11 . . . . . 6K **51**
EN2: Enf 4J **23**
IG6: Ilf 2G **53**
IG8: Wfd G 4D **36**
N8 . . . . . 4A **48**
N10 . . . . . 1E **46**
SE2 . . . . . 3C **108**
SM1: Sutt 4J **165**
SW20 . . . . . 2F **153**
Sydney Rd. TW9: Rich 4E **114**
TW11: Tedd 5K **131**
TW14: Felt 1J **129**
W13 . . . . . 1A **96**
Sydney Russell Leisure Cen. 5E **72**
Sydney St. SW3 . . . . . 5C **16** (5C **100**)
Sylvana Cl. UB10: Hil 1B **74**
Sylvan Av. N3 . . . . . 2J **45**
N22 . . . . . 7E **32**
NW7 . . . . . 6F **29**
RM6: Chad H 6F **55**
Sylvan Ct. N12 . . . . . 3E **30**
NW6 . . . . . *1K* **81**
(off Abbey Rd.)
Sylvan Est. SE19 . . . . . 1F **157**
Sylvan Gdns. KT6: Surb 7D **150**
Sylvan Gro. NW2 . . . . . 4F **63**
SE15 . . . . . 6H **103**
Sylvan Hill SE19 . . . . . 1E **156**
Sylvan Rd. E7 . . . . . 6K **69**
E11 . . . . . 5J **51**
Sylvan Rd. E17 . . . . . 5C **50**
IG1: Ilf 2G **71**
SE19 . . . . . 1F **157**
Sylvan Ter. *SE15* *6H* **103**
(off Sylvan Gro.)
Sylvan Wlk. BR1: Brom 3D **160**
Sylvan Way BR4: W W'ck 4G **171**
RM8: Dag 4B **72**
Sylverdale Rd. CR0: C'don 3B **168**
Sylvester Av. BR7: Chst 6D **142**
Sylvester Path E8 . . . . . 6H **67**
Sylvester Rd. E8 . . . . . 6H **67**
E17 . . . . . 7B **50**
HA0: Wemb 5C **60**
N2 . . . . . 2A **46**
Sylvestrus Cl. KT1: King T 1G **151**
Sylvia Ct. HA9: Wemb 7H **61**
N1 . . . . . *2D* **84**
(off Wenlock St.)
Sylvia Gdns. HA9: Wemb 7H **61**
Sylvia Pankhurst Ho.
RM10: Dag *3G* **73**
(off Wythenshawe Rd.)
Symes M. NW1 . . . . . 2G **83**
Symington Ho. *SE1* *3D* **102**
(off Deverell St.)
Symington M. E9 . . . . . 5K **67**
Symister M. N1 . . . . . 2G **9**
Symons Cl. SE15 . . . . . 2J **121**
Symons St. SW3 . . . . . 4F **17** (4D **100**)
Symphony Cl. HA8: Edg 7C **28**
Symphony M. W10 . . . . . 3G **81**
Syon Ct. E11 . . . . . 5K **51**
Syon Ga. Way TW8: Bford 7A **96**
Syon House 1C **114**
Syon La. TW7: Isle 6J **95**
Syon Lodge SE12 . . . . . 7J **123**
Syon Pk. 1B **114**
Syon Pk. Gdns. TW7: Isle 7K **95**
Syringa Ho. SE4 . . . . . 3B **122**

T

Tabard Ct. *E14* *6E* **86**
(off Lodore St.)
Tabard Gdn. Est. SE1 . . . . . 7E **14** (3D **102**)
Tabard Ho. *SE1* *7F* **15**
(off Manciple St.)
Tabard St. SE1 . . . . . 6D **14** (2D **102**)
Tabernacle Av. E13 . . . . . 4J **87**
Tabernacle St. EC2 . . . . . 4F **9** (4D **84**)
Tableer Av. SW4 . . . . . 5G **119**
Tabley Rd. N7 . . . . . 4J **65**
Tabor Ct. SM3: Cheam 6G **165**
Tabor Gdns. SM3: Cheam 6H **165**
Tabor Gro. SW19 . . . . . 7H **135**
Tabor Rd. W6 . . . . . 3D **98**
Tachbrook Est. SW1 . . . . . 6C **18** (5H **101**)
Tachbrook M. SW1 . . . . . 3A **18** (4G **101**)
Tachbrook Rd. TW14: Felt 7H **111**
UB2: S'hall 4B **94**
UB7: W Dray 1A **92**
Tachbrook St. SW1 . . . . . 4B **18** (4G **101**)
(not continuous)
Tack M. SE4 . . . . . 3C **122**
Tadema Ho. NW8 . . . . . 4B **4**
Tadema Rd. SW10 . . . . . 7A **100**
Tadlow *KT1: King T* *3G* **151**
(off Washington Rd.)
Tadmor Cl. TW16: Sun 4H **147**
Tadmor St. W12 . . . . . 1F **99**
Tadworth Av. KT3: N Mald 4B **152**
Tadworth Ho. SE1 . . . . . 7A **14**
Tadworth Rd. NW2 . . . . . 2C **62**
Taeping St. E14 . . . . . 4D **104**
Taff Ho. *KT2: King T* *1D* **150**
(off Henry Macaulay Av.)
Taffrail Ho. *E14* *5D* **104**
(off Burrells Wharf Sq.)
Taffy's Row CR4: Mitc 3C **154**
Taft Way E3 . . . . . 3D **86**
Taggs Ho. *KT1: King T* *2D* **150**
(off Wadbrook St.)
Taggs Island TW12: Hamp 2H **149**
Tailor Ho. *WC1* *4F* **7**
(off Colonnade)
Tailworth St. *E1* *6K* **9**
(off Chicksand St.)
Tait Ct. *E3* *1B* **86**
(off St Stephen's Rd.)
SW8 . . . . . *1J* **119**
(off Lansdowne Grn.)
Tait Ho. *SE1* *5K* **13**
(off Greet St.)
Tait Rd. CR0: C'don 7E **156**
Tait Rd. Ind. Est. *CR0: C'don* *7E* **156**
(off Tait Rd.)
Takeley Cl. RM5: Col R 2K **55**
Takhar M. SW11 . . . . . 2C **118**
Talacre Community Sports Cen. 6E **64**
Talacre Rd. NW5 . . . . . 6E **64**
Talbot Av. N2 . . . . . 3B **46**
Talbot Cl. N15 . . . . . 4F **49**
Talbot Ct. EC3 . . . . . 2F **15**
NW9 . . . . . 3K **61**
Talbot Cres. NW4 . . . . . 5C **44**
Talbot Gdns. IG3: Ilf 2A **72**
Talbot Gro. Ho. *W11* *6G* **81**
(off Lancaster Rd.)
Talbot Ho. *E14* *6D* **86**
(off Girauld St.)
N7 . . . . . 3A **66**
Talbot Pl. SE3 . . . . . 2G **123**
Talbot Rd. CR7: Thor H 4D **156**
E6 . . . . . 2E **88**
E7 . . . . . 4J **69**
HA0: Wemb 6D **60**
HA3: W'stone 2K **41**
N6 . . . . . 6E **46**
N15 . . . . . 4F **49**
N22 . . . . . 2G **47**
RM9: Dag 6F **73**
SE22 . . . . . 4E **120**
SM5: Cars 5E **166**
TW2: Twick 1J **131**
TW7: Isle 4A **114**
TW15: Ashf 5A **128**
UB2: S'hall 4C **94**
W2 . . . . . 6H **81**
W11 . . . . . 6H **81**
(not continuous)
W13 . . . . . 1A **96**
Talbot Sq. W2 . . . . . 1B **10** (6B **82**)
Talbot Wlk. NW10 . . . . . 6A **62**
W11 . . . . . 6G **81**
Talbot Yd. SE1 . . . . . 5E **14** (1D **102**)
Talcott Path SW2 . . . . . 1A **138**
Talfourd Pl. SE15 . . . . . 1F **121**
Talfourd Rd. SE15 . . . . . 1F **121**
Talgarth Mans. *W14* *5G* **99**
(off Talgarth Rd.)
Talgarth Rd. W6 . . . . . 5F **99**
W14 . . . . . 5F **99**
Talgarth Wlk. NW9 . . . . . 5A **44**
Talia Ho. *E14* *3E* **104**
(off Manchester Rd.)
Talina Cen. SW6 . . . . . 1A **118**
Talisman Cl. IG3: Ilf 1B **72**
Talisman Sq. SE26 . . . . . 4G **139**
Talisman Way HA9: Wemb 3F **61**
Tallack Cl. HA3: Hrw W 7D **26**
Tallack Rd. E10 . . . . . 1B **68**
Tall Elms Cl. BR2: Brom 5H **159**
Talleyrand Ho. *SE5* *2C* **120**
(off Lilford Rd.)
Tallis Cl. E16 . . . . . 6K **87**
Tallis Gro. SE7 . . . . . 6K **105**
Tallis St. EC4 . . . . . 2K **13** (7A **84**)
Tallis Vw. NW10 . . . . . 6K **61**
Tallow Rd. TW8: Bford 6C **96**
Tall Trees SW16 . . . . . 3K **155**
Talma Gdns. TW2: Twick 6J **113**
Talmage Cl. SE23 . . . . . 7J **121**
Talman Gro. HA7: Stan 6J **27**
Talma Rd. SW2 . . . . . 4A **120**
Talwin St. E3 . . . . . 3D **86**
Tamar Cl. E3 . . . . . 1B **86**
Tamar Ho. *E14* *2E* **104**
(off Plevna St.)
SE11 . . . . . *5K* **19**
(off Kennington La.)
Tamarind Ct. SE1 . . . . . 6K **15**
W8 . . . . . *3K* **99**
(off Stone Hall Gdns.)
Tamarind Ho. *SE15* *7G* **103**
(off Reddins Rd.)
Tamarind Yd. *E1* *1G* **103**
(off Kennet St.)
Tamarisk Sq. W12 . . . . . 7B **80**
Tamar Sq. IG8: Wfd G 6E **36**
Tamar St. SE7 . . . . . 3C **106**
Tamar Way N17 . . . . . 3F **49**
Tamesis Gdns. KT4: Wor Pk 2A **164**
Tamian Ind. Est.
TW4: Houn 4A **112**
Tamian Way TW4: Houn 4A **112**
Tamworth N7 . . . . . 6J **65**
Tamworth Av. IG8: Wfd G 6B **36**
Tamworth La. CR4: Mitc 2F **155**
Tamworth Pk. CR4: Mitc 4F **155**
Tamworth Pl. CR0: C'don 2C **168**
Tamworth Rd. CR0: C'don 2B **168**
Tamworth St. SW6 . . . . . 6J **99**
Tamworth Vs.
CR4: Mitc 4F **155**
Tancred Rd. N4 . . . . . 6B **48**
Tandem Cen. SW19 . . . . . 1B **154**
Tandem Way SW19 . . . . . 1B **154**
Tandridge Dr. BR6: Orp 1H **173**
Tandridge Pl. BR6: Orp 1H **173**
Tanfield Av. NW2 . . . . . 4B **62**
Tanfield Rd. CR0: C'don 4C **168**
Tangerine Ho. *SE1* *7F* **15**
(off Long La.)
Tangier Rd. TW10: Rich 4G **115**
Tangleberry Cl. BR1: Brom 4D **160**
Tangle Tree Cl. N3 . . . . . 2K **45**
Tanglewood Cl. CR0: C'don 3J **169**
HA7: Stan 2D **26**
UB10: Hil 4C **74**
Tanglewood Way TW13: Felt 3K **129**
Tangley Gro. SW15 . . . . . 6B **116**
Tangley Pk. Rd. TW12: Hamp 5D **130**
Tanglyn Av. TW17: Shep 5D **146**
Tangmere *N17* *2D* **48**
(off Willan Rd.)
WC1 . . . . . *2G* **7**
(off Sidmouth St.)

Tangmere Gdns. UB5: Yead 2A 76
(not continuous)
Tangmere Gro. KT2: King T 5D 132
Tangmere Way NW9 2A 44
Tanhouse Fld. *NW5* *5H 65*
(*off Torriano Av.*)
Tanhurst Ho. *SW2* *7K 119*
(*off Redlands Way*)
Tanhurst Wlk. *SE2* *3D 108*
(*off Alsike Rd.*)
Tankerton Ho's. *WC1* *2F 7*
(*off Tankerton St.*)
Tankerton Rd. KT6: Surb 2F 163
Tankerton St. WC1 2F 7 (3J 83)
Tankerton Ter. CR0: C'don 6K 155
Tankerville Ct.
TW3: Houn 3G 113
Tankerville Rd. SW16 7H 137
Tankridge Rd. NW2 2D 62
Tanner Ho. *SE1* *7H 15*
(*off Tanner St.*)
Tanneries, The *E1* *4J 85*
(*off Cephas Av.*)
Tanner Point *E13* *1J 87*
(*off Pelly Rd.*)
Tanners Cl. KT12: Walt T 6K 147
Tanners End La. N18 4K 33
Tanner's Hill SE8 1B 122
Tanners La. IG6: Ilf 3G 53
Tanner St. IG11: Bark 6G 71
SE1 7H 15 (2E 102)
(not continuous)
Tannery, The *SE1* *2E 102*
(*off Black Swan Yd.*)
Tannery Cl. BR3: Beck 5K 157
RM10: Dag 3H 73
Tannington Ter. N5 3B 66
Tannsfeld Rd. SE26 5K 139
Tansley Cl. N7 5H 65
Tanswell St. SE1 7J 13 (2A 102)
Tansy Cl. E6 6E 88
Tantallon Rd. SW12 1E 136
Tant Av. E16 6H 87
Tantony Gro. RM6: Chad H 3D 54
Tanworth Gdns. HA5: Pinn 2K 39
Tanyard Ho. *TW8: Bford* *7C 96*
(*off High St.*)
Tanyard La. DA5: Bexl 7G 127
Tanza Rd. NW3 4D 64
Tapestry Cl. SM2: Sutt 7K 165
Tapley Ho. *SE1* *7K 15*
(*off Wolseley St.*)
Taplow NW3 7B 64
SE17 *5D 102*
(*off Thurlow St.*)
Taplow Ct. CR4: Mitc 4C 154
Taplow Ho. *E2* *2J 9*
(*off Palissy St.*)
Taplow Rd. N13 4H 33
Taplow St. N1 1D 8 (2C 84)
Tappesfield Rd. SE15 3J 121
Tapping Cl. KT2: King T 7G 133
Tapp St. E1 4H 85
Tapster St. EN5: Barn 3C 20
Tara Arts Cen. 1A 136
Tara Ct. BR3: Beck 2D 158
Tara M. N8 6J 47
Taransay Wlk. N1 6D 66
Taranto Ho. *E1* *5K 85*
(*off Master's St.*)
Tarbert M. N15 5E 48
Tarbert Rd. SE22 5E 120
Tarbert Wlk. E1 7J 85
Target Cl. TW14: Felt 6G 111
Target Ho. *W13* *1B 96*
(*off Sherwood Cl.*)
TARGET RDBT. 1D 76
Tariff Cres. SE8 4B 104
Tariff Rd. N17 6B 34
Tarleton Ct. N22 2A 48
Tarleton Gdns. SE23 2H 139
Tarling Cl. DA14: Sidc 3B 144
Tarling Ho. *E1* *6H 85*
(*off Tarling St.*)
Tarling Rd. E16 6H 87
N2 2A 46
Tarling St. E1 6H 85
Tarling St. Est. E1 6J 85
Tarmac Way UB7: Harm 3C 174
Tarnbank EN2: Enf 5D 22
Tarnbrook Ct. *SW1* *4G 17*
(*off Whittaker St.*)
Tarns, The *NW1* *1A 6*
(*off Varndell St.*)
Tarn St. SE1 3C 102
Tarnwood Pk. SE9 7D 124
Tarplett Ho. *SE14* *6K 103*
(*off John Williams Cl.*)
Tarquin Ho. *SE26* *4G 139*
(*off High Level Dr.*)
Tarragon Cl. SE14 7A 104
Tarragon Ct. IG1: Ilf 2J 71
Tarragon Gro. SE26 6K 139
Tarranbrae NW6 7G 63
Tarrant Ho. *E2* *3J 85*
(*off Roman Rd.*)
W14 *3G 99*
(*off Russell Rd.*)
Tarrant Pl. W1 6E 4 (5D 82)
Tarrington Cl.
SW16 3H 137
Tartan Ho. *E14* *6E 86*
(*off Dee St.*)
Tarver Rd. SE17 5B 102
Tarves Way SE10 7D 104
(not continuous)
Tash Pl. N11 5A 32
Tasker Cl. UB3: Harl 7E 92
Tasker Ho. *E14* *5B 86*
(*off Wallwood St.*)
IG11: Bark 2H 89
Tasker Lodge *W8* *2J 99*
(*off Campden Hill*)
Tasker Rd. NW3 5D 64
Tasman Ct. *E14* *4D 104*
(*off Westferry Rd.*)
TW16: Sun 7G 129
Tasman Ho. *E1* *1H 103*
(*off Clegg St.*)
Tasmania Ter. N18 6H 33
Tasman Rd. SW9 3J 119
Tasman Wlk. E16 6B 88
Tasso Rd. W6 6G 99
Tasso Yd. *W6* *6G 99*
(*off Tasso Rd.*)
Tatam Rd. NW10 7K 61
Tatchbury Ho.
SW15 *6B 116*
(*off Tunworth Cres.*)
Tate Britain 4E 18 (4J 101)
Tate Ho. *E2* *2K 85*
(*off Mace St.*)
Tate Modern 4B 14 (1B 102)
Tate Rd. E16 1D 106
(not continuous)
SM1: Sutt 5J 165
Tatham Pl. NW8 2B 82
Tatnell Rd. SE23 6A 122
Tatsfield Ho. *SE1* *7F 15*
(*off Pardoner St.*)
Tattersall Cl. SE9 5C 124
Tatton Cres. N16 7F 49
Tatum St. SE17 4D 102
Tauheed Cl. N4 2C 66
Taunton Av. SW20 2D 152
TW3: Houn 2G 113
Taunton Cl. DA7: Bex 2K 127
SM3: Sutt 1J 165
Taunton Dr. EN2: Enf 3F 23
N2 2A 46
Taunton Ho. *W2* *6A 82*
(*off Hallfield Est.*)
Taunton M. NW1 4E 4 (4D 82)
Taunton Pl. NW1 3E 4 (4D 82)
Taunton Rd. SE12 5G 123
UB6: G'frd 1F 77
Taunton Way
HA7: Stan 2E 42
Tavern Cl. SM5: Cars 7C 154
Tavern Ct. *SE1* *3C 102*
(*off New Kent Rd.*)
Taverners Cl. W11 1G 99
Taverners Ct. *E3* *3A 86*
(*off Grove Rd.*)
Taverner Sq. N5 4C 66
Taverners Way E4 1B 36
Tavern La. SW9 2A 120
Tavern Quay SE16 4A 104
Tavistock Av. E17 3K 49
NW7 7A 30
UB6: G'frd 2A 78
Tavistock Cl. N16 5E 66
TW18: Staines 7A 128
Tavistock Ct. *CR0: C'don* *1D 168*
(*off Tavistock Rd.*)
WC1 *3D 6*
(*off Tavistock Sq.*)
WC2 *2F 13*
(*off Tavistock St.*)
Tavistock Cres. CR4: Mitc 4J 155
W11 5H 81
(not continuous)
Tavistock Gdns. IG3: Ilf 4J 71
Tavistock Ga. CR0: C'don 1D 168
Tavistock Gro. CR0: C'don 7D 156
Tavistock Ho. IG8: Wfd G 6K 37
WC1 3D 6 (4H 83)
Tavistock M. W11 6H 81
Tavistock Pl. N14 6A 22
WC1 3E 6 (4J 83)
Tavistock Rd. BR2: Brom 4H 159
CR0: C'don 1D 168
DA16: Well 1C 126
E7 4H 69
E15 6H 69
E18 3J 51
HA8: Edg 1G 43
N4 6D 48
NW10 2B 80
SM5: Cars 1B 166
UB7: Yiew 1A 92
UB10: Ick 5F 57
W11 6H 81
(not continuous)
Tavistock Sq. WC1 3D 6 (4H 83)
Tavistock St. WC2 2F 13 (7J 83)
Tavistock Ter. N19 3H 65
Tavistock Twr. SE16 3A 104
Tavistock Wlk. SM5: Cars 1B 166
Taviton St. WC1 3C 6 (4H 83)
Tavy Bri. SE2 2C 108
Tavy Cl. SE11 5K 19
Tawney Rd. SE28 7B 90
Tawny Cl. TW13: Felt 3J 129
W13 1B 96
Tawny Way SE16 4K 103
Tayben Av. TW2: Twick 6J 113
Taybridge Rd. SW11 3E 118
Tay Bldgs. SE1 7G 15
Tayburn Cl. E14 6E 86
Tay Ct. *E2* *3K 85*
(*off Meath Cres.*)
SE1 *3E 102*
(*off Decima St.*)
Tayfield Cl. UB10: Ick 3F 57
Tayler Ct. NW8 1B 82
Taylor Av. TW9: Kew 2H 115
Taylor Cl. BR6: Orp 4K 173
N17 7B 34
SE8 6B 104
Taylor Cl. TW3: Houn 1G 113
TW12: Ham H 5G 131
Taylor Ct. *SE20* *2J 157*
(*off Elmers End Rd.*)
Taylor Rd. CR4: Mitc 7C 136
SM6: Wall 5F 167
Taylors Bldgs. SE18 4F 107
Taylors Cl. DA14: Sidc 3K 143
Taylors Ct. TW13: Felt 2J 129
Taylors Grn. W3 6A 80
Taylors La. EN5: Barn 1C 20
NW10 6A 62
SE26 4H 139
Taylorsmead NW7 5H 29
Taymount Grange SE23 2J 139
Taymount Ri. SE23 2J 139
Tayport Cl. N1 7J 65
Tayside Ct. SE5 4D 120
Tayside Dr. HA8: Edg 3C 28
Taywood Rd. UB5: N'olt 4D 76
Teak Cl. SE16 1A 104
Tealby Ct. *N7* *5K 65*
(*off George's Rd.*)
Teal Cl. E16 5B 88
Teal Ct. *E1* *3K 15*
(*off Star Pl.*)
NW10 6K 61
SE8 *6B 104*
(*off Abinger Gro.*)
SM6: Wall 5G 167
Teal Dr. HA6: Nwood 1E 38
Teale St. E2 2G 85
Tealing Dr. KT19: Ewe 4K 163
Teal Pl. SM1: Sutt 5H 165
Teal St. SE10 3H 105
Teasel Cl. CR0: C'don 1K 169
Teasel Cres. SE28 1J 107
Teasel Way E15 3G 87
Teather St. *SE5* *7E 102*
(*off Southampton Way*)
Tea Trade Wharf *SE1* *6K 15*
(*off Shad Thames*)
Tebworth Rd. N17 7A 34
Technology Pk., The NW9 3A 44
Teck Cl. TW7: Isle 2A 114
Tedder Cl. HA4: Ruis 5J 57
KT9: Chess 5C 162
UB10: Uxb 7B 56
Tedder Rd. CR2: Sels 7J 169
TEDDINGTON 5A 132
Teddington Bus. Pk.
TW11: Tedd *6K 131*
(*off Station Rd.*)
Teddington Pk. TW11: Tedd 5K 131
Teddington Pk. Rd. TW11: Tedd 4K 131
Teddington Pool & Fitness Cen. 5A 132
Teddington Sports Cen. 6D 132
Teddy Bear Mus. *6K 135*
(*within Polka Theatre for Children*)
Ted Hennem Ho. RM10: Dag 3H 73
Ted Roberts Ho. *E2* *2H 85*
(*off Parmiter St.*)
Tedworth Gdns. SW3 6E 16 (5D 100)
Tedworth Sq. SW3 6E 16 (5D 100)
Tee, The W3 6A 80
Tees Av. UB6: G'frd 2J 77
Tees Ct. *W7* *6H 77*
(*off Hanway Rd.*)
Teesdale Av. TW7: Isle 1A 114
Teesdale Cl. E2 2G 85
Teesdale Gdns. SE25 2E 156
TW7: Isle 1A 114
Teesdale Rd. E11 6H 51
Teesdale St. E2 2H 85
Teesdale Yd. *E2* *2H 85*
(*off Teesdale St.*)
Teeswater Ct. DA18: Erith 3D 108
Teevan Cl. CR0: C'don 7G 157
Teevan Rd. CR0: C'don 1G 169
Tegan Cl. SM2: Sutt 7J 165

Teignmouth Cl. HA8: Edg 2F 43
SW4 4H 119
Teignmouth Gdns. UB6: G'frd 2A 78
Teignmouth Pde. UB6: G'frd 2A 78
Teignmouth Rd. DA16: Well 2C 126
NW2 5F 63
Telcote Way HA4: Ruis 7A 40
Telegraph Hill NW3 3K 63
Telegraph La. KT10: Clay 4A 162
Telegraph M. IG3: Ilf 1A 72
Telegraph Pas. SW2 7J 119
(off New Pk. Rd.)
Telegraph Path BR7: Chst 5F 143
Telegraph Pl. E14 4D 104
Telegraph Quarters SE10 5F 105
(off Park Row)
Telegraph Rd. SW15 7D 116
Telegraph St. EC2 7E 8 (6D 84)
Telemann Sq. SE3 4K 123
Telephone Pl. SW6 6H 99
Telfer Cl. W3 2J 97
Telfer Ho. EC1 2B 8
Telferscot Rd. SW12 1H 137
Telford Av. SW2 1H 137
Telford Cl. E17 7A 50
SE19 6F 139
Telford Dr. KT12: Walt T 7A 148
Telford Ho. SE1 3C 102
(off Tiverton St.)
W10 5G 81
(off Portobello Rd.)
Telford Rd. N11 5B 32
NW9 6C 44
SE9 2H 143
TW2: Whitt 7E 112
UB1: S'hall 7F 77
W10 5G 81
Telfords Yd. E1 7G 85
Telford Ter. SW1 7A 18 (6G 101)
Telford Way UB4: Yead 5C 76
W3 5A 80
Telham Rd. E6 2E 88
Tell Gro. SE22 4F 121
Tellson Av. SE18 1B 124
Telscombe Cl. BR6: Orp 2J 173
Temair Ho. SE10 7D 104
(off Tarves Way)
Temeraire Pl. TW8: Bford 5F 97
Temeraire St. SE16 2J 103
Tempelhof Av. NW2 7E 44
NW4 7E 44
Temperley Rd. SW12 7E 118
Templar Ct. NW8 2A 4
RM7: Mawney 4H 55
Templar Dr. SE28 6D 90
Templar Ho. HA2: Harr 2G 59
NW2 6H 63
RM13: Rain 2K 91
Templar Pl. TW12: Hamp 7E 130
Templars Av. NW11 6H 45
Templars Cres. N3 2J 45
Templars Dr. HA3: Hrw W 6C 26
Templars Ho. E16 7F 89
(off University Way)
Templar St. SE5 2B 120
Temple Av. CR0: C'don 2B 170
EC4 2K 13 (7A 84)
N20 7G 21
RM8: Dag 1G 73
Temple Bar 1J 13
Temple Bar Gate 1B 14
(off Paternoster Sq.)
Temple Chambers EC4 2K 13
Temple Cl. E11 7G 51
N3 2H 45
SE28 3G 107
Templecombe Rd.
E9 1J 85
Templecombe Way
SM4: Mord 5G 153
Temple Ct. E1 5K 85
(off Rectory Sq.)
SW8 7J 101
(off Thorncroft St.)
Templecroft TW15: Ashf 6F 129
Temple Dwellings E2 2H 85
(off Temple St.)
TEMPLE FORTUNE 5H 45
Temple Fortune Hill NW11 5J 45
Temple Fortune La. NW11 6H 45
Temple Fortune Pde.
NW11 5H 45
Temple Gdns. EC4 2J 13
N21 2G 33
NW11 6H 45
RM8: Dag 3D 72
Temple Gro. EN2: Enf 2G 23
NW11 6J 45
Temple Hall Ct. E4 2A 36
Temple La. EC4 1K 13 (6A 84)
Templeman Rd. W7 5K 77
Temple Mead Cl.
HA7: Stan 6G 27
Templemead Cl. W3 6A 80
Templemead Ho. E9 4A 68
Temple Mill La. E10 4D 68
(not continuous)
E15 4E 68
TEMPLE MILLS 4D 68
Temple Mills E10 3E 68
Temple of Mithras (remains) 1E 14
(off Queen Victoria St.)
Temple Pde. EN5: New Bar 7G 21
(off Netherlands Rd.)
Temple Pk. UB8: Hil 3C 74
Temple Pl. WC2 2H 13 (7K 83)
Temple Rd. CR0: C'don 4D 168
E6 1C 88
N8 4K 47
NW2 4E 62
TW3: Houn 4F 113
TW9: Rich 2F 115
W4 3J 97
W5 3D 96
Temple Sheen SW14 4J 115
Temple Sheen Rd. SW14 4H 115
Temple St. E2 2H 85
Temple Ter. N22 2A 48
(off Vincent Rd.)
Templeton Av. E4 4H 35
Templeton Cl. N15 6D 48
N16 5E 66
SE19 1D 156
Templeton Ct. EN3: Enf W 1D 24
Templeton Pl. SW5 4J 99
Templeton Rd. N15 6D 48
Temple Way SM1: Sutt 3B 166
Temple West M. SE11 3B 102
Templewood W13 5B 78
Templewood Av. NW3 3K 63
Templewood Gdns. NW3 3K 63
Templewood Point
NW2 2H 63
(off Granville Rd.)
Temple Yd. E2 2H 85
(off Temple St.)
Tempo Ho. UB5: N'olt 3B 76
Tempsford Cl. EN2: Enf 4H 23
Tempsford Ct. HA1: Harr 6K 41
Tempus Ct. E18 1J 51
Tempus Wharf SE16 2G 103
(off Bermondsey Wall W.)
Temsford Cl. HA2: Harr 2G 41
Tenbury Cl. E7 5B 70
Tenbury Ct. SW2 1H 137
Tenby Av. HA3: Kent 2B 42
Tenby Cl. N15 4F 49
RM6: Chad H 6E 54
Tenby Ct. E17 5A 50
Tenby Gdns. UB5: N'olt 6E 58
Tenby Ho. UB3: Harl 3E 92
W2 6A 82
(off Hallfield Est.)
Tenby Mans. W1 5H 5
(off Nottingham St.)
Tenby Rd. DA16: Well 1D 126
E17 5A 50
EN3: Pond E 4D 24
HA8: Edg 1F 43
RM6: Chad H 6E 54
Tench St. E1 1H 103
Tenda Rd. SE16 4H 103
Tendring Way RM6: Chad H 5C 54
Tenham Av. SW2 1H 137
Tenison Ct. W1 2A 12 (7G 83)
Tenison Way SE1 5H 13 (1K 101)
Tenniel Cl. W2 7A 82
Tennis Ct. La. KT8: E Mos 3K 149
Tennison Rd. SE25 4F 157
Tennis St. SE1 6E 14 (2D 102)
Tenniswood Rd. EN1: Enf 1K 23
Tennyson N8 3J 47
(off Boyton Cl.)
Tennyson Av. E11 7J 51
E12 7C 70
KT3: N Mald 5D 152
Tennyson Av. NW9 3J 43
TW1: Twick 1K 131
Tennyson Cl. DA16: Well 1J 125
EN3: Pond E 5E 24
TW14: Felt 6H 111
Tennyson Ct. SW6 1A 118
(off Imperial Rd.)
Tennyson Ho. DA17: Belv 5F 109
SE17 5C 102
(off Browning St.)
Tennyson Mans. SW1 5J 17
(off Sutherland St.)
SW3 7C 16
(off Lordship Pl.)
W14 6H 99
(off Queen's Club Gdns.)
Tennyson Rd. E10 1D 68
E15 7G 69
E17 6B 50
NW6 1H 81
NW7 5H 29
SE20 7K 139
SW19 6A 136
TW3: Houn 2G 113
TW15: Ashf 5A 128
W7 7K 77
Tennyson St. SW8 2F 119
Tensing Ct. TW19: Stanw 1A 128
Tensing Rd. UB2: S'hall 3E 94
Tentelow La. UB2: S'hall 5E 94
Tenterden Cl. NW4 3F 45
SE9 4D 142
Tenterden Dr. NW4 3F 45
Tenterden Gdns.
CR0: C'don 7G 157
NW4 3F 45
Tenterden Gro. NW4 3F 45
Tenterden Ho. SE17 5E 102
(off Surrey Gro.)
Tenterden Rd. CR0: C'don 7G 157
N17 7A 34
RM8: Dag 2F 73
Tenterden St. W1 1K 11 (6F 83)
Tenter Ground E1 6J 9 (5F 85)
Tenter Pas. E1 1K 15
(off Nth. Tenter St.)
Tent Peg La. BR5: Pet W 5G 161
Tent St. E1 4H 85
Tequila Wharf E14 6A 86
Terborch Way SE22 5E 120
Teredo St. SE16 3K 103
Terence Ct. DA17: Belv 6F 109
(off Stream Way)
Terence McMillan Stadium 4B 88
Terence Messenger Twr. E10 2D 68
(off Alpine Rd.)
Teresa M. E17 4C 50
Teresa Wlk. N10 5F 47
Terling Cl. E11 3H 69
Terling Ho. W10 5E 80
(off Sutton Way)
Terling Rd. RM8: Dag 2G 73
Terling Wlk. N1 1C 84
(off Popham St.)
Terminal 4 Rdbt. TW6: H'row A 6E 110
Terminal 5 Rdbt. TW6: H'row A 5C 174
Terminal Ho. HA7: Stan 5J 27
Terminus Pl. SW1 2K 17 (3F 101)
Terrace, The E2 3J 85
(off Old Ford Rd.)
E4 3B 36
(off Newgate St.)
EC4 1K 13
IG8: Wfd G 6D 36
N3 2H 45
NW6 1J 81
SE8 4B 104
(off Longshore)
SE23 7A 122
SW13 2A 116
Terrace Apartments N5 5A 66
Terrace Av. NW10 4E 80
Terrace Gdns. SW13 2B 116
Terrace Hill CR0: C'don 3B 168
(off Hanover St.)
Terrace La. TW10: Rich 6E 114
Terrace Rd. E9 7J 67
E13 2J 87
KT12: Walt T 7J 147
Terraces, The NW8 2B 82
(off Queen's Ter.)
Terrace Wlk. RM9: Dag 5E 72
SW11 7D 100
(off Albert Bri. Rd.)
SW11 7H 17 (6E 100)
(Carriage Dr. Nth.)
Terrano Ho. TW9: Kew 7H 97
Terrapin Rd. SW17 3F 137
Terretts Pl. N1 7B 66
(off Upper St.)
Terrick Rd. N22 1J 47
Terrick St. W12 6D 80
Terrilands HA5: Pinn 3D 40
Territorial Ho. SE11 4K 19
Terront Rd. N15 4C 48
Tersha St. TW9: Rich 4F 115
Tessa Sanderson Pl. SW8 3F 119
(off Daley Thompson Way)
Tessa Sanderson Way
UB6: G'frd 5H 59
Testerton Rd. W11 7F 81
(off Hurstway Rd.)
Testerton Wlk. W11 7F 81
Testwood Ct. W7 7J 77
Tetbury Pl. N1 1B 84
Tetcott Rd. SW10 7A 100
(not continuous)
Tetherdown N10 3E 46
Tetty Way BR2: Brom 2J 159
Tevatree Ho. SE1 5G 103
(off Avondale Sq.)
Teversham La. SW8 1J 119
Teviot Cl. DA16: Well 1B 126
Teviot Est. E14 5D 86
Teviot St. E14 4E 86
Tewkesbury Av. HA5: Pinn 5C 40
SE23 1H 139
Tewkesbury Cl. EN4: E Barn 4G 21
N15 6D 48
Tewkesbury Gdns. NW9 3H 43
Tewkesbury Rd. N15 6D 48
SM5: Cars 1B 166
W13 1A 96
Tewkesbury Ter. N11 6B 32

Tewson Rd. SE18 5J 107
Teynham Av. EN1: Enf 6J 23
Teynham Ct. BR3: Beck 3D 158
Teynham Grn. BR2: Brom 5J 159
Teynton Ter. N17 1C 48
Thackeray Av. N17 2G 49
Thackeray Cl. SW19 7F 135
TW7: Isle 2A 114
UB8: Hil 6D 74
Thackeray Ct. *NW6* *7A 64*
(off Fairfax Rd.)
SW3 *5E 16*
(off Elystan Pl.)
W5 *6F 79*
(off Hanger Va. La.)
W14 *3G 99*
(off Blythe Rd.)
Thackeray Dr. RM6: Chad H 7A 54
Thackeray Ho. WC1 3E 6
Thackeray Lodge
TW14: Bedf 6F 111
Thackeray M. E8 6G 67
Thackeray Rd. E6 2B 88
SW8 2F 119
Thackeray St. W8 3K 99
Thackery Ct. *EC1* *5A 8*
(off Turnmill St.)
Thackrah Cl. *N2* *2A 46*
(off Sims Gdns.)
Thakeham Cl. SE26 4H 139
Thalia Cl. SE10 6F 105
Thalia Ct. *E8* *7F 67*
(off Albion Dr.)
Thame Rd. SE16 2K 103
Thames Av. RM9: Dag, Rain 4H 91
SW10 1A 118
UB6: G'frd 2K 77
Thames Bank SW14 2J 115
Thamesbank Pl. SE28 6C 90
Thames Barrier Ind. Area
SE18 *3B 106*
(off Faraday Way)
Thames Barrier Pk. 2A 106
Thames Barrier Vis. Cen. 3B 106
Thamesbrook SW3 6C 16
Thames Circ. E14 4C 104
Thames Cl. TW12: Hamp 2F 149
Thames Cotts. KT7: T Ditt 6B 150
Thames Ct. KT8: W Mole 2F 149
SE15 *7F 103*
(off Daniel Gdns.)
W7 *6J 77*
(off Hanway Rd.)
Thames Cres. W4 7A 98
THAMES DITTON 6A 150
Thames Ditton Miniature Railway 1A 162
Thames Dr. HA4: Ruis 6E 38
Thames Exchange Bldg. EC4 3D 14
Thames Eyot TW1: Twick 1A 132
Thamesfield Ct. TW17: Shep 7E 146
Thamesfield M. TW17: Shep 7E 146
Thamesgate Cl. TW10: Ham 4B 132
Thames Gateway RM9: Dag 2F 91
RM13: Rain 2F 91
Thames Gateway Pk. RM9: Dag 3F 91
Thames Haven KT6: Surb 5D 150
Thames Hgts. *SE1* *6J 15*
(off Gainsford St.)
Thameshill Av. RM5: Col R 2J 55
Thames Ho. *EC4* *2D 14*
(off Up. Thames St.)
KT1: King T *4D 150*
(off Surbiton Rd.)
SW1 *3E 18*
(off Millbank)
Thameside KT8: W Mole 3F 149
TW11: Tedd 7D 132
Thameside Cen. TW8: Bford 6F 97
Thameside Community Nature Reserve 4A 90
Thameside Ind. Est. E16 2B 106
Thameside Pk. City Farm 3A 90
Thameside Pl. KT1: Ham W 1D 150
Thameside Wlk. SE28 6A 90
Thames Lock KT12: Walt T 3A 148
THAMESMEAD 1B 108
Thamesmead KT12: Walt T 6J 147
THAMESMEAD CENTRAL 1A 108
THAMESMEAD EAST 2G 109
THAMESMEAD NORTH 6D 90
Thames Mdw. KT8: W Mole 2E 148
TW17: Shep 7F 147
THAMESMEAD SOUTH 2D 108
THAMESMEAD SOUTH WEST 2K 107
THAMESMEAD WEST 3G 107
Thamesmere Dr. SE28 7A 90
Thamesmere Leisure Cen. 7A 90
Thames Path SE10 1G 105
Thames Pl. SW15 3F 117
(not continuous)
Thames Point SW6 2A 118
Thamespoint TW11: Tedd 7D 132
Thames Quay E14 2D 104
SW10 *1A 118*
(off Chelsea Harbour)
Thames Reach SE28 2J 107
W6 *6E 98*
(off Rainville Rd.)
Thames Rd. E16 1B 106
IG11: Bark 3K 89
W4 6G 97
Thames Rd. Ind. Est. E16 2B 106
Thames Side KT1: King T 1D 150
KT7: T Ditt 6B 150
Thames St. KT1: King T 2D 150
(not continuous)
KT12: Walt T 7H 147
SE10 6D 104
TW12: Hamp 1F 149
TW16: Sun 4J 147
Thames Tunnel Mills SE16 2J 103
Thames Va. Cl. TW3: Houn 3E 112
Thames Valley University
Ealing Campus 1D 96
Paragon Campus *5C 96*
(off Boston Mnr. Rd.)
Spesom House 7C 78
Westel House 7C 78
Thamesview Bus. Cen.
RM13: Rain 5K 91
Thamesview Ho's. KT12: Walt T 6J 147
Thames Vw. Lodge IG11: Bark 3J 89
Thames Village W4 1J 115
Thames Wlk. SW11 7C 100
Thames Wharf Studios
W6 *6E 98*
(off Rainville Rd.)
Thanescroft Gdns. CR0: C'don 3E 168
Thanet Ct. W3 6G 79
Thanet Dr. BR2: Kes 3B 172
Thanet Ho. *CR0: C'don* *4C 168*
(off Coombe Rd.)
WC1 *2E 6*
(off Thanet St.)
Thanet Lodge *NW2* *6G 63*
(off Mapesbury Rd.)
Thanet Pl. CR0: C'don 4C 168
Thanet Rd. DA5: Bexl 7G 127
Thanet St. WC1 2E 6 (3J 83)
Thanet Wharf *SE8* *6D 104*
(off Copperas St.)
Thane Vs. N7 3K 65
Thane Works N7 3K 65
Thanington Ct. SE9 6J 125
Thant Cl. E10 3D 68
Tharp Rd. SM6: Wall 5H 167
Thatcham Ct. N20 7F 21
Thatcham Gdns. N20 7F 21
Thatcher Cl. UB7: W Dray 2A 92
Thatchers Way TW7: Isle 5H 113
Thatches Gro. RM6: Chad H 4E 54
Thavie's Inn EC4 7K 7 (6A 84)
Thaxted Ct. *N1* *1F 9*
(off Murray Gro.)
Thaxted Ho. RM10: Dag 7H 73
SE16 *4J 103*
(off Abbeyfield Est.)
Thaxted Pl. SW20 7F 135
Thaxted Rd. IG9: Buck H 1H 37
SE9 3G 143
Thaxton Rd. W14 6H 99
Thayers Farm Rd. BR3: Beck 1A 158
Thayer St. W1 6H 5 (6E 82)
The
Names prefixed with 'The' for example 'The Acacias' are indexed under the main name such as 'Acacias, The'
Theatrerites 2K 135
Theatre Royal
Stratford 7F 69
Theatre Sq. E15 6F 69
Theatre St. SW11 3D 118
Theatro Technis *1G 83*
(off Crowndale Rd.)
Theberton St. N1 1A 84
Theed St. SE1 5K 13 (1A 102)
Thelma Gdns. SE3 1B 124
Thelma Gro. TW11: Tedd 6A 132
Theobald Cres. HA3: Hrw W 1G 41
Theobald Rd. CR0: C'don 2B 168
E17 7B 50
Theobalds Av. N12 4F 31
Theobalds Ct. N4 3C 66
Theobald's Rd. WC1 5G 7 (5K 83)
Theobald St. SE1 3D 102
Theodora Way HA5: Eastc 3H 39
Theodore Ct. SE13 6F 123
Theodore Rd. SE13 6F 123
Therapia La. CR0: Bedd 7H 155
CR0: C'don 6J 155
Therapia Rd. SE22 6J 121
Theresa Rd. W6 4C 98
Therfield Ct. N4 2C 66
Thermopylae Ga. E14 4D 104
Theseus Wlk. N1 1B 8 (2B 84)
Thesiger Rd. SE20 7K 139
Thessaly Ho. *SW8* *7G 101*
(off Thessaly Rd.)
Thessaly Rd. SW8 7G 101
(not continuous)
Thesus Ho. *E14* *6E 86*
(off Blair St.)
Thetford Cl. N13 6G 33
Thetford Gdns. RM9: Dag 7E 72
Thetford Ho. *SE1* *7J 15*
(off St Saviour's Est.)
Thetford Rd. KT3: N Mald 6K 151
RM9: Dag 7D 72
TW15: Ashf 4A 128
Thetis Ter. TW9: Kew 6G 97
Theydon Gro. IG8: Wfd G 6F 37
Theydon Rd. E5 2J 67
Theydon St. E17 7B 50
Thicket, The UB7: Yiew 6A 74
Thicket Cres. SM1: Sutt 4A 166
Thicket Gro. RM9: Dag 6C 72
SE20 7G 139
Thicket Rd. SE20 7G 139
SM1: Sutt 4A 166
Third Av. E12 4C 70
E13 3J 87
E17 5C 50
EN1: Enf 5A 24
HA9: Wemb 2D 60
RM6: Chad H 6C 54
RM10: Dag 1H 91
UB3: Hayes 1H 93
W3 1B 98
W10 3G 81
Third Cl. KT8: W Mole 4G 149
Third Cross Rd. TW2: Twick 2H 131
Third Way HA9: Wemb 4H 61
Thirleby Rd. HA8: Edg 1K 43
SW1 2B 18 (3G 101)
Thirlestane Ct. N10 2E 46
Thirlmere *NW1* *1K 5*
(off Cumberland Mkt.)
Thirlmere Av. UB6: G'frd 3C 78
Thirlmere Gdns. HA9: Wemb 1C 60
Thirlmere Ho. *N16* *4D 66*
(off Howard Rd.)
TW7: Isle 5K 113
Thirlmere Ri. BR1: Brom 6H 141
Thirlmere Rd. DA7: Bex 1J 127
N10 1F 47
SW16 4H 137
Thirsk Cl. UB5: N'olt 6E 58
Thirsk Rd. CR4: Mitc 7E 136
SE25 4D 156
SW11 3E 118
Thirza Ho. *E1* *6J 85*
(off Devonport St.)
Thistlebrook SE2 3C 108
Thistlebrook Ind. Est. SE2 3C 108
Thistlecroft Gdns. HA7: Stan 1D 42
Thistledene KT7: T Ditt 6J 149
Thistledene Av. HA2: Harr 3C 58
Thistlefield Cl. DA5: Bexl 1D 144
Thistle Gro. SW10 6A 16 (5A 100)
Thistle Ho. *E14* *6E 86*
(off Dee St.)
Thistlemead BR7: Chst 2F 161
Thistlewaite Rd. E5 3H 67
Thistlewood Cl. N7 2K 65
Thistleworth Cl. TW7: Isle 7H 95
Thistleworth Marina
TW7: Isle *4B 114*
(off Railshead Rd.)
Thistley Cl. N12 6H 31
Thistley Ct. SE8 6D 104
Thomas A'Beckett Cl.
HA0: Wemb 4K 59
Thomas Baines Rd. SW11 3B 118
Thomas Burt Ho. *E2* *3H 85*
(off Canrobert St.)
Thomas Cribb M. E6 6E 88
Thomas Darby Ct. *W11* *6G 81*
(off Lancaster Rd.)
Thomas Dean Rd. SE26 4B 140
Thomas Dinwiddy Rd.
SE12 2K 141
Thomas Doyle St. SE1 7A 14 (3B 102)
Thomas England Ho.
RM7: Rom *6K 55*
(off Waterloo Gdns.)
Thomas Frye Ct. *E15* *2D 86*
(off High St.)
Thomas Hardy Ho. N22 7E 32
Thomas Hewlett Ho. HA1: Harr 4J 59
Thomas Hollywood Ho. *E2* *2J 85*
(off Approach Rd.)
Thomas Ho. SM2: Sutt 7K 165
Thomas Jacomb Pl. E17 4B 50
Thomas La. SE6 7C 122
Thomas Lodge E17 5D 50
Thomas More Highwalk *EC2* *6C 8*
(off Barbican)
Thomas More Ho. EC2 6C 8
HA4: Ruis 1G 57
Thomas More Sq. *E1* *7G 85*
(off Thomas More St.)
Thomas More St. E1 7G 85
Thomas More Way N2 3A 46
Thomas Neal's Cen. WC2 1E 12 (6J 83)
Thomas Nth. Ter. *E16* *5H 87*
(off Barking Rd.)
Thomas Pl. W8 3K 99
Thomas Rd. E14 6B 86
Thomas Rd. Ind. Est. E14 5C 86
Thomas St. SE18 4F 107

Thomas Turner Path CR0: C'don 2C 168
(off George St.)
Thomas Wall Cl. SM1: Sutt 5K 165
Thomas Watson Cott. Homes
EN5: Barn 4B 20
(off Leecroft Rd.)
Thompson Av. TW9: Rich 3G 115
Thompson Cl. IG1: Ilf 2G 71
SM3: Sutt 1J 165
Thompson Ho. SE14 6K 103
(off John Williams Cl.)
W10 4G 81
(off Wornington Rd.)
Thompson Rd. RM9: Dag 3F 73
SE22 6F 121
TW3: Houn 4F 113
UB10: Uxb 1A 74
Thompson's Av. SE5 7C 102
Thomson Cres. CR0: C'don 1A 168
Thomson Ho. E14 6C 86
(off Saracen St.)
SE17 4E 102
(off Tatum St.)
SW1 6D 18
UB1: S'hall 7C 76
(off The Broadway)
Thomson Rd. HA3: W'stone 3J 41
Thorburn Ho. SW1 7F 11
(off Kinnerton St.)
Thorburn Sq. SE1 4G 103
Thorburn Way SW19 1B 154
Thoresby St. N1 1D 8 (3C 84)
Thorkhill Gdns. KT7: T Ditt 1A 162
Thorkhill Rd. KT7: T Ditt 1A 162
Thornaby Gdns. N18 6B 34
Thornaby Ho. E2 3H 85
(off Canrobert St.)
Thorn Av. WD23: B Hea 1B 26
Thornbill Ho. SE15 7G 103
(off Bird in Bush Rd.)
Thornbury NW4 4D 44
(off Prince of Wales Cl.)
Thornbury Av. TW7: Isle 7H 95
Thornbury Cl. N16 5E 66
NW7 7A 30
Thornbury Ct. CR2: S Croy 5D 168
(off Blunt Rd.)
TW7: Isle 7J 95
W11 7J 81
(off Chepstow Vs.)
Thornbury Lodge
EN2: Enf 3G 23
Thornbury Rd. SW2 6J 119
TW7: Isle 7H 95
Thornbury Sq. N6 1G 65
Thornby Rd. E5 3J 67
Thorncliffe Rd. SW2 6J 119
UB2: S'hall 5D 94
Thorn Cl. BR2: Brom 6E 160
UB5: N'olt 3D 76
Thorncombe Rd. SE22 5E 120
Thorncroft Rd.
SM1: Sutt 5K 165
Thorncroft St. SW8 7J 101
Thorndean St. SW18 2A 136
Thorndene SE28 7B 90
Thorndene Av. N11 1K 31
Thorndike Av. UB5: N'olt 1B 76
Thorndike Cl. SW10 7A 100
Thorndike Ho. SW1 5C 18
(off Vauxhall Bri. Rd.)
Thorndike St. SW1 4C 18 (4H 101)
Thorndon Cl. BR5: St P 2K 161
Thorndon Gdns. KT19: Ewe 5A 164
Thorndon Rd. BR5: St P 2K 161
Thorne Cl. DA8: Erith 6H 109
E11 4F 69
E16 6J 87
KT10: Clay 7A 162
TW15: Ashf 7E 128
Thorne Ho. E2 3J 85
(off Roman Rd.)
E14 3E 104
(off Launch St.)
Thorneloe Gdns. CR0: Wadd 5A 168
Thorne Pas. SW13 2A 116
Thorne Rd. SW8 7J 101
Thornes Cl. BR3: Beck 3E 158
Thorne St. SW13 3A 116
Thornet Wood Rd.
BR1: Brom 3E 160
Thornewill Ho. E1 7J 85
(off Cable St.)
Thorney Ct. W8 2A 100
(off Palace Ga.)
Thorney Cres. SW11 7B 100
Thorneycroft Cl. KT12: Walt T 6A 148
Thorney Hedge Rd. W4 4H 97
Thorney St. SW1 3E 18 (4J 101)
Thornfield Av. NW7 1G 45
Thornfield Ct. NW7 1G 45
Thornfield Ho. E14 7C 86
(off Rosefield Gdns.)
Thornfield Pde. NW7 7B 30
(off Holders Hill Rd.)
Thornfield Rd. W12 2D 98
(not continuous)
Thornford Rd. SE13 5E 122
Thorngate Rd. W9 4J 81
Thorngrove Rd. E13 1K 87
Thornham Gro. E15 5F 69
Thornham Ind. Est. E15 6F 69
Thornham St. SE10 6D 104
Thornhaugh M. WC1 4D 6 (4H 83)
Thornhaugh St. WC1 4D 6 (4H 83)
Thornhill Av. KT6: Surb 2E 162
SE18 7J 107
Thornhill Bri. Wharf N1 1K 83
Thornhill Cres. N1 7K 65
Thornhill Gdns. E10 2D 68
IG11: Bark 7J 71
Thornhill Gro. N1 7K 65
Thornhill Ho. W4 5A 98
(off Wood St.)
Thornhill Ho's. N1 7A 66
Thornhill M. SW15 4H 117
Thornhill Rd. CR0: C'don 7C 156
E10 2D 68
KT6: Surb 2E 162
N1 7A 66
UB10: Ick 4B 56
Thornhill Sq. N1 7K 65
Thornhill Way TW17: Shep 5C 146
Thornicroft Ho. SW9 2K 119
(off Stockwell Rd.)
Thornlaw Rd. SE27 4A 138
Thornley Cl. N17 7B 34
Thornley Dr. HA2: Harr 2F 59
Thornley Pl. SE10 5G 105
Thornsbeach Rd. SE6 1E 140
Thornsett Pl. SE20 2H 157
Thornsett Rd. SE20 2H 157
SW18 1K 135
Thornsett Ter. SE20 2H 157
(off Croydon Rd.)
Thorn Ter. SE15 3J 121
Thornton Av. CR0: C'don 6K 155
SW2 1H 137
UB7: W Dray 3B 92
W4 4A 98
Thornton Cl. UB7: W Dray 3B 92
Thornton Dene BR3: Beck 2C 158
Thornton Gdns. SW12 1H 137
Thornton Health Leisure Cen. 4C 156
THORNTON HEATH 4C 156
THORNTON HEATH POND 5A 156
Thornton Hill SW19 7G 135
Thornton Ho. SE17 4E 102
(off Townsend St.)
Thornton Pl. W1 5F 5 (5D 82)
Thornton Rd. BR1: Brom 5J 141
CR0: C'don 7K 155
CR7: Thor H 7K 155
DA17: Belv 4H 109
E11 2F 69
EN5: Barn 3B 20
IG1: Ilf 4F 71
N18 3D 34
SM5: Cars 1B 166
SW12 7H 119
SW14 4K 115
SW19 6F 135
Thornton Rd. E. SW19 6F 135
Thornton Rd. Ind. Est.
CR0: C'don 6K 155
Thornton Row CR7: Thor H 5A 156
Thornton's Farm Av. RM7: Rush G 1J 73
Thornton St. SW9 2A 120
Thornton Way NW11 5K 45
Thorntree Ct. W5 5E 78
Thorntree Rd. SE7 5B 106
Thornville Gro. CR4: Mitc 2B 154
Thornville St. SE8 1C 122
Thornwell Ct. W7 2J 95
(off Du Burstow Ter.)
Thornwood Cl. E18 2K 51
Thornwood Gdns. W8 2J 99
Thornwood Ho. IG9: Buck H 1H 37
Thornwood Lodge W8 2J 99
(off Thornwood Gdns.)
Thornwood Rd. SE13 5G 123
Thornycroft Ho. W4 5A 98
(off Fraser St.)
Thorogood Gdns. E15 5G 69
Thorogood Way RM13: Rain 1K 91
Thorold Ho. SE1 6C 14
(off Pepper St.)
Thorold Rd. IG1: Ilf 2F 71
N22 7D 32
Thorparch Rd. SW8 1H 119
Thorpebank Rd. W12 1C 98
Thorpe Cl. BR6: Orp 2J 173
SE26 4K 139
W10 6G 81
Thorpe Ct. EN2: Enf 3G 23
Thorpe Cres. E17 2B 50
Thorpedale Gdns. IG2: Ilf 4E 52
IG6: Ilf 4E 52
Thorpedale Rd. N4 2J 65
Thorpe Hall Rd. E17 1E 50
Thorpe Ho. N1 1K 83
(off Barnsbury Est.)
Thorpe Rd. E6 1D 88
E7 4H 69
E17 2E 50
IG11: Bark 7H 71
KT2: King T 7E 132
N15 6E 48
Thorpewood Av. SE26 2H 139
Thorpland Av. UB10: Ick 3E 56
Thorsden Way SE19 5E 138
Thorverton Rd. NW2 3G 63
Thoydon Rd. E3 2A 86
Thrale Rd. SW16 4G 137
Thrale St. SE1 5D 14 (1C 102)
Thrasher Cl. E8 1F 85
Thrawl St. E1 6K 9 (5F 85)
Thrayle Ho. SW9 3K 119
(off Benedict Rd.)
Threadgold Ho. N1 6D 66
(off Dovercourt Est.)
Threadneedle St. EC2 1F 15 (6D 84)
Three Barrels Wlk. EC4 3D 14
(off Queen St. Pl.)
Three Bridges Bus. Cen.
UB2: S'hall 2G 95
Three Colt Cnr. E2 3K 9
Three Colts La. E2 4H 85
Three Colt St. E14 6B 86
Three Corners DA7: Bex 2H 127
Three Cranes Wlk. EC4 3D 14
Three Cups Yd. WC1 6H 7
Three Kings Yd. W1 2J 11 (7F 83)
Three Mdws. M. HA3: Stan 1K 41
Three Mill La. E3 3E 86
(not continuous)
Three Mills 3E 86
Three Nun Ct. EC2 6C 84
(off Aldermanbury)
Three Oak La. SE1 6J 15 (2F 103)
Three Oaks Cl. UB10: Ick 3B 56
Three Quays EC3 3H 15
Three Quays Wlk. EC3 3H 15 (7E 84)
Threshers Pl. W11 7G 81
Thriffwood SE26 3J 139
Thrigby Rd. KT9: Chess 6F 163
Thring Ho. SW9 2K 119
(off Stockwell Rd.)
Throckmorten Rd. E16 6K 87
Throgmorton Av. EC2 7F 9 (6D 84)
(not continuous)
Throgmorton St. EC2 7F 9 (6D 84)
Throwley Cl. SE2 3C 108
(not continuous)
Throwley Rd. SM1: Sutt 5K 165
Throwley Way SM1: Sutt 4K 165
Thrupp Cl. CR4: Mitc 2F 155
Thrush Grn. HA2: Harr 4E 40
Thrush St. SE17 5C 102
Thurbarn Rd. SE6 5D 140
Thurland Ho. SE16 4H 103
(off Camilla Rd.)
Thurland Rd. SE16 3G 103
Thurlby Cl. HA1: Harr 6A 42
IG8: Wfd G 5J 37
Thurlby Cft. NW4 3E 44
(off Mulberry Cl.)
Thurlby Rd. HA0: Wemb 6D 60
SE27 4A 138
Thurleigh Av. SW12 6E 118
Thurleigh Ct. SW12 6E 118
Thurleigh Rd. SW12 7D 118
Thurleston Av. SM4: Mord 5G 153
Thurlestone Av. IG3: Bark, Ilf 4K 71
N12 6J 31
Thurlestone Cl. TW17: Shep 6E 146
Thurlestone Ct. UB1: S'hall 6F 77
(off Howard Rd.)
Thurlestone Pde. TW17: Shep 6E 146
(off High St.)
Thurlestone Rd. SE27 3A 138
Thurloe Cl. SW7 3C 16 (4C 100)
Thurloe Ct. SW3 4C 16
(off Fulham Ct.)
Thurloe Pl. SW7 3B 16 (4B 100)
Thurloe Pl. M. SW7 3B 16
Thurloe Sq. SW7 3C 16 (4C 100)
Thurloe St. SW7 3B 16 (4B 100)
Thurlow Cl. E4 6K 35
Thurlow Gdns. HA0: Wemb 5D 60
Thurlow Hill SE21 1C 138
Thurlow Ho. SW16 3J 137
Thurlow Pk. Rd. SE21 2B 138
Thurlow Rd. NW3 5B 64
W7 2A 96
Thurlow St. SE17 5D 102
(not continuous)
Thurlow Ter. NW5 5E 64
Thurlow Wlk. SE17 5E 102
(not continuous)
Thurlstone Rd. HA4: Ruis 3J 57
Thurnby Ct. TW2: Twick 3J 131
Thurnscoe NW1 1G 83
(off Pratt St.)
Thursland Rd. DA14: Sidc 5E 144
Thursley Cres. CR0: New Ad 7E 170
Thursley Gdns. SW19 2F 135
Thursley Ho. SW2 7K 119
(off Holmewood Gdns.)
Thursley Rd. SE9 3D 142

Thurso Ho. NW6 2K 81
Thurso St. SW17 4B 136
Thurstan Dwellings *WC2* *7F 7*
(off Newton St.)
Thurstan Rd. SW20 7D 134
Thurston Ho. BR3: Beck 6D 140
Thurston Ind. Est. SE13 3D 122
Thurston Rd. SE13 2D 122
UB1: S'hall 6D 76
Thurtle Rd. E2 1F 85
Thwaite Cl. DA8: Erith 6J 109
Thyer Cl. BR6: Farnb 4G 173
Thyme Cl. SE3 3A 124
Thyme Ct. NW7 1G 45
Thyra Gro. N12 6E 30
Tibbatt's Rd. E3 4D 86
Tibbenham Pl. SE6 2C 140
Tibbenham Wlk. E13 2H 87
Tibberton Sq. N1 1C 84
Tibbet's Cl. SW19 1F 135
TIBBET'S CORNER 7F 117
Tibbet's Ride SW15 7F 117
Tiber Cl. E3 1C 86
Tiber Gdns. N1 1J 83
Ticehurst Cl. BR5: St P 7A 144
Ticehurst Rd. SE23 2A 140
Tickford Cl. SE2 2C 108
Tickford Ho. NW8 2C 4 (3C 82)
Tidal Basin Rd. E16 7H 87
(not continuous)
Tidbury Ct. *SW8* *7G 101*
(off Stewart's Rd.)
Tideham Ho. SE28 1H 107
Tidelea Twr. SE28 2G 107
Tidenham Gdns. CR0: C'don 3E 168
Tideside Ct. SE18 3C 106
Tideslea Path SE28 1H 107
Tideswell Rd. CR0: C'don 3C 170
SW15 4E 116
Tideway Cl. TW10: Ham 4B 132
Tideway Ct. SE16 1K 103
Tideway Ho. *E14* *2C 104*
(off Strafford St.)
Tideway Ind. Est.
SW8 6G 101
Tideway Wlk. SW8 7B 18 (6G 101)
Tidey St. E3 5C 86
Tidford Rd. DA16: Well 2K 125
Tidlock Ho. SE28 2H 107
Tidworth Rd. E3 4C 86
Tiepigs La. BR2: Hayes 2G 171
BR4: W W'ck 2G 171
Tierney Ct. CR0: C'don 2E 168
Tierney Rd. SW2 1J 137
Tiffany Hgts. SW18 7J 117
Tiffin School Sports Hall 2F 151
Tiffins Girls Community Sports Cen.
6E 132
Tiger Ho. *WC1* *2D 6*
(off Burton St.)
Tiger La. BR2: Brom 4K 159
Tiger Way E5 4H 67
Tigris Cl. N9 2D 34
Tilbrook Rd. SE3 3A 124
Tilbury Cl. HA5: Hat E 1D 40
SE15 7F 103
Tilbury Ho. *SE14* *6K 103*
(off Myers La.)
Tilbury Rd. E6 2D 88
E10 7E 50
Tildesley Rd. SW15 6E 116
Tile Farm Rd. BR6: Orp 3H 173
Tilehurst NW1 2K 5
Tilehurst Point SE2 2D 108
(Blewbury Ho.)
SE2 2C 108
(Tavy Bri.)
Tilehurst Rd.
SM3: Cheam 5G 165
SW18 1B 136
Tile Kiln La. DA5: Bexl 2J 145
N6 1F 65
N13 5H 33
UB9: Hare 7D 38
Tile Kiln Studios N6 7G 47
Tile Yd. E14 6B 86
Tileyard Rd. N7 7J 65
Tilford Av. CR0: New Ad 7E 170
Tilford Gdns. SW19 1F 135
Tilford Ho. *SW2* *7K 119*
(off Holmewood Gdns.)
Tilia Cl. SM1: Sutt 5H 165
Tilia Rd. E5 4H 67
Tilia Wlk. SW9 4B 120
Tiller Ho. *N1* *1E 84*
(off Whitmore Est.)
Tiller Leisure Cen., The 3C 104
Tiller Rd. E14 3C 104
Tillett Cl. NW10 6J 61
Tillett Sq. SE16 2A 104
Tillet Way E2 3G 85
Tilley Rd. TW13: Felt 1J 129
Tillingbourne Gdns. N3 3H 45
Tillingbourne Grn.
BR5: St M Cry 4K 161 & 5K 161
Tillingbourne Way N3 4H 45
Tillingham Way N12 4D 30
Tilling Rd. NW2 1E 62
Tillings Cl. SE5 1C 120
Tilling Way HA9: Wemb 2D 60
Tillman St. E1 6H 85
Tilloch St. N1 7K 65
Tillotson Ct. *SW8* *7H 101*
(off Wandsworth Rd.)
Tillotson Rd. HA3: Hrw W 7A 26
IG1: Ilf 7E 52
N9 2A 34
Tilney Ct. EC1 3D 8 (4C 84)
IG9: Buck H 2D 36
Tilney Dr. IG9: Buck H 2D 36
Tilney Gdns. N1 6D 66
Tilney Rd. RM9: Dag 6F 73
(not continuous)
UB2: S'hall 4A 94
Tilney St. W1 4H 11 (1E 100)
Tilson Cl. SE15 7E 102
Tilson Gdns. SW2 7J 119
Tilson Ho. SW2 7J 119
Tilson Rd. N17 1G 49
Tilston Cl. E11 3H 69
Tiltman Pl. N7 3K 65
Tilton St. SW6 6G 99
Tiltwood, The W3 7J 79
Tilt Yd. App. SE9 6D 124
Timber Cl. BR7: Chst 2E 160
Timbercroft KT19: Ewe 4A 164
Timbercroft La. SE18 6J 107
Timberdene NW4 2F 45
Timberdene Av. IG6: Ilf 1G 53
Timberland Cl. SE15 7G 103
Timberland Rd. E1 6H 85
Timber Mill Way SW4 3H 119
Timber Pond Rd. SE16 1K 103
Timbers, The SM3: Cheam 6G 165
Timberslip Dr.
SM6: Wall 7H 167
Timber St. EC1 3C 8 (4C 84)
Timber Wharf E2 1F 85
Timberwharf Rd. N16 6G 49
Timber Wharves Est. *E14* *4C 104*
(off Charnwood Gdns.)
E14 *4C 104*
(off Copeland Dr.)
Timber Yd., The *N1* *2H 9*
(off Drysdale St.)
Timbrell Pl. SE16 1B 104
Time Sq. E8 5F 67
Times Sq. SM1: Sutt 5K 165
Timor Ho. *E1* *4A 86*
(off Duckett St.)
Timothy Cl. DA6: Bex 5E 126
SW4 5G 119
Timothy Ho. *DA18: Erith* *2E 108*
(off Kale Rd.)
Timothy Pl. KT8: W Mole 5D 148
Timothy Rd. E3 5B 86
Timperley Ct. SW19 1G 135
Timsbury Wlk. SW15 1C 134
Tina Ct. SE6 7B 122
Tindal St. SW9 1B 120
Tinderbox All. SW14 3K 115
Tinniswood Cl. N5 5A 66
Tinsley Cl. SE25 3H 157
Tinsley Rd. E1 5J 85
Tintagel Cres. SE22 4F 121
Tintagel Dr. HA7: Stan 4J 27
Tintagel Gdns. SE22 4F 121
Tintangel Ct. *EC1* *3A 8*
(off St John St.)
Tintern Av. NW9 3H 43
Tintern Cl. SW15 5G 117
SW19 6A 136
Tintern Ct. W13 7A 78
Tintern Gdns. N14 7D 22
Tintern Ho. *NW1* *1K 5*
(off Augustus St.)
SW1 *4J 17*
(off Abbots Mnr.)
Tintern Path *NW9* *6A 44*
(off Fryent Gro.)
Tintern Rd. N22 1C 48
SM5: Cars 1B 166
Tintern St. SW4 4J 119
Tintern Way HA2: Harr 1F 59
Tinto Rd. E16 4J 87
Tinworth St. SE11 5F 19 (5J 101)
Tippett Ct. E6 2D 88
Tippetts Cl. EN2: Enf 1H 23
Tipthorpe Rd. SW11 3E 118
Tipton Dr. CR0: C'don 4E 168
Tiptree *NW1* *7F 65*
(off Castlehaven Rd.)
Tiptree Cl. E4 3K 35
Tiptree Cres. IG5: Ilf 2E 52
Tiptree Dr. EN2: Enf 4J 23
Tiptree Rd. HA4: Ruis 4K 57
Tirlemont Rd. CR2: S Croy 7C 168
Tirrell Rd. CR0: C'don 6C 156
Tisbury Ct. W1 2C 12
Tisbury Rd. SW16 2J 155
Tisdall Ho. *SE17* *4D 102*
(off Catesby St.)
Tisdall Pl. SE17 4D 102
Tissington Ct. SE16 4J 103
Titan Bus. Est. *SE8* *7C 104*
(off Ffinch St.)
Titan Ct. TW8: Bford 5F 97
Titchborne Row W2 1D 10 (6C 82)
Titchfield Rd. NW8 1C 82
SM5: Cars 1B 166
Titchfield Wlk. SM5: Cars 7B 154
Titchwell Rd. SW18 1B 136
Tite St. SW3 6E 16 (5D 100)
Tithe Barn Cl. KT2: King T 1F 151
Tithe Barn Way
UB5: Yead 2K 75
Tithe Cl. KT12: Walt T 6K 147
NW7 1C 44
UB4: Hayes 5H 75
Tithe Farm Av. HA2: Harr 3E 58
Tithe Farm Cl. HA2: Harr 3E 58
Tithe Wlk. NW7 1C 44
Titian Av. WD23: B Hea 1D 26
Titley Cl. E4 5H 35
Titmus Cl. UB8: Hil 6E 74
Titmuss Av. SE28 7B 90
Titmuss St. W12 2E 98
Tivendale N8 3J 47
Tiverton Av. IG5: Ilf 3E 52
Tiverton Cl. CR0: C'don 7F 157
Tiverton Dr. SE9 1G 143
Tiverton Ho. EN3: Enf H 3E 24
Tiverton Rd. HA0: Wemb 2E 78
HA4: Ruis 3J 57
HA8: Edg 2F 43
N15 6D 48
N18 5K 33
NW10 1F 81
TW3: Houn 2G 113
Tiverton St. SE1 3C 102
Tiverton Way KT9: Chess 5D 162
NW7 7A 30
Tivoli Ct. SE16 1B 104
Tivoli Gdns. SE18 4C 106
(not continuous)
Tivoli Rd. N8 5H 47
SE27 5C 138
TW4: Houn 4C 112
Toad La. TW4: Houn 4D 112
Tobacco Dock E1 7H 85
Tobacco Quay E1 7H 85
Tobago St. E14 2C 104
Tobin Cl. NW3 7C 64
Toby Ct. *N9* *7D 24*
(off Tramway Av.)
Toby La. E1 4A 86
Toby Way KT5: Surb 2H 163
Todber Ho. *W14* *3G 99*
(off Russell Rd.)
Todd Ho. *N2* *2B 46*
(off The Grange)
Todds Wlk. N7 2K 65
Todhunter Ter. EN5: New Bar 4D 20
Tokenhouse Yd. EC2 7E 8 (6D 84)
Token Yd. SW15 4G 117
TOKYNGTON 6H 61
Tokyngton Av. HA9: Wemb 6G 61
Toland Sq. SW15 5C 116
Tolcairn Ct. DA17: Belv 5G 109
Tolcarne Dr. HA5: Eastc 2J 39
Tolchurch *W11* *6H 81*
(off Dartmouth Cl.)
Toley Av. HA9: Wemb 7E 42
Tolhurst Dr. W10 3G 81
Tollard Ho. W14 3G 99
Toll Bar Ct. SM2: Sutt 7K 165
Tollbridge Cl. W10 4G 81
Tollesbury Gdns. IG6: Ilf 3H 53
Tollet St. E1 4K 85
Tollgate Ct. CR2: S Croy 5D 168
Tollgate Dr. SE21 2E 138
UB4: Yead 7B 76
Tollgate Gdns. NW6 2K 81
Tollgate Ho. *NW6* *2K 81*
(off Tollgate Gdns.)
Tollgate Rd. E6 5A 88
E16 5A 88
Tollgate Sq. E6 5D 88
Tollhouse Way N19 2G 65
Tollington Pk. N4 2K 65
Tollington Pl. N4 2K 65
Tollington Rd. N7 4K 65
Tollington Way N7 3J 65
Tolmers Sq. NW1 3B 6 (4G 83)
(not continuous)
Tolpaide Ho. SE11 4J 19
Tolpuddle Av. *E13* *1A 88*
(off Queens Rd.)
Tolpuddle St. N1 2A 84
Tolsford Rd. E5 5H 67
Tolson Rd. TW7: Isle 3A 114
Tolverne Rd. SW20 1E 152
TOLWORTH 2H 163
Tolworth B'way. KT6: Surb 1H 163
Tolworth Cl. KT6: Surb 1H 163
Tolworth Gdns. RM6: Chad H 5D 54
TOLWORTH JUNC. (TOBY JUG) 2H 163
Tolworth Pde. RM6: Chad H 5E 54
Tolworth Pk. Rd. KT6: Surb 2F 163
Tolworth Recreation Cen. 3F 163

Tolworth Ri. Nth. KT5: Surb 1H 163
Tolworth Ri. Sth. KT5: Surb 2H 163
Tolworth Rd. KT6: Surb 2E 162
Tolworth Twr. KT6: Surb 2H 163
Tomahawk Gdns. UB5: N'olt 3B 76
Tom Allen Arts Cen. 6F 69
Tom Blau Gallery 6J 15
(off Queen Elizabeth St.)
Tom Coombs Cl. SE9 4C 124
Tom Cribb Rd. SE28 3G 107
Tom Groves Cl. E15 5F 69
Tom Hood Cl. E15 5F 69
Tom Jenkinson Rd.
E16 1J 105
Tomkyns Ho. SE11 3J 19
Tomline Ho. SE1 5C 14
(off Union St.)
Tomlins All. TW1: Twick 1A 132
Tomlin's Gro. E3 3C 86
Tomlinson Cl. E2 2K 9 (3F 85)
W4 5H 97
Tomlins Orchard IG11: Bark 1G 89
Tomlins Ter. E14 6A 86
Tomlins Wlk. N7 2K 65
Tom Mann Cl. IG11: Bark 1J 89
Tom Nolan Cl. E15 2G 87
Tom Oakman Cen. E4 2A 36
Tompion Ho. EC1 3B 8
(off Percival St.)
Tompion St. EC1 2A 8 (3B 84)
(not continuous)
Tom Smith Cl. SE10 6G 105
Tomson Ho. SE1 7J 15
(off St Saviour's Est.)
Tomswood Ct. IG6: Ilf 1G 53
Tomswood Hill IG6: Ilf 6K 37 & 1F 53
Tomswood Rd. IG7: Chig 6K 37
Tom Williams Ho. SW6 6H 99
(off Clem Attlee Ct.)
Tonbridge Cres. HA3: Kent 4E 42
Tonbridge Ho's. WC1 2E 6
(off Tonbridge St.)
Tonbridge Rd. KT8: W Mole 4D 148
Tonbridge St. WC1 1E 6 (3J 83)
Tonbridge Wlk. WC1 1E 6
Toneborough NW8 1K 81
(off Abbey Rd.)
Tonfield Rd. SM3: Sutt 1H 165
Tonge Cl. BR3: Beck 5C 158
Tonsley Hill SW18 5K 117
Tonsley Pl. SW18 5K 117
Tonsley Rd. SW18 5K 117
Tonsley St. SW18 5K 117
Tonstall Rd. CR4: Mitc 2E 154
Tony Cannell M. E3 3B 86
Tony Law Ho. SE20 1H 157
Tooke Cl. HA5: Pinn 1C 40
Tookey Cl. HA3: Kent 7F 43
Took's Ct. EC4 7J 7 (6A 84)
Tooley St. SE1 4F 15 (1D 102)
Toomy Cen. E16 1K 105
(off Evelyn Rd.)
Toorack Rd. HA3: Hrw W 2H 41
TOOTING 5C 136
TOOTING BEC 3D 136
Tooting Bec Gdns. SW16 4H 137
(not continuous)
Tooting Bec Lido 4G 137
Tooting Bec Rd. SW16 3E 136
SW17 3E 136
Tooting B'way. SW17 5C 136
TOOTING GRAVENEY 6D 136
Tooting Gro. SW17 5C 136
Tooting High St. SW17 6C 136
Tooting Leisure Cen. 4B 136
Tooting Mkt. SW17 4D 136
Tootswood Rd. BR2: Brom 5G 159
Topaz Ct. E11 1G 69
Topaz Wlk. NW2 7F 45
Topcliffe Dr. BR6: Farnb 4H 173
Topham Ho. SE10 7E 104
(off Prior St.)
Topham Sq. N17 1C 48
Topham St. EC1 3J 7 (4A 84)
Top Ho. Ri. E4 7K 25
Topiary Sq. TW9: Rich 3F 115
Topley St. SE9 4A 124
Topmast Point E14 2C 104
Top Pk. BR3: Beck 5G 159
Topp Wlk. NW2 2E 62
Topsfield Cl. N8 5H 47
Topsfield Pde. N8 5J 47
(off Tottenham La.)
Topsfield Rd. N8 5J 47
Topsham Rd. SW17 3D 136
Tora Ct. IG9: Buck H 2F 37
Torbay Ct. NW1 7F 65
Torbay Mans. NW6 1H 81
(off Willesden La.)
Torbay Rd. HA2: Harr 2C 58
NW6 7H 63
Torbay St. NW1 7F 65
Torbitt Way IG2: Ilf 5K 53
Torbridge Cl. HA8: Edg 7K 27
Torbrook Cl. DA5: Bexl 6E 126
Tor Ct. W8 2J 99
Torcross Dr. SE23 2J 139
Torcross Rd. HA4: Ruis 3K 57
Tor Gdns. W8 2J 99
Tor Gro. SE28 1J 107
Tor Ho. N6 6F 47
Tormead Cl. SM1: Sutt 6J 165
Tormount Rd. SE18 6J 107
Tornay Ho. E9 7J 67
N1 2K 83
(off Priory Grn. Est.)
Toronto Av. E12 4D 70
Toronto Rd. IG1: Ilf 1F 71
Torquay Gdns. IG4: Ilf 4B 52
Torquay St. W2 5K 81
Torrance Cl. SE7 6B 106
Torrens Ct. SE5 3D 120
Torrens Rd. E15 6H 69
SW2 5K 119
Torrens Sq. E15 6H 69
Torrens St. EC1 2A 84
Torres Sq. E14 5C 104
Torre Wlk. SM5: Cars 1C 166
Torrey Dr. SW9 2A 120
Torriano Av. NW5 5H 65
Torriano Cotts. NW5 5G 65
Torriano M. NW5 5G 65
Torridge Gdns. SE15 4J 121
Torridge Rd. CR7: Thor H 5B 156
Torridon Ho. NW6 2K 81
(off Randolph Gdns.)
Torridon Rd. SE6 7F 123
SE13 7G 123
Torrington Av. N12 5G 31
Torrington Cl. N12 4G 31
Torrington Ct. SE26 5G 139
(off Crystal Pal. Pk. Rd.)
Torrington Dr. HA2: Harr 4F 59
Torrington Gdns. N11 6B 32
UB6: G'frd 1C 78
Torrington Gro. N12 5H 31
Torrington Pk. N12 5F 31
Torrington Pl. E1 1G 103
WC1 5C 6 (5H 83)
Torrington Rd. E18 3J 51
HA4: Ruis 3J 57
RM8: Dag 1F 73
UB6: G'frd 1C 78
Torrington Sq. CR0: C'don 7D 156
WC1 4D 6 (4H 83)
Torrington Way SM4: Mord 6J 153
Tor Rd. DA16: Well 1C 126
Torr Rd. SE20 7K 139
Tortington Ho. SE15 7G 103
(off Friary Est.)
Torver Rd. HA1: Harr 4J 41
Torver Way BR6: Orp 3H 173
Torwood Rd. SW15 5C 116
Tothill Ho. SW1 3D 18
(off Page St.)
Tothill St. SW1 7D 12 (2H 101)
Totnes Rd. DA16: Well 7B 108
Totnes Vs. N11 5B 32
(off Telford Rd.)
Totnes Wlk. N2 4B 46
Tottan Ter. E1 6K 85
Tottenhall NW1 7E 64
(off Ferdinand St.)
Tottenhall Rd. N13 6F 33
TOTTENHAM 1F 49
Tottenham Community Sports Cen. 1F 49
Tottenham Ct. Rd. W1 4B 6 (4G 83)
Tottenham Ent. Cen. N17 2F 49
Tottenham Grn. E. N15 4F 49
Tottenham Green Leisure Cen. 4F 49
TOTTENHAM HALE 2G 49
TOTTENHAM HALE GYRATORY 4G 49
Tottenham Hale Retail Pk.
N15 4G 49
Tottenham Hotspur FC 7B 34
Tottenham La. N8 6J 47
Tottenham M. W1 5B 6 (5G 83)
Tottenham Rd. N1 6E 66
Tottenham St. W1 6B 6 (5G 83)
Totterdown St. SW17 4D 136
TOTTERIDGE 1C 30
Totteridge Comn. N20 2H 29
Totteridge Grn. N20 2D 30
Totteridge Ho. SW11 2B 118
(off Yelverton Rd.)
Totteridge La. N20 2D 30
Totteridge Village N20 1B 30
Totternhoe Cl. HA3: Kent 5C 42
Totton Rd. CR7: Thor H 3A 156
Touchard Ho. N1 2F 9
Toulmin St. SE1 7C 14 (2C 102)
Toulon St. SE5 7C 102
Toulouse Ct. SE16 5H 103
(off Rossetti Rd.)
Tounson Ct. SW1 4D 18
(off Montaigne Cl.)
Tourist Info. Cen.
Bexley 6J 127
Bexleyheath 4G 127
City of London 1C 14 (6C 84)
Croydon 3C 168
Greenwich 6E 104
Hackney 6H 67
Hammersmith 4E 98
Harrow 4J 41
Heathrow Central 3D 110
Hounslow 3F 113
Ilford 3F 71
King's Cross 1E 6
Kingston upon Thames 2D 150
Leicester Sq. 3D 12 (7H 83)
Lewisham 4E 122
London-Heathrow Airport,
Terminal 1 2D 110
Terminal 2 3D 110
Terminal 3 3C 110
Regent St. 4C 12
Richmond 5D 114
Somers Town 3J 83
Southwark 4D 14 (1C 102)
Tate Modern 4B 14 (1B 102)
Twickenham 1B 132
Victoria Station 2K 17
Waterloo Station 2A 102
Tournay Rd. SW6 7H 99
Tours Pas. SW11 4A 118
Toussaint Wlk. SE16 3G 103
Tovil Cl. SE20 2H 157
Tovy Ho. SE1 5G 103
(off Avondale Sq.)
Towcester Rd. E3 4D 86
Tower 42 7G 9 (6E 84)
Tower Bri. E1 5J 15
SE1 5J 15 (1F 103)
Tower Bri. App. E1 4J 15 (1F 103)
Tower Bri. Bus. Complex
SE16 3G 103
Tower Bri. Bus. Sq. SE16 4H 103
Tower Bridge Exhibition 4J 15
Tower Bri. M. HA1: Harr 4K 59
Tower Bri. Plaza SE1 5J 15 (1F 103)
Tower Bri. Rd. SE1 7H 15 (3E 102)
Tower Bri. Sq. SE1 6J 15
Tower Bri. Wharf E1 5K 15 (1G 103)
Tower Bldgs. E1 1H 103
(off Brewhouse La.)
Tower Cl. BR6: Orp 2K 173
NW3 5B 64
SE20 7H 139
Tower Ct. E5 7F 49
N1 7C 66
(off Canonbury St.)
NW8 2C 82
(off Mackennal St.)
WC2 1E 12
Tower Gdns. KT10: Clay 7A 162
Tower Gdns. Rd. N17 1C 48
Towergate SE1 4E 102
(off Page's Wlk.)
Towergate Cl. UB8: Uxb 5A 56
Tower Gym 2A 34
Tower Hamlets Rd. E7 4H 69
E17 3C 50
TOWER HILL 7F 85
Tower Hill EC3 3H 15 (7E 84)
Tower Hill Ter. EC3 3H 15
Tower Ho. E1 5G 85
(off Fieldgate St.)
Tower La. HA9: Wemb 3D 60
Tower M. E5 4A 68
E17 4C 50
Tower Mill Rd. SE15 7E 102
Tower of London, The 3J 15 (7F 85)
Tower of London Vis. Cen., The
3H 15 (7E 84)
Tower Pl. EC3 3H 15 (7E 84)
Tower Pl. E. EC3 3H 15
(off Lwr. Thames St.)
Tower Pl. W. EC3 3H 15
(off Lwr. Thames St.)
Tower Point EN2: Enf 4J 23
Tower Ri. TW9: Rich 3E 114
Tower Rd. BR6: Orp 2K 173
DA7: Bex 4G 127
DA17: Belv 4J 109
NW10 7C 62
TW1: Twick 3K 131
Tower Royal EC4 2E 14 (7D 84)
Towers Av. UB10: Hil 3E 74
Towers Bus. Pk.
HA9: Wemb 4J 61
(off Carey Way)
Towers Ct. UB10: Hil 3E 74
Towers Pl. TW9: Rich 5E 114
Towers Rd. HA5: Pinn 1C 40
UB1: S'hall 4E 76
Tower St. WC2 1E 12 (6J 83)
Tower Ter. N22 2K 47
Tower Vw. CR0: C'don 7A 158
WD23: B Hea 1D 26
Tower Wlk. SE1 4E 102
(off Aberdour St.)
Tower Wharf SE1 6J 15
(off Tooley St.)
Tower Yd. TW10: Rich 5F 115
Towfield Ct. TW13: Hanw 2D 130
Towfield Rd. TW13: Hanw 2D 130
Town, The EN2: Enf 3J 23
Towncourt Cres. BR5: Pet W 5G 161
Towncourt La. BR5: Pet W 6H 161

Towncourt Path N4 . . . . 1C 66
Town End Pde. KT1: King T 3D 150
(off High St.)
Towney Mead UB5: N'olt 2D 76
Towney Mead Ct. UB5: N'olt 2D 76
Townfield Rd. UB3: Hayes 1H 93
Townfield Sq. UB3: Hayes 7H 75
Town Fld. Way TW7: Isle 2A 114
Town Hall App. Rd. N15 . . . . 4F 49
Town Hall Av. W4 . . . . 5K 97
Town Hall Rd. SW11 . . . . 3D 118
Town Hall Wlk. N16 . . . . 4D 66
(off Albion Rd.)
Townholm Cres. W7 . . . . 3K 95
Town La. TW19: Stanw 1A 128
(not continuous)
Townley Ct. E15 . . . . 6H 69
Townley Rd. DA6: Bex 5F 127
SE22 . . . . 5E 120
Townley St. SE17 . . . . 5D 102
(not continuous)
Townmead Bus. Cen. SW6 . . . . 3A 118
Town Mdw. TW8: Bford 6D 96
Town Mdw. Rd. TW8: Bford 7D 96
Townmead Rd. SW6 . . . . 3K 117
TW9: Kew 2H 115
Town Quay IG11: Bark 1F 89
Town Quay Wharf IG11: Bark 1F 89
Town Rd. N9 . . . . 2C 34
Townsend Av. N14 . . . . 4C 32
Townsend Ho. SE1 . . . . 4G 103
(off Strathnairn St.)
Townsend Ind. Est. NW10 . . . . 2J 79
Townsend La. NW9 . . . . 7K 43
Townsend M. SW18 . . . . 2A 136
Townsend Rd. N15 . . . . 5F 49
TW15: Ashf 5A 128
UB1: S'hall 1C 94
Townsend St. SE17 . . . . 4E 102
Townsend Way HA6: Nwood 1H 39
Townsend Yd. N6 . . . . 1F 65
Townshend Cl. DA14: Sidc 6B 144
Townshend Ct. NW8 . . . . 2C 82
(off Townshend Rd.)
Townshend Est. NW8 . . . . 2C 82
Townshend Rd. BR7: Chst 5F 143
NW8 . . . . 1C 82
(not continuous)
TW9: Rich 4F 115
Townshend Ter. TW9: Rich 4F 115
Towns Ho. SW4 . . . . 3H 119
Townson Av. UB5: Yead 2J 75
Townson Way UB5: Yead 2J 75
Town Sq. TW7: Isle 3B 114
(off Swan St.)
Town Tree Rd. TW15: Ashf 5C 128
Town Wharf TW7: Isle 3B 114
Towpath KT12: Walt T 5J 147
TW17: Shep 7B 146
Towpath, The SW10 . . . . 1B 118
Towpath Rd. N18 . . . . 6E 34
Towpath Wlk. E9 . . . . 5B 68
Towpath Way CR0: C'don 6F 157
Towton Rd. SE27 . . . . 2C 138
Toynbec Cl. BR7: Chst 4F 143
Toynbee Rd. SW20 . . . . 1G 153
Toynbee St. E1 . . . . 6J 9 (5F 85)
Toynbee Studios 7K 9
Toyne Way N6 . . . . 6D 46
Tracey Av. NW2 . . . . 5E 62
Tracy Ct. HA7: Stan 7H 27
Trade Cl. N13 . . . . 4F 33
Trader Rd. E6 . . . . 6F 89
Tradescant Ho. E9 . . . . 7J 67
(off Frampton Pk. Rd.)
Tradescant Rd. SW8 . . . . 7J 101
Tradewind Hgts. SE16 . . . . 1K 103
(off Rotherhithe St.)
Tradewinds Ct. E1 . . . . 7G 85
Trading Est. Rd. NW10 . . . . 4J 79
Trafalgar Av. KT4: Wor Pk 1F 165
N17 . . . . 6K 33
SE15 . . . . 5F 103
Trafalgar Bus. Cen. IG11: Bark 4K 89
Trafalgar Chambers SW3 . . . . 5B 16
(off South Pde.)
Trafalgar Cl. SE16 . . . . 3A 104
Trafalgar Ct. E1 . . . . 1J 103
(off Wapping Wall)
Trafalgar Gdns. E1 . . . . 5K 85
W8 . . . . 3K 99
Trafalgar Gro. SE10 . . . . 6F 105
Trafalgar Ho. SE17 . . . . 5C 102
(off Bronti Cl.)
Trafalgar M. E9 . . . . 6B 68
Trafalgar Pl. E11 . . . . 4J 51
N18 . . . . 5B 34
Trafalgar Point N1 . . . . 7D 66
(off Downham Rd.)
Trafalgar Rd. SE10 . . . . 6F 105
SW19 . . . . 7K 135
TW2: Twick 2H 131
Trafalgar Square 4E 12 (1J 101)
Trafalgar Sq. WC2 . . . . 4D 12 (1H 101)
(not continuous)
Trafalgar St. SE17 . . . . 5D 102
Trafalgar Studios 4E 12
(off Whitehall)
Trafalgar Ter. HA1: Harr 1J 59
Trafalgar Trad. Est.
EN3: Brim 4F 25
Trafalgar Way CR0: Wadd 2A 168
E14 . . . . 1E 104
Trafford Ho. N1 . . . . 2D 84
(off Cranston Est.)
Trafford Rd. CR7: Thor H 5K 155
Traherne Lodge TW11: Tedd 5K 131
Trahorn Cl. E1 . . . . 4H 85
Traitors' Gate 4J 15
Tralee Ct. SE16 . . . . 5H 103
(off Masters Dr.)
Tram Cl. SE24 . . . . 3B 120
(off Milkwood Rd.)
Tramlink, The SW19 . . . . 2A 154
Tramsheds, The CR0: Bedd 7H 155
Tramway Av. E15 . . . . 7G 69
N9 . . . . 7C 24
Tramway Cl. SE20 . . . . 1J 157
Tramway Path CR4: Mitc 4C 154
(not continuous)
Tranley M. NW3 . . . . 4C 64
(off Fleet Rd.)
Tranmere Ct. SM2: Sutt 7A 166
Tranmere Rd. N9 . . . . 7A 24
SW18 . . . . 2A 136
TW2: Whitt 7F 113
Tranquil Pas. SE3 . . . . 2H 123
(off Montpelier Va.)
Tranquil Va. SE3 . . . . 2G 123
Transept St. NW1 . . . . 6D 4 (5C 82)
Transmere Cl. BR5: Pet W 6G 161
Transmere Rd. BR5: Pet W 6G 161
Transom Cl. SE16 . . . . 4A 104
Transom Sq. E14 . . . . 5D 104
Transport Av. TW8: Bford 5A 96
Tranton Rd. SE16 . . . . 3G 103
Trappes Ho. SE16 . . . . 4H 103
(off Camilla Rd.)
Traps La. KT3: N Mald 1A 152
Traq Motor Racing 6F 155
Travellers Way TW4: Cran 2A 112
Travers Cl. E17 . . . . 1K 49
Travers Ho. SE10 . . . . 6F 105
(off Trafalgar Gro.)
Travers Rd. N7 . . . . 3A 66
Travis Ho. SE10 . . . . 1E 122
Treacy Cl. WD23: B Hea 2B 26
Treadgold Ho. W11 . . . . 7F 81
(off Bomore Rd.)
Treadgold St. W11 . . . . 7F 81
Treadway St. E2 . . . . 2H 85
Treasury Cl. SM6: Wall 5H 167
Treasury Pas. SW1 . . . . 6E 12
Treaty Cen. TW3: Houn 3F 113
Treaty St. N1 . . . . 1K 83
Trebeck St. W1 . . . . 4J 11 (1F 101)
Trebovir Rd. SW5 . . . . 5J 99
Treby St. E3 . . . . 4B 86
Trecastle Way N7 . . . . 4H 65
Tredegar M. E3 . . . . 3B 86
Tredegar Rd. E3 . . . . 2B 86
N11 . . . . 7C 32
Tredegar Sq. E3 . . . . 3B 86
Tredegar Ter. E3 . . . . 3B 86
Trederwen Rd. E8 . . . . 1G 85
Tredown Rd. SE26 . . . . 5J 139
Tredwell Cl. BR2: Brom 4C 160
SW2 . . . . 2K 137
Tredwell Rd. SE27 . . . . 4B 138
Tree Cl. TW10: Ham 1D 132
Treen Av. SW13 . . . . 3B 116
Tree Rd. E16 . . . . 6A 88
Treeside Cl. UB7: W Dray 4A 92
Tree Top M. RM10: Dag 6K 73
Treetops Cl. SE2 . . . . 5E 108
Treeview Cl. SE19 . . . . 1E 156
Treewall Gdns. BR1: Brom 4K 141
Trefgarne Rd. RM10: Dag 2G 73
Trefil Wlk. N7 . . . . 4J 65
Trefoil Ho. DA18: Erith 2E 108
(off Kale Rd.)
Trefoil Rd. SW18 . . . . 5A 118
Trefusis Ct. TW5: Cran 1K 111
Tregaron Av. N8 . . . . 6J 47
Tregaron Gdns. KT3: N Mald 4A 152
Tregarvon Rd. SW11 . . . . 4E 118
Tregenna Av. HA2: Harr 4E 58
Tregenna Cl. N14 . . . . 5B 22
Tregenna Ct. HA2: Harr 4E 58
Tregony Rd. BR6: Chels 4K 173
Trego Rd. E9 . . . . 7C 68
Tregothnan Rd. SW9 . . . . 3J 119
Tregunter Rd. SW10 . . . . 6K 99
Trehearn Rd. IG6: Ilf 1H 53
Treherne Ct. SW9 . . . . 1B 120
SW17 . . . . 4E 136
Trehern Rd. SW14 . . . . 3K 115
Trehurst St. E5 . . . . 5A 68
Trelawney Est. E9 . . . . 6J 67
Trelawney Ho. SE1 . . . . 5C 14
(off Union St.)
Trelawney Rd. IG6: Ilf 1H 53
Trelawn Rd. E10 . . . . 3E 68
SW2 . . . . 5A 120
Trelawny Cl. E17 . . . . 4D 50
Trellick Twr. W10 . . . . 4H 81
(off Golborne Rd.)
Trellis Ho. SW19 . . . . 7A 136
Trellis Sq. E3 . . . . 3B 86
Treloar Gdns. SE19 . . . . 6D 138
Tremadoc Rd. SW4 . . . . 4H 119
Tremaine Cl. SE4 . . . . 2C 122
Tremaine Rd. SE20 . . . . 2H 157
Trematon Ho. SE11 . . . . 5K 19
(off Kennings Way)
Trematon Pl. TW11: Tedd 7C 132
Tremlett Gro. N19 . . . . 3G 65
Trenance Gdns. IG3: Ilf 3A 72
Trenchard Av. HA4: Ruis 4K 57
Trenchard Cl. HA7: Stan 6F 27
NW9 . . . . 1A 44
Trenchard Ct. NW4 . . . . 5C 44
SM4: Mord 6J 153
Trenchard St. SE10 . . . . 5F 105
Trenchold St. SW8 . . . . 6J 101
Trendell Ho. E14 . . . . 6C 86
(off Dod St.)
Trenear Cl. BR6: Chels 4K 173
Trenholme Cl. SE20 . . . . 7H 139
Trenholme Rd. SE20 . . . . 7H 139
Trenholme Ter. SE20 . . . . 7H 139
Trenmar Gdns. NW10 . . . . 3D 80
Trent Av. W5 . . . . 3C 96
Trent Ct. CR2: S Croy 5C 168
(off Nottingham Rd.)
Trent Gdns. N14 . . . . 6A 22
Trentham Ho. W3 . . . . 5K 79
Trentham St. SW18 . . . . 1J 135
Trent Ho. KT2: King T 1D 150
SE15 . . . . 4J 121
Trent Pk. Country Pk. 1A 22
Trent Pk. Sports Cen. 4B 22
Trent Rd. IG9: Buck H 1E 36
SW2 . . . . 5K 119
Trent Way KT4: Wor Pk 3E 164
UB4: Hayes 2G 75
Trentwood Side EN2: Enf 3E 22
Treport St. SW18 . . . . 7K 117
Tresco Cl. BR1: Brom 6G 141
Trescoe Gdns. HA2: Harr 7C 40
Tresco Gdns. IG3: Ilf 2A 72
Tresco Ho. SE11 . . . . 5J 19
Tresco Rd. SE15 . . . . 4H 121
Tresham Cres. NW8 . . . . 3D 4 (4C 82)
Tresham Ho. WC1 . . . . 5K 83
(off Red Lion Sq.)
Tresham Rd. IG11: Bark 7K 71
Tresham Wlk. E9 . . . . 5J 67
Tresidder Ho. SW4 . . . . 7H 119
Tresilian Av. N21 . . . . 5E 22
Tressell Cl. N1 . . . . 7B 66
Tressillian Cres. SE4 . . . . 3C 122
Tressillian Rd. SE4 . . . . 4B 122
Tress Pl. SE1 . . . . 4A 14
Trestis Cl. UB4: Yead 4B 76
Treswell Rd. RM9: Dag 1E 90
Tretawn Gdns. NW7 . . . . 4F 29
Tretawn Pk. NW7 . . . . 4F 29
Trevanion Rd. W14 . . . . 4G 99
Treve Av. HA1: Harr 7H 41
Trevelyan Av. E12 . . . . 4D 70
Trevelyan Ct.
KT3: N Mald 7A 152
Trevelyan Cres. HA3: Kent 7D 42
Trevelyan Gdns. NW10 . . . . 1E 80
Trevelyan Ho. E2 . . . . 3K 85
(off Morpeth St.)
SE5 . . . . 7B 102
(off John Ruskin St.)
Trevelyan Rd. E15 . . . . 4H 69
SW17 . . . . 5C 136
Trevenna Ho. SE23 . . . . 3K 139
(off Dacres Rd.)
Trevera Ct. EN3: Pond E 4F 25
Treveris St. SE1 . . . . 5B 14 (1B 102)
Treverton St. W10 . . . . 4F 81
Treverton Towers W10 . . . . 5F 81
(off Treverton St.)
Treves Cl. N21 . . . . 5E 22
Treves Ho. E1 . . . . 4G 85
(off Vallance Rd.)
Treville St. SW15 . . . . 7D 116
Treviso Rd. SE23 . . . . 2K 139
Trevithick Cl. TW14: Felt 1H 129
Trevithick Ho. SE16 . . . . 4H 103
(off Rennie Est.)
Trevithick St. SE8 . . . . 6C 104
Trevone Ct. SW2 . . . . 7J 119
(off Doverfield Rd.)
Trevone Gdns.
HA5: Pinn 6C 40
Trevor Cl. BR2: Hayes 7H 159
EN4: E Barn 6G 21
HA3: Hrw W 7E 26
TW7: Isle 5K 113
UB5: Yead 2A 76
Trevor Cres. HA4: Ruis 4H 57
Trevor Gdns. HA4: Ruis 4J 57
HA8: Edg 1K 43
UB5: Yead 2A 76

Trevor Pl. SW7 .....7D **10** (2C **100**)
Trevor Rd. HA8: Edg 1K **43**
IG8: Wfd G 7D **36**
SW19 .....7G **135**
UB3: Hayes 2G **93**
Trevor Sq. SW7 .....7E **10** (2D **100**)
Trevor St. SW7 .....7D **10** (2C **100**)
Trevor Wlk. *SW7* *7E* ***10***
(off Lancelot Pl.)
SW7 .....*7D* ***10***
(off Trevor Pl., not continuous)
Trevose Ho. *SE11* *5H* ***19***
(off Orsett St.)
Trevose Rd. E17 .....1F **51**
Trewenna Dr. KT9: Chess 5D **162**
Trewince Rd. SW20 .....1E **152**
Trewint St. SW18 .....2A **136**
Trewsbury Ho. SE2 .....1D **108**
Trewsbury Rd. SE26 .....5K **139**
Triandra Way UB4: Yead 5B **76**
Triangle, The *DA15: Sidc* *7A* ***126***
(off Burnt Oak La.)
E8 .....1H **85**
EC1 .....3B **8**
IG11: Bark 6G **71**
KT1: King T 2H **151**
N13 .....4E **32**
Triangle Bus. Cen., The
NW10 .....3B **80**
Triangle Cen. UB1: S'hall 1H **95**
Triangle Ct. E16 .....5B **88**
SE1 .....*1C* ***102***
(off Redcross Way)
Triangle Est. *SE11* *6J* ***19***
(off Kennington La.)
SE11 .....*5A* ***102***
(off Kennington Rd.)
Triangle Ho. *SE1* *6J* ***15***
(off Three Oak La.)
Triangle Pas. EN4: E Barn 4F **21**
Triangle Pl. SW4 .....4H **119**
Triangle Rd. E8 .....1H **85**
Triangle Way W3 .....3G **97**
Trickett Ho. SM2: Sutt 7K **165**
Tricorn Ho. SE28 .....1J **107**
Tricycle Cinema 7H **63**
Tricycle Theatre 7H **63**
Trident Bus. Cen. SW17 .....5D **136**
Trident Gdns. UB5: N'olt 3B **76**
Trident Ho. *E14* *6E* ***86***
(off Blair St.)
SE28 .....1H **107**
TW19: Stanw *7A* ***110***
(off Clare Rd.)
Trident Pl. *SW3* *7B* ***16***
(off Old Church St.)
Trident St. SE16 .....4K **103**
Trident Way UB2: S'hall 3K **93**
Trig La. EC4 .....2C **14** (7C **84**)
Trigon Rd. SW8 .....7K **101**
Trilby Rd. SE23 .....2K **139**
Trillo Ct. IG2: Ilf 7J **53**
Trimdon NW1 .....1G **83**
Trimmer Wlk.
TW8: Bford 6E **96**
Trim St. SE14 .....6B **104**
Trinder Gdns. N19 .....1J **65**
Trinder M. TW11: Tedd 5A **132**
Trinder Rd. EN5: Barn 5A **20**
N19 .....1J **65**
Tring Av. HA9: Wemb 6G **61**
UB1: S'hall 6D **76**
W5 .....1F **97**
Tring Cl. IG2: Ilf 5H **53**
Tring Ct. TW1: Twick 4A **132**
Trinidad Gdns.
RM10: Dag 7K **73**
Trinidad Ho. *E14* *7B* ***86***
(off Gill St.)
Trinidad St. E14 .....7B **86**
Trinity Av. EN1: Enf 6A **24**
N2 .....3B **46**
Trinity Buoy Wharf *E14* *7G* ***87***
(off Orchard Pl.)
Trinity Bus. Pk. E4 .....6G **35**
Trinity Chu. Pas. SW13 .....6D **98**
Trinity Chu. Rd. SW13 .....6D **98**
Trinity Chu. Sq. SE1 .....7D **14** (3C **102**)
Trinity Cl. BR2: Brom 1C **172**
CR2: Sande 7E **168**
E8 .....6F **67**
E11 .....2G **69**
NW3 .....4B **64**
SE13 .....4F **123**
SW4 .....4G **119**
TW4: Houn 4C **112**
Trinity College of Music 6E **104**
Trinity Cotts. TW9: Rich 3F **115**
Trinity Ct. CR0: C'don 2C **168**
EN2: Enf 2H **23**
N1 .....*1E* ***84***
(off Downham Rd.)
NW2 .....5E **62**
SE7 .....4B **106**
SE8 .....*5A* ***104***
(off Evelyn St.)
SE25 .....6E **156**
SE26 .....3J **139**
SW9 .....3K **119**
W2 .....*6A* ***82***
(off Gloucester Ter.)
WC1 .....3G **7**
Trinity Cres. SW17 .....2D **136**
Trinity Dr. UB8: Hil 5E **74**
Trinity Gdns. E16 .....5H **87**
(not continuous)
SW9 .....4K **119**
Trinity Grn. E1 .....4J **85**
Trinity Gro. SE10 .....1E **122**
Trinity Hospital (Almshouses)
SE10 .....5F **105**
Trinity Ho. EC3 .....2J **15**
SE1 .....*3C* ***102***
(off Bath Ter.)
Trinity M. *E1* *5J* ***85***
(off Redman's Rd.)
SE20 .....1H **157**
W10 .....6F **81**
Trinity Path SE23 .....3J **139**
Trinity Pl. DA6: Bex 4F **127**
EC3 .....2J **15** (7F **85**)
Trinity Ri. SW2 .....1A **138**
Trinity Rd. IG6: Ilf 3G **53**
N2 .....3B **46**
N22 .....7D **32**
(not continuous)
SW17 .....4A **118**
SW18 .....4A **118**
SW19 .....6J **135**
TW9: Rich 3F **115**
UB1: S'hall 1C **94**
Trinity Sq. EC3 .....3H **15** (7E **84**)
Trinity St. E16 .....5H **87**
EN2: Enf 2H **23**
SE1 .....7D **14** (2C **102**)
(not continuous)
Trinity Twr. *E1* *7G* ***85***
(off Vaughan Way)
Trinity Wlk. NW3 .....6A **64**
Trinity Way E4 .....6G **35**
W3 .....7A **80**
Trio Pl. SE1 .....7D **14** (2C **102**)
Tristan Ct. *SE8* *6B* ***104***
(off Dorking Cl.)
Tristan Sq. SE3 .....3G **123**
Tristram Cl. E17 .....3F **51**
Tristram Dr. N9 .....3B **34**
Tristram Rd. BR1: Brom 4H **141**
Triton Ho. *E14* *4D* ***104***
(off Cahir St.)
Triton Sq. NW1 .....3A **6** (4G **83**)
Tritton Av. CR0: Bedd 4J **167**
Tritton Rd. SE21 .....3D **138**
Triumph Cl. UB3: Harl 1E **110**
Triumph Ho. IG11: Bark 3A **90**
Triumph Rd. E6 .....6D **88**
Triumph Trad. Est. N17 .....6B **34**
Trocadero Cen. 2C **12** (7H **83**)
Trocette Mans. *SE1* *3E* ***102***
(off Bermondsey St.)
Trojan Ct. NW6 .....7G **63**
Trojan Ind. Est. NW10 .....6B **62**
Trojan Way CR0: Wadd 3K **167**
Troon Cl. SE16 .....5H **103**
SE28 .....6D **90**
Troon Ho. *E1* *6A* ***86***
(off White Horse Rd.)
Troon St. E1 .....6A **86**
Tropical Ct. *W10* *3F* ***81***
(off Kilburn La.)
Trosley Rd. DA17: Belv 6G **109**
Trossachs Rd. SE22 .....5E **120**
Trothy Rd. SE1 .....4G **103**
Trotman Ho. *SE14* *1J* ***121***
(off Pomeroy St.)
Trott Rd. N10 .....7J **31**
Trott St. SW11 .....1C **118**
Trotwood Ho. *SE16* *2H* ***103***
(off Wilson Gro.)
Troughton Rd. SE7 .....5K **105**
Troutbeck NW1 .....2K **5**
Troutbeck Rd. SE14 .....1A **122**
Trout Rd. UB7: Yiew 7A **74**
Trouville Rd. SW4 .....6G **119**
Trowbridge Rd. E9 .....6B **68**
Trowlock Av. TW11: Tedd 6C **132**
Trowlock Island TW11: Tedd 6D **132**
Trowlock Way TW11: Tedd 6D **132**
Troy Ct. SE18 .....4F **107**
W8 .....*3J* ***99***
(off Kensington High St.)
Troy Ind. Est. HA1: Harr 5K **41**
Troy Rd. SE19 .....6D **138**
Troy Town SE15 .....3G **121**
Trubshaw Rd. UB2: S'hall 3F **95**
Trueman Cl. HA8: Edg 7C **28**
Truesdale Rd. E6 .....6D **88**
Trulock Ct. N17 .....7B **34**
Trulock Rd. N17 .....7B **34**
Trumans Rd. N16 .....5F **67**
Trumble Gdns. *CR7: Thor H* *4B* ***156***
(off Brigstock Rd.)
Trumpers Way W7 .....3J **95**
Trumpington Rd. E7 .....4H **69**
Trump St. EC2 .....1D **14** (6C **84**)
Trundle Ho. *SE1* *2C* ***102***
(off Trundle St.)
Trundlers Way WD23: B Hea 1D **26**
Trundle St. SE1 .....6C **14** (2C **102**)
Trundleys Rd. SE8 .....5K **103**
Trundley's Ter. SE8 .....4K **103**
Truro Gdns. IG1: Ilf 7C **52**
Truro Ho. HA5: Hat E 1D **40**
W2 .....*5J* ***81***
(off Westbourne Pk. Rd.)
Truro Rd. E17 .....4B **50**
N22 .....7D **32**
Truro St. NW5 .....6E **64**
Truro Way UB4: Hayes 3G **75**
Truslove Rd. SE27 .....5A **138**
Trussley Rd. W6 .....3E **98**
Trust Wlk. SE21 .....1B **138**
Tryfan Cl. IG4: Ilf 5B **52**
Tryon Cres. E9 .....1J **85**
Tryon St. SW3 .....5E **16** (5D **100**)
Trystings Cl. KT10: Clay 6A **162**
Tuam Rd. SE18 .....6H **107**
Tubbenden Cl. BR6: Orp 3J **173**
Tubbenden Dr. BR6: Orp 4H **173**
Tubbenden La. BR6: Orp 4H **173**
Tubbenden La. Sth. BR6: Farnb 5H **173**
Tubbs Rd. NW10 .....2B **80**
Tucklow Wlk. SW15 .....7B **116**
Tudor Av. KT4: Wor Pk 3D **164**
TW12: Hamp 6E **130**
Tudor Cl. BR7: Chst 1D **160**
HA5: Eastc 5J **39**
IG7: Chig 4K **37**
IG8: Wfd G 5E **36**
KT9: Chess 5E **162**
N6 .....7G **47**
NW3 .....5C **64**
NW7 .....6H **29**
NW9 .....2J **61**
SM3: Cheam 5F **165**
SM6: Wall 7G **167**
SW2 .....6K **119**
TW12: Ham H 5G **131**
TW15: Ashf 4A **128**
Tudor Ct. DA14: Sidc 3A **144**
E17 .....7B **50**
N1 .....6E **66**
N22 .....7D **32**
SE9 .....4C **124**
SE16 .....*1K* ***103***
(off Princes Riverside Rd.)
TW11: Tedd 6K **131**
TW13: Hanw 4A **130**
TW19: Stanw 6A **110**
W3 .....2G **97**
Tudor Ct. Nth. HA9: Wemb 5G **61**
Tudor Ct. Sth.
HA9: Wemb 5G **61**
Tudor Cres. EN2: Enf 1H **23**
Tudor Dr. KT2: King T 5D **132**
SM4: Mord 6F **153**
Tudor Ent. Pk.
HA1: Harr 3K **59**
HA3: W'stone 3H **41**
Tudor Est. NW10 .....2H **79**
Tudor Gdns. BR4: W W'ck 3E **170**
HA3: Hrw W 2H **41**
NW9 .....2J **61**
SW13 .....3A **116**
TW1: Twick 1K **131**
W3 .....5G **79**
Tudor Gro. E9 .....7J **67**
Tudor Ho. E9 .....7J **67**
E16 .....*1K* ***105***
(off Wesley Av.)
HA5: Pinn *2A* ***40***
(off Pinner Hill Rd.)
W14 .....*4F* ***99***
(off Windsor Way)
Tudor M. E17 .....4B **50**
Tudor Pde. RM6: Chad H 7D **54**
SE9 .....4C **124**
Tudor Pl. CR4: Mitc 7C **136**
SE19 .....7F **139**
Tudor Rd. BR3: Beck 3E **158**
E4 .....6J **35**
E6 .....1A **88**
E9 .....1H **85**
EN5: New Bar 3D **20**
HA3: Hrw W, W'stone 2H **41**
HA5: Pinn 2A **40**
IG11: Bark 1K **89**
KT2: King T 7G **133**
N9 .....7C **24**
SE19 .....7F **139**
SE25 .....5H **157**
TW3: Houn 4H **113**
TW12: Hamp 7E **130**
TW15: Ashf 6F **129**
UB1: S'hall 7C **76**
UB3: Hayes 6F **75**
Tudor Sq. UB3: Hayes 5F **75**
Tudor Stacks SE24 .....4C **120**
Tudor St. EC4 .....2K **13** (7A **84**)
Tudor Wlk. DA5: Bexl 6E **126**

Tudor Way BR5: Pet W 6H 161
N14 1C 32
UB10: Hil 6C 56
W3 2G 97
Tudor Well Cl. HA7: Stan 5G 27
Tudor Works UB4: Yead 1A 94
Tudway Rd. SE3 3K 123
TUFNELL PARK 4G 65
Tufnell Pk. Rd. N7 4G 65
N19 4G 65
Tufton Ct. *SW1* *2E 18*
(off Tufton St.)
Tufton Gdns.
KT8: W Mole 2F 149
Tufton Rd. E4 4H 35
Tufton St. SW1 1E 18 (3J 101)
Tugboat St. SE28 2J 107
Tugela Rd. CR0: C'don 6D 156
Tugela St. SE6 2B 140
Tugmutton Cl. BR6: Farnb 4F 173
Tulip Cl. CR0: C'don 1K 169
E6 5D 88
TW12: Hamp 6D 130
UB2: S'hall 2G 95
Tulip Gdns. E4 3A 36
IG1: Ilf 6F 71
Tullis Ho. *E9* *7J 67*
(off Frampton Pk. Rd.)
Tull St. CR4: Mitc 7D 154
Tulse Cl. BR3: Beck 3E 158
TULSE HILL 1B 138
Tulse Hill SW2 6A 120
Tulse Hill Est. SW2 6A 120
Tulse Ho. SW2 6A 120
Tulsemere Rd. SE27 2C 138
Tumbling Bay KT12: Walt T 6J 147
Tummons Gdns. SE25 2E 156
Tump Ho. SE28 1J 107
Tunbridge Ho. EC1 1K 7
Tuncombe Rd. N18 4K 33
Tunis Rd. W12 1E 98
Tunley Grn. E14 5B 86
Tunley Rd. NW10 1A 80
SW17 1E 136
Tunmarsh La. E13 3K 87
Tunnan Leys E6 6E 88
Tunnel App. E14 7A 86
SE10 2G 105
SE16 2J 103
Tunnel Av. SE10 2F 105
(not continuous)
Tunnel Av. Trad. Est. SE10 2F 105
Tunnel Gdns. N11 7B 32
Tunnel Link Rd. TW6: H'row A 5C 110
Tunnel Rd. SE16 2J 103
Tunnel Rd. E. TW6: H'row A 1D 110
Tunnel Rd. W. TW6: H'row A 1C 110
Tunstall Cl. BR6: Orp 4J 173
Tunstall Rd. CR0: C'don 1E 168
SW9 4K 119
Tunstall Wlk. TW8: Bford 6E 96
Tunstock Way DA17: Belv 3E 108
Tunworth Cl. NW9 6J 43
Tunworth Cres. SW15 6B 116
Tun Yd. *SW8* *2F 119*
(off Silverthorne Rd.)
Tupelo Rd. E10 2D 68
Tupman Ho. *SE16* *2G 103*
(off Scott Lidgett Cres.)
Tuppy St. SE28 3G 107
Turenne Cl. SW18 4A 118
Turin Rd. N9 7D 24
Turin St. E2 2K 9 (3G 85)
Turkey Oak Cl. SE19 1E 156
Turks Boatyard KT1: King T 1D 150
Turks Cl. UB8: Hil 3C 74
Turk's Head Yd. EC1 5A 8 (5B 84)
Turk's Row SW3 5F 17 (5D 100)
Turle Rd. N4 2K 65
SW16 2J 155
Turlewray Cl. N4 1K 65
Turley Cl. E15 1G 87
Turnagain La. EC4 7A 8
Turnage Rd. RM8: Dag 1E 72
Turnant Rd. N17 1C 48
Turnberry Cl. NW4 2F 45
SE16 5H 103
Turnberry Quay E14 3D 104
Turnberry Way
BR6: Orp 1H 173
Turnbull Ho. N1 1B 84
Turnbury Cl. SE28 6D 90
Turnchapel M. SW4 3F 119
Turner Av. CR4: Mitc 1D 154
N15 4E 48
TW2: Twick 3G 131
Turner Cl. HA0: Wemb 6D 60
NW11 6K 45
SW9 7B 102
UB4: Hayes 2E 74
Turner Ct. *SE16* *2J 103*
(off Albion St.)
Turner Dr. NW11 6K 45
Turner Ho. *E14* *2C 104*
(off Cassilis Rd.)
NW6 *5A 64*
(off Dresden Cl.)
NW8 *2C 82*
(off Townshend Est.)
SW1 *4D 18*
(off Herrick St.)
TW1: Twick *6D 114*
(off Clevedon Rd.)
Turner M. SM2: Sutt 7K 165
Turner Pl. SW11 5C 118
Turner Rd. E17 3E 50
HA8: Edg 2E 42
KT3: N Mald 7K 151
Turners Cl. N20 3J 31
Turners Ct. N15 5D 48
Turners Mdw. Way BR3: Beck 1B 158
Turners Rd. E3 5B 86
Turner St. E1 5H 85
E16 6H 87
Turner's Way CR0: Wadd 2A 168
Turners Wood NW11 7A 46
Turneville Rd. W14 6H 99
Turney Rd. SE21 7C 120
TURNHAM GREEN 4A 98
Turnham Grn. Ter. W4 4A 98
Turnham Grn. Ter. M. W4 4A 98
Turnham Rd. SE4 5A 122
Turnmill St. EC1 4A 8 (4B 84)
Turnour Ho. *E1* *6H 85*
(off Walburgh St.)
Turnpike Cl. SE8 7B 104
Turnpike Ct. DA6: Bex 4D 126
Turnpike Ho. EC1 2B 8 (3B 84)
Turnpike La. N8 4K 47
SM1: Sutt 5A 166
UB10: Uxb 3A 74
Turnpike Link CR0: C'don 2E 168
Turnpike M. *N8* *3A 48*
(off Turnpike La.)
Turnpike Pde. *N15* *3B 48*
(off Green Lanes)
Turnpike Way TW7: Isle 1A 114
Turnpin La. SE10 6E 104
Turnstone Cl. E13 3J 87
NW9 2A 44
UB10: Ick 5D 56
Turnstone Ho. *E1* *3K 15*
(off Star Pl.)
Turpentine La. SW1 5K 17 (5F 101)
Turpin Cl. E1 7K 85
Turpington Cl. BR2: Brom 6C 160
Turpington La. BR2: Brom 7C 160
Turpin Ho. SW11 1F 119
Turpin Rd. TW14: Felt 6H 111
Turpin's La. IG8: Wfd G 5J 37
Turpins Yd. SE10 7E 104
Turpin Way N19 2H 65
SM6: Wall 7F 167
Turquand St. SE17 4C 102
Turret Gro. SW4 3G 119
Turton Rd. HA0: Wemb 5E 60
Turville Ho. *NW8* *3C 4*
(off Grendon St.)
Turville St. E2 3J 9 (4F 85)
Tuscan Ho. *E2* *3J 85*
(off Knottisford St.)
Tuscan Rd. SE18 5H 107
Tuscany Ho. E17 2B 50
Tuskar St. SE10 6G 105
Tustin Est. SE15 6J 103
Tuttlebee La. IG9: Buck H 2D 36
Tuttle Ho. *SW1* *6C 18*
(off Aylesford St.)
Tweed Ct. *W7* *6J 77*
(off Hanway Rd.)
Tweeddale Gro. UB10: Ick 3E 56
Tweeddale Rd. SM5: Cars 1B 166
Tweed Glen RM1: Rom 1K 55
Tweed Grn. RM1: Rom 1K 55
Tweed Ho. *E3* *2E 86*
(off Teviot St.)
Tweedmouth Rd. E13 2K 87
Tweed Way RM1: Rom 1K 55
Tweedy Cl. EN1: Enf 5A 24
Tweedy Rd. BR1: Brom 1J 159
Tweezer's All. WC2 2J 13
Twelvetrees Bus. Pk. E3 4F 87
Twelvetrees Cres. E3 4E 86
(not continuous)
E16 4E 86
Twentyman Cl. IG8: Wfd G 5D 36
TWICKENHAM 1A 132
Twickenham Baths 1A 132
Twickenham Bri. TW1: Twick 5C 114
TW9: Rich 5C 114
Twickenham Cl. CR0: Bedd 3K 167
Twickenham Gdns. HA3: Hrw W 7D 26
UB6: G'frd 5A 60
Twickenham Rd. E11 2E 68
TW7: Isle 5A 114
TW9: Rich 4C 114
TW11: Tedd 4A 132
(not continuous)
TW13: Hanw 3D 130
Twickenham Rugby Union Football Ground 6J 113
Twickenham Stoop, The 7J 113
Twickenham Trad. Est.
TW1: Twick 6K 113
Twig Folly Cl. E2 2K 85
Twigg Cl. DA8: Erith 7K 109
Twilley St. SW18 7K 117
Twin Bridges Bus. Pk.
CR2: S Croy 6D 168
Twine Cl. IG11: Bark 3B 90
Twine Ct. E1 7J 85
Twineham Grn. N12 4D 30
Twine Ter. *E3* *4B 86*
(off Ropery St.)
Twining Av. TW2: Twick 3G 131
Twinn Rd. NW7 6B 30
Twin Tumps Way SE28 7A 90
Twisden Rd. NW5 4F 65
Twybridge Way NW10 7J 61
Twycross M. SE10 5G 105
Twyford Abbey Rd. NW10 3F 79
Twyford Av. N2 3D 46
W3 7G 79
Twyford Ct. *HA0: Wemb* *2E 78*
(off Vicars Bri. Cl.)
N10 3E 46
Twyford Cres. W3 1G 97
Twyford Ho. N5 3B 66
N15 *6E 48*
(off Chisley Rd.)
Twyford Pl. WC2 7G 7 (6K 83)
Twyford Rd. HA2: Harr 1F 59
IG1: Ilf 5G 71
SM5: Cars 1B 166
Twyford Sports Cen. 1H 97
Twyford St. N1 1K 83
Twynholm Mans. *SW6* *7G 99*
(off Lillie Rd.)
Tyas Rd. E16 4H 87
Tybenham Rd. SW19 3J 153
Tyberry Rd. EN3: Enf H 3C 24
Tyburn La. HA1: Harr 7K 41
Tyburn Tree (site of) 1F 11
Tyburn Way W1 2F 11 (7D 82)
Tye La. BR6: Farnb 5G 173
Tyers Est. SE1 6G 15
Tyers Ga. SE1 7G 15 (2E 102)
Tyers St. SE11 6G 19 (5K 101)
Tyers Ter. SE11 6G 19 (5K 101)
Tyeshurst Cl. SE2 5E 108
Tylecroft Rd. SW16 2J 155
Tylehurst Gdns. IG1: Ilf 5G 71
Tyler Cl. DA8: Erith 7H 109
E2 2F 85
Tyler Rd. UB2: S'hall 3F 95
Tylers Ct. *E17* *4C 50*
(off Westbury Rd.)
HA0: Wemb 2E 78
W1 1C 12
Tylers Ga. HA3: Kent 6E 42
Tylers Path SM5: Cars 4D 166
Tyler St. SE10 5G 105
(not continuous)
Tylney Av. SE19 5F 139
(not continuous)
Tylney Ho. *E1* *6H 85*
(off Nelson St.)
Tylney Rd. E7 4A 70
Tynamara *KT1: King T* *4D 150*
(off Portsmouth Rd.)
Tynan Cl. TW14: Felt 1J 129
Tyndale Ct. *E14* *5D 104*
(off Transom Sq.)
Tyndale Ho. *N1* *7B 66*
(off Tyndale La.)
Tyndale La. N1 7B 66
Tyndale Mans. *N1* *7B 66*
(off Upper St.)
Tyndale Ter. N1 7B 66
Tyndall Gdns. E10 2E 68
Tyndall Rd. DA16: Well 3K 125
E10 2E 68
Tyne Ct. *W7* *6J 77*
(off Hanway Rd.)
Tyneham Cl. SW11 3E 118
Tyneham Rd. SW11 2E 118
Tyne Ho. KT2: King T 1D 150
Tynemouth Cl. E6 6F 89
Tynemouth Dr. EN1: Enf 1B 24
Tynemouth Rd. CR4: Mitc 7E 136
N15 4F 49
SE18 5J 107
Tynemouth St. SW6 2A 118
Tyne St. E1 7K 9 (6F 85)
Tynley Rd. BR1: Brom 2B 160
Tynsdale Rd. NW10 6A 62
Tynwald Ho. SE26 3G 139
Type St. E2 2K 85
Typhoon Way
SM6: Wall 7J 167
Tyrawley Rd. SW6 1K 117
Tyre La. NW9 4A 44
Tyrell Cl. HA1: Harr 4J 59
Tyrell Ct. SM5: Cars 4D 166
Tyrell Ho. *BR3: Beck* *5D 140*
(off Beckenham Hill Rd.)
Tyrols Rd. SE23 1K 139
Tyrone Rd. E6 2D 88
Tyron Way DA14: Sidc 4J 143
Tyrrell Av. DA16: Well 5A 126

Tyrrell Ho. SW1 . . . . .7B 18
(off Churchill Gdns.)
Tyrrell Rd. SE22 . . . . .4G 121
Tyrrell Sq. CR4: Mitc 1C 154
Tyrrel Way NW9 . . . . .7B 44
Tyrwhitt Rd. SE4 . . . . .3C 122
Tysoe St. EC1 . . . . .2K 7 (3A 84)
Tyson Gdns. SE23 . . . . .7J 121
Tyson Rd. SE23 . . . . .7J 121
Tyssen Pas. E8 . . . . .6F 67
Tyssen Rd. N16 . . . . .3F 67
Tyssen St. E8 .6F 67
N1 . . . . .2E 84
Tytherton E2 .2J 85
(off Cyprus St.)
Tytherton Rd. N19 . . . . .3H 65

U

Uamvar St. E14 . . . . .5D 86
Uckfield Gro. CR4: Mitc 7E 136
Udall St. SW1 . . . . .4B 18 (4G 101)
Udimore Ho. W10 . . . . .5E 80
(off Sutton Way)
Udney Pk. Rd. TW11: Tedd 6A 132
Uffington Rd. NW10 . . . . .1C 80
SE27 . . . . .4A 138
Ufford Cl. HA3: Hrw W 7A 26
Ufford Rd. HA3: Hrw W 7A 26
Ufford St. SE1 . . . . .6K 13 (2A 102)
Ufton Ct. UB5: Yead 3B 76
Ufton Gro. N1 .7D 66
Ufton Rd. N1 . . . . .7D 66
(not continuous)
Uhura Sq. N16 .3E 66
Ujima Ct. SW16 . . . . .4J 137
Ullathorne Rd. SW16 . . . . .4G 137
Ulleswater Rd. N14 . . . . .3D 32
Ullin St. E14 . . . . .5E 86
Ullswater E18 .2J 51
Ullswater Cl. BR1: Brom 7G 141
SW15 . . . . .4K 133
UB4: Hayes 2G 75
Ullswater Ct. HA2: Harr 7E 40
Ullswater Cres. SW15 . . . . .4K 133
Ullswater Ho. SE15 . . . . .6J 103
(off Hillbeck Cl.)
Ullswater Rd. SE27 . . . . .2B 138
SW13 . . . . .7C 98
Ulster Gdns. N13 . . . . .4H 33
Ulster Pl. NW1 . . . . .4J 5 (4F 83)
Ulster Ter. NW1 . . . . .3H 5 (4F 83)
Ulundi Rd. SE3 . . . . .6G 105
Ulva Rd. SW15 . . . . .5F 117
Ulverscroft Rd. SE22 . . . . .5F 121
Ulverstone Rd. SE27 . . . . .2B 138
Ulverston Rd. E17 . . . . .2F 51
Ulysses Rd. NW6 . . . . .5H 63
Umberston St. E1 . . . . .6G 85
Umbria St. SW15 . . . . .6C 116
Umfreville Rd. N4 . . . . .6B 48
Undercliff Rd. SE13 . . . . .3C 122
UNDERHILL 5D 20
Underhill EN5: Barn 5D 20
Underhill Ct. EN5: Barn 5D 20
Underhill Ho. E14 . . . . .5C 86
(off Burgess St.)
Underhill Pas. NW1 . . . . .1F 83
(off Camden High St.)
Underhill Rd. SE22 . . . . .5G 121
Underhill Stadium 5D 20
Underhill St. NW1 . . . . .1F 83
Underne Av. N14 . . . . .2A 32
Undershaft EC3 . . . . .1G 15 (6E 84)
Undershaw Rd. BR1: Brom 3H 141
Underwood CR0: New Ad 5E 170
Underwood, The SE9 . . . . .2D 142
Underwood Ct. E10 . . . . .1D 68
(off Leyton Grange Est.)
Underwood Ho. KT8: W Mole 5E 148
(off Approach Rd.)
W6 . . . . .3D 98
(off Sycamore Gdns.)
Underwood Rd. E1 . . . . .4G 85
E4 . . . . .5J 35
IG8: Wfd G 7F 37
Underwood Row N1 . . . . .1D 8 (3C 84)
Underwood St. N1 . . . . .1D 8 (3C 84)
Undine Rd. E14 . . . . .4D 104
Undine St. SW17 . . . . .5D 136
Uneeda Dr. UB6: G'frd 1H 77
Unicorn Bldg. E1 . . . . .7K 85
(off Jardine Rd.)
Unicorn Theatre 1E 102
Unicorn Works N17 . . . . .7D 34
Union Canal Wlk.
W10 . . . . .4E 80
(off Canal Way)
Union Cl. E11 . . . . .4F 69
Union Cotts. E15 . . . . .7G 69
Union Ct. EC2 . . . . .7G 9
SW4 . . . . .2J 119
TW9: Rich 5E 114
W9 . . . . .5J 81
(off Elmfield Way)
Union Dr. E1 . . . . .4A 86
Union Gro. SW8 . . . . .2H 119
Union M. SW9 .2J 119
Union Pk. SE10 . . . . .5H 105
(off Calvert Rd.)
Union Rd. BR2: Brom 5B 160
CR0: C'don 7C 156
HA0: Wemb 6E 60
N11 . . . . .6C 32
RM7: Rush G 6K 55
Union Rd. SW4 . . . . .2H 119
SW8 . . . . .2H 119
UB5: N'olt 2E 76
Union Sq. N1 . . . . .1C 84
Union St. E15 . . . . .1F 87
EN5: Barn 3B 20
KT1: King T 2D 150
SE1 . . . . .5A 14 (1B 102)
Union Theatre .5B 14
Union Wlk. E2 . . . . .1H 9 (3E 84)
Union Wharf N1 . . . . .1C 84
(Arlington Av.)
N1 . . . . .2C 84
(off Wenlock Rd.)
UB7: Yiew 1A 92
(off Bentinck Rd.)
Union Yd. W1 . . . . .1K 11 (6F 83)
Unitair Cen. TW14: Bedf 6E 110
United Ho. SE16 . . . . .2J 103
(off Brunel Rd.)
Unit Workshops E1 . . . . .6G 85
(off Adler St.)
Unity Cl. CR0: New Ad 7D 170
NW10 . . . . .6C 62
SE19 . . . . .5C 138
Unity Ct. SE1 .5F 103
(off Fortune Pl.)
Unity M. NW1 . . . . .2H 83
Unity Ter. HA2: Harr 1F 59
Unity Trad. Est.
IG8: Wfd G 2B 52
Unity Way SE18 . . . . .3B 106
Unity Wharf SE1 . . . . .6K 15
(off Mill St.)
Universal Ho. UB1: S'hall 7C 76
University Cl. NW7 . . . . .7G 29
University College London
Campbell Ho. 4H 83
Campbell House 3C 6
(off Taviton St.)
Chemistry Building 3C 6 (4H 83)
Department of Geological
Sciences Collection 4C 6
(off Gower St.)
University College London
Gower St. 3C 6 (4H 83)
University Gdns. DA5: Bexl 7F 127
University of East London
Barking Campus 4A 72
Docklands Campus 7E 88
Maryland House 6G 69
Stratford Campus 6G 69
University of Greenwich
Avery Hill Campus 6G 125
Maritime Greenwich Campus
. . . . .6E 104
Thomas Spencer Hall of Residence
. . . . .4E 106
(off Grand Depot Rd.)
(Woolwich Campus)
Wellington St. 4E 106
Woolwich High St. 3E 106
University of London
College Hall 4C 6 (5H 83)
Institute of Education &
Institute of Advanced Legal Studies
. . . . .4D 6 (4H 83)
School of Oriental & African Studies
. . . . .4D 6
Senate House 5D 6 (5H 83)
Warburg Institute 4D 6 (4H 83)
University of London Observatory 6G 29
University of London Union 4D 6
University of North London
Highbury Cres. 6A 66
Highbury Gro. 5C 66
Hornsey Rd. 4A 66
University of Surrey
St Mary's College 3K 131
University of Westminster
(Cavendish Campus)
Bolsover St. 5K 5 (5F 83)
Hanson St. 5A 6 (5G 83)
Harrow Campus 7A 42
Marylebone Campus . . .5G 5 (5E 82)
(Regent Campus)
Lit. Titchfield St. 6A 6
Regent St. 7K 5
School of Languages . . .3A 6 (4G 83)
Wells St. 7B 6
University of Westminster and Library
Holborn 6G 7
University of Westminster Sports Cen.
. . . . .7A 42
University Pl. DA8: Erith 7J 109
University Rd. SW19 . . . . .6B 136
University St. WC1 . . . . .4B 6 (4G 83)
University Way E16 . . . . .7E 88
Unwin Av. TW14: Felt 5F 111
Unwin Cl. SE15 . . . . .6G 103
Unwin Mans. W14 . . . . .6H 99
(off Queen's Club Gdns.)
Unwin Rd. SW7 . . . . .1A 16 (3B 100)
TW7: Isle 3J 113
Upbrook M. W2 . . . . .1A 10 (6A 82)
Upcerne Rd. SW10 . . . . .7A 100
Upchurch Cl. SE20 . . . . .7H 139
Upcott Ho. E9 . . . . .7J 67
(off Frampton Pk. Rd.)
Upcroft Av. HA8: Edg 5D 28
Updale Rd. DA14: Sidc 4K 143
Upfield CR0: C'don 3H 169
Upfield Rd. W7 .5K 77
Upgrove Mnr. Way
SW2 . . . . .7A 120
Uphall Rd. IG1: Ilf 5F 71
Upham Pk. Rd. W4 . . . . .4A 98
Uphill BR2: Brom 4H 159
(off Westmoreland Rd.)
Uphill Dr. NW7 .5F 29
NW9 . . . . .5J 43
Uphill Gro. NW7 . . . . .4F 29
Uphill Rd. NW7 .4F 29
Upland M. SE22 . . . . .5G 121
Upland Rd. CR2: S Croy 5D 168
DA7: Bex 3F 127
E13 . . . . .4J 87
SE22 . . . . .5G 121
SM2: Sutt 7B 166
Uplands BR3: Beck 2C 158
Uplands, The HA4: Ruis 1J 57
Uplands Av. E17 . . . . .2K 49
Uplands Bus. Pk. E17 . . . . .3K 49
Uplands Cl. SW14 . . . . .5H 115
Uplands Ct. N21 . . . . .7F 23
(off The Green)
Uplands End IG8: Wfd G 7H 37
Uplands Pk. Rd. EN2: Enf 2F 23
Uplands Rd. EN4: E Barn 1K 31
IG8: Wfd G 7H 37
N8 . . . . .5K 47
RM6: Chad H 3D 54
Uplands Way N21 . . . . .5F 23
Upnall Ho. SE15 . . . . .6J 103
Upney La. IG11: Bark 6J 71
Upnor Way SE17 . . . . .5E 102
Uppark Dr. IG2: Ilf 6G 53
Up. Abbey Rd. DA17: Belv 4F 109
Up. Addison Gdns. W14 . . . . .2G 99
Up. Bank St. E14 . . . . .1D 104
(not continuous)
Up. Bardsey Wlk. N1 . . . . .6C 66
(off Douglas Rd. Nth.)
Up. Belgrave St. SW1 . . . . . . .1H 17 (3E 100)
Up. Berenger Wlk.
SW10 . . . . .7B 100
(off Berenger Wlk.)
Up. Berkeley St. W1 . . . . .1E 10 (6D 82)
Up. Beulah Hill SE19 . . . . .1E 156
Up. Blantyre Wlk. SW10 . . . . .7B 100
(off Blantyre Wlk.)
Up. Brighton Rd. KT6: Surb 6D 150
Up. Brockley Rd. SE4 . . . . .3B 122
(not continuous)
Up. Brook St. W1 . . . . .2G 11 (7E 82)
Upper Butts TW8: Bford 6C 96
Up. Caldy Wlk. N1 . . . . .6C 66
(off Caldy Wlk.)
Up. Camelford Wlk.
W11 . . . . .6G 81
(off Cambourne M.)
W11 . . . . .6G 81
(off St Mark's Rd.)
Up. Cavendish Av. N3 . . . . .3J 45
Up. Cheyne Row SW3 . . . . .7C 16
UPPER CLAPTON 2H 67
Up. Clapton Rd. E5 . . . . .1H 67
Up. Clarendon Wlk. W11 . . . . .6G 81
(off Clarendon Rd.)
Up. Dartrey Wlk. SW10 . . . . .7A 100
(off Whistler Wlk.)
Up. Dengie Wlk. N1 . . . . .1C 84
(off Baddow Wlk.)
UPPER EDMONTON 5B 34
UPPER ELMERS END 5B 158
Up. Elmers End Rd.
BR3: Beck 4A 158
Up. Farm Rd. KT8: W Mole 4D 148
Upper Feilde W1 . . . . .2G 11
(off Park St.)
Upper Fosters NW4 . . . . .4E 44
(off New Brent St.)
Upper Grn. E. CR4: Mitc 3D 154
Upper Grn. W. CR4: Mitc 2D 154
(not continuous)
Up. Grosvenor St. W1 . . . . .3G 11 (7E 82)
Up. Grotto Rd.
TW1: Twick 2K 131
Upper Ground SE1 . . . . .4J 13 (1A 102)
Upper Gro. SE25 . . . . .4E 156
Upper Gro. Rd. DA17: Belv 6F 109
Up. Gulland Wlk. N1 . . . . .7C 66
(off Church Rd.)
UPPER HALLIFORD 4G 147

Up. Halliford By-Pass
TW17: Shep 5G 147
Up. Halliford Grn. TW17: Shep 4G 147
Up. Halliford Rd. TW17: Shep 3G 147
Up. Hampstead Wlk. NW3 4A 64
Up. Ham Rd. KT2: King T 4D 132
TW10: Ham 4D 132
Up. Handa Wlk. *N1* *6D 66*
(off Handa Wlk.)
Up. Hawkwell Wlk. *N1* *1C 84*
(off Baddow Wlk.)
UPPER HOLLOWAY 2G 65
Up. Holly Hill Rd. DA17: Belv 5H 109
Up. James St. W1 2B 12 (7G 83)
Up. John St. W1 2B 12 (7G 83)
Up. Lismore Wlk. *N1* *6C 66*
(off Clephane Rd.)
Upper Lodge *W8* *1K 99*
(off Palace Grn.)
Upper Mall W6 5C 98
(not continuous)
Upper Marsh SE1 1H 19 (3K 101)
Up. Montagu St. W1 5E 4 (5D 82)
Up. Mulgrave Rd. SM2: Cheam 7G 165
Upper Nth. St. E14 5C 86
UPPER NORWOOD 1E 156
Up. Park Rd. BR1: Brom 1K 159
DA17: Belv 4H 109
KT2: King T 6G 133
N11 5A 32
NW3 5D 64
Up. Phillimore Gdns. W8 2J 99
Up. Ramsey Wlk. *N1* *6D 66*
(off Ramsey Wlk.)
Up. Rawreth Wlk. *N1* *1C 84*
(off Basire St.)
Up. Richmond Rd. SW15 4B 116
Up. Richmond Rd. W. SW14 4G 115
TW10: Rich 4G 115
Upper Rd. E13 3J 87
SM6: Wall 5H 167
UPPER RUXLEY 7G 145
Up. St Martin's La. WC2 2E 12 (7J 83)
Up. Selsdon Rd. CR2: Sande, Sels 7F 169
Up. Sheridan Rd. DA17: Belv 4G 109
UPPER SHIRLEY 4K 169
Up. Shirley Rd. CR0: C'don 2J 169
Upper Sq. TW7: Isle 3A 114
Upper St. N1 2A 84
Up. Sunbury Rd. TW12: Hamp 1C 148
Up. Sutton La. TW5: Hest 7E 94
UPPER SYDENHAM 3H 139
Up. Tachbrook St. SW1 3B 18 (4G 101)
Up. Talbot Wlk. *W11* *6G 81*
(off Talbot Wlk.)
Up. Teddington Rd. KT1: Ham W 7C 132
Upper Ter. NW3 3A 64
Up. Thames St. EC4 2B 14 (7B 84)
Up. Tollington Pk. N4 1A 66
(not continuous)
Upperton Rd. DA14: Sidc 5K 143
Upperton Rd. E. E13 3A 88
Upperton Rd. W. E13 3A 88
UPPER TOOTING 4D 136
Up. Tooting Pk. SW17 2D 136
Up. Tooting Rd. SW17 4D 136
Up. Town Rd. UB6: G'frd 4F 77
Up. Tulse Hill SW2 7K 119
Up. Vernon Rd. SM1: Sutt 5B 166
UPPER WALTHAMSTOW 4F 51
Up. Walthamstow Rd. E17 4E 50
Up. Whistler Wlk. *SW10* *7A 100*
(off Worlds End Est.)
Up. Wickham La. DA16: Well 7B 108
Up. Wimpole St. W1 5H 5 (5E 82)
Up. Woburn Pl. WC1 2D 6 (3H 83)
Uppingham Av. HA7: Stan 1B 42
Upsdell Av. N13 6F 33
Upshire Ho. E17 2B 50
Upstall St. SE5 1B 120

UPTON
DA6 5D 126
E7 7J 69
Upton Av. E7 7J 69
Upton Cl. DA5: Bexl 6F 127
NW2 3G 63
Upton Ct. *SE20* *7J 139*
(off Blean Gro.)
Upton Dene SM2: Sutt 7K 165
Upton Gdns. HA3: Kent 5B 42
Upton Hgts. E7 7J 69
Upton La. E7 7J 69
Upton Lodge E7 6J 69
Upton Lodge Cl. WD23: Bush 1B 26
UPTON PARK 1B 88
Upton Pk. 2A 88
Upton Pk. Boleyn Cinema 2B 88
Upton Pk. Rd. E7 7K 69
Upton Rd. CR7: Thor H 2D 156
DA5: Bexl 4E 126
DA6: Bex 4E 126
N18 5B 34
SE18 6G 107
TW3: Houn 3E 112
Upton Rd. Sth. DA5: Bexl 6F 127
Upton Vs. DA6: Bex 4E 126
Upway N12 6H 31
Upwey Ho. N1 1E 84
Upwood Rd. SE12 6J 123
SW16 1J 155
Urban M. N4 6B 48
Urlwin St. SE5 6C 102
Urlwin Wlk. SW9 1A 120
Urmston Dr. SW19 1G 135
Urmston Ho. *E14* *4E 104*
(off Seyssel St.)
Urquhart Ct. BR3: Beck 7B 140
Ursula Lodges DA14: Sidc 5B 144
Ursula M. N4 1C 66
Ursula St. SW11 1C 118
Urswick Gdns. RM9: Dag 7E 72
Urswick Rd. E9 5J 67
RM9: Dag 7D 72
Usborne M. SW8 7K 101
Usher Rd. E3 1B 86
Usk Rd. SW11 4A 118
Usk St. E2 3K 85
Utah Bldg. *SE10* *1D 122*
(off Deal's Gateway)
Utopia Village NW1 7E 64
Uvedale Rd. EN2: Enf 5J 23
RM10: Dag 3G 73
Uverdale Rd. SW10 7A 100
UXBRIDGE 1A 74
Uxbridge Ct. *KT1: King T* *5D 150*
(off Uxbridge Rd.)
Uxbridge Rd. HA3: Hrw W 1E 40
HA5: Hat E, Pinn 2A 40
HA7: Stan 1E 40
KT1: King T 4D 150
TW12: Hamp, Ham H 4E 130
TW13: Felt 2A 130
UB1: S'hall 1E 94
UB4: Hayes, Yead 5G 75
UB10: Hil 3C 74
W3 7E 78
W5 7E 78
W7 1K 95
W12 1C 98
W13 1B 96
Uxbridge Rd. Retail Pk. UB4: Yead 7A 76
Uxbridge St. W8 1J 99
Uxendon Cres. HA9: Wemb 1E 60
Uxendon Hill HA9: Wemb 1F 61

V

Vaine Ho. E9 6A 68
Vaizeys Wharf SE7 3K 105
Valance Av. E4 1B 36
Valan Leas BR2: Brom 3G 159
Vale, The CR0: C'don 2K 169
HA4: Ruis 4A 58
IG8: Wfd G 7D 36
N10 1E 46
N14 7C 22
NW11 3F 63
SW3 7A 16 (6B 100)
TW5: Hest 6C 94
TW14: Felt 6K 111
TW16: Sun 6J 129
W3 1K 97
Vale Cl. BR6: Farnb 4E 172
N2 3D 46
TW1: Twick 3A 132
W9 3A 82
Vale Cotts. SW15 3A 134
Vale Ct. EN5: New Bar 4E 20
W3 1B 98
W9 3A 82
Vale Cres. SW15 4A 134
Vale Cft. HA5: Pinn 5C 40
Vale Dr. EN5: Barn 4C 20
Vale End SE22 4F 121
Vale Est., The W3 1A 98
Vale Farm Sports Cen. 4B 60
Vale Gro. N4 7C 48
W3 2K 97
Vale La. W3 5G 79
Vale Lodge SE23 2J 139
Valence Av. RM8: Dag 1D 72
Valence Cir. RM8: Dag 3D 72
Valence House Mus. & Gallery 3E 72
Valence Rd. DA8: Erith 7K 109
Valence Wood Rd. RM8: Dag 3D 72
Valencia Rd. HA7: Stan 4H 27
Valentia Pl. SW9 4A 120
Valentine Av. DA5: Bexl 2E 144
Valentine Ct. SE23 2K 139
(not continuous)
Valentine Pl. SE1 6A 14 (2B 102)
Valentine Rd. E9 6K 67
HA2: Harr 3F 59
Valentine Row SE1 7A 14 (2B 102)
Valentines Rd. IG1: Ilf 1F 71
Valentine's Way RM7: Rush G 2K 73
VALE OF HEALTH 3A 64
Vale of Health NW3 3B 64
Vale Pde. SW15 3A 134
Valerian Wlk. N11 2K 31
Valerian Way E15 3G 87
Valerie Ct. SM2: Sutt 7K 165
WD23: Bush 1B 26
Vale Ri. NW11 1H 63
Vale Rd. BR1: Brom 1E 160
CR4: Mitc 3H 155
E7 6K 69
KT4: Wor Pk 3B 164
KT19: Ewe 4B 164
N4 7C 48
SM1: Sutt 4K 165
Vale Rd. Nth. KT6: Surb 2E 162
Vale Rd. Sth. KT6: Surb 2E 162
Vale Row N5 3B 66
Vale Royal N7 7J 65
Vale Royal Ho. *WC2* *2D 12*
(off Charing Cross Rd.)
Valery Pl. TW12: Hamp 7E 130
Valeside Ct.
EN5: New Bar 4E 20
Vale St. SE27 3D 138
Valeswood Rd. BR1: Brom 5H 141
Vale Ter. N4 6C 48
Valetta Gro. E13 2J 87
Valetta Rd. W3 2A 98
Valette Ct. *N10* *4F 47*
(off St James's La.)
Valette Ho. E9 6J 67
Valette St. E9 6J 67

Valiant Cl. RM7: Mawney 2H 55
UB5: N'olt 3B 76
Valiant Ho. *E14* *2E 104*
(off Plevna St.)
SE7 5A 106
Valiant Path NW9 1A 44
(not continuous)
Valiant Way E6 5D 88
Vallance Rd. E1 3G 85
E2 3G 85
N22 2G 47
Vallentin Rd. E17 4E 50
Valley, The 5A 106
Valley Av. N12 4G 31
Valley Cl. HA5: Pinn 2K 39
Valley Dr. NW9 6G 43
Valleyfield Rd. SW16 5K 137
Valley Flds. Cres. EN2: Enf 2F 23
Valley Gdns. HA0: Wemb 7F 61
SW19 7B 136
Valley Gro. SE7 5A 106
Valley Leisure Cen., The 5A 106
Valley Leisure Pk. CR0: Wadd 1J 167
Valleylink Est. EN3: Pond E 6F 25
Valley M. TW1: Twick 2K 131
Valley Point Ind. Est. CR0: Bedd 7J 155
Valley Rd. BR2: Brom 2G 159
BR5: St P 7B 144
DA8: Erith 4J 109
DA17: Belv 4H 109
SW16 5K 137
UB10: Uxb 2A 74
Valley Side E4 2H 35
SE7 5B 106
Valley Side Pde. E4 2H 35
Valley Trade Pk. *CR0: Bedd* *7J 155*
(off Therapia La.)
Valley Vw. EN5: Barn 6B 20
Valley Wlk. CR0: C'don 2J 169
Valliere Rd. NW10 3C 80
Valliers Wood Rd.
DA15: Sidc 1J 143
Vallis Way KT9: Chess 4D 162
W13 5A 78
Val McKenzie Av. N7 3A 66
Valmar Rd. SE5 1C 120
Valmar Trad. Est. SE5 1C 120
Valnay St. SW17 5D 136
Valognes Av. E17 1A 50
Valois Ho. *SE1* *3F 103*
(off St Saviour's Est.)
Valonia Gdns. SW18 6H 117
Vambery Rd. SE18 6G 107
Vanbrough Cres. UB5: N'olt 1A 76
Vanbrugh Castle *SE10* *6G 105*
(off Maze Hill)
Vanbrugh Cl. E16 5B 88
Vanbrugh Ct. SE11 4K 19
Vanbrugh Dr. KT12: Walt T 7A 148
Vanbrugh Flds. SE3 6H 105
Vanbrugh Hill SE3 5H 105
SE10 5H 105
Vanbrugh Ho. *E9* *7J 67*
(off Loddiges Rd.)
Vanbrugh M. KT12: Walt T 7A 148
Vanbrugh Pk. SE3 7H 105
Vanbrugh Pk. Rd. SE3 7H 105
Vanbrugh Pk. Rd. W.
SE3 7H 105
Vanbrugh Rd. W4 3K 97
Vanbrugh Ter. SE3 1H 123
Vanburgh Cl. BR6: Orp 1J 173
Vanburgh Ho. *E1* *5J 9*
(off Folgate St.)
Vancouver Cl. BR6: Chels 4K 173
Vancouver Ho. *E1* *1H 103*
(off Reardon Path)
Vancouver Mans. HA8: Edg 1H 43
Vancouver Rd. HA8: Edg 1H 43
SE23 2A 140

Vancouver Rd. TW10: Ham 4C 132
UB4: Yead 4K 75
Vanderbilt Rd. SW18 1K 135
Vanderbilt Vs. *W12* *2F 99*
(off Sterne St.)
Vanderville Gdns. N2 2B 46
Vandome Cl. E16 6K 87
Vandon Ct. *SW1* *1B 18*
(off Petty France)
Vandon Pas. SW1 1B 18 (3G 101)
Vandon St. SW1 1B 18 (3G 101)
Van Dyck Av. KT3: N Mald 7K 151
Vandyke Cl. SW15 7F 117
Vandyke Cross SE9 5C 124
Vandy St. EC2 4G 9 (4E 84)
Vane Cl. HA3: Kent 6F 43
NW3 5B 64
Vanessa Cl. DA17: Belv 5G 109
Vanessa Way DA5: Bexl 3K 145
Vane St. SW1 3B 18 (4G 101)
Vange Ho. *W10* *5E 80*
(off Sutton Way)
Van Gogh Cl. TW7: Isle 3A 114
Van Gogh Ct. E14 3F 105
Vanguard NW9 7F 29
Vanguard Bldg. E14 2B 104
Vanguard Cl. CR0: C'don 1B 168
E16 5J 87
RM7: Mawney 2G 55
Vanguard Ct. SE5 1E 120
Vanguard Ho. E8 7H 67
Vanguard St. SE8 1C 122
Vanguard Trad. Est. E15 1E 86
Vanguard Way SM6: Wall 7J 167
TW6: H'row A 2G 111
Vanneck Sq. SW15 5C 116
Vanoc Gdns. BR1: Brom 4J 141
Vanquish Cl. TW2: Whitt 7E 112
Vansittart Rd. E7 4H 69
Vansittart St. SE14 7A 104
Vanston Pl. SW6 7J 99
Vantage Ct. UB3: Harl 7G 93
Vantage M. *E14* *1E 104*
(off Preston's Rd.)
Vantage Pl. TW14: Felt 6J 111
W8 3J 99
Vantage Point CR2: Sande 7D 168
Vantage W. TW8: Bford 4F 97
Vantrey Ho. SE11 4J 19
Vant Rd. SW17 5D 136
Varcoe Rd. SE16 5H 103
Vardens Rd. SW11 4B 118
Varden St. E1 6H 85
Vardon Cl. W3 6K 79
Vardon Ho. SE10 1E 122
Varley Ho. NW6 1J 81
Varley Pde. NW9 4A 44
Varley Rd. E16 6K 87
Varley Way CR4: Mitc 2B 154
Varna Rd. SW6 7G 99
TW12: Hamp 1F 149
Varndell St. NW1 1A 6 (3G 83)
Varnishers Yd. *N1* *1F 7*
(off York Rd.)
Varsity Dr. TW1: Twick 5J 113
Varsity Row SW14 2J 115
Vartry Rd. N15 6D 48
Vascroft Est. NW10 4H 79
Vassall Ho. *E3* *3A 86*
(off Antill Rd.)
Vassall Rd. SW9 7A 102
Vat Ho. *SW8* *7J 101*
(off Rita Rd.)
Vauban Est. SE16 3F 103
Vauban St. SE16 3F 103
Vaudeville Ct. N4 2A 66
Vaudeville Theatre 3F 13
(off Strand)
Vaughan Almshouses *TW15: Ashf* *5D 128*
(off Feltham Hill Rd.)
Vaughan Av. NW4 5C 44
W6 4B 98
Vaughan Cl. TW12: Hamp 6C 130
Vaughan Est. E2 1J 9
Vaughan Gdns. IG1: Ilf 7D 52
Vaughan Ho. *SE1* *6A 14*
(off Blackfriars Rd.)
SW4 7G 119
Vaughan Rd. DA16: Well 2K 125
E15 6H 69
HA1: Harr 6G 41
KT7: T Ditt 7B 150
SE5 2C 120
Vaughan St. SE16 2B 104
Vaughan Way E1 7G 85
Vaughan Williams Cl. SE8 7C 104
VAUXHALL 5H 19 (6J 101)
Vauxhall Bri. SE1 6E 18 (5J 101)
SW1 6E 18 (5J 101)
Vauxhall Bri. Rd. SW1 2A 18 (3G 101)
VAUXHALL CROSS 6F 19 (5J 101)
Vauxhall Distribution Pk.
SW8 7C 18 (6H 101)
Vauxhall Gdns. CR2: S Croy 6C 168
Vauxhall Gro. SW8 7G 19 (6K 101)
Vauxhall St. SE11 5H 19 (5K 101)
Vauxhall Wlk. SE11 5G 19 (5K 101)
Vawdrey Cl. E1 4J 85
Veals Mead CR4: Mitc 1C 154
Vectis Gdns. SW17 6F 137
Vectis Rd. SW17 6F 137
Veda Rd. SE13 4C 122
Vega Rd. WD23: Bush 1B 26
Veitch Cl. TW14: Felt 7H 111
Veldene Way HA2: Harr 3D 58
Velde Way SE22 5E 120
Velletri Ho. *E2* *2K 85*
(off Mace St.)
Vellum Dr. SM5: Cars 3E 166
Venables Cl. RM10: Dag 4H 73
Venables St. NW8 5B 4 (4B 82)
Vencourt Pl. W6 4C 98
Venetian Rd. SE5 2C 120
Venetia Rd. N4 6B 48
W5 2D 96
Venice Ct. *NW8* *3B 4*
(off Fisherton St.)
SE5 *7C 102*
(off Bowyer St.)
Venner Rd. SE26 6J 139
(not continuous)
Venners Cl. DA7: Bex 2K 127
Venn Ho. *N1* *1K 83*
(off Barnsbury Est.)
Venn St. SW4 4G 119
Ventnor Av. HA7: Stan 1B 42
Ventnor Dr. N20 3E 30
Ventnor Gdns. IG11: Bark 6J 71
Ventnor Rd. SE14 7K 103
SM2: Sutt 7K 165
Venture Cl. DA5: Bexl 7E 126
Venture Ct. SE12 7J 123
Venture Ho. *W10* *6F 81*
(off Bridge Cl.)
Venue St. E14 5E 86
Venus Ho. *E14* *4C 104*
(off Westferry Rd.)
Venus M. CR4: Mitc 3C 154
Venus Rd. SE18 3D 106
Vera Av. N21 5F 23
Vera Lynn Cl. E7 4J 69
Vera Rd. SW6 1G 117
Verbena Cl. E16 4H 87
UB7: W Dray 1E 174
Verbena Gdns. W6 5C 98
Verdant Ct. *SE6* *7G 123*
(off Verdant La.)
Verdant La. SE6 7G 123
Verdayne Av. CR0: C'don 2K 169
Verdi Cres. W10 2G 81
Verdun Rd. SE18 6A 108
SW13 6C 98
Vere Ct. *W2* *6K 81*
(off Westbourne Gdns.)
Vereker Dr. TW16: Sun 3J 147
Vereker Rd. W14 5G 99
Vere St. W1 1J 11 (6F 83)
Veritas Ho. *DA15: Sidc* *2A 144*
(off Station Rd.)
Verity Cl. W11 7G 81
Vermeer Ct. E14 3F 105
Vermeer Gdns. SE15 4J 121
Vermont Cl. EN2: Enf 4G 23
Vermont Ho. E17 2B 50
Vermont Rd. SE19 6D 138
SM1: Sutt 3K 165
SW18 6K 117
Verne Ct. *W3* *3J 97*
(off Vincent Rd.)
Verney Gdns. RM9: Dag 4E 72
Verney Ho. NW8 3B 4
Verney Rd. RM9: Dag 4E 72
(not continuous)
SE16 6G 103
Verney St. NW10 3K 61
Verney Way SE16 5H 103
Vernham Rd. SE18 6G 107
Vernon Av. E12 4D 70
IG8: Wfd G 7E 36
SW20 2F 153
Vernon Cl. KT19: Ewe 6J 163
TW19: Stanw 1A 128
Vernon Ct. HA7: Stan 1B 42
NW2 3H 63
W5 7C 78
Vernon Cres. EN4: E Barn 6K 21
Vernon Dr. HA7: Stan 1A 42
Vernon Ho. SE11 6H 19
WC1 *6F 7*
(off Vernon Pl.)
Vernon Mans. *W14* *6H 99*
(off Queen's Club Mans.)
Vernon M. E17 5B 50
W14 4G 99
Vernon Pl. WC1 6F 7 (5J 83)
Vernon Ri. UB6: G'frd 5H 59
WC1 1H 7 (3K 83)
Vernon Rd. E3 2B 86
E11 1G 69
E15 7G 69
E17 5B 50
IG3: Ilf 1K 71
N8 3A 48
SM1: Sutt 5A 166
SW14 3K 115
TW13: Felt 2H 129
Vernon Sq. WC1 1H 7 (3K 83)
Vernon St. W14 4G 99
Vernon Yd. W11 7H 81
Veroan Rd. DA7: Bex 2E 126
Verona Ct. *SE14* *6K 103*
(off Myers La.)
TW15: Ashf 4D 128
W4 5A 98
Verona Dr. KT6: Surb 2E 162
Verona Rd. E7 7J 69
Veronica Gdns. SW16 1G 155
Veronica Ho. SE4 3B 122
Veronica Rd. SW17 2F 137
Veronique Gdns. IG6: Ilf 5G 53
Verran Rd. SW12 7F 119
Versailles Rd. SE20 7G 139
Verulam Av. E17 6B 50
Verulam Bldgs. WC1 5H 7
Verulam Ct. NW9 7C 44
UB1: S'hall *6G 77*
(off Haldane Rd.)
Verulam Ho. *W6* *2E 98*
(off Hammersmith Gro.)
Verulam Rd. UB6: G'frd 4E 76
Verulam St. WC1 5J 7 (5A 84)
Vervian Ho. *SE15* *7G 103*
(off Reddins Rd.)
Verwood Dr. EN4: Cockf 3J 21
Verwood Ho. *SW8* *7K 101*
(off Cobbett St.)
Verwood Lodge *E14* *3F 105*
(off Manchester Rd.)
Verwood Rd. HA2: Harr 2G 41
Veryan Ct. N8 5H 47
Vesage Ct. *EC1* *6K 7*
(off Leather La.)
Vesey Path E14 6D 86
Vespan Rd. W12 2C 98
Vesta Ct. SE1 7G 15
Vesta Rd. SE4 2A 122
Vestris Rd. SE23 2K 139
Vestry Ct. *SW1* *2D 18*
(off Monck St.)
Vestry House Mus. 4D 50
Vestry M. SE5 1E 120
Vestry Rd. E17 4D 50
SE5 1E 120
Vestry St. N1 1E 8 (3D 84)
Vevey St. SE6 2B 140
Veysey Gdns.
RM10: Dag 3G 73
Viaduct, The E18 2J 51
HA0: Wemb 1E 78
N10 4F 47
Viaduct Bldgs. EC1 6K 7 (5A 84)
Viaduct Pl. E2 3H 85
Viaduct Rd. N2 2B 46
Viaduct St. E2 3H 85
Vian St. SE13 3D 122
Viant Ho. *NW10* *7K 61*
(off Fawood Av.)
Vibart Gdns. SW2 7K 119
Vibart Wlk. *N1* *1J 83*
(off Outram Pl.)
Vibia Cl. TW19: Stanw 7A 110
Vicarage Av. SE3 7J 105
Vicarage Cl. DA8: Erith 6J 109
HA4: Ruis 7F 39
KT4: Wor Pk 1A 164
UB5: N'olt 7D 58
Vicarage Ct. BR3: Beck 3A 158
IG1: Ilf 5F 71
TW14: Bedf 7E 110
W8 2K 99
Vicarage Cres. SW11 1B 118
Vicarage Dr. BR3: Beck 1C 158
IG11: Bark 7G 71
SW14 5K 115
Vicarage Farm Ct. TW5: Hest 7D 94
Vicarage Farm Rd. TW3: Houn 2C 112
TW5: Hest 1C 112
Vicarage Flds. KT12: Walt T 6A 148
Vicarage Fld. Shop. Cen.
IG11: Bark 7G 71
Vicarage Gdns. CR4: Mitc 3C 154
SW14 5J 115
W8 1J 99
Vicarage Ga. W8 1K 99
Vicarage Gro. SE5 1D 120
Vicarage Ho. *KT1: King T* *2F 151*
(off Cambridge Rd.)
Vicarage La. E6 3D 88
E15 7G 69
IG1: Ilf 1H 71
KT17: Ewe 7C 164
(not continuous)
Vicarage M. NW9 2K 61
Vicarage Pde. N15 4C 48
Vicarage Pk. SE18 5G 107
Vicarage Path N8 7J 47
Vicarage Rd. CR0: Wadd 3A 168
DA5: Bexl 1H 145
E10 7C 50
E15 7H 69

Vicarage Rd. IG8: Wfd G 7H 37
KT1: Ham W 1C 150
KT1: King T 2D 150
N17 1G 49
NW4 6C 44
RM10: Dag 7H 73
SE18 5G 107
(not continuous)
SM1: Sutt 3K 165
SW14 5J 115
TW2: Twick 2J 131
TW2: Whitt 6G 113
TW11: Tedd 5A 132
TW16: Sun 5H 129
Vicarage Wlk. KT12: Walt T 7J 147
SW11 1B 118
Vicarage Way HA2: Harr 7E 40
NW10 3K 61
Vicars Bri. Cl. HA0: Wemb 2E 78
Vicars Cl. E9 1J 85
E15 1J 87
EN1: Enf 2K 23
Vicar's Hill SE13 4D 122
Vicars Moor La. N21 7F 23
Vicars Oak Rd. SE19 6E 138
Vicar's Rd. NW5 5E 64
Vicars Wlk. RM8: Dag 3B 72
Viceroy Cl. *N2* *4C 46*
(off East End Rd.)
Viceroy Ct. CR0: C'don 1D 168
NW8 *2C 82*
(off Prince Albert Rd.)
Viceroy Pde. *N2* *4C 46*
(off High Rd.)
Viceroy Rd. SW8 1J 119
Vickers Cl. SM6: Wall 7K 167
Vickers Ct. *TW19: Stanw* *6A 110*
(off Whitley Cl.)
Vickers Rd. DA8: Erith 5K 109
Vickers Way TW4: Houn 5C 112
Vickery Ct. *EC1* *3D 8*
(off Mitchell St.)
Vickery's Wharf E14 6C 86
Victor Cazalet Ho. *N1* *1B 84*
(off Gaskin St.)
Victor Gro. HA0: Wemb 7E 60
Victoria & Albert Mus. 2B 16 (3B 100)
Victoria Arc. *SW1* *2K 17*
(off Victoria St.)
Victoria Av. E6 1B 88
EC2 6H 9 (5E 84)
EN4: E Barn 4G 21
HA9: Wemb 6H 61
KT6: Surb 6D 150
KT8: W Mole 3F 149
N3 1H 45
SM6: Wall 3E 166
TW3: Houn 5E 112
UB10: Hil 6D 56
Victoria Bldgs. *E8* *1H 85*
(off Mare St.)
Victoria Chambers *EC2* *3G 9*
(off Luke St.)
Victoria Cl. EN4: E Barn 4G 21
HA1: Harr 6K 41
KT8: W Mole 3E 148
UB3: Hayes 6F 75
Victoria Colonnade
WC1 *6F 7*
(off Southampton Row)
Victoria Cotts. *E1* *5G 85*
(off Deal St.)
N10 2E 46
TW9: Kew 1F 115
Victoria Ct. E18 3K 51
HA9: Wemb 6G 61
SE1 *4E 102*
(off Hendre Rd.)
SE26 6J 139
W3 2G 97
Victoria Cres. N15 5E 48
SE19 6E 138
SW19 7H 135
Victoria Dock Rd. E16 6H 87
Victoria Dr. SW19 7F 117
Victoria Emb. EC4 6F 13 (7K 83)
SW1 6F 13 (2J 101)
WC2 6F 13 (2J 101)
Victoria Gdns. TW5: Hest 1C 112
W11 1J 99
Victoria Gro. N12 5G 31
W8 3A 100
Victoria Gro. M. W2 7J 81
Victoria Hall *E16* *1J 105*
(off Wesley Av., not continuous)
Victoria Ho. E6 6E 88
HA8: Edg 6C 28
SW1 *5J 17*
(off Ebury Bri. Rd.)
SW1 *3B 18*
(off Francis St.)
SW8 *7J 101*
(off Sth. Lambeth Rd.)
Victoria Ind. Est. W3 5A 80
Victoria La. EN5: Barn 4C 20
UB3: Harl 5F 93
Victoria Mans. NW10 7D 62
SW8 *7J 101*
(off Sth. Lambeth Rd.)
W14 *6H 99*
(off Queen's Club Mans.)
Victoria M. E8 6G 67
NW6 1J 81
SW4 4F 119
SW18 1A 136
UB2: S'hall 3C 94
Victoria Mills Studios E15 1F 87
Victorian Gro. N16 4E 66
Victorian Hgts. *SW8* *2F 119*
(off Thackeray Rd.)
Victorian Rd. N16 3E 66
Victoria Palace Theatre *2A 18*
(off Victoria St.)
Victoria Pde. *TW9: Kew* *1G 115*
(off Sandycombe Rd.)
Victoria Pk. Ct. *E9* *7J 67*
(off Well St.)
Victoria Pk. Ind. Cen. *E9* *7C 68*
(off Rothbury Rd.)
Victoria Pk. Rd. E9 1J 85
Victoria Pk. Sq. E2 3J 85
Victoria Pas. NW8 3B 4
Victoria Pl. TW9: Rich 5D 114
Victoria Pl. Shop. Cen. SW1 3K 17
Victoria Point *E13* *2J 87*
(off Victoria Rd.)
Victoria Retail Pk. HA4: Ruis 5B 58
Victoria Ri. *NW6* *7A 64*
(off Hilgrove Rd.)
SW4 3F 119
Victoria Rd. BR2: Brom 5B 160
BR7: Chst 5E 142
CR4: Mitc 7C 136
DA6: Bex 4G 127
DA8: Erith 6K 109
(not continuous)
DA15: Sidc 3K 143
E4 1B 36
E11 4G 69
E13 2J 87
E17 2E 50
E18 2K 51
EN4: E Barn 4G 21
HA4: Ruis 1J 57
IG9: Buck H 2G 37
IG11: Bark 6F 71
KT1: King T 2F 151
KT6: Surb 6D 150
N4 7K 47
N9 4A 34
Victoria Rd. N15 4G 49
N18 4A 34
N22 1G 47
NW4 4E 44
NW6 2H 81
NW7 5G 29
NW10 5K 79
RM10: Dag 5H 73
SM1: Sutt 5B 166
SW14 3K 115
TW1: Twick 7B 114
TW11: Tedd 6A 132
TW13: Felt 1K 129
UB2: S'hall 3D 94
W3 5K 79
W5 5B 78
W8 3A 100
WD23: Bush 1A 26
Victoria Sq. SW1 1K 17 (3F 101)
Victoria St. DA17: Belv 5F 109
E15 7G 69
SW1 2K 17 (3G 101)
Victoria Ter. HA1: Harr 1J 59
N4 1A 66
NW10 4B 80
W5 1D 96
Victoria Vs. TW9: Rich 3F 115
Victoria Way HA4: Ruis 5B 58
SE7 5K 105
Victoria Wharf *E2* *2K 85*
(off Palmers Rd.)
E14 7A 86
SE8 *5B 104*
(off Dragoon Rd.)
Victoria Works NW2 2D 62
Victoria Yd. E1 6G 85
Victor Rd. HA2: Harr 3G 41
NW10 3D 80
SE20 7K 139
TW11: Tedd 4J 131
Victors Dr. TW12: Hamp 6C 130
Victors Way EN5: Barn 3C 20
Victor Vs. N9 3J 33
Victor Wlk. NW9 2A 44
Victor Wharf *SE1* *4E 14*
(off Clink St.)
Victory Av. SM4: Mord 5A 154
Victory Bus. Cen. TW7: Isle 4K 113
Victory Cl. TW19: Stanw 1A 128
Victory Ct. IG11: Bark 4B 90
W9 *4J 81*
(off Hermes Cl.)
Victory Pk. HA9: Wemb 3D 60
Victory Pl. E14 7A 86
SE17 4D 102
SE19 7E 138
Victory Rd. E11 4J 51
SW19 7A 136
Victory Rd. M. *SW19* *7A 136*
(off Victory Rd.)
Victory Wlk. SE8 1C 122
Victory Way RM7: Mawney 2H 55
SE16 2A 104
TW5: Cran 5A 94
Video Ct. N4 7K 47
Vidler Cl. KT9: Chess 6C 162
Vienna Cl. IG5: Ilf 2B 52
View, The SE2 5E 108
View Cl. HA1: Harr 4H 41
N6 7D 46
View Ct. SE12 3A 142
View Cres. N8 5H 47
Viewfield Cl. HA3: Kent 7E 42
Viewfield Rd. DA5: Bexl 1C 144
SW18 6H 117
Viewland Rd. SE18 5K 107
View Rd. N6 7D 46
Viga Rd. N21 6F 23
Vigilant Cl. SE26 4G 139
Vignoles Rd. RM7: Rush G 7G 55
Vigo St. W1 3A 12 (7G 83)
Viking Bus. Cen. RM7: Rush G 7J 55
Viking Cl. E3 2A 86
Viking Ct. SW6 6J 99
Viking Gdns. E6 4C 88
Viking Ho. *SE5* *2C 120*
(off Denmark Rd.)
SE18 *4C 106*
(off Pett St.)
Viking Pl. E10 1B 68
Viking Rd. UB1: S'hall 7C 76
Viking Way DA8: Erith 3J 109
Villacourt Rd. SE18 7A 108
Village, The NW3 2A 64
SE7 6A 106
Village Arc. E4 1A 36
Village Cl. E4 5K 35
NW3 *5B 64*
(off Belsize La.)
Village Ct. *E17* *5D 50*
(off Eden Rd.)
SE3 *3G 123*
(off Hurren Cl.)
Village Ga. TW17: Shep 5D 146
Village Hgts. IG8: Wfd G 5C 36
Village M. NW9 2K 61
Village Mt. *NW3* *4A 64*
(off Perrins Ct.)
Village Pk. Cl. EN1: Enf 6K 23
Village Rd. EN1: Enf 5K 23
N3 2G 45
Village Row SM2: Sutt 7J 165
Village Way BR3: Beck 2C 158
HA5: Pinn 7C 40
IG6: Ilf 4G 53
NW10 4K 61
SE21 6D 120
TW15: Ashf 4B 128
Village Way E. HA2: Harr 7E 40
Villa Rd. SW9 3A 120
Villas on the Heath
NW3 3A 64
Villas Rd. SE18 5G 107
(not continuous)
Villa St. SE17 5D 102
Villa Wlk *SE17* *5D 102*
(off Villa St.)
Villiers Av. KT5: Surb 5F 151
TW2: Whitt 1D 130
Villiers Cl. E10 2C 68
KT5: Surb 4F 151
Villiers Gro. SM2: Cheam 7F 165
Villiers M. NW2 6C 62
Villiers Path KT6: Surb 5E 150
Villiers Rd. BR3: Beck 2K 157
KT1: King T 4F 151
NW2 6C 62
TW7: Isle 2J 113
UB1: S'hall 1D 94
Villiers St. WC2 3E 12 (1J 101)
Vimy Cl. TW4: Houn 5D 112
Vincam Cl. TW2: Whitt 7E 112
Vince Ct. N1 2F 9 (3D 84)
Vincennes Est.
SE27 4D 138
Vincent Av. KT5: Surb 2J 163
Vincent Cl. BR2: Brom 4K 159
DA15: Sidc 1J 143
EN5: New Bar 3E 20
SE16 2A 104
UB7: Sip 6C 92
Vincent Ct. HA6: Nwood 1H 39
N4 1J 65
NW4 4F 45
SW9 1K 119
W1 *7E 4*
(off Seymour Pl.)
Vincent Dr. TW17: Shep 3G 147
UB10: Uxb 1B 74
Vincent Gdns. NW2 3B 62

Vincent Ho. *SW1* . . . 3D 18
(off Regency St.)
SW1 . . . 4C 18
(off Vincent Sq.)
Vincent M. E3 . . . 2C 86
Vincent Rd. CR0: C'don . . . 7E 156
E4 . . . 6A 36
HA0: Wemb . . . 7F 61
KT1: King T . . . 3G 151
N15 . . . 4C 48
N22 . . . 2A 48
RM9: Dag . . . 7E 72
SE18 . . . 4F 107
TW4: Houn . . . 2B 112
TW7: Isle . . . 1H 113
W3 . . . 3J 97
Vincent Row
TW12: Ham H . . . 6G 131
Vincents Path *UB5: N'olt* . . . 6C 58
(off Arnold Rd.)
Vincent Sq. N22 . . . 2A 48
SW1 . . . 3C 18 (4H 101)
Vincent Sq. Mans. *SW1* . . . 3B 18
(off Walcott St.)
Vincent St. E16 . . . 5H 87
SW1 . . . 3C 18 (4H 101)
Vincent Ter. N1 . . . 2B 84
Vince St. EC1 . . . 2F 9 (3D 84)
Vine Cl. KT5: Surb . . . 6F 151
SM1: Sutt . . . 3A 166
TW19: Stan M . . . 7B 174
UB7: W Dray . . . 4C 92
Vine Cotts. *E1* . . . 6J 85
(off Sidney Sq.)
W7 . . . 1J 95
Vine Ct. E1 . . . 5G 85
HA3: Kent . . . 6E 42
Vinegar All. E17 . . . 4D 50
Vine Gdns. IG1: Ilf . . . 5G 71
Vinegar St. E1 . . . 1H 103
Vinegar Yd. SE1 . . . 6G 15 (2E 102)
Vine Gro. UB10: Hil . . . 7C 56
Vine Hill EC1 . . . 4J 7 (4A 84)
Vine La. SE1 . . . 5H 15 (1E 102)
UB10: Hil . . . 1B 74
Vine Pl. TW3: Houn . . . 4F 113
W5 . . . 1E 96
(off St Mark's Rd.)
Viner Cl. KT12: Walt T . . . 6A 148
Vineries, The EN1: Enf . . . 3K 23
N14 . . . 6B 22
SE6 . . . 1C 140
Vineries Bank NW7 . . . 5J 29
Vineries Cl. RM9: Dag . . . 6F 73
UB7: Sip . . . 6C 92
Vine Rd. BR6: Chels . . . 6K 173
E15 . . . 7H 69
KT8: E Mos . . . 4G 149
SW13 . . . 3B 116
Vinery Row W6 . . . 3D 98
Vines Av. N3 . . . 1K 45
Vine Sq. *W14* . . . 5H 99
(off Star Rd.)
Vine St. EC3 . . . 1J 15 (6F 85)
RM7: Rom . . . 4J 55
W1 . . . 3B 12 (7G 83)
Vine St. Bri. EC1 . . . 4K 7 (4A 84)
Vine Yd. SE1 . . . 6D 14
Vineyard, The TW10: Rich . . . 5E 114
Vineyard Av. NW7 . . . 7B 30
Vineyard Cl. KT1: King T . . . 3F 151
SE6 . . . 1C 140
Vineyard Gro. N3 . . . 1K 45
Vineyard Hill Rd. SW19 . . . 4H 135
Vineyard M. TW10: Rich . . . 5E 114
Vineyard Pas. TW10: Rich . . . 5E 114
Vineyard Path *SW14* . . . 3K 115
(off Church Path)
SW14 . . . 3K 115
(Sheen La.)
Vineyard Rd. TW13: Felt . . . 3J 129
Vineyard Row KT1: Ham W . . . 1C 150
Vineyards, The *TW13: Felt* . . . 3J 129
(off High St.)
TW16: Sun . . . 3J 147
Vineyard Wlk. EC1 . . . 3J 7 (4A 84)
Viney Bank CR0: Sels . . . 7B 170
Viney Rd. SE13 . . . 3D 122
Vining St. SW9 . . . 4A 120
Vinlake Av. UB10: Ick . . . 3B 56
Vinopolis . . . 4D 14 (1C 102)
Vinson Cl. BR6: Orp . . . 1K 173
Vinson Ho. *N1* . . . 2D 84
(off Cranston Est.)
Vintage M. E4 . . . 4H 35
Vinter Ct. TW17: Shep . . . 5C 146
Vintner's Ct. EC4 . . . 3D 14 (7C 84)
Vintner's Pl. EC4 . . . 2D 14 (7C 84)
Vintry M. E17 . . . 4C 50
Viola Av. SE2 . . . 4B 108
TW14: Felt . . . 6A 112
TW19: Stanw . . . 1A 128
Viola Sq. W12 . . . 7B 80
Violet Av. EN2: Enf . . . 1J 23
UB8: Hil . . . 5B 74
Violet Cl. E16 . . . 4G 87
SE8 . . . 6B 104
SM3: Sutt . . . 1G 165
SM6: Wall . . . 1E 166
Violet Gdns. CR0: Wadd . . . 5B 168
Violet Hill NW8 . . . 2A 82
Violet Hill Ho. *NW8* . . . 2A 82
(off Violet Hill)
Violet La. CR0: Wadd . . . 6B 168
Violet Rd. E3 . . . 4D 86
E17 . . . 6C 50
E18 . . . 2K 51
Violet St. E2 . . . 4H 85
VIP Trading Est.
SE7 . . . 4A 106
Virgil Pl. W1 . . . 6E 4 (5D 82)
Virgil St. SE1 . . . 1H 19 (3K 101)
Virgin Active Health Club
Bromley . . . 4B 160
Mill Hill East . . . 7B 30
South Wimbledon . . . 6A 136
Stockley Pk. . . . 7E 74
Sunbury . . . 1J 147
Virginia Cl. KT3: N Mald . . . 4J 151
RM5: Col R . . . 1J 55
Virginia Ct. *SE16* . . . 2K 103
(off Eleanor Cl.)
WC1 . . . 3D 6
(off Burton St.)
Virginia Gdns. IG6: Ilf . . . 2G 53
Virginia Ho. *E14* . . . 7E 86
(off Newby Pl.)
TW11: Tedd . . . 5B 132
Virginia Rd. CR7: Thor H . . . 1B 156
E2 . . . 2J 9 (3F 85)
Virginia St. E1 . . . 7G 85
Virginia Wlk. SW2 . . . 6K 119
Viridian Apartments
SW8 . . . 7G 101
Visage *NW3* . . . 7B 64
(off Winchester Rd.)
Viscount Cl. N11 . . . 6A 32
Viscount Ct. *W2* . . . 6J 81
(off Pembridge Vs.)
Viscount Dr. E6 . . . 5D 88
Viscount Gro. UB5: N'olt . . . 3B 76
Viscount Rd. TW19: Stanw . . . 1A 128
Viscount St. EC1 . . . 4C 8 (4C 84)
Viscount Way
TW6: H'row A . . . 4G 111
Vista, The DA14: Sidc . . . 5K 143
SE9 . . . 6B 124
Vista Av. EN3: Enf H . . . 2E 24
Vista Bldg. SE18 . . . 4E 106
Vista Dr. IG4: Ilf . . . 5B 52
Vista Ho. *SW19* . . . 1B 154
(off Chapter Way)
Vista Way HA3: Kent . . . 6E 42
Vitae Apartments W6 . . . 3C 98
Vittoria Ho. *N1* . . . 1K 83
(off High Rd.)
Viveash Cl. UB3: Hayes . . . 3H 93
Vivian Av. HA9: Wemb . . . 5G 61
NW4 . . . 5D 44
Vivian Comma Cl. N4 . . . 3B 66
Vivian Ct. N12 . . . 5E 30
NW6 . . . 2K 81
Vivian Gdns. HA9: Wemb . . . 5G 61
Vivian Mans. *NW4* . . . 5D 44
(off Vivian Av.)
Vivian Rd. E3 . . . 2A 86
Vivian Sq. SE15 . . . 3H 121
Vivian Way N2 . . . 5B 46
Vivien Cl. KT9: Chess . . . 7E 162
Vivienne Cl. TW1: Twick . . . 6D 114
Vixen M. *E8* . . . 7F 67
(off Haggerston Rd.)
Voce Rd. SE18 . . . 7H 107
Voewood Cl. KT3: N Mald . . . 6B 152
Vogans Mill SE1 . . . 6K 15 (2F 103)
Vogler Ho. *E1* . . . 7J 85
(off Cable St.)
Vogue Ct. BR1: Brom . . . 1K 159
Vollasky Ho. *E1* . . . 5K 9
(off Daplyn St.)
Volta Cl. N9 . . . 3D 34
Voltaire Rd. SW4 . . . 3H 119
Voltaire Way UB3: Hayes . . . 7G 75
Volt Av. NW10 . . . 3A 80
Volta Way CR0: Wadd . . . 1K 167
Voluntary Pl. E11 . . . 6J 51
Vorley Rd. N19 . . . 2G 65
Voss Ct. SW16 . . . 6J 137
Voss St. E2 . . . 3G 85
Voyager Bus. Est.
SE16 . . . 3G 103
(off Spa Rd.)
Voyagers Cl. SE28 . . . 6C 90
Voysey Cl. N3 . . . 3G 45
Vue Cinema
Croydon, High St. . . . 3C 168
Croydon, Purley Way . . . 1K 167
Dagenham . . . 1E 90
Fallow Corner . . . 7G 31
Finchley Rd. . . . 6A 64
(in O2 Cen.)
Fulham Broadway . . . 7J 99
Harrow . . . 6J 41
(in St George's Shop. & Leisure Cen.)
Islington . . . 2A 84
Leicester Sq. . . . 2D 12
(off Cranbourn St.)
Romford . . . 6K 55
Royale Leisure Pk. . . . 4G 79
Shepherds Bush . . . 2F 99
The O2 . . . 1G 105
(in The O2)
Vulcan Cl. E6 . . . 6E 88
Vulcan Ga. EN2: Enf . . . 2F 23
Vulcan Rd. SE4 . . . 2B 122
Vulcan Sq. E14 . . . 4D 104
Vulcan Ter. SE4 . . . 2B 122
Vulcan Way N7 . . . 6K 65
SM6: Wall . . . 7J 167
Vyne, The DA7: Bex . . . 3H 127
Vyner Rd. W3 . . . 7K 79
Vyner St. E2 . . . 1H 85
Vyner's Way UB10: Ick . . . 5C 56

W

Wadbrook St. KT1: King T . . . 2D 150
Wadding St. SE17 . . . 4D 102
Waddington Cl. EN1: Enf . . . 4K 23
Waddington Rd. E15 . . . 5F 69
Waddington St. E15 . . . 6F 69
Waddington Way SE19 . . . 7C 138
WADDON . . . 3A 168
Waddon Cl. CR0: Wadd . . . 3A 168
Waddon Ct. Rd. CR0: Wadd . . . 3A 168
Waddon Marsh Way
CR0: Wadd . . . 1K 167
Waddon New Rd. CR0: C'don . . . 3B 168
Waddon Pk. Av. CR0: Wadd . . . 4A 168
Waddon Rd. CR0: C'don, Wadd . . . 3A 168
Waddon Way CR0: Wadd . . . 6A 168
Wade Ct. N10 . . . 7A 32
Wade Ho. EN1: Enf . . . 5J 23
SE1 . . . 7K 15
(off Parkers Row)
Wades Gro. N21 . . . 7F 23
Wades Hill N21 . . . 6F 23
Wades La. TW11: Tedd . . . 5A 132
Wades M. N21 . . . 7F 23
Wadeson St. E2 . . . 2H 85
Wade's Pl. E14 . . . 7D 86
Wadeville Av. RM6: Chad H . . . 6E 54
Wadeville Cl. DA17: Belv . . . 5G 109
Wadham Av. E17 . . . 7J 35
Wadham Cl. TW17: Shep . . . 7E 146
Wadham Gdns. NW3 . . . 1C 82
UB6: G'frd . . . 6H 59
Wadham Ho. N18 . . . 5A 34
Wadham Rd. E17 . . . 7J 35
SW15 . . . 4G 117
Wadhurst Cl. SE20 . . . 2H 157
Wadhurst Rd. SW8 . . . 1G 119
W4 . . . 3K 97
Wadley Rd. E11 . . . 7G 51
Wadsworth Bus. Cen.
UB6: G'frd . . . 2C 78
Wadsworth Cl. EN3: Pond E . . . 5E 24
UB6: G'frd . . . 2C 78
Wadsworth Rd. UB6: G'frd . . . 2B 78
Wager St. E3 . . . 4B 86
WAGGONERS RDBT. . . . 1K 111
Waggon La. N17 . . . 6B 34
Waggon M. N14 . . . 1B 32
Waghorn Rd. E13 . . . 1A 88
HA3: Kent . . . 3D 42
Waghorn St. SE15 . . . 3G 121
Wagner M. *KT6: Surb* . . . 5E 150
(off Avenue Elmers)
Wagner St. SE15 . . . 7J 103
Wagstaff Gdns. RM9: Dag . . . 7C 72
Wagtail Cl. EN1: Enf . . . 1C 24
NW9 . . . 2A 44
Wagtail Rd. TW6: H'row A . . . 5C 174
Wagtail Wlk. BR3: Beck . . . 5E 158
Waight's Ct. KT2: King T . . . 1E 150
Wainfleet Av. RM5: Col R . . . 2J 55
Wainford Cl. SW19 . . . 1F 135
Wainwright Gro. TW7: Isle . . . 4H 113
Wainwright Ho. *E1* . . . 1J 103
(off Garnet St.)
Wait Ct. *CR0: C'don* . . . 6B 156
(off Goodman Ct.)
Waite Davies Rd. SE12 . . . 7H 123
Waite St. SE15 . . . 6F 103
Waithman St. *EC4* . . . 1A 14
(off Apothecary St.)
Wakefield Ct. SE26 . . . 6J 139
Wakefield Gdns. IG1: Ilf . . . 6C 52
SE19 . . . 7E 138
Wakefield Ho. SE15 . . . 1G 121
Wakefield M. WC1 . . . 2F 7 (3J 83)
Wakefield Rd. N11 . . . 5C 32
N15 . . . 5F 49
TW10: Rich . . . 5D 114
Wakefield St. E6 . . . 1B 88
N18 . . . 5B 34
WC1 . . . 2F 7 (3J 83)
Wakeford Cl. SW4 . . . 5G 119
Wakehams Hill HA5: Pinn . . . 3D 40

Wakeham St. N1 . . . 6D 66
Wakehurst Rd. SW11 . . . 5C 118
Wakeling Rd. W7 . . . 5K 77
Wakeling St. E14 . . . 6A 86
Wakelin Ho. *N1* . . . 7B 66
(off Sebbon St.)
SE23 . . . 7A 122
(off Brockley Pk.)
Wakelin Rd. E15 . . . 2G 87
Wakeman Ho. *NW10* . . . 3F 81
(off Wakeman Rd.)
Wakeman Rd. NW10 . . . 3E 80
Wakemans Hill Av. NW9 . . . 5K 43
Wakering Rd. IG11: Bark . . . 7G 71
Wakerings, The
IG11: Bark . . . 6G 71
(off Wakering Rd.)
Wakerley Cl. E6 . . . 6D 88
Wakley St. EC1 . . . 1A 8 (3B 84)
Walberswick St. SW8 . . . 7J 101
Walbrook EC4 . . . 2E 14 (7D 84)
(not continuous)
Walbrook Ct. *N1* . . . 2E 84
(off Hemsworth St.)
Walbrook Ho. *N9* . . . 2D 34
(off Huntingdon Rd.)
Walbrook Wharf *EC4* . . . 3D 14
(off Bell Wharf La.)
Walburgh St. E1 . . . 6H 85
Walcorde Av. SE17 . . . 4C 102
Walcot Gdns. SE11 . . . 3J 19
Walcot Rd. EN3: Brim . . . 2G 25
Walcot Sq. SE11 . . . 3K 19 (4A 102)
Walcott St. SW1 . . . 3B 18 (4G 101)
Waldair Ct. E16 . . . 2F 107
Waldeck Gro. SE27 . . . 3B 138
Waldeck Rd. N15 . . . 4B 48
SW14 . . . 3J 115
W4 . . . 6G 97
W13 . . . 6B 78
Waldeck Ter. *SW14* . . . 3J 115
(off Waldeck Rd.)
Waldegrave Ct. IG11: Bark . . . 1H 89
Waldegrave Gdns. TW1: Twick . . . 2K 131
Waldegrave Pk.
TW1: Twick . . . 4K 131
Waldegrave Rd. BR1: Brom . . . 4C 160
N8 . . . 3A 48
RM8: Dag . . . 2C 72
SE19 . . . 7F 139
TW1: Twick . . . 4K 131
TW11: Tedd . . . 4K 131
W5 . . . 7F 79
Waldegrove CR0: C'don . . . 3F 169
Waldemar Av. SW6 . . . 1G 117
W13 . . . 1C 96
Waldemar Rd. SW19 . . . 5J 135
Walden Av. BR7: Chst . . . 4D 142
N13 . . . 4H 33
RM13: Rain . . . 2K 91
Walden Cl. DA17: Belv . . . 5F 109
Walden Ct. SW8 . . . 1H 119
Walden Gdns. CR7: Thor H . . . 3K 155
Walden Ho. *SW1* . . . 4H 17
(off Pimlico Rd.)
SW11 . . . 1E 118
(off Dagnall St.)
Walden Pde. BR7: Chst . . . 6D 142
(not continuous)
Walden Rd. BR7: Chst . . . 6D 142
N17 . . . 1D 48
Waldenshaw Rd. SE23 . . . 1J 139
Walden St. E1 . . . 6H 85
(not continuous)
Walden Way NW7 . . . 6A 30
Waldo Cl. SW4 . . . 5G 119
Waldo Ho. *NW10* . . . 3D 80
(off Waldo Rd.)
Waldo Ind. Est. BR1: Brom . . . 3B 160
Waldo Pl. CR4: Mitc . . . 7C 136
Waldorf Cl. CR2: S Croy . . . 7B 168
Waldo Rd. BR1: Brom . . . 3B 160
NW10 . . . 3C 80
(not continuous)
Waldram Cres. SE23 . . . 1J 139
Waldram Pk. Rd. SE23 . . . 1K 139
Waldram Pl. SE23 . . . 1J 139
Waldrist Way DA18: Erith . . . 2F 109
Waldron Gdns. BR2: Brom . . . 3F 159
Waldronhyrst CR2: S Croy . . . 4B 168
Waldron M. SW3 . . . 7B 16 (6B 100)
Waldron Rd. HA1: Harr . . . 1J 59
HA2: Harr . . . 1J 59
SW18 . . . 3A 136
Waldrons, The CR0: C'don . . . 4B 168
Waldron's Path CR2: S Croy . . . 4C 168
Waldrons Yd. HA2: Harr . . . 2H 59
Waldstock Rd. SE28 . . . 7A 90
Waleran Cl. HA7: Stan . . . 5E 26
Walerand Rd. SE13 . . . 2E 122
Waleran Flats SE1 . . . 4E 102
Wales Av. SM5: Cars . . . 5C 166
Wales Cl. SE15 . . . 6H 103
Wales Farm Rd. W3 . . . 5K 79
Waleton Acres SM6: Wall . . . 6G 167
Waley St. E1 . . . 5A 86
Walfield Av. N20 . . . 7E 20
Walford Ho. E1 . . . 6G 85
Walford Rd. N16 . . . 4E 66
Walfrey Gdns. RM9: Dag . . . 7E 72
WALHAM GREEN . . . 1J 117
Walham Grn. Ct. *SW6* . . . 7K 99
(off Waterford Rd.)
Walham Gro. SW6 . . . 7J 99
Walham Ri. SW19 . . . 6G 135
Walham Yd. SW6 . . . 7J 99
Walk, The *N13* . . . 3F 33
(off Fox La.)
TW16: Sun . . . 7H 129
Walkato Lodge IG9: Buck H . . . 1F 37
Walkden Rd. BR7: Chst . . . 5E 142
Walker Cl. N11 . . . 4B 32
SE18 . . . 4G 107
TW12: Hamp . . . 6D 130
TW14: Felt . . . 7H 111
W7 . . . 1J 95
Walker Ho. NW1 . . . 1C 6 (2H 83)
Walker M. SW2 . . . 5A 120
Walker's Ct. W1 . . . 2C 12
Walkerscroft Mead SE21 . . . 1C 138
Walkers Lodge *E14* . . . 2E 104
(off Manchester Rd.)
Walkers Pl. SW15 . . . 4G 117
Walkinshaw Ct. *N1* . . . 7C 66
(off Rotherfield St.)
Walks, The N2 . . . 3B 46
Wallace Cl. SE28 . . . 7D 90
TW17: Shep . . . 4F 147
UB10: Uxb . . . 2A 74
Wallace Collection . . . 7H 5 (6E 82)
Wallace Ct. *NW1* . . . 6D 4
(off Old Marylebone Rd.)
Wallace Cres. SM5: Cars . . . 5D 166
Wallace Ho. *N7* . . . 6K 65
(off Caledonian Rd.)
Wallace Rd. N1 . . . 6C 66
Wallace Way *N19* . . . 2H 65
(off St John's Way)
RM1: Rom . . . 1K 55
Wallasey Cres. UB10: Ick . . . 2C 56
Wallbrook Bus. Cen.
TW4: Houn . . . 3K 111
Wallbutton Rd. SE4 . . . 2A 122
Wallcote Av. NW2 . . . 1F 63
Wall Ct. *N4* . . . 1K 65
(off Stroud Grn. Rd.)
Walled Gdn. Cl. BR3: Beck . . . 4D 158
WALLEND . . . 1E 88
Wall End Ct. *E6* . . . 1E 88
(off Wall End Rd.)
Wall End Rd. E6 . . . 7E 70
Waller Dr. HA6: Nwood . . . 2J 39
Waller Rd. SE14 . . . 1K 121
Wallers Cl. IG8: Wfd G . . . 6J 37
RM9: Dag . . . 1E 90
Waller Way SE10 . . . 7D 104
Wallflower St. W12 . . . 7B 80
Wallgrave Rd. SW5 . . . 4K 99
Wallingford Av. W10 . . . 5F 81
WALLINGTON . . . 6F 167
Wallington Cl. HA4: Ruis . . . 6E 38
Wallington Cnr. *SM6: Wall* . . . 4F 167
(off Manor Rd. Nth.)
Wallington Ct. *SM6: Wall* . . . 6F 167
(off Stanley Pk. Rd.)
WALLINGTON GREEN . . . 4F 167
Wallington Rd. IG3: Ilf . . . 7K 53
Wallington Sq. SM6: Wall . . . 6F 167
Wallis All. SE1 . . . 6D 14
Wallis Cl. SW11 . . . 3B 118
Wallis Ho. HA4: Ruis . . . 1F 57
SE14 . . . 1A 122
Wallis M. *N8* . . . 3A 48
(off Courcy Rd.)
Wallis Rd. E9 . . . 6B 68
TW6: H'row A . . . 5C 174
UB1: S'hall . . . 6F 77
Wallis's Cotts. SW2 . . . 7J 119
Wallman Pl. N22 . . . 1K 47
Wallorton Gdns. SW14 . . . 4K 115
Wallside EC2 . . . 6D 8
Wall St. N1 . . . 6D 66
Wallwood Rd. E11 . . . 7F 51
Wallwood St. E14 . . . 5B 86
Walmar Cl. EN4: Had W . . . 1G 21
Walmer Cl. BR6: Farnb . . . 4H 173
E4 . . . 2J 35
RM7: Mawney . . . 2H 55
Walmer Ct. *KT5: Surb* . . . 5E 150
(off Cranes Pk.)
Walmer Gdns. W13 . . . 2A 96
Walmer Ho. *W10* . . . 6F 81
(off Bramley Rd.)
Walmer Pl. W1 . . . 5E 4
Walmer Rd. W10 . . . 6E 80
W11 . . . 7G 81
Walmer St. W1 . . . 5E 4 (5D 82)
Walmer Ter. SE18 . . . 4G 107
Walmgate Rd. UB6: G'frd . . . 1B 78
Walmington Fold N12 . . . 6D 30
Walm La. NW2 . . . 6E 62
Walney Wlk. N1 . . . 6C 66
Walnut Av. UB7: W Dray . . . 3C 92
Walnut Cl. IG6: Ilf . . . 4G 53
SE8 . . . 6B 104
SM5: Cars . . . 5D 166
UB3: Hayes . . . 7G 75
Walnut Ct. E17 . . . 4E 50
W5 . . . 2E 96
W8 . . . 3K 99
(off St Mary's Ga.)
Walnut Flds. KT17: Ewe . . . 7B 164
Walnut Gdns. E15 . . . 5G 69
Walnut Gro. EN1: Enf . . . 5J 23
Walnut M. *N22* . . . 3A 48
(off High Rd.)
SM2: Sutt . . . 7A 166
Walnut Rd. E10 . . . 2C 68
Walnut Tree Av.
CR4: Mitc . . . 3C 154
(off Dearn Gdns.)
Walnut Tree Cl. BR7: Chst . . . 1H 161
SW13 . . . 1B 116
TW17: Shep . . . 3E 146
Walnut Tree Cotts. SW19 . . . 5G 135
Walnut Tree Ho. *SW10* . . . 6K 99
(off Tregunter Rd.)
Walnut Tree Rd. RM8: Dag . . . 2E 72
SE10 . . . 5G 105
(not continuous)
Walnut Tree Rd. TW5: Hest . . . 6D 94
TW8: Bford . . . 6E 96
TW17: Shep . . . 2E 146
Walnut Tree Wlk. SE11 . . . 3J 19 (4A 102)
Walnut Way HA4: Ruis . . . 6A 58
IG9: Buck H . . . 3G 37
Walpole Av. TW9: Kew . . . 2F 115
Walpole Cl. W13 . . . 2C 96
Walpole Ct. *NW6* . . . 7A 64
(off Fairfax Rd.)
TW2: Twick . . . 2J 131
W14 . . . 3F 99
(off Blythe Rd.)
Walpole Cres. TW11: Tedd . . . 5K 131
Walpole Gdns. TW2: Twick . . . 2J 131
W4 . . . 5J 97
Walpole Ho. *KT8: W Mole* . . . 5E 148
(off Approach Rd.)
SE1 . . . 7J 13
(off Westminster Bri. Rd.)
Walpole Lodge W13 . . . 1C 96
Walpole M. NW8 . . . 1B 82
SW19 . . . 6B 136
Walpole Pk. Summer Theatre . . . 1C 96
Walpole Pl. SE18 . . . 4F 107
TW11: Tedd . . . 5K 131
Walpole Rd. BR2: Brom . . . 5B 160
CR0: C'don . . . 2D 168
E6 . . . 7A 70
E17 . . . 4A 50
E18 . . . 1H 51
KT6: Surb . . . 7E 150
N17 . . . 2C 48
(not continuous)
SW19 . . . 6B 136
TW2: Twick . . . 2J 131
TW11: Tedd . . . 5K 131
Walpole St. SW3 . . . 5E 16 (5D 100)
Walrond Av. HA9: Wemb . . . 5E 60
Walsham Cl. N16 . . . 1G 67
SE28 . . . 7D 90
Walsham Ho. SE14 . . . 2K 121
SE17 . . . 5D 102
(off Blackwood St.)
Walsham Rd. SE14 . . . 2K 121
TW14: Felt . . . 7K 111
Walsingham NW8 . . . 1B 82
Walsingham Gdns. KT19: Ewe . . . 4A 164
Walsingham Lodge SW13 . . . 1C 116
Walsingham Mans. *SW6* . . . 7K 99
(off Fulham Rd.)
Walsingham Pk. BR7: Chst . . . 2H 161
Walsingham Pl. SW4 . . . 6E 118
Walsingham Rd. CR4: Mitc . . . 5D 154
E5 . . . 3G 67
EN2: Enf . . . 4J 23
W13 . . . 1A 96
Walsingham Wlk. DA17: Belv . . . 6G 109
Walston Ho. *SW1* . . . 5C 18
(off Aylesford St.)
Walter Besant Ho. *E1* . . . 3K 85
(off Bancroft Rd.)
Walter Ct. *W3* . . . 6J 79
(off Lynton Ter.)
Walter Grn. Ho. *SE15* . . . 1J 121
(off Lausanne Rd.)
Walter Ho. *SW10* . . . 7B 100
(off Riley St.)
Walter Hurford Pde. *E12* . . . 4E 70
(off Walton Rd.)
Walter Langley Ct. *SE16* . . . 2J 103
(off Brunel Rd.)
Walter Rodney Cl. E6 . . . 6D 70
Walter Savil Twr. *E17* . . . 6C 50
(off Colchester Rd.)
Walters Cl. *SE17* . . . 4D 102
(off Brandon St.)
UB3: Hayes . . . 2H 93
Walters Ho. *SE17* . . . 6B 102
(off Otto St.)

Walter Sickert Hall *N1* *1C 8*
(off Graham St.)
Walters Rd. EN3: Pond E 4D **24**
SE25 . . . . 4E **156**
Walter St. E2 . . . . 3K **85**
KT2: King T 1E **150**
Walters Way SE23 . . . . 6K **121**
Walters Yd. BR1: Brom 2J **159**
Walter Ter. E1 . . . . 6K **85**
Walterton Rd. W9 . . . . 4H **81**
Walter Wlk. HA8: Edg 6D **28**
Waltham Av. NW9 . . . . 6G **43**
UB3: Harl 3E **92**
Waltham Dr. HA8: Edg 2G **43**
Waltham Forest Pool & Track 2D **50**
Waltham Forest Theatre 2C **50**
Waltham Ho. NW8 . . . . 1A **82**
Waltham Pk. Way E17 . . . . 1C **50**
Waltham Rd. IG8: Wfd G 6H **37**
SM5: Cars 7B **154**
UB2: S'hall 3C **94**
WALTHAMSTOW 3C **50**
Walthamstow Av. E4 . . . . 6G **35**
Walthamstow Bus. Cen. E17 . . . . 2E **50**
Walthamstow Stadium (Greyhound) . . . 7J **35**
Waltham Way E4 . . . . 3G **35**
Waltheof Av. N17 . . . . 1D **48**
Waltheof Gdns. N17 . . . . 1D **48**
Walton Av. HA2: Harr 5D **58**
HA9: Wemb 3H **61**
KT3: N Mald 4B **152**
SM3: Cheam 3H **165**
Walton Bri. KT12: Walt T 7G **147**
TW17: Shep 7G **147**
Walton Bri. Rd. TW17: Shep 7G **147**
Walton Cl. *E5* *3K 67*
(off Orient Way)
HA1: Harr 4H **41**
NW2 . . . . 2D **62**
SW8 . . . . 7J **101**
Walton Ct. *CR2: S Croy* *5C 168*
(off Warham Rd.)
EN5: New Bar 5F **21**
NW6 . . . . *7A 64*
(off Fairfax Rd.)
Walton Cft. HA1: Harr 4J **59**
Walton Dr. HA1: Harr 4H **41**
NW10 . . . . 6K **61**
Walton Gdns. HA9: Wemb 2E **60**
TW13: Felt 4H **129**
W3 . . . . 5H **79**
Walton Grn. CR0: New Ad 7D **170**
Walton Ho. *E2* *3K 9*
(off Montclare St.)
E4 . . . . *5H 35*
(off Chingford Mt. Rd.)
E17 . . . . *3D 50*
(off The Drive)
SW1 . . . . *2E 16*
(off Walton St.)
Walton La. KT13: Weyb . . . . 7F **147** & 7G **147**
TW17: Shep 7F **147**
WALTON-ON-THAMES 7K **147**
Walton Pl. SW3 . . . . 1E **16** (3D **100**)
Walton Rd. DA14: Sidc 2C **144**
E12 . . . . 4E **70**
(not continuous)
E13 . . . . 2A **88**
HA1: Harr 4H **41**
KT8: W Mole, E Mos 4D **148**
KT12: Walt T 5A **148**
N15 . . . . 4F **49**
RM5: Col R 1F **55**
Walton Screen Cinema 7J **147**
Walton St. EN2: Enf 1J **23**
SW3 . . . . 3D **16** (4C **100**)
Walton Vs. *N1* *7E 66*
(off Downham Rd.)
Walton Way CR4: Mitc 4G **155**
W3 . . . . 5H **79**
Walt Whitman Cl. SE24 . . . . 4B **120**
WALWORTH 5C **102**
Walworth Pl. SE17 . . . . 5C **102**
Walworth Rd. SE1 . . . . 4C **102**
SE17 . . . . 4C **102**
Walwyn Av. BR1: Brom 3B **160**
Wanborough Dr. SW15 . . . . 1D **134**
Wanderer Dr. IG11: Bark 3C **90**
Wandle Bank CR0: Bedd 3J **167**
SW19 . . . . 7B **136**
Wandle Ct. CR0: Bedd 3J **167**
KT19: Ewe 4J **163**
Wandle Ct. Gdns. CR0: Bedd 3J **167**
Wandle Ho. BR1: Brom 5F **141**
NW8 . . . . *5C 4*
(off Penfold St.)
Wandle Industrial Mus.
(within The Vestry Hall Annexe)
. . . . 3D **154**
Wandle Meadow Nature Pk. 5A **136**
Wandle Pk. Trad. Est., The
CR0: C'don 1B **168**
Wandle Recreation Cen. 6K **117**
Wandle Rd. CR0: Bedd 3J **167**
CR0: C'don 3C **168**
SM4: Mord 4A **154**
SM6: Wall 3F **167**
SW17 . . . . 2C **136**
Wandle Side CR0: Wadd 3K **167**
SM6: Wall 3F **167**
Wandle Technology Pk.
CR4: Mitc 7D **154**
Wandle Trad. Est. CR4: Mitc 7D **154**
Wandle Way CR4: Mitc 5D **154**
SW18 . . . . 1K **135**
Wandon Rd. SW6 . . . . 7K **99**
(not continuous)
Wandsdown Pl. SW6 . . . . 7K **99**
WANDSWORTH 5K **117**
Wandsworth Bri. SW6 . . . . 3K **117**
Wandsworth Bri. Rd. SW6 . . . . 1K **117**
WANDSWORTH COMMON 1D **136**
Wandsworth Comn. W. Side
SW18 . . . . 5A **118**
WANDSWORTH GYRATORY 5K **117**
Wandsworth High St. SW18 . . . . 5J **117**
Wandsworth Mus. 5K **117**
Wandsworth Plain SW18 . . . . 5K **117**
Wandsworth Rd. SW8 . . . . . . 7E **18** (3F **119**)
Wangey Rd. RM6: Chad H 7D **54**
Wangford Ho. *SW9* *4B 120*
(off Loughborough Pk.)
Wanless Rd. SE24 . . . . 3C **120**
Wanley Rd. SE5 . . . . 4D **120**
Wanlip Rd. E13 . . . . 4K **87**
Wannock Gdns. IG6: Ilf 1F **53**
Wansbeck Ct. *EN2: Enf* *3G 23*
(off Waverley Rd.)
Wansbeck Rd. E9 . . . . 7B **68**
Wansey St. SE17 . . . . 4C **102**
Wansford Rd. IG8: Wfd G 1A **52**
WANSTEAD 6K **51**
Wanstead Cl. BR1: Brom 2A **160**
Wanstead Gdns. IG4: Ilf 6B **52**
Wanstead La. IG1: Ilf 6B **52**
Wanstead Leisure Cen. 6A **52**
Wanstead Pk. Av. E12 . . . . 1B **70**
Wanstead Pk. Rd. IG1: Ilf 6B **52**
Wanstead Pl. E11 . . . . 6J **51**
Wanstead Rd. BR1: Brom 2A **160**
Wansunt Rd. DA5: Bexl 1J **145**
Wantage Rd. SE12 . . . . 5H **123**
Wantz Rd. RM10: Dag 4H **73**
WAPPING 1H **103**
Wapping Dock St. E1 . . . . 1H **103**
Wapping High St. E1 . . . . 1G **103**
Wapping La. E1 . . . . 7H **85**
Wapping Wall E1 . . . . 1J **103**
Warbank La. KT2: King T 7B **134**
Warbeck Rd. W12 . . . . 2D **98**
Warberry Rd. N22 . . . . 1K **47**
Warboys App. KT2: King T 6H **133**
Warboys Cres. E4 . . . . 5K **35**
Warboys Rd. KT2: King T 6H **133**
Warburton Cl. HA3: Hrw W 6C **26**
N1 . . . . *6E 66*
(off Culford Rd.)
Warburton Ct. HA4: Ruis 2J **57**
Warburton Ho. *E8* *1H 85*
(off Warburton St.)
Warburton Rd. E8 . . . . 1H **85**
TW2: Whitt 1F **131**
Warburton St. E8 . . . . 1H **85**
Warburton Ter. E17 . . . . 2D **50**
Wardalls Gro. SE14 . . . . 7J **103**
Wardalls Ho. *SE8* *6B 104*
(off Staunton St.)
Ward Cl. CR2: S Croy 6E **168**
DA8: Erith 6K **109**
Wardell Cl. NW7 . . . . 7F **29**
Wardell Fld. NW9 . . . . 1A **44**
Wardell Ho. *SE10* *6E 104*
(off Welland St.)
Warden Av. HA2: Harr 1D **58**
Warden Rd. NW5 . . . . 6E **64**
Wardens Fld. Cl.
BR6: Chels 6J **173**
Wardens Gro. SE1 . . . . 5C **14** (1C **102**)
Wardle St. E9 . . . . 5K **67**
Wardley St. SW18 . . . . 7K **117**
Wardo Av. SW6 . . . . 1G **117**
Wardour M. W1 . . . . 1B **12**
Wardour St. W1 . . . . 7B **6** (6G **83**)
Ward Point
SE11 . . . . 4J **19** (4A **102**)
Ward Rd. E15 . . . . 1F **87**
N19 . . . . 3G **65**
SW19 . . . . 1A **154**
Wardrobe, The *TW9: Rich* *5D 114*
(off Old Palace Rd.)
Wardrobe Pl. EC4 . . . . 1B **14**
Wardrobe Ter. EC4 . . . . 2B **14**
Wards Rd. IG2: Ilf 7H **53**
Wards Wharf App. E16 . . . . 1B **106**
Ware Ct. HA8: Edg 4K **27**
SM1: Sutt 4H **165**
Wareham Cl. TW3: Houn 4F **113**
Wareham Ct. *N1* *7E 66*
(off Hertford Rd.)
Wareham Ho. SW8 . . . . 7K **101**
Warehouse Theatre 2D **168**
Warehouse Way E16 . . . . 7K **87**
Waremead Rd. IG2: Ilf 5F **53**
Warepoint Dr. SE28 . . . . 2H **107**
Warfield Rd. NW10 . . . . 3F **81**
TW12: Hamp 1F **149**
TW14: Felt 7G **111**
Warfield Yd. *NW10* *3F 81*
(off Warfield Rd.)
Wargrave Av. N15 . . . . 6F **49**
Wargrave Ho. *E2* *2J 9*
(off Navarre St.)
Wargrave Rd. HA2: Harr 3G **59**
Warham Rd. CR2: S Croy 5B **168**
HA3: W'stone 2K **41**
N4 . . . . 5A **48**
Warham St. SE5 . . . . 7B **102**
Waring & Gillow Est.
W3 . . . . 4G **79**
Waring Cl. BR6: Chels 6K **173**
Waring Dr. BR6: Chels 6K **173**
Waring Rd. DA14: Sidc 6C **144**
Waring St. SE27 . . . . 4C **138**
Warkworth Gdns.
TW7: Isle 7A **96**
Warkworth Rd. N17 . . . . 7J **33**
Warland Rd. SE18 . . . . 7H **107**
Warley Av. RM8: Dag 7F **55**
UB4: Hayes 6J **75**
Warley Cl. E10 . . . . 1B **68**
Warley Rd. IG5: Ilf 1E **52**
IG8: Wfd G 7E **36**
N9 . . . . 2D **34**
UB4: Hayes 6J **75**
Warley St. E2 . . . . 3K **85**
Warlingham Ct. SE13 . . . . 6E **122**
Warlingham Rd. CR7: Thor H 4B **156**
Warlock Rd. W9 . . . . 4H **81**
Warlters Cl. N7 . . . . 4J **65**
Warlters Rd. N7 . . . . 4J **65**
Warltersville Mans. N19 . . . . 7J **47**
Warltersville Rd. N19 . . . . 7J **47**
Warmington Cl. E5 . . . . 3K **67**
Warmington Rd. SE24 . . . . 6C **120**
Warmington St. E13 . . . . 4J **87**
Warmington Twr. SE14 . . . . 1A **122**
Warminster Gdns. SE25 . . . . 2G **157**
Warminster Rd. SE25 . . . . 2F **157**
Warminster Sq. SE25 . . . . 2G **157**
Warminster Way CR4: Mitc 1F **155**
Warmsworth *NW1* *1G 83*
(off Pratt St.)
Warmwell Av. NW9 . . . . 1A **44**
Warndon St. SE16 . . . . 4K **103**
Warneford Rd. HA3: Kent 3D **42**
Warneford St. E9 . . . . 1H **85**
Warne Pl. DA15: Sidc 6B **126**
Warner Av. SM3: Cheam 2G **165**
Warner Cl. E15 . . . . 5G **69**
NW9 . . . . 7B **44**
TW12: Hamp 5D **130**
UB3: Harl 7F **93**
Warner Ho. BR3: Beck 6D **140**
NW8 . . . . 3A **82**
SE13 . . . . *2D 122*
(off Russett Way)
Warner Pl. E2 . . . . 2G **85**
Warner Rd. BR1: Brom 7H **141**
E17 . . . . 4A **50**
N8 . . . . 4H **47**
SE5 . . . . 1C **120**
Warners Cl. IG8: Wfd G 5D **36**
Warners La. KT2: King T 4D **132**
Warners Path
IG8: Wfd G 5D **36**
Warner St. EC1 . . . . 4J **7** (4A **84**)
Warner Ter. *E14* *5D 86*
(off Broomfield St.)
Warner Yd. EC1 . . . . 4J **7**
Warnford Ct. *EC2* *7F 9*
(off Throgmorton Av.)
Warnford Ho. *SW15* *6A 116*
(off Tunworth Cres.)
Warnford Ind. Est. UB3: Hayes 2G **93**
Warnford Rd. BR6: Chels 5K **173**
Warnham *WC1* *2G 7*
(off Sidmouth St.)
Warnham Ct. Rd.
SM5: Cars 7D **166**
Warnham Ho. *SW2* *7K 119*
(off Up. Tulse Hill)
Warnham Rd. N12 . . . . 5H **31**
Warple M. W3 . . . . 2A **98**
Warple Way W3 . . . . 2A **98**
(not continuous)
Warren, The E12 . . . . 4C **70**
KT4: Wor Pk 4K **163**
SE7 . . . . 6A **106**
TW5: Hest 7D **94**
UB4: Hayes 6J **75**
Warren Av. BR1: Brom 7G **141**
BR6: Chels 5K **173**
CR2: Sels 7K **169**
E10 . . . . 3E **68**
TW10: Rich 4H **115**
Warren Cl. DA6: Bex 5G **127**
HA9: Wemb 2D **60**
N9 . . . . 7E **24**
SE21 . . . . 7C **120**
UB4: Yead 5A **76**

Warren Ct. BR3: Beck ... 7C 140
CR0: C'don ... 1E 168
N17 ... *3G 49*
(off High Cross Rd.)
NW1 ... *3B 6*
(off Warren St.)
W5 ... 5C 78
Warren Cres. N9 ... 7A 24
Warren Cutting KT2: King T ... 7K 133
Warrender Rd. N19 ... 3G 65
Warrender Way HA4: Ruis ... 7J 39
Warren Dr. HA4: Ruis ... 7B 40
UB6: G'frd ... 4F 77
Warren Dr., The E11 ... 7A 52
Warren Dr. Nth. KT5: Surb ... 1H 163
Warren Dr. Sth. KT5: Surb ... 1J 163
Warren Farm Cotts.
RM6: Chad H ... 4F 55
Warren Farm Sports Cen. ... 3H 95
Warren Flds. HA7: Stan ... 4H 27
Warren Footpath TW1: Twick ... 1C 132
Warren Gdns. BR6: Chels ... 5K 173
E15 ... 5F 69
Warren Ho. *N17* ... *3G 49*
(off High Cross Rd.)
W14 ... *4H 99*
(off Beckford Cl.)
Warren La. HA7: Stan ... 2F 27
SE18 ... 3F 107
Warren La. Ga. SE18 ... 3F 107
Warren M. W1 ... 4A 6 (4G 83)
Warren Pk. KT2: King T ... 6J 133
Warren Pk. Rd. SM1: Sutt ... 6B 166
Warren Pl. *E1* ... *6K 85*
(off Caroline St.)
Warren Pond Rd. E4 ... 1C 36
(not continuous)
Warren Ri. KT3: N Mald ... 1K 151
Warren Rd. BR2: Hayes ... 2J 171
BR6: Chels ... 5K 173
CR0: C'don ... 1E 168
DA6: Bex ... 5G 127
DA14: Sidc ... 3C 144
E4 ... 2K 35
E10 ... 3E 68
E11 ... 6A 52
(not continuous)
IG6: Ilf ... 5H 53
KT2: King T ... 6J 133
NW2 ... 2B 62
Warren Rd. SW19 ... 6C 136
TW2: Whitt ... 6G 113
TW15: Ashf ... 7G 129
UB10: Ick ... 4A 56
WD23: B Hea ... 1B 26
Warren Sports Cen. ... 5F 55
Warrens Shawe La. HA8: Edg ... 2C 28
Warren St. W1 ... 4A 6 (4G 83)
Warren Ter. RM6: Chad H ... 4D 54
Warren Wlk. SE7 ... 6A 106
Warren Way HA8: Edg ... 2H 43
NW7 ... 6B 30
Warren Wood Cl. BR2: Hayes ... 2H 171
Warriner Dr. N9 ... 3B 34
Warriner Gdns. SW11 ... 1D 118
Warrington Ct. *CR0: Wadd* ... *3B 168*
(off Warrington Rd.)
Warrington Cres. W9 ... 4A 82
Warrington Gdns. W9 ... 4A 82
Warrington Rd. CR0: Wadd ... 3B 168
HA1: Harr ... 5J 41
RM8: Dag ... 2D 72
TW10: Rich ... 5D 114
Warrington Sq. RM8: Dag ... 2D 72
Warrior Cl. SE28 ... 1H 107
Warrior Sq. E12 ... 4E 70
Warsaw Cl. HA4: Ruis ... 6K 57
Warspite Ho. *E14* ... *4D 104*
(off Cahir St.)
Warspite Rd. SE18 ... 3C 106
Warton Rd. E15 ... 1E 86
Warwall E6 ... 6F 89
Warwark Ct. KT6: Surb ... 2E 162
Warwick *W14* ... *4H 99*
(off Kensington Village)
Warwick Av. HA2: Harr ... 4D 58
HA8: Edg ... 3C 28
W2 ... 4A 82
W9 ... 4K 81
Warwick Bldg. SW8 ... 6F 101
Warwick Chambers *W8* ... *3J 99*
(off Pater St.)
Warwick Cl. DA5: Bexl ... 7F 127
EN4: E Barn ... 5G 21
TW12: Hamp ... 7G 131
W8 ... *3H 99*
(off Kensington High St.)
WD23: B Hea ... 1D 26
Warwick Ct. BR2: Brom ... 2G 159
EC4 ... *1B 14*
(off Warwick La.)
EN5: New Bar ... *5E 20*
(off Station Rd.)
HA3: W'stone ... 3J 41
N11 ... 6C 32
UB5: N'olt ... *5E 58*
(off Newmarket Av.)
W7 ... *6K 77*
(off Copley Cl.)
WC1 ... 6H 7 (5K 83)
Warwick Cres. UB4: Hayes ... 4H 75
W2 ... 5A 82
Warwick Dene W5 ... 1E 96
Warwick Dr. SW15 ... 3D 116
Warwick Est. W2 ... 5K 81
Warwick Gdns. CR7: Thor H ... 3A 156
EN5: Barn ... 1C 20
IG1: Ilf ... 1F 71
KT7: T Ditt ... 5K 149
N4 ... 5C 48
W14 ... 3H 99
Warwick Gro. E5 ... 1H 67
KT5: Surb ... 7F 151
Warwick Ho. *E16* ... *1J 105*
(off Wesley Av.)
KT2: King T ... *1E 150*
(off Acre Rd.)
SW9 ... 2A 120
Warwick Ho. St. SW1 ... 4D 12 (1H 101)
Warwick La. EC4 ... 7B 8 (6B 84)
Warwick Lodge TW2: Twick ... 3F 131
Warwick Mans *SW5* ... *4J 99*
(off Cromwell Cres.)
Warwick Pde. HA3: Kent ... 2B 42
Warwick Pas. *EC4* ... *7B 8*
(off Old Bailey)
Warwick Pl. KT7: T Ditt ... 6A 150
W5 ... 2D 96
W9 ... 5A 82
Warwick Pl. Nth. SW1 ... 4A 18 (4G 101)
Warwick Rd. CR7: Thor H ... 3A 156
DA14: Sidc ... 5B 144
DA16: Well ... 3C 126
E4 ... 5H 35
E11 ... 5K 51
E12 ... 5C 70
E15 ... 6H 69
E17 ... 1B 50
EN5: New Bar ... 4E 20
KT1: Ham W ... 1C 150
KT3: N Mald ... 3J 151
KT7: T Ditt ... 5K 149
N11 ... 6C 32
N18 ... 4K 33
SE20 ... 3H 157
SM1: Sutt ... 4A 166
SW5 ... 4H 99
TW2: Twick ... 1J 131
TW4: Houn ... 3K 111
TW6: H'row A ... 5C 174
Warwick Rd. TW15: Ashf ... 5A 128
UB2: S'hall ... 3D 94
UB7: W Dray ... 2A 92
W5 ... 2D 96
W14 ... 4H 99
Warwick Row SW1 ... 1K 17 (3F 101)
Warwickshire Path SE8 ... 7B 104
Warwickshire Rd. N16 ... 4E 66
Warwick Sq. EC4 ... 7B 8 (6B 84)
SW1 ... 5A 18 (5G 101)
(not continuous)
Warwick Sq. M. SW1 ... 4A 18 (4G 101)
Warwick St. W1 ... 2B 12 (7G 83)
Warwick Ter. *E17* ... *5F 51*
(off Lea Bri. Rd.)
SE18 ... 6H 107
Warwick Way SW1 ... 5J 17 (5F 101)
Warwick Yd. EC1 ... 4D 8 (4C 84)
Wasdale *NW1* ... *3F 83*
(off Cumberland Mkt.)
Washbourne Ct. *N9* ... *2B 34*
(off Acton Cl.)
Washington Av. E12 ... 4D 70
Washington Bldg. *SE10* ... *1D 122*
(off Deal's Gateway)
Washington Cl. E3 ... 3D 86
Washington Ho. *E17* ... *2B 50*
(off Priory Ct.)
SW3 ... *7E 10*
(off Basil St.)
Washington Rd. E6 ... 7A 70
E18 ... 2H 51
KT1: King T ... 2G 151
KT4: Wor Pk ... 2D 164
SW13 ... 7C 98
Wasp Rd. TW6: H'row A ... 5C 174
Wastdale Rd. SE23 ... 1K 139
Watch, The N12 ... 4F 31
Watchfield Ct. W4 ... 5J 97
Watcombe Cotts. TW9: Kew ... 6G 97
Watcombe Pl. SE25 ... 5H 157
Watcombe Rd. SE25 ... 5H 157
Waterbank Rd. SE6 ... 3D 140
Waterbeach Rd. RM9: Dag ... 6C 72
Water Brook La. NW4 ... 5E 44
Watercress Pl. N1 ... 7E 66
Waterdale Rd. SE2 ... 6A 108
Waterden Ct. W11 ... 1G 99
Waterden Rd. E15 ... 5C 68
Waterer Ho. SE6 ... 4E 140
Waterer Ri. SM6: Wall ... 6H 167
Waterfall Cl. N14 ... 3B 32
Waterfall Cotts. SW19 ... 6B 136
Waterfall Rd. N11 ... 4A 32
N14 ... 4A 32
SW19 ... 6B 136
Waterfall Ter. SW17 ... 6C 136
Waterfall Wlk. N14 ... 1A 32
Waterfield Cl. DA17: Belv ... 3G 109
SE28 ... 1B 108
Waterfield Gdns. SE25 ... 4D 156
Waterford Ho. *W11* ... *7H 81*
(off Kensington Pk. Rd.)
Waterford Rd. SW6 ... 7K 99
(not continuous)
Waterford Way NW10 ... 5D 62
Waterfront W6 ... 6E 98
Waterfront Leisure Cen.
Woolwich ... 3E 106
Waterfront Studios Bus. Cen.
E16 ... *1J 105*
(off Dock Rd.)
Water Gdns. HA7: Stan ... 6G 27
Water Gdns., The W2 ... 7D 4 (6C 82)
Watergardens, The KT2: King T ... 6J 133
Watergate EC4 ... 2A 14 (7B 84)
Watergate St. SE8 ... 6C 104
Watergate Wlk. WC2 ... 4F 13 (1J 101)
Waterhall Av. E4 ... 4B 36
Waterhall Cl. E17 ... 1K 49
Waterhead *NW1* ... *1A 6*
(off Varndell St.)
Waterhouse Cl. E16 ... 5B 88
NW3 ... 5B 64
W6 ... 4F 99
Waterhouse Sq. EC1 ... 6J 7 (5A 84)
Wateridge Cl. E14 ... 3C 104
Water La. DA14: Sidc ... 2F 145
E15 ... 6G 69
EC3 ... 3H 15 (7E 84)
IG3: Ilf ... 3J 71
KT1: King T ... 1D 150
N9 ... 1C 34
NW1 ... 7F 65
SE14 ... 7J 103
TW1: Twick ... 1A 132
TW9: Rich ... 5D 114
Water Lily Cl. UB2: S'hall ... 2G 95
Waterloo Bri. SE1 ... 7K 83
WC2 ... 3G 13 (7K 83)
Waterloo Cl. E9 ... 5J 67
TW14: Felt ... 1H 129
Waterloo Gdns. E2 ... 2J 85
N1 ... 7B 66
RM7: Rom ... 6K 55
Waterloo Pas. NW6 ... 7H 63
Waterloo Pl. *SM5: Cars* ... *3D 166*
(off Wrythe La.)
SW1 ... 4C 12 (1H 101)
TW9: Rich ... 4E 114
Waterloo Rd. E6 ... 7A 70
E7 ... 5H 69
E10 ... 7C 50
IG6: Ilf ... 2G 53
NW2 ... 1C 62
RM7: Rom, Rush G ... 5K 55
SE1 ... 4H 13 (1K 101)
SM1: Sutt ... 5B 166
Waterloo Ter. N1 ... 7B 66
Waterlow Ct. NW11 ... 7K 45
Waterlow Rd. N19 ... 1G 65
Waterman Bldg. E14 ... 2B 104
Watermans Art Cen., Cinema & Theatre
... 6E 96
Watermans Cl. KT2: King T ... 7E 132
Watermans Ct. *TW8: Bford* ... *6D 96*
(off High St.)
Watermans M. W5 ... 7E 78
Waterman's Quay SW6 ... 2A 118
Waterman St. SW15 ... 3F 117
Watermans Wlk. EC4 ... 3E 14
SE16 ... 2A 104
Waterman Way E1 ... 1H 103
Watermark Ct. *RM6: Chad H* ... *6B 54*
(off Quarles Pk. Rd.)
Watermead TW14: Felt ... 1G 129
Watermead Ho. E9 ... 5A 68
Watermead La. SM5: Cars ... 7D 154
Watermead Lodge *SE16* ... *1K 103*
(off Princes Riverside Rd.)
Watermeadow La. SW6 ... 2A 118
Watermead Rd. SE6 ... 4E 140
Watermead Way N17 ... 3H 49
Watermen's Sq. SE20 ... 7J 139
Water M. SE15 ... 4J 121
Watermill Bus. Cen. EN3: Brim ... 2G 25
Watermill Cl. TW10: Ham ... 3C 132
Water Mill Ho.
TW13: Hanw ... 2E 130
Watermill La. N18 ... 5K 33
Watermill Way SW19 ... 1A 154
TW13: Hanw ... 2D 130
Watermint Quay N16 ... 7G 49
Water Rd. HA0: Wemb ... 1F 79
Water's Edge *SW6* ... *1E 116*
(off Palemead Cl.)
Watersedge KT19: Ewe ... 4J 163
Watersfield Way
HA8: Edg ... 7J 27
Waters Gdns. RM10: Dag ... 5G 73

Waterside BR3: Beck 1B 158
E17 6J 49
N1 2C 84
UB7: Harm 3D 174
W2 6A 4
Waterside Av. *BR3: Beck* *5E 158*
(off Adamson Way)
Waterside Bus. Cen. TW7: Isle 4B 114
Waterside Cl. E3 1B 86
IG11: Bark 4A 72
KT6: Surb 2E 162
SE16 2G 103
SE28 1K 107
UB5: N'olt 3D 76
Waterside Ct. *SM5: Cars* *3E 166*
(off Millpond Pl.)
Waterside Dr. KT12: Walt T 5J 147
Waterside Ho. *E14* *2D 104*
(off Admirals Way)
Waterside Pl. NW1 1E 82
Waterside Point SW11 7C 100
Waterside Rd. UB2: S'hall 3E 94
Waterside Twr. *SW6* *2A 118*
(off The Boulevard)
Waterside Trad. Cen. W7 3J 95
Waterside Way SW17 4A 136
Watersmeet Way SE28 6C 90
Waterson St. E2 1H 9 (3E 84)
Waters Pl. SW15 2E 116
Watersplash Cl. KT1: King T 3E 150
Watersplash La. TW5: Cran 5K 93
UB3: Harl 4J 93
Watersplash Rd.
TW17: Shep 5C 146
Waters Rd. KT1: King T 2H 151
SE6 3G 141
Waters Sq. KT1: King T 3H 151
Water St. WC2 2J 13
Water Twr. Cl. UB8: Uxb 5A 56
Water Twr. Hill CR0: C'don 4D 168
Water Twr. Pl. N1 1A 84
Waterview Cl. DA6: Bex 5D 126
Waterview Ho. *E14* *5A 86*
(off Carr St.)
Waterway Av. SE13 3D 122
Waterways Bus. Cen.
EN3: Enf L 1G 25
WATERWORKS CORNER 1G 51
Waterworks La. E5 2K 67
Waterworks Rd. SW2 6K 119
Waterworks Yd. *CR0: C'don* *3C 168*
(off Surrey St.)
Watery La. DA14: Sidc 6B 144
SW20 2H 153
UB3: Harl 5G 93
(not continuous)
UB5: Yead 2A 76
Wates Way CR4: Mitc 6D 154
Wateville Rd. N17 1C 48
Watford By-Pass HA8: Edg 1G 27
Watford Cl. SW11 1C 118
Watford Rd. E16 5J 87
HA0: Wemb 2A 60
HA1: Harr 7A 42
Watford Way NW4 4C 44
NW7 4F 29
Watkin Rd. HA9: Wemb 3H 61
Watkins Cl. HA6: Nwood 1H 39
Watkins Ho. *E14* *2E 104*
(off Manchester Rd.)
Watkinson Rd. N7 6K 65
WATLING 7E 28
Watling Av. HA8: Edg 1J 43
Watling Ct. EC4 1D 14
Watling Farm Cl.
HA7: Stan 1H 27
Watling Gdns. NW2 6G 63
Watling Ga. NW9 4A 44
Watling Ho. *SE1* *4C 102*
(off New Kent Rd.)
Watlings Cl. CR0: C'don 6A 158
Watling St. DA6: Bex 4H 127
(not continuous)
EC4 1D 14 (6C 84)
SE15 6E 102
Watlington Gro. SE26 5A 140
Watney Cotts. SW14 3J 115
Watney Mkt. E1 6H 85
Watney Rd. SW14 3J 115
Watney's Rd. CR4: Mitc 5H 155
Watney St. E1 6H 85
Watson Av. E6 7E 70
SM3: Cheam 2G 165
Watson Cl. N16 5D 66
SW19 6C 136
Watson's M. W1 6D 4 (5C 82)
Watsons Rd. N22 1K 47
Watsons St. SE8 7C 104
Watson St. E13 2K 87
Wattisfield Rd. E5 3J 67
Watts Cl. N15 5E 48
Wattsdown Cl. E13 1J 87
Watts Gro. E3 5C 86
Watts Ho. *W10* *5G 81*
(off Wornington Rd.)
Watts La. BR7: Chst 1F 161
TW11: Tedd 5A 132
Watts Point *E13* *1J 87*
(off Brooks Rd.)
Watts Rd. KT7: T Ditt 7A 150
Watts St. E1 1H 103
SE15 1F 121
Wat Tyler Ho. *N8* *3J 47*
(off Boyton Rd.)
Wat Tyler Rd. SE3 2E 122
SE10 2E 122
Wauthier Cl. N13 5G 33
Wavel Ct. *CR0: C'don* *5D 168*
(off Hurst Rd.)
E1 *1J 103*
(off Garnet St.)
Wavelengths Leisure Pool 7C 104
Wavell Dr. DA15: Sidc 6J 125
Wavel M. N8 4H 47
NW6 7K 63
Wavel Pl. SE26 4F 139
Wavendon Av. W4 5K 97
Waveney Av. SE15 4H 121
Waveney Cl. E1 1G 103
Waveney Ho. SE15 4H 121
Waverley Av. E4 4G 35
E17 3F 51
HA9: Wemb 5F 61
KT5: Surb 6H 151
SM1: Sutt 2K 165
TW2: Whitt 1D 130
Waverley Cl. BR2: Brom 5B 160
E18 1A 52
KT8: W Mole 5E 148
UB3: Harl 4F 93
Waverley Ct. EN2: Enf 3G 23
NW3 6D 64
NW6 7G 63
SE26 5J 139
Waverley Cres. SE18 5H 107
Waverley Gdns. E6 5C 88
HA6: Nwood 1J 39
IG6: Ilf 2G 53
IG11: Bark 2J 89
NW10 2F 79
Waverley Gro. N3 3F 45
Waverley Ind. Est.
HA1: Harr 3H 41
Waverley Pl. N4 2B 66
NW8 2B 82
Waverley Rd. E17 3E 50
E18 1A 52
EN2: Enf 3G 23
HA2: Harr 2C 58
KT17: Ewe 5D 164
Waverley Rd. N8 6J 47
N17 7C 34
SE18 5G 107
SE25 4H 157
UB1: S'hall 7E 76
Waverley Vs. N17 2F 49
Waverley Way SM5: Cars 6C 166
Waverton Ho. E3 1B 86
Waverton Rd. SW18 7A 118
Waverton St. W1 4J 11 (1E 100)
Wavertree Ct. SW2 1J 137
Wavertree Rd. E18 2J 51
SW2 1K 137
Waxham NW3 5D 64
Waxlow Cres. UB1: S'hall 6E 76
Waxlow Ho. UB4: Yead 5B 76
Waxlow Rd. NW10 2J 79
Waxlow Way UB5: N'olt 4D 76
Waxwell Cl. HA5: Pinn 2B 40
Waxwell Farm Ho. HA5: Pinn 2B 40
Waxwell La. HA5: Pinn 2B 40
Wayborne Gro. HA4: Ruis 6E 38
Waye Av. TW5: Cran 1J 111
Wayfarer Rd.
TW6: H'row A 5C 174
UB5: N'olt 3B 76
Wayfield Link SE9 6H 125
Wayford St. SW11 2C 118
Wayland Av. E8 5G 67
Wayland Ho. *SW9* *2A 120*
(off Robsart St.)
Waylands UB3: Hayes 5F 75
Waylands Mead BR3: Beck 1D 158
Waylett Ho. SE11 6J 19
Waylett Pl. HA0: Wemb 4D 60
SE27 3B 138
Wayman Ct. E8 6H 67
Wayne Cl. BR6: Orp 3K 173
Wayne Kirkum Way NW6 5H 63
Waynflete Av. CR0: Wadd 3B 168
Waynflete Ho. *SE1* *5C 14*
(off Union St.)
Waynflete Sq. W10 7F 81
Waynflete St. SW18 2A 136
Wayside CR0: New Ad 6D 170
NW11 1G 63
SW14 5J 115
Wayside Cl. N14 6B 22
Wayside Commercial Cen.
IG11: Bark 1K 89
Wayside Ct. HA9: Wemb 3G 61
TW1: Twick 6C 114
Wayside Gdns. RM10: Dag 5G 73
Wayside Gro. SE9 4D 142
Wayside M. IG2: Ilf 5E 52
Weald, The BR7: Chst 6D 142
Weald Cl. BR2: Brom 2C 172
SE16 5H 103
Weald La. HA3: Hrw W 2H 41
Weald Ri. HA3: Hrw W 7E 26
Weald Rd. UB10: Hil 2C 74
Weald Sq. E5 2G 67
WEALDSTONE 3J 41
Wealdstone Rd.
SM3: Sutt 2H 165
Weald Way RM7: Rom 6H 55
UB4: Hayes 3G 75
Wealdwood Gdns.
HA5: Hat E 6A 26
Weale Rd. E4 3A 36
Weall Ct. HA5: Pinn 4C 40
Weardale Gdns. EN2: Enf 1J 23
Weardale Rd. SE13 4F 123
Wearmouth Ho. *E3* *5B 86*
(off Joseph St.)
Wear Pl. E2 3H 85
(not continuous)
Wearside Rd. SE13 4D 122
Weatherbury *W2* *6J 81*
(off Talbot Rd.)
Weatherbury Ho. *N19* *3H 65*
(off Wedmore St.)
Weatherley Cl. E3 5B 86
Weaver Cl. CR0: C'don 4F 169
E6 7F 89
Weavers Almshouses *E11* *6H 51*
(off Cambridge Rd.)
Weavers Cl. TW7: Isle 4J 113
Weavers Ho. *E11* *6J 51*
(off New Wanstead)
Weavers La. SE1 5H 15 (1E 102)
Weavers Ter. *SW6* *6J 99*
(off Micklethwaite Rd.)
Weaver St. E1 4G 85
Weavers Way NW1 1H 83
Weaver Wlk. SE27 4C 138
Webb Cl. W10 4E 80
Webb Ct. *SE28* *7B 90*
(off Attlee Rd.)
Webber Ho. *IG11: Bark* *7G 71*
(off North St.)
Webber Row SE1 1K 19 (3A 102)
Webber St. SE1 6K 13 (2A 102)
Webb Est. E5 7G 49
Webb Gdns. E13 4J 87
Webb Ho. *RM10: Dag* *3G 73*
(off Kershaw Rd.)
SW8 7H 101
TW13: Hanw 3C 130
Webb Pl. NW10 3B 80
Webb Rd. SE3 6H 105
Webbscroft Rd. RM10: Dag 4H 73
Webbs Rd. SW11 4D 118
UB4: Yead 3K 75
Webb St. SE1 3E 102
Webheath NW6 7H 63
(not continuous)
Webster Gdns. W5 1D 96
Webster Rd. E11 3E 68
SE16 3G 103
Weddell Ho. *E1* *4K 85*
(off Duckett St.)
Wedderburn Ho. *SW1* *5G 17*
(off Lwr. Sloane St.)
Wedderburn Rd. IG11: Bark 1J 89
NW3 5B 64
Wedgewood Ct. *BR2: Brom* *3H 159*
(off Cumberland Rd.)
DA5: Bexl 7F 127
Wedgewood Ho. *SW1* *6K 17*
(off Churchill Gdns.)
Wedgewood M. W1 1D 12 (6H 83)
Wedgwood Ho. *E2* *3K 85*
(off Warley St.)
SE11 2J 19
Wedgwood Wlk. *NW6* *5K 63*
(off Dresden Cl.)
Wedgwood Way SE19 7C 138
Wedlake St. W10 4G 81
Wedmore Av. IG5: Ilf 1E 52
Wedmore Gdns. N19 2H 65
Wedmore M. N19 3H 65
Wedmore Rd. UB6: G'frd 3H 77
Wedmore St. N19 3H 65
Weech Rd. NW6 4J 63
Weedington Rd. NW5 5E 64
Weedon Ho. W12 6C 80
Weekley Sq. SW11 3B 118
Weigall Rd. SE12 5J 123
Weighhouse St. W1 1H 11 (6E 82)
Weighton M. SE20 2H 157
Weighton Rd. HA3: Hrw W 1H 41
SE20 2H 157
Weihurst Ct. SM1: Sutt 5C 166
Weihurst Gdns.
SM1: Sutt 5B 166
Weimar St. SW15 3G 117
Weirdale Av. N20 2J 31
Weir Hall Av. N18 6J 33
Weir Hall Gdns. N18 5J 33

Weir Hall Rd. N17 5J 33
N18 5J 33
Weir Rd. DA5: Bexl 7H 127
KT12: Walt T 6J 147
SW12 7G 119
SW19 3K 135
Weir's Pas. NW1 1D 6 (3H 83)
Weiss Rd. SW15 3F 117
Welbeck Av. BR1: Brom 4J 141
DA15: Sidc 1A 144
UB4: Yead 4K 75
Welbeck Cl. KT3: N Mald 5B 152
KT17: Ewe 7C 164
N12 5G 31
Welbeck Ct. W14 4H 99
(off Addison Bri. Pl.)
Welbeck Ho. W1 7J 5
(off Welbeck St.)
Welbeck Rd. E6 3B 88
EN4: E Barn 6H 21
HA2: Harr 1F 59
SM1: Sutt 2B 166
SM5: Cars 2B 166
Welbeck St. W1 6H 5 (5E 82)
Welbeck Vs. N21 2H 33
Welbeck Wlk. SM5: Cars 1B 166
Welbeck Way W1 7J 5 (6F 83)
Welbury Ct. E8 7E 66
(off Kingsland Rd.)
Welby Ho. N19 7H 47
Welby St. SE5 1B 120
Welch Pl. HA5: Pinn 1A 40
Welcome Ct. E17 7C 50
(off Boundary Rd.)
Weldon Cl. HA4: Ruis 6K 57
Weldon Ct. N21 5E 22
Weldon Dr. KT8: W Mole 4D 148
Weld Pl. N11 5A 32
(not continuous)
Welfare Rd. E15 7G 69
Welford Cl. E5 3K 67
Welford Ct. NW1 7F 65
(off Castlehaven Rd.)
SW8 2G 119
W9 5J 81
(off Elmfield Way)
Welford Ho. UB5: N'olt 4D 76
Welford Pl. SW19 4G 135
Welham Rd. SW16 5E 136
SW17 5E 136
Welhouse Rd. SM5: Cars 1C 166
Wellacre Rd. HA3: Kent 6B 42
Wellan Cl. DA15: Sidc 5B 126
Welland Ct. SE6 2B 140
(off Oakham Cl.)
Welland Gdns. UB6: G'frd 2K 77
Welland Ho. SE15 4J 121
Welland M. E1 1G 103
Welland Rd. TW6: H'row A 5C 174
Wellands Cl. BR1: Brom 2D 160
Welland St. SE10 6E 104
Well App. EN5: Barn 5A 20
Wellbrook Rd. BR6: Farnb 4E 172
Wellby Cl. N9 1B 34
Wellby Ct. E13 1A 88
Well Cl. HA4: Ruis 3C 58
SW16 4K 137
Wellclose Sq. E1 7G 85
(not continuous)
Wellclose St. E1 7G 85
E3 2A 86
(off Driffield Rd)
Wellcome Collection 3C 6
Wellcome Mus., The 7H 7
(within Royal College of Surgeons)
Well Cott. Cl. E11 6A 52
Well Ct. EC4 1D 14 (6C 84)
(not continuous)
Welldon Ct. HA1: Harr 5J 41
Welldon Cres. HA1: Harr 5J 41
Weller Ct. W11 1H 99
(off Ladbroke Rd.)
Weller Ho. SE16 2G 103
(off George Row)
Weller M. BR2: Brom 4K 159
Weller St. SE1 6C 14 (2C 102)
Welles Ct. E14 7C 86
(off Premiere Pl.)
Wellesley Av. W6 3D 98
Wellesley Cl. SE7 5A 106
Wellesley Ct. NW2 2C 62
SM3: Sutt 1G 165
W9 3A 82
Wellesley Ct. Rd. CR0: C'don 2D 168
Wellesley Cres. TW2: Twick 2J 131
Wellesley Gro. CR0: C'don 2D 168
Wellesley Ho. NW1 2D 6
(off Wellesley Pl.)
SW1 5J 17
(off Ebury Bri. Rd.)
Wellesley Mans. W14 5H 99
(off Edith Vs.)
Wellesley Pde. TW2: Twick 3J 131
Wellesley Pk. M. EN2: Enf 2G 23
Wellesley Pas. CR0: C'don 2C 168
Wellesley Pl. NW1 2C 6 (3H 83)
NW5 5E 64
Wellesley Rd. CR0: C'don 1C 168
E11 5J 51
E17 6C 50
HA1: Harr 5J 41
IG1: Ilf 2F 71
N22 2A 48
NW5 5E 64
SM2: Sutt 6A 166
(not continuous)
TW2: Twick 3H 131
W4 5G 97
Wellesley St. E1 5K 85
Wellesley Ter. N1 1D 8 (3C 84)
Wellfield Av. N10 3F 47
Wellfield Rd. SW16 4J 137
Wellfield Wlk. SW16 4K 137
Wellfit St. SE24 3B 120
Wellgarth UB6: G'frd 6B 60
Wellgarth Rd. NW11 1K 63
Well Gro. N20 1F 31
Well Hall Pde. SE9 4D 124
Well Hall Rd. SE9 3C 124
WELL HALL RDBT. 4C 124
Wellhouse La. EN5: Barn 4A 20
Wellhouse Rd. BR3: Beck 4C 158
Wellhurst Cl. BR6: Chels 7K 173
WELLING 3B 126
Welling High St. DA16: Well 3B 126
Wellings Ho. UB3: Hayes 1K 93
Welling Sq. N1 1J 83
Wellington N8 4J 47
(not continuous)
Wellington Arch 6H 11 (2E 100)
Wellington Av. DA15: Sidc 6A 126
E4 2H 35
HA5: Hat E 1D 40
KT4: Wor Pk 3E 164
N9 3C 34
N15 6F 49
TW3: Houn 5E 112
Wellington Bldgs. SW1 6H 17 (5E 100)
Wellington Cl. KT12: Walt T 7H 147
RM10: Dag 7J 73
SE14 1K 121
W11 6J 81
Wellington Ct. HA5: Hat E 1D 40
(off Wellington Rd.)
NW8 2B 82
(off Wellington Rd.)
SW1 7E 10
(off Knightsbridge)
SW6 1K 117
(off Maltings Pl.)
Wellington Ct. TW12: Ham H 5H 131
TW15: Ashf 5A 128
TW19: Stanw 7A 110
Wellington Cres.
KT3: N Mald 3J 151
Wellington Dr. RM10: Dag 7J 73
Wellington Gdns. SE7 6A 106
TW2: Twick 4H 131
Wellington Gro. SE10 7F 105
Wellington Ho. E16 1J 105
(off Pepys Cres.)
NW3 6D 64
(off Eton Rd.)
SE17 6C 102
(off Arnside St.)
UB5: N'olt 7E 58
(off The Farmlands)
W5 3E 78
Wellington Mans. E10 1C 68
SE7 5A 106
(off Wellington Gdns.)
W14 6H 99
(off Queen's Club Mans.)
Wellington M. N7 6K 65
(off Roman Way)
SE7 6A 106
SE22 4G 121
SW16 3H 137
Wellington Monument 6H 11
Wellington Mus. 6H 11 (2E 100)
Wellington Pde. DA15: Sidc 5A 126
Wellington Pk. Est. NW2 2C 62
Wellington Pas. E11 5J 51
(off Wellington Rd.)
Wellington Pl. N2 5C 46
NW8 1B 4 (3B 82)
Wellington Rd. BR2: Brom 4A 160
CR0: C'don 7B 156
DA5: Bexl 5D 126
DA17: Belv 5F 109
E6 1D 88
E7 4H 69
E10 1A 68
E11 5J 51
E17 4A 50
EN1: Enf 5K 23
HA3: W'stone 3J 41
HA5: Hat E 1D 40
NW8 1B 4 (2B 82)
NW10 3F 81
SW19 2J 135
TW2: Twick 5H 131
TW6: H'row A 5C 174
(off Wallis Rd.)
TW6: H'row A 6D 174
(off Whittle Rd.)
TW12: Ham H 5H 131
TW14: Felt 5G 111
TW15: Ashf 5A 128
W5 3C 96
Wellington Rd. Nth.
TW4: Houn 3D 112
Wellington Rd. Sth.
TW4: Houn 4D 112
Wellington Row E2 1K 9 (3F 85)
Wellington Sq. SW3 5E 16 (5D 100)
Wellington St. IG11: Bark 1G 89
SE18 4E 106
WC2 2G 13 (7K 83)
Wellington Ter. E1 1H 103
HA1: Harr 1H 59
N8 3A 48
(off Turnpike La.)
W2 7J 81
Wellington Way E3 3C 86
Welling United FC (Park View Road)
3C 126
Welling Way DA16: Well 3G 125
SE9 3G 125
Well La. SW14 5J 115
Wellmeadow Rd. SE13 6G 123
(not continuous)
W7 4A 96
Wellow Wlk. SM5: Cars 1B 166
Well Pl. NW3 3B 64
Well Rd. EN5: Barn 5A 20
NW3 3B 64
Wells, The N14 7C 22
Wells Cl. CR2: S Croy 5E 168
UB5: Yead 3A 76
Wells Ct. BR2: Brom 2F 159
NW6 2J 81
(off Cambridge Av.)
Wells Dr. NW9 1K 61
Wells Gdns. IG1: Ilf 7C 52
RM10: Dag 5H 73
Wells Ho. BR1: Brom 5K 141
(off Pike Cl.)
EC1 1K 7
(off Spa Grn. Est.)
IG11: Bark 7A 72
(off Margaret Bondfield Av.)
SE16 3J 103
(off Howland Est.)
W5 1D 96
(off Grove Rd.)
W10 4G 81
(off Wornington Rd.)
Wells Ho. Rd. NW10 5A 80
Wellside Cl. EN5: Barn 4A 20
Wellside Gdns. SW14 4J 115
Wells M. W1 6B 6 (5G 83)
Wellsmoor Gdns. BR1: Brom 3E 160
Wells Pk. Rd. SE26 3G 139
Wells Path UB4: Hayes 3G 75
Wells Pl. SW18 7A 118
Wellspring Cres. HA9: Wemb 3H 61
Wells Ri. NW8 1D 82
Wells Rd. BR1: Brom 2D 160
W12 2E 98
Wells Sq. WC1 2G 7 (3K 83)
Wells St. W1 6A 6 (5G 83)
Wellstead Av. N9 7E 24
Wellstead Rd. E6 2E 88
Wells Ter. N4 2A 66
Well St. E9 7J 67
E15 6G 69
Wells Way SE5 6D 102
SW7 1A 16 (3B 100)
Wells Yd. N7 5A 66
Well Wlk. NW3 4B 64
Wellwood Rd. IG3: Ilf 1A 72
Welmar M. SW4 5H 119
(off Clapham Pk. Rd.)
Welsby Ct. W5 5C 78
Welsford St. SE1 4G 103
(not continuous)
Welsh Cl. E13 3J 87
Welsh Harp Nature Reserve 1A 62
Welsh Ho. E1 1H 103
(off Wapping La.)
Welshpool Ho. E8 1G 85
(off Welshpool St.)
Welshpool St. E8 1G 85
(not continuous)
Welshside NW9 6A 44
(off Ruthin Cl.)
Welshside Wlk. NW9 6A 44
Welstead Ho. E1 6H 85
(off Cannon St. Rd.)
Welstead Way W4 4B 98
Weltje Rd. W6 4C 98
Welton Ct. SE5 1E 120
Welton Ho. E1 5K 85
(off Stepney Way)
Welton Rd. SE18 7J 107
Welwyn Av. TW14: Felt 6H 111
Welwyn St. E2 3J 85
Welwyn Way UB4: Hayes 4G 75
WEMBLEY 5E 60

Wembley Arena 4G 61
Wembley Commercial Cen.
HA9: Wemb 2D 60
Wembley Hill Rd. HA9: Wemb 3F 61
WEMBLEY PARK 4F 61
Wembley Pk. Blvd.
HA9: Wemb 4G 61
Wembley Pk. Bus. Cen.
HA9: Wemb 4H 61
Wembley Pk. Dr. HA9: Wemb 4F 61
Wembley Rd. TW12: Hamp 1E 148
Wembley Stadium 4G 61
Wembley Stadium Ind. Est.
HA9: Wemb 4H 61
Wembley Way HA9: Wemb 6H 61
Wemborough Rd. HA7: Stan 1B 42
Wembury M. N6 7G 47
Wembury Rd. N6 7F 47
Wemyss Rd. SE3 2H 123
Wendela Ct. HA1: Harr 2J 59
Wendell Rd. W12 3B 98
Wenderholme CR2: S Croy 5D 168
(off South Pk. Hill Rd.)
Wendle Ct. SW8 7E 18 (6J 101)
Wendling NW5 5D 64
Wendling Rd. SM1: Sutt 1B 166
Wendon St. E3 1B 86
Wendover SE17 5E 102
(not continuous)
Wendover Cl. UB4: Yead 4C 76
Wendover Ct. BR2: Brom 3K 159
(off Wendover Rd.)
NW2 3J 63
NW10 4H 79
W1 6G 5
(off Chiltern St.)
Wendover Dr. KT3: N Mald 6B 152
Wendover Ho. W1 6G 5
(off Chiltern St.)
Wendover Rd. BR2: Brom 4K 159
NW10 2B 80
SE9 3B 124
Wendover Way DA16: Well 5A 126
Wendy Cl. EN1: Enf 6A 24
Wendy Way HA0: Wemb 1E 78
Wenham Ho. SW8 7G 101
Wenlake Ho. EC1 3C 8
(off Old St.)
Wenlock Barn Est. N1 2D 84
(off Wenlock St.)
Wenlock Ct. N1 1F 9 (2D 84)
Wenlock Gdns. NW4 4D 44
Wenlock Rd. HA8: Edg 7C 28
N1 1D 8 (2C 84)
Wenlock St. N1 1D 8 (2C 84)
Wennington Rd. E3 2K 85
Wensdale Ho. E5 2G 67
Wensley Av. IG8: Wfd G 7C 36
Wensley Cl. N11 6K 31
SE9 6D 124
Wensleydale Av. IG5: Ilf 2C 52
Wensleydale Gdns.
TW12: Hamp 7F 131
Wensleydale Pas.
TW12: Hamp 1E 148
Wensleydale Rd.
TW12: Hamp 6E 130
Wensley Rd. N18 6C 34
Wentland Cl. SE6 2F 141
Wentland Rd. SE6 2F 141
Wentway Ct. W13 4K 77
(off Ruislip Rd. E.)
Wentworth Av. N3 7D 30
Wentworth Cl. BR2: Hayes 2J 171
BR6: Farnb 5J 173
KT6: Surb 2D 162
N3 7E 30
SE28 6D 90
SM4: Mord 7J 153
TW15: Ashf 4D 128
Wentworth Ct. SW18 6K 117
(off Garratt La.)
TW2: Twick 3J 131
W6 6G 99
(off Paynes Wlk.)
Wentworth Cres. SE15 7G 103
UB3: Harl 3F 93
Wentworth Dr. HA5: Eastc 5J 39
Wentworth Dwellings E1 7J 9
(off Wentworth St.)
Wentworth Flds. UB4: Hayes 2F 75
Wentworth Gdns. N13 3G 33
Wentworth Hill HA9: Wemb 1F 61
Wentworth M. E3 4A 86
W3 6A 80
Wentworth Pk. N3 7D 30
Wentworth Pl. HA7: Stan 6G 27
Wentworth Rd. CR0: C'don 7A 156
E12 4B 70
EN5: Barn 3A 20
NW11 6H 45
UB2: S'hall 4A 94
Wentworth St. E1 7J 9 (6F 85)
Wentworth Way HA5: Pinn 4C 40
Wenvoe Av. DA7: Bex 2H 127
Wepham Cl. UB4: Yead 5B 76
Wernbrook St. SE18 6G 107
Werndee Rd. SE25 4G 157
Werneth Hall Rd.
IG5: Ilf 3D 52
Werrington St. NW1 1B 6 (2G 83)
Werter Rd. SW15 4G 117
Wesleyan Pl. NW5 4F 65
Wesley Av. E16 1J 105
NW10 3K 79
TW3: Houn 2C 112
Wesley Cl. HA2: Harr 2G 59
N7 2K 65
SE17 4B 102
Wesley Ct. SE16 3H 103
Wesley Rd. E10 7E 50
N2 1C 46
NW10 1J 79
UB3: Hayes 7J 75
Wesley's Chapel & Mus. of Methodism
3F 9 (4D 84)
Wesley's House 3F 9 (4D 84)
Wesley Sq. W11 6G 81
Wesley St. W1 6H 5 (5E 82)
Wessex Av. SW19 3J 153
Wessex Cl. IG3: Ilf 6J 53
KT1: King T 1H 151
Wessex Ct. BR3: Beck 1A 158
EN5: Barn 4A 20
HA9: Wemb 2F 61
TW19: Stanw 6A 110
Wessex Dr. HA5: Hat E 1C 40
Wessex Gdns. NW11 1G 63
Wessex Ho. SE1 5F 103
Wessex La. UB6: G'frd 3H 77
Wessex St. E2 3J 85
Wessex Wlk. DA2: Dart 2K 145
Wessex Way NW11 1G 63
Wesson Mead SE5 7C 102
(off Camberwell Rd.)
West 12 W12 2F 99
Westacott UB4: Hayes 5G 75
Westacott Cl. N19 1H 65
WEST ACTON 6G 79
West App. BR5: Pet W 5G 161
W. Arbour St. E1 6K 85
West Av. E17 4D 50
HA5: Pinn 6D 40
N2 4K 45
N3 6D 30
NW4 5F 45
SM6: Wall 5J 167
UB1: S'hall 7D 76
UB3: Hayes 7H 75
West Av. Rd. E17 4C 50
West Bank EN2: Enf 2H 23
IG11: Bark 1F 89
N16 7E 48
Westbank Rd. TW12: Ham H 6G 131
WEST BARNES 5D 152
W. Barnes La. KT3: N Mald 3D 152
WEST BECKTON 6B 88
WEST BEDFONT 6B 110
Westbeech Rd. N22 3A 48
Westbere Dr. HA7: Stan 5J 27
Westbere Rd. NW2 4G 63
West Block SE1 7H 13
(off Addington St.)
Westbourne Av. SM3: Cheam 2G 165
W3 6K 79
Westbourne Bri. W2 5A 82
Westbourne Cl. UB4: Yead 4A 76
Westbourne Ct. W2 5A 82
Westbourne Cres. W2 2A 10 (7B 82)
Westbourne Cres. M. W2 2A 10
Westbourne Dr. SE23 2K 139
Westbourne Gdns. W2 6K 81
WESTBOURNE GREEN 6H 81
Westbourne Gro. W2 6J 81
W11 7H 81
Westbourne Gro. M. W11 6J 81
Westbourne Gro. Ter. W2 6K 81
Westbourne Ho. SW1 5J 17
(off Ebury Bri. Rd.)
TW5: Hest 6E 94
Westbourne Pde. UB10: Hil 4D 74
Westbourne Pk. Pas. W2 5J 81
(not continuous)
Westbourne Pk. Rd. W2 5J 81
W11 6G 81
Westbourne Pk. Vs. W2 5J 81
Westbourne Pl. N9 3C 34
Westbourne Rd.
CR0: C'don 6F 157
DA7: Bex 7D 108
N7 6K 65
SE26 6K 139
TW13: Felt 3H 129
UB8: Hil 4D 74
Westbourne St. W2 2A 10 (7B 82)
Westbourne Ter. SE23 2K 139
(off Westbourne Dr.)
W2 1A 10 (6A 82)
Westbourne Ter. M. W2 6A 82
Westbourne Ter. Rd. W2 5K 81
Westbourne Ter. Rd. Bri.
W2 5A 82
(off Westbourne Ter. Rd.)
Westbridge Cl. W12 2C 98
Westbridge Rd. SW11 1B 118
WEST BROMPTON 6A 100
Westbrook Av. TW12: Hamp 7D 130
Westbrook Cl. EN4: Cockf 3G 21
Westbrook Cres. EN4: Cockf 3G 21
Westbrooke Cres. DA16: Well 3C 126
Westbrooke Rd. DA15: Sidc 2H 143
DA16: Well 3B 126
Westbrook Ho. E2 3J 85
(off Victoria Pk. Sq.)
Westbrook Rd. CR7: Thor H 1D 156
SE3 1K 123
TW5: Hest 7D 94
Westbrook Sq. EN4: Cockf 3G 21
Westbury Av. HA0: Wemb 7E 60
N22 3B 48
UB1: S'hall 4E 76
Westbury Cl. HA4: Ruis 7J 39
TW17: Shep 6D 146
Westbury Ct. IG11: Bark 1H 89
(off Westbury Rd.)
Westbury Gro. N12 6D 30
Westbury Ho. E17 4B 50
W11 5J 81
(off Aldridge Rd. Vs.)
Westbury La. IG9: Buck H 2E 36
Westbury Lodge Cl. HA5: Pinn 3B 40
Westbury Pl. TW8: Bford 6D 96
Westbury Rd. BR1: Brom 1B 160
BR3: Beck 3A 158
CR0: C'don 6D 156
E7 6K 69
E17 4B 50
HA0: Wemb 7E 60
IG1: Ilf 2E 70
IG9: Buck H 2F 37
IG11: Bark 1H 89
KT3: N Mald 4K 151
N11 6D 32
N12 6D 30
SE20 1K 157
TW13: Felt 1B 130
W5 6E 78
Westbury St. SW8 2G 119
(off Portslade Rd.)
Westbury Ter. E7 6K 69
Westbush Ct. W12 2D 98
(off Goldhawk M.)
W. Carriage Dr. W2 3C 10 (7C 82)
(North Ride)
W2 6B 10 (2B 100)
(The Ring)
W. Central St. WC1 7E 6 (6J 83)
West Cen. Av. NW10 4D 80
West Chantry HA3: Hrw W 1F 41
Westchester Dr. NW4 3F 45
Westcliffe Apartments W2 6B 4 (5B 82)
West Cl. EN4: Cockf 4K 21
HA9: Wemb 1F 61
N9 3A 34
TW12: Hamp 6C 130
TW15: Ashf 4A 128
UB6: G'frd 2G 77
Westcombe Av. CR0: C'don 7J 155
Westcombe Ct. SE3 7H 105
Westcombe Dr. EN5: Barn 5D 20
Westcombe Hill SE3 7J 105
SE10 7J 105
Westcombe Lodge Dr. UB4: Hayes 5G 75
Westcombe Pk. Rd. SE3 6G 105
West Comn. Rd. BR2: Hayes 1J 171
BR2: Kes 1J 171
UB8: Uxb 5A 56
Westcoombe Av. SW20 1B 152
Westcote Ri. HA4: Ruis 7E 38
Westcote Rd. SW16 5G 137
West Cotts. NW6 5J 63
Westcott Cl. BR1: Brom 5D 160
CR0: New Ad 7D 170
N15 6F 49
Westcott Cres. W7 6J 77
Westcott Ho. E14 7C 86
Westcott Rd. SE17 6B 102
West Ct. E17 4C 50
HA0: Wemb 2C 60
TW7: Isle 7G 95
Westcroft Cl. EN3: Enf W 1D 24
NW2 4G 63
Westcroft Est. NW2 4G 63
Westcroft Gdns. SM4: Mord 3H 153
Westcroft Leisure Cen. 4E 166
Westcroft Rd. SM5: Cars 4E 166
SM6: Wall 4E 166
Westcroft Sq. W6 4C 98
Westcroft Way NW2 4G 63
W. Cromwell Rd. SW5 5H 99
W14 5H 99
W. Cross Cen. TW8: Bford 6A 96
W. Cross Route W10 7F 81
W11 7F 81
W12 7F 81
W. Cross Way TW8: Bford 6B 96
Westdale Pas. SE18 6F 107
Westdale Rd. SE18 6F 107
Westdean Av. SE12 1K 141
Westdean Cl. SW18 6K 117

West Dene SM3: Cheam 6G 165
Westdown Rd. E15 4E 68
SE6 7C 122
WEST DRAYTON 2A 92
W. Drayton Pk. Av. UB7: W Dray 3A 92
W. Drayton Rd. UB8: Hil 6D 74
West Dr. HA3: Hrw W 6C 26
SM2: Cheam 7F 165
SW16 4G 137
West Dr. Gdns. HA3: Hrw W 6C 26
WEST DULWICH 2D 138
WEST EALING 1B 96
W. Ealing Bus. Cen. W13 7A 78
W. Eaton Pl. SW1 3G 17 (4E 100)
W. Eaton Pl. M. SW1 2G 17
W. Ella Rd. NW10 7A 62
WEST END 2B 76
West End Av. E10 5F 51
HA5: Pinn 4B 40
Westend Cl. NW10 7J 61
West End Ct. HA5: Pinn 4B 40
NW6 7K 63
West End Gdns. UB5: Yead 2A 76
West End La. EN5: Barn 4A 20
HA5: Pinn 3B 40
NW6 5J 63
(not continuous)
UB3: Harl 7E 92
West End Quay W2 6B 4
West End Rd. HA4: Ruis 2G 57
UB1: S'hall 1C 94
UB5: N'olt 7A 58
Westerdale Rd. SE10 5J 105
Westerfield Rd. N15 5F 49
Westergate W5 5E 78
Westergate Ho. *KT1: King T* *4D 150*
(off Portsmouth Rd.)
Westergate Rd. SE2: Belv 6E 108
Westerham *NW1* *1G 83*
(off Bayham St.)
Westerham Av. N9 3J 33
Westerham Dr. DA15: Sidc 6B 126
Westerham Ho. *SE1* *3D 102*
(off Law St.)
Westerham Lodge *BR3: Beck* *7C 140*
(off Park Rd.)
Westerham Rd. BR2: Kes 6B 172
E10 7D 50
Westerley Cres. SE26 5B 140
Westerley Ware *TW9: Kew* *6G 97*
(off Waterloo Pl.)
Western Av. HA4: Ruis 5A 56
NW11 6F 45
RM10: Dag 6J 73
UB5: N'olt 7A 58
UB6: G'frd 2H 77
UB10: Hil 5A 56
W3 4F 79
W5 4F 79
Western Av. Bus. Pk. W3 4H 79
Western Beach Apartments E16 7J 87
Western Ct. N3 6D 30
NW6 2H 81
W3 6K 79
Western Dr. TW17: Shep 6F 147
Western Gdns. W5 7G 79
Western Gateway E16 7J 87
Western Intl. Mkt. UB2: S'hall 4K 93
Western La. SW12 7E 118
Western Mans. *EN5: New Bar* *5E 20*
(off Great Nth. Rd.)
Western M. W9 4H 81
Western Pde. EN5: New Bar 5D 20
Western Perimeter Rd.
TW6: H'row A 5C 174
TW6: Lford, H'row A 5C 174
Western Pl. SE16 2J 103
Western Rd. CR4: Mitc 1B 154
E13 2A 88
E17 5E 50
Western Rd. N2 4D 46
N22 2K 47
NW10 4J 79
SM1: Sutt 5J 165
SW9 3A 120
SW19 1B 154
UB2: S'hall 4A 94
W5 7D 78
Western Ter. *W6* *5C 98*
(off Chiswick Mall)
Western Vw. UB3: Hayes 2H 93
Westernville Gdns. IG2: Ilf 7G 53
Western Way EN5: Barn 6D 20
SE28 3H 107
WEST EWELL 7K 163
Westferry Cir. E14 1B 104
Westferry Rd. E14 7B 86
Westfield W12 1E 98
Westfield Cl. EN3: Enf H 3F 25
NW9 3J 43
SM1: Sutt 4H 165
SW10 7A 100
Westfield Ct. *KT6: Surb* *5D 150*
(off Portsmouth Rd)
NW10 *3F 81*
(off Chamberlayne Rd.)
Westfield Dr. HA3: Kent 4D 42
Westfield Gdns. HA3: Kent 4D 42
RM6: Chad H 6C 54
Westfield Ho. *SE16* *4K 103*
(off Rotherhithe New Rd.)
SW10 *7B 100*
(off Cremorne Est.)
SW18 1K 135
Westfield La. HA3: Kent 5D 42
(not continuous)
Westfield Pk. HA5: Hat E 1D 40
Westfield Pk. Dr. IG8: Wfd G 6H 37
Westfield Rd. BR3: Beck 2B 158
CR0: C'don 2B 168
CR4: Mitc 2C 154
DA7: Bex 3J 127
KT6: Surb 5D 150
KT12: Walt T 7C 148
NW7 3E 28
RM9: Dag 4E 72
SM1: Sutt 4H 165
W13 1A 96
Westfields SW13 3B 116
Westfields Av. SW13 3A 116
Westfields Rd. W3 5H 79
Westfield St. SE18 3B 106
Westfield Way E1 3A 86
HA4: Ruis 3G 57
West Gdn. Pl. W2 1D 10 (6C 82)
West Gdns. E1 7H 85
SW17 6C 136
Westgate W5 3E 78
Westgate Cen., The *E8* *1H 85*
(off Bocking St.)
Westgate Ct. *SE12* *1J 141*
(off Burnt Ash Hill)
SW9 *3A 120*
(off Canterbury Cres.)
Westgate Est. TW14: Bedf 1D 128
Westgate Ho. TW7: Isle 2H 113
Westgate M. *W10* *4G 81*
(off West Row)
Westgate Rd. BR3: Beck 1E 158
SE25 4H 157
Westgate St. E8 1H 85
Westgate Ter. SW10 6K 99
Westglade Ct. HA3: Kent 5D 42
WEST GREEN 4B 48
West Grn. Pl. UB6: G'frd 1H 77
West Grn. Rd. N15 4B 48
West Gro. IG8: Wfd G 6F 37
SE10 1E 122
Westgrove La. SE10 1E 122
W. Halkin St. SW1 1G 17 (3E 100)
West Hallowes SE9 1B 142
W. Hall Rd. TW9: Kew 1H 115
WEST HAM 1H 87
W. Ham La. E15 7F 69
(not continuous)
WEST HAMPSTEAD 6K 63
W. Hampstead M. NW6 6K 63
West Ham United FC 2A 88
W. Harding St. EC4 7K 7 (6A 84)
WEST HARROW 7G 41
W. Hatch Mnr. HA4: Ruis 1H 57
Westhay Gdns. SW14 5H 115
WEST HEATH 6D 108
W. Heath Av. NW11 1J 63
W. Heath Cl. NW3 3J 63
W. Heath Ct. NW11 1J 63
W. Heath Dr. NW11 1J 63
W. Heath Gdns. NW3 2J 63
W. Heath Rd. NW3 2J 63
SE2 6C 108
WEST HENDON 7C 44
W. Hendon Broadway
NW9 6B 44
WEST HILL 6H 117
West Hill CR2: Sande 7E 168
HA2: Harr 2J 59
HA9: Wemb 1F 61
SW15 7F 117
SW18 7F 117
W. Hill Ct. N6 3E 64
Westhill Ct. *W11* *7H 81*
(off Denbigh Rd.)
W. Hill Pk. N6 2D 64
(not continuous)
W. Hill Rd. SW18 6H 117
W. Hill Way N20 1E 30
Westholm NW11 4K 45
West Holme DA8: Erith 1J 127
Westholme BR6: Orp 7J 161
Westholme Gdns.
HA4: Ruis 1J 57
Westhope Ho. *E2* *4G 85*
(off Derbyshire St.)
Westhorne Av. SE9 7J 123
SE12 7J 123
Westhorpe Gdns. NW4 3E 44
Westhorpe Rd. SW15 3E 116
West Ho. IG11: Bark 6F 71
West Ho. Cl. SW19 1G 135
West Ho. Cotts.
HA5: Pinn 4B 40
Westhurst Dr. BR7: Chst 5F 143
W. India Av. E14 1C 104
W. India Dock Rd. E14 7B 86
(not continuous)
W. India Ho. *E14* *7C 86*
(off W. India Dock Rd.)
W. Kensington Ct. *W14* *5H 99*
(off Edith Vs.)
W. Kensington Mans.
W14 *5H 99*
(off Beaumont Cres.)
WEST KILBURN 3H 81
Westlake *SE16* *4J 103*
(off Rotherhithe New Rd.)
Westlake Cl. N13 3F 33
UB4: Yead 4C 76
Westlake Rd. HA9: Wemb 2D 60
Westland Cl. TW19: Stanw 6A 110
Westland Ct. *UB5: N'olt* *3B 76*
(off Seasprite Cl.)
Westland Dr. BR2: Hayes 2H 171
Westland Ho. *E16* *1E 106*
(off Rymill St.)
Westland Pl. N1 1E 8 (3D 84)
Westlands Cl. UB3: Harl 4J 93
Westlands Ct. KT8: E Mos 4H 149
Westlands Ter. SW12 6G 119
West La. SE16 2H 103
Westlea Rd. W7 3A 96
Westleigh Av. SW15 5D 116
Westleigh Ct. *CR2: S Croy* *4E 168*
(off Birdhurst Rd.)
E11 5J 51
Westleigh Dr. BR1: Brom 1C 160
Westleigh Gdns. HA8: Edg 1G 43
West Links HA0: Wemb 3D 78
Westlinton Cl. NW7 6C 30
West Lodge *E16* *1J 105*
(off Britannia Ga.)
W. Lodge Av. W3 1G 97
W. Lodge Ct. W3 1G 97
W. London Crematorium
NW10 4D 80
Westmacott Dr. TW14: Felt 1H 129
Westmacott Ho. *NW8* *4B 4*
(off Hatton St.)
West Mall *W8* *1J 99*
(off Palace Gdns. Ter.)
Westmark Point *SW15* *1D 134*
(off Norley Vale)
West Mead HA4: Ruis 4A 58
KT19: Ewe 6A 164
Westmead SW15 6D 116
Westmead Cnr. SM5: Cars 4C 166
Westmead Ho. SM1: Sutt 4B 166
Westmead Rd. SM1: Sutt 4B 166
Westmere Dr. NW7 3E 28
W. Mersea Cl. E16 1K 105
West M. N17 7C 34
SW1 4A 18
WESTMINSTER 7E 12 (2J 101)
Westminster Abbey 7E 12 (3H 101)
Westminster Abbey Chapter House *1E 18*
(in Westminster Abbey)
Westminster Abbey Mus. *1E 18*
(in Westminster Abbey)
Westminster Abbey Pyx Chamber *1E 18*
(in Westminster Abbey)
Westminster Av. CR7: Thor H 2B 156
Westminster Boating Base & Pier
7C 18 (6H 101)
Westminster Bri. SW1 7F 13 (2J 101)
Westminster Bri. Rd. SE1 7G 13 (2K 101)
Westminster Bus. Sq. SE11 7H 19
Westminster Children's Sports Cen., The
5A 4 (4B 82)
Westminster Cl. IG6: Ilf 2H 53
TW11: Tedd 5A 132
TW14: Felt 1J 129
Westminster Ct. *E11* *6J 51*
(off Cambridge Pk.)
NW8 *4A 4*
(off Aberdeen Pl.)
SE16 *1K 103*
(off King & Queen Wharf)
Westminster Dr. N13 5D 32
Westminster Gdns. E4 1B 36
IG6: Ilf 2G 53
IG11: Bark 2J 89
SW1 *3E 18*
(off Marsham St.)
Westminster Hall 7E 12
Westminster Ho. HA3: Hrw W 7E 26
Westminster Ind. Est. SE18 3B 106
Westminster Mans. *SW1* *2D 18*
(off Gt. Smith St.)
Westminster Pal. Gdns.
SW1 2C 18
Westminster RC Cathedral 2A 18 (3G 101)
Westminster Rd. N9 1C 34
SM1: Sutt 2B 166
W7 1J 95
Westmoat Cl. BR3: Beck 7E 140
WEST MOLESEY 4E 148
Westmoor Gdns. EN3: Enf H 2E 24
Westmoor Rd. EN3: Enf H 2E 24
Westmoor St. SE7 3A 106
Westmore Ct. SW15 5G 117
Westmoreland Av. DA16: Well 3J 125

Westmoreland Dr. SM2: Sutt 7K 165
Westmoreland Ho. E16 1J 105
(off Gatcombe Rd.)
Westmoreland Pl. BR1: Brom 3J 159
SW1 6K 17 (5F 101)
W5 5D 78
Westmoreland Rd. BR2: Brom 5G 159
NW9 3F 43
SE17 6D 102
(not continuous)
SW13 1B 116
Westmoreland St. W1 6H 5 (5E 82)
Westmoreland Ter. SE20 7H 139
SW1 6K 17 (5F 101)
Westmoreland Wlk. SE17 6D 102
(not continuous)
Westmorland Cl. E12 2B 70
TW1: Twick 6B 114
Westmorland Ct. KT6: Surb 7D 150
Westmorland Rd. E17 6C 50
HA1: Harr 5F 41
Westmorland Sq. CR4: Mitc 5J 155
(off Westmorland Way)
Westmorland Way CR4: Mitc 4H 155
Westmount Ct. W5 6F 79
Westmount Rd. SE9 2D 124
WEST NORWOOD 4C 138
West Norwood Crematorium
SE27 3C 138
West Oak BR3: Beck 1F 159
Westoe Rd. N9 2C 34
Weston Av. KT7: T Ditt 7J 149
KT8: W Mole 3C 148
Westonbirt Ct. SE15 6F 103
(off Ebley Cl.)
Weston Ct. KT1: King T 3E 150
(off Grove Cres.)
N4 3C 66
N20 7F 21
(off Farnham Cl.)
Weston Dr. HA7: Stan 1B 42
West One Ho. W1 6A 6
(off Wells St.)
Westone Mans. IG11: Bark 7K 71
(off Upney La.)
W. One Shop. Cen. W1 1H 11
Weston Gdns. TW7: Isle 1J 113
WESTON GREEN 7K 149
Weston Grn. KT7: T Ditt 7J 149
RM9: Dag 4F 73
Weston Grn. Rd.
KT7: T Ditt 7J 149
KT10: Esh 7J 149
Weston Gro. BR1: Brom 1H 159
Weston Ho. E9 1J 85
(off King Edward's Rd.)
NW6 7G 63
Weston London Heliport 2B 118
Weston Pk. KT1: King T 2E 150
KT7: T Ditt 7J 149
N8 6J 47
Weston Ri. WC1 1H 7 (3K 83)
Weston Rd. BR1: Brom 7H 141
EN2: Enf 2J 23
RM9: Dag 4E 72
W4 3J 97
Weston St. SE1 7F 15 (2E 102)
(not continuous)
Weston Wlk. E8 7H 67
Westover Hill NW3 2J 63
Westover Rd. SW18 7A 118
Westow Hill SE19 6E 138
Westow St. SE19 6E 138
West Pk. SE9 2C 142
West Pk. Av. TW9: Kew 1G 115
West Pk. Cl. RM6: Chad H 5D 54
TW5: Hest 6D 94
West Pk. Rd. TW9: Kew 1G 115
UB2: S'hall 1G 95
West Parkside SE10 2G 105
West Pl. SW19 5E 134
West Point E14 7B 86
(off Grenade St.)
SE1 5G 103
Westpoint Apartments N8 3K 47
W. Point Cl. TW3: Houn 3D 112
(off Grosvenor Rd.)
Westpoint Trad. Est. W3 5H 79
Westpole Av. EN4: Cockf 4K 21
Westport Ct. UB4: Yead 4A 76
Westport Rd. E13 4K 87
Westport St. E1 6K 85
W. Poultry Av. EC1 6A 8 (5B 84)
West Quarters W12 6C 80
West Quay SW10 1A 118
W. Quay Dr. UB4: Yead 5C 76
West Ramp TW6: H'row A 1C 110
West Reservoir Cen. 1C 66
W. Ridge Gdns. UB6: G'frd 2G 77
West Ri. W2 2D 10
West Rd. E15 1H 87
EN4: E Barn 1K 31
KT2: King T 1J 151
N2 2B 46
N17 6C 34
RM6: Chad H 6D 54
RM7: Rush G 7K 55
SE1 6H 13 (2K 101)
SW3 6F 17 (5D 100)
SW4 5H 119
TW14: Bedf 6F 111
UB7: W Dray 3B 92
W5 5E 78
West Row W10 4G 81
Westrow SW15 6E 116
Westrow Dr. IG11: Bark 5A 72
Westrow Gdns. IG3: Ilf 2K 71
WEST RUISLIP 2E 56
W. Ruislip Ct. HA4: Ruis 2F 57
(off Ickenham Rd.)
W. Sheen Va. TW9: Rich 4F 115
West Side NW4 2D 44
Westside N2 3D 46
Westside Apartments IG1: Ilf 3E 70
(off Roden St.)
W. Side Comn. SW19 5E 134
Westside Ct. W9 4J 81
(off Elgin Av.)
Westside Lawn Tennis Club 7E 134
West Smithfield EC1 6A 8 (5B 84)
West Sq. E10 7D 50
SE11 2K 19 (3B 102)
West St. BR1: Brom 1J 159
CR0: C'don 4C 168
DA7: Bex 3F 127
DA8: Erith 4K 109
E2 2H 85
E11 3G 69
E17 5D 50
HA1: Harr 1H 59
SM1: Sutt 5K 165
SM5: Cars 3D 166
West St. TW8: Bford 6C 96
WC2 1D 12 (6H 83)
West St. La. SM5: Cars 4D 166
(not continuous)
West St. Pl. CR0: C'don 4C 168
(off West St.)
W. Temple Sheen SW14 5H 115
W. Tenter St. E1 1K 15 (6F 85)
West Ter. DA15: Sidc 1J 143
W. Thamesmead Bus. Pk. SE28 3J 107
(not continuous)
West Towers HA5: Pinn 5B 40
Westvale M. W3 2A 98
West Vw. NW4 4E 44
TW14: Bedf 7E 110
Westview W7 6J 77
West Vw. Cl. NW10 5B 62
Westview Cl. W10 6E 80
Westview Ct. N20 1F 31
Westview Cres. N9 7K 23
Westview Dr. IG8: Wfd G 2B 52
Westville Rd. KT7: T Ditt 1A 162
W12 2C 98
West Wlk. EN4: E Barn 7K 21
NW9 1A 44
UB3: Hayes 1J 93
W5 5E 78
Westward Rd. E4 5G 35
(not continuous)
Westward Way HA3: Kent 6E 42
W. Warwick Pl. SW1 4A 18 (4G 101)
West Way BR4: W W'ck 6F 159
CR0: C'don 2A 170
HA4: Ruis 1H 57
HA5: Pinn 4B 40
HA8: Edg 6C 28
NW10 3K 61
TW5: Hest 1D 112
TW17: Shep 6F 147
Westway BR5: Pet W 5H 161
N18 4J 33
SW20 3D 152
UB6: G'frd 1J 77
W2 6A 4 (5H 81)
W9 5H 81
W10 5H 81
W12 7B 80
Westway Cl. SW20 3D 152
Westway Ct. UB5: N'olt 1E 76
Westway Est. W3 5A 80
West Way Gdns. CR0: C'don 2K 169
Westway Lodge W9 5J 81
(off Amberley Rd.)
West Ways HA6: Nwood 2J 39
Westways KT19: Ewe 4B 164
Westway Sports Cen. 6F 81
Westway Travellers Site W12 7F 81
(off Stable Way)
Westwell M. SW16 6J 137
Westwell Rd. SW16 6J 137
Westwell Rd. App. SW16 6J 137
Westwick KT1: King T 2G 151
(off Chesterton Ter.)
Westwick Gdns. TW4: Cran 2K 111
W14 2F 99
WEST WICKHAM 1E 170
West Wickham Leisure Cen. 1E 170
Westwood Av. HA2: Harr 4F 59
SE19 1C 156
Westwood Bus. Cen. NW10 4A 80
Westwood Cl. BR1: Brom 2B 160
HA4: Ruis 6D 38
Westwood Ct. EN1: Enf 6K 23
(off Village Rd.)
HA0: Wemb 4B 60
UB6: G'frd 5H 59
Westwood Gdns. SW13 3B 116
Westwood Hill SE26 5G 139
Westwood Ho. W12 1E 98
(off Wood La.)
Westwood La. DA15: Sidc 5A 126
DA16: Well 3K 125
Westwood Pk. SE23 7H 121
Westwood Pk. Trad. Est. W3 5H 79
Westwood Pl. SE26 4G 139
Westwood Rd. E16 1K 105
IG3: Ilf 1K 71
SW13 3B 116
West Woodside DA5: Bexl 7E 126
Wetheral Dr. HA7: Stan 1B 42
Wetherby Cl. UB5: N'olt 6F 59
Wetherby Gdns. SW5 4A 100
Wetherby Mans. SW5 5K 99
(off Earls Ct. Sq.)
Wetherby M. SW5 5K 99
Wetherby Pl. SW7 4A 100
Wetherby Rd. EN2: Enf 1H 23
Wetherby Way KT9: Chess 7E 162
Wetherden St. E17 7B 50
Wetherell Rd. E9 1K 85
Wetherill Rd. N10 1E 46
Wevco Wharf SE15 6H 103
Wevell Ho. N6 7E 46
(off Hillcrest)
Wexford Ho. E1 5J 85
(off Sidney St.)
Wexford Rd. SW12 7D 118
Weybourne St. SW18 2A 136
Weybridge Ct. SE16 5H 103
(off Argyle Way)
Weybridge Point SW11 2D 118
Weybridge Rd. CR7: Thor H 4A 156
Wey Ct. KT19: Ewe 4J 163
Weydown Cl. SW19 1G 135
Weyhill Rd. E1 6G 85
Wey Ho. NW8 4B 4
(off Church St. Est.)
Weylands Cl. KT12: Walt T 7D 148
Weylond Rd. RM8: Dag 3F 73
Weyman Rd. SE3 1A 124
Weymarks, The N17 6J 33
Weymouth Av. NW7 5F 29
W5 3C 96
Weymouth Cl. E6 6F 89
Weymouth Ct. E2 2F 85
(off Weymouth Ter.)
SM2: Sutt 7J 165
Weymouth Ho. BR2: Brom 2H 159
(off Beckenham La.)
SW8 7K 101
(off Bolney St.)
Weymouth M. W1 5J 5 (5F 83)
Weymouth Rd. UB4: Hayes 3G 75
Weymouth St. W1 6H 5 (5E 82)
Weymouth Ter. E2 1K 9 (2F 85)
Weymouth Vs. N4 2K 65
(off Moray Rd.)
Weymouth Wlk. HA7: Stan 6F 27
Whadcoat St. N4 2A 66
Whalebone Av. RM6: Chad H 6F 55
Whalebone Ct. EC2 7E 8
Whalebone Gro. RM6: Chad H 6F 55
Whalebone La. E15 7G 69
Whalebone La. Nth.
RM6: Chad H, Col R 1E 54
Whalebone La. Sth.
RM6: Chad H, Dag 7F 55
RM8: Dag 7F 55
Whales Yd. E15 7G 69
(off W. Ham La.)
Wharf, The EC3 4H 15 (1F 103)
Wharfdale Cl. N11 6K 31
Wharfdale Rd. N1 2J 83
Wharfedale Ct. E5 4K 67
Wharfedale Gdns. CR7: Thor H 4K 155
Wharfedale Ho. NW6 1K 81
(off Kilburn Va.)
Wharfedale St. SW10 5K 99
Wharfedale Yard N1 2J 83
(off Wharfedale Rd.)
Wharf La. TW1: Twick 1A 132
Wharf Pl. E2 1H 85
Wharf Rd. EN3: Pond E 6F 25
N1 1C 8 (2C 84)
(Baldwin Ter.)
N1 1H 83
(Camley St.)
Wharf Rd. Ind. Est.
EN3: Pond E 6F 25
Wharfside Rd. E16 5G 87
Wharf St. E16 5G 87
Wharf Vw. Ct. E14 6E 86
(off Athol Sq.)
Wharncliffe Dr. UB1: S'hall 1H 95
Wharncliffe Gdns. SE25 2E 156
Wharncliffe Rd. SE25 2E 156
Wharton Cl. NW10 6A 62
Wharton Cotts. WC1 2J 7 (3A 84)

Wharton Ho. SE1 7J 15
(off St Saviour's Est.)
Wharton Rd. BR1: Brom 1K 159
Wharton St. WC1 2H 7 (3K 83)
Whatcott's Yd. N16 4E 66
Whateley Rd. SE20 7K 139
SE22 5F 121
Whatley Av. SW20 3F 153
Whatman Ho. E14 6B 86
(off Wallwood St.)
Whatman Rd. SE23 7K 121
Wheatcroft Ct. SM1: Sutt 1K 165
(off Cleeve Way)
Wheatfield Ho. W9 3J 81
(off Kilburn Pk. Rd.)
Wheatfields E6 6F 89
EN3: Enf H 1F 25
Wheatfield Way KT1: King T 2E 150
Wheathill Ho. SE20 2H 157
(off Croydon Rd.)
Wheathill Rd. SE20 3H 157
Wheatland Ho. SE22 3E 120
Wheatlands TW5: Hest 6E 94
Wheatlands Rd. SW17 3E 136
Wheatley Cl. NW4 2C 44
Wheatley Cres. UB3: Hayes 7J 75
Wheatley Gdns. N9 2K 33
Wheatley Ho. SW15 7C 116
(off Ellisfield Dr)
Wheatley Mans. IG11: Bark 7A 72
(off Bevan Av.)
Wheatley Rd. TW7: Isle 3K 113
Wheatley's Eyot TW16: Sun 5J 147
Wheatley St. W1 6H 5 (5E 82)
Wheat Sheaf Cl. E14 4D 104
Wheatsheaf Cl. UB5: N'olt 5C 58
Wheatsheaf La. SW6 7E 98
SW8 7J 101
Wheatsheaf Ter. SW6 7H 99
Wheatstone Cl. CR4: Mitc 1C 154
Wheatstone Ho. W10 5G 81
(off Telford Rd.)
Wheatstone Rd. DA8: Erith 5K 109
W10 5G 81
Wheeler Cl. IG8: Wfd G 6J 37
Wheeler Gdns. N1 1J 83
(off Outram Pl.)
Wheeler Pl. BR2: Brom 4K 159
Wheelers Cross IG11: Bark 2H 89
Wheelers Dr. HA4: Ruis 6E 38
Wheeler's St. SM1: Sutt 3J 165
Wheel Farm Dr. RM10: Dag 3J 73
Wheel Ho. E14 5D 104
(off Burrells Wharf Sq.)
Wheelock Cl. DA8: Erith 7H 109
Wheelwright St. N7 7K 65
Whelan Way SM6: Bedd 3H 167
Wheler Ho. E1 4J 9
(off Quaker St.)
Wheler St. E1 4J 9 (4F 85)
Whellock Rd. W4 3A 98
Whenman Av. DA5: Bexl 2J 145
Whernside Cl. SE28 7C 90
WHETSTONE 2F 31
Whetstone N20 2F 31
Whetstone Cl. N20 2G 31
Whetstone Pk. WC2 7G 7 (6K 83)
Whetstone Rd. SE3 2A 124
Whewell Rd. N19 2J 65
Whidborne Bldgs. WC1 2F 7
(off Whidborne St.)
Whidborne Cl. SE8 2C 122
Whidborne St. WC1 2F 7 (3J 83)
(not continuous)
Whimbrel Cl. SE28 7C 90
Whimbrel Way UB4: Yead 5B 76
Whinchat Rd. SE28 3H 107
Whinfell Cl. SW16 5H 137
Whinyates Rd. SE9 3C 124
Whippendell Way BR5: St P 7B 144
Whipps Cross E17 5F 51
Whipps Cross Ho. E17 5F 51
(off Wood St.)
Whipps Cross Rd. E11 5F 51
(not continuous)
Whiskin St. EC1 2A 8 (3B 84)
Whisperwood Cl. HA3: Hrw W 1J 41
Whistler Gdns. HA8: Edg 2F 43
Whistler M. RM8: Dag 5B 72
(off Fitzstephen Rd.)
SE15 7F 103
Whistlers Av. SW11 7B 100
Whistler St. N5 5B 66
Whistler Twr. SW10 7A 100
(off Worlds End Est.)
Whistler Wlk. SW10 7B 100
Whiston Ho. N1 7B 66
(off Richmond Gro.)
Whiston Rd. E2 2F 85
Whitacre M. SE11 6K 19 (5A 102)
Whitakers Lodge EN2: Enf 1J 23
Whitbread Cl. N17 1G 49
Whitbread Rd. SE4 4A 122
Whitburn Rd. SE13 4D 122
Whitby Av. NW10 3H 79
Whitby Ct. N7 4J 65
Whitby Gdns. NW9 3G 43
SM1: Sutt 2B 166
Whitby Ho. NW8 1A 82
(off Boundary Rd.)
Whitby Pde. HA4: Ruis 2A 58
Whitby Rd. HA2: Harr 3G 59
HA4: Ruis 3K 57
SE18 4D 106
SM1: Sutt 2B 166
Whitby St. E1 3J 9 (4F 85)
(not continuous)
Whitcher Cl. SE14 6A 104
Whitcher Pl. NW1 6G 65
Whitchurch Av. HA8: Edg 7A 28
Whitchurch Cl. HA8: Edg 6A 28
Whitchurch Gdns. HA8: Edg 6A 28
Whitchurch Ho. W10 6F 81
(off Kingsdown Cl.)
Whitchurch La. HA8: Edg 7J 27
Whitchurch Pde. HA8: Edg 7B 28
Whitchurch Rd. W11 7F 81
Whitcomb Ct. WC2 3D 12
Whitcombe M. TW9: Kew 1H 115
Whitcomb St. WC2 3D 12 (7H 83)
Whitcome M. TW9: Kew 1H 115
Whiteadder Way E14 4D 104
Whitear Wlk. E15 6F 69
Whitebarn La. RM10: Dag 1G 91
Whitebeam Av. BR2: Brom 7E 160
Whitebeam Cl. SW9 7K 101
White Bear Pl. NW3 4B 64
White Bear Yd. EC1 4J 7
(off Clerkenwell Rd.)
White Bri. Av. CR4: Mitc 3B 154
Whitebridge Cl. TW14: Felt 6H 111
White Butts Rd. HA4: Ruis 3B 58
WHITECHAPEL 5G 85
Whitechapel Art Gallery 7K 9 (6F 85)
Whitechapel High St. E1 7K 9 (6F 85)
Whitechapel Rd. E1 7K 9 (5G 85)
Whitechapel Sports Cen. 5H 85
White Church La. E1 7K 9 (6G 85)
White Church Pas. E1 7K 9
(off White Church La.)
WHITE CITY 7D 80
WHITE CITY 6E 80
White City Cl. W12 7E 80
White City Est. W12 7D 80
White City Rd. W12 7E 80
White Conduit St. N1 2A 84
Whitecote Rd. UB1: S'hall 6G 77
Whitecroft Cl. BR3: Beck 4F 159
Whitecroft Way BR3: Beck 5E 158
Whitecross Pl. EC2 5F 9 (5D 84)
Whitecross St. EC1 3D 8 (4C 84)
Whitefield Av. NW2 1E 62
Whitefield Cl. SW15 6G 117
Whitefoot La. BR1: Brom 4E 140
(not continuous)
Whitefoot Ter. BR1: Brom 3H 141
Whitefriars Av. HA3: W'stone 2J 41
Whitefriars Ct. N12 5G 31
Whitefriars Dr. HA3: Hrw W 2H 41
Whitefriars St. EC4 1K 13 (6A 84)
Whitefriars Trad. Est.
HA3: W'stone 3H 41
White Gables Ct. CR2: S Croy 5E 168
White Gdns. RM10: Dag 6G 73
Whitegate Gdns.
HA3: Hrw W 7E 26
White Gates KT7: T Ditt 7A 150
Whitehall 6G 165
Whitehall SW1 5E 12 (1J 101)
Whitehall Ct. SW1 5E 12 (1J 101)
(not continuous)
Whitehall Cres. KT9: Chess 5D 162
Whitehall Gdns. E4 1B 36
SW1 5E 12
W3 1G 97
W4 6H 97
Whitehall La. IG9: Buck H 2D 36
Whitehall Lodge N10 3E 46
Whitehall Pk. N19 1G 65
Whitehall Pk. Rd. W4 6H 97
Whitehall Pl. E7 5J 69
SM6: Wall 4F 167
SW1 5E 12 (1J 101)
Whitehall Rd. BR2: Brom 5B 160
CR7: Thor H 5A 156
E4 2B 36
HA1: Harr 7J 41
IG8: Wfd G 2B 36
W7 2A 96
Whitehall St. N17 7A 34
White Hart Av. SE18 4K 107
SE28 4K 107
White Hart Cl. UB3: Harl 6F 93
White Hart Ct. EC2 6G 9
White Hart Lane 7B 34
White Hart La. N17 7H 33
N22 1K 47
NW10 6B 62
RM7: Col R, Mawney 1G 55
SW13 3A 116
White Hart Rd. SE18 4J 107
White Hart Rdbt. UB5: N'olt 2B 76
White Hart School Sports Cen. 7G 33
White Hart Slip BR1: Brom 2J 159
White Hart St. EC4 7B 8 (6B 84)
SE11 5K 19 (5A 102)
White Hart Yd. SE1 5E 14 (1D 102)
Whitehaven Cl. BR2: Brom 4J 159
Whitehaven St. NW8 4C 4 (4C 82)
Whitehead Cl. N18 5J 33
SW18 7A 118
Whiteheads Gro. SW3 4D 16 (4C 100)
White Heart Av. UB8: Hil 5E 74
Whiteheath Av. HA4: Ruis 7E 38
White Heather Ho. WC1 2F 7
(off Cromer St.)
White Heron M.
TW11: Tedd 6K 131
White Horse All. EC1 5A 8
White Horse Hill BR7: Chst 4E 142
White Horse La. E1 4K 85
Whitehorse La. SE25 4D 156
Whitehorse M. SE1 1K 19 (3A 102)
White Horse Rd. E1 5A 86
(not continuous)
E6 3D 88
Whitehorse Rd. CR0: C'don 7C 156
CR7: Thor H 7C 156
White Horse St. W1 5K 11 (1F 101)
White Horse Yd. EC2 7E 8 (6D 84)
White Ho. SW4 7H 119
(off Clapham Pk. Est.)
SW11 1B 118
White House, The NW1 3K 5
Whitehouse Apartments SE1 1K 101
White Ho. Ct. N14 2D 32
White Ho. Dr. HA7: Stan 4H 27
IG8: Wfd G 6C 36
Whitehouse Est. E10 6E 50
White Ho. La. EN2: Enf 1H 23
Whitehouse Way N14 2A 32
Whitehurst Dr. N18 5E 34
White Kennett St. E1 7H 9 (6F 85)
Whitelands Cres. SW18 7G 117
Whitelands Ho. SW3 5F 17
(off Cheltenham Ter.)
Whiteledges W13 6C 78
Whitelegg Rd. E13 2H 87
Whiteley Rd. SE19 5D 138
Whiteleys Cen. (Shop. Cen.)
W2 6K 81
Whiteleys Pde. UB10: Hil 4D 74
Whiteley's Way TW13: Hanw 3E 130
White Lion Ct. EC3 1G 15
SE15 6J 103
TW7: Isle 3B 114
White Lion Hill EC4 2B 14 (7B 84)
White Lion St. N1 2A 84
White Lodge SE19 7B 138
W5 5C 78
White Lodge Cl. N2 6B 46
SM2: Sutt 7A 166
TW7: Isle 2A 114
White Lodge Ct. TW16: Sun 1A 148
White Lyon Ct. EC2 5C 8
Whiteoak Ct. BR7: Chst 6E 142
White Oak Dr. BR3: Beck 2E 158
White Oak Gdns. DA15: Sidc 7K 125
Whiteoaks La. UB6: G'frd 3H 77
White Orchards HA7: Stan 5F 27
N20 1C 30
White Post La. E9 7B 68
White Post St. SE15 7J 103
White Rd. E15 7G 69
Whiterose Trad. Est. EN4: E Barn 5G 21
(off Margaret Rd.)
Whites Av. IG2: Ilf 6J 53
White's Grounds SE1 7H 15 (2E 102)
White's Grounds Est. SE1 6H 15
White's Mdw. BR1: Brom 4E 160
White's Row E1 6J 9 (5F 85)
Whites Sq. SW4 4H 119
Whitestile Rd. TW8: Bford 5C 96
Whitestone La. NW3 3A 64
Whitestone Wlk. NW3 3A 64
White St. UB1: S'hall 2B 94
White Swan M. W4 5A 98
Whitethorn Av. UB7: Yiew 7A 74
Whitethorn Gdns. CR0: C'don 2H 169
EN2: Enf 5J 23
Whitethorn Ho. E1 1J 103
(off Prusom St.)
Whitethorn Pas. E3 4C 86
(off Whitethorn St.)
Whitethorn Pl. UB7: Yiew 1B 92
Whitethorn St. E3 5C 86
Whitewebbs Way BR5: St P 1K 161
Whitfield Ct. IG1: Ilf 7D 52
Whitfield Ho. NW8 4C 4
(off Salisbury St.)
Whitfield Pl. W1 4A 6
Whitfield Rd. DA7: Bex 7F 109
E6 7A 70
SE3 1F 123
Whitfield St. W1 4A 6 (4G 83)
Whitford Gdns. CR4: Mitc 3D 154
Whitgift Av. CR2: S Croy 5B 168
Whitgift Cen. CR0: C'don 2C 168
Whitgift Ct. CR2: S Croy 5C 168
(off Nottingham Rd.)

Whitgift Ho. SE11 3G 19 (4K 101)
SW11 1C 118
Whitgift Sq. CR0: C'don 2C 168
Whitgift St. CR0: C'don 3C 168
SE11 3G 19 (4K 101)
Whiting Av. IG11: Bark 7F 71
Whitings IG2: Ilf 5J 53
Whitings Rd. EN5: Barn 5A 20
Whitings Way E6 5E 88
Whitland Rd. SM5: Cars 1B 166
Whitley Cl. TW19: Stanw 6A 110
Whitley Ho. *SW1* *7B 18*
(off Churchill Gdns.)
Whitley Rd. N17 2E 48
Whitlock Dr. SW19 7G 117
Whitman Ho. *E2* *3J 85*
(off Cornwall Av.)
Whitman Rd. E3 4A 86
Whitmead Cl. CR2: S Croy 6E 168
Whitmore Cl. N11 5A 32
Whitmore Est. N1 1E 84
Whitmore Gdns. NW10 2E 80
Whitmore Ho. *N1* *1E 84*
(off Whitmore Est.)
Whitmore Rd. BR3: Beck 3B 158
HA1: Harr 7G 41
N1 1E 84
Whitmore Sports Cen. 1G 59
Whitnell Way SW15 5E 116
Whitney Av. IG4: Ilf 4B 52
Whitney Rd. E10 7D 50
Whitney Wlk. DA14: Sidc 6E 144
Whitstable Cl. BR3: Beck 1B 158
HA4: Ruis 2G 57
Whitstable Ho. *W10* *6F 81*
(off Silchester Rd.)
Whitstable Pl. CR0: C'don 4C 168
Whitstone La. BR3: Beck 5D 158
Whittaker Av. TW9: Rich 5D 114
Whittaker Pl. *TW9: Rich* *5D 114*
(off Whittaker Av.)
Whittaker Rd. E6 7A 70
SM3: Sutt 3H 165
Whittaker St. SW1 4G 17 (4E 100)
Whittaker Way SE1 4G 103
Whitta Rd. E12 4B 70
Whittell Gdns. SE26 3J 139
Whittingham N17 7C 34
Whittingham Ct. W4 7A 98
Whittingstall Rd. SW6 1H 117
Whittington Av. EC3 1G 15 (6E 84)
UB4: Hayes 5H 75
Whittington Ct. N2 5D 46
Whittington M. N12 4F 31
Whittington Rd. N22 7D 32
Whittington Way HA5: Pinn 5C 40
Whittlebury Cl. SM5: Cars 7D 166
Whittle Cl. E17 6A 50
UB1: S'hall 6F 77
Whittle Rd. TW5: Hest 7A 94
TW6: H'row A 6C 174
UB2: S'hall 2F 95
Whittlesea Cl. HA3: Hrw W 7B 26
Whittlesea Path HA3: Hrw W 1G 41
Whittlesea Rd. HA3: Hrw W 7B 26
Whittlesey St. SE1 5J 13 (1A 102)
WHITTON 7G 113
Whitton NW3 7D 64
Whitton Av. E. UB6: G'frd 5J 59
Whitton Av. W. UB5: N'olt 5F 59
UB6: G'frd 5F 59
Whitton Cl. UB6: G'frd 6B 60
Whitton Dene TW3: Houn 5G 113
TW7: Isle 6H 113
Whitton Dr. UB6: G'frd 6A 60
Whitton Mnr. Rd. TW7: Isle 6G 113
Whitton Rd. TW1: Twick 6K 113
TW2: Twick 6J 113
TW3: Houn 4F 113
WHITTON ROAD RDBT. 6K 113
Whitton Sports & Fitness Cen. 2F 131
Whitton Wlk. E3 3C 86
Whitton Waye TW3: Houn 6E 112
Whitwell Rd. E13 3J 87
Whitworth Ho. SE1 3C 102
Whitworth Rd. SE18 7E 106
SE25 3E 156
Whitworth St. SE10 5G 105
Whorlton Rd. SE15 3H 121
Whychcote Point *NW2* *1E 62*
(off Whitefield Av.)
Whymark Av. N22 3A 48
Whytecroft TW5: Hest 7B 94
Whyte M. SM3: Cheam 7G 165
Whyteville Rd. E7 6K 69
Whytlaw Ho. *E3* *5B 86*
(off Baythorne St.)
Wickersley Rd. SW11 2E 118
Wickers Oake SE19 4F 139
Wicker St. E1 6H 85
Wicket, The CR0: Addtn 5C 170
Wicket Rd. UB6: G'frd 3A 78
Wickets, The TW15: Ashf 4A 128
Wickfield Ho. *SE16* *2H 103*
(off Wilson Gro.)
Wickford Ho. *E1* *4J 85*
(off Wickford St.)
Wickford St. E1 4J 85
Wickford Way E17 4K 49
Wickham Av. CR0: C'don 2A 170
SM3: Cheam 5E 164
Wickham Chase BR4: W W'ck 1F 171
Wickham Cl. E1 5J 85
EN3: Enf H 3C 24
KT3: N Mald 6B 152
Wickham Ct. *KT5: Surb* *5F 151*
(off Cranes Pk.)
Wickham Ct. Rd. BR4: W W'ck 2E 170
Wickham Cres. BR4: W W'ck 2E 170
Wickham Gdns. SE4 3B 122
Wickham Ho. *N1* *1E 84*
(off New Era Est.)
Wickham La. DA16: Well 5A 108
SE2 5A 108
Wickham M. SE4 2B 122
Wickham Rd. BR3: Beck 2D 158
CR0: C'don 2K 169
E4 7K 35
HA3: Hrw W 2H 41
SE4 4B 122
Wickham St. DA16: Well 2J 125
SE11 5G 19 (5K 101)
Wickham Theatre Cen. 2F 171
Wickham Way BR3: Beck 4E 158
Wick Ho. *KT1: Ham W* *1D 150*
(off Station Rd.)
Wick La. E3 1C 86
Wickliffe Av. N3 2G 45
Wickliffe Gdns. HA9: Wemb 2H 61
Wicklow Ho. N16 1F 67
Wicklow St. WC1 1G 7 (3K 83)
Wick M. E9 6A 68
Wick Rd. E9 6K 67
TW11: Tedd 7B 132
Wicks Cl. SE9 4B 142
Wick Sq. E9 6B 68
Wicksteed Cl. DA5: Bexl 3K 145
Wicksteed Ho. SE1 3C 102
TW8: Bford 5F 97
Wickway Ct. *SE15* *6F 103*
(off Cator St.)
Wickwood St. SE5 2B 120
Widdecombe Av. HA2: Harr 2C 58
Widdenham Rd. N7 4K 65
Widdin St. E15 7G 69
Widecombe Gdns. IG4: Ilf 4C 52
Widecombe Rd. SE9 3C 142
Widecombe Way N2 5B 46
Widegate St. E1 6H 9 (5E 84)
Widenham Cl. HA5: Eastc 5A 40
Wide Way CR4: Mitc 3H 155
Widewing Cl. TW11: Tedd 7B 132
Widford *NW1* *6F 65*
(off Lewis St.)
Widford Ho. *N1* *2B 84*
(off Colebrooke Rd.)
Widgeon Cl. E16 6K 87
Widgeon Rd. TW6: H'row A 5C 174
Widley Rd. W9 3J 81
Widmer Ct. TW3: Houn 2C 112
WIDMORE 3A 160
WIDMORE GREEN 2B 160
Widmore Lodge Rd. BR1: Brom 2B 160
Widmore Rd. BR1: Brom 2J 159
UB8: Hil 4D 74
Wigan Ho. E5 1H 67
Wigeon Path SE28 3H 107
Wigeon Way UB4: Yead 6C 76
Wiggins La. TW10: Ham 2C 132
Wiggins Mead NW9 7G 29
Wigginton Av. HA9: Wemb 6H 61
Wight Ho. *KT1: King T* *3D 150*
(off Portsmouth Rd.)
Wightman Rd. N4 4A 48
N8 4A 48
Wighton M. TW7: Isle 2J 113
Wigley Rd. TW13: Felt 2B 130
Wigmore Ct. *W13* *1A 96*
(off Singapore Rd.)
Wigmore Hall 7J 5
Wigmore Pl. W1 7J 5 (6F 83)
Wigmore Rd. SM5: Cars 2B 166
Wigmore St. W1 7H 5 (6E 82)
Wigmore Wlk. SM5: Cars 2B 166
Wigram Ho. *E14* *7D 86*
(off Wade's Pl.)
Wigram Rd. E11 6A 52
Wigram Sq. E17 3E 50
Wigston Cl. N18 5K 33
Wigston Rd. E13 4K 87
Wigton Gdns. HA7: Stan 1E 42
Wigton Pl. SE11 6K 19 (5A 102)
Wigton Rd. E17 1B 50
Wilberforce Ct. BR2: Kes 7B 172
HA8: Edg *4A 28*
(off King's Dr.)
Wilberforce M. SW4 4H 119
Wilberforce Rd. N4 2B 66
(not continuous)
NW9 6C 44
Wilberforce Wlk. E15 5G 69
Wilberforce Way SW19 6F 135
Wilbraham Ho. *SW8* *7J 101*
(off Wandsworth Rd.)
Wilbraham Mans. *SW1* *3G 17*
(off Wilbraham Pl.)
Wilbraham Pl. SW1 3F 17 (4D 100)
Wilbrahams Almshouses
EN5: Barn 2C 20
Wilbury Way N18 5J 33
Wilby M. W11 1H 99
Wilcox Cl. SW8 7J 101
(not continuous)
Wilcox Gdns. TW17: Shep 3A 146
Wilcox Ho. *E3* *5B 86*
(off Ackroyd Dr.)
Wilcox Pl. SW1 2B 18 (3G 101)
Wilcox Rd. SM1: Sutt 4K 165
SW8 7J 101
TW11: Tedd 4H 131
Wildberry Cl. W7 4A 96
Wildcat Rd. TW6: H'row A 6C 174
Wild Ct. WC2 1G 13 (6K 83)
(not continuous)
Wildcroft Gdns. HA8: Edg 6J 27
Wildcroft Mnr. SW15 7E 116
Wildcroft Rd. SW15 7E 116
Wilde Cl. E8 1G 85
Wilde Ho. *W2* *7B 82*
(off Gloucester Ter.)
Wilde Pl. N13 6G 33
SW18 7B 118
Wilder Cl. HA4: Ruis 1K 57
Wilderness, The
KT8: W Mole, E Mos 5G 149
TW12: Ham H 4F 131
Wilderness Island Nature Reserve 2E 166
Wilderness M. SW4 4F 119
Wilderness Rd. BR7: Chst 7F 143
Wilde Rd. DA8: Erith 7H 109
Wilderton Rd. N16 7E 48
Wildfell Rd. SE6 7D 122
Wild Goose Dr. SE14 1J 121
Wild Hatch NW11 6J 45
Wild's Rents SE1 7G 15 (3E 102)
Wild St. WC2 1F 13 (6J 83)
Wildwood Cl. SE12 7H 123
Wildwood Gro. NW3 1A 64
Wildwood Ri. NW11 1A 64
Wildwood Rd. NW11 6K 45
Wildwood Ter. NW3 1A 64
Wilford Cl. EN2: Enf 3J 23
Wilford Rd. CR0: C'don 6C 156
Wilfred Ct. *N15* *5D 48*
(off South Gro.)
Wilfred Owen Cl.
SW19 6A 136
Wilfred St. SW1 1A 18 (3G 101)
Wilfrid Gdns. W3 5J 79
Wilkes Rd. TW8: Bford 6E 96
Wilkes St. E1 5K 9 (5F 85)
Wilkie Ho. *SW1* *5D 18*
(off Cureton St.)
Wilkins Cl. CR4: Mitc 1C 154
UB3: Harl 5H 93
Wilkins Ho. *SW1* *7A 18*
(off Churchill Gdns.)
Wilkinson Cl. UB10: Hil 1D 74
Wilkinson Ct. SW17 4B 136
Wilkinson Gdns. SE25 1E 156
Wilkinson Ho. *N1* *2D 84*
(off Cranston Est.)
Wilkinson Rd. E16 6A 88
Wilkinson St. SW8 7K 101
Wilkinson Way W4 2K 97
Wilkin St. NW5 6E 64
Wilkin St. M. NW5 6F 65
Wilks Gdns. CR0: C'don 1A 170
Wilks Pl. N1 2E 84
Willan Rd. N17 2D 48
Willan Wall E16 7H 87
Willard St. SW8 3F 119
Willcocks Cl. KT9: Chess 3E 162
Willcott Rd. W3 1H 97
Will Crooks Gdns. SE9 4A 124
Willenfield Rd. NW10 2J 79
Willenhall Av. EN5: New Bar 6F 21
Willenhall Ct. EN5: New Bar 6F 21
Willenhall Dr. UB3: Hayes 7G 75
Willenhall Rd. SE18 5F 107
Willersley Av. BR6: Orp 3H 173
DA15: Sidc 1K 143
Willersley Cl. DA15: Sidc 1K 143
WILLESDEN 6C 62
Willesden Belle Vue Cinema *6D 62*
(within Library)
WILLESDEN GREEN 6E 62
Willesden La. NW2 6E 62
NW6 6E 62
Willesden Section Ho.
NW6 *6F 63*
(off Willesden La.)
Willesden Sports Cen. 1D 80
Willesden Sports Stadium 1D 80
Willes Rd. NW5 6F 65
Willett Cl. BR5: Pet W 6J 161
UB5: Yead 3A 76
Willett Ho. *E13* *2K 87*
(off Queens Rd. W.)
Willett Pl. CR7: Thor H 5A 156

Willett Rd. CR7: Thor H 5A 156
Willett Way BR5: Pet W 5H 161
William IV St. WC2 3E 12 (7J 83)
William Allen Ho. HA8: Edg 7A 28
William Ash Cl. RM9: Dag 6B 72
William Banfield Ho. *SW6* *2H 117*
(off Munster Rd.)
William Barefoot Dr. SE9 4E 142
William Blake Ho. SW11 1C 118
William Bonney Est. SW4 4H 119
William Booth Rd. SE20 1G 157
William Carey Way HA1: Harr 6J 41
William Caslon Ho. *E2* *2H 85*
(off Patriot Sq.)
William Channing Ho. *E2* *3H 85*
(off Canrobert St.)
William Cl. N2 3B 46
RM5: Col R 1J 55
SE13 3E 122
UB2: S'hall 2G 95
William Cobbett Ho. *W8* *3K 99*
(off Scarsdale Pl.)
William Ct. W5 5C 78
William Covell Cl. EN2: Enf 1E 22
William Dr. HA7: Stan 6F 27
William Dromey Ct. NW6 7H 63
William Dunbar Ho. *NW6* *2H 81*
(off Albert Rd.)
William Dyce M. SW16 4H 137
William Ellis Way *SE16* *3G 103*
(off St James's Rd.)
William Evans Ho. *SE8* *4K 103*
(off Bush Rd.)
William Farm La. SW15 3D 116
William Fenn Ho. *E2* *1K 9*
(off Shipton Rd.)
William Foster La. DA16: Well 2A 126
William Gdns. SW15 5D 116
William Gibbs Ct. *SW1* *2C 18*
(off Old Pye St.)
William Gunn Ho. NW3 5C 64
William Guy Gdns. E3 3D 86
William Harvey Ho. *SW19* *1G 135*
(off Whitlock Dr.)
William Henry Wlk. SW8 7C 18 (6H 101)
William Hunt Mans. SW13 6E 98
William Margrie Cl. SE15 2G 121
William M. SW1 7F 11 (2D 100)
William Morley Cl. E6 1B 88
William Morris Cl. E17 3B 50
William Morris Gallery 3C 50
William Morris Ho. W6 6F 99
William Morris Way SW6 3A 118
William Perkin Ct. UB6: G'frd 6J 59
William Pike Ho. *RM7: Rom* *6K 55*
(off Waterloo Gdns.)
William Pl. E3 2B 86
William Rathbone Ho. *E2* *3H 85*
(off Florida St.)
William Rd. NW1 2A 6 (3G 83)
SM1: Sutt 5A 166
SW19 7G 135
William Rushbrooke Ho.
SE16 *4G 103*
(off Rouel Rd.)
Williams Av. E17 1B 50
William Saville Ho. *NW6* *2H 81*
(off Denmark Rd.)
William's Bldgs. E2 4J 85
Williams Cl. N8 6H 47
SW6 7G 99
Williams Dr. TW3: Houn 4E 112
Williams Gro. KT6: Surb 6C 150
N22 1A 48
Williams Ho. *E9* *1H 85*
(off King Edward's Rd.)
NW2 *3E 62*
(off Stoll Cl.)
SW1 *4D 18*
(off Regency St.)
Williams La. SM4: Mord 5A 154
SW14 3J 115
William Smith Ho. *DA17: Belv* *3G 109*
(off Ambrooke Rd.)
Williamson Cl. SE10 5H 105
Williamson Ct. SE17 5C 102
Williamson Rd. N4 6B 48
Williamson St. N7 4J 65
Williamson Way NW7 6B 30
William Sq. *SE16* *7A 86*
(off Sovereign Cres.)
Williams Rd. UB2: S'hall 4C 94
W13 1A 96
Williams Ter. CR0: Wadd 6A 168
William St. E10 6D 50
IG11: Bark 7G 71
N17 7A 34
SM5: Cars 3C 166
SW1 7F 11 (2D 100)
Williams Way DA2: Dart 2K 145
William White Ct. *E13* *1A 88*
(off Green St.)
William Wood Ho. *SE26* *3J 139*
(off Shrublands Cl.)
Willifield Way NW11 4H 45
Willingale Cl. IG8: Wfd G 6F 37
Willingdon Rd. N22 2B 48
Willingham Cl. NW5 5G 65
Willingham Ter. NW5 5G 65
Willingham Way
KT1: King T 3G 151
Willington Ct. E5 3A 68
Willington Rd. SW9 3J 119
Willis Av. SM2: Sutt 6C 166
Willis Ct. BR4: W W'ck 2F 171
CR7: Thor H 6A 156
Willis Ho. *E14* *7D 86*
(off Hale St.)
Willis Rd. CR0: C'don 7C 156
DA8: Erith 4J 109
E15 2H 87
Willis St. E14 6D 86
Willis Yd. N14 7C 22
Will Miles Ct. SW19 7A 136
Willmore End SW19 1K 153
Willoughby Av. CR0: Bedd 4K 167
Willoughby Dr. RM13: Rain 7K 73
Willoughby Gro. N17 7C 34
Willoughby Highwalk *EC2* *6E 8*
(off Moor La.)
Willoughby Ho. *E1* *1H 103*
(off Reardon Path)
EC2 5E 8
Willoughby La. N17 6C 34
Willoughby M. N17 7C 34
SW4 *4F 119*
(off Wix's La.)
Willoughby Pk. Rd. N17 7C 34
Willoughby Pas. *E14* *1C 104*
(off W. India Av.)
Willoughby Rd. KT2: King T 1F 151
N8 3A 48
Willoughby Rd. NW3 4B 64
TW1: Twick 5C 114
(not continuous)
Willoughbys, The SW14 3A 116
Willoughby St. WC1 6E 6
Willoughby Way SE7 4K 105
Willow Av. DA15: Sidc 6A 126
SW13 2B 116
UB7: Yiew 7B 74
Willow Bank KT7: T Ditt 1A 162
SW6 3G 117
TW10: Ham 3B 132
Willowbay Cl. EN5: Barn 6A 20
Willow Bri. Rd. N1 6C 66
(not continuous)
Willowbrook TW12: Ham H 5F 131
Willowbrook Est. SE15 7G 103
Willow Brook Rd. SE15 7F 103
Willowbrook Rd.
TW19: Stanw 2A 128
UB2: S'hall 3E 94
Willow Bus. Cen., The
CR4: Mitc 6D 154
Willow Bus. Pk. SE26 3J 139
Willow Cl. BR2: Brom 5D 160
DA5: Bexl 6F 127
IG9: Buck H 3G 37
SE6 1H 141
TW8: Bford 6C 96
Willow Cotts. TW9: Kew 6G 97
TW13: Hanw 3C 130
Willow Ct. *E11* *2G 69*
(off Trinity Cl.)
EC2 3G 9
HA3: Hrw W 1K 41
HA8: Edg 4K 27
N12 4E 30
NW6 7G 63
SM6: Wall *7F 167*
(off Willow Rd.)
TW16: Sun *7G 129*
(off Staines Rd. W.)
W4 *7A 98*
(off Corney Reach Way)
W9 *5J 81*
(off Admiral Wlk.)
Willowcourt Av. HA3: Kent 5B 42
Willow Dene HA5: Pinn 2B 40
WD23: B Hea 1D 26
Willowdene N6 7D 46
SE15 7H 103
Willowdene Cl. TW2: Whitt 7G 113
Willowdene Ct. *N20* *7F 21*
(off High Rd.)
Willow Dr. EN5: Barn 4B 20
Willow End KT6: Surb 1E 162
N20 2D 30
Willowfields Cl. SE18 5J 107
Willow Gdns. HA4: Ruis 2H 57
TW3: Houn 1E 112
Willow Grange DA14: Sidc 3B 144
Willow Grn. NW9 1A 44
Willow Gro. BR7: Chst 6E 142
E13 2J 87
HA4: Ruis 2H 57
Willowhayne Ct. *KT12: Walt T* *7K 147*
(off Willowhayne Dr.)
Willowhayne Dr. KT12: Walt T 7K 147
Willowhayne Gdns. KT4: Wor Pk 3E 164
Willow Ho. BR2: Brom 2G 159
SE1 *4F 103*
(off Curtis St.)
W10 *4F 81*
(off Maple Wlk.)
Willow La. CR4: Mitc 5D 154
SE18 4D 106
Willow Lodge SW6 1F 117
TW16: Sun *7H 129*
(off Forest Dr.)
Willowmead Cl. W5 4D 78
Willow Mt. CR0: C'don 3E 168
Willow Pl. SW1 3B 18 (4G 101)
Willow Rd. E12 3D 70
EN1: Enf 3K 23
KT3: N Mald 4J 151
NW3 4B 64
RM6: Chad H 6E 54
SL3: Poyle 5A 174
SM6: Wall 7F 167
W5 2E 96
Willows, The BR3: Beck 1C 158
E6 7D 70
Willows Av.
SM4: Mord 5K 153
Willows Cl. HA5: Pinn 2A 40
Willowside Ct. EN2: Enf 3G 23
Willows Ter. *NW10* *2B 80*
(off Rucklidge Av.)
Willow St. E4 1A 36
EC2 3G 9 (4E 84)
RM7: Rom 4J 55
Willow Tree Cl. E3 1B 86
SW18 1K 135
UB4: Yead 4A 76
UB5: N'olt 6D 58
Willowtree Cl. UB10: Ick 3E 56
Willow Tree Ct. DA14: Sidc 5A 144
HA0: Wemb 5D 60
Willow Tree La. UB4: Yead 4A 76
Willow Tree Rdbt. UB4: Yead 5B 76
Willow Tree Wlk. BR1: Brom 1K 159
Willowtree Way CR7: Thor H 1A 156
Willow Va. BR7: Chst 6F 143
W12 1C 98
Willow Vw. SW19 1B 154
Willow Wlk. BR6: Farnb 3F 173
E17 5B 50
IG1: Ilf 2F 71
N2 2B 46
N15 4B 48
N21 6E 22
SE1 3E 102
SM3: Sutt 3H 165
Willow Way HA0: Wemb 3A 60
KT19: Ewe 6K 163
N3 7E 30
SE26 3J 139
TW2: Twick 2F 131
TW16: Sun 4J 147
W11 7F 81
Willow Wood Cres. SE25 6E 156
Willow Wren Wharf
UB2: S'hall 4K 93
Willrose Cres. SE2 5B 108
Willsbridge Ct. SE15 6E 102
Wills Cres. TW3: Houn 6F 113
Wills Gro. NW7 5H 29
(not continuous)
Wilman Gro. E8 7G 67
Wilmar Cl. UB4: Hayes 4F 75
Wilmar Gdns. BR4: W W'ck 1D 170
Wilmcote Ho. *W2* *5K 81*
(off Woodchester Sq.)
Wilment Ct. NW2 3E 62
Wilmer Cl. KT2: King T 5F 133
Wilmer Cres. KT2: King T 5F 133
Wilmer Gdns. N1 1E 84
(not continuous)
Wilmer Lea Cl. E15 7E 68
Wilmer Pl. N16 2F 67
Wilmers Ct. *NW10* *1K 79*
(off Lawrence Av.)
Wilmer Way N14 5C 32
Wilmington Av. W4 7K 97
Wilmington Ct.
SW16 7J 137
Wilmington Gdns.
IG11: Bark 6H 71
Wilmington Sq. WC1 2J 7 (3A 84)
(not continuous)
Wilmington St. WC1 2J 7 (3A 84)
Wilmot Cl. N2 2A 46
SE15 7G 103
Wilmot Pl. *NW1* *7G 65*
(off St Pancras Way)
NW1 7G 65
(Rochester Rd.)
W7 1J 95
Wilmot Rd. E10 2D 68
N17 3D 48
SM5: Cars 5D 166
Wilmot St. E2 4H 85
Wilmount St. SE18 4F 107
Wilna Rd. SW18 7A 118
Wilsham St. W11 1F 99
Wilshaw Cl. NW4 3C 44
Wilshaw Ho. SE8 7C 104
Wilshaw St. SE14 1C 122

Wilsmere Dr. HA3: Hrw W 7D 26
UB5: N'olt 6C 58
Wilson Av. CR4: Mitc 7C 136
Wilson Cl. CR2: S Croy 5D 168
HA9: Wemb 7F 43
Wilson Ct. RM7: Rush G 6K 55
(off Union Rd.)
SE28 .... 3G 107
Wilson Dr. HA9: Wemb 7F 43
Wilson Gdns. HA1: Harr 7G 41
Wilson Gro. SE16 .... 2H 103
Wilson Ho. NW6 .... 7A 64
(off Goldhurst Ter.)
Wilson Rd. E6 .... 3B 88
IG1: Ilf 7D 52
KT9: Chess 6F 163
SE5 .... 1E 120
Wilson's Av. N17 .... 2F 49
Wilson's Pl. E14 .... 6B 86
Wilson's Rd. W6 .... 5F 99
Wilson St. E17 .... 5E 50
EC2 .... 5F 9 (5D 84)
N21 .... 7F 23
Wilson Wlk. W4 .... 4B 98
(off Prebend Gdns.)
W6 .... 4B 98
(off Prebend Gdns.)
Wilstone Cl. UB4: Yead 4C 76
Wiltern Ct. NW2 .... 6G 63
Wilthorne Gdns. RM10: Dag 7H 73
Wilton Av. W4 .... 5A 98
Wilton Cl. UB7: Harm 2E 174
Wilton Ct. E1 .... 6H 85
(off Cavell St.)
Wilton Cres. SW1 .... 7G 11 (2E 100)
SW19 .... 7H 135
Wilton Dr. RM5: Col R 1J 55
Wilton Est. E8 .... 6G 67
Wilton Gdns. KT8: W Mole 3E 148
Wilton Gro. KT3: N Mald 6B 152
SW19 .... 1H 153
Wilton Ho. CR2: S Croy 5C 168
(off Nottingham Rd.)
Wilton M. E8 .... 6H 67
SW1 .... 1H 17 (3E 100)
Wilton Pde. TW13: Felt 2J 129
Wilton Pl. HA1: Harr 6K 41
SW1 .... 7G 11 (2E 100)
Wilton Rd. EN4: Cockf 4J 21
N10 .... 2E 46
SE2 .... 4C 108
SW1 .... 2A 18 (3F 101)
SW19 .... 7C 136
TW4: Houn 3B 112
Wilton Row SW1 .... 7G 11 (2E 100)
Wilton Sq. N1 .... 1D 84
Wilton St. SW1 .... 1J 17 (3F 101)
Wilton Ter. SW1 .... 1G 17 (3E 100)
Wilton Vs. N1 .... 1D 84
(off Wilton Sq.)
Wilton Way E8 .... 6G 67
Wiltshire Cl. NW7 .... 5G 29
SW3 .... 3E 16 (4D 100)
Wiltshire Ct. CR2: S Croy 5C 168
IG1: Ilf 6G 71
N4 .... 1K 65
(off Marquis Rd.)
Wiltshire Gdns. N4 .... 6C 48
TW2: Twick 1G 131
Wiltshire La. HA5: Eastc 3H 39
Wiltshire Rd. BR6: Orp 7K 161
CR7: Thor H 3A 156
SW9 .... 3A 120
Wiltshire Row N1 .... 1D 84
Wilverley Cres. KT3: N Mald 6A 152
Wimbart Rd. SW2 .... 7K 119
WIMBLEDON 6G 135
Wimbledon
All England Lawn Tennis & Croquet Club 4G 135
Wimbledon Bri. SW19 .... 6H 135
Wimbledon Cl. SW20 .... 7F 135
Wimbledon Common 4C 134
Wimbledon Hill Rd. SW19 .... 6G 135
Wimbledon Lawn Tennis Mus. 3G 135
Wimbledon Leisure Cen. 6K 135
Wimbledon Mus. of Local History 6G 135
WIMBLEDON PARK 3J 135
Wimbledon Pk. Ct. SW19 .... 1H 135
Wimbledon Pk. Rd. SW18 .... 2G 135
SW19 .... 2G 135
Wimbledon Pk. Side SW19 .... 3F 135
Wimbledon Rd. SW17 .... 4A 136
Wimbledon Stadium Bus. Cen.
SW17 .... 3K 135
Wimbledon Stadium (Greyhound) 4A 136
Wimbledon Theatre 7J 135
Wimbledon Windmill Mus. 2D 134
Wimbolt St. E2 .... 3G 85
Wimborne Av. BR5: St P 4K 161
BR7: Chst 4K 161
UB2: S'hall 4E 94
UB4: Yead 6K 75
Wimborne Cl. IG9: Buck H 2E 36
KT4: Wor Pk 1E 164
SE12 .... 5H 123
Wimborne Ct. SW12 .... 3G 137
UB5: N'olt 6E 58
Wimborne Dr. HA5: Pinn 7B 40
NW9 .... 3G 43
Wimborne Gdns. W13 .... 5B 78
Wimborne Ho. E16 .... 7H 87
(off Victoria Dock Rd.)
NW1 .... 4D 4
(off Harewood Av.)
SW8 .... 7K 101
(off Dorset Rd.)
SW12 .... 3G 137
Wimborne Rd. N9 .... 2B 34
N17 .... 2E 48
Wimborne Way BR3: Beck 3K 157
Wimbourne Ct. N1 .... 2D 84
(off Wimbourne St.)
Wimbourne St. N1 .... 2D 84
Wimpole Cl. BR2: Brom 4A 160
KT1: King T 2F 151
Wimpole M. W1 .... 5J 5 (5F 83)
Wimpole Rd. UB7: Yiew 1A 92
Wimpole St. W1 .... 6J 5 (5F 83)
Wimshurst Cl. CR0: Wadd 1J 167
Winans Wlk. SW9 .... 2A 120
Winant Ho. E14 .... 7D 86
(off Simpson's Rd.)
Wincanton Ct. N11 .... 6K 31
(off Martock Gdns.)
Wincanton Cres.
UB5: N'olt 5E 58
Wincanton Gdns.
IG6: Ilf 3F 53
Wincanton Rd. SW18 .... 7H 117
Winchcombe Rd.
SM5: Cars 7B 154
Winchcomb Gdns. SE9 .... 3B 124
Winchelsea Av. DA7: Bex 7F 109
Winchelsea Cl. SW15 .... 5F 117
Winchelsea Ho. SE16 .... 2J 103
(off Swan Rd.)
Winchelsea Rd. E7 .... 3J 69
N17 .... 3E 48
NW10 .... 1K 79
Winchelsey Ri. CR2: S Croy 6F 169
Winchendon Rd. SW6 .... 1H 117
TW11: Tedd 4H 131
Winchester Av. NW6 .... 1G 81
NW9 .... 3G 43
TW5: Hest 6D 94
Winchester Cl. BR2: Brom 3H 159
E6 .... 6D 88
EN1: Enf 5K 23
KT2: King T 7H 133
Winchester Cl. SE17 .... 4B 102
SL3: Poyle 4A 174
Winchester Ct. W8 .... 2J 99
(off Vicarage Ga.)
Winchester Dr. HA5: Pinn 5B 40
Winchester Ho. IG11: Bark 7A 72
(off Keir Hardie Way)
SE18 .... 7B 106
(off Portway Gdns.)
SW3 .... 7B 16
SW9 .... 7A 102
W2 .... 6A 82
(off Hallfield Est.)
Winchester M. KT4: Wor Pk 2F 165
Winchester Pk. BR2: Brom 3H 159
Winchester Pl. E8 .... 5F 67
N6 .... 1F 65
Winchester Rd. BR2: Brom 3H 159
DA7: Bex 2D 126
E4 .... 7K 35
HA3: Kent 4E 42
HA6: Nwood 2H 39
IG1: Ilf 3H 71
KT12: Walt T 7J 147
N6 .... 7F 47
N9 .... 1A 34
NW3 .... 7B 64
TW1: Twick 6B 114
TW13: Hanw 3D 130
UB3: Harl 7G 93
Winchester Sq. SE1 .... 4E 14
Winchester St. SW1 .... 5K 17 (5F 101)
W3 .... 1J 97
Winchester Wlk. SE1 .... 4E 14 (1D 102)
Winchester Wharf
SE1 .... 4E 14
(off Clink St.)
Winchet Wlk. CR0: C'don 6J 157
Winchfield Cl. HA3: Kent 6C 42
Winchfield Ho. SW15 .... 6B 116
Winchfield Rd. SE26 .... 5A 140
Winch Ho. E14 .... 3D 104
(off Tiller Rd.)
SW10 .... 7A 100
(off King's Rd.)
Winchilsea Cres. KT8: W Mole 2G 149
Winchilsea Ho. NW8 .... 2B 4
(off St John's Wood Rd.)
WINCHMORE HILL 7F 23
Winchmore Hill Rd.
N14 .... 1C 32
N21 .... 1C 32
Winchmore Vs. N21 .... 7E 22
(off Winchmore Hill Rd.)
Winchstone Cl. TW17: Shep 4B 146
Winckley Cl. HA3: Kent 5F 43
Winckworth Ct. N1 .... 2F 9
(off Brunswick Pl.)
Wincott Pde. SE11 .... 4A 102
(off Wincott St.)
Wincott St. SE11 .... 4K 19 (4A 102)
Wincrofts Dr. SE9 .... 4H 125
Windall Cl. SE19 .... 1G 157
Windborough Rd. SM5: Cars 7E 166
Windermere NW1 .... 2K 5
(off Albany St.)
Windermere Av. HA4: Ruis 7A 40
HA9: Kent, Wemb 7C 42
N3 .... 3J 45
NW6 .... 1G 81
SW19 .... 3K 153
Windermere Cl. BR6: Farnb 3F 173
TW14: Felt 1H 129
TW19: Stanw 1A 128
Windermere Ct. HA9: Wemb 7C 42
SM5: Cars 3E 166
SW13 .... 6B 98
Windermere Gdns. IG4: Ilf 5C 52
Windermere Gro. HA9: Wemb 1C 60
Windermere Hall HA8: Edg 5A 28
Windermere Ho. E3 .... 4B 86
EN5: New Bar 4E 20
TW7: Isle 5K 113
Windermere Point SE15 .... 7J 103
(off Old Kent Rd.)
Windermere Rd. BR4: W W'ck 2G 171
CR0: C'don 1F 169
DA7: Bex 2J 127
N10 .... 1F 47
N19 .... 2G 65
SW15 .... 4A 134
SW16 .... 1G 155
UB1: S'hall 5D 76
W5 .... 3C 96
Windermere Way UB7: Yiew 1A 92
Winders Rd. SW11 .... 2C 118
(not continuous)
Windfield Cl. SE26 .... 4K 139
Windham Rd. TW9: Rich 3F 115
Winding, The W2 .... 6B 4
Winding Way RM8: Dag 3C 72
Windlass Pl. SE8 .... 4A 104
Windlesham Gro. SW19 .... 1F 135
Windley Cl. SE23 .... 2J 139
Windmill WC1 .... 5G 7
(off New North St.)
Windmill Av. UB2: S'hall 1G 95
Windmill Bri. Ho. CR0: C'don 1E 168
(off Freemasons Rd.)
Windmill Bus. Village
TW16: Sun 1G 147
Windmill Cl. KT6: Surb 1C 162
SE1 .... 4G 103
(off Beatrice Rd.)
SE13 .... 2E 122
TW16: Sun 7G 129
Windmill Ct. NW2 .... 6G 63
W5 .... 4C 96
(off Windmill Rd.)
Windmill Dr. BR2: Kes 4A 172
NW2 .... 3G 63
SW4 .... 5F 119
Windmill Gdns. EN2: Enf 3F 23
Windmill Grn. TW17: Shep 7G 147
(off Walton La.)
Windmill Gro. CR0: C'don 6C 156
Windmill Hill EN2: Enf 3G 23
HA4: Ruis 7H 39
NW3 .... 3A 64
Windmill Ho. E14 .... 4C 104
SE1 .... 5K 13
(off Windmill Wlk.)
Windmill La. E15 .... 6F 69
KT6: Surb 6B 150
TW7: Isle 1G 95
UB2: S'hall 1G 95
UB6: G'frd 6G 77
WD23: B Hea 1D 26
Windmill M. W4 .... 4A 98
Windmill Pas. W4 .... 4A 98
Windmill Pl. Bus. Cen.
UB2: S'hall 1G 95
Windmill Ri. KT2: King T 7H 133
Windmill Rd. CR0: C'don 7C 156
CR4: Mitc 5G 155
N18 .... 4J 33
SW18 .... 6B 118
SW19 .... 2D 134
Windmill Rd. TW8: Bford 4C 96
TW12: Ham H 5F 131
TW16: Sun 1G 147
W4 .... 4A 98
W5 .... 4C 96
Windmill Rd. W.
TW16: Sun 2G 147
Windmill Row SE11 .... 6J 19 (5A 102)
Windmill St. W1 .... 6C 6 (5H 83)
(not continuous)
WD23: B Hea 1D 26
Windmill Ter. TW17: Shep 7G 147

Windmill Wlk. SE1 . . . 5K 13 (1A 102)
Windmill Way HA4: Ruis . . . 1H 57
Windmore Cl.
HA0: Wemb . . . 5A 60
Windrose Cl. SE16 . . . 2K 103
Windrush KT3: N Mald . . . 4H 151
SE28 . . . 1B 108
Windrush Cl. E8 . . . 7G 67
N17 . . . 1E 48
SW11 . . . 4B 118
UB10: Ick . . . 4B 56
W4 . . . 1J 115
Windrush Ho. NW8 . . . 5B 4
(off Church St. Est.)
Windrush La. SE23 . . . 3K 139
Windrush Rd. NW10 . . . 1K 79
Windsock Cl. SE16 . . . 4B 104
Windsor Av. E17 . . . 2A 50
HA8: Edg . . . 4C 28
KT3: N Mald . . . 5J 151
KT8: W Mole . . . 3E 148
SM3: Cheam . . . 3G 165
SW19 . . . 1A 154
UB10: Hil . . . 1D 74
Windsor Cen., The N1 . . . 1B 84
(off Windsor St.)
Windsor Cl. BR7: Chst . . . 5F 143
HA2: Harr . . . 3E 58
HA6: Nwood . . . 2J 39
N3 . . . 2G 45
SE27 . . . 4C 138
TW6: H'row A . . . 6D 174
(off Whittle Rd.)
TW8: Bford . . . 6B 96
Windsor Cotts. SE14 . . . 7B 104
(off Amersham Gro.)
Windsor Ct. HA5: Pinn . . . 3B 40
KT1: King T . . . 4D 150
(off Palace Rd.)
N11 . . . 5J 31
N14 . . . 7B 22
NW3 . . . 4J 63
NW11 . . . 6G 45
(off Golders Grn. Rd.)
SE16 . . . 7K 85
(off King & Queen Wharf)
SW3 . . . 5D 16
(off Jubilee Pl.)
SW11 . . . 2B 118
TW16: Sun . . . 7J 129
W2 . . . 7K 81
(off Moscow Rd.)
W10 . . . 6F 81
(off Bramley Rd.)
WD23: Bush . . . 1B 26
(off Catsey La.)
Windsor Cres. HA2: Harr . . . 3E 58
HA9: Wemb . . . 3H 61
Windsor Dr. BR6: Chels . . . 6K 173
EN4: E Barn . . . 6J 21
Windsor Gdns. CR0: Bedd . . . 3J 167
UB3: Harl . . . 3F 93
W9 . . . 5J 81
Windsor Gro. SE27 . . . 4C 138
Windsor Hall E16 . . . 1K 105
(off Wesley Av.)
Windsor Ho. E2 . . . 3K 85
(off Knottisford St.)
N1 . . . 2C 84
Windsor Ho. NW1 . . . 1K 5
NW2 . . . 6G 63
(off Chatsworth Rd.)
UB5: N'olt . . . 6E 58
(off The Farmlands)
Windsor M. SE6 . . . 1E 140
SE23 . . . 1A 140
SW18 . . . 7A 118
(off Wilna Rd.)
Windsor Pk. Rd. UB3: Harl . . . 7H 93
Windsor Pl. SW1 . . . 3B 18 (3G 101)
Windsor Rd. CR7: Thor H . . . 2B 156
DA6: Bex . . . 4E 126
E4 . . . 4J 35
E7 . . . 5K 69
E10 . . . 2D 68
E11 . . . 1J 69
EN5: Barn . . . 6A 20
HA3: Hrw W . . . 1G 41
IG1: Ilf . . . 4F 71
KT2: King T . . . 7E 132
KT4: Wor Pk . . . 2C 164
N3 . . . 2G 45
N7 . . . 3J 65
N13 . . . 3F 33
N17 . . . 2G 49
NW2 . . . 6D 62
RM8: Dag . . . 3E 72
TW4: Cran . . . 2K 111
TW9: Kew . . . 2F 115
TW11: Tedd . . . 5H 131
TW16: Sun . . . 6J 129
UB2: S'hall . . . 3D 94
W5 . . . 7E 78
(not continuous)
Windsors, The IG9: Buck H . . . 2H 37
Windsor St. N1 . . . 1B 84
Windsor Ter. N1 . . . 1D 8 (3C 84)
Windsor Wlk. SE5 . . . 2D 120
Windsor Way W14 . . . 4F 99
Windsor Wharf E9 . . . 6C 68
Windspoint Dr. SE15 . . . 6H 103
Windus Rd. N16 . . . 1F 67
Windus Wlk. N16 . . . 1F 67
Windy Ridge BR1: Brom . . . 1C 160
Windy Ridge Cl. SW19 . . . 5F 135
Wine Cl. E1 . . . 7J 85
(not continuous)
Wine Office Ct.
EC4 . . . 7K 7 (6A 84)
Winery La. KT1: King T . . . 3F 151
Winey Cl. KT9: Chess . . . 7C 162
Winford Ct. SE15 . . . 1H 121
Winford Ho. E3 . . . 7B 68
Winford Pde. UB1: S'hall . . . 6F 77
(off Marconi Way)
Winforton St. SE10 . . . 1E 122
Winfrith Rd. SW18 . . . 7A 118
Wingate Cres. CR0: C'don . . . 6J 155
Wingate Rd. DA14: Sidc . . . 6C 144
IG1: Ilf . . . 5F 71
W6 . . . 3D 98
Wingate Trad. Est. N17 . . . 7A 34
Wingfield Ct. DA15: Sidc . . . 2K 143
E14 . . . 7F 87
(off John Smith M.)
Wingfield Ho. E2 . . . 2J 9
(off Virginia Rd.)
NW6 . . . 2K 81
(off Tollgate Gdns.)
Wingfield M. SE15 . . . 3G 121
Wingfield Rd. E15 . . . 4G 69
E17 . . . 5D 50
KT2: King T . . . 6F 133
Wingfield St. SE15 . . . 3G 121
Wingfield Way HA4: Ruis . . . 6K 57
Wingford Rd. SW2 . . . 6J 119
Wingmore Rd. SE24 . . . 3C 120
Wingrad Ho. E1 . . . 5J 85
(off Jubilee St.)
Wingrave SE17 . . . 4D 102
Wingrave Rd. W6 . . . 6E 98
Wingreen NW8 . . . 1K 81
(off Abbey Rd.)
Wingrove E4 . . . 7H 25
Wingrove Ct. RM7: Rom . . . 5J 55
Wingrove Rd. SE6 . . . 2G 141
Wings Cl. SM1: Sutt . . . 4J 165
Wings Rd. TW6: H'row A . . . 6C 174
Wing Yip Bus. Cen.
NW2 . . . 2D 62
Winicotte Ho. W2 . . . 5B 4
(off Paddington Grn.)
Winifred Pl. N12 . . . 5F 31
Winifred Rd. DA8: Erith . . . 5K 109
RM8: Dag . . . 2E 72
SW19 . . . 1J 153
TW12: Ham H . . . 4E 130
Winifred St. E16 . . . 1D 106
Winifred Ter. E13 . . . 2J 87
(off Upper Rd.)
EN1: Enf . . . 7A 24
Winkfield Rd. E13 . . . 2K 87
N22 . . . 1A 48
Winkley Ct. HA2: Harr . . . 3E 58
N10 . . . 4F 47
(off St James's La.)
Winkley St. E2 . . . 2H 85
Winkworth Cotts. E1 . . . 4J 85
(off Cephas St.)
Winlaton Rd. BR1: Brom . . . 4F 141
Winmill Rd. RM8: Dag . . . 3F 73
Winnett St. W1 . . . 2C 12 (7H 83)
Winningales Ct. IG5: Ilf . . . 2C 52
Winnings Wlk. UB5: N'olt . . . 6C 58
Winnington Cl. N2 . . . 6B 46
Winnington Ho. SE5 . . . 7C 102
(off Wyndham Est.)
W10 . . . 4G 81
(off Southern Row)
Winnington Rd. N2 . . . 6B 46
Winnipeg Dr. BR6: Chels . . . 6K 173
Winnock Rd. UB7: Yiew . . . 1A 92
Winn Rd. SE12 . . . 1J 141
Winns Av. E17 . . . 3B 50
Winns Comn. Rd. SE18 . . . 6J 107
Winns M. N15 . . . 4E 48
Winns Ter. E17 . . . 3C 50
Winsbeach E17 . . . 2F 51
Winscombe Cres. W5 . . . 4D 78
Winscombe St. N19 . . . 2F 65
Winscombe Way HA7: Stan . . . 5F 27
Winsford Rd. SE6 . . . 3B 140
Winsford Ter. N18 . . . 5J 33
Winsham Gro. SW11 . . . 5E 118
Winsham Ho. NW1 . . . 1D 6
(off Churchway)
Winslade Rd. SW2 . . . 5J 119
Winslade Way SE6 . . . 7D 122
Winsland M. W2 . . . 7A 4 (6B 82)
Winsland St. W2 . . . 7A 4 (6B 82)
Winsley St. W1 . . . 7B 6 (6G 83)
Winslow SE17 . . . 5E 102
Winslow Cl. HA5: Eastc . . . 6K 39
NW10 . . . 3A 62
Winslow Gro. E4 . . . 2B 36
Winslow Rd. W6 . . . 6E 98
Winslow Way TW13: Hanw . . . 3B 130
Winsmoor Ct. EN2: Enf . . . 3G 23
WINSOR PARK . . . 5F 89
Winsor Ter. E6 . . . 5E 88
Winstanley Est. SW11 . . . 3B 118
Winstanley Rd. SW11 . . . 3B 118
(not continuous)
Winstead Gdns. RM10: Dag . . . 5J 73
Winston Av. NW9 . . . 7A 44
Winston Cl. HA3: Hrw W . . . 6E 26
RM7: Mawney . . . 4H 55
Winston Ct. BR1: Brom . . . 1K 159
(off Widmore Rd.)
HA3: Hrw W . . . 7A 26
Winston Ho. W13 . . . 2A 96
(off Balfour Rd.)
WC1 . . . 3D 6
Winston Rd. N16 . . . 4D 66
Winston Wlk. W4 . . . 3K 97
Winston Way IG1: Ilf . . . 3F 71
Winter Av. E6 . . . 1C 88
Winterborne Av. BR6: Orp . . . 3H 173
Winterbourne Ho. W11 . . . 7G 81
(off Portland Rd.)
Winterbourne Rd. CR7: Thor H . . . 4A 156
RM8: Dag . . . 2C 72
SE6 . . . 1B 140
Winter Box Wlk. TW10: Rich . . . 5F 115
Winterbrook Rd. SE24 . . . 6C 120
Winterburn Cl. N11 . . . 6K 31
Winterfold Cl. SW19 . . . 2G 135
Wintergreen Cl. E6 . . . 5C 88
Winterleys NW6 . . . 2H 81
(off Denmark Rd.)
Winter Lodge SE16 . . . 5G 103
(off Fern Wlk.)
Winter's Ct. E4 . . . 3J 35
Winterslow Ho. SE5 . . . 2C 120
(off Flaxman Rd.)
Winters Rd. KT7: T Ditt . . . 7B 150
Winterstoke Gdns. NW7 . . . 5H 29
Winterstoke Rd. SE6 . . . 1B 140
Winterton Ct. KT1: Ham W . . . 1D 150
(off Lwr. Teddington Rd.)
SE20 . . . 2G 157
Winterton Ho. E1 . . . 6J 85
(off Deancross St.)
Winterton Pl. SW10 . . . 7A 16 (6A 100)
Winterwell Rd. SW2 . . . 5J 119
Winthorpe Rd. SW15 . . . 4G 117
Winthrop Ho. W12 . . . 7D 80
(off White City Est.)
Winthrop St. E1 . . . 5H 85
Winthrop Wlk. HA9: Wemb . . . 3E 60
(off Everard Way)
Winton Av. N11 . . . 7B 32
Winton Cl. N9 . . . 7E 24
Winton Ct. N1 . . . 2K 83
(off Calshot St.)
Winton Gdns. HA8: Edg . . . 7A 28
Winton Rd. BR6: Farnb . . . 4F 173
Winton Way SW16 . . . 5A 138
Wireworks Ct. SE1 . . . 7C 14
(off Gt. Sufolk St.)
Wirrall Ho. SE26 . . . 3G 139
Wirral Wood Cl. BR7: Chst . . . 6E 142
Wirra Way TW6: H'row A . . . 5C 174
Wisbeach Rd. CR0: C'don . . . 5D 156
Wisbech N4 . . . 1K 65
(off Lorne Rd.)
Wisborough Rd. CR2: Sande . . . 7F 169
Wisden Ho. SW8 . . . 7H 19 (6K 101)
Wisdom Ct. TW7: Isle . . . 3A 114
(off South St.)
Wisdons Cl. RM10: Dag . . . 1H 73
Wise La. NW7 . . . 5H 29
UB7: W Dray . . . 1E 174
Wiseman Rd. E10 . . . 2C 68
Wise Rd. E15 . . . 1F 87
Wiseton Rd. SW17 . . . 1C 136
Wishart Rd. SE3 . . . 2B 124
Wishaw Wlk. N13 . . . 6D 32
Wisley Ho. SW1 . . . 5C 18
(off Rampayne St.)
Wisley Rd. BR5: St P . . . 7A 144
SW11 . . . 5E 118
Wistaria Cl. BR6: Farnb . . . 2F 173
Wisteria Cl. IG1: Ilf . . . 5F 71
NW7 . . . 6G 29
Wisteria Gdns. IG8: Wfd G . . . 5D 36
Wisteria Rd. SE13 . . . 4F 123
Wistow Ho. E2 . . . 1G 85
(off Whiston Rd.)
Witanhurst La. N6 . . . 1E 64
Witan St. E2 . . . 3H 85
Witchwood Ho. SW9 . . . 3A 120
(off Gresham Rd.)
Witham Ct. E10 . . . 3D 68
SW17 . . . 3D 136
Witham Rd. RM10: Dag . . . 5G 73
SE20 . . . 3J 157
TW7: Isle . . . 1H 113
W13 . . . 1A 96
Witherby Cl. CR0: C'don . . . 5E 168

Witherington Rd. N5 5A 66
Withers Cl. KT9: Chess 6C 162
Withers Mead NW9 1B 44
Withers Pl. EC1 3D 8 (4C 84)
Witherston Way SE9 2E 142
Withycombe Rd. SW19 7F 117
Withy Ho. *E1* *4K 85*
(off Globe Rd.)
Withy La. HA4: Ruis 5E 38
Withy Mead E4 3A 36
Witley Ct. WC1 4E 6
Witley Cres. CR0: New Ad 6E 170
Witley Gdns. UB2: S'hall 4D 94
Witley Ho. SW2 7J 119
Witley Ind. Est. UB2: S'hall 4D 94
Witley Point *SW15* *1D 134*
(off Wanborough Dr.)
Witley Rd. N19 2G 65
Witney Cl. UB10: Ick 4B 56
Witney Path SE23 3K 139
Wittenham Way E4 3A 36
Wittering Cl. KT2: King T 5D 132
Wittersham Rd. BR1: Brom 5H 141
Witts Ho. *KT1: King T* *3F 151*
(off Winery La.)
Wivenhoe Cl. SE15 3H 121
Wivenhoe Ct. TW3: Houn 4D 112
Wivenhoe Rd. IG11: Bark 2A 90
Wiverton Rd. SE26 6J 139
Wixom Ho. SE3 4A 124
Wix Rd. RM9: Dag 1D 90
Wix's La. SW4 3F 119
Woburn *W13* *5B 78*
(off Clivedon Ct.)
Woburn Cl. SE28 6D 90
SW19 6A 136
Woburn Ct. CR0: C'don 1C 168
E18 2J 51
SE16 *5H 103*
(off Masters Dr.)
WC1 *4J 83*
(off Bernard St.)
Woburn Mans. *WC1* *5C 6*
(off Torrington Pl.)
Woburn M. WC1 4D 6 (4H 83)
Woburn Pl. WC1 4E 6 (4J 83)
Woburn Rd. CR0: C'don 1C 168
SM5: Cars 1C 166
Woburn Sq. WC1 4D 6 (4H 83)
Woburn Twr. *UB5: Yead* *3B 76*
(off Broomcroft Av.)
Woburn Wlk. WC1 2D 6 (3H 83)
Wodeham Gdns. E1 5G 85
Wodehouse Av. SE5 1F 121
Wodehouse Ct. *W3* *3J 97*
(off Vincent Rd.)
Woffington Cl. KT1: Ham W 1C 150
Woking Cl. SW15 4B 116
Wolcot Ho. *NW1* *1B 6*
(off Aldenham St.)
Woldham Pl. BR2: Brom 4A 160
Woldham Rd. BR2: Brom 4A 160
Wolds Dr. BR6: Farnb 4E 172
Wolfe Cl. BR2: Hayes 6J 159
UB4: Yead 3K 75
Wolfe Cres. SE7 5B 106
SE16 2K 103
Wolfe Ho. *W12* *7D 80*
(off White City Est.)
Wolferton Rd. E12 4D 70
Wolffe Gdns. E15 6H 69
Wolfington Rd. SE27 4B 138
Wolfram Cl. SE13 5G 123
Wolftencroft Cl. SW11 3C 118
Wollaston Cl. SE1 4C 102
Wollaton Ho. *N1* *2A 84*
(off Batchelor St.)
Wollett Ct. *NW1* *7G 65*
(off St Pancras Way)
Wolmer Cl. HA8: Edg 4B 28
Wolmer Gdns. HA8: Edg 3B 28
Wolseley Av. SW19 2J 135
Wolseley Gdns. W4 6H 97
Wolseley Rd. CR4: Mitc 7E 154
E7 7K 69
HA3: W'stone 3J 41
N8 6H 47
N22 1K 47
RM7: Rush G 7K 55
W4 4J 97
Wolseley St. SE1 7K 15 (2G 103)
Wolsey Av. E6 3E 88
E17 3B 50
KT7: T Ditt 5K 149
Wolsey Cl. KT2: King T 1H 151
KT4: Wor Pk 4C 164
SW20 7D 134
TW3: Houn 4G 113
UB2: S'hall 3G 95
Wolsey Ct. NW6 7A 64
SW11 *1C 118*
(off Westbridge Rd.)
Wolsey Cres. CR0: New Ad 7E 170
SM4: Mord 7G 153
Wolsey Dr. KT2: King T 5E 132
KT12: Walt T 7B 148
Wolsey Gro. HA8: Edg 7E 28
Wolsey M. BR6: Chels 5K 173
NW5 6G 65
Wolsey Rd. EN1: Enf 2C 24
KT8: E Mos 4H 149
N1 5D 66
TW12: Ham H 6F 131
TW15: Ashf 4A 128
TW16: Sun 7H 129
Wolsey St. E1 5J 85
Wolsey Way KT9: Chess 5G 163
Wolsternholme HA7: Stan 5G 27
Wolstonbury N12 5D 30
Wolvercote Rd. SE2 2D 108
Wolverley St. E2 3H 85
Wolverton SE17 5E 102
Wolverton Av. KT2: King T 1G 151
Wolverton Gdns. W5 7F 79
W6 4F 99
Wolverton Rd. HA7: Stan 6G 27
Wolverton Way N14 5B 22
Wolves La. N13 7F 33
N22 7F 33
Womersley Rd. N8 6K 47
Wonersh Way
SM2: Cheam 7F 165
Wonford Cl. KT2: King T 1A 152
Wontner Cl. N1 7C 66
Wontner Rd. SW17 2D 136
Wooburn Cl. UB8: Hil 4D 74
Woodall Av. EN3: Pond E 6E 24
Woodall Cl. E14 7D 86
KT9: Chess 7C 162
Woodall Ho. N22 1A 48
Woodall Rd. EN3: Pond E 6E 24
Woodbank Rd. BR1: Brom 3H 141
Woodbastwick Rd.
SE26 5K 139
Woodberry Av. HA2: Harr 4F 41
N21 2F 33
Woodberry Cl. NW7 7A 30
TW16: Sun 6J 129
Woodberry Cres. N10 3F 47
Woodberry Down N4 7C 48
Woodberry Down Est. N4 1C 66
(Spring Pk. Dr.)
N4 7C 48
(Woodberry Gro.)
Woodberry Gdns. N12 6F 31
Woodberry Gro. DA5: Bexl 3K 145
N4 7C 48
N12 6F 31
Woodberry Way E4 7K 25
N12 6F 31
Woodbine Cl. TW2: Twick 2H 131
Woodbine Gro. EN2: Enf 1J 23
SE20 7H 139
Woodbine La. KT4: Wor Pk 3D 164
Woodbine Pl. E11 6J 51
Woodbine Rd. DA15: Sidc 1J 143
Woodbines Av. KT1: King T 3D 150
Woodbine Ter. E9 6J 67
Woodborough Rd. SW15 4D 116
Woodbourne Av. SW16 3H 137
Woodbourne Cl. SW16 3J 137
Woodbourne Gdns. SM6: Wall 7F 167
Woodbridge Cl. N7 2K 65
NW2 3C 62
Woodbridge Ct. IG8: Wfd G 7H 37
Woodbridge Ho. E11 1H 69
Woodbridge Rd. IG11: Bark 5K 71
Woodbridge St. EC1 3A 8 (4B 84)
(not continuous)
Woodbridge Ter. RM6: Chad H 6B 54
Woodbrook Rd. SE2 6A 108
Woodburn Cl. NW4 5F 45
Woodbury Cl. CR0: C'don 2F 169
E11 4K 51
Woodbury Ho. SE26 3G 139
Woodbury Pk. Rd. W13 4B 78
Woodbury Rd. E17 4D 50
Woodbury St. SW17 5C 136
Woodchester Sq. W2 5K 81
Woodchurch Cl. DA14: Sidc 3H 143
Woodchurch Dr. BR1: Brom 7B 142
Woodchurch Rd. NW6 7J 63
Wood Cl. E2 4G 85
HA1: Harr 7H 41
NW9 7K 43
Woodclyffe Dr. BR7: Chst 2E 160
Woodcock Ct. HA3: Kent 7E 42
Woodcock Dell Av. HA3: Kent 7D 42
Woodcock Hill HA3: Kent 5C 42
Woodcock Ho. *E14* *5C 86*
(off Burgess St.)
Woodcock Rd.
TW6: H'row A 7C 174
Woodcocks E16 5A 88
Woodcombe Cres. SE23 1J 139
Woodcote Av. CR7: Thor H 4B 156
NW7 6K 29
SM6: Wall 7F 167
Woodcote Cl. EN3: Pond E 6D 24
KT2: King T 5F 133
Woodcote Dr. BR6: Orp 1H 173
Woodcote Grn. SM6: Wall 7G 167
Woodcote Ho. *SE8* *6B 104*
(off Prince St.)
Woodcote M. SM6: Wall 6F 167
Woodcote Pl. SE27 5B 138
Woodcote Rd. E11 7J 51
SM6: Wall 6F 167
Woodcote Vs. *SE27* *5C 138*
(off Woodcote Pl.)
Wood Crest *SM2: Sutt* *7A 166*
(off Christchurch Pk.)
Woodcroft N21 1F 33
SE9 3D 142
UB6: G'frd 6A 60
Woodcroft Av. HA7: Stan 1A 42
NW7 6F 29
Woodcroft Cres. UB10: Hil 1D 74
Woodcroft M. SE8 4A 104
Woodcroft Rd.
CR7: Thor H 5B 156
Wood Dene *SE15* *1H 121*
(off Queen's Rd.)
Wood Dr. BR7: Chst 6C 142
Woodedge Cl. E4 1C 36
WOOD END
UB4 5H 75
UB5 5G 59
Wood End UB3: Hayes 6G 75
Wood End, The SM6: Wall 7F 167
Woodend SE19 6C 138
SM1: Sutt 2A 166
Wood End Av. HA2: Harr 4F 59
Wood End Cl. UB5: N'olt 5H 59
Wood End Gdns. UB5: N'olt 5G 59
Woodend Gdns. EN2: Enf 4D 22
WOOD END GREEN 5F 75
Wood End Grn. Rd. UB3: Hayes 5F 75
Wood End La. UB5: N'olt 6F 59
(not continuous)
Wood End Rd. HA1: Harr 4H 59
Woodend Rd. E17 2E 50
Wood End Way UB5: N'olt 5G 59
Wooder Gdns. E7 4J 69
Wooderson Cl. SE25 4E 156
Woodfall Av. EN5: Barn 5C 20
Woodfall Rd. N4 2A 66
Woodfall St. SW3 6E 16 (5D 100)
Woodfarrs SE5 4D 120
Wood Fld. NW3 5D 64
Woodfield Av. HA0: Wemb 3C 60
NW9 4A 44
SM5: Cars 6E 166
SW16 3H 137
W5 4C 78
Woodfield Cl. EN1: Enf 4K 23
SE19 7C 138
Woodfield Cres. W5 4C 78
Woodfield Dr. EN4: E Barn 1K 31
Woodfield Gdns. KT3: N Mald 5B 152
Woodfield Gro. SW16 3H 137
Woodfield Ho. *SE23* *3K 139*
(off Dacres Rd.)
Woodfield La. SW16 3H 137
Woodfield Pl. W9 4H 81
Woodfield Ri. WD23: Bush 1C 26
Woodfield Rd. TW4: Cran 2K 111
W5 4C 78
W9 5H 81
Woodfield Way N11 7C 32
WOODFORD 6F 37
Woodford Av. IG2: Ilf 5D 52
IG4: Ilf, Wfd G 3B 52
WOODFORD BRIDGE 6H 37
Woodford Bri. Rd. IG4: Ilf 3B 52
Woodford Ct. *W12* *2F 99*
(off Shepherd's Bush Grn.)
Woodford Cres. HA5: Pinn 2K 39
Woodforde Ct. UB3: Harl 5F 93
WOODFORD GREEN 6D 36
Woodford Hall Path E18 1H 51
Woodford Ho. E18 4J 51
Woodford New Rd. E17 4G 51
E18 1G 51
IG8: Wfd G 1G 51
Woodford Pl. HA9: Wemb 1E 60
Woodford Rd. E7 3K 69
E18 4J 51
WOODFORD SIDE 5C 36
Woodford Trad. Est. IG8: Wfd G 2B 52
WOODFORD WELLS 3E 36
Woodgate Av. KT9: Chess 5D 162
Woodgate Dr. SW16 7H 137
Woodger Rd. W12 2E 98
Woodget Cl. E6 6C 88
Woodgrange Av. EN1: Enf 6B 24
HA3: Kent 5C 42
N12 6G 31
W5 1G 97
Woodgrange Cl. HA3: Kent 5D 42
Woodgrange Gdns. EN1: Enf 6B 24
Woodgrange Ho. *W5* *1F 97*
(off Woodgrange Av.)
Woodgrange Mans. HA3: Kent 5D 42
Woodgrange Rd. E7 5K 69
Woodgrange Ter. EN1: Enf 6B 24
WOOD GREEN 2K 47
Wood Green Shop. City N22 2A 48
Woodhall *NW1* *2A 6*
(off Robert St.)

Woodhall Av. HA5: Pinn 1C **40**
SE21 3F **139**
Woodhall Cl. UB8: Uxb 5A **56**
Woodhall Dr. HA5: Pinn 1B **40**
SE21 3F **139**
Woodhall Ga. HA5: Pinn 1B **40**
Woodhall Ho. SW18 6B **118**
Woodham Ct. E18 4H **51**
Woodham Rd. SE6 3E **140**
Woodhatch Cl. E6 5C **88**
Woodhaven Gdns.
IG6: Ilf 4G **53**
Woodhayes Rd. SW19 7E **134**
Woodhead Dr. BR6: Orp 3J **173**
Woodheyes Rd. NW10 5K **61**
Woodhill SE18 4C **106**
Woodhill Cres. HA3: Kent 6D **42**
Wood Ho. *NW6* *2H* ***81***
(off Albert Rd.)
Woodhouse Av. UB6: G'frd 2K **77**
Woodhouse Cl. UB3: Harl 3G **93**
UB6: G'frd 1K **77**
Woodhouse Gro. E12 6C **70**
Woodhouse Rd. E11 3H **69**
N12 6G **31**
Woodhurst Av. BR5: Pet W 6G **161**
Woodhurst Rd. SE2 5A **108**
W3 7J **79**
Woodington Cl. SE9 6E **124**
Woodknoll Dr. BR7: Chst 1D **160**
Woodland App. UB6: G'frd 6A **60**
Woodland Av. E12 3C **70**
Woodland Cl. IG8: Wfd G 3E **36**
KT19: Ewe 6A **164**
NW9 6J **43**
SE19 6E **138**
UB10: Ick 2D **56**
Woodland Ct. *E11* *6J* ***51***
(off New Wanstead)
Woodland Cres. SE10 6G **105**
SE16 2K **103**
Woodland Gdns. N10 5F **47**
TW7: Isle 3J **113**
Woodland Gro. SE10 5G **105**
Woodland Hill SE19 6E **138**
Woodland M. SW16 3J **137**
Woodland Ri. N10 4F **47**
UB6: G'frd 6A **60**
Woodland Rd.
CR7: Thor H 4A **156**
E4 1K **35**
N11 5A **32**
SE19 5E **138**
WOODLANDS 3J **113**
Woodlands BR2: Brom 4H **159**
DA6: Bex 5H **127**
HA2: Harr 4E **40**
NW11 5G **45**
SW20 4E **152**
Woodlands, The HA1: Harr 2J **59**
HA7: Stan 5G **27**
N5 4C **66**
N12 6F **31**
N14 1A **32**
SE13 7F **123**
SE19 7C **138**
SM6: Wall 7F **167**
TW7: Isle 2K **113**
Woodlands Art Gallery 6J **105**
Woodlands Av. DA15: Sidc 1J **143**
E11 1K **69**
HA4: Ruis 7A **40**
KT3: N Mald 1J **151**
Woodlands Av. KT4: Wor Pk 2B **164**
N3 7F **31**
RM6: Chad H 6E **54**
W3 1H **97**
Woodlands Cl. BR1: Brom 2D **160**
KT10: Clay 7A **162**
NW11 5G **45**
Woodlands Ct. BR1: Brom 1H **159**
HA1: Harr 5K **41**
NW10 *1F* ***81***
(off Wrentham Av.)
SE23 7H **121**
Woodlands Dr. HA7: Stan 6E **26**
TW16: Sun 2A **148**
Woodlands Gdns. E17 4G **51**
Woodlands Ga. *SW15* *5H* ***117***
(off Woodlands Way)
Woodlands Gro. TW7: Isle 2J **113**
Woodlands Hgts. *SE3* *6H* ***105***
(off Vanburgh Hill)
Woodlands Pde. TW15: Ashf 6E **128**
Woodlands Pk. DA5: Bexl 4K **145**
Woodlands Pk. Rd. N15 5B **48**
SE10 6G **105**
(not continuous)
Woodlands Rd. BR1: Brom 2C **160**
BR6: Chels 6K **173**
DA7: Bex 3E **126**
E11 2G **69**
E17 3E **50**
EN2: Enf 1J **23**
HA1: Harr 5K **41**
IG1: Ilf 3G **71**
KT6: Surb 7D **150**
N9 1D **34**
SW13 3B **116**
TW7: Isle 3H **113**
UB1: S'hall 1B **94**
Woodlands St. SE13 7F **123**
Woodland St. E8 6F **67**
Woodlands Way SW15 5H **117**
Woodland Ter. SE7 4C **106**
Woodland Wlk. BR1: Brom 4F **141**
(not continuous)
KT19: Ewe 6G **163**
NW3 5C **64**
SE10 5G **105**
Woodland Way BR4: W W'ck 4D **170**
BR5: Pet W 4G **161**
CR0: C'don 1A **170**
CR4: Mitc 7E **136**
IG8: Wfd G 3E **36**
KT5: Surb 2H **163**
N21 2F **33**
NW7 6F **29**
SE2 4D **108**
SM4: Mord 4H **153**
Wood La. HA4: Ruis 1F **57**
HA7: Stan 3F **27**
IG8: Wfd G 4C **36**
N6 6F **47**
NW9 7K **43**
RM8: Dag 4C **72**
RM9: Dag 4C **72**
RM10: Dag 2G **73**
TW7: Isle 6J **95**
W12 6E **80**
Wood Lane Sports Cen. 1H **73**
Woodlawn Cl. SW15 5H **117**
Woodlawn Cres. TW2: Whitt 2F **131**
Woodlawn Dr. TW13: Felt 2B **130**
Woodlawn Rd. SW6 7F **99**
Woodlawns KT19: Ewe 7K **163**
Woodlea Dr. BR2: Brom 5G **159**
Woodlea Rd. N16 3E **66**
Woodleigh E18 1J **51**
Woodleigh Av. N12 6H **31**
Woodleigh Gdns. SW16 3J **137**
Woodley Cl. SW17 7D **136**
Woodley La. SM5: Cars 3C **166**
Wood Lodge Gdns. BR1: Brom 7C **142**
Wood Lodge La. BR4: W W'ck 3E **170**
Woodman M. TW9: Kew 1H **115**
Woodman Pde. *E16* *1E* ***106***
(off Woodman St.)
Woodmans Gro. NW10 5B **62**
Woodman's M. W12 5D **80**
Woodmansterne Rd. SM5: Cars 7C **166**
SW16 7G **137**
Woodman St. E16 1E **106**
(not continuous)
Wood Mead N17 6B **34**
Woodmere SE9 1D **142**
Woodmere Av. CR0: C'don 7J **157**
Woodmere Cl. CR0: C'don 7K **157**
SW11 3E **118**
Woodmere Ct. N14 7A **22**
Woodmere Gdns. CR0: C'don 7K **157**
Woodmere Way BR3: Beck 5F **159**
Woodnook Rd. SW16 5F **137**
Woodpecker Cl. HA3: Hrw W 1K **41**
N9 6C **24**
WD23: Bush 1B **26**
Woodpecker M. *SE13* *4F* ***123***
(off Freshfield Cl.)
Woodpecker Mt. CR0: Sels 7A **170**
Woodpecker Rd. SE14 6A **104**
SE28 7C **90**
Wood Point *E16* *5J* ***87***
(off Fife Rd.)
Woodquest Av. SE24 5C **120**
Wood Retreat SE18 7H **107**
Wood Ride BR5: Pet W 4H **161**
EN4: Had W 1G **21**
Woodridge Cl. EN2: Enf 1F **23**
Woodridings Av. HA5: Hat E 1D **40**
Woodridings Cl. HA5: Hat E 1C **40**
Woodridings Ct. N22 1H **47**
Woodriffe Rd. E11 7F **51**
Wood Ri. HA5: Eastc 5J **39**
Wood Rd. NW10 7J **61**
TW17: Shep 4C **146**
Woodrow SE18 4D **106**
Woodrow Av. UB4: Hayes 5H **75**
Woodrow Cl. UB6: G'frd 7B **60**
Woodrow Ct. N17 7C **34**
Woodrush Cl. SE14 7A **104**
Woodrush Way RM6: Chad H 4D **54**
Woods, The UB10: Ick 4D **56**
Wood's Bldgs. *E1* *5H* ***85***
(off Winthrop St.)
Woodseer St. E1 5K **9** (5F **85**)
Woodsford *SE17* *5D* ***102***
(off Portland St.)
Woodsford Sq. W14 2G **99**
Woodshire Rd. RM10: Dag 3H **73**
WOODSIDE 6G **157**
Wood Side NW11 5J **45**
Woodside IG9: Buck H 2F **37**
N10 3E **46**
SW19 6H **135**
Woodside Av. BR7: Chst 5G **143**
HA0: Wemb 1E **78**
KT10: Esh 7J **149**
N6 5D **46**
N10 5D **46**
N12 4E **30**
SE25 6H **157**
Woodside Cl. DA7: Bex 4K **127**
HA0: Wemb 1E **78**
HA4: Ruis 6F **39**
HA7: Stan 5G **27**
KT5: Surb 7J **151**
Woodside Ct. E12 1A **70**
N12 4E **30**
W5 1E **96**
Woodside Ct. Rd. CR0: C'don 7G **157**
Woodside Cres. DA15: Sidc 3J **143**
Woodside Dr. DA2: Dart 4K **145**
Woodside End HA0: Wemb 1E **78**
Woodside Gdns. E4 6J **35**
N17 2E **48**
Woodside Grange Rd. N12 4E **30**
Woodside Grn. SE25 6G **157**
(not continuous)
Woodside Gro. N12 3F **31**
Woodside Ho. SW19 6H **135**
Woodside La. DA5: Bexl 6D **126**
N12 3F **31**
Woodside M. SE22 5F **121**
Woodside Pde. DA15: Sidc 3J **143**
WOODSIDE PARK 4D **30**
Woodside Pk. SE25 6H **157**
Woodside Pk. Av. E17 4F **51**
Woodside Pk. Rd. N12 4E **30**
Woodside Pl. HA0: Wemb 1E **78**
Woodside Rd. BR1: Brom 5C **160**
DA7: Bex 4K **127**
DA15: Sidc 3J **143**
E13 4A **88**
IG8: Wfd G 4D **36**
KT2: King T 7E **132**
KT3: N Mald 2K **151**
N22 7E **32**
SE25 6H **157**
SM1: Sutt 3A **166**
Woodside Way CR0: C'don 6J **157**
CR4: Mitc 1F **155**
Woods M. W1 2G **11** (7E **82**)
Woodsome Rd. NW5 3E **64**
Woods Pl. SE1 3E **102**
Woodspring Rd. SW19 2G **135**
Woods Rd. SE15 1H **121**
Woodstar Ho. *SE15* *7G* ***103***
(off Reddins Rd.)
Woodstead Gro. HA8: Edg 6K **27**
WOODSTOCK, THE 7H **153**
Woodstock Av. NW11 7G **45**
SM3: Sutt 7H **153**
TW7: Isle 5A **114**
UB1: S'hall 3D **76**
W13 3A **96**
Woodstock Cl. DA5: Bexl 7F **127**
HA7: Stan 2E **42**
Woodstock Ct. SE11 5H **19** (5K **101**)
SE12 6J **123**
Woodstock Cres. N9 6C **24**
Woodstock Dr. UB10: Ick 4A **56**
Woodstock Gdns. BR3: Beck 1D **158**
IG3: Ilf 2A **72**
UB4: Hayes 5H **75**
Woodstock Grange W5 1E **96**
Woodstock Gro. W12 2F **99**
Woodstock La. KT9: Chess 4B **162**
Woodstock La. Nth. KT6: Surb 2C **162**
Woodstock La. Sth.
KT9: Chess 5B **162**
KT10: Clay 5B **162**
Woodstock M. W1 6H **5**
Woodstock Ri. SM3: Sutt 7H **153**
Woodstock Rd. CR0: C'don 3D **168**
E7 7A **70**
E17 2F **51**
HA0: Wemb 1F **79**
N4 1A **66**
NW11 7H **45**
SM5: Cars 5E **166**
W4 4A **98**
Woodstock St. W1 1J **11** (6F **83**)
Woodstock Studios *W12* *2F* ***99***
(off Woodstock Gro.)
Woodstock Ter. E14 7D **86**
Woodstock Way CR4: Mitc 2F **155**
Woodstone Av. KT17: Ewe 5C **164**
WOOD STREET 3E **50**
Wood St. CR4: Mitc 7E **154**
E17 3E **50**
EC2 7D **8** (6C **84**)
(not continuous)
EN5: Barn 4A **20**
Wood St. KT1: King T 2D **150**
(not continuous)
W4 5A **98**
Woodsyre SE26 4F **139**
Wood Ter. NW2 3D **62**
Woodthorpe Rd. SW15 4D **116**
TW15: Ashf 5A **128**

Woodtree Cl. NW4 .2F **45**
Wood Va. N10 .5G **47**
SE23 .1H **139**
Woodvale Av. SE25 .3F **157**
Woodvale Ct. *BR1: Brom* .*1K* ***159***
(off Widmore Rd.)
Wood Va. Est. SE23 .7J **121**
Woodvale Wlk. SE27 .5C **138**
Woodvale Way NW11 .3F **63**
Woodview Av. E4 .4K **35**
Woodview Cl. BR6: Farnb .2G **173**
N4 .7B **48**
SW15 .4K **133**
Woodville SE3 .7K **105**
Woodville, The *W5* .*6D* ***78***
(off Woodville Rd.)
Woodville Cl. SE12 .5J **123**
TW11: Tedd .4A **132**
Woodville Ct. N14 .5B **22**
SE19 .1F **157**
Woodville Gdns. HA4: Ruis .7E **38**
IG6: Ilf .3F **53**
KT6: Surb .7D **150**
NW11 .7F **45**
W5 .6E **78**
Woodville Gro. DA16: Well .3A **126**
Woodville Ho. *SE1* .*3F* ***103***
(off St Saviour's Est.)
Woodville Rd. CR7: Thor H .4C **156**
E11 .1H **69**
E17 .4B **50**
E18 .2K **51**
EN5: New Bar .3E **20**
N16 .5E **66**
NW6 .2H **81**
NW11 .7F **45**
SM4: Mord .4J **153**
TW10: Ham .3B **132**
W5 .6D **78**
Woodville St. SE18 .4C **106**
Woodward Av. NW4 .5C **44**
Woodward Cl. KT10: Clay .6A **162**
Woodwarde Rd. SE22 .6E **120**
Woodward Gdns. HA7: Stan .7E **26**
RM9: Dag .7C **72**
Woodward Rd. RM9: Dag .7B **72**
Woodward's Footpath
TW2: Whitt .6G **113**
Wood Way BR6: Farnb .2E **172**
Woodway Cres. HA1: Harr .6A **42**
Woodwell St. SW18 .5A **118**
Wood Wharf SE10 .6D **104**
Wood Wharf Bus. Pk. E14 .1D **104**
(not continuous)
Woodyard Cl. NW5 .5E **64**
Woodyard La. SE21 .7E **120**
Woodyates Rd. SE12 .6J **123**
Woody Bay Station
Ruislip Lido Railway .5F 39
Woolacombe Rd. SE3 .1A **124**
Woolacombe Way
UB3: Harl .4G **93**
Woolcombes Ct. *SE16* .*1K* ***103***
(off Princes Riverside Rd.)
Wooldridge Cl. TW14: Bedf .1E **128**
Wooler St. SE17 .5D **102**
Woolf Cl. SE28 .1B **108**
Woolf Ct. *W3* .*3J* ***97***
(off Vincent Rd.)
Woolf M. *WC1* .*3D* ***6***
(off Burton Pl.)
Woolford Ct. *SE5* .*2C* ***120***
(off Coldharbour La.)
Woolgar M. *N16* .*5E* ***66***
(off Gillett St.)
Woollaston Rd. N4 .6B **48**
Woolley Ho. *SW9* .*3B* ***120***
(off Loughborough Rd.)
Woollon Ho. *E1* .*6J* ***85***
(off Clark St.)
Woolmead Av. NW9 .7C **44**
Woolmer Gdns. N18 .6B **34**
Woolmer Rd. N18 .5B **34**
Woolmore St. E14 .7E **86**
Woolneigh St. SW6 .3K **117**
Woolridge Way E9 .7J **67**
Wool Rd. SW20 .6D **134**
Woolstaplers Way SE16 .3G **103**
Woolston Cl. E17 .2K **49**
Woolstone Ho. *E2* .*1G* ***85***
(off Whiston Rd.)
Woolstone Rd. SE23 .2A **140**
WOOLWICH .3E **106**
Woolwich Chu. St. SE18 .3C **106**
Woolwich Comn. SE18 .6E **106**
Woolwich Dockyard Ind. Est.
SE18 .3C **106**
Woolwich High St. SE18 .3E **106**
Woolwich Mnr. Way E6 .4D **88**
E16 .2F **107**
Woolwich New Rd. SE18 .5E **106**
Woolwich Rd. DA7: Bex .3G **127**
DA17: Belv .5F **109**
SE2 .6D **108**
SE7 .5H **105**
SE10 .5H **105**
Woolwich Trad. Pk. SE28 .3H **107**
Wooster Gdns. E14 .6F **87**
Wooster M. HA2: Harr .3G **41**
Wooster Pl. *SE1* .*4D* ***102***
(off Searles Rd.)
Wootton Gro. N3 .1J **45**
Wootton St. SE1 .5K **13** (1A **102**)
Worbeck Rd. SE20 .2H **157**
Worcester Av. N17 .7B **34**
Worcester Cl. CR0: C'don .2C **170**
CR4: Mitc .2E **154**
NW2 .3D **62**
Worcester Ct. HA1: Harr .3J **41**
KT4: Wor Pk .3A **164**
N12 .5E **30**
W7 .*6K* ***77***
(off Copley Cl.)
W9 .*5J* ***81***
(off Elmfield Way)
Worcester Cres. IG8: Wfd G .4F **37**
NW7 .3F **29**
Worcester Dr. TW15: Ashf .5D **128**
W4 .2A **98**
Worcester Gdns. IG1: Ilf .7C **52**
KT4: Wor Pk .3A **164**
SW11 .*5D* ***118***
(off Grandison Rd.)
UB6: G'frd .6H **59**
Worcester Ho. *SE11* .*2J* ***19***
(off Kennington Rd.)
SW9 .*7A* ***102***
(off Cranmer Rd.)
W2 .*6A* ***82***
(off Hallfield Est.)
Worcester M. NW6 .6K **63**
WORCESTER PARK .1C **164**
Worcester Pk. Rd. KT4: Wor Pk .3K **163**
Worcester Rd. E12 .4D **70**
E17 .2K **49**
SM2: Sutt .7J **165**
SW19 .5H **135**
Worcesters Av. EN1: Enf .1B **24**
Wordsworth Av. E12 .7C **70**
E18 .3H **51**
UB6: G'frd .3H **77**
Wordsworth Ct. HA1: Harr .7J **41**
Wordsworth Dr. SM3: Cheam .4E **164**
Wordsworth Ho. *NW6* .*3J* ***81***
(off Stafford Rd.)
SE18 .*6E* ***106***
(off Woolwich Comn.)
Wordsworth Mans. *W14* .*6H* ***99***
(off Queens Club Gdns.)
Wordsworth Pde. N8 .4B **48**
Wordsworth Pl. NW5 .5D **64**
Wordsworth Rd. DA16: Well .1J **125**
N16 .4E **66**
SE1 .4F **103**
SE20 .7K **139**
SM6: Wall .6G **167**
TW12: Hamp .4D **130**
Wordsworth Wlk. NW11 .4J **45**
Wordsworth Way UB7: W Dray .4A **92**
Worfield St. SW11 .7C **100**
Worgan St. SE11 .5G **19** (5K **101**)
SE16 .4K **103**
Worland Rd. E15 .7G **69**
World Bus. Cen. TW6: H'row A .1E **110**
WORLD'S END .3E **22**
Worlds End Est. SW10 .7B **100**
Worlds End La. BR6: Chels .6K **173**
EN2: Enf .5E **22**
N21 .5E **22**
World's End Pas. *SW10* .*7B* ***100***
(off Worlds End Est.)
World's End Pl. *SW10* .*7B* ***100***
(off Worlds End Est.)
Worleys Dr. BR6: Orp .4H **173**
Worlidge St. W6 .5E **98**
Worlingham Rd. SE22 .4F **121**
Wormholt Rd. W12 .7C **80**
Wormwood St. EC2 .7G **9** (6E **84**)
Wornington Rd. W10 .4G **81**
(not continuous)
Woronzow Rd. NW8 .1B **82**
Worple Av. SW19 .7F **135**
TW7: Isle .5A **114**
Worple Cl. HA2: Harr .1D **58**
Worple Rd. SW19 .2E **152**
SW20 .2E **152**
TW7: Isle .4A **114**
Worple Rd. M. SW19 .6H **135**
Worple St. SW14 .3K **115**
Worple Way HA2: Harr .1D **58**
TW10: Rich .5E **114**
Worship St. EC2 .4F **9** (4D **84**)
Worslade Rd. SW17 .4B **136**
Worsley Bri. Rd. BR3: Beck .7C **140**
SE26 .4B **140**
Worsley Grange BR7: Chst .6G **143**
Worsley Gro. E5 .4G **67**
Worsley Ho. SE23 .2J **139**
Worsley Rd. E11 .4G **69**
Worsopp Dr. SW4 .5G **119**
Worth Cl. BR6: Orp .4J **173**
Worthfield Cl. KT19: Ewe .7K **163**
Worth Gro. SE17 .5D **102**
Worthing Cl. E15 .1G **87**
Worthing Rd. TW5: Hest .6D **94**
Worthington Cl. CR4: Mitc .4F **155**
Worthington Ho. *EC1* .*1K* ***7***
(off Myddelton Pas.)
Worthington Rd. KT6: Surb .1F **163**
Wortley Rd. CR0: C'don .7A **156**
E6 .7B **70**
Worton Ct. TW7: Isle .4J **113**
Worton Gdns. TW7: Isle .2H **113**
Worton Hall Ind. Est. TW7: Isle .4J **113**
Worton Rd. TW7: Isle .4H **113**
Worton Way TW3: Houn .2H **113**
TW7: Houn, Isle .2H **113**
Wotton Ct. *E14* .*7F* ***87***
(off Jamestown Way)
Wotton Rd. NW2 .3E **62**
SE8 .6B **104**
Wouldham Rd. E16 .6H **87**
Wragby Rd. E11 .3G **69**
Wrampling Pl. N9 .1B **34**
Wrangthorn Wlk. CR0: Wadd .4A **168**
Wray Av. IG5: Ilf .3E **52**
Wrayburn Ho. *SE16* .*2G* ***103***
(off Llewellyn St.)
Wray Cres. N4 .2J **65**
Wrayfield Rd. SM3: Cheam .3F **165**
Wray Rd. SM2: Cheam .7H **165**
Wraysbury Cl. TW4: Houn .5C **112**
Wrays Way UB4: Hayes .4G **75**
Wrekin Rd. SE18 .7G **107**
Wren Av. NW2 .4E **62**
UB2: S'hall .4D **94**
Wren Cl. E16 .6H **87**
N9 .1E **34**
TW6: H'row A .6C **174**
Wren Ct. *CR0: C'don* .*4D* ***168***
(off Coombe Rd.)
Wren Cres. WD23: Bush .1B **26**
Wren Gdns. RM9: Dag .5D **72**
Wren Ho. *E3* .*2A* ***86***
(off Gernon Rd.)
KT1: Ham W .*2D* ***150***
(off High St.)
SW1 .*6C* ***18***
(off Aylesford St.)
Wren Landing E14 .1C **104**
Wrenn Ho. SW13 .6E **98**
Wren Path SE28 .3H **107**
Wren Rd. DA14: Sidc .4C **144**
RM9: Dag .5D **72**
SE5 .1D **120**
Wren's Av. TW15: Ashf .4E **128**
Wren's Pk. Ho. E5 .2H **67**
Wren St. WC1 .3H **7** (4K **83**)
Wrentham Av. NW10 .2F **81**
Wrenthorpe Rd. BR1: Brom .4G **141**
Wren Vw. N6 .7G **47**
Wrenwood Way HA5: Eastc .4K **39**
Wrestlers Ct. EC3 .7G **9**
Wrexham Rd. E3 .2C **86**
Wricklemarsh Rd. SE3 .2K **123**
(not continuous)
Wrigglesworth St. SE14 .7K **103**
Wright Cl. SE13 .4F **123**
Wright Gdns. TW17: Shep .5C **146**
Wright Rd. N1 .6E **66**
TW5: Hest .7A **94**
Wrights All. SW19 .6E **134**
Wrights Cl. RM10: Dag .4H **73**
Wrights Grn. SW4 .4H **119**
Wright's La. W8 .3K **99**
Wrights Pl. NW10 .6J **61**
Wrights Rd. E3 .2B **86**
(not continuous)
SE25 .3E **156**
Wrights Row SM6: Wall .4F **167**
Wrights Wlk. SW14 .3K **115**
Wright Way TW6: H'row A .5C **174**
Wrigley Cl. E4 .5A **36**
Writtle Ho. NW9 .2B **44**
Wrotham Ho. *BR3: Beck* .*7B* ***140***
(off Sellindge Cl.)
SE1 .*3D* ***102***
(off Law St.)
Wrotham Rd. DA16: Well .1C **126**
EN5: Barn .2B **20**
NW1 .7G **65**
W13 .1C **96**
Wrottesley Rd. NW10 .2C **80**
SE18 .6G **107**
Wroughton Rd. SW11 .5D **118**
Wroughton Ter. NW4 .4D **44**
Wroxall Rd. RM9: Dag .6C **72**
Wroxham Gdns. N11 .7C **32**
Wroxham Rd. SE28 .7D **90**
Wroxham Way IG6: Ilf .1F **53**
Wroxton Rd. SE15 .2J **121**
WRYTHE, THE .3D **166**
Wrythe Grn. SM5: Cars .3D **166**
Wrythe Grn. Rd. SM5: Cars .3D **166**
Wrythe La. SM5: Cars .1A **166**
Wulfstan St. W12 .5B **80**
Wyatt Cl. SE16 .2B **104**
TW13: Felt .1B **130**
UB4: Hayes .5J **75**
WD23: Bush .1C **26**

Wyatt Ct. HA0: Wemb .7E 60
Wyatt Dr. SW13 .6D 98
Wyatt Ho. NW8 .4B 4
(off Frampton St.)
SE3 .2H 123
TW1: Twick .6D 114
Wyatt Pk. Rd. SW2 .2J 137
Wyatt Point SE28 .2G 107
Wyatt Rd. E7 .6J 69
N5 .3C 66
Wyatts La. E17 .3E 50
Wybert St. NW1 .3A 6 (4G 83)
Wyborne Ho. NW10 .7J 61
Wyborne Way NW10 .7J 61
Wyburn Av. EN5: Barn .3C 20
Wychcombe Studios NW3 .6D 64
Wyche Gro. CR2: S Croy .7D 168
Wych Elm Lodge BR1: Brom .7H 141
Wych Elm Pas. KT2: King T .7F 133
Wycherley Cl. SE3 .7H 105
Wycherley Cres. EN5: New Bar .6E 20
Wychwood Av. CR7: Thor H .3C 156
HA8: Edg .6J 27
Wychwood Cl. HA8: Edg .6J 27
TW16: Sun .6J 129
Wychwood End N6 .7G 47
Wychwood Gdns. IG5: Ilf .4D 52
Wychwood Way SE19 .6D 138
Wyclif Ct. EC1 .2A 8
(off Wyclif St.)
Wycliffe Cl. DA16: Well .1K 125
Wycliffe Rd. SW11 .2E 118
SW19 .6K 135
Wyclif St. EC1 .2A 8 (3B 84)
Wycombe Gdns. NW11 .2J 63
Wycombe Ho. NW8 .3C 4
(off Grendon St.)
Wycombe Pl. SW18 .6A 118
Wycombe Rd. HA0: Wemb .1G 79
IG2: Ilf .5D 52
N17 .1G 49
Wycombe Sq. W8 .1H 99
Wydehurst Rd. CR0: C'don .7G 157
Wydell Cl. SM4: Mord .6F 153
Wydeville Mnr. Rd. SE12 .4K 141
Wye Cl. BR6: Orp .7K 161
HA4: Ruis .6E 38
TW15: Ashf .4D 128
Wye Ct. W13 .5B 78
(off Malvern Way)
Wyemead Cres. E4 .2B 36
Wye St. SW11 .2B 118
Wyevale Cl. HA5: Eastc .3J 39
Wyfields IG5: Ilf .1F 53
Wyfold Ho. SE2 .2D 108
(off Wolvercote Rd.)
Wyfold Rd. SW6 .7G 99
Wyhill Wlk. RM10: Dag .6J 73
Wyke Cl. TW7: Isle .6K 95
Wyke Gdns. W7 .3A 96
Wykeham Av. RM9: Dag .6C 72
Wykeham Cl. UB7: Sip .6C 92
Wykeham Ct. NW4 .5E 44
(off Wykeham Rd.)
Wykeham Grn. RM9: Dag .6C 72
Wykeham Hill HA9: Wemb .1F 61
Wykeham Ho. SE1 .5C 14
(off Union St.)
Wykeham Ri. N20 .1B 30
Wykeham Rd. HA3: Kent .4B 42
NW4 .4E 44
Wyke Rd. E3 .7C 68
SW20 .2E 152
Wylchin Cl. HA5: Eastc .3H 39
Wyldes Cl. NW11 .1A 64
Wyldfield Gdns. N9 .2A 34
Wyld Way HA9: Wemb .6H 61
Wyleu St. SE23 .7A 122
Wylie Rd. UB2: S'hall .3E 94
Wyllen Cl. E1 .4J 85
Wymans Way E7 .4A 70
Wymering Mans. W9 .3J 81
(off Wymering Rd.)
Wymering Rd. W9 .3J 81
Wymondham Ct. NW8 .1B 82
(off Queensmead)
Wymond St. SW15 .3E 116
Wynan Rd. E14 .5D 104
Wynash Gdns. SM5: Cars .5C 166
Wynaud Ct. N22 .6E 32
Wyncham Av. DA15: Sidc .1J 143
Wyncham Ho. DA15: Sidc .2A 144
(off Longlands Rd.)
Wynchgate HA3: Hrw W .7D 26
N14 .1C 32
N21 .1C 32
UB5: N'olt .5C 58
Wyncroft Cl. BR1: Brom .3D 160
Wyndale Av. NW9 .6G 43
Wyndcliff Rd. SE7 .6K 105
Wyndcroft Cl. EN2: Enf .3G 23
Wyndham Cl. BR6: Farnb .1G 173
SM2: Sutt .7J 165
Wyndham Ct. W7 .4A 96
Wyndham Cres. N19 .3G 65
TW4: Houn .6E 112
Wyndham Deedes Ho. E2 .2G 85
(off Hackney Rd.)
Wyndham Est. SE5 .7C 102
Wyndham Ho. E14 .2D 104
(off Marsh Wall)
SW1 .4G 17
(off Sloane Sq.)
Wyndham M. W1 .6E 4 (5D 82)
Wyndham Pl. W1 .6E 4 (5D 82)
Wyndham Rd. E6 .7B 70
EN4: E Barn .1J 31
KT2: King T .7F 133
(not continuous)
SE5 .7C 102
W13 .3B 96
Wyndhams Ct. E8 .7F 67
(off Celandine Dr.)
Wyndham's Theatre .2E 12
(off Charing Cross Rd.)
Wyndham St. W1 .5E 4 (5D 82)
Wyndham Yd. W1 .6E 4 (5D 82)
Wyndhurst Cl. CR2: S Croy .7B 168
Wyneham Rd. SE24 .5D 120
Wynell Rd. SE23 .3K 139
Wynford Ho. N1 .2K 83
(off Wynford Rd.)
Wynford Pl. DA17: Belv .6G 109
Wynford Rd. N1 .2K 83
Wynford Way SE9 .3D 142
Wynlie Gdns. HA5: Pinn .2K 39
Wynn Bri. Cl. IG8: Wfd G .1B 52
Wynndale Rd. E18 .1K 51
Wynne Ho. SE14 .1K 121
Wynne Rd. SW9 .2A 120
Wynn's Av. DA15: Sidc .5K 125
Wynnstay Gdns. W8 .3J 99
Wynter St. SW11 .4A 118
Wynton Gdns. SE25 .5F 157
Wynton Pl. W3 .6H 79
Wynyard Ho. SE11 .5H 19
Wynyard Ter. SE11 .5H 19 (5K 101)
Wynyatt St. EC1 .2A 8 (3B 84)
Wyre Gro. HA8: Edg .3C 28
UB3: Harl .4J 93
Wyresdale Cres.
UB6: G'frd .3K 77
Wyteleaf Cl. HA4: Ruis .6E 38
Wytham Ho. NW8 .4B 4
(off Church St. Est.)
Wythburn Ct. W1 .7E 4
(off Wythburn Pl.)
Wythburn Pl. W1 .1E 10 (6D 82)
Wythenshawe Rd. RM10: Dag .3G 73
Wythens Wlk. SE9 .6F 125
Wythes Cl. BR1: Brom .2D 160
Wythes Rd. E16 .1C 106
Wythfield Rd. SE9 .6D 124
Wyvenhoe Rd. HA2: Harr .4G 59
Wyvern Est. KT3: N Mald .4C 152
Wyvil Rd. SW8 .7J 101
Wyvis St. E14 .5D 86

X

XS Superbowl .5E 88
Xylon Ho. KT4: Wor Pk .2D 164

Y

Yabsley St. E14 .1E 104
Yaldham Ho. SE17 .4E 102
(off Massinger St.)
Yalding Rd. SE16 .3G 103
Yale Cl. TW4: Houn .5D 112
Yale Ct. NW6 .5K 63
Yarborough Rd. SW19 .1B 154
Yard, The N1 .1F 7
(off Caledonian Rd.)
Yardley Cl. E4 .5J 25
Yardley Ct. SM3: Cheam .4E 164
Yardley La. E4 .5J 25
Yardley St. WC1 .2J 7 (3A 84)
(not continuous)
Yarlington Ct. N11 .5K 31
(off Sparkford Gdns.)
Yarmouth Cres. N17 .5H 49
Yarmouth Pl. W1 .5J 11 (1F 101)
Yarnfield Sq. SE15 .1G 121
Yarnton Way
DA18: Belv, Erith .3F 109
SE2 .2C 108
Yarrell Mans. W14 .6H 99
(off Queen's Club Mans.)
Yarrow Cres. E6 .5C 88
Yarrow Ho. E14 .3E 104
(off Stewart St.)
W10 .5E 80
(off Sutton Way)
Yateley St. SE18 .3B 106
Yates Ct. NW2 .6F 63
(off Willesden La.)
Yates Ho. E2 .3G 85
(off Roberta St.)
Yatton Ho. W10 .5E 80
(off Sutton Way)
YEADING .4A 76
Yeading Av. HA2: Harr .2C 58
Yeading Ct. UB4: Yead .4A 76
Yeading Fork UB4: Yead .5A 76
Yeading Gdns. UB4: Yead .5K 75
Yeading Ho. UB4: Yead .5B 76
Yeading La. UB4: Yead .6K 75
UB5: Yead .6K 75
Yeading Wlk. HA2: Harr .5D 40
Yeadon Ho. W10 .5E 80
(off Sutton Way)
Yeames Cl. W13 .6A 78
Yearby Ho. W10 .4E 80
(off Sutton Way)
Yeate St. N1 .7D 66
Yeatman Rd. N6 .6D 46
Yeats Cl. NW10 .5A 62
SE13 .2F 123
W7 .7K 77
Yeend Cl. KT8: W Mole .4E 148
Yeldham Ho. W6 .5F 99
(off Yeldham Rd.)
Yeldham Rd. W6 .5F 99
Yeldham Vs. W6 .5F 99
(off Yeldham Rd.)
Yellowhammer Ct. NW9 .2A 44
(off Eagle Dr.)
Yelverton Lodge TW1: Twick .7C 114
(off Richmond Rd.)
Yelverton Rd. SW11 .2B 118
Ye Market CR2: S Croy .5D 168
(off Selsdon Rd.)
Yenston Cl. SM4: Mord .6J 153
Yeoman Cl. E6 .7F 89
SE27 .3B 138
Yeoman Ct. TW5: Hest .7D 94
Yeoman Dr. TW19: Stanw .1A 128
Yeoman Rd. UB5: N'olt .7C 58
Yeomans Acre HA4: Ruis .6J 39
Yeomans M. TW7: Isle .6H 113
Yeoman's Row SW3 .2D 16 (3C 100)
Yeoman St. SE8 .4A 104
Yeomans Way
EN3: Enf H .2D 24
Yeoman's Yd. E1 .2K 15
Yeo St. E3 .5D 86
Yeovil Cl. BR6: Orp .2J 173
Yeovil Ho. W10 .4E 80
(off Sutton Way)
Yeovilton Pl. KT2: King T .5C 132
Yerbury Rd. N19 .3H 65
(not continuous)
Yester Dr. BR7: Chst .7C 142
Yester Pk. BR7: Chst .7D 142
Yester Rd. BR7: Chst .7C 142
Yetev Lev Ct. E5 .1G 67
Yew Av. UB7: Yiew .7A 74
Yew Cl. IG9: Buck H .2G 37
Yewdale Cl. BR1: Brom .6G 141
Yewfield Rd. NW10 .6B 62
Yew Gro. NW2 .4F 63
Yew Ho. SE16 .2K 103
(off Woodland Cres.)
Yews, The TW15: Ashf .4D 128
Yew Tree Cl. KT4: Wor Pk .1A 164
N21 .7F 23
SE13 .3E 122
Yewtree Cl. DA16: Well .1A 126
HA2: Harr .4F 41
N22 .1G 47
Yew Tree Ct. NW11 .5H 45
(off Bridge La.)
SM2: Sutt .7A 166
(off Walnut M.)
Yew Tree Gdns.
RM6: Chad H .5E 54
RM7: Rom .5K 55
Yew Tree Lodge RM7: Rom .5K 55
(off Yew Tree Gdns.)
SW16 .4G 137
Yew Tree Rd. BR3: Beck .3B 158
UB10: Uxb .1B 74
W12 .7B 80
Yew Trees TW17: Shep .4B 146
Yew Tree Wlk. TW4: Houn .5D 112
Yew Tree Way CR0: Sels .7B 170
(not continuous)
Yew Wlk. HA1: Harr .1J 59
YIEWSLEY .1A 92
Yiewsley Ct. UB7: Yiew .1A 92
Yiewsley Swimming Pool .7A 74
YMCA Hawker Cen.
(Health & Fitness) .5D 132
Yoakley Rd. N16 .2E 66
Yoga Way KT4: Wor Pk .2C 164
Yoke Cl. N7 .6J 65
Yolande Gdns. SE9 .5C 124
Yonge Pk. N4 .3A 66
York Av. DA15: Sidc .2J 143
HA7: Stan .1B 42
SE17 .5C 102
SW14 .5J 115
York Av.
UB3: Hayes .5E 74
W7 .1J 95
York Bri. NW1 .3G 5 (4E 82)
York Bldgs. WC2 .3F 13 (7J 83)

York Cl. E6 ....6D **88**
SE5 ....*2C* ***120***
(*off Lilford Rd.*)
SM4: Mord 4K **153**
W7 ....1J **95**
York Ct. N14 ....3D **32**
York Ga. N14 ....7D **22**
NW1 ....4G **5** (4E **82**)
York Gro. SE15 ....1J **121**
York Hill SE27 ....3B **138**
York Ho. *E16* *1J* ***105***
(*off De Quincey M.*)
EN2: Enf 1J **23**
HA9: Wemb 4G **61**
KT2: King T *7F* ***133***
(*off Elm Rd.*)
SE1 ....2H **19** (3K **101**)
SW3 ....5F **17**
W1 ....*5E* ***4***
(*off York St.*)
W8 ....*2K* ***99***
(*off York Ho. Pl.*)
York Ho. Pl. W8 ....2K **99**
Yorkland Av. DA16: Well 3K **125**
Yorkley Ho. *W10* *4E* ***80***
(*off Sutton Way*)
York Mans. *SE17* *5C* ***102***
(*off Browning St.*)
SW5 ....*5K* ***99***
(*off Earls Ct. Rd.*)
SW11 ....*1E* ***118***
(*off Prince of Wales Dr.*)
W1 ....*5G* ***5***
(*off Chiltern St.*)
York M. IG1: Ilf 3E **70**
NW5 ....5F **65**
York Pde. *NW9* *6C* ***44***
(*off The Broadway*)
TW8: Bford 5D **96**
York Pas. *W8* *2K* ***99***
(*off York Ho. Pl.*)
York Pl. IG1: Ilf 2E **70**
RM10: Dag 6J **73**
SW11 ....3B **118**
WC2 ....3F **13**
York Pl. Mans. *W1* *5F* ***5***
(*off Baker St.*)
York Ri. BR6: Orp 2J **173**
NW5 ....3F **65**
York Rd. CR0: C'don 7A **156**
E4 ....4H **35**
E7 ....6J **69**
E10 ....3E **68**
E17 ....5K **49**
EN5: New Bar 5F **21**
HA6: Nwood 2J **39**
IG1: Ilf 3E **70**
KT2: King T 7F **133**
N11 ....6C **32**
N18 ....6C **34**
N21 ....7J **23**
RM13: Rain 7K **73**
SE1 ....6H **13** (2K **101**)
SM1: Sutt 6J **165**
SM2: Sutt 6J **165**
SW11 ....4A **118**
SW18 ....4A **118**
SW19 ....6A **136**
TW3: Houn 3F **113**
TW8: Bford 5D **96**
TW10: Rich 5F **115**
TW11: Tedd 4J **131**
W3 ....6J **79**
W5 ....3C **96**
York Rd. Bus. Cen.
SW11 ....2B **118**
Yorkshire Cl. N16 ....3E **66**
Yorkshire Gdns. N18 ....5C **34**
YORKSHIRE GREY **5B 124**
Yorkshire Grey Pl. NW3 ....4A **64**
Yorkshire Grey Yd. WC1 ....6G **7**
Yorkshire Rd. CR4: Mitc 5J **155**
E14 ....6A **86**
York Sq. E14 ....6A **86**
York St. CR4: Mitc 7E **154**
TW1: Twick 1A **132**
W1 ....6E **4** (5D **82**)
York St. Chambers *W1* *6E* ***4***
(*off York St.*)
York Ter. DA8: Erith 1J **127**
EN2: Enf 1H **23**
York Ter. E. NW1 ....4H **5** (4E **82**)
York Ter. W. NW1 ....4G **5** (4E **82**)
Yorkton St. E2 ....2G **85**
York Way KT9: Chess 7E **162**
N1 ....1F **7** (6J **65**)
N7 ....6H **65**
N20 ....3J **31**
TW13: Hanw 3D **130**
(not continuous)
York Way Ct. N1 ....1J **83**
York Way Est. N7 ....6J **65**
Young Ct. NW6 ....7G **63**
Youngmans Cl.
EN2: Enf 1H **23**
Young Rd. E16 ....6A **88**
Youngs Bldgs. EC1 ....3D **8**
Youngs Ct. SW11 ....1E **118**
Youngs Rd. IG2: Ilf 5H **53**
Young St. W8 ....2K **99**
Young Vic Theatre, The
.......6K **13**
Yoxall Ho. *W10* *4E* ***80***
(*off Sutton Way*)
Yoxford Ct. RM6: Chad H 5B **54**
Yoxley App. IG2: Ilf 6G **53**
Yoxley Dr. IG2: Ilf 6G **53**
Yukon Rd. SW12 ....7F **119**
Yunus Khan Cl. E17 ....5C **50**

Z

Zambezie Dr. N9 ....3D **34**
Zampa Rd. SE16 ....5J **103**
Zander Ct. E2 ....3G **85**
Zangwill Ho. *NW6* *2H* ***81***
(*off Denmark Rd.*)
Zangwill Rd. SE3 ....1B **124**
Zapotec Ho. *SE8* *4K* ***103***
(*off Chilton Gro.*)
Zealand Av. UB7: Harm 3E **174**
Zealand Ho. *SE5* *2C* ***120***
(*off Denmark Rd.*)
SE18 ....4C **106**
Zealand Rd. E3 ....2A **86**
Zenith Lodge N3 ....7E **30**
Zennor Rd. SW12 ....1G **137**
Zennor Rd. Ind. Est.
SW12 ....1G **137**
Zenobia Mans. *W14* *6H* ***99***
(*off Queen's Club Mans.*)
Zenoria St. SE22 ....4F **121**
Zermatt Rd. CR7: Thor H 4C **156**
Zetland Ho. *W8* *3K* ***99***
(*off Marloes Rd.*)
Zetland St. E14 ....5D **86**
Zion Ho. *E1* *6J* ***85***
(*off Jubilee St.*)
Zion Pl. CR7: Thor H 4D **156**
Zion Rd. CR7: Thor H 4D **156**
Zoar St. SE1 ....4C **14** (1C **102**)
Zodiac Ct. CR0: C'don 1B **168**
Zoffany St. N19 ....2H **65**
Zoroastrian Ho. *NW6* *6K* ***63***
(*off Compayne Gdns.*)

HOSPITALS, TREATMENT CENTRES, WALK-IN CENTRES and HOSPICES covered by this atlas.

N.B. Where it is not possible to name these facilities on the map, the reference given is for the road in which they are situated.

ASHFORD HOSPITAL 2A **128**
London Road
ASHFORD TW15 3AA
Tel: 01784 884488

BARKHAM LONDON CLINIC 1K **19** (3A **102**)
22 Barkham Terrace
LONDON SE1 7PW
Tel: 020 7928 5633

BARKING HOSPITAL 7K **71**
Upney Lane
BARKING IG11 9LX
Tel: 0845 130 4204

BARNES HOSPITAL 3A **116**
South Worple Way
LONDON SW14 8SU
Tel: 020 88784981

BARNET HOSPITAL 4A **20**
Wellhouse Lane
BARNET EN5 3DJ
Tel: 0845 111 4000

BECKENHAM HOSPITAL 2B **158**
379 Croydon Road
BECKENHAM BR3 3QL
Tel: 01689 863000

BECKTON CYGNET HOSPITAL 6E **88**
23 Tunnan Leys
LONDON E6 6ZB
Tel: 0207 5112299

BELVEDERE DAY HOSPITAL 1C **80**
341 Harlesden Road
LONDON NW10 3RX
Tel: 020 8459 3562

BELVEDERE PRIVATE HOSPITAL 5C **108**
Knee Hill
LONDON SE2 0GD
Tel: 020 8310 8866

BETHLEM ROYAL HOSPITAL 7C **158**
Monks Orchard Road
BECKENHAM BR3 3BX
Tel: 020 32286000

BLACKHEATH BMI HOSPITAL, THE 3H **123**
40-42 Lee Terrace
LONDON SE3 9UD
Tel: 020 8318 7722

BRITISH HOME, THE 5B **138**
Crown Lane
LONDON SW16 3JB
Tel: 020 8670 8261

BROMLEY PRIVATE PATIENT UNIT 3E **172**
Princess Royal University Hospital
Farnborough Common
ORPINGTON BR6 8ND
Tel: 01689 863739

BUSHEY SPIRE HOSPITAL 1E **26**
Heathbourne Road
Bushey Heath
BUSHEY WD23 1RD
Tel: 020 8950 9090

CAMDEN MEWS DAY HOSPITAL 7G **65**
1-5 Camden Mews
LONDON NW1 9DB
Tel: 020 7530 4780

CARSHALTON WAR MEMORIAL HOSPITAL 6D **166**
The Park
CARSHALTON SM5 3DB
Tel: 020 8647 5534

CASSEL HOSPITAL, THE 4D **132**
1 Ham Common
RICHMOND TW10 7JF
Tel: 020 8940 8181

CASUALTY PLUS WALK-IN CENTRE (BRENTFORD) 5C **96**
1010 Great West Road
BRENTFORD TW8 9BA
Tel: 0845 677 7999

CENTRAL MIDDLESEX HOSPITAL 3J **79**
Acton Lane
LONDON NW10 7NS
Tel: 020 8965 5733

CHARING CROSS HOSPITAL 6F **99**
Fulham Palace Road
LONDON W6 8RF
Tel: 020 8846 1234

CHASE FARM HOSPITAL 1F **23**
127 The Ridgeway
ENFIELD EN2 8JL
Tel: 0845 111 4000

CHELSEA & WESTMINSTER HOSPITAL 6A **100**
369 Fulham Road
LONDON SW10 9NH
Tel: 020 8746 8000

CHILDREN'S HOSPITAL, THE (LEWISHAM) 5D **122**
Lewisham High Street
LONDON
SE13 6LH
Tel: 020 8333 3000

CLAYPONDS HOSPITAL 4E **96**
Sterling Place
LONDON W5 4RN
Tel: 020 8560 4011

CLEMENTINE CHURCHILL BMI HOSPITAL, THE 3K **59**
Sudbury Hill
HARROW HA1 3RX
Tel: 020 8872 3872

CROMWELL HOSPITAL, THE 4K **99**
162-174 Cromwell Road
LONDON SW5 0TU
Tel: 020 7460 2000

DULWICH COMMUNITY HOSPITAL 4E **120**
East Dulwich Grove
LONDON SE22 8PT
Tel: 020 7346 6444

EALING CYGNET HOSPITAL 5E **78**
22 Corfton Road
LONDON W5 2HT
Tel: 0208 9916699

EALING HOSPITAL 1H **95**
Uxbridge Road
SOUTHALL UB1 3HW
Tel: 020 8967 5000

EASTMAN DENTAL HOSPITAL & DENTAL INSTITUTE, THE 3G **7** (4K **83**)
256 Gray's Inn Road
LONDON WC1X 8LD
Tel: 020 7915 1000

EDGWARE COMMUNITY HOSPITAL 7C **28**
Burnt Oak Broadway
EDGWARE HA8 0AD
Tel: 020 8952 2381

ELIZABETH GARRETT ANDERSON & OBSTETRIC HOSPITAL, THE 4B **6** (4G **83**)
Huntley Street
LONDON WC1E 6DH
Tel: 0845 155 5000

ERITH & DISTRICT HOSPITAL 6K **109**
Park Crescent
ERITH DA8 3EE
Tel: 020 8308 3131

EVELINA CHILDREN'S HOSPITAL 1G **19** (3K **101**)
St Thomas' Hospital
Lambeth Palace Road
LONDON SE1 7EH
Tel: 020 7188 7188

FINCHLEY MEMORIAL HOSPITAL 7F **31**
Granville Road
LONDON N12 0JE
Tel: 020 8349 7500

GARDEN BMI HOSPITAL, THE 3E **44**
46-50 Sunny Gardens Road
LONDON NW4 1RP
Tel: 020 8457 4500

GOODMAYES HOSPITAL 5A **54**
Barley Lane
ILFORD IG3 8XJ
Tel: 0844 600 1200

GORDON HOSPITAL 4C **18** (4H **101**)
Bloomburg Street
LONDON SW1V 2RH
Tel: 020 8746 8733

GREAT ORMOND STREET HOSPITAL FOR CHILDREN 4F **7** (4J **83**)
Great Ormond Street
LONDON WC1N 3JH
Tel: 020 7405 9200

GREENWICH & BEXLEY COTTAGE HOSPICE 5C **108**
185 Bostall Hill
LONDON SE2 0GB
Tel: 020 8312 2244

GUY'S HOSPITAL 5F **15** (1D **102**)
St Thomas Street
LONDON SE1 9RT
Tel: 020 7188 7188

GUY'S NUFFIELD HOUSE 6E **14** (2D **102**)
Newcomen Street
LONDON SE1 1YR
Tel: 020 7188 5292

HAMMERSMITH HOSPITAL 6C **80**
Du Cane Road
LONDON W12 0HS
Tel: 020 8383 1000

HARLEY STREET CLINIC 5J **5** (5F **83**)
35 Weymouth Street
LONDON W1G 8BJ
Tel: 020 7935 7700

HARLINGTON HOSPICE
(THE REG HOPKINS DAY CARE HOSPICE) 5F **93**
St Peters Way
HAYES UB3 5AB
Tel: 020 8759 0453 / 1700

HARRIS HOSPISCARE 4K **173**
Tregony Road
ORPINGTON BR6 9XA
Tel: 01689 825755

HAVEN HOUSE FOUNDATION (HOSPICE) 6C **36**
High Road
Woodford Green
WOODFORD GREEN IG8 9LB
Tel: 020 8505 9944

HAYES GROVE PRIORY HOSPITAL, THE 2J **171**
Prestons Road
Hayes
BROMLEY BR2 7AS
Tel: 020 8462 7722

HEART HOSPITAL, THE 6H **5** (5E **82**)
16-18 Westmoreland Street
LONDON W1G 8PH
Tel: 020 7573 8888

HEATHVIEW DAY CENTRE 6C **108**
Lodge Hill
LONDON SE2 0AY
Tel: 020 8319 7166

HIGHGATE HOSPITAL 6D **46**
17 View Road
LONDON N6 4DJ
Tel: 020 8341 4182

HIGHGATE MENTAL HEALTH CENTRE 2F **65**
Dartmouth Park Hill
LONDON N19 5NX
Tel: 020 7561 4000

HILLINGDON HOSPITAL 5B **74**
Pield Heath Road
UXBRIDGE UB8 3NN
Tel: 01895 238282

HOLLY HOUSE HOSPITAL 2E **36**
High Road
BUCKHURST HILL IG9 5HX
Tel: 020 8505 3311

HOMERTON UNIVERSITY HOSPITAL 5K **67**
Homerton Row
LONDON E9 6SR
Tel: 020 8510 5555

HOSPITAL FOR TROPICAL DISEASES 4B **6** (4G **83**)
Mortimer Market,
Capper Street
LONDON WC1E 6AU
Tel: 0845 155 5000

HOSPITAL OF ST JOHN & ST ELIZABETH 2B **82**
60 Grove End Road
LONDON NW8 9NH
Tel: 020 7806 4000

KING EDWARD VII'S HOSPITAL SISTER AGNES .. 5H **5** (5E **82**)
5-10 Beaumont Street
LONDON W1G 6AA
Tel: 020 7486 4411

KING GEORGE HOSPITAL 5A **54**
Barley Lane
ILFORD IG3 8YB
Tel: 0845 130 4204

KING'S COLLEGE HOSPITAL 2D **120**
Denmark Hill
LONDON SE5 9RS
Tel: 0203 299 9000

KING'S OAK BMI HOSPITAL, THE 1F **23**
The Ridgeway
ENFIELD EN2 8SD
Tel: 020 8370 9500

KINGSTON HOSPITAL 1H **151**
Galsworthy Road
KINGSTON UPON THAMES KT2 7QB
Tel: 020 8546 7711

LAMBETH HOSPITAL 3K **119**
108 Landor Road
LONDON SW9 9NT
Tel: 020 32286000

LATIMER DAY HOSPITAL 5A **6** (5G **83**)
40 Hanson Street
LONDON W1W 6UL
Tel: 020 7612 1645

LEWISHAM UNIVERSITY HOSPITAL 5D **122**
Lewisham High Street
LONDON SE13 6LH
Tel: 020 8333 3000

LISTER HOSPITAL, THE 6J **17** (5F **101**)
Chelsea Bridge Road
LONDON SW1W 8RH
Tel: 020 7730 7733

LONDON BRIDGE HOSPITAL 4F **15** (1D **102**)
27 Tooley Street
LONDON SE1 2PR
Tel: 020 7407 3100

LONDON CHEST HOSPITAL 2J **85**
Bonner Road
LONDON E2 9JX
Tel: 020 7377 7000

LONDON CLINIC, THE 4H **5** (4E **82**)
20 Devonshire Place
LONDON W1G 6BW
Tel: 020 7935 4444

LONDON INDEPENDENT BMI HOSPITAL, THE
.... 5K **85**
1 Beaumont Square
LONDON E1 4NL
Tel: 020 7780 2400

LONDON WELBECK HOSPITAL 6J **5** (5F **83**)
27 Welbeck Street
LONDON W1G 8EN
Tel: 020 7224 2242

MARGARET CENTRE (HOSPICE) 6G **51**
Whipps Cross University Hospital
Whipps Cross Road
LONDON E11 1NR
Tel: 020 8535 6605

MARIE CURIE HOSPICE, HAMPSTEAD 5B **64**
11 Lyndhurst Gardens
LONDON NW3 5NS
Tel: 020 7853 3400

MAUDSLEY HOSPITAL, THE 2D **120**
Denmark Hill
LONDON SE5 8AZ
Tel: 020 32286000

MAYDAY UNIVERSITY HOSPITAL 6B **156**
530 London Road
THORNTON HEATH CR7 7YE
Tel: 020 8401 3000

MEADOW HOUSE HOSPICE 2H **95**
Ealing Hospital
Uxbridge Road
SOUTHALL UB1 3HW
Tel: 020 8967 5179

MEMORIAL HOSPITAL 2E **124**
Shooters Hill
LONDON SE18 3RZ
Tel: 020 8836 8500

MILDMAY MISSION HOSPITAL (HOSPICE) 2J **9** (3F **85**)
Hackney Road
LONDON E2 7NA
Tel: 020 7613 6300

MILE END HOSPITAL 4K **85**
Bancroft Road
LONDON E1 4DG
Tel: 020 7377 7000

MOLESEY HOSPITAL 5E **148**
High Street
WEST MOLESEY KT8 2LU
Tel: 020 8941 4481

MOORFIELDS EYE HOSPITAL 2E **8** (3D **84**)
162 City Road
LONDON EC1V 2PD
Tel: 020 7253 3411

NATIONAL HOSPITAL FOR NEUROLOGY & NEUROSURGERY, THE
.... 4F **7** (4J **83**)
Queen Square
LONDON WC1N 3BG
Tel: 0845 155 5000

NELSON HOSPITAL 2H **153**
Kingston Road
LONDON SW20 8DB
Tel: 020 8251 1111

NEWHAM UNIVERSITY HOSPITAL 4A **88**
Glen Road
LONDON E13 8SL
Tel: 020 7476 4000

NEW VICTORIA HOSPITAL 1A **152**
184 Coombe Lane West
KINGSTON UPON THAMES KT2 7EG
Tel: 020 8949 9000

NHS WALK-IN CENTRE (ASHFORD) 2A **128**
London Road
ASHFORD TW15 3AA
Tel: 01784 884488

NHS WALK-IN CENTRE (BARKING & DAGENHAM) 6K **71**
132 Upney Lane
BARKING IG11 9YD
Tel: 020 8924 6633

NHS WALK-IN CENTRE (BROAD STREET) 1G **91**
Broad Street Centre
Morland Road
DAGENHAM RM10 9HU
Tel: 020 8596 4400

NHS WALK-IN CENTRE (CANARY WHARF) 2C **104**
30 Marsh Wall
LONDON E14 9TP
Tel: 020 7517 3300

NHS WALK-IN CENTRE (CHARING CROSS) 5F **99**
Fulham Palace Road
LONDON W6 8RF
Tel: 020 8846 1234

NHS WALK-IN CENTRE (CROYDON) 3C **168**
45 High Street
CROYDON CR0 1QD
Tel: 020 8666 0555

NHS WALK-IN CENTRE (EDGWARE) 7C **28**
Burnt Oak Broadway
EDGWARE HA8 0AD
Tel: 020 8732 6459

NHS WALK-IN CENTRE (FINCHLEY) 7F **31**
Granville Road
LONDON N12 0JE
Tel: 020 8349 7471

NHS WALK-IN CENTRE (HACKNEY) 5K **67**
Homerton Row
LONDON E9 6SR
Tel: 020 8510 5342

NHS WALK-IN CENTRE (LEYTONSTONE) 5F **51**
Whipps Cross Road
LONDON E11 1NR
Tel: 020 8539 5522

NHS WALK-IN CENTRE (LIVERPOOL STREET) 5H **9** (5E **84**)
Exchange Arcade
Bishopsgate
LONDON EC2M 3WA
Tel: 0845 880 1242

NHS WALK-IN CENTRE (NEW CROSS) 7A **104**
40 Goodwood Road
LONDON SE14 6BL
Tel: 020 7206 3100

NHS WALK-IN CENTRE (NEWHAM) 4A **88**
Glen Road
LONDON E13 8SH
Tel: 020 7363 9200

NHS WALK-IN CENTRE
(NORTH MIDDLESEX UNIVERSITY HOSPITAL) ...5A **34**
Sterling Way
LONDON N18 1QX
Tel: 020 8887 2680

NHS WALK-IN CENTRE (PARSONS GREEN) 1J **117**
5-7 Parsons Green
LONDON SW6 4UL
Tel: 020 8846 6758

NHS WALK-IN CENTRE (SOHO) 1C **12** (6H **83**)
1 Frith Street
LONDON W1D 3HZ
Tel: 020 7534 6500

NHS WALK-IN CENTRE (TEDDINGTON) 6J **131**
Hampton Road
TEDDINGTON TW11 0JL
Tel: 020 8714 4004

NHS WALK-IN CENTRE
(TOLLGATE LODGE PRIMARY CARE CENTRE) 1F **67**
57 Stamford Hill
LONDON N16 5SR
Tel: 020 7689 3140

NHS WALK-IN CENTRE (TOOTING) 5C **136**
Blackshaw Road
LONDON SW17 0QT
Tel: 020 8700 0505

NHS WALK-IN CENTRE (VICTORIA) 1C **18** (3H **101**)
63 Buckingham Gate
LONDON SW1E 6AS
Tel: 020 7340 1190

NHS WALK-IN CENTRE (WEMBLEY) 6D **60**
Wembley Centre for Health & Care
116 Chaplin Road
WEMBLEY HA0 4UZ
Tel: 0208 795 6000

NHS WALK-IN CENTRE (WHITECHAPEL) 5H **85**
174 Whitechapel Road
LONDON E1 1BZ
Tel: 020 7943 1333

NHS WALK-IN CENTRE (WHITTINGTON) 2G **65**
Highgate Hill
LONDON N19 5NF
Tel: 020 7272 3070

NIGHTINGALE DAY HOSPITAL 5D **4** (5C **82**)
1b Harewood Row
LONDON NW1 6SE
Tel: 020 7725 9940

NIGHTINGALE HOSPITAL (ENFORD STREET) 5E **4** (5D **82**)
23-24 Enford Street
LONDON W1H 1DG
Tel: 020 7723 3635

NIGHTINGALE HOSPITAL (LISSON GROVE) 5D **4** (5C **82**)
11-19 Lisson Grove
LONDON NW1 6SH
Tel: 020 7535 7700

NIGHTINGALE HOSPITAL (RADNOR WALK) 6D **16** (5C **100**)
1-5 Radnor Walk
LONDON SW3 4BP
Tel: 020 7349 3900

NORTH LONDON CLINIC 2B **34**
15 Church Street
LONDON N9 9DY
Tel: 020 8956 1234

NORTH LONDON (ENFIELD) NUFFIELD HOSPITAL 2F **23**
Cavell Drive
ENFIELD EN2 7PR
Tel: 020 8366 2122

NORTH LONDON HOSPICE 3F **31**
47 Woodside Avenue
LONDON N12 8TT
Tel: 020 8343 8841

NORTH LONDON PRIORY HOSPITAL 1D **32**
The Bourne
Southgate
LONDON N14 6RA
Tel: 020 8882 8191

NORTH MIDDLESEX UNIVERSITY HOSPITAL 5K **33**
Sterling Way
LONDON N18 1QX
Tel: 020 8887 2000

NORTHWICK PARK HOSPITAL 7A **42**
Watford Road
HARROW HA1 3UJ
Tel: 020 8864 3232

ORPINGTON HOSPITAL 4K **173**
Sevenoaks Road
ORPINGTON BR6 9JU
Tel: 01689 863000

PARKSIDE HOSPITAL 3F **135**
53 Parkside
LONDON SW19 5NX
Tel: 020 8971 8000

PEMBRIDGE PALLIATIVE CARE CENTRE, THE 5F **81**
Exmoor Street
LONDON W10 6DZ
Tel: 020 8962 4410 / 4411

PENNY SANGAM DAY HOSPITAL 3D **94**
Osterley Park Road
SOUTHALL UB2 4EU
Tel: 020 8571 9676

PLAISTOW DAY HOSPITAL 2A **88**
Samson Street
LONDON E13 9EH
Tel: 020 8586 6200

PORTLAND HOSPITAL FOR WOMEN & CHILDREN, THE
...................................4K **5** (4F **83**)
205-209 Great Portland Street
LONDON W1W 5AH
Tel: 020 7580 4400

PRINCESS GRACE HOSPITAL 5G **5** (5E **82**)
42-52 Nottingham Place
LONDON W1U 5NY
Tel: 020 7486 1234

PRINCESS GRACE HOSPITAL (OUTPATIENTS) ...5H **5** (5E **82**)
30 Devonshire Street
LONDON W1G 6PU
Tel: 020 7908 3602

PRINCESS ROYAL UNIVERSITY HOSPITAL 3E **172**
Farnborough Common
ORPINGTON BR6 8ND
Tel: 01689 863000

QUEEN CHARLOTTE'S & CHELSEA HOSPITAL 6C **80**
Du Cane Road
LONDON W12 0HS
Tel: 020 8383 1111

QUEEN ELIZABETH HOSPITAL 7C **106**
Stadium Road
LONDON SE18 4QH
Tel: 020 8836 6000

QUEEN MARY'S HOSPITAL 5A **144**
Frognal Avenue
SIDCUP DA14 6LT
Tel: 020 8302 2678

QUEEN MARY'S HOSPITAL FOR CHILDREN 1A **166**
Wrythe Lane
CARSHALTON SM5 1AA
Tel: 020 8296 2000

QUEEN MARY'S HOSPITAL, ROEHAMPTON 6C **116**
Roehampton Lane
LONDON SW15 5PN
Tel: 020 8487 6000

QUEEN MARY'S HOUSE 3A **64**
23 East Heath Road
LONDON NW3 1DU
Tel: 020 7431 4111

QUEEN'S HOSPITAL 7K **55**
Rom Valley Way
ROMFORD RM7 0AG
Tel: 0845 130 4204

RICHARD DESMOND CHILDREN'S EYE CENTRE ...2E **8** (3D **84**)
Moorfields Eye Hospital
162 City Road
LONDON EC1V 2PD
Tel: 020 7253 3411

RICHARD HOUSE CHILDREN'S HOSPICE 7B **88**
Richard House Drive
LONDON E16 3RG
Tel: 020 7511 0222

RICHMOND ROYAL HOSPITAL 3E **114**
Kew Foot Road
RICHMOND TW9 2TE
Tel: 020 8940 3331

RODING SPIRE HOSPITAL 3B **52**
Roding Lane South
ILFORD IG4 5PZ
Tel: 020 8551 1100

ROEHAMPTON HUNTERCOMBE HOSPITAL 7C **116**
Holybourne Avenue
LONDON SW15 4JL
Tel: 020 8780 6155

ROEHAMPTON PRIORY HOSPITAL 4B **116**
Priory Lane
LONDON SW15 5JJ
Tel: 020 8876 8261

ROYAL BROMPTON HOSPITAL 5C **16** (5C **100**)
Sydney Street
LONDON SW3 6NP
Tel: 020 7352 8121

ROYAL BROMPTON HOSPITAL (FULHAM WING)
..................................5B **16** (5B **100**)
Fulham Road
LONDON SW3 6HP
Tel: 020 7352 8121

ROYAL FREE HOSPITAL, THE 5C **64**
Pond Street
LONDON NW3 2QG
Tel: 020 7794 0500

ROYAL HOSPITAL FOR NEURO-DISABILITY 6G **117**
West Hill
LONDON SW15 3SW
Tel: 020 8780 4500

ROYAL LONDON HOMOEOPATHIC HOSPITAL 5F **7** (5J **83**)
Great Ormond Street
LONDON WC1N 3HR
Tel: 0845 155 5000

ROYAL LONDON HOSPITAL, THE 5H **85**
Whitechapel Road
LONDON E1 1BB
Tel: 020 7377 7000

ROYAL MARSDEN HOSPITAL (FULHAM), THE ...5B **16** (5B **100**)
Fulham Road
LONDON SW3 6JJ
Tel: 020 7352 8171

ROYAL NATIONAL ORTHOPAEDIC HOSPITAL 2G **27**
Brockley Hill
STANMORE HA7 4LP
Tel: 020 8954 2300

ROYAL NATIONAL ORTHOPAEDIC HOSPITAL (CENTRAL LONDON OUTPATIENT DEPT.) ...4K **5** (4F **83**)
45-51 Bolsover Street
LONDON W1W 5AQ
Tel: 020 7387 5070

ROYAL NATIONAL THROAT, NOSE & EAR HOSPITAL 1G **7** (3K **83**)
330 Gray's Inn Road
LONDON WC1X 8DA
Tel: 020 7915 1300

ST ANDREW'S AT HARROW (BOWDEN HOUSE) 2J **59**
London Road
HARROW HA1 3JL
Tel: 020 8966 7000

ST ANN'S HOSPITAL 5C **48**
St Ann's Road
LONDON N15 3TH
Tel: 020 8442 6000

ST ANTHONY'S HOSPITAL 1F **165**
London Road
SUTTON SM3 9DW
Tel: 020 8337 6691

ST BARTHOLOMEW'S HOSPITAL 6B **8** (5B **84**)
West Smithfield
LONDON EC1A 7BE
Tel: 020 7377 7000

ST BERNARD'S HOSPITAL 2H **95**
Uxbridge Road
SOUTHALL UB1 3EU
Tel: 020 8967 5000

ST CHARLES HOSPITAL 5F **81**
Exmoor Street
LONDON W10 6DZ
Tel: 020 8969 2488

ST CHRISTOPHER'S HOSPICE 5J **139**
51-59 Lawrie Park Road
LONDON SE26 6DZ
Tel: 020 8768 4500

ST CLEMENT'S HOSPITAL 3B **86**
2A Bow Road
LONDON E3 4LL
Tel: 020 7377 7000

ST GEORGE'S HOSPITAL (TOOTING) 5C **136**
Blackshaw Road
LONDON SW17 0QT
Tel: 020 8672 1255

ST HELIER HOSPITAL 1A **166**
Wrythe Lane
CARSHALTONSM5 1AA
Tel: 020 8296 2000

ST JOHN'S AND AMYAND HOUSE 7A **114**
Strafford Road
TWICKENHAM TW1 3AD
Tel: 020 8744 9943

ST JOHN'S HOSPICE 1A **4** (2B **82**)
Hospital of St John & St Elizabeth
60 Grove End Road
LONDON NW8 9NH
Tel: 020 7806 4040

ST JOSEPH'S HOSPICE 1H **85**
Mare Street
LONDON E8 4SA
Tel: 020 8525 6000

ST LUKE'S HOSPICE 5D **42**
Kenton Road
HARROW HA3 0YG
Tel: 020 8382 8000

ST LUKE'S HOSPITAL FOR THE CLERGY 4A **6** (4G **83**)
14 Fitzroy Square
LONDON W1T 6AH
Tel: 020 7388 4954

ST LUKE'S WOODSIDE HOSPITAL 4E **46**
Woodside Avenue
LONDON N10 3HU
Tel: 020 8219 1800

ST MARK'S HOSPITAL 7B **42**
Watford Road
HARROW HA1 3UJ
Tel: 020 8864 3232

ST MARY'S HOSPITAL 7B **4** (6B **82**)
Praed Street
LONDON W2 1NY
Tel: 020 7725 6666

ST MICHAEL'S PRIMARY CARE CENTRE 1J **23**
Gater Drive
ENFIELD EN2 0JB
Tel: 020 8375 2894

ST PANCRAS HOSPITAL 1H **83**
4 St Pancras Way
LONDON NW1 0PE
Tel: 020 7530 3500

ST RAPHAEL'S HOSPICE 2F **165**
St. Anthony's Hospital
London Road
SUTTON SM3 9DX
Tel: 020 8335 4575

ST THOMAS' HOSPITAL 1G **19** (3K **101**)
Lambeth Palace Road
LONDON SE1 7EH
Tel: 020 7188 7188

SHIRLEY OAKS BMI HOSPITAL 7J **157**
Poppy Lane
CROYDON CR9 8AB
Tel: 020 8655 5500

SHOOTING STAR HOUSE, CHILDREN'S HOSPICE 6D **130**
The Avenue
HAMPTON TW12 3RA
Tel: 020 8783 2000

SLOANE BMI HOSPITAL, THE 1F **159**
125 Albemarle Road
BECKENHAM BR3 5HS
Tel: 020 8466 4000

SPRINGFIELD UNIVERSITY HOSPITAL 3C **136**
61 Glenburnie Road
LONDON SW17 7DJ
Tel: 020 8682 6000

SURBITON HOSPITAL 6E **150**
Ewell Road
SURBITON KT6 6EZ
Tel: 020 8399 7111

TEDDINGTON MEMORIAL HOSPITAL 6J **131**
Hampton Road
TEDDINGTON TW11 0JL
Tel: 020 8714 4000

THORPE COOMBE HOSPITAL 3E **50**
714 Forest Road
LONDON
E17 3HP
Tel: 020 8520 8971

TOLWORTH HOSPITAL 2G **163**
Red Lion Road
SURBITON KT6 7QU
Tel: 020 8390 0102

TRINITY HOSPICE 4F **119**
30 Clapham Common North Side
LONDON SW4 0RN
Tel: 020 7787 1000

UNIVERSITY COLLEGE HOSPITAL 3B **6** (4G **83**)
235 Euston Road
LONDON NW1 2BU
Tel: 0845 155 5000

UPTON CENTRE 4E **126**
14 Upton Road
BEXLEYHEATH DA6 8LQ
Tel: 020 8301 7900

WELLINGTON HOSPITAL, THE 1B **4** (3B **82**)
8a Wellington Place
LONDON NW8 9LE
Tel: 020 7586 5959

WESTERN EYE HOSPITAL 5E **4** (5D **82**)
171 Marylebone Road
LONDON NW1 5QH
Tel: 020 7886 6666

WEST HAMPSTEAD DAY HOSPITAL 5H **63**
85-87 Fordwych Road
LONDON NW2 3TL
Tel: 020 8208 1612

WEST MIDDLESEX UNIVERSITY HOSPITAL 2A **114**
Twickenham Road
ISLEWORTH TW7 6AF
Tel: 020 8560 2121

WHIPPS CROSS UNIVERSITY HOSPITAL 5F **51**
Whipps Cross Road
LONDON E11 1NR
Tel: 020 8539 5522

WHITTINGTON HOSPITAL 2G **65**
Highgate Hill
LONDON N19 5NF
Tel: 020 7272 3070

WILLESDEN CENTRE FOR HEALTH & CARE 7C **62**
Robson Avenue
LONDON NW10 3RY
Tel: 020 8438 7000

WOODBURY UNIT 6G **51**
178 James Lane
LONDON E11 1NU
Tel: 020 8535 6478

RAIL, CROYDON TRAMLINK, DOCKLANDS LIGHT RAILWAY, RIVERBUS AND LONDON UNDERGROUND AND OVERGROUND STATIONS

with their map square reference

A

Abbey Wood (Rail) .3C 108
Acton Central (Overground) .1K 97
Acton Main Line (Rail) .6J 79
Acton Town (Underground) .2G 97
Addington Village Stop (CT) .6C 170
Addiscombe Stop (CT) .1G 169
Albany Park (Rail) .2D 144
Aldgate (Underground) .1J 15 (6F 85)
Aldgate East (Underground) .7K 9 (6F 85)
Alexandra Palace (Rail) .2J 47
All Saints (DLR) .7D 86
Alperton (Underground) .1D 78
Ampere Way Stop (CT) .1K 167
Anerley (Rail) .1H 157
Angel (Underground) .2A 84
Angel Road (Rail) .5D 34
Archway (Underground) .2G 65
Arena Stop (CT) .5J 157
Arnos Grove (Underground) .5B 32
Arsenal (Underground) .3A 66
Ashford (Rail) .4B 128
Avenue Road Stop (CT) .2K 157

B

Baker Street (Underground) .4F 5 (4D 82)
Balham (Rail & Underground) .1F 137
Bank (Underground & DLR) .1E 14 (6D 84)
Bankside Pier (Riverbus) .3C 14 (7C 84)
Barbican (Rail & Underground) .5C 8 (5C 84)
Barking (Rail & Underground) .7G 71
Barkingside (Underground) .3H 53
Barnehurst (Rail) .2J 127
Barnes (Rail) .3C 116
Barnes Bridge (Rail) .2B 116
Barons Court (Underground) .5G 99
Battersea Park (Rail) .7F 101
Bayswater (Underground) .7K 81
Beckenham Hill (Rail) .5E 140
Beckenham Junction (Rail & CT) .1C 158
Beckenham Road Stop (CT) .1A 158
Beckton (DLR) .5E 88
Beckton Park (DLR) .7D 88
Becontree (Underground) .6D 72
Beddington Lane Stop (CT) .6G 155
Belgrave Walk Stop (CT) .4B 154
Bellingham (Rail) .3D 140
Belsize Park (Underground) .5C 64
Belvedere (Rail) .3H 109
Bermondsey (Underground) .3G 103
Berrylands (Rail) .4H 151
Bethnal Green (Rail) .4H 85
Bethnal Green (Underground) .3J 85
Bexley (Rail) .1G 145
Bexleyheath (Rail) .2E 126
Bickley (Rail) .3C 160
Birkbeck (Rail & CT) .3J 157
Blackfriars (Rail & Underground) .2A 14 (7B 84)
Blackfriars Millennium Pier (Riverbus) .2A 14 (7A 84)
Blackheath (Rail) .3H 123
Blackhorse Lane Stop (CT) .7G 157
Blackhorse Road (Underground) .4K 49
Blackwall (DLR) .7E 86
Bond Street (Underground) .1J 11 (6F 83)
Borough (Underground) .7D 14 (2C 102)
Boston Manor (Underground) .4A 96
Bounds Green (Underground) .6C 32
Bow Church (DLR) .3C 86
Bowes Park (Rail) .7D 32
Bow Road (Underground) .3C 86
Brent Cross (Underground) .7F 45
Brentford (Rail) .6C 96
Brimsdown (Rail) .3F 25
Brixton (Rail & Underground) .4A 120
Brockley (Rail) .3A 122
Bromley-by-Bow (Underground) .3D 86
Bromley North (Rail) .1J 159
Bromley South (Rail) .3J 159
Brondesbury (Overground) .7H 63
Brondesbury Park (Overground) .1G 81
Bruce Grove (Rail) .2F 49
Buckhurst Hill (Underground) .2G 37
Burnt Oak (Underground) .1J 43
Bush Hill Park (Rail) .6A 24

C

Cadogan Pier (Riverbus) .7D 16 (6C 100)
Caledonian Road (Underground) .6K 65
Caledonian Road & Barnsbury (Overground) .7K 65
Cambridge Heath (Rail) .2H 85
Camden Road (Overground) .7G 65
Camden Town (Underground) .1F 83
Canada Water (Underground) .2J 103
Canary Wharf (DLR & Underground) .1C 104
Canary Wharf Pier (Riverbus) .1B 104
Canning Town (Underground & DLR) .6G 87
Cannon Street (Rail & Underground) .2E 14 (7D 84)
Canonbury (Overground) .5C 66
Canons Park (Underground) .7K 27
Carshalton (Rail) .4D 166
Carshalton Beeches (Rail) .6D 166
Castle Bar Park (Rail) .5K 77
Catford (Rail) .7C 122
Catford Bridge (Rail) .7C 122
Centrale Stop (CT) .2C 168
Chadwell Heath (Rail) .7D 54
Chalk Farm (Underground) .7E 64
Chancery Lane (Underground) .6J 7 (5A 84)
Charing Cross (Rail & Underground) .4E 12 (1J 101)
Charlton (Rail) .5A 106
Cheam (Rail) .7G 165
Chelsea Harbour Pier (Riverbus) .1B 118
Chessington North (Rail) .5E 162
Chessington South (Rail) .7D 162
Chigwell (Underground) .3K 37
Chingford (Rail) .1B 36
Chislehurst (Rail) .2E 160
Chiswick (Rail) .7J 97
Chiswick Park (Underground) .4J 97
Church Street Stop (CT) .2C 168
City Thameslink (Rail) .7A 8 (6B 84)
Clapham Common (Underground) .4G 119
Clapham High Street (Rail) .3H 119
Clapham Junction (Rail & Overground) .3C 118
Clapham North (Underground) .3J 119
Clapham South (Underground) .6F 119
Clapton (Rail) .2H 67
Clock House (Rail) .1A 158
Cockfosters (Underground) .4K 21
Colindale (Underground) .3A 44
Colliers Wood (Underground) .7B 136
Coombe Lane Stop (CT) .5J 169
Covent Garden (Underground) .2F 13 (7J 83)
Cricklewood (Rail) .4F 63
Crofton Park (Rail) .5B 122
Crossharbour (DLR & Underground) .3D 104
Crouch Hill (Overground) .7K 47
Crystal Palace (Rail) .6G 139
Custom House for ExCeL (DLR) .7K 87
Cutty Sark for Maritime Greenwich (DLR) .6E 104
Cyprus (DLR) .7E 88

D

Dagenham Dock (Rail) .2F 91
Dagenham East (Underground) .5J 73
Dagenham Heathway (Underground) .6F 73
Dalston Kingsland (Overground) .5E 66
Denmark Hill (Rail) .2D 120
Deptford (Rail) .7C 104
Deptford Bridge (DLR) .1C 122
Devons Road (DLR) .4D 86
Dollis Hill (Underground) .5C 62
Drayton Green (Rail) .6K 77
Drayton Park (Rail) .4A 66
Dundonald Road Stop (CT) .7H 135

E

Ealing Broadway (Rail & Underground) .7D 78
Ealing Common (Underground) .1F 97
Earl's Court (Underground) .4K 99
Earlsfield (Rail) .1A 136
East Acton (Underground) .6B 80
Eastcote (Underground) .7A 40
East Croydon (Rail & CT) .2D 168
East Dulwich (Rail) .4E 120
East Finchley (Underground) .4C 46
East Ham (Underground) .7C 70
East India (DLR) .7F 87
East Putney (Underground) .5G 117
Eden Park (Rail) .5C 158
Edgware (Underground) .6C 28
Edgware Road (Underground) .5C 4 (5C 82)
Edmonton Green (Rail) .2B 34
Elephant & Castle (Rail & Underground) .4C 102
Elmers End (Rail & CT) .4K 157
Elmstead Woods (Rail) .6C 142
Eltham (Rail) .5D 124
Elverson Road (DLR) .2D 122
Embankment (Underground) .4F 13 (1J 101)
Embankment Pier (Riverbus) .4G 13 (1J 101)
Enfield Chase (Rail) .3H 23
Enfield Town (Rail) .3K 23
Erith (Rail) .5K 109
Essex Road (Rail) .7C 66
Euston (Rail & Underground) .2C 6 (3G 83)
Euston Square (Underground) .3B 6 (4G 83)
Ewell West (Rail) .7A 164

F

Fairlop (Underground) .1H 53
Falconwood (Rail) .4H 125
Farringdon (Rail & Underground) .5A 8 (5B 84)
Feltham (Rail) .1K 129
Fenchurch Street (Rail) [illegible] (7F 85)
Festival Pier (Riverbus) [illegible]
Fieldway Stop (CT) [illegible]
Finchley Central (Underground) [illegible]
Finchley Road (Underground) [illegible]
Finchley Road & Frognal (Overgro[illegible]
Finsbury Park (Rail & Undergrou[illegible]
Forest Gate (Rail) [illegible]

Forest Hill (Rail) 2J 139
Fulham Broadway (Underground) 7J 99
Fulwell (Rail) 4H 131

G

Gallions Reach (DLR) 7F 89
Gants Hill (Underground) 6E 52
George Street Stop (CT) 2C 168
Gipsy Hill (Rail) 5E 138
Gloucester Road (Underground) 4A 100
Golders Green (Underground) 1J 63
Goldhawk Road (Underground) 2E 98
Goodge Street (Underground) 5C 6 (5H 83)
Goodmayes (Rail) 1A 72
Gordon Hill (Rail) 1G 23
Gospel Oak (Overground) 4E 64
Grange Park (Rail) 5G 23
Gravel Hill Stop (CT) 6A 170
Great Portland Street (Underground) 4K 5 (4F 83)
Greenford (Rail & Underground) 1H 77
Greenland Pier (Riverbus) 3B 104
Green Park (Underground) 4K 11 (1G 101)
Greenwich (Rail & DLR) 7D 104
Greenwich Pier (Riverbus) 5E 104
Grove Park (Rail) 3K 141
Gunnersbury (Underground) 5H 97

H

Hackbridge (Rail) 2F 167
Hackney Central (Overgroundl) 6H 67
Hackney Downs (Rail) 5H 67
Hackney Wick (Overground) 6C 68
Hadley Wood (Rail) 1F 21
Hammersmith (Underground) 4E 98
Hampstead (Underground) 4A 64
Hampstead Heath (Overground) 4C 64
Hampton (Rail) 1E 148
Hampton Court (Rail) 4J 149
Hampton Wick (Rail) 1C 150
Hanger Lane (Underground) 3E 78
Hanwell (Rail) 7J 77
Harlesden (Overground & Underground) 2K 79
Harringay (Rail) 6A 48
Harringay Green Lanes (Overground) 6B 48
Harrington Road Stop (CT) 3J 157
Harrow-on-the-Hill (Rail & Underground) 6J 41
Harrow & Wealdstone (Underground) 4J 41
Hatch End (Overground) 1E 40
Hatton Cross (Underground) 4H 111
Haydons Road (Rail) 5A 136
Hayes (Rail) 1J 171
Hayes & Harlington (Rail) 3H 93
Headstone Lane (Overground) 1F 41
Heathrow Central (Rail) 3C 110
Heathrow Terminals 1, 2 & 3 (Underground) 3D 110
Heathrow Terminal 4 (Rail) 6E 110
Heathrow Terminal 4 (Underground) 5E 110
Heathrow Terminal 5 (Rail & Underground) 6D 174
Hendon (Rail) 6C 44
Hendon Central (Underground) 5D 44
Herne Hill (Rail) 6B 120
Heron Quays (DLR) 1C 104
Highams Park (Rail) 6A 36
High Barnet (Underground) 4D 20
Highbury & Islington (Underground) 6B 66
Highgate (Underground) 6F 47
High Street Kensington (Underground) 2K 99
Hillingdon (Underground) 5D 56
Hilton Docklands Pier (Riverbus) 1B 104
Hither Green (Rail) 6G 123
Holborn (Underground) 6G 7 (6K 83)
Holland Park (Underground) 1H 99
Holloway Road (Underground) 5K 65
Homerton (Overground) 6K 67
Honor Oak Park (Rail) 6K 121
…sey (Rail) 4K 47
Hounslow (Rail) 5F 113
Hounslow Central (Underground) 3F 113
Hounslow East (Underground) 2G 113
Hounslow West (Underground) 2C 112
Hyde Park Corner (Underground) 6H 11 (2E 100)

I

Ickenham (Underground) 4E 56
Ikea Ampere Way Stop (CT) 7K 155
Ilford (Rail) 3E 70
Island Gardens (DLR) 5E 104
Isleworth (Rail) 2K 113

K

Kempton Park (Rail) 7K 129
Kennington (Underground) 5B 102
Kensal Green (Underground) 3E 80
Kensal Rise (Overground) 2F 81
Kensington Olympia (Underground) 3G 99
Kent House (Rail) 1A 158
Kentish Town (Rail & Underground) 5G 65
Kentish Town West (Overground) 6F 65
Kenton (Overground & Underground) 6B 42
Kew Bridge (Rail) 5F 97
Kew Gardens (Underground) 1G 115
Kidbrooke (Rail) 3K 123
Kilburn (Underground) 6H 63
Kilburn High Road (Overground) 1K 81
Kilburn Park (Underground) 2J 81
King George V (DLR) 1E 106
Kingsbury (Underground) 5G 43
King's Cross (Rail & Underground) 1F 7 (2J 83)
King's Cross St Pancras (Underground) 1E 6 (3J 83)
Kingston (Rail) 1E 150
Knightsbridge (Underground) 7F 11 (2D 100)

L

Ladbroke Grove (Underground) 6G 81
Ladywell (Rail) 5D 122
Lambeth North (Underground) 1J 19 (3A 102)
Lancaster Gate (Underground) 2A 10 (7B 82)
Langdon Park (DLR) 6D 86
Latimer Road (Underground) 7F 81
Lebanon Road Stop (CT) 2E 168
Lee (Rail) 6J 123
Leicester Square (Underground) 2D 12 (7J 83)
Lewisham (Rail & DLR) 3E 122
Leyton (Underground) 3E 68
Leyton Midland Road (Overground) 7E 50
Leytonstone (Underground) 1G 69
Leytonstone High Road (Overground) 2G 69
Limehouse (Rail & DLR) 6A 86
Liverpool Street (Rail & Underground) 6G 9 (5E 84)
Lloyd Park Stop (CT) 4F 169
London Bridge (Rail & Underground) 5F 15 (1D 102)
London Bridge City Pier (Riverbus) 4F 15 (1E 102)
London City Airport (DLR) 1C 106
London Fields (Rail) 7H 67
Loughborough Junction (Rail) 3B 120
Lower Sydenham (Rail) 5B 140

M

Maida Vale (Underground) 3K 81
Malden Manor (Rail) 7A 152
Manor House (Underground) 7C 48
Manor Park (Rail) 4B 70
Mansion House (Underground) 2D 14 (7C 84)
Marble Arch (Underground) 1F 11 (6D 82)
Maryland (Rail) 6G 69
Marylebone (Rail & Underground) 4E 4 (4D 82)
Masthouse Terrace Pier (Riverbus) 5C 104
Maze Hill (Rail) 6G 105
Merton Park Stop (CT) 1J 153
Mile End (Underground) 4B 86
Millbank Millennium Pier (Riverbus) 4F 19 (4J 101)
Mill Hill Broadway (Rail) 6F 29
Mill Hill East (Underground) 7B 30
Mitcham Stop (CT) 4C 154
Mitcham Junction (Rail & CT) 5E 154
Monument (Underground) 2F 15 (7D 84)
Moorgate (Rail & Underground) 6E 8 (5D 84)
Morden (Underground) 3K 153
Morden Road Stop (CT) 2K 153
Morden South (Rail) 5J 153
Mornington Crescent (Underground) 2G 83
Mortlake (Rail) 3J 115
Motspur Park (Rail) 5D 152
Mottingham (Rail) 1D 142
Mudchute (DLR) 4D 104

N

Neasden (Underground) 5A 62
New Barnet (Rail) 5G 21
New Beckenham (Rail) 7B 140
Newbury Park (Underground) 6H 53
New Cross (Rail & Underground) 7B 104
New Cross Gate (Rail & Underground) 1A 122
New Eltham (Rail) 1F 143
New Malden (Rail) 3A 152
New Southgate (Rail) 5A 32
Norbiton (Rail) 1G 151
Norbury (Rail) 1K 155
North Acton (Underground) 5K 79
North Dulwich (Rail) 5D 120
North Ealing (Underground) 6F 79
Northfields (Underground) 3C 96
North Greenwich (Underground) 2G 105
North Harrow (Underground) 5F 41
Northolt Park (Rail) 4F 59
Northolt (Underground) 6E 58
North Sheen (Rail) 4G 115
Northumberland Park (Rail) 7C 34
North Wembley (Overground & Underground) 3D 60
Northwick Park (Underground) 7B 42
Northwood Hills (Underground) 2J 39
Norwood Junction (Rail) 4G 157
Notting Hill Gate (Underground) 1J 99
Nunhead (Rail) 2J 121

O

Oakleigh Park (Rail) 7G 21
Oakwood (Underground) 5B 22
Old Street (Rail & Underground) 2F 9 (4D 84)
Orpington (Rail) 2J 173
Osterley (Underground) 7H 95
Oval (Underground) 6A 102
Oxford Circus (Underground) 1A 12 (6G 83)

P

Paddington (Rail & Underground) 7A 4 (6B 82)
Palmers Green (Rail) 4E 32
Park Royal (Underground) 4G 79
Parsons Green (Underground) 1J 117
Peckham Rye (Rail) 2G 121
Penge East (Rail) 6J 139
Penge West (Rail) 6H 139
Perivale (Underground) 2A 78
Petts Wood (Rail) 5G 161
Phipps Bridge Stop (CT) 3B 154
Piccadilly Circus (Underground) 3C 12 (7H 83)
Pimlico (Underground) 5C 18 (5H 101)
Pinner (Underground) 4C 40
Plaistow (Underground) 2H 87
Plumstead (Rail) 4H 107
Ponders End (Rail) 5F 25
Pontoon Dock (DLR) 1A 106

Poplar (DLR) 7D 86
Preston Road (Underground) 1E 60
Prince Regent (DLR) 7A 88
Pudding Mill Lane (DLR) 1D 86
Putney (Rail) 4G 117
Putney Bridge (Underground) 3H 117
Putney Pier (Riverbus) 3G 117

Q

Queensbury (Underground) 3F 43
Queen's Park (Underground) 2H 81
Queens Road (Peckham) (Rail) 1J 121
Queenstown Road (Battersea) (Rail) 1F 119
Queensway (Underground) 7K 81

R

Ravensbourne (Rail) 7F 141
Ravenscourt Park (Underground) 4D 98
Rayners Lane (Underground) 7D 40
Raynes Park (Rail) 2E 152
Rectory Road (Rail) 3F 67
Redbridge (Underground) 6B 52
Reeves Corner Stop (CT) 2B 168
Regent's Park (Underground) 4J 5 (4F 83)
Richmond (Rail & Underground) 4E 114
Roding Valley (Underground) 4G 37
Rotherhithe (Underground) 2J 103
Royal Albert (DLR) 7C 88
Royal Arsenal Woolwich Pier (Riverbus) 3F 107
Royal Oak (Underground) 5K 81
Royal Victoria (DLR) 7J 87
Ruislip (Underground) 1G 57
Ruislip Gardens (Underground) 4J 57
Ruislip Manor (Underground) 1J 57
Russell Square (Underground) 4E 6 (4J 83)

S

St Helier (Rail) 6J 153
St James's Park (Underground) 1C 18 (2H 101)
St James Street (Rail) 5A 50
St Johns (Rail) 2C 122
St John's Wood (Underground) 2B 82
St Katharine's Pier (Riverbus) 4K 15 (1F 103)
St Margarets (Rail) 6B 114
St Pancras International (Rail) 1E 6 (3J 83)
St Paul's (Underground) 7C 8 (6C 84)
Sanderstead (Rail) 7D 168
Sandilands Stop (CT) 2F 169
Savoy Pier (Riverbus) 3G 13 (7K 83)
Selhurst (Rail) 5E 156
Seven Kings (Rail) 1J 71
Seven Sisters (Rail & Underground) 5E 48
Shadwell (Underground & DLR) 7H 85
Shepherd's Bush (Underground) 2F 99
Shepherd's Bush Market (Underground) 1E 98
Shepperton (Rail) 5E 146
Shortlands (Rail) 2G 159
Sidcup (Rail) 2A 144
Silver Street (Rail) 4A 34
Sloane Square (Underground) 4G 17 (4E 100)
Snaresbrook (Underground) 5J 51
South Acton (Overground) 3J 97
Southall (Rail) 2D 94
South Bermondsey (Rail) 5J 103
Southbury (Rail) 4C 24
South Croydon (Rail) 5D 168
South Ealing (Underground) 3D 96
Southfields (Underground) 1H 135
Southgate (Underground) 1C 32
South Greenford (Rail) 3J 77
South Hampstead (Overground) 7A 64
South Harrow (Underground) 3G 59
South Kensington (Underground) 3B 16 (4B 100)
South Kenton (Overground & Underground) 1C 60
South Merton (Rail) 3H 153
South Quay (DLR) 2D 104
South Ruislip (Rail & Underground) 5A 58
South Tottenham (Overground) 5F 49
Southwark (Underground) 5A 14 (1B 102)
South Wimbledon (Underground) 7K 135
South Woodford (Underground) 2K 51
Stamford Brook (Underground) 4B 98
Stamford Hill (Rail) 7E 48
Stanmore (Underground) 4J 27
Stepney Green (Underground) 4K 85
Stockwell (Underground) 1J 119
Stoke Newington (Rail) 2F 67
Stonebridge Park (Underground) 7H 61
Stoneleigh (Rail) 5C 164
Stratford (Rail) 6F 69
Stratford International (Rail) 6E 68
Stratford Low Level (Overground, Underground & DLR) 7F 69
Strawberry Hill (Rail) 3K 131
Streatham (Rail) 5H 137
Streatham Common (Rail) 6H 137
Streatham Hill (Rail) 2J 137
Sudbury & Harrow Road (Rail) 5B 60
Sudbury Hill (Underground) 4J 59
Sudbury Hill Harrow (Rail) 4J 59
Sudbury Town (Underground) 6B 60
Sunbury (Rail) 1J 147
Sundridge Park (Rail) 7K 141
Surbiton (Rail) 6E 150
Surrey Quays (Underground) 4K 103
Sutton (Rail) 6A 166
Sutton Common (Rail) 2K 165
Swiss Cottage (Underground) 7B 64
Sydenham (Rail) 4J 139
Sydenham Hill (Rail) 3F 139
Syon Lane (Rail) 7A 96

T

Teddington (Rail) 6A 132
Temple (Underground) 2J 13 (7K 83)
Thames Ditton (Rail) 7K 149
Therapia Lane Stop (CT) 7J 155
Thornton Heath (Rail) 4C 156
Tolworth (Rail) 2H 163
Tooting (Rail) 6D 136
Tooting Bec (Underground) 3E 136
Tooting Broadway (Underground) 5C 136
Tottenham Court Road (Underground) 7D 6 (6H 83)
Tottenham Hale (Rail & Underground) 3H 49
Totteridge & Whetstone (Underground) 2F 31
Tower Gateway (DLR) 2J 15 (7F 85)
Tower Hill (Underground) 2J 15 (7F 85)
Tower Millennium Pier (Riverbus) 4H 15 (1E 102)
Tufnell Park (Underground) 4G 65
Tulse Hill (Rail) 2B 138
Turnham Green (Underground) 4A 98
Turnpike Lane (Underground) 3B 48
Twickenham (Rail) 7A 114

U

Upney (Underground) 7K 71
Upper Halliford (Rail) 2G 147
Upper Holloway (Overground) 2H 65
Upton Park (Underground) 1A 88

V

Vauxhall (Rail & Underground) 6F 19 (5J 101)
Victoria (Rail & Underground) 3K 17 (4F 101)
Victoria Coach (Bus) 4J 17 (4F 101)

W

Waddon (Rail) 4A 168
Waddon Marsh Stop (CT) 2A 168
Wallington (Rail) 6F 167
Walthamstow Central (Rail & Underground) 5C 50
Walthamstow Queens Road (Overground) 5C 50
Wandle Park Stop (CT) 2A 168
Wandsworth Common (Rail) 1D 136
Wandsworth Road (Rail) 2G 119
Wandsworth Town (Rail) 4K 117
Wanstead (Underground) 6K 51
Wanstead Park (Overground) 4K 69
Wapping (Underground) 1J 103
Warren Street (Underground) 3A 6 (4G 83)
Warwick Avenue (Underground) 4A 82
Waterloo (Rail & Underground) 6J 13 (2A 102)
Waterloo East (Rail) 5K 13 (1A 102)
Waterloo Millennium Pier (Riverbus) 6G 13 (2K 101)
Wellesley Road Stop (CT) 2D 168
Welling (Rail) 2A 126
Wembley Central (Overground & Underground) 5E 60
Wembley Park (Underground) 3G 61
Wembley Stadium (Rail) 5F 61
West Acton (Underground) 6G 79
Westbourne Park (Underground) 5H 81
West Brompton (Underground) 6J 99
Westcombe Park (Rail) 5J 105
West Croydon (Rail & CT) 1C 168
West Drayton (Rail) 1A 92
West Dulwich (Rail) 2D 138
West Ealing (Rail) 7B 78
Westferry (DLR) 7C 86
West Finchley (Underground) 6E 30
West Hampstead (Overground) 6J 63
West Hampstead (Underground) 6K 63
West Hampstead Thameslink (Rail) 6J 63
West Ham (Rail & Underground) 3G 87
West Harrow (Underground) 6G 41
West India Quay (DLR) 7C 86
West Kensington (Underground) 5H 99
Westminster Millennium Pier (Riverbus) 6F 13 (2J 101)
Westminster (Underground) 7F 13 (2J 101)
West Norwood (Rail) 4B 138
West Ruislip (Rail & Underground) 2E 56
West Silvertown (DLR) 1J 105
West Sutton (Rail) 4J 165
West Wickham (Rail) 7E 158
Whitechapel (Underground) 5H 85
White City (Underground) 7E 80
White Hart Lane (Rail) 7A 34
Whitton (Rail) 7G 113
Willesden Green (Underground) 6E 62
Willesden Junction (Rail, Underground & Overground) 3B 80
Wimbledon (Rail, Underground & CT) 6H 135
Wimbledon Chase (Rail) 2G 153
Wimbledon Park (Underground) 3J 135
Winchmore Hill (Rail) 7G 23
Woodford (Underground) 6E 36
Woodgrange Park (Overground) 5B 70
Wood Green (Underground) 2A 48
Wood Lane (Underground) 7E 80
Woodside Stop (CT) 6H 157
Woodside Park (Underground) 4E 30
Wood Street Walthamstow (Rail) 4F 51
Woolwich Arsenal (Rail) 4F 107
Woolwich Dockyard (Rail) 4D 106
Worcester Park (Rail) 1C 164

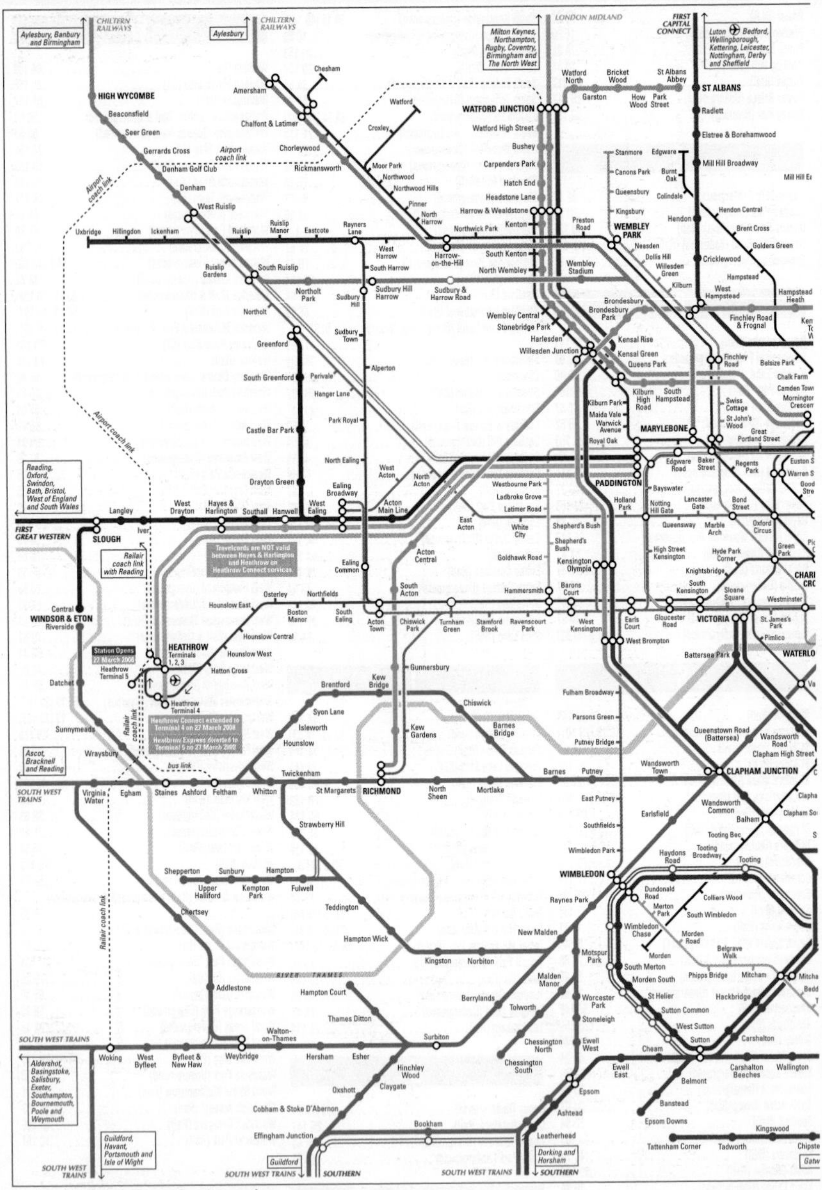

National Rail Train Operating Companies

Chiltern Railways		London Midland	
c2c		London Overground	
First Capital Connect		'one' Railway	
First Great Western		Southern	
Heathrow Connect		Southeastern	
Heathrow Express		South West Trains	

Limited service lines and/or stations (in outline in Train Company colours)

Interchange stations

Bus and coach links

NOTES: This map is a guide to services provided by the train operators on weekdays but does not guarantee direct trains between the stations shown; some peak period services are omitted. A few services do not operate and some stations are not served in the early mornings and late evenings, or at weekends and on public holidays.
Improvement work to track and signalling can affect services and may apply for extended periods in some instances. It is recommended that journey details are checked prior to travel.

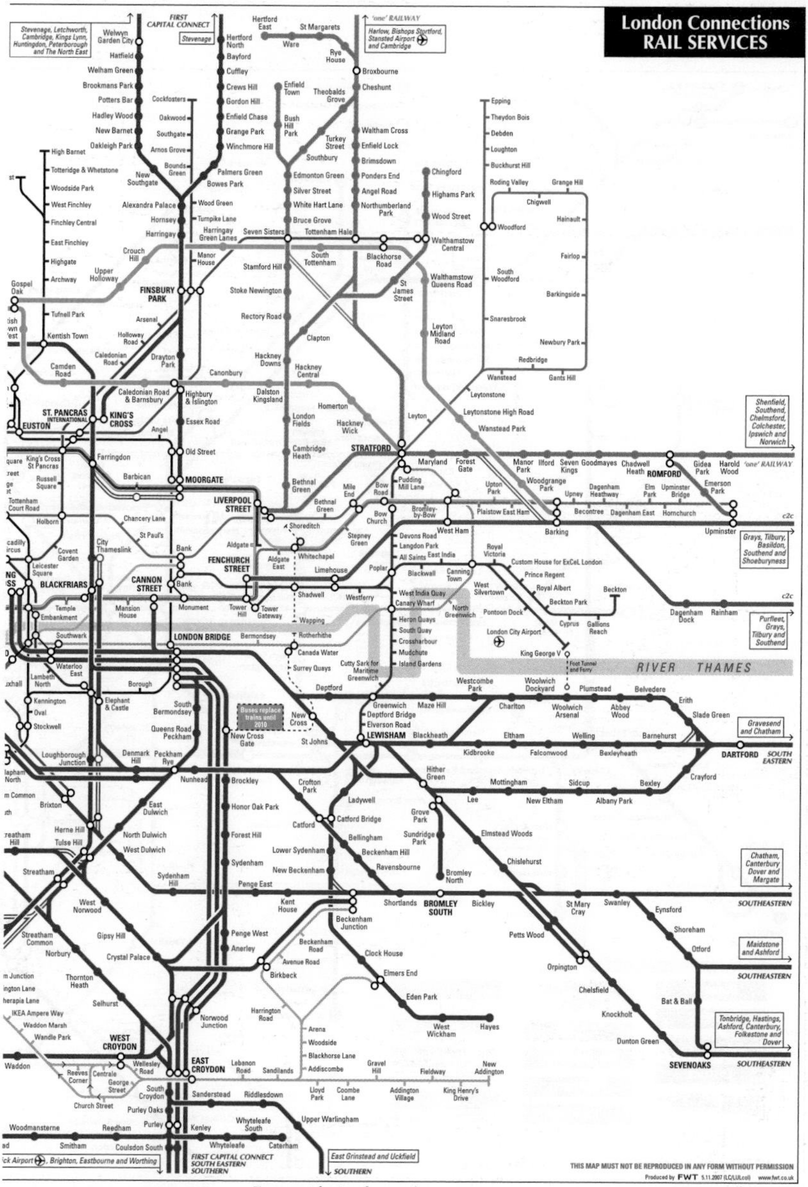

Rail Franchises or Train Company trading names may change during the currency of this publication. Every effort has been made to ensure the information shown is correct at the time of going to press: December 2007. For further information and prices of Travelcards, train times and fares, contact your local station, telephone National Rail Enquiries on 08457 48 49 50, or visit: www. nationalrail.co.uk © Association of Train Operating Companies – DECEMBER 2007

Transport for London services (thinner lines)

- Bakerloo Line
- Central Line
- Circle Line
- Croydon Tramlink
- District Line
- Docklands Light Railway
- East London Line (buses replace trains until 2010)
- Hammersmith & City Line
- Jubilee Line
- Metropolitan Line
- Northern Line
- Piccadilly Line
- Victoria Line
- Waterloo & City

Chesham
Chalfont & Latimer
Amersham
Chorleywood
Rickmansworth
Watford
Croxley
Moor Park
Northwood
Northwood Hills
Pinner
North Harrow
Harrow-on-the-Hill
West Harrow
West Ruislip
Hillingdon
Ruislip
Ruislip Manor
Eastcote
Uxbridge
Ickenham
Rayners Lane
Ruislip Gardens
South Ruislip
South Harrow
Northolt
Sudbury Hill
Sudbury Hill Harrow (no weekend service) 150m
Sudbury Town
Greenford
(no Sunday service)
Alperton
Perivale
Hanger Lane
Park Royal
North Ealing
Ealing Broadway
West Acton
North Acton
Ealing Common
South Acton
Acton Town
South Ealing
Northfields
Boston Manor
Osterley
Hounslow East
Hounslow Central
Hounslow West
Hatton Cross
Heathrow Terminals 1, 2, 3
Heathrow Terminal 4
Heathrow Terminal 5
opens Spring 2008
Chiswick Park
Turnham Green
Gunnersbury
Kew Gardens
Richmond
Watford Junction
Watford High Street
Bushey
Carpenders Park
Hatch End
Headstone Lane
Harrow & Wealdstone
Kenton
South Kenton
North Wembley
Wembley Central
Stonebridge Park
Harlesden
Willesden Junction
Northwick Park
Preston Road
Wembley Park
Stanmore
Canons Park
Queensbury
Kingsbury
Neasden
Dollis Hill
Willesden Green
Kilburn
West Hampstead
Thameslink 200m
Brondesbury Park
Brondesbury
Kensal Rise
Kensal Green
Queen's Park
Kilburn High Road
South Hampstead
Finchley Road
Swiss Cottage
St. John's Wood
Maida Vale
Kilburn Park
Warwick Avenue
Royal Oak
Westbourne Park
Paddington
Edgware Road
Marylebone
Baker Street
Great Portland Street
Euston
Ladbroke Grove
Latimer Road
White City
Holland Park
Notting Hill Gate
Bayswater
Lancaster Gate
Bond Street
Oxford Circus
Warren Street
Regent's Park
Goodge Street
Tottenham Court Road
East Acton
Wood Lane
station under construction
Shepherd's Bush
London Overground station under construction
Queensway
Marble Arch
High Street Kensington
Hyde Park Corner
Green Park
Piccadilly Circus
Acton Central
Shepherd's Bush
Kensington (Olympia)
Goldhawk Road
Knightsbridge
Hammersmith
Barons Court
Gloucester Road
Sloane Square
St. James's Park
Stamford Brook
Ravenscourt Park
West Kensington
Earl's Court
South Kensington
Victoria
Westminster
West Brompton
Fulham Broadway
Parsons Green
Putney Bridge
River Thames
East Putney
Southfields
Wimbledon Park
Wimbledon
Clapham Junction
Pimlico
Vauxhall
Waterloo
International rail services now depart from King's Cross St. Pancras
Kennington
Oval
Stockwell
Clapham North
Clapham High Street 100m
Brixt
Clapham South
Clapham Common
Balham
Tooting Bec
Tooting Broadway
Colliers Wood
South Wimbledon
Morden
Edgware
Burnt Oak
Colindale
Hendon Central
Brent Cross
Golders Green
Hampstead
Hampstead Heath
Finchley Road & Frognal
Belsize Park
Chalk Farm
Camden Town
Mornington Crescent
Mill Hi
Bakerloo
Central
Circle
District
East London
line closed, replacement bus services operate
Hammersmith & City
Jubilee
Metropolitan
Northern
Piccadilly
Heathrow Terminal 5 opens Spring 2008
Victoria
Waterloo & City
Overground
DLR
under construction
© Transport for London
Reg. user No. 08/1020/LS
MAYOR OF LONDON
Website
tfl.gov.uk
24 hour
020

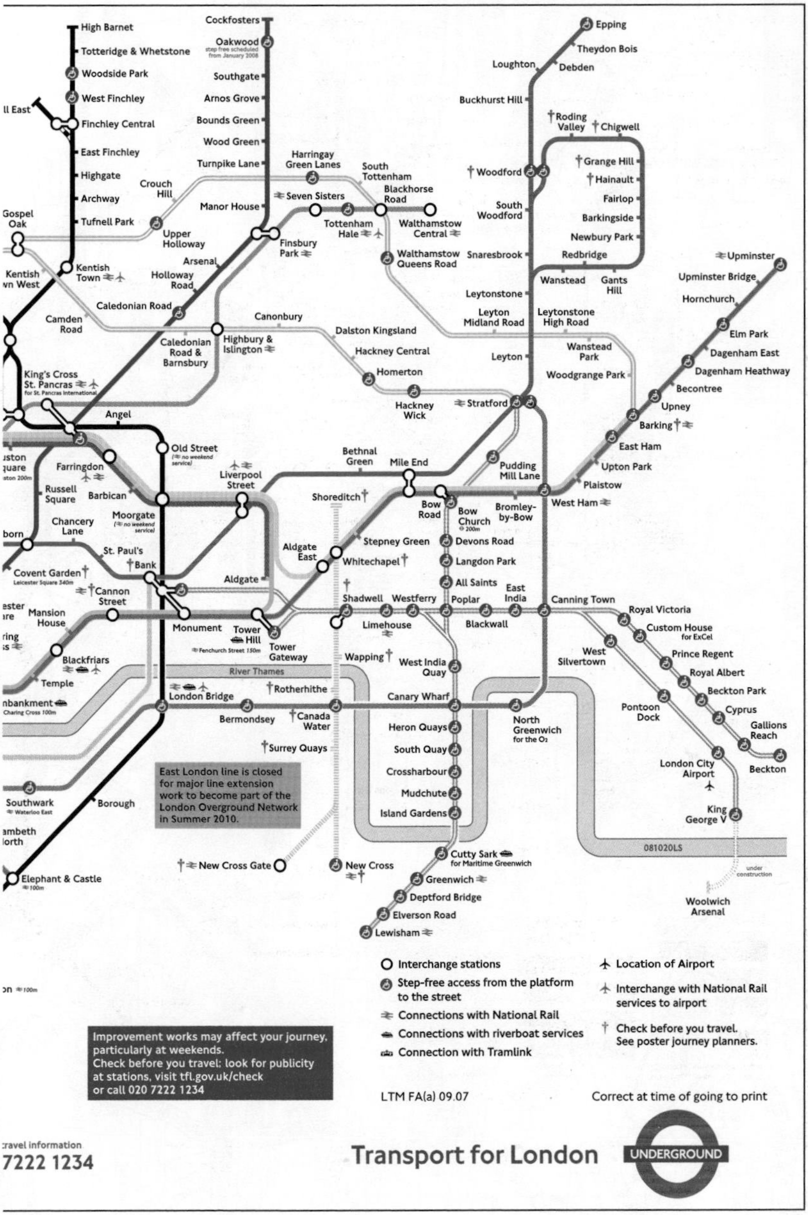

High Barnet
Totteridge & Whetstone
Woodside Park
West Finchley
Finchley Central
East Finchley
Highgate
Archway
Tufnell Park
Gospel Oak
Kentish Town
Kentish Town West
Camden Road
Crouch Hill
Upper Holloway
Cockfosters
Oakwood
step free scheduled from January 2008
Southgate
Arnos Grove
Bounds Green
Wood Green
Turnpike Lane
Manor House
Harringay Green Lanes
South Tottenham
Seven Sisters
Blackhorse Road
Tottenham Hale
Walthamstow Central
Walthamstow Queens Road
Finsbury Park
Arsenal
Holloway Road
Caledonian Road
Caledonian Road & Barnsbury
Highbury & Islington
Canonbury
Dalston Kingsland
Hackney Central
Homerton
Hackney Wick
King's Cross St. Pancras
for St. Pancras International
Angel
Old Street
no weekend service
Farringdon
Barbican
Russell Square
Chancery Lane
Moorgate
no weekend service
Liverpool Street
Bethnal Green
Mile End
Shoreditch
St. Paul's
Bank
Covent Garden
Leicester Square 340m
Cannon Street
Mansion House
Monument
Aldgate
Aldgate East
Whitechapel
Stepney Green
Tower Hill
Fenchurch Street 150m
Tower Gateway
Blackfriars
Temple
Embankment
Charing Cross 100m
London Bridge
River Thames
Bermondsey
Rotherhithe
Canada Water
Surrey Quays
Southwark
Waterloo East
Borough
Lambeth North
Elephant & Castle
100m
New Cross Gate
New Cross
East London line is closed for major line extension work to become part of the London Overground Network in Summer 2010.
Epping
Theydon Bois
Loughton
Debden
Buckhurst Hill
Roding Valley
Chigwell
Woodford
Grange Hill
Hainault
Fairlop
Barkingside
Newbury Park
South Woodford
Snaresbrook
Redbridge
Wanstead
Gants Hill
Leytonstone
Leyton Midland Road
Leytonstone High Road
Wanstead Park
Woodgrange Park
Leyton
Stratford
Pudding Mill Lane
Bow Road
Bow Church
200m
Bromley-by-Bow
West Ham
Devons Road
Langdon Park
All Saints
Shadwell
Westferry
Poplar
East India
Blackwall
Limehouse
Wapping
West India Quay
Canary Wharf
Heron Quays
South Quay
Crossharbour
Mudchute
Island Gardens
Cutty Sark
for Maritime Greenwich
Greenwich
Deptford Bridge
Elverson Road
Lewisham
Canning Town
North Greenwich
for the O2
Royal Victoria
Custom House
for ExCel
Prince Regent
Royal Albert
Beckton Park
Cyprus
Gallions Reach
Beckton
West Silvertown
Pontoon Dock
London City Airport
King George V
under construction
Woolwich Arsenal
081020LS
Upminster
Upminster Bridge
Hornchurch
Elm Park
Dagenham East
Dagenham Heathway
Becontree
Upney
Barking
East Ham
Upton Park
Plaistow
Interchange stations
Step-free access from the platform to the street
Connections with National Rail
Connections with riverboat services
Connection with Tramlink
Location of Airport
Interchange with National Rail services to airport
Check before you travel. See poster journey planners.
Improvement works may affect your journey, particularly at weekends. Check before you travel; look for publicity at stations, visit tfl.gov.uk/check or call 020 7222 1234
LTM FA(a) 09.07
Correct at time of going to print
travel information
7222 1234
Transport for London
UNDERGROUND

14 Fanny BR5 1EC

CONGESTION CHARGING ZONE
CONGESTION CHARGING ZONE
City
West End
Westminster
Peckham
Camden Town
Kilburn
Dalston
Islington
Bloomsbury
Mayfair
Soho
Pimlico
Belgravia
Chelsea
Kensington
Notting Hill
Paddington
Hyde Park
Regent's Park
Battersea
Clapham
Kennington
Walworth
Camberwell
Bermondsey
Rotherhithe
Wapping
Whitechapel
Shoreditch
Hoxton
Haggerston
Stepney
Shepherds Bush
Hammersmith
Fulham
Barnes
White City
HOLLAND PARK ROUNDABOUT
HAMMERSMITH FLYOVER
EUSTON UNDERPASS
MARYLEBONE FLYOVER
ELEPHANT & CASTLE
HYDE PARK CORNER
MARBLE ARCH
VAUXHALL CROSS
KENNINGTON OVAL
CANAL BRIDGE
TOWER HILL
ALDGATE
ANGEL
KINGS CROSS
BAKER STREET
BRITANNIA JUNCTION
SWISS COTTAGE
FULHAM BROADWAY
HAMMERSMITH BROADWAY
WHITE CITY
BRICKLAYER'S ARMS
CAMBERWELL GREEN